CHAMBERS

LARGE PRINT DICTIONARY

CHAMBERS

CHAMBERS
An imprint of Chambers Harrap Publishers Ltd
7 Hopetoun Crescent
Edinburgh, EH7 4AY

www.chambers.co.uk

Previous edition published by Chambers Harrap Publishers Ltd 1999
This edition published by Chambers Harrap Publishers Ltd 2005

A CIP catalogue record for this book is available from the British Library.

ISBN 0550 10164 0

Designed and typeset by Chambers Harrap Publishers Ltd, Edinburgh
Printed and bound in Germany by Bercker

Contents

Contributors

Editor
Mary O'Neill

Editorial assistance
Ian Brookes

Kay Cullen

Alice Grandison

Michael Munro

Camilla Rockwood

Publishing manager
Patrick White

Prepress manager
Sharon McTeir

Prepress controller
David Reid

Preface

Chambers Large Print Dictionary has been designed and compiled with the advice of the Royal National Institute for the Blind and the British Dyslexia Association, to ensure that it meets the needs of users for whom larger, clearer print is desirable or essential. The text is presented in a large, clear font on an uncluttered, well-spaced page, while the inclusion of over 100,000 references and definitions means that the dictionary is thoroughly comprehensive and up to date.

Definitions are given in clear, straightforward English, and there is help with irregular verbs, irregular plurals and the comparatives and superlatives of adjectives. Geographical and register labels indicate the contexts in which a word is typically used. Idioms and phrasal verbs are grouped alphabetically at the ends of entries, marked by a bold ◆ symbol. Such devices have been kept to a minimum, and are easy to see.

In creating this dictionary, the specific needs of the large print dictionary user have been carefully considered, resulting in easy-to-read pages without the loss of important information. **Chambers Large Print Dictionary** will be a reliable companion wherever English is written or spoken.

Model of dictionary layout

Irregular forms are shown where the spelling could cause a problem. —————

Usage examples illustrate meaning. ——————

Idioms and phrasal verbs are grouped alphabetically at the end of some entries. These are indicated by the symbol ◆. —————

Related words are included in the entry if the meaning is straightforward. ——————

Labels indicate when words and senses are restricted to certain areas of language.

Parts of speech are shown by traditional abbreviations, in small capitals. A change within an entry is signalled by an arrow, on a new line.

mean[1] VB (*meant*) **1** to express or intend to express, show or indicate something. **2** to intend something; to have it as a purpose: didn't mean any harm. **3** to be serious or sincere about something: **He means what he says**. **4** to be important to the degree specified; to represent something: **Your approval means a lot to me**. **5** to entail something necessarily; to involve or result in it: **War means hardship**. **6** to foretell or portend something: **This means war**.
◆ **mean well** to have good intentions.

mean[2] ADJ **1** not generous. **2** low; despicable. **3** poor; shabby; characterized by inferior quality. **4** COLLOQ, esp N AMER vicious; malicious; bad-tempered. **5** COLLOQ good; skilful: **plays a mean guitar**. ■ **meanly** ADV. ■ **meanness** N.

mean[3] ADJ **1** midway. **2** average.
➤ N **1** a midway position or course, etc between two extremes. **2** MATH, STATISTICS a mathematical average.

meander VB, INTR **1** of a river: to bend and curve. **2** (also **meander about**) to wander randomly or aimlessly.
➤ N (often **meanders**) a bend; a winding course.

meanie or **meany** N (**-ies**) COLLOQ **1** a selfish or ungenerous person. **2** esp N AMER a malicious or bad-tempered person.

meaning N **1** the sense in which a statement, action, word, etc is intended to be understood. **2** significance, importance or purpose, esp when hidden or special.

meaningful ADJ **1** having meaning; significant. **2** full of significance; expressive.

meaningless ADJ without meaning or reason.

Abbreviations used in the dictionary

ABBREV	abbreviation	MED	medicine
ADJ	adjective	METEOROL	meteorology
ADV	adverb	MIL	military
AFR	African	MUS	music
AGRIC	agriculture	MYTHOL	mythology
AMER	American	N	North, Northern
ANAT	anatomy	NAUT	nautical
ARCHIT	architecture	NZ	New Zealand
ASTROL	astrology	orig	originally
ASTRON	astronomy	ORNITHOL	ornithology
AUSTRAL	Australian	PA P	past participle
BIOCHEM	biochemistry	PA T	past tense
BIOL	biology	PATHOL	pathology
BOT	botany	PFX	prefix
BRIT	British	PHILOS	philosophy
c	century (eg 15c)	PHOTOG	photography
CHEM	chemistry	PHYS	physics
CINEMATOG	cinematography	PHYSIOL	physiology
C OF E	Church of England	PL	plural
COLLOQ	colloquial	POL	politics
COMB	combining	PREP	preposition
COMP	computing	PR P	present participle
CONJ	conjunction	PR T	present tense
DEROG	derogatory	PSYCHOANAL	psychoanalysis
E	East, Eastern	PSYCHOL	psychology
ECOL	ecology	RC	Roman Catholic
ECON	economics	RELIG	religion
eg	for example	S	South, Southern
ELEC	electricity, electrical	S AFR	South African
ENG	engineering	sb	somebody
ENTOMOL	entomology	SCOT	Scottish
esp	especially	SFX	suffix
EU	European Union	SING	singular
EXCLAM	exclamation	sth	something
GEOG	geography	TELECOMM	telecommunications
GEOL	geology	THEAT	theatre
GEOM	geometry	TR	transitive
GR	Greek	TRIG	trigonometry
GRAM	grammar	TV	television
HIST	history, historical	US	United States
HORTIC	horticulture	usu	usually
INTR	intransitive	VB	verb
LING	linguistics	VET	veterinary
MATH	mathematics	W	West, Western
MECH	mechanics	ZOOL	zoology

Aa

A¹ or **a** N (*As, A's* or *a's*) **1** the first letter of the English alphabet. **2** (usu **A**) the highest grade or quality, or a mark indicating this. **3** (**A**) MUS the sixth note on the scale of C major.
- ◆ **from A to B** from one place to another.
- ◆ **from A to Z** from beginning to end.

A² ABBREV ampere(s).

a (before a consonant or consonant sound, eg **a boy, a one**) or **an** (before a vowel or vowel sound, eg **an egg, an hour**) INDEFINITE ARTICLE **1** used with a singular noun where the thing referred to has not been mentioned before, or where it is not a specific example: **a dozen eggs**. **3 a** any or every: **A fire is hot**; **b** (used after **not** or **never**): any at all: **not a chance**. **4** each or every; per: **once a day**.

a-¹ PFX, SIGNIFYING **1** to or towards: **ashore**. **2** in the process or state of something: **asleep** • **a-roving**.

a-² or (BEFORE A VOWEL, AND IN SCIENTIFIC COMPOUNDS BEFORE **h**) **an-** PFX, SIGNIFYING not; without; opposite to: **amoral** • **anhydrous**.

AA ABBREV **1** Alcoholics Anonymous. **2** anti-aircraft. **3** BRIT Automobile Association.

aardvark N a nocturnal African mammal.

AB ABBREV, BRIT able seaman.

aback ADV (always **taken aback**) surprised or shocked.

abacus N a calculating device consisting of several rows of beads mounted in a frame.

abalone N a marine gastropod mollusc.

abandon VB **1** to give something up completely: **abandon hope**. **2** to leave or desert (a person, responsibility, etc).
- ➤ N uncontrolled or uninhibited behaviour.
- ■ **abandonment** N.
- ◆ **abandon oneself to sth** to let oneself be overcome by (strong emotion etc).

abandoned ADJ **1** deserted. **2** having no sense of shame or morality.

abase VB to humiliate or degrade (someone or oneself). ■ **abasement** N.

abashed ADJ embarrassed.

abate VB, TR & INTR to become or make less strong or severe. ■ **abatement** N.

abattoir N a slaughterhouse.

abbess N a woman in charge of an abbey.

abbey N **1** a monastery or convent under an abbot or abbess. **2** a church associated with it.

abbot N a man in charge of an abbey.

abbreviate VB to shorten, esp to represent (a word) by a shortened form. ■ **abbreviation** N.

ABC N (*ABCs* or *ABC's*) **1** the alphabet. **2** the basic facts about a subject.

abdicate VB **1** TR & INTR to give up one's right to (the throne). **2** to refuse or fail to carry out (one's responsibilities). ■ **abdication** N.

abdomen N, ZOOL, ANAT **1** in vertebrates: the lower part of the body, containing the stomach and reproductive organs. **2** in arthropods: the rear part of the body. ■ **abdominal** ADJ.

abduct VB to take someone away illegally by force. ■ **abduction** N. ■ **abductor** N.

aberrant ADJ departing from what is normal or

standard. ■ **aberrance** N.

aberration N a temporary change from what is normal or standard.

abet VB (-*tt*-) to encourage someone to commit an offence. See also **aid and abet** at **aid**.

abeyance N of laws, customs, etc: the condition of not being followed.

abhor VB to hate or dislike (usu something one considers morally wrong) very much.

abhorrent ADJ (esp **abhorrent to sb**) hated by them. ■ **abhorrence** N.

abide VB (*abided* or *abode*) to tolerate someone or something: cannot abide dishonesty.
◆ **abide by sth** to follow (a rule etc).

abiding ADJ lasting for a long time.

ability N (-*ies*) **1** the power or skill to do something. **2** great skill or intelligence.

abject ADJ **1** of living conditions, etc: extremely sad, miserable or poor. **2** showing lack of courage or pride, etc. ■ **abjectly** ADV.

abjure VB, FORMAL to promise to stop believing or doing something. ■ **abjuration** N.

ablaze ADJ **1** burning strongly. **2** brightly lit.

able ADJ **1** having the knowledge, power, etc to do something. **2** clever or skilful. ■ **ably** ADV.

able-bodied ADJ fit and healthy.

able seaman N a sailor able to perform all duties.

ablution N (usu **ablutions**) COLLOQ or FACETIOUS the ordinary washing of oneself.

abnegation N, FORMAL **1** the act of giving up something one has or would like to have. **2** the act of renouncing a doctrine, etc.

abnormal ADJ not normal; different from what is expected or usual. ■ **abnormality** N (-*ies*).
■ **abnormally** ADV.

aboard ADV, PREP on, on to, in or into (a ship, train, aircraft, etc).

abode N, FORMAL a house; a dwelling.

abolish VB to put an end to (laws etc).

abolition N the act of abolishing something; the state of being abolished. ■ **abolitionist** N.

A-bomb short for **atom bomb**

abominable ADJ greatly disliked or found loathsome. ■ **abominably** ADV.

abominable snowman N a yeti.

abominate VB to dislike or hate something greatly. ■ **abomination** N.

aboriginal ADJ **1** of inhabitants: earliest known; indigenous. **2** of the Aborigines of Australia or their languages.
➤ N (**Aboriginal**) an Aborigine.

aborigine N **1** (**Aborigine**) a member of a people who were the orginal inhabitants of Australia. **2** a member of any people who were the first to live in a country or region.

abort VB **1** INTR to expel (an embryo or fetus) spontaneously from the uterus before it is capable of surviving independently. **2** to induce termination of a pregnancy. **3** TR & INTR to stop (a plan, etc), or to be stopped, before a successful conclusion. ■ **abortion** N.

abortive ADJ unsuccessful.

abound VB, INTR to exist in large numbers.

about PREP **1** concerning or relating to someone or something. **2** near to something. **3** around or centring on something. **4** all around or surrounding someone or something.
➤ ADV **1** approximately. **2** nearby. **3** here and there. **4** all around; in all directions. **5** in or to the opposite direction: turn about.
◆ **about to do sth** on the point of doing it.

about turn and **about face** N a complete change of direction.

above PREP **1** higher than or over something. **2** more or greater than something in quantity or degree. **3** higher or superior to someone in rank, importance, ability, etc. **4** too good or great for a specified thing: above the law.
➤ ADV **1** at, in or to a higher position, place, rank, etc. **2 a** in an earlier passage of text; **b** IN COMPOUNDS: above-mentioned.

➤ ADJ appearing or mentioned in an earlier passage of text.

➤ N (**the above**) something already mentioned.

◆ **above all** more than anything else.

above-board ADJ honest; open; not secret.

abrasion N 1 an area of skin, rock, etc which has been worn away by scraping or rubbing. 2 the act of scraping or rubbing away.

abrasive ADJ 1 of a material: capable of wearing something away by rubbing. 2 of a material: used to smooth or polish by rubbing. 3 of people or actions: harsh and rude.

➤ N any abrasive material.

abreast ADV side by side and facing in the same direction.

◆ **abreast of sth** up to date concerning it.

abridge VB to make (a book, etc) shorter.

abroad ADV 1 in or to a foreign country. 2 in circulation; at large. 3 over a wide area.

abrogate VB to cancel (a law, agreement, etc) formally or officially. ■ **abrogation** N.

abrupt ADJ 1 sudden and unexpected. 2 esp of speech, etc: rather sharp and rude. ■ **abruptly** ADV. ■ **abruptness** N.

abscess N, PATHOL a collection of pus in a cavity surrounded by inflamed tissue.

abscond VB, INTR to depart or leave quickly and usu secretly.

abseil VB, INTR to go backwards down a steep drop using a rope wound round the body.

absence N 1 the state of being away. 2 the time when a person is away. 3 the state of not existing or of being lacking.

absent ADJ 1 not present. 2 not existing, esp where expected. ■ **absently** ADV.

absentee N someone who is not present at a particular place or required time.

absent-minded ADJ preoccupied or forgetful. ■ **absent-mindedly** ADV.

absolute ADJ 1 complete; total. 2 not relative: an absolute standard. 3 pure.

➤ N a rule, standard, etc which is thought to be true or right in all situations.

absolutely ADV 1 completely. 2 independently of anything else. 3 COLLOQ in actual fact; very much.

absolute majority N in an election: a number of votes for a candidate which is greater than the number of votes for all the other candidates put together.

absolution N the formal forgiving of a person's sins, esp by a priest.

absolve VB 1 (usu **absolve sb from** or **of sth**) to release them or pronounce them free from a promise, duty, blame, etc. 2 of a priest: to forgive someone formally for their sins.

absorb VB 1 to take in or suck up (knowledge, etc). 2 SCIENTIFIC to take up or receive (matter or energy, eg water or radiation). 3 to receive or take something in as part of oneself or itself. 4 to engage all of (someone's attention or interest). 5 to reduce or lessen (the shock, force, impact, etc of something). ■ **absorbent** ADJ.

absorption N 1 the act of absorbing, or the process of being absorbed. 2 the state of having all one's interest or attention occupied.

abstain VB, INTR (usu **abstain from sth** or **from doing sth**) 1 to choose not to take, have or do it. 2 to formally record one's intention not to vote in an election.

abstemious ADJ of people, habits, etc: taking food, alcohol, etc in very limited amounts.

abstention N 1 the act of choosing not to do something. 2 an abstaining from voting.

abstinence N the practice or state of choosing not to do or take something, esp to drink alcohol. ■ **abstinent** ADJ.

abstract ADJ 1 referring to something which exists only as an idea or quality. 2 concerned with ideas and theory rather than with things which really exist or could exist. 3 of an art form, esp painting: that represents the subject by shapes and patterns, etc rather than in the shape or form it actually has. 4 GRAM of a noun: denoting a quality, condition or action.

➤ N **1** a summary. **2** an abstract idea, theory, etc. **3** an example of abstract painting, etc.

abstracted ADJ preoccupied; inattentive. ■ **abstractedly** ADV.

abstraction N **1** the act, or an example, of abstracting something. **2** something which exists as a general idea rather than as an actual example. **3** the state of being abstracted.

abstruse ADJ hard to understand.

absurd ADJ **1** not at all suitable or appropriate. **2** ridiculous; silly. ■ **absurdity** N (*-ies*). ■ **absurdly** ADV.

abundance N **1** a large amount. **2** wealth. ■ **abundant** ADJ. ■ **abundantly** ADV.

abuse VB **1** to use (one's position, power, etc) wrongly. **2** to treat someone or something cruelly or wrongly. **3** to speak rudely or insultingly to or about someone.
➤ N **1** wrong use of one's position, power, etc. **2** bad or cruel treatment of someone or something. **3** an evil or corrupt practice. **4** rude or insulting words.

abusive ADJ insulting or rude; using insulting or rude language. ■ **abusively** ADV.

abut VB (*-tt-*) INTR of areas of land, buildings, etc: to join, touch or lean against another.

abysmal ADJ, COLLOQ extremely bad. ■ **abysmally** ADV.

abyss N **1** a very large and deep chasm. **2** anything that seems to be bottomless.

AC ABBREV alternating current.

acacia N a tree or shrub which bears clusters of small yellow flowers.

academia N the scholarly world or life.

academic ADJ **1** to do with learning, study, education or teaching. **2** to do with a university or college. **3** theoretical rather than practical. **4** of no practical importance. **5** of a person: fond of or having an aptitude for intellectual pursuits.
➤ N a member of the teaching or research staff at a university or college.

academy N (*-ies*) **1** a school or college that gives training in a particular subject or skill. **2** a society which encourages the study of science, literature, art or music.

ACAS ABBREV, BRIT Advisory, Conciliation and Arbitration Service.

accede VB, INTR (often **accede to sth**) **1** to take office, esp (as **accede to the throne**) to become king or queen. **2** to agree.

accelerate VB **1** TR & INTR to increase the speed of something. **2** to make something happen sooner. ■ **acceleration** N.

accelerator N **1** ENG, AUTOS a pedal or lever designed to control the speed of an electric motor or engine. **2** PHYS a device used to increase the velocity of atomic particles.

accent N **1** the particular way words are pronounced by people who live in a particular place, belong to a particular social group, etc. **2** emphasis or stress put on a particular syllable in speaking. **3** a mark put over a vowel to show how it is pronounced.
➤ VB to emphasize or stress.

accentuate VB to emphasize or stress. ■ **accentuation** N.

accept VB **1** to agree or be willing to take or receive (something offered). **2** TR & INTR to agree to (a suggestion, proposal, etc). **3** to agree to do (a job, etc) or take on (a responsibility, etc). **4** to believe something to be true or correct. **5** to be willing to listen to and follow (advice, etc). **6** to be willing to suffer or take (blame, etc). **7** to allow someone into a group. **8** to tolerate something.

acceptable ADJ **1** worth accepting; welcome. **2** good enough, but usu only just; tolerable. ■ **acceptability** N. ■ **acceptably** ADV.

acceptance N **1** the act or state of accepting something. **2** favourable reception of something.

access N **1** a means of approaching or entering a place. **2** the right, opportunity or ability to use, approach, meet with or enter something.
➤ VB to locate or retrieve (information, etc).

accessible ADJ **1** able to be reached easily. **2** easy to understand. ■ **accessibility** N.

accession N the act or process of taking up a new office or responsibility.

accessory N (*-ies*) **1** something additional to, but less important than, something else. **2** an item of dress, such as a bag, hat, etc which goes with a dress, coat, etc. **3** LAW someone who helps a criminal do something wrong.

accident N **1** an unexpected event which causes damage or harm. **2** something which happens without planning or intention; chance: **managed it by accident**.

accidental ADJ happening or done by accident; not planned. ■ **accidentally** ADV.

acclaim VB **1** (usu **acclaim sb as sth**) to declare them to be a specified thing, with noisy enthusiasm. **2** to receive or welcome someone or something with noisy enthusiasm. ➢ N acclamation.

acclamation N approval or agreement demonstrated by applause or shouting.

acclimatize or **-ise** VB, TR & INTR to make or become accustomed to a new situation, climate, etc. ■ **acclimatization** N.

accolade N a sign or expression of great praise or approval.

accommodate VB **1** to provide someone with a place in which to stay. **2** to be large enough to hold something. **3** to oblige someone; to do them a favour.

accommodating ADJ helpful; willing to do what another person wants.

accommodation N **1** a room or rooms in a house or hotel in which to live. **2** willingness to accept other people's wishes, etc.

accompaniment N **1** something that happens or exists at the same time as something else, or which comes with something else. **2** music played to accompany a singer or another instrument.

accompanist N someone who plays a musical accompaniment.

accompany VB (*-ies, -ied*) **1** to come or go with someone. **2** to be done or found with something. **3** to play a musical accompaniment for.

accomplice N someone who helps another commit a crime.

accomplish VB to manage to do something.

accomplished ADJ **1** expert or skilled. **2** completed or finished.

accomplishment N **1** a social or other skill developed through practice. **2** something special or remarkable which has been done. **3** the finishing or completing of something.

accord VB, rather FORMAL to give someone (a welcome, etc) or grant them (permission, etc). ➢ N agreement or harmony. ◆ **of one's own accord** willingly.

accordance N agreement or harmony: **in accordance with the law**.

according ADV **1** (usu **according to sb**) as said or told by them. **2** (usu **according to sth**) **a** in agreement with it: **live according to one's principles**; **b** in proportion to it: **Give to each according to his need**.

accordingly ADV **1** in an appropriate way: **act accordingly**. **2** therefore; for that reason.

accordion N a musical instrument with metal reeds blown by bellows, the melody being produced by means of buttons or a keyboard. ■ **accordionist** N.

accost VB to approach someone and speak to them, esp boldly or in a threatening way.

account N **1** a description or report. **2** an explanation, esp of one's behaviour. **3 a** an arrangement by which a bank or building society allows a person to have banking or credit facilities; **b** a deposit of money in a bank or building society. **4** a statement of the money owed to a person or company for goods or services. **5** (usu **accounts**) a record of money received and spent. **6** an arrangement by which a shop allows a person to buy goods on credit and pay for them later. ◆ **account for sth 1** to give a reason or explanation for it. **2** to make or give a reckoning of (money spent, etc).

◆ **by all accounts** according to general opinion.

◆ **on account of sth** because of it.

◆ **take sth into account** or **take account of sth** to make allowances for or consider (another factor) when making a decision.

accountable ADJ responsible; having to explain one's actions. ■ **accountability** N.

accountant N a person whose profession is to prepare, keep or audit the accounts of a business company, etc. ■ **accountancy** N.

accounting N the skill or practice of preparing or keeping the accounts of a company, etc.

accoutrements PL N equipment.

accredit VB to state officially that something is of a satisfactory standard.

accrue VB **1** INTR **a** to come in addition, as a product, result or development; **b** to be added as interest. **2** to collect: *accrued a collection of antique vases.*

◆ **accrue to sb** or **sth** to fall to them or it naturally.

accumulate VB **1** to collect or gather something in an increasing quantity. **2** INTR to grow greater in number or quantity.

accumulation N **1** the activity or process of accumulating. **2** a heap or mass. ■ **accumulative** ADJ.

accumulator N, ELEC ENG a storage battery that can be recharged by passing a current through it from an external direct current supply.

accuracy N (*-ies*) the state of being absolutely correct and making no mistakes.

accurate ADJ **1** absolutely correct; making no mistakes. **2** agreeing exactly with the truth or a standard. ■ **accurately** ADV.

accursed ADJ **1** COLLOQ disliked or hated. **2** having been cursed.

accusation N **1** the act of accusing someone of having done something wrong. **2** LAW a statement charging a person with having

committed a crime. ■ **accusatory** ADJ.

accusative N, GRAM **1** in certain languages: the form or case of a noun, pronoun or adjective when it is the object of an action. **2** a noun, etc in this case.

accuse VB (USU **accuse sb of sth**) to charge them with (an offence).

◆ **the accused** the person or people accused of an offence.

accustom VB (USU **accustom sb** or **oneself to sth**) to make them or oneself familiar with it.

accustomed ADJ usual; customary.

ace N **1** CARDS the card in each of the four suits with a single symbol on it. **2** COLLOQ someone who is extremely good at something. **3** a fighter pilot who has shot down many enemy aircraft. **4** TENNIS a serve that the opposing player cannot hit back.
➤ ADJ, COLLOQ excellent.

acerbic ADJ **1** bitter and sour in taste. **2** bitter and harsh in manner, etc. ■ **acerbity** N.

acetate N **1** a salt or ester of acetic acid. **2** any synthetic fibres made from cellulose acetate.

acetic ADJ consisting of or like vinegar.

acetic acid N a clear colourless pungent liquid present in vinegar.

acetone N, CHEM a colourless flammable volatile liquid.

acetylene N, CHEM a colourless highly flammable gas.

ache VB, INTR **1** to feel a dull continuous pain. **2** to be the source of a dull continuous pain.
➤ N a dull continuous pain.

achieve VB to reach, realize or attain (a goal, ambition, etc), esp through hard work.

achievement N **1** the gaining of something, usu after working hard for it. **2** something that has been done or gained by effort.

Achilles' heel N a person's weak or vulnerable point.

Achilles' tendon N, ANAT the tendon that

connects the muscles in the calf of the leg to the heelbone.

acid N **1** CHEM any of a group of compounds that have a sour or sharp taste, turn blue litmus paper red, and react with bases to form salts. **2** any sour substance. **3** SLANG **LSD**.
➤ ADJ **1** sour to taste. **2** of remarks, etc: expressing bitterness or anger. **3** CHEM containing or having the properties of an acid. ■ **acidic** ADJ. ■ **acidly** ADV.

acidify VB (*-ies, -ied*) TR & INTR to make or become acid.

acidity N (*-ies*) **1** the quality of being acid or sour. **2** CHEM the extent to which a given solution is acid, as indicated by its pH value.

acid rain N, ECOL rain containing dissolved pollutants from the atmosphere.

acknowledge VB **1** to admit or accept the truth of (a fact or situation). **2** to report that one has received (what has been sent). **3** to express thanks for something. **4** to show that one has noticed or recognized someone.

acknowledgement or **acknowledgment** N **1** the act of acknowledging. **2** something done, given or said to acknowledge something.

acme N the highest point of achievement, etc.

acne N, PATHOL a skin disorder caused by overactivity of the sebaceous glands.

acolyte N an assistant or attendant.

acorn N the nut-like fruit of the oak tree, which has a cup-shaped outer case.

acoustic ADJ **1** relating to, producing or operated by sound. **2** relating to the sense of hearing. **3** of a musical instrument, eg a guitar or piano: not using an electrical amplifier. ■ **acoustically** ADV.

acoustics PL N the characteristics of a room, theatre, etc that determine the nature and quality of sounds heard within it.
➤ SING N the scientific study of sound.

acquaint VB now only in phrases.
◆ **acquaint sb with sth** to make them aware of or familiar with it.
◆ **be acquainted with sb** to know them personally but only slightly.
◆ **be acquainted with sth** to be familiar with it.

acquaintance N **1** slight knowledge. **2** someone whom one knows slightly.

acquiesce VB, INTR (USU **acquiesce in** or **to sth**) to accept it or agree to it without objection. ■ **acquiescence** N. ■ **acquiescent** ADJ.

acquire VB to get or develop something, esp through skill or effort. ■ **acquirement** N.

acquisition N **1** something obtained or acquired, esp through hard work or effort. **2** the act of obtaining or developing a skill, etc.

acquisitive ADJ very eager to obtain things.

acquit VB (*-tt-*) (often **acquit sb of sth**) of a court or jury, etc: to declare a person accused of a crime to be innocent. ■ **acquittal** N.

acre N a measure of land area equal to 4840 square yards (4047 square metres).

acreage N the acres in a piece of land.

acrid ADJ **1** having a very bitter and pungent smell or taste. **2** of speech, manner, etc: sharp or bitter. ■ **acridity** N.

acrimony N bitterness in feeling, temper or speech. ■ **acrimonious** ADJ.

acrobat N an entertainer who performs skilful balancing acts and other athletic tricks. ■ **acrobatic** ADJ. ■ **acrobatically** ADV.

acrobatics SING N the art or skill of an acrobat.
➤ PL N acrobatic movements.

acronym N a word made from the first letters or syllables of other words, and usu pronounced as a word, eg NATO.

across PREP **1** to, at or on the other side of something. **2** from one side of something to the other. **3** so as to cross something: **arms folded across the chest**.
➤ ADV **1** to, at or on the other side. **2** from one side to the other.

acrostic N a poem or puzzle in which the first,

last or middle letters in each line, or a combination of these, form a word or proverb.

acrylic N any of various synthetic products derived from acrylic acid.
➤ ADJ relating to, containing or derived from acrylic acid.

acrylic acid N, CHEM a colourless liquid with a pungent odour and acidic properties.

act N 1 a thing done; a deed. 2 the process of doing something: **caught in the act.**
3 behaviour that is not a sincere expression of feeling: **Her shyness is just an act. 4 a** a short piece of entertainment, usu in a variety show; **b** the person or people performing this.
5 a major division of a play, opera, etc.
➤ VB 1 INTR to behave or function in a specified way: **act tough. 2** INTR to do something: **need to act fast. 3** INTR to perform in a play or film.
4 a to perform in a play or film; **b** to perform (a play). **5** to play the part of someone or something: **to act the fool. 6** INTR to show feelings one does not really have.
◆ **act on** or **upon sth** to follow (advice, instructions, etc).

acting N the profession or art of performing in a play or film.
➤ ADJ temporarily doing someone else's job or duties: **the acting headmaster.**

action N 1 the process of doing something: **put ideas into action. 2** something done. **3** activity, force or energy: **a woman of action.**
4 a movement or gesture. **5** the working part of a machine, etc; a mechanism. **6** a battle; fighting: **saw action in Korea. 7** a legal case.
◆ **out of action** not working.

action replay N on television: the repeating of a piece of recorded action, eg the scoring of a goal in football, usu in slow motion.

activate VB to make something start working.

active ADJ 1 of a person, etc: full of energy. 2 of a machine, etc: operating; working. 3 having an effect: **the active ingredients. 4** of a volcano: liable to erupt; not extinct. **5** PHYS radioactive. **6** GRAM **a** denoting or relating to a verbal construction in which the subject

performs the action or has the state described by the verb, as in **the man fell, smoking kills you** and **God exists; b** denoting or relating to the verb in such a construction.

activist N someone who is very active, esp as a member of a political group. ■ **activism** N.

activity N (**-ies**) 1 the state of being active or busy. 2 (often **activities**) something that people do, esp for pleasure, exercise, etc.

actor N a man or woman who performs in plays or films, esp as their profession.

actress N a female actor.

actual ADJ 1 existing as fact; real. 2 not imagined, estimated or guessed. 3 current.

actuality N (**-ies**) fact; reality.

actually ADV 1 really; in fact. 2 usu said in surprise or disagreement: as a matter of fact.

actuary N (**-ies**) someone who calculates insurance risks, and gives advice to insurance companies, etc on what premiums to set.

actuate VB to make (a mechanism, etc) go into action.

acuity N sharpness or acuteness.

acumen N the ability to judge quickly and well; keen insight.

acupuncture N, ALT MED a traditional Chinese method of healing in which symptoms are relieved by the insertion of needles at specified points beneath the skin. ■ **acupuncturist** N.

acute ADJ 1 of the senses: keen, good or sharp; penetrating. 2 of mental powers, etc: quick and very good. 3 of a disease or symptoms: arising suddenly and often severe: **acute pain • acute bronchitis. 4** extremely severe: **acute drought.**
5 MATH of an angle: less than 90°.
➤ N (also **acute accent**) a sign placed above a vowel to indicate a particular pronunciation, as with **é** in French, or, as in Spanish, to indicate stress. ■ **acutely** ADV.

AD ABBREV in dates: **Anno Domini** (Latin), in the year of our Lord, used together with a figure to indicate a number of years after that in which Christ was once thought to have been born.

ad N, COLLOQ an advertisement.

adage N a proverb or maxim.

adagio MUS, ADV slowly.
➤ N a piece of music to be played in this way.

adamant ADJ completely determined; not likely to change one's mind or opinion.

Adam's apple N, ANAT the projection of the thyroid cartilage at the front of the throat.

adapt VB 1 TR & INTR to change something, oneself, etc so as to fit new circumstances, etc; to make something suitable for a new purpose. 2 to alter or modify something. ■ **adaptable** ADJ. ■ **adaptation** N.

adaptor N 1 a device connecting two parts of different sizes. 2 a device that enables a plug and socket with incompatible terminals to be connected, or that connects more than one electrical appliance to a single socket.

add VB 1 (also **add sth together**) to put together or combine (two or more things). 2 (also **add sth up**) **a** to calculate the sum of two or more numbers or quantities in order to obtain their total value; **b** INTR (also **add up**) to carry out the process of addition. 3 to say or write something further.

addendum N (PL -*da*) 1 an addition. 2 an extra piece of text added to the end of a book.

adder N a poisonous snake with a dark zigzag line running down its back.

addict N 1 someone who is dependent on the habitual intake of a drug. 2 COLLOQ someone who is extremely fond of a hobby, etc: a chess addict. ■ **addictive** ADJ.

addicted ADJ 1 (esp **addicted to sth**) dependent on it (esp a drug). 2 unable to give it up, eg a habit. ■ **addiction** N.

addition N 1 the act of adding. 2 someone or something that is added. 3 MATH the combination of two or more numbers in such a way as to obtain their sum.
◆ **in addition (to)** as well (as); besides.
■ **additional** ADJ. ■ **additionally** ADV.

additive N any chemical substance that is deliberately added to another substance, usu in small quantities, for a specific purpose.

addle VB 1 to confuse or muddle. 2 INTR of an egg: to go bad. ■ **addled** ADJ.

address N 1 the number or name of the house or building, and the name of the street and town, where a person lives or works. 2 rather FORMAL a speech or lecture.
➤ VB 1 to put the name and address on (an envelope, etc). 2 to make a speech, give a lecture, etc to (a group of people). 3 to speak to someone. 4 to give one's attention to (a problem, etc).

addressee N the person to whom a letter, etc is addressed.

adduce VB to mention (a fact) as a supporting reason, piece of evidence, etc.

adenoids PL N, ANAT a pair of lymph glands in the upper part of the throat.

adept ADJ (often **adept at sth**) skilful at it.

adequate ADJ 1 sufficient. 2 only just satisfactory. ■ **adequacy** N. ■ **adequately** ADV.

adhere VB, INTR (often **adhere to sth**) 1 to stick to something. 2 to remain loyal to (a religion, etc). 3 to follow (a plan, rule, etc) exactly.

adherent N a follower; a supporter.
➤ ADJ sticking or adhering. ■ **adherence** N.

adhesion N 1 the process of adhering. 2 the sticking together of two surfaces.

adhesive ADJ sticky; able to make things stick together.
➤ N any substance that is used to bond two surfaces together.

ad hoc ADJ, ADV for one particular purpose, situation, etc only: on an ad hoc basis.

adieu N (*adieus* or *adieux*) a goodbye.
➤ EXCLAM goodbye.

ad infinitum ADV for ever; without limit.

adipose ADJ, TECHNICAL relating to fat.

adjacent ADJ (often **adjacent to sth**) lying beside or next to it. ■ **adjacency** N.

adjective N, GRAM a word that describes or modifies a noun or pronoun, as **dark** describes hair in She has dark hair. ■ **adjectival** ADJ.

adjoin VB to be next to and joined to something. ■ **adjoining** ADJ.

adjourn VB **1** to put off (a meeting, etc) to another time. **2** to finish (a meeting, etc), intending to continue it at another time or place. ■ **adjournment** N.

adjudge VB to declare or judge officially.

adjudicate VB **1** INTR to act as judge in a court, competition, etc. **2** to give a decision on (a disagreement between two parties, etc). ■ **adjudication** N. ■ **adjudicator** N.

adjunct N something attached or added to something else but not an essential part of it.

adjure VB, FORMAL to request, beg or command someone formally. ■ **adjuration** N.

adjust VB **1** to change something or oneself, etc slightly. **2** to change or alter something, esp only slightly, to make it more correct or accurate. **3** INTR (often **adjust to sth**) to change so that one becomes suited to it. ■ **adjustable** ADJ. ■ **adjustment** N.

adjutant N an army officer who does administrative work.

ad-lib VB (-bb-) TR & INTR **1** to say something without preparation. **2** to improvise (music, etc). ➤ ADJ of speeches, etc: improvised. ➤ ADV (**ad lib**) without preparation.

administer VB **1** to manage, govern or direct (one's affairs, an organization, etc). **2** to give out something formally: **administer justice**. **3** to supervise a person taking (an oath). **4** to apply or provide (medicine).

administrate VB, TR & INTR to administer.

administration N **1** the directing, managing or governing of a company's affairs, etc. **2** a period of government by a particular party, etc. **3** the group of people who manage a company's affairs or run the business of government. ■ **administrative** ADJ.

administrator N someone who manages

the affairs of an organization, etc.

admirable ADJ **1** worthy of being admired. **2** very good; excellent. ■ **admirably** ADV.

admiral N **1** a high-ranking officer in the navy. **2** a species of butterfly: **red admiral**.

admire VB to regard with respect or approval. ■ **admiration** N. ■ **admirer** N.

admissible ADJ that can be allowed or accepted, esp as proof in a court of law.

admission N **1** the act of allowing someone or something in or of being allowed in. **2** the cost of entry. **3 a** an act of admitting the truth of something; **b** something admitted.

admit VB (-tt-) **1** TR & INTR to confess the truth of something. **2** (also **admit to sth**) to agree that one is responsible for (a deed or action). **3** to allow someone to enter. **4** (also **admit sb to sth**) to allow them to take part in it; to accept them as a member or patient of it.

admittance N **1** the right to enter; permission to enter. **2** the act of entering; entry.

admittedly ADV as is known to be true; as one must admit.

admonish VB to scold someone firmly but mildly. ■ **admonition** N. ■ **admonitory** ADJ.

ad nauseam ADV **1** to a disgusting or objectionable extent. **2** excessively.

ado N difficulty or trouble. ◆ **without more** or **further ado** without any more delay.

adolescent ADJ **1** of a young person: between puberty and adulthood. **2** relating to or typical of this state. ➤ N a young person between puberty and adulthood. ■ **adolescence** N.

adopt VB **1** TR & INTR to take (a child of other parents) into one's own family, becoming its legal parent. **2** to take up (a habit, position, policy, etc). **3** to take (an idea, etc) over from someone else. ■ **adoption** N.

adoptive ADJ that adopts or is adopted.

adorable ADJ, COLLOQ charming and attractive.

adore VB 1 to love someone deeply. 2 COLLOQ to like something very much. 3 to worship (a god). ■ **adoration** N.

adorn VB 1 to decorate. 2 to add beauty to something. ■ **adornment** N.

adrenal gland N, ZOOL, ANAT either of two glands, situated above the kidneys, that secrete adrenalin.

adrenalin or **adrenaline** N, BIOL a hormone secreted by the adrenal glands which increases heartbeat and blood pressure.

adrift ADJ, ADV 1 of a boat: not tied up. 2 without help or guidance. 3 COLLOQ off course.

adroit ADJ quick and clever in action or thought.

adulation N excessive praise or flattery.

adult ADJ 1 fully grown; mature. 2 typical of, or suitable for, a fully grown person.
➢ N a fully grown person, animal, bird or plant.
■ **adulthood** N.

adulterate VB to debase something by mixing it with something inferior or harmful.
■ **adulteration** N.

adultery N sexual relations between a married person and a person who is not their spouse. ■ **adulterous** ADJ.

advance VB 1 TR & INTR to put or move forward. 2 INTR to make progress. 3 to help the progress of something. 4 to suggest (an idea, etc).
➢ N 1 progress. 2 a payment made before it is due. 3 money lent to someone. 4 (esp **advances**) a friendly or sexual approach.
➢ ADJ done, made or given beforehand.
◆ **in advance** ahead in time, place or development.

advanced ADJ 1 having progressed or developed well or far. 2 new or revolutionary.

Advanced level see **A level**

Advanced Supplementary level see **AS level**

advantage N 1 a favourable circumstance; benefit. 2 a circumstance that may help one to succeed, win, etc. 3 superiority over another.
➢ VB to benefit someone or improve their position. ■ **advantageous** ADJ.
◆ **take advantage of sb** or **sth** to make use of a situation, a person's good nature, etc in such a way as to benefit oneself.
◆ **to advantage** in such a way as to emphasize the good qualities: **shows off her figure to advantage**.

advent N 1 coming or arrival; first appearance. 2 (**Advent**) CHRISTIANITY the period which includes the four Sundays before Christmas.

adventitious ADJ happening by chance.

adventure N 1 an exciting and often dangerous experience. 2 the excitement of risk or danger: **a sense of adventure**.

adventurer and **adventuress** N 1 a man or woman who is willing to use unscrupulous means to make money, obtain power, etc. 2 a man or woman who is eager for adventure.

adventurous ADJ enterprising; daring.

adverb N, GRAM a word which describes or adds to the meaning of a verb, adjective or another adverb, such as **very** and **quietly** in talking very quietly. ■ **adverbial** ADJ.

adversary N (-*ies*) 1 an opponent in a competition, etc. 2 an enemy.

adverse ADJ 1 unfavourable to one's interests. 2 disapproving. 3 hurtful. ■ **adversely** ADV.

adversity N (-*ies*) 1 circumstances that cause trouble or sorrow. 2 a misfortune.

advert N, COLLOQ an advertisement.

advertise VB 1 to draw attention to or describe (goods for sale, services offered, etc) to encourage people to buy or use them. 2 (usu **advertise for sth** or **sb**) to ask for or seek it or them by putting a notice in a newspaper, etc.

advertisement N 1 a public notice, etc, which advertises something. 2 a short television film advertising something.

advice N suggestions or opinions given to someone about what they should do in a particular situation.

advisable ADJ of action to be taken, etc: to be recommended; sensible. ■ **advisability** N.

advise VB **1** to give advice to someone. **2** to recommend something. **3** (usu **advise sb of sth**) to inform them about it. ■ **adviser** or **advisor** N.

advisedly ADV after careful thought.

advisory ADJ appointed to give advice.

advocacy N (**-ies**) recommendation or active support of an idea, etc.

advocate N **1** esp in Scotland: a lawyer who speaks for the defence or prosecution in a trial. **2** someone who supports or recommends an idea, proposal, etc.
➢ VB to recommend or support (an idea, proposal, etc), esp in public.

adze or (US) **adz** N a tool with a blade at right angles to its handle, used for shaping wood.

aegis N protection or patronage.

aeon see **eon**

aerate VB to charge (a liquid) with carbon dioxide or some other gas. ■ **aeration** N.

aerial N a wire, rod or other device, esp on a radio or television receiver, used to receive or transmit signals.
➢ ADJ **1** relating to or found in the air. **2** like air.

aerobatics PL N spectacular or dangerous manoeuvres in an aircraft or glider.

aerobics SING N a system of physical exercise aimed at increasing the supply of oxygen in the blood and strengthening the heart and lungs.

aerodrome N, BRIT a small airport.

aerodynamics SING N the study of the movement of air relative to moving objects.
➢ PL N the qualities required for fast and efficient movement through the air.
■ **aerodynamic** ADJ.

aeronautics SING N the scientific study of travel through the Earth's atmosphere.

aeroplane N a powered machine used for travelling in the air, that is heavier than air and supported in its flight by fixed wings.

aerosol N a can containing a product with a propellant, that can be released in a fine spray.

aerospace N the Earth's atmosphere and the space beyond it.

aesthete or (US) **esthete** N someone who has a special appreciation of art and beauty.

aesthetic or (US) **esthetic** ADJ **1** able to appreciate beauty. **2** artistic; tasteful.
■ **aesthetically** ADV.

aesthetics SING N **1** the branch of philosophy concerned with the study of the principles of beauty, esp in art. **2** the principles of good taste and the appreciation of beauty.

afar ADV at a distance.

affable ADJ pleasant and friendly in manner.
■ **affability** N. ■ **affably** ADV.

affair N **1** a concern, matter or thing to be done. **2** an event or connected series of events. **3** a sexual relationship between two people, usu when at least one of them is married to someone else. **4** (**affairs**) matters of importance and public interest: **current affairs**. **5** (**affairs**) private or public business matters.

affect[1] VB **1** to have an effect on someone or something. **2** to cause someone to feel strong emotions, esp sadness or pity. **3** of diseases: to attack or infect. ■ **affecting** ADJ.

affect[2] VB **1** to pretend to feel or have (eg an illness or emotion). **2** to use, wear, etc something in a way that is intended to attract attention.

affectation N unnatural behaviour or pretence which is intended to impress people.

affected ADJ **1** not genuine; pretended. **2** put on to impress people.

affection N **1** a feeling of love or strong liking. **2** (**affections**) feelings.

affectionate ADJ showing love or fondness.

affidavit N, LAW a written statement for use as evidence in a court of law.

affiliate VB, TR & INTR (usu **be affiliated with** or **to sth**) to connect or associate a person or organization with a group or a larger organization.
➢ N a person or organization, etc that has an

association with a group or larger body.
■ **affiliation** N.

affinity N (*-ies*) **1** a strong natural liking for or feeling of attraction or closeness towards someone or something. **2** (usu **affinity with sb**) relationship to them, esp by marriage. **3** similarity in appearance, structure, etc, esp one that suggests relatedness.

affirm VB **1** to state something as a fact. **2** to uphold or confirm (an idea, belief, etc).
■ **affirmation** N.

affirmative ADJ expressing agreement; giving the answer 'yes'.
➤ N an affirmative word or phrase.

affix VB to attach or fasten.

afflict VB to cause someone suffering.

affliction N **1** suffering. **2** a cause of this.

affluent ADJ having more than enough money; rich. ■ **affluence** N.

afford VB **1** (USED WITH **can, could, be able to**) **a** to have enough money, time, etc to spend on something; **b** to be able to do something, or allow it to happen, without risk. **2** to give; to provide: **a room affording a view of the sea.**

affray N a fight in a public place.

affront N an insult, esp one delivered in public.
➤ VB **1** to insult someone, esp in public. **2** to offend the pride of someone.

Afghan N **1** a citizen or inhabitant of, or person born in, Afghanistan. **2** (also **Afghan hound**) a type of tall thin dog with long silky hair.

aficionado N an enthusiast for a particular sport or pastime.

afield ADV to or at a distance.

aflame ADJ **1** in flames; burning. **2** very excited.

afloat ADJ, ADV **1** floating. **2** at sea; aboard ship. **3** out of debt; financially secure.

afoot ADJ, ADV being prepared or already in progress or operation: **There is trouble afoot.**

aforethought ADJ premeditated.

afraid ADJ **1** (often **afraid of sb** or **sth**) frightened of them or it. **2** (usu **afraid to do sth**) reluctant to do it out of fear or concern for the consequences. **3** as a polite formula of regret: sorry: **I'm afraid we're going to be late.**

afresh ADV again, esp from the start.

African-American N an American whose ancestors orig came from Africa.
➤ ADJ of African-Americans.

Afrikaans N one of the official languages of S Africa, developed from Dutch.

Afrikaner N a white inhabitant of S Africa, esp one of Dutch descent.

Afro- COMB FORM, SIGNIFYING African.

Afro-American same as **African-American**

Afro-Caribbean N a person living in the Caribbean whose ancestors orig came from Africa.
➤ ADJ of Afro-Caribbeans.

aft ADV, ADJ, chiefly NAUT at or towards the rear.

after PREP **1** coming later in time than something. **2** following someone or something in position. **3** next to and following something in importance, order, etc. **4** because of something; considering: **You can't expect to be promoted after that mistake. 5** in spite of something: **He's still no better after all that medicine. 6** about someone or something: **ask after her. 7** in pursuit of someone or something: **run after him. 8** of a painting or other work of art: in the style or manner of (someone else). **9** with a name derived from that of (someone else): **called her Mary after her aunt.**
➤ ADV **1** later in time. **2** behind in place.
➤ CONJ after the time when.
➤ ADJ later: **in after years.**
◆ **after all 1** in spite of all that has happened or has been said or done. **2** contrary to what is or was expected.

afterbirth N, ZOOL, MED the placenta, blood and ruptured membranes expelled from the uterus after the birth of a mammal.

after-effect N a circumstance or event that follows as the result of something.

afterlife N the continued existence of one's spirit or soul after one's death.

aftermath N circumstances that follow and are a result of something.

afternoon N the period of the day between noon and the evening.

afters SING N, BRIT COLLOQ dessert; pudding.

aftershave N a perfumed lotion for a man to put on his face after shaving.

aftertaste N the taste in the mouth after one has eaten or drunk something.

afterthought N an idea thought of after the main plan, etc has been formed.

afterwards and (esp US) **afterward** ADV later.

again ADV 1 once more; another time. 2 back to (a previous condition or situation, etc): **get well again. 3** in addition: **twice as much again. 4** however; on the other hand: **He might come, but then again he might not. 5** further; besides.

against PREP 1 close to or leaning on something. 2 into collision with something or someone. 3 in opposition to something. 4 in contrast to something: **against a dark background. 5** with a bad or unfavourable effect on someone or something: **His age counts against him. 6** as a protection from someone or something.

agape ADJ 1 of the mouth: gaping; open wide. 2 of a person: very surprised.

agate N, MINERALOGY a variety of chalcedony consisting of concentrically arranged bands of two or more colours.

age N 1 the period of time during which a person, animal or thing has lived or existed. 2 a stage in life: **old age. 3** the fact or time of being old. 4 in the Earth's history: an interval of time during which specific life forms, physical conditions, geological events, etc were dominant: **the Ice Age. 5** (usu **ages**) COLLOQ a very long time.
➤ VB (*ageing* or *aging*) INTR 1 to show signs of growing old. 2 to grow old. 3 to mature.
◆ **come of age** to become legally old enough to have an adult's rights and duties.

aged ADJ 1 having a specified age. 2 very old. 3 (**the aged**) old people as a group.

ageism N the practice of treating people differently, and usu unfairly, on the grounds of age only. ■ **ageist** N, ADJ.

ageless ADJ never growing old or fading.

agency N (*-ies*) 1 an office or business that provides a particular service. 2 an active part played by someone or something in bringing something about.

agenda SING N 1 a list of things to be done or discussed. 2 a written list of subjects to be dealt with at a meeting, etc.

agent N 1 **a** someone who represents an organization and acts on its behalf; **b** someone who deals with someone else's business matters, etc. 2 (also **secret agent**) a spy. 3 a substance that produces a particular effect. 4 someone who is the cause of something.

agent provocateur N (*agents provocateurs*) someone employed to lead others in illegal acts for which they will be punished.

agglomerate VB, TR & INTR to make into or become a mass. ■ **agglomeration** N.

aggrandize or **-ise** VB to make someone or something seem greater than they really are. ■ **aggrandizement** N.

aggravate VB to make (a bad situation, an illness, etc) worse. ■ **aggravation** N.

aggregate N 1 a collection of separate units brought together; a total. 2 CIVIL ENG, BUILDING any material, esp sand, gravel or crushed stone, that is mixed with cement to form concrete.
➤ ADJ formed of separate units combined.
➤ VB, TR & INTR to combine or be combined into a single unit or whole. ■ **aggregation** N.

aggression N 1 the act of attacking another person or country without being provoked. 2 an instance of hostile behaviour towards someone. 3 the tendency to make unprovoked attacks. 4 hostile feelings or behaviour.

aggressive ADJ **1** always ready to attack; hostile. **2** strong and determined.

aggrieved ADJ angry, hurt or upset.

aghast ADJ filled with fear or horror.

agile ADJ able to move, change direction, etc quickly and easily; nimble. ■ **agility** N.

agitate VB **1** to excite or trouble (a person, their feelings, etc). **2** INTR to stir up public opinion for or against an issue. **3** to stir or shake (a liquid) vigorously. ■ **agitation** N. ■ **agitator** N.

aglow ADJ shining with colour or warmth.

AGM ABBREV annual general meeting.

agnostic N someone who believes that nothing can be known about God. ➤ ADJ relating to this view. ■ **agnosticism** N.

ago ADV in the past; earlier.

agog ADJ very interested; eager to know more.

agonize or **-ise** VB, INTR (esp **agonize about** or **over sth**) to worry intensely or suffer great anxiety about it. ■ **agonized** ADJ.

agony N (**-ies**) severe bodily or mental pain.

agoraphobia N, PSYCHOL an irrational fear of open or public places. ■ **agoraphobic** ADJ, N.

agrarian ADJ relating to land or agriculture.

agree VB (**agreed, agreeing**) USU INTR **1** (often **agree with sb** or **sth** or **about sth**) to be of the same opinion as them about it. **2** (usu **agree to sth**) to say yes to (a suggestion, request or instruction). **3** (usu **agree on** or **upon sth**) to reach a joint decision about it. **4** to reach agreement about something.

agreeable ADJ **1** of things: pleasant. **2** of people: friendly. **3** (usu **agreeable to sth**) of people: willing to accept (a suggestion, etc). ■ **agreeably** ADV.

agreement N **1** a contract or promise. **2** a joint decision. **3** the state of agreeing.

agriculture N the cultivation of the land in order to grow crops or raise animal livestock. ■ **agricultural** ADJ. ■ **agriculturalist** N.

aground ADJ, ADV of ships: stuck on the bottom of the sea or rocks, usu in shallow water.

ague N **1** a fit of shivering. **2** malaria.

AH ABBREV used in the Islamic dating system: anno Hegirae (Latin), in the year of the Hegira, ie counting from AD 622.

ahead ADV **1** at or in the front; forwards. **2** earlier in time; before: **arrived ahead of me**. **3** in the lead; advanced: **ahead on points**.

ahem EXCLAM a sound made in the back of the throat, used to gain people's attention.

ahoy EXCLAM, NAUT a shout to greet or attract the attention of another ship.

aid N **1** help. **2** help or support in the form of money, supplies or services. **3** (often IN COMPOUNDS) a person or thing that helps do something: **a hearing-aid**. ➤ VB to help or support someone. ◆ **aid and abet** LAW to help and encourage someone to disobey the law.

aide N a confidential assistant or adviser.

aide-de-camp N (**aides-de-camp**) an officer in the armed forces who acts as assistant to a senior officer.

AIDS or **Aids** ABBREV acquired immune deficiency (or immunodeficiency) syndrome, a disease which destroys the immune system.

ail VB **1** INTR to be ill and weak. **2** OLD USE to cause pain or trouble to someone.

aileron N, AERONAUTICS one of a pair of hinged flaps at the rear edge of each wing of an aircraft, used to control roll.

ailing ADJ ill; in poor health.

ailment N an illness, esp a minor one.

aim VB **1** TR & INTR (USU **aim at** or **for sb** or **sth**) to point or direct a weapon, remark, etc at them or it. **2** INTR to plan, intend or try. ➤ N **1** what a person, etc intends to do; the achievement aimed at. **2** the ability to hit what is aimed at: **good aim**. ◆ **take aim** to point a weapon at a target.

aimless ADJ without any purpose. ■ **aimlessly** ADV.

ain't CONTRACTION, COLLOQ **1** am not; is not; are not. **2** has not; have not.

air N **1** the invisible odourless tasteless mixture of gases that forms the atmosphere surrounding the Earth, consisting mainly of nitrogen and oxygen. **2** the space above and around the Earth, where birds and aircraft fly. **3** moving air; a light breeze. **4** an appearance, look or manner: a nonchalant air. **5** (**airs**) behaviour intended to impress others, to show off, etc: put on airs. **6** a tune. **7** IN COMPOUNDS **a** relating to air or the air; **b** relating to aircraft.
➤ VB **1** TR & INTR to hang (laundry) in a warm dry place to make it completely dry or to remove unpleasant smells. **2** TR & INTR to let fresh air into (a room, etc). **3** to make (one's thoughts, opinions, etc) known publicly.

air bag N in a vehicle: a safety device consisting of a bag that inflates automatically in a collision to protect the occupants.

airborne ADJ **1** of aircraft, etc: flying in the air. **2** transported by air.

air brick N a brick with small holes, put into the side of a building to allow ventilation.

airbrush N a device for painting which uses compressed air to form a spray.

air-conditioning N any system that is used to control the temperature, relative humidity or purity of air, and to circulate it in an enclosed space such as a room, building or motor vehicle. ■ **air-conditioned** ADJ.

aircraft SING OR PL N any machine that is designed for travelling through air, eg an aeroplane or helicopter.

aircraft carrier N a large naval warship with a flat deck which aircraft can use.

airfield N an open expanse that is used by aircraft for landing and take-off.

air force N that part of a country's defence forces which uses aircraft for fighting.

airgun N a gun that uses air under pressure to fire small pellets.

air hostess N, BRIT a female flight attendant.

airless ADJ **1** of the weather: unpleasantly warm, with no wind. **2** of a room: stuffy.

airlift N the transporting of large numbers of people or large amounts of goods in aircraft when other routes are blocked.
➤ VB to transport (people, etc) in this way.

airline N a company or organization which provides a regular transport service for passengers or cargo by aircraft.

airliner N a large passenger aircraft.

airlock N **1** a bubble of air or gas that obstructs or blocks the flow of liquid through a pipe. **2** an airtight chamber with two entrances, on either side of which are different air pressures, eg between a space vehicle and outer space.

airmail N **1** the system of carrying mail by air. **2** mail carried by air.

airman and **airwoman** N a member of the crew of an aeroplane, esp in an air force.

airplane N, N AMER an aeroplane.

airport N a place where civil aircraft arrive and depart, with facilities for passengers and cargo, etc.

air raid N an attack by enemy aircraft.

air-rifle N a rifle that is fired by pressured air.

airship N a power-driven aircraft that consists of an envelope containing helium gas, with an engine and a gondola suspended from it.

airspace N the part of the atmosphere above a country, claimed by that country.

airstrip N a strip of ground where aircraft can land and take off but which has no facilities.

airtight ADJ **1** of a container, etc: which air cannot get into, out of, or through. **2** of an opinion, argument, etc: having no weak points.

airtime N on TV or radio: the length of time given to a particular item, programme or topic.

airwaves PL N, INFORMAL the radio waves used for radio and television broadcasting.

airway N in the body: the route by which oxygen reaches the lungs, from the nose or mouth via the windpipe.

airwoman see **airman**

airy ADJ (*-ier, -iest*) **1** with plenty of fresh cool air. **2** unconcerned. ■ **airily** ADV.

aisle N **1** a passage between rows of seats, eg in an aircraft, theatre, etc. **2** the side part of the inside of a church.

ajar ADJ, ADV partly open.

AKA or **aka** ABBREV also known as.

akimbo ADJ, ADV with hands on hips and elbows bent outward.

akin ADJ **1** similar; being of the same kind. **2** related by blood.

alabaster N a type of white stone used for ornaments, etc.

à la carte ADV, ADJ of a meal in a restaurant: with each dish priced and ordered separately.

alacrity N quick and cheerful enthusiasm.

à la mode ADJ, ADV in fashion.

alarm N **1** sudden fear produced by awareness of danger. **2** a noise warning of danger. **3** a bell, etc which sounds to warn of danger or, eg on a clock, to wake a person from sleep. **4** an alarm clock.
➤ VB **1** to frighten. **2** to warn someone of danger. ■ **alarming** ADJ.

alarm clock N a clock that can be set to sound at a particular time, usu to wake someone up.

alarmist N someone who spreads unnecessary alarm.
➤ ADJ causing unnecessary alarm.

alas EXCLAM, OLD OR LITERARY expressing grief or misfortune.

albatross N **1** a large seabird with very long wings. **2** GOLF a score of three under par.

albeit CONJ even if; although.

albino N a person or animal with abnormally white skin and hair and pink irises.

album N **1** a book with blank pages for holding photographs, stamps, etc. **2** a record, CD, etc which contains multiple tracks.

albumen N, ZOOL the white of an egg.

alchemy N the forerunner of modern chemistry, which attempted to convert ordinary metals into gold. ■ **alchemist** N.

alcohol N **1** CHEM any of numerous organic chemical compounds containing one or more hydroxyl groups. **2** ethanol, esp when used as an intoxicant in alcoholic beverages. **3** any drink containing this liquid, such as wine or beer.

alcoholic ADJ **1** relating to or containing alcohol. **2** relating to alcoholism.
➤ N a person suffering from alcoholism.

alcoholism N, PATHOL a condition in which habitual and extensive consumption of alcohol impairs physical and mental health.

alcove N a recess in a wall.

alder N any of various deciduous trees and shrubs with toothed leaves and catkins.

alderman N in England and Wales until 1974: a member of a town, county or borough council elected by fellow councillors.

ale N **1** a light-coloured beer, higher in alcohol content than lager and with a fuller body, flavoured with hops. **2** beer.

aleatory ADJ depending on chance.

alert ADJ **1** thinking and acting quickly. **2** (esp **alert to sth**) aware of (a danger, etc).
➤ N **1** a warning of danger. **2** the period of time covered by such a warning.
➤ VB (usu **alert sb to sth**) to warn them of (a danger); to make them aware of (a fact or circumstance).

A level (in full **Advanced level**) N **1** an examination in a single subject in England, Wales and N Ireland for which students study until about the age of 18. **2** a pass in such an examination. Also as ADJ: A-level pass.

alfalfa N a plant of the pulse family widely cultivated as a forage crop.

alfresco ADV, ADJ in the open air.

algae PL N (SING *alga*) a large and very diverse group of mainly aquatic organisms.

algebra N the branch of mathematics that uses letters and symbols to represent variable quantities and numbers, and to express generalizations about them. ■ **algebraic** ADJ.

algorithm N any procedure involving a series of steps that is used to solve a specific problem, eg to solve a mathematical equation.

alias N a false or assumed name.
➤ ADV also known as: John Smith, alias Mr X.

alibi N 1 a plea of being somewhere else when a crime was committed. 2 COLLOQ an excuse.

Alice band N a wide hair-band.

alien N 1 a foreign-born resident of a country who has not adopted that country's nationality. 2 an inhabitant of another planet.
➤ ADJ 1 foreign. 2 (usu **alien to sb** or **sth**) not in keeping with them or it; unfamiliar.

alienable ADJ, LAW of property: able to be transferred to another owner.

alienate VB 1 to make someone become unfriendly or estranged. 2 to make someone feel unwelcome or isolated. 3 LAW to transfer ownership of (property) to another person. ■ **alienation** N.

alight[1] ADJ 1 on fire. 2 lighted up; excited.

alight[2] VB (*alighted* or *alit*) INTR 1 (often **alight from sth**) to get down from or out of (a vehicle). 2 of a bird, etc: to land.

align VB 1 to put something in a straight line or bring it into line. 2 to bring (someone, a country, etc) into agreement with others, or with a political belief, cause, etc. 3 INTR to come into alignment with someone or something. ■ **alignment** N.

alike ADJ like one another; similar.
➤ ADV in a similar manner.

alimentary ADJ 1 relating to digestion. 2 relating to food, diet or nutrition.

alimentary canal N, ANAT a tubular organ extending from the mouth to the anus, along which food passes, and in which it is digested.

alimony N, LAW money for support paid by a man to his wife or by a woman to her husband,

when they are legally separated or divorced.

alive ADJ 1 living; having life; in existence. 2 lively. 3 (usu **alive to sth**) aware of it. 4 (usu **alive with sth**) full of it.

alkali N, CHEM a hydroxide of any of various metallic elements that dissolves in water to produce an alkaline solution, and neutralizes acids to form salts. ■ **alkaline** ADJ.

all ADJ 1 the whole amount, number or extent of something. 2 the greatest possible: with all speed. 3 any whatever: beyond all doubt.
➤ N 1 every one of the people or things concerned; the whole of something. 2 one's whole strength, resources, etc: give one's all.
➤ ADV 1 entirely; quite. 2 COLLOQ very: go all shy. 3 used in giving the score in various games: on each side: 30 all.
◆ **all along** the whole time.
◆ **all for sth** extremely enthusiastic about it.
◆ **at all** WITH NEGATIVES AND IN QUESTIONS 1 in the least. 2 in any way.
◆ **in all** all together.

allay VB to make (pain, fear, etc) less intense.

all clear N a signal or statement that the threat of danger is over.

allegation N an unsupported claim.

allege VB to claim or declare something to be the case, usu without proof.

alleged ADJ presumed and claimed, but not proved, to be as stated. ■ **allegedly** ADV.

allegiance N commitment and duty to obey and be loyal to a government, sovereign, etc.

allegory N (-*ies*) a story, play, poem, picture, etc in which the characters represent moral or spiritual ideas or messages. ■ **allegorical** ADJ. ■ **allegorize** or **-ise** VB.

allegretto MUS, ADV in a fairly quick and lively manner (less brisk than allegro).
➤ ADJ fairly quick and lively.
➤ N a piece of music to be played in this way.

allegro MUS, ADV in a quick lively manner.
➤ ADJ quick and lively.
➤ N a piece of music to be played in this way.

allergen N, MED any substance that induces an allergic reaction in someone.

allergic ADJ 1 (**allergic to sth**) having an allergy caused by abnormal sensitivity to it. 2 relating to or caused by an allergy: **an allergic reaction**.

allergy N (*-ies*) 1 PATHOL a hypersensitive reaction of the body to certain substances, eg dust or pollen. 2 COLLOQ a dislike.

alleviate VB to make (pain, a problem, suffering, etc) less severe. ■ **alleviation** N.

alley N 1 (also **alleyway**) a narrow passage behind or between buildings. 2 a long narrow channel used for bowling or skittles.

alliance N 1 the state of being allied. 2 an agreement or treaty by which people, countries, etc ally themselves with one another.

allied ADJ 1 a joined by political agreement or treaty; b (**Allied**) belonging or referring to Britain and her allies in World Wars I and II: **Allied troops**. 2 similar; related.

alligator N a large reptile similar to a crocodile but with a broader head.

alliteration N the repetition of the same sound at the beginning of each word or each stressed word in a phrase, as in **sing a song of sixpence**. ■ **alliterate** VB. ■ **alliterative** ADJ.

allocate VB to give, set apart or assign something to someone or for some particular purpose. ■ **allocation** N.

allot VB (*-tt-*) 1 to give (a share of or place in something) to each member of a group. 2 to assign something to a specific purpose.

allotment N 1 BRIT a small piece of land rented by an individual to grow vegetables, etc on. 2 the act of allotting. 3 an amount allotted.

allotrope N, CHEM any of the two or more structural forms in which some elements can exist. ■ **allotropic** ADJ.

all-out ADJ using all one's strength, powers, etc. Also AS ADV (**all out**).

allow VB 1 to permit (someone to do something, something to happen, etc). 2 to assign or

allocate: **allow £10 for food**. 3 to admit or agree to (a point, claim, etc).
◆ **allow for sth** to take it into consideration.

allowance N 1 a fixed sum of money, amount of something, etc given regularly. 2 money given for expenses. 3 something allowed.

alloy N a material consisting of a mixture of two or more metals, or a metal and a non-metal.
➤ VB to mix (one metal with another).

all right or sometimes **alright** ADJ 1 unhurt; safe; feeling fine. 2 just about adequate, satisfactory, etc. 3 (**all-right**) COLLOQ genuine; cool: **an all-right kind of a guy**.
➤ EXCLAM used to signal agreement.
➤ ADV 1 satisfactorily; properly. 2 COLLOQ used to reinforce what has just been said: **It's broken all right**.

all-round ADJ 1 having many different skills: **an all-round player**. 2 including everyone or everything: **an all-round education**.

all-rounder N someone who has a lot of different skills.

allspice N an aromatic spice prepared from the dried unripe berries of a small tropical evergreen tree, used to flavour foods.

allude VB, INTR (USU **allude to sth**) to mention it indirectly or speak about it in passing.

allure N attractiveness, appeal or charm.
➤ VB to attract, charm or fascinate.

allusion N any indirect reference to something else. ■ **allusive** ADJ.

alluvium N (*-via*) fine particles of silt, clay, mud and sand, carried by rivers. ■ **alluvial** ADJ.

ally N (*-ies*) a country, state, etc that has formally agreed to help and support another.
➤ VB (*-ies, -ied*) 1 of a country, state, etc: to join or become joined politically or militarily with another. 2 of an individual or group: to join or become joined with another.

alma mater N the school, college or university that someone used to attend.

almanac N a book, published yearly, with a calendar, information about the phases of the Moon and stars, dates of public holidays, etc.

almighty ADJ **1** having complete power: Almighty God. **2** COLLOQ very great: **an almighty crash**.
➤ N (**the Almighty**) CHRISTIANITY God.

almond N **1** a small tree related to the peach. **2** the nut-like seed from the fruit of this tree.

almost ADV nearly but not quite.

alms PL N, HIST charity donations to the poor.

aloe N **1** a plant with fleshy spiny leaves. **2** (usu **aloes**) the dried juice of the leaves of this plant, formerly used as a purgative drug known as **bitter aloes**.

aloe vera N **1** a species of aloe plant. **2** the juice of the leaves of this plant, used in skin lotions, shampoos, etc.

aloft ADV in the air; overhead.

alone ADJ, ADV **1** by oneself. **2** without anyone else: **The idea was mine alone**. **3** lonely.

along ADV **1** in some direction: **chugging along**. **2** in the company of someone else or with others: **went along with him to the gig**. **3** into a more advanced state: **coming along nicely**.
➤ PREP **1** by the side of something or near something. **2** down the length of or down part of the length of something: **The shops are just along that street**.
◆ **along with sth** or **sb 1** in addition to it or them. **2** in conjunction with it or them.

alongside PREP close to the side of something.
➤ ADV to or at the side.

aloof ADJ unfriendly and distant.

alopecia N, PATHOL baldness.

aloud ADV loud enough to be heard.

alp N **1** a high mountain. **2** in Switzerland: pasture land on a mountainside.

alpaca N a S American mammal, closely related to the llama, reared mainly for its long straight fleece.

alpha N the first letter of the Greek alphabet (A, α).

◆ **alpha and omega** the beginning and the end.

alphabet N a set of letters, characters, symbols, etc, usu arranged in a fixed order that, by convention, are used to represent the spoken form of a language in writing and printing. ■ **alphabetical** ADJ. ■ **alphabetize** or **-ise** VB.

alpine ADJ **1** of alps or high mountains. **2** (**Alpine**) of the Alps.

already ADV **1** before the present time or the time in question: **We've already paid**. **2** so soon or so early: **It's already lunchtime**.

alright ADJ an alternative spelling of **all right**.

Alsatian N a German shepherd dog.

also ADV in addition; as well as; besides.

altar N **1** a table, raised structure, etc where sacrifices are made to a god. **2** CHRISTIANITY the table at the front of a church, consecrated for use during communion.

altarpiece N a religious picture or carving that is placed above and behind an altar.

alter VB, TR & INTR to change; to become, or make something or someone become, different. ■ **alteration** N.

altercate VB, INTR to argue or dispute, esp angrily, heatedly, etc. ■ **altercation** N.

alter ego N **1** someone's second or alternative character. **2** a close and trusted friend.

alternate ADJ **1** of two feelings, states, conditions, etc: arranged or coming one after the other in turn: **alternate layers of pasta and sauce**. **2** every other; one out of two.
➤ VB, TR & INTR of two things: to succeed or make them succeed each other by turns: **they alternate their days off**. ■ **alternately** ADV. ■ **alternation** N.

alternate angles PL N, GEOM a pair of angles that lie on opposite sides and at opposite ends of a line that cuts two other lines.

alternating current N an electric current that reverses its direction of flow at constant regular intervals.

alternative ADJ **1** of two or more possibilities: secondary or different, esp in terms of being less favourable as a choice: **had to make alternative travel plans. 2** of a lifestyle, etc: outside the conventionally accepted ways of doing something.
➤ N **1** the option to choose between two or more things: **We had no alternative but to take the train. 2** something that represents another possible option.
■ **alternatively** ADV.

alternative medicine and **complementary medicine** N the treatment of diseases and disorders using procedures other than those traditionally practised in orthodox medicine.

alternator N, ELEC ENG an electricity generator that produces alternating current.

although CONJ in spite of the fact that; apart from the fact that; though.

altimeter N, AERONAUTICS a device used in aircraft for measuring altitude.

altitude N height, esp above sea level, of a mountain, aircraft, etc.

alto N **1** the lowest female singing voice. **2** the highest male singing voice. **3** someone with either of these types of singing voice.
➤ ADJ of a musical instrument, etc: having a high pitch: **alto sax.**

altogether ADV **1** completely. **2 a** on the whole: **Altogether it was a wonderful holiday; b** taking everything into consideration: **Altogether the holiday cost £500.**

altruism N an unselfish concern for others.
■ **altruist** N. ■ **altruistic** ADJ.

alum N, CHEM aluminium potassium sulphate, a white crystalline compound used in dyeing and tanning, and as a medical astringent.

aluminium or (N AMER) **aluminum** N, CHEM a silvery-white light metallic element that forms strong alloys.

alumnus N (-ni) a former pupil or student of a school, college or university.

always ADV **1** on every occasion.

2 continually; time and time again. **3** whatever happens; if necessary.

alyssum N a bushy plant with white, yellow or purple cross-shaped flowers.

Alzheimer's disease N, PATHOL a disease in which degeneration of the brain cells results in gradual loss of memory, confusion, etc, eventually leading to dementia.

am VB (used with I): the first person singular of the present tense of **be.**

a.m. or **am** ABBREV ante meridiem.

amalgam N **1** a mixture or blend. **2** CHEM an alloy of mercury with one or more other metals.

amalgamate VB **1** TR & INTR to join together to form a single unit, etc. **2** INTR of metals: to form an alloy with mercury. ■ **amalgamation** N.

amaranth N **1** any of various species of plant with spikes of small brightly coloured flowers. **2** POETIC a fabled flower that never fades.

amaryllis N any of various plants, esp a S African species with large pink or white trumpet-shaped scented flowers.

amass VB to gather or collect (money, possessions, etc), esp in great quantity.

amateur N **1** someone who takes part in a sport, pastime, etc as a hobby and without being paid for it. **2** someone who is not very skilled in an activity, etc. **3** AS ADJ **a** unskilled or non-professional; **b** for or done by those who are not professional: **amateur dramatics.**
■ **amateurish** ADJ. ■ **amateurism** N.

amatory ADJ belonging or relating to, or showing, sexual love or desire.

amaze VB to surprise someone greatly.
■ **amazement** N. ■ **amazing** ADJ.

Amazon N **1** a member of a legendary nation of women warriors, eg from Scythia. **2** (usu **amazon**) any tall, well-built, strong woman.

ambassador N **1** a diplomat of the highest rank permanently appointed by a government, head of state, sovereign, etc to act on their behalf or to be their official representative in some foreign country, etc. **2** a representative,

messenger or agent. ■ **ambassadorial** ADJ.
■ **ambassadorship** N.

amber N, GEOL **1** a transparent yellow or reddish fossilized resin, often carved and polished and used to make jewellery. **2** the yellow or reddish–brown colour of this. Also AS ADJ. **3** a traffic light that acts as a cautionary signal between green for 'go' and red for 'stop'.

ambergris N a waxy substance produced in the intestines of sperm whales, and widely used until recently in the perfume industry.

ambidextrous ADJ able to use both hands equally well.

ambience or **ambiance** N the surroundings or atmosphere of a place.

ambiguity N (-*ies*) **1** uncertainty of meaning. **2** a word or statement that can be interpreted in more than one way.

ambiguous ADJ having more than one possible meaning. ■ **ambiguously** ADV.

ambition N **1** a strong desire for success, fame or power. **2** a thing someone wants to do or achieve.

ambitious ADJ **1** having a strong desire for success, etc. **2** enterprising or daring, but requiring hard work: **an ambitious plan**.

ambivalence N, orig PSYCHOL the concurrent adherence to two opposite or conflicting views, feelings, etc about someone or something. ■ **ambivalent** ADJ.

amble VB, INTR **1** to walk without hurrying; to stroll. **2** of a horse, etc: to walk in a smooth, flowing way.
➤ N **1** a leisurely walk. **2** a horse's ambling walk.

ambrosia N **1** GR MYTHOL the food of the gods, believed to give them eternal youth.
2 something with a delicious taste or smell.

ambulance N a specially equipped vehicle for carrying sick or injured people to hospital.

ambulatory ADJ **1** of, relating to or designed for walking. **2** moving from place to place.

ambush N **1** the act of lying in wait to attack

someone by surprise. **2** an attack made in this way.
➤ VB to attack someone in this way.

ameba an alternative US spelling of **amoeba**.

ameliorate VB, TR & INTR to make or become better. ■ **amelioration** N.

amen EXCLAM usu said at the end of a prayer, hymn, etc: so be it.

amenable ADJ (esp **amenable to sth**) ready to accept (someone else's idea, proposal, advice, guidance, etc).

amend VB to correct, improve or make minor changes to (esp a book, document, etc).
◆ **make amends for sth** to make up for or compensate for (some injury, insult, etc).

amendment N **1** an addition or alteration, esp to a motion, official document, etc. **2** an act of correcting or improving something.

amenity N (-*ies*) **1** a valued public facility. **2** anything that makes life more comfortable.

American ADJ **1** of the United States of America. **2** of the American continent.
➤ N a citizen or inhabitant of, or person born in, the United States of America, or the American continent. ■ **Americanize** or **-ise** VB.

American Indian and **Amerindian** ADJ of the indigenous peoples of America.
➤ N a member of an indigenous people of America.

Americanism N a word, phrase, custom, etc that is characteristic of Americans.

amethyst N **1** a pale- to deep–purple transparent or translucent variety of the mineral quartz used as a gemstone. **2** the purple or violet colour of this gemstone.

amiable ADJ friendly, pleasant and good-tempered. ■ **amiability** N. ■ **amiably** ADV.

amicable ADJ **1** friendly. **2** done in a reasonably friendly manner: **an amicable parting**. ■ **amicability** N. ■ **amicably** ADV.

amid and **amidst** PREP in the middle of something; among.

amidships ADV in or near the middle of a ship.

amine N, CHEM any member of a class of organic compounds in which one or more of the hydrogen atoms of ammonia has been replaced by an organic group.

amino acid N any of a group of water-soluble organic compounds that contain an amino ($-NH_2$) group and a carboxyl ($-COOH$) group.

amiss ADJ wrong; out of order.
➤ ADV wrongly.
◆ **take sth amiss** to be upset or offended by it.

amity N friendship; friendliness.

ammeter N, ELEC ENG a device used for measuring electric current in a circuit.

ammonia N, CHEM **1** a colourless pungent gas formed naturally by the bacterial decomposition of proteins, etc. **2** an alkaline solution of ammonia in water, used as a bleach and cleaning agent.

ammonite N the fossilized shell of an extinct marine cephalopod mollusc.

ammunition N **1** bullets, shells, bombs, etc made to be fired from a weapon. **2** anything that can be used against someone in an argument, etc.

amnesia N, PATHOL the loss or impairment of memory. ■ **amnesiac** N.

amnesty N (-*ies*) **1** a general pardon, esp for people convicted or accused of political crimes. **2** a period of time when people can admit to crimes, hand in weapons, etc in the knowledge that they will not be prosecuted.

amniotic fluid N, ZOOL the clear fluid that surrounds and protects the embryo.

amoeba or (N AMER) **ameba** N (-*bae* or -*bas*) ZOOL a microscopic animal that inhabits water or damp soil and has no fixed shape.

amok or **amuck** ADV.
◆ **run amok** or **amuck** to rush about violently and out of control.

among and **amongst** PREP used of more than two things, people, etc: **1** in the middle of them: **among friends**. **2** between them: **divide it among them**. **3** in the group or number of them: **among his best plays**. **4** with one another: **decide among yourselves**.

amoral ADJ having no moral standards or principles. ■ **amorality** N.

amorous ADJ showing, feeling or relating to love, esp sexual love.

amorphous ADJ **1** without definite shape or structure. **2** without any clearly defined or thought-out purpose, identity, etc.

amortize or **-ise** VB to gradually pay off (a debt) by regular payments of money.

amount N a quantity; a total or extent: **a large amount of money**.
➤ VB (always **amount to sth**) to be equal to it or add up to it in size, number, significance, etc.

amour N, OLD USE a love affair.

amp N **1** an ampere. **2** COLLOQ an amplifier.

amperage N the magnitude or strength of an electric current expressed in amperes.

ampere N the SI unit of electric current.

ampersand N the symbol &, meaning 'and'.

amphetamine N, MED a potentially addictive synthetic drug, used illegally as a stimulant.

amphibian N **1** ZOOL a cold-blooded animal, eg frog, toad and newt, which live on land but return to water to lay their eggs. **2** a vehicle that can operate on land and in water.

amphibious ADJ **1** ZOOL of a living organism: capable of living both on land and in water. **2** of vehicles, equipment, etc: designed to be operated or used both on land and on or in water. **3** of a military operation: using troops that have been conveyed across the sea.

amphitheatre N an oval or round building without a roof, with tiers of seats built around a central open area.

amphora N (-*ras* or -*rae*) ARCHAEOL a large narrow-necked Greek or Roman jar with two handles.

ample ADJ **1** more than enough; plenty. **2** abundant. ■ **amply** ADV.

amplifier N an electronic device that strengthens an electrical or radio signal.

amplify VB (*-ies, -ied*) **1** to increase the strength of (an electrical or radio signal). **2** TR & INTR to add details or further explanation to an account, story, etc. ■ **amplification** N.

amplitude N **1** spaciousness, wide range or extent. **2** abundance. **3** PHYS in any quantity that varies in periodic cycles, such as a wave or vibration: the maximum displacement from its mean position.

ampoule or (US) **ampule** N, MED a small sealed container containing one sterile dose of a drug for injection.

amputate VB, SURGERY to remove (all or part of a limb). ■ **amputation** N. ■ **amputee** N.

amuck see **amok**

amulet N a small object or jewel worn to protect the wearer from evil, disease, etc.

amuse VB **1** to make someone laugh. **2** to keep someone entertained and interested. ■ **amusing** ADJ.

amusement N **1** the state of being amused. **2** something that amuses.

an see **a**

an- see **a-²**

anabolic steroid N, BIOCHEM a synthetic hormone that increases muscle strength.

anabolism N, BIOCHEM in the cells of living organisms: the process whereby complex molecules are made from smaller molecules.

anachronism N **1** the attribution of something to a historical period in which it did not exist. **2** a person, thing or attitude that is or appears to be out of date. ■ **anachronistic** ADJ.

anaconda N a non–venomous S American snake of the boa family.

anaemia or (N AMER, esp US) **anemia** N, PATHOL an abnormal reduction in the amount of haemoglobin in the red blood cells.

anaemic ADJ **1** suffering from anaemia. **2** pale or weak. **3** spiritless; lacking in energy.

anaesthesia or (US) **anes-** N a reversible loss of sensation in all or part of the body, usu induced by drugs.

anaesthetic or (US) **anes-** N any agent, esp a drug, capable of producing anaesthesia. ➢ ADJ denoting anaesthesia.

anaesthetist or (US) **anes-** N someone who has been specifically trained in the administration of anaesthetics to patients.

anaesthetize, -ise or (US) **anes-** VB to give an anaesthetic to someone.

anagram N a word, phrase or sentence that is formed by changing the order of the letters of another word, phrase or sentence.

analgesia N, PHYSIOL a reduction in or loss of the ability to feel pain.

analgesic N a drug or other agent that relieves pain. ➢ ADJ having the effect of relieving pain.

analogous ADJ similar or alike in some way.

analogue or (US) **analog** N something regarded in terms of its similarity or parallelism to something else.

analogy N (*-ies*) **1** a similarity in some ways. **2** a way of reasoning which makes it possible to explain one thing or event by comparing it with something else. ■ **analogical** ADJ.

analyse or (US) **analyze** VB **1** to examine the structure or content of something in detail. **2** to resolve or separate something into its component parts. **3** to detect and identify the chemical compounds present in (a mixture).

analysis N (*-ses*) **1** a detailed examination of the structure and content of something. **2** a statement of the results of such an examination.

analyst N someone who is skilled in analysis.

analytic and **analytical** ADJ concerning or involving analysis. ■ **analytically** ADV.

anaphylaxis N, MED a sudden severe hypersensitive reaction to a particular foreign substance or antigen. ■ **anaphylactic** ADJ.

anarchist N **1** someone who believes that governments and laws are unnecessary and should be abolished. **2** someone who tries to overthrow the government by violence. **3** someone who tries to cause disorder. ■ **anarchism** N. ■ **anarchistic** ADJ.

anarchy N **1** confusion and lack of order, esp because of the failure or breakdown of law and government. **2** the absence of law and government. ■ **anarchic** ADJ.

anathema N **1** someone or something that is detested or abhorred. **2** a curse.

anatomy N (**-ies**) **1** the scientific study of the structure of plants and animals. **2** the physical structure of a plant or animal, esp the internal structure. **3** any close examination, analysis or study of something. ■ **anatomical** ADJ. ■ **anatomist** N.

ancestor N **1** someone, usu more distant than a grandparent, from whom a person is descended. **2** a plant or animal that another type of plant or animal has evolved from.

ancestral ADJ belonging to or inherited from one's ancestors: **the ancestral home.**

ancestry N (**-ies**) lineage or family descent.

anchor N **1** a heavy piece of metal attached by a cable to a ship and put overboard to restrict the ship's movement. **2** anything that acts as a weight to secure something else. **3** anything that gives security or stability. ➢ VB **1** to fasten (a ship) using an anchor. **2** to fasten anything securely. **3** INTR to drop an anchor and become moored by it; to be moored by an anchor.

anchorage N a place where a ship may anchor.

anchorite N someone who lives separate from other people, usu for religious reasons.

anchorman N, TV, RADIO the person in the studio who provides the links with outside broadcast reporters, etc.

anchovy N (**-ies**) a small fish related to the herring, with a pungent flavour.

ancient ADJ **1** dating from very long ago. **2** very old. **3** dating from before the end of the Western Roman Empire in AD 476.

ancillary ADJ **1** helping or giving support to something else. **2** being used as an extra.

and CONJ **1 a** used to show addition: **dogs and cats**; **b** used in sums of addition: **two and two make four. 2 a** used to connect an action that follows as a result or reason of a previous one: **fall and bang one's head**; **b** used to connect an action that follows sequentially on from another: **boil the kettle and make the tea. 3** used to show repetition or duration: **She cried and cried. 4** used to show progression: **get bigger and bigger. 5** used to show variety or contrast: **the ins and outs of it. 6** used after some verbs instead of **to**: **come and try.**

andante ADV, ADJ, MUS in a slow, steady manner. ➢ N a piece of music to be played in this way.

andiron N an iron bar, usu one of a pair, for supporting logs and coal in a fireplace.

androgynous ADJ **1** BIOL denoting an animal or plant that shows both male and female characteristics, esp one that possesses both male and female sex organs. **2** showing both male and female traits, eg a woman who resembles a man in appearance.

android N a robot that resembles a human being in form or features.

anecdote N a short entertaining account of an incident. ■ **anecdotal** ADJ.

anemia an alternative N AMER, ESP US spelling of **anaemia.**

anemone N **1** BOT any of several plants of the buttercup family, esp with red, purple, blue or white cup-shaped flowers. **2** ZOOL short form of **sea anemone.**

anesthesia etc an alternative N AMER, ESP US spelling of **anaesthesia** etc.

aneurysm or **aneurism** N, PATHOL a balloon-like swelling in the wall of an artery.

anew ADV **1** again. **2** in a different way.

angel N 1 a messenger or attendant of God. 2 a representation of this in the form of a human being with a halo and wings. 3 COLLOQ a good, helpful, pure or beautiful person. 4 COLLOQ someone who puts money into an enterprise, esp a theatrical production.

angelfish N a S American freshwater fish with elongated pectoral fins.

angelic ADJ of someone's face, expression, behaviour, etc: like that of an angel, esp in being innocent, beautiful, etc. ■ **angelically** ADV.

angelica N a tall plant whose stem and leaf stalks are crystallized in sugar and used as a food flavouring and cake decoration.

angelus N, CHRISTIANITY a Roman Catholic prayer said in the morning, at noon and at sunset.

anger N a feeling of great annoyance. ➤ VB to cause this kind of feeling in someone.

angina N, PATHOL severe pain behind the chest-bone, usu induced by insufficient blood supply to the heart muscle during exertion.

Angle N a member of a N German tribe who settled in N and E England in the 5c.

angle[1] N 1 MATH a measure of the rotation of a line about a point, usu measured in degrees, radians or revolutions. 2 the point where two lines or planes intersect. 3 the extent to which one line slopes away from another. 4 a corner. 5 a point of view. ➤ VB 1 TR & INTR to move in or place at an angle. 2 to present a news story, information, etc from a particular point of view.

angle[2] VB to use a rod and line for catching fish. ■ **angler** N. ■ **angling** N.

Anglican ADJ relating to the Church of England or another Church in communion with it. ➤ N a member of an Anglican Church. ■ **Anglicanism** N.

Anglicism N 1 a specifically English word, phrase or idiom. 2 a custom or characteristic that is peculiar to the English.

Anglo- COMB FORM, DENOTING 1 English: Anglophobic. 2 British: Anglo-American.

Anglo-Norman N 1 a blending of Norman French and English, used in England after the Norman conquest. 2 someone of Norman descent who settled in England, Scotland or Wales after 1066. Also AS ADJ.

anglophile or **Anglophile** N someone who admires England and the English.

anglophobe or **Anglophobe** N someone who hates or fears England and the English. ■ **anglophobia** N.

anglophone or **Anglophone** N someone who speaks English.

Anglo-Saxon N 1 a member of any of the Germanic tribes who settled in England in the 5c. 2 the English language before about 1150. Also called **Old English**. 3 English thought of in terms of its plain, usu monosyllabic, words including taboo ones. 4 any English-speaking White person, usu of Germanic descent. ➤ ADJ 1 a of the Germanic peoples who settled in England; b of the early form of the English language. 2 of any English speech or writing: blunt and to the point. 3 of the shared cultural, legal, political, etc aspects of British and American life: **Anglo-Saxon values**.

angora N the wool or cloth made from the soft silky wool of the Angora goat or rabbit. ➤ ADJ denoting a breed of domestic goat, rabbit or domestic cat with long white silky hair.

angry ADJ (**-ier, -iest**) 1 feeling or showing annoyance, resentment, wrath, disapproval, etc. 2 irritable, cross, etc: **an angry expression**. 3 of a wound, rash, etc: red and sore. 4 dark and stormy: **an angry sea**. ■ **angrily** ADV.

angst N a feeling of apprehension or anxiety.

anguish N severe mental distress or torture.

angular ADJ 1 of someone or part of someone's body, etc: thin and bony. 2 having sharp edges or corners. 3 measured by an angle: **angular distance**. ■ **angularity** N.

anhydrous ADJ containing no water.

aniline N a colourless oily highly toxic liquid organic compound, used in the manufacture of rubber, plastics, drugs and dyes.

animal N 1 a ZOOL any member of the kingdom of organisms that are capable of voluntary movement, have specialized sense organs that allow rapid response to stimuli; **b** any of these excluding human beings. **2** someone who behaves in a rough uncivilized way.
➢ ADJ **1** belonging or relating to, from or like, an animal: **animal fat**. **2** relating to physical desires; brutal; sensual: **animal passions**.

animality N **1** someone's animal nature or behaviour. **2** the state of being an animal.

animate VB **1** to give life to someone or something. **2** to make something lively. **3** to record (drawings) on film in such a way as to make the images seem to move.
➢ ADJ alive.

animated ADJ **1** lively; spirited: **an animated discussion**. **2** living. **3** moving as if alive: **animated cartoons**. ■ **animatedly** ADV.

animation N **1** liveliness; vivacity. **2 a** the techniques used to record still drawings on film in such a way as to make the images seem to move; **b** any sequence of these images.

animator N someone who makes animated films or cartoons.

animism N the belief that plants and natural phenomena such as rivers, mountains, etc have souls. ■ **animist** N. ■ **animistic** ADJ.

animosity N (-ies) a strong dislike or hatred.

animus N a feeling of strong dislike or hatred.

anion N, CHEM any negatively charged ion.
■ **anionic** ADJ.

anise N an annual plant with aromatic fruits containing liquorice-flavoured seeds.

aniseed N the liquorice-flavoured seeds of the anise plant, used as a food flavouring.

ankh N the ancient Egyptian symbol of life in the form of a T-shaped cross with a loop above the horizontal bar.

ankle N **1** the joint that connects the leg and the foot. **2** the part of the leg just above the foot.

anklet N a chain or ring worn around the ankle.

annals PL N **1 a** yearly historical records of events; **b** recorded history in general. **2** regular reports of the work of an organization.
■ **annalist** N.

anneal VB, ENG to heat (a material such as metal or glass) and then slowly cool it in order to make it softer, less brittle and easier to work.

annex VB **1** to take possession of land or territory, esp by conquest or occupation. **2** to add or attach something to something larger.
■ **annexation** N.

annexe N **1** an additional room, building, area, etc. **2** anything that has been added to something else, esp an extra clause, appendix, etc in a document.

annihilate VB **1** to destroy something completely. **2** to defeat, crush or humiliate someone. ■ **annihilation** N.

anniversary N (-ies) **1** a date on which some event took place in a previous year. **2** the celebration of this event on the same date.

Anno Domini or **anno Domini** see **AD**.

annotate VB to add notes and explanations to (a book, article, etc). ■ **annotation** N.

announce VB **1** to make something known publicly. **2** to make (an arrival, esp of a guest or some form of transport) known. **3** to declare in advance. **4** to be a sign of something.
■ **announcement** N.

announcer N someone who introduces programmes or reads the news on radio or TV.

annoy VB **1** to anger or distress. **2** to harass or pester. ■ **annoyance** N. ■ **annoying** ADJ.

annual ADJ **1** done or happening once a year or every year. **2** lasting for a year.
➢ N **1** BOT a plant that germinates, flowers, produces seed, and dies within a period of one year. **2** a book published every year.
■ **annually** ADV.

annuity N (-ies) **1** a yearly grant or allowance. **2** money that has been invested to provide a fixed amount of interest every year.

annul VB (-ll-) to declare publicly that a

marriage, legal contract, etc is no longer valid. ■ **annulment** N.

annular ADJ ring-shaped.

anode N in an electrolytic cell: the positive electrode.

anodize or **-ise** VB to coat (an object made of metal, esp aluminium) with a thin protective oxide film by making it the anode in a cell.

anodyne N 1 a medicine or drug that relieves or alleviates pain. 2 anything that has a palliative effect.
➤ ADJ able to relieve pain or distress.

anoint VB to put oil or ointment on (someone's head, feet, etc), usu as part of a religious ceremony, eg baptism. ■ **anointment** N.

anomalous ADJ different from the usual; irregular; peculiar.

anomaly N (*-ies*) 1 something that is unusual or different from what is expected. 2 divergence from what is usual or expected.

anon¹ ABBREV anonymous.

anon² ADV, OLD USE some time soon.

anonymous ADJ 1 having no name. 2 from or by someone whose name is not known or not given. 3 without character; nondescript. ■ **anonymity** N.

anorak N a hooded waterproof jacket.

anorexia N 1 loss of appetite. 2 the common name for **anorexia nervosa**.

anorexia nervosa N a psychological disorder characterized by a refusal to eat because of an obsessive desire to lose weight. ■ **anorexic** N, ADJ.

another ADJ, PRONOUN 1 one more. 2 one of a different kind: **let me try another.**

answer N 1 something said or done in response to a question, request, letter, particular situation, etc. 2 (**the answer**) **a** the solution: **the answer to all our problems; b** the solution to a mathematical problem.
➤ VB 1 TR & INTR to make a spoken or written reply to something or someone. 2 to react or respond to something (esp a doorbell, the telephone, etc). 3 to solve (esp a maths problem), write in response to (an exam question), etc. 4 to put up a defence to or offer an explanation for something.

answerable ADJ (usu **answerable to sb for sth**) accountable to them for it.

ant N a small often wingless social insect.

antacid N, MED an alkaline substance that neutralizes acidity in the stomach.

antagonism N openly expressed hostility.

antagonist N an opponent or enemy. ■ **antagonistic** ADJ.

antagonize or **-ise** VB 1 to make someone feel anger or hostility. 2 to irritate.

Antarctic N (**the Antarctic**) the area round the South Pole.
➤ ADJ of this area.

ante N 1 a stake put up by a player before receiving any cards. 2 an advance payment.

ante- PFX before in place or time: **anteroom** • **antenatal.**

anteater N a mammal that has a long snout and a bushy tail.

antecedent N 1 an event or circumstance which precedes another. 2 (usu **antecedents**) **a** someone's past history; **b** someone's ancestry.
➤ ADJ going before in time.

antechamber N an anteroom.

antedate VB 1 to belong to an earlier period than (some other date). 2 to put a date (on a document, letter, etc) that is earlier than the actual date.

antediluvian ADJ 1 belonging to the time before the flood as described in the Bible. 2 FACETIOUS very old or old-fashioned.

antelope N (*antelope* or *antelopes*) any of various species of hoofed mammal, usu with paired horns, found mainly in Africa.

ante meridiem ADJ indicating the time from midnight to midday.

antenatal ADJ 1 before birth. 2 during pregnancy.

antenna N 1 (-*nae*) in esp insects and crustaceans: one of a pair of long slender jointed structures on the head which act as feelers. 2 (*antennas*) an aerial.

anterior ADJ 1 earlier in time. 2 at the front.

anteroom N a small room which opens into another, more important, room.

anthem N 1 a song of praise or celebration, esp a national anthem. 2 a piece of music for a church choir, usu set to a Biblical text.

anther N the structure at the tip of the stamen which contains the pollen sacs.

anthology N (-*ies*) a collection of poems, usu by different authors but with some kind of thematic link. ■ **anthologist** N.

anthracite N a hard shiny black coal that generates much heat but little or no smoke.

anthrax N, PATHOL an acute infectious disease, mainly affecting sheep and cattle, which can be transmitted to humans.

anthropoid ADJ like a human being in form. ➢ N (also **anthropoid ape**) any of the apes closely resembling a human.

anthropology N the study of the origins and characteristics of human beings and their societies, customs and beliefs. ■ **anthropological** ADJ. ■ **anthropologist** N.

anti ADJ, INFORMAL opposed to. ➢ N someone who is opposed to something.

anti- PFX, SIGNIFYING 1 opposed to: anti–war. 2 opposite to: anticlockwise. 3 mainly of drugs, etc: counteracting, resisting or reversing: antidepressant. 4 preventing; having a counteracting effect: antifreeze. 5 set up as a rival or alternative: Antichrist.

antibiotic N a substance that can selectively destroy or inhibit other bacteria or fungi. ➢ ADJ of or relating to antibiotics.

antibody N (-*ies*) a protein produced in the blood, part of the body's immune response.

antic N (often **antics**) a playful caper or trick.

Antichrist N 1 an enemy of Christ. 2 CHRISTIANITY the great enemy of Christ.

anticipate VB 1 to see what will be needed or wanted in the future and do what is necessary in advance. 2 to predict something and then act as though it is bound to happen. 3 to expect something. 4 to look forward to something. 5 to know beforehand. 6 TR & INTR to mention or think something before the proper time. 7 to foil or preclude: anticipated the attack. ■ **anticipation** N. ■ **anticipatory** ADJ.

anticlimax N a dull or disappointing end to an event, a film, etc. ■ **anticlimactic** ADJ.

anticlockwise ADV, ADJ in the opposite direction to that of the hands of a clock.

anticyclone N, METEOROL an area of relatively high atmospheric pressure from which light winds spiral outward.

antidepressant N, MED any drug that prevents or relieves the symptoms of depression. ➢ ADJ having or relating to this effect.

antidote N 1 any agent, eg a drug, that counteracts or prevents the action of a poison. 2 anything that acts as a means of preventing, or counteracting something bad.

antifreeze N any substance that is added to water or some other liquid to lower its freezing point, used eg in the radiators of motor vehicles.

antigen N, BIOL any foreign substance that stimulates the body's immune system to produce antibodies.

antihero N (-*oes*) a principal character in a novel, play, film, etc who lacks the conventional qualities of a hero.

antihistamine N, MED a drug that counteracts the effects of histamines produced in allergic reactions such as hay fever.

anti-lock ADJ of a braking system: fitted with a special sensor that prevents the wheels of a vehicle locking when the brakes are applied.

antimacassar N a covering for the back of a

chair to stop it getting dirty.

antimony N, CHEM a brittle bluish–white metallic element used to increase the hardness of lead alloys.

antinomy N (-*ies*) **1** a contradiction between two laws or beliefs that are reasonable in themselves. **2** a conflict of authority.

antipathy N (-*ies*) a feeling of strong dislike.

antiperspirant N a substance applied to the skin in order to reduce perspiration.

antiphon N a hymn or psalm sung alternately by two groups of singers.

antipodes PL N (usu **the Antipodes**) two points on the Earth's surface that are diametrically opposite each other, esp Australia and New Zealand as being opposite Europe. ■ **antipodean** ADJ, N.

antipope N a pope elected in opposition to one already canonically chosen.

antiquarian ADJ of or dealing in antiques or rare books.
➤ N an antiquary.

antiquary N (-*ies*) someone who collects, studies or deals in antiques or antiquities.

antiquated ADJ old-fashioned.

antique N a piece of furniture, china, etc which is old and often valuable.
➤ ADJ **1** old and often valuable. **2** COLLOQ old-fashioned.

antiquity N **1** ancient times. **2** great age. **3** (**antiquities**) objects from ancient times.

antirrhinum N a bushy plant with large brightly coloured two-lipped flowers. Also called **snapdragon**.

anti-semite N someone who is hostile to or prejudiced against Jews. ■ **antisemitic** ADJ. ■ **antisemitism** N.

antiseptic ADJ killing or inhibiting the growth of bacteria and other micro-organisms.
➤ N a drug or other substance with this effect.

antisocial ADJ **1** reluctant to mix socially with other people. **2** of behaviour: harmful or annoying to the community in general.

antithesis N (-*ses*) **1** a direct opposite of something. **2** the placing together of contrasting ideas, words or themes in an argument. ■ **antithetic** or **antithetical** ADJ.

antitoxin N, MED an antibody which neutralizes a toxin.

antler N either of a pair of usu branched solid bony outgrowths on the head of a deer.

antonym N a word that in certain contexts is the opposite in meaning to another word.

anus N the opening at the end of the alimentary canal, through which the faeces are expelled from the body. ■ **anal** ADJ.

anvil N a heavy iron block on which metal objects can be hammered into shape.

anxiety N (-*ies*) **1** a strong feeling of fear or distress. **2** INFORMAL a worry.

anxious ADJ **1** worried, nervous or fearful. **2** causing worry, fear or uncertainty: **an anxious moment. 3** very eager: **anxious to do well.**

any ADJ **1** one, no matter which: **can't find any answer. 2** some, no matter which: **have you any apples? 3** WITH NEGATIVES AND IN QUESTIONS even a very small amount of something: **won't tolerate any nonsense. 4** indefinitely large: **have any number of dresses. 5** every, no matter which: **Any child could tell you.**
➤ PRONOUN any one or any amount.
➤ ADV, WITH NEGATIVES AND IN QUESTIONS in any way whatever: **It isn't any better.**

anybody PRONOUN **1** any person. **2** an important person: **everybody who is anybody. 3** some ordinary person: **not just anybody.**

anyhow ADV **1** anyway. **2** carelessly.

anyone PRONOUN anybody.

anything PRONOUN a thing of any kind; a thing, no matter which.
➤ ADV in any way: **not anything like her sister.**

anyway CONJ used as a sentence connector or when resuming an interrupted piece of dialogue: and so: **Anyway, you'll never guess**

what he did next.
> ADV **1** nevertheless; in spite of what has been said, done, etc. **2** in any way or manner: **Do it anyway you can.**

anywhere ADV in, at or to any place.
> PRONOUN any place.

AOB or **a.o.b.** ABBREV any other business on the agenda for a meeting.

aorta N, ANAT the main artery in the body, which carries oxygenated blood from the heart to the smaller arteries. ■ **aortic** ADJ.

apace ADV, LITERARY quickly.

Apache N a member of a Native N American people.

apart ADV **1** in or into pieces: **come apart. 2** separated by a certain distance or time: **about 6 miles apart. 3** to or on one side: **set apart. 4** disregarded, not considered, etc: **joking apart. 5** distinguished by some unique quality: **a breed apart.**
◆ **apart from sb** or **sth** not including them or it.

apartheid N an official state policy of keeping different races segregated.

apartment N **1** a single room in a house or flat. **2** (**apartments**) a set of rooms used for accommodation. **3** N AMER a flat.

apathy N **1** lack of interest or enthusiasm. **2** lack of emotion. ■ **apathetic** ADJ.

ape N **1** any of several species of primate that resemble humans in that they have a highly developed brain, lack a tail and can walk upright. **2** an ugly, stupid or clumsy person.
> VB to imitate (someone or an action).

apeman N any of various extinct primates thought to have been intermediate between humans and the higher apes.

aperient ADJ having a mild laxative effect.

aperitif N an alcoholic drink taken before a meal to stimulate the appetite.

aperture N **1** a small hole or opening. **2** the opening through which light enters an optical instrument such as a camera or telescope.

apex N (*-es* or *apices*) the highest point or tip.

aphelion N (*-lia*) the point in a planet's orbit when it is farthest from the Sun.

aphid or **aphis** N (*-s* or *aphides*) a small insect which sucks sap from plants.

aphorism N a short and often clever or humorous saying.

aphrodisiac N a food, drink or drug that is said to stimulate sexual desire.
> ADJ sexually exciting or arousing.

apiary N (*-ies*) a place where honey bees are kept. ■ **apiarist** N.

apical ADJ belonging to, at or forming an apex.

apiece ADV to, for, by or from each one.

aplomb N calm self-assurance.

apocalypse N **1** (**Apocalypse**) the last book of the New Testament, also called the revelation of St John. **2** any revelation of the future, esp future destruction or violence.
■ **apocalyptic** ADJ.

apocryphal ADJ **1** being of doubtful authenticity. **2** of a story, etc: unlikely to be true.

apogee N, ASTRON the point in the orbit of the Moon or a satellite around the Earth when it is at its greatest distance from the Earth.

apolitical ADJ not interested in politics.

apologetic ADJ showing regret for a mistake or offence. ■ **apologetically** ADV.

apologist N someone who formally defends a belief or cause.

apologize or **-ise** VB, INTR to acknowledge a mistake or offence and express regret for it.

apology N (*-ies*) an expression of regret for a mistake or offence.

apoplectic ADJ **1** of or causing apoplexy. **2** COLLOQ red-faced and seething with anger.

apoplexy N the former name for a stroke caused by a cerebral haemorrhage.

apostasy N (*-ies*) the rejection of one's religion or principles or political affiliation, etc.

apostate N someone who rejects a religion, belief, political affiliation, etc that they previously held.

a posteriori ADJ, ADV of an argument or reasoning: working from effect to cause.

apostle N 1 CHRISTIANITY (often **Apostle**) someone sent out to preach about Christ in the early church, esp one of the twelve disciples. 2 any enthusiastic supporter of a cause.

apostolic ADJ 1 relating to the apostles or to their teaching. 2 relating to the Pope.

apostrophe N a punctuation mark (') that is used to show that there has been an omission of a letter or letters, eg I'm for I am, or as a signal for the possessive, eg Ann's book.

apotheosis N (-ses) 1 the action of raising someone to the rank of a god. 2 a glorification or idealization of someone or something; b an ideal embodiment.

appal or (N AMER) **appall** VB (-ll-) to shock, dismay or horrify.

appalling ADJ 1 causing shock or horror. 2 COLLOQ extremely bad. ■ **appallingly** ADV.

apparatus N (*apparatuses* or *apparatus*) 1 the equipment needed for a specified purpose, esp in a science laboratory, gym, etc. 2 an organization or system.

apparel N, OLD USE, FORMAL clothing.

apparent ADJ 1 easy to see or understand; obvious. 2 seeming to be real but perhaps not actually so. ■ **apparently** ADV.

apparition N 1 a sudden unexpected appearance, esp of a ghost. 2 a ghost.

appeal N 1 a an urgent or formal request for help, money, medical aid, etc; b a request made in a pleading or heartfelt way. 2 LAW a an application or petition to a higher authority or law court to carry out a review of a decision taken by a lower one; b a review and its outcome as carried out by such an authority or court. 3 the quality of being attractive, interesting, pleasing, etc.
➤ VB, INTR 1 to make an urgent or formal request: appealed for calm. 2 LAW to request a higher authority or law court to review a decision given by a lower one. 3 to be attractive, interesting, pleasing, etc.

appear VB, INTR 1 to become visible or come into sight. 2 to develop. 3 to seem. 4 to present oneself formally or in public, eg on stage. 5 to be present in a law court as either accused or counsel. 6 to be published.

appearance N 1 an act or instance of appearing. 2 the outward or superficial look of someone or something. 3 illusion; pretence: the appearance of being a reasonable person. 4 (**appearances**) the outward show or signs by which someone or something is judged or assessed: appearances can be deceptive.

appease VB 1 to calm, quieten, pacify, etc, esp by making some kind of concession. 2 to satisfy or allay (a thirst, appetite, doubt, etc).
■ **appeasement** N.

appellant N, LAW someone who makes an appeal to a higher court.

appellation N, FORMAL a name or title.

append VB to add or attach something to a document, esp as a supplement, footnote, etc.

appendage N anything added or attached to a larger or more important part.

appendectomy or **appendicectomy** N (-ies) SURGERY an operation to remove the appendix.

appendicitis N, PATHOL inflammation of the appendix.

appendix N (-es or -dices) 1 extra information, notes, etc at the end of a book or document. 2 ANAT a short tube-like sac attached to the large intestine.

appertain VB, INTR (usu **appertain to sth**) to belong or relate to it.

appetite N 1 a natural physical desire, esp for food. 2 the extent to which someone enjoys their food: he has a very poor appetite.

appetizer or **-iser** N a small amount of food or drink taken before a meal to stimulate the appetite.

appetizing or **-ising** ADJ stimulating the appetite, esp by looking or smelling delicious.

applaud VB **1** INTR to show approval by clapping. **2** to express approval of something.

applause N approval or appreciation shown by clapping.

apple N **1** a small deciduous tree with pink or white flowers and edible fruit. **2** the firm round edible fruit of this tree.

appliance N any electrical device that is used to perform a specific task, esp in the home.

applicable ADJ relevant; appropriate.

applicant N someone who has applied for a job, a university place, a grant, etc.

application N **1** a formal written or verbal request, proposal or submission, eg for a job. **2 a** the act of putting something on (something else); **b** something put on (something else): **an application of oil**. **3** the act of using something for a particular purpose: **the application of statistics to interpret the data**.

applicator N a device designed for putting something on to or into something else.

applied ADJ of a skill, theory, etc: put to practical use: **applied linguistics**.

appliqué N a decorative technique whereby pieces of differently textured and coloured fabrics are stitched onto each other.

apply VB (**-ies, -ied**) **1** INTR to make a formal request, proposal or submission, eg for a job. **2** to put something on to something else. **3** to put or spread something on a surface. **4** INTR to be relevant or suitable. **5** to put (a skill, rule, theory, etc) to practical use.

appoint VB **1** TR & INTR to give someone a job or position. **2** to fix or agree on (a date, time or place). **3** to equip or furnish. ■ **appointee** N.

appointment N **1** an arrangement to meet someone. **2 a** the act of giving someone a job or position; **b** the position someone is given; **c** the person who is given a position.

apportion VB to share out fairly or equally.

apposite ADJ suitable; appropriate.

appraisal N **1** evaluation; estimation of quality. **2** any method of doing this.

appraise VB to decide the value or quality of (someone's skills, ability, etc).

appreciable ADJ noticeable; significant: **an appreciable difference**.

appreciate VB **1** to be grateful or thankful for something. **2** to be aware of the value, quality, etc of something. **3** to understand or be aware of something. **4** usu INTR to increase in value. ■ **appreciative** ADJ. ■ **appreciatively** ADV.

appreciation N **1** gratitude or thanks. **2** sensitive understanding and enjoyment of something. **3** the state of knowing or being aware of something. **4** an increase in value.

apprehend VB **1** to arrest. **2** to understand.

apprehension N **1** fear or anxiety. **2** the act of capturing and arresting someone or something. **3** understanding.

apprehensive ADJ anxious or worried.

apprentice N someone, usu a young person, who works for an agreed period of time in order to learn a craft or trade. ■ **apprenticeship** N.

apprise VB (usu **apprise sb of sth**) to give them information about it.

appro N.
◆ **on appro** COLLOQ on approval.

approach VB **1** TR & INTR to come near or nearer in space, time, etc. **2** to begin to deal with, think about, etc (a problem, subject, etc). **3** to contact someone.
➤ N **1** the act of coming near. **2** a way to, or means of reaching, a place. **3** a suggestion or proposal. **4** a way of considering or dealing with a problem, etc. ■ **approachable** ADJ.

approbation N approval; consent.

appropriate ADJ suitable or proper.
➤ VB to take something as one's own, esp without permission. ■ **appropriately** ADV.

approval N **1** a favourable opinion; esteem.

2 official permission.

◆ **on approval** of goods for sale: able to be returned if not satisfactory.

approve VB **1** to agree to or permit. **2** INTR (**approve of sb** or **sth**) to be pleased with or think well of them or it.

approximate ADJ almost exact or accurate. ➤ VB, TR & INTR to come close to something in value, accuracy, etc. ■ **approximately** ADV. ■ **approximation** N.

appurtenance N (usu **appurtenances**) an accessory to, or detail of, something larger.

apricot N **1** a small deciduous tree with oval toothed leaves and white or pale pink flowers. **2** the small edible fruit of this plant. **3** the colour of this fruit. **Also** AS ADJ.

April N the fourth month of the year.

April fool N **1** someone who has had a practical joke played on them on 1 April. **2** a practical joke played on this date.

a priori ADJ, ADV of an argument or reasoning: working from cause to effect.

apron N **1** a piece of cloth, plastic, etc worn over the front of clothes to protect them. **2** a hard-surface area at an airport where aircraft are loaded.

apropos ADJ of remarks: suitable or to the point. ➤ ADV by the way; appropriately. ◆ **apropos of sth** with reference to it.

apse N a semicircular recess, esp when arched and domed and at the east end of a church.

apt ADJ **1** suitable. **2** clever or quick to learn. ◆ **apt to do sth** inclined or likely to do it.

aptitude N **1** (usu **aptitude for sth**) a natural skill or talent. **2** intelligence; speed in learning or understanding.

aqualung N a device that enables a diver to breathe under water, consisting of a mouth tube connected to cylinders of compressed air.

aquamarine N **1** GEOL a transparent bluish-green gemstone. **2** the colour of this gemstone.

aquaplane N a board on which the rider is towed along at high speed by a motor boat. ➤ VB, INTR **1** to ride on an aquaplane. **2** of a vehicle: to slide along out of control on a thin film of water.

aquarium N (-**iums** or -**ia**) a glass tank that fish and other water animals are kept in so that they can be observed or displayed.

Aquarius N, ASTROL the eleventh sign of the zodiac (the Water-bearer).

aquatic ADJ **1** living or growing in, on or near water. **2** of sports: taking place in water. ➤ N **1** an aquatic animal or plant. **2** (**aquatics**) water sports.

aqueduct N a channel or canal that carries water, esp one that is in the form of a tall bridge across a valley, river, etc.

aqueous ADJ **1** relating to water. **2** denoting a solution that contains water, or in which water is the solvent.

aqueous humour N, ANAT the clear liquid between the lens and the cornea of the eye.

aquiline ADJ **1** of or like an eagle. **2** of a nose: curved like an eagle's beak.

Arab N a member of a Semitic people living in the Middle East and N Africa. ➤ ADJ of the Arabs.

arabesque N, BALLET a position with one leg stretched out backwards and the body bent forwards from the hips.

Arabian ADJ of Arabia or the Arabs. ➤ N an Arab.

Arabic N the Semitic language of the Arabs. ➤ ADJ of Arabs.

Arabic numeral N any of the symbols 0, 1, 2, 3, 4, 5, 6, 7, 8 and 9.

arable ADJ, AGRIC of land: suitable or used for ploughing and growing crops.

arachnid N any eight-legged invertebrate animal belonging to the class which includes spiders, scorpions and ticks.

Aramaic N any of a group of northern Semitic languages.

arbiter N someone who has the authority or influence to settle arguments or disputes.

arbitrary ADJ 1 capricious; whimsical. 2 based on subjective factors or random choice and not objective. ■ **arbitrarily** ADV.

arbitrate VB, INTR to submit to or settle by arbitration. ■ **arbitrator** N.

arbitration N the settling of a dispute between two or more groups by some neutral person who is acceptable to all concerned.

arboreal ADJ 1 relating to or resembling a tree. 2 denoting an animal that lives mainly in trees.

arboretum N (-*ta*) BOT a botanical garden where trees and shrubs are grown.

arbour N a shady area in a garden formed by trees or climbing plants, usu with a seat.

arc N 1 a continuous section of a circle or other curve. 2 a continuous electric discharge, giving out heat and light, that is maintained across the space between two electrodes. ➤ VB 1 to form an arc. 2 to move in an arc.

arcade N 1 a covered walk or passage, usu lined with shops. 2 a row of arches supporting a roof, wall, etc.

Arcadian ADJ characterized by simple rural pleasures.

arcane ADJ mysterious, secret or obscure.

arch¹ N 1 a curved structure forming an opening, used to sustain an overlying weight such as a roof or bridge, or for ornament. 2 anything shaped like an arch. 3 the bony structure of the foot between the heel and the toes, normally having an upward curve. ➤ VB 1 to form an arch. 2 to span something like an arch.

arch² ADJ 1 (USU IN COMPOUNDS) chief; principal: arch enemy. 2 cunning; knowing: an arch look. 3 self-consciously playful. ■ **archly** ADV.

arch- or **archi-** COMB FORM 1 chief; most important: archduke. 2 most esteemed, feared, extreme, etc of its kind: **arch-criminal**.

archaeology or (US) **archeology** N the study of the physical remains of earlier civilizations, esp buildings and artefacts. ■ **archaeological** or **archeological** ADJ. ■ **archaeologist** or **archeologist** N.

archaic ADJ 1 relating or referring to, or from, a much earlier period. 2 out of date; old-fashioned. 3 no longer in general use.

archaism N an archaic expression or style.

archangel N an angel of the highest rank.

archbishop N a chief bishop of an area.

archbishopric N 1 the office of an archbishop. 2 the area that is governed by an archbishop.

archdeacon N, C OF E a member of the clergy who ranks just below a bishop.

archdiocese N, C OF E the area under the control of an archbishop.

archduchess N the wife of an archduke.

archduke N the title of some princes.

archeology an alternative US spelling of **archaeology.**

archery N the art or sport of shooting with a bow and arrow. ■ **archer** N.

archetype N 1 an original model. 2 a perfect example. ■ **archetypal** ADJ.

archi- see **arch-**

archipelago N, GEOG a group of islands.

architect N 1 someone who is professionally qualified to design buildings and other large structures. 2 someone responsible for creating or initiating something.

architecture N 1 the art, science and profession of designing and constructing buildings, ships and other large structures. 2 a a specified style of building design: Victorian architecture; b the buildings of any particular style. ■ **architectural** ADJ.

archive N (usu **archives**) a a collection of old public documents, records, etc; b a place where such documents are kept.

archivist N someone who collects, keeps, catalogues, records, etc archives.

archway N a passage or entrance under an arch or arches.

Arctic N (**the Arctic**) the area round the North Pole.
➤ ADJ of this area.

Arctic Circle N the imaginary circular line at a latitude of 66° 32′ north, which forms a boundary around the area of the north pole.

ardent ADJ 1 enthusiastic; eager. 2 burning; passionate. ■ **ardently** ADV.

ardour N a great enthusiasm or passion.

arduous ADJ 1 difficult; needing a lot of work, effort or energy. 2 steep.

are[1] VB used with **you, we** and **they**: the second person singular and first, second and third person plural of the present tense of **be**.

are[2] N a unit of land measure equal to 100 square metres.

area N 1 a measure of the size of any surface, measured in square units. 2 a region or part. 3 any space set aside for a particular purpose. 4 the range of a subject, activity or topic.

arena N 1 an area surrounded by seats, for sports contests, etc. 2 a place of great activity, esp conflict: **the political arena**. 3 the open area in the middle of an amphitheatre.

aren't CONTRACTION 1 are not: **They aren't coming**. 2 IN QUESTIONS am not: **Aren't I lucky?**

areola N (**-lae** or **-s**) ANAT the ring of pigmented tissue surrounding a nipple.

argon N, CHEM a colourless odourless inert gas.

argot N slang that is only used and understood by a particular group of people.

argue VB 1 TR & INTR to put forward one's case, esp in a clear and well-ordered manner. 2 INTR to quarrel. 3 to show or be evidence for something: **It argues a degree of enthusiasm**. ■ **arguable** ADJ. ■ **arguably** ADV.

argument N 1 a quarrel. 2 a reason for or against an idea, etc.

argumentation N methodical reasoning.

argumentative ADJ fond of arguing.

aria N, MUS a long accompanied song for one voice, esp in an opera or oratorio.

arid ADJ 1 having very low rainfall. 2 uninteresting. ■ **aridity** N.

Aries N, ASTROL the first sign of the zodiac (the Ram).

arise VB (**arose**, **arisen**) INTR 1 to come into being. 2 to get up. 3 to come to notice.

aristocracy N (**-ies**) 1 the highest social class. 2 government by this class.

aristocrat N a member of the aristocracy.

aristocratic ADJ 1 referring or relating to the aristocracy. 2 proud and noble-looking.

arithmetic N 1 the branch of mathematics that uses numbers to solve theoretical or practical problems, mainly by the processes of addition, subtraction, multiplication and division. 2 any calculation that involves the use of numbers. ■ **arithmetically** ADV.

ark N, BIBLE the vessel built by Noah in which his family and animals survived the Flood.

arm[1] N 1 a in humans: either of the two upper limbs from the shoulders to the hands; b a limb of an octopus, squid, etc. 2 anything shaped like or similar to this: **the arm of the record player**. 3 the sleeve of a garment. 4 the part of a chair, etc that supports a person's arm. ■ **armful** N.
◆ **arm in arm** with arms linked together.
◆ **at arm's length** at a distance, esp to avoid becoming too friendly.

arm[2] N (usu **arms**) 1 a weapon: **nuclear arms**. 2 fighting; soldiering. 3 heraldic insignia.
➤ VB 1 to equip (with weapons). 2 to prepare (a bomb) for use.
◆ **up in arms** openly angry and protesting.

armada N a fleet of ships.

armadillo N a small nocturnal burrowing American mammal covered with horny plates.

Armageddon N a large-scale and bloody battle, esp the final battle between good and evil, as described in the New Testament (Revelation 16.16).

armament N 1 (**armaments**) weapons or military equipment. 2 preparation for war.

armchair N 1 a comfortable chair with arms at each side. 2 AS ADJ taking no active part: **an armchair detective.**

armed forces N the military forces of a country thought of collectively.

armhole N the opening at the shoulder of a garment where the arm goes through.

armistice N an agreement between warring factions to suspend all fighting.

Armistice Day N the anniversary of the day when World War I ended, 11 November 1918.

armlet N a band or bracelet round the arm.

armorial ADJ of heraldry or coats of arms.

armour or (US) **armor** N 1 HIST a metal or chainmail, etc suit or covering worn by men or horses to protect them against injury in battle. 2 metal covering to protect ships, tanks, etc. 3 armoured fighting vehicles as a group. ■ **armoured** ADJ.

armourer N someone whose job is to make or repair suits of armour, weapons, etc.

armour-plate N strong metal or steel for protecting ships, tanks, etc. ■ **armour-plated** ADJ.

armoury N (*-ies*) 1 a place where arms are kept. 2 a collection of arms and weapons.

armpit N the hollow under the arm at the shoulder.

army N (*-ies*) 1 a large number of people armed and organized for fighting on land. 2 the military profession. 3 a large number.

A-road N in the UK: a main or principal road that can be a dual or a single carriageway.

aroma N a distinctive, usu pleasant, smell.

aromatherapy N a form of therapy involving the use of essential plant oils, usu in combination with massage. ■ **aromatherapist** N.

aromatic ADJ 1 having a strong, but sweet or pleasant smell. 2 CHEM of an organic compound: having carbon atoms arranged in one or more rings rather than in chains.

around ADV 1 on every side; in every direction: **threw his money around.** 2 here and there; in different directions; in or to different places; with or to different people, etc: **could see for miles around.** 3 approximately: **This cinema seats around 100.** 4 somewhere in the vicinity: **waited around.**
➤ PREP 1 on all sides of something. 2 in all directions from (a specified point): **The land around here is very fertile.** 3 over; in all directions: **Toys were scattered around the floor.** 4 so as to surround or encircle. 5 reached by making a turn or partial turn about: **around the corner.** 6 somewhere in or near. 7 approximately in or at; about.

arouse VB 1 to cause or produce (an emotion, reaction, response, etc). 2 to cause to become awake or active. ■ **arousal** N.

arraign VB 1 to bring (usu a prisoner) to a court of law to answer a criminal charge or charges. 2 to accuse someone. ■ **arraignment** N.

arrange VB 1 to put into the proper or desired order. 2 to settle the plans for something: **arranged their holiday.** 3 to make a mutual agreement. 4 to make (a piece of music) suitable for particular voices or instruments.

arrangement N 1 a plan or preparation for some future event. 2 the act of putting things into a proper order. 3 an agreement.

array N 1 a large and impressive number, display or collection. 2 a well-ordered arrangement, esp a military one.
➤ VB to put in order.

arrears PL N an amount or quantity which still needs to be done or paid back.
◆ **in arrears** late in paying back money.

arrest VB 1 to take someone into custody. 2 to stop or slow down the progress of (growth, development, etc). 3 to catch or attract (someone's attention).
➤ N 1 the act of taking, or state of being taken,

into custody, esp by the police. **2** a stopping. **3** a halting or slowing down in the progress, development or growth of something.

arresting ADJ strikingly individual or attractive.

arrival N **1a** the act of coming to a destination; **b** AS ADJ: the arrival lounge. **2** someone or something that has arrived.

arrive VB, INTR **1** to reach a place during a journey or come to a destination at the end of a journey. **2** COLLOQ to be successful or to attain recognition. **3** of a thing: to be brought, delivered, etc. **4** to come about or occur at last.

arrogant ADJ having or showing too high an opinion of one's own abilities or importance. ■ **arrogance** N.

arrogate VB to claim a responsibility, power, etc without having any legal right to do so.

arrow N **1** a thin straight stick with a sharp point at one end and feathers at the other, which is fired from a bow. **2** any arrow-shaped symbol or sign, esp one showing the way to go.

arrowhead N the pointed tip of an arrow.

arrowroot N a fine-grained starch obtained from the tubers of a tropical plant.

arse or (N AMER) **ass** N, SLANG the buttocks.

arsehole or (N AMER) **asshole** N, SLANG **1** the anus. **2** someone whose behaviour, opinion, etc is not highly regarded.

arsenal N **1** a store for weapons, explosives, etc. **2** a factory or workshop where weapons are made, repaired or serviced. **3** the weapons, etc available to a country or group.

arsenic N **1** a metalloid chemical element. **2** a powerful poison, an oxide of arsenic.

arson N the crime of deliberately setting fire to a building, etc. ■ **arsonist** N.

art N **1a** the creation of works of beauty, esp visual ones; **b** such creations thought of collectively. **2** human skill and work as opposed to nature. **3** a skill, esp one gained through practice: the lost art of conversation.

art deco or **Art Deco** N a style of interior design, orig of the 1920s and 1930s, with geometric shapes and strong colours.

artefact or **artifact** N a handcrafted object, eg a tool, esp one that is historically or archaeologically interesting.

arterial ADJ **1** of or like an artery or arteries. **2** of a road, etc: connecting towns or cities.

artery N (**-ies**) **1** ANAT a blood vessel that carries blood from the heart to the body tissues. **2** a main road, railway or shipping lane.

artesian well N, GEOL a deep well that is drilled so that the water trapped there under pressure is forced to flow upward in the well.

artful ADJ **1** cunning, esp in achieving what one wants. **2** skilful. ■ **artfully** ADV.

arthritis N, PATHOL inflammation of a joint, characterized by swelling, pain and often restricted movement. ■ **arthritic** N, ADJ.

arthropod N, ZOOL any invertebrate animal such as an insect, crustacean or arachnid.

artichoke N a thistle-like plant with an edible flower-head.

article N **1** a thing or object. **2** a short written composition in a newspaper, magazine, etc. **3** a clause or paragraph in a document, legal agreement, etc. **4** GRAM the definite article 'the' or the indefinite article 'a' or 'an'.

articled ADJ of a trainee lawyer, accountant, etc: bound by a legal contract while working in an office to learn the job.

articulate VB **1** TR & INTR to pronounce (words) or speak clearly and distinctly. **2** to express (thoughts, feelings, ideas, etc) clearly. ➢ ADJ **1a** skilled at expressing one's thoughts clearly; **b** of a speech or a piece of writing: clearly presented, well-argued and to the point. **2** having joints. ■ **articulately** ADV.

articulated lorry N a large lorry with two or more separate parts, joined by a pivot.

articulation N **1** the act of speaking or expressing an idea in words. **2** PHONETICS **a** the process of uttering separate speech sounds; **b** the speech sound produced. **3** a joint.

artifact see **artefact**

artifice N 1 a clever trick or plan. 2 cunning.

artificial ADJ 1 made by human effort; not occurring naturally. 2 imitating something natural, esp in order to become a cheaper substitute for the natural product. 3 of someone, their behaviour, etc: not genuine or sincere. ■ **artificiality** N. ■ **artificially** ADV.

artificial insemination N, MED the introduction of semen into the vagina of a woman or female animal by artificial means.

artificial intelligence N the development and use of computer systems that can perform some of the functions normally associated with human intelligence, such as problem-solving.

artificial respiration N respiration that is stimulated and maintained manually or mechanically.

artillery N (-ies) 1 large guns for use on land. 2 the part of an army equipped with such guns.

artisan N someone who does skilled work with their hands.

artist N 1 someone who produces works of art, esp paintings. 2 someone who is skilled at some particular thing. 3 an artiste. ■ **artistic** ADJ. ■ **artistically** ADV. ■ **artistry** N.

artiste N a professional performer, esp a singer or dancer, in a theatre, circus, etc.

artless ADJ 1 simple and natural in manner. 2 honest, not deceitful. ■ **artlessly** ADV.

art nouveau N a style of art, architecture and interior design that flourished towards the end of the 19c, with flowing curved lines and highly stylized flowers and leaves.

artwork N any illustrations, drawings, designs, etc in a book, magazine etc.

arty ADJ (-ier, -iest) COLLOQ affectedly or ostentatiously artistic.

arum lily N a plant with large leaves shaped like arrow-heads and a yellow cylindrical spadix surrounded by a white, yellow or pink petal-like spathe.

as CONJ 1 when; while; during: met him as I was leaving the shop. 2 because; since: didn't go as it was raining. 3 in the manner that: fussing as only a mother can. 4 that which; what: Do as you're told. 5 to the extent that: Try as he might, he still couldn't reach. 6 for instance: large books, as this one for example. 7 in the same way that: married late in life, as his father had done. 8 used to refer to something previously said, done, etc: like; just like: As Frank says, the job won't be easy.
➤ PREP in the role of something: speaking as her friend.
➤ ADV equally: not as hot today.
◆ **as … as …** used in similes and for comparison: denoting that the things compared are the same: as sly as a fox.
◆ **as for** or **to sth** or **sb** with regard to it or them; concerning it or them.
◆ **as if** or **as though** as he, she, etc would if: behaved as if nothing had happened.
◆ **as well** also.

ASAP or **asap** ABBREV as soon as possible.

asbestos N, GEOL a fibrous silicate mineral that is highly resistant to heat.

ascend VB 1 TR & INTR to climb, go or rise up. 2 INTR to slope upwards. 3 INTR to rise to a higher level, rank, etc.

ascendancy N controlling or dominating power.

ascendant or **ascendent** ADJ having more influence or power.
◆ **in the ascendant** showing an increase in power, domination, authority, wealth, etc.

ascension N an act of climbing or moving upwards.

ascent N 1 the act of climbing, ascending or rising. 2 an upward slope.

ascertain VB to find out; to discover.

ascetic N someone who abstains from all physical comfort and pleasure, esp in solitude and for religious reasons.
➤ ADJ characterized by the abstinence from physical pleasure and comfort; self-denying.

ascribe VB to attribute; assign.

asexual ADJ 1 denoting reproduction that does not involve sexual processes. 2 without functional sexual organs. ■ **asexually** ADV.

ash¹ N 1 the dusty residue that remains after something has been burnt. 2 the powdery dust that is put out by an erupting volcano. 3 (**ashes**) the remains of a body after cremation.

ash² N 1 a deciduous tree or shrub with strong grey bark. 2 the timber of this tree.

ashamed ADJ 1 troubled by feelings of guilt, embarrassment, etc. 2 (usu **ashamed of sb** or **sth**) embarrassed or humiliated by them or it. 3 hesitant or reluctant (to do something) because of embarrassment, guilt, etc.

ashen ADJ of a face: very pale, usu from shock.

ashlar or **ashler** N a large square-cut stone that is used for building or facing walls.

ashore ADV to, towards or onto the land.

ashtray N a dish or other container for the ash, butts, etc from cigarettes, etc.

Ash Wednesday N, CHRISTIANITY the first day of Lent, so called because of the practice of sprinkling ashes on the heads of penitents.

Asian ADJ of Asia.
➤ N 1 an inhabitant of, or person born in, Asia. 2 someone of Asian descent.

Asiatic ADJ of Asia or Asians.

aside ADV 1 on, to, towards or over to one side. 2 away from everyone else: **took him aside**. 3 in a direction away from oneself: **tossed the magazine aside**. 4 out of mind, consideration, etc: **put his worries aside**.
➤ N 1 words said by a character in a play which the audience can hear, but which the other characters cannot. 2 a remark that is not related to the main subject of a conversation.

asinine ADJ 1 relating to or resembling an ass. 2 stupid; idiotic; stubborn.

ask VB 1 TR & INTR to question someone about something: **asked her name**. 2 to call for an answer to (a question): **asked what qualifications she had**. 3 to inquire about: ask

the way. 4 to invite. 5 to expect: **I don't ask a lot of him**.
◆ **ask after sb** to show concern about them.

askance ADV sideways.
◆ **look askance at sb** or **sth** to consider them or it with suspicion or disapproval.

askew ADV, ADJ squint; not straight or level.

asleep ADJ 1 in a sleeping state. 2 of limbs, hands, feet, etc: numb.
➤ ADV into a sleeping state: **fall asleep**.

AS level or (in full) **Advanced Supplementary level** N 1 an examination designed to provide supplementary A-level study. 2 a pass in such an examination.

asp N 1 a small venomous S European snake. 2 the Egyptian cobra.

asparagus N 1 a plant with cylindrical green shoots or 'spears' that function as leaves. 2 the edible shoots of this plant.

aspartame N an artificial sweetener.

aspect N 1 a particular part or element of a problem, subject, etc. 2 a particular way of considering a matter. 3 **a** the appearance something has to the eye: **a lush green aspect**; **b** a look or appearance, esp of a face: **a worried aspect**. 4 the direction something faces: **a southern aspect**.

aspen N a tree of the poplar family.

asperity N (**-ies**) roughness, esp of temper.

aspersion N
◆ **cast aspersions on sb** or **sth** to make a damaging or spiteful remark.

asphalt N a dark semi-solid bituminous material used in roofing and road-surfacing.
➤ VB to cover with asphalt.

asphodel N a plant of the lily family with yellow or white star-shaped flowers.

asphyxia N suffocation caused by any factor that interferes with respiration and prevents oxygen from reaching the body tissues, such as choking or drowning.

asphyxiate VB, TR & INTR 1 to stop or cause to

stop breathing. **2** to suffocate.
■ **asphyxiation** N.

aspic N a savoury jelly made from meat or fish stock, used as a mould for terrines, eggs, etc.

aspidistra N a house plant with broad leaves and bell-shaped flowers.

aspirate PHONETICS, N the sound represented in English by the letter **h**.
➤ VB to pronounce a word with an **h** sound as opposed to 'dropping' it.

aspiration N eager desire; ambition.

aspire VB (USU **aspire to** or **after sth**) to have a strong desire to achieve or reach (an objective or ambition): aspired to greatness.

aspirin N **1** an analgesic drug that is widely used to relieve pain and to reduce inflammation and fever. **2** a tablet of this drug.

ass[1] N **1** a hoofed mammal resembling, but smaller than, a horse, with longer ears.
2 COLLOQ a stupid person.

ass[2] N, N AMER, ESP US SLANG arse.

assail VB **1** to make a strong physical attack. **2** to criticize fiercely. **3** to agitate, esp mentally.
■ **assailant** N.

assassin N someone who kills someone else, esp for political or religious reasons.

assassinate VB to murder, esp for political or religious reasons. ■ **assassination** N.

assault N **1** a violent physical or verbal attack. **2** LAW any act that causes someone to feel physically threatened.
➤ VB to attack someone or something.

assault and battery N, LAW the act of threatening to physically attack someone which is then followed by a physical attack.

assay N, METALLURGY the analysis of the composition and purity of a metal in an ore or mineral, or of a chemical compound.
➤ VB to perform such an analysis on, or to determine the commercial value of (an ore or mineral) on the basis of such an analysis.

assemblage N **1** a collection of people or

things. **2** the act of gathering together.

assemble VB **1** TR & INTR to gather or collect together. **2** to put together (the parts of something, such as a machine).

assembly N (-*ies*) **1** a group of people gathered together, esp for a meeting. **2 a** the act of assembling; **b** the state of being assembled. **3** the procedure of putting together the parts of something.

assembly line N a continuous series of machines and workers that an article passes along in the stages of its manufacture.

assent N consent or approval, esp official.
➤ VB (often **assent to sth**) to agree to it.

assert VB **1** to state firmly. **2** to insist on or defend (one's rights, opinions, etc).
◆ **assert oneself** to state one's wishes, etc confidently and vigorously.

assertion N **1** a positive or strong statement or claim. **2** the act of making such a claim or statement.

assertive ADJ expressing wishes and opinions in a firm and confident manner. ■ **assertively** ADV. ■ **assertiveness** N.

assess VB **1** to judge the quality or importance of something. **2** to estimate the cost, value, etc of something. **3** to fix the amount of (a fine or tax). ■ **assessment** N.

assessor N someone who assesses the value, importance or quality of something.

asset N anything that is considered valuable or useful, such as a skill, quality, person, etc.

assets PL N, ACCOUNTING the total value of the property of a person or company.

asset-stripping N the practice of buying an unsuccessful company at a low price and selling off its assets separately for a profit.

asseverate VB to state solemnly.

asshole see **arsehole**

assiduous ADJ **1** hard-working. **2** done carefully and exactly. ■ **assiduity** N.

assign VB **1** to give (a task, etc) to someone.

2 to appoint someone to a position or task. **3** to fix (a time, place, etc) for a purpose. **4** to attribute or ascribe.

assignation N a secret appointment to meet.

assignment N **1 a** a task or duty that has been selected for someone to do; **b** an exercise that is set for students, etc. **2** the act of assigning.

assimilate VB **1** to become familiar with and understand (information, etc) completely. **2** TR & INTR to become part of, or make (people) part of, a larger group, esp when they are of a different race, etc. ■ **assimilation** N.

assist VB, TR & INTR to help. ■ **assistance** N.

assistant N **1** a person whose job is to help someone of higher rank, position, etc. **2** a person whose job is to serve customers in a shop: **sales assistant**.

associate VB **1** to connect in the mind: **associate lambs with spring**. **2** INTR to mix socially: **don't associate with him**. **3** to involve (oneself) in a group because of shared aims. ➤ N **1** a business partner or colleague. **2** a companion or friend. ➤ ADJ joined with another, esp in a business: **an associate director**.

association N **1** an organization or club. **2** a friendship or partnership. **3** a connection in the mind. **4** the act of associating.

Association Football see under **football**

assonance N, PROSODY a correspondence or resemblance in the sounds of words or syllables, either between their vowels, eg in **meet** and **bean**, or between their consonants, eg in **keep** and **cape**.

assorted ADJ **1** mixed; consisting of various different kinds. **2** arranged in sorts; classified.

assortment N a mixed collection.

assuage VB to make (a pain, sorrow, hunger, etc) less severe.

assume VB **1** to accept something without proof; to take for granted. **2** to take on (a responsibility, duty, etc). **3** to take on or adopt (an appearance, quality, etc). **4** to pretend to have or feel.

assumed ADJ not genuine: **an assumed name**.

assumption N **1** something that is accepted as true without proof. **2** the act of accepting something as true without proof. **3** the act of assuming in other senses.

assurance N **1** a promise, guarantee or statement that something is true. **2** confidence and poise. **3** BRIT insurance, esp life insurance.

assure VB **1** to state positively and confidently; to guarantee. **2** to make (an event, etc) certain: **Her hard work assured her success**. **3** BRIT to insure something (esp one's life). ■ **assurer** N.

assured ADJ **1** of someone or their attitude, behaviour, etc: confident and poised. **2** certain to happen. ■ **assuredly** ADV.

astatine N, CHEM a radioactive chemical element that occurs naturally in trace amounts and is produced artificially.

aster N a plant with blue, purple, pink or white daisy-like flowers.

asterisk N a star-shaped symbol (*) used in printing and writing to mark a cross-reference to a footnote, an omission, etc.

astern ADV, ADJ **1** in or towards the stern. **2** backwards. **3** behind.

asteroid N any of thousands of small rocky objects that orbit around the Sun.

asthma N a respiratory disorder in which breathlessness and wheezing occur. ■ **asthmatic** N, ADJ

astigmatism N a defect in a lens, esp abnormal curvature of the lens or cornea of the eye. ■ **astigmatic** ADJ.

astir ADJ, ADV **1** awake and out of bed. **2** in a state of motion or excitement.

astonish VB to surprise greatly. ■ **astonishment** N.

astound VB to amaze or shock.

astray ADJ, ADV out of the right way.

astride ADV **1** with a leg on each side. **2** with

legs apart.
➤ PREP **1** with a leg on each side of something. **2** stretching across.

astringent ADJ **1** severe and harsh. **2** causing cells to shrink.
➤ N an astringent substance.

astro- COMB FORM, DENOTING stars or space.

astrolabe N, ASTRON, FORMERLY a navigational instrument used to measure the altitude of the Sun and bright stars.

astrology N the study of the movements of the stars and planets, and on how they are thought to exert influences on people's lives, character traits, etc. ■ **astrologer** N.
■ **astrological** ADJ.

astronaut N someone who is trained to travel in space.

astronautics SING N the science of travel in space. ■ **astronautical** or **astronautic** ADJ.

astronomical and **astronomic** ADJ **1** very large; vast. **2** relating to astronomy.
■ **astronomically** ADV.

astronomy N the scientific study of celestial bodies and the universe as a whole.

astrophysics SING N the application of physical laws and theories to astronomical objects and phenomena. ■ **astrophysical** ADJ. ■ **astrophysicist** N.

astute ADJ mentally perceptive; shrewd.
■ **astutely** ADV. ■ **astuteness** N.

asunder ADV apart or into pieces.

asylum N **1** a place of safety or protection. **2** HIST a mental hospital.

asymmetry N a lack of symmetry.
■ **asymmetric** and **asymmetrical** ADJ.

at PREP **1** used to indicate position or place: in, within, on, near, etc: **worked at a local factory**. **2** towards, in the direction of something: **working at getting fit**. **3** used to indicate a position in time: **a** around; on the stroke of: **The train arrives at six**; **b** having reached the age of: **At 17 you can start to drive**. **4** with, by, in reference to etc: **annoyed at her • good at**

games. **5** engaged in; occupied with: **children at play**. **6** for; in exchange for: **sold it at a profit**. **7** in a state of: **at liberty**.

atavism N reversion to an earlier type.
■ **atavistic** ADJ.

ate PAT OF **eat**

atheism N the belief that there is no god.
■ **atheist** N.

athlete N **1** someone who trains for and competes in field and track events. **2** someone who is good at sports.

athlete's foot N a fungal foot infection.

athletic ADJ **1** of someone or their build: physically fit and strong. **2** relating to athletics.
■ **athletically** ADV. ■ **athleticism** N.

athletics SING N competitive track and field sports such as running, jumping, etc.

Atlantic ADJ of the Atlantic Ocean, an ocean bounded by Europe and Africa to the East, and by N and S America to the West.

atlas N a book of maps.

ATM ABBREV automated or automatic telling machine. See **cash machine.**

atmosphere N **1** the layer of gas surrounding a planet, esp the Earth, and held to it by gravity. **2** the air in a particular place. **3** the mood of a book, film, painting, piece of music, etc. **4** the general or prevailing climate or mood. **5** a unit of pressure equal to normal air pressure at sea level. ■ **atmospheric** ADJ.
■ **atmospherically** ADV.

atoll N a circle of coral reef that surrounds a lagoon, and is itself surrounded by open sea.

atom N **1** the smallest unit of a chemical element that can display the properties of that element, and which is capable of combining with other atoms to form molecules. **2** NON-TECHNICAL a very small amount.

atom bomb and **atomic bomb** N a powerful explosive device that derives its force from the sudden release of enormous amounts of nuclear energy during nuclear fission. Also called **nuclear bomb.**

atomic ADJ 1 relating to atoms. 2 obtained by atomic phenomena, esp nuclear fission.

atomic energy see **nuclear energy**

atomize or **-ise** VB 1 to reduce to atoms or small particles. 2 to reduce (a liquid) to a spray or mist of fine droplets by passage through a nozzle or jet under pressure.

atomizer or **-iser** N a container that releases liquid, containing eg perfume, as a fine spray.

atonal ADJ, MUS lacking tonality; not written in a particular key. ■ **atonality** N.

atone VB (also **atone for sth**) to make amends for (a wrongdoing, crime, sin, etc).

atonement N an act of making amends for, making up for, or paying for a wrongdoing, etc.

atop ADV on top; at the top.
➤ PREP on top of, or at the top of, something.

atrium N (*-ia* or *-iums*) 1 a central court or entrance hall in an ancient Roman house. 2 a court in a public space, such as an office block, hotel, etc, that has galleries around it, and is often several storeys high. 3 ANAT either of the two upper chambers of the heart.

atrocious ADJ 1 COLLOQ very bad. 2 extremely cruel or wicked. ■ **atrociously** ADV.

atrocity N (*-ies*) 1 wicked or cruel behaviour. 2 an act of wickedness or cruelty.

atrophy VB (*-ies, -ied*) TR & INTR to diminish or die away; to cause to diminish or die away.
➤ N the process of atrophying.

attach VB 1 to fasten or join. 2 to associate (oneself) with or join. 3 to attribute or assign.
◆ **be attached to sb** or **sth** to be fond of them or it.

attaché N someone who is connected to a diplomatic department.

attaché-case N a small rigid leather case for holding documents, etc.

attachment N 1 a an act or means of fastening; b the state of being fastened. 2 liking or affection. 3 an extra part that can be fitted to a machine, often used to change its function.

attack VB 1 to make a sudden violent attempt to hurt, damage or capture. 2 to criticize strongly in speech or writing. 3 INTR to make an attack. 4 to begin to do something with enthusiasm or determination. 5 INTR to take the initiative in a game, contest, etc to attempt to score.
➤ N 1 an act or the action of attacking. 2 a sudden spell of illness: **an attack of flu**.
■ **attacker** N.

attain VB 1 to complete successfully; to achieve. 2 to reach: **attained the summit**.

attainment N 1 achievement, esp after some effort. 2 the act of achieving something. 3 something that is achieved.

attempt VB 1 to try. 2 to try to master, tackle, answer, etc (a problem, etc).
➤ N an effort; an endeavour.

attend VB 1 TR & INTR to be present at something. 2 to go regularly to (eg school, church, etc). 3 to wait upon; to serve: **attended the princess**.
◆ **attend to sb** or **sth** to take care of them or it or to take action over them or it.

attendance N 1 the act of attending. 2 the number of people attending. 3 regularity of attending.

attendant N 1 someone whose job is to help, guide or give some other service, esp to the public: **museum attendant**. 2 someone who serves or waits upon someone else.
➤ ADJ 1 being in or giving attendance. 2 accompanying: **attendant responsibilities**.

attention N 1 the act of concentrating or directing the mind. 2 notice; awareness: **The problem has recently come to my attention**. 3 special care: **attention to detail**.

attentive ADJ 1 showing close concentration; alert. 2 considerate; polite and courteous.
■ **attentively** ADV. ■ **attentiveness** N.

attenuated ADJ 1 thin. 2 thinned; diluted. 3 tapering.

attest VB 1 to affirm or be proof of the truth or validity of something. 2 to be evidence of something. ■ **attestation** N.

attic N a space or room at the top of a house under the roof.

attire N clothes, esp formal or elegant ones.

attitude N 1 a way of thinking or behaving. 2 a hostile or resentful manner. 3 a position of the body. 4 a pose, esp for dramatic effect.

attorney N 1 someone able to act for another in legal or business matters. 2 N AMER a lawyer.

attract VB 1 to cause (attention, notice, a crowd, interest, etc) to be directed towards oneself, itself, etc. 2 of a magnet: to draw or pull (towards itself), esp by exerting some force or power. 3 to arouse liking or admiration in someone; to be attractive to them.

attraction N 1 the act or power of attracting. 2 someone or something that attracts.

attractive ADJ 1 appealing; enticing: **an attractive salary**. 2 appealing in looks or character. ■ **attractiveness** N.

attribute VB (always **attribute sth to sb** or **sth**) to think of it as being written, said, or caused by them or it; to ascribe it to them or it. ➤ N a quality, characteristic, feature, etc. ■ **attributable** ADJ ■ **attribution** N.

attributive ADJ, GRAM of an adjective or noun: placed before the noun it modifies, eg the adjective 'young' in **young girl**.

attrition N 1 a rubbing together; friction. 2 MIL a relentless wearing down of an enemy's strength, morale, etc, esp by continual attacks.

attune VB (often **attune to** or **become attuned to sth**) to adjust to or prepare for (a situation, etc).

atypical ADJ not typical, representative, usual, etc. ■ **atypically** ADV.

aubergine N 1 a bushy plant widely cultivated for its edible fruit. 2 the large egg-shaped fruit of this plant, with a smooth skin that is usu deep purple in colour. N Amer & Austral equivalent **eggplant**.

aubrietia N a dwarf plant with purple, lilac, blue or pink flowers.

auburn ADJ of hair: reddish–brown.

auction N a public sale in which each item is sold to the person who offers the most money. ➤ VB to sell something in an auction.

auctioneer N a person whose job is to conduct an auction.

audacious ADJ 1 bold and daring. 2 disrespectful; impudent. ■ **audacity** N.

audible ADJ loud enough to be heard. ■ **audibility** N. ■ **audibly** ADV.

audience N 1 a group of people watching a performance, eg of a play, concert, etc. 2 the people reached by a film, TV or radio broadcast, book, magazine, etc. 3 a formal interview with an important person.

audio ADJ 1 relating to hearing or sound. 2 relating to the recording and broadcasting of sound.

audio– COMB FORM, DENOTING 1 sound, esp broadcast sound. 2 hearing.

audiovisual ADJ of a device or teaching method: using both sound and vision.

audit N an official inspection of an organization's accounts by an accountant. ➤ VB to examine (accounts) officially.

audition N a test of the suitability of an actor, singer, musician, etc for a particular part or role, by way of a short performance. ➤ VB, TR & INTR to test or be tested by audition.

auditor N a person who is professionally qualified to audit accounts.

auditorium N (-*iums* or -*ia*) the part of a theatre, hall, etc where the audience sits.

auditory ADJ belonging, relating or referring to hearing or the organs involved in hearing.

au fait ADJ (usu **au fait with sth**) well informed about or familiar with it.

auger N a hand–tool for boring holes.

augment VB, TR & INTR to make or become greater in size, number, strength, amount, etc. ■ **augmentation** N.

augur VB, INTR (usu **augur well** or **ill**) to be a

good or bad sign for the future.

augury N (*-ies*) **1** a sign or omen. **2** the practice of predicting the future.

August N the eighth month of the year.

august ADJ noble; imposing.

auk N a species of small diving seabird with black and white plumage, and short wings.

aunt N **1** the sister of one's father or mother. **2** the wife of one's uncle.

auntie or **aunty** N (*-ies*) COLLOQ an aunt.

Aunt Sally N (*Aunt Sallies*) **1** a game in which sticks or balls are thrown at a dummy. **2** any target of abuse.

au pair N a young person from abroad, usu female, who, in order to learn the language, helps with housework, looking after children, etc in return for board and lodging.

aura N (*-ras* or *-rae*) a distinctive character or quality around a person or in a place.

aural ADJ relating to the sense of hearing or to the ears. ■ **aurally** ADV.

aureole and **aureola** N **1** a bright disc of light that surrounds the head of a holy figure in Christian painting and iconography. **2** ASTRON a halo surrounding the Sun or Moon.

au revoir EXCLAM goodbye.

auricle N, ANAT **1** the outer part of the ear. **2** the ear-shaped tip of the atrium of the heart. ■ **auricular** ADJ.

auriferous ADJ containing or yielding gold.

aurora N (*-ras* or *-rae*) **1** ASTRON the appearance of bands of coloured lights in the night sky above the northern (**aurora borealis**) or southern (**aurora australis**) magnetic pole. **2** POETIC the dawn.

auscultation N, MED the practice of listening, esp with a stethoscope, to the sounds produced within the heart, lungs, etc, in order to diagnose any abnormalities.

auspice N.
◆ **under the auspices of sb** or **sth** with their or its help, support and guidance.

auspicious ADJ promising future success; favourable.

Aussie N, ADJ, COLLOQ Australian.

austere ADJ **1** severely simple and plain. **2** serious; severe; stern. **3** severe in self-discipline.

austerity N (*-ies*) **1** the state of being austere. **2** severe simplicity of dress, lifestyle, etc.

Australasian ADJ of Australia, New Zealand and the nearby Pacific islands.

authentic ADJ **1** genuine. **2** reliable; trustworthy; true to the original. ■ **authentically** ADV. ■ **authenticity** N.

authenticate VB to prove something to be true or genuine. ■ **authentication** N.

author N **1** the writer of a book, article, play, etc. **2** the creator or originator of an idea, event, etc: **the author of the peace plan.** ➤ VB to be the author of (a book, article, etc).

authoritarian ADJ in favour of, insisting on, characterized by, etc strict authority. ➤ N an authoritarian person. ■ **authoritarianism** N.

authoritative ADJ **1** accepted as a reliable source of knowledge. **2** having authority; official. ■ **authoritatively** ADV.

authority N (*-ies*) **1** the power or right to control or judge others, or to have the final say in something. **2** a position which has such a power or right. **3** (sometimes **authorities**) the person or people who have power. **4** the ability to influence others, usu as a result of knowledge or expertise. **5** well-informed confidence: **She delivered her lecture with authority. 6** an expert.

authorize or **-ise** VB **1** to give someone the power or right to do something. **2** to give permission for something. ■ **authorization** N.

authorship N **1** the origin of a particular piece of writing. **2** the profession of writing.

autism N, PSYCHOL a mental disorder that develops in early childhood and is characterized by inability to relate to other people and the outside world. ■ **autistic** ADJ.

auto N, N AMER a motor car.

auto- or (BEFORE A VOWEL) **aut-** COMB FORM
1 self; same; by or of the same person or thing:
autobiography. 2 self-acting: automatic.
3 self-induced.

autobiography N (-ies) someone's own
account of their life. ■ **autobiographer** N.
■ **autobiographical** ADJ.

autocracy N (-ies) 1 absolute government by
one person; dictatorship. 2 the rule of such a
person. 3 a country, state, society, etc that is
governed by one person.

autocrat N 1 a ruler with absolute power. 2 an
authoritarian person. ■ **autocratic** ADJ.

Autocue N, TRADEMARK, TV a screen hidden from
the camera from which a newscaster or
speaker can read a script.

autograph N someone's signature, esp that
of a famous person.
➤ VB to sign (a photograph, book, poster, etc).

automat N, N AMER a vending machine.

automate VB to apply automation to (a
technical process).

automatic ADJ 1 of a machine or device:
capable of operating on its own and requiring
little human control. 2 of an action: done
without thinking. 3 happening as a necessary
result: an automatic driving ban. 4 of a
firearm: able to reload itself and so fire
continuously. 5 of a motor vehicle: having
automatic transmission.
➤ N 1 an automatic firearm. 2 a vehicle with
automatic transmission. 3 a washing machine
that operates automatically.
■ **automatically** ADV.

automatic pilot and **autopilot** N an
electronic control device that automatically
steers a vehicle.

automation N the use of automatic
machinery in manufacturing and data-
processing.

automaton N (-tons or -ta) 1 a machine or

robot that has been programmed to perform
specific actions in a manner imitative of a
human or animal. 2 someone who acts like a
machine, to routine and without thinking.

automobile N, N AMER a motor car.

automotive ADJ 1 of motor vehicles. 2 self-
propelling.

autonomous ADJ 1 of a country, state, etc:
self-governing. 2 independent of others.

autonomy N (-ies) 1 the power or right of self-
government, administering one's own affairs,
etc. 2 freedom from the intervention of others.
3 personal freedom or independence.

autopilot see **automatic pilot**

autopsy N (-ies) a postmortem.

autumn N 1 (also **Autumn**) the season of the
year between summer and winter. 2 a period
of maturity before decay. ■ **autumnal** ADJ.

auxiliary ADJ 1 helping or supporting.
2 additional or extra.
➤ N (-ies) 1 a helper. 2 (**auxiliaries**) foreign
troops that fight for another nation.

auxiliary verb N, GRAM a verb, such as **be**,
do, **have**, **can**, **shall**, **may** or **must**, used with
other verbs to indicate tense, mood, voice, etc,
as in **you will go**.

avail VB, TR & INTR to help or be of use.
➤ N use; advantage.
◆ **avail oneself of sth** to make use of it or
take advantage of it.

available ADJ able or ready to be obtained or
used. ■ **availability** N.

avalanche N 1 the rapid movement of a large
mass of snow or ice down a mountain slope.
2 a sudden appearance or a large amount of
something: an avalanche of criticism.

avant-garde N the writers, painters,
musicians, etc whose ideas and techniques are
considered the most modern or advanced of
their time, regarded collectively.
➤ ADJ of a work of art, idea, movement, etc:
characterized by daring modernity; innovative.

avarice N excessive desire for money,

possessions, etc; greed. ■ **avaricious** ADJ.

Ave[1] ABBREV used in addresses: Avenue.

Ave[2] and **Ave Maria** N a prayer to the Virgin Mary.

avenge VB to carry out some form of retribution for (some previous wrong-doing).

avenue N **1a** a broad road or street, often with trees along the sides; **b** (**Avenue**) a street title in an address. **2** a tree-lined approach to a house. **3** a means, way or approach.

aver VB (-*rr*-) to state firmly and positively.

average N **1** the usual or typical amount, extent, quality, number, etc. **2** STATISTICS any number that is representative of a group of numbers or other data, esp the arithmetic mean. ➤ ADJ **1** usual or ordinary. **2** estimated by taking an average. **3** mediocre. ➤ VB **1** to obtain the numerical average of (several numbers). **2** to amount to on average: Her speed averaged 90 miles per hour on the motorway.

averse ADJ (always **averse to sth**) reluctant about or opposed to it.

aversion N **1** a strong dislike. **2** something or someone that is the object of strong dislike.

avert VB **1** to turn away: **avert one's eyes**. **2** to prevent (esp danger).

aviary N (-*ies*) a large enclosed area where birds are kept. ■ **aviarist** N.

aviation N **1** the science or practice of mechanical flight through the air, esp by powered aircraft. **2** the production, design and operation of aircraft. **3** the aircraft industry.

aviator N, OLD USE an aircraft pilot.

avid ADJ very enthusiastic: **an avid film-goer**. ■ **avidity** N. ■ **avidly** ADV.

avocado N **1** a tropical evergreen tree of the laurel family, with a pear-shaped fruit. **2** the edible pear-shaped fruit of this tree, which has greenish-brown skin and creamy flesh.

avocet N any of various large wading birds with long legs and an upward curving bill.

avoid VB **1** to keep away from (a place, person, action, etc). **2** to stop, prevent, manage not to do, or escape something. ■ **avoidable** ADJ. ■ **avoidably** ADV. ■ **avoidance** N.

avoirdupois N a system of units of mass based on a pound consisting of 16 ounces.

avow VB to state openly. ■ **avowal** N. ■ **avowed** ADJ. ■ **avowedly** ADV.

avuncular ADJ relating to or like an uncle, esp in being kind and caring.

await VB **1** FORMAL to wait for something. **2** to be in store for someone.

awake VB (**awoke, awoken**) TR & INTR **1** to stop sleeping or cause to stop sleeping. **2** to become active or cause to become active. ➤ ADJ **1** not sleeping. **2** alert or aware.

awaken VB, TR & INTR **1** to wake up. **2** to arouse (feelings, etc). **3** to stir or evoke.

award VB (always **award sth to sb** or **award sb sth**) to present or grant them it. ➤ N a payment, prize, etc, esp one given in recognition of an achievement, etc.

aware ADJ **1** (often **aware of sth** or **sb**) acquainted with or mindful of it or them. **2** (**aware that**) conscious that. **3** well informed. ■ **awareness** N.

awash ADJ, ADV, COLLOQ covered or flooded with water.

away ADV **1** from one place, position, person or time towards another; off. **2** in or to the usual or proper place: **put the books away**. **3** into the distance; into extinction: **fade away**. **4** apart; remote: **stay away from the city**. **5** continuously; repeatedly: **talk away**. **6** in another direction: **looked away**. **7** of a sporting event: on the opponent's ground. ➤ ADJ **1** not present; not at home. **2** distant: **not far away**. **3** of a sporting event: played on the opponent's ground: **away game**. ◆ **right** or **straight away** immediately.

awe N admiration, fear and wonder. ➤ VB to fill with awe.

aweigh ADV, NAUT of an anchor: in the process of being raised from the bottom of the sea.

awe-inspiring ADJ **1** causing or deserving awe. **2** COLLOQ wonderful.

awesome ADJ **1** causing awe; dreaded. **2** COLLOQ completely and utterly wonderful.

awful ADJ **1** COLLOQ very bad. **2** COLLOQ very great: *an awful shame*. **3** terrible or shocking. ➤ ADV, NON-STANDARD very: *I'm awful busy*. ■ **awfully** ADV.

awhile ADV for a short time.

awkward ADJ **1** clumsy and ungraceful. **2** embarrassed or embarrassing. **3** difficult and dangerous: *an awkward turning*. **4** difficult or inconvenient to deal with.

awl N a pointed tool for boring small holes.

awning N a plastic or canvas covering over the entrance or window of a shop, etc, that can be extended to give shelter from the sun or rain.

awoke, **awoken** see under **awake**

AWOL ABBREV absent without leave, temporarily absent, esp in the armed forces, without official permission.

awry ADJ, ADV **1** twisted to one side. **2** wrong.

axe or (US) **ax** N a hand-tool with a long handle and a heavy metal blade, used for cutting down trees, chopping wood, etc. ➤ VB **1** to get rid of, dismiss or put a stop to something. **2** to reduce (costs, services, etc). ◆ **have an axe to grind** to have a personal reason for being involved in something.

axes plural of **axe**, **axis**

axial ADJ of, forming or placed along an axis.

axiom N **1** a proposition, fact, principle, etc which, because it is long-established, is generally accepted as true. **2** a self-evident statement. ■ **axiomatic** ADJ.

axis N (**axes**) **1** an imaginary straight line around which an object, eg a planet, rotates. **2** an imaginary straight line around which an object is symmetrical. **3** GEOM one of the lines of reference used to specify the position of points on a graph. ■ **axial** ADJ. ■ **axially** ADV.

axle N a rod designed to carry a wheel or one or more pairs of wheels which may be attached to it, driven by it, or rotate freely on it.

ayatollah N a Shi'ite religious leader in Iran.

aye or **ay** ADV, chiefly DIALECT yes. ➤ N **1** a vote in favour of something. **2** someone who votes in favour of something.

azalea N a deciduous shrub with large clusters of funnel-shaped flowers.

Aztec N **1** a group of Mexican Indian peoples whose great empire was overthrown by the Spanish in the 16c. **2** an individual belonging to this group of peoples. **3** their language. ➤ ADJ of this group or their language.

azure N **1** a deep blue colour. **2** POETIC the sky.

Bb

B or **b** N (*Bs, B's* or *b's*) **1** the second letter of the English alphabet. **2** (usu **B**) the second highest grade or quality, or a mark indicating this. **3** (**B**) MUS the seventh note on the scale of C major.

BA ABBREV Bachelor of Arts.

baa N the cry of a sheep. ➤ VB, INTR to bleat.

babble VB **1** TR & INTR to talk or say something quickly, esp so that it is hard to understand. **2** INTR, COLLOQ to talk foolishly. **3** INTR of a

stream, etc: to make a low murmuring sound.
4 to give away (a secret) carelessly.

babe N **1** N AMER COLLOQ a girl or young woman. **2** LITERARY a baby. **3** someone who is stunningly sexy and beautiful, esp a woman.

baboon N a large ground-dwelling monkey, with a long muzzle, large teeth and long tail.

baby N (-ies) **1** a newborn or very young child or animal. **2** an unborn child. **3** the youngest member of a group. **4** DEROG a childish person. **5** COLLOQ a person's own particular project, etc. **6** COLLOQ, esp N AMER a term of affection for a girl or woman.
➢ VB (-ies, -ied) to treat someone as a baby.
■ **babyhood** N. ■ **babyish** ADJ.

baby-sit VB, TR & INTR to look after a child, usu in its own home, while the parents are out.
■ **baby-sitter** N. ■ **baby-sitting** N.

baccalaureate N **1** FORMAL a bachelor's degree. **2** a diploma.

baccarat N a card game in which players bet money against the banker.

bacchanalia PL N drunken celebrations; orgies. ■ **bacchanalian** ADJ.

baccy N (-ies) COLLOQ tobacco.

bachelor N **1** an unmarried man.
2 (**Bachelor**) a person with a first university degree. ■ **bachelorhood** N.

bacillus N (-li) BIOL any of a large group of rod-shaped bacteria.

back N **1 a** the rear part of the human body from the neck to the base of the spine; **b** the spinal column itself. **2** the upper part of an animal's body. **3** the part of an object that is opposite to or furthest from the front: **the back of the house**. **4** the side of an object that is not normally seen or used. **5** the upright part of a chair. **6** SPORT a player whose usual position is behind the forwards.
➢ ADJ **1** located or situated behind or at the back: **the back door**. **2** concerning, belonging to or from an earlier date: **back pay**. **3** away from or behind something, esp something more important: **back roads**.

➢ ADV **1** to or towards the rear. **2** in or into an original position or condition: **get back from holiday**. **3** in return or in response: **hit back**. **4** in or into the past: **look back to happier days**.
➢ VB **1** to help or support someone or something, usu with money. **2** TR & INTR (usu **back away, out** or **out of sth**, or **up**) to move or cause something to move backwards, away from or out of something. **3** to bet on the success of (a horse, etc). **4** (sometimes **back sb** or **sth up**) to provide support for them. **5** to accompany (a singer) with music.
◆ **back down** to concede an argument or claim, esp under pressure or opposition.
◆ **back off 1** to move backwards or retreat. **2** to back down.
◆ **back out of sth** to withdraw from (a promise or agreement, etc).
◆ **back to front 1** with the back where the front should be. **2** in the wrong order.

backbench N a seat in the House of Commons for members who do not hold an official position either in the government or in the opposition. ■ **backbencher** N.

backbite VB, INTR, COLLOQ to speak unkindly about someone who is absent.

backbone N **1** the spine. **2** in both physical and abstract senses: the main support of something: **the backbone of a company**. **3** strength of character.

backbreaking ADJ extremely hard or tiring.

backchat N, BRIT impertinent or rude replies.

backcloth and **backdrop** N the painted cloth at the back of a stage.

backcomb VB to comb (the hair) towards the roots to make it look thicker.

backdate VB **1** to put a date on (a document, etc) that is earlier than the actual date. **2** to make (something) effective from a past date.

backdoor ADJ applied to an activity done secretly and often dishonestly.
➢ N (usu **the back door**) a clandestine or illicit means of achieving an objective.

backer N a person who gives financial support to a project, etc.

backfire VB, INTR **1** of an engine or vehicle: to make a loud bang caused when unburnt gases in the exhaust or inlet system explode. **2** of a plan, etc: to go wrong and have a bad effect on the person who originated it.

backgammon N a board game for two players, with pieces moved according to the throws of a dice.

background N **1** the space behind the main figures of a picture. **2** the events or circumstances that precede and help to explain an event, etc. **3** a person's social origins or education, etc. **4** a less noticeable or less public position: **stay in the background**.

backhand N, TENNIS, SQUASH, **etc** a stroke made with the back of the hand turned towards the ball.

backhanded ADJ **1** TENNIS of a stroke: made with or as a backhand. **2** of a compliment: ambiguous or doubtful in effect.

backing N **1** support, esp financial support. **2** material, etc that supports the back of something. **3** music accompanying a singer. Also AS ADJ: **backing group**.

backlash N a sudden violent reaction to an action or situation, etc.

backlog N an amount of uncompleted work, etc.

back number N a copy of a newspaper or magazine issued earlier than the current one.

backpack N, N AMER, ESP US a rucksack. ➤ VB, INTR to go travelling with a pack on one's back. ■ **backpacker** N. ■ **backpacking** N.

back-pedal VB, INTR **1** to turn the pedals on a bicycle backwards. **2** to withdraw rapidly or suddenly from one's previous course of action.

backside N, COLLOQ the buttocks.

backslide VB, INTR to relapse into former bad behaviour, habits, etc. ■ **backslider** N.

backspin N, SPORT the spinning of a ball in the opposite direction to the way it is travelling, which reduces its speed when it hits a surface.

backstage ADV behind a theatre stage.

➤ ADJ not seen by the public.

backstreet ADJ secret or illicit.

backstroke N a swimming stroke performed on the back.

backtrack VB, INTR **1** to return the way one came. **2** to reverse one's course of action.

backup N **1** support; assistance. **2** COMP **a** a procedure for backing up data for security; **b** a copy made by this procedure.

backward ADJ **1** directed behind or towards the back. **2** less advanced than normal in mental, physical or intellectual development. **3** reluctant or shy. ➤ ADV backwards.

backwards or sometimes **backward** ADV **1** towards the back or rear. **2** with one's back facing the direction of movement. **3** in reverse order: **counting backwards**. **4** in or into a worse state: **felt her career going backwards**.

backwater N **1** a pool of stagnant water connected to a river. **2** DEROG an isolated place, not affected by events elsewhere.

backyard N **1** BRIT a yard at the back of a house. **2** N AMER a garden at the rear of a house.

bacon N meat from the back and sides of a pig. ◆ **bring home the bacon** COLLOQ **1** to earn the money. **2** to accomplish a task successfully. ◆ **save sb's bacon** COLLOQ to rescue them from a difficult situation.

bacteria PL N (SING *bacterium*) BIOL an extremely diverse group of microscopic organisms. ■ **bacterial** ADJ.

bacteriology N the scientific study of bacteria. ■ **bacteriologist** N.

bad ADJ (*worse, worst*) **1** not good. **2** wicked; immoral. **3** naughty. **4** (**bad at sth**) not skilled or clever (at some activity). **5** (**bad for sb**) harmful to them. **6** unpleasant; unwelcome. **7** rotten; decayed. **8** serious; severe: **a bad cold**. **9** unhealthy; injured; painful: **a bad leg**. **10** sorry, upset or ashamed. **11** not valid; worthless: **a bad cheque**. ➤ ADV, N AMER COLLOQ badly; greatly; hard: **needs the money bad**.

➢ N **1** evil; badness. **2** unpleasant events.
■ **badness** N.
◆ **not bad** COLLOQ quite good.
◆ **too bad** COLLOQ unfortunate; regrettable.

bad blood N angry or bitter feelings.

baddy N (-*ies*) COLLOQ a criminal or villain, esp one in a film or book, etc.

badge N **1** a small emblem or mark worn to show rank, membership of a society, etc. **2** any distinguishing feature or mark.

badger N a stocky burrowing mammal with black and white stripes on its head.
➢ VB to pester someone.

badinage N playful bantering talk.

bad language N coarse words.

badly ADV (*worse, worst*) **1** poorly.
2 unfavourably: **came off badly**. **3** extremely; severely: **badly in arrears**.

badminton N a game played with rackets and a shuttlecock which is hit across a high net.

bad-tempered ADJ easily made angry.

baffle VB **1** to confuse or puzzle. **2** to hinder or frustrate (plans, etc).
➢ N a device for controlling the flow of gas, liquid or sound through an opening.
■ **baffling** ADJ.

bag N **1** a container made of a soft material with an opening at the top, for carrying things.
2 (also **bagful**) the amount a bag can hold.
3 an amount of fish or game caught. **4** (**bags**, esp **bags of sth**) COLLOQ a large amount of it.
➢ VB (-*gg*-) **1** TR & INTR (also **bag sth up**) to put (something) into a bag. **2** to kill (game): **bagged six pheasants**. **3** COLLOQ to obtain or reserve (a seat, etc).

bagatelle N **1** a game played on a board with holes into which balls are rolled. **2** an unimportant thing. **3** a short piece of light music.

bagel N a hard, ring–shaped bread roll.

baggage N a traveller's luggage.

baggy ADJ (-*ier, -iest*) hanging loose.

bagpipes PL N a wind instrument consisting of

a bag into which air is blown through a reed pipe (the chanter) by means of which the melody is also created.

baguette N a long narrow French loaf.

bah EXCLAM expressing displeasure, scorn, etc.

bail¹ N **1** the temporary release of a person awaiting trial, secured by the payment of money and/or the imposition of special conditions. **2** money required as security for such a release.
➢ VB (usu **bail sb out**) **1** to provide bail for them. **2** COLLOQ to help them out of difficulties, esp by lending them money.

bail² or **bale** VB (usu **bail out** or **bale out**)
1 TR & INTR to remove (water) from a boat with a bucket or scoop. **2** INTR to escape from an aeroplane by jumping out.

bail³ N (usu **bails**) CRICKET one of the cross-pieces laid on top of the stumps.

bailiff N an officer of a lawcourt, esp one with the power to seize the property of a person who has not paid money owed to the court.

bairn N, DIALECT a child.

bait N **1** food put on a hook or in a trap to attract fish or animals. **2** anything intended to attract.
➢ VB **1** to put food on or in (a hook or trap). **2** to harass or tease (a person or animal) wilfully.

baize N a woollen cloth, usu green and used as a covering on snooker and card tables, etc.

bake VB **1** TR & INTR to cook (cakes, bread, vegetables, etc) using dry heat in an oven. **2** TR & INTR to dry or harden by heat from the sun or a fire. **3** INTR, COLLOQ to be extremely hot.

Bakelite N, TRADEMARK a type of plastic formerly used to make dishes, etc.

baker N a person who bakes or sells bread and cakes, etc, esp as their profession.

baker's dozen N thirteen.

bakery N (-*ies*) a place where bread, cakes, etc are made or sold.

baking powder and **baking soda** see under **bicarbonate of soda**

baksheesh N in some Eastern countries: money given as a tip or present.

balaclava and **balaclava helmet** N a knitted hat that covers the head and neck, with an opening for the face.

balalaika N a Russian stringed musical instrument with a triangular body.

balance N 1 a state of physical stability in which the weight of a body is evenly distributed. 2 an instrument for weighing. 3 the amount by which the two sides of a financial account differ. 4 an amount left over. 5 a state of mental or emotional stability. 6 a state existing when two opposite forces are equal. 7 something needed to create such equality. ➢ VB 1 TR & INTR to be in, or put (something) into, a state of physical balance. 2 to compare two or more things in one's mind; to compare their advantages and disadvantages. 3 to find the difference between money put into an account and money taken out of it, and to make them equal. 4 INTR (also **balance out**) to be or become equal in amount. ■ **balanced** ADJ. ◆ **in the balance** not yet decided.

balcony N (-ies) 1 a platform surrounded by a wall or railing, projecting from the wall of a building. 2 an upper tier in a theatre or cinema.

bald ADJ 1 of a person: having little or no hair on their head. 2 of birds or animals: **a** not having any feather or fur; **b** having white markings on the face. 3 bare or plain: the bald truth. ■ **balding** ADJ. ■ **baldly** ADV. ■ **baldness** N.

bale¹ N a large tied bundle of a commodity such as hay or cloth. ➢ VB to make (hay, etc) into bales.

bale² see **bail²**

baleful ADJ 1 evil; harmful. 2 threatening; gloomy. ■ **balefully** ADV.

balk or **baulk** VB 1 INTR (usu **balk at sth**) to hesitate, or refuse to go on, because of some obstacle. 2 to check or block.

ball¹ N 1 a round or roundish object used in some sports. 2 anything round or nearly round in shape: a ball of wool. 3 the act of throwing a ball, or the way a ball is thrown. 4 a rounded fleshy part of the body: the ball of the foot. 5 (usu **balls**) COARSE SLANG a testicle. ➢ VB, TR & INTR to form or gather into a ball. ◆ **on the ball** COLLOQ well-informed; alert.

ball² N 1 a formal social meeting for dancing. 2 COLLOQ an enjoyable time: We had a ball.

ballad N 1 a slow, usu romantic song. 2 a poem or song which tells a popular story.

ballast N 1 heavy material used to stabilize a ship or a hot-air balloon. 2 broken rocks used as a base for roads and railway lines.

ball-bearing N 1 a set of small steel balls between moving parts of some machines, to help reduce friction. 2 one of these balls.

ballcock N a floating ball that rises and falls with the water level in a tank or cistern, which operates a valve controlling the inflow.

ballerina N a female ballet-dancer.

ballet N 1 a classical style of dancing and mime, using set steps and body movements. 2 a single performance or work in this style. ■ **balletic** ADJ.

ballistic missile N a type of missile which is initially guided but drops on its target under the force of gravity.

balloon N 1 a rubber pouch with a neck, inflated with air or gas and used as a toy or decoration, etc. 2 a large bag made of light material and filled with a light gas or hot air, designed to float in the air carrying people, etc in a basket underneath. 3 a balloon-shaped outline in a cartoon. ➢ VB 1 INTR to travel by balloon. 2 INTR to increase dramatically. ■ **balloonist** N.

ballot N 1 **a** a method or system of voting, usu in secret, by putting a marked paper into a box or other container; **b** an act or occasion of voting by this system. 2 the total number of votes recorded in an election. ➢ VB 1 to take the vote or ballot of (a group of people). 2 INTR (esp **ballot for sth**) to vote by ballot (in favour of it).

ball park N, orig US 1 a baseball field. 2 a sphere of activity.

➢ ADJ (USU **ballpark**) approximate.

ballpoint and **ballpoint pen** N a pen which has a tiny ball as the writing point.

ballroom N a large room with a spacious dance floor, in which balls are held.

balls SING N, COARSE SLANG **1** N AMER courage or bravery. **2** rubbish; nonsense. Also AS EXCLAM.

balls-up N, BRIT, COARSE SLANG a mess; something confused or bungled.

ballyhoo N, COLLOQ **1** a noisy confused situation. **2** noisy or sensational publicity.

balm N **1** an oil obtained from certain types of trees, having a pleasant smell and used in healing or reducing pain. **2** a fragrant and healing ointment. **3** an aromatic plant, esp one of the mint family. **4** something comforting.

balmy ADJ (*-ier, -iest*) of the air: warm and soft.

baloney or **boloney** N, SLANG nonsense.

balsa N **1** a tropical American tree. **2** (also **balsa-wood**) the very lightweight wood of this tree.

balsam N **1** an aromatic thick sticky substance obtained from some trees and plants. **2** a tree or plant from which this substance is obtained.
■ **balsamic** ADJ.

balti N in Indian cookery: a style of curry cooked in a two-handled wok-like dish.

baluster N any one of a series of posts or pillars supporting a rail.

balustrade N a row of posts or pillars, joined by a rail, on the edge of a staircase, bridge, etc.

bamboo N (PL only in sense 1) **1** a tall tropical grass with hollow stems. **2** its stems.

bamboozle VB, COLLOQ **1** to cheat (someone). **2** to confuse (someone).

ban N an official order stating that something is not allowed.
➢ VB (*-nn-*) **1** to forbid (something). **2** to forbid (someone) from doing something.

banal ADJ commonplace; unoriginal.
■ **banality** N.

banana N **1** a large tropical treelike plant. **2** the long curved fruit of this plant.

band[1] N **1** a flat narrow strip of cloth, metal, paper, etc used to hold things together or as a decoration. **2** a stripe of colour or strip of material differing from its background or surroundings. **3** a group or range of values between two limits.

band[2] N **1** a group of people with a common purpose or interest. **2** a group of musicians who play music other than classical music.
➢ VB (USU **band together**) to act as a group.

bandage N a strip of cloth for winding round a wound or a broken limb.
➢ VB to wrap in a bandage.

bandana or **bandanna** N a large brightly-coloured cotton or silk square, folded and worn around the neck or head.

bandbox N a light round box for holding hats.

bandeau N (*-deaux*) a narrow band of material worn around the head.

bandicoot N an Australian marsupial with elongated hindlegs and a long flexible snout.

bandit N an armed robber.

bandoleer or **bandolier** N a leather shoulder belt, esp for carrying bullets.

band-saw N a saw consisting of a blade with teeth attached to a metal band which moves around two wheels.

bandstand N a platform with a roof, often in a park, where bands play music.

bandwagon N.
◆ **jump on the bandwagon** to join or show interest in something only because it is fashionable or likely to succeed.

bandy[1] VB (*-ies, -ied*) (USU **bandy about** or **around**) **1** to pass (a story, etc) from one person to another. **2** to mention (someone's name) in rumour.

bandy[2] ADJ (*-ier, -iest*) of legs: curved or bending wide apart at the knees.

bane N the cause of trouble or evil: **the bane**

of my life. ■ **baneful** ADJ.

bang N **1** a sudden loud explosive noise. **2** a heavy blow.
➤ VB, TR & INTR **1** to make, or cause (something) to make, a loud noise by hitting, dropping or closing (it) violently, etc. **2** to hit (something) sharply, esp by accident: **banged her elbow**. **3** to make, or cause (something) to make, the sound of an explosion.
➤ ADV, COLLOQ **1** exactly: **bang on time**. **2** suddenly.

banger N **1** COLLOQ a sausage. **2** COLLOQ an old car, usu in poor condition. **3** a loud firework.

bangle N a piece of jewellery in the form of a solid band, worn round the arm or leg.

banish VB **1** to send (someone) away from a place. **2** to put (thoughts, etc) out of one's mind. ■ **banishment** N.

banister or **bannister** N (usu **banisters**) a row of posts and the hand-rail they support, running up the side of a staircase.

banjo N (-**os** or -**oes**) a stringed musical instrument with a long neck and a round body, played like a guitar. ■ **banjoist** N.

bank¹ N **1** a financial organization which keeps money in accounts for its clients, lends money, etc. **2** a box in which money can be saved, esp by children. **3** a place where something is stored or collected for later use. Also IN COMPOUNDS: **databank**.
➤ VB **1** to put (money) into a bank. **2** INTR to have a bank account: **We bank with Lloyds**.
◆ **bank on sth** to rely on it or expect it.

bank² N **1** the side or slope of a hill. **2** the ground at the edge of a river or lake, etc. **3** a long raised pile of earth or snow, etc.
➤ VB **1** to enclose something with a bank, or form a bank to it. **2** TR & INTR of an aircraft: to change direction, with one wing higher than the other. **3** (also **bank up**) to cover (a fire) with coal to keep it burning slowly for a long time.

bank³ N a collection of similar things arranged in rows: **a bank of switches**.

bank card and **banker's card** N a cheque card or debit card.

banker N a person who owns or manages a bank.

banker's order see **standing order**

bank holiday N in the UK: any one of several days in the year on which banks are closed, usu observed as a public holiday.

banknote N a special piece of paper, issued by a bank, which serves as money.

bankrupt N someone who is recognized as not being able to pay their debts.
➤ ADJ **1** not having money to pay one's debts; insolvent. **2** exhausted of or lacking (some quality, etc): **bankrupt of ideas**.
➤ VB (PA P **bankrupt**) to make (someone) bankrupt. ■ **bankruptcy** N (-**ies**).

banner N a large piece of cloth or cardboard, with a design or slogan, carried or displayed at public meetings and parades.

banns PL N the public announcement of an intended marriage.

banquet N a sumptuous formal dinner.
➤ VB, INTR to eat or take part in a banquet.

banshee N, FOLKLORE a wailing female spirit.

bantam N a small breed of farm chicken.

bantamweight N a class for boxers, wrestlers and weightlifters, between featherweight and flyweight.

banter N light-hearted friendly talk.
➤ VB, INTR to engage in banter.

Bantu N (PL **Bantu**) **1** a group of languages spoken in southern and central Africa. **2** PL the group of peoples who speak these languages.
➤ ADJ of the Bantu languages or people.

banyan N an Indian fruit tree.

bap N, DIALECT a large flat bread roll.

baptism N the religious ceremony of baptizing a person by immersion in, or sprinkling with, water. ■ **baptismal** ADJ.

Baptist N a member of a Christian group which believes that only adults should be baptized, and only by complete immersion in water.

baptize or -**ise** VB **1** to immerse (someone) in,

or sprinkle (them) with, water as a sign of them having become a member of the Christian Church. **2** to give a name to (someone).

bar N **1** a block of some solid substance: **bar of soap**. **2** a rod or long piece of a strong rigid material used as a weapon, obstruction, etc. **3** anything that prevents, restricts or hinders. **4** a line or band of colour or light, etc, esp a stripe on a heraldic shield. **5** a room or counter in a restaurant or hotel, etc, or a separate establishment, where alcoholic drinks are sold and drunk. **6 a** (also **bar-line**) a vertical line marked on music, dividing it into sections of equal value; **b** one of these sections. **7** the rail in a law court where the accused person stands. **8** (**the Bar**) the profession of barristers.
➤ VB (-**rr**-) **1** to fasten (something) with a bar. **2** (often **bar sb from sth**) to forbid, prohibit, prevent them from entering, eg a place or event, doing something, etc. **3** to hinder, obstruct or prevent progress.
➤ PREP except; except for: **interviewed every suspect, bar one**.

barb N **1** a point on a hook facing in the opposite direction to the main point. **2** a humorous but hurtful remark. ■ **barbed** ADJ.

barbarian N **1** someone who is cruel and wild in behaviour. **2** an uncivilized and uncultured person. Also AS ADJ. ■ **barbaric** ADJ.

barbarism N **1** the state of being uncivilized, coarse, etc. **2** a cruel, coarse or ignorant act.

barbarity N (-**ies**) barbarism (senses 1 and 2).

barbarous ADJ **1** uncultured and uncivilized. **2** extremely cruel or brutal.

barbecue N **1** a frame on which food is grilled over an open fire. **2** food cooked in this way. **3** a party held out of doors at which food is cooked on a barbecue.
➤ VB to cook (food) on a barbecue.

barbed wire N wire with sharp twisted points, used for making fences, etc.

barbell N a bar with heavy metal weights at each end, used for weightlifting exercises.

barber N someone who cuts and styles men's hair and shaves their beards.

barbican N a tower over the outer gate of a castle or town, for the purpose of defence.

barbie N, orig AUSTRAL COLLOQ a barbecue.

barbiturate N, MED a salt or ester of barbituric acid, used as a source of sedative drugs.

bar chart and **bar graph** N a graph which shows values or amounts in vertical bars.

bar code N a series of numbers and parallel lines of varying thickness on product labels, that represents information about the product.

bard N, LITERARY a poet.

bare ADJ **1** not covered by clothes; naked. **2** without the usual or natural covering: **bare trees**. **3** empty. **4** simple; plain: **the bare facts**. **5** basic; essential: **the bare necessities**.
➤ VB to uncover. ■ **bareness** N.

bareback ADV, ADJ on a horse without a saddle.

barefaced ADJ having no shame or regret; impudent: **a barefaced lie**.

barefoot or **barefooted** ADJ, ADV not wearing shoes or socks.

barely ADV **1** scarcely or only just. **2** plainly or simply: **barely furnished**.

bargain N **1** an agreement made between people buying and selling things, offering services, etc: **strike a bargain**. **2** something offered for sale, or bought, at a low price.
➤ VB INTR (often **bargain with sb**) to discuss the terms for buying or selling, etc.
◆ **bargain for** or **on sth** to expect it.
◆ **into the bargain** in addition; besides.

barge N a long flat-bottomed boat used on rivers and canals.
➤ VB, INTR (esp **barge about** or **around**) to move in a clumsy ungraceful way.
◆ **barge in** to interrupt, esp rudely or abruptly.
◆ **barge into sb** or **sth** to hit or knock them or it roughly.

baritone N, MUS **1** the second lowest male singing voice, between bass and tenor. **2** a singer with such a voice.
➤ ADJ referring to a baritone.

barium N, CHEM a soft silvery–white metallic element.

bark[1] N the short sharp cry of a dog, fox, etc. ➤ VB, INTR **1** to make this sound. **2** to speak loudly and sharply. **3** to cough harshly.

bark[2] N, BOT the tough protective outer layer consisting mainly of dead cells, that covers the stems and roots of woody plants, eg trees. ➤ VB **1** to scrape the skin from (one's leg, etc). **2** to strip or remove the bark from (a tree, etc).

barley N (-eys) **1** a cereal of the grass family with a dense head of grains. **2** (also **barleycorn**) these grains.

barmaid and **barman** N a woman or man who serves drinks in a bar or public house.

bar mitzvah N a Jewish ceremony in which a boy (usu aged 13) formally accepts full religious responsibilities.

barmy ADJ (-ier, -iest) COLLOQ crazy.

barn N a building in which grain or hay, etc is stored, or for housing cattle, etc.

barnacle N a marine crustacean which clings firmly to rocks, hulls of boats, etc.

barney N (-eys) COLLOQ a rough noisy quarrel.

barnstorm VB, INTR to tour a district, giving theatrical performances or making political speeches. ■ **barnstorming** N.

barnyard N the area around a barn.

barometer N, METEOROL an instrument which measures atmospheric pressure, used to predict changes in the weather or to estimate height above sea level. ■ **barometric** ADJ.

baron N **1** a man holding the lowest rank of the British nobility. **2** a powerful businessman: oil baron. ■ **baronial** ADJ.

baroness N **1** a baron's wife. **2** a woman holding the title of baron in her own right.

baronet N in the UK: **a** a hereditary title ranking below that of baron; **b** a man holding such a title. ■ **baronetcy** N (-ies).

baroque (also **Baroque**) N a decorative style of architecture, art and music, popular in Europe from the late 16c to the early 18c. ➤ ADJ **1** in such a style. **2** of ornamentation, etc: flamboyant or extravagant.

barrack[1] N (usu **barracks**) a building or group of buildings for housing soldiers.

barrack[2] VB, TR & INTR, chiefly BRIT to shout and laugh rudely or hostilely at (a speaker, sports team, etc). ■ **barracking** N.

barracuda N (barracuda or barracudas) a large tropical sea fish which feeds on other fish.

barrage N **1** MIL a long burst of gunfire which keeps an enemy back. **2** a large number of things coming in quickly one after the other. **3** an artificial barrier across a river.

barre N, BALLET a rail fixed to a wall at waist level, which dancers use while exercising.

barrel N **1** a large round container with a flat top and bottom and curving out in the middle, usu made of planks of wood held together with metal bands. **2** (also **barrelful**) the amount a barrel can hold. **3** a measure of capacity, esp of industrial oil. **4** the long hollow tube–shaped part of a gun or pen, etc.

barren ADJ **1** of a woman or female animal: not able to bear offspring. **2** of land or soil, etc: not able to produce crops or fruit, etc. **3** not producing results. ■ **barrenness** N.

barricade N a barrier, esp an improvised one. ➤ VB to block or defend (something) with a barricade.

barrier N **1** a fence, gate or bar, etc put up to defend, block, protect, separate, etc. **2** something that separates people, items, etc.

barring PREP except for; leaving a specified thing out of consideration.

barrister N in England and Wales: a lawyer who acts for someone in the higher law courts.

barrow[1] N **1** a one–wheeled cart used to carry earth, etc. **2** a larger wheeled cart, from which goods are sold in the street.

barrow[2] N, ARCHAEOL a pile of earth over an ancient grave.

bartender N, N AMER someone who serves

drinks in a bar; a barperson.

barter VB, TR & INTR to trade or exchange (goods or services) without using money. ➤ N trade by exchanging goods.

baryon N, PHYS a heavy subatomic particle.

barytes N, GEOL the mineral form of barium sulphate, the chief ore of barium.

basal ADJ 1 at, referring to or forming a base. 2 at the lowest level.

basalt N, GEOL a fine-grained dark volcanic rock. ■ **basaltic** ADJ.

base[1] N 1 the lowest part or bottom; the part which supports something or on which something stands. 2 the origin, root or foundation of something. 3 the headquarters or centre of activity or operations. 4 a starting point. 5 the main part of a mixture. 6 CHEM any of a group of chemical compounds that can neutralize an acid to form a salt and water. 7 BASEBALL any one of four fixed points on the pitch which players run between. ➤ VB to make or form a base for (something or someone).

base[2] ADJ 1 lacking morals; wicked. 2 not pure. 3 low in value.

baseball N 1 a team game using a truncheon-shaped bat and a ball, in which the person batting attempts to run as far as possible round a diamond-shaped pitch formed by four bases aiming to get back to the home plate to score a run. 2 the ball used in this game.

baseless ADJ having no cause or foundation.

basement N the lowest floor of a building, usu below ground level.

base metal N any metal that readily corrodes, tarnishes or oxidizes.

bash COLLOQ, VB 1 to strike or smash. 2 to attack harshly or maliciously with words. ➤ N 1 a heavy blow or knock. 2 a mark made by a heavy blow. 3 an attempt. ■ **bashing** N.

bashful ADJ lacking confidence; shy; self-conscious. ■ **bashfulness** N.

basic ADJ 1 referring to or forming the base or

basis of something. 2 belonging to, or at, a very simple or low level. 3 without additions. 4 CHEM referring or relating to, or forming, a base or bases. ➤ N (usu **the basics**) the essential parts or facts; the simplest principles. ■ **basically** ADV.

basil N an aromatic plant used as a herb.

basilica N 1 an ancient Roman public hall, with a rounded wall at one end and pillars along each side. 2 a church shaped like this.

basin N 1 a wide open dish, esp one for holding water. 2 a bowl or sink in a bathroom, etc for washing oneself in. 3 (also **basinful**) the amount a basin holds. 4 a valley or area of land drained by a river, or by the streams running into a river. 5 the deep part of a harbour; a dock.

basis N (PL **-ses**) 1 a principle on which an idea or theory, etc is based. 2 a foundation or starting point: a basis for discussion.

bask VB, INTR 1 to lie in comfort, esp in warmth or sunshine. 2 to enjoy and take great pleasure: basking in her success.

basket N 1 a container made of plaited or interwoven twigs, rushes, canes, etc. 2 (also **basketful**) the amount a basket holds. 3 BASKETBALL **a** either of the nets used to score a goal; **b** a goal scored.

basketball N 1 a team game in which players score by throwing a ball into nets fixed high up at each end of the court. 2 the ball used.

basmati rice N a type of long-grain rice.

basque N a tight-fitting bodice for women.

bas-relief N, ART sculpture in which the relief figures are only slightly raised.

bass[1] N, MUS 1 the lowest male singing voice. 2 a singer with such a voice. 3 a musical part written for such a voice or for an instrument of the lowest range. 4 COLLOQ a bass instrument, esp a bass guitar or a double-bass. ➤ ADJ of a musical instrument, voice or sound: low in pitch and range. ■ **bassist** N.

bass[2] N (**bass** or **basses**) 1 an edible marine fish. 2 a similar freshwater fish.

bass clef N, MUS a sign (𝄢) placed at the beginning of a piece of written music.

basset and **basset hound** N a breed of dog with a long body, smooth hair, short legs and long drooping ears.

bassoon N a large woodwind instrument with a very low sound. ■ **bassoonist** N.

bastard N 1 DATED, often OFFENSIVE a child born of parents not married to each other. 2 COARSE SLANG a specified kind of person: **rotten bastard** • **lucky bastard** • **poor bastard**.
➢ ADJ of a person: illegitimate.

baste[1] VB to pour hot fat, butter or juices over (esp roasting meat), during cooking.

baste[2] VB to sew (eg a seam) with temporary loose stitches.

bastion N 1 a kind of tower which sticks out from a castle wall. 2 a person, place or thing regarded as a defender of a principle, etc.

bat[1] N 1 a shaped piece of wood for hitting the ball in cricket, baseball, etc. 2 chiefly CRICKET a batsman or batswoman.
➢ VB (-tt-) 1 INTR, CRICKET, BASEBALL, etc to take a turn at hitting a ball with a bat. 2 to hit with, or as if with, a bat.
◆ **off one's own bat** without prompting.

bat[2] N any of various small nocturnal flying mammals.

bat[3] VB (-tt-) to open and close (one's eyelids) quickly.
◆ **not bat an eyelid** COLLOQ to show no surprise or emotion.

batch N a number of things or people dealt with at the same time.
➢ VB to arrange or treat (something) in batches.

bated ADJ.
◆ **with bated breath** hushed and tense with excitement, fear or anxiety.

bath N 1 a large open container for water, in which to wash the whole body while sitting in it. 2 an act of washing the body in a bath. 3 the water filling a bath. 4 (**the baths**) a public swimming pool.
➢ VB to wash (someone or something) in a bath.

bathe VB 1 INTR to swim in the sea, etc for pleasure. 2 INTR, chiefly N AMER to wash (oneself) in a bath; to take a bath. 3 to wash or treat (part of the body, etc) with water, or with a liquid, etc to clean it or to lessen pain. 4 of light, etc: to cover and surround (someone or something); to suffuse.
➢ N an act of swimming in the sea, etc; a swim or dip. ■ **bather** N.

bathos N in speech or writing: a sudden descent from very important, serious or beautiful ideas to very ordinary or trivial ones. ■ **bathetic** ADJ.

bathrobe N a loose towelling coat used esp before and after taking a bath.

bathroom N 1 a room containing a bath and now usu other washing facilities, a lavatory, etc. 2 esp N AMER a room with a lavatory.

bathyscaphe or **bathyscape** N a crewed vessel with an observation cabin on its underside, for exploring the ocean depths.

bathysphere N a deep-sea observation chamber, consisting of a steel sphere that is lowered and raised from a surface vessel.

batik N 1 a method of printing cloth by covering those parts not to be coloured with wax. 2 cloth coloured by this method.

batman N an army officer's personal servant.

baton N 1 a light thin stick used by the conductor of an orchestra or choir, etc to direct them. 2 a short heavy stick carried by a policeman as a weapon. 3 a short stick passed from one runner to another in a relay race. 4 a stick tossed and twirled, etc.

baton round N a plastic or rubber bullet.

batsman N, chiefly CRICKET (also **batswoman**) a person who bats or is batting.

battalion N an army unit made up of several companies and forming part of a brigade.

batten N 1 a long flat piece of wood used for keeping other pieces in place. 2 a strip of wood used to fasten the covers over the hatches in a ship's deck, etc.
➢ VB to fasten, strengthen or shut with battens.

batter[1] VB 1 TR & INTR to strike or hit hard and often, or continuously. 2 to damage or wear out through continual use. ■ **battering** N.

batter[2] N a mixture of eggs, flour and either milk or water, used in cooking.

batter[3] N, esp BASEBALL a person who bats.

battering-ram N a large wooden beam, formerly used in war for breaking down walls.

battery N (-ies) 1 a device that converts chemical energy into electrical energy in the form of direct current. 2 a long line of small tiered cages in which hens are kept. 3 LAW intentional physical attack on a person. 4 a a group of heavy guns with their equipment; b the place where they are mounted.

battle N 1 a fight between opposing armies, naval or air forces, etc or people. 2 a competition between opposing groups or people. 3 a long or difficult struggle. ➣ VB, INTR 1 to fight. 2 to struggle.

battle-cry N 1 a shout given by soldiers charging into battle. 2 a slogan used to arouse support for a cause, etc.

battledress N a soldier's ordinary uniform.

battlefield and **battleground** N 1 the place at which a battle is or was fought. 2 a site or area of intense disagreement.

battlement N a low wall around the top of a castle, etc with gaps for shooting through.

battle royal N (*battles royal*) 1 a general brawl or melée. 2 a long heated argument.

battleship N the largest type of warship.

batty ADJ (-ier, -iest) COLLOQ crazy; eccentric.

bauble N 1 a small cheap trinket. 2 a round coloured decoration hung on Christmas trees.

baulk see **balk**

bauxite N, GEOL a clay-like substance which is the main ore of aluminium.

bawdy ADJ (-ier, -iest) of language or writing, etc: containing coarsely humorous references to sex. ■ **bawdily** ADV. ■ **bawdiness** N.

bawl VB, INTR to cry or shout loudly. ➣ N a loud shout.

bay[1] N a body of water that forms a wide-mouthed indentation in the coastline.

bay[2] N 1 an enclosed or partly enclosed area within a building, vessel, etc for storage or some other purpose. 2 IN COMPOUNDS a compartment for storing or carrying, eg in an aircraft: bomb bay. 3 a a parking bay; b a loading bay.

bay[3] ADJ of a horse: reddish-brown in colour. ➣ N a bay-coloured horse.

bay[4] N any of various evergreen trees of the laurel family with shiny dark-green leaves.

bay[5] VB 1 INTR esp of large dogs: to make a deep howling bark or cry. 2 INTR of a crowd, etc: to howl or shout loudly.

bayonet N 1 a steel knife that fixes to the muzzle of a soldier's rifle. 2 (also **bayonet fitting**) a fitting for a light bulb or camera lens, etc in which prongs on its side fit into slots. ➣ VB to stab with a bayonet.

bay window N a three-sided or rounded window that juts out from the wall of a building.

bazaar N 1 a sale of goods, etc usu in order to raise money for a particular organization or purpose. 2 in Eastern countries: a market place or exchange.

bazooka N a portable anti-tank gun which fires small rockets.

BC ABBREV in dates: before Christ.

BCE ABBREV in dates: before the Common Era, sometimes used instead of **BC**, as a culturally neutral notation.

BCG or **bcg** ABBREV bacillus Calmette-Guérin, a vaccine to prevent tuberculosis.

be VB (*been, being*; PR T *am, are, is*; PA T *was, were*) INTR 1 to exist or live: I think, therefore I am. 2 to occur or take place: Lunch is in an hour. 3 to occupy a position in space: She is at home. 4 IN PA T to go: He's never been to Italy. 5 to remain or continue without change: Let it be. 6 (as a copula) used to link a subject and what is said about it: She is a doctor • He is ill.

7 used with the infinitive form of a verb to express a possibility, command, intention, outcome, etc: **if it were to rain • It was not to be.**
➢ AUXILIARY VERB **1** used with a past participle to form a passive construction: **The film was shown last night. 2** used with a present participle to form the progressive tenses: **He was running.**

beach N the sandy or stony shore of a sea.
➢ VB to push, pull or drive on to a beach.

beachhead N, MIL an area of shore captured from the enemy.

beacon N **1** a warning or guiding device for aircraft or ships. **2** a fire on a hill, mountain or high ground, lit as a signal.

bead N **1** a small ball strung with others, eg in a necklace. **2** (**beads**) a string of beads worn as jewellery, or one used when praying. **3** a small drop of liquid. **4** beading. ■ **beaded** ADJ.

beading N thin strips of patterned wood used to decorate the edges of furniture or walls, etc.

beadle N, BRIT **1** a person who leads formal processions in church or in some other institutions. **2** in Scotland: a church officer who attends the minister.

beady ADJ (**-ier, -iest**) USU DEROG of a person's eyes: small, round and bright.

beagle N a breed of small hunting-dog with a short-haired coat.

beak N **1** the horny projecting jaws of a bird. **2** any pointed projection that resembles this, eg the jaws of certain fishes. **3** SLANG a nose, esp a big pointed one.

beaker N **1** a large cup without a handle. **2** a glass container used in laboratory work.

beam N **1** a long straight thick piece of wood, used eg as a main structural component in a building. **2** a ray of light. **3** a broad radiant smile. **4** the widest part of a ship or boat. **5** a horizontal wooden bar on which gymnasts perform balancing exercises. **6** PHYS a directed flow of electromagnetic radiation or particles.
➢ VB **1** INTR to smile broadly. **2** INTR (often **beam**

down or **out**) to shine. **3** to send out or transmit (eg rays of light, radio waves, etc).

bean N **1** the edible seed of plants belonging to the pea family. **2** any plant belonging to the pea family that bears such seeds. **3** (usu **beans**) a seed or young pod of such a plant, used as food. **4** any seed that resembles those of the pea family, eg coffee bean.

bean bag N **1** a small bag filled with dried beans, used like a ball. **2** a large filled cushion used as seating.

beansprout and **beanshoot** N a young shoot of a bean plant eaten as a vegetable.

bear¹ VB (PA T **bore,** PA P **borne** or (in sense 7b) **born**) **1** to support or sustain (a weight or load). **2** to take or accept: **bear the blame. 3** to put up with or tolerate. **4 a** to allow; to be fit or suitable for (something): **It doesn't bear thinking about; b** to stand up to or be capable of withstanding: **will not bear close scrutiny. 5** to bring, take or carry: **bearing gifts. 6** to produce. **7a** to give birth to: **She has borne five sons; b** in the passive using past participle born: **He was born in 1990. 8** to carry in one's thought or memory: **bearing grudges. 9** to have: **bears no resemblance to his father. 10** to show or be marked by: **Her cheeks bore the traces of tears. 11** INTR to turn slightly in a given direction: **bear left. ■ bearable** ADJ.

bear² N (**bears** or **bear**) **1** any of various large carnivorous animals with a heavily built body, covered with thick fur. **2** a rough ill-mannered person. **3** a teddy bear. **4** STOCK EXCHANGE someone who sells shares, hoping to buy them back later at a much lower price.

beard N **1** the hair that grows on a man's chin. **2** a beard-like growth on some animals.

bearer N a person or thing that bears, carries or brings something.

bearing N **1** the way a person stands, walks, behaves, etc. **2** relevance. **3 a** the horizontal direction of a fixed point, or the path of a moving object, measured from a reference point on the Earth's surface; **b** (usu **bearings**) position or a calculation of position: **compass**

bearing. **4** (**bearings**) COLLOQ a sense or awareness of one's own position or surroundings. **5** any part of a machine or device that supports another part, and allows free movement between the two parts.

beast N **1** any large animal, esp a wild one. **2** COLLOQ a cruel brutal person.

beastly ADJ (**-ier, -iest**) COLLOQ unpleasant; disagreeable.

beat VB (PA T *beat,* PA P *beaten* or (now RARE) *beat*) **1** to hit (a person, animal, etc) violently and repeatedly. **2** to strike (something) repeatedly, eg to remove dust or make a sound. **3** INTR to knock or strike repeatedly. **4** to defeat. **5** to be too difficult to be solved or understood by (someone): **it beats me. 6** to mix thoroughly. **7** to shape or flatten by beating: **beat the hot metal with a hammer. 8** INTR to move in a regular pattern of strokes, etc: **heard my heart beating. 9** TR & INTR to move rhythmically up and down: **beating its wings. 10** (usu **beat time** or **beat out time**) to mark or show (musical time or rhythm) with the hand or a baton, etc. **11** (**beat back** or **down** or **off**) to push, drive or force away.
➤ N **1** a regular recurrent stroke, or its sound: **the beat of my heart. 2 a** in music and poetry, etc: the basic pulse, unit of rhythm or accent: **two beats to the bar; b** the conductor's stroke of the hand or baton indicating such a pulse; **c** in popular music: a strong rhythmic pulse. **3** a regular course: **a policeman's beat.**
➤ ADJ, COLLOQ, esp US worn out; exhausted.
■ **beating** N.
◆ **beat it** SLANG to go away.
◆ **beat up** or (US) **beat up on** to punch, kick or hit severely and repeatedly.

beaten ADJ **1** defeated or outmanoeuvred. **2** made smooth or hard by beating or treading: **beaten path. 3** shaped and made thin by beating: **beaten gold.**

beater N a person or thing that beats, eg a person who rouses game for shooting.

beatific ADJ expressing or revealing supreme peaceful happiness.

beatify VB (**-ies, -ied**) RC CHURCH to declare the blessed status of (a dead person), the first step towards canonization. ■ **beatification**.

beatitude N **1** (**the Beatitudes**) BIBLE the statements made by Christ about the kinds of people who receive God's blessing. **2** a state of blessedness.

beau N (*beaux* or *beaus*) **1** US OR DATED BRIT a boyfriend or male lover. **2** OLD USE a dandy.

Beaufort scale N, METEOROL a system for estimating wind speeds.

beauteous ADJ, POETIC beautiful.

beautician N a person who gives beauty treatments.

beautiful ADJ **1** having an appearance or qualities which please the senses or give rise to admiration in the mind. **2** COLLOQ very enjoyable; excellent. ■ **beautifully** ADV.

beautify VB (**-ies, -ied**) to make (something or someone) beautiful; to adorn or grace.

beauty N (**-ies**) **1** a quality pleasing to the senses, esp to the eye or ear, or giving aesthetic pleasure generally. **2** COLLOQ an excellent example: **a beauty of a black eye. 3** a benefit or advantage: **The beauty of the plan is its flexibility. 4** a beautiful woman or girl.

beauty spot N a place of great beauty.

beaver N **1** a large semi-aquatic rodent with dark-brown fur, large incisor teeth, webbed hind feet and a broad flat scaly tail. **2** its fur. **3** a hat made of beaver fur.
➤ VB, INTR (esp **beaver away at sth**) COLLOQ, chiefly BRIT to work hard and persistently at something.

becalmed ADJ of a sailing ship: motionless and unable to move because of lack of wind.

because CONJ for the reason that.

beck N.
◆ **at sb's beck and call** having to be always ready to carry out their wishes.

beckon VB, TR & INTR to summon (someone) with a gesture.

become VB (PA T *became,* PA P *become*) **1** INTR

to come or grow to be, or develop into (something). **2** FORMAL esp of clothing: to suit, look good on or befit (someone).
◆ **become of sb** or **sth** to happen to them.

becoming ADJ **1** attractive. **2** suitable.

becquerel N, PHYS the SI unit of activity of a radioactive source per second.

bed N **1** a piece of furniture for sleeping on. **2** a place in which eg an animal sleeps or rests. **3** COLLOQ sleep or rest: **ready for bed**. **4** the bottom of a river, lake or sea. **5** an area in a garden for growing plants. **6** a flat surface or base on which something can be supported or laid down. **7** a layer, eg of oysters, sedimentary rock, etc. **8** a place available for occupancy in a residential home, nursing home or hospital. ➤ VB (**-dd-**) **1** TR & INTR (usu **bed down**) to go to bed, or put (someone) in bed or in a place to sleep: **bedded down on the sofa**. **2** (usu **bed out**) to plant (something) in the soil, in a garden, etc. **3** to place or fix (something) firmly. **4** COLLOQ to have sex with (someone).

bed and breakfast N **1** at a guest-house, hotel, etc: overnight accommodation with breakfast included in the price. **2** a guest-house, etc that provides accommodation and breakfast.

bedbug N any of various species of pest that infest bedding and feed on human blood.

bedclothes PL N blankets, etc for a bed.

bedding N **1** bedclothes, and sometimes also a mattress and pillows, etc. **2** straw or hay, etc for animals to sleep on. **3** GEOL stratification.

bedeck VB to cover (something or someone) with decorations; to adorn.

bedevil VB (**-ll-**; US **-l-**) **1** to cause continual difficulties or trouble to (someone or something). **2** to throw (something or someone) into confusion. ■ **bedevilment** N.

bedfellow N **1** a partner or associate. **2** a person with whom one shares a bed.

bedlam N, COLLOQ a very noisy confused place or situation.

bed linen N sheets and pillowcases for a bed.

Bedouin N (**Bedouin** or **Bedouins**) a member of a nomadic tent-dwelling Arab tribe that lives in the deserts of the Middle East.

bedpan N a wide shallow pan used as a toilet by someone who is unable to get out of bed.

bedraggled ADJ very wet and untidy.

bedridden ADJ not able to get out of bed.

bedrock N **1** solid rock forming the lowest layer under soil and rock fragments. **2** the basic principle, etc on which something rests.

bedroom N a room for sleeping in.

bedsitting-room, **bedsit** and **bedsitter** N, BRIT a single room combining bedroom and sitting-room.

bedsore N an ulcer on a person's skin, caused by lying in bed for long periods.

bedspread N a top cover for a bed.

bedstead N the frame of a bed.

bee[1] N any of numerous four-winged insects, some species of which live in colonies and are kept for their honey.

bee[2] N, N AMER a meeting of friends to work on a particular task together (eg a **quilting bee**) or in competition (eg a **spelling-bee**).

beech N **1** (also **beech tree**) a deciduous tree or shrub with smooth grey bark. **2** (also **beechwood**) the hard wood of this tree.

beef N (PL in sense 3 **beefs**, in sense 4 **beeves**) **1** the flesh of a bull, cow or ox, used as food. **2** COLLOQ muscle; vigorous muscular force or strength. **3** SLANG a complaint or argument. ➤ VB, INTR, SLANG to complain or grumble.

beefburger N a piece of minced beef made into a flat round shape and grilled or fried.

beefeater or **Beefeater** N, BRIT a yeoman guard at the Tower of London.

beefy ADJ (**-ier, -iest**) **1** made of or like beef. **2** COLLOQ eg of a person: fleshy or muscular. ■ **beefiness** N.

beehive N a box or hut in which bees are kept.

beekeeper N a person who keeps bees for

their honey, as a hobby, etc. ■ **beekeeping** N.

beeline N.
◆ **make a beeline for sth** or **sb** to go directly or purposefully to it or them.

beep N a short high-pitched sound, like that made by a car horn.
➤ VB, TR & INTR to produce a beep on or with (something).

beer N 1 an alcoholic drink brewed by the slow fermentation of malted cereal grains, usu barley, flavoured with hops. 2 a glass, can or bottle of this drink. ■ **beery** (**-ier, -iest**) ADJ.

beeswax N 1 a solid yellowish substance produced by bees for their combs. 2 this substance, refined and used esp as a polish.

beet N any of several types of edible plant with large round or carrot-shaped roots which are also used for making sugar (**beet sugar**).

beetle N an insect with thickened forewings modified to form rigid horny cases which cover and protect the hindwings.

beetroot N a type of plant with a round red root which is cooked and used as a vegetable.

befit VB (**-tt-**) FORMAL to be suitable or right for. ■ **befitting** ADJ.

before PREP 1 earlier than something: **before noon. 2** ahead of or in front of someone or something. **3** in the presence of, or for the attention of, someone: **The question before us. 4** rather than or in preference to someone or something: **put money before friendship.**
➤ CONJ 1 earlier than the time when something occurs: **Tidy up before dinner. 2** rather than doing something: **I'd die before I'd surrender.**
➤ ADV previously; in the past.

beforehand ADV 1 before a particular time or event. 2 in preparation or anticipation.

befriend VB to become the friend of or be friendly and helpful towards (someone).

beg VB (**-gg-**) TR & INTR 1 to ask for (money or food, etc). 2 to ask earnestly or humbly. 3 esp of an animal: to sit up on the hindquarters, with paws raised.

◆ **go begging** COLLOQ to be unused or unwanted.

beggar N 1 a person who lives by begging. 2 COLLOQ, chiefly BRIT a person: **cheeky beggar.** ■ **beggarly** ADJ.

begin VB (PA T **began**, PA P **begun**, PR P **beginning**) 1 TR & INTR to start. 2 TR & INTR to bring or come into being. 3 INTR to start speaking. 4 INTR to be the first or to take the first step. 5 INTR, COLLOQ to have the ability or possibility to do something: **I can't even begin to understand.**

beginner N someone who is just starting to learn, or is still learning, how to do something.

beginning N 1 the point or occasion at which something begins. 2 an opening or first part of something.

begone EXCLAM, POETIC OR OLD USE go away!

begonia N a tropical plant with brightly coloured waxy flowers.

begrudge VB 1 to do, give or allow (something) unwillingly or with regret. 2 (**begrudge sb sth**) to resent them for it.

beguile VB to charm or captivate. ■ **beguiling** ADJ.

behalf N interest, part or benefit.
◆ **on** or (N AMER) **in behalf of sb** or **sth** and **on** or (N AMER) **in sb's** or **sth's behalf 1** as a representative of them or it. **2** in the interest of them or it.

behave VB 1 INTR to act in a specified way. 2 TR & INTR (**behave oneself**) to act or conduct oneself in a suitable, polite or orderly way.

behaviour or (US) **behavior** N way of behaving; manners. ■ **behavioural** ADJ.

behead VB to cut off the head of (someone), usu as a form of capital punishment.

behemoth N something huge or monstrous.

behind PREP 1 at or towards the back or the far side. 2 later or slower than something; after in time: **behind schedule. 3** supporting: **We're all behind you. 4** in the past: **Those problems are all behind me now. 5** not as far advanced:

Technologically, they are behind the Japanese. **6** being the cause or precursor: reasons behind the decision.
➤ ADV **1** in or to the back or far side. **2** remaining; in a place, etc that is or was being left or departed from: **Wait behind after class. 3** following: **The dog was running behind. 4** in or into arrears: **fell behind with the rent.**
➤ ADJ **1** not up to date; late: **behind with the payments. 2** not having progressed enough: **I got behind with my work.**
➤ N, COLLOQ the buttocks.

behold LITERARY OR OLD USE, VB (PA T & PA P *beheld*) to see; to look at (something or someone).
➤ EXCLAM see!; look! ■ **beholder** N.

beholden ADJ (**beholden to**) FORMAL owing a debt or favour to (someone or something).

beige N a very pale pinkish-brown or yellowish-brown colour.

being N **1** existence; life: **come into being. 2** a living person or thing. **3** essence; essential self: **She was like part of my very being.**

bejewelled ADJ decorated with jewels.

belabour or (US) **belabor** VB **1** to argue about or discuss (something) at excessive length. **2** to attack or batter (someone or something), either physically or with words.

belated ADJ happening or coming late, or too late. ■ **belatedly** ADV.

belay VB **1** MOUNTAINEERING to make (a climber) safe by tying their rope to a rock, etc. **2** NAUT to make (a rope) secure by winding it round a hook, etc.

belch VB **1** INTR to give out air noisily from the stomach through the mouth; to burp. **2** (also **belch out**) to send out (eg smoke) forcefully or in quantity.
➤ N an act of belching.

beleaguer VB **1** to cause (someone) bother or worry; to beset. **2** to lay siege to (eg a city).
■ **beleaguered** ADJ.

belfry N (*-ies*) **1** the part of a tower or steeple, where the bells are hung. **2** a bell tower.

belie VB (*belying*) **1** to show (something) to be

untrue or false. **2** to give a false idea or impression of (something): **Her cheerful face belied the seriousness of the situation.**

belief N **1** a principle or idea, etc accepted as true, esp without proof. **2** trust or confidence. **3** a person's religious faith. **4** a firm opinion.

believe VB **1** to accept (something) as true. **2** to accept what is said or proposed as true. **3** to think or suppose: **I believe you're right.**
■ **believable** ADJ. ■ **believer** N.
◆ **believe in sb** to have trust or confidence in them.
◆ **believe in sth** or **sb 1** to be convinced of the existence of it or them: **believe in ghosts. 2** to have religious faith about God or a supreme being, etc.
◆ **believe in sth** to consider it right or good.

belittle VB to treat (something or someone) as unimportant, or of little or no significance; to speak or write disparagingly about (it or them).

bell N **1** a deep hollow object, usu one made of metal, rounded at one end and wide and open at the other, which makes a ringing sound when struck by the small clapper fixed inside it. **2** any other device which makes a ringing or buzzing sound. **3** the sound made by such an object or device.

belladonna N **1** deadly nightshade. **2** a compound, used medicinally, obtained from the deadly nightshade plant.

bellboy and (N AMER) **bellhop** N a hotel worker who carries guests' bags, delivers messages, etc.

belle N, DATED a beautiful woman.

bellicose ADJ likely to, or seeking to, cause an argument or war; aggressive; warlike.

belligerent ADJ **1** aggressive; ready to argue. **2** engaged in conflict or war.
➤ N a person, faction or country fighting a war.
■ **belligerence** N.

bell jar N a bell-shaped glass cover used esp in a laboratory.

bellow VB **1** INTR to make a loud deep cry like a bull. **2** TR & INTR to shout loudly.

➤ N **1** the roar of a bull. **2** a deep loud cry.

bellows SING OR PL N (also **a pair of bellows**) a device for creating a current of air, used eg to fan a fire.

belly N (-*ies*) **1** the part of the human body below the chest, containing the organs used for digesting food. **2** the stomach. **3** the lower or under part of an animal's body, which contains the stomach and other organs. **4** the deep interior of something. **5** a swelling part of something, eg the underside of a plane, etc. ➤ VB (-*ies*, -*ied*) TR & INTR (usu **belly out**) to bulge out, or make (something) bulge out.

belly button N, COLLOQ the navel.

belly dance N a sensual dance performed by women, in which the belly and hips are moved in a circling motion. ➤ VB (**belly-dance**) INTR to perform a belly dance. ■ **belly-dancer** N.

bellyful N **1** enough to eat. **2** SLANG more than enough, or more than one can bear.

belong VB, INTR **1 a** to have a proper place, or have the right qualities to fit (esp with or in something or someone); to go along or together (with something or someone); **b** to be properly classified. **2** to be entirely acceptable; to be at home, or to fit in. ◆ **belong to sb** or **sth** to be their or its property or right. ◆ **belong to sth** to be a member of a group, club, etc or a native of a place.

belongings PL N personal possessions.

beloved ADJ much loved; very dear. ➤ N, chiefly LITERARY a person who is much loved.

below PREP **1** lower in position, rank, amount, degree, number or status, etc than a specified thing. **2** not worthy of someone; beneath them. **3** under the surface of something. ➤ ADV **1** at, to or in a lower place, point or level. **2** further on in a book, etc: See below.

belt N **1** a long narrow piece of leather or cloth worn around the waist. **2** a seat belt. **3** an area or zone: **a belt of rain**. **4** a band of rubber, etc moving the wheels, or round the wheels, of a machine. Often IN COMPOUNDS: **fan belt**

• **conveyor belt**. **5** SLANG a hard blow. ➤ VB **1** to put a belt around. **2** to beat with a belt. **3** TR & INTR, COLLOQ to hit someone. **4** INTR (esp **belt along**) COLLOQ to move fast. ◆ **belt up** COLLOQ **1** to stop talking; to be quiet. **2** to fasten one's seat-belt. ◆ **under one's belt** COLLOQ acquired; in one's possession.

beluga N **1** a kind of large sturgeon. **2** caviar from this sturgeon. **3** a white whale.

bemoan VB to express great sadness or regret about (something).

bemused ADJ bewildered; confused.

ben N, SCOT esp in place names: a mountain or mountain peak: **Ben Nevis**.

bench N **1** a long seat for seating several people. **2** a work-table for a carpenter, scientist, etc. **3** (**the bench** or **the Bench**) **a** the place where the judge or magistrate sits in court; **b** judges and magistrates as a group.

benchmark N anything taken or used as a standard or point of reference.

bend VB (*bent*) **1** TR & INTR to make or become angled or curved. **2** INTR to move or stretch in a curve. **3** INTR (usu **bend down** or **over**) to move the top part of the body forward and down towards the ground. **4** TR & INTR to submit or force (someone or something) to submit: **bent them to his will**. **5** to aim or direct (one's attention, etc) towards something. ➤ N **1** a curve or bent part. **2** the act of curving or bending. ■ **bendy** ADJ. ◆ **round the bend** COLLOQ mad; crazy.

the bends SING OR PL N decompression sickness.

beneath PREP **1** under; below. **2** not worthy of (someone or something). ➤ ADV, RATHER FORMAL OR ARCHAIC below.

Benedictine N **1** a Christian religious order that follows the teachings of St Benedict. **2** a liqueur first made by Benedictine monks.

benediction N, CHRISTIANITY **1** a prayer giving blessing. **2** RC CHURCH a service in which the congregation is blessed. ■ **benedictory** ADJ.

benefactor N a person who gives help, esp financial help, to an institution, cause or person. Also (if a female benefactor) **benefactress**.

benefice N a position as a priest, or other church office, and its income.

beneficent ADJ kind and generous. ■ **beneficence** N.

beneficial ADJ having benefits; advantageous.

beneficiary N (-*ies*) 1 a person who benefits from something. 2 LAW a a person who is entitled to estate or interest held for them by trustees; b a person who receives property or money, etc in a will, or benefits under an insurance policy, etc. Also AS ADJ.

benefit N 1 something good gained or received. 2 advantage or sake. 3 (often **benefits**) a payment made by a government or company insurance scheme, usu to someone who is ill or out of work. 4 a concert, match, etc from which the profits are given to a particular cause, person or group in need.
➤ VB (-*t*-; US also -*tt*-) 1 INTR (esp **benefit from** or **by**) to gain an advantage from (something). 2 to do good to (someone).

benevolence N 1 the desire to do good; kindness; generosity. 2 an act of kindness or generosity. ■ **benevolent** ADJ.

benign ADJ 1 kind; gentle. 2 MED a of a disorder: not having harmful effects; of a mild form; b of a cancerous tumour: not invading and destroying the surrounding tissue. 3 favourable; promising. ■ **benignly** ADV.

benignant ADJ 1 MED of a disease, etc: not fatal; a less common word for **benign**. 2 kind. 3 favourable. ■ **benignancy** N (-*ies*).

bent ADJ 1 not straight; curved or having a bend. 2 BRIT SLANG dishonest; corrupt. 3 BRIT, DEROG SLANG homosexual. 4 (usu **bent on** or **upon sth**) having all one's attention or energy directed on it, or on doing it: **bent on revenge**.
➤ N a natural inclination, liking or aptitude.

benumb VB 1 to make numb. 2 to stupefy.

benzene N, CHEM an inflammable colourless liquid hydrocarbon widely used as a solvent.

benzine or **benzin** N a volatile mixture of hydrocarbons distilled from petroleum, used as a motor fuel and solvent, etc.

bequeath VB 1 to leave (personal property) in a will (to someone). 2 to pass on.

bequest N 1 an act of leaving personal property in a will. 2 anything left or bequeathed in someone's will.

berate VB to scold (someone) severely.

bereaved ADJ deprived of a close relative or friend by death. ■ **bereavement** N.

bereft ADJ (usu **bereft of sth**) deprived of it.

beret N a round flat cap made of soft material.

bergamot N 1 a small citrus tree bearing acidic pear-shaped fruits. 2 (also **bergamot oil**) oil extracted from the rind of this fruit.

berk or **burk** N, BRIT SLANG a fool or twit.

berry N (-*ies*) 1 BOT an indehiscent fleshy fruit whose seeds are not surrounded by a stony protective layer, eg grape, cucumber, tomato. 2 any of the various small fleshy edible fruits that are not true berries, eg strawberry.

berserk ADJ (esp **go berserk**) 1 violently angry. 2 COLLOQ & FACETIOUS furious; crazy.

berth N 1 a sleeping-place in a ship or train, etc. 2 a place in a port where a ship or boat can be tied up.
➤ VB 1 to tie up (a ship) in its berth. 2 INTR of a ship: to moor.

beryl N, GEOL a hard mineral, used as a source of beryllium and as a gemstone.

beryllium N, CHEM a silvery-grey metal, obtained from the mineral beryl.

beseech VB (*besought* or *beseeched*) FORMAL OR LITERARY to ask (someone) earnestly.

beset VB (*beset, besetting*) now chiefly LITERARY OR FORMAL 1 to worry or harass (someone). 2 to beseige (a person or people).

beside PREP 1 next to, by the side of or near. 2 not relevant: **beside the point**. 3 as compared with: **All beauty pales beside hers**.

◆ **beside oneself** in a state of uncontrollable anger, excitement, etc.

besides PREP **1** in addition to. **2** apart from. ➤ ADV **1** also; as well. **2** moreover; in any case.

besiege VB **1** to surround (a town or stronghold) with an army in order to force it to surrender. **2** to gather round (something or someone) in a crowd; to surround. **3** to inundate or overwhelm (someone): besieged with offers of help.

besotted ADJ foolishly infatuated (with or by someone or something).

bespatter VB to cover with splashes.

bespeak VB, FORMAL **1** to claim, engage or order (something) in advance. **2** to show or be evidence of (something). **3** to indicate (something) in advance; to foretell.

bespectacled ADJ wearing spectacles.

bespoke ADJ, now rather FORMAL **1** of clothes: made to fit a particular person. **2** of a tailor: making clothes to order, to fit individual customers and their requirements.

best ADJ (SUPERLATIVE OF **good**) **1** most excellent, suitable or desirable. **2** most successful, clever, able or skilled, etc. **3** the greatest or most: the best part of an hour.
➤ ADV (SUPERLATIVE OF **well**[1]) **1** most successfully or skilfully, etc: Who did best in the test? **2** more than, or better than, all others: Which hat looks best?
➤ N **1** (**the best**) the most excellent or suitable person or thing; the most desirable quality or result, etc: the best of the bunch. **2** the greatest effort; one's utmost: Do your best. **3** a person's finest clothes: Sunday best. **4** (**the best**) victory or success: get the best of an argument. **5** (usu **the best of sth**) a winning majority from (a given number, etc).
➤ VB, COLLOQ to beat or defeat (someone).
◆ **at best** considered in the most favourable way; in the best of circumstances.

bestial ADJ **1** DEROG cruel; savage; brutish. **2** rude; unrefined; uncivilized. **3** sexually depraved. **4** like an animal.

bestiality N (**-ies**) **1** disgusting or cruel behaviour. **2** sexual intercourse between a human and an animal.

bestir VB (**bestir oneself**) to make an effort to become active; to get oneself moving or busy.

best man N a bridegroom's chief attendant at a wedding.

bestow VB (**bestow on**) FORMAL to give (a title, etc) to (someone). ■ **bestowal** N.

bestseller N a book or other item which sells in large numbers. ■ **bestselling** ADJ.

bet VB (*bet* or *betted, betting*) **1** TR & INTR to risk (a sum of money or other asset) on predicting the outcome or result of a future event, esp a race or other sporting event. **2** (usu **bet sb sth**) to make a bet (with someone) of (a specified amount). **3** COLLOQ to feel sure or confident: I bet they've forgotten.
➤ N **1** an act of betting. **2** a sum of money, or other asset, betted. **3** COLLOQ an opinion or guess. **4** COLLOQ a choice of action or way ahead: Our best bet is to postpone the trip.
◆ **you bet** SLANG certainly; of course.

beta N the second letter of the Greek alphabet (Β, β).

beta-blocker N, MED a drug used to treat high blood pressure and angina.

betacarotene N, BIOCHEM a form of carotene, found in yellow and orange fruits and vegetables, converted to vitamin A in the body.

betel N an Asian palm, the fruit of which (the **betel nut**) is chewed as a mild stimulant.

bête noire N (*bêtes noires*) a person or thing that esp bothers, annoys or frightens someone.

betray VB **1** to hand over or expose (a friend or one's country, etc) to an enemy. **2** to give away or disclose (a secret, etc). **3** to break (a promise, etc) or to be unfaithful to (someone). **4** to be evidence of: Her face betrayed her unhappiness. ■ **betrayal** N. ■ **betrayer** N.

betrothal N, FORMAL engagement to be married.

betrothed FORMAL OR FACETIOUS, ADJ of a person: engaged to marry someone.

➤ N a person to whom someone is betrothed.

better ADJ (COMPARATIVE OF **good**) **1** more excellent, suitable or desirable, etc. **2** (usu **better at sth**) more successful, skilful, etc in doing it. **3** (COMPARATIVE OF **well**[1]) (esp **be** or **feel** or **get better**) improved in health. **4** greater: the better part of a day.
➤ ADV (COMPARATIVE OF **well**[1]) **1** more excellently, successfully or fully, etc. **2** in or to a greater degree.
➤ N **1** (esp **betters**) a person superior in quality or status, etc. **2** (**the better**) the thing or person that is the more excellent or suitable, etc of two comparable things or people.
➤ VB **1** to beat or improve on (something). **2** to make (something) more suitable or desirable.
◆ **get the better of sb** to gain the advantage over them; to outwit them.

betterment N improvement or advancement.

betting N gambling by predicting the outcome of some future event, eg a sporting event.

betting-shop N, BRIT a licensed establishment where bets can be placed; a bookmaker's.

between PREP **1** in, to, through or across the space dividing (two people, places, times, etc). **2** to and from: travelling between Leeds and Bradford. **3** in combination; acting together: They bought it between them. **4** shared out among: Divide the money between you. **5** involving a choice between alternatives: choose between right and wrong. **6** including; involving: a fight between rivals.
➤ ADV (also **in between**) in or into the middle of (two points in space or time, etc): time between appointments.

bevel N a sloping edge to a surface, meeting another surface at an angle.
➤ VB (-*ll*-; US -*l*-) **1** to give a bevel to (eg a piece of wood). **2** INTR to slope at an angle.

beverage N, FORMAL a prepared drink.

bevvy or **bevy** N (-*ies*) COLLOQ **1** alcoholic drink, or an individual alcoholic drink. **2** a drinking session.

bevy N (-*ies*) **1** a group of women or girls. **2** a flock of larks, quails or swans.

beware VB (only in imperative and infinitive) **1** INTR (usu **beware of**) to be careful of (something); to be on one's guard. **2** OLD USE OR LITERARY to be on one's guard against (something or someone).

bewilder VB to confuse, disorientate or puzzle thoroughly. ■ **bewildering** ADJ.

bewitch VB **1** to charm, fascinate or enchant. **2** to cast a spell on (someone or something).

beyond PREP **1** on the far side of: beyond the hills. **2** farther on in time or place. **3** out of the range, reach, understanding, possibility, etc of. **4** greater or better in amount, size, or level: beyond all our expectations. **5** other than: unable to help beyond giving money.
➤ ADV farther away; to or on the far side of.
➤ N (**the beyond**) the unknown, esp life after death.

bezel N **1** the sloped surface of a cutting tool. **2** a grooved rim which holds eg a gem in its setting. **3** an oblique side or face of a cut gem.

bhangra N a style of pop music created from a mix of traditional Punjabi and Western pop.

biannual ADJ occurring or produced, etc twice a year. ■ **biannually** ADV.

bias N **1** an inclination to favour or disfavour one side against another in a dispute, competition, etc; a prejudice. **2** a tendency or principal quality in a person's character.
➤ VB (-*s*-; also -*ss*-) **1** to influence or prejudice, esp unfairly. **2** to give a bias to (something).
■ **biased** or **biassed** ADJ.

biathlon N an outdoor sporting event involving skiing and shooting.

bib N **1** a piece of cloth or plastic fastened under a baby's or child's chin to protect its clothes while eating or drinking. **2** the top part of an apron or overalls.

Bible N **1 a** (**the Bible**) the sacred writings of the Christian Church, consisting of the Old and New Testaments; **b** (sometimes **bible**) a copy of these writings. **2 a** (**the Bible**) the Jewish Scriptures; the Old Testament or Hebrew Bible; **b** (sometimes **bible**) a copy of these. **3** (usu **bible**) an authoritative and comprehensive book on a particular subject. ■ **biblical** ADJ.

bibliography N (-*ies*) **1** a list of books by one author or on one subject. **2** a list of the books used as sources by a writer. **3** the study, description or knowledge of books.
■ **bibliographer** N.

bibliophile N an admirer of books.

bicameral ADJ of a legislative body: made up of two chambers.

bicarbonate of soda N, COLLOQ sodium bicarbonate, a white powder used in baking (as **baking soda** and **baking powder**), and as an indigestion remedy.

bicentenary N (-*ies*) esp BRIT a two-hundredth anniversary of an event.

biceps N (PL *biceps*) the muscle at the front of the upper arm.

bicker VB, INTR, COLLOQ to argue or quarrel in a petty way (esp about or over something trivial).

bicycle N a vehicle consisting of a metal frame with two wheels one behind the other and a saddle, which is driven by turning pedals with the feet and steered by handlebars attached to the front wheel.

bid¹ VB (*bid, bidding*) **1** TR & INTR to offer (an amount of money) when trying to buy something, esp at an auction. **2** TR & INTR, CARDS to state in advance (the number of tricks one will try to win). **3** INTR (esp **bid for sth**) to state a price one will charge for work to be done.
➤ N **1** an offer of an amount of money in payment for something, esp at an auction.
2 CARDS a statement of how many tricks one proposes to win. **3** COLLOQ an attempt to obtain or achieve something: **a bid for freedom**.
■ **bidder** N.

bid² VB (PA T *bade*, PA P *bidden*, PR P *bidding*) FORMAL, ARCHAIC OR LITERARY **1** to express (a wish or greeting, etc): **We bid you welcome**. **2** (with an imperative) to command, request or invite: **The king bade him kneel**.

biddable ADJ compliant; obedient; docile.

bidding N.
◆ **do sb's bidding** to obey their orders.

bide VB (PA T *bided* or *bode*) INTR, SCOT OR OLD USE to wait or stay.
◆ **bide one's time** to wait patiently for a good opportunity or for the right moment.

bidet N a small low basin with taps, for washing the genital and anal areas.

biennial ADJ **1** occurring once in every two years. **2** esp of a plant: lasting two years.
➤ N **1** BOT a plant which takes two years to complete its life cycle. **2** an event which takes place, or is celebrated, every two years.

bier N a movable stand on which a coffin rests or is transported.

bifocal ADJ of a lens: **1** having two different focal lengths. **2** having two separate sections with different focal lengths, one for near vision, and one for viewing distant objects.

bifocals PL N glasses with bifocal lenses.

bifurcate VB, INTR, FORMAL to divide into two parts or branches; to fork.
➤ ADJ forked or branched. ■ **bifurcation** N.

big ADJ **1** large or largest in size, amount, weight, number, power, etc. **2** significant or important to someone. **3** important, powerful or successful. **4** elder: **my big sister**. **5** grown-up: **not big enough to go**. **6** often IRONIC generous or magnanimous: **That was big of him**.
7 boastful; ambitious: **big ideas**.
➤ ADV, COLLOQ in a boastful, extravagant or ambitious way: **act big**.
◆ **in a big way** COLLOQ very much; strongly and enthusiastically.

bigamy N (-*ies*) the crime of being married to two wives or husbands at the same time.
■ **bigamist** N. ■ **bigamous** ADJ.

Big Bang N the theory that the universe originated from a gigantic explosion.

Big Brother N an all-powerful government or organization, etc, or its leader.

big game N large animals, such as lions, tigers and elephants, etc hunted for sport.

bighead N, COLLOQ, DEROG a conceited or arrogant person. ■ **bigheaded** ADJ.

bight N 1 a stretch of gently curving coastline. 2 a loose curve or loop in a rope.

big noise and (chiefly BRIT) **big shot** N, COLLOQ an important or powerful person.

bigot N someone who is persistently prejudiced and refuses to tolerate the opinions of others. ■ **bigoted** ADJ. ■ **bigotry** N (-*ies*).

bigwig N, COLLOQ an important person.

bijou N (*bijoux* or *bijous*) a small delicate jewel or trinket.
➤ ADJ small and elegant.

bike N, COLLOQ 1 a bicycle. 2 a motorcycle.
➤ VB, INTR to ride a bicycle or motorcycle.
■ **biker** N.

bikini N a two-piece swimsuit for women.

bilateral ADJ 1 of a treaty, talks, etc: involving two countries, parties or groups, etc. 2 referring to, or on, two sides. ■ **bilaterally** ADV.

bilberry N 1 a small deciduous shrub. 2 its edible round black berry.

bile N 1 BIOL a yellowish-green alkaline liquid produced by the liver to aid the digestion of fats. 2 LITERARY anger, irritability or bad temper.

bilge N 1 (usu **bilges**) the lowermost parts on the inside of a ship's hull. 2 (also **bilge-water**) the dirty water that collects in the bilges.

biliary ADJ of bile, the bile ducts or the gall bladder.

bilingual ADJ written in, spoken in, or able to speak two languages. ■ **bilingualism** N.

bilious ADJ 1 affected by a disorder relating to the secretion of bile. 2 of a colour: unpleasant and sickly. 3 peevish; bad-tempered.

bilk VB 1 to avoid paying (someone) money owed. 2 to cheat (someone).

bill¹ N 1 a a printed or written statement of the amount of money owed for goods or services received; an invoice; b such a statement for food and drink received in a restaurant, etc; c the amount of money owed. 2 a written plan or draft for a proposed law. 3 N AMER, ESP US a banknote. 4 an advertising poster.

5 a programme of entertainment.
➤ VB 1 to send or give a bill to (someone), requesting payment for goods, etc. 2 to advertise (a person or event) in a poster, etc.

bill² N 1 the beak of a bird. 2 any structure which resembles this. 3 a long thin piece of land that extends into the sea.

billabong N, AUSTRAL 1 a pool of water left when a river or stream dries up. 2 a branch of a river with no outflow.

billboard N, esp N AMER a hoarding.

billet N a house, often a private home, where soldiers are lodged temporarily.
➤ VB to give or assign lodging to (soldiers, etc).

billet-doux N (*billets-doux*) often HUMOROUS a love-letter.

billhook N a cutting tool with a long curved blade, used for pruning, lopping, etc.

billiards SING N an indoor game played with a cue and coloured balls on a covered table.

billion N (*billions* or after a number *billion*) 1 a thousand million. 2 FORMERLY in the UK and France, etc: a million million. 3 (usu **a billion** or **billions of sth**) COLLOQ a great number; lots. ■ **billionth** N, ADJ.

billionaire and **billionairess** N a person who has over a billion pounds, dollars, etc.

bill of exchange N (*bills of exchange*) FINANCE esp in international trade: a document promising payment of a specified sum of money.

bill of fare N (*bills of fare*) a menu.

billow VB, INTR 1 eg of smoke: to move in large waves or clouds. 2 (usu **billow out**) to swell or bulge, like a sail in the wind.
➤ N a rolling upward-moving mass of smoke or mist, etc. ■ **billowing** or **billowy** ADJ.

billposter and **billsticker** N a person who puts up advertising posters on hoardings, etc.

billy and **billycan** N (*billies*) BRIT & ESP AUSTRAL a metal cooking pot with a lid and wire handle used esp when camping.

billy goat N a male goat.

bimbo N, DEROG SLANG a young woman who is physically attractive, but empty-headed.

bimetallic ADJ made of or using two metals.

bimonthly ADJ **1** occurring or produced, etc once every two months. **2** occurring or produced, etc twice a month. Also AS ADV.

bin N **1** a container for depositing or storing rubbish. **2** a container for storing some kinds of food. **3** a large industrial container. **4** a stand or case for storing bottles of wine.

binary ADJ **1** consisting of or containing two parts or elements. **2** COMP, MATH denoting a system that consists of two components, esp a number system which uses the digits 0 and 1.
➤ N (-*ies*) **1** a thing made up of two parts.
2 ASTRON a binary star.

bind VB (*bound*) **1** to tie or fasten tightly.
2 (often **bind up**) to tie or pass strips of cloth or bandage, etc around (something). **3** to control or prevent (someone or something) from moving; to restrain (them or it). **4** to make (someone) promise to do something. **5** to require or oblige (someone) to do something: He is legally bound to reply. **6** to fasten together and put a cover on (the separate pages of a book). **7** to put a strip of cloth on the edge of (something) to strengthen it. **8** to cause (dry ingredients) to stick together.
➤ N, COLLOQ a tedious or annoying situation; something that limits or hampers one.

binder N **1** a hard book-like cover in which papers can be kept in order. **2** a person or business that binds books. **3** a reaping machine which ties cut grain into bundles.

bindery N (-*ies*) a place where books are bound.

binding N **1** the part of a book cover on to which the pages are stuck. **2** cloth or tape, etc used to bind something.
➤ ADJ formally or legally obliging someone to do something: **a binding contract**.

bindweed N convolvulus, or any of several other plants with twining habit.

binge N, COLLOQ a bout of over-indulgence, usu in eating and drinking.
➤ VB (*bingeing* or *binging*) INTR to indulge in a binge.

bingo N a game in which each player has a card with a set of numbers on it, each number, if called, being marked off until one player has the winning sequence.

binnacle N, NAUT a case for a ship's compass.

binoculars PL N an optical instrument designed for viewing distant objects, consisting of two small telescopes side by side.

biochemistry N the scientific study of the chemical compounds and chemical reactions that occur within the cells of living organisms.
■ **biochemical** ADJ. ■ **biochemist** N.

biodegradable ADJ capable of being broken down by bacteria, fungi or other living organisms.

bioengineering N **1** MED the application of engineering methods and technology to biology and medicine, esp in designing and manufacturing artificial limbs, hip joints, pacemakers, etc. **2** BIOL the application of engineering methods and technology to the biosynthesis of plant and animal products.

biography N (-*ies*) **1** an account of a person's life. **2** biographies as a genre. ■ **biographer** N. ■ **biographical** ADJ.

biological ADJ **1** relating to biology.
2 physiological. **3** of a detergent: containing enzymes that remove dirt of organic origin, eg blood or grass. ■ **biologically** ADV.

biological control N, BIOL the control of plant or animal pests by the introduction of natural predators or parasites, etc.

biological warfare N the use of toxins and micro-organisms as weapons of war.

biology N the scientific study of living organisms. ■ **biologist** N.

biomass N, BIOL, ECOL **1** the total mass of living organisms in an ecosystem, population or designated area at a given time. **2** plant material that can be converted into useful fuel.

bionic ADJ 1 using, or belonging or relating to, bionics. 2 COLLOQ, SCIENCE FICTION having extraordinary superhuman powers.

bionics SING N 1 the study of how living organisms function, and the application of the principles observed to develop computers and other machines. 2 the replacement of damaged parts of the body, such as limbs and heart valves, by electronic devices.

biophysics SING N the application of the ideas and methods of physics to the study of biological processes. ■ **biophysicist** N.

biopic N a film telling the life-story of a famous person.

biopsy N (-ies) PATHOL the removal and examination of a small piece of living tissue from an organ or part of the body in order to determine the nature of any suspected disease.

biorhythm N, BIOL 1 a periodic change in the behaviour or physiology of many animals and plants. 2 any of three cyclical patterns believed to influence aspects of human behaviour.

biosphere N that part of the earth's surface and its atmosphere with living organisms.

biotechnology N, BIOL the use of living organisms (eg bacteria) in industrial manufacture.

bipartisan ADJ involving two groups or political parties.

bipartite ADJ 1 of or divided into two parts. 2 involving or agreed by two parties.

biped N an animal with two feet.
➤ ADJ (also **bipedal**) having or walking on two feet.

biplane N an early type of aeroplane with two sets of wings, one above the other.

bipolar ADJ having two poles or extremes.
■ **bipolarity** N.

birch N 1 a slender deciduous tree or shrub with silvery-white bark. 2 (also **birchwood**) the strong fine-textured wood of this tree.
➤ ADJ made of birch wood.

bird N 1 any member of a class of warm-blooded vertebrate animals that have feathers, front limbs modified to form wings, and projecting jaws modified to form a beak. 2 BRIT SLANG, often considered OFFENSIVE a girl or woman. 3 COLLOQ, OLD USE a person, esp a strange or unusual one: *He's a funny old bird.*

birdie N 1 COLLOQ a little bird. 2 GOLF a score of one stroke under par for a particular hole.
➤ VB (*birdying*) TR & INTR, GOLF to complete (a hole) with a birdie score.

bird of paradise N (*birds of paradise*) any of various brilliantly coloured birds, native to New Guinea and Australia.

bird of prey N (*birds of prey*) any bird that hunts and kills animals for food.

bird's-eye view N 1 a wide general overall view from above. 2 a general impression.

birdwatcher N a person who studies wild birds in their natural habitat, esp as a hobby.

biretta N a stiff square cap worn by Roman Catholic clergy.

biriani or **biryani** N, COOKERY a spicy Indian dish of rice, with meat or vegetables, etc.

Biro N, BRIT TRADEMARK a type of ballpoint pen.

birth N 1 the act or process of bearing offspring. 2 the act or process of being born. 3 ancestry; descent: **of humble birth**. 4 beginning; origins: **the birth of socialism**.
◆ **give birth** to bear or produce (offspring).
◆ **give birth to sth** to produce or be the cause or origin of it.

birth certificate N an official document that records the date and place of a person's birth.

birth control N the prevention of pregnancy, esp by means of contraception.

birthday N the anniversary of the day on which a person was born.

birthmark N a blemish or mark that is present on the skin at birth; a naevus.

birthplace N the place where a person was born or where something important.

birthright N the rights conferred by being born into a particular family or social class, etc.

biscuit N 1 esp BRIT **a** a small sweet cake, in any of numerous varieties or flavours, etc; **b** a small thin crisp plain or savoury cake. **2** a pale golden brown or pale tan colour.

bisect MATH, etc, VB to divide (something) into two equal parts. ■ **bisection** N.

bisexual ADJ **1** sexually attracted to both males and females. **2** having the sexual organs of both sexes.
➢ N a bisexual person or organism, etc.
■ **bisexuality** N.

bishop N **1** (often **Bishop**) a senior priest or minister in the Roman Catholic, Anglican and Orthodox Churches, in charge of a group of churches in an area or a diocese. **2** CHESS a piece shaped like a bishop's mitre at the top, which may only be moved diagonally.

bishopric N **1** the post or position of bishop. **2** the area under the charge of a bishop.

bismuth N, CHEM a hard silvery-white metallic element with a pinkish tinge.

bison N (PL **bison**) either of two species of large hoofed mammal with a dark-brown coat, broad humped shoulders and long shaggy hair on its head, neck, shoulders and forelegs.

bisque[1] N, COOKERY a thick rich shellfish soup.

bisque[2] N a type of baked clay or china, which has not been glazed; biscuit.

bistro N a small bar or informal restaurant.

bit[1] N a small piece, part or amount.
◆ **a bit** COLLOQ **1** a short time or distance: Wait a bit. **2** a little: feel a bit of a fool. **3** a lot: takes a bit of doing.

bit[2] N **1** a small metal bar which a horse holds in its mouth as part of the bridle with which it is controlled. **2** (also **drill bit**) a tool with a cutting edge, which can be fitted into a drill.

bit[3] N, COMP a binary digit with a value of either 0 or 1, the smallest piece of information that can be dealt with by a computer.

bitch N **1** a female of the dog family. **2** OFFENSIVE OR DEROG SLANG an unpleasant or spiteful woman. **3** SLANG a difficult or unpleasant thing: Life's a bitch.
➢ VB, INTR (also **bitch about**) to talk maliciously or complain (about someone or something).

bitchy ADJ (**-ier, -iest**) COLLOQ spiteful; bad-tempered or malicious. ■ **bitchiness** N.

bite VB (PA T **bit**, PA P **bitten**) **1** TR & INTR (sometimes **bite sth away** or **off** or **out**) to grasp, seize or tear with the teeth. **2** TR & INTR of snakes and insects: to puncture (a victim's skin) with the fangs, mouthparts, etc. **3** TR & INTR to smart or sting, or to make (something) do so. **4** COLLOQ to annoy or worry: What's biting him? **5** INTR to start to have an effect, usu an adverse one. **6** INTR, ANGLING of fish: to be caught on the hook on a fishing line, by taking the bait.
➢ N **1** an act or an instance of biting. **2** a wound or sting caused by biting. **3** COLLOQ a small amount of food; a mouthful. **4** strength, sharpness or bitterness of taste. **5** ANGLING of a fish: an act or an instance of biting at the bait.

biting ADJ **1** bitterly and painfully cold. **2** of a remark: sharp and hurtful; sarcastic.

bits and pieces and **bits and bobs** PL N, BRIT COLLOQ odds and ends.

bitter ADJ **1** having a sharp, acid and often unpleasant taste. **2** feeling or causing sadness or pain: bitter memories. **3** difficult to accept: a bitter disappointment. **4** showing an intense persistent feeling of dislike, hatred or opposition: bitter resentment. **5** of words, etc: sharp; acrimonious. **6** of the weather, etc: extremely and painfully cold.
➢ N, BRIT a type of beer. ■ **bitterness** N.

bittern N a wading bird, the male of which has a distinctive booming call.

bitters PL N a liquid made from bitter herbs or roots, used to flavour certain alcoholic drinks.

bittersweet ADJ pleasant and unpleasant, or bitter and sweet, at the same time.

bitty ADJ (**-ier, -iest**) COLLOQ consisting of small unrelated bits or parts; scrappy; disjointed.

bitumen N any of various black solid or tarry flammable substances used for surfacing roads, etc. ■ **bituminous** ADJ.

bivalve ZOOL, ADJ of a mollusc: having a shell composed of two valves hinged together.
➤ N any of numerous species of such shells.

bivouac N a temporary camp or camping place without tents.
➤ VB (*-acked, -acking*) INTR to camp out temporarily at night without a tent.

bizarre ADJ weirdly odd or strange.
■ **bizarrely** ADV.

blab VB (*-bb-*) **1** TR & INTR (usu **blab sth out**) to tell or divulge (a secret, etc). **2** INTR to chatter foolishly or indiscreetly.

blabber VB, INTR to talk nonsense.

blabbermouth N, SLANG, orig US a person who talks foolishly and indiscreetly.

black ADJ **1** having the darkest colour, the same colour as coal; reflecting no light. **2** without any light; totally dark. **3** (now usu **Black**) used of people: dark-skinned, esp of African or Australian Aboriginal origin. **4** (usu **Black**) of Black people. **5** of coffee or tea: without milk. **6** angry; threatening. **7** dirty; soiled. **8** sad or depressed; dismal. **9** promising trouble: **The future looks black**. **10** wicked or sinister; grim or macabre: **black comedy**.
➤ N **1** the colour of coal, etc, the darkest colour, or absence of colour. **2** anything which is black in colour. **3** (usu **Black**) a dark-skinned person. **4** black clothes worn when in mourning. **5** a black dye. **6** the credit side of an account.
➤ VB **1** to blacken. **2** to clean (shoes, etc) with black polish. **3** of a trade union: to forbid work to be done on or with (certain goods).
■ **blackness** N.
◆ **black out 1** to deprive (something) of light; to extinguish or cover (lights), or all lights in (a place). **2** to prevent (information) from being broadcast. **3** to lose consciousness.

black and blue ADJ, COLLOQ of a person or of a person's skin: covered in bruises.

black and white ADJ used of photographs or TV images: having no colours except black, white, and shades of grey.

blackball VB to vote against (a candidate for membership of something), orig by putting a black ball in the ballot box.

blackberry N a thorny shrub or one of the dark purple-coloured berries it produces.

blackbird N a small European bird, the male of which is black with a yellow beak.

blackboard N a black or dark-coloured board for writing on with chalk.

black box N a flight recorder.

blackcurrant N a widely cultivated shrub or one of the small round black fruits it produces.

blacken VB **1** TR & INTR (also **black**) to become or cause (something) to become black. **2** to damage (someone's reputation).

black eye N an eye with darkened bruised swollen skin around it, usu caused by a blow.

blackguard N, DATED OR FACETIOUS a rogue.

blackhead N a small black spot on the skin caused by a blocked pore.

black hole N, ASTRON a region in space with such a strong gravitational pull that not even light waves can escape from it.

black ice N a transparent layer of ice that forms on road surfaces.

blackleg N, chiefly BRIT DEROG a person who refuses to take part in a strike, or who works in a striker's place during a strike.

blacklist N a list of people convicted or suspected of something, or not approved of, to be boycotted or excluded, etc.
➤ VB to put (someone) on such a list.

black magic N magic which supposedly invokes the power of the devil to perform evil.

blackmail VB **1** to extort money, etc illegally from (someone) by threatening to reveal harmful information about them. **2** to try to influence (someone) by pressure or threats.
➤ N an act of blackmailing someone.
■ **blackmailer** N.

black mark N a sign or record of discredit.

black market N the illegal trading of goods which are scarce, strictly regulated or in great demand. ■ **black-marketeer** N.

blackout N 1 an enforced period of darkness, eg as a precaution during an air raid at night. 2 an electrical power-failure or power-cut. 3 a sudden loss of memory or of consciousness. 4 a suppression or stoppage of news, information, communications, etc.

black pudding N a dark sausage made from pig's blood and fat, cereal, etc.

black sheep N a member of a family or group who is disapproved of in some way.

blacksmith N a craftsman who makes and repairs things in iron.

black spot N, chiefly BRIT 1 a dangerous stretch of road where accidents often occur. 2 an area where an adverse social condition is prevalent: **an unemployment black spot**.

blackthorn N a thorny shrub or small tree with rounded bluish-black fruits (sloes).

black widow N a venomous spider, the female of which eats the male after mating.

bladder N 1 ANAT in all mammals, and some fish, amphibians and reptiles: a hollow sac-shaped organ in which urine is stored. 2 any of various similar hollow organs in which liquid or gas is stored, eg the swim bladder of fish.

blade N 1 the cutting part of a knife or sword, etc. 2 the flat, usu long and narrow, part of a leaf, petal or sepal. 3 the wide flat part of an oar, bat or propeller, etc. 4 a broad flat bone, eg the shoulder blade. 5 the runner of an ice-skate, that slides on the ice.

blag VB (-**gg**-) SLANG 1 to rob or steal (something). 2 to scrounge (something); to get (something) for nothing. ■ **blagger** N.

blame VB 1 to consider (someone) as responsible for (something bad, wrong or undesirable). 2 to find fault with (someone). ➤ N (esp **the blame**) responsibility for something bad, wrong or undesirable. ■ **blameless** ADJ. ■ **blameworthy** ADJ. ◆ **be to blame for** to be responsible for.

blameworthy ADJ deserving blame.

blanch VB 1 to make (something) white by removing the colour. 2 usu INTR to become pale or white, esp out of fear. 3 COOKERY to prepare (vegetables or meat) by boiling in water for a few seconds.

blancmange N a jelly-like milk pudding.

bland ADJ, DEROG 1 of food: having a very mild taste; tasteless. 2 insipid; lacking interest.

blandish VB to persuade (someone) by gentle flattery; to coax or cajole.

blandishments PL N flattery intended to persuade.

blank ADJ 1 of paper: not written or printed on. 2 of magnetic tape, etc: with no sound or pictures yet recorded on it. 3 with spaces left for details, information, a signature, etc: **a blank form**. 4 not filled in; empty: **Leave that space blank**. 5 showing no expression or interest. 6 having no thoughts or ideas: **My mind went blank**. 7 without a break or relieving feature: **a blank wall**. 8 sheer; absolute: **blank refusal**. ➤ N 1 an empty space; a void. 2 an empty space left (on forms, etc) to be filled in. 3 a cartridge containing an explosive but no bullet. ➤ VB 1 to ignore (someone). 2 to obscure or hide (something); to blot or cross (something) out. ■ **blankly** ADV.

blanket N 1 a thick covering of wool or other material. 2 a thick layer or mass which covers or obscures: **a blanket of fog**. ➤ ADJ general; applying to or covering all. ➤ VB 1 to cover (something) with, or as if with, a blanket. 2 to cover or apply (something) in a comprehensive or indiscriminate way.

blank verse N, PROSODY unrhymed poetry.

blare VB (often **blare out**) 1 INTR to make a sound like a trumpet. 2 TR & INTR to sound or say loudly and harshly. ➤ N a loud harsh sound.

blarney N flattering words used to persuade, deceive or cajole.

blasé ADJ lacking enthusiasm or interest.

blaspheme VB 1 TR & INTR to show disrespect for (God or sacred things) in speech. 2 INTR to swear or curse using the name of God or referring to sacred things. ■ **blasphemer** N.

blasphemy N (*-ies*) **1** speaking about God or sacred matters in a disrespectful or rude way. **2** an action, word or sign that insults God, or something sacred. ■ **blasphemous** ADJ.

blast N **1** an explosion, or the strong shock waves spreading out from it. **2** a strong sudden stream or gust (of air or wind, etc). **3** a sudden loud sound. **4** a sudden and violent outburst of anger or criticism. **5** COLLOQ something highly enjoyable or exciting.
➣ VB **1** to blow up (a tunnel or rock, etc) with explosives. **2** TR & INTR (esp **blast out**) to make or cause (something) to make a loud or harsh sound. **3** to criticize (someone) severely.
◆ **blast off** of a spacecraft: to take off from its launching pad.

blasted ADJ, COLLOQ (often used as an intensifier) annoying; damned; stupid.

blast furnace N a tall furnace that is used to extract iron from iron ores.

blast-off N **1** the moment at which a spacecraft or rocket-propelled missile is launched. **2** the launching of a spacecraft or rocket-propelled missile.

blatant ADJ **1** very obvious and without shame. **2** very noticeable. ■ **blatantly** ADV.

blaze[1] N **1** a bright strong fire or flame. **2** a brilliant display. **3** a sudden and sharp bursting out of feeling or emotion. **4** an intense burst or spate: **a blaze of publicity**.
➣ VB, INTR **1** to burn or shine brightly. **2** COLLOQ to be furious. **3** (often **blaze away**) INTR to fire rapidly and without stopping.

blaze[2] N **1** a white mark or band on an animal's face. **2** a mark made on the bark of a tree, esp to show a route or path.
➣ VB to mark (a tree or path, etc) with blazes.

blazer N a light jacket.

blazon VB (often **blazon abroad**) to make (something) public.
➣ N, HERALDRY a shield or coat of arms.

bleach VB, TR & INTR to whiten or remove colour from (a substance) by exposure to sunlight or certain chemicals.
➣ N a liquid chemical used to bleach.

bleak ADJ **1** exposed and desolate. **2** cold and unwelcoming. **3** offering little or no hope. ■ **bleakly** ADV. ■ **bleakness** N.

bleary ADJ (*-ier, -iest*) **1** of eyes: red and dim, usu from tiredness or through crying. **2** blurred, indistinct and unclear. ■ **blearily** ADV.

bleat VB, INTR to cry like a sheep or goat.

bleed VB (*bled*) **1** INTR to lose or let out blood. **2** to remove or take blood from (someone, etc). **3** INTR of plants, etc: to lose juice or sap. **4** to empty liquid or air from (a radiator, hydraulic brakes, etc).

bleep N a short high-pitched burst of sound, usu made by an electronic machine.
➣ VB, INTR of an electronic machine, etc: to give out a short high-pitched sound.

blemish N a stain, mark or fault.
➣ VB to stain or spoil the beauty of (something).

blench VB, INTR to start back or flinch.

blend VB **1** to mix (different sorts or varieties) into one. **2** INTR (often **blend in,** also **blend with**) to form a mixture or harmonious combination; to go well together. **3** to mix together. **4** INTR esp of colours: to shade gradually into another.
➣ N a mixture or combination.

blender N a machine for mixing food or esp for making it into a liquid or purée.

bless VB (PA P *blessed* or *blest*) **1** to ask for divine favour or protection for (someone or something). **2 a** to make or pronounce (someone or something) holy; **b** to make the sign of the cross over (someone or something) or to cross (oneself). **3** to praise; to give honour or glory to (a deity). **4** to thank or be thankful for (something): **I bless the day I met him**.

blessed ADJ **1 a** (also **blest**) holy; **b** consecrated. **2** RC CHURCH pronounced holy by the Pope, usu as the first stage towards becoming a saint. **3** EUPHEMISTIC, COLLOQ damned; confounded: **This blessed zip's stuck.**

4 very fortunate or happy.

blessing N **1** a wish or prayer for happiness or success. **2** RELIG **a** an act which invites the goodness of God to rest upon someone; **b** a short prayer said before or after a meal or church service, etc. **3** a cause of happiness, or sometimes of relief or comfort; a benefit or advantage. **4** approval or good wishes.

blether VB, INTR (chiefly SCOT) **1** to talk foolishly and long-windedly. **2** to chat.
➢ N **1** long-winded nonsense. **2** a chat or gossip. ■ **blethering** N, ADJ.

blight N **1** a fungal disease of plants. **2** a fungus that causes blight. **3** something or someone that has a damaging or destructive effect on something. **4** often IN COMPOUNDS an ugly or neglected state or condition: **urban blight**.
➢ VB **1** to affect (something) with blight. **2** to harm or destroy (someone or something). **3** to disappoint or frustrate (someone or something).

blimp N a type of large balloon or airship.

blind ADJ **1** not able to see. **2** (always **blind to sth**) unable or unwilling to understand or appreciate something. **3** without reason or purpose: **blind hatred**. **4** hidden from sight: **blind entrance**. **5** not allowing sight of what is beyond: **blind summit**. **6** of flying, navigating, etc: relying completely on instruments. **7** having no openings or windows, etc: **blind wall**. **8** closed at one end: **blind alley**.
➢ ADV **1** blindly. **2** without proper knowledge of the item concerned: **bought the car blind**.
➢ N **1** a screen to stop light coming through a window. **2** a person, action or thing which hides the truth or deceives.
➢ VB **1** to make (someone) blind. **2** to make (someone) unreasonable or foolish, etc. ■ **blinding** ADJ. ■ **blindly** ADV. ■ **blindness** N.

blindfold N a piece of cloth used to cover the eyes to prevent a person from seeing.
➢ ADJ, ADV with one's eyes covered with a blindfold.
➢ VB to cover the eyes of (someone) to prevent them from seeing.

blind spot N **1** on the retina of the eye: a small

area from which no visual images can be transmitted. **2** a place where sight or vision is obscured. **3** any subject which a person either cannot or will not understand.

blindworm N a slowworm.

blink VB **1** INTR to shut and open the eyes again quickly, esp involuntarily. **2** to shut and open (an eyelid or an eye) very quickly. **3** INTR of a light: to flash on and off; to shine unsteadily.
➢ N **1** an act of blinking. **2** a gleam or quick glimmer of light.

blinker N (usu **blinkers**) one of two small flat pieces of leather attached to a horse's bridle to prevent it from seeing sideways.
➢ VB **1** to put blinkers on (a horse). **2** to limit the vision or awareness of (a person, etc).

blip N **1** a sudden sharp sound produced by a machine such as a monitor or radar screen. **2** a spot of bright light on a radar screen, showing the position of an object. **3** a short interruption, pause or irregularity in the expected pattern or course of something.

bliss N **1** very great happiness. **2** happiness in heaven. ■ **blissful** ADJ. ■ **blissfully** ADV.

blister N **1** a small swelling on or just beneath the surface of the skin, containing watery fluid. **2** a bubble in a thin surface coating of paint or varnish, etc.
➢ VB **1** to make a blister or blisters occur on (something). **2** INTR of hands or feet, etc: to come up in blisters. ■ **blistering** ADJ.

blithe ADJ **1** happy; without worries or cares. **2** thoughtless; casual. ■ **blithely** ADV.

blitz N **1** a sudden strong attack, or period of such attacks, esp from the air. **2** (esp **have a blitz on sth**) COLLOQ a period of hard work, etc to get something finished or done quickly.
➢ VB **1** to attack, damage or destroy (something) as if by an air raid. **2** COLLOQ to work hard at (something) for a short period.

blizzard N a severe snowstorm characterized by low temperatures and strong winds.

bloat VB **1** TR & INTR to swell or make (something) swell or puff out with air, pride, food, etc, esp unpleasantly or uncomfortably. **2** to prepare (fish, esp herring) by salting and half-drying in smoke. ■ **bloated** ADJ.

blob N 1 a small soft round mass of something. 2 a small drop of liquid.

bloc N a group of countries or people, etc that have a common interest, purpose or policy.

block N 1 a mass of solid wood, stone, ice or other hard material, usu with flat sides. 2 a piece of wood or stone, etc used for chopping and cutting on. 3 a wooden or plastic cube, used as a child's toy. 4 SLANG a person's head. 5 a large building containing offices, flats, etc. 6 a group of buildings with roads on all four sides. 7 a compact mass, group or set. 8 a group of seats, tickets, votes, data, shares, etc. 9 an obstruction. 10 ENG a pulley or set of pulleys mounted in a case.
➤ VB to obstruct or impede; to put an obstacle in the way of (someone or something).

blockade N the closing off of a port or region, etc by surrounding it with troops, ships and/or air-power, to prevent people or goods, etc from passing in and out.
➤ VB to impose a blockade.

blockage N 1 anything that causes a pipe or roadway, etc to be blocked. 2 the state of being blocked or the act of blocking.

block and tackle N, MECH, ENG a device used for lifting heavy objects, consisting of a case containing a pulley or system of pulleys and a rope or chain passed over it.

blockbuster N, COLLOQ a highly popular and successful film, book or TV drama, etc.

blockhead N, DEROG COLLOQ a stupid person.

bloke N, BRIT COLLOQ a man or chap.

blond and (THE FEMININE FORM) **blonde** ADJ 1 of a person or people: having light-coloured hair and usu fair or pale skin and blue or grey eyes. 2 of a person's hair: light-coloured; fair.
➤ N a person with fair hair.

blood N 1 a fluid tissue that circulates in the arteries veins, and capillaries of the body. 2 relationship through belonging to the same family or race, etc; descent: **of royal blood**.

3 near family: **my own flesh and blood.** 4 bloodshed or murder; violence. 5 **a** life or vitality; lifeblood; **b** (esp **new blood** and **young blood**) a group of people seen as adding new strength, youth, young ideas, etc. ◆ **in cold blood** deliberately or cruelly; showing no concern.

blood bank N a place where blood collected from donors is stored.

bloodbath N a massacre.

blood count N, MED a numerical calculation to determine the number of red or white blood cells in a known volume of blood.

bloodcurdling ADJ causing a chilling fear.

blood group and **blood type** N, MED any one of the various types into which human blood is classified.

bloodhound N 1 a large breed of dog, known for its keen sense of smell. 2 COLLOQ a detective, or anyone who follows a trail intently.

bloodless ADJ 1 without bloodshed. 2 pale and lifeless; weak and sickly. 3 dull and tedious; without emotion or spirit.

bloodletting N killing; bloodshed.

blood poisoning N the presence of either bacterial toxins or large numbers of bacteria in the bloodstream.

blood pressure N the pressure of the blood within the arteries.

blood relation and **blood relative** N a person related to one by birth.

bloodshed N the killing of people; slaughter.

bloodshot ADJ of the eyes: red and irritated.

blood sports PL N sports that involve the killing of animals, eg fox-hunting.

bloodstream N the flow of blood through the arteries, veins and capillaries.

bloodthirsty ADJ eager for or fond of killing or violence.

blood transfusion N, MED the introduction of a volume of donated blood directly into a person's bloodstream.

blood type see **blood group**

blood vessel N any tubular structure through which blood flows.

bloody ADJ (*-ier, -iest*) **1** stained or covered with blood. **2** involving or including much killing. **3** SLANG used as an intensifier expressing annoyance, etc. **4** murderous or cruel.
➤ ADV, SLANG used as an intensifier: bloody angry.
➤ VB (*-ies,-ied*) to stain or cover (something) with blood. ■ **bloodiness** N.

bloody-minded ADJ, DEROG deliberately unco-operative.

bloom N **1 a** a flower; **b** flowers or blossoms collectively. **2** the state of being in flower. **3** a state of perfection or beauty: **in the full bloom of youth**. **4** a glow or flush on the skin. **5** a powdery coating on the surface of fruits.
➤ VB, INTR **1** of a plant: to be in or come into flower. **2** to be in a state of great beauty or perfection. **3** to be healthy; to flourish.

bloomer[1] N, BRIT COLLOQ an embarrassing mistake.

bloomer[2] N, BRIT a crusty loaf of white bread.

bloomers PL N COLLOQ, FACETIOUS OR OLD USE women's knickers, esp large or baggy ones.

blooming ADJ **1** of a plant: flowering. **2** of someone or something: healthy and flourishing. **3** SLANG used as an intensifier.
➤ ADV, SLANG used as an intensifier.

blossom N **1** a flower or mass of flowers, esp on a fruit tree. **2** the state of being in flower.
➤ VB, INTR **1** to produce blossom. **2** to grow well or develop successfully.

blot N **1** a spot or stain, esp of ink. **2** a spot or blemish which spoils the beauty of something.
➤ VB (*-tt-*) **1** to make a spot or stain on (something), esp with ink. **2 a** to dry (something) with blotting-paper; **b** (sometimes **blot up**) to soak up (excess liquid) by pressing eg a cloth, towel or tissue against it.
◆ **blot out 1** to hide (something) from sight. **2** to refuse to think about (a painful memory). **3** to destroy or obliterate (something).

blotch N a large irregular-shaped coloured patch or mark on the skin, etc.
➤ VB to mark (something) with blotches.
■ **blotchy** ADJ.

blotter N a large pad of blotting paper.

blotting paper N soft thick unsized paper for absorbing excess ink.

blouse N **1** a woman's garment very similar to a shirt. **2** esp FORMERLY a loose jacket belted or gathered in at the waist, forming part of a soldier's or airman's uniform.

blouson N a loose jacket or top gathered in tightly at the waist.

blow[1] VB (PA T *blew*, PA P *blown* or (ONLY IN SENSE 12) *blowed*, PR P *blowing*) **1** INTR of an air current or wind, etc: to be moving, esp rapidly. **2** TR & INTR to move or cause (something) to move by a current of air or wind, etc. **3** to send (a current of air) from the mouth. **4** to form or shape (eg bubbles, glass) by blowing air from the mouth. **5** to shatter or destroy (something) by an explosion. **6** to produce a sound from (an instrument, etc) by blowing. **7** to clear (something) by blowing through it: **blow one's nose**. **8** COLLOQ **a** to make (an electric fuse) melt and so interrupt the circuit; **b** (also **blow out**) INTR of an electric fuse: to melt, causing an interruption in the flow of current. **9** to break into (a safe, etc) using explosives. **10** SLANG to spoil or bungle (an opportunity, etc). **11** SLANG to spend (money), esp quickly or recklessly.
➤ N an act or example of blowing.
◆ **blow out 1** of a tyre: to burst; to puncture suddenly and forcibly when in use; **2** of an electric fuse: to melt or blow. **3** to put out (a flame, etc) by blowing.
◆ **blow up 1** COLLOQ of a person: to explode in anger. **2** to fill up or swell up with air or gas. **3** to explode. **4** to inflate (eg a balloon). **5** to produce a larger version of (a photograph, etc). **6** COLLOQ to make (something) seem more serious or important than it really is. **7** to destroy (something) by way of an explosion.

blow[2] N **1** a forceful stroke or knock with the hand or with a weapon. **2** a sudden shock or misfortune.

blow-dry VB to dry (hair) in a particular style using a hand-held hairdrier.
> N an act or process of blow-drying.
■ **blow-drier** N.

blower N 1 a device that blows out air. 2 (**the blower**) BRIT COLLOQ the telephone.

blowfly N any of various flies whose eggs are laid in rotting flesh or excrement.

blowhole N 1 a hole in an area of surface ice, where marine mammals, eg seals, can go to breathe. 2 a hole on top of a whale's head.

blowlamp and (esp N AMER) **blowtorch** N a small portable burner, that produces an intense hot flame.

blow-out N 1 COLLOQ a tyre-burst. 2 COLLOQ a large meal at which one overindulges.

blow-up N 1 COLLOQ an enlargement of a photograph. 2 COLLOQ an explosion of temper.

blowy ADJ (*-ier, -iest*) blustery; windy.

blowzy or **blowsy** ADJ (*-ier, -iest*) DEROG, COLLOQ of a woman: 1 fat and red-faced or flushed. 2 dirty and dishevelled; slovenly.

blubber N 1 the fat of sea animals such as the whale. 2 COLLOQ excessive body fat; flab.
> VB, INTR, DEROG COLLOQ to weep, esp noisily.

bludgeon N a stick or club with a heavy end.
> VB 1 to hit (someone or something) with or as if with a bludgeon. 2 (usu **bludgeon sb into sth**) to force or bully them into doing it.

blue ADJ 1 with the colour of a clear cloudless sky; having any of the shades of this colour. 2 sad or depressed. 3 indecent. 4 politically conservative. 5 with a skin which is pale blue or purple because of the cold or from bruising, etc.
> N the colour of a clear cloudless sky; any blue shade or hue.
> VB (*bluing* or *blueing*) to make (something) blue. ■ **blueness** N.
◆ **out of the blue** unexpectedly.

bluebell N 1 a bulbous spring-flowering plant with clusters of bell-shaped flowers that are usu blue. 2 SCOT, N ENGLISH the harebell.

blueberry N 1 any of various deciduous shrubs, native to N America, with white or pinkish flowers and edible berries. 2 the bluish-black edible berry produced by this plant.

bluebird N any of various birds of the thrush family, the male of which has bright blue plumage on its back.

blue blood N royal or aristocratic ancestry.

bluebottle N a large blowfly whose abdomen has a metallic blue sheen.

blue cheese N cheese with veins of blue mould running through it.

blue-collar ADJ of workers: doing manual or unskilled work.

blueprint N 1a a pattern, model or prototype; b a detailed original plan of work to be done to develop an idea, project or scheme, etc. 2 TECHNICAL a photographic print of plans, engineering or architectural designs, etc consisting of white lines on a blue background.

blues SING OR PL N (usu **the blues**) 1 a feeling of sadness or depression. 2 slow melancholy jazz music of Black American origin.

blue tit N a small bird with a bright blue crown, wings and tail, and yellow underparts.

blue whale N a rare whale, the largest living animal, which has a bluish body.

bluff[1] VB, TR & INTR to deceive (someone) by pretending to be stronger, cleverer or more determined, etc than one really is.
> N an act of bluffing.
◆ **call sb's bluff** to challenge them to prove the genuineness of their claim, threat, etc.

bluff[2] ADJ rough, cheerful and honest; outspoken and hearty.
> N a steep cliff or high bank of ground.

blunder N a foolish or thoughtless mistake.
> VB 1 INTR to make a blunder. 2 INTR to act or move about awkwardly and clumsily.

blunderbuss N, HIST a type of musket with a wide barrel and a flared muzzle.

blunt ADJ 1 of a pencil, knife or blade, etc: having no point or sharp edge. 2 dull;

imperceptive. **3** direct in a rough way.
➤ VB to make (something) blunt or less sharp.
■ **bluntly** ADV. ■ **bluntness** N.

blur N **1** a thing not clearly seen or heard, or
happening too fast or too distantly, etc to be
clearly seen, comprehended or recognized.
2 a smear or smudge.
➤ VB (**-rr-**) **1** TR & INTR to become or cause
(something) to become less clear or distinct.
2 to rub over and smudge (something). **3** to
make (one's memory or judgement, etc) less
clear.

blurb N a brief description of a book, usu
printed on the jacket in order to promote it.

blurt VB (usu **blurt out**) to say (something)
suddenly or without thinking.

blush VB, INTR to become red or pink in the face
because of shame, excitement, joy, etc.
➤ N (*blushes*) **1** a red or pink glow on the skin of
the face, caused by shame, embarrassment.
2 esp LITERARY a pink rosy glow.

bluster VB **1** INTR to speak in a boasting, angry
or threatening way. **2** INTR of the wind or
waves, etc: to blow or move roughly.
➤ N speech that is ostentatiously boasting,
angry or threatening. ■ **blustery** ADJ.

b.o. ABBREV (also **BO**) body odour.

boa N **1** a **boa constrictor** or any similar
snake that kills by crushing its prey in its coils.
2 a woman's long scarf, usu of feathers or fur.

boar N (*boars* or *boar*) **1** a wild ancestor of
the domestic pig. **2** a mature male pig.

board N **1** a long flat strip of wood. **2** often IN
COMPOUNDS a piece of material resembling this,
made from fibres compressed together:
chipboard. **3** often IN COMPOUNDS **a** a flat piece
of wood or other hard solid material: **ironing
board**; **b** a slab, table or other flat surface for
playing a game on: **chessboard**. **4** thick stiff
card used eg for binding books. **5** a person's
meals, provided in return for money: **bed and
board**. **6 a** a group of people controlling or
managing an organization, etc, or examining or
interviewing candidates: **a board of
examiners**; **b** (also **board of directors**) a

group of directors appointed by a company,
who are responsible for its management.
➤ VB **1** to enter or get on to (a ship, aeroplane,
bus, etc). **2** (usu **board up**) to cover (a gap or
entrance) with boards. **3** INTR **a** to receive
accommodation and meals in someone else's
house, in return for payment; **b** to receive
accommodation and meals at school; to attend
school as a boarder. **4** to provide (someone)
with accommodation and meals in return for
payment.
◆ **go by the board** COLLOQ to be given up.
◆ **on board** on or into a ship or aeroplane,
etc.

boarder N a pupil who lives at school during
term time.

board game N a game (such as chess or
draughts) played with pieces or counters that
are moved on a specially designed board.

boarding house N a house in which people
live and take meals as paying guests.

boarding school N a school at which all or
most of the pupils live during term time.

boardroom N a room in which the directors
of a company meet.

boardwalk N, N AMER, ESP US a footpath made
of boards, esp on the seafront.

boast VB **1** INTR (often **boast about** or **of**) to
talk with excessive pride about (one's own
abilities or achievements, etc). **2** to own or have
(something it is right to be proud of): **The hotel
boasts magnificent views**.
➤ N **1** an act of boasting; a brag. **2** a thing one
is proud of. ■ **boastful** ADJ.

boat N **1** a small vessel for travelling over water.
2 COLLOQ, LOOSELY a larger vessel; a ship.
◆ **in the same boat** in the same difficult
circumstances.

boathouse N a building in which boats are
stored, esp by a lake or river.

boating N the sailing or rowing, etc of boats.

boatman N a man who is in charge of, or hires
out, etc a boat or boats.

boatswain or **bosun** N a warrant officer in

the navy, or the foreman of a crew, who is in charge of a ship's equipment.

bob¹ VB (-*bb*-) **1** INTR (sometimes **bob along** or **past,** etc) to move up and down quickly. **2** INTR (usu **bob for**) to try to catch (esp an apple floating on water or suspended on a string) with one's teeth, as a game.
➤ N a quick up-and-down bouncing movement.

bob² N **1** a short hairstyle for women and children, with the hair cut evenly all round the head. **2** a hanging weight on a clock's pendulum or plumbline, etc.
➤ VB (-*bb*-) to cut (hair) in a bob.

bob³ N (PL *bob*) BRIT COLLOQ **1** OLD USE a shilling. **2** LOOSELY (usu **a few bob** or **a bob or two**) a sum of money, esp a large amount.

bobbin N a small cylindrical object on which thread or yarn, etc is wound.

bobble N **1** a small ball, often fluffy or made of tufted wool, used to decorate clothes or furnishings, etc. **2** a little ball formed on the surface of a fabric through rubbing, etc.

bobby N (-*ies*) BRIT COLLOQ a policeman.

bobcat N a solitary nocturnal type of cat.

bobsleigh and (esp US) **bobsled** N, SPORT a sledge for racing on an ice-covered track.
➤ VB, INTR to ride or race on a bobsleigh.

bode VB.
◆ **bode ill** or **well** to be a bad or good sign for the future.

bodice N **1** the close-fitting upper part of a woman's dress, from shoulder to waist. **2** FORMERLY a similar tight-fitting stiffened undergarment for women.

bodily ADJ of the body.
➤ ADV as a whole; taking the whole body: carried me bodily to the car.

bodkin N a large blunt needle.

body N (-*ies*) **1** the whole physical structure of a person or animal. **2** the physical structure of a person or animal excluding the head and limbs. **3** a corpse. **4** the main or central part of

anything, such as the main part of a vehicle. **5** a person's physical needs and desires as opposed to spiritual concerns. **6** a substantial section or group: a body of opinion. **7** a group of people regarded as a single unit. **8** a quantity or mass: a body of water. **9** a distinct mass or object: a foreign body. **10** applied to wine, music, etc: a full or strong quality or tone; fullness. **11** thickness; substantial quality. **12** COLLOQ a person.

body bag N a bag in which a dead body is transported.

body blow N **1** BOXING a blow to the torso. **2** a serious setback or misfortune.

body-building N physical exercise to develop the muscles. ■ **bodybuilder** N.

bodyguard N a person or group of people whose job is to accompany and give physical protection to an important person, etc.

body language N communication by means of conscious or unconscious gestures, facial expressions, etc, rather than by words.

body politic N (usu **the body politic**) all the people of a nation in their political capacity.

body warmer N a padded sleeveless jacket.

bodywork N the shell of a motor vehicle.

Boer N a descendant of the early Dutch settlers in S Africa.

boffin N, BRIT COLLOQ a research scientist.

bog N **1** an area of wet spongy poorly-drained ground. **2** BRIT SLANG a toilet.
➤ VB (-*gg*-) (usu **bog down**) **1** to become or cause to become stuck. **2** to hinder or hold up the progress of. ■ **bogginess** N. ■ **boggy** ADJ (-*ier,* -*iest*).

bogey¹ or **bogy** N (*bogeys* or *bogies*) **1** an evil or mischievous spirit. **2** a bugbear. **3** SLANG a piece of nasal mucus.

bogey² N (*bogeys*) GOLF a score of one over par on a specific hole.
➤ VB to complete (a hole) in one over par.

bogeyman or **bogyman** N a cruel or

frightening person or creature.

boggle VB, INTR, COLLOQ **1** to be amazed or unable to understand or imagine: **the mind boggles**. **2** (usu **boggle at**) to hesitate over (something), out of surprise or fright, etc.

bogie or **bogey** N, mainly BRIT a frame with four or six wheels used as part of a pivoting undercarriage, supporting a railway carriage.

bog-standard ADJ, COLLOQ ordinary.

bogus ADJ false; not genuine.

bohemian ADJ ignoring standard customs and rules of social behaviour.
➤ N someone who lives in this way.

boil[1] VB **1** INTR of a liquid: to change rapidly to a vapour on reaching a temperature known as the boiling point. **2** INTR of a container, eg a kettle: to have contents that are boiling. **3 a** to make (a liquid) reach its boiling point rapidly; **b** to boil the contents of (a container). **4** TR to cook (food) by heating in boiling liquid. **5** (sometimes **boil up**) to bring (a container or its contents) to boiling point. **6** (usu **be boiling**) COLLOQ **a** to be very hot: **It's boiling in the car**; **b** to be extremely angry.
➤ N (usu **a boil** or **the boil**) the act or point of boiling.
◆ **boil over** of a liquid: to boil and flow over the edge of its container.

boil[2] N a reddened pus-filled swelling in the skin, caused by bacterial infection.

boiler N **1** any closed vessel that is used to convert water into steam, in order to drive machinery. **2** an apparatus for heating a building's hot water supply.

boilersuit N a one-piece suit worn over normal clothes to protect them while doing manual or heavy work.

boiling point N the temperature at which a substance changes from a liquid to a vapour.

boisterous ADJ of people, behaviour, etc: very lively, noisy and cheerful.

bold ADJ **1** daring or brave; confident and courageous. **2** not showing respect; impudent. **3** striking and clearly marked; noticeable.

■ **boldly** ADV. ■ **boldness** N.

bole N the trunk of a tree.

bolero N **1** a traditional Spanish dance. **2** a short open jacket.

boll N a rounded capsule containing seeds, esp of a cotton or flax plant.

bollard N **1** BRIT a small post used to mark a traffic island or to keep traffic away from a certain area. **2** a short but strong post on a ship or quay, etc around which ropes are fastened.

boloney see **baloney**

bolshie or **bolshy** ADJ (*-ier, -iest*) BRIT DEROG COLLOQ **1** bad-tempered and unco-operative; difficult or rebellious. **2** left-wing.

bolster VB (often **bolster sth up**) to support it, make it stronger or hold it up.
➤ N **1** a long narrow pillow. **2** any pad or support.

bolt[1] N **1** a bar or rod that slides into a hole or socket to fasten a door, etc. **2** a small thick round bar of metal, with a screw thread, used with a nut to fasten things together. **3** a sudden movement or dash away. **4** a flash of lightning. **5** a short arrow fired from a crossbow.
➤ VB **1** to fasten (a door, etc) with a bolt. **2** to fasten (two or more things) together with bolts. **3** to eat (a meal, etc) very quickly. **4** INTR to run or dash away suddenly and quickly. **5** INTR of a horse: to run away out of control.

bolt[2] or **boult** VB **1** to pass (flour, etc) through a sieve. **2** to examine or sift (information, etc).

bolthole N, BRIT COLLOQ a secluded private place to hide away in.

bomb N **1** a hollow case or other device containing a substance capable of causing an explosion, fire or smoke, etc. **2** (**a bomb**) BRIT COLLOQ a lot of money. **3** N AMER COLLOQ a failure, flop or fiasco.
➤ VB **1** to attack or damage, etc (something) with a bomb or bombs. **2** (esp **bomb along** or **off**, etc) INTR, COLLOQ to move or drive quickly. **3** INTR, N AMER COLLOQ to fail or flop badly.
■ **bombing** N.

bombard VB **1** to attack (a place, target, etc)

with large, heavy guns or bombs. **2** to direct questions or abuse at (someone) rapidly and continuously. **3** to batter or pelt (something or someone) heavily and persistently.
■ **bombardment** N.

bombardier N **1** BRIT a noncommissioned officer in the Royal Artillery. **2** the member of a bomber's crew who releases the bombs.

bombast N pretentious, boastful or insincere words having little real force or meaning.
■ **bombastic** ADJ.

bomber N **1** an aeroplane designed for carrying and dropping bombs. **2** a person who bombs something or who plants bombs.

bombshell N **1** a piece of surprising and usu devastating news. **2** COLLOQ a stunningly attractive woman.

bona fide ADJ genuine or sincere; done or carried out in good faith: **a bona fide offer**.
➤ ADV genuinely or sincerely.

bonanza N **1** an unexpected and sudden source of good luck or wealth. **2** N AMER a rich vein of precious ore such as gold or silver.

bond N **1** something used for tying, binding or holding. **2** (usu **bonds**) something which restrains or imprisons someone. **3** something that unites or joins people together: **a bond of friendship**. **4** a binding agreement or promise. **5** FINANCE a debenture. **6** LAW a written agreement.
➤ VB **1** to join, secure or tie (two or more things) together. **2** INTR to hold or stick together securely.

bondage N **1** slavery. **2** the state of being confined or imprisoned, etc; captivity.

bone N **1** the hard dense tissue that forms the skeleton of vertebrates. **2** any of the components of the skeleton, made of this material. **3** (**bones**) the skeleton. **4** a substance similar to human bone, such as ivory and whalebone, etc.
➤ VB **1** to take bone out of (meat, etc). **2** to make (a piece of clothing, eg a corset or bodice) stiff by adding strips of bone or some other hard substance.

◆ **bone up on** COLLOQ to learn or collect information about (a subject).

bone china N a type of fine china made from clay mixed with ash from bones.

bone-dry ADJ completely dry.

bone-idle ADJ, COLLOQ utterly lazy.

bonfire N a large outdoor fire.

bongo N (**-os** or **-oes**) each of a pair of small drums held between the knees and played with the hands.

bonhomie N cheerful friendliness.

bonk VB, TR & INTR **1** to hit (something or someone). **2** COARSE SLANG to have sexual intercourse with (someone).
➤ N **1** a blow. **2** COARSE SLANG an act of sexual intercourse.

bonkers ADJ, chiefly BRIT SLANG mad or crazy.

bon mot N (**bons mots**) a short clever remark.

bonnet N **1** a type of hat fastened under the chin with ribbon, worn esp by babies. **2** BRIT the hinged cover over a motor vehicle's engine.

bonny ADJ (**-ier, -iest**) **1** chiefly SCOT & N ENGLISH attractive; pretty. **2** looking very healthy.

bonsai N (PL **bonsai**) a miniature tree.

bonus N **1** an extra sum of money given on top of what is due as wages, interest or dividend, etc. **2** an unexpected extra benefit gained or given with something else. **3** INSURANCE an additional sum of money payable to the holder of a policy when it matures.

bony ADJ (**-ier, -iest**) **1** consisting of, made of or like bone. **2** full of bones. **3** thin, so that the bones are very noticeable.

boo EXCLAM, N a sound expressing disapproval, or made to frighten or surprise someone.
➤ VB, TR & INTR to shout 'boo' to express disapproval (or someone or something).

boob[1] N, COLLOQ (also **booboo**) a stupid or foolish mistake.
➤ VB, INTR, COLLOQ to make a foolish mistake.

boob[2] N, SLANG a woman's breast.

booby N (-ies) 1 any of various seabirds of the gannet family. 2 OLD USE, COLLOQ a stupid or foolish person.

booby prize N a prize (usu a joke prize) for the lowest score in a competition.

booby trap N 1 a bomb or mine which is disguised so that it is set off by the victim. 2 a trap, esp one intended as a practical joke. ➢ VB (**booby-trap**) to put a booby trap in or on (a place).

boogie COLLOQ, VB (-gieing or -gying) INTR to dance to pop, rock or jazz music. ➢ N 1 a dance, or dancing, to pop, rock or jazz music. 2 boogie-woogie.

boo-hoo EXCLAM, N the sound of noisy weeping. ➢ VB, INTR to weep noisily.

book N 1 a number of printed pages bound together along one edge and protected by covers. 2 a piece of written work intended for publication, eg a novel, etc. 3 a number of sheets of blank paper bound together. 4 (usu **the books**) a record or formal accounts of the business done by a company, society, etc. 5 a record of bets made with different people. 6 (usu **Book**) a major division of a long literary work. 7 a number of stamps, matches or cheques, etc bound together. ➢ VB 1 TR & INTR to reserve (a ticket, seat, etc), or engage (a person's services) in advance. 2 of a police officer, etc: to record the details of (a person who is being charged with an offence). 3 FOOTBALL of a referee: to enter (a player's name) in a notebook as a record of an offence. ■ **bookable** ADJ. ◆ **book in** esp BRIT to report one's arrival at a hotel, etc.

bookcase N a piece of furniture with shelves for books.

book end N each of a pair of supports used to keep a row of books standing upright.

bookie N, mainly BRIT COLLOQ a bookmaker.

booking N 1 a reservation of a theatre seat, hotel room, etc. 2 esp in sport: the recording of an offence with details of the offender. 3 an engagement for the services of a person or company.

bookish ADJ, often DEROG 1 fond of reading and books. 2 having knowledge based on books rather than experience.

bookkeeper N a person who keeps a record of the financial transactions of a business or organization, etc. ■ **bookkeeping** N

booklet N a small book with a paper cover.

bookmaker N, mainly BRIT (often shortened to **bookie**) 1 a person whose job is to take bets on horse-races, etc and pay out winnings. 2 COLLOQ a shop or premises used by a bookmaker. ■ **bookmaking** N.

bookmark N a strip of leather, card, etc put in a book, esp to mark one's place.

bookstall N a small shop in a station, etc selling books, newspapers, magazines, etc.

bookworm N 1 COLLOQ a person who is extremely fond of reading. 2 a type of small insect which feeds on books.

boom[1] N a deep resounding sound. ➢ VB, INTR to make a deep resounding sound.

boom[2] N 1 a sudden increase or growth in business, prosperity, activity, etc. 2 a period of such rapid growth or activity, etc. ➢ VB, INTR esp of a business: to become rapidly and suddenly prosperous.

boom[3] N 1 NAUT a pole to which the bottom of a ship's sail is attached, keeping the sail stretched tight. 2 a heavy pole or chain, or a barrier of floating logs, etc across the entrance to a harbour or across a river. 3 CINEMA, TV, etc a long pole with a microphone, camera or light attached to one end.

boomerang N a piece of flat curved wood used by Australian Aborigines for hunting. ➢ VB, INTR of an act or statement, etc: to go wrong and harm the perpetrator.

boon[1] N an advantage, benefit or blessing.

boon[2] ADJ close, convivial, intimate or favourite: **a boon companion**.

boor N, DEROG a coarse person with bad manners. ■ **boorish** ADJ.

boost VB 1 to improve or encourage (something or someone). 2 to make (something) greater or increase it; to raise: **boost profits**. 3 to promote (something) by advertising.
➤ N 1 a piece of help or encouragement, etc. 2 a push upwards. 3 a rise or increase.

booster N 1 (also **booster shot**) a dose of vaccine that is given in order to renew or increase the immune response to a previous dose of the same vaccine. 2 AEROSPACE an engine in a rocket that provides additional thrust. 3 (also **booster rocket**) a rocket that is used to launch a space vehicle, before another engine takes over.

boot N 1 an outer covering, made of leather or rubber, etc, for the foot and lower part of the leg. 2 BRIT a compartment for luggage in a car, usu at the back. 3 COLLOQ a hard kick. 4 (**the boot**) COLLOQ dismissal from a job.
➤ VB 1 to kick (something or someone). 2 (usu **boot sb** or **sth out**) to throw them or it out, or remove them or it by force.

bootee N a soft knitted boot for a baby.

booth N 1 a small temporary roofed structure or tent, esp a covered stall at a fair or market. 2 a small partly-enclosed compartment.

bootleg VB (-**gg**-) 1 to make, sell or transport (alcoholic drink) illegally, esp in a time of prohibition. 2 to make or deal in (illicit goods such as unofficial recordings of copyright music, videos, etc).
➤ N illegally produced, sold or transported goods. ■ **bootlegger** N.

booty N (-**ies**) valuable goods taken in wartime or by force; plunder.

booze SLANG, N alcoholic drink.
➤ VB, INTR to drink a lot of alcohol, or too much of it. ■ **boozer** N. ■ **boozy** ADJ (-**ier**, -**iest**).

bop COLLOQ, VB (-**pp**-) INTR to dance to popular music.
➤ N a dance to popular music.

borage N a plant with hairy leaves widely cultivated for use in salads and medicinally.

borax N a colourless crystalline salt, found in saline lake deposits, used in the manufacture of glass and as a mild antiseptic.

border N 1 a band or margin along the edge of something. 2 the boundary of a country or political region, etc. 3 the land on either side of a country's border. 4 a narrow strip of ground planted with flowers, surrounding a lawn. 5 any decorated or ornamental edge or trimming.
➤ ADJ belonging or referring to the border, or on the border.
➤ VB 1 to be a border to, adjacent to, or on the border of (something). 2 to provide (something) with a border.

borderland N 1 land at or near a country's border. 2 the undefined margin or condition between two states.

borderline N the border between one thing, country, etc and another.
➤ ADJ on the border between one thing, state, etc and another; marginal: **a borderline result**.

bore¹ VB 1 to make a hole in (something) by drilling. 2 to produce (a borehole, tunnel or mine, etc) by drilling.
➤ N 1 the hollow barrel of a gun, or the cavity inside any such tube. 2 a IN COMPOUNDS the diameter of the hollow barrel of a gun, esp to show which size bullets the gun requires: **12-bore shotgun**; b the diameter of the cavity inside any such tube or pipe. 3 a borehole.

bore² VB to make (someone) feel tired and uninterested, by being dull, tedious, etc.
➤ N a dull, uninteresting or tedious person or thing. ■ **boredom** N. ■ **boring** ADJ.

borehole N a deep narrow hole made by boring, esp to find oil or water, etc.

boric and **boracic** ADJ containing boron.

born ADJ 1 brought into being by birth. 2 having a specified quality or ability as a natural attribute: **a born leader**. 3 (**born to sth**) destined to do it: **born to lead men**.

born-again ADJ converted or re-converted, esp to a fundamentalist or Christian faith.

boron N, CHEM a non-metallic element found only in compounds, eg borax and boric acid.

borough N 1 (also **parliamentary borough**) in England: a town or urban area represented by at least one member of Parliament. 2 HIST in England: a town with its own council and special rights granted by royal charter. 3 a division of a large town for local-government purposes.

borrow VB 1 to take (something) temporarily, usu with permission and with the intention of returning it. 2 INTR to get (money) in this way, from a bank, etc. 3 to take, adopt or copy (words or ideas, etc) from another language or person, etc. ■ **borrower** N. ■ **borrowing** N.

borscht, bortsch or **borsh** N a Russian and Polish beetroot soup.

borstal N, BRIT, FORMERLY an institution to which young criminals were sent.

bosom N 1 a person's chest or breast, now esp that of a woman. 2 (sometimes **bosoms**) COLLOQ a woman's breasts. 3 a loving or protective centre: **the bosom of one's family**.

boss COLLOQ, N a person who employs others, or who is in charge of others.
➤ VB 1 (esp **boss sb about** or **around**) to give them orders in a domineering way 2 to manage or control (someone).

boss-eyed ADJ, BRIT COLLOQ 1 having only one good eye. 2 cross-eyed. 3 crooked; squint.

bossy ADJ (**-ier, -iest**) COLLOQ inclined to give orders like a boss; disagreeably domineering. ■ **bossiness** N.

bosun see **boatswain**

botany N (**-ies**) the branch of biology concerned with the scientific study of plants. ■ **botanic** or **botanical** ADJ. ■ **botanist** N.

botch COLLOQ, VB (esp **botch up**) 1 to do (something) badly and unskilfully. 2 to repair (something) carelessly or badly.
➤ N (also **botch-up**) a badly or carelessly done piece of work, repair, etc.

both ADJ, PRONOUN (sometimes **both of sth**) the two; the one and the other.
➤ ADV as well.

bother VB 1 to annoy, worry or trouble (someone or something). 2 TR & INTR (usu **bother about sth**) to worry about it. 3 INTR (esp **bother about** or **with sth**) to take the time or trouble to do it or consider it, etc.
➤ N 1 a minor trouble or worry. 2 a person or thing that causes bother.

bothersome ADJ causing bother or annoyance.

bottle N 1 a hollow glass or plastic container with a narrow neck, for holding liquids. 2 (also **bottleful**) the amount a bottle holds. 3 a baby's feeding bottle or the liquid in it. 4 BRIT, SLANG courage, nerve or confidence 5 (usu **the bottle**) SLANG drinking of alcohol.
➤ VB to put (something) into a bottle.
◆ **bottle up** to suppress (one's feelings).

bottle-feed VB to feed (a baby) with milk from a bottle rather than the breast.

bottle green N a dark-green colour.

bottleneck N 1 a place or thing which impedes the movement of traffic, esp a narrow or partly-blocked part of a road. 2 something which is an obstacle to progress.

bottom N 1 the lowest position or part. 2 the point farthest away from the front, top, most important or most successful part: **the bottom of the garden** • **bottom of the class**. 3 the buttocks. 4 the base on which something stands or rests. 5 the ground underneath a sea, river or lake.
➤ ADJ lowest or last.

bottomless ADJ extremely deep or plentiful.

bottom line N 1 COLLOQ the essential factor or truth in a situation. 2 the last line of a financial statement, showing profit or loss.

botulism N, PATHOL a severe form of food poisoning, caused by a bacterial toxin.

boudoir N, DATED a woman's private sitting-room or bedroom.

bouffant ADJ esp of a hairstyle: very full.

bougainvillea N a S American climbing shrub with flower-heads surrounded by large brightly coloured bracts.

bough N a branch of a tree.

bouillon N a thin clear soup or stock.

boulder N a large piece of rock that has been rounded and worn smooth by erosion.

boulevard N a broad street in a town or city.

boult see **bolt²**

bounce VB **1** INTR of a ball, etc: to spring or jump back from a solid surface. **2** to make (a ball, etc) spring or jump back from a solid surface. **3** INTR to move or spring suddenly. **4** (often **bounce in** or **out**) to rush noisily, angrily or with a lot of energy, etc. **5** COLLOQ **a** of a bank, etc: to return (a cheque) to the payee because of insufficient funds in the drawer's account; **b** INTR of a cheque: to be returned to the payee in this way. ➤ N **1** the ability to spring back or bounce well; springiness. **2** COLLOQ energy and liveliness. **3** a jump or leap. **4** the act of springing back from a solid surface. ■ **bouncy** ADJ (*-ier, -iest*).

bouncer N, COLLOQ a person employed by a club or restaurant, etc to stop unwanted guests entering, and to throw out troublemakers.

bouncing ADJ strong, healthy, and lively.

bound¹ ADJ **1** tied with or as if with a rope or other binding. **2** IN COMPOUNDS restricted to or by the specified thing: housebound • snowbound. **3** obliged. **4** of a book: fastened with a permanent cover.
◆ **bound to do sth** certain or obliged to do it.

bound² ADJ **1 a** (usu **bound for**) on the way to or going towards; **b** FOLLOWING AN ADV: homeward bound. **2** IN COMPOUNDS going in a specified direction: southbound.

bound³ N **1** (usu **bounds**) a limit or boundary. **2** (usu **bounds**) a limitation or restriction. **3** (**bounds**) land generally within certain understood limits; the district. ➤ VB to form a boundary to or of (something); to surround. ■ **boundless** ADJ.
◆ **out of bounds** not to be visited or entered, etc; outside the permitted area or limits.

bound⁴ N **1** a jump or leap upwards. **2** a bounce (eg of a ball). ➤ VB, INTR **1** (often **bound across, in, out,** over** or **up,** etc) to spring or leap in the specified direction; to move energetically. **2** to move with leaps. **3** of a ball: to bounce back.

boundary N (*-ies*) **1** a line marking the farthest limit of an area, etc. **2** a limit to anything: the boundary of good taste.

bountiful ADJ, now chiefly LITERARY **1** of a person, etc: generous. **2** ample; plentiful.

bounty N (*-ies*) **1** a reward or premium given, esp by a government. **2** chiefly LITERARY generosity. **3** a generous gift.

bouquet N **1** a bunch of flowers arranged in an artistic way. **2** the delicate smell of wine, etc.

bourbon N a type of whisky made from maize and rye, popular in the US.

bourgeois N (PL **bourgeois**) USU DEROG **1** a member of the middle class (**the bourgeoisie**), esp someone regarded as politically conservative and socially self-interested. **2** a person with capitalist, materialistic or conventional values. ➤ ADJ of the middle class or bourgeoisie.

bout N **1** a period or turn of some activity; a spell or stint. **2** an attack or period of illness. **3** a boxing or wrestling match.

boutique N a small shop, esp one selling fashionable clothes and accessories.

bovine ADJ **1** of or relating to, or characteristic of, cattle. **2** DEROG of people: dull or stupid.

bow¹ VB **1** (also **bow down**) to bend (the head or the upper part of the body) forwards and downwards. **2** (ALSO **bow down before sb** or **sth**) INTR to bend the head or the upper part of the body forwards and downwards, usu as a sign of greeting, respect, shame, etc or to acknowledge applause. **3** (usu **bow to**) to accept or submit to (something), esp unwillingly. ➤ N an act of bowing.
◆ **bow out** to stop taking part; to retire or withdraw.

bow² N **1 a** a knot made with a double loop, to fasten the two ends of a lace or string, etc; **b** a lace or string, etc tied in such a knot; **c** a looped knot of ribbons, etc used to decorate anything.

2 a weapon made of a piece of flexible wood or other material, bent by a string stretched between its two ends, for shooting arrows. **3** a long, thin piece of wood with horsehair along its length, for playing the violin, etc. ➤ VB, TR & INTR to bend or make (something) bend into a curved shape.

bow³ N, NAUT (often **bows**) the front part of a ship or boat.

bowdlerize or **-ise** VB to remove passages or words from (a book or play, etc), esp on moral and social rather than aesthetic grounds.

bowel N **1** an intestine, esp the large intestine in humans. **2** (usu **bowels**) the depths or innermost part: **the bowels of the earth**.

bower N a place in a garden, etc which is enclosed and shaded from the sun.

bowl¹ N **1** a round deep dish for mixing or serving food, or for holding liquids, etc. **2** (also **bowlful**) the amount a bowl holds. **3** the round hollow part of a spoon, lavatory, etc.

bowl² N **a** a heavy wooden ball for rolling, esp one for use in the game of bowls; **b** a similar metal ball used in tenpin bowling. ➤ VB **1** to roll (a ball or hoop, etc) smoothly along the ground. **2** INTR to play bowls, or tenpin bowling, etc. **3** TR & INTR, CRICKET to throw (the ball) towards the person batting at the wicket. **4** (often **bowl sb out**) CRICKET to put (the batsman) out by hitting the wicket with the ball. **5** INTR to roll or trundle along the ground. ◆ **bowl along** to move smoothly and quickly. ◆ **bowl sb over 1** COLLOQ to surprise, delight or impress them thoroughly. **2** to knock them over.

bow legs PL N legs which curve out at the knees. ■ **bow-legged** ADJ.

bowler¹ N **1** a person who bowls the ball in cricket, etc. **2** a person who plays bowls or goes bowling.

bowler² N (also **bowler hat**) a hard felt hat, with a rounded crown and curved brim.

bowling N **1** the game of bowls. **2** a game (eg esp tenpin bowling) played indoors, in which a ball is rolled along an alley at a group of skittles.

3 CRICKET the act of throwing the ball.

bowls SING N a game played on smooth grass with bowls, the object being to roll these as close as possible to a smaller ball (the jack).

bowsprit N, NAUT a strong spar projecting from the front of a ship.

bowstring N, ARCHERY the string on a bow.

bow tie N a necktie tied in a double loop to form a horizontal bow at the collar.

bow window N an outward-curving window.

box¹ N **1** a container made from wood, cardboard or plastic, etc, usu square or rectangular and with a lid. **2** (also **boxful**) the amount a box holds. **3 a** IN COMPOUNDS a small enclosed area, shelter or kiosk, etc for a specified purpose: **telephone box** • **witness box**; **b** in a theatre, etc: a separate compartment for a group of people, containing several seats; **c** (often **horse-box**) an enclosed area for a horse in a stable or vehicle. **4** an area in a field, pitch, road, printed page, etc marked out by straight lines. **5** (**the box**) BRIT COLLOQ **a** the television; **b** FOOTBALL the penalty box. **6** an individually allocated pigeonhole or similar container at a newspaper office or other agency, in which mail is collected for the person it is intended for. ➤ VB **1** (also **box up**) to put (something) into a box or boxes. **2** (**box sb** or **sth in** or **up**) to confine or enclose them or it. ■ **boxlike** ADJ.

box² VB **1** TR & INTR to fight (someone) with the hands formed into fists. **2** COLLOQ to hit (esp someone's ears) with the fist or the hand.

boxer N **1** a person who boxes, esp as a sport. **2** a breed of dog with a muscular body and a short broad muzzle with pronounced jowls.

boxing N the sport of fighting with the fists.

Boxing Day N in the UK and the Commonwealth: the first weekday after Christmas, observed as a public holiday.

box office N an office at which theatre, cinema or concert tickets, etc are sold.

box pleat N a large double pleat formed by

two pleats facing in opposite directions.

boxroom N, chiefly BRIT a small room, usu without a window, used esp for storage.

boy N 1 a male child. 2 a son: *He's our youngest boy*. 3 a young man, esp one regarded as still immature. 4 (**the boys**) COLLOQ a group of male friends with whom a man regularly socializes. ■ **boyhood** N. ■ **boyish** ADJ.

boycott VB 1 to refuse to have any business or social dealings with (a company or a country, etc), usu as a form of disapproval or coercion. 2 to refuse to handle or buy (goods), as a way of showing disapproval, exerting pressure, etc. ➤ N an act or instance of boycotting.

boyfriend N a regular male friend and companion, esp as a partner in a romantic or sexual relationship.

bra N a woman's undergarment which supports and covers the breasts.

brace N 1 a device, usu made from metal, which supports, strengthens or holds two things together. 2 (**braces**) BRIT straps worn over the shoulders, for holding trousers up. 3 a wire device worn on the teeth to straighten them. 4 BUILDING, etc a tool used by carpenters and metalworkers to hold a bit and enable it to be rotated. 5 (IN PL ALSO **brace**) a pair or couple, esp of game birds.
➤ VB 1 to make (something) tight or stronger, usu by supporting it in some way. 2 (**brace oneself**) to prepare and steady oneself for a blow or shock, etc.

bracelet N a band or chain worn as a piece of jewellery round the arm or wrist.

bracing ADJ of the wind, air, etc: stimulatingly cold and fresh.

bracken N a common fern with tall fronds.

bracket N 1 NON-TECHNICAL either member of several pairs of symbols, (), [ ], { }, ‹ ›, used to group together or enclose words, figures, etc. 2 USU IN COMPOUNDS a group or category falling within a certain range: *out of my price bracket*. 3 an L-shaped piece of metal or strong plastic, used for attaching shelves, etc to walls.

➤ VB to enclose (words, etc) together in brackets.
◆ **bracket sb** or **sth together** to put them or it into the same group or category.

brackish ADJ of water: slightly salty.

bract N, BOT a modified leaf, usu smaller than a true leaf and green in colour, in which an inflorescence develops.

brag VB (**-gg-**) INTR, DEROG to talk boastfully about oneself.
➤ N 1 a boastful statement or boastful talk. 2 a card game similar to poker.

braggart N someone who brags a lot.
➤ ADJ boastful.

braid N 1 a band or tape, often made from threads of gold and silver twisted together, used as a decoration on uniforms, etc. 2 now chiefly N AMER a length of interwoven hair.
➤ VB to interweave (several lengths of thread or hair, etc) together. ■ **braiding** N.

Braille or **braille** N a system of printing for the blind, consisting of dots read by touch.

brain N 1 the highly developed mass of nervous tissue that co-ordinates and controls the activities of the central nervous system of animals. 2 (esp **brains**) COLLOQ cleverness; intelligence. 3 (esp **brains** or **the brains**) COLLOQ a very clever person.
➤ VB, COLLOQ to hit (someone) hard on the head. ■ **brainless** ADJ.

brainchild N a person's original idea or plan.

brain death N the functional death of the centres in the brain that control breathing and other vital reflexes. ■ **brain-dead** ADJ.

brain drain N, COLLOQ the steady loss of scientists, academics, professionals, etc to another country.

brainstorm N, COLLOQ a sudden loss of the ability to think clearly and act sensibly.
➤ VB to try to solve problems or develop new ideas by intensive group discussion.

brainwash VB to force (someone) to change their beliefs or ideas, etc by applying continual and prolonged mental pressure.

brainwave N, COLLOQ a sudden, bright or clever idea.

brainy ADJ, COLLOQ clever; intelligent.

braise VB to cook (meat, vegetables, etc) slowly with a little liquid in a closed dish.

brake N 1 a device used to slow down or stop a moving vehicle or machine, or to prevent the movement of a parked vehicle. 2 anything which makes something stop or prevents or slows down progress, etc.
➤ VB to apply or use a brake.

bramble N 1 (also **bramble-bush**) a blackberry bush. 2 any other wild prickly shrub. 3 esp SCOT a blackberry. ■ **brambly** ADJ.

bran N the outer covering of cereal grain.

branch N 1 an offshoot arising from the trunk of a tree or the main stem of a shrub. 2 a main division of a railway line, river, road or mountain range. 3 a local office of a large company or organization. 4 a subdivision or section in a family, subject, group of languages, etc.
➤ VB, INTR (esp **branch off**) 1 to divide from the main part. 2 to send out branches.
◆ **branch out** to expand or diversify.

brand N 1 a distinctive maker's name or trademark, symbol or design, etc used to identify a product. 2 a variety or type. 3 an identifying mark on cattle, etc, usu burned on with a hot iron. 4 (also **branding-iron**) a metal instrument used for branding animals. 5 a sign or mark of disgrace or shame.
➤ VB 1 to mark (cattle, etc) with a hot iron. 2 to give (someone) a bad name or reputation.

brandish VB to flourish or wave (a weapon, etc) as a threat or display.

brand-new ADJ completely new.

brandy N (-ies) 1 a strong alcoholic drink distilled from grape wine. 2 a glass of this drink.

brash ADJ 1 very loud, flashy or showy. 2 impudent, overbearingly forward.
■ **brashness** N.

brass N (PL **brasses** in senses 2 and 4) 1 an alloy of copper and zinc. 2 an ornament, tool or other object made of brass, or such objects collectively. 3 (SING OR PL N) **a** wind instruments made of brass, such as the trumpet and horn; **b** the people who play brass instruments in an orchestra. 4 a piece of flat engraved brass, usu found in a church, in memory of someone who has died. 5 (also **top brass**) COLLOQ people in authority or of high military rank collectively.
➤ ADJ made of brass.

brass band N a band consisting mainly of brass instruments.

brassica N any vegetable of the cabbage family, including cauliflower, broccoli, turnip.

brassière N the full name for **bra**.

brass tacks PL N, COLLOQ the essential details.

brassy ADJ (-ier, -iest) 1 esp of colour: like brass in appearance. 2 of sound: hard, sharp or strident. 3 flashy or showy.

brat N, DEROG a child, esp a badly-behaved one.

bravado N (-os or -oes) a display of confidence or daring, often insincere.

brave ADJ having or showing courage; daring or fearless.
➤ N, FORMERLY a warrior, esp one from a Native American tribe.
➤ VB to meet or face up to (danger, pain, etc) boldly or resolutely; to defy. ■ **bravery** N.

bravo EXCLAM shouted to express one's appreciation at the end of a performance, etc.
➤ N a cry of 'bravo'.

bravura N 1 a display of great spirit, dash or daring. 2 MUS esp in vocal music: virtuosity, spirit or brilliance in performance. Also AS ADJ.

brawl N a noisy quarrel or fight, esp in public.
➤ VB, INTR to quarrel or fight noisily.

brawn N muscle; muscular or physical strength. ■ **brawny** ADJ.

bray VB 1 INTR of a donkey: to make its characteristic loud harsh cry. 2 to talk in a loud harsh voice.
➤ N 1 the sound made by a donkey. 2 any loud harsh cry or sound.

brazen ADJ 1 bold; shameless. 2 made of

brass. ■ **brazenly** ADV.

brazier N a portable metal container for holding burning coal or charcoal.

Brazil nut or **brazil** N an edible nut with a hard three-sided shell.

breach N 1 an act of breaking, esp a law or promise, etc. 2 a serious disagreement. 3 a gap, break or hole.
➤ VB 1 to break (a promise, etc). 2 to make an opening in (something).

bread N 1 a staple food prepared from flour mixed with water or milk, kneaded into a dough with a leavening agent, eg yeast, and baked. 2 (often **daily bread**) food and the other things one needs to live. 3 SLANG money.

bread and butter N a means of earning a living.

breadline N.
◆ **on the breadline** having hardly enough food and money to live on.

breadth N 1 the measurement from one side of something to the other. 2 extent, size.

breadwinner N the person who earns money to support a family.

break VB (PA T *broke*, PA P *broken*) 1 TR & INTR to divide or cause (something) to become divided into two or more parts as a result of stress or a blow. 2 to damage or become damaged. 3 to fracture a bone in (a limb, etc). 4 to burst or cut (the skin, etc). 5 to do something not allowed by (a law, agreement, promise, etc); to violate (something). 6 to exceed or improve upon (a sporting record, etc). 7 INTR to stop work, etc for a short period of time. 8 to interrupt (a journey, one's concentration, etc). 9 INTR of a boy's voice: to become lower in tone at puberty. 10 to defeat or destroy (something): **break a strike**. 11 to force (something) open with explosives: **break a safe**. 12 INTR of a storm: to begin violently. 13 INTR (also **break up**) to disperse or scatter. 14 to reduce the force of (a fall or a blow, etc). 15 INTR of waves, etc: to collapse into foam. 16 to lose or disrupt the order or form of (something): **break ranks**. 17 INTR of the weather: to change suddenly. 18 INTR to come

into being: **day breaking**. 19 TR & INTR to make or become weaker. 20 to destroy (someone) financially. 21 to decipher (a code, etc). 22 to interrupt the flow of electricity in (a circuit).
➤ N 1 an act or result of breaking. 2 a a pause, interval or interruption in some ongoing activity or situation; b (also **breaktime**) a short interval in work or lessons, etc. 3 a change from the usual or overall trend: **a break in the weather**. 4 a sudden rush, esp to escape: **make a break for it**. 5 COLLOQ a piece of luck. ■ **breakable** ADJ.
◆ **break away** INTR 1 to escape from control, esp suddenly or forcibly. 2 to put an end to one's connection with a group or custom, etc.
◆ **break down** 1 to stop working properly; to fail. 2 to collapse, disintegrate or decompose. 3 to give way to emotions; to burst into tears. 4 to suffer a nervous breakdown.
◆ **break sth down** 1 to use force to crush, demolish or knock it down. 2 to divide it into separate parts and analyse it.
◆ **break even** to make neither a profit nor a loss in a transaction.
◆ **break in** 1 to enter a building by force, esp to steal things inside. 2 (also **break in on sth**) to interrupt (a conversation, etc).
◆ **break sb in** to train or familiarize them in a new job or role.
◆ **break off** 1 to become detached by breaking. 2 to come to an end abruptly. 3 to stop talking.
◆ **break sth off** 1 to detach it by breaking. 2 to end a relationship, etc abruptly.
◆ **break out** 1 to escape from a prison, etc using force. 2 to begin suddenly: **war broke out**. 3 (esp **break out in sth**) to become suddenly covered in (spots or a rash, etc).
◆ **break through** 1 to force a way through. 2 to make a new discovery or be successful.
◆ **break up** 1 to break into pieces. 2 to come to an end. 3 to end a relationship or marriage.

breakage N 1 the act of breaking. 2 a broken object; damage caused by breaking.

breakaway N an act of breaking away or escaping. Also AS ADJ.

breakdown N 1 a a failure in a machine or device; b AS ADJ esp of a road vehicle used in connection with a breakdown: **a breakdown van**. **2** a failure or collapse of a process. **3** (also **nervous breakdown**) a failure or collapse in a person's mental health.

breaker N a large wave which breaks on rocks or on the beach.

breakfast N the first meal of the day.
➢ VB, INTR to have breakfast.

break-in N an illegal entry by force into a building, esp to steal property inside.

breaking point N the point at which something can no longer stand up to a stress or strain, and breaks down.

breakneck ADJ of speed: extremely fast.

breakout N an act or instance of breaking out.

breakthrough N **1** a decisive advance or discovery. **2** an act of breaking through.

breakwater N a wall or barrier built out from a beach to break the force of the waves.

bream N (PL **bream**) any of various freshwater fish of the carp family.

breast N **1** ANAT in women: each of the two mammary glands, which form soft protuberances on the chest. **2** the front part of the body between the neck and the belly. **3** the part of a garment covering the breast.
➢ VB to come to the top of (a hill, wave, etc).

breastbone N, NON-TECHNICAL the sternum.

breastfeed VB, TR & INTR to feed (a baby) with milk from the breast.

breastplate N a piece of armour which protects the chest.

breaststroke N a style of swimming breast–downwards in the water.

breath N **1** PHYSIOL the air drawn into, and then expelled from, the lungs. **2** exhaled air as odour, vapour or heat. **3** a single inhalation of air: **a deep breath**. **4** a faint breeze. **5** a slight hint or rumour. **6** a slight trace of perfume, etc. **7** life: **not while I have breath in my body**.
◆ **catch one's breath** to stop doing

something until one's normal breathing returns.
◆ **out of** or **short of breath** breathless.

breathe VB **1** TR & INTR to respire by alternately drawing air into and expelling it from the lungs. **2** TR & INTR to say, speak or sound quietly. **3** INTR to rest or pause: **haven't had a moment to breathe**. **4** INTR of fabric: to allow air and moisture, etc to pass through. **5** INTR of wine: to develop flavour when exposed to the air. **6** to live. **7** INTR to blow softly.

breather N, COLLOQ a short rest or break.

breathing-space N a brief respite.

breathless ADJ **1** having difficulty in breathing normally. **2** very eager or excited. **3** with no wind or fresh air. ■ **breathlessness** N.

breathtaking ADJ very surprising or impressive.

breathy ADJ (**-ier, -iest**) of a voice: accompanied by a sound of breathing.

breech N the back part of a gun barrel.

breeches or (chiefly N AMER) **britches** PL N short trousers fastened usu just below the knee.

breed VB (**bred**) **1** INTR of animals and plants: to reproduce sexually. **2** to make (animals or plants) reproduce sexually. **3** to make or produce (something): **Dirt breeds disease**. **4** to train, bring up or educate (children, etc).
➢ N **1** a subdivision within an animal species, produced by selective breeding, eg Friesian cattle. **2** a race or lineage. **3** a kind or type.
■ **breeder** N.

breeding N **1** BIOL the process of controlling the manner in which plants or animals reproduce. **2** the result of a good education and training, social skills, manners, etc; upbringing. **3** the act of producing offspring.

breeze N **1** a gentle wind. **2** COLLOQ, esp N AMER a pleasantly simple task. **3** cinders.
➢ VB, INTR, COLLOQ to move briskly, in a cheery and confident manner.

breezeblock N a type of brick made from cinders, sand and cement.

breezy ADJ (**-ier, -iest**) **1** rather windy. **2** lively, confident and casual: bright and breezy.

brethren see under **brother**

breviary N (-ies) RC CHURCH a book of the hymns, prayers and psalms of the daily service.

brevity N (-ies) the use of few words.

brew VB 1 to make (eg beer) by mixing, boiling and fermenting. 2 (also **brew up**) TR & INTR to make (tea, etc) by mixing the leaves, grains, etc with boiling water. 3 INTR to be in the process of brewing. 4 INTR to get stronger and threaten: There's a storm brewing.
➤ N 1 a drink produced by brewing.
2 a concoction or mixture. ■ **brewer** N.
■ **brewery** N.

briar or **brier** N 1 a prickly shrub, esp a wild rose bush. 2 a S European shrub or small tree with a woody root. 3 a tobacco pipe made from this root.

bribe N 1 a gift offered to persuade someone to do something illegal or improper.
2 something offered to someone in order to persuade them to behave in a certain way.
➤ VB 1 USU TR to offer or promise a bribe, etc to (someone). 2 to gain co-operation from (someone) by a bribe. ■ **bribery** N.

bric-à-brac N small objects of little financial value kept as decorations or ornaments.

brick N 1 a rectangular block of baked clay used for building. 2 the material used for making bricks. 3 a child's building block.
4 something in the shape of a brick.
➤ ADJ made of brick or of bricks.

bricklayer N a tradesman who builds with bricks. Often (COLLOQ) shortened to **brickie**.

bridal ADJ relating to a bride or a wedding.

bride and **bridegroom** N a woman, or man, who has just been, or is about to be, married.

bridesmaid N a girl or unmarried woman who attends the bride at a wedding.

bridge[1] N 1 a structure that spans a river, road, railway, etc, providing a continuous route across it. 2 anything that joins or connects two separate things or parts of something. 3 on a

ship: the narrow raised platform from which the captain and officers direct its course. 4 the hard bony upper part of the nose. 5 in a pair of spectacles: the part of the frame that rests on the bridge of the nose. 6 on a violin or guitar, etc: a thin, movable, upright piece of wood, etc which supports the strings.
➤ VB 1 to form or build a bridge over (eg a river). 2 to make a connection across (something), or close the two sides of (a gap, etc).

bridge[2] N, CARDS a game which developed from whist, for four people playing in pairs.

bridgehead N, MIL a fortified position held at the end of a bridge nearest to the enemy.

bridle N 1 the leather straps put on a horse's head which help the rider to control the horse.
2 anything used to control or restrain.
➤ VB 1 to put a bridle on (a horse). 2 to bring (something) under control. 3 (esp **bridle at sth** or sometimes **bridle up**) INTR to show anger or resentment, esp by moving the head upwards proudly or indignantly.

brief ADJ 1 lasting only a short time. 2 short or small: a brief stint. 3 using few words; concise.
➤ N 1 LAW a a summary of the facts and legal points of a case, prepared for a barrister; b a case taken by a barrister; c COLLOQ a barrister.
2 (also **briefing**) instructions given for a job or task. 3 (**briefs**) close-fitting underpants without legs.
➤ VB to prepare (someone) by giving them instructions in advance. ■ **briefly** ADV.
◆ **in brief** in few words; briefly.

briefcase N a case for carrying papers, etc.

brier see **briar**

brig N a two-masted square-rigged sailing ship.

brigade N 1 a subdivision of the army, consisting eg of a group of regiments. 2 esp IN COMPOUNDS a group of people organized for a specified purpose: the fire brigade.

brigadier N an officer of a brigade.

bright ADJ 1 giving out or shining with much light.
2 of a colour: strong, light and clear. 3 lively; cheerful. 4 COLLOQ clever and quick to learn.

5 full of hope or promise: **a bright future**.
➤ ADV brightly. ■ **brightly** ADV. ■ **brightness** N.

brighten VB, TR & INTR (often **brighten up**) **1** to become, or make, bright or brighter. **2** to become or make happier or more cheerful.

brilliant ADJ **1** very bright and sparkling. **2** of a colour: bright and vivid. **3** showing outstanding intelligence or talent. **4** COLLOQ excellent; exceptionally good.
➤ N a diamond or other gem. ■ **brilliance** N.

brim N **1** the top edge or lip of a cup, bowl, etc. **2** the projecting edge of a hat.
➤ VB (**-mm-**) INTR to be, or become, full to the brim. ■ **brimful** or **brimfull** ADJ.
◆ **brim over** INTR to begin to overflow.

brimstone N, OLD USE sulphur.

brindled ADJ brown or grey, and marked with streaks or patches of a darker colour.

brine N **1** very salty water, used for preserving food. **2** LITERARY the sea.

bring VB (**brought**) **1** to carry or take (something or someone) to a stated or implied place or person. **2** to make (someone or something) be in, or reach, a certain state: **It brought him to his senses**. **3** to make or result in: **War brings misery**. **4** (esp **bring oneself**) USU WITH NEGATIVES to persuade, make or force oneself (to do something unpleasant). **5** (esp **bring in**) to be sold for (a stated price); to produce (a stated amount) as income.
◆ **bring about** to make (something) happen.
◆ **bring sb down 1** to make them sad or disappointed, etc. **2** to demean them.
◆ **bring forward 1** to move (an arrangement, etc) to an earlier date or time. **2** BOOKKEEPING to transfer (a partial sum) to the next column.
◆ **bring sb round** to cause them to recover consciousness.
◆ **bring sb up** to care for and educate them when young.
◆ **bring up 1** to introduce (a subject) for discussion. **2** to regurgitate (something eaten).

brink N **1** the edge or border of a steep dangerous place or of a river. **2** the point immediately before something dangerous, unknown or exciting, etc starts or occurs.

brinkmanship and **brinksmanship** N the art or practice of going to the very edge of a dangerous situation (eg war) before moving back or withdrawing.

briny ADJ (**-ier, -iest**) of water: very salty.
➤ N (**the briny**) COLLOQ the sea.

brisk ADJ **1** lively, active or quick: **a brisk walk**. **2** pleasantly cold and fresh. ■ **briskly** ADV.

brisket N meat from the breast of a bull or cow.

bristle N **1** a short stiff hair on an animal or plant. **2** something similar to this but artificial, used eg for brushes.
➤ VB **1** TR & INTR of hair: to stand upright and stiff. **2** (usu **bristle with**) INTR to show obvious anger or rage, etc. **3** (usu **bristle with**) INTR to be covered or closely-packed with (upright objects). ■ **bristly** ADJ.

Brit N, COLLOQ a British person.

britches see **breeches**

British ADJ **1** of Great Britain. **2** of or relating to the British Empire or to the Commonwealth. **3** (**the British**) the people of Great Britain.

British Summer Time N the system of time (one hour ahead of Greenwich Mean Time) used in Britain during the summer to give extra daylight in the evenings.

Briton N **1** a British person. **2** (also **ancient Briton**) HIST one of the Celtic people living in Southern Britain before the Roman conquest.

brittle ADJ **1** hard but easily broken. **2** sharp or hard in quality: **a brittle laugh**.

broach VB **1** to raise (a subject) for discussion. **2** to open (a bottle, barrel, etc) to remove liquid.

broad ADJ **1** large in extent from one side to the other. **2** wide and open; spacious. **3** general, not detailed: **a broad inquiry**. **4** clear; full: **in broad daylight**. **5** strong; obvious: **a broad hint**. **6** main; concentrating on the main elements rather than on detail: **the broad facts**. **7** strongly marked by local dialect or features:

broad Scots. **8** rather rude and vulgar.
■ **broadly** ADV.

B-road N in the UK: a secondary road.

broadband ADJ **1** TELECOMM across, involving or designed to operate across a wide range of frequencies. **2** COMP capable of accommodating data from a variety of input sources, such as voice, telephone, TV, etc.

broad bean N one of the large flattened pale green edible seeds growing in pods on an annual plant.

broadcast VB **1** TR & INTR to transmit (a radio or TV programme, speech, etc) to the public. **2** INTR to take part in a radio or TV broadcast. **3** to make (something) widely known. **4** to sow (seeds) by scattering them in all directions.
➤ N a radio or TV programme.
➤ ADJ communicated or sent out by radio or TV.
■ **broadcaster** N. ■ **broadcasting** N.

broaden VB (also **broaden out**) TR & INTR to become or make (something) broad.

broad-minded ADJ tolerant; liberal.

broadsheet N a newspaper printed on large sheets of paper.

broadside N **1** a strongly critical verbal attack. **2** NAVY **a** all of the guns on one side of a warship; **b** the firing of these simultaneously.

broadsword N, OLD USE a heavy sword with a broad blade.

brocade N a heavy silk fabric with a raised design.

broccoli N a type of cultivated cabbage or its immature flower buds eaten as a vegetable.

brochure N a booklet, esp one giving information about holidays, products, etc.

brogue N **1** a strong heavy-soled leather shoe, with decorative punched holes. **2** a strong but gentle accent.

broil VB **1** chiefly N AMER to grill (food). **2** INTR to be extremely hot.

broke ADJ, COLLOQ having no money.

broken ADJ **1** smashed; fractured. **2** disturbed

or interrupted. **3** not working properly. **4** of a promise, agreement or law, etc: not kept; violated. **5** of a marriage or family, etc: split apart by divorce. **6** of language, esp speech: not perfect or fluent. **7** weakened and tired out. **8** of a horse: broken-in. **9** with an uneven surface: **broken ground**.

broken-down ADJ **1** not in working order. **2** not in good condition, spirits or health.

broken-hearted ADJ deeply hurt emotionally, or overwhelmed with sadness.

broker N **1** IN COMPOUNDS a person who acts as an agent in buying and selling goods or property. **2** a negotiator or middleman.

brolly N (-*ies*) chiefly BRIT COLLOQ an umbrella.

bromide N CHEM a compound of bromine, esp one used medicinally as a sedative.

bromine N a non-metallic element, a dark-red corrosive liquid with a pungent smell.

bronchial ADJ, ANAT of the bronchi.

bronchitis N, PATHOL inflammation of the mucous membrane of the bronchi.

bronchus N (*bronchi*) either of the two main airways to the lungs that branch off the lower end of the trachea.

brontosaurus N (-*ri*) a huge herbivorous dinosaur with a small head and a long neck.

bronze N **1** an alloy of copper and tin. **2** the dark orangey-brown colour of bronze. **3** a bronze medal. **4** a work of art made of bronze.
➤ ADJ made of or the colour of bronze.
➤ VB **1** to give a bronze colour, surface or appearance to. **2** INTR to become the colour of bronze, or tanned.

bronze medal N in athletics, etc: a medal given to the competitor who comes third.

brooch N a piece of jewellery with a hinged pin at the back for fastening it to clothes.

brood N **1** a number of young animals, esp birds, produced or hatched at the same time. **2** COLLOQ, USU HUMOROUS all the children in a family. **3** a kind, breed or race of something.
➤ VB, INTR **1** of a bird: to sit on (eggs) in order to

hatch them. **2** (often **brood about, on** or **over**) to think anxiously or resentfully about (something). ■ **brooding** ADJ.

broody ADJ (*-ier, -iest*) **1** of a bird: ready and wanting to brood. **2** introspective; moody.

brook[1] N a small stream.

brook[2] VB, FORMAL, USU WITH NEGATIVES to tolerate or accept (something).

broom N **1** a long-handled sweeping brush. **2** any of various deciduous shrubby plants of the pea family.

broomstick N the long handle of a broom.

Bros ABBREV (ESP IN A COMPANY NAME) Brothers.

broth N, COOKERY a thin clear soup made by boiling meat, fish or vegetables, etc in water.

brothel N a house where men can go to have sexual intercourse with prostitutes for money.

brother N **1** a boy or man with the same natural parents as another person or people. **2** a man belonging to the same group, trade union, etc as another or others. **3** (PL *brethren*) a man who is a member of a religious group, esp a monk. ■ **brotherly** ADJ.

brotherhood N **1** an association of men formed for, esp a religious, purpose. **2** friendliness, or a sense of companionship or unity, etc felt towards other people. **3** the state of being a brother.

brother-in-law N (*brothers-in-law*) **1** the brother of one's husband or wife. **2** the husband of one's sister. **3** the husband of the sister of one's own wife or husband.

brouhaha N noisy, excited and confused activity; a commotion or uproar.

brow N **1** (usu **brows**) an eyebrow. **2** the forehead. **3** the top of a hill, road or pass, etc. **4** the edge of a cliff, etc.

browbeat VB to intimidate (someone) by speaking angrily or sternly, or by looking fierce.

brown ADJ **1** having the colour of dark soil or wood, or any of various shades of this colour. **2** of bread, etc: made from wholemeal flour.

3 having a dark skin or complexion. **4** having a sun-tanned skin.
➤ N **1** any of various dark earthy colours, like those of bark, tanned skin or coffee, etc. **2** brown paint, dye, pigment, material or clothes.
➤ VB, TR & INTR to become or cause (something) to become brown.

brownie N **1** FOLKLORE a friendly goblin or fairy, said to help with domestic chores. **2** esp US a small square piece of chewy chocolate cake.

Brownie Guide and **Brownie** N a young girl belonging to the junior section of the Guides Association in Britain, or of the Girl Scouts in the US.

browning N, COOKERY, chiefly BRIT a substance used to turn gravy a rich brown colour.

browse VB, TR & INTR **1** to look through a book, etc, or look around a shop, etc in a casual, relaxed or haphazard way. **2** of certain animals, eg deer: to feed by nibbling on young buds, shoots, leaves, etc.
➤ N an act of browsing.

brucellosis N, VET MED an infectious disease, mainly affecting cattle.

bruise N **1** an area of skin discoloration and swelling caused by the leakage of blood from damaged blood vessels following injury. **2** a similar injury to a fruit or plant, shown as a soft discoloured area.
➤ VB **1** to mark and discolour (the surface of the skin or of a fruit, etc) in this way. **2** INTR to develop bruises. **3** TR & INTR to hurt (someone's feelings, pride, etc) or be hurt emotionally.

bruiser N, COLLOQ a big strong person, esp one who likes fighting or who looks aggressive.

brunch N, COLLOQ a meal that combines breakfast and lunch.

brunette N a woman or girl with brown hair.
➤ ADJ of hair colour: brown.

brunt N (esp **the brunt of**) the main force or shock of (a blow, attack, etc).

brush N **1** a tool with lengths of stiff nylon, wire, hair, bristles, etc set into it, used for tidying the hair, cleaning, painting, etc. **2** an act of

brushing. **3** a light grazing contact. **4** a short encounter: **a brush with the law. 5** a fox's bushy tail. **6** brushwood.
➤ VB **1** to sweep, groom or clean (the hair, teeth, a floor, etc) with a brush. **2** (also **brush against**) TR & INTR to touch (someone or something) lightly in passing.
◆ **brush off** to ignore or refuse to listen to.
◆ **brush up (on)** to improve or refresh one's knowledge of (a language or subject, etc).

brush-off N (usu **the brush-off**) COLLOQ an act of ignoring, rebuffing or dismissing someone or something in an abrupt or offhand manner.

brushwood N **1** dead, broken or lopped-off branches and twigs, etc from trees and bushes. **2** small trees and bushes on rough land. **3** rough land covered by such trees and bushes.

brushwork N a particular technique a painter uses to apply the paint to a canvas, etc.

brusque ADJ blunt and often impolite; curt. ■ **brusquely** ADV. ■ **brusqueness** N.

Brussels sprout or **brussels sprout** N (usu as PL **Brussels sprouts** or (COLLOQ) **sprouts**) a type of cabbage or one of its buds cooked and eaten as a vegetable.

brutal ADJ **1** savagely cruel or violent. **2** ruthlessly harsh or unfeeling. **3** of or like a brute. ■ **brutality** N (-**ies**).

brutalize or **-ise** VB to make brutal or treat brutally. ■ **brutalization** N.

brute N **1** a cruel, brutal or violent person. **2** an animal other than a human; a beast.
➤ ADJ **1** instinctive, not involving rational thought: **brute force. 2** coarse, crudely sensual or animal-like. ■ **brutish** ADJ.

bryony N (-**ies**) a climbing plant with highly poisonous red berries.

BSc ABBREV Bachelor of Science.

BSE ABBREV bovine spongiform encephalopathy, a fatal brain disease of cattle.

BST ABBREV British Summer Time.

bubble N **1** a thin film of liquid forming a sphere filled with air or gas. **2** a ball of air or gas which has formed in a solid or liquid. **3** a dome made of clear plastic or glass.
➤ VB, INTR **1** to form or give off bubbles. **2** to make a sound like bubbling liquid.

bubble and squeak N, COOKERY, chiefly BRIT cooked cabbage and potatoes fried together.

bubble gum N a type of chewing gum which can be blown into bubbles.

bubbly ADJ (-**ier, -iest**) **1** being like bubbles. **2** very lively and cheerful.

bubo N (-**oes**) PATHOL a swollen tender lymph node, esp in the armpit or groin.

bubonic plague N, PATHOL the commonest form of plague, characterized by the development of buboes.

buccaneer N, HIST & LITERARY a pirate.

buck[1] N (*bucks* or only in sense 1 *buck*) **1** a male animal, esp a male deer, goat, rabbit, hare or kangaroo. **2** an act of bucking.
➤ VB **1** INTR of a horse, etc: to make a series of rapid jumps into the air, with the back arched and legs held stiff. **2** of a horse, etc: to throw (a rider) from its back in this way. **3** COLLOQ to oppose or resist (an idea or trend, etc).

buck[2] N, COLLOQ **1** N AMER, AUSTRAL, NZ, etc a dollar. **2** S AFR a rand.

buck[3] N.
◆ **pass the buck** COLLOQ to give someone else the responsibility for something.

bucket N **1** a round open-topped container for holding or carrying liquids and solids. **2** (also **bucketful**) the amount a bucket holds. **3** COLLOQ a rubbish-bin. **4** the scoop of a dredging machine.

buckle N a flat piece of metal or plastic, etc usu attached to one end of a strap or belt, with a pin in the middle which goes through a hole in the other end of the strap or belt to fasten it.
➤ VB, TR & INTR **1** to fasten (something) with a buckle. **2** to bend (metal, etc) out of shape, using or as a result of great heat or force.

buckshot N a large type of lead shot.

buckskin N a strong greyish-yellow

leather made from deerskin.

buckthorn N any of various shrubs or small trees, esp a thorny shrub with black berries.

bucktooth N a large front tooth which sticks out. ■ **bucktoothed** ADJ.

buckwheat N 1 a fast-growing plant bearing triangular seeds. 2 the seeds of this plant.

bucolic ADJ concerned with the countryside or people living there; pastoral; rustic.

bud N 1 in a plant: an immature knob-like shoot that will develop into a leaf or flower. 2 a flower or leaf that is not yet fully open. ➤ VB (-*dd*-) INTR of a plant, etc: to put out or develop buds. ◆ **nip sth in the bud** to put a stop to it, or destroy it, at a very early stage.

Buddhism N a world religion that originated in ancient India, founded by the Buddha, Siddhartha Gautama, in the 6c BC, and based on his teachings. ■ **Buddhist** N and ADJ.

budding ADJ of a person: developing; beginning to show talent in a specified area.

buddleia N any of various deciduous shrubs with fragrant flowers which attract butterflies.

buddy N (-*ies*) COLLOQ, esp N AMER **a** a friend or companion; **b** a term of address used to a man.

budge VB, TR & INTR 1 to move, or cause to move. 2 to change one's mind or opinions, or make (someone) change their mind or opinions.

budgerigar N (also COLLOQ **budgie**) a type of small Australian parrot.

budget N 1 a plan, esp for a particular period of time, specifying how money coming in will be spent and allocated. 2 (**the Budget**) BRIT an annual programme for national revenue and expenditure, proposed by the government. 3 the amount of money set aside for a purpose. 4 AS ADJ low in cost; economical. ➤ VB 1 INTR to draw up a budget. 2 (usu **budget for**) INTR to plan, arrange or allow for (a specific expense). 3 to provide (an amount of money, or sometimes time, etc) in a budget. ■ **budgetary** ADJ.

buff[1] N, COLLOQ, USU IN COMPOUNDS a knowledgeable enthusiast: an opera buff.

buff[2] N 1 a dull-yellowish colour. 2 a soft undyed leather. 3 (sometimes **buffer**) a cloth or pad, used for polishing. ➤ ADJ 1 dull yellow in colour: a buff envelope. 2 made of buff (N sense 2). ➤ VB 1 (also **buff up**) to polish (something) with a buff. 2 to make (leather) soft like buff.

buffalo N (*buffalo* or *buffaloes*) 1 a member of the cattle family, native to S and E Africa, with a heavy black or brown body and thick upward-curving horns. 2 a member of the cattle family, native to SE Asia. 3 GENERALLY the American bison.

buffer N 1 an apparatus designed to take the shock when an object such as a railway carriage or a ship hits something. 2 a person or thing which protects from harm or shock, etc, or makes its impact less damaging or severe.

buffer state and **buffer zone** N a neutral country or zone situated between two others.

buffet[1] N 1 a meal set out on tables from which people help themselves. 2 a place, room or counter, etc where light meals and drinks may be bought and eaten.

buffet[2] N 1 a blow with the hand or fist. 2 a stroke or blow: a sudden buffet of wind. ➤ VB 1 to strike or knock with the hand or fist. 2 to knock about; to batter repeatedly.

buffoon N 1 a person who amuses people with comic behaviour; a clown. 2 a fool. ■ **buffoonery** N.

bug N 1 the common name for any insect with a flattened oval body and mouthparts for piercing and sucking. 2 N AMER a popular name for any kind of insect. 3 COLLOQ a bacterium or virus that causes infection or illness. 4 COLLOQ a small hidden microphone. 5 COLLOQ a fault in a machine or computer program. ➤ VB (-*gg*-) 1 COLLOQ to hide a microphone in (a room, telephone, etc) to listen in to what is said. 2 SLANG to annoy or worry (someone).

bugbear N an object of fear, dislike or annoyance.

bugger COARSE SLANG, N **1** a person who practises anal sex. **2** a difficult or awkward person or thing. **3** a person one feels affection or pity for: **poor bugger.**
➤ VB **1** to practise anal sex with (someone). **2** (also **bugger up**) to ruin (something).

buggery N anal sex.

buggy N (*-ies*) **1** a light open carriage pulled by one horse. **2** a light folding pushchair. **3** (also **baby buggy**) N AMER a pram. **4** a small motorized vehicle.

bugle N a brass or copper instrument similar to a small trumpet, used mainly for sounding military calls. ■ **bugler** N.

build VB (*built*) **1** to make or construct (something) from parts. **2** (also **build up**) INTR to increase gradually in size, strength, amount, intensity, etc; to develop. **3** to make (something) in a specified way or for a specified purpose: **built to last. 4** to control the building of (something); to have (something) built.
➤ N physical form, esp that of the human body.
◆ **build sth up** to build or amass it gradually.

builder N a person who builds houses, etc.

building N **1** the business, process or art of constructing houses, etc. **2** a structure with walls and a roof, such as a house.

building society N, BRIT a finance company that lends money to its members.

build-up N **1** a gradual increase. **2** a gradual approach to a climax.

built-in ADJ **1** built to form part of the main structure or design of something. **2** included as a necessary part of something. **3** inherent.

built-up ADJ of land, etc: covered with buildings, esp houses.

bulb N **1** in certain plants, eg tulip and onion: a swollen underground organ that functions as a food store. **2** a light-bulb.

bulbous ADJ **1** like a bulb in shape; fat, bulging or swollen. **2** having or growing from a bulb.

bulge N **1** a swelling, esp where one would expect to see something flat. **2** a sudden and usu temporary increase, eg in population.
➤ VB, INTR to swell outwards.

bulghur or **bulgur** N wheat that has been boiled, dried, lightly milled and cracked.

bulimia N, MED (in full **bulimia nervosa**) a psychological disorder in which episodes of excessive eating are followed by self-induced vomiting or laxative abuse. ■ **bulimic** N, ADJ.

bulk N **1** size, esp when large and awkward. **2** the greater or main part of something. **3** a large body, shape or person. **4** a large quantity: **buy in bulk.** ■ **bulky** (*-ier, -iest*) ADJ.
◆ **bulk large** to be or seem important.

bulkhead N a wall in a ship or aircraft, etc which separates one section from another.

bull[1] N **1** the uncastrated male of animals in the cattle family. **2** the male of the elephant, whale and some other large animals. **3** STOCK EXCHANGE someone who buys shares hoping to sell them at a higher price at a later date. **4** COLLOQ a bull's-eye.
➤ ADJ **1** male: **a bull walrus. 2** STOCK EXCHANGE of a market: favourable to the bulls; rising.

bull[2] N, SLANG nonsense; meaningless talk.

bull[3] N an official letter from the Pope.

bulldog N a breed of dog with a heavy body and a square head with a flat upturned muzzle.

bulldoze VB **1** to use a bulldozer to move, flatten or demolish (something). **2** (**bulldoze sb into sth**) to force them to do something they do not want to do. **3** to force or push (something) through against all opposition.

bulldozer N a large, powerful, heavy tractor with a vertical blade at the front.

bullet N a small metal cylinder with a pointed or rounded end, for firing from a gun.

bulletin N **1** a short official news statement. **2** a short printed newspaper or leaflet.

bullet-proof ADJ of a material, etc: strong enough to prevent bullets passing through.

bullfight N a public show, esp in Spain and Portugal, etc in which people bait, and usu ultimately kill, a bull. ■ **bullfighter** N.

bullfinch N a small bird of the finch family, the male having a conspicuous red breast.

bullfrog N a large frog with a loud call.

bullion N gold or silver that has not been coined, esp in large bars, or in mass.

bullock N a castrated bull.

bullring N an arena for bullfighting.

bull's-eye N 1 the small circular centre of a target used in shooting or darts, etc. 2 DARTS, etc a shot which hits this. 3 COLLOQ anything which hits its target or achieves its aim, etc.

bullshit N, COARSE SLANG 1 nonsense. 2 deceptive, insincere or pretentious talk.

bull terrier N a breed of dog with a heavy body and a short smooth coat.

bully N (*-ies*) a person who hurts, frightens or torments weaker or smaller people.
➢ VB (*-ies, -ied*) 1 to act like a bully towards (someone); to threaten or persecute (them). 2 (**bully sb into sth**) to force them to do something. ■ **bullying** N.

bulrush N a tall waterside plant with spikes of tightly packed dark-brown flowers.

bulwark N 1 a wall built as a defence, often one made of earth; a rampart. 2 something that defends a cause or way of life, etc. 4 (esp **bulwarks**) NAUT the side of a ship projecting above the deck.

bum¹ N, BRIT COLLOQ 1 the buttocks. 2 the anus.

bum² COLLOQ, esp N AMER & AUSTRAL, N 1 someone who lives by begging; a tramp. 2 someone who is lazy and irresponsible.
➢ ADJ worthless; dud or useless.
➢ VB (*-mm-*) 1 to get (something) by begging, borrowing or cadging: **bum a lift**. 2 (usu **bum around** or **about**) INTR to spend one's time doing nothing in particular.

bumble VB, INTR 1 to move in an awkward or clumsy way. 2 to speak in a confused or confusing way. ■ **bumbling** ADJ.

bumble-bee N a large bee.

bumf or **bumph** N, BRIT COLLOQ miscellaneous useless papers or documents, etc.

bump VB 1 TR & INTR to knock or hit (someone or something), esp heavily or with a jolt. 2 to hurt or damage (eg one's head) by hitting or knocking it. 3 INTR of two moving objects: to collide. 4 INTR to move or travel with jerky or bumpy movements.
➢ N 1 a knock, jolt or collision. 2 a dull sound caused by a knock or collision, etc. 3 a lump or swelling on the body, caused by a blow. 4 a lump on a road surface. ■ **bumpy** ADJ.
◆ **bump into sb** COLLOQ to meet them by chance.

bumper N 1 BRIT a bar on the front or back of a motor vehicle which lessens the shock or damage if it hits anything. 2 US a railway buffer. 3 a large example or measure.
➢ ADJ exceptionally large: **a bumper edition**.

bumpkin N, COLLOQ, USU DEROG an awkward, simple or stupid person, esp a simple fellow who lives in the country.

bump-start VB to start (a car) by pushing it and engaging the gears while it is moving.
➢ N (**bump start**) an act or instance of this.

bumptious ADJ conceited or self-important.

bun N 1 esp BRIT a a small, round, usu sweetened, roll; b a small round cake of various types. 2 a mass of hair fastened in a round shape on the back of the head.

bunch N 1 a number of things fastened or growing together. 2 (usu **bunches**) two sections of hair tied separately at each side or the back of the head. 3 COLLOQ a group.
➢ VB, TR & INTR (sometimes **bunch up**) to group (people or things) together in, or to form a bunch or bunches.

bundle N 1 a number of things loosely fastened or tied together. 2 a loose parcel, esp one contained in a cloth.
➢ VB 1 (often **bundle up**) to make (something) into a bundle or bundles. 2 (usu **bundle into**) to put (someone or something) somewhere quickly and unceremoniously.

bung N a small round piece of wood, rubber or

cork, etc used to close a hole eg in the top of a jar or other container.
➤ VB **1** (esp **bung up**) **a** to block (a hole) with a bung; **b** COLLOQ, esp IN PASSIVE to block, plug or clog (something): **My nose is bunged up.** **2** SLANG to throw or put (something) somewhere in a careless way.

bungalow N a single-storey house.

bungee jumping N the sport in which a person jumps from a height with strong rubber ropes or cables attached to their ankles.

bungle VB, TR & INTR to spoil or mismanage (a job or procedure).
➤ N a mistake or foul-up. ■ **bungler** N.
■ **bungling** N, ADJ.

bunion N a painful swelling on the first joint of the big toe.

bunk[1] N **1** a narrow bed attached to the wall in a cabin in a ship, caravan, etc. **2** a bunk bed.
➤ VB, INTR, COLLOQ **1** (esp **bunk down**) to lie down and go to sleep, esp in some improvised place. **2** to occupy a bunk.

bunk[2] N, BRIT SLANG (usu **do a bunk**) the act of leaving the place where one ought to be, usu furtively: **He did a bunk from gym.**

bunk bed N each of a pair of single beds fixed one on top of the other.

bunker N **1** an obstacle on a golf course consisting of a hollow area containing sand. **2** a large container or compartment for storing fuel. **3** an underground bombproof shelter.

bunkum N, COLLOQ nonsense; foolish talk; claptrap. Often shortened to **bunk**.

bunny N (-**ies**) (also **bunny rabbit**) a pet name or child's word for a rabbit.

Bunsen burner N an adjustable gas burner, used mainly in chemistry laboratories.

bunting[1] N a row of small cloth or paper flags on a string; streamers or other similar decorations hung on string.

bunting[2] N any of various small finch-like birds with a short stout bill and a sturdy body.

buoy N a floating object fastened to the bottom of the sea by an anchor, to warn ships of rocks, etc or to mark channels, etc.
➤ VB **1** to mark (eg a channel) with a buoy or buoys. **2** (usu **buoy up**) to raise or lift the spirits of (someone); to encourage, cheer or excite (them). **3** (often **buoy up**) to sustain, support or boost (something).

buoyant ADJ **1** able to float in or on the surface of a liquid. **2** able to keep an object afloat. **3** cheerful; resilient. ■ **buoyancy** N (-**ies**).

bur or **burr** N any seed or fruit with hooks or prickles, or any plant with such seeds or fruits.

burble VB **1** (often **burble on** or **away**) INTR to speak at length but with little meaning or purpose. **2** INTR of a stream, etc: to make a bubbling murmuring sound.
➤ N a bubbling murmuring sound.

burbot N (*burbot* or *burbots*) a large fish, the only freshwater species in the cod family.

burden N **1** something to be carried; a load. **2** a duty, etc which is time-consuming, difficult, costly, exacting or hard to endure. **3** the carrying of a load or loads: **a beast of burden**.
➤ VB to weigh (someone) down (with a burden, etc); to trouble or impose upon (them).
■ **burdensome** ADJ.

bureau N (-**reaux** or -**reaus**) **1** BRIT a desk for writing at, with drawers and usu a front flap which provides the writing surface. **2** N AMER, ESP US a chest of drawers. **3** an office or department for business, esp for collecting and supplying information. **4** N AMER a government or newspaper department.

bureaucracy N (-**ies**) **1** a system of government by non-elected officials who are responsible to their department heads. **2** these officials as a group, esp when regarded as oppressive. **3** any system of administration with complex procedures and trivial rules.

bureaucrat N **1** a government official. **2** an official who follows rules rigidly, so creating delays and difficulties. ■ **bureaucratic** ADJ.

burgeon VB, INTR **1** to grow or develop quickly; to flourish. **2** of a plant: to bud or sprout.

burger N **1** a hamburger. **2** esp IN COMPOUNDS

a hamburger covered or flavoured with something: **cheeseburger**.

burglar N, LAW a person who commits the crime of burglary.

burglary N (-*ies*) LAW the crime of entering a building illegally, esp in order to steal.

burgle VB **1** to enter (a building, etc) illegally and steal from it. **2** INTR to commit burglary.

burgundy N (-*ies*) **1** a French wine made in the Burgundy region, esp a red wine. **2** any similar red wine. **3** a deep or purplish red colour.

burial N the burying of a dead body.

burk see **berk**

burlesque N a piece of literature, acting or some other presentation which exaggerates, demeans or mocks a serious subject or art form. ➤ VB to make fun of (something) using burlesque.

burly ADJ (-*ier*, -*iest*) strong and heavy in build.

burn[1] VB (*burned* or *burnt*) **1** TR & INTR to be on fire or set (something) on fire. **2** TR & INTR to damage or injure (someone or something), or be damaged or injured, by fire or heat. **3** to use (something) as fuel. **4** TR & INTR to char or scorch (someone or something), or become charred or scorched. **5** to make (a hole, etc) by or as if by fire or heat, etc. **6** INTR to be or feel hot. **7** TR & INTR to feel or make (something) feel a hot or stinging pain. **8** to use (coal, oil, etc) as fuel. ➤ N **1** an injury or mark caused by fire, heat, acid, friction, etc. **2** an act of firing the engines of a space rocket so as to produce thrust.

burn[2] N, chiefly SCOT a small stream.

burner N **1** the part of a gas lamp or stove, etc which produces the flame. **2** a piece of equipment, etc for burning something.

burning ADJ **1** on fire. **2** feeling extremely hot. **3** very strong or intense. **4** very important or urgent: **the burning question**.

burnish VB to make (metal) shiny by polishing. ➤ N polish; lustre.

burnous N (*burnouses* or *burnous*) a long cloak with a hood, worn by Arabs.

burp COLLOQ, VB INTR to let air escape noisily from one's stomach through one's mouth. ➤ N a belch.

burr[1] N **1** in some English accents: a rough 'r' sound pronounced at the back of the throat. **2** a continual humming sound.

burr[2] see **bur**

burrow N a hole in the ground, esp one dug by a rabbit or other animal for shelter or defence. ➤ VB **1** (esp **burrow in** or **into** or **through** or **under sth**) TR & INTR to make (a hole) or tunnel in or under it. **2** INTR of an animal: to make burrows or live in a burrow. **3** INTR to search or investigate deeply into it.

bursary N (-*ies*) **1** an award or grant of money made to a student; a scholarship. **2** the bursar's room in a school, college, etc.

burst VB (*burst*) **1** TR & INTR to break or fly open or into pieces, usu suddenly and violently, or to cause to do this. **2** INTR to make one's way suddenly or violently into or out of, etc: **burst into the room**. **3** INTR to appear suddenly and be immediately important: **burst on to the political scene**. **4** INTR to begin suddenly and violently, or unexpectedly: **burst into flames/ tears/song** • **burst out laughing**. **5** INTR **a** to be completely full; **b** to break open; to overflow, etc: **My suitcase is bursting**; **c** to be unable to contain one's emotion. ➤ N **1** an instance of bursting or breaking open. **2** the place where something has burst or broken open, or the hole or break, etc made by it bursting. **3** a sudden, brief or violent period of some activity, eg speed, gunfire, applause.

bury VB (-*ies*, -*ied*) **1** to place (a dead body) in a grave, the sea, etc. **2** to hide (something) in the ground. **3** to put something out of sight; to cover: **bury one's face in one's hands**. **4** to put (something) out of one's mind or memory; to blot out: **Let's bury our differences**.

bus N (*buses* or (chiefly US) *busses*) a road vehicle which carries passengers to and from established stopping points along a fixed route for payment. ➤ VB (-*s*- or -*ss*-) **1** (also **bus it**) INTR to go by bus. **2** esp US to transport (children) by bus to a school in a different area.

busby N (*-ies*) **1** a tall fur hat worn as part of some military uniforms. **2** COLLOQ a bearskin.

bush[1] N **1** a low woody perennial plant, esp one having many separate branches originating at or near ground level. **2** (usu **the bush**) wild uncultivated land covered with shrubs or small trees. **3** something like a bush, esp in density. ■ **bushy** (*-ier, -iest*) ADJ.

bush[2] N a sheet of thin metal lining a cylinder in which an axle revolves.

bush-baby N an agile nocturnal African primate with thick fur, large eyes and a long tail.

bushel N **1** in the imperial system: a unit for measuring dry or liquid goods by volume, equal to 8 gallons or 36.4 litres in the UK (35.2 litres in the USA). **2** a container with this capacity.

bushman N **1** AUSTRAL, NZ someone who lives or travels in the bush. **2** (**Bushman**) a member of an almost extinct, small-statured, aboriginal race of nomadic hunters in S Africa.

bushranger N, AUSTRAL, HIST an outlaw or escaped convict living in the bush.

business N **1** the buying and selling of goods and services. **2** a shop, firm or commercial company, etc. **3** a regular occupation, trade or profession. **4** the things that are one's proper or rightful concern: **mind your own business**. **5** serious work or activity: **get down to business**. **6** an affair or matter: **a nasty business**. **7** COLLOQ a difficult or complicated problem. **8** (**the business**) SLANG exactly what is required. **9** economic or commercial dealings, activity, custom or contact: **I have some business with his company**.
◆ **go out of business** to fold or go bankrupt.

business card N a card carried by a person in business showing their name, etc.

businesslike ADJ practical and efficient; methodical.

businessman and **businesswoman** N a man or woman working in trade or commerce.

busk VB, INTR, chiefly BRIT to sing, play music, etc in the street for money. ■ **busker** N.

busman's holiday N leisure time spent doing what one normally does at work.

bus stop N **1** a stopping place for a bus. **2** a post or sign marking such a place.

bust[1] N **1** the upper, front part of a woman's body; breasts or bosom. **2** a sculpture of a person's head, shoulders and upper chest.

bust[2] COLLOQ, VB (*bust* or *busted*) **1** TR & INTR to break or burst (something). **2** of the police: to arrest (someone). **3** to raid or search (someone or somewhere), esp in a search for illegal drugs.
➢ ADJ **1** broken or burst. **2** having no money left; bankrupt or ruined.

bustard N a large ground-dwelling bird with speckled grey or brown plumage.

bustle[1] VB **1** (usu **bustle about**) INTR to busy oneself in a brisk, energetic and/or noisy manner. **2** to make (someone) hurry or work hard, etc: **bustled her out of the room**.
➢ N hurried, noisy and excited activity.
■ **bustling** ADJ.

bustle[2] N, HIST a frame or pad for holding a skirt out from the back of the waist.

bust-up N, COLLOQ a quarrel; the ending of a relationship or partnership.

busty ADJ (*-ier, -iest*) COLLOQ of a woman: having large breasts.

busy ADJ (*-ier, -iest*) **1** fully occupied; having much work to do. **2** full of activity: **a busy street**. **3** N AMER, ESP US of a telephone line, etc: in use. **4** constantly working. **5** of a person: fussy and tending to interfere in the affairs of others. **6** too full of detail: **a busy pattern**. ■ **busily** ADV.
◆ **busy sb** or **oneself** (**with sth**) to occupy them or oneself (with a task, etc); to make them or oneself busy.

busybody N someone who is always interfering in other people's affairs.

but CONJ **1** contrary to expectation: **She fell down but didn't hurt herself**. **2** in contrast: **You've been to Spain but I haven't**. **3** other than: **You can't do anything but wait**. **4** used to emphasize the word that follows it: **Nobody, but nobody, must go in there**.

➤ PREP except: **They are all here but him.**
➤ ADV only: **I can but try.**
➤ N an objection or doubt: **no buts about it.**
◆ **but for** were it not for; without.

butane N a colourless highly flammable gas used in liquid form as a fuel.

butch ADJ, SLANG of a person: tough and strong-looking; aggressively masculine.

butcher N **1** a person or shop that sells meat. **2** someone whose job is slaughtering animals and preparing the carcasses for use as food. **3** a person who kills people needlessly and savagely.
➤ VB **1** to kill and prepare (an animal) for sale as food. **2** to kill (esp a large number of people or animals) cruelly or indiscriminately. **3** COLLOQ to ruin or make a botch of (something).

butchery N (-**ies**) **1** the preparing of meat for sale as food; the trade of a butcher. **2** senseless, cruel or wholesale killing. **3** a slaughterhouse.

butler N the chief male servant in a house.

butt[1] VB, TR & INTR **1** to push or hit (someone or something) hard or roughly with the head, in the way a ram or goat might. **2** (esp **butt against** or **on sth**) to join or be joined end to end with it.
➤ N **1** a blow with the head or horns. **2** the place where two edges join.
◆ **butt in** COLLOQ to interrupt or interfere.

butt[2] N **1** the unused end of a finished cigar or cigarette, etc. **2** the thick, heavy or bottom end of a tool or weapon: **a rifle butt**. **3** chiefly N AMER COLLOQ the buttocks.

butt[3] N **1** a person who is often a target of jokes, ridicule or criticism, etc. **2** a mound of earth behind a target on a shooting range.

butt[4] N a large barrel for beer or rainwater, etc.

butte N, GEOL an isolated flat-topped hill with steep sides.

butter N **1** a solid yellowish edible food, made from the fats in milk by churning, and used for spreading on bread, and in cooking. **2** IN COMPOUNDS any of various substances that resemble this food in appearance or texture:

peanut butter.
➤ VB to put butter on or in (something).
■ **buttery** ADJ.

butter bean N any of several varieties of lima bean plants or one of their large edible seeds.

buttercup N any of various plants with bright yellow cup-shaped flowers.

butterfingers SING N, COLLOQ a person who often drops things, or who fails to catch things.

butterfly N **1** an insect which has four broad, often brightly-coloured wings, and a long proboscis for sucking nectar from flowers. **2** (**butterflies**) COLLOQ a nervous or fluttering feeling in the stomach.

buttermilk N the slightly sharp-tasting liquid left after all the butter has been removed from milk after churning.

butterscotch N **1** a kind of hard toffee made from butter and sugar. **2** a flavouring made from butterscotch or similar to it.

buttock N (usu **buttocks**) each of the fleshy parts of the body between the base of the back and the top of the legs.

button N **1** a small round piece of metal or plastic, etc sewn on to a piece of clothing, which fastens it by being passed through a buttonhole. **2** (sometimes **push button**) a small round disc pressed to operate a door, bell, electrical appliance, etc. **3** a small round object worn as decoration or a badge. **4** any small round object more or less like a button.
➤ VB **1** (also **button up**) to fasten or close (something) using a button or buttons. **2** INTR to be capable of being fastened with buttons or a button: **This dress buttons at the back**.

buttonhole N **1** a small slit or hole through which a button is passed to fasten a garment. **2** a flower or flowers worn in a buttonhole or pinned to a lapel.
➤ VB **1** to stop (someone), and force conversation on them. **2** to make buttonholes in (something).

buttress N **1** ARCHIT, CIVIL ENG a projecting support made of brick or masonry, etc built on to the outside of a wall. **2** any support or prop.

➤ VB **1** to support (a wall, etc) with buttresses. **2** to support or encourage (an argument, etc).

butty N (*-ies*) BRIT, esp N ENGLISH, COLLOQ a sandwich; a piece of bread and butter.

buxom ADJ of a woman: **1** attractively plump, lively and healthy–looking. **2** having large or plumply rounded breasts; busty.

buy VB (*bought*) **1** to obtain (something) by paying a sum of money for it. **2** to be a means of obtaining (something): **There are some things money can't buy**. **3** to obtain (something) by giving up or sacrificing something else: **success bought at the expense of happiness**. **4** COLLOQ to believe (something): **I didn't buy his story**.
➤ N (USU IN **a good buy** or **a bad buy**) a thing bought.
◆ **buy off** to get rid of (a threatening person, etc) by paying them money.
◆ **buy time** COLLOQ to gain more time before a decision or action, etc is taken.
◆ **buy sth up** to buy the whole stock of it.

buyer N **1** a person who buys. **2** a person employed to buy goods on behalf of a large shop, etc.

buy-out N, COMMERCE the purchase of all the shares in a company in order to get control of it.

buzz VB **1** INTR to make a continuous, humming or rapidly vibrating sound, like that made by the wings of an insect such as the bee. **2** INTR to be filled with activity or excitement. **3** COLLOQ to call (someone) using a buzzer. **4** COLLOQ to call someone on the telephone. **5** COLLOQ of an aircraft: to fly very low over or very close to (another aircraft or a building, etc).
➤ N **1** a humming or rapidly vibrating sound, such as that made by a bee. **2** COLLOQ a telephone call. **3** COLLOQ a very pleasant, excited, or exhilarated feeling; a kick or thrill. **4** a low murmuring sound such as that made by many people talking. **5** COLLOQ a rumour.
◆ **buzz off** COLLOQ to go away.

buzzard N **1** any of several large hawks that resemble eagles in their effortless gliding flight. **2** N AMER a vulture.

buzzer N an electrical device which makes a buzzing sound.

by PREP **1** next to, beside or near: **standing by the door**. **2** past: **drive by the house**. **3** through, along or across: **enter by the window**. **4** used to indicate the person or thing that does, causes or produces, etc something: **destroyed by fire**. **5** used to show method or means: **sent by registered post**. **6** not later than: **Be home by 10pm**. **7** during: **escape by night**. **8** used to show extent or amount: **worse by far**. **9** used in stating rates of payment, etc: **paid by the hour**. **10** according to: **It's 8.15 by my watch**. **11** used to show the part of someone or something held, taken or used, etc: **pulling me by the hand**. **12** used to show the number which performs a mathematical operation on another: **multiply three by four**. **13** used in giving measurements and compass directions, etc: **a room measuring six feet by ten**. **14** used to show a specific quantity or unit, etc that follows another to bring about an increase or progression: **two by two**. **15** with regard to someone or something: **do his duty by them**. **16** in oaths, etc: in the name of, or strictly 'in the presence of' (a specified deity, thing or person): **By God, you're right!**
➤ ADV **1** near: **live close by**. **2** past: **drive by without stopping**. **3** aside; away; in reserve: **put money by**.
➤ N same as **bye**[1].
◆ **by and by** after a short time.
◆ **by and large** generally.
◆ **by oneself 1** alone: **sit by yourself**. **2** without anyone else's help: **can do it by myself**.

bye[1] N **1** SPORT, etc a pass into the next round of a competition, given to a competitor or team not given an opponent in the current round. **2** CRICKET a run scored from a ball which the batsman has not hit or touched.

bye[2] or **bye-bye** EXCLAM, COLLOQ goodbye.

by-election N an election held during the sitting of parliament, in order to fill a vacant seat.

bygone ADJ former: **in bygone days**.
➤ N (**bygones**) events, troubles or arguments which occurred in the past.

by-law or **bye-law** N, BRIT a law or rule made by a local authority or other body, rather than by the national government.

byline N 1 a line in a newspaper article giving the name of the writer. 2 FOOTBALL the touchline.

bypass N 1 a major road carrying traffic on a route that avoids a city centre, town or congested area. 2 MED the redirection of blood flow so as to avoid a blocked or diseased coronary artery.
➤ VB 1 to avoid (a congested or blocked place) by taking a route which goes round or beyond it. 2 to avoid (a step in a process), or ignore and not discuss something with (a person).

by-product N 1 a secondary product that is formed at the same time as the main product. 2 an unexpected or extra result; a side effect.

byroad and **byway** N a minor, secondary or secluded road.

bystander N a person who happens to be standing by, who sees but does not take part in what is happening; an onlooker.

byte N, COMP a group of adjacent binary digits handled as a single unit, esp a group of eight.

byword N 1 a person or thing that is well known as an example of something: **a byword for luxury**. 2 a common saying or proverb.

Byzantine ADJ 1 HIST of Byzantium or the eastern part of the Roman Empire from AD 395 to 1453. 2 of the style of architecture and painting, etc developed in the Byzantine Empire. 3 secret; extremely intricate and complex. 4 rigidly hierarchic; inflexible.
➤ N, HIST an inhabitant of Byzantium.

Cc

C[1] or **c** N (**Cs, C's** or **c's**) 1 the third letter of the English alphabet. 2 (usu **C**) the third highest grade or a mark indicating this. 3 (**C**) MUS a musical key with the note C as its base.

C[2] ABBREV 1 Celsius. 2 centigrade. 3 century.
➤ SYMBOL (also **c**) the Roman numeral for 100.

c. ABBREV 1 cent. 2 century. 3 chapter. 4 (also **ca**) circa (Latin), approximately.

cab N 1 a taxi. 2 the driver's compartment in a lorry, railway engine, etc.

cabal N 1 a small group formed within a larger one, for secret, esp political, discussion, etc. 2 a political plot or conspiracy.

cabaret N entertainment with songs, dancing, etc at a nightclub, etc.

cabbage N 1 a vegetable with a compact head of green, white or red edible leaves. 2 DEROG a dull inactive person.

cabby or **cabbie** N (**-ies**) COLLOQ a taxi-driver.

cabin N 1 a small house, esp one made of wood. 2 a small room on a ship for living, sleeping or working in. 3 the section of a plane for passengers or crew. 4 a driver's cab.

cabinet N 1 a piece of furniture with shelves and doors, for storing or displaying items. 2 (often **the Cabinet**) a body of senior ministers in charge of government departments.

cabinet-maker N a craftsman who makes and repairs fine furniture.

cable N 1 a strong wire cord or rope. 2 electrical wires bound together but separated from each other by insulating

material, used to carry electricity, television signals, etc. **3** (also **cablegram**) a telegram sent by cable. **4** short for **cable television**.
➤ VB **1** to tie up or provide with a cable or cables. **2** TR & INTR to send a cable, or send (a message) to someone by cable.

cable car N a small carriage suspended from a continuous moving cable, for carrying passengers up or down a steep mountain, etc.

cable television and **cable TV** N a TV broadcasting system in which signals are relayed to individual subscribers by cables.

cacao N the seed of a small evergreen tree, used to make chocolate and cocoa.

cache N **1** a hiding-place, eg for weapons. **2** a collection of hidden things.
➤ VB to put or collect in a cache.

cachet N **1** something which brings one respect or admiration. **2** a distinguishing mark.

cackle N **1** the sound made by a hen or a goose. **2** DEROG a raucous laugh. **3** shrill, silly chatter.
➤ VB, INTR **1** to laugh raucously. **2** to chatter noisily. **3** to utter as a cackle.

cacophony N (*-ies*) a mixture of harsh loud noises. ■ **cacophonous** ADJ.

cactus N (*-ti* or *-tuses*) any, usu spiny, plant which stores water in fleshy stems.

cad N, BRIT a man who behaves dishonourably.

cadaver N, MED a human corpse.

cadaverous ADJ corpse-like; pale and gaunt.

caddie or **caddy** N (*-ies*) someone who carries the golf clubs around the course for a golf-player.
➤ VB (*-ies, -ied*) INTR to act as a caddie.

caddy N (*-ies*) a small container for loose tea.

cadence N **1** the rising and falling of the voice in speaking. **2** rhythm or beat.

cadenza N, MUS an elaborate virtuoso passage given by a solo performer.

cadet N a trainee for the army or police.

cadge VB, TR & INTR, COLLOQ to get (esp money or

food) by scrounging or begging. ■ **cadger** N.

cadmium N, CHEM a soft bluish-white metallic element.

caesarean (**section**) or (US) **cesarean** (**section**) N a surgical operation in which a baby is delivered through an incision in the lower abdomen. Also spelt **caesarian** or (US) **cesarian**.

caesium or (US) **cesium** N, CHEM a soft silvery-white metallic element.

café or **cafe** N a usu small restaurant that serves light meals or snacks.

cafeteria N a self-service restaurant.

cafetière N a coffee-pot with a plunger for separating the grounds from the liquid.

caffeine N a bitter-tasting stimulant alkaloid, found in coffee, tea and cola nuts.
■ **caffeinated** ADJ.

caftan N a long loose-fitting robe.

cage N an enclosure, usu of bars or wires, in which eg captive birds and animals are kept.
➤ VB (also **cage sb in**) to put them in a cage; to confine them. ■ **caged** ADJ.

cagey or **cagy** ADJ (*-ier, -iest*) COLLOQ secretive and cautious; not forthcoming.

cagoule N a lightweight hooded anorak.

cahoots PL N.
♦ **in cahoots with sb** USU DEROG, COLLOQ working closely with them.

cairn N a heap of stones piled up to mark something, eg a grave or pathway.

cairngorm N, GEOL a yellow or smoky-brown variety of quartz, often used as a gemstone.

cajole VB to persuade with flattery, promises, etc; to coax. ■ **cajolery** N.

cake N **1** a solid food made by baking a mixture of flour, fat, eggs, sugar, etc. **2** a portion of some other food pressed into a particular shape: **fish cake**. **3** a solid block, eg of soap.
➤ VB **1** INTR to dry as a thick hard crust. **2** to cover in a thick crust: **skin caked with blood**.

calamari PL N squid.

calamine N a fine pink powder containing zinc oxide and ferric oxide.

calamity N (-*ies*) a catastrophe, disaster or serious misfortune. ■ **calamitous** ADJ.

calciferous ADJ 1 CHEM containing lime. 2 BIOL containing or producing calcium salts.

calcify VB (-*ies*, -*ied*) TR & INTR to harden by the deposit of calcium salts. ■ **calcification** N.

calcite N, GEOL a white or colourless mineral, composed of crystalline calcium carbonate.

calcium N, CHEM a soft, silvery-white metallic element occurring mainly in the form of calcium carbonate minerals such as chalk.

calcium carbonate N, CHEM a white powder or colourless crystals, occurring naturally as limestone, marble, chalk, etc.

calculate VB 1 to work out, find out or estimate, esp by mathematical means. 2 (often **calculate on sth**) INTR to make plans that depend on or take into consideration some probability or possibility. 3 to intend or aim.

calculated ADJ intentional; deliberate.

calculating ADJ, DEROG scheming and selfish.

calculation N the act, process or result of calculating.

calculator N a small electronic device used to perform numerical calculations.

calculus N (-*luses* or -*li*) 1 the branch of mathematics concerned with the differentiation and integration of functions. 2 MED a hard stone-like mass that forms within body structures such as the kidney or gall bladder.

Caledonian ADJ of Scotland or its inhabitants.

calendar N 1 any system by which the beginning, length and divisions of the year are fixed. 2 a booklet, chart, etc showing this. 3 a timetable or list of important dates, events, etc.

calender N a machine through which paper or cloth is passed to give it a smooth shiny finish. ➤ VB to give a smooth finish to (paper or cloth) using a calender.

calf¹ N (*calves*) 1 the young of any bovine animal, esp domestic cattle. 2 the young of other mammals, eg the elephant and whale.

calf² N (*calves*) the thick fleshy part of the back of the leg, below the knee.

calibrate VB to mark a scale on (a measuring instrument) so that it can be used to take readings in suitable units. ■ **calibration** N.

calibre N 1 the internal diameter of a gun barrel. 2 the outer diameter of a bullet or other projectile. 3 quality; standard; ability.

calico N (-*oes*) a kind of cotton cloth, usu plain white or in its natural unbleached state.

caliph N a Muslim civil and religious leader.

call VB 1 TR & INTR (also **call out**) to shout or speak loudly in order to attract attention. 2 to ask someone to come, esp with a shout: **called us in to tea**. 3 to summon someone: **call the doctor**. 4 TR & INTR to telephone. 5 INTR to make a visit: **call at the grocer's**. 6 to name someone or something. 7 to regard or consider something as something specified: **I call that strange**. 8 (often **call for**) TR & INTR to make a demand or appeal for: **call a strike**. 9 INTR of a bird, etc: to make its typical sound. ➤ N 1 a shout or cry. 2 the cry of a bird or animal. 3 an invitation; a summons. 4 a demand, request or appeal. 5 a claim on something: **too many calls on my time**. 6 a brief visit. 7 an act of telephoning someone; a telephone conversation. 8 a need or reason: **not much call for Latin teachers**. ■ **caller** N. ◆ **call sth off** to cancel a meeting, arrangement, etc. ◆ **on call** available if needed.

call box N a public telephone box.

calligraphy N 1 handwriting as an art. 2 beautiful decorative handwriting. ■ **calligrapher** N.

calling N 1 a trade or profession. 2 an urge to follow a particular profession, eg the ministry.

calliper N 1 a measuring device consisting of hinged prongs attached to a scale. 2 a metal splint for supporting a leg.

callisthenics PL N a system of physical

exercises to increase the strength and grace of the body. ■ **callisthenic** ADJ.

callous ADJ unconcerned for the feelings of others; deliberately cruel. ■ **callously** ADV.

callow ADJ young and inexperienced.

callus N a thickened hardened pad of skin.

calm ADJ 1 relaxed and in control; not anxious, angry, etc. 2 of the weather, etc: still, quiet. ➤ N 1 peace and quiet. 2 stillness of weather. ➤ VB, TR & INTR (usu **calm down**) to make or become calm. ■ **calmly** ADV. ■ **calmness** N.

calorie N a metric unit denoting the amount of heat required to raise the temperature of one gram of water by 1°C.

calumniate VB to slander.

calumny N (-ies) an untrue and malicious spoken statement about a person.

calve VB, INTR 1 to give birth to (a calf). 2 of a glacier or iceberg: to release (masses of ice).

calypso N a type of West Indian popular song.

calyx N (-lyces or -lyxes) BOT the outermost set of petals of a flower, that protects the developing flower bud.

cam N, ENG an irregular projection on a wheel or rotating shaft, which transmits regular movement to another part in contact with it.

camaraderie N a feeling of friendship.

camber N a slight convexity on a road.

camcorder N a portable video camera used to record images and sound.

camel N a large mammal with a long neck and legs, and one or two humps on its back.

cameo N 1 a gemstone with a raised design carved on it. 2 (also **cameo role**) a small part in a play or film performed by a well-known actor.

camera N 1 an optical device that records images as photographs. 2 a device in a television system that converts visual images into electrical signals for transmission.

cameraman N in TV or film-making: someone who operates a camera.

camisole N a woman's loose vest-like undergarment, with narrow shoulder straps.

camomile or **chamomile** N 1 a strongly scented plant with white and yellow daisy-like flowers. 2 its dried crushed flowers or leaves, used esp as a herbal tea.

camouflage N 1 any means of disguising or concealing a person or animal, or of deceiving an adversary, esp by adopting the colour, texture, etc, of natural surroundings. 2 the use of such methods to conceal or disguise military troops, equipment, vehicles or buildings. 3 the colour pattern or other features that enable an animal to blend with its environment and so avoid detection by predators. ➤ VB to disguise or conceal with camouflage.

camp¹ N 1 a piece of ground on which tents have been erected. 2 a collection of buildings, huts, tents, etc used as temporary accommodation. 3 a permanent site where troops are housed or trained. 4 a group having a particular set of opinions, beliefs, etc. ➤ VB, INTR to stay in a tent. ■ **camping** N.

camp² ADJ, COLLOQ, SOMETIMES DEROG 1 effeminate, esp in an exaggerated way. 2 homosexual.

campaign N 1 an organized series of actions intended to build up support for or opposition to a particular practice, group, etc. 2 the operations of an army in a particular area. ➤ VB, INTR (usu **campaign for** or **against sth**) to organize or take part in a campaign. ■ **campaigner** N.

campanology N the art of bell-ringing. ■ **campanologist** N.

camp bed N a light portable folding bed.

camper N 1 someone who camps. 2 a motor vehicle equipped for sleeping in.

camphor N a white or colourless crystalline compound with a strong aromatic odour.

campsite N a piece of land on which people are allowed to camp.

campus N (*campuses*) the grounds of a college or university.

camshaft N, ENG a shaft to which one or more cams are attached.

can[1] VB (PAT *could*) **1** to be able to: **Can you lift that? 2** to know how to: **He can play the guitar. 3** to feel able to; to feel it right to: **How can you believe that? 4** to have permission to: **Can I take an apple? 5** used when asking for help, etc: **Can you give me the time?**

can[2] N **1** a sealed container, usu of tin plate or aluminium, used for food and esp fizzy drinks. **2** a large container made of metal or another material, for holding liquids, eg oil or paint. ➤ VB (*-nn-*) to seal (food or drink) in metal containers to preserve it.

canal N **1** an artificial channel or waterway, usu constructed for navigation or irrigation. **2** ANAT any tubular channel that conveys food, air or fluids from one part of the body to another.

canalize or **-ise** VB **1** to make or convert into a canal or system of canals. **2** to channel. ■ **canalization** N.

canapé N a small piece of bread or toast topped with something savoury.

canard N a false report or piece of news.

canary N (*-ies*) a small finch with bright yellow plumage, very popular as a caged bird.

canasta N a card game similar to rummy played with two packs of cards.

cancan N a lively dance usu performed by dancing girls, who execute high kicks, raising their skirts to reveal their petticoats.

cancel VB (*-ll-*) **1** to stop (something already arranged) from taking place. **2** to stop (something in progress) from continuing. **3** to delete or cross out something. **4** to put an official stamp on (eg a cheque or postage stamp) so that it cannot be re-used. **5** MATH to strike out (equal quantities) from opposite sides of an equation, or (common factors) from the numerator and denominator of a fraction. **6** (usu **cancel sth out**) to remove the effect of it, by

having an exactly opposite effect. ■ **cancellation** N.

Cancer N, ASTROL the fourth sign of the zodiac (the Crab).

cancer N **1** PATHOL any form of malignant tumour that develops when the cells of a tissue or organ multiply in an uncontrolled manner. **2** PATHOL a disease caused by the spread of a malignant tumour. **3** an evil that gradually destroys or corrupts. ■ **cancerous** ADJ.

candela N the SI unit of luminous intensity.

candelabrum or (SOMETIMES USED WRONGLY AS SING) **candelabra** N (*-rums, -ra* or *-ras*) a candle-holder with branches for several candles, or a similar light-fitting.

candid ADJ **1** honest and open about what one thinks; outspoken. **2** COLLOQ of a photograph: taken without the subject's knowledge so as to catch them unawares.

candidate N **1** someone who is competing with others for a job, prize, parliamentary seat, etc. **2** someone taking an examination. **3** a person or thing considered suitable for a particular purpose or likely to suffer a particular fate. ■ **candidacy** or **candidature** N.

candle N a piece of wax formed around a wick, which is burnt to provide light.

candlelight N the light given by a candle or candles. ■ **candlelit** ADJ.

candlestick N a holder for a candle.

candlewick N a cotton fabric with a tufted surface formed by cut loops of thread.

candour N the quality of being candid; frankness and honesty.

candy N (*-ies*) N AMER **1** a sweet. **2** sweets or confectionery. ➤ VB (*-ies, -ied*) to preserve (fruit, etc) by boiling in sugar. ■ **candied** ADJ.

candy floss N a fluffy mass of coloured spun sugar served on a stick.

cane N **1** the long jointed stem of certain plants, eg rattan, bamboo and sugar cane. **2** sugar cane. **3** thin stems or strips cut from stems, eg of

rattan, for weaving into baskets, etc. **4** a walking-stick. **5** a slim stick for beating people as a punishment.
➤ VB to beat (someone) with a cane.

cane-sugar N sucrose, esp that obtained from sugar cane.

canine ADJ **1** of or like a dog. **2** relating to the dog family in general.
➤ N **1** any animal belonging to the dog family. **2** a canine tooth.

canine tooth N a long sharp pointed tooth located between the incisors and premolars.

canister N a metal or plastic container for storing tea or other dry foods.

canker N **1** a fungal, bacterial or viral disease of trees and woody shrubs, eg fruit trees. **2** a destructive influence, etc. ■ **cankerous** ADJ.

cannabis N a narcotic drug, prepared from the leaves and flowers of the hemp plant.

canned ADJ **1** contained in cans. **2** COLLOQ previously recorded: **canned laughter**.

cannelloni PL N pasta in the form of large tubes, served with a filling of meat, etc.

cannibal N **1** someone who eats human flesh. **2** an animal that eats others of its own kind. ■ **cannibalism** N.

cannibalize or **-ise** VB, COLLOQ to take parts from (a machine, etc) for use in repairing another.

cannon N (**cannons** or in senses 1 and 2 **cannon**) **1** HIST a large gun mounted on wheels. **2** a rapid-firing gun fitted to an aircraft or ship. **3** in billiards, pool etc: a shot in which the cue ball strikes one object ball and then another.

cannonade N a continuous bombardment by heavy guns.

cannonball N, HIST a ball, usu of iron, for shooting from a cannon.

cannot VB can not.

canny ADJ (**-ier, -iest**) **1** wise and alert; shrewd. **2** careful; cautious. ■ **cannily** ADV.

canoe N a light narrow boat propelled by one

or more paddles. ■ **canoeist** N.

canon N **1** a basic law, rule or principle. **2 a** a member of the clergy attached to a cathedral; **b** C OF E a member of the clergy with special rights regarding the election of bishops. **3** an officially accepted collection of writing, or work considered to be by a particular writer. **4** a list of saints.

canonical ADJ **1** according to, or of the nature of, a canon. **2** orthodox or accepted.

canonize or **-ise** VB to officially declare someone to be a saint. ■ **canonization** N.

canon law N the law of the Christian church.

canoodle VB, INTR, COLLOQ to cuddle.

canopy N (**-ies**) **1** an ornamental covering hung over a bed, throne, etc. **2** a covering hung or held up over something or someone, usu for shelter. **3** BOT the topmost layer of a wood or forest.

cant[1] N **1** DEROG insincere talk, esp with a false display of moral or religious principles. **2** the special slang or jargon of a particular group.
➤ VB, INTR to use cant.

cant[2] N a slope.
➤ VB, TR & INTR to tilt or slope.

can't CONTRACTION cannot.

cantaloup or **cantaloupe** N a melon with a thick ridged skin and orange-coloured flesh.

cantankerous ADJ bad-tempered; irritable.

cantata N a musical work for singers, with parts for chorus and soloists.

canteen N **1** a restaurant at a factory, office, etc for the use of employees. **2** a case for cutlery or the full set of cutlery it contains.

canter N a horse-riding pace between trotting and galloping.
➤ VB to move at this pace.

canticle N a non-metrical hymn or chant.

cantilever N a beam or other support that projects from a wall.

cantilever bridge N a bridge with two outer spans supporting a central span.

canto N a section of a long poem.

canton N a division of a country, esp one of the separately governed regions of Switzerland.

cantor N 1 JUDAISM a man who chants the liturgy and leads the congregation in prayer. 2 CHRISTIANITY someone who leads the choir.

canvas N 1 a thick heavy coarse cloth, made from hemp or flax, used to make sails, tents, etc and for painting pictures on. 2 a painting done on a piece of canvas.

canvass VB 1 TR & INTR to ask for votes or support from (someone). 2 to find out the opinions of (voters, etc).
➤ N a solicitation of information, votes, opinions, etc. ■ **canvasser** N.

canyon N a deep gorge or ravine.

cap N 1 any of various types of hat, eg with a flat or rounded crown and a peak. 2 a lid, cover or top, eg for a bottle or pen. 3 (also **percussion cap**) a little metal or paper case containing a small amount of gunpowder that explodes when struck, used eg to make a noise in toy guns. 4 a protective or cosmetic covering fitted over a damaged or decayed tooth. 5 the top or top part. 6 (also **Dutch cap** or **diaphragm**) a contraceptive device consisting of a rubber cover that fits over the cervix.
➤ VB (-pp-) 1 to put a cap on, or cover the top or end of, (something) with a cap. 2 to be or form the top of. 3 to do better than, improve on or outdo. 4 to set an upper limit to (a tax), or to the tax–gathering powers of (a local authority).

capability N (-ies) 1 ability or efficiency. 2 a power or ability.

capable ADJ 1 clever; able; efficient. 2 (**capable of sth**) having the ability or disposition to do it. ■ **capably** ADV.

capacious ADJ, FORMAL roomy.

capacitance N, ELEC the ability of a capacitor to store electric charge.

capacitor N, ELEC a device that can store electric charge.

capacity N (-ies) 1 the amount that something

can hold. 2 the amount that a factory, etc can produce. 3 (**capacity for sth**) the ability or power to achieve it. 4 function; role.

cape N 1 a short cloak. 2 a part of the coast that projects into the sea.

caper VB, INTR to jump or dance about playfully.
➤ N 1 a playful jump. 2 a young flower bud of a small deciduous shrub, pickled in vinegar and used as a condiment.

capillary N (-ies) 1 a tube, usu made of glass, which has a very small diameter. 2 the narrowest type of blood vessel.

capital N 1 the chief city of a country. 2 a capital letter. 3 the total amount of money or wealth possessed by a person or business, etc. 4 ARCHIT a slab of stone, etc forming the top section of a column.
➤ ADJ 1 principal; chief. 2 of a letter of the alphabet: in its large form, as used eg at the beginnings of names. Also called **upper-case**. 3 of a crime: punishable by death.

capitalism N an economic system based on private, rather than state, ownership of businesses, services, etc, with free competition.

capitalist N 1 someone who believes in capitalism. 2 DEROG a wealthy person, esp one who is obviously making a great deal of personal profit from business, etc. Also AS ADJ.

capitalize or **-ise** VB 1 to write with a capital letter or in capital letters. 2 to sell (property, etc) in order to raise money. 3 to supply (a business, etc) with needed capital. ■ **capitalization** N.
◆ **capitalize on sth** to exploit (an asset, achievement, etc) to one's advantage.

capital punishment N punishment by death.

capitulate VB, INTR 1 to surrender formally, usu on agreed conditions. 2 to give in to argument or persuasion. ■ **capitulation** N.

capon N a male chicken fattened for eating.

cappuccino N coffee made with frothy milk.

caprice N 1 a sudden change of mind for no good or obvious reason. 2 the tendency to have caprices. ■ **capricious** ADJ.

Capricorn N, ASTROL the tenth sign of the zodiac (the Goat).

caprine ADJ of or characteristic of, a goat.

capsicum N the hollow red, green or yellow fruit of a tropical plant.

capsize VB 1 INTR to tip over completely; to overturn. 2 to cause (a boat) to capsize.

capstan N a cylinder-shaped apparatus turned to wind a heavy rope or cable, eg that of a ship's anchor.

capsule N 1 a soluble case containing a single dose of a powdered drug to be taken orally. 2 (also **space capsule**) a small spacecraft or a compartment within a spacecraft that contains the instruments and crew. 3 ANAT a membranous structure that surrounds an organ or tissue. 4 BOT a dry fruit that splits to release the seeds.

captain N 1 a leader or chief. 2 the commander of a ship. 3 the commander of a company of troops. 4 a naval officer below a commodore and above a commander in rank. 5 an army officer of the rank below major. 6 the chief pilot of a civil aircraft. 7 the leader of a team or side, or chief member of a club. ➤ VB to be captain of something. ■ **captaincy** N (-**ies**).

caption N 1 the words that accompany a photograph, cartoon, etc. 2 a heading given to a chapter, article, etc. 3 wording on a television or cinema screen as part of a film or broadcast.

captious ADJ inclined to criticize and find fault.

captivate VB to delight, charm or fascinate. ■ **captivating** ADJ. ■ **captivation** N.

captive N a person or animal that has been caught or taken prisoner. ➤ ADJ 1 kept prisoner. 2 held so as to be unable to get away. ■ **captivity** N (-**ies**).

captor N someone who takes a person or animal captive.

capture VB 1 to catch; to take prisoner; to gain control of someone or something. 2 to succeed in recording (a subtle quality, etc). ➤ N 1 the capturing of someone or something.

2 the person or thing captured.

car N 1 (also **motor car**) a self-propelled four-wheeled road vehicle designed to carry passengers and powered by an internal combustion engine. 2 N AMER a railway carriage or van: **dining car**.

carafe N a wide-necked flask for wine, etc.

caramel N 1 a brown substance made by heating sugar solution, used as a food colouring and flavouring. 2 a toffee-like sweet made from sugar, animal fat and milk or cream. 3 the pale yellowish brown colour of this.

caramelize or **-ise** VB 1 to change (sugar) into caramel. 2 INTR to turn into caramel.

carapace N, ZOOL the hard thick shell that covers the upper part of the body of some tortoises, turtles and crustaceans.

carat N 1 a unit of mass, equal to 0.2 grams, used to measure the mass of gemstones. 2 a unit expressing the purity of gold in an alloy with another metal, equal to the number of parts of gold in 24 parts of the alloy.

caravan N 1 a vehicle fitted for living in, designed for towing by a motor vehicle. 2 HIST a group of travellers, merchants, etc, crossing the desert as a large company for safety.

carbide N, CHEM any chemical compound consisting of carbon and another element (except for hydrogen), usu a metallic one.

carbine N a short light rifle.

carbohydrate N any of a group of organic compounds, present in the cells of all living organisms and formed in green plants during photosynthesis.

carbolic acid see **phenol**

carbon N 1 a non-metallic element that occurs in all organic compounds, and as two crystalline allotropes, namely diamond and graphite. 2 a sheet of carbon paper.

carbonaceous ADJ containing large amounts of, or resembling, carbon.

carbonate N, CHEM any salt of carbonic acid. ➤ VB to combine (eg a liquid) with carbon dioxide, to make it fizzy. ■ **carbonated** ADJ.

carbon copy N an exact duplicate.

carbon dioxide N, CHEM a colourless odourless tasteless gas, present in the atmosphere and formed during respiration.

carbonic ADJ containing carbon.

carboniferous ADJ producing carbon.

carbonize or **-ise** VB 1 TR & INTR to convert or reduce (a substance containing carbon) into carbon, either by heating or by natural methods such as fossilization. 2 to coat (a substance) with a layer of carbon. ■ **carbonization** N.

carbon monoxide N, CHEM a poisonous colourless odourless gas formed by the incomplete combustion of carbon.

carbon paper N paper coated on one side with an ink-like substance containing carbon, used to make copies.

carbuncle N a boil on the skin.

carburettor N the part of an internal combustion engine in which the liquid fuel and air are mixed and vaporized.

carcass or **carcase** N 1 the dead body of an animal. 2 COLLOQ the body of a living person.

carcinogen N, PATHOL any substance capable of causing cancer in a living tissue. ■ **carcinogenic** ADJ.

carcinoma N, PATHOL any cancer that occurs in the skin or in the tissue that lines the internal organs, and may spread via the bloodstream.

card[1] N 1 a kind of thick, stiff paper or thin cardboard. 2 (also **playing card**) a rectangular piece of card bearing a design, usu one of a set, used eg for playing games, fortune-telling, etc. 3 a small rectangular piece of card or plastic, showing eg one's identity, job, membership of an organization, etc. 4 a small rectangular piece of stiff plastic issued by a bank, etc to a customer, used when making payments, as a guarantee for a cheque, for operating a cash machine, etc. 5 a piece of card, usu folded double and bearing a design, used to send greetings to someone.

card[2] N a comb-like device with sharp teeth for pulling across cloth to make it fluffy. ➤ VB to treat (wool, fabric) with a card.

cardboard N a stiff material made from pulped waste paper, used for making boxes, etc.

cardiac ADJ relating to or affecting the heart.

cardiac arrest N, PATHOL the stopping of the pumping action of the heart.

cardigan N a long-sleeved knitted jacket that fastens down the front.

cardinal N, RC CHURCH one of a group of leading clergy, who elect and advise the pope. ➤ ADJ highly important; principal.

cardinal number N one of a series of numbers expressing quantity (eg 1, 2, 3, …).

cardiography N the branch of medicine concerned with the recording of the movements of the heart. ■ **cardiographer** N.

cardiology N the branch of medicine concerned with the study of the structure, function and diseases of the heart. ■ **cardiologist** N.

cardiovascular ADJ, ANAT relating to the heart and blood vessels.

care N 1 attention and thoroughness. 2 caution; regard for safety. 3 the activity of looking after someone or something, or the state of being looked after. 4 worry. 5 a cause for worry. ➤ VB, INTR 1 to mind or be upset by something, or the possibility of something. 2 (usu **care about** or **for sb** or **sth**) to concern oneself about them or be interested in them. 3 to wish or be willing: **Would you care to come?**
◆ **care for** 1 to look after. 2 to be fond of or love. 3 to like or approve of. 4 to have a wish or desire for: **Would you care for a drink?**
◆ **take care** to be cautious or thorough.
◆ **take care of** 1 to look after. 2 to attend to or organize.

career N 1 one's professional life; one's progress in one's job. 2 a job, occupation or profession. 3 one's progress through life. ➤ VB, INTR to rush in an uncontrolled way.

careerist N someone who is chiefly interested in the advancement or promotion of their career. ■ **careerism** N.

carefree ADJ having few worries; cheerful.

careful ADJ 1 giving or showing care and attention; thorough. 2 watchful; cautious. 3 taking care to avoid harm or damage.

careless ADJ 1 not careful or thorough enough; inattentive. 2 lacking or showing a lack of a sense of responsibility.

carer N the person who has the responsibility for looking after an ill or dependent person.

caress VB to touch or stroke gently and lovingly. ➤ N a gentle loving touch or embrace.

caretaker N 1 a person whose job is to look after a house or a public building. 2 AS ADJ temporary; stopgap: **caretaker president**.

careworn ADJ worn out with or marked by worry and anxiety.

cargo N (-oes) the goods carried by a ship, aircraft or other vehicle.

Caribbean ADJ of **the Caribbean**, the part of the Atlantic and its islands between the West Indies and Central and S America.

caribou N (*caribous* or *caribou*) a large deer found in N America and Siberia.

caricature N 1 a representation, esp a drawing, of someone with their most noticeable and distinctive features exaggerated for comic effect. 2 a ridiculously poor attempt at something. ➤ VB to make or give a caricature of someone. ■ **caricaturist** N.

caring ADJ 1 showing concern for others; sympathetic and helpful. 2 professionally concerned with social, medical, etc welfare.

carmine N a deep red colour; crimson.

carnage N great slaughter.

carnal ADJ 1 of the body or the flesh, as opposed to the spirit or intellect. 2 sexual.

carnation N a plant with strongly scented flowers.

carnelian see **cornelian**

carnival N 1 a period of public festivity with eg street processions, colourful costumes, singing and dancing. 2 a circus or fair.

carnivore N an animal that feeds mainly on the flesh of other animals. ■ **carnivorous** ADJ.

carol N a religious song sung at Christmas. ➤ VB (-ll-) 1 INTR to sing carols. 2 to sing joyfully.

carotid N (also **carotid artery**) either of the two major arteries that supply blood to the head and neck.

carouse VB, INTR to take part in a noisy drinking party.

carousel N 1 a revolving belt in an airport, etc onto which luggage is unloaded so that passengers can collect it as it passes by. 2 N AMER a merry-go-round.

carp N (*carps* or *carp*) a deep-bodied freshwater fish. ➤ VB, INTR (often **carp at sb** or **sth**) to complain, find fault or criticize.

carpel N, BOT the female reproductive part of a flowering plant. ■ **carpellary** ADJ.

carpenter N someone skilled in working with wood. ■ **carpentry** N.

carpet N 1 a covering for floors and stairs, made of heavy fabric. 2 something that covers a surface: **a carpet of leaves**. ➤ VB to cover something with or as if with a carpet.

carpus N (-*pi*) ANAT the eight small bones that form the wrist.

carriage N 1 a four-wheeled horse-drawn passenger vehicle. 2 a railway coach for carrying passengers. 3 a moving section of a machine, eg a typewriter. 4 the way one holds oneself when standing or walking.

carriageway N the part of a road used by vehicles.

carrier N 1 a person or thing that carries. 2 a person or firm that transports goods. 3 an individual who may transmit a disease or hereditary disorder to other individuals.

carrier bag N a plastic or paper bag with handles.

carrion N dead and rotting animal flesh.

carrot N 1 a plant with a large fleshy orange root eaten as a vegetable. 2 COLLOQ something offered as an incentive.

carroty ADJ of hair: of a strong reddish colour.

carry VB (*-ies, -ied*) 1 to hold something in one's hands, have it in a pocket, bag, etc, or support its weight on one's body, while moving from one place to another. 2 to bring, take or convey something. 3 to have on one's person. 4 to be the means of spreading (a disease, etc). 5 to be pregnant with (a baby or babies). 6 to hold (oneself or a part of one's body) in a specified way: **She carries herself well**. 7 to bear the burden or expense of something. 8 to do the work of (someone who is not doing enough). 9 to print or broadcast: **carry the story**. 10 INTR of a sound: to be able to be heard a distance away. 11 to take to a certain point: **carry it too far**. 12 MATH to transfer (a figure) in a calculation from one column to the next.
➤ N (*-ies*) an act of carrying.
◆ **be** or **get carried away** COLLOQ to become over-excited or over-enthusiastic.
◆ **carry sth off** 1 to manage (an awkward situation, etc) well. 2 to win (a prize, etc). 3 to take something away by force.
◆ **carry on** 1 to continue; to keep going. 2 COLLOQ to make a noisy or unnecessary fuss.
◆ **carry sth out** to accomplish it successfully.
◆ **carry sth through** to complete it.

carrycot N a light box-like cot with handles, for carrying a baby.

carry-on N an excitement or fuss.

cart N 1 a two- or four-wheeled, horse-drawn vehicle for carrying goods or passengers. 2 a light vehicle pushed or pulled by hand.
➤ VB 1 to carry in a cart. 2 (often **cart sth around** or **off**, etc) COLLOQ to carry it.

carte blanche N freedom of action.

cartel N a group of firms that agree, esp illegally, on similar prices for their products, so as to reduce competition and keep profits high.

carthorse N a large strong horse.

cartilage N a tough flexible material that forms the skeleton of the embryo, but is largely converted into bone before adulthood.

cartography N the art of making maps. ■ **cartographer** N. ■ **cartographic** ADJ.

carton N 1 a plastic or cardboard container in which certain foods or drinks are packaged for sale. 2 a cardboard box.

cartoon N 1 a humorous drawing in a newspaper, etc. 2 (also **animated cartoon**) a film made by photographing a series of drawings, each showing the subjects in a slightly altered position, giving the impression of movement when the film is run at normal speed. 3 (also **strip cartoon**) a strip of drawings in a newspaper, etc showing a sequence of events. ■ **cartoonist** N.

cartridge N 1 a metal case containing the propellant charge for a gun. 2 the part of the pick-up arm of a record-player containing the stylus. 3 a small plastic tube containing ink for a fountain pen. 4 a plastic container holding a continuous loop of magnetic tape inserted into a tape deck, video recorder, etc. 5 a plastic container holding photographic film.

cartridge paper N a type of thick rough-surfaced paper for drawing or printing on.

cartwheel N 1 the wheel of a cart. 2 an acrobatic movement in which the body is thrown sideways with a turning action.
➤ VB, INTR to perform a cartwheel.

carve VB 1 to cut (wood, stone, etc) into a shape. 2 to make something from wood, stone, etc by cutting into it. 3 TR & INTR to cut (meat) into slices; to cut (a slice) of meat. ■ **carver** N.

carving N a figure or pattern, etc produced by carving wood, stone, etc.

cascade N 1 a waterfall or series of waterfalls. 2 something resembling a waterfall. 3 a large number of things arriving suddenly.
➤ VB, INTR to fall like a waterfall.

case[1] N 1 often IN COMPOUNDS a box, container or cover, used for storage, transportation, etc.

2 an outer covering, esp a protective one.
➤ VB to put something in a case.

case² N **1** a particular occasion, situation or set of circumstances. **2** an example, instance or occurrence. **3** someone receiving some sort of treatment or care. **4** a matter requiring investigation. **5** a matter to be decided in a law court. **6** (sometimes **case for** or **against sth**) the argument for or against something, with the relevant facts fully stated. **7** GRAM **a** the relationship of a noun, pronoun or adjective to other words in a sentence; **b** the form or category indicating this.
◆ **in any case** whatever happens; no matter what happens.
◆ **in case** so as to be prepared or safe (if a certain thing should happen).

casein N a milk protein that is the main constituent of cheese.

case law N law based on decisions made about similar cases in the past.

casement N a window with vertical hinges that opens outwards like a door.

cash N **1** coins or paper money, as distinct from cheques, credit cards, etc. **2** COLLOQ money in any form.
➤ VB to obtain or give cash in return for (a cheque, postal order, etc).

cash-and-carry N (-*ies*) a large shop where registered customers pay for goods in cash and take them away immediately.

cash crop N a crop grown for sale.

cash desk N a desk in a shop, etc at which one pays for goods.

cashew N (also **cashew nut**) the curved edible seed of a small evergreen tree.

cash flow N the amount of money coming into and going out of a business, etc.

cashier N in a bank, etc: any person who receives, pays out and deals with the cash.
➤ VB to dismiss (an officer) from the armed forces in disgrace.

cash machine and **cash dispenser** N an electronic machine from which one can obtain cash using one's personal cash card. Also called **ATM**.

cashmere N very fine soft wool from a long-haired Asian goat or a fabric made from this.

cash register N a machine in a shop, etc that records the amount of each sale.

casing N a protective covering.

casino N a building or room for gambling.

cask N a barrel for holding liquids.

casket N **1** a small case for holding jewels, etc. **2** N AMER a coffin.

casserole N **1** an ovenproof dish with a lid. **2** the food cooked in this kind of dish.

cassette N **1** a plastic case containing magnetic tape wound around two reels, that can be inserted into a suitable audio or video tape recorder. **2** a small lightproof cartridge containing photographic film.

cassock N a long garment worn by clergymen and male members of a church choir.

cast VB (PA T & PA P *cast*) **1** to throw. **2** to direct (one's eyes, a glance, etc) on or over something. **3** to throw off or shed something. **4** to project; to cause to appear: **cast a shadow**. **5** TR & INTR to throw (a fishing-line) out into the water. **6** to let down (an anchor). **7** (usu **cast sth off, aside** or **out**) to throw it off or away; to get rid of it. **8** to give (an actor) a part in a play or film; to distribute the parts in a film, play, etc. **9** to shape (molten metal, plastic, etc) by pouring it into a mould and allowing it to set. **10** to give or record (one's vote).
➤ N **1** a throw; an act of throwing (eg dice, a fishing-line). **2** an object shaped by pouring metal, plastic, etc, into a mould and allowing it to set. **3** (also **plaster cast**) a rigid casing, usu of plaster, moulded round a broken limb or other body part while the plaster is still wet.
4 the set of performers in a play, opera, etc.
◆ **cast off 1** to untie a boat ready to sail away. **2** to finish off and remove knitting from the needles.
◆ **cast on** to form (stitches) in knitting, etc by looping and securing wool, etc over the needles.

castanets PL N a musical instrument consisting of two pieces of wood which are held in the palm and struck together.

castaway N someone who has been shipwrecked.

caste N 1 any of the four hereditary social classes of Hindu society. 2 this system of class division or any system of social division based on inherited rank or wealth.

castellated ADJ of a building: having turrets and battlements like those of a castle.

caster see **castor**

caster sugar N finely crushed white sugar.

castigate VB to criticize or punish severely. ■ **castigation** N.

cast iron N any of a group of hard heavy alloys of iron, containing more carbon than steels, and cast into shape when molten.
➤ ADJ (**cast-iron**) 1 made of cast iron. 2 of a rule or decision: firm; not to be altered.

castle N 1 a large, fortified building with battlements and towers. 2 a large mansion. 3 CHESS a piece that is moved any number of squares forwards or backwards, but not diagonally.

cast-off N something discarded or no longer wanted. Also AS ADJ.

castor or **caster** N a small swivelling wheel fitted to the legs or underside of a piece of furniture so that it can be moved easily.

castor oil N oil from the seeds of a tropical African plant, used as a lubricant and laxative.

castrate VB 1 to remove the testicles of a male person or animal. 2 to deprive of vigour or strength. ■ **castrated** ADJ. ■ **castration** N.

casual ADJ 1 happening by chance. 2 showing no particular interest or concern. 3 without serious intention or commitment: **casual sex**. 4 of clothes: informal. ■ **casually** ADV. ■ **casualness** N.

casualty N (**-ies**) 1 someone killed or hurt in an accident or war. 2 the casualty department of a hospital. 3 something lost, destroyed, sacrificed, etc as a result of some event.

casuist N someone who uses cleverly misleading arguments, esp to make things that are morally wrong seem acceptable. ■ **casuistic** ADJ. ■ **casuistry** N.

cat N 1 any of a wide range of carnivorous mammals, including the lion, leopard and tiger, and the domestic cat. 2 cat-o'-nine-tails.

cataclysm N 1 an event causing tremendous change or upheaval. 2 a terrible flood or other disaster. ■ **cataclysmic** ADJ.

catabolism N, BIOCHEM in the cells of living organisms: the process by which complex compounds are broken down into simple molecules.

catacomb N (usu **catacombs**) an underground burial place, often a system of tunnels with recesses for the tombs.

catafalque N a temporary platform on which the body of an important person lies in state.

catalepsy N (**-ies**) a trance-like state characterized by the abnormal maintenance of rigid body postures. ■ **cataleptic** ADJ, N.

catalogue N 1 a list of items arranged in a systematic order. 2 a brochure, booklet, etc containing a list of goods for sale. 3 a list or index of all the books in a library.
➤ VB (**-guing**) 1 to make a catalogue of (a library, books, etc). 2 to enter (an item) in a catalogue. 3 to list or mention one by one.

catalyse or (US) **-lyze** VB of a catalyst: to alter the rate of (a chemical reaction) without itself undergoing any permanent chemical change.

catalysis N (**-ses**) CHEM the process effected by a catalyst. ■ **catalytic** ADJ.

catalyst N 1 CHEM any substance that accelerates a chemical reaction. 2 something or someone that causes change.

catalytic converter N a device fitted to a motor vehicle's exhaust system that reduces polluting emissions from the engine.

catamaran N a sailing-boat with two

hulls parallel to each other.

catapult N 1 a Y-shaped stick with an elastic or rubber band fitted between its prongs, used esp by children for firing stones, etc. 2 HIST a weapon of war designed to fire boulders. ➤ VB 1 to fire or send flying with, or as if with, a catapult. 2 INTR to be sent flying.

cataract N 1 PATHOL an opaque area within the lens of the eye that produces blurring of vision. 2 an immense rush of water.

catarrh N inflammation of the membranes lining the nose and throat, causing an excessive discharge of thick mucus.

catastrophe N a terrible blow, calamity or disaster. ■ **catastrophic** ADJ.

catatonia N, PATHOL a mental state characterized either by stupor or by excessive excitement. ■ **catatonic** ADJ, N.

catcall N a long shrill whistle expressing disagreement or disapproval.

catch VB (PA T, PA P *caught*) 1 to stop (a moving object) and hold it. 2 to manage to get hold of or trap, esp after a hunt or chase. 3 to be in time to get, reach, see, etc something: **catch the last post. 4** to overtake or draw level with someone or something. 5 to discover someone or something in time to prevent, or encourage, the development of something: **The disease can be cured if caught early. 6** to surprise someone doing something wrong or embarrassing. 7 to trick or trap. 8 to become infected with (a disease, etc). 9 TR & INTR to become or cause to become accidentally attached or held: **My dress caught on a nail. 10** to manage to hear, see or understand something: **I didn't quite catch your third point. 11** CRICKET to put (a batsman) out by gathering the ball he has struck before it touches the ground. ➤ N 1 an act of catching. 2 a small device for keeping a lid, door, etc closed. 3 something caught. 4 the total amount of eg fish caught. 5 a hidden problem or disadvantage; a snag. 6 someone or something that it would be advantageous to get hold of.
◆ **catch fire** to start burning.
◆ **catch on** COLLOQ 1 to become popular.

2 (often **catch on to sth**) to understand it.
◆ **catch sb out 1** to trick them into making a mistake. **2** to take them unawares in embarrassing circumstances.
◆ **catch up 1** (often **catch up to sb**) to draw level with someone ahead. **2** (also **catch up on sth**) to bring oneself up to date with eg one's work, news, etc.

catching ADJ 1 infectious. 2 captivating.

catchment area N 1 the area served by a particular school, hospital, etc. 2 (also **drainage basin**) the area of land whose rainfall feeds a particular river, lake or reservoir.

catchphrase N a well-known phrase.

catchword N a much-repeated well-known word or phrase.

catchy ADJ (*-ier, -iest*) of a song, etc: tuneful and easily remembered.

catechism N a series of questions and answers about the Christian religion.

catechize or **-ise** VB to instruct someone in the Christian faith, esp by means of a catechism.

categorical and **categoric** ADJ 1 of a statement, refusal, denial, etc: absolute or definite. 2 relating or belonging to a category. ■ **categorically** ADV.

categorize or **-ise** VB to put something into a category or categories. ■ **categorization** N.

category N (*-ies*) a group of things, people or concepts classed together because of some quality or qualities they have in common.

cater VB only in phrases.
◆ **cater for sb** or **sth 1** to supply food, accommodation, etc for them. **2** to make provision for them; to take them into account.
◆ **cater to sth** to indulge or pander to (unworthy desires, etc).

caterer N a person whose professional occupation is to provide food, etc for social occasions. ■ **catering** N.

caterpillar N 1 the larva of a butterfly or moth. 2 (usu **Caterpillar**) TRADEMARK a a continuous band or track made up of metal plates, used on heavy vehicles for travelling over rough surfaces; **b** a vehicle fitted with such tracks.

caterwaul VB, INTR **1** of a cat: to make a loud high wailing noise. **2** to wail or shriek in this way.

catfish N a freshwater fish with long whisker-like sensory barbels around the mouth.

catgut N a strong cord made from the dried intestines of sheep and other animals.

catharsis N (**-ses**) the emotional relief that results from allowing repressed thoughts and feelings to surface. ■ **cathartic** ADJ.

cathedral N the principal church of a diocese, in which the bishop has his throne.

catheter N, MED a hollow slender flexible tube that can be introduced into a narrow opening or body cavity, usu to drain a liquid, esp urine.

cathode N **1** in an electrolytic cell: the negative electrode, towards which positively charged ions, usu in solution, are attracted. **2** the positive terminal of a battery.

cathode rays PL N a stream of electrons emitted from a cathode in a vacuum tube.

cathode-ray tube N an evacuated glass tube in which streams of cathode rays are produced, used to display images in television sets, visual display units, etc.

catholic ADJ **1** (**Catholic**) of the Roman Catholic Church. **2** esp of a person's interests and tastes: broad; wide-ranging. ➤ N (**Catholic**) a member of the Roman Catholic Church.

Catholicism N the faith, dogma, etc of the Catholic Church.

catkin N, BOT in certain tree species: a flowering shoot that bears many small unisexual flowers, adapted for wind pollination.

catmint and **catnip** N, BOT a plant with oval toothed leaves and spikes of white two-lipped flowers spotted with purple.

catnap N a short sleep. ➤ VB, INTR to doze; to sleep briefly.

cat-o'-nine-tails N (PL **cat-o'-nine-tails**)

HIST a whip with nine knotted rope lashes.

CAT scanner ABBREV, MED (often **CT scanner**) computer-assisted, or computed axial, tomography scanner, a machine that produces X-ray images of soft body tissues.

Catseye N, TRADEMARK a small glass reflecting device, set into the surface of a road.

catsuit N a close-fitting one-piece garment, combining trousers and top.

cattle PL N large grass-eating mammals, including wild species and the domestic varieties farmed for their milk, meat and hides.

cattle grid N a grid of parallel metal bars covering a trench in a road, designed to prevent the passage of livestock.

catty ADJ (**-ier, -iest**) INFORMAL malicious; spiteful. ■ **cattily** ADV. ■ **cattiness** N.

catwalk N the narrow raised stage along which models walk at a fashion show.

Caucasian ADJ of one of the light- or white-skinned races of mankind.

caucus N **1** a small group of people taking decisions within a larger organization. **2** N AMER, ESP US a group or meeting of members of a political party.

caul N, ANAT a membrane that sometimes surrounds an infant's head at birth.

cauldron or **caldron** N a very large metal pot, often with handles, for heating liquids.

cauliflower N a type of cabbage, made up of white florets.

causal ADJ **1** relating to or being a cause. **2** relating to cause and effect. ■ **causally** ADV.

causation N the process of causing.

causative ADJ making something happen; producing an effect.

cause N **1** something which produces an effect; the person or thing through which something happens. **2** a reason or justification: **no cause for concern**. **3** an ideal, principle, aim, etc, that people support and work for. ➤ VB to produce as an effect; to bring about.

cause célèbre N (*causes célèbres*) a legal case, etc, that attracts much attention.

causeway N **1** a raised roadway crossing low-lying marshy ground or shallow water. **2** a stone-paved pathway.

caustic ADJ **1** CHEM of a chemical substance: strongly alkaline and corrosive to living tissue. **2** of remarks, etc: sarcastic; cutting; bitter. ➢ N a caustic substance. ■ **caustically** ADV.

cauterize or **-ise** VB to destroy (living tissue) by the direct application of a heated instrument or a caustic chemical. ■ **cauterization** N.

caution N **1** care in avoiding danger; prudent wariness. **2** a warning. **3** a formal reprimand for an offence, with a warning not to repeat it. ➢ VB, TR & INTR to warn or admonish someone. ■ **cautionary** ADJ.

cautious ADJ having or showing caution; careful; wary. ■ **cautiously** ADV. ■ **cautiousness** N.

cavalcade N **1** a ceremonial procession of cars, riders, etc. **2** any procession or parade.

cavalier N **1** a courtly gentleman. **2** (**Cavalier**) HIST a supporter of Charles I during the 17c English Civil War. ➢ ADJ, DEROG thoughtless, offhand, casual or disrespectful.

cavalry N (*-ies*) soldiers on horseback or in armoured vehicles. ■ **cavalryman** N.

cave N a large natural hollow chamber either underground or in the side of a mountain or cliff. ◆ **cave in 1** of walls, a roof, etc: to collapse inwards. **2** COLLOQ of a person: to give way to persuasion.

caveat N a warning.

cave-in N **1** a collapse. **2** a surrender.

caveman N **1** (also **cave-dweller**) a person of prehistoric times, who lived in caves, etc. **2** DEROG a crude, brutish man.

cavern N a large cave.

cavernous ADJ of a space: deep and vast.

caviar or **caviare** N the salted roe of the sturgeon, considered a delicacy.

cavil VB (*-ll-*) INTR (usu **cavil at** or **about sth**) to make trivial objections to something. ➢ N a trivial objection.

caving N the sport of exploring caves.

cavity N (*-ies*) a hollow or hole.

cavort VB, INTR to jump or caper about.

cay see **key**²

cayenne and **cayenne pepper** N a hot spice made from capsicum seeds.

cayman or **caiman** N a reptile closely related to the alligator.

CD ABBREV compact disc.

CD-i or **CDI** ABBREV compact disc interactive.

CD-ROM ABBREV compact disc read-only memory.

cease VB, TR & INTR to bring or come to an end.

ceasefire N a break in the fighting during a war, agreed to by all sides.

ceaseless ADJ continuous; going on without a pause or break. ■ **ceaselessly** ADV.

cedar N **1** a tall coniferous tree with widely spreading branches and reddish-brown bark. **2** (also **cedarwood**) the sweet-smelling wood of this tree.

cede VB to give up something formally.

cedilla N **1** in French and Portuguese: a diacritic put under **c** in some words, eg *façade*, to show that it is to be pronounced like **s**, not like **k**. **2** the same mark used in other languages.

ceilidh N in Scotland and Ireland: a social gathering with traditional music and dancing.

ceiling N **1** the inner roof of a room, etc. **2** an upper limit.

celebrant N someone who performs a religious ceremony.

celebrate VB **1** to mark (an occasion, esp a birthday or anniversary) with festivities. **2** INTR to do something enjoyable to mark a happy occasion, anniversary, etc. **3** to give public praise or recognition to someone or something, eg in the form of a poem. **4** to conduct (a religious ceremony, eg a marriage or mass). ■ **celebration** N. ■ **celebratory** ADJ.

celebrated ADJ famous; renowned.

celebrity N (*-ies*) **1** a famous person. **2** fame.

celeriac N a variety of celery, cultivated for the swollen base of its stem, which is eaten as a vegetable.

celery N (*-ies*) a plant with deeply grooved leaf stalks that are eaten as a vegetable.

celestial ADJ **1** of the sky: **celestial bodies**. **2** heavenly; divine: **celestial voices**.

celibate ADJ **1** unmarried, esp in obedience to a religious vow. **2** having no sexual relations. ➤ N someone who is unmarried, esp because of a religious vow. ■ **celibacy** N.

cell N **1** a small room occupied by an inmate in a prison or monastery. **2** BIOL the basic structural unit of all living organisms. **3** ELEC a device consisting of two electrodes, for converting chemical energy into electrical energy. **4** one of the compartments in a honeycomb or in a similarly divided structure.

cellar N **1** a room, usu underground, for storage, eg of wine. **2** a stock of wines.

cello N a large stringed musical instrument of the violin family. ■ **cellist** N.

Cellophane N, TRADEMARK a thin transparent wrapping material.

cellphone N, RADIO a portable telephone for use in a cellular radio system.

cellular ADJ composed of cells or divided into cell-like compartments.

cellular radio N a system of radio communication based on a network of geographical areas, each of which is served by a transmitter.

cellulite N deposits of fat cells which give the skin a dimpled, pitted appearance.

celluloid N, TRADEMARK **1** a transparent highly flammable plastic material made from cellulose nitrate and camphor. **2** cinema film.

cellulose N a complex carbohydrate, the main constituent of plant cell walls, used in the manufacture of paper, rope, textiles, etc.

Celsius scale N a scale of temperature in which the freezing point of water is 0°C and its boiling point is 100°C.

Celt N a member of one of the ancient peoples of Europe in pre-Roman and Roman times, or of the peoples descended from them, eg in Scotland, Wales and Ireland.

Celtic ADJ of the Celts or their languages.

cement N **1** a fine powder, composed of a mixture of clay and limestone, that hardens when mixed with water, and is used to make mortar and concrete. **2** any of various substances used as adhesives. ➤ VB **1** to stick together with cement. **2** to apply cement. **3** to bind or make firm (eg a friendship).

cemetery N (*-ies*) a burial ground.

cenotaph N a tomb-like monument in honour of a person or persons buried elsewhere.

censer N a container in which incense is burnt. Also called **thurible**.

censor N an official who examines books, films, etc, with the power to cut out any politically sensitive or offensive parts, and to forbid publication or showing altogether. ➤ VB **1** to alter or cut out parts of something, or forbid its publication, showing or delivery. **2** to act as a censor. ■ **censorship** N.

censorious ADJ inclined to find fault; critical.

censure N severe criticism or disapproval. ➤ VB to criticize severely or express strong disapproval of someone or something.

census N an official count of a population, carried out at periodic intervals.

cent N a currency unit of several countries, worth one hundredth of the standard unit.

centaur N, GR MYTHOL a creature with a man's head, arms and trunk, joined to the body and legs of a horse.

centenarian N someone who is 100 years old or more.
➤ ADJ **1** 100 years old or more. **2** relating to a centenarian.

centenary N (*-ies*) the one-hundredth anniversary of some event, or its celebration.
➤ ADJ **1** occurring every 100 years. **2** relating to a period of 100 years.

centennial N, N AMER a centenary.
➤ ADJ **1** relating to a period of 100 years. **2** occurring every 100 years. **3** lasting 100 years.

centigrade ADJ, N the former name for the Celsius scale of temperature.

centimetre N one hundredth of a metre.

centipede N any of numerous terrestrial arthropods with a long segmented body and usu a pair of legs for each segment.

central ADJ **1** at or forming the centre of something. **2** near the centre of a city, etc; easy to reach. **3** principal or most important. ■ **centrality** N. ■ **centrally** ADV.

central heating N a system for heating a whole building, by means of pipes, radiators, etc connected to a central source of heat.

centralism N the policy of bringing the administration of a country under central control. ■ **centralist** N, ADJ.

centralize or **-ise** VB, TR & INTR to bring under central control. ■ **centralization** N.

central reservation N, BRIT a narrow strip dividing the two sides of a motorway.

centre or (N AMER) **center** N **1** a part at the middle of something. **2** a point inside a circle or sphere that is an equal distance from all points on the circumference or surface, or a point on a line at an equal distance from either end. **3** a point or axis round which a body revolves or rotates. **4** a central area. **5** chiefly IN COMPOUNDS a place where a specified activity is concentrated or specified facilities, etc are available: **a sports centre**. **6** a focus. **7** a point or place from which activities are controlled. **8** a position that is at neither extreme, esp in politics. **9** in some field sports, eg football: **a** a position in the middle of the field; **b** a player in this position.
➤ ADJ at the centre; central.
➤ VB **1** to place in or at the centre. **2** TR & INTR (often **centre on sth**) to concentrate on it.

centrepiece N **1** a central or most important item. **2** an ornament or decoration for the centre of a table.

centrifugal force N an apparent force that seems to exert an outward pull on an object that is moving in a circular path.

centrifuge N a device using rotation to separate particles of different densities.

centripetal force N the force that keeps an object moving in a circular path.

centrist ADJ having moderate, non-extreme political opinions.
➤ N someone holding such opinions.

centurion N, HIST in the army of ancient Rome: an officer in charge of a century.

century N (*centuries*) **1** a period of 100 years. **2** a score of 100. **3** HIST in the army of ancient Rome: a company of 100 soldiers.

cephalopod N any invertebrate animal with a head and many tentacles surrounding its mouth, eg squid, octopus.

ceramic N **1** any of a number of hard brittle materials produced by baking or firing clays at high temperatures. **2** an object made from such a material. Also AS ADJ.

ceramics SING N the art and technique of making pottery.

cereal N **1** a grass cultivated as a food crop for its nutritious edible seeds, ie grains, eg barley, wheat, rice, etc. **2** the grain produced. **3** a breakfast food prepared from this grain.
➤ ADJ relating to edible grains.

cerebellum N (*-bella*) ANAT in vertebrates: the main part of the back of the brain, concerned primarily with the co-ordination of movement.

cerebral ADJ **1** relating to or in the region of the

brain. **2** often FACETIOUS intellectual; using the brain rather than appealing to the emotions.

cerebral palsy N, PATHOL a failure of the brain to develop normally in young children due to brain damage before or around the time of birth, resulting in weakness and lack of co-ordination of the limbs.

cerebrospinal ADJ relating to the brain and spinal cord together: **cerebrospinal fluid**.

cerebrum N (-*rums* or -*ra*) ANAT in higher vertebrates: the front part of the brain, which controls thinking and emotions.

ceremonial ADJ relating to, used for or involving a ceremony.
➤ N a system of rituals. ■ **ceremonially** ADV.

ceremonious ADJ excessively formal.

ceremony N (-*ies*) **1** a ritual performed to mark a particular, esp public or religious, occasion. **2** formal politeness.

cerise N a bright cherry-red colour.

cerium N, CHEM a soft silvery-grey metallic element used in catalytic converters, alloys, etc.

certain ADJ **1** proved or known beyond doubt. **2** (sometimes **certain about** or **of sth**) having no doubt about it; absolutely sure. **3** definitely going to happen, etc; able to rely on or be relied on. **4** not named or specified: **a certain person. 5** some: **true to a certain extent**.

certainly ADV **1** without any doubt. **2** definitely. **3** in giving permission: of course.

certainty N (-*ies*) **1** something that cannot be doubted or is bound to happen. **2** freedom from doubt; the state of being sure.

certificate N an official document that formally acknowledges or witnesses a fact, an achievement or qualification, or one's condition.
➤ VB to provide with a certificate.

certified ADJ **1** possessing a certificate. **2** endorsed or guaranteed. **3** insane.

certify VB (-*ies*, -*ied*) **1** TR & INTR to declare or confirm officially. **2** to declare someone legally insane. **3** to declare to have reached a required standard, passed certain tests, etc.

certitude N a feeling of certainty.

cervical ADJ of or in the region of the cervix.

cervix N (-*vixes* or -*vices*) ANAT **1** the neck of the uterus. **2** the neck.

cessation N a stopping or ceasing; a pause.

cession N the giving up or yielding of territories, rights, etc to someone else.

cesspit N **1** a pit for the collection and storage of sewage. **2** a foul and squalid place.

cesspool N a tank, well, etc for the collection and storage of sewage and waste water.

cetacean N any animal belonging to the order which includes dolphins and whales.
➤ ADJ of this group.

cf ABBREV: **confer** (Latin), compare.

CFC ABBREV chlorofluorocarbon.

cha-cha and **cha-cha-cha** N a Latin American dance.

chador N a thick veil worn by Muslim women.

chafe VB **1** TR & INTR to make or become sore or worn by rubbing. **2** INTR (also **chafe at** or **under sth**) to become angry or impatient.

chafer N any of various species of large slow-moving nocturnal beetle.

chaff[1] N **1** the husks that form the outer covering of cereal grain, and are separated from the seeds during threshing. **2** worthless material.

chaff[2] N light-hearted joking or teasing.
➤ VB to tease or make fun of someone in a good-natured way.

chaffinch N a finch with a blue crown.

chagrin N acute annoyance or disappointment.
➤ VB to annoy or embarrass someone.

chain N **1** a series of interconnecting links or rings, esp of metal, used for fastening, binding or holding, or, eg in jewellery, for ornament. **2** a series or progression: **a chain of events**. **3** a number of shops, hotels, etc under common ownership or management. **4** (**chains**) something that restricts or frustrates.

➤ VB (often **chain sb** or **sth up** or **down**) to fasten, bind or restrict with, or as if with, chains.

chainmail see **mail**²

chain reaction N **1** a nuclear or chemical reaction that is self-sustaining. **2** a series of events, each causing the next.

chainsaw N a portable power-driven saw with cutting teeth in a continuous chain.

chain-smoke VB, TR & INTR to smoke (cigarettes, etc) continuously. ■ **chain-smoker** N.

chair N **1** a seat for one person, with a back-support and usu four legs. **2** the office of chairman or chairwoman at a meeting, etc, or the person holding this office.
3 a professorship.
➤ VB to control or conduct (a meeting) as chairman or chairwoman.

chairlift N a series of seats suspended from a moving cable, for carrying skiers, etc up a mountain.

chairman, **chairwoman** and **chairperson** N **1** someone who controls a meeting or debate. **2** someone who presides over a committee, board of directors, etc.

chaise N, HIST a light open two-wheeled horse-drawn carriage.

chaise longue N (*chaises longues*) a long seat with a back and one arm-rest.

chalcedony N (-*ies*) GEOL a fine-grained variety of quartz, eg agate, jasper, onyx.

chalet N **1** a style of house typical of Alpine regions, built of wood. **2** a small cabin for holiday accommodation.

chalice N a wine cup; a goblet.

chalk N **1** a soft fine-grained porous rock, composed of calcium carbonate. **2** a material similar to this, usu calcium sulphate, in stick form, either white or coloured, and used for writing and drawing, esp on a blackboard.
➤ VB to write or mark in chalk. ■ **chalky** ADJ.

challenge VB **1** to call on someone to settle a matter by any sort of contest. **2** to cast doubt on something or call it in question. **3** to test, esp in a stimulating way. **4** to order someone to stop and show official proof of identity, etc.
➤ N **1** an invitation to a contest. **2** the questioning or doubting of something. **3** a problem or task that stimulates effort and interest. **4** an order to stop and prove identity. ■ **challenger** N. ■ **challenging** ADJ.

challenged ADJ, USU IN COMPOUNDS a supposedly neutral term, denoting some kind of handicap or disability: **vertically challenged**.

chamber N **1** OLD USE a room, esp a bedroom. **2** a hall for the meeting of an assembly, esp a legislative body. **3** one of the houses of which a parliament consists. **4** (**chambers**) a suite of rooms used by eg a judge or lawyer. **5** an enclosed space or hollow; a cavity. **6** the compartment in a gun into which the cartridge is loaded. **7** a room with a particular function: a decompression chamber.

chambermaid N a woman who cleans bedrooms in a hotel, etc.

chamber of commerce N an association of business people that promotes local trade.

chamberpot N a receptacle for urine, etc for use in a bedroom.

chameleon N a lizard whose granular skin changes colour rapidly in response to changes in its environment.

chamois N (PL *chamois*) **1** SING AND PL an agile antelope, native to S Europe and Asia. **2** soft suede leather, formerly made from the skin of this animal, but now usu made from the hides of sheep, lambs or goats. **3** a piece of this used as a polishing cloth for glass, etc. Also written **shammy** (-*ies*) and **shammy leather** or **chamois leather**.

chamomile see **camomile**

champ¹ VB, TR & INTR to munch noisily.
➤ N the sound of munching.

champ² N, COLLOQ a champion.

champagne N, STRICTLY a sparkling white wine made in the Champagne district of France.
➤ ADJ **1** of or for champagne: **champagne**

bottle. **2** denoting an extravagant way of life: champagne **lifestyle**.

champion N **1** a competitor who has defeated all others. **2** the supporter or defender of a person or cause.
➤ VB to strongly support or defend (a person or cause). ■ **championship** N.

chance N **1** the way that things happen unplanned and unforeseen. **2** fate or luck; fortune. **3** an unforeseen and unexpected occurrence. **4** a possibility or probability. **5** a possible or probable success. **6** an opportunity. **7** risk; a gamble.
➤ VB **1** to risk something. **2** INTR to do or happen by chance: I chanced to meet her.
◆ **take one's chances** to risk an undertaking; to accept whatever happens.

chancel N the eastern part of a church containing the altar.

chancellery or **chancellory** N (-ies) **1** the rank of chancellor. **2** a chancellor's department.

chancellor N **1** the head of the government in certain European countries. **2** a state or legal official of various kinds. **3** in the UK: the honorary head of a university. **4** in the USA: the president of a university or college.
■ **chancellorship** N.

chancre N, PATHOL a small hard growth that develops in the primary stages of syphilis and certain other diseases.

chancy ADJ (-ier, -iest) risky; uncertain.

chandelier N an ornamental light-fitting hanging from the ceiling, with branching holders for candles or light-bulbs.

chandler N a dealer in candles, oil, groceries, etc. ■ **chandlery** n (-ies).

change VB **1** TR & INTR to make or become different. **2** to give, leave or substitute one thing for another. **3** to exchange (usu one's position) with another person, etc. **4** TR & INTR to remove (clothes, sheets, a baby's nappy, etc) and replace them with clean or different ones. **5** TR & INTR (sometimes **change into sth**) to make into or become something different. **6** TR & INTR to put a vehicle engine into (another gear).

➤ N **1** the process of changing or an instance of it. **2** the replacement of one thing with another. **3** a variation, esp a welcome one, from one's regular habit, etc. **4** a fresh set (of clothes) for changing into. **5** (also **small** or **loose change**) coins as distinct from notes. **6** coins or notes given in exchange for ones of higher value. **7** money left over or returned from the amount given in payment. ■ **changeable** ADJ.
◆ **change one's mind** or **tune** to adopt a different intention or opinion.

change of life N the menopause.

channel N **1** any natural or artificially constructed water course. **2** the part of a river, waterway, etc, that is deep enough for navigation by ships. **3** a wide stretch of water, esp between an island and a continent. **4** ELECTRONICS the frequency band that is assigned for sending or receiving a clear radio or television signal. **5** a groove, furrow or any long narrow cut, esp one along which something moves. **6** (often **channels**) a means by which information, etc is communicated, obtained or received.
➤ VB (-ll-) **1** to make a channel or channels in something. **2** to convey (a liquid, information, etc) through a channel. **3** to direct (a resource, eg energy, money) into a course, project, etc.

chant VB, TR & INTR **1** to recite in a singing voice. **2** to keep repeating, esp rhythmically.
➤ N **1** a type of singing used in religious services for passages in prose, with a simple melody and several words sung on one note. **2** a phrase constantly repeated, esp loudly and rhythmically. ■ **chanting** N, ADJ.

chanter N on a set of bagpipes: the pipe on which the melody is played.

chanty another spelling of **shanty**²

chaos N complete confusion or disorder.
■ **chaotic** ADJ. ■ **chaotically** ADV.

chap¹ N, COLLOQ (also **chappie**) a man or boy.

chap² VB (-pp-) TR & INTR of the skin: to make or become cracked, roughened and red as a result of rubbing or exposure to cold.
➤ N a roughened red patch on the skin.

chapati or **chapatti** N (*-ti, -tis* or *-ties*) in Indian cooking: a thin flat portion of unleavened bread.

chapel N 1 a recess within a church or cathedral, with its own altar. 2 a place of worship attached to a house, school, etc. 3 in England and Wales: a place of Nonconformist worship. 4 in Scotland and N Ireland: a Roman Catholic or Episcopalian place of worship.

chaperone or **chaperon** N 1 FORMERLY an older woman accompanying a younger unmarried one on social occasions. 2 an older person accompanying and supervising a young person or group of young people. ➤ VB to act as chaperone to someone.

chaplain N a member of the clergy attached to a school, hospital or other institution, or to the armed forces. ■ **chaplaincy** N (*-ies*).

chapped ADJ of the skin: dry and cracked.

chappie see **chap**[1]

chapter N 1 one of the numbered or titled sections into which a book is divided. 2 a period associated with certain happenings: **an exciting chapter in my life.** 3 a sequence or series: **a chapter of accidents.** 4 N AMER a branch of a society. 5 the body of canons of a cathedral, or of members of a religious order.

char[1] VB (*-rr-*) TR & INTR to blacken or be blackened by burning; to scorch.

char[2] or **charr** N (*char, charr, chars* or *charrs*) a fish related to and resembling the salmon, native to cool northern lakes and rivers.

charabanc N, DATED a single-decker coach.

character N 1 the combination of qualities that makes up a person's nature or personality. 2 the combination of qualities that typifies anything. 3 type or kind. 4 strong admirable qualities such as determination, etc. 5 interesting qualities that make for individuality: **a house with character.** 6 someone in a story or play. 7 an odd or amusing person. 8 reputation. 9 a letter, number or other written or printed symbol.
◆ **in** or **out of character** typical or untypical of a person's nature.

characteristic N 1 a distinctive quality or feature. 2 MATH the integral part of a logarithm. ➤ ADJ indicative of a distinctive quality or feature; typical. ■ **characteristically** ADV.

characterize or **-ise** VB to describe, give or be the chief qualities of someone or something. ■ **characterization** N.

charade N 1 DEROG a ridiculous pretence; a farce. 2 (**charades**) a party game in which one player mimes each syllable of a word, or each word of a book title, etc, while others try to guess the complete word or title.

charcoal N 1 a black form of carbon produced by heating organic material, esp wood, in the absence of air. 2 a stick of this used for drawing. 3 a drawing done in charcoal. 4 (also **charcoal grey**) a dark grey colour. ➤ ADJ charcoal-coloured.

charge VB 1 to ask for an amount as the price of something. 2 to ask someone to pay an amount for something. 3 to accuse someone officially of a crime. 4 INTR to rush at someone or something in attack. 5 to rush. 6 FORMAL to officially order someone to do something: **She was charged to appear in court.** 7 to load (a gun, furnace, etc) with explosive, fuel, etc. 8 FORMAL & OLD USE to fill up: **charge your glasses.** 9 INTR of a battery, capacitor, etc: to take up or store electricity. 10 to cause (a battery, capacitor, etc) to take up or store electricity.
➤ N 1 an amount of money charged. 2 control, care or responsibility: **in charge of repairs.** 3 supervision or guardianship: **take charge.** 4 something or someone that is in one's care. 5 something of which one is accused: **a charge of murder.** 6 a rushing attack. 7 (also **electrical charge**) a deficiency or excess of electrons on a particular object, giving rise to a positive or negative charge, respectively. 8 the total amount of electricity stored by eg an accumulator or capacitor. 9 an amount of explosive, fuel, etc, for loading into a gun, furnace, etc. 10 a debt or financial liability.
■ **chargeable** ADJ.

charge card N a small card issued by a store, used to buy goods on credit.

charge hand N a foreman's deputy.

charge nurse N a nurse in charge of a hospital ward.

chariot N, HIST a two-wheeled vehicle pulled by horses, used in ancient times for warfare or racing. ■ **charioteer** N.

charisma N a strong ability to attract people, and inspire loyalty. ■ **charismatic** ADJ.

charitable ADJ 1 having a kind and understanding attitude to others. 2 generous in assisting people in need. 3 of, or in the nature of a charity. ■ **charitably** ADV.

charity N (-ies) 1 assistance given to those in need. 2 an organization established to provide such assistance. 3 a kind and understanding attitude towards other people.

charlatan N, DEROG someone posing as an expert in some profession, esp medicine.

charm N 1 the power of delighting, attracting or fascinating. 2 (**charms**) delightful qualities possessed by a person, place, thing, etc. 3 an object believed to have magical powers. 4 a magical saying or spell. 5 a small ornament, esp of silver, worn on a bracelet.
➤ VB 1 to delight, attract or fascinate someone. 2 to influence or persuade them by charm.
■ **charmer** N. ■ **charmless** ADJ.

charming ADJ delightful; pleasing; attractive; enchanting. ■ **charmingly** ADV.

chart N 1 a map, esp one designed as an aid to navigation by sea or air. 2 a table, graph or diagram of information.
➤ VB 1 to make a chart of something. 2 to plot (the course or progress of something).

charter N 1 a formal deed guaranteeing the rights and privileges of subjects, issued by a sovereign or government. 2 a document stating the constitution and principles of an organization. 3 a document creating a borough or burgh. 4 the hire of aircraft or ships for private use, or a contract for this.
➤ VB 1 to hire (an aircraft, etc) for private use. 2 to grant a charter to someone.

chartered ADJ 1 qualified according to the rules of a professional body that has a royal charter: **chartered accountant**. 2 having been granted a charter: **a chartered plane**.

chary ADJ (-ier, -iest) 1 cautious or wary. 2 sparing; rather mean: **chary of praise**.

chase VB 1 (often **chase after sb**) to follow or go after them in an attempt to catch them. 2 (often **chase sb away** or **off,** etc) to drive or force them away, off, etc. 3 INTR to rush; to hurry. 4 COLLOQ to try to obtain or achieve something, esp with difficulty. 5 COLLOQ to pursue a particular matter urgently with someone. 6 COLLOQ to pursue (a desired partner).
➤ N a pursuit.

chasm N 1 a deep opening in the ground. 2 a very wide difference in opinion, etc.

chassis N (PL *chassis*) the structural framework of a vehicle, to which the body and movable working parts are attached.

chaste ADJ 1 sexually virtuous or pure. 2 modest; decent. ■ **chastely** ADV. ■ **chasteness** N.

chasten VB 1 to free someone from faults by punishing them. 2 to moderate or restrain something.

chastise VB 1 to scold someone. 2 to punish someone severely, esp by beating. ■ **chastisement** N.

chastity N the state of being chaste.

chat VB (-*tt*-) INTR to talk in a friendly way. ➤ N informal familiar talk.

château N (-*teaux*) a French castle.

chat show N a TV or radio programme in which well-known people are interviewed informally.

chattel N any kind of movable property.

chatter VB, INTR 1 to talk rapidly and unceasingly. 2 of the teeth: to keep clicking together as a result of cold or fear. 3 to make rapid continuous high-pitched noises.
➤ N 1 a sound similar to this. 2 idle talk or gossip.

chatterbox N, DEROG someone who is inclined to chatter.

chatty ADJ (*-ier, -iest*) COLLOQ **1** given to amiable chatting. **2** of writing: friendly and informal. ■ **chattily** ADV. ■ **chattiness** N.

chauffeur N someone employed to drive a car for someone else.
➤ VB, TR & INTR to act as a driver for someone.

chauvinism N, DEROG an unreasonable belief in the superiority of one's own nation, sex, etc. ■ **chauvinist** N, ADJ. ■ **chauvinistic** ADJ.

cheap ADJ **1** low in price; inexpensive. **2** being or charging less than the usual. **3** low in price but of poor quality. **4** having little worth. **5** vulgar or nasty.
➤ ADV, COLLOQ cheaply: **Houses don't come cheap.** ■ **cheaply** ADV. ■ **cheapness** N.

cheapen VB **1** to cause to appear cheap. **2** TR & INTR to make or become cheaper.

cheapskate N, COLLOQ DEROG a mean person.

cheat VB **1** to trick, deceive or swindle. **2** (usu **cheat sb of** or **out of sth**) to deprive them of it by deceit or trickery. **3** INTR to act dishonestly so as to gain an advantage: **cheat at cards.**
➤ N **1** someone who cheats. **2** a dishonest trick.

check VB **1** TR & INTR to establish that something is correct or satisfactory, esp by investigation or enquiry; to verify. **2** to hold back or prevent. **3** COLLOQ to reproach or rebuke someone.
➤ N **1** an inspection or investigation made to find out about something or to ensure that something is as it should be. **2** a standard or test by means of which to check something. **3** a stoppage in, or control on, progress or development. **4** a pattern of squares. **5** N AMER a restaurant bill. **6** CHESS the position of the king when directly threatened by an opposing piece. ■ **checker** N.
◆ **check in** to report one's arrival at an air terminal or hotel.
◆ **check out 1** to register one's departure, esp from a hotel. **2** of information, etc: to be satisfactory or consistent.
◆ **check sb** or **sth out** to investigate them or it.

checked ADJ having a squared pattern.

check-in N at an air terminal: the desk at which passengers' tickets are checked and luggage weighed and accepted for loading.

checklist N a list of things to be done or systematically checked.

checkmate CHESS, N a winning position, putting one's opponent's king under inescapable attack.
➤ VB to put the (opposing king) into checkmate.

checkout N the pay desk in a supermarket.

check-up N a thorough examination, esp a medical one.

cheek N **1** either side of the face below the eye; the fleshy wall of the mouth. **2** impudence. **3** COLLOQ either of the buttocks.

cheekbone N either of a pair of bones that lie beneath the prominent part of the cheeks.

cheeky ADJ (*-ier, -iest*) impudent or disrespectful. ■ **cheekily** ADV.

cheep VB, INTR to make high-pitched noises.
➤ N a sound of this sort.

cheer N **1** a shout of approval or encouragement. **2** OLD USE disposition; frame of mind: **be of good cheer.**
➤ VB, TR & INTR to show approval or encouragement of someone or something by shouting.
◆ **cheer up** to become more cheerful.
◆ **cheer sb up** to make them more cheerful.

cheerful ADJ **1** happy; optimistic. **2** bright and cheering. **3** willing; glad; ungrudging.

cheering ADJ bringing comfort; making one feel glad or happier.

cheerio EXCLAM, BRIT COLLOQ goodbye.

cheerleader N someone who leads organized cheering, applause, etc, esp at sports events.

cheerless ADJ dismal, depressing or dreary.

cheers EXCLAM, BRIT COLLOQ **1** used as a toast before drinking. **2** thank you. **3** goodbye.

cheery ADJ (*-ier, -iest*) cheerful; lively; jovial. ■ **cheerily** ADV. ■ **cheeriness** N.

cheese N **1** a creamy food made from the

curds of milk. **2** a solid mass of this.

cheesecake N a sweet cake with a pastry base, topped with cream cheese, sugar, etc.

cheesecloth N a loosely woven cloth used for shirts, etc.

cheesy ADJ (*-ier, -iest*) **1** like cheese eg in smell, flavour, etc. **2** COLLOQ cheap, inferior. **3** of a smile: wide, but probably insincere.

cheetah N a large member of the cat family with a tawny or grey coat with black spots.

chef N a cook in a restaurant etc.

chemical ADJ **1** relating to or used in the science of chemistry. **2** relating to a substance or substances that take part in or are formed by reactions in which atoms or molecules undergo changes. **3** relating to chemicals. ➤ N a substance that has a specific molecular composition, and takes part in or is formed by reactions in which atoms or molecules undergo changes. ■ **chemically** ADV.

chemical warfare N warfare using toxic chemical substances, eg mustard gas.

chemise N a woman's shirt or loose dress.

chemist N **1** a scientist who specializes in chemistry. **2** someone qualified to dispense medicines; a pharmacist. **3** a shop dealing in medicines, toiletries, cosmetics, etc.

chemistry N (*-ies*) the scientific study of the composition, properties, and reactions of chemical elements and their compounds.

chemotherapy N, MED the treatment of a disease or disorder by means of drugs.

cheque N a printed form instructing one's bank to pay a specified sum of money from one's account to another account.

cheque card N a card issued to customers by a bank, guaranteeing payment of their cheques up to a stated amount.

chequered ADJ **1** patterned with squares or patches of alternating colour. **2** of a person's life, career, etc: eventful, with alternations of good and bad fortune.

chequers or (US) **checkers** SING N the game of draughts.

cherish VB **1** to care for lovingly. **2** to cling fondly to (a hope, belief or memory).

cherry N (*-ies*) **1** a small round red or purplish fruit containing a small stone surrounded by pulpy flesh. **2** any of various small deciduous trees which bear this fruit. **3** a bright red colour.

cherub N **1** (PL ALSO *cherubim*) **a** an angel, represented as a winged child; **b** an angel of the second-highest rank. **2** a sweet, innocent and beautiful child. ■ **cherubic** ADJ.

chervil N a plant that is widely cultivated for its aromatic leaves.

chess N a game of skill played on a chequered board, a **chessboard**, by two people, each with 16 playing-pieces, **chessmen**, the object of which is to trap the opponent's king.

chest N **1** the front part of the body between the neck and the waist. **2** a large strong box.

chesterfield N a padded leather-covered sofa with arms and back of the same height.

chestnut N **1** (also **sweet chestnut**) a deciduous tree with toothed glossy leaves and prickly globular fruits containing large edible nuts. **2** the large reddish-brown nut of this tree. **3** (also **horse chestnut**) a large deciduous tree bearing brown shiny inedible seeds, popularly known as conkers. **4** the hard timber of either of these trees. **5** a reddish-brown colour. **6** a reddish-brown horse.

chest of drawers N a piece of furniture fitted with drawers.

chesty ADJ (*-ier, -iest*) BRIT, COLLOQ liable to, suffering from or caused by illness affecting the lungs: *a chesty cough.* ■ **chestiness** N.

chevron N **1** a V-shaped mark or symbol, esp one worn on the sleeve of a uniform to indicate non-commissioned rank. **2** on a road sign: a horizontal row of black and white V-shapes indicating a sharp bend ahead.

chew VB **1** TR & INTR to use the teeth to break up (food) inside the mouth before swallowing. **2** TR & INTR (sometimes **chew at** or **on sth**) to

keep biting or nibbling it.
> N **1** an act of chewing. **2** something for chewing, eg a sweet.

chewy ADJ (*-ier, -iest*) COLLOQ requiring a lot of chewing. ■ **chewiness** N.

chic ADJ appealingly elegant or fashionable.
> N stylishness; elegance.

chicane N, MOTOR SPORT on a motor-racing circuit: a series of sharp bends.

chicanery N (*-ies*) **1** clever talk intended to mislead. **2** trickery; deception.

chick N **1** the young of a bird, esp a domestic fowl. **2** SLANG a young woman.

chicken N **1** the domestic fowl, bred for its meat and eggs. **2** the flesh of this animal used as food. **3** DEROG a cowardly person.
> ADJ, DEROG cowardly.
◆ **chicken out of sth** to avoid or withdraw from (an activity or commitment) from lack of nerve or confidence.

chickenfeed N **1** food for poultry. **2** a small and insignificant sum of money.

chickenpox N an infectious viral disease which mainly affects children, characterized by a fever and an itchy rash of dark red spots.

chicken wire N wire netting.

chickpea N a plant with yellow pea-like edible seeds.

chickweed N a sprawling plant with oval pointed leaves and tiny white flowers.

chicory N (*-ies*) **1** a plant with a long stout tap root. **2** the dried root, which is often ground, roasted and blended with coffee. **3** the leaves of this plant, eaten raw as a salad vegetable.

chide VB (PA T *chided* or *chid*, PA P *chidden* or *chided*) chiefly LITERARY to scold or rebuke.

chief N **1** the head of a tribe, clan, etc. **2** a leader. **3** any person in charge.
> ADJ **1** used in titles, etc: first in rank; leading: chief inspector. **2** main; most important.

chiefly ADV **1** mainly. **2** especially; above all.

chieftain N the head of a tribe or clan.

chiffchaff N an insect-eating warbler.

chiffon N a very fine transparent silk.

chignon N a soft bun or coil of hair.

chihuahua N a tiny dog with a large head, eyes and ears.

chilblain N a painful itchy swelling on the skin caused by exposure to cold.

child N (*children*) **1** a boy or girl between birth and physical maturity. **2** one's son or daughter. **3** DEROG an innocent or naive person. **4** someone seen as a typical product of a particular period, etc: a child of his time. ■ **childless** ADJ. ■ **childlike** ADJ.

childbearing N giving birth to a child.

childbirth N the process whereby a mother gives birth to a child.

childhood N the state or time of being a child.

childish ADJ **1** DEROG silly; immature. **2** relating to children or childhood; like a child.

childminder N an officially registered person who is paid to look after children.

childproof and **child-resistant** ADJ designed so as not to be able to be opened, operated, damaged, etc by a child.

child's play N, COLLOQ a basic or simple task.

chill N **1** a feeling of coldness. **2** a cold that causes shivering, chattering teeth, etc, commonly caused by exposure to a cold damp environment. **3** a feeling, esp sudden, of depression or fear.
> VB **1** TR & INTR to make or become cold. **2** to cause to feel cold. **3** to scare or discourage.

chilled ADJ **1** made cold. **2** hardened by chilling. **3** preserved by chilling.

chilli or **chili** N (*chillis* or *chillies*) **1** the fruit or pod of a variety of capsicum, which has a hot spicy flavour and is used in cooking, often in powdered form. **2** chilli con carne.

chilli con carne N a spicy Mexican dish of minced meat and beans, flavoured with chilli.

chilling ADJ frightening. ■ **chillingly** ADV.

chilly ADJ (*-ier, -iest*) **1** rather cold. **2** COLLOQ unfriendly; hostile. ■ **chilliness** N.

chime N the sound made by a clock, set of tuned bells, etc.
➢ VB **1** INTR of bells: to ring. **2** TR & INTR of a clock: to indicate (the time) by chiming.

chimera N a wild or impossible idea.

chimney N **1** a vertical structure that carries smoke, steam, fumes or heated air away from a fireplace, stove, furnace or engine. **2** the top part of this, rising from a roof.

chimneypot N a short hollow rounded fitting that sits in the opening at the top of a chimney.

chimney-sweep N someone who cleans soot out of chimneys, esp for a living.

chimp N, COLLOQ a chimpanzee.

chimpanzee N the most intelligent of the apes, found in tropical rainforests of Africa.

chin N the front protruding part of the lower jaw.
◆ **keep one's chin up** COLLOQ to stay cheerful in spite of misfortune or difficulty.

china SING N **1** articles made from a fine translucent earthenware, orig from China. **2** articles made from similar materials.
➢ ADJ made of china.

chinchilla N **1** a small S American mammal with a thick soft grey coat, a bushy tail and large round ears. **2** its soft grey fur.

chine N **1** the backbone. **2** a cut, esp of pork, which includes part of the backbone.

chink N **1** a small slit or crack. **2** a narrow beam of light shining through such a crack.

chinless ADJ, DEROG having a weak indecisive character.

chinos PL N trousers made from **chino**, a strong twilled cotton.

chintz N a cotton patterned fabric with bright colours printed on a light background.

chintzy ADJ (*-ier, -iest*) DEROG sentimentally or quaintly showy.

chinwag N, COLLOQ a chat.

chip VB (*-pp-*) **1** (sometimes **chip at sth**) to knock or strike small pieces off (a hard object or material). **2** INTR to be broken off in small pieces; to have small pieces broken off. **3** to shape by chipping. **4** TR & INTR, GOLF, FOOTBALL to strike the ball so that it goes high up in the air over a short distance.
➢ N **1** a small piece chipped off. **2** a place from which a piece has been chipped off: **a chip in the vase**. **3** BRIT (usu **chips**) strips of deep-fried potato. **4** N AMER (also **potato chip**) a potato crisp. **5** in gambling: a plastic counter used as a money token. **6** COMP a silicon chip. **7** a small piece of stone. **8** GOLF, FOOTBALL a short high shot or kick. ■ **chipped** ADJ.
◆ **chip in** COLLOQ **1** to interrupt. **2** TR & INTR to contribute (eg money).

chipboard N thin solid board made from compressed wood chips.

chipmunk N a small ground squirrel with reddish-brown fur, found esp in N America.

chipolata N a small sausage.

chipper ADJ, COLLOQ cheerful and lively.

chiropodist N someone who treats minor disorders of the feet. ■ **chiropody** N.

chiropractic N a method of treating pain by manual adjustment of the spinal column, etc, so as to release pressure on the nerves.
■ **chiropractor** N.

chirp VB **1** INTR of birds, grasshoppers, etc: to produce a short high-pitched sound. **2** TR & INTR to chatter or say something merrily.
➢ N a chirping sound.

chirpy ADJ (*-ier, -iest*) COLLOQ lively and merry.
■ **chirpiness** N.

chirrup VB, INTR of some birds and insects: to chirp, esp in little bursts.
➢ N a burst of chirping.

chisel N a hand tool which has a strong metal blade with a cutting edge at the tip, used for cutting and shaping wood or stone.
➢ VB (*-ll-*) to cut or shape (wood or stone) with a chisel.

chit[1] or **chitty** N **1** a short note or voucher

recording money owed or paid. **2** a note.

chit² N, DEROG **1** a cheeky girl. **2** a mere child.

chitchat N, COLLOQ **1** chatter. **2** gossip.
➤ VB, INTR to gossip idly.

chivalrous ADJ **a** gallant; **b** courteous.

chivalry N **1** courtesy and protectiveness, esp as shown by men towards women. **2** HIST a code of moral and religious behaviour followed by medieval knights.

chive N a plant of the onion family with thin hollow leaves used as a flavouring or garnish.

chivvy or **chivy** VB (**-ies, -ied**) to harass or pester someone.

chloride N, CHEM **a** a compound of chlorine with another element or radical; **b** a salt of hydrochloric acid.

chlorinate VB to treat (eg water) with, or cause (a substance) to combine with, chlorine. ■ **chlorination** N.

chlorine N, CHEM a greenish-yellow poisonous gas with a pungent smell, widely used as a disinfectant and bleach.

chlorofluorocarbon N, CHEM a compound of chlorine, fluorine and carbon, formerly used as an aerosol propellant and refrigerant, but now widely banned because of its damaging effects on the ozone layer.

chloroform N, CHEM a sweet-smelling liquid, formerly used as an anaesthetic.

chlorophyll N, BOT the green pigment, found in all green plants, that absorbs light energy from the Sun during photosynthesis.

chock N a heavy block or wedge used to prevent movement of a wheel, etc.

chock-a-block and **chock-full** ADJ tightly jammed; crammed full.

chocolate N **1** a food product, made from cacao beans. **2** an individual sweet made from or coated with this substance. **3** a hot drink prepared from this substance. **4** a dark-brown colour.
➤ ADJ **1** made from or coated with chocolate.

2 dark brown. ■ **chocolaty** or **chocolatey** ADJ.

choice N **1** the act or process of choosing. **2** the right, power, or opportunity to choose. **3** something or someone chosen. **4** a variety of things available for choosing between.
➤ ADJ select; worthy of being chosen.

choir N **1** an organized group of trained singers, esp one that performs in church. **2** the area, esp in a church, occupied by a choir.

choke VB **1** TR & INTR to prevent or be prevented from breathing by an obstruction in the throat. **2** to stop or interfere with breathing in this way. **3** (often **choke up**) to fill up, block or restrict something. **4** to restrict the development of.
➤ N **1** the sound or act of choking. **2** ENG a valve in the carburettor of a petrol engine that reduces the air supply and so gives a richer fuel/air mixture while the engine is still cold.

cholera N, PATHOL an acute and potentially fatal bacterial infection of the small intestine.

cholesterol N a sterol present in most body tissues, and associated with hardening of the arteries when present at high levels in the blood.

chomp VB, TR & INTR to munch noisily.
➤ N an act or sound of chomping.

choose VB (**chose, chosen**) **1** TR & INTR to take or select (one or more things or persons) from a larger number. **2** to decide; to think fit. **3** INTR to be inclined; to like: **I will leave when I choose.**

choosy ADJ (**-ier, -iest**) COLLOQ difficult to please; fussy.

chop¹ VB (**-pp-**) **1** to cut with a vigorous downward or sideways slicing action, with an axe, knife, etc. **2** to hit (a ball) with a sharp downwards stroke.
➤ N **1** a slice of pork, lamb or mutton containing a bone, esp a rib. **2** a chopping action or stroke. **3** a sharp downward stroke given to a ball. **4** in boxing, karate etc: a short sharp blow.

chop² VB (**-pp-**) to change direction or have a change of mind.

chopper N **1** COLLOQ a helicopter. **2** COLLOQ a

motorcycle with high handlebars. **3** a short-handled axe. **4** (**choppers**) COLLOQ the teeth.

choppy ADJ (*-ier, -iest*) of the sea, weather etc: rather rough. ■ **choppiness** N.

chops PL N the jaws or mouth, esp of an animal.

chopsticks PL N a pair of slender sticks used for eating with, chiefly in Oriental countries.

choral ADJ relating to, or to be sung by, a choir or chorus.

chorale or **choral** N a hymn tune with a slow dignified rhythm.

chord¹ N, MUS a combination of musical notes played together.

chord² N **1** ANAT another spelling of **cord**. **2** MATH a straight line joining two points on a curve or curved surface.

chore N **1** a domestic task. **2** a boring or unenjoyable task.

chorea N, PATHOL either of two disorders of the nervous system that cause rapid involuntary movements of the limbs.

choreograph VB to plan the choreography for (a dance, ballet, etc).

choreography N **1** the arrangement of the sequence and pattern of movements in dancing. **2** the steps of a dance or ballet. ■ **choreographer** N.

chorister N a singer in a choir.

chortle VB, INTR to laugh joyfully. ➤ N a joyful laugh.

chorus N **1** a set of lines in a song, sung as a refrain after each verse. **2** a large choir. **3** a piece of music for such a choir. **4** the group of singers and dancers supporting the soloists in an opera or musical show. **5** something uttered by a number of people at the same time: **a chorus of 'No's'**. **6** GR THEAT a group of actors, always on stage, who comment on developments in the plot. ➤ VB to say, sing or utter simultaneously.

choux pastry N a very light pastry.

chowder N, chiefly N AMER a thick soup or stew made from clams or fish with vegetables.

Christ N **1** the Messiah whose coming is prophesied in the Old Testament. **2** Jesus of Nazareth, or Jesus Christ, believed by Christians to be the Messiah. **3** a figure or picture of Jesus.

christen VB **1** to give a person, esp a baby, a name as part of the religious ceremony of receiving them into the Christian Church. **2** to give a name or nickname to someone. **3** HUMOROUS, COLLOQ to use something for the first time. ■ **christening** N.

Christendom N all Christian people and parts of the world.

Christian N someone who believes in, and follows the teachings of, Jesus Christ. ➤ ADJ **1** of Jesus Christ, the Christian religion or Christians. **2** COLLOQ showing virtues exemplified by Christ, such as kindness, tolerance and generosity. ■ **Christianity** N.

christian name N **1** LOOSELY anyone's first or given name; a forename. **2** the personal name given to a Christian at baptism.

Christmas N the annual Christian festival held on 25 December, which commemorates the birth of Christ. ■ **Christmassy** ADJ.

chromatic ADJ **1** relating to colours; coloured. **2** MUS relating to the chromatic scale.

chromatic scale N, MUS a scale which proceeds by semitones.

chrome N, NON-TECHNICAL chromium, esp when used as a silvery plating for other metals. ➤ VB **1** in dyeing: to treat with a chromium solution. **2** to plate with chrome.

chromium N, CHEM a hard silvery metallic element that is resistant to corrosion, used in electroplating and to make stainless steel.

chromosome N in the nucleus of a cell: any of a number of microscopic thread-like structures which contain, in the form of DNA, all the genetic information needed for the development of the cell and the organism.

chronic ADJ **1** of a disease or symptoms: long-lasting and often difficult to treat: **chronic pain**.

2 BRIT COLLOQ very bad; severe: *The film was chronic.* **3** habitual: *a chronic dieter*.

chronicle N (often **chronicles**) a record of historical events year by year in the order in which they occurred.
➤ VB to record (an event) in a chronicle.

chronological ADJ **1** according to the order of occurrence. **2** relating to chronology.

chronology N (*-ies*) **1** the study or science of determining the correct order of historical events. **2** the arrangement of events in order of occurrence. **3** a table or list showing events in order of occurrence. ■ **chronologist** N.

chronometer N a type of watch or clock, used esp at sea, which is designed to keep accurate time in all conditions.

chrysalis or **chrysalid** N (*-lises* or *-lides*) **1** the pupa of insects that undergo metamorphosis, eg butterflies. **2** the protective case that surrounds the pupa.

chrysanthemum N a garden plant of the daisy family, with large bushy flowers.

chubby ADJ (*-ier, -iest*) plump, esp in a childishly attractive way. ■ **chubbiness** N.

chuck[1] VB **1** COLLOQ to throw or fling. **2** to give (someone) an affectionate tap under the chin.
➤ N **1** COLLOQ a toss, fling or throw. **2** an affectionate tap under the chin.
◆ **chuck sth out** COLLOQ to get rid of it.

chuck[2] N a device for holding a piece of work in a lathe, or for holding the blade or bit in a drill.

chuckle VB, INTR to laugh quietly, esp in a half-suppressed private way.
➤ N an amused little laugh.

chuffed ADJ, BRIT COLLOQ very pleased.

chug VB (*-gg-*) INTR of a motor boat, motor car, etc: to progress with a quiet thudding noise.

chum N, COLLOQ a close friend. ■ **chummy** ADJ (*-ier, -iest*).

chump N, COLLOQ an idiot; a fool.

chunk N **1** a thick, esp irregularly shaped,

piece. **2** COLLOQ a considerable amount.

chunky ADJ (*-ier, -iest*) **1** thick-set; stockily or strongly built. **2** of clothes, fabrics, etc: thick; bulky. **3** solid and strong.

church N **1** a building for public Christian worship. **2** the religious services held in a church. **3** (**the Church**) the clergy as a profession or considered as a political group. **4** (usu **Church**) any of many branches of Christians with their own doctrines, etc.

churchgoer N someone who regularly attends church services.

churchman and **churchwoman** N a member of the clergy or of a church.

churchyard N the burial ground round a church.

churlish ADJ ill-mannered or rude.

churn N **1** a machine in which milk is vigorously shaken to make butter. **2** a large milk can.
➤ VB **1a** to make (butter) in a churn; **b** to turn (milk) into butter in a churn. **2** (often **churn sth up**) to shake or agitate it violently.
◆ **churn sth out** to keep producing things of tedious similarity in large quantities.

chute N **1** a sloping channel down which to send water, rubbish, etc. **2** a slide in a children's playground or swimming-pool. **3** a waterfall or rapid. **4** COLLOQ short for **parachute**.

chutney N a type of pickle, orig from India, made with fruit, vinegar, spices, sugar, etc.

chutzpah N, chiefly N AMER COLLOQ self-assurance bordering on impudence.

ciabatta N (*-tas* or *-te*) **1** Italian bread made with olive oil. **2** a loaf of this.

cicada N (*-das* or *-dae*) a large insect of mainly tropical regions, the male of which is noted for its high-pitched warbling whistle.

cider N an alcoholic drink made from apples.

cigar N a long slender roll of tobacco leaves for smoking.

cigarette N a tube of finely cut tobacco rolled in thin paper, for smoking.

cinch N, COLLOQ **1** an easily accomplished task. **2** a certainty.

cinder N **1** a piece of burnt coal or wood. **2** (**cinders**) ashes.

Cinderella N someone or something whose charms or merits go unnoticed.

cinema N **1** a theatre in which motion pictures are shown. **2** (usu **the cinema**) **a** motion pictures or films generally; **b** the art or business of making films. ■ **cinematic** ADJ.

cinematography N the art of making motion pictures. ■ **cinematographer** N.

cinnabar N **1** a bright red form of mercury sulphide. **2** a bright orange-red colour.

cinnamon N a spice obtained from the cured dried bark of a SE Asian tree.

cipher or **cypher** N **1** a secret code. **2** something written in code. **3** the key to a code. **4** an interlaced set of initials; a monogram. **5** MATH, OLD USE the symbol 0, used to fill blanks in writing numbers, but of no value itself. **6** a person or thing of no importance. ➤ VB to write (a message, etc) in code.

circa PREP (abbrev **c.** and **ca.**) used esp with dates: about; approximately: circa 1250.

circle N **1** a perfectly round two-dimensional figure that is bordered by the circumference, every point of which is an equal distance from the centre. **2** anything in the form of a circle. **3** a circular route. **4** in a theatre, auditorium etc: a gallery of seats above the main stalls. **5** a series or chain of events, steps or developments, ending at the point where it began. **6** a group of people associated in some way. ➤ VB **1** TR & INTR **a** to move in a circle; **b** to move in a circle round something. **2** to draw a circle round something.

circlet N **1** a simple band or hoop of gold, silver, etc worn on the head. **2** a small circle.

circuit N **1** a complete course, journey or route round something. **2** a race track, running-track, etc. **3** (sometimes **electric circuit**) a path consisting of various electrical devices joined together by wires, to allow an electric current to flow continuously through it. **4** a round of places made by a travelling judge. **6** SPORT a round of tournaments.

circuitous ADJ indirect.

circuitry N (-*ies*) ELEC **1** a plan or system of circuits used in a particular electronic or electrical device. **2** the equipment or components making up such a system.

circular ADJ **1** having the form of a circle. **2** moving or going round in a circle, leading back to the starting-point. **3** of reasoning, etc: illogical, since the truth of the premise cannot be proved without reference to the conclusion. **4** of a letter, etc: addressed and copied to a number of people. ➤ N a circular letter or notice. ■ **circularity** N.

circularize or **-ise** VB to send circulars.

circulate VB **1** TR & INTR to move or cause to move round freely, esp in a fixed route. **2** TR & INTR to spread; to pass round: circulate the report. **3** INTR to move around talking to different people. ■ **circulatory** ADJ.

circulation N **1** the act or process of circulating. **2** ANAT in most animals: the system of blood vessels that supplies oxygenated blood pumped by the heart to all parts of the body, and that transports deoxygenated blood to the lungs. **3 a** the distribution of a newspaper or magazine; **b** the number of copies sold.

circumcise VB to cut away all or part of the foreskin of the penis of (a male), as a religious rite or medical necessity. ■ **circumcision** N.

circumference N **1** GEOM the length of the boundary of a circle. **2** the boundary of any area. **3** the distance represented by these.

circumflex N in some languages, eg French: a mark placed over a vowel, eg ô, û, as an indication of pronunciation, length or the omission of a letter formerly pronounced.

circumlocution N an unnecessarily long or indirect way of saying something. ■ **circumlocutory** ADJ.

circumnavigate VB to sail or fly round, esp the world. ■ **circumnavigation** N.

circumscribe VB 1 to put a boundary, or draw a line, round something. 2 to limit or restrict something. ■ **circumscription** N.

circumspect ADJ cautious; prudent; wary. ■ **circumspection** N.

circumstance N 1 (usu **circumstances**) a fact, occurrence or condition, esp when relating to an act or event: **died in mysterious circumstances**. 2 (**circumstances**) one's financial situation. 3 events that one cannot control; fate. 4 ceremony.

circumstantial ADJ 1 relating to or dependent on circumstance. 2 of an account of an event: full of detailed description, etc.

circumvent VB 1 to find a way of getting round or evading (a rule, law, etc). 2 to outwit or frustrate someone. ■ **circumvention** N.

circus N 1 **a** a travelling company of performers including acrobats, clowns and often trained animals, etc; **b** a performance by such a company. 2 in ancient Rome: an open-air stadium for chariot-racing, etc.

cirrhosis N, PATHOL a progressive disease of the liver, esp alcohol related.

cirrus N (-ri) METEOROL a common type of high cloud with a wispy appearance.

cissy see **sissy**

cistern N a tank storing water.

citadel N a fortress built close to or within a city, for its protection and as a place of refuge.

citation N 1 the quoting or citing of something as example or proof. 2 a passage quoted from a book, etc. 3 a special official commendation or award for merit, bravery, etc.

cite VB 1 to quote or mention as an example, illustration or proof. 2 LAW to summon someone to appear in court. 3 to commend someone in an official report: **cited for bravery**.

citizen N 1 an inhabitant of a city or town. 2 a native of a country or state, or a naturalized member of it.

citizenry N (-ies) the citizens of a place.

citizenship N 1 the status or position of a citizen. 2 the rights and duties of a citizen.

citric acid N, CHEM an organic acid present in the juice of citrus fruit, used as a food flavouring and antioxidant.

citrus N (also **citrus fruit**) any of a group of edible fruits with a tough outer peel enclosing juicy flesh, eg oranges and lemons.

city N (-ies) 1 any large town. 2 in the UK: a town with a royal charter and usu a cathedral. 3 the body of inhabitants of a city. 4 (**the City**) the business centre of a city, esp London.

city hall N **a** the local government of a city; **b** the building in which it is housed.

civet N 1 (also **civet cat**) a small spotted and striped carnivorous mammal found in Asia and Africa. 2 a strong-smelling fluid secreted by this animal, used to make perfumes last.

civic ADJ relating to a city, citizen or citizenship.

civics SING N the study of local government and of the rights and duties of citizenship.

civil ADJ 1 relating to the community: **civil affairs**. 2 relating to or occurring between citizens: **civil disturbances**. 3 **a** relating to ordinary citizens; **b** not military, legal or religious. 4 LAW relating to cases about individual rights, etc, not criminal cases. 5 polite. ■ **civilly** ADV.

civil engineering N the branch of engineering concerned with the design, construction, and maintenance of roads, bridges, railways, tunnels, docks, etc.

civilian N anyone who is not a member of the armed forces or the police force.

civility N (-ies) 1 politeness. 2 **a** an act of politeness; **b** a polite remark or gesture.

civilization or **-isation** N 1 a stage of development in human society that is socially, politically, culturally and technologically advanced. 2 the parts of the world that have reached such a stage. 3 the state of having achieved such a stage. 4 usu HIST a people and their society and culture: **the Minoan**

civilization. **5** intellectual or spiritual enlightenment, as opposed to brutishness.

civilize or **-ise** VB **1** to lead out of a state of barbarity to a more advanced stage of social development. **2** to enlighten morally, intellectually and spiritually. ■ **civilized** ADJ.

civil service N the body of officials employed by a government to administer the affairs of a country. ■ **civil servant** N.

civil war N a war between citizens of the same state.

CJD ABBREV Creutzfeldt–Jakob disease.

clack N a sharp noise made by one hard object striking another.
➤ VB, TR & INTR to make or cause something to make this kind of noise.

clad ADJ, LITERARY **1** clothed. **2** covered. Also IN COMPOUNDS: **velvet–clad • stone–clad.**
➤ VB (*clad, cladding*) to cover eg brick or stonework with a different material, esp to form a protective layer.

claim VB **1** to state something firmly, insisting on its truth. **2** to declare oneself (to be, to have done, etc). **3** to assert that one has something. **4** TR & INTR to demand as a right. **5** to take or use up something. **6 a** to need; **b** to have a right to. **7** to declare that one is the owner of something.
➤ N **1** a statement of something as a truth. **2** a demand, esp for something to which one has, or believes one has, a right: **lay claim to the throne. 3** a right to or reason for something: **a claim to fame. 4** something one has claimed, eg a piece of land or a sum of money. **5** a demand for compensation, in accordance with an insurance policy, etc. ■ **claimant** N.

clairvoyance or **clairvoyancy** N the alleged ability to see into the future, or know things that cannot be discovered through the normal range of senses. ■ **clairvoyant** N, ADJ.

clam N any of various bivalve shellfish.

clamber VB, INTR to climb using one's hands as well as one's feet.

clammy ADJ (*-ier, -iest*) **1** moist or damp, esp unpleasantly so. **2** of the weather: humid.

clamour N **1** a noise of shouting or loud talking. **2** loud protesting or loud demands.
➤ VB, INTR to make a loud continuous outcry.

clamp N **1** a tool with adjustable jaws for gripping things firmly or pressing parts together. **2** (usu **wheel clamp**) a heavy metal device fitted to the wheels of an illegally parked car, to prevent it being moved.
➤ VB **1** to fasten together or hold with a clamp. **2** to fit a clamp to a wheel of (a parked car). **3** to hold, grip or shut tightly.
◆ **clamp down on sth** or **sb** to put a stop to or to control it or them strictly.

clampdown N **1** a suppressive measure. **2** repression of activity: **clampdown on drugs.**

clan N **1** a group of families, often with the same surname, and (esp formerly) led by a chief. **2** HUMOROUS one's family or relations. **3** a group of people with similar interests, etc.

clandestine ADJ kept secret; furtive; surreptitious. ■ **clandestinely** ADV.

clang VB, TR & INTR to ring or make something ring loudly and deeply.
➤ N this ringing sound.

clank N a sharp metallic sound like pieces of metal striking together.
➤ VB, TR & INTR to make or cause something to make such a sound.

clannish ADJ, DEROG of a group of people: closely united, with little interest in others.

clap VB (*-pp-*) **1** TR & INTR to strike the palms of (one's hands) together in order to mark (a rhythm), gain attention, etc. **2** TR & INTR to applaud someone or something by clapping. **3** to strike someone softly with the palm of the hand, usu as a friendly gesture. **4** to place forcefully.
➤ N **1** an act of clapping. **2** the sudden loud noise made by thunder.

clapper N the dangling piece of metal inside a bell that strikes against the sides to make it ring.

claptrap N meaningless talk.

claret N **1** a French red wine, esp from the Bordeaux area in SW France. **2** the deep reddish–purple colour of this wine.

clarify VB (*-ies, -ied*) TR & INTR **1** to make or become clearer or easier to understand. **2** of butter, fat, etc: to make or become clear by heating. ■ **clarification** N.

clarinet N, MUS a woodwind instrument with a single reed. ■ **clarinettist** N.

clarion N, chiefly POETIC, HIST an old kind of trumpet with a shrill sound: **a clarion call**.

clarity N the quality of being clear.

clash N **1** a loud noise, like that of metal objects striking each other. **2** a serious disagreement. **3** a fight, battle or match.
➤ VB **1** TR & INTR of metal objects, etc: to strike against each other noisily. **2** (often **clash with sb**) to fight; to have a battle; to disagree violently. **3** INTR of commitments, etc: to coincide, usu not fortuitously. **4** INTR of colours, etc: to be unharmonious together.

clasp N **1** a fastening on jewellery, a bag, etc made of two parts that link together. **2** a firm grip, or act of gripping.
➤ VB **1** to hold or take hold of someone or something firmly. **2** to fasten or secure something with a clasp.

class N **1** a lesson or lecture. **2** a number of pupils taught together. **3** esp US the body of students that begin or finish university or school in the same year: **class of '94**. **4** a category, kind or type. **5** a grade or standard. **6** any of the social groupings into which people fall according to their job, wealth, etc. **7** the system by which society is divided into such groups. **8** COLLOQ **a** stylishness in dress, behaviour, etc; **b** good quality.
➤ VB **a** to regard someone or something as belonging to a certain class; **b** to put into a category.

classic ADJ **1** made of or belonging to the highest quality; established as the best. **2** entirely typical. **3** simple, neat and elegant, esp in a traditional style.
➤ N **1** an established work of literature. **2** an outstanding example of its type. **3** something, eg an item of clothing, which will always last,

irrespective of fashions and fads.
■ **classically** ADV.

classical ADJ **1** of literature, art, etc: **a** from ancient Greece and Rome; **b** in the style of ancient Greece and Rome. **2** of architecture or the other arts: showing the influence of ancient Greece and Rome. **3** of music and related arts: having an established, traditional style and form. **4** simple; pure; without complicated decoration. **5** of education: concentrating on Latin, Greek and the humanities.

classicism N in art and literature: a simple, elegant style based on the Roman and Greek principles of beauty, restraint and clarity.

classics SING N (often **the Classics**) **a** the study of Latin and Greek; **b** the study of ancient Greece and Rome.

classification N **1** arrangement and division of things and people into classes. **2** a group or class into which a person or thing is put.

classified ADJ **1** arranged in groups or classes. **2** of information: secret or restricted.

classify VB (*-ies, -ied*) **1** to put into a category. **2** of information: to declare it secret.

classless ADJ of a community, society etc: not divided into social classes.

classmate N a fellow pupil or student in one's class at school or college.

classroom N a room in a school or college where classes are taught.

classy ADJ (*-ier, -iest*) COLLOQ **a** stylish or fashionable; **b** superior.

clatter N a loud noise made by hard objects striking each other.
➤ VB, TR & INTR to make or cause to make this noise.

clause N **1** GRAM **a** a group of words that includes a subject and its related finite verb, and which may or may not constitute a sentence; **b** a group of words with a similar grammatical function, but which has no expressed subject or finite verb. **2** LAW a paragraph or section in a contract, will or act of parliament.

claustrophobia N an irrational fear of being in confined spaces. ■ **claustrophobic** ADJ.

clavichord N an early keyboard instrument.

clavicle N either of two slender bones linking the shoulder-blades with the breastbone.

claw N 1 a hard curved pointed nail on the end of each digit of the foot in birds, most reptiles and many mammals. 2 the foot of an animal or bird with a number of such nails. 3 something resembling a claw, eg part of a device.
➤ VB, TR & INTR (often **claw at sth**) to tear or scratch it with claws, nails or fingers.
◆ **claw sth back** 1 of a government: to recover money given away in benefits and allowances by imposing a new tax. 2 to regain something with difficulty.

clay N 1 GEOL a poorly draining soil which is pliable when wet and is used to make pottery, bricks, ceramics, etc. 2 earth or soil generally. 3 POETIC the substance of the human body.

claymore N, HIST a two-edged broadsword used by Scottish highlanders.

clean ADJ 1 free from dirt or contamination. 2 not containing anything harmful to health; pure. 3 pleasantly fresh: **a clean taste**. 4 recently washed. 5 hygienic in habits. 6 unused; unmarked. 7 neat and even: **a clean cut**. 8 simple and elegant. 9 clear of legal offences: **a clean driving licence**. 10 morally pure; innocent. 11 of humour, etc: not offensive or obscene. 12 fair: **a clean fight**. 13 absolute; complete: **a clean break**.
➤ ADV 1 COLLOQ completely: **I clean forgot**. 2 straight or directly.
➤ VB, TR & INTR to make or become free from dirt.
➤ N an act of cleaning.

clean-cut ADJ 1 pleasingly regular in outline or shape. 2 neat; respectable.

cleaner N 1 someone employed to clean inside buildings, offices, etc. 2 a machine or substance used for cleaning. 3 (usu **cleaners**) a shop where clothes, etc are cleaned.

cleanly ADV 1 in a clean way. 2 tidily; efficiently; easily. ■ **cleanliness** N.

cleanse VB 1 to clean or get rid of dirt from someone or something. 2 to purify someone or something. ■ **cleanser** N.

clean-shaven ADJ of men: without facial hair.

clear ADJ 1 transparent; easy to see through. 2 of weather, etc: not misty or cloudy. 3 of the skin: healthy; unblemished by spots, etc. 4 a easy to see, hear or understand; b lucid. 5 bright; sharp; well-defined: **a clear photograph**. 6 of vision: not obstructed. 7 certain; having no doubts or confusion. 8 definite; free of doubt, ambiguity or confusion. 9 evident; obvious. 10 free from obstruction: **a clear path**. 11 well away from something; out of range of or contact with it: **well clear of the rocks**. 12 free of it; no longer affected by it. 13 of the conscience, etc: free from guilt, etc. 14 free of appointments, etc.
➤ ADV 1 in a clear manner. 2 completely: **get clear away**. 3 N AMER all the way: **see clear to the hills**. 4 well away from something; out of the way of it: **steer clear of trouble**.
➤ VB 1 TR & INTR to make or become clear, free of obstruction, etc. 2 to remove or move out of the way. 3 to prove or declare to be innocent or free from suspicion. 4 to get over or past something without touching: **clear the fence**. 5 to make as profit over expenses. 6 to pass inspection by (customs). 7 to give or get official permission for (a plan, etc). 8 to approve someone for a special assignment, access to secret information, etc. 9 to pay a debt. 10 TR & INTR to give or receive clearance.
◆ **clear off** or **out** COLLOQ to go away.
◆ **clear sth out** to rid it of rubbish, etc.
◆ **clear up** 1 of the weather: to brighten after rain, a storm, etc. 2 to get better.
◆ **clear sth up** 1 to tidy up a mess, room, etc. 2 to solve a mystery, etc.

clearance N 1 the act of clearing. 2 the distance between one object and another passing beside or under it. 3 permission.

clear-cut ADJ clear; sharp.

clearing N an area in a forest, etc that has been cleared of trees, etc.

clearly ADV 1 in a clear manner: **speak clearly**. 2 obviously: **Clearly, he's wrong**.

clear-out N a clearing out of something, eg rubbish, possessions, etc.

clear-sighted ADJ capable of, or showing, accurate observation and good judgement.

clearway N a stretch of road on which cars may not stop except in an emergency.

cleavage N 1 COLLOQ the hollow between a woman's breasts. 2 GEOL a the splitting of rocks into thin parallel sheets; b the splitting of a crystal to give smooth surfaces.

cleave[1] VB (PAT *clove, cleft* or *cleaved*, PAP *cloven, cleft* or *cleaved*) TR & INTR, FORMAL OR LITERARY 1 to split or divide. 2 to cut or slice.

cleave[2] VB, INTR to cling or stick.

cleaver N a knife with a large square blade, used esp by butchers for chopping meat.

clef N, MUS a symbol placed on a stave to indicate the pitch of the notes written on it.

cleft N a split, wide crack or deep indentation. ➤ ADJ split; divided.

cleft palate N, PATHOL a split in the palate caused by the failure of the two sides of the mouth to fuse together in the fetus.

clemency N 1 the quality of being clement. 2 mercy.

clement ADJ of the weather: mild.

clementine N a citrus fruit, a hybrid of a tangerine and an orange.

clench VB 1 to close one's teeth or one's fists tightly, esp in anger. 2 to hold or grip firmly.

clergy SING OR PL N (*-ies*) the ministers of the Christian church, or the priests of any religion. ■ **clergyman** and **clergywoman** N.

cleric N a clergyman.

clerical ADJ 1 relating to clerks, office workers or office work. 2 relating to the clergy.

clerihew N a humorous poem about a famous person, consisting of two short couplets.

clerk N 1 in an office or bank: someone who deals with accounts, records, files, etc. 2 in a law court: someone who keeps records or accounts. 3 a public official in charge of the records and business affairs of the town council. 4 N AMER a shop assistant or hotel receptionist. ■ **clerkship** N.

clever ADJ 1 good or quick at learning and understanding. 2 skilful, dexterous, nimble or adroit. 3 well thought out; ingenious. ■ **cleverly** ADV. ■ **cleverness** N.

cliché N, DEROG a once striking and effective phrase or combination of words which has become stale and hackneyed through overuse. ■ **clichéd** or **cliché'd** ADJ.

click N a short sharp sound like that made by two parts of a mechanism locking into place. ➤ VB 1 TR & INTR to make or cause to make a click. 2 INTR, COLLOQ to become clear or understood. 3 COMP to press and release one of the buttons on a mouse. 4 INTR of two or more people: to instantly get along very well.

client N 1 someone using the services of a professional institution, eg a bank. 2 a customer.

clientele N the clients of a professional person, customers of a shopkeeper, etc.

cliff N a high steep rock face.

cliffhanger N a story that keeps one in suspense up to the end.

climate N 1 the average weather conditions of a particular region of the world over a long period of time. 2 a part of the world considered from the point of view of its weather conditions. 3 a current trend in general feeling, opinion, policies, etc. ■ **climatic** ADJ.

climax N 1 the high point or culmination of events or of an experience. 2 a sexual orgasm. ➤ VB, TR & INTR 1 to come or bring to a climax. 2 INTR to experience orgasm. ■ **climactic** ADJ.

climb VB 1 (often **climb up**) to mount or ascend (a hill, ladder, etc), often using hands and feet. 2 TR & INTR to rise or go up. 3 INTR to increase. 4 INTR to slope upwards. 5 of plants: to grow upwards using tendrils, etc. ➤ N 1 an act of climbing. 2 a slope to be climbed. ■ **climbable** ADJ. ■ **climbing** N.
◆ **climb down** 1 to descend. 2 to concede

one's position on some issue, etc.

climb-down N a dramatic change of mind or concession, often humiliating.

climber N 1 a climbing plant. 2 a mountaineer.

clinch VB 1 to settle something finally and decisively, eg an argument, deal, etc. 2 INTR, COLLOQ to embrace.
➤ N 1 an act of clinching. 2 BOXING, WRESTLING an act of clinging to each other to prevent further blows, etc. 3 COLLOQ an embrace.

clincher N a point, argument or circumstance that finally settles or decides a matter.

cling VB (*clung*) INTR 1 to hold firmly or tightly; to stick. 2 to be emotionally over-dependent. 3 to refuse to let go. ■ **clingy** ADJ (*-ier, -iest*).

clingfilm N a thin clear plastic material that adheres to itself, used for wrapping food, etc.

clinic N 1 a private hospital or nursing home that specializes in the treatment of particular diseases or disorders. 2 a department of a hospital or a health centre which specializes in one particular area. 3 the instruction given to medical students, usu at the patient's bedside in a hospital ward. 4 a session in which an expert is available for consultation.

clinical ADJ 1 relating to, or like, a clinic or hospital. 2 of medical studies: based on, or relating to, direct observation and treatment of the patient. 3 cold; impersonal; unemotional or detached. 4 severely plain and simple, with no personal touches. ■ **clinically** ADV.

clink N a short sharp ringing sound.
➤ VB, TR & INTR to make or cause to make such a sound.

clinker N a mass of fused ash or slag left unburnt in a furnace.

clip[1] VB (*-pp-*) 1 to cut (hair, wool, etc). 2 to trim or cut off the hair, wool or fur of (an animal). 3 to punch out a piece from (a ticket) to show that it has been used. 4 to cut (an article, etc) from a newspaper, etc. 5 COLLOQ to hit or strike someone or something sharply.
➤ N 1 an act of clipping. 2 a short sequence extracted from a film. 3 COLLOQ a sharp blow.

4 COLLOQ speed; rapid speed: **moving at a fair clip.**

clip[2] N 1 often IN COMPOUNDS any of various devices, usu small ones, for holding things together or in position: **paper clip. 2** (also **cartridge clip**) a container for bullets attached to a gun, that feeds bullets into it.
➤ VB (*-pp-*) to fasten something with a clip.

clipboard N a firm board with a clip at the top for holding paper, forms, etc.

clipped ADJ 1 of the form of a word: shortened, eg **deli** from **delicatessen. 2** of speaking style: **a** tending to shorten vowels, omit syllables, etc; **b** curt and distinct.

clippers PL N, often IN COMPOUNDS a clipping device: **nail clippers.**

clipping N 1 a piece clipped off: **hair clippings. 2** a cutting from a newspaper, etc.

clique N, DEROG a group of people who stick together and are hostile towards outsiders.

clitoris N, ANAT a small highly sensitive organ located in front of the opening of the vagina. ■ **clitoral** ADJ.

cloak N 1 a loose outdoor garment, usu sleeveless, fastened at the neck. 2 a covering: **a cloak of mist.**
➤ VB to cover up or conceal something.

cloak-and-dagger ADJ full of adventure, mystery, plots, spying, etc.

cloakroom N **a** a room where coats, hats, etc may be left; **b** a room containing a WC.

clobber VB, COLLOQ 1 to beat or hit someone very hard. 2 to defeat someone completely. 3 to criticize someone severely.

cloche N 1 a covering for protecting young plants from frost, etc. 2 a woman's close-fitting dome-shaped hat.

clock N 1 a device for measuring and indicating time, usu by means of a digital display or pointers on a dial. 2 a device that synchronizes the timing in switching circuits, transmission systems, etc. 3 (**the clock**) COLLOQ **a** a mileometer; **b** a speedometer. 4 (in full

time clock) a device for recording the arrival and departure times of employees.
➤ VB **1** to measure or record (time) using such a device. **2** to record with a stopwatch the time taken by (a racer, etc) to complete a distance, etc. **3** COLLOQ to travel at (a speed as shown on a speedometer).

clockwise ADJ, ADV moving, etc in the same direction as the hands of a clock move.

clockwork N a mechanism like that of some clocks, working by means of gears and a spring that must be wound periodically.
➤ ADJ operated by clockwork.
◆ **like clockwork** without difficulties.

clod N **1** a lump of earth, clay, etc. **2** COLLOQ a stupid person.

clodhopper N, COLLOQ **1** a clumsy person. **2** a large heavy boot or shoe.

clog N a shoe carved entirely from wood, or having a thick wooden sole.
➤ VB (*-gg-*) TR & INTR to obstruct or become obstructed so that movement is difficult.

cloister N **1** a covered walkway built around a garden or quadrangle. **2** a place of religious retreat, eg a monastery or convent.
➤ VB to keep someone away from the problems of normal life in the world.
■ **cloistered** ADJ.

clone N **1** BIOL any of a group of genetically identical cells or organisms derived from a single parent cell or organism by asexual reproduction. **2** BIOL any of a large number of identical copies of a gene produced by genetic engineering. **3** COLLOQ a person or thing that looks like someone or something else.
➤ VB **1** to produce a set of identical cells or organisms from (a single parent cell or organism). **2** to produce many identical copies of (a gene) by genetic engineering. **3** to produce replicas of, or to copy something.

close[1] ADJ **1** near in space or time; at a short distance. **2 a** near in relationship: **a close relation; b** intimate. **3** touching or almost touching. **4** tight; dense or compact; with little space between: **a close fit. 5** near to the surface. **6** thorough; searching: **a close reading. 7** of a contest, etc: with little difference between entrants, etc. **8** (often **close to sth**) about to happen, on the point of doing it, etc: **close to tears. 9** similar to the original, or to something else: **a close resemblance.** **10** uncomfortably warm; stuffy. **11** secretive. **12** mean. **13** heavily guarded: **close arrest.**
➤ ADV **1** often IN COMPOUNDS in a close manner; closely: **follow close behind. 2** at close range.
■ **closely** ADV. ■ **closeness** N.

close[2] VB **1** TR & INTR to shut. **2** (sometimes **close sth off**) to block (a road, etc) so as to prevent use. **3** TR & INTR of shops, etc: to stop or cause to stop being open to the public for a period of time. **4** TR & INTR of a factory, business, etc: to stop or cause to stop operating permanently. **5** TR & INTR to conclude. **6** TR & INTR to join up or come together; to cause edges, etc, of something to come together. **7** to settle or agree on something: **close a deal.**
➤ N an end or conclusion.
◆ **close down** to close permanently.

closed ADJ **1** shut; blocked. **2** of a community or society: exclusive, with membership restricted to a chosen few.

closed-circuit television N a TV system serving a limited number of receivers, eg within a building.

closed shop N a workplace which requires employees to be members of a trade union.

close-knit ADJ of a group, community, etc: closely bound together.

close-range ADJ **1** in, at or within a short distance. **2** eg of a gun: fired from close by.

close shave and **close call** N a narrow or lucky escape.

closet N **1** chiefly N AMER a cupboard. **2** OLD USE a small private room. **3** AS ADJ not openly declared: **a closet gambler.**
➤ VB to shut away in private, eg for discussion.

close-up N a photograph, television shot, etc taken at close range.

closure N the act of closing something, eg a business or a transport route.

clot N **1** a soft semi-solid mass, esp one formed in blood. **2** BRIT COLLOQ a fool.
➤ VB (*-tt-*) TR & INTR to form into clots.

cloth N **1** woven, knitted or felted material. **2** often IN COMPOUNDS a piece of fabric for a special use: **tablecloth**. **3** (**the cloth**) the clergy.

clothe VB (PA T, PA P *clothed* or *clad*) **1** to cover or provide someone with clothes. **2** to dress someone. **3** to cover, conceal or disguise someone or something: **hills clothed in mist**.

clothes PL N **1** articles of dress for covering the body. **2** bedclothes.

clothesline N a rope, usu suspended outdoors, on which washed clothes, etc are hung to dry.

clothing N clothes collectively.

cloud N **1** METEOROL a visible floating mass of small water droplets or ice crystals suspended in the atmosphere above the Earth's surface. **2** a visible mass of particles of dust or smoke in the atmosphere. **3** a circumstance that causes anxiety. **4** a state of gloom or suspicion.
➤ VB **1** TR & INTR (usu **cloud over** or **cloud sth over**) to make or become misty or cloudy. **2** INTR (often **cloud over**) of the face: to develop a troubled expression. **3** to make dull or confused. **4** to spoil. ■ **cloudless** ADJ.
◆ **with one's head in the clouds** COLLOQ preoccupied with one's own thoughts.

cloudburst N a sudden heavy downpour of rain over a small area.

cloudy ADJ (*-ier, -iest*) **1** full of clouds; overcast. **2** not clear; muddy.

clout COLLOQ, N **1** a blow or cuff. **2** influence or power.
➤ VB to hit or cuff.

clove N **1** the strong-smelling dried flower-bud of a tropical evergreen tree, used as a spice. **2** one of the sections into which a compound bulb, esp of garlic, naturally splits.

cloven hoof and **cloven foot** N the partially divided hoof of various mammals.

clover N a small plant with leaves divided into three leaflets and small red or white flowers.

clown N **1** in a circus or pantomime, etc: a comic performer, usu wearing ridiculous clothes and make-up. **2** someone who behaves comically. **3** DEROG a fool.
➤ VB, INTR to play the clown.

cloy VB **1** INTR to become distasteful through excess, esp of sweetness. **2** to satiate to the point of disgust. ■ **cloying** ADJ.

club N **1** a stick, usu thicker at one end, used as a weapon. **2** in various sports, esp golf: a stick with a specially shaped head, used to hit the ball. **3** a society or association. **4** the place where such a group meets. **5** a building with dining and sleeping facilities for its members. **6** a nightclub. **7** CARDS **a** (**clubs**) one of the four suits of playing-cards, with a black cloverleaf-shaped symbol (♣); **b** a playing-card of this suit.
➤ VB (*-bb-*) to beat (a person, animal, etc) with a club.

club foot N a congenital deformity in which the foot is twisted down and turned inwards.

cluck N the sound made by a hen.
➤ VB, INTR **1** of a hen: to make such a sound. **2** to express disapproval by making a similar sound.

clue N **1** a fact or circumstance which helps towards the solution of a crime or a mystery. **2** in a crossword puzzle: a word or words representing a problem to be solved.

clueless ADJ, DEROG incompetent or ignorant.

clump N **1** a group or cluster of something, eg trees or people standing close together. **2** a dull heavy sound, eg of treading feet. **3** a shapeless mass: **a clump of weeds**.
➤ VB **1** INTR to walk with a heavy tread. **2** TR & INTR to form into clumps.

clumsy ADJ (*-ier, -iest*) **1** unskilful with the hands or awkward and ungainly in movement. **2** badly or awkwardly made. ■ **clumsily** ADV. ■ **clumsiness** N.

clunk N the sound of a heavy object, esp a metal one, striking something.
➤ VB, TR & INTR to make or cause to make such a sound.

cluster N 1 a small group or gathering. 2 a number of flowers growing on one stem. ➤ VB, TR & INTR to form into a cluster or clusters.

clutch[1] VB 1 to grasp something tightly. 2 INTR (usu **clutch at sth**) to try to grasp it. ➤ N 1 (usu **clutches**) control or power. 2 any device for connecting and disconnecting two rotating shafts, esp the device in a motor vehicle that transmits the driving force from engine to gearbox. 3 in a motor vehicle: the pedal operating this device. 4 a grasp.

clutch[2] N 1 a number of eggs laid at the same time. 2 a brood of newly hatched birds.

clutter N an untidy accumulation of objects, or the confused overcrowded state caused by it. ➤ VB (often **clutter sth up**) to overcrowd it or make it untidy with accumulated objects. ■ **cluttered** ADJ.

coach N 1 a railway carriage. 2 a bus designed for long-distance travel. 3 HIST a closed horse-drawn carriage. 4 a trainer. ➤ VB, TR & INTR to train or instruct. ■ **coaching** N.

coachwork N the painted outer bodywork of a motor or rail vehicle.

coagulate VB, TR & INTR of a liquid: to become clotted or curdled, or to form a soft semi-solid mass. ■ **coagulation** N. ■ **coagulant** N.

coal N 1 a hard brittle carbonaceous rock, formed from partially decomposed plant material and used as a fuel. 2 a piece of this.

coalesce VB, INTR to come together to form a single mass. ■ **coalescence** N.

coalition N a temporary alliance.

coal tar N a thick black liquid obtained as a by-product during the manufacture of coke, and used in the manufacture of drugs, dyes, etc.

coarse ADJ 1 rough or open in texture. 2 rough or crude; not refined. 3 rude or offensive. ■ **coarsely** ADV. ■ **coarseness** N.

coarse fish N a freshwater fish, other than trout and salmon. ■ **coarse fishing** N.

coarsen VB, TR & INTR to make or become coarse.

coast N the zone of land that borders the sea. ➤ VB, INTR 1 to travel downhill, eg on a bicycle or in a motor vehicle, relying on gravity or momentum rather than power. 2 to progress smoothly and satisfactorily without much effort. ■ **coastal** ADJ.

coaster N 1 a vessel that sails along the coast. 2 a small mat or tray placed under a cup, glass, etc to protect the table surface.

coastguard N 1 an official organization stationed on the coast which rescues people at sea, etc. 2 a member of this organization.

coastline N the shape of the coast.

coat N 1 an outer garment with long sleeves, typically reaching below the waist. 2 any similar garment, eg a jacket. 3 the hair, fur or wool of an animal. 4 a covering or application of something eg paint, dust, sugar, etc. ➤ VB to cover with a layer of something. ■ **coating** N.

coat-hanger N a shaped piece of wood, plastic or metal with a hook, on which to hang clothes.

coat of arms N (*coats of arms*) a heraldic shield bearing the special insignia of a particular person, family, organization or town.

coat-tails PL N the two long pieces hanging down at the back of a man's tailcoat.

coax VB 1 (often **coax sb into** or **out of sth**) to persuade them, using flattery, promises, kind words, etc. 2 to get something by coaxing. 3 to manipulate something patiently.

cob N 1 a short-legged sturdy horse used for riding. 2 a male swan. 3 a corncob. 4 BRIT a loaf with a rounded top.

cobalt N, CHEM a hard silvery-white metallic element commonly used in alloys to produce cutting tools and magnets.

cobber N, AUSTRAL & NZ COLLOQ a pal or mate.

cobble[1] and **cobblestone** N a rounded stone used esp formerly to surface streets. ➤ VB to pave with these. ■ **cobbled** ADJ.

cobble[2] VB 1 to mend (shoes). 2 (often **cobble**

sth together or **up**) to assemble or put it together roughly or hastily.

cobbler N someone who mends shoes.

cobra N any of various species of venomous snake found in Africa and Asia.

cobweb N 1 a web of fine sticky threads spun by a spider. 2 a single thread from this.

coca N 1 either of two S American shrubs whose leaves contain cocaine. 2 the leaves of the shrub chewed as a stimulant.

cocaine N, MED an addictive narcotic drug obtained from the leaves of the coca plant.

coccyx N (**-cyges**) ANAT in humans and certain apes: a small triangular tail-like bone at the base of the spine.

cochineal N a bright red pigment widely used as a food colouring.

cochlea N (**-leae**) ANAT in the inner ear of vertebrates: a hollow spirally coiled structure which converts the vibrations of sound waves into nerve impulses. ■ **cochlear** ADJ.

cock N 1 an adult male bird. 2 a stopcock. 3 the hammer of a gun which, when raised and let go by the trigger, produces the discharge. 4 COARSE SLANG the penis. ➢ VB 1 to turn in a particular direction: **cock an ear**. 2 to draw back the hammer of a gun. 3 to set (one's hat) at an angle.

cockade N, HIST a feather or a rosette of ribbon worn on the hat as a badge.

cock-a-hoop ADJ, COLLOQ 1 jubilant; exultant. 2 boastful.

cockatoo N a light-coloured parrot with a brightly coloured erectile crest on its head.

cock-crow N dawn; early morning.

cocked hat N, HIST a three-cornered hat with upturned brim.

cockerel N a young cock.

cock-eyed ADJ, COLLOQ 1 crooked; lopsided. 2 senseless; crazy; impractical.

cockle N an edible bivalve shellfish with a rounded and ribbed shell.

cockney N 1 (often **Cockney**) a LOOSELY a native of London, esp of the East End; **b** STRICTLY someone born within the sound of Bow Bells. 2 the dialect used by Cockneys.

cockpit N 1 in an aircraft: the compartment for the pilot and crew. 2 in a racing-car: the driver's seat. 3 NAUT the part of a small yacht, etc which contains the wheel and tiller.

cockroach N a large insect which infests houses, etc.

cocksure ADJ foolishly over-confident.

cocktail N 1 a mixed drink of spirits and other liquors. 2 a mixed dish esp of seafood and mayonnaise. 3 a mixture of different things.

cocktail stick N a short thin pointed stick for serving small items of food at parties, etc.

cock-up N, SLANG a mess or muddle resulting from incompetence.

cocky ADJ (**-ier, -iest**) DEROG cheekily self-confident. ■ **cockily** ADV. ■ **cockiness** N.

cocoa N 1 the seed of the cacao tree. 2 a powder prepared from the seeds after they have been fermented and roasted. 3 a drink made with this powder and hot milk.

cocoa bean N a seeds from the cacao tree.

cocoa butter N a pale yellow fat obtained from cocoa beans.

coconut N 1 (also **coconut palm, coco**) a tropical palm tree cultivated for its edible fruit. 2 the large single-seeded fruit of this tree, with a thick fibrous outer husk and a woody inner shell enclosing a layer of white edible flesh.

cocoon N 1 the protective silky covering that many animals, eg spiders, spin around their eggs. 2 a similar covering that a larva spins around itself before it develops into a pupa. ➢ VB 1 to wrap someone or something up as if in a cocoon. 2 to protect someone from the problems of everyday life.

cod N (PL **cod**) a large food fish, found mainly in the N Atlantic Ocean.

c.o.d. ABBREV cash on delivery.

coda N, MUS a passage added at the end of a movement or piece.

code N 1 a system of words, letters or symbols, used in place of those really intended, for secrecy's or brevity's sake. 2 a set of signals for sending messages, etc. 3 COMP the set of instructions or statements that make up a computer program. 4 a set of principles of behaviour. 5 an organized set of laws. ➤ VB to put something into a code.

codeine N, MED a morphine derivative that relieves pain and has a sedative effect.

codicil N, LAW a supplement to a will.

codify VB (-ies, -ied) to arrange something into a systematic code. ■ **codification** N.

cod-liver oil N a medicinal oil obtained from the livers of cod, rich in vitamins A and D.

codswallop N, BRIT SLANG nonsense.

co-ed ABBREV, COLLOQ coeducation(al).

coeducation N the teaching of pupils of both sexes in the same school or college. ■ **coeducational** ADJ.

coelacanth N a primitive bony fish.

coelenterate N, ZOOL any member of the phylum of invertebrate animals, eg jellyfish, which have a single body cavity and usu show radial symmetry.

coeliac ADJ relating to the abdomen.

coerce VB (often **coerce sb into sth**) to force them to do it. ■ **coercion** N. ■ **coercive** ADJ.

co-exist VB, INTR 1 to exist together, or simultaneously. 2 to live peacefully side by side in spite of differences, etc. ■ **co-existence** N.

coffee N 1 an evergreen tree or shrub with oval leaves, white fragrant flowers and red fleshy fruits. 2 the seeds, or beans, of this plant, roasted whole or ground to a powder. 3 a drink prepared from roasted and ground coffee.

coffee table N a small low table.

coffer N 1 a large chest for holding valuables. 2 (**coffers**) a treasury or supply of funds.

coffin N a box in which a corpse is cremated or buried.

cog N 1 one of a series of teeth on the edge of a wheel or bar which engage with another series of teeth to bring about motion. 2 a small gear wheel. 3 someone unimportant in, though necessary to, a process or organization.

cogent ADJ of arguments, etc: strong; persuasive; convincing. ■ **cogency** N.

cogitate VB, INTR to think deeply; to ponder. ■ **cogitation** N. ■ **cogitative** ADJ.

cognac N a quality French brandy.

cognate ADJ 1 descended from or related to a common ancestor. 2 of words or languages: derived from the same original form. 3 related. ➤ N something that is related to something else.

cognition N, PSYCHOL the mental processes, such as perception, reasoning, etc, which enable humans to experience and process knowledge and information. ■ **cognitive** ADJ.

cognizance or **cognisance** N 1 knowledge; understanding. 2 the range or scope of awareness or knowledge. ■ **cognizant** ADJ. ◆ **take cognizance of sth** to take it into consideration.

cognomen N (-mens or -mina) a nickname or surname.

cognoscenti PL N knowledgeable people.

cogwheel N a toothed wheel.

cohabit VB, INTR to live together as husband and wife, usu without being married. ■ **cohabitation** N.

cohere VB, INTR 1 to stick together. 2 to be consistent; to have a clear logical connection.

coherent ADJ 1 of a description or argument: logical and consistent. 2 speaking intelligibly. 3 sticking together; cohering. ■ **coherence** N.

cohesion N sticking together. ■ **cohesive** ADJ.

cohort N 1 HIST in the ancient Roman army: one of the ten divisions of a legion. 2 a group of people sharing a common quality or belief.

coiffeur and **coiffeuse** N a male and female hairdresser respectively.

coiffure N a hairstyle.

coil VB, TR & INTR (sometimes **coil up**) to wind round in loops to form rings or a spiral.
➤ N **1** something looped into rings or a spiral: a **coil of rope**. **2** a single loop in such an arrangement. **3** ELEC a conducting wire wound into a spiral. **4** NON-TECHNICAL an IUD.

coin N **1** a small metal disc stamped for use as currency. **2** coins generally.
➤ VB **1 a** to manufacture(coins) from metal; **b** to make (metal) into coins. **2** to invent (a new word or phrase).

coinage N **1** the process of coining. **2** coins.

coincide VB, INTR **1** to happen at the same time. **2** to be the same; to agree. **3** to occupy the same position.

coincidence N **1** the striking occurrence of events together without any causal connection. **2** the fact of being the same.

coincident ADJ **1** coinciding in space or time. **2** in agreement.

coincidental ADJ happening by coincidence. ■ **coincidentally** ADV.

coir N fibre from coconut shells, used for making ropes, matting, etc.

coition and **coitus** N sexual intercourse. ■ **coital** ADJ.

coke[1] N a brittle greyish-black solid left after gases have been extracted from coal.

coke[2] N, COLLOQ cocaine.

col N, GEOL a pass between two adjacent peaks, or the lowest point in a ridge.

cola N **1** a tropical tree cultivated for its seeds, **cola nuts**. **2** a soft drink flavoured with the extract obtained from cola seeds.

colander N a perforated bowl used to drain the water from cooked vegetables, etc.

cold ADJ **1** low in temperature. **2** lower in temperature than is normal, comfortable or pleasant. **3** cooked, but not eaten hot: **cold**
meat. **4** unfriendly. **5** comfortless; depressing. **6** COLLOQ unenthusiastic. **7** without warmth or emotion. **8** sexually unresponsive. **9** COLLOQ unconscious: **out cold**. **10** dead. **11** of a trail or scent: not fresh.
➤ ADV without preparation or rehearsal.
➤ N **1** lack of heat or warmth; cold weather. **2** a highly contagious viral infection whose symptoms include a sore throat, coughing and sneezing, and a congested nose. ■ **coldly** ADV. ■ **coldness** N.

cold-blooded ADJ **1** having a body temperature that varies with the temperature of the surrounding environment. **2 a** lacking emotion; **b** callous or cruel.

cold front N, METEOROL the leading edge of an advancing mass of cold air moving under a retreating mass of warm air.

cold-hearted ADJ unkind.

cold sore N a patch of small blister-like spots on or near the lips, caused by a herpes virus.

cold war N a state of hostility and antagonism between nations, without actual warfare.

coleslaw N a salad made with finely-cut raw vegetables bound with mayonnaise.

coley N a large edible fish of the cod family.

colic N, PATHOL severe abdominal pain.

colitis N inflammation of the colon.

collaborate VB, INTR **1** to work together with another or others on something. **2** DEROG to co-operate or collude with an enemy. ■ **collaboration** N. ■ **collaborative** ADJ. ■ **collaborator** N.

collage N **1** a design or picture made up of pieces of paper, cloth, photographs, etc glued onto a background surface. **2** the art of making such works. ■ **collagist** N.

collapse VB **1** INTR of buildings, etc: to fall or cave in. **2** INTR of people: **a** to fall or drop in a state of unconsciousness; **b** to drop in a state of exhaustion or helplessness. **3** INTR to break down emotionally. **4** INTR to fail suddenly and completely. **5** TR & INTR to fold up compactly.
➤ N **1** a process or act of collapsing.

2 a breakdown. ■ **collapsible** ADJ.

collar N **1 a** a band or flap of any of various shapes, folded over or standing up round the neck of a garment; **b** the neck of a garment generally. **2** something worn round the neck. **3** a band of leather, etc worn round the neck by an animal. **4** a distinctively coloured ring of fur or feathers round the neck of certain mammals and birds. **5** a ring-shaped fitting for joining two pipes, etc together.
➤ VB, COLLOQ to catch someone or something.

collarbone N the clavicle.

collate VB **1** to study and compare. **2** to check and arrange (sheets of paper) in order.

collateral ADJ **1** descended from a common ancestor, but through a different branch of the family. **2** additional; secondary in importance.
➤ N **1** a collateral relative. **2** assets offered to a creditor as security for a loan.

colleague N a fellow-worker.

collect VB **1** TR & INTR to bring or be brought together. **2** to build up a collection of things of a particular type: **collect stamps**. **3** to call for someone or something. **4** TR & INTR to get something from people, eg money owed or voluntary contributions, etc.

collection N **1** the act of collecting. **2** an accumulated assortment of things of a particular type: **a stamp collection**. **3** an amount of money collected.

collective ADJ of, belonging to or involving all the members of a group: **a collective effort**.
➤ N an organized group or unit who run some kind of business, etc.

collective noun N a singular noun which refers to a group of people, animals, things, etc, such as **cast, flock, gang**.

collectivize or **-ise** VB to group (farms, factories, etc) into larger units and bring them under state control and ownership.
■ **collectivization** N.

collector N, often IN COMPOUNDS, DENOTING someone who collects, as a job or hobby.

college N **1** an institution, either self-contained

or part of a university, which provides higher education, further education or professional training. **2** one of a number of self-governing establishments that make up certain universities. **3** the staff and students of a college. **4** the buildings of a college. **5** an official body of members of a profession.

collegiate ADJ **1** of, relating to or belonging to a college. **2** having the form of a college. **3** of a university: consisting of individual colleges.

collide VB, INTR to crash together or crash into someone or something.

collie N a long-haired breed of dog.

collier N **1** a coal-miner. **2** a ship that transports coal.

colliery N (*-ies*) a coal mine and its buildings.

collision N **1** a violent meeting of objects; a crash. **2** a disagreement or conflict.

collocate VB **1** to arrange or group together in some kind of order. **2** GRAM of a word: to occur frequently alongside another word.
■ **collocation** N.

colloid N, CHEM a state in which fine particles of one substance are spread evenly throughout another.

colloquium N (*-quia* or *-quiums*) an academic conference; a seminar.

colloquy N (*-quies*) a conversation; talk.

collude VB, INTR to plot secretly with someone, esp with a view to committing fraud. .

collusion N secret and illegal co-operation.
■ **collusive** ADJ.

collywobbles PL N (usu **the collywobbles**) COLLOQ **1** pain or discomfort in the abdomen. **2** nervousness; apprehensiveness.

cologne see **eau de Cologne**

colon[1] N a punctuation mark (:), used to introduce a list, an example or an explanation.

colon[2] N, ANAT in vertebrates: the large intestine lying between the caecum and rectum. ■ **colonic** ADJ.

colonel N a senior army officer, in charge of a

regiment. ■ **colonelcy** N (*-ies*).

colonial ADJ **1** relating to, belonging to or living in a colony or colonies. **2** possessing colonies. ➤ N an inhabitant of a colony.

colonize or **-ise** VB **1** TR & INTR to establish a colony in (an area or country). **2** to settle (people) in a colony. ■ **colonist** N. ■ **colonization** N.

colonnade N, ARCHIT a row of columns placed at regular intervals. ■ **colonnaded** ADJ.

colony N (*-ies*) **1 a** a settlement abroad established and controlled by the founding country; **b** the settlers living there; **c** the territory they occupy. **2** a group of the same nationality or occupation forming a distinctive community within a city, etc: **writers' colony**. **3** ZOOL a group of animals or plants of the same species living together in close proximity.

colorant or **colourant** N a substance used for colouring.

coloration or **colouration** N arrangement or combination of colours.

colossal ADJ huge; vast.

colossus N (*-si* or *-suses*) **1** a gigantic statue. **2** a very powerful person or organization.

colostomy N (*-ies*) an operation in which part of the colon is brought to the surface of the body through an incision in the abdomen.

colour or (US) **color** N **1 a** the visual sensation produced when light of different wavelengths is absorbed by the cones of the retina and relayed, in the form of nerve impulses, to the brain; **b** the particular visual sensation produced in this way, depending upon the wavelength. **2** any of these variations or colours, often with the addition of black and white. **3** PHOTOG, ART the use of some or all colours, as distinct from black and white only. **4** a colouring substance, esp paint. **5** the shade of a person's skin, as related to race. **6** pinkness of the face or cheeks, usu indicating healthiness. **7** lively or convincing detail: **add colour**. ➤ VB **1 a** to put colour on to something; **b** to paint or dye. **2** (often **colour sth in**) to fill in (an

outlined area or a black and white picture) with colour. **3** to influence. **4** INTR to blush.

colour-blind ADJ unable to distinguish between certain colours, most commonly red and green. ■ **colour-blindness** N.

coloured ADJ **1** ALSO IN COMPOUNDS having colour, or a specified colour: **coloured paper**. **2 a** belonging to a dark-skinned race; **b** non-white. **3** (**Coloured**) S AFR being of mixed white and non-white descent. ➤ N **1** someone of a dark-skinned race. **2** (**Coloured**) S AFR a person of mixed white and non-white descent.

colour-fast ADJ of fabrics: dyed with colours that will not run or fade when washed.

colourful ADJ **1** full of esp bright colour. **2** lively; vivid. ■ **colourfully** ADV.

colouring N **1** a substance used to give colour, eg to food. **2** the applying of colour. **3** arrangement of colour. **4** facial complexion, or this in combination with eye and hair colour.

colourless ADJ **1** without or lacking colour. **2** uninteresting; dull; lifeless. **3** pale.

colours PL N **1** the flag of a nation, regiment or ship. **2** the coloured uniform or other distinguishing badge awarded to team-members in certain games. **3** a badge of ribbons in colours representing a particular party, etc, worn to show support for it.

colt N a young male horse or pony.

columbine N a wild flower related to the buttercup.

column N **1** ARCHIT a vertical pillar, usu cylindrical, with a base and a capital. **2** a long and more or less cylindrical mass. **3** a vertical row of numbers. **4** a vertical strip of print on a newspaper page, etc. **5** a regular section in a newspaper concerned with a particular topic, or by a regular writer. **6** a troop of soldiers or vehicles standing or moving a few abreast. ■ **columnar** ADJ.

columnist N someone who writes a regular section of a newspaper.

coma N a prolonged state of deep

unconsciousness from which a person cannot be awakened, caused by head injury, etc.

comatose ADJ in a coma.

comb N 1 a a rigid toothed device for tidying and arranging the hair; b a similar device worn in the hair to keep it in place. 2 a toothed implement or part of a machine for disentangling and cleaning wool or cotton. 3 an act of combing. 4 a honeycomb. 5 the fleshy serrated crest on the head of a fowl. ➤ VB 1 to arrange, smooth or clean something with a comb. 2 to search (a place) thoroughly.

combat N fighting; a struggle or contest. ➤ VB to fight against someone or something.

combatant ADJ involved in or ready for a fight. ➤ N someone involved in or ready for a fight.

combative ADJ inclined to fight or argue.

combination N 1 the process of combining or the state of being combined. 2 a two or more things, people, etc combined; b the resulting mixture or union. 3 a sequence of numbers or letters for opening a kind of lock.

combine VB, TR & INTR 1 to join together. 2 CHEM to coalesce or make things coalesce so as to form a new compound. ➤ N 1 a group of people or businesses associated for a common purpose. 2 COLLOQ a combine harvester.

combine harvester N, AGRIC a machine used to both reap and thresh crops.

combustible ADJ liable to catch fire.

combustion N the process of catching fire and burning.

come VB (PA T *came,* PA P *come*) INTR in most senses 1 to move in the direction of speaker or hearer. 2 to reach a place; to arrive. 3 (usu **come to** or **into sth**) to reach (a certain stage or state). 4 to travel or traverse (a distance, etc). 5 to enter one's consciousness or perception: **come into view.** 6 to occupy a specific place in order, etc: **In 'ceiling', 'e' comes before 'i'.** 7 to be available; to exist or be found: **These jeans come in several sizes.** 8 to become: **come undone.** 9 INTR, COLLOQ to have a sexual orgasm. 10 on the arrival of (a particular point in time): **Come next Tuesday, I'll be free.** ➤ EXCLAM used to reassure or admonish: **Oh, come now, don't exaggerate.**

◆ **come about** to happen.

◆ **come across sth** or **sb** to meet or discover them accidentally.

◆ **come back** 1 to be recalled to mind. 2 to become fashionable again.

◆ **come by sth** to obtain it, esp accidentally.

◆ **come down with sth** to develop (an illness).

◆ **come in** 1 to arrive; to be received. 2 to have a particular role, function or use: **This is where you come in.** 3 to become fashionable.

◆ **come in for sth** to deserve or incur it.

◆ **come off** 1 to become detached. 2 to succeed. 3 INFORMAL to take place.

◆ **come on** 1 to start. 2 to prosper or make progress. 3 to make an entrance on stage.

◆ **come out** 1 to become known; to become public. 2 to be removed. 3 to be released or made available. 4 to go on strike. 5 to emerge in a specified position or state: **come out well from the affair.** 6 COLLOQ to declare openly that one is a homosexual.

◆ **come out with sth** to make a remark, etc.

◆ **come over** 1 to change one's opinion or side. 2 to make a specified impression: **comes over well on TV.**

◆ **come round** 1 to regain consciousness. 2 to change one's opinion.

◆ **come through** 1 to survive. 2 to emerge successfully.

◆ **come to** to regain consciousness.

◆ **come up** 1 to occur; to happen. 2 to be considered or discussed.

◆ **come up against sb** or **sth** to be faced with them as an opponent, challenge, etc.

◆ **come up with sth** to put it forward.

◆ **come upon sth** or **sb** to discover it or them by chance.

comeback N 1 a return to former success, or to the stage, etc after retirement, etc. 2 a retort.

comedian or **comedienne** N 1 a male or female entertainer who tells jokes, performs comic sketches, etc. 2 an actor in comedy.

comedown N 1 a decline in social status. 2 an anticlimax.

comedy N (-*ies*) 1 a light amusing play or film. 2 in earlier literature: a play with a fortunate outcome. 3 funny incidents.

comely ADJ (-*ier*, -*iest*) DATED of a person: attractive. ■ **comeliness** N.

comestible N (usu **comestibles**) AFFECTED something to eat.

comet N, ASTRON a small body which follows an elliptical orbit around the Sun, leaving a trail.

come-uppance N, COLLOQ justified punishment or retribution.

comfort N 1 a state of contentedness or wellbeing. 2 relief from suffering, or consolation in grief. 3 a person or thing that provides such relief or consolation. 4 (usu **comforts**) something that makes for ease and physical wellbeing.
➤ VB to relieve from suffering; to console.

comfortable ADJ 1 in a state of wellbeing, esp physical. 2 at ease. 3 providing comfort. 4 COLLOQ financially secure. 5 of a hospital patient, etc: in a stable condition.
■ **comfortably** ADV.

comforter N 1 someone who comforts. 2 OLD USE a warm scarf. 3 OLD USE a baby's dummy.

comfrey N a bristly plant with tubular white, pink or purple flowers, used medicinally.

comfy ADJ (-*ier*, -*iest*) COLLOQ comfortable.

comic ADJ 1 characterized by or relating to comedy. 2 funny.
➤ N 1 a comedian. 2 a paper or magazine which includes strip cartoons, etc.

comical ADJ funny; amusing; humorous; ludicrous. ■ **comically** ADV.

comic strip N in a newspaper, magazine, etc: a brief story or episode told through a short series of cartoon drawings.

coming N an arrival or approach.
➤ ADJ 1 COLLOQ likely to succeed: **the coming man**. 2 approaching: **in the coming months**.

comma N a punctuation mark (,) indicating a slight pause or break.

command VB 1 to order formally. 2 to have authority over or be in control of someone or something. 3 to deserve or be entitled to something. 4 to look down over something.
➤ N 1 an order. 2 control; charge. 3 knowledge of and ability to use something. 4 a military unit or a district under one's command. 5 COMP an instruction.

commandant N a commanding officer, esp of a prisoner-of-war camp.

commandeer VB 1 to seize (property) for military use. 2 to seize without justification.

commander N 1 in the British navy: an officer just below captain in rank. 2 a high-ranking police officer.

commanding ADJ 1 powerful; leading. 2 in charge. 3 inspiring respect or awe.

commandment N a divine command.

commando N 1 a unit of soldiers specially trained to carry out dangerous and difficult attacks or raids. 2 a member of such a unit.

commemorate VB 1 to honour the memory of (a person or event) with a ceremony, etc. 2 to be a memorial to someone or something.
■ **commemoration** N.
■ **commemorative** ADJ.

commence VB, TR & INTR to begin.
■ **commencement** N.

commend VB to praise someone.
■ **commendable** ADJ. ■ **commendation** N. ■ **commendatory** ADJ.

commensurate ADJ 1 in equal proportion to something; appropriate to it. 2 equal in extent, quantity, etc to something.

comment N 1 a remark or observation, esp a critical one. 2 talk, discussion or gossip. 3 an explanatory or analytical note on a text.
➤ VB, TR & INTR (often **comment on sth**) to make observations, remarks, etc.

commentary N (-*ies*) 1 an ongoing description of an event, eg a football match, as it happens. **2** a set of notes in a text, etc.

commentator N a broadcaster who gives a commentary on an event, etc. ■ **commentate** VB.

commerce N the buying and selling of commodities and services.

commercial ADJ **1** relating to, engaged in or used for commerce. **2** profitable; having profit as the main goal. **3** paid for by advertising. ➤ N a radio or TV advertisement.

commiserate VB, TR & INTR (often **commiserate with sb**) to express one's sympathy for them. ■ **commiseration** N.

commission N **1 a** a formal or official request to someone to perform a task or duty; **b** the authority to perform such a task or duty; **c** the task or duty performed. **2** a military rank above the level of officer. **3** an order for a piece of work, esp a work of art. **4** a board or committee entrusted with a task. **5** a fee or percentage given to an agent for arranging a sale, etc. ➤ VB **1** to give a commission or authority to someone. **2** to grant a military rank above a certain level to someone. **3** to request someone to do something. **4** to place an order for something, eg a work of art, etc. **5** to prepare (a ship) for active service.

commissionaire N, chiefly BRIT a uniformed attendant at the door of a building.

commissioned officer N a military officer who holds a commission.

commissioner N **1** a representative of the government in a district, department, etc. **2** a member of a commission.

commit VB (-*tt*-) **1** to carry out or perpetrate (a crime, offence, error, etc). **2** to have someone put in prison or a mental institution. **3** to promise or engage, esp oneself, for some undertaking, etc. **4** to dedicate oneself to a cause, etc from a sense of conviction. ■ **commitment** N.

committee N a group of people selected by and from a larger body, eg a club, to undertake certain duties on its behalf.

commode N a chair with a hinged seat,

designed to conceal a chamber pot.

commodity N (-*ies*) **1** something that is bought and sold, esp a manufactured product or raw material. **2** something, eg a quality, from the point of view of its value or importance.

commodore N in the navy: an officer just below a rear admiral in rank.

common ADJ **1** frequent; familiar: *a common mistake*. **2** shared by two or more people, things, etc: *characteristics common to both animals*. **3** publicly owned. **4** widespread: *common knowledge*. **5** DEROG lacking taste or refinement; vulgar. **6 a** of the ordinary type: *the common cold*; **b** esp of plants and animals: general or ordinary: *common toad*. ➤ N a piece of land that is publicly owned or available for public use. ■ **commonly** ADV. ◆ **in common** shared.

common denominator N **1** MATH a whole number that is a multiple of each of the denominators of two or more vulgar fractions. **2** something that enables comparison, agreement, etc between people or things.

commoner N someone who is not a member of the nobility.

Common Era N a culturally neutral term for the present era, reckoned since the birth of Christ, sometimes used instead of Anno Domini.

common law N **1** law based on custom and decisions by judges, in contrast to statute law. **2** ADJ (**common-law**) denoting the relationship of two people who live together as husband and wife but are not married.

commonplace ADJ **1** ordinary; everyday. **2** DEROG unoriginal; lacking individuality; trite. ➤ N **1** DEROG a trite comment; a cliché. **2** an everyday occurrence.

commons PL N, HIST (**the commons**) the ordinary people. ➤ SING N (**the Commons**) the House of Commons.

common sense N practical wisdom and understanding. ■ **common-sense** ADJ.

commonwealth N **1** a country or state. **2** an

association of states that have joined together for their common good. **3** a state in which the people hold power; a republic.

commotion N **1** a disturbance; an upheaval. **2** noisy confusion.

communal ADJ **1** relating or belonging to a community. **2** relating to a commune or communes. ■ **communally** ADV.

commune[1] N a number of unrelated families and individuals living together as a mutually supportive community, with shared accommodation, responsibilities, etc.

commune[2] VB, INTR **1** to communicate intimately. **2** to get close to or relate spiritually to (eg nature).

communicable ADJ **1** of a disease: that can be easily transmitted from one organism to another. **2** capable of being communicated.

communicate VB **1** TR & INTR **a** to impart (information, ideas, etc); to make something known or understood; **b** to get in touch. **2** to pass on or transmit (a feeling, etc). **3** INTR to understand someone; to have a comfortable social relationship. ■ **communicative** ADJ.

communication N **1 a** the process or act of communicating; **b** the exchanging or imparting of ideas and information, etc. **2** a piece of information, a letter or a message. **3** social contact. **4** (**communications**) the various means by which information is conveyed.

communion N **1** the sharing of thoughts or feelings. **2** a group of people sharing the same religious beliefs. **3** (also **Holy Communion**) CHRISTIANITY a church service at which bread and wine symbolize Christ's body and blood.

communiqué N an official announcement.

communism N a political ideology advocating a classless society where all sources of wealth and production are collectively owned and controlled by the people. ■ **communist** N.

community N (*-ies*) **1** the group of people living in a particular place. **2** a group of people bonded together by a common religion,

nationality or occupation. **3** a group of states with common interests. **4** the public; society.

commute VB **1** INTR to travel regularly between two places which are a significant distance apart, esp between home and work. **2** to alter (a criminal sentence) to one less severe.

commuter N someone who regularly travels a significant distance to work.

compact[1] ADJ **1** firm and dense in form or texture. **2** small, but with all essentials neatly contained. **3** concise.
➤ VB to compress.
➤ N a small case for women's face powder, usu including a mirror. ■ **compactness** N.

compact[2] N a contract or agreement.

compact disc N a small aluminium disc used to record audio and/or visual information in the form of digital data.

companion N a friend or frequent associate. ■ **companionship** N.

companionable ADJ friendly; sociable.

companionway N on a ship: a staircase from a deck to a cabin, or between decks.

company N (*-ies*) **1** the presence of another person or other people; companionship. **2** the presence of guests or visitors, or the people involved: **expecting company**. **3** one's friends or associates: **get into bad company**. **4** a business organization. **5** a troop of actors or entertainers. **6** a military unit of about 120 men.

comparable ADJ **1** being of the same or equivalent kind. **2** able to be compared. ■ **comparability** N.

comparative ADJ **1** as compared with others. **2** relating to, or using the method of, comparison. **3** relative: **their comparative strengths**. **4** GRAM of adjectives and adverbs: in the form denoting a greater degree of the quality in question (but not the greatest).

compare VB **1** to examine (items, etc) to see what differences or similarities they have. **2** INTR (often **compare with sth** or **sb**) to be comparable with it or them. **3** INTR to relate (well, badly, etc) when examined.

comparison N the process of, an act of, or a reasonable basis for comparing.

compartment N a separated-off or enclosed section.

compass N 1 any device for finding direction, esp one consisting of a magnetized needle that swings freely on a pivot and points to magnetic north, from which true north can be calculated. 2 (usu **compasses**) a device consisting of two hinged legs, for drawing circles, measuring distances on maps, etc. 3 range or scope. ➤ VB 1 to pass or go round. 2 to surround or enclose. 3 to accomplish or obtain.

compassion N a feeling of sorrow and pity for someone in trouble.■ **compassionate** adj. ■ **compassionately** ADV.

compatible ADJ (often **compatible with sth** or **sb**) 1 able to associate or coexist agreeably. 2 consistent or congruous. 3 COMP of a program or device: capable of being used with a particular system. ■ **compatibility** N.

compatriot N someone from one's own country; a fellow-citizen.

compel VB (-*ll*-) 1 to force; to drive. 2 to elicit.

compelling ADJ 1 powerful; forcing one to agree, etc. 2 irresistibly fascinating.

compendium N (-*iums* or -*ia*) 1 a concise summary; an abridgement. 2 a collection of board games, puzzles, etc in a single container.

compensate VB 1 to make amends to someone for loss, injury or wrong, esp by a suitable payment. 2 INTR (often **compensate for sth**) to make up for (a disadvantage, loss, imbalance, etc). ■ **compensatory** ADJ.

compensation N 1 the process of compensating. 2 something that compensates. 3 a sum of money awarded to make up for loss, injury, etc.

compere or **compère** N someone who hosts a stage, radio or television show. ➤ VB, TR & INTR to act as compere for (a show).

compete VB, INTR 1 to take part in a contest. 2 to strive or struggle. ■ **competitor** N.

competent ADJ 1 efficient. 2 having sufficient skill or training to do something. 3 legally capable. ■ **competence** or **competency** N.

competition N 1 an event in which people compete. 2 the process or fact of competing. 3 rivals, eg in business or their products.

competitive ADJ 1 involving rivalry. 2 characterized by competition; aggressive; ambitious. 3 of a price or product: reasonably cheap; comparing well with those of market rivals. ■ **competitiveness** N.

compile VB 1 to collect and organize (information, etc) from different sources. 2 to produce (a list, reference book, etc) from information collected. ■ **compilation** N. ■ **compiler** N.

complacent ADJ 1 self-satisfied; smug. 2 too easily satisfied; disinclined to worry. ■ **complacence** or **complacency** N.

complain VB, INTR to express dissatisfaction. ◆ **complain of sth** to say that one is suffering from (a pain, disease, etc).

complaint N 1 the act of complaining. 2 an expression of dissatisfaction. 3 a grievance. 4 a disorder, illness, etc.

complaisant ADJ eager to please; obliging; amenable. ■ **complaisance** N.

complement N 1 something that completes or perfects; something that provides a needed balance or contrast. 2 the number or quantity required to make something complete, eg the crew of a ship. ➤ VB to be a complement to something.

complementary ADJ 1 serving as a complement to something. 2 of two or more things: complementing each other.

complete ADJ 1 whole; finished; with nothing missing. 2 thorough; absolute. 3 perfect. ➤ VB 1 **a** to finish; **b** to make complete or perfect. 2 to fill in (a form). ■ **completely** ADV. ■ **completion** N.

complex ADJ 1 composed of many interrelated parts. 2 complicated; involved; tangled. ➤ N 1 something made of interrelating parts, eg a multi–purpose building: **a leisure complex**. **2** PSYCHOANAL a set of repressed thoughts and emotions that strongly influence an individual's behaviour and attitudes.

complexion N **1** the appearance of the skin, esp of the face. **2** character or appearance.

complexity N (*-ies*) **1** the quality of being complex. **2** a complication; an intricacy.

compliance N **1** yielding. **2** agreement; assent. **3** submission. ■ **compliant** ADJ.

complicate VB to add difficulties to something; to make complex or involved.

complicated ADJ **1** difficult to understand or deal with. **2** intricate; complex.

complication N **1** a circumstance that causes difficulties. **2** PATHOL a second and possibly worse disease or disorder that arises during the course of an existing one.

complicity N the state of being an accomplice in a crime or wrongdoing.

compliment N **1** an expression of praise, admiration or approval. **2** a gesture implying approval: **paid her the compliment of dancing with her**. **3** (**compliments**) formal regards accompanying a gift, etc.
➤ VB (often **compliment sb on sth**) **1** to congratulate them for it. **2** to praise them; to pay them a compliment.

complimentary ADJ **1** paying a compliment; admiring or approving. **2** given free.

comply VB (*-ies, -ied*) INTR (usu **comply with sth**) to act in obedience to an order, command, request, etc; to agree.

component N any of the parts or elements that make up a machine, engine, instrument, etc.
➤ ADJ functioning as a part of something.

compose VB **1** TR & INTR to create (music). **2** to write (a poem, letter, article, etc). **3** to make up or constitute something. **4** to arrange as a balanced, artistic whole. **5** to calm (oneself); to bring (thoughts, etc) under control.

composed ADJ of a person: calm; controlled.

composer N someone who composes.

composite ADJ **1** made up of different parts, materials or styles. **2** of a plant: with flower heads made up of many small flowers.

composition N **1** something composed, esp a musical or literary work. **2** the process of composing. **3** ART arrangement, esp with regard to balance and visual effect: **photographic composition**. **4** the constitution of something.

compos mentis ADJ, LAW sound in mind.

compost N a mixture of decomposed organic substances such as rotting vegetable matter, used to enrich soil and nourish plants.
➤ VB **1** to treat with compost. **2** to convert (decaying organic matter) into compost.

composure N mental and emotional calmness; self–control.

compound[1] N **1** (in full **chemical compound**) CHEM a substance composed of two or more elements combined in fixed proportions and held together by chemical bonds. **2** something composed of two or more ingredients or parts. **3** a word made up of two or more words, eg **tablecloth**.
➤ ADJ made of a number of parts or ingredients.
➤ VB **a** to make (something) much worse; **b** to complicate or add to (an error, etc).

compound[2] N an enclosed area.

compound fracture N, MED a type of bone fracture in which the overlying skin is pierced by the broken bone.

compound interest N interest calculated on the original sum of money borrowed and on any interest already accumulated.

comprehend VB **1** to understand; to grasp with the mind. **2** to include.
■ **comprehensible** ADJ.

comprehension N **a** the process or power of understanding; **b** the scope or range of someone's knowledge or understanding.

comprehensive ADJ **1** covering or including a large area or scope. **2** of a school or education: providing teaching for pupils of all abilities aged between 11 and 18.
➤ N a comprehensive school.

compress VB 1 to press, squeeze or squash together. 2 to reduce in bulk; to condense. ➤ N a cloth or pad soaked in water and pressed against a part of the body to reduce swelling, bleeding, etc. ■ **compression** N.

compressor N, ENG a device that uses pressure to reduce the volume of eg a gas.

comprise VB 1 to contain, include or consist of something specified. 2 to go together to make up something.

compromise N 1 a settlement of differences agreed upon after concessions have been made on each side. 2 anything which comes halfway between two opposing stages. ➤ VB 1 INTR to make concessions; to reach a compromise. 2 to endanger or expose to scandal, by acting indiscreetly.

compulsion N 1 the act of compelling or condition of being compelled. 2 an irresistible urge to perform a certain action.

compulsive ADJ 1 having the power to compel. 2 resulting from a compulsion. 3 acting on a compulsion. 4 holding the attention; fascinating. ■ **compulsively** ADV.

compulsory ADJ required by the rules or law.

compunction N a feeling of guilt or regret.

computation N 1 the process or act of calculating or computing. 2 a result calculated or computed. ■ **computational** ADJ.

compute VB, TR & INTR 1 to calculate or estimate, esp with the aid of a computer. 2 to carry out (a computer operation).

computer N an electronic device which processes data at great speed.

computerize or **-ise** VB a to transfer (a procedure, system, etc) to control by computer; b to organize (information, data, etc) by computer; c to install (computers) for this purpose. ■ **computerization** N.

computing N the process of using a computer.

comrade N 1 a a friend or companion; b an associate, fellow worker, etc. 2 a fellow communist or socialist. ■ **comradeship** N.

con[1] COLLOQ, N a confidence trick. ➤ VB (**-nn-**) to swindle or trick someone, esp after winning their trust.

con[2] N an argument against something.

concave ADJ curving inwards, like the inside of a bowl. ■ **concavity** N.

conceal VB 1 to hide. 2 to keep secret. ■ **concealer** N. ■ **concealment** N.

concede VB 1 to admit to be true or correct. 2 to give or grant. 3 to yield or give up. 4 INTR to admit defeat in (a contest, etc) before the end.

conceit N a an inflated opinion of oneself; b vanity.

conceited ADJ a having too good an opinion of oneself; b vain. ■ **conceitedness** N.

conceivable ADJ imaginable; possible. ■ **conceivably** ADV.

conceive VB 1 TR & INTR to become pregnant. 2 TR & INTR (often **conceive of sth**) to think of or imagine (an idea, etc).

concentrate VB 1 INTR (often **concentrate on sth** or **sb**) to give full attention and energy to them or it. 2 to focus: **concentrate our efforts**. 3 CHEM to increase the strength of (a dissolved substance in a solution). ➤ N a concentrated liquid or substance. ■ **concentrated** ADJ.

concentration N 1 intensive mental effort. 2 the act of concentrating or the state of being concentrated.

concentration camp N a prison camp used to detain civilians, esp as in Nazi Germany.

concentric ADJ, GEOM of circles, spheres, etc: having a common centre.

concept N an abstract or general idea.

conception N 1 an idea or notion. 2 the origin or start of something, esp something intricate. 3 the act or an instance of conceiving. 4 BIOL the fertilization of an ovum by a sperm, representing the start of pregnancy.

conceptualize or **-ise** VB to form a

concept or idea of something.

concern VB **1** to have to do with someone or something; to be about someone or something. **2** (often **be concerned about sth** or **sb**) to worry, bother or interest. **3** to affect; to involve. ➢ N **1 a** worry or a cause of worry; **b** interest or a subject of interest. **2** someone's business or responsibility. **3** a company or business.

concerned ADJ worried.
◆ **concerned with sth** or **sb** having to do with it or them; involving it or them.

concerning PREP regarding; relating to; about.

concert N **1** a musical performance given before an audience. **2** agreement; harmony. ➢ VB to endeavour or plan by arrangement.
◆ **in concert 1** jointly. **2** in a live performance.

concerted ADJ planned and carried out jointly.

concertina N a musical instrument like a small accordion.

concerto N (**-tos** or **-ti**) MUS a composition for an orchestra and one or more solo performers.

concession N **1** the act of conceding. **2** something conceded or allowed. **3** the right, granted under government licence, to extract minerals, etc in an area. **4** the right to conduct a business from within a larger concern. **5** a reduction in ticket prices, fares, etc for categories such as students, the elderly, etc. ■ **concessionary** ADJ.

conch N (**conchs** or **conches**) **1** any of a family of large marine snails, native to warm shallow tropical waters, with large colourful shells. **2** the shell of this animal often used as a trumpet.

concierge N a caretaker of a block of flats.

conciliate VB **1** to overcome the hostility of someone. **2** to reconcile (people in dispute, etc). ■ **conciliation** N. ■ **conciliatory** ADJ.

concise ADJ brief but comprehensive. ■ **conciseness** or **concision** N.

conclave N **1** a private or secret meeting. **2** RC CHURCH the body of cardinals gathered to elect a new pope.

conclude VB **1** TR & INTR to come or bring to an end. **2** to reach an opinion based on reasoning. **3** to settle or arrange.

conclusion N **1** an end. **2** a reasoned judgement; an opinion based on reasoning: draw a conclusion. **3** LOGIC a statement validly deduced from a previous premise. **4** a result or outcome (of a discussion, event, etc).

conclusive ADJ leaving no room for doubt.

concoct VB **1** to make something, esp ingeniously from a variety of ingredients. **2** to invent (a story, excuse, etc). ■ **concoction** N.

concomitant ADJ accompanying because of or as a result of something else.

concord N **1** agreement; peace or harmony. **2** GRAM agreement. ■ **concordant** ADJ.

concordance N **1** a state of harmony. **2** a book containing an alphabetical index of principal words used in a major work.

concourse N **1** in a railway station, airport, etc: a large open area where people can gather. **2** a throng; a gathering.

concrete N a building material consisting of a mixture of cement, sand, gravel and water, which forms a hard rock–like mass when dry. ➢ ADJ **1** relating to such a material. **2** relating to items which can be felt, touched, seen, etc: concrete objects. **3** definite or positive: concrete evidence.

concubine N, HIST a woman who lives with a man and has sexual intercourse with him, without being married to him.

concupiscence N strong desire, esp sexual. ■ **concupiscent** ADJ.

concur VB (**-rr-**) INTR **1** to agree. **2** to happen at the same time; to coincide.

concurrent ADJ **1** happening or taking place simultaneously. **2** of lines: meeting or intersecting. **3** in agreement. ■ **concurrence** N. ■ **concurrently** ADV.

concuss VB to cause concussion in someone.

concussion N a violent shaking or jarring of the brain, caused by injury to the head and usu resulting in temporary loss of consciousness.

condemn VB 1 to declare something to be wrong or evil. 2 to pronounce someone guilty; to convict someone. 3 (usu **condemn sb to sth**) **a** to sentence them to (a punishment, esp death); **b** to force into (a disagreeable fate). 4 to show the guilt of someone; to betray someone. 5 to declare (a building) unfit to be used or lived in. ■ **condemnation** N. ■ **condemnatory** ADV.

condensation N, CHEM the process whereby a gas or vapour turns into a liquid by cooling.

condense VB 1 to decrease the volume, size or density of (a substance). 2 to concentrate something. 3 TR & INTR to undergo or cause to undergo condensation. 4 to express something more briefly; to summarize.

condescend VB, INTR 1 to act in a gracious manner towards those one regards as inferior. 2 to be gracious enough to do something, esp as though it were a favour. ■ **condescending** ADJ. ■ **condescension** N.

condiment N any seasoning or sauce, eg salt, mustard, etc, added to food at the table.

condition N 1 a particular state of existence. 2 a state of health, fitness or suitability for use: **out of condition**. 3 an ailment or disorder: **a heart condition**. 4 (**conditions**) circumstances. 5 a requirement or qualification. ➤ VB 1 to accustom or train someone or something to behave or react in a particular way; to influence them or it. 2 to prepare or train (a person or animal) for a certain activity or for certain conditions of living. 3 to affect or control; to determine. 4 to improve (the physical state of hair, skin, fabrics, etc) by applying a particular substance.

conditional ADJ 1 dependent on a particular condition, etc. 2 GRAM expressing a condition on which something else is dependent, as in the first clause in 'If it rains, I'll stay at home'.

conditioner N a substance which improves the condition of something.

condolence N (usu **condolences**) an expression of sympathy. ■ **condole** VB.

condom N a thin rubber sheath worn on the penis during sexual intercourse, to prevent conception and infection.

condone VB 1 to pardon or overlook (an offence or wrong). 2 LOOSELY to tolerate.

condor N either of two species of large American vulture.

conducive ADJ (often **conducive to sth**) likely to achieve a desirable result; encouraging.

conduct VB 1 to lead or guide. 2 to manage; to control. 3 TR & INTR to direct an orchestra or choir by movements of the hands or by using a baton. 4 to transmit (heat or electricity) by conduction. 5 to behave (oneself) in a specified way: **conduct oneself with dignity**. ➤ N 1 behaviour. 2 the managing or organizing of something.

conduction N 1 the transmission of heat through a material from a region of higher temperature to one of lower temperature, without any movement of the material itself. 2 the flow of electricity through a material under the influence of an electric field, without any movement of the material itself.

conductivity N 1 a measure of the ability of a material to conduct electricity. 2 the ability of a material to conduct heat.

conductor N 1 the person who conducts a choir or orchestra. 2 a material that conducts heat or electricity. 3 someone who collects fares from passengers on a bus, etc.

conduit N a channel, pipe, tube or duct through which a fluid, a liquid or a gas, may pass.

cone N 1 GEOM a solid, three-dimensional figure with a flat base in the shape of a circle or ellipse, and a curved upper surface that tapers to a fixed point. 2 something similar to this in shape. 3 BOT the oval fruit of a coniferous tree, consisting of overlapping woody scales. 4 a plastic cone-shaped bollard placed on the road temporarily, to divert traffic, etc.

confab N, COLLOQ a conversation.

confection N any sweet food, eg a cake, sweet, biscuit or pudding.

confectioner N someone who makes or sells sweets or cakes.

confectionery N (-*ies*) 1 sweets, biscuits and cakes. 2 the work or art of a confectioner.

confederacy N (-*ies*) a league of states.

confederate N 1 a member of a confederacy. 2 a friend or an ally. ➤ ADJ allied; united.

confederation N 1 the uniting of states into a league. 2 the league so formed.

confer VB (-*rr*-) 1 INTR to consult or discuss together. 2 (usu **confer sth on sb**) to grant them (an honour). ■ **conferment** N.

conference N 1 a formally organized gathering for the discussion of matters of common interest or concern. 2 consultation: in conference with the Prime Minister.

confess VB 1 TR & INTR **a** to own up to (a fault, wrongdoing, etc); **b** to admit (a disagreeable fact, etc) reluctantly. 2 TR & INTR, CHRISTIANITY to declare (one's sins) to a priest or directly to God, in order to gain absolution.

confession N 1 the admission of a sin, fault, crime, distasteful or shocking fact, etc. 2 CHRISTIANITY the formal act of confessing one's sins to a priest.

confessional N the small enclosed stall in a church where a priest hears confessions. ➤ ADJ relating to a confession.

confetti N tiny pieces of coloured paper traditionally thrown over the bride and groom by wedding guests.

confidant or **confidante** N a close friend (male or female, respectively) with whom one discusses personal matters.

confide VB to tell (a secret, etc) to someone.

confidence N 1 trust or belief in a person or thing. 2 faith in one's own ability; self-assurance. 3 a secret, etc confided to someone. 4 a relationship of mutual trust. ◆ **in confidence** in secret; confidentially.

confidence trick N a swindle in which the swindler first wins the trust of the victim.

confident ADJ 1 (sometimes **confident of sth**) certain; sure. 2 self-assured.

confidential ADJ 1 secret; not to be divulged. 2 trusted with private matters. 3 indicating privacy or secrecy. ■ **confidentiality** N.

configuration N 1 the positioning or distribution of the parts of something, relative to each other. 2 an outline or external shape.

confine VB 1 to restrict or limit. 2 to keep prisoner. 3 to restrict someone's movement.

confinement N the state of being shut up or kept in an enclosed space.

confirm VB 1 to provide support for the truth or validity of something. 2 to finalize or make definite (a booking, arrangement etc). 3 of an opinion, etc: to strengthen it or become more convinced in it. 4 CHRISTIANITY to accept someone formally into full membership of the Church. ■ **confirmation** N.

confiscate VB to take away something from someone, usu as a penalty. ■ **confiscation** N.

conflagration N a large destructive blaze.

conflate VB to blend or combine (two things) into a single whole. ■ **conflation** N.

conflict N 1 disagreement; fierce argument; a quarrel. 2 a clash. 3 a struggle or battle. ➤ VB INTR to be incompatible or in opposition.

confluence N the point where two rivers flow into one another. ■ **confluent** ADJ.

conform VB, INTR (often **conform to**) to behave, dress, etc according to some standard considered normal by the majority. ■ **conformist** N. ■ **conformity** N.

confound VB 1 to puzzle; to baffle. 2 to mix up or confuse (one thing with another).

confront VB 1 to face someone, esp defiantly or accusingly. 2 to prepare to deal firmly with something. 3 of an unpleasant prospect: to present itself to someone. ■ **confrontation** N.

confuse VB 1 to put into a muddle or mess. 2 to mix up or fail to distinguish (things, ideas, people, etc). 3 to puzzle, bewilder or muddle. 4 to complicate. ■ **confusion** N.

conga N a dance performed by people moving in single file.
➢ VB (*-gaed, -gaing*) INTR to dance the conga.

congeal VB, TR & INTR of a liquid, eg blood: to thicken or coagulate, esp through cooling.

congenial ADJ 1 compatible; having similar interests. 2 pleasant or agreeable.
■ **congeniality** N.

congenital ADJ 1 of a disease or deformity: present at or before birth, but not inherited. 2 complete, as if from birth: **congenital liar**.

conger N a large marine eel.

congest VB, TR & INTR 1 to excessively crowd or become excessively crowded. 2 to accumulate or make something accumulate with blood, often causing inflammation. 3 to block up with mucus. ■ **congestion** N.

conglomerate N 1 a miscellaneous collection or mass. 2 a business group of a large number of firms. ■ **conglomeration** N.

congratulate VB 1 to express pleasure to someone at their success, good fortune, happiness, etc. 2 to consider (oneself) lucky or clever to have managed something.
■ **congratulatory** ADJ.

congratulations PL N an expression used to congratulate someone.

congregate VB, TR & INTR to gather together into a crowd.

congregation N a gathering or assembly of people, esp for worship in church.
■ **congregational** ADJ.

congress N 1 a large, esp international, assembly of delegates. 2 in some countries: the law-making body.

congressman and **congresswoman** N someone who is a member of a congress.

congruent ADJ 1 GEOM identical in size and shape. 2 (often **congruent with**) suitable or appropriate to.

conic and **conical** ADJ, GEOM **a** relating to a cone; **b** resembling a cone.

conifer N an evergreen tree or shrub which produces pollen and seeds in cones and has narrow needle-like leaves. ■ **coniferous** ADJ.

conjecture N 1 an opinion based on incomplete evidence. 2 the process of forming such an opinion.
➢ VB, INTR to make a conjecture. ■ **conjectural** ADJ.

conjoin VB, TR & INTR to join together or unite.

conjoined twins N (also **Siamese twins**) twins who are physically joined from birth.

conjugal ADJ relating to marriage.

conjugate VB, GRAM **a** to give the inflected parts of (a verb), indicating number, person, tense, mood and voice; **b** INTR of a verb: to undergo inflection.

conjugation N 1 GRAM **a** the inflection of a verb to indicate number, person, tense, mood and voice; **b** a particular class of verbs having the same set of inflections. 2 a uniting or fusing.

conjunction N 1 GRAM a word used to link sentences, clauses or other words, eg **and, but, if, or, because**, etc. 2 a joining together; combination. 3 the coinciding of events.

conjunctiva N (*-as* or *-ae*) ANAT the thin mucous membrane that lines the eyelids and covers the cornea.

conjunctivitis N inflammation of the conjunctiva.

conjure VB 1 INTR to perform magic tricks, esp ones which deceive the eye or seem to defy nature. 2 to summon (a spirit, demon, etc) to appear. ■ **conjurer** or **conjuror** N.
◆ **conjure sth up** 1 to produce it as though from nothing. 2 to call up, evoke or stir.

conk[1] N, SLANG 1 the nose. 2 the head.

conk[2] VB, INTR, SLANG (usu **conk out**) 1 to break down. 2 to collapse with fatigue, etc.

conker N, COLLOQ the brown shiny seed of the horse chestnut tree.

con man N, COLLOQ a swindler.

connect VB (usu **connect to** or **with sb** or

sth) **1** TR & INTR to join; to link. **2** to associate or involve: **is connected with advertising**. **3** to join by telephone. **4** to relate by marriage or birth. **5** INTR of aeroplanes, trains, buses, etc: to be timed to allow transfer from one to another. ■ **connective** ADJ. ■ **connector** or **connecter** N.

connection or **connexion** N **1** something that connects; a link. **2** a relationship through marriage or birth. **3** an esp influential person whom one meets through one's job, etc; a contact. **4** a train, bus, etc timed so as to allow transfer to it from another passenger service. ◆ **in connection with** to do with; concerning.

connive VB, INTR (often **connive with sb**) to conspire or plot. ■ **connivance** N.

connoisseur N someone who is knowledgeable about and a good judge of a particular subject, eg the arts, wine, food, etc.

connotation N an idea, association or implication additional to the main idea or object expressed. ■ **connote** VB.

connubial ADJ pertaining to marriage.

conquer VB **1** to gain possession or dominion over (territory) by force. **2** to defeat or overcome. **3** to overcome or put an end to (a failing, difficulty, evil, etc). ■ **conqueror** N.

conquest N **1** the act of conquering. **2** something won by effort or force.

conquistador N (-*dores* or -*dors*) one of the 16th-century Spanish conquerors of Peru and Mexico.

consanguinity N relationship by blood. ■ **consanguine** or **consanguineous** ADJ.

conscience N the moral sense of right and wrong that determines someone's thoughts and behaviour.

conscientious ADJ **1** painstaking. **2** guided by conscience. ■ **conscientiousness** N.

conscious ADJ **1** awake, alert and aware of one's thoughts and one's surroundings. **2** knowing: **conscious that someone was watching**. **3** deliberate: **a conscious effort**.

➤ N the part of the human mind which is responsible for such awareness, and is concerned with perceiving and reacting to external objects and events. ■ **consciously** ADV. ■ **consciousness** N.

conscript VB to enlist for military service. ➤ N someone conscripted. ■ **conscription** N.

consecrate VB to set something apart for a holy use; to make sacred. ■ **consecration** N.

consecutive ADJ following one after the other; in sequence. ■ **consecutively** ADV.

consensus N general feeling or agreement; the majority view.

consent VB **1** INTR (often **consent to**) to give permission for. **2** to agree to do something. ➤ N agreement; assent; permission.

consequence N **1** something that follows from, or is caused by, an action or set of circumstances. **2** importance or significance: **of no consequence**.

consequent ADJ **1** following as a result. **2** following as an inference.

consequential ADJ **1** significant or important. **2** following as a result.

consequently ADV as a result; therefore.

conservancy N (-*ies*) an area under special environmental protection.

conservation N **1** the act of conserving; the state of being conserved. **2** the protection and preservation of the environment, its wildlife and its natural resources. **3** the preservation of historical artefacts. ■ **conservationist** N.

conservative ADJ **1** favouring that which is established or traditional, with an opposition to change. **2** of an estimate or calculation: deliberately low, for the sake of caution. **3** of tastes, clothing, etc: restrained or modest. ➤ N **1** a traditionalist. **2** (**Conservative**) a member or supporter of a political party with 'Conservative' in its title. ■ **conservatism** N.

conservatoire N a school specializing in the teaching of music. Also called **conservatory**.

conservatory N (-*ies*) **1 a** a greenhouse for

plants; **b** a similar room used as a lounge. **2** a conservatoire.

conserve VB **1** to keep safe from damage, deterioration, loss or undesirable change. **2** to preserve (fruit, etc) with sugar.
➤ N a jam, esp one containing chunks of fruit.

consider VB **1** to go over something in one's mind. **2** to look at someone or something thoughtfully. **3** to call to mind for comparison, etc. **4** to contemplate doing something. **5** to regard as something specified: **considered him to be his best friend. 6** to think.

considerable ADJ **1** large; great. **2** worthy. ■ **considerably** ADV.

considerate ADJ thoughtful; kind.

consideration N **1** thoughtfulness on behalf of others. **2** careful thought. **3** a fact, circumstance, etc to be taken into account.

considered ADJ **1** carefully thought about. **2** thought of in a specified way.

considering PREP in view of.
➤ CONJ taking into account.
➤ ADV taking the circumstances into account.

consign VB **1** to hand over; to entrust. **2** to send, commit or deliver formally. **3** to send (goods).

consignment N **1** a load of goods, etc sent or delivered. **2** the act of consigning.

consist VB, INTR **1** (always **consist of**) to be composed or made up of several elements or ingredients. **2** (always **consist in** or **of**) to have as an essential feature.

consistency or **consistence** N (**-ies**) **1** texture or composition, with regard to firmness, thickness, etc. **2** agreement; harmony.

consistent ADJ **1** (usu **consistent with sth**) in agreement or in keeping with it. **2** reliable; regular; steady. **3** of people or their actions: not contradictory. ■ **consistently** ADV.

console[1] VB to comfort in distress, grief or disappointment. ■ **consolation** N.

console[2] N **1** MUS the part of an organ with the keys, pedals and panels of stops. **2** a panel of dials, switches, etc for operating electronic equipment.

consolidate VB, TR & INTR **1** to make or become solid or strong. **2** of businesses, etc: to combine or merge into one. ■ **consolidation** N.

consommé N a type of thin clear soup.

consonant N **a** any speech-sound produced by obstructing the passage of the breath in any of several ways; **b** a letter of the alphabet representing such a sound.

consort N a wife or husband, esp of a reigning sovereign.
◆ **consort with sb** (usu with unfavourable implications) to associate with them.

consortium N (**-ia** or **-iums**) an association or combination of several banks, businesses, etc.

conspicuous ADJ **1** visibly noticeable or obvious. **2** notable; striking; glaring.

conspiracy N (**-ies**) **1** the act of plotting in secret. **2** a plot.

conspire VB, INTR **1** to plot secretly together, esp for an unlawful purpose. **2** of events: to seem to be working together to achieve a certain end. ■ **conspirator** N. ■ **conspiratorial** ADJ.

constable N a police officer of the most junior rank.

constabulary N (**-ies**) a police force.

constant ADJ **1** never stopping. **2** frequently recurring. **3** unchanging. **4** faithful; loyal.
➤ N, MATH a symbol representing an unspecified number, which remains unchanged. ■ **constancy** N. ■ **constantly** ADV.

constellation N, ASTRON a named group of stars seen as forming a recognizable pattern.

consternation N anxiety or dismay.

constipation N a condition in which bowel movements occur infrequently or with pain or difficulty. ■ **constipated** ADJ.

constituency N (**-ies**) **1** the district represented by a member of parliament or other representative in a legislative body. **2** the voters in that district.

constituent ADJ forming part of a whole.

➤ N **1** a necessary part; a component. **2** a resident in a constituency.

constitute VB **1** to be; to make up. **2** to establish formally.

constitution N **1** a set of rules governing an organization. **2** the supreme laws and rights upon which a country or state is founded. **3** one's physical make-up, health, etc.

constitutional ADJ **1** legal according to a given constitution. **2** relating to, or controlled by, a constitution. **3** relating to one's physical make-up, health, etc.

constrain VB **1** to force; to compel. **2** to limit the freedom, scope or range of someone.

constraint N **1** a limit or restriction. **2** force; compulsion. **3** awkwardness or inhibition.

constrict VB **1 a** to squeeze or compress; **b** to enclose tightly, esp too tightly. **2** to inhibit. ■ **constriction** N. ■ **constrictive** ADJ.

constrictor N a snake that kills by coiling around its prey and suffocating it.

construct VB **1** to build. **2** to form, compose or put together. **3** GEOM to draw (a figure). ➤ N something constructed.

construction N **1** the process of building or constructing. **2** something built or constructed. **3** GRAM the arrangement of words in a particular relationship. **4** interpretation.

constructive ADJ helping towards progress or development; useful.

construe VB to interpret or explain.

consul N an official representative of a state, stationed in a foreign country. ■ **consular** ADJ. ■ **consulate** N.

consult VB **1** to ask the advice of. **2** to refer to (a map, book, etc). **3** INTR (often **consult with sb**) to have discussions with them.

consultant N **1** someone who gives professional advice. **2** a doctor or surgeon holding the most senior post in a particular field of medicine. ■ **consultancy** N (**-ies**).

consultation N **1** the act or process of

consulting. **2** a meeting for the obtaining of advice or for discussion. ■ **consultative** ADJ.

consume VB **1** to eat or drink. **2** to use up. **3** to destroy. **4** to devour or overcome completely.

consumer N someone who buys goods and services for personal use or need.

consummate VB **1** to finish, perfect or complete something. **2** to complete (a marriage) in its full legal sense through the act of sexual intercourse. ➤ ADJ **1** supreme; very skilled. **2** complete; utter. ■ **consummation** N.

consumption N **1** the act or process of consuming. **2** the amount consumed. **3** the buying and using of goods.

contact N **1** the condition of touching physically. **2** communication or a means of communication. **3** an acquaintance whose influence or knowledge may prove useful. **4** a connection made of a conducting material that allows the passage of an electric current by forming a junction with another conducting part. ➤ VB to get in touch with someone; to communicate with someone.

contact lens N a small lens placed in direct contact with the eyeball to correct vision.

contagion N the transmission of a disease by physical contact with an infected person.

contagious ADJ **1** of a disease: only able to be transmitted by direct contact with or close proximity to an infected individual. **2** of a mood, laughter, etc: spreading easily from person to person.

contain VB **1** to hold or be able to hold. **2** to consist of something specified. **3** to control, limit, check or prevent the spread of something. **4** to control (oneself or one's feelings). **5** to enclose or surround. ■ **containable** ADJ.

container N **1** an object designed for holding or storing, such as a box, tin, etc. **2** a huge metal box for carrying goods by lorry or ship.

containment N the action of preventing the expansion of a hostile power, etc.

contaminate VB **1** to pollute or infect (a

substance). **2** to make something radioactive.
■ **contaminant** N. ■ **contamination** N.

contemplate VB **1** TR & INTR to think about; to
meditate. **2** to look thoughtfully at something.
3 to consider something as a possibility.
■ **contemplation** N.

contemplative ADJ thoughtful; meditative.

contemporaneous ADJ existing or
happening at the same time.

contemporary ADJ **1** (often
contemporary with) belonging to the same
period or time as. **2** (often **contemporary
with**) around the same age as. **3** modern.
➤ N (*-ies*) **1** someone who lives or lived at the
same time as another. **2** someone of about the
same age as another.

contempt N **1** scorn. **2** LAW disregard of or
disobedience to the rules of a court of law.

contemptible ADJ despicable; vile.

contemptuous ADJ (often **contemptuous
of**) showing contempt or scorn.

contend VB **1** INTR (often **contend with**) to
fight or compete. **2** INTR to argue earnestly. **3** to
maintain or assert something. ■ **contender** N.

content[1] ADJ (often **content with**) satisfied.
➤ VB to satisfy or make satisfied.
➤ N peaceful satisfaction; peace of mind.
■ **contented** ADJ. ■ **contentment** N.

content[2] N **1** the subject matter of a book,
speech, etc. **2** the proportion in which a
particular ingredient is present in something.
3 (**contents**) **a** the text of a book, divided into
chapters; **b** a list of these chapters.

contention N a point that one asserts or
maintains in an argument.

contentious ADJ **1** likely to cause argument or
quarrelling. **2** quarrelsome or argumentative.

contest N **1** a competition. **2** a struggle.
➤ VB **1** to enter the competition or struggle for
something. **2** TR & INTR to dispute (a claim, a will,
etc). ■ **contestable** ADJ.

contestant N a competitor.

context N **1** the parts of a passage
surrounding a particular word, phrase, etc
which contribute to the full meaning of the word,
phrase, etc in question. **2** circumstances,
background or setting. ■ **contextual** ADJ.

contiguous ADJ touching.

continent[1] N **1 a** any of the seven main land
masses of the world; **b** the mainland portion of
one of these land masses. **2** (**the Continent**)
the mainland of Europe, as regarded from the
British Isles. ■ **continental** ADJ.

continent[2] ADJ able to control one's bowels
and bladder. ■ **continence** N.

continental breakfast N a light breakfast
of rolls and coffee.

continental quilt N a duvet.

contingency N (*-ies*) **1** something liable, but
not certain, to occur. **2** something dependent
on a chance future happening.

contingent N **1** a body of troops. **2** any
identifiable body of people.
➤ ADJ **1** (USU **contingent on** or **upon**)
dependent on some uncertain circumstance.
2 liable but not certain to occur. **3** accidental.

continual ADJ **1** constantly happening or done;
frequent. **2** constant. ■ **continually** ADV.

continuance N the act or state of continuing.

continue VB **1** TR & INTR to go on without
stopping. **2** TR & INTR to last or cause to last. **3** TR &
INTR to start again. **4** INTR to keep moving in the
same direction. ■ **continuation** N.

continuous ADJ **1** incessant. **2** unbroken;
uninterrupted. ■ **continuously** ADV.

contort VB, TR & INTR to twist violently out of
shape. ■ **contorted** ADJ. ■ **contortion** N.

contortionist N an entertainer able to twist
their body into unnatural positions.

contour N **1** (often **contours**) the distinctive
outline of something. **2** a line on a map joining
points of the same height or depth.

contraband N smuggled goods.
➤ ADJ **1** prohibited from being imported or

exported. **2** smuggled.

contraception N the deliberate prevention of pregnancy by artificial or natural means.

contraceptive N a drug or device that prevents pregnancy.
➤ ADJ preventing pregnancy.

contract N **1** an agreement, esp a legally binding one. **2** a document setting out the terms of such an agreement.
➤ VB **1** TR & INTR to make or become smaller. **2** TR & INTR of muscles: to make or become shorter. **3** to catch (a disease). **4** to enter into (an alliance or marriage). **5** TR & INTR to reduce to a short form: 'Are not' is contracted to 'aren't'.
◆ **contract in** or **out** to arrange to participate, or not to participate, eg in a pension scheme.
◆ **contract sth out** of a company, etc: to arrange for (part of) a job to be done by another company.

contraction N **1** the process of contracting or state of being contracted. **2** a decrease in length, size or volume. **3** a tightening of the muscles caused by a shortening in length of the muscle fibres. **4** (**contractions**) the regular painful spasms of the muscles of the uterus that occur during labour.

contractor N a person or firm that undertakes work on contract.

contractual ADJ relating to a contract or binding agreement.

contradict VB **1** to assert the opposite of or deny (a statement, etc) made by (a person). **2** of a statement, action, etc: to disagree or be inconsistent with another. ■ **contradiction** N. ■ **contradictory** ADJ.

contraflow N a form of traffic diversion whereby traffic moving in opposite directions share the same carriageway.

contralto N (**-tos** or **-ti**) **1** the female singing voice that is lowest in pitch. **2** a singer with this voice. **3** a part to be sung by this voice.

contraption N, COLLOQ a machine or apparatus which is usu ingenious rather than effective.

contrariwise ADV **1** on the other hand. **2** the opposite way round or in the opposite direction.

contrary ADJ **1** opposite; quite different; opposed. **2** of a wind: blowing against one; unfavourable. **3** obstinate, perverse, self-willed or wayward.
➤ N (**-ies**) **1** an extreme opposite. **2** either of a pair of opposites. ■ **contrariness** N.
◆ **on the contrary** in opposition or contrast to what has just been said.
◆ **to the contrary** to the opposite effect; giving the contrasting position.

contrast N **1** difference or dissimilarity between things or people that are being compared. **2** a person or thing strikingly different from another. **3** the degree of difference in tone between the light and dark parts, of a photograph or television picture.
➤ VB **1** to compare so as to reveal differences. **2** (often **contrast with sth**) to show the difference.

contravene VB to break or disobey (a law or rule, etc). ■ **contravention** N (often **in contravention of**) infringement of a law, etc.

contretemps N (PL **contretemps**) **1** an awkward or embarrassing moment, situation, etc. **2** a slight disagreement.

contribute VB (USU **contribute to**) **1** TR & INTR to give (money, time, etc) for some joint purpose. **2** INTR to be one of the causes of something. **3** to supply (an article, etc) for publication in a magazine, etc. ■ **contribution** N. ■ **contributor** N. ■ **contributory** ADJ.

contrite ADJ **1** sorry for something one has done. **2** resulting from a feeling of guilt: a contrite apology. ■ **contrition** N.

contrivance N **1** the act or power of contriving. **2** a device or apparatus, esp an ingenious one. **3** a scheme; a piece of cunning.

contrive VB **1** to manage or succeed. **2** to bring about something: **contrive one's escape**. **3** to make or construct something.

contrived ADJ forced or artificial.

control N **1** authority or charge; power to

influence or guide: **take control. 2** a means of limitation. **3** (**controls**) a device for operating, regulating, or testing (a machine, system, etc). **4** the people in control of some operation. **5** the place where something is checked.
➤ VB (-**ll**-) **1** to have or exercise power over someone or something. **2** to regulate. **3** to limit. ■ **controllable** ADJ.

controller N **1** a person or thing that controls. **2** someone in charge of the finances of an enterprise, etc.

controversy N (-**ies**) a dispute or argument. ■ **controversial** ADJ.

contumely N (-**ies**) FORMAL **1** scornful or insulting words. **2** a contemptuous insult.

contusion N, TECHNICAL a bruise.

conundrum N **1** a confusing problem. **2** a riddle, esp one involving a pun.

conurbation N an extensive cluster of towns merging into one another.

convalesce VB, INTR to recover one's strength after an illness, operation or injury, esp by resting. ■ **convalescence** N. ■ **convalescent** N, ADJ.

convection N the process by which heat is transferred through a liquid or gas.

convene VB, TR & INTR to assemble or summon to assemble.

convener or **convenor** N someone who convenes or chairs a meeting.

convenience N **1** the quality of being convenient. **2** something useful. **3** BRIT EUPHEMISTIC a lavatory, esp a public one.
◆ **at one's convenience** when and where it suits one.

convenient ADJ **1** not causing trouble or difficulty. **2** useful; saving time and trouble. **3** at hand. ■ **conveniently** ADV.

convent N **a** a community of nuns; **b** the building they occupy.

convention N **1** a large and formal conference or assembly. **2** a formal treaty or agreement. **3** a custom or generally accepted practice. **4** US POL a meeting of party delegates to nominate a candidate for office.

conventional ADJ **1** traditional; normal; customary. **2** conservative or unoriginal. **3** of weapons: non-nuclear.

converge VB, INTR **1** (often **converge on** or **upon**) to move towards or meet at one point. **2** eg of opinions: to tend towards one another; to coincide. ■ **convergence** N.

conversant ADJ (usu **conversant with**) having a thorough knowledge of.

conversation N informal talk.

conversational ADJ relating to conversation. ■ **conversationalist** N.

converse[1] VB, INTR, FORMAL **1** to hold a conversation; to talk. **2** to commune spiritually.

converse[2] ADJ reverse; opposite.
➤ N opposite. ■ **conversely** ADV.

conversion N **1** the act of converting. **2** something converted to another use.

convert VB **1** TR & INTR to change the form or function of one thing into another. **2** TR & INTR to win over, or be won over, to another religion, opinion, etc.
➤ N someone who has been converted to a new religion, practice, etc.

convertible ADJ capable of being converted.
➤ N a car with a fold-down top.

convex ADJ outward-curving, like the surface of the eye. ■ **convexity** N.

convey VB **1** to carry; to transport. **2** to communicate. **3** LAW to transfer the ownership of (property). ■ **conveyable** ADJ. ■ **conveyor** N.

conveyance N **1** the process of conveying. **2** a vehicle of any kind. **3** LAW **a** the transfer of the ownership of property; **b** the document setting out such a transfer. ■ **conveyancer** N.

conveyor belt N an endless moving rubber or metal belt for transporting articles.

convict VB to prove or declare someone guilty (of a crime).

➤ N someone serving a prison sentence.

conviction N 1 the act of convicting; an instance of being convicted. 2 the state of being convinced; a strong belief.

convince VB to persuade someone of something; to make or cause to make them believe it. ■ **convincing** ADJ.

convivial ADJ 1 lively, jovial, sociable and cheerful. 2 festive. ■ **conviviality** N.

convocation N 1 the act of summoning together. 2 an assembly.

convoke VB to call together; to assemble.

convoluted ADJ 1 coiled and twisted. 2 complicated; difficult to understand.

convolution N 1 a twist. 2 a complication.

convolvulus N (-*luses* or -*li*) a trailing or twining plant with funnel-shaped flowers.

convoy N a group of vehicles or merchant ships travelling together, or under escort.

convulse VB, TR & INTR to jerk or distort violently by or as if by a spasm. ■ **convulsive** ADJ.

convulsion N (often **convulsions**) a violent involuntary contraction of the muscles of the body, or a series of such contractions.

coo N the soft murmuring call of a dove.
➤ VB (**cooed, cooing**) 1 INTR to make this sound. 2 TR & INTR to murmur affectionately.
➤ EXCLAM, BRIT COLLOQ used to express amazement.

cook VB, TR & INTR to prepare (food) or be prepared by heating.
➤ N someone who cooks or prepares food.
◆ **cook sth up** COLLOQ to concoct or invent it.

cooker N an apparatus for cooking food; a stove.

cookery N the art or practice of cooking food.

cookie N 1 chiefly N AMER a biscuit. 2 COLLOQ a person: a smart cookie.

cool ADJ 1 between cold and warm; fairly cold. 2 pleasantly fresh; free of heat. 3 calm; laid-back. 4 lacking enthusiasm; unfriendly: a cool response. 5 of a large sum: exact; at least:

made a cool million. 6 COLLOQ excellent.
➤ N 1 a cool part or period; coolness. 2 COLLOQ self-control; composure.
➤ VB, TR & INTR (often **cool down** or **off**) 1 to become cool. 2 to become less interested or enthusiastic. ■ **coolly** ADV. ■ **coolness** N.

coolant N a liquid or gas used as a cooling agent, eg in a car radiator, nuclear reactor, etc.

coolie N, OFFENSIVE 1 an unskilled native labourer in Eastern countries. 2 S AFR an Indian.

coomb or **combe** N 1 in S England: a short deep valley. 2 a deep hollow in a hillside.

coop N 1 a cage for hens. 2 any confined or restricted space.
➤ VB (usu **coop up**) to confine in a small space.

cooper N someone who makes barrels.

co-operate VB, INTR 1 (often **co-operate with**) to work together with. 2 to be willing to fit in with the plans of others. ■ **co-operation** N.

co-operative ADJ 1 relating to or giving co-operation. 2 willing to fit in with others' plans, etc. 3 jointly owned by workers, with profits shared equally.
➤ N a co-operative business.

co-opt VB to elect an additional member, by the votes of the existing ones.

co-ordinate VB 1 to integrate and adjust (a number of different parts or processes) so as to relate smoothly one to another. 2 to bring (one's limbs or bodily movements) into a smoothly functioning relationship.
➤ N 1 (usu **coordinate**) MATH, GEOG either of a pair of numbers taken from a vertical and horizontal axis which together establish the position of a fixed point on a map. 2 GEOM any of a set of numbers used to define the position of a point, line or surface by reference to axes drawn through a fixed point at right angles to each other. ■ **co-ordination** N.

coot N an aquatic bird with dark plumage, a characteristic white shield above the bill and large feet with lobed toes.

cop N, SLANG 1 a policeman. 2 an arrest.
➤ VB (-*pp*-) 1 to catch. 2 to grab; to seize. 3 to

suffer (a punishment, etc).
- ◆ **cop it** SLANG to be punished.
- ◆ **cop out** COLLOQ to avoid a responsibility.

cope VB, INTR to manage; to get by.
- ◆ **cope with sth** to deal with (a difficulty or problem, etc) successfully.

copier N a person or machine which copies.

co-pilot N the assistant pilot of an aircraft.

coping N a capping along the top row of stones in a wall.

copious ADJ plentiful. ■ **copiously** ADV.

cop-out N, COLLOQ an avoidance of a responsibility.

copper[1] N **1** CHEM a soft reddish-brown metallic element. **2** (usu **coppers**) any coin of low value made of copper or bronze. **3** a large metal vessel for boiling water in. **4** a reddish-brown colour.
- ➤ ADJ **1** made from copper. **2** copper-coloured.

copper[2] N, SLANG, chiefly BRIT a policeman.

copperplate N **1** a copper plate used for engraving or etching, or a print made from it. **2** fine handwriting of the style formerly used on copperplates.

coppice N, BOT an area of woodland in which trees are regularly cut back to ground level to encourage the growth of side shoots.

copra N the dried kernel of the coconut.

copse N a coppice.

copula N (*-las* or *-lae*) GRAM a verb that links the subject and complement of a sentence, eg is in **She is a doctor** or grew in **It grew dark**.

copulate VB, INTR to have sexual intercourse.
■ **copulation** N.

copy N (*-ies*) **1** an imitation or reproduction. **2** one of the many specimens of a book or of a particular issue of a magazine, newspaper, etc. **3** written material for printing. **4** the wording of an advertisement.
- ➤ VB (*-ies, -ied*) **1** to imitate. **2** to make a copy of something; to transcribe.

copycat N, COLLOQ DERISIVE an imitator or person who copies the work of another.

copyist N **1** someone who copies (documents, etc) in writing. **2** an imitator.

copyright N the sole right, granted by law, to reproduce an original artistic work.
- ➤ ADJ protected by copyright.
- ➤ VB to secure the copyright of something.

coquette N a flirtatious woman.
■ **coquettish** ADJ.

coracle N a small oval rowing-boat made of wickerwork covered with waterproof material.

coral N **1** a tiny invertebrate marine animal, consisting of a hollow tube with a mouth surrounded by tentacles at the top. **2** a hard chalky substance of various colours, formed from the skeletons of this animal.

cor anglais (*cors anglais*) N, MUS a woodwind instrument similar to the oboe.

corbel N, ARCHIT a piece of stone or timber, projecting from a wall.

cord N **1** a thin rope or string consisting of several separate strands twisted together. **2** ANAT any long flexible structure resembling this: **umbilical cord**. **3** N AMER the cable of an electrical appliance. **4** a ribbed fabric, esp corduroy. **5** (**cords**) corduroy trousers.

cordial ADJ **1** warm and affectionate. **2** heartfelt; profound.
- ➤ N a concentrated fruit-flavoured drink, which is usu diluted. ■ **cordially** ADV.

cordite N any of various smokeless explosive materials used as a propellant for guns, etc.

cordless ADJ operating without a flex connecting it to the mains: **cordless phone**.

cordon N a line of police or soldiers, or a system of road blocks, encircling an area so as to prevent or control passage into or out of it.
- ➤ VB (often **cordon sth off**) to close off (an area) with a cordon.

cordon bleu ADJ of a cook or cookery: being of the highest standard.

corduroy N **1** a thick ribbed cotton fabric.

2 (**corduroys**) trousers made of corduroy.
➤ ADJ made from corduroy.

core N **1** the fibrous case at the centre of some fruits, eg apples and pears, containing the seeds. **2** the innermost, central, essential or unchanging part. **3** the central region of a star or planet, or of a nuclear reactor.
➤ VB to remove the core of (an apple, etc).

corgi N a sturdy short-legged breed of dog with a thick coat and fox-like head.

coriander N **1** a plant with narrowly lobed leaves and globular aromatic fruits. **2** the leaves and dried ripe fruit of this plant, widely used as a flavouring in cooking.

cork N **1** BOT a layer of tissue that forms below the epidermis in the stems and roots of woody plants, eg trees. **2** a piece of this used as a stopper for a bottle, etc.
➤ VB to stop up (a bottle, etc) with a cork.

corkage N the fee charged by a restaurant for serving customers wine, etc that they have bought off the premises.

corkscrew N a tool with a spiral spike for screwing into bottle corks to remove them.
➤ VB, TR & INTR to move spirally.

corm N, BOT in certain plants, eg crocus: a swollen underground stem.

cormorant N a black or dark brown seabird with a long snakelike neck.

corn[1] N **1** in the UK: the most important cereal crop of a particular region, esp wheat in England, and oats in Scotland and Ireland. **2** in N America, Australia and New Zealand: maize. **3** the harvested seed of cereal plants.

corn[2] N a small painful area of hard thickened skin, usu on or between the toes.

corncob N the woody core of an ear of maize, to which the rows of kernels are attached.

corncrake N a bird which has light brown streaky plumage and chestnut wings.

cornea N (-neas or -neae) in vertebrates: the convex transparent membrane that covers the front of the eyeball. ■ **corneal** ADJ.

corned beef N beef that has been cooked, salted and then canned.

cornelian or **carnelian** N, GEOL a red and white form of agate, a semi-precious stone.

corner N **1 a** a point or place where lines or surface-edges meet; **b** the inside or outside of the angle so formed. **2** an intersection between roads. **3** a quiet or remote place. **4** an awkward situation: **in a tight corner**. **5** BOXING either of the angles of the ring used as a base between bouts by contestants. **6** FOOTBALL, ETC a free kick from a corner of the field.
➤ VB **1** to force into a position from which escape is difficult. **2** to gain control of (a market) by obtaining a monopoly. **3** INTR of a driver or vehicle: to turn a corner.

cornerstone N **1** a stone in the corner of the foundation of a building. **2** a crucial part.

cornet N **1** MUS a brass instrument similar to the trumpet. **2** an edible cone-shaped holder for ice cream. ■ **cornetist** or **cornettist** N.

cornflakes PL N toasted maize flakes, usu as a breakfast cereal.

cornflour N, COOKERY a finely ground flour used for thickening sauces, etc.

cornflower N a plant with deep blue flowers.

cornice N **1** a decorative border of moulded plaster round a ceiling. **2** ARCHIT the projecting section of an entablature.

Cornish ADJ of Cornwall.

cornucopia N **1** ART a horn full to overflowing with fruit and other produce, used as a symbol of abundance. **2** an abundant supply.

corny ADJ (-ier, -iest) COLLOQ **1** of a joke: old and stale. **2** old-fashioned or sentimental.

corolla N, BOT the collective name for the petals of a flower.

corona N (-nae or -nas) ASTRON the outer atmosphere of the Sun, consisting of a halo of hot luminous gases.

coronary ADJ, PHYSIOL denoting vessels, nerves, etc which encircle a part or organ, esp the arteries which supply blood to the heart.

➢ N (*-ies*) PATHOL a coronary thrombosis.

coronary thrombosis N, PATHOL the formation of a blood clot in a coronary artery.

coronation N the ceremony of crowning a monarch or consort.

coroner N a public official whose chief responsibility is the investigation of sudden, suspicious or accidental deaths.

coronet N a small crown.

corporal[1] N a non-commissioned officer in the army or air force.

corporal[2] ADJ of the body.

corporal punishment N physical punishment such as beating or caning.

corporate ADJ 1 shared by members of a group; joint. 2 belonging or relating to a corporation. 3 formed into a corporation.

corporation N 1 a body of people acting jointly, eg for administration or business purposes. 2 the council of a town or city.

corporeal ADJ relating to the body as distinct from the soul; physical.

corps N (PL *corps*) 1 a military body or division forming a tactical unit. 2 a body of people engaged in particular work: **diplomatic corps**.

corpse N the dead body of a human.

corpulent ADJ fat; fleshy; obese. ■ **corpulence** or **corpulency** N.

corpus N (*-pora*) a body of writings, eg by a particular author. 2 a body of written and/or spoken material for language research.

corpuscle N, ANAT any small particle or cell within a tissue or organ, esp a red or white blood cell. ■ **corpuscular** ADJ.

corral chiefly N AMER, N 1 an enclosure for driving horses or cattle into. 2 a defensive ring of wagons.
➢ VB (*-ll-*) to herd or pen into a corral.

correct VB 1 to set or put right; to remove errors from something. 2 to mark the errors in. 3 to adjust or make better.
➢ ADJ 1 free from error; accurate.

2 appropriate; conforming to accepted standards. ■ **correctly** ADV. ■ **correctness** N.

correction N 1 the act of correcting. 2 an alteration that improves something. ■ **correctional** ADJ.

corrective ADJ having the effect of correcting.

correlate VB 1 TR & INTR to have a connection or correspondence. 2 to combine, compare or show relationships between (information, reports, etc). ■ **correlation** N.

correlative ADJ mutually linked.

correspond VB, INTR 1 (usu **correspond to**) to be similar or equivalent. 2 (usu **correspond with** or **to**) to be compatible or in agreement; to match. 3 to communicate, esp by letter. ■ **corresponding** ADJ.

correspondence N 1 similarity; equivalence. 2 agreement. 3 a communication by letters; b the letters received or sent.

correspondent N 1 someone with whom one exchanges letters. 2 someone employed by a newspaper, etc to send reports from some part of the world or on some topic.

corridor N a passageway.

corrie N in the Scottish Highlands: a semicircular hollow on a hillside.

corroborate VB to confirm (eg someone's statement), esp by providing evidence. ■ **corroboration** N. ■ **corroborative** ADJ.

corrode VB 1 TR & INTR to eat or be eaten away, esp by rust or chemicals. 2 to destroy gradually.

corrosion N 1 the process of corroding, eg of a metal or alloy. 2 a corroded part or patch.

corrosive ADJ 1 tending to cause corrosion. 2 of language: hurtful, sarcastic.
➢ N a corrosive thing or substance.

corrugate VB to fold into parallel ridges, so as to make stronger. ■ **corrugated** ADJ. ■ **corrugation** N.

corrupt VB 1 TR & INTR to change for the worse, esp morally. 2 to spoil, deform or make impure. 3 to bribe.

➤ ADJ **1** morally evil. **2** involving bribery.
■ **corruptive** ADJ.

corruptible ADJ capable of being or liable to be corrupted.

corruption N **1** the process of corrupting or condition of being corrupt. **2** a deformed or altered form of a word or phrase: 'Santa Claus' is a corruption of 'Saint Nicholas'.

corsage N a small spray of flowers for pinning to the bodice of a dress.

corset N a tightly fitting undergarment stiffened by strips of bone or plastic, and used for shaping or controlling the figure, or for supporting an injured back. ■ **corsetry** N.

cortège N a funeral procession.

cortisone N, BIOCHEM a naturally occurring steroid hormone which, in synthetic form, is used to treat rheumatoid arthritis, certain eye and skin disorders, etc.

corundum N, GEOL a hard aluminium oxide mineral used as an abrasive, and whose crystalline forms include ruby and sapphire.

coruscate VB, INTR to sparkle; to give off flashes of light. ■ **coruscating** ADJ.

corvette N a small warship for escorting larger vessels.

cos[1] and **cos lettuce** N a type of lettuce with crisp slim leaves.

cos[2] ABBREV cosine.

cosh N a club used as a weapon.
➤ VB, COLLOQ to hit with a cosh.

cosine N, TRIG in a right-angled triangle: a function, that is the ratio of the length of the side adjacent to the angle to the length of the hypotenuse.

cosmetic N (often **cosmetics**) any application to improve the appearance of the body.
➤ ADJ **1** used to beautify the face, body or hair. **2** improving superficially, for the sake of appearance only. ■ **cosmetically** ADV.

cosmic ADJ **1** relating to the Universe; universal. **2** coming from outer space: **cosmic rays**.

cosmology N (-ies) **1** the scientific study of the origin, nature, structure and evolution of the Universe. **2** a particular theory or model of the origin and structure of the Universe.
■ **cosmological** ADJ. ■ **cosmologist** N.

cosmonaut N an astronaut from any of the countries of the former Soviet Union.

cosmopolitan ADJ **1** free of national prejudices; international in experience and outlook. **2** composed of people from all different parts of the world.

cosmos N the Universe seen as an ordered system.

cosset VB (-*tt*-) to pamper.

cost VB (in senses 1 and 2 PA T, PA P **cost**) **1** to be obtainable at a certain price. **2** TR & INTR to involve the loss or sacrifice of someone or something. **3** (PA T, PA P **costed**) to estimate or decide the cost of something.
➤ N **1** what something costs. **2** loss or sacrifice.

co-star N a fellow star in a film, play, etc.
➤ VB **1** INTR to appear alongside another star. **2** to feature as fellow stars: **co-starring Gielgud and Olivier**.

cost-effective ADJ giving acceptable financial return in relation to initial outlay.

costermonger N, BRIT someone who sells fruit and vegetables from a barrow.

costly ADJ (-ier, -iest) **1** involving much cost; expensive. **2** involving major losses or sacrifices. ■ **costliness** N.

cost of living N the expense of ordinary necessities such as food, clothing, fuel, etc.

costume N **1** a set of clothing of a special kind, esp of a particular historical period or country. **2** a garment or outfit for a special activity: **a swimming-costume**.

costume jewellery N inexpensive jewellery made from artificial materials.

cosy ADJ (-ier, -iest) **1** warm and comfortable. **2** friendly, intimate and confidential: **a cosy chat**.
➤ N (-ies) a cover to keep something warm, esp

a teapot. ■ **cosily** ADV. ■ **cosiness** N.

cot N **1** a small bed with high, barred sides for a child. **2** a portable bed.

cot death N Sudden Infant Death Syndrome.

coterie N a small exclusive group of people who have the same interests.

cotoneaster N a shrub with clusters of white or pink flowers, then red or orange berries.

cottage N a small house, esp one in a village or the countryside. ■ **cottager** N.

cottage cheese N soft white cheese made from the curds of skimmed milk.

cottage industry N a craft industry employing workers in their own homes.

cotton N **1** a shrubby plant cultivated for the creamy-white downy fibres which surround its seeds. **2** the soft white fibre from this plant, used in the production of textiles. **3** the cloth or yarn woven from these fibres.
➢ ADJ made from cotton. ■ **cottony** ADJ.

cotton wool N soft fluffy wadding made from cotton fibre.

cotyledon N, BOT in flowering plants: one of the leaves produced by the embryo.

couch[1] N **1** a sofa or settee. **2** a bed-like seat with a headrest, eg for patients to lie on when being treated by a doctor or psychiatrist.

couch[2] and **couch grass** N a grass with rough dull green or bluish-green leaves.

couch potato N, COLLOQ someone who spends a lot of time watching television.

cougar N, N AMER a puma.

cough VB **1** INTR to expel air, mucus, etc from the throat or lungs with a rough sharp noise. **2** INTR of an engine, etc: to make a similar noise.
➢ N **1** an act or sound of coughing. **2** a condition of lungs or throat causing coughing.
◆ **cough up** SLANG to provide (money, information, etc), esp reluctantly.

could VB **1** PA T OF **can**: I found I could lift it. **2** used to express a possibility: You could be right. **3** used to express a possible course of action: You could try telephoning her. **4** used in making requests: Could you help me? **5** to feel like doing something or able to do something: I could have strangled him.

couldn't CONTRACTION could not.

coulis N (PL **coulis**) a purée of fruit, vegetables, etc often served as a sauce.

coulomb N the SI unit of electric charge.

council N **1 a** a body of people whose function is to advise, administer, organize, discuss or legislate; **b** the people making up such a body. **2** the elected body of people that directs the affairs of a town, borough, district, region, etc.

council house N a house built, owned and rented out by a local council.

councillor N an elected member of a council.

counsel N **1** advice. **2** consultation or discussion. **3** a lawyer or group of lawyers that gives legal advice and fights cases in court.
➢ VB (**-ll-**) to advise.

counsellor or (N AMER) **counselor** N **1** an adviser. **2** N AMER a lawyer.

count[1] VB **1** INTR to recite numbers in ascending order. **2** to find the total amount of (items), by adding up. **3** to include: Did you count Iain? **4** INTR to be important: Good contacts count. **5** to consider: Count yourself lucky.
➢ N **1** an act of counting. **2** the number counted. **3** a charge brought against an accused person.
◆ **count on sb** or **sth** to rely on it or them.

count[2] N a European nobleman.

countdown N a count backwards from a certain number to zero, the moment for action.

countenance N face; expression or appearance.
➢ VB to allow; to tolerate.

counter[1] N **1** a long flat-topped fitting in a shop, cafeteria, bank, etc over which goods are sold, food is served or business is transacted. **2** a small flat disc used as a playing-piece. **3** a disc-shaped token used as a substitute coin.

counter[2] VB, TR & INTR to oppose or hit back.

➤ ADV (often **counter to sth**) in the opposite direction to it; in contradiction of it.
➤ ADJ contrary; opposing.
➤ N **1** a return blow; an opposing move. **2** an opposite or contrary.

counteract VB to reduce or prevent the effect of something.

counter-attack N an attack in reply to an attack.
➤ VB, TR & INTR to attack in return.

counterbalance N a weight, force, etc that balances another or cancels it out.
➤ VB to act as a counterbalance to.

counter-espionage N activities undertaken to frustrate spying by an enemy.

counterfeit ADJ **1** made in imitation of a genuine article, esp with the purpose of deceiving; forged. **2** not genuine; insincere.
➤ N an imitation, esp one designed to deceive.
➤ VB **1** to copy for a dishonest purpose; to forge. **2** to pretend.

counterfoil N the section of a cheque, ticket, etc retained by the person who issues it.

counter-intelligence N another name for **counter-espionage**.

countermand VB to cancel or revoke (an order or command).

counter-measure N an action taken to counteract a dangerous development or move.

counterpane N, DATED a bedspread.

counterpart N **1** one of two parts which form a corresponding pair. **2** a person or thing which is not exactly the same as another, but which is equivalent to it in a different place or context.

counterpoint N, MUS **1** the combining of two or more melodies sung or played simultaneously into a harmonious whole. **2** a part or melody combined with another.
➤ VB to set in contrast to.

counterpoise N **1** a weight which balances another weight. **2** a state of equilibrium.
➤ VB to balance with something of equal weight.

counter-productive ADJ having the opposite effect to that intended.

countersign VB to sign (a document, etc already signed) by way of confirmation.
➤ N a sign or signal given in response to another sign or signal.

countersink VB to widen the upper part of (a screw hole) so that the top of the screw will be level with the surrounding surface.

counterweight N a counterbalancing weight.

countess N **1** the wife or widow of an earl or count. **2** a woman with the rank of earl or count.

countless ADJ too many to count.

country N (**-ies**) **1** an area of land distinguished from other areas by its culture, inhabitants, political boundary, etc. **2** the population of such an area of land. **3** a nation or state. **4** one's native land. **5** (often **the country**) open land, away from the towns and cities, usu characterized by hills, fields, etc.

country and western N a style of popular music characterized by its use of instruments like banjos, fiddles and pedal steel guitar.

country dance N any one of many traditional British dances in which partners face each other in lines or sometimes form circles.

countryman and **countrywoman** N **1** someone who lives in a rural area. **2** someone belonging to a particular country, esp the same country as oneself.

country music N a category of popular music, including country and western.

countryside N rural land situated outside or away from towns.

county N (**-ies**) **1** any of the geographical divisions within England, Wales and Ireland that form the larger units of local government. **2** in the USA: an administrative subdivision within a state.

coup N **1** a successful move; a masterstroke. **2** a coup d'état.

coup d'état N (**coups d'état**) the sudden, usu

violent, overthrow of a government.

coupé N a car with four seats, two doors and a sloping rear.

couple N 1 a pair of people attached in some way, often romantically. 2 a pair of partners, eg for dancing. 3 (usu **a couple of**) two, or a few. ➤ VB 1 to associate; to link. 2 to connect (two things). 3 INTR to have sexual intercourse.

couplet N a pair of consecutive lines of verse.

coupling N a link for joining things together.

coupon N a slip of paper entitling one to something, eg a discount.

courage N 1 bravery. 2 cheerfulness or resolution in coping with setbacks.

courageous ADJ having or showing courage. ■ **courageously** ADV.

courgette N a variety of small marrow.

courier N 1 a guide who travels with and looks after, parties of tourists. 2 a messenger, esp one delivering special or urgent messages or items.

course N 1 the path in which anyone or anything moves. 2 a direction taken or planned: **go off course**. 3 the channel of a river, etc. 4 the normal progress of something. 5 the passage of a period of time: **in the course of a year**. 6 a line of action. 7 **a** a series of lessons, etc; a curriculum; **b** the work covered in such a series. 8 a prescribed treatment over a period. 9 any of the successive parts of a meal. 10 often IN COMPOUNDS the ground over which a game is played or a race run: **golf course**. ➤ VB, INTR to move or flow.
◆ **in due course** at the appropriate time.
◆ **in the course of sth** during it.
◆ **a matter of course** a natural or expected action or result.
◆ **of course** 1 as expected. 2 naturally; certainly; without doubt.

court N 1 the judge, law officials and members of the jury gathered to hear and decide on a legal case. 2 the room or building used for such a hearing. 3 an area marked out for a particular game or sport, or a division of this: **basketball court**. 4 an open space or square surrounded by houses or by sections of a building. 5 the palace, household, attendants, and advisers of a sovereign. ➤ VB 1 TR & INTR, OLD USE to try to win the love of someone. 2 to try to win the favour of someone. 3 to risk or invite: **court danger**.

courteous ADJ polite; considerate; respectful.

courtesan N, HIST a prostitute with wealthy or noble clients.

courtesy N (**-ies**) 1 courteous behaviour; politeness. 2 a courteous act.

courthouse N a building in which the lawcourts are held.

courtier N 1 someone in attendance at a royal court. 2 an elegant flatterer.

courtly ADJ 1 having fine manners. 2 flattering.

court-martial N (**courts-martial** or **court-martials**) a military court which tries members of the armed forces. ➤ VB (**-ll-**) to try by court-martial.

courtroom N a room in which a lawcourt is held.

courtship N, DATED 1 the courting or wooing of an intended spouse. 2 the period of this.

courtyard N an open space surrounded by buildings or walls.

couscous N a N African dish of crushed semolina.

cousin N a son or daughter of one's uncle or aunt. Also called **first cousin**.

couture N the designing, making and selling of fashionable clothes.

cove N a small and usu sheltered bay or inlet on a rocky coast.

coven N a gathering of witches.

covenant N 1 LAW a formal sealed agreement to do something, eg pay money regularly to a charity. 2 a formal binding agreement. ➤ VB, TR & INTR to agree by covenant to do something. ■ **covenanter** N.

cover VB 1 to form a layer over someone or something. 2 to protect or conceal someone or

something by putting something over them or it. **3** to clothe. **4** to extend over something. **5** to strew, sprinkle, spatter, mark all over, etc. **6** to deal with (a subject). **7** of a reporter, etc: to investigate or report on (a story). **8** to have as one's area of responsibility. **9** to travel (a distance). **10** to be adequate to pay. **11** to insure; to insure against something. **12** to shield with a firearm at the ready or with actual fire. **13** INTR (usu **cover for**) to take over the duties of an absent colleague, etc.
➤ N **1** something that covers. **2** a lid, top, protective casing, etc. **3** the covering of something. **4** (**covers**) the sheets and blankets on a bed. **5** the paper or board binding of a book, magazine, etc; one side of this. **6** an envelope: *a first-day cover.* **7** shelter or protection. **8** insurance. **9** service: *emergency cover.* **10** a pretence; a screen; a false identity. **11** armed protection; protective fire.

coverage N **1** an amount covered. **2** the extent to which a news item is reported.

cover charge N in a restaurant, café, etc: a service charge made per person.

cover girl N a girl or woman whose photograph is shown on a magazine cover.

covering N something that covers.

covering letter N a letter explaining the documents or goods it accompanies.

coverlet N a thin top cover for a bed.

cover note N a temporary insurance certificate, giving cover until the policy is issued.

covert ADJ secret; concealed.
➤ N **1** a thicket providing cover for game. **2** a shelter for animals. ■ **covertly** ADV.

cover-up N an act of concealing something suspect or illicit.

cover version N a recording of a song, which has already been recorded by another artist.

covet VB to long to possess something (esp something belonging to someone else).

covetous ADJ envious; greedy.

covey N **1** a small flock of birds, esp partridge

or grouse. **2** a small group of people.

cow[1] N **1** the mature female of any bovine animal, esp domesticated cattle. **2** the mature female of certain other mammals, eg the elephant, whale and seal. **3** loosely used to refer to any domestic breed of cattle.

cow[2] VB to frighten someone or something into submission.

coward N someone easily frightened, or lacking courage to face danger or difficulty. ■ **cowardice** N. ■ **cowardly** ADV.

cowboy N **1** in the western USA: a man who tends cattle, usu on horseback. **2** SLANG, DEROG someone who undertakes building or other work without proper training or qualifications.

cower VB, INTR to shrink away in fear.

cowhide N leather made from the hide of a cow.

cowl N **1** a monk's large loose hood or hooded habit. **2** any large loose hood.

cowling N the streamlined metal casing that houses the engine of an aircraft, etc.

cowpat N a flat deposit of cow dung.

cowrie or **cowry** N (*-ries*) **1** a marine snail, found mainly in tropical waters. **2** the brightly coloured egg-shaped shell of this animal.

cowslip N a plant with a cluster of yellow sweet-smelling flowers.

cox N short for **coxswain**.
➤ VB, TR & INTR to act as cox of (a boat).

coxswain or **cockswain** N someone who steers a small boat.

coy ADJ **1** shy; modest; affectedly bashful. **2** irritatingly uncommunicative. ■ **coyly** ADV. ■ **coyness** N.

coyote N (*coyotes* or *coyote*) a small N American wolf.

coypu N (*coypus* or *coypu*) **1** a large rat-like aquatic rodent with a broad blunt muzzle and webbed hind feet. **2** its soft fur.

CPU ABBREV, COMP central processing unit.

crab[1] N 1 a marine crustacean with a hard flattened shell and five pairs of jointed legs, the front pair being developed into pincers. **2 a** the **crab louse**; **b** (**crabs**) infestation by this.

crab[2] N 1 short for **crab apple**. 2 a grumpy or irritable person.

crab apple N 1 a deciduous shrub or small tree with thorny branches and white flowers. 2 the small hard sour fruit of this tree.

crabbed ADJ 1 bad-tempered; grouchy. 2 of handwriting: cramped and hard to decipher.

crabby ADJ (-*ier*, -*iest*) COLLOQ bad-tempered.

crab louse N a crab-shaped parasitic louse which infests the hair of the human pubic area.

crack VB 1 TR & INTR to fracture or cause to fracture without breaking into pieces. 2 TR & INTR to split or make something split. 3 TR & INTR to make or cause to make a sudden sharp noise. 4 to strike sharply. 5 TR & INTR to give way or make someone or something give way. 6 to force open (a safe). 7 to solve (a problem etc). 8 to tell (a joke). 9 INTR of the voice: to change pitch or tone suddenly and unintentionally. ➤ N 1 a sudden sharp sound. 2 a partial fracture in a material produced by an external force or internal stress. 3 a narrow opening. 4 a resounding blow. 5 SLANG (in full **crack cocaine**) a highly addictive derivative of cocaine. ➤ ADJ, COLLOQ expert: **a crack shot**.
◆ **at the crack of dawn** COLLOQ at daybreak; very early.
◆ **crack down on sb** or **sth** COLLOQ to take firm action against them or it.
◆ **crack up** COLLOQ 1 to suffer an emotional breakdown. 2 to collapse with laughter.
◆ **have a crack at sth** COLLOQ to attempt it.

crackdown N a firm action taken against someone or something.

cracked ADJ 1 COLLOQ crazy. 2 of a voice: harsh; uneven. 3 damaged by splitting.

cracker N 1 a thin crisp unsweetened biscuit. 2 a party toy in the form of a paper tube usu containing a paper hat, gift and motto, that pulls apart with a bang. 3 a small, noisy firework.
4 COLLOQ an exceptional person or thing.

crackers ADJ, COLLOQ mad.

crackle VB, INTR to make a faint continuous cracking or popping sound. ➤ N this kind of sound. ■ **crackly** ADJ.

crackling N the crisp skin of roast pork.

crackpot COLLOQ, ADJ crazy. ➤ N a crazy person.

cradle N 1 a cot for a small baby, esp one that can be rocked. 2 a place of origin; the home or source of something: **the cradle of civilization**. 3 a suspended platform or cage for workmen working on a ship or building. ➤ VB 1 to rock or hold gently. 2 to nurture.

craft N 1 a skill, trade or occupation, esp one using the hands. 2 skilled ability. 3 cunning. ➤ PL N, often IN COMPOUNDS boats, ships, air or space vehicles collectively. ➤ VB to make something skilfully.

craftsman and **craftswoman** N someone skilled at a craft.

craftsmanship N the skill of a craftsman or craftswoman.

crafty ADJ (-*ier*, -*iest*) clever, shrewd, cunning or sly. ■ **craftily** ADV. ■ **craftiness** N.

crag N a rocky peak or jagged outcrop of rock. ■ **craggy** ADJ. (-*ier*, -*est*).

cram VB (-*mm*-) 1 to stuff full. 2 to pack it tightly.

cramp N 1 a painful involuntary prolonged contraction of a muscle or group of muscles. 2 (**cramps**) severe abdominal pain. ➤ VB to restrict with or as with a cramp.

cramped ADJ 1 overcrowded; closed in. 2 of handwriting: small and closely written.

crampon N a spiked iron attachment for climbing boots, to improve grip on ice or rock.

cranberry N 1 a shrub with oval pointed leaves, pink flowers and red berries. 2 the sour-tasting fruit of this plant.

crane N 1 a machine with a long pivoted arm from which lifting gear is suspended, allowing heavy weights to be moved. 2 a large wading

bird with a long neck and long legs.
➤ VB, TR & INTR to stretch (one's neck), or lean forward, in order to see better.

cranefly N a long-legged, two-winged insect. Also (COLLOQ) called **daddy-long-legs**.

cranial ADJ relating to the skull.

cranium N (-*ia* or -*iums*) 1 the dome-shaped part of the skull that encloses and protects the brain. 2 the skull.

crank N 1 a device consisting of an arm connected to and projecting at right angles from the shaft of an engine or motor. 2 a handle bent at right angles and incorporating such a device, used to start an engine or motor by hand. 3 DEROG an eccentric person.
◆ **crank sth up** 1 to rotate (a shaft) using a crank. 2 to start (an engine, a machine, etc) using a crank.

crankshaft N the main shaft of an engine or other machine, used to transmit power from the cranks to the connecting rods.

cranky ADJ (-*ier*, -*iest*) 1 COLLOQ eccentric or faddy. 2 N AMER bad-tempered.

cranny N (-*ies*) a cleft or crevice.

crap COARSE SLANG, N 1 faeces. 2 nonsense; rubbish.
➤ VB (-*pp*-) INTR to defecate.

crape see **crêpe** (N sense 1)

crapulent or **crapulous** ADJ 1 suffering from sickness caused by overdrinking. 2 of or resulting from intemperance. ■ **crapulence** N.

crash VB 1 TR & INTR to fall or strike with a banging or smashing noise. 2 TR & INTR (often **crash into sth**) of a vehicle: to collide or cause it to collide with something. 3 INTR to make a deafening noise. 4 INTR to move noisily. 5 INTR of a business or stock exchange: to collapse. 6 INTR of a computer or program: to fail completely. 7 SLANG to gatecrash (a party, etc). 8 (often **crash out**) SLANG to fall asleep.
➤ N 1 a violent impact or breakage, or the sound of it. 2 a deafening noise. 3 a traffic or aircraft accident. 4 the collapse of a business or

the stock exchange. 5 the failure of a computer.

crash barrier N a protective metal barrier along the edge of a road, carriageway, etc.

crash helmet N a protective helmet worn eg by motor-cyclists, motor-racing drivers, etc.

crash-land VB, TR & INTR of an aircraft or pilot: to land or cause (an aircraft) to land, usu without lowering the undercarriage and with the risk of crashing. ■ **crash-landing** N.

crass ADJ 1 gross; vulgar. 2 colossally stupid. 3 utterly tactless or insensitive.

crate N a strong wooden, plastic or metal case with partitions, for storing or carrying breakable or perishable goods.

crater N 1 the bowl-shaped mouth of a volcano or geyser. 2 a hole left in the ground where a meteorite has landed, or a bomb or mine has exploded. 3 ASTRON a circular, rimmed depression in the surface of the Moon or other planets. ■ **cratered** ADJ.

cravat N a formal style of men's neckerchief.

crave VB 1 to long for (something). 2 OLD USE, FORMAL to ask for politely; to beg. ■ **craving** N.

craven ADJ cowardly; cringing.

crawl VB, INTR 1 of insects, worms, etc: to move along the ground slowly. 2 of a human: to move along on hands and knees. 3 eg of traffic: to progress very slowly. 4 to be, or feel as if, covered or overrun with something. 5 (often **crawl to sb**) DEROG COLLOQ to behave in a fawning way.
➤ N 1 a crawling motion. 2 a very slow pace. 3 SWIMMING a stroke with an alternate overarm action together with a kicking leg action.

crawler N 1 someone or something which crawls. 2 DEROG COLLOQ someone who behaves in a fawning and ingratiating way.

crayfish and **crawfish** N an edible, freshwater crustacean, similar to a small lobster.

crayon N 1 a pencil or stick made from coloured wax, chalk or charcoal and used for drawing. 2 a drawing made using crayons.

craze N an intense but passing fashion.

crazy ADJ (*-ier, -iest*) **1** mad; insane. **2** foolish; absurd. ■ **crazily** ADV. ■ **craziness** N.
◆ **like crazy** COLLOQ keenly; fast and furious.

crazy paving N a type of paving made up of irregularly shaped slabs of stone or concrete.

creak N a shrill squeaking noise made typically by an unoiled hinge or loose floorboard.
➤ VB, INTR to make or seem to make this noise.
■ **creaky** ADJ.

cream N **1** the yellowish fatty substance that rises to the surface of milk, and yields butter when churned. **2** any food that resembles this substance in consistency or appearance. **3** any cosmetic substance that resembles cream in texture or consistency. **4** the best part of something. **5** a yellowish-white colour.
➤ VB (often **cream sth off**) to select or take away (the best part). ■ **creamy** ADJ.

cream cheese N a soft cheese made from soured milk or cream.

cream of tartar N a white crystalline powder, used in baking powder, laxatives, etc.

crease N **1** a line made by folding, pressing or crushing. **2** a wrinkle, esp on the face.
➤ VB, TR & INTR to make a crease or creases in (paper, fabric, etc); to develop creases.

create VB **1** to form or produce from nothing. **2** to bring into existence. **3** to cause. **4** to produce or contrive. **5** TR & INTR said of an artist, etc: to use one's imagination to make something. **6** INTR, BRIT COLLOQ to make a fuss.

creation N **1** the act of creating. **2** something created, particularly something special or striking. **3** the universe. **4** (often **the Creation**) CHRISTIANITY God's act of creating the universe.

creative ADJ **1** having the ability to create. **2** inventive or imaginative. ■ **creativity** N.

creator N **1** someone who creates. **2** (**the Creator**) CHRISTIANITY God.

creature N **1** a bird, beast or fish. **2** a person. **3** a slavish underling or puppet.

crèche N **1** a nursery where babies can be left and cared for while their parents are at work, shopping, exercising, etc. **2** a model representing the scene of Christ's nativity.

credence N faith placed in something.

credentials PL N **1** personal qualifications and achievements that can be quoted as evidence of one's trustworthiness, competence, etc. **2** documents or other evidence of these.

credible ADJ **1** capable of being believed. **2** reliable; trustworthy. ■ **credibility** N.

credit N **1** faith placed in something. **2** honour or a cause of honour: **To her credit, she didn't say anything**. **3** acknowledgement, recognition or praise. **4** (**credits**) a list of acknowledgements to those who have helped in the preparation of a book or film. **5** trust given to someone promising to pay later for goods already supplied: **buy goods on credit**. **6** one's financial reliability, esp as a basis for such trust. **7** the amount of money available to one at one's bank. **8 a** an entry in a bank account acknowledging a payment; **b** the side of an account on which such entries are made.
➤ VB **1** to believe; to place faith in someone or something. **2** to enter a sum as a credit on someone's account, or allow someone a sum as credit. **3** (often **credit sb with sth**) to attribute a quality or achievement to someone.

creditable ADJ praiseworthy; laudable.

credit card N a card issued by a bank, finance company, etc authorizing the holder to purchase goods or services on credit.

creditor N a person or company to whom one owes money.

creditworthy ADJ judged as deserving financial credit. ■ **creditworthiness** N.

credo N a belief or set of beliefs.

credulous ADJ apt to be too ready to believe something, without sufficient evidence.
■ **credulity** N. ■ **credulously** ADV.

creed N **1** (often **Creed**) a statement of the main points of Christian belief. **2** any set of beliefs or principles.

creek N **1** a small narrow inlet or bay in the shore of a lake, river, or sea. **2** N AMER, AUSTRAL, NZ a small natural stream or tributary.

creel N a large wicker basket for carrying fish.

creep VB (**crept**) INTR **1** to move slowly, with stealth or caution. **2** to move with the body close to the ground. **3** of a plant: to grow along the ground, up a wall, etc. **4** esp of the flesh: to have a strong tingling sensation as a response to fear or disgust. **5** to act in a fawning way.
➤ N **1** an act of creeping. **2** DEROG an unpleasant person. ■ **creeping** ADJ.
◆ **give sb the creeps** COLLOQ to disgust or frighten them.

creeper N a creeping plant.

creepy ADJ (**-ier, -iest**) COLLOQ slightly scary.

cremate VB to burn (a corpse) to ashes. ■ **cremation** N.

crematorium N (**-ia** or **-iums**) a place where corpses are cremated.

crème de la crème N the very best.

creole N **1** a pidgin language that has become the accepted language of a community or region. **2** (**Creole**) the French-based creole spoken in the US states of the Caribbean Gulf. **3** (**Creole**) a native-born West Indian or Latin American of mixed European and Negro blood. **4** (**Creole**) a French or Spanish native of the US Gulf states.

creosote N **1** a thick dark oily liquid, obtained by distilling coal tar, used as a wood preservative. **2** a colourless or pale yellow oily liquid with a penetrating odour, obtained by distilling wood tar, used as an antiseptic.

crêpe or **crepe** N **1** (also **crape**) a thin finely-wrinkled silk fabric. **2** rubber with a wrinkled surface, used for shoe soles. **3** a thin pancake.

crêpe paper N a type of thin paper with a wrinkled elastic texture.

crepuscular ADJ **1** relating to or like twilight; dim. **2** denoting animals that are active before sunrise or at dusk.

crescendo N **1** a gradual increase in loudness. **2** a musical passage of increasing loudness. **3** a high point or climax.

crescent N **1** the curved shape of the Moon when less than half is illuminated. **2** something similar in shape to this.

cress N a plant cultivated for its seed leaves eaten raw in salads, sandwiches, etc.

crest N **1** a comb or a tuft of feathers or fur on top of the head of certain birds and mammals. **2** a ridge of skin along the top of the head of certain reptiles and amphibians. **3** a plume on a helmet. **4** the topmost part of something, esp a hill, mountain or wave.
➤ VB **1** to reach the top of (a hill, mountain, etc). **2** to crown; to cap. **3** INTR of a wave: to rise or foam up into a crest. ■ **crested** ADJ.

crestfallen ADJ dejected as a result of a blow to one's pride or ambitions.

cretaceous ADJ, GEOL (**Cretaceous**) of the period during which the first flowering plants appeared, and dinosaurs and many other reptiles became extinct.

cretin N, OFFENSIVE an idiot. ■ **cretinous** ADJ.

cretonne N a strong cotton material, usu with a printed design, used for curtains, etc.

Creutzfeldt-Jakob disease N, PATHOL a usu fatal disease caused by viral infection and characterized by dementia, muscle wastage and neurological abnormalities.

crevasse N, GEOL a deep vertical crack in a glacier.

crevice N a narrow crack or opening.

crew N **1** the team of people manning a ship, aircraft, train, bus, etc. **2** a ship's company excluding the officers. **3** a team engaged in some operation: **camera crew**. **4** COLLOQ, USU DEROG a bunch of people: **a strange crew**.
➤ VB, INTR to serve as a crew member.

crewcut N a closely cropped hairstyle.

crew neck N a round neckline on a sweater. ➤ ADJ (**crew-neck**).

crib N **1** a baby's cot or cradle. **2** a manger. **3** a model of the nativity, with the infant Christ in a manger. **4** a literal translation of a text, used as an aid by students. **5** something copied or plagiarized from another's work.

➤ VB (*-bb-*) TR & INTR to copy or plagiarize.

cribbage N a card game for two to four players, who each try to be first to score a certain number of points.

crick COLLOQ, N a painful spasm or stiffness of the muscles, esp in the neck.
➤ VB to wrench (eg one's neck or back).

cricket[1] N an outdoor game played using a ball, bats and wickets, between two sides of eleven players, the object of which is for one team to score more runs than the other by the end of the period of play. ■ **cricketer** N.

cricket[2] N a species of mainly nocturnal insect related to the grasshopper, whose males can produce a distinctive chirping sound by rubbing their forewings together.

crime N 1 an illegal act. 2 such acts collectively. 3 an act which is wrong in a moral sense. 4 COLLOQ a shame.

criminal N someone guilty of a crime or crimes.
➤ ADJ 1 against the law. 2 relating to crime or criminals, or their punishment. 3 COLLOQ very wrong; wicked. ■ **criminality** N.
■ **criminally** ADV.

criminology N the scientific study of crime and criminals. ■ **criminologist** N.

crimp VB 1 to press into small regular ridges; to corrugate. 2 to wave or curl (hair) with crimping-irons. 3 US to thwart or hinder.
➤ N a curl or wave in the hair. ■ **crimped** ADJ.

Crimplene N, TRADEMARK a crease-resistant fabric made from a thick polyester yarn.

crimson N a deep purplish red colour.

cringe VB, INTR 1 to cower away in fear. 2 DEROG to behave in a submissive, over-humble way. 3 LOOSELY to wince in embarrassment, etc.
➤ N an act of cringing.

crinkle VB, TR & INTR to wrinkle or crease.
➤ N a crease. ■ **crinkly** ADJ (*-ier, -iest*).

crinoline N, HIST a petticoat fitted with hoops to make the skirts stick out.

cripple VB 1 to make lame; to disable. 2 to

damage, weaken or undermine.
➤ N 1 someone who is lame or badly disabled. 2 someone damaged psychologically.

crisis N (*-ses*) 1 a crucial or decisive moment. 2 a turning-point, eg in a disease. 3 a time of difficulty or distress. 4 an emergency.

crisp ADJ 1 dry and brittle. 2 firm and fresh. 3 fresh; bracing. 4 firm; decisive; brisk. 5 clean.
➤ N, BRIT (usu **crisps**) thin deep-fried slices of potato, usu flavoured. ■ **crispness** N.

crispbread N a brittle unsweetened biscuit made from wheat or rye.

criss-cross ADJ 1 of lines: crossing one another in different directions. 2 of a pattern, etc: consisting of criss-cross lines.
➤ ADV in a criss-cross way or pattern.
➤ VB, TR & INTR to form, mark with or move in a criss-cross pattern.

criterion N (*criteria*) a standard or principle on which to base a judgement.

critic N 1 a professional reviewer of literature, art, drama, music, etc. 2 someone who finds fault with or disapproves of something.

critical ADJ 1 fault-finding; disapproving. 2 relating to a critic or criticism. 3 involving analysis and assessment. 4 relating to a crisis; decisive; crucial. 5 urgent; vital. 6 of a patient: to be at risk of dying. ■ **critically** ADV.

criticism N 1 fault-finding. 2 reasoned analysis and assessment, esp of art, literature, music, drama, etc. 3 the art of such assessment. 4 a critical comment or piece of writing.

criticize or **-ise** VB, TR & INTR 1 to find fault; to express disapproval of someone or something. 2 to analyse and assess.

critique N a critical analysis.

croak N the harsh throaty noise typically made by a frog or crow.
➤ VB 1 INTR to make this sound. 2 to utter with a croak. 3 INTR, SLANG to die.

crochet N decorative work consisting of intertwined loops, made with wool or thread and a hooked needle.
➤ VB TR & INTR to make this kind of work.

crock¹ N, COLLOQ a decrepit person or an old vehicle, etc.

crock² N an earthenware pot.

crockery N earthenware or china dishes collectively.

crocodile N a large amphibious reptile.

crocus N a small plant with yellow, purple or white flowers and an underground corm.

croft N esp in the Scottish Highlands: a small piece of farmland attached to a house.

croissant N a flaky crescent–shaped bread roll, made from puff pastry or leavened dough.

crone N, DEROG an old woman.

crony N (-*ies*) a close friend.

crook N 1 a bend or curve. 2 a shepherd's or bishop's hooked staff. 3 COLLOQ a criminal.
➢ ADJ, AUSTRAL & NZ COLLOQ 1 ill. 2 not working properly. 3 nasty; unpleasant.
➢ VB to bend or curve.

crooked ADJ 1 bent, curved, angled or twisted. 2 not straight; tipped at an angle. 3 COLLOQ dishonest. ■ **crookedly** ADV.

croon VB, TR & INTR to sing in a subdued tone and sentimental style. ■ **crooner** N.

crop N 1 AGRIC a plant that is cultivated to produce food for people, fodder for animals, or raw materials, eg cereals, barley, etc. 2 AGRIC the total yield produced by or harvested from such a plant, or from a certain area of cultivated land, such as a field. 3 a batch; a bunch: **this year's crop of graduates**. 4 a very short style of haircut. 5 **a** a whip handle; **b** a horserider's short whip.
➢ VB (-*pp*-) 1 to trim; to cut short. 2 of animals: to feed on grass, etc. 3 to reap or harvest a crop.
◆ **crop up** COLLOQ to appear unexpectedly.

croquet N a game played on a lawn, in which the players use mallets to drive wooden balls through a sequence of hoops.

croquette N a round cake made from eg fish, potato, etc coated in breadcrumbs.

crosier or **crozier** N a bishop's hooked staff,

carried as a symbol of office.

cross N 1 **a** a mark, structure or symbol composed of two lines, one crossing the other in the form + or ×; **b** the mark × indicating a mistake or cancellation. 2 a vertical post with a shorter horizontal bar fixed to it, on which criminals were crucified in antiquity. 3 (**the Cross**) CHRISTIANITY **a** the cross on which Christ was crucified, or a representation of it; **b** this as a symbol of Christianity. 4 a variation of this symbol, eg the Maltese cross. 5 a burden or affliction. 6 **a** a monument in the form of a cross; **b** as a place name: the site of such a monument. 7 a medal in the form of a cross. 8 a plant or animal produced by crossing two different strains, breeds or varieties of a species. 9 a mixture or compromise: **a cross between a bedroom and a living room**.
➢ VB 1 TR & INTR (often **cross over**) to move, pass or get across (a road, a path, etc). 2 to place one across the other: **cross one's legs**. 3 INTR to meet; to intersect. 4 INTR of letters between two correspondents: to be in transit simultaneously. 5 to make the sign of the Cross upon someone or on oneself, usu as a blessing. 6 to make (a cheque) payable only through a bank by drawing two parallel lines across it. 7 (usu **cross out, off** or **through**) to delete or cancel something by drawing a line through it. 8 to cross–breed (two different strains, breeds or varieties of a species of animal or plant). 9 to frustrate or thwart.
➢ ADJ 1 angry; in a bad temper. 2 IN COMPOUNDS **a** across: **cross–country**; **b** intersecting or at right angles: **crossbar**; **c** contrary: **cross purposes**; **d** intermingling: **cross–breeding**.
◆ **cross sb's mind** to occur to them.

crossbar N 1 a horizontal bar, esp between two posts. 2 the horizontal bar on a bicycle.

crossbeam N a beam which stretches across from one support to another.

crossbill N a finch with a beak in which the points cross instead of meeting.

crossbones PL N a pair of crossed femurs appearing beneath the skull in the sign of the skull and crossbones.

crossbow N a bow placed crosswise on a stock, with a crank to pull back the bow and a trigger to release arrows.

cross-breed BIOL, VB to mate (two animals or plants of different pure breeds) to produce offspring in which the best characteristics of both parents are combined.
➢ N an animal or plant bred in this way.

cross-country ADJ, ADV across fields, etc rather than on roads.

cross-dress VB, INTR esp of men: to dress in the clothes of the opposite sex. ■ **cross-dressing** N.

cross-examine VB 1 LAW to question (esp a witness for the opposing side) so as to develop or throw doubt on his or her statement. 2 to question closely. ■ **cross-examination** N.

cross-eyed ADJ 1 squinting. 2 having an abnormal condition in which one or both eyes turn inwards towards the nose.

crossfire N 1 gunfire coming from different directions. 2 a bitter or excited exchange of opinions, arguments, etc.

crossing N 1 the place where two or more things cross each other. 2 a place for crossing a river, road, etc. 3 a journey across something, esp the sea: **a rough crossing**.

cross-legged ADJ, ADV sitting, usu on the floor, with the ankles crossed and knees wide apart.

cross-ply ADJ of a tyre: having fabric cords in the outer casing that run diagonally to stiffen and strengthen the side walls.

cross-pollination N, BOT the transfer of pollen from the anther of one flower to the stigma of another flower of the same species, by wind dispersal, pollen tubes, etc.

cross-purposes PL N confusion in a conversation or action by misunderstanding.

cross-refer VB, TR & INTR to direct (the reader) from one part of something, esp a text, to another. ■ **cross-reference** N.

crossroads SING N 1 the point where two or more roads cross or meet. 2 a point at which an important choice has to be made.

cross section N 1 a the surface revealed when a solid object is sliced through, esp at right angles to its length; b a diagram representing this. 2 a representative sample.

crosswise and **crossways** ADJ, ADV 1 lying or moving across. 2 in the shape of a cross.

crossword and **crossword puzzle** N a puzzle in which numbered clues are solved and their answers in words inserted into their correct places in a grid of squares.

crotch N (also **crutch**) a the place where the body or a pair of trousers forks into the two legs; b the human genital area.

crotchet N, MUS a note equal to two quavers or half a minim in length.

crotchety ADJ, COLLOQ irritable; peevish.

crouch VB, INTR (sometimes **crouch down**) 1 to bend low or squat with one's knees and thighs against one's chest and often also with one's hands on the ground. 2 of animals: to lie close to the ground ready to spring up.
➢ N a crouching position or action.

croup[1] N a condition in young childen characterized by inflammation and narrowing of the larynx, resulting in a hoarse cough, difficulty in breathing and fever.

croup[2] N the rump or hindquarters of a horse.

croupier N in a casino: someone who presides over a gaming-table.

croûton N a small cube of fried or toasted bread, served in soup, etc.

crow N 1 a large black bird, usu with a powerful black beak and shiny feathers. 2 the shrill drawn-out cry of a cock.
➢ VB (PA T **crowed** or **crew**) INTR 1 of a cock: to cry shrilly. 2 of a baby: to make happy inarticulate sounds. 3 (usu **crow over sb** or **sth**) to triumph gleefully over them; to gloat.

crowbar N a heavy iron bar with a bent flattened end, used as a lever.

crowd N 1 a large number of people gathered together. 2 spectators or audience. 3 (usu

crowds) COLLOQ a large number of people. **4** (**the crowd**) the general mass of people.
➤ VB **1** INTR to gather or move in a large, usu tightly-packed, group. **2** to fill. **3** to pack; to cram. **4** to press round, or supervise someone too closely. ■ **crowded** ADJ.

crown N **1** the circular, usu jewelled, gold headdress of a sovereign. **2** (**the Crown**) **a** the sovereign as head of state; **b** the authority or jurisdiction of a sovereign or of the government representing a sovereign.
3 a wreath for the head or other honour, awarded for victory or success. **4** a highest point of achievement: **the crown of one's career**. **5** the top, esp of something rounded. **6 a** the part of a tooth projecting from the gum; **b** an artificial replacement for this.
➤ VB **1** to place a crown ceremonially on the head of someone, thus making them a monarch. **2** to be on or round the top of someone or something. **3** to reward; to make complete or perfect: **efforts crowned with success**. **4** to put an artificial crown on (a tooth). **5** COLLOQ to hit on the head.

crown jewels PL N the crown, sceptre and other ceremonial regalia of a sovereign.

crow's feet PL N the wrinkles at the outer corner of the eye.

crow's nest N at the top of a ship's mast: a lookout platform.

crozier see **crosier**

crucial ADJ **1** decisive; critical. **2** very important; essential. ■ **crucially** ADV.

crucible N **1** an earthenware pot in which to heat metals, etc. **2** a severe test or trial.

crucifix N a representation, esp a model, of Christ on the cross.

crucifixion N **1** execution by crucifying.
2 (**Crucifixion**) CHRISTIANITY the crucifying of Christ, or a representation of this.

cruciform ADJ cross-shaped.

crucify VB (**-ies, -ied**) **1** to put to death by fastening or nailing to a cross by the hands and feet. **2** SLANG to defeat or humiliate utterly.

crude ADJ **1** in its natural unrefined state. **2** rough or undeveloped. **3** vulgar; tasteless.

crude oil N petroleum in its unrefined state.

cruel ADJ (**crueller, cruellest**) **1** deliberately causing pain or suffering. **2** painful; distressing: a cruel blow. ■ **cruelly** ADV. ■ **cruelty** N.

cruet N a small container which holds salt, pepper, mustard, vinegar, etc, for use at table.

cruise VB **1** TR & INTR to sail about for pleasure, calling at a succession of places. **2** INTR eg of a vehicle or aircraft: to go at a steady speed.
➤ N an instance of cruising.

cruiser N **1** a large fast warship. **2** (also **cabin-cruiser**) a large, esp luxurious motor boat with living quarters.

crumb N **1** a particle of dry food, esp bread. **2** a small amount. ■ **crumby** ADJ.

crumble VB **1** TR & INTR to break into crumbs or powdery fragments. **2** INTR to collapse, decay or disintegrate.
➤ N a baked dessert of stewed fruit covered with a crumbled mixture of sugar, butter and flour. ■ **crumbly** ADJ.

crummy ADJ (**-ier, -iest**) COLLOQ, DEROG shoddy, dingy, dirty or generally inferior.

crumpet N a thick round cake made of soft light dough, eaten toasted and buttered.

crumple VB **1** TR & INTR to make or become creased or crushed. **2** INTR to pucker in distress. **3** INTR to collapse; to give way.

crunch VB **1** TR & INTR to crush or grind noisily between the teeth or under the foot. **2** INTR to produce a crunching sound.
➤ N **1** a crunching action or sound. **2** (**the crunch**) COLLOQ the moment of crisis.
■ **crunchy** ADJ.

crusade N a strenuous campaign in aid of a cause.
➤ VB, INTR to engage in a crusade; to campaign.
■ **crusader** N.

crush VB **1** to break, damage, bruise, injure or distort by compressing violently. **2** to grind or pound into powder, crumbs, etc. **3** TR & INTR to

crumple or crease. **4** to defeat or subdue.
➤ N **1** violent compression. **2** a dense crowd.
3 a drink made from the juice of crushed fruit:
orange crush. **4** COLLOQ an amorous passion,
usu an unsuitable one. ■ **crushing** ADJ.

crust N **1 a** the hard-baked outer surface of a
loaf of bread; **b** a piece of this; a dried-up
piece of bread. **2** the pastry covering a pie, etc.
3 a crisp or brittle covering.
➤ VB, TR & INTR to cover with or form a crust.

crustacean N, ZOOL any invertebrate animal
which typically possesses two pairs of
antennae and a segmented body covered in a
carapace, eg crabs, lobsters, woodlice, etc.

crusty ADJ (**-ier, -iest**) **1** having a crisp crust.
2 irritable or cantankerous. ■ **crustiness** N.

crutch N **1** a stick, usu one of a pair, used as a
support by a lame person. **2** a support, help or
aid. **3** BRIT another word for **crotch**.

crux N (**cruces** or **cruxes**) a decisive, essential
or crucial point.

cry VB (**cries, cried**) **1** INTR to shed tears; to
weep. **2** INTR (often **cry out**) to shout or shriek,
eg in pain or fear, or to get attention or help.
3 (often **cry out**) to exclaim (words, news, etc).
4 INTR of an animal or bird: to utter its
characteristic noise.
➤ N (**cries**) **1** a shout or shriek. **2** an excited
utterance or exclam. **3** an appeal or demand.
4 a bout of weeping. **5** the characteristic
utterance of an animal or bird.
◆ **cry off** COLLOQ to cancel an engagement or
agreement.
◆ **cry out for sth** to be in obvious need of it.

crybaby N, DEROG, COLLOQ a person, esp a
child, who weeps at the slightest upset.

crying ADJ demanding attention: **a crying
need**.

cryogenics SING N the branch of physics
concerned with very low temperatures.

crypt N an underground chamber or vault, esp
one beneath a church, often used for burials.

cryptic ADJ **1** puzzling, mysterious, obscure or
enigmatic. **2** secret or hidden. **3** of a crossword

puzzle: with clues in the form of riddles, puns,
anagrams, etc. ■ **cryptically** ADV.

cryptography N the study of writing in and
deciphering codes. ■ **cryptographer** N.
■ **cryptographic** ADJ.

crystal N **1** (also **rock crystal**) colourless
transparent quartz. **2 a** a brilliant, highly
transparent glass used for cut glass; **b** cut-glass
articles. **3** CHEM any solid substance consisting
of a regularly repeating arrangement of atoms,
ions or molecules.
➤ ADJ relating to, or made of, crystal.

crystal ball N a globe of rock crystal or glass
into which a fortune-teller gazes.

crystalline ADJ **1** composed of or having the
clarity of crystal. **2** CHEM displaying the
properties or structure of crystals.

crystallize or **-ise** VB **1** TR & INTR to form
crystals. **2** to coat or preserve (fruit) in sugar.
3 TR & INTR of plans, etc: to make or become
clear and definite. ■ **crystallization** N.

crystallography N the scientific study of the
structure, forms and properties of crystals.

CS gas N an irritant vapour which causes a
burning sensation in the eyes, choking, nausea
and vomiting, used in riot control.

cub N **1** the young of certain carnivorous
mammals, such as the fox, wolf, lion and bear.
2 (**Cub**) a member of the junior branch of the
Scout Association. Also called **Cub Scout**.

cubbyhole N, COLLOQ **1** a tiny room.
2 a cupboard, nook or recess.

cube N **1** MATH a solid figure having six square
faces of equal area. **2** a block of this shape.
3 MATH the product of any number or quantity
multiplied by its square, ie the third power of a
number or quantity.
➤ VB **1** to raise (a number or quantity) to the third
power. **2** to form or cut into cubes.

cubic ADJ **1** of or resembling a cube. **2** having
three dimensions. **3** MATH of or involving a
number or quantity that is raised to the third
power. **4** MATH of a unit of volume: equal to that
contained in a cube of specified dimensions.

cubicle N a small compartment for sleeping or undressing in, screened for privacy.

Cubism N, ART an early-20c movement in painting which represented natural objects as geometrical shapes. ■ **Cubist** N, ADJ.

cuboid ADJ (also **cuboidal**) like a cube.
➢ N, MATH a solid body having six rectangular faces, the opposite faces of which are equal.

Cub Scout see **cub** (N sense 2)

cuckoo N an insectivorous bird which lays its eggs in the nests of other birds.
➢ ADJ, COLLOQ insane; crazy.

cuckoo clock N a clock from which a model cuckoo springs on the hour, uttering the appropriate number of cries.

cuckoo spit N a frothy mass found on plants, secreted by the larvae of some insects.

cucumber N 1 a creeping plant cultivated for its edible fruit. 2 a long green fruit of this plant, containing juicy white flesh, which is often used raw in salads, etc.

cud N in ruminant animals: partially digested food that is regurgitated from the first stomach into the mouth to be chewed again.

cuddle VB 1 TR & INTR to hug or embrace affectionately. 2 (usu **cuddle in** or **up**) to lie close and snug; to nestle.
➢ N a hug. ■ **cuddly** ADJ (-*ier*, -*iest*).

cudgel N a heavy stick used as a weapon.
➢ VB (-*ll*-) to beat with a cudgel.

cue[1] N 1 the end of an actor's speech, or something else said or done by a performer, that serves as a prompt for another to say or do something. 2 anything that serves as a signal or hint to do something.
➢ VB (*cueing*) to give a cue to someone.
◆ **on cue** at precisely the right moment.

cue[2] N in snooker, etc: a stick tapering almost to a point, used to strike the ball.

cue ball N in snooker, etc: the ball which is struck by the cue.

cuff[1] N 1 a band or folded-back part at the lower end of a sleeve, usu at the wrist. 2 N AMER the turned-up part of a trouser leg.
◆ **off the cuff** COLLOQ without preparation.

cuff[2] N a blow with the open hand.
➢ VB to hit with an open hand.

cufflink N one of a pair of decorative fasteners for shirt cuffs, used in place of buttons.

cuisine N 1 a style of cooking. 2 the range of food prepared and served at a restaurant, etc.

cul-de-sac N (*culs-de-sac* or *cul-de-sacs*) a street closed at one end; a blind alley.

culinary ADJ relating to cookery or the kitchen.

cull VB 1 to gather or pick up (information or ideas). 2 to select and kill (weak or surplus animals) from a group, eg seals or deer, in order to keep the population under control.
➢ N an act of culling.

culminate VB, TR & INTR (often **culminate in** or **with sth**) to reach the highest point or climax. ■ **culmination** N.

culottes PL N wide-legged trousers for women, intended to look like a skirt.

culpable ADJ to blame. ■ **culpability** N.

culprit N someone guilty of a misdeed.

cult N 1 **a** a system of religious belief; **b** the sect following such a system. 2 an esp extravagant admiration for a person, idea, etc. ■ **cultic** ADJ.

cultivate VB 1 to prepare and use (land or soil) for growing crops. 2 to grow (a crop, plant, etc). 3 to develop or improve: **cultivate a taste for literature**. 4 to try to develop a friendship, a relationship, etc with (someone).

cultivated ADJ well bred and knowledgeable.

cultivation N 1 the act of cultivating. 2 education, breeding and culture.

cultivator N 1 a tool for breaking up the surface of the ground. 2 someone or something which cultivates.

cultural ADJ 1 relating to a culture. 2 relating to the arts. ■ **culturally** ADV.

culture N 1 the customs, ideas, values, etc of a particular civilization, society or social group. 2 appreciation of art, music, literature, etc.

3 improvement and development through care and training: **beauty culture. 4** BIOL a population of micro-organisms (esp bacteria), cells or tissues grown usu for scientific study or medical diagnosis.

cultured ADJ **1** well-educated; having refined tastes and manners. **2** grown in a culture medium.

culvert N a covered drain or channel carrying water or cables underground, eg under a road.

cumbersome ADJ awkward or unwieldy.

cumin or **cummin** N an umbelliferous Mediterranean plant whose seeds are used as an aromatic herb or flavouring.

cummerbund N a wide sash worn around the waist, esp one worn with a dinner jacket.

cumulative ADJ increasing in amount or effect with each addition.

cumulus N (-*li*) METEOROL a fluffy heaped cloud with a rounded white upper surface and a flat base.

cuneiform ADJ **1** relating to any of several ancient Middle-Eastern scripts with wedge-shaped characters. **2** wedge-shaped.

cunning ADJ **1** clever, sly or crafty. **2** ingenious, skilful or subtle.
➤ N **1** slyness; craftiness. **2** skill; expertise.

cunt N **1** TABOO the female genitals. **2** OFFENSIVE SLANG an unpleasant person.

cup N **1** a small, round, open container, usu with a handle, used to drink from. **2** the amount a cup will hold, used as a measure in cookery. **3** a container or something else shaped like a cup: **egg cup. 4** an ornamental trophy awarded as a prize in sports competitions, etc. **5** a competition in which the prize is a cup.
➤ VB (-*pp*-) **1** to form (one's hands) into a cup shape. **2** to hold something in cupped hands.

cupboard N a piece of furniture or a recess for storing provisions, etc.

cupboard love N an insincere show of affection towards someone or something in return for some kind of material gain.

cupidity N greed for wealth and possessions.

cupola N **1** a small dome or turret on a roof. **2** a domed roof or ceiling.

cupro-nickel N an alloy of copper and nickel used to make silver-coloured coins in the UK.

cur N, DEROG, OLD USE **1** a surly mongrel dog. **2** a scoundrel.

curable ADJ capable of being cured.

curacy N (-*ies*) the office of a curate.

curare N a poisonous black resin obtained from certain tropical plants in South America, which has medicinal uses as a muscle relaxant.

curate N, C OF E a clergyman who acts as assistant to a vicar or rector.

curate's egg N anything of which some parts are excellent and some parts are bad.

curative ADJ able or tending to cure.
➤ N a substance that cures.

curator N the custodian of a museum, etc.

curb N **1** something that restrains or controls. **2 a** a chain or strap passing under a horse's jaw, attached at the sides to the bit; **b** a bit with such a fitting. **3** N AMER a kerb.
➤ VB **1** to restrain. **2** to put a curb on (a horse).

curd N **1** (often **curds**) the clotted protein substance, as opposed to the liquid component, formed when fresh milk is curdled, and used to make cheese, etc. **2** any of several substances of similar consistency.

curdle VB, TR & INTR to turn into curd; to clot.

cure VB **1** to restore someone to health or normality. **2** to get rid of (an illness, harmful habit, etc). **3** to preserve (food) by salting, smoking, etc. **4** to preserve (leather, tobacco, etc) by drying. **5** to vulcanize (rubber).
➤ N **1** something that cures or remedies. **2** restoration to health. **3** a course of healing or remedial treatment.

cure-all N a universal remedy.

curettage N the process of using a curette.

curette or **curet** N, SURGERY a spoon-shaped device used to scrape tissue from the inner

surface of an organ or body cavity.
➤ VB to scrape with a curette.

curfew N **a** an official order restricting people's movements, esp after a certain hour at night; **b** the time at which such an order applies.

curio N an article valued for its rarity or unusualness.

curiosity N (-ies) **1** inquisitiveness. **2** something strange, rare, exotic or unusual.

curious ADJ **1** strange; odd. **2** eager or interested. **3** inquisitive. ■ **curiously** ADV.

curl VB **1** to twist, roll or wind (hair) into coils or ringlets. **2** INTR to grow in coils or ringlets. **3** TR & INTR to move in or form into a spiral, coil or curve.
➤ N **1** a small coil or ringlet of hair. **2** a twist, spiral, coil or curve.

curler N **1** a type of roller for curling the hair. **2** a participant in the sport of curling.

curlew N a large wading bird, with a slender down-curved bill and long legs.

curlicue N **a** a fancy twist or curl; **b** a flourish made with a pen.

curling N a team game played on ice with smooth heavy stones with handles, that are slid towards a circular target.

curly ADJ (-ier, -iest) **1** having curls; full of curls. **2** tending to curl.

curmudgeon N a bad-tempered or mean person. ■ **curmudgeonly** ADJ.

currant N a small dried seedless grape.

currency N (-ies) **1** the system of money, or the coins and notes, in use in a country. **2** general acceptance or popularity, esp of a theory, etc.

current ADJ **1** generally accepted. **2** belonging to the present. **3** in circulation; valid.
➤ N **1** the continuous steady flow of a body of water, air, heat, etc, in a particular direction. **2** the rate of flow of electric charge per unit time. **3** an electric current. ■ **currently** ADV.

current account N a bank account from which money can be drawn without notice.

curriculum N (-la or -lums) **1** a course of study,

esp at school or university. **2** a list of all the courses available at a school, university, etc. ■ **curricular** ADJ.

curriculum vitae N (curricula vitae) (abbrev **CV**) a written summary of one's personal details, education and career.

curry[1] N (-ies) a dish, orig Indian, of meat, fish, or vegetables usu cooked with hot spices.
➤ VB (-ies, -ied) to prepare (food) using curry powder or a curry sauce.

curry[2] VB to groom (a horse).
◆ **curry favour with sb** to ingratiate oneself with them.

curse N **1** a blasphemous or obscene expression, usu of anger; an oath. **2** an appeal to God or some other divine power to harm someone. **3** the resulting harm suffered by someone: **under a curse. 4** an evil; a cause of harm or trouble.
➤ VB **1** to utter a curse against; to revile. **2** INTR to use violent language; to swear.

cursed ADJ **1** under a curse. **2** OLD USE hateful.

cursive ADJ of handwriting: having letters which are joined up rather than separate.

cursor N **1** on a VDU: an underline character or a rectangular box that flashes on and off to indicate where the next character to be entered on the keyboard will appear. **2** the transparent movable part of a measuring device, esp a slide rule.

cursory ADJ hasty; superficial; not thorough. ■ **cursorily** ADV.

curt ADJ rudely brief; dismissive; abrupt. ■ **curtly** ADV. ■ **curtness** N.

curtail VB to reduce; to cut short. ■ **curtailment** N.

curtain N **1** a hanging cloth over a window, round a bed, etc for privacy or to exclude light. **2** THEAT a hanging cloth in front of the stage to screen it from the auditorium. **3** THEAT (often **the curtain**) the rise of the curtain at the beginning, or fall of the curtain at the end, of a stage performance, act, scene, etc. **4** something resembling a curtain: **a curtain of thick dark**

hair. **5** (**curtains**) COLLOQ the end; death.
➢ VB **1** (often **curtain sth off**) to surround or enclose it with a curtain. **2** to supply (windows, etc) with curtains.

curtsy or **curtsey** N (**-sies** or **-seys**) a slight bend of the knees with one leg behind the other, performed as a formal gesture of respect by women.
➢ VB (**-ies, -ied**) INTR to perform a curtsy.

curvaceous ADJ, COLLOQ of a woman: having a shapely figure.

curvature N **a** the condition of being curved; **b** the degree of curvedness.

curve N **1** a line no part of which is straight, or a surface no part of which is flat. **2** any smoothly arched line or shape, like part of a circle or sphere. **3** (**curves**) COLLOQ the rounded contours and shapes of a woman's body. **4** any line representing data on a graph.
➢ VB, TR & INTR to form or form into a curve; to move in a curve. ■ **curvy** ADJ (**-ier, -iest**).

cushion N **1** a fabric case stuffed with soft material, used for making a seat comfortable, for kneeling on, etc. **2** a thick pad or something having a similar function. **3** something that gives protection from shock, reduces unpleasant effects, etc. **4** the inner rim of a billiard table.
➢ VB **1** to reduce the unpleasant or violent effect of something. **2** to protect from shock, injury or the extremes of distress.

cushy ADJ (**-ier, -iest**) COLLOQ comfortable; easy; undemanding.

cusp N **1** ANAT a sharp raised point on the grinding surface of a molar tooth. **2** ASTROL the point of transition between one sign of the zodiac and the next.

cuss OLD USE, COLLOQ, N a curse.
➢ VB, TR & INTR to curse or swear.

custard N **1** a sauce made with sugar, milk and cornflour. **2** (also **egg custard**) a baked dish or sauce of eggs and sweetened milk.

custodian N someone who has care of something, eg a public building.

custody N (**-ies**) **1** protective care, esp the guardianship of a child, awarded to someone by a court of law. **2** arrest or imprisonment. ■ **custodial** ADJ.

custom N **1** a traditional activity or practice. **2** a personal habit. **3** the body of established practices of a community; convention. **4** an established practice having the force of a law. **5** the trade or business that one gives to a shop, etc by regular purchases.
➢ ADJ made to order.

customary ADJ usual; traditional; according to custom. ■ **customarily** ADV.

custom-built and **custom-made** ADJ built or made to a customer's requirements.

customer N **1** someone who purchases goods from a shop, uses the services of a business, etc. **2** COLLOQ someone with whom one has to deal: **an awkward customer.**

customs PL N taxes or duties paid on imports.
➢ SING N **1** the government department that collects these taxes. **2** the place at a port, airport or frontier where baggage is inspected for taxed and illegal goods.

cut VB (**cut, cutting**) **1** TR & INTR (also **cut sth off** or **out**) to slit, pierce, slice or sever (a person or thing) using a sharp instrument. **2** (often **cut sth up**) to divide something by cutting. **3** to trim (hair, nails, etc). **4** to reap or mow (corn, grass, etc). **5** to prune (plants). **6** (sometimes **cut sth out**) to make or form it by cutting. **7** to shape the surface of (a gem) into facets, or decorate (glass) by cutting. **8** to shape the pieces of (a garment). **9** to make (a sound recording). **10** to hurt. **11** to reduce (eg prices, wages, interest rates, working hours, etc). **12** to shorten or abridge (eg a book or play). **13** to delete or omit. **14** INTR, CINEMA of a film or camera: to change directly to another shot, etc. **15** COLLOQ to absent oneself from something: **cut classes.** **16** to switch off (an engine, etc). **17** of a baby: to grow (teeth). **18** INTR (usu **cut across** or **through**) to go off in a certain direction; to take a short route.
➢ N **1** an act of cutting; a cutting movement or stroke. **2** a slit, incision or injury made by cutting. **3** a reduction. **4** a deleted passage in a play,

etc. **5** the stoppage of an electricity supply, etc. **6** SLANG one's share of the profits. **7** a piece of meat cut from an animal. **8** the style in which clothes or hair are cut.

◆ **a cut above sth** COLLOQ superior to it.

◆ **cut across sth 1** to go against (normal procedure, etc). **2** to take a short cut through it, eg a field, etc.

◆ **cut and dried** decided; definite; settled.

◆ **cut and run** COLLOQ to escape smartly.

◆ **cut back on sth** to reduce spending, etc.

◆ **cut down on sth** to reduce one's use of it; to do less of it.

◆ **cut in 1** to interrupt. **2** of a vehicle: to squeeze in front of another vehicle.

◆ **cut it out** SLANG to stop doing something.

◆ **cut sth off 1** to separate or isolate it. **2** to stop it or cut it short.

◆ **cut out 1** of an engine, etc: to stop working. **2** of an electrical device: to switch off or stop automatically, usu as a safety precaution.

◆ **cut sth out 1** to remove or delete it. **2** to clip pictures, etc out of a magazine, etc. **3** COLLOQ to stop doing it.

◆ **cut out for** or **to be sth** having the qualities needed for it.

cutaway ADJ of a diagram, etc: having outer parts omitted so as to show the interior.

cutback N a reduction in spending, use of resources, etc.

cute ADJ, COLLOQ **1** attractive; pretty. **2** clever; cunning; shrewd. ■ **cuteness** N.

cuticle N, ANAT the dead hardened skin at the base of fingernails and toenails.

cutlass N, HIST a short, broad, slightly curved sword with one cutting edge.

cutlery N knives, forks and spoons.

cutlet N **1** a small piece of meat with a bone attached, usu cut from a rib or the neck; **b** a piece of food in this shape, not necessarily containing meat: **nut cutlet**. **2** a slice of veal. **3** a rissole of minced meat or flaked fish.

cut-off N **1** the point at which something is cut off or separated. **2** a stopping of a flow or supply.

cut-out N something which has been cut out of something else, eg a newspaper clipping.

cutter N **1** a person or thing that cuts. **2** a small single-masted sailing ship.

cut-throat ADJ of competition, etc: very keen and aggressive.
➤ N **1** a murderer. **2** (also **cut-throat razor**) a long-bladed razor that folds into its handle.

cutting N **1** an extract, article or picture cut from a newspaper, etc. **2** HORTIC a piece cut from a plant for eg rooting. **3** a narrow excavation made through high ground for a road or railway.
➤ ADJ **1** hurtful; sarcastic. **2** of wind: penetrating.

cutting edge N a part or area (of an organization, branch of study, etc) that breaks new ground, effects development, etc.

cuttlefish N a mollusc related to the squid and octopus, which has a shield-shaped body containing an inner chalky plate, and a small head bearing eight arms and two tentacles.

CV or **cv** ABBREV (**CVs**, **cvs**) curriculum vitae.

cyan N a greenish blue colour.

cyanide N any of the poisonous salts of hydrocyanic acid, which smell of bitter almonds, esp potassium cyanide.

cybernetics SING N the comparative study of communication and automatic control processes in mechanical or electronic systems, eg computers. ■ **cybernetic** ADJ.

cyberspace N the three-dimensional artificial environment of virtual reality, generated by computer, that gives the user the impression of physically interacting with it.

cyclamen N a plant with heart-shaped leaves and white, pink or red flowers.

cycle N **1** a constantly repeating series of events or processes. **2** a recurring period of years; an age. **3** short for **a** bicycle; **b** motorcycle; **c** tricycle.
➤ VB, TR & INTR to ride a bicycle.

cyclic and **cyclical** ADJ **1** relating to, containing, or moving in a cycle. **2** recurring in cycles.

cyclist N the rider of a bicycle, motorcycle, etc.

cyclometer N a device for recording the revolutions of a wheel, used on a bicycle to measure the distance travelled.

cyclone N **1** METEOROL (also **depression** or **low**) an area of low atmospheric pressure, often associated with stormy weather, in which winds spiral inward towards the centre. **2** a violent, often destructive, tropical storm. ■ **cyclonic** ADJ.

cygnet N a young swan.

cylinder N **1** GEOM a solid figure of uniform circular cross-section, in which the curved surface is at right angles to the base. **2** a container, machine part or other object of this shape. **3** ENG in an internal combustion engine: the tubular cylinder within which the chemical energy of the burning fuel is converted to the mechanical energy of a moving piston. ■ **cylindrical** ADJ.

cymbal N a thin plate-like brass percussion instrument, either beaten with a drumstick, or used as one of a pair that are struck together.

Cymric ADJ of Wales.

cynic N someone who takes a pessimistic view of human goodness or sincerity.

cynical ADJ disinclined to believe in the goodness or sincerity of others. ■ **cynically** ADV.

cynicism N **1** the attitude, beliefs or behaviour of a cynic. **2** a cynical act, remark, etc.

cypher see **cipher**

cypress N **a** a dark-green coniferous tree; **b** the wood of this tree.

Cyrillic ADJ of the alphabet used for Russian, Bulgarian and other Slavonic languages.

cyst N **1** PATHOL an abnormal sac that contains fluid, semi-solid material or gas. **2** ANAT any normal sac or closed cavity.

cystic fibrosis N, PATHOL a hereditary disease in which the exocrine glands produce abnormally thick mucus that blocks the bronchi, pancreas and intestinal glands, causing respiratory problems.

cystitis N, PATHOL inflammation of the bladder characterized by a desire to pass urine frequently, accompanied by a burning sensation.

cytology N the scientific study of the structure and function of individual cells in plants and animals. ■ **cytological** ADJ. ■ **cytologist** N.

cytoplasm N, BIOL the part of a living cell enclosed by the cell membrane.

czar, etc see **tsar**, etc.

Dd

D¹ or **d** N (*Ds, D's* or *d's*) **1** the fourth letter of the English alphabet. **2** (**D**) MUS the second note on the scale of C major. **3** (usu **D**) the fourth highest grade.

D² SYMBOL the Roman numeral for 500.

'd CONTRACTION **1** would: I'd go. **2** had: He'd gone. **3** COLLOQ did: Where'd they go?

dab¹ VB (*-bb-*) TR & INTR (often **dab at sth**) to touch something lightly with a cloth, etc. ➢ N **1** a small amount of something creamy or liquid. **2** a light touch.

dab² N a small flatfish with rough scales.

dab³ N (usu **a dab hand**) an expert.

dabble VB **1** TR & INTR to move or shake (a hand, foot, etc) about in water. **2** INTR (often **dabble at, in** or **with sth**) to do or study something without serious effort. ■ **dabbler** N.

dace N (*dace* or *daces*) a small river fish.

dachshund N a small dog with a long body and short legs.

dactyl N, PROSODY a foot consisting of a long or stressed syllable followed by two short or unstressed ones. ■ **dactylic** ADJ.

dad or **daddy** N (*-ies*) COLLOQ father.

daddy-long-legs N (PL *daddy-long-legs*) BRIT, AUSTRAL, NZ COLLOQ a cranefly.

dado N (*-oes* or *-os*) the lower part of an indoor wall when different from the upper part.

daemon N same as **demon**.

daffodil N a plant with yellow trumpet-shaped flowers.

daft ADJ, COLLOQ **1** silly; foolish. **2** mad. **3** (**daft about** or **on sth**) enthusiastic about it.

dag N, AUSTRAL COLLOQ a scruffy, untidy person. ■ **daggy** ADJ.

dagger N **1** a pointed knife for stabbing. **2** PRINTING the symbol †.

dahlia N, BOT a garden plant with large, brightly coloured flowers.

daily ADJ **1** happening, appearing, etc every day. **2** relating to a single day.
➤ ADV every day, or every weekday.
➤ N (*-ies*) a newspaper published every day except Sunday.

dainty ADJ (*-ier, -iest*) small, pretty or delicate.
➤ N (*-ies*) something small and nice to eat. ■ **daintily** ADV. ■ **daintiness** N.

dairy N (*-ies*) **1** a farm building where milk is stored or where butter and cheese are made. **2** a business or factory that bottles and distributes milk and manufactures dairy

products. **3** a shop which sells milk, butter, etc. **4** AS ADJ of milk production or milk products: *a dairy farm* • *dairy products*.

dais N a platform in a hall, eg for speakers.

daisy N (*-ies*) a small flower with heads consisting of a yellow centre and white petals.

dal or **dhal** N **1** an edible dried split pea-like seed. **2** a cooked dish made of these.

dalai lama N the head of Tibetan Buddhism.

dale N a valley.

dally VB (*-ies, -ied*) INTR **1** to waste time idly or frivolously. **2** (often **dally with sb**) OLD USE to flirt with them. ■ **dalliance** N.

dam¹ N **1** a barrier built to hold back water. **2** the water confined behind such a structure.
➤ VB (*-mm-*) to hold back (water, etc) with a dam.

dam² N of horses, sheep, etc: a female parent.

damage N **1** harm or injury, or loss caused by injury. **2** (**damages**) LAW payment due for loss or injury.
➤ VB to cause harm, injury or loss to someone or something. ■ **damaging** ADJ.

damask N a patterned silk or linen cloth, used for tablecloths, curtains, etc.

dame N **1** a woman who has been honoured by the Queen or the Government for service or merit. **2** N AMER SLANG a woman. **3** a comic female character in a pantomime, usu played by a man.

damn VB **1** RELIG to sentence someone to punishment in hell. **2** to declare someone or something to be useless or worthless. **3** to prove someone's guilt.
➤ EXCLAM (often **damn it**) expressing annoyance.
➤ ADJ, COLLOQ annoying: **the damn cold**.
➤ ADV, COLLOQ used for emphasis: **It's damn cold**. ■ **damning** ADJ.
◆ **not give a damn** COLLOQ not to care at all.

damnable ADJ **1** hateful; awful. **2** annoying.

damnation N, RELIG punishment in hell.
➤ EXCLAM expressing annoyance.

damned ADJ **1** RELIG sentenced to damnation. **2** COLLOQ annoying, hateful, etc.
➤ ADV, COLLOQ extremely; very: **damned cold.**

damp ADJ slightly wet.
➤ N slight wetness, esp if unpleasant.
➤ VB to wet something slightly. ■ **damply** ADV. ■ **dampness** N.
◆ **damp sth down 1** to make (emotions, interest, etc) less strong. **2** to make (a fire) burn more slowly.

damp-course and **damp-proof course** N a layer of material in a wall of a building which stops damp rising up the wall.

dampen VB **1** to make something slightly wet. **2** TR & INTR **a** of emotions, interest, etc: to make or become less strong; **b** to make (a fire) burn more slowly.

damsel N, OLD USE OR LITERARY a young woman.

damson N **1** a small purple plum. **2** the tree it grows on.

dance VB **1** INTR & TR to make rhythmic steps or movements (usu in time to music). **2** INTR (usu **dance about** or **around**) to move or jump about quickly.
➤ N **1** a pattern of rhythmic steps, usu in time to music. **2** a social gathering for dancing. **3** music played for dancing. **4** AS ADJ: **dance-band.** ■ **dancer** N. ■ **dancing** N.

D and C ABBREV, MED dilatation and curettage.

dandelion N a plant with notched leaves and yellow flowerheads on hollow stems.

dander N (only **get one's** or **sb's dander up**) COLLOQ to become angry, or make someone angry.

dandle VB to bounce or dance (usu a small child) on one's knee.

dandruff N whitish flakes of dead skin shed from the scalp.

dandy N (**-ies**) a man who is concerned to dress very fashionably or elegantly.
➤ ADJ, COLLOQ (**-ier, -iest**) good; fine.

Dane N **1** a citizen or inhabitant of, or person born in, Denmark. **2** HIST a Viking.

danger N **1** a situation or state of possible harm, injury, loss or unpleasantness. **2** a possible cause of harm, injury or loss.

dangerous ADJ likely or able to cause harm or injury. ■ **dangerously** ADV.

dangle VB, TR & INTR to hang loosely.

Danish pastry N a flat cake of rich light pastry, with a sweet filling or topping.

dank ADJ unpleasantly wet and cold.

dapper ADJ smart and lively.

dappled ADJ with spots or patches of a different, usu darker, colour.

dapple-grey ADJ of a horse: pale-grey with darker spots.
➤ N a dapple-grey horse.

dare VB **1** INTR, AUXILIARY VERB to be brave enough to do something. **2** to challenge someone to do something dangerous, etc.
➤ N a challenge to do something.

dare-devil N a recklessly daring person.
➤ ADJ of actions, etc: daring and dangerous.

daring ADJ **1** courageous or adventurous. **2** intended to shock or surprise.
➤ N boldness, courage.

dark ADJ **1** without light. **2** closer to black than to white. **3** of a person or skin or hair colour: not light or fair. **4** sad or gloomy. **5** evil or sinister. **6** mysterious and unknown.
➤ N **1** (usu **the dark**) the absence of light. **2** the beginning of night-time. ■ **darkly** ADV. ■ **darkness** N.

the Dark Ages N the period of European history from about the 5c to the 11c.

darken VB, TR & INTR to make or become dark.

dark horse N someone who keeps their past, life, abilities, etc secret.

darkroom N a darkened room used for developing photographs.

darling N **1** a dearly loved person. **2** a lovable person or thing.
➤ ADJ **1** well loved. **2** COLLOQ delightful.

darn[1] VB to mend (a hole, a garment, etc) with

rows of stitches which cross each other.
➤ N a darned place.

darn² EXCLAM a substitute for **damn**.

dart N **1** a narrow pointed missile that can be thrown or fired. **2** a sudden quick movement. **3** a fold sewn into a piece of clothing.
➤ VB **1** INTR to move suddenly and quickly. **2** to send or give (a look or glance) quickly.

dartboard N a circular target at which darts are thrown in the game of darts.

darts SING N a game in which darts are thrown at a dartboard.

dash VB **1** INTR to run quickly. **2** INTR to crash or smash. **3** to hit or smash into something violently. **4** to put an end to (hopes, etc).
➤ N **1** a quick run or sudden rush. **2** a small amount of something, esp a liquid. **3** a patch of colour. **4** a short line (–) used in writing to show a break in a sentence, etc. **5** in Morse code: the longer of the two lengths of signal element. **6** confidence and stylishness. **7** a dashboard.
◆ **dash sth off** to produce or write it hastily.

dashboard N a panel with dials, switches, etc in front of the driver's seat in a car, boat, etc.

dashing ADJ **1** smart; stylish. **2** lively.

DAT ABBREV digital audio tape.

data N (orig pl of **datum** but now generally treated as **sing**) **1** information or facts, esp if obtained by scientific observation or experiment. **2** information that can be supplied to, stored in or processed by a computer.

database N, COMP a collection of computer data.

data processing N, COMP the processing of data by a computer system.

date¹ N **1** the day of the month and/or the year, given as a number or numbers. **2** the day on which a letter, etc was written, sent, etc, an event took place or is planned to take place, etc. **3** a particular period of time in history. **4** COLLOQ a planned meeting or social outing, usu with a person one is romantically attached to. **5** esp N AMER, COLLOQ a person whom one is meeting or going out with, esp romantically.

➤ VB **1** to put a date on (a letter, etc). **2** to find, decide on or guess the date of something. **3** to show the age of someone or something; to make (esp a person) seem old. **4** INTR to become old-fashioned. **5** TR & INTR, COLLOQ to go out with someone, esp regularly for romantic reasons.

date² N the fruit of the date palm.

dated ADJ old-fashioned.

dateline N a line, usu at the top of a newspaper article, which gives the date and place of writing.

date palm N a tall tree with a crown of leaves, cultivated for its edible fruit.

datum N (*data*) a piece of information.

daub VB **1** to spread something roughly or unevenly onto a surface. **2** to cover (a surface) with a soft sticky substance or liquid. **3** TR & INTR, DEROG to paint carelessly or without skill.
➤ N **1** soft, sticky material such as clay, often used as a covering for walls. **2** DEROG, COLLOQ a carelessly done painting.

daughter N **1** a female child. **2** a woman closely associated with, involved with or influenced by a person, thing or place.
■ **daughterly** ADJ.

daughter-in-law N (*daughters-in-law*) the wife of one's son.

daunting ADJ intimidating; discouraging.

dauntless ADJ fearless; not discouraged.

davit N either of a pair of crane-like devices on a ship on which a lifeboat is hung.

Davy Jones's locker N the bottom of the sea.

dawdle VB, INTR **1** to walk unnecessarily slowly. **2** to waste time.

dawn N **1** daybreak. **2** the beginning of (a new period of time, etc).
➤ VB, INTR of the day: to begin.
◆ **dawn on sb** to begin to be realized by them.

day N **1** a period of 24 hours, esp from midnight

to midnight. **2** the period from sunrise to sunset. **3** the period in any 24 hours normally spent doing something: **the working day**. **4** (**day** or **days**) a particular period of time, usu in the past: **childhood days**. **5** time of success, influence, power, etc: **Their day will come**.
◆ **at the end of the day** when all is said and done.
◆ **call it a day** to leave off doing something.

daybreak N first light in the morning.

day care N supervision and care given to young children, the elderly or handicapped people during the day.

daydream N pleasant thoughts which take one's attention away from what one is doing.
➤ VB, INTR to be engrossed in daydreams.
■ **daydreamer** N.

dayglo ADJ luminously brilliant.

daylight N **1** the light given by the Sun. **2** the time when light first appears in the sky.
◆ **in broad daylight 1** during the day.
2 openly.

daylight robbery N, COLLOQ greatly overcharging for something.

daylight-saving time N time, usu one hour ahead of standard time, adopted, usu in summertime, to increase the hours of daylight at the end of the day.

day release N a system by which employees are given time off work (usu one day a week) to study at college, etc.

day return N a ticket at a reduced price for a journey both ways on the same day.

daytime N the time from sunrise to sunset.

day-to-day ADJ daily; routine.

daze VB to make someone confused or unable to think clearly (eg by a blow or shock).
➤ N a confused, forgetful or inattentive state of mind. ■ **dazed** ADJ.

dazzle VB **1** to make someone unable to see properly, with or because of a strong light. **2** to impress someone greatly by one's beauty, skill, etc. ■ **dazzling** ADJ. ■ **dazzlingly** ADV.

D-Day N the date of the Allied invasion of Europe in World War II, 6 June 1944.

DDT ABBREV dichlorodiphenyltrichloroethane, a highly toxic insecticide.

de- PFX, SIGNIFYING **1** down or away: **debase**. **2** reversal or removal: **decriminalize**.

deacon N **1** a member of the lowest rank of clergy in the Roman Catholic and Anglican churches. **2** in some other churches: a person with certain duties such as looking after the church's financial affairs.

deactivate VB to remove the capacity of (something such as a bomb) to function.

dead ADJ **1** no longer living. **2** not alive. **3** no longer in existence. **4** with nothing living or growing in or on it. **5** not, or no longer, functioning; not connected to a source of power. **6** no longer burning. **7** no longer in everyday use: **a dead language**. **8** no longer of importance: **a dead issue**. **9** having little or no excitement or activity. **10** without feeling; numb. **11** complete; absolute. **12** of a sound: dull. **13** SPORT of a ball: out of play.
➤ ADV, SLANG absolutely; very: **dead drunk**.
◆ **the dead of night** the middle of the night.
◆ **the dead of winter** the middle of winter.

deadbeat N, COLLOQ a useless person; a down-and-out.

dead beat ADJ, COLLOQ exhausted.

deaden VB **1** to lessen or weaken something or make it less sharp, strong, etc. **2** to make something soundproof.

dead end N **1** a passage, road, etc, closed at one end. **2** a situation or activity with no possibility of further progress or movement.
➤ ADJ (**dead-end**) allowing no progress.

deadhead N, chiefly N AMER an ineffective unproductive person.
➤ VB to remove dead flowers from (plants).

dead heat N the result when competitors produce equally good performances or finish a race in exactly the same time.

deadline N a time or date for completion.

deadlock N a situation in which no further progress towards an agreement is possible.

dead loss N, COLLOQ someone or something that is totally useless.

deadly ADJ (*-ier, -iest*) **1** causing or likely to cause death. **2** COLLOQ very dull. **3** very great: in deadly earnest.
➤ ADV very; absolutely.

deadly nightshade N a poisonous plant with purple flowers and black berries.

dead march N, MUS solemn music played at funeral processions, esp those of soldiers.

dead-nettle N any of various plants superficially like a nettle but without a sting.

deadpan ADJ showing no emotion or feeling, esp when joking but pretending to be serious.

deaf ADJ **1** unable to hear at all or to hear well. **2** (usu **deaf to sth**) not willing to listen to (advice, appeals, etc). ■ **deafness** N.

deafblind ADJ both deaf and blind.

deafen VB to make someone deaf or temporarily unable to hear. ■ **deafening** ADJ.

deaf-mute N, often considered OFFENSIVE someone who can neither hear nor speak.
➤ ADJ unable to hear or speak.

deal¹ N **1** a bargain, agreement or arrangement. **2** particular treatment of or behaviour towards someone: a rough deal. **3** the act of, or a player's turn of, sharing out cards among the players in a card game.
➤ VB (PA T & PA P *dealt*) TR & INTR **1** (also **deal out**) to divide the cards among the players in a card game. **2** (also **deal out**) to give something out to a number of people, etc.
◆ **a good** or **great deal 1** a large quantity. **2** very much or often.
◆ **deal in sth** to buy and sell it.
◆ **deal with sth** or **sb 1** to take action regarding them. **2** to be concerned with them.

deal² N a plank or planks of fir or pine wood.

dealer N **1** a person or firm dealing in retail goods. **2** the player who deals in a card game. **3** someone who sells illegal drugs.

dealings PL N **1** one's manner of acting towards others. **2** business, etc, transactions.

dean N **1** a senior clergyman in an Anglican cathedral. **2** a senior official in a university or college. **3** the head of a university or college faculty.

dear ADJ **1** high in price; charging high prices. **2** lovable; attractive. **3** used in addressing someone at the start of a letter. **4** (usu **dear to sb**) greatly loved by, or very important or precious to, them.
➤ N **1** a charming or lovable person. **2** used esp as a form of address: a person one likes.
➤ EXCLAM used as an expression of dismay, etc: Dear me! ■ **dearly** ADV.
◆ **cost sb dear** to result in a lot of trouble.

dearth N a scarceness or lack.

death N **1** the time, act or manner of dying; the state of being dead. **2** often HUMOROUS something which causes a person to die: His antics will be the death of me. **3** the end or destruction of something. ■ **deathly** ADJ.
◆ **at death's door** near death.
◆ **put sb to death** to kill them or have them killed.
◆ **to death** extremely: bored to death.

deathbed N the bed in which a person died or is about to die.

death certificate N a certificate stating the time and cause of someone's death.

death duty N (often **death duties**) BRIT the former name for inheritance tax.

death knell N an action, announcement, etc that heralds the end or destruction of (hopes, plans, etc).

death penalty N punishment of a crime by death.

deathtrap N a building, vehicle, place, etc which is very unsafe.

death warrant N an official order for a death sentence to be carried out.

deathwatch beetle N a beetle which makes a ticking sound once believed to herald a death.

death wish N a desire to die, or that someone else should die.

deb N, COLLOQ a debutante.

debacle or **débâcle** N total disorder, defeat, collapse of organization, etc.

debar VB to stop someone from joining, taking part in, doing, etc something.

debase VB 1 to lower the value, quality, or status of something. 2 to lower the value of (a coin) by adding metal of a lower value. ■ **debasement** N.

debatable ADJ not agreed; uncertain.

debate N 1 a formal discussion. 2 a general discussion.
➤ VB, TR & INTR 1 to hold or take part in a debate. 2 to consider the arguments for or against something.

debauch VB to cause or persuade someone to take part in immoral, esp sexual, activities or excessive drinking. ■ **debauched** ADJ. ■ **debauchery** N.

debenture N, FINANCE a type of loan to a company or government agency which is usu made for a set period of time.

debilitate VB to make someone weak or weaker. ■ **debilitation** N. ■ **debility** N.

debit N 1 an entry in an account recording what is owed or has been spent. 2 a sum taken from a bank, etc account.
➤ VB 1 to take from (an account, etc). 2 to record something in a debit entry.

debit card N a plastic card used by a purchaser to transfer money directly from their account to the retailer's.

debonair ADJ esp of a man: cheerful, charming, elegant and well-mannered.

debrief VB to gather information from (a diplomat, astronaut, soldier, etc) after a battle, event, mission, etc. ■ **debriefing** N.

debris N 1 what remains of something destroyed. 2 rubbish. 3 small pieces of rock.

debt N 1 something owed. 2 the state of owing.

◆ **in sb's debt** under an obligation to them.

debtor N someone owing money.

debug VB 1 to remove secret microphones from (a room, etc). 2 to remove faults in (a computer program).

debunk VB to show (a person's claims, good reputation, etc) to be false or unjustified.

debut or **début** N the first public appearance of a performer.

debutante or **débutante** N a young woman making her first formal appearance as an adult in upper-class society.

deca- and (BEFORE A VOWEL) **dec-** COMB FORM, SIGNIFYING ten: decagon.

decade N 1 a period of ten years. 2 a group or series of ten things, etc.

decadence N 1 a falling to low standards in morals, art, etc. 2 the state of having low or immoral standards of behaviour, etc. ■ **decadent** ADJ ■ **decadently** ADV.

decaff or **decaf** COLLOQ, ADJ decaffeinated.
➤ N decaffeinated coffee.

decaffeinate VB to remove the caffeine from (eg coffee). ■ **decaffeinated** ADJ.

decagon N, GEOM a polygon with ten sides. ■ **decagonal** ADJ.

decahedron N a solid figure with ten faces. ■ **decahedral** ADJ.

decamp VB, INTR 1 to go away suddenly, esp secretly. 2 to break camp.

decant VB to pour (wine, etc) from one container to another.

decanter N an ornamental bottle with a stopper, used for decanted wine, sherry, etc.

decapitate VB to cut off the head of someone. ■ **decapitation** N.

decathlon N an athletic competition involving 10 events over two days. ■ **decathlete** N.

decay VB 1 TR & INTR to make or become rotten, ruined, weaker in health or power, etc. 2 INTR, PHYS of a radioactive substance: to break down into radioactive or non-radioactive isotopes. ➤ N **1** the natural breakdown of dead organic matter. **2** PHYS the breakdown of a radioactive substance into one or more isotopes. **3** a gradual decrease in health, power, quality, etc. **4** rotten matter in a tooth, etc.

decease N, FORMAL, LAW death.

deceased ADJ, FORMAL, LAW **1** dead, esp recently dead. **2** (**the deceased**) the dead person or dead people in question.

deceit N **1** an act of deceiving. **2** dishonesty; willingness to deceive. ■ **deceitful** ADJ.

deceive VB **1** to mislead or lie to someone. **2** to convince (oneself) that something untrue is true.

decelerate VB, TR & INTR to slow down, or make something slow down. ■ **deceleration** N.

December N the twelfth month of the year.

decency N (-*ies*) **1** decent behaviour or character. **2** (**decencies**) the generally accepted rules of moral behaviour.

decent ADJ **1** respectable; not vulgar or immoral. **2** kind, tolerant or likeable. **3** fairly good; adequate. ■ **decently** ADV.

deception N **1** deceiving or being deceived. **2** something which deceives. ■ **deceptive** ADJ. ■ **deceptiveness** N.

decibel N a unit equal to one tenth of a bel, used for comparing levels of power, esp sound.

decide VB **1** to settle something, or make its final result certain. **2** (**decide to do sth**) to make up one's mind to do it. **3** to make someone decide in a certain way. **4** to make a formal judgement.

decided ADJ **1** definite. **2** determined; showing no doubt. ■ **decidedly** ADV.

decider N **1** someone or something that decides. **2** something that decides a result, eg a winning goal.

deciduous ADJ, BOT shedding leaves once a year.

decimal ADJ **1** based on the number 10 or powers of 10. **2** denoting a system of units related to each other by multiples of 10.

➤ N a decimal fraction.

decimal fraction N a fraction in which tenths, hundredths, etc are written in figures after a decimal point, eg 0.5 = five tenths.

decimalize or **-ise** VB to convert (numbers, etc) to a decimal form. ■ **decimalization** N.

decimal point N the point which precedes the decimal fraction.

decimate VB to destroy a large part or number of something. ■ **decimation** N.

decipher VB **1** to translate (eg a message in code) into ordinary language. **2** to work out the meaning of something obscure or difficult to read. ■ **decipherable** ADJ.

decision N **1** the act of deciding. **2** something decided. **3** the ability to make decisions and act on them firmly.

decisive ADJ **1** putting an end to doubt or dispute. **2** having or showing decision. ■ **decisively** ADV. ■ **decisiveness** N.

deck[1] N **1** a platform forming a floor or covering across a ship. **2** a floor or platform in a bus, etc. **3** US a pack of playing-cards.

deck[2] VB (usu **deck sth out**) to decorate or embellish it.

deck chair N a light folding chair made of wood and a length of heavy fabric.

declaim VB **1** TR & INTR to make (a speech) in an impressive and dramatic manner. **2** INTR (usu **declaim against sth**) to protest about it forcefully. ■ **declamatory** ADJ.

declare VB **1** to announce something publicly or formally. **2** to say something firmly or emphatically. **3** to make known (goods on which duty must be paid, income on which tax should be paid, etc). ■ **declaration** N. ■ **declaratory** ADJ. ◆ **declare for** or **against sth** to state one's support or opposition regarding it.

declassify VB to state that (an official document, etc) is no longer on the secret list.

decline VB **1** to refuse (an invitation, etc), esp politely. **2** INTR to become less, less strong, less

healthy or less good.
➤ N a lessening of health, quality, quantity, etc.

declutch VB, INTR to release the clutch of (a motor vehicle).

decoct VB to extract the essence, etc of (a substance) by boiling. ■ **decoction** N.

decode VB to translate (a coded message) into ordinary language. ■ **decoder** N.

décolletage N a low-cut neckline on a woman's dress, etc.

décolleté ADJ of a dress, etc: low-cut.

decommission VB to take (eg a warship or atomic reactor) out of use or operation.

decompose VB 1 INTR of a dead organism: to rot. 2 TR & INTR, TECHNICAL to separate or break down into smaller or simpler elements.
■ **decomposition** N.

decompression sickness N a disorder caused by a person who has been breathing air under high pressure returning too quickly to normal atmospheric pressure.

decongestant MED, N a drug which reduces nasal congestion.
➤ ADJ relieving congestion.

decontaminate VB to remove poisons, radioactivity, etc from something.
■ **decontamination** N.

décor N 1 scenery, etc; a theatre set. 2 the style of decoration, etc in a room or house.

decorate VB 1 to beautify something with ornaments, etc. 2 to put paint or wallpaper on (a wall, etc). 3 to give a medal to someone as an honour. ■ **decorative** ADJ. ■ **decorator** N.

decoration N 1 something used to decorate. 2 the act of decorating. 3 the state of being decorated. 4 a medal.

decorous ADJ socially correct or acceptable; showing proper respect. ■ **decorously** ADV.

decorum N correct behaviour.

decoy VB to lead or lure into a trap.
➤ N someone or something used to lure (a person or animal) into a trap.

decrease VB TR & INTR to make or become less.
➤ N a lessening or loss. ■ **decreasing** ADJ.
■ **decreasingly** ADV.

decree N 1 a formal order or ruling. 2 LAW a ruling made in a law court.
➤ VB (-*eed, -eeing*) to order something by decree.

decrepit ADJ 1 weak or worn out because of old age. 2 in a very poor state because of age or long use. ■ **decrepitude** N.

decriminalize or **-ise** VB, LAW to make (something) no longer a criminal offence.
■ **decriminalization** N.

decry VB to express disapproval of.

dedicate VB (USU **dedicate oneself** or **sth to sb** or **sth**) 1 to give or devote (oneself or one's time, money, etc) to some purpose, cause, etc. 2 to devote or address (a book, piece of music, etc) to someone.

dedicated ADJ 1 committing a great deal of time and effort to something. 2 committed to a cause, etc.

dedication N 1 the quality of being dedicated. 2 the act of dedicating. 3 the words dedicating a book, etc to someone.

deduce VB to think out or judge on the basis of what one knows. ■ **deducible** ADJ.

deduct VB to take away (a number, amount, etc). ■ **deductible** ADJ.

deduction N 1 the act or process of deducting or deducing. 2 something, esp money, which has been or will be deducted. 3 something that has been deduced. ■ **deductive** ADJ.

deed N 1 something done. 2 a brave action or notable achievement. 3 LAW a signed statement recording an agreement.

deed poll N, LAW a deed made by one person only, esp when changing their name.

deem VB FORMAL, OLD USE to judge or consider.

deep ADJ 1 far down from the top or surface; with a relatively great distance from the top or

surface to the bottom. **2** far in from the outside surface or edge. **3** USU IN COMPOUNDS far down by a specified amount: **knee-deep in mud**. **4** in a specified number of rows or layers: **lined up four deep**. **5** coming from or going far down; long and full: **a deep sigh**. **6** very great: **deep trouble**. **7** of a colour: strong and relatively dark. **8** low in pitch: **deep-toned**. **9** of emotions, etc: strongly felt. **10** obscure; hard to understand: **deep thoughts**. **11** of a person: mysterious; keeping secret thoughts.
➤ ADV **1** deeply. **2** far down or into. **3** late on in or well into (a period of time).
➤ N (**the deep**) the ocean. ■ **deeply** ADV.

deepen VB, TR & INTR to make or become deeper, greater, more intense, etc.

deep-freeze N a refrigeration unit, or a compartment in a refrigerator, designed for storing perishables below − 18°C (0°F).
➤ VB to preserve perishable material, esp food, by storing it in a frozen state.

deep-rooted and **deep-seated** ADJ of ideas, etc: deeply and firmly established.

deer N (PL **deer**) a ruminant mammal, the male of which has antlers.

deerstalker N a hat with peaks at the front and back and earflaps.

deface VB to deliberately spoil the appearance of something. ■ **defacement** N.

de facto ADJ, ADV actual or actually, though not necessarily legally so.

defame VB to attack someone's reputation.
■ **defamation** N. ■ **defamatory** ADJ.

default VB, INTR (usu **default on sth**) to fail to do what one should do, esp to pay a due.
➤ N a failure to do or pay what one should.
■ **defaulter** N.
◆ **by default** because of someone's failure to do something.

defeat VB **1** to beat someone, eg in a war, competition, game or argument. **2** to make (plans, etc) fail.
➤ N defeating or being defeated.

defeatism N a state of mind in which one too

readily expects or accepts defeat or failure.
■ **defeatist** ADJ, N.

defecate VB to empty the bowels of waste matter. ■ **defecation** N.

defect N a flaw or fault.
➤ VB INTR to leave one's country, political party, etc, esp to go to or join an opposing one.
■ **defection** N. ■ **defector** N.

defective ADJ having a defect or defects.

defence or (US) **defense** N **1** the act of defending against attack. **2** the method or equipment used to protect against attack or when attacked. **3** the armed forces of a country. **4** (**defences**) fortifications. **5** a person's answer to an accusation, justifying or denying what they have been accused of. **6** (**the defence**) LAW the person or people on trial and the lawyer or lawyers acting for them.
■ **defenceless** ADJ.

defend VB **1** to guard or protect someone or something against attack or when attacked. **2** to explain, justify or argue in support of the actions of someone accused of doing wrong. **3** to be the lawyer acting on behalf of (the accused) in a trial. ■ **defender** N.

defendant N someone against whom a charge is brought in a law-court.

defensible ADJ able to be defended or justified. ■ **defensibility** N.

defensive ADJ **1** defending or ready to defend. **2** attempting to justify one's actions when criticized or when expecting criticism.
■ **defensively** ADV. ■ **defensiveness** N.

defer[1] VB (**-rr-**) to put off something until a later time. ■ **deferment** or **deferral** N.

defer[2] VB (**-rr-**) INTR (usu **defer to sb,** etc) to yield to their wishes, opinions or orders.

deference N willingness to consider or respect the wishes, etc of others.
■ **deferential** ADJ. ■ **deferentially** ADV.

defiance N open disobedience or opposition.
■ **defiant** ADJ. ■ **defiantly** ADV.

deficiency N (**-ies**) **1** a lack in quality or

amount. **2** the thing or amount lacking.

deficient ADJ not good enough; not having all that is needed.

deficit N the difference between what is required and what is available.

defile VB **1** to make something dirty or polluted. **2** to take away or spoil the goodness, holiness, etc of something. ■ **defilement** N.

define VB **1** to fix or state the exact meaning of (a word, etc). **2** to fix, describe or explain (opinions, duties, the qualities or limits of something, etc). **3** to make clear the outline or shape of something. ■ **definable** ADJ.

definite ADJ **1** fixed or firm; not liable to change. **2** sure; certain. **3** clear and precise. **4** having clear outlines. ■ **definitely** ADV.

definite article N, GRAM the word **the**, or any equivalent word in other languages.

definition N **1** a statement of the meaning of a word or phrase. **2** the act of defining a word or phrase. **3** the quality of having clear precise limits or form.

definitive ADJ **1** settling a matter once and for all. **2** complete and authoritative.

deflate VB **1** TR & INTR to collapse or grow smaller by letting out gas. **2** to reduce or take away the hopes, excitement, feelings of self-confidence, etc of someone.

deflation N **1** deflating or being deflated. **2** the state of feeling deflated. ■ **deflationary** ADJ.

deflect VB, TR & INTR to turn aside from the correct or intended course. ■ **deflection** N.

deflower VB, LITERARY to take away someone's virginity.

defoliant N, TECHNICAL a herbicide that causes the leaves to fall off plants. ■ **defoliate** VB. ■ **defoliation** N.

deforest VB, AGRIC to clear forested land, eg for agriculture. ■ **deforestation** N.

deform VB to change the shape of something, making it look ugly, unpleasant,

unnatural or spoiled. ■ **deformed** ADJ.

deformity N (-**ies**) **1** being deformed. **2** ugliness; disfigurement; an ugly feature.

defraud VB (usu **defraud sb of sth**) to dishonestly prevent someone getting or keeping something which belongs to them.

defrock VB to remove (a priest) from office.

defrost VB, TR & INTR **1** to remove ice from something. **2** to thaw or unfreeze.

deft ADJ skilful, quick and neat. ■ **deftly** ADV. ■ **deftness** N.

defunct ADJ no longer living, existing, active, usable or in use.

defuse VB **1** to remove the fuse from (a bomb, etc). **2** to make (a situation, etc) harmless.

defy VB (-**ies, -ied**) **1** to resist or disobey someone boldly and openly. **2** to dare or challenge someone. **3** FORMAL to make something impossible: **defy explanation**.

degenerate ADJ physically, morally or intellectually worse than before.
➤ N a degenerate person or animal.
➤ VB INTR to become degenerate.
■ **degeneracy** N. ■ **degeneration** N.

degrade VB **1** to disgrace or humiliate someone. **2** to reduce someone or something in rank, status, etc. ■ **degradation** N. ■ **degrading** ADJ.

degree N **1** an amount or extent. **2** PHYS (symbol °) a unit of temperature. **3** GEOM (symbol °) a unit by which angles are measured. **4** an award given by a university or college.

dehiscent ADJ, BOT bursting open to release seeds or pollen. ■ **dehiscence** N.

dehydrate VB **1** to remove water from (a substance or organism). **2** TR & INTR to lose or make someone or something lose too much water from the body. ■ **dehydration** N.

de-ice VB to make or keep something free of ice. ■ **de-icer** N.

deify VB (-**ies, -ied**) to regard someone or

something as a god. ■ **deification** N.

deign VB, INTR to do something in a way that shows that one considers the matter unimportant or beneath one's dignity.

deity N (-*ies*) FORMAL 1 a god or goddess. 2 the state of being divine. 3 (**the Deity**) God.

déjà vu N the feeling that one has experienced something before when one is actually experiencing it for the first time.

dejected ADJ sad; miserable. ■ **dejectedly** ADV. ■ **dejection** N.

de jure ADV, ADJ according to law.

dekko N (usu **take a dekko**) SLANG a look.

delay VB 1 to slow someone or something down or make them late. 2 to put off to a later time. 3 INTR to be slow in doing something. ➤ N 1 delaying or being delayed. 2 the amount of time by which something is delayed.

delectable ADJ delightful; delicious.

delectation N, FORMAL delight or enjoyment.

delegate VB 1 to give (part of one's work, power, etc) to someone else. 2 to send or name someone as the one to do a job, etc. ➤ N someone chosen to represent others.

delegation N 1 a group of delegates. 2 delegating or being delegated.

delete VB to rub out, score out or remove something. ■ **deletion** N.

deleterious ADJ, FORMAL harmful.

deli N a delicatessen.

deliberate ADJ 1 done on purpose. 2 slow and careful. ➤ VB TR & INTR to think about something carefully. ■ **deliberately** ADV.

deliberation N 1 careful thought. 2 (**deliberations**) formal and thorough discussion. 3 slowness and carefulness.

delicacy N (-*ies*) 1 being delicate. 2 something considered particularly delicious to eat.

delicate ADJ 1 easily damaged or broken. 2 not strong or healthy. 3 having fine texture or workmanship. 4 small and attractive. 5 small, neat and careful: delicate movements. 6 requiring tact and careful handling: a delicate situation. 7 careful not to offend others. 8 of colours, flavours, etc: light; not strong. ■ **delicately** ADV.

delicatessen N a shop or counter selling eg cheeses, cooked meats, and unusual foods.

delicious ADJ 1 with a very pleasing taste or smell. 2 giving great pleasure.

delight VB 1 to please greatly. 2 INTR (**delight in sth**) to take great pleasure from it. ➤ N 1 great pleasure. 2 something or someone that gives great pleasure. ■ **delightful** ADJ.

delimit VB to mark or fix the limits of (powers, etc). ■ **delimitation** N.

delineate VB 1 to show something by drawing. 2 to describe something in words. ■ **delineation** N.

delinquent N someone, esp a young person, guilty of a minor crime. ➤ ADJ guilty of a minor crime or misdeed. ■ **delinquency** N (-*ies*).

delirious ADJ 1 affected by delirium. 2 very excited or happy. ■ **deliriously** ADV.

delirium N 1 a state of madness or mental confusion and excitement, often caused by fever, drugs, etc. 2 extreme excitement or joy.

delirium tremens N delirium caused by chronic alcoholism.

deliver VB 1 to carry (goods, letters, etc) to a person or place. 2 to give or make (a speech, etc). 3 to help (a woman) at the birth of (a child). 4 TR & INTR, COLLOQ to keep or fulfil (a promise or undertaking).

delivery N (-*ies*) 1 the carrying of (goods, letters, etc) to a person or place. 2 the thing or things being delivered. 3 the process or manner of giving birth to a child. 4 the act of making, or the manner of making, a speech, etc. 5 the act or manner of throwing a ball.

dell N a small valley or hollow, usu wooded.

delphinium N (-*iums* or -*ia*) a garden plant

with tall spikes of usu blue flowers.

delta N **1** the fourth letter of the Greek alphabet (Δ,δ). **2** an area of silt, sand, gravel or clay, often roughly triangular, at a river mouth.

delude VB to deceive or mislead someone.

deluge N **1** a flood. **2** a downpour of rain. **3** a great quantity of anything pouring in. ➢ VB **1** FORMAL to flood. **2** to overwhelm.

delusion N **1** the act of deluding or the state of being deluded. **2** PSYCHOL a false or mistaken belief. ■ **delusive** and **delusory** ADJ.

de luxe or **deluxe** ADJ **1** very luxurious or elegant. **2** with special features or qualities.

delve VB, INTR (usu **delve into sth**) to search it for information.

demagogue N, DEROG someone who tries to win power or support by appealing to people's emotions and prejudices. ■ **demagogic** ADJ.

demand VB **1** to ask or ask for firmly, forcefully or urgently. **2** to require or need something. **3** to claim something as a right. ➢ N **1** a forceful request or order. **2** an urgent claim for action or attention: **demands on one's time**. **3** people's desire or ability to buy or obtain goods, etc. **4** ECON the amount of any article, etc, which consumers will buy. ◆ **in demand** frequently asked for. ◆ **on demand** when asked for.

demanding ADJ requiring a lot of effort, ability, attention, etc: **a demanding job/child**.

demean VB to lower the dignity of or lessen respect for (esp oneself).

demeanour or (US) **demeanor** N way of behaving.

demented ADJ mad; out of one's mind.

dementia N, PSYCHOL a loss or severe lessening of normal mental ability and functioning, esp in the elderly.

demerara and **demerara sugar** N a form of crystallized brown sugar.

demi- COMB FORM, SIGNIFYING half or partly: demigod.

demigod N, MYTHOL someone part human and part god.

demilitarize or **-ise** VB to remove armed forces from (an area). ■ **demilitarization** N.

demi-monde N **1** women in an unrespectable social position. **2** any group considered not completely respectable.

demise N **1** FORMAL OR EUPHEMISTIC death. **2** a failure or end.

demist VB to free (a vehicle's windscreen, etc) from condensation. ■ **demister** N.

demo N, COLLOQ **1** a public display of opinion on a political or moral issue. **2** (also **demo tape**) a recording made usu by as yet unsigned musicians to demonstrate their music.

demob VB, BRIT COLLOQ (**-bb-**) to demobilize.

demobilize or **-ise** VB to release someone from service in the armed forces.

democracy N (**-ies**) **1** a form of government in which the people elect representatives to govern them. **2** a country, state or other body with such a form of government.

democrat N **1** someone who believes in democracy. **2** (**Democrat**) a member or supporter of a political party with Democratic in its title.

democratic ADJ **1** concerned with or following the principles of democracy. **2** believing in or providing equal rights and privileges for all. ■ **democratically** ADV.

demography N, TECHNICAL the scientific study of population. ■ **demographic** ADJ.

demolish VB **1** to pull down (a building, etc). **2** to destroy (an argument, etc). **3** FACETIOUS to eat up. ■ **demolition** N.

demon N **1** an evil spirit. **2** a cruel or evil person. **3** someone who has great energy or skill: **a demon at football**. ■ **demonic** ADJ.

demoniac and **demoniacal** ADJ **1** of or like a demon. **2** frenzied or very energetic.

demonstrate VB **1** to show or prove something by reasoning or evidence. **2** TR & INTR to show how something is done, operates, etc. **3** TR & INTR to show (support, opposition, etc) by protesting, marching, etc in public. ■ **demonstration** N.

demonstrative ADJ **1** showing one's feelings openly. **2** (usu **demonstrative of sth**) showing evidence of it.

demonstrator N **1** someone who demonstrates equipment, etc. **2** someone who takes part in a public demonstration.

demoralize or **-ise** VB to take away the confidence, courage or enthusiasm of someone. ■ **demoralization** N.

demote VB to reduce someone to a lower rank or grade. ■ **demotion** N.

demotic ADJ of a language: colloquial. ➢ N colloquial language.

demur VB (**-rr-**) INTR (often **demur at sth**) to object mildly to it or be reluctant to do it.

demure ADJ quiet, modest and well-behaved. ■ **demurely** ADV. ■ **demureness** N.

den N **1** a wild animal's home. **2** a centre (often secret) of illegal or immoral activity.

denationalize or **-ise** VB to transfer (an industry) to private ownership from state ownership. ■ **denationalization** N.

dengue N an acute tropical viral fever transmitted by mosquitos.

denial N **1** declaring something not to be true. **2** an act of refusing something to someone. **3** a refusal to acknowledge connections with somebody or something.

denier N the unit of weight of silk, rayon or nylon thread, usu used as a measure of the fineness of stockings or tights.

denigrate VB to attack or belittle someone's reputation or worth. ■ **denigration** N.

denim N **1** a hard-wearing twilled cotton cloth. **2** (**denims**) jeans made of denim.

denizen N, FORMAL an inhabitant.

denomination N **1** a religious group with its own beliefs, organization and practices. **2** a

particular unit of value of a postage stamp, coin or banknote, etc. ■ **denominational** ADJ.

denominator N, MATH in a vulgar fraction, the number below the line.

denote VB **1** to mean; to be the name of or sign for something. **2** to be a sign, mark or indication of something. ■ **denotation** N.

denouement N the final part of a story or plot, in which uncertainties are explained and problems and mysteries resolved.

denounce VB **1** to inform against or accuse someone publicly. **2** to condemn (an action, proposal, etc) strongly and openly.

dense ADJ **1** closely packed or crowded together. **2** thick: **dense fog**. **3** COLLOQ stupid; slow to understand. ■ **densely** ADV.

density N (**-ies**) **1** the state of being dense; the degree of denseness. **2** the ratio of the mass of a substance to its volume. **3** the number of items within a specific area or volume.

dent N a hollow made by pressure or a blow. ➢ VB to make a dent in something.

dental ADJ of the teeth or dentistry.

dentine N, ANAT the hard material that forms the bulk of a tooth.

dentist N someone who diagnoses, treats and prevents diseases of the oral cavity and teeth. ■ **dentistry** N.

denture N a false tooth or (usu **dentures**) set of false teeth.

denude VB **1** to make someone or something completely bare. **2** to strip (land) through weathering and erosion. ■ **denudation** N.

denunciation N a public condemnation or accusation.

deny VB (**-ies, -ied**) **1** to declare something not to be true. **2** to refuse to give or allow something to someone. **3** to refuse to acknowledge.

deodorant N a substance that prevents or conceals unpleasant smells, esp on the body.

deodorize or **-ise** VB to remove, conceal or

absorb the unpleasant smell of something.

deoxyribonucleic acid N, BIOCHEM see DNA.

depart VB, INTR 1 to leave. 2 (usu **depart from sth**) to stop following or decline to follow a planned or usual course of action.

departed ADJ, FORMAL dead.

department N 1 a section of an organization. 2 something which is someone's special skill or responsibility. ■ **departmental** ADJ.

department store N a large shop with many departments selling a wide variety of goods.

departure N 1 an act of going away or leaving. 2 a change from a planned or usual course of action.

depend VB, INTR (usu **depend on** or **upon sb** or **sth**) 1 to trust or rely on them or it. 2 to rely on financial or other support from someone. 3 to be decided by something else.

dependable ADJ trustworthy; reliable. ■ **dependability** N. ■ **dependably** ADV.

dependant N a person who is kept or supported financially by another.

dependence N (usu **dependence on sth** or **sb**) 1 the state of being dependent on them. 2 trust and reliance.

dependency N (-ies) 1 a country governed or controlled by another. 2 excessive dependence on someone or something.

dependent ADJ (often **dependent on sth** or **sb**) relying on it or them for support.

depict VB 1 to paint or draw something. 2 to describe something. ■ **depiction** N.

depilate VB to remove hair from (a part of the body). ■ **depilatory** N, ADJ.

deplete VB to reduce greatly in number, quantity, etc; to use up (money, resources, etc). ■ **depletion** N.

deplorable ADJ very bad.

deplore VB to feel or express great disapproval of or regret for something.

deploy VB, TR & INTR to position (troops) ready for battle. ■ **deployment** N.

depopulate VB to greatly reduce the number of people living in (an area, country, etc). ■ **depopulation** N.

deport VB to legally remove or expel (a person) from a country. ■ **deportation** N.

depose VB to remove someone from a high office or powerful position.

deposit VB 1 to put down or leave something. 2 to put (money, etc) in a bank, etc. 3 to give (money) as the first part of the payment for something. 4 to pay (money) as a guarantee against loss or damage.
➤ N 1 money, etc, deposited in a bank, etc. 2 money given as part payment for something or as a guarantee against loss or damage. 3 solid matter that has settled at the bottom of a liquid, or is left behind by a liquid. 4 GEOL a layer (of coal, minerals, etc) occurring in rock.

deposit account N a bank account in which money gains interest but which cannot be used for money transfers by eg cheque.

deposition N 1 deposing or being deposed. 2 the act of depositing or process of being deposited. 3 LAW a written statement made under oath and used as evidence in a court.

depot N 1 a storehouse or warehouse. 2 a place where buses, trains and other vehicles are kept and repaired. 3 N AMER a bus or railway station.

depraved ADJ morally corrupted. ■ **depravity** N.

deprecate VB to express or feel disapproval of something. ■ **deprecatory** ADJ.

depreciate VB 1 TR & INTR to fall, or make something fall, in value. 2 to belittle someone or something. ■ **depreciatory** ADJ.

depreciation N 1 ECON a fall in value of a currency against the value of other currencies. 2 the reduction in the value of assets through use or age. 3 the process of depreciating.

depredation N (often **depredations**) damage, destruction or violent robbery.

depress VB **1** to make someone sad and gloomy. **2** FORMAL to make (prices, etc) lower. **3** FORMAL to press down. **4** to weaken.
■ **depressing** ADJ. ■ **depressingly** ADV.

depressant ADJ, MED able to reduce mental or physical activity.
➢ N a depressant drug.

depressed ADJ **1** sad and gloomy. **2** PSYCHOL suffering from depression. **3** of a region, etc: suffering from high unemployment and low standards of living. **4** of a market, trade, etc: reduced; not flourishing.

depression N **1** PSYCHOL a mental state characterized by prolonged feelings of sadness, pessimism, apathy, low self-esteem and despair. **2** a period of low business and industrial activity accompanied by a rise in unemployment. **3** METEOROL a cyclone. **4** a hollow, esp in the ground.

depressive ADJ **1** depressing. **2** suffering from frequent bouts of depression.
➢ N someone who suffers from depression.

deprive VB (usu **deprive sb of sth**) to prevent them from having or using it. ■ **deprivation** N.

deprived ADJ **1** lacking money, reasonable living conditions, etc. **2** of a district, etc: lacking good housing, schools, medical facilities, etc.

depth N **1** the distance from the top downwards, from the front to the back or from the surface inwards. **2** intensity or strength. **3** extensiveness: **depth of knowledge**. **4** (usu **the depths**) somewhere far from the surface or edge of somewhere: **the depths of the ocean**. **5** (usu **the depths**) an extreme feeling (of despair, etc) or great degree (of deprivation, etc). **6** (often **the depths**) the middle and most intense part (of winter, etc). **7** of sound: lowness of pitch.

depth charge N a bomb which explodes underwater, used to attack submarines.

deputation N a group of people appointed to represent and speak on behalf of others.

deputize or **-ise** VB, INTR (often **deputize for sb**) to act as their deputy.

deputy N (*-ies*) a person appointed to act on behalf of, or as an assistant to, someone else.

derail VB, TR & INTR to leave or make (a train, etc) leave the rails. ■ **derailment** N.

derange VB **1** to make someone insane. **2** to disrupt or throw into disorder or confusion.
■ **deranged** ADJ. ■ **derangement** N.

derby[1] N (*-ies*) **1** (**the Derby**) a horse race held annually at Epsom Downs. **2** a race or a sports event, esp a contest between teams from the same area.

derby[2] N (*-ies*) N AMER a bowler hat.

derelict ADJ abandoned; in ruins.
➢ N a tramp with no home or money.

dereliction N **1** (usu **dereliction of duty**) neglect or failure. **2** the state of being abandoned.

deride VB to laugh at or make fun of someone. ■ **derision** N.

de rigueur ADJ required by fashion or custom.

derisive ADJ scornful. ■ **derisively** ADV.

derisory ADJ ridiculous and insulting, esp ridiculously small.

derivation N **1** deriving or being derived. **2** the source or origin (esp of a word).

derivative ADJ not original; derived from or copying something else.
➢ N something derived from something else.

derive VB now only in phrases.
◆ **derive from sth** to have it as a source.
◆ **derive sth from sth else 1** to obtain or produce one thing from another. **2** to trace something back to (a source or origin).

dermatitis N, MED inflammation of the skin.

dermatology N the study of the skin and treatment of its diseases. ■ **dermatologist** N.

derogatory ADJ showing, or intended to show, disapproval, dislike or lack of respect.

derrick N **1** a type of crane with a movable arm. **2** a framework built over an oil-well, for raising and lowering the drill.

derv N, BRIT diesel oil used as a fuel for road vehicles.

dervish N a Muslim ascetic, noted for performing spinning dances as a religious ritual.

descale VB to remove encrusted deposits from (a pipe, kettle, etc).

descant MUS, N a melody played or harmony sung above the main tune.
➤ ADJ of a musical instrument: having a higher pitch and register than others of the same type.

descend VB 1 TR & INTR to move from a higher to a lower place or position. 2 INTR to lead or slope downwards. 3 INTR (often **descend on sb** or **sth**) to invade or attack them or it.
◆ **be descended from sb** to have them as an ancestor.

descendant N a person or animal, etc that is the child, grandchild, etc of another.

descent N 1 the act or process of coming or going down. 2 a slope downwards. 3 family ancestry. 4 a sudden invasion or attack.

describe VB 1 to say what something is like. 2 TECH, GEOM to draw or form (eg a circle).

description N 1 the act of describing. 2 a statement of what someone or something is like. 3 COLLOQ a sort, type or kind: **toys of every description**.

descriptive ADJ describing, esp describing vividly. ■ **descriptively** ADV.

descry VB (-ies, -ied) FORMAL 1 to catch sight of something. 2 to discover by looking carefully.

desecrate VB to treat or use (a sacred object) or behave in (a holy place) in a way that shows a lack of respect. ■ **desecration** N.

desegregate VB to end segregation, esp racial segregation in (public places, schools, etc). ■ **desegregation** N.

deselect VB not to reselect (eg a sitting MP or councillor, an athlete). ■ **deselection** N.

desensitize or **-ise** VB to make someone or something less sensitive to light, pain, suffering, etc. ■ **desensitization** N.

desert[1] VB 1 to leave or abandon (a place or person). 2 INTR to leave (esp a branch of the armed forces) without permission. ■ **deserter** N. ■ **desertion** N.

desert[2] N an area of land with little rainfall and scarce vegetation.

deserts PL N (usu **just deserts**) what one deserves, usu something bad.

deserve VB to have earned or be worthy of (a reward or punishment, etc). ■ **deservedly** ADV.

deserving ADJ (usu **deserving of sth**) worthy of being given support, a reward, etc.

desiccate VB to dry or remove the moisture from something, esp food. ■ **desiccation** N.

design VB 1 to make a preparatory plan, drawing or model of something. 2 FORMAL to plan, intend or develop something for a particular purpose.
➤ N 1 a plan, drawing or model showing how something is to be made. 2 the art or job of making such drawings, plans, etc. 3 the way in which something has been made. 4 a decorative picture, pattern, etc. 5 a plan, purpose or intention.

designate VB 1 to choose or specify someone or something for a purpose or duty. 2 to mark or indicate something. 3 to be a name or label for someone or something. ■ **designation** N.

designedly ADV intentionally.

designer N someone who makes plans, patterns, drawings, etc.
➤ ADJ designed by and bearing the name of a famous fashion designer: **designer dresses**.

designing ADJ cunning, deceitful.

desirable ADJ 1 worth having. 2 sexually attractive. ■ **desirability** N.

desire N 1 a longing or wish. 2 strong sexual interest and attraction.
➤ VB 1 FORMAL to want. 2 to feel sexual desire for someone.

desist VB, INTR, FORMAL to stop.

desk N 1 a table, often with drawers, for sitting at while writing, reading, etc. 2 a service counter in a public building. **3** a section of a newspaper, etc office with responsibility for a particular subject: **news desk**.

desktop ADJ small enough to fit on the top of a desk.
➤ N a desktop computer.

desktop publishing N the preparation and production of typeset material using a computer and printer.

desolate ADJ **1** barren and lonely. **2** very sad. **3** lacking pleasure or comfort: **a desolate life**. **4** lonely; alone.
➤ VB **1** to overwhelm someone with sadness. **2** to lay waste (an area). ■ **desolation** N.

despair VB, INTR (often **despair of sth** or **despair of doing sth**) to lose or lack hope.
➤ N the state of having lost hope.

despatch see **dispatch**

desperado N (-**os** or -**oes**) a bandit or outlaw.

desperate ADJ **1** extremely anxious, fearful or despairing. **2** willing to take risks because of hopelessness and despair. **3** very serious, difficult, dangerous and almost hopeless: **a desperate situation**. **4** dangerous and likely to be violent: **a desperate criminal**. **5** extreme and carried out as a last resort: **desperate measures**. **6** very great: **desperate need**. **7** very anxious or eager: **desperate to go**.
■ **desperately** ADV. ■ **desperation** N.

despicable ADJ contemptible; mean.

despise VB to scorn or have contempt for someone or something.

despite PREP in spite of.

despondent ADJ sad; dejected.
■ **despondency** N. ■ **despondently** ADV.

despot N someone who has great or total power, esp if cruel or oppressive. ■ **despotic** ADJ. ■ **despotically** ADV.

despotism N complete or absolute power.

dessert N a sweet course of a meal.

destination N the place to which someone or something is going.

destine VB, FORMAL (usu **be destined for sth** or **to do sth**) to have it as one's fate.

destiny N (-**ies**) **1** the future as arranged by fate or God. **2** (also **Destiny**) fate.

destitute ADJ very poor. ■ **destitution** N.

destroy VB **1** to break something into pieces, completely ruin it, etc. **2** to put an end to something. **3** to defeat someone totally. **4** to ruin the reputation, health, etc of someone. **5** to kill (an animal).

destroyer N **1** someone or something that destroys. **2** a type of small fast warship.

destruction N **1** the act or process of destroying or being destroyed. **2** something that destroys. ■ **destructible** ADJ.

destructive ADJ **1** causing destruction or serious damage. **2** of criticism, etc: pointing out faults, etc without suggesting improvements.

desuetude N disuse.

desultory ADJ jumping from one thing to another with no plan, purpose or logical connection. ■ **desultorily** ADV.

detach VB **1** TR & INTR to unfasten or separate. **2** MIL to select (soldiers, etc) from a larger group. ■ **detachable** ADJ.

detached ADJ **1** of a building: not joined to another on either side. **2** feeling no personal or emotional involvement.

detachment N **1** the state of being emotionally detached. **2** a group (eg of soldiers) detached for a purpose.

detail N **1** a small feature, fact or item. **2** something considered unimportant. **3** all the small features and parts of something: **an eye for detail**. **4** a part of a painting, map, etc considered separately. **5** MIL a group of eg soldiers given a special task.
➤ VB **1** to describe or list fully. **2** to appoint someone to do a particular task.
◆ **in detail** giving or looking at all the details.

detailed ADJ **1** of a list, etc: itemized. **2** of a story, picture, etc: intricate.

detain VB **1** to delay someone or something.

2 of the police, etc: to keep someone in a cell, prison, etc. ■ **detainee** N. ■ **detainment** N.

detect VB **1** to see or notice. **2** to discover, and usu indicate, the presence of (something). ■ **detectable** ADJ. ■ **detector** N.

detection N **1** detecting or being detected. **2** the work of a detective.

detective N a police officer whose job is to solve crime.

détente N a lessening of tension, esp between countries.

detention N **1** the act of detaining or the state of being detained, esp in prison or police custody. **2** a punishment in which a pupil is kept at school after most pupils have gone home.

deter VB (**-rr-**) to discourage or prevent someone from doing something.

detergent N a soap–like cleansing agent.
➤ ADJ having the power to clean.

deteriorate VB, INTR to grow worse. ■ **deterioration** N.

determinant N a determining factor or circumstance.

determinate ADJ having definite fixed limits.

determination N **1** firmness or strength of will, purpose or character. **2** the act of determining or process of being determined.

determine VB **1** to fix or settle the exact limits or nature of something. **2** to find out or reach a conclusion about something by gathering facts, making measurements, etc. **3** TR & INTR to decide or make someone decide. **4** to be the main or controlling influence on someone or something.

determined ADJ **1** (**determined to do sth**) firmly intending to do it. **2** having or showing a strong will. ■ **determinedly** ADV.

determiner N, GRAM a word that precedes a noun and limits its meaning in some way, eg **a**, **the**, **this**, **every**, **some**.

deterrent N something which deters.
➤ ADJ capable of deterring. ■ **deterrence** N.

detest VB to dislike someone or something

intensely. ■ **detestable** ADJ hateful.

dethrone VB **1** to remove from the throne or from a position of power or authority.

detonate VB, TR & INTR to explode or make something explode. ■ **detonation** N.

detonator N an explosive substance or a device used to make a bomb, etc explode.

detour N a route away from and longer than a planned or more direct route.

detoxify VB (**-ies, -ied**) to remove poison, drugs or harmful substances from (a person, etc); to treat (a patient) for alcoholism or drug addiction. ■ **detoxification** N. Often shortened to **detox**.

detract VB, INTR (chiefly **detract from sth**) to take away from it or lessen it. ■ **detraction** N.

detriment N harm or loss. ■ **detrimental** ADJ. ■ **detrimentally** ADV.

detritus N bits and pieces of rubbish left over.

deuce N **1** TENNIS a score of forty points each in a game or five games each in a match. **2** a card, dice throw, etc, of the value two.

deuterium N, CHEM one of the three isotopes of hydrogen.

devalue VB **1** TR & INTR to reduce the value of (a currency) in relation to other currencies. **2** to make (a person, action, etc) seem less valuable or important. ■ **devaluation** N.

devastate VB **1** to cause great destruction in or to something. **2** to overwhelm someone with grief or shock. ■ **devastated** ADJ. ■ **devastating** ADJ. ■ **devastation** N.

develop VB **1** TR & INTR to make or become more mature, advanced, complete, organized, detailed, etc. **2** to change to a more complex structure. **3** to begin to have, or to have more, of something: **develop an interest in politics**. **4** TR & INTR to appear and grow; to have or suffer from something which has appeared and grown: **developing a cold**. **5** to convert an invisible image on (exposed photographic film or paper) into a visible image. **6** to bring into fuller use (the natural resources, etc of a country or region). **7** to build on (land) or prepare (land) for being built on.

developer N **1** a chemical used to develop film. **2** someone who builds on land.

development N **1** the act of developing or the process of being developed. **2** a new stage, event or situation. **3** a result or consequence. ■ **developmental** ADJ.

deviant ADJ not following the normal patterns, accepted standards, etc.
➤ N someone who behaves in a way not considered normal or acceptable, esp sexually.
■ **deviance** N.

deviate VB, INTR to move away from what is considered a correct or normal course, standard of behaviour, way of thinking, etc.
■ **deviation** N.

device N **1** a tool or instrument. **2** a plan or scheme, sometimes involving trickery or deceit. **3** HERALDRY a sign or symbol eg on a crest.

devil N **1** (**the Devil**) RELIG the most powerful evil spirit; Satan. **2** any evil spirit. **3** COLLOQ a mischievous or bad person. **4** COLLOQ a person: **lucky devil**. **5** someone or something difficult to deal with. **6** someone who excels at something. **7** (**the devil**) used for emphasis in exclamations: **What the devil is it?**

devilish ADJ **1** of or like a devil. **2** very wicked.
➤ ADV, OLD USE very.

devil-may-care ADJ cheerfully heedless of danger, etc.

devilment N mischievous fun.

devilry N (**-ies**) **1** mischievous fun. **2** wickedness or cruelty. **3** black magic.

devil's advocate N someone who argues for or against something simply to encourage discussion or argument.

devious ADJ **1** not totally open or honest. **2** cunning, often deceitfully. **3** not direct: **came by a devious route**. ■ **deviously** ADV.

devise VB to think up (a plan, etc).

devoid ADJ (always **devoid of sth**) lacking it.

devolution N the giving of certain powers to a regional government by a central government. ■ **devolutionist** N, ADJ.

devolve VB (usu **devolve to** or **on** or **upon sb**) TR & INTR of duties, power, etc: to be transferred or to transfer them to someone else.

devote VB to use or give up (eg time or money) to a purpose.

devoted ADJ **1** (usu **devoted to sb**) loving and loyal to them. **2** (usu **devoted to sth**) given up to it; totally occupied by it.
■ **devotedly** ADV.

devotee N **1** a keen follower or enthusiastic supporter. **2** a keen believer in a religion.

devotion N **1** great love or loyalty. **2** devoting or being devoted. **3** religious enthusiasm and piety. **4** (**devotions**) RELIG prayers.

devour VB **1** to eat up something greedily. **2** to completely destroy something. **3** to read (a book, etc) eagerly. **4** (usu **be devoured**) to be taken over totally: **devoured by guilt**.

devout ADJ **1** sincerely religious. **2** deeply felt; earnest. ■ **devoutly** ADV.

dew N tiny droplets of water deposited on eg leaves close to the ground on cool clear nights.
■ **dewy** ADJ (**-ier, -iest**).

dewclaw N a small functionless toe or claw on the legs of some dogs and other animals.

dewlap N a flap of loose skin hanging down from the throat of certain cattle, dogs, etc.

dexterity N **1** skill in using one's hands. **2** quickness of mind.

dexterous ADJ having, showing or done with dexterity. ■ **dexterously** ADV.

dextrose N a type of glucose.

dhal see **dal**

di- PFX **1** two or double: **dicotyledon**. **2** CHEM containing two atoms of the same type: **dioxide**.

diabetes N, MED a metabolic disorder in which insulin is not produced sufficiently.

diabetic N someone suffering from diabetes.

➤ ADJ **1** of or suffering from diabetes. **2** for people who have diabetes.

diabolic ADJ **1** satanic; devilish. **2** very wicked.

diabolical ADJ, BRIT COLLOQ very shocking, annoying, bad, difficult, etc.

diaconal ADJ of a deacon.

diacritic N a mark over, under or through a letter to show that it has a particular sound, as in é, è, ç, ñ.

diadem N a crown or jewelled headband.

diaeresis or (N AMER) **dieresis** N (-ses) a mark (¨) placed over a vowel to show that it is to be pronounced separately, as in **naïve**.

diagnosis N (-ses) MED the identification of a medical disorder on the basis of its symptoms. ■ **diagnose** VB. ■ **diagnostic** ADJ.

diagonal ADJ **1** MATH of a straight line: joining non-adjacent corners of a polygon or vertices not on the same face in a polyhedron. **2** sloping or slanting. ➤ N a diagonal line. ■ **diagonally** ADV.

diagram N a drawing that shows something's structure or the way in which it functions. ■ **diagrammatic** ADJ.

dial N **1** a plate on a clock, radio, meter, etc with numbers or symbols on it and a movable indicator, used to indicate eg measurements or selected settings. **2** the movable round numbered plate on some telephones. ➤ VB (-*ll*-; US -*l*-) TR & INTR to use a telephone dial or keypad to call (a number).

dialect N a form of a language spoken in a particular region or by a certain social group.

dialectic N, PHILOS **1** (also **dialectics**) the establishing of truth by discussion. **2** (also **dialectics**) a debate which aims to resolve the conflict between two opposing theories rather than to disprove either of them. **3** the art of arguing logically. ■ **dialectical** ADJ.

dialogue or sometimes (US) **dialog** N **1** a conversation, esp a formal one. **2** the words spoken by the characters in a play, book, etc. **3** a discussion with a view to resolving conflict or achieving agreement.

dialysis N (-ses) **1** CHEM the separation of particles in a solution by diffusion through a semi-permeable membrane. **2** MED the removal of toxic substances from the blood by such a process in an artificial kidney machine.

diamanté ADJ decorated with small sparkling ornaments.

diameter N, GEOM **1** a straight line drawn across a circle through its centre. **2** the length of this line.

diametric and **diametrical** ADJ **1** relating to or along a diameter. **2** of opinions, etc: directly opposed. ■ **diametrically** ADV.

diamond N **1** a colourless crystalline form of carbon, the hardest mineral and a gemstone. **2** a rhombus. **3** CARDS **a** (**diamonds**) one of the four suits of playing-cards, with red rhombus-shaped symbols ◆; **b** a playing-card of this suit. **4** a baseball pitch. ➤ ADJ **1** resembling, made of or marked with diamonds. **2** rhombus-shaped.

diamond wedding N the sixtieth wedding anniversary.

diaper N, N AMER a baby's nappy.

diaphanous ADJ of cloth: light and fine, and almost transparent.

diaphragm N **1** ANAT the sheet of muscle that separates the thorax from the abdomen. **2** OPTICS an opaque disc with an adjustable aperture that is used to control the amount of light entering eg a camera or microscope. **3** same as **cap** (N sense 6).

diarist N a person who writes a diary.

diarrhoea or (N AMER) **diarrhea** N, MED a condition in which the bowels are emptied frequently and the faeces are very soft.

diary N (-ies) **1 a** a written record of daily events in a person's life; **b** a book containing this. **2** BRIT a book with separate spaces for each day in which appointments, daily notes and reminders may be written.

the Diaspora N **1** the scattering of the Jewish

people to various countries following their exile in Babylon in the 6c BC. **2** (also **diaspora**) a dispersion of people of the same nation or culture.

diatribe N a bitter or abusive critical attack.

dibble N a short pointed hand–tool used for making holes in the ground for seeds, etc.

dice N (PL *dice*) a small cube with one to six spots on each of its faces, used in games of chance. See also **die²**.
➤ VB to cut (vegetables, etc) into small cubes.

dicey ADJ (*-cier, -ciest*) COLLOQ risky.

dichotomy N (*-ies*) a division into two groups or parts, esp when sharply opposed or contrasted. ■ **dichotomous** ADJ.

dick N, COARSE SLANG the penis.

dickens N, COLLOQ (usu **the dickens**) the devil, used esp for emphasis: **What the dickens are you doing?**

Dickensian ADJ **1** resembling the 19c English social life depicted in the novels of Charles Dickens, eg the poor living and working conditions. **2** of Charles Dickens or his writings.

dicotyledon N, BOT a flowering plant with two cotyledons.

dicta see **dictum**

Dictaphone N, TRADEMARK a small tape–recorder for use esp when dictating letters.

dictate VB **1** to say or read out something for someone else to write down. **2** to state or lay down (rules, terms, etc) forcefully or with authority. **3** TR & INTR, DEROG to give orders to or try to impose one's wishes on someone.
➤ N (usu **dictates**) **1** an order or instruction. **2** a guiding principle. ■ **dictation** N.

dictator N **1** a ruler with total power. **2** someone who behaves in a dictatorial manner. ■ **dictatorship** N.

dictatorial ADJ fond of using one's power and authority and imposing one's wishes on or giving orders to other people.

diction N the way in which one speaks.

dictionary N (*-ies*) **1** a book containing the words of a language arranged alphabetically with their meanings, etc, or with the equivalent words in another language. **2** an alphabetically arranged book of information.

dictum N (*-tums* or *-ta*) **1** a formal statement of opinion. **2** a popular saying.

didactic ADJ intended to teach or instruct. ■ **didactically** ADV. ■ **didacticism** N.

diddle VB, COLLOQ to cheat or swindle.

didgeridoo N, MUS a native Australian tubular wind instrument.

didn't CONTRACTION OF did not.

die¹ VB (*dies, died, dying*) INTR **1** to stop living. **2** to come to an end or fade away. **3** of an engine, etc: to stop working suddenly. **4** (usu **die of sth**) to suffer or be overcome by the effects of it: **die of laughter**.
◆ **be dying for sth** or **to do sth** COLLOQ to have a strong desire or need for it or to do it.
◆ **die down** to lose strength or force.
◆ **die off** to die one after another; to die in large numbers.
◆ **die out** to cease to exist anywhere.

die² N **1** (PL *dies*) **a** a metal tool or stamp for cutting or shaping metal or making designs on coins, etc. **b** a metal device for shaping a semisoft solid material. **2** (PL *dice*) a dice.

diehard N a person who stubbornly refuses to accept new ideas or changes. **Also AS ADJ.**

dielectric PHYS, ADJ not conducting electricity.
➤ N a dielectric material.

dieresis an alternative N AMER, ESP US spelling of **diaeresis**.

diesel N **1** diesel fuel. **2** a diesel engine. **3** a train, etc driven by a diesel engine.

diesel engine N a type of engine in which fuel is ignited by heat produced by compression of air in the cylinder.

diesel fuel and **diesel oil** N, ENG liquid fuel for use in a diesel engine.

diet¹ N **1** the food and drink habitually consumedby a person or animal. **2** a planned

or prescribed selection of food and drink, eg for weight loss. **3** AS ADJ containing less sugar than the standard version: **diet lemonade**.
➢ VB, INTR to restrict the quantity or type of food that one eats, esp in order to lose weight. ■ **dietary** ADJ. ■ **dieter** N.

diet[2] N a legislative assembly.

dietetics SING N the scientific study of diet and nutrition. ■ **dietician** or **dietitian** N.

differ VB, INTR **1** to be different or unlike in some way. **2** (often **differ with sb**) to disagree.

difference N **1** something that makes one thing or person unlike another. **2** the state of being unlike. **3** a change from an earlier state, etc. **4** the amount by which one quantity or number is greater or less than another. **5** a quarrel or disagreement.

different ADJ **1** (usu **different from** or **to sth** or **sb**) not the same; unlike. **2** separate; distinct; various. **3** COLLOQ unusual. ■ **differently** ADV.

differential ADJ constituting, showing, relating to or based on a difference.
➢ N a difference in the rate of pay between one category of worker and another.

differential gear N an arrangement of gears that allows the wheels on either side of a vehicle to rotate at different speeds.

differentiate VB **1** TR & INTR to establish a difference between things. **2** to constitute a difference between things. **3** to become different. ■ **differentiation** N.

difficult ADJ **1** requiring great skill, intelligence or effort. **2** not easy to please; unco-operative. **3** of a problem, situation, etc: embarrassing; hard to resolve or get out of.

difficulty N (*-ies*) **1** the state or quality of being difficult. **2** a difficult thing to do or understand. **3** a problem, obstacle or objection. **4** (usu **difficulties**) trouble or embarrassment, esp financial trouble.

diffident ADJ lacking in confidence; too modest or shy. ■ **diffidence** N.

diffraction N, PHYS the spreading out of waves (eg light or sound waves) as they

emerge from a small opening. ■ **diffract** VB.

diffuse VB, TR & INTR to spread or send out in all directions.
➢ ADJ **1** widely spread; not concentrated. **2** using too many words. ■ **diffuser** N.

diffusion N diffusing or being diffused.

dig VB (*dug, digging*) **1** TR & INTR to turn up or move (earth, etc) esp with a spade. **2** to make (a hole, etc) by digging. **3** TR & INTR to poke. **4** OLD SLANG to appreciate or understand.
➢ N **1** a remark intended to irritate, criticize or make fun of someone. **2** a place where archaeologists are digging. **3** a poke. **4** an act of digging.
◆ **dig in 1** COLLOQ to start to eat. **2** to work hard.
◆ **dig sth out 1** to get it out by digging. **2** COLLOQ to find it by extensive searching.

digest[1] VB **1** TR & INTR to break down (food), or be broken down, in the stomach, intestine, etc into a form which the body can use. **2** to hear and consider the meaning and implications of (information). ■ **digestible** ADJ.

digest[2] N **1** a collection of summaries or shortened versions of news stories or current literature, etc. **2** a summary or shortened version.

digestion N the process whereby food is broken down in the alimentary canal.

digestive ADJ concerned with or for digestion.

digger N **1** a machine for digging and excavating. **2** someone who digs, esp a gold-miner. **3** COLLOQ an Australian or New Zealander.

digit N **1** any of the figures 0 to 9. **2** TECHNICAL a finger or toe.

digital ADJ **1** showing numerical information in the form of digits, rather than by a pointer on a dial. **2** operating by processing information supplied and stored in the form of a series of binary digits: **digital recording**. **3** ELECTRONICS denoting an electronic circuit that responds to and produces signals which at any given time are in one of two possible states.

digital audio tape N, ELECTRONICS a magnetic audio tape on which sound has been recorded after it has been converted into a binary code.

digital compact cassette N a digital audio tape in standard cassette format.

digitalis N, MED a drug that stimulates the heart muscle, orig obtained from foxglove leaves.

dignified ADJ 1 showing or consistent with dignity. 2 stately; noble; serious.

dignify VB (-ies, -ied) to make something impressive or dignified.

dignitary N (-ies) someone of high rank or position.

dignity N 1 stateliness, seriousness and formality of manner and appearance. 2 nobility of character. 3 calmness and self-control. 4 high rank or position.

digress VB, INTR to wander from the point or from the main subject. ■ **digression** N.

digs PL N, BRIT COLLOQ lodgings.

dike see **dyke**¹, **dyke**²

dilapidated ADJ falling to pieces; in great need of repair. ■ **dilapidation** N.

dilatation and curettage N, MED an operation in which the cervix is dilated and a curette is inserted to scrape the uterus lining.

dilate VB, TR & INTR to make or become larger, wider or further open. ■ **dilatation** or **dilation** N.

dilatory ADJ inclined to or causing delay.

dildo N an object shaped like an erect penis, used for sexual pleasure.

dilemma N a situation in which one must choose between two or more courses of action, both/all equally undesirable.

dilettante N (-s or -ti) often DEROG someone interested in a subject but who does not study it in depth. ■ **dilettantism** N.

diligent ADJ 1 hard-working and careful. 2 showing or done with care and serious effort. ■ **diligence** N. ■ **diligently** ADV.

dill N a herb used in flavouring.

dilly-dally VB (-ies, -ied) INTR, COLLOQ 1 to be slow. 2 to be unable to make up one's mind.

dilute VB 1 to decrease the concentration of a solute in a solution by adding more solvent, eg water. 2 to reduce the strength, influence or effect of something.
➤ ADJ, CHEM of a solution: containing a relatively small amount of solute compared to the amount of solvent present. ■ **dilution** N.

dim ADJ 1 not bright or distinct. 2 lacking enough light to see clearly. 3 faint; not clearly remembered: **a dim memory**. 4 COLLOQ not very intelligent. 5 of eyes: not able to see well.
➤ VB (-mm-) TR & INTR to make or become dim. ■ **dimly** ADV. ■ **dimness** N.

dime N 1 a coin of the USA and Canada worth ten cents. 2 ten cents.

dimension N 1 a measurement of length, width or height. 2 (often **dimensions**) size or extent. 3 a particular aspect of a problem, situation, etc. ■ **dimensional** ADJ.

diminish VB 1 TR & INTR to become or make something less or smaller. 2 to make someone or something seem less important or valuable.

diminution N a lessening or decrease.

diminutive ADJ very small.

dimmer and **dimmer switch** N a control used to modify the brightness of a light.

dimple N a small hollow, esp in the skin.
➤ VB to form into dimples.

dimwit N, COLLOQ a stupid person. ■ **dim-witted** ADJ.

din N a loud, continuous and unpleasant noise.
➤ VB (-nn-) (usu **din sth into sb**) to repeat something forcefully to someone over and over again so that it will be remembered.

dinar N the standard unit of currency in Serbia and Montenegro, and several Arab countries.

dine VB, FORMAL 1 INTR to eat dinner. 2 to give dinner to someone.

diner N 1 someone who dines. 2 a restaurant

car on a train. **3** N AMER a small restaurant.

ding-dong N **1** the sound of bells ringing. **2** COLLOQ a heated argument or fight.

dinghy N (-*ies*) a small open boat.

dingo N (-*oes*) an Australian wild dog.

dingy ADJ (-*ier*, -*iest*) **1** faded and dirty–looking: *dingy clothes*. **2** dark and rather dirty: *a dingy room*. ■ **dinginess** N.

dining-car see **restaurant car**

dining-room N a room in a house, hotel, etc, used for eating in.

dinkum ADJ, AUSTRAL & NZ COLLOQ real; genuine; honest. **Also** AS ADV.

dinky ADJ (-*ier*,-*iest*) COLLOQ neat; dainty.

dinner N **1** the main meal of the day, eaten in the middle of the day or in the evening. **2** a formal meal, esp in the evening.

dinner-jacket N a man's usu black formal jacket for evening wear.

dinner service and **dinner set** N a complete set of dishes for serving dinner.

dinosaur N **1** a prehistoric reptile. **2** often JOCULAR a chance survivor from past times.

dint N a dent.
◆ **by dint of sth** by means of it.

diocese N the district over which a bishop has authority. ■ **diocesan** ADJ.

diode N, ELECTRONICS an electronic device containing an anode and a cathode, allowing current to flow in one direction only.

dioxide N, CHEM a compound formed by combining two atoms of oxygen with one atom of another element.

dip VB (-*pp*-) **1** to put something briefly into a liquid. **2** INTR to go briefly under the surface of a liquid. **3** INTR to drop below a surface or level. **4** TR & INTR to go, or push something, down briefly and then up again. **5** INTR to slope downwards. **6** to immerse (an animal) in disinfectant that kills parasites. **7** BRIT to lower the beam of (a vehicle's headlights).
➢ N **1** an act of dipping. **2** a downward slope or hollow (eg in a road). **3** a short swim or bathe. **4** a chemical liquid for dipping animals. **5** a type of thick sauce into which biscuits, raw vegetables, etc are dipped.
◆ **dip into sth 1** to take or use part of it. **2** to look briefly at a book or subject.

diphtheria N, MED a disease which affects the throat, causing difficulty in breathing.

diphthong N two vowel sounds pronounced as one syllable, such as **ou** in **sounds**.

diploma N a document certifying that one has completed a course of study.

diplomacy N **1** the art or profession of making agreements, treaties, etc between countries, or of representing and looking after the affairs and interests of one's own country in a foreign country. **2** skill and tact in dealing with people.

diplomat N **1** a government official or representative engaged in diplomacy. **2** a very tactful person.

diplomatic ADJ **1** of diplomacy. **2** tactful. ■ **diplomatically** ADV.

diplomatic immunity N the privilege granted to members of the diplomatic corps by which they may not be taxed, arrested, etc by the country in which they are working.

dipper N **1** a type of ladle. **2** a small songbird which feeds on river–beds.

dipsomania N, MED an insatiable craving for alcoholic drink. ■ **dipsomaniac** N.

dipstick N a stick used to measure the level of a liquid in a container, esp the oil in a car engine.

diptych N a work of art, esp on a church altar, consisting of a pair of pictures painted on hinged wooden panels.

dire ADJ **1** dreadful; terrible. **2** extreme; very serious; very difficult. ■ **direly** ADV.

direct ADJ **1** following the shortest path. **2** open, straightforward and honest. **3** actual: *the direct cause*. **4** not working or communicating through other people, organizations, etc. **5** exact; complete: *a direct opposite*. **6** in an unbroken line of descent from parent to child to

grandchild, etc: **a direct descendant**.
➤ VB **1** to point, aim or turn something in some direction. **2** to show the way to someone. **3** TR & INTR to give orders or instructions. **4** to manage or be in charge of something. **5** TR & INTR to supervise the production of (a play or film).
➤ ADV by the quickest or shortest path.
■ **directness** N.

direct current N electric current which flows in one direction.

direct debit N, FINANCE an order to one's bank which allows someone else to withdraw sums of money from one's account.

direction N **1** the place or point towards which one is moving or facing. **2** the way in which someone or something is developing. **3** (usu **directions**) information, instructions or advice, eg on how to operate a piece of equipment. **4** (**directions**) instructions about how to reach a place. **5** management or supervision. **6** the act, style, etc of directing a play or film.

directional ADJ relating to direction in space.

directive N an official instruction issued by a higher authority.

directly ADV **1** in a direct manner. **2** by a direct path. **3** at once. **4** very soon. **5** exactly.

director N **1** a senior manager of a business firm. **2** the person in charge of an organization, institution or special activity. **3** the person directing a play, film, etc. ■ **directorial** ADJ.
■ **directorship** N.

directorate N **1** the directors of a business firm. **2** the position or office of director.

directory N (**-ies**) a book with a (usu alphabetical) list of names and addresses.

direct speech N, GRAM speech reported in the actual words of the speaker, eg 'Hello' in the sentence 'Hello', said Henry.

direct tax N a tax paid directly to the government, eg income tax.

dirge N a funeral song or hymn.

dirk N a small knife or dagger.

dirt N **1** mud, dust, etc. **2** soil; earth.

3 EUPHEMISTIC excrement. **4** COLLOQ scandal.

dirt-cheap ADJ, ADV, COLLOQ very cheap.

dirty ADJ (**-ier, -iest**) **1** marked with dirt; soiled. **2** making one become soiled with dirt: **a dirty job**. **3** unfair; dishonest: **dirty tricks**. **4** obscene, lewd or pornographic: **dirty films**. **5** of weather: rainy or stormy. **6** of a colour: dull. **7** showing dislike or disapproval: **a dirty look**. **8** unsportingly rough or violent: **a dirty tackle**.
➤ VB (**-ies,-ied**) to make dirty.
➤ ADV **1** dirtily: **fight dirty**. **2** very: **dirty great stains**. ■ **dirtiness** N.

dirty work N **1** work that makes a person or their clothing dirty. **2** COLLOQ unpleasant or dishonourable tasks.

dis- PFX, FORMING WORDS DENOTING **1** the opposite of the base word: **disagree** • **dislike**. **2** reversal of the action of the base word: **disassemble**. **3** removal or undoing: **disrobe**.

disability N (**-ies**) **1** the state of being disabled. **2** a physical or mental handicap.

disable VB **1** to deprive someone of a physical or mental ability. **2** to make (eg a machine) unable to work. ■ **disablement** N.

disabled ADJ **1** having a physical or mental handicap. **2** designed or intended for people with physical disabilities.

disabuse VB (always **disabuse sb of sth**) to rid them of a mistaken idea or impression.

disadvantage N **1** a difficulty, drawback or weakness. **2** an unfavourable situation.
➤ VB to put someone at a disadvantage.
■ **disadvantageous** ADJ.

disadvantaged ADJ in an unfavourable position; deprived of normal benefits.

disaffected ADJ dissatisfied and no longer loyal or committed. ■ **disaffection** N.

disagree VB, INTR **1** to have conflicting opinions. **2** to conflict with each other.
◆ **disagree with sb 1** to have a different opinion from them. **2** of food: to give them digestive problems.

disagreeable ADJ **1** unpleasant. **2** bad–

tempered; unfriendly. ■ **disagreeably** ADV.

disagreement N 1 the state of disagreeing. 2 EUPHEMISTIC a quarrel.

disallow VB 1 to formally refuse to allow something. 2 to judge something to be invalid.

disappear VB, INTR 1 to vanish. 2 to cease to exist. 3 to go missing. ■ **disappearance** N.

disappoint VB to fail to fulfil the hopes of someone. ■ **disappointed** ADJ. ■ **disappointing** ADJ. ■ **disappointment** N.

disapprobation N, FORMAL disapproval.

disapprove VB, INTR (usu **disapprove of sth** or **sb**) to think it or them bad or wrong. ■ **disapproval** N. ■ **disapproving** ADJ. ■ **disapprovingly** ADV.

disarm VB 1 to take weapons away from someone. 2 INTR to reduce or destroy one's own military capability. 3 to take the fuse out of (a bomb). 4 to take away someone's anger.

disarmament N the reduction or destruction by a nation of its own military forces.

disarming ADJ taking away anger. ■ **disarmingly** ADV.

disarrange VB to make something untidy or disordered. ■ **disarrangement** N.

disarray N a state of disorder or confusion.

disassociate VB, TR & INTR to dissociate. ■ **disassociation** N.

disaster N 1 an event causing great damage, injury or loss of life. 2 a total failure. ■ **disastrous** ADJ. ■ **disastrously** ADV.

disavow VB, FORMAL to deny knowledge of or responsibility for something or someone.

disband VB, TR & INTR to stop operating as a group; to break up. ■ **disbandment** N.

disbelieve VB 1 to believe something to be false or someone to be lying. 2 INTR to have no religious faith. ■ **disbelief** N.

disburse VB to pay out (a sum of money), esp from a fund. ■ **disbursement** N.

disc N 1 a flat thin circular object. 2 a recording medium, such as a record or compact disc. 3 ANAT a plate of fibrous tissue between vertebrae. 4 COMP see **disk**.

discard VB to get rid of something.

disc brake N a brake in which pads are pressed against a metal disc on the wheel.

discern VB to perceive, notice or make out something; to judge. ■ **discernible** ADJ.

discerning ADJ having or showing good judgement. ■ **discernment** N.

discharge VB 1 to allow someone to leave; to dismiss or send away (a person). 2 to perform or carry out (eg duties). 3 TR & INTR to flow out or make something flow out. 4 LAW to release someone from custody. 5 TR & INTR to fire (a gun). ➤ N 1 the act of discharging. 2 something discharged. 3 FORMAL, LAW release or dismissal.

disciple N 1 someone who believes in, and follows, the teachings of another. 2 one of the twelve close followers of Christ.

disciplinarian N someone who enforces strict discipline.

disciplinary ADJ of or enforcing discipline.

discipline N 1 a strict training, or the enforcing of rules, intended to produce controlled behaviour; b the ordered behaviour resulting from this. 2 punishment designed to create obedience. 3 an area of learning or study, or a branch of sport. ➤ VB 1 to train or force (oneself or others) to behave in a controlled way. 2 to punish someone.

disc jockey N someone who presents recorded pop music on the radio, at a disco, etc.

disclaim VB to deny (eg involvement with or knowledge of something).

disclaimer N 1 a written statement denying legal responsibility. 2 a denial.

disclose VB to make something known or visible. ■ **disclosure** N.

disco N 1 a discotheque. 2 a party with dancing to recorded music.

discolour or (US) **discolor** VB, TR & INTR to stain or dirty something. ■ **discoloration** N.

discomfit VB to make someone feel uneasy. ■ **discomfiture** N.

discomfort N a slight pain or uneasiness.

disconcert VB to make someone feel anxious, uneasy or flustered. ■ **disconcerting** ADJ.

disconnect VB 1 to break the connection between (esp an electrical device and a power supply). 2 to stop the supply of (eg gas) to (a building, etc). ■ **disconnection** N.

disconsolate ADJ deeply sad or disappointed; not able to be consoled.

discontent N lack of contentment. ■ **discontented** ADJ. ■ **discontentedly** ADV.

discontinue VB 1 TR & INTR to stop or cease. 2 to stop producing something.

discord N 1 disagreement; conflict. 2 unharmonious noise. ■ **discordant** ADJ. ■ **discordantly** ADV.

discotheque N a night–club where people dance to recorded pop music.

discount N 1 an amount deducted from the normal price. 2 the rate or percentage of the deduction granted. ➤ VB 1 to disregard as unlikely, untrue or irrelevant. 2 to make a deduction from (a price).

discourage VB 1 to deprive someone of confidence, hope or the will to continue. 2 to seek to prevent (a person or an action) with advice or persuasion. ■ **discouragement** N. ■ **discouraging** ADJ.

discourse N 1 a formal speech or essay on a particular subject. 2 serious conversation. ➤ VB INTR to speak or write at length.

discourteous ADJ impolite. ■ **discourtesy** N (-*ies*).

discover VB 1 to be the first person to find something or someone. 2 to find by chance. 3 to learn or become aware of for the first time.

discovery N (-*ies*) 1 the act of discovering. 2 a person or thing discovered.

discredit N loss of good reputation, or the cause of it. ➤ VB 1 to make someone or something be disbelieved or regarded with doubt or suspicion. 2 to damage the reputation of someone. ■ **discreditable** ADJ.

discreet ADJ 1 careful to prevent suspicion or embarrassment, eg by keeping a secret. 2 avoiding notice; inconspicuous.

discrepancy N (-*ies*) a failure (eg of sets of information) to correspond or be the same.

discrete ADJ separate; distinct.

discretion N 1 behaving discreetly. 2 the ability to make wise judgements. 3 the freedom or right to make decisions and do as one thinks best. ■ **discretional** or **discretionary** ADJ.

discriminate VB, INTR 1 to see a difference between two people or things. 2 (usu **discriminate in favour of** or **against sb**) to give different treatment to different people or groups, esp without justification and on political, racial or religious grounds. ■ **discrimination** N. ■ **discriminatory** ADJ.

discursive ADJ of spoken or written style: wandering from the main point.

discus N (-*ses* or -*sci*) a heavy disc thrown in athletic competitions.

discuss VB 1 to examine or consider something in speech or writing. 2 to talk or argue about something in conversation. ■ **discussion** N.

disdain N dislike due to a feeling that something is not worthy of attention; contempt. ➤ VB 1 to refuse or reject someone or something out of disdain. 2 to regard someone or something with disdain. ■ **disdainful** ADJ.

disease N a disorder or illness caused by infection. ■ **diseased** ADJ.

disembark VB, TR & INTR to take or go from a ship on to land. ■ **disembarkation** N.

disembodied ADJ 1 separated from the body; having no physical existence. 2 seeming not to come from, or be connected to, a body.

disembowel VB (-*ll*-) to remove the internal

organs of someone or something.

disenchanted ADJ dissatisfied or discontented. ■ **disenchantment** N.

disfavour or (N AMER) **disfavor** N 1 a state of being disliked, unpopular or disapproved of. 2 dislike or disapproval.

disfigure VB to spoil the appearance of something. ■ **disfigurement** N.

disgorge VB 1 TR & INTR to vomit. 2 to discharge or pour out something.

disgrace N a shame or loss of favour or respect; b the cause of it; c an example of it.
➤ VB to bring shame upon someone.
■ **disgraceful** ADJ.
◆ **in disgrace** out of favour.

disgruntled ADJ annoyed and dissatisfied.

disguise VB 1 to hide the identity of someone or something by a change of appearance. 2 to conceal the true nature of (eg intentions).
➤ N 1 a disguised state. 2 clothes, make-up, etc intended to disguise.

disgust VB to sicken; to provoke intense dislike or disapproval in someone.
➤ N intense dislike; loathing. ■ **disgusting** ADJ.

dish N 1 a shallow container in which food is served or cooked. 2 its contents, or the amount it can hold. 3 anything shaped like this. 4 a particular kind of food, esp food prepared for eating. 5 (**dishes**) used plates and other utensils. 6 a dish-shaped aerial. 7 COLLOQ a physically attractive person.
➤ VB to put (food) into a dish for serving.
◆ **dish sth out** COLLOQ 1 to distribute it. 2 to give it out. 3 (esp **dish it out**) to give out punishment.

disharmony N disagreement; lack of harmony. ■ **disharmonious** ADJ.

dishcloth N a cloth for washing or drying dishes.

dishearten VB to dampen the courage, hope or confidence of someone.

dishevelled ADJ of clothes or hair: untidy.

dishonest ADJ not honest; likely to deceive or

cheat. ■ **dishonestly** ADV. ■ **dishonesty** N.

dishonour or (US) **dishonor** N a shame or loss of honour; b the cause of it.
➤ VB 1 to bring dishonour on someone or something. 2 to treat someone or something with no respect. ■ **dishonourable** ADJ.

dishwasher N a machine or person that washes dishes.

dishwater N 1 water in which dirty dishes have been washed. 2 any liquid like it.

dishy ADJ (-ier, -iest) COLLOQ sexually attractive.

disillusion VB to correct the mistaken beliefs or illusions of someone.
➤ N (also **disillusionment**) a state of being disillusioned.

disincentive N something that discourages or deters.

disinclined ADJ unwilling. ■ **disinclination** N.

disinfect VB to clean with a substance that kills germs. ■ **disinfectant** N, ADJ.

disinformation N false information intended to deceive or mislead.

disingenuous ADJ not entirely sincere or open. ■ **disingenuously** ADV.

disinherit VB to legally deprive someone of an inheritance. ■ **disinheritance** N.

disintegrate VB, TR & INTR to break into tiny pieces; to shatter or crumble. 2 to break up. ■ **disintegration** N.

disinterested ADJ 1 not having an interest in a matter; impartial, objective. 2 COLLOQ showing no interest; uninterested. ■ **disinterest** N.

disjointed ADJ esp of speech: not properly connected; incoherent.

disk N 1 COMP a magnetic disk. See also **floppy disk**, **hard disk**. 2 esp US a disc.

disk drive N, COMP the mechanism for reading or writing the data stored on a floppy disk.

dislike VB to consider someone or something unpleasant or unlikeable.

➤ N **1** mild hostility; aversion. **2** something disliked.

dislocate VB **1** to dislodge (a bone) from its normal position. **2** to disturb or disrupt something. ■ **dislocation** N.

dislodge VB to force something or someone out of a fixed or established position.

disloyal ADJ not loyal. ■ **disloyalty** N.

dismal ADJ **1** not cheerful; causing or suggesting sadness. **2** COLLOQ third-rate; of poor quality. ■ **dismally** ADV.

dismantle VB **1** to take something to pieces. **2** to abolish or close down something.

dismay N a feeling of sadness, discouragement or alarm.
➤ VB to make someone sad, discouraged or alarmed.

dismember VB **1** to tear or cut the limbs from (the body). **2** to divide up (esp land). ■ **dismemberment** N.

dismiss VB **1** to refuse to consider or accept (an idea, claim, etc). **2** to put someone out of one's employment. **3** to send someone away; to allow them to leave. **4** to close (a court case). ■ **dismissal** N. ■ **dismissive** ADJ.

dismount VB, INTR to get off a horse, bicycle, etc.

disobedient ADJ refusing or failing to obey. ■ **disobedience** N.

disobey VB to act contrary to the orders of someone; to refuse to obey (a law, etc).

disorder N **1** lack of order; confusion or disturbance. **2** unruly or riotous behaviour. **3** a disease or illness. ■ **disordered** ADJ.

disorderly ADJ **1** not neatly arranged; disorganized. **2** causing trouble in public.

disorganize or **-ise** VB to disturb the order or arrangement of something. ■ **disorganization** N. ■ **disorganized** ADJ.

disorientate and **disorient** VB to make someone lose all sense of position, direction or time. ■ **disorientation** N.

disown VB to deny having any relationship to, or connection with, someone or something.

disparage VB to speak of someone or something with contempt. ■ **disparaging** ADJ.

disparate ADJ completely different; too different to be compared. ■ **disparity** N (**-ies**).

dispassionate ADJ not influenced by personal feelings; impartial. ■ **dispassionately** ADV.

dispatch or **despatch** VB **1** to send (mail, a person, etc) to a place. **2** to finish off or deal with something quickly: *dispatch a meal.* ➤ N **1** (often **dispatches**) an official (esp military or diplomatic) report. **2** a journalist's report sent to a newspaper. **3** the act of dispatching; the fact of being dispatched.

dispel VB (**-ll-**) to drive away or banish (thoughts or feelings).

dispensable ADJ able to be done without.

dispensary N (**-ies**) a place where medicines are given out or dispensed.

dispensation N **1** special exemption from a rule or obligation. **2** the act of dispensing.

dispense VB **1** to give out (eg advice). **2** to prepare and distribute (medicine). **3** to administer (eg the law). ■ **dispenser** N. ◆ **dispense with sth** to do without it.

disperse VB, TR & INTR **1** to spread out over a wide area. **2** to break up, or make (a crowd) break up. **3** to vanish or make something vanish. ■ **dispersal** N. ■ **dispersion** N.

dispirit VB to dishearten or discourage someone. ■ **dispirited** ADJ.

displace VB **1** to put or take something or someone out of the usual place. **2** to remove someone from a post.

displaced person N someone forced to leave their home through war or persecution.

displacement N **1** the act of displacing. **2** TECHNICAL the quantity of liquid, gas, etc displaced by an immersed object, eg of water by a floating ship.

display VB 1 to put someone or something on view. 2 to show or betray (eg feelings). ➤ N 1 the act of displaying. 2 an exhibition or show, eg of talent or work. 3 the showing of information on a screen, calculator, etc, or the information shown.

displease VB to annoy or offend someone. ■ **displeasure** N.

disposable ADJ 1 intended to be thrown away or destroyed after one use. 2 of income or assets: remaining after tax and other commitments are paid, so available for use.

disposal N getting rid of something. ◆ **at the disposal of sb** available for them.

dispose VB to place something in an arrangement or order. ◆ **dispose of sth** 1 to get rid of it. 2 to deal with or settle it.

disposition N 1 temperament; personality; a tendency. 2 arrangement; position; distribution.

dispossess VB (always **dispossess sb of sth**) to take (esp property) away from them. ■ **dispossessed** ADJ. ■ **dispossession** N.

disproportion N lack of balance or equality.

disproportionate ADJ unreasonably large or small in comparison with something else. ■ **disproportionately** ADV.

disprove VB to prove something to be wrong.

dispute VB 1 to question or deny the accuracy or validity of (a statement, etc). 2 to quarrel over rights to or possession of something. 3 TR & INTR to argue about something. ➤ N an argument. ■ **disputable** ADJ. ■ **disputation** N. ■ **disputatious** ADJ.

disqualify VB 1 to ban someone from doing something. 2 to make someone or something unsuitable or ineligible. ■ **disqualification** N.

disquiet N anxiety or uneasiness. ➤ VB to make someone anxious, uneasy, etc. ■ **disquieting** ADJ. ■ **disquietude** N.

disregard VB 1 to pay no attention to someone or something. 2 to dismiss something as unworthy of consideration. ➤ N dismissive lack of attention or concern.

disrepair N bad condition or working order, showing a need for repair and maintenance.

disreputable ADJ not respectable; having a bad reputation. ■ **disrepute** N.

disrespect N lack of respect; impoliteness; rudeness. ■ **disrespectful** ADJ.

disrobe VB, TR & INTR, LITERARY to undress.

disrupt VB to disturb the order or peaceful progress of (an activity, process, etc). ■ **disruption** N. ■ **disruptive** ADJ.

dissatisfied ADJ discontented. ■ **dissatisfaction** N.

dissect VB 1 to cut open (a plant or dead body) for scientific or medical examination. 2 to examine something in minute detail, esp critically. ■ **dissection** N.

dissemble VB, TR & INTR to conceal or disguise (true feelings or motives). ■ **dissemblance** N.

disseminate VB to make (eg news or theories) widely known. ■ **dissemination** N.

dissension N disagreement.

dissent N 1 disagreement, esp open or hostile. 2 separation, esp from an established church. ➤ VB, INTR (often **dissent from sb** or **sth**) to disagree with them. ■ **dissenter** N. ■ **dissenting** ADJ.

dissertation N 1 a long essay. 2 a formal lecture.

disservice N a wrong; a bad turn.

dissident N someone who disagrees publicly, esp with a government. ➤ ADJ disagreeing; dissenting.

dissimilar ADJ (often **dissimilar to sth**) unlike; different. ■ **dissimilarity** N.

dissimulate VB, TR & INTR to hide or disguise (esp feelings). ■ **dissimulation** N.

dissipate VB 1 TR & INTR to separate and scatter. 2 to squander something. ■ **dissipation** N.

dissipated ADJ over-indulging in pleasure.

dissociate VB 1 to regard something or

someone as separate. **2** to declare someone or oneself to be unconnected with someone or something else. ■ **dissociation** N.

dissolute ADJ indulging in pleasures considered immoral. ■ **dissoluteness** N.

dissolution N **1** the breaking up of a meeting or assembly. **2** the ending of a formal or legal partnership. **3** abolition, eg of the monarchy. **4** breaking up into parts.

dissolve VB **1** TR & INTR to merge with a liquid. **2** to bring (an assembly) to a close. **3** to end (a legal partnership). **4** TR & INTR to disappear or make something disappear. **5** INTR (often **dissolve into laughter, tears,** etc) to be overcome emotionally.

dissonance N **1** MUS an unpleasant combination of sounds. **2** disagreement; incompatibility. ■ **dissonant** ADJ.

dissuade VB (usu **dissuade sb from doing sth**) to deter them by advice or persuasion. ■ **dissuasion** N.

distance N **1** the length between two points in space. **2** the fact of being apart. **3** any faraway point or place; the furthest visible area. **4** coldness of manner.
➤ VB **1** to put someone or something at a distance. **2** (usu **distance oneself from sb** or **sth**) to declare oneself to be unconnected or unsympathetic to something.
◆ **keep one's distance** to stay away or avoid friendship or familiarity.

distant ADJ **1** far away or far apart in space or time. **2** not closely related. **3** cold and unfriendly. ■ **distantly** ADV.

distaste N dislike. ■ **distasteful** ADJ.

distemper[1] N any of several infectious diseases of animals, esp **canine distemper**, an often fatal viral infection of dogs.

distemper[2] N a water–based paint, esp one mixed with glue or size.

distend VB, TR & INTR to make or become swollen, inflated or stretched. ■ **distension** N.

distil or (N AMER) **distill** VB (*-ll-*) **1** to purify a liquid by heating it to boiling point and

condensing the vapour formed. **2** to produce alcoholic spirits in this way. ■ **distillation** N.

distillery N (*-ies*) a place where alcoholic spirits are distilled. ■ **distiller** N.

distinct ADJ **1** clear or obvious. **2** noticeably different or separate. ■ **distinctly** ADV.

distinction N **1** exceptional ability or achievement, or an honour awarded in recognition of it. **2** the act of differentiating. **3** the state of being noticeably different.

distinctive ADJ easily recognized because very individual. ■ **distinctiveness** N.

distinguish VB **1** (often **distinguish one thing from another**) to mark or recognize them as different. **2** INTR (often **distinguish between things** or **people**) to see the difference between them. **3** to make out or identify something. **4** (always **distinguish oneself**) often IRONIC to be outstanding because of some achievement.
■ **distinguishable** ADJ. ■ **distinguishing** ADJ.

distinguished ADJ **1** famous (and usu well respected). **2** with a dignified appearance.

distort VB **1** to twist something out of shape. **2** to change the meaning of (a statement, etc) by inaccurate retelling. ■ **distortion** N.

distract VB **1** (usu **distract sb** or **sb's attention from sth**) to divert their attention from it. **2** to entertain or amuse someone.

distraction N **1** something that diverts the attention. **2** an amusement; recreation. **3** anxiety; anger. **4** madness.

distraught ADJ extremely distressed.

distress N **1** mental or emotional pain. **2** financial difficulty; hardship. **3** great danger; peril: **a ship in distress.**
➤ VB to upset someone. ■ **distressing** ADJ.

distribute VB **1** to give out something. **2** to supply or deliver (goods). **3** to spread (something) widely.

distribution N **1** the process of distributing or being distributed. **2** the placing of things spread out. ■ **distributive** ADJ.

distributor N 1 a person or company that distributes goods, esp between manufacturer and retailer. 2 a device in a vehicle ignition system that directs pulses of electricity to the spark plugs.

district N an area or region; an administrative or geographical unit.

district nurse N a nurse who treats patients in their homes.

distrust VB to have no trust in someone or something; to doubt them or it.
➤ N suspicion; lack of trust. ■ **distrustful** ADJ.

disturb VB 1 to interrupt someone. 2 to inconvenience someone. 3 to upset the arrangement or order of something. 4 to upset someone's peace of mind. ■ **disturbing** ADJ.

disturbance N 1 an outburst of noisy or violent behaviour. 2 an interruption.

disturbed ADJ, PSYCHOL emotionally upset or confused; maladjusted.

disunite VB to cause disagreement between (people) or within (a group). ■ **disunity** N.

disuse N the state of no longer being used or observed; neglect. ■ **disused** ADJ.

ditch N a narrow channel dug in the ground.
➤ VB 1 SLANG to get rid of or abandon someone or something. 2 TR & INTR, COLLOQ of an aircraft or a pilot: to bring or come down in the sea.

dither VB, INTR to act in a nervously uncertain manner; to waver.
➤ N a state of indecision. ■ **dithery** ADJ.

ditto N the same thing; that which has just been said.
➤ ADV likewise; the same.

ditto marks N a symbol (″) written immediately below a word, etc in a list to mean 'same as above'.

ditty N (-ies) a short simple song or poem.

diuretic MED, N a drug or other substance that increases the volume of urine excreted.
➤ ADJ increasing the excretion of urine.

diurnal FORMAL, TECHNICAL, ADJ 1 daily. 2 during the day. 3 active during the day.

diva N (-vas or -ve) a great female singer.

divalent ADJ, CHEM of an atom: able to combine with two atoms of hydrogen or the equivalent.

divan N 1 a sofa with no back or sides. 2 a bed without a headboard or footboard.

dive VB (PA T & PA P **dived** or (N AMER) **dove**) INTR 1 to throw oneself into water, or plunge down through water. 2 of a submarine, etc: to become submerged. 3 to descend or fall steeply through the air. 4 to throw oneself to the side or to the ground. 5 to move quickly and suddenly out of sight: **diving behind a tree**.
➤ N 1 an act of diving. 2 SLANG any dirty or disreputable place, esp a bar or club.

diver N 1 someone who dives. 2 someone who works underwater. 3 a diving bird.

diverge VB, INTR 1 to separate and go in different directions. 2 to differ. ■ **divergence** N. ■ **divergent** ADJ.

diverse ADJ 1 various; assorted. 2 different.

diversify VB (-ies, -ied) 1 TR & INTR to become or make something diverse. 2 INTR to engage in new and different activities. ■ **diversification** N.

diversion N 1 the act of diverting; the state of being diverted. 2 a detour from a usual route. 3 something intended to draw attention away. 4 amusement. ■ **diversionary** ADJ.

diversity N (-ies) variety; being different.

divert VB 1 to make someone or something change direction. 2 to draw away (esp attention). 3 to amuse someone.

divest VB (usu **divest sb of sth**) 1 to take away or get rid of it. 2 rather FORMAL to take something off: **divested herself of her jacket**.

divide VB 1 TR & INTR to split up or separate into parts. 2 (also **divide sth up**) to share. 3 MATH a to determine how many times one number is contained in (another); b INTR of a number: to be a number of times greater or smaller than another: **3 divides into 9**. 4 to bring about a

disagreement among (people). **5** to serve as a boundary between something.
➤ N **1** a disagreement. **2** a gap or split.

dividend N **1** a portion of a company's profits paid to a shareholder. **2** a benefit: **Meeting her would pay dividends. 3** MATH a number divided by another number.

dividers PL N a V-shaped device with movable arms ending in points, used in geometry, etc for measuring.

divination N the practice of foretelling the future by, or as if by, supernatural means.

divine ADJ **1** belonging or relating to, or coming from God or a god. **2** COLLOQ extremely good, pleasant or beautiful.
➤ VB **1** to foretell something. **2** to realize something by intuition. **3** TR & INTR to search for (underground water) with a divining-rod.
➤ N a member of the clergy who is expert in theology. ■ **divinely** ADV. ■ **diviner** N.

diving board N a narrow platform from which swimmers can dive into a pool, etc.

diving suit N a diver's waterproof suit, esp one with a helmet and heavy boots.

divining rod and **dowsing rod** N a stick held when divining for water, which moves when a discovery is made.

divinity N (*-ies*) **1** theology. **2** a god. **3** the state of being God or a god.

divisible ADJ able to be divided.

division N **1** dividing or being divided. **2** something that divides or separates. **3** one of the parts into which something is divided. **4** a major unit of an organization such as an army or police force. **5** MATH the process of determining how many times one number is contained in another. ■ **divisional** ADJ.

division sign N the symbol ÷, representing division in calculations.

divisive ADJ tending to cause disagreement.

divorce N **1** the legal ending of a marriage. **2** a complete separation.
➤ VB **1** TR & INTR to legally end marriage to

someone. **2** to separate.

divorcee N someone who has been divorced.

divot N a piece of grass and earth.

divulge VB to make something known; to reveal (a secret, etc). ■ **divulgence** N.

Diwali N a Hindu festival held in honour of Lakshmi, goddess of wealth and good fortune.

DIY ABBREV do-it-yourself.

dizzy ADJ (*-ier, -iest*) **1** experiencing or causing a spinning sensation in the head. **2** COLLOQ silly; not responsible. **3** COLLOQ bewildered.
➤ VB (*-ies, -ied*) **1** to make someone dizzy. **2** to bewilder someone. ■ **dizziness** N.

DJ ABBREV **1** SLANG dinner jacket. **2** disc jockey.

DNA ABBREV deoxyribonucleic acid, the nucleic acid that forms the material that chromosomes and genes are composed of.

do¹ VB (*does,* PA T *did,* PA P *done,* PR P *doing*) **1** to carry out, perform or commit something. **2** to finish or complete something. **3** TR & INTR (also **do for sb**) to be enough or suitable. **4** to work at or study: **Are you doing maths? 5** INTR to be in a particular state: **Business is doing well. 6** to put in order or arrange. **7** INTR to act or behave. **8** to provide something as a service: **do lunches. 9** to bestow (honour, etc). **10** to cause or produce. **11** to travel (a distance). **12** to travel at (a speed). **13** COLLOQ to cheat someone. **14** COLLOQ to assault someone. **15** COLLOQ to spend (time) in prison. **16** COLLOQ to convict someone. **17** INTR, COLLOQ to happen: **nothing doing. 18** SLANG to take (drugs).
➤ AUXILIARY VERB **1** used in questions and negative statements or commands, as in **Do you smoke?**, **I don't like wine** and **Don't go! 2** used to avoid repetition of a verb, as in **She eats as much as I do. 3** used for emphasis, as in **She does know you've arrived.**
➤ N (*dos* or *do's*) COLLOQ **1** a party or other gathering. **2** something done as a rule or custom: **dos and don'ts.**
◆ **could do with sth** or **sb** would benefit from having it or them.
◆ **do away with sb** or **sth 1** to murder them or it. **2** to abolish (an institution, etc).

◆ **do sb** or **sth down** to speak of them or it disparagingly.

◆ **do sb in** COLLOQ 1 to kill them. 2 to exhaust them.

◆ **do sb out of sth** to deprive them of it.

◆ **do sth up** COLLOQ 1 to repair, clean or improve the decoration of (a building, etc). 2 to fasten it; to tie or wrap it up.

◆ **do without sth** to manage without it.

◆ **have** or **be to do with sb** or **sth** 1 to be related to or connected with something: *What has that to do with me?* 2 to be partly or wholly responsible for something: *I had nothing to do with it.*

do² see **doh**

Dobermann N a large breed of dog with a smooth black-and-tan coat.

doc N, COLLOQ a doctor.

docile ADJ easy to manage or control.
■ **docilely** ADV. ■ **docility** N.

dock¹ N 1 a harbour where ships are loaded, unloaded, and repaired. 2 (**docks**) the area surrounding this.
➤ VB, TR & INTR 1 to bring or come into a dock. 2 of space vehicles: to link up in space.

dock² VB 1 to cut off all or part of (an animal's tail). 2 to make deductions from (eg someone's pay). 3 to deduct (an amount).

dock³ N a weed with large broad leaves.

dock⁴ N the enclosure in a court of law where the accused sits or stands.

docker N a labourer who loads ships.

docket N a label or note accompanying a parcel or package, eg detailing contents or recording receipt.

dockyard N a shipyard, esp a naval one.

doctor N 1 someone qualified to practise medicine. 2 someone holding a doctorate.
➤ VB 1 to falsify (eg information). 2 to tamper with something; to drug (food or drink). 3 COLLOQ to sterilize or castrate (an animal).

doctorate N a high academic degree, awarded esp for research.

doctrinaire ADJ, DEROG adhering too rigidly to theories or principles.

doctrine N something taught; a religious or political belief. ■ **doctrinal** ADJ.

document N 1 any piece of writing of an official nature. 2 COMP a text file.
➤ VB 1 to record something, esp in written form. 2 to provide written evidence to support or prove something.

documentary N (*-ies*) a film or television or radio programme presenting real people in real situations.
➤ ADJ 1 connected with, or consisting of, documents: **documentary evidence**. 2 of the nature of a documentary; undramatized.

documentation N documents.

dodder VB, INTR to move in an unsteady trembling fashion, usu as a result of old age.
■ **dodderer** N. ■ **doddery** ADJ.

doddle N, COLLOQ something easily done or achieved.

dodecagon N a flat geometric figure with 12 sides and angles.

dodecahedron N a solid geometric figure with twelve faces.

dodge VB 1 to avoid (a blow, a person, etc) by moving quickly away. 2 to escape or avoid something by cleverness or deceit.
➤ N 1 a sudden movement aside. 2 a trick to escape or avoid something.

dodgy ADJ (*-ier*, *-iest*) COLLOQ 1 difficult or risky. 2 untrustworthy; dishonest, or dishonestly obtained. 3 unstable; slightly broken.

dodo N (*dodos* or *dodoes*) a large extinct flightless bird.

doe N (*does* or *doe*) an adult female rabbit, hare or small deer.

does see under **do¹**

doesn't CONTRACTION OF does not.

doff VB, OLD USE, LITERARY 1 to lift (one's hat) in greeting. 2 to take off (a piece of clothing).

dog N 1 a carnivorous mammal such as a wolf,

jackal or fox. **2** a domestic species of this family. **3** the male of any such animal.
➤ VB (*-gg-*) **1** to follow someone very closely. **2** to trouble or plague someone.
◆ **dog eat dog** ruthless pursuit of one's own interests.

dog collar N **1** a collar for a dog. **2** COLLOQ a stiff collar worn by certain clergy.

doge N the chief magistrate of Venice or Genoa.

dog-eared ADJ of a book: with its pages turned down at the corners; shabby; scruffy.

dog-end N, SLANG a cigarette end.

dogfight N a battle at close quarters between two fighter aircraft.

dogfish N any of various kinds of small shark

dogged ADJ determined; resolute.
■ **doggedly** ADV. ■ **doggedness** N.

doggerel N badly written poetry.

doggo ADV.
◆ **lie doggo** COLLOQ to hide; to lie low.

doggy ADJ (*-ier, -iest*) COLLOQ **1** belonging to, like or relating to dogs. **2** fond of dogs.
➤ N (*-ies*) a child's word for a dog. Also **doggie**.

doggy-bag N a bag in which a customer at a restaurant can take home uneaten food.

doggy-paddle and **dog-paddle** N a basic swimming stroke with short paddling movements.

doghouse N, now chiefly N AMER a kennel.
◆ **in the doghouse** COLLOQ out of favour.

dog in the manger N someone who has no need of something but refuses to let others use it.

dogleg N a sharp bend, esp on a golf course.

dogma N (*-mas* or *-mata*) **1** a belief or principle laid down by an authority as unquestionably true. **2** such beliefs or principles in general.

dogmatic ADJ **1** of an opinion: forcefully and arrogantly stated as if unquestionable. **2** of a

person: tending to make such statements of opinion. ■ **dogmatically** ADV.
■ **dogmatism** N.

do-gooder N, COLLOQ an enthusiastic helper of other people.

dog-paddle see under **doggy-paddle**

dogsbody N, COLLOQ someone who does menial tasks for someone else.

doh or **do** N, MUS in sol–fa notation: the first note of the major scale.

doily or **doyley** N (*-ies* or *-eys*) a small decorative napkin of lace or lace–like paper laid on plates under sandwiches, cakes, etc.

doings 1 PL N activities; behaviour. **2** SING N, COLLOQ something whose name cannot be remembered or is left unsaid.

do-it-yourself N the practice of doing one's own household repairs, etc.

Dolby N, TRADEMARK a system of noise reduction in audio recording, used to reduce the background hissing heard during replay, and to improve stereophonic sound in cinemas.

the doldrums PL N **1** a depressed mood; low spirits. **2** a state of inactivity. **3** (also **the Doldrums**) METEOROL a hot humid region on either side of the Equator.

dole N, COLLOQ (**the dole**) unemployment benefit.
➤ VB, INTR (always **dole sth out**) to hand it out or give it out.

doleful ADJ sad; mournful. ■ **dolefully** ADV.

doll N **1** a toy in the form of a small model of a human being. **2** SLANG, often OFFENSIVE any girl or woman, esp when considered pretty.
3 COLLOQ a term of endearment, esp for a girl.
➤ VB (always **doll oneself up**) to dress smartly or showily.

dollar N (symbol $) the standard unit of currency in the US, Canada, Australia and other countries, divided into 100 cents.

dollop N, COLLOQ a small shapeless mass.

dolly N (*-ies*) COLLOQ a doll.

dolphin N a small toothed variety of whale.

dolphinarium N (*-ia* or *-iums*) a large open–air aquarium in which dolphins are kept.

dolt N, DEROG a stupid person. ■ **doltish** ADJ.

domain N 1 the scope of any subject or area of interest. 2 a territory owned or ruled by one person or government.

dome N 1 a hemispherical roof. 2 anything of similar shape. ■ **domed** ADJ.

domestic ADJ 1 belonging or relating to the home, the family or private life. 2 kept as a pet or farm animal. 3 within or relating to one's country: **domestic sales**. 4 enjoying home life. ➢ N a servant. ■ **domestically** ADV.

domesticate VB to train (an animal) to live with people. ■ **domestication** N.

domesticity N home life, or a liking for it.

domestic science N training in household skills, esp cooking; home economics.

domicile N a legally recognized place of permanent residence. ■ **domiciliary** ADJ.

dominant ADJ 1 most important, evident or active. 2 tending or seeking to command or influence others. 3 of a building, etc: overlooking others from an elevated position. ■ **dominance** N.

dominate VB, TR & INTR 1 to have command or influence over someone. 2 to be the most important, evident or active of (a group). 3 to stand above (a place). ■ **domination** N.

domineering ADJ overbearing; arrogant.

Dominican N a member of a Christian order of friars and nuns orig founded by St Dominic. ➢ ADJ belonging or relating to this order.

dominion N 1 rule; power; influence. 2 a territory or country governed by a single ruler or government.

domino N (*-oes*) 1 any of the small rectangular tiles marked, in two halves, with varying numbers of spots. 2 (**dominoes**) a game in which these tiles are laid down, with matching halves end to end. 3 a black

cloak with a hood and mask.

don[1] N a university lecturer.

don[2] VB (*-nn-*) to put on (clothing).

donate VB to give. ■ **donation** N.

done ADJ 1 finished; completed. 2 fully cooked. 3 socially acceptable. 4 used up. 5 COLLOQ exhausted. ➢ EXCLAM expressing completion of a deal. ◆ **done for** COLLOQ facing ruin or death.

Don Juan N a man who seduces women.

donkey N 1 a hoofed herbivorous mammal related to but smaller than the horse. 2 COLLOQ a stupid person.

donkey's years PL N, COLLOQ a very long time.

donkey-work N 1 heavy manual work. 2 preparation; groundwork.

donor N 1 someone who donates something, esp money. 2 a person or animal that provides blood, semen or organs for medical use.

donor card N a card indicating that its carrier is willing, in the event of sudden death, to have their healthy organs removed for transplant.

don't CONTRACTION OF do not. ➢ N, COLLOQ something that must not be done: **dos and don'ts**.

doodle VB, INTR to scribble meaninglessly. ➢ N a meaningless scribble.

doom N inescapable death, ruin or other unpleasant fate. ➢ VB to condemn someone to death or some other dire fate.

doomsday N the last day of the world.

door N 1 a movable barrier opening and closing an entrance. 2 an entrance. 3 a house considered in relation to others: **three doors away**. 4 a means of entry; an opportunity to gain access: **opened the door to stardom**.

doorjamb and **doorpost** N one of the two vertical side pieces of a door frame.

doorknocker see **knocker**

doorman N a man employed to guard the entrance to a hotel, club, etc and assist guests or customers.

doormat N a mat for wiping shoes on before entering.

doorstep N a step in front of a building's door. ➤ VB 1 to go from door to door canvassing. 2 of journalists, etc: to pester someone by waiting at their door.

doorstop N 1 a device, eg a wedge, for holding a door open. 2 a device, eg a fixed knob, for preventing a door opening too far.

door-to-door ADJ, ADV 1 going from house to house. 2 between departure and arrival.

doorway N the space where there is or might be a door; an entrance.

dope N 1 COLLOQ a drug taken for pleasure, esp cannabis. 2 COLLOQ a drug given to athletes, dogs or horses to affect performance. 3 COLLOQ a stupid person. ➤ VB to give or apply drugs to.

dopey or **dopy** ADJ, COLLOQ (-*ier*, -*iest*) 1 sleepy or inactive, as if drugged. 2 stupid.

doppelgänger N an apparition or double of a person.

Doric ADJ, ARCHIT denoting an order of classical architecture, characterized by fluted columns.

dormant ADJ 1 temporarily quiet, inactive or out of use. 2 BIOL in a resting state. ■ **dormancy** N.

dormer and **dormer window** N a window fitted vertically into an extension built out from a sloping roof.

dormitory N (-*ies*) 1 a large bedroom for several people. 2 esp US a hall of residence in a college or university.

dormitory town and **dormitory suburb** N a town or suburb from which most residents travel to work elsewhere.

dormouse N a small nocturnal rodent with large eyes and a bushy tail.

dorp N, S AFR a small town or village.

dorsal ADJ, BIOL, PHYSIOL relating to the back.

dory N (-*ies*) a golden-yellow fish of the mackerel family. Also called **John Dory**.

DOS ABBREV, COMP disk-operating system, a program for handling information on a disk.

dos and **do's** see under **do**[1]

dose N 1 MED the measured quantity of medicine, etc that is prescribed by a doctor to be administered to a patient. 2 the amount of radiation a person is exposed to over a specified period of time. 3 COLLOQ a bout, esp of an illness or something unpleasant. ➤ VB (also **dose sb up with sth**) to give them medicine, esp in large quantities. ■ **dosage** N.

doss VB, INTR, SLANG (often **doss down**) to settle down to sleep, esp on an improvised bed.

dossier N a file of papers containing information on a person or subject.

dot N 1 a spot; a point. 2 in Morse code: the shorter of the two lengths of signal element. ➤ VB (-*tt*-) 1 to put a dot on something. 2 to scatter; to cover with: **dotted with daisies**. ◆ **on the dot** exactly on time.

dotage N feeble-mindedness owing to old age.

dote VB, INTR to be foolish or weak-minded, esp because of old age. ■ **doting** ADJ. ◆ **dote on sb** or **sth** to show a foolishly excessive fondness for them.

dotty ADJ (-*ier*, -*iest*) COLLOQ silly; crazy. ■ **dottiness** N.

double ADJ 1 made up of two similar parts; paired; in pairs. 2 twice the weight, size, etc, or twice the usual weight, size, etc. 3 for two people: **a double bed**. 4 ambiguous: **double meaning**. 5 of a musical instrument: sounding an octave lower: **double bass**. ➤ ADV 1 twice. 2 with one half over the other: **folded double**. ➤ N 1 a double quantity. 2 a duplicate or lookalike. 3 an actor's stand-in. 4 a double measure of alcoholic spirit. See also **doubles**. ➤ VB 1 TR & INTR to make or become twice as

large in size, number, etc. **2** INTR to have a second use or function: **The spare bed doubles as a couch. 3** INTR to turn round sharply.
- ◆ **double back** to turn and go back.
- ◆ **double for sb** to act as their substitute.
- ◆ **double sth over** to fold one half of it over the other.
- ◆ **double up 1** to bend sharply at the waist, esp through pain. **2** (also **double up with sb**) to share a bedroom with another person.

double agent N a spy working for one country while apparently spying for another.

double-barrelled or (N AMER) **-barreled** ADJ **1** having two barrels. **2** of a surname: made up of two names.

double bass N the largest and lowest in pitch of the orchestral stringed instruments.

double-breasted ADJ of a coat or jacket: having overlapping front flaps.

double chin N a chin with an area of loose flesh underneath.

double cream N thick cream with a high fat content.

double-cross VB to cheat or deceive (esp a colleague or ally).
➤ N such a deceit.

double-dealing N cheating; treachery.

double-decker N **1** a bus with two decks. **2** COLLOQ anything with two levels or layers.

double Dutch N, COLLOQ nonsense; incomprehensible jargon.

double-edged ADJ **1** having two cutting edges. **2** having two possible meanings or purposes.

double entendre N a remark having two possible meanings, one of them usu sexually suggestive.

double figures PL N the numbers between 10 and 99 inclusive.

double-glazing N windows constructed with two panes separated by a vacuum.

double-jointed ADJ having extraordinarily flexible body joints.

double negative N an expression containing two negative words, esp where only one is needed: **He hasn't never asked.**

doubles SING N a competition in tennis, etc between two teams of two players each.

double standard N (often **double standards**) a principle or rule applied firmly to one person or group and loosely or not at all to another, esp oneself.

doublet N **1** HIST a close-fitting man's jacket. **2** a pair of objects of any kind.

double take N an initial inattentive reaction followed swiftly by a sudden full realization.

double-talk N ambiguous talk, or talk that seems relevant but is really meaningless.

doublethink N simultaneous belief in, or acceptance of, two opposing ideas.

double time N **1** a rate of pay equal to double the basic rate. **2** MUS a time twice as fast as the previous time. **3** MUS duple time.

doubloon N a gold coin formerly used in Spain and S America.

doubly ADV **1** to twice the extent; very much more. **2** in two ways.

doubt VB **1** to feel uncertain about something; to be suspicious or show mistrust of it. **2** to be inclined to disbelieve something.
➤ N **1** a feeling of uncertainty, suspicion or mistrust. **2** an inclination to disbelieve; a reservation. ■ **doubter** N.
- ◆ **beyond doubt** certain; certainly.
- ◆ **in doubt** not certain.
- ◆ **no doubt** surely; probably.

doubtful ADJ **1** feeling doubt. **2** uncertain; able to be doubted. **3** likely not to be the case.

doubtless ADV probably; certainly.
■ **doubtlessly** ADV.

douche N a powerful jet of water that is used to clean a body orifice, esp the vagina.

dough N **1** a mixture of flour, liquid (water or milk) and yeast, used in the preparation of bread, pastry, etc. **2** SLANG money.

doughnut N a portion of sweetened dough fried in deep fat, usu with a hole in the middle.

dour ADJ stern; sullen. ∎ **dourness** N.

douse or **dowse** VB **1** to throw water over something; to plunge something into water. **2** to extinguish (a light or fire).

dove N **1** any of various pigeons. **2** POL a person favouring peace rather than hostility.

dovecote or **dovecot** N a building or shed in which domestic pigeons are kept.

dovetail N a joint, esp in wood, made by fitting V-shaped parts into corresponding slots. Also called **dovetail joint**.
➤ VB, TR & INTR **1** to fit using one or more dovetails. **2** to fit or combine neatly.

dowdy ADJ (*-ier, -iest*) dull, plain and unfashionable. ∎ **dowdily** ADV. ∎ **dowdiness** N.

dowel N a wooden peg, esp used to join two pieces by fitting into holes in each.

down[1] ADV **1** towards or in a low or lower position, level or state; on or to the ground. **2** from a greater to a lesser size, level, etc: **scaled down**. **3** towards or in a more southerly place. **4** in writing; on paper: **take down notes**. **5** as a deposit: **put down five pounds**. **6** to an end stage or finished state: **hunt someone down**. **7** from earlier to later times: **handed down through generations**. **8** to a state of exhaustion, defeat, etc: **worn down by illness**. **9** not vomited up: **keep food down**.
➤ PREP **1** in a lower position on something. **2** along; at a further position on, by or through: **down the road**. **3** along in the direction of the current of a river. **4** from the top to or towards the bottom.
➤ ADJ **1** sad; in low spirits. **2** going towards or reaching a lower position: **a down pipe**. **3** made as a deposit: **a down payment**. **4** reduced in price. **5** of a computer, etc: out of action, esp temporarily.
➤ VB **1** to drink something quickly, esp in one gulp. **2** to force someone to the ground.
➤ N **1** an unsuccessful or otherwise unpleasant

period: **Life has its ups and downs**. **2** (**downs**) an area of rolling (esp treeless) hills.
◆ **down under** COLLOQ in or to Australia and/or New Zealand.
◆ **down with...**! let us get rid of...!

down[2] N fine feathers or hair. ∎ **downy** ADJ.

down-and-out ADJ homeless and penniless.
➤ N a down-and-out person.

down-at-heel ADJ shabby.

downbeat ADJ **1** pessimistic; cheerless. **2** calm; relaxed.

downcast ADJ **1** glum; dispirited. **2** of eyes: looking downwards.

downfall N failure or ruin, or its cause.

downgrade VB to reduce to a lower grade.

downhearted ADJ dispirited; discouraged.

downhill ADV **1** downwards. **2** to or towards a worse condition.
➤ ADJ downwardly sloping.
➤ N a ski race down a hillside.

down-in-the-mouth ADJ unhappy.

download VB, COMP to transfer (data) from one computer to another.

down-market ADJ cheap, lacking prestige.

down payment N a deposit.

downpour N a very heavy fall of rain.

downright ADJ utter.
➤ ADV utterly.

Down's syndrome N, PATHOL a congenital disorder which results in mental retardation, flattened facial features, and slight slanting of the eyes.

downstairs ADV to or towards a lower floor; down the stairs.
➤ ADJ on a lower or ground floor.

downstream ADJ, ADV further along a river towards the sea; with the current.

downtime N time during which work ceases because a machine is not working.

down-to-earth ADJ sensible and practical.

downtown ADJ, ADV in or towards either the lower part of the city or the city centre.

downtrodden ADJ oppressed.

downturn N a decline in economic activity.

downward ADJ leading or moving down.
➤ ADV downwards. ■ **downwardly** ADV.
■ **downwards** ADV.

downwind ADV in or towards the direction in which the wind is blowing.
➤ ADJ moving with, or sheltered from, the wind.

dowry N (**-ies**) an amount of wealth handed over by a woman's family to her husband on marriage.

dowse[1] VB, INTR to search for underground water with a divining-rod. ■ **dowser** N.

dowse[2] see **douse**

doyen N, LITERARY the most senior and most respected member of a group or profession.

doyley see **doily**

doze VB, INTR to sleep lightly.
➤ N a brief period of light sleep.
◆ **doze off** to fall into a light sleep.

dozen N (*dozens* or, following a number, *dozen*) 1 a set of twelve. 2 (often **dozens**) COLLOQ very many. ■ **dozenth** ADJ.

dozy ADJ (**-ier, -iest**) 1 sleepy. 2 COLLOQ stupid; slow to understand; not alert.

Dr ABBREV Doctor.

drab ADJ (*drabber, drabbest*) 1 dull; dreary. 2 of a dull brown colour. ■ **drabness** N.

drachm N a unit of liquid volume equal to one eighth of a fluid ounce.

draconian ADJ of a law, etc: harsh; severe.

draft N 1 a written plan; a preliminary sketch. 2 a written order requesting a bank to pay out money, esp to another bank. 3 a group of people drafted. 4 esp US conscription.
➤ VB 1 to set something out in preliminary sketchy form. 2 to select and send off (personnel) to perform a specific task. 3 esp US to conscript.

drag VB (**-gg-**) 1 to pull someone or something along roughly, violently, slowly and with force. 2 TR & INTR to move or make something move along scraping the ground. 3 COLLOQ (usu **drag sb away**) to force or persuade them to come away. 4 to search (eg a lake) with a hook or dragnet.
➤ N 1 an act of dragging; a dragging effect. 2 a person or thing that makes progress slow. 3 COLLOQ a draw on a cigarette. 4 COLLOQ a dull or tedious person or thing. 5 COLLOQ women's clothes worn by a man.

dragnet N a heavy net pulled along the bottom of a river, etc in a search for something.

dragon N a mythical, fire-breathing, reptile-like creature with wings and a long tail.

dragonfly N an insect with a long slender brightly coloured body and gauzy wings.

dragoon N, HIST but still used in regimental titles: a heavily armed mounted soldier.
➤ VB to force or bully someone into doing something.

drain VB 1 to empty (a container) by causing or allowing liquid to escape. 2 (**drain sth of liquid**) to remove liquid from it. 3 to drink the total contents of (a glass, etc). 4 to use up the strength, emotion or resources of (someone). 5 of a river: to carry away surface water from (land).
➤ N a device for carrying away liquid.

drainage N the process or a method or system of draining.

draining board N a sloping, and often channelled, surface at the side of a sink allowing water from washed dishes, etc to drain away.

drainpipe N a pipe carrying waste water or rainwater, esp water from a roof into a drain below ground.

drake N a male duck.

dram N 1 COLLOQ a small amount of alcoholic spirit, esp whisky. 2 a measure of weight equal to one sixteenth of an ounce.

drama N 1 a play. 2 plays in general. 3 the art

of producing, directing and acting in plays. **4** excitement and emotion; an exciting situation.

dramatic ADJ **1** relating to plays, the theatre or acting in general. **2** exciting. **3** sudden and striking; drastic. **4** of a person or behaviour: flamboyantly emotional. ■ **dramatically** ADV.

dramatics 1 SING N OR PL N activities associated with the staging and performing of plays. **2** PL N exaggeratedly emotional behaviour.

dramatist N a writer of plays.

dramatize or **-ise** VB **1** to make something into a work for public performance. **2** to treat something as, or make it seem, more exciting or important. ■ **dramatization** N.

drape VB **1** to hang cloth loosely over something. **2** to arrange (cloth, etc) loosely.

drastic ADJ extreme. ■ **drastically** ADV.

draught N **1** a current of air, esp indoors. **2** a quantity of liquid swallowed in one go. **3** any of the discs used in the game of draughts. Also called **draughtsman**. **4** COLLOQ draught beer. **5** a dose of medicine.
➢ ADJ **1** of beer: pumped direct from the cask to the glass. **2** of an animal: esp IN COMPOUNDS used for pulling loads..

draughts SING N a game for two people played with 24 discs on a chequered board (a **draughtboard**).

draughtsman N **1** someone skilled in drawing. **2** someone employed to produce detailed technical drawings. **3** see **draught** (N sense 3). ■ **draughtsmanship** N.

draughty ADJ (**-ier, -iest**) prone to or suffering draughts of air.

draw VB (PA T **drew**, PA P **drawn**, PR P **drawing**) **1** TR & INTR to make a picture of something or someone, esp with a pencil. **2** to pull out or take out something: **draw water from a well**. **3** INTR to move or proceed steadily in a specified direction: **draw nearer**. **4** to pull someone along or into a particular position: **drawing her closer to him**. **5** to open or close (curtains). **6** to attract (eg attention or criticism). **7** TR & INTR (also

draw with sb) to end a game equal with an opponent. **8** to choose or be given as the result of random selection. **9** to arrive at or infer (a conclusion). **10 a** INTR (also **draw on**) to suck air through (a cigarette); **b** of a chimney: to make air flow through a fire, allowing burning. **11** to write (a cheque).
➢ N **1** a result in which neither side is the winner. **2 a** the making of a random selection, eg of the winners of a competition; **b** a competition with winners chosen at random. **3** the potential to attract many people, or a person or thing having this. **4** the act of drawing a gun.
◆ **draw a blank** to get no result.
◆ **draw back** to retreat; to recoil.
◆ **draw in** of nights: to start earlier, making days shorter.
◆ **draw on sth** to make use of assets.
◆ **draw up** to come to a halt.
◆ **draw sth up** to plan and write (a contract or other document).

drawback N a disadvantage.

drawbridge N a bridge that can be lifted to prevent access across or allow passage beneath.

drawer N **1** a sliding lidless storage box fitted as part of a desk or other piece of furniture. **2** someone who draws. **3** (**drawers**) OLD USE knickers, esp large ones.

drawing N **1** a picture made up of lines. **2** the act or art of making such pictures.

drawing-pin N a short pin with a flat head.

drawing-room N a sitting-room.

drawl VB, TR & INTR to speak or say in a slow lazy manner, esp with prolonged vowel sounds.

drawn[1] ADJ showing signs of mental strain or tiredness.

drawn[2] ADJ, IN COMPOUNDS pulled by: **horse-drawn**.

drawstring N a cord sewn inside a hem eg on a bag, closing up the hem when pulled.

dread N great fear or apprehension.
➢ VB to look ahead to something with dread.

dreadful ADJ **1** inspiring great fear; terrible.

2 LOOSELY very bad. ■ **dreadfully** ADV.

dreadlocks PL N thin braids of hair tied tightly all over the head.

dream N **1** thoughts and mental images experienced during sleep. **2** complete engrossment in one's own thoughts. **3** a distant ambition, esp if unattainable. **4** COLLOQ an extremely pleasing person or thing: He's a dream to work with. **5** COLLOQ, AS ADJ ideal. ➢ VB (PA T & PA P *dreamed* or *dreamt*) **1** TR & INTR to have thoughts and visions during sleep. **2** (usu **dream of sth**) **a** to have a distant ambition or hope; **b** to imagine or conceive of something. **3** INTR to have extravagant and unrealistic thoughts or plans. **4** INTR to be lost in thought. ■ **dreamer** N.
◆ **dream sth up** to devise or invent something unusual or absurd.

dreamy ADJ (*-ier, -iest*) **1** unreal, as if in a dream. **2** having or showing a wandering mind. **3** COLLOQ lovely.

dreary ADJ (*-ier, -iest*) **1** dull and depressing. **2** unintersting. ■ **drearily** ADV. ■ **dreariness** N.

dredge[1] VB, TR & INTR to clear the bottom of or deepen (the sea or a river) by bringing up mud and waste. ■ **dredger** N.

dredge[2] VB to sprinkle (food), eg with sugar or flour. ■ **dredger** N.

dregs PL N **1** solid particles in a liquid that settle at the bottom. **2** worthless elements.

drench VB to make something or someone soaking wet.

dress VB **1** TR & INTR to put clothes on; to wear, or make someone wear, clothes (of a certain kind). **2** to treat and bandage (wounds). **3** to prepare, or add seasoning or a sauce to (food). ➢ N **1** a woman's garment with top and skirt in one piece. **2** clothing; wear: **in evening dress.** ➢ ADJ formal; for evening wear: **dress jacket.**
◆ **dress up 1** to put on fancy dress. **2** to dress in smart or formal clothes.
◆ **get dressed** to dress.

dressage N the training of a horse in, or

performance of, set manoeuvres signalled by the rider.

dresser N **1** a free-standing kitchen cupboard with shelves above. **2** US a chest of drawers or dressing-table.

dressing N **1** COOKERY any sauce added to food, esp salad. **2** a covering for a wound. **3** AGRIC an application of fertilizer.

dressing down N a reprimand.

dressing gown N a loose robe worn informally indoors, esp over nightclothes.

dressing room N a room used when changing clothing.

dressing table N a piece of bedroom furniture typically with drawers and a mirror.

dressmaking N the craft or business of making women's clothes. ■ **dressmaker** N.

dress rehearsal N, THEAT the last rehearsal of a performance, with full costumes, lighting, etc.

dress shirt N a man's formal shirt worn with a dinner-jacket.

dressy ADJ (*-ier, -iest*) **1** dressed or dressing stylishly. **2** of clothes: for formal wear; elegant. ■ **dressily** ADV.

dribble VB **1** INTR to fall or flow in drops. **2** INTR to allow saliva to run slowly down from the mouth. **3** TR & INTR, FOOTBALL, HOCKEY, etc to move along keeping (a ball) in close control with frequent short strokes. ➢ N **1** a small quantity of liquid. **2** FOOTBALL, HOCKEY, etc an act of dribbling a ball.

dribs and drabs PL N very small quantities.

drier or **dryer** N a device or substance that dries clothing, hair, paint, etc.

drift N **1** a general movement or tendency to move. **2** degree of movement off course caused by wind or a current. ➢ VB, INTR **1** to float or be blown along or into heaps. **2** to move aimlessly from one place or occupation to another. **3** to move off course.

drifter N someone who moves aimlessly from place to place.

driftwood N wood floating near, or washed up on, a shore.

drill[1] N **1** a tool for boring holes. **2** a training session. **3** COLLOQ correct procedure.
➤ VB **1** to make (a hole) in something with a drill. **2** to exercise or teach through repetition.

drill[2] N thick strong cotton cloth.

drill[3] N **1** a shallow furrow in which seeds are sown. **2** the seeds sown or plants growing in a row. **3** a machine for sowing seeds in rows.

drilling platform N a floating or fixed offshore structure supporting a **drilling rig,** the apparatus required for drilling an oil well.

drink VB (PA T *drank,* PA P *drunk*) **1** TR & INTR to take in (a liquid) by swallowing. **2** INTR to drink alcohol; to drink alcohol to excess.
➤ N **1** an act of drinking. **2** liquid for drinking. **3** alcohol of any kind; the habit of drinking alcohol to excess. **4** a glass or amount of drink. **5** (**the drink**) COLLOQ the sea. ■ **drinkable** ADJ. ■ **drinker**.
◆ **drink sth in** to listen to it eagerly.

drink-driving N driving while under the influence of alcohol. ■ **drink-driver** N.

drip VB (*-pp-*) **1** TR & INTR to release or fall in drops. **2** INTR to release a liquid in drops.
➤ N **1** the action or noise of dripping. **2** a device for passing a liquid solution slowly and continuously into a vein. Also called **drip-feed**. **3** DEROG, COLLOQ someone who lacks spirit or character.

drip-dry ADJ requiring little or no ironing if hung up to dry by dripping.
➤ VB, TR & INTR to dry in this way.

drip-feed N same as **drip** (N sense 2).
➤ VB to feed something or someone with a liquid using a drip.

dripping N fat from roasted meat.

drive VB (PA T *drove,* PA P *driven*) **1 a** to control the movement of (a vehicle); **b** to be legally qualified to do so. **2** INTR to travel in a vehicle. **3** to take or transport someone or something in a vehicle. **4** to urge or force someone or something to move: **boats driven on to the**
beach by the storm. **5** to make someone or something get into a particular state or condition: **It drove me crazy. 6** to force by striking: **drove the nail into the wood. 7** to produce motion in something; to make it operate: **machinery driven by steam. 8** to conduct or dictate: **drive a hard bargain.**
➤ N **1** a trip in a vehicle by road. **2** a path for vehicles, leading from a private residence to the road outside. Also called **driveway**. **3** (**Drive**) a street title in an address. **4** energy and enthusiasm. **5** an organized campaign; a group effort: **an economy drive. 6** operating power, or a device supplying this. **7** a united movement forward, esp by a military force. ■ **driver** N.
◆ **be driven by sth** to be motivated by it.
◆ **be driving at sth** to intend or imply it as a meaning or conclusion.

drive-in ADJ providing a service or facility for customers remaining in vehicles. Also AS NOUN.

drivel N nonsense.
➤ VB (*-ll-*) INTR **1** to talk nonsense. **2** to dribble.

drive-through N, esp N AMER a shop, restaurant, etc from a window of which drivers can be served without leaving their cars.

driveway see under **drive**

drizzle N fine light rain.
➤ VB, INTR to rain lightly. ■ **drizzly** ADJ.

droll ADJ oddly amusing or comical.
■ **drollery** N. ■ **drolly** ADV.

dromedary N (*-ies*) a single-humped camel.

drone VB, INTR to make a low humming noise.
➤ N **1** a deep humming sound. **2** a male honeybee whose sole function is to mate with the queen. **3** a lazy person.

drool VB, INTR to dribble or slaver.

droop VB, INTR **1** to hang loosely; to sag. **2** to be or grow weak with tiredness.
➤ N a drooping state. ■ **droopy** ADJ.

drop VB (*-pp-*) **1** TR & INTR to fall or allow to fall. **2** TR & INTR to decline or make something decline; to lower or weaken. **3** to give up or abandon (eg a friend or a habit). **4** to stop

discussing (a topic). **5** (also **drop sb** or **sth off**) to set them down from a vehicle; to deliver or hand them in. **6** to leave or take out someone or something. **7** to mention something casually: **drop a hint. 8** to fail to pronounce (a consonant): **drop one's h's.**
➤ N **1** a small round or pear-shaped mass of liquid; a small amount (of liquid). **2** a descent; a fall. **3** a vertical distance. **4** a decline or decrease. **5** any small round or pear-shaped object, eg an earring or boiled sweet. **6** (**drops**) liquid medication administered in small amounts. **7** a delivery.
◆ **drop in** or **by** to pay a brief unexpected visit.
◆ **drop off 1** COLLOQ to fall asleep. **2** to become less; to diminish; to disappear.
◆ **drop out 1** (often **drop out of sth**) to withdraw from an activity. **2** COLLOQ to adopt an alternative lifestyle as a reaction against traditional social values.

drop-dead ADJ, SLANG stunning or breathtaking, particularly in a sexual way: drop-dead gorgeous.

drop goal N, RUGBY a goal scored by a drop kick.

drop kick RUGBY, N a kick in which the ball is released from the hands and struck as it hits the ground.
➤ VB (**drop-kick**) to kick (a ball) in this way.

droplet N a tiny drop.

dropout N **1** a student who quits before completing a course of study. **2** a person whose alternative lifestyle is a reaction against traditional social values.

dropper N a short narrow glass tube with a rubber bulb on one end, for applying liquid in drops.

droppings PL N animal or bird faeces.

dross N **1** waste coal. **2** scum that forms on molten metal. **3** DEROG COLLOQ rubbish.

drought N a prolonged lack of rainfall.

drove N **1** a moving herd of animals, esp cattle. **2** a large moving crowd.

drown VB **1** INTR to die by suffocation as a result of inhaling liquid, esp water, into the lungs. **2** to kill by suffocation in this way.
◆ **drown sth out** to suppress the effect of one sound with a louder one.

drowse VB, INTR to sleep lightly for a short while.

drowsy ADJ (*-ier, -iest*) **1** sleepy; causing sleepiness. **2** quiet and peaceful. ■ **drowsily** ADV. ■ **drowsiness** N.

drub VB (*-bb-*) **1** to defeat severely. **2** to beat; to thump. ■ **drubbing** N.

drudge VB, INTR to do tedious or menial work.
➤ N a servant; a labourer. ■ **drudgery** N.

drug N **1** a medicine. **2** an illegal addictive substance; a narcotic. **3** anything craved for.
➤ VB (*-gg-*) **1** to administer a drug to (a person or animal). **2** to poison or stupefy with drugs. **3** to mix or season (food) with drugs.

drug addict N someone who has become dependent on drugs. ■ **drug addiction** N.

drugstore N, N AMER, ESP US a chemist's shop, esp one also selling refreshments.

druid or **Druid** N **1** a Celtic priest in pre-Christian times. **2** an eisteddfod official. ■ **druidic** or **druidical** ADJ.

drum N **1** a percussion instrument consisting of a hollow frame with a membrane stretched tightly across it, sounding when struck. **2** any object resembling this in shape. **3** an eardrum.
➤ VB (*-mm-*) **1** INTR to beat a drum. **2** TR & INTR to make or cause to make continuous tapping or thumping sounds. ■ **drummer** N.
◆ **drum sth in** or **into sb** to force it into their mind through constant repetition.
◆ **drum sth up** COLLOQ to achieve or attract it by energetic persuasion.

drumbeat N the sound made by a drum.

drum major N the leader of a marching (esp military) band.

drum majorette see **majorette**

drumstick N **1** a stick used for beating a drum. **2** the lower leg of a cooked fowl, esp a chicken.

drunk ADJ lacking control in movement, speech, etc after consuming too much alcohol.
➤ N a drunk person, esp one regularly so.

drunkard N someone who is often drunk.

drunken ADJ 1 drunk. 2 relating to, or brought on by, alcoholic intoxication. ■ **drunkenly** ADV. ■ **drunkenness** N.

dry ADJ (*drier, driest*) 1 free from or lacking moisture or wetness. 2 with little or no rainfall. 3 from which all the water has evaporated or been taken: **a dry well**. 4 thirsty. 5 of an animal: no longer producing milk. 6 of wine, etc: not sweet. 7 not buttered: **dry toast**. 8 of humour: expressed in a quietly sarcastic or matter-of-fact way. 9 forbidding the sale and consumption of alcohol. 10 of eyes: without tears. 11 dull; uninteresting.
➤ VB (*dries, dried*) 1 TR & INTR to make or become dry. 2 TR to preserve (food) by removing all moisture. ■ **drily** or **dryly** ADV. ■ **dryness** N.
◆ **dry out** to become completely dry.
◆ **dry sth out** to dry it completely.
◆ **dry up** 1 to dry thoroughly or completely. 2 to cease to produce or be produced. 3 COLLOQ of a speaker or actor: to run out of words; to forget lines while on stage.

dry-clean VB to clean (esp clothes) with liquid chemicals, not water. ■ **dry-cleaner** N. ■ **dry-cleaning** N.

dry dock N a dock from which the water can be pumped out to allow work on a ship's lower parts.

dry rot N, BOT a serious type of timber decay caused by a fungus common in damp, poorly ventilated buildings, which ultimately reduces the wood to a dry brittle mass.

dry run N 1 a rehearsal, practice or test. 2 MIL a practice exercise.

dry-stone ADJ of a wall: made of stones wedged together without mortar.

DT and **DTs** ABBREV delirium tremens.

dual ADJ 1 consisting of or representing two separate parts. 2 double. ■ **duality** N.

dual carriageway N a road on which traffic moving in opposite directions is separated by a central barrier or strip of land.

dual-purpose ADJ serving two purposes.

dub¹ VB (-*bb*-) to give a name, esp a nickname, to someone.

dub² VB (-*bb*-) 1 to add a new soundtrack to (eg a film), esp in a different language. 2 to add sound effects or music to (eg a film).

dubbin N a wax-like mixture for softening and waterproofing leather.

dubiety N, FORMAL dubiousness; doubt.

dubious ADJ 1 feeling doubt; unsure; uncertain. 2 arousing suspicion; potentially dishonest or dishonestly obtained. ■ **dubiously** ADV. ■ **dubiousness** N.

ducal ADJ belonging or relating to a duke.

duchess N 1 the wife or widow of a duke. 2 a woman of the same rank as a duke.

duchy N (-*ies*) the territory owned or ruled by a duke or duchess.

duck¹ N 1 a water bird with short legs, webbed feet, and a large flattened beak. 2 the flesh of this bird used as food. 3 the female of such a bird, as opposed to the male drake. 4 CRICKET a batsman's score of zero.

duck² VB 1 INTR to lower the head or body suddenly, esp to avoid notice or a blow. 2 to push someone briefly under water.
◆ **duck out of sth** COLLOQ to avoid something unpleasant or unwelcome.

duck-billed platypus see **platypus**

duckling N a young duck.

duckweed N a plant with broad flat leaves that grows on the surface of water.

ducky COLLOQ, N (-*ies*) a term of endearment.
➤ ADJ (-*ier, -iest*) excellent; pleasing.

duct N 1 ANAT a tube in the body, esp one for carrying glandular secretions. 2 a casing or shaft for pipes or electrical cables, or a tube used for ventilation and air-conditioning.

ductile ADJ denoting metals that can be drawn

out into a thin wire without breaking.

dud COLLOQ, N **1** a counterfeit article. **2** a bomb, firework, etc that fails to go off. **3** any useless or ineffectual person or thing. **4** (**duds**) clothes.
➤ ADJ **1** useless. **2** counterfeit.

dude N, COLLOQ, N AMER, ESP US, orig SLANG **1** a man; a guy. **2** a city man, esp an Easterner holidaying in the West. **3** a man preoccupied with dressing smartly.

dudgeon N (usu **in high dudgeon**) the condition of being very angry or resentful.

due ADJ **1** owed; payable. **2** expected, esp according to timetable. **3** proper.
➤ N **1** what is owed; something that can be rightfully claimed or expected. **2** (**dues**) subscription fees.
➤ ADV directly: **due north**.
◆ **due to sth** or **sb 1** caused by it or them. **2** because of it or them.

duel N **1** a pre-arranged fight between two people to settle a matter of honour. **2** any serious conflict between two people or groups.
➤ VB (**-ll-**) INTR to fight a duel. ■ **duellist** or **dueller** N.

duet N **1** a piece of music for two singers or players. **2** a pair of musical performers.

duff ADJ, COLLOQ useless; broken.

duffel or **duffle** N a thick woollen fabric.

duffel bag N a cylindrical canvas shoulder bag with a drawstring fastening.

duffel coat N a heavy, esp hooded, coat made of duffel.

duffer N, COLLOQ a clumsy or incompetent person.

dug N an animal's udder or nipple.

dugong N a seal-like tropical sea mammal.

dugout N **1** a canoe made from a hollowed-out log. **2** a soldier's rough shelter dug into a slope or bank or in a trench. **3** a covered shelter at the side of a sports field, for the trainer, substitutes, etc.

duke N **1** a nobleman of the highest rank. **2** the ruler of a small state or principality.

dukedom N the title or property of a duke.

dulcet ADJ, LITERARY of sounds: sweet and pleasing to the ear.

dull ADJ **1** of colour or light: lacking brightness or clearness. **2** of sounds: deep and low; muffled. **3** of weather: cloudy; overcast. **4** of pain: not sharp. **5** of a person: slow to learn or understand. **6** uninteresting; lacking liveliness. **7** of a blade: blunt.
➤ VB, TR & INTR to make or become dull.
■ **dullness** N. ■ **dully** ADV.

duly ADV **1** in the proper way. **2** at the proper time.

dumb ADJ **1** temporarily or permanently unable to speak. **2** of animals: not having human speech. **3** silent; not expressed in words. **4** COLLOQ, esp US foolish; unintelligent.

dumbbell N a short metal bar with a weight on each end, used in muscle exercises.

dumbfound or **dumfound** VB to astonish someone; to leave someone speechless.

dumbstruck ADJ silent with astonishment or shock.

dumb waiter N **1** a small lift for transporting laundry, dirty dishes, etc between floors in a restaurant or hotel. **2** a movable shelved stand for food. **3** a revolving food tray.

dumdum N a bullet that expands on impact, causing severe injury.

dummy N (**-ies**) **1** a life-size model of the human body, eg used for displaying clothes. **2** a realistic copy, esp one substituted for something. **3** a rubber teat sucked by a baby for comfort. **4** COLLOQ, chiefly N AMER a stupid person. **5** SPORT an act of dummying with the ball.
➤ ADJ false; sham; counterfeit.
➤ VB (**-ies, -ied**) TR & INTR, SPORT **a** to make as if to move one way before sharply moving the other, in order to deceive (an opponent); **b** to do so with (a ball).

dummy run N a practice; a try-out.

dump VB **1** to put something down heavily or carelessly. **2** TR & INTR to dispose of (rubbish), esp in an unauthorized place. **3** SLANG to break off a romantic relationship with someone.
➤ N **1** a place where rubbish may be dumped. **2** a military store, eg of weapons or food. **3** COLLOQ a dirty or dilapidated place.

dumpbin N a display stand or a container.

dumper truck and **dumptruck** N a lorry which can be emptied by raising one end of the carrier to allow the contents to slide out.

dumpling N **1** a baked or boiled ball of dough served with meat. **2** a rich fruit pudding.

dumps PL N only in phrase below.
◆ **down in the dumps** COLLOQ in low spirits.

dumpy ADJ (*-ier, -iest*) short and plump.

dun ADJ (*dunner, dunnest*) greyish-brown.
➤ N **1** a dun colour. **2** a horse of this colour.

dunce N a stupid person; a slow learner.

dune N a ridge or hill of windblown sand.

dung N animal excrement.

dungarees PL N loose trousers with a bib and shoulder straps attached.

dungeon N a prison cell, esp underground.

dungheap and **dunghill** N **1** a pile of dung. **2** any squalid situation or place.

dunk VB **1** to dip (eg a biscuit) into tea or a similar beverage. **2** to submerge or be submerged.

dunlin N a small brown wading bird.

dunno COLLOQ, CONTRACTION OF I do not know.

dunnock N the hedge sparrow.

duo N **1** a pair of musicians or other performers. **2** any two people considered a pair. **3** MUS a duet.

duodecimal ADJ relating to or based on the number twelve, or multiples of it.

duodenum N (*-na* or *-nums*) ANAT the first part of the small intestine, into which food passes after leaving the stomach. ■ **duodenal** ADJ.

duologue or (sometimes US) **duolog** N **1** a dialogue between two actors. **2** a play for two actors.

dupe VB to trick or deceive.
➤ N a person who is deceived.

duple ADJ **1** double; twofold. **2** MUS having two beats in the bar.

duplex ADJ double; twofold.

duplicate ADJ identical to another.
➤ N **1** an exact copy. **2** another of the same kind.
➤ VB **1** to make or be an exact copy or copies of something. **2** to repeat something.
■ **duplication** N. ■ **duplicator** N.
◆ **in duplicate** in two exact copies.

duplicity N (*-ies*) FORMAL deception; trickery; double-dealing. ■ **duplicitous** ADJ.

durable ADJ **1** lasting a long time without breaking; sturdy. **2** long-lasting; enduring.
➤ N a durable item. ■ **durability** N (*-ies*).

duration N the length of time that something lasts or continues.

duress N the influence of force or threats; coercion.

during PREP **1** throughout the time of something. **2** in the course of something.

dusk N twilight; the period of semi-darkness before night.

dusky ADJ (*-ier, -iest*) **1** dark; shadowy. **2** dark-coloured; dark-skinned. ■ **duskily** ADV. ■ **duskiness** N.

dust N **1** earth, sand or household dirt in the form of fine powder. **2** a cloud of this. **3** any substance in powder form.
➤ VB **1** to remove dust from (furniture, etc). **2** to sprinkle something with powder.

dustbin N a large lidded container for household rubbish.

dust bowl N an area of land from which the topsoil has been removed by winds and drought.

dustcart N a vehicle in which

household rubbish is collected.

dust cover N **1** a dust jacket. **2** a dust sheet.

duster N a cloth for removing household dust.

dust jacket and **dust cover** N a loose protective paper cover on a book, carrying the title and other information.

dustman N someone employed to collect household rubbish.

dustpan N a handled container into which dust is swept, like a flattish open-ended box with a shovel edge.

dust sheet and **dust cover** N a cloth or plastic sheet used to protect furniture from dust or paint.

dusty ADJ (*-ier, -iest*) **1** covered with or containing dust. **2** of a colour: dull. **3** old-fashioned; dated. ■ **dustiness** N.

Dutch ADJ of the Netherlands.
➢ N **1** the official language of the Netherlands. **2** (**the Dutch**) the people of the Netherlands.
◆ **go Dutch** COLLOQ each person to pay their own share of a meal, etc.

Dutch cap see **cap** (N sense 6)

Dutch courage N artificial courage gained by drinking alcohol.

Dutch elm disease N, BOT a serious disease of elm trees, caused by a fungus and spread by a beetle.

Dutchman and **Dutchwoman** N a native or citizen of, or a person born in, the Netherlands.

dutiable ADJ of goods: on which duty is payable.

duty N (*-ies*) **1** an obligation or responsibility, or the awareness of it. **2** a task, esp part of a job. **3** tax on goods, esp imports. ■ **dutiful** ADJ. ■ **dutifully** ADV.
◆ **off duty** not on duty.
◆ **on duty** working; liable to be called upon to go into action.

duty-free ADJ of goods, esp imports: non-taxable.

duvet N a thick quilt filled with feathers or man-made fibres, for use on a bed.

dwarf N (*dwarfs* or less often *dwarves*) **1** an abnormally small person. **2 a** an animal or plant that is much smaller or shorter than others of its species, usu as a result of selective breeding; **b** AS ADJ: dwarf rabbits. **3** a mythical man-like creature with magic powers.
➢ VB to make something seem small or unimportant.

dwell VB (PA T & PA P *dwelt* or *dwelled*) INTR, FORMAL, LITERARY to reside. ■ **dweller** N.
◆ **dwell on sth** to think or speak about it obsessively.

dwelling N, FORMAL, LITERARY a place of residence.

dwindle VB, INTR to shrink in size, number etc.

dye VB (*dyeing*) TR & INTR to colour or stain something, or undergo colouring or staining.
➢ N **1** a coloured substance that is used in solution to give colour to a material. **2** the solution used for dyeing. **3** the colour produced by dyeing. ■ **dyer** N.

dyed-in-the-wool ADJ of firmly fixed opinions.

dying ADJ **1** expressed or occurring immediately before death: **her dying breath**. **2** final: **the dying seconds of the match**.

dyke[1] or **dike** N **1** a wall or embankment built to prevent flooding. **2** esp SCOT a wall, eg surrounding a field.

dyke[2] or **dike** N, OFFENSIVE SLANG a lesbian.

dynamic ADJ **1** full of energy, enthusiasm and new ideas. **2** relating to dynamics. ■ **dynamically** ADV.

dynamics 1 SING N the branch of mechanics that deals with motion and the forces that produce motion. **2** PL N **a** movement or change in any sphere; **b** the forces causing this: **political dynamics**.

dynamism N limitless energy and enthusiasm.

dynamite N **1** a powerful explosive. **2** COLLOQ a thrilling person or thing.

➤ VB to explode something with dynamite.

dynamo N an electric generator that converts mechanical energy into electrical energy.

dynasty N (-*ies*) **1** a succession of rulers from the same family. **2** their period of rule. **3** a succession of members of a powerful family or other connected group. ■ **dynastic** ADJ.

dysentery N, MED severe infection and inflammation of the intestines.

dysfunction N impairment or abnormality of functioning. ■ **dysfunctional** ADJ.

dyslexia N, PSYCHOL, MED a disorder characterized by difficulty in reading, writing and spelling correctly. ■ **dyslexic** ADJ, N.

dyspepsia N, PATHOL indigestion. ■ **dyspeptic** ADJ.

dystrophy N (-*ies*) MED a disorder of organs or tissues, esp muscle, arising from an inadequate supply of nutrients.

Ee

E¹ or **e** N (*Es, E's* or *e's*) **1** the fifth letter and second vowel of the English alphabet. **2** MUS (**E**) the third note in the scale of C major.

E² ABBREV **1** East. **2** Ecstasy. **3** (also **e**) electronic: E-mail.

each ADJ applied to every one of two or more people or items considered separately.
➤ PRONOUN every single one of two or more people, animals or things.
➤ ADV to, for or from each one: **Have one each.**
◆ **each other** used when an action takes place between two (or more than two) people, etc: **They talked to each other.**

eager ADJ **1** feeling or showing enthusiasm; keen to do or get something. **2** excited by desire or expectancy: **an eager glance.** ■ **eagerly** ADV. ■ **eagerness** N.

eagle N **1** any of various kinds of large birds of prey. **2** GOLF a score of two under par.

eagle eye N **1** exceptionally keen eyesight. **2** careful supervision. ■ **eagle-eyed** ADJ.

ear¹ N **1** the sense organ concerned with hearing. **2** the external part of the ear. **3** the ability to hear and appreciate the difference between sounds: **an ear for music.**

ear² N the part of a cereal plant that contains the seeds.

earache N pain in the inner part of the ear.

eardrum N the small thin membrane inside the ear, which transmits vibrations.

earful N, COLLOQ **1** a long complaint or telling-off. **2** as much talk or gossip as one can stand.

earl N a male member of the British nobility ranking below a marquess and above a viscount. ■ **earldom** N.

earlobe N the soft, loosely hanging piece of flesh which forms the lower part of the ear.

early ADV, ADJ (-*ier, -iest*) **1** of or near the beginning of (a period of time, period of development, etc). **2** sooner than others, sooner than usual, or sooner than expected. **3** in the near future. **4** in the distant past.

earmark VB to set aside for a particular purpose.

earn VB **1** TR & INTR to gain (money, one's living,

etc) by working. **2** to gain. **3** to deserve.
■ **earner** N.

earnest ADJ serious or over-serious.
■ **earnestly** ADV. ■ **earnestness** N.
◆ **in earnest 1** serious or seriously. **2** sincere.
3 not as a joke.

earnings PL N money earned.

earphones PL N headphones.

ear-piercing ADJ loud and sharp; shrill.

earplug N a piece of wax or rubber, etc
placed in the ear as a protection.

earring N a piece of jewellery worn on the
ear.

earshot N the distance at which sound can be
heard: **out of earshot**.

ear-splitting ADJ extremely loud; deafening.

earth N **1** (often **the Earth**) the planet on
which we live. **2** the land and sea, as opposed
to the sky. **3** dry land; the land surface; the
ground. **4** soil. **5** a hole in which an animal lives,
esp a fox. **6** an electrical connection with the
ground, or a wire that provides this.
➢ VB, ELECTRONICS to connect to the ground.

earthbound ADJ **1** attached or restricted to
the earth. **2** moving towards the Earth.

earthen ADJ made of earth or baked clay.

earthenware N pottery made of baked
clay.

earthly ADJ (*-ier, -iest*) **1** LITERARY of or
belonging to this world; not spiritual. **2** COLLOQ,
WITH NEGATIVES used for emphasis: **have no
earthly chance**.

earthquake N a succession of vibrations that
shake the Earth's surface, caused by shifting
movements in the Earth's crust.

earth-shattering ADJ, COLLOQ being of great
importance. ■ **earth-shatteringly** ADV.

earthworm N any of several types of worm
which live in and burrow through the soil.

earthy ADJ (*-ier, -iest*) **1** of, relating to, or like
earth or soil. **2** coarse or crude.

earwig N an insect with pincers at the end of
its body.

ease N **1** freedom from pain, anxiety or
constraint. **2** absence of difficulty. **3** absence
of restriction. **4** leisure; relaxation.
➢ VB **1** to free someone from pain, trouble or
anxiety. **2** to make someone comfortable. **3** to
relieve or calm something. **4** to loosen
something. **5** to make something less difficult:
ease his progress. **6** INTR (often **ease off** or
up) to become less intense. **7** INTR to move
gently or very gradually.

easel N a stand for supporting a blackboard or
an artist's canvas, etc.

easily ADV **1** without difficulty. **2** clearly;
beyond doubt; by far. **3** very probably.

east N **1** (also **East** or **the East**) the direction
from which the sun rises at the equinox. **2** the
direction that is directly opposite west, ie 180°
from the west and 90° from both north and
south. **3** any part of the Earth, a country or a
town, etc lying in that direction.
➢ ADJ **1** on the side which is on or nearest the
east. **2** facing or toward the east. **3** of a wind:
coming from the east.
➢ ADV towards the east.

eastbound ADJ going towards the east.

Easter N, CHRISTIANITY a religious festival
celebrating the resurrection of Christ, held in
spring, on **Easter Day** or **Easter Sunday**.

easterly ADJ **1** of a wind, etc: coming from the
east. **2** being, lying, etc towards the east.
➢ ADV **1** to or towards the east. **2** from the east.
➢ N (*-ies*) an easterly wind.

eastern ADJ situated in, directed towards or
belonging to the east or the East.
■ **easternmost** ADJ.

easterner N a person who lives in or comes
from the east.

eastward and **eastwards** ADJ, ADV
towards the east.

easy ADJ (*-ier, -iest*) **1** not difficult. **2** free from
pain, trouble, anxiety, etc. **3** not stiff or formal;
friendly. **4** tolerant. **5** not tense or strained.

➤ ADV, COLLOQ in a slow, calm or relaxed way: take it easy. ■ **easiness** N.

◆ **go easy** (**on** or **with**) **1** to deal with gently. **2** to use sparingly.

easy-going ADJ relaxed, tolerant or placid.

eat VB (*ate*, *eaten*) **1** to bite, chew and swallow (food). **2** INTR to take in food; to take a meal. **3** to eat into something. **4** COLLOQ to trouble or worry someone: What's eating you?

◆ **eat into** or **through 1** to use up gradually. **2** to waste. **3** to destroy or corrode.

◆ **eat up 1** to finish food. **2** to destroy.

eatable ADJ fit to be eaten.

eau de Cologne N a mild type of perfume.

eaves PL N the part of a roof that sticks out beyond the wall, or the underside of it.

eavesdrop VB, INTR to listen secretly to a private conversation. ■ **eavesdropper** N.

ebb VB, INTR **1** of the tide: to move back from the land. **2** (also **ebb away**) to grow smaller or weaker.

➤ N **1** the movement of the tide away from the land. **2** a decline.

◆ **at a low ebb** in a poor or weak state, mentally or physically.

ebony N (*-ies*) a hard, almost black wood.
➤ ADJ **1** made from this wood. **2** black.

ebullient ADJ very high-spirited; full of cheerfulness or enthusiasm. ■ **ebullience** N.

eccentric ADJ **1** odd; unusual or unconventional. **2** of a wheel, etc: not having the axis at the centre. **3** of circles: not having a common centre; not concentric. **4** of an orbit: not circular.
➤ N an eccentric person. ■ **eccentricity** N.

ecclesiastic ADJ (also **ecclesiastical**) of the church or the clergy.

echelon N **1 a** a level or rank in an organization, etc; **b** the people at that level. **2** a V-shaped formation, used by planes, birds in flight, etc.

echinoderm N a sea animal having a body wall strengthened by plates, eg starfish.

echo N (*-oes*) **1** the repeating of a sound caused by the sound waves striking a surface

and coming back. **2** a sound repeated in this way. **3** an imitation or repetition. **4** something which brings to mind thoughts of something else.
➤ VB (*-oes*, *-oed*) **1** to send back an echo of something. **2** to repeat (a sound or a statement). **3** to imitate or in some way be similar to something. **4** INTR to resound; to reverberate.

éclair N a long cake of choux pastry with a cream filling and chocolate icing.

eclectic ADJ selecting material or ideas from a wide range of sources or authorities. ■ **eclectically** ADV. ■ **eclecticism** N.

eclipse N **1** the total or partial obscuring of one planet or heavenly body by another, eg of the Sun when the Moon comes between it and the Earth. **2** a loss of fame or importance.
➤ VB **1** to cause an eclipse of (a heavenly body). **2** to surpass or outshine. **3** to obscure.

eco-friendly ADJ not harmful to or threatening the environment.

E. coli ABBREV Escherichia coli.

ecology N **1** the relationship between living things and their surroundings. **2** the study of plants, animals, peoples and institutions, in relation to environment. ■ **ecologic** or **ecological** ADJ. ■ **ecologist** N.

economic ADJ **1** of or concerned with economy or economics. **2** relating to industry or business. **3** operated at, or likely to bring, a profit. **4** economical. **5** COLLOQ cheap; not expensive.

economical ADJ not wasting money or resources. ■ **economically** ADV.

economics SING N **1** the study of the production, distribution and consumption of money, goods and services. **2** the financial aspects of something. ■ **economist** N.

economize or **-ise** VB, INTR to cut down on spending or waste.

economy N (*-ies*) **1** the organization of money and resources within a nation or community, etc, esp in terms of the production, distribution and

consumption of goods and services.
2 a system in which these are organized in a specified way: **a socialist economy. 3** careful management of money or resources. **4** (usu **economies**) an instance of economizing; a saving. **5** efficient or sparing use of something: **economy of movement. 6** AS ADJ **a** of the cheapest kind; **b** (also **economy-size** or **economy-sized**) larger than the standard or basic size, and proportionally cheaper.

ecotourism N tourism in areas of unspoiled natural beauty, managed so that the environment is preserved. ■ **ecotourist** N.

ecru N an off-white or greyish-yellow colour.

ecstasy N **1** (*-ies*) a feeling of immense joy; rapture. **2** (**Ecstasy**) SLANG a powerful hallucinatory drug. ■ **ecstatic** ADJ.

ectopic pregnancy N, PATHOL the development of a fetus outside the uterus.

ectoplasm N the substance thought to be given off by a medium during a trance.

ecumenical ADJ **1** bringing together different branches of the Christian church. **2** working towards the unity of the Christian church. **3** referring to or consisting of the whole Christian church: **an ecumenical council.** ■ **ecumenicism** or **ecumenism** N.

eczema N, PATHOL a skin disorder in which itchy red blisters form on the skin.

eddy N (*-ies*) **1** a current of water running back against the main stream or current, forming a small whirlpool. **2** a movement of air, smoke or fog, etc similar to this.
➢ VB (*-ies, -ied*) TR & INTR to move or make something move in this way.

Eden N the garden where, according to the Bible, the first man and woman lived.

edge N **1** the part farthest from the middle of something; a border or boundary; the rim. **2** the area beside a cliff or steep drop. **3** the cutting side of something sharp, eg a knife. **4** sharpness or severity: **take the edge off his hunger. 5** bitterness: **There was an edge to his criticism.**
➢ VB **1** to form or make a border to something.

2 to shape the edge or border of something. **3** TR & INTR to move gradually and carefully, esp sideways. ■ **edging** N.
◆ **on edge** uneasy; nervous and irritable.

edgeways and **edgewise** ADV
1 sideways. **2** with the edge uppermost or forwards.

edgy ADJ (*-ier, -iest*) COLLOQ easily annoyed; anxious, nervous or tense. ■ **edginess** N.

edible ADJ fit to be eaten; suitable to eat.
■ **edibility** N.

edict N an order issued by any authority.

edifice N, FORMAL a building.

edify VB (*-ies, -ied*) FORMAL to improve the mind or morals of someone. ■ **edification** N.

edit VB **1** to prepare (a book, newspaper, film, etc) for publication or broadcasting, esp by making corrections or alterations. **2** to be in overall charge of the process of producing (a newspaper, etc). **3** to compile (a reference work). **4** (usu **edit out sth**) to remove (parts of a work) before printing or broadcasting, etc. **5** to prepare (a cinema film, or a TV or radio programme) by putting together material previously photographed or recorded.
➢ N a period or instance of editing.

edition N **1** the total number of copies of a book, etc printed at one time. **2** one of a series of printings of a book or periodical, etc, produced with alterations and corrections. **3** the form in which a book, etc is published: **paperback edition.**

editor N **1** a person who edits. **2** a person in charge of a newspaper or magazine, etc, or one section of it. **3** a person in charge of a radio or TV programme made up of different items, eg a news programme. **4** a person who puts together the various sections of a film, etc. ■ **editorship** N.

editorial ADJ relating to editors or editing.
➢ N an article written by the editor of a newspaper or magazine, usu one offering an opinion on a current topic. ■ **editorially** ADV.

educate VB **1** to train and teach. **2** to provide

school instruction for someone. **3** to train and improve (one's taste, etc). ■ **educative** ADJ.

educated ADJ **1** having received an education, esp to a level higher than average. **2** produced by an education, usu a good one. **3** based on experience: **an educated guess**.

education N **1** the process of teaching. **2** the instruction received. **3** the process of training and improving (one's taste, etc).
■ **educational** ADJ.

Edwardian ADJ of or characteristic of Britain in the years 1901–10, the reign of Edward VII.

eel N a fish with a long smooth snake-like body and very small fins.

eerie ADJ strange and disturbing or frightening.
■ **eerily** ADV. ■ **eeriness** N.

efface VB **1** to rub or wipe out something. **2** to block out (a memory, etc). **3** to avoid drawing attention to (oneself). ■ **effacement** N.

effect N **1** a result. **2** an impression given or produced. **3** operation; a working state: **The ban comes into effect today. 4** (usu **effects**) FORMAL property. **5** (usu **effects**) devices used to create a particular impression in a film or on a stage, etc.
➤ VB, FORMAL to do something; to make something happen, or to bring it about.
◆ **in effect** in reality; practically speaking.
◆ **take effect** to come into force.

effective ADJ **1** producing a desired result. **2** producing a pleasing effect. **3** impressive; striking. **4** in, or coming into, operation. **5** actual, rather than theoretical. ■ **effectiveness** N.

effectual ADJ **1** producing the intended result. **2** of a document, etc: valid. ■ **effectually** ADV.

effeminate ADJ of a man: having features of behaviour or appearance more typical of a woman; not manly. ■ **effeminacy** N.

effervesce VB, INTR **1** to give off bubbles of gas. **2** to behave in a lively or energetic way.
■ **effervescence** N. ■ **effervescent** ADJ.

effete ADJ, DEROG lacking strength or energy.

efficacious ADJ, FORMAL producing, or certain to produce, the intended result. ■ **efficacy** N.

efficient ADJ **1** producing satisfactory results with an economy of effort and a minimum of waste. **2** capable of competent work within a relatively short time. **3** IN COMPOUNDS economical in the use or consumption of a specified resource: **energy-efficient.**
■ **efficiency** N (**-ies**).

effigy N (**-ies**) a crude model representing a person, used as an object of hatred.

effloresce VB, INTR **1** BOT to produce flowers. **2** CHEM to form a powdery substance.
■ **efflorescence** N.

effluent N **1** liquid industrial waste or sewage released into a river, etc. **2** GEOG, etc a stream flowing from a larger body of water.

effort N **1** hard mental or physical work, or something that requires it. **2** an act of trying hard. **3** the result of an attempt; an achievement. ■ **effortless** ADJ.

effrontery N (**-ies**) shameless rudeness.

effusion N **1** the act of pouring or flowing out. **2** something that is poured out.

effusive ADJ, DEROG expressing feelings, esp happiness or enthusiasm, in an excessive or very showy way. ■ **effusiveness** N.

eg ABBREV: **exempli gratia** (Latin), for example.

egalitarian ADJ of, promoting or believing in the principle that all human beings are equal and should enjoy the same rights.
➤ N a person who upholds this principle.
■ **egalitarianism** N.

egg N **1** the reproductive cell produced by a female animal, bird, etc, from which the young one develops. Also called **ovum.**
2 a reproductive cell or developing embryo produced and deposited in a hard shell by female birds, reptiles, and certain animals.
3 a hen's egg, used as food.
➤ VB (usu **egg sb on**) COLLOQ to urge or encourage them.

eggcup N a small cup-shaped container for holding a boiled egg while it is being eaten.

egghead N, COLLOQ an intellectual.

eggplant N, N AMER, ESP US an aubergine.

eggshell N the hard porous covering of an egg.

ego N 1 personal pride. 2 PSYCHOANAL the part of a person that is conscious and thinks. 3 one's image of oneself.

egocentric ADJ, DEROG interested in oneself only.

egoism N 1 PHILOS the principle that self-interest is the basis of morality. 2 selfishness. 3 egotism. ■ **egoist** N. ■ **egoistic** or **egoistical** ADJ.

egomania N, PSYCHOL extreme self-interest. ■ **egomaniac** N.

egotism N, DEROG the fact of having a very high opinion of oneself. ■ **egotist** N. ■ **egotistic** or **egotistical** ADJ.

egregious ADJ, FORMAL outrageous; shockingly bad.

egress N, FORMAL or LAW 1 the act of leaving an enclosed place. 2 an exit. 3 the right to depart.

egret N any of various white wading birds similar to herons.

eh EXCLAM 1 used to request that a remark, etc be repeated. 2 added to a question, often implying that agreement is expected. 3 used to express surprise.

eider N a large sea duck.

eiderdown N 1 the down or soft feathers of the eider. 2 a quilt filled with this material.

eight N 1 a the cardinal number 8; b the quantity that this represents, being one more than seven. 2 any symbol for this, eg 8, VIII. 3 something, eg a garment, whose size is denoted by the number 8. 4 the eighth hour after midnight or midday: **Come at eight.** ➤ ADJ 1 totalling eight. 2 aged eight.

eighteen N 1 a the cardinal number 18; b the quantity that this represents, being one more than seventeen. 2 any symbol for this, eg 18, XVIII. 3 something, esp a garment, or a person, whose size is denoted by the number 18. 4 (written **18**) a film classified as suitable for people aged 18 and over. ➤ ADJ 1 totalling eighteen. 2 aged eighteen. ■ **eighteenth** ADJ, N.

eightfold ADJ 1 equal to eight times as much. 2 divided into or consisting of eight parts. ➤ ADV by eight times as much.

eighth (often written **8ᵗʰ**) ADJ 1 in counting: a next after seventh; b last of eight. 2 in eighth position. ➤ N 1 one of eight equal parts. 2 a fraction equal to one divided by eight.

eighties (often written **80s** or **80's**) PL N 1 (**one's eighties**) the period of time between one's eightieth and ninetieth birthdays. 2 (**the eighties**) the range of temperatures between eighty and ninety degrees. 3 (**the eighties**) the period of time between the eightieth and ninetieth years of a century.

eighty N (-*ies*) 1 a the cardinal number 80; b the quantity that this represents, being one more than seventy-nine, or the product of ten and eight. 2 any symbol for this, eg 80, LXXX. ➤ ADJ 1 totalling eighty. 2 aged eighty. ■ **eightieth** ADJ, N.

eisteddfod N a Welsh festival with competitions for poetry, drama, etc.

either ADJ 1 any one of two. 2 each of two: **on either side.** ➤ PRONOUN any one of two things or people. ➤ ADV, WITH NEGATIVES 1 also; as well: **I thought him rather unpleasant, and I didn't like his wife either.** 2 what is more; besides: **He plays golf, and he's not bad, either.**

ejaculate VB 1 TR & INTR of a male animal: to discharge (semen). 2 to exclaim. ■ **ejaculation** N.

eject VB 1 to throw out someone or something with force. 2 to force someone to leave. ■ **ejection** N. ■ **ejector** N.

eke VB (always **eke sth out**) 1 to make (a supply) last longer, eg by adding something else to it or by careful use. 2 to manage with difficulty to make (a living, etc).

elaborate ADJ **1** complicated in design; complex. **2** carefully planned or worked out. ➤ VB **1** INTR (usu **elaborate on** or **upon sth**) to add detail to it. **2** to work out something in great detail. ■ **elaboration** N.

élan N energetic style; dash.

elapse VB, INTR of time: to pass.

elastic ADJ **1** of a material: able to return to its original shape or size after being pulled or pressed out of shape. **2** of a force: caused by, or causing, such an ability. **3** flexible. **4** made of elastic.
➤ N stretchable fabric woven with strips of rubber. ■ **elasticated** ADJ. ■ **elasticity** N.

elastic band N a thin loop of rubber for keeping papers, etc together.

elate VB **1** to make someone intensely happy. **2** to fill someone with pride or optimism. ■ **elated** ADJ. ■ **elation** N.

elbow N **1** the joint where the human arm bends. **2** the part of a garment which covers this joint. **3** the corresponding joint in animals. ➤ VB **1** to push or strike something with the elbow. **2** to make (one's way through) by pushing with the elbows.

elbow-room N enough space for moving or doing something.

elder[1] ADJ **1** older. **2** (**the elder**) used before or after a person's name to distinguish them from a younger person of the same name. ➤ N **1** a person who is older. **2** (often **elders**) an older person, esp one with authority.

elder[2] N a bush or small tree with white flowers and purple-black or red berries (**elderberries**).

elderly ADJ **1** rather old. **2** bordering on old age. **3** (**the elderly**) old people as a group.

eldest ADJ oldest.
➤ N someone who is the oldest of three or more.

elect VB **1** to choose someone to be an official or representative by voting. **2** to choose something in preference to other options.
➤ ADJ, FOLLOWING ITS NOUN elected to, but not yet occupying a position: **president elect**.

election N **1** the process or act of choosing by taking a vote. **2** an instance of this.

electioneer VB, INTR to work for the election of a candidate, esp in a political campaign. ■ **electioneering** N, ADJ.

elective ADJ **1** of an office, etc: to which someone is appointed by election. **2** optional: **elective surgery**.

elector N someone who has the right to vote at an election. ■ **electoral** ADJ.

electorate N all the electors of a city or country, etc.

electric ADJ **1** (also **electrical**) relating to, produced by, worked by or generating electricity. **2** of a musical instrument: amplified electronically. **3** causing great excitement, tension or expectation. ■ **electrically** ADV.

electrical engineering N the branch of engineering concerned with the practical applications of electricity and magnetism.

electric blanket N a blanket incorporating an electric element, used for warming a bed.

electric chair N a chair used for executing criminals using a powerful electric current.

electric current N the flow of electric charge through a conductor.

electric eel N an eel-like fish, able to give electric shocks by means of an organ in its tail.

electrician N a person whose job is to install, maintain and repair electrical equipment.

electricity N **1** the energy which exists in a negative form in electrons and in a positive form in protons, and also as a flowing current usu of electrons. **2** an electric charge or current. **3** a supply of this energy to a household, etc. **4** excitement, tension or expectation.

electrify VB (**-ies**, **-ied**) **1** to give an electric charge to something. **2** to equip (eg a railway system) for the use of electricity as a power supply. **3** to cause great excitement in (eg a crowd). ■ **electrification** N.

electrocardiogram N, MED the diagram or tracing produced by an electrocardiograph.

electrocardiograph N, MED an apparatus which registers the electrical variations of the beating heart, as a diagram or tracing.

electrocute VB 1 to kill by electric shock. 2 to carry out a death sentence by means of electricity. ■ **electrocution** N.

electrode N either of the two conducting points by which electric current enters or leaves a battery or other electrical apparatus.

electroencephalogram N, MED a diagram produced by an electroencephalograph.

electroencephalograph N, MED an apparatus which registers the electrical activity of the brain, as a diagram or tracing.

electrolysis N the removal of tumours or hair roots by means of an electric current.

electrolyte N, CHEM a chemical solution that conducts electricity. ■ **electrolytic** ADJ.

electromagnet N, PHYS a piece of soft metal, usu iron, made magnetic by the passage of an electric current through a coil of wire wrapped around the metal. ■ **electromagnetic** ADJ.

electron N, PHYS a particle, present in all atoms, having a negative electric charge and responsible for carrying electricity in solids.

electronic ADJ 1 operated by means of electrical circuits, usu several very small ones. 2 produced or operated, etc, using electronic apparatus. 3 concerned with electronics. ■ **electronically** ADV.

electronic mail see under **e-mail**

electronics SING N the science that deals with the study of the behaviour of electronic circuits and their applications in machines, etc. ➤ PL N the electronic parts of something.

electron microscope N a microscope using a beam of electrons rather than a beam of light, capable of very high magnification.

electroplate VB to coat (an object) with metal, esp silver, by electrolysis.

elegant ADJ 1 having or showing good taste in dress or style, combined with dignity and gracefulness. 2 graceful. 3 simple and ingenious. ■ **elegance** N. ■ **elegantly** ADV.

elegiac ADJ, FORMAL, LITERARY mournful.

elegy N (*-ies*) a mournful or thoughtful song or poem, esp about death or loss.

element N 1 a part of anything; a component. 2 CHEM, PHYS any substance that cannot be split by chemical means into simpler substances. 3 a person or small group within a larger group. 4 a slight amount. 5 the wire coil through which an electric current is passed to produce heat in electrical appliances. 6 any one of the four substances (earth, air, fire and water) from which, according to ancient philosophy, everything is formed. 7 (**the elements**) weather conditions, esp when severe. 8 (**the elements**) basic facts or skills. 9 (**the elements**) bread and wine representing Christ's body and blood in the Eucharist. ◆ **in one's element** in the surroundings that one finds most natural and enjoyable.

elemental ADJ 1 basic or primitive. 2 of or relating to the forces of nature, esp the four elements (earth, air, fire and water). 3 immense; referring to the power of a force of nature.

elementary ADJ 1 dealing with simple or basic facts; rudimentary. 2 belonging or relating to the elements or an element.

elementary particle N, CHEM, PHYS any of the particles which make up an atom.

elephant N (*elephants* or *elephant*) the largest living land animal, with thick greyish skin, a long trunk, and two curved tusks.

elevate VB 1 to raise or lift. 2 to give a higher rank or status to someone or something. 3 to improve (a person's mind, etc).

elevated ADJ 1 very high; important. 2 intellectually advanced or very moral. 3 raised above the surrounding level.

elevation N 1 the act of elevating or state of being elevated. 2 TECHNICAL height, eg of a place above sea-level.

elevator N N AMER, ESP US a lift.

eleven N 1 a the cardinal number 11; b the quantity that this represents, being one more than ten. 2 any symbol for this, eg 11, XI. 3 something, eg a garment or a person, whose size is denoted by the number 11. 5 the eleventh hour after midnight or midday: Come at eleven.
➤ ADJ 1 totalling eleven. 2 aged eleven.
■ **eleventh** ADJ, N.

elevenses PL N (OFTEN USED WITH SING VERB) COLLOQ a mid-morning snack.

elf N (*elves*) a tiny mischievous supernatural being in human form. ■ **elfin** ADJ.

elicit VB to cause something to happen; to bring something out into the open.

elide VB, GRAM to omit (a vowel or syllable), as in I'm and we're. ■ **elision** N.

eligible ADJ 1 suitable, or deserving to be chosen (for a job, as a husband, etc). 2 having a right to something. ■ **eligibility** N.

eliminate VB 1 to get rid of or exclude. 2 to expel (waste matter) from the body. 3 to exclude someone or something from a competition by defeat. 4 SLANG to kill someone. ■ **elimination** N. ■ **eliminator** N.

elite or **élite** N 1 the best, most important or most powerful people within society. 2 the best of a group or profession.

elitism N 1 the belief in the need for a powerful social elite. 2 the belief in the natural social superiority of some people. ■ **elitist** ADJ, N.

elixir N 1 in medieval times: a liquid preparation believed to give people everlasting life or to turn base metals into gold. 2 any medical preparation claimed to cure all illnesses.

Elizabethan ADJ of the reign of Elizabeth I of England (1558–1603).
➤ N a person living during this time.

elk N (*elks* or *elk*) 1 in Europe and Asia: the moose. 2 N AMER the wapiti.

ellipse N, GEOM a regular oval, as formed by a diagonal cut through a cone above the base.

elliptical or **elliptic** ADJ 1 GEOM relating to, or having the shape of, an ellipse. 2 of speech or writing: so concise as to be unclear.

elm N 1 a tall deciduous tree with broad leaves. 2 (also **elmwood**) the wood of this tree.

elocution N the art of speaking clearly and effectively. ■ **elocutionist** N.

elongate VB to lengthen or stretch something out. ■ **elongation** N.

elope VB, INTR to run away secretly in order to get married. ■ **elopement** N.

eloquence N 1 the art or power of using speech to impress, move or persuade. 2 persuasive, fine and effectual language. ■ **eloquent** ADJ.

else ADV, ADJ different from or in addition to something or someone known or already mentioned: Where else can you buy it?

elsewhere ADV somewhere else.

elucidate VB to make clear; to shed light on. ■ **elucidation** N.

elude VB 1 to escape or avoid something by quickness or cleverness. 2 to fail to be understood or remembered by someone.

elusive ADJ 1 difficult to find or catch. 2 difficult to understand or remember. ■ **elusiveness** N.

elver N a young eel.

emaciated ADJ made extremely thin, esp through illness or starvation. ■ **emaciation** N.

e-mail or **email** N (in full **electronic mail**) 1 a system for transmitting messages and computer files electronically from one computer to another, eg over the Internet. 2 correspondence sent in this way.
➤ VB to send someone an electronic message.

emanate VB, INTR 1 to emerge or originate. 2 to flow; to issue. ■ **emanation** N.

emancipate VB to set someone free from slavery, or from some other social or political restraint. ■ **emancipation** N.

emasculate VB 1 to reduce the force, strength or effectiveness of. 2 to castrate (a man or male animal). ■ **emasculation** N.

embalm VB **1** to preserve (a dead body) from decay. **2** to preserve something unchanged.

embankment N **1** a bank or wall of earth made to enclose a waterway. **2** a mound built to carry a road or railway over a low-lying place. **3** a slope of grass, earth, etc which rises from either side of a road or railway.

embargo N (-oes) **1** an official order forbidding something, esp trade with another country. **2** any restriction or prohibition.
➤ VB (-oes, -oed) to place under an embargo.

embark VB, TR & INTR to go on board a ship or aircraft. ■ **embarkation** N.
◆ **embark on sth** to begin (a task, etc).

embarrass VB **1** TR & INTR to make someone feel, or become anxious, self-conscious or ashamed. **2** to confuse or perplex.
■ **embarrassed** ADJ. ■ **embarrassing** ADJ.
■ **embarrassment** N.

embassy N (-ies) **1** the official residence of an ambassador. **2** an ambassador and his or her staff.

embed VB (-dd-) (also **imbed**) to set or fix something firmly and deeply.

embellish VB **1** to make (a story, etc) more interesting by adding extra details. **2** to beautify something with decoration.
■ **embellishment** N.

ember N **1** a piece of glowing or smouldering coal or wood. **2** (**embers**) the smouldering remains of a fire.

embezzle VB to take or use dishonestly (eg money with which one has been entrusted).
■ **embezzlement** N. ■ **embezzler** N.

embitter VB to make someone feel bitter.

emblazon VB to decorate with a coat of arms or some other bright design.

emblem N an object chosen to represent an idea, a country, etc. ■ **emblematic** ADJ.

embody VB (-ies, -ied) **1** to be an expression or a representation of something in words, actions or form; to typify or personify. **2** to

include or incorporate. ■ **embodiment** N.

embolism N, PATHOL the blocking of a blood vessel by an air bubble, a blood clot, etc.

emboss VB to carve or mould a raised design on (a surface).

embrace VB **1** to hold someone closely in the arms, affectionately or as a greeting. **2** to take (eg an opportunity) eagerly, or accept (eg a religion) wholeheartedly. **3** to include.
➤ N **1** an act of embracing. **2** a loving hug.

embrocation N a lotion for rubbing into the skin, eg to soothe sore or pulled muscles.

embroider VB **1** to decorate (cloth) with sewn designs. **2** to make (a story, etc) more interesting by adding details, usu untrue ones.
■ **embroidery** N.

embroil VB to involve in a dispute or argument.

embryo N, BIOL **1** in animals: the developing young organism until hatching or birth. **2** in humans: the developing young organism during the first seven weeks after conception.
■ **embryonic** ADJ.

embryology N the study of embryos.

emend VB to edit (a text), removing errors and making improvements. ■ **emendation** N.

emerald N **1** a deep green gemstone. **2** (also **emerald green**) its colour.

emerge VB, INTR **1** to come out from hiding or into view. **2** to become known or apparent.
■ **emergence** N. ■ **emergent** ADJ.

emergency N (-ies) **1** an unexpected and serious happening which calls for immediate action. **2 a** a serious injury needing immediate treatment; **b** a patient suffering such an injury.

emery N (-ies) a hard mineral, usu used in powder form, for polishing or abrading.

emery board N a strip of card coated with emery or other abrasive, for filing one's nails.

emetic ADJ, MED making one vomit.
➤ N an emetic medicine.

emigrate VB, INTR to leave one's native country and settle in another. ■ **emigrant**

N, ADJ. ■ **emigration** N.

émigré N (*émigrés*) a person who has emigrated, usu for political reasons.

eminence N 1 honour, distinction or prestige. 2 an area of high ground.
◆ **Your Eminence** a title of honour used in speaking to a cardinal.

eminent ADJ 1 famous and admired. 2 distinguished; outstanding.

eminently ADV 1 very. 2 obviously.

emir N a title given to various Muslim rulers.■ **emirate** N.

emissary N (*-ies*) a person sent on a mission, esp on behalf of a government.

emission N 1 the act of emitting. 2 something emitted.

emit VB (*-tt-*) to give out (light, heat, a smell, etc).

emollient ADJ, MED soothing the skin.
➤ N, MED a substance which soothes the skin.

emolument N, FORMAL money gained through employment, eg salary or fees.

emotion N a strong feeling.

emotional ADJ 1 referring or relating to the emotions. 2 causing or expressing emotion. 3 tending to express emotions easily or excessively. 4 based on emotions, rather than rational thought. ■ **emotionally** ADV.

emotive ADJ tending to excite emotion.

empathize or **-ise** VB, INTR (usu **empathize with sb**) to share their feelings.

empathy N the ability to share, understand and feel another person's feelings.
■ **empathetic** or **empathic** ADJ.

emperor N the male ruler of an empire.

emphasis N (*-ses*) 1 (usu **emphasis on sth**) special importance or attention given to it. 2 greater force or loudness on certain words to show that they are significant. 3 force or firmness of expression.

emphasize or **-ise** VB to put emphasis on something.

emphatic ADJ 1 expressed with or expressing emphasis. 2 speaking firmly and forcefully.
■ **emphatically** ADV.

emphysema N, PATHOL the presence of air in the body tissues.

empire N 1 a group of nations or states under the control of a single ruling power. 2 the period of time during which such control is exercised. 3 a large commercial or industrial organization controlling many separate firms.

empirical and **empiric** ADJ based on experiment, observation or experience, rather than on theory. ■ **empirically** ADV.

employ VB 1 to give work, usu paid work, to someone. 2 to use.

employee N a person who works for another in return for payment.

employer N a person or company that employs workers.

employment N 1 the act of employing or the state of being employed. 2 an occupation, esp regular paid work.

emporium N (*-iums* or *-ia*) FORMAL a shop, esp a large one that sells a wide variety of goods.

empower VB (usu **empower sb to do sth**) to give them authority or power to do it.

empress N 1 the female ruler of an empire. 2 the wife or widow of an emperor.

empty ADJ (*-ier, -iest*) 1 having nothing inside. 2 not occupied, inhabited or furnished. 3 not likely to be carried out: **empty promises**. 4 completely without it: **empty of meaning**.
➤ VB (*-ies, -ied*) TR & INTR 1 to make or become empty. 2 to tip, pour or fall out of a container.
➤ N (*-ies*) COLLOQ an empty container, esp a bottle. ■ **emptiness** N.

empty-headed ADJ foolish or frivolous.

emu N a large flightless Australian bird.

emulate VB 1 to try hard to equal or be better than. 2 to imitate. ■ **emulation** N.

emulsify VB (*-ies, -ied*) TR & INTR to make or become an emulsion. ■ **emulsifier** N.

emulsion N 1 CHEM a colloid consisting of a stable mixture of two immiscible liquids (such as oil and water), in which small droplets of one liquid are dispersed uniformly throughout the other. 2 PHOTOG the light–sensitive material used to coat photographic film and paper, etc. 3 water-based paint.
➤ VB, COLLOQ to apply emulsion paint to something.

enable VB 1 to make someone able; to give them the necessary means or authority (to do something). 2 to make something possible.

enact VB 1 to act or perform something on stage or in real life. 2 to establish by law.

enamel N 1 a hardened coloured glass–like substance applied as a decorative or protective covering to metal or glass. 2 any paint or varnish which gives a finish similar to this. 3 the hard white covering of the teeth.
➤ VB (-ll-; US -l-) to cover or decorate something with enamel.

enamoured or (US) **enamored** ADJ 1 (USU **enamoured with**) in love with. 2 (USU **enamoured of**) very fond of.

encamp VB, TR & INTR to settle in a camp. ■ **encampment** N.

encapsulate VB 1 to express concisely the main points or ideas of something, or capture its essence. 2 to enclose something in a capsule. ■ **encapsulation** N.

encase VB 1 to enclose something in, or as if in, a case. 2 to surround or cover.

encephalitis N, PATHOL inflammation of the brain.

enchant VB 1 to charm or delight. 2 to put a magic spell on. ■ **enchanted** ADJ. ■ **enchanting** ADJ. ■ **enchantment** N.

enchilada N a Mexican flour tortilla with a filling, served with a chilli–flavoured sauce.

encircle VB to surround, or form a circle round, something. ■ **encirclement** N.

enclave N a small country or state entirely surrounded by foreign territory.

enclose VB 1 to put something inside a letter or in its envelope. 2 to shut in or surround.

enclosure N 1 the process of enclosing or being enclosed, esp with reference to common land. 2 land surrounded by a fence or wall. 3 an enclosed space at a sporting event. 4 an additional item included with a letter.

encompass VB 1 to include or contain something. 2 to surround something.

encore N an additional performance after the end of a concert, etc.
➤ EXCLAM an enthusiastic call from the audience for such a performance.

encounter VB 1 to meet, esp unexpectedly. 2 to meet with (difficulties, etc).
➤ N 1 a chance meeting. 2 a fight or battle.

encourage VB 1 to give support, confidence or hope to someone. 2 to urge someone to do something. ■ **encouragement** N.

encroach VB, INTR 1 to intrude or extend gradually (on someone else's land, etc). 2 to overstep proper or agreed limits. ■ **encroachment** N.

encrust VB to cover something with a thick hard coating. ■ **encrustation** N.

encrypt VB to put information (eg computer data or TV signals) into a coded form.

encumber VB 1 to hamper or impede. 2 to burden with a load or debt.

encumbrance N a hindrance or burden.

encyclopedia or **encyclopaedia** N a reference work containing information on every branch of knowledge, or on one particular branch, usu arranged in alphabetical order. ■ **encyclopedic** ADJ.

end N 1 the point or part farthest from the beginning, or either of the points or parts farthest from the middle, where something stops. 2 a finish or conclusion. 3 (**the end**) COLLOQ the last straw; the limit. 4 a piece left over: **a cigarette end**. 5 death or destruction: **meet one's end**. 6 an object or purpose: **The end justifies the means.**
➤ VB, TR & INTR 1 to finish or cause something to

finish. **2** INTR to reach a conclusion.

◆ **end up** COLLOQ to arrive or find oneself eventually or finally.

◆ **on end 1** vertical; standing straight up. **2** continuously; without a pause.

endanger VB to put in danger; to expose to possible loss or injury.

endangered species N any plant or animal species in danger of extinction.

endear VB (usu **endear sb to**) to make them beloved or liked. ■ **endearing** ADJ.

endearment N **1** a word or phrase expressing affection. **2** a caress.

endeavour or (US) **endeavor** VB to try to do, esp seriously and with effort.
➤ N a determined attempt.

endemic ADJ regularly occurring in a particular area or among a particular group of people.

ending N the end, esp of a story or poem, etc.

endive N a plant, related to chicory, whose crisp leaves are used in salads.

endless ADJ having no end, or seeming to have no end. ■ **endlessly** ADV.

endocrine ADJ of a gland: secreting hormones directly into the bloodstream.

endorphin N, BIOCHEM any of a group of naturally-occurring chemical compounds in the brain that have similar pain-relieving properties to morphine.

endorse VB **1** to sign the back of (a document, esp the back of a cheque) to specify oneself or another person as payee. **2** to make a note of an offence on (a driving licence). **3** to state one's approval of or support for something.
■ **endorsement** N.

endoscope N, MED an instrument for viewing internal body cavities and organs.

endoskeleton N, ZOOL invertebrates: an internal skeleton made of bone or cartilage.

endow VB **1** to provide a source of income for (a hospital or place of learning, etc), often by a bequest. **2** (often **be endowed with sth**) to have a quality or ability, etc.

endowment N **1** a sum endowed. **2** a quality or skill, etc with which a person is endowed.

endure VB **1** to bear something patiently; to put up with it. **2** INTR, FORMAL to continue to exist; to last. ■ **endurance** N. ■ **enduring** ADJ.

endways and (esp N AMER) **endwise** ADV **1** with the end forward or upward. **2** end to end.

enema N (**-mas** or **-mata**) MED **1** the injection of a liquid into the rectum, eg to clean it out or to introduce medication. **2** the liquid injected.

enemy N (**-ies**) **1** a person who is actively opposed to someone else. **2** a hostile nation or force, or a member of it. **3** an opponent or adversary. **4** a person or thing that opposes or acts against someone or something.
➤ ADJ hostile.

energize or **-ise** VB **1** to stimulate, invigorate or enliven. **2** to provide energy for the operation of (a machine, etc). ■ **energizer** N.

energy N (**-ies**) **1** the capacity for vigorous activity; liveliness or vitality. **2** force or forcefulness. **3** PHYS the capacity to do work.
■ **energetic** ADJ.

enervate VB **1** to take energy or strength from something. **2** to deprive someone of moral or mental vigour. ■ **enervation** N.

enfeeble VB, FORMAL to make someone weak.

enfold VB **1** to wrap up. **2** to embrace.

enforce VB **1** to cause (a law or decision) to be carried out. **2** to press (an argument). **3** to persist in (a demand). ■ **enforceable** ADJ.
■ **enforcement** N.

enfranchise VB, FORMAL to give someone the right to vote in elections.

engage VB **1** to take someone on as a worker. **2** to book or reserve (eg a table or room). **3** TR & INTR, MIL to come or bring into battle: **engage with the enemy**. **4** TR & INTR to cause part of a machine to fit into and lock with another part.

engaged ADJ **1** bound by a promise to marry. **2** not free or vacant; occupied; in use.

engagement N **1** the act of engaging. **2** a firm agreement between two people to marry. **3** an arrangement made in advance; an appointment. **4** MIL a battle.

engaging ADJ charming; attractive.

engender VB to produce or cause (esp feelings or emotions).

engine N **1** a machine used to convert some form of energy into mechanical energy. **2** a railway locomotive.

engineer N **1** someone who designs, makes, or works with machinery, including electrical equipment. **2** an officer in charge of a ship's engines. **3** someone who contrives to bring something about.
➤ VB **1** often DEROG to arrange or bring something about by skill or deviousness. **2** to design or construct something as an engineer.

engineering N the application of scientific knowledge, esp to practical problems of design, construction, operation and maintenance of devices.

English ADJ **1** of England. **2** relating to English, the language.
➤ N **1** (**the English**) the citizens or inhabitants of, or people born in, England. **2** the native language of Britain, N America, much of the Commonwealth and some other countries.

engrained a variant of **ingrained**

engrave VB **1** to carve (letters or designs) on stone, metal, etc. **2** to decorate (stone, etc) in this way. **3** to fix or impress something deeply on the mind, etc. ■ **engraver** N.

engraving N **1** the art or process of carving or incising designs on wood or metal, etc, esp for the purpose of printing. **2** a print taken from an engraved metal plate, etc.

engross VB to take up someone's attention completely.

engulf VB **1** to swallow something up completely. **2** to overwhelm.

enhance VB to improve or increase the value, quality or intensity of something (esp something already good). ■ **enhancement** N.

enigma N **1** a puzzle or riddle. **2** a mysterious person, thing or situation. ■ **enigmatic** ADJ.

enjoy VB **1** to find pleasure in something. **2** to have, experience or have the benefit of something good. ■ **enjoyable** ADJ. ■ **enjoyment** N.

enlarge VB **1** TR & INTR to make or become larger. **2** to reproduce (a photograph, etc) in a larger form. ■ **enlargement** N.

enlighten VB **1** to give more information to someone. **2** to free someone from ignorance or superstition.

enlightenment N **1** the act of enlightening. **2** freedom from ignorance or superstition.

enlist VB **1** INTR to join one of the armed forces. **2** to obtain the support and help of someone; to obtain (support and help). ■ **enlistment** N.

enliven VB to make active or cheerful.

enmesh VB to catch or trap something in a net, or as if in a net; to entangle.

enmity N (*-ies*) **1** the state or quality of being an enemy. **2** ill-will; hostility.

ennoble VB **1** to make noble or dignified. **2** to make a member of the nobility.

ennui N, LITERARY boredom or discontent caused by a lack of activity or excitement.

enormity N (*-ies*) **1** outrageousness or wickedness. **2** an outrageous or wicked act.

enormous ADJ extremely large; huge.

enough ADJ in the number or quantity needed; sufficient: **enough food to eat**.
➤ ADV **1** to the necessary degree or extent. **2** fairly: **She's pretty enough, I suppose.** **3** quite: **Oddly enough, I can't remember.**
➤ PRONOUN the amount needed.

enquire, enquiring, enquiry variants of **inquire**, etc.

enrage VB to make someone extremely angry.

enrapture VB to give intense pleasure or joy to someone. ■ **enraptured** or **enrapt** ADJ.

enrich VB **1** to make something rich or richer, esp in quality, value or flavour, etc. **2** to make wealthy or wealthier. **3** to fertilize (soil, etc). ■ **enriched** ADJ. ■ **enrichment** N.

enrol or (US) **enroll** VB (*-ll-*) **1** to add the name of (a person) to a list or roll, eg of members or pupils. **2** to secure the membership or participation of someone. **3** INTR to add one's own name to such a list; to become a member. ■ **enrolment** N.

en route ADV on the way.

ensconce VB (often **be ensconced**) **1** to settle comfortably or safely. **2** to hide safely.

ensemble N **1** a small group of musicians who regularly perform together. **2** an outfit. **3** all the parts of a thing considered as a whole.

enshrine VB to enter and protect (a right or idea) in the laws or constitution of a state, etc.

ensign N **1** the flag of a nation or regiment. **2** a coloured flag with a smaller union flag in one corner.

enslave VB to make someone into a slave. ■ **enslavement** N.

ensnare VB to catch in, or as if in, a trap; to trick or lead dishonestly (into doing something).

ensue VB INTR **1** to follow; to happen after. **2** to result from. ■ **ensuing** ADJ.

en suite ADV, ADJ forming, or attached as part of, a single unit or set.

ensure VB to make something certain.

entail VB **1** to have something as a necessary result or requirement. **2** LAW to bequeath (property) to one's descendants, not allowing them the option to sell it. ■ **entailment** N.

entangle VB **1** to cause to get caught in some obstacle, eg a net. **2** to involve in difficulties. **3** to make something complicated or confused. ■ **entanglement** N.

enter VB **1** TR & INTR to go or come in or into (eg a room). **2** TR & INTR to register or join in a competition. **3** to record in a book, diary, etc. **4** to join (a profession or society, etc). **5** to submit or present: **enter a complaint**. **6** INTR, THEAT to come on to the stage.
◆ **enter into 1** to begin to take part in. **2** to

become involved in; to participate actively or enthusiastically in.

enteritis N, PATHOL inflammation of the intestines, esp the small intestine.

enterprise N **1** a project or undertaking, esp one that requires boldness and initiative. **2** boldness and initiative. **3** a business firm.

enterprising ADJ showing initiative.

entertain VB **1** to provide amusement or recreation for someone. **2** TR & INTR to give hospitality to (a guest), esp in the form of a meal. **3** to consider or be willing to adopt (an idea or suggestion, etc). ■ **entertainer** N.

entertaining ADJ interesting and amusing.

entertainment N **1** something that entertains, eg a theatrical show. **2** the act of entertaining. **3** amusement or recreation.

enthral or (esp US) **enthrall** VB (*-ll-*) to fascinate; to hold the attention or grip the imagination of someone. ■ **enthralment** N.

enthrone VB to place someone on a throne.

enthuse VB, TR & INTR to be or make enthusiastic.

enthusiasm N lively or passionate interest.

enthusiast N someone filled with enthusiasm, esp for a particular subject; a fan or devotee. ■ **enthusiastic** ADJ. ■ **enthusiastically** ADV.

entice VB to tempt or persuade, by arousing hopes or desires or by promising a reward. ■ **enticement** N. ■ **enticing** ADJ.

entire ADJ **1** whole or complete. **2** absolute or total. ■ **entirely** ADV.

entirety N (*-ies*) completeness; the whole.

entitle VB to give a title or name to (a book, etc). ■ **entitlement** N.
◆ **entitle to** to give a right to have or to do something.

entity N (*-ies*) **1** something that has a physical existence, as opposed to a quality or mood. **2** the essential nature of something.

entomb VB to put (a body) in a tomb.

entomology N the scientific study of insects.

■ **entomological** ADJ. ■ **entomologist** N.

entourage N a group of followers.

entrails PL N **1** the internal organs of a person or animal. **2** LITERARY the inner parts of anything.

entrance¹ N **1** a way in, eg a door. **2** FORMAL the act of entering. **3** the right to enter.

entrance² VB **1** to grip or captivate someone's attention and imagination. **2** to put someone into a trance. ■ **entrancement** N.

entrancing ADJ gripping the imagination; fascinating; delightful.

entrant N someone who enters something, esp an examination or competition.

entrap VB **1** to catch in a trap. **2** to trick into doing something. ■ **entrapment** N.

entreat VB, TR & INTR to ask passionately or desperately; to beg. ■ **entreaty** N (*-ies*).

entrée N **1** a small dish served after the fish course and before the main course at a formal dinner. **2** chiefly US a main course.

entrench VB **1** to fix or establish something firmly, often too firmly. **2** to fortify something with trenches dug around.

entrepreneur N someone who engages in business enterprises, often with some personal financial risk. ■ **entrepreneurial** ADJ.

entropy N (*-ies*) PHYS a measure of the amount of disorder in a system.

entrust VB (usu **entrust sth to sb,** or **sb with sth**) to give it to them to deal with.

entry N (*-ies*) **1** the act of coming or going in. **2** the right to enter. **3** a place of entering. **4** an item written on a list or in a book, etc.

entwine VB to wind or twist (two or more things) together.

enumerate VB **1** to list one by one. **2** to count. ■ **enumeration** N.

enunciate VB **1** TR & INTR to pronounce words clearly. **2** to state something formally. ■ **enunciation** N.

envelop VB **1** to cover or wrap completely. **2** to obscure or conceal. ■ **envelopment** N.

envelope N **1** a thin flat sealable paper packet or cover, esp for a letter. **2** a cover or wrapper of any kind.

enviable ADJ likely to cause envy; highly desirable. ■ **enviably** ADV.

envious ADJ feeling or showing envy.

environment N **1** the surroundings or conditions within which something or someone exists or operates. **2** (usu **the environment**) the combination of external conditions that surround and influence a living organism. ■ **environmental** ADJ.

environmentalist N someone concerned about the harmful effects of human activity on the environment. ■ **environmentalism** N.

environs PL N surrounding areas, esp the outskirts of a town or city.

envisage VB **1** to picture something in the mind. **2** to consider as likely in the future.

envoy N **1** a diplomat ranking next below an ambassador. **2** a messenger or agent.

envy N (*-ies*) **1** a feeling of resentment or regretful desire for another person's qualities, better fortune or success. **2** anything that arouses envy: She is the envy of his friends. ➤ VB (*-ies, -ied*) **1** feel envy towards someone. **2** to covet. **3** (**envy sb sth**) to feel envy towards them on account of (their success, etc).

enzyme N a specialized protein molecule that acts as a catalyst for biochemical reactions in living cells. ■ **enzymatic** or **enzymic** ADJ.

eon or **aeon** N **1** an endless or immeasurable period of time. **2** GEOL the largest unit of geological time, consisting of a number of eras.

epaulette or (chiefly US) **epaulet** N a decoration on the shoulder.

épée N a sword with a narrow flexible blade.

ephemeral ADJ lasting a short time.

epic N **1** a long narrative poem of heroic acts, the birth and death of nations, etc. **2** a long adventure story or film.

➤ ADJ of or like an epic.

epicentre N the point on the Earth's surface which is directly above the focus of an earthquake.

epicure N someone who has refined taste, esp one who enjoys good food and drink.
■ **epicurism** N.

epicurean N someone who likes pleasure and good living; an epicure. Also AS ADJ.

epidemic N 1 a sudden outbreak of infectious disease which spreads rapidly and affects large numbers in a particular area for a limited period of time. 2 a sudden and extensive spread of anything undesirable.
➤ ADJ of or like an epidemic.

epidermis N, BIOL the outermost layer of a plant or animal, which serves to protect the underlying tissues from infection, injury and water loss. ■ **epidermal** ADJ.

epidural N, MED (in full **epidural anaesthetic**) the injection of an anaesthetic to remove all sensation below the waist.

epigram N 1 a witty or sarcastic saying. 2 a short poem with such an ending.
■ **epigrammatic** ADJ.

epigraph N an inscription on a building.

epilepsy N, PATHOL any of a group of disorders of the nervous system characterized by recurring attacks that involve impairment, or sudden loss, of consciousness.

epileptic ADJ of or suffering from epilepsy.
➤ N someone who suffers from epilepsy.

epilogue or (US) **epilog** N 1 the closing section of a book or programme, etc. 2 a speech at the end of a play.

Epiphany N (-*ies*) CHRISTIANITY a festival on 6 January which commemorates the showing of Christ to the three wise men.

episcopacy N (-*ies*) 1 government by bishops. 2 bishops as a group. 3 the position or period of office of a bishop.

episcopal ADJ 1 of or belonging to bishops. 2 governed by bishops.

episcopalian ADJ 1 of or belonging to an episcopal church. 2 advocating church government by bishops.
➤ N a member of an episcopal church.
■ **episcopalianism** N.

episode N 1 one of several events or distinct periods making up a longer sequence. 2 one of the separate parts of a serial.

episodic ADJ 1 consisting of several distinct periods. 2 occurring at intervals; sporadic.

epistle N 1 LITERARY a letter. 2 (usu **Epistle**) CHRISTIANITY each of the letters written by Christ's Apostles, which form part of the New Testament. ■ **epistolary** ADJ.

epitaph N 1 an inscription on a gravestone. 2 a short commemorative speech or piece of writing in a similar style.

epithet N an adjective or short descriptive phrase which captures the particular quality of the person or thing it describes.

epitome N a person or thing that is the embodiment or a perfect example of a quality.

epitomize or **-ise** VB to typify or personify.

epoch N 1 a major division or period of history, or of a person's life, etc, usu marked by some important event. 2 GEOL an interval of geological time representing a subdivision of a period, and during which a particular series of rocks was formed. ■ **epochal** ADJ.

epoch-making ADJ highly significant or decisive.

eponymous ADJ of a character in a story, etc: having the name used as the title.

epoxy N (-*ies*) (also **epoxy resin**) CHEM any of a group of synthetic resins, that form strong adhesive bonds.

Epsom salts SING OR PL N a magnesium sulphate, used as a medicine.

equable ADJ 1 never showing great variations or extremes. 2 even-tempered.

equal ADJ 1 the same in size, amount or value, etc. 2 evenly balanced. 3 having the same status; having or entitled to the same rights.

➤ N a person or thing of the same age, rank, ability, etc.

➤ VB (*-ll-*) **1** to be the same in amount, value, size, etc as someone or something. **2** to be as good as someone or something; to match. **3** to achieve something which matches (a previous achievement or achiever). ■ **equality** N (*-ies*). ■ **equally** ADV.
◆ **equal to sth** having the necessary ability for it.

equalize or **-ise** VB **1** TR & INTR to make or become equal. **2** INTR to reach the same score as an opponent, after being behind. ■ **equalization** N. ■ **equalizer** N.

equanimity N composure.

equate VB (usu **equate with sth**) to be equivalent to it.

equation N **1** MATH a mathematical statement of the equality between two expressions involving constants and/or variables. **2** the act of equating.

equator N **1** (often **the Equator**) the imaginary great circle that passes around the Earth at latitude 0 at an equal distance from the North and South Poles. **2** ASTRON the celestial equator. ■ **equatorial** ADJ.

equerry N (*-ies*) an official who acts as attendant to a member of a royal family.

equestrian ADJ of or relating to horse–riding or horses. ■ **equestrianism** N.

equidistant ADJ equally distant.

equilateral ADJ having all sides of equal length.

equilibrium N (*-ia* or *-iums*) **1** a calm and composed state of mind. **2** a state of balance.

equine ADJ, FORMAL of or like a horse or horses.

equinoctial ADJ happening on or near an equinox.

equinox N either of the two occasions on which the Sun crosses the equator, making night and day equal in length, occurring about 21 March and 23 September.

equip VB (*-pp-*) to fit out or provide someone or something with the necessary tools, supplies, abilities, etc.

equipment N the clothes, machines, tools or instruments, etc necessary for a particular kind of work or activity.

equitable ADJ fair and just. ■ **equitably** ADV.

equity N (*-ies*) **1** fair or just conditions or treatment. **2** LAW the concept of natural justice, as opposed to common law or statute law. **3** the excess in value of a property over the mortgage and other charges held on it.

equivalent ADJ equal in value, power, meaning, etc.
➤ N an equivalent thing or amount, etc. ■ **equivalence** N.

equivocal ADJ **1** ambiguous; of doubtful meaning. **2** of an uncertain nature. **3** questionable, suspicious or mysterious. ■ **equivocally** ADV.

equivocate VB, INTR to use ambiguous words in order to deceive or to avoid answering a question. ■ **equivocation** N.

era N **1** a distinct period in history marked by or beginning at an important event. **2** GEOL the second largest unit of geological time, representing a subdivision of an eon.

eradicate VB to get rid of something completely. ■ **eradication** N.

erase VB **1** to rub out (pencil marks, etc). **2** to remove all trace of something. **3** to destroy (a recording) on audio or video tape. ■ **erasable** ADJ. ■ **eraser** N. ■ **erasure** N.

ere PREP, CONJ, now only POETIC before.

erect ADJ **1** upright; not bent or leaning. **2** PHYSIOL of the penis, clitoris or nipples: enlarged and rigid through being filled with blood.
➤ VB **1** to put up or to build something. **2** to set or put (a pole or flag, etc) in a vertical position. **3** to establish something. ■ **erection** N.

ergo ADV, FORMAL OR LOGIC therefore.

ermine N (**ermine** or **ermines**) **1** the stoat in its winter phase, when its fur has turned white.

2 the fur of this animal.

erode VB, TR & INTR to wear away, destroy or be destroyed gradually.

erogenous ADJ of areas or zones of the body: sensitive to sexual stimulation.

erosion N the loosening, fragmentation and transport from one place to another of rock material by various means.

erotic ADJ arousing; referring or relating to sexual desire, or giving sexual pleasure. ■ **erotically** ADV.

erotica PL N erotic literature or pictures, etc.

eroticism N **1** interest in, or pursuit of, sexual sensations. **2** the use of erotic images and symbols in art and literature, etc.

err VB, INTR **1** to make a mistake, be wrong, or do wrong. **2** to sin.

errand N **1** a short journey made in order to get or do something, esp for someone else. **2** the purpose of such a journey.

errant ADJ, LITERARY **1** doing wrong; erring. **2** wandering in search of adventure.

erratic ADJ **1** irregular; having no fixed pattern or course. **2** unpredictable in behaviour. ■ **erratically** ADV.

erratum N (-*ta*) FORMAL an error in writing or printing.

erroneous ADJ wrong or mistaken.

error N **1** a mistake, inaccuracy or misapprehension. **2** the state of being mistaken. **3** the possible discrepancy between an estimate and an actual value or amount: *a margin of error.*

ersatz ADJ, DEROG substitute; imitation.

erstwhile ADJ, FORMAL former; previous.

erudite ADJ showing or having a great deal of knowledge. ■ **erudition** N.

erupt VB, INTR **1** of a volcano: to throw out lava, ash and gases. **2** to break out suddenly and violently. **3** of a skin blemish or rash: to appear suddenly and in a severe form. ■ **eruption** N.

escalate VB, TR & INTR to increase or be increased rapidly in scale or degree, etc. ■ **escalation** N. ■ **escalatory** ADJ.

escalator N a type of conveyor belt which forms a continuous moving staircase.

escalope N, COOKERY a thin slice of boneless meat, esp veal.

escapade N a daring, adventurous or unlawful act.

escape VB **1** INTR to gain freedom. **2** to manage to avoid (punishment or disease, etc). **3** not to be noticed or remembered by someone. **4** INTR of a gas or liquid, etc: to leak out or get out. ➤ N **1** an act of escaping. **2** a means of escape. **3** the avoidance of danger or harm: *a narrow escape.* **4** a leak or release.

escapee N someone who has escaped, esp from prison.

escapism N the means of escaping, or the tendency to escape, from unpleasant reality into daydreams or fantasy. ■ **escapist** ADJ, N.

escapology N the art of freeing oneself from chains and other constraints, esp as theatrical entertainment. ■ **escapologist** N.

escarpment N, GEOL a more or less continuous line of very steep slopes.

Escherichia coli N, BIOL a bacterium that occurs in the intestines of vertebrates including humans, and which sometimes causes disease.

eschew VB, FORMAL to avoid, keep away from, or abstain from. ■ **eschewal** N.

escort N **1** one or more people or vehicles, etc accompanying another or others for protection, guidance, or as a mark of honour. **2** someone of the opposite sex asked or hired to accompany another at a social event. ➤ VB to accompany as an escort.

escutcheon N a shield decorated with a coat of arms.
◆ **a blot on the escutcheon** FACETIOUS a stain on one's good reputation.

Eskimo N (*Eskimos* or *Eskimo*) Inuit. Also ADJ.

esoteric ADJ understood only by those few

people who have special knowledge.

ESP ABBREV extra-sensory perception.

espadrille N a type of light canvas shoe.

especial ADJ special.

especially ADV more than in other cases.

Esperanto N a language invented in 1887 for international use. **Also** AS ADJ.

espionage N the activity of spying, or the use of spies to gather information.

esplanade N a long wide pavement next to a beach.

espouse VB 1 FORMAL to adopt or give one's support to. 2 OLD USE to marry, or to give in marriage. ■ **espousal** N.

espresso or **expresso** N coffee made by forcing boiling water through ground coffee beans.

esprit de corps N loyalty to, or concern for the honour of, a group to which one belongs.

esquire N a title used after a man's name when no other form of address is used, esp when addressing letters.

essay N a short formal piece of writing, usu on a single subject. ■ **essayist** N.

essence N 1 the basic distinctive part or quality of something, which determines its nature or character. 2 a liquid obtained from a plant or drug, etc, which has its properties in concentrated form.

essential ADJ 1 absolutely necessary. 2 of the basic or inner nature of something.
➤ N 1 something necessary. 2 (often **the essentials**) a basic or fundamental element, principle or piece of information.
■ **essentially** ADV.

establish VB 1 to settle someone firmly in a position, place or job, etc. 2 to set up (eg a university or a business). 3 to find, show or prove something.

establishment N 1 the act of establishing. 2 a business, its premises or its staff. 3 a public or government institution: **a research**

establishment. 4 (**the Establishment**) the group of people in a country, society or community who hold power.

estate N 1 a large piece of land owned by a person or group of people. 2 an area of land on which development of a particular kind has taken place: **housing estate • industrial estate**. 3 LAW a person's total possessions (property or money, etc), esp at death. 4 an estate car.

estate agent N a person whose job is the buying and selling of property.

estate car N a car with a large area behind the rear seats for luggage, etc, and a rear door.

esteem VB to value, respect or think highly of someone or something.
➤ N high regard or respect. ■ **esteemed** ADJ.

estimable ADJ worthy of respect.

estimate VB 1 to judge or calculate (size, amount or value, etc) roughly or without measuring. 2 to have or form an opinion (that …); to think. 3 to submit to a possible client a statement of (the likely cost) of a job.
➤ N 1 a rough assessment (of size, etc).
2 a calculation of the probable cost of a job.
■ **estimation** N. ■ **estimator** N.

estrange VB to cause someone to break away from a previously friendly state or relationship. ■ **estrangement** N.

estuary N (**-ies**) the broad mouth of a river that flows into the sea, where fresh water mixes with tidal sea water. ■ **estuarine** ADJ.

et al. ABBREV 1 et alia (Latin), and other things. 2 et alibi (Latin), and other people. 3 et alii (Latin), and in other places.

et cetera or **etcetera** ADV 1 and the rest; and so on. 2 and/or something similar.

etch VB 1 TR & INTR to make designs on (metal or glass, etc) using an acid to eat out the lines. 2 to make a deep or irremovable impression.
■ **etcher** N. ■ **etching** N.

eternal ADJ 1 without beginning or end; everlasting. 2 unchanging. 3 COLLOQ frequent or endless. ■ **eternally** ADV.

eternity N (-ies) **1** time regarded as having no end. **2** the state of being eternal. **3** RELIG a timeless existence after death. **4** COLLOQ an extremely long time.

ethane N, CHEM a colourless odourless flammable gas found in natural gas.

ethanol N, CHEM a colourless volatile flammable alcohol produced by fermentation of the sugar in fruit or cereals.

ethene N, CHEM ethylene.

ether N **1** any of a group of organic chemical compounds formed by the dehydration of alcohols, that are volatile and highly flammable. **2** (also **diethyl ether**) the commonest ether, widely used as a solvent.

ethereal ADJ **1** having an unreal lightness or delicateness; fairy–like. **2** heavenly or spiritual.

ethic N the moral system or set of principles particular to a certain person or group, etc.

ethical ADJ **1** relating to or concerning morals, justice or duty. **2** morally right. ■ **ethically** ADV.

ethics SING N the study or the science of morals. ➤ PL N rules or principles of behaviour.

ethnic ADJ **1** relating to or having a common race or cultural tradition: **an ethnic group**. **2** associated with or resembling an exotic, esp non–European, racial or tribal group: **ethnic clothes**. **3** seen from the point of view of race, rather than nationality: **ethnic Asians**.

ethnic cleansing N genocide or forced removal inflicted by one ethnic group on all others in a particular area.

ethnology N the scientific study of different races and cultural traditions. ■ **ethnological** ADJ. ■ **ethnologist** N.

ethos N the typical spirit, character or attitudes (of a group or community, etc).

ethylene N, CHEM a colourless flammable gas with a sweet smell.

etiquette N conventions of correct or polite social behaviour.

étude N, MUS a short piece written for a single instrument, often intended as an exercise.

etymology N (-ies) **1** the study of the origin and development of words and their meanings. **2** an explanation of the history of a particular word. ■ **etymological** ADJ.

EU ABBREV European Union.

eucalyptus N (-tuses or -ti) **1** an evergreen tree, native to Australia. **2** the hard durable wood of this tree. **3** the medicinal oil of this tree.

Eucharist N, CHRISTIANITY **1** the sacrament of the Last Supper. **2** the Lord's Supper. **3** the elements of the sacrament, the bread and wine. ■ **Eucharistic** ADJ.

Euclidean or **Euclidian** ADJ of or based on the geometrical system devised by Euclid, a Greek mathematician who lived in c.300 BC.

eulogy N (-ies) **1** a speech or piece of writing in praise of someone or something. **2** high praise. ■ **eulogize** or **-ise** VB.

eunuch N **1** a man who has been castrated. **2** esp FORMERLY such a man employed as a guard of a harem in Eastern countries.

euphemism N **1** a mild or inoffensive term used in place of one considered offensive or unpleasantly direct. **2** the use of such terms. ■ **euphemistic** ADJ. ■ **euphemistically** ADV.

euphonium N a four–valved brass instrument of the tuba family.

euphony N (-ies) **1** a pleasing sound, esp in speech. **2** pleasantness of sound. ■ **euphonious** or **euphonic** ADJ.

euphoria N a feeling of wild happiness and well–being. ■ **euphoric** ADJ.

Eurasian ADJ **1** of mixed European and Asian descent. **2** of or relating to Europe and Asia. ➤ N a Eurasian person.

eureka EXCLAM expressing triumph at finding something or solving a problem, etc.

European ADJ of Europe. ➤ N a citizen or inhabitant of Europe.

Eurosceptic N someone who is not in favour of the UK's continuing political and economic integration with other states of the EU.

euthanasia N the practice of ending the life of a person suffering from an incurable illness.

evacuate VB 1 to leave (a place), esp because of danger. 2 to make (people) evacuate a place. ■ **evacuee** N. ■ **evacuation** N.

evade VB 1 to escape or avoid by trickery or skill. 2 to avoid answering (a question).

evaluate VB 1 to form an idea or judgement about the worth of. 2 MATH to calculate the value of. ■ **evaluation** N.

evanesce VB, INTR, LITERARY to disappear gradually. ■ **evanescent** ADJ.

evangelical ADJ 1 based on the Gospels. 2 of or denoting any of various groups within the Protestant church stressing the authority of the Bible. 3 enthusiastically advocating a particular cause, etc. ■ **evangelicalism** N.

evangelism N 1 the act or practice of evangelizing. 2 evangelicalism.

evangelist N 1 a person who preaches Christianity. 2 (usu **Evangelist**) any of the writers of the four Biblical Gospels.

evangelize or **-ise** VB 1 TR & INTR to attempt to persuade someone to adopt Christianity. 2 INTR to preach Christianity. ■ **evangelization** N.

evaporate VB, TR & INTR 1 to change or cause to change from a liquid into a vapour. 2 to disappear or make disappear. ■ **evaporation** N.

evaporated milk N unsweetened milk concentrated by evaporation.

evasion N 1 the act of evading, esp evading a commitment or responsibility. 2 a trick or excuse used to evade (a question, etc).

evasive ADJ 1 intending or intended to evade something, esp trouble or danger. 2 not honest or open. ■ **evasiveness** N.

eve N 1 esp IN COMPOUNDS the evening or day before some event: **New Year's Eve**. 2 the period immediately before: **the eve of war**.

even[1] ADJ 1 smooth and flat. 2 constant or regular: travelling at an even 50mph. 3 MATH of a number: divisible by two, with nothing left over. 4 designated or marked by an even number: **the even houses in the street**. 5 (usu **even with sth**) level, on the same plane or at the same height as it. 6 (often **even with sb**) having no advantage over or owing no debt to them. 7 calm: **even-tempered**. 8 equal.
➢ ADV 1 used with a comparative to emphasize a comparison with something else: **He's good, but she's even better**. 2 used with an expression stronger than a previous one: **He looked sad, even depressed**. 3 used to introduce a surprising piece of information: **Even John was there!** 4 used to indicate a lower extreme in an implied comparison: **Even a child would have known that!**
➢ VB (often **even sth up**) to make it equal. ■ **evenly** ADV. ■ **evenness** N.
◆ **even out** to make or become level or regular.
◆ **get even with sb** to be revenged on them.

even[2] N, OLD USE OR POETIC evening.

even-handed ADJ fair; impartial.

evening N 1 the last part of the day, usu from late afternoon until bedtime. 2 often IN COMPOUNDS a party or other social gathering held at this time: **a poetry evening**. 3 POETIC the latter part of something: **the evening of her life**.
➢ ADJ of or during the evening.

evening dress N clothes worn on formal occasions in the evening.

evensong N, C OF E evening prayer.

event N 1 something that occurs or happens; an incident, esp a significant one. 2 an item in a programme of sports, etc.

eventful ADJ full of significant events.

eventual ADJ happening after or at the end of a period of time or a process, etc.

eventuality N (**-ies**) a possible happening or result: **plan for every eventuality**.

eventually ADV after an indefinite period of time; in the end.

ever ADV 1 at any time. 2 a FORMAL always;

continually; **b** IN COMPOUNDS: **ever-hopeful**.
◆ **for ever 1** always. **2** COLLOQ for a long time.

evergreen ADJ, BOT denoting plants that bear leaves all the year round, eg pines or firs. ➢ N an evergreen tree or shrub.

everlasting ADJ **1** without end; continual. **2** lasting a long time, esp so as to become tiresome. ■ **everlastingly** ADV.

evermore ADV for all time to come.

every ADJ **1** each one or single of a number or collection; omitting none. **2** the greatest or best possible: **making every effort**.
➢ ADV at, in, or at the end of, each stated period of time or distance, etc: **every six inches**.
◆ **every bit** the whole; all of it; entirely.
◆ **every last** (USED FOR EMPHASIS) every.
◆ **every other** or **every second** one out of every two (things) repeatedly (the first, third, fifth, etc or second, fourth, sixth, etc): **comes every other day**.

everybody PRONOUN every person.

everyday ADJ **1** happening, done or used, etc daily, or on ordinary days, rather than on special occasions. **2** common or usual.

everyone PRONOUN every person.

everything PRONOUN **1** all things; all. **2** the most important thing: **Fitness is everything**.

everywhere ADV in or to every place.

evict VB to put someone out of a house, etc or off land by force of law. ■ **eviction** N.

evidence N **1** information, etc that gives grounds for belief; that which points to, reveals or suggests something. **2** written or spoken testimony used in a court of law.

evident ADJ clear to see or understand.

evidently ADV **1** obviously. **2** as it appears.

evil ADJ **1** morally bad or offensive. **2** harmful. **3** COLLOQ very unpleasant: **an evil stench**.
➢ N **1** wickedness or moral offensiveness, or the source of it. **2** harm, or a cause of harm; a harmful influence. **3** anything bad or unpleasant, eg crime or disease. ■ **evilly** ADV.

evince VB, FORMAL to show or display something (usu a personal quality) clearly.

evoke VB **1** to cause or produce (a response or reaction, etc). **2** to bring (a memory or emotion, etc) into the mind. ■ **evocation** N. ■ **evocative** ADJ.

evolution N **1** the process of evolving. **2** a gradual development. **3** BIOL the cumulative changes in the characteristics of living organisms from generation to generation. ■ **evolutionary** ADJ.

evolve VB **1** TR & INTR to develop or produce gradually. **2** INTR to develop from a primitive into a more complex or advanced form.

ewe N a female sheep.

ewer N a large water-jug with a wide mouth.

ex N, COLLOQ a person who is no longer what he or she was, esp a former spouse or lover.

ex- PFX, SIGNIFYING **1** former: **ex-president** • **ex-wife**. **2** outside: **ex-directory**.

exacerbate VB to make (a bad situation, etc) worse or more severe. ■ **exacerbation** N.

exact ADJ **1** absolutely accurate or correct. **2** insisting on accuracy or precision in even the smallest details. **3** dealing with measurable quantities or values.
➢ VB **1** (usu **exact sth from** or **of sb**) to demand (payment, etc) from them. **2** to insist on (a right, etc). ■ **exactness** N.

exacting ADJ making difficult demands.

exactitude N, FORMAL accuracy or correctness.

exactly ADV **1** just; quite, precisely or absolutely. **2** with attention to detail.

exaggerate VB **1** TR & INTR to regard or describe something as being greater or better than it really is. **2** to emphasize something or make it more noticeable. **3** to do something in an excessive or affected way. ■ **exaggeration** N.

exalt VB **1** to praise (eg God) highly. **2** to fill someone with great joy. **3** to give a higher rank

or position to someone or something.
■ **exaltation** N.

exalted ADJ 1 noble; very moral.
2 exaggerated; too high. ■ **exaltedly** ADV.

exam N, COLLOQ an examination.

examination N 1 a set of tasks, esp in written form, designed to test knowledge or ability. 2 an inspection of a person's state of health, carried out by a doctor. 3 the act of examining, or process of being examined.

examine VB 1 to inspect, consider or look into something closely. 2 to check the health of someone. 3 to test the knowledge or ability of (a person), esp in a formal examination.
■ **examinee** N. ■ **examiner** N.

example N 1 someone or something that is a typical specimen. 2 something that illustrates a fact or rule. 3 a person or pattern of behaviour, etc as a model to be, or not to be, copied: **set a good example**.
◆ **for example** as an example or illustration.

exasperate VB to make someone annoyed and frustrated. ■ **exasperating** ADJ.
■ **exasperation** N.

excavate VB 1 to dig up or uncover something (esp historical remains). 2 to dig up (a piece of ground, etc); to make (a hole) by doing this.
■ **excavator** N.

excavation N 1 esp ARCHAEOL the process of excavating or digging up ground. 2 an excavated area or site.

exceed VB 1 to be greater than someone or something. 2 to go beyond; to do more than is required by something. ■ **exceedingly** ADV.

excel VB (-ll-) INTR (usu **excel in** or **at sth**) to be exceptionally good at it.

excellence N great worth; very high or exceptional quality.

Excellency N (-ies) a title of honour given to certain people of high rank, eg ambassadors.

excellent ADJ of very high quality; extremely good. ■ **excellently** ADV.

except PREP (also **excepting**) not including.

➤ VB to leave out or exclude.
◆ **except for sth** apart from it.

exception N 1 someone or something not included. 2 someone or something that does not, or is allowed not to, follow a general rule. 3 an act of excluding.
◆ **take exception to sth** to object to it; to be offended by it.

exceptional ADJ 1 remarkable or outstanding. 2 being or making an exception.

excerpt N a short piece from a book, film, etc.
➤ VB to select extracts from (a book, etc).

excess N 1 the act of going, or the state of being, beyond normal limits. 2 an amount or extent greater than is usual, necessary or wise. 3 the amount by which one quantity, etc exceeds another; an amount left over.
➤ ADJ 1 greater than is usual, necessary or permitted. 2 additional; required to make up for an amount lacking: **excess postage** • **excess fare**. ■ **excessive** ADJ. ■ **excessively** ADV.

exchange VB 1 to give, or give up, something, in return for something else. 2 to give and receive in return: **exchange gifts**.
➤ N 1 the giving and taking of one thing for another. 2 a thing exchanged. 3 an argument or conversation, esp a brief one. 4 the act of exchanging the currency of one country for that of another. 5 a place where shares are traded, or international financial deals carried out. 6 (also **telephone exchange**) a central telephone system where lines are connected, or the building housing this.

exchequer N (often **Exchequer**) the government department in charge of the financial affairs of a nation.

excise[1] N the tax or duty payable on goods, etc produced and sold within a country, and on certain trading licences: **excise duty**.

excise[2] VB 1 to remove (eg a passage from a text). 2 to cut out something, or cut off something by surgery. ■ **excision** N.

excite VB 1 to make someone feel lively expectation or a pleasant tension and thrill. 2 to arouse (feelings, emotions or sensations, etc).

3 to provoke (eg action). ■ **excitable** ADJ.
■ **excited** ADJ. ■ **excitedly** ADV.

excitement N **1** the state of being excited.
2 objects and events that produce such a state,
or the quality they have which produces it.

exciting ADJ arousing a lively expectation or a
pleasant tension and thrill. ■ **excitingly** ADV.

exclaim VB, TR & INTR to call or cry out suddenly
and loudly, eg in surprise or anger.

exclamation N **1** a word or expression
uttered suddenly and loudly. **2** the act of
exclaiming. ■ **exclamatory** ADJ.

exclamation mark N the punctuation mark
(!), used to indicate an exclamation.

exclude VB **1** to prevent someone from sharing
or taking part. **2** to shut someone or something
out, or to keep them out. **3** to omit someone or
something or leave them out of consideration.
4 to make something impossible.

excluding PREP not counting; without including.

exclusion N the act of excluding, or the state
of being excluded.

exclusive ADJ **1** involving the rejection or denial
of something else or everything else. **2** limited
to, given to, found in, etc only that place, group
or person. **3** not including a specified thing.
4 not readily accepting others: **an exclusive
club**. **5** fashionable and expensive: **an
exclusive restaurant**.
➤ N a report or story published in only one
newspaper or magazine. ■ **exclusiveness** or
exclusivity N.

excommunicate VB, CHRISTIANITY to exclude
someone from membership of a church.
■ **excommunication** N.

excrement N waste matter passed out of the
body, esp faeces. ■ **excremental** ADJ.

excrete VB to eliminate (waste products).
■ **excretion** N.

excruciating ADJ **1** causing great physical or
mental pain. **2** COLLOQ extremely bad or
irritating. ■ **excruciatingly** ADV.

exculpate VB, FORMAL to free someone from

guilt or blame. ■ **exculpation** N.

excursion N a short trip, usu for pleasure.

excuse VB **1** to pardon or forgive someone. **2** to
offer justification for (a wrongdoing). **3** to free
someone from (an obligation or duty, etc). **4** to
allow someone to leave a room, etc, eg in order
to go to the lavatory.
➤ N **1** an explanation for a wrongdoing,
offered as an apology or justification. **2** DEROG
a very poor example.
◆ **excuse me** an expression of apology, or
one used to attract attention.

ex-directory ADJ not included in the
telephone directory at the request of the
subscriber.

execrable ADJ **1** detestable. **2** dreadful; of
very poor quality. ■ **execrably** ADV.

execute VB **1** to put someone to death by order
of the law. **2** to perform or carry out something.
3 to produce something, esp according to a
design. **4** LAW to make something valid by
signing. **5** LAW to carry out instructions
contained in (a will or contract). ■ **executable**
ADJ. ■ **executer** N.

execution N **1** the act, or an instance, of
putting someone to death by law. **2** the act or
skill of carrying something out; an instance or
the process of carrying something out.
■ **executioner** N.

executive ADJ **1** in a business organization,
etc: concerned with management or
administration. **2** for the use of managers and
senior staff. **3** LAW, POL relating to the carrying
out of laws: **executive powers**.
➤ N **1** someone in an organization, etc who has
power to direct or manage. **2** (**the
executive**) the branch of government that puts
laws into effect.

executor N, LAW a male or female person
appointed to carry out instructions stated in a
will. ■ **executorship** N. ■ **executory** ADJ.

exegesis N (**-ses**) an explanation of a text.

exemplar N **1** a person or thing worth
copying; a model. **2** a typical example.

exemplary ADJ 1 worth following as an example. 2 serving as an illustration or warning.

exemplify VB (*-ies*, *-ied*) 1 to be an example of something. 2 to show as or by means of an example. ■ **exemplification** N.

exempt VB to free someone from a duty or obligation that applies to others.
➤ ADJ free from some obligation; not liable.
■ **exemption** N.

exercise N 1 physical training or exertion for health or pleasure. 2 an activity intended to develop a skill. 3 a task designed to test ability.
➤ VB 1 TR & INTR to give exercise to (oneself, or someone or something else). 2 to use something or bring it into use: **exercised his right to appeal.**

exert VB 1 to bring something into use or action forcefully. 2 to force oneself to make a strenuous, esp physical, effort. ■ **exertion** N.

exfoliate VB, TR & INTR of bark, rocks or skin, etc: to shed or peel off in flakes or layers.
■ **exfoliation** N. ■ **exfoliative** ADJ.

ex gratia ADV, ADJ given as a favour, not in recognition of any obligation.

exhale VB, TR & INTR 1 to breathe out. 2 to give off or be given off. ■ **exhalation** N.

exhaust VB 1 to make (a person or animal) very tired. 2 to use something up completely.
➤ N 1 the escape of waste gases from an engine, etc. 2 the gases themselves. 3 the part or parts of an engine, etc through which the waste gases escape. ■ **exhausted** ADJ.
■ **exhausting** ADJ. ■ **exhaustion** N.

exhaustive ADJ complete; comprehensive or very thorough. ■ **exhaustively** ADV.

exhibit VB 1 to present or display something for public appreciation. 2 to show or manifest (a quality, etc).
➤ N an object displayed in a museum.

exhibition N 1 a display, eg of works of art, to the public. 2 the act or an instance of showing something, eg a quality.

exhibitionism N, DEROG the tendency to behave so as to attract attention to oneself.
■ **exhibitionist** N.

exhilarate VB to fill someone with a lively cheerfulness. ■ **exhilarating** ADJ.
■ **exhilaration** N.

exhort VB to urge or advise someone strongly and sincerely. ■ **exhortation** N.

exhume VB, FORMAL to dig up (a body) from a grave. ■ **exhumation** N.

exile N 1 enforced or regretted absence from one's country or town. 2 someone who suffers such absence.
➤ VB to send someone into exile.

exist VB, INTR 1 to be, esp to be present in the real world or universe rather than in story or imagination. 2 to occur or be found. 3 to manage to stay alive; to live with only the most basic necessities of life. ■ **existent** ADJ.

existence N 1 the state of existing. 2 a life, or a way of living. 3 everything that exists.

existentialism N a philosophy that emphasizes freedom of choice and personal responsibility for one's own actions.

exit N 1 a way out of a building, etc. 2 going out or departing. 3 an actor's departure from the stage. 4 a place where vehicles can leave a motorway or main road.
➤ VB INTR 1 FORMAL to go out, leave or depart. 2 THEAT **a** to leave the stage; **b** as a stage direction: (**exit …**) he or she leaves the stage.

exit poll N a poll of a sample of voters in an election, taken as they leave a polling-station.

exocrine ADJ, PHYSIOL of a gland: discharging its secretions through a duct.

exodus N a mass departure of people.

ex officio ADV, ADJ by virtue of one's official position.

exonerate VB to free someone from blame, or acquit them of a criminal charge.
■ **exoneration** N. ■ **exonerative** ADJ.

exorbitant ADJ of prices or demands: very high, excessive or unfair. ■ **exorbitantly** ADV.

exorcize or **-ise** VB in some beliefs: **1** to drive away (an evil spirit or influence) with prayer or holy words. **2** to free (a person or place) from the influence of an evil spirit in this way. ■ **exorcism** N. ■ **exorcist** N.

exoskeleton N, ZOOL in some invertebrates: an external skeleton forming a rigid covering that is external to the body. ■ **exoskeletal** ADJ.

exotic ADJ **1** introduced from a foreign country, esp a distant and tropical country: **exotic plants**. **2** interestingly different or strange, and suggestive of a distant land.
➤ N an exotic person or thing. ■ **exotically** ADV. ■ **exoticism** N.

expand VB **1** TR & INTR to make or become greater in size, extent or importance. **2** INTR, FORMAL to become more at ease or more open and talkative. ■ **expandable** ADJ.
◆ **expand on** or **upon sth** to give additional information; to enlarge on (a description, etc).

expanse N a wide area or space.

expansion N **1** the act or state of expanding. **2** the amount by which something expands.

expansionism N the act or practice of increasing territory or political influence or authority, usu at the expense of other nations or bodies. ■ **expansionist** N, ADJ.

expansive ADJ **1** ready or eager to talk; open or effusive. **2** wide-ranging. **3** able or tending to expand. ■ **expansiveness** N.

expat N, COLLOQ an expatriate.

expatriate ADJ **1** living abroad, esp for a long but limited period. **2** exiled.
➤ N a person living or working abroad.

expect VB **1** to think of something as likely to happen or come. **2** COLLOQ to suppose: I expect you're tired.
◆ **be expecting** COLLOQ to be pregnant.
◆ **expect sth from** or **of** to require it; to regard it as normal or reasonable.

expectancy N (**-ies**) **1** the act or state of expecting. **2** a future chance or probability.

expectant ADJ **1** eagerly waiting; hopeful.

2 not yet, but expecting to be something (esp a mother or father). ■ **expectantly** ADV.

expectation N **1** the state, or an attitude, of expecting. **2** (often **expectations**) something expected, whether good or bad.

expectorant MED, ADJ causing the coughing up of phlegm.
➤ N an expectorant medicine.

expectorate VB, TR & INTR, MED to cough up and spit out (phlegm). ■ **expectoration** N.

expedient ADJ **1** suitable or appropriate. **2** practical or advantageous.
➤ N a suitable method or solution, esp one quickly thought of to meet an urgent need. ■ **expediency** (**-ies**) or **expedience** N.

expedite VB to speed up or assist the progress of something.

expedition N **1** an organized journey with a specific purpose. **2** a group making such a journey. ■ **expeditionary** ADJ.

expel VB (**-ll-**) **1** to dismiss from or deprive someone of membership of (a club or school, etc), usu permanently. **2** to get rid of something; to force it out.

expend VB to use or spend (time, effort, etc).

expendable ADJ **1** that may be given up or sacrificed for some purpose or cause. **2** not valuable enough to be worth preserving.

expenditure N **1** the act of expending. **2** an amount expended, esp of money.

expense N **1** the act of spending money, or the amount of money spent. **2** something on which money is spent. **3** (**expenses**) a sum of one's own money spent doing one's job, or this sum of money or an allowance paid by one's employer to make up for this.
◆ **at the expense of sth** or **sb 1** with the loss or sacrifice of them. **2** causing damage to their pride or reputation: **a joke at my expense**.

expensive ADJ involving much expense; costing a great deal. ■ **expensiveness** N.

experience N **1** practice in an activity. **2** knowledge or skill gained through practice.

3 wisdom gained through long and varied observation of life. **4** an event which affects or involves one.
➤ VB **1** to have practical acquaintance with someone or something. **2** to feel or undergo. ■ **experienced** ADJ.

experiment N **1** a trial carried out in order to test a theory, a machine's performance, etc or to discover something. **2** the carrying out of such trials. **3** an attempt at something original.
➤ VB, INTR (USU **experiment on** or **with sth**) to carry out an experiment.

experimental ADJ **1** consisting of or like an experiment. **2** relating to, or used in, experiments. **3** trying out new styles and techniques. ■ **experimentally** ADV.

expert N someone with great skill in, or extensive knowledge of, a particular subject.
➤ ADJ **1** highly skilled or extremely knowledgeable. **2** relating to or done by an expert or experts. ■ **expertly** ADV.

expertise N special skill or knowledge.

expire VB, INTR **1** to come to an end or cease to be valid. **2** to breathe out. **3** to die.
■ **expiration** N.

expiry N (*-ies*) the ending of the duration or validity of something.

explain VB, TR & INTR **1** to make something clear or easy to understand. **2** to give, or be, a reason for or account for. **3** (**explain oneself**) **a** to justify (oneself or one's actions); **b** to clarify one's meaning or intention. ■ **explanation** N.

explanatory ADJ serving to explain.

expletive N a swear-word or curse.

explicable ADJ able to be explained.

explicate VB **1** to explain in depth. **2** to unfold or develop (an idea or theory, etc).
■ **explication** N.

explicit ADJ **1** stated or shown fully and clearly. **2** speaking openly. ■ **explicitly** ADV.

explode VB **1** INTR of a substance: to undergo an explosion. **2** to cause something to undergo an explosion. **3** INTR to undergo a violent

explosion as a result of a chemical or nuclear reaction. **4** INTR to suddenly show a strong or violent emotion, esp anger. **5** INTR esp of population: to increase rapidly.

exploit N (USU **exploits**) an act or feat, esp a bold or daring one.
➤ VB **1** to take unfair advantage of something or someone so as to achieve one's own aims. **2** to make good use of something. ■ **exploitation** N. ■ **exploitative** ADJ. ■ **exploiter** N.

exploratory ADJ **1** serving to establish procedures or rules. **2** aiming to establish the nature of a complaint rather than treat it.

explore VB **1** to search or travel through (a place) for the purpose of discovery. **2** to examine something carefully: **explore every possibility**. ■ **exploration** N. ■ **explorer** N.

explosion N **1** CHEM a sudden and violent increase in pressure, which generates large amounts of heat and destructive shock waves. **2** the sudden loud noise that accompanies such a reaction. **3** a sudden display of strong feelings, etc. **4** a sudden great increase.

explosive ADJ **1** likely, tending or able to explode. **2** likely to become marked by violence or emotional outbursts. **3** likely to result in violence or an outburst of feeling.
➤ N any substance that is capable of producing an explosion. ■ **explosively** ADV.

expo N, COLLOQ a large public exhibition.

exponent N **1** someone able to perform some art or activity, esp skilfully. **2** someone who explains and promotes (a theory or belief, etc).

export VB to send or take (goods, etc) to another country, esp for sale.
➤ N **1** the act or business of exporting. **2** something exported. ■ **exportation** N. ■ **exporter** N.

expose VB **1** to remove cover, protection or shelter from something, or to allow this to be the case: **exposed to the wind** • **exposed to criticism**. **2** to discover something (eg a criminal or crime) or make it known. **3** to allow light to fall on (a photographic film or paper) when taking or printing a photograph.

◆ **expose oneself** to display one's sexual organs in public.

exposé N 1 a formal statement of facts, esp one that introduces an argument. 2 an article or programme which exposes a scandal, etc.

exposition N 1 an in-depth explanation or account (of a subject). 2 the act of presenting such an explanation, or a viewpoint. 3 a large public exhibition.

expostulate VB, INTR (usu **expostulate with sb about sth**) to argue or reason with them. ■ **expostulation** N. ■ **expostulatory** ADJ.

exposure N 1 the act of exposing or the state of being exposed. 2 the harmful effects on the body of extreme cold. 3 the number or regularity of someone's appearances in public, eg on TV. 4 the act of exposing photographic film or paper to light. 5 the amount of light to which a film or paper is exposed, or the length of time for which it is exposed. 6 the amount of film exposed or to be exposed in order to produce one photograph.

expound VB 1 to explain something in depth. 2 (often **expound on sth**) INTR to talk at length about it.

express VB 1 to put something into words. 2 to indicate or represent something with looks, actions, symbols, etc. 3 to show or reveal. 4 to press or squeeze out something.
➤ ADJ 1 of a train, etc: travelling esp fast, with few stops. 2 belonging or referring to, or sent by, a fast delivery service. 3 clearly stated: **his express wish**. 4 particular; clear: **with the express purpose of insulting him**.
➤ N an express train.
➤ ADV by express delivery service.
■ **expressible** ADJ. ■ **expressly** ADV.
◆ **express oneself** to put one's thoughts into words.

expression N 1 the act of expressing. 2 a look on the face that displays feelings. 3 a word or phrase. 4 the indication of feeling, eg in a manner of speaking or a way of playing music. ■ **expressionless** ADJ.

expressive ADJ 1 showing meaning or feeling in a clear or lively way. 2 (always **expressive of sth**) expressing a feeling or emotion. ■ **expressiveness** N.

expresso see **espresso**

expropriate VB, FORMAL OR LAW esp of the state: to take (property, etc) from its owner for some special use. ■ **expropriation** N.

expulsion N 1 the act of expelling from school or a club, etc. 2 the act of forcing or driving out.

expunge VB 1 to cross out or delete something (eg a passage from a book). 2 to cancel out or destroy something.

expurgate VB 1 to revise (a book) by removing objectionable or offensive words or passages. 2 to remove (such words or passages). ■ **expurgation** N.

exquisite ADJ 1 extremely beautiful or skilfully produced. 2 able to exercise sensitive judgement: **exquisite taste**. 3 of pain or pleasure, etc: extreme. ■ **exquisitely** ADV.

extant ADJ still existing; surviving.

extempore ADV, ADJ without planning or preparation; impromptu. ■ **extemporaneous** or **extemporary** ADJ.

extemporize or **-ise** VB, TR & INTR to speak or perform without preparation.

extend VB 1 to make something longer or larger. 2 TR & INTR to reach or stretch in space or time. 3 to hold out or stretch out (a hand, etc). 4 to offer (kindness or greetings, etc) to someone. 5 to increase something in scope. 6 to exert someone to their physical or mental limit: **extend oneself**. ■ **extendable**, **extendible**, **extensible** or **extensile** ADJ.

extension N 1 the process of extending something, or the state of being extended. 2 an added part, that makes the original larger or longer. 3 a subsidiary or extra telephone, connected to the main line. 4 an extra period beyond an original time limit. 5 range or extent.

extensive ADJ large in area, amount, range or effect. ■ **extensively** ADV.

extent N 1 the area over which something

extends. **2** amount, scope or degree.

extenuate VB to reduce the seriousness of (an offence) by giving an explanation that partly excuses it. ■ **extenuation** N.

extenuating ADJ esp of a circumstance: reducing the seriousness of an offence by partially excusing it.

exterior ADJ **1** on, from, or for use on the outside. **2** relating to foreign nations. ➤ N **1** an outside part or surface. **2** an outward appearance, esp when intended to deceive.

exterminate VB to get rid of or completely destroy (something living). ■ **extermination** N. ■ **exterminator** N.

external ADJ **1** belonging to, for, from or on the outside. **2** being of the world, as opposed to the mind: **external realities**. **3** foreign; involving foreign nations: **external affairs**. **4** of a medicine: to be applied on the outside of the body. **5** taking place, or coming from, outside one's school or university, etc: **an external examination**. ■ **externally** ADV.

extinct ADJ **1** of a species: no longer in existence. **2** of a volcano: no longer active.

extinction N **1** the process of making or becoming extinct; elimination or disappearance. **2** BIOL the total elimination or dying out of any plant or animal species.

extinguish VB to put out (a fire, etc). ■ **extinguishable** ADJ. ■ **extinguisher** N.

extirpate VB, FORMAL **1** to destroy completely. **2** to uproot. ■ **extirpation** N.

extol VB (-*ll*-) to praise enthusiastically.

extort VB to obtain (money or information, etc) by threats or violence. ■ **extortion** N.

extortionate ADJ of a price or demand, etc: unreasonably high or great.

extra ADJ **1** additional; more than is usual, necessary or expected. **2** for which an additional charge is made. ➤ N **1** an additional or unexpected thing. **2 a** an extra charge; **b** an item for which this is made. **3** an actor employed for a small, usu non-

speaking, part in a film. **4** a special edition of a newspaper containing later news. ➤ ADV unusually or exceptionally.

extract VB **1** to pull or draw something out, esp by force or with effort. **2** to separate (a substance) from a liquid or solid mixture. **3** to derive (pleasure, etc). ➤ N **1** a passage selected from a book, etc. **2** CHEM a substance that is separated from a liquid or solid mixture by using heat, solvents or distillation, etc. ■ **extractable** ADJ.

extraction N **1** the act of extracting. **2** the process whereby a metal is obtained from its ore. **3** the removal of a tooth from its socket. **4** family origin; descent: **of Dutch extraction**.

extra-curricular ADJ in addition to the subjects studied in a curriculum.

extradite VB to return (a person accused of a crime) for trial in the country where the crime was committed. ■ **extradition** N.

extramarital ADJ esp of sexual relations: taking place outside marriage.

extramural ADJ of courses, etc: for people who are not full-time students at a college, etc.

extraneous ADJ **1** not belonging; not relevant or related. **2** coming from outside.

extraordinary ADJ **1** unusual; surprising or remarkable. **2** additional; not part of the regular pattern or routine: **extraordinary meeting**. ■ **extraordinarily** ADV.

extrasensory ADJ achieved using means other than the senses of sight, hearing, touch, taste and smell: **extrasensory perception**.

extraterrestrial ADJ of a being or creature, etc: coming from outside the Earth. ➤ N an extraterrestrial being.

extravagant ADJ **1** using, spending or costing too much. **2** unreasonably or unbelievably great: **extravagant praise**. ■ **extravagance** N. ■ **extravagantly** ADV.

extravaganza N a spectacular display.

extravert N a variant of **extrovert**

extreme ADJ **1** very high, or highest, in degree

or intensity. **2** very far, or furthest, in any direction, esp out from the centre. **3** very violent or strong. **4** not moderate; severe.
➤ N **1** either of two people or things as far, or as different, as possible from each other. **2** the highest limit; the greatest degree of any state or condition. ■ **extremely** ADV.

extremist N someone who has extreme opinions, esp in politics.
➤ ADJ relating to, or favouring, extreme measures. ■ **extremism** N.

extremity N (-*ies*) **1** the furthest point. **2** an extreme degree; the quality of being extreme. **3** a situation of great danger. **4** (**extremities**) the hands and feet.

extricate VB to free someone or something from difficulties; to disentangle.

extrovert or **extravert** N **1** PSYCHOL someone who is more concerned with the outside world and social relationships than with their inner thoughts and feelings. **2** someone who is sociable, outgoing and talkative.
➤ ADJ having the temperament of an extrovert; sociable or outgoing. ■ **extroverted** ADJ.

extrude VB to squeeze something or force it out. ■ **extrusion** N.

exuberant ADJ **1** in very high spirits. **2** enthusiastic and energetic. **3** of health, etc: excellent. **4** of plants, etc: growing abundantly. ■ **exuberance** N.

exude VB **1** to give off or give out (an odour or sweat). **2** to show or convey (a quality or characteristic, etc) by one's behaviour. **3** INTR to ooze out. ■ **exudate** N. ■ **exudation** N.

exult VB, INTR **1** (often **exult in** or **at sth**) to be intensely joyful about it. **2** (often **exult over sth**) to show or enjoy a feeling of triumph. ■ **exultant** ADJ. ■ **exultation** N.

eye N **1** the organ of vision, usu one of a pair. **2** the area of the face around the eye. **3** (often **eyes**) sight; vision: Surgeons need good eyes. **4** attention, gaze or observation: catch someone's eye • in the public eye. **5** the ability to appreciate and judge: an eye for beauty. **6** a look or expression: a hostile eye. **7** BOT the

bud of a tuber such as a potato. **8** an area of calm and low pressure at the centre of a tornado, etc. **9** any rounded thing, esp when hollow, eg the hole in a needle.
➤ VB (**eyeing** or **eying**) to look at something carefully. ■ **eyeless** ADJ.
◆ **an eye for an eye** retaliation; justice enacted in the same way or to the same degree as the crime.
◆ **be all eyes** COLLOQ to be vigilant.
◆ **eye sb** or **sth up** COLLOQ to assess their worth or attractiveness.
◆ **have one's eye on sth** to be eager to acquire it.
◆ **in one's mind's eye** in one's imagination.
◆ **in the eyes of sb** in their opinion.
◆ **keep an eye on sb** or **sth** COLLOQ to keep them or it under observation.
◆ **see eye to eye with sb** to be in agreement with them.
◆ **with an eye to sth** having it as a purpose or intention.
◆ **with one's eyes open** with full awareness of what one is doing.

eyeball N the nearly spherical body of the eye.

eyebath and (esp US) **eye-cup** N a small vessel for holding and applying medication or cleansing solution, etc to the eye.

eyebrow N the arch of hair on the bony ridge above each eye.

eyecatching ADJ drawing attention, esp by being strikingly attractive. ■ **eye-catcher** N.

eyeful N, COLLOQ **1** an interesting or beautiful sight. **2** a look or view.

eyeglass N **1** a single lens in a frame, to assist weak sight. **2** (**eyeglasses**) chiefly US spectacles.

eyelash N any of the short protective hairs that grow from the edges of the eyelids.

eyelet N **1** a small hole in fabric, etc through which a lace, etc is passed. **2** the metal, etc ring reinforcing such a hole.

eyelid N a protective fold of skin and muscle, lined with a membrane, that can be moved to cover or uncover the front of the eyeball.

eyeliner N a cosmetic used to outline the eye.

eyepiece N, OPTICS the lens or lenses nearest to the eye in an optical instrument.

eyeshade N a visor.

eyeshadow N a coloured cosmetic for the eyelids.

eyesight N the ability to see; power of vision.

eyesore N, DEROG an ugly thing, esp a building.

eyestrain N tiredness or irritation of the eyes.

eye tooth N a canine tooth.

eyewash N 1 liquid for soothing sore eyes. 2 COLLOQ, DEROG nonsense; insincere talk.

eyewitness N someone who sees something happen, esp a crime.

eyrie N the nest of an eagle or other bird of prey, built in a high inaccessible place.

Ff

F¹ or **f** N (*Fs, F's* or *f's*) 1 the sixth letter of the English alphabet. 2 (**F**) MUS the fourth note in the scale of C major.

F² ABBREV 1 Fahrenheit. 2 farad. 3 PHYS force.

fa see **fah**

fable N 1 a story with a moral, usu with animals as characters. 2 a false story. ■ **fabled** ADJ.

fabric N 1 woven, knitted or felted cloth. 2 quality; texture. 3 the walls, floor and roof of a building. 4 structure: **the fabric of society**.

fabricate VB 1 to invent or make up (a story, evidence, etc). 2 to make something. 3 to forge (a document, etc). ■ **fabrication** N.

fabulous ADJ 1 a COLLOQ marvellous; wonderful; excellent; b immense; amazing. 2 legendary; mythical.

façade or **facade** N 1 the front of a building. 2 a false outer appearance; a mask.

face N 1 the front part of the head, from forehead to chin. 2 the features or facial expression. 3 a surface or side, eg of a mountain, gem, geometrical figure, etc. 4 the important or working side, eg of a golf-club

head. 5 a in a mine or quarry: the exposed surface from which coal, etc is mined; b on a cliff: the exposed surface, usu vertical; c IN COMPOUNDS: **coalface • cliff-face**. 6 the dial of a clock, watch, etc. 7 the side of a playing card that is marked with numbers, symbols, etc. 8 general look or appearance. 9 an aspect. ➤ VB 1 TR & INTR to be opposite to something or someone; to turn to look at or look in some direction. 2 to have something unpleasant before one: **face ruin**. 3 to confront, brave or cope with (problems, etc). 4 to accept (the unpleasant truth, etc). 5 to present itself to someone: **the scene that faced us**. 6 to cover with a surface: **bricks faced with plaster**. ◆ **face up to sth** or **sb** to accept an unpleasant fact, etc; to deal with it or them bravely. ◆ **in the face of sth** in spite of a known circumstance, etc.

face card N a court card.

faceless ADJ 1 of a person: with identity concealed. 2 of bureaucrats, etc: impersonal.

facelift N 1 a surgical operation to remove facial wrinkles by tightening the skin. 2 any procedure for improving the external appearance of something.

facet N 1 a face of a cut jewel. 2 an aspect, eg of a problem, topic or someone's personality.

facetious ADJ of a person or remark, etc: amusing or witty, esp unsuitably so.

facial ADJ of or relating to the face: facial hair. ➣ N a beauty treatment for the face.

facile ADJ 1 too easily achieved. 2 over-simple.

facilitate VB to make something easy or easier to do. ■ **facilitation** N.

facility N (-ies) 1 skill, talent or ability. 2 fluency; ease. 3 an arrangement, feature, etc that enables someone to do something. 4 (chiefly **facilities**) a building, service or piece of equipment for a particular activity.

facsimile N 1 an exact copy made, eg of a manuscript, picture, etc. 2 electronic copying of a document and its transmission by telephone line. 3 a copy made by facsimile.

fact N 1 a thing known to be true, to exist or to have happened. 2 truth or reality, as distinct from mere statement or belief.

faction[1] N 1 an active or trouble-making group within a larger organization. 2 argument or dissent within a group. ■ **factional** ADJ.

faction[2] N 1 a play, programme, piece of writing, etc that is a mixture of fact and fiction. 2 this type of writing, etc as a genre.

fact of life N 1 an unavoidable truth, esp if unpleasant. 2 (**the facts of life**) basic information on sex and reproduction.

factor N 1 a circumstance that contributes to a result. 2 MATH one of two or more numbers that, when multiplied together, produce a given number: 4 is a factor of 12.

factory N (-ies) a building with equipment for the large-scale manufacture of goods.

factotum N a person employed to do a large number of different jobs.

factual ADJ 1 concerned with, or based on, facts. 2 actual. ■ **factually** ADV.

faculty N (-ies) 1 a mental or physical power.

2 a particular talent or aptitude for something. 3 **a** a section of a university, comprising a number of departments; **b** the professors and lecturers belonging to such a section. 4 N AMER the staff of a college, school or university.

fad N, COLLOQ 1 a shortlived fashion. 2 an odd belief or practice. ■ **faddy** (-ier, -iest) ADJ.

fade VB 1 TR & INTR to lose, or cause something to lose, strength, freshness, colour, etc. 2 INTR to disappear gradually.
◆ **fade in** or **out** CINEMATOG, BROADCASTING to become gradually louder and more distinct, or gradually fainter and disappear.

faeces or (N AMER) **feces** PL N waste matter discharged from the body through the anus. ■ **faecal** or **fecal** ADJ.

fag[1] N 1 COLLOQ a cigarette. 2 COLLOQ a piece of drudgery; a bore.
➣ VB (-gg-) to tire out or exhaust.
◆ **fagged out** very tired; exhausted.

fag[2] N, SLANG, OFFENSIVE a gay man.

faggot or (N AMER) **fagot** N 1 a ball or roll of chopped pork and liver mixed with breadcrumbs and herbs, and fried or baked. 2 a bundle of sticks, twigs, etc, used for fuel, fascines, etc. 3 SLANG, OFFENSIVE a gay man.

fah or **fa** N, MUS in sol-fa notation: the fourth note of the major scale.

Fahrenheit N a scale of temperature on which water boils at 212° and freezes at 32°. ➣ ADJ on or of this scale.

fail VB 1 TR & INTR (often **fail in sth**) not to succeed; to be unsuccessful in (an undertaking). 2 to judge (a candidate) not good enough to pass a test, etc. 3 INTR to stop working or functioning. 4 INTR not to manage (to do something). 5 not to bother (doing something). 6 to let (someone) down; to disappoint. 7 of courage, strength, etc: to desert (one) at the time of need. 8 INTR to become gradually weaker. 9 INTR to collapse; to become insolvent or bankrupt.
➣ N a failure, esp in an exam.
◆ **without fail** for certain; with complete regularity and reliability.

failing N a fault; a weakness.
➤ ADJ becoming weak or weaker.
➤ PREP should (something) not happen.

fail-safe ADJ designed to return to a safe condition if something goes wrong.

failure N 1 an act of failing; lack of success. 2 someone or something that is unsuccessful. 3 a stoppage in functioning, eg of a machine, system, etc. 4 a poor result. 5 an instance of something not being done or not happening.

faint ADJ 1 pale; dim; indistinct; slight. 2 physically weak; on the verge of losing consciousness. 3 feeble; timid; unenthusiastic.
➤ VB, INTR to lose consciousness; to collapse.
➤ N a sudden loss of consciousness.

faint-hearted ADJ timid; cowardly; spiritless.

fair[1] ADJ 1 just; not using dishonest methods or discrimination. 2 in accordance with the rules. 3 **a** of hair and skin: light-coloured; **b** having light-coloured hair and skin. 4 OLD USE beautiful. 5 quite good; reasonable. 6 sizeable; considerable. 7 of weather: fine.
➤ ADV 1 in a fair way. 2 DIALECT completely.
■ **fairness** N.
◆ **fair-and-square** 1 absolutely; exactly.

fair[2] N 1 a collection of sideshows and amusements, often set up temporarily on open ground and travelling from place to place. 2 HIST a market. 3 an indoor trade exhibition.

fairground N the piece of land on which sideshows and amusements are set up.

fairly ADV 1 justly; honestly. 2 quite; rather.

fair play N honourable behaviour; just treatment.

fairway N, GOLF a broad strip of short grass extending from the tee to the green.

fairy N (-ies) 1 MYTHOL a supernatural being, usu with magical powers and of diminutive human form. 2 SLANG, OFFENSIVE a gay man.

fairy tale and **fairy story** N 1 a story about fairies, magic and other supernatural things. 2 EUPHEMISTIC, COLLOQ a lie.
➤ ADJ (**fairy-tale**) beautiful, magical or marvellous.

fait accompli N (*faits accomplis*) something done and unalterable.

faith N 1 trust or confidence. 2 strong belief, eg in God. 3 a specified religion: the Jewish faith. 4 any set or system of beliefs. 5 loyalty to a promise, etc: break faith. ■ **faithless** ADJ.

faithful ADJ 1 having or showing faith. 2 loyal and true. 3 accurate. 4 loyal to a sexual partner. 5 reliable; constant.
➤ PL N 1 (**the Faithful**) the believers in a particular religion, esp Islam. 2 (**the faithful**) loyal supporters, esp of a sports team.
■ **faithfully** ADV. ■ **faithfulness** N.

faith healing N the curing of illness through religious faith. ■ **faith healer** N.

fake N someone or something, or an act that is not genuine.
➤ ADJ not genuine; false; counterfeit.
➤ VB 1 TR to alter something dishonestly; to falsify something or make something up. 2 TR & INTR to pretend to feel (an emotion) or have (an illness).

fakir N a wandering mendicant Hindu or Muslim holy man.

falcon N a long-winged bird of prey that can be trained to hunt small birds and animals.

falconry N 1 the breeding and training of falcons for hunting. 2 the sport of using falcons to hunt prey. ■ **falconer** N.

fall VB (*fell, fallen*) INTR 1 to descend or drop freely and involuntarily, esp accidentally, by force of gravity. 2 (also **fall over** or **down**) of someone, or something upright: to drop to the ground after losing balance. 3 to collapse. 4 to come down from the sky; to precipitate. 5 of hair, etc: to hang down. 6 (usu **fall on sth**) to land. 7 to go naturally or easily into position. 8 to lose power; to be no longer able to govern. 9 to be captured: the city fell. 10 to be lowered or broken down. 11 to die or be badly wounded in battle, etc. 12 to give in to temptation; to sin. 13 to become less. 14 to diminish. 15 to intervene. 16 to arrive: **night fell**. 17 to pass into a certain state; to begin to be in that state: **fall asleep** • **fall in love**. 18 to be

grouped or classified in a certain way: **falls into two categories. 19** to occur at a certain time or place: **The accent falls on the first syllable. 20** to show disappointment: **her face fell.**
➤ N **1** an act or way of falling. **2** something, or an amount, that falls. **3** (often **falls**) a waterfall. **4** a drop in quality, value, etc. **5** a defeat or collapse. **6** (also **Fall**) N AMER autumn.
◆ **fall apart 1** to break in pieces. **2** to fail; to collapse.
fall away 1 of land: to slope downwards. **2** to become fewer or less. **3** to disappear.
fall behind to fail to keep up with someone, with one's work, with paying rent, etc.
fall down of an argument, etc: to be shown to be invalid.
fall for sb to fall in love with them.
fall for sth to be deceived or taken in by it.
fall in 1 of a roof, etc: to collapse. **2** of a soldier, etc: to take his or her place in a parade.
fall off to decline in quality or quantity.
fall out with sb to quarrel with them.
fall through of a plan, etc: to fail.
fall to pieces or **bits 1** to break up; to disintegrate. **2** to be unable to function.

fallacy N (**-ies**) **1** a mistaken notion. **2** a mistake in reasoning that spoils a whole argument. ■ **fallacious** ADJ.

fallible ADJ capable of making mistakes. ■ **fallibility** N (**-ies**).

Fallopian tube N in female mammals: either of the two long slender tubes through which the egg cells pass from the ovaries to the uterus.

fallout N **1** a cloud of radioactive dust caused by a nuclear explosion. **2** (**fall-out** and **falling-out**) a quarrel.

fallow ADJ of land: left unplanted after ploughing, to recover its natural fertility.

fallow deer N a small deer with a reddish-brown coat spotted with white in summer.

false ADJ **1** untrue. **2** mistaken. **3** artificial; not genuine. **4** insincere. **5** treacherous; disloyal.
➤ ADV in a false manner; incorrectly; dishonestly. ■ **falsely** ADJ. ■ **falseness** N.
■ **falsity** N (**-ies**).

false alarm N an alarm given unnecessarily.

falsehood N **1** dishonesty. **2** a lie.

false start N **1** a failed attempt to begin something. **2** an invalid start to a race, in which one competitor begins before the signal.

falsetto N (someone using) an artificially high voice, esp a tenor singing above his normal range.

falsify VB (**-ies, -ied**) to alter (accounts, evidence, etc) dishonestly, or make something up, in order to deceive or mislead. ■ **falsification** N.

falter VB **1** INTR to move unsteadily; to stumble. **2** INTR to start functioning unreliably. **3** INTR to lose strength or conviction. **4** TR & INTR to speak, or say something, hesitantly. ■ **faltering** ADJ.

fame N the condition of being famous.

famed ADJ very well known.

familiar ADJ **1** well known or recognizable. **2** frequently met with. **3** (**familiar with**) well acquainted with something. **4** friendly; close. **5** over-friendly.
➤ N a close friend. ■ **familiarity** N.
■ **familiarly** ADV.

familiarize or **-ise** VB **1** (usu **familiarize with sth**) to make (someone) familiar with it. **2** to make something well known or familiar.

family N (**-ies**) **1** a group consisting of a set of parents and children. **2** a group of people related to one another by blood or marriage. **3** a person's children. **4** a household of people. **5** all those descended from a common ancestor. **6** a related group, eg of languages, etc. **7** AS ADJ: belonging to, concerning, or suitable for a family or families: **family car • family pub • family matters.** ■ **familial** ADJ.

family planning N birth control.

family tree N the relationships within a family throughout the generations, or a diagram showing these.

famine N a severe shortage, esp of food.

famished ADJ **1** starving. **2** COLLOQ hungry.

famous ADJ **1** well known; celebrated; renowned. **2** great; glorious: **a famous victory**. ■ **famously** ADV.

fan¹ N **1** a hand-held device, usu semicircular, and made of silk or paper, for creating a cool current of air. **2** any mechanical or electrical device that creates air currents, esp for ventilation. **3** any structure that can be spread into the shape of a fan, eg a bird's tail.
➢ VB (-nn-) **1** to cool or ventilate with a fan. **2** to kindle (flames, resentment, etc).

fan² N an enthusiastic supporter or admirer, esp of a pop group, a football team, a sport, etc.

fanatic N someone with an extreme or excessive enthusiasm for something.
➢ ADJ (also **fanatical**) extremely or excessively enthusiastic about something.
■ **fanaticism** N.

fancier N, esp IN COMPOUNDS someone with a special interest in, or knowledge of, a specified bird, animal or plant: **pigeon fancier**.

fanciful ADJ **1** imaginative or over-imaginative. **2** imaginary. **3** designed in a curious or fantastic way. ■ **fancifully** ADV.

fancy N (-ies) **1** the imagination. **2** an image, idea or whim. **3** a sudden liking or desire.
➢ ADJ (-ier, -iest) **1** elaborate. **2** COLLOQ special, unusual or superior, esp in quality.
➢ VB (-ies, -ied) **1** to think or believe something. **2** to have a desire for something. **3** COLLOQ to be physically attracted to someone. **4** to consider likely to win or do well. **5** TR & INTR to imagine: **Fancy him getting married at last!**
➢ EXCLAM (also **fancy that!**) expressing surprise. ■ **fanciable** ADJ. ■ **fancily** ADV.

fancy dress N clothes for dressing up in.

fancy-free ADJ **1** not in love. **2** free to do as one pleases.

fanfare N a short piece of trumpet music to announce an important event or arrival.

fang N **1** a sharp pointed tooth, esp a large canine tooth of a carnivorous animal. **2** a tooth of a poisonous snake.

fanny N (-ies) **1** BRIT TABOO SLANG a woman's genitals. **2** N AMER SLANG the buttocks.

fantasize or **-ise** VB, INTR (often **fantasize about sth**) to indulge in fantasies.

fantastic and **fantastical** ADJ **1** COLLOQ splendid; excellent. **2** COLLOQ enormous; amazing. **3** absurd; unlikely; incredible. **4** fanciful; strange. ■ **fantastically** ADV.

fantasy N (-ies) **1** a pleasant daydream. **2** something longed-for but unlikely to happen. **3** a mistaken notion. **4** the activity of imagining. **5** a fanciful piece of writing, music, etc.

fanzine N a magazine produced by and for a particular group of fans.

FAQ ABBREV, COMP frequently asked question.

far (*farther, farthest* or *further, furthest*) ADV **1** at, to or from a great distance. **2** to or by a great extent: **My guess wasn't far out**. **3** at or to a distant time.
➢ ADJ **1** distant; remote. **2** the more distant of two things. **3** extreme: **the far Right**.
◆ **as far as** up to a certain place or point.
◆ **far from** the opposite of; not at all.
◆ **go far** to achieve great things.
◆ **in so far as** to the extent that.

farad N, ELECTRONICS the SI unit of electrical capacitance.

faraway ADJ **1** distant. **2** dreamy; abstracted.

farce N **1 a** a comedy involving ridiculously unlikely turns of events; **b** comedies of this type. **2** an absurd situation; something ludicrously badly organized. ■ **farcical** ADJ.

fare N **1** the price paid by a passenger to travel on a bus, train, etc. **2** a taxi passenger. **3** food or the provision of food.
➢ VB, INTR, FORMAL to get on (in a specified way): **She fared well.**

the Far East N a loosely-used term for the countries of E and SE Asia. ■ **Far Eastern** ADJ.

farewell EXCLAM, OLD USE goodbye!
➢ N an act of saying goodbye; an act of departure.
➢ ADJ parting; final: **a farewell party**.

far-fetched ADJ unlikely; unconvincing.

far-flung ADJ 1 extensive. 2 distant.

farm N 1 a piece of land with its buildings, used for growing crops, breeding livestock, etc. 2 a farmer's house and the buildings round it. 3 a place specializing in the rearing or growing of a specified type of livestock, crop, etc: **dairy farm** • **fish farm**.
➤ VB 1 a TR to prepare and use (land) for crop-growing, animal-rearing, etc. b INTR to be a farmer. 2 (also **farm out**) a to hand over (a child, old person, etc) temporarily to a carer; b to hand over (work, etc) to another to do.

farmer N someone who earns a living by managing or operating a farm.

farming N the business of running a farm.

far-off ADJ, ADV distant; remote.

far-reaching ADJ extensive in scope, influence, etc.

farrier N a person who shoes horses.

far-sighted ADJ 1 (also **far-seeing**) wise; prudent; forward-looking. 2 long-sighted.

fart COARSE SLANG, VB, INTR to emit wind from the anus.
➤ N 1 an emission of this kind. 2 a term of abuse for a person: **a boring old fart**.

farther ADJ, ADV further (with reference to physical distance).

farthest ADJ, ADV furthest (with reference to physical distance).

fascia (-*iae* or -*ias*) N 1 the board above a shop entrance, bearing the shop name and logo, etc. 2 BRIT the dashboard of a motor vehicle. 3 ARCHIT a long flat band or surface.

fascinate VB 1 to interest strongly; to intrigue. 2 to hold spellbound; to enchant irresistibly. ■ **fascinating** ADJ. ■ **fascination** N.

fascism N a political system characterized by extreme right-wing or nationalistic views. ■ **fascist** N, ADJ. ■ **fascistic** ADJ.

fashion N 1 style, esp the latest style, in clothes, music, lifestyle, etc. 2 a currently popular style or practice; a trend. 3 a manner of doing something. 4 sort, type or kind.
➤ VB 1 to form or make something into a particular shape, esp with the hands. 2 to mould or influence something.

fashionable ADJ 1 following the latest fashion. 2 used by or popular with fashionable people.

fast[1] ADJ 1 moving, or able to move, quickly. 2 taking a relatively short time. 3 of a clock, etc: showing a time in advance of the correct time. 4 allowing or intended for rapid movement: **the fast lane**. 5 firmly fixed or caught; steadfast. 6 of friends: firm; close. 7 of fabric colours: not liable to run or fade.
➤ ADV 1 quickly; rapidly. 2 in quick succession: **coming thick and fast**. 3 firmly; tight: **The glue held fast**. 4 deeply; thoroughly: **fast asleep**.

fast[2] VB, INTR to go without food.
➤ N a period of fasting.

fasten VB 1 to make something firmly closed or fixed. 2 to attach something to something else. 3 INTR to become fastened. 4 to be capable of being fastened. ■ **fastener** or **fastening** N.
◆ **fasten on** or **upon** to concentrate on eagerly; to dwell on.

fast food N ready-prepared food, such as hamburgers, fried fish, chips, etc.

fastidious ADJ 1 very particular in matters of taste and detail. 2 easily disgusted.

fastness N the quality of being firmly fixed.

fat N 1 any of a group of organic compounds that occur naturally in animals and plants, are solid at room temperature, and are insoluble in water. 2 a in mammals: a layer of tissue beneath the skin and between various organs, that serves as a thermal insulator and as a means of storing energy; b an excess of this.
➤ ADJ (**fatter, fattest**) 1 plump; overweight. 2 containing a lot of fat. 3 thick or wide. 4 COLLOQ of a fee, etc: large. 5 fertile; profitable. 6 FACETIOUS, SLANG none at all: **a fat chance**.

fatal ADJ 1 causing death; deadly. 2 bringing ruin; disastrous: **a fatal mistake**. 3 destined; unavoidable. ■ **fatally** ADV.

fatalism N 1 a belief or doctrine that all events are predestined and cannot be altered. 2 a defeatist attitude or outlook.

■ **fatalist** N. ■ **fatalistic** ADJ.

fatality N (*-ies*) **1** an accidental or violent death. **2** a person who has been killed in an accident, etc. **3** the quality of being fatal.

fate N **1** (also **Fate**) the apparent power that determines the course of events, over which humans have no control. **2** the individual destiny or fortune of a person or thing. **3** ultimate outcome. **4** death, downfall, destruction or doom.

fateful ADJ **1** of a remark, etc: prophetic. **2** decisive; critical; having significant results. **3** bringing calamity. ■ **fatefully** ADV.

father N **1** a male parent. **2** (**fathers**) one's ancestors. **3** a founder, inventor, originator, pioneer or early leader. **4** (**Father**) a title or form of address for a priest. **5** (**Father**) CHRISTIANITY the first person of the Trinity; God. ➤ VB **1** to be the father of (a child); to beget (offspring); to procreate. **2** to invent or originate (an idea, etc). ■ **fatherhood** N.

father-in-law N (*fathers-in-law*) the father of one's wife or husband.

fatherland N one's native country.

fatherly ADJ benevolent, protective and encouraging. ■ **fatherliness** N.

fathom N an imperial unit of measurement of the depth of water, equal to 6 feet. ➤ VB (also **fathom sth out**) **1** to work out a problem; to get to the bottom of a mystery. **2** to measure the depth of water.

fatigue N (PL in sense 3 only) **1** tiredness after work or effort; exhaustion. **2** weakness, esp in metals, caused by variations in stress. **3** (**fatigues**) military clothing. ➤ VB, TR & INTR to exhaust or become exhausted.

fatten VB, TR & INTR (also **fatten up**) to make or become fat. ■ **fattening** ADJ, N.

fatty ADJ (*-ier, -iest*) **1** containing fat. **2** greasy.

fatuous ADJ foolish, esp in a self-satisfied way; empty-headed; inane. ■ **fatuity** N (*-ies*).

fatwa or **fatwah** N a formal legal opinion or decree issued by a Muslim authority.

faucet N **1** a tap fitted to a barrel. **2** N AMER a tap on a bath, etc.

fault N **1** a weakness or failing in character. **2** a flaw or defect in an object or structure. **3** a misdeed or slight offence. **4** responsibility for something wrong: **all my fault**. **5** GEOL a break or crack in the Earth's crust. **6** TENNIS, ETC an incorrectly placed or delivered serve. ➤ VB **1** INTR to commit a fault. **2** to blame someone. ■ **faultless** ADJ.
◆ **at fault** culpable; to blame.

faulty ADJ (*-ier, -iest*) **1** having a fault or faults. **2** not working correctly.

faun N a mythical creature with a man's head and body and a goat's horns, hind legs and tail.

fauna N (*-as* or *-ae*) the wild animals of a particular region or time period. ■ **faunal** ADJ.

faux pas N (PL *faux pas*) an embarrassing blunder, esp a social one.

favour or (N AMER) **favor** N **1** a kind action. **2** approval or goodwill. **3** unfair preference. ➤ VB **1** to regard someone or something with goodwill. **2** to treat someone or something with preference, or over-indulgently. **3** to prefer; to support. **4** of circumstances: to give an advantage to someone or something.
◆ **in favour of 1** having a preference for. **2** to the benefit of. **3** in support or approval of.

favourable or (N AMER) **favorable** ADJ **1** showing or giving agreement or consent. **2** pleasing; likely to win approval. **3** advantageous or helpful. **4** of a wind: following. ■ **favourably** ADV.

favourite or (N AMER) **favorite** ADJ best-liked; preferred. ➤ N **1** a favourite person or thing. **2** someone unfairly preferred. **3** SPORT a horse or competitor expected to win.

favouritism or (N AMER) **favoritism** N the practice of giving unfair preference, help or support to someone or something.

fawn[1] N **1** a young deer of either sex. **2** a yellowish-beige colour. ➤ ADJ of this colour.

fawn[2] VB, INTR (often **fawn on** or **upon sb**) to flatter or behave over-humbly towards someone, in order to win approval.

fax N 1 a machine that scans documents electronically and transmits a photographic image of them to a receiving machine by telephone line. 2 a faxed document.
➤ VB 1 to transmit (a document) by this means. 2 to send a communication by fax.

faze VB, COLLOQ to disturb, worry or fluster.

FBI ABBREV Federal Bureau of Investigation.

fear N 1 anxiety and distress caused by the awareness of danger or expectation of pain. 2 a cause of this feeling.
➤ VB 1 to be afraid of (someone or something). 2 to think or expect (something) with dread. 3 to regret; to be sorry to say something: **I fear you have misunderstood.**
◆ **fear for sth** to be frightened or anxious about it: **feared for their lives.** ■ **fearless** ADJ.

fearful ADJ 1 afraid. 2 frightening. 3 COLLOQ very bad: **a fearful mess.** ■ **fearfully** ADJ.

fearsome ADJ 1 causing fear. 2 frightening.

feasible ADJ 1 capable of being done or achieved; possible. 2 LOOSELY probable; likely. ■ **feasibility** N (*-ies*). ■ **feasibly** ADV.

feast N 1 a large rich meal, esp one prepared to celebrate something. 2 a pleasurable abundance of something. 3 RELIG a regularly occurring celebration.
➤ VB, INTR to take part in a feast.

feat N a deed or achievement.

feather N 1 any of the light growths that form the soft covering of a bird. 2 something with a featherlike appearance. 3 plumage.
➤ VB to provide, cover or line with feathers.

featherbrain N a silly, feckless or empty-headed person. ■ **feather-brained** ADJ.

featherweight N 1 a class for boxers, etc of not more than a specified weight (57 kilograms or 126 pounds in professional boxing). 2 a boxer, etc of this weight class.

feature N 1 any of the parts of the face, eg eyes, nose, mouth, etc. 2 (**features**) the face. 3 a characteristic. 4 a noticeable part or quality of something. 5 an extended article in a newspaper, discussing a particular issue. 6 an article or item appearing regularly in a newspaper. 7 (also **feature film**) a main film in a cinema programme.
➤ VB 1 to have as a feature or make a feature of something. 2 to give prominence to (an actor, a well-known event, etc) in a film.
◆ **feature in sth** to play an important part or role in (a film, documentary, etc).

febrile ADJ relating to fever; feverish.

February N the second month of the year.

feckless ADJ 1 helpless; clueless. 2 irresponsible; aimless.

fecund ADJ fruitful; fertile; richly productive.

federal ADJ 1 of or relating to a country consisting of a group of states independent in local matters but united for other purposes, eg defence, foreign policy. 2 relating to the central government of a federation. ■ **federalism** N. ■ **federalist** N.

federation N 1 a federal union of states, ie a group of states united politically by a treaty. 2 a union of business organizations, institutions, etc. 3 the act of uniting in a league.

fed up ADJ bored; irritated.

fee N 1 a charge made for professional services, eg by a doctor or lawyer. 2 a charge for eg membership of a society, sitting an examination, entrance to a museum, etc. 3 (usu **fees**) a payment for education or instruction. 4 a payment made to a football club for the transfer of one of its players.

feeble ADJ 1 lacking strength. 2 lacking power or effectiveness. ■ **feebly** ADV.

feed VB (*fed*) 1 to give or supply food to (animals, etc). 2 to give something as food (to animals, etc). 3 to administer food (to an infant, young animal). 4 IN COMPOUNDS to administer food to someone in a specified way: **breast-feed.** 5 INTR of animals: to eat food. 6 to supply a machine, etc with fuel or other material.
➤ N 1 an act or session of feeding. 2 food for

livestock, etc. **3** the channel or mechanism by which a machine is supplied with fuel, etc.

feedback N **1** responses and reactions that provide guidelines for adjustment and development. **2** in a public-address system, etc: the partial return of the sound output to the microphone, producing a high-pitched whistle or howl.

feel VB (*felt*) **1** to become aware of something through the sense of touch. **2** TR & INTR to have a physical or emotional sensation of something; to sense. **3** TR & INTR to find out or investigate with the hands, etc. **4** TR & INTR to have (an emotion). **5** TR & INTR to react emotionally to something or be emotionally affected by something: **feels the loss very deeply. 6** INTR to give the impression of being (soft, hard, rough, etc) when touched. **7** INTR to be or seem (well, ill, happy, etc). **8** to instinctively believe in something: **She feels that this is a good idea. 9** to seem to oneself to be: **feel a fool.**
➤ N **1** a sensation or impression produced by touching. **2** an impression or atmosphere created by something. **3** an act of feeling with the fingers, etc. **4** an instinct, touch or knack.
◆ **feel like sth 1** to seem to oneself to be like something, to perceive oneself as something. **2** to have an inclination or desire for it.

feeler N **1** a tentacle. **2** either of a pair of structures, sensitive to touch, on the head of certain invertebrate animals.

feeling N **1** the sense of touch, a sensation or emotion. **2** emotion as distinct from reason. **3** strong emotion. **4** a belief or opinion. **5** (usu **a feeling for sth**) a natural ability for, or understanding of, an activity, etc. **6** affection. **7** mutual interactive emotion between two people, such as **bad feeling** (resentment), **good feeling** (friendliness), etc. **8** (often **feeling for sth**) an instinctive grasp or appreciation of it. **9** (**feelings**) one's attitude to something: **have mixed feelings. 10** (**feelings**) sensibilities: **hurt his feelings.**

feign VB to pretend to have (eg an illness) or feel (an emotion, etc); to invent.

feint N **1** in boxing, fencing, etc: a movement intended to deceive or distract one's opponent. **2** a misleading action or appearance.
➤ VB, INTR to make a feint.
➤ ADJ of paper: ruled with pale horizontal lines.

feisty ADJ (*-ier, -iest*) COLLOQ **1** spirited; lively. **2** irritable; quarrelsome.

feldspar or **felspar** N, GEOL a mineral found in most igneous and many metamorphic rocks. ■ **feldspathic** or **felspathic** ADJ.

felicitation N **1** the act of congratulating. **2** (**felicitations**) congratulations.

felicitous ADJ **1** of wording: elegantly apt; well-chosen; appropriate. **2** pleasant; happy.

felicity N (*-ies*) **1** happiness. **2** a cause of happiness. **3** elegance or aptness of wording.

feline ADJ **1** relating to the cat or cat family. **2** like a cat, esp in terms of stealth or elegance.
➤ N a member of the cat family.

fell¹ VB **1** to cut down (a tree). **2** to knock down someone or something.

fell² N (often **fells**) a hill, moor or an upland tract of pasture or moorland.

fellow N **1** a companion or equal. **2** (also COLLOQ **fella, fellah** or **feller**) **a** a man or boy; **b** COLLOQ a boyfriend. **3** a senior member of a college or university. **4** (**Fellow**) a member of a learned society. **5** one of a pair. **6** AS ADJ relating to a person in the same situation or condition as oneself, or having the same status, etc: **a fellow worker.**

fellowship N **1** friendly companionship. **2** commonness or similarity of interests between people. **3** a society or association.

felon N, LAW a person guilty of felony.

felony N (*-ies*) LAW a serious crime. ■ **felonious** ADJ.

felt N a fabric formed by matting or pressing fibres, esp wool, together.

felt pen, felt-tip pen and **felt tip** N a pen with a nib made of felt.

female ADJ **1** belonging or relating to the sex that gives birth to young, produces eggs, etc.

2 denoting the reproductive structure of a plant that contains an egg cell. **3** of or characteristic of a woman.
➤ N **1** a woman or girl. **2** a female animal.

feminine ADJ **1** typically belonging or relating to, or characteristic of, a woman. **2** having or reflecting qualities considered typical of a woman; effeminate. ■ **femininity** N.

feminism N a belief or movement advocating women's rights, particularly equal rights with men. ■ **feminist** N.

femur N (*femurs* or *femora*) **1** the longest bone of the human skeleton, from hip to knee. **2** the corresponding bone in the hind limb of four-limbed vertebrates. ■ **femoral** ADJ.

fen or **fenland** N a wet area of lowland, dominated by grasses, sedges and rushes.

fence N **1** a barrier, eg of wood or wire, for enclosing or protecting land. **2** a barrier for a horse to jump.
➤ VB **1** (also **fence sth in** or **off**) to enclose or separate with a fence, or as if with a fence. **2** INTR to practise fencing. **3** to build fences.

fencing N **1** the sport of attack and defence with a foil, épée or sabre. **2** material used for constructing fences. **3** fences collectively.

fend VB **1** (usu **fend sth** or **sb off**) to defend oneself from (blows, questions, etc). **2** INTR (esp **fend for sb**) to provide for, esp oneself.

fender N **1** a low guard fitted round a fireplace to keep ash, coals, etc within the hearth. **2** N AMER the wing or mudguard of a car. **3** a bundle of rope, tyres, etc hanging from a ship's side to protect it when in contact with piers, etc.

feng shui N the process of making the correct decision about the siting of a building, placing of furniture, etc to bring good luck.

fennel N a strong-smelling plant, whose seeds and leaves are used in cooking.

fenugreek N a plant with strong-smelling seeds, used as animal fodder and in cooking.

feral ADJ living or growing wild.

ferment N **1** fermentation. **2** a state of agitation or excitement.
➤ VB **1** INTR to undergo fermentation. **2** to be, or make something be, in a state of excitement.

fermentation N, CHEM a biochemical process in which micro-organisms break down an organic compound, usu a carbohydrate, in the absence of oxygen.

fern N a flowerless feathery-leaved plant that reproduces by spores. ■ **ferny** ADJ (*-ier, -iest*).

ferocious ADJ savagely fierce; cruel; savage ■ **ferocity** N.

ferret N a small, half-tame type of polecat.
➤ VB, TR & INTR to hunt (rabbits, etc) with a ferret.
◆ **ferret sth out** to find it out through persistent investigation.

ferric ADJ, CHEM denoting a compound that contains iron in its trivalent state.

ferrous ADJ, CHEM denoting a chemical compound that contains iron in its divalent state.

ferrule N a metal ring or cap at the tip of a walking-stick or umbrella.

ferry N (*-ies*) **1** (also **ferryboat**) a boat that carries passengers and often cars across a river or strip of water, esp as a regular service. **2** the service thus provided. **3** the place or route where a ferryboat runs.
➤ VB (*-ies, -ied*) **1** TR & INTR (sometimes **ferry across**) to transport or go by ferry. **2** to convey (passengers, goods, etc) in a vehicle.

fertile ADJ **1** containing the nutrients required to support an abundant growth of crops, plants, etc. **2** producing or capable of producing babies, young or fruit. **3** of an egg or seed: capable of developing into a new individual. **4** rich in ideas; very productive. ■ **fertility** N.

fertilize or **-ise** VB **1** of a male gamete, esp a sperm cell: to fuse with (a female gamete, esp an egg cell) to form a zygote. **2** of a male animal: to inseminate or impregnate (a female animal). **3** of flowering/cone-bearing plants: to transfer (pollen) by the process of pollination. **4** to supply (soil) with extra nutrients in order to increase its fertility. ■ **fertilization** N.

fertilizer or **fertiliser** N a substance added

to soil to improve fertility.

fervent ADJ enthusiastic; earnest or ardent.

fervid ADJ fervent; full of fiery passion or zeal.

fervour or (N AMER) **fervor** N passionate enthusiasm; intense eagerness or sincerity.

fest N, IN COMPOUNDS a gathering or festival for a specified activity: **filmfest • thrill fest**.

fester VB 1 INTR to form or discharge pus. 2 to continue unchecked. 3 INTR to rot or decay.

festival N 1 a day or period of celebration, esp one kept traditionally. 2 RELIG a feast or saint's day. 3 a season or series of performances (of musical, theatrical or other cultural events).

festive ADJ 1 relating to a festival. 2 celebratory; joyous; lively; cheerful.

festivity N (-*ies*) 1 a lighthearted event; celebration, merrymaking. 2 (**festivities**) festive activities; celebrations.

festoon N a decorative chain of flowers, ribbons, etc looped between two points. ➢ VB to hang or decorate with festoons.

fetch VB 1 to go and get something, and bring it back. 2 to be sold for (a certain price). 3 INFORMAL to deal someone (a blow, slap, etc). 4 to bring forth (tears, blood, a sigh, etc). ◆ **fetch up** COLLOQ to arrive; to end up.

fetching ADJ, COLLOQ attractive, charming.

fête or **fete** N 1 an outdoor event with entertainment, competitions, stalls, etc, usu to raise money for a charity. 2 a festival or holiday, esp to mark the feast day of a saint. ➢ VB to entertain or honour someone lavishly.

fetid ADJ having a strong disgusting smell.

fetish N 1 an object worshipped for its perceived magical powers. 2 a procedure or ritual followed obsessively, or an object of obsessive devotion. ■ **fetishism** N. ■ **fetishist** N.

fetlock N the thick projection at the back of a horse's leg just above the hoof.

fetter N (usu **fetters**) a chain or shackle fastened to a prisoner's ankle.

➢ VB to put someone in fetters.

fettle N spirits; condition; state of health.

fetus or **foetus** N 1 the embryo of a viviparous mammal during the later stages of development in the uterus. 2 a human embryo from the end of the eighth week after conception until birth. ■ **fetal** ADJ.

feud N a long-drawn-out bitter quarrel between families, individuals or clans. ➢ VB, INTR (often **feud with sb**) to carry on a feud with them. ■ **feuding** N, ADJ.

feudal ADJ relating to feudalism.

feudalism and **feudal system** N a social system in the Middle Ages, in which powerful land-owning lords granted degrees of privilege and protection to lesser subjects holding a range of positions within a rigid hierarchy.

fever N 1 an abnormally high body temperature, often accompanied by shivering, thirst and headache. 2 a disease in which this is a marked symptom, eg scarlet fever, yellow fever. 3 an extreme state of agitation or excitement. ■ **feverish** ADJ.

few ADJ not many; a small number; hardly any. ➢ PRONOUN (USED AS A PL) hardly any things, people, etc. ◆ **a few** a small number; some. ◆ **a good few** or **quite a few** INFORMAL a fairly large number; several.

fey ADJ 1 strangely fanciful; whimsical. 2 able to foresee future events.

fez N (**fezzes** or **fezes**) a hat shaped like a flat-topped cone, with a tassel.

fiancé or **fiancée** N respectively, a man or woman to whom one is engaged to be married.

fiasco N (-**os** or -**oes**) a humiliating failure.

fib COLLOQ, N a trivial lie. ➢ VB (-**bb**-) INTR to tell fibs. ■ **fibber** N.

fibre or (N AMER) **fiber** N 1 a fine thread or thread-like cell of a natural or artificial substance, eg cellulose, nylon. 2 a material composed of fibres. 3 the indigestible parts of edible plants or seeds, that help to move food quickly through the body: **dietary fibre**. **4** strength of character; stamina: **moral fibre**.

fibreglass or (N AMER) **fiberglass** N **1** a strong light plastic strengthened with glass fibres, which is resistant to heat, fire and corrosion. **2** material consisting of fine, tangled fibres of glass, used for insulation.

fibre optics or (N AMER) **fiber optics** SING N the use of flexible strands of glass or plastic to carry information in the form of light signals.

fibrous ADJ of, containing or like fibre.

fibula N (*-ae* or *-as*) **1** the outer and narrower of the two bones in the lower leg, between the knee and the ankle. **2** the corresponding bone in the hind limb of four–limbed vertebrates.

fickle ADJ changeable in affections, loyalties or intentions. ■ **fickleness** N.

fiction N **1** literature concerning imaginary characters or events, eg a novel or story. **2** a pretence; a lie. **3** LAW a misrepresentation of the truth, accepted for convenience. ■ **fictional** ADJ. ■ **fictionalize** VB.

fictitious ADJ imagined; invented; not real.

fiddle N **1** a violin, esp when used to play folk music or jazz. **2** COLLOQ a dishonest arrangement; a fraud. **3** a manually delicate or tricky operation.
➤ VB **1** INTR (often **fiddle with sth**) to play about aimlessly with it; to tinker, toy or meddle with it. **2** TR & INTR to falsify (accounts, etc); to manage or manipulate dishonestly. **3** TR & INTR to play a violin or fiddle; to play (a tune) on one. ■ **fiddler** N.

fiddling ADJ unimportant; trifling.

fiddly ADJ (*-ier, -iest*) awkward to handle or do.

fidelity N (*-ies*) faithfulness.

fidget VB **1** INTR to move about restlessly. **2** (often **fidget with sth**) to touch and handle it aimlessly.
➤ N **1** a person who fidgets. **2** (**the fidgets**) nervous restlessness. ■ **fidgety** ADJ.

field N **1** a piece of land enclosed for crop-growing or pasturing animals. **2** a piece of open grassland. **3** an area marked off as a ground for a sport, etc. **4** IN COMPOUNDS an area rich in a specified mineral, etc: **coalfield** • **oilfield**. **5** IN COMPOUNDS an expanse of something specified, usu from the natural world: **snowfields** • **poppy fields**. **6** an area of knowledge or study; speciality. **7** PHYS a region of space in which one object exerts force on another: **force field**. **8** the area included in something; the range over which a force, etc extends; the area visible to an observer at any one time: **field of vision**. **9 a** the contestants in a race, competition, etc; **b** all contestants except for the favourite; the rivals of a particular contestant. **10** a battlefield: **fell on the field**. **11** any place away from the classroom, office, etc where practical experience is gained.
➤ VB **1** TR & INTR, SPORT, esp CRICKET **a** of a team: to be the team whose turn it is to retrieve balls hit by the batting team; **b** TR & INTR of a player: to retrieve the ball from the field; **c** INTR of a player: to play in the field. **2** to put forward as (a team or player) for a match. **3** to enter someone in a competition. **4** to deal with a succession of (inquiries, etc): **to field questions**.

field day N **1** a day spent on some specific outdoor activity, such as a nature study. **2** INFORMAL any period of exciting activity.

fielder N, SPORT a member of the fielding side.

field glasses PL N binoculars.

field marshal N an army officer of high rank.

field sports PL N sports carried out in the countryside, such as hunting, fishing, etc.

fieldwork N practical work or research done away from the laboratory or place of study.

fiend N **1** a devil; an evil spirit. **2** COLLOQ a spiteful person. **3** COLLOQ an enthusiast for something specified: **sun fiend**.

fiendish ADJ **1** like a fiend. **2** devilishly cruel. **3** extremely difficult or unpleasant.

fierce ADJ **1** violent and aggressive. **2** intense; strong: **fierce competition**. **3** severe; extreme: **a fierce storm**. ■ **fiercely** ADV.

fiery ADJ (*-ier, -iest*) **1** consisting of fire; like fire. **2** easily enraged: **a fiery temper**. **3** passionate; spirited; vigorous: **fiery oratory**. **4** of food: hot-tasting. ■ **fieriness** N.

fiesta N esp in Spanish-speaking communities: a religious festival or carnival.

fife N a small type of flute.

fifteen N **1 a** the cardinal number 15; **b** the quantity that this represents, being one more than fourteen or the sum of ten and five. **2** any symbol for this, eg **15** or **XV**. **3** something, esp a garment, or a person, whose size is denoted by the number 15. **4** (**15**) BRIT a film classified as suitable for people aged 15 and over. ➤ ADJ **1** totalling fifteen. **2** aged fifteen. ■ **fifteenth** N, ADJ.

fifth (often written **5th**) ADJ **1** in counting: **a** next after fourth; **b** last of five. **2** in fifth position. ➤ N **1** one of five equal parts. **2** a fraction equal to one divided by five.

fifth column N a body of citizens prepared to co-operate with an invading enemy. ■ **fifth columnist** N.

fifties (often written **50s** or **50's**) PL N **1** (**one's fifties**) the period of time between one's fiftieth and sixtieth birthdays. **2** (**the fifties**) the range of temperatures between fifty and sixty degrees. **3** (**the fifties**) the period of time between the fiftieth and sixtieth years of a century.

fifty N (*-ies*) **1 a** the cardinal number 50; **b** the quantity that this represents, being one more than forty-nine, or the product of ten and five. **2** any symbol for this, eg **50** or **L**. **3** a set or group of fifty people or things. ➤ ADJ **1** totalling fifty. **2** aged fifty. ■ **fiftieth** N, ADJ.

fifty-fifty ADJ **1** of a chance: equal either way. **2** half-and-half. ➤ ADV divided equally between two.

fig N **1** a tropical and sub-tropical tree or shrub with a soft pear-shaped fruit. **2** its fruit.

fight VB (*fought*) **1** TR & INTR to attack or engage (an enemy, army, etc) in combat. **2** to take part in or conduct (a battle, campaign, etc). **3** TR & INTR (sometimes **fight against**) to oppose (eg an enemy, a person, an illness, a cause, etc) vigorously. **4** INTR to quarrel; to disagree. **5** INTR (often **fight for sth** or **sb**) to struggle or campaign on its or their behalf. **6** INTR to make (one's way) with a struggle. ➤ N **1** a battle; a physically violent struggle. **2** a quarrel; a dispute; a contest. **3** resistance. **4** the will to resist. **5** a boxing-match. **6** a campaign or crusade. ■ **fighter** N.
◆ **fight back** to counter an attack.
◆ **fight sb off** to repulse them (esp an attacker).
◆ **fight sth off** to get rid of or resist (an illness).

fighting chance N a chance to succeed dependent chiefly on determination.

figment N something imagined or invented.

figurative ADJ **1** metaphorical; not literal. **2** of writing, etc: full of figures of speech, esp metaphor. **3** representing a figure; representing using an emblem or symbol, etc. **4** of art: showing things as they actually look.

figure N **1** the form of anything in outline. **2** a symbol representing a number; a numeral. **3** a number representing an amount; a price. **4** an indistinctly seen or unidentified person. **5** a representation of the human form, esp in painting or sculpture. **6** (**figures**) arithmetical calculations; statistics. **7** a well-known person. **8** a specified impression that a person has or makes. **9** a diagram or illustration, esp in a text. **10** the shape of a person's body. **11** a geometrical shape, formed from a combination of points, lines, curves or surfaces. ➤ VB **1** N AMER to think; to reckon. **2** to imagine; to envisage. **3** INTR, COLLOQ to be probable or predictable; to make sense: **That figures!**
◆ **figure sb out** to understand how they are thinking or what their motivation is, etc.
◆ **figure sth out** to work it out; to begin to understand it.

figurehead N **1** a leader in name only. **2** a carved figure fixed to a ship's prow.

figure of speech N a device such as a metaphor, simile, etc that enlivens language.

figure skating N ice skating where

prescribed patterns are performed. ■ **figure skater** N.

figurine N a small carved or moulded figure.

filament N a fine thread, stalk, wire or fibre.

filbert N 1 the nut of the cultivated hazel. 2 (also **filbert tree**) the tree bearing the nut.

filch VB to steal something small or trivial.

file¹ N 1 a folder or box in which to keep loose papers. 2 a collection of papers so kept, esp dealing with a particular subject. 3 COMP an organized collection of data that can be accessed as a single unit. 4 a line of people or things, esp soldiers, positioned or moving one behind the other: single file.
➢ VB 1 (often **file sth away**) to put (papers, etc) into a file. 2 (often **file for sth**) to make a formal application to a law court on (a specified matter). 3 to place (a document) on official or public record. 4 INTR to march or move along one behind the other.

file² N 1 a steel hand tool with a rough surface consisting of fine parallel grooves with sharp cutting edges, used to smooth or rub away wood, metal, etc. 2 a small object of metal or emeryboard used for shaping fingernails.
➢ VB to smooth or shape (a surface) using a file.

filial ADJ of or resembling, a son or daughter.

filibuster N esp in the US Senate: **a** the practice of making long speeches to delay the passing of laws; **b** a person who does this.

filigree N 1 delicate work in gold or silver wire, used in jewellery, etc. 2 any delicate thing.

filing cabinet N a set of drawers for holding collections of papers and documents.

filings PL N particles rubbed off with a file.

fill VB 1 (also **fill sth up**) to make it full. 2 INTR (also **fill up**) to become full. 3 to take up all the space in something. 4 to satisfy (a need); to perform (a role) satisfactorily. 5 (sometimes **fill up**) to occupy (time). 6 (also **fill sth in** or **up**) to put material into (a hole, cavity, etc) to level the surface. 7 to appoint someone to (a position or post of employment). 8 **a** to take up (a position or post of employment); **b** to work in (a job), sometimes temporarily.
➢ N 1 anything used to fill something. 2 SOMETIMES IN COMPOUNDS material used to fill a space to a required level: rock-fill. ■ **filler** N.
◆ **eat one's fill** to consume enough to satisfy.
◆ **fill sb in** to inform them fully; to brief them.
◆ **fill sth in** to write information as required on to (a form, etc).
◆ **fill in for sb** to take over their work temporarily.
◆ **fill out** to put on weight and become fatter.
◆ **fill sth up** 1 to fill in (a form, etc). 2 to make it full.

fillet N **a** a piece of meat without bone, taken as a cut of the sirloin, or the fleshy part of the thigh: pork fillet; **b** (in full **fillet steak**) the most highly valued cut of beef, cut from the lowest part of the loin.
➢ VB 1 to cut fillets from (meat or fish). 2 to remove the bones from (a fish).

filling N 1 DENTISTRY a substance inserted into a cavity in a decaying tooth. 2 food put inside a pie, sandwich, etc.
➢ ADJ of food, a meal, etc: satisfying.

fillip N something that has a stimulating or brightening effect; a boost.

filly N (-ies) a young female horse or pony.

film N 1 a strip of thin flexible light-sensitive plastic, etc, exposed inside a camera to produce still or moving pictures. 2 a series of images recorded and edited to tell a story, present a subject, etc, and shown in the cinema or on TV. 3 a fine skin or coating.
➢ VB 1 TR & INTR to record any series of images, usu moving objects, using a TV camera, cine camera, video camera, camcorder, etc. 2 INTR to make a motion picture.

filmy ADJ (-ier, -iest) of a fabric, etc: thin, light and transparent.

filo N (in full **filo pastry**) a type of Greek flaky pastry made in thin sheets.

filter N 1 a porous substance that allows liquid, gas, smoke, etc through, but traps solid matter, impurities, etc. 2 a device containing this. 3 a fibrous pad at the unlit end of a cigarette,

and some types of cigars, that traps some of the smoke's impurities, eg tar. **4** a transparent tinted disc used to reduce the strength of certain colour frequencies in the light entering a camera or emitted by a lamp. **5** BRIT a traffic signal at traffic lights that allows vehicles going in some directions to proceed while others are stopped.
➢ VB **1** TR & INTR to pass something through a filter, often to remove impurities, particles, etc. **2** INTR to go past little by little.
◆ **filter sth out** to remove (impurities, etc) from (liquids, gases, etc) by filtering.
◆ **filter through** or **out** INTR of news: to leak out, often gradually.

filth N **1** repulsive dirt; any foul matter. **2** anything perceived as obscene.

filthy ADJ (*-ier, -iest*) **1** extremely dirty. **2** obscenely vulgar. **3** offensive or vicious: *a filthy lie*. **4** INFORMAL OR DIALECT extremely unpleasant: *filthy weather*.
➢ ADV, COLLOQ used for emphasis: *filthy rich*.

fin N **1** a thin wing–like projection on a fish's body for propelling it through the water, balancing, steering, etc. **2** anything that resembles a fin in appearance or function, eg the vertical projection in the tail of an aircraft.

final ADJ **1** occurring at the end. **2** completed. **3** of a decision, etc: not to be altered.
➢ N **1 a** the last part of a competition at which the winner is decided; **b** (**finals**) the last round or group of contests resulting in a winner. **2** (**finals**) the examinations held at the end of a degree course, etc. ■ **finality** N. ■ **finally** ADV.

finale N **1** the grand conclusion to a show, etc. **2** the last or closing movement of a symphony or other piece of music.

finalist N someone who reaches the final round in a competition.

finalize or **-ise** VB to decide on or finally agree to something.

finance N **1** money affairs and the management of them. **2** the money or funds needed or used to pay for something.

3 (**finances**) a person's financial state.
➢ VB to provide funds for something.
■ **financial** ADJ.

financier N someone engaged in large financial transactions.

finch N a songbird, eg a sparrow, goldfinch, etc, with a short beak adapted for cracking seeds.

find VB (*found*) **1** to discover through search, enquiry, mental effort or chance. **2** to seek out and provide something. **3** to realize or discover something. **4** to experience something as being (easy, difficult, etc). **5** to consider; to think. **6** to get or experience. **7** to become aware of something or someone: *found her beside him*. **8** to succeed in getting (time, courage, money, etc for something). **9** to see or come across.
➢ N something or someone that is found.
◆ **find out about sth** to discover or get information about it.

finder N someone who finds something.

finding N **1** LAW a decision or verdict reached as the result of a judicial inquiry. **2** (usu **findings**) conclusions reached as the result of some research or investigation.

fine[1] ADJ **1** of high quality; excellent; splendid. **2** beautiful; handsome. **3** grand; superior: *her fine relations*. **4** of weather: bright; not rainy. **5** well; healthy. **6** quite satisfactory: *That's fine by me*. **7** pure; refined. **8** thin; delicate. **9** close-set in texture or arrangement. **10** consisting of tiny particles. **11** intricately detailed: *fine embroidery*. **12** slight; subtle: *fine adjustments*.
➢ ADV **1** COLLOQ satisfactorily. **2** finely; into fine pieces. ■ **finely** ADV. ■ **fineness** N.

fine[2] N an amount of money to be paid as a penalty for breaking a regulation or law.
➢ VB to impose a fine on someone.

fine art N **1** art produced for its aesthetic value. **2** (usu **fine arts**) painting, drawing, sculpture and architecture.

finery N showy clothes, jewellery, etc.

finespun ADJ delicate; over–subtle.

finesse N **1** skilful elegance or expertise. **2** tact and poise in handling situations.

finger N 1 a one of the five jointed extremities of the hand; b any of the four of these other than the thumb; c AS ADJ: finger buffet; d IN COMPOUNDS: fingerprint. 2 the part of a glove that fits over a finger. 3 anything resembling or similar to a finger in shape. 4 a measure or quantity of alcoholic spirits in a glass, filling it to a depth which is equal to the width of a finger. ➤ VB to touch or feel something with the fingers: He fingered the velvet.

fingerboard N the part of a violin, guitar, etc against which the strings are pressed by the fingers to change the note.

fingering N 1 the correct positioning of the fingers for playing a particular musical instrument or piece of music. 2 the written or printed notation indicating this.

fingernail N the nail at the tip of one's finger.

fingerprint N the print or inked impression made by the pattern of minute swirling ridges on the surface of the end joints of the fingers and thumbs.

fingertip N the end or tip of one's finger.
◆ **have sth at one's fingertips** to have information readily available.

finicky ADJ 1 too concerned with detail. 2 of a task: intricate; tricky. 3 fussy; faddy.

finish VB (often **finish off** or **up**) 1 TR & INTR to bring something to an end, or come to an end; to reach a natural conclusion. 2 to complete or perfect something. 3 to use, eat, drink, etc the last of something. 4 INTR to reach or end up in a certain position or situation. 5 to give a particular treatment to the surface of (cloth, wood, etc). ➤ N 1 the last stage; the end. 2 the last part of a race, etc. 3 perfecting touches put to a product. 4 the surface texture given to cloth, wood, etc.
◆ **finish with sb** 1 to end a relationship with them. 2 to stop dealing with them.

finishing touch N (also **finishing touches**) a last minor improvement or detail that makes something perfect.

finite ADJ 1 having an end or limit. 2 MATH having a fixed, countable number of elements. 3 GRAM of a verb: being in a form that reflects person, number, tense, etc, as distinct from being an infinitive or participle.

fiord see **fjord**

fir N 1 a coniferous evergreen tree, with silvery or bluish foliage and leathery needle-like leaves. 2 any of various related trees, eg the Douglas fir. 3 the wood of any of these trees.

fire N (PL in senses 2, 3 and 4 only) 1 flames coming from something that is burning. 2 an occurrence of destructive burning of something: a forest fire. 3 mainly in homes: a mass of burning wood, coal or other fuel, usu in a grate, etc, used for warmth or cooking. 4 a gas or electric room-heater. 5 the discharge of firearms. 6 the launching of a missile. 7 heat and light produced by something burning or some other source. 8 enthusiasm; passion. ➤ VB 1 TR & INTR to discharge (a gun); to send off (a bullet or other missile) from a gun, catapult, bow, etc: fired the gun. 2 to launch (a rocket, missile, etc). 3 to detonate (an explosive). 4 of a gun, missile, etc: to be discharged, launched, etc: The gun fired. 5 to direct (eg questions) in quick succession at someone. 6 COLLOQ to dismiss someone from employment. 7 INTR of a vehicle engine, boiler, etc: to start working when a spark causes the fuel to burn: The motor fired. 8 to put fuel into (a furnace, etc). 9 to inspire or stimulate someone. 10 POTTERY to bake (pottery, bricks, etc) in a kiln, usu at a very high temperature. ➤ EXCLAM 1 a cry, warning others of a fire. 2 the order to start firing weapons, etc.
◆ **fire at** or **on sb** to discharge a gun at them.
◆ **set fire to sth** or **set sth on fire** to make it burn; to set light to it.

firearm N (often **firearms**) a gun, pistol, revolver or rifle.

fireball N 1 a mass of hot gases at the centre of a nuclear explosion. 2 COLLOQ a lively energetic person.

firebomb N an incendiary bomb. ➤ VB to attack something with firebombs.

firebrand N 1 a piece of burning wood. 2 someone who stirs up unrest.

fire brigade N, chiefly BRIT a team of people employed to prevent and extinguish fires.

firedamp N an explosive mixture of methane gas and air.

fire door N a fire-resistant door between two parts of a building to prevent the spread of fire.

fire engine N a vehicle which carries firefighters and their equipment to a fire.

fire escape N an external metal staircase which can be used to escape from a burning building.

fire extinguisher N a portable device containing water, liquid carbon dioxide under pressure, foam, etc, for spraying on to a fire to put it out.

firefighter N a person who is trained to put out large fires. ■ **firefighting** N, ADJ.

firefly N (-ies) a small, winged, nocturnal beetle that emits light in a series of brief flashes.

fireguard N a metal or wire-mesh protective screen for putting round an open fire.

fire irons PL N a set of tools for tending a coal or log fire, usu a poker, tongs, brush and shovel.

firelighter N a block of flammable material used to help light a coal or log fire.

fireman N 1 a male member of a fire brigade, officially called a firefighter. 2 on steam trains or steamboats: a person who stokes the fire or furnace.

fireplace N a recess for a coal or log fire or a tiled, marble, etc structure surrounding it.

fire-power N, MIL the destructive capacity of an artillery unit.

fire-raiser N someone who deliberately sets fire to buildings, etc. ■ **fire-raising** N.

firewood N wood for burning as fuel.

firework N 1 a device that, when lit, produces coloured sparks, flares, etc, often with accompanying loud bangs. 2 (**fireworks** or **firework display**) a show at which such devices are let off for entertainment. 3 (**fireworks**) COLLOQ a show of anger.

firing squad N a detachment of soldiers with the job of shooting a condemned person.

firkin N, BREWING a measure equal to 9 gallons (c. 40 litres).

firm¹ ADJ 1 strong; compact; steady. 2 solid; not soft or yielding. 3 definite: a firm offer. 4 of prices, markets, etc: steady or stable, with a slight upward trend. 5 determined; resolute. 6 of a mouth or chin: suggesting determination.
➤ ADV in a determined and unyielding manner; with resolution: hold firm to a promise.
➤ VB to make something firm or secure.
■ **firmly** ADV. ■ **firmness** N.

firm² N a business or company.

firmament N, LITERARY, OLD USE the sky; heaven.

first (often written **1st**) ADJ 1 in counting: before all others; before the second and following ones. 2 earliest in time or order; the starting object of a series of objects. 3 basic; fundamental: first principles.
➤ ADV 1 before anything or anyone else. 2 foremost: got in feet first. 3 before doing anything else: first make sure of the facts. 4 for the first time: since he first saw him. 5 preferably; rather: I'd die first. 6 firstly.
➤ N 1 COLLOQ a first occurrence of something; something never done before: That's a first for me! 2 the beginning; the start: from first to last. 3 (**a first**) EDUCATION, chiefly BRIT first-class honours in a university degree.
◆ **at first** at the start of something; early on in the course of something.

first-born LITERARY OR OLD USE, N the eldest child in a family.
➤ ADJ eldest.

first-class ADJ 1 referring to the best or highest grade in terms of value, performance or quality. 2 excellent. 3 referring to the most comfortable grade of accommodation in a train, plane, etc. 4 chiefly BRIT the category of mail most speedily delivered. Also AS NOUN.
➤ ADV (**first class**) by first-class mail, etc.

first cousin see **cousin**

first-degree ADJ 1 MED denoting the least severe type of burn in which only the outer layer of the skin is damaged. **2** N AMER LAW denoting the most serious level of murder.

first floor N **1** the floor directly above the ground floor. **2** US the ground floor.

first-hand ADJ, ADV direct; from the original source; without an intermediary.

firstly ADV used to introduce a list of things: before all others; in the first place; to begin with.

first name N a personal name as distinct from a family name or surname.

first person see under **person**

first-rate ADJ **1** being of the highest quality, as opposed to second-rate, etc. **2** excellent; fine.

firth N a river estuary or an inlet.

fiscal ADJ **1** of or relating to government finances or revenue. **2** of or relating to financial matters generally. ■ **fiscally** ADV.

fish N (*fish* or *fishes*) **1** a cold-blooded aquatic vertebrate that breathes by means of gills, and has a bony or cartilaginous skeleton, a body covered with scales, and that swims using fins. **2** IN COMPOUNDS any of various creatures that inhabit water: **shellfish** • **jellyfish**. **3** the flesh of fish used as food.
➤ VB **1** INTR to catch or try to catch fish. **2** to catch or try to catch fish in (a river, lake, etc). **3** INTR to search or grope. **4** INTR to seek information, compliments, etc by indirect means.

fisherman N a person who fishes as a job or hobby.

fishery N (*-ies*) **1** an area of water where fishing takes place, particularly sea waters; a fishing ground. **2** the business or industry of catching, processing and selling fish.

fish finger N an oblong piece of filleted or minced fish coated in breadcrumbs.

fishing N the sport or business of catching fish.

fishing-rod N a long flexible rod to which a fishing-line, and usu a reel, is attached.

fishmonger N a retailer of fish.

fishnet N **1** a net for catching fish. **2** AS ADJ having an open mesh, like netting: **fishnet tights**.

fish slice N a kitchen utensil with a flat slotted head, for lifting and turning food.

fishy ADJ (*-ier, -iest*) **1 a** of, like or consisting of fish. **2** COLLOQ dubious; questionable.

fission N a splitting or division into pieces.

fissure N, GEOL a long narrow crack.

fist N a tightly closed or clenched hand with the fingers and thumb doubled back into the palm. ■ **fistful** N.

fisticuffs PL N, HUMOROUS fighting with fists.

fit[1] VB (*fitted* or (N AMER) *fit*) **1** TR & INTR to be the right shape or size for something or someone. **2** to be suitable or appropriate for something. **3** TR & INTR to be consistent or compatible with something. **4** to install or put something new in place. **5** to equip. **6** to make or be suitable. **7** to try clothes on someone to see where adjustment is needed.
➤ N the way something fits according to its shape or size: **a tight fit**.
➤ ADJ (*fitter, fittest*) **1 a** healthy; feeling good. **b** healthy, esp because of exercise. **2** about to do something: **looked fit to drop**.
➤ ADV enough to do something: **laughed fit to burst**. ■ **fitly** ADV. ■ **fitness** N.
◆ **fit for sth** suited to it; good enough for it.
◆ **fit in 1** of someone in a social situation: to behave in a suitable or accepted way. **2** to conform to certain arrangements.
◆ **fit sb** or **sth in** to find time to deal with them or it.
◆ **fit sth together** or **fit sth in** to insert or place it in position.

fit[2] N **1** a sudden involuntary attack, of convulsions, coughing, fainting, hysterics, etc. **2** a burst, spell or bout: **a fit of giggles**.

fitful ADJ irregular, spasmodic or intermittent; not continuous. ■ **fitfully** ADV.

fitment N a piece of equipment or furniture which is fixed to a wall, floor, etc.

fitted ADJ **1** made to fit closely: **fitted sheets**. **2** of a carpet: covering the floor entirely. **3** fixed; built-in: **fitted cupboards**. **4** of a kitchen, etc: with built-in cupboards, appliances, etc.

fitter N a person who installs, adjusts or repairs machinery, equipment, etc.

fitting ADJ suitable; appropriate.
➤ N 1 an accessory or part: **a light fitting**. 2 (**fittings**) fitted furniture or equipment. 3 an act of trying on a specially made piece of clothing, to see where adjustment is necessary.

five N 1 a the cardinal number 5; b the quantity that this represents, being one more than four. 2 any symbol for this number, eg 5 or V. 3 something, esp a garment, or a person, whose size is denoted by the number 5. 4 the fifth hour after midnight or midday: **The meeting starts at five**.
➤ ADJ 1 totalling five. 2 aged five.

fivefold ADJ 1 equal to five times as much or many. 2 divided into, or consisting of, five parts.
➤ ADV by five times as much.

fiver N, BRIT, COLLOQ a five-pound note.

fix VB 1 to attach or place something firmly. 2 to mend or repair something. 3 to direct; to concentrate: **fixed his eyes on her**. 4 to arrange or agree (a time, etc). 5 to establish (the time of an occurrence). 6 COLLOQ to arrange (the result of a race, trial, etc) dishonestly. 7 COLLOQ to thwart, punish or kill someone. 8 PHOTOG to make (the image in a photograph) permanent by the use of chemicals. 9 COLLOQ to prepare (a meal, etc): **I'll fix breakfast**.
➤ N, COLLOQ a situation which is difficult to escape from; a predicament.
◆ **fix sth up** 1 to arrange a meeting, etc. 2 to get a place ready for some purpose.

fixation N 1 an (often abnormal) attachment, preoccupation or obsession. 2 PSYCHOL a strong attachment of a person to another person, an object or a particular means of gratification during childhood. ■ **fixated** ADJ.

fixative N 1 a liquid sprayed on a drawing, painting or photograph to preserve and protect it. 2 a liquid used to hold eg dentures in place. 3 a substance added to perfume to stop it evaporating.

fixed ADJ 1 fastened; immovable. 2 unvarying; unchanging; set or established: **fixed ideas**.

3 steady; concentrated; rigid. 4 stationary. 5 permanent: **fixed address**. ■ **fixedly** ADV.

fixer N, PHOTOG a chemical solution that fixes photographic images.

fixture N 1 a permanently fixed piece of furniture or equipment. 2 a a match, horse-race or other event in a sports calendar; b the date for such an event. 3 someone or something permanently established in a place.

fizz VB, INTR 1 of a liquid: to give off bubbles of carbon dioxide with a hissing sound. 2 to hiss.
➤ N 1 a hiss or spluttering sound; fizziness. 2 vivacity. 3 the bubbly quality of a drink; effervescence. 4 any effervescent drink.
■ **fizziness** N. ■ **fizzy** ADJ.

fizzle VB, INTR to make a faint hiss.
➤ N a faint hissing sound.
◆ **fizzle out** to come to a feeble end; to come to nothing, esp after an enthusiastic start.

fjord or **fiord** N a long narrow steep-sided inlet of the sea in a mountainous coast.

flab N, COLLOQ excess flesh or fat on the body.

flabbergast VB, COLLOQ to astonish.

flabby ADJ (*-ier, -iest*) DEROG 1 a of flesh: sagging, not firm; b of a person: having excess or sagging flesh. 2 lacking vigour; feeble; ineffective. ■ **flabbiness** N.

flaccid ADJ limp and soft; not firm.

flag[1] N a piece of cloth with a distinctive design, flown from a pole to represent a country, political party, etc, or used for signalling.
➤ VB (*-gg-*) to mark something with a flag, tag or symbol.
◆ **flag sb** or **sth down** to signal, usu with a hand, to a vehicle or driver to stop.

flag[2] VB (*-gg-*) INTR to grow weak or tired after a period of intense work or activity.

flag[3] N (also **flagstone**) a large flat stone for paving.

flagellate VB to whip someone or oneself, for the purposes either of religious penance or for sexual stimulation.

flagellation N an act or the practice of whipping, for religious or sexual purposes.

flageolet N 1 a small pale green kidney bean. 2 a high-pitched woodwind instrument similar to the recorder.

flagon N a large bottle or jug with a narrow neck, usu with a spout and handle.

flagpole and **flagstaff** N a pole from which a flag is flown.

flagrant ADJ brazen or barefaced. ■ **flagrancy** N. ■ **flagrantly** ADJ.

flagship N 1 the ship that carries and flies the flag of the fleet commander. 2 the leading ship in a shipping-line. 3 a commercial company's leading product, model, etc.

flail N a long-handled threshing tool with a free-swinging wooden or metal bar attached to the end.
➢ VB to beat with or as if with a flail.

flair N 1 (often **flair for sth**) a natural ability or talent for something: **a flair for maths**. 2 stylishness; elegance: **dresses with flair**.

flak N 1 anti-aircraft fire. 2 COLLOQ unfriendly or adverse criticism.

flake N, often IN COMPOUNDS 1 a small flat particle which has broken away or is breaking away from a larger object: **flakes of plaster**. 2 a small piece or particle: **snowflake**.
➢ VB 1 INTR to come off in flakes. 2 to break (eg cooked fish) into flakes.
◆ **flake out** COLLOQ to collapse or fall asleep from exhaustion.

flaky ADJ (*-ier, -iest*) made of flakes or tending to form flakes.

flambé ADJ of food: soaked in a spirit, usu brandy, and set alight before serving.

flamboyant ADJ of a person or behaviour: colourful, exuberant, and showy. ■ **flamboyance** N.

flame N 1 a hot luminous flickering tongue shape of burning gases coming from something that is on fire. 2 a a strong passion or affection; b COLLOQ a boyfriend or girlfriend.
➢ VB 1 INTR to burn with flames; to blaze. 2 INTR to shine brightly. 3 INTR to explode with anger. 4 INTR to get red and hot: **Her cheeks flamed with anger**. 5 to apply a flame to (an object or substance).

flamenco N 1 a rhythmical emotionally stirring type of Spanish gypsy music, usu played on the guitar. 2 the dance performed to it.

flame-thrower N a gun that discharges a stream of burning liquid.

flaming ADJ 1 blazing. 2 bright; glowing, particularly a brilliant red. 3 COLLOQ very angry; furious. 4 COLLOQ damned: **That flaming dog!**

flamingo N (*-os* or *-oes*) a large wading bird with white or pinkish plumage, a long neck and long legs.

flammable ADJ liable to catch fire; inflammable. ■ **flammability** N.

flan N an open pastry or sponge case with a savoury or fruit filling.

flange N a broad flat projecting rim added for strength or for connecting with another object.

flank N 1 a the side of an animal, between the ribs and hip; b the corresponding part of the human body. 2 a cut of beef from the flank, consisting of the abdominal muscles. 3 the side of anything, eg a mountain, building, etc. 4 of a body of things, esp of troops or a fleet drawn up in formation: the left or right extremities.
➢ VB 1 to be on the edge of (an object, a body of things, etc). 2 to move around the sides of a body of things.

flannel N 1 soft woollen cloth with a slight nap used to make clothes. 2 (also **face flannel**) a small square of towelling for washing with. Also called **face cloth**. 3 COLLOQ flattery or meaningless talk.
➢ VB (*-ll-*; N AMER *-l-*) TR & INTR to flatter or persuade by flattery, or to talk flannel.

flap VB (*-pp-*) 1 TR & INTR to wave something up and down, or backwards and forwards. 2 TR & INTR of a bird: to move (the wings) up and down; to fly with pronounced wing movements.
➢ N 1 a broad piece or part of something attached along one edge and hanging loosely,

usu as a cover to an opening: **pocket flaps.**
2 an act, sound or impact of flapping. **3** COLLOQ
a panic; a flustered state. **4** a hinged section on
an aircraft wing adjusted to control speed.

flapjack N **1** a thick biscuit made with oats and
syrup. **2** N AMER a pancake.

flare VB **1** INTR to burn with sudden brightness.
2 INTR to explode into anger. **3** TR & INTR to widen
towards the edge.
➤ N **1** a sudden blaze of bright light. **2** a device
composed of combustible material that
produces a sudden blaze of intense light. **3** in
chemical plants and oil refineries: a device for
burning off superfluous combustible gas or oil.
4 a widening out towards the edges: **sleeves
with a wide flare.**
◆ **flare up 1** to explode into anger. **2** to burst
into a blaze suddenly.

flares PL N, COLLOQ trousers with legs which are
tight at the top but widen out below the knee.

flare-up N **1** COLLOQ a sudden explosion of
emotion or violence. **2** a sudden burst into
flames.

flash N **1** a sudden brief blaze of light. **2** an
instant; a very short length of time. **3** a brief but
intense occurrence: **a flash of inspiration.**
4 a fleeting look on a face or in the eyes: **a flash
of joy. 5** PHOTOG **a** a bulb or electronic device
attached to a camera which produces a
momentary bright light as a picture is taken;
b the bright light produced by it.
➤ VB **1** TR & INTR to shine briefly or intermittently.
2 TR & INTR to appear or cause to appear briefly;
to move or pass quickly. **3** INTR of the eyes: to
brighten with anger, etc. **4** to give (a smile or
look) briefly. **5** TR & INTR to operate (a light) as a
signal. **6** INTR, COLLOQ (usu **flash at sb**) of a
man: to expose his genitals in a public place.
➤ ADJ **1** sudden and severe: **flash floods.**
2 quick: **flash freezing. 3** COLLOQ smart and
expensive.

flashback N esp in a film, novel, etc: a scene
depicting earlier events.

flashbulb N a small light bulb used to produce
a brief bright light in photography.

flash flood N a sudden, severe and brief
flood caused by a heavy rainstorm.

flashlight N, N AMER a torch.

flash point N a stage in a tense situation, etc
where people become angry or violent.

flashy ADJ (*-ier, -iest*) COLLOQ ostentatiously
smart and gaudy. ■ **flashily** ADV.
■ **flashiness** N.

flask N **1** (also **hip flask**) a small flat pocket
bottle for alcoholic spirits. **2** a vacuum flask.
3 a narrow-necked bottle used in chemical
experiments, etc.

flat[1] ADJ (*flatter, flattest*) **1** level; horizontal;
even. **2** without hollows or prominences.
3 lacking the usual prominence: **a flat nose.**
4 not bent or crumpled. **5** of feet: having little
arch to the instep. **6** of shoes: not having a
raised heel. **7** bored; depressed. **8** dull; not
lively. **9** toneless and expressionless. **10** COLLOQ
definite; downright; emphatic: **a flat refusal.**
11 MUS **a** of an instrument, voice, etc: lower than
the correct pitch; **b** FOLLOWING ITS NOUN
lowering the specified note by a semitone: C
flat. **12** of a tyre: having too little air in it. **13** of a
drink: having lost its fizziness. **14** of a battery:
having little or no charge remaining.
➤ ADV **1** stretched out rather than curled up,
crumpled, etc. **2** into a flat compact shape:
folds flat for storage. 3 exactly: **in two minutes
flat. 4** bluntly and emphatically: **I can tell you
flat. 5** MUS at lower than the correct pitch.
➤ N **1** something flat; a flat surface or part.
2 (**flats**) **a** an area of flat land; **b** a mud bank
exposed at low tide. **3** COLLOQ a punctured tyre
on a vehicle. **4** MUS **a** a sign (♭) that lowers a
note by a semitone from the note that it refers to;
b a note lowered in this way. ■ **flatly** ADV
emphatically: **She flatly refused to go.**
■ **flatness** N.
◆ **flat out** COLLOQ with maximum effort.

flat[2] N a set of rooms for living in as a self-
contained unit, in a building or tenement with a
number of such units.

flatfish N a flat-bodied fish, with both eyes on
the upper surface, eg a sole, plaice, etc.

flat-footed ADJ **1** having flat feet. **2** DEROG clumsy or tactless.

flat racing N the sport of racing horses on courses with no obstacles. ■ **flat race** N.

flatten VB **1** TR & INTR to make or become flat or flatter. **2** COLLOQ **a** to knock someone to the ground in a fight; **b** to overcome, crush or subdue someone utterly.

flatter VB **1** to compliment someone excessively or insincerely, esp in order to win a favour from them. **2** of a picture or description: to represent someone or something over-favourably. **3** to show something off well: a dress that flatters the figure. **4** to make someone feel honoured; to gratify.

flattery N (-ies) **1** the act of flattering. **2** excessive or insincere praise.

flatulence N an accumulation of gas formed during digestion in the stomach or intestines, causing discomfort. ■ **flatulent** ADJ.

flatworm N a type of worm with a flattened body, eg the tapeworm.

flaunt VB to display or parade oneself or something, esp one's clothes, in an ostentatious way, in the hope of being admired.

flautist and (chiefly N AMER) **flutist** N someone skilled in playing the flute.

flavour or (N AMER) **flavor** N **1** a sensation perceived when eating or drinking which is a combination of taste and smell. **2** any substance added to food, etc to give it a particular taste. **3** a characteristic quality. ➤ VB to add something (usu to food) to give it a particular flavour or quality. ■ **flavourless** ADJ.

flavouring or (N AMER) **flavoring** N any substance added to food, etc to give it a particular taste.

flaw N a fault, defect, imperfection or blemish. ■ **flawed** ADJ. ■ **flawless** ADJ.

flax N **1** a slender herbaceous plant that is cultivated for the fibre of its stem and for its seeds. **2** this fibre used to make thread and woven into linen fabrics.

flaxen ADJ **1** of hair: very fair. **2** made of or resembling flax.

flaxseed N linseed.

flay VB **1** to strip the skin from (an animal or a person). **2** to whip or beat violently. **3** to criticize harshly.

flea N **1** a wingless blood-sucking jumping insect, that lives as a parasite on mammals (including humans) and some birds. **2** IN COMPOUNDS referring to small crustaceans which leap like fleas: **sand flea** • **water flea**.

flea market N, COLLOQ a street market that sells second-hand goods or clothes.

fleck N **1** a spot or marking: white with flecks of gray. **2** a speck or small bit: a fleck of dirt.

fledged ADJ **1** of a young bird: able to fly because the feathers are fully developed. **2** qualified; trained: a fully-fledged doctor.

fledgling or **fledgeling** N **1** a young bird that has just grown its feathers and is still unable to fly. **2** an inexperienced person. **Also** AS ADJ: a fledgling company.

flee VB **1** INTR to run away quickly. **2** to hurriedly run away from or escape from (danger or a dangerous place).

fleece N **1** a sheep's woolly coat. **2** a sheep's wool cut from it at one shearing. **3** sheepskin or a fluffy fabric for lining garments, etc. **4** a garment made of fluffy thermal fabric. ➤ VB **1** to cut wool from (sheep); to shear (sheep). **2** SLANG to rob, swindle or overcharge. ■ **fleecy** ADJ.

fleet N **1** a number of ships under one command and organized as a tactical unit. **2** a navy; all the ships of a nation. **3** a number of buses, aircraft, etc operating under the same ownership or management.

fleeting ADJ passing swiftly; brief; short-lived: a fleeting smile. ■ **fleetingly** ADV.

flesh N **1** in animals: the soft tissues covering the bones, consisting chiefly of muscle. **2** the meat of animals, as distinct from that of fish, used as food. **3** the pulp of a fruit or vegetable. **4** the body as distinct from the soul or spirit; bodily

needs. **5** a yellowish-pink colour.
◆ **flesh sth out** to add descriptive detail to it.

flesh-coloured ADJ yellowish pink.

flesh wound N a wound, not deep enough to damage bone or a bodily organ.

fleshy ADJ (*-ier, -iest*) **1** plump. **2** relating to or like flesh. **3** of leaves, etc: thick and pulpy. ■ **fleshiness** N.

flex¹ VB **1** to bend (a limb or joint). **2** to contract or tighten (a muscle) so as to bend a joint.

flex² N flexible insulated electrical cable.

flexible ADJ **1** bending easily; pliable. **2** readily adaptable. ■ **flexibility** N. ■ **flexibly** ADV.

flexitime N a system which allows workers to choose when they put in their hours, usu including certain hours (**core time**) each day when everyone must be at work.

flibbertigibbet N a frivolous or over-talkative person.

flick VB **1** to move or touch something with a quick light movement. **2** to move the hand or finger quickly and jerkily against something small, eg a speck of dust, to remove it.
➤ N **1** a flicking action. **2** COLLOQ (often PL) a cinema film.
◆ **flick through sth** to glance quickly through (a book, a video, etc), in order to get a rough impression of it.

flicker VB **1** INTR to burn or shine unsteadily by alternately flashing bright and dying away again. **2** to cause something to flicker.
➤ N **1** a brief or unsteady light. **2** a fleeting appearance or occurrence: **a flicker of hope**.

flier or **flyer** N **1** a leaflet used to advertise a product, etc. **2** an aviator or pilot. **3** COLLOQ a flying start. **4** someone or something that flies or moves fast.

flight¹ N **1** the practice or an act of flying with wings or in an aeroplane or other vehicle. **2** the movement of eg a vehicle, bird or projectile through the air. **3** a flock of birds flying together. **4** a regular air journey made by an aircraft. **5** a journey of a spacecraft. **6** a group of aircraft involved in a joint mission. **7** a set of

steps or stairs. **8** a feather or something similar attached to the end of a dart or arrow.
◆ **in flight** flying.

flight² N the act of fleeing; escape.

flight attendant N a member of the cabin crew on a passenger aircraft.

flightless ADJ unable to fly.

flight lieutenant N an officer in the Royal Air Force.

flight recorder N an electronic recording device fitted to an aircraft often used in determining the cause of an air crash.

flighty ADJ (*-ier, -iest*) irresponsible; frivolous; flirtatious. ■ **flightiness** N.

flimsy ADJ (*-ier, -iest*) **1** of clothing, etc: light and thin. **2** of a structure: insubstantially made; frail. **3** of an excuse, etc: inadequate or unconvincing. ■ **flimsily** ADV. ■ **flimsiness** N.

flinch VB, INTR to start or jump in pain, fright, etc.
◆ **flinch from sth** to shrink back from or avoid something difficult such as a task, duty, etc.

fling VB (*flung*) **1** to throw something, esp violently or vigorously. **2** sometimes INTR to throw oneself or one's body about.
➤ N **1** an act of flinging. **2** COLLOQ a sexual relationship with someone for a short period of time. **3** COLLOQ a spell of enjoyable self-indulgence. **4** a lively reel.

flint N **1** GEOL a crystalline form of quartz. **2** ARCHAEOL a trimmed piece of this used as a tool. **3** a piece of a hard metal alloy from which a spark can be struck. ■ **flinty** ADJ (*-ier, -iest*).

flip VB (*-pp-*) **1** to toss (eg a coin) so that it turns over in mid-air. **2** INTR, COLLOQ (also **flip one's lid**) to lose one's temper.
➤ N **1** a flipping action. **2** a somersault, esp performed in mid-air. **3** an alcoholic drink made with beaten egg.
➤ ADJ, COLLOQ flippant; over-smart.

flip-flop N, COLLOQ a sandal consisting of a sole held on to the foot by a thong.

flippant ADJ not serious enough about grave matters; disrespectful; irreverent; frivolous.

■ **flippancy** N. ■ **flippantly** ADV.

flipper N 1 a limb adapted for swimming, eg in a whale, seal, penguin, etc. 2 a rubber foot-covering worn for underwater swimming.

flipping ADJ, ADV, COLLOQ used as an intensifier or to express annoyance.

flirt VB, INTR (usu **flirt with sb**) to behave in a playful sexual manner (towards them).
➤ N someone who flirts. ■ **flirtation** N.
■ **flirtatious** ADJ. ■ **flirty** ADJ.
◆ **flirt with sth** 1 to consider it briefly. 2 to treat death, danger, etc lightly.

flit VB (-tt-) INTR 1 a to move about lightly and quickly from place to place; b to fly silently or quickly from place to place. 2 SCOT & N ENGLISH to move house.
➤ N an act of flitting.

float VB 1 TR & INTR to rest or move, or make something rest or move, on the surface of a liquid. 2 INTR to drift about or hover in the air. 3 INTR to move about in an aimless or disorganized way. 4 to start up or launch (a company, scheme, etc).
➤ N 1 something that floats or is designed to keep something afloat. 2 ANGLING a floating device fixed to a fishing-line, that moves to indicate a bite. 3 a low-powered delivery vehicle: **milk float**. 4 a vehicle decorated as an exhibit in a street parade. 5 an amount of money set aside each day for giving change, etc in a shop at the start of business.

floatation see **flotation**

floating ADJ 1 not fixed; moving about: a floating population. 2 of a voter: not committed to supporting any one party.

flock[1] N 1 a group of creatures, esp birds or sheep. 2 a crowd of people. 3 a body of people under the care of a priest or minister.
➤ VB, INTR to gather or move in a group.

flock[2] N 1 a tuft of wool, etc. 2 fine particles of wool or nylon fibre applied to paper or cloth to give a raised velvety surface.

floe N a sheet of ice floating in the sea.

flog VB (-gg-) 1 to beat; to whip repeatedly, particularly as a form of punishment. 2 COLLOQ to sell something.

flood N 1 an overflow of water from rivers, lakes or the sea on to dry land. 2 any overwhelming flow or quantity of something. 3 the rising of the tide. 4 COLLOQ a floodlight.
➤ VB 1 to overflow or submerge (land) with water. 2 to fill something too full or to overflowing. 3 (usu **flood sb out**) to force them to leave a building, etc because of floods. 4 INTR to become flooded, esp frequently. 5 INTR to move in a great mass. 6 INTR to flow or surge. 7 to supply (a market) with too much of a commodity. 8 to supply (an engine) with too much petrol so that it cannot start.

floodgate N a gate for controlling the flow of a large amount of water.

floodlight N (also **floodlamp**) a powerful light used to illuminate extensive areas.
➤ VB (*floodlit*) to illuminate with floodlights.

floor N 1 the lower interior surface of a room or vehicle. 2 all the rooms, etc on the same level in a building; the storey of a building. 3 usu IN COMPOUNDS the lowest surface of some open areas, eg the ground in a forest or cave. 4 the debating area in a parliamentary assembly or the open area of a stock exchange.
➤ VB 1 to construct the floor of (a room, etc). 2 COLLOQ to knock someone down. 3 COLLOQ to baffle someone completely.

flooring N material for constructing floors.

floor show N a series of performances at a nightclub or restaurant.

floosie, floozie or **floozy** N (-sies or -zies) COLLOQ, often FACETIOUS a woman or girl, esp a disreputable or immodestly dressed one.

flop VB (-pp-) 1 INTR to fall, drop, move or sit limply and heavily. 2 INTR of eg hair: to hang or sway about loosely. 3 INTR, COLLOQ of a play, project, business, etc: to fail dismally.
➤ N 1 a flopping movement or sound. 2 COLLOQ a complete failure.

floppy ADJ (-ier, -iest) tending to flop; loose.
➤ N (-ies) COMP a floppy disk.

floppy disk N, COMP a flexible plastic disc,

coated with magnetic material and enclosed in a hard rectangular plastic casing, which is used to store data.

flora N (*-as* or *-ae*) BOT the wild plants of a particular region, country or time period.

floral ADJ 1 consisting of or relating to flowers: a floral tribute. 2 patterned with flowers.

floret N, BOT 1 a small flower; one of the single flowers in the head of a composite flower, such as a daisy or sunflower. 2 each of the branches in the head of a cauliflower or of broccoli.

florid ADJ 1 over-elaborate: a florid speech. 2 of a complexion: pink or ruddy.

florist N someone who grows, sells or arranges flowers.

floss N 1 loose strands of fine silk which are not twisted together, used in embroidery, for tooth-cleaning (**dental floss**), etc. 2 any fine silky substance. ■ **flossy** ADJ.

flotation or **floatation** N the act of floating.

flotilla N a small fleet, or a fleet of small ships.

flotsam N goods lost by shipwreck and found floating on the sea.
◆ **flotsam and jetsam** odds and ends.

flounce VB, INTR to move in a way expressive of impatience or indignation.
➢ N 1 a flouncing movement. 2 a deep frill on a dress, etc.

flounder VB, INTR 1 to thrash about helplessly, as if caught in a bog. 2 to stumble helplessly in thinking or speaking.
➢ N 1 an act of floundering. 2 a type of European flatfish.

flour N 1 the finely ground meal of wheat or other cereal grain. 2 a dried powdered form of any other vegetable material: **potato flour**.
■ **floury** ADJ.

flourish VB 1 INTR to be strong and healthy; to grow well. 2 INTR to do well; to develop and prosper. 3 INTR to be at one's most productive, or at one's peak. 4 to adorn with flourishes or ornaments. 5 to wave or brandish something.
➢ N 1 a decorative twirl in handwriting. 2 an

elegant sweep of the hand. 3 a showy piece of music. 4 a piece of fancy language.

flout VB to defy (an order, convention, etc) openly; to disrespect (authority, etc).

flow VB, INTR 1 to move along like water. 2 of blood or electricity: to circulate. 3 to keep moving steadily. 4 of hair: to hang or ripple in a loose shining mass. 5 of words or ideas: to come readily to mind or in speech or writing. 6 to be present in abundance. 7 of the tide: to advance or rise.
➢ N 1 the action of flowing. 2 the rate of flowing. 3 a continuous stream or outpouring. 4 the rising of the tide.

flower N 1 in a flowering plant: the structure that bears the reproductive organs. 2 a plant that bears flowers, esp if cultivated for them. 3 the best part; the cream. 4 the most distinguished person or thing.
➢ VB 1 INTR to produce flowers; to bloom. 2 INTR to reach a peak; to develop to full maturity.

flower-bed N a garden bed planted with flowering plants.

flowerpot N a clay or plastic container for growing plants in.

flowery ADJ 1 decorated or patterned with flowers. 2 of language or gestures: excessively elaborate. ■ **floweriness** N.

flowing ADJ 1 moving as a fluid. 2 smooth and continuous; fluent.

flu N, COLLOQ (often **the flu**) influenza.

fluctuate VB, INTR of prices etc: to rise and fall.
■ **fluctuation** N.

flue N 1 an outlet for smoke or gas, eg through a chimney. 2 a pipe or duct for conveying heat.

fluent ADJ 1 having full command of a foreign language: **fluent in French**. 2 spoken or written with ease: **speaks fluent Russian**. 3 speaking or writing in an easy flowing style. 4 of a movement: smooth, easy or graceful.
■ **fluency** N.

fluff N small bits of soft woolly material.
➢ VB 1 (usu **fluff sth out** or **up**) to shake or arrange it into a soft mass. 2 TR & INTR of an

actor, speaker, etc: to make a mistake in (lines, etc); to bungle. ■ **fluffy** ADJ. ■ **fluffiness** N.

fluid N a substance which can move about with freedom and has no fixed shape.
➤ ADJ **1** able to flow like a liquid; unsolidified. **2** of movements, etc: smooth and graceful. **3** altering easily; adaptable. ■ **fluidity** N.

fluid ounce N **1** in the UK: a unit of liquid measurement, equal to one twentieth of a British or imperial pint. **2** in the USA: a unit of liquid measurement, equal to one sixteenth of a US pint.

fluke[1] N a success achieved by accident or chance. ■ **flukey** or **fluky** ADJ.

fluke[2] N **1** a parasitic flatworm. **2** a flounder.

flume N **1** a descending chute with flowing water. **2** an artificial channel for water, used in industry, eg for transporting logs.

flummox VB, COLLOQ to confuse someone; to bewilder someone.

flunk VB, esp N AMER COLLOQ **1** TR & INTR to fail (a test, examination, etc). **2** of an examiner: to fail (a candidate).

flunkey or **flunky** N (*-eys* or *-ies*) **1** a uniformed manservant, eg a footman. **2** DEROG a slavish follower.

fluorescence N, PHYS **1** the emission of light and other radiation by an object after it has absorbed electrons or radiation of a different wavelength. **2** the radiation emitted as a result of fluorescence. ■ **fluoresce** VB.

fluoride N, CHEM any chemical compound consisting of fluorine and another element.

fluorine N, CHEM a highly corrosive poisonous yellow gas of the halogen group, used in the manufacture of organic compounds.

fluorspar, **fluorite** and **fluor** N, GEOL calcium fluoride, a mineral used in glass and some cements, and in the plastic industry.

flurry N (*-ies*) **1** a sudden commotion; a sudden bustle or rush: **a flurry of activity**. **2** a brief shower of rain, snow, etc: **a flurry of snowflakes**.
➤ VB (*-ies*, *-ied*) to agitate, confuse or bewilder someone.

flush[1] VB **1** USU INTR to blush or make someone blush or go red. **2** to clean out (esp a lavatory pan) with a rush of water.
➤ N **1** a redness or rosiness, esp of the cheeks or face; a blush. **2** a rush of water that cleans a lavatory pan. **3** high spirits: **in the first flush of enthusiasm**. **4** freshness; bloom; vigour: **the flush of youth**.

flush[2] ADJ **1** (often **flush with sth**) level or even with an adjacent surface. **2** COLLOQ having plenty of money.
➤ ADV so as to be level with an adjacent surface: **flush with the wall**.

flush[3] N, CARDS a hand made up of cards from a single suit.

flush[4] VB, HUNTING to startle (game birds) so that they rise from the ground.

fluster VB to agitate, confuse or upset.
➤ N a state of confused agitation.

flute N **1** a wind instrument consisting of a wooden or metal tube with holes stopped by the fingertips or by keys, which is held horizontally and played by breathing across the hole in the mouthpiece. **2** ARCHIT a rounded concave groove in wood or stone, eg running vertically down a pillar. **3** a tall narrow glass.
➤ VB to produce or utter (sounds) like the high shrill tones of a flute. ■ **fluty** ADJ.

fluted ADJ ornamented by grooves.

fluting N a series of parallel grooves cut into wood or stone.

flutist N, N AMER a flautist.

flutter VB **1** TR & INTR of a bird, etc: to flap (its wings) lightly and rapidly; to fly with a rapid wing movement. **2** INTR of a flag, etc: to flap repeatedly in the air. **3** INTR to drift with a twirling motion. **4** INTR of the heart: to race.
➤ N **1** a quick flapping or vibrating motion. **2** agitation; excitement. **3** COLLOQ a bet.

fluvial ADJ relating to or found in rivers.

flux N **1** a flow of matter; a process or act of flowing. **2** constant change; instability. **3** any substance added to another in order to aid the process of melting. **4** in the smelting of metal ores: any substance added so that it will combine with impurities which can then be removed.

fly[1] N (*flies*) **1** a two-winged insect, esp the common housefly. **2** IN COMPOUNDS any of various other flying insects: **dragonfly**. **3** ANGLING a fish hook tied with colourful feathers to look like a fly, used in fly-fishing.

fly[2] VB (3RD PERSON PR T *flies*, PA T *flew*, PA P *flown*) **1** INTR **a** of birds, bats, insects and certain other animals: to move through the air using wings or structures resembling wings; **b** of an aircraft or spacecraft: to travel through the air or through space. **2** TR & INTR to travel or convey in an aircraft. **3** to operate and control (an aircraft, kite, etc); to cause it to fly. **4** to cross (an area of land or water) in an aircraft: **They flew the Atlantic to New York. 5 a** to raise (a flag). **b** INTR of a flag: to blow or flutter in the wind. **6** INTR to move or pass rapidly: **fly into a temper** • **rumours flying around. 7** INTR, COLLOQ to depart quickly: **I must fly.** ➤ N (*flies*) **1** (chiefly **flies**) a zip or set of buttons fastening a trouser front, or the flap covering these. **2** a flap covering the entrance to a tent.

fly[3] ADJ, COLLOQ cunning; smart.

flyblown ADJ **1** of food: covered with blowfly eggs and, therefore, unfit to eat; contaminated. **2** shabby, dirty or dingy.

fly-by-night ADJ, DEROG not trustworthy. ➤ N an unreliable person, esp one who avoids debts by disappearing overnight.

flyer see **flier**

fly-fish VB, INTR to fish using artificial flies as bait. ■ **fly-fishing** N.

flying ADJ **1** hasty; brief: **a flying visit. 2** designed or organized for fast movement. **3** able to fly or glide. ➤ N **1** flight. **2** the activity of piloting, or travelling in, an aircraft.

flying colours PL N triumphant success.

flying fish N a fish with stiff, greatly enlarged pectoral fins that enable it to leap out of the water and glide for considerable distances.

flying officer N an officer in the air force.

flying picket N a picket travelling from place to place during any strike.

flying saucer N an unidentified circular flying object reported in the sky, believed by some to be a craft from outer space.

flying squad N a body of police specially trained for quick response and fast action.

flyleaf N a blank page at the beginning or end of a book.

flyover N a bridge that takes a road or railway over another.

flypaper N a strip of paper with a sticky poisonous coating that traps and kills flies.

flypast N a ceremonial flight of aircraft.

flyposting N the putting up of advertising or political posters, etc illegally.

flysheet N a protective outer sheet for a tent.

flyspray N a liquid poisonous to flies, sprayed from an aerosol can.

fly-tipping N unauthorized disposal of waste.

flytrap N **1** a device for catching flies. **2** BOT a plant that traps flies and digests them.

flyweight N **1** a class for boxers, etc of not more than a specified weight (51 kilograms or 112 pounds in professional boxing). **2** a boxer, etc of this weight class.

flywheel N a heavy wheel on a revolving shaft that regulates the action of a machine.

foal N the young of a horse, donkey, etc. ➤ VB, INTR to give birth to a foal.

foam N **1** a mass of tiny bubbles on the surface of liquids. **2** a substance composed of tiny bubbles formed by passing gas through it. **3** frothy saliva or perspiration. **4** a light cellular material used for packaging, insulation, etc. ➤ VB, TR & INTR (sometimes **foam up**) to produce or make something produce foam.

fob¹ VB (*-bb-*) now only in phrases below.
- ◆ **fob sb off** to dismiss or ignore them.
- ◆ **fob sb off with sth** to provide them with something inferior (eg a poor substitute, or an inadequate explanation).
- ◆ **fob sth off on sb** to manage to sell or pass off something inferior to someone.

fob² N **1** a chain attached to a watch. **2** a decorative attachment to a key ring, etc.

focaccia N a flat round of Italian bread topped with olive oil and herbs or spices.

fo'c'sle N, NAUT a spelling of **forecastle** suggested by its pronunciation.

focus N (*focuses* or *foci*) **1** the point at which rays of light or sound waves converge or appear to diverge. **2 a** the condition in which an image is sharp; **b** the state of an instrument producing this image. **3** the centre of an earthquake. **4** a centre of interest or attention. **5** special attention paid to something.
➢ VB (*-s-*; or *-ss-*) **1** TR & INTR to bring or be brought into focus; to meet or make something meet or converge at a focus. **2** to adjust the thickness of the lens of (the eye) or to move the lens of (an optical instrument) so as to obtain the sharpest possible image of a particular object. **3** (often **focus sth on sth**) TR & INTR to concentrate attention, etc on it: **focused her energies on the problem.** ■ **focal** ADJ.

fodder N **1** any bulk feed, esp hay and straw, for cattle and other animal livestock. **2** COLLOQ something that is constantly made use of: **fodder for the popular press.**

foe N, LITERARY, OLD USE an enemy.

foetid ADJ another spelling of **fetid**.

foetus N another spelling of **fetus**.

fog N **1** a suspension of tiny water droplets or ice crystals forming a cloud close to the ground surface. **2** a blur; cloudiness. **3** a state of confusion or bewilderment.
➢ VB (*-gg-*) TR & INTR (often **fog over** or **up**) to obscure or become obscured with, or as if with, fog or condensation.

fogey or **fogy** N (*-eys* or *-ies*) someone with boring, old-fashioned attitudes.

foggy ADJ (*-ier, -iest*) **1** covered with or thick with fog; misty, damp. **2** not clear; confused.
- ◆ **not have the foggiest** or **not have the foggiest idea** COLLOQ not to know at all.

foghorn N a horn that sounds at regular intervals to ships in fog as a warning of danger.

foible N a slight personal eccentricity.

foil¹ VB to prevent, thwart or frustrate someone or something.

foil² N **a** metal beaten or rolled out into thin sheets; **b** ALSO IN COMPOUNDS: tinfoil • gold foil.

foil³ N, FENCING a fencing sword with a blunt edge and a point protected by a button.

foist VB.
- ◆ **foist sth on sb** to inflict or impose something unwanted on them.

fold¹ VB **1** to double (something) over so that one part lies on top of another. **2** INTR to be able to be folded, or closed up so that it takes up less space, usu making it flat. **3** of an insect, etc: to bring in (wings) close to its body. **4** to arrange (clothes, etc) for storage by laying them flat and doubling each piece of clothing over on itself. **5** INTR of flower petals: to close. **6** to clasp (someone) in one's arms, etc. **7** COLLOQ of a business, etc: to collapse; to fail.
➢ N **1** a doubling of one layer over another. **2** a rounded or sharp bend made by this, particularly the inside part of it; a crease. **3** a hollow in the landscape.

fold² N **1** a walled or fenced enclosure or pen for sheep or cattle. **2** the body of believers within the protection of a church.

folder N a cardboard or plastic cover in which to keep loose papers.

foliage N the green leaves on a tree or plant.

folio N **1** a leaf of a manuscript, etc, numbered on one side. **2 a** a sheet of paper folded once to make two leaves for a book; **b** a book composed of such sheets.
➢ ADJ of a book: composed of folios: **a folio edition.**

folk PL N **1** people in general. **2** (ALSO COLLOQ **folks**) a person's family: **going to visit the folks.**

3 people belonging to a particular group, nation, etc: **country folk**.
> ADJ traditional among, or originating from, a particular group of people or nation: **folk tale**.

folklore N **1** the customs, beliefs, stories, traditions, etc of a particular group of people, usu passed down through the oral tradition. **2** the study of these.

folk music N **1** music which is played on traditional instruments or sung in the tradition style. **2** contemporary music of a similar style.

folk song N any song or ballad originating among the people and traditionally handed down from generation to generation.

follicle N a small cavity or sac within a tissue or organ: **hair follicle**. ■ **follicular** ADJ.

follow VB **1** TR & INTR (also **follow after**) to go or come after (someone or something), either immediately or shortly afterwards. **2** to secretly go after (someone or something); to pursue stealthily. **3** to accept someone as leader or authority. **4** INTR (sometimes **follow from**) to result from or be a consequence of (something). **5** to go along (a road, etc), alongside (a river, etc) or on the path marked by (signs). **6** to watch (someone or something moving). **7** to do (something) in a particular way; to practise (something). **8** to conform to (something): **follows a familiar pattern**. **9** to obey (advice, etc). **10** TR & INTR to copy. **11** TR & INTR to understand: **Do you follow me?** **12** to take a keen interest in (a sport, etc).
◆ **follow suit** to do what someone else has done without thinking much about it.
◆ **follow sth through** or **up** to pursue (an idea, a project, etc) beyond its early stages, and often to fruition; to investigate or test it.

follower N **1** someone or something that follows or comes after others. **2** an avid supporter or devotee. **3** a disciple.

following N **1** a body of supporters, devotees, etc. **2** (**the following**) the thing or things, or the person or people, about to be mentioned or referred to.
> ADJ **1** coming after; next. **2** about to be mentioned: **deal with the following points**. **3** of

a wind, currents, etc: blowing in the direction in which a ship, etc is travelling.
> PREP after.

follow-up N continuing something that is not completed; further action or investigation.

folly N (**-ies**) **1** foolishness; a foolish act. **2** a mock temple, castle, ruin, etc.

foment VB to encourage or foster (ill-feeling, etc). ■ **fomentation** N.

fond ADJ **1** loving; tender: **fond glances**. **2** happy: **fond memories**. **3** impractical: **a fond hope**. ■ **fondly** ADV. ■ **fondness** N.

fondant N a soft sweet paste made with sugar and water.

fondle VB to touch, stroke or caress someone or something lovingly, affectionately or lustfully.

fondue N, COOKERY a dish consisting of hot cheese into which bits of bread are dipped.

font[1] N a basin in a church that holds water for baptisms.

font[2] see **fount**[1]

food N **1** a substance taken in by a living organism that provides it with energy and materials for growth and repair of tissues. **2** something that provides stimulation: **food for thought**.

foodie N, COLLOQ a person who is greatly or excessively interested in cookery and food.

food poisoning N an illness caused by eating contaminated food or drinking water.

food processor N an electrical domestic apparatus for chopping, liquidizing, etc, food.

foodstuff N a substance used as food.

fool[1] N **1** someone who lacks common sense or intelligence. **2** someone made to appear ridiculous. **3** HIST a jester.
> VB to deceive someone so that they appear foolish or ridiculous.
◆ **fool sb into** or **out of sth** to persuade them by deception to do something or not to do it.

◆ **fool about** or **around** to behave stupidly or playfully.

fool² N a dessert of puréed fruit mixed with cream or custard.

foolhardy ADJ taking foolish risks; rash; reckless. ■ **foolhardiness** N.

foolish ADJ 1 unwise; senseless. 2 ridiculous; silly. ■ **foolishly** ADV. ■ **foolishness** N.

foolproof ADJ of a plan, etc: designed so that it is very unlikely to go wrong.

foolscap N a large size of printing- or writing-paper, measuring 432×343 millimetres.

fool's errand N a pointless or unprofitable task or venture; a futile journey.

fool's gold see under **pyrite**

fool's paradise N a state of happiness or confidence based on false expectations.

foot N (PL USU **feet** but see sense 7) 1 the part of the leg on which a human being or animal stands or walks. 2 in molluscs: a muscular organ used for locomotion. 3 the part of a sock, stocking, etc that fits over the foot. 4 the bottom or lower part of something. 5 the part on which something stands; anything functioning as or resembling a foot. 6 the end of a bed where the feet go, as opposed to the head. 7 (PL **feet** or often **foot**) in the imperial system: a unit of length equal to 12 inches.
◆ **on foot** walking.
◆ **put one's foot down** to be firm about something.
◆ **put one's foot in it** COLLOQ to cause offence or embarrassment.
◆ **under foot** on the ground.

footage N 1 measurement or payment by the foot. 2 a the length of exposed cine film measured in feet; b a clip from a film, etc.

football N 1 a team game played with a large ball that players try to kick or head into the opposing team's goal. Also called **Association Football** and **soccer**. 2 the ball used in the game. ■ **footballer** N.

footbridge N a bridge for pedestrians.

footed ADJ 1 having a foot or feet. 2 IN COMPOUNDS a having a specified number or type of feet: four-footed; b having a specified manner of walking: light-footed.

footfall N the sound of a footstep.

foothill N (usu **foothills**) a lower hill on the approach to a mountain or mountain range.

foothold N 1 a place to put one's foot when climbing. 2 a firm starting position.

footing N 1 the stability of one's feet on the ground: lost my footing. 2 basis or status: on a friendly footing.

footlights PL N, THEAT a row of lights set along the front edge of a stage to illuminate it.

footloose ADJ free to go where, or do as, one likes; not hampered by any ties.

footman N a uniformed male attendant.

footnote N a comment printed at the bottom of a page.

footpath N 1 a path or track for walkers, usu in the countryside, eg alongside fields, through a wood, etc: public footpath. 2 a pavement.

footprint N the mark or impression of a foot or shoe left eg in sand, soft ground, etc.

footsore ADJ having sore and tired feet.

footwear SING N shoes, boots, socks, etc.

footwork N the agile use of the feet.

fop N a man who is very consciously elegant in his dress and manners. ■ **foppish** ADJ.

for PREP 1 intended to be given or sent to someone: This is for you. 2 towards: heading for home. 3 throughout (a time or distance): was writing for half an hour. 4 in order to have, get, etc: meet for a chat • fight for freedom. 5 at a cost of something: said he'd do it for £10. 6 as reward, payment or penalty appropriate to something: got six months for stealing • charge for one's work. 7 with a view to something: train for the race. 8 representing; on behalf of someone: the MP for Greenfield • speaking for myself. 9 to the benefit of someone or something: What can I do for

you? **10** in favour of someone: **for or against the proposal**. **11** proposing to oneself: **I'm for bed**. **12** because of something: **couldn't see for tears**. **13** on account of something: **famous for its confectionery**. **14** suitable to the needs of something: **books for children**. **15** having as function or purpose: **scissors for cutting hair**. **16** on the occasion of something: **got it for my birthday**. **17** in place of; in exchange with something: **replacements for the breakages • translated word for word**. **18** up to someone: **It's for him to decide**. **19** as being: **took you for someone else • know for a fact**. **20** considering what one would expect: **serious for his age • warm for winter**. **21** about; aimed at: **proposals for peace • a desire for revenge**. **22** in spite of something: **quite nice for all his faults**. **23** available to be disposed of or dealt with by: **not for sale**. **24** with reference to time: **a** at or on: **an appointment for 12 noon on Friday**; **b** so as to be starting by: **7.30 for 8.00**; **c** throughout (a time): **in jail for 15 years**.
◆ **as for** as far as concerns.

forage N (also **forage crop**) a crop, eg grass, kale, swede, etc, grown as feed for livestock.
➢ VB **1** INTR to search around, esp for food. **2** to rummage about (for something).

foray N **1** a raid or attack. **2** a venture.

forbear¹ VB (PA T *forbore*, PA P *forborne*) **1** ARCHAIC to tolerate something. **2** INTR (usu **forbear from** or **forbear to do**) to stop oneself going as far as; to refrain from: **forbear to mention it**. ■ **forbearance** N.

forbear² see **forebear**

forbid VB (PA T *forbade* or *forbad*, PA P *forbidden* or *forbid*, PR P *forbidding*) to order not; to refuse to allow; to prohibit.

forbidden ADJ prohibited; not allowed.

forbidding ADJ **1** threatening; grim. **2** uninviting; sinister; unprepossessing.

force N **1** strength; power; impact or impetus. **2** compulsion, esp with threats or violence. **3** military power. **4** passion or earnestness. **5** strength or validity. **6** meaning. **7** influence. **8** a person or thing seen as an influence. **9** PHYS (SI unit newton) **a** any external agent that produces a change in the speed or direction of a moving object, or that makes a stationary object move: **the force of gravity**; **b** any external agent that produces a strain on a static object. **10** any irresistible power or agency: **the forces of nature**. **11** the term used in specifying an index between 0 and 12 on the Beaufort Scale, each of which corresponds to a different wind speed: **a gale of force 8 • a force-10 gale**. **12 a** a military body; **b** (**the forces**) a nation's armed services.
➢ VB **1** to make or compel (someone to do something). **2** to obtain (something) by effort, strength, threats, violence, etc. **3** to produce (something) with an effort. **4** to inflict (eg views, opinions etc) (on someone).
◆ **in force 1** of a law, etc: valid; effective. **2** in large numbers: **Protesters arrived in force**.

forced ADJ **1** of a smile, laugh, etc: unnatural; unspontaneous. **2** done or provided under compulsion: **forced labour**. **3** carried out as an emergency: **a forced landing**.

force-feed VB to feed (a person or animal) forcibly.

forceful ADJ powerful; effective; influential. ■ **forcefully** ADV. ■ **forcefulness** N.

forceps SING N (PL **forceps**) BIOL, MED, etc an instrument like pincers, for gripping firmly.

forcible ADJ **1** done by or involving force. **2** powerful. ■ **forcibly** ADV.

ford N a crossing-place in a river, where a road or track passes through shallow water.
➢ VB to ride, drive or wade across (a stream, river, etc) by passing through shallow water.

fore N the front part.

fore-and-aft ADJ, NAUT **1** at the front and rear of a vessel: **fore-and-aft rig**. **2** set lengthways, pointing to the bow and stern.

forearm N the lower part of the arm between wrist and elbow.

forebear or **forbear** N an ancestor.

foreboding N a feeling of impending doom.

forecast VB (**forecast** or sometimes

forecasted) TR & INTR **1** to give warning of something; to predict something. **2** to gauge or estimate (weather, statistics, etc) in advance. ➢ N a warning, prediction or advance estimate. ■ **forecaster** N.

forecastle N a short raised deck at the front of a vessel. Often shortened to **fo'c'sle**.

foreclose VB of a mortgager, bank, etc: to repossess a property because of failure on the part of the mortgagee to repay agreed amounts of the loan. ■ **foreclosure** N.

forecourt N a courtyard or paved area in front of a building, eg a filling-station.

forefather N an ancestor.

forefinger N the index finger.

forefront N **1** the very front. **2** the most prominent or active position.

forego[1] VB (*-goes, -went, -gone*) TR & INTR to precede.

forego[2] see **forgo**

foregoing ADJ just mentioned. ➢ N the thing or person just mentioned.

foregone conclusion N an inevitable or predictable result or conclusion.

foreground N **1** the part of a picture or view nearest to the observer. **2** a position where one is noticeable.

forehand ADJ, TENNIS, SQUASH, etc of a stroke: with the palm in front, as opposed to backhand. ➢ N, TENNIS, SQUASH, etc a forehand stroke.

forehead N the part of the face between the eyebrows and hairline; the brow.

foreign ADJ **1** concerned with or relating to, or coming from another country. **2** not belonging where found: **a foreign body in my eye**. ◆ **foreign to sb 1** unfamiliar: **the technique was foreign to them**. **2** uncharacteristic: **Envy was foreign to his nature**.

foreigner N a person from another country.

foreknowledge N knowledge of something before it happens; foresight.

foreleg N either of the two front legs of a four-legged animal.

forelock N a lock of hair growing or falling over the brow.

foreman, forewoman and **foreperson** N **1** someone in charge of a department or group of workers. **2** LAW the chairperson or spokesperson of a jury.

foremost ADJ leading; best. ➢ ADV leading; coming first.

forename N one's personal name as distinct from one's family name or surname.

forensic ADJ **1** belonging or relating to courts of law, or to the work of a lawyer in court. **2** INFORMAL concerned with the scientific side of legal investigations: **forensic laboratory**.

foreordain VB to determine (events, etc) in advance; to destine.

foreplay N sexual stimulation, often leading up to sexual intercourse.

forerunner N **1** a person or thing that goes before; a predecessor. **2** a sign of what is to come. **3** an advance messenger.

foresee VB to see that something will happen in advance, or know in advance, often by circumstantial evidence. ■ **foreseeable** ADJ.

foreshore N the area on the shore between the positions that the high and low tides reach.

foresight N **1** the ability to foresee. **2** wise forethought; prudence. **3** consideration taken or provision made for the future.

foreskin N, ANAT the retractable fold of skin that covers the tip of the penis.

forest N **1** a large area of land dominated by trees. **2** the trees growing on such an area. **3** a large number or dense arrangement of objects.

forestall VB **1** to prevent something by acting in advance. **2** to anticipate (an event) or anticipate the action of (someone).

forestry N the science or management of forests and woodlands. ■ **forester** N.

foretaste N a brief experience of what is to come.

foretell VB to predict.

forethought N 1 provision made for the future. 2 deliberate or conscious intent.

forever ADV (also **for ever**) 1 always; eternally; for all time. 2 continually: **forever whining**. 3 INFORMAL for a very long time. ➤ N 1 an endless or indefinite length of time. 2 a very long time.

forewarn VB to warn beforehand.

foreword N an introduction to a book, often by a writer other than the author; a preface.

forfeit N 1 something that is surrendered, usu as a penalty. 2 a penalty or fine. ➤ VB to lose (the right to something), or to hand (something) over, as a penalty. ■ **forfeiture** N.

forge N 1 a furnace for heating metal prior to shaping it. 2 the workshop of a blacksmith. ➤ VB 1 to shape metal by heating and hammering, or by heating and applying pressure more gradually. 2 to make an imitation of (a signature, banknote, etc) for a dishonest or fraudulent purpose. ■ **forger** N.

forgery N (-*ies*) 1 the act or an instance of making a copy of a picture, document, signature, banknote, etc for a fraudulent purpose. 2 a copy of this kind.

forget VB (*forgot, forgotten*) TR & INTR 1 to fail to remember or be unable to remember (something). 2 to stop being aware of (something): **forgot his headache in the excitement**. 3 to neglect or overlook (something). 4 to leave (something) behind accidentally. 5 COLLOQ to dismiss something from one's mind. 6 to lose control over (oneself).

forgetful ADJ inclined to forget.

forget-me-not N a plant with small blue flowers.

forgive VB (*forgave, forgiven*) 1 to stop being angry with (someone who has done something wrong) or about (an offence). 2 to pardon someone. ■ **forgivable** ADJ. ■ **forgiving** ADJ.

forgiveness N 1 the act of forgiving or state of being forgiven. 2 readiness to forgive.

forgo or **forego** VB (*-goes, -went, -gone, -going*) to do or go without (something); to sacrifice (something) or give (something) up.

fork N 1 an eating or cooking implement with prongs. 2 a pronged digging or lifting tool. 3 a a division in a road, etc with two branches; b one such branch: **take the left fork**. ➤ VB 1 INTR of a road, etc: to divide into two branches. 2 INTR to follow one such branch: **fork left at the church**.

forked ADJ 1 dividing into two branches or parts; shaped like a fork. 2 of lightning: forming zigzagged lines.

fork-lift truck N a small vehicle equipped with two horizontal prongs that can be raised and lowered to move or stack goods.

forlorn ADJ 1 exceedingly unhappy; miserable. 2 deserted; forsaken. 3 desperate.

form N 1 shape. 2 figure or outward appearance. 3 kind, type, variety or manifestation. 4 a document with printed text and spaces for the insertion of information. 5 the correct way of doing or saying something. 6 structure and organization in a piece of writing or work of art. 7 one's potential level of performance, eg in sport: **soon find your form again**. 8 a school class. ➤ VB 1 to organize or set something up. 2 INTR to come into existence; to take shape. 3 to shape; to make (a shape). 4 to take on the shape or function of. 5 to make up; to constitute. 6 to develop. 7 to influence or mould.

formal ADJ 1 relating to or involving etiquette, ceremony or conventional procedure generally: **formal dress**. 2 stiffly polite rather than relaxed and friendly. 3 valid; official; explicit: **a formal agreement**. 4 of language: strictly correct, as distinct from conversational. 5 organized and methodical. 6 precise and symmetrical in design: **a formal garden**. ■ **formally** ADV.

formaldehyde N, CHEM a colourless pungent gas widely used as a preservative.

formality N (-*ies*) 1 a procedure gone through as a requirement of etiquette, ceremony, the law, etc. **2** a procedure gone through merely for the sake of correctness. **3** attention to the rules of social behaviour.

formalize or **-ise** VB **1** to make precise or give definite form to. **2** to make official, eg by putting in writing, etc. ■ **formalization** N.

format N **1** the size and shape of something, esp a book or magazine. **2** the style in which a television programme, radio programme, etc is organized and presented.
➤ VB (*-tt-*) **1** to design, shape or organize in a particular way. **2** to organize (data) for input into a particular computer.

formation N **1** the process of forming, making, developing or establishing something.
2 a a particular arrangement, pattern or order, particularly of troops, aircraft, players of a game, etc: **flew in formation**; **b** a shape or structure. **3** GEOL a mass or area of rocks which have common characteristics.

formative ADJ **1** relating to development or growth: **the formative years**. **2** having an effect on development.

former ADJ **1** belonging to or occurring at an earlier time. **2** of two people or things: mentioned, considered, etc first. **3** having once or previously been: **her former partner**.

formerly ADV previously; in the past.

formidable ADJ **1** awesomely impressive. **2** of problems, etc: enormous; difficult to overcome. ■ **formidably** ADV.

formula N (*-ae* or *-as*) **1** the combination of ingredients used in manufacturing something. **2** a method or rule, esp a successful one. **3** CHEM a combination of chemical symbols that represents the chemical composition of a particular substance. **4** MATH, PHYSICS a mathematical equation or expression, or a physical law, that represents the relationship between various quantities, etc. **5** an established piece of wording used by convention. **6** a classification for racing cars acccording to engine size. ■ **formulaic** ADJ.

formulate VB **1** to express something in terms of a formula. **2** to express something in

systematic terms. **3** to express something precisely and clearly. ■ **formulation** N.

fornicate VB, INTR to have sexual intercourse outside marriage. ■ **fornication** N.

forsake VB (*forsook, forsaken*) **1** to desert; to abandon. **2** to renounce, or no longer follow or indulge in. ■ **forsaken** ADJ.

forswear VB (*forswore, forsworn*) OLD USE **1** to give up or renounce (one's foolish ways, etc). **2** to perjure (oneself).

fort N a fortified military building or position.

forte[1] N something one is good at.

forte[2] MUS, ADV in a loud manner.
➤ ADJ loud.

forth ADV, OLD USE except in certain set phrases **1** into existence or view: **bring forth children**. **2** forwards: **back and forth**. **3** out: **set forth on a journey**. **4** onwards: **from this day forth**.

forthcoming ADJ **1** happening or appearing soon. **2** of a person: willing to talk; communicative. **3** available.

forthright ADJ straightforward and decisive.

forthwith ADV immediately; at once.

forties (often written **40s** or **40's**) PL N **1** (**one's forties**) the period of time between one's fortieth and fiftieth birthdays. **2** (**the forties**) the range of temperatures between forty and fifty degrees. **3** (**the forties**) the period of time between the fortieth and fiftieth years of a century.

fortification N **1** the process of fortifying. **2** (**fortifications**) walls and other defensive structures built in preparation for an attack.

fortify VB (*-ies, -ied*) **1** to strengthen (a building, city, etc) in preparation for an attack. **2** to add extra alcohol to (wine) during production, in order to produce sherry, port, etc.

fortitude N uncomplaining courage in pain or misfortune.

fortnight N a period of 14 days; two weeks.

fortnightly ADJ occurring, appearing, etc once every fortnight; bi–monthly.

➤ ADV once a fortnight.
➤ N (*-ies*) a publication which comes out every two weeks.

fortress N a fortified town or a large fort.

fortuitous ADJ happening by chance; accidental. ■ **fortuitously** ADV.

fortunate ADJ 1 lucky; favoured by fate. 2 timely; opportune. ■ **fortunately** ADV.

fortune N 1 chance as a force in human affairs; fate. 2 luck. 3 (**fortunes**) unpredictable happenings that swing affairs this way or that. 4 (**fortunes**) the state of one's luck. 5 one's destiny. 6 a large sum of money.

forty N (*-ies*) 1 a the cardinal number 40; b the quantity that this represents, being one more than thirty–nine, or the product of ten and four. 2 any symbol for this, eg 40 or XL. 3 something, esp a garment or a person, whose size is denoted by the number 40.
➤ ADJ 1 totalling forty. 2 aged forty. ■ **fortieth** ADJ, N.

forum N (PL *fora*) 1 HIST a public square or market place, esp in ancient Rome. 2 a meeting to discuss topics of public concern. 3 a place, programme or publication where opinions can be expressed and openly discussed.

forward ADV 1 (also **forwards**) in the direction in front or ahead of one. 2 (also **forwards**) progressing from first to last. 3 on or onward; to a later time. 4 to an earlier time.
➤ ADJ 1 in the direction in front or ahead. 2 at the front. 3 advanced in development. 4 concerning the future. 5 DEROG inclined to push oneself forward.
➤ N, SPORT a player whose task is to attack.
➤ VB to send (mail) on to another address from the one to which it arrived.

fossil N an impression or cast of an animal or plant preserved within a rock.
➤ ADJ of, like or in the form of a fossil.

fossilize or **-ise** VB, TR & INTR to change or be changed into a fossil.

foster VB 1 TR & INTR to bring up (a child that is not one's own). 2 to put (a child) into the care of someone who is not its parent, usu for a temporary period of time. 3 to encourage the development of (ideas, feelings, etc).
➤ ADJ 1 concerned with or offering fostering: **foster home**. 2 related through fostering rather than by birth: **foster mother**.

foul ADJ 1 disgusting: **a foul smell**. 2 soiled; filthy. 3 contaminated: **foul air**. 4 COLLOQ very unkind or unpleasant. 5 of language: offensive or obscene. 6 unfair or treacherous: **by fair means or foul**. 7 of weather: stormy. 8 clogged. 9 entangled.
➤ N, SPORT a breach of the rules.
➤ VB 1 TR & INTR, SPORT to commit a foul against (an opponent). 2 to make something dirty or polluted. 3 to contaminate or pollute something. 4 TR & INTR a (also **foul up**) to become entangled; b to become entangled with something so as to hinder its movement.
➤ ADV in a foul manner; unfairly. ■ **foully** ADV. ■ **foulness** N.

foul-mouthed and **foul-spoken** ADJ of a person: using offensive or obscene language.

foul play N 1 treachery or criminal violence, esp murder. 2 SPORT a breach of the rules.

found VB 1 to start or establish (an organization, institution, city, etc). 2 to lay the foundation of (a building). ■ **founder** N.

foundation N 1 a an act or the process of founding or establishing an institution, etc; b an institution, etc founded or the fund providing for it. 2 (usu **foundations**) the underground structure on which a building is supported and built. 3 the basis on which a theory, etc rests.

founder VB, INTR 1 of a ship: to sink. 2 of a car, etc: to get stuck in mud, etc. 3 of a horse: to go lame. 4 of a business, scheme, etc: to fail.

foundry N (*-ies*) a place where metal or glass is melted and cast.

fount[1] or **font** N, PRINTING a set of printing type of the same design and size.

fount[2] N 1 a spring or fountain. 2 a source.

fountain N 1 a a jet or jets of water for ornamental effect; b a structure supporting this, consisting of a basin and statues, etc. 2 a structure housing a jet of drinking water, eg, in an office, shopping mall or other public place. **3** a spring of water. **4** a source of wisdom, etc.

fountain pen N a metal-nibbed pen equipped with a cartridge or reservoir of ink.

four N **1 a** the cardinal number 4; **b** the quantity that this represents, being one more than three. **2** any symbol for this, eg **4** or **IV**. **3** something, esp a garment, or a person, whose size is denoted by the number 4. **4** the fourth hour after midnight or midday: *Tea's at four.*
➤ ADJ **1** totalling four. **2** aged four.
◆ **on all fours** on hands and knees.

fourfold ADJ **1** equal to four times as much or many. **2** divided into, or consisting of, four parts.
➤ ADV by four times as much.

four-letter word N a short obscene word.

four-poster N a large bed with a post at each corner to support curtains and a canopy.

foursome N a set or group of four people.

four-square ADJ **1** strong; solidly based. **2** of a building: square and solid-looking.
➤ ADV steadily; squarely.

fourteen N **1 a** the cardinal number 14; **b** the quantity that this represents, being one more than thirteen, or the sum of ten and four. **2** any symbol for this, eg **14** or **XIV**. **3** something, esp a garment, or a person, whose size is denoted by the number 14.
➤ ADJ **1** totalling fourteen. **2** aged fourteen.
■ **fourteenth** ADJ, N.

fourth (often written **4th**) ADJ **1** in counting: **a** next after third; **b** last of four. **2** in fourth position. **3** (**the fourth**)
➤ N **1** one of four equal parts. Usu called **quarter**. **2** a fraction equal to one divided by four. Usu called **quarter**.

fowl N (*fowls* or *fowl*) **1** a farmyard bird, eg a chicken or turkey. **2** the flesh or meat of one of these birds used as food.

fox N **1** a carnivorous mammal of the dog family, with a pointed muzzle, large pointed ears and a long bushy tail. **2** the fur of this animal. **3** COLLOQ a cunning person.

➤ VB **1** to puzzle, confuse or baffle. **2** to deceive, trick or outwit.

foxglove N a plant that produces tall spikes with many purple or white flowers.

foxhole N, MIL a hole from which a soldier may shoot while protected from the enemy's guns.

foxhound N a breed of dog bred and trained to chase foxes.

fox hunt N **1** a hunt for a fox by people on horseback using hounds. **2** a group of people who meet to hunt foxes. ■ **foxhunting** N.

foxtrot N a ballroom dance with gliding steps, alternating between quick and slow.

foxy ADJ (*-ier, -iest*) **1** foxlike. **2** cunning; sly.

foyer N an entrance hall of a theatre, hotel, etc.

fracas N (*fracas*) a noisy quarrel; a brawl.

fraction N **1** MATH an expression that indicates one or more equal parts of a whole, usu represented by a pair of numbers separated by a horizontal or diagonal line. **2** a portion; a small part of something. ■ **fractionally** ADV.

fractious ADJ cross and quarrelsome; inclined to quarrel and complain. ■ **fractiously** ADV.

fracture N **1** the breaking or cracking of anything hard, esp bone, rock or mineral. **2** the medical condition resulting from this.
➤ VB **1** to break or crack something, esp a bone. **2** INTR of a bone, etc: to break or crack.

fragile ADJ **1** easily broken; liable to break. **2** easily destroyed. **3** delicate. **4** in a weakened state of health. ■ **fragility** N.

fragment N **1** a piece broken off; a small piece of something that has broken. **2** something incomplete; a small part.
➤ VB, TR & INTR to break into pieces.
■ **fragmentation** N.

fragmentary and **fragmented** ADJ consisting of small pieces; in fragments.

fragrance N **1** sweetness of smell. **2** a sweet smell or odour. ■ **fragrant** ADJ.

frail ADJ **1** easily broken or destroyed; delicate; fragile. **2** in poor health; weak. **3** morally

weak; easily tempted. ■ **frailness** N.
■ **frailty** N (*-ies*).

frame N 1 a hard main structure or basis to something, round which something is built or to which other parts are added. 2 a structure that surrounds and supports something. 3 something that surrounds. 4 a body, esp a human one, as a structure of a certain size and shape. 5 one of the pictures that make up a strip of film. 6 a single television picture, eg a still picture seen when the pause button on a video player is pressed. 7 one of the pictures in a comic strip. 8 a low glass or semi-glazed structure for protecting young plants growing out of doors. Also called **cold frame**. 9 the rigid part of a bicycle, usu made of metal tubes.
➤ VB 1 to put a frame round something. 2 to be a frame for something. 3 to compose or design something. 4 to shape or direct (one's thoughts, actions, etc) for a particular purpose. 5 COLLOQ to dishonestly direct suspicion for a crime, etc at (an innocent person).

framework N 1 a basic supporting structure. 2 a basic plan or system.

franc N the unit of currency of various countries, including Switzerland and formerly France.

franchise N 1 the right to vote. 2 a right, privilege, exemption from a duty, etc, granted to a person or organization. 3 an agreement by which a business company gives someone the right to market its products in an area.
➤ VB to grant a franchise to (a person, a company, etc).

francophone N (sometimes **Francophone**) a French-speaking person.
➤ ADJ speaking French.

frank ADJ 1 open and honest in speech or manner; candid. 2 bluntly outspoken. 3 undisguised; openly visible.
➤ VB to mark (a letter), either cancelling the stamp or, in place of a stamp, to show that postage has been paid.
➤ N a franking mark on a letter. ■ **frankly** ADV.
■ **frankness** N.

frankfurter N a type of spicy smoked sausage.

frankincense N an aromatic gum resin obtained from E African or Arabian trees.

frantic ADJ 1 desperate, eg with fear or anxiety. 2 hurried; rushed. ■ **frantically** ADV.

fraternal ADJ 1 concerning a brother; brotherly. 2 of twins: developed from two zygotes or fertilized eggs. ■ **fraternally** ADV.

fraternity N (*-ies*) 1 a religious brotherhood. 2 a group of people with common interests. 3 the fact of being brothers; brotherly feeling.

fraternize or **-ise** VB, INTR (often **fraternize with sb**) to meet or associate together as friends. ■ **fraternization** N.

fratricide N the murder of a brother.

fraud N 1 an act or instance of deliberate deception, with the intention of gaining some benefit. 2 COLLOQ someone who dishonestly pretends to be something they are not.

fraudster N a cheat; a swindler.

fraudulent ADJ intended to deceive.

fraught ADJ, COLLOQ causing or feeling worry.
◆ **fraught with danger**, etc full of or laden down with danger, etc.

fray VB, TR & INTR 1 of cloth or rope: to wear away along an edge or at a point of friction, so that individual threads come loose. 2 of tempers, etc: to make or become strained.
➤ N 1 a fight, quarrel or argument. 2 any scene of lively action.

frazzle N 1 a state of nervous and physical exhaustion. 2 a scorched and brittle state.

freak N 1 a person, animal or plant of abnormal shape or form. 2 someone or something odd or unusual. 3 esp IN COMPOUNDS someone highly enthusiastic about the specified thing: **health freak • film freak**. 4 a drug addict: **an acid freak**. 5 a whim or caprice: **a freak of fancy**.
➤ ADJ abnormal: **a freak storm**.

freckle N a small yellowish-brown benign mark on the skin.
➤ VB, TR & INTR to mark, or become marked, with freckles. ■ **freckled** or **freckly** ADJ.

free ADJ 1 allowed to move as one pleases; not

shut in. **2** not tied or fastened. **3** allowed to do as one pleases; not restricted, controlled or enslaved. **4** of a country: independent. **5** costing nothing. **6** open or available to all. **7** not working, busy, engaged or having another appointment. **8** not occupied; not being used. **9** of a translation: not precisely literal. **10** smooth and easy. **11** without obstruction. **12** IN COMPOUNDS **a** not containing the specified ingredient, substance, factor, etc (which is usu considered to be undesirable): **sugar-free • nuclear-free**; **b** free from, or not affected or troubled by, the specified thing: **stress-free weekend • carefree**; **c** not paying or exempt from the specified thing: **rent-free • tax-free**.
➤ ADV **1** without payment: **free of charge**. **2** freely; without restriction: **wander free**.
➤ VB (**freed**) to allow someone to move without restriction after a period in captivity, prison, etc; to set or make someone free; to liberate someone. ■ **freely** ADV.
◆ **free of** or **from sth** without; not or no longer having or suffering: **free from pain**.
◆ **free sb of sth 1** to make them free from it; to release them. **2** to rid or relieve them of it.
◆ **free with sth** open, generous, lavish or liberal: **free with her money**.

freebie N, COLLOQ something given or provided without charge.

freedom N **1** the condition of being free to act, move, etc without restriction. **2** personal liberty or independence, eg from slavery, serfdom, etc. **3** a right or liberty. **4** (often **freedom from sth**) the state of being without or exempt (from something). **5** autonomy, self-government or independence. **6** unrestricted access to or use of something. **7** honorary citizenship of a place, entitling one to certain privileges.

free enterprise N business carried out without interference by the government.

free fall N **1** the fall of something acted on by gravity alone. **2** the part of a descent by parachute before the parachute opens.

free-for-all N a fight, argument, or discussion in which everybody present feels free to join.

free-form ADJ freely flowing; spontaneous.

freehand ADJ, ADV of a drawing, etc: done without the help of a ruler, compass, etc.

free hand N complete freedom of action.

freehold ADJ of land, property, etc: belonging to the owner by fee simple, fee tail, or for life and without limitations.
➤ N ownership of such land, property, etc.
■ **freeholder** N.

free kick N, FOOTBALL a kick awarded to one side with no tackling from the other, following an infringement of the rules.

freelance N **1** a self-employed person offering their services where needed, not under contract to any single employer. Also called **freelancer**. **2** AS ADJ: freelance journalist.
➤ ADV as a freelance: **She works freelance**.
➤ VB, INTR to work as a freelance.

freeload VB, INTR, COLLOQ to eat, live, enjoy oneself, etc at someone else's expense.
■ **freeloader** N.

Freemason and **Mason** N a member of an international secret male society.
■ **Freemasonry** N.

free radical N, CHEM an uncharged atom or group of atoms containing at least one unpaired electron.

free-range ADJ **1** of poultry and pigs: allowed some freedom to move about and graze or feed naturally; not kept in a battery. **2** of eggs: laid by free-range poultry.

freesia N a plant of the iris family with fragrant trumpet-shaped flowers.

free speech N the right to express any opinion freely, particularly in public.

free-standing ADJ not attached to or supported by a wall or other structure.

freestyle SPORT, ADJ **1 a** denoting a competition or race in which competitors are allowed to choose their own style or programme; **b** SWIMMING denoting the front crawl stroke, as being the fastest. **2** denoting all-in wrestling.

3 of a competitor: taking part in freestyle competitions, etc.
➤ N a freestyle competition or race.

free trade N trade between or amongst countries without protective tariffs.

freeway N, N AMER a toll-free highway.

freewheel VB, INTR **1** to travel, usu downhill, without using mechanical power. **2** to act or drift about unhampered by responsibilities.

free will N **1** the power of making choices without the constraint of some uncontrollable force, regarded as a human characteristic. **2** a person's independent choice.

freeze VB (*freezes, froze, frozen*) **1** TR & INTR to change (a liquid) into a solid by cooling it to below its freezing point, eg to change water into ice. **2** of a liquid: to change into a solid when it is cooled to below its freezing point. **3** TR & INTR (often **freeze together**) to stick or cause to stick together by frost. **4** INTR of the weather, temperature, etc: to be at or below the freezing-point of water. **5** TR & INTR, COLLOQ to be or make very cold. **6** INTR to die of cold. **7** TR & INTR of food: to preserve, or be suitable for preserving, by refrigeration below freezing-point. **8** TR & INTR to make or become motionless or unable to move, because of fear, etc. **9** to fix (prices, wages, etc) at a certain level.
➤ N **1** a period when temperatures are below freezing-point. **2** a period during which wages, prices, etc are controlled.

freeze-dry VB to preserve (perishable material, esp food and medicines) by rapidly freezing it and then drying it.

freezer N a refrigerated cabinet or compartment in which to store or preserve food at a temperature below freezing-point.

freezing point N **1** the temperature at which the liquid form of a particular substance turns into a solid. **2** (also **freezing**) the freezing point of water (0°C at sea level).

freight N **1** transport of goods by rail, road, sea or air. **2** the goods transported in this way. **3** the cost of such transport.
➤ VB **1** to transport (goods) by rail, road, sea or air. **2** to load (a vehicle, etc) with goods for transport.

freighter N a ship or aircraft that carries cargo rather than passengers.

French ADJ of France.
➤ N **1** the official language of France and one of the official languages of Canada, Switzerland and several other countries. **2** (**the French**) the people of France.

French bean N a widely cultivated species of bean with seeds known as haricot beans.

French bread, **French loaf** and **French stick** N white bread in the form of a long narrow loaf with a thick crisp crust.

French dressing N a salad dressing made from oil, vinegar, herbs, etc.

French fries and **fries** PL N, chiefly N AMER & BRIT INFORMAL long thin strips of potato deep-fried in oil, usu longer and thinner than chips.

French horn N an orchestral horn.

French polish N a varnish for furniture, consisting of shellac dissolved in alcohol.
➤ VB (**French-polish**) to varnish with French polish.

French windows PL N a pair of glass doors that open on to a garden, etc.

frenetic ADJ frantic, distracted, hectic or wildly energetic. ■ **frenetically** ADV.

frenzy N (**-ies**) **1** wild agitation or excitement. **2** a frantic burst of activity. **3** a state of violent mental disturbance. ■ **frenzied** ADJ.

frequency N (**-ies**) **1** the condition of happening often. **2** the rate at which a happening, phenomenon, etc, recurs. **3** PHYS (SI unit hertz) a measure of the rate at which a complete cycle of wave motion is repeated per unit time. **4** RADIO the rate of sound waves per second at which a radio signal is sent out.

frequent ADJ **1** recurring at short intervals. **2** habitual.
➤ VB to visit or attend (a place, an event, etc) often. ■ **frequently** ADV.

fresco N (**-oes** or **-os**) a picture painted on a

wall, usu while the plaster is still damp.

fresh ADJ **1** newly made, gathered, etc. **2** having just finished doing something or just had some experience, etc: **fresh from university**. **3** new; additional: **a fresh sheet of paper** • **fresh supplies**. **4** original: **a fresh approach**. **5** not tinned, frozen, dried, salted or otherwise preserved. **6** not tired; bright and alert. **7** cool; refreshing: **a fresh breeze**. **8** of water: not salty. **9** of air: cool and uncontaminated; invigorating. **10** youthfully healthy; ruddy. **11** not worn or faded.

freshen VB **1** to make something fresh or fresher. **2** TR & INTR (also **freshen up** or **freshen oneself** or **sb up**) to get washed and tidy; to wash and tidy (oneself or someone). **3** INTR of a wind: to become stronger.

freshwater ADJ consisting of or living in fresh as opposed to salt water: **freshwater lake** • **freshwater fish**.

fret[1] VB (*-tt-*) **1** INTR (also **fret about** or **over sth**) to worry, esp unnecessarily; to show or express anxiety. **2** to wear something away or consume something by rubbing or erosion.

fret[2] N any of the narrow metal ridges across the neck of a guitar or similar musical instrument.

fretful ADJ anxious and unhappy; tending to fret; peevish. ■ **fretfully** ADV.

fretwork N decorative carved openwork in wood or metal.

Freudian slip N an error or unintentional action, esp a slip of the tongue, taken as revealing an unconscious thought.

friar N a male member of any of various religious orders of the Roman Catholic Church.

friary N (*-ies*) **1** a building inhabited by a community of friars. **2** the community itself.

friction N **1** the rubbing of one thing against another. **2** PHYS the force that opposes the relative motion of two bodies or surfaces that are in contact with each other. **3** quarrelling; disagreement; conflict. ■ **frictional** ADJ.

Friday N the sixth day of the week.

fridge N, COLLOQ a refrigerator.

friend N **1** someone whom one knows and likes, and to whom one shows loyalty and affection; a close or intimate acquaintance. **2** someone who gives support or help. **3** an ally as distinct from an enemy or foe. **4** someone or something already encountered or mentioned: **our old friend the ant**. ■ **friendless** ADJ.

friendly ADJ (*-ier, -iest*) **1** kind; behaving as a friend. **2** (**friendly with sb**) on close or affectionate terms with them. **3** relating to, or typical of, a friend. **4** being a colleague, helper, partner, etc rather than an enemy: **friendly nations**. **5** SPORT of a match, etc: played for enjoyment or practice and not as part of a formal competition. **6** IN COMPOUNDS, FORMING ADJS **a** denoting things that are made easy or convenient for those for whom they are intended: **user-friendly**; **b** indicating that something causes little harm to something, particularly something related to the environment: **eco-friendly**.
➢ N (*-ies*) SPORT a friendly match.
■ **friendliness** N. ■ **friendship** N.

frier see **fryer**

frieze N **1** a decorative strip running along a wall. **2** ARCHIT **a** a horizontal band between the cornice and capitals of a classical temple; **b** the sculpture which fills this space.

frigate N **1** a naval escort vessel, smaller than a destroyer. **2** HIST a small sailing warship.

fright N **1** sudden fear; a shock. **2** COLLOQ a person or thing of ludicrous appearance.

frighten VB to make someone afraid; to alarm them. ■ **frightened** ADJ. ■ **frightening** ADJ.

frightful ADJ **1** ghastly; frightening. **2** COLLOQ bad; awful. **3** COLLOQ great; extreme. ■ **frightfully** ADV.

frigid ADJ **1** cold and unfriendly; without spirit or feeling. **2** of a woman: not sexually responsive. **3** GEOG intensely cold. ■ **frigidity** N.

frill N **1** a gathered or pleated strip of cloth attached to a garment, etc as a trimming. **2** (usu **frills**) something extra serving no very useful purpose. ■ **frilled** ADJ. ■ **frilly** ADJ (*-ier, -iest*).

fringe N 1 a border of loose threads on a carpet, tablecloth, garment, etc. 2 hair cut to hang down over the forehead but above the eyeline. 3 the part farthest from the main area or centre. 4 bordering, or just outside, the recognized or orthodox form.
➤ VB 1 to decorate something with a fringe. 2 to form a fringe round something.

frippery N (-ies) 1 showy but unnecessary finery or adornment. 2 trifles; trivia.

frisk VB 1 INTR (also **frisk about**) to jump or run about happily and playfully. 2 SLANG to search someone for concealed weapons, drugs, etc.

frisky ADJ (-ier, -iest) lively; playful; high-spirited; frolicsome. ■ **friskily** ADV.

frisson N a shiver of fear or excitement.

fritter[1] N a piece of meat, fruit, etc coated in batter and fried: **spam fritter** • **banana fritter**.

fritter[2] VB (chiefly **fritter sth away**) to waste (time, money, energy, etc) on unimportant things; to squander something.

frivolous ADJ 1 silly; not sufficiently serious. 2 trifling or unimportant. ■ **frivolity** N.

frizz N of hair: a mass of tiny tight curls.
➤ VB, TR & INTR to form or make into a frizz.

frizzy ADJ (-ier, -iest) tightly curled.

frock N 1 a woman's or girl's dress. 2 a priest's or monk's long garment, with large open sleeves. 3 a loose smock.

frog N a tailless amphibian with a moist smooth skin, protruding eyes, powerful hind legs for swimming and leaping, and webbed feet.
◆ **a frog in one's throat** a throat irritation that temporarily interferes with one's speech.

frogman N an underwater swimmer wearing a rubber suit and using breathing equipment.

frogmarch VB to force someone forward, holding them firmly by the arms.

frogspawn N a mass of frogs' eggs encased in protective nutrient jelly.

frolic VB (-icked, -icking) INTR to frisk or run about playfully; to gambol about.
➤ N 1 a spell of happy playing or frisking; a gambol. 2 something silly done as a joke; a prank. ■ **frolicsome** ADJ.

from PREP, INDICATING 1 a starting-point in place or time: **from London to Glasgow** • **crippled from birth**. 2 a lower limit: **tickets from £12 upwards**. 3 repeated progression: **trail from shop to shop**. 4 movement out of: **took a letter from the drawer**. 5 distance away: **16 miles from Dover**. 6 a viewpoint: **can see the house from here**. 7 separation; removal: **took it away from her**. 8 point of attachment: **hanging from a nail**. 9 exclusion: **omitted from the sample**. 10 source or origin: **made from an old curtain**. 11 change of condition: **translate from French into English**. 12 cause: **ill from overwork**. 13 deduction as a result of observation: **see from her face she's angry**. 14 distinction: **can't tell one twin from the other**. 15 prevention, protection, exemption, immunity, release, escape, etc: **safe from harm** • **excused from attending** • **released from prison**.

fromage frais N a creamy low-fat cheese, often used for desserts.

frond N, BOT a large compound leaf, esp of a fern or palm.

front N 1 the side or part of anything that is furthest forward or nearest to the viewer; the most important side or part, eg the side of a building where the main door is. 2 any side of a large or historic building. 3 the part of a vehicle, etc that faces or is closest to, the direction in which it moves. 4 THEAT the auditorium of a theatre, etc. 5 the cover or first pages of a book. 6 a road or promenade in a town that runs beside the sea, or large lake, etc; sea front. 7 in war, particularly when fought on the ground: the area where the soldiers are nearest to the enemy: **eastern front**. 8 a matter of concern or interest: **no progress on the job front**. 9 METEOROL the boundary between two air masses that have different temperatures. 10 an outward appearance.
➤ VB 1 TR & INTR of a building: to have its front facing or beside something specified: **The house fronts on to the main road**. 2 to be the leader or representative of (a group, etc). 3 to

present (a radio or television programme).
➤ ADJ relating to, or situated at or in the front.

◆ **in front 1** on the forward-facing side. **2** ahead.

◆ **in front of sb** or **sth 1** at or to a position in advance of them or it. **2** in their presence.

frontage N the front of a building, esp in relation to the street, etc along which it extends.

frontal ADJ **1** relating to the front. **2** aimed at the front; direct: *a frontal assault*.

frontier N **1 a** the part of a country bordering onto another country; **b** a line, barrier, etc marking the boundary between two countries. **2** (**frontiers**) limits: *the frontiers of knowledge*.

frontiersman and **frontierswoman** N someone who lives on the frontier of a country.

frontispiece N a picture at the beginning of a book, facing the title page.

front line N in a war, particularly when fought on the ground: **a** the area of a front where soldiers are physically closest to the enemy; **b** AS ADJ (**front-line**) belonging or relating to the front line: *front-line soldiers*.

front-runner N the person most likely or most favoured to win a competition, election, etc.

frost N **1** a deposit of ice crystals formed when water vapour comes into contact with a surface whose temperature is below the freezing point of water. **2** an air temperature below freezing-point: *12 degrees of frost*.
➤ VB, TR & INTR (also **frost up** or **over**) to cover or become covered with frost.

frostbite N damage to body tissues caused by very low temperatures. ■ **frostbitten** ADJ.

frosted ADJ **1** covered by frost. **2** of glass: patterned or roughened as though with frost.

frosting N, N AMER cake icing.

frosty ADJ (**-ier, -iest**) **1** covered with frost. **2** cold enough for frost to form. **3** cold; unfriendly; unwelcoming. ■ **frostily** ADV.

froth N **1** a mass of tiny bubbles forming eg on the surface of a liquid, or round the mouth in certain diseases. **2** writing, talk, etc that has no serious content or purpose. **3** glamour; something frivolous or trivial.
➤ VB, TR & INTR to produce or make something produce froth. ■ **frothy** ADJ (**-ier, -iest**).

frown VB, INTR to wrinkle one's forehead and draw one's eyebrows together in worry, disapproval, deep thought, etc.
➤ N **1** the act of frowning. **2** a disapproving expression or glance.

◆ **frown on** or **at sth** to disapprove of it.

frowsy or **frowzy** ADJ (**-ier, -iest**) **1** untidy, dishevelled or slovenly. **2** stuffy; stale-smelling.

frozen ADJ **1** preserved by keeping at a temperature below freezing point. **2** very cold. **3** stiff and unfriendly.

fructose N, BIOCHEM a sugar found in fruit and honey.

frugal ADJ **1** thrifty; economical; not generous; careful, particularly in financial matters. **2** not large; costing little: *a frugal meal*. ■ **frugality** N. ■ **frugally** ADV.

fruit N **1** the fully ripened ovary of a flowering plant, containing one or more seeds. **2** an edible part of a plant that is generally sweet and juicy, esp the ovary, but sometimes extended to include other parts. **3** plant products generally: *the fruits of the land*. **4** (also **fruits**) whatever is gained as a result of hard work, etc: *the fruit of his labour*.
➤ VB, INTR to produce fruit.

◆ **bear fruit 1** to produce fruit. **2** to produce good results.

fruitcake N **1** a cake containing dried fruit, nuts, etc. **2** COLLOQ a slightly mad person.

fruiterer N a person who sells or deals in fruit.

fruitful ADJ producing useful results; productive; worthwhile. ■ **fruitfully** ADV.

fruition N **1** the achievement of something that has been aimed at and worked for: *The project finally came to fruition*. **2** the bearing of fruit.

fruitless ADJ **1** useless; unsuccessful; done in vain. **2** not producing fruit. ■ **fruitlessly** ADV.

fruity ADJ (**-ier, -iest**) **1** full of or tasting like fruit. **2** of a voice: deep and rich in tone.

frump N a woman who dresses in a dowdy way. ■ **frumpish** ADJ. ■ **frumpy** ADJ (*-ier, -iest*).

frustrate VB 1 to prevent (someone from doing something or from getting something); to thwart or foil (a plan, attempt, etc). 2 to make (someone) feel disappointed, useless, lacking a purpose in life, etc. ■ **frustration** N.

fry[1] VB (*fries, fried*) TR & INTR to cook (food) in hot oil or fat.
➣ N (*fries*) 1 a dish of anything fried. 2 a fry-up.

fry[2] PL N 1 young or newly spawned fish. 2 salmon in their second year.

fryer or **frier** N 1 a pan for frying. 2 someone who fries something (esp fish).

frying-pan N a shallow long-handled pan for frying food.

fuchsia N a shrub with purple, red or white hanging flowers.

fuck TABOO SLANG, VB, TR & INTR to have sex (with someone).
➣ N 1 an act of sexual intercourse. 2 a sexual partner.
➣ EXCLAM an expression of anger, frustration, etc. ■ **fucking** ADJ, N, ADV.
◆ **fuck off** to go away.
◆ **fuck up** or **fuck sth up** to ruin or spoil it.

fuddle VB to confuse or stupefy.

fuddy-duddy COLLOQ, ADJ old-fashioned or prim.
➣ N (*-ies*) a fuddy-duddy person.

fudge[1] N a soft toffee made from butter, sugar and milk.

fudge[2] VB, COLLOQ 1 to invent or concoct (an excuse, etc). 2 to distort or obscure (figures, an argument, etc). 3 to dodge or evade something. 4 INTR to avoid stating a clear opinion.
➣ N an act of obscuring, distorting an issue, etc.

fuel N 1 any material that releases energy when it is burned, which can be used as a source of heat or power. 2 material that is used to release energy by nuclear fission in a nuclear reactor.
➣ VB (*-ll-*) 1 to fill or feed with fuel. 2 INTR to take on or get fuel. 3 to inflame (anger or other passions).

fug N a stale-smelling stuffy atmosphere, often very hot and airless. ■ **fuggy** (*-ier, -iest*) ADJ.

fugitive N a person who is fleeing someone or something, usually some kind of authority.
➣ ADJ 1 fleeing away. 2 lasting only briefly.

fugue N, MUS a style of composition in which a theme is introduced in one part and developed as successive parts take it up. ■ **fugal** ADJ.

fulcrum N (*-rums* or *-ra*) 1 TECHNICAL the point on which a lever turns, balances or is supported. 2 a support; a means to an end.

fulfil or (N AMER) **fulfill** VB (*-ll-*) 1 to carry out or perform (a task, promise, etc). 2 to satisfy (requirements). 3 to achieve (an aim, ambition, etc). ■ **fulfilment** N.

full ADJ 1 (also **full of sth**) holding, containing or having as much as possible, or a large quantity. 2 complete: do a full day's work. 3 detailed; thorough; including everything necessary: a full report. 4 occupied: My hands are full. 5 having eaten till one wants no more. 6 plump: the fuller figure • full lips. 7 of clothes: made with a large amount of material: a full skirt. 8 rich and varied: a full life. 9 of the Moon: at the stage when it is seen as a fully-illuminated disc.
➣ ADV 1 completely; at maximum capacity: Is the radiator full on? 2 exactly; directly: hit him full on the nose. ■ **fullness** or (N AMER OR DATED) **fulness** N.
◆ **be full up** 1 to be full to the limit. 2 to have had enough to eat.
◆ **full of oneself** having too good an opinion of oneself.
◆ **full well** perfectly well.
◆ **in full** 1 completely. 2 at length; in detail.
◆ **to the full** to the greatest possible extent.

full-blast ADV with maximum energy.

full-blooded ADJ 1 of pure breed; thoroughbred. 2 enthusiastic; whole-hearted.

full-blown ADJ having all the features of the specified thing: a full-blown war.

full-bodied ADJ rich in flavour.

full-circle ADV 1 round in a complete revolution. 2 back to the starting position.

full-length ADJ 1 complete; of the usual or standard length. 2 showing the whole body: a full-length mirror. 3 of maximum length; long: a full-length skirt.

full moon N 1 one of the four phases of the Moon, when it is seen as a fully-illuminated disc. 2 the time when the Moon is full.

full-scale ADJ 1 of a drawing, etc: the same size as the subject. 2 using all possible resources, means, etc; complete or exhaustive.

full stop N a punctuation mark (.) used to indicate the end of a sentence or to mark an abbreviation.

full time N the end of the time normally allowed for a sports match, etc.

full-time ADJ occupied for or extending over the whole of the working week.
➤ ADV (**full time**): working full time.

fully ADV 1 to the greatest possible extent. 2 completely: fully qualified.

fully-fledged ADJ 1 of a person: completely trained or qualified. 2 of a bird: old enough to have grown feathers.

fulminate VB, INTR to utter angry criticism or condemnation. ■ **fulmination** N.

fulsome ADJ of praise, compliments, etc: so overdone as to be distasteful.

fumble VB 1 INTR to grope, clumsily. 2 to say or do awkwardly. 3 to fail to manage, because of clumsy handling.
➤ N an act of fumbling.

fume N 1 (often **fumes**) smoke, gases or vapour, esp if strong-smelling or toxic, emanating from heated materials, operating engines or machinery, etc. 2 the pungent toxic vapours given off by solvents or concentrated acids. 3 a rage; fretful excitement.
➤ VB 1 INTR to be furious; to fret angrily. 2 INTR to give off smoke, gases or vapours. 3 INTR of gases or vapours: to come off in fumes, esp during a chemical reaction.

fumigate VB to disinfect (a room, a building, etc) with fumes, in order to destroy pests. ■ **fumigation** N. ■ **fumigator** N.

fun N 1 enjoyment; merriment. 2 a source of amusement or entertainment.
➤ ADJ, COLLOQ for amusement: fun run.

function N 1 the special purpose or task of a machine, person, bodily part, etc. 2 a an organized event such as a party, reception, meeting, etc; b Also AS ADJ: function room. 3 a duty particular to someone in a particular job. 4 MATH, LOGIC a mathematical procedure that relates one or more variables to one or more other variables.
➤ VB, INTR 1 to work; to operate. 2 to fulfil a function. 3 to serve or act as something. ■ **functionality** N.

functional ADJ 1 designed for efficiency rather than decorativeness. 2 in working order.

functionary N (*-ies*) DEROG someone who works as a minor official, eg in government.

fund N 1 a sum of money on which some enterprise is founded or on which the expenses of a project are supported. 2 a large store or supply: a fund of jokes. 3 (**funds**) COLLOQ money available for spending.
➤ VB to provide money for a particular purpose: fund the project.
◆ **in funds** COLLOQ having plenty of cash.

fundamental ADJ 1 basic; underlying: fundamental rules of physics. 2 large; important: fundamental differences. 3 essential; necessary.
➤ N 1 (usu **fundamentals**) a basic principle or rule. 2 MUS the lowest note of a chord.

fundamentalism N in religion, politics, etc: strict adherence to traditional teachings. ■ **fundamentalist** N.

funeral N the ceremonial burial or cremation of a dead person.
➤ ADJ relating to funerals.

funeral director N an undertaker.

funeral parlour N 1 an undertaker's place of business. 2 a room that can be hired for funeral ceremonies.

funerary ADJ relating to or used for funerals.

funereal ADJ 1 associated with or suitable for funerals. 2 mournful; dismal. 3 extremely slow.

funfair N a collection of sideshows, amusements, rides, etc, often set up temporarily on open ground and moving from town to town.

fungicide N a chemical that kills or limits the growth of fungi. ■ **fungicidal** ADJ.

fungus N (*fungi* or *funguses*) an organism that superficially resembles a plant, but does not have leaves and roots, and lacks chlorophyll, so that it must obtain its nutrients from other organisms. ■ **fungal** ADJ. ■ **fungoid** ADJ.

funicular ADJ of a mountain railway: operating by a machine-driven cable, with two cars, one of which descends while the other ascends.

funk¹ N, COLLOQ jazz or rock music with a strong rhythm and repeating bass pattern, with a down-to-earth bluesy feel.

funk² COLLOQ, N 1 a (also **blue funk**) a state of fear or panic; **b** shrinking back or shirking because of a loss of courage. 2 a coward. ➢ VB to balk at something or shirk from fear.

funky ADJ (*-ier, -iest*) COLLOQ 1 of jazz or rock music: strongly rhythmical and emotionally stirring. 2 trendy; good. 3 earthy; smelly.

funnel N 1 a tube with a cone-shaped opening through which liquid, etc can be poured into a narrow-necked container. 2 a vertical exhaust pipe on a steamship or steam engine through which smoke escapes. ➢ VB (*-ll-*; (US) *-l-*) 1 INTR to rush through a narrow space: **wind funnelling through the streets**. 2 to transfer (liquid, etc) from one container to another using a funnel.

funny ADJ (*-ier, -iest*) 1 amusing; causing laughter. 2 strange; odd; mysterious. 3 COLLOQ dishonest; shady; involving trickery. 4 COLLOQ ill: **feeling a bit funny**. 5 COLLOQ slightly crazy. ➢ N (*-ies*) COLLOQ a joke. ■ **funnily** ADV.

fur N 1 the thick fine soft coat of a hairy animal. 2 **a** the skin of such an animal with the hair attached, used to make, line or trim garments; **b** a synthetic imitation of this. 3 a coat, cape or jacket made of fur or an imitation of it. 4 a whitish coating on the tongue. ➢ VB (*-rr-*) 1 TR & INTR (often **fur up** or **fur sth up**) to coat or become coated with a fur-like deposit. 2 to cover, trim or line with fur. ■ **furry** ADJ (*-ier, -iest*).

furious ADJ 1 violently or intensely angry. 2 raging; stormy. 3 frenzied; frantic. ■ **furiously** ADV.

furl VB, TR & INTR of flags, sails or umbrellas: to roll up.

furlong N a measure of distance equal to one eighth of a mile, or 220 yards (201.2 metres).

furlough N leave of absence.

furnace N 1 an enclosed chamber in which heat is produced, eg for smelting metal or burning rubbish. 2 COLLOQ a very hot place.

furnish VB 1 to provide (a house, etc) with furniture. 2 to supply (what is necessary). ■ **furnished** ADJ. ◆ **furnish sb with sth** to supply or equip them with what they require.

furnishings PL N articles of furniture, fittings, carpets, curtains, etc.

furniture N movable household equipment such as tables, chairs, beds, etc.

furore or (esp N AMER) **furor** N a general outburst of excitement or indignation.

furrier N someone who makes or sells furs.

furrow N 1 a groove or trench cut into the earth by a plough; a rut. 2 a wrinkle. ➢ VB 1 to plough (land) into furrows. 2 INTR to become wrinkled.

further ADJ 1 more distant or remote (than something else). 2 more extended than was orig expected: **further delay**. 3 additional. ➢ ADV 1 at or to a greater distance or more distant point. 2 to or at a more advanced point. 3 to a greater extent or degree. 4 moreover; furthermore. ➢ VB to help the progress of something. ■ **furtherance** N. ◆ **further to** following on from (a telephone conversation, letter, etc).

further education N, BRIT formal education at a college, usu on a vocational course, for school-leavers or mature students.

furthermore ADV in addition to what has already been said; moreover.

furthermost ADJ most distant or remote; farthest.

furthest ADJ most distant or remote.
➤ ADV **1** at or to the greatest distance or most distant point. **2** at or to the most advanced point; to the greatest extent or degree.

furtive ADJ stealthy; sly. ■ **furtively** ADV.

fury N (-*ies*) **1** (an outburst of) violent anger. **2** violence: the fury of the wind. **3** a frenzy.

furze N gorse.

fuse[1] N, ELEC a safety device consisting of a wire which melts when the current exceeds a certain value, thereby breaking the circuit.
➤ VB, TR & INTR **1** to melt as a result of the application of heat. **2** (also **fuse together**) to join by, or as if by, melting together. **3** of an electric circuit or appliance: to cease to function as a result of the melting of a fuse.

fuse[2] N a cord or cable containing combustible material, used for detonating a bomb or explosive charge.
➤ VB to fit with such a device.

fuselage N the main body of an aircraft, to which the wings and tail unit are attached.

fusilier N, HIST an infantryman armed with a **fusil**, a light musket.

fusillade N a continuous discharge of firearms; an onslaught.

fusion N **1** CHEM the process of melting, whereby a substance changes from a solid to a liquid. **2** the act of joining together.

fuss N **1** agitation and excitement, esp over something trivial. **2** a commotion, disturbance or bustle. **3** a show of fond affection.
➤ VB, INTR (also **fuss over** or **about sth**) **1** to worry needlessly. **2** to concern oneself too much with trivial matters. **3** to agitate.
◆ **make a fuss** or **make a fuss about sth** to complain about it.
◆ **make a fuss of sb** COLLOQ to give them a lot of affectionate or amicable attention.

fusspot N COLLOQ someone who makes too much of trivial things.

fussy ADJ (-*ier, -iest*) **1** choosy; discriminating. **2** over-concerned with details or trifles; finicky. **3** bustling and officious. **4** over-elaborate.

fusty ADJ (-*ier, -iest*) **1** stale-smelling; old and musty. **2** old-fashioned. ■ **fustiness** N.

futile ADJ vain or pointless. ■ **futility** N.

futon N a thin cloth-filled mattress.

future N **1** the time to come; events that are still to occur. **2** GRAM **a** the future tense; **b** a verb in the future tense. **3** prospects: must think about one's future. **4** likelihood of success: no future in that.
➤ ADJ **1** yet to come or happen. **2** about to become: my future wife. **3** GRAM of the tense of a verb: indicating actions or events yet to happen, in English formed with the auxiliary verb **will** and infinitive without **to**, as in She will see him tomorrow.
◆ **in future** from now on.

futurism N an artistic movement concerned with expressing the dynamism of modern technology. ■ **futurist** N.

futuristic ADJ **1** of design, etc: so modern or original as to seem appropriate to the future. **2** relating to futurism.

futurity N (-*ies*) **1** the future. **2** a future event.

fuzz N **1** a mass of fine fibres or hair. **2** a blur.

fuzzy ADJ (-*ier, -iest*) **1** covered with fuzz. **2** forming tight curls. **3** indistinct; blurred.

Gg

G or **g** N (**Gs, G's** or **g's**) **1** the seventh letter of the English alphabet. **2** (**G**) MUS the fifth note on the scale of C major.

g ABBREV **1** gallon. **2** gram or gramme. **3** gravity.

gab COLLOQ, N idle talk; chat.
➤ VB (-**bb**-) INTR (also **gab on** or **away**) to talk idly, esp at length.

gabble VB, TR & INTR to talk or say something quickly and unclearly.

gable N **1** the triangular upper part of a side wall between the sloping parts of a roof. **2** a triangular canopy above a door or window.

gad VB (-**dd**-) INTR, COLLOQ (usu **gad about** or **around**) to go from place to place busily, esp in the hope of finding amusement.

gadabout N, COLLOQ, DEROG a person who gads about.

gadget N any small device, esp one more ingenious than necessary. ■ **gadgetry** N.

Gaelic N any of the closely related Celtic languages spoken in the Scottish Highlands and Islands , or Ireland or the Isle of Man.
➤ ADJ of these languages or the people who speak them, or to their customs.

gaffe N a socially embarrassing action or remark.

gaffer N, COLLOQ a boss or foreman.

gag[1] VB (-**gg**-) **1** to silence someone by putting something in or over their mouth. **2** to deprive someone of free speech. **3** INTR to retch. **4** INTR to choke.
➤ N **1** something put into or over a person's mouth to silence them. **2** any suppression of free speech.

gag[2] COLLOQ, N a joke or trick.
➤ VB (-**gg**-) INTR to tell jokes.

gaga ADJ, COLLOQ **1** weak–minded through old age; senile. **2** silly; foolish.

gaggle N **1** a flock of geese. **2** COLLOQ a group of noisy people.

gaiety N **1** the state of being merry or bright. **2** attractively bright appearance. **3** fun.

gaily ADV **1** in a light–hearted, merry way. **2** brightly; colourfully.

gain VB **1** to get or obtain. **2** to win (esp a victory or prize). **3** to have or experience an increase in something: **gain speed**. **4** TR & INTR of a clock, etc: to go too fast by (a specified amount of time).
➤ N **1** (often **gains**) something gained, eg profit. **2** an increase, eg in weight.
◆ **gain on sb** or **sth** to come closer to them or it; to catch them up.

gainful ADJ **1** profitable. **2** of employment: paid. ■ **gainfully** ADV.

gainsay VB (**gainsaid**) FORMAL to deny or contradict. ■ **gainsayer** N.

gait N **1** a way of walking. **2** the leg movements of an animal travelling at a specified speed.

gaiter N a leather or cloth covering for the lower leg and ankle.

gala N **1 a** a public festivity of some kind, eg a carnival; **b** AS ADJ: **gala night**. **2** a meeting for sports competitions, esp swimming.

galactic ADJ relating to a galaxy.

galaxy N (*-ies*) **1** a huge collection of stars, dust and gas. **2** (**the Galaxy**) the vast spiral arrangement of stars to which our solar system belongs, known as the Milky Way. **3** a fabulous gathering, eg of famous people.

gale N **1 a** LOOSELY any very strong wind; **b** TECHNICAL a wind that blows with a speed of 51.5 to 101.4 kilometres per hour, corresponding to force 7 to 10 on the Beaufort scale. **Also** AS ADJ: *gale warning*. **2** (usu **gales**) a sudden loud burst, eg of laughter.

gall[1] N **1** COLLOQ impudence; cheek. **2** bitterness or spitefulness.

gall[2] N a small round abnormal growth on the stem or leaf of a plant, usu caused by invading parasitic fungi, or by insects.

gall[3] N **1** a sore or painful swelling on the skin caused by chafing. **2** something annoying or irritating. **3** a state of being annoyed. ➢ VB **1** to annoy. **2** to chafe (skin).

gallant ADJ **1** brave. **2** LITERARY OR OLD USE splendid, grand or fine. **3** of a man: courteous and attentive to women. ➢ N, OLD USE a handsome young man.

gallantry N **1** bravery. **2** OLD USE politeness and attentiveness to women.

gall bladder N, ANAT a small muscular pear-shaped sac that lies beneath the liver. Its function is to store bile produced by the liver.

galleon N, HIST a large Spanish ship.

gallery N (*-ies*) **1** a room or building used to display works of art. **2** a balcony in a church or hall, providing extra seating or reserved for musicians, etc. **3 a** the upper floor in a theatre, usu containing the cheapest seats; **b** the part of the audience seated there. **4** a long corridor. **5** a covered walkway.

galley N **1** HIST a long single-deck ship propelled by sails and oars. **2** HIST a Greek or Roman warship. **3** NAUT the kitchen on a ship.

Gallic ADJ **1** typically French. **2** HIST relating to ancient Gaul or the Gauls.

galling ADJ irritating.

gallium N a soft silvery metallic element found in zinc blende, bauxite and kaolin.

gallivant VB, INTR, HUMOROUS OR DEROG, COLLOQ to go out looking for amusement.

gallon N (abbrev **gal.**) in the imperial system: a unit of liquid measurement equal to four quarts or eight pints.

gallop VB **1** INTR to move at a gallop. **2** INTR to ride a horse, etc at a gallop. **3** to read, talk or do something quickly. **4** INTR, COLLOQ to move, progress or increase very quickly. ➢ N **1** the fastest pace at which a horse or similar animal moves. **2** a period of riding at this pace. **3** an unusually fast speed.

gallows SING N a wooden frame on which criminals are hanged.

gallstone N, PATHOL a small hard mass that is formed in the gall bladder or one of its ducts.

galore ADV (placed after the noun) in large amounts or numbers: *I read books galore*.

galosh or **golosh** N, USU IN PL a waterproof overshoe.

galvanize or **-ise** VB **1** TECHNICAL to coat a metallic surface with a thin layer of zinc, in order to protect it from corrosion. **2** to stimulate by electricity. ■ **galvanization** N.

gambit N **1** CHESS a chess move made early in a game, in which a pawn or other piece is sacrificed. **2** an initial action or remark inviting a response or establishing a point of view. **3** a piece of trickery; a stratagem.

gamble VB **1** TR & INTR to bet (usu money) on the result of a card game, horse race, etc. **2** (also **gamble sth away**) to lose (money, etc) through gambling. ➢ N **1** an act of gambling; a bet. **2** a risk or a situation involving risk: *take a gamble*. ■ **gambler** N. ■ **gambling** N.

gambol VB (*-ll-*; or US ALSO *-l-*) INTR to jump around playfully. ➢ N jumping around playfully; a frolic.

game N **1** an amusement or pastime. **2** the equipment used for this, eg a board, cards, dice, etc. **3** a competitive activity with rules,

involving some form of skill. **4** in some sports, eg tennis: a division of a match. **5** (**games**) an event consisting of competitions in various activities, esp sporting ones: **the Commonwealth games. 6** COLLOQ a type of, esp business, activity: **in the advertising game. 7** DEROG an activity undertaken light-heartedly: **War is just a game to him. 8 a** certain birds and animals which are killed for sport; **b** their flesh. **9** DEROG, COLLOQ a scheme, trick or intention: **What's your game?**
➤ ADJ, COLLOQ **1** (also **game for sth**) ready and willing to undertake it. **2** OLD USE having plenty of fighting spirit; plucky. **3** OLD USE lame.
■ **gamely** ADV bravely, sportingly.
■ **gameness** N.
◆ **play the game** to behave fairly.

gamekeeper N a person employed to look after and manage game on a country estate.

game show N a TV quiz or other game, usu with prizes.

gamesmanship N, DEROG the practice of winning games by trying to upset one's opponent.

gamete N, BIOL in sexual reproduction: a specialized sex cell, esp an ovum or sperm, which fuses with one of the opposite type.

gaming N gambling.

gamma N the third letter of the Greek alphabet (Γ, γ).

gamma rays PL N, PHYS high-frequency electromagnetic radiation, consisting of high-energy photons, often produced during radioactive decay. Also called **gamma radiation**.

gammon N **1** cured meat from the upper leg and hindquarters of a pig. **2** the whole back part of a side of bacon.

gamut N the whole range of anything.

gander N **1** a male goose. **2** COLLOQ a look.

gang N **1** a group, esp of criminals or troublemakers. **2** a group of friends, esp children. **3** an organized group of workers.

◆ **gang up on** or **against** to act as a group against.
◆ **gang up with** to join in or form a gang with.

gangland N the world of organized crime.

gangling and **gangly** ADJ (**-ier, -iest**) tall and thin, and usu awkward in movement.

gangplank N a movable plank serving as a gangway for a ship.

gangrene N, PATHOL the death and decay of part of the body due to restriction of the blood supply to that region as a result of disease, injury, frostbite, etc. ■ **gangrenous** ADJ.

gangster N a member of a gang of violent criminals. ■ **gangsterism** N.

gangway N **1 a** a small movable bridge used for getting on and off a ship; **b** the opening on the side of a ship into which this fits. **2** a passage between rows of seats.
➤ EXCLAM make way!

gannet N **1** a large white seabird that performs spectacular dives into the water to catch fish, etc. **2** COLLOQ a greedy person.

gantry N (**-ies**) a large metal supporting framework, eg serving as a bridge for a travelling crane, overhead for railway signals, or used at the side of a rocket's launch pad.

gaol and **gaoler** N variants of **jail** and **jailer**.

gap N **1** a break or open space, eg in a fence, etc. **2** a break in time; an interval. **3** a difference or disparity: **the generation gap.**

gape VB, INTR **1** to stare with the mouth open. **2** to be or become wide open. **3** to open the mouth wide.
➤ N **1** a wide opening. **2** an open-mouthed stare. ■ **gaping** ADJ.

garage N **1** a building in which motor vehicles are kept. **2** an establishment where motor vehicles are bought, sold and repaired, often also selling petrol, etc. **3** a filling station.
➤ VB to put or keep (a car, etc) in a garage.

garb N, LITERARY clothing, esp as worn by people in a particular job or position: **priestly garb.**

garbage N 1 N AMER, esp US domestic waste; refuse. 2 DEROG worthless or poor quality articles or matter. 3 DEROG nonsense.

garble VB to give muddled information, intentionally or unintentionally. ■ **garbled** ADJ.

garden N an area of land, where grass, trees, flowers, fruit, vegetables, etc, are grown.
➤ ADJ 1 of a plant: cultivated, not wild. 2 of or for use in a garden, or in gardening: **garden fork**.
➤ VB, INTR to cultivate, work in or take care of a garden, esp as a hobby. ■ **gardener** N. ■ **gardening** N.

gardenia N 1 an evergreen shrub with glossy leaves and large, usu white, fragrant flowers. 2 the flower produced by this plant.

gargantuan ADJ enormous; colossal.

gargle VB, TR & INTR to cleanse the mouth and throat with a medicinal liquid without swallowing.
➤ N 1 the sound produced while gargling. 2 the liquid used.

gargoyle N a grotesque carved open-mouthed head or figure acting as a rainwater spout from a roof gutter, esp on a church.

garish ADJ, DEROG unpleasantly bright or colourful; very gaudy. ■ **garishly** ADV.

garland N a circular arrangement of flowers or leaves.

garlic N 1 a plant of the onion family. 2 the bulb of this plant, widely used in cooking.

garment N, FORMAL an article of clothing.

garner VB, FORMAL OR LITERARY to collect and usu store (information, knowledge, etc).

garnet N any of various silicate minerals, esp a red variety used as a semi-precious stone.

garnish VB to decorate (esp food).
➤ N a decoration, esp one added to food.

garret N an attic room, often a dingy one.

garrison N 1 a body of soldiers stationed in a town or fortress. 2 the building they occupy.

garrotte or **garotte** N 1 a wire loop or metal collar tightened around the neck to cause strangulation. 2 this method of execution.
➤ VB to kill someone with a garrotte.

garrulous ADJ 1 tending to talk a lot, esp about trivial things. 2 DEROG of a speech, etc: long and wordy. ■ **garrulousness** N.

garter N a band of tight material, usu elastic, worn on the leg to hold up a stocking or sock.

gas N 1 a form of matter that has no fixed shape, is easily compressed, and which will expand to occupy all the space available. 2 a substance or mixture of substances which is in this state at ordinary temperatures, eg hydrogen, air. 3 a natural gas used as a source of fuel for heating, lighting or cooking; b AS ADJ: **gas cooker**. 4 a particular gas used as an anaesthetic or weapon of war. 5 COLLOQ gasoline; petrol.
➤ VB (-ss-) 1 to poison or kill (people or animals) with gas. 2 INTR, DEROG, COLLOQ to chat, esp at length, boastfully or about trivial things. ■ **gassy** ADJ (-ier, -iest).

gas chamber N a sealed room filled with poisonous gas to kill people or animals.

gaseous ADJ in the form of, or like, gas.

gash N a deep open cut or wound.
➤ VB to make a gash in something.

gasket N a compressible ring or sheet that fits tightly in the join between two metal surfaces to form an airtight seal.

gaslight N 1 a lamp powered by gas. 2 the light from such a lamp.

gas mask N a mask used in warfare and certain industries to filter out poisonous gases.

gasoline N, N AMER petrol.

gasometer N a gas holder, a large metal tank used for storing coal gas or natural gas before it is distributed to customers.

gasp VB 1 INTR to take a sharp breath in, through surprise, sudden pain, etc. 2 INTR to breathe in with difficulty, eg because of illness, exhaustion, etc. 3 (also **gasp sth out**) to say it breathlessly.
➤ N a sharp intake of breath.

gastric ADJ, MED, etc relating to the stomach.

gastroenteritis N, MED inflammation of the lining of the stomach and intestine.

gastronomy N the appreciation and enjoyment of good food and wine. ■ **gastronomic** ADJ.

gastropod N, BIOL a mollusc, eg snail, that typically has a large, flat muscular foot and a coiled shell.

gasworks SING N a place where gas is manufactured from coal.

gate N **1** a door or barrier, usu a hinged one, across an entrance in a wall, fence, etc. **2** at an airport: any of the numbered exits from which passengers can board or leave a plane. **3** the total number of people attending a sports event, etc. **4** (also **gate money**) the total money paid in admission fees to an entertainment.

gateau N (-*teaux*, -*teaus*) a large rich cake, esp one filled with cream.

gatecrash VB, TR & INTR to attend (a party, meeting, etc) uninvited. ■ **gatecrasher** N.

gatehouse N a building at or above the gateway to a city, castle, etc.

gatepost N either of the posts on each side of a gate.

gateway N **1** an entrance with a gate across it. **2** a way in or to something: **the gateway to success**.

gather VB **1** TR & INTR (also **gather together**) to bring or come together in one place. **2** (also **gather sth in**) to collect, pick or harvest it. **3** to pick something up. **4** to increase in (speed or force). **5** to accumulate or become covered with (eg dust). **6** to learn or understand something from information received. **7** to pull someone or something close to oneself: **She gathered the child into her arms**. ➤ N a small fold in material, often stitched.

gathering N **1** a meeting or assembly. **2** a series of gathers in material.

gauche ADJ awkward in social situations.

■ **gauchely** ADV. ■ **gaucheness** N.

gaucho N a modern cowboy of the S American plains.

gaudy ADJ (-*ier*, -*iest*) DEROG coarsely and brightly coloured. ■ **gaudiness** N.

gauge VB **1** to measure something accurately. **2** to estimate or guess (a measurement, size, etc). **3** to judge or appraise. ➤ N **1** any of various instruments that are used to measure a quantity: **pressure gauge**. **2** each of the standard sizes used in measuring articles such as wire, bullets or knitting needles. **3** on a railway: **a** the distance between the inner faces of the rails on a line; **b** the distance between wheels on an axle. **4** a standard against which other things are judged.

gaunt ADJ thin or thin-faced; lean, haggard. ■ **gauntness** N.

gauntlet N **1** HIST a metal or metal-plated glove worn by medieval soldiers. **2** a heavy protective leather glove.

gauze N **1** thin transparent fabric, esp cotton muslin as used to dress wounds. **2** thin wire mesh. ■ **gauzy** ADJ (-*ier*, -*iest*).

gavel N a small hammer used by a judge, auctioneer, etc to call attention.

gawk VB, INTR, COLLOQ to stare blankly.

gawky ADJ (-*ier*, -*iest*) COLLOQ, DEROG awkward-looking, ungainly, and usu tall and thin. ■ **gawkiness** N.

gawp VB, INTR, COLLOQ to stare stupidly, esp open-mouthed; to gape.

gay ADJ **1** homosexual; relating to, frequented by, or intended for, homosexuals. **2** happily carefree. **3** bright and attractive. **4** fun-loving. ➤ N a homosexual.

gaze VB, INTR (esp **gaze at sth** or **sb**) to stare fixedly. ➤ N a fixed stare.

gazebo N (-*os* or -*oes*) a small summerhouse usu offering pleasant views.

gazelle N (*gazelles* or *gazelle*) a fawn-coloured antelope with a white rump and belly found in Africa and Asia.

gazette N an official newspaper giving lists of government, military and legal notices.

gazetteer N a book or part of a book which lists place names and describes the places.

gazump VB, COLLOQ to raise the price that has already been verbally agreed (with a prospective buyer of property), usu because someone else has offered a higher price.

GB ABBREV Great Britain.

GBH or **gbh** ABBREV grievous bodily harm.

GCSE ABBREV General Certificate of Secondary Education.

gear N 1 (also **gearwheel**) a toothed wheel or disc that engages with another wheel or disc having a different number of teeth, and turns it, so transmitting motion from one rotating shaft to another. 2 the specific combination of such wheels or discs that is being used: **second gear** • **low gear** • **to change gear**. 3 COLLOQ the equipment or tools needed for a particular job, sport, etc. 4 COLLOQ personal belongings. 5 COLLOQ clothes, esp young people's current fashion. 6 SLANG drugs.

gearbox N 1 the set or system of gears that transmits power from the engine to the road wheels. 2 the metal casing that encloses such a set or system of gears.

gearing N a set of gearwheels as a means of transmission of motion.

gear lever and **gear stick** and (N AMER) **gearshift** N a lever for engaging and disengaging gears, esp in a motor vehicle.

gecko N (**-os** or **-oes**) a nocturnal lizard.

gee[1] EXCLAM (usu **gee up**) used to encourage a horse to move, or to go faster.
➤ VB (**geed, geeing**) to encourage (a horse, etc) to move or move faster.

gee[2] EXCLAM, COLLOQ expressing surprise, admiration or enthusiasm. Also **gee whiz**.

geek N, N AMER SLANG 1 a creep or misfit. 2 an obsessive enthusiast, esp about computers.

geese plural of **goose**

geezer N, COLLOQ a man.

Geiger counter N, PHYS an instrument that is used to detect and measure radiation.

geisha N (*geisha* or *geishas*) a Japanese girl or woman who is trained to entertain men with music, dancing, conversation, etc.

gel N 1 a colloid consisting of a solid and a liquid that are dispersed evenly throughout a material and have set to form a jellylike mass, eg gelatine. 2 (also **hair gel**) such a substance used in styling the hair or fixing it in place.
➤ VB (**-ll-**) 1 TR & INTR to become or cause something to become a gel. 2 to style (hair) using gel. 3 to jell.

gelatine or **gelatin** N a clear protein extracted from animal bones and hides and used in food thickenings, etc.

gelatinous ADJ like jelly.

geld VB to castrate (a male animal, esp a horse) by removing its testicles. ■ **gelding** N.

gelignite N a powerful explosive.

gem N 1 (also **gemstone**) a semi-precious or precious stone or crystal, esp one that has been cut and polished for use in jewellery. 2 COLLOQ someone or something that is valued.

Gemini SING N, ASTROL the third sign of the zodiac (the Twins).

gemsbok N a large S African antelope with long straight horns.

gen N, COLLOQ (esp **the gen**) the required or relevant information.

gendarme N a member of an armed police force in France and other French-speaking countries.

gender N 1 the condition of being male or female; one's sex. 2 GRAM a a system of dividing nouns and pronouns into different classes; b any of these classes.

gene N the basic unit of inheritance by which one or more specific characteristics are passed on from parents to offspring.

genealogy N (*-ies*) **1 a** a person's direct line of descent from an ancestor; **b** a diagram or scheme showing this. **2** the study of the history and lineage of families. **3** the study of the development of plants and animals into present-day forms. ■ **genealogical** ADJ. ■ **genealogist** N.

genera plural of **genus**

general ADJ **1** widespread, not specific, limited, or localized: **as a general rule. 2** not detailed or definite; vague: **general description. 3** not specialized: **general knowledge.** ➤ N **1** an officer in the army. **2** the commander of a whole army. **3** any leader, esp when regarded as competent. ■ **generality** N. ◆ **in general** usually; mostly.

general election N a national election in which the voters of every constituency in the country elect a member of parliament.

generalize or **-ise** VB **1** INTR to speak in general terms or form general opinions. **2** to make something more general. ■ **generalization** N.

generally ADV **1** usually. **2** without considering details; broadly. **3** as a whole; collectively.

general practitioner N a community doctor who treats most illnesses and complaints. ■ **general practice** N.

general strike N a strike by workers in all or most of the industries in a country.

generate VB to produce or create something. ■ **generative** ADJ.

generation N **1** the act of producing something, eg electricity or ideas. **2** the act of producing offspring. **3** all the individuals produced at a particular stage in the natural descent of humans or animals: **the younger generation. 4** the average period between the birth of a person or animal and the birth of their offspring, which, in humans, is usu about 30 years. **5 a** a single stage in a person's descent; **b** AS ADJ AND IN COMPOUNDS: **second-generation American.**

generator N, ELEC a machine that converts mechanical energy into electrical energy.

generic ADJ **1** belonging, referring or relating to any member of a general class or group. **2 a** esp of a drug: not protected by a trademark and sold as a specific brand: **generic aspirin**; **b** applied to supermarket products: sold without a brand-name. **3** applied to a product name that was orig a trademark, eg hoover: now used as the general name.

generous ADJ **1** giving or willing to give or help unselfishly. **2** eg of a donation: large and given unselfishly. **3** large; ample; plentiful: **generous portions. 4** kind; willing to forgive: **of generous spirit.** ■ **generosity** N. ■ **generously** ADV.

genesis N (*-ses*) **1** a beginning or origin. **2** (**Genesis**) the first book in the Old Testament.

genetic ADJ **1** of or relating to genes or genetics: **a genetic defect. 2** belonging or relating to origin. ■ **genetically** ADV.

genetics SING N the scientific study of heredity and of the mechanisms by which characteristics are transmitted from one generation to the next. ■ **geneticist** N.

genial ADJ **1** cheerful; friendly; sociable. **2** of climate: pleasantly warm or mild. ■ **geniality** N. ■ **genially** ADV.

genie N (*-nies* or *-nii*) a spirit with the power to grant wishes.

genital ADJ **1** relating to or affecting the genitals. **2** relating to reproduction.

genitals or **genitalia** PL N the external sexual organs.

genius N **1** someone who has outstanding creative or intellectual ability. **2** such ability. **3** a person who exerts a powerful influence on another (whether good or bad).

genocide N the deliberate killing of a whole nation or people. ■ **genocidal** ADJ.

genre N **1** a particular type or kind of literature, music or other artistic work. **2** (in full **genre painting**) ART a type of painting featuring scenes from everyday life.

genteel ADJ **1** DEROG polite or refined in an artificial, affected way approaching snobbishness. **2** well-mannered.

gentian N a low-growing plant with funnel-shaped flowers, often deep blue in colour.

gentile N (often **Gentile**) used esp by Jews: a person who is not Jewish.
➤ ADJ (often **Gentile**) used esp by Jews: not Jewish.

gentility N good manners and respectability.

gentle ADJ **1** mild-mannered, not stern, coarse or violent. **2** light and soft; not harsh, loud, strong, etc: **a gentle breeze**. **3** moderate; mild: **a gentle reprimand**. **4** of hills, etc: rising gradually. ■ **gentleness** N. ■ **gently** ADV.

gentleman N **1** (esp as a term of reference or address) a polite name for a man: **Ask that gentleman**. **2** a polite, well-mannered, respectable man. **3** a man from the upper classes. ■ **gentlemanly** ADJ.

gentry PL N (esp **the gentry**) people of the class directly below the nobility.

gents SING N a men's public toilet.

genuflect VB, INTR to bend one's knee in worship or as a sign of respect.
■ **genuflection** N.

genuine ADJ **1** authentic, not artificial or fake. **2** honest; sincere.

genus N (-*nera* or -*nuses*) **1** BIOL in taxonomy: any of the groups into which a family is divided and which in turn is subdivided into one or more species. **2** a class divided into several subordinate classes.

geo- COMB FORM, SIGNIFYING **1** the Earth. **2** geography or geographical.

geocentric ADJ of a system, esp the universe or the solar system: having the Earth as its centre.

geodesic and **geodetic** ADJ **1** relating to or determined by the Earth's shape and size. **2** denoting a structure composed of a large number of identical components, esp a dome.

geography N (-*ies*) **1** the scientific study of the Earth's surface, esp its physical features, climate, resources, population, etc. **2** COLLOQ the layout of a place. ■ **geographer** N.
■ **geographical** ADJ.

geology N **1** the scientific study of the origins and structure, composition, etc of the Earth, esp its rocks. **2** the distinctive geological features of an area, country, etc. ■ **geological** ADJ.
■ **geologist** N.

geometric or **geometrical** ADJ **1** relating to or using the principles of geometry. **2** of a pattern, design, style of architecture, etc: using or consisting of lines, points, or simple figures.

geometry N the branch of mathematics dealing with lines, angles, shapes, etc and their relationships. ■ **geometrician** N.

Georgian ADJ typical of the reigns of King George I, II, III and IV, ie the period 1714–1830.

geostationary ADJ, TECHNICAL of an artificial satellite above the Earth's equator: taking exactly 24 hours to complete one orbit and so appearing to remain stationary above a fixed point on the Earth's surface.

geothermal ADJ, TECHNICAL relating to the internal heat of the Earth.

geranium N, BOT a plant or shrub with divided leaves and large flowers with five pink or purplish petals.

gerbil N a small burrowing rodent with long hind legs and a long furry tail.

geriatric ADJ **1** for or dealing with old people; relating to geriatrics: **geriatric medicine**. **2** DEROG, COLLOQ very old.
➤ N an old person.

geriatrics SING N the branch of medicine concerned with the health of the elderly.

germ N **1** a micro-organism, esp a bacterium or virus that causes disease. Also AS ADJ: **germ warfare**. **2** the embryo of a plant, esp of wheat. **3** an origin or beginning: **the germ of a plan**.

Germanic N a branch of the Indo-European family of languages.
➤ ADJ **1** of these languages or the people speaking them. **2** typical of Germany or the Germans.

German measles SING N rubella.

germicide N any agent that destroys

disease-causing micro-organisms.
■ **germicidal** ADJ.

germinate VB 1 INTR, BIOL of a seed or spore: to show the first signs of development into a new individual. 2 **a** to make (a seed, an idea, etc) begin to grow; **b** INTR to come into being or existence. ■ **germination** N.

germ warfare N the use of bacteria to inflict disease on an enemy in war.

gerontology N the scientific study of old age and the ageing process.

gerrymander VB, DEROG 1 to change the boundaries of electoral constituencies to favour one political party. 2 to manipulate (eg data, etc) unfairly. ■ **gerrymandering** N.

gerund N, GRAM a noun formed from a verb and which refers to an action. In English gerunds end in **–ing**, eg 'the BAKING of bread'.

gesso N (-oes) plaster for sculpting with or painting on.

gestate VB, TR & INTR 1 ZOOL to carry (young) or be carried in the uterus, and to undergo physical development, in the period from fertilization to birth. 2 to develop (an idea, etc) slowly in the mind. ■ **gestation** N.

gesticulate VB 1 INTR to make gestures, esp when speaking. 2 to express (eg feelings) by gestures. ■ **gesticulation** N.

gesture N 1 a movement of a part of the body as an expression of meaning, esp when speaking. 2 something done to communicate feelings or intentions, esp friendly ones. 3 DEROG something done as a formality.
➢ VB 1 INTR to make gestures. 2 to express (eg feelings) with gestures. ■ **gestural** ADJ.

get VB (*got*, PA P *got* or (US) *gotten, getting*) 1 to receive or obtain. 2 to have or possess. 3 TR & INTR (also **get across** or **get sb across** or **away, to, through,** etc) to go or make them go, move, travel or arrive as specified: **tried to get past him • Will you get him to bed at 8? • got to Paris on Friday.** 4 (often **get sth down, in, out,** etc) to fetch, take, or bring it as specified: **Get it down from the shelf.** 5 to put into a particular state or condition: **Don't get it**

wet • **got him into trouble.** 6 INTR to become: **I got angry.** 7 to catch (a disease, etc): **She got measles.** 8 to order or persuade: **Get him to help us.** 9 COLLOQ to receive (a broadcast, etc): **can't get the World Service.** 10 COLLOQ to make contact with someone, esp by telephone: **never get him at home.** 11 COLLOQ to arrive at (a number, etc) by calculation. 12 INTR, COLLOQ to receive permission (to do something): **Can you get to stay out late?** 13 COLLOQ to prepare (a meal): **I'll get the breakfast.** 14 COLLOQ to buy something: **got her some flowers.** 15 COLLOQ to suffer: **got a broken arm.** 16 COLLOQ to receive something as punishment: **got ten years for armed robbery.** 17 (**get sb**) COLLOQ to attack or punish them: **I'll get you for that!** 18 COLLOQ to annoy someone: **It really gets me.** 19 COLLOQ to understand something. 20 COLLOQ to hear something: **I didn't quite get his name.** 21 COLLOQ to affect someone emotionally. 22 COLLOQ to baffle someone: **You've got me there.**

◆ **get sth across** to make it understood.
◆ **get ahead** to make progress; to be successful.
◆ **get along with sb** COLLOQ to be on friendly terms with them.
◆ **get at sb** COLLOQ 1 to criticize or victimize them persistently. 2 COLLOQ to influence them by dishonest means, eg bribery.
◆ **get at sth** 1 to reach or take hold of it. 2 COLLOQ to suggest or imply it.
◆ **get away with sth** to commit (an offence etc) without being caught or punished.
◆ **get by** COLLOQ to manage to live.
◆ **get sb down** COLLOQ to make them sad.
◆ **get down to sth** to apply oneself to (a task).
◆ **get in** of a political party: to be elected to power.
◆ **get off** or **get sb off** COLLOQ to escape, or cause them to escape, with no punishment or with only the stated punishment.
◆ **get on** COLLOQ to make progress; to be successful.
◆ **get on with sb** to have a friendly relationship with them.
◆ **get over sb** or **sth** to be no longer emotionally affected by them or it.

◆ **get over sth** to recover from (an illness, disappointment, etc).

◆ **get sth over** to explain it successfully.

◆ **get sth over with** to deal with (something unpleasant) as quickly as possible.

◆ **get round sb** COLLOQ to persuade them or win their approval or permission.

◆ **get round sth** to successfully pass by or negotiate (a problem, etc).

◆ **get round to sth** or **sb** to deal with it or them eventually.

◆ **get through sth** 1 to complete (a task, piece of work, etc). 2 to use it steadily until it is finished. 3 COLLOQ to pass (a test, etc).

◆ **get through to sb** 1 to make contact with them by telephone. 2 to make them understand.

◆ **get to sb** COLLOQ to annoy them.

◆ **get up to sth** COLLOQ to do it.

getaway N an escape, esp after committing a crime. Also AS ADJ: **getaway car**.

get-out N a means or instance of escape.

get-together N,COLLOQ an informal meeting.

get-up N,COLLOQ an outfit or clothes, esp when considered strange or remarkable.

get-up-and-go N,COLLOQ energy.

geyser N 1 GEOL a type of hot spring that intermittently spouts hot water and steam. 2 a domestic appliance for heating water.

ghastly ADJ (-*ier, -iest*) 1 extremely frightening, hideous or horrific. 2 COLLOQ very bad. 3 COLLOQ very ill.
➢ ADV,COLLOQ extremely; unhealthily: **ghastly pale**. ■ **ghastliness** N.

ghee N in Indian cookery: clarified butter.

gherkin N 1 a variety of cucumber that bears very small fruits. 2 a small or immature fruit of a cucumber, used for pickling.

ghetto N (-*os* or -*oes*) 1 DEROG a poor area densely populated by people from a deprived social group, esp a racial minority. 2 HIST a part of a city to which Jews were formerly restricted.

ghost N 1 the spirit of a dead person when it is visible in some form to a living person. See also **spectre**. 2 a hint or trace. 3 a faint shadow

attached to the image on a television screen.

ghost town N a deserted town.

ghost writer N someone who writes books, speeches, etc on behalf of another person who is credited as their author.

ghoul N 1 someone who is interested in morbid or disgusting things. 2 **a** in Arab mythology: a demon that robs graves and eats dead bodies; **b** an evil spirit or presence. ■ **ghoulish** ADJ.

GI N,COLLOQ a soldier in the US army, esp during World War II.

giant N 1 in stories: a huge, extremely strong creature of human form. 2 COLLOQ an unusually large person or animal. 3 a person, group, etc of exceptional ability, importance or size.
➢ ADJ 1 COLLOQ huge: **giant portions**. 2 belonging to a particularly large species: **giant tortoise**. ■ **giantess** N.

gibber VB, INTR 1 to talk so fast that one cannot be understood. 2 DEROG to talk foolishly.

gibberish N 1 speech that is meaningless or difficult to understand. 2 utter nonsense.

gibbet N, HIST 1 a gallows-like frame on which the bodies of executed criminals were hung as a public warning. 2 a gallows.

gibbon N an ape with very long arms, and the only one to walk upright habitually.

gibe[1] or **jibe** VB, INTR to mock, scoff or jeer.
➢ N a jeer.

gibe[2] see **gybe**

giblets PL N the heart, liver and other edible internal organs of a chicken or other fowl.

giddy ADJ (-*ier, -iest*) 1 suffering an unbalancing spinning sensation. 2 causing such a sensation. 3 light-hearted and carefree. ■ **giddily** ADV. ■ **giddiness** N.

gift N 1 something given; a present. 2 a natural ability. 3 the act or process of giving: **the gift of a book**. 4 COLLOQ something easily obtained, made easily available or simply easy.
➢ VB, FORMAL to give something as a present.

gifted ADJ having a great natural ability.

gig[1] N **1** HIST a small open two-wheeled horse-drawn carriage. **2** a small rowing boat.

gig[2] COLLOQ, N **1** a pop, jazz or folk concert. **2** a musician's booking to perform.
➤ VB (*-gg-*) INTR to play a gig or gigs.

gigabyte N, COMP a unit of storage capacity roughly equal to a thousand million bytes.

gigantic ADJ huge; enormous.
■ **gigantically** ADV.

giggle VB, INTR to laugh quietly in short bursts or in a nervous or silly way.
➤ N **1** such a laugh. **2** (**the giggles**) a fit of giggling. **3** COLLOQ a funny person, situation, thing, activity, etc: **the film was a right giggle.**
■ **giggly** ADJ (*-ier, -iest*).

gigot N a leg of lamb or mutton.

gild VB (*gilded* or *gilt*) **1** to cover something with a thin coating of gold or something similar. **2** to give something a falsely attractive or valuable appearance.

gill[1] N in all fishes and many other aquatic animals: a respiratory organ that extracts dissolved oxygen from the surrounding water.

gill[2] N in the UK: a unit of liquid measure equal to 142.1 millilitres or a quarter of a pint.

gilt ADJ covered with a thin coating of gold or apparently so covered; gilded.
➤ N **1** gold or a gold-like substance used in gilding. **2** (**gilts**) gilt-edged securities.

gilt-edged ADJ **1** of a book: having pages with gilded edges. **2** of the highest quality. **3** of government securities with a fixed rate of interest: able to be sold at face value.

gimcrack ADJ, DEROG cheap, showy and badly made.

gimlet N a T-shaped hand-tool for boring holes in wood.

gimmick N, DEROG a scheme or object used to attract attention or publicity, esp to bring in customers. ■ **gimmickry** N. ■ **gimmicky** ADJ.

gin[1] N an alcoholic spirit made from barley, rye or maize and flavoured with juniper berries.

gin[2] N (also **gin trap**) a wire noose laid as a snare or trap for catching game.

ginger N **1** an aromatic spicy swollen root widely used as a flavouring, or preserved in syrup. **2** the tropical plant from which this root is obtained. **3** a reddish-brown colour.
➤ ADJ **1** flavoured with ginger. **2** of hair: reddish-orange in colour.

gingerly ADV with delicate caution.
➤ ADJ very cautious or wary.

gingham N striped or checked cotton cloth.

gingivitis N, MED inflammation of the gums.

gin rummy N, CARDS a type of rummy in which players can end the round at any time when their unmatched cards count ten or less.

ginseng N **1 a** a plant cultivated in China for its roots; **b** a similar American species. **2** the aromatic root of either of these plants used for its stimulant and aphrodisiac qualities.

Gipsy N a variant spelling of **Gypsy**.

giraffe N (*giraffes* or *giraffe*) a very tall African mammal with an extremely long neck and legs, a small head, and large eyes.

girder N a large beam of wood, iron or steel used to support a floor, wall, road or bridge.

girdle[1] N a woman's close-fitting elasticated undergarment that covers from waist to thigh.
➤ VB **1** to put a girdle on someone or something. **2** LITERARY to surround something.

girdle[2] see **griddle**

girl N **1** a female child. **2** a daughter. **3** often OFFENSIVE a young woman, esp an unmarried one. **4** often OFFENSIVE a woman of any age. **5** COLLOQ a sweetheart. ■ **girlish** ADJ.

girlfriend N **1** a female sexual or romantic partner. **2** a female friend.

girlie or **girly** ADJ, COLLOQ **1** of a magazine, etc: featuring naked or nearly naked young women in erotic poses. **2** DEROG girlish, esp in being stereotypically feminine.

giro N **1** a banking system by which money can be transferred from one account directly to another. **2** BRIT COLLOQ a social security benefit received in the form of a cheque.

girth N **1** the distance round something such as a tree or a person's waist. **2** the strap round a horse's belly that holds a saddle in place.
➤ VB to put a girth on (a horse).

gismo or **gizmo** N, COLLOQ a gadget.

gist N the general meaning or main point of something said or written.

git N, DEROG SLANG a contemptible person.

give VB (*gave, given*) **1** to transfer ownership of something; to transfer possession of something temporarily: Give me your bags. **2** to provide or administer: give advice. **3** to produce: Cows give milk. **4** to perform (an action, service, etc): She gave a lecture on beetles. **5** to pay: gave £20 for it. **6** INTR to make a donation: Please give generously. **7** (also **give sth up**) to sacrifice it. **8** to be the cause or source of something: gives me pain. **9** INTR to yield or break: give under pressure. **10** to organize something at one's own expense: give a party. **11** to have something as a result: four into twenty gives five. **12** to reward or punish with something: was given 20 years.
➤ N capacity to yield; flexibility: a board with plenty of give.
◆ **give sb away 1** to betray (someone). **2** to present (the bride) to the bridegroom at a wedding ceremony.
◆ **give sth away 1** to hand over as a gift. **2** to sell at an incredibly low price.
◆ **give in to** to yield to; to admit defeat.
◆ **give sth off** to produce or emit (eg a smell).
◆ **give sth out 1** to announce or distribute it. **2** to emit (a sound, smell, etc).
◆ **give up** to admit defeat.
◆ **give oneself up** to surrender.
◆ **give sth up** to renounce or quit (a habit, etc): give up smoking.
◆ **give way 1** to allow priority. **2** to collapse under pressure.

give-and-take N mutual willingness to accept the other's point of view.

given ADJ **1** stated or specified. **2** admitted, assumed or accepted as true.
➤ PREP, CONJ accepting (a specified thing); assuming: given that he is illegitimate.
➤ N something that is admitted, assumed or accepted as true: His illegitimacy is a given.
◆ **given to sth** prone to it.

giving ADJ generous; liberal.

gizzard N in birds, earthworms and certain other animals: a muscular chamber specialized for grinding up indigestible food.

glacé ADJ candied: glacé cherries.

glacial ADJ **1** GEOL, GEOG **a** relating to or resembling a glacier; **b** caused by the action of a glacier. **2** referring or relating to ice or its effects. **3** hostile: a glacial stare.

glaciation N **1** the process by which land or rocks are eroded by glaciers or ice sheets. **2** the formation of glaciers and ice sheets.

glacier N a large slow-moving body of ice, formed by compacted snow.

glad ADJ (*gladder, gladdest*) **1** (sometimes **glad about sth**) happy or pleased. **2** (**glad of sth**) grateful for it. **3** very willing: glad to help. **4** OLD USE bringing happiness: glad tidings. ■ **gladness** N.

gladden VB to make someone (or their heart, etc) happy or pleased.

glade N, LITERARY an open space in a wood.

gladiator N in ancient Rome: a man trained to fight against other men or animals in an arena. ■ **gladiatorial** ADJ.

glamorize or **-ise** VB **1** to make someone or something glamorous. **2** to romanticize. ■ **glamorization** N.

glamorous ADJ full of glamour.

glamour N **1** the quality of being fascinatingly, if falsely, attractive. **2** great beauty or sexual charm, esp when created by make-up, etc.

glance VB, USU INTR **1** (often **glance at sth** or **sb**) to look quickly or indirectly at it or them. **2** TR & INTR (often **glance off**) **a** of a blow or weapon: to be deflected; to hit (a target) obliquely; **b** of light: to shine or reflect in flashes.
➤ N **1** a brief (and often indirect) look.

2 a deflection. **3** LITERARY a brief flash of light.

gland N **1** ZOOL in humans and animals: an organ that produces a specific chemical substance (eg a hormone) for use inside the body. **2** BOT in plants: a specialized cell or group of cells involved in the secretion of plant products such as nectar, oils and resins.

glandular ADJ, ZOOL, BOT, **etc** relating to, containing or affecting a gland or glands.

glans N (*glandes*) ANAT an acorn-shaped part of the body.

glare VB **1** INTR to stare angrily. **2** INTR to be unpleasantly bright or shiny. **3** to express something with a glare.
➤ N **1** an angry stare. **2** dazzling light.

glaring ADJ **1** unpleasantly bright. **2** very obvious. ■ **glaringly** ADV.

glass N **1** a hard brittle non-crystalline material that is usu transparent or translucent, used to make windows, bottles and other containers, lenses, etc. **2** a drinking vessel made from this. **3** (also **glassful**) the amount held by a glass. **4** (also **glassware**) articles made of glass. **5** (**glasses**) spectacles.
➤ VB to supply or cover something with glass.

glass-blowing N the process of shaping molten glass by blowing air into it.

glass fibre N glass that has been melted and then drawn out into extremely fine fibres used in combination with resin to make strong lightweight materials.

glasshouse N a building constructed mainly or entirely of glass, and with the internal temperature maintained at a constant level, used for growing plants.

glassy ADJ (*-ier, -iest*) **1** like glass. **2** expressionless: **glassy eyes**.

glaucoma N, MED, OPHTHALMOLOGY, **etc** an eye disease which causes impaired vision and can lead to blindness.

glaze VB **1** to fit glass panes into (a window, door, etc). **2** to achieve a glaze on or apply a glaze to (pottery). **3** in painting: to apply a glaze to something. **4** INTR (usu **glaze over**) of

the eyes: to become fixed and expressionless. **5** to apply a glaze to (eg pastry).
➤ N **1** a hard glassy coating on pottery or the material for this coating before it is applied or fired. **2** in painting: a thin coat of semi-transparent colour. **3 a** a shiny coating of milk, eggs or sugar on food; **b** the material for this coating before it is applied or baked.

glazier N someone whose job is to fit glass in windows, doors, etc.

gleam N **1** a gentle glow. **2** a brief flash of light, esp reflected light. **3** a brief appearance or sign: **a gleam of excitement in his eyes**.
➤ VB, INTR **1** to glow gently. **2** to shine with brief flashes of light.

glean VB **1** to collect (information, etc) bit by bit, often with difficulty. **2** TR & INTR to collect (loose grain and other useful remnants of a crop left in a field) after harvesting.

glee N great delight; joy.

gleeful ADJ joyful; merry. ■ **gleefully** ADV. ■ **gleefulness** N.

glen N esp in Scotland: a long narrow valley.

glib ADJ (*glibber, glibbest*) DEROG speaking or spoken readily and persuasively, but neither sincere nor reliable: **glib explanations**. ■ **glibly** ADV. ■ **glibness** N.

glide VB, INTR **1** to move smoothly without visible effort: **glide along the ice**. **2** of an aircraft: to travel through the air or to land without engine power. **3** to travel through the air by glider. **4** to pass gradually: **glide into sleep**.
➤ N **1** a gliding movement. **2** the controlled descent of an aircraft without engine power.

glider N a fixed-wing aircraft designed to glide and soar in air currents without using any form of engine power.

glimmer VB, INTR to glow faintly.
➤ N **1** a faint glow; a twinkle. **2** a hint or trace: **a glimmer of hope**. ■ **glimmering** N, ADJ.

glimpse N a very brief look.
➤ VB to see something momentarily.

glint VB, INTR to give off tiny flashes of light.
➤ N a brief flash of light.

glisten VB, INTR often of something wet or icy: to shine or sparkle. ■ **glistening** ADJ.

glitch N, COLLOQ a sudden brief irregularity or failure to function.

glitter VB, INTR **1** to shine with bright flashes of light; to sparkle. **2** COLLOQ to be sparklingly attractive or resplendent: *a party glittering with famous film stars.*
➤ N **1** sparkle. **2** COLLOQ bright attractiveness, often superficial. **3** tiny pieces of shiny material used for decoration. ■ **glittering** ADJ.
■ **glittery** ADJ.

glitz N showiness; garishness. ■ **glitzy** ADJ.

gloaming N, POETIC OR SCOT dusk; twilight.

gloat VB, INTR (often **gloat over sth**) to feel or show smug or vindictive satisfaction, esp in one's own success or in another's misfortune.
➤ N an act of gloating.

global ADJ **1** affecting the whole world. **2** total; including everything. ■ **globally** ADV.

global warming N, ECOL a gradual increase in the average temperature of the Earth's surface and its atmosphere which has been attributed to the greenhouse effect.

globe N **1** (**the globe**) the Earth. **2** a sphere with a map of the world on it. **3** any spherical object. ■ **globular** ADJ.

globetrotter N, COLLOQ someone who travels all over the world. ■ **globetrotting** N.

globule N a small drop. ■ **globular** ADJ.

glockenspiel N a musical instrument consisting of tuned metal plates held in a frame, played with two small hammers.

gloom N **1** near-darkness. **2** sadness.

gloomy ADJ (-ier, -iest) **1** dark; dimly lit. **2** causing gloom. **3** sad or depressed.
■ **gloomily** ADV. ■ **gloominess** N.

glorified ADJ, DEROG given a fancy name or appearance: *a glorified skivvy.*

glorify VB (-ied) **1** to exaggerate the beauty, importance, etc of something or someone. **2** to praise or worship (God). **3** to make someone or something glorious. ■ **glorification** N.

glorious ADJ **1** having or bringing glory. **2** splendidly beautiful. **3** COLLOQ excellent. **4** HUMOROUS, COLLOQ very bad: *glorious mess.*

glory N (-ies) **1** great honour and prestige. **2** great beauty or splendour. **3** praise given to God. **4** a greatly-admired asset.
➤ VB (-ies, ied) INTR (usu **glory in sth**) to feel or show great delight or pride in it.

gloss[1] N **1** shiny brightness on a surface. **2** a superficial attractiveness. **3** (in full **gloss paint**) paint which produces a shiny finish. **4** a substance which adds shine.
➤ VB **1** to give a shiny finish to something. **2** to paint (a surface, etc) with gloss.
◆ **gloss over sth** to disguise (a deficiency, etc), esp by treating a subject briefly.

gloss[2] N a short explanation of a difficult word, phrase, etc in a text, eg in the margin.

glossary N (-ies) a list of explanations of words, etc, often at the end of a book.

glossy ADJ (-ier, -iest) **1** smooth and shiny. **2** superficially attractive. **3** of a magazine: printed on glossy paper. ■ **glossily** ADV.
■ **glossiness** N.

glove N **1** a covering for the hand which usu has individual casings for each finger. **2** a similar padded hand covering used in sports such as boxing, baseball, etc.

glove compartment N a small compartment in the front of a car, usu part of the dashboard, where small articles can be kept.

glow VB, INTR **1** to give out a steady heat or light without flames. **2** to shine brightly, as if very hot. **3** to feel or communicate a sensation of intense contentment or well-being: *glow with pride.* **4** of the complexion: to be rosy or tanned, and healthy-looking.
➤ N **1** a steady flameless heat or light. **2** bright, shiny appearance. **3** intensity of feeling, esp pleasant feeling. **4** a healthy colour of complexion.

glower VB, INTR to stare angrily.
➤ N an angry stare; a scowl.

glowing ADJ commendatory; full of praise.

glow-worm N a small nocturnal beetle, the wingless female of which attracts the male by giving out a bright greenish light from the underside of her abdomen.

glucose N, BIOCHEM a monosaccharide found in living cells, and in animals the main form in which energy derived from carbohydrates is transported around the bloodstream.

glue N 1 any adhesive obtained by extracting natural substances, esp from bone, in boiling water. 2 any adhesive made by dissolving synthetic substances such as rubber or plastic in a suitable solvent. ➤ VB (*glueing* or *gluing*) to use such an adhesive to stick (two materials or parts) together. ■ **gluey** ADJ (*gluier, gluiest*).

glum ADJ (*glummer, glummest*) in low spirits; sullen. ■ **glumness** N.

glut N an excessive supply of goods, etc.

gluten N, BIOCHEM a mixture of two plant storage proteins occurring in wheat flour that gives bread dough elastic properties.

glutinous ADJ like glue; sticky. ■ **glutinously** ADV. ■ **glutinousness** N.

glutton N 1 DEROG someone who eats too much. 2 someone whose behaviour suggests an eagerness (for something unpleasant): a glutton for hard work. ■ **gluttonous** ADJ. ■ **gluttony** N.

glycerine or **glycerin** N, NON- TECHNICAL glycerol.

glycerol N, CHEM a colourless viscous sweet-tasting liquid that is a by-product in the manufacture of soap.

GMT ABBREV Greenwich Mean Time.

gnarled ADJ twisted, with knotty swellings, usu as a result of age.

gnash VB, TR & INTR to grind (the teeth) together, esp in anger or pain.

gnat N a small biting fly.

gnaw VB (PA P *gnawed* or *gnawn*) 1 (also **gnaw at** or **gnaw away at sth**) to bite it with a scraping action, causing a gradual wearing away. 2 to make (eg a hole) in this way. 3 TR & INTR (also **gnaw at**) of pain, etc: to trouble persistently. ■ **gnawing** ADJ.

gneiss N, GEOL a coarse metamorphic rock.

gnome N 1 a fairy-tale creature, usu in the form of a little old man, who lives underground, often guarding treasure. 2 a statue of such a creature used as a garden ornament.

gnomic ADJ, FORMAL of speech or writing: 1 expressed in or containing short pithy aphorisms. 2 often DEROG moralizing.

gnostic ADJ relating to knowledge, esp mystical or religious knowledge.

gnu N (*gnus* or *gnu*) a wildebeest.

go VB (*goes, went, gone*) USU INTR 1 (often **go about** or **by** or **down,** etc) to walk, move or travel in the direction specified. 2 to lead or extend: **The road goes all the way to the farm.** 3 to visit or attend, once or regularly: **go to the cinema • go to school.** 4 **a** to leave or move away; **b** (ONLY AS EXCLAM) begin the race! 5 to be destroyed or taken away; to disappear: **The old door had to go.** 6 to proceed or fare: **The scheme is going well.** 7 to be used up: **All his money went on drink.** 8 to be given or sold for a stated amount: **went for £20. 9** to leave or set out for a stated purpose: **go on holiday • gone fishing. 10** TR & INTR to perform (an action) or produce (a sound): **go bang. 11** COLLOQ to break, break down, or fail: **His eyes have gone. 12** to work or be in working order: **get it going. 13** to become; to pass into a certain condition: **go mad. 14** to belong; to be placed correctly: **Where does this go? 15** to fit, or be contained: **Four into three won't go. 16** to be or continue in a certain state: **go hungry. 17** of time: to pass. **18** of a story or tune: to run: **How does it go? 19** (often **go for sb** or **sth**) to apply to them; to be valid or accepted for them: **The same goes for you. 20** COLLOQ to carry authority: **What she says goes. 21** (often **go with sth**) of colours, etc: to match or blend. **22** to subject oneself: **go to much trouble. 23** to adopt a specified system: **go metric.**

➤ N **1** a turn or spell: **It's my go. 2** energy; liveliness: **She lacks go. 3** COLLOQ busy activity: **It's all go. 4** COLLOQ a success: **make a go of it.**

◆ **go about 1** to circulate: **a rumour going about. 2** NAUT to change course.

◆ **go about sth** to attempt or tackle it.

◆ **go against sb** to be decided unfavourably for them.

◆ **go against sth** to be contrary to it.

◆ **go all out for** to make a great effort to obtain or achieve (something).

◆ **go along with** to agree with and support.

◆ **go back on sth** to break (an agreement, etc).

◆ **go down 1** to decrease. **2** COLLOQ to be received: **The joke went down well.**

◆ **go down with sth** to contract an illness.

◆ **go for** COLLOQ **1** to attack. **2** to be attracted by. **3** to choose. **4** (usu **go for it**) COLLOQ to try very hard to achieve something.

◆ **go in for sth** COLLOQ **1** to take up (a profession). **2** to enter (a contest). **3** to be interested or attracted by something, as a rule.

◆ **go into 1** to take up or join (a profession). **2** to discuss or investigate (something).

◆ **go off 1** to explode. **2** COLLOQ of perishables, eg food: to become rotten.

◆ **go on 1** to continue or proceed. **2** COLLOQ to talk too much.

◆ **go out 1** to become extinguished. **2** to be broadcast.

◆ **go out with sb** to spend time with someone socially or (esp) romantically.

◆ **go over sth 1** to examine it. **2** to revise or rehearse it.

◆ **go over to** to transfer support to.

◆ **go through sth 1** to use it up. **2** to revise or rehearse it. **3** to examine it. **4** to suffer it: **went through hell. 5** to search it: **went through all our bags.**

◆ **go through with sth** to carry it out to the end.

◆ **go up 1** to increase. **2** of a building, etc: to be erected.

◆ **have a go** COLLOQ to try; to make an attempt.

◆ **have a go at** to attack verbally.

◆ **on the go** COLLOQ busily active.

goad VB (usu **goad sb into sth** or **to do sth**) to urge or provoke them to action.
➤ N **1** a sharp-pointed stick used for driving cattle, etc. **2** anything that provokes or incites.

go-ahead COLLOQ, ADJ energetically ambitious and far-sighted.
➤ N (**the go-ahead**) permission to start.

goal N **1 a** in various sports, esp football: a set of posts with a crossbar, through which the ball is struck to score points; **b** the area in which the goal stands. **2 a** an act of scoring in this way; **b** the point or points scored. **3** an aim. **4** a destination, etc: **Paris was our goal.**
■ **goalless** ADJ.

goalie N, COLLOQ a goalkeeper.

goalkeeper N in various sports: the player who guards the goal and tries to prevent the opposition from scoring.

goalpost N in various sports: each of two upright posts forming the goal.

goat N **1** an herbivorous mammal, noted for its physical agility and sure-footedness. **2** DEROG COLLOQ a man, esp an old one, who makes unwanted sexual advances to women. **3** DEROG, COLLOQ a foolish person.

◆ **get sb's goat** COLLOQ to annoy them.

goatee N a pointed beard growing only on the front of the chin.

goatherd N someone who looks after goats.

gobble[1] VB, TR & INTR (usu **gobble sth up** or **down**) to eat hurriedly and noisily.

gobble[2] VB, INTR of a male turkey: to make a loud gurgling sound in the throat.
➤ N this loud gurgling sound.

gobbledygook or **gobbledegook** N, COLLOQ, usu DEROG **1** official jargon, meaningless to ordinary people. **2** nonsense; rubbish.

go-between N a messenger between two people or sides; an intermediary.

goblet N a drinking-cup with a base and stem but no handles.

goblin N in folk-tales: an evil or mischievous spirit in the form of a small man.

god N 1 (**God**) in the Christian and other monotheistic religions: the unique supreme being, creator and ruler of the universe. **2** in other religions: a superhuman male being with power over nature and humanity; a male object of worship. **3** a man greatly admired, esp for his fine physique or wide influence. **4** often DEROG an object of excessive worship or influence. **5** (**the gods**) superhuman beings collectively. ■ **godlike** ADJ.

godchild N a child that a godparent is responsible for.

goddaughter N a female godchild.

goddess N 1 a superhuman female being who has power over nature and humanity; a female object of worship. **2** a woman greatly admired for her beauty.

godfather N 1 a male godparent. **2** the head of a criminal group, esp in the Mafia.

godforsaken ADJ, DEROG of a place: remote and desolate.

godless ADJ 1 not religious. **2** having no god. **3** immoral. ■ **godlessness** N.

godly ADJ (*-ier, -iest*) religious; pious. ■ **godliness** N.

godmother N a female godparent.

godparent N someone who takes on the responsibility of the religious education of a child and agrees to supervise its upbringing in the event of the death of its parents.

godsend N someone or something whose arrival is unexpected but very welcome.

godson N a male godchild.

go-getter N, COLLOQ an ambitious enterprising person. ■ **go-getting** ADJ.

goggle VB 1 INTR to look with staring eyes. **2** to roll (the eyes). **3** INTR of the eyes: to stick out.

goggles PL N 1 protective spectacles that fit closely against the face. **2** COLLOQ spectacles.

going N 1 leaving; a departure: **comings and goings of the lodgers**. **2** HORSE-RACING the condition of the track. **3** progress: **made good**

going. **4** COLLOQ general situation or conditions: **when the going gets tough**. **5** IN COMPOUNDS the act or practice of making visits, esp regular ones, to specified places: **theatre-going**. ➤ VB, PR P OF **go** 1 about or intending (to do something). **2** IN COMPOUNDS in the habit of visiting: **the cinema-going public**. ➤ ADJ 1 flourishing, successful: **a going concern**. **2** usual or accepted: **the going rate**.

going-over N (*goings-over*) COLLOQ 1 a beating. **2** a close inspection.

goings-on PL N, COLLOQ events or happenings, esp if they are strange or disapproved of.

go-kart N a low racing vehicle consisting of a frame with wheels, engine and steering gear.

gold N 1 a soft yellow precious metallic element used for making jewellery, coins, etc. **2** articles made from it. **3** its value, used as a standard for the value of currency. **4** its deep yellow colour. **5** COLLOQ a gold medal. **6** precious or noble quality: **heart of gold**. **7** monetary wealth. ➤ ADJ 1 made of gold. **2** gold-coloured.

golden ADJ 1 gold-coloured. **2** made of or containing gold. **3** happy; prosperous or thriving: **golden age**. **4** excellent; extremely valuable: **golden opportunity**. **5** greatly admired or favoured: **golden girl**. **6** denoting a 50th anniversary: **golden wedding**.

golden age N 1 an imaginary past time of innocence and happiness. **2** the period of highest achievement in any sphere.

golden mean N the midpoint between two extremes.

golden rule N any essential principle or rule.

goldfinch N a European finch with a broad yellow bar across each wing.

goldfish N a yellow, orange or golden-red freshwater fish, often kept as a pet.

gold leaf N gold in very thin sheets.

gold medal N a medal awarded to the winner of a contest.

gold mine or **goldmine** N 1 a place where gold is mined. **2** COLLOQ a source of wealth.

gold plate N 1 a thin coating of gold, esp on silver. 2 articles such as spoons and dishes made of gold.
➤ VB (**gold-plate**) to coat (another metal) with gold. ■ **gold-plated** ADJ.

gold rush N a frantic scramble by large numbers of people to prospect in a newly-discovered source of gold.

goldsmith N someone who makes articles out of gold.

golf N a game played on a golf course, the object being to hit a small ball into each of a series of nine or eighteen holes using a set of clubs, taking as few strokes as possible.
➤ VB, INTR to play this game. ■ **golfer** N.

golf club N 1 any of the set of long-handled clubs used to play golf. 2 **a** an association of players of golf; **b** its premises with a golf course attached.

golf course N an area of specially prepared ground on which golf is played.

golliwog or **gollywog** N a child's doll with a black face, bristling hair and bright clothes.

golly EXCLAM, OLD USE expressing surprise or admiration.

gondola N 1 a long narrow flat-bottomed boat with pointed upturned ends, used to transport passengers on the canals of Venice. 2 the passenger cabin suspended from an airship, balloon or cable-railway.

gone ADJ 1 departed. 2 COLLOQ of time: past: gone six. 3 used up. 4 lost. 5 dead.

gong N 1 a hanging metal plate that makes a resonant sound when struck: a dinner gong. 2 SLANG a medal.

gonorrhoea or (N AMER) **gonorrhea** N, PATHOL a sexually transmitted disease.

goo N (PL in sense 1 **goos**) COLLOQ 1 any sticky substance. 2 DEROG excessive sentimentality.

good ADJ (**better, best**) 1 **a** having desirable or necessary (positive) qualities; admirable; **b** PATRONIZING used when addressing or referring to someone: my good man • your good lady.

2 **a** virtuous; **b** (**the good**) virtuous people in general. 3 kind and generous. 4 bringing happiness or pleasure: good news. 5 well-behaved. 6 wise; advisable: a good buy. 7 thorough. 8 finest compared with others: my good china. 9 adequate; satisfactory: a good supply. 10 enjoyable: having a good time. 11 valid. 12 well-respected. 13 sound; giving use; serviceable: The roof is good for another winter. 14 financially sound: a good investment. 15 considerable; at least: waited a good while. 16 certain to provide the desired result: good for a laugh. 17 used to introduce exclamations expressing surprise, dismay, or exasperation: good heavens • good grief.
➤ N 1 moral correctness; virtue. 2 benefit; advantage: do you good.
◆ **as good as ...** almost ...; virtually ...
◆ **good morning** or **good afternoon** or **good evening** traditional expressions used when either meeting or parting from someone at the specified time of day.
◆ **good night** a traditional expression used when parting from someone in the evening.
◆ **make sth good** 1 to repair it. 2 to carry it out or fulfil it.

goodbye EXCLAM used when parting from someone.
➤ N an act or instance of saying goodbye.

good-for-nothing ADJ lazy and irresponsible.
➤ N a lazy and irresponsible person.

Good Friday N a Christian festival in memory of Christ's crucifixion.

goodies PL N, COLLOQ things considered pleasant or desirable.

goodly ADJ (**-ier, -iest**) OLD USE OR JOCULAR quite large: a goodly measure of beer.

good nature N natural goodness and mildness of disposition. ■ **good-natured** ADJ.

goodness N 1 the state or quality of being good; generosity; kindness; moral correctness. 2 EUPHEMISTIC used in exclamations: God: goodness knows. 3 nourishing quality: all the goodness of the grain.
➤ EXCLAM expressing surprise or relief:

Goodness! What a mess!

goods PL N **1** articles for sale; merchandise. **2** freight. Often AS ADJ: goods train. **3** COLLOQ the required result: deliver the goods.

goodwill N **1** a feeling of kindness towards others. **2** the good reputation of an established business, seen as having an actual value.

goody N (-ies) COLLOQ a hero in a film, book, etc.

gooey (gooier, gooiest) COLLOQ ADJ sticky.

goof chiefly N AMER COLLOQ, N **1** a silly or foolish person. **2** a stupid mistake.
➤ VB, INTR to make a stupid mistake.

goofy ADJ (-ier, -iest) COLLOQ **1** silly; crazy. **2** of teeth: protruding.

googly N (-ies) CRICKET a ball bowled so that it changes direction unexpectedly on bouncing.

goon N **1** COLLOQ a silly person. **2** SLANG a hired thug.

goose N (geese in senses 1 to 4, gooses in sense 5) **1** any of numerous large wild or domesticated waterfowl, with a stout body, long neck, webbed feet and a broad flat bill. **2** the female of this, as opposed to the male (the gander). **3** the flesh of a goose cooked as food. **4** COLLOQ, OLD USE a silly person. **5** COLLOQ a poke or pinch on the buttocks.
➤ VB, COLLOQ to poke or pinch someone on the buttocks.

gooseberry N (-ies) **1** a low-growing deciduous shrub with spiny stems. **2** one of the small sour-tasting yellowish-green or reddish berries produced by this plant.

goose pimples and **goose bumps** PL N and **goose flesh** SING N a physical manifestation of cold or fear, causing pimples to appear on the skin and a bristling feeling.

goose-step N a marching step in which the legs are kept rigid and swung very high.
➤ VB, INTR to march with this step.

gopher N a small burrowing rodent with a stocky body, short legs and large teeth.

gore[1] N blood from a wound.

gore[2] VB to pierce something or someone with a horn or tusk.

gorge N **1** a deep narrow valley, usu containing a river. **2** the contents of the stomach.
➤ VB **1** TR & INTR to eat or swallow greedily. **2** (usu **gorge oneself**) to stuff oneself with food.

gorgeous ADJ extremely beautiful or attractive; magnificent. ■ **gorgeously** ADV. ■ **gorgeousness** N.

gorgon N, MYTHOL any of the three female monsters with live snakes for hair who were capable of turning people to stone.

gorilla N **1** the largest of the apes, native to African rainforests, having a heavily built body and jet black skin covered with dense fur. **2** COLLOQ a brutal-looking man.

gormless ADJ, DEROG COLLOQ stupid; dim.

gorse N an evergreen shrub with leaves reduced to very sharp deeply furrowed spines and bright yellow flowers.

gory ADJ (-ier, -iest) **1** causing or involving bloodshed. **2** COLLOQ unpleasant: gory details. **3** covered in gore. ■ **goriness** N.

gosh EXCLAM, COLLOQ expressing mild surprise.

gosling N a young goose.

go-slow N an instance or the process of deliberately working slowly so as to encourage an employer to negotiate.

gospel N **1** the life and teachings of Christ: preach the gospel. **2** (**Gospel**) each of the New Testament books ascribed to Matthew, Mark, Luke and John. **3** (also **gospel truth**) COLLOQ the absolute truth. **4** (also **gospel music**) lively religious music of Black American origin.

gossamer N **1** fine spider-woven threads seen on hedges or floating in the air. **2** any soft fine material.

gossip N **1** DEROG talk or writing about the private affairs of others, often spiteful and untrue. **2** DEROG someone who engages in or spreads such talk. **3** casual and friendly talk.

➢ VB, INTR **1** to engage in, or pass on, malicious gossip. **2** to chat. ■ **gossipy** ADJ.

Gothic ADJ **1** belonging or relating to the Goths, a Germanic people, or to their language. **2** of a style of architecture featuring high pointed arches. **3** of a type of literature dealing with mysterious or supernatural events, popular in the 18c.
➢ N **1** Gothic architecture or literature. **2** Gothic lettering.

gouge N **1** a chisel with a rounded hollow blade, used for cutting grooves or holes in wood. **2** a groove or hole made using this.
➢ VB to cut something out with or as if with a gouge.
◆ **gouge sth out 1** to use a gouge on it. **2** to force or press it out of position.

gourd N **1 a** a climbing plant that produces a large fruit with a hard woody outer shell; **b** the large fruit of this plant. **2** the hard durable shell of this fruit, often used as a cup, bowl, etc.

gourmand N **1** a greedy eater; a glutton. **2** a gourmet.

gourmet N someone who has expert knowledge of, and a passion for, good food and wine.

gout N, MED, PATHOL a disease causing acute arthritis, esp of the big toe.

govern VB **1** TR & INTR to control and direct the affairs of (a country, state, or organization). **2** to guide or influence; to control or restrain: **govern his temper**. ■ **governable** ADJ.

governess N, chiefly FORMERLY a woman employed to teach, and perhaps look after, children, usu while living in their home.

government N **1** a body of people, usu elected, with the power to control the affairs of a country or state. **2 a** the way in which this is done; **b** the particular system used. **3** the act or practice of ruling. ■ **governmental** ADJ.

governor N **1** the elected head of a US state. **2** the head of an institution, eg a prison. **3** a member of a governing body of a school, hospital, college, etc. **4** the head of a colony or province, esp the monarch's representative.

5 MECH a device for maintaining uniform speed in an engine. ■ **governorship** N.

gown N **1** a woman's long formal dress. **2** an official robe worn by clergymen, lawyers and academics. **3** a protective overall worn eg by surgeons, patients, hairdressers' clients, etc.

grab VB (-*bb*-) **1** TR & INTR (also **grab at sth**) to seize suddenly and often with violence. **2** to take something greedily. **3** to take something hurriedly or without hesitation: **grab a snack** • **grab an opportunity**. **4** COLLOQ to impress or interest someone: **How does that grab you?**
➢ N **1** an act or an instance of grabbing something. **2** a mechanical device with scooping jaws, used eg for excavation.

grace N **1** elegance and beauty of form or movement. **2** decency; politeness. **3** a short prayer of thanks to God said before or after a meal. **4** a delay allowed, esp to a debtor, as a favour. **5** a pleasing or attractive characteristic: **social graces** • **a saving grace**. **6 a** RELIG the mercy and favour shown by God to mankind; **b** RELIG the condition of a person's soul when they have been made free from sin by God. **7** (**His** or **Her Grace** or **Your Grace** a title used of or to a duke, duchess or archbishop.
➢ VB **1** often FACETIOUS to honour (an occasion, person, etc), eg with one's presence. **2** to add beauty or charm to something.

graceful ADJ showing elegance and beauty of form or movement. ■ **gracefully** ADV.

graceless ADJ **1** awkward. **2** bad-mannered. ■ **gracelessly** ADV.

grace note N, MUS a note introduced as an embellishment and not essential to the melody.

gracious ADJ **1** kind and polite. **2** of God: merciful. **3** having qualities of luxury, elegance, comfort and leisure: **gracious living**.
➢ EXCLAM expressing surprise. ■ **graciously** ADV. ■ **graciousness** N.

grade N **1** a stage or level on a scale of quality, rank, size, etc. **2** a mark indicating this.
➢ VB **1** to arrange (things or people) in different grades. **2** to award a mark indicating grade, eg on a piece of written work, essay, etc. **3** to

produce a gradual merging of (esp colours).
◆ **make the grade** COLLOQ to succeed; to reach the required or expected standard.

gradient N 1 the steepness of a slope. 2 FORMAL a slope. 3 MATH the slope of a line or a tangent to a curve at a particular point.

gradual ADJ 1 developing or happening slowly, by degrees. 2 of a slope: not steep; gentle. ■ **gradually** ADV.

graduate VB 1 INTR to receive an academic degree from a higher-education institution. 2 INTR, N AMER to receive a diploma at the end of high school. 3 INTR to move up from a lower to a higher level, often in stages. 4 to mark with units of measurement or other divisions. 5 to arrange something into regular groups, according to size, type, etc.
➤ N someone who has a higher-education degree or (N AMER) a high-school diploma. ■ **graduation** N.

graffiti PL N, sometimes used as SING (SING ALSO *graffito*) words or drawings scratched or painted on walls, etc in public places.

graft[1] N 1 HORTIC a piece of plant tissue that is inserted into a cut in the outer stem of another plant, resulting in fusion of the tissues and growth of a single plant. 2 SURGERY the transfer or transplantation of an organ or tissue from one individual to another, or to a different site within the same individual. 3 a transplanted organ.
➤ VB 1 (also **graft in** or **into** or **on** or **together**) a to attach a graft in something or someone; b to attach something as a graft. 2 INTR to attach grafts.

graft[2] N 1 COLLOQ hard work. 2 SLANG a the use of illegal or unfair means to gain profit or advantage, esp by politicians or officials; b the profit or advantage gained.
➤ VB, INTR 1 COLLOQ to work hard. 2 SLANG to practise graft. ■ **grafter** N.

grail or **Grail** N 1 (in full **Holy Grail**) the plate or cup used by Christ at the Last Supper, the object of quests by medieval knights. 2 a cherished ambition or goal.

grain N 1 a single small hard fruit, resembling a seed. 2 such fruits referred to collectively. 3 any of the cereal plants that produce such fruits, eg wheat, corn. 4 a small hard particle of anything. 5 a very small amount: **a grain of truth**. 6 a the arrangement of the fibres in wood, leather, etc b the pattern formed as a result of this arrangement. 7 the main direction of the fibres in paper or the threads in a woven fabric.
➤ VB 1 TR & INTR to form into grains. 2 to give a rough appearance or texture to something. ■ **grainy** ADJ (*-ier*, *-iest*).

gram or **gramme** N in the metric system: the basic unit of mass, equal to one thousandth of a kilogram (0.035 ounces).

grammar N 1 the accepted rules by which words are formed and combined into sentences. 2 the branch of language study dealing with these. 3 a a description of these rules applied to a particular language; b a book containing this. ■ **grammatical** ADJ.

grammar school N, BRIT, esp FORMERLY a secondary school which emphasizes the study of academic rather than technical subjects.

gramophone N, DATED a record-player.

granary N (*-ies*) 1 a building where grain is stored. 2 a region that produces large quantities of grain.

grand ADJ 1 large or impressive in size, appearance or style. 2 sometimes considered DEROG dignified; self-important. 3 intended to impress or gain attention: **a grand gesture**. 4 complete; in full: **grand total**. 5 COLLOQ very pleasant; excellent. 6 greatest; highest ranking: **Grand Master**. 7 highly respected: **grand old man**. 8 main; principal: **the grand entrance**. 9 IN COMPOUNDS indicating a family relationship that is one generation more remote than that of the base word: **grandson**.
➤ N (PL **grand**) SLANG a thousand dollars or pounds. ■ **grandly** ADV. ■ **grandness** N.

grandad or **granddad** N, COLLOQ 1 a grandfather. 2 OFFENSIVE an old man.

grandchild N a child of one's son or daughter.

granddaughter N a daughter of one's son or daughter.

grandee N 1 a Spanish or Portuguese nobleman of the highest rank. 2 any well-respected or high-ranking person.

grandeur N 1 greatness of character, esp nobility. 2 impressive beauty; magnificence.

grandfather N the father of one's father or mother.

grandfather clock N a clock driven by a system of weights and a pendulum contained in a tall free-standing wooden case.

grandiloquent ADJ, DEROG speaking, or spoken or written, in a pompous, self-important style. ■ **grandiloquence** N.

grandiose ADJ 1 DEROG exaggeratedly impressive or imposing, esp on a ridiculously large scale. 2 splendid; magnificent; impressive.

grandma N, COLLOQ a grandmother.

grandmother N the mother of one's father or mother.

grandpa N, COLLOQ a grandfather.

grandparent N either parent of one's father or mother.

grand piano N a large, harp-shaped piano that has its strings arranged horizontally.

grand prix N (PL *grands prix*) 1 any of a series of races held annually in various countries to decide the motor racing championship of the world. 2 in other sports: any competition of similar importance.

grand slam N 1 SPORT, EG TENNIS, RUGBY the winning in one season of all major competitions. 2 CARDS, esp BRIDGE the winning of all thirteen tricks by one player or side.

grandson N a son of one's son or daughter.

grandstand N a large covered sports-ground stand that has tiered seating and which provides a good view for spectators.

grange N a country house with farm buildings.

granite N a coarse-grained igneous rock.

granny or **grannie** N (-*ies*) COLLOQ a grandmother.

grant VB 1 to give, allow or fulfil. 2 to admit something to be true.
➤ N 1 something granted, esp an amount of money from a public fund for a purpose. 2 LAW the transfer of property by deed.

granted VB, PA P OF **grant** (USED AS A SENTENCE SUBSTITUTE) an admission that something is true or valid: She's a good writer. Granted. But rather limited.
➤ CONJ though it is admitted that: granted you gave it back later.
➤ PREP though (a specified thing) is admitted: Granted his arrogance, still he gets results.
◆ **take sb for granted** to treat them casually and without appreciation.
◆ **take sth for granted** to assume it to be true; to accept it without question.

granular ADJ, TECHNICAL 1 made of or containing tiny particles or granules. 2 of appearance or texture: rough.

granule N a small particle or grain.

grape N a pale green or purplish-black juicy edible berry which may be eaten fresh, pressed to make wine or dried to form currants, raisins, etc.

grapefruit N (*grapefruit* or *grapefruits*) 1 an evergreen tree cultivated for its large fruits. 2 the round fruit produced by this tree which has acidic pale yellow or pink flesh.

grapevine N 1 a vine on which grapes grow. 2 (**the grapevine**) COLLOQ an informal means of spreading information through conversation.

graph N 1 a diagram that illustrates the way in which one quantity varies in relation to another. 2 a symbolic diagram.
➤ VB to represent something with or as a graph.

graphic and **graphical** ADJ 1 described or shown vividly and in detail. 2 referring to or composed in a written medium. 3 referring to the **graphic arts**, ie those concerned with drawing, printing and lettering: graphic design. 4 relating to graphs; shown by means of a graph. ■ **graphically** ADV.

graphics SING N the art or science of drawing according to mathematical principles.

➤ PL N **1** the photographs and illustrations used in a magazine. **2** COMP **a** the use of computers to display and manipulate information in graphical or pictorial form; **b** the images that are produced by this.

graphite N a soft black allotrope of carbon used as a lubricant and electrical contact, and mixed with clay to form the 'lead' in pencils.

graphology N the study of handwriting.

graph paper N paper covered in small squares, used for drawing graphs.

grapnel N a large multi-pointed hook on one end of a rope, used for securing a heavy object on the other end.

grapple VB **1** struggle and fight, esp at close quarters, eg in hand-to-hand combat. **2** to secure something with a hook, etc.
➤ N **1** a hook or other device for securing. **2** an act of gripping, as in wrestling; a way of gripping.
◆ **grapple with** to struggle mentally with (a difficult problem).

grasp VB **1** to take a firm hold of something or someone; to clutch. **2** (often **grasp at** or **after sth**) to make a movement as if to seize it. **3** to understand.
➤ N **1** a grip or hold. **2** power or control; ability to reach, achieve or obtain: **within her grasp**. **3** ability to understand: **beyond their grasp**.

grasping ADJ, DEROG greedy, esp for wealth.

grass N **1** flowering plants (eg cereals, bamboos, etc) that have long narrow leaves and flowers (with no petals) borne alternately on both sides of an axis. **2** an area planted with or growing such plants, eg a lawn or meadow. **3** lawn or pasture. **4** SLANG marijuana.
➤ VB **1** to plant something with grass or turf. **2** to feed (animals) with grass; to provide pasture for them. ■ **grassy** ADJ (*-ier*, *-iest*).

grasshopper N a large brown or green jumping insect, the male of which produces a characteristic chirping sound.

grass roots PL N **1** esp POL ordinary people, as opposed to those in a position of power. **2** bare essentials; fundamental principles.

grass snake N a small non-venomous snake.

grate[1] VB **1** to cut (eg vegetables or cheese) into shreds by rubbing them against a rough or sharp perforated surface. **2** TR & INTR to make, or cause something to make, a harsh grinding sound. ■ **grater** N. ■ **grating** ADJ, N.
◆ **grate on sb** to irritate or annoy them.

grate[2] N **1** a framework of iron bars for holding coal, etc in a fireplace or furnace. **2** the fireplace or furnace itself.

grateful ADJ **a** feeling thankful; **b** showing or giving thanks. ■ **gratefully** ADV.

gratify VB (*-ied*) **1** to please someone. **2** to satisfy (eg a desire). ■ **gratification** N.

grating N a framework of metal bars.

gratis ADV, ADJ free; without charge.

gratitude N the state or feeling of being grateful; thankfulness.

gratuitous ADJ **1** done without good reason; unnecessary or unjustified: **gratuitous violence**. **2** given or received without charge; voluntary.

gratuity N (*-ies*) a sum of money given as a reward for good service; a tip.

grave[1] N **1** a deep trench dug in the ground for burying a dead body. **2** the site of an individual burial. **3** (**the grave**) LITERARY death.

grave[2] ADJ **1** giving cause for great concern; very dangerous. **2** very important; serious. **3** solemn in manner. ■ **gravely** ADV.

gravel N a mixture of small loose rock fragments and pebbles found on beaches and in the beds of rivers, streams and lakes.

gravelly ADJ **1** full of, or containing, small stones. **2** of a voice: rough and deep.

gravestone N a stone marking a grave, usu having the dead person's name and dates of birth and death engraved on it.

graveyard N a burial place; a cemetery.

gravid ADJ, MED pregnant.

gravitas N seriousness of manner; solemnity, authoritativeness; weight.

gravitate VB, INTR **1** to fall or be drawn under the force of gravity. **2** to move or be drawn gradually, as if attracted by some force.

gravitation N **1** PHYS the force of attraction that exists between any two bodies on account of their mass. **2** the process of moving or being drawn, either by this force or some other influence. ■ **gravitational** ADJ.

gravity N **1** the observed effect of the force of attraction that exists between two massive bodies. **2** the name commonly used to refer to the force of attraction between any object situated within the Earth's gravitational field, and the Earth itself. **3** seriousness; dangerous nature. **4** serious attitude; solemnity.

gravy N (-*ies*) **1** the juices released by meat as it is cooking. **2** a sauce made by thickening and seasoning these juices, or an artificial substitute.

grayling N (*grayling* or *graylings*) a freshwater fish that has silvery scales and a large purplish spiny dorsal fin.

graze[1] VB **1** TR & INTR of animals: to eat grass. **2 a** to feed (animals) on grass; **b** to feed animals on (an area of pasture). ■ **grazing** N.

graze[2] VB **1** to suffer a break in (the skin of eg a limb), through scraping against a hard rough surface. **2** to brush against something lightly. ➤ N **1** an area of grazed skin. **2** the action of grazing skin.

grease N **1** animal fat softened by melting or cooking. **2** any thick oily substance, esp a lubricant for the moving parts of machinery. ➤ VB to lubricate something with grease.

greaseproof ADJ impermeable to grease.

greasy ADJ (-*ier*, -*iest*) **1** containing, or covered in, grease. **2** having an oily appearance or texture. **3** slippery, as if covered in grease. ■ **greasily** ADV. ■ **greasiness** N.

great ADJ **1** outstandingly talented and much admired and respected. **2** very large in size, quantity, intensity or extent. **3** (**greater**) (added to the name of a large city) indicating the wider area surrounding the city as well as the city itself: Greater Manchester. **4** (also **greater**) BIOL larger in size than others of the same kind, species, etc: great tit. **5** IN COMPOUNDS indicating a family relationship that is one generation more remote than that of the base word: great-grandmother. **6** COLLOQ very enjoyable; excellent or splendid. **7** (also **great at sth**) COLLOQ clever; talented. **8** (also **great for sth**) COLLOQ very suitable or useful. **9** most important: the great advantage of it. **10** enthusiastic; keen: a great reader. **11** COLLOQ used to emphasize other adjectives describing size, esp **big**: a great big dog. **12** (**the Great**) in names and titles: indicating an importance or reputation of the highest degree: Alexander the Great. ➤ N a person who has achieved lasting fame, deservedly or not: one of the all-time greats. ➤ ADV, COLLOQ very well. ■ **greatly** ADV. ■ **greatness** N.

greatcoat N a heavy overcoat.

grebe N any of various waterfowl with short wings, a pointed bill and almost no tail.

Grecian ADJ in the style of ancient Greece.

greed N **1** an excessive desire for, or consumption of, food. **2** selfish desire. ■ **greedy** ADJ (-*ier*, -*iest*). ■ **greedily** ADV.

green ADJ **1** like the colour of the leaves of most plants. **2** covered with grass, bushes, etc: green areas of the city. **3** consisting mainly of leaves: green salad. **4** of fruit: not yet ripe. **5** COLLOQ of a person: young, inexperienced or easily fooled. **6** showing concern for, or designed to be harmless to, the environment. ➤ N **1** the colour of the leaves of most plants. **2** something of this colour. **3** an area of grass, esp one in a public place: the village green. **4** an area of prepared turf: bowling green • putting green. **5** (**greens**) vegetables with edible green leaves and stems. **6** (sometimes **Green**) someone who supports actions or policies designed to protect or benefit the environment. ■ **greenness** N.

green bean N any variety of bean, such as the French bean, etc, of which the green unripe pod and contents can be eaten whole.

green belt N open land near a town or city, where building is strictly controlled.

greenery N green plants or their leaves.

greenfield site N a site which is to be developed for the first time.

green fingers PL N, COLLOQ natural skill at growing plants successfully.

greenfly N (*greenfly* or *greenflies*) any of various species of aphid.

greengage N 1 a cultivated variety of tree, sometimes regarded as a subspecies of the plum. 2 the small green plum-like edible fruit produced by this tree.

greengrocer N a person or shop that sells fruit and vegetables.

greenhouse N a glasshouse, esp one with little or no artificial heating.

greenhouse effect N, METEOROL, ECOL, etc the warming of the Earth's surface as a result of the trapping of long-wave radiation by carbon dioxide, ozone, etc in the atmosphere.

greenhouse gas N any of various gases, eg carbon dioxide, present in the atmosphere and contributing to the greenhouse effect.

greenkeeper N someone who maintains a golf course or bowling green.

green light N 1 a signal to drivers of cars, trains, etc that they can move forward. 2 COLLOQ permission to proceed.

green party N a political party concerned with promoting policies for the protection and benefit of the environment.

green pepper N a green sweet pepper.

greenstick fracture N a fracture where the bone is partly broken and partly bent.

green tea N a sharp-tasting light-coloured tea made from leaves that have been dried quickly without fermenting.

Greenwich Mean Time N the local time at the line of 0° longitude, which passes through Greenwich in England.

greet VB 1 to address or welcome someone, esp in a friendly way. 2 to receive or respond to something in a specified way: His remarks were greeted with dismay. 3 to be immediately noticeable to someone: smells of cooking greeted me.

greeting N 1 a friendly expression or gesture used on meeting or welcoming someone. 2 (**greetings**) a good or fond wish; a friendly message.

gregarious ADJ 1 liking the company of other people; sociable. 2 of animals: living in groups.

gremlin N an imaginary mischievous creature blamed for faults in machinery or equipment.

grenade N a small bomb thrown by hand or fired from a rifle.

grenadier N a member of a regiment of soldiers formerly trained in the use of grenades.

grenadine N a syrup made from pomegranate juice, used to flavour drinks.

grey or (esp N AMER) **gray** ADJ 1 of a colour between black and white. 2 dull and cloudy. 3 **a** of hair: turning white; **b** of a person: having grey hair. 4 COLLOQ of or relating to elderly people: the grey population.
➤ N 1 a colour between black and white. 2 grey material or clothes: dressed in grey. 3 dull light. 4 an animal, esp a horse, that is grey or whitish in colour.
➤ VB, TR & INTR to make or become grey.
■ **greyish** ADJ. ■ **greyness** N.

grey area N an unclear situation or subject.

greyhound N a tall dog with a slender body, renowned for its speed and raced for sport.

grid N 1 a network of evenly spaced horizontal and vertical lines. 2 such a network used for constructing a chart. 3 (**the grid** or **the national grid**) the network of power transmission lines. 4 a network of underground pipes. 5 a framework of metal bars, esp one covering the opening to a drain.

griddle or (SCOT) **girdle** N a flat iron plate that is heated for baking or frying.

gridiron N 1 a frame of iron bars used for grilling food over a fire. 2 AMER FOOTBALL the field of play.

gridlock N 1 a jammed-up situation, in which no progress is possible, esp a severe traffic jam. ■ **gridlocked** ADJ.

grief N 1 a great sorrow and unhappiness, esp at someone's death; **b** an event that is the source of this. 2 COLLOQ trouble or bother.
◆ **come to grief** COLLOQ 1 to end in failure. 2 to have an accident.

grief-stricken ADJ crushed with sorrow.

grievance N 1 a real or perceived cause for complaint, esp unfair treatment at work. 2 a formal complaint, esp one made in the workplace.

grieve VB 1 INTR **a** to feel grief, esp at a death; **b** to mourn. 2 to upset or distress someone: It grieves me to learn that he's still on drugs.

grievous ADJ 1 very severe or painful. 2 causing or likely to cause grief. 3 showing grief. 4 of a fault, etc: extremely serious. ■ **grievously** ADV.

griffin or **gryphon** N, MYTHOL a winged monster with an eagle's head and a lion's body.

grill VB 1 to cook over or, more usu, under radiated heat. 2 COLLOQ to interrogate someone, esp at length.
➢ N 1 a device on a cooker which radiates heat downwards. 2 a metal frame for cooking food over a fire; a gridiron. 3 a dish of grilled food: mixed grill. 4 (also **grillroom**) a restaurant or part of a restaurant which specializes in grilled food.

grille or **grill** N a protective framework of metal bars or wires, eg over a window.

grim ADJ (*grimmer, grimmest*) 1 stern and unsmiling. 2 terrible; horrifying. 3 resolute; dogged: grim determination. 4 depressing; gloomy. 5 COLLOQ unpleasant. ■ **grimly** ADV. ■ **grimness** N.

grimace N an ugly twisting of the face that expresses pain or amusement.
➢ VB, INTR to make a grimace.

grime N thick ingrained dirt. ■ **grimy** ADJ.

grin VB (-*nn*-) 1 INTR to smile broadly, showing the teeth. 2 to express (eg pleasure) in this way.
➢ N a broad smile, showing the teeth. ■ **grinning** ADJ, N.

grind VB (*ground*) 1 to crush something into powder. 2 to sharpen, smooth or polish something by rubbing against a hard surface. 3 TR & INTR to rub something together with a jarring noise. 4 to press something hard with a twisting action: ground his heel into the dirt. 5 to operate something by turning a handle: grinding his barrel-organ.
➢ N 1 COLLOQ steady, dull and laborious routine. 2 the act or sound of grinding. ■ **grinder** N.
◆ **grind sb down** to crush their spirit.
◆ **grind to a halt** to stop completely.

grinding ADJ crushing; oppressive.

grindstone N a revolving stone wheel used for sharpening and polishing.

grip VB (-*pp*-) 1 to take or keep a firm hold of something. 2 to capture the imagination or attention of a person.
➢ N 1 a firm hold; the action of taking a firm hold. 2 a way of gripping. 3 a handle or part that can be gripped. 4 a U-shaped wire pin for keeping the hair in place. 5 N AMER, ESP US a holdall. 6 COLLOQ understanding. 7 COLLOQ control; mastery: lose one's grip.
◆ **get to grips with sth** to begin to deal successfully with it.

gripe VB 1 INTR, COLLOQ to complain persistently. 2 TR & INTR to feel, or cause someone to feel, intense stomach pain.
➢ N, COLLOQ a complaint.

gripping ADJ holding the attention; exciting.

grisly ADJ (-*ier, -iest*) horrible; ghastly; gruesome. ■ **grisliness** N.

grist N grain that is to be, or that has been, ground into flour.
◆ **grist to the mill** anything profitable.

gristle N cartilage, esp in meat. ■ **gristly** ADJ.

grit N 1 small particles of a hard material, esp of stone or sand. 2 COLLOQ courage and determination.
➢ VB (-*tt*-) 1 to spread grit on (icy roads, etc). 2 to clench (the teeth), eg to overcome pain.

grits PL N ground grain with the husks removed.

gritty ADJ (*-ier, -iest*) **1** full of or covered with grit. **2** like grit. **3** determined; dogged.

grizzled ADJ **1** of the hair or a beard: grey or greying. **2** of a person: having such hair.

grizzly ADJ (*-ier, -iest*) grey or greying. ➢ N (*-ies*) COLLOQ a grizzly bear.

grizzly bear N the largest of the bears, so called because its fur is frosted with white.

groan VB **1** INTR to make a long deep sound in the back of the throat, expressing pain, distress, disapproval, etc. **2** to utter or express something with a groan. **3** INTR to creak loudly. **4** INTR to be weighed down or almost breaking: **tables groaning with food**. ➢ N an act, or the sound, of groaning.

grocer N **1** someone whose job is selling food and household goods. **2** a grocer's shop.

grocery N (*-ies*) **1** the trade or premises of a grocer. **2** (**groceries**) merchandise, esp food, sold in a grocer's shop.

groggy ADJ (*-ier, -iest*) COLLOQ weak, dizzy and unsteady on the feet, eg from the effects of illness or alcohol. ■ **groggily** ADV.

groin N the part of the body where the lower abdomen joins the upper thigh.

grommet N **1** a rubber or plastic ring around a hole in metal. **2** MED a small tube passed through the eardrum to drain the middle ear.

groom N **1** someone who looks after horses and cleans stables. **2** a bridegroom. **3** a title given to various officers in a royal household. ➢ VB **1** to clean, brush and generally smarten (animals, esp horses). **2** to keep (a person) clean and neat, esp regarding clothes and hair. **3** to train or prepare someone for a specified office, stardom or success in any sphere.

groove N **1** a long narrow channel. **2** the continuous track cut into the surface of a record. **3** COLLOQ a set routine, esp a monotonous one. ➢ VB **1** to cut a groove in something. **2** INTR, DATED SLANG to enjoy oneself.

groovy ADJ (*-ier, -iest*) SLANG excellent,

attractive or fashionable.

grope VB **1** INTR to search by feeling about with the hands, eg in the dark. **2** INTR to search uncertainly or with difficulty: **groping for answers**. **3** to find (one's way) by feeling. **4** COLLOQ to fondle someone sexually. ➢ N, COLLOQ an act of sexual fondling.

gross ADJ (*grosser, grossest*, except in sense 1) **1** total, with no deductions: **gross weight**. **2** very great; flagrant; glaring: **gross negligence**. **3** DEROG vulgar. **4** DEROG unattractively fat. **5** COLLOQ, DEROG very unpleasant. ➢ N **1** (PL **gross**) twelve dozen, 144. **2** (PL **grosses**) the total amount or weight, without deductions. ■ **grossly** ADV. ■ **grossness** N.

grotesque ADJ **1** very unnatural or strange–looking, so as to cause fear or laughter. **2** exaggerated; ridiculous; absurd. ■ **grotesquely** ADV. ■ **grotesqueness** N.

grotto N (*-os* or *-oes*) **1** a cave, esp a small one. **2** a man–made cave–like structure.

grotty ADJ (*-ier, -iest*) COLLOQ **1** DEROG unpleasantly dirty or shabby. **2** ill. ■ **grottiness** N.

grouch COLLOQ VB, INTR to grumble or complain. ➢ N **1** a complaining person. **2 a** a bad–tempered complaint; **b** the cause of it.

grouchy ADJ (*-ier, -iest*) bad–tempered; tending to grumble. ■ **grouchiness** N.

ground N **1** the solid surface of the Earth, or any part of it; soil; land. **2** (often **grounds**) an area of land, usu extensive, attached to or surrounding a building. **3** an area of land used for a specified purpose: **football ground**. **4** distance covered or to be covered. **5** the substance of discussion: **cover a lot of ground**. **6** a position or standpoint, eg in an argument: **stand or shift one's ground**. **7** progress relative to that made by an opponent; advantage: **lose or gain ground**. **8** (usu **grounds**) a reason or justification. **9** (**grounds**) sediment or dregs. ➢ VB **1** TR & INTR to hit or cause (a ship) to hit the seabed or shore and remain stuck. **2** to refuse to allow (a pilot or aeroplane) to fly. **3** to forbid (eg teenagers) to go out socially. **4** to lay (eg

weapons) on the ground.
➤ ADJ on or relating to the ground: **ground forces.**
◆ **give ground** to give way; to retreat.
◆ **go to ground 1** of an animal: to go into a burrow to escape from hunters. **2** to go into hiding, eg from the police.

groundbreaking ADJ innovative.

ground floor N, BRIT the floor of a building that is at street level.

grounding N a basic knowledge.

groundless ADJ having no justification.

ground rule N a basic principle.

groundsheet N a waterproof sheet spread on the ground to give protection against damp.

groundsman N someone whose job is to maintain a sports field.

groundswell N **1** a broad high swell of the sea, often caused by a distant storm or earthquake. **2** a rapidly growing indication of public or political feeling.

group N **1** a number of people or things gathered, placed or classed together. **2** a number of business companies under single ownership and central control. **3** a band of musicians and singers.
➤ VB, TR & INTR to form into a group.

group captain N an officer in the air force.

groupie N, COLLOQ an ardent follower, esp of a touring pop star or group.

grouse[1] N (PL *grouse*) a bird with a plump body, hunted as game.

grouse[2] COLLOQ, VB, INTR to complain.
➤ N **1** a complaint. **2** a moaner. ■ **grouser** N.

grout N thin mortar applied to the joints between bricks or esp ceramic tiles.
➤ VB to apply grout to joints. ■ **grouting** N.

grove N **1** a small group of trees, often planted for shade or ornament. **2** an area planted with fruit trees, esp citrus and olive.

grovel VB (*-ll-* or (US) *-l-*) INTR **1** to act with exaggerated (and usu insincere) respect or

humility, esp to gain the favour of a superior. **2** to lie or crawl face down, in fear or respect.
■ **groveller** N. ■ **grovelling** ADJ.

grow VB (*grew, grown*) **1** INTR of a living thing: to develop into a larger more mature form. **2** TR & INTR to increase, or allow (hair, nails, etc) to increase, in length. **3** INTR to increase in size, intensity or extent. **4** to cultivate (plants). **5 a** to become … gradually: **They grew lazy; b** (usu **grow to …**) to come gradually to (have a specified feeling): **grew to hate him.**
◆ **grow into sth 1** to develop and become (a specified form). **2** to become big enough to wear (clothes that were orig too large).
◆ **grow on sb** to come to be liked by them.
◆ **grow out of sth 1** to become too big to wear (clothes that were orig the right size). **2** to lose a liking for it, or the habit of doing it, with age. **3** to originate in it: **The plan grew out of an idea of mine.**
◆ **grow up 1** to become, or be in the process of becoming, an adult. **2** to behave in an adult way. **3** to come into existence; to develop.

growl VB **1** INTR of animals: to make a deep rough sound in the throat, showing hostility. **2** TR & INTR of people: to make a similar sound showing anger or displeasure; to speak or say something angrily.
➤ N an act or the sound of growling.

grown ADJ **1** mature. **2** IN COMPOUNDS developed to a specified degree: **fully grown.**

grown-up COLLOQ, ADJ adult.
➤ N an adult.

growth N **1 a** the process or rate of growing; **b** the increase in size, weight and complexity of a living organism that takes place as it develops to maturity. **2** an increase. **3** MED a benign or malignant tumour.

grub N **1** the worm-like larva of an insect, esp a beetle. **2** food.
➤ VB (*-bb-*) **1** INTR (usu **grub about**) to dig or search in the soil. **2** INTR (usu **grub around**) to search or rummage.

grubby ADJ (*-ier, -iest*) COLLOQ dirty.
■ **grubbily** ADV. ■ **grubbiness** N.

grudge N a feeling of resentment.
➤ VB **1** (esp **grudge doing sth**) to be unwilling to do it; to do it unwillingly. **2** (**grudge sb sth**) **a** to be unwilling to give them it; to give them it unwillingly; **b** to feel envy or resentment at their good fortune.

grudging ADJ **1** resentful. **2** unwilling.
■ **grudgingly** ADV.

gruel N thin porridge.

gruelling ADJ exhausting; punishing.

gruesome ADJ inspiring horror or disgust; sickening; macabre. ■ **gruesomely** ADV.

gruff ADJ **1** of a voice: deep and rough. **2** rough, unfriendly or surly in manner. ■ **gruffly** ADV. ■ **gruffness** N.

grumble VB, INTR **1** to complain in a bad-tempered way. **2** to make a rumbling sound.
➤ N **1** a complaint. **2** a rumbling sound.
■ **grumbler** N. ■ **grumbling** N, ADJ.

grumpy ADJ (*-ier, -iest*) bad-tempered; surly.
■ **grumpily** ADV. ■ **grumpiness** N.

grunt VB **1** INTR of animals, esp pigs: to make a low rough sound in the back of the throat. **2** INTR of people: to make a similar sound, eg indicating disgust or unwillingness to speak fully. **3** to utter something with this sound.
➤ N an act or the sound of grunting.

G-string N (also **gee-string**) a garment which barely covers the pubic area, consisting of a strip of cloth attached to a waistband.

guacamole N a traditional Mexican dish of mashed avocado mixed with spicy seasoning.

guano N the accumulated droppings of large colonies of bats, fish-eating seabirds or seals.

guarantee N **1 a** a formal agreement, usu in writing, that a product, service, etc will conform to specified standards for a particular period of time; **b** a document that records this kind of agreement. **2** an assurance that something will have a specified outcome, condition, etc: **no guarantee that there wouldn't be more pay cuts. 3** LAW an agreement under which one person, the guarantor, becomes liable for the debt or default of another.

➤ VB (*-teed, -teeing*) **1** to provide (eg a product, service, etc) with a guarantee. **2** to ensure something. **3** to assure or promise. **4** to act as a guarantor for something.

guarantor N someone who gives a guarantee.

guard VB **1** to protect someone or something from danger or attack. **2** to watch over someone in order to prevent their escape. **3** to control or check: **guard your tongue. 4** to control passage through (eg a doorway).
➤ N **1** a person or group whose job is to provide protection, eg from danger or attack, or to prevent escape. **2** BRIT a person in charge of a railway train. **3** a state of readiness to give protection or prevent escape: **keep guard. 4** BOXING, CRICKET, etc a defensive posture. **5** esp IN COMPOUNDS anything that gives protection from or to something: **fireguard. 6** the act or duty of protecting. **7** (often **Guard**) a soldier in any of certain army regiments orig formed to protect the sovereign.
◆ **off guard** or **off one's guard** not on the alert; unwary: **caught you off guard.**
◆ **on guard 1** on sentry duty. **2** (also **on one's guard**) on the alert; wary.

guarded ADJ cautious. ■ **guardedly** ADV.

guardhouse and **guardroom** N a building or room for guards on duty.

guardian N **1** someone who is legally responsible for the care of another, esp an orphaned child. **2** a guard, defender or protector. ■ **guardianship** N.

guardian angel N an angel believed to watch over a particular person.

guardsman N **1** BRIT a member of a regiment of Guards. **2** US a member of the National Guard.

guava N **1** a small tropical tree cultivated for its edible fruits. **2** its yellow pear-shaped fruit.

gubernatorial ADJ, FORMAL, esp US of or relating to a governor.

guernsey N a hand-knitted woollen pullover.

guerrilla or **guerilla** N a member of a small,

independent armed force making surprise attacks, eg against government troops. ALSO AS ADJ: **guerrilla warfare**.

guess VB 1 TR & INTR to make an estimate or form an opinion about something, based on little or noinformation. **2** to estimate something correctly. **3** to think or suppose: **I guess so.** ➤ N an estimate based on guessing.

guesstimate COLLOQ, N a very rough estimate, based on guesswork. ➤ VB to estimate something using a guess.

guesswork N the process or result of guessing.

guest N 1 someone who receives hospitality in the home of, or at the expense of, another. **2** someone who stays at a hotel, boarding-house, etc. **3** a person specially invited to take part: **tonight's guests are ...** ➤ VB, INTR to appear as a guest, eg on a television show.

guesthouse N a private home that offers accommodation to paying guests.

guff N, COLLOQ, DEROG nonsense.

guffaw N a loud coarse laugh. ➤ VB, INTR to laugh in this way.

guidance N 1 help, advice or counselling; the act or process of guiding. **2** direction or leadership. **3** AS ADJ: **guidance teacher**.

guide VB 1 to lead, direct or show the way to someone. **2** to control or direct the movement or course of something. **3** to advise or influence: **be guided by your parents.** ➤ N 1 someone who leads the way for eg tourists or mountaineers. **2** any device used to direct movement. **3** a guidebook. **4** (**Guide**) a member of a worldwide youth organization for girls. Also called **Girl Guide**. **5** someone or something, esp a quality, which influences another person's decisions or behaviour.

guidebook N a book containing information or instructions.

guided missile N a jet- or rocket-propelled projectile that can be electronically directed to its target by remote control.

guide dog N a dog specially trained to guide a blind person safely.

guideline N (often **guidelines**) an indication of what future action is required.

guild N 1 a medieval association of merchants or craftsmen. **2** a name used by various modern societies, clubs, etc.

guile N 1 the ability to deceive or trick. **2** craftiness or cunning. ■ **guileless** ADJ.

guillemot N a seabird with black and white plumage and a long narrow bill.

guillotine N 1 an instrument for beheading. **2** a device for cutting paper or metal. ➤ VB to use a guillotine.

guilt N 1 a feeling of shame or remorse resulting from a sense of having done wrong. **2** the state of having done wrong or having broken a law. **3** blame. **4** LAW liability to a penalty.

guiltless ADJ innocent. ■ **guiltlessly** ADV.

guilty ADJ (*-ier, -iest*) (often **guilty of sth**) **1** responsible for a crime or wrongdoing, or judged to be so. **2** feeling, showing or involving guilt: **a guilty look**. **3** able to be justly accused of something: **guilty of working too hard**.

guinea N 1 an obsolete British gold coin worth 21 shillings (£1.05). **2** its value, still used as a monetary unit in some professions.

guinea pig N 1 a tailless rodent, widely kept as a domestic pet and also used as a laboratory animal. **2** a person used as the subject of an experiment.

guise N 1 assumed appearance; pretence. **2** external appearance in general.

guitar N a musical instrument with a body generally shaped like a figure eight, a long fretted neck and usu six strings that are plucked or strummed. ■ **guitarist** N.

gulch N, N AMER, ESP US a narrow rocky ravine with a fast-flowing stream running through it.

gulf N 1 a very large and deeply indented inlet of the sea extending far into the land. **2** a vast difference or separation, eg between points of view, etc. **3** a deep hollow in the ground; a chasm. **4 (the Gulf) a** the region around the Persian Gulf in the Middle East; **b** the area around the Gulf of Mexico in Central America.

gull N an omnivorous seabird with a stout body and predominantly white or greyish plumage.

gullet N the oesophagus or throat.

gullible ADJ easily tricked. ■ **gullibility** N.

gully or **gulley** N (*gullies* or *gulleys*) a small channel or cutting with steep sides.

gulp VB **1** TR & INTR (also **gulp down**) to swallow (food, drink, etc) eagerly or in large mouthfuls. **2** INTR to make a swallowing motion, eg because of fear.
➤ N **1** a swallowing motion. **2** an amount swallowed at once; a mouthful.

gum[1] N the firm fibrous flesh surrounding the roots of the teeth.

gum[2] N **1** a substance found in certain plants, esp trees, that produces a sticky solution or gel when added to water. **2** this or any similar substance used as glue. **3** COLLOQ a sweet, sticky substance for chewing.
➤ VB (*-mm-*) to smear or glue something with gum.

gumboil N a small abscess on the gum.

gumboot N a wellington boot.

gummy[1] ADJ (*-ier, -iest*) toothless.

gummy[2] ADJ (*-ier, -iest*) **1** sticky. **2** producing gum.

gumption N, COLLOQ **1** common sense; initiative. **2** courage.

gun N **1** any weapon which fires bullets or shells from a metal tube. **2** any instrument which forces something out under pressure: spray gun.
➤ VB (*-nn-*) COLLOQ to rev up (a car engine) noisily.
◆ **gun sb** or **sth down** to shoot them or it with a gun.

gunboat N a small warship with large guns.

gun dog N a dog specially trained to flush birds or small mammals and to retrieve them when they have been shot by a hunter.

gunfire N **1** the act of firing guns. **2** the bullets fired. **3** the sound of firing.

gunge N, COLLOQ any messy substance.

gunk N, COLLOQ any slimy or oily substance.

gunman N **1** an armed criminal. **2** an assassin. **3** a terrorist.

gunner N **1** any member of an armed force who operates a heavy gun. **2** a soldier in an artillery regiment.

gunnery N **1** the use of guns. **2** the science of designing guns.

gunpoint N.
◆ **at gunpoint** threatening, or being threatened, with a gun.

gunpowder N the oldest known explosive, a mixture of potassium nitrate, sulphur and charcoal.

gunrunning N the act of smuggling arms into a country. ■ **gunrunner** N.

gunshot N **1** bullets fired from a gun. **2** the distance over which a gun can fire a bullet: within gunshot. **3** a sound of firing.

gunsmith N someone whose job is to make and/or repair firearms.

gunwale or **gunnel** N the upper edge of a ship's side.

guppy N (*-ies*) a small brightly coloured freshwater fish that is a popular aquarium fish.

gurgle VB **1** INTR of water: to make a bubbling noise when flowing. **2** INTR to make a bubbling noise in the throat. **3** to utter with a gurgle.
➤ N the sound of gurgling.

guru N **1** a Hindu or Sikh spiritual leader or teacher. **2** sometimes FACETIOUS any greatly respected and influential leader or adviser.

gush VB **1** TR & INTR of a liquid: to flood out or make it flood out suddenly and violently. **2** INTR, DEROG, COLLOQ to speak or act with affected and exaggerated emotion or enthusiasm.
➤ N **1** a sudden violent flooding-out. **2** DEROG, COLLOQ exaggerated emotion or enthusiasm.

■ **gushing** ADJ, N. ■ **gushingly** ADV.

gusset N, DRESSMAKING a piece of material sewn into a garment, eg at the crotch.

gust N 1 a sudden blast or rush, eg of wind or smoke. 2 an emotional outburst.
➢ VB, INTR of the wind: to blow in gusts.

gusto N enthusiastic enjoyment; zest.

gusty ADJ (-ier, -iest) 1 blowing in gusts; stormy. 2 fitfully irritable or upset. ■ **gustily** ADV.

gut N 1 ANAT the alimentary canal or part of it. 2 (**guts**) COLLOQ the insides of a person or animal. 3 COLLOQ the stomach or abdomen. 4 COLLOQ a fat stomach. 5 (**guts**) COLLOQ courage or determination. 6 a catgut; b a fibre obtained from silkworms, used for fishing tackle.
➢ VB (-tt-) 1 to take the guts out of (an animal, esp fish). 2 to destroy the insides of something; to reduce to a shell: **Fire gutted the building**.

gutless ADJ, DEROG cowardly.

gutsy ADJ (-ier, -iest) COLLOQ 1 courageous and determined. 2 gluttonous.

gutter N 1 a channel for carrying away rainwater, fixed to the edge of a roof or built between a pavement and a road. 2 TEN-PIN BOWLING either of the channels at the sides of a lane. 3 (**the gutter**) a state of poverty and social deprivation or of degraded living.
➢ VB 1 INTR of a candle: to have its melted wax, etc suddenly pour down a channel which forms on its side. 2 of a flame: to flicker and threaten to go out. ■ **guttering** N.

guttural ADJ 1 NON-TECHNICAL of sounds: produced in the throat or the back of the mouth. 2 having or using such sounds; harsh-sounding. ■ **gutturally** adv.

guy[1] N 1 COLLOQ a man or boy. 2 COLLOQ, orig US a a person; b (**guys**) used to address or refer to a group of people: **What do you guys think?** 3 a crude model of Guy Fawkes that is burnt on a bonfire on Guy Fawkes Day.

guy[2] N (in full **guy rope**) a rope or wire used to hold something, esp a tent, firm or steady.

guzzle VB, TR & INTR to eat or drink greedily.

gybe, **gibe** or **jibe** VB, TR & INTR, NAUT 1 of a sail: to swing, or make it swing, over from one side of a boat to the other. 2 of a boat: to change or make it change course in this way.
➢ N an act of gybing.

gym N, COLLOQ 1 gymnastics. 2 gymnasium.

gymkhana N a local public event consisting of competitions in sports, esp horse-riding.

gymnasium N (PL -iums or -ia) a building or room with equipment for physical exercise.

gymnast N someone skilled in gymnastics.

gymnastic ADJ 1 relating to gymnastics. 2 athletic; agile. ■ **gymnastically** ADV.

gymnastics SING N physical training designed to improve agility.
➢ PL N 1 feats of agility. 2 exercises that test or demonstrate ability: **mental gymnastics**.

gym shoe N a plimsoll.

gym slip N a belted pinafore dress worn (esp FORMERLY) by schoolgirls.

gynaecology or (US) **gynecology** N the branch of medicine concerned with the diagnosis and treatment of diseases and disorders that affect the reproductive organs of the female body. ■ **gynaecological** ADJ. ■ **gynaecologist** N.

gypsum N a soft mineral composed of calcium sulphate, used to make plaster, cement, rubber and paper.

Gypsy or **Gipsy** N (-ies) a member of a travelling people, orig from NW India, now scattered throughout Europe and N America. Also called **Romany**.

gyrate VB, INTR to move with a circular or spiralling motion. ■ **gyration** N.

gyroscope N a device consisting of a small flywheel with a heavy rim, mounted so that once in motion it resists any changes in the direction of motion. ■ **gyroscopic** ADJ.

Hh

H or **h** N (*Hs, H's* or *h's*) the eighth letter of the English alphabet.

haar N, SCOT & NE ENGLISH DIALECT a cold mist or fog coming off the North Sea.

habeas corpus N, LAW a writ requiring a person to be brought into court for a judge to decide if their imprisonment is legal.

haberdasher N, BRIT a person or shop that deals in items such as ribbons, needles, buttons, etc. ■ **haberdashery** N (*-ies*).

habit N 1 a tendency to behave, think, etc in a specific way. 2 a usual practice or custom. 3 an addiction. 4 a long loose garment worn by monks and nuns.

habitable or **inhabitable** ADJ suitable for living in; fit to live in.

habitat N the natural home of an animal or plant.

habitation N 1 the act of living in a particular dwelling place. 2 a house or home.

habitual ADJ 1 done regularly. 2 done by habit. 3 usual. ■ **habitually** ADV.

habituate VB to accustom. ■ **habituation** N.

habitué N a regular visitor to a place.

háček N a diacritic (ˇ) placed over a letter in some Slavonic and Baltic languages.

hacienda N in Spanish-speaking countries: a ranch or large estate.

hack[1] VB 1 to cut or chop roughly. 2 INTR, COLLOQ (often **hack into**) to use a computer to obtain unauthorized access to (computer files, etc). 3 SLANG to bear, tolerate, etc. 4 FOOTBALL, RUGBY to kick the shin of (an opponent). ➤ N 1 a kick on the shins. 2 a wound or rough cut. 3 a short dry cough. 4 a chop or blow.

hack[2] N 1 a horse kept for general riding. 2 a writer who produces dull or routine work.

hacker N, COLLOQ someone who uses computers to gain unauthorized access to data, other computers, etc.

hackles PL N the hairs or feathers on the back of the neck of some animals and birds, which are raised when they are angry.

hackney cab and **hackney carriage** N 1 HIST a carriage for public hire. 2 a taxi.

hackneyed ADJ of a word, phrase, etc: meaningless and trite through too much use.

hacksaw N a saw for cutting metals.

haddock N (*haddock* or *haddocks*) a commercially important N Atlantic sea-fish.

hadn't CONTRACTION had not.

haemal or **hemal** ADJ, MED relating to the blood or blood-vessels.

haematology or (US) **hematology** N the branch of medicine concerned with the blood and its diseases. ■ **haematologist** N.

haemoglobin or **hemoglobin** N, BIOCHEM a protein in red blood cells that carries oxygen.

haemophilia or (US) **hemophilia** N a hereditary disease, usu only affecting males, in which the blood does not clot as it should. ■ **haemophiliac** N.

haemorrhage or **hemorrhage** N, MED the escape of profuse amounts of blood, esp

from a ruptured blood vessel.
➢ VB, INTR to lose copious amounts of blood.

haemorrhoids or (US) **hemorrhoids** PL N, MED swollen veins in the anus; piles.

hafnium N CHEM a metallic element found in zirconium minerals and used in electrodes.

haft N a handle of a knife, sword, axe, etc.

hag N 1 OFFENSIVE an ugly old woman. 2 a witch.

haggard ADJ looking very tired and upset, esp because of pain, worry, etc.

haggis N a Scottish dish made from sheep's or calf's offal mixed with suet and oatmeal.

haggle VB, INTR (often **haggle over** or **about**) to bargain over (a price, etc).

hagiography N (-ies) the writing of the lives of saints. ■ **hagiographer** N.

ha-ha[1] or **haw-haw** EXCLAM 1 a conventional way of representing the sound of laughter. 2 expressing triumph, scorn, etc.

ha-ha[2] N a wall or a fence built into a bank or ditch to avoid interrupting a view.

hail[1] N 1 grains of ice which fall from the clouds. 2 a large quantity (of words, missiles, etc). ➢ VB INTR of hail: to fall from the clouds.

hail[2] VB 1 to attract attention by shouting or making gestures. 2 to greet someone, esp enthusiastically. 3 to recognize someone as being something: **hailed a hero**. ➢ N the act or an instance of hailing. ◆ **hail from** to come from (a place).

hail-fellow-well-met ADJ friendly and familiar, esp overly so.

hail Mary N (*hail Marys*) a prayer to the Virgin Mary.

hailstone N a single grain of hail.

hair N 1 a thread-like structure growing from the skin of animals. 2 a mass or growth of such strands, esp on a person's head. 3 BOT a thread-like structure growing from the surface of a plant. 4 a locking mechanism on a firearm.
◆ **get in sb's hair** COLLOQ to annoy them.

◆ **not turn a hair** to remain calm and show no surprise, anger, etc.
◆ **split hairs** to make unnecessary petty distinctions or quibbles.

haircut N 1 the cutting of someone's hair. 2 the shape or style in which it is cut.

hairdo N, COLLOQ a woman's haircut, esp after styling and setting.

hairdresser N 1 a person whose job is cutting, styling, etc hair. 2 an establishment where this takes place. ■ **hairdressing** N.

hairdryer or **hairdrier** N an electrical device that dries hair by blowing hot air over it.

hairline N 1 the line along the forehead where the hair begins to grow. 2 a very fine line.

hairnet N a fine-meshed net for keeping the hair in place.

hairpiece N a wig or piece of false hair.

hair-raising ADJ extremely frightening.

hair's-breadth N a very small margin.

hair shirt N a shirt made of rough cloth usu worn next to the skin as a religious penance.

hairspray N lacquer for holding the hair in place.

hairspring N a very small spiral spring which regulates a watch.

hairstyle N the way in which someone's hair is cut or shaped. ■ **hair-stylist** N.

hair trigger N a device in a firearm that responds to very light pressure.

hairy ADJ (-ier, -iest) 1 covered in hair. 2 COLLOQ a dangerous, frightening or exciting; b difficult or tricky. ■ **hairiness** N.

hajj or **hadj** N the Muslim pilgrimage to Mecca.

hake N (*hake* or *hakes*) an edible sea fish.

halal N meat from an animal which has been killed according to Muslim holy law.

halcyon ADJ peaceful, calm and happy.

hale ADJ strong and fit: **hale and hearty**.

half N (*halves*) **1 a** one of two equal parts which together form a whole; **b** a quantity which equals such a part. **2** a fraction equal to one divided by two. **3** COLLOQ a half pint, esp of beer. **4** SCOT a measure of spirits. **5** one of two equal periods of play in a match. **6** FOOTBALL, HOCKEY, etc the half of the pitch considered to belong to one team. **7** GOLF an equal score with an opponent. **8** a half-hour. **9** SPORT a halfback. **10** a half-price ticket.
➤ ADJ forming or equal to half of something: *a half chicken* • *half dozen*.
➤ ADV **1** to the extent or amount of one half: *half finished*. **2** almost; partly: *half dead*. **3** thirty minutes past the hour: *half three*.
◆ **by half** COLLOQ excessively: *He's too clever by half*.
◆ **by halves** without being thorough: *never do things by halves*.
◆ **not half** COLLOQ very: *It isn't half cold*.

half-and-half ADV, ADJ in equal parts; in part one thing, in part another.

halfback N **1** FOOTBALL, HOCKEY, etc a player or position immediately behind the forwards and in front of the fullbacks. **2** RUGBY either the stand-off half or the scrum half.

half-baked ADJ COLLOQ of a scheme, etc: **a** not properly thought out; **b** unrealistic.

half-breed N, often OFFENSIVE someone with parents of different races.

half-brother N a brother with whom one has only one parent in common.

half-caste N, often OFFENSIVE a person who has parents of different races.

half-cock N.
◆ **to go off half-cocked** or **at half-cock** to start too soon.

half-cut ADJ, SLANG drunk.

half-day N a day on which someone only works, etc in the morning or in the afternoon.

half-hearted ADJ not eager; without enthusiasm. ■ **half-heartedly** ADV.

half-hitch N a simple knot formed by passing the end of a piece of rope around the rope and through the loop made in the process.

half-hour N **1** a period of thirty minutes. **2** the moment that is thirty minutes after the start of an hour. ■ **half-hourly** ADJ, ADV.

half-life N, PHYS the period of time required for half the original number of atoms of a radioactive substance to undergo decay.

half mast N the lower-than-normal position at which a flag flies as a sign of mourning.

half-moon N **1** the Moon when only half of it can be seen. **2** the time when this occurs.

half nelson N a hold in which a wrestler puts an arm under one of their opponent's arms from behind, and pushes on the back of their neck.

half-note N, N AMER a minim.

halfpenny or **ha'penny** (*-ies* or *halfpence*) N, HIST an old British coin worth half an old penny.

half-sister N a sister with whom one only has one parent in common.

half-term N, BRIT EDUCATION a short holiday halfway through an academic term.

half-time N, SPORT an interval between the two halves of a match.

half-title N a short title on the right-hand page of a book which precedes the title page.

half-tone N **1** an illustration made up of dots of different sizes. **2** N AMER a semitone.

half volley N, SPORT a stroke in which the ball is hit immediately after, or as, it bounces.

halfway ADJ, ADV **1** at a point equally far from two others. **2** in an incomplete manner.
◆ **meet sb halfway** to come to a compromise with them.

halfwit N a foolish or stupid person. ■ **halfwitted** ADJ. ■ **halfwittedly** ADV.

halibut N (*halibut* or *halibuts*) a large edible flatfish found in the N Atlantic and N Pacific.

halitosis N unpleasant-smelling breath.

hall N **1** a room or passage just inside the entrance to a house, which usu allows access to other rooms and the stairs. **2** a building or large room, used for concerts, public meetings, etc. **3** (usu **Hall**) a large country house or manor. **4** BRIT (IN FULL **hall of residence**) a building where university or college students live.

hallelujah or **halleluia** and **alleluia** EXCLAM expressing praise to God.

hallmark N **1** a series of marks stamped on gold, silver and platinum articles to guarantee their authenticity. **2** a distinctive feature. ➤ VB to stamp with a hallmark.

hallo see **hello**

hallow VB to make or regard as holy.

Hallowe'en or **Halloween** N the evening of 31 October, the eve of All Saints' Day.

hallucinate VB, INTR to see something that is not actually present. ■ **hallucination** N. ■ **hallucinatory** ADJ.

hallucinogen N a drug that causes hallucination. ■ **hallucinogenic** ADJ.

hallway N an entrance hall or corridor.

halo N (**-os** or **-oes**) **1** in paintings etc: a ring of light around the head of a saint, etc. **2** a ring of light that can be seen around the sun or moon. ➤ VB (**-oes, -oed**) to put a halo round someone or something.

halogen N, CHEM any of the elements fluorine, chlorine, bromine, iodine and astatine, which form salts when in union with metals.

halt N **1** an interruption or stop to movement, progression or growth. **2** BRIT a small railway station without a building. ➤ VB, TR & INTR to come or bring to a halt.

halter N **1** a rope or strap for holding and leading a horse by its head. **2** a halterneck.

halterneck N a woman's top or dress held in place by a strap which goes round the neck.

halting ADJ unsure; hesitant. ■ **haltingly** ADV.

halve VB **1** to divide into two equal parts or halves. **2** TR & INTR to reduce by half. **3** GOLF to take the same number of strokes as an opponent over (a hole or match).

halyard or **halliard** N a rope for raising or lowering a sail or flag on a ship.

ham¹ N **1** the top part of the back leg of a pig. **2** the meat from this part, salted and smoked. **3** INFORMAL the back of the thigh.

ham² N, COLLOQ **1** a bad actor, esp one who overacts. **2** an amateur radio operator. ➤ VB (**-mm-**) TR & INTR (also **ham up**) to overact or exaggerate. ■ **hammy** ADJ (**-ier, -iest**).

hamburger N a flat round cake of finely chopped beef, usu served in a soft bread roll.

ham-fisted and **ham-handed** ADJ, COLLOQ clumsy; lacking skill or grace.

hamlet N a small village.

hammer N **1** a tool with a heavy metal head on the end of a handle, used for driving nails into wood, breaking hard substances, etc. **2** the part of a bell, piano, etc that hits against some other part, making a noise. **3** the part of a gun that causes the bullet to be fired. **4** (the sport of throwing) a metal ball on a long steel chain. ➤ VB **1** TR & INTR to strike or hit with or as if with a hammer. **2** INTR to make a noise as of a hammer. **3** BRIT COLLOQ to criticize or beat severely. **4** COLLOQ to defeat.
◆ **come** or **go under the hammer** to be sold at auction.
◆ **hammer and tongs** COLLOQ with a lot of enthusiasm, effort or commotion.
◆ **hammer out 1** to shape or remove with, or as if with, a hammer. **2** to settle (problems, differences, etc) through effort and discussion.

hammock N a piece of canvas or net hung by the corners, used as a bed.

hamper N **1** a large basket with a lid, used esp for carrying food. **2** BRIT the food and drink packed in such a basket. ➤ VB to hinder the progress or movement of.

hamster N a small nocturnal rodent with a short tail and pouches in its mouth.

hamstring N **1** in humans: a tendon at the back of the knee attached to muscles in the thigh. **2** in horses: the large tendon at the back of the hind leg. ➤ VB (**hamstrung** or **hamstringed**) **1** to make powerless. **2** to lame by cutting the hamstring.

hand N **1** the extremity of the arm below the wrist. **2** AS ADJ relating to or involving the hand: hand grenade • hand lotion • hand saw. **3** IN COMPOUNDS made by hand rather than by a machine: hand-crafted • hand-knitted. **4** control or influence: the hand of fate. **5** (**a hand**) assistance: He gave us a hand. **6** a needle or pointer on a clock or gauge. **7** COLLOQ a round of applause: He got a big hand. **8** a manual worker or assistant: farm hand. **9** a specified way of doing something: She has a light hand at baking. **10** CARDS **a** the cards dealt to a player in one round of a game; **b** one round of a card game. **11** someone's style of handwriting. **12** in measuring the height of horses: a unit equal to 4 inches (about 10 centimetres).
➤ VB **1** (often **hand sth back** or **in** or **out** or **round, etc**) to give it using the hand or hands. **2** to help in a specified direction with the hand or hands: handed her into the carriage.
◆ **at hand** near by; about to happen.
◆ **hand in glove** very closely associated.
◆ **hand it to sb** COLLOQ to give them credit.
◆ **hand over fist** COLLOQ in large amounts and quickly: making money hand over fist.
◆ **in hand 1** under control. **2** being done or prepared. **3** in reserve: with an hour in hand.
◆ **keep one's hand in** COLLOQ to continue to have some involvement in an activity.
◆ **live from hand to mouth** to live with only enough food and money for immediate needs.
◆ **on hand** near; available if required.
◆ **out of hand 1** beyond control. **2** immediately and without thinking: to dismiss it out of hand.
◆ **to hand** within reach.
◆ **try one's hand at sth** to attempt to do it.

handbag N a small bag, often with a strap, for carrying personal articles.

handball N **1** a game in which two or four players hit a small ball against a wall with their hands or the ball used in this game. **2** FOOTBALL the offence of a player other than a goalkeeper touching the ball with their hand.

handbill N a small printed notice.

handbook N **1** a manual that gives guidelines on maintenance or repair, eg of a car. **2** a guidebook that lists brief facts on a subject.

handbrake N a brake on a motor vehicle, operated by a lever.

handcart N a small light cart which can be pushed or pulled by hand.

handcuff N (**handcuffs**) a pair of steel rings, joined by a short chain, for locking round the wrists of prisoners, etc.
➤ VB to put handcuffs on someone.

handed ADJ, IN COMPOUNDS **1** using one hand in preference to the other: left-handed. **2** having or using hands as specified: one-handed.

handful N **1** the amount that can be held in one hand. **2** a small number. **3** COLLOQ **a** someone who is difficult to control; **b** a difficult task.

handicap N **1** a physical or mental impairment. **2** something that impedes or hinders. **3 a** a disadvantage or advantage imposed on a competitor in a contest, race, etc, so that everyone has an equal chance of winning; **b** a race or competition in which competitors are given a handicap. **4** the number of strokes by which a golfer's averaged score exceeds par for a course.
➤ VB (-*pp*-) **1** to impede or hamper someone. **2** to impose special disadvantages or advantages on (a player, horse, etc) in order to make a better contest. ■ **handicapped** ADJ, N.

handicraft N **1** an activity which requires skilful use of the hands, eg pottery. **2** (usu **handicrafts**) the work so produced.

handiwork N **1** work, esp skilful work, produced by hand. **2** often DEROG the outcome of someone's action or efforts.

handkerchief N (-*chiefs* or -*chieves*) a piece of cloth used for wiping the nose, face, etc.

handle N **1** the part of a utensil, door, etc by which it is held so that it may be used, moved, picked up, etc. **2** SLANG a person's name or title.
➤ VB **1** to touch or operate with the hands. **2** to deal with, control, discuss, etc: She handles all the accounts. **3** to buy or sell: handle stolen goods. **4** INTR to respond in a specified way to

being operated: **handles very smoothly**.
◆ **fly off the handle** COLLOQ to become suddenly very angry.

handlebars PL N, SOMETIMES SING a bar for steering a bicycle, motorcycle, etc.

handler N 1 someone who trains an animal. 2 IN COMPOUNDS someone who handles something specified: **a baggage handler**.

handmade ADJ made by a person's hands or with hand-held tools.

hand-me-down N, COLLOQ something passed down from one person to another.

handout N 1 money, food, etc given to people who need it. 2 a leaflet, free sample, etc.

handover N the transfer of power, etc from one person or group of people to another.

hand-pick VB to choose carefully, esp for a particular purpose. ■ **hand-picked** ADJ.

handset N a telephone mouthpiece and earpiece together in a single unit.

handshake N an act of holding or shaking a person's hand, eg as a greeting.

hands-off ADJ 1 not touched or operated by the hands. 2 deliberately avoiding involvement.

handsome ADJ 1 of a man: good-looking. 2 of a woman: attractive in an imposing way. 3 well-proportioned; impressive. 4 generous: **a handsome donation**. 5 noble: **a handsome gesture**. ■ **handsomely** ADV.

hands-on ADJ involving practical experience rather than just information or theory.

handspring N a somersault in which one lands first on one's hands and then on one's feet.

handstand N the act of balancing one's body on one's hands with one's legs in the air.

hand-to-hand ADJ of fighting: involving direct physical contact with the enemy.

handwriting N 1 writing with a pen or pencil. 2 the characteristic way a person writes. ■ **handwritten** ADJ.

handy ADJ (*-ier, -iest*) 1 conveniently placed. 2 easy to use or handle. 3 clever with one's

hands. ■ **handily** ADV. ■ **handiness** N.

handyman N a man skilled at, or employed to do, odd jobs around the house.

hang VB (*hung* or (IN SENSE 3) *hanged*) 1 TR & INTR to fasten or be fastened from above. 2 TR & INTR of a door, etc: to fasten or be fastened with hinges. 3 TR & INTR to suspend or be suspended by a rope around the neck until dead. 4 (sometimes **hang over**) to be suspended or hover, esp in the air or in a threatening way. 5 TR & INTR to droop or make something droop: **hang one's head**. 6 to fix (wallpaper) to a wall. 7 to display or be displayed on a wall. 8 to suspend pictures or other hangings on or in (a wall, room, etc). 9 COMP to stop functioning.
◆ **get the hang of sth** COLLOQ to learn or begin to understand how to do it.
◆ **hang about** or **around** COLLOQ 1 to waste time; to stand doing nothing. 2 to remain.
◆ **hang back** to be unwilling or reluctant to do something.
◆ **hang fire** 1 to delay taking action. 2 to cease to develop or progress.
◆ **hang on** COLLOQ 1 to wait: **I'll hang on for a bit**. 2 to carry on bravely, in spite of difficulties.
◆ **hang on sth** 1 to depend on it: **It all hangs on the weather**. 2 to listen closely to it: **hanging on her every word**.
◆ **hang on to sth** to keep a hold of it.
◆ **hang out** 1 to lean or bend out (eg of a window, etc). 2 COLLOQ to frequent a place: **He hangs out in local bars**.
◆ **hang together** 1 of two people: to support each other. 2 to be consistent.
◆ **hang up** to finish a telephone conversation by replacing the receiver.

hangar N a large shed or building in which aircraft are kept.

hangdog ADJ ashamed, guilty or downcast.

hanger N 1 (in full **coat-hanger**) a fame on which clothes are hung to keep their shape. 2 a someone who hangs something; b IN COMPOUNDS a person or contraption that hangs a specified thing: **paper-hanger**.

hanger-on N (*hangers-on*) a dependant or follower, esp one who is not wanted.

hang-glider N **1** a type of glider which has a large light metal frame with cloth stretched across it and a harness hanging below it for the pilot. **2** the pilot of this. ■ **hang-gliding** N.

hanging N **1 a** the execution of someone by suspending their body by the neck; **b** AS ADJ: a hanging offence. **2** (usu **hangings**) curtains, tapestries, etc hung on walls.
➤ ADJ suspended; overhanging.

hangman N an official who carries out executions by hanging.

hangnail N a piece of loose skin partly torn away from the base or side of a fingernail.

hang-out N, COLLOQ a place where one lives or spends much time.

hangover N **1** unpleasant physical symptoms that may follow a period of heavy drinking. **2** someone or something left over from or influenced by an earlier time.

hang-up N, COLLOQ an emotional or psychological problem or preoccupation.

hank N a loop or skein of rope, wool, etc.

hanker VB, INTR (usu **hanker after** or **for sth**) to have a longing for it. ■ **hankering** N.

hankie or **hanky** N (*-ies*) COLLOQ a handkerchief.

hanky-panky N, COLLOQ **1** slightly improper sexual behaviour. **2** dubious or foolish conduct.

hansom cab N, HIST a two-wheeled horse-drawn carriage.

ha'penny see **halfpenny**

haphazard ADJ **1** careless. **2** random.
➤ ADV at random. ■ **haphazardly** ADV.

hapless ADJ unlucky; unfortunate.

haploid BIOL, ADJ of a cell nucleus: having a single set of unpaired chromosomes.

happen VB, INTR **1** to take place or occur. **2** to have the good or bad luck (to do something): I happened to see it in the shop window.

happening N an event.

happy ADJ (*-ier, -iest*) **1** feeling or showing pleasure or contentment: a happy smile. **2** causing pleasure. **3** fortunate: a happy coincidence. **4** appropriate; reasonable: a happy medium. **5** IN COMPOUNDS overcome with the thing specified: power-happy. ■ **happily** ADV. ■ **happiness** N.

happy-go-lucky ADJ carefree.

hara-kiri or **hari-kari** N ritual suicide by cutting one's belly open, formerly practised in Japan to avoid dishonour.

harangue N a forceful speech attacking people or trying to influence them.
➤ VB to address (someone) in this way.

harass VB to pester, torment or trouble (someone). ■ **harassed** ADJ. ■ **harassment** N.

harbinger N a person or thing that announces something to come; a forerunner.

harbour or (N AMER) **harbor** N **1** a place of shelter for ships. **2** a refuge or safe place.
➤ VB **1** to give shelter or protection to (someone, esp to a criminal). **2** to have (a feeling, etc) in one's head: harbour a grudge.

hard ADJ **1** of a substance: resistant to scratching or indentation; firm; solid. **2** toughened; not soft or smooth: hard skin. **3** difficult to do, understand, solve or explain. **4** using, needing or done with a great deal of effort. **5** demanding: a hard master. **6** harsh; cruel: hard times. **7** tough or violent: a hard man. **8** forceful: a hard knock. **9** uncompromising: a long hard look at sales figures. **10** proven and reliable: hard facts. **11** of water: tending to produce an insoluble scum instead of a lather with soap. **12** of a drug: highly addictive. **13** of an alcoholic drink: very strong, esp a spirit. **14** PHONETICS, NON-TECHNICAL of certain consonants: produced as a stop, as eg the **c** in **cat**. **15** of currency: in strong demand due to having a stable value. **16** of pencil leads: indicating durable quality and faintness in use.
➤ ADV **1** with great effort or energy: work hard. **2** IN COMPOUNDS achieved in the specified way with difficulty: hard-earned results. **3** with great intensity: It hit us hard. ■ **hardness** N.

◆ **be hard put to do sth** to have difficulty doing it.

◆ **hard at it** working hard; very busy.

◆ **hard by** close by.

◆ **hard done by** COLLOQ unfairly treated.

◆ **hard of hearing** partially deaf.

◆ **hard up** COLLOQ in need of money.

hard-and-fast ADJ of a rule or principle: that can never be changed.

hardback N a book with a hard cover.

hardball N no-nonsense tough tactics.

hard-bitten ADJ, COLLOQ tough and ruthless.

hardboard N light strong board made by compressing wood pulp.

hard-boiled ADJ 1 of eggs: boiled until the yolk is solid. 2 COLLOQ of a person: cynical.

hard cash N coins and banknotes, as opposed to cheques and credit cards.

hard copy N information from a computer printed on paper.

hardcore N 1 pieces of broken brick, stone, etc used as a base for a road. 2 (also **hard core**) the central, most important group within an organization, resistant to change. ➤ ADJ (often **hard-core**) 1 of pornography: sexually explicit. 2 having strong and unchanging beliefs: hard-core fans.

hard disk or **hard disc** N, COMP a rigid aluminium disk, coated with magnetic material and normally permanently sealed within a disk drive, with a large capacity for storing data.

harden VB 1 TR & INTR to make or become hard or harder. 2 TR & INTR to become or make less sympathetic. ■ **hardener** N.

hardened ADJ 1 rigidly set, eg in a behavioural pattern. 2 toughened through experience and not likely to change: a hardened criminal.

hard-headed ADJ tough, realistic or shrewd.

hard-hearted ADJ feeling no pity.

hardihood N courage or daring.

hard labour N, LAW a punishment involving heavy physical work and imprisonment.

hard line N an uncompromising course, opinion, decision or policy. ■ **hardliner** N.

hardly ADV 1 barely; scarcely: hardly knew him. 2 only just: could hardly keep her eyes open. 3 often IRONIC certainly not: They'll hardly come now.

hard-nosed ADJ, COLLOQ 1 tough and shrewd. 2 influenced by reason, not emotion.

hard-on N, COARSE SLANG an erection of the penis.

hard palate N the bony front part of the palate.

hard-pressed ADJ 1 having problems; in difficulties. 2 threatened by severe competition or attack. 3 closely pursued.

hardship N 1 conditions that are difficult to endure. 2 severe suffering or a cause of this.

hard shoulder N, BRIT a hard verge along the side of a motorway.

hardware N 1 metal goods such as pots, cutlery, tools, etc. 2 COMP the electronic, electrical, magnetic and mechanical components of a computer system. 3 military or mechanical equipment, components, etc.

hard-wearing ADJ designed to last and stay in good condition despite regular use.

hard-wired ADJ, COMP having functions that are controlled by hardware and cannot be altered by software programs.

hardwood N the wood of a slow-growing deciduous tree, such as the oak or mahogany.

hardy ADJ (*-ier, -iest*) 1 strong; able to bear difficult conditions. 2 of a plant: able to survive outdoors in winter. ■ **hardiness** N.

hare N a herbivorous mammal like a rabbit but slightly larger and with longer legs and ears. ➤ VB, INTR COLLOQ to run very fast or wildly.

harebell N a wild plant with violet-blue bell-shaped flowers. Also called **bluebell**.

hare-brained ADJ foolish; rash; heedless.

harelip N a deformity of the upper lip.

harem N a traditional Muslim house in which

wives, concubines, etc live.

haricot N a small white dried bean.

hari-kari see **hara-kiri**

hark VB.
◆ **hark back to sth** to refer again to a past time, topic, etc: *hark back to one's childhood.*

harken see **hearken**

harlequin N, THEAT a masked character who wears a brightly-coloured, diamond-patterned costume.
➤ ADJ in varied bright colours.

harlot N, OLD USE a prostitute. ■ **harlotry** N.

harm N physical, emotional, etc damage.
➤ VB to injure or damage. ■ **harmful** ADJ.
■ **harmless** ADJ.

harmonic ADJ **1** of or producing harmony; harmonious. **2** MUS of harmony.
➤ N, MUS an overtone of a fundamental note.
■ **harmonically** ADV.

harmonica N a mouth organ, a small wind instrument played by being held against the mouth, and blown or sucked.

harmonious ADJ **1** pleasant-sounding and tuneful. **2** forming a pleasing whole. **3** without disagreement. ■ **harmoniously** ADV.

harmonium N a keyboard instrument with bellows pumped by the feet.

harmonize or **-ise** VB **1** TR & INTR to be in or bring into musical harmony. **2** TR & INTR to form or be made to form a pleasing whole. **3** to add notes to (a tune) to form harmonies. **4** INTR to sing in harmony. ■ **harmonization** N.

harmony N (*-ies*) **1** MUS a pleasing combination of notes or sounds produced simultaneously. **2** a pleasing arrangement of parts or things. **3** agreement in opinions, etc.

harness N **1** a set of straps used to attach a cart to a horse, and to control the horse's movements. **2** a similar set of straps for attaching to a person's body, eg to hold a child.
➤ VB **1** to put a harness on (a horse, person, etc).
2 to attach (a draught animal to a cart, etc). **3** to control (resources) so as to make use of the

potential energy or power they contain.

harp N a large upright musical instrument with strings stretched vertically across it.
➤ VB, INTR to play the harp. ■ **harpist** N.
◆ **harp on about sth** COLLOQ to talk or write repeatedly and tediously about it.

harpoon N a barbed spear fastened to a rope, used for catching whales, etc.
➤ VB to strike (a whale, etc) with a harpoon.

harpsichord N a triangular-shaped keyboard instrument. ■ **harpsichordist** N.

harpy N (*-ies*) **1** MYTHOL an evil creature with the head and body of a woman and the wings and feet of a bird. **2** a cruel, grasping person.

harridan N a scolding old woman; a nag.

harrier N **1** a diurnal bird of prey with broad wings and long legs. **2** a cross-country runner. **3** a hound used orig for hunting horses.

harrow N a heavy metal framed farm implement with spikes or teeth, used to break up clods of soil and cover seed.
➤ VB to pull a harrow over (land).

harrowing ADJ extremely distressing.

harry VB (*-ies*, *-ied*) to annoy or worry someone.

harsh ADJ **1** rough; grating. **2** strict, cruel or severe. ■ **harshly** ADV. ■ **harshness** N.

hart N a male deer.

harum-scarum ADJ wild and reckless.
➤ ADV recklessly.

harvest N **1** the gathering in of ripened crops, usu in late summer or early autumn. **2** the season when this takes place. **3** the crop or crops gathered.
➤ VB **1** TR & INTR to gather (a ripened crop). **2** to reap (benefits, consequences, etc).
■ **harvester** N.

harvest moon N the full moon nearest to the autumnal equinox.

has-been N, COLLOQ someone who was once, but is no longer, successful or influential.

hash N **1** a dish of cooked meat and

vegetables chopped up together. **2** COLLOQ a mess. **3** SLANG hashish.
➤ VB **1** to chop into small pieces. **2** to mess up.

hashish or **hasheesh** N cannabis.

hasn't CONTRACTION has not.

hasp N a hinged metal fastening.

hassle COLLOQ, N **1** trouble or inconvenience, or a cause of this. **2** a fight or argument.
➤ VB **1** to annoy or bother someone, esp repeatedly; to harass. **2** INTR to argue or fight.

hassock N **1** a firm cushion for kneeling on, esp in church. **2** a tuft of grass.

haste N speed, esp in an action.
➤ VB to hasten.

hasten VB **1** TR & INTR to hurry or cause to hurry. **2** (always **hasten to do sth**) to do it eagerly and promptly.

hasty ADJ (**-ier, -iest**) **1** hurried; swift; quick. **2** without enough thought or preparation. ■ **hastily** ADV. ■ **hastiness** N.

hat N a type of covering for the head.
◆ **keep sth under one's hat** COLLOQ to keep it secret.
◆ **take one's hat off to sb** COLLOQ to admire or praise them.

hatch[1] N **1** a door covering an opening in a ship's deck. **2** a hatchway. **3** a door in an aircraft or spacecraft. **4** an opening in a wall between a kitchen and dining-room.

hatch[2] VB **1** INTR (also **hatch out**) to break out of an egg. **2** INTR of an egg: to break open, allowing young animals or birds to be born. **3** to produce (young animals or birds) from eggs. **4** to plan or devise (a plot, scheme, etc).

hatch[3] VB to shade (the surface of a map, drawing, engraving, etc) with close parallel or crossed lines. ■ **hatching** N.

hatchback N a sloping rear end of a car with a single door which opens upwards.

hatchery N (**-ies**) a place where eggs, esp fish eggs, are hatched under artificial conditions.

hatchet N a small axe held in one hand.

hatchway N **1** an opening in a ship's deck for loading cargo through. **2** a similar opening in a wall, ceiling, floor, etc.

hate VB to dislike intensely.
➤ N (an instance or target of) intense dislike.

hateful ADJ loathsome; detestable.

hatred N intense dislike; enmity; ill-will.

hatstand N a piece of furniture with pegs for hanging hats, coats, etc on.

hatter N someone who makes or sells hats.

hat trick N the scoring of three points, goals, victories, etc in a single match, etc.

haughty ADJ (**-ier, -iest**) very proud; arrogant. ■ **haughtily** ADV. ■ **haughtiness** N.

haul VB **1** TR & INTR to pull with great effort or difficulty. **2** to transport by road, eg in a lorry. **3** (usu **haul up**) to bring (someone before some authority) for punishment, reprimand etc.
➤ N **1** a distance to be travelled: **a short haul** • **a long haul**. **2** an amount gained or seized, eg of items stolen or contraband.

haulage N **1** the act or labour of hauling. **2** the business of transporting goods by road.

haulier N a person or company that transports goods by road, esp in lorries.

haunch N **1** the fleshy part of the buttock or thigh. **2** the leg and loin as a cut of meat.

haunt VB **1** of a ghost or spirit: to visit (a person or place) regularly. **2** of unpleasant thoughts, etc: to keep coming back to someone's mind: **haunted by the memory of his death**.
➤ N **1** a place visited frequently. **2** the habitation or usual feeding-ground of deer, game, fowls, etc. ■ **haunted** ADJ.

haute couture N the leading fashion designers or their products, collectively.

haute cuisine N cookery, esp French cookery, of a very high standard.

hauteur N haughtiness; arrogance.

have VB (PR T **has**, PA T AND PA P **had**, PR P **having**)
1 to possess: **They have a big house** • **He has**

brown eyes. **2** to receive, obtain or take: **have a drink. 3** to think of or hold in the mind: **have an idea. 4** to experience, enjoy or suffer: **have a good time • had my car stolen. 5** to be in a specified state: **has a screw loose. 6** to arrange or hold: **having a party. 7** to cause, order or invite something to be done: **have your hair cut. 8** to gain an advantage over or control of someone: **You have me on that point. 9** COLLOQ to cheat or deceive: **You've been had. 10** WITH NEGATIVES to accept or tolerate: **I won't have that! 11** to receive as a guest: **have people to dinner. 12** to give birth to (a baby, etc): **She had a boy. 13** COARSE SLANG to have sexual intercourse with someone.
➤ AUXILIARY VERB used with a past participle to show that the action or actions described have been completed, as in **I have made the cake** and **She has been there many times.**
◆ **have had it** COLLOQ to be dead or ruined.
◆ **have it off** BRIT, COARSE SLANG to have sexual intercourse.
◆ **have it out** to settle a disagreement by arguing or discussing it frankly.
◆ **have sb on** COLLOQ to trick or tease them.
◆ **have sth on sb** to have information about them.

haven N **1** a place of safety or rest. **2** a harbour or other sheltered spot for ships.

haven't CONTRACTION have not.

haver VB, INTR, esp SCOT & N ENGLISH to babble; to talk nonsense.

haversack N a canvas bag carried over one shoulder or on the back.

havoc N **1** great destruction or damage. **2** COLLOQ chaos; confusion.
◆ **play havoc with sth** to cause a great deal of damage or confusion to it.

haw¹ see **hum and haw** at **hum**

haw² N **1** a hawthorn berry. **2** the hawthorn.

haw-haw see **ha-ha¹**

hawk¹ N **1** a relatively small bird of prey with short rounded wings and very good eyesight. **2** POL a person favouring force rather than peaceful means of settling disputes.

➤ VB INTR to hunt with a hawk. ■ **hawkish** ADJ. ■ **hawklike** ADJ.

hawk² VB to carry (goods) round, usu from door to door, trying to sell them. ■ **hawker** N.

hawk³ VB, INTR to clear the throat noisily.

hawthorn N a thorny tree or shrub with pink or white flowers and red berries.

hay N grass, clover, etc that has been cut and dried before being baled and stored.
◆ **make hay while the sun shines** to take advantage of an opportunity while one can.

hay fever N, NON-TECHNICAL an allergic response to pollen.

haystack and **hayrick** N a large firm stack of hay built in an open field.

haywire ADJ, COLLOQ (often **go haywire**) of things: out of order; not working properly.

hazard N **1** a risk of harm or danger. **2** something which is likely to cause harm or danger. **3** chance; accident.
➤ VB **1** to put forward (a guess, suggestion, etc). **2** to risk. ■ **hazardous** ADJ.

haze N **1** a thin mist, vapour or shimmer in the atmosphere which obscures visibility. **2** a feeling of confusion or of not understanding.
➤ VB, TR & INTR to make or become hazy.

hazel N **1** a small deciduous shrub or tree with edible nuts. **2** its wood. **3** a hazelnut. **4** a greenish-brown colour.

hazelnut N the edible nut of the hazel tree, with a smooth hard shiny shell.

hazy ADJ (*-ier, -iest*) **1** misty. **2** vague; not clear. ■ **hazily** ADV. ■ **haziness** N.

he PRONOUN **1** a male person or animal already referred to. **2** a person or animal of unstated sex, esp after pronouns such as 'whoever'.
➤ N a male person or animal.

head N **1** the uppermost or foremost part of an animal's body, containing the brain, skull etc. **2** the head thought of as the seat of intelligence, ability, etc: **a head for heights. 3** something like a head in form, eg the top of a tool. **4** the person with the most authority in an organization, country, etc. **5** COLLOQ a head teacher or principal teacher. **6** the top or upper end of something. **7** the front of something, eg a queue. **8** (PL *head*) a person, animal or individual considered as a unit: **The meal cost £10 a head. 9** COLLOQ a headache. **10** the source of a river, lake, etc. **11** the height or length of a head, used as a measurement: **He won by a head. 12** a headland: **Beachy Head. 13** pressure: **a full head of steam. 14** an electromagnetic device in a tape recorder, etc for recording, playing back and erasing. **15** (**heads**) the side of a coin bearing the head of a monarch, etc. **16** AS ADJ **a** for or belonging to the head: **headband • head cold; b** chief; principal: **head gardener; c** at, or coming from, the front: **head wind.**

➤ VB **1** to be at the front of or top of something: **to head the queue. 2** to be in charge of, or in the most important position. **3** TR & INTR to move or cause to move in a certain direction: **heading home. 4** to provide with or be (a headline or heading) at the beginning of a chapter, letter, etc. **5** FOOTBALL to hit (the ball) with the head. ■ **headless** ADJ.

  bring or **come to a head** to reach or cause to reach a climax or crisis.

  give sb his or **her head** to allow them to act freely and without restraint.

  go to one's head 1 of alcoholic drink: to make one slightly intoxicated. **2** of praise, success, etc: to make one conceited.

  head off to leave.

  head sb off to get ahead of them so as to intercept them and force them to turn back.

  head sth off to prevent or hinder it.

  head over heels completely.

◆ **not make head or tail of sth** to be unable to understand it.

  off one's head COLLOQ mad; crazy.

  off the top of one's head COLLOQ without much thought or calculation.

◆ **over sb's head 1** without considering the obvious candidate: **He was promoted over the head of his supervisor. 2** referring to a higher authority without consulting them. **3** too difficult for them to understand.

◆ **turn sb's head 1** to make them vain and conceited. **2** to attract their attention.

headache N **1** a continuous pain felt in the head. **2** COLLOQ something that causes worry or annoyance. ■ **headachy** ADJ.

headbanger N, COLLOQ **1** a fan of heavy-metal music. **2** a stupid or fanatical person.

headboard N a panel at the top of a bed.

head case N, COLLOQ **1** someone who behaves in a wild or irrational way. **2** a person suffering from a psychiatric disorder.

headdress N a covering for the head, esp a highly decorative one used in ceremonies.

headed ADJ **1** having a heading: **headed notepaper. 2** IN COMPOUNDS: **clear-headed.**

header N **1** COLLOQ a fall or dive forward. **2** FOOTBALL the hitting of the ball with the head. **3** a heading for a chapter, article, etc.

headfirst ADV **1** moving esp quickly with one's head in front or bent forward. **2** rashly.

headgear N anything worn on the head.

headhunting N **1** the practice in certain societies of taking the heads of one's dead enemies as trophies. **2** the practice of trying to attract a person away from their present job to work for one's own or a client's company. ■ **headhunt** VB. ■ **headhunter** N.

heading N a title at the top of a page, letter, section of a report, etc.

headland N a strip of land which sticks out into a sea or other expanse of water.

headlight and **headlamp** N a powerful light on the front of a vehicle.

headline N **1** a title or heading of a newspaper article, written above the article in large letters. **2** (**headlines**) the most important points in a news broadcast, read out before the full broadcast.
➤ VB, TR & INTR to have top billing in (a show, etc).

headlong ADJ, ADV headfirst.

headmaster and **headmistress** N, OLD USE the principal teacher in a school.

head on ADV **1** with the front of one vehicle hitting the front of another. **2** in direct confrontation. **Also** AS ADJ: **a head–on crash.**

headphones PL N a device consisting of two small sound receivers for the ears.

headquarters SING OR PL N the control centre of an organization or group.

headrest N a cushion which supports the head, fitted to the top of a car seat, etc.

headroom N the space overhead, below an obstacle, etc.

headset N a pair of headphones, often with a microphone attached.

head start N an initial advantage.

headstone N **1** a gravestone. **2** ARCHIT a keystone.

headstrong ADJ **1** difficult to persuade; determined; obstinate. **2** heedless; rash.

head to head ADV, INFORMAL in direct competition. **Also** AS ADJ: **a head-to-head clash.**
➤ N a competition with two people, teams, etc.

headwaters PL N the tributary streams of a river, which flow from the area in which it rises.

headway N **1** progress. **2** a ship's movement forward.

heady ADJ (**-ier, -iest**) **1** very exciting. **2** rash.

heal VB **1** TR & INTR to become or cause (a person, wound, etc) to become healthy again. **2** to make (sorrow, etc) less painful. **3** to settle (disputes, etc). ■ **healer** N. ■ **healing** N, ADJ.

health N **1** a state of physical, mental and social well–being. **2** a person's general mental or physical condition: **in poor health.** **3** soundness, esp financial soundness.
■ **healthful** ADJ.

health farm N a place where people go to improve their health through diet and exercise.

health food N any food that is considered to be natural and beneficial to health.

health service N a public service providing medical care, usu without charge.

health visitor N a trained nurse who visits

people in their homes to check on their health.

healthy ADJ (**-ier, -iest**) **1** having or showing good health: **feeling healthy • a healthy appetite. 2** causing good health. **3** in a good state: **a healthy economy. 4** COLLOQ considerable: **a healthy sum.** ■ **healthily** ADV.
■ **healthiness** N.

heap N **1** a collection of things in an untidy pile or mass. **2** (usu **heaps**) COLLOQ a large amount or number: **heaps of time. 3** COLLOQ something that is very old and not working properly.
➤ VB, TR & INTR (also **heap up**) to collect or be collected together in a heap.
➤ ADV (**heaps**) COLLOQ very much.

hear VB (**heard**) **1** TR & INTR to perceive (sounds) with the ear. **2** INTR to be informed. **3** INTR (usu **hear from**) to be contacted (by them). **4** LAW to listen to and judge (a case). ■ **hearer** N.
◆ **hear! hear!** an expression of agreement.
◆ **not hear of sth** not to allow it to happen.

hearing N **1** the sense that involves the perception of sound. **2** the distance within which something can be heard: **within hearing. 3** an opportunity to state one's case: **gave him a fair hearing. 4** a judicial investigation and listening to evidence etc, esp without a jury.

hearing aid N a small electronic device worn in or behind the ear by a partially deaf person to help them hear more clearly.

hearken or (sometimes US) **harken** VB, INTR (often **hearken to**) OLD USE to listen or pay attention (to someone or something).

hearsay N rumour; gossip.

hearse N a vehicle for carrying a coffin.

heart N **1** a muscular organ that contracts and pumps blood round the body. **2** this organ considered as the centre of thoughts, emotions, conscience, etc. **3** courage and enthusiasm: **take heart. 4** the central part: **the heart of the town. 5** the most important part: **the heart of the problem. 6** a symbol (♥) representing the heart. **7** CARDS **a** (**hearts**) one of the four suits of playing-cards, with the heart-shaped (♥) symbols on them; **b** a playing-card of this suit.

◆ **break sb's heart** to cause them great sorrow.

◆ **by heart** by or from memory.

◆ **take sth to heart** to pay great attention to it or be very affected by it.

heartache N great sadness.

heart attack N, NON-TECHNICAL a sudden severe chest pain caused by failure of part of the heart muscle to function.

heartbeat N 1 the pulsation of the heart. 2 a single pumping action of the heart.

heartbreak N very great sorrow or grief. ■ **heartbreaking** ADJ. ■ **heart-broken** ADJ.

heartburn N a burning feeling caused by indigestion.

hearten VB, TR & INTR to make or become happier, more cheerful or encouraged. ■ **heartening** ADJ.

heart failure N a condition in which the heart fails to pump sufficient blood.

heartfelt ADJ sincerely and deeply felt.

hearth N 1 the floor of a fireplace, or the area surrounding it. 2 the home.

heartland N a central or important area.

heartless ADJ cruel; very unkind. ■ **heartlessly** ADV. ■ **heartlessness** N.

heart-rending ADJ causing great sorrow.

heart-searching N the close examination of one's deepest feelings and conscience.

heartstrings PL N a person's deep emotions.

heart-throb N, COLLOQ someone, esp a male actor or singer, many people find attractive.

heart-to-heart N an intimate and candid conversation. Also ADJ.

heart-warming ADJ gratifying; pleasing.

hearty ADJ (*-ier, -iest*) 1 very friendly and warm in manner. 2 strong or enthusiastic: **hale and hearty**. 3 large: **a hearty breakfast**. ■ **heartily** ADV. ■ **heartiness** N.

heat N 1 a form of energy that is stored as the energy of vibration or motion of the atoms or molecules of a material. 2 a high temperature; warmth; the state of being hot. 3 intensity of feeling: **the heat of anger**. 4 SPORT **a** a preliminary contest which eliminates some competitors; **b** a single section in a contest. ➤ VB, TR & INTR 1 to make or become hot or warm. 2 to make or become intense or excited. ◆ **in** or **on heat** of some female mammals: ready to mate.

heated ADJ 1 having been made hot or warm. 2 angry or excited. ■ **heatedly** ADV.

heater N 1 an apparatus for heating a room, water in a tank, etc. 2 US SLANG a pistol.

heath N 1 an area of open land, usu with acidic soil, dominated by low-growing evergreen shrubs, esp heathers. 2 a low evergreen shrub found esp on open moors and heaths.

heathen N (*heathens* or *heathen*) someone who does not adhere to a particular religion, esp when regarded by a community that does follow that religion. **Also** AS ADJ.

heather N a low evergreen moor or heath shrub with small bell-shaped flowers.

Heath-Robinson ADJ of a machine or device: ludicrously impractical in design.

heating N a system for maintaining the temperature inside a room or building at a level higher than that of the surroundings.

heatstroke N a condition caused by overexposure to heat, characterized by lassitude, fainting and high fever.

heatwave N a prolonged period of unusually hot dry weather.

heave VB (*heaved* or (IN NAUT SENSES) *hove*) 1 to lift or pull with great effort. 2 COLLOQ to throw something heavy. 3 INTR to rise and fall heavily. 4 INTR, COLLOQ to retch or vomit. ➤ N an act or instance of heaving. ◆ **the heave** or **the heave-ho** COLLOQ dismissal or rejection.

heaven N 1 the place believed to be the abode of God, angels and the righteous after death. 2 (usu **the heavens**) the sky. 3 a place or the state of great happiness or bliss.

heavenly ADJ 1 COLLOQ very pleasant; beautiful. 2 situated in or coming from heaven or the sky. 3 holy. ■ **heavenliness** N.

heaven-sent ADJ very lucky or timely.

heavy ADJ (-*ier, -iest*) 1 having great weight. 2 of breathing: loud, because of excitement, exhaustion, etc. 3 great in amount, size, intensity, etc: **heavy traffic** • **heavy fighting** • **heavy rain** • **heavy artillery**. 4 ungraceful and coarse: **heavy features**. 5 of food: difficult to digest: **a heavy meal**. 6 having a great or relatively high density: **a heavy metal**. 7 of the sky: dark and cloudy. 8 needing a lot of physical or mental effort. 9 of literature, music, etc: serious in tone and content. 10 physically and mentally slow. 11 of soil: wet and soft. ➤ N (-*ies*) 1 SLANG a large, violent man; a villain in a play, film, etc. 2 SCOT a dark beer. ■ **heavily** ADV. ■ **heaviness** N.

heavy-duty ADJ designed to resist or withstand very hard wear or use.

heavy going N difficult or slow progress. ➤ ADJ (**heavy-going**) difficult to deal with or to get further with.

heavy-handed ADJ 1 clumsy and awkward. 2 too severe or strict; oppressive. ■ **heavy-handedly** ADV. ■ **heavy-handedness** N.

heavy industry N a factory or factories involving the use of large or heavy equipment, eg coal-mining, ship-building, etc.

heavy metal N loud repetitive rock music.

heavyweight N 1 the class for the heaviest competitors in boxing, wrestling and weightlifting. 2 a boxer, etc of this weight class. 3 COLLOQ a powerful or influential person.

hebdomadal ADJ weekly.

Hebrew N 1 the ancient language of the Hebrews and its modern form spoken by Jews in Israel. 2 a member of an ancient people claiming descent from Abraham. ➤ ADJ of the Hebrew language or people.

heckle VB, TR & INTR to interrupt (a speaker) with critical shouts and jeers. ■ **heckler** N.

hectare N in the metric system: a metric unit of land measurement, equivalent to 100 ares, or 10 000 square metres (2.471 acres).

hectic ADJ agitated; very excited, flustered or rushed. ■ **hectically** ADV.

hector VB, TR & INTR to bully or threaten.

he'd CONTRACTION 1 he had. 2 he would.

hedge N a boundary formed by bushes and shrubs planted close together. ➤ VB 1 to surround with a hedge. 2 to avoid making a decision or giving a clear answer.

hedgehog N a small, prickly-backed, insectivorous, nocturnal mammal that can roll itself into a tight ball for protection.

hedgerow N a row of bushes, hedges or trees forming a boundary.

hedonism N 1 the belief that pleasure is the most important achievement or the highest good in life. 2 the pursuit of and devotion to pleasure. ■ **hedonist** N. ■ **hedonistic** ADJ.

the heebie-jeebies PL N, SLANG feelings or fits of nervousness or anxiety.

heed VB to pay attention to or take notice of (something, esp advice or a warning, etc). ➤ N careful attention. ■ **heedful** ADJ.

heedless ADJ taking no care; careless. ■ **heedlessly** ADV.

hee-haw N the bray of a donkey. ➤ VB, INTR to bray.

heel[1] N 1 the rounded back part of the foot below the ankle. 2 the part of a sock, stocking and tights that covers the heel. 3 the part of a shoe, boot and other such footwear which supports the heel. 4 anything shaped or functioning like the heel, eg that part of the palm near the wrist. 5 the end of a loaf. 6 SLANG a despicable person. ➤ VB 1 to strike using the heel. 2 to repair or fit a new heel on (a shoe, etc). ◆ **cool** or **kick one's heels** to be kept waiting. ◆ **dig one's heels in** to behave stubbornly. ◆ **down at heel** untidy; in poor condition or circumstances. ◆ **take to one's heels** to run away.

◆ **to heel 1** esp of a dog: walking obediently at the heels of the person in charge of it. **2** under control; submissive.

heel² VB **1** INTR (often **heel over**) to lean over to one side; to list. **2** to cause to tilt.

hefty ADJ (**-ier, -iest**) COLLOQ **1** of a person: strong, robust or muscular. **2** of an object, blow, etc: large, heavy or powerful. ■ **heftily** ADV. ■ **heftiness** N.

hegemony N (**-ies**) authority or control, esp of one state over another within a confederation.

heifer N a cow over one year old that has either not calved, or has calved only once.

height N **1** the condition of being high. **2** the distance from the base of something to the top. **3** a high place or location. **4** the highest point of elevation; the summit. **5** the most intense part or climax: **the height of battle**. **6** an extreme example: **the height of stupidity**.

heighten VB to make higher, greater, etc.

heinous ADJ extremely wicked or evil; odious.

heir N **1** someone who by law receives or is entitled to receive property, wealth, a title, etc when the previous owner or holder dies. **2** someone who is successor to a position, eg leadership. ■ **heirless** ADJ.

heir apparent N (**heirs apparent**) LAW an heir whose claim to an inheritance cannot be challenged, even by the birth of another heir.

heiress N a female heir.

heirloom N an object that has been handed down through a family over many generations.

heir presumptive N (**heirs presumptive**) LAW an heir whose claim to an inheritance may be challenged by the birth of another heir.

heist N, N AMER, SLANG a robbery. ➤ VB to steal or rob in a heist.

helical ADJ relating to or like a helix; coiled.

helicopter N an aircraft that is lifted and propelled by rotating blades above its body.

heliograph N an instrument which uses mirrors to reflect light from the Sun in flashes as a way of sending messages.

heliotrope N a garden plant with small fragrant lilac–blue flowers.

helium N, CHEM a colourless odourless gas.

helix N (**-ices** or **-ixes**) **1** a spiral or coiled structure. **2** GEOM a spiral–shaped curve on the lateral surface of a cylinder or cone.

hell N **1** the place or state of infinite punishment for the wicked after death. **2** any place or state which causes extensive pain and misery. ➤ EXCLAM, COLLOQ expressing annoyance.
◆ **a hell of a** or **one hell of a** COLLOQ a very great or significant: **one hell of a row**.
◆ **as hell** absolutely; extremely: **mad as hell**.
◆ **for the hell of it** COLLOQ for the sake of it.
◆ **give sb hell** COLLOQ **1** to punish or rebuke them severely. **2** to make things extremely difficult for them.
◆ **hell for leather** COLLOQ extremely fast.
◆ **like hell 1** very much, fast, etc: **ran like hell**. **2** not in any circumstances: **Like hell I will**.
◆ **what the hell 1** what does it matter?; who cares? **2** an expression of surprise and amazement: **What the hell are you doing?**

he'll CONTRACTION **1** he will. **2** he shall.

hellbent ADJ (usu **hellbent on sth**) COLLOQ recklessly determined or intent about it.

hellhole N a disgusting, evil, etc place.

hellish ADJ **1** relating to or resembling hell. **2** COLLOQ horrifying or difficult.

hello, hallo or **hullo** EXCLAM **1** used as a greeting, to attract attention or to start a telephone conversation. **2** used to express discovery: **Hello! What's going on here?**

hellraiser N, COLLOQ a boisterously debauched person.

helm N, NAUT the steering apparatus of a boat or ship, such as a wheel or tiller.

helmet N a protective head covering, worn eg by firefighters, soldiers, motorcyclists, etc.

helmsman N someone who steers a boat.

help VB **1** to contribute towards the success of something; to assist or aid. **2** to give the means

to do something. **3** to relieve a difficult situation or burden. **4** to refrain: **I couldn't help laughing**. **5** to prevent: **I can't help the bad weather**. **6** INTR to give assistance.
➤ N **1** an act of helping. **2** means or strength given to another for a particular purpose. **3** someone who is employed to help. **4** a remedy or relief. ■ **helper** N.
◆ **help (sb) out** to offer help.
◆ **help oneself (to sth) 1** to take (a serving of food, etc) for oneself. **2** to take (it) without permission or without having any right to.

helpful ADJ giving help or aid; useful.

helping N a single portion of food.

helpless ADJ **1** unable or unfit to do anything for oneself. **2** weak and defenceless.

helpline N a telephone service that people with a particular problem can call in order to contact qualified advisers.

helpmate N a friend or partner.

helter-skelter ADJ hurried and disorderly.
➤ ADV in a hurried and disorientated manner.
➤ N, BRIT a spiral slide on the outside of a tower in a fairground or playground.

hem[1] N a bottom edge or border of a garment, piece of cloth, etc, folded over and sewn down.
➤ VB (**-mm-**) TR & INTR to form a border or edge on a garment, piece of cloth, etc.
◆ **hem sth** or **sb in** to surround it or them.

hem[2] EXCLAM a slight clearing of the throat or cough to show hesitation or to draw attention.
➤ N such a sound.
➤ VB (**-mm-**) INTR to utter this kind of sound.

hemisphere N **1** one half of a sphere. **2** either half of the Earth's sphere, when divided into the northern and southern hemispheres, or into the eastern and western hemispheres.

hemline N the level of a hem on a skirt, etc.

hemlock N **1** a poisonous umbelliferous plant with small white flowers and a spotted stem. **2** the poison extracted from this plant.

hemp N **1** (in full **Indian hemp**) an Asian plant grown commercially for its stem fibres, a drug and an oil. **2** any drug obtained from this plant,

eg cannabis or marijuana. **3** the coarse fibre obtained from the stem of this plant, used to make rope, tough cloth, etc. ■ **hempen** ADJ.

hen N a female bird, esp a domestic fowl.

hence ADV **1** for this reason. **2** from this time onwards. **3** OLD USE from this place or origin.

henceforth ADV from now on.

henchman N a faithful supporter or right-hand man.

henna N reddish-brown dye obtained from the leaves of a small Asian and N African shrub, used for colouring the hair and decorating the skin.

hen party and **hen night** N a party attended by women only, esp one to celebrate the future marriage of one of the group.

henpecked ADJ, COLLOQ usu of a man: dominated by a wife, girlfriend, etc.

henry N (*henry, henrys* or *henries*) in the SI system: the unit of electrical inductance.

hepatic ADJ **1** of the liver. **2** liver-coloured.

hepatitis N inflammation of the liver, usu caused by a viral infection.

heptagon N a plane figure with seven angles and sides. ■ **heptagonal** ADJ.

heptathlon N an athletic contest, usu restricted to women, comprising seven events.

her PRONOUN **1** the object form of **she**: We all like her • send it to her. **2** the possessive form of **she**: Her car is outside.
➤ ADJ referring to a female person or animal, or something personified as female, eg a ship: went to her house • gave the cat her milk.

herald N **1** a person who announces important news, or an officer whose task it is to make public proclamations. **2** someone or something that is a sign of what is to come. **3** an officer responsible for keeping a record of the genealogies of noble families.
➤ VB to be a sign of the approach of something: clouds heralding a storm. ■ **heraldic** ADJ.

heraldry N the art of recording genealogies,

and blazoning coats of arms.

herb N **1** a flowering plant which has no woody stem above the ground. **2** an aromatic plant such as rosemary, mint and parsley, used in cookery or in herbal medicine. ■ **herbal** ADJ.

herbaceous ADJ of a plant: relating to or having the characteristics of a herb.

herbage N herbaceous vegetation covering a large area, esp for use as pasture.

herbalist and **herbist** N **1** a person who researches, collects and sells herbs and plants. **2** a person who practises herbal medicine. ■ **herbalism** N.

herbarium N (-*ia* or -*iums*) a classified collection of preserved plants.

herbicide N a substance used to kill weeds, etc. ■ **herbicidal** ADJ.

herbivore N an animal that feeds on plants. ■ **herbivorous** ADJ.

herculean ADJ requiring great strength or an enormous effort: *a herculean task*.

herd N **1** a company of animals, esp large ones, that habitually remain together. **2** a collection of livestock or domestic animals, esp cows or pigs. **3** (ALSO IN COMBINATION) a person who looks after a herd: *a goatherd*. **4** a large crowd of people. **5** (**the herd**) people in general, esp behaving in an unimaginative way.
➤ VB **1** INTR to gather in a crowd like an animal in a herd. **2** to look after or tend a herd of (animals). **3** to group (animals) together.

here ADV **1** at, in or to this place. **2** at this point, stage or time. **3** used with **this, these**, etc for emphasis: *this chair here*.
➤ N this place or location.
➤ EXCLAM **1** calling for attention. **2** calling attention to one's own presence.
◆ **here and there** in various places; thinly.
◆ **here's to** used when proposing a toast: *Here's to the happy couple*.
◆ **neither here nor there** of no particular importance or relevance.

hereabouts or **hereabout** ADV around or near this place; within this area.

hereafter ADV, FORMAL **1** after this time. **2** LAW from this point on.
◆ **the hereafter** a future stage; the afterlife.

hereby ADV, FORMAL **1** not far off. **2** as a result of this or by this.

hereditary ADJ **1** descending or acquiring by inheritance. **2** passed down or transmitted genetically to offspring: *a hereditary disease*.

heredity N (-*ies*) **1** the transmission of recognizable and genetically based characteristics from one generation to the next. **2** the total of such characteristics inherited.

herein ADV **1** FORMAL in this case or respect. **2** LAW & FORMAL contained within this letter or document, etc.

hereinafter ADV, LAW & FORMAL later in this document or form, etc.

hereof ADV, LAW & FORMAL concerning this.

hereon ADV, FORMAL on, upon or to this point.

heresy N (-*ies*) **1** an opinion or belief contrary to the authorized teaching of a particular religion. **2** an opinion that contradicts a conventional or traditional belief.

heretic N **1** someone who believes in, endorses or practises heresy. **2** someone who has views and opinions that conflict with those commonly held. ■ **heretical** ADJ. ■ **heretically** ADV.

hereto ADV, LAW & FORMAL **1** to this place or document. **2** for this purpose.

heretofore ADV, LAW & FORMAL before or up to this time; formerly.

hereupon ADV, LAW & FORMAL **1** on this. **2** immediately after or as a result of this.

herewith ADV, LAW & FORMAL with this; enclosed or together with this letter, etc.

heritable ADJ **1** of property: able to be inherited or passed down. **2** of people: able or in a position to inherit property.

heritage N **1** something that is inherited. **2** the characteristics, qualities, property, etc inherited at birth. **3** the buildings, countryside, cultural traditions, etc of a people or country.

hermaphrodite N a person, plant or animal that has both male and female reproductive organs. Also AS ADJ. ■ **hermaphroditic** ADJ.

hermetic and **hermetical** ADJ perfectly closed or airtight. ■ **hermetically** ADV.

hermit N **1** an ascetic who leads an isolated life for religious reasons. **2** someone who lives a solitary life. ■ **hermitic** ADJ.

hermitage N **1** the dwelling-place of a hermit. **2** a secluded place or abode; a retreat.

hernia N the protrusion of an organ (esp part of the viscera) through an opening or weak spot in the wall of its surroundings.

hero N (-oes) **1** a man distinguished by his bravery or his achievements. **2** in novels, plays, films, etc: a principal male character.

heroic ADJ **1** supremely courageous and brave. **2** of heroes or heroines. ■ **heroically** ADV.

heroics PL N **1** overdramatic or extravagant speech. **2** excessively bold behaviour.

heroin N a powerful analgesic drug produced from morphine.

heroine N **1** a woman distinguished by her bravery or her achievements. **2** in novels, plays, films, etc: a principal female character.

heroism N heroic qualities or behaviour.

heron N a large wading bird with a long neck and legs, and usu with grey and white plumage.

hero-worship N an excessive fondness and admiration for someone.
➤ VB to have great admiration for someone.

herpes N any of various contagious skin diseases caused by a virus and giving rise to watery blisters. ■ **herpetic** ADJ.

herring N (*herring* or *herrings*) a small edible silvery sea-fish, found in northern waters.

herringbone N a zigzag pattern, like the spine of a herring, woven into cloth.

hers PRONOUN the one or ones belonging to **her**.
◆ **of hers** relating to or belonging to **her**.

herself PRONOUN **1** the reflexive form of **her** and **she**: She made herself a dress. **2** used for emphasis: the Queen herself. **3** her normal self or true character: She isn't feeling herself. **4** (also **by herself**) alone; without help.

hertz N (PL *hertz*) in the SI system: the unit of frequency, equal to one cycle per second.

he's CONTRACTION **1** he is. **2** he has.

hesitant ADJ holding back; doubtful. ■ **hesitance** and **hesitancy** N. ■ **hesitantly** ADV.

hesitate VB, INTR **1** to falter or delay in speaking, acting or making a decision. **2** to be unwilling to do or say something. ■ **hesitatingly** ADV. ■ **hesitation** N.

hessian N a coarse cloth, similar to sacking, made from hemp or jute.

heterodoxy N a belief, esp a religious one, that is different from the one most commonly accepted. ■ **heterodox** ADJ.

heterogeneous ADJ composed of parts, people, things, etc not related to each other, or of different kinds. ■ **heterogeneity** N.

heterologous ADJ not homologous; different in form and origin. ■ **heterology** N.

heterosexual ADJ **1** having a sexual attraction to people of the opposite sex. **2** of a relationship: between a man and a woman.
➤ N a heterosexual person.
■ **heterosexuality** N.

het up ADJ, COLLOQ angry; agitated.

heuristic ADJ serving or leading to discover.

hew VB (PA P *hewn*) **1** to cut, fell or sever something using an axe, sword, etc. **2** to carve or shape something from wood or stone.

hex N **1** a witch, wizard or wicked spell. **2** anything that brings bad luck.
➤ VB to bring misfortune; to bewitch.

hexad N any group or series of six.

hexadecimal ADJ, COMP relating to or being a number system with a base of 16.
➤ N **1** such a system. **2** the notation used in the system. **3** a number so expressed.

hexagon N a plane figure with six sides and angles. ■ **hexagonal** ADJ.

hexameter N a line or verse with six feet.

hey EXCLAM, COLLOQ **1** a shout of surprise or dismay. **2** a call to attract attention.

heyday N a period of great success, power, prosperity, popularity, etc.

HGV ABBREV, BRIT heavy goods vehicle.

hi EXCLAM, COLLOQ a casual form of greeting.

hiatus N (*hiatus* or *hiatuses*) a gap.

hibernate VB, INTR of certain animals: to pass the winter sleeping. ■ **hibernation** N.

Hibernian LITERARY, ADJ relating to Ireland. ➢ N a native of Ireland.

hibiscus N a tropical tree or shrub with large brightly coloured flowers.

hiccup and **hiccough** N **1 a** an involuntary spasm of the diaphragm; **b** a burping sound caused by this. **2** COLLOQ a temporary and usu minor setback, difficulty or interruption. ➢ VB **1** INTR to produce a hiccup or hiccups. **2** INTR to falter, hesitate or malfunction.

hick N, COLLOQ **1** someone from the country. **2** an unsophisticated person.

hickory N (*-ies*) **1** a N American tree of the walnut family. **2** its heavy strong wood.

hide[1] VB (*hid, hidden*) **1** to put, keep or conceal (something) from sight. **2** to keep secret. **3** INTR to conceal (oneself). ➢ N a concealed shelter. ■ **hidden** ADJ.

hide[2] N the skin of an animal, esp a large one.

hide-and-seek N a game in which one person seeks the others who have hidden.

hideaway and **hideout** N a refuge or retreat; concealment.

hidebound ADJ, DEROG reluctant to accept new ideas or opinions.

hideous ADJ **1** of a person or thing: dreadful; revolting. **2** frightening; horrific; ghastly.

hiding N **1** the state of being hidden or concealed. **2** COLLOQ a severe beating.

◆ **be on a hiding to nothing** COLLOQ to be in a situation in which a favourable outcome is impossible.

hie VB (*hied, hieing* or *hying*) ARCHAIC **1** INTR to hasten or hurry. **2** to urge.

hierarchy N (*-ies*) **1** a system that classifies people or things according to rank, importance, etc. **2** the operation of such a system or the people who control it. ■ **hierarchical** or **hierarchic** ADJ.

hieroglyph and **hieroglyphic** N a character or symbol representing a word, syllable, sound or idea, esp in ancient Egyptian.

hi-fi ADJ of high fidelity. ➢ N a set of equipment, usu consisting of an amplifier, tape deck, CD player, etc.

higgledy-piggledy ADV, ADJ, COLLOQ haphazard; in confusion; disorderly.

high ADJ **1** elevated; tall; towering: **high buildings**. **2** being a specific height: **a hundred feet high**. **3** far up from a base point: **a high branch • a high mountain**. **4** intense or advanced: **a high wind**. **5** at the peak or climax: **high summer**. **6** of sound: acute in pitch. **7** of meat: partially decomposed or tainted. **8** elated; over-excited. **9** COLLOQ under the influence of drugs or alcohol: **high on E**. ➢ ADV at or to a height; in or into an elevated position: **The plane flew high**. ➢ N **1** a high point or level. **2** the maximum or highest level. **3** COLLOQ a state of ecstasy and euphoria, often produced by drugs or alcohol: **on a high**. **4** METEOROL an anticyclone.
◆ **high and dry 1** stranded or helpless; defenceless. **2** of boats: out of the water.
◆ **on one's high horse** COLLOQ having an attitude imagined superiority.

highball N, chiefly N AMER an alcoholic drink of spirits and soda served with ice in a long glass.

highbrow often DEROG, N an intellectual or learned person. ➢ ADJ of art, literature, etc: intellectual; cultured.

high-chair N a tall chair with a small attached table for young children.

high-class ADJ **1** of very high quality.

2 superior and distinguished.

high court N **1** a supreme court. **2** (**the High Court**) the supreme court for civil cases in England and Wales.

high-density ADJ, COMP of a disk: having a very compact data-storage capacity.

higher education N, BRIT education beyond secondary school level, eg at university.

high explosive N a detonating explosive of immense power and rapid action, eg dynamite.

highfalutin and **highfaluting** ADJ, INFORMAL ridiculously pompous or affected.

high fidelity N an accurate and high quality reproduction of sound.

high-five N, esp N AMER a sign of greeting or celebration, involving the slapping together of raised palms.

high-flier or **high-flyer** N **1** an ambitious person, likely to achieve their goals. **2** someone skilled in their career. ■ **high-flying** ADJ.

high-flown ADJ often of language: sounding grand but lacking real substance; rhetorical.

high frequency N a radio frequency between 3 and 30 megahertz.

high-handed ADJ overbearing and arrogant.

high jump N **1** an athletic event where competitors jump over a high bar. **2** COLLOQ a severe punishment or reproof: He's for the high jump. ■ **high-jumper** N.

highland N **1** (often **highlands**) a mountainous area of land. **2** (**the Highlands**) the mountainous area of northern Scotland. ➤ ADJ of or characteristic of highland regions.

high-level language N, COMP a programming language which allows users to employ instructions that more closely resemble their own language, rather than machine code.

high life N (usu **the high life**) luxurious living associated with the very wealthy.

highlight N **1** the most memorable or outstanding feature, event, etc. **2** (**highlights**) lighter patches or streaks in the hair. ➤ VB **1** to draw attention to or emphasize something. **2** to overlay sections of (a text) with a bright colour for special attention. **3** to put highlights in (someone's hair).

highly ADV **1** very; extremely: highly gratified. **2** with approval: speak highly of her. **3** at or to a high degree: He is rated highly in his office.

highly strung and **highly-strung** ADJ excitable; easily upset or sensitive.

high-minded ADJ having or showing noble and moral ideas and principles, etc.

highness N **1** (**Highness**) an address used for royalty, usu as **Her Highness, His Highness** and **Your Highness**. **2** the state of being high.

high point N the most memorable, successful, etc moment or occasion.

high-powered ADJ **1** very powerful or energetic. **2** very important or responsible.

high-pressure ADJ **1** having or using air, water, etc at a pressure higher than that of the atmosphere: high-pressure water reactor. **2** COLLOQ forceful: high-pressure negotiations. **3** involving considerable stress or intense activity: a high-pressure job.

high priest and **high priestess** N the chief priest or priestess of a cult.

high-rise ADJ of a building: having many storeys: high-rise flats. ➤ N, COLLOQ a building with many storeys.

high road N a public or main road.

high school N a secondary school in the UK.

high seas PL N the open ocean not under the control of any country.

high society N fashionable wealthy society.

high spirits PL N a positive, happy and exhilarated frame of mind.

high spot N an outstanding feature or event.

high street N **1** (also **High Street**) the main shopping street of a town. **2** (**the high street**) shops generally; the retail trade.

hightail VB, N AMER COLLOQ (usu **hightail it**) to hurry away: Let's hightail it out of here.

high tea N, BRIT a meal served in the late afternoon.

high-tech, **hi-tech** or **hi-tec** ADJ using, designed by, etc sophisticated technology.

high-tension ADJ carrying high-voltage electrical currents.

high tide and **high water** N 1 the highest level of a tide. 2 the time when this occurs.

high time ADV, COLLOQ the right or latest time by which something ought to have been done: It's high time you went home.

high treason N treason or betrayal against one's sovereign or country.

high-water mark N 1 a the highest level reached by a tide, river, etc; b a mark indicating this. 2 the highest point reached by anything.

highway N, chiefly N AMER 1 a public road. 2 the main or normal way or route.

highwayman N, HIST a robber, usu on horseback, who robs people travelling by road.

high wire N a tightrope stretched high above the ground for performing.

hijack VB 1 to take control of a vehicle, esp an aircraft, and force it to go somewhere. 2 to stop and rob (a vehicle). 3 to steal (goods) in transit. ■ **hijacker** N. ■ **hijacking** N.

hike N a long walk or tour, usu in the country. ➤ VB 1 INTR to go on or for a hike. 2 (often **hike sth up**) to pull up, raise or lift it. ■ **hiker** N.

hilarious ADJ extravagantly funny. ■ **hilariously** ADV. ■ **hilarity** N.

hill N 1 a raised area of land, smaller than a mountain. 2 an incline on a road. ■ **hilly** ADJ. ◆ **over the hill** COLLOQ past one's peak.

hillbilly N (-ies) esp US DEROG any unsophisticated person, particularly from a remote, mountainous or rustic area.

hillock N 1 a small hill. 2 a small heap or pile.

hillwalking N the activity of walking in hilly or mountainous country. ■ **hillwalker** N.

hilt N the handle, esp of a sword, dagger, etc.

him PRONOUN the object form of **he**: We saw him • We gave it to him.

himself PRONOUN 1 the reflexive form of **him** and **he**: He made himself a drink. 2 used for emphasis: the Pope himself. 3 his normal self: He's still not feeling himself after the flu. 4 (also **by himself**) alone; without help.

hind[1] ADJ in the area behind: hind legs.

hind[2] N (*hind* or *hinds*) a female red deer, usu older than three years of age.

hinder[1] VB to delay or hold back; to prevent the progress of something.

hinder[2] ADJ at the back.

Hindi N 1 one of the official languages of India, a literary form of Hindustani. 2 a group of Indo-European languages spoken in N India.

hindquarters PL N the rear parts of an animal.

hindrance N 1 an obstacle or prevention. 2 the act or an instance of hindering.

hindsight N knowledge after an event.

Hindu N 1 someone who practises Hinduism. 2 a native or citizen of Hindustan or India. ➤ ADJ of or referring to Hindus or Hinduism.

Hinduism N the main religion of India, that includes the worship of several gods and the arrangement of society into a caste system.

hinge N 1 the movable hook or joint by which a door is fastened to a door-frame or a lid is fastened to a box, etc. 2 BIOL the pivoting point from which a bivalve opens and closes. ➤ VB (*hinging*) to provide a hinge or hinges for something. ◆ **hinge on sth** to depend on it: Everything hinges on their decision.

hinny N (-ies) the offspring of a stallion and a female donkey or ass.

hint N 1 a distant or indirect indication or allusion; an insinuation or implication. 2 a helpful suggestion or tip. 3 a small amount; a slight impression or suggestion of something: a hint of perfume. ➤ VB to indicate indirectly.

hinterland N 1 the region lying inland from the coast or a river. 2 an area dependent on a nearby port, commercial site, etc.

hip[1] N 1 the haunch or upper fleshy part of the thigh just below the waist. 2 the joint between the thigh bone and the pelvis.

hip[2] N the red fruit of a rose, esp a wild variety.

hip[3] EXCLAM used to encourage a united cheer: Hip, hip, hooray!

hip[4] ADJ (*hipper, hippest*) COLLOQ informed about current fashions in music, clothes, etc.

hip bath N a bath for sitting in.

hip flask N a flask, esp for alcoholic drink, small enough to be carried in the hip pocket.

hip-hop N a popular culture movement originating in the USA, incorporating rap music and graffiti art.

hippie or **hippy** N (*-ies*) COLLOQ esp in the 1960s: someone, typically young, with long hair and wearing brightly-coloured clothes, rebelling against the more conservative standards and values of society.

hippo N, COLLOQ short for **hippopotamus**.

hippodrome N 1 a variety theatre or circus. 2 in ancient Greece and Rome: a racecourse.

hippopotamus N (*-muses* or *-mi*) a hoofed mammal with a large head and muzzle, and short stout legs, found in parts of Africa.

hipsters PL N trousers which hang from the hips rather than the waist.

hire VB 1 to procure the temporary use of (something) in exchange for payment. 2 to employ (someone) for wages.
➤ N 1 payment for the use or hire of something. 2 wages paid for services. 3 an act of hiring. ■ **hirable** or **hireable** ADJ. ■ **hirer** N.
◆ **for hire** ready for hiring.

hireling N, DEROG 1 a hired servant. 2 someone whose work is motivated solely by money.

hire-purchase N, BRIT a system where a hired article becomes owned by the hirer after a specified number of payments.

hirsute ADJ hairy; shaggy. ■ **hirsuteness** N.

his ADJ the possessive form of **he**: His car is outside.
➤ PRONOUN the one or ones belonging to **him**.
◆ **of his** relating or belonging to **him**.

Hispanic ADJ of or from Spain, the Spanish or Spanish-speaking communities.

hiss N a sharp sibilant sound like a sustained **s**.
➤ VB 1 INTR of an animal, such as a snake or goose, or a person: to make such a sound. 2 to show (disapproval of something) by hissing.

histamine N, BIOCHEM a chemical compound released by body tissues during allergic reactions, injury, etc.

histogram N a statistical graph with vertical rectangles of differing heights.

histology N the study of the microscopic structure of cells and tissues of living organisms. ■ **histologist** N.

historian N a person who studies history.

historic ADJ famous or significant in history.

historical ADJ 1 relevant to or about history. 2 of the study of a subject: based on its development over a period of time. 3 referring to something that actually existed or took place; authentic. ■ **historically** ADV.

historicism N 1 the idea that historical events are determined by natural laws. 2 the theory that sociological circumstances are historically determined. ■ **historicist** N, ADJ.

historicity N historical truth or actuality.

history N (*-ies*) 1 an account of past events and developments. 2 the knowledge of past events associated with a particular nation, the world, a person, etc. 3 the academic discipline of understanding and interpreting past events.
◆ **be history** COLLOQ to be finished, dead, etc.
◆ **make history** to do something significant.

histrionic ADJ of behaviour, etc: theatrical.
➤ N (**histrionics**) theatrical behaviour done to get attention. ■ **histrionically** ADV.

hit VB (PA T, PA P *hit*, PR P *hitting*) 1 to strike (someone or something). 2 to affect suddenly

and severely. **3** to reach: **hit an all-time low.**
➤ N **1** a stroke or blow. **2** SPORT a successful stroke or shot. **3** COLLOQ something of extreme popularity or success. **4** SLANG a murder, esp one by organized gangs. **5** SLANG a shot of a hard drug.
◆ **hit it off** (**with sb**) to get on well (with them).

hit-and-miss or **hit-or-miss** ADJ, COLLOQ without any order or planning; random.

hitch VB **1** to move (something) jerkily. **2** (also **hitch up**) to hook, fasten or tether: **hitched the caravan to the car. 3** COLLOQ **a** INTR to hitchhike; **b** to obtain (a lift) as a hitchhiker.
➤ N **1** a small temporary setback or difficulty. **2** a jerk; a sudden movement. **3** a knot for attaching two pieces of rope together.
◆ **get hitched** COLLOQ to get married.

hitchhike VB, INTR to travel by obtaining lifts from passing vehicles. ■ **hitchhiker** N.

hi-tec and **hi-tech** see **high tech**

hither ADV, OLD USE to this place.
◆ **hither and thither** this way and that.

hitherto ADV up to this or that time.

hit list N, COLLOQ a list of targeted victims.

hit man N, COLLOQ someone hired to assassinate or attack others.

HIV ABBREV human immunodeficiency virus, which often leads to AIDS.

hive N **1** a box or basket for housing bees. **2** a colony of bees living in such a place. **3** a scene of extreme animation: **a hive of activity.**
◆ **hive sth off** to separate (a company, etc) from a larger organization.

hives PL N, NON-TECHNICAL urticaria.

hiya EXCLAM, SLANG a familiar greeting.

HM ABBREV Her or His Majesty or Majesty's.

ho EXCLAM **1** a call or shout to attract attention or indicate direction or destination. **2** (esp **ho-ho**) representation of laughter.

hoar ADJ, esp POETIC white or greyish-white.

hoard N a store of money, food or treasure, usu

one hidden away for use in the future.
➤ VB, TR & INTR to store or gather (food, money or treasure), often secretly. ■ **hoarder** N.

hoarding N **1** a screen of light boards, esp round a building site. **2** a similar wooden surface for displaying advertisements, etc.

hoarfrost N the white morning frost on grass, leaves, etc formed by freezing dew.

hoarse ADJ **1** of the voice: rough and husky. **2** of a person: having a hoarse voice.
■ **hoarsely** ADV. ■ **hoarseness** N.

hoary ADJ (**-ier, -iest**) **1** white or grey with age. **2** ancient. **3** overused; trite. ■ **hoariness** N.

hoax N a deceptive trick.
➤ VB to deceive with a hoax. ■ **hoaxer** N.

hob N the flat surface on which pots are heated.

hobble VB **1** INTR to walk awkwardly and unsteadily by taking short unsteady steps. **2** to loosely tie the legs of (a horse) together, to inhibit its movement. **3** to hamper or impede.
➤ N **1** an awkward and irregular gait. **2** something used to hamper an animal's feet.

hobbledehoy N an awkward youth.

hobby[1] N (**-ies**) an activity or occupation carried out in one's spare time for amusement.

hobby[2] N (**-ies**) a small species of falcon.

hobby-horse N **1** a child's toy consisting of a long stick with a horse's head. **2** a subject which a person talks about frequently.

hobgoblin N a mischievous or evil spirit.

hobnail N a short nail with a large strong head for protecting the soles of boots, shoes and horseshoes. ■ **hobnailed** ADJ.

hobnob VB (**-bb-**) INTR (also **hobnob with**) to spend time socially (with someone).

hobo N (**-os** or **-oes**) N AMER **1** a tramp. **2** an itinerant worker, esp an unskilled one.

Hobson's choice N the choice of taking the thing offered, or nothing at all.

hock[1] N **1** the joint on the hind leg of horses and other hoofed mammals, corresponding to the ankle-joint on a human leg. Also called **hamstring**. **2** the joint of meat extending upwards from the hock-joint.

hock² VB, COLLOQ to pawn.

hockey N **1** a ball game played by two teams of eleven players with long clubs curved at one end, each team attempting to score goals. **2** N AMER short for **ice hockey**.

hocus-pocus N, COLLOQ **1** the skill of trickery or deception. **2** a conjurer's chant.

hod N an open V-shaped box on a pole, used for carrying bricks, etc.

hodgepodge see **hotchpotch**

hoe N a long-handled tool with a narrow blade, used for loosening soil, weeding, etc. ➢ VB (*hoed, hoeing*) **1** to dig or weed (the ground, etc) using a hoe. **2** INTR to use a hoe.

hoedown N, esp US **1** a country dance. **2** a gathering for performing such dances.

hog N **1** N AMER, ESP US a pig. **2** a castrated boar. **3** a pig reared for slaughter. **4** COLLOQ an inconsiderate and often coarse person. ➢ VB (-*gg-*) COLLOQ to use, occupy, etc selfishly. ◆ **go the whole hog** to carry out or do something completely.

hogback and **hog's-back** N a steep-sided hill-ridge.

Hogmanay N, SCOT New Year's Eve.

hogshead N **1** a large cask for liquids. **2** a liquid or dry measure of capacity (usu about 63 gallons or 238 litres).

hogtie VB **1** to tie (someone) up by fastening all four limbs together. **2** to obstruct or impede.

hogwash N, COLLOQ worthless nonsense.

hoi see **hoy**

hoick or **hoik** VB, COLLOQ to lift up abruptly.

hoi polloi PL N (usu **the hoi polloi**) the masses; the common people.

hoist VB to lift or heave up. ➢ N **1** COLLOQ the act of hoisting. **2** equipment for hoisting heavy articles.

hoity-toity ADJ arrogant; haughty.

hokum N, N AMER SLANG **1** nonsense. **2** pretentious or over-sentimental material in a play, film, etc.

hold¹ VB (PA T & PA P *held*) **1** to have or keep in one's hand or hands. **2** to have in one's possession. **3** to think or believe. **4** to retain or reserve. **5** TR & INTR to keep or stay in a specified state or position: **hold firm**. **6** to detain or restrain. **7** to contain or be able to contain: **This bottle holds three pints**. **8** to conduct or carry on: **hold a meeting**. **9** INTR to continue to be valid or apply: **The law still holds**. **10** to cease or stop: **hold fire**. **11** MUS to continue (a note or pause). **12** INTR of a telephone caller: to wait without hanging up while the person being called comes on the line. ➢ N **1** an act of holding. **2** a power or influence: **They have a hold over him**. **3** a way of holding someone in certain sports, eg judo. **4** a place of confinement. **5** an object to hold on to. ◆ **hold sth down** to manage to keep it: **hold down a job**. ◆ **hold good** or **hold true** to remain true or valid; to apply. ◆ **hold off** or **hold off doing sth** to delay or not begin to do it; to refrain from doing it. ◆ **hold on** COLLOQ to wait. ◆ **hold one's own** to maintain one's position. ◆ **hold one's peace** or **tongue** to remain silent. ◆ **hold out 1** to stand firm, esp resisting difficulties. **2** to endure or last. ◆ **hold out for sth** to wait persistently for something one wants or has demanded. ◆ **hold out on sb** COLLOQ to keep back money, information, etc from them. ◆ **hold sth over** to postpone or delay it. ◆ **hold sb** or **sth up as sth** to exhibit them or it as an example. ◆ **hold sb up 1** to delay or hinder them. **2** to stop and rob them. ◆ **hold sth up 1** to support it. **2** to delay it. ◆ **hold with sth** (WITH NEGATIVES AND IN QUESTIONS) to endorse or approve of it. ◆ **on hold** in a state of suspension; temporarily postponed: **She put the trip on hold**.

◆ **with no holds barred** without any restrictions.

hold² N a storage place in ships and aeroplanes.

holdall N a large strong bag for carrying miscellaneous articles.

holder N 1 someone or something that holds or grips. 2 LAW someone who has ownership or control of something, eg a shareholder.

holding N 1 land held by lease. 2 land, shares, etc owned by a person or company.

hold-up N 1 a delay or setback. 2 a robbery, usu with violence or threats of violence.

hole N 1 a hollow area or cavity in something solid. 2 a gap in or through something: **a hole in the sock**. 3 an animal's nest or refuge. 4 COLLOQ an unpleasant place. 5 GOLF a hollow in the middle of each green, into which the ball is hit.
➢ VB 1 to make a hole in something. 2 to hit or play (a ball, etc) into a hole.
◆ **hole up** COLLOQ to go to earth; to hide.
◆ **pick holes in sth** to find fault with it.

hole-and-corner ADJ secret; underhand.

hole in one N, GOLF a single hit of the ball which results in it going straight into the hole.

holey ADJ (*-ier, -iest*) full of holes.

holiday N 1 (often **holidays**) a period of recreational time spent away from work, study, etc. 2 a day when no work is done.
➢ VB, INTR to spend or go away for a holiday in a specified place or at a specified time: **They holiday every year in Cornwall**.

holidaymaker N a person on holiday.

holier-than-thou ADJ of a person, attitude, etc: self-righteous, esp patronizingly so.

holiness N 1 the state of being holy; sanctity. 2 (**Holiness**) a title of the Pope in the form of **Your Holiness** and **His Holiness**.

holism N, PHILOS 1 the theory that a complex entity or system is more than merely the sum of its parts or elements. 2 the treatment of a disease, etc by taking social, economic, etc factors into consideration. ■ **holistic** ADJ.

hollandaise sauce N a sauce made from egg yolks, butter and lemon juice or vinegar.

holler VB, TR & INTR, COLLOQ to shout or yell.
➢ N a shout or yell.

hollow ADJ 1 containing an empty space within or below; not solid. 2 sunken or depressed: **hollow cheeks**. 3 of a sound: echoing as if made in a hollow place. 4 without any great significance: **a hollow victory**.
➢ N 1 a hole or cavity in something. 2 a valley or depression in the land.
➢ ADV, COLLOQ completely: **beat hollow**.
➢ VB (usu **hollow out**) to make hollow.

holly N (*-ies*) an evergreen tree or shrub with dark shiny prickly leaves and red berries.

hollyhock N a tall garden plant with thick hairy stalks and colourful flowers.

holocaust N 1 a large-scale slaughter or destruction of life, often by fire. 2 (**the Holocaust**) the mass murder of Jews by the German Nazis during World War II.

hologram N, PHOTOG a photograph produced without a lens which, when suitably illuminated, shows a three-dimensional image.

holograph ADJ of a document: completely in the handwriting of the author.
➢ N a holograph document.

holography N the study of producing or using holograms. ■ **holographic** ADJ.

hols PL N, COLLOQ holidays.

holster N a leather case for a handgun.

holt N an animal's den, esp that of an otter.

holy ADJ (*-ier, -iest*) 1 associated with God or gods; sanctified or sacred. 2 morally pure and perfect; saintly. ■ **holily** ADV.

the Holy Ghost and **the Holy Spirit** N, CHRISTIANITY the third person in the Trinity.

holy of holies N any place or thing regarded as especially sacred.

holy orders PL N the office of an ordained member of the clergy.

the Holy See N, RC CHURCH the see or

office of the pope in Rome.

holy war N a war waged in the name of or in support of a religion.

homage N a display of great respect towards someone or something.

home N **1** the place where one lives, often with one's family. **2** the country or area one orig comes from. **3** a place where something first occurred, or was first invented. **4** an institution for people who need care or rest, eg the elderly, orphans, etc. **5** the den, base or finishing point in some games and races.
➤ ADJ **1** being at or belonging to one's home, country, family, sports ground, etc. **2** made or done at home or in one's own country: **home baking**. **3** of a sporting event: played on one's own ground, etc: **a home match**.
➤ ADV **1** to or at one's home. **2** to the target place, position, etc: **hit the point home**.
➤ VB **1** INTR of an animal, esp a bird: to return home safely. **2** to give a home to.
◆ **bring sth home to sb** to make it clear or obvious to them.
◆ **home and dry** having met one's goal.
◆ **home in on sth** to identify a target, destination, etc and focus on reaching it.

home-brew N beer, etc brewed at home.

homecoming N an arrival home, usu of someone who has been away for a long time.

home economics SING N the study of household skills and management.

home farm N, BRIT a farm, usu one of several on a large estate, set aside to produce food, etc for the owner of the estate.

home help N, BRIT a person who is hired, often by the local authority, to help sick, aged, etc people with domestic chores.

homeland N one's native country.

homeless ADJ of a person: without a home and living, sleeping, etc in public places or squats. ■ **homelessness** N.

homely ADJ (**-ier, -iest**) **1** relating to home; familiar. **2** making someone feel at home. **3** of a person: honest and unpretentious; pleasant.

4 N AMER of a person: plain and unattractive.

home movie N a motion picture made by an amateur, usu using a cine camera or camcorder.

homeopathy or **homoeopathy** N a system of alternative medicine where a disease is treated by small doses of drugs which produce symptoms similar to those of the disease itself. ■ **homeopath** N.
■ **homeopathic** ADJ.

homer N **1** a breed of pigeon that can be trained to return home from a distance. **2** BASEBALL a home run. **3** COLLOQ a job illicitly done by a tradesman for cash payment.

home rule N the government of a country and its internal affairs by its own citizens.

homesick ADJ pining for one's home and family when away from them. ■ **homesickness** N.

homespun ADJ of character, advice, thinking, etc: artless, simple and straightforward.

homestead N a dwelling-house and its surrounding land and buildings.

home truth N (usu **home truths**) a true but unwelcome fact, usu about oneself.

homeward ADJ going home.
➤ ADV (also **homewards**) towards home.

homework N **1** work or study done at home, esp for school. **2** paid work done at home.

homey or **homy** ADJ (**-ier, -iest**) homely.

homicide N **1** the murder or manslaughter of one person by another. **2** a person who kills another person. ■ **homicidal** ADJ.

homily N (**-ies**) a sermon.

homing ADJ **1** of animals, esp pigeons: trained to return home. **2** of navigational devices: guiding towards a target.

hominid N a primate belonging to the family which includes modern humans.

hominoid ADJ resembling a human.
➤ N any animal resembling a human.

hominy N, N AMER coarsely ground maize boiled with milk or water to make a porridge.

homoeopathy see **homeopathy**

homogeneous ADJ **1** made up of parts or elements that are all of the same kind or nature. **2** made up of similar parts or elements.
■ **homogeneity** N.

homogenize or **-ise** VB **1** to make or become homogeneous. **2** to break up the fat droplets of (a liquid, esp milk) into smaller particles so that they are evenly distributed.

homograph N a word with the same spelling as another, but with a different meaning, origin, and sometimes a different pronunciation, eg **tear** (rip) and **tear** (teardrop).

homologous ADJ having a related or similar function or position. ■ **homology** N (*-ies*).

homonym N a word with the same sound and spelling as another, but with a different meaning, eg **kind** (helpful) and **kind** (sort).

homophobe N a person with a strong aversion to or hatred of homosexuals.
■ **homophobia** N. ■ **homophobic** ADJ.

homophone N **1** a word which sounds the same as another word but is different in spelling and/or meaning, eg **bear** and **bare**.
2 a character or characters that represent the same sound as another, eg **f** and **ph**.

homophony N, MUS a style of composition in which one part or voice carries the melody, and other parts or voices add texture.

homosexual N a person who is sexually attracted to people of the same sex.
➤ ADJ **1** having a sexual attraction to people of the same sex. **2** relating to a homosexual or homosexuals. ■ **homosexuality** N.
■ **homosexually** ADV.

honcho N, N AMER COLLOQ an important person.

hone N a stone used for sharpening tools.
➤ VB to sharpen with or as if with a hone.

honest ADJ **1** not inclined to steal, cheat or lie. **2** fair or justified: **an honest wage**.

honestly ADV **1** in an honest way. **2** in truth.
➤ EXCLAM **1** expressing annoyance.
2 expressing disbelief.

honesty N **1** the state of being honest and truthful. **2** integrity and candour. **3** a common garden plant with silvery leaf-like pods.

honey N **1** a sweet viscous fluid made by bees from flower nectar, and stored in honeycombs, used as a food and sweetener. **2** a yellow or golden-brown colour like that of honey.

honeycomb N **1** the structure made up of rows of hexagonal wax cells in which bees store honey. **2** anything like a honeycomb.

honeyed or **honied** ADJ of a voice, words, etc: sweet, flattering or soothing.

honeymoon N **1** the first weeks after marriage, often spent on holiday. **2** a period of unusual or temporary goodwill at the start eg of a new business relationship.
➤ VB, INTR to spend time on a honeymoon, usu on holiday. ■ **honeymooner** N.

honeysuckle N a climbing garden shrub with sweet-scented flowers.

honk N **1** the cry of a wild goose. **2** the sound made by a car horn.
➤ VB, TR & INTR to make or cause something to make a honking noise.

honky or **honkie** N (*-ies*) N AMER, BLACK SLANG, OFFENSIVE a white person.

honky-tonk N, COLLOQ **1** a style of jangly popular piano music based on ragtime.
2 N AMER SLANG a cheap seedy nightclub.

honorarium N (*-iums* or *-ia*) a fee paid to a professional person for voluntary services.

honorary ADJ **1** bestowing honour. **2** of a title, etc: given as a mark of respect, and without the usual functions, dues, etc. **3** of an official position: receiving no payment.

honorific ADJ showing or giving honour.
➤ N a form of title, address or mention.

Honour N (as **Your**, **His** or **Her Honour**) a title of respect given to judges, mayors, etc.

honour or (US) **honor** N **1** the esteem or respect earned by or paid to a worthy person. **2** a source of credit, or an award in recognition of this. **3** a scrupulous sense of what is right.

4 a pleasure or privilege.
➤ VB **1** to respect or venerate; to hold in high esteem. **2** to confer an award, title, etc on someone. **3** to keep or meet (a promise etc).
◆ **do the honours** COLLOQ to perform or carry out a task, esp that of a host.

honourable or (US) **honorable** ADJ **1** deserving or worthy of honour. **2** having high moral principles. **3** (**Honourable**) a prefix to the names of certain people as a courtesy title. ■ **honourableness** N. ■ **honourably** ADV.

honour-bound ADJ obliged to do something by duty or by moral considerations.

honours PL N **1** a higher grade of university degree with distinction for specialized or advanced work. **2** a mark of civility or respect.

hooch or **hootch** N, N AMER COLLOQ any strong alcoholic drink.

hood¹ N **1** a flexible covering for the whole head and back of the neck, often attached to a coat at the collar. **2** a folding and often removable roof or cover on a car, pushchair, etc. **3** N AMER a car bonnet.
➤ VB to cover with a hood; to blind.

hood² N, SLANG a hoodlum.

hoodlum N **1** N AMER a small-time criminal. **2** a violent or destructive youth.

hoodoo N **1** voodoo. **2** a jinx or bad luck.

hoodwink VB to trick or deceive.

hooey N, SLANG nonsense.

hoof N (*hoofs* or *hooves*) the horny structure that grows beneath and covers the ends of the digits in the feet of certain mammals, eg horses.
◆ **hoof it** SLANG **1** to go on foot. **2** to dance.
◆ **on the hoof** of cattle, horses, etc: alive.

hoo-ha or **hoo-hah** N, COLLOQ commotion.

hook N **1** a curved piece of metal or similar material, used for catching or holding things. **2** a curved tool used for cutting grain, etc. **3** a sharp bend or curve. **4** BOXING a swinging punch with the elbow bent. **5** SPORT a method of striking the ball causing it to curve in the air. **6** POP MUS a catchy phrase.

➤ VB **1** to catch, fasten or hold with or as if with a hook. **2** to ensnare, trap, attract, etc. **3 a** GOLF, CRICKET to hit (the ball) out round the other side of one's body; **b** of the ball: to curve in this direction. **4** in a rugby scrum: to catch (the ball) with the foot and kick it backwards. **5** TR & INTR to bend or curve.
◆ **by hook or by crook** by some means.
◆ **hook, line and sinker** COLLOQ completely.
◆ **off the hook** COLLOQ out of trouble or difficulty; excused of the blame for something.

hookah or **hooka** N an oriental tobacco pipe consisting of a tube which passes through water, used to cool the smoke.

hooked ADJ **1** curved like a hook. **2** COLLOQ physically, emotionally, etc dependent.

hooker N **1** COLLOQ a prostitute. **2** RUGBY the forward who hooks the ball out of a scrum.

hookey or **hooky** N, N AMER COLLOQ unauthorized absence from school.

hook-up N a temporary link-up of different broadcasting stations, for a transmission.

hookworm N a parasitic worm with hook-like parts in its mouth, which lives in the intestines of animals and humans.

hooligan N a violent, destructive or badly-behaved youth. ■ **hooliganism** N.

hoop N **1** a thin ring of metal, wood, etc. **2** anything similar to this in shape. **3** a horizontal band of colour round a shirt, etc.
➤ VB to bind or surround with a hoop or hoops.
◆ **go** or **be put through hoops** COLLOQ to undergo or suffer a thorough and difficult test.

hoop-la N, BRIT a fairground game in which small rings are thrown at objects.

hoorah and **hooray** see under **hurrah**

hoot N **1** the call of an owl, or a similar sound. **2** the sound of a car horn, siren, etc. **3** a loud shout of laughter or disapproval. **4** COLLOQ a hilarious person or thing.
➤ VB **1** INTR of an owl: to make a hoot. **2** to sound (a car horn, etc). **3** INTR of a person: to shout or laugh loudly.

hooter N **1** a person or thing that makes a

hooting sound. **2** BRIT COLLOQ a nose.

Hoover N, TRADEMARK (also **hoover**) a vacuum cleaner.
➤ VB (**hoover**) TR & INTR to clean (a carpet, etc) with or as if with a vacuum cleaner.

hooves see **hoof**

hop¹ VB (-*pp*-) **1** INTR of a person: to jump up and down on one leg. **2** INTR of certain small birds, animals and insects: to move by jumping on both or all legs. **3** to jump over something. **4** INTR (usu **hop in**, **out**, etc) COLLOQ to move in a lively or agile way in the specified direction.
➤ N **1** an act of hopping; a jump on one leg. **2** COLLOQ a distance travelled in an aeroplane without stopping; a short journey by air. **3** OLD USE, COLLOQ an informal dance.
◆ **catch sb on the hop** COLLOQ to catch them unawares or by surprise.
◆ **hop it** BRIT SLANG to take oneself off; to leave.

hop² N **1** a climbing plant of the mulberry family. **2** (usu **hops**) the female flower of this plant, which contains the bitter flavours used in brewing and in medicine.

hope N **1** a desire for something, with some confidence or expectation of success. **2** a person, thing or event that gives one good reason for hope. **3** something hoped for.
➤ VB (also **hope for sth**) to wish or desire that something may happen, esp with some reason to believe that it will.

hopeful ADJ feeling, or full of, hope.
➤ N a person who is ambitious or expected to succeed. ■ **hopefulness** N.

hopefully ADV **1** in a hopeful way. **2** COLLOQ it is to be hoped, if all goes according to plan.

hopeless ADJ **1** without hope. **2** having no reason or cause to expect a good outcome or success. **3** COLLOQ having no ability; incompetent: *He is hopeless at maths.* **4** unresolvable. ■ **hopelessly** ADV. ■ **hopelessness** N.

hopper N **1** a person, animal or insect that hops. **2** a funnel–like device used to feed material into a container, or on to the ground.

hopscotch N a children's game in which players take turns at throwing a stone into one of a series of squares marked on the ground, and hopping in the others around it.

horde N **1** often DEROG a huge crowd or multitude. **2** a group of nomads.

horizon N **1** the line at which the Earth and the sky seem to meet. **2** the limit of a person's knowledge, interests or experience.

horizontal ADJ **1** at right angles to vertical. **2** relating to or parallel to the horizon; level or flat. **3** measured in the plane of the horizon.
➤ N a horizontal line, position or object. ■ **horizontally** ADV.

hormone N **1** a substance secreted by an endocrine gland, and carried in the bloodstream to organs and tissues located elsewhere in the body, where it performs a specific physiological action. **2** an artificially manufactured chemical compound which has the same function as such a substance. **3** a substance in plants which influences their growth and development. ■ **hormonal** ADJ.

horn N **1** one of a pair of hard hollow outgrowths on the heads of many animals, such as cattle, sheep, etc. **2** the bony substance (keratin) of which horns are made. **3** something resembling a horn in shape. **4** MUS a wind instrument orig made from horn, now usu made of brass, specifically: **a** BRIT a French horn; **b** JAZZ any wind instrument. **5** an apparatus for making a warning sound, esp on motor vehicles.
➤ ADJ made of horn. ■ **horned** ADJ.

hornbeam N a tree similar to a beech.

hornblende N a dark green or black mineral.

hornet N a large social wasp, with a brown and yellow striped body.

horn of plenty N a cornucopia.

hornpipe N a lively solo jig, conventionally regarded as popular amongst sailors.

horny ADJ (-*ier*, -*iest*) **1** of or resembling horn, esp in hardness. **2** SLANG sexually excited.

horology N the art of measuring time or of

making clocks. ■ **horologist** N.

horoscope N 1 an astrologer's prediction of someone's future based on the position of the stars and planets at the time of their birth. 2 a map or diagram showing the positions of the stars and planets at a particular moment in time, eg at the time of someone's birth.

horrendous ADJ causing great shock or fear.

horrible ADJ 1 causing horror, dread or fear. 2 COLLOQ unpleasant, detestable or foul. ■ **horribleness** N. ■ **horribly** ADV.

horrid ADJ 1 revolting; detestable or nasty. 2 COLLOQ unpleasant; distasteful. 3 spiteful.

horrific ADJ 1 terrible or frightful. 2 COLLOQ very bad. ■ **horrifically** ADV.

horrify VB (-ies, -ied) to shock greatly; to cause a reaction of horror. ■ **horrified** ADJ. ■ **horrifying** ADJ.

horror N 1 intense fear, loathing or disgust. 2 someone or something causing horror. 3 COLLOQ a distasteful person or thing. ➢ ADJ of literature, films, etc: with horrifying or frightening themes: a horror film.

hors d'oeuvre N (PL *hors d'oeuvre* or *hors d'oeuvres*) a savoury appetizer.

horse N 1 a large hoofed mammal, with a long neck, a mane and long legs, used in many countries for pulling and carrying loads, and for riding. 2 GYMNASTICS a piece of apparatus used for vaulting over, etc. 3 IN COMPOUNDS a supporting apparatus: clothes-horse. ◆ **horse about** or **around** COLLOQ to fool about.

horseback N the back of a horse.

horsebox N a trailer for transporting horses.

horse chestnut see under **chestnut**

horsefly N a large biting fly. Also called **cleg**.

horseman and **horsewoman** N 1 a horse rider. 2 a person skilled in riding and managing horses. ■ **horsemanship** N.

horseplay N rough boisterous play.

horsepower N 1 in the imperial system: the

unit of power, replaced in the SI system by the watt. 2 the power of a vehicle's engine.

horseradish N a plant whose long white pungent root is used to make a sauce.

horse sense N, COLLOQ plain common sense.

horseshoe N a piece of curved iron nailed to the bottom of a horse's hoof to protect the foot.

horse-trading N hard bargaining.

horsewhip N a long whip. ➢ VB to beat, esp severely, with a horsewhip.

horsey or **horsy** ADJ (-ier, -iest) 1 of or relating to horses. 2 often DEROG of people: like a horse, esp in appearance. 3 BRIT COLLOQ very interested in or devoted to horses.

hortative and **hortatory** ADJ giving advice or encouragement.

horticulture N 1 the intensive cultivation of fruit, vegetables, flowers and ornamental shrubs. 2 the art of gardening or cultivation. ■ **horticultural** ADJ. ■ **horticulturist** N.

hosanna N, EXCLAM a shout praise to God.

hose[1] N (also **hosepipe**) a flexible tube for conveying water, eg for watering plants. ➢ VB (often **hose down**) to water, clean or soak with a hose.

hose[2] N (*hose*) a covering for the legs and feet, such as stockings, socks and tights.

hosiery N 1 stockings, socks and tights collectively. 2 knitted underwear.

hospice N 1 a home that specializes in the care of the sick, esp the terminally ill. 2 HIST a hospital.

hospitable ADJ welcoming towards guests. ■ **hospitableness** N. ■ **hospitably** ADV.

hospital N an institution for the treatment and care of the sick or injured.

hospitality N (-ies) the friendly welcome and entertainment of guests or strangers.

hospitalize or **-ise** VB 1 to take or admit (someone) to hospital for treatment. 2 to injure (someone) so badly that hospital treatment is necessary. ■ **hospitalization** N.

host¹ N **1** someone who entertains someone. **2** OLD USE an innkeeper. **3** someone who introduces participants, chairs discussions, etc on a TV or radio show. **4** BIOL a plant or animal on which a parasite lives. **5** MED the recipient of a tissue graft or organ transplant.
➤ VB to be the host of (an event, show, etc).

host² N **1** a very large number; a multitude. **2** OLD USE an army.

host³ N, RC CHURCH the consecrated bread of the Eucharist.

hostage N someone who is held prisoner as a guarantee or security that the captor's demands and conditions are carried out.

hostel N **1** a residence providing shelter for the homeless. **2** a residence for students, nurses, etc. **3** a youth hostel.

hosteller or (US) **hosteler** N **1** someone who lives in or regularly uses a hostel, esp a youth hostel. **2** ARCHAIC the keeper of a hostel or inn.

hostelry N (-ies) an inn or public house.

hostess N **1** a female host. **2** a woman employed as a man's companion for the evening at a nightclub, dance hall, etc.

hostile ADJ **1** expressing aggression or angry opposition. **2** relating or belonging to an enemy. **3** harsh, forbidding or inhospitable.

hostility N (-ies) **1** aggression or opposition. **2** (**hostilities**) acts of warfare; battles.

hot ADJ (*hotter, hottest*) **1** having or producing a great deal of heat. **2** having a high temperature. **3** of food: spicy or fiery. **4** excitable or passionate: **a hot temper**. **5** of a contest or fight: intense. **6** of news: recent. **7** strongly favoured: **a hot favourite**. **8** of a colour: bright and fiery. **9** SLANG of goods: illegally acquired. **10** COLLOQ of a situation: difficult or dangerous: **make life hot for him**. **11** in certain games, etc: very close to guessing the answer or finding the thing sought.
➤ ADV in a hot way; hotly: **a dish served hot**.
■ **hotly** ADV. ■ **hotness** N.
◆ **have** or **get the hots for sb** SLANG to have a strong sexual desire or attraction for them.

◆ **hot on sth** interested in, skilled at or well-informed about it.
◆ **hot under the collar** COLLOQ indignant or annoyed; uncomfortable.
◆ **hot (sth) up** to increase or cause something to increase in excitement or danger.

hot air N, COLLOQ empty or boastful talk.

hotbed N **1** a glass-covered bed of earth heated by a layer of fermenting manure, to encourage rapid plant growth. **2** a place where something, esp something undesirable, flourishes: **a hotbed of discontent**.

hot-blooded ADJ having strong and passionate feelings; high-spirited.

hotchpotch and **hodgepodge** N a confused mass or jumble.

hot cross bun N a fruit bun marked with a pastry cross.

hot dog N a sausage in a long soft bread roll.

hotel N a commercial building providing accommodation, meals and other services to visitors for payment.

hotelier N a person who manages a hotel.

hotfoot COLLOQ, ADV as fast as possible.
➤ VB (usu **hotfoot it**) to rush or hasten.

hothead N **1** an easily angered or agitated person. **2** an impetuous or headstrong person. ■ **hotheaded** ADJ. ■ **hotheadedness** N.

hothouse N **1** a greenhouse which is kept warm for growing tender or tropical plants. **2** any establishment or environment promoting rapid growth or development.

hot line N **1** a direct and exclusive telephone link, eg, between leaders of governments, allowing prompt communication in an emergency. **2** an emergency telephone number for inquiries about a particular incident.

hotplate N **1** the flat top surface of a cooker on which food is cooked. **2** a portable heated surface for keeping food, dishes, etc hot.

hotpot N chopped meat and vegetables cooked slowly in a sealed pot.

hot potato N, COLLOQ a controversial problem.

hot rod N a motor car modified for extra speed by increasing the engine power.

the hot seat N, COLLOQ an uncomfortable or difficult situation.

hotshot N, chiefly US a person who is, often boastfully or pretentiously, successful or skilful.

hot spot N 1 an area with higher than normal temperature. 2 COLLOQ a popular or trendy nightclub. 3 an area of potential trouble.

hot water N, COLLOQ trouble; bother.

hot-wire VB, COLLOQ to start (a vehicle engine) by touching electrical wires together.

hound N 1 COLLOQ a dog. 2 a type of dog used in hunting. 3 COLLOQ a despicable man. 4 often IN COMPOUNDS **a** a hunting dog: **foxhound**; **b** an addict or devotee: **news-hound**.
➤ VB to chase or bother relentlessly.

hound's-tooth N a textile pattern of small broken checks. Also called **dog's-tooth**.

hour N 1 sixty minutes, or a twenty-fourth part of a day. 2 the time indicated by a clock or watch. 3 an occasion or a point in time: **an early hour**. 4 (**hours**) the time allowed or fixed for a specified activity: **office hours**.
◆ **at the eleventh hour** at the last moment.
◆ **on the hour** at one, two, etc, o'clock.

hourglass N an instrument that measures time, consisting of two reversible glass containers and filled with sand that takes a specified time to pass from one container to the other.

hourly ADJ 1 happening or done every hour. 2 measured by the hour: **an hourly wage**.
➤ ADV 1 every hour. 2 frequently.

house N 1 a building in which people, esp a single family, live. 2 IN COMPOUNDS a building used for a specified purpose: **an opera-house**. 3 a business firm: **a publishing house**. 4 the audience in a theatre, a theatre itself or a performance given there. 5 the legislative body that governs a country, esp either chamber in a bicameral system. 6 (**House**) a family, esp a noble or royal one: **the House of Hanover**. 7 BRIT one of several divisions of pupils

at a large school. 8 house music.
➤ VB 1 to provide with a house or similar shelter. 2 to store. 3 to protect by covering.
◆ **bring the house down** COLLOQ to evoke loud applause; to be a great success.
◆ **like a house on fire** COLLOQ very well: **get on like a house on fire**.
◆ **on the house** of food, drink, etc: at the expense of the manager or owner; free.
◆ **put** or **set one's house in order** to organize or settle one's affairs.

house arrest N confinement in one's own home instead of imprisonment.

houseboat N a barge or boat with a deck-cabin designed and built for living in.

housebound ADJ confined to one's house because of illness, carer's duties, etc.

housebreaking N the act of unlawfully breaking into and entering a house with the intention of stealing. ■ **housebreaker** N.

housecoat N a woman's long loose garment similar to a dressing-gown, worn in the home.

household N the people who live together in a house, making up a family.
➤ ADJ relating to the house or family living there.

householder N 1 the owner or tenant of a house. 2 the head of a family or household.

household name and **household word** N a familiar name, word or saying.

housekeeper N a person who is paid to manage a household.

housekeeping N 1 the management of a household. 2 money set aside for this.

housemaid N a maid employed to keep a house clean and tidy.

houseman N a recently qualified doctor holding a junior resident post in a hospital.

housemaster and **housemistress** N in Britain: a male or female teacher in charge of a house in a school, esp a boarding-school.

house music N a style of dance music that is produced electronically.

house-parent N a man or woman in charge of children in an institution.

house-proud ADJ taking pride in the condition and appearance of one's house.

houseroom N.
◆ **not give sth houseroom** to refuse to have anything to do with it.

house-sit VB, INTR to look after someone's house by living in it while they are away.
■ **housesitter** N.

housetrain VB to train (a puppy, kitten, etc) to urinate and defecate outside or in a special tray, etc. ■ **housetrained** ADJ.

house-warming N a party given to celebrate moving into a new house.

housewife N a woman who takes on most of a household's domestic and caring duties.

housework N the work involved in keeping a house clean and tidy.

housing N 1 houses and accommodation collectively. 2 anything designed to cover, contain or protect machinery, etc.

housing estate N a planned residential estate, esp one built by a local authority.

housing scheme N, SCOT a local-authority housing estate.

hovel N a small, dirty, run-down dwelling.

hover VB, INTR 1 of a bird, helicopter, etc: to remain in the air without moving in any direction. 2 to linger, esp anxiously or nervously. 3 to be undecided (usu between two options). ➤ N 1 an act or state of hovering. 2 a condition of uncertainty or indecision.

hovercraft N a vehicle able to move over land or water, supported by a cushion of air.

hoverfly N a wasp-like fly that hovers.

how ADV 1 in what way; by what means: How did it happen? 2 to what extent: How old is he? • How far is it? 3 in what condition: How is she feeling now? 4 to what extent or degree is something good, successful, etc: How was your holiday? 5 for what cause or reason; why: How can you behave like that? ➤ N a manner or means of doing something: The hows and whys of it.
◆ **how about** would you like; what do you think of.
◆ **how come?** COLLOQ for what reason?

howdah or **houdah** N a seat, usu with a sunshade, for riding on an elephant's back.

howdy EXCLAM, N AMER, COLLOQ hello.

however ADV, CONJ 1 in spite of that; nevertheless. 2 by whatever means: Do it however you like. 3 to no matter what extent: however long it takes.

howitzer N a short heavy gun which fires shells high in the air and at a steep angle.

howl N 1 a long mournful cry of a wolf or dog. 2 a loud cry made by the wind, etc. 3 a cry of pain or distress. 4 a loud peal of laughter. ➤ VB, INTR to make a howl.

howler N 1 the largest of the S American monkeys, with black, brown or reddish fur. 2 COLLOQ an outrageous and amusing blunder.

howling ADJ, COLLOQ very great; tremendous.

howzat EXCLAM, CRICKET an appeal to the umpire to give the batsman out.

hoy or **hoi** EXCLAM used to attract attention.

hoyden N a wild lively girl; a tomboy.

HP or **hp** ABBREV 1 high pressure. 2 BRIT hire purchase. 3 horsepower.

HQ or **hq** ABBREV headquarters.

http ABBREV in Web addresses: hypertext transfer protocol.

hub N 1 the centre of a wheel. 2 the focal point of activity, interest, discussion, etc.

hubbub N 1 a confused noise of many sounds, esp voices. 2 uproar; commotion.

hubby N (-ies) COLLOQ an affectionate contraction of **husband**.

hubris N arrogance or pride. ■ **hubristic** ADJ.

huckleberry N 1 a low-growing American woodland plant. 2 its dark blue or blackish fruit.

huckster N an aggressive seller.

huddle VB 1 TR & INTR (USU **huddle together** or **up**) to nestle or crowd closely, eg because of cold. 2 INTR to sit curled up or curl oneself up. ➤ N 1 a confused mass or crowd. 2 COLLOQ a secret or private conference: **go into a huddle.**

hue N 1 a colour, tint or shade. 2 the feature of a colour that distinguishes it from other colours.

hue and cry N a loud public protest or uproar.

huff N a fit of annoyance or offended dignity. ➤ VB 1 INTR to blow or puff loudly. 2 TR & INTR to give or take offence.

huffy and **huffish** ADJ (-*ier*, -*iest*) 1 offended. 2 easily offended; touchy. ■ **huffily** or **huffishly** ADV. ■ **huffiness** N.

hug VB (-*gg*-) 1 TR & INTR to hold tightly in one's arms. 2 to keep close to something. ➤ N a tight grasp with the arms.

huge ADJ very large or enormous. ■ **hugely** ADV. ■ **hugeness** N.

hugger-mugger ADJ, ADV 1 secret; in secret. 2 confused; in confusion or disorder.

hula and **hula-hula** N a Hawaiian dance involving swaying hip movements.

hula hoop N a light hoop, usu made of plastic, which is kept spinning round the waist by a swinging movement of the hips.

hulk N 1 the dismantled body of an old ship. 2 a ship which is or looks unwieldy or difficult to steer. 3 DEROG, COLLOQ a large, awkward and ungainly person or thing.

hull[1] N 1 the frame or body of a ship or airship. 2 the armoured body of a tank, missile, etc.

hull[2] N the husk of certain fruit and seeds. ➤ VB to remove the hulls from (strawberries, etc).

hullabaloo N, COLLOQ an uproar or clamour.

hum VB (-*mm*-) 1 INTR to make a low, steady murmuring sound. 2 TR & INTR to sing (a tune) with closed lips. 3 INTR, COLLOQ to be full of activity: **The building was humming.** 4 INTR, SLANG to have an unpleasant smell. ➤ N 1 a humming sound. 2 an inarticulate sound or murmur. 3 SLANG a bad smell.

◆ **hum and haw** to make inarticulate sounds expressing doubt, uncertainty or hesitation.

human ADJ 1 of or belonging to people. 2 having the qualities and limitations typical of a person. 3 having or showing the better qualities of people. ➤ N a human being. ■ **humanness** N.

human being N a man, woman or child.

humane ADJ 1 kind and sympathetic. 2 of a killing: done with as little pain and suffering as possible. ■ **humanely** ADV.

humanism N a system of thought that rejects the divine in favour of the notion that human beings are paramount. ■ **humanist** N.

humanitarian ADJ concerned with improving people's lives and welfare: **humanitarian aid.** ➤ N a person who tries to improve the quality of people's lives by means of reform, charity, etc; a philanthropist. ■ **humanitarianism** N.

humanity N (-*ies*) 1 humans as a species or a collective group. 2 the typical qualities of human beings, eg kindness, mercy, etc. 3 (**humanities**) the subjects involving the study of human culture, esp language, literature, philosophy, and Latin and Greek.

humanize or **-ise** VB 1 to render, make or become human. 2 to make humane.

humankind N 1 the human species. 2 people generally or collectively.

humanly ADV by human agency or means: **if it is humanly possible.**

humanoid N 1 any of the ancestors from which modern human beings are descended. 2 something with human characteristics.

human resources PL N 1 people collectively in terms of their skills, etc in the workplace. 2 the workforce of an organization.

humble ADJ 1 having a low opinion of oneself and one's abilities, etc. 2 having a low position in society. 3 lowly, modest or unpretentious. ➤ VB to make humble or modest. ■ **humbleness** N. ■ **humbling** ADJ. ■ **humbly** ADV.

humble pie N.
- ◆ **eat humble pie** to be forced to humble or abase oneself, or to make a humble apology.

humbug N 1 a trick or deception. 2 nonsense or rubbish. 3 BRIT a hard, mint-flavoured sweet.

humdinger N, SLANG an exceptionally good person or thing.

humdrum ADJ dull or monotonous; ordinary.

humerus N (-*ri*) the bone in the upper arm.

humid ADJ damp; moist. ■ **humidness** N.

humidifier N a device for increasing or maintaining the humidity of a room, etc.

humidity N 1 the amount of water vapour in the atmosphere, usu expressed as a percentage. 2 moisture; dampness.

humiliate VB to injure (someone's pride), or make (someone) feel ashamed or look foolish, esp in the presence of others. ■ **humiliating** ADJ. ■ **humiliatingly** ADV. ■ **humiliation** N.

humility N (-*ies*) 1 the quality or state of being humble. 2 modesty or meekness.

hummingbird N a small S American bird with brilliant plumage.

hummock N a hillock. ■ **hummocky** ADJ.

hummus N a Middle-Eastern dip made from puréed cooked chickpeas.

humongous or **humungous** ADJ, COLLOQ huge or enormous.

humorist N someone with a talent for talking or writing humorously.

humorous ADJ funny or amusing.
■ **humorously** ADV. ■ **humorousness** N.

humour or (US) **humor** N 1 the quality of being amusing. 2 the ability to appreciate something amusing. 3 a specified state of mind: **good humour**. 4 a specified type of fluid in the body: **aqueous humour**.
➤ VB to please or gratify someone by doing what they wish. ■ **humourless** ADJ.

hump N 1 a large rounded lump of fat on the back of a camel. 2 an abnormal curvature of the spine. 3 a rounded raised area of a road.
➤ VB 1 to hunch or bend in a hump. 2 (usu **hump about** or **around**) to shoulder or carry (esp something awkward or heavy) with difficulty. 3 TR & INTR, COARSE SLANG to have sexual intercourse with. ■ **humpy** ADJ.
- ◆ **have** or **give sb the hump** to be in, or put someone in, a bad mood or sulk.

humus N dark-brown organic material produced in the topmost layer of soil.

hunch N 1 an idea, guess or belief based on feelings, suspicions or intuition rather than on actual evidence. 2 a hump.
➤ VB 1 to bend or arch; to hump. 2 INTR (also **hunch up** or **over**) to sit with the body hunched or curled up.

hunchback N someone with a large rounded lump on their back. ■ **hunchbacked** ADJ.

hundred N (*hundreds* or, AFTER A NUMBER, *hundred*) 1 the number which is ten times ten. 2 a numeral, figure or symbol representing this, eg 100 or C. 3 a set of 100 people or things: **one hundred pounds**. 4 a score of 100 points. 5 (**hundreds**) COLLOQ a large but indefinite number: **hundreds of people**. 6 (**hundreds**) IN COMPOUNDS the 100 years of a specified century: **the thirteen-hundreds**.
➤ ADJ 1 totalling or to the number of 100. 2 COLLOQ very many. ■ **hundredfold** ADJ. ■ **hundredth** ADJ, N.

hundredweight N (*hundredweight* or *hundredweights*) 1 BRIT a measure of weight equal to 112 pounds. 2 N AMER a measure of weight equal to 100 pounds. 3 a metric measure equal to 50 kilograms.

hung ADJ of a parliament or jury: with neither side having a majority.
- ◆ **be hung up on** or **about sb** or **sth** COLLOQ 1 to be extremely anxious or upset about it. 2 to be obsessed with them or it.

hunger N 1 the desire or need for food. 2 a strong desire for anything.
➤ VB, INTR (usu **hunger for** or **after**) to crave.

hungry ADJ (-*ier*, -*iest*) 1 having a need or craving for food. 2 (usu **hungry for**) having a great desire (for something): **He is hungry for**

success. **3** eager; greedy: **hungry eyes**.
■ **hungrily** ADV. ■ **hungriness** N.

hunk N **1** a lump or piece. **2** COLLOQ a muscular, attractive man. ■ **hunky** ADJ (*-ier, -iest*).

hunky-dory ADJ, COLLOQ fine; excellent.

hunt VB, TR & INTR to chase and kill (wild birds or animals) for food or sport.
➤ N **1** an act of hunting. **2** a group of people meeting together to hunt animals for sport.
3 a search. ■ **hunting** N.

hunter N **1 a** someone who hunts; **b** esp IN COMPOUNDS someone who seeks someone or something out: **bounty hunter**. **2** an animal that hunts (usu other animals) for food. **3** a horse used in hunting, esp fox–hunting.

hunter-gatherer N a member of a society which lives by hunting animals from the land and sea, and by gathering wild plants.

hurdle N **1** ATHLETICS, HORSE-RACING one of a series of portable frames, hedges or barriers to be jumped in a race. **2** an obstacle, problem or difficulty to be overcome. **3** (**hurdles**) a race with hurdles. **4** a light frame with bars or wire across it, used as a temporary fence.
➤ VB, TR & INTR to jump over (a hurdle in a race, an obstacle, etc). ■ **hurdler** N. ■ **hurdling** N.

hurl VB **1** to fling violently. **2** to utter with force.
➤ N an act of hurling.

hurling and **hurley** N a traditional Irish game resembling hockey.

hurly-burly N noisy activity; uproar.

hurrah, **hoorah** or **hooray** EXCLAM a shout of joy, enthusiasm or victory.

hurricane N an intense, often devastating, cyclonic tropical storm.

hurry VB (*-ies, -ied*) **1** to make (someone or something) move or act quickly. **2** INTR to move or act with haste.
➤ N **1** great haste or speed. **2** the necessity for haste or speed. ■ **hurried** ADJ.
◆ **in a hurry 1** rushed; in haste. **2** readily; willingly: **I won't do that again in a hurry**.

hurt VB (PA T & PA P *hurt*) **1** to injure or cause

physical pain to. **2** to cause emotional pain to. **3** INTR to be injured or painful: **The wound hurts**.
➤ N **1** an injury or wound. **2** mental or emotional pain or suffering.
➤ ADJ **1** injured. **2** aggrieved; upset.

hurtful ADJ causing mental pain.

hurtle VB, TR & INTR to move or throw very quickly or noisily.

husband N a man to whom a woman is married.

husbandry N **1** the farming business. **2** the wise management of money, resources, etc.

hush EXCLAM silence!; be still!
➤ N silence or calm, esp after noise.
➤ VB, TR & INTR to make or become silent, calm or still. ■ **hushed** ADJ.

hush-hush ADJ, COLLOQ top–secret.

husk N **1** the thin dry covering of certain fruits and seeds. **2** a case, shell or covering.

husky[1] ADJ (*-ier, -iest*) **1** of a voice: rough and dry in sound. **2** COLLOQ usu of a man: big and strong. ■ **huskily** ADV. ■ **huskiness** N.

husky[2] N (*-ies*) a dog with a thick coat and curled tail, used as a sledge–dog in the Arctic.

hussar N a soldier in a cavalry regiment who carries only light weapons.

hussy N (*-ies*) DEROG a forward, immoral or promiscuous girl or woman.

hustings SING OR PL N speeches, campaigning, etc prior to a political election, or a platform, etc from which such speeches are given.

hustle VB **1** to push or shove quickly and roughly; to jostle. **2** to act hurriedly or hastily. **3** COLLOQ to coerce someone to act quickly. **4** to earn money or one's living illicitly.
➤ N **1** lively activity. **2** SLANG a swindle.

hustler N, SLANG **1** a lively or energetic person. **2** a swindler. **3** a prostitute.

hut N **1** a small and crudely built house, usu made of wood. **2** a small temporary dwelling.

hutch N a box, usu made of wood and with a wire–netting front, in which eg rabbits, are kept.

hyacinth N a bulbous spring plant with sweet-smelling clusters of blue, pink or white flowers.

hybrid N 1 an animal or plant produced by crossing two different species, varieties, etc. 2 something composed of disparate elements. ➢ ADJ bred or produced by combining elements from different sources. ■ **hybridize** VB.

hydra N (-ras or -rae) 1 a freshwater polyp with a tube-like body and tentacles round the mouth. 2 any manifold or persistent evil.

hydrant N a pipe connected to the main water supply, esp in a street.

hydrate CHEM, N a compound containing water which is chemically combined. ➢ VB 1 to form (such a compound) by combining with water. 2 to cause something to absorb water. ■ **hydration** N.

hydraulic ADJ 1 relating to hydraulics. 2 worked by the pressure of fluid carried in pipes: hydraulic brakes. 3 relating to something that sets in water: hydraulic cement.

hydraulics SING N, ENG the science of the mechanical properties of fluids, esp water.

hydride N a chemical compound of hydrogen with another element or radical.

hydro N, BRIT a hotel or clinic, often situated near a spa, providing hydropathy.

hydrocarbon N, CHEM an organic chemical compound containing carbon and hydrogen.

hydrochloric acid N, CHEM a strong corrosive acid.

hydrodynamics SING N the science of the movement, equilibrium and power of liquids.

hydroelectricity N electricity generated by turbines driven by water. ■ **hydroelectric** ADJ.

hydrofoil N a device on a boat which raises it out of the water as it accelerates.

hydrogen N a flammable colourless odourless gas which is the lightest of all known substances. ■ **hydrogenous** ADJ.

hydrogen bomb and **H-bomb** N a bomb which releases vast amounts of energy as a result of hydrogen nuclei being converted into helium nuclei by fusion.

hydrogen peroxide N, CHEM an unstable colourless viscous liquid used as an oxidant and a bleach.

hydrography N the science of charting and mapping seas, rivers and lakes, and of studying tides, currents, winds, etc. ■ **hydrographer** N.

hydrology N the scientific study of the occurrence, movement and properties of water on the Earth's surface, and in the atmosphere.

hydrolysis N the chemical decomposition of organic compounds caused by the action of water. ■ **hydrolytic** ADJ.

hydrometer N, PHYS a device used for measuring the density of a liquid.

hydropathy N the treatment of disease or illness using large amounts of water.

hydrophilic ADJ, CHEM of a substance that absorbs, attracts or has an affinity for water.

hydrophobia N 1 a fear or horror of water. 2 the inability to swallow water, a symptom of rabies. 3 rabies. ■ **hydrophobic** ADJ.

hydroplane N a motorboat with a flat bottom or hydrofoils which, at high speeds, skims along the surface of the water.

hydrosphere N the water, such as seas and rivers, on the surface of the Earth.

hydrotherapy N, MED the treatment of diseases and disorders by the external use of water, esp through exercising in water.

hydrous ADJ of a substance: containing water.

hydroxide N, CHEM a chemical compound containing one or more hydroxyl (OH) groups.

hyena N a carrion-feeding doglike mammal.

hygiene N 1 the practice or study of preserving health and preventing the spread of disease. 2 sanitary principles and practices. ■ **hygienic** ADJ. ■ **hygienically** ADV.

hymen N, ANAT a thin membrane partially covering the opening of the vagina.

hymn N a song of praise, esp to God.

hymnal N a book containing hymns.

hype COLLOQ, N **1** intensive, exaggerated or artificially induced excitement about, or enthusiasm for, something or someone. **2** exaggerated publicity or advertising. ➤ VB to promote or advertise intensively.

hyped up ADJ, SLANG artificially stimulated or highly excited, eg with drugs.

hyper ADJ, COLLOQ of a person: over-excited.

hyperactive ADJ of, esp, a child: abnormally or pathologically active. ■ **hyperactivity** N.

hyperbola N (*-las* or *-lae*) GEOM the curve produced when a plane cuts through a cone so that the angle between the base of the cone and the plane is greater than the angle between the base and the sloping side of the cone. ■ **hyperbolic** ADJ.

hyperbole N, RHETORIC an overstatement or exaggeration used for effect. ■ **hyperbolic** ADJ. ■ **hyperbolically** ADV.

hypercritical ADJ overly critical.

hyperglycaemia or (N AMER) **hyperglycemia** N, PATHOL a condition in which blood sugar is abnormally high.

hyperlink N, COMP a link between pieces of information in hypertext.

hypersensitive ADJ abnormally sensitive.

hypersonic ADJ **1** of speeds: greater than Mach number 5 (about five times the speed of sound in the same medium and in the same environment). **2** AERONAUTICS of an aircraft or rocket: capable of flying at such speeds. **3** of sound waves: having a frequency greater than 1000 million hertz. ■ **hypersonics** PL N.

hypertension N, PATHOL a condition in which the blood pressure is abnormally high.

hypertext N, COMP computer-readable text in which cross-reference links (hyperlinks) have been inserted, enabling the user to call up relevant data from other files.

hyperventilation N a condition in which the speed and depth of breathing becomes abnormally rapid. ■ **hyperventilate** VB.

hyphen N a punctuation mark (–) used to join two words, or to split a word between the end of one line and the beginning of the next. ➤ VB to hyphenate.

hyphenate VB to join or separate (two words or parts of words) with a hyphen. ■ **hyphenated** ADJ. ■ **hyphenation** N.

hypnosis N (*-ses*) an induced sleeplike state in which a person is deeply relaxed, and in which the mind responds to external suggestion.

hypnotherapy N the treatment of illness or altering of habits, eg smoking, by hypnosis. ■ **hypnotherapist** N.

hypnotic ADJ **1** relating to, causing or caused by, hypnosis. **2** causing sleepiness; soporific. ➤ N **1** a drug that produces sleep. **2** someone in a state of hypnosis. ■ **hypnotically** ADV.

hypnotism N the science or practice of hypnosis. ■ **hypnotist** N.

hypnotize or **-ise** VB **1** to put someone in a state of hypnosis. **2** to fascinate or bewitch.

hypo N, COLLOQ a hypodermic syringe.

hypochondria and **hypochondriasis** N a condition characterized by excessive or morbid concern over one's health. ■ **hypochondriac** N, ADJ.

hypocrisy N (*-ies*) **1** the practice of pretending to have feelings, beliefs or principles which one does not actually have. **2** an act or instance of this.

hypocrite N a person who practises hypocrisy. ■ **hypocritical** ADJ. ■ **hypocritically** ADV.

hypodermic ADJ **a** of a drug: injected under the skin; **b** of a syringe; designed for such use. ➤ N a hypodermic injection or syringe.

hypoglycaemia or **hypoglycemia** N, PATHOL a condition in which the sugar content of the blood is abnormally low. ■ **hypoglycaemic** ADJ.

hypotenuse N, MATH the longest side of a right-angled triangle, opposite the right angle.

hypothalamus N (*-mi*) ANAT the region of

the brain which is involved in the regulation of involuntary functions. ■ **hypothalamic** ADJ.

hypothermia N a condition where the body temperature becomes abnormally and sometimes dangerously low.

hypothesis N (*-ses*) **1** a statement or proposition assumed to be true for the sake of argument. **2** a statement or theory to be proved or disproved by reference to evidence or facts.

hypothesize or **-ise** VB **1** INTR to form a hypothesis. **2** to assume as a hypothesis.

hypothetical and **hypothetic** ADJ based on hypothesis. ■ **hypothetically** ADV.

hysterectomy N (*-ies*) the surgical

removal of the womb.

hysteresis N, PHYS the delay or lag between the cause of an effect, and the effect itself. ■ **hysteretic** ADJ.

hysteria N **1** any state of emotional instability. **2** any extreme emotional state.

hysteric N **1** (**hysterics**) PSYCHOL a bout of hysteria. **2** (**hysterics**) COLLOQ a bout of uncontrollable laughter.

hysterical ADJ **1** relating to, suffering from, or characterized by hysteria. **2** COLLOQ extremely funny or amusing. ■ **hysterically** ADV.

Hz ABBREV hertz.

I¹ or **i** N (*Is, I's* or *i's*) the ninth letter of the English alphabet.

I² PRONOUN used to refer to oneself.

I³ SYMBOL as a Roman numeral: one.

iambus and **iamb** N (*-buses, -bi*) PROSODY a metrical foot of a short or unstressed syllable followed by a long or stressed one. ■ **iambic** ADJ.

Iberian ADJ of Portugal and Spain.

ibex N (*ibex, ibexes* or *ibices*) a wild mountain goat with backward-curving horns.

ibis N (*ibis* or *ibises*) a large wading bird with a long downward-curving beak.

ice N **1** solid frozen water. **2** ice cream or water ice, or a portion of this. **3** coldness of manner.
➤ VB **1** to cover (a cake) with icing. **2** INTR (usu **ice over** or **up**) to become covered with ice. **3** to cool or mix something with ice.

◆ **on ice 1** to be used later. **2** awaiting further attention.

ice age N, GEOL any period when ice sheets and glaciers covered large areas of the Earth.

iceberg N **1** a huge mass of ice floating in the sea. **2** a type of firm crisp lettuce.

icebox N **1** a refrigerator compartment where food is kept frozen and ice is made. **2** a container packed with ice for keeping food, drink, etc cold. **3** N AMER a refrigerator.

icebreaker N **1** a ship that cuts channels through ice. **2** something or someone that breaks down shyness or formality.

icecap N a thick permanent covering of ice.

ice cream N a sweet creamy frozen dessert.

iced ADJ **1** covered or cooled with, or affected by, ice. **2** covered with icing.

ice floe N a sheet of ice floating on the sea.

ice hockey N a form of hockey played on ice, with a puck instead of a ball.

ice lolly N, BRIT COLLOQ a portion of flavoured water or ice cream frozen on a small stick.

ice pack N 1 MED a bag of crushed ice, used to reduce swelling, lower a patient's temperature, etc. 2 GEOG an area of pack ice.

ichthyology N the study of fishes. ■ **ichthyological** ADJ. ■ **ichthyologist** N.

icicle N a long hanging spike of ice.

icing N a sugar-based coating for cakes, etc.

icon or (sometimes) **ikon** N 1 RELIG ART an image of Christ, the Virgin Mary or a saint. 2 a person or thing uncritically revered or admired. 3 COMP a symbol on a computer screen. ■ **iconic** ADJ.

iconoclast N 1 esp CHURCH HIST someone who destroys religious images. 2 someone who is opposed to, and attacks, traditional and cherished beliefs. ■ **iconoclasm** N. ■ **iconoclastic** ADJ.

icy ADJ (-ier, -iest) 1 very cold. 2 covered with ice. 3 unfriendly. ■ **icily** ADV. ■ **iciness** N.

ID ABBREV identification or identity.

id N, PSYCHOANAL the unconscious source of primitive biological instincts and urges.

I'd CONTRACTION 1 I had. 2 I would.

idea N 1 a thought, image or concept formed by the mind. 2 a plan or notion. 3 an aim or purpose. 4 an opinion, belief, or vague fancy. 5 someone's conception of something.

ideal ADJ 1 perfect; best possible or conceivable. 2 existing only in the mind. 3 theoretical; conforming to theory. ➤ N 1 the highest standard of behaviour, perfection, etc. 2 someone or something considered perfect. ■ **ideally** ADV.

idealism N 1 a tendency to see or present things in an idealized form. 2 the practice of forming, and living by, ideals. 3 impracticality. ■ **idealist** N. ■ **idealistic** ADJ.

idealize or **-ise** VB to regard or treat someone or something as perfect or ideal.

identical ADJ 1 exactly alike in every respect. 2 being the very same one. 3 of twins: developed from a single fertilized egg. ■ **identically** ADV.

identification parade N, BRIT a line containing a person suspected of a crime and others innocent of it, from which a witness tries to identify the suspect.

identify VB (-ies, -ied) 1 to recognize or establish someone or something as being a particular person or thing. 2 to associate (one person, thing or group) closely with another. 3 to pinpoint (a problem, method, solution, etc). ■ **identifiable** ADJ. ■ **identification** N.

identity N (-ies) 1 who or what a person or thing is: The winner's identity is not yet known. 2 AS ADJ serving to identify the wearer or holder or to give information about them: identity bracelet. 3 the characteristics by which a person or thing can be identified.

ideogram and **ideograph** N a symbol for a concept or object.

ideology N (-ies) 1 the ideas and beliefs which form the basis for a social, economic or political system. 2 the opinions, beliefs and way of thinking characteristic of a particular person, group or nation. ■ **ideological** ADJ.

idiocy N (-ies) 1 a foolish action or foolish behaviour. 2 NON-TECHNICAL the state of being extremely retarded mentally.

idiom N 1 an expression with a meaning which cannot be derived from the meanings of the words which form it. 2 the forms of expression peculiar to a language, dialect, group, etc. 3 the characteristic style or expression of a particular artistic or musical school, etc. ■ **idiomatic** ADJ.

idiosyncrasy N (-ies) a personal peculiarity or eccentricity. ■ **idiosyncratic** ADJ.

idiot N 1 COLLOQ a foolish or stupid person. 2 NON-TECHNICAL a severely retarded person. ■ **idiotic** ADJ. ■ **idiotically** ADV.

idle ADJ 1 not in use. 2 not wanting to work; lazy. 3 worthless: idle chatter. 4 without cause or good reason: an idle rumour. 5 having no

effect or result: **an idle threat.**
➤ VB **1** to spend (time) idly. **2** INTR to do nothing or be idle. **3** INTR of an engine, machinery, etc: to run gently while out of gear or without doing any work. ■ **idleness** N. ■ **idly** ADV.

idol N **1** an image used as an object of worship. **2** an object of excessive devotion.

idolatry N (**-ies**) **1** the worship of idols. **2** excessive honour, admiration or devotion. ■ **idolater** N. ■ **idolatrous** ADJ.

idolize or **-ise** VB **1** to love, honour, admire, etc someone or something too much. **2** to make an idol of someone or something.

idyll N **1** a short poem or prose work describing a simple, pleasant, usu rural or pastoral scene. **2** a story, episode or scene of happy innocence or love. ■ **idyllic** ADJ.

ie or **i.e.** ABBREV: **id est** (Latin), that is (to say).

if CONJ **1** in the event that; on condition that; supposing that. **2** although; even though: **very enjoyable, if overpriced. 3** whenever: **She jumps if the phone rings. 4** whether. **5** (usu **if only**) used to express a wish. **6** used to make a polite request or suggestion: **if you would wait. 7** used in exclamations, to express surprise or annoyance: **Well, if it isn't John!**
➤ N **1** a condition or supposition: **ifs and buts. 2** an uncertainty.

iffy ADJ (**-ier, -iest**) COLLOQ uncertain; dubious.

igloo N a dome-shaped Inuit house built with blocks of snow and ice.

igneous ADJ **1** of or like fire. **2** GEOL of a rock: formed by the solidification of molten magma.

ignite VB **1** to set fire to something or heat it to the point of combustion. **2** INTR to catch fire. **3** to excite (feelings, emotions, etc).

ignition N **1** CHEM the point at which combustion begins. **2** a system that produces the spark which ignites the mixture of fuel and air in an internal-combustion engine.

ignoble ADJ **1** dishonourable; mean. **2** of humble or low birth; not noble. ■ **ignobly** ADV.

ignominy N (**-ies**) **1** public shame, disgrace or

dishonour. **2** dishonourable conduct. ■ **ignominious** ADJ.

ignoramus N an ignorant person.

ignorant ADJ **1** knowing very little; uneducated. **2** (usu **ignorant of sth**) knowing little or nothing about it. **3** rude; ill-mannered. ■ **ignorance** N.

ignore VB to take no notice of.

iguana N (**iguanas** or **iguana**) a large lizard with a crest of spines along its back.

ikebana N the Japanese art of flower-arranging.

ikon see **icon**

ileum N (**ilea**) ANAT the lowest part of the small intestine.

ilium N (**ilia**) ANAT one of the bones that form the upper part of the pelvis.

ilk N type; kind; class.

ill ADJ (**worse, worst**) **1** unwell. **2** of health: not good. **3** bad; harmful: **ill effects. 4** hostile; unfriendly: **ill feeling. 5** causing or heralding bad luck: **an ill omen. 6** incorrect; improper.
➤ ADV (**worse, worst**) **1** badly; wrongly: **ill-fitting. 2** harshly; unfavourably: **speak ill of. 3** with difficulty: **ill able to afford it.**
➤ N **1** evil; trouble. **2** an injury, ailment or misfortune.
◆ **ill at ease** uneasy; uncomfortable.

I'll CONTRACTION I will or I shall.

ill-advised ADJ foolish.

ill-bred ADJ badly brought up or educated.

ill-considered ADJ not well planned.

ill-disposed ADJ unfriendly; unsympathetic.

illegal ADJ **1** not legal. **2** not authorized by law. ■ **illegality** N (**-ies**). ■ **illegally** ADV.

illegible ADJ difficult or impossible to read. ■ **illegibility** N. ■ **illegibly** ADV.

illegitimate ADJ **1** born of unmarried parents. **2** illegal. **3** improper. ■ **illegitimacy** N.

ill-equipped ADJ poorly provided with the necessary tools, skills, etc.

ill-fated ADJ ending in ruin; doomed.

ill-favoured ADJ unattractive.

ill-founded ADJ without sound basis.

ill-gotten ADJ obtained dishonestly.

illiberal ADJ 1 narrow-minded; prejudiced. 2 not generous.

illicit ADJ not permitted by law or rule.

ill-informed ADJ lacking knowledge.

illiterate ADJ 1 unable to read and write. 2 uneducated; ignorant of some subject. ➢ N an illiterate person. ■ **illiteracy** N.

ill-judged ADJ done without proper consideration.

ill-mannered ADJ rude.

illness N 1 a disease. 2 the state of being ill.

illogical ADJ 1 not based on careful reasoning. 2 against the principles of logic. ■ **illogicality** N. ■ **illogically** ADV.

ill-timed ADJ done at an unsuitable time.

ill-treat VB to abuse; to maltreat. ■ **ill-treatment** N.

illuminance N, PHYS the luminous flux on a given surface per unit area.

illuminate VB 1 to light something up or make it bright. 2 to decorate something with lights. 3 to decorate (a manuscript) with elaborate designs. 4 to make something clearer and more easily understood. 5 to enlighten someone spiritually or intellectually. ■ **illuminating** ADJ.

illumination N 1 illuminating or being illuminated. 2 any source of light; lighting. 3 (usu **illuminations**) decorative lights hung in streets and towns, eg at times of celebration. 4 the art of decorating manuscripts with elaborate designs and letters.

illusion N 1 a deceptive appearance: an optical illusion. 2 a false belief.

illusionist N a conjurer who plays tricks, performs optical illusions, etc.

illusive and **illusory** ADJ 1 seeming to be or like an illusion. 2 deceptive; unreal.

illustrate VB 1 to provide or create pictures and/or diagrams for (a book, lecture, etc). 2 to make (a statement, etc) clearer by providing examples. 3 to be an example of, or an analogy for, something. ■ **illustrated** ADJ. ■ **illustrative** ADJ. ■ **illustrator** N.

illustration N 1 a picture or diagram. 2 an example. 3 illustrating or being illustrated.

illustrious ADJ distinguished; renowned.

ill will N hostile or unfriendly feeling.

I'm CONTRACTION I am.

image N 1 a likeness of a person or thing, esp a portrait or statue. 2 someone or something that closely resembles another: He's the image of his father. 3 an idea or picture in the mind. 4 the visual display produced by a television. 5 the public impression of someone's character, etc. ➢ VB 1 to form a likeness or image of something or someone. 2 MED to produce a pictorial representation of (a body part) using eg X-ray or ultrasound scanning. ■ **imaging** N.

imagery N (-ies) 1 figures of speech in writing, literature, etc that produce a particular effect. 2 mental images. 3 statues, carvings, etc.

imaginary ADJ existing only in the mind or imagination; not real.

imagination N 1 the forming or ability to form mental images of things, people, events, etc that one has not seen or of which one has no direct knowledge. 2 the creative ability of the mind.

imaginative ADJ 1 showing or done with imagination. 2 having a lively imagination.

imagine VB 1 to form a mental picture of something. 2 to see, hear or think something which is not true or does not exist. 3 to think, suppose or guess. 4 INTR to use the imagination. ■ **imaginable** ADJ. ■ **imaginings** PL N.

imago N (-gos or -gines) ENTOMOL a sexually mature adult insect.

imam N, ISLAM 1 a leader of prayers in a mosque. 2 (**Imam**) a title given to various Muslim leaders.

imbalance N a lack of balance or proportion.

imbecile N 1 someone of extremely low intelligence. 2 COLLOQ a fool. ➤ ADJ. ■ **imbecility** N (-ies).

imbibe VB, now FACETIOUS OR FORMAL to drink, esp alcoholic drinks.

imbroglio N a confused and complicated situation.

imbue VB (-bued, -buing) 1 (esp **imbue sb with sth**) to fill or inspire someone, esp with ideals or principles. 2 to soak or saturate something, esp with dye.

imitate VB 1 to copy the behaviour, appearance, etc of someone. 2 to make a copy of something. ■ **imitator** N.

imitation N 1 an act of imitating. 2 something which is produced by imitating; a copy or counterfeit. ■ **imitative** ADJ.

immaculate ADJ 1 perfectly clean and neat. 2 free from blemish, flaw or error. 3 free from any moral stain or sin. ■ **immaculately** ADV.

immanent ADJ existing or remaining within something; inherent. ■ **immanence** N.

immaterial ADJ 1 not important or relevant. 2 not formed of matter.

immature ADJ 1 not fully grown or developed; not mature or ripe. 2 childish. ■ **immaturity** N.

immeasurable ADJ too great to be measured; very great; immense.

immediacy N (-ies) the quality of being immediate. Also **immediateness**.

immediate ADJ 1 happening or done at once and without delay. 2 nearest or next in space, time, relationship, etc: **the immediate family**. 3 belonging to the current time; urgent: **deal with the immediate problems first**. 4 having a direct effect: **the immediate cause of death**.

immediately ADV 1 without delay. 2 without anything between: **immediately next to me**. ➤ CONJ as soon as: **Immediately he arrived, the meeting began**.

immemorial ADJ extending far back in time, beyond anyone's memory or written records.

immense ADJ 1 very or unusually large or great. 2 DATED COLLOQ very good; splendid. ■ **immenseness** or **immensity** N (-ies).

immerse VB to dip into a liquid completely. ■ **immersible** ADJ. ■ **immersion** N.

immigrant N someone who has immigrated. ➤ ADJ of or relating to immigrants.

immigrate VB, INTR to come to a foreign country with the intention of settling in it.

immigration N 1 a the process of immigrating; b AS ADJ: **immigration control**. 2 COLLOQ a the immigration checkpoint at an airport, seaport b the immigration authorities.

imminent ADJ likely to happen in the near future. ■ **imminence** N. ■ **imminently** ADV.

immiscible N, CHEM of liquids, eg oil and water: not mixing when shaken together.

immobile ADJ 1 not able to move or be moved. 2 motionless. ■ **immobility** N.

immobilize or **-ise** VB to make something or someone immobile. ■ **immobilization** N.

immoderate ADJ excessive or extreme.

immodest ADJ 1 shameful; indecent. 2 boastful and conceited; forward.

immolate VB to kill or offer as a sacrifice. ■ **immolation** N.

immoral ADJ 1 morally wrong or bad. 2 not conforming to the sexual standards of society. 3 unscrupulous; unethical. ■ **immorality** N.

immortal ADJ 1 living forever. 2 lasting forever. ➤ N someone who will live forever or who will always be remembered. ■ **immortality** N.

immortalize or **-ise** VB 1 to make (a person, etc) famous for ever, eg in a work of art or literature. 2 to make someone immortal.

immovable or **immoveable** ADJ impossible to move; not meant to be moved. ■ **immovability** N.

immune ADJ 1 having a natural resistance to or protected by inoculation from (a particular disease). 2 protected from or unaffected by: **immune to criticism**. 4 PHYSIOL relating to or concerned with producing immunity: **the immune system. ■ immunity** N.

immunize or **-ise** VB, MED to produce artificial immunity to a disease by injecting with eg a treated antigen. **■ immunization** N.

immunodeficiency N, PHYSIOL, MED a deficiency in the body's ability to fight infection.

immunology N the scientific study of immunity and the defence mechanisms that the body uses to resist infection and disease.

immunotherapy N the treatment of disease, esp cancer, by antigens which stimulate the patient's own natural immunity.

immure VB 1 to enclose or imprison someone within walls. 2 to shut someone away.

immutable ADJ unable to be changed.

imp N 1 a small mischievous or evil spirit. 2 a mischievous or annoying child. **■ impish** ADJ.

impact N 1 the collision of an object with another object. 2 the force of such a collision. 3 a strong effect or impression.
➤ VB 1 a to press (two objects) together with force; b to force (one object) into (another). 2 INTR to come forcefully into contact with another body or surface, etc. 3 to have an impact or effect on. **■ impaction** N.

impair VB to damage or weaken something. **■ impairment** N.

impala N (*impalas* or *impala*) an antelope of S and E Africa.

impale VB 1 to pierce with, or as if with, a long, pointed object or weapon. 2 to put someone to death by this method. **■ impalement** N.

impart VB 1 to make (information, knowledge, etc) known. 2 to transmit (a particular quality).

impartial ADJ fair and unbiased. **■ impartiality** N. **■ impartially** ADV.

impassable ADJ not able to be travelled along. **■ impassability** N.

impasse N a situation with no possible progress or escape.

impassioned ADJ 1 fervent, zealous or animated. 2 deeply moved by emotion.

impassive ADJ 1 incapable of feeling and expressing emotion. 2 showing no emotion.

impasto N, ART in painting and pottery: **a** the technique of laying paint or pigment on thickly; **b** paint applied thickly.

impatient ADJ 1 unwilling to wait or delay; lacking patience. 2 intolerant; showing a lack of patience. 3 restlessly eager and anxious. **■ impatience** N. **■ impatiently** ADV.

impeach VB 1 BRIT LAW to charge someone with a serious crime, esp against the state. 2 N AMER to accuse (a serving public official) of misconduct. 3 to cast doubt upon (eg a person's honesty). **■ impeachment** N.

impeccable ADJ faultless; perfect; flawless.

impecunious ADJ having little or no money.

impedance N, ELEC the effective resistance of an electric circuit or component.

impede VB to prevent or delay the start or progress of; to hinder.

impediment N 1 an obstacle or hindrance. 2 a defect in a person's speech.

impel VB (*-ll-*) 1 to drive or urge something forward. 2 to urge someone into action.

impend VB, INTR 1 to be about to happen. 2 to be threateningly close.

impenetrable ADJ 1 incapable of being entered or seen or passed through. 2 not capable of being understood or explained.

impenitent ADJ not sorry for having done something wrong. **■ impenitence** N.

imperative ADJ 1 absolutely essential; urgent. 2 having or showing authority; commanding: **an imperative manner.** 3 GRAM of the mood of a verb: used for giving orders.
➤ N 1 GRAM a mood of verbs used for giving orders. 2 a verb form of this kind. 3 something imperative, esp a command or order.

imperceptible ADJ not able to be perceived by the senses. **■ imperceptibly** ADV.

imperfect ADJ 1 having faults; spoilt. 2 lacking

the full number of parts; incomplete or unfinished. **3** GRAM of the tense of a verb: expressing a continuing state or incomplete action in the past. **4** MUS reduced by a semitone. ➤ N, GRAM **a** the imperfect tense; **b** a verb in the imperfect tense. ■ **imperfection** N.

imperial ADJ **1** relating to an empire, emperor or empress. **2** having supreme authority. **3** commanding; august. **4** regal; magnificent. **5** BRIT of a non−metric system: fixed by parliament. ■ **imperially** ADV.

imperialism N **1** the power of, or rule by, an emperor. **2** the policy or principle of having or extending control over other nations. ■ **imperialist** N, ADJ. ■ **imperialistic** ADJ.

imperil VB (*-ll-*; US *-l-*) to endanger.

imperious ADJ arrogant, haughty and domineering. ■ **imperiously** ADV.

imperishable ADJ not subject to decay.

impermeable ADJ not allowing substances, esp liquids, to pass through.

impersonal ADJ **1** having no reference to any particular person; objective. **2** without personal feelings, sympathy, etc. **3** without personality. **4** GRAM **a** of a verb: used without a subject or with a purely formal one (as in *It's snowing*). **b** of a pronoun: not referring to a particular person; indefinite.

impersonate VB to pretend to be, or copy the behaviour and appearance of, someone, esp in order to entertain or deceive other people. ■ **impersonation** N. ■ **impersonator** N.

impertinent ADJ disrespectful; impudent. ■ **impertinence** N.

imperturbable ADJ always calm and unruffled. ■ **imperturbability** N.

impervious ADJ of a substance or material, etc: not allowing (eg water) to pass through or penetrate it; impermeable.

impetigo N, PATHOL a contagious skin disease.

impetuous ADJ **1** acting or done hurriedly and without due consideration. **2** moving or acting with great energy. ■ **impetuosity** N.

impetus N **1** the force or energy with which something moves. **2** a driving force. **3** an incentive or encouragement.

impinge VB (*impinging*) INTR (usu **impinge on sth** or **sb**) **1** to interfere with or encroach on it or them. **2** to make an impression on it or them.

impious ADJ lacking respect or proper reverence. ■ **impiety** N (*-ies*).

implacable ADJ unyielding.

implant VB **1** to fix or plant something securely; to embed it. **2** SURGERY to insert or graft (an object, tissue, etc) into the body. ➤ N, SURGERY an implanted object, tissue, etc.

implausible ADJ not easy to believe; not likely to be true. ■ **implausibly** ADV.

implement N a tool or utensil. ➤ VB to fulfil or perform. ■ **implementation** N.

implicate VB **1** to show or suggest that someone is or was involved in eg a crime. **2** to imply. ■ **implicative** ADJ.

implication N **1** implicating someone or being implicated. **2** implying something or being implied. **3** something that is implied.

implicit ADJ **1** implied but not stated directly. **2** present, although not explicit or immediately discernible. **3** unquestioning; complete.

implode VB, TR & INTR to collapse or make something collapse inwards.

implore VB to entreat or beg someone.

imply VB (*-ies, -ied*) **1** to suggest or express something indirectly; to hint at it. **2** to suggest or involve something as a necessary result or consequence.

impolite ADJ rude, disrespectful.

impolitic ADJ unwise; not advisable.

imponderable ADJ that cannot be assessed. ➤ N something imponderable.

import VB **1** to bring (goods, etc) into a country from another country. **2** to bring something in from an external source. **3** COMP to load (a file, text, data, etc) into a program. **4** FORMAL OR OLD

USE to signify, imply or portend.
➤ N **1** an imported commodity, article, etc. **2** AS ADJ: import duty. **3** FORMAL importance: a matter of great import. **4** FORMAL OR OLD USE meaning. ■ **importation** N. ■ **importer** N.

important ADJ **1** having great value, influence or significance. **2** having high social rank. ■ **importance** N. ■ **importantly** ADV.

importunate ADJ, FORMAL **1** persistent or excessively demanding. **2** pressing.

importune VB, TR & INTR, FORMAL to make persistent and usu annoying requests of someone. ■ **importunity** N (-**ies**).

impose VB **1** to make payment of (a tax, fine, etc) or performance of (a duty) compulsory. **2** to force one's opinions, company, etc on others. **3** (esp **impose on** or **upon sb** or **sth**) INTR to take advantage of them or it. ■ **imposition** N.

imposing ADJ impressive, esp in size, dignity, handsome appearance, etc.

impossible ADJ **1** not capable of happening, being done, etc. **2** not capable of being true; difficult to believe. **3** COLLOQ intolerable. ■ **impossibility** N. ■ **impossibly** ADV.

impostor or **imposter** N someone who pretends to be someone else in order to deceive others. ■ **imposture** N.

impotent ADJ **1** powerless. **2** of a male: **a** unable to maintain a sexual erection; **b** unable to have an orgasm. ■ **impotence** N.

impound VB **1** to shut (eg an animal) up in, or as if in, a pound. **2** to take legal possession of something; to confiscate it.

impoverish VB to make poor or poorer. ■ **impoverished** ADJ.

impracticable ADJ not able to be done, put into practice, used, etc. ■ **impracticability** N.

impractical ADJ **1** not effective in actual use. **2** of a person, plan, etc: lacking common sense. ■ **impracticality** N (-**ies**).

imprecation N, FORMAL OR OLD USE a curse.

imprecise ADJ inaccurate. ■ **imprecision** N.

impregnable ADJ not able to be taken by force.

impregnate VB **1** to make (a woman or female animal) pregnant; to fertilize (eg a female cell or plant). **2** to permeate or fill something completely. ■ **impregnation** N.

impresario N **1** someone who organizes public concerts, etc. **2** the manager of an opera or theatre company.

impress VB **1** to produce a strong and usu favourable impression on someone. **2** (esp **impress sth on** or **upon sb**) to make it very clear or emphasize it to them. **3** to make or stamp (a mark, pattern, etc) on something by pressure. **4** (often **impress sth on** or **upon sb**) to fix (a fact, belief, etc) firmly or deeply in their mind or memory.
➤ N **1** the act or process of impressing. **2** something made by impressing. ■ **impressible** ADJ.

impression N **1** an idea or effect, esp a favourable one, produced in the mind or made on the senses. **2** a vague or uncertain idea, notion or belief: I got the impression he was lying. **3** an act or the process of impressing. **4** a mark or stamp produced by, or as if by, pressure. **5** an imitation of a person, thing or sound, done for entertainment. **6** the copies of a book, newspaper, etc printed at one time.

impressionable ADJ easily impressed or influenced. ■ **impressionability** N.

Impressionism N (sometimes **impressionism**) in art, music or literature: a 19c style aiming to give a general impression of feelings and events rather than a formal treatment of them. ■ **Impressionist** N, ADJ.

impressionistic ADJ based on impressions or feelings rather than facts or knowledge.

impressive ADJ capable of making a deep impression on a person's mind, feelings, etc. ■ **impressively** ADV.

imprimatur N approval; permission.

imprint N **1** a mark made by pressure. **2** a permanent effect, eg on the mind. **3** a publisher's name and address, as printed eg at the opening of a book.

➤ VB (usu **imprint sth on sth**) **1** to mark or print an impression of it on (eg a surface). **2** to fix it firmly in (the mind, etc).

imprison VB **1** to put in prison. **2** to confine or restrain as if in a prison. ■ **imprisonment** N.

improbable ADJ **1** unlikely to happen or exist. **2** hard to believe. ■ **improbability** N (*-ies*).

improbity N (*-ies*) dishonesty; wickedness.

impromptu ADJ made or done without preparation or rehearsal.
➤ ADV without preparation; spontaneously.

improper ADJ **1** not conforming to accepted standards of modesty and moral behaviour. **2** not correct; wrong: **improper use of funds**. **3** not suitable. ■ **improperly** ADV.

impropriety N (*-ies*) **1** an improper act. **2** the state of being improper.

improve VB **1** TR & INTR to make or become better or of higher quality or value; to make or cause something to make progress. **2** (esp **improve on sth**) to produce something better, or of higher quality or value, than a previous example.

improvement N **1** improving or being improved. **2** someone or something considered better than a previous example. **3** something that improves, esp by adding value, beauty, etc: **home improvements**.

improvident ADJ **1** not providing for likely future needs. **2** careless; thoughtless; rash. ■ **improvidence** N. ■ **improvidently** ADV.

improvise VB **1** TR & INTR to compose, recite or perform (music, verse, etc) without advance preparation. **2** to make something quickly, using materials to hand. ■ **improvisation** N.

imprudent ADJ lacking good sense or caution. ■ **imprudence** N.

impudent ADJ rude, insolent or impertinent. ■ **impudence** N.

impugn VB to call into question (the honesty, integrity, etc of someone or something).

impulse N **1** a sudden push forwards; a force producing sudden movement forwards. **2** the movement produced by such a force or push. **3** a sudden desire or urge to do something: **bought the dress on impulse**. **4** an instinctive or natural tendency. **5** PHYSIOL an electrical signal that travels along a nerve fibre.

impulsive ADJ **1** tending or likely to act suddenly and without considering the consequences. **2** done without consideration of consequences. **3** having the power to urge or push forwards, into motion or into action.

impunity N freedom or exemption from punishment, injury, loss, etc.

impure ADJ **1** mixed with something else; adulterated . **2** dirty. **3** immoral; not chaste. **4** RELIG ritually unclean. ■ **impurity** N (*-ies*).

impute VB (usu **impute sth to sb** or **sth**) to regard (something unfavourable or unwelcome) as being brought about by them or it. ■ **imputable** ADJ. ■ **imputation** N.

in PREP **1** used to express position with regard to what encloses, surrounds or includes someone or something. **2** into. **3** after (a period of time): **Come back in an hour**. **4** during; while: **lost in transit**. **5** used to express arrangement or shape: **in a square**. **6** from; out of something: **one in every eight**. **7** by the medium or means of, or using, something: **in code**. **8** wearing (something). **9** used to describe a state or manner: **in a hurry**. **10** used to state an occupation: **She's in banking**. **11** used to state a purpose: **in memory of his wife**.
➤ ADV **1** to or towards the inside; indoors. **2** at home or work: **Is John in?** **3** so as to be added or included: **beat in the eggs**. **4** so as to enclose or conceal: **The fireplace was bricked in**. **5** in or into political power or office. **6** in or into fashion. **7** in favour: **kept in with the boss**. **8** in certain games: batting. **9** into a proper, required or efficient state: **run a new car in**. **10** of the tide: at its highest point.
➤ ADJ **1** inside; internal; inwards: **the in door**. **2** fashionable: **the in colour**. **3** IN COMPOUNDS used for receiving things coming in: **an in-tray**. **4** IN COMPOUNDS shared by a particular group of people: **an in-joke**.

in as far as or **in so far as ...** to the degree that ...

in as much as ... or **inasmuch as ...** because ...; considering that ...

in itself essentially; considered on its own.

in on sth COLLOQ sharing in it.

ins and outs the complex and detailed facts of a matter; intricacies.

insomuch that or **insomuch as 1** in as much as. **2** to such an extent that.

in that ... for the reason that ...

inability N the lack of sufficient power, means or ability.

inaccessible ADJ **1** difficult or impossible to approach, reach or obtain. **2** difficult to understand; unapproachable.

inaccurate ADJ containing errors.
■ **inaccuracy** N (-*ies*). ■ **inaccurately** ADV.

inaction N lack of action; inactivity.

inactive ADJ **1** taking little or no exercise. **2** no longer operating or functioning. **3** not taking part in or available for duty or operations. **4** CHEM of a substance: showing little or no chemical reactivity. ■ **inactivity** N.

inadequate ADJ **1** not sufficient or adequate. **2** not competent or capable. ■ **inadequacy** N (-*ies*).

inadmissible ADJ not allowable.

inadvertent ADJ **1** not deliberate; unintentional. **2** not paying attention; heedless.

inadvisable ADJ not wise; not advisable.

inalienable ADJ not capable of being taken or given away: **an inalienable right**.

inane ADJ **1** without meaning or point. **2** silly or senseless. ■ **inanity** N.

inanimate ADJ **1** not living. **2** dull; spiritless.

inappropriate ADJ not suitable.

inarticulate ADJ **1** unable to express oneself clearly or to speak distinctly. **2** badly expressed; not spoken or pronounced clearly.

inasmuch see under **in**

inattentive ADJ not paying attention;

neglectful; not attentive. ■ **inattention** or **inattentiveness** N.

inaudible ADJ not loud enough to be heard.

inaugural ADJ officially marking the beginning of something.

inaugurate VB **1** to place (a person) in office with a formal ceremony. **2** to mark the beginning of (some activity) with a formal ceremony, etc. ■ **inauguration** N.

inauspicious ADJ not promising future success; unlucky.

inboard ADJ, ADV esp of a boat's motor or engine: situated inside the hull.

inborn ADJ of an attribute or characteristic: possessed from birth; innate or hereditary.

inbred ADJ **1** inborn. **2** BIOL of a plant or animal: produced by inbreeding.

inbreed VB (PA T & PA P *inbred*) BIOL to allow or be involved in reproduction between closely related individuals. ■ **inbreeding** N.

in-built ADJ integral; built–in.

incalculable ADJ **1** not able to be estimated or reckoned in advance; unpredictable. **2** too great to be measured. ■ **incalculably** ADV.

in camera ADV in secret; in private.

incandescent ADJ **1** glowing with intense heat. **2** luminous. ■ **incandescence** N.

incantation N **1** a spell. **2** the use of spells and magical formulae.

incapable ADJ lacking the ability, power, character, etc to do something.

incapacitate VB (often **incapacitate sb for sth**) **1** to take away strength or ability; to make unfit (eg for work). **2** to disqualify someone.

incapacity N (-*ies*) **1** a lack of the necessary strength, power, ability, etc; inability or disability. **2** legal disqualification.

incarcerate VB to shut in or keep in prison. ■ **incarceration** N.

incarnate ADJ (usu placed after a noun) **1** in bodily, esp human, form: **God incarnate**.

2 personified; typified.

incarnation N **1** the bodily form, esp human form, taken by a spirit or god. **2** someone or something that typifies a quality or idea. **3** a period spent in a particular form or state.

incendiary ADJ **1** relating to the deliberate and illegal burning of property or goods. **2** capable of catching fire and burning readily. **3** causing, or likely to cause, trouble or violence.
➤ N (**-ies**) **1** someone who deliberately and illegally sets fire to buildings or property. **2** (also **incendiary bomb**) a device containing a highly inflammable substance, designed to burst into flames on striking its target.

incense[1] N a spice or other substance which gives off a pleasant smell when burned.

incense[2] VB to make someone very angry.

incentive N something, such as extra money, that encourages an action, work, etc.

inception N beginning; outset.

incessant ADJ going on without stopping; continual. ■ **incessantly** ADV.

incest N sexual intercourse between people who are too closely related to be allowed to marry. ■ **incestuous** ADJ.

inch N **1** a unit of length equal to one twelfth of a foot. **2** METEOROL a unit of pressure equal to the amount of atmospheric pressure required to balance the weight of a column of mercury one inch high. **3** (also **inches**) a small amount or distance. **4** (**inches**) stature.
➤ VB, TR & INTR (esp **inch along, forward, out, etc**) to move or be moved slowly, carefully and by small degrees.

inchoate ADJ, FORMAL OR TECHNICAL at the earliest stage of development; just beginning.

incidence N **1** the frequency with which something happens or the extent of its influence. **2** PHYS the way in which something moving in a line (eg a ray of light) comes into contact with a surface or plane.

incident N **1** an event or occurrence. **2** a brief violent conflict or disturbance.

incidental ADJ **1** happening, etc by chance in connection with something else, and of secondary or minor importance: incidental expenses. **2** occurring or likely to occur as a minor consequence of it. **3** (usu **incidental on** or **upon sth**) following or depending upon it, or caused by it, as a minor consequence.
➤ N **1** anything that occurs incidentally. **2** (**incidentals**) minor expenses, details, items, etc. ■ **incidentally** ADV.

incidental music N music which accompanies the action of a film, play, etc.

incinerate VB, TR & INTR to burn to ashes. ■ **incineration** N.

incinerator N a furnace for burning rubbish.

incipient ADJ beginning to exist or appear.

incise VB, esp TECHNICAL **1** to cut into, esp precisely with a sharp tool. **2** to engrave (an inscription, stone, etc).

incision N **1** a cut, esp one made by a surgeon. **2** an act of cutting, esp by a surgeon.

incisive ADJ clear and sharp; to the point; acute. ■ **incisively** ADV. ■ **incisiveness** N.

incisor N in mammals: a sharp chisel-edged tooth in the front of the mouth, used for biting.

incite VB (esp **incite sb to sth**) to stir up or provoke to action, etc. ■ **incitement** N.

incivility N (**-ies**) **1** rudeness. **2** an uncivil act.

inclement ADJ, FORMAL of weather: stormy or severe.

inclination N **1** a tendency or feeling; a liking, interest or preference. **2** the degree to which an object slopes. **3** a bow or nod of (the head, etc). **4** the act of inclining; being inclined.

incline VB **1** TR & INTR (esp **incline to** or **towards sth**) to lean or make someone lean towards or be disposed towards (a particular opinion or conduct). **2** TR & INTR to slope or make something slope. **3** to bow or bend (the head, one's body, etc) forwards or downwards.
➤ N a slope; an inclined plane. ■ **inclined** ADJ.

include VB **1** to count, take in or consider something or someone as part of a group. **2** to contain or be made up of something, or to have it as a part of the whole.

inclusion N **1** including or being included. **2** something that is included.

inclusive ADJ **1** (usu **inclusive of sth**) incorporating it; taking it in. **2** counting the items or terms forming the limits. **3** comprehensive.

incognito ADJ, ADV keeping one's identity secret, eg by using a disguise and a false name. ➤ N **1** the disguise and false name of a person who wishes to keep their identity secret. **2** someone who is incognito.

incoherent ADJ **1** not expressed clearly or logically; difficult to understand. **2** unable to speak clearly and logically.

income N money received over a period of time as salary or wages, interest or profit.

incomer N someone who comes to live in a place, not having been born there.

incoming ADJ **1** coming in; approaching: the incoming train. **2** next or following. **3** of an official, politician, etc: coming into office.

incommodious ADJ, FORMAL inconvenient or uncomfortable; too small.

incommunicado ADV, ADJ not able or allowed to communicate with other people.

incomparable ADJ **1** having no equal. **2** not comparable; lacking a basis for comparison.

incompatible ADJ **1** unable to live, work or get on together in harmony. **2** (often **incompatible with sth**) not in agreement; inconsistent. **3** not able to be combined or used together. ■ **incompatibility** N.

incompetent ADJ lacking the necessary skill, ability or qualifications, esp for a job. ➤ N an incompetent person. ■ **incompetence** N. ■ **incompetently** ADV.

incomplete ADJ not complete or finished.

incomprehensible ADJ difficult or impossible to understand.

inconceivable ADJ **1** unable to be imagined, believed or conceived by the mind. **2** COLLOQ

extremely unlikely. ■ **inconceivability** N.

inconclusive ADJ not leading to a definite conclusion, or decision.

incongruous ADJ out of place; unsuitable; inappropriate. ■ **incongruity** N (**-ies**).

inconsequent ADJ **1** not following logically or reasonably; illogical. **2** irrelevant. **3** (also **inconsequential**) not connected or related.

inconsequential ADJ **1** of no importance, value or consequence. **2** inconsequent.

inconsiderable ADJ small in amount, value, etc: a not inconsiderable sum.

inconsiderate ADJ thoughtless, esp in not considering the feelings, rights, etc of others. ■ **inconsiderateness** N.

inconsistent ADJ **1** not in agreement or accordance with. **2** containing contradictions. **3** not consistent in thought, speech, behaviour, etc; changeable. ■ **inconsistency** N (**-ies**).

inconsolable ADJ not able to be comforted.

inconspicuous ADJ not easily noticed.

incontestable ADJ indisputable; undeniable.

incontinent ADJ **1** unable to control one's bowels and/or bladder. **2** FORMAL OR OLD USE unable to control oneself, esp one's sexual desires. ■ **incontinence** N.

incontrovertible ADJ not able to be disputed or doubted. ■ **incontrovertibly** ADV.

inconvenience N **1** trouble or difficulty. **2** something that causes trouble or difficulty. ➤ VB to cause trouble or difficulty to someone. ■ **inconvenient** ADJ. ■ **inconveniently** ADV.

incorporate VB **1** TR & INTR to include or contain something, or be included, as part of a whole. **2** TR & INTR to combine something, or be united thoroughly, in a mass. **3** to admit someone to membership of a legal corporation. **4** to form into a legal corporation. ■ **incorporation** N. ➤ ADJ (also **incorporated**) **1** united as a single whole. **2** forming a legal corporation.

incorporeal ADJ **1** without bodily or material form or substance. **2** spiritual.

incorrect ADJ 1 not accurate; containing errors or faults. 2 not in accordance with normal or accepted standards; improper.

incorrigible ADJ not able to be improved, corrected or reformed.

incorruptible ADJ 1 incapable of being bribed or morally corrupted. 2 not liable to decay. ■ **incorruptibility** N.

increase VB TR & INTR to make or become greater in size, intensity or number.
➤ N 1 increasing or becoming increased; growth. 2 the amount by which something increases or is increased. ■ **increasing** ADJ.

incredible ADJ 1 difficult or impossible to believe. 2 COLLOQ amazing; unusually good. ■ **incredibility** N. ■ **incredibly** ADV.

incredulous ADJ 1 showing or expressing disbelief. 2 (often **incredulous of sth**) unwilling to believe or accept that it is true. ■ **incredulity** N. ■ **incredulously** ADV.

increment N 1 an increase, esp of one point or level on a scale, eg a regular increase in salary. 2 the amount by which something is increased. 3 MATH a small positive or negative change in the value of a variable. ■ **incremental** ADJ.

incriminate VB 1 (sometimes **incriminate sb in sth**) **a** to show that they were involved in it (esp in a crime); **b** to involve or implicate them (esp in a crime). 2 to charge someone with a crime or fault. ■ **incriminating** or **incriminatory** ADJ. ■ **incrimination** N.

incubate VB 1 TR & INTR of birds: to hatch (eggs) by sitting on them to keep them warm. 2 to encourage (germs, bacteria, etc) to develop, eg in a culture medium in a laboratory. 3 INTR of germs, etc: to remain inactive in an organism before the first signs of disease appear. ■ **incubation** N.

incubator N 1 MED a transparent boxlike container in which a premature baby can be nurtured under controlled conditions. 2 a cabinet or room maintained at a constant temperature, used for hatching eggs, etc.

incubus N (*-buses, -bi*) FOLKLORE an evil male spirit which is supposed to have sexual intercourse with sleeping women.

inculcate VB (esp **inculcate sth in** or **into** or **upon sb**) rather FORMAL to teach or fix (ideas, habits, a warning, etc) firmly in their mind by constant repetition. ■ **inculcation** N.

inculpate VB, FORMAL to blame someone or show them to be guilty of a crime.

incumbent ADJ, rather FORMAL 1 (esp **incumbent on** or **upon sb**) imposed as a duty or responsibility on them: *incumbent upon me to defend him.* 2 currently occupying a position or office: *the incumbent bishop.*
➤ N a holder of an office, esp a church office or benefice. ■ **incumbency** N (*-ies*).

incur VB (*-rr-*) 1 to bring (something bad) upon oneself. 2 to become liable for (debts, etc).

incurable ADJ 1 not curable. 2 incapable of changing. ■ **incurably** ADV.

incursion N 1 a brief or sudden attack made into enemy territory. 2 a damaging invasion into or using up of something.

indebted ADJ (USU **indebted to sb**) 1 having reason to be grateful or obliged to them. 2 owing them money. ■ **indebtedness** N.

indecent ADJ 1 offensive to accepted standards of morality or sexual behaviour. 2 in bad taste; improper. ■ **indecency** N (*-ies*).

indecipherable ADJ unable to be read, deciphered or understood.

indecisive ADJ 1 not producing a clear or definite decision or result; inconclusive. 2 of a person: unable to make a firm decision; hesitating. ■ **indecision** N. ■ **indecisively** ADV. ■ **indecisiveness** N.

indecorous ADJ, FORMAL in bad taste; improper or unseemly.

indeed ADV 1 without any question. 2 in fact. 3 used for emphasis: *very wet indeed.*
➤ EXCLAM expressing irony, surprise, disbelief, disapproval, etc, or simple acknowledgement of a previous remark: *'I'm going whether you like it or not.' 'Indeed?'*

indefatigable ADJ 1 without tiring;

unflagging. **2** never stopping; unremitting.

indefensible ADJ **1** unable to be excused or justified. **2** of an opinion, position, etc: untenable; unable to be defended. **3** LITERALLY not possible to defend against attack.
■ **indefensibility** N. ■ **indefensibly** ADV.

indefinable ADJ unable to be exactly defined or described. ■ **indefinably** ADV.

indefinite ADJ **1** without fixed or exact limits or clearly marked outline. **2** uncertain; vague; imprecise. **3** GRAM not referring to a particular person or thing. ■ **indefinitely** ADV.

indefinite article N, GRAM in English, the words **a** or **an**, or any equivalent word in another language.

indelible ADJ **1** unable to be removed or rubbed out. **2** designed to make an indelible mark. ■ **indelibly** ADV.

indelicate ADJ **1** tending to embarrass or offend. **2** slightly coarse; rough. ■ **indelicacy** N (*-ies*). ■ **indelicately** ADV.

indemnify VB (*-ies, -ied*) **1** (esp **indemnify sb against** or **from sth**) to provide them with security or protection against (loss or misfortune). **2** (usu **indemnify sb for sth**) to pay them compensation for (esp loss or damage). ■ **indemnification** N.

indemnity N (*-ies*) **1 a** compensation for loss or damage; **b** money paid in compensation. **2** security or protection from loss or damage; insurance. **3** legal exemption from penalties.

indent[1] VB **1** PRINTING, TYPING to begin (a line or paragraph) further in from the margin than the main body of text. **2** to divide (a document drawn up in duplicate in two columns) along a zigzag line. **3** to draw up (a document, deed, etc) in duplicate. **4** to notch (eg a border).
➤ N **1** PRINTING, TYPING an indented line or paragraph. **2** a notch.

indent[2] VB to form a dent in something.
➤ N a hollow, depression or dent.

indentation N **1** a cut or notch. **2** a deep, inward curve or recess, eg in a coastline. **3** the act or process of indenting. **4** indention.

indention N, PRINTING, TYPING **1** the indenting of a line or paragraph. **2** the blank space at the beginning of a line caused by indenting.

indenture N (usu **indentures**) a contract binding an apprentice to a master.
➤ VB, chiefly OLD USE **1** to bind (eg an apprentice) by indentures. **2** to bind (eg another party) by an indented contract or agreement.

independent ADJ (sometimes **independent of sth** or **sb**) **1 a** not under the control or authority of others; **b** self-governing. **2** not relying on others for financial support, care, help or guidance. **3** thinking and acting for oneself and not under an obligation to others. **4** MATH, **etc** not dependent on something else for value, purpose or function. **5** of two or more people or things: not related to or affected by the others. **6** large enough to make it unnecessary to work for a living: **a man of independent means**.
➤ N an independent person or thing.
■ **independence** N. ■ **independently** ADV.

in-depth ADJ thorough; exhaustive.

indescribable ADJ unable to be put into words, esp because too extreme, too difficult, too vague, etc. ■ **indescribably** ADV.

indestructible ADJ not able to be destroyed.

indeterminate ADJ **1** not precisely fixed or settled. **2** doubtful; vague.

index N (*indexes* or TECHNICAL *indices*) **1** an alphabetical list of names, subjects, etc dealt with in a book, with the page numbers on which each item appears. **2** in a library, etc: a catalogue or set of reference cards which lists each book, magazine, etc alphabetically and gives details of where it is shelved. **3** anything which points to, identifies or highlights a particular trend or condition. **4** a scale of numbers which shows changes in price, wages, etc: **retail price index**. **5** MATH an exponent.
➤ VB **1** to provide (a book, etc) with an index. **2** to list something in an index. ■ **indexation** N. ■ **indexer** N.

index finger N the finger next to the thumb. Also called **forefinger**.

index-linked ADJ, ECON of prices, wages, rates of interest, etc: rising or falling by the same amount as the cost of living.

Indian summer N a period of unusually warm dry weather in late autumn.

indicate VB 1 to point out or show. 2 to be a sign or symptom of something. 3 INTR to use an indicator on a motor vehicle. ■ **indication** N.

indicative ADJ 1 (also **indicatory**) (usu **indicative of sth**) serving as a sign or indication of it. 2 GRAM **a** of the mood of a verb: used to state facts, describe events or ask questions; **b** of a verb, tense, etc: in this mood. ➢ N, GRAM 1 the indicative mood. 2 a verb form of this kind. ■ **indicatively** ADV.

indicator N 1 **a** an instrument or gauge that shows the level of temperature, fuel, pressure, etc; **b** a needle or pointer on such a device. 2 a flashing light on a motor vehicle which shows that the vehicle is about to change direction. 3 any sign, situation, etc which shows or indicates something: **an economic indicator**.

indict VB, LAW to accuse someone of, or charge them formally with, a crime, esp in writing. ■ **indictable** ADJ. ■ **indictment** N.

indie N, COLLOQ 1 a small independent and usu non-commercial record or film company. 2 AS ADJ not mainstream or commercial: **indie music**.

indifferent ADJ 1 (esp **indifferent to** or **towards sth** or **sb**) showing no interest in or concern for it or them. 2 neither good nor bad; average; mediocre. 3 fairly bad; inferior. 4 unimportant. 5 neutral. ■ **indifference** N. ■ **indifferently** ADV.

indigenous ADJ 1 BIOL belonging naturally to or occurring naturally in a country or area. 2 born in a region, area, country, etc.

indigent ADJ, FORMAL very poor; needy. ■ **indigence** N.

indigestible ADJ 1 difficult or impossible to digest. 2 not easily understood.

indigestion N discomfort or pain in the abdomen or lower region of the chest caused by difficulty in digesting food.

indignant ADJ feeling or showing anger or a sense of having been treated unjustly or wrongly. ■ **indignation** N.

indignity N (-*ies*) 1 any act or treatment which makes someone feel shame or humiliation. 2 a feeling of shame, disgrace or dishonour.

indigo N (-*os* or -*oes*) 1 a violet-blue dye. 2 a plant whose leaves yield this dye. 3 the deep violet-blue colour of this dye.

indirect ADJ 1 of a route, line, etc: not direct or straight. 2 not going straight to the point; not straightforward or honest. 3 not directly aimed at or intended: **indirect consequences**.

indirect object N, GRAM a noun, phrase or pronoun which is affected indirectly by the action of a verb.

indirect speech N, GRAM a speaker's words as reported by another person, eg **We will come** becomes **They said they would come**.

indirect tax N a tax levied on goods and services when they are purchased.

indiscernible ADJ unable to be noticed or recognized as being distinct.

indiscipline N lack of discipline.

indiscreet ADJ 1 giving away too many secrets or too much information. 2 not wise or cautious. ■ **indiscreetly** ADV. ■ **indiscretion** N.

indiscriminate ADJ 1 making no distinctions; not making careful choice or showing discrimination. 2 confused; not differentiated.

indispensable ADJ necessary; essential. ■ **indispensability** N. ■ **indispensably** ADV.

indisposed ADJ, rather FORMAL 1 slightly ill. 2 (esp **indisposed to do sth**) reluctant or unwilling to do it. ■ **indisposition** N.

indisputable ADJ beyond doubt.

indistinct ADJ not clear. ■ **indistinctly** ADV. ■ **indistinctness** N.

indistinguishable ADJ not able to be distinguished or told apart from something.

individual ADJ 1 intended for or relating to a

single person or thing: **individual portions**.
2 particular to one person; showing or having a particular person's unique qualities or characteristics. **3** separate; single.
➤ N **1** a particular person, animal or thing, esp in contrast to the group to which it belongs.
2 COLLOQ a person. ■ **individually** ADV.

individualism N **1 a** the belief that individual people should lead their lives as they want and should be independent; **b** behaviour governed by this belief. **2** self-centredness; egoism.
■ **individualist** N. ■ **individualistic** ADJ.

individuality N (*-ies*) the qualities which distinguish one person or thing from others.

indivisible ADJ **1** not able to be separated.
2 MATH of a number: not divisible (by a given number) without leaving a remainder.

indoctrinate VB to teach (an individual or group) to accept and believe a particular set of beliefs, etc uncritically. ■ **indoctrination** N.

indolent ADJ lazy. ■ **indolence** N.

indomitable ADJ unable to be conquered or defeated. ■ **indomitably** ADV.

indoor ADJ used, belonging, done, happening, etc inside a building.

indoors ADV in or into a building.

indubitable ADJ certain. ■ **indubitably** ADV.

induce VB **1** to persuade, influence or cause someone to do something. **2** OBSTETRICS to initiate or hasten (labour) by artificial means.
3 to make something happen or appear. **4** to produce or transmit (an electromotive force) by induction. **5** LOGIC to infer (a general conclusion) from particular cases. ■ **inducible** ADJ.

inducement N an incentive or motive.

induct VB **1** to place (eg a priest) formally and often ceremonially in an official position. **2** to initiate someone as a member of eg a society.

inductance N, PHYS the property of an electric circuit that causes an electromotive force to be generated when a changing current is present.

induction N **1** inducting or being inducted, esp into office. **2** OBSTETRICS the initiation of labour

by artificial means. **3** ELEC the production of an electric current in a conductor as a result of its close proximity to a varying magnetic field.
4 ELEC magnetization caused by close proximity either to a magnetic field or to the electromagnetic field of a current-carrying conductor. ■ **inductional** ADJ.

inductor N **1** ELEC a component of an electrical circuit that shows inductance. **2** someone or something that inducts.

indulge VB **1** TR & INTR (esp **indulge in sth** or **indulge sb in sth**) to allow oneself or someone else pleasure or the pleasure of (a specified thing). **2** to allow someone to have or do anything they want. **3** to give in to (a desire, taste, wish, etc) without restraint.

indulgence N **1** generosity; favourable or tolerant treatment. **2** an act or the process of indulging a person, desire, etc. **3** a pleasure that is indulged in. **4** RC CHURCH a remission from the punishment due for a sin.

indulgent ADJ quick or too quick to overlook or forgive faults or gratify the wishes of others; too tolerant or generous. ■ **indulgently** ADV.

industrial ADJ **1** of or suitable for industry.
2 having highly developed industry.

industrial action N, BRIT action taken by workers as a protest.

industrialism N a social system in which industry (rather than agriculture) forms the basis of commerce and the economy.

industrialist N someone who owns or runs a large industrial organization.

industrialize or **-ise** VB, TR & INTR to develop industrially; to introduce industry to (a place).
■ **industrialization** N.

industrious ADJ busy and hard-working.
■ **industriously** ADV. ■ **industriousness** N.

industry N (*-ies*) **1** the business of producing goods. **2** a branch of manufacturing and trade which produces a particular product: **the coal industry**. **3** organized commercial exploitation or use of natural or national assets: **the tourist industry**. **4** hard work or effort.

inebriate VB to make someone drunk.
➤ ADJ (now usu **inebriated**) drunk, esp habitually drunk.
➤ N, FORMAL someone who is drunk, esp regularly so. ■ **inebriation** N.

inedible ADJ not fit or suitable to be eaten.

ineffable ADJ, esp LITERARY OR FORMAL unable to be expressed in words. ■ **ineffably** ADV.

ineffective ADJ having no effect; not able to produce a result. ■ **ineffectiveness** N.

ineffectual ADJ 1 not producing a result or the intended result. 2 lacking the ability needed to achieve results. ■ **ineffectually** ADV.

inefficient ADJ lacking the power or skill to do or produce something in the best, most economical, etc way. ■ **inefficiency** N.

inelegant ADJ lacking grace or refinement.
■ **inelegance** N. ■ **inelegantly** ADV.

ineligible ADJ not suitable to be chosen.

ineluctable ADJ, esp LITERARY OR FORMAL unavoidable, irresistible or inescapable.

inept ADJ 1 awkward; done without, or not having, skill. 2 not suitable or fitting; out of place. 3 silly; foolish. ■ **ineptitude** N.

inequable ADJ 1 not fair or just. 2 changeable.

inequality N (-*ies*) a lack of equality, fairness or evenness, or an instance of this.

inequity N (-*ies*) rather FORMAL 1 an unjust action. 2 lack of fairness or equity.

inert ADJ 1 PHYS tending to remain in a state of rest or uniform motion in a straight line unless acted upon by an external force. 2 not wanting to move, act or think. 3 CHEM unreactive or showing only a limited ability to react with other chemical elements.

inert gas see **noble gas**

inertia N 1 PHYS the tendency of an object to be inert. 2 the state of not wanting to move, act or think. ■ **inertial** ADJ.

inescapable ADJ inevitable; unable to be avoided. ■ **inescapably** ADV.

inestimable ADJ, rather FORMAL too great, or of too great a value, to be estimated, measured or fully appreciated. ■ **inestimably** ADV.

inevitable ADJ 1 certain to happen. 2 COLLOQ tiresomely regular or predictable.
➤ N (esp **the inevitable**) something that is certain to happen and is unavoidable. ■ **inevitability** N. ■ **inevitably** ADV.

inexact ADJ not quite correct or true.

inexcusable ADJ too bad to be excused, justified or tolerated. ■ **inexcusably** ADV.

inexhaustible ADJ 1 incapable of being used up. 2 tireless; never failing or giving up.

inexorable ADJ 1 refusing to change opinion, course of action, etc; unrelenting. 2 unable to be altered or avoided. ■ **inexorably** ADV.

inexpensive ADJ reasonable in price.

inexperience N lack of knowledge gained from experience. ■ **inexperienced** ADJ.

inexpert ADJ (often **inexpert at** or **in sth**) unskilled at it. ■ **inexpertly** ADV.

inexplicable ADJ impossible to explain or understand. ■ **inexplicably** ADV.

inexpressible ADJ unable to be expressed or described. ■ **inexpressibly** ADV.

in extremis ADV 1 at, or as if at, the point of death or ultimate failure. 2 in desperate circumstances; in serious difficulties.

inextricable ADJ 1 of a situation, etc: unable to be escaped from. 2 of a knot, etc: unable to be disentangled. ■ **inextricably** ADV.

infallible ADJ 1 of a person: incapable of error. 2 of a plan, method, etc: always, or bound to be, successful or effective. ■ **infallibility** N.

infamous ADJ 1 notoriously bad. 2 FORMAL vile; disgraceful. ■ **infamy** N (-*ies*).

infancy N (-*ies*) 1 the state or time of being an infant. 2 an early period of existence, growth and development. 3 LAW minority.

infant N 1 a very young child. 2 BRIT a schoolchild under the age of seven or eight.
➤ ADJ at an early stage of development.

infanticide N 1 the murder of a child. 2 a child

murderer. ■ **infanticidal** ADJ.

infantile ADJ **1** relating to infants or infancy.
2 very childish; immature.

infantry N (*-ies*) soldiers trained and
equipped to fight on foot.

infantryman N a soldier in the infantry.

infarction N, PATHOL the death of a localized
area of tissue as a result of the blocking of its
blood supply.

infatuate VB to make someone feel intense
love or admiration. ■ **infatuation** N.

infect VB (often **infect sth** or **sb with sth**)
1 BIOL, MED, etc to contaminate (an organism)
with a bacterium, virus, etc and thereby cause
disease. **2** to taint or contaminate (eg water,
food or air) with a bacterium, pollutant, etc.

infection N **1** infecting or being infected.
2 BIOL, MED, etc the invasion of a human, animal
or plant by disease-causing micro-organisms.
3 a disease caused by such micro-organisms.

infectious ADJ **1** of a disease: caused by
bacteria, viruses or other micro-organisms, and
therefore capable of being transmitted through
air, water, etc. **2** eg of a person: capable of
infecting others; causing infection. **3** of an
emotion, etc: likely to be passed on to others.

infer VB (*-rr-*) **1** TR & INTR to conclude or judge
from facts, observation and deduction.
■ **inference** N. ■ **inferential** ADJ.

inferior ADJ (often **inferior to sth** or **sb**)
1 poor or poorer in quality. **2** low or lower in
value, rank or status. **3** low or lower in position.
➤ N someone or something which is inferior.
■ **inferiority** N.

inferiority complex N a general feeling of
inadequacy or worthlessness.

infernal ADJ **1** of or relating to the underworld.
2 of or relating to hell. **3** COLLOQ extremely
annoying, unpleasant, etc.

inferno N **1** a raging fire. **2** a place or situation
of horror and confusion.

infertile ADJ **1** lacking the nutrients required to
support the growth of crops, etc. **2** unable to

produce offspring. ■ **infertility** N.

infest VB **1** of fleas, lice, etc: to invade and
occupy an animal or plant. **2** of someone or
something harmful or unpleasant: to exist in
large numbers or quantities. ■ **infestation** N.

infidel N **1** someone who rejects a particular
religion, esp Christianity or Islam. **2** someone
who rejects all religions.
➤ ADJ relating to unbelievers; unbelieving.

infidelity N (*-ies*) unfaithfulness, esp of a
sexual nature, or an instance of this.

infield N **1** CRICKET **a** the area of the field close
to the wicket; **b** the players positioned there.
2 BASEBALL **a** the diamond-shaped area of the
pitch enclosed by the four bases; **b** the players
positioned there. ■ **infielder** N.

in-fighting N fighting or competition
between members of the same group, etc.

infill N (also **infilling**) **1** the act of filling or
closing gaps, holes, etc. **2** the material used to
fill a gap, hole, etc.
➤ VB to fill in (a gap, hole, etc).

infiltrate VB **1** of troops, agents, etc: to get into
(territory or an organization) secretly to gain
influence or information. **2** to filter (eg liquid or
gas) slowly through the pores (of a substance).
3 INTR eg of liquid or gas: to filter in.
■ **infiltration** N. ■ **infiltrator** N.

infinite ADJ **1** having no limits in size, extent, time
or space. **2** too great to be measured or
counted. **3** very great; vast. **4** MATH of a
number, series, etc: having an unlimited number
of elements or terms. **5** all-encompassing.
➤ N anything which has no limits, boundaries,
etc. ■ **infinitely** ADV. ■ **infinitude** N.

infinitesimal ADJ **1** infinitely small; with a value
too close to zero to be measured. **2** COLLOQ
extremely small. ■ **infinitesimally** ADV.

infinitive N, GRAM a verb form which
expresses an action but which does not refer to
a particular subject or time, in English often used
with **to** (eg **go** in **Tell him to go** • **Let her go**).
➤ ADJ of a verb: having this form.

infinity N (*-ies*) **1** space, time, distance or

quantity that is without limit or boundaries. **2** LOOSELY a quantity, etc that is too great to be measured. **3** MATH **a** a number that is larger than any finite value; **b** the reciprocal of zero. **4** the quality or state of being infinite.

infirm ADJ **1** weak or ill, esp from old age. **2** (**the infirm**) weak or ill people.

infirmary N (*-ies*) **1** a hospital. **2** a room or ward, eg in a boarding school, monastery, etc, where the sick and injured are treated.

infirmity N (*-ies*) **1** the state or quality of being sick, weak or infirm. **2** a disease or illness.

inflame VB **1** to arouse strong or violent emotion in someone or something. **2** to make something more heated or intense; to exacerbate it. **3** TR & INTR to become or to make (part of the body) red, swollen and painful.

inflammable ADJ **1** easily set on fire. **2** easily excited or angered. ■ **inflammability** N.

inflammation N **1** PATHOL a response of body tissues to injury, infection, etc in which the affected part becomes inflamed. **2** inflaming or being inflamed.

inflammatory ADJ **1** likely to cause violent emotion. **2** PATHOL relating to, causing, or caused by, inflammation of part of the body.

inflatable ADJ able to be inflated for use. ➤ N an inflatable object.

inflate VB **1** TR & INTR to swell or cause something to swell or expand with air or gas. **2** ECON **a** to increase (prices generally) by artificial means; **b** to increase (the volume of money in circulation). **3** to exaggerate the importance or value of something. **4** to raise (the spirits, etc).

inflation N **1** ECON a general increase in the level of prices caused by an increase in the amount of money available. **2** inflating or being inflated. ■ **inflationary** ADJ.

inflect VB **1** GRAM to change the form of (a word) to show eg tense, number, gender or grammatical case. **2** to vary the tone or pitch of (the voice, a note, etc). **3** to bend inwards. ■ **inflection** or **inflexion** N.

inflexible ADJ **1** incapable of being bent.

2 DEROG unyielding; obstinate. **3** unable to be changed. ■ **inflexibility** N. ■ **inflexibly** ADV.

inflict VB to impose something unpleasant.

inflorescence N, BOT the flower-head and stem of a flowering plant.

inflow N **1** the act or process of flowing in. **2** something that flows in. ■ **inflowing** N, ADJ.

influence N **1** (esp **influence on** or **over sb** or **sth**) the power that one person or thing has to affect another. **2** a person or thing that has such a power. **3** power resulting from political or social position, wealth, ability, etc. ➤ VB **1** to have an effect on (a person, their work, events, etc). **2** to exert influence on someone or something; to persuade.

influential ADJ **1** having influence or power. **2** (esp **influential in sth**) making an important contribution. ■ **influentially** ADV.

influenza N, PATHOL a viral infection, with symptoms including headache, fever, a sore throat, catarrh and muscular aches and pains.

influx N **1** a continual arrival of large numbers of people or things. **2** a flowing in or inflow.

info N, COLLOQ information.

inform VB **1** TR & INTR (esp **inform sb about** or **of sth**) to tell them about it. **2** LITERARY OR FORMAL to animate, inspire, or give life to something. ◆ **inform against** or **on sb** to give incriminating evidence about them to the authorities.

informal ADJ **1** without ceremony or formality; relaxed and friendly. **2** of language, clothes, etc: suitable for relaxed, everyday situations. ■ **informality** N (*-ies*). ■ **informally** ADV.

informant N someone who informs or gives information.

information N knowledge gained or given.

information technology N, COMP the use, study or production of technologies to store, process and transmit information.

informative ADJ giving useful or interesting information. ■ **informatively** ADV.

informed ADJ 1 having or showing knowledge, esp in being educated and intelligent. 2 based on sound information; showing knowledge or experience. Also IN COMPOUNDS: well-informed.

informer N someone who informs against another, esp to the police.

infraction N, FORMAL the breaking of a law, rule, etc.

infrared or (sometimes) **infra-red** ADJ 1 of electromagnetic radiation: with a wavelength between the red end of the visible spectrum and microwaves and radio waves. 2 relating to, using, producing or sensitive to radiation of this sort: infrared camera. ➤ N 1 infrared radiation. 2 the infrared part of the spectrum.

infrasonic ADJ having a frequency or frequencies below the range normally heard by the human ear, less than 20 hertz.

infrastructure N 1 the basic inner structure of a society, organization or system. 2 the roads, railways, bridges, factories, schools, etc needed for a country to function properly.

infrequent ADJ occurring rarely or occasionally. ■ **infrequency** N.

infringe VB 1 to break or violate (eg a law or oath). 2 INTR (esp **infringe on** or **upon sth**) to encroach or trespass; to interfere with (a person's rights, freedom, etc) in such a way as to limit or reduce them. ■ **infringement** N.

infuriate VB to make someone very angry. ■ **infuriating** ADJ.

infuse VB, TR & INTR to soak, or cause (eg herbs or tea) to be soaked, in hot water to release flavour or other qualities.

infusion N 1 an act or the process of infusing something. 2 a solution produced by infusing.

ingenious ADJ showing or having skill, originality and inventive cleverness. ■ **ingeniously** ADV. ■ **ingenuity** N.

ingenuous ADJ innocent and childlike, esp in being frank and honest. ■ **ingenuously** ADV.

ingest VB to take (eg food or liquid) into the body. ■ **ingestible** ADJ. ■ **ingestion** N.

ingot N a brick-shaped block of metal, esp of gold or silver.

ingrained ADJ 1 difficult to remove or wipe off or out. 2 fixed firmly; instilled or rooted deeply.

ingratiate VB (esp **ingratiate oneself with sb**) to gain or try to gain their favour or approval. ■ **ingratiating** ADJ.

ingratitude N lack of due gratitude.

ingredient N a component of a mixture.

ingress N, FORMAL 1 the act of going in or entering. 2 the power or right to go in or enter.

ingrowing ADJ esp of a toenail: growing inwards so that it becomes embedded in the flesh. ■ **ingrown** ADJ.

inhabit VB to live in or occupy (a place). ■ **inhabitable** ADJ. ■ **inhabitant** N.

inhalant N a medicinal preparation in the form of a vapour or aerosol, to be inhaled.

inhale VB to draw (air, tobacco smoke, etc) into the lungs; to breathe in. ■ **inhalation** N.

inhaler N, MED a small, portable device used for inhaling certain medicinal preparations.

inharmonious ADJ 1 not sounding well together. 2 not agreeing; not compatible.

inhere VB, FORMAL, INTR of character, a quality, etc: to be an essential or permanent part.

inherent ADJ of a quality, etc: existing as anessential, natural or permanent part.

inherit VB 1 to receive (money, property, a title, etc) after someone's death. 2 to receive (genetically transmitted characteristics) from the previous generation. ■ **inheritable** ADJ. ■ **inheritor** N.

inheritance N 1 something (eg money, property, a title, a physical or mental characteristic) that is or may be inherited. 2 the legal right to inherit something. 3 heredity.

inhibit VB 1 to make someone feel unable to act freely or spontaneously. 2 to hold back, restrain or prevent (an action, desire, progress, etc). 3 to prohibit or forbid someone from doing something. ■ **inhibited** ADJ. ■ **inhibitor** or **inhibiter** N. ■ **inhibition** N.

inhospitable ADJ **1** not friendly or welcoming to others. **2** of a place: bleak or barren.

in-house ADV, ADJ within a particular company, organization, etc.

inhuman ADJ **1** cruel and unfeeling. **2** not human. ■ **inhumanity** N (*-ies*).

inhumane ADJ showing no kindness, sympathy or compassion.

inimical ADJ, FORMAL **1** tending to discourage; unfavourable. **2** hostile or in opposition.

inimitable ADJ too good, skilful, etc to be satisfactorily imitated by others; unique.

iniquity N (*-ies*) **1** an unjust, wicked or sinful act. **2** sinfulness. ■ **iniquitous** ADJ.

initial ADJ relating to or at the beginning.
➤ N the first letter of a word, esp of a name.
➤ VB (*-ll-*; (N AMER) *-l-*) to mark or sign something with the initials of one's name.

initially ADV **1** at first. **2** as a beginning.

initiate VB **1** to begin (eg a relationship, project, conversation, etc). **2** (usu **initiate sb into sth**) to accept (a new member) into a society, organization, etc, esp with secret ceremonies. **3** (usu **initiate sb in sth**) to give them instruction in the basics of a skill, science, etc.
➤ N someone who has recently been or is soon to be initiated. ■ **initiation** N.

initiative N **1** the ability to initiate things, take decisions or act resourcefully. **2** (esp in **take the initiative**) a first step or move towards an end or aim. **3** the power to begin something.

inject VB **1** to introduce (a liquid, eg medicine) into the body using a hypodermic syringe. **2** to force (fuel) into an engine. **3** to introduce (a quality, element, etc): **inject a note of optimism.** ■ **injectable** ADJ. ■ **injection** N.

injudicious ADJ not wise.

injunction N, LAW an official court order that forbids or commands.

injure VB **1** to do physical harm or damage to someone or something. **2** to harm or spoil something: **His pride was injured. 3** to do an injustice or wrong to someone.

injurious ADJ causing injury or damage.

injury N (*-ies*) **1 a** physical harm or damage; **b** an instance of this: **did herself an injury. 2** a wound: **has a serious head injury. 3** something that harms or spoils something. **4** now chiefly LAW a wrong or injustice.

injustice N **1** unfairness or lack of justice. **2** an unfair or unjust act.

ink N **1** a coloured liquid used for writing, drawing or printing. **2** BIOL a dark liquid ejected by octopus, squid, etc to confuse predators.
➤ VB **1** to mark something with ink. **2** to cover (a surface to be printed) with ink.

inkling N a vague or slight idea or suspicion.

inky ADJ (*-ier, -iest*) **1** covered with ink. **2** like ink; black or very dark. ■ **inkiness** N.

inland ADJ **1** not beside the sea. **2** esp BRIT not abroad; domestic.
➤ ADV in or towards the parts of a country away from the sea.

in-laws PL N, COLLOQ relatives by marriage, esp one's mother– and father–in-law.

inlay VB (PA T & PA P *inlaid*) **1** to set or embed (eg pieces of wood, metal, etc) flush in another material. **2** to decorate (eg a piece of furniture) by inlaying pieces of coloured wood, ivory, metal, etc in its surface.
➤ N **1** a decoration or design made by inlaying. **2** the pieces used to create an inlaid design. **3** DENTISTRY a filling shaped to fit a tooth cavity.

inlet N **1** GEOG a narrow arm of water running inland from a sea coast or lake shore. **2** a narrow opening or valve through which a gas or liquid enters a device.

inmate N someone living in or confined to an institution, esp a prison or a hospital.

in memoriam PREP in memory of.

inn N, esp BRIT a public house or small hotel providing food and accommodation.

innards PL N, COLLOQ **1** the inner organs of a person or animal, esp the stomach and intestines. **2** the inner workings of a machine.

innate ADJ **1** existing from birth; inherent. **2** natural or instinctive, rather than learnt or acquired. ■ **innately** ADV.

inner ADJ **1** further in; situated inside, close or closer to the centre: **inner ear**. **2** of thoughts, feelings, etc: secret, hidden and profound, or more secret, profound, etc.

innermost and **inmost** ADJ **1** furthest within; closest to the centre. **2** most secret or hidden.

inning N in a baseball game: any of the nine divisions per game in which a team may bat.

innings N **1** CRICKET **a** a team's or player's turn at batting; **b** the runs scored during such a turn. **2** BRIT a period during which someone has an opportunity for action or achievement.

innocent ADJ **1** free from sin; pure. **2** not guilty, eg of a crime. **3** not causing, or intending to cause, harm or offence: **an innocent remark**. **4** simple and trusting; guileless. **5** lacking, free or deprived of something: **innocent of all knowledge of the event**.
➤ N an innocent person. ■ **innocence** N.
■ **innocently** ADV.

innocuous ADJ harmless; inoffensive.

innovate VB, INTR to introduce new ideas, methods, etc. ■ **innovation** N. ■ **innovative** ADJ. ■ **innovator** N. ■ **innovatory** ADJ.

innuendo N (-os or -oes) **a** an indirectly unpleasant, critical or spiteful remark; **b** a rude or smutty allusion or insinuation.

innumerable ADJ too many to be counted.

innumerate ADJ having no understanding of mathematics or science. ■ **innumeracy** N.

inoculate VB **1** MED to inject a harmless form of an antigen into (a person or animal). **2** BIOL, etc to introduce a micro-organism into (a medium) in order to start a culture, or into another organism in order to produce antibodies.
■ **inoculation** N.

inoffensive ADJ harmless; not objectionable.

inoperable ADJ, MED of a disease or condition: not able to be treated by surgery.

inoperative ADJ not working or functioning.

inopportune ADJ badly-timed.

inordinate ADJ greater than or beyond what is normal or acceptable.

inorganic ADJ not composed of living or formerly living material.

inpatient N a patient temporarily living in hospital while receiving treatment there.

input N **1** COMP the data that is transferred from a disk, tape, keyboard, etc into the main memory of a computer. **2** something which is put or taken in, eg a contribution to a discussion. **3** the money, power, materials, labour, etc required to produce something; the power or electrical current put into a machine. **4** an act or process of putting something in. Also AS ADJ.
➤ VB to transfer (data) from a disk, keyboard, etc into the main memory of a computer.

inquest N a coroner's investigation.

inquire or **enquire** VB, TR & INTR to seek or ask for information.

inquiring or **enquiring** ADJ **1** eager to discover things: **an inquiring mind**. **2** appearing to be asking a question. ■ **inquiringly** ADV.

inquiry or **enquiry** N (-ies) **1** an act or the process of asking for information. **2** an investigation, esp a formal one.

inquisition N **1** a searching or intensive inquiry or investigation. **2** an official or judicial inquiry. ■ **inquisitional** ADJ.

inquisitive ADJ **1** over-eager to find out things, esp about other people's affairs. **2** curious. ■ **inquisitively** ADV. ■ **inquisitiveness** N.

inquisitor N someone who carries out an inquisition or inquiry. ■ **inquisitorial** ADJ.

inroad N **1** (usu **inroads into sth**) a large or significant using up or consumption of it, or encroachment on it. **2** a hostile attack or raid.

insane ADJ **1** mad; mentally ill. **2** COLLOQ esp of

actions: extremely foolish. **3** relating to the mentally ill. ■ **insanely** ADV. ■ **insanity** N.

insatiable ADJ not able to be satisfied; extremely greedy.

inscribe VB **1** to write, print or engrave (words) on (paper, metal, stone, etc). **2** to enter (a name) on a list or in a book; to enrol. **3** to dedicate or address (a book, etc) to someone.

inscription N words written, printed or engraved, eg on a gravestone.

inscrutable ADJ hard to understand or explain; enigmatic. ■ **inscrutability** N.

insect N, ZOOL an invertebrate animal, such as a fly, beetle, ant or bee, typically with a segmented body and two pairs of wings.

insecticide N any substance used to kill insects. ■ **insecticidal** ADJ.

insectivore N **1** an animal or bird that feeds on insects. **2** a plant that traps and digests insects. ■ **insectivorous** ADJ.

insecure ADJ **1** not firmly fixed; unstable. **2** lacking confidence; anxious about possible loss or danger. **3** under threat or likely to be so: insecure jobs. ■ **insecurity** N (-ies).

inseminate VB **1** to introduce semen into (a female). **2** FORMAL OR LITERARY to sow (seeds, ideas, attitudes, etc). ■ **insemination** N.

insensate ADJ, FORMAL OR LITERARY not able to perceive physical sensations; inanimate.

insensible ADJ, FORMAL OR LITERARY **1** not able to feel pain; not conscious. **2** (usu **insensible of** or **to sth**) unaware of it; not caring about it. **3** incapable of feeling emotion. **4** too small to be noticed. ■ **insensibility** N.

insensitive ADJ **1** not aware of, or not capable of responding sympathetically or thoughtfully to, other people's feelings, etc. **2** not feeling or reacting to (stimulation, eg touch or light).

inseparable ADJ **1** incapable of being separated. **2** unwilling to be apart; constantly together. ■ **inseparability** N.

insert VB **1** to put or fit something inside something else. **2** to introduce (text, words, etc)

into the body of other text, words, etc. ➤ N something inserted, esp a loose sheet in a book or magazine, or piece of material in a garment. ■ **insertion** N.

in-service ADJ carried on while a person is employed.

inset N something set in or inserted, eg a piece of lace or cloth set into a garment. ➤ VB (**inset, insetting**) to put in, add or insert something.

inshore ADV, ADJ in or on water, but near or towards the shore: inshore shipping.

inside N **1** the inner side, surface or part of something. **2** the side of a road nearest to the buildings, pavement, etc (as opposed to the other lane or lanes of traffic). **3** the part of a pavement or path away from the road. **4** SPORT the inside track, or the equivalent part of any racetrack. **5** (**insides**) COLLOQ the inner organs, esp the stomach and bowels. **6** COLLOQ a position which gains one the confidence of and otherwise secret information from people in authority: Those on the inside knew his plans. ➤ ADJ **1a** being on, near, towards or from the inside; **b** indoor. **2** COLLOQ coming from, concerned with, or planned by people within a specific organization: inside knowledge. ➤ ADV **1** to, in or on the inside or interior. **2** indoors. **3** COLLOQ in or into prison. ➤ PREP **1** to or on the interior or inner side of something; within. **2** in less than (a specified time).

insider N a member of an organization or group who has access to confidential or exclusive information about it.

inside out ADV (also **outside in**) with the inside surface turned out.

insidious ADJ **1** developing gradually without being noticed but causing great harm. **2** attractive but harmful; treacherous.

insight N **1** the ability to gain a relatively rapid, clear and deep understanding of the real, often hidden and usu complex nature of a situation, problem, etc. **2** an instance or example of this.

insignia SING OR PL N (**insignia** or **insignias**)

badges or emblems of office or honour.

insignificant ADJ 1 of little or no meaning, value or importance. 2 relatively small in size or amount. ■ **insignificance** N.

insincere ADJ not genuine; false; hypocritical. ■ **insincerely** ADV. ■ **insincerity** N (*-ies*).

insinuate VB 1 to suggest or hint in an indirect way. 2 to introduce in an indirect, subtle or devious way. ■ **insinuation** N.

insipid ADJ 1 having little or no interest or liveliness; boring. 2 having little or no taste or flavour. ■ **insipidness** or **insipidity** N.

insist VB 1 TR & INTR to maintain or assert something firmly. 2 (usu **insist on** or **upon sth**) to demand it firmly.

insistent ADJ 1 making continual forceful demands. 2 demanding attention; compelling. ■ **insistence** or **insistency** N.

in situ ADV in the natural or original position.

insole N an inner sole in a shoe or boot.

insolent ADJ rude or insulting; showing a lack of respect. ■ **insolence** N. ■ **insolently** ADV.

insoluble ADJ 1 not able to be dissolved in a particular solvent (esp water). 2 not able to be solved or resolved. ■ **insolubility** N.

insolvent ADJ not having enough money to pay debts, etc. ■ **insolvency** N.

insomnia N the chronic inability to sleep or to have enough sleep. ■ **insomniac** N, ADJ.

insomuch see under **in**

insouciant ADJ without cares or worries; light-hearted. ■ **insouciance** N.

inspect VB 1 to look at or examine closely, often to find faults. 2 to look at or examine (a body of soldiers, etc) ceremonially. ■ **inspection** N.

inspector N 1 someone whose job is to inspect something. 2 (often **Inspector**) BRIT a police officer below a superintendent in rank.

inspectorate N a body of inspectors.

inspiration N 1 someone or something that inspires. 2 the state of being inspired.

3 a brilliant idea. 4 PHYSIOL **a** the act of drawing breath into the lungs; **b** a breath taken in this way. ■ **inspirational** ADJ.

inspire VB 1 (often **inspire sb to sth** or **to do sth**) to stimulate them into activity, esp into artistic or creative activity. 2 to fill someone with a feeling of confidence, encouragement and exaltation. 3 (esp **inspire sb with sth** or **inspire sth into sb**) to create (a particular feeling) in them. 4 to be the origin or source of (a poem, piece of music, etc). 5 TR & INTR to breathe in (air, etc); to inhale.

instability N lack of physical or mental steadiness or stability.

install or (sometimes) **instal** VB (*-ll-*) 1 to put (equipment, machinery, etc) in place and make it ready for use. 2 to place (a person) in office with a formal ceremony. 3 to place (something, oneself, etc) in a particular position, condition or place. ■ **installation** N.

instalment or (US) **installment** N 1 one of a series of parts into which a debt is divided for payment. 2 one of several parts published, issued, broadcast, etc at regular intervals.

instance N 1 an example, esp one of a particular condition or circumstance. 2 a particular stage in a process or a situation: in the first instance. 3 FORMAL request; urging: at the instance of your partner. ◆ **for instance** for example.

instant ADJ 1 immediate. 2 of food and drink, etc: quickly and easily prepared, esp by the addition of boiling water. 3 present; current. ➤ N 1 a particular moment in time. 2 a moment.

instantaneous ADJ done, happening or occurring at once, very quickly or in an instant.

instantly ADV immediately.

instead ADV as a substitute or alternative; in place of something or someone.

instep N 1 the arched middle section of the human foot, between the ankle and the toes. 2 the part of a shoe, sock, etc that covers this.

instigate VB 1 to urge someone on or incite

them, esp to do something wrong or evil. **2** to set in motion or initiate (eg an inquiry). ■ **instigation** N. ■ **instigator** N.

instil or (US) **instill** VB (-*ll*-) (esp **instil sth in** or **into sb**) to impress, fix or plant (ideas, feelings, etc) slowly or gradually in their mind.

instinct N **1** in animal behaviour: an unlearned and inherited response to a stimulus. **2** in humans: a basic natural drive that urges a person towards a specific goal, such as survival or reproduction. **3** intuition.

instinctive ADJ **1** prompted by instinct. **2** involuntary; automatic. ■ **instinctively** ADV.

institute N **1** a society or organization which promotes research, education or a particular cause. **2** a building or group of buildings used by an institute. **3** an established law, principle, rule or custom.
➤ VB, rather FORMAL **1** to set up, establish or organize something: **instituted a trust fund. 2** to initiate something or cause it to begin.

institution N **1** an organization or public body founded for a special purpose, esp an educational purpose or as a hospital.
2 a hospital, old people's home, etc, regarded as impersonal or bureaucratic. **3** something which is well-established: **the institution of marriage.** ■ **institutional** ADJ.

institutionalize or **-ise** VB **1** to place someone in an institution. **2** to cause someone to lose their individuality and ability to cope with life by keeping them in (eg a long-stay hospital or prison) for too long.

instruct VB **1 a** to teach or train someone in a subject or skill; **b** (usu **instruct sb in sth**) to give them information about or practical knowledge of it. **2** to direct or order, eg someone to do something. **3** LAW to engage (a lawyer) to act in a case.

instruction N **1** (often **instructions**) a direction or command. **2** teaching. **3** COMP a command that activates a specific operation. **4** (**instructions**) guidelines on eg how to operate a piece of equipment.
■ **instructional** ADJ.

instructive ADJ giving knowledge or information.

instructor N someone who gives instruction.

instrument N **1** a tool, esp one used for delicate scientific work or measurement. **2** (also **musical instrument**) a device used to produce musical sounds. **3** a device which measures, shows and controls speed, temperature, direction, etc. **4** a means of achieving or doing something: **the instrument of his downfall. 5** a legal document.

instrumental ADJ **1** (often **instrumental in** or **to sth**) being responsible for it or an important factor in it. **2** of music: performed by or for musical instruments only. **3** relating to or done with an instrument or tool.
➤ N a piece of music for or performed by musical instruments only.

instrumentalist N someone who plays a musical instrument.

instrumentation N **1** the way in which a piece of music is written or arranged to be played by instruments. **2** the use, design or provision of instruments or tools.

insubordinate ADJ refusing to take orders or submit to authority. ■ **insubordination** N.

insubstantial ADJ not solid, strong or satisfying; flimsy: **insubstantial evidence.**

insufferable ADJ too unpleasant, annoying, etc to tolerate. ■ **insufferably** ADV.

insufficient ADJ not enough or not adequate.
■ **insufficiency** N. ■ **insufficiently** ADV.

insular ADJ narrow-minded. ■ **insularity** N.

insulate VB **1** to surround (a body, device or space) with a material that prevents or slows down the flow of heat, electricity or sound. **2** to remove or set someone or something apart; to isolate. ■ **insulation** N. ■ **insulator** N.

insulin N a hormone which controls the concentration of sugar in the blood.

insult VB **1** to speak rudely or offensively to or about someone or something. **2** to behave in a way that offends or affronts.

➢ N **1** a rude or offensive remark or action. **2** an affront: **an insult to the intelligence**.

insuperable ADJ too difficult to be overcome.

insupportable ADJ **1** intolerable. **2** not justifiable.

insurance N **1** an agreement by which a company promises to pay a person, etc money in the event of loss, theft, damage to property, injury or death, etc. **2** the contract for such an agreement. **3** the protection offered by such a contract. **4** an insurance premium. **5** the sum which will be paid according to such an agreement. **6** the business of providing such contracts for clients. **7** any measure taken to try to prevent possible loss, etc.

insure VB **1** TR & INTR to arrange for the payment of an amount of money in the event of the loss or theft of or damage to (property) or injury to or the death of (a person), etc by paying regular amounts of money to an insurance company. **2** to take measures to try to prevent (an event leading to loss, damage, difficulties, etc). ■ **insurable** ADJ. ■ **insurer** N.

insurgence or **insurgency** N (-**ces** or -**cies**) an uprising or rebellion.

insurgent ADJ opposed to and fighting against the government of the country. ➢ N a rebel.

insurmountable ADJ too difficult to be dealt with; impossible to overcome.

insurrection N a rebellion against authority.

intact ADJ whole; not broken or damaged.

intaglio N **1** the art or process of engraving designs into the surface of objects, esp jewellery. **2** an engraved design or gem.

intake N **1** a thing or quantity taken in or accepted. **2 a** a number or the amount taken in; **b** the people, etc taken in. **3** an opening through which liquid or gas (eg air) enters a pipe, etc.

intangible ADJ **1** not perceptible by touch. **2** difficult for the mind to grasp. **3** of eg a business asset: having value but no physical existence.

integer N **1** MATH a positive or negative whole number. **2** any whole or complete entity.

integral ADJ **1** being a necessary part of a whole. **2** forming a whole. **3** whole; complete. **4** MATH, DENOTING an integer.

integrate VB **1** to fit (parts) together to form a whole. **2** TR & INTR to mix (people) or cause (people) to mix freely with other groups in society, etc. **3** to end racial segregation in something. **4** MATH **a** to find the integral of (a function or equation); **b** to find the total or mean value of (a variable). ■ **integration** N.

integrated circuit N, ELECTRONICS a circuit on a chip of semiconductor material, usu silicon.

integrity N **1** moral uprightness. **2** the quality or state of being whole and unimpaired.

intellect N **1** the part of the mind that thinks, reasons and understands. **2** the capacity to use this part of the mind. **3** someone who has great mental ability.

intellectual ADJ **1** involving or appealing to the intellect. **2** having a highly developed ability to think, reason and understand. ➢ N an intellectual person.

intelligence N **1** the ability to use one's mind to solve problems, etc. **2** news or information. **3** the gathering of information about an enemy.

intelligence quotient N a measure of a person's intellectual ability.

intelligent ADJ **1** having highly developed mental ability. **2** of a machine, computer, weapon, etc: able to vary its behaviour according to the situation. ■ **intelligently** ADV.

intelligentsia N (usu **the intelligentsia**) the most highly educated people in a society.

intelligible ADJ able to be understood. ■ **intelligibility** N. ■ **intelligibly** ADV.

intemperate ADJ **1** going beyond reasonable limits. **2** having extreme and severe temperatures. ■ **intemperance** N.

intend VB **1** to have in mind as one's purpose or aim. **2** to set aside or destine for. **3** to mean.

intense ADJ **1** very great or extreme. **2** feeling

or expressing emotion deeply. **3** very deeply felt: intense happiness. ■ **intensely** ADV.

intensifier N, GRAM an adverb or adjective which adds emphasis to the word or phrase which follows it, eg **very**.

intensify VB (**-ies**, **-ied**) TR & INTR to make or become intense or more intense. ■ **intensification** N.

intensity N (**-ies**) **1** the quality or state of being intense. **2** PHYS the rate per unit area at which power or energy is transmitted.

intensive ADJ **1** often IN COMPOUNDS using, done with or requiring considerable amounts of thought, effort, time, etc within a relatively short period: **labour-intensive**. **2** thorough; intense; concentrated. **3** using large amounts of capital and labour (rather than more land or raw materials) to increase production: **intensive farming**. **4** GRAM of an adverb or adjective: adding force or emphasis, eg **extremely, quite**. ➤ N, GRAM an intensifier. ■ **intensively** ADV.

intensive care N **1** the care of critically ill patients who require continuous attention. **2** a hospital unit that provides such care.

intent N **1** an aim, intention or purpose. **2** LAW the purpose of committing a crime. ➤ ADJ **1** (usu **intent on** or **upon sth**) firmly determined to do it. **2** (usu **intent on sth**) having one's attention fixed on it. **3** showing concentration; absorbed: **an intent look**. ■ **intently** ADV. ■ **intentness** N. ◆ **to all intents and purposes** virtually.

intention N **1** an aim or purpose. **2** (**intentions**) COLLOQ a man's purpose with regard to marrying a particular woman.

intentional ADJ said, done, etc on purpose. ■ **intentionally** ADV.

inter VB (**-rr-**) to bury (a dead person, etc).

interact VB, INTR to act with or on one another. ■ **interaction** N.

interactive ADJ **1** characterized by interaction. **2** denoting a continuous exchange of information between a computer and its user.

interbreed VB, TR & INTR **1** to breed within a single family or strain so as to control the appearance of certain characteristics in the offspring. **2** to cross-breed.

intercede VB, INTR **1** to act as a peacemaker between (two people, groups, etc). **2** (usu **intercede for sb**) to make an appeal on their behalf. ■ **intercession** N.

intercept VB **1 a** to stop or catch (eg a person, missile, aircraft, etc) on their or its way from one place to another; **b** to prevent (a missile, etc) from arriving at its destination, often by destroying it. **2** MATH to mark or cut off (a line, plane, curve, etc) with another line, plane, etc that crosses it. ■ **interception** N. ■ **interceptive** ADJ.

interchange VB, TR & INTR to change or cause to change places with something or someone. ➤ N **1** an act of interchanging; an exchange. **2** a road junction consisting of roads and bridges designed to prevent streams of traffic from directly crossing one another. ■ **interchangeable** ADJ. ■ **interchangeably** ADV.

intercom N a system which allows communication within a building, aircraft, etc.

interconnect VB, TR & INTR to connect (two things) or be connected with one another.

intercontinental ADJ travelling between or connecting different continents.

intercourse N **1** sexual intercourse. **2** communication, connection or dealings between people, groups, etc.

interdenominational ADJ involving (members of) different religious denominations.

interdepartmental ADJ involving (members of) different departments.

interdependent ADJ depending on one another. ■ **interdependence** N.

interdict N **1** an order forbidding someone to do something. **2** SCOTS LAW an injunction. ■ **interdiction** N. ■ **interdictory** ADJ.

interest N **1** the desire to learn or know about someone or something; curiosity. **2** the power to attract attention and curiosity. **3** something

which arouses attention and curiosity; a hobby or pastime. **4** a charge for borrowing money or using credit. **5** (often **interests**) advantage, benefit or profit, esp financial. **6** a share or claim in a business and its profits, or a legal right to property. **7** (also **interest group**) a group of people or organizations with common, esp financial, aims and concerns.
➤ VB **1** to attract the attention and curiosity of someone. **2** (often **interest sb in sth**) to cause them to take a part in or be concerned about some activity.

interested ADJ **1** showing concern or having an interest. **2** personally involved; not impartial or disinterested. ■ **interestedly** ADV.

interesting ADJ attracting interest; holding the attention. ■ **interestingly** ADV.

interface N **1** a surface forming a common boundary between two regions, things, etc. **2** a common boundary or meeting–point. **3** COMP a link between a computer and a peripheral device, such as a printer, or a user.

interfacing N a piece of stiff fabric sewn between two layers of material to give shape.

interfere VB, INTR **1** (often **interfere with** or **in sth**) **a** of a person: to meddle with something not considered their business; **b** of a thing: to hinder or adversely affect something else: The weather is interfering with picture reception. **2** PHYS of sound waves, rays of light, etc: to combine together to cause disturbance or interference. ■ **interfering** ADJ.

interference N **1** the act or process of interfering. **2** PHYS the interaction between two or more waves of the same frequency. **3** TELECOMM the distortion of transmitted signals by an external power source.

intergalactic ADJ between galaxies.

interim ADJ provisional, temporary.
◆ **in the interim** in the meantime.

interior ADJ **1** on, of, suitable for, happening or acting in, or coming from the inside; inner: interior design. **2** away from the shore or frontier; inland. **3** concerning the domestic or internal affairs of a country. **4** belonging to or

existing in the mind or spirit; belonging to the mental or spiritual life.
➤ N **1** an internal or inner part; the inside. **2** the part of a country or continent that is furthest from the coast. **3** the internal or home affairs of a country. **4** a picture or representation of the inside of a room or building, esp with reference to its decoration or style.

interject VB to say or add abruptly.

interjection N **1** an exclamation of surprise, pain, etc. **2** an act of interjecting.

interlace VB **1** TR & INTR to join by lacing or by crossing over. **2** to mix or blend with something.

interlard VB to add foreign words, quotations, unusual phrases, etc to (a speech or piece of writing), esp to do so excessively.

interlay VB to lay (eg layers) between.

interline VB to put an extra lining between the first lining and the fabric (of a garment), esp for stiffness. ■ **interlining** N.

interlink VB, TR & INTR to join together.

interlock VB, TR & INTR to fit, fasten or connect together, esp by the means of teeth or parts which fit into each other.
➤ ADJ of a fabric or garment: knitted with closely locking stitches. ■ **interlocking** ADJ.

interlocutor N someone who takes part in a conversation or dialogue.

interloper N someone who meddles in or interferes with other people's affairs, or goes to places where they have no right to be.

interlude N **1** a short period of time between two events. **2** a short break between the acts of a play or opera or between items of music. **3** a short piece of music, or short item of entertainment, played during such a break.

intermarry VB, INTR **1** of different races, social or religious groups, etc: to become connected by marriage. **2** to marry someone from one's own family. ■ **intermarriage** N.

intermediary N (*-ies*) **1** someone who mediates between two people or groups, eg to try to settle a dispute or get agreement.

2 any intermediate person or thing.

intermediate ADJ in the middle; placed between two points, stages or extremes.
➤ N an intermediate thing.
➤ VB, INTR to act as an intermediary.

interment N burial.

intermezzo N (*-zi* or *-zos*) MUS a short instrumental piece usu performed between the sections of a symphonic work, opera, etc.

interminable ADJ seemingly without an end, esp because of being extremely dull.

intermingle VB, TR & INTR to mingle or mix.

intermission N a short period of time between two parts, eg of a film, play, etc.

intermittent ADJ happening occasionally; not continuous. ■ **intermittently** ADV.

intern VB **1** to confine within a country, restricted area or prison, esp during a war. **2** INTR, chiefly US to train or work as an intern.
➤ N (also **interne**) **1** chiefly US an advanced student or graduate who gains practical experience by working, eg in a hospital. **2** an inmate. ■ **internee** N. ■ **internment** N.
■ **internship** N.

internal ADJ **1** on, in, of or suitable for the inside; inner. **2** on, in, belonging to or suitable for the inside of the body. **3** relating to domestic affairs. **4** for, belonging to or coming from within. **5** relating to the inner nature or feelings or of the mind or soul. ■ **internally** ADV.

internal-combustion engine N an engine that produces power by burning a mixture of fuel and air.

internalize or **-ise** VB **1** to make (a type of behaviour, a characteristic, etc) part of one's personality. **2** to keep (an emotion, etc) inside oneself rather than express it.

international ADJ involving or affecting two or more nations.
➤ N **1** a sports match or competition between two national teams. **2** (also **internationalist**) someone who takes part in, or has taken part in, such a match or competition.

internationalism N the view that the nations of the world should co-operate and work towards greater mutual understanding.
■ **internationalist** N.

internationalize or **-ise** VB to make international.

internecine ADJ of a conflict or struggle: within a group or organization.

the Internet N a global computer communications network.

interplanetary ADJ **1** relating to the solar system. **2** happening or existing in the space between the planets.

interplay N the action and influence of two or more things on each other.

interpolate VB **1** to add (words) to a book or manuscript, esp in order to make the text misleading or corrupt. **2** to interrupt a conversation, a person speaking, etc with (a remark or comment). ■ **interpolation** N.

interpose VB **1** TR & INTR to put something, or come, between two other things. **2** INTR to intervene. ■ **interposition** N.

interpret VB **1** to explain the meaning of (a foreign word, dream, etc). **2** INTR to act as an interpreter. **3** to consider or understand (behaviour, a remark, etc). **4** to convey one's idea of the meaning of (eg a dramatic role, piece of music) in one's performance.
■ **interpretation** N. ■ **interpretative** or **interpretive** ADJ.

interpreter N someone who translates foreign speech as the words are spoken.

interregnum N (*-nums* or *-na*) the time between two monarchs' reigns when the throne is unoccupied.

interrelate VB, TR & INTR to be in or be brought into a dependent or reciprocal relationship.

interrogate VB **1** to question closely and thoroughly. **2** of a radar set, etc: to send out signals to (a radio beacon) to work out a position. ■ **interrogation** N.
■ **interrogator** N. ■ **interrogatory** ADJ, N.

interrogative ADJ like a question; asking or seeming to ask a question.
➤ N an interrogative word or construction.

interrupt VB 1 TR & INTR to break into (a conversation or monologue) by asking a question or making a comment. 2 TR & INTR to make a break in the continuous activity of (an event), or to disturb someone from some action. 3 to destroy (a view, eg of a clear sweep of land) by getting in the way. ■ **interruption** N.

intersect VB 1 to divide (lines, an area, etc) by passing or cutting through or across. 2 INTR esp of lines, roads, etc: to cut across each other.

intersection N 1 a place where things meet or intersect, esp a road junction. 2 the act of intersecting. 3 GEOM the point or set of points where two or more lines or plane surfaces cross each other. 4 GEOM a set of points common to two or more geometrical figures. 5 MATH the set of elements formed by the elements common to two or more other sets.

intersperse VB to scatter or insert something here and there. ■ **interspersion** N.

interstate ADJ between two or more states.
➤ N, esp US a major road that crosses a state boundary.

interstice N a very small gap or space.

intertwine VB, TR & INTR to twist or be twisted together.

interval N 1 a period of time between two events. 2 a space or distance between two things. 3 BRIT a short break between the acts of a play or opera, or between parts of a concert or long film. 4 MUS the difference in pitch between two notes or tones.
◆ **at intervals** 1 here and there; now and then. 2 with a stated distance between.

intervene VB, INTR 1 (often **intervene in sth**) to involve oneself in something which is happening in order to affect the outcome. 2 to involve oneself or interfere in a dispute between other people in order to settle it or prevent more serious conflict. 3 to come or occur between two things in place or time.
■ **intervention** N.

interview N 1 a formal meeting and discussion with someone, esp one at which an employer meets and judges a prospective employee. 2 a conversation or discussion, esp one for broadcasting or publication in which a famous or important person is questioned.
➤ VB to hold an interview. ■ **interviewee** N. ■ **interviewer** N.

interweave VB, TR & INTR to weave or be woven together.

intestate LAW, ADJ of a person: not having made a valid will before their death.
➤ N someone who dies without making a valid will. ■ **intestacy** N.

intestine N the muscular tube-like part of the alimentary canal between the stomach and the anus. ■ **intestinal** ADJ.

intimacy N (-ies) 1 warm close personal friendship. 2 an intimate or personal remark. 3 EUPHEMISTIC sexual intercourse. 4 the state or quality of being intimate.

intimate[1] ADJ 1 marked by or sharing a close and affectionate friendship. 2 very private or personal. 3 of a place: small and quiet with a warm, friendly atmosphere. 4 (often **intimate with sb**) sharing a sexual relationship with them. 5 of knowledge: deep and thorough.
➤ N a close friend. ■ **intimately** ADV.

intimate[2] VB to announce or make known.
■ **intimation** N.

intimidate VB 1 to coerce, esp with threats. 2 to frighten or overawe. ■ **intimidation** N.

into PREP 1 to or towards the inside or middle of sth. 2 against; making contact or colliding with something or someone. 3 used to express a change of state or condition: **get into difficulties**. 4 having reached a certain period of time: **into extra time**. 5 MATH used to express division: **Four into twenty makes five**. 6 COLLOQ involved with, interested in or enthusiastic about: **into golf in a big way**.

intolerable ADJ too bad, difficult, painful, etc to be put up with. ■ **intolerably** ADV.

intolerant ADJ refusing or unwilling to accept ideas, beliefs, behaviour, etc different from one's own. ■ **intolerance** N.

intonation N 1 the rise and fall of the pitch of the voice in speech. 2 an act of intoning. 3 the correct pitching of musical notes.

intone VB, TR & INTR 1 to recite (a prayer, etc) in a solemn monotonous voice or in singing tones. 2 to say something with a particular intonation.

intoxicate VB 1 to make drunk. 2 to excite or elate. ■ **intoxicant** N, ADJ. ■ **intoxicating** ADJ. ■ **intoxication** N.

intractable ADJ 1 difficult to control or influence; obstinate. 2 difficult to solve, cure or deal with. ■ **intractability** N.

intransigent ADJ refusing to compromise one's beliefs. ■ **intransigence** N.

intransitive ADJ, GRAM of a verb: not taking or having a direct object.

intrauterine ADJ, MED within the uterus.

intravenous ADJ, MED within a vein or veins.

in-tray N, BRIT a tray, eg on a desk, etc, that incoming mail, etc is put in before it is dealt with.

intrepid ADJ bold and daring; brave. ■ **intrepidity** N. ■ **intrepidly** ADV.

intricate ADJ full of complicated, interrelating or tangled details or parts and therefore difficult to understand, analyse or sort out. ■ **intricacy** N (-ies). ■ **intricately** ADV.

intrigue N 1 secret plotting. 2 a secret plot or plan. 3 a secret illicit love affair.
➤ VB (*intrigued, intriguing*) 1 to arouse the curiosity or interest of someone. 2 INTR to plot secretly. ■ **intriguing** ADJ.

intrinsic ADJ being an inherent and essential part. ■ **intrinsically** ADV.

intro N, COLLOQ an introduction, esp to a piece of music.

introduce VB 1 (usu **introduce sb to sb else**) to present them to one another by name. 2 to announce or present (eg a radio or television programme) to an audience. 3 to bring (something) into a place, situation, etc for the first time. 4 to bring into operation, practice

or use. 5 to put forward or propose (a possible law or bill) for consideration or approval. 6 to cause someone to experience or discover something for the first time. 7 to start or preface. 8 to insert or put something into something else. ■ **introductory** ADJ.

introduction N 1 a presentation of one person to another or others. 2 a section at the beginning of a book which explains briefly what it is about, why it was written, etc. 3 a book which outlines the basic principles of a subject. 4 a short passage of music beginning a piece or song, or leading up to a movement. 5 something which has been introduced.

introspection N examination of one's own thoughts, feelings, etc. ■ **introspective** ADJ.

introvert N 1 PSYCHOL someone who is more interested in the self and inner feelings than in the outside world and social relationships. 2 someone who tends not to socialize and who is uncommunicative and withdrawn.
➤ ADJ (also **introverted**) concerned more with one's own thoughts and feelings than with other people and outside events. ■ **introversion** N. ■ **introverted** ADJ.

intrude VB, TR & INTR to force or impose (oneself, one's presence or something) without welcome or invitation. ■ **intruder** N. ■ **intrusion** N.

intrusive ADJ 1 tending to intrude. 2 of rock: formed by molten magma being forced under pressure into pre-existing rock.

intuition N 1 the power of understanding or realizing something without conscious rational thought or analysis. 2 something understood or realized in this way. ■ **intuitive** ADJ. ■ **intuitively** ADV. ■ **intuitiveness** N.

Inuit N (PL *Inuit*) 1 a member of a people of the Arctic and sub-Arctic regions of Canada, Greenland and Alaska. 2 their language.
➤ ADJ of this people or their language.

inundate VB 1 to overwhelm with water. 2 to swamp. ■ **inundation** N.

inure VB (often **inure sb to sth**) to accustom them to something unpleasant or unwelcome.

invade VB 1 TR & INTR to enter (a country) by

force with an army. **2** TR & INTR to attack or overrun. **3** to interfere with (a person's rights, privacy, etc). ■ **invader** N.

invalid[1] N someone who is constantly ill or who is disabled.
➢ ADJ suitable for or being an invalid.
➢ VB to discharge (a soldier, etc) from service because of illness. ■ **invalidity** N.

invalid[2] ADJ **1** of a document, agreement, etc: having no legal force. **2** based on false reasoning or a mistake and therefore not valid, correct or reliable. ■ **invalidity** N.

invalidate VB to make invalid.

invaluable ADJ having a value that is too great to be measured.

invariable ADJ not prone to change or alteration. ■ **invariably** ADV.

invasion N **1** invading, or being invaded, eg by a hostile country or by something harmful. **2** an encroachment or violation. ■ **invasive** ADJ.

invective N **1** sarcastic or abusive language. **2** a critical attack using such words.

inveigh VB, INTR (usu **inveigh against sb** or **sth**) to speak strongly against them or it.

inveigle VB (usu **inveigle sb into sth**) to trick, deceive or persuade them into doing it. ·

invent VB **1** to be the first person to make or use (a machine, game, method, etc). **2** to think or make up (an excuse, false story, etc).
■ **invention** N. ■ **inventive** ADJ.
■ **inventiveness** N. ■ **inventor** N.

inventory N (-**ies**) **1** a list of the articles, goods, etc in a particular place. **2** the items on such a list.

inverse ADJ opposite or reverse in order, sequence, direction, effect, etc.
➢ N a direct opposite. ■ **inversely** ADV.

invert VB **1** to turn upside down or inside out. **2** to reverse in order, sequence, direction, effect, etc. ■ **inversion** N.

invertebrate N, ZOOL any animal that does not possess a backbone, such as an insect, worm, snail or jellyfish.

➢ ADJ (also **invertebral**) relating to an animal without a backbone.

inverted commas see **quotation marks**

invest VB **1** TR & INTR to put (money) into a company or business, eg by buying shares in it, in order to make a profit. **2** TR & INTR to devote (time, effort, energy, etc) to something. **3** (often **invest sb with sth**) to give them the symbols of power, rights, rank, etc officially. **4** (usu **invest sth in sb**) to place power, rank, a quality or feeling, etc in sb. **5** to clothe or adorn. **6** MIL to besiege (a stronghold). ■ **investor** N.
◆ **invest in sth** COLLOQ to buy it.

investigate VB, TR & INTR to carry out a thorough and detailed inquiry into or examination of something or someone.
■ **investigation** N. ■ **investigative** or **investigatory** ADJ. ■ **investigator** N.

investiture N a formal ceremony giving a rank or office to someone.

investment N **1** a sum of money invested. **2** something, such as a business, house, etc in which one invests money, time, effort, etc. **3** the act of investing.

inveterate ADJ of a habit, etc: firmly established. ■ **inveterately** ADV.

invidious ADJ likely to cause envy, resentment or indignation, esp by being or seeming to be unfair. ■ **invidiously** ADV. ■ **invidiousness** N.

invigilate VB, TR & INTR, BRIT to keep watch over people sitting an examination, esp to prevent cheating. ■ **invigilation** N. ■ **invigilator** N.

invigorate VB to give fresh life, energy and health to something or someone.

invincible ADJ unable to be defeated.
■ **invincibility** N. ■ **invincibly** ADV.

inviolable ADJ not to be broken or violated.

inviolate ADJ not broken, violated or injured.

invisible ADJ **1** not able to be seen. **2** unseen. **3** ECON relating to services (eg insurance, tourism) rather than goods: invisible exports.
➢ N an invisible item of trade. ■ **invisibility** N.

invitation N **1** a request to a person to come

or go somewhere, eg to a party, meal, etc. **2** the form such a request takes, eg written on a card, etc. **3** an act of inviting.

invite VB **1** to request the presence of someone at one's house, at a party, etc. **2** to ask politely or formally for (eg comments, advice, etc). **3** to bring on or encourage (something undesirable). **4** to attract or tempt.
➤ N, COLLOQ an invitation.

inviting ADJ attractive or tempting.

in vitro ADJ, ADV, BIOL performed outside a living organism in an artificial environment, eg in a test-tube: in-vitro fertilization.

invoice N a list of goods supplied, delivered with the goods and giving details of price and quantity, usu treated as a request for payment.
➤ VB **1** to send an invoice to (a customer). **2** to provide an invoice for (goods).

invoke VB **1** to make an appeal to (God, some deity, a Muse, authority, etc) for help, support or inspiration. **2** to appeal to (a law, principle, etc) as an authority or reason for eg one's behaviour. **3** to put (a law, decision, etc) into effect. ■ **invocation** N.

involuntary ADJ done without being controlled by the will; not able to be controlled by the will; unintentional. ■ **involuntarily** ADV.

involute ADJ **1** entangled; intricate. **2** BOT of petals, etc: rolled in at the edges. **3** of shells: curled up in a spiral shape.
➤ VB, INTR to become involute.

involve VB **1** to require as a necessary part. **2** (usu **involve sb in sth**) to cause them to take part or be implicated in it. **3** to have an effect on someone or sth. **4** (often **involve oneself in sth**) to become emotionally concerned in it. ■ **involved** ADJ. ■ **involvement** N.

invulnerable ADJ incapable of being hurt, damaged or attacked.

inward ADJ **1** placed or being within. **2** moving towards the inside. **3** relating or belonging to the mind or soul.
➤ ADV (also **inwards**) **1** towards the inside or the centre. **2** into the mind or soul.

inwardly ADV **1** on the inside; internally. **2** in one's private thoughts; secretly.

iodine N **1** CHEM a non-metallic element consisting of dark-violet crystals that form a violet vapour when heated. **2** MED a solution of iodine in ethanol, used as an antiseptic.

iodize or **-ise** VB to treat something with iodine, esp common salt.

ion N, CHEM an atom or group of atoms that has acquired a net positive charge as a result of losing one or more electrons, or a net negative charge as a result of gaining one or more electrons. ■ **ionic** ADJ.

ionize or **-ise** VB, TR & INTR, CHEM to produce or make something produce ions.

ionosphere N the layer of the Earth's atmosphere from about 50 kilometres to about 80 kilometres above the Earth's surface to an indefinite height.

iota N **1** the ninth letter of the Greek alphabet (I, ι). **2** a very small amount; a jot.

IOU N (*IOUs, IOU's*) COLLOQ a written and signed note as an acknowledgement of a debt.

IQ ABBREV (*IQs, IQ's*) intelligence quotient.

irascible ADJ easily made angry; irritable. ■ **irascibility** N. ■ **irascibly** ADV.

irate ADJ very angry; enraged. ■ **irately** ADV. ■ **irateness** N.

ire N, LITERARY anger.

iridescent ADJ having many bright rainbow-like colours which seem to shimmer and change constantly. ■ **iridescence** N.

iridium N, CHEM a silvery metallic element resistant to corrosion, used in hard alloys.

iris N **1** (*irises*) a plant that has flattened sword-shaped leaves and large brilliantly coloured flowers. **2** ANAT an adjustable pigmented ring of muscle lying in front of the lens of the eye, surrounding the pupil.

Irish ADJ of Ireland.
➤ N the Celtic language of Ireland.
➤ PL N (**the Irish**) the people of Ireland.

irk VB to annoy or irritate, esp persistently.

irksome ADJ annoying, irritating or boring.

iron N **1** a strong hard greyish metallic element, naturally magnetic and thought to be the main component of the Earth's core. **2** a tool, weapon or other implement made of iron. **3** a triangular, flat-bottomed, now usu electrical, household tool used for smoothing out creases and pressing clothes. **4** GOLF any of various clubs with an angled iron head. **5** great strength. **6** (**irons**) chains; fetters.
➤ ADJ **1** made of iron. **2** very strong, inflexible, unyielding, etc: **iron determination**.
➤ VB to smooth the creases out of or press (eg clothes) with an iron.
◆ **iron sth out** to remove or put right (difficulties, problems, etc) so that progress becomes easier.

ironclad ADJ **1** covered with protective iron plates. **2** inflexible; set firm.

ironic and **ironical** ADJ **1** containing, characterized by or expressing irony. **2** of a person: given to frequent use of irony.
■ **ironically** ADV.

ironing N **1** clothes and household linen, etc which need to be or have just been ironed. **2** the act or process of ironing.

ironmonger N, BRIT a dealer in articles made of metal, eg tools, locks, etc, and other household hardware. ■ **ironmongery** N.

ironstone N hard, white earthenware.

ironwork N **1** articles made of iron, such as gates and railings. **2** (**ironworks**) a factory where iron is smelted.

irony N (-*ies*) **1** a linguistic device or form of humour that takes its effect from stating the opposite of what is meant. **2** a dramatic device by which information is given to the audience that is not known to all the characters, or in which words convey different meanings to the audience and to the characters.

irradiation N **1** MED exposure of part of the body to electromagnetic radiation or a radioactive source, for diagnostic or therapeutic purposes. **2** a method of preserving food by exposing it to ultraviolet or ionizing radiation. ■ **irradiate** VB.

irrational ADJ **1** not the result of clear, logical thought. **2** unable to think logically and clearly. **3** MATH of a quantity or root: unable to be expressed as a ratio of whole numbers.
■ **irrationality** N. ■ **irrationally** ADV.

irreconcilable ADJ **1** not agreeing or able to be brought into agreement; incompatible. **2** hostile and opposed; unwilling to be friendly.
■ **irreconcilably** ADV.

irrecoverable ADJ **1** not able to be recovered or regained. **2** not able to be corrected.

irredeemable ADJ **1** of a person: too evil to be saved. **2** incapable of being recovered.

irreducible ADJ **1** unable to be reduced or made simpler. **2** unable to be brought from one state into another. ■ **irreducibly** ADV.

irrefutable ADJ not able to be proved false.
■ **irrefutability** N. ■ **irrefutably** ADV.

irregular ADJ **1** not happening or occurring at regular or equal intervals. **2** not smooth, even or balanced. **3** not conforming to rules, custom, accepted or normal behaviour, or to routine. **4** GRAM of a word: not changing its form (eg to show tenses or plurals) according to the usual patterns in the language. **5** of troops: not belonging to the regular army.
➤ N an irregular soldier. ■ **irregularity** N.

irrelevant ADJ not connected with or applying to the subject in hand. ■ **irrelevance** N.
■ **irrelevantly** ADV.

irreligious ADJ **1** lacking religion. **2** showing hostility towards religion.

irremovable ADJ not able to be removed.
■ **irremovability** N. ■ **irremovably** ADV.

irreparable ADJ not able to be restored or put right. ■ **irreparably** ADV.

irreplaceable ADJ not able to be replaced.
■ **irreplaceably** ADV.

irrepressible ADJ not able to be controlled, restrained or repressed. ■ **irrepressibly** ADV.

irreproachable ADJ free from faults;

blameless. ■ **irreproachably** ADV.

irresistible ADJ 1 too strong to be resisted. 2 very attractive. ■ **irresistibly** ADV.

irresolute ADJ not able to take firm decisions. ■ **irresoluteness** or **irresolution** N.

irrespective ADJ (always **irrespective of sth**) without taking it into account. ➤ ADV, COLLOQ nevertheless; regardless.

irresponsible ADJ 1 done without, or showing no, concern for the consequences; reckless; careless. 2 not reliable or trustworthy. ■ **irresponsibility** N. ■ **irresponsibly** ADV.

irretrievable ADJ not able to be recovered or put right. ■ **irretrievably** ADV.

irreverent ADJ lacking respect or reverence (eg for things considered sacred or for important people). ■ **irreverence** N.

irreversible ADJ 1 not able to be changed back to a former or original state; permanent. 2 not able to be recalled or annulled. ■ **irreversibility** or **irreversibleness** N. ■ **irreversibly** ADV.

irrevocable ADJ unable to be changed, stopped, or undone. ■ **irrevocability** N. ■ **irrevocably** ADV.

irrigate VB 1 to provide (land) with a supply of water. 2 MED to wash out (the eye, a wound, body cavity, etc), with a liquid. ■ **irrigation** N.

irritable ADJ 1 easily annoyed, angered or excited. 2 extremely or excessively sensitive. ■ **irritability** N. ■ **irritably** ADV.

irritant N 1 any chemical, physical or biological agent that causes irritation of a tissue, esp inflammation of the skin or eyes. 2 something or someone that causes irritation.

irritate VB 1 to make someone angry or annoyed. 2 to make (part of the body, an organ, etc) sore and swollen or itchy. ■ **irritating** ADJ. ■ **irritation** N.

irrupt VB, INTR to burst into or enter (a place, etc) suddenly. ■ **irruption** N.

isinglass N gelatine from the dried swim bladders of certain fish, used in glues and inks.

Islam N the religion of the Muslims, which teaches that people should be obedient to the will of Allah as set forth in the Koran. ■ **Islamic** ADJ.

island N 1 a piece of land, smaller than a continent, surrounded by water. 2 anything like an island, esp in being detached.

islander N someone who lives on an island.

isle N an island, esp a small one.

islet N 1 a small island. 2 any small group of cells which has a different nature and structure to the cells surrounding it.

isn't CONTRACTION is not.

isobar N a line on a weather chart connecting points that have the same atmospheric pressure. ■ **isobaric** ADJ.

isolate VB 1 to separate from others; to cause to be alone. 2 to place in quarantine. 3 to separate or detach, esp to allow closer examination. 4 to separate so as to obtain in a pure or uncombined form. ■ **isolation** N.

isolated ADJ 1 placed or standing alone or apart. 2 separate. 3 solitary.

isomer N 1 CHEM one of two or more chemical compounds that have the same molecular composition but different three-dimensional structures. 2 PHYS one of two or more atomic nuclei with the same atomic number and mass number, but with different energy states and radioactive properties. ■ **isomeric** ADJ.

isometric ADJ 1 having equal size or measurements. 2 of a three-dimensional drawing: having all three axes equally inclined to the surface of the drawing and all lines drawn to scale. 3 PHYSIOL relating to muscular contraction that generates tension but does not produce shortening of the muscle fibres.

isometrics SING OR PL N a system of exercises for strengthening and toning the body.

isomorph N any object or substance that is similar or identical in structure or shape to another object. ■ **isomorphic** ADJ.

isosceles ADJ of a triangle: having two sides of equal length.

isotherm N a line on a weather map connecting places where the temperature is the same.

isotonic ADJ, PHYSIOL, DENOTING of muscles: having the same tension.

isotope N, CHEM one of two or more atoms of the same chemical element that contain the same number of protons but different numbers of neutrons in their nuclei. ■ **isotopy** N.

issue N 1 the giving out, publishing or making available of something, eg stamps, a magazine, etc. 2 something given out, published or made available. 3 one item in a regular series. 4 a subject for discussion or argument. 5 a result or consequence. 6 FORMAL offspring. 7 an act of going or flowing out. ➤ VB (*issued, issuing*) to give or send out, distribute, publish or make available, esp officially or formally. ◆ **at issue 1** in dispute or disagreement. **2** under discussion. ◆ **join** or **take issue with sb** to disagree with them.

isthmus N a narrow strip of land, bounded by water on both sides, that joins two larger areas.

IT ABBREV information technology.

it PRONOUN 1 the thing, animal, baby or group already mentioned. 2 the person in question: Who is it? 3 used as the subject with impersonal verbs and when describing the weather or distance or telling the time: It's a bit blustery today. 4 used as the grammatical subject of a sentence when the real subject comes later, eg It's very silly to run away. 5 used to refer to a general situation or state of affairs: How's it going? 6 used to emphasize a certain word or phrase in a sentence: When is it that her train's due? 7 exactly what is needed, suitable or available: That's it! 8 used with many verbs and prepositions as an object with little meaning: run for it. ➤ N 1 the person in a children's game who has to oppose all the others, eg by trying to catch them. 2 OLD USE, COLLOQ sex appeal.

Italian ADJ of Italy. ➤ N 1 a citizen or inhabitant of, or person born in, Italy. 2 the official language of Italy. 3 COLLOQ a a restaurant that serves Italian food; b a meal in one of these restaurants.

italic ADJ of a typeface: containing characters which slope upwards to the right. ➤ N 1 (usu **italics**) a typeface with characters which slope upwards to the right. 2 a character written or printed in this typeface.

italicize or **-ise** VB to print or write in italics; to change (characters, words, etc in normal typeface) to italics. ■ **italicization** N.

itch N 1 an unpleasant or ticklish irritation on the surface of the skin which makes one want to scratch. 2 COLLOQ a strong or restless desire. 3 a skin disease or condition which causes a constant unpleasant irritation, esp scabies. ➤ VB 1 INTR to have an itch and want to scratch. 2 TR & INTR to cause someone to feel an itch. 3 INTR, COLLOQ to feel a strong or restless desire. ■ **itchiness** N. ■ **itchy** ADJ.

itchy feet N, COLLOQ the strong desire to leave, move or travel.

it'd CONTRACTION 1 it had. 2 it would.

item N 1 a separate object or unit, esp one on a list. 2 a separate piece of information or news. 3 INFORMAL a couple regarded as having a romantic or sexual relationship.

itemize or **-ise** VB to list (things) separately, eg on a bill. ■ **itemization** N. ■ **itemizer** N.

iterate VB to say or do again. ■ **iteration** N. ■ **iterative** ADJ.

itinerant ADJ travelling from place to place. ➤ N a person whose work involves going from place to place or who has no fixed address.

itinerary N (*-ies*) 1 a planned route for a journey or trip. 2 a diary or record of a journey. 3 a guidebook. ➤ ADJ belonging or relating to journeys.

it'll CONTRACTION 1 it will. 2 it shall.

its ADJ belonging to it. ➤ PRONOUN the one or ones belonging to it.

it's CONTRACTION **1** it is. **2** INFORMAL it has.

itself PRONOUN **1** the reflexive form of **it**. **2** used for emphasis: **His behaviour itself was bad**. **3** its usual or normal state: **The dog was itself again**. **4** (also **by itself**) alone; without help.

itsy-bitsy and **itty-bitty** ADJ, COLLOQ very small.

IUD ABBREV intrauterine device, a contraceptive device inserted into the womb.

I've CONTRACTION I have.

ivory N (-*ies*) **1** a hard white material that forms the tusks of the elephant, walrus, etc. **2** the creamy-white colour of this substance. **3** an article made from this substance. **4** (**ivories**) COLLOQ the keys on a piano.
➤ ADJ ivory-coloured, often with the implication of smoothness: ivory skin.

ivory tower N a hypothetical place where the unpleasant realities of life can be ignored.

ivy N (-*ies*) **1** a woody evergreen climbing or trailing plant. **2** any of several other climbing plants, such as poison ivy.

Jj

J or **j** N (*Js, J's* or *j's*) the tenth letter of the English alphabet.

jab VB (-*bb*-) **1** to poke or prod (someone or something). **2** to strike (someone or something) with a short quick punch.
➤ N **1** a poke or prod. **2** COLLOQ an injection.

jabber VB, TR & INTR to talk or utter rapidly and indistinctly.

jack N **1** a device for raising a heavy weight, such as a car, off the ground. **2** a winch. **3** a socket with two or more terminals into which a **jack plug** can be inserted to make or break a circuit or circuits. **4** CARDS the court card of least value, bearing a picture of a page. **5** BOWLS the small white ball that the players aim at.
➤ VB to raise (something) with a jack.
◆ **jack up** to increase (prices, etc).

jackal N a carnivorous mammal, related to the dog and wolf, that lives in Asia and Africa.

jackass N **1** a male ass or donkey. **2** COLLOQ a fool.

jackboot N **1** a tall knee-high military boot. **2** this as a symbol of oppressive military rule.

jackdaw N a bird of the crow family.

jacket N **1** a short coat, esp a long-sleeved, hip-length one. **2** something worn over the top half of the body: **life jacket**. **3** a dust jacket.

jack-in-the-box N (*jack-in-the-boxes*) a box containing a doll attached to a spring, which jumps out when the lid is opened.

jackknife N a large pocket knife with a folding blade.
➤ VB, INTR of an articulated vehicle: to go out of control in such a way that the trailer swings round against the cab.

jack-of-all-trades N someone who does a variety of different jobs.

jackpot N the maximum win, to be made in a lottery, card game, etc.

Jacobean ADJ of the reign of James I of England (also VI of Scotland).

Jacobite BRIT HIST, N an adherent of the **Jacobites**, supporters of James II, his son or

grandson, the Stuart claimants to the British throne.
➤ ADJ relating to the Jacobites.

jacquard N **1** a piece of equipment that can be fitted to a loom to produce a fabric with an intricate woven pattern. **2** the fabric produced.

Jacuzzi N, TRADEMARK a bath or pool with underwater jets that massage the body.

jade N **1** GEOL a very hard, green, white, brown or yellow semi-precious stone. **2** the intense green colour of jade.

jaded ADJ fatigued; dull and bored.

jag N **1** a sharp projection. **2** SCOT an injection. ■ **jaggy** ADJ.

jagged ADJ having a rough or sharp uneven edge. ■ **jaggedness** N.

jaguar N the largest of the American big cats, with a tawny coat covered with black spots.

jail or **gaol** N prison.
➤ VB to imprison. ■ **jailer**, **jailor** and **gaoler** N.

jalopy N (-*ies*) COLLOQ a worn-out old car.

jam¹ N a thick sticky food made from fruit boiled with sugar.

jam² VB (-*mm*-) **1** often IN PASSIVE to stick or wedge (something) so as to make it immovable. **2** TR & INTR of machinery, etc: to stick or make it stick and stop working. **3** to push or shove (something); to cram, press or pack. **4** (also **jam up**) to fill (eg a street) so full that movement comes to a stop. **5** to cause interference to (a radio signal, etc).

jamb N the vertical post at the side of a door, window or fireplace.

jamboree N **1** a large rally of Scouts, Guides, etc. **2** COLLOQ a large and lively gathering.

jammy ADJ (-*ier*, -*iest*) **1** covered or filled with jam. **2** COLLOQ of a person: lucky.

jam-packed ADJ, COLLOQ packed tight.

jangle VB **1** TR & INTR to make or cause (something) to make an irritating, discordant ringing noise. **2** to upset or irritate (a person's nerves).

janitor N **1** N AMER, SCOT a caretaker, esp of a school. **2** a doorkeeper.

January N the first month of the year.

japan N a hard glossy black lacquer, orig from Japan, used to coat wood and metal.
➤ VB (-*nn*-) to lacquer (something) with japan.

jape N, OLD USE a trick, prank or joke.

jar¹ N **1** a wide-mouthed cylindrical container, usu made of glass **2** COLLOQ a glass of beer.

jar² VB (-*rr*-) **1** INTR to have a harsh effect; to grate. **2** TR & INTR to jolt or vibrate. **3** INTR (esp **jar with**) to clash or conflict (with something).
➤ N a jarring sensation, shock or jolt.

jargon N **1** the specialized vocabulary of a particular trade, profession, group or activity. **2** DEROG language which uses such vocabulary in a pretentious or meaningless way.

jasmine N a shrub or vine with fragrant flowers.

jasper N, GEOL a semi-precious gemstone.

jaundice N, PATHOL a condition which turns the skin and the whites of the eyes a yellowish colour, caused by an excess of bile pigments in the blood.

jaundiced ADJ **1** suffering from jaundice. **2** of a person or attitude: bitter or resentful; cynical.

jaunt N a short journey for pleasure.
➤ VB, INTR to go for a jaunt.

jaunty ADJ (-*ier*, -*iest*) **1** breezy and exuberant. **2** smart. ■ **jauntily** ADV. ■ **jauntiness** N.

javelin N **1** a light spear for throwing. **2** (**the javelin**) the athletic event of throwing the javelin.

jaw N **1** ZOOL, BIOL in most vertebrates: either of the two bony structures that form the framework of the mouth and in which the teeth are set. **2** the lower part of the face round the mouth and chin. **3** (**jaws**) the mouth, esp of an animal. **4** (**jaws**) a threshold, esp of something terrifying: **the jaws of death**. **5** (**jaws**) in a machine or tool: a pair of opposing parts used for gripping, crushing, etc.
➤ VB, INTR, COLLOQ to chatter, gossip or talk.

jay N a bird of the crow family which has pinkish-brown plumage and blue, black and white bands on its wings.

jaywalk VB, INTR to cross streets wherever one likes, regardless of traffic signals.

jazz N 1 popular music of Black American origin, with strong catchy rhythms, performed with much improvisation. 2 COLLOQ talk; nonsense; business, stuff, etc.
➤ VB (usu **jazz up**) COLLOQ to enliven or brighten (something).

jazzy ADJ (-ier, -iest) 1 in the style of, or like, jazz. 2 COLLOQ showy; stylish. ■ **jazzily** ADV.

JCB N, TRADEMARK a mobile excavator with a hydraulic shovel and a digging arm.

jealous ADJ (often **jealous of sb**) 1 envious (of someone else). 2 suspicious and resentful (of possible rivals); possessive. 3 anxiously protective (of something one has). 4 caused by jealousy: a jealous fury. ■ **jealously** ADV. ■ **jealousy** N (-ies).

jeans PL N casual trousers made esp of denim.

Jeep N, TRADEMARK a light military vehicle capable of travelling over rough country.

jeer VB 1 to mock or deride (a speaker, performer, etc). 2 INTR (**jeer at**) to laugh unkindly at.
➤ N a taunt, insult or hoot of derision.

jejune ADJ, DEROG 1 dull, unoriginal and empty of imagination. 2 childish; naïve.

jejunum N, ANAT the part of the small intestine between the duodenum and the ileum.

jell or **gel** VB, INTR 1 to become firm; to set. 2 COLLOQ to take definite shape.

jellied ADJ set in jelly: jellied eels.

jelly N (-ies) 1 a wobbly, transparent, fruit-flavoured dessert set with gelatine. 2 a clear jam made by boiling and straining fruit. 3 any jelly-like substance.

jellyfish N, ZOOL any of various marine coelenterates, usu having an umbrella-shaped body and stinging tentacles.

jemmy N (-ies) a small crowbar.

jenny N (-ies) a name given to the female of certain animals, esp the donkey, ass and wren.

jeopardize or **-ise** VB to put (something) at risk of harm, loss or destruction.

jeopardy N 1 danger of harm, loss or destruction. 2 US LAW the danger of trial and punishment faced by a person accused on a criminal charge.

jeremiad N, COLLOQ a lengthy tale of woe.

jerk N 1 a quick tug or pull. 2 a sudden movement; a jolt. 3 DEROG SLANG a useless or idiotic person.
➤ VB 1 to pull or tug (something) sharply. 2 INTR to move with sharp suddenness.

jerkin N a sleeveless jacket, short coat or close-fitting waistcoat.

jerky ADJ (-ier, -iest) making sudden movements or jerks. ■ **jerkily** ADV. ■ **jerkiness** N.

jerry-built ADJ cheaply and quickly built.

jerry can N a flat-sided can used for carrying water, petrol, etc.

jersey N (-eys) 1 a knitted garment, pulled on over the head. 2 a fine slightly stretchy fabric, usu machine-knitted.

jest N a joke or prank.
➤ VB, INTR to make a jest; to joke.

jester N, HIST a professional clown, employed by a king or noble to amuse the court.

jet[1] N, GEOL a hard black variety of lignite used to make jewellery and ornaments.

jet[2] N 1 a strong continuous stream of liquid gas, forced under pressure from a narrow opening. 2 an orifice or nozzle through which such a stream is forced. 3 any device powered by such a stream of liquid or gas. 4 (also **jet aircraft**) an aircraft powered by a jet engine.
➤ VB (-tt-) TR & INTR, COLLOQ to travel or transport (something) by jet aircraft.

jet-black ADJ deep glossy black.

jet engine N any engine which generates

forward thrust by ejecting a jet of gases formed as a result of fuel combustion.

jet lag N the tiredness and lethargy that result from the body's inability to adjust to the changes of time zone in high-speed, long-distance air travel. ■ **jet-lagged** ADJ.

jet propulsion N the forward thrust of a body brought about by means of a force produced by ejection of a jet of gas or liquid to the rear of the body. ■ **jet-propelled** ADJ.

jetsam N goods jettisoned from a ship and washed up on the shore.

jet ski N a powered craft adapted for skimming across water on a ski-like keel. ■ **jet-ski** VB.

jettison VB **1** to throw (cargo) overboard to lighten a ship, aircraft, etc in an emergency. **2** COLLOQ to abandon, reject or get rid of.

jetty N (-ies) **1** a stone or wooden landing-stage. **2** a stone barrier built out into the sea to protect a harbour from high waves.

Jew N **1** a member of the Hebrew race. **2** someone who practises Judaism. ■ **Jewish** ADJ.

jewel N **1** a precious stone. **2** a personal ornament made with precious stones and metals. **3** a gem used in the machinery of a watch. **4** someone or something greatly prized.

jeweller or (US) **jeweler** N a person who deals in, makes or repairs jewellery.

jewellery or (US) **jewelry** N articles worn for personal adornment.

jib[1] N, NAUT a small three-cornered sail in front of the mainsail of a yacht.
➤ VB (-bb-) (**jib at sth**) INTR of a person: to object to it.

jib[2] N the projecting arm of a crane from which the lifting gear hangs.

jibe see **gybe**

jiffy or **jiff** N (*jiffies* or *jiffs*) COLLOQ a moment.

jig N **1** a lively country dance or folk dance.

2 a jerky movement. **3** MECH a device that holds a piece of work in position and guides the tools being used on it.
➤ VB (-gg-) **1** INTR to dance a jig. **2** TR & INTR to jerk rapidly up and down.

jiggered ADJ, COLLOQ exhausted.

jiggery-pokery N, COLLOQ trickery or deceit.

jiggle VB, TR & INTR to jump or make (something) jump or jerk about.
➤ N a jiggling movement.

jigsaw N **1** (also **jigsaw puzzle**) a picture, mounted on wood or cardboard and cut into interlocking irregularly shaped pieces, to be fitted together again. **2** a fine-bladed saw for cutting intricate patterns.

jihad N a holy war, against infidels, fought by Muslims on behalf of Islam.

jilt VB to leave and abruptly discard (a lover).

jingle N **1** a light ringing or clinking sound. **2** a simple rhyming verse, song or tune.
➤ VB, TR & INTR to make, or cause (something) to make, a ringing or clinking sound.

jingoism N over-enthusiastic or aggressive patriotism. ■ **jingoist** N. ■ **jingoistic** ADJ.

jink VB **1** INTR to dodge. **2** to elude (someone or something).
➤ N a dodge; a jinking movement.

jinni or **djinni** and **djinn** N (PL *jinn* or *djinn*) in Muslim folklore: a supernatural being able to adopt human or animal form.

jinx N **1** (usu **a jinx on sth** or **sb**) an evil spell or influence, held responsible for misfortune. **2** someone or something that appears to bring bad luck.
➤ VB to bring bad luck to (someone or something). ■ **jinxed** ADJ.

jitter COLLOQ, VB INTR to behave in an agitated or nervous way.
➤ N (usu **the jitters**) an attack of nervousness: He's got the jitters. ■ **jittery** ADJ.

jitterbug N, US an energetic dance like the **jive**, popular in the 1940s.

➤ VB (-**gg**-) INTR to dance the jitterbug.

jive N **1** a lively style of jazz music or swing, popular in the 1950s. **2** the style of dancing done to this music.
➤ VB, INTR to dance in this style.

Jnr or **jnr** ABBREV Junior or junior.

job N **1** a person's regular paid employment. **2** a piece of work. **3** a completed task: **made a good job of the pruning**. **4** a function or responsibility. **5** COLLOQ a problem; difficulty: **had a job finding it**. **6** a crime, esp a burglary: **an inside job**.

jobless ADJ unemployed.
➤ N (**the jobless**) unemployed people as a group.

job lot N a mixed collection of objects sold as one item at an auction, etc.

jock N, US COLLOQ a male athlete.

jockey N (-**eys**) a rider in horse races.
◆ **jockey for position** to seek an advantage over rivals.

jockstrap N a garment for supporting the genitals, worn by male athletes.

jocose ADJ FORMAL playful; humorous.

jocular ADJ **1** given to joking; good-humoured. **2** intended as a joke. ■ **jocularity** N.

jocund ADJ, FORMAL cheerful; merry; good-humoured. ■ **jocundity** N.

jodhpurs PL N riding-breeches that are loose-fitting over the buttocks and thighs, and tight-fitting from knee to calf.

joey N **1** AUSTRAL a young animal, esp a kangaroo. **2** NZ an opossum.

jog VB (-**gg**-) **1** to knock or nudge (someone or something) slightly. **2 a** to remind (someone); **b** to prompt (a person's memory). **3** INTR (also **jog along** or **on**) to progress slowly and steadily; to plod. **4** INTR to run at a slowish steady pace.
➤ N **1** a period or spell of jogging: **go for a jog**. **2** a nudge, knock or jolt. ■ **jogger** N.

joggle VB, TR & INTR to jolt, shake or wobble.

johnny N (-**ies**) **1** BRIT COLLOQ, OLD USE a chap; a fellow. **2** a condom.

joie de vivre N enthusiasm for living.

join VB **1** to connect, attach, link or unite. **2** TR & INTR to become a member of (a society, firm, etc). **3** TR & INTR of roads, rivers, etc: to meet. **4** to come together (with someone or something); to enter the company of (a person or group of people): **joined them for supper**. **5** to take part in (something) or do the same as others.
➤ N a seam or joint.
◆ **join in** to take part.
◆ **join up** to enlist as a member of an armed service.

joiner N a craftsman who makes and fits wooden doors, window frames, stairs, shelves, etc. ■ **joinery** N.

joint N **1** the place where two or more pieces join. **2** ANAT the point of contact or articulation between two or more bones. **3** a piece of meat, usu containing a bone, for cooking or roasting. **4** SLANG a cheap shabby café, bar or nightclub, etc. **5** SLANG a cannabis cigarette.
➤ VB **1** to connect to (something) by joints. **2** to divide (a bird or animal) into, or at, the joints for cooking.
➤ ADJ owned or done, etc in common; shared: **joint responsibility**. ■ **jointly** ADV.
◆ **out of joint 1** of a bone: dislocated. **2** in disorder.

joist N any of the beams supporting a floor or ceiling.

jojoba N a shrub whose edible seeds contain a waxy oil, used in cosmetics.

joke N **1** a short humorous story. **2** anything said or done in jest. **3** an amusing situation.
➤ VB, INTR **1** to make jokes. **2** to speak in jest, not in earnest. ■ **jokey** ADJ. ■ **jokingly** ADV.

joker N **1** CARDS an extra card in a pack, usu bearing a picture of a jester. **2** a cheerful person, always full of jokes. **3** COLLOQ an irresponsible or incompetent person.

jollify VB (-**ies**, -**ied**) to make (something) jolly. ■ **jollification** N.

jollity N **1** merriment. **2** (**jollities**) festivities.

jolly ADJ (*-ier, -iest*) **1** good-humoured; cheerful. **2** happy; enjoyable; convivial.
➤ ADV, BRIT COLLOQ very: **jolly good**.
➤ VB (*-ies, -ied*) (**jolly along**) to keep going in a cheerful way.

jolt VB **1** INTR to move along jerkily. **2** to shock (someone) emotionally.
➤ N **1** a jarring shake. **2** an emotional shock.

joss-stick N a stick of dried scented paste, burnt as incense.

jostle VB **1** INTR to push and shove. **2** to push against (someone) roughly.

jot N (USU WITH NEGATIVES) the least bit: **not a jot of sympathy**.
➤ VB (*-tt-*) (**jot sth down**) to write it down hastily. ■ **jotting** N.

jotter N a school notebook for rough work.

joule N, PHYS in the SI system: the unit of work and energy.

journal N **1** a magazine or periodical. **2** a diary in which one recounts one's daily activities.

journalese N, DEROG the language typically used in newspapers and magazines.

journalism N the profession of writing for newspapers and magazines, or for radio and television. ■ **journalist** N. ■ **journalistic** ADJ.

journey N (*-eys*) **1** a process of travelling from one place to another. **2** the distance covered by, or time taken for, a journey.
➤ VB, INTR to make a journey.

journeyman N a craftsman qualified in a particular trade and working for an employer.

joust N, HIST a contest between two knights on horseback armed with lances.

jovial ADJ good-humoured; merry; cheerful. ■ **joviality** N. ■ **jovially** ADV.

jowl N **1** the lower jaw. **2** the cheek. **3** (USU **jowls**) loose flesh under the chin.

joy N **1** intense gladness. **2** someone or something that causes delight.

joyful ADJ **1** happy; full of joy. **2** expressing or

resulting in joy. ■ **joyfully** ADV.

joyous ADJ filled with, causing or showing joy. ■ **joyously** ADV. ■ **joyousness** N.

joyride N a jaunt, esp a reckless drive in a stolen vehicle.
➤ VB, INTR to go for such a jaunt. ■ **joyrider** N. ■ **joyriding** N.

joystick N, COLLOQ the controlling lever of an aircraft, machine etc or a lever for controlling a moving image on a VDU screen.

jubilant ADJ showing and expressing triumphant joy; rejoicing. ■ **jubilantly** ADV.

jubilation N triumphant rejoicing.

jubilee N a special anniversary of a significant event, esp the 25th (**silver jubilee**) or 50th (**golden jubilee**).

Judaic ADJ of the Jews or Judaism.

Judaism N the Jewish religion, based on a belief in one God, or way of life.

Judas N a traitor.

judder VB, INTR to jolt, shake, shudder or vibrate.
➤ N an intense jerking motion.

judge N **1** a public officer who hears and decides cases in a law court. **2** a person appointed to decide the winner of a contest. **3** someone qualified to assess something.
➤ VB **1** to try (a legal case) in a law court as a judge; to decide (questions of guiltiness, etc). **2** to decide the winner of (a contest). **3** INTR to act as judge or adjudicator. **4** to form an opinion about. **5** to consider or state (to be the case), after consideration.

judgement or **judgment** N **1** the decision of a judge in a court of law. **2** the act or process of judging. **3** the ability to make wise or sensible decisions; good sense: **I value his judgement**. **4** an opinion: **in my judgement**.

judgemental or **judgmental** ADJ apt to pass judgement, esp moral judgements.

judicial ADJ of a court of law, judges or the decisions of judges. ■ **judicially** ADV.

judiciary N (*-ies*) **1** the branch of government

concerned with the law and the administration of justice. **2** a country's body of judges.

judicious ADJ shrewd, sensible, wise or tactful.

judo N a Japanese sport and physical discipline based on unarmed self-defence.

jug N **1** a deep container for liquids, with a handle and a shaped lip for pouring. **2** (also **jugful**) the amount a jug holds. **3** SLANG prison.

juggernaut N **1** BRIT COLLOQ a very large articulated lorry. **2** a mighty force sweeping away and destroying everything in its path.

juggle VB to keep several objects simultaneously in the air by skilful throwing and catching. ■ **juggler** N.

jugular N, ANAT any of several veins that carry blood from the head to the heart.

juice N **1** the liquid or sap from fruit or vegetables. **2** a natural fluid in the body.

juicy ADJ (*-ier, -iest*) **1** full of juice. **2** COLLOQ of gossip: intriguing; spicy. ■ **juiciness** N.

ju-jitsu N a martial art founded on the ancient Japanese system of combat and self-defence without weapons.

jujube N a soft fruit-flavoured sweet.

jukebox N a coin-operated machine that plays the record or CD one selects.

julep N **1** a sweet drink, often a medicated one. **2** esp in N America: an iced drink of spirits and sugar, flavoured esp with mint.

julienne N a clear soup, with shredded vegetables.
➤ ADJ of vegetables: in thin strips; shredded.

July N the seventh month of the year.

jumble VB **1** to mix or confuse, physically or mentally. **2** to throw together untidily.
➤ N **1** a confused mass. **2** unwanted possessions for a jumble sale.

jumble sale N a sale of unwanted possessions, usu to raise money for charity.

jumbo ADJ, COLLOQ extra-large.

jump VB **1** INTR to spring off the ground, pushing

off with the feet. **2** to get over or across (something) by jumping. **3** to make (esp a horse) leap. **4** INTR to rise abruptly. **5** INTR to make a startled movement. **6** INTR to twitch, jerk or bounce. **7** TR & INTR to omit or skip (something): **jump the next chapter**. **8** COLLOQ to pounce on someone or something. **9** COLLOQ of a car: to pass through (a red traffic light).
➤ N **1** an act of jumping. **2** an obstacle to be jumped. **3** the height or distance jumped. **4** a jumping contest. **5** a sudden rise in amount, cost or value. **6** an abrupt change or move. **7** a startled movement; a start.
◆ **jump down sb's throat** COLLOQ to snap at them impatiently.
◆ **jump the gun** to act prematurely.

jumped-up ADJ, DEROG COLLOQ having an inflated view of one's importance.

jumper N **1** a knitted garment for the top half of the body. **2** N AMER a pinafore dress.

jumpsuit N a one-piece garment combining trousers and top.

jumpy ADJ (*-ier, -iest*) nervy; anxious.

junction N a place where roads or railway lines meet or cross; an intersection.

juncture N **1** a joining; a union. **2** a point in time.

June N the sixth month of the year.

jungle N **1** an area of dense vegetation, esp in a tropical region. **2** a mass of complexities difficult to penetrate: **the jungle of building regulations**. **3** a complex or hostile environment: **the concrete jungle**. **4** fast rhythmic music characterized by very low bass lines and complex percussion breaks.

junior ADJ **1 a** low or lower in rank; **b** younger. **2** relating or belonging to, or for, schoolchildren aged between 7 and 11: **junior schools**. **3** used after the name of a person with the same forename as their father.
➤ N **1** a person of low or lower rank in a profession, organization, etc. **2** a pupil in a junior school. **3** N AMER, ESP US a third-year college or high-school student. **4** a person younger than the one in question.

juniper N an evergreen coniferous tree or

shrub with purple berry-like cones.

junk¹ COLLOQ, N **1** worthless material; rubbish. **2** nonsense. **3** SLANG narcotic drugs.
➢ VB to discard (something) as useless.

junk² N a flat-bottomed square-sailed boat, from the Far East.

junket N **1** a dessert made from sweetened and curdled milk. **2** a feast or celebration. **3** a trip made by a government official, etc which they do not pay for themselves.

junk food N food with little nutritional value.

junkie or **junky** N (*-ies*) **1** SLANG a drug addict or drug-pusher. **2** COLLOQ someone who is addicted to something: **a TV junkie**.

junk mail N unsolicited mail.

junta N a group, usu of army officers, in control of a country after a coup d'état.

Jupiter N, ASTRON the fifth planet from the Sun, and the largest in the solar system.

juridical ADJ relating to the law or the administration of justice. ■ **juridically** ADV.

jurisdiction N **1** the right or authority to apply laws and administer justice. **2** the district or area over which this authority extends.

jurisprudence N **1** knowledge of or skill in law. **2** a speciality within law.

jurist N **1** an expert in the science of law. **2** US a lawyer.

juror N a member of a jury in a court of law.

jury N (*-ies*) **1** a body of people sworn to give an honest verdict on the evidence presented to a court of law on a particular case. **2** a group of people selected to judge a contest.

just¹ ADJ **1** fair; impartial. **2** reasonable; based on justice. **3** deserved. ■ **justly** ADV.

just² ADV **1** exactly; precisely. **2** a short time before: **just gone**. **3** at this or that very moment: **just leaving**. **4** and no earlier, more, etc: **just enough**. **5** barely; narrowly: **just missed him**. **6** only; merely; simply: **just a brief note**. **7** COLLOQ used for emphasis: **just not true**. **8** COLLOQ absolutely: **just great**.
◆ **just about** almost: **I'm just about ready**.
◆ **just about to** on the point of.
◆ **just so 1** a formula of agreement. **2** neat and tidy.
◆ **just the same** nevertheless.

justice N **1** the quality of being just; fairness. **2** the quality of being reasonable. **3** the law, or administration of or conformity to the law: **a miscarriage of justice**. **4** a justice of the peace. **5** N AMER, ESP US a judge.
◆ **bring sb to justice** to arrest and try them.

justice of the peace N (*justices of the peace*) a person authorized to judge minor criminal cases.

justifiable ADJ able to be justified.

justify VB (*-ies, -ied*) **1** to prove (something) to be right, just or reasonable. **2** PRINTING to arrange (text) so that the margins are even-edged. ■ **justification** N.

jut VB (*-tt-*) INTR (also **jut out**) to stick out; to project. ■ **jutting** ADJ.

jute N fibre from certain types of tropical bark.

juvenile ADJ **1** young; youthful. **2** suitable for young people. **3** DEROG childish; immature.
➢ N a young person.

juxtapose VB to place (things) side by side. ■ **juxtaposition** N.

Kk

K¹ or **k** N (*Ks*, *K's* or *k's*) the eleventh letter of the English alphabet.

K² N (PL **K**) COLLOQ one thousand, esp £1000.

k ABBREV **1** karat or carat. **2** kilo.

kaftan another spelling of **caftan**

kagoule another spelling of **cagoule**

Kaiser N, HIST any of the emperors of Germany, Austria or the Holy Roman Empire.

kale or **kail** N a variety of cabbage with loose wrinkled or curled leaves.

kaleidoscope N **1** an optical toy consisting of long mirrors fixed inside a tube containing small pieces of coloured plastic, glass or paper, so that multiple reflections produce random regular patterns when the tube is viewed through an eyepiece and rotated. **2** any colourful and constantly changing scene or succession of events. ■ **kaleidoscopic** ADJ.

kamikaze N **1** in World War II: a Japanese plane loaded with explosives that the pilot would deliberately crash into an enemy target. **2** the pilot of this kind of plane.
➤ ADJ **1** of such an attack or the pilot concerned. **2** COLLOQ suicidally dangerous.

kangaroo N a marsupial mammal with a thick muscular tail and large powerful hind legs adapted for leaping, native to Australasia.
➤ VB, INTR, COLLOQ of a car: to move forward in jerks because of poor clutch control.

kangaroo court N a court with no legal status and usu delivering unfair judgements.

kaolin N a soft white clay used for making fine porcelain, and medicinally to treat diarrhoea

and vomiting. Also called **china clay**.

kapok N the light waterproof silky fibres that surround the seeds of certain trees.

karaoke N a form of entertainment in which amateur performers sing to the accompaniment of pre-recorded music.

karat see **carat**

karate N a system of unarmed self-defence, using blows and kicks.

karma N, BUDDHISM, HINDUISM **1** the sum of someone's lifetime's actions, seen as governing their fate in the next life. **2** destiny; fate. **3** POPULARLY an aura or quality perceived to be given off by someone or something.

kart N, COLLOQ a go-kart. ■ **karting** N.

kayak N **1** a sealskin-covered canoe used by the Inuit. **2** a similar craft used in the sport of canoeing.

kazoo N a crude wind instrument which makes a buzzing sound when blown.

kebab N (in full **shish kebab**) a dish of pieces of meat and vegetable grilled on a skewer.

kedge VB, TR & INTR to manoeuvre by means of a hawser attached to a light anchor.
➤ N a light anchor used for kedging.

kedgeree N, COOKERY a dish consisting of rice, fish and eggs.

keek SCOT & N ENGLISH, N a peep.
➤ VB, INTR to take a peep.

keel N the timber or metal strut extending from stem to stern along the base of a ship.
◆ **keel over 1** of a ship: to tip over sideways.

2 COLLOQ to fall over.
◆ **on an even keel** calm and steady.

keelhaul VB to drag someone under the keel of a ship from one side to the other.

keen[1] ADJ **1** eager; willing. **2** fierce. **3** bitter. **4** sharp. **5** quick; acute. **6** competitive.

keen[2] VB, TR & INTR to lament or mourn in a loud wailing voice.
➤ N a lament for the dead.

keep VB (*kept*) **1** to have; to possess. **2** to continue to have something; not to part with it. **3** to maintain or retain. **4** to store. **5** TR & INTR to remain or cause something to remain in a certain state, position, place, etc. **6** INTR to continue or be frequently doing something: **keep smiling**. **7** to have something regularly in stock. **8** to own and look after (an animal, etc). **9** to own or run (a shop, boarding-house, etc). **10** to look after something: **keep this for me**. **11** INTR of food: to remain fit to be eaten. **12** to preserve (a secret). **13** to stick to (a promise or appointment). **14** to celebrate (a festival, etc) in the traditional way; to follow (a custom). **15** to support someone financially.
➤ N **1** the cost of one's food and other daily expenses: **earn one's keep**. **2** the central tower or stronghold in a Norman castle.
◆ **for keeps** COLLOQ permanently; for good.
◆ **keep at** to persevere at or persist in.
◆ **keep sth back** to conceal information, etc.
◆ **keep sb down** to oppress them; to prevent their development or progress, etc.
◆ **keep down 1** to control or limit (prices, etc). **2** to manage not to vomit (food, etc).
◆ **keep off 1** to avoid (a harmful food, awkward topic, etc). **2** to stay away from: Keep off my books!
◆ **keep sb on** to continue to employ them.
◆ **keep on at** to nag or harass.
◆ **keep sth up 1** to prevent (eg spirits, morale, etc) from falling. **2** to maintain (a habit, friendship, pace, etc). **3** to maintain (a house, garden, etc) in good condition.
◆ **keep up with 1** not to be left behind by. **2** to maintain the pace or standard set by.

keeper N **1** a person who looks after something, eg a collection in a museum.

2 a gamekeeper. **3** COLLOQ a goalkeeper. **4** a wicketkeeper.

keep fit N a series or system of exercises to improve the circulation, suppleness and stamina, etc. Also AS ADJ: **keep-fit classes**.

keeping N care or charge.
◆ **in keeping with sth** in harmony with it.

keepsake N something kept in memory of the giver, or of a particular event or place.

keg N a small barrel, usu for transporting and storing beer.

kelp N a common name for any large brown seaweed that grows below the low-tide mark.

kelson N a timber fixed along a ship's keel for strength.

kelvin N, PHYS in the SI system: a unit of thermodynamic or absolute temperature.

ken VB (*kent* or *kenned, kenning*) SCOT & N ENGLISH DIALECT **1** to know. **2** to understand.
➤ N range of knowledge; perception.

kendo N a Japanese art of fencing using bamboo staves or sometimes real swords, while observing strict ritual.

kennel N **1** a small shelter for a dog. **2** (**kennels**) an establishment where dogs are boarded or bred.
➤ VB (*-ll-*; N AMER *-l-*) to put or keep (an animal) in a kennel.

keratin N, BIOCHEM a tough fibrous protein forming the main component of hair, nails, claws, horns, feathers and the dead outer layers of skin cells. ■ **keratinous** ADJ.

kerb or (esp N AMER) **curb** N **1** the row of stones or concrete edging forming the edge of a pavement. **2** a kerbstone.

kerbstone N one of the stones forming a kerb.

kerchief N a square of cloth or a scarf for wearing over the head or round the neck.

kerfuffle N, COLLOQ fuss; a commotion.

kernel N **1** the inner part of a seed, eg the edible part of a nut. **2** in cereal plants such as corn: the entire grain or seed. **3** the important, essential part of anything.

kerosine N 1 a combustible oily mixture of hydrocarbons obtained mainly by distillation of petroleum, used as a fuel. 2 N AMER paraffin.

kestrel N a small falcon with a long tail and broad pointed wings.

ketch N a small two-masted sailing boat.

ketchup N, POPULARLY a thick sauce made from tomatoes, vinegar, spices, etc.

ketone N any of a class of organic chemical compounds formed by the oxidation of secondary alcohols.

kettle N 1 a container with a spout, lid and handle, for boiling water. 2 a metal container for heating liquids. ■ **kettleful** N.

kettledrum N a large copper or brass cauldron-shaped drum with a skin stretched over the top, tuned by adjusting screws that alter the tension of the skin.

key[1] N 1 a device for opening or closing a lock, or for winding up, turning, tuning, tightening or loosening. 2 one of a series of buttons or levers pressed to sound the notes on a musical instrument, or to print or display a character on a computer, typewriter, calculator, etc. 3 a system of musical notes related to one another in a scale. 4 pitch, tone or style. 5 something that provides an answer or solution. 6 a means of achievement: **the key to success**. 7 a table explaining signs and symbols used on a map, etc. 8 a pin or wedge for fixing something.
➤ ADJ centrally important: **key questions**.
➤ VB 1 (also **key sth in**) to enter (data) into a computer, calculator, etc by means of a keyboard. 2 to lock or fasten with a key.
◆ **keyed up** COLLOQ excited; tense; anxious.
◆ **under lock and key 1** safely stored. 2 in prison.

key[2] or **cay** N a small low island or reef formed of sand, coral, rock or mud.

keyboard N 1 the set of keys on a piano, etc. 2 the bank of keys for operating a typewriter or computer. 3 MUS an electronic musical instrument with a keyboard.
➤ VB 1 INTR to operate the keyboard of a computer. 2 to set (text) using a computer keyboard. ■ **keyboarder** N.

keyhole N 1 the hole through which a key is inserted into a lock. 2 any small hole similar to this in shape or purpose.

keyhole surgery N a technique that involves internal surgical operations being performed with minimal external excision.

keynote N 1 the note on which a musical scale or key is based; the tonic. 2 a central theme, principle or controlling thought.

keypad N a small device with push-button controls.

key signature N, MUS the sharps and flats indicating the key a piece of music is to be played in.

keystone N, ARCHIT the central supporting stone at the high point of an arch.

keystroke N a single press of a key on a keyboard, etc.

keyword N a word that sums up or gives an indication of the nature of the passage in which it occurs.

khaki N 1 a dull brownish-yellow or brownish-green colour. 2 **a** cloth of this colour; **b** military uniform made of such cloth.

khan N the title of a ruler or prince in central Asia.

kibbutz N (*kibbutzim*) in Israel: a communal farm or other concern owned and run jointly as a co-operative by its workers.

kibosh or **kybosh** N, COLLOQ rubbish; nonsense.
◆ **put the kibosh on sth** to put an end to it; to ruin it.

kick VB 1 to hit with the foot. 2 to propel something with the foot: **kicks the ball**. 3 INTR to strike out or thrust with one or both feet, eg when swimming, struggling, etc. 4 TR & INTR esp in dancing: to jerk (the leg) vigorously or swing it high. 5 INTR of a gun, etc: to recoil when fired. 6 INTR (sometimes **kick against sth**) to resist it. 7 to get rid of (a habit, etc).

➤ N **1** a blow or fling with the foot. **2** any of various movements of the leg, in dancing, swimming, etc. **3** the recoil of a gun, etc after firing. **4** COLLOQ a thrill of excitement. **5** COLLOQ the effect of certain drugs or strong drink.
◆ **for kicks** for thrills.
◆ **kick about** or **around** COLLOQ **1** to lie around unused and neglected. **2** to pass time idly or to little purpose.
◆ **kick in** to take effect.
◆ **kick in the teeth** COLLOQ a humiliating snub.
◆ **kick off 1** to start, or restart, a football game by kicking the ball away from the centre. **2** COLLOQ to begin a discussion or other activity involving several people.
◆ **kick out** COLLOQ to dismiss or get rid of.
◆ **kick the bucket** COLLOQ to die.
◆ **kick up a fuss**, **row** or **stink** COLLOQ to complain or disapprove strongly and vociferously.

kick-off N **1** the start or restart of a football match. **2** COLLOQ the start of anything.

kick-start N **1** (also **kick-starter**) a pedal on a motorcycle that is kicked vigorously downwards to start the engine. **2** the starting of an engine with this pedal.
➤ VB **1** to start (a motorcycle) using this pedal. **2** to give an advantageous, and sometimes sudden, impulse to something.

kid¹ N **1** COLLOQ a child; a young person. **2** a young goat, antelope or other related animal. **3** the smooth soft leather made from the skin of such an animal.
➤ ADJ, COLLOQ younger: **my kid sister**.
➤ VB (-*dd*-) INTR of a goat, etc: to give birth to young.

kid² VB (-*dd*-) COLLOQ (sometimes **kid on** or **along**) **1** to fool or deceive, esp light-heartedly or in fun. **2** INTR to bluff; to pretend.
◆ **kid oneself** to fool oneself.

kiddie or **kiddy** N (-*ies*) COLLOQ a small child.

kid glove N a glove made of kid skin.
◆ **handle sb with kid gloves** to treat them with special care or caution.

kidnap VB (-*pp*-; N AMER -*p*-) to seize and hold someone prisoner illegally, usu demanding a ransom for their release. ■ **kidnapper** N.

kidney N **1** ANAT either of a pair of organs at the back of the abdomen whose function is to remove waste products from the blood. **2** animal kidneys as food.

kilim N a woven rug without any pile.

kill VB **1** TR & INTR to cause the death of (an animal or person); to murder; to destroy someone or something. **2** COLLOQ to cause severe pain to someone. **3** COLLOQ to cause something to fail; to put an end to it. **4** to defeat (a parliamentary bill); to veto (a proposal). **5** COLLOQ to deaden (pain, noise, etc). **6** to pass (time) while waiting for some later event. **7** COLLOQ to overwhelm someone with admiration, laughter, etc.
➤ N **1** an act of killing. **2** the prey killed by any creature. **3** game killed. ■ **killer** N.
◆ **kill two birds with one stone** to accomplish two things by one action.

killing N an act of slaying.
➤ ADJ, COLLOQ **1** exhausting. **2** highly amusing. **3** deadly; fatal.
◆ **make a killing** COLLOQ to make a large amount of money, esp quickly.

killjoy N someone who spoils the pleasure of others.

kiln N an oven or furnace used for drying timber, grain or hops, or for firing bricks, pottery, etc.

kilo N **1** a kilogram. **2** a kilometre.

kilobyte N, COMP a unit of memory equal to 1024 bytes.

kilogram or **kilogramme** N in the SI system: the basic unit of mass, equal to 1000 grams (2.205 pounds).

kilohertz N (PL *kilohertz*) an SI unit of frequency equal to 1000 hertz or 1000 cycles per second, used to measure the frequency of sound and radio waves.

kilojoule N 1000 joules, an SI unit used to measure energy, work and heat.

kilolitre N a metric unit of liquid measure equal to 1000 litres.

kilometre or (N AMER) **kilometer** N a metric unit of length equal to 1000 metres (0.62 miles).

kiloton or **kilotonne** N a metric unit of explosive power equal to that of 1000 tonnes of TNT.

kilovolt N an SI unit: 1000 volts.

kilowatt N an SI unit of electrical power equal to 1000 watts or about 1.34 horsepower.

kilt N **1** a pleated tartan knee-length wraparound skirt, worn by men as part of traditional Scottish Highland dress. **2** any similar garment.

kilter N good condition.
♦ **out of kilter** out of order; not working properly; out of condition.

kimono N a long, loose, wide-sleeved Japanese garment fastened by a sash.

kin N **1** one's relatives. **2** people belonging to the same family.

kind¹ N **1** a group, class, sort, race or type. **2** a particular variety or a specimen belonging to a specific variety. **3** nature, character or distinguishing quality: **differ in kind**.
♦ **in kind 1** of payment: in goods instead of money. **2** of repayment or retaliation: in the same form as the treatment received.
♦ **of a kind 1** of the same sort: **three of a kind**. **2** of doubtful worth: **an explanation of a kind**.

kind² ADJ **1** friendly, helpful, generous or considerate. **2** warm; cordial: **kind regards**.
■ **kindness** N.

kindergarten N a school for young children.

kindle VB, TR & INTR to start burning.

kindling N materials for starting a fire, eg dry twigs or leaves, sticks, etc.

kindly ADV **1** in a kind manner. **2** please: Kindly remove your feet from the desk.
➤ ADJ (-ier, -iest) kind, friendly, generous or good-natured. ■ **kindliness** N.

kindred N **1** one's relatives; family. **2** relationship by blood.
➤ ADJ **1** related. **2** having qualities in common: kindred arts.

kinematics SING N, PHYS the study of the motion of objects. ■ **kinematic** ADJ.

kinetic ADJ **1** PHYS relating to or producing motion. **2** CHEM relating to the speed of chemical reactions. ■ **kinetically** ADV.

kinetics SING N, PHYS the branch of mechanics concerned with the relationship between moving objects, their masses and the forces acting on them.

kinfolk and **kinfolks** see **kinsfolk**

king N **1** a male ruler of a nation. **2** a ruler or chief. **3** a creature considered supreme in strength, ferocity, etc: **king of beasts**. **4** ESP AS ADJ a large, or the largest, variety of something: **king prawns**. **5** a leading or dominant figure in a specified field: **king of jazz**. **6** CARDS the court card bearing a picture of a king. **7** CHESS the most important piece, which must be protected from checkmate. ■ **kingship** N.

kingdom N **1** a region, state or people ruled, or previously ruled, by a king or queen. **2** BIOL any of the divisions corresponding to the highest rank in the classification of plants and animals. **3** the domain of, or area associated with, something: **the kingdom of the imagination**.

kingfisher N a brightly coloured fish-eating bird with a long pointed bill and short wings.

kingpin N **1** the most important person in an organization, team, etc. **2** MECH a bolt serving as a pivot.

king post N, ARCHIT a perpendicular beam in the frame of a roof.

king-size and **king-sized** ADJ of a large or larger-than-standard size.

kink N **1** a bend or twist in hair or in a string, rope, wire, etc. **2** COLLOQ an oddness of personality; an eccentricity.
➤ VB, TR & INTR to develop, or cause something to develop, a kink.

kinky ADJ (-ier, -iest) **1** COLLOQ interested in or practising unusual or perverted sexual acts.

2 COLLOQ eccentric; crazy. ■ **kinkiness** N.

kinsfolk, (N AMER) **kinfolk** and **kinfolks** PL N one's relations.

kinship N **1** family relationship. **2** a state of having common properties or characteristics.

kinsman and **kinswoman** N a relative.

kiosk N **1** a small booth or stall for the sale of newspapers, etc. **2** a public telephone box.

kip N **1** sleep or a sleep. **2** somewhere to sleep; a bed.
➤ VB (*-pp-*) INTR **1** to sleep. **2** (also **kip down**) to go to bed; to doss down.

kipper N a fish, esp a herring, that has been split open, salted and smoked.
➤ VB to cure by salting and smoking.

kirk N, SCOT **1** a church. **2** (**the Kirk**) the Church of Scotland.

kirsch N a clear liqueur distilled from black cherries.

kismet N **1** ISLAM the will of Allah. **2** fate or destiny.

kiss VB **1** to touch someone with the lips, or to press one's lips against them, as a greeting, sign of affection, etc. **2** INTR to kiss one another on the lips. **3** to express something by kissing. **4** INTR of billiard or snooker balls: to touch each other gently while moving.
➤ N **1** an act of kissing. **2** a gentle touch.
◆ **kiss sth goodbye** or **kiss goodbye to sth** to lose it, esp through mismanagement, etc.

kiss curl N a flat curl of hair pressed against the cheek or forehead.

kisser N, SLANG the mouth or face.

kiss of death N, COLLOQ someone or something that brings failure or ruin.

kiss of life N **1** mouth-to-mouth. **2** a means of restoring vitality or vigour.

kit[1] N **1** a set of instruments, equipment, etc needed for a purpose. **2** a set of special clothing and personal equipment. **3** a set of parts ready for assembling.
➤ VB (*-tt-*) (also **kit out**) to provide with the clothes and equipment necessary for a particular occupation, assignment, etc.

kit[2] N **1** a kitten. **2** the young of various smaller fur-bearing animals, eg the ferret or fox.

kitbag N a soldier's or sailor's bag, usu cylinder-shaped and made of canvas.

kitchen N a room or an area in a building where food is prepared and cooked.

kitchenette N a small kitchen, or a section of a room serving as a kitchen.

kite N **1** a bird of prey of the hawk family with long pointed wings and a deeply forked tail. **2** a light frame covered in paper or other light material, with a long holding string attached to it, for flying in the air. **3** SLANG an aircraft.

kith N friends.
◆ **kith and kin** friends and relations.

kitsch N sentimental, pretentious or vulgar tastelessness in art, design, writing, film-making, etc. Also AS ADJ. ■ **kitschy** ADJ (*-ier,-iest*).

kitten N **1** a young cat. **2** the young of various other small mammals, eg the rabbit.
➤ VB, TR & INTR of a cat: to give birth.

kittenish ADJ **1** like a kitten; playful. **2** of a woman: affectedly playful; flirtatious.

kittiwake N a type of gull with white plumage, dark-grey back and wings, a yellow bill and black legs.

kitty[1] N (*-ies*) **1** a fund contributed to jointly, for communal use by a group of people. **2** CARDS a pool of money used in certain games.

kitty[2] N an affectionate name for a cat.

kiwi N **1** a nocturnal flightless bird, found in New Zealand, with hair-like brown or grey feathers, a long slender bill and no tail. **2** COLLOQ a New Zealander.

kiwi fruit N an oval edible fruit with green juicy flesh enclosed by a brown hairy skin.

klaxon N a loud horn used as a warning signal.

kleptomania N an irresistible urge to steal, esp objects that are not desired for themselves. ■ **kleptomaniac** N, ADJ.

klutz N, US SLANG an idiot; an awkward person.

knack N 1 the ability to do something effectively and skilfully. 2 a habit or tendency.

knacker N a buyer of worn-out old horses for slaughter.
➤ VB, COLLOQ 1 to exhaust. 2 to wear out.

knapsack N a hiker's or traveller's bag for clothes, etc, carried on the back.

knave N, OLD USE 1 CARDS the jack. 2 a scoundrel. ■ **knavish** ADJ.

knead VB 1 to work (dough) with one's fingers and knuckles into a uniform mass. 2 to massage (flesh) with firm finger-movements.

knee N 1 in humans: the joint in the middle of the leg. 2 a the corresponding joint in the hind limb of other vertebrates; b in a horse's foreleg: the joint corresponding to the wrist. 3 the area surrounding this joint. 4 the lap. 5 the part of a garment covering the knee.
➤ VB (*kneed, kneeing*) to hit, nudge or shove someone or something with the knee.
◆ **bring sb to their knees** to defeat, prostrate, humiliate or ruin them utterly.

kneecap N a small plate of bone situated in front of and protecting the knee joint.
➤ VB to shoot or otherwise damage someone's kneecaps as a form of revenge or torture.

knee-deep ADJ, ADV 1 rising or reaching to someone's knees. 2 sunk to the knees: standing knee-deep in mud. 3 deeply involved.

knee-high ADJ rising or reaching to the knees: knee-high grass.

knee-jerk N an involuntary kick of the lower leg, caused by a reflex response.
➤ ADJ of a response or reaction: automatic; unthinking; predictable.

kneel VB (*knelt* or *kneeled*) INTR (often **kneel down**) to support one's weight on, or lower oneself onto, one's knees.

knee-length ADJ coming down or up as far as the knees: knee-length skirt.

knees-up N, BRIT COLLOQ a riotous party or dance; an uninhibited celebration.

knell N 1 the tolling of a bell announcing a death or funeral. 2 something that signals the end of anything.

knickerbockers and (US) **knickers** PL N baggy trousers tied just below the knee or at the ankle.

knickers PL N an undergarment with two separate legs or legholes, worn by women, and covering the lower abdomen and buttocks.

knick-knack N a little trinket or ornament.

knife N (*knives*) a cutting instrument, typically in the form of a blade fitted into a handle or into machinery, and sometimes also used for spreading.
➤ VB 1 to cut. 2 to stab or kill with a knife.

knife edge N.
◆ **on a knife edge** in a state of extreme uncertainty; at a critical point.

knifepoint N.
◆ **at knifepoint** under threat of injury from a knife.

knight N 1 a man who has been awarded the highest or second highest class of distinction in any of the four British orders of chivalry. 2 HIST in medieval Europe: a man-at-arms of high social status, usu mounted, serving a feudal lord. 3 HIST the armed champion of a lady, devoted to her service. 4 CHESS a piece shaped like a horse's head.
➤ VB to make someone a knight; to confer a knighthood on someone. ■ **knighthood** N.
■ **knightly** ADJ (*-ier, -iest*).

knit VB (*-tt-*) 1 TR & INTR to produce a fabric composed of interlocking loops of yarn, using knitting needles or a knitting machine. 2 to make (garments, etc) by this means. 3 to unite something. 4 TR & INTR of broken bones: to grow or make them grow together again. 5 to draw (one's brows) together. ■ **knitting** N.

knitwear N knitted clothing.

knives plural of **knife**

knob N 1 a hard rounded projection. 2 a handle, esp a rounded one, on a door or drawer. 3 a button that is pressed or rotated to operate a piece of equipment. 4 a small roundish lump: **a knob of butter**.

knobbly ADJ (*-ier, -iest*) covered with or full of knobs; knotty.

knock VB 1 INTR to tap or rap with the knuckles or some object. 2 to strike and so push someone or something, esp accidentally. 3 to put someone or something into a specified condition by hitting them or it: **knocked him senseless**. 4 TR & INTR (usu **knock against** or **on** or **into sth** or **sb**) to strike, bump or bang against it or them. 5 COLLOQ to find fault with or criticize someone or something, esp unfairly. ➤ N 1 an act of knocking. 2 a tap or rap. 3 a push or shove. 4 COLLOQ a personal misfortune, blow, setback, calamity, etc. ◆ **knock about** or **around** COLLOQ to lie about unused; to be idle: **knocking about the streets**. ◆ **knock sb about** or **around** COLLOQ to treat them roughly; to hit or batter them. ◆ **knock back** 1 to rebuff or reject; to turn down. 2 COLLOQ to eat or drink quickly. ◆ **knock down** 1 to strike to the ground: **knocked down by a car**. 2 to demolish (a building). 3 COLLOQ to reduce its price: **knocked these down to a fiver each**. ◆ **knock off** 1 COLLOQ to finish work. 2 SLANG to kill. 3 COLLOQ to produce at speed or in quick succession, apparently quite easily: **knocks off several books a year**. 3 COLLOQ to deduct (a certain amount): **knocked off £15**. ◆ **knock on** RUGBY to commit the foul of pushing the ball forward with the hand. ◆ **knock out** 1 to make unconscious. 2 to defeat in a knockout competition. 3 COLLOQ to amaze; to impress greatly. ◆ **knock up** 1 to wake (someone) by knocking. 2 COLLOQ to make hurriedly.

knockabout ADJ of comedy: boisterous; slapstick. ➤ N 1 a boisterous performance with horseplay. 2 someone who performs such turns.

knock-back N a setback; a rejection or refusal.

knockdown ADJ, COLLOQ very low; cheap: **knockdown prices**.

knocker N 1 a heavy piece of metal fixed to a door by a hinge and used for knocking. 2 someone who knocks.

knock knee or **knock knees** N a condition in which the lower legs curve inwards, so that the knees touch when standing with the feet slightly apart. ■ **knock-kneed** ADJ.

knockout N 1 COLLOQ someone or something stunning. 2 a competition in which the defeated competitors are dropped after each round. ➤ ADJ 1 of a competition: in which the losers in each round are eliminated. 2 of a punch, etc: leaving the victim unconscious. 3 COLLOQ stunningly attractive; excellent.

knoll N a small round, usu grassy hill.

knot N 1 a join or tie in string, etc made by looping the ends around each other and pulling tight. 2 a bond or uniting link. 3 a coil or bun in the hair. 4 a decoratively tied ribbon, etc. 5 a tangle in hair, string, etc. 6 a difficulty or complexity. 7 a hard mass of wood at the point where a branch has grown out from a tree trunk. 8 a unit of speed equal to one nautical mile (1.85km) per hour. 9 a tight feeling, eg in the stomach, caused by nervousness. ➤ VB (*-tt-*) 1 to tie something in a knot. 2 TR & INTR to tangle; to form knots. 3 INTR eg of the stomach: to become tight with nervousness, etc. ■ **knotty** ADJ (*-ier, -iest*). ◆ **at a rate of knots** COLLOQ very fast. ◆ **tie sb** or **oneself in knots** to bewilder, confuse or perplex them or oneself.

knothole N a hole left in a piece of wood where a knot has fallen out.

know VB (*knew, known*) 1 TR & INTR (usu **know sth** or **know of** or **about sth**) to be aware of it; to be certain about it. 2 to have learnt and remembered something. 3 to have an understanding or grasp of something. 4 to be familiar with someone or something: **know her well**. 5 to be able to recognize or identify someone or something. **6** to be able to distinguish someone or something, or to tell them apart. **7** INTR to have enough experience or training. **8** to experience or be subject to something. ■ **knowable** ADJ.

◆ **in the know** COLLOQ **1** having information not known to most people. **2** initiated.

◆ **know sth backwards** COLLOQ to know it thoroughly.

◆ **know the ropes** to understand the detail or procedure.

◆ **there's no knowing** it's impossible to predict.

know-all N, DEROG someone who seems, or claims, to know more than others.

know-how N **1** COLLOQ ability; adroitness; skill. **2** specialized skill.

knowing ADJ **1** shrewd; canny; clever. **2** of a glance, etc: signifying secret awareness. **3** deliberate. ■ **knowingly** ADV.

knowledge N **1** the fact of knowing; awareness; understanding. **2** information one has acquired. **3** learning; the sciences: a branch of knowledge. **4** specific information about a subject.

◆ **to one's** or **to the best of one's knowledge** as far as one knows.

knowledgeable or **knowledgable** ADJ well-informed.

known ADJ **1** widely recognized. **2** identified by the police: a known thief.

knuckle N **1** a joint of a finger. **2** COOKERY the knee or ankle joint of an animal, esp with the surrounding flesh, as food.

◆ **knuckle down to** to begin to work hard at.

◆ **knuckle under** COLLOQ to submit or yield.

knuckle-duster N a set of metal links worn over the knuckles as a weapon.

KO or **k.o.** ABBREV (*KO's* or *k.o.'s*) **1** kick-off. **2** knockout.

koala N an Australian tree-climbing marsupial with thick grey fur and bushy ears.

kohl N a cosmetic for darkening the eyelids.

kohlrabi N (*kohlrabis* or *kohlrabi*) a variety

of cabbage with a short swollen green or purple edible stem.

kookaburra N a large kingfisher, found in Australia and New Guinea and known for its chuckling cry.

Koran N the holy book of Islam. ■ **Koranic** ADJ.

korma N in Indian cookery: a mild-flavoured dish of meat or vegetables braised in stock, yoghurt or cream.

kosher ADJ **1** in accordance with Jewish law. **2** of food: prepared as prescribed by Jewish dietary laws. **3** COLLOQ legitimate.

kowtow VB, INTR (usu **kowtow to sb**) COLLOQ **1** to defer to them, esp in an over-submissive or obsequious way. **2** to touch the forehead to the ground in a gesture of submission. ➤ N an act of kowtowing.

kraal N **1** a S African village of huts surrounded by a fence. **2** S AFR an enclosure for cattle, etc.

kraft and **kraft paper** N a type of strong brown wrapping paper.

kremlin N the citadel of a Russian town, esp (**the Kremlin**) that of Moscow.

krill N (PL *krill*) a shrimp-like crustacean that feeds on plankton.

krona N (*kronor*) the standard unit of currency of Sweden.

krone N (*kroner*) the standard unit of currency of Norway.

krugerrand N a S African one-ounce (or 28-gram) gold coin minted only for investment. Also called **rand**.

krypton N a colourless, odourless, tasteless noble gas that is almost inert, used in lasers, fluorescent lamps, etc.

kudos N credit, honour or prestige.

kudu N a striped African antelope, the male having long spiral horns.

kümmel N a German liqueur flavoured with cumin and caraway seeds.

kumquat N **1** a spiny evergreen shrub or tree,

native to China. **2** its small round orange fruit.

kung fu N a Chinese martial art with similarities to karate and judo.

kybosh see **kibosh**

kyle N, SCOT a channel, strait or sound, a common element in placenames.

L[1] or **l** N (*Ls, L's* or *l's*) the twelfth letter of the English alphabet.

L[2] ABBREV learner driver.

L[3] SYMBOL, the Roman numeral for 50.

la see **lah**

lab CONTRACTION short form of **laboratory**.

label N **1** a tag, sticker, etc attached to something and specifying its contents, etc or how to use it, etc. **2** a descriptive word or short phrase. **3** a small strip of material on a garment, etc with the name of the maker or designer. **4** a recording company's trademark.
➣ VB (-*ll*-; or US ALSO -*l*-) **1 a** to mark in a specified way with a special tag, etc; **b** to attach a tag, sticker, etc to (something). **2** to call by a specified name.

labial ADJ of or beside the lips.

labium N (-*ia*) **1** a lip or lip-like structure. **2** (usu **labia**) one section of the two pairs of folds which form part of the vulva.

laboratory N (-*ies*) a room or building specially equipped for scientific experiments, research, the preparation of drugs, etc.

laborious ADJ of a task, etc: requiring hard work or much effort. ■ **laboriously** ADV.

labour or (N AMER) **labor** N **1** strenuous and prolonged work. **2** (usu **labours**) the amount of effort put in to doing something. **3** working people or their productive output regarded collectively. **4** the process of giving birth.
➣ VB, INTR **1** to work hard or with difficulty. **2** to progress slowly and with difficulty. **3** to spend time and effort achieving something.
◆ **labour a** or **the point** to spend excessive time on one particular subject, etc.

laboured or (esp N AMER) **labored** ADJ **1** showing signs of effort or difficulty. **2** not natural or spontaneous.

labourer or (esp N AMER) **laborer** N someone employed to do physical work.

labour-saving ADJ having the effect of reducing the amount of work or effort needed: labour-saving devices.

Labrador N a medium-sized retriever dog with a short black or golden coat.

laburnum N a small tree with hanging clusters of yellow flowers and poisonous seeds.

labyrinth N **1** a network of interconnected passages. **2** anything that is complicated, intricate or difficult to negotiate.
■ **labyrinthine** ADJ.

lac N a resinous substance produced by certain tropical Asian insects.

lace N **1** a delicate material made of thread woven into open intricate patterns. **2** a string or cord used for fastening shoes, etc.
➣ VB **1** TR & INTR to fasten or be fastened with a lace or laces. **2** to put a lace or laces into (shoes, etc). **3** to flavour, strengthen, adulterate, etc (with alcohol, drugs, poison, etc).

lacerate VB **1** to tear or cut (esp flesh) roughly.

2 to wound or hurt (someone's feelings). ■ **lacerated** ADJ. ■ **laceration** N.

lace-up N a shoe fastened with a lace. ➤ ADJ of a shoe: fastened with a lace or laces.

lachrymal ADJ (also **lacrimal**) ANAT of tears or the glands that secrete them.

lachrymose ADJ, LITERARY **1** prone to crying. **2** of a novel, play, film, etc: likely to make someone cry. ■ **lachrymosely** ADV.

lack N a deficiency or want: **a lack of understanding**. ➤ VB to be without or to have too little of (something). ■ **lacking** ADJ.

lackadaisical ADJ **1** showing little energy, enthusiasm, etc. **2** lazy or idle.

lackey N **1** DEROG a grovelling or servile follower. **2** OLD USE a male servant.

lacklustre or (US) **lackluster** ADJ lacking energy, enthusiasm, brightness, etc.

laconic ADJ **1** of speech or writing: using few words. **2** of someone: laconic in speech or writing. ■ **laconically** ADV.

lacquer N **1** a substance made of natural or man-made resins and used to form a hard, shiny covering on wood and metal. **2** the sap from some trees, used as a varnish. **3** hairspray. ➤ VB to cover with lacquer. ■ **lacquered** ADJ.

lacrimal see under **lachrymal**

lacrosse N a team game similar to hockey but played with a stick with a netted pocket.

lactate VB, INTR of mammary glands: to secrete milk. ■ **lactation** N.

lactic ADJ relating to, derived from or containing milk.

lactose N, BIOCHEM a white crystalline sugar found in milk.

lacuna N (*-nae* or *-nas*) a gap or a space where something is missing, esp in printed text.

lacy ADJ (*-ier, -iest*) like, made of or trimmed with lace.

lad N **1** a boy or youth. **2 a** a male of any age, esp one of a group who drink together on a regular basis: **out with the lads**; **b** a male of any age, esp one considered to be high-spirited: **a bit of a lad**. **3** someone who works in a stable, regardless of their age or sex.

ladder N **1** a piece of equipment used for climbing up or down, consisting of a set of parallel horizontal rungs or steps set between two vertical supports. **2** chiefly BRIT a long narrow flaw, esp in a stocking or tights where a row of stitches has broken. **3** a hierarchical or graded route of advancement or progress. ➤ VB, chiefly BRIT **a** to cause a ladder to appear in (a stocking, etc); **b** INTR of a stocking, etc: to develop a ladder.

lade VB (PA T *laded*, PA P *laden*, PR P *lading*) **1 a** to load cargo on to (a ship); **b** INTR of a ship: to take cargo on board. **2** to put a burden, esp one of guilt, on (someone).

laden ADJ **1** of a ship: loaded with cargo. **2** heavily loaded, weighed down, burdened.

ladies SING N a women's public lavatory.

lading N the cargo or load of a ship, etc.

ladle N a large spoon with a long handle and deep bowl, for serving or transferring liquid. ➤ VB to serve or transfer with a ladle.

lady N (*-ies*) **1** a woman who is regarded as having good manners and refined behaviour. **2** a polite word for a woman. **3** HIST a woman of the upper classes. **4** (**Lady**) BRIT a title used for peeresses, wives and daughters of peers and knights, etc.

ladybird and (N AMER) **ladybug** N a small beetle whose body is usu red or yellow with black spots.

lady-in-waiting N (*ladies-in-waiting*) a woman who attends a queen, princess, etc.

ladykiller N, COLLOQ a man who is, or who thinks he is, irresistibly attractive to women.

ladylike ADJ showing attributes, eg refinement, appropriate to a lady.

Ladyship N (usu **Your** or **Her Ladyship**) a title used to address or refer to peeresses and the wives and daughters of peers and knights, etc.

lag[1] VB (-*gg*-) INTR (usu **lag behind**) to move or progress so slowly as to become separated. ➤ N a delay or the length of a delay.

lag[2] VB (-*gg*-) to cover (a boiler, water pipes, etc) with thick insulating material.

lager N a light effervescent beer.

laggard N someone who lags behind.

lagging N insulating cover for boilers, etc.

lagoon N a relatively shallow body of water separated from the open sea by a barrier such as a reef or a narrow bank of sand.

lah or **la** N, MUS in sol-fa notation: the sixth note of the major scale.

laid-back ADJ, COLLOQ relaxed; easy-going.

laid-up ADJ confined to bed because of illness or injury.

lair N 1 a wild animal's den. 2 COLLOQ a place of refuge or hiding.

laird N, SCOT someone who owns a large country estate.

laissez-faire or **laisser-faire** N a policy of not interfering in what others are doing.

laity N (usu **the laity**) the people who are not members of the clergy.

lake[1] N a large area of water, enclosed by land.

lake[2] N 1 a reddish dye, usu obtained from cochineal. 2 a dye, used in the textile industry, made by combining pigment with a metallic oxide or earth.

lama N a Buddhist priest or monk in Tibet and Mongolia.

lamb N 1 a young sheep. 2 the flesh of a lamb used as food. 3 COLLOQ a kind, gentle, good, sweet, etc person. ➤ VB, INTR of a ewe: to give birth to a lamb.

lambaste or **lambast** VB 1 to beat severely. 2 to criticize or scold severely.

lambent ADJ 1 of a flame or light: flickering over a surface. 2 of wit, writing style, etc: playfully light and clever. ■ **lambency** N.

lame ADJ 1 not able to walk properly, esp due to an injury or defect. 2 of an excuse, etc: not convincing; weak; ineffective. ➤ VB to make lame.

lamé N a fabric which has metallic threads, usu gold or silver, woven into it.

lame duck N someone who depends on the help of others to an excessive extent.

lament VB, TR & INTR to feel or express regret or sadness. ➤ N 1 an expression of sadness, grief, etc. 2 a poem, song, etc which expresses great grief, mourning, etc. ■ **lamentation** N.

lamentable ADJ 1 regrettable, shameful or deplorable. 2 inadequate.

lamented ADJ of a dead person: sadly missed; mourned for: **her late lamented father**.

lamina N (-*nae*) a thin plate or layer, esp of bone, rock or metal.

laminate VB 1 to beat (a material, esp metal) into thin sheets. 2 to form (a composite material) by bonding or gluing together two or more sheets of that material. 3 to cover or overlay (a surface) with a thin sheet of protective material, eg transparent plastic film. ➤ N a laminated sheet, material, etc. ➤ ADJ of a material: composed of layers or beaten into thin sheets. ■ **lamination** N.

lamp N 1 a piece of equipment designed to give out light. 2 any device that produces ultraviolet or infrared radiation and is used to treat certain medical conditions.

lampblack N soot obtained from burning carbon and used as a pigment.

lampoon N an attack, usu in the form of satirical prose or verse, on someone. ➤ VB to satirize (someone or their writing style, etc). ■ **lampooner** or **lampoonist** N.

lamppost N a tall post that supports a streetlamp.

lamprey N, ZOOL a primitive eel-like fish with a sucker-like mouth.

lampshade N a shade placed over a lamp to

soften or direct the light coming from it.

lance N a long spear used as a weapon by charging horsemen.
➤ VB **1** to cut open (a boil, abscess, etc) with a lancet. **2** to pierce with, or as if with, a lance.

lance corporal N the lowest rank of non-commissioned officer in the British army.

lanceolate ADJ shaped like a spear-head, tapering at both ends.

lancer N, FORMERLY a cavalry soldier belonging to a regiment armed with lances.

lancet N a small pointed surgical knife which has both edges sharpened.

land N **1** the solid part of the Earth's surface as opposed to the area covered by water.
2 ground or soil, esp with regard to its use or quality: **farm land**. **3** ground that is used for agriculture. **4** a country, state or region: **native land**. **5** (**lands**) estates.
➤ VB **1** TR & INTR to come or bring to rest after flight through the air. **2** INTR to end up in a specified place or position, esp after a fall, etc. **3** to bring on to the land from a ship: **landed the cargo**. **4** to bring (a fish, esp one caught on a line) out of the water. **5** COLLOQ to be successful in getting (a job, etc).
◆ **land up** COLLOQ to come to be in a specified position or situation: **landed up homeless**.

landau N a four-wheeled horse-drawn carriage with a removable top.

landed ADJ **1** owning land or estates.
2 consisting of land: **landed estates**.

landfall N **1** an approach to land after an air or sea voyage. **2** the land approached.

landfill N **1** a site where rubbish is disposed of by burying it. **2** the rubbish disposed of in this way.

landing N **1** the act of coming or being put ashore or of returning to the ground. **2** a place for disembarking. **3** a level part of a staircase between flights of steps, or at the very top.

landing-gear N the wheels, etc which allow an aircraft to land and take off.

landlady N **1** a woman who rents property out to a tenant or tenants. **2** a woman who owns or runs a public house or hotel.

landlocked ADJ of a country or a piece of land: almost or completely enclosed by land.

landlord N **1** a man who rents property out to a tenant or tenants. **2** a man who owns or runs a public house or hotel.

landlubber N someone who has no sailing or sea-going experience.

landmark N **1** a distinctive feature, esp one used by sailors or travellers as an indication of where they are. **2** an event of importance.

landmass N an area of land unbroken by seas.

land mine N an explosive device that is laid on or near the surface of the ground and which detonates if it is disturbed from above.

landowner N someone who owns land.

landscape N **1** the area and features of land that can be seen in a broad view.
2 a a painting, drawing, photograph, etc of the countryside; **b** this genre of art. **3** an orientation of a page, illustration, etc that is wider than it is tall or deep.
➤ VB to improve the look of (a garden, park, etc) by enhancing the existing natural features.

landslide N **1** (also **landslip**) a sudden downward movement of a mass of soil and rock material. **2** an overwhelming victory in an election.

lane N **1** a narrow road or street. **2** a division of a road for a single line of traffic.
3 a regular course taken by ships across the sea, or by aircraft through the air: **shipping lane**. **4** a marked subdivision of a running track or swimming pool for one competitor.

language N **1** a formalized system of communication, esp one that uses sounds or written symbols which the majority of a particular community will readily understand.
2 the speech and writing of a particular nation or social group. **3** the faculty of speech.
4 a specified style of speech or verbal

expression: **elegant language. 5** any other way of communicating or expressing meaning: **sign language. 6** professional or specialized vocabulary: **legal language.**

languid ADJ **1** lacking in energy or vitality. **2** sluggish; slow-moving.

languish VB, INTR **1** to spend time in hardship or discomfort. **2** to grow weak; to lose energy or vitality. **3** to pine. ■ **languishment** N.

languor N **1** a lack of energy. **2** a stuffy suffocating atmosphere or stillness. ■ **languorous** ADJ.

lank ADJ **1** long and thin. **2** of hair, etc: long, straight and dull.

lanky ADJ (*-ier, -iest*) thin and tall, esp in an awkward and ungainly way. ■ **lankiness** N.

lanolin N a fat that occurs in sheep's wool.

lantern N **1** a light contained in a transparent case. **2** the top part of a lighthouse, where the light is kept. **3** a structure, esp on the top of a dome, that admits light and air.

lantern jaws PL N long thin jaws. ■ **lantern-jawed** ADJ.

lanthanide N, CHEM any of a group of 15 highly reactive metallic elements with atomic numbers ranging from 57 to 71.

lanyard N **1** a cord for hanging a knife, whistle, etc round the neck, esp as worn by sailors. **2** NAUT a short rope for fastening rigging, etc.

lap[1] VB (*-pp-*) **1** usu of an animal: to drink (milk, water, etc) using the tongue. **2** TR & INTR of water, etc: to wash or flow against (a shore or other surface) with a light splashing sound. ➤ N the sound, act or process of lapping.

lap[2] N **1** the front part of the body from the waist to the knees, when in a sitting position. **2** the part of someone's clothing which covers this part of the body.

lap[3] N **1** one circuit of a racecourse etc. **2** one section of a journey. **3** a part which overlaps or the amount it overlaps by. ➤ VB **1** to get ahead of (another competitor in a race) by one or more laps. **2** to make

(something) overlap (something else). **3** INTR to lie with an overlap.

lapdog N a small pet dog.

lapel N the part of a collar on a coat that is folded back towards the shoulders.

lapidary ADJ relating to stones, especially gemstones.

lapis lazuli N **1** GEOL a deep-blue mineral used as a gemstone. **2** a bright-blue colour.

lap of honour N (*laps of honour*) a ceremonial circuit of a racecourse by the winner.

lapse N **1** a slight mistake or failure. **2** a perceived decline in standards of behaviour, etc. **3** a passing of time. **4** LAW the loss of a right or privilege because of failure to renew a claim to it. ➤ VB, INTR **1** to fail to behave in what is perceived as a proper way. **2** to turn away from a faith or belief. **3** LAW of a right, privilege, etc: to become invalid because the claim to it has not been renewed. **4** of a membership of a club, etc: to become invalid. ■ **lapsed** ADJ. ◆ **lapse into** to pass into or return to (a specified state).

laptop N a portable personal computer, small enough to be used on someone's lap.

lapwing N a crested bird of the plover family. Also called **peewit**.

larceny N (*-ies*) LAW, OLD USE theft of personal property. ■ **larcenist** N.

larch N **1** a deciduous coniferous tree with short needles. **2** the wood of this tree.

lard N a soft white preparation made from pig fat, used in cooking. ➤ VB **1** to coat (meat, etc) in lard. **2** to insert strips of bacon or pork into (lean meat) in order to make it more moist and tender once it is cooked. **3** to sprinkle (a piece of writing, etc) with technical details or over-elaborate words.

larder N a cool room or cupboard for storing food, orig bacon.

large ADJ **1** occupying a comparatively big

space. **2** comparatively big in size, extent, amount, etc. **3** broad in scope; wide-ranging; comprehensive. **4** generous.
➤ ADV importantly; prominently: **loom large**.
■ **largeness** N.
◆ **as large as life** COLLOQ in person.
◆ **at large 1** of prisoners, etc: free and threatening. **2** in general: **people at large**.

large intestine N in mammals: the part of the alimentary canal comprising the caecum, colon and rectum.

largely ADV **1** mainly. **2** to a great extent.

large-scale ADJ **1** of maps, models, etc: made on a relatively large scale. **2** extensive; widespread.

largesse or **largess** N **1** generosity. **2** gifts, money, etc given generously.

largo MUS, ADV slowly and with dignity.
➤ ADJ slow and dignified.
➤ N a piece of music to be played in this way.

lariat N **1** a lasso. **2** a rope used for tethering animals.

lark¹ N a gregarious, brownish bird, such as the skylark.

lark² COLLOQ, N **1** a joke or piece of fun. **2** BRIT a job or activity: **I'm really getting into this gardening lark now.**
➤ VB, INTR (usu **lark about**) to play or fool about frivolously.

larkspur N a plant with blue, white or pink flowers, related to the delphinium.

larva N (**-vae**) ZOOL the immature stage in the life cycle of many insects between the egg and pupa stages. ■ **larval** ADJ.

laryngeal ADJ relating to the larynx.

laryngitis N inflammation of the larynx.

larynx N (**larynges** or **-xes**) the upper part of the trachea containing the vocal cords.

lasagne or **lasagna** N **1** pasta in the form of thin flat sheets. **2** a dish made of layers of lasagne, minced beef or vegetables in a tomato sauce, and cheese sauce.

lascivious ADJ of behaviour, thoughts, etc: lewd; lecherous.

laser N a device that produces a very powerful narrow beam of coherent light of a single wavelength.

lash¹ N **1** a stroke made by a whip. **2** the flexible part of a whip. **3** an eyelash.
➤ VB **1** to hit or beat with a lash. **2** TR & INTR to move suddenly, restlessly, etc. **3** to attack with criticism. **4** INTR to make a sudden whip-like movement. **5** TR & INTR of waves or rain: to beat with great force. **6** to urge on as if with a whip.
◆ **lash out 1** to speak or hit out angrily. **2** COLLOQ to spend money extravagantly.

lash² VB to fasten with a rope or cord.

lashing N **1** a beating with a whip. **2** (**lashings**) a generous amount.

lass N, SCOT & N ENGLISH DIALECT a girl.

lassie N, SCOT & N ENGLISH DIALECT, COLLOQ a girl.

lassitude N physical or mental tiredness; a lack of energy and enthusiasm.

lasso N (**-os** or **-oes**) a long rope with a sliding noose at one end used for catching cattle, etc.
➤ VB (**-oes, -oed**) to catch with a lasso.

last¹ ADJ **1** being, coming or occurring at the end of a series or after all others. **2** most recent; happening immediately before the present (week, month, year, etc). **3** only remaining after all the rest have gone or been used up. **4** least likely, desirable, suitable, etc: **the last person you'd expect help from. 5** final: **administered the last rites.**
➤ ADV **1** most recently: **When did you see her last?. 2** lastly; at the end.
➤ N **1** a person or thing that is at the end or behind the rest. **2** (**the last**) the end; a final moment, part, etc: **That's the last of the milk. 3** (**the last**) the final appearance or mention: **We haven't heard the last of him.**
◆ **at last** or **at long last** in the end, esp after a long delay.

last² VB, TR & INTR **1** to take (a specified amount of time) to complete, happen, come to an end, etc. **2** to be adequate: **enough water to last us a week. 3** to be or keep fresh or in good condition: **The bread will last one more day.**

last³ N a foot-shaped piece of wood or metal used in making and repairing shoes, etc.

last-ditch ADJ done as a last resort.

lasting ADJ existing or continuing for a long time or permanently: **had a lasting effect.**

lastly ADV used to introduce the last item or items in a series or list: finally.

the last post N, MIL **1** a bugle call given to signal that it is time to retire at night. **2** a farewell bugle call at military funerals.

the last rites PL N, CHRISTIANITY the ceremonial acts performed for someone who is dying.

latch N **1** a door catch consisting of a bar which is lowered or raised from its notch by a lever or string. **2** a door lock by which a door may be opened from the inside using a handle, and from the outside by using a key.
➤ VB, TR & INTR to fasten or be fastened with a latch.
◆ **latch on to sth** COLLOQ to cling to it, often obsessively.

latchkey child N a child who comes home from school while the parent or parents are still out at work.

late ADJ **1** coming, arriving, etc after the expected or usual time. **2 a** far on in the day or night: **late afternoon; b** IN COMPOUNDS occurring towards the end of a specified historical period, etc: **late-Georgian architecture; c** written, painted, etc towards the end of someone's life or career: **a late Picasso.** **3** happening, growing, etc at a relatively advanced time: **Let's go to the late showing.** **4** dead: **his late father. 5** former: **the late prime minister. 6** recent: **a late model of car.**
➤ ADV **1** after the expected or usual time. **2** far on in the day or night: **He arrived late on Thursday. 3** at an advanced time: **flower late in the season. 4** recently: **The letter was sent as late as this morning. 5** formerly, but no longer: **late of Glasgow. ■ lateness** N.

lateen ADJ, NAUT of a ship: having a triangular sail on a long sloping yard.

lately ADV in the recent past; not long ago.

latent ADJ of a characteristic, tendency, etc: present or existing in an undeveloped or hidden form. ■ **latency** N.

later ADJ more late.
➤ ADV at some time after, or in the near future.

lateral ADJ at, from or relating to a side or the side of something: **lateral fins. ■ laterally** ADV.

lateral thinking N an indirect or seemingly illogical approach to problem-solving.

latest ADJ **1** most recent. **2** (**the latest**) the most recent news, occurrence, fashion, etc.
◆ **at the latest** not later than a specified time.

latex N **1** a thick milky juice produced by some plants and used in the manufacture of rubber. **2** a synthetic product, similar to rubber.

lath N a thin narrow strip of wood.

lathe N a machine used to shape a piece of metal, wood or plastic that is rotated against its cutting edge.

lather N **1** a foam made by mixing water and soap or detergent. **2** foamy sweat.
➤ VB **1** INTR to form a lather. **2** to cover (something) with lather. ■ **lathery** ADJ.
◆ **in a lather** COLLOQ agitated or excited.

Latin N **1** the language of ancient Rome and its empire. **2** a person of Italian, Spanish or Portuguese extraction.
➤ ADJ **1** relating to, or in, the Latin language. **2** applied to languages derived from Latin, esp Italian, Spanish and Portuguese. **3** of a person: Italian, Spanish or Portuguese in origin.

Latin American N an inhabitant of Latin America, the areas in America where Spanish and Portuguese are spoken. ■ **Latin-American** ADJ.

latitude N **1** GEOG the angular distance north or south of the equator. **2** (usu **latitudes**) GEOG a region or area thought of in terms of its distance from the equator or its climate: **warm latitudes. 3** scope for freedom of action or choice. ■ **latitudinal** ADJ.

latitudinarian N someone who is liberal.

latrine N a lavatory, esp in a barracks or camp.

latter ADJ 1 nearer the end than the beginning. 2 used when referring to two people or things: mentioned, considered, etc second.
◆ **the latter** of two people or things: the second one mentioned.

latter-day ADJ recent or modern.

latterly ADV 1 recently. 2 towards the end.

lattice PL N 1 (also **lattice-work**) an open frame made by crossing narrow strips of wood or metal over each other. 2 (also **lattice window**) a window with small diamond-shaped panels of glass held in place with strips of lead.

laud VB, FORMAL to praise.

laudable ADJ worthy of praise; commendable. ■ **laudability** N. ■ **laudably** ADV.

laudanum N a solution of morphine in alcohol, prepared from raw opium.

laudatory ADJ expressing praise.

laugh VB 1 INTR to make spontaneous sounds associated with happiness, amusement, scorn, etc. 2 to express (a feeling, etc) by laughing: laughed his contempt.
➤ N 1 an act or sound of laughing. 2 COLLOQ someone or something that is good fun, amusing, etc.
◆ **have the last laugh** COLLOQ to win or succeed in the end; to be finally proved right.

laughable ADJ 1 deserving to be laughed at. 2 absurd; ludicrous. ■ **laughably** ADV.

laughing gas N nitrous oxide, esp when used as an anaesthetic.

laughing-stock N someone or something that is the object of ridicule, mockery, etc.

laughter N the act or sound of laughing.

launch[1] VB 1 **a** to send (a ship or boat, etc) into the water at the beginning of a voyage; **b** to send (a newly-built ship or boat) into the water for the first time. 2 to send (a spacecraft, missile, etc) into space or into the air. 3 to start (someone or something) off in a specified direction. 4 to bring (a new product) on to the market, esp with promotions and publicity. 5 to begin (an attack, etc).
➤ N 1 the action or an instance of a ship, spacecraft, missile, etc being sent off into the water or into the air. 2 the start of something.
◆ **launch into sth** 1 to begin an undertaking with enthusiasm. 2 to begin a story, song, etc.

launch[2] N a large powerful motorboat.

launching-pad and **launch pad** N the area for launching a spacecraft or missile.

launder VB 1 to wash and iron (clothes, linen, etc). 2 COLLOQ to transfer (illegally obtained money, etc) to cover up its origins.

launderette or **laundrette** N a place where clothes can be washed and dried using coin-operated machines.

laundry N (-ies) 1 a place where clothes, linen, etc are washed. 2 clothes, linen, etc for washing or newly washed.

laureate ADJ crowned with laurel leaves as a sign of honour or distinction.
➤ N someone honoured for artistic or intellectual achievement.

laurel N 1 a small evergreen tree with smooth dark shiny leaves. 2 a crown of laurel leaves worn as a symbol of victory or mark of honour. 3 (**laurels**) honour; praise.
◆ **look to one's laurels** to beware of losing one's reputation by being outclassed.
◆ **rest on one's laurels** to be satisfied with one's past successes and so not bother to achieve anything more.

lava N 1 GEOL magma that has erupted from a volcano. 2 the solid rock that forms as a result of cooling and solidification of this material.

lavatorial ADJ of humour, jokes, etc: rude, esp in making use of references to excrement.

lavatory N (-ies) 1 a bowl-shaped receptacle where urine and faeces are deposited and flushed away by water. 2 a room containing one or more of these.

lavender N 1 a shrub with sweet-smelling

pale bluish-purple flowers. **2** a pale bluish-purple colour.

lavish ADJ **1** spending or giving generously. **2** gorgeous or luxurious: **lavish decoration**. **3** extravagant or excessive.
➤ VB to spend (money) or give (praise, etc) freely or generously. ■ **lavishly** ADV.

law N **1** a customary rule recognized as allowing or prohibiting certain actions. **2** a collection of such rules according to which people live or a country or state is governed. **3** the control which such rules exercise: **law and order**. **4** a controlling force: **Their word is law**. **5** a collection of laws as a social system or a subject for study. **6** the legal system as a recourse; litigation. **7** a rule in science, etc, based on practice or observation.
◆ **the law 1** people who are knowledgeable about law, esp professionally. **2** COLLOQ the police or a member of the police.

law-abiding ADJ obeying the law.

lawcourt N (also **court of law**) a place where people accused of crimes are tried and legal disagreements settled.

lawful ADJ **1** allowed by or according to law. **2** just or rightful. ■ **lawfully** ADV.

lawless ADJ **1** ignoring or breaking the law, esp violently. **2** having no laws. ■ **lawlessness** N.

lawn¹ N an area of smooth mown cultivated grass, esp as part of a garden or park.

lawn² N fine linen or cotton.

lawnmower N a machine for cutting grass.

lawn tennis N see **tennis** (sense 1).

lawsuit N an argument or disagreement taken to a court of law to be settled.

lawyer N a person employed in the legal profession, esp a solicitor.

lax ADJ **1** showing little care or concern over behaviour, morals, etc. **2** loose, slack or flabby. **3** negligent. ■ **laxity** N. ■ **laxly** ADV.

laxative ADJ inducing movement of the bowels.
➤ N a laxative medicine.

lay¹ VB (**laid**) **1** to place on a surface, esp in a horizontal position. **2** to put or bring to a stated position or condition: **laid her hand on his arm**. **3** to design, arrange or prepare: **lay plans**. **4** to put plates and cutlery, etc on (a table) ready for a meal. **5** to prepare (a fire) by putting coal, etc in the grate. **6** TR & INTR to produce (eggs). **7** to present. **8** to set down as a basis: **laid the ground rules**. **9** to deal with or remove. **10** COLLOQ to place (a bet): **I'll lay 20 quid you can't do it**. **11** SLANG to have sexual intercourse with.
➤ N the way or position in which something is lying.
◆ **lay bare** to reveal or explain (a plan or intention that has been kept secret).
◆ **lay sth down 1** to put it on the ground or some other surface. **2** to give it as a deposit, pledge, etc. **3** to give it up or sacrifice it: **lay down one's life**. **4** to formulate or devise: **lay down a plan**. **5** to store (wine) in a cellar.
◆ **lay sth in** to get and store a supply of it.
◆ **lay into sb** COLLOQ to attack or scold them severely.
◆ **lay off** to dismiss (an employee) when there is no work available.
◆ **lay off sth** COLLOQ to stop it.
◆ **lay sth on** to provide a supply of it.
◆ **lay sth out 1** to plan and arrange esp land or natural features. **2** to spread it out or display it. **3** COLLOQ to spend it.
◆ **lay waste** to destroy or devastate completely.

lay² ADJ **1** relating to or involving people who are not members of the clergy. **2** not having specialized or professional knowledge of a particular subject.

lay³ N a short narrative or lyric poem.

layabout N, COLLOQ a habitually lazy person.

lay-by N (**lay-bys**) BRIT an area off to the side of a road where cars can stop safely.

layer N **1** a thickness or covering, esp one of several on top of each other. **2** IN COMPOUNDS someone or something that lays something specified: **bricklayer**. **3** a hen that regularly lays eggs. **4** a shoot from a plant fastened into the soil so that it can take root while still

attached to the parent plant.
➤ VB **1** to arrange or cut in layers. **2** to produce (a new plant) by preparing a layer from the parent plant. ■ **layered** ADJ.

layette N, OLD USE a complete set of clothes, blankets, etc for a new baby.

layman, **laywoman** and **layperson** N **1** someone who is not a member of the clergy. **2** someone who does not have specialized or professional knowledge of a subject.

lay-off N a dismissal of employees when there is no work available.

layout N **1** an arrangement or plan of how land, buildings, pages of a book, etc are to be set out. **2** the things displayed or arranged in this way. **3** the general appearance of a printed page.

laze VB, INTR to be idle or lazy.
➤ N a period of time spent lazing.

lazy ADJ (*-ier, -iest*) **1** disinclined to work or do anything requiring effort. **2** idle. **3** appropriate to idleness. **4** of a river: slow-moving; sluggish. ■ **lazily** ADV. ■ **laziness** N.

lazy-bones N (PL *lazy-bones*) COLLOQ someone who is lazy.

lbw or **l.b.w.** ABBREV, CRICKET leg before wicket.

lea N, POETIC a field or meadow.

leach VB **1** CHEM to wash (a soluble substance) out of (a solid) by allowing a suitable liquid solvent to percolate through it. **2** to make (liquid) seep through (ash, soil, etc), in order to remove substances from that material.

lead[1] VB (*led*) **1** TR & INTR to guide by going in front. **2** to precede. **3** to guide or make (someone or something) go in a certain direction by holding or pulling with the hand, etc. **4** to guide. **5** to conduct. **6** to induce. **7** to cause to live or experience. **8** TR & INTR to direct or be in control of (something). **9** to cause (someone) to act, feel or think in a certain way. **10** to live, pass or experience: **lead a miserable existence**. **11** TR & INTR to go or take (someone) in a certain direction: **The road leads to the village**. **12** TR & INTR to be foremost or first; to be the most important or influential in (a group, etc). **13** INTR (usu **lead with** or **on**) of a newspaper: to have (a particular story) as its most important article. **14** TR & INTR, CARDS to begin a round of cards by playing (the first card, esp of a particular suit).
➤ N **1** an instance of guidance given by leading. **2** the first, leading, or most prominent place; leadership. **3** the amount by which someone or something, etc is in front of others in a race, contest, etc. **4** a strap or chain for leading or holding a dog, etc. **5** an initial clue or piece of information which might help solve a problem, mystery, etc. **6** the principal part in a play, film, etc; the actor playing this role. **7** the most important story in a newspaper. **8** a precedent or example. **9** precedence. **10** an indication. **11** direction. **12** initiative. **13** a wire or conductor taking electricity from a source to an appliance. **14** CARDS the act or right of playing first, the first card played or the turn of someone who plays first.
◆ **lead sb on** to deceive or mislead them.
◆ **lead up to sth** to approach a topic of conversation, etc reluctantly or gradually.

lead[2] N **1** a soft, heavy, bluish-grey, highly toxic metallic element. **2** graphite. **3** a thin stick of graphite used in pencils. **4** a lump of lead used for measuring the depth of water. **5** (**leads**) a sheet of lead for covering roofs; a roof covered with lead sheets. **6** a lead frame for a small window-pane, eg in stained glass windows.
➤ VB **1** to fit, set or surround with lead. **2** to cover or weight with lead. **3** PRINTING to separate (lines of type) with lead or leads.

leaden ADJ **1** made of lead. **2** dull grey in colour. **3** heavy or slow. **4** depressing; dull.

leader N **1** someone or something that leads or guides others. **2** someone who organizes or is in charge of a group. **3 a** BRIT the principal violinist in an orchestra; **b** US an alternative name for a conductor of an orchestra, etc. **4** BRIT (also **leading article**) an article in a newspaper, etc giving the opinions of the editor. ■ **leadership** N.

lead-in N an introduction, opening, etc.

leading ADJ chief; most important.

leading light N someone who is very important and influential in a particular field.

leading question N a question asked in such a way as to suggest the answer wanted.

leaf N (*leaves*) **1** an expanded outgrowth from the stem of a green plant. **2** anything like a leaf, such as a scale or a petal. **3** a single sheet of paper forming two pages in a book. **4** a very thin sheet of metal: **gold leaf. 5** a hinged or sliding extra part or flap on a table, etc.
➢ VB of plants: to produce leaves.
◆ **leaf through sth** to turn the pages of a book, magazine, etc quickly and cursorily.
◆ **turn over a new leaf** to begin a new and better way of behaving or working.

leaflet N **1** a single sheet of paper, or several sheets of paper folded together, giving information, advertising products, etc, usu given away free. **2** a small or immature leaf.
➢ VB, TR & INTR to distribute leaflets.

leaf mould N earth formed from rotted leaves, used as a compost for plants.

leafy ADJ (*-ier, -iest*) **1** having or covered with leaves. **2** shaded by leaves. **3** like a leaf.

league[1] N **1** a union of people, nations, etc formed for the benefit of the members. **2** a group of sports clubs which compete over a period for a championship. **3** a class or group, considered in terms of ability, etc.
➢ VB, TR & INTR to form or be formed into a league.
◆ **in league with sb** acting or planning with them, usu for some underhand purpose.

league[2] N, OLD USE a unit of distance, usu taken to be about 4.8 kilometres (3 miles).

leak N **1 a** an unwanted crack or hole in a container, pipe, etc where liquid or gas can pass in or out; **b** the act or fact of liquid or gas escaping in this way; **c** liquid or gas which has escaped in this way. **2 a** a revelation of secret information, esp when unauthorized; **b** information revealed in this way; **c** someone who reveals information in this way.
➢ VB **1 a** INTR of liquid, gas, etc: to pass accidentally in or out of an unwanted crack or hole; **b** to allow (liquid, gas, etc) to pass accidentally in or out. **2 a** to reveal (secret information) without authorization; **b** INTR of secret information: to become known.
■ **leaky** ADJ.

leakage N **1** an act or instance of leaking. **2** the result of leaking.

lean[1] VB (*leant* or *leaned*) **1** TR & INTR to slope or be placed in a sloping position. **2** TR & INTR to rest or be rested against something for support. **3** INTR (usu **lean towards**) to have an inclination to or a preference for.
➢ N **1** an act or condition of leaning. **2** a slope.

lean[2] ADJ **1** of a person or animal: thin. **2** of meat: containing little or no fat. **3** producing very little food, money, etc: **lean years.**
➢ N meat with little or no fat. ■ **leanness** N.

leaning N a liking or preference; tendency.

lean-to N a shed or other light construction built against another building or a wall.

leap VB (*leapt* or *leaped*) **1** INTR to jump or spring suddenly or with force. **2** to jump over (something). **3** INTR of prices: to go up by a large amount suddenly and quickly.
➢ N an act of leaping or jumping.
◆ **by leaps and bounds** extremely rapidly.
◆ **leap at sth** COLLOQ to accept it eagerly.

leap-frog N a game in which each player in turn jumps over the back of the stooping player in front.
➢ VB (*-gg-*) TR & INTR to jump over (someone's back) in this way.

leap year N a year, occurring once in every four years, of 366 days, with an extra day on 29 February.

learn VB (*learnt* or *learned*) **1** TR & INTR to be or become informed of or to hear of (something). **2** TR & INTR to gain knowledge of or skill in (something) through study, teaching, instruction or experience. **3** to get to know by heart; to memorize. ■ **learner** N.
◆ **learn about** or **of sth** to hear about or of it.

learned ADJ **1** having great knowledge or learning, esp through years of study. **2** scholarly.

learning N knowledge gained through study.

lease N a contract by which the owner of a house, etc agrees to let someone else use it for a stated period of time in return for payment. ➤ VB **1** of an owner: to allow someone else to use (a house, land, etc) under the terms of a lease. **2** of an occupier: to borrow (a house, land, etc) from the owner under the terms of a lease.

leasehold N **1** the holding of land or buildings by lease. **2** the land or buildings held by lease.

leash N a strip of leather or chain used for leading or holding a dog or other animal. ➤ VB **1** to put a leash on (a dog, etc). **2** to control or restrain.

least ADJ smallest; slightest. ➤ ADV in the smallest or lowest degree. ➤ PRONOUN the smallest amount: **I think he has least to offer.** ◆ **at least 1** if nothing else; at any rate. **2** not less than: **at least half an hour late.** ◆ **not in the least** or **not in the least bit** not at all.

leather N **1** the skin of an animal made smooth by tanning. **2** a small piece of leather for polishing or cleaning. **3** (usu **leathers**) clothes made of leather. ➤ VB **1** to cover or polish with leather. **2** COLLOQ OR DIALECT to thrash.

leathery ADJ **1** tough. **2** like leather.

leave[1] VB (*left*) **1** INTR to go away from (someone or somewhere). **2** to allow (something) to remain behind, esp by mistake: **left the keys at home. 3** to move out of (an area). **4** to abandon. **5** to resign or quit. **6** to allow (someone or something) to be or remain in a particular state etc: **leave the window open. 7** to deliver to or deposit: **I'll leave the keys with a neighbour. 8** to cause: **It may leave a scar. 9** to have as a remainder: **Three minus one leaves two. 10** to make a gift of in a will. **11** to be survived by: **leaves a wife and daughter. 12** to cause (esp food or drink) to remain unfinished: **She left half her dinner. 13** to hand or turn (something) over to (someone else): **left the driving to her.**

◆ **leave sb** or **sth alone** to allow them or it to remain undisturbed.
◆ **leave sb** or **sth behind** to go without taking them or it.
◆ **leave sb** or **sth out** to exclude or omit it or them.

leave[2] N **1** permission to do something. **2 a** permission to be absent, esp from work or military duties; **b** permitted absence from work or military duties; **c** the length of time this lasts.
◆ **on leave** officially absent from work.
◆ **take one's leave** FORMAL, OLD USE to depart.

leaven N a substance, esp yeast, added to dough to make it rise. ➤ VB to cause (dough) to rise with leaven.

leaves plural of **leaf**

lecherous ADJ having or showing great or excessive sexual desire. ■ **lecher** N. ■ **lechery** N.

lectern N a stand with a sloping surface for holding notes, etc for someone to read from.

lecture N **1** a formal talk on a particular subject given to an audience. **2** a lesson or period of instruction, esp as delivered at a college or university. **3** a long and tedious scolding or warning. ➤ VB **1** TR & INTR to give or read a lecture or lectures (to a group of people). **2** to scold (someone) at length. **3** to instruct by lectures, esp in a college or university. ■ **lecturer** N.

LED ABBREV, ELECTRONICS light-emitting diode, a semiconductor diode used in the displays of calculators, digital watches, etc.

ledge N **1** a narrow horizontal shelf or shelf-like part. **2** a ridge or shelf of rock.

ledger N the chief book of accounts of an office or shop.

lee N **1** shelter given by a neighbouring object. **2** the sheltered side, away from the wind.

leech N **1** a blood-sucking worm formerly used medicinally. **2** a person who befriends another in the hope of personal gain.

leek N a long thin vegetable with broad flat

leaves and a white base, related to the onion.

leer N **1** a lecherous look or grin. **2** a sideways look.
➤ VB, INTR **1** to look or grin lecherously. **2** to look sideways.

lees PL N **1** sediment at the bottom of wine bottles, etc. **2** the worst part or parts.

leeward NAUT, ADJ, ADV in or towards the direction in which the wind blows.
➤ N the sheltered side.

leeway N **1** scope for freedom of movement or action. **2** NAUT a ship's drift sideways.

left ADJ **1** referring, relating to, or indicating the side facing west from the point of view of someone or something facing north.
2 relatively liberal, democratic, progressive, innovative in disposition, political outlook, etc.
3 inclined towards socialism or communism.
➤ ADV on or towards the left side.
➤ N **1** the left side, part, direction, etc. **2** the region to the left side. **3** (**the Left**) people, political parties, etc in favour of socialism. **4** the left hand: **a boxer who leads with his left.**
5 a blow with the left hand.

left-hand ADJ **1** relating to, on or towards the left. **2** done with the left hand.

left-handed ADJ **1** having the left hand stronger and more skilful than the right. **2** for use by the left hand. **3** awkward; clumsy. **4** anti-clockwise. ■ **left-hander** N.

leftism N principles and policies of the political left. ■ **leftist** N, ADJ.

left-luggage N **1** (in full **left-luggage office**) in an airport or railway station: an area with lockers where luggage can be stored for collection at a later time. **2** luggage so stored.

left wing N **1** the members of a political party or group who are most inclined towards a socialist viewpoint. **2** SPORT **a** the extreme left side of a pitch or team in a field game; **b** (also **left-winger**) a player playing on this side.
■ **left-wing** ADJ.

lefty N (**-ies**) COLLOQ, often DEROG **1** a person with socialist leanings. **2** a left-handed person.

leg N **1** one of the limbs on which animals, birds and people walk and stand. **2** an animal's or bird's leg used as food. **3** the part of a piece of clothing that covers one of these limbs. **4** a long narrow support of a table, chair, etc. **5** one stage in a journey. **6** a section of a competition or lap of a race.
◆ **not have a leg to stand on** COLLOQ to have no way of excusing behaviour or supporting an argument, etc.

legacy N (**-ies**) **1** an amount of property or money left in a will. **2** something handed on or left unfinished by a past owner or predecessor.

legal ADJ **1** allowed by the law. **2** of the law or lawyers. **3** created by law. ■ **legally** ADV.

legal aid N financial assistance for those who cannot afford to pay for legal costs.

legalese N technical legal jargon.

legalism N the tendency to observe the letter or form of the law rather than the spirit.
■ **legalist** N, ADJ. ■ **legalistic** ADJ.

legality N (PL in sense 2 only **-ies**) **1** the state of being legal; lawfulness. **2** a legal obligation.

legalize or **-ise** VB to make (something) legal or lawful. ■ **legalization** N.

legal tender N currency which, by law, must be accepted in payment of a debt.

legate N an ambassador, esp from the Pope.

legatee N the recipient of a legacy.

legation N **1** a diplomatic mission or group of delegates. **2** the official residence of such a mission or group.

legato MUS, ADV smoothly, with the notes running into each other.
➤ ADJ smooth and flowing.
➤ N **1** a piece of music to be played in this way.
2 a legato style of playing.

legend N **1** a traditional story, popularly regarded as true, but not confirmed as such.
2 such stories collectively. **3** someone famous about whom popularly-believed stories are told. **4** words accompanying a map or picture, etc which explain the symbols used. **5** an

inscription on a coin, medal or coat of arms.

legendary ADJ **1** relating to or in the nature of legend. **2** described or spoken about in legend. **3** COLLOQ very famous.

leggings PL N close-fitting coverings for the legs, worn by girls and women.

leggy ADJ (*-ier, -iest*) **1** having long slim legs. **2** of a plant: having a long stem.

legible ADJ clear enough to be read. ■ **legibly** ADV.

legion N **1** HIST a unit in the ancient Roman army, containing between three and six thousand soldiers. **2** a very great number. **3** a military force: **the French Foreign Legion**.
➤ ADJ great in number: **Books on this subject are legion**. ■ **legionary** N, ADJ.

legionnaire N a member of a legion.

Legionnaire's Disease N, PATHOL a disease caused by a bacterial infection of the lungs.

legislate VB, INTR to make laws. ■ **legislator** N.

legislation N **1** the process of legislating. **2** a group of laws.

legislative ADJ **1** relating to or concerned with law-making. **2** having the power to make laws: **a legislative assembly**.

legislature N the part of the government which has the power to make laws.

legitimate ADJ **1** lawful. **2** born to parents who are married to each other. **3** of an argument, conclusion, etc: reasonable or logical.
➤ VB **1** to make lawful or legitimate. **2** to justify. ■ **legitimacy** N. ■ **legitimately** ADV.

legitimize or **-ise** VB **1** to make legitimate. **2** to make (an argument, etc) valid.

legless ADJ **1** COLLOQ drunk. **2** having no legs.

legroom N the amount of space available for someone's legs, eg in a car, etc.

legume N **1** a flowering plant with fruit in the form of a pod, eg pea, bean, lentil. **2** the fruit of such a plant. **3** an edible seed of this plant. ■ **leguminous** ADJ.

lei N a garland of flowers worn round the neck.

leisure N free time, esp when a person can relax, pursue a hobby, etc.

leisurely ADJ not hurried; relaxed.
➤ ADV without hurrying. ■ **leisureliness** N.

leitmotif or **leitmotiv** N a recurring theme, image, etc in a piece of music, novel, etc.

lemming N a small rodent which occasionally participates in migrations once believed to result in mass drownings at sea.

lemon N **1** a small oval citrus fruit with tough yellow rind and sour-tasting juicy flesh. **2** the small evergreen tree that produces this fruit. **3** a pale yellow colour.
➤ ADJ pale yellow in colour. ■ **lemony** ADJ.

lemonade N a fizzy or still drink flavoured with or made from lemons.

lemon sole N a European flatfish.

lemur N a nocturnal tree-dwelling primate, now confined to Madagascar, with large eyes and a long bushy tail.

lend VB (*lent*) **1** to allow (someone) to use (something) on the understanding that it (or its equivalent) will be returned. **2** to give (someone) the use of (usu money), esp in return for interest paid on it. **3** to give or add (interest, beauty, etc) to. ■ **lender** N.
◆ **lend itself to sth** to be suitable for a purpose, etc.

length N **1** the distance from one end of an object to the other. **2** often IN COMPOUNDS the distance something extends. **3** the quality of being long. **4** a long piece of something or a stated amount of something long: **a length of rope**. **5** the extent from end to end of a horse, boat, etc, as a way of measuring one participant's lead over another in a race: **won by two lengths**. **6** (often **in length**) a stretch or extent. **7** SWIMMING **a** the longer measurement of a swimming pool; **b** this distance swum. **8 a** an extent of time; **b** PHONETICS, MUSIC the amount of time a vowel, note, etc sounds.
◆ **at length 1** at last. **2** in great detail.

lengthen VB, TR & INTR to make or become longer.

lengthways and **lengthwise** ADV, ADJ in the direction of something's length.

lengthy ADJ (*-ier, -iest*) **1** of great, often excessive, length. **2** of speech, etc: long and tedious. ■ **lengthily** ADV. ■ **lengthiness** N.

lenient ADJ mild and tolerant, not severe. ■ **lenience** or **leniency** N. ■ **leniently** ADV.

lens N **1 a** an optical device consisting of a piece of glass, clear plastic, etc curved on one or both sides, used for converging or diverging a beam of light; **b** a contact lens. **2** in a camera: a mechanical equivalent of the lens of an eye.

Lent N, CHRISTIANITY the time, lasting from Ash Wednesday to Easter Sunday, of fasting or going without something. ■ **Lenten** ADJ.

lentil N **1** a small orange, brown or green seed used as food. **2** a leguminous plant which produces these seeds.

lento MUS, ADV slowly.
➤ ADJ slow.

Leo N, ASTROL the fifth sign of the zodiac (the Lion).

leonine ADJ relating to or like a lion.

leopard N a large member of the cat family with a black-spotted tawny coat or a completely black coat. **Also called panther**.

leotard N a stretchy one-piece tight-fitting garment worn for dancing, exercise, etc.

leper N **1** MED someone who has leprosy. **2** DEROG someone who is avoided.

lepidopterous ADJ relating or belonging to the order of insects that includes butterflies and moths. ■ **lepidopteran** ADJ, N.

lepidopterist N a person who studies butterflies and moths.

leprechaun N, IRISH FOLKLORE a small mischievous elf.

leprosy N an infectious disease of the skin, mucous membranes and nerves. ■ **leprous** ADJ.

lesbian N a woman who is sexually attracted to other women.
➤ ADJ for or of lesbians. ■ **lesbianism** N.

lesion N **1** an injury or wound. **2** PATHOL an abnormal change in the structure of an organ or tissue as a result of disease or injury.

less ADJ **1** smaller in size, quantity, duration, etc. **2** COLLOQ fewer in number: **smoke less cigars**.
➤ ADV not so much; to a smaller extent: **exercises less nowadays**.
➤ PRONOUN a smaller amount or number: **tried to eat less**.
➤ PREP without; minus: **£100 less the discount**.

lessee N someone granted the use of property by lease.

lessen VB, TR & INTR to make or become less.

lesser ADJ smaller in size, quantity or importance: **lesser celandine**.

lesson N **1** an amount taught or learned at one time. **2** a period of teaching. **3** (**lessons**) instruction given over a period of time. **4** an experience or example which one should take as a warning or encouragement.

lessor N someone who rents out property by lease.

lest CONJ, FORMAL OR LITERARY in case: **speak quietly lest they hear us**.

let[1] VB (*let, letting*) **1 a** to allow, permit, or cause: **let her daughter borrow the car**; **b** used in commands, orders, warnings, etc: **let him go**. **2** BRIT to give the use of (rooms, a building, or land) in return for payment.
➤ N, BRIT **1** the leasing of a property, etc: **got the let of the cottage for £100 a week**. **2** the period of time for which a property, etc is leased: **a two-week let**.
◆ **let down 1** to disappoint or fail to help (someone). **2** to lower. **3** to allow the air to escape from (something inflated).
◆ **let sb off 1** to allow them to go without punishment, etc. **2** to release them from work, duties, etc.
◆ **let sth off** to fire a gun or explode a bomb, etc.
◆ **let sth out 1** to enlarge it: **let out the waist of**

the jeans. **2** to emit a sound.
◆ **let up** to stop or to become less strong or violent: **The rain let up at last.**

let² N, SPORT esp in racket games: an obstruction during service that requires the ball, etc to be served again.

let-down N a disappointment.

lethal ADJ causing or enough to cause death.
■ **lethally** ADV.

lethargy N **1** lack of energy and vitality. **2** PATHOL a state of abnormal drowsiness.
■ **lethargic** ADJ. ■ **lethargically** ADV.

let-out N a chance to escape, avoid keeping an agreement, contract, etc.

let's CONTRACTION let us: **let's go.**

letter N **1** a conventional written or printed mark, usu part of an alphabet, used to represent a speech sound or sounds. **2** a written or printed message usu sent by post. **3** (**the letter**) the strict literal meaning of words, or how such words can be interpreted: **according to the letter of the law. 4** printing type.
➤ VB to write or mark letters on. ■ **lettering** N.
◆ **to the letter** exactly.

letter box N, BRIT **1** a slot in a door through which letters are delivered. **2** a large box, with a slot in the front, for people to post letters. Also called **pillar box, post box**.

lettered ADJ well educated; literary.

letterhead N a printed heading on notepaper giving a company's or an individual's name, address, etc.

lettuce N a green plant with large edible leaves used in salads.

let-up N end; respite; relief.

leucocyte or **leukocyte** N, ANAT a white blood cell or corpuscle.

leukaemia or (esp US) **leukemia** N a malignant disease which affects the bone marrow etc.

levee N, US **1** a natural or artificial embankment along a watercourse. **2** a quay.

level N **1** a horizontal plane or line. **2** a specified height, value or extent. **3** position, status, or importance in a scale of values. **4** a stage or degree of progress. **5** any device for checking whether a surface is horizontal or not: **spirit level. 6** (**the level**) a flat area of land. **7** a storey of a building.
➤ ADJ **1** having a flat smooth even surface. **2** horizontal. **3** having or being at the same height (as something else). **4** having the same standard (as something else); equal. **5** steady; constant; regular. **6** COOKERY of measurements: filled so as to be even with the rim: **3 level tablespoons.**
➤ VB (**-ll-**) **1** to make flat, smooth or horizontal. **2** to make equal. **3** to pull down or demolish.
◆ **level sth at sb** to point a gun, etc at them.
◆ **level sth at** or **against sb** to direct an accusation, criticism, etc at them.

level crossing N, BRIT, AUSTRAL & NZ a place where a road and a railway line, or two railway lines, cross at the same level.

level-headed ADJ sensible; well-balanced.

leveller N someone or something that flattens or makes equal: **Death is the great leveller.**

lever N **1** a simple device for lifting and moving heavy loads, consisting of a rigid bar supported by and pivoting about a fulcrum at some point along its length, so that an effort applied at one point can be used to move an object (the load) at another point. **2** a strong bar for moving heavy objects, prising things open, etc. **3** a handle for operating a machine. **4** anything that can be used to gain an advantage.
➤ VB to move or open using a lever.

leverage N **1** the mechanical power or advantage gained through using a lever. **2** the action of a lever. **3** power or advantage.

leveret N a young hare.

leviathan N **1** BIBLE a sea-monster. **2** anything which is large or powerful.

levitate VB, TR & INTR to float or cause to float in the air, esp by invoking some supernatural power or through spiritualism. ■ **levitation** N.

levity N a lack of seriousness; silliness.

levy VB (*-ies, -ied*) **1** to calculate and then collect (a tax, etc). **2** to raise (an army or the money needed to fund a war).
➢ N (*-ies*) **1** the collection of a tax, etc. **2** the amount of money raised by collecting a tax, etc. **3** soldiers or money collected in preparation for a war.

lewd ADJ **1** feeling, expressing or designed to stimulate crude sexual desire or lust. **2** obscene; indecent. ■ **lewdly** ADV. ■ **lewdness** N.

lexical ADJ **1** of the words in a language. **2** of a lexicon. ■ **lexically** ADV.

lexicography N the writing, compiling and editing of dictionaries. ■ **lexicographer** N.

lexicon N **1** a dictionary, esp one for Arabic, Greek, Hebrew or Syriac. **2** the vocabulary of terms as used in a particular branch of knowledge or by a particular group, etc.

liability N (*-ies*) **1** the state of being legally liable or responsible for something. **2** a debt or obligation. **3** someone or something one is responsible for. **4** someone or something that is a problem or that causes a problem.

liable ADJ **1** legally bound or responsible. **2** given or inclined: She is liable to outbursts of temper. **3** likely. **4** susceptible.

liaise VB, TR & INTR (usu **liaise with** or **between**) to communicate with or be in contact with (someone).

liaison N **1** communication or co-operation between individuals or groups. **2** an adulterous or illicit sexual or romantic relationship.

liar N someone who tells lies.

libation N **1** the pouring out of wine, etc in honour of a god. **2** a drink so poured.

libel N **1** BRIT, LAW **a** the publication of a statement which has the potential to damage someone's reputation and which is claimed to be false; **b** the act of publishing this kind of statement. **2** any false or potentially damaging description.
➢ VB (*-ll-* or US *-l-*) **1** LAW to publish a libellous statement about (someone). **2** to accuse wrongly and spitefully. ■ **libellous** or (US) **libelous** ADJ.

liberal ADJ **1** given or giving generously, freely or abundantly. **2** tolerant of different opinions; open-minded. **3** lavish; extensive. **4** in favour of social and political reform, progressive. **5** of education: aiming to develop general cultural interests and to broaden the mind: a **liberal arts student**. **6** free from restraint; not rigorous.
➢ N someone who has liberal views, either politically or in general. ■ **liberalism** N. ■ **liberally** ADV.

liberality N **1** the quality of being generous. **2** the quality of being open-minded.

liberalize or **-ise** VB, TR & INTR to make or become more liberal or less strict. ■ **liberalization** N.

liberate VB, TR & INTR **1** to set free. **2** to free (a country from enemy occupation). **3** to free from accepted moral or social conventions. ■ **liberation** N. ■ **liberator** N.

liberated ADJ **1** not bound by traditional ideas. **2** freed from enemy occupation.

libertine N, OLD USE someone who leads a licentious life.

liberty N (*-ies*) **1** freedom from captivity, slavery, restrictions, etc. **2** freedom to act and think as one pleases. **3** (usu **liberties**) a natural right or privilege. **4** an action or utterance thought of as over-familiar or presumptuous.
◆ **take liberties** to treat someone with too much familiarity; to be too presumptuous.

libidinous ADJ lustful; lewd.

libido N sexual urge or desire. ■ **libidinal** ADJ.

Libra N, ASTROL the seventh sign of the zodiac (the Balance).

librarian N someone who works in or is in charge of a library. ■ **librarianship** N.

library N (*-ies*) **1** a room, rooms or building where books, films, records, etc are kept for study, reference or for lending. **2** a collection of books, films, etc for public or private use. **3** a group of books published as a series.

libretto N (-*ti* or -*tos*) the words or text of an opera, oratorio, or musical. ■ **librettist** N.

lice plural of **louse**

licence or (US) **license** N 1 an official document that allows someone to own something, eg, a dog, gun, etc, or that gives permission to do something, eg, use a television set. 2 permission or leave in general. 3 freedom of action or speech. 4 a departure from a rule or convention, esp by writers and artists, for effect: **poetic licence**.

license VB 1 to give a licence or permit for (something). 2 to give a licence or permit (to someone) to do something such as drive, etc.

licensee N someone who has been given a licence, esp to sell alcohol.

licentiate N someone who holds a certificate of competence to practise a profession.

licentious ADJ immoral or promiscuous. ■ **licentiousness** N.

lichee see **lychee**

lichen N a primitive plant form, usu found on rocks, walls or tree trunks.

lichgate or **lychgate** N a roofed gateway to a churchyard.

licit ADJ lawful; permitted.

lick VB 1 to pass the tongue over in order to moisten, taste or clean. 2 of flames, etc: to flicker over or around. 3 COLLOQ to defeat. 4 COLLOQ to beat or hit repeatedly. ➢ N 1 an act of licking with the tongue. 2 COLLOQ a small amount. 3 COLLOQ a quick speed: **drove away at some lick**. 4 COLLOQ a sharp blow.

licorice see **liquorice**

lid N 1 a removable or hinged cover for a pot, box, etc. 2 an eyelid. ■ **lidded** ADJ. ◆ **put the lid on it** to put an end to something.

lido N a public open-air swimming pool.

lie[1] N 1 a false statement made with the intention of deceiving. 2 anything misleading; a fraud. ➢ VB (*lied, lying*) INTR 1 to say things that are not true with the intention of deceiving. 2 to give a wrong or false impression. ◆ **give the lie to** to show to be false.

lie[2] VB (PA T *lay*, PA P *lain*, PR P *lying*) INTR 1 to be in or take on a flat or more or less horizontal position on a supporting surface. 2 to be situated: **The village lies to the west of here**. 3 to stretch or be spread out to view: **The harbour lay before us**. 4 of subjects for discussion: to remain undiscussed: **let matters lie**. 5 **a** to be or remain in a particular state: **lie dormant**; **b** to be buried: **Morrison's remains lie in a cemetery in Paris**. ➢ N 1 the way or direction in which something is lying. 2 an animal's or bird's hiding-place. ◆ **lie down** to take a flat or horizontal position, esp to sleep or have a short rest. ◆ **lie in** to stay in bed later than usual. ◆ **lie in wait** (**for sb** or **sth**) to hide before ambushing (them or it). ◆ **lie low** to stay quiet or hidden. ◆ **take sth lying down** OFTEN WITH NEGATIVES to accept a rebuke or disappointment, etc meekly and without protest.

liege ADJ 1 of a feudal lord: entitled to receive service, etc from a vassal. 2 of a vassal: bound to give service, etc to a feudal lord. ➢ N 1 (also **liege lord**) a feudal superior, lord or sovereign. 2 a feudal subject or vassal.

lie-in N a longer than usual stay in bed.

lien N, LAW a right to keep someone's property until a debt has been paid.

lie of the land N the current state of affairs.

lieu N 1 (**in lieu**) instead. 2 (**in lieu of**) in place of.

lieutenant N 1 a deputy acting for a superior. 2 an officer in the British army and navy. 3 US a police officer with the rank immediately below captain.

life N (*lives*) 1 the quality or state which distinguishes living animals and plants, characterized by the ability to grow, develop and reproduce. 2 **a** the period between birth and death; **b** the period between birth and the present time: **has led a very sheltered life**; **c** the

period between the present time and death.
3 the length of time a thing exists or is able to function: **a long shelf life**. **4** living things in general or as a group: **marine life**. **5** a living thing, esp a human: **many lives lost in war**. **6** a way or manner of living: **leads a very busy life**. **7** IN COMPOUNDS a specified aspect of someone's life: **her love-life**. **8** liveliness; energy; high spirits: **full of life**. **9** a source of liveliness, energy or high spirits: **the life and soul of the party**. **10** a written account of someone's life. **11** COLLOQ a life sentence. **12** any of a number of chances a player has of remaining in a game: **got to level six without losing a life**. ◆ **not on your life!** COLLOQ certainly not!

life-and-death ADJ extremely serious.

lifebelt N a ring or belt used to support someone who is in danger of drowning.

lifeblood N **1** the blood necessary for life. **2** anything that is an essential part or factor.

lifeboat N **1** a boat for rescuing people who are in trouble at sea. **2** a small boat carried on a larger ship for use in emergencies.

lifebuoy N a float for supporting someone in the water until they are rescued.

life-cycle N the sequence of stages through which a living organism passes.

lifeguard N an expert swimmer employed at a swimming-pool or beach to rescue people in danger of drowning.

life jacket N an inflatable sleeveless jacket for supporting someone in the water.

lifeless ADJ **1** dead. **2** unconscious. **3** having no energy or vivacity; dull. ■ **lifelessly** ADV.

lifelike ADJ of a portrait, etc: very like the person or thing represented.

lifeline N **1** a rope for support in dangerous operations or for saving lives. **2** a vital means of communication or support.

lifelong ADJ lasting the length of a life.

lifer N, SLANG someone sent to prison for life.

life raft N a raft kept on a ship, for use in emergencies.

life sciences PL N botany, zoology, etc regarded as a collective branch of study.

life sentence N, BRIT a prison sentence for life.

life-size and **life-sized** ADJ having the same size as the original.

lifestyle N the particular way a group or individual lives.

life-support ADJ of machines, etc: allowing someone to remain alive, eg when seriously ill.

lifetime N the duration of someone's life.

lift VB **1** TR & INTR to raise or rise to a higher position. **2** to move (esp one's eyes or face) upwards. **3** to take and carry away; to remove. **4** to raise to a better or more agreeable level: **lift one's spirits**. **5** INTR **a** of cloud, fog, etc: to clear; **b** of winds: to become less strong. **6** to remove or annul. **7** to dig up (potatoes, etc). **8** COLLOQ to plagiarize from someone else's work. **9** SLANG to arrest. **10** COLLOQ to steal. ➢ N **1** an act of lifting. **2** lifting power. **3** the upward force of the air on an aircraft, etc. **4** BRIT a device for moving people and goods between floors of a building. **5** BRIT a ride in a person's car or other vehicle. **6** a boost to the spirits or sudden feeling of happiness.

lift-off N the vertical launching of a spacecraft or rocket.

ligament N, ANAT a band of tough connective tissue that holds two bones together at a joint.

ligature N **1** anything that binds or ties. **2** MUS a slur. **3** PRINTING a character formed from two or more characters joined together, eg æ.

light[1] N **1** a form of electromagnetic radiation that travels freely through space, and can be absorbed and reflected, esp that part of the spectrum which can be seen with the human eye. **2** any source of this, such as the Sun, a lamp, a candle, etc. **3** an appearance of brightness; a shine or gleam: **see a light in the distance**. **4** (**the lights**) traffic lights: **turn left at the lights**. **5** the time during the day when it is daylight. **6** dawn. **7** a particular quality or amount of light: **a good light for taking photographs**. **8** a flame or spark for igniting. **9** a means of producing a flame for igniting,

such as a match. **10** a way in which something is thought of or regarded: **see the problem in a new light**. **11** a glow in the eyes or on the face as a sign of energy, liveliness, happiness or excitement. **12** someone who is well regarded in a particular field: **a leading light**. **13** an opening in a wall that lets in light.
➤ ADJ **1** having light; not dark. **2** of a colour: pale; closer to white than black.
➤ VB (PA T & PA P **lit** or **lighted,** PR P **lighting**) **1** to provide light for: **lit the stage**. **2** TR & INTR to begin to burn or make (something) begin to burn: **light the fire**. **3** to guide or show someone (the way) using a light or torch. **4** TR & INTR to make or become bright, sparkling with liveliness, happiness or excitement.
◆ **come to light** to be made known or discovered.
◆ **in a good** or **bad light** putting a favourable or unfavourable construction on something.
◆ **in light of sth** taking it into consideration.

light² ADJ **1** weighing little; easy to lift or carry. **2** low in weight, amount or density: **light rain**. **3** not pressing heavily; gentle: **a light touch**. **4** easy to bear, suffer or do: **light work**. **5** weighing less than is correct or proper. **6** equipped with only hand-held weapons: **light infantry**. **7** without problems, sorrow, etc; cheerful: **a light heart**. **8** graceful and quick; nimble: **a light skip**. **9** not serious or profound, but for amusement only: **light reading**. **10** thoughtless or trivial: **a light remark**. **11** not thinking clearly or seriously; giddy: **a light head**. **12** easily digested: **a light meal**.
➤ ADV **1** in a light manner. **2** with little luggage: **travel light**. ■ **lightly** ADV. ■ **lightness** N.

light³ VB (PA T & PA P **lit** or **lighted,** PR P **lighting**) of birds, etc: to come to rest after flight.
◆ **light on** or **upon sth** to come upon or find it by chance: **suddenly lit upon the idea**.

light bulb N an airtight glass bulb with an electric filament which emits light.

lighten¹ VB **1** TR & INTR to make or become brighter. **2** to cast light on. **3** INTR to shine.

lighten² VB **1** TR & INTR to make or become less heavy. **2** TR & INTR to make or become happier or

more cheerful. **3** to make less: **lighten her sadness**. ■ **lightening** N.

lighter¹ N a device for lighting cigarettes, etc.

lighter² N a large open boat used for transferring goods between ships, or between a ship and a wharf.

light-fingered ADJ having a habitual tendency to steal.

light-headed ADJ having a dizzy feeling in the head.

light-hearted ADJ **1** of entertainment, etc: not serious; cheerful and amusing. **2** happy and carefree.

lighthouse N a building on the coast with a flashing light to guide or warn ships.

lighting N **1** equipment for providing light. **2** light, usu of a specified kind: **soft lighting**.

lightning N, METEOROL a bright flash of light produced by the discharge of static electricity between clouds, or between a cloud and the Earth's surface.
➤ ADJ very quick and sudden: **a lightning dash to catch the bus**.

lightning-conductor and **lightning-rod** N a metal rod designed to divert lightning directly to earth.

light pen N, COMP a light-sensitive pen-like device that can be used to generate or modify images and move them about on a computer screen by touching the screen with the device.

lights PL N the lungs of an animal, used as food.

lightship N a ship with a beacon, that acts as a lighthouse.

lightweight ADJ **1** light in weight. **2** DEROG having little importance or authority.
➤ N **1** a person or thing of little physical weight. **2** DEROG a person or thing having little importance or authority. **3** a class for boxers, wrestlers and weightlifters, between welterweight and featherweight.

light-year N the distance travelled by a beam of light in one year, equal to about 9.46 trillion kilometres or 5.88 trillion miles.

ligneous ADJ **1** of a plant: with woody parts. **2** resembling or composed of wood.

lignite N, GEOL a soft low-grade form of coal.

like¹ ADJ **1** similar; resembling: **as like as two peas**. **2** typical of: **It's just like them to forget**. **3** used in asking someone for a description of someone or something: **What's he like?**
➢ PREP **1** in the same manner as; to the same extent as: **run like a deer**. **2** such as: **animals like cats and dogs**.
➢ ADV **1** COLLOQ approximately. **2** COLLOQ as it were: **It was magic, like**.
➢ CONJ, COLLOQ **1** as if; as though: **It's like I've been here before**. **2** in the same way as: **not pretty like you are**.
◆ **the like 1** things of the same kind: **TVs, radios and the like are on the third floor**. **2** WITH NEGATIVES AND IN QUESTIONS anything similar: **never see the like again**.

like² VB **1** to enjoy or be pleased with (something). **2** to be fond of (someone or something). **3** to prefer: **She likes her tea without sugar**. **4** to wish, or wish for: **if you like**.
➢ N (**likes**) things that someone has a preference for: **likes and dislikes**. ■ **likeable** or **likable** ADJ.

likelihood and **likeliness** N probability.

likely ADJ **1** probable. **2** useful for a particular purpose. **3** IRONIC credible: **a likely tale**.
➢ ADV probably.
◆ **not likely** COLLOQ absolutely not: **Invite him? Not likely!**

like-minded ADJ sharing a similar outlook, opinion, taste, purpose, etc.

liken VB to compare or point to the similarities between (two things or people).

likeness N **1** a similarity: **a family likeness**. **2** FORMERLY a portrait or formal photograph.

likewise ADV **1** in the same or a similar manner. **2** also; in addition.

liking N **1** a fondness: **a liking for chocolates**. **2** taste; preference: **Is it to your liking?**

lilac N **1** a small tree or shrub with white or pale pinkish-purple sweet-smelling flowers.

2 a pale pinkish-purple colour.

Lilliputian N someone or something very small.
➢ ADJ (also **lilliputian**) very small.

Lilo or **Li-lo** N (**-os**) TRADEMARK a type of inflatable mattress.

lilt N **1** a light graceful swinging rhythm. **2** a tune, song or voice with such a rhythm.
➢ VB, INTR to speak, sing or move with a lilt.
■ **lilting** ADJ.

lily N (**-ies**) **1** STRICTLY a plant with an underground bulb, narrow leaves, and white or brightly coloured flowers. **2** LOOSELY any of various other plants, eg water lily.

lily-livered ADJ cowardly.

lily-of-the-valley N (**lilies-of-the-valley**) a spring plant with small white bell-shaped flowers that have a sweet smell.

limb N **1** an arm, leg or wing. **2** a projecting part. **3** a main branch on a tree. ■ **limbless** ADJ.
◆ **out on a limb** exposed or isolated.

limber ADJ flexible and supple.
◆ **limber up** to warm up before taking exercise.

limbo¹ N **1** CHRISTIANITY an area between heaven and hell reserved for the unbaptized dead. **2** a place of oblivion or neglect.
◆ **in limbo** in a state of uncertainty or waiting.

limbo² N a West Indian dance in which the object is to lean backwards and shuffle under a rope or bar which is gradually lowered.

lime¹ N **1** LOOSELY calcium oxide, a white chemical compound used in producing other calcium compounds, eg slaked lime, and in agriculture to reduce acidity in soil. **2** LOOSELY slaked lime. **3** LOOSELY limestone. **4** bird-lime.

lime² N **1** a small citrus fruit with a sour taste. **2** a small evergreen tree that bears this fruit. **3** the colour of this fruit.

lime³ N (also **lime-tree**) a deciduous tree with fragrant flowers. Also called **linden**.

limelight N **1** formerly used in theatres: a bright white light produced by heating a block of lime in a flame. **2** the glare of publicity.

limerick N a humorous poem with five lines rhyming **aabba**.

limestone N, GEOL a sedimentary rock composed mainly of calcium carbonate.

limey N N AMER, AUSTRAL & NZ SLANG **1** a British person. **2** FORMERLY a British sailor or ship.

limit N **1** a point, degree, amount or boundary, esp one which cannot or should not be passed. **2** a restriction or boundary. **3** (**the limit**) COLLOQ someone or something that is intolerable or extremely annoying. ➤ VB **1** to be a limit or boundary to. **2** to restrict. ■ **limitable** ADJ.

limitation N **1** an act of limiting or the condition of being limited. **2** (often **limitations**) someone's weakness, lack of ability, etc.

limited ADJ **1** having a limit or limits. **2** narrow; restricted: **a limited understanding**.

limited company N a company owned by its shareholders, who have liability for debts, etc only to the extent of their stake in the company.

limo N, COLLOQ short form of **limousine**.

limousine N a large, luxurious motor car.

limp[1] VB, INTR **1** to walk with an awkward or uneven step. **2** to move with difficulty. ➤ N the walk of someone who limps.

limp[2] ADJ **1** not stiff or firm; hanging loosely. **2** without energy or vitality; drooping. **3** of a book: with a soft cover. ■ **limply** ADV.

limpet N a marine gastropod mollusc with a conical shell that clings to rock surfaces, etc by a muscular foot.

limpid ADJ of water, eyes, etc: clear; transparent. ■ **limpidity** N.

linage N the number of lines in a piece of printed matter.

linchpin N **1** a pin-shaped rod passed through an axle to keep a wheel in place. **2** someone or something essential to a business, plan, etc.

linctus N, BRIT a syrupy medicine taken by mouth to relieve coughs, etc.

linden see under **lime**[3]

line[1] N **1** a long narrow mark, streak or stripe. **2** often IN COMPOUNDS a length of thread, rope, wire, etc used for specified purposes: **a washing line**. **3** a wrinkle or furrow, esp on the skin. **4** MATH something that has length but no breadth or thickness. **5** the path which a moving object is considered to leave behind it, having length but no breadth. **6** a row. **7** a row of words or printed or written characters. **8** (**lines**) the words of an actor's part. **9** (often **lines**) an outline or shape: **a car of stylish lines**. **10** (**lines**) a punishment at school where a phrase or sentence has to be written out a set number of times. **11** COLLOQ a short letter or note: **drop him a line**. **12** a series or group of people coming one after the other: **from a long line of doctors**. **13** a field of activity, interest, study or work: **his line of business**. **14** a course or way of acting, behaving, thinking or reasoning: **think along different lines**. **15** the rules or limits of acceptable behaviour: **cross the line**. **16** a group or class of goods for sale: **a new line in tonic water**. **17** a production line. **18** one of several white marks outlining a pitch, race-track, etc on a field: **goal line**. **19 a** a single track for trains or trams; **b** a branch or route of a railway system. **20** a route, track or direction of movement: **line of fire**. **21 a** a continuous system, eg of telephone cables, connecting one place with another; **b** a telephone connection; **c** IN COMPOUNDS a telephone number for some kind of special service: **called the ticket line**. **22** a company running regular services of ships, buses or aircraft between two or more places. **23** an arrangement of troops or ships side by side and ready to fight. **24** (always **lines**) a connected series of military defences: **behind enemy lines**. **25** N AMER a queue. **26** SLANG a remark, usu insincere, that someone uses to get some kind of benefit: **He spun her a line**. ➤ VB **1** to mark or cover (something) with lines. **2** to form a line along (something): **Crowds lined the streets**.

◆ **get a line on sb** or **sth** COLLOQ to get information about them or it.

◆ **in line for sth** likely to get it: in line for promotion.
◆ **lay it on the line** to speak frankly.
◆ **lay** or **put sth on the line** to risk one's reputation or career over it.
◆ **line sth up** to organize it: lined up a new job.

line² VB **1** to cover the inside of (clothes, boxes, curtains, etc) with some other material. **2** to cover as if with a lining: **line the walls with books**. **3** COLLOQ to fill, esp with large amounts.
◆ **line one's pocket** or **pockets** to make a profit, esp by dishonest means.

lineage N ancestry.

lineal ADJ of family descent: in a direct line.

lineament N (usu **lineaments**) a distinguishing feature, esp on the face.

linear ADJ **1** referring to, consisting of or like a line or lines. **2** long and very narrow with parallel sides. ■ **linearity** N.

line drawing N a drawing in pen or pencil using lines only.

linen N **1** cloth made from flax. **2** articles such as sheets, tablecloths, underclothes, etc. ➤ ADJ made of or like linen.

liner¹ N a large passenger ship or aircraft.

liner² N, often IN COMPOUNDS something used for lining: **bin-liner**.

liner³ N, often IN COMPOUNDS colouring used to outline the eyes or the lips.

linesman N an official in some sports who indicates when the ball has gone out of play.

line-up N **1** an arrangement of things or people in line. **2** a list of people selected for a sports team. **3** the artistes appearing in a show.

ling¹ N (*ling* or *lings*) a long slender edible marine fish, related to the cod.

ling² N same as **heather**.

linger VB, INTR **1** to remain for a long time. **2** to be slow or reluctant to leave. **3** to die very slowly.

lingerie N women's underwear and nightclothes.

lingo N, COLLOQ **1** a foreign language. **2** the specialized vocabulary of a particular group.

lingua franca N (*lingua francas*) a language used as a means of communication amongst the speakers of different languages.

lingual ADJ **1** of the tongue. **2** relating to speech or language. ■ **lingually** ADV.

linguist N someone skilled in languages.

linguistic ADJ **1** relating to language. **2** relating to linguistics. ■ **linguistically** ADV.

linguistics SING N the study of language.

liniment N a thin oily cream applied to the skin to ease muscle pain, etc.

lining N **1** material used for lining something. **2** an inner covering, eg, of a bodily organ, etc.

link N **1** a ring of a chain or in chain-mail. **2** someone or something that connects. **3** a means of communication or travel. ➤ VB **1** to connect or join. **2** INTR to be or become connected.

links PL N **1** a stretch of more or less flat ground near the sea. **2** a golf course by the sea.

link-up N esp of spacecraft, military manoeuvres, and telecommunications: a connection, esp of two different systems.

linnet N a small brown songbird.

lino N, COLLOQ linoleum.

linocut N **1** a design cut in relief in linoleum. **2** a print made from this.

linoleum N, DATED a smooth hard-wearing covering for floors, made by impregnating a fabric with a mixture of substances such as linseed oil and cork.

linseed N a seed of the flax plant.

linseed oil N oil extracted from linseed and used in paints, varnishes, enamels, etc.

lint N **1** linen or cotton with a raised nap on one side, for dressing wounds. **2** fine, very small pieces of wool, cotton, etc; fluff.

lintel N a horizontal wooden or stone supporting beam over a doorway or window.

lion N **1** a large member of the cat family, found mainly in Africa, with a tawny coat, a tufted tail, and, in the male, a thick mane. **2** the male of this species, as opposed to the female. **3** someone who is brave.

lioness N a female lion.

lionize or **-ise** VB to treat (someone) as a celebrity or hero.

lip N **1** either of the two fleshy parts which form the edge of the mouth. **2** the edge or rim of something: **the lip of the jug. 3** COLLOQ cheek.

lipid N, BIOCHEM any of a group of organic compounds, mainly oils and fats, that occur naturally in living organisms.

liposuction N a surgical process where excess fat is removed from the body by sucking it out through an incision in the skin.

lip-read VB of a deaf person: to make sense of (what someone is saying) by watching the movement of their lips.

lip-service N insincere or feigned approval, acceptance, etc.

lipstick N cosmetic colouring for the lips.

liquefy VB (*-fies, -fied*) TR & INTR to make or become liquid. ■ **liquefaction** N.

liqueur N a sweet alcoholic drink.

liquid N **a** a state of matter between solid and gas, where the volume remains constant, but the shape depends on that of its container; **b** any substance in a water–like state.
➤ ADJ **1** of a substance: able to flow and change shape. **2** like water in appearance. **3** flowing and smooth. **4** of assets: able to be easily changed into cash. ■ **liquidity** N.

liquidate VB **1** to bring to an end the trading of (an individual or a company), and have debts and assets calculated. **2** to turn (assets) into cash. **3** to pay off (a debt). **4** COLLOQ to get rid of (someone) by killing. ■ **liquidation** N. ■ **liquidator** N.

liquidize or **-ise** VB **1** to make liquid. **2** to make (food, etc) into a purée. ■ **liquidizer** N.

liquor N **1** strong alcoholic, esp distilled, drink. **2** any fluid substance.

liquorice or **licorice** N **1** a plant with roots used in sweets and medicine. **2** a black sticky sweet made from the roots of this plant.

lira N (*lire* or *liras*) the standard unit of currency in Turkey and formerly Italy.

lisle N fine smooth cotton thread.

lisp VB **1** INTR to pronounce the sounds of **s** and **z** in the same way as the **th** sounds in **thin** and **this** respectively. **2** to say or pronounce (words, an answer, etc) in this way.
➤ N a speech defect distinguished by lisping.

lissom or **lissome** ADJ graceful and supple.

list[1] N **1** a series of names, numbers, prices, etc printed out, written down or said one after the other. **2** COMP an arrangement of data in a file.
➤ VB **1** to make a list of (something). **2** to add (an item, etc) to a list. **3** to include in a list.

list[2] VB, INTR to lean over to one side.
➤ N an act of listing or a listing position.

listed building N a building which is protected because of its historical interest.

listen VB, INTR **1** to try to hear. **2** to pay attention to. **3** to follow advice. ■ **listener** N.

listeria N a bacterium sometimes found in certain foods, which if not killed in cooking may cause the serious disease **listeriosis**.

listing N **1** a list. **2** a position in a list. **3** (**listings**) a guide to what is available in entertainment.

listless ADJ tired and lacking energy or interest. ■ **listlessly** ADV.

litany N (*-ies*) **1** CHRISTIANITY a series of prayers or supplications with a response which is repeated several times by the congregation. **2** a long tedious recital or list.

liter see **litre**

literacy N the ability to read and write.

literal ADJ **1** of words or a text: following the exact meaning, without allegorical or metaphorical interpretation. **2** of a translation: following the words of the original exactly. **3** true; exact: **the literal truth.**

➤ N, PRINTING a misprint of one letter.

literalism N strict adherence to the literal meaning of words. ■ **literalist** N.

literary ADJ 1 referring or relating to, or concerned with, literature or writing. 2 of a person: knowing a great deal about canonical literature. 3 of a word: formal; used in literature.

literate ADJ 1 able to read and write. 2 educated. 3 IN COMPOUNDS competent in something specified: **computer-literate**. ➤ N someone who is literate.

literati PL N literary or learned people.

literature N 1 written material, such as novels, poems and plays, that is valued for its language, content, etc. 2 the whole body of written works of a particular country, period in time, subject, etc: **American literature**. 3 COLLOQ any printed matter.

lithe ADJ supple and flexible.

lithium N, CHEM a soft silvery metallic element.

litho N 1 a lithograph. 2 lithography. ➤ ADJ lithographic. ➤ VB (**-os** or **-oes, -oed**) to lithograph.

lithograph N a print made by lithography. ➤ VB to print (images, etc) using lithography. ■ **lithographic** ADJ. ■ **lithographically** ADV.

lithography N a method of printing using a stone or metal plate which has been treated so that the ink adheres only to the design or image to be printed. ■ **lithographer** N.

litigant N someone involved in a lawsuit.

litigate VB 1 INTR to be involved in a lawsuit. 2 to contest (a point, claim, etc) in a lawsuit. ■ **litigation** N. ■ **litigator** N.

litigious ADJ inclined to take legal action.

litmus N, CHEM a dye obtained from certain lichens, which turns red in acid solutions, and blue in alkaline solutions.

litmus paper N, CHEM paper that has been treated with litmus, and which is used to test for acidity and alkalinity.

litmus test N, COLLOQ an event or action that serves as a definitive test or trial of something.

litotes N, RHETORIC understatement used for effect, esp by negating the opposite, as in **not a little angry** meaning **furious**.

litre or (N AMER, esp US) **liter** N 1 in the metric system: the basic unit of volume, equal to one cubic decimetre (10 000 cubic centimetres) or about 1.76 pints. 2 IN COMPOUNDS, DENOTING the capacity of the cylinders of a motor vehicle engine: **a three-litre engine**.

litter N 1 discarded paper, rubbish, etc lying in a public place. 2 a number of animals born to the same mother at the same time. 3 any scattered or confused collection of objects. 4 a straw, hay, etc used as bedding for animals; b absorbent material put in a tray for an indoor cat to urinate and defecate in. 5 OLD USE a framework consisting of cloth stretched tight between two long poles, used to carry sick or wounded people. 6 OLD USE a framework consisting of a couch covered by curtains for transporting a single passenger. ➤ VB 1 to make (something) untidy by spreading litter or objects about. 2 of objects: to lie untidily around (a room, etc).

litter-lout N, BRIT COLLOQ someone who deliberately drops litter outside.

little ADJ (often having connotations of affection or another emotion and used instead of the more formal **small**) 1 small in size, extent or amount. 2 young; younger: **a little girl**. 3 small in importance: **a little mishap**. 4 trivial. 5 petty: **a little quarrel**. 6 used as a way of detracting from a potentially disparaging implication: **funny little ways**. ➤ ADV (**less, least**) not much or at all: **They little understood the implications**. ➤ PRONOUN not much: **little to be gained**. ◆ **a little** (with a noun such as **bit, while, way** understood but not expressed) 1 a small amount or extent. 2 a short time or distance. ◆ **little by little** gradually; by degrees. ◆ **make little of sth** to treat it as unimportant.

littoral ADJ of, on or near the shore.

liturgy N (**-ies**) 1 the standard form of service in a church. 2 Holy Communion in the Eastern

Orthodox Church. ■ **liturgical** ADJ.

live[1] VB **1** INTR to have life. **2** INTR to be alive. **3** INTR to continue to be alive. **4** INTR to survive or to escape death. **5** INTR to have a home or dwelling: **We live in a small flat. 6** INTR to lead life in a certain way: **live well. 7** to pass or spend: **live a happy life in the country. 8** INTR to enjoy life passionately or to the full: **They really know how to live. 9** to express (something) through a way of living: **lived a lie.**
◆ **live and let live** COLLOQ to be tolerant of others and expect toleration in return.
◆ **live sth down** to carry on living until something in the past has been forgotten or forgiven in the eyes of other people.
◆ **live off sb** or **sth** to be supported by them or it: **live off the land.**
◆ **live up to sb** to become as respected as them: **could never live up to his brother.**
◆ **live up to sth** to turn out in a manner worthy of them or it: **tried to live up to expectations.**

live[2] ADJ **1** having life; not dead. **2** of a radio or TV broadcast: heard or seen as the event takes place. **3** of a record, video, etc: recorded during a performance. **4** of a wire: connected to a source of electrical power.
➤ ADV at, during, or as a live performance: **They had to perform live on stage.**

liveable ADJ fit to live in.

live-in ADJ **1** living at a workplace: **a live-in nanny. 2** of a sexual partner: sharing the same home: **a live-in lover.**

livelihood N a means of earning a living.

livelong ADJ, POETIC of the day or night: complete: **the livelong day.**

lively ADJ (**-ier, -iest**) **1** active and full of life, energy and high spirits. **2** brisk. **3** vivid or bright. **4** interesting or stimulating. ■ **liveliness** N.

liven VB, TR & INTR (USU **liven up**) to make or become lively.

liver[1] N **1** a large dark red glandular organ whose main function is to regulate the chemical composition of the blood. **2** this organ in certain animals, used as food.

liver[2] N someone who lives in a specified

way: **a riotous liver.**

liverish ADJ **1** OLD USE suffering from a disordered liver. **2** disgruntled or irritable.

liverwort N a small spore-bearing plant closely related to mosses.

livery N (**-ies**) **1** a distinctive uniform worn by male servants or by the members of a particular trade guild, etc. **2** the feeding, care, stabling and hiring out of horses for money.

lives plural of **life**

livestock SING OR PL N domesticated farm animals.

live wire N, COLLOQ someone who is full of energy and enthusiasm.

livid ADJ **1** COLLOQ extremely angry. **2** of a bruise: black and blue.

living ADJ **1** having life; alive. **2** currently in existence, use or activity. **3** of a likeness: exact.
➤ N **1** livelihood or means of subsisting. **2** a manner of life: **riotous living. 3** (**the living**) people who are alive.

lizard N a reptile closely related to the snake.

'll VB, CONTRACTION OF **shall** and **will**: I'll • they'll.

llama N a domesticated S American mammal kept for its wool, and as a beast of burden.

lo EXCLAM, OLD USE look! see!

loach N a small edible freshwater fish.

load N **1** something that is carried or transported. **2 a** an amount that is or can be carried or transported at one time; **b** IN COMPOUNDS: **lorryload of bricks. 3** a burden. **4** a cargo. **5** a specific quantity, varying according to the type of goods. **6** the weight carried by a structure, etc. **7** (**loads**) COLLOQ a large amount: **loads of time. 8** something, eg, a duty, etc, oppressive or difficult to bear: **a load off my mind. 9** an amount or number of things to be dealt with at one time. **10** the power carried by an electric circuit. **11** the power output of an engine. **12** the amount of work expected of someone: **a heavy teaching load.**
➤ VB **1** to put (cargo, passengers, etc) on (a ship, vehicle, plane, etc). **2** to fill: **load the**

dishwasher. **3** PHOTOG to put (film) in (a camera). **4** to weigh down or overburden. **5** to be a weight on or burden to someone or something; to oppress. **6** COMP **a** to put (a disk, computer tape, etc) into a drive, so that it may be used; **b** to transfer (a program or data) into main memory, so that it may be used. **7** to put (ammunition) into (a gun). **8** to give weight or bias to (dice, a roulette wheel, a question, etc).
◆ **get a load of sth** SLANG to pay attention to, listen to, or look at it.

loaded ADJ **1** carrying a load. **2** of a gun: containing bullets. **3** of a camera: containing film. **4** COLLOQ very wealthy.

loaded question N a question designed to bring out a specific response.

loadline N a line on a ship's side to mark the depth to which her cargo may be allowed to sink her. Also called **plimsoll line**.

loadstar see **lodestar**

loadstone see **lodestone**

loaf[1] N (*loaves*) **1** a shaped lump of dough, esp after it has been baked. **2** IN COMPOUNDS a quantity of food formed into a regular shape: meatloaf. **3** COLLOQ the head or brains.

loaf[2] VB, INTR to loiter idly.

loafer N **1** someone who loafs about. **2** a light casual shoe like a moccasin.

loam N a dark fertile easily-worked soil.

loan N **1** something lent, esp money lent at interest. **2** an act or the state of lending or being lent.
➤ VB to lend (esp money).
◆ **on loan** given as a loan.

loath or **loth** ADJ unwilling; reluctant.

loathe VB to dislike intensely.

loathing N intense dislike or disgust.

loathsome ADJ causing loathing.

loaves plural of **loaf**[1]

lob N **1** TENNIS a ball hit in a high overhead path. **2** CRICKET a slow high underhand ball. **3** SPORT any high looping ball.

➤ VB (*-bb-*) **1** to hit, kick or throw (a ball) in this way. **2** to send a high ball over (an opponent).

lobby N (*-ies*) **1** an entrance-hall, passage or waiting-room. **2** an antechamber of a legislative hall. **3** BRIT (also **division lobby**) either of two corridors in the House of Commons that members pass into when they vote. **4** a group of people who try to influence politicians, etc to favour their particular cause.
➤ VB (*-ies, -ied*) **1** to try to influence (politicians, etc) to favour a particular cause. **2** INTR to frequent a parliamentary lobby. ■ **lobbyist** N.

lobe N **1** (also **earlobe**) the soft lower part of the outer ear. **2** a division of an organ or gland in the body, esp the lungs, brain or liver. **3** a division of a leaf. ■ **lobed** ADJ.

lobelia N a garden plant with red, white, purple, blue or yellow flowers.

lobotomy N (*-ies*) SURGERY an operation that involves cutting into a lobe of an organ or gland.

lobster N **1** an edible marine crustacean with two pincer-like claws. **2** its flesh used as food.

local ADJ **1** relating or belonging to a particular place. **2** relating or belonging to someone's home area or neighbourhood. **3** of a train or bus: stopping at all the stops. **4** MED affecting a small area of the body: a local infection.
➤ N **1** someone who lives in a particular area. **2** BRIT someone's nearest and most regularly visited pub. **3** a local anaesthetic. ■ **localize** or **-ise** VB. ■ **localization** N. ■ **locally** ADV.

local authority N the elected local government body in an area.

locale N a scene of some event or occurrence.

local government N government of town or county affairs by a locally elected authority.

locality N (*-ies*) **1** a district or neighbourhood. **2** the position of a thing.

locate VB **1** to set in a particular place or position. **2** to find the exact position of.

location N **1** a position or situation. **2** the act of locating or process of being located. **3** COMP a position in a memory which can hold a unit of information.

◆ **on location** CINEMA at an authentic site as opposed to in the studio.

loc. cit. ABBREV: loco citato (Latin), in the passage just quoted.

loch N, SCOT **1** a lake. **2** (also **sea loch**) a long narrow arm of the sea surrounded by land on three sides.

loci plural of **locus**

lock¹ N **1** a mechanical device, usu consisting of a sliding bolt moved by turning a key, dial, etc, that secures a door, lid, machine, etc. **2** an enclosed section of a canal or river in which the water level can be altered by means of gates. **3** a state of being jammed or fixed together, and completely immovable. **4** the part of a gun that explodes the charge. **5** WRESTLING a tight hold which prevents an opponent from moving. **6** the full amount by which the front wheels of a vehicle will turn. **7** (also **lock forward**) RUGBY either of the two inside players in the second row of a scrum.
➤ VB **1** to fasten (a door, box, etc) with a lock. **2** INTR of a door, etc: to become or have the means of becoming locked. **3** to shut up or secure (a building, etc) by locking all doors and windows. **4** TR & INTR to jam or make (something) jam. **5** TR & INTR to fasten or make (something) be fastened so as to prevent movement.
◆ **lock on** (**to sth**) of a radar beam, etc: to track (it) automatically.
◆ **lock out 1** to prevent (someone or something) from getting into a building, room, etc by locking the doors. **2** to exclude (employees) from a workplace.
◆ **lock up 1** to confine (someone or something). **2** to lock (a building, etc) securely.

lock² N **1** a section or curl of hair. **2** (**locks**) hair.

locker N a small lockable cupboard for storage, eg of luggage at a station.

locket N a small case for holding a photograph or memento, worn on a chain round the neck.

lockout N the exclusion of employees by the management from their place of work.

locksmith N someone who makes and mends locks.

lockup N, BRIT **1** a building, etc that can be locked up. **2** a small shop with no living quarters attached.

locomotion N the power, process or capacity of moving from one place to another.

locomotive N a railway engine used for pulling trains.
➤ ADJ relating to, capable of or causing locomotion.

locum someone who temporarily stands in for someone else, esp in the medical and clerical professions.

locus N (-*ci*) **1** LAW an exact place or location. **2** MATH the set of points or values that satisfy an equation or a particular set of conditions.

locust N a grasshopper noted for its tendency to form dense migratory swarms that eat all the vegetation in their path, including crops.

locution N a style of speech.

lode N a vein containing metallic ore.

lodestar or **loadstar** N **1** a star used as a guide by sailors and astronomers, esp the Pole Star. **2** any guide or guiding principle.

lodestone or **loadstone** N **1** a form of magnetite with magnetic properties. **2** a magnet. **3** something that attracts.

lodge N **1** a cottage at the gateway to the grounds of a large house or mansion. **2** a small house in the country orig used by people taking part in field sports: **a hunting lodge**. **3** a porter's room in a university or college, etc. **4 a** the meeting-place of a local branch of certain societies; **b** the members of a branch of one of these societies. **5** a beaver's nest.
➤ VB **1** INTR to live, usu temporarily, in rented accommodation, esp in someone else's home. **2** TR & INTR **a** to become or cause (something) to become firmly fixed; **b** of feelings, ideas, thoughts, etc: to become implanted. **3 a** to bring (a charge or accusation) against someone; **b** to make (a complaint) officially. **4** to provide with rented accommodation, esp in one's home.

lodger N someone who rents accommodation

in someone else's home, often temporarily.

lodging N 1 (usu **lodgings**) a room or rooms rented in someone else's home. 2 temporary accommodation.

loess N, GEOL a deposit of fine wind–blown dust found esp in river basins.

loft N 1 a room or space under a roof. 2 a gallery in a church or hall: **an organ loft**. 3 a room used for storage, esp one over a stable for storing hay. 4 a room or shed where pigeons are kept. 5 GOLF the relative backward slant of the face of a golf club. 6 GOLF **a** a stroke that causes a golf ball to rise up high; **b** the amount of height that a player gives a ball. ➢ VB to strike, kick or throw high up in the air.

lofty ADJ (**-ier, -iest**) 1 very tall; of imposing height. 2 high or noble in character. 3 haughty or proud. ■ **loftily** ADV. ■ **loftiness** N.

log N 1 **a** part of a tree trunk or branch that has been cut, esp for firewood; **b** a tree trunk or large branch that has fallen to the ground. 2 a detailed record of events occurring during the voyage of a ship or aircraft, etc. 3 a logbook. 4 a float, orig made of wood, attached by a line to a ship and used for measuring its speed. ➢ VB (**-gg-**) 1 **a** to record (distances covered on a journey, events, etc) in a book or logbook; **b** to record (speed) over a distance. 2 to cut (trees or branches) into logs. 3 INTR to cut logs. ◆ **log in** or **on** COMP to start a session on a computer system, often by typing a password. ◆ **log out** or **off** COMP to end a session on a computer system.

logarithm N (often **log**) MATH the power to which a real number, called the base, must be raised in order to give another number or variable, eg the logarithm of 100 to the base 10 is 2. ■ **logarithmic** ADJ.

logbook N a book containing an official record of a voyage.

loggerhead N (in full **loggerhead turtle**) a large sea turtle. ◆ **at loggerheads** disagreeing fiercely.

logic N 1 **a** PHILOS the exploration of the validity or otherwise of arguments and reasoning; **b** MATH the analysis of the principles on which mathematical systems are based. 2 rationalized thinking: **Logic dictated that she should go.** ■ **logical** ADJ. ■ **logician** N.

logistics SING OR PL N 1 the organizing of everything needed for any large–scale operation. 2 the art of moving and supplying troops and military equipment. ■ **logistic** ADJ. ■ **logistical** ADJ. ■ **logistically** ADV.

logo N an emblem used by a company, etc.

loin N 1 (**loins**) the area of the body in humans and some animals, stretching from the bottom rib to the pelvis. 2 a cut of meat from the lower back area of an animal.

loincloth N a piece of material worn round the hips.

loiter VB, INTR 1 to wait around, esp furtively; to skulk. 2 to stand around doing nothing.

loll VB, INTR 1 (often **loll about**) to lie or sit about lazily. 2 of the tongue: to hang down or out.

lollipop N a sweet on a stick.

lollipop lady and **lollipop man** N someone employed to see that children get across busy roads safely.

lollop VB INTR, COLLOQ to bound around, esp with big ungainly strides.

lolly N (**-ies**) 1 COLLOQ a lollipop or an ice lolly. 2 SLANG money.

lone ADJ 1 without a partner, spouse or companion: **a lone parent**. 2 only: **the lone car in the carpark**. 3 of a place: isolated.

lonely ADJ (**-ier, -iest**) 1 of a person: sad because they have no companions or friends. 2 solitary and without companionship: **a lonely existence**. 3 of a place: isolated and unfrequented: **a lonely street**. ■ **loneliness** N.

loner N a person who prefers to be alone.

lonesome ADJ 1 sad and lonely. 2 causing feelings of loneliness.

long[1] ADJ 1 **a** measuring a great distance in space from one end to the other; **b** of time: lasting for an extensive period. 2 often IN

COMPOUNDS **a** measuring a specified amount: six centimetres long; **b** lasting a specified time: a three-hour-long movie. **3** having a large number of items: a long list. **4 a** measuring more than is usual, expected or wanted: She has really long hair; **b** lasting a greater time than is usual, expected or wanted: The breakdown made it a really long journey. **5** of someone's memory: able to recall things that happened a considerable time ago. **6** having greater length than breadth. **7 a** of a dress or skirt: reaching down to the feet; **b** of trousers: covering the whole of the legs. **8** of a drink: large. ➢ ADV **1** for, during or by a long period of time: They had long expected such news. **2** throughout the whole time: all night long. ➢ N **1** a comparatively long time: won't be there for long. **2** a syllable that takes a comparatively long time to pronounce. ◆ **as long as** or **so long as 1** provided that. **2** while; during the time that.

long² VB, INTR (often **long for** or **to**) to desire very much: longed to hear from her.

longboat N, FORMERLY the largest boat carried by a sailing ship.

longbow N a large bow, drawn by hand, used for hunting and as a weapon.

long-distance ADJ covering, travelling, operating, etc between or over long distances. ➢ ADV over a long distance: called New York long-distance.

long-drawn-out ADJ taking too long: a long-drawn-out argument.

longevity N great length of life.

longhand N ordinary handwriting as opposed to shorthand or typing.

longing N an intense desire or yearning. ➢ ADJ having or exhibiting this feeling: a longing look. ■ **longingly** ADV.

longitude N, GEOG the angular distance east or west of the meridian.

longitudinal ADJ **1** relating to longitude; measured by longitude. **2** relating to length. **3** lengthways. ■ **longitudinally** ADV.

long johns PL N underpants with long legs.

long jump N an athletics event in which competitors try to jump as far as possible, usu into a sandy pit. ■ **long-jumper** N.

long-life ADJ of food and drink: treated so that, even without refrigeration, it may be stored for a long time in an unopened container.

long-lived ADJ having a long life.

long-playing ADJ denoting a record where each side lasts approximately 25 minutes.

long-range ADJ **1** of predictions, etc: looking well into the future. **2** of a missile or weapon: able to reach remote or far-off targets.

long-running ADJ continuing over a long period.

longship N, HIST a long narrow Viking warship.

long shot N **1** COLLOQ **a** a guess, attempt, etc which is unlikely to be successful; **b** a bet made in the knowledge that there is only a slim chance of winning. **2** CINEMATOG a camera shot that makes viewers feel they are at a considerable distance from the scene.

long-sighted ADJ only able to see distant objects clearly. ■ **long-sightedness** N.

long-standing ADJ having existed or continued for a long time.

long-suffering ADJ patiently tolerating difficulties, hardship, etc.

long-term ADJ of a plan, etc: occurring in or concerning the future.

long wave N an electromagnetic wave with a wavelength greater than 1000 metres.

longways ADV, ADJ in the direction of a thing's length; lengthways

long-winded ADJ of a speaker or speech: tediously using or having far more words than are necessary. ■ **long-windedness** N.

loo N, BRIT COLLOQ a lavatory.

loofah N the dried inner part of a tropical gourd-like fruit, used as a kind of rough sponge.

look VB **1** INTR to direct one's sight: looked out of

the window. **2** to seem to be; to have the appearance of being: *She looked much younger than she was.* **3** INTR to face or be turned in a specified direction: *The window looks south.* **4** to express by a look: *She was looking daggers at him.* **5** to consider or realize: *Just look what you've done!*

➤ N **1 a** an act or the action of looking; a glance or view: *had a look through his photos;* **b** a glance or stare that conveys a particular feeling or emotion: *gave her an impatient look.* **2** (sometimes **looks**) the outward appearance of something or someone: *She always has that tired look: She didn't like the looks of the restaurant.* **3** (**looks**) beauty; attractiveness. **4** a particular way of dressing, etc, esp one that is different or particularly up-to-date: *went for a punk look.* **5 a** a search: *I'll have another look for that missing CD;* **b** a browse.

look after sb or **sth** to attend to or take care of them or it.

look at 1 to turn the eyes in a certain direction so as to see; to use one's sight. **2** to think about something: *We have to look at all the implications.* **3** COLLOQ to be expecting, hoping, facing, etc something or to do something: *was looking at five years for the robbery.*

look back to think about the past.

look down on or **upon sb** or **sth** to consider them or it inferior or contemptible.

look for sb or **sth 1** to search for them or it. **2** COLLOQ to be hoping for it: *He was looking for around £100 for the bike.*

look forward to sth to anticipate it with pleasure.

look in on sb to visit them briefly.

look into sth to investigate it.

look on or **upon sb** or **sth in a certain way** to think of or consider them or it in that way: *look on it as a bonus.*

look oneself to seem to be as healthy as usual: *He doesn't quite look himself yet.*

look out 1 to keep watch and be careful. **2** used as an exclamation warning of imminent danger.

look out sth to find it by searching: *I'll look out that magazine for you.*

look out for sb or **sth 1** to be alert about

finding them or it. **2** COLLOQ to protect: *He has always looked out for his younger brother.*

◆ **look over sth** to check it.

◆ **look sharp** COLLOQ to hurry up.

◆ **look to sb** or **sth** to rely on, turn to or refer to them or it: *looked to her for support.*

◆ **look up** to show signs of improving.

◆ **look sb up** COLLOQ to visit or get in touch with them.

◆ **look sth up** to search for an item of information, etc in a reference book, etc.

◆ **look up to sb** to respect them.

lookalike N someone or something that looks very much like someone or something else.

look-in N a chance of joining in or doing something: *never gives her a look-in.*

looking-glass N, OLD USE a mirror.

lookout N **1** a careful watch. **2** a place from which such a watch can be kept. **3** someone who has to keep watch, eg on board ship. **4** COLLOQ a personal concern or problem: *That's your lookout.*

loom[1] N a machine that weaves thread into fabric.

loom[2] VB, INTR **1** to appear indistinctly and in an enlarged or threatening form. **2** of an event: to be imminent, esp in a menacing way.

loony SLANG, N (**-ies**) someone who is mad.
➤ ADJ (**-ier, -iest**) crazy; mad.

loop N **1** a rounded or oval-shaped single coil in a piece of thread, string, rope, chain, etc, formed as it crosses over itself. **2** any similar oval-shaped or U-shaped bend. **3** a manoeuvre in which an aircraft describes a complete vertical circle in the sky. **4** a strip of magnetic tape or film whose ends have been spliced together to form a loop.
➤ VB **1** to fasten with or enclose in a loop. **2** to form into a loop or loops.

loophole N a means of escaping or evading a responsibility, duty, obligation, etc.

loopy ADJ (**-ier, -iest**) SLANG mad; crazy.

loose ADJ **1** not or no longer tied up or attached to something else; free. **2** of clothes, etc: not

tight or close- fitting. **3 a** not held together; not fastened or firmly fixed in place; **b** not packaged. **4** not tightly-packed or compact: **loose soil. 5** vague or inexact: **loose translation. 6** usu of a woman: promiscuous. **7** indiscreet: **loose talk. 8** SPORT of a ball: in play but not under a player's control. **9** droopy; baggy. **10** of the bowels: moving frequently and producing softer faeces than is usual.
➢ ADV in an unrestrained way: **The dog can run loose in the park.**
➢ N (**the loose**) a state of freedom: **a prisoner on the loose.**
➢ VB **1** to release or set free. **2** to unfasten or untie. **3** to make less tight, compact or dense. ■ **loosely** ADV. ■ **looseness** N.
◆ **at a loose end** lacking something to do.

loose box N a part of a stable or horse-box where horses are kept untied.

loose-leaf ADJ of a folder, etc: allowing pages to be taken out or put in.

loosen VB **1** TR & INTR to make or become loose or looser. **2** to free; to cause to become free or freer: **Drink always loosened his tongue.**
◆ **loosen up** COLLOQ to become more relaxed.

loot VB, INTR **1** to steal from shops, warehouses, etc, often during or following rioting. **2** to steal from an enemy in wartime.
➢ N **1** stolen money, goods or supplies; plunder. **2** SLANG money. ■ **looter** N.

lop VB (-pp-) to cut off (esp the branches of a tree).

lope VB, INTR to run with long bounding steps.
➢ N a bounding leap.

lop-eared ADJ of animals: having ears that droop.

lopsided ADJ **1** with one side lower or lighter than the other. **2** leaning over to one side.

loquacious ADJ talkative. ■ **loquacity** N.

lord N **1** a master or ruler. **2** FEUDALISM someone who is in a superior position. **3** chiefly BRIT **a** a man who is a member of the aristocracy; **b** (**Lord**) a title used to address certain members of the aristocracy. **4** (**My Lord** or **my lord**) **a** a conventional way for lawyers, etc to address a judge in court; **b** a formal way of addressing certain members of the clergy and aristocracy. **5** (**Lord** or **Our Lord** or **the Lord**) CHRISTIANITY a way of addressing or referring to God or Jesus Christ. **6** (**Lord**) IN COMPOUNDS forming part of the titles of some high-ranking officials: **Lord Provost. 7** (**Lord!**) expressing shock, surprise, dismay, etc.
◆ **lord it over sb** to have an overbearing manner towards them.

lordly ADJ (-ier, -iest) **1** grand or haughty. **2** belonging, relating or suitable to a lord or lords. ■ **lordliness** N.

the Lords SING N short for House of Lords.

Lordship N (**His** or **Your Lordship**) a title used to address bishops, judges and peers.

lore N the whole body of knowledge on a particular subject, esp the kind of knowledge that has been enhanced by legends, etc.

lorgnette N a pair of spectacles that are held up to the eyes using a long handle.

lorry N (-ies) BRIT a large road vehicle for heavy loads. N Amer equivalent **truck.**

lose VB (*lost*) **1 a** to fail to keep or obtain (something), esp because of a mistake, carelessness, etc: **lost his money through a hole in his pocket; b** to stop or begin to stop having (some distinguishing quality, characteristic or property): **She was losing her nerve. 2 a** to misplace (something), esp temporarily: **I've lost the car keys; b** to be unable to find (something). **3 a** to suffer the loss of (usu a close friend or relative) through death; **b** to suffer the loss of (an unborn baby) through miscarriage or stillbirth; **c** to fail to save the life of (esp a patient); **d** to be deprived of (life, possessions, etc), esp in a war, fire, natural disaster, etc; **e** (**be lost**) to be killed or drowned, esp at sea. **4** to fail to use or get; to miss (an opportunity, etc). **5 a** TR & INTR to fail to win (a game, vote, proposal, election, battle, bet, etc); **b** to give away; to forfeit: **lost £50 on the horses. 6** to confuse or bewilder (someone): **Sorry, you've lost me there. 7** to escape or get away from (someone or something). **8** of a clock or watch: to become slow by (a specified amount).

◆ **lose face** to be humiliated or discredited.

◆ **lose one's mind** or **reason** to behave irrationally, esp temporarily.

◆ **lose out** COLLOQ **1** to suffer loss or be at a disadvantage. **2** to fail to get something one wants.

◆ **lose sight of sb** or **sth 1** to be unable or no longer able to see them or it. **2** to forget or ignore the importance of them or it: They lost sight of their original aims.

◆ **lose one's temper** to become angry.

◆ **lose one's** or **the way** to stray from one's intended route by mistake.

loser N **1** someone or something that is defeated. **2** COLLOQ someone who is habitually unsuccessful.

losing ADJ failing; never likely to be successful: fighting a losing battle.

loss N **1** an act or instance of losing or being lost. **2** the thing, amount, etc lost: His loss of hearing was severe. **3** the disadvantage that results when someone or something goes: a great loss to the company.

◆ **at a loss 1** puzzled; uncertain; unable to understand. **2** of a selling price, etc: lower than the buying price: sold the house at a loss. **3** of a company, etc: losing more money than it is making: trading at a loss.

loss leader N, COMMERCE an item on sale at a loss, as a means of attracting customers.

lost cause N an aim, ideal, person, etc that has no chance of success.

lot N **1** COLLOQ (usu **a lot** or **lots**) a large number or amount of something: an awful lot of work to do: lots of children. **2** a (**the lot**) everything; the total; the whole number or amount: ate the lot; **b** (**one's lot**) COLLOQ all one is getting. **3** a group of people or things that have something, often a specified attribute or quality, in common: Get a move on, you lazy lot. **4** a a straw, slip of paper, etc that is drawn from a group of similar objects, in order to reach a fair and impartial decision: draw lots to see who'd

go first; **b** the use of lots to arrive at a decision, choice, etc: made their selection by lot. **5** someone's destiny, plight, etc: the lot of the homeless. **6** an item or set of items for sale by auction, usu identified by a number: Lot 49 looks intriguing. **7** N AMER an area of land for a specified purpose: parking lot. **8** the area around a film studio used for outside filming.

◆ **cast** or **throw in one's lot with sb** to decide to share their fortunes.

loth see **loath**

lotion N any liquid, used either as a medicine or a cosmetic, for healing or cleaning the skin.

lottery N (**-ies**) **1** a system for raising money which involves randomly drawing numbered tickets from a drum, etc and giving prizes to those who hold the tickets with the same numbers. **2** anything which is thought of as being a matter of chance.

lotus N **1** GR MYTHOL a fruit which was thought to produce a state of blissful and dreamy forgetfulness. **2** a water lily traditionally associated with Buddhism and Hinduism.

lotus-eater N someone who lives a lazy and indulgent life.

loud ADJ **1** making a relatively great sound; noisy. **2** capable of making a relatively great sound: a loud horn. **3** emphatic and insistent: loud complaints. **4** of colours, clothes, designs, etc: bright or gaudy. **5** of someone or their behaviour: aggressively noisy and coarse.

➤ ADV in a loud manner. ■ **loudly** ADV.

loudhailer N a portable device for amplifying the voice.

loudmouth N, COLLOQ someone who is very noisy and boastful. ■ **loud-mouthed** ADJ.

loudspeaker (often just **speaker**) N an electronic device that converts electrical signals into audible sound waves.

lough N, IRISH a loch.

lounge VB, INTR **1** to lie, sit, stand, recline etc in a relaxed and comfortable way. **2** to pass the time without doing very much.

➤ N **1** a sitting-room in a private house.

2 a large room in a public building, such as a hotel, where people can sit and relax. **3** (also **departure lounge**) an area or large room in an airport, ferry terminal, etc, where passengers can relax prior to being called to board the aeroplane, ferry, etc. **4** BRIT (also **lounge bar**) the more up-market bar of a pub or hotel.

lounge suit N, BRIT a man's suit for everyday wear.

lour or **lower** VB, INTR **1** of the sky: to darken or threaten rain or storms. **2** to scowl or look angry or gloomy. ■ **loury** ADJ.

louse N **1** (PL *lice*) a wingless parasitic insect infesting human hair and skin. **2** (PL *louses*) SLANG a scornful term of abuse for a person.
◆ **louse sth up** SLANG to spoil or ruin it.

lousy ADJ (*-ier, -iest*) **1** having lice. **2** SLANG very bad, unpleasant, or disgusting.

lout N a bad-mannered and aggressive person. ■ **loutish** ADJ.

louvre or (N AMER) **louver** N **1** any one of a set of overlapping slats in a door, etc which let air in but keep rain and light out. **2** a dome-like structure on a roof for letting smoke out and light and air in. ■ **louvred** ADJ.

lovage N a S European flowering plant used medicinally and for flavouring.

lovat N **1** a palish dusky green colour. **2** a tweed suit in this colour.

love VB **1** to feel great affection for (someone). **2 a** to enjoy very much: **I love to boogie**; **b** to like very much: **I love chocolate biscuits.**
➤ N **1** a feeling of great affection: **brotherly love. 2** a strong liking: **a love of the outdoors. 3** used as an affectionate term of address: **my love. 4** TENNIS, SQUASH, WHIST, **etc** no score.
■ **lovable** or **loveable** ADJ.
◆ **make love to** or **with 1** to have sexual intercourse. **2** OLD USE to woo.

love affair N a romantic or sexual relationship, esp one that is fleeting or illicit.

lovebird N a small parrot.

love-child N, OLD USE an illegitimate child.

loveless ADJ devoid of love.

lovelorn ADJ sad or pining because the love felt for someone else is not returned.

lovely ADJ (*-ier, -iest*) **1** strikingly attractive; beautiful. **2** COLLOQ delightful or pleasing.
➤ N (*-ies*) COLLOQ a pretty woman.

love-making N **1** FORMERLY courting. **2** any form of sexual activity.

lover N **1** someone who is in love with someone else, esp in a romantic or sexual way. **2** (**lovers**) two people who are in love with one another or who are sharing a sexual relationship. **3** someone who enjoys or is fond of a specified thing: **a cat lover.**

lovesick ADJ **1** infatuated with someone. **2** lovelorn.

loving ADJ **1** affectionate and caring. **2** IN COMPOUNDS enjoying, valuing or appreciating a specified thing: **fun-loving.** ■ **lovingly** ADV.

low[1] ADJ **1** measuring comparatively little from top to bottom. **2** close to the ground, sea-level, the horizon, etc: **low cloud. 3** measuring comparatively less than is usual or average: **The river is low. 4** having little value; not costing very much. **5** of numbers: small. **6** not near the top: **Shopping was low on her list of priorities. 7** coarse, rude, vulgar, etc. **8** being of humble rank or position. **9** not very advanced; unsophisticated: **a low form of animal life. 10** of the neckline of a garment: leaving the neck and upper part of the chest bare. **11** of a sound, note, voice, etc: **a** quiet; soft; **b** having a deep pitch. **12 a** weak; lacking in vitality; **b** depressed; dispirited. **13** unfavourable: **a low opinion. 14** underhanded; unprincipled: **How low can you get? 15** giving a relatively slow engine speed: **a low gear. 16** subdued: **low lighting. 17** not prominent or conspicuous: **keeping a low profile.**
➤ ADV **1** in or to a low position, state or manner: **aimed low and fired • brought low by his gambling debts. 2** in a small quantity or to a small degree. **3** of a sound, etc: **a** quietly; **b** with or in a deep pitch. **4** IN COMPOUNDS **a** not measuring much in a specified respect: **low-voltage; b** not far off the ground: **low-slung;**

c deeply: **low-cut**; **d** lowly: **low-born**.
➤ N **1** a depth, position, level, etc which is low or lowest: **an all-time low**. **2** METEOROL a cyclone.
■ **lowness** N.
◆ **lay sb low** of an illness: to affect them severely.

low² VB, INTR of cattle: to make a gentle mooing sound.
➤ N the gentle mooing sound made by cattle.

lowbrow ADJ lacking cultural or intellectual values.
➤ N a lowbrow person.

the lowdown N, COLLOQ information about someone or something.

low-down ADJ, COLLOQ mean and dishonourable: **a low-down dirty trick**.

lower¹ ADJ **1** not as high in position, status, height, value, etc: **lower middle class**. **2** of an animal or plant: less highly developed than other species. **3** in place names: **a** relatively far south; **b** geographically not so high.
➤ ADV in or to a lower position.
➤ VB **1** to lessen or become less in amount, value, status, sound, etc. **2 a** to pull down: **We'd better lower the window**; **b** to cause to come down: **lowered the lifeboat**. **3** to reduce or cause to be reduced.

lower² see **lour**

lower case PRINTING, ADJ of small letters as opposed to capitals.
➤ N a letter or letters of this kind.

lowest common denominator N, MATH in a group of fractions, the lowest common multiple of all the denominators.

low frequency N a radio band where the number of cycles per second is between 30 and 300 kilohertz.

low-key ADJ restrained or subdued.

lowland N (also **lowlands**) land which is comparatively low-lying and flat.
➤ ADJ of lowlands. ■ **lowlander** N.

lowly ADJ (**-ier, -iest**) **1** humble in rank, status or behaviour. **2** simple, modest and unpretentious.
■ **lowliness** N.

low-pitched ADJ **1** of a sound: low in pitch. **2** of a roof: having a gentle slope.

low profile N a deliberate avoidance of publicity and attention. ■ **low-profile** ADJ.

low-spirited ADJ dejected or depressed.

low-tech ADJ, COLLOQ not involving the use of the latest technology.

low tide N the tide at its lowest level or the time when this occurs. Also called **low water**.

loyal ADJ **1** faithful and true. **2** expressing or showing loyalty. ■ **loyally** ADV.

loyalist N a loyal supporter, esp of a sovereign or an established government. ■ **loyalism** N.

loyalty N (**-ies**) **1** the state or quality of being loyal. **2** (often **loyalties**) a feeling of loyalty or duty: **divided loyalties**.

lozenge N **1** a small sweet or tablet, esp one with some kind of medicinal property, which dissolves in the mouth. **2** MATH a less common term for a **rhombus**.

LP ABBREV **1** long-playing **2** long-playing record.

L-plate N, BRIT a small square white sign with a red letter L on it which, by law, a learner driver must display on the back and front of a car.

LSD ABBREV lysergic acid diethylamide, an illegal hallucinatory drug. Also called **acid**.

Ltd or **Ltd.** ABBREV Limited.

lubricant N oil, etc used to reduce friction.

lubricate VB **1** to coat (engine parts, etc) with oil, grease, etc in order to reduce friction. **2** INTR to act as a lubricant. ■ **lubrication** N.

lucerne N, BRIT alfalfa.

lucid ADJ **1** clearly presented and easily understood. **2** not confused, esp in contrast to bouts of insanity or delirium. ■ **lucidity** N.
■ **lucidly** ADV. ■ **lucidness** N.

luck N **1** chance, esp as it is perceived as influencing someone's life at specific points in time: **luck was on his side**. **2** good fortune. **3** events in life which cannot be controlled and seem to happen by chance: **She's had nothing but bad luck**. ■ **luckless** ADJ.

◆ **down on one's luck** experiencing problems or suffering hardship.

◆ **no such luck** COLLOQ unfortunately not.

lucky ADJ (**-ier, -iest**) **1** having good fortune. **2** bringing good fortune. **3** happening by chance, esp when the outcome is advantageous. ■ **luckily** ADV.

lucky dip N a tub or container in which prizes are drawn out at random.

lucrative ADJ profitable. ■ **lucratively** ADV.

lucre N, DEROG profit or financial gain.

Luddite N **1** (**the Luddites**) HIST a group which, in the early 19c, destroyed machinery in protest against mechanization. **2** anyone who opposes new technology.

ludicrous ADJ completely ridiculous or absurd.

ludo N, BRIT a game played with dice and counters on a board.

lug¹ VB (**-gg-**) to carry, pull or drag with effort.

lug² N **1** DIALECT OR COLLOQ an ear. **2** a protruding part on something.

luggage N, BRIT suitcases, bags, etc.

lugger N a small vessel with square sails.

lugubrious ADJ sad and gloomy; mournful.

lugworm N a large marine worm used as fishing bait.

lukewarm ADJ **1** of liquids: moderately warm. **2** of interest, support, response, etc: not enthusiastic; indifferent.

lull VB **1** to soothe or induce a feeling of well-being in (someone): **lulled the baby to sleep. 2** to allay (suspicions), esp falsely. **3** to deceive (someone): **lulled them into a false sense of security.**
➤ N a period of calm and quiet.

lullaby N (**-ies**) a soft soothing song to help send a child to sleep.

lumbago N chronic pain in the lower back.

lumbar ADJ, ANAT in the lower back.

lumber¹ N disused articles of furniture.
◆ **lumber sb with** COLLOQ to burden them with (something or someone unwanted, difficult, etc).

lumber² VB, INTR to move about heavily and clumsily. ■ **lumbering** ADJ.

lumberjack N someone who works at felling trees, sawing them up and moving them.

luminary N (**-ies**) **1** someone who is an expert or authority in a particular field. **2** a famous or prominent member of a group.

luminescence N, PHYS the emission of light by a substance, usu a solid, in the absence of a rise in temperature. ■ **luminescent** ADJ.

luminous ADJ **1** full of or giving out light. **2** NON-TECHNICAL glowing in the dark: **a luminous clock face.** ■ **luminosity** N (**-ies**).

lump N **1** a small solid mass that has no definite shape: **a lump of coal. 2** a swelling or tumour. **3** a number of things taken as a single whole.
◆ **a lump in one's throat** a sensation of tightness in one's throat, usu caused by emotion.
◆ **lump together** to gather (esp dissimilar things) into a group or pile.

lumpectomy N (**-ies**) SURGERY the removal of a lump, esp a tumour from the breast.

lumpish ADJ heavy, dull or awkward.

lump sum N a large single payment.

lumpy ADJ (**-ier, -iest**) full of lumps. ■ **lumpiness** N.

lunacy N (**-ies**) **1** insanity. **2** great foolishness or stupidity; a misguided or misjudged action: **It would be sheer lunacy to do that.**

lunar ADJ relating to or caused by the Moon.

lunatic ADJ **1 a** FORMERLY insane; **b** LAW of unsound mind and so not legally responsible for any actions taken. **2** foolish, stupid or wildly eccentric.
➤ N **1** someone who is foolish or highly eccentric. **2 a** FORMERLY someone who is considered insane; **b** LAW someone who is deemed lunatic.

lunatic asylum N, OLD USE a psychiatric home or hospital.

lunatic fringe N the most extreme, fanatical or eccentric members of any group.

lunch N a light meal in the middle of the day.
➤ VB, INTR to eat lunch.

luncheon N 1 a formal meal served in the middle of the day. 2 FORMAL lunch.

lung N one of a pair of respiratory organs in air–breathing vertebrates.

lunge N 1 a sudden plunge forwards.
2 FENCING a sudden thrust with a sword.
➤ VB, INTR 1 to make a sudden strong or thrusting movement forwards. 2 FENCING to make a sudden forward movement with a sword.

lupin N a garden plant with long spikes of brightly coloured flowers.

lupine ADJ relating to or like a wolf.

lurch VB, INTR 1 of a person: to stagger unsteadily: **He lurched towards the bar.** 2 of ships, etc: to make a sudden roll to one side.
➤ N 1 an act of staggering: **made a lurch for the door.** 2 a sudden roll to one side.
◆ **leave sb in the lurch** COLLOQ to abandon them in a difficult situation.

lure VB to tempt or entice, often by the offer of some reward.
➤ N 1 someone or something which tempts, attracts or entices: **left teaching for the lure of more money.** 2 FALCONRY a piece of meat used for encouraging a bird to return to its falconer.

lurid ADJ 1 glaringly bright, esp when the surroundings are dark: **a lurid light in the sky.**
2 horrifying or sensational: **lurid details.**
■ **luridly** ADV.

lurk VB 1 to lie in wait, esp in ambush. 2 to linger unseen or furtively; to be latent: **The idea lurked at the back of his mind.**

luscious ADJ 1 of a smell, taste, etc: richly sweet; delicious. 2 voluptuously attractive.

lush[1] ADJ 1 green and growing abundantly.
2 ripe and succulent.

lush[2] N, SLANG someone who frequently or regularly drinks a lot of alcohol.

lust N 1 strong sexual desire. 2 enthusiasm; relish: **a lust for life.**
➤ VB, INTR (usu **lust after**) to have a strong desire for. ■ **lustful** ADJ. ■ **lustfully** ADV.

lustre or (US) **luster** N 1 the shiny appearance of something in reflected light. 2 shine, brightness or gloss. 3 splendour and glory.
■ **lustrous** ADJ.

lusty ADJ (-**ier**, -**iest**) 1 vigorous or loud:
a baby's lusty cries. 2 strong and healthy.

lute N, MUS a stringed instrument with a long neck and a pear–shaped body.

luvvie or **luvvy** N (-**ies**) BRIT, FACETIOUS someone, orig in the theatre, who speaks and behaves in an overly pretentious manner.

lux N (PL **lux**) PHYS in the SI system: a unit of illuminance.

luxe see **de luxe**

luxuriant ADJ 1 of plants, etc: growing abundantly; lush. 2 of someone's writing, imagination, etc: full of metaphors and very elaborate. 3 of material things: ornate; overwrought. ■ **luxuriance** N.
■ **luxuriantly** ADV.

luxuriate VB, INTR to live in comfort or luxury.
◆ **luxuriate in sth** to revel in it.

luxurious ADJ 1 expensive and opulent.
2 enjoying luxury. ■ **luxuriously** ADV.

luxury N (-**ies**) 1 expensive, rich and extremely comfortable surroundings and possessions.
2 indulgence in or enjoyment of luxurious surroundings. 3 something that is pleasant and enjoyable but not essential.

lychee or **lichee** N a small fruit with sweet white juicy flesh enclosing a single seed.

lychgate see **lichgate**

Lycra N, TRADEMARK a stretchy fabric.

lye N 1 an alkaline solution made by leaching water through wood ash, etc. 2 a strong solution of sodium or potassium hydroxide.

lymph N, ANAT in animals: a colourless fluid which contains lymphocytes and antibodies.
■ **lymphatic** ADJ.

lymphatic system N, ANAT the network of vessels that transports lymph around the body.

lymphocyte N a type of white blood cell.

lymphoma N (*-mas* or *-mata*) PATHOL any tumour of the lymphatic tissues.

lynch VB of a group of people: to execute (someone thought guilty of a crime), usu by hanging, without recourse to the law.

lynx N (*-es* or *lynx*) a wild cat with a stubby tail with a black tip, and tufted ears.

lyre N a small stringed musical instrument.

lyric ADJ 1 POETRY expressing personal, private or individual emotions. 2 having the form of a song; intended for singing, orig to the lyre. ➤ N 1 a short poem or song, usu written in the first person and expressing emotion: a love lyric. 2 (**lyrics**) the words of a song.

lyrical ADJ 1 song-like. 2 full of enthusiastic praise: waxing lyrical. ■ **lyrically** ADV.

lyricism N 1 the state or quality of being lyrical. 2 an affected pouring out of emotions.

lyricist N 1 someone who writes the words to songs. 2 a lyric poet.

Mm

M[1] or **m** N (*Ms, M's* or *m's*) the thirteenth letter of the English alphabet.

M[2] ABBREV 1 Master. 2 million. 3 BRIT Motorway, followed by a number, as in **M1**. ➤ SYMBOL, as a Roman numeral: 1000.

MA ABBREV Master of Arts.

ma'am CONTRACTION madam.

mac or **mack** N short form of **mackintosh**.

macabre ADJ ghastly; gruesome.

macadam N 1 a road-making material consisting of layers of broken stones, usu bound with tar. 2 a road surface made with this.

macadamia N the round edible oily nut of an Australian evergreen tree.

macaque N a short-tailed or tailless monkey of Asia and Africa, with large cheek-pouches.

macaroni N (*-nis* or *-nies*) pasta in the form of short narrow tubes.

macaroon N a sweet cake or biscuit made with sugar, eggs and crushed almonds.

macaw N any of the large brilliantly-coloured parrots with long tails and strong beaks, found mainly in the forests of Central and S America.

mace[1] N 1 a ceremonial staff carried by some public officials. 2 HIST a heavy club, usu with a spiked head, used as a weapon.

mace[2] N a spice made from the layer around the nutmeg seed, dried and ground up.

macerate VB, TR & INTR, TECHNICAL to break up or make something break up or become soft by soaking. ■ **maceration** N.

machete N a long heavy broad-bladed knife used as a weapon or cutting tool.

Machiavellian ADJ crafty, amoral and opportunist. ■ **Machiavellianism** N.

machinations PL N a crafty scheme or plot.

machine N 1 a device with moving parts, and usu powered, designed to perform a particular task: sewing machine. 2 a group of people or institutions under a central control: **the party's political machine. 3** COLLOQ a motor vehicle. ➢ VB to make, shape or cut with a machine.

machine-gun N a portable gun that fires a continuous rapid stream of bullets.

machinery N (*-ies*) **1** machines in general. **2** the working or moving parts of a machine. **3** the combination of processes, systems or people that keeps anything working, or that produces the desired result.

machinist N **1** someone who operates a machine. **2** someone who makes or repairs machines.

machismo N, USU DEROG exaggerated manliness.

Mach number N (often shortened to **Mach**) a ratio of the speed of an object to the speed of sound in the same medium.

macho ADJ, often DEROG exaggeratedly or aggressively manly. **Also** AS N.

mack see **mac**

mackerel N (*mackerels* or *mackerel*) an important food fish with a streamlined body that is blue-green above and silvery below.

mackintosh or **macintosh** N **1** chiefly BRIT a waterproof raincoat. **2** a kind of rubberized waterproof material.

macramé N **1** the art of knotting string or coarse thread into patterns. **2** decorative articles made in this way.

macro N, COMP a single instruction that brings a set of instructions into operation.

macrobiotics SING N the science of devising diets using grains and organically-grown fruit and vegetables. ■ **macrobiotic** ADJ.

macrocosm N **1** the universe as a whole. **2** any large or complex system or structure made up of similar smaller systems or structures.

macron N a straight horizontal bar (−) placed over a vowel to show that it is long or stressed.

macroscopic ADJ, TECHNICAL large enough to be seen by the naked eye.

macula N (*-lae*) TECHNICAL a spot, discoloured mark or blemish, eg a freckle. ■ **macular** ADJ.

mad ADJ (*madder, maddest*) **1** mentally disturbed; insane. **2** foolish or senseless; extravagantly carefree. **3** COLLOQ very angry; furious. **4** COLLOQ (USU **mad about** or **on**) extremely enthusiastic; fanatical. **5** marked by extreme confusion, haste or excitement: **a mad dash**. ■ **madly** ADV. ■ **madness** N.

madam N (PL in sense 1 *mesdames* or in other senses *madams*) **1** a polite form of address to any woman. **2** a form of address to a woman in authority: **Madam Chairman**. **3** a woman who manages a brothel.

madcap ADJ foolishly impulsive or wild. ➢ N a foolishly impulsive person.

madden VB to make (a person, etc) mad, esp to enrage them. ■ **maddening** ADJ.

madder N **1** a plant with yellow flowers and a red root. **2** a dark red dye, orig made from the root of this plant.

made ADJ **1** (esp **made from, in** or **of sth**) artificially produced or formed. **2** IN COMPOUNDS, DENOTING produced, constructed or formed in a specified way or place: **handmade. 3** of a person, etc: whose success or prosperity is certain: **a made man**. ◆ **have it made** COLLOQ to enjoy, or be assured of, complete success, happiness, etc.

made up ADJ **1** wearing make-up. **2** of a story, etc: not true; invented. **3** COLLOQ of a person: extremely pleased; chuffed.

madman and **madwoman** N **1** an insane person. **2** a very foolish person.

Madonna N (**the Madonna**) esp RC CHURCH the Virgin Mary, mother of Christ.

madras N a kind of medium-hot curry.

madrigal N, MUS an unaccompanied part song, popular in the 16c and 17c.

maelstrom N, esp LITERARY **1** a place or state of uncontrollable confusion or destruction. **2** a violent whirlpool.

maestro N (*-ros* or *-ri*) someone specially

gifted in a specified art.

Mafia N (**the Mafia**) a secret international criminal organization that controls numerous illegal activities, esp in Italy and the USA.

mag N, COLLOQ a magazine or periodical.

magazine N 1 a paperback periodical publication, usu a heavily illustrated one, containing articles, stories, etc by various writers. 2 TV, RADIO a regular broadcast in which reports are presented on a variety of subjects. 3 in some automatic firearms: a metal container for several cartridges. 4 a storeroom for ammunition, explosives, etc. 5 PHOTOG a removable container for slides or film.

maggot N the worm-like larva of various flies. ■ **maggoty** ADJ.

magi see under **magus**

magic N 1 the supposed art or practice of using the power of supernatural forces, spells, etc to affect people, objects and events. 2 the art or practice of performing entertaining illusions and conjuring tricks. 3 the quality of being wonderful, charming or delightful. 4 a secret or mysterious power over the imagination or will. ➤ ADJ 1 of, relating to, used in, or done by, sorcery or conjuring. 2 causing wonderful, startling or mysterious results. ➤ VB (-**icked, -icking**) to produce something by using, or as if by using, sorcery or conjuring. ■ **magical** ADJ. ■ **magically** ADV.

magician N 1 an entertainer who performs conjuring tricks, illusions, etc. 2 someone who practises black or white magic.

magisterial ADJ 1 of or relating to, or administered by, a magistrate. 2 authoritative; dictatorial. ■ **magisterially** ADV.

magistracy N (-**ies**) 1 the rank or position of a magistrate. 2 (usu **the magistracy**) all magistrates. Also called **magistrature**.

magistrate N 1 in England and Wales: a judge who presides in a lower court of law (**Magistrates' Court**), dealing with minor criminal and civil cases. 2 any public official administering the law.

magma N (-**mas** or -**mata**) GEOL hot molten rock material generated deep within the Earth's crust or mantle. ■ **magmatic** ADJ.

magnanimous ADJ having great generosity of spirit towards others. ■ **magnanimity** N.

magnate N someone of high rank or great power, esp in industry.

magnesia N, CHEM a white light powder, magnesium oxide.

magnesium N, CHEM a reactive silvery-grey metallic element that burns with a dazzling white flame.

magnet N 1 a piece of metal, esp a piece of iron, with the power to attract and repel iron. 2 someone or something that attracts.

magnetic ADJ 1 belonging to, having the powers of, or operated by, a magnet or magnetism. 2 of a metal, etc: able to be made into a magnet. 3 of a person, etc: extremely charming or attractive.

magnetic field N, PHYS the region surrounding a magnet, electromagnetic wave or current-carrying conductor, within which magnetic forces may be detected.

magnetic north N the direction in which a compass's magnetic needle always points.

magnetic pole N, GEOL either of two points on the Earth's surface to or from which a magnetic needle points.

magnetism N 1 the properties of attraction possessed by magnets. 2 the scientific study of the properties of magnets and magnetic phenomena. 3 strong personal charm.

magnetite N, GEOL a black, strongly magnetic mineral form of iron oxide, an ore of iron.

magnetize or -**ise** VB 1 to make something magnetic. 2 to attract something or someone.

magneto N, ELEC a simple electric generator consisting of a rotating magnet that induces an alternating current in a coil surrounding it, used to provide the ignition spark in petrol engines without batteries.

magnetron N, PHYS a device for generating

microwaves, widely used in microwave ovens.

magnification N 1 OPTICS the extent to which an image of an object is enlarged or reduced. 2 the action of magnifying, or the state of being magnified.

magnificent ADJ 1 splendidly impressive in size, extent or appearance. 2 COLLOQ excellent; admirable. ■ **magnificence** N. ■ **magnificently** ADV.

magnify VB (*-ies, -ied*) 1 to make something appear larger, eg by using a microscope or telescope. 2 to exaggerate something.

magnifying glass N a convex lens through which objects appear larger.

magniloquent ADJ of speech: in a grand or pompous style. ■ **magniloquence** N.

magnitude N 1 importance or extent. 2 physical size; largeness. 3 ASTRON the degree of brightness of a star.

magnolia N 1 a a tree or shrub with large sweet-smelling usu white or pink flowers; b one of its flowers. 2 a very pale, pinkish-white or beige colour.

magnum N a wine bottle that holds approx 1.5 litres or twice the amount of a standard bottle.

magpie N 1 a black-and-white bird of the crow family, known for its habit of collecting shiny objects. 2 a person who collects small objects.

magus N (*magi*) (usu **the Magi**) CHRISTIANITY the three wise men who brought gifts to the infant Jesus, guided by a star.

maharajah or **maharaja** N, HIST an Indian prince.

maharani or **maharanee** N 1 the wife or widow of a maharajah. 2 a woman of the same rank as a maharajah in her own right.

maharishi N a Hindu religious teacher or spiritual leader.

mahatma N a wise and holy Hindu leader.

mah-jong or **mah-jongg** N an old game of Chinese origin, usu played by four players using a set of 144 small patterned tiles.

mahogany N (*-ies*) 1 a tall evergreen tropical tree. 2 the hard wood of this tree. 3 the colour of the wood, a dark reddish-brown. ➤ ADJ 1 made from this wood. 2 dark reddish-brown.

mahout N someone who drives, trains and looks after elephants.

maid N 1 a female servant. 2 LITERARY & OLD USE an unmarried woman.

maiden N 1 LITERARY a young, unmarried woman. 2 LITERARY a virgin. 3 HORSE-RACING a horse that has never won a race. 4 CRICKET an over from which no runs are scored. ➤ ADJ 1 first ever: **maiden voyage**. 2 unmarried: **maiden aunt**. ■ **maidenly** ADJ.

maidenhair N a fern with delicate, fan-shaped leaves.

maiden name N the surname of a married woman at birth, ie before she married.

maid of honour N (*maids of honour*) the principal bridesmaid at a wedding.

maidservant N, OLD USE a female servant.

mail[1] N 1 the postal system. 2 letters, parcels, etc sent by post. 3 a single collection or delivery of letters, etc. 4 same as **e-mail**. ➤ VB, esp N AMER to send (a letter, etc) by post.

mail[2] N flexible armour made of small linked metal rings. Also called **chainmail**.

mailbox N 1 esp N AMER a letterbox or postbox. 2 COMP a facility that allows electronic mail from one user to be stored in the file of another.

mailman N, esp N AMER a postman.

mail order N a system of buying and selling goods by post.

mailshot N an unrequested item sent by post, esp a piece of advertising material.

maim VB to wound (a person or animal) seriously, esp to disable or cripple them.

main ADJ most important; chief; leading.

➢ N **1** (often **the mains**) the chief pipe, conduit or cable in a branching system: **not connected to the mains. 2** (usu **the mains**) chiefly BRIT the network by which power, water, etc is distributed. **3** (always **mains**) AS ADJ relating to the mains (senses 1 and 2): **mains supply.**
◆ **in the main** on the whole.

mainbrace N, NAUT the rope controlling the movement of a ship's mainsail.

mainframe N, COMP a large powerful computer that is capable of handling very large amounts of data at high speed.

mainland N (esp **the mainland**) a country's principal mass of land, as distinct from its nearby islands. **Also** AS ADJ: **mainland Britain.**

mainline VB, TR & INTR, SLANG to inject (a drug) into a principal vein.

main line N **1** the principal railway line between two places. **2** US a principal route, road, etc. **3** SLANG a major vein.

mainly ADV chiefly; for the most part; largely.

mainmast N, NAUT the principal mast of a sailing ship.

mainsail N, NAUT the largest and lowest sail on a sailing ship.

mainspring N **1** the chief spring in a watch or clock, or other piece of machinery, that gives it motion. **2** a chief motive, reason or cause.

mainstay N **1** NAUT a rope stretching forward and down from the top of the mainmast. **2** a chief support.

mainstream N the chief trend, or direction of development, in any activity, business, etc.
➢ ADJ **1** of or relating to the mainstream. **2** in accordance with what is normal or standard.

maintain VB **1** to continue; to keep something in existence. **2** to keep something in good condition. **3** to pay the expenses of someone or something. **4** to affirm or assert (eg an opinion, one's innocence, etc).

maintenance N **1** the process of keeping something in good condition. **2** money paid by one person to support another, eg money paid

to an ex-wife and/or children, following a divorce. **3** the process of continuing something or keeping it in existence.

maisonette or **maisonnette** N a flat within a larger block, esp one on two floors.

maître d' N the manager or head waiter of a hotel or restaurant.

maize N **1** a tall cereal plant, grown for its edible yellow grain which grows in large spikes called corncobs. **2** the grain of this plant, eaten as a vegetable (sweetcorn).

majestic ADJ stately, dignified or grand in manner, style, appearance, etc.

majesty N (*-ies*) **1** great and impressive dignity, sovereign power or authority. **2** splendour; grandeur. **3 His, Her** or **Your Majesty** the title used when speaking of or to a king or queen.

majolica N colourfully glazed earthenware.

major ADJ **1** great, or greater, in number, size, extent, value, importance, etc. **2** MUS **a** of a scale: having two full tones between the first and third notes; **b** of a key, chord, etc: based on such a scale.
➢ N **1 a** an officer in the army; **b** an officer who is in charge of a military band: **pipe major. 2** MUS a major key, chord or scale. **3** esp N AMER **a** a student's main or special subject of study; **b** a student studying such a subject. **4** someone who has reached the age of full legal responsibility.
➢ VB, INTR (always **major in sth**) esp US to specialize in (a particular subject of study).

major-domo N a chief servant or steward in charge of the management of a household.

majorette N a member of a group of girls who march in parades, performing elaborate displays of baton-twirling, etc.

majority N (*-ies*) **1** the greater number; the largest group. **2** the difference between the greater and the lesser number. **3** the winning margin of votes in an election. **4** the age at which someone legally becomes an adult.

make VB (*made*) **1** to form, create, manufacture

or produce something by combining or shaping materials: **make the tea**. **2** to cause, bring about or create something by one's actions, etc: **make trouble**. **3** to force, induce or cause someone to do something: **He makes me laugh**. **4** to cause to change into something else; to transform or convert: **make grass into hay**. **5** to cause something or someone to be, do or become a specified thing: **made me cross**. **6** to be capable of turning or developing into (a specified thing); to have the appropriate qualities for something: **This box makes a good table**. **7** to appoint somebody as something: **They made her deputy head**. **8** to cause to appear to be, or to represent as being (a specified thing): **Long hair makes her look younger**. **9** to gain, earn or acquire something: **makes £400 a week**. **10** to add up to or amount to something; to constitute: **4 and 4 makes 8**. **11** to calculate, judge or estimate something to be (a specified thing): **I make it three o'clock**. **12** to arrive at or reach something, or to succeed in doing so: **can't make the party**. **13** to score or win (points, runs, card tricks, etc). **14** to tidy (a bed) after use. **15** to bring about or ensure the success of something; to cap or complete something: **It made my day**. **16** to propose something or propose something to someone: **make me an offer**. **17** to perform, carry out or produce something: **make a speech**.
➤ N a manufacturer's brand: **What make of car is it?** ■ **maker** N.
◆ **make do** COLLOQ to manage or get by.
◆ **make do with sth** COLLOQ to manage with a second or inferior choice.
◆ **make for sth** or **sb** to go towards it or them, esp rapidly, purposefully or suddenly.
◆ **make it** COLLOQ **1** to be successful: **make it in show business**. **2** to survive.
◆ **make it up to sb** to compensate or repay them for difficulties one has caused them or kindness which they have shown to one.
◆ **make of sth** or **sb** to understand by it or them: **What do you make of their comments?**
◆ **make off** to leave, esp in a hurry or secretly.
◆ **make off** or **away with sth** or **sb** to run off with it or them; to steal or kidnap it or them.
◆ **make out 1** COLLOQ to progress or get

along: **How did you make out in the exam?** **2** COLLOQ, chiefly N AMER to manage, succeed or survive: **It's been tough, but we'll make out**.
◆ **make out sth** or **that sth** to pretend or claim that it is so: **He made out that he was ill**.
◆ **make out sth** or **make sth out 1** to begin to discern it, esp to see or hear it. **2** to fill in a document, etc: **made out a cheque for £20**.
◆ **make sth** or **sb out to be sth** to portray them, or cause them to seem to be, what they are not: **They made us out to be liars**.
◆ **make over sth** or **make sth over** to transfer ownership of it: **made over my shares to her when I retired**.
◆ **make up for sth** to compensate or serve as an apology for it.
◆ **make up to sb** COLLOQ to seek their friendship or favour.
◆ **make up with sb** to resolve a disagreement with someone.
◆ **make sth up 1** to fabricate or invent it: **made up the story**. **2** to prepare or assemble it: **made up a food parcel**. **3** to constitute it; to be the parts of it: **The three villages together make up a district**. **4** to complete something: **make up our quota**.

make-believe N pretence.
➤ ADJ pretended; imaginary.

makeover N **1** a complete change in a person's style of dress, appearance, make-up, hair, etc. **2** a remake or reconstruction.

makeshift ADJ serving as a less adequate substitute for something: **a makeshift bed**.

make-up N **1** cosmetics applied to the face, esp by women or actors. **2** the combination of characteristics or ingredients that form something: **Greed is not in his make-up**.

making N.
◆ **be the making of sb** to ensure their success.
◆ **in the making** in the process of being made, formed or developed.

makings PL N.
◆ **have the makings of sth** to have the ability to become a specified thing.

malachite N, GEOL a bright green copper

mineral used as a gemstone.

maladjusted ADJ psychologically unable to deal with everyday situations and relationships. ■ **maladjustment** N.

maladminister VB to manage (eg public affairs) badly, dishonestly or incompetently. ■ **maladministration** N.

maladroit ADJ, rather FORMAL clumsy; tactless; unskilful. ■ **maladroitness** N.

malady N (*-ies*) an illness or disease.

malaise N a feeling of uneasiness, discontent, general depression or despondency.

malapropism N the unintentional misuse of a word, usu with comic effect, through confusion with another word that sounds similar.

malaria N an infectious disease that produces recurring bouts of fever, caused by the bite of the mosquito. ■ **malarial** ADJ.

malarkey or **malarky** N, COLLOQ nonsense; rubbish; absurd behaviour or talk.

malcontent N a dissatisfied person.

male ADJ **1** denoting the sex that produces sperm and fertilizes the egg cell produced by the female. **2** denoting the reproductive structure of a plant that produces the male gamete. **3** of or characteristic of men; masculine: **male hormones. 4** for or made up of men or boys: **male college.**
➤ N a male person, animal or plant.

male chauvinist N, DEROG a man who believes in the superiority of men over women. ■ **male chauvinism** N.

malediction N, LITERARY OR FORMAL a curse or defamation.

malefactor N, LITERARY OR FORMAL a criminal; an evil-doer or wrongdoer.

malevolent ADJ wishing to do evil to others; malicious. ■ **malevolence** N.

malfeasance N, LAW wrongdoing; the committing of an unlawful act, esp by a public official. ■ **malfeasant** ADJ.

malformation N **1** the state or condition of

being badly or wrongly formed or shaped. **2** a badly or wrongly formed part.

malfunction VB, INTR to work imperfectly; to fail to work.
➤ N failure of, or a fault or failure in, the operation of a machine, etc.

malice N the desire or intention to harm or hurt another or others. ■ **malicious** ADJ.

malign VB to say or write bad or unpleasant things about someone, esp falsely or spitefully.
➤ ADJ of a person: evil in nature or influence.

malignant ADJ **1** of a person: feeling or showing hatred or the desire to do harm to another or others; malicious. **2** MED esp of a cancerous tumour: of a type that destroys the surrounding tissue and may spread elsewhere. ■ **malignancy** N.

malinger VB, INTR to pretend to be ill, esp in order to avoid work. ■ **malingerer** N.

mall N a shopping centre, street or area, etc with shops, that is closed to vehicles.

mallard N (*mallard* or *mallards*) a common wild duck, the male of which has a green head.

malleable ADJ **1** of certain metals and alloys, etc: able to be beaten into a different shape, etc without breaking. **2** easily influenced.

mallet N **1** a hammer with a large head. **2** in croquet, polo, etc: a long-handled wooden hammer used to strike the ball.

mallow N a plant with pink, purple or white flowers.

malnourished ADJ suffering from malnutrition.

malnutrition N, MED a disorder resulting from inadequate food intake, an unbalanced diet or inability to absorb nutrients from food.

malodorous ADJ, FORMAL foul-smelling.

malpractice N, LAW improper, careless, illegal or unethical professional conduct.

malt N **1** BREWING a mixture prepared from barley or wheat grains that have been soaked in water, allowed to sprout and then

dried in a kiln. **2** malt whisky.
➤ VB to make (a grain) into malt. ■ **malted** ADJ.
■ **malty** ADJ.

maltreat VB to treat someone or something roughly or cruelly. ■ **maltreatment** N.

malt whisky N whisky made entirely from malted barley.

mama or (chiefly US) **mamma** and **mammy** N (*mamas, mammas* or *mammies*) rather DATED mother.

mamba N a large, poisonous, black or green African snake.

mambo N **1** a rhythmic Latin-American dance resembling the rumba. **2** music for this dance.

mammal N, ZOOL any warm-blooded, vertebrate animal having, in the female, mammary glands which secrete milk to feed its young. ■ **mammalian** ADJ.

mammary ADJ, BIOL, MED of or relating to the breasts or other milk-producing glands.

mammography N, MED the process of X-raying the breast (called a **mammograph** or **mammogram**).

mammon N, chiefly LITERARY wealth when considered as the source of evil and immorality.

mammoth N an extinct shaggy-haired, prehistoric elephant, with long curved tusks.
➤ ADJ huge; giant-sized.

man N (*men*) **1** an adult male human being. **2** human beings as a whole or as a genus; the human race: **when man first walked the Earth**. **3** any subspecies of, or type of creature belonging to, the human genus **Homo. 4** a person: **the right man for the job. 5** in various board games: one of the movable pieces.
➤ VB (-*nn*-) to provide (eg a ship, industrial plant, fortress, etc) with men, ie workers, operators, defenders.

manacle N a handcuff; a shackle for the hand or wrist.
➤ VB to restrain someone with manacles.

manage VB **1** to be in overall control or charge of, or the manager of, something or someone.

2 to deal with something successfully or competently: **I can manage my own affairs.** **3** TR & INTR to succeed in doing or producing something: **Can you manage the food if I organize the drink? 4** to have, or to be able to find, enough room, time, etc for something: **Can you manage another sandwich?**
■ **manageable** ADJ.

management N **1** the skill or practice of controlling, directing or planning something. **2** the managers of a company, etc, as a group. **3** manner of directing or using something.

manager N **1** someone who manages a commercial enterprise, organization, project, etc. **2** someone who manages esp actors, musicians, sportsmen and sportswomen, or a particular team, etc. ■ **managerial** ADJ.

manageress N a female manager of a business, etc.

managing director N a director in overall charge of an organization and its day-to-day running.

man-at-arms N (*men-at-arms*) HIST a soldier, esp a heavily-armed, mounted soldier.

manatee N a large plant-eating marine mammal of tropical waters.

mandarin N **1** (also **mandarin orange**) a small citrus fruit, similar to the tangerine. **2** a high-ranking official or bureaucrat, esp one who is thought to be outside political control. **3** HIST a senior official belonging to any of the nine ranks of officials in the Chinese Empire.

mandate N a right or authorization given to a nation, person, etc to act on behalf of others.
➤ VB **1** to give authority or power to someone or something. **2** to assign (territory) to a nation under a mandate.

mandatory ADJ **1** not allowing any choice; compulsory. **2** referring to the nature of, or containing, a mandate or command.

mandible N, ZOOL **1** the lower jaw of a vertebrate. **2** the upper or lower part of a bird's beak. **3** one of a pair of jawlike mouthparts in insects, crustaceans, etc.

mandolin or **mandoline** N a musical instrument with eight metal strings tuned in pairs.

mandrake N a plant with a forked root, formerly thought to have magical powers.

mandrel or **mandril** N the rotating shaft on a lathe or the axle of a circular saw.

mandrill N a large W African baboon with distinctive red and blue striped markings.

mane N 1 on a horse, lion or other animal: the long hair growing from and around the neck. 2 on a human: a long, thick head of hair.

maneuver, **maneuvered**, etc the N AMER spellings of **manoeuvre**, etc.

man Friday N (*man Fridays*) a faithful or devoted manservant or male assistant.

manful ADJ brave and determined. ■ **manfully** ADV.

manganese N, CHEM a hard brittle pinkish–grey metallic element, used to make alloys.

mange N, VET MED a skin disease that affects hairy animals such as cats and dogs, causing itching and loss of hair. ■ **mangy** ADJ.

mangel-wurzel N a variety of beet with a large yellow root, used as cattle food.

manger N an open box or trough from which cattle or horses feed.

mangetout N a variety of garden pea with an edible pod.

mangle[1] VB 1 to damage or destroy something or someone by cutting, crushing, tearing, etc. 2 to spoil, ruin or bungle something.

mangle[2] N, DATED a device consisting of two large heavy rotating rollers which have wet laundry fed between them so as to squeeze most of the water out.

mango N (**-os** or **-oes**) a heavy fruit with a central stone surrounded by sweet, soft orange flesh and a thick, green, yellow or red skin.

mangrove N a tropical evergreen tree that grows in salt marshes and on mudflats.

manhandle VB 1 to treat someone or something roughly; to push or shove them or it.

2 to move or transport something using manpower, not machinery.

manhole N an opening large enough to allow a person through, esp an access to a sewer.

manhood N the state of being an adult male.

man-hour N a unit of work equal to the work done by one person in one hour.

manhunt N an intensive organized search for someone, esp a criminal or fugitive.

mania N 1 PSYCHOL a mental disorder characterized by great excitement or euphoria and violence. 2 LOOSELY a craze or obsession.

maniac N 1 COLLOQ a person who behaves wildly. 2 an extremely keen enthusiast.

manic ADJ 1 PSYCHOL characteristic of, relating to or suffering from mania. 2 COLLOQ very energetic or active. ■ **manically** ADV.

manic-depressive ADJ, PSYCHIATRY affected by an illness which produces phases of extreme elation and severe depression.

manicure N the care and cosmetic treatment of the hands, esp the fingernails. ➤ VB to carry out a manicure on.

manifest VB, FORMAL 1 to show or display something clearly. 2 (usu **manifest itself**) to reveal or declare itself. ➤ ADJ easily seen; obvious: a manifest lie. ➤ N 1 a customs document that gives details of a ship or aircraft, its cargo and destination. 2 a passenger list, for an aeroplane, etc. ■ **manifestation** N. ■ **manifestly** ADV.

manifesto N (**-os** or **-oes**) a written public declaration of policies, intentions, opinions etc, esp one by a political party or candidate.

manifold ADJ, FORMAL OR LITERARY many and various: manifold pleasures.

manikin N 1 a model of the human body. 2 OLD USE an abnormally small person.

manila or **manilla** N a type of thick strong brown paper.

manipulate VB 1 to handle something, or move or work it with the hands, esp in a skilful

way. **2** to control or influence someone or something cleverly and unscrupulously, esp to one's own advantage. **3** to give false appearance to something, etc.
■ **manipulation** N. ■ **manipulative** ADJ.

mankind N **1** human beings collectively. **2** human males collectively.

manly ADJ (**-ier, -iest**) **1** displaying qualities considered admirable in a man, such as strength, determination, courage, etc. **2** considered suitable for or characteristic of a man. ■ **manliness** N.

man-made ADJ made by humans.

manna N **1** in the Old Testament: the food provided by God for the Israelites in the wilderness. **2** any unexpected gift or windfall.

manned ADJ of a ship, machine, spacecraft, etc: provided with men, operators, crew, etc.

mannequin N **1** a fashion model, esp a woman, employed to model clothes, etc. **2** a life-size dummy of the human body, used in the making or displaying of clothes.

manner N **1** way; fashion: **an unusual manner of walking. 2** (often **manners**) behaviour towards others: **has a very pleasant manner. 3** (**manners**) good or polite social behaviour. **4** FORMAL kind or kinds: **all manner of things**.

mannered ADJ, FORMAL **1** USU DEROG unnatural; affected. **2** IN COMPOUNDS displaying a specified kind of behaviour: **bad-mannered**.

mannerism N **1** an individual characteristic, such as a gesture or facial expression. **2** DEROG esp in art or literature: noticeable or excessive use of an individual or mannered style.

mannerly ADJ, OLD USE polite; showing good manners. ■ **mannerliness** N.

mannish ADJ of a woman: having an appearance more typical of a man.

manoeuvre or (N AMER) **maneuver** N **1** a movement requiring, or performed with, skill or intelligence. **2** a clever or skilful handling of affairs, often one involving deception or inventiveness. **3** MIL, NAVY **a** (usu **manoeuvres**) a large-scale battle-training exercise by

armed forces; **b** a skilful or clever tactical movement of troops or ships, etc.
➤ VB **1** TR & INTR to move something accurately and with skill. **2** TR & INTR to use ingenuity in handling something or someone.
■ **manoeuvrable** ADJ.

man-of-war or **man-o'-war** N, HIST an armed sailing ship used as a warship.

manor N **1** (also **manor-house**) the principal residence on a country estate. **2** HIST in medieval Europe: an area of land under the control of a lord. **3** BRIT, COLLOQ the area in which a particular person or group, esp a police unit or a criminal, operates.

manpower N the number of available employees or people fit and ready to work.

manqué ADJ, FOLLOWING ITS NOUN, LITERARY having once had the ambition or potential to be a specified kind of person, without achieving it; unfulfilled: **an artist manqué**.

mansard N, ARCHIT a four-sided roof, each side of which is in two parts, the lower part sloping more steeply.

manse N esp in Scotland: the house of a religious minister.

manservant N (**menservants**) OLD USE a male servant, esp a valet.

mansion N **1** a large house, usu a grand one. **2** (**mansions** or **Mansions**) BRIT a large building divided into luxury apartments.

manslaughter N, LAW the crime of homicide without premeditation, eg as a result of provocation or diminished responsibility.

mantel N, chiefly OLD USE a mantelpiece.

mantelpiece N the ornamental frame around a fireplace.

mantilla N a scarf worn by women over the hair and shoulders, esp in Spain.

mantis N (**mantises** or **mantes**) a tropical insect-eating insect that sits in wait for prey with its two front legs raised. Also called **praying mantis**.

mantle N **1** a cloak or loose outer garment.

2 LITERARY a covering. **3** GEOL the part of the Earth between the crust and the core. **4** a fireproof mesh around a gas or oil lamp, that glows when the lamp is lit. **5** LITERARY a position of responsibility.
➤ VB, LITERARY to cover, conceal or obscure.

man-to-man ADJ open and frank.
➤ ADV in an open and frank manner; honestly.

mantra N, HINDUISM, BUDDHISM a sacred phrase, word or sound chanted repeatedly as part of meditation and prayer.

manual ADJ **1** of or relating to the hand or hands: **manual skill**. **2** using the body, rather than the mind. **3** operated by hand.
➤ N **1** a book of instructions, eg for repairing a car or operating a machine. **2** an organ keyboard or a key played by hand not by foot.

manufacture VB **1** to make something from raw materials, esp in large quantities using machinery. **2** to invent or fabricate something.
➤ N **1** the practice, act or process of manufacturing something. **2** anything manufactured. ■ **manufacturer** N.
■ **manufacturing** ADJ, N.

manumit VB (-*tt*-) FORMAL to release (a person) from slavery; to set someone free.
■ **manumission** N.

manure N any substance, esp animal dung, used on soil as a fertilizer.
➤ VB to apply manure to (land, soil, etc).

manuscript N **1** an author's handwritten or typed version of a book, play, etc. **2** a book or document written by hand.

many ADJ (*more, most*) **1** (sometimes **a great many** or **good many**) consisting of a large number; numerous: **Many teenagers smoke**. **2** (**the many**) the majority or the crowd; ordinary people, not nobility or royalty.
➤ PRONOUN a great number: **The sweets were so rich that I couldn't eat many**.

map N **1** a diagram of any part of the Earth's surface, showing geographical and other features. **2** a similar diagram of the surface of the Moon or a planet. **3** a diagram showing the position of the stars in the sky. **4** a diagram of the layout of anything.
➤ VB (-*pp*-) to make a map of something.
◆ **map sth out** to plan (a route, course of action, etc) in detail.
◆ **put sth** or **sb on the map** COLLOQ to cause to become well-known or important.

maple N **1** (also **maple tree**) a broad-leaved deciduous tree of northern regions whose seeds float by means of winglike growths. **2** its hard light-coloured wood.

marabou N **1** a large black-and-white African stork. **2** its feathers.

maraca N a hand-held percussion instrument, usu one of a pair, consisting of a gourd filled with dried beans, pebbles, etc.

maraschino N a liqueur made from cherries.

marathon N **1** (sometimes **marathon race**) a long-distance race on foot, usu 42.195 kilometres. **2** any lengthy and difficult task.
➤ ADJ **1** of or relating to a marathon race. **2** requiring or displaying great powers of endurance or stamina: **a marathon effort**.

maraud VB **1** INTR to wander in search of people to attack and property to steal or destroy. **2** to plunder (a place). ■ **marauder** N. ■ **marauding** ADJ, N.

marble N **1** a GEOL a hard, metamorphic rock, white when pure but usu mottled or streaked; **b** any such rock that can be highly polished, used in building and sculpture. **2** in children's games: a small hard ball, now usu made of glass, but orig made of marble.
➤ VB to stain or paint something (esp paper) to resemble marble.

marbles SING N any of several children's games played with marbles.

marc N **1** TECHNICAL the leftover skins and stems of grapes used in winemaking. **2** a kind of brandy made from these.

marcasite N **1** GEOL a pale yellow mineral, a compound of iron, formerly used in jewellery. **2** a polished gemstone made from this.

March N the third month of the year.

march[1] VB **1** INTR to walk in a stiff, upright, formal

manner, usu at a brisk pace. **2** to make or force someone, esp a soldier or troop of soldiers, to walk in this way. **3** INTR to walk in a purposeful way. **4** INTR to advance or continue, steadily or irresistibly: **events marched on**.
➤ N **1** an act of marching. **2** a distance travelled by marching. **3** a brisk walking pace. **4** a procession of people moving steadily forward. **5** MUS a piece of music written in a marching rhythm. **6** steady and unstoppable progress or movement: **the march of time**.

march² N **1** a border. **2** a border district.

marchioness N **1** the wife or widow of a marquis. **2** a woman who holds the rank of marquis in her own right.

mare N an adult female horse, ass, zebra, etc.

mare's nest N a discovery that proves to be untrue or without value; a hoax.

margarine N a food, usu made from vegetable oils with water, flavourings, colourings, etc, used as a substitute for butter.

margin N **1** the blank space around a page of writing or print. **2** any edge, border or fringe. **3** an extra amount, eg of time or money, beyond what should strictly be needed. **4** an amount by which one thing exceeds another: **win by a large margin**. **5** BUSINESS the difference between the selling and buying price; profit.

marginal ADJ **1** small and unimportant or insignificant. **2** near to the lower limit; barely sufficient. **3** chiefly BRIT of a political constituency: whose current MP or other representative was elected by only a small majority of votes at the last election. **4** of a note, mark, design, etc: appearing in the margin of a page of text. **5** in, on, or of a margin.
➤ N, chiefly BRIT a marginal constituency or seat. ■ **marginality** N. ■ **marginally** ADV.

marginalize or **-ise** VB to push something or someone to the edges of anything, in order to reduce its or their effect, relevance, significance, etc. ■ **marginalization** N.

marigold N a plant with bright orange or yellow flowers and strongly-scented leaves.

marijuana or **marihuana** N cannabis.

marimba N a type of xylophone consisting of hardwood strips which, when struck with hammers, vibrate metal plates underneath.

marina N a harbour for berthing private pleasure boats.

marinade N, COOKERY any liquid mixture, esp a mixture of oil, herbs, spices, vinegar or wine, etc, in which food is soaked before cooking.
➤ VB, TR & INTR to soak (meat or fish, etc) in a marinade. Also called **marinate**.

marine ADJ **1** of or concerned with the sea: **marine landscape**. **2** inhabiting, found in or obtained from the sea: **marine mammal**. **3** of or relating to ships, shipping trade or the navy: **marine insurance**.
➤ N (often **Marine**) **a** a soldier trained to serve on land or at sea; **b** a member of the Royal Marines or the US Marine Corps.

mariner N a seaman.

marionette N a puppet with jointed limbs moved by strings.

marital ADJ belonging or relating to marriage: **marital status**. ■ **maritally** ADV.

maritime ADJ **1** of or relating to the sea or ships, sea-trade, etc: **maritime communications**. **2** of plants, etc: living or growing near the sea.

marjoram N (in full **wild marjoram**) a pungent plant used to season food, esp pasta dishes. Also called **oregano**.

mark N **1** a visible blemish, such as a scratch or stain. **2** a grade or score awarded according to the proficiency of a student or competitor, etc. **3** a sign or symbol: **a question mark**. **4** an indication or representation: **a mark of respect**. **5** the position from which a competitor starts in a race. **6** a target or goal: **It fell wide of the mark**. **7** a required or normal standard: **up to the mark**. **8** an impression, characteristic or influence: **Your work bears his mark**.
➤ VB **1** TR & INTR to spoil something with, or become spoiled by, a mark. **2 a** to read, correct and award (a grade) to a piece of written work, etc; **b** to allot a score to someone or something. **3** to show; to be a sign of something: **events marking a new era**. **4** to pay

close attention to something: **mark my words.**
5 SPORT to stay close to (an opposing player) in order to try and prevent them from getting or passing the ball. **6** to characterize or label: **This incident marks him as a criminal.**
◆ **make** or **leave one's mark** to make a strong or permanent impression.
◆ **mark sth down 1** to reduce its price: a jacket marked down from £75 to £55.
2 to note or record it.
◆ **mark time** merely to keep things going, without making progress or speeding up.
◆ **mark sth up** to increase its price; to make a profit for the seller on it.
◆ **off the mark 1** not on target; off the subject or target. **2** of an athlete, etc: getting away from the mark in a race, etc: **slow off the mark.**
◆ **on your marks** or **mark** ATHLETICS said to the runners before a race begins: get into your position, ready for the starting signal.

marked ADJ **1** obvious or noticeable: a marked change. **2** of a person: watched with suspicion; selected as the target for an attack: a marked man. ■ **markedly** ADV.

marker N **1** a pen with a thick point. Also called **marker pen. 2** anything used to mark the position of something.

market N **1** a gathering of people that takes place periodically, where stalls, etc are set up allowing them to buy and sell a variety of goods or a specified type of goods. **2** a public place, square, building, etc in which this regularly takes place. **3** a particular region, country or section of the population, considered as a potential customer. **4** buying and selling; a level of trading: **The market is slow. 5** opportunity for buying and selling; demand: **no market for these goods. 6** esp N AMER a shop or supermarket.
➢ VB **1** to offer something for sale; to promote (goods, etc). **2** INTR to trade or deal, esp at a market. **3** INTR, esp US to shop; to buy provisions.
◆ **on the market** on sale; able to be bought.

marketeer N, ECON someone involved with a particular market: **black marketeer.**

market garden N an area of land, usu near a large town or city, used commercially to grow produce, esp vegetables, salad crops, etc.

marketing N, BUSINESS the techniques or processes by which a product or service is sold, including responsibility for its promotion, distribution and development.

market-place N **1** the open space in a town, etc in which a market is held. **2** (**the market-place**) the commercial world of buying and selling.

market research N analysis of the habits, needs and preferences of customers.

market town N a town, often at the centre of a farming area, where a market is held regularly, usu on the same day every week.

marking N (often **markings**) a distinctive pattern of colours on an animal or plant.

marksman N someone who can shoot a gun accurately. ■ **marksmanship** N.

mark-up N, COMMERCE an increase in price, esp in determining level of profit.

marl N, GEOL a mixture of clay and limestone.

marlin N (*marlin* or *marlins*) a large fish found in warm and tropical seas which has a long spear-like upper jaw. Also called **spearfish.**

marlinspike N, NAUT a pointed metal tool for separating the strands of rope to be spliced.

marmalade N jam made from the pulp and rind of any citrus fruit, esp oranges.

marmoreal ADJ, FORMAL OR LITERARY like marble or made of marble.

marmoset N a S American monkey with a long bushy tail and tufts of hair around the ears.

marmot N a stout, coarse-haired, burrowing rodent of Europe, Asia and N America.

maroon[1] N a dark brownish-red or purplish-red colour.

maroon[2] VB **1** to leave someone in isolation in a deserted place, esp on a desert island. **2** to leave someone helpless or without support.

marque N a brand or make.

marquee N a very large tent used for circuses, parties, etc.

marquess N, BRIT a member of the nobility.

marquetry N (-ies) the art or practice of making decorative patterns out of pieces of different-coloured woods, ivory, etc.

marquis N (*marquis* or *marquises*) in various European countries: a nobleman next in rank above a count.

marquise N 1 in various European countries: a marchioness. 2 a gemstone cut to form a pointed oval.

marram grass N a coarse grass that grows on sandy shores.

marriage N 1 the state or relationship of being husband and wife. 2 the act, or legal contract, of becoming husband and wife. 3 a wedding. 4 a joining together; a union.

marriageable ADJ of a woman, or sometimes a man: suitable for or of the legal age for marriage. ■ **marriageability** N.

married ADJ 1 having a husband or wife. 2 belonging or relating to marriage: **married life**. 3 (esp **married to sth**) joined inseparably or intimately to it: **He's married to his work**.

marrow N 1 (also **bone marrow**) the soft tissue that fills the internal cavities of bones. 2 (also **vegetable marrow**) **a** a plant with large prickly leaves, cultivated worldwide for its large, oblong, edible fruit; **b** the fruit of this plant which has soft white flesh, and is cooked as a vegetable.

marrowfat pea N 1 a variety of large, edible pea. 2 the plant that bears it.

marry VB (-ies, -ied) 1 to take someone as one's husband or wife. 2 to perform the ceremony of marriage between two people: **My uncle married us**. 3 INTR to become joined in marriage: **We married last June**. 4 INTR (also **marry sth up**) to fit together, join up, or match (usu two things) correctly.
◆ **marry sb off** COLLOQ to find a husband or wife for them.

Mars N, ASTRON the fourth planet from the Sun, and the nearest planet to the Earth.

marsh N a poorly-drained, low-lying, often flooded area of land. ■ **marshland** N. ■ **marshy** ADJ.

marshal N 1 (often **Marshal**) IN COMPOUNDS **a** a high-ranking officer in the armed forces: **Air Vice-Marshal**; **b** BRIT a high-ranking officer of State: **Earl Marshal**. 2 an official who organizes parades etc, or controls crowds at large public events. 3 US in some states: a chief police or fire officer.
➤ VB (-ll-; US -l-) 1 to arrange (troops, competitors, facts, etc) in order. 2 to direct, lead or show the way to (a crowd, procession, etc), esp in a formal or precise way.

marshalling-yard N a place where railway wagons are arranged into trains.

marsh gas N methane.

marshmallow N a spongy sweet.

marsupial N, ZOOL a mammal, such as the kangaroo or koala, in which the young is carried and suckled in an external pouch on the mother's body until more mature.
➤ ADJ of or like a marsupial.

mart N a trading place; a market or auction.

martello tower N a small circular fortified tower used for coastal defence.

marten N 1 a small, tree-dwelling, predatory mammal with a long thin body and a bushy tail. 2 its soft black or brown fur.

martial ADJ belonging or relating to, or suitable for, war or the military; warlike; militant.

martial art N a fighting sport or self-defence technique of Far Eastern origin.

martial law N law and order strictly enforced by the military powers.

Martian ADJ of or relating to the planet Mars.

martin N a small bird of the swallow family, with a square or slightly forked tail.

martinet N a strict disciplinarian.

martingale N a strap passed between a

horse's forelegs and fastened to the head harness, used to keep the horse's head down.

martini N a cocktail of gin and vermouth.

martyr N **1** someone who chooses to be put to death, rather than abandon his or her religious beliefs. **2** someone who suffers or dies, esp for their beliefs, or for a particular cause. **3** (usu **a martyr to sth**) COLLOQ someone who suffers greatly on account of something: **a martyr to arthritis**.
➤ VB to put someone to death as a martyr.
■ **martyrdom** N.

marvel VB (**-ll-**; US **-l-**) INTR (esp **marvel at sth**) to be filled with astonishment or wonder.
➤ N an astonishing or wonderful person or thing; a wonder.

marvellous or (US) **marvelous** ADJ **1** so wonderful or astonishing as to be almost beyond belief. **2** COLLOQ excellent; extremely pleasing. ■ **marvellously** ADV.

marzipan N a sweet paste made of ground almonds, sugar and egg whites.

masala N, COOKERY **1** a blend of spices ground into a powder or paste used in Indian cookery. **2** a dish using this: **chicken tikka masala**.

mascara N a cosmetic for lengthening and thickening the eyelashes, applied with a brush.

mascarpone N a soft Italian cream cheese.

mascot N a person, animal or thing thought to bring good luck and adopted for this purpose by a person, team, etc.

masculine ADJ **1** belonging to, typical of, or suitable for a man or the male sex; male. **2** of a woman: mannish. ■ **masculinity** N.

maser N a device for increasing the strength of microwaves.

mash VB (also **mash sth up**) to beat or crush it into a pulpy mass.
➤ N **1** a boiled mixture of grain and water used to feed farm animals. **2** any soft or pulpy mass. **3** COLLOQ mashed potatoes.

mask N **1 a** any covering for the face or for part of the face, worn for protection or as a disguise:

Hallowe'en mask. **b** a covering for the mouth and nose, eg an oxygen mask or a surgical mask worn by surgeons. **2** anything that disguises the truth, eg false behaviour. **3** a moulded or sculpted cast of someone's face: **death-mask**. **4** a cosmetic face pack.
➤ VB **1** to put a mask on someone or something. **2** to disguise, conceal or cover. **3** to protect something with a mask.

masking tape N adhesive tape, used esp to cover the edges to be left unpainted.

masochism N **1** PSYCHOL the practice of deriving sexual pleasure from pain or humiliation inflicted by another person. **2** COLLOQ pleasure in one's own suffering. ■ **masochist** N. ■ **masochistic** ADJ.

mason N **1** a stonemason. **2** a Freemason. ■ **masonic** ADJ.

masonry N **1** stonework and brickwork. **2** the craft of a mason.

masque N, HIST a kind of entertainment performed to music by masked actors.

masquerade N **1** a pretence or false show. **2** a formal dance at which the guests wear masks and costumes.
➤ VB, INTR (esp **masquerade as sb** or **sth**) **1** to disguise oneself. **2** to pretend to be someone or something else.

mass[1] N **1** PHYS the amount of matter that an object contains, which is a measure of its inertia. **2** a large quantity, usu a shapeless quantity, gathered together; a lump. **3** (often **masses**) COLLOQ a large quantity or number: **masses of books**. **4** (usu **the mass of sth**) the majority or bulk of it. **5** TECHNICAL a measure of the quantity of matter in a body. **6** (**the masses**) ordinary people; the people as a whole.
➤ ADJ **a** involving a large number of people: **mass meeting**; **b** of or relating to a mass, or to large quantities or numbers: **mass production**.
➤ VB, chiefly INTR to gather or form in a large quantity or number.

mass[2] or **Mass** N **1** in the Roman Catholic and Orthodox Churches: **a** the Eucharist, a celebration of the Last Supper; **b** the ceremony in which this occurs. **2** a part of the Roman Catholic liturgy set to music and sung.

massacre N **1** a cruel and indiscriminate killing of large numbers of people or animals. **2** COLLOQ an overwhelming defeat.
➤ VB **1** to kill (people or animals) cruelly, indiscriminately and in large numbers. **2** COLLOQ to defeat (the opposition or enemy, etc) overwhelmingly.

massage N a technique of easing pain or stiffness in the body, esp the muscles, by rubbing, kneading and tapping with the hands.
➤ VB **1** to perform massage on someone. **2** to alter something (esp data) to produce a more favourable result.

masseur and **masseuse** N someone who is trained to carry out massage.

massif N, GEOL a mountainous plateau that differs from the surrounding lowland.

massive ADJ **1** very big, bulky, solid and heavy. **2** COLLOQ very large; of great size or power: a massive explosion. ■ **massively** ADV. ■ **massiveness** N.

mass market N, ECON the market for goods that have been mass–produced.

mass-produce VB to produce (goods, etc) in a standard form in great quantities. ■ **mass production** N.

mast[1] N any upright wooden or metal supporting pole, esp one carrying the sails of a ship, or a radio or television aerial.

mast[2] N the nuts of various forest trees, esp beech, oak and chestnut, used as food for pigs.

mastaba N, ARCHAEOL an ancient Egyptian tomb with sloping sides and a flat roof.

mastectomy N (-ies) SURGERY the surgical removal of a woman's breast.

master N **1** someone esp a man, who commands or controls. **2** the owner, esp a male owner, of a dog, slave, etc. **3** someone with outstanding skill in a particular activity, eg art. **4** a fully qualified craftsman or tradesman, allowed to train and direct others. **5** rather DATED a male teacher. **6** the commanding officer on a merchant ship. **7** (**Master**) a a degree of the level above bachelor. Usually called **Masters**; b someone who holds this degree: Master of Science. **8** (**Master**) a title for a boy too young to be called Mr.
➤ ADJ **1** fully qualified; highly skilled; expert: master craftsman. **2** main; principal: master bedroom. **3** controlling: master switch.
➤ VB **1** to overcome or defeat (eg feelings or an opponent). **2** to become skilled in something.

masterful ADJ showing the authority, skill or power of a master. ■ **masterfully** ADV.

masterly ADJ showing the skill of a master.

mastermind N **1** someone who has great intellectual ability. **2** the person responsible for devising a complex scheme or plan.
➤ VB to be the mastermind of (a scheme, etc); to originate, think out and direct something.

master of ceremonies N (*masters of ceremonies*) an announcer, esp one who announces the speakers at a formal dinner.

masterpiece N a skilful piece of work, esp the greatest work of an artist or writer.

mastery N (-*ies*) **1** (usu **mastery of sth**) great skill or knowledge in it. **2** (esp **mastery over sb** or **sth**) control over them or it.

masthead N **1** NAUT the top of a ship's mast. **2** JOURNALISM the title of a newspaper, etc, printed at the top of its front page.

mastic N **1** a gum obtained from a Mediterranean tree, used in making varnish. **2** a putty–like paste used as a filler.

masticate VB, TR & INTR, FORMAL OR TECHNICAL to chew (food). ■ **mastication** N.

mastiff N a large powerful breed of dog.

mastitis N inflammation of a woman's breast or an animal's udder.

mastodon N any of several, now extinct, mammals from which elephants are thought to have evolved.

mastoid ANAT, ADJ like a nipple or breast.
➤ N the raised area of bone behind the ear.

masturbate VB, TR & INTR to rub or stroke the

genitals of (oneself or someone else) so as to produce sexual arousal, usu to the point of orgasm or ejaculation. ■ **masturbation** N.

mat N 1 a flat piece of any carpet-like material, used as a decorative or protective floor-covering, for wiping shoes on to remove dirt, or absorbing impact on landing or falling in gymnastics, etc. 2 a smaller piece of fabric, or a harder material, used under a plate, vase, etc to protect a surface from heat or scratches. ➤ VB (*-tt-*) TR & INTR to become, or make something become, tangled or interwoven into a dense untidy mass. ■ **matted** ADJ.

matador N the principal toreador who kills the bull in bullfighting.

match[1] N 1 a formal contest or game. 2 (esp **a match for sb** or **sth**) a person or thing that is similar or identical to, or combines well with, another. 3 a person or thing able to equal, or surpass, another: **met his match**. 4 a partnership or pairing; a suitable partner. 5 a condition of exact agreement, compatibility or close resemblance. ➤ VB 1 TR & INTR (also **match up** or **match sth up**) to combine well; to be compatible or exactly alike. 2 to set (people or things) in competition; to hold them up in comparison. 3 to be equal to something: **cannot match the offer**. ■ **matching** ADJ.

match[2] N a short thin piece of wood or strip of card coated on the tip with a substance that ignites when rubbed against a rough surface.

matchless ADJ having no equal; superior to all.

matchmaker N someone who tries to arrange romantic partnerships or marriages between people. ■ **matchmaking** N, ADJ.

match play N, GOLF scoring according to holes won and lost.

matchstick N the stem of a wooden match.

mate N 1 an animal's breeding partner. 2 COLLOQ a person's sexual partner. 3 a COLLOQ a companion or friend; b used as a form of address, esp to a man: **alright, mate**. 4 IN COMPOUNDS a person someone shares something with: **workmate • flatmate**.

5 a tradesman's assistant: **plumber's mate**. 6 one of a pair. 7 NAUT any officer below the rank of master on a merchant ship: **first mate**. ➤ VB 1 INTR of animals: to copulate. 2 to bring (animals) together for breeding. 3 TR & INTR to marry. 4 to join (two things) as a pair.

material N 1 any substance out of which something is, or may be, made. 2 cloth; fabric. 3 (**materials**) instruments or tools needed for a particular activity or task. 4 information that provides the substance from which a book, TV programme, etc is prepared. 5 someone who is suitable for a specified occupation, training, etc: **He is management material**. ➤ ADJ 1 relating to or consisting of solid matter, physical objects, etc: **the material world**. 2 (usu **material to sth**) TECHNICAL significant.

materialism N 1 often DEROG excessive interest in or devotion to material possessions and financial success. 2 PHILOS the theory stating that only material things exist, esp denying the existence of a soul or spirit. ■ **materialist** N, ADJ. ■ **materialistic** ADJ.

materialize or **-ise** VB 1 INTR to become real, visible or tangible; to appear or take shape. 2 INTR, LOOSELY to become fact; to happen. ■ **materialization** N.

matériel N materials and equipment.

maternal ADJ 1 belonging to, typical of or like a mother. 2 of a relative: related on the mother's side of the family: **my maternal grandfather**.

maternity N 1 the state of being or becoming a mother; motherhood. 2 AS ADJ relating to pregnancy or giving birth: **maternity wear**. 3 the qualities typical of a mother.

matey or **maty** ADJ (*matier, matiest*) COLLOQ friendly or familiar.

mathematical ADJ 1 of or relating to, or using, mathematics. 2 of calculations, etc: very exact or accurate. ■ **mathematically** ADV.

mathematician N someone who specializes in or studies mathematics.

mathematics SING N the science dealing with measurements, numbers, quantities, and shapes, usu expressed as symbols.

maths SING N, BRIT COLLOQ mathematics.

matinée or **matinee** N an afternoon performance of a play or showing of a film.

matins SING OR PL N, C OF E the daily morning prayer or service. ■ **matinal** ADJ.

matriarch N the female head of a family, community or tribe. ■ **matriarchal** ADJ.

matriarchy N (*-ies*) a social system in which women are the heads of families or tribes.

matricide N the killing of a mother by her own child. ■ **matricidal** ADJ.

matriculate VB, INTR to register as a student at a university, college, etc. ■ **matriculation** N.

matrimony N, FORMAL the state of being married. ■ **matrimonial** ADJ.

matrix N (*matrices* or *matrixes*) MATH a square or rectangular arrangement of symbols or numbers, in rows or columns, used to summarize relationships between different quantities, etc.

matron N **1** the former title of the head of the nursing staff in a hospital. Now usu called **senior nursing officer**. **2** a woman in charge of nursing and domestic arrangements in an institution such as a boarding school. **3** any dignified, worthy or respectable middle-aged or elderly woman, esp a married one. ■ **matronly** ADJ.

matt or (sometimes) **matte** ADJ eg of paint: having a dull surface without gloss or shine.

matter N **1** the substance from which all physical things are made; material. **2** material of a particular kind: **reading matter**. **3** a subject or topic; a concern, affair or question: **it's a matter of money**. **4** content, as distinct from style or form. **5** (usu **a matter of sth**) **a** an approximate quantity or amount of (time, etc): **I'll be there in a matter of minutes**; **b** used in saying what is involved or necessary: **It's just a matter of asking her to do it**. **6** (**the matter** or **the matter with sb** or **sth**) something that is wrong; the trouble or difficulty: **What is the matter? 7** MED pus or discharge.
➤ VB, INTR to be important or significant.

◆ **as a matter of fact** in fact; actually.
◆ **for that matter** as far as that is concerned.
◆ **no matter** it is not important.
◆ **no matter how** or **what**, etc regardless of how or what, etc.

matter-of-fact ADJ calm and straightforward; not excited or emotional.

matting N material of rough woven fibres.

mattock N a tool with a blade flattened at one end, used for breaking up soil.

mattress N a large flat fabric-covered pad, used for sleeping on.

mature ADJ **1** fully grown or developed. **2** having or showing adult good sense, social and emotional development, etc. **3** of cheese, wine, etc: having a fully developed flavour. **4** of bonds, insurance policies, etc: paying out, or beginning to pay out, money to the holder.
➤ VB **1** TR & INTR to make or become fully developed or adult in outlook. **2** INTR of a life insurance policy, etc: to begin to produce a return. ■ **maturation** N. ■ **maturity** N.

matzo N **1** unleavened bread. **2** a wafer or cracker made of this.

maudlin ADJ foolishly sad or sentimental.

maul VB **1** to attack someone or something fiercely, usu tearing the flesh. **2** to handle someone or something roughly or clumsily. **3** to subject someone to fierce criticism.

maunder VB, INTR **1** (also **maunder on**) to talk in a rambling way; to drivel. **2** to wander about, or behave, in an aimless way.

mausoleum N (*-leums* or *-lea*) a grand or monumental tomb.

mauve N a pale purple colour.

maverick N **1** N AMER, ESP US an unbranded stray animal, esp a calf. **2** a determinedly independent person; a nonconformist.

maw N the jaws, throat or stomach of a voracious animal.

mawkish ADJ **1** weakly sentimental, maudlin or insipid. **2** sickly or disgusting.

maxi ADJ, often IN COMPOUNDS of a skirt, coat, etc: **1** extra long; full length. **2** extra large.
➤ N a maxi garment.

maxilla N (*lae*) BIOL the upper jaw or jawbone in animals. ■ **maxillary** ADJ.

maxim N **1** a saying that expresses a general truth. **2** a general rule or principle.

maximal ADJ having the greatest possible size, value, etc.

maximize or **-ise** VB to make as high or great, etc as possible. ■ **maximization** N.

maximum ADJ greatest possible.
➤ N (*-mums* or *-ma*) the greatest or most; the greatest possible number, quantity, degree, etc.

maxwell N, PHYS an old unit of magnetic flux, equal to 10^{8-} weber.

May N the fifth month of the year.

may[1] AUXILIARY VERB (PAT *might*) **1** used to express permission: **You may go now.**
2 (sometimes **may well**) used to express a possibility: **I may come with you if I get this finished. 3** used to express an offer: **May I help you? 4** FORMAL used to express a wish: **May you prosper! 5** FORMAL & OLD USE used to express purpose or result: **Listen, so that you may learn. 6** AFFECTED, OLD USE OR FACETIOUS used to express a question: **And who may you be? 7** used to express the idea of 'although': **You may be rich, but you're not happy.**
◆ **be that as it may** in spite of that.
◆ **come what may** whatever happens.

may[2] N **1** the blossom of the hawthorn tree. Also called **mayflower. 2** any variety of hawthorn tree. Also called **may tree.**

maybe ADV it is possible; perhaps.
➤ N a possibility.

mayday or **Mayday** N the international distress signal sent out by ships and aircraft.

mayfly N (*-ies*) an insect with transparent wings, which appears briefly in spring.

mayhem N **1** a state of great confusion and disorder; chaos. **2** US & FORMERLY LAW the crime of maiming someone.

mayn't CONTRACTION, COLLOQ may not.

mayonnaise N, COOKERY a cold, creamy sauce made of egg yolk, oil, vinegar or lemon juice and seasoning. Sometimes (COLLOQ) shortened to **mayo.**

mayor N **1** in England, Wales and N Ireland: the head of the local council in a city, town or borough. **2** in other countries: the head of any of various communities. ■ **mayoral** ADJ.

mayoress N **1** a mayor's wife. **2** OLD USE a female mayor.

maypole N a tall, decorated pole traditionally set up for dancing round on May Day.

maze N **1** a confusing network of paths bordered by high walls or hedges, laid out in a garden as a puzzling diversion in which a person might become lost or disorientated. **2** any confusingly complicated system, procedure, etc.

mazurka N a lively Polish dance in triple time.

MC ABBREV master of ceremonies.

MD ABBREV managing director.

ME ABBREV, MED myalgic encephalomyelitis.

me[1] PRONOUN **1** the object form of **I**, used by a speaker or writer to refer to himself or herself: **asked me a question. 2** used for **I** after the verb **be** or when standing alone: **It's only me.**

me[2] or **mi** N, MUS in sol–fa notation: the third note of the major scale.

mea culpa INTERJ, LITERARY OR FACETIOUS I am to blame.

mead[1] N an alcoholic drink made by fermenting honey and water.

mead[2] N, POETIC OR OLD USE a meadow.

meadow N **1** a low–lying field of grass, used for grazing animals or making hay. **2** any moist, grassy area near a river.

meagre or (US) **meager** ADJ **1** lacking in quality or quantity; inadequate. **2** of a person: thin, esp unhealthily so.

meal[1] N **1** an occasion on which food is eaten, eg lunch, supper, dinner, etc. **2** an amount of food eaten on one such occasion.

meal² N, often IN COMPOUNDS **1** the edible parts of a grain ground to a coarse powder: oatmeal. **2** any other food substance in ground form: bone meal. ■ **mealy** ADJ.

meal ticket N, COLLOQ a person or situation that provides a source of income.

mealy-mouthed ADJ, DEROG afraid to speak plainly or openly; not frank or sincere.

mean¹ VB (*meant*) **1** to express or intend to express, show or indicate something. **2** to intend something; to have it as a purpose: didn't mean any harm. **3** to be serious or sincere about something: He means what he says. **4** to be important to the degree specified; to represent something: Your approval means a lot to me. **5** to entail something necessarily; to involve or result in it: War means hardship. **6** to foretell or portend something: This means war. ◆ **mean well** to have good intentions.

mean² ADJ **1** not generous. **2** low; despicable. **3** poor; shabby; characterized by inferior quality. **4** COLLOQ, esp N AMER vicious; malicious; bad-tempered. **5** COLLOQ good; skilful: plays a mean guitar. ■ **meanly** ADV. ■ **meanness** N.

mean³ ADJ **1** midway. **2** average. ➤ N **1** a midway position or course, etc between two extremes. **2** MATH, STATISTICS a mathematical average.

meander VB, INTR **1** of a river: to bend and curve. **2** (also **meander about**) to wander randomly or aimlessly. ➤ N (often **meanders**) a bend; a winding course.

meanie or **meany** N (-*ies*) COLLOQ **1** a selfish or ungenerous person. **2** esp N AMER a malicious or bad-tempered person.

meaning N **1** the sense in which a statement, action, word, etc is intended to be understood. **2** significance, importance or purpose, esp when hidden or special.

meaningful ADJ **1** having meaning; significant. **2** full of significance; expressive.

meaningless ADJ without meaning or reason.

means SING OR PL N **1** the instrument or method used to achieve some object. **2** wealth; resources.
◆ **by all means** rather FORMAL yes, of course.
◆ **by no means** or **not by any means** not at all; definitely not.

meantime N (esp **in the meantime**) the time or period in between; the intervening time. ➤ ADV meanwhile.

meanwhile ADV **1** during the time in between. **2** at the same time.

measles SING N a highly infectious viral disease characterized by fever, a sore throat and a blotchy red rash.

measly ADJ (-*ier, -iest*) **1** DEROG, COLLOQ of an amount, value, etc: very small; miserable; paltry. **2** relating to, or suffering from, measles. ■ **measliness** N.

measure N **1** size, volume, etc determined by comparison with something of known size, etc, usu an instrument graded in standard units. **2** such an instrument for taking a measurement of something. **3** a standard unit of size, etc; a standard amount: a measure of whisky. **4** a system of such units: metric measure. **5** (usu **measures**) an action; a step: We must take drastic measures. **6** a limited, or appropriate, amount or extent: a measure of politeness. **7** an enactment or bill. ➤ VB **1** TR & INTR to determine the size, volume, etc of, usu with a specially made instrument. **2** INTR to be a specified size. **3** (also **measure off sth** or **measure sth off** or **out**) to mark or divide something into units of a given size, etc. **4** to set something in competition with something else: measure his strength against mine. ■ **measurable** ADJ. ■ **measuring** N.
◆ **for good measure** as something extra, or above the minimum necessary.
◆ **measure up to sth** to reach the required standard; to be adequate.

measured ADJ **1** slow and steady. **2** carefully chosen or considered. ■ **measuredly** ADV.

measurement N **1** (often **measurements**) a size, amount, etc determined by measuring.

2 (often **measurements**) the size of a part of the body.

meat N **1** the flesh of any animal used as food. **2** the basic or most important part; the essence.

meaty ADJ (*-ier, -iest*) **1** full of or resembling meat. **2** full of interesting information or ideas.

mecca or **Mecca** N **1** a city in Saudi Arabia to which Muslims make pilgrimage. **2** any place of outstanding importance or significance to a particular group of people, esp one which they feel they have to visit.

mechanic N a skilled worker who repairs, maintains or constructs machinery.

mechanical ADJ **1** of or concerning machines or mechanics. **2** worked by, or performed with, machinery or a mechanism. **3** of an action or movement, etc: done without or not requiring much thought. ■ **mechanically** ADV.

mechanics SING N **1** the branch of physics that deals with the motion of bodies and the forces that act on them. **2** the art or science of machine construction.
➤ PL N **1** the system on which something works. **2** COLLOQ routine procedures.

mechanism N **1** a working part of a machine or its system of working parts. **2** the arrangements and action by which something is produced or achieved. ■ **mechanistic** ADJ.

mechanize or **-ise** VB **1** to change (the production of something, a procedure, etc) from a manual to a mechanical process. **2** MIL to provide (troops etc) with armoured armed vehicles. ■ **mechanization** N.

medal N a flat piece of metal decorated with a design or inscription and awarded, eg to a soldier, sportsperson, etc, or produced in celebration of an occasion. ■ **medallist** N.

medallion N **1** a large medal-like piece of jewellery, usu worn on a chain. **2** in architecture or on textiles: an oval or circular decorative feature. **3** COOKERY a thin circular cut of meat.

meddle VB, INTR **1** (usu **meddle in sth**) to interfere in it. **2** (usu **meddle with sth**) to tamper with it. ■ **meddler** N.

■ **meddlesome** ADJ.

media SING OR PL N (usu **the media** or **the mass media**) the means by which news and information, etc is communicated to the public, usu considered to be TV, radio and the press.

mediaeval another spelling of **medieval**.

median N **1** a middle point or part. **2** GEOM a straight line between any vertex of a triangle and the centre of the opposite side. **3** STATISTICS **a** the middle value in a set of numbers or measurements arranged from smallest to largest, eg the median of 1, 5 and 11 is 5; **b** of an even number of measurements: the average of the middle two measurements.
➤ ADJ **1** situated in or passing through the middle. **2** STATISTICS belonging or relating to the median.

mediate VB **1 a** INTR to act as the agent seeking to reconcile the two sides in a disagreement; **b** to intervene in or settle (a dispute) in this way. **2** INTR to hold an intermediary position. ■ **mediation** N. ■ **mediator** N.

medic N, COLLOQ a doctor or medical student.

medical ADJ **1** belonging or relating to doctors or the science or practice of medicine. **2** concerned with medicine, or treatment by medicine, rather than surgery.
➤ N a medical examination to discover a person's physical health. ■ **medically** ADV.

medicament N, FORMAL a medicine.

medicate VB **1** to treat someone with medicine. **2** to add a healing or health-giving substance to something. ■ **medication** N.

medicinal ADJ having healing qualities.
■ **medicinally** ADV.

medicine N **1** any substance used to treat or prevent disease or illness, esp one taken internally. **2** the science or practice of treating or preventing illness, esp using prepared substances rather than surgery.

medicine man N a person believed to have magic powers, used for healing or sorcery.

medieval or **mediaeval** ADJ **1** of or relating to the Middle Ages. **2** DEROG, COLLOQ extremely old and primitive. ■ **medievalist** N.

mediocre ADJ only ordinary or average; rather inferior. ■ **mediocrity** N (-*ies*).

meditate VB **1** INTR to spend time in deep religious or spiritual thought, often with the mind in a practised state of emptiness. **2** (often **meditate about** or **on sth**) to think deeply about something. ■ **meditative** ADJ.

meditation N **1** the act or process of meditating. **2** deep thought; contemplation, esp on a spiritual or religious theme.

medium N (PL in all senses except 2 and 5 *mediums* or, in all senses except 3, *media*) **1** something by or through which an effect is produced. **2** someone through whom the spirits of dead people are said to communicate with the living. **3** ART a particular category of materials seen as a means of expression, eg watercolours, photography or clay. **4** COMP (usu **media**) any material on which data is recorded, eg magnetic disk. **5** a middle position or course: **a happy medium**. ➤ ADJ **1** intermediate; midway; average. **2** moderate. **3** of meat, esp steak: cooked through so that it is not bloody when cut open.

medium wave N a radio wave with a wavelength between 200 and 1000 metres.

medlar N a small brown apple-like fruit eaten only when already decaying.

medley N **1** a piece of music made up of pieces from other songs, tunes, etc. **2** a mixture or miscellany. **3** a race in stages with each stage a different length or, in swimming, with each stage swum using a different stroke.

medulla N (-*ae* or *as*) BIOL the central part of an organ or tissue, when this differs in structure or function from the outer layer.

medusa N (-*as* or -*ae*) ZOOL a jellyfish.

meek ADJ **1** having a mild and gentle temperament. **2** submissive. ■ **meekly** ADV.

meerkat N any of several species of mongoose-like carnivores native to S Africa.

meerschaum N **1** a fine, clay-like mineral. **2** a tobacco pipe with a bowl made of this.

meet[1] VB (*met*) **1** TR & INTR to be introduced to someone for the first time. **2** TR & INTR **a** (also **meet up with sb** or US **meet with sb**) to come together with them by chance or by arrangement; **b** of two people, groups, etc: to come together, either by chance or arrangement. **3** to be present at the arrival of (a vehicle, etc): **met the train**. **4** TR & INTR to join; to come into contact with something: **where the path meets the road**. **5** to satisfy: **meet your requirements**. **6** to pay: **meet costs**. **7** to come into the view, experience or presence of something: **the sight that met my eyes**. **8** (also **meet with sth**) to encounter or experience it: **met with disaster**. ➤ N **1** the assembly of hounds and huntsmen and huntswomen before a foxhunt begins. **2** a sporting event, esp a series of competitions. ◆ **more to sth than meets the eye** more complicated, etc than it first appears.

meet[2] ADJ, OLD USE proper, correct or suitable.

meeting N **1** an act of coming together. **2** an assembly or gathering at a prearranged time, usu to discuss specific topics. **3** a sporting event, esp an athletics or horse-racing event.

megabyte N, COMP a unit of storage capacity equal to 1 048 576 bytes.

megahertz N (PL *megahertz*) a unit of frequency equal to of one million hertz.

megalith N, ARCHAEOL a very large stone, esp one that forms part of a prehistoric monument.

megalomania N an exaggerated sense of one's own importance and power. ■ **megalomaniac** N, ADJ.

megaphone N a funnel-shaped device which amplifies the voice.

megaton N **1** a unit of weight equal to one million tons. **2** a unit of explosive power equal to one million tons of TNT.

meiosis N (-*ses*) BIOL a type of cell division in which four daughter nuclei are produced, each containing half the number of chromosomes of the parent nucleus and resulting in the formation of male and female gametes. ■ **meiotic** ADJ.

melamine N, CHEM a white crystalline organic

compound used to form artificial resins that are resistant to heat, water and many chemicals.

melancholia N, OLD USE mental depression.

melancholy N (-*ies*) **1** a tendency to be gloomy or depressed. **2** prolonged sadness. **3** a sad, pensive state of mind.
➤ ADJ sad; causing or expressing sadness.
■ **melancholic** ADJ.

melange N a mixture, esp a confused one.

melanin N, PHYSIOL, CHEM the black or dark brown pigment found to varying degrees in the skin, hair and eyes of humans and animals.

melanoma N (-*mas* or -*mata*) MED a cancerous tumour, usu of the skin, that may spread to other parts of the body.

meld VB, TR & INTR to merge or blend.

melee or **mêlée** N a riotous brawl involving large numbers of people.

mellifluous or **mellifluent** ADJ of sounds: having a smooth sweet flowing quality.

mellow ADJ **1** of a person: calm and relaxed. **2** of sound, colour, light, etc: soft, rich and pure. **3** of wine, cheese, etc: well matured.
➤ VB, TR & INTR to make or become mellow.

melodeon or **melodion** N **1** a small reed–organ; a harmonium. **2** a kind of accordion.

melodic ADJ **1** relating or belonging to melody. **2** pleasant–sounding; tuneful; melodious.

melodious ADJ **1** pleasant to listen to; tuneful. **2** having a recognizable melody.

melodrama N **1** a play or film containing sensational events, and also usu appealing to the emotions. **2** DEROG excessively dramatic behaviour. ■ **melodramatic** ADJ.

melody N (-*ies*) **1** MUS the sequence of single notes forming the core of a tune. **2** pleasantness of sound; tuneful music.

melon N **1** any of several plants of the gourd family, cultivated for their fruits. **2** the large rounded edible fruit of any of these plants.

melt VB, TR & INTR **1** to make or become soft or liquid, esp through the action of heat; to dissolve (something solid). **2** (often **melt into sth**) to combine or fuse, or make something combine or fuse with something else, causing a loss of distinctness. **3** (also **melt away**) to disappear or make something disappear or disperse. **4** COLLOQ to make or become emotionally or romantically tender or submissive: Her smile melted my heart.
➤ N **1** the act of melting. **2** the quantity or material melted. ■ **meltingly** ADV.
◆ **melt down** to turn (metal) to a liquid state so that the raw material can be reused.

meltdown N, COLLOQ a major disaster or failure.

melting point N the temperature at which a substance changes from a solid to a liquid.

melting-pot N a place or situation in which varying cultures, races, etc come together.

member N **1** someone who belongs to a group or organization. **2** (often **Member**) an elected representative of a governing body, eg a Member of Parliament, or of a local council, etc. **3** a part of a whole, esp a limb of an animal or a petal of a plant. **4** a plant or animal belonging to a specific class or group.

membership N **1** the state of being a member. **2 a** the members of an organization collectively; **b** the number of members.

membrane N a thin sheet of tissue that lines a body cavity or surrounds a body part, organ, cell, etc. ■ **membranous** ADJ.

memento N (-*os* or -*oes*) a thing that serves as a reminder of the past; a souvenir.

memo N a short note.

memoir N **1** a written record of events in the past, esp one based on personal experience. **2** (usu **memoirs**) a person's written account of his or her own life; an autobiography.

memorabilia PL N souvenirs.

memorable ADJ worth remembering; easily remembered.

memorandum N (-*dums* or -*da*) **1** a written statement or record, esp one circulated for the attention of colleagues at work. **2** a note of something to be remembered.

memorial N a thing that honours or commemorates a person or an event. ➤ ADJ serving to preserve the memory of a person or event: **a memorial fund.**

memorize or **-ise** VB to learn something thoroughly, so as to be able to reproduce it exactly from memory.

memory N (**-ies**) **1** the ability of the mind to remember. **2** the mind's store of remembered events, impressions, knowledge and ideas. **3** the mental processes of memorizing information, retaining it, and recalling it on demand. **4** any such impression reproduced in the mind: **have no memory of the event. 5** COMP the part of a computer that is used to store data and programs. **6** the limit in the past beyond which one's store of mental impressions does not extend. **7** the act of remembering; commemoration: **in memory of old friends. 8** reputation after death: **Her memory lives on.**

men plural of **man**

menace N **1** a source of threatening danger. **2** a threat; a show of hostility. ➤ VB, TR & INTR to threaten; to show an intention to damage or harm someone. ■ **menacing** ADJ.

menagerie N **a** a collection of wild animals caged for exhibition; **b** the place where they are kept.

mend VB **1** to repair something. **2** INTR to heal or recover. **3** to improve or correct something: **mend one's ways.** ➤ N on a garment, etc: a repaired part or place.

mendacious ADJ lying, or likely to lie. ■ **mendacity** N.

mendicant ADJ **1** dependent on charity. **2** FORMAL begging.

menfolk PL N men collectively, esp the male members of a particular group, family, etc.

menhir N a monumental prehistoric single upright standing stone.

menial ADJ of work: unskilled, uninteresting and of low status. ➤ N, DEROG a domestic servant.

meninges PL N (SING **meninx**) the three membranes covering the brain and spinal cord.

meningitis N, PATHOL inflammation of the meninges, usu caused by infection.

meniscus N (**-scuses** or **-sci**) PHYS the curved upper surface of a liquid in a partly-filled narrow tube, caused by surface tension.

menopause N the period in a woman's life when menstruation ceases and pregnancy is no longer possible. ■ **menopausal** ADJ.

menorah N a seven-branched candelabrum regarded as a symbol of Judaism.

menses PL N, BIOL, MED the fluids discharged from the womb during menstruation.

menstrual ADJ relating to or involving menstruation: **the menstrual cycle.**

menstruation N, BIOL **1** in women of childbearing age: the discharge through the vagina of blood and fragments of mucous membrane, that takes place at approximately monthly intervals if fertilization of an ovum has not occurred. **2** the time or occurrence of menstruating. ■ **menstruate** VB.

mensuration N, TECHNICAL the application of geometric principles to the calculation of measurements.

menswear N clothing for men.

mental ADJ **1** of or relating to, or done by using, the mind or intelligence: **mental arithmetic. 2** OLD USE of, or suffering from, an illness or illnesses of the mind: **a mental patient. 3** COLLOQ foolish; stupid. **4** COLLOQ ridiculous. ■ **mentally** ADV.

mentality N (**-ies**) **1** an outlook; a certain way of thinking. **2** intellectual ability.

menthol N a sharp-smelling substance obtained from peppermint oil, used as a decongestant and a painkiller. ■ **mentholated** ADJ.

mention VB **1** to speak of or make reference to something or someone. **2** to remark on something or someone, usu briefly or indirectly. ➤ N a remark, usu a brief reference.

◆ **don't mention it** COLLOQ no apologies or words of thanks are needed.

◆ **not to mention sth** used to introduce (a subject or facts that the speaker is about to mention), usu for emphasis.

mentor N a trusted teacher or adviser.

menu N **1 a** the range of dishes available in a restaurant, etc; **b** a list of these dishes. **2** COMP a set of options displayed on a computer screen.

meow, **meowed** and **meowing** see under **miaow**

mercantile ADJ, FORMAL of or relating to trade or traders; commercial.

mercenary ADJ **1** DEROG excessively concerned with the desire for personal gain, esp money. **2** hired for money.
➢ N (-*ies*) a soldier available for hire.

mercerize or **-ise** VB to treat a material, esp cotton, with a substance which strengthens it and gives it a silky appearance.

merchandise N commercial goods.
➢ VB, TR & INTR **1** to trade; to buy and sell. **2** to plan the advertising or supplying of (a product). ■ **merchandising** N.

merchant N **1** a trader, esp a wholesale trader. **2** N AMER, ESP US & SCOT a shopkeeper. **3** COLLOQ someone who indulges in an activity, esp one that is generally not acceptable or appropriate: gossip merchant.
➢ ADJ commercial: merchant ship.

merchant bank N a bank whose main activities are financing international trade, lending money to industry, etc.

merchantman N a ship that carries merchandise; a trading ship. Also called **merchant ship**.

merchant navy and **merchant service** N the ships and crews that are employed in a country's commerce.

merciful ADJ showing mercy; forgiving.

merciless ADJ without mercy; cruel; pitiless.
■ **mercilessly** ADV.

mercurial ADJ **1** relating to or containing mercury. **2** lively and unpredictable.

mercury N **1** a dense, silvery-white metallic element, and the only metal that is liquid at room temperature. **2** (**Mercury**) ASTRON the closest planet to the Sun.

mercy N (-*ies*) **1** kindness or forgiveness shown when punishment is possible or justified. **2** an act or circumstance in which these qualities are displayed, esp by God. **3** a tendency to be forgiving. **4** a piece of good luck; a welcome happening: grateful for small mercies.
◆ **at the mercy of sb** or **sth** wholly in their or its power; liable to be harmed by them or it.

mere[1] ADJ nothing more than; no better than: but he's a mere boy. ■ **merely** ADV.

mere[2] N often in English place names: a lake or pool.

meretricious ADJ, FORMAL bright or attractive on the surface, but of no real value.

merge VB, TR & INTR (often **merge with sth**) to blend, combine or join with something else.
◆ **merge into sth** to become part of it and therefore impossible to distinguish from it.

merger N a joining together, esp of business firms. Also called **amalgamation**.

meridian N, GEOG **a** an imaginary line on the Earth's surface passing through the poles at right angles to the equator; **b** a representation of this, eg on a map. ■ **meridional** ADJ.

meringue N **1** a crisp, cooked mixture of sugar and egg-whites. **2** a cake or dessert made from this, often with a filling of cream.

merino N **1** a type of sheep bred for its long, fine wool. **2** fine yarn or fabric made from its wool. Also AS ADJ: merino shawl.

merit N worth, excellence or praiseworthiness.
➢ VB to deserve; to be worthy of or entitled to something.

meritocracy N (-*ies*) a social system based on leadership by people of great talent or intelligence, rather than of wealth or noble birth. ■ **meritocrat** N. ■ **meritocratic** ADJ.

meritorious ADJ, FORMAL deserving reward or

praise; having merit. ■ **meritoriously** ADV.

merlin N a small, dark-coloured falcon.

mermaid N, FOLKLORE a mythical sea creature with a woman's head and upper body and a fish's tail. ■ **merman** N.

merry ADJ (*-ier, -iest*) **1** cheerful and lively. **2** COLLOQ slightly drunk. **3** causing or full of laughter. ■ **merrily** ADV. ■ **merriment** N. ■ **merriness** N.

merry-go-round N **1** a fairground ride with a revolving platform fitted with rising and falling seats in the form of horses or other figures. Sometimes called **roundabout**. **2** a whirl of activity.

merrymaking N cheerful celebration; revelry. ■ **merrymaker** N.

mescaline or **mescalin** N a hallucinogenic drug obtained from the mescal cactus.

mesdames plural of **madam**

mesh N **1** netting, or a piece of netting. **2** each of the openings between the threads of a net. **3** (usu **meshes**) a network.
➤ VB **1** INTR, TECHNICAL of the teeth on gear wheels: to engage. **2** INTR (often **mesh with sth**) to fit or work together. **3** INTR to become entangled.

mesmerize or **-ise** VB **1** to grip the attention of someone; to fascinate. **2** OLD USE to hypnotize someone. ■ **mesmerism** N.

meson N, PHYS any of a group of unstable elementary particles, with a mass between that of an electron and a nucleon.

mesosphere N, METEOROL the layer of the Earth's atmosphere above the stratosphere and below the thermosphere.

mess N **1** an untidy or dirty state: The kitchen's in a mess. **2** a state of disorder or confusion: The accounts are in a mess. **3** a badly damaged state. **4** something or someone in a damaged, disordered or confused state: My hair is a mess. **5** a communal dining room, esp in the armed forces: the sergeants' mess.
➤ VB **1** (often **mess sth up**) to put or get it into an untidy, dirty, confused or damaged state; to

spoil. **2** INTR of soldiers, etc: to eat, or live, together. ■ **messy** ADJ (*-ier, -iest*).
◆ **mess about** or **around** COLLOQ to behave in an annoyingly foolish way.

message N **1** a spoken or written communication sent from one person to another. **2** the instructive principle contained within a story, poem, religious teaching, work of art, etc. **3** (usu **messages**) chiefly SCOT household shopping.

messenger N someone who carries communications between people.

Messiah N (usu **the Messiah**) **1** CHRISTIANITY Jesus Christ. **2** JUDAISM the king of the Jews still to be sent by God. **3** someone who sets a country or a people free.

Messianic ADJ **1** belonging or relating to, or associated with, a Messiah. **2** relating to any popular or inspirational leader, esp a liberator.

Messrs plural of **Mr**

metabolism N, BIOCHEM the sum of all the chemical reactions that occur within the cells of a living organism, including both anabolism and catabolism of complex organic compounds. ■ **metabolic** ADJ.

metabolize or **-ise** VB, TR & INTR, BIOCHEM to break down complex organic compounds into simpler molecules.

metacarpus N (*-pi*) ANAT the set of five bones in the human hand between the wrist and the knuckles. ■ **metacarpal** ADJ.

metal N **1** any of a class of chemical elements with certain shared characteristic properties, most being shiny, malleable, ductile and good conductors of heat and electricity, and all (except mercury) being solid at room temperature. **2** road metal, broken rock for making and mending roads.
➤ ADJ made of, or mainly of, metal.

metallic ADJ **1** made of metal. **2** characteristic of metal, eg in sound or appearance.

metalloid N, CHEM a chemical element that has both metallic and non-metallic properties, eg silicon and arsenic.

metallurgy N the scientific study of the nature and properties of metals. ■ **metallurgical** ADJ. ■ **metallurgist** N.

metalwork N 1 the craft, process or practice of shaping metal and making items of metal. 2 articles made of metal. ■ **metalworker** N.

metamorphic ADJ 1 of metamorphosis. 2 GEOL formed by metamorphism.

metamorphism N, GEOL the transformation of the structure of rock by the action of the Earth's crust.

metamorphose VB, TR & INTR to undergo or cause something to undergo metamorphosis.

metamorphosis N (-ses) 1 a change of form, appearance, character, etc; a transformation. 2 BIOL the change of physical form that occurs during the development into adulthood of some creatures, eg butterflies.

metaphor N 1 an expression in which the person, action or thing referred to is described as if it really were what it merely resembles, eg a rejection as 'a slap in the face'. 2 such expressions in general. ■ **metaphorical** ADJ. ■ **metaphorically** ADV.

metaphysical ADJ 1 relating to metaphysics. 2 abstract. ■ **metaphysically** ADV.

metaphysics SING N 1 the branch of philosophy dealing with the nature of existence and the basic principles of truth and knowledge. 2 COLLOQ any type of abstract discussion, writing or thinking.

metastasis N (-ses) MED the spread of a malignant tumour.

metatarsus N (-si) ANAT the set of five long bones in the human foot between the ankle and the toes. ■ **metatarsal** ADJ.

metazoan N, ZOOL any multicellular animal that has specialized differentiated body tissues.

mete VB, rather FORMAL (now always **mete sth out** or **mete out sth**) to give out or dispense something, esp punishment.

meteor N, ASTRON the streak of light seen when a meteoroid enters into the Earth's atmosphere, where it burns up as a result of friction.

meteoric ADJ 1 of or relating to meteors. 2 of success, etc: very rapid; very short-lived. ■ **meteorically** ADV.

meteorite N, ASTRON the remains of a meteoroid which has survived burn-up in its passage through the Earth's atmosphere as a meteor. ■ **meteoritic** ADJ.

meteoroid N, ASTRON in interplanetary space: a small, moving, solid object or dust particle, which becomes visible as a meteorite or a meteor if it enters the Earth's atmosphere.

meteorology N the scientific study of weather and climate over a relatively short period. ■ **meteorological** ADJ. ■ **meteorologist** N.

meter[1] N 1 an instrument for measuring and recording, esp quantities of electricity, gas, water, etc used. 2 a parking-meter.

meter[2] the US spelling of **metre**[1], **metre**[2]

methadone N a drug similar to morphine, but less addictive.

methanal N, CHEM formaldehyde.

methane N, CHEM a colourless odourless gas, the main component of natural gas.

methanol N, CHEM a colourless flammable toxic liquid used as a solvent and antifreeze, and which can be converted to petrol. Also called **methyl alcohol**.

methinks VB (*methought*) OLD USE OR HUMOROUS it seems to me (that).

method N 1 a way of doing something, esp an ordered set of procedures or an orderly system. 2 good planning; efficient organization. 3 (often **methods**) a technique used in a particular activity: **farming methods**.

methodical ADJ efficient and orderly; done in a systematic way. ■ **methodically** ADV.

methodology N (-ies) 1 the system of methods and principles used in a particular activity, science, etc. 2 the study of method and procedure.

meths SING N, COLLOQ, esp BRIT methylated spirits.

methyl alcohol see under **methanol**

methylate VB to mix or impregnate something with methanol.

methylated spirits or **methylated spirit** SING N ethanol with small quantities of methanol and pyridine and often blue or purple dye added, used as a fuel and solvent.

meticulous ADJ paying, or showing, very careful attention to detail; scrupulously careful. ■ **meticulously** ADV. ■ **meticulousness** N.

métier N 1 a person's business or line of work. 2 the field in which one is especially skilled.

metonymy N (-ies) LING the use of a word referring to an element or attribute of something to mean the thing itself, eg **the bottle** for 'the drinking of alcohol'.

metre[1] or (US) **meter** N in the SI system: the principal unit of length, equal to 39.37 inches or 1.094 yards.

metre[2] or (US) **meter** N 1 POETRY the arrangement of words and syllables, or feet, in a rhythmic pattern according to their length and stress; a particular pattern or scheme. 2 MUS **a** the basic pattern of beats; **b** tempo.

metric ADJ relating to or based on the metre or the metric system. ■ **metrically** ADV.

metrical or **metric** ADJ, TECHNICAL 1 in or relating to verse as distinct from prose. 2 of or relating to measurement.

metricate VB, TR & INTR to convert (a non-metric measurement, system, etc) to a metric one. ■ **metrication** N.

metric system N a standard system of measurement, based on decimal units, in which each successive multiple of a unit is 10 times larger than the one before it. Technical equivalent **SI**.

metro N an urban railway system, usu one that is mostly underground.

metronome N a device that indicates musical tempo by means of a ticking pendulum that can be set to move at different speeds.

metropolis N (-ses) a large city.

metropolitan ADJ 1 of or relating to a large city. 2 belonging or referring to a country's mainland.

mettle N, LITERARY 1 courage, determination and endurance. 2 character; personal qualities: show one's mettle.
◆ **put sb on their mettle** LITERARY to encourage them to make their best effort.

mew VB, INTR to make the cry of a cat; to miaow.
➤ N a cat's cry.

mews SING N a set of stables around a yard or square, esp one converted into residential accommodation or garages.

mezzanine N, ARCHIT in a building: a small storey between two main floors.

mezzo ADV, MUS moderately, quite or rather, as in **mezzo-forte** rather loud.

mezzo-soprano N, MUS a singing voice with a range between soprano and contralto.

mezzotint N, chiefly HIST 1 a method of engraving a copper plate, by polishing and scraping to produce areas of light and shade. 2 a print made from a plate so engraved.

mi see **me**[2]

miaow or **meow** VB, INTR to make the cry of a cat.
➤ N a cat's cry. Also called **mew**.

miasma N (-mata or -mas) LITERARY 1 a thick foul-smelling vapour. 2 an evil influence or atmosphere.

mica N, GEOL any of a group of silicate minerals that split easily into thin flexible sheets and are poor conductors of heat and electricity.

mice plural of **mouse**

mickey N.
◆ **take the mickey** or **take the mickey out of sb** COLLOQ to tease or make fun of them.

mickle or **muckle** ARCHAIC OR N ENGLISH DIALECT & SCOT, ADJ & ADV much or great.
➤ N a great quantity.

micro N, COLLOQ **1** a microcomputer or microprocessor. **2** a microwave oven.

microbe N, LOOSELY any micro-organism, esp a bacterium that is capable of causing disease. ■ **microbial** or **microbic** ADJ.

microbiology N the branch of biology dealing with the study of micro-organisms.

microchip see under **silicon chip**

microcircuit N an electronic circuit with components formed in one microchip.

microcomputer N a personal computer.

microcosm N **1** any structure or system which contains, in miniature, all the features of the larger structure or system that it is part of. **2** PHILOS humankind regarded as a model or epitome of the universe. ■ **microcosmic** ADJ.

microdot N a photograph, eg of secret documents, reduced to the size of a pinhead.

microelectronics SING N the branch of electronics dealing with the design and use of small-scale electrical circuits.

microfibre N a synthetic, very closely woven fabric.

microfiche N, PHOTOG a flat sheet of film with printed text on it that has been reduced photographically, used for storing library catalogues, newspaper texts, etc.

microfilm N a length of thin photographic film on which printed material is stored in miniaturized form.

microlight N a lightweight, small-engined aircraft, like a powered hang-glider.

micrometer N an instrument used for accurately measuring very small distances.

microminiaturize or **-ise** VB to reduce to an extremely small size.

micron N the former name for the micrometre.

micro-organism N any organism that can only be observed through a microscope.

microphone N an electromagnetic transducer that converts sound waves into electrical signals.

microphotography N photography in the form of greatly-reduced images of small area (**microphotograph**s) which have to be viewed by magnification.

microprocessor N, COMP a single circuit performing most of the functions of a CPU.

microscope N an instrument consisting of a system of lenses which produce a magnified image of objects that are too small to be seen with the naked eye. ■ **microscopy** N.

microscopic ADJ **1** too small to be seen without the aid of a microscope. **2** COLLOQ extremely small. ■ **microscopically** ADV.

microsecond N in the SI or metric system: a millionth part of a second.

microsurgery N, MED any intricate surgical procedure performed on very small body structures by means of a powerful microscope.

microwave N **1** a form of electromagnetic radiation with wavelengths between those of infrared and radio waves, used in radar, communications and cooking. Also called **microwave radiation**. **2** a microwave oven. ➤ VB to cook something in a microwave oven.

microwave oven N an oven that uses microwaves to cook food rapidly.

micturate VB, INTR, FORMAL to urinate.

mid[1] ADJ, often IN COMPOUNDS (sometimes with hyphen) referring to the middle point or in the middle of something: **mid-March**.

mid[2] or **'mid** PREP, POETIC a short form of **amid**.

mid-air N any area or point above the ground: **caught it in mid-air**.

midday N the middle of the day; twelve o'clock.

midden N **1** chiefly OLD USE OR DIALECT a rubbish heap; a pile of dung. **2** COLLOQ an untidy mess.

middle ADJ **1** at, or being, a point or position between two others, usu two ends or extremes, and esp the same distance from each. **2** intermediate; not at the top or at the bottom end of the scale: **middle income**. **3** moderate; as a compromise: **middle ground**.

➤ N **1** the middle point or part of something: **the middle of the night. 2** COLLOQ the waist.

middle age N the years between youth and old age, usu thought of as between the ages of 40 and 60. ■ **middle-aged** ADJ.

middlebrow DEROG, ADJ intended for, or appealing to, people with conventional tastes and average intelligence.
➤ N a middlebrow person.

middle class N (esp **the middle class**) a social class between the working class and the upper class, traditionally thought of as being made up of educated people with professional or business careers.
➤ ADJ (**middle-class**) belonging or relating to, or characteristic of, the middle class.

middle distance N in a painting, photograph, etc: the area between the foreground and the background.
➤ ADJ (**middle-distance**) **1** of an athlete: competing in races of distances of 400, 800 and 1500 metres. **2** of a race: run over any of these distances.

middle ear N, ANAT an air-filled cavity between the eardrum and the inner ear.

middleman N a dealer who buys from a producer or manufacturer and sells to shopkeepers or to the public.

middle-of-the-road ADJ, often DEROG not extreme; moderate; boringly average.

middle school N, ENGLAND & WALES a school for children between 8 or 9 and 12 or 13.

middleweight N a class for boxers, wrestlers and weightlifters of not more than a specified weight (73kg or 161 lb in professional boxing).

middling COLLOQ, ADJ average; mediocre.
➤ ADV esp of a person's health: fairly good; moderately: **middling good.**

midfield N, FOOTBALL the middle area of the pitch, not close to the goal of either team. ■ **midfielder** N.

midge N a small biting insect that gathers with others near water.

midget N **1** an unusually small person whose limbs are of normal proportions. **2** any thing that is smaller than others of its kind.

midland ADJ belonging or relating to the central, inland part of a country.

midmost LITERARY, ADV in the very middle.
➤ ADJ nearest the middle.

midnight N twelve o'clock at night.

midpoint N a point at or near the middle.

midriff N **1** the part of the body between the chest and waist. **2** the diaphragm.

midshipman N, NAUT a trainee naval officer, stationed on land.

midships see **amidships**

midst N **1** (always **in the midst of sth**) **a** among it or in the centre of it; **b** at the same time as something; during it. **2** (always **in sb's midst**) among or in the same place as them.

midstream N the area of water in the middle of a river or stream, away from its banks.
◆ **in midstream** before a sentence, action, etc is finished: **She cut him off in midstream.**

midsummer N the period of time in the middle of summer, or near the summer solstice.

midterm N **1** the middle of an academic term or term of office, etc. **2** the middle of a particular period of time, esp of a pregnancy.

midway ADJ, ADV halfway between two points in distance or time.

midweek N the period of time in the middle of the week, esp Wednesday.

midwife N a nurse, esp a female one, trained to assist women in childbirth. ■ **midwifery** N.

midwinter N the period of time in the middle of winter, or near the winter solstice.

mien N, FORMAL OR LITERARY an appearance, expression or manner, esp one that reflects a mood: **her thoughtful mien.**

miff VB, INTR, COLLOQ (usu **miffed at, about** or **with sb** or **sth**) to be offended. ■ **miffed** ADJ.

might¹ AUXILIARY VERB **1** PA T OF **may¹**: He asked if he might be of assistance. **2** (sometimes **might well**) used to express a possibility: He might win if he tries hard. **3** used to request permission: Might I speak to you a moment?

might² N power or strength.

mightn't CONTRACTION might not.

mighty ADJ (*-ier, -iest*) **1** having great strength or power. **2** very large. **3** very important.
➤ ADV, N AMER, ESP US, COLLOQ very: **mighty pretty**. ■ **mightily** ADV. ■ **mightiness** N.

migraine N a throbbing headache accompanied by blurred vision.

migrant N a person or animal that migrates.
➤ ADJ regularly moving from place to place.

migrate VB, INTR **1** of animals, esp birds: to travel from one region to another at certain times of the year. **2** of people: to leave one place and settle in another, esp another country, often regularly. ■ **migration** N. ■ **migratory** ADJ.

mike CONTRACTION, COLLOQ short for **microphone**.

milady N (*-ies*) DATED a term formerly used to address, or to refer to, a rich English woman.

milch ADJ of cattle: producing milk.

mild ADJ **1** gentle in temperament or behaviour. **2** not sharp or strong in flavour or effect. **3** not great or severe. **4** of climate, etc: not characterized by extremes; rather warm.
➤ N (also **mild ale**) dark beer less flavoured with hops than bitter beer. ■ **mildly** ADV. ■ **mildness** N.

mildew N **a** a parasitic fungus that produces a fine white powdery coating on the surface of infected plants; **b** similar white or grey patches on the surface of paper which has been exposed to damp conditions.

mile N **1** in the imperial system: a unit of distance equal to 1760 yards. **2** a race over this distance, esp a race on foot. **3** COLLOQ a great distance; a large margin: **missed by a mile**.
➤ ADV (**miles**) **a** at a great distance: **lives miles away**; **b** COLLOQ very much: **miles better**.

mileage N **1** the number of miles travelled or to

be travelled. **2 a** the number of miles a motor vehicle will travel on a fixed amount of fuel; **b** the total number of miles a car has done since new, as shown on the mileometer. **3** COLLOQ use; benefit; advantage: **We can get a lot of mileage out of that story.**

mileometer or **milometer** N in a motor vehicle: an instrument for recording the total number of miles travelled.

milestone N **1** a very important event; a significant point or stage. **2** a stone at a roadside showing distances to various places.

milieu N (*milieus* or *milieux*) LITERARY a social environment or set of surroundings.

militant ADJ **1** taking, or ready to take, strong or violent action; aggressively active. **2** FORMAL engaged in warfare.
➤ N a militant person. ■ **militancy** N.

militarism N, often DEROG **1** an aggressive readiness to engage in warfare. **2** the vigorous pursuit of military aims and ideals. ■ **militarist** N. ■ **militaristic** ADJ.

militarize or **-ise** VB **1** to provide (a country, body, etc) with a military force. **2** to make something military in nature or character. ■ **militarization** N.

military ADJ **1** by, for, or belonging or relating to the armed forces or warfare: **military encounter**. **2** characteristic of members of the armed forces: **military bearing**.
➤ N (*-ies*) (usu **the military**) the armed forces. ■ **militarily** ADV.

militate VB, INTR (usu **militate for** or **against sth**) to have a strong influence or effect.

militia N a civilian fighting force used to supplement a regular army in emergencies. ■ **militiaman** N.

milk N **1** a whiteish liquid that is secreted by the mammary glands of female mammals to provide their young with nourishment. **2** the whiteish, milk-like juice or sap of certain plants: **coconut milk**. **3** any preparation that resembles milk: **milk of magnesia**.
➤ VB **1** to take milk from (an animal). **2** to extract or draw off a substance (eg venom or sap) from

something. **3** COLLOQ to obtain a benefit from someone or something, cleverly or relentlessly; to exploit: **milked the scandal for all it was worth. 4** INTR of cattle: to yield milk. ■ **milkiness** N. ■ **milky** ADJ.

milk chocolate N chocolate containing milk.

milk float N, BRIT a vehicle, usu an electrically–powered one, used for delivering milk.

milkman N, BRIT a man who delivers milk to people's houses.

milkshake N a drink consisting of a mixture of milk, flavouring and sometimes ice cream, whipped together until creamy.

milksop N, DEROG, OLD USE a weak, effeminate or ineffectual man or youth.

milk tooth N any of a baby's first set of teeth. Also called **baby tooth**.

mill N **1 a** a large machine that grinds grain into flour; **b** a building containing such a machine: **windmill. 2** a smaller machine or device for grinding a particular thing: **a pepper mill. 3** a factory, esp one with one or more large machines that press, roll or otherwise shape something: **a woollen mill.**
➤ VB **1** to grind (grain, etc). **2** to shape (eg metal) in a mill. **3** to cut grooves into the edge of (a coin). **4** INTR, COLLOQ (esp **mill about** or **around**) to move in an aimless or confused manner. ■ **miller** N.
◆ **go** or **put sb** or **sth through the mill** to undergo or make them or it undergo an unpleasant experience or difficult test.

millennium N (-*iums* or -*ia*) a period of a thousand years. ■ **millennial** ADJ.

millepede see **millipede**

millesimal ADJ **1** thousandth. **2** consisting of or relating to thousandths.
➤ N a thousandth part.

millet N a cereal grass which is grown as an important food crop, and also widely used as animal fodder.

millibar N, PHYS, METEOROL, etc a unit of atmospheric pressure equal to one thousandth of a bar.

milligram or **milligramme** N a unit of weight equal to one thousandth of a gram.

millilitre or (US) **milliliter** N a unit of volume equal to one thousandth of a litre.

millimetre or (US) **millimeter** N a unit of length equal to one thousandth of a metre.

milliner N someone who makes or sells women's hats. ■ **millinery** N.

million N (*millions* or after a number *million*) **1** the number or quantity 10^6, a thousand thousands. **2** a numeral, figure or symbol representing this, eg 1,000,000. **3** (often **millions**) COLLOQ a great number.
➤ ADJ one million in number. ■ **millionth** N, ADJ.

millionaire N someone whose wealth amounts to a million pounds, etc.

millionairess N a female millionaire.

millipede or **millepede** N (*millipedes* or *millepede*) a small creature with a many-jointed body and numerous pairs of legs.

millisecond N a unit of time equal to one thousandth of a second.

millpond N a pond containing water which is used for driving a mill.
◆ **like** or **as calm as a millpond** of water: completely smooth and calm.

millstone N **1** either of the large, heavy stones between which grain is ground in a mill. **2** (esp **a millstone around sb's neck**) any heavy burden which someone has to bear and which inhibits/slows their progress.

millstream N a stream of water that turns a millwheel.

millwheel N a wheel, esp a waterwheel, used to drive a mill.

milometer see **mileometer**

milord N, DATED a term formerly used on the continent to address a rich English gentleman.

milt N the testis or sperm of a fish.

mime N **1** the theatrical art of conveying meaning without words through gesture, movement and facial expression. **2** a play or dramatic sequence performed in this way. **3** an actor who practises this art.

➤ VB, TR & INTR to act or express (feelings, etc) without words through gesture, movement and facial expression.

mimeograph N **1** a machine that produces copies of printed or handwritten material from a stencil. **2** a copy produced in this way.

➤ VB to make a copy of something in this way.

mimesis N in art or literature: imitative representation. ■ **mimetic** ADJ.

mimic VB (*-icked, -icking*) **1** to imitate someone or something, esp for comic effect. **2** to copy. **3** to simulate.

➤ N someone who is skilled at imitating other people, esp in a comic manner.

➤ ADJ **1** imitative. **2** mock. ■ **mimicry** N (*-ies*).

mimosa N (*-as* or *-ae*) a tropical shrub or tree which has leaves that droop when touched, and clusters of flowers, typically yellow ones.

minaret N a tower on or attached to a mosque, with a balcony from which the muezzin calls Muslims to prayer.

minatory ADJ, FORMAL threatening.

mince VB **1** to cut or shred something (esp meat) into very small pieces. **2** (esp **mince one's words**), chiefly WITH NEGATIVES to soften the impact of (one's words, opinion, etc) when addressing someone. **3** INTR, usu DEROG to walk or speak with affected delicateness.

➤ N minced meat. ■ **mincer** N.

mincemeat N a spiced mixture of dried fruits, candied peel, etc, used as a filling for pies.

◆ **make mincemeat of sb** or **sth** COLLOQ to destroy or defeat them or it thoroughly.

mince pie N a pie filled with mincemeat or with minced meat.

mind N **1** the power of thinking and understanding; the intelligence. **2** the place where thoughts, feelings and creative reasoning exist; the intellect. **3** memory; recollection: **call something to mind**. **4** opinion; judgement: **It's unjust, to my mind**. **5** attention: **keep your mind on the job**. **6** wish; inclination: **I have a mind to go**. **7** a very intelligent person:

great minds agree.

➤ VB **1** to look after or care for something or someone: **Stay here and mind the luggage**. **2** TR & INTR to be upset or offended by something or someone: **I don't mind the noise**. **3** to be careful or wary of it: **Mind where you step**. **4** to take notice of or pay attention to something or someone: **Mind your own business**. **5** to take care to control something: **Mind your language**. **6** TR & INTR to take care to protect something or someone: **Mind my foot!**

◆ **bear sth in mind** to consider it.

◆ **do you mind!** an exclamation expressing disagreement or objection.

◆ **in one's mind's eye** in one's imagination.

◆ **make up one's mind** to come to a decision.

◆ **mind you** an expression used when adding a qualification to something already said.

◆ **on one's mind** referring to something that is being thought about, worried about, etc.

◆ **take one's** or **sb's mind off sth** to distract one's or someone's thoughts from it.

minder N **1** IN COMPOUNDS someone who takes care of or supervises someone or something: **childminder**. **2** COLLOQ a bodyguard.

mindful ADJ (usu **mindful of sth**) keeping it in mind.

mindless ADJ **1** DEROG senseless; done without a reason: **mindless violence**. **2** DEROG needing no effort of mind. **3** (usu **mindless of sth**) taking no account of it: **mindless of his duties**.

mine¹ PRONOUN **1** something or someone belonging to, or connected with, me; the thing or things, etc belonging to me: **that coat is mine**. **2** my family or people: **as long as it doesn't affect me or mine**.

➤ ADJ, OLD USE, POETIC used in place of **my** before a vowel sound or **h**: **mine host**.

mine² N **1** an opening or excavation in the ground, used to remove minerals, metal ores, coal, etc, from the Earth's crust. **2** an explosive device that is placed just beneath the ground surface or in water, designed to destroy tanks, ships, etc, when detonated. **3** a rich source: **He's a mine of information**.

➤ VB TR & INTR **1** to dig for (minerals, etc). **2** to lay exploding mines in (land or water): The beach has been mined. ■ **mining** N.

minefield N **1** an area of land or water in which mines have been laid. **2** a subject or situation that presents many problems or dangers, esp hidden ones.

miner N someone who mines or works in a mine, esp a coal mine.

mineral N **1** TECHNICAL a naturally occurring substance that is inorganic, and has characteristic physical and chemical properties by which it may be identified. **2** LOOSELY any substance obtained by mining, including fossil fuels although they are organic. **3** any inorganic substance.
➤ ADJ of or relating to the nature of a mineral; containing minerals.

mineralogy N the scientific study of minerals. ■ **mineralogical** ADJ. ■ **mineralogist** N.

mineral water N water containing small quantities of dissolved minerals.

minestrone N a clear soup containing a variety of chunky vegetables and pasta.

minesweeper N a ship equipped to clear mines from an area. ■ **minesweeping** N.

mingle VB (often **mingle with sth** or **sb**) **1** TR & INTR to become or make something become blended or mixed. **2** INTR to move from person to person at a social engagement.

mingy ADJ (*-ier, -iest*) BRIT DEROG, COLLOQ ungenerous; mean; meagre.

mini ADJ small or short of its kind; miniature.

mini- PFX, FORMING NOUNS, DENOTING smaller or shorter than the standard size.

miniature N **1** a small copy, model or breed of anything. **2** a very small painting.
➤ ADJ minute or small-scale; referring to the nature of a miniature.
◆ **in miniature** on a small scale.

miniaturize or **-ise** VB **1** to make (eg technical equipment) on a small scale. **2** to make something very small.

minibus N a small bus.

minicab N a taxi that is ordered by telephone from a private company, not one that can be stopped in the street.

minim N **1** MUS a note half the length of a semibreve. **2** a unit of liquid volume, equal to one sixtieth of a fluid drachm.

minimal ADJ very little indeed; negligible: caused minimal damage. ■ **minimally** ADV.

minimalism N esp in art, music and design: the policy of using the minimum means, eg the fewest and simplest elements, to achieve the desired result. ■ **minimalist** N, ADJ.

minimize or **-ise** VB **1** to reduce something to a minimum. **2** to treat something as being of little importance or significance.

minimum N (*-mums* or *-ma*) **1** the lowest possible number, value, quantity or degree. **2** the lowest number, value, quantity or degree reached or allowed.
➤ ADJ **1** relating or referring to the nature of a minimum; lowest possible: minimum waste. **2** lowest reached or allowed: minimum age.

minion N, DEROG an employee or follower, esp one who is fawning or subservient.

miniskirt N a very short skirt.

minister N **1** the political head of, or a senior politician with responsibilities in, a government department. **2** a member of the clergy in certain branches of the Christian church. **3** a high-ranking diplomat, esp the next in rank below an ambassador.
➤ VB, INTR, FORMAL (esp **minister to sb**) to provide someone with help or service; to take care of them. ■ **ministerial** ADJ.

ministration N, FORMAL **1** the act or process of ministering. **2** (usu **ministrations**) help or service given.

ministry N (*-ies*) **1 a** a government department; **b** the premises it occupies. **2** (**the ministry**) **a** the profession, duties or period of service of a religious minister; **b** religious ministers collectively. **3** the act of ministering.

mink N (PL *mink*) **1** a European or N American

mammal with a slender body, webbed feet and thick fur. **2** the highly valued fur of this animal.

minnow N a small freshwater fish.

minor ADJ **1** not as great in importance or size; fairly or relatively small or insignificant: **only a minor problem. 2** MUS **a** of a scale: having a semitone between the second and third, fifth and sixth, and seventh and eighth notes; **b** of a key, chord, etc: based on such a scale. **3** of a person: below the age of legal adulthood.
➤ N **1** someone who is below the age of legal majority. **2** MUS a minor key, chord or scale. **3** esp US **a** a student's minor or subsidiary subject of study; **b** a student studying such a subject: **a history minor.**
➤ VB, esp US (always **minor in sth**) to study as a subsidiary subject at college or university.

minority N (**-ies**) **1** a small number, or the smaller of two numbers, sections or groups. **2** a group of people who are different, esp in terms of race or religion, from most of the people in a country, region, etc. **3** the state of being the smaller or lesser of two groups: **in a minority. 4** the state of being below the age of legal adulthood.

minster N a large church or cathedral, esp one orig attached to a monastery: **York Minster.**

minstrel N, HIST in the Middle Ages: a travelling singer, musician and reciter of poetry, etc.

mint[1] N **1** an aromatic plant with paired leaves, widely grown as a garden herb. **2** the pungent-smelling leaves of this plant, used as a flavouring. **3** a sweet flavoured with mint or a synthetic substitute. ■ **minty** ADJ (**-ier, -iest**).

mint[2] N **1** a place where coins are produced under government authority. **2** COLLOQ a very large sum of money: **must be worth a mint.**
◆ **in mint condition** as if brand new.

minuet N a slow formal dance with short steps in triple time, popular in the 17c and 18c.

minus PREP **1** with the subtraction of (a specified number): **Eight minus six equals two. 2** COLLOQ without: **arrived minus his wife.**
➤ ADJ **1** negative or less than zero. **2** of a student's grade: indicating a level slightly below that indicated by the letter: **got a B minus for my essay. 3** COLLOQ characterized by being a disadvantage: **a minus point.**
➤ N **1** a sign (–) indicating a negative quantity or that the quantity which follows it is to be subtracted. Also called **minus sign. 2** COLLOQ a negative point; a disadvantage.

minuscule ADJ extremely small.

minute[1] N **1** a unit of time equal to one sixtieth of an hour; 60 seconds. **2** COLLOQ a short while: **Wait a minute. 3** a particular point in time: **At that minute the phone rang. 4** the distance that can be travelled in a minute: **five minutes away. 5** (usu **the minutes**) the official written record of what is said at a formal meeting. **6** GEOM a unit of angular measurement equal to one sixtieth of a degree; 60 seconds.
➤ VB to make an official written record of what is said in (eg a meeting); to take or record something in the minutes of (eg a meeting).
◆ **up to the minute** or **up-to-the-minute** very modern or recent; the latest.

minute[2] ADJ **1** tiny. **2** precise; detailed.

minutiae PL N small details.

minx N, HUMOROUS OR RATHER DATED a cheeky, playful, sly or flirtatious young woman.

miracle N **1** an act or event that breaks the laws of nature, and is therefore thought to be caused by the intervention of God or another supernatural force. **2** COLLOQ a fortunate happening; an amazing event. **3** COLLOQ an amazing example or achievement of something: **a miracle of modern technology.**

miraculous ADJ **1** brought about by, relating to, or like a miracle. **2** COLLOQ wonderful; amazing; amazingly fortunate: **a miraculous escape.**
■ **miraculously** ADV.

mirage N **1** an optical illusion that usu resembles a pool of water on the horizon reflecting light from the sky, commonly experienced in deserts, and caused by the refraction of light by very hot air near to the ground. **2** anything illusory or imaginary.

mire N **1** deep mud; a boggy area. **2** trouble; difficulty; anything unpleasant and messy.

➤ VB, TR & INTR to sink, or to make something or someone sink, in a mire.

mirror N 1 a smooth highly-polished surface, such as glass, coated with a thin layer of metal, such as silver, that reflects an image of what is in front of it. 2 any surface that reflects light. 3 a faithful representation or reflection: **when art is a mirror of life**.
➤ VB 1 to represent or depict something faithfully. 2 to reflect something as in a mirror.

mirth N laughter; merriment. ■ **mirthful** ADJ. ■ **mirthless** ADJ.

misadventure N, FORMAL 1 an unfortunate happening. 2 LAW an accident, with total absence of negligence or intent to commit crime: **death by misadventure**.

misalign VB to align something wrongly. ■ **misalignment** N.

misanthrope or **misanthropist** N someone who has an irrational hatred or distrust of people in general. ■ **misanthropic** ADJ. ■ **misanthropy** N.

misapply VB 1 to apply something wrongly. 2 to use something for the wrong purpose.

misapprehend VB, FORMAL to misunderstand something. ■ **misapprehension** N.

misappropriate VB, FORMAL, esp LAW to put something (eg funds) to a wrong use.

misbegotten ADJ 1 LITERARY ill-conceived. 2 OLD USE illegitimate.

misbehave VB, INTR to behave badly. ■ **misbehaviour** or (US) **misbehavior** N.

miscalculate VB, TR & INTR to calculate or estimate wrongly. ■ **miscalculation** N.

miscall VB to call by the wrong name.

miscarriage N 1 MED the expulsion of a fetus from the uterus before it is capable of independent survival, ie at any time up to about the 24th week of pregnancy. Also called **spontaneous abortion**. 2 an act or instance of failure or error.

miscarry VB, INTR 1 to have a miscarriage. 2 FORMAL of a plan, etc: to go wrong or fail.

miscellaneous ADJ made up of various kinds.

miscellany N (-*ies*) a mixture of various kinds.

mischance N 1 bad luck. 2 an instance of bad luck.

mischief N 1 behaviour that annoys or irritates people but does not mean or cause any serious harm. 2 damage or harm; an injury: **You'll do yourself a mischief**.

mischievous ADJ 1 of a child, etc: tending to make mischief. 2 of behaviour: playfully troublesome. 3 rather DATED of a thing: damaging or harmful. ■ **mischievously** ADV.

miscible ADJ, FORMAL, CHEM of a liquid or liquids: capable of mixing with each other.

misconceive VB 1 TR & INTR (also **misconceive of sth**) to have the wrong idea or impression about it; to misunderstand it. 2 to plan or think something out badly.

misconception N a wrong or misguided attitude, opinion or view.

misconduct N improper or unethical behaviour.

misconstrue VB to interpret something wrongly or mistakenly.

miscreant N, LITERARY OR OLD USE a malicious person; a villain or scoundrel.

misdeed N, LITERARY OR FORMAL an example of bad or criminal behaviour; a wrongdoing.

misdemeanour or (US) **misdemeanor** N 1 FORMAL a wrongdoing; a misdeed. 2 OLD USE, LAW a crime less serious than a felony.

misdirect VB, FORMAL to give wrong directions to someone; to direct, address or instruct something or someone wrongly.

miser N someone who stores up their wealth and hates to spend any of it. ■ **miserly** ADJ.

miserable ADJ 1 of a person: **a** very unhappy; **b** habitually bad-tempered or depressed. 2 causing unhappiness or discomfort: **miserable weather**. 3 marked by poverty or squalor: **miserable living conditions**. 4 DIALECT ungenerous; mean. ■ **miserably** ADV.

misericord N in a church: a ledge on the underside of a seat in the choir stalls which a standing person can use as a support.

misery N (*-ies*) **1** great unhappiness or suffering. **2** a cause of unhappiness. **3** poverty or squalor: living in misery.

misfire VB, INTR **1** of a gun, etc: to fail to fire, or to fail to fire properly. **2** of an engine or vehicle: to fail to ignite the fuel at the right time. **3** to be unsuccessful; to produce the wrong effect.

misfit N someone who is not suited to the situation, job, environment, etc that they are in.

misfortune N **1** bad luck. **2** an unfortunate incident.

misgiving N (often **misgivings**) a feeling of uneasiness, doubt or suspicion.

misguided ADJ acting from or showing mistaken ideas or bad judgement.

mishandle VB to deal with something or someone carelessly or without skill.

mishap N an unfortunate accident, esp a minor one; a piece of bad luck.

mishmash N, COLLOQ a jumbled mixture.

misinform VB to give someone incorrect or misleading information. ■ **misinformation** N.

misinterpret VB to understand or explain something incorrectly or misleadingly.

misjudge VB to judge something or someone wrongly, or to have an unfairly low opinion of them. ■ **misjudgement** or **misjudgment** N.

mislay VB to lose something, usu temporarily, esp by forgetting where it was put.

mislead VB to cause someone to have a false impression or belief. ■ **misleading** ADJ.

mismanage VB to manage or handle something or someone badly or carelessly.

mismatch VB to match (things or people) unsuitably or incorrectly.
➤ N an unsuitable or incorrect match.

misnomer N **1** a wrong or unsuitable name. **2** the use of an incorrect name or term.

misogyny N hatred of women.
■ **misogynist** N.

misplace VB **1** to lose something, usu temporarily, esp by forgetting where it was put. **2** to give (trust, affection, etc) inappropriately.

misprint N a mistake in printing, eg an incorrect or damaged character.

mispronounce VB to pronounce (a word, etc) incorrectly. ■ **mispronunciation** N.

misquote VB to quote inaccurately.

misread VB **1** to read something incorrectly. **2** to misunderstand or misinterpret something.

misrepresent VB to represent something or someone falsely, esp to give a false or misleading account or impression of it or them, often intentionally. ■ **misrepresentation** N.

misrule N, FORMAL bad or unjust government.
➤ VB to govern in a disorderly or unjust way.

miss¹ VB **1** TR & INTR to fail to hit or catch something: missed the ball. **2** to fail to get on something: missed my train. **3** to fail to take advantage of something: missed your chance. **4** to feel or regret the absence or loss of someone or something: I miss you when you're away. **5** to notice the absence of someone or something. **6** to fail to hear or see something: missed his last remark. **7** to refrain from going to (a place or an event): miss the next class.
➤ N a failure to hit or catch something, etc.
◆ **miss out** to fail to benefit from something enjoyable or worthwhile, etc.
◆ **miss out on sth** to fail to benefit from it or participate in it.
◆ **miss sth out** or **miss out sth** to fail to include it; to leave it out.
◆ **miss the boat** or **bus** COLLOQ to miss an opportunity, esp by being too slow to act.

miss² N **1** a girl or unmarried woman. **2** (**Miss**) a term used when addressing an unmarried woman (esp in front of her surname).

missal N, RC CHURCH a book containing all the texts used in the service of mass.

misshapen ADJ badly shaped; deformed.

missile N **1** a self-propelled flying bomb.

2 any weapon or object that is thrown or fired.

missing ADJ **1** absent; lost; not able to be found. **2** of a soldier, military vehicle, etc: not able to be located, but not known to be dead or destroyed.
◆ **go missing** to disappear, esp unexpectedly and inexplicably.

mission N **1** a purpose for which a person or group of people is sent. **2 a** a journey made for a scientific, military or religious purpose; **b** a group of people sent on such a journey. **3** a flight with a specific purpose, such as a bombing raid or a task assigned to the crew of a spacecraft. **4** a group of people sent somewhere to have discussions, esp political ones. **5** (USU **mission in life**) someone's chosen, designated or assumed purpose in life or vocation. **6** a centre run by a charitable or religious organization.

missionary N (*-ies*) a member of a religious organization seeking to carry out charitable works and religious teaching.

missive N, LITERARY OR LAW, etc a letter, esp a long or official one.

misspell VB to spell something incorrectly.
■ **misspelling** N.

missy N (*-ies*) COLLOQ, OLD USE, USU FACETIOUS OR DEROG a term used to address a girl.

mist N **1** condensed water vapour in the air near the ground; thin fog or low cloud. **2** a mass of tiny droplets of liquid, eg one forced from a pressurized container. **3** condensed water vapour on a surface.
➤ VB, TR & INTR (also **mist up** or **over**) to cover or become covered with mist, or as if with mist.
■ **misty** ADJ.

mistake N **1** an error. **2** a regrettable action. **3** an act of understanding or interpreting something wrongly.
➤ VB (*mistook, mistaken*). **1** to misinterpret or misunderstand something: **I mistook your meaning**. **2** to make the wrong choice of something: **He mistook the turning in the fog.**
■ **mistakable** ADJ.
◆ **by mistake** accidentally.

mistaken ADJ **1** understood, thought, named, etc wrongly; incorrect: **mistaken identity**. **2** guilty of, or displaying, a failure to understand correctly: **You are mistaken in saying that he's English.** ■ **mistakenly** ADV.

mister N **1** (**Mister**) the full form of the abbrev **Mr**. **2** COLLOQ a term used when addressing an adult male stranger.

mistletoe N an evergreen shrub that produces clusters of white berries in winter.

mistreat VB to treat someone or something cruelly or without care. ■ **mistreatment** N.

mistress N **1** the female lover of a man married to another woman. **2** rather DATED a female teacher: **She is the French mistress**. **3** a woman in a commanding or controlling position; a female head or owner.

mistrial N, LAW a trial not conducted properly according to the law and declared invalid.

mistrust VB to have no trust in, or to be suspicious of, someone or something.
➤ N a lack of trust. ■ **mistrustful** ADJ.

misunderstand VB, TR & INTR to fail to understand something or someone properly.

misunderstanding N **1** a failure to understand properly. **2** a slight disagreement.

misunderstood ADJ not properly understood or appreciated as regards character, feelings, intentions, purpose, etc.

misuse N improper or inappropriate use.
➤ VB **1** to put something to improper or inappropriate use. **2** to treat something or someone badly.

mite N **1** a small, often microscopic, animal with a simple rounded body and eight legs. **2** any small person or animal.

miter the US spelling of **mitre**.

mitigate VB to make (pain, anger, etc) less severe. ■ **mitigation** N. ■ **mitigating** ADJ.

mitochondrion N (*-dria*) BIOL in the cytoplasm of most cells: a specialized oval structure, consisting of a central matrix surrounded by two membranes.

■ **mitochondrial** ADJ.

mitosis N (**-ses**) BIOL a type of cell division in which two new nuclei are produced, each containing the same number of chromosomes as the parent nucleus.

mitre or (US) **miter** N 1 the ceremonial headdress of a bishop or abbot, a tall pointed hat with separate front and back sections. 2 in joinery, etc: a corner joint between two lengths of wood, etc made by fitting together two 45° sloping surfaces cut into their ends.

mitt N 1 COLLOQ a hand: Keep your mitts off! 2 a thick loosely-shaped glove designed for a specific purpose: oven mitt. 3 a mitten.

mitten N a glove with one covering for the thumb and a large covering for all the other fingers together.

mix VB 1 (esp **mix sth with sth else**, or **mix sth and sth else together** or **up together**) to put (things, substances, etc) together or to combine them to form one mass. 2 to prepare or make something by doing this: mix a cake. 3 INTR to blend together into one mass: Water and oil do not mix. 4 INTR of a person: a to meet with people socially; b to feel at ease in social situations. 5 to do something at the same time as something else; to combine: I'm mixing business with pleasure. 6 to drink (different types of alcoholic drink) on one occasion: don't mix your drinks! 7 TECHNICAL to adjust (separate sound elements) electronically to create an overall balance or particular effect.
➤ N 1 a collection of people or things mixed together. 2 a collection of ingredients, esp dried ingredients, from which something is prepared: cake mix.
◆ **be mixed up** COLLOQ to be upset or emotionally confused.
◆ **be mixed up in sth** or **with sth** or **sb** COLLOQ to be involved in it or with them, esp when it is something illicit or suspect.
◆ **mix sth** or **sb up** 1 to confuse it or them for something else. 2 COLLOQ to upset or put into a state of confusion.

mixed ADJ 1 consisting of different and often opposite kinds of things, elements, characters, etc: a mixed reaction. 2 done, used, etc by people of both sexes: mixed bathing. 3 mingled or combined by mixing.

mixed metaphor N a combination of two or more metaphors which produces an inconsistent or incongruous mental image, eg There are concrete steps in the pipeline.

mixed-up ADJ 1 mentally or emotionally confused. 2 badly-adjusted socially.

mixer N 1 a machine used for mixing: a cement mixer. 2 a soft drink for mixing with alcoholic drinks. 3 COLLOQ someone considered in terms of their ability to mix socially: a good mixer.

mixture N 1 a blend of ingredients prepared for a particular purpose: cake mixture • cough mixture. 2 a combination: a mixture of sadness and relief. 3 the act of mixing.

mix-up N a confusion or misunderstanding.

mizzenmast N, NAUT on a ship with three or more masts: the third mast from the front.

mnemonic N a device or form of words, often a short verse, used as a memory aid.
➤ ADJ serving to help the memory.

mo N, chiefly BRIT COLLOQ a moment.

moa N an extinct flightless ostrich-like bird of New Zealand.

moan N 1 a low prolonged sound expressing sadness or pain. 2 any similar sound, eg made by an engine. 3 COLLOQ a complaint. 4 COLLOQ someone who complains a lot.
➤ VB 1 INTR to utter or produce a moan. 2 INTR, COLLOQ to complain, esp without good reason. 3 to utter something with a moan or moans.
■ **moaner** N. ■ **moaning** ADJ, N.

moat N a deep defensive trench, often filled with water, round a castle, etc.

mob N 1 a large, disorderly crowd. 2 COLLOQ any group or gang. 3 (**the mob**) COLLOQ ordinary people; the masses. 4 (**the mob**) an organized gang of criminals, esp the Mafia.
➤ VB (**-bb-**) 1 to attack something or someone as a mob. 2 to crowd round someone or something, esp curiously or admiringly. 3 esp N AMER to crowd into (a building, shop, etc).

mobile ADJ 1 able to be moved easily; not fixed. 2 set up inside a vehicle travelling from place to place: **mobile shop**. 3 of a face: that frequently changes expression. 4 moving, or able to move, from one social class to another. ➤ N a hanging decoration or sculpture, etc made up of parts that are moved around by air currents. ■ **mobility** N.

mobile phone N a portable telephone that operates by means of a cellular radio system.

mobilize or **-ise** VB 1 to organize or prepare something or someone for use, action, etc. 2 a to assemble and make (forces, etc) ready for war; b INTR of forces, etc: to become ready for war. ■ **mobilization** N.

mobster N, SLANG a member of a gang or an organized group of criminals, esp the Mafia.

moccasin N 1 a soft leather shoe with a continuous sole and heel, as worn by Native Americans. 2 any slipper or shoe in this style.

mocha N 1 a flavouring made from coffee and chocolate. 2 a deep brown colour. 3 dark brown coffee of fine quality.

mock VB 1 TR & INTR (also **mock at sb** or **sth**) to speak or behave disparagingly, derisively, or contemptuously towards someone or something. 2 to mimic someone, usu in a way that makes fun of them. ➤ ADJ 1 false; sham: **mock sincerity**. 2 serving as practice for the similar but real or true thing, event, etc: **a mock examination**.

mockers PL N.
◆ **put the mockers on sth** or **sb** COLLOQ to spoil or end its or their chances of success.

mockery N (**-ies**) 1 an imitation, esp a contemptible or insulting one. 2 any ridiculously inadequate person, action or thing. 3 ridicule.

mock-up N a full-size model or replica of something, built for experimental purposes.

modal ADJ 1 GRAM belonging or concerning mood or a mood. 2 of music: using or relating to a particular mode. ■ **modality** N.

mod cons PL N, COLLOQ modern household conveniences, eg central heating, etc.

mode N 1 rather FORMAL a way of doing something: **a new mode of transport**. 2 a fashion or style, eg in clothes or art. 3 COMP a method of operation as provided by the software: **print mode**.

model N 1 a small-scale representation of something that serves as a guide in constructing the full-scale version. 2 a small-scale replica. 3 one of several types or designs of manufactured article: **the latest model of car**. 4 a person whose job is to display clothes to potential buyers by wearing them. 5 a person who is the subject of an artist's or photographer's work, etc. 6 a thing from which something else is to be derived; a basis. 7 a an excellent example; an example to be copied: **a model of loyalty**; b AS ADJ: **a model boss**. ➤ VB (**-ll-**; US **-l-**) 1 TR & INTR to display (clothes) by wearing them. 2 INTR to work as a model for an artist, photographer, etc. 3 TR & INTR to make models of something. 4 (esp **model sth on sth else**) to plan, build or create it according to a model. ■ **modelling** or (US) **modeling** N.

modem N, COMP an electronic device that transmits information from one computer to another along a telephone line, converting digital data into audio signals and back again.

moderate ADJ 1 not extreme; not strong or violent. 2 average: **moderate intelligence**. ➤ N someone who holds moderate views. ➤ VB 1 TR & INTR to make or become less extreme, violent or intense. 2 INTR (also **moderate over sth**) to act as a moderator in any sense, eg over an assembly. ■ **moderately** ADV.

moderation N 1 the quality or state of being moderate. 2 an act of becoming or making something moderate or less extreme. 3 lack of excess; self-control.

moderator N 1 someone who settles disputes. Also called **mediator**. 2 a person or thing that moderates in any other sense.

modern ADJ 1 belonging to the present or to recent times; not old or ancient. 2 of techniques, equipment, etc: involving, using or being the very latest available: **modern transport**. ➤ N a person living in modern times, esp someone who follows the latest trends. ■ **modernity** N.

modernism N 1 modern spirit or character. 2 a modern usage, expression or trait. ■ **modernist** N, ADJ.

modernize or **-ise** VB to bring something up to modern standards, or adapt it to modern style, conditions, etc. ■ **modernization** N.

modest ADJ 1 not having or showing pride; humble; not pretentious or showy. 2 not large; moderate: a modest income. 3 unassuming; shy or diffident. ■ **modesty** N.

modicum N, FORMAL OR FACETIOUS a small amount.

modifier N 1 GRAM a word or phrase that modifies or identifies the meaning of another word, eg **in the green hat** in the phrase **the man in the green hat**. 2 a person or thing that modifies in any sense.

modify VB (**-ies, -ied**) 1 to change the form or quality of something. 2 GRAM to act as a modifier of (a word). ■ **modification** N.

modish ADJ, rather FORMAL stylish; fashionable. ■ **modishly** ADV. ■ **modishness** N.

modulate VB 1 TECHNICAL to alter the tone or volume of (a sound, or one's voice). 2 FORMAL to change or alter. ■ **modulator** N.

modulation N 1 the act or process of, or an instance of, modulating something. 2 TECHNICAL in radio transmission: the process whereby the frequency or amplitude, etc of a carrier wave is increased or decreased in response to variations in the signal being transmitted.

module N 1 a separate self-contained unit that combines with others to form a larger unit, structure or system. 2 in a space vehicle: a separate self-contained part used for a particular purpose: **lunar module**. 3 EDUCATION a set course forming a unit in a training scheme, degree programme, etc. ■ **modular** ADJ.

moggy or **moggie** N (**-ies**) BRIT COLLOQ a cat.

mogul N 1 an important, powerful, or influential person: a movie mogul. 2 (**Mogul**) HIST a Muslim ruler of India between the 16c and 19c.

mohair N 1 the long soft hair of the Angora goat. 2 a yarn or fabric made of this, either pure or mixed with wool.

mohican N a hairstyle in which the head is partially shaved, leaving a central band of hair.

moiety N (**-ies**) LITERARY OR LAW a half; one of two parts or divisions.

moist ADJ 1 damp or humid; slightly wet or watery. 2 of a climate: rainy. ■ **moistness** N.

moisten VB, TR & INTR to make something moist, or become moist.

moisture N liquid in vapour or spray form, or condensed as droplets.

moisturize or **-ise** VB to make something less dry; to add moisture to it. ■ **moisturizer** N.

molar N any of the large back teeth in humans and other mammals.

molasses SING N 1 the thickest kind of treacle, left over at the very end of the process of refining raw sugar. 2 N AMER treacle.

mold, molder, molding, moldy, etc the N AMER spelling of **mould, moulder, moulding, mouldy,** etc.

mole[1] N 1 a small insectivorous burrowing mammal with velvety greyish-black fur and strong front legs with very broad feet adapted for digging. 2 COLLOQ a spy who works inside an organization and passes secret information to people outside it.

mole[2] N a dark, permanent spot on the skin.

mole[3] N, CHEM the SI unit of amount of substance.

mole[4] N 1 a pier, causeway or breakwater made of stone. 2 a harbour protected by any of these.

molecule N 1 CHEM, PHYSICS the smallest particle of an element or compound that can exist independently and participate in a reaction, consisting of two or more atoms bonded together. 2 LOOSELY a tiny particle. ■ **molecular** ADJ.

molehill N a little pile of earth thrown up

by a burrowing mole.

moleskin N **1** mole's fur. **2 a** a heavy twilled cotton fabric with a short nap. **b** (**moleskins**) trousers made of this fabric.

molest VB **1** to attack or interfere with someone sexually. **2** FORMAL to attack someone, causing them physical harm. ■ **molestation** N.

moll N, SLANG, OLD USE a gangster's girlfriend.

mollify VB (-**ies**, -**ied**) **1** to make someone calmer or less angry. **2** to soothe, ease, or soften something (eg someone's anger, etc). ■ **mollification** N. ■ **mollifier** N.

mollusc N, ZOOL an invertebrate animal with a soft unsegmented body, often protected by a hard, chalky shell, eg the snail, mussel, etc.

mollycoddle VB, COLLOQ to treat someone with fussy care and protection.

molt the N AMER spelling of **moult**

molten ADJ in a melted state; liquefied.

molybdenum N, CHEM a hard silvery metallic element that is used as a hardening agent in various alloys, etc.

moment N **1** a short while: It will only take a moment. Sometimes shortened to **mo**. **2** a particular point in time: at that moment. **3** (**the moment**) the present point, or the right point, in time: cannot be disturbed at the moment. **4** FORMAL importance or significance: a literary work of great moment.

momentarily ADV **1** for a moment: paused momentarily. **2** every moment: kept pausing momentarily. **3** N AMER at any moment.

momentary ADJ lasting for only a moment.

momentous ADJ describing something of great importance or significance.

momentum N (-**tums** or -**ta**) **1 a** a continuous speed of progress; impetus: The campaign gained momentum; **b** the force that an object gains in movement. **2** PHYS the product of the mass and the velocity of a moving object.

monarch N a king, queen or other non-elected sovereign with a hereditary right to

rule. ■ **monarchic** or **monarchical** ADJ.

monarchism N **1** the principles of monarchic government. **2** support for monarchy. ■ **monarchist** N.

monarchy N (-**ies**) **1** a form of government in which the head of state is a monarch. **2** a country which has this form of government.

monastery N (-**ies**) the home of a community of monks.

monastic ADJ **1** belonging or relating to monasteries, monks or nuns. **2** marked by simplicity and self-discipline, like life in a monastery. ■ **monasticism** N.

Monday N the second day of the week, and the beginning of the working week.

monetarism N, ECON the theory or practice of basing an economy on, and curbing inflation by, control of the money supply rather than by fiscal policy. ■ **monetarist** N, ADJ.

monetary ADJ belonging or relating to, or consisting of, money.

money N (PL in sense 1b **monies** or **moneys**) **1 a** coins or banknotes used as a means of buying things; **b** any currency used as legal tender. **2** wealth in general. **3** COLLOQ a rich person; rich people. **4** COMMERCE, LAW (always **monies** or **moneys**) sums of money. ■ **moneyed** or **monied** ADJ. ◆ **be in the money** COLLOQ to be wealthy. ◆ **money for old rope** COLLOQ money obtained without any effort. ◆ **money talks** an expression used to convey the idea that people with money have power and influence over others.

moneybags SING N, COLLOQ a rich person.

money-grubber N, DEROG, COLLOQ someone who greedily acquires as much money as possible. ■ **money-grubbing** ADJ, N.

moneylender N a person or small business that lends money to people at interest, esp at rates higher than general commercial interest rates. ■ **moneylending** N.

money-spinner N, COLLOQ an idea or project, etc that brings in large sums of money.

mongoose N (*mongooses*) a small mammal that preys on snakes, etc, and has a long, slender body, pointed muzzle and a bushy tail.

mongrel N 1 an animal, esp a dog, of mixed breeding. 2 DEROG a person or thing of mixed origin or nature.
➤ ADJ characterized by being of mixed breeding, origin or nature.

monied and **monies** see under **money**

moniker N, SLANG a nickname.

monism N, PHILOS the theory that reality exists in one form only. ■ **monist** N. ■ **monistic** ADJ.

monitor N 1 any instrument designed to check, record or control something on a regular basis. 2 a high-quality screen used in closed-circuit television systems, in TV studios, etc to view the picture being transmitted, etc. 3 the visual display unit of a computer. 4 someone whose job is to monitor eg a situation, process, etc.
➤ VB to check, record, track or control something on a regular basis; to observe or act as a monitor of something. ■ **monitorial** ADJ. ■ **monitorship** N.

monk N a member of a religious community of men living disciplined austere lives devoted primarily to worship.

monkey N 1 any mammal belonging to the primates other than a human, ape, chimpanzee, gibbon, orang utan or lemur, with a hairy coat, nails instead of claws and usu tree-dwelling. 2 COLLOQ a mischievous child.
➤ VB, INTR, COLLOQ (esp **monkey about** or **around with sth**) to play, fool, etc with it.

monkey business N, COLLOQ mischief; illegal or dubious activities.

monkey nut N a peanut in its shell.

monkey wrench N a spanner-like tool with movable jaws; an adjustable spanner.

monochrome ADJ 1 using or having one colour, or in black and white only. 2 using shades of one colour only.
➤ N a monochrome picture, photograph, drawing, etc.

monocle N a lens for correcting the sight in one eye only, held in place between the bones of the cheek and brow. ■ **monocled** ADJ.

monocracy N (*-ies*) government by one person only.

monoculture N, AGRIC the practice of growing the same crop each year on a given area of land.

monogamy N the state or practice of having only one husband or wife at any one time. ■ **monogamist** N. ■ **monogamous** ADJ.

monoglot N a person who speaks only one language.

monogram N a design composed from letters, usu a person's initials, often used on personal belongings, clothing, etc.

monograph N a book or essay dealing with one particular subject or a specific aspect of it.

monolingual ADJ 1 of a person: able to speak one language only. 2 expressed in, or dealing with, a single language.

monolith N 1 a single, tall block of stone, esp one shaped like or into a column or pillar. 2 anything resembling one of these in its uniformity, immovability or massiveness. ■ **monolithic** ADJ.

monologue or (US) **monolog** N, THEAT, etc a a long speech by one actor in a film or play; b a drama for one actor.

monomania N, PSYCHOL domination of the mind by a single subject, to an excessive degree. ■ **monomaniac** N, ADJ.

monomer N, CHEM a simple molecule that can be joined to many others to form a much larger molecule known as a polymer.

monophthong N a single vowel sound.

monoplane N an aeroplane with a single set of wings.

monopolize or **-ise** VB 1 to have a monopoly or exclusive control of trade in (a commodity or service). 2 to dominate (eg a conversation or a person's attention), while excluding all others. ■ **monopolization** N.

monopoly N (-*ies*) **1** the right to be, or the fact of being, the only supplier of a specified commodity or service. **2** a business that has such a monopoly. **3** a commodity or service controlled in this way. **4** exclusive possession or control of anything.

monorail N a railway system in which the trains run on, or are suspended from, a single rail.

monosaccharide N, BIOCHEM a simple sugar, eg glucose, that cannot be broken down into smaller units.

monosodium glutamate N a white crystalline chemical substance used to enhance the flavour of many processed foods.

monosyllable N a word consisting of only one syllable. ■ **monosyllabic** ADJ.

monotheism N the belief that there is one God. ■ **monotheist** N. ■ **monotheistic** ADJ.

monotone N **1** in speech or sound: a single unvarying tone. **2** a sequence of sounds of the same tone. **3** esp in colour: lack of variety. ➤ ADJ **1** lacking in variety; unchanging. **2** in monotone.

monotonous ADJ **1** lacking in variety; tediously unchanging. **2** of speech or sound, etc: in one unvaried tone.

monotony N (-*ies*) **1** the quality of being monotonous. **2** routine or dullness or sameness.

monovalent ADJ, CHEM of an atom of an element: with a valency of one; capable of comb with one atom of hydrogen or its equivalent. Also called **univalent**. ■ **monovalence** or **monovalency** N.

monoxide N, CHEM a compound that contains one oxygen atom in each molecule.

Monsignor N (*Monsignors* or *Monsignori*) a title given to various high-ranking male members of the Roman Catholic church.

monsoon N **1** esp in India, etc and S Asia: a wind that blows from the NE in winter (the **dry monsoon**) and from the SW in summer (the **wet monsoon**). **2** in India: the heavy rains that accompany the summer monsoon.

monster N **1** esp in fables and folklore: any large and frightening imaginary creature. **2** a cruel or evil person. **3** any unusually large thing. ➤ ADJ huge; gigantic: **monster portions**.

monstrosity N (-*ies*) any very ugly or outrageous thing; a monster or freak.

monstrous ADJ **1** like a monster; huge and horrible. **2** outrageous. **3** extremely cruel.

montage N **1 a** the process of creating a picture by assembling and piecing together elements from other pictures, photographs, etc, and mounting them on to canvas, etc; **b** a picture made in this way. **2** the process of editing film material. **3** CINEMA, TV a film sequence made up of short clips, or images superimposed, dissolved together, etc.

month N **1** any of the 12 named divisions of the year, which vary in length between 28 and 31 days. **2** a period of roughly four weeks or 30 days. **3** the period between identical dates in consecutive months.

monthly ADJ **1** happening, published, etc once a month. **2** lasting one month. ➤ ADV once a month. ➤ N (-*ies*) **1** a monthly periodical. **2** COLLOQ a menstrual period.

monument N **1** something, eg a statue, built to preserve the memory of a person or event. **2** any ancient building or structure preserved for its hist value. **3** FORMAL a tombstone.

monumental ADJ **1** like a monument, esp huge and impressive. **2** belonging or relating to, or taking the form of, a monument. **3** COLLOQ very great; extreme: **monumental arrogance**.

moo N the low sound made by a cow, ox, etc. ➤ VB, INTR to make this sound. ■ **mooing** N.

mooch VB, COLLOQ **1** INTR (usu **mooch about** or **around**) to wander around aimlessly. **2** TR & INTR to cadge or scrounge.

mood¹ N **1** a state of mind at a particular time. **2** (esp **the mood**) a suitable or necessary state of mind: **not in the mood**. **3** a temporary grumpy state of mind: **in a mood**. **4** an atmosphere: **The mood is tense**.

mood² N, GRAM each of several forms of a verb, indicating whether the verb is expressing a fact, a wish, possibility or doubt, or a command.

moody ADJ (*-ier, -iest*) **1** tending to change mood often. **2** frequently bad-tempered or sulky. ■ **moodily** ADV. ■ **moodiness** N.

moon¹ N **1** (often **Moon**) the Earth's natural satellite, illuminated to varying degrees by the Sun depending on its position and often visible in the sky, esp at night. **2** a natural satellite of any planet. **3** LITERARY OR OLD USE a month.

moon² VB, INTR (usu **moon about** or **around**) to wander around aimlessly; to spend time idly.

moonlit ADJ illuminated by moonlight.

moonshine N, COLLOQ **1** foolish talk; nonsense. **2** chiefly N AMER smuggled or illegally-distilled alcoholic spirit.

moonshot N a launching of an object, craft, etc to orbit or land on the moon.

moonstone N, GEOL a transparent or opalescent, silvery or bluish feldspar, used as a semi-precious gemstone.

moor¹ N a large area of open, uncultivated upland with a peaty soil. ■ **moorland** N.

moor² VB **1** to fasten (a ship or boat) by a rope, cable or anchor. **2** INTR of a ship, etc: to be fastened in this way. ■ **moorage** N.

moorhen N a small black water bird.

mooring N **1** a place where a boat is moored. **2** (**moorings**) the ropes, anchors, etc used to moor a boat.

moose N (PL *moose*) a large deer with flat, rounded antlers, found in N America. Also called **elk**.

moot VB to suggest.
➢ ADJ open to argument: *a moot point*.

mop N **1** a tool for washing or wiping floors, consisting of a large sponge or a set of thick threads fixed on to the end of a long handle. **2** a similar smaller tool for washing dishes. **3** COLLOQ a thick or tangled mass of hair.

➢ VB (*-pp-*) **1** to wash (eg a floor) with a mop. **2** to wipe or dab (eg a sweaty brow).
◆ **mop up** or **mop sth up 1** to clean something up (eg a spillage) with a mop. **2** COLLOQ to deal with or get rid of (anything that remains).

mope VB, INTR **1** (esp **mope about** or **around**) to behave in a depressed, sulky or aimless way. **2** to move in a listless, aimless or depressed way. ■ **mopy** ADJ.

moped N a small-engined motorcycle, esp one that is started by using pedals.

moraine N, GEOL a ridge of rock and earth formed by the gradual movement of a glacier down a valley.

moral ADJ **1** of or relating to the principles of good and evil, or right and wrong. **2** conforming to what is considered by society to be good, right or proper. **3** having a psychological rather than a practical effect: *moral support*. **4** capable of distinguishing between right and wrong.
➢ N **1** a principle or practical lesson that can be learned from a story or event. **2** (**morals**) a sense of right and wrong, or a standard of behaviour based on this. ■ **morally** ADV.

morale N the level of confidence or optimism in a person or group; spirits.

moralist N someone who advocates strict moral principles. ■ **moralistic** ADJ.

morality N (*-ies*) **1** the quality of being moral. **2** behaviour in relation to accepted moral standards. **3** a system of moral standards.

moralize or **-ise** VB **1** INTR to write or speak, esp critically, about moral standards. **2** to explain something in terms of morals. **3** to make someone or something moral or more moral. ■ **moralization** N.

morass N **1** an area of swampy ground. **2** LITERARY a dangerous or confused situation.

moratorium N (*-iums* or *-ia*) an agreed temporary break in an activity.

moray N a sharp-toothed eel.

morbid ADJ **1** displaying an unhealthy interest in

unpleasant things, esp death. **2** MED relating to, or indicating the presence of, disease. ■ **morbidity** N. ■ **morbidly** ADV.

mordant ADJ sharply sarcastic or critical.
➤ N **1** a chemical compound used to fix colour on textiles, etc that cannot be dyed directly. **2** a corrosive substance. ■ **mordancy** N.

more (USED AS THE COMPARATIVE OF **many** and **much**) ADJ greater; additional: We need more bags.
➤ ADV **1** used to form the comparative form of many adjectives and most adverbs, esp those of two or more syllables: a more difficult problem. **2** to a greater degree; with a greater frequency: I miss him more than ever. **3** again: Do it once more.
➤ PRONOUN a greater, or additional, number or quantity of people or things: If we run out, I'll have to order more.
◆ **more or less 1** almost: more or less finished. **2** roughly.

moreish or **morish** ADJ, BRIT COLLOQ esp of a food: so tasty, delicious, etc that one wants to keep eating more of it.

morel N, BOT an edible fungus whose body has a pale stalk and a ridged head.

morello N a bitter-tasting, dark-red cherry.

moreover ADV, slightly FORMAL OR OLD USE also; besides; and what is more important.

mores PL N, FORMAL social customs that reflect the basic moral and social values of a society.

morganatic ADJ denoting a marriage between a person of high social rank and one of low rank, and allowing neither the lower-ranking person nor any child from the marriage to inherit the title or property of the higher-ranking person.

morgue N **1** a mortuary. **2** in a newspaper office, etc: a place where miscellaneous information is stored for reference.

moribund ADJ **1** dying; near the end of existence. **2** lacking strength or vitality.

morn N, POETIC morning.

mornay ADJ (following its noun) COOKERY served in a cheese sauce: cod mornay.

morning N **1** the part of the day from sunrise to midday, or from midnight to midday. **2** dawn.

mornings ADV, COLLOQ, DIALECT OR US in the morning: I don't work mornings.

morocco N a type of soft fine goatskin leather. Also called **morocco leather**.

moron N **1** DEROG, COLLOQ a very stupid person. **2** now very OFFENSIVE a person with a mild degree of mental handicap. ■ **moronic** ADJ.

morose ADJ silently gloomy or bad-tempered.

morpheme N, LING any of the non-divisible grammatically or lexically meaningful units forming a word. ■ **morphemic** ADJ.

morphine N a highly-addictive, narcotic drug obtained from opium, used medicinally as a powerful analgesic and as a sedative. Also (FORMERLY) called **morphia**.

morphing N, CINEMATOG the use of computer graphics to blend one screen image into another.

morphology N **1** LING the study of morphemes and the rules by which they combine to form words. **2** BIOL the scientific study of the structure of plants and animals. ■ **morphological** ADJ. ■ **morphologist** N.

Morse and **Morse code** N a code used for sending messages, each letter of a word being represented as a series of short or long radio signals or flashes of light.

morsel N a small piece of something, esp of food.

mortal ADJ **1** esp of human beings: certain to die at some future time. **2** causing or resulting in death: mortal combat. **3** extreme: mortal fear. **4** characterized by intense hostility: mortal enemies. **5** used for emphasis: conceivable; single: every mortal thing.
➤ N a mortal being, esp a human being. ■ **mortally** ADV.

mortality N (-ies) **1** the state of being mortal. **2** the number of deaths, eg in a war or epidemic; the death-rate. Also called **mortality rate**.

mortar N **1** BUILDING a mixture of sand, water and cement or lime, used to bond bricks or stones. **2** the small heavy dish in which substances are ground with a pestle. **3** a type of short-barrelled artillery gun for firing shells over short distances.
➤ VB **1** to fix something (esp bricks) in place with mortar. **2** to plaster (eg a wall) with mortar. **3** to bombard (a place or target, etc) using a mortar.

mortarboard N **1** BUILDING a flat board used by bricklayers to carry mortar. **2** a black cap with a hard, square, flat top, worn by academics at formal occasions.

mortgage N **1 a** a legal agreement by which a building society or bank, etc (the **mortgagee**) grants a client (the **mortgagor** or **mortgager**) a loan for the purpose of buying property, ownership of the property being held by the mortagee until the loan is repaid; **b** the deed that brings such a contract into effect. **2 a** the money borrowed for this; **b** the regular amounts of money repaid.
➤ VB to give ownership of (property) as security for a loan.

mortician N, N AMER, ESP US an undertaker.

mortify VB (*-ies, -ied*) **1** to make someone feel humiliated or ashamed. **2** RELIG to control (physical desire) through self-discipline or self-inflicted hardship: **mortify the flesh**.
■ **mortification** N.

mortise lock N a lock fitted into a hole cut in the side edge of a door.

mortuary N (*-ies*) a building or room in which dead bodies are laid out for identification or kept until they are buried or cremated.

mosaic N **1** a design or piece of work formed by fitting together lots of small pieces of coloured stone, glass, etc. **2** anything that resembles a mosaic.

mosey VB, INTR (USU **mosey along**) COLLOQ to walk in a leisurely way; to saunter.

Moslem see **Muslim**

mosque N a Muslim place of worship.

mosquito N (*-os* or *-oes*) a type of small two-winged insect with thin, feathery antennae and a slender body, the female of which has piercing mouthparts for sucking blood.

moss N **1** the common name for a type of small spore-bearing plant, typically found growing in dense, spreading clusters in moist shady habitats. **2** DIALECT, esp SCOT & N ENGLISH an area of boggy ground. ■ **mossy** ADJ (*-ier, -iest*).

most (USED AS THE SUPERLATIVE OF **many** and **much**) ADJ, DENOTING the greatest number, amount, etc: **Most people enjoy parties**.
➤ ADV **1** (also **the most**) used to form the superlative of many adjectives and most adverbs, esp those of more than two syllables: **the most difficult problem of all**. **2** (also **the most**) to the greatest degree; with the greatest frequency: **I miss him most at Christmas**. **3** extremely: **a most annoying thing**.
➤ PRONOUN the greatest number or quantity, or the majority of people or things: **Most of them are here**.
◆ **at the most** or **at most** certainly not more than (a specified number).
◆ **for the most part** mostly.
◆ **make the most of sth** to take the greatest possible advantage of it.

mostly ADV **1** mainly; almost completely. **2** usually.

mote N a speck, esp a speck of dust.

motel N a hotel situated near a main road and intended for overnight stops by motorists.

motet N a short piece of sacred music for several voices.

moth N the common name for one of many winged insects belonging to the same order as butterflies but generally night-flying.

mothball N a small ball of camphor or naphthalene that is hung in wardrobes, etc to keep away clothes moths.
➤ VB **1** to postpone work on something (eg a project), or to lay it aside, esp for an indefinitely long time. **2** to put (clothes, linen, etc), with mothballs, into a place for long-term storage.

mother N 1 a female parent. 2 (also **Mother**) as a term of address or a title for: one's female parent or stepmother, foster-mother, etc. 3 the cause or origin; the source from which other things have sprung or developed.
➤ VB 1 to give birth to or give rise to someone or something. 2 to treat someone with care and protection, esp excessively so. ■ **motherhood** N. ■ **motherless** ADJ. ■ **motherly** ADJ.

motherboard N, COMP the printed circuit board which holds the principal components in a computer.

mother-in-law N (*mothers-in-law*) the mother of one's husband or wife.

mother-of-pearl N a hard iridescent substance that forms the inner layer of the shell of some molluscs (eg oysters) and is used to make buttons, beads, etc. Also called **nacre**.

mother tongue N one's native language.

mothproof ADJ of cloth: treated with chemicals which resist attack by clothes moths.
➤ VB to treat (fabric) in this way.

motif N 1 on clothing, etc: a design or symbol. 2 a shape repeated within a pattern. Also called **motive**. 3 in the arts: something that is repeated throughout a work or works.

motile ADJ, BIOL capable of independent spontaneous movement. ■ **motility** N.

motion N 1 the act, state, process or manner of moving. 2 a single movement, esp one made by the body; a gesture or action. 3 the ability to move a part of the body. 4 a proposal for formal discussion at a meeting. 5 LAW an application made to a judge during a court case for an order or ruling to be made. 6 BRIT **a** an act of discharging faeces from the bowels; **b** (**motions**) faeces.
➤ VB, TR & INTR (often **motion to sb**) to give a signal or direction. ■ **motionless** ADJ.
◆ **go through the motions** 1 to pretend to do something; to act something out. 2 to perform a task mechanically or half-heartedly.
◆ **in motion** moving; operating.

motivate VB 1 to be the motive of something or

someone. 2 to cause or stimulate (a person) to act; to be the underlying cause of (an action). ■ **motivation** N.

motive N 1 a reason for, or underlying cause of, action of a certain kind. 2 see **motif** (sense 2).
➤ ADJ causing motion: motive force.

motley ADJ 1 made up of many different kinds: a motley crew. 2 many-coloured.

motocross N a form of motorcycle racing in rough terrain.

motor N 1 an engine, esp the internal-combustion engine of a vehicle or machine. 2 COLLOQ a car. 3 a device that converts electrical energy into mechanical energy.
➤ ADJ 1 ANAT **a** of a nerve: transmitting impulses from the central nervous system to a muscle or gland; **b** of a nerve cell: forming part of such a nerve. 2 giving or transmitting motion.
➤ VB, INTR 1 to travel by motor vehicle, esp by private car. 2 COLLOQ to move or work, etc fast and effectively. ■ **motoring** N. ■ **motorist** N.

motorbike N, COLLOQ a motorcycle.

motorcade N a procession of cars.

motorcycle N any two-wheeled vehicle powered by an internal combustion engine that runs on petrol. ■ **motorcyclist** N.

motorize or **-ise** VB to fit a motor or motors to something. ■ **motorization** N.

motorway N, BRIT, AUSTRAL & NZ a major road for fast-moving traffic.

mottled ADJ having a pattern of different coloured blotches or streaks.

motto N (-os or -oes) 1 a phrase adopted by a person, family, etc as a principle of behaviour. 2 a printed phrase or verse in a paper cracker. 3 a quotation at the beginning of a book or chapter, hinting at what is to follow.

mould¹ or (N AMER) **mold** N 1 a fungus that produces an abundant woolly network of threadlike strands which may be white, grey-green or black in colour. 2 a woolly growth of this sort on foods, plants, etc.

mould² or (N AMER) **mold** N 1 a hollow, shaped container into which a liquid substance, eg jelly, is poured so that it takes on the container's shape when it cools and sets. 2 nature, character or personality: **We need a leader in the traditional mould.**
➤ VB 1 to shape something in or using a mould. 2 a to shape (a substance) with the hands: **moulded the clay in her hands**; b to form something by shaping a substance with the hands: **moulded a pot out of the clay. 3** TR & INTR to fit, or make something fit, tightly: **The dress was moulded to her body. 4** (esp **mould sth** or **sb into sth**) to exercise a controlling influence over their development.

mould³ or (N AMER) **mold** N loose soft soil that is rich in decayed organic matter.

moulder or (N AMER) **molder** VB, INTR (also **moulder away**) to decay.

moulding or (N AMER) **molding** N a shaped, decorative strip.

mouldy or (N AMER) **moldy** ADJ (-ier, -iest) 1 covered with mould. 2 old and stale.

moult or (N AMER) **molt** VB, INTR, ZOOL of an animal: to shed feathers, hair or skin to make way for a new growth.
➤ N 1 the act or process of moulting. 2 the time taken for this.

mound N 1 any small hill, or bank of earth or rock. 2 a heap or pile.

mount¹ VB 1 TR & INTR to go up: **mounting the stairs. 2** TR & INTR to get up on to (a horse, bicycle, etc). 3 INTR (also **mount up**) to increase in level or intensity: **when pressure mounts up. 4** to put (a picture, slide, etc) in a frame or on a background for display; to hang or put something up on a stand or support. 5 to organize or hold (a campaign, etc).
➤ N 1 a support or backing on which something is placed for display or use, etc. 2 a horse that is ridden. ■ **mounted** ADJ.

mount² N, chiefly POETIC OR OLD USE a mountain. Also **Mount** in place names.

mountain N 1 a very high, steep hill, often one of bare rock. 2 (also **mountains of sth**) COLLOQ a large heap or mass: **a mountain of washing. 3** a huge surplus of some commodity: **a butter mountain.** ■ **mountainous** ADJ.

mountain ash N the rowan.

mountain bike N a sturdy bicycle designed for riding in hilly terrain.

mountaineer N someone who climbs mountains. ■ **mountaineering** N.

mountebank N, LITERARY, DEROG 1 FORMERLY a medically unqualified person who sold supposed medicines from a public platform. 2 any person who swindles or deceives.

mourn VB 1 TR & INTR (esp **mourn for** or **over sb** or **sth**) to feel or show deep sorrow at the death or loss of them or it. 2 INTR to be in mourning or wear mourning. ■ **mourner** N.

mournful ADJ 1 feeling or expressing grief. 2 suggesting sadness or gloom: **mournful music.** ■ **mournfully** ADV.

mourning N 1 grief felt or shown over a death. 2 a symbol of grief, esp black clothing. 3 a period of time during which someone is officially mourning a death.

mouse N (*mice* or in sense 3 *mouses*) 1 a small rodents with a grey or brown coat, pointed muzzle, bright eyes and a long hairless tail. 2 COLLOQ a very shy, quiet or timid person. 3 COMP an input device which can be moved around on a flat surface, causing a cursor to move around the computer screen in response.

mousse N, COOKERY a a dessert made from a whipped mixture of cream, eggs and flavouring, eaten cold: **strawberry mousse**; b a similar but savoury dish, made with meat, fish, etc: **salmon mousse.**

moustache and (N AMER) **mustache** N unshaved hair growing across the top of the upper lip. ■ **moustached** ADJ.

mousy or **mousey** ADJ (-ier, -iest) 1 like a mouse, or belonging or relating to a mouse. 2 of hair: light dullish brown in colour. 3 of a person: shy, quiet or timid. ■ **mousiness** N.

mouth N 1 in humans, animals, etc: an opening in the head through which food is taken in and speech or sounds emitted, and containing the teeth, gums, tongue, etc. **2** the lips; the outer visible parts of the mouth. **3** an opening, eg of a bottle. **4** the part of a river that widens to meet the sea. **5** a person considered as a consumer of food: **five mouths to feed**. **6** DEROG, COLLOQ boastful talk: **He's all mouth.**

➢ VB **1** to form (words) without actually speaking. **2** TR & INTR, DEROG to speak (words) pompously or insincerely.

◆ **mouth off** SLANG, esp US **1** to express opinions forcefully or loudly. **2** to boast or brag.

mouthful N **1** as much food or drink as fills the mouth or is in one's mouth. **2** a small quantity, esp of food. **3** COLLOQ a word or phrase that is difficult to pronounce. **4** COLLOQ an outburst of forceful and often abusive language.

mouth organ see under **harmonica**

mouthpiece N **1** the part of a musical instrument, telephone receiver, etc that is held in or against the mouth. **2** a person or publication that is used to express the views of a group.

mouthwash N an antiseptic liquid used for gargling or for rinsing or freshening the mouth.

mouth-watering ADJ **1** of food: having a delicious appearance or smell. **2** COLLOQ highly desirable.

movable or **moveable** ADJ **1** not fixed in one place; portable. **2** esp SCOTS LAW of property: able to be removed; personal. **3** of a religious festival: taking place on a different date each year: **Easter is a movable feast.**

move VB **1** TR & INTR to change position or make something change position or go from one place to another. **2** INTR to make progress of any kind: **move towards a political solution**. **3** chiefly INTR (often **move on, out** or **away, etc**) to change one's place of living, working, operating, etc. **4** to affect someone's feelings or emotions. **5** (usu **move sb to do sth**) to prompt them or affect them in such a way that they do it: **What moved him to say that? 6** TR & INTR to change the position of (a piece in a board game). **7** TR & INTR to propose or request something formally, at a meeting, etc. **8** INTR to spend time; to associate with people: **move in**

fashionable circles. **9** INTR, COLLOQ to take action; to become active or busy: **must move on this matter straight away**. **10** INTR, COLLOQ to travel or progress fast: **That bike can really move**. **11 a** INTR of the bowels: to be evacuated; **b** to cause (the bowels) to evacuate.

➢ N **1** an act of moving the body; a movement. **2** an act of changing homes or premises: **How did your move go? 3** GAMES **a** an act of moving a piece on the board; **b** a particular player's turn to move a piece. ■ **mover** N.

◆ **make a move 1** COLLOQ to start on one's way; to leave. **2** to begin to proceed.

◆ **on the move 1** moving from place to place. **2** advancing or making progress.

movement N **1** a process of changing position or going from one point to another. **2** an act or manner of moving: **made a sudden, jerky movement. 3** an organization, association or group, esp one that promotes a particular cause. **4** a general tendency or current of opinion, taste, etc. **5** MUS a section of a large-scale piece, esp a symphony. **6** (**movements**) a person's actions during a particular time. **7 a** an act of evacuating the bowels; **b** the waste matter evacuated. **8** the moving parts of a watch or clock.

movie N, esp US **1** a cinema film. **2** (esp **the movies**) cinema films in general.

moving ADJ **1** having an effect on the emotions; touching; stirring: **a moving story**. **2** in motion; not static: **a moving staircase**.

mow VB (**mown**) to cut (grass, a lawn, crop, etc) by hand or with a machine. ■ **mower** N.

◆ **mow sb down** to kill them in large numbers.

mozzarella N a white, Italian curd cheese.

MP ABBREV **1** Member of Parliament. **2** Military Police.

mpg ABBREV miles per gallon.

Mr N (**Messrs**) the standard title given to a man, used as a prefix before his surname.

Mrs N the standard title given to a married woman, used as a prefix before her surname.

Ms N the standard title given to a woman,

married or not, used as a prefix before her surname in place of Mrs or Miss.

MSc ABBREV Master of Science.

MSG ABBREV monosodium glutamate.

much ADJ, PRONOUN (*more, most*) esp with negatives and in questions: **1** a great amount or quantity of something: **You don't have much luck. 2** (as PRONOUN) a great deal; anything of significance or value: **Can you see much?**
➤ ADV **1** by a great deal: **That looks much prettier. 2** to a great degree: **don't like her much. 3** (often **much the same**) nearly the same; almost: **Things look much as I left them.**
◆ **a bit much** COLLOQ rather more that can be tolerated or accepted.
◆ **(as) much as** although: **I cannot come, much as I would like to.**
◆ **make much of sth** or **sb 1** to cherish or take special interest in them or it, or to treat them or it as very important. **2** WITH NEGATIVES to succeed in understanding them or it: **couldn't make much of what he was saying.**
◆ **not much of a sth** COLLOQ not a very good example of it: **I'm not much of a singer.**
◆ **not up to much** COLLOQ not much good.
◆ **too much** COLLOQ more than can be tolerated or accepted.
◆ **too much for sb** more than a match for them.

mucilage N, BOT a gum–like substance that becomes viscous and slimy when added to water, present in or secreted by various plants. ■ **mucilaginous** ADJ.

muck N **1** COLLOQ dirt, esp wet or clinging dirt. **2** manure. **3** DEROG, COLLOQ anything disgusting or of very poor quality.
➤ VB to treat (soil) with manure.
◆ **muck about** or **around** COLLOQ to behave foolishly.
◆ **muck about** or **around with sth** COLLOQ to interfere, tinker or fiddle about with it.
◆ **muck sb about** or **around** to treat them inconsiderately; to try their patience.
◆ **muck in** or **muck in with sb** COLLOQ to take a share of responsibilities with others.
◆ **muck out** or **muck sth out** to clear dung from (a farm building, etc).

◆ **muck sth up** COLLOQ **1** to do it badly or wrongly; to ruin or spoil it. **2** to make it dirty.

muckle see **mickle**

muck-raking N, COLLOQ the practice of searching for and exposing scandal, esp about famous people. ■ **muck-raker** N.

mucky ADJ (*-ier, -iest*) COLLOQ very dirty.

mucous membrane N, ZOOL, ANAT in vertebrates: the moist, mucus–secreting lining of various internal cavities of the body.

mucus N the thick slimy substance that protects and lubricates the surface of mucous membranes and traps bacteria and dust.

mud N **1** soft, wet earth. **2** COLLOQ insults; slanderous attacks: **throw mud at someone.**

muddle VB (also **muddle sth** or **sb up**) **1** to put it or them into a disordered or confused state. **2 a** to confuse the mind of someone: **You'll muddle him with all those figures; b** to confuse (different things) in the mind.
➤ N a state of disorder or mental confusion.
◆ **muddle along** COLLOQ to manage or make progress slowly and haphazardly.
◆ **muddle through** COLLOQ to succeed by persevering in spite of difficulties.

muddy ADJ (*-ier, -iest*) **1** covered with or containing mud. **2** dull, cloudy or dirty. **3** of thoughts, etc: not clear; vague.
➤ VB (*-ies, -ied*) to make something muddy, esp to make it unclear or difficult to understand. ■ **muddiness** N.

mudflap N a flap of rubber, etc fixed behind the wheel of a vehicle to prevent mud, etc being thrown up behind.

mudflat N (often **mudflats**) a relatively flat area of land which is covered by a shallow layer of water at high tide.

mudguard N a curved, metal guard over the upper half of a wheel to keep rain or mud from splashing up.

mud-slinging N, COLLOQ the act or process of making slanderous personal attacks. ■ **mud-slinger** N.

muesli N a mixture of crushed grain, nuts and dried fruit, eaten with milk.

muezzin N, ISLAM the Muslim official who calls worshippers to prayer, usu from a minaret.

muff N a wide fur tube which the wearer places their hands inside for warmth.

muffin N **1** BRIT a small round flat breadlike cake, usu eaten toasted or hot with butter. **2** N AMER a cup-shaped sweet cake.

muffle VB **1** to make something quieter; to suppress (sound). **2** to prevent someone from saying something.

muffler N **1** a thick scarf. **2** US a silencer.

mufti N, OLD USE civilian clothes when worn by people who usu wear a uniform.

mug[1] N **1** a drinking-vessel with a handle, used without a saucer. **2** (also **mugful**) the amount a mug will hold. **3** COLLOQ a face or mouth. **4** COLLOQ someone who is easily fooled. ➤ VB (-**gg**-) to attack and rob someone violently. ■ **mugger** N. ■ **mugging** N.

mug[2] VB (-**gg**-) TR & INTR (esp **mug sth up** or **mug up on sth**) COLLOQ to study or revise (a subject, etc) thoroughly, esp for an examination.

muggy ADJ (-**ier, -iest**) of the weather: unpleasantly warm and damp; close.

mugshot N, COLLOQ, orig US a photograph of a criminal's face, taken for police records.

mulberry N **1** a tree that produces small edible purple berries. **2** such a berry. **3** a dark purple colour.

mulch N straw, compost, shredded bark, etc laid on the soil around plants to retain moisture and prevent the growth of weeds. ➤ VB to cover (soil, etc) with mulch.

mule[1] N **1** the offspring of a male donkey and a female horse. **2** a stubborn person.

mule[2] N a shoe or slipper with no back part covering the heel.

muleteer N someone who drives mules.

mulish ADJ stubborn; obstinate.

mull[1] VB (now always **mull sth over**) to consider it carefully; to ponder on it.

mull[2] VB to spice, sweeten and warm (wine or beer). ■ **mulled** ADJ.

mullah N a Muslim scholar and adviser in Islamic religion and sacred law.

mullet N any of a family of thick-bodied edible marine fish.

mulligatawny N, COOKERY a thick curry-flavoured meat soup.

mullion N, ARCHIT a vertical bar or post separating the panes or casements of a window. ■ **mullioned** ADJ.

multicellular ADJ, BIOL made up of many cells.

multicoloured ADJ having many colours.

multicultural ADJ esp of a society, community, etc: made up of, involving or relating to several distinct racial or religious cultures, etc.

multifarious ADJ, FORMAL very varied.

multigym N an apparatus with weights and levers, designed for exercising and toning up all the muscles of the body.

multilateral ADJ **1** involving or affecting several people, groups, parties or nations: a multilateral treaty. **2** many-sided.

multilingual ADJ **1** written or expressed in several different languages. **2** of a person: able to speak several different languages.

multimedia ADJ **1** in entertainment, education, etc: involving the use of a combination of different media, eg TV, radio, slides, hi-fi, visual arts. **2** COMP of a computer system: able to present and manipulate data in a variety of forms, eg text, graphics and sound.

multinational ADJ esp of a large business: operating in several different countries. ➤ N a multinational corporation, business or organization.

multiparous ADJ, ZOOL of a mammal: producing several young at one birth.

multipartite ADJ divided into many parts.

multiple ADJ **1** having, involving or affecting many parts. **2** many, esp more than several.

3 multiplied or repeated.
➢ N, MATH a number or expression for which a given number or expression is a factor, eg 24 is a multiple of 12.

multiple-choice ADJ of a test, exam or question: giving a list of possible answers from which the candidate has to try to select one.

multiplex N a large cinema building divided into several smaller cinemas.
➢ ADJ, FORMAL having very many parts; manifold; complex.

multiplicand N, MATH a number to be multiplied by a second number (the multiplier).

multiplication N, MATH **a** an operation in which one number is added to itself as many times as is indicated by a second number, written using the multiplication sign; **b** the process of performing this operation.

multiplication sign N, MATH the symbol $\times$ used between two numbers to indicate that they are to be multiplied.

multiplicity N (-ies) FORMAL a great number and variety.

multiplier N **1** MATH a number indicating by how many times another number (the multiplicand), to which it is attached by a multiplication sign, is to be multiplied. **2** a person or thing that multiplies.

multiply VB (-ies, -ied) **1** (esp **multiply sth by sth**) **a** to add (one number or amount) to itself a specified number of times: Two multiplied by two equals four; **b** (sometimes **multiply sth and sth together**) to combine (two numbers) by the process of multiplication. **2** INTR to increase in number, esp by breeding.

multipurpose ADJ having many uses.

multiracial ADJ for, including, or consisting of, people of many different races.

multistorey ADJ of a building: having many floors or levels.

multitasking N, COMP the action of running several processes or jobs simultaneously.

multitude N **1** a great number of people or things. **2** (**the multitude**) ordinary people. ■ **multitudinous** ADJ.

mum[1] N **1** COLLOQ a mother. **2** a term used to address or refer to one's own mother.

mum[2] ADJ, COLLOQ silent; not speaking: keep mum about it.

mumble VB, TR & INTR to speak or say something unclearly, esp with the mouth partly closed.

mumbo-jumbo N, COLLOQ **1** foolish talk, esp of a religious or spiritual kind. **2** baffling jargon.

mummer N, HIST in medieval England: one of a group of masked actors who visited houses during winter festivals, distributing gifts and performing dances, etc. ■ **mummery** N.

mummify VB (-ies, -ied) to preserve (a corpse) as a mummy. ■ **mummification** N.

mummy[1] N (-ies) chiefly BRIT a child's word for mother.

mummy[2] N (-ies) a corpse preserved with embalming spices and bandaged.

mumps SING N (also **the mumps**) MED an infectious viral disease causing fever, headache and painful swelling of the salivary glands on one or both sides of the face.

mumsy ADJ (-ier, -iest) COLLOQ **1** homely; comfy. **2** maternal.

munch VB, TR & INTR to chew with a steady movement of the jaws, esp noisily.

mundane ADJ **1** ordinary; dull; everyday. **2** belonging or relating to this world.

mung bean N **1** an E Asian plant that produces beans and beansprouts. **2** the edible green or yellow bean of this plant.

municipal ADJ of or relating to, or controlled by, the local government of a town or region.

municipality N (-ies) a town or region that has its own local government.

munificent ADJ, FORMAL extremely generous. ■ **munificence** N.

muniments PL N, LAW official papers that prove ownership, esp title deeds to property.

munitions PL N military equipment.

muon N, PHYS an elementary particle that behaves like a heavy electron, but decays to form an electron and neutrino. ■ **muonic** ADJ.

mural N (also **mural painting**) a painting that is painted directly on to a wall.

murder N 1 the act of unlawfully and intentionally killing a person. 2 COLLOQ something that causes hardship or difficulty: The traffic in town was murder today. ➤ VB 1 TR & INTR to kill someone unlawfully and intentionally. 2 COLLOQ to spoil or ruin something (eg a piece of music), by performing it very badly. 3 COLLOQ to defeat someone easily. ■ **murderer** N. ■ **murderess** N.

murderous ADJ 1 of a person, weapon, etc: intending, intended for, or capable of, causing or committing murder. 2 COLLOQ very unpleasant; causing hardship or difficulty.

murk or (rarely) **mirk** N darkness; gloom.

murky ADJ (-ier, -iest) 1 dark; gloomy. 2 of water: dark and dirty. 3 suspiciously vague or unknown; shady: her murky past. ■ **murkily** ADV. ■ **murkiness** N.

murmur N 1 a quiet, continuous sound, eg of running water or low voices. 2 anything said in a low, indistinct voice. 3 a complaint, esp a subdued, muttering one. 4 MED an abnormal rustling sound made by the heart. ➤ VB, TR & INTR to speak (words) softly.

muscle N 1 an animal tissue composed of bundles of fibres that are capable of contracting to produce movement of part of the body. 2 a body structure or organ composed of this tissue. 3 bodily strength. 4 power or influence of any kind: financial muscle. ➤ VB, COLLOQ (always **muscle in on sth**) to force one's way into it.

muscle-bound ADJ having over-enlarged muscles that are stiff and difficult to move.

muscular ADJ 1 belonging or relating to, or consisting of, muscle. 2 having well-developed muscles; strong; brawny. ■ **muscularity** N.

musculature N the arrangement, or degree of development, of muscles in a body or organ.

Muse N, GR MYTHOL any of the nine goddesses of the arts, said to be a source of creative inspiration to all artists, esp poets.

muse VB 1 INTR (often **muse on sth**) to reflect or ponder silently. 2 to say something in a reflective way. 3 INTR to gaze contemplatively.

museum N a place where objects of artistic, scientific or historical interest are displayed to the public, preserved and studied.

mush[1] N a soft half-liquid mass of anything.

mush[2] EXCLAM, N AMER used esp to a team of dogs: go on! go faster!

mushroom N 1 a a type of fungus which consists of a short white stem supporting an umbrella-shaped cap with numerous spore-bearing gills on the underside. b the edible species of such fungi. 2 anything resembling this in shape. 3 anything resembling this in the speed of its growth or development. ➤ VB, INTR to increase with alarming speed.

mushy ADJ (-ier, -iest) 1 in a soft half-liquid state. 2 sentimental in a sickly way.

music N 1 the art of making sound in a rhythmically organized, harmonious form, either sung or produced with instruments. 2 such sound, esp that produced by instruments. 3 a any written form or composition in which such sound is expressed; b musical forms or compositions collectively. 4 the performance of musical compositions. 5 pleasing, harmonious or melodic sound.

musical ADJ 1 consisting of, involving, relating to or producing music. 2 melodious. 3 having a talent or aptitude for music. ➤ N a play or film that features singing and dancing. ■ **musicality** N. ■ **musically** ADV.

music hall N 1 variety entertainment. 2 a theatre for variety entertainment.

musician N someone who is skilled in music, esp in performing or composing it.

musicology N the academic study of music in all its aspects. ■ **musicologist** N.

musk N a strong-smelling substance much used in perfumes, secreted by the glands of various animals, esp the male musk deer. ■ **musky** ADJ (*-ier, -iest*).

musket N, HIST an early rifle-like gun that was loaded through the barrel and fired from the shoulder. ■ **musketeer** N.

muskrat and **musquash** N 1 a large, N American water rodent, which produces a musky smell. 2 its thick brown fur.

Muslim and **Moslem** N a follower of the religion of Islam.
➤ ADJ of or relating to Muslims or to Islam.

muslin N a fine gauze-like cotton cloth.

mussel N an edible marine bivalve mollusc.

must¹ AUXILIARY VERB 1 used to express necessity: I must earn some extra money. 2 used to express duty or obligation: You must help him. 3 used to express certainty: You must be Charles. 4 used to express determination: I must remember to smile. 5 used to express probability: She must be there by now. 6 used to express inevitability: We must all die. 7 used to express an invitation or suggestion: You must come and see us soon.
➤ N (always **a must**) a necessity.

must² N the juice of grapes or other fruit before it is completely fermented to become wine.

mustache the N AMER spelling of **moustache**.

mustang N a small wild or half-wild horse native to the plains of the western US.

mustard N 1 a plant with bright yellow flowers. 2 a hot-tasting paste used as a condiment or seasoning, made from powdered or crushed whole seeds of black or white mustard or both, mixed with water or vinegar. 3 a light yellow or brown colour.
➤ ADJ having a light yellow or brown colour.

mustard gas N a highly poisonous gas that causes severe blistering of the skin, used as a chemical warfare agent.

muster VB 1 TR & INTR esp of soldiers: to gather together for duty or inspection, etc. 2 (also **muster up**) to summon or gather (eg courage or energy).
◆ **pass muster** to be accepted as satisfactory, eg at an inspection.

mustn't CONTRACTION must not.

musty ADJ (*-ier, -iest*) 1 mouldy or damp. 2 smelling or tasting stale. ■ **mustiness** N.

mutable ADJ subject to or able to change; variable. ■ **mutability** N.

mutagen N, BIOL a chemical agent that induces or increases the frequency of mutations in organisms. ■ **mutagenic** ADJ.

mutant N a living organism or cell that carries a specific mutation of a gene.
➤ ADJ of an organism or cell: carrying or resulting from a mutation.

mutate VB, TR & INTR 1 BIOL to undergo or cause to undergo mutation. 2 FORMAL to change.

mutation N 1 GENETICS in a living organism: a change in the structure of a single gene, the arrangement of genes on a chromosome or the number of chromosomes, which may result in a change in the appearance or behaviour of the organism. 2 FORMAL a change of any kind.

mute ADJ 1 unable to speak; dumb. 2 silent. 3 felt, but not expressed in words: mute anger.
➤ N 1 MED someone who is physically unable to speak. 2 a device that softens or deadens the sound of a musical instrument.
➤ VB to soften the sound of (a musical instrument). ■ **mutely** ADV. ■ **muteness** N.

muted ADJ 1 not loud or harsh; soft. 2 mildly expressed; not outspoken.

mutilate VB 1 to cause severe injury to (a person or animal), esp by removing a limb or organ. 2 to damage something severely, esp to alter (eg a text, song, etc) beyond recognition. ■ **mutilation** N. ■ **mutilator** N.

mutinous ADJ 1 having mutinied or likely to mutiny. 2 of or relating to mutiny.

mutiny N (*-ies*) rebellion, or an act of rebellion, against authority, esp in the armed services.
➤ VB (*-ies, -ied*) INTR to engage in mutiny. ■ **mutineer** N.

mutt N, SLANG a dog, esp a mongrel.

mutter VB **1** TR & INTR to utter (words) in a quiet, barely audible voice. **2** INTR to grumble or complain, esp in a low voice.
➤ N **1** a soft, barely audible or indistinct tone of voice. **2** a muttered complaint.

mutton N the flesh of a sheep, used as food.

mutual ADJ **1** felt by each of two or more people about the other or others; reciprocal. **2** to, towards or of each other: **mutual supporters**. **3** COLLOQ shared by each of two or more; common: **a mutual friend**. ■ **mutuality** N. ■ **mutually** ADV.

muzak N piped music.

muzzle N **1** the projecting jaws and nose of an animal, eg a dog. **2** an arrangement of straps fitted round an animal's jaws to prevent it biting. **3** the open end of a gun barrel.
➤ VB **1** to put a muzzle on (eg a dog). **2** to prevent someone from speaking or being heard.

muzzy ADJ (**-ier, -iest**) **1** not thinking clearly; confused. **2** blurred; hazy.

my ADJ **1** belonging or relating to **me**: **my book**. **2** used with nouns in various exclams: **My goodness!: My foot!** **3** used in respectful terms of address such as **my lord**.
➤ EXCLAM (also **my word, my goodness** or, more strongly, **my God**) expressing surprise or amazement.

myalgia N, MED muscle pain. ■ **myalgic** ADJ.

mycelium N (**-lia**) BIOL in multicellular fungi: a mass of threadlike filaments formed when the non-reproductive tissues are growing.

mycology N, BIOL the study of fungi.

myna or **mynah** N a bird of the starling family which can imitate human speech.

myopia N, OPHTHALMOLOGY short-sightedness, in which distant objects appear blurred. ■ **myopic** ADJ.

myriad N an exceedingly great number.
➤ ADJ numberless; innumerable.

myriapod N, ZOOL a crawling, many-legged arthropod, eg the centipede or millipede.

myrmidon N LITERARY **1** a hired thug; a henchman. **2** a follower.

myrrh N the brown resin produced by an African and Asian tree, used in perfumes, etc.

myrtle N an evergreen shrub with pink or white flowers and dark blue, aromatic berries.

myself PRONOUN **1** the reflexive form of **I** (USED INSTEAD OF **me** when the speaker or writer is the object of an action he or she performs): **I burnt myself**. **2** used with **I** or **me**, to add emphasis or to clarify something: **I prefer tea myself**. **3** my normal self: **I am not myself today**. **4** (also **by myself**) alone; without help: **I did it myself**.

mysterious ADJ **1** difficult or impossible to understand or explain; deeply curious. **2** creating, containing or suggesting mystery.

mystery N (**-ies**) **1** an event or phenomenon that cannot be, or has not been, explained. **2** someone about whom very little is known. **3** a story about a crime that is difficult to solve.

mystic N, RELIG someone whose life is devoted to meditation or prayer in an attempt to achieve communication with and knowledge of God.
➤ ADJ mystical.

mystical ADJ (also **mystic**) **1** RELIG **a** relating to or involving truths about the nature of God and reality revealed only to those people with a spiritually-enlightened mind; esoteric; **b** relating to the mysteries or to mysticism. **2** mysterious. **3** wonderful or awe-inspiring.

mysticism N **1** RELIG the practice of gaining direct communication with God through prayer and meditation. **2** the belief in the existence of a reality hidden from human understanding.

mystify VB (**-ies, -ied**) **1** to puzzle or bewilder. **2** to make something mysterious or obscure. ■ **mystification** N.

mystique N a mysterious or compelling quality possessed by a person or thing.

myth N **1** an ancient story that deals with gods and heroes, esp one used to explain some natural phenomenon. **2** such stories in general; mythology. **3** a commonly-held, false notion.

4 a non-existent, fictitious person or thing. ■ **mythical** ADJ.

mythology N (*-ies*) **1** myths in general. **2** a collection of myths, eg about a specific subject.

3 the study of myths. ■ **mythological** ADJ.

myxomatosis N, VET MED, BIOL an infectious, usu fatal, viral disease of rabbits, causing the growth of numerous tumours through the body.

Nn

N¹ or **n** N (*Ns, N's* or *n's*) the fourteenth letter of the English alphabet.

N² ABBREV North.

n/a ABBREV not applicable.

nab VB (*-bb-*) COLLOQ **1** to catch someone doing wrong. **2** to arrest someone. **3** to grab or take something.

nachos PL N, COOKERY tortilla chips topped with chillis, melted cheese, etc.

nadir N **1** ASTRON the point on the celestial sphere directly opposite the zenith. **2** the lowest point; the depths.

naevus or (US) **nevus** N (*-vi*) a birthmark.

naff ADJ, SLANG **1** stupid; foolish. **2** tasteless; vulgar. **3** of poor quality; worthless.

nag¹ N **1** DEROG a broken-down old horse. **2** a small riding-horse.

nag² VB (*-gg-*) **1** (also **nag at sb**) TR & INTR to keep finding fault with them. **2** (also **nag at sb**) INTR to worry them or cause them anxiety. **3** INTR of pain: to persist.
➢ N someone who nags. ■ **nagging** ADJ.

naiad N (*-ades* or *-ads*) GR MYTHOL a water nymph.

nail N **1** the hard structure at the tip of a finger or toe. **2** a metal spike for hammering into something, eg to join two objects together.
➢ VB **1** to fasten something with, or as if with, a nail or nails. **2** COLLOQ to catch, trap or corner

someone. **3** to expose (a lie, deception, etc).
◆ **hit the nail on the head 1** to pinpoint a problem. **2** to sum something up precisely.
◆ **nail sb down** COLLOQ to extract a definite decision or promise from them.
◆ **nail sth down 1** to fix it down with nails. **2** to define or identify it clearly.
◆ **on the nail** COLLOQ immediately.

nail-biting ADJ excitingly full of suspense.

naive or **naïve** ADJ **1** innocent or unsophisticated. **2** DEROG too trusting. ■ **naively** ADV. ■ **naivety** or **naïveté** N.

naked ADJ **1** wearing no clothes. **2** without fur, feathers or foliage. **3** barren; blank; empty. **4** simple; without decoration; artless. **5** undisguised; blatant: **naked greed**. **6** of a light or flame: uncovered; exposed. **7** of the eye: unaided by an optical instrument. **8** LITERARY vulnerable; defenceless. ■ **nakedness** N.

name N **1** a word or words by which a person, place or thing is identified and referred to. **2** reputation: **get a bad name**. **3** a famous or important person, firm, etc: **the big names in fashion**.
➢ VB, TR & INTR **1** to give a name to someone or something. **2** to mention or identify someone or something by name. **3** to specify or decide on someone or something. **4** to choose or appoint.
◆ **call sb names** to insult them verbally.
◆ **in all but name** in practice, but not officially.

◆ **in name only** officially, but not in practice.

◆ **make a name for oneself** to become famous.

◆ **name after** or (N AMER) **for** to give (eg a child or a place) the same name as someone, as an honour or commemoration.

◆ **the name of the game** COLLOQ the essential aspect or aim of some activity.

◆ **to one's name** belonging to one.

name-dropping N, DEROG the practice of referring to well-known people as if they were friends, to impress one's hearers. ■ **name-dropper** N.

nameless ADJ **1** having no name. **2** unidentified. **3** anonymous; undistinguished. **4** too awful to specify.

namely ADV used to introduce an expansion or explanation of what has just been mentioned.

nameplate N a plate on or beside a door, bearing the name, etc of the occupant.

namesake N someone with the same name as, or named after, another person.

nan or **naan** and **nan bread** N a slightly leavened Indian bread.

nanny N (-*ies*) a children's nurse.
➢ ADJ, DEROG protective to an intrusive extent.
➢ VB (-*ies*,-*ied*) to over-protect.

nanny goat N an adult female goat.

nap¹ N a short sleep.
➢ VB (-*pp*-) INTR to have a nap.

nap² N a woolly surface on cloth.

nap³ N **1** a card game like whist. **2** HORSE-RACING a tip that is claimed to be a certainty.
➢ VB (-*pp*-) HORSE-RACING to name (a particular horse) as certain to win.

napalm N an incendiary agent used in bombs and flame-throwers.

nape N the back of the neck.

naphthalene N, CHEM a white crystalline hydrocarbon, used eg in mothballs and dyes.

napkin N (also **table napkin**) a piece of cloth or paper for wiping one's mouth and fingers or to protect one's clothing at mealtimes.

nappy N (-*ies*) a pad secured round a baby's bottom to absorb urine and faeces.

narcissism N excessive admiration for oneself. ■ **narcissistic** ADJ.

narcissus N (-*suses* or -*si*) a plant similar to the daffodil, with white or yellow flowers.

narcosis N (-*ses*) PATHOL unconsciousness or other effects produced by a narcotic.

narcotic N **1** a drug which causes numbness, drowsiness and unconsciousness, deadens pain or produces a sense of well-being. **2** LOOSELY any addictive or illegal drug.
➢ ADJ **1** relating to narcotics or the users of narcotics. **2** relating to narcosis.

nark N, SLANG **1** a spy or informer working for the police. **2** a habitual grumbler.
➢ VB, COLLOQ **1** TR & INTR to annoy. **2** INTR to grumble. **3** INTR to inform or spy, esp for the police. ■ **narky** ADJ (-*ier*, -*iest*) COLLOQ irritable.

narrate VB, TR & INTR **1** to tell (a story). **2** to give a running commentary on (a film, etc).
■ **narration** N. ■ **narrator** N.

narrative N **1** an account of events. **2** those parts of a book, etc that recount events.
➢ ADJ **1** telling a story; recounting events. **2** relating to the telling of stories.

narrow ADJ **1** not wide. **2** restricted; limited. **3** illiberal, unenlightened, intolerant or bigoted. **4** restricted to the precise or original meaning. **5** only just achieved, etc: *a narrow escape*.
➢ N **1** a narrow part or place. **2** (**narrows**) a narrow part of a channel, river, etc.
➢ VB, TR & INTR **1** to make or become narrow. **2** (also **narrow sth down**) to reduce or limit (eg a range of possibilities). ■ **narrowness** N.

narrow boat N a canal barge.

narrowly ADV **1** only just; barely. **2** with close attention: *eyed him narrowly*. **3** in a narrow or restricted way.

narrow-minded ADJ, DEROG **1** intolerant. **2** prejudiced. ■ **narrow-mindedness** N.

narwhal N an arctic whale, the male of which has a long spiral tusk.

nasal ADJ 1 relating to the nose. 2 pronounced through, or partly through, the nose. 3 of a voice, etc: full of nasal sounds.
➤ N 1 a nasal sound. 2 a letter representing such a sound. ■ **nasalize** or **-ise** VB.

nascent ADJ coming into being; in the early stages of development. ■ **nascency** N.

nasturtium N a climbing garden plant with brightly-coloured trumpet-like flowers.

nasty ADJ (**-ier, -iest**) 1 unpleasant; disgusting. 2 malicious; ill-natured. 3 worrying; serious: a nasty wound. 4 of weather: wet or stormy.
➤ N (**-ies**) someone or something unpleasant, disgusting or offensive: a video nasty. ■ **nastily** ADV. ■ **nastiness** N.

natal ADJ connected with birth.

nation N 1 the people of a single state. 2 a race of people of common descent, language, culture, etc. ■ **nationhood** N.

national ADJ 1 belonging to a particular nation. 2 concerning the whole nation.
➤ N 1 a citizen of a particular nation. 2 a national newspaper. ■ **nationally** ADV.

national anthem N a nation's official song.

national insurance N, BRIT state insurance to which employers and employees contribute, to provide for the sick, unemployed, etc.

nationalism N 1 great pride in or loyalty to one's nation; patriotism. 2 extreme or fanatical patriotism. 3 a policy of, or movement aiming at, national independence. ■ **nationalist** N, ADJ. ■ **nationalistic** ADJ.

nationality N (**-ies**) 1 citizenship of a particular nation. 2 a group that has the character of a nation. 3 the racial or national group to which one belongs.

nationalize or **-ise** VB 1 to bring (eg an industry) under state ownership and control. 2 to make national. ■ **nationalization** N.

national service N compulsory service in the armed forces.

nationwide ADJ extending over the whole of a nation.
➤ ADV over the whole of a nation.

native ADJ 1 being or belonging to the place of one's upbringing. 2 born a citizen of a particular place. 3 inborn or innate: native wit. 4 being a person's first language. 5 originating in a particular place: native to Bali. 6 belonging to the original inhabitants of a country: native Balinese music. 7 natural; in a natural state.
➤ N 1 someone born in a certain place. 2 a plant or animal originating in a particular place. 3 often DEROG an original inhabitant of a place as distinct from later, esp European, settlers.

nativity N (**-ies**) 1 birth, advent or origin. 2 (**Nativity**) a the birth of Christ; b a picture representing it; c Christmas.

natter COLLOQ, VB, INTR to chat busily.
➤ N an intensive chat.

natterjack N, ZOOL a European toad with a yellow stripe down its spine.

natty ADJ (**-ier, -iest**) COLLOQ 1 of clothes: flashily smart. 2 clever; ingenious.

natural ADJ 1 normal; unsurprising. 2 instinctive; not learnt. 3 born in one; innate. 4 being such because of inborn qualities. 5 of manner, etc: simple, easy and direct; not artificial. 6 of looks: not, or apparently not, improved on artificially. 7 relating to nature: natural sciences • areas of natural beauty. 8 following the normal course of nature. 9 derived from plants and animals; not manufactured. 10 wild; uncultivated or uncivilized. 11 related by blood: one's natural parents. 12 MUS not sharp or flat.
➤ N 1 COLLOQ someone with an inborn feel for something. 2 an obvious choice for something. 3 someone or something that is assured of success; a certainty. 4 MUS a a sign (♮) indicating a note that is not to be played sharp or flat; b such a note. ■ **naturalness** N.

naturalism N realistic treatment of subjects in art, sculpture, etc. ■ **naturalistic** ADJ.

naturalist N 1 someone who studies animal and plant life. 2 a follower of naturalism.

naturalize or **-ise** VB **1** to confer citizenship on (a foreigner). **2** TR & INTR to gradually consider (a word of foreign origin), or come to be considered, as part of a language. **3** to gradually admit (a custom) among established traditions. **4** to make (an introduced species) adapt to the local environment. **5** INTR of a plant or animal: to adapt to a new environment.

naturally ADV **1** of course; not surprisingly. **2** by nature; as a natural characteristic. **3** by means of a natural process, as opposed to a man–made process. **4** in a relaxed or normal manner.

natural selection N the process by which plant and animal species that adapt most successfully to their environment survive.

nature N **1** (also **Nature**) the physical world and the forces that have formed and control it. **2** animal and plant life as distinct from human life. **3** what something is or consists of. **4** a fundamental tendency; essential character; attitude or outlook. **5** a kind, sort or type.

nature reserve N an area of land specially managed to preserve the flora and fauna in it.

naturism N nudism. ■ **naturist** N.

naught N, OLD USE nothing.

naughty ADJ (**-ier, -iest**) **1** mischievous; disobedient. **2** mildly shocking or indecent; titillating. ■ **naughtily** ADV. ■ **naughtiness** N.

nausea N **1** a feeling that one is about to vomit. **2** disgust.

nauseate VB **1** to make someone feel nausea. **2** to disgust someone. ■ **nauseating** ADJ.

nauseous ADJ **1** sickening; disgusting. **2** affected by nausea.

nautical ADJ of ships, sailors or navigation.

nautical mile N a measure of distance traditionally used at sea, equal to about 1.85 kilometres.

nautilus N (**-luses** or **-li**) a sea creature related to the squid and octopus.

naval ADJ relating to a navy or to ships.

nave N, ARCHIT the main central part of a church.

navel N **1** the small hollow or scar at the point where the umbilical cord was attached to the fetus. **2** the central point of something.

navigable ADJ **1** able to be sailed along or through. **2** seaworthy. **3** steerable.

navigate VB **1** INTR to direct the course of a ship, aircraft or other vehicle. **2** INTR to find one's way and hold one's course. **3** to steer (a ship or aircraft). **4 a** to manage to sail along or through (a river, channel, etc); **b** to find one's way through, along, over or across something, etc. ■ **navigator** N.

navigation N **1** the act, skill or science of navigating. **2** the movement of ships and aircraft. ■ **navigational** ADJ.

navvy N (**-ies**) a labourer. ➢ VB (**-ies, -ied**) INTR to work as or like a navvy.

navy N (**-ies**) **1** (often **the Navy**) **a** the warships of a state, and their personnel; **b** the organization to which they belong. **2** a body or fleet of ships with their crews. **3** (also **navy blue**) a dark blue colour. ➢ ADJ (also **navy-blue**) having a navy blue colour.

nay EXCLAM, OLD USE OR DIALECT **1** no. **2** rather; to put it more strongly. ➢ N **1** the word 'no'. **2** FORMAL **a** someone who casts a negative vote; **b** a vote against.

NB ABBREV (also **nb**) nota bene (Latin), note well.

Neanderthal ADJ **1** denoting a primitive type of man. **2** COLLOQ primitive or old–fashioned.

neap tide and **neap** N a tide at the first and last quarters of the Moon, when there is the least variation between high and low water.

near PREP close to (someone or something). ➢ ADV **1** close: **came near to hitting her. 2** COLLOQ almost; nearly: **She damn near died.** ➢ ADJ **1** being a short distance away; close. **2** closer of two. **3** similar; comparable: **the nearest thing to a screwdriver. 4** closely related to one. **5** almost amounting to, or almost turning into, the specified thing. ➢ VB, TR & INTR to approach. ■ **nearness** N.

◆ **near at hand** conveniently close.

nearby ADJ, ADV a short distance away.

nearly ADV almost.
◆ **not nearly** very far from; nothing like.

near miss N **1** something not quite achieved, eg a shot that almost hits the target. **2** something (eg a collision) only just avoided.

nearside N the side of a vehicle nearer the kerb. Also AS ADJ.

near-sighted ADJ short-sighted.

near thing N a narrow escape.

neat ADJ **1** tidy; clean; orderly. **2** pleasingly small or regular. **3** elegantly or cleverly simple. **4** esp of an alcoholic drink: undiluted. ■ **neatness** N.

neaten VB to make something neat and tidy.

nebula N (-ae or -as) ASTRON a luminous or dark patch in space representing a mass of dust or particles. ■ **nebular** ADJ.

nebulizer N, MED a device with a mouthpiece or facemask, through which a drug is administered as a fine mist.

nebulous ADJ vague; lacking distinct shape.

necessarily ADV as a necessary result.

necessary ADJ **1** needed; essential; indispensable. **2** inevitable; inescapable. **3** logically required or unavoidable. **4** of eg an agent: not free.
➢ N (-ies) **1** (usu **necessaries**) something that is necessary. **2** (**the necessary**) HUMOROUS, COLLOQ **a** money needed for a purpose; **b** action that must be taken.

necessitate VB to make something necessary.

necessity N (-ies) **1** something necessary or essential. **2** circumstances that make something necessary or unavoidable. **3** a pressing need. **4** poverty; want; need.

neck N **1** the part of the body between the head and the shoulders. **2** the part of a garment at or covering the neck. **3** a narrow part; a narrow connecting part. **4** HORSE-RACING a head-and-neck's length: **won by a neck**.

5 meat from the neck of an animal. **6** COLLOQ impudence; boldness.
➢ VB, TR & INTR, SLANG to hug and kiss amorously.
◆ **get it in the neck** COLLOQ to be severely rebuked or punished.
◆ **neck and neck** of competitors: exactly level.

necklace N a string of beads, chain, etc, worn round the neck as jewellery.

neckline N the edge of a garment at the neck, or its shape.

neck of the woods N, HUMOROUS a neighbourhood or locality.

necromancy N **1** divination or prophecy through communication with the dead. **2** black magic; sorcery. ■ **necromancer** N.

necrophilia N obsessive interest, esp of an erotic kind, in dead bodies. ■ **necrophiliac** or **necrophile** N. ■ **necrophilic** ADJ.

necropolis N a cemetery or burial site.

necrosis N (-ses) PATHOL the death of living tissue or bone. ■ **necrotic** ADJ.

nectar N **1** a sugary substance produced in flowers, collected by bees to make honey. **2** GR MYTHOL the special drink of the gods. **3** any delicious drink.

nectarine N a variety of peach with a shiny downless skin.

née or **nee** ADJ used in giving a married woman's maiden name: born.

need VB **1** to lack; to require. **2** INTR (also AS AUXILIARY VERB) to be obliged to do something.
➢ N **1** something one requires. **2** (**need of** or **for sth**) a condition of lacking or requiring it; an urge or desire. **3** (**need for sth**) necessity or justification for it.
◆ **if need** or **needs be** if necessary.
◆ **in need** needing help or financial support.

needful ADJ necessary.
➢ N (**the needful**) COLLOQ **1** whatever action is necessary. **2** money needed.

needle N **1** a slender pointed sewing instrument with a hole for the thread. **2** a longer,

thicker implement without a hole, for knitting, etc. **3** a hypodermic syringe. **4** a gramophone stylus. **5** the pointer on a compass or other instrument. **6** anything slender, sharp and pointed. **7** the needle-shaped leaf of a tree such as the pine or fir. **8** (**the needle**) COLLOQ **a** provocation; **b** irritation; anger; **c** dislike. ➤ VB, TR & INTR, COLLOQ to provoke or irritate someone, esp deliberately.
◆ **look for a needle in a haystack** to undertake a hopeless search.

needlepoint N **1** embroidery on canvas. **2** lace made with needles over a pattern.

needless ADJ unnecessary. ■ **needlessly** ADV.

needlework N sewing and embroidery.

needn't CONTRACTION, COLLOQ need not.

needy ADJ (*-ier, -iest*) in severe need.

ne'er-do-well ADJ good-for-nothing. ➤ N an idle irresponsible useless person.

nefarious ADJ wicked; evil.

negate VB **1** to cancel the effect of something. **2** to deny the existence of something. ■ **negation** N. ■ **negator** N.

negative ADJ **1** meaning or saying 'no'. **2** unenthusiastic or pessimistic. **3** MATH less than zero. **4** contrary to, or cancelling the effect of, whatever is regarded as positive. **5** MATH opposite to positive. **6** ELEC having an electric charge produced by an excess of electrons. **7** PHOTOG of film: having the light and shade of the actual image reversed. ➤ N **1** a word, statement or grammatical form expressing 'no' or 'not'. **2** a photographic film with a negative image, from which prints are made. ■ **negativeness** or **negativity** N.

negative equity N, ECON the situation when the market value of property is less than the value of the mortgage on it.

negativism N a tendency to deny and criticize without offering anything positive. ■ **negativist** N, ADJ. ■ **negativistic** ADJ.

neglect VB **1** not to give proper care and attention to someone or something. **2** to leave (duties, etc) undone. **3** to fail or omit (to do something). ➤ N **1** lack of proper care. **2** a state of disuse or decay. ■ **neglectful** ADJ.

négligée or **negligee** N a woman's thin light dressing-gown.

negligent ADJ **1** not giving proper care and attention. **2** offhand. ■ **negligence** N.

negligible ADJ small enough to ignore.

negotiable ADJ **1** open to discussion. **2** able to be got past or through.

negotiate VB **1** INTR to confer; to bargain. **2** to bring about (an agreement), or arrange (a treaty, price, etc), by conferring. **3** to pass safely (a hazard on one's way, etc). **4** COLLOQ to cope with something successfully. ■ **negotiation** N. ■ **negotiator** N.

neigh N the cry of a horse. ➤ VB, INTR to make this cry or a sound like it.

neighbour or (N AMER) **neighbor** N **1** someone near or next door to one. **2** an adjacent territory, person, etc. **3** OLD USE a fellow human: **Love your neighbour.**

neighbourhood or (N AMER) **neighborhood** N **1** a district or locality. **2** the local community. **3** the area near something or someone.
◆ **in the neighbourhood of** approximately.

neighbouring ADJ **1** nearby. **2** adjoining.

neighbourly or (N AMER) **neighborly** ADJ friendly, esp to the people around one.

neither ADJ, PRONOUN not the one nor the other thing or person. ➤ CONJ (USED TO INTRODUCE THE FIRST OF TWO OR MORE ALTERNATIVES) not: **I neither know nor care.** ➤ ADV nor; also not: **If you won't, then neither will I.**
◆ **neither here nor there** irrelevant.

nematode N, ZOOL a long thin worm, a parasite in plants and animals.

nemesis N (*-ses*) **1** retribution or just punishment. **2** something bringing this.

neoclassical ADJ of artistic or architectural style, esp in the late 18c and early 19c: imitating or adapting the styles of the ancient classical world. ■ **neoclassicism** N.

neologism N a new word or expression.

neon N, CHEM an element, a colourless gas that glows red when electricity is passed through it, used eg in illuminated signs. Also AS ADJ.

neonatal ADJ relating to newly born children. ■ **neonate** N.

neon lamp and **neon light** N a neon-filled glass tube used for lighting.

neophyte N 1 a beginner. 2 a new convert to a religious faith. 3 a novice in a religious order.

nephew N the son of one's brother or sister, or of the brother or sister of one's wife or husband.

nephrite N, GEOL a hard glistening mineral that occurs in a wide range of colours; jade. ■ **nephritic** ADJ.

nephritis N, PATHOL inflammation of a kidney. ■ **nephritic** ADJ.

nepotism N the favouring of one's relatives or friends, esp in making official appointments. ■ **nepotistic** ADJ. ■ **nepotist** N.

nerd or **nurd** N, DEROG SLANG someone foolish or annoying, esp one who is wrapped up in something that isn't thought by others to be worthy of such interest. ■ **nerdy** ADJ.

nerve N 1 a cord that carries instructions and information between the brain or spinal cord and other parts of the body. 2 courage; assurance. 3 COLLOQ cheek; impudence. 4 (**nerves**) COLLOQ nervousness; tension. 5 (usu **nerves**) COLLOQ one's capacity to cope with stress. 6 BOT a leaf-vein or rib. ◆ **get on sb's nerves** COLLOQ to annoy them.

nerveless ADJ 1 lacking feeling or strength; inert. 2 fearless.

nerve-racking or **nerve-wracking** ADJ making one feel tense and anxious.

nervous ADJ 1 timid; easily agitated. 2 uneasy; apprehensive. 3 relating to the nerves.

4 consisting of nerves. ■ **nervously** ADV. ■ **nervousness** N.

nervous system N the brain, nerves and spinal cord collectively.

nervy ADJ (**-ier, -iest**) 1 excitable. 2 nervous.

ness N a headland.

nest N 1 a structure built by birds, rats, wasps, etc in which to lay eggs or give birth to and look after young. 2 a cosy habitation or retreat. 3 a den or haunt, eg of thieves, or secret centre, eg of vice. 4 a swarm, gang, etc. 5 a set of things that fit together: **a nest of tables**. ➤ VB 1 INTR to build and occupy a nest. 2 TR & INTR to fit things together one inside another.

nest egg N, COLLOQ a sum of money saved up for the future.

nestle VB, INTR to lie or settle snugly.

nestling N a young bird still unable to fly.

net[1] N 1 an open material made of thread, cord, etc knotted, twisted or woven to form mesh. 2 a piece of this, eg for catching fish, confining hair, dividing a tennis court, etc. 3 SPORT the net-backed goal in hockey, football, etc. 4 (**the net**) short for **the Internet**. ➤ ADJ made of or like net. ➤ VB (**-tt-**) 1 to catch something in a net. 2 to cover something with a net.

net[2] ADJ 1 of profit: remaining after all expenses, etc have been paid. 2 of weight: excluding the packaging or container. ➤ VB (**-tt-**) to produce, or earn, (an amount) as clear profit.

netball N a game in which a ball is thrown through a net at the top of a pole.

nether ADJ, LITERARY OR OLD USE lower or under. ■ **nethermost** ADJ lowest; farthest down.

netting N any material with meshes, made by knotting or twisting thread, cord or wire, etc.

nettle N a plant covered with stinging hairs. ◆ **grasp the nettle** to deal boldly with a difficult situation.

nettle rash N, NON-TECHNICAL urticaria.

network N **1** any system that resembles a mass of criss-crossing lines. **2** any co-ordinated system involving large numbers of people or branches, etc. **3** COMP a linked set of computers capable of sharing power or storage facilities.
➤ VB **1** to broadcast something on a network. **2** INTR to build or maintain relationships with a network of people. **3** to link (computer terminals, etc) to operate interactively.

neural ADJ relating to the nerves or nervous system. ■ **neurally** ADV.

neuralgia N, PATHOL spasmodic pain along the course of a nerve. ■ **neuralgic** ADJ.

neuritis N, PATHOL inflammation of a nerve.

neurology N, MED the study of the central nervous system, and the peripheral nerves. ■ **neurological** ADJ. ■ **neurologist** N.

neurone or **neuron** N, ANAT a specialized cell that transmits nerve impulses from one part of the body to another. Also called **nerve cell**.

neurosis N (**-ses**) **1** a mental disorder that causes obsessive fears, depression and unreasonable behaviour. **2** COLLOQ an anxiety or obsession.

neurotic ADJ **1** relating to, or suffering from, a neurosis. **2** COLLOQ obsessive.
➤ N someone suffering from a neurosis.

neuter ADJ sexless or apparently sexless.
➤ VB to castrate (an animal).

neutral ADJ **1** not taking sides in a quarrel or war. **2** not belonging or relating to either side: **neutral ground**. **3** of colours: indefinite enough to blend easily with brighter ones. **4** with no strong or noticeable qualities; not distinctive. **5** ELEC with no positive or negative electrical charge. **6** CHEM neither acidic nor alkaline.
➤ N **1** a neutral person or nation, not allied to any side. **2** the disengaged position of an engine's gears, when no power is transmitted to the moving parts. ■ **neutrality** N.

neutralize or **-ise** VB to cancel out the effect of something.

neutrino N, PHYS a stable subatomic particle that has no electric charge, virtually no mass, and travels at or near the speed of light.

neutron N, PHYS one of the electrically uncharged particles in the nucleus of an atom.

never ADV **1** not ever; at no time. **2** not: **I never realized that**. **3** emphatically not: **This will never do**.

never-never N, COLLOQ hire-purchase.

nevertheless ADV in spite of that.

nevus see **naevus**

new ADJ **1** recently made, bought, built, opened, etc. **2** recently discovered. **3** never having existed before; just invented, etc. **4** fresh; additional: **a new consignment**. **5** recently arrived, installed, etc. **6** (chiefly **new to sb** or **sth**) unfamiliar; experienced, or experiencing something, for the first time. **7** changed physically, mentally or morally for the better. **8** renewed: **gave us new hope**. **9** modern: **the new generation**. **10** used in naming a place after an older one: **New York**.
➤ ADV, USU IN COMPOUNDS **1** only just; freshly: **new-baked bread**. **2** anew.
➤ N **1** COLLOQ something which is new. **2** newness. ■ **newness** N.

new blood see **blood** (N sense 5b)

newborn ADJ just or very recently born.

newcomer N **1** someone recently arrived. **2** a beginner.

newel N **1** the central spindle round which a spiral stair winds. **2** (also **newel post**) a post at the top or bottom of a flight of stairs, supporting the handrail.

newfangled ADJ, USU DEROG modern.

newly ADV **1** only just; recently: **newly-weds**. **2** again; anew: **newly awakened desire**.

new moon N **1** the moon when it is visible as a narrow waxing crescent. **2** the time of this.

news SING N **1** information about recent events, esp as reported in newspapers, on radio or TV, or via the Internet. **2** (**the news**) a radio or TV broadcast report of news. **3** any fresh interesting information.

news agency N an agency that collects news stories and supplies them to newspapers.

newsagent N (the proprietor of) a shop that sells newspapers.

newscast N a radio or TV broadcast of news items. ■ **newscaster** N. ■ **newscasting** N.

news conference see **press conference**

newsflash N an announcement of important news that interrupts a radio or TV broadcast.

newsletter N a sheet containing news, issued to members of an organization, etc.

newspaper N a daily or weekly publication composed of folded sheets, containing news, topical articles, correspondence, etc.

newsprint N 1 the paper on which newspapers are printed. 2 the ink used to print newspapers.

newsreader N a radio or TV news announcer.

newsreel N a film of news events, once a regular cinema feature.

newsroom N an office in a newspaper office or broadcasting station where news stories are received and edited.

news stand N a stall or kiosk that sells newspapers and magazines, etc.

newsworthy ADJ interesting or important enough to be reported as news.

newsy ADJ (-ier, -iest) full of news, esp gossip.

newt N a small amphibious animal with a long body and tail and short legs.

New Testament N the part of the Bible concerned with the teachings of Christ.

newton N, PHYS an SI unit of force equivalent to that which gives a one kilogram mass an acceleration of one second every second.

next ADJ 1 following in time or order. 2 following this one: **next week**. 3 adjoining; neighbouring: **in the next room**. 4 first, counting from now: **the next person I meet**.
➤ N someone or something that is next.
➤ ADV 1 immediately after that or this. 2 on the next occasion: **when I next saw her**.
3 following, in order of degree: **It's the next best thing to flying**.

next-door ADJ occupying or belonging to the next room, house, shop, etc.
➤ ADV (**next door**) to or in the next room, etc.

next of kin N one's closest relative.

nexus N (*nexus* or *nexuses*) 1 a connected series or group. 2 a bond or link.

nib N 1 the writing-point of a pen, esp a metal one with a divided tip. 2 a point or spike.

nibble VB, TR & INTR 1 to take very small bites of something. 2 to bite gently.

nibs SING N (usu **his** or **her nibs**) a derogatory title for an important person.

nice ADJ 1 pleasant; respectable. 2 often IRONIC good; satisfactory. 3 IRONIC nasty: **a nice mess**. 4 fine; subtle: **nice distinctions**. 5 exacting; particular: **nice in matters of etiquette**.
■ **niceness** N.

nicely ADV 1 in a nice or satisfactory way. 2 precisely; carefully. 3 suitably; effectively.

nicety N (-ies) 1 precision. 2 a subtle point.
◆ **to a nicety** exactly.

niche N 1 a shallow recess in a wall. 2 a position in life in which one feels fulfilled or at ease. 3 a small specialized group identified as a market for a range of products or services. Also AS ADJ: **niche marketing**.

nick N 1 a small cut; a notch. 2 COLLOQ a prison or police station.
➤ VB 1 to make a small cut in something. 2 SLANG to arrest (a criminal). 3 SLANG to steal.
◆ **in good nick** COLLOQ in good condition.
◆ **in the nick of time** just in time.

nickel N 1 CHEM a greyish-white metallic element used esp in alloys and for plating. 2 an American or Canadian coin worth five cents.
➤ ADJ made of or with nickel.

nickelodeon N, US OLD USE 1 an early form of jukebox. 2 a type of pianola.

nickname N a name given to a person or place in fun, affection or contempt.

➤ VB to give a nickname to someone.

nicotine N a poisonous alkaline substance contained in tobacco.

niece N the daughter of one's sister or brother, or the sister or brother of one's husband or wife.

niff SLANG, N a bad smell.
➤ VB, INTR to smell bad. ■ **niffy** ADJ.

nifty ADJ (-*ier*, -*iest*) 1 clever; adroit; agile. 2 stylish. ■ **niftily** ADV.

niggardly ADJ 1 stingy; miserly. 2 meagre. ■ **niggard** N. ■ **niggardliness** N.

niggle VB, INTR 1 to complain about small or unimportant details. 2 to irritate slightly.
➤ N 1 a slight nagging worry. 2 a small complaint or criticism. ■ **niggling** ADJ.

nigh ADV, OLD USE, DIALECT OR POETIC near.
◆ **nigh on** or **well nigh** nearly; almost.

night N 1 the time of darkness between sunset and sunrise. 2 the time between going to bed and getting up in the morning. 3 evening: **last night**. 4 nightfall. 5 POETIC darkness.
➤ ADJ 1 belonging to, occurring, or done in the night: **the night hours**. 2 working or on duty at night: **the night shift**. ■ **nightly** ADJ done or happening at night or every night.
➤ ADV at night; every night. ■ **nights** ADV, COLLOQ at night; most nights or every night.

nightcap N 1 a drink, esp an alcoholic one, taken before going to bed. 2 OLD USE a cap worn in bed at night.

nightclub N a club open in the evening and into the night for drinking, dancing, etc.

nightdress N a loose garment for sleeping in.

nightfall N the beginning of night; dusk.

nightie or **nighty** N (-*ties*) COLLOQ a nightdress.

nightingale N a small brown thrush known for its melodious song, heard esp at night.

nightjar N a nocturnal bird of the swift family.

nightlife N entertainment available in a city or resort, etc, late into the night.

nightmare N 1 a frightening dream. 2 an intensely distressing or frightful experience or situation. ■ **nightmarish** ADJ.

night owl N someone who likes to stay up late at night or who is active, etc, at night.

night school N educational classes held in the evening.

nightshade N any of various wild plants, some with poisonous berries.

night shift N 1 a session of work during the night. 2 the staff working during this period.

nightshirt N a loose garment for sleeping in.

night spot N, COLLOQ a nightclub.

nihilism N the rejection of moral and religious principles. ■ **nihilist** N. ■ **nihilistic** ADJ.

nil N, GAMES, SPORT, etc a score of nothing; zero.

nimble ADJ 1 quick and light in movement; agile. 2 of wits: sharp; alert. ■ **nimbly** ADV.

nimbus N (-*buses* or -*bi*) 1 METEOROL a heavy dark type of cloud bringing rain or snow. 2 a luminous mist surrounding a god or goddess.

nincompoop N a fool; an idiot.

nine N 1 a the cardinal number 9; b the quantity that this represents, being one more than eight. 2 any symbol for this, eg 9, IX. 3 something whose size is denoted by the number 9. 5 the ninth hour after midnight or midday: **opens at nine**.
➤ ADJ 1 totalling nine. 2 aged nine.
◆ **dressed up to the nines** COLLOQ elaborately dressed.

ninefold ADJ 1 equal to nine times as much or many. 2 divided into, or consisting of, nine parts.
➤ ADV by nine times as much.

ninepins SING N a game in which a wooden ball is used to knock down nine skittles.

nineteen N 1 a the cardinal number 19; b the quantity that this represents, being one more than eighteen, or the sum of ten and nine. 2 any symbol for this, eg 19, XIX. 3 something whose size is denoted by the number 19.
➤ ADJ 1 totalling nineteen. 2 aged nineteen.
■ **nineteenth** ADJ, N.

◆ **talk nineteen to the dozen** COLLOQ to chatter away animatedly.

nineties (often written **90s** or **90's**) PL N **1** (**one's nineties**) the period of time between one's ninetieth and hundredth birthdays. **2** (**the nineties**) the range of temperatures between ninety and a hundred degrees. **3** (**the nineties**) the period of time between the ninetieth and hundredth years of a century.

ninety N **1 a** the cardinal number 90; **b** the quantity that this represents, being one more than eighty-nine, or the product of ten and nine. **2** any symbol for this, eg 90, XC. ➤ ADJ **1** totalling ninety. **2** aged ninety. ■ **ninetieth** ADJ, N.

ninja N (**ninja** or **ninjas**) esp in medieval Japan: a professional assassin trained in martial arts.

ninny N (**-ies**) a foolish person.

ninth (often written **9th**) ADJ **1** in counting: **a** next after eighth; **b** last of nine. **2** in ninth position. ➤ N **1** one of nine equal parts. **2** a fraction equal to one divided by nine.

nip[1] VB (**-pp-**) **1** to pinch or squeeze something or someone sharply. **2** to give a sharp little bite to something. **3** (often **nip off sth**) to remove or sever it by pinching or biting. **4** TR & INTR to sting; to cause smarting. ➤ N **1** a pinch or squeeze. **2** a sharp little bite. **3** a sharp biting coldness, or stinging quality. ◆ **nip sth in the bud** to halt its growth or development at an early stage.

nip[2] N a small quantity of alcoholic spirits.

nip and tuck ADJ, ADV, N AMER neck and neck.

nipper N **1** the large claw of a crab, lobster, etc. **2** (**nippers**) any gripping or severing tool. **3** OLD COLLOQ USE a small child.

nipple N **1** the deep-coloured pointed projection on a breast. **2** N AMER the teat on a baby's feeding-bottle. **3** MECH any small projection with a hole through which a flow is regulated or machine parts lubricated.

nippy ADJ (**-ier, -iest**) COLLOQ **1** cold; chilly. **2** quick-moving; nimble. **3** pungent or biting.

nirvana N, COLLOQ a place or state of bliss.

nit[1] N the egg of a louse, found eg in hair.

nit[2] N, SLANG an idiot.

nit-picking N petty criticism or fault-finding. ➤ ADJ fussy. ■ **nit-picker** N.

nitrate N, CHEM **1** a salt or ester of nitric acid. **2** sodium nitrate or potassium nitrate used as a soil fertilizer.

nitre N, CHEM potassium nitrate; saltpetre.

nitric ADJ, CHEM of or containing nitrogen.

nitrify VB (**-ies, -ied**) TR & INTR, CHEM to convert or be converted into nitrates or nitrites through the action of bacteria. ■ **nitrification** N.

nitrite N, CHEM a salt or ester of nitrous acid.

nitrogen N CHEM an element, the colourless, odourless and tasteless gas making up four-fifths of air. ■ **nitrogenous** ADJ.

nitroglycerine or **nitroglycerin** N, CHEM an explosive liquid compound.

nitrous ADJ, CHEM relating to or containing nitrogen in a low valency.

nitrous oxide N, CHEM an anaesthetic compound, popularly known as laughing gas.

the nitty-gritty N, COLLOQ the fundamental issue or essential part of something.

nitwit N a stupid person.

No, No. or **no.** ABBREV number.

no EXCLAM **1** used as a negative reply, expressing denial, refusal or disagreement. **2** COLLOQ used as a question tag expecting agreement: **It's a deal, no? 3** used as an astonished rejoinder: **No! You don't say!** ➤ ADV **1** not any: **no bigger than one's thumb. 2** used to indicate a negative alternative: not: **willing or no.** ➤ ADJ **1** not any. **2** certainly not or far from something specified: **He's no fool. 3** hardly any: **do it in no time. 4** not allowed: **no smoking.** ➤ N (**noes**) a negative reply or vote: **The noes have it.** ◆ **no more 1** destroyed; dead. **2** never again.

♦ **no way** COLLOQ no; definitely not.

nob¹ N, SLANG someone of high social rank.

nob² N, SLANG the head.

nobble VB, COLLOQ **1** to drug or interfere with (a horse) to stop it winning. **2** to persuade someone by bribes or threats. **3** to catch (a criminal). **4** to swindle someone.

nobility N (-*ies*) **1** the quality of being noble. **2** (**the nobility**) people of noble birth.

noble ADJ **1** honourable. **2** generous. **3** of high birth or rank. **4** splendid in appearance. ➤ N a person of noble rank. ■ **nobly** ADV.

noble gas N, CHEM any of the gases helium, neon, argon, krypton, xenon and radon. Also called **inert gas**.

nobleman and **noblewoman** N a member of the nobility.

noble metal N a metal such as gold, silver or platinum that does not easily tarnish.

nobody PRONOUN no person; no one. ➤ N (-*ies*) someone of no significance.

nocturnal ADJ **1** of animals, etc: active at night. **2** happening at night. **3** of the night.

nocturne N **1** a dreamy piece of music, usu for the piano. **2** ART a night or moonlight scene.

nod VB (-*dd*-) **1** TR & INTR to make a brief bowing gesture with (the head) in agreement, greeting, etc. **2** INTR to let the head droop with sleepiness; to become drowsy. **3** INTR to make a mistake through momentary loss of concentration. **4** to indicate or direct by nodding. **5** INTR of flowers, plumes, etc: to sway or bob about. ➤ N a quick bending forward of the head as a gesture of assent, greeting or command. ♦ **nod off** INTR to fall asleep. ♦ **nod sb** or **sth through** to pass something without a discussion, vote, etc. ♦ **on the nod** COLLOQ of the passing of a proposal, etc: by general agreement, without the formality of a vote.

noddle N, COLLOQ the head or brain.

node N **1** a knob, lump, swelling or knotty mass.

2 BOT a swelling where a leaf is attached to a stem. **3** GEOM the point where a curve crosses itself. ■ **nodal** ADJ.

nodule N **1** a small round lump. **2** BOT a swelling in a root of a leguminous plant, inhabited by nitrogen-converting bacteria. ■ **nodular** ADJ.

Noel or **Noël** N Christmas.

no-frills ADJ basic, not elaborate or fancy.

nog N an alcoholic drink made with whipped eggs.

noggin N **1** a small measure or quantity of alcoholic spirits. **2** a small mug or wooden cup. **3** COLLOQ one's head.

no-go area N an area to which normal access is prevented.

noise N **1** a sound. **2** a harsh disagreeable sound; a din. **3** RADIO interference in a signal. **4** COMP meaningless material appearing in output. **5** something one says as a conventional response, vague indication of inclinations, etc: make polite noises. ➤ VB (usu **noise abroad** or **about**) to make something generally known; to spread (a rumour, etc). ■ **noiseless** ADJ.

noisette N **1** a small piece of meat (usu lamb) cut off the bone and rolled. **2** a nutlike or nut-flavoured sweet.

noisome ADJ **1** disgusting; offensive; stinking. **2** harmful; poisonous.

noisy ADJ (-*ier, -iest*) **1** making a lot of noise. **2** full of noise. ■ **noisily** ADV.

nomad N **1** a member of a people who travel from place to place seeking food and pasture. **2** a wanderer. ■ **nomadic** ADJ.

no-man's-land N **1** neutral territory between opposing armies or between two countries with a common border. **2** a state or situation that is neither one thing nor another.

nom-de-plume or **nom de plume** N (*noms-de-plume* or *noms de plume*) a pseudonym used by a writer.

nomenclature N **1** a classified system of names, esp in science. **2** a set of names.

nominal ADJ 1 in name only; so called, but not actually. 2 very small in comparison to actual cost or value: *a nominal rent*. 3 GRAM being or relating to a noun. 4 being or relating to a name. ➤ N, GRAM a noun, or a phrase, etc standing as a noun. ■ **nominally** ADV.

nominate VB 1 (usu **nominate sb for sth**) to propose them formally as a candidate for election, a job, etc. 2 (usu **nominate sb to sth**) to appoint them to (a post or position). 3 to specify (eg a date). ■ **nomination** N.

nominative GRAM, N 1 in certain languages: the form or case used to mark the subject of a verb. 2 a noun, etc in this case.

nominee N someone nominated to, or as a candidate for, a job, position, etc.

nonagenarian N someone between the ages of 90 and 99 years old. Also AS ADJ.

nonagon N, GEOM a nine-sided figure.

non-aligned ADJ not allied to any of the major power blocs in world politics; neutral. ■ **non-alignment** N.

nonce N.
♦ **for the nonce** for the present.

nonchalant ADJ calmly or indifferently unconcerned. ■ **nonchalance** N.

non-committal ADJ avoiding expressing a definite opinion or decision.

non compos mentis ADJ not of sound mind.

nonconformist N someone who refuses to conform to generally accepted practice. Also AS ADJ. ■ **non-conformity** N.

non-contributory ADJ of a pension scheme: paid for by the employer, without contributions from the employee.

non-denominational ADJ not linked with any particular religious denomination.

nondescript ADJ with no strongly noticeable characteristics or distinctive features. ➤ N a nondescript person or thing.

none PRONOUN (with SING or PL verb) 1 not any. 2 no one; not any people: *None were*
as kind as she.
♦ **none but** only
♦ **none other than sb** or **sth** the very person or thing mentioned or thought of.
♦ **none the** (followed by a COMPARATIVE) not any: *none the worse for his adventure*.
♦ **none too** by no means: *none too clean*.
♦ **none the less** or **nonetheless** nevertheless; in spite of that.

nonentity N (*-ies*) 1 DEROG someone of no significance, character, ability, etc. 2 DEROG a thing of no importance. 3 a thing which does not exist. 4 the state of not being.

nones PL N in the Roman calendar: the seventh day of March, May, July and October, and the fifth day of other months.

nonesuch or **nonsuch** N, LITERARY a unique, unparalleled or extraordinary thing.

nonet N, MUS 1 a composition for nine instruments or voices. 2 a group of nine instrumentalists or singers.

nonetheless see under **none**

non-event N an event that turns out to be insignificant or a disappointment.

non-fiction ADJ of a literary work: factual. Also AS NOUN.

non-flammable ADJ not liable to catch fire or burn easily.

non-invasive ADJ of medical treatment: not involving surgery or the insertion of instruments, etc into the patient.

non-negotiable ADJ 1 not open to negotiation. 2 of a cheque, etc: not negotiable.

no-no N (*no-nos* or *no-noes*) COLLOQ 1 something which must not be done, said, etc. 2 something impossible.

nonpareil ADJ having no equal; matchless. ➤ N a person or thing without equal.

nonplus VB (*-ss-*; US *-s-*) to puzzle; to disconcert.

nonsense N 1 words or ideas that do not make sense. 2 foolishness; silly behaviour. ➤ EXCLAM you're quite wrong.

◆ **make a nonsense of sth** to destroy the effect of it; to make it pointless.

nonsensical ADJ making no sense; absurd.

non sequitur N **1** an illogical step in an argument. **2** a conclusion that does not follow from the premisses.

non-specific ADJ **1** not specific. **2** of a disease: not caused by any identifiable agent.

non-standard ADJ **1** not standard. **2** of language: not used by educated speakers.

non-starter N **1** a person, thing or idea, etc that has no chance of success. **2** a horse which, though entered for a race, does not run.

non-stick ADJ of a pan, etc: that has a coating to which food does not stick during cooking.

non-stop ADJ, ADV without a stop; which does not stop.

nonsuch see **nonesuch**

non-violence N the ideal or practice of refraining from violence on grounds of principle. ■ **non-violent** ADJ.

noodle N **1** (usu **noodles**) COOKERY a thin strip of pasta, often made with egg. **2** COLLOQ a simpleton; a blockhead.

nook N **1** a secluded retreat. **2** a corner or recess.
◆ **every nook and cranny** everywhere.

noon N midday; twelve o'clock.

noonday N midday.
➤ ADJ relating to midday.

no one or **no-one** N no person.

noose N **1** a loop made in the end of a rope, etc, with a sliding knot. **2** any snare or bond.

nope EXCLAM, SLANG emphatic form of **no**.

nor CONJ **1** (USED TO INTRODUCE ALTERNATIVES AFTER **neither**): He neither knows nor cares. **2** and not: It didn't look appetizing, nor was it.
➤ ADV not either: If you won't, nor shall I.

nor' ADJ, IN COMPOUNDS, NAUT north: a nor'-wester.

norm N **1** (**the norm**) a typical pattern or

situation. **2** an accepted way of behaving, etc. **3** a standard.

normal ADJ **1** usual; typical; not extraordinary. **2** mentally or physically sound: a normal baby.
➤ N what is average or usual. ■ **normality** and (N AMER) **normalcy** N. ■ **normalize** or **-ise** VB. ■ **normally** ADV.

Norman N **1** a person from Normandy in N France, esp one of the invaders and conquerers of England in 1066. **2** Norman French.
➤ ADJ of the Normans or Normandy.

normative ADJ establishing a guiding standard or rules.

Norse ADJ **1** of or relating to ancient or medieval Scandinavia. **2** Norwegian.
➤ N **1** the Germanic language group of Scandinavia. **2** the language of this group used in medieval Norway and its colonies.

north N (also **North** or **the North**) **1** the direction to one's left when one faces the rising sun. **2** the direction that is directly opposite south, ie 180° from the south and 90° from both east and west. **3** any part of the Earth, a country or a town, etc that lies in this direction.
➤ ADJ (also **North**) **1** on the side that is on or nearest the north. **2** of a wind: blowing from the north.
➤ ADV towards the north.

northbound ADJ going towards the north.

north-east N **1** the direction midway between north and east. **2** an area lying in this direction.
➤ ADJ **1** in the north-east. **2** from the direction of the north-east: a north-east wind.
➤ ADV in this direction. ■ **north-easterly** ADJ, ADV, N. ■ **north-eastern** ADJ.

north-easter or **nor'-easter** N a strong wind or storm from the north-east.

northerly ADJ **1** of a wind, etc: coming from the north. **2** being, looking, etc towards the north.
➤ ADV **1** to or towards the north. **2** from the north.
➤ N (**-ies**) a northerly wind.

northern ADJ **1** of or relating to the north. **2** in the north or in the direction toward it. **3** of winds, etc: coming from the north. ■ **northernmost** ADJ situated furthest north.

the northern lights PL N the aurora borealis.

northerner N a person who lives in or comes from the north.

northing N, chiefly NAUT **1** motion, distance or tendency northward. **2** distance of a heavenly body from the equator northward. **3** difference of latitude made by a ship in sailing. **4** deviation towards the north.

northward and **northwards** ADJ, ADV towards the north.

north-west N **1** the direction midway between north and west. **2** an area lying in this direction.
➢ ADJ **1** in the north-west. **2** from the direction of the north-west: a north-west wind.
➢ ADV in this direction. ■ **north-westerly** ADJ, ADV, N. ■ **north-western** ADJ.

north-wester N a strong wind from the north-west.

nose N **1** the projecting organ above the mouth, with which one smells and breathes. **2** an animal's snout or muzzle. **3** the sense of smell. **4** a scent or aroma, esp a wine's bouquet. **5** the front part of anything, eg a motor vehicle.
➢ VB **1** TR & INTR to move carefully forward: nosed the car out of the yard. **2** to detect something by smelling. **3** of an animal: to sniff at something or nuzzle it.
   nose about or **around** COLLOQ to pry.
   a nose for sth a facility for detecting or recognizing something.
   cut off one's nose to spite one's face to act from resentment in a way that causes injury to oneself.
◆ **get up sb's nose** COLLOQ to annoy them.
   keep one's nose clean COLLOQ to avoid doing anything that might get one into trouble.
   look down or **turn up one's nose at sth** or **sb** COLLOQ to show disdain for it or them.
   pay through the nose COLLOQ to pay an exorbitant price.
   put sb's nose out of joint COLLOQ to affront them.
   under one's (very) nose in full view and very obviously in front of one.

nosedive N **1** a steep nose-downward plunge by an aircraft. **2** a sharp plunge or fall. **3** a sudden drop, eg in prices.
➢ VB, INTR to plunge or fall suddenly.

nosegay N, OLD USE a posy of flowers.

nosey see **nosy**

nosh SLANG, N food.
➢ VB, INTR to eat.

nostalgia N **1** a yearning for the past. **2** homesickness. ■ **nostalgic** ADJ. ■ **nostalgically** ADV.

nostril N either of the two openings in the nose.

nostrum N a patent medicine; a panacea.

nosy or **nosey** ADJ (*nosier, nosiest*) DEROG inquisitive; prying.
➢ N (*nosies* or *noseys*) a prying person. ■ **nosiness** N.

not ADV (often shortened to **-n't**) **1** used to make a negative statement, etc. **2** used in place of a negative clause or predicate: We might be late, but I hope not. **3** (indicating surprise, an expectation of agreement, etc) surely it is the case that: Haven't you heard? **4** used to contrast the untrue with the true: It's a cloud, not a mountain. **5** barely: not two feet away.
◆ **not a** absolutely no: not a hope.
◆ **not at all** don't mention it.

notable ADJ worth noting; significant.
➢ N a notable person. ■ **notability** N. ■ **notably** ADV.

notary N (*-ies*) (in full **notary public**) (PL *notaries public*) a public official with the legal power to draw up and witness official documents, and to administer oaths, etc.

notation N the representation of quantities, musical sounds or movements, etc by symbols.

notch N **1** a small V-shaped cut or indentation. **2** a nick. **3** COLLOQ a step or level.
➢ VB **1** to cut a notch in something. **2** to record something with, or as if with, a notch. **3** to fit (an arrow) to a bowstring. ■ **notched** ADJ.

◆ **notch sth up 1** to record it as a score. **2** to achieve it.

note N **1** (often **notes**) a brief written record made for later reference. **2** a short informal letter. **3** a brief comment explaining a textual point, etc. Often IN COMPOUNDS: a footnote. **4** a short account or essay. **5 a** a banknote; **b** a promissory note. **6** esp in diplomacy: a formal communication. **7** attention; notice: **buildings worthy of note. 8** distinction; eminence. **9** MUS **a** a written symbol indicating the pitch and length of a musical sound; **b** the sound itself; **c** a key on a keyboard instrument. **10** esp POETIC the call or cry of a bird or animal. **11** a hint or touch: **with a note of panic in her voice.**
➤ VB **1** (also **note sth down**) to write it down. **2** to notice something. **3** to pay close attention to something. **4** to mention or to remark upon something. **5** to annotate something.
◆ **compare notes** to exchange ideas and opinions, esp about a particular event, etc.
◆ **strike the right note** to act or speak appropriately.
◆ **take note** (**of sth**) to observe it carefully.

notebook N **1** a small book for notes, etc. **2** a portable computer, smaller than a laptop.

noted ADJ famous; eminent; notorious.

noteworthy ADJ worthy of notice.

nothing N **1** no thing; not anything. **2 a** zero; **b** the figure 0. **3 a** very little; **b** something of no importance or not very impressive; **c** no difficulty or trouble. **4** an absence of anything.
➤ ADV not at all: **nothing daunted.**
◆ **be nothing to do with sb** or **sth 1** to be unconnected with them. **2** to be of no concern to them.
◆ **come to nothing** to fail or peter out.
◆ **have nothing to do with sb** or **sth 1** to avoid them. **2** to be unconnected with them. **3** to be of no concern to them.
◆ **make nothing of sb** or **sth** not to understand them or it.
◆ **nothing if not** primarily, above all, or very: **nothing if not keen.**
◆ **nothing like** by no means: **nothing like good enough.**
◆ **nothing much** very little.

◆ **nothing short of** or **less than sth 1** downright; absolute: **They were nothing less than criminals. 2** only: **will accept nothing less than an apology.**
◆ **nothing to it** or **in it** straightforward; easy.
◆ **think nothing of sth 1** to regard it as normal or straightforward. **2** to feel no hesitation, guilt or regret about it.
◆ **to say nothing of sth** as well as it.

notice N **1** an announcement displayed or delivered publicly. **2** one's attention: **It escaped my notice. 3 a** a warning or notification given: **will continue until further notice. b** warning or notification given before leaving, or dismissing someone from, a job. **4** a review of a book, etc.
➤ VB **1** to observe; to become aware of something. **2** to remark on something. **3** to show signs of recognition of someone, etc. **4** to treat someone with polite attention.
◆ **at short notice** with little warning.

noticeable ADJ easily seen; clearly apparent.
■ **noticeably** ADV.

noticeboard N a board on which notices are displayed.

notifiable ADJ of infectious diseases: that must be reported to the public health authorities.

notify VB (**-ies, -ied**) to tell or to inform.
■ **notification** N.

notion N **1** an impression, conception or understanding. **2** a belief or principle. **3** an inclination, whim or fancy.

notional ADJ **1** existing in imagination only. **2** theoretical. **3** hypothetical. ■ **notionally** ADV.

notorious ADJ famous, usu for something disreputable. ■ **notoriety** N.

notwithstanding PREP in spite of.
➤ ADV in spite of that; however.
➤ CONJ although.

nougat N a chewy sweet containing chopped nuts, cherries, etc.

nought N **1** the figure 0; zero. **2** OLD USE nothing; naught.

noun N, GRAM a word used as the name of a

person, animal, thing, place or quality.

nourish VB **1** to supply someone or something with food. **2 a** to encourage the growth of something; **b** to foster (an idea, etc).
■ **nourishing** ADJ. ■ **nourishment** N.

nous N, COLLOQ gumption.

nova N (*-ae* or *-as*) ASTRON a faint star that suddenly brightens and then fades again.

novel[1] N **1** a book-length fictional story. **2** (**the novel**) such writing as a literary genre.
■ **novelist** N.

novel[2] ADJ new; original.

novelette N, DEROG a short novel, esp one that is trite or sentimental.

novella N a short story or short novel.

novelty N (*-ies*) **1** the quality of being new and intriguing. **2** something new and strange. **3** a small, cheap toy or souvenir.

November N the eleventh month of the year.

novena N, RC CHURCH a series of prayers and services held over nine days.

novice N **1** someone new in anything; a beginner. **2** a probationary member of a religious community. **3** HORSE-RACING a horse that has not won a race in a season prior to the current season.

now ADV **1** at the present time or moment. **2** immediately. **3** in narrative: then: *He now turned from journalism to fiction.* **4** in these circumstances; as things are: *I planned to go, but now I can't.* **5** up to the present: *has now been teaching 13 years.* **6** used in conversation to accompany explanations, warnings, commands, rebukes, words of comfort, etc: *Now, this is what happened.*
➤ N the present time.
➤ CONJ (also **now that**) because at last; because at this time: *Now we're all here, we'll begin.*
◆ **any day** or **moment** or **time now** at any time soon.
◆ **as of now** from this time onward.
◆ **for now** until later; for the time being.
◆ **just now 1** a moment ago. **2** at this moment.

◆ **now and again** or **now and then** sometimes; occasionally.
◆ **now for** used in anticipation, or in turning from one thing to another: *Now for some fun!*
◆ **now, now! 1** used to comfort someone: *Now, now, don't cry!* **2** (also **now then!**) a warning or rebuke: *Now, now! Stop that!*

nowadays ADV in these present times.

nowhere ADV in or to no place; not anywhere.
➤ N a non-existent place.
◆ **from** or **out of nowhere** suddenly and inexplicably.
◆ **get nowhere** COLLOQ to make no progress.
◆ **in the middle of nowhere** COLLOQ remote from towns or cities, etc.
◆ **nowhere near** COLLOQ not nearly.
◆ **nowhere to be found** or **seen** lost.

nowt N, COLLOQ OR DIALECT nothing.

noxious ADJ harmful; poisonous.

nozzle N an outlet tube or spout, esp as a fitting attached to the end of a hose, etc.

nth ADJ **1** denoting an indefinite position in a sequence: **to the nth degree**. **2** many times removed from the first; umpteenth: **I'm telling you for the nth time**.

nuance N a subtle variation.

the nub N the central and most important issue.

nubile ADJ of a young woman: **1** sexually mature. **2** sexually attractive.

nuclear ADJ **1** having the nature of, or like, a nucleus. **2** relating to atoms or their nuclei: *nuclear physics.* **3** relating to or produced by the fission or fusion of atomic nuclei.

nuclear bomb see **atom bomb**

nuclear disarmament N a country's act of giving up its nuclear weapons.

nuclear energy N energy produced through a nuclear reaction. Also called **atomic energy**.

nuclear family N the basic family unit, mother, father and children.

nuclear fission N a reaction in which an

atomic nucleus of a radioactive element splits and releases large amounts of energy.

nuclear fusion N a thermonuclear reaction in which two atomic nuclei combine with a release of large amounts of energy.

nuclear power N power, esp electricity, obtained from reactions by nuclear fission or nuclear fusion. ■ **nuclear-powered** ADJ.

nuclear reactor N an apparatus for producing nuclear energy by means of sustained and controlled nuclear fission.

nuclear weapon N a weapon that derives its destructive force from the energy released during nuclear fission or nuclear fusion.

nuclear winter N a period without light, heat or growth, as a likely after-effect of nuclear war.

nuclei plural of **nucleus**

nucleic acid N a complex compound, either DNA or RNA, found in all living cells.

nucleon N, PHYS a proton or neutron.

nucleus N (-*clei*) **1** PHYS the central part of an atom, consisting of neutrons and protons. **2** BIOL the central part of a plant or animal cell, containing genetic material. **3** a core round which things grow or accumulate.

nude ADJ **1** wearing no clothes; naked. **2** uncovered; bare.
➢ N **1** a representation of one or more naked figures in painting or sculpture, etc. **2** someone naked. **3** the state of nakedness: **in the nude**. ■ **nudity** N.

nudge VB **1** to poke or push someone gently, esp with the elbow, to get attention, etc. **2** to give someone a gentle reminder or persuasion. ➢ N a gentle prod.

nudism N the practice of not wearing clothes, as a matter of principle. ■ **nudist** N, ADJ.

nugatory ADJ, FORMAL **1** worthless; trifling; valueless. **2** ineffective; futile. **3** invalid.

nugget N **1** a lump, esp of gold. **2** a small piece of something precious: **nuggets of wisdom**.

nuisance N an annoying or troublesome person, thing or circumstance.

nuke SLANG, VB to attack with nuclear weapons.
➢ N a nuclear weapon.

null ADJ **1** legally invalid: **declared null and void**. **2** with no significance or value. **3** MATH of a set: with no members; empty. ■ **nullness** N.

nullify VB (-*ies, -ied*) **1** to cause or declare something to be legally invalid. **2** to make something ineffective; to cancel it out.

numb ADJ **1** deprived completely, or to some degree, of sensation. **2** too stunned to feel emotion; stupefied: **numb with shock**.
➢ VB **1** to make something numb. **2** to deaden something. ■ **numbly** ADV. ■ **numbness** N.

number N **1** the system by which things are counted. **2** an arithmetical symbol representing such a quantity, eg 5 or V. **3** a numeral or set of numerals identifying something or someone within a series: **telephone numbers**. **4** a single one of a series, eg an issue of a magazine. **5** a quantity of individuals. **6** an act or turn in a programme. **7** a piece of popular music or jazz. **8** COLLOQ an article or person considered appreciatively. **9** a group or set: **one of our number**. **10** (**numbers**) numerical superiority: **overwhelmed by sheer weight of numbers**.
➢ VB **1** to give a number to something; to mark it with a number. **2** to amount to (a specified number). **3** TR & INTR to list; to enumerate.
◆ **any number of sth** many of it.
◆ **get** or **have sb's number** COLLOQ to have sized them up.
◆ **number among**, **in** or **with sth** to include.
◆ **one's days are numbered** one is soon to die or be removed, disposed of, etc.
◆ **one's number is up** COLLOQ one is about to suffer some unpleasant fate, eg death or ruin.
◆ **without number** countless.

number one N, COLLOQ, IRONIC oneself.

number plate N a plate on a motor vehicle bearing its registration number.

numbskull see **numskull**

numeral N an arithmetical symbol or group of

symbols used to express a number, eg **5** or **V**, **29** or **XXIX**.

numerate ADJ **1** able to perform arithmetical operations. **2** having some understanding of mathematics and science. ■ **numeracy** N.

numerator N the number above the line in a fraction.

numeric and **numerical** ADJ relating to, using, or consisting of, numbers.

numerology N the study of numbers as supposed to predict future events or influence human affairs. ■ **numerologist** N.

numerous ADJ many.

numismatics and **numismatology** N the study or collecting of coins and medals.

numskull or **numbskull** N, COLLOQ a stupid person.

nun N a member of a female religious order living in obedience to certain vows.

nuncio N an ambassador from the pope.

nunnery N (**-ies**) a house in which a group of nuns live; a convent.

nuptial ADJ **1** relating to marriage. **2** ZOOL relating to mating.
➤ N (usu **nuptials**) a marriage ceremony.

nurd see **nerd**

nurse N **1** someone trained to look after sick, injured or feeble people. **2** a woman who looks after small children in a household, etc.
➤ VB **1** to look after (sick or injured people). **2** INTR to follow a career as a nurse. **3** TR & INTR **a** to breastfeed a baby; **b** of a baby: to feed at the breast. **4** to hold with care: **nursing a bag of meringues**. **5** to tend something with concern: **was at home nursing a cold**. **6** to encourage or indulge (a feeling) in oneself: **nursing her jealousy**. ■ **nursing** ADJ, N.

nursemaid and **nurserymaid** N a children's nurse in a household.

nursery N (**-ies**) **1a** a place where children are looked after while their parents are at work, etc; **b** a nursery school. **2** a room in a house,

etc, set apart for young children. **3** a place where plants are grown for sale. **4** a place where young animals are reared or tended. **5** a place where the growth of anything is promoted. Also AS ADJ.

nurseryman N someone who grows plants for sale.

nursery rhyme N a short simple traditional rhyme or song for young children.

nursery school N a school for young children, usu those under five.

nursery slopes PL N, SKIING the lower, more gentle slopes, used for practice by beginners.

nursing home N a small private hospital or home, esp one for old people.

nurture N care and nourishment given to a growing child, animal or plant.
➤ VB **1** to nourish and tend (a growing child, animal or plant). **2** to encourage the development of (a project, idea or feeling, etc).

nut N **1** POPULARLY **a** a fruit consisting of a kernel contained in a hard shell, eg a hazelnut or walnut; **b** the kernel itself. **2** BOT a hard dry indehiscent one-seeded fruit. **3** POPULARLY a roasted peanut. **4** a small piece of metal with a hole through it, for screwing on the end of a bolt. **5** COLLOQ a person's head. **6** COLLOQ (also **nutter**) a crazy person. **7** COLLOQ, usu IN COMPOUNDS an enthusiast: **a football nut**. **8** (**nuts**) COLLOQ testicles.
◆ **a hard** or **tough nut to crack** COLLOQ **1** a difficult problem to solve. **2** an awkward person to deal with.
◆ **off one's nut** COLLOQ mad.

nutcase N, COLLOQ a crazy person.

nutcracker N (usu **nutcrackers**) a utensil for cracking nuts.

nutmeg N the hard aromatic seed of an E Indian tree, used ground or grated as a spice.

nutrient N any nourishing substance.
➤ ADJ nourishing.

nutriment N nourishment; food.

nutrition N **1** the act or process of nourishing.

2 the study of the body's dietary needs.
3 food. ■ **nutritional** ADJ. ■ **nutritionist** N.

nutritious ADJ nourishing; providing nutrition.

nutritive ADJ **1** nourishing. **2** of nutrition.

nuts COLLOQ, ADJ insane; crazy.

the nuts and bolts PL N, COLLOQ the essential or practical details.

nutshell N.
◆ **in a nutshell** concisely expressed.

nutty ADJ (*-ier, -iest*) **1** full of, or tasting of, nuts. **2** COLLOQ crazy. ■ **nuttiness** N.

nuzzle VB, TR & INTR **1** to push or rub someone or something with the nose. **2** (usu **nuzzle up to** or **against sb**) to snuggle up against them.

nylon N **1** a polymeric amide that can be formed into fibres, bristles or sheets. **2** a yarn or cloth made of nylon.

nymph N **1** MYTHOL a goddess that inhabits mountains, water, trees, etc. **2** POETIC a beautiful young woman. **3** ZOOL the immature larval form of certain insects.

nymphet N a sexually attractive and precocious girl in early adolescence.

nymphomania N in women: overpowering sexual desire. ■ **nymphomaniac** N, ADJ.

O or **o** N (**Oes, Os**, or **o's**) the fifteenth letter of the English alphabet.

oaf N a stupid, awkward or loutish person. ■ **oafish** ADJ.

oak N **1** any tree or shrub which produces acorns, and usu has lobed leaves. **2** the hard durable wood of this tree.

oakum N pieces of old, usu tarred, rope untwisted and pulled apart, used to fill small holes and cracks in wooden boats and ships.

OAP ABBREV, BRIT old age pensioner.

oar N a long pole with a broad flat blade at one end, used for rowing a boat.

oasis N (**oases**) **1** a fertile area in a desert, where water is found and plants grow. **2** any place or period of rest or calm, etc.

oast N a kiln for drying hops or, formerly, malt.

oat N **1** a cereal and type of grass cultivated as a food crop. **2** (**oats**) the grains of this plant, used as food.

◆ **sow one's (wild) oats** COLLOQ to indulge in excessive promiscuity, etc during youth and before settling down.

oatcake N a thin dry savoury biscuit made from oatmeal.

oath N **1** a solemn promise to tell the truth or to be loyal, etc, often naming God as a witness. **2** swear-word, obscenity or blasphemy.

oatmeal N meal ground from oats.

obbligato N, MUS (*-tos* or *-ti*) an accompaniment that forms an essential part of a piece of music.

obdurate ADJ **1** hard-hearted. **2** stubborn. ■ **obduracy** N.

obedient ADJ obeying; willing to obey. ■ **obedience** N. ■ **obediently** ADV.

obeisance N a bow, act or other expression of obedience or respect. ■ **obeisant** ADJ.

obelisk N **1** a tall tapering, usu four-sided, stone pillar with a pyramidal top. **2** an obelus.

obelus N (PL -*li*) PRINTING a dagger-shaped mark (†) used esp for referring to footnotes.

obese ADJ very fat. ■ **obesity** N.

obey VB 1 to do what one is told to do by someone. 2 to carry out (a command).

obfuscate VB 1 to darken or obscure (something). 2 to make (something) difficult to understand. ■ **obfuscation** N.

obituary N (-*ies*) a notice or announcement, esp in a newspaper, of a person's death.

object N 1 a material thing that can be seen or touched. 2 an aim or purpose. 3 a person or thing to which action, feelings or thought are directed. 4 GRAM **a** a word or phrase affected by the action of the verb. **b** a word or phrase affected by a preposition.
➤ VB 1 INTR (usu **object to** or **against sth**) to feel or express dislike or disapproval for it. 2 to state something as a ground for disapproval or objection. ■ **objector** N.

objection N 1 the act of or a cause for objecting. 2 an expression or feeling of disapproval, opposition or dislike, etc.

objectionable ADJ unpleasant; offensive.

objective ADJ 1 **a** not depending on personal opinions or prejudices; **b** relating to external facts, etc as opposed to internal thoughts or feelings. 2 PHILOS **a** having existence outside the mind; **b** based on fact or reality.
➤ N 1 a goal. 2 something independent of or external to the mind. ■ **objectivity** or **objectiveness** N.

object lesson N an instructive experience.

oblate ADJ, GEOM of something approximately spherical: flattened at the poles, like the Earth.

oblation N a religious or charitable offering.

obligate VB to bind or oblige (someone) by contract, duty or moral obligation.

obligation N 1 a moral or legal duty or tie. 2 the binding power of such a duty or tie.

obligatory ADJ 1 legally or morally binding. 2 compulsory. ■ **obligatorily** ADV.

oblige VB 1 to bind (someone) morally or legally; to compel. 2 to bind (someone) by a service or favour. 3 to please or do a favour for (someone): Oblige me by listening.

obliging ADJ ready to help others.

oblique ADJ 1 sloping; not vertical or horizontal. 2 GEOM not at a right angle. 3 indirect.
➤ N 1 an oblique line; a solidus (/). 2 anything oblique. ■ **obliqueness** or **obliquity** N.

obliterate VB to destroy or blot out completely. ■ **obliteration** N.

oblivion N the state of having forgotten, being forgotten, or being unconscious.

oblivious ADJ unaware, unconscious or forgetful. ■ **obliviousness** N.

oblong ADJ rectangular with adjacent sides of unequal length; with a greater breadth than height.
➤ N this shape; a rectangular figure.

obloquy N (-*quies*) abuse, blame or censure.

obnoxious ADJ offensive; objectionable.

oboe N (*oboes*) a double-reed treble woodwind instrument. ■ **oboist** N.

obscene ADJ offensive to accepted standards of behaviour or morality. ■ **obscenity** N.

obscure ADJ 1 dark; dim. 2 not clear; hidden. 3 not well known. 4 difficult to understand.
➤ VB 1 to make (something) dark, dim or invisible. 2 to make (something) difficult to understand. ■ **obscurity** N (-*ies*).

obsequies PL N funeral rites.

obsequious ADJ submissively obedient; fawning. ■ **obsequiousness** N.

observance N the fact or an act of obeying rules or keeping customs, etc.

observant ADJ quick to notice; perceptive.

observation N 1 the ability to observe; perception. 2 a remark or comment. 3 the noting of behaviour, symptoms or phenomena, etc as they occur. ■ **observational** ADJ.

observatory N (-*ies*) a room or building, etc for making observations of natural phenomena, esp the stars and other celestial objects.

observe VB **1** to notice or become conscious of (something). **2** to watch (something) carefully; to pay close attention to it. **3** TR & INTR to examine and note (behaviour, symptoms, etc). **4** to obey, follow or keep (a law, custom or religious rite, etc). **5** TR & INTR to remark or comment. ■ **observable** ADJ. ■ **observer** N.

obsess VB **1** to occupy (someone's thoughts or mind) completely, persistently or constantly.

obsession N **1** a persistent or dominating thought, idea, feeling, etc. **2** PSYCHOL a recurring thought, feeling or impulse, that preoccupies a person against their will and is a source of constant anxiety. **3** the act of obsessing or state of being obsessed. ■ **obsessional** ADJ.

obsessive ADJ **1** relating to or resulting from obsession. **2** affected by an obsession. ➤ N an obsessive person.

obsolescent ADJ going out of use; becoming out of date. ■ **obsolescence** N.

obsolete ADJ no longer in use or in practice.

obstacle N someone or something that obstructs, or hinders or prevents advance.

obstetrics SING N the branch of medicine and surgery that deals with pregnancy, childbirth and the care of the mother. ■ **obstetrician** N.

obstinate ADJ **1** stubborn. **2** difficult to defeat or remove. ■ **obstinacy** N.

obstreperous ADJ unruly.

obstruct VB **1** to block or close (a passage or opening, etc). **2** to prevent or hinder the movement or progress of (someone or something). ■ **obstruction** N.

obstructive ADJ causing or designed to cause an obstruction. ■ **obstructively** ADV.

obtain VB **1** to get (something); to become the owner, or come into possession, of (something). **2** INTR to be established, exist or hold good.

obtrude VB, INTR to be or become unpleasantly noticeable or prominent.

obtrusive ADJ unpleasantly noticeable or

prominent. ■ **obtrusiveness** N.

obtuse ADJ **1** stupid and slow to understand. **2** blunt; not pointed or sharp; rounded at the tip. **3** GEOM of an angle: greater than 90° and less than 180°. ■ **obtuseness** N.

obverse N **1** the side of a coin with the head or main design on it. **2** an opposite or counterpart.

obviate VB to prevent or remove (a potential difficulty or problem, etc) in advance.

obvious ADJ easily seen or understood. ➤ N (**the obvious**) something which is obvious. ■ **obviously** ADV.

occasion N **1** a particular event or happening, or the time at which it occurs: **met on three occasions**. **2** a special event or celebration. **3** a reason; grounds: **no occasion to be angry**. ➤ VB to bring something about, esp incidentally. ◆ **on occasion** from time to time.

occasional ADJ **1** happening irregularly and infrequently. **2** produced on or for a special occasion. ■ **occasionally** ADV.

Occident N (**the Occident**) the countries in the west. ■ **Occidental** ADJ.

occipital ADJ, ANAT relating to or in the region of the back of the head.

occlude VB, TECHNICAL **1** to block up or cover (an opening or passage). **2** to shut (something) in or out. ■ **occlusion** N.

occult ADJ **1** involving, using or dealing with that which is magical, mystical or supernatural. **2** beyond ordinary understanding. ➤ N (**the occult**) the knowledge and study of magical, mystical or supernatural things. ■ **occultism** N.

occupancy N (**-ies**) **1** the act or condition of occupying (a house or flat, etc), or the fact of its being occupied. **2** the period of time during which a house, etc is occupied.

occupant N someone who occupies or holds property, a particular position, etc.

occupation N **1** a person's job or profession. **2** an activity that occupies a person's attention or free time, etc. **3** the act of occupying or state of being occupied. **4** the act of taking and keeping control of a foreign country by military power. ■ **occupational** ADJ.

occupier N someone who lives in a building, either as a tenant or owner.

occupy VB (*-ies, -ied*) **1** to have possession of or live in (a house, etc). **2** to be in or fill (time or space, etc). **3** to take possession of (a country, etc) by force. **4** to enter and take possession of (a building, etc). **5** to hold (a post or office).

occur VB (*-rr-*) INTR **1** to happen or take place. **2** to be found or exist.
◆ **occur to sb** to come into their mind.

occurrence N **1** anything that occurs; an event. **2** the act or fact of occurring.

ocean N **1** the continuous expanse of salt water that covers about 70% of the Earth's surface. **2** any one of its five main divisions: the Atlantic, Indian, Pacific, Arctic and Antarctic. **3** the sea. **4** (often **oceans**) a very large number, amount or expanse. ■ **oceanic** ADJ.

ocean-going ADJ of a ship, etc: suitable for sailing across oceans.

oceanography N the scientific study of the oceans. ■ **oceanographic** or **oceanographical** ADJ.

ocelot N **1** a medium-sized wild cat of Central and S America. **2** its fur.

ochre or (N AMER) **ocher** N **1** a fine earth or clay used as a red, yellow or brown pigment. **2** a pale brownish-yellow colour.
➤ ADJ with the colour of ochre.

o'clock ADV after a number from one to twelve: used in specifying the time, indicating the number of hours after midday or midnight.

octagon N a plane figure with eight straight sides and eight angles. ■ **octagonal** ADJ.

octahedron or **octohedron** N (*-ra* or *-rons*) a solid figure with eight plane faces.

octane N, CHEM a liquid present in petroleum.

octave N, MUS the series of notes between the first and the eighth notes of a major or minor scale, eg from C to the C above.

octet or **octette** N **1** any group of eight people or things. **2** MUS **a** a group of eight musicians or singers who perform together; **b** a piece of music for eight instruments or voices.

October N the tenth month of the year.

octogenarian N someone who is 80 years old, or between 80 and 89 years old.

octopus N (*octopuses*) a marine mollusc with no external shell and eight arms with suckers.

octuplet N **1** MUS a group of eight notes to be played in the time of six. **2** one of eight children or animals born at one birth.

ocular ADJ of or in the region of the eye.

oculist N a specialist in diseases and defects of the eye; an optician or ophthalmologist.

OD SLANG, N (*ODs* or *OD's*) an overdose of drugs.
➤ VB (*OD's, OD'd, OD'ing*) INTR to take a drug overdose.

odd ADJ **1** left over when others are put into groups or pairs; remaining. **2** not matching: **odd socks**. **3** not one of a complete set. **4** MATH of a whole number: not exactly divisible by two. **5** unusual; strange. ■ **oddly** ADV. ■ **oddness** N.
◆ **against all (the) odds** in spite of great difficulty or disadvantage.
◆ **at odds** in disagreement or dispute.
◆ **odd man** or **odd one out** someone that is in some way different from others in a group.
◆ **over the odds** more than is normal, required or expected, etc.

oddball orig US COLLOQ, N an eccentric person.

oddity N (*-ies*) **1** a strange or odd person or thing. **2** a peculiarity. **3** the state of being odd or unusual; strangeness.

odd job N (usu **odd jobs**) casual or occasional pieces of work.

oddment N something left over or remaining from a greater quantity: **oddments of fabric**.

odds PL N **1** the chance or probability, expressed as a ratio, that something will or will not happen: **The odds are 10—1 against**. **2** the difference, expressed as a ratio, between the amount placed as a bet and the money which might be won: **offer odds of 2 to 1. 3** an advantage that is thought to exist, esp in favour of one competitor over another: **The odds are in her favour. 4** likelihood: **The odds are he'll be late again.**

odds and ends PL N, COLLOQ miscellaneous objects or pieces of things, etc.

odds-on ADJ very likely to succeed, win, etc.

ode N a poem addressed to a person or thing.

odious ADJ repulsive; extremely unpleasant.

odium N hatred, strong dislike, or disapproval.

odometer N, N AMER a device for measuring distance travelled.

odour or (N AMER) **odor** N **1** a distinctive smell; scent. **2** a characteristic or quality.
■ **odourless** ADJ. ■ **odorous** ADJ.

odyssey N a long and adventurous journey.

oedema or **edema** N (-*mata* or -*mas*) PATHOL an abnormal accumulation of fluid within body tissues or body cavities.

oenology N the study of wine.

oesophagus or (esp N AMER) **esophagus** N (-*gi*) ANAT the narrow muscular tube from the mouth to the stomach. ■ **oesophageal** ADJ.

oestrogen or (N AMER) **estrogen** N a female sex hormone.

oestrus or (N AMER) **estrus** N, ZOOL, PHYSIOL a regular period of sexual receptivity in most female mammals. ■ **oestrous** ADJ.

of PREP **1** used to show origin or cause: **people of Glasgow. 2** belonging to or connected with. **3** used to specify a component, ingredient or characteristic, etc: **built of bricks. 4** at a given distance or amount of time from something: **within a minute of arriving. 5** about; concerning: **tales of Rome. 6** belonging to or forming a part of something: **most of the story. 7** existing or happening, etc, at, on, in or during: **Battle of Hastings. 8** used with words denoting loss, removal or separation, etc: **cured of cancer. 9** used to show the connection

between a verbal noun and the person or thing that is performing, or that is the object of, the action stated: **the eating of healthy food. 10** aged: **a boy of twelve.**

off ADV **1** away; at or to a distance. **2** in or into a position which is not attached; separate: **The handle came off. 3** in or into a state of not being on: **Turn the radio off. 4** in or into a state of being stopped: **The match was rained off. 5** in or into a state of sleep: **nodded off. 6** so as to be completely finished: **Finish the work off. 7** away from work or one's duties: **Take an hour off. 8** situated as regards money: **badly off.**
➤ ADJ **1** not functioning or operating; disconnected; not on: **The radio was off. 2** not taking place: **The meeting's off. 3** not good; not up to standard: **an off day. 4** no longer available as a choice: **Peas are off. 5** in a state of decay; gone bad or sour: **The milk was off.**
➤ PREP **1** from or away from: **Lift it off the shelf. 2** removed from or no longer attached. **3** opening out of, leading from, or not far from: **a side street off the main road. 4** not wanting or no longer attracted by: **off one's food. 5** no longer using: **be off the tablets.**
➤ N (usu **the off**) the start: **ready for the off.**
◆ **off and on** now and then; occasionally.

offal N the heart, brains, liver and kidneys, etc of an animal, used as food.

offbeat ADJ unconventional; eccentric.

off-colour ADJ **1** BRIT slightly unwell; not in good health. **2** chiefly N AMER (**off-color**) of humour: rude; smutty.

offcut N a small piece of eg wood or cloth, etc cut off or left over from a larger quantity.

offence or (chiefly US) **offense** N **1 a** the breaking of a rule or law, etc; **b** a crime. **2** any cause of anger, annoyance or displeasure.
◆ **give offence** to cause annoyance.
◆ **take offence at sth** to be offended by it.

offend VB **1** to make (someone) feel hurt or angry; to insult (them). **2** to be unpleasant or annoying to (someone). **3** INTR (usu **offend against sb** or **sth**) to commit a sin or crime against them. ■ **offender** N.

offensive ADJ 1 giving or likely to give offence; insulting. 2 unpleasant, disgusting and repulsive: **an offensive smell**. 3 SPORT, MILITARY, ETC used for attacking: **offensive weapons**. ➤ N 1 an aggressive action or attitude: **go on the offensive**. 2 an attack. ■ **offensiveness** N.

offer VB 1 to put forward for acceptance, refusal or consideration. 2 FORMAL to provide: **a site offering the best view**. 3 INTR to state one's willingness (to do something). 4 to present (something) for sale. 5 to provide (an opportunity) (for something): **a job offering rapid promotion**. 6 INTR to present itself; to occur: **if opportunity offers**. 7 TR & INTR to propose (a sum of money) as payment (to someone): **offer him £250 for the car**. ➤ N 1 an act of offering. 2 something that is offered.

offering N 1 the act of making an offer. 2 anything offered, esp a gift. 3 a gift of money given to a church, usu during a religious service. 4 a sacrifice made to God, a saint.

offertory N (-ies) CHRISTIANITY 1 the offering of bread and wine during a Eucharist. 2 money collected during a church service.

offhand and **offhanded** ADJ casual or careless.

office N 1 the room, set of rooms or building in which the business of a firm is done, or in which a particular kind of business, clerical work, etc is done. 2 a local centre or department of a large business. 3 a position of authority, esp in the government or in public service: **run for office**. 4 a the length of time for which an official position is held; b of a political party: the length of time for which it forms the government: **hold office**. 5 the group of people working in an office. 6 a function or duty. 7 (usu **offices**) an act of kindness or service.

officer N 1 someone in a position of authority and responsibility in the armed forces. 2 someone with an official position in an organization or government department. 3 a policeman or policewoman.

official ADJ 1 of or relating to an office or position of authority. 2 given or authorized by a person in authority: **an official report**. 3 characteristic of people holding office: **official dinners**. ■ **officially** ADV.

officialdom N 1 officials and bureaucrats as a group. 2 officialism.

officiate VB, INTR 1 a to act in an official capacity; b to perform official duties. 2 to conduct a religious service. ■ **officiation** N.

officious ADJ too ready to offer advice, etc, esp when it is not wanted. ■ **officiousness** N.

offing N.
◆ **in the offing** not far off.

off-key ADJ, ADV, MUS a in the wrong key; b out of tune.

off-limits ADJ not to be entered. ➤ ADV (**off limits**) in or into an area that is out of bounds.

off-line ADJ, COMP of a peripheral device: 1 not connected to the central processing unit, and therefore not controlled by it. 2 not connected; switched off. Also AS ADV: **went off-line at 2pm**.

offload VB 1 TR & INTR to unload. 2 to get rid of (something, esp something unpleasant or unwanted) by passing it on to someone else.

off-peak ADJ used at a time when there is little demand, and therefore usu cheaper.

off-putting ADJ, COLLOQ 1 disconcerting; distracting. 2 unpleasant; repulsive.

off-road ADJ 1 of vehicle use: not on public roads; esp on rough ground or terrain. 2 of a vehicle: suitable for such use. ■ **off-roader** N.

off-season N the less busy period in a particular business or for a particular activity. ➤ ADJ relating to such a period: **off-season reductions**.

offset N 1 a start; the outset. 2 a side-shoot on a plant, used for developing new plants. 3 PRINTING a process in which an image is inked on to a rubber roller which then transfers it to paper, etc. ➤ VB 1 to counter-balance or compensate for (something): **price rises offset by tax cuts**. 2 to print (something) using an offset process.

offshoot N anything which is a branch of, or has developed from, something else.

offshore ADV, ADJ **1** situated in, at, or on the sea, not far from the coast: **offshore industries**. **2** of the wind: blowing away from the coast.

offside ADJ, ADV, FOOTBALL, RUGBY, etc in an illegal forward position.
➤ N the side of a vehicle or horse nearest the centre of the road, in the UK the right side.

offspring N (PL *offspring*) **1** a person's child or children. **2** the young of an animal.

off-stage ADJ, ADV, THEAT not on the stage and so unable to be seen by the audience.

off-the-peg ADJ of clothing: ready to wear.

often ADV **1** many times. **2** in many cases.
◆ **every so often** sometimes; now and then.
◆ **more often than not** in most of the cases.

ogle VB to look at or eye (someone) in an amorous or lecherous way.

ogre and **ogress** N **1** in fairy stories: a frightening, cruel, ugly giant. **2** a cruel, frightening or ugly person.

oh EXCLAM expressing surprise, admiration, pleasure, anger or fear, etc.

ohm N the SI unit of electrical resistance.

oil N **1** any greasy, viscous and usu flammable substance, insoluble in water but soluble in organic compounds, that is derived from animals, plants or mineral deposits, or manufactured artificially, and used as a fuel, lubricant or food. **2** petroleum. **3 a** (often **oils**) oil paint; **b** an oil painting.
➤ VB to apply oil to (something); to lubricate or treat (something) with oil.

oilcloth N cloth, often cotton, treated with oil to make it waterproof; oilskin.

oilfield N an area of land or sea bed that contains reserves of petroleum.

oil-fired ADJ using oil as a fuel.

oil paint N paint made by mixing ground pigment with oil, often linseed oil.

oilskin N **1** cloth treated with oil to make it

waterproof. **2** (often **oilskins**) an outer garment made of oilskin.

oily ADJ (*-ier, -iest*) **1 a** like oil; greasy; **b** containing or consisting of oil. **2** soaked in or covered with oil. **3** DEROG smooth; unctuous; servile and flattering. ■ **oiliness** N.

oink N the grunting noise made by a pig.

ointment N any greasy or oily semi–solid preparation, usu medicated, applied externally to the skin in order to heal, soothe or protect it.

OK or **okay** COLLOQ, ADJ all correct; all right; satisfactory: **an okay song**.
➤ ADV well; satisfactorily.
➤ EXCLAM expressing agreement or approval; yes; certainly: OK! I'll do it!
➤ NOUN (**OKs, OK's** or **okays**) approval, sanction or agreement.
➤ VERB (**OK'd** or **OK'ed, OK'ing**; **okayed, okaying**) to approve or pass (something) as satisfactory.

okapi N (*okapis* or *okapi*) a ruminant animal related to the giraffe, but with a shorter neck.

okey-doke or **okey-dokey** ADV, ADJ, EXCLAM, COLLOQ OK; fine.

okra N **1** a tall plant that has red and yellow flowers. **2** the edible fruit of this plant, consisting of long green seed pods, used in stews, etc. Also called **gumbo, lady's finger**.

old ADJ (*older* or *elder, oldest* or *eldest*) **1** advanced in age; that has existed for a long time; not young. **2** having a stated age: **five years old**. **3** belonging or relating to the end period of a long life or existence: **old age**. **4** worn out or shabby through long use: **old shoes**. **5** no longer in use; out of date; old–fashioned. **6** belonging to the past. **7** former or previous; earliest of two or more things: **went back to see their old house**. **8** of long standing or long existence: **an old member of the society**. **9** with the characteristics, eg experience, maturity or appearance, of age: **be old beyond one's years**. **10** (**Old**) of a language: relating to or denoting its earliest form: **Old English**. **11** COLLOQ, JOCULAR used in expressions of familiar affection or contempt,

etc: **silly old fool.**
➤ N an earlier time: **men of old.**

old age pension N a retirement pension.
■ **old age pensioner** N.

olden ADJ, ARCHAIC former; past: **in olden days.**

Old English see under **Anglo-Saxon**

old-fashioned ADJ **1** of or in a style common some time ago; out of date. **2** in favour of the habits and moral views of the past.

old flame N, COLLOQ a former boyfriend or girlfriend.

old hand N, COLLOQ an experienced person.

old hat ADJ, COLLOQ tediously familiar.

oldie N, COLLOQ an old person, song or film.

old maid N, DEROG, COLLOQ **1** a spinster.
2 a woman or man who is prim and fussy.

old school N a group of people or section of society with traditional or old-fashioned ways. Also (**old-school**) AS ADJ.

Old Testament N the first part of the Christian Bible.

old-time ADJ of or typical of the past.

old wives' tale N an old belief, superstition or theory considered foolish and unscientific.

old-world ADJ belonging to earlier times, esp when quaint or charming: **old-world charm.**

oleaginous ADJ **1** like or containing oil; oily.
2 producing oil. **3** unctuous.

olfactory ADJ relating to the sense of smell.

oligarchy N (**-ies**) **1** government by a small group of people. **2** a state or organization so governed. **3** a small group of people which forms a government. ■ **oligarch** N.
■ **oligarchic** or **oligarchical** ADJ.

oligopoly N (**-ies**) ECON a situation in which there are few sellers of a particular product or service, and a small number of competitive firms control the market.

olive N **1** a small evergreen tree cultivated mainly in the Mediterranean region for its fruit and the oil obtained from the fruit. **2** the small

green or black oval edible fruit of this tree. **3** the wood of this tree. **4** (also **olive green**) a dull yellowish-green colour.
➤ ADJ **1** (also **olive-green**) dull yellowish-green in colour. **2** of a complexion: sallow.

olive branch N a sign or gesture that indicates a wish for peace or reconciliation.

olive oil N the pale-yellow oil obtained by pressing ripe olives.

oloroso N a medium-sweet sherry.

ombudsman N an official appointed to investigate complaints against public authorities and government departments.

omega N **1** the twenty-fourth and last letter of the Greek alphabet (Ω, ω). **2** the last of a series.

omelette or (N AMER) **omelet** N, COOKERY a dish made of beaten eggs fried in a pan.

omen N **1** a circumstance, etc regarded as a sign of a future event. **2** threatening or prophetic character: **bird of ill omen.**

ominous ADJ threatening; containing a warning of something evil or bad.

omission N **1** something that has been left out or neglected. **2** the act of leaving something out or neglecting it. ■ **omissive** ADJ.

omit VB (**-tt-**) **1** to leave out, either by mistake or on purpose. **2** to fail to do (something).

omnibus N **1** OLD USE OR FORMAL a bus.
2 a book that contains reprints of a number of works by a single author, or several works on the same subject or of a similar type. **3** a TV or radio programme made up of or edited from the preceding week's editions of a particular serial.

omnipotent ADJ all-powerful.
■ **omnipotence** N.

omnipresent ADJ esp of a god: present everywhere at the same time.
■ **omnipresence** N.

omniscient ADJ **1** with infinite knowledge or understanding. **2** knowing everything.
■ **omniscience** N.

omnivore N a person or animal that eats any type of food. ■ **omnivorous** ADJ.

on PREP **1** touching, supported by, attached to, covering, or enclosing. **2** in or into (a vehicle, etc): **got on the bus. 3** COLLOQ carried with (a person): **I've got no money on me. 4** very near to or along the side of something: **on the shore. 5** at or during (a certain day or time, etc): **on Monday. 6** immediately after, at or before: **on his return. 7** within the (given) limits of something: **on page nine. 8** about: **a book on Jane Austen. 9** through contact with or as a result of something: **cut himself on the broken bottle. 10** in the state or process of something: **on fire. 11** using as a means of transport: **goes to work on the bus. 12** using as a means or medium: **talk on the telephone. 13** having as a basis or source: **on good authority. 14** working for or being a member of something: **on the committee. 15** at the expense of or to the disadvantage of something or someone: **treatment on the National Health. 16** supported by something: **live on bread and cheese. 17** regularly taking or using something: **on tranquillizers. 18** staked as a bet: **put money on a horse.**
➤ ADV **1** esp of clothes: in or into contact or a state of enclosing, covering, or being worn, etc: **have no clothes on. 2** ahead, forwards or towards in space or time: **later on. 3** continuously; without interruption: **keep on about something. 4** in or into operation or activity: **put the radio on.**
➤ ADJ **1** working, broadcasting or performing: **You're on in two minutes. 2** taking place: **Which films are on this week? 3** COLLOQ possible, practicable or acceptable: **That just isn't on. 4** COLLOQ talking continuously, esp to complain or nag: **always on at him. 5** in favour of a win: **odds of 3 to 4 on.**
◆ **be on to sb** or **sth** COLLOQ **1** to realize their or its importance or intentions. **2** to be in touch with them: **He's been on to his MP.**
◆ **get on to sb** COLLOQ to get in touch with them.
◆ **on and off** now and then; occasionally.
◆ **on and on** continually; at length.

onager N a variety of wild ass found in C Asia.

onanism N **1** coitus interruptus. **2** masturbation. ■ **onanist** N.

once ADV **1 a** a single time: **I'll say this only once; b** on one occasion: **They came once. 2** multiplied by one. **3** at some time in the past; formerly: **lived in London once. 4** by one degree of relationship: **a cousin once removed.**
➤ CONJ as soon as: **Once you have finished you can go out.**
➤ N one time or occasion: **just this once.**
◆ **at once 1** immediately; without any delay. **2** all at the same time; simultaneously.
◆ **once (and) for all** now and never again.

once-over N, COLLOQ a quick examination.

oncology N the branch of medicine that deals with the study of tumours, esp cancerous ones. ■ **oncologist** N.

oncoming ADJ approaching; advancing.

one N **1 a** the cardinal number 1; **b** the quantity that this represents, being a single unit. **2** a unity or unit. **3** any symbol for this, eg 1, I. **4** the first hour after midnight or midday.
➤ ADJ **1** being a single unit, number or thing. **2** being a particular person or thing: **lift one leg and then the other. 3** being a particular but unspecified instance or example: **visit him one day soon. 4** being the only such: **the one woman who can beat her. 5** same; identical: **of one mind. 6** undivided; forming a single whole: **They sang with one voice. 7** first: **page one. 8** COLLOQ an exceptional example or instance of something: **That was one big fellow. 9** totalling one. **10** aged one.
➤ PRONOUN **1** (often referring to a noun already mentioned or implied) an individual person, thing or instance: **buy the blue one. 2** anybody: **One simply doesn't. 3** FORMAL OR FACETIOUS I; me: **One doesn't like to pry.**
◆ **at one with sb** or **sth** in complete agreement or harmony with them or it.
◆ **for one** as one person: **I for one object.**
◆ **one and all** everyone without exception.
◆ **one and only** used for emphasis: only.
◆ **one another** used as the object of a verb or preposition when an action takes place between two (or more than two) people, etc:

Chris and Pat love one another.
◆ **one by one** one after the other; individually.

one-armed bandit N a fruit machine with a long handle at the side which is pulled down hard to make the machine work.

one-horse race N a race or competition, etc in which one particular competitor or participant is certain to win.

one-liner N, COLLOQ a short amusing remark or joke made in a single sentence.

one-night stand N 1 COLLOQ a sexual encounter that lasts only one night. 2 a performance given only once in any place, the next performance taking place elsewhere.

one-off ADJ, COLLOQ, chiefly BRIT made or happening, etc on one occasion only.
➤ N something that is one-off.

one-piece ADJ of a garment: made as a single piece as opposed to separate parts.
➤ N a garment made in such a way.

onerous ADJ heavy; difficult to do or bear.

oneself and **one's self** PRONOUN 1 the reflexive form of **one**: to help oneself. 2 the emphatic form of **one**: One hasn't been there oneself. 3 one's normal self: not feeling oneself.

one-sided ADJ 1 of a competition, etc: with one side having a great advantage over the other. 2 seeing, accepting, representing or favouring only one side of a subject or argument, etc. 3 limited to one side only.

one-stop ADJ able to provide the complete range of goods that a customer might require.

one-time ADJ former; past: one-time lover.

one-to-one ADJ 1 with one person or thing exactly corresponding to or matching another. 2 in which a person is involved with only one other person: one-to-one teaching.

one-track ADJ, COLLOQ **a** incapable of dealing with more than one subject or activity, etc at a time; **b** obsessed with one idea.

one-upmanship N, INFORMAL the art of gaining advantages over other people.

one-way ADJ 1 **a** of a road or street, etc: on which traffic is allowed to move in one direction only; **b** relating to or indicating such a traffic system: one-way sign. 2 of a feeling or relationship: not returned or reciprocated. 3 N AMER, ESP US of a ticket: valid for travel in one direction only.

ongoing ADJ in progress; going on.

onion N 1 a plant belonging to the lily family. 2 the pungent bulb of this plant eaten raw, cooked or pickled. ■ **oniony** ADJ.

on-line ADJ 1 COMP of a peripheral device, eg a printer: connected to and controlled by the central processor of a computer. Also AS ADV. 2 of a service, etc: run with a direct connection to a computer: on-line shopping.

onlooker N someone who watches and does not take part; an observer. ■ **onlooking** ADJ.

only ADJ 1 without any others of the same type. 2 of someone: having no brothers or sisters. 3 COLLOQ best: the only way to travel.
➤ ADV 1 not more than; just. 2 alone; solely. 3 not longer ago than; not until: only a minute ago. 4 merely; with no other result than: I arrived only to find him gone.
➤ CONJ 1 but; however: Come if you want to, only don't complain if you're bored. 2 if it were not for the fact that: I'd come too, only I know I'd slow you down.
◆ **if only** I wish.
◆ **only too** extremely: only too ready to help.

o.n.o. ABBREV or near offer; or nearest offer.

onomatopoeia N the formation of words whose sounds imitate the sound they represent, eg hiss, squelch. ■ **onomatopoeic** ADJ.

onset N 1 an attack; an assault. 2 a beginning, esp of something unpleasant.

onshore ADV towards, on, or on to the shore.
➤ ADJ found or occurring on the shore or land.

onside ADJ, ADV, FOOTBALL, RUGBY, ETC of a player: in a position where the ball may legally be played; not offside. Also written **on-side**.

onslaught N a fierce attack; an onset.

onto PREP on to.
◆ **be onto sb** to be suspicious or aware of their (usu underhand) actions.

ontology N, PHILOS the study of the nature and essence of things or of existence.

onus N a responsibility or burden: **The onus is on you to prove it.**

onward ADJ moving forward in place or time.
➤ ADV (also **onwards**) **1** towards or at a place or time which is advanced or in front; ahead. **2** continuing to move forwards or progress.

onyx N, GEOL a very hard variety of agate.

oodles PL N, COLLOQ lots; a great quantity.

ooh EXCLAM expressing pleasure, surprise, excitement or pain.

oops EXCLAM, COLLOQ (also **oops-a-daisy**) expressing surprise or apology, eg when one makes a mistake or drops something, etc.

ooze VB **1** INTR to flow or leak out gently or slowly. **2** INTR of a substance: to give out moisture. **3** to give out (a liquid, etc) slowly. **4** to overflow with (a quality or feeling); to exude: **oozed charm.**
➤ N **1** a slow gentle leaking or oozing. **2** mud or slime. ■ **oozy** ADJ.

opacity N **1** opaqueness. **2** the state of having an obscure meaning and being difficult to understand. **3** dullness; obtuseness.

opal N, GEOL a usu milky-white stone often with flecks and shimmering flashes.

opalescent ADJ reflecting different colours as the surrounding light changes, like an opal.
■ **opalescence** N.

opaque ADJ **1** not transparent or translucent. **2** difficult to understand; obscure.
■ **opaqueness** N.

open ADJ **1 a** not closed or locked; **b** allowing people or things to go in or out; with its door or gate, etc not closed or locked. **2 a** not sealed or covered; **b** with the insides visible: **an open cupboard. 3** not enclosed, confined or restricted: **the open sea. 4** not covered, guarded or protected: **an open wound.**

5 spread out or unfolded: **an open newspaper. 6** receiving customers; ready for business. **7** MUS **a** of a string: not stopped by a finger; **b** of a note: played on an open string, or without holes on the instrument being covered. **8** generally known; public. **9** (usu **open to sth**) liable or susceptible to it; defenceless against it: **open to abuse. 10** allowing anyone to take part, esp both amateurs and professionals. **11** free from restraint or restrictions of any kind: **open market. 12** unprejudiced: **have an open mind. 13** (usu **open to**) amenable to or ready to receive (eg new ideas or impressions): **open to suggestion. 14** of a person: candid.
➤ VB **1 a** to unfasten or move (eg a door or barrier) to allow access; **b** INTR of a door or barrier, etc: to become unfastened to allow access. **2** TR & INTR to become or make (something) become open or more open, eg by removing obstructions, etc. **3** (also **open out**) TR & INTR to spread (something) out or become spread out or unfolded, esp so as to make or become visible. **4** TR & INTR to start or begin working: **The office opens at nine. 5** to declare (something) open with an official ceremony: **open the new hospital. 6** TR & INTR to begin (something) or start speaking or writing, etc: **opened his talk with a joke.**
➤ NOUN **1** (**the open**) an area of open country; an area not obstructed by buildings, etc. **2** (**the open**) public notice or attention.
■ **opener** N. ■ **openly** ADV. ■ **openness** N.
◆ **open fire** to start shooting.
◆ **with open arms** warmly; cordially.

open-and-shut ADJ easily decided.

opencast ADJ of a mine: mined by removing the overlying layers of material.

open day N a day when members of the public can visit an institution usu closed to them.

open-ended ADJ **1** with an open end or ends. **2** not limited to strictly 'yes' or 'no' answers; allowing for free expression of opinion.

open-handed ADJ generous.

open-hearted ADJ **1** honest, direct and hiding nothing; candid. **2** kind; generous.

open house N the state of being willing to

welcome and entertain visitors at any time.

opening N 1 the act of making or becoming open. 2 a hole or gap. 3 a beginning or first stage of something. 4 THEAT the first performance of a play or opera, etc. 5 an opportunity or chance. 6 a vacancy.
➤ ADJ relating to or forming an opening; first.

open-minded ADJ willing to receive new ideas; unprejudiced.

open-plan ADJ with few internal walls and with large undivided rooms.

open prison N a prison which allows prisoners greater freedom of movement than in normal prisons.

open question N a matter that is undecided.

open secret N something that is supposedly a secret but that is in fact widely known.

opera[1] N 1 a dramatic work set to music, in which the singers are usu accompanied by an orchestra. 2 operas as an art form. ■ **operatic** ADJ.

opera[2] plural of **opus**

operable ADJ 1 MED of a disease or injury, etc: that can be treated by surgery. 2 that can be operated.

opera glasses N small binoculars used at the theatre or opera, etc.

operand N, MATH, LOGIC a quantity on which an operation is performed.

operate VB 1 INTR to function or work. 2 to make (a machine, etc) function or work; to control the functioning of (something). 3 to manage, control or direct (a business, etc). 4 (usu **operate on sb**) INTR to perform a surgical operation on them. 5 INTR to perform military, naval or police, etc operations.

operating theatre and **operating room** N the room in a hospital, etc where surgical operations are performed.

operation N 1 an act, method or process of working or operating. 2 the state of working or being active: **The factory is not yet in operation.** 3 an activity; something done. 4 an action or series of actions which have a particular effect. 5 MED any surgical procedure that is performed in order to treat a damaged or diseased part of the body. 6 (often **operations**) one of a series of military, naval or police, etc actions, usu involving a large number of people, performed as part of a much larger plan. 7 COMP a series of actions that are specified by a single computer instruction.

operational ADJ 1 relating to an operation or operations. 2 able or ready to work or perform an intended function.

operative ADJ 1 working; in action; having an effect. 2 of a word: esp important or significant: '**Must**' **is the operative word.** 3 relating to a surgical operation.
➤ N a worker, esp one with special skills.

operator N 1 someone who operates a machine or apparatus. 2 someone who operates a telephone switchboard, connecting calls, etc. 3 someone who runs a business.

operetta N a short light opera, with spoken dialogue and often dancing.

ophthalmic ADJ relating to the eye.

ophthalmology N, MED the study, diagnosis and treatment of diseases and defects of the eye. ■ **ophthalmologist** N.

opiate N a drug containing or derived from opium.

opine VB, FORMAL to suppose or express (something) as an opinion.

opinion N 1 a belief or judgement which seems likely to be true, but which is not based on proof. 2 (usu **opinion on** or **about sth**) what one thinks about it. 3 a professional judgement given by an expert: **medical opinion.** 4 estimation or appreciation: **a high opinion of himself.**

opinionated ADJ with very strong opinions that one refuses or is very unwilling to change.

opinion poll see under **poll**

opium N a highly addictive narcotic drug.

opossum N (**opossums** or **opossum**) 1 a small

tree-dwelling American marsupial with a hairless prehensile tail. **2** any similar marsupial, native to Australasia. Also called **possum**.

opponent N someone who belongs to the opposing side in an argument, contest, etc.

opportune ADJ suitable; proper.

opportunist N someone whose actions are governed by the circumstances of the moment rather than being based on settled principles. ➤ ADJ referring to such actions or opinions. ■ **opportunistic** ADJ. ■ **opportunism** N.

opportunity N (-*ies*) **1** an occasion offering a possibility; a chance. **2** favourable or advantageous conditions.

opposable ADJ of a digit, esp the thumb: able to be placed in a position so that it faces and can touch the ends of the other digits.

oppose VB **1** to resist or fight against (someone or something) by force or argument. **2** INTR to compete in a game or contest, etc against another person or team; to act in opposition. ■ **opposer** N. ■ **opposing** ADJ. ◆ **as opposed to** in contrast to.

opposite ADJ **1** placed or being on the other side of, or at the other end of, a real or imaginary line or space. **2** facing in a directly different direction: **opposite sides of the coin**. **3** completely or diametrically different. **4** referring to something that is the other of a matching or contrasting pair: **the opposite sex**. ➤ N an opposite person or thing. ➤ ADV in or into an opposite position: **live opposite**. ➤ PREP **1** (also **opposite to sb** or **sth**) in a position across from and facing them or it: **a house opposite the station**. **2** of an actor: co-starring with another actor: **played opposite Olivier**.

opposite number N someone with an equivalent position in another company, etc.

opposition N **1** the act of fighting against someone or something by force or argument; resistance. **2** the state of being hostile or in conflict. **3** a person or group of people who are opposed to something.

oppress VB **1** to govern with cruelty and injustice. **2** to worry, trouble or make (someone) anxious. **3** to distress or afflict (someone). ■ **oppression** N. ■ **oppressor** N.

oppressive ADJ **1** cruel, tyrannical and unjust. **2** causing worry or mental distress; weighing heavily on the mind. **3** heavy, hot and sultry. ■ **oppressiveness** N.

opprobrium N public shame, disgrace or loss of favour; infamy. ■ **opprobrious** ADJ.

oppugn VB to call into question; to dispute.

opt VB, INTR (usu **opt for sth** or **to do sth**) to decide between several possibilities. ◆ **opt in** to choose to take part in something. ◆ **opt out** to choose not to take part in something.

optic ADJ relating to the eye or vision.

optical ADJ **1** relating to sight or to what one sees. **2** relating to light or optics. **3** of a lens: designed to improve vision. ■ **optically** ADV.

optical illusion N **1** something that has an appearance which deceives the eye. **2** a misunderstanding caused by such a deceptive appearance.

optician N someone who fits and sells glasses and contact lenses but is not qualified to prescribe them.

optics SING N, PHYS the study of light and its applications in a range of devices and systems.

optimal ADJ most favourable; optimum.

optimism N **1** the tendency to take a bright, hopeful view of things and expect the best possible outcome. **2** the theory that good will ultimately triumph over evil. ■ **optimist** N. ■ **optimistic** ADJ. ■ **optimistically** ADV.

optimize or **-ise** VB to make the most or best of (a particular situation or opportunity, etc).

optimum N (-*mums* or -*ma*) the condition, situation, amount or level, etc that is the most favourable or gives the best results. ➤ ADJ best or most favourable.

option N **1** an act of choosing. **2** that which is or which may be chosen. **3** the power or right

to choose: **You have no option. 4** COMMERCE the exclusive right to buy or sell something at a fixed price and within a specified time-limit.
➢ VB, chiefly US **1** to buy or sell (something) under option. **2** to have or grant an option on (something).

optional ADJ left to choice; not compulsory.

opt-out N **1 a** the action or an act of opting out of something; **b** of a school or hospital: the act of leaving local authority control.

opulent ADJ **1** rich; wealthy. **2** abundant.
■ **opulence** N. ■ **opulently** ADV.

opus N (*opuses* or *opera*) an artistic work, esp a musical composition, often used with a number to show the order in which a composer's works were written or catalogued.

or CONJ used to introduce: **1** alternatives: **red or pink. 2** a synonym or explanation: **a puppy or young dog. 3** the second part of an indirect question: **Ask her whether she thinks he'll come or not. 4** or else: **Run or you'll be late.**
◆ **or else 1** otherwise. **2** COLLOQ expressing a threat or warning: **Give it to me or else!**
◆ **or so** about; roughly: **two hours or so.**

oracle N someone who is believed to be capable of prophesying the future.
■ **oracular** ADJ.

oral ADJ **1** spoken; not written. **2** relating to or used in the mouth. **3** taken in through the mouth.
➢ N a spoken examination. ■ **orally** ADV.

orange N **1** a round citrus fruit with a tough reddish-yellow outer rind or peel filled with sweet or sharp-tasting juicy flesh. **2** the evergreen tree, cultivated in most subtropical regions, that bears this fruit. **3** a reddish-yellow colour like that of the skin of an orange. **4** an orange-flavoured drink.
➢ ADJ **1** orange-coloured. **2** orange-flavoured. ■ **orangey** ADJ.

orangery N (*-ies*) a greenhouse or other building in which orange trees can be grown.

orang-utan or **orang-outang** N a tree-dwelling great ape, of Borneo and Sumatra, with long reddish hair and long strong arms.

oration N a formal public speech.

orator N someone skilled in public speaking.

oratorio N a musical composition, usu based on a religious theme or story, sung by soloists and a chorus accompanied by an orchestra.

oratory[1] N (*-ies*) a chapel or small place set aside for private prayer.

oratory[2] N **1** the art of public speaking; rhetoric. **2** rhetorical style or language.

orb N **1** a globe with a cross on top that is decorated with jewels and is part of a monarch's regalia. **2** anything in the shape of a globe.

orbit N **1** ASTRON in space: the elliptical path of one celestial body around another, or of an artificial satellite or spacecraft, etc around a celestial body. **2** a sphere of influence or action. **3** ANAT an eye socket.
➢ VB of a spacecraft, etc: to circle (the Earth or another planet, etc) in space.

orbital ADJ **1** relating to or going round in an orbit. **2** of a road: forming a complete circle or loop round a city.

orchard N a garden or piece of land where fruit trees are grown.

orchestra N a large group of instrumentalists who play together as an ensemble.
■ **orchestral** ADJ.

orchestrate VB **1** to arrange, compose or score (a piece of music) for an orchestra. **2** to organize or arrange (elements of a plan or a situation, etc) so as to get the desired or best result. ■ **orchestration** N. ■ **orchestrator** N.

orchid N a plant which is best known for its complex and exotic flowers.

ordain VB **1** CHRISTIANITY to appoint or admit (someone) as priest or vicar, etc. **2** to order, command or decree (something) formally.

ordeal N a difficult or testing experience.

order N **1** a state in which everything is in its proper place; tidiness. **2** an arrangement of objects according to importance, value or position, etc. **3** a command, instruction or

direction. **4** a state of peace and harmony in society, characterized by the absence of crime and the general obeying of laws. **5** the condition of being able to function properly: **in working order**. **6** a social class or rank making up a distinct social group: **the lower orders**. **7** a kind or sort: **of the highest order**. **8** an instruction to a manufacturer, supplier or waiter, etc to provide something. **9** the goods or food, etc supplied. **10** an established system of society: **a new world order**. **11** BIOL in taxonomy: any of the groups into which a class is divided, and which is in turn subdivided into one or more families. **12** COMMERCE a written instruction to pay money. **13** the usual procedure followed at esp official meetings and during debates: **a point of order**. **14** (**Order**) a religious community living according to a particular rule and bound by vows. Also called **religious order**. **15** any of the different grades of the Christian ministry. ➢ VB **1** to give a command to (someone). **2** to command (someone) to go to a specified place: **order the regiment to Germany**. **3** to instruct a manufacturer, supplier or waiter, etc to provide (something): **ordered the fish**. **4** to arrange or regulate: **order one's affairs**.
◆ **a tall order** COLLOQ a difficult task.
◆ **in order 1** in accordance with the rules; properly arranged. **2** suitable or appropriate. **3** in the correct sequence.
◆ **in the order of** approximately (the number specified).
◆ **in order that** so that.
◆ **in order to do sth** so as to be able to do it.
◆ **order sb about** or **around** to give them orders continually and officiously.
◆ **out of order** not correct, proper or suitable.
◆ **to order** according to a customer's particular or personal requirements.
◆ **under orders** having been commanded or instructed (to do something).

orderly ADJ **1** in good order; well arranged. **2** well behaved; quiet. ➢ N (**-ies**) **1** an attendant, usu without medical training, who does various jobs in a hospital, such as moving patients. **2** MIL a soldier who carries an officer's orders and

messages. ■ **orderliness** N.

ordinal number N a number which shows a position in a sequence, eg **first**, **second**, etc.

ordinance N a law, order or ruling.

ordinary ADJ **1** of the usual everyday kind; unexceptional. **2** plain; uninteresting.
■ **ordinarily** ADV usually; normally.
◆ **out of the ordinary** unusual; strange.

ordination N the act or ceremony of ordaining a priest or minister of the church.

ordnance N heavy guns and military supplies.

ordure N excrement.

ore N, GEOL a solid naturally occurring mineral deposit from which valuable substances, esp metals, can be extracted.

oregano N a sweet-smelling herb, used as a flavouring in cooking.

organ N **1** a part of a body or plant which has a special function, eg a kidney. **2** a musical instrument with a keyboard and pedals, in which sound is produced by air being forced through pipes of different lengths. **3** any similar instrument without pipes, such as one producing sound electronically. **4** a means of spreading information, esp a newspaper or journal of a particular group.

organdie N a very fine stiffened cotton fabric.

organic ADJ **1** BIOL relating to, derived from, or with the characteristics of a living organism. **2** AGRIC **a** of farming practices that avoid the use of synthetic fertilizers and pesticides, etc; **b** of food produced in this way. **3** systematically organized. ■ **organically** ADV.

organism N **1** any living structure, such as a plant, animal, fungus or bacterium. **2** any establishment, system or whole made up of parts that depend on each other.

organist N a person who plays an organ.

organize or **-ise** VB **1** to give an orderly structure to (something): **organized the books into a neat pile**. **2** to arrange, provide or prepare (something): **organized the tickets**. **3** to form or enrol (people or a person) into a

society or organization. ■ **organizer** N.
■ **organization** N. ■ **organizational** ADJ.

organza N a very fine stiff dress material made of silk or synthetic fibres.

orgasm N the climax of sexual excitement. ■ **orgasmic** ADJ.

orgy N (-*ies*) a wild party or celebration involving indiscriminate sexual activity.

oriel N a small room or recess with a polygonal bay window.

orient N (**the Orient**) the countries in the east, esp those of E Asia regarded as culturally distinct from western countries (the Occident). ➤ VB to place (something) in a definite position in relation to the points of the compass or some other known point. ■ **oriental** or **Oriental** ADJ. ■ **orientation** N.

orientate VB to orient. ■ **orientation** N.

orienteering N a cross-country sport in which contestants race on foot and on skis, etc, finding their way to official check points using a map and compass. ■ **orienteer** VB.

orifice N a usu small opening or hole, esp one in the body or body cavity.

origami N the Japanese art of folding paper into decorative shapes and figures.

origin N 1 a beginning or starting-point; a source. 2 (usu **origins**) a person's family background or ancestry.

original ADJ 1 relating to an origin or beginning. 2 existing from the beginning; earliest; first. 3 of an idea or concept, etc: not thought of before; fresh or new. 4 of a person: creative or inventive. 5 being the first form from which copies, reproductions or translations are made; not copied or derived, etc from something else. ➤ N 1 something which is copied, reproduced or translated to produce others, but which is not itself copied or derived, etc from something else. 2 a work of art or literature that is not a copy, reproduction or imitation. ■ **originality** N. ■ **originally** ADV.

originate VB, TR & INTR to bring or come into being; to start. ■ **originator** N.

oriole N a songbird with bright yellow and black plumage.

ormolu N a gold-coloured alloy.

ornament N 1 something that decorates or adds grace or beauty to a person or thing. 2 embellishment or decoration. 3 a small, usu decorative object. ➤ VB to decorate (something) with ornaments or serve as an ornament to (something); to adorn. ■ **ornamental** ADJ. ■ **ornamentation** N.

ornate ADJ 1 highly or excessively decorated. 2 of language: flowery; using many elaborate words or expressions. ■ **ornately** ADV.

ornithology N the scientific study of birds and their behaviour. ■ **ornithological** ADJ. ■ **ornithologist** N.

orotund ADJ 1 of the voice: full, loud and grand. 2 of speech or writing: boastful or self-important; pompous. ■ **orotundity** N.

orphan N a child whose parents are dead. ➤ VB, USU IN PASSIVE to make (a child) an orphan.

orphanage N a home for orphans.

orrery N (-*ies*) a clockwork model of the Sun and the planets which revolve around it.

orris N the dried sweet-smelling rhizome of a species of iris, used in perfumes.

orthodontics SING N, DENTISTRY the branch of dentistry concerned with the prevention and correction of irregularities in the alignment of the teeth or jaws. ■ **orthodontist** N.

orthodox ADJ believing in, living according to, or conforming with established or generally accepted opinions; conventional.

orthography N (-*ies*) 1 correct or standard spelling. 2 a particular system of spelling. 3 the study of spelling.

orthopaedics or (US) **orthopedics** SING N, MED the correction by surgery or manipulation, etc of deformities arising from injury or disease of the bones and joints. ■ **orthopaedic** ADJ.

oryx N (**oryxes** or **oryx**) an antelope with very long slender horns.

oscillate VB **1** TR & INTR to swing or make (something) swing backwards and forwards like a pendulum. **2** TR & INTR to vibrate. **3** INTR to waver between opinions, choices, courses of action, etc. **4** INTR of an electrical current: to vary regularly in strength or direction between certain limits. ■ **oscillation** N. ■ **oscillator** N.

oscilloscope N a device that measures an oscillating electrical current over time, and displays the varying electrical signals graphically on the screen of a cathode-ray tube. Also called **cathode-ray oscilloscope**.

osmosis N, CHEM the movement of a solvent, eg water, across a semi-permeable membrane from a more dilute solution to a more concentrated one. ■ **osmotic** ADJ.

osprey N a large fish-eating bird of prey.

ossify VB (-*ies*, -*ied*) **1** TR & INTR to turn into or make (something) turn into bone or a bonelike substance. **2** INTR to become rigid, fixed or inflexible. ■ **ossification** N.

ostensible ADJ of reasons, etc: stated or claimed, but not necessarily true; apparent.

ostentation N pretentious display of wealth or knowledge, etc, esp to attract attention or admiration. ■ **ostentatious** ADJ.

osteoarthritis N, PATHOL a chronic non-inflammatory degenerative disease of bones. ■ **osteoarthritic** ADJ.

osteopathy N, MED a system of healing or treatment involving manipulation of the bones and joints and massage of the muscles. ■ **osteopath** N.

osteoporosis N, PATHOL a disease in which the bones become porous and brittle.

ostler N, HIST someone who attends to horses at an inn.

ostracize or **-ise** VB to exclude (someone) from a group or society, etc. ■ **ostracism** N.

ostrich N (*ostriches* or *ostrich*) the largest living bird, native to Africa, having a long neck and legs, and only two toes on each foot.

other ADJ **1** remaining from a group of two or more when one or some have been specified already: Now close the other eye. **2** different from the one or ones already mentioned, understood or implied: other people. **3** additional; further: need to buy one other thing. **4** opposite: the other side of the world. ➤ PRONOUN **1 a** another person or thing; **b** (**others**) other people or things. **2** (**others**) further or additional ones: I'd like to see some others. **3** (usu **the others**) the remaining people or things of a group. ➤ ADV (usu **other than**) otherwise; differently: couldn't do other than hurry home. ➤ N someone or something considered separate, different, additional to, apart from, etc the rest. ■ **otherness** N.
◆ **every other** each alternate; every second: see him every other week.
◆ **in other words** this means.
◆ **other than 1** except; apart from: Other than that, there's no news. **2** different from: do something other than watch TV.
◆ **the other day** or **week, etc** a few days or weeks, etc ago.

otherwise CONJ or else; if not. ➤ ADV **1** in other respects. **2** in a different way. **3** under different circumstances. ➤ ADJ different: The truth is otherwise.

otherworldly ADJ relating to, or resembling, a world supposedly inhabited after death.

otiose ADJ, FORMAL serving no useful function.

OTT ABBREV, SLANG over the top.

otter N (*otters* or *otter*) a carnivorous semi-aquatic mammal with a long body, short smooth fur, and large webbed hind feet.

ouch EXCLAM expressing sudden sharp pain.

ought AUXILIARY VERB used to express: **1** duty or obligation: You ought to help. **2** advisability: You ought to see a doctor. **3** probability or expectation: She ought to be here soon. **4** shortcoming or failure: He ought to know better. **5** enthusiastic desire on the part of the speaker: You really ought to read this book. **6** logical consequence.

Ouija board N, TRADEMARK a board with the letters of the alphabet printed round the edge, used at séances to spell out messages supposed to be from the dead.

ounce N **1** in the imperial system: a unit of weight equal to one sixteenth of a pound. **2** short form of **fluid ounce**. **3** a small amount or quantity.

our ADJ **1** relating or belonging to, associated with, or done by us: **our children**. **2** relating or belonging to people in general: **our planet**.

ours PRONOUN the one or ones belonging to us.

ourself PRONOUN, ARCHAIC formerly used by monarchs: myself.

ourselves PRONOUN **1** reflexive form of **we**; us: **We helped ourselves to cakes**. **2** our normal self: **We can relax and be ourselves**. **3** (also **by ourselves**) a alone: **went by ourselves**; **b** without anyone else's help: **did it all by ourselves**.

oust VB to force (someone) out of a position and take their place.

out ADV **1** away from the inside; not in or at a place. **2** not in one's home or place of work: **you were out**. **3** to or at an end; to or into a state of being completely finished, exhausted, etc: **The milk has run out**. **4** aloud: **cried out**. **5** with care or taking care: **watch out**. **6** in all directions from a central point: **Share out the sweets**. **7** to the fullest extent or amount: **Spread the blanket out**. **8** to public attention or notice; revealed: **The secret is out**. **9** SPORT no longer able to bat, eg because of having the ball caught by an opponent. **10** in or into a state of being removed, omitted or forgotten: **Rub it out**. **11** not to be considered; rejected: **That idea's out**. **12** removed; dislocated: **have a tooth out**. **13** not in authority; not having political power: **voted out of office**. **14** into unconsciousness: **pass out in the heat**. **15** in error: **Your total is out by three**. **16** COLLOQ existing: **the best car out**. **17** in bloom. **18** published. **19** visible: **the moon's out**. **20** no longer in fashion: **Drainpipes are out**. **21** on strike: **called the miners out**.
➤ ADJ **1** external. **2** directing or showing

direction outwards.
➤ N a way out, a way of escape; an excuse.
➤ VB **1** INTR to become publicly known: **Murder will out**. **2** to make public the homosexuality of (someone who has tried to keep it secret).
◆ **be out for sth** COLLOQ to be determined to achieve it: **out for revenge**.
◆ **out and about** active outside the house, esp after an illness.
◆ **out of sth 1** from inside it: **drive out of the garage**. **2** not in or within it: **be out of the house**. **3** having exhausted a supply of it: **we're out of butter**. **4** from among several: **two out of three cats**. **5** from a material: **made out of wood**. **6** because of it: **out of anger**. **7** beyond the range, scope or bounds of it: **out of reach**. **8** excluded from it: **leave him out of the team**. **9** no longer in a stated condition: **out of practice**. **10** at a stated distance from a place: **a mile out of town**. **11** so as to be without something: **cheat him out of his money**.
◆ **out of date** obsolete.
◆ **out of it 1** COLLOQ not part of, or wanted in, a group or activity, etc. **2** SLANG unable to behave normally or control oneself.
◆ **out of pocket** having spent more money than one can afford.
◆ **out of the way 1** difficult to reach or arrive at. **2** unusual; uncommon.

outage N a period of time during which a power supply fails to operate.

out-and-out ADJ complete; utter; thorough.

outback N isolated remote areas of a country, esp in Australia.

outboard ADJ of a motor or engine: designed to be attached to the outside of a boat's stern.
➤ ADV, ADJ nearer or towards the outside of a ship or aircraft.
➤ N **1** an outboard motor or engine. **2** a boat equipped with an outboard motor or engine.

outbound ADJ of a vehicle, flight, etc: going away from home or a station, etc; departing.

outbreak N a sudden, usu violent beginning or occurrence, eg of a disease.

outbuilding N a building such as a barn, stable, etc that is separate from the main building of a house but within its grounds.

outburst N **1** a sudden violent expression of strong emotion. **2** an eruption or explosion.

outcast N someone who has been rejected by their friends or by society.

outclass VB to be or become of a much better quality or class than (something else).

outcome N the result of some action or situation, etc; consequence.

outcrop N a rock or group of rocks which sticks out above the surface of the ground.

outcry N a widespread and public show of anger or disapproval.

outdated ADJ no longer useful or in fashion.

outdo VB to do much better than (someone or something else); to surpass.

outdoor ADJ done, taking place, situated or for use, etc in the open air: **outdoor pursuits**.

outdoors ADV (also **out-of-doors**) in or into the open air; outside a building.
➤ SING N the open air.

outer ADJ **1** external; belonging to or for the outside. **2** further from the centre or middle.

outermost ADJ nearest the edge.

outer space N any region of space beyond the Earth's atmosphere.

outfield N **1** CRICKET the area of the pitch far from the part where the stumps, etc are laid out. **2** BASEBALL the area of the field beyond the diamond-shaped pitch where the bases are laid out. ■ **outfielder** N.

outfit N **1** a set of clothes worn together, esp for a particular occasion. **2** a set of articles, tools or equipment, etc for a particular task. **3** COLLOQ a group of people working as a single unit or team. ■ **outfitter** N.

outflank VB **1** MIL to go round the side or sides of (an enemy's position). **2** to get the better of (someone), esp by a surprise action.

outfox VB to get the better of (someone) by being more cunning; to outwit (someone).

outgoing ADJ **1** friendly and sociable; extrovert. **2** leaving; departing.

outgoings PL N money spent; expenditure.

outgrow VB to grow too large or too old for.

outhouse N a building, usu a small one such as a shed, etc built close to a house.

outing N a short pleasure trip or excursion.

outlandish ADJ of appearance, etc: very strange; odd; bizarre.

outlaw N **1** orig someone excluded from, and deprived of the protection of, the law. **2** a criminal who is a fugitive from the law.
➤ VB **1** to make (someone) an outlaw. **2** to forbid (something) officially.

outlay N money, or occasionally time, spent on something; expenditure.

outlet N **1** a vent or way out, esp for water or steam. **2** a way of releasing or using energy, talents or strong feeling, etc. **3** a market for the goods produced by a particular manufacturer.

outline N **1** a line that forms or marks the outer edge of an object. **2** a drawing with only the outer lines and no shading. **3** the main points, etc without the details: **an outline of the plot**.
➤ VB **1** to draw the outline of (something). **2** to give a brief description of the main features of (something).

outlive VB to live longer than (someone or something else).

outlook N **1** a view from a particular place. **2** someone's mental attitude or point of view. **3** a prospect for the future.

outmoded ADJ no longer in fashion.

outpatient N a patient who receives treatment at a hospital or clinic but does not stay there overnight.

outpost N, MIL a group of soldiers stationed at a distance from the main body.

outpouring N **1** (usu **outpourings**) a powerful or violent show of emotion. **2** the amount that pours out.

output N **1** the quantity or amount of something

produced. **2** COMP data transferred from the main memory of a computer to a disk, tape or output device such as a VDU or printer.
➤ VB, COMP to transfer (data from the main memory of a computer) to a disk or tape, or to an output device.

outrage N **1** an act of great cruelty or violence. **2** an act which breaks accepted standards of morality, honour and decency. **3** great anger or resentment.
➤ VB to shock or anger (someone) greatly.

outrageous ADJ **1** not moderate in behaviour; extravagant. **2** greatly offensive to accepted standards of morality, honour and decency.

outrank VB to have a higher rank than (someone); to be superior to (them).

outrider N an attendant or guard who rides a horse or motorcycle at the side or ahead of a vehicle conveying an important person.

outright ADV **1** completely: **be proved outright. 2** immediately; at once: **killed outright. 3** openly; honestly: **ask outright.**
➤ ADJ **1** complete: **an outright fool. 2** clear: **the outright winner.**

outset N a beginning or start.

outside N **1** the outer surface; the external parts. **2** everything that is not inside or within the bounds of something. **3** the farthest limit.
➤ ADJ **1** relating to, on or near the outside. **2** not forming part of a group, organization or one's regular job, etc: **outside interests. 3** unlikely.
➤ ADV **1** on or to the outside; outdoors. **2** SLANG not in prison.
➤ PREP **1** on or to the outside of something. **2** beyond the limits of something. **3** apart from.
◆ **at the outside** at the most.

outside broadcast N a radio or TV programme that is recorded or filmed somewhere other than in a studio.

outsider N **1** someone who is not part of a group, etc or who refuses to accept the general values of society. **2** in a race or contest, etc: a competitor who is not expected to win.

outsize ADJ (also **outsized**) over normal or standard size.

outskirts PL N the outer parts or area.

outsmart VB, COLLOQ to outwit.

outsource VB, orig US of a business, company, etc: to subcontract (work) to another company; to contract (work) out. ■ **outsourcing** N.

outspoken ADJ **1** of a person: saying exactly what they think; frank. **2** of a remark or opinion, etc: candid; frank. ■ **outspokenness** N.

outspread ADJ spread out widely or fully.

outstanding ADJ **1** excellent; superior; remarkable. **2** not yet paid or done, etc: **outstanding debts.** ■ **outstandingly** ADV.

outstay VB **1** to stay longer than the length of (one's invitation, etc): **outstay one's welcome. 2** to stay longer than (other people).

outstretch VB **1** to stretch or spread out; to expand. **2** to reach or stretch out (esp one's hand); to extend. ■ **outstretched** ADJ.

outstrip VB **1** to go faster than (someone or something else). **2** to leave behind; to surpass.

outtake N, CINEMA, TV a section of film or tape removed from the final edited version.

outward ADJ **1** on or towards the outside. **2** of a journey: away from a place. **3** apparent or seeming: **outward appearances.**
➤ ADV (also **outwards**) towards the outside; in an outward direction. ■ **outwardly** ADV.

outweigh VB **1** to be greater than (something) in weight. **2** to be greater than (something) in value, importance or influence.

outwit VB to get the better of or defeat (someone) by being cleverer than they are.

outworn ADJ no longer useful or in fashion; out of date; obsolete.

ouzo N a Greek alcoholic drink flavoured with aniseed.

ova plural of **ovum**

oval ADJ **1** having the outline of an egg; shaped like an egg. **2** LOOSELY elliptical.
➤ NOUN any egg-shaped figure or object.

ovary N (-ies) **1** in a female animal: the reproductive organ in which the ova are

produced. **2** BOT the hollow base of the carpel of a flower, which contains the ovules.
■ **ovarian** ADJ.

ovate ADJ egg-shaped.

ovation N sustained applause or cheering.

oven N a closed compartment in which food is cooked, clay dried, etc.

oven-ready ADJ of food: ready for cooking in the oven immediately after purchase.

over ADV **1** above and across. **2** outwards and downwards: **knock him over**. **3** across a space: **fly over from Australia**. **4** from one person, side or condition to another: **turn the card over**. **5** through, from beginning to end, usu with concentration: **think it over**. **6** again; in repetition: **do it twice over**. **7** at an end: **The game is over**. **8** so as to cover completely: **paper the cracks over**. **9** beyond a limit; in excess (of): **go over budget**. **10** remaining: **left over**.
➤ PREP **1** in or to a position which is above or higher in place, importance, authority, value or number, etc. **2** above and from one side to another: **fly over the sea**. **3** so as to cover: **flopped over his eyes**. **4** out and down from: **fall over the edge**. **5** throughout the extent of something: **read over that page again**.
6 during a specified time or period: **sometime over the weekend**. **7** until after a specified time: **stay over Monday night**. **8** more than: **over a year ago**. **9** concerning; about: **argue over who would pay**. **10** while occupied with something: **chat about it over coffee**.
11 occupying time with something: **spend a day over the tasks**. **12** recovered from the effects of something: **she's over the accident**.
13 by means of something: **hear about it over the radio**. **14** divided by: **Six over three is two**.
➤ ADJ **1** upper; higher. **2** outer. **3** excessive.
➤ N, CRICKET **1** a series of six balls bowled by the same bowler from the same end of the pitch.
2 play during such a series of balls.
◆ **over again** once more.
◆ **over and above sth** in addition to it.
◆ **over and over again** repeatedly.
◆ **over the top** COLLOQ excessive.

overact VB, TR & INTR to act (a part) with too much expression or emotion.

overall N **1** BRIT a loose-fitting coat-like garment worn over ordinary clothes to protect them. **2** (**overalls**) a one-piece garment with trouser legs, worn to protect clothes.
➤ ADJ **1** including everything: **the overall total**.
2 from end to end: **the overall length**.
➤ ADV as a whole; in general.

overawe VB to subdue or restrain (someone) by filling them with awe, fear or astonishment.

overbalance VB to lose balance and fall.

overbearing ADJ **1** domineering. **2** having particularly great importance.

overblown ADJ overdone; excessive.

overboard ADV over the side of a ship or boat into the water: **fall overboard**.
◆ **go overboard** COLLOQ to be very or too enthusiastic.

overcast ADJ of the sky or weather: cloudy.

overcharge VB **1** TR & INTR to charge (someone) too much. **2** to overfill or overload (something).

overcoat N a warm heavy coat.

overcome VB **1** to defeat (someone or something); to succeed in a struggle against (them or it). **2** to deal successfully with (something): **overcame his problems**.

overdo VB **1** to do (something) too much; to exaggerate. **2** to cook (food) for too long. **3** to use too much of (something).

overdose N an excessive dose of a drug, etc.
➤ VB, TR & INTR to take an overdose or give an excessive dose to (someone).

overdraft N **1** a state in which one has taken more money out of one's bank account than was in it. **2** the excess of money taken from one's account over the sum that was in it.

overdraw VB, TR & INTR to draw more money from (one's bank account) than is in it.
■ **overdrawn** ADJ.

overdrive N a high gear in a motor vehicle's

gearbox, which reduces wear on the engine.

overdue ADJ of bills or work, etc: not yet paid, done or delivered, etc, although the date for doing this has passed.

overestimate VB to estimate or judge, etc (something) too highly.
➤ N too high an estimate.

overflow VB 1 to flow over (a brim) or go beyond (the limits or edge of something). 2 INTR of a container, etc: to be so full that the contents spill over or out. 3 (**overflow with sth**) INTR to be full of it: overflowing with pride.
➤ N 1 something that overflows. 2 a pipe or outlet for surplus water.

overgrown ADJ 1 of a garden, etc: dense with plants that have grown too large and thick. 2 grown too large or beyond the normal size.

overhang VB, TR & INTR to project or hang out over (something).
➤ N a piece of rock or part of a roof, etc that overhangs.

overhaul VB 1 to examine carefully and repair (something). 2 to overtake.
➤ N a thorough examination and repair.

overhead ADV, ADJ above; over one's head.
➤ N (**overheads**) the regular costs of a business, such as rent, wages and electricity.

overhear VB, TR & INTR to hear (a person or remark, etc) without the speaker knowing.

overheat VB 1 to heat (something) excessively. 2 INTR to become too hot.

overjoyed ADJ very glad; elated.

overkill N action, behaviour or treatment, etc that is far in excess of what is required.

overlap VB 1 of part of an object: to partly cover (another object). 2 INTR of two parts: to have one part partly covering the other. 3 INTR of two things: to partly coincide.
➤ N an overlapping part.

overlay VB to lay (one thing) on or over (another).
➤ N a covering; something that is laid over something else.

overleaf ADV on the other side of the page.

overload VB to load (something) too heavily.
➤ N too great an electric current flowing through a circuit.

overlook VB 1 to give a view of (something) from a higher position: overlooks the garden. 2 to fail to see or notice (something). 3 to allow (a mistake or crime, etc) to go unpunished.

overlord N a ruler with supreme power.

overly ADV too; excessively.

overnight ADV 1 during the night. 2 for the duration of the night. 3 suddenly: Success came overnight.
➤ ADJ 1 done or occurring in the night. 2 sudden: an overnight success. 3 for use overnight: an overnight bag.

overplay VB 1 to exaggerate or overemphasize (the importance of something). 2 TR & INTR to exaggerate (an emotion, etc); to act in an exaggerated way.

overpower VB 1 to defeat or subdue (someone or something) by greater strength. 2 to reduce (someone or something) to helplessness. ■ **overpowering** ADJ.

overrate VB to assess or value too highly.

overreach VB to strain (oneself) by trying to reach too far or do too much.

overreact VB, INTR to react excessively or too strongly. ■ **overreaction** N.

override VB 1 to ride over; to cross (an area) by riding. 2 to dominate or assume superiority over (someone). 3 to annul something or set it aside. 4 to take manual control of (a normally automatically controlled operation).
■ **overriding** ADJ.

overrule VB to cancel (esp a previous decision or judgement) by higher authority.

overrun VB 1 to spread over or through (something): overrun with weeds. 2 to occupy an area, country, etc quickly and by force.

overseas ADV in or to a land beyond the sea; abroad: working overseas.
➤ ADJ (also **oversea**) across or from beyond

the sea; foreign: *an overseas posting*.

oversee VB to supervise (someone or something). ■ **overseer** N.

overshadow VB to seem much more important than (someone or something else).

overshoot VB to shoot or go farther than (a target aimed at).

oversight N a mistake or omission, esp one made through a failure to notice something.

oversize ADJ (also **oversized**) larger then normal.

overspill N, BRIT the people leaving an overcrowded town area to live elsewhere.

overstate VB to state (something) too strongly; to exaggerate. ■ **overstatement** N.

overstep VB (esp **overstep the mark**) to go beyond (a certain limit).

oversubscribe VB to apply for or try to purchase (eg shares, etc) in larger quantities than are available.

overt ADJ open; public. ■ **overtly** ADV.

overtake VB **1** TR & INTR, chiefly BRIT to catch up with and go past (a car or a person, etc) moving in the same direction. **2** to draw level with and begin to do better than (someone). **3** to come upon (someone) suddenly or without warning: *overtaken by bad weather*.

overtax VB **1** to demand too much tax from (someone). **2** to put too great a strain on (someone or oneself).

over-the-counter ADJ of eg drugs and medicines: legally sold directly to the customer.

overthrow VB to defeat completely (an established order or a government, etc). ➤ N the act of overthrowing or state of being overthrown.

overtime N **1** time spent working beyond the regular hours. **2** money paid for this. ➤ ADV during overtime; in addition to regular hours: *work overtime*.

overtone N **1** (often **overtones**) a subtle hint, quality or meaning; a nuance: *political*

overtones. **2** MUS a tone that contributes towards a musical sound and adds to its quality.

overture N **1** MUS **a** an orchestral introduction to an opera, oratorio or ballet; **b** a one-movement orchestral composition in a similar style. **2** (usu **overtures**) a proposal intended to open a discussion, or a relationship, etc.

overturn VB, TR & INTR to turn or cause (something) to be turned over or upside down.

overview N a brief general account or description of a subject, etc; a summary.

overweening ADJ **1** of a person: arrogant; conceited. **2** of pride: inflated and excessive.

overweight ADJ above the desired, required or usual weight.

overwhelm VB **1** to crush mentally; to overpower (a person's emotions or thoughts, etc). **2** to defeat completely by superior force or numbers. ■ **overwhelming** ADJ.

overwind VB to wind (a watch, etc) too far.

overwork VB **1** INTR to work too hard. **2** to make (someone) work too hard. **3** to make too much use of (something).

overwrite VB **1** to write on top of (something else). **2** COMP to record new information over (existing data), thereby destroying (it).

overwrought ADJ very nervous or excited.

oviform ADJ egg-shaped.

ovine ADJ relating to sheep; sheeplike.

oviparous ADJ, ZOOL laying eggs that develop and hatch outside the mother's body.

ovoid ADJ, chiefly ZOOL & BOT egg-shaped.

ovoviviparous ADJ, ZOOL producing eggs that hatch within the body of the mother.

ovulate VB, INTR, PHYSIOL **1** to release an ovum or egg cell from the ovary. **2** to form or produce ova. ■ **ovulation** N.

ovule N, BOT in flowering plants: the structure that develops into a seed after fertilization.

ovum N (**ova**) an unfertilized egg or egg cell.

owe VB **1** TR & INTR to be under an obligation to

pay (money) (to someone): **owes him £5. 2** to feel required by duty or gratitude to do or give (someone) (something).

owing ADJ still to be paid; due.
◆ **owing to sth** because of it; on account of it.

owl N a nocturnal bird of prey with a flat face, large forward–facing eyes and a short hooked beak. ■ **owlish** ADJ.

own ADJ often used for emphasis: belonging to or for oneself or itself: **my own sister**.
➤ PRONOUN one belonging (or something belonging) to oneself or itself: **lost his own, so I lent him mine**.
➤ VB **1** to have (something) as a possession or property. **2** (usu **own to sth**) INTR to admit or confess to it: **owned to many weaknesses**. ■ **owner** N. ■ **ownership** N.
◆ **come into one's own** to realize one's potential.
◆ **hold one's own** to maintain one's position, esp in spite of difficulty or opposition, etc.
◆ **on one's own 1** alone. **2** without help.
◆ **own up** or **own up to sth** to confess; to admit a wrongdoing, etc.

own goal N **1** SPORT a goal scored by mistake for the opposing side. **2** COLLOQ an action that turns out to be to the disadvantage of the person who took it.

ox N (**oxen**) an adult castrated bull.

oxbow N (also **oxbow lake**) a shallow curved lake on a river's flood plain formed when one of the meanders of the river has been cut off.

oxen plural of **ox**

oxidation N, CHEM the process of oxidizing.

oxide N, CHEM any compound of oxygen and another element.

oxidize or **-ise** VB, TR & INTR, CHEM **1** to undergo, or cause (a substance) to undergo, a chemical reaction with oxygen. **2** to become, or make (something) become, rusty. ■ **oxidization** N.

oxtail N the tail of an ox used as food.

oxyacetylene N a mixture of oxygen and acetylene which burns with an extremely hot flame and is used in torches for welding.

oxygen N a colourless odourless tasteless gas, which is an essential requirement of most forms of plant and animal life.

oxygenate VB to combine, treat, supply or enrich (eg the blood) with oxygen.

oxymoron N a rhetorical figure of speech in which contradictory terms are used together, often for emphasis or effect, eg **horribly good**.

oyster N a marine mollusc with a soft fleshy body enclosed by a hinged shell.

ozone N, CHEM an allotrope of oxygen formed when an electric spark acts on oxygen.

ozone layer and **ozonosphere** N a layer of the upper atmosphere where ozone is formed, which filters, and protects the Earth from, harmful ultraviolet radiation from the Sun.

Pp

P¹ or **p** N (*Ps, P's* or *p's*) the sixteenth letter of the English alphabet.
◆ **mind one's p's and q's** COLLOQ to

behave with the etiquette suitable to a situation.

P² ABBREV as a street sign: parking.

p ABBREV 1 page. Also written **pg**. 2 penny or pence.

PA ABBREV 1 personal assistant. 2 public-address system.

p.a. ABBREV per annum.

pace N 1 a single step. 2 the distance covered by one step when walking. 3 rate of walking or running, etc: **at a slow pace**. 4 rate of movement or progress: **at your own pace**. 5 any of the gaits used by a horse.
➤ VB 1 TR & INTR (often **pace about** or **around**) to keep walking about, in a preoccupied way. 2 to set the pace for (others) in a race, etc.
◆ **keep pace with sb** to go as fast as them.
◆ **put sb through their paces** to test them in some activity.

pacemaker N, MED an electronic device that stimulates the heart muscle to contract at a specific and regular rate.

pachyderm N any large thick-skinned non-ruminant mammal, such as the elephant.

pacific ADJ tending to make peace or keep the peace; peaceful; peaceable.

pacifist N someone who believes that violence is unjustified and refuses to take part in making war. ■ **pacifism** N.

pacify VB (-ies, -ied) 1 to calm, soothe or appease someone. 2 to restore something to a peaceful condition. ■ **pacification** N.

pack N 1 a collection of things tied into a bundle for carrying. 2 a rucksack; a backpack. 3 a set of playing cards, usu 52. 4 a group of animals living and hunting together. 5 a compact package, eg of equipment for a purpose: **a first-aid pack**. 6 DEROG a collection or bunch: **a pack of lies**. 7 a group of Brownie Guides or Cub Scouts. 8 RUGBY the forwards in a team. 9 a skin preparation: **a face pack**.
➤ VB 1 to stow (goods, clothes, etc) compactly in cases, boxes, etc for transport or travel. 2 INTR to put one's belongings into a suitcase, rucksack, travel bag, etc, ready for a journey. 3 to put (goods, etc) into a container, or to wrap them, ready for sale. 4 INTR to be capable of being formed into a compact shape. 5 to fill

something tightly or compactly. 6 to fill (a jury, meeting, etc) illicitly with one's supporters.
◆ **pack sth in 1 a** to push and cram it into something that is already quite full; **b** to cram (a great deal of activity) into a limited period. **2** to give something up or stop doing it.
◆ **pack sb off** to send them off hastily.
◆ **pack up 1** to stop work at the end of the day. **2** COLLOQ of machinery, etc: to break down.
◆ **send sb packing** COLLOQ to send them away unceremoniously.

package N 1 something wrapped and secured with string, adhesive tape, etc; a parcel. 2 a container for packing goods in.

packaging N the wrappers or containers in which goods for sale are packed.

pack animal N an animal, eg a donkey, mule or horse, used to carry luggage.

packet N 1 a wrapper or container made of paper, cardboard or plastic, with its contents: **packet of biscuits**. 2 a small pack or package. 3 a mailboat that also carries cargo and passengers, and plies a fixed route. Also called **packet-boat**. 4 COLLOQ a large sum of money.

pact N an agreement reached between two or more parties, states, etc for mutual advantage.

pad N 1 a wad of material used to cushion, protect, shape or clean. 2 a quantity of sheets of paper fixed together into a block. 3 a rocket-launching platform. 4 the soft fleshy underside of an animal's paw. 5 SLANG the place where someone lives.
➤ VB (-dd-) 1 to cover, fill, stuff, cushion or shape something with layers of soft material. 2 (also **pad sth out**) DEROG to include unnecessary or irrelevant material in (a piece of writing, speech, etc) for the sake of length. 3 INTR to walk softly or with a quiet or muffled tread. 4 TR & INTR to tramp along (a road); to travel on foot.

padding N 1 material for cushioning, shaping or filling. 2 DEROG irrelevant or unnecessary matter in a speech or piece of writing, added to extend it to the desired length.

paddle[1] VB, INTR to walk about barefoot in

shallow water.

➤ N a spell of paddling.

paddle² N **1** a short light oar with a blade at one or both ends, used to propel and steer a canoe, kayak, etc. **2** a paddle-shaped instrument or bat.

➤ VB, TR & INTR **1** to propel (a canoe, kayak, etc) with paddles. **2** INTR (also **paddle along**) to move through water using, or as if using, a paddle or paddles.

paddock N a small enclosed field for a horse.

paddy N (-ies) **1** (also **paddy field**) a field filled with water in which rice is grown. **2** COLLOQ a fit of rage.

padlock N a detachable lock with a U-shaped bar that pivots at one side, so that it can be passed through a ring and locked.

➤ VB to fasten (a door, etc) with a padlock.

padre N a chaplain in the armed services.

paean or (US) **pean** N a song of triumph, praise or thanksgiving.

paediatrics or (N AMER) **pediatrics** SING N, MED the branch of medicine concerned with the health and care of children. ■ **paediatric** or (N AMER) **pediatric** ADJ. ■ **paediatrician** or (N AMER) **pediatrician** N.

paedophilia N sexual attraction to children. ■ **paedophile** N.

paella N, COOKERY a Spanish rice dish of fish or chicken with vegetables and saffron.

pagan ADJ **1 a** not a Christian, Jew, or Muslim; **b** belonging or relating to a religion in which a number of gods are worshipped. **2** without religious belief.

➤ N a pagan person; a heathen. ■ **paganism** N.

page N **1** one side of a leaf in a book, etc. **2** a leaf of a book, etc. **3** LITERARY an episode or incident in history, one's life, etc. **4** HIST a boy attendant serving a knight and training for knighthood. **5** a boy attending the bride at a wedding. **6** a boy who carries messages or luggage, etc in hotels, clubs, etc.

➤ VB to summon someone by calling their name

out loud, or through a pager.

pageant N **1** a series of tableaux or dramatic scenes, depicting eg local historical events. **2** any colourful and varied spectacle.

pageantry N splendid display; pomp.

pager N, TELECOMM a small radio receiver that enables its user to receive a signal.

paginate VB to give consecutive numbers to the pages of (a text). ■ **pagination** N.

pagoda N **1** a Buddhist shrine or memorial, esp in the form of a tall tower with many storeys. **2** an ornamental building imitating this.

paid VB.

◆ **put paid to sth** to destroy any chances of success in it.

paid-up ADJ of a society member, etc: having paid a membership fee.

pail N **1** a bucket. **2** the amount contained in a pail: *a pail of milk*. ■ **pailful** N.

pain N **1** an uncomfortable, distressing or agonizing sensation caused by the stimulation of specialized nerve endings by heat, cold, pressure or other strong stimuli. **2** emotional suffering. **3** (**pains**) trouble taken or efforts made in doing something.

➤ VB, rather FORMAL to cause distress to someone.

◆ **on pain of sth** at the risk of incurring it as a punishment.

painful ADJ **1** causing pain: *a painful injury*. **2** of a body part: affected by some injury, etc which causes pain. **3** causing distress: *a painful duty*. **4** laborious and slow. ■ **painfully** ADV.

painkiller N any drug or other agent that relieves pain; an analgesic.

painstaking ADJ conscientious and thorough, ie taking pains or care: **painstaking work**.

paint N **1** colouring matter, esp in the form of a liquid, which dries forming a hard surface. **2** a dried coating of this.

➤ VB **1** to apply a coat of paint to (walls, woodwork, etc). **2** to turn something a certain

colour by this means: **paint the door yellow**. **3** TR & INTR to make (pictures) using paint. **4** to depict in paint. **5** to describe as if in paint.
◆ **paint the town red** to go out and celebrate something lavishly.

painter N **1** someone who decorates houses with paint. **2** an artist who paints pictures. **3** a rope for fastening a boat.

painting N **1** a painted picture. **2** the art or process of applying paint to walls, etc. **3** the art of creating pictures in paint.

pair N **1** a set of two identical or corresponding things, eg shoes or gloves, intended for use together. **2** something consisting of two joined and corresponding parts: **a pair of trousers** • **a pair of scissors**. **3** one of a matching pair: **Where's this earring's pair? 4** two people associated in a relationship; a couple. **5** two mating animals, birds, fishes, etc. **6** two horses harnessed together: **a coach and pair**. **7** two playing cards of the same denomination.
➤ VB, TR & INTR to divide into groups of two; to sort out in pairs. ■ **paired** ADJ.
◆ **in pairs** in twos.
◆ **pair off** COLLOQ to get together with someone romantically, sexually, etc.
◆ **pair sth** or **sb off** to sort them into pairs.

pajamas see **pyjamas**

pal COLLOQ, N a friend; a mate.
➤ VB (*-ll-*) INTR (usu **pal up with sb**) to make friends with them. ■ **pally** ADJ.

palace N **1** the official residence of a sovereign, bishop, archbishop or president. **2** a magnificent residence or other building.

paladin N, HIST a knight errant; a champion of a sovereign.

palaeontology N, GEOL the scientific study of the structure, distribution, environment and evolution of extinct life forms by interpretation of their fossil remains. ■ **palaeontologist** N.

palamino see **palomino**

palanquin or **palankeen** N, HIST a light covered litter used in the Orient.

palatable ADJ **1** having a pleasant taste;

appetizing. **2** acceptable; agreeable.

palate N **1** the roof of the mouth. **2** the sense of taste. ■ **palatal** ADJ.

palatial ADJ like a palace.

palatine ADJ **1** referring to a palace. **2** having royal privileges or jurisdiction.

palaver N **1** a long, boring, complicated and seemingly pointless exercise; an unnecessary fuss: **What a palaver! 2** idle chatter.

pale¹ ADJ **1** having less colour than normal. **2** of a colour: whitish; closer to white than black; light: **pale-green**.
➤ VB, INTR **1** to become pale. **2** to fade or become weaker or less significant: **My worries pale by comparison**. ■ **paleness** N.

pale² N a wooden or metal post or stake used for making fences.
◆ **beyond the pale** outside the limits of acceptable behaviour; intolerable.

palette N **1** a hand-held board with a thumb-hole, on which an artist mixes colours. **2** the range of colours used by a particular artist.

palimpsest N a parchment re-used after the original content has been erased.

palindrome N a word or phrase that reads the same backwards and forwards, eg Hannah. ■ **palindromic** ADJ.

paling N **1** the act of constructing a fence with pales. **2** a fence of this kind. **3** an upright stake or board in a fence.

palisade N a tall fence of pointed wooden stakes fixed edge to edge.

pall N **1 a** the cloth that covers a coffin at a funeral; **b** the coffin itself. **2** anything spreading or hanging over: **a pall of smoke**.
➤ VB **1** INTR to begin to bore or seem tedious. **2** to cloy; to bore.

pall-bearer N one of the people carrying the coffin or walking beside it at a funeral.

pallet N **1** a small wooden platform on which goods can be stacked for lifting and transporting, esp by forklift truck. **2** a flat-bladed wooden tool used for shaping pottery.

3 a straw bed. **4** a small makeshift bed.

palliate VB **1** to ease the symptoms of (a disease) without curing it. **2** to serve to lessen the gravity of (an offence, etc); to mitigate.

palliative N anything used to reduce pain or anxiety.
➤ ADJ having the effect of reducing pain.

pallid ADJ **1** pale, esp unhealthily so. **2** lacking vigour or conviction.

pallor N paleness, esp of complexion.

palm[1] N the inner surface of the hand between the wrist and the fingers.
➤ VB to conceal something in the palm of the hand.
◆ **in the palm of one's hand** in one's power.
◆ **palm sth off on sb** or **palm sb off with sth** COLLOQ to give them something unwanted or unwelcome, esp by trickery.

palm[2] N a tropical tree with a woody unbranched trunk bearing a crown of large fan-shaped or feather-shaped leaves.

palmate ADJ, BOT resembling an open hand.

palmetto N (-**os** or -**oes**) a small palm tree.

palmistry N the art of telling someone's fortune by reading the lines on the palm of their hand. Also called **chiromancy**. ■ **palmist** N.

palm oil N cooking oil obtained from the outer pulp of the fruit of some palm trees.

palmy ADJ (-**ier**, -**iest**) effortlessly successful and prosperous: **one's palmy days**.

palomino or **palamino** N (-**os**) a golden or cream horse, largely of Arab blood.

palpable ADJ **1** easily detected; obvious. **2** MED eg of an internal organ: able to be felt.

palpate VB, MED to examine (the body or a part of it) by touching or pressing.

palpitate VB, INTR **1** MED of the heart: to beat abnormally rapidly. **2** to tremble or throb. ■ **palpitation** N.

palsy N (-**ies**) paralysis, or loss of control or feeling in a part of the body.

paltry ADJ (-**ier**, -**iest**) worthless; trivial; meagre; insignificant or insultingly inadequate.

pampas grass N a large S American grass with large plume-like panicles.

pamper VB to treat (a person or animal) over-indulgently; to cosset or spoil them.

pamphlet N a booklet or leaflet providing information or dealing with a current topic.

pan[1] N **1** a pot, usu made of metal, used for cooking. **2** a panful, the amount a pan will hold. **3** often IN COMPOUNDS a vessel, usu shallow, used for domestic, industrial and other purposes: **dustpan**. **4** the bowl of a lavatory. **5** either of the two dishes on a pair of scales. **6** a shallow hollow in the ground: **a salt pan**.
➤ VB (-**nn**-) **1** (often **pan for sth**) TR & INTR to wash (river gravel) in a shallow metal vessel in search for (eg gold). **2** COLLOQ to criticize something harshly.
◆ **pan out** to result or turn out.

pan[2] VB (-**nn**-) TR & INTR of a film camera, camcorder, etc: to swing round so as to follow a moving object or show a panoramic view.
➤ N a panning movement or shot.

panacea N a universal remedy.

panache N flamboyant self-assurance.

panama and **panama hat** N a lightweight brimmed hat for men.

panatella N a long slim cigar.

pancake N a thin cake made from a batter of eggs, flour and milk, cooked on both sides in a frying-pan or on a griddle.

panchromatic ADJ, PHOTOG of a film: sensitive to all colours.

pancreas N, ANAT a large carrot-shaped gland lying between the duodenum and the spleen. ■ **pancreatic** ADJ.

panda N **1** (also **giant panda**) a black-and-white bearlike animal, native to China. **2** (also **red panda**) a related species, smaller and with a reddish-brown coat, native to S Asia.

pandemic ADJ, MED describing a widespread epidemic of a disease, one that affects a whole country, continent, etc.

pandemonium N any very disorderly or noisy place or assembly.

pander N someone who obtains a sexual partner for someone else.
◆ **pander to sb** or **sth** to indulge them.

Pandora's box N any source of great and unexpected troubles.

pane N a sheet of glass, esp one fitted into a window or door.

panegyric N a speech or piece of writing in praise of someone or something; a eulogy.

panel N 1 a rectangular wooden board forming a section, esp an ornamentally sunken or raised one, of a wall or door. 2 one of several strips of fabric making up a garment. 3 any of the metal sections forming the bodywork of a vehicle. 4 a board bearing the instruments and dials for controlling an aircraft, etc: **control panel**. 5 rectangular divisions on the page of a book, esp for illustrations. 6 a team of people selected to judge a contest, or to participate in a discussion, quiz or other game before an audience. 7 the people serving on a jury.

panel-beating N the removal of dents from metal using a soft-headed hammer. ■ **panel-beater** N.

panelling or (N AMER) **paneling** N 1 panels covering a wall, usu as decoration. 2 material for making these.

panellist or (N AMER) **panelist** N a member of a panel of people, esp in a panel game.

pang N a brief but painfully acute feeling of hunger, guilt, remorse, etc: **a pang of guilt**.

pangolin N a toothless mammal that is covered with large overlapping horny plates and can curl into an armoured ball.

panic N a sudden overpowering fear.
➤ VB (**-icked, -icking**) TR & INTR to feel panic, or make someone feel panic. ■ **panicky** ADJ.

panicle N, BOT a branched flower-head, common in grasses, in which the youngest flowers are at the tip of the flower-stalk.

panic-stricken ADJ struck with sudden fear.

pannier N 1 one of a pair of baskets carried over the back of a pack animal. 2 one of a pair of bags carried on either side of the wheel of a bicycle, etc.

panoply N (**-ies**) the full assemblage got together for a ceremony, etc.

panorama N an open and extensive or all-round view. ■ **panoramic** ADJ.

panpipes, **Pan pipes** or **Pan's pipes** PL N a musical instrument, made of reeds of different lengths bound together and played by blowing across their open ends.

pansy N (**-ies**) a garden plant which has flat flowers with five white, yellow or purple petals.

pant VB 1 INTR to breathe in and out with quick, shallow, short gasps as a result of physical exertion. 2 to say something breathlessly.
➤ N a gasping breath. ■ **panting** N, ADJ.

pantaloons PL N baggy trousers gathered at the ankle.

pantechnicon N a large furniture-removal van.

pantheism N 1 the belief that equates all the matter and forces in the Universe with God. 2 readiness to believe in all or many gods.
■ **pantheistic** or **pantheistical** ADJ.

pantheon N 1 all the gods of a particular people: **the ancient Greek pantheon**. 2 a temple sacred to all the gods.

panther N a leopard, esp a black one, formerly believed to be a different species.

panties PL N thin light knickers, mainly for women and children.

pantile N, BUILDING a roofing tile with an S-shaped cross section. ■ **pantiled** ADJ.

panto N, COLLOQ short form of **pantomime**.

pantomime N 1 a Christmas entertainment usu based on a popular fairy tale, with songs, dancing, comedy acts, etc. 2 a farcical or confused situation.

pantry N (**-ies**) a small room or cupboard for

storing food, cooking utensils, etc; a larder.

pants PL N **1** BRIT an undergarment worn over the buttocks and genital area; underpants. **2** N AMER trousers.

panty hose or **pantihose** PL N, N AMER women's tights.

pap N **1** soft semi-liquid food for babies and sick people. **2** DEROG trivial or worthless reading matter or entertainment. ■ **pappy** ADJ.

papa N a child's word for father.

papacy N (-ies) **1** the position or period of office of a pope. **2** government by popes.

papal ADJ referring or relating to the pope or the papacy.

paparazzo N (-zi) a newspaper photographer who follows famous people about in the hope of photographing them.

papaw or **pawpaw** N a large oblong yellow or orange fruit, which has sweet orange flesh and a central cavity filled with black seeds. Sometimes called **papaya**.

paper N **1** a material manufactured in thin sheets from pulped wood, rags, or other forms of cellulose, used for writing and printing on, wrapping things, etc. **2** a loose piece of paper, eg a wrapper or printed sheet. **3** other material used for a similar purpose or with a similar appearance, eg papyrus, rice paper. **4** wallpaper. **5 a** a newspaper; **b** (**the papers**) newspapers collectively; the press. **6** a set of questions on a certain subject for a written examination. **7 a** a written article dealing with a certain subject, esp for reading to an audience at a meeting, conference, etc; **b** an essay written eg by a student. **8** (**papers**) personal documents establishing one's identity, etc. ➢ ADJ **1** consisting of or made of paper. **2** paper-like, esp thin like paper. **3** on paper. ➢ VB **1** to decorate (a wall, a room, etc) with wallpaper: **paper the hall**. **2** to cover something with paper. ■ **papery** ADJ. ◆ **on paper 1** in theory. **2** in written form. ◆ **paper over sth** to conceal or avoid (an awkward fact, mistake, etc).

paperback N a book with a thin flexible paper binding. **Also** AS ADJ.

paper clip N a metal clip formed from bent wire, for holding papers together.

paperless ADJ using esp electronic means, rather than paper, for recording, etc.

paperweight N a heavy, usu ornamental, object kept on a desk for holding papers down.

paperwork N routine written work, eg filling out forms, keeping files and writing letters.

papier-mâché N a light hard material consisting of pulped paper mixed with glue, moulded into shape while wet and left to dry, and used to make boxes, jewellery, etc.

papilla N (-ae) ANAT, BIOL a small nipple-like projection from the surface of a structure. ■ **papillary** ADJ.

papoose N a Native American baby.

pappadom see **poppadum**

paprika N a powdered hot spice made from red peppers.

papyrus N (-ri or -ruses) **1** a tall plant, common in ancient Egypt. **2** the writing material prepared from the pith of the flowering stems of this plant, used by the ancient Egyptians, Greeks and Romans. **3** an ancient manuscript written on this material.

par N **1** a normal level or standard. **2** GOLF the standard number of strokes that a good golfer would take for a certain course or hole. ◆ **below** or **not up to par** COLLOQ **1** not up to the usual or required standard. **2** slightly unwell. ◆ **par for the course** COLLOQ only to be expected; typical.

para N, COLLOQ a paratrooper.

parable N a story intended to convey a moral or religious lesson.

parabola N, GEOM a conic section produced when a plane intersects a cone and the plane is parallel to the cone's sloping side.

paracetamol N a mild analgesic drug, used to relieve pain or to reduce fever.

parachute N 1 an umbrella-shaped apparatus consisting of light fabric, with a harness for attaching to, and slowing the fall of, a person or package dropped from an aircraft. 2 any structure that serves a similar purpose. ➤ VB, TR & INTR to drop from the air by parachute. ■ **parachutist** N.

parade N 1 a ceremonial procession of people, vehicles, etc. 2 of soldiers, etc: **a** the state of being drawn up in rank for formal marching or inspection; **b** a group or body of soldiers, etc drawn up in this way. 3 a self-advertising display. ➤ VB 1 TR & INTR to walk or make (a body of soldiers, etc) walk or march in procession, eg across a square, etc. 2 to display; to flaunt.

paradigm N an example, model or pattern.

paradise N 1 heaven. 2 a place of utter bliss.

paradox N 1 a statement that seems to contradict itself, eg **More haste, less speed**. 2 a situation involving apparently contradictory elements. 3 LOGIC a proposition that is essentially absurd or leads to an absurd conclusion. ■ **paradoxical** ADJ.

paraffin N 1 a fuel oil obtained from petroleum or coal and used in aircraft, domestic heaters, etc. 2 any of a series of saturated aliphatic hydrocarbons derived from petroleum. Now more commonly called an **alkane**.

paragliding N a sport in which the participant, wearing a modified parachute, is towed through the air by a light aircraft then released to glide. ■ **paraglider** N.

paragon N someone who is a model of excellence or perfection.

paragraph N 1 a section of a piece of writing of variable length, starting on a fresh, often indented, line, and dealing with a distinct point or idea. 2 a short report in a newspaper. 3 (also **paragraph mark**) PRINTING a sign (¶), indicating the start of a new paragraph. ➤ VB to divide (text) into paragraphs.

parakeet N a small brightly-coloured parrot.

parallax N, PHYS the apparent change in the position of an object, relative to a distant background, when it is viewed from two different positions. ■ **parallactic** ADJ.

parallel ADJ (often **parallel to sth**) 1 of lines, planes, etc: the same distance apart at every point; alongside and never meeting or intersecting. 2 similar; exactly equivalent; corresponding; analogous: **parallel careers**. ➤ ADV (often **parallel to sth**) alongside and at an unvarying distance from it. ➤ N 1 GEOM a line or plane parallel to another. 2 a corresponding or equivalent instance of something. 3 any of the lines of latitude circling the Earth parallel to the equator. ➤ VB (-l-) 1 to correspond to or be equivalent to something. 2 to run parallel to something. ◆ **without parallel** unequalled.

parallelism N 1 the state of being parallel. 2 resemblance in corresponding details.

parallelogram N, GEOM a two-dimensional four-sided figure in which opposite sides are parallel and equal in length, and opposite angles are equal.

paralyse or (N AMER) **paralyze** VB 1 to affect (a person or bodily part) with paralysis. 2 to have an immobilizing effect.

paralysis N (-ses) 1 a temporary or permanent loss of muscular function or sensation in any part of the body, usu caused by nerve damage, eg as a result of disease or injury. 2 a state of immobility; a standstill.

paralytic ADJ 1 relating to or suffering from paralysis. 2 COLLOQ helplessly drunk. ➤ N a person affected by paralysis.

paramedic N someone whose work supplements and supports that of the medical profession. ■ **paramedical** ADJ.

parameter N 1 MATH a constant or variable that, when altered, affects the form of a mathematical expression in which it appears. 2 a limiting factor that serves to define the scope of a task, project, discussion, etc.

paramilitary ADJ organized like a professional military force and often reinforcing it, but not a professional military force. ➤ N (-ies) 1 a group organized in this way.

2 a member of such a group.

paramount ADJ foremost; supreme; of supreme importance.

paramour N a male or female lover.

paranoia N **1** PSYCHOL a rare mental disorder, characterized by delusions of persecution by others. **2** a strong, usu irrational, feeling that one is being persecuted by others.

paranoid, **paranoiac** and **paranoic** ADJ of or affected by paranoia.
➤ N a person affected by paranoia.

paranormal ADJ of beyond the normal scope of scientific explanation, and therefore not possible to explain in terms of current understanding of scientific laws.
➤ N (**the paranormal**) paranormal events.

parapet N **1** a low wall along the edge of a bridge, balcony, roof, etc. **2** an embankment of earth or sandbags above a military trench.

paraphernalia PL N, SOMETIMES USED AS SING N equipment and accessories.

paraphrase N a restatement of something using different words, esp in order to clarify.
➤ VB to express something in other words.

paraplegia N, MED paralysis of the lower half of the body, usu caused by injury or disease of the spinal cord. ■ **paraplegic** ADJ, N.

parapsychology N the study of mental phenomena, such as telepathy and clairvoyance. ■ **parapsychologist** N.

parasite N a plant or animal that for all or part of its life obtains food and physical protection from a living organism of another species which never benefits from its presence. ■ **parasitic** or **parasitical** ADJ. ■ **parasitically** ADV. ■ **parasitism** N.

parasitology N, ZOOL the scientific study of parasites. ■ **parasitologist** N.

parasol N a light umbrella used as a protection against the Sun; a sunshade.

paratroops PL N a division of soldiers trained to parachute from aircraft into enemy territory or a battle zone. ■ **paratrooper** N.

paratyphoid N, MED an infectious disease, similar to but milder than typhoid fever.

parboil VB to boil something until it is partially cooked.

parcel N **1** something wrapped in paper, etc and secured with string or sticky tape; a package. **2** a portion of something, eg of land. **3** a group of people, etc. **4** a lot or portion of goods for sale; a deal or transaction.
➤ VB (**-ll-**) **1** (also **parcel sth up**) to wrap it up in a parcel. **2** (also **parcel sth out**) to divide it into portions and share it out.

parch VB **1** to dry something up; to deprive (soil, plants, etc) of water. **2** to make something or someone hot and very dry.

parched ADJ **1** COLLOQ very thirsty. **2** very dry.

parchment N **a** a material formerly used for bookbinding and for writing on, made from goatskin, calfskin or sheepskin; **b** a piece of this, or a manuscript written on it.

pardon VB **1** to forgive or excuse someone for a fault or offence: **pardon me for interrupting**. **2** to allow someone who has been sentenced to go without the punishment.
➤ N **1** forgiveness. **2** the cancellation of a punishment; remission. ■ **pardonable** ADJ.

pare VB **1** to trim off (skin, etc) in layers. **2** to cut (fingernails or toenails). **3** to peel (fruit). **4** (also **pare sth down**) to reduce (expenses, funding, etc) gradually, in order to economize.

parent N **1** a father or mother. **2** the adopter or guardian of a child. **3** an animal or plant that has produced offspring. **4** something from which anything is derived; a source or origin.
➤ VB, TR & INTR to be or act as a parent.
■ **parentage** N. ■ **parental** ADJ.
■ **parenthood** N. ■ **parenting** N.

parenthesis N (**-ses**) **1** a word or phrase inserted into a sentence as a comment, usu marked off by brackets or dashes. **2** (**parentheses**) a pair of round brackets ( ), used to enclose such a comment.

parenthetic or **parenthetical** ADJ **1** referring to the nature of a parenthesis. **2** using parenthesis. ■ **parenthetically** ADV.

pariah N someone avoided by others.

parietal ADJ, MED, ANAT relating to, or forming, the wall of a bodily cavity, eg the skull: **the parietal bones**.

parish N **1** a district or area served by its own church and priest or minister. **2** esp in England: the smallest unit of local government. Also called **civil parish**. **3** the inhabitants of a parish.
➤ ADJ **1** of or relating to a parish. **2** employed or supported by the parish. ■ **parishioner** N.

parity N (-**ies**) **1** equality in status, eg in pay. **2** exact equivalence or correspondence.

park N **1** an area in a town with grass and trees, for public recreation. **2** an area of land kept in its natural condition as a nature reserve, etc. **3** the woodland and pasture forming the estate of a country house. **4** a place where vehicles can be left temporarily; a car park. **5** an area containing buildings housing related enterprises: **a science park**. **7** chiefly N AMER a sports field or stadium. **8** (**the park**) COLLOQ the pitch in use in a football game.
➤ VB **1** TR & INTR **a** to leave (a vehicle) temporarily at the side of the road or in a car park; **b** to manoeuvre (a vehicle) into such a position. (**park oneself**) COLLOQ to sit or install oneself.

parka N a windproof jacket, esp a quilted one with a fur-trimmed hood; an anorak.

Parkinson's disease N, MED an incurable disorder caused by degeneration of brain cells.

parkland N pasture and woodland forming part of a country estate.

parky ADJ (-**ier**, -**iest**) BRIT COLLOQ of the weather: somewhat cold; chilly.

parlance N a particular style or way of using words: **in legal parlance**.

parley VB, INTR to discuss peace terms, etc with an enemy, esp under truce.
➤ N a meeting with an enemy to discuss peace terms, etc.

parliament N **1** the highest law-making assembly of a nation. **2** (**Parliament**) in the UK: the Houses of Commons and Lords.

■ **parliamentary** ADJ.

parliamentarian N **1** an expert in parliamentary procedure. **2** an experienced parliamentary debater.

parlour N **1** USU IN COMPOUNDS a shop or commercial premises providing specified goods or services: **an ice-cream parlour**. **2** DATED a sitting-room for receiving visitors.

parlous ADJ, ARCHAIC OR FACETIOUS perilous.

Parmesan N a hard dry Italian cheese made from skimmed milk mixed with rennet.

parochial ADJ **1** DEROG of tastes, attitudes, etc: concerned only with local affairs; narrow, limited or provincial in outlook. **2** referring or relating to a parish. ■ **parochialism** N.

parody N (-**ies**) **1** a comic or satirical imitation of a work, or the style, of a particular writer, composer, etc. **2** a poor attempt at something; a mockery or travesty.
➤ VB (-**ies**, -**ied**) to ridicule something through parody; to mimic satirically. ■ **parodist** N.

parole N **1 a** the release of a prisoner before the end of their sentence, on promise of good behaviour: **released on parole**; **b** the duration of this conditional release. **2** the promise of a prisoner so released to behave well.
➤ VB to release or place (a prisoner) on parole.

parotid N the **parotid gland**, a salivary gland in front of the ear.

paroxysm N **1** a sudden emotional outburst, eg of rage or laughter. **2** a spasm, convulsion or seizure, eg of coughing or acute pain.
■ **paroxysmal** ADJ.

parquet N flooring composed of small inlaid blocks of wood.

parquetry N inlaid work in wood arranged in a geometric pattern, used esp to cover floors or to decorate furniture, etc.

parr N (*parr* or *parrs*) a young salmon aged up to two years, before it becomes a smolt.

parricide N **1** killing one's own parent or near relative. **2** someone who commits this act.

parrot N **1** a brightly-coloured bird, native to

forests of warmer regions, with a large head and a strong hooked bill. **2** a person who merely imitates or mimics others.
➤ VB to repeat or mimic (another's words, etc) unthinkingly.

parrot-fashion ADV by mindless, unthinking repetition.

parry VB (*-ies, -ied*) to fend off (a blow).
➤ N (*-ies*) an act of parrying, esp in fencing.

parse VB, TR & INTR **1** GRAM to analyse (a sentence) grammatically; to explain the grammatical role of (a word). **2** COMP to analyse (a string of input symbols) in terms of the computing language being used.

parsec N, ASTRON a unit of astronomical measurement equal to 3.26 light years or 3.09 $\times 10^{13}$ kilometres.

parsimony N meanness with money.
■ **parsimonious** ADJ.

parsley N a plant with finely-divided bright green curly aromatic leaves, used as a herb.

parsnip N a plant widely grown for its thick fleshy tap root, eaten as a vegetable.

parson N **1** a parish priest in the Church of England. **2** any clergyman.

parsonage N the residence of a parson.

part N **1** a portion, piece or bit; some but not all. **2** one of a set of equal divisions or amounts that compose a whole: **five parts cement to two of sand. 3** an essential piece; a component: **vehicle spare parts. 4** a section of a book; any of the episodes of a story, etc issued or broadcast as a serial. **5 a** a performer's role in a play, opera, etc; **b** the words, actions, etc belonging to the role. **6** the melody, etc given to a particular instrument or voice in a musical work. **7** one's share, responsibility or duty in something: **do one's part. 8** (usu **parts**) a region: **foreign parts. 9** (**parts**) talents; abilities: **a man of many parts.**
➤ VB **1** to divide; to separate. **2** INTR to become divided or separated. **3** to separate (eg curtains, combatants, etc). **4** INTR of more than one person: to leave one another. **5** to put a parting in (hair). **6** INTR to come or burst apart.

➤ ADJ in part; partial: **part payment.**
◆ **for the most part** mostly or mainly.
◆ **for my part** as far as I am concerned.
◆ **take sb's part** to support them.

partake VB (*partook, partaken*) INTR (USU **partake in** or **of sth**) **1** to participate in it. **2** to eat or drink.

parterre N a formal flower-garden.

Parthian shot see **parting shot**

partial ADJ **1** incomplete; in part only. **2** (always **partial to sth**) having a liking for it. **3** biased. ■ **partially** ADV.

partiality N **1** being partial. **2** favourable bias or prejudice. **3** fondness.

participate VB, INTR (often **participate in sth**) to take part or be involved in it. ■ **participant** N. ■ **participation** N.

participle N, GRAM a word formed from a verb, which has adjectival qualities as well as verbal ones. There are two participles in English, the **present participle**, formed with the ending –ing, as in **going**, SWIMMING or **shouting**, and the **past participle**, generally ending in –d, –ed, –t or –n, as in **chased, shouted, kept** and **shown**, but also with irregular forms such as **gone**, swum, etc. ■ **participial** ADJ.

particle N **1** a tiny piece. **2** PHYS a tiny unit of matter such as a molecule, atom or electron.

particoloured ADJ partly one colour, partly another; variegated.

particular ADJ **1** specific; single; individually known or referred to: **that particular day. 2** especial: **took particular care. 3** difficult to satisfy; fastidious; exacting: **He's very particular. 4** exact; detailed.
➤ N **1** a detail. **2** (**particulars**) personal details, eg name, date of birth, etc.
◆ **in particular** especially.

particularity N **1** the quality of being particular. **2** minuteness of detail.

particularize or **-ise** VB **1** to specify individually. **2** to give specific examples of something. **3** INTR to go into detail.

particularly ADV **1** more than usually: particularly good. **2** specifically; especially: particularly wanted red.

parting N **1** the act of taking leave. **2** a divergence or separation. **3** a line of exposed scalp that divides sections of hair brushed in opposite directions.
➤ ADJ referring to, or at the time of, leaving; departing: **a parting comment**.

parting shot N a final hostile remark made on departing. Also called **Parthian shot**.

partisan N **1** an enthusiastic supporter of a party, person, cause, etc. **2** a member of an armed resistance group in a country occupied by an enemy.
➤ ADJ strongly loyal to one side, esp blindly so; biased. ■ **partisanship** N.

partition N **1** something which divides an object into parts. **2** a screen or thin wall dividing a room. **3** the dividing of a country into two or more independent states.
➤ VB **1** to divide (a country) into independent states. **2** (also **partition sth off**) to separate it off with a partition.

partly ADV in part, or in some parts; to a certain extent, not wholly.

partner N **1** one of two or more people who jointly own or run a business or other enterprise on an equal footing. **2** a person with whom one has a sexual relationship, esp a long-term one. **3** a person one dances with: **dance partner**.
➤ VB to join as a partner with someone; to be the partner of someone.

partnership N **1** a relationship in which two or more people or groups operate together. **2** the status of a partner. **3** a business jointly owned or run by two or more people, etc.

part of speech N (*parts of speech*) GRAM any of the grammatical classes of words, eg noun, adjective, verb or preposition.

partridge N (*partridge* or *partridges*) a plump ground-dwelling gamebird, with brown or grey plumage, and a very short tail.

part-time ADJ done, attended, etc during only part of the full working day.

➤ ADV: studying part-time. ■ **part-timer** N.

parturient ADJ, MED **1** referring or relating to childbirth. **2** giving birth or about to give birth.

parturition N, MED the process of giving birth.

party N (*-ies*) **1** a social gathering, esp of invited guests, for enjoyment or celebration. **2** a group of people involved in a certain activity together: **search party**. **3** LAW each of the individuals or groups concerned in a contract, agreement, lawsuit, etc.

parvenu and **parvenue** N (*parvenus* or *parvenues*) DEROG respectively a man or woman who has recently acquired wealth but lacks social refinement. **Also** AS ADJ.

pascal N in the SI system: a unit of pressure, equal to one newton per square metre.

pass VB **1** TR & INTR to come alongside and progress beyond something or someone. **2** INTR to run, progress, etc. **3** TR & INTR (also **pass through, into, etc sth** or **pass sth through, into, etc sth**) to go or make it go, penetrate, etc: **pass through a filter**. **4** TR & INTR to move lightly across, over, etc something. **5** INTR to move from one state or stage to another. **6** to exceed: **pass the target**. **7** TR & INTR of a vehicle: to overtake. **8 a** TR & INTR to achieve the required standard in (a test, etc); **b** to award (a student, etc) the marks required for success in a test, etc. **9** INTR to take place: **what passed between them**. **10** TR & INTR of time: to go by; to use up (time) in some activity, etc. **11** TR & INTR (usu **pass down** or **pass sth down**) to be inherited; to hand it down. **12** TR & INTR, SPORT to throw or kick (the ball, etc) to another player in one's team. **13** TR & INTR to agree to (a proposal or resolution) or be agreed to; to vote (a law) into effect. **14** of a judge or law court: to pronounce (judgement). **15** INTR to go away after a while. **16** INTR to be accepted, tolerated or ignored: **let it pass**.
➤ N **1** a route through a gap in a mountain range. **2** an official card or document permitting one to enter somewhere, be absent from duty, etc. **3** a successful result in an examination. **4** SPORT a throw, kick, hit, etc to another player in one's team. **5** a state of affairs: **came to a sorry pass**.

come or **be brought to pass** to happen.
make a pass at sb to make a casual sexual advance towards them.
pass away or **on** EUPHEMISTIC to die.
pass sth or **sb by** to overlook them.
pass off 1 of a sickness or feeling, etc: to go away; to diminish. **2** of an arranged event: to take place with the result specified: **The party passed off very well.**
pass sth off to successfully present (something which is fraudulent).
pass out to faint.
pass over sth to overlook it; to ignore it.
◆ **pass the time of day** to exchange an ordinary greeting with someone.
pass sth up COLLOQ to neglect or sacrifice (an opportunity).

passable ADJ **1** COLLOQ fairly good. **2** able to be travelled along, crossed, etc.

passage N **1** a route through; a corridor, narrow street, or channel. **2** a tubular vessel in the body. **3** a piece of a text or musical composition of moderate length. **4** the process of passing: **the passage of time. 5 a** a journey, esp by ship or aeroplane; **b** the cost of such a journey. **6** permission or freedom to pass through a territory, etc.

passageway N a narrow passage or way, etc, usu with walls on each side.

passenger N **1** a traveller in a vehicle, boat, aeroplane, etc, driven, sailed or piloted by someone else. **2** DEROG someone not doing their share of the work in a joint project, etc.

passer-by N (*passers-by*) someone who is walking past a house, shop, incident, etc.

passerine ORNITHOLOGY, ADJ of or relating to the largest order of birds, which includes the songbirds.
➢ N any bird belonging to this order.

passim ADV of a word, reference, etc: occurring frequently throughout the literary or academic work in question.

passing ADJ lasting only briefly.
➢ N **1** a coming to the end. **2** EUPHEMISTIC death.
in passing while dealing with something else; casually; by allusion rather than directly.

passion N **1** a violent emotion, eg anger or envy. **2** a fit of anger. **3** sexual love or desire. **4** an enthusiasm: **has a passion for bikes.**

passionate ADJ **1** easily moved to passion; strongly emotional. **2** keen; enthusiastic; intense. ■ **passionately** ADV.

passion fruit N the round yellow or purple edible fruit of the passion flower.

passive ADJ **1** lacking positive or assertive qualities; submissive. **2** lethargic; inert. **3** GRAM **a** denoting or relating to a verbal construction which in English consists of **be** and the past participle, which carries a meaning in which the subject undergoes, rather than performs, the action of the verb, such as '**the letter**' in **The letter was written by John**; **b** denoting or relating to the verb in such a construction.
■ **passively** ADV. ■ **passivity** N.

passive smoking N the breathing in of tobacco-smoke by non-smokers.

passport N an official document issued by a government, giving proof of the holder's identity, and permission to travel abroad.

password N **1** esp MIL a secret word allowing entry to a high-security area or past a checkpoint, etc. **2** COMP a set of characters personal to a user which they input to gain access to a computer or network.

past ADJ **1** referring to an earlier time; of long ago; bygone. **2** recently ended; just gone by: **the past year. 3** over; finished. **4** former; previous: **past presidents. 5** GRAM of the tense of a verb: indicating an action or condition which took place or began in the past.
➢ PREP **1** up to and beyond: **went past me.**
2 after in time or age: **past your bedtime.**
3 beyond: **the corner past the library • past help.**
➢ ADV **1** so as to pass by: **watched me go past.**
2 ago: **two months past.**
➢ N **1** (usu **the past**) **a** the time before the present; **b** events, etc belonging to this time. **2** one's earlier life or career. **3** a disreputable period earlier in life: **a woman with a past.**

◆ **not put it past sb** COLLOQ to believe them quite liable or disposed to do a certain thing.

pasta N a dough made with flour, water and eggs, shaped into a variety of forms such as spaghetti, macaroni, lasagne, etc.

paste N **1** a stiff moist mixture made from a powder, traditionally flour, and water, and used as an adhesive: **wallpaper paste**. **2** a spread for sandwiches, etc made from ground meat or fish, etc. **3** any fine, often sweet, dough-like mixture: **almond paste**. **4** a hard brilliant glass used in making imitation gems.
➢ VB **1** to stick something with paste. **2** (also **paste sth up**) PRINTING to mount (text, illustrations, etc) on a backing as a proof for printing from or photographing, etc. **3** WORD PROCESSING to insert text, etc which has been copied or cut from another part of the document, etc. **4** COLLOQ to beat soundly.

pastel N **1** a chalk-like crayon. **2** a picture drawn with pastels.
➢ ADJ **1** of colours: delicately pale; soft, quiet. **2** drawn with pastels.

pastern N the part of a horse's foot between the hoof and the fetlock.

pasteurize or **-ise** VB to partially sterilize (food, esp milk) by heating it to a specific temperature for a short period before rapidly cooling it. ■ **pasteurization** N.

pastiche N a musical, artistic or literary work in someone else's style, or in a mixture of styles.

pastille N **1** a small fruit-flavoured sweet. **2** a cone of fragrant paste, burned as incense.

pastime N a spare-time pursuit; a hobby.

pasting N, COLLOQ a thrashing.

past master N an expert.

pastor N a member of the clergy, esp in churches other than Anglican and Catholic.

pastoral ADJ **1 a** relating to the countryside or country life; **b** of a poem, painting, musical work, etc: depicting the countryside or country life, esp in an idealized way. **2** relating to a member of the clergy or their work. **3** relating to a shepherd or their work.

pastrami N a smoked highly-seasoned beef.

pastry N (**-ies**) **1** dough made with flour, fat and water, used for piecrusts. **2** a sweet baked article made with this; a pie, tart, etc.

pasturage N **1** an area of land where livestock can graze. **2** grass for feeding.

pasture N an area of grassland suitable or used for the grazing of livestock.

pasty[1] N (**-ies**) a pie consisting of pastry folded round a savoury or sweet filling: **Cornish pasty**.

pasty[2] ADJ (**-ier, -iest**) **1** like a paste in texture. **2** of the complexion: unhealthily pale. ■ **pastiness** N.

pat VB (**-tt-**) **1** to strike (a person or animal) lightly or affectionately with the palm of one's hand. **2** to shape something by striking it lightly with the palm or a flat instrument: **pat it into shape**.
➢ N **1** a light blow, esp an affectionate one, with the palm of the hand. **2** a round flat mass.
➢ ADV immediately and fluently, as if memorized: **Their answers came too pat**.
➢ ADJ of answers, etc: quickly and easily supplied.

patch N **1** a piece of material sewn on or applied, eg to a garment or piece of fabric, etc, so as to cover a hole or reinforce a worn area. **2** a plot of earth: **a vegetable patch**. **3** a pad or cover worn as protection over an injured eye. **4** a small expanse contrasting with its surroundings: **patches of ice**. **5** scrap or shred. **6** COLLOQ a phase: **go through a bad patch**.
➢ VB **1** to mend (a hole or garment) by sewing a patch or patches on or over it. **2** (also **patch sth up**) to repair it hastily and temporarily. **3** COMP to make a temporary correction in (a program). ■ **patchy** ADJ (**-ier, -iest**).
◆ **not a patch on sb** or **sth** COLLOQ not nearly as good as them.
◆ **patch sth up** COLLOQ to settle (a quarrel, etc).

patchwork N **1** needlework done by sewing together small pieces of contrastingly patterned fabric. **2 a** a piece of work produced in this way; **b** AS ADJ: **patchwork quilt**.

pate N, OLD USE OR FACETIOUS the head or skull.

pâté N a spread made from ground or chopped meat, fish or vegetables.

patella N (-ae or -as) ANAT the kneecap.

patent N 1 an official licence from the government granting a person or business the sole right, for a certain period, to make and sell a particular article. 2 the right so granted. 3 the invention so protected.
➤ VB to obtain a patent for (an invention, etc).
➤ ADJ 1 very evident: a patent lie. 2 concerned with the granting of, or protection by, patents. 3 of a product: protected under patent. 4 open for inspection: letters patent. ■ **patentable** ADJ. ■ **patently** ADV.

patent leather N leather made glossy by varnishing.

paternal ADJ 1 referring, relating, or appropriate to a father. 2 related on one's father's side: paternal grandmother.

paternalism N governmental or managerial benevolence towards its citizens, employees, etc taken to the extreme of overprotectiveness and authoritarianism. ■ **paternalistic** ADJ.

paternity N 1 the quality or condition of being a father; fatherhood. 2 the relation of a father to his children.

path N 1 (also **pathway**) a track trodden by, or specially surfaced for, walking. 2 the line along which something is travelling: the path of Jupiter. 3 a course of action: the path to ruin.

pathetic ADJ 1 moving one to pity; touching, heart-rending, poignant or pitiful: her pathetic sobs. 2 DEROG, COLLOQ hopelessly inadequate. ■ **pathetically** ADV.

pathogen N, PATHOL any micro-organism, esp a bacterium or virus, that causes disease in a living organism. ■ **pathogenic** ADJ.

pathological ADJ 1 relating to pathology. 2 caused by, or relating to, illness. 3 COLLOQ compulsive; habitual. ■ **pathologically** ADV.

pathology N (-ies) the branch of medicine concerned with the study of the nature of diseases. ■ **pathologist** N.

pathos N a quality in a situation, etc, esp in literature, that moves one to pity.

patience N 1 the ability to endure delay, trouble, pain or hardship in a calm way. 2 tolerance. 3 perseverance.

patient ADJ having or showing patience.
➤ N a person who is being treated by, or is registered with, a doctor, dentist, etc.

patina N 1 a coating formed on a metal surface by oxidation. 2 a mature shine on wood resulting from continual polishing and handling. ■ **patinated** ADJ. ■ **patination** N.

patio N an open paved area beside a house.

patisserie N 1 a shop or café selling fancy cakes, sweet pastries, etc. 2 such cakes.

patois N (PL patois) the local dialect of a region, used usu in informal everyday situations.

patriarch N 1 the male head of a family or tribe. 2 in the Eastern Orthodox Church: a high-ranking bishop. 3 in the RC Church: the pope. 4 in the Old Testament: any of the ancestors of the human race or of the tribes of Israel, eg Adam, Abraham or Jacob. 5 a venerable old man. ■ **patriarchal** ADJ.

patriarchy N (-ies) a social system in which a male is head of the family and descent is traced through the male line.

patrician N 1 HIST a member of the aristocracy of ancient Rome. 2 an aristocrat.
➤ ADJ belonging or relating to the aristocracy, esp that of ancient Rome.

patricide N the act of killing one's own father.

patrimony N (-ies) 1 property inherited from one's father or ancestors. 2 something inherited; a heritage.

patriot N someone who loves and serves their fatherland or country devotedly. ■ **patriotic** ADJ. ■ **patriotically** ADV. ■ **patriotism** N.

patrol VB (-ll-) 1 TR & INTR to make a regular systematic tour of (an area) to maintain security or surveillance. 2 INTR of a police officer: to be on duty on a beat.
➤ N 1 the act of patrolling: on patrol. 2 a person or group of people performing this duty.

3 a body of aircraft, etc carrying out this duty.

patron N **1** someone who gives financial support and encouragement eg to an artist, the arts, a movement or charity: **a patron of the arts**. **2** a regular customer of a shop, attender at a theatre, etc. ■ **patronal** ADJ.

patronage N **1** the support given by a patron. **2** regular custom given to a shop, theatre, etc. **3** the power of bestowing, or recommending people for, offices.

patronize or **-ise** VB **1** to treat someone condescendingly. **2** to act as a patron towards (an organization, etc). **3** to give regular custom to (a shop, etc). ■ **patronizing** ADJ.

patron saint N the guardian saint of a country, profession, craft, etc.

patronymic N a name derived from one's father's or other male ancestor's name, usu with a suffix or prefix, as in **Donaldson**.

patsy N (**-ies**) SLANG, chiefly N AMER an easy victim; a sucker; a scapegoat or fall guy.

patter¹ VB, INTR **1** to make a light rapid tapping noise. **2** to move with light rapid footsteps. ➣ N the light rapid tapping of footsteps or rain.

patter² N **1** the fast persuasive talk of a salesman, or the quick speech of a comedian. **2** the speech of a particular group or area.

pattern N **1** a model, guide or set of instructions for making something: **a dress pattern**. **2** a decorative design, often consisting of repeated motifs. **3** a piece, eg of fabric, as a sample. **4** any excellent example suitable for imitation. **5** a coherent series of occurrences or set of features.
➣ VB (usu **pattern sth on another thing**) to model it on another type, design, etc.

paucity N (**-ies**) smallness of quantity; fewness; a scarcity or lack; dearth.

paunch N a protruding belly, esp in a man. ■ **paunchy** ADJ (**-ier, -iest**).

pauper N **1** a poverty-stricken person. **2** HIST someone living on charity.

pause N a relatively short break in some activity, etc.
➣ VB, INTR **1** to stop briefly. **2** to hesitate.
◆ **give sb pause** to make them hesitate before acting.

pave VB to surface (esp a footpath, but also a street, etc) with stone slabs, cobbles, etc.
◆ **pave the way for sth** or **sb** to prepare for and make way it.

pavement N **1** a raised footpath edging a road, etc, often but not always paved. **2** a paved road, area, expanse, etc. **3** a road surface; road-surfacing material.

pavilion N **1** a building in a sports ground in which players change their clothes, store equipment, etc. **2** a summerhouse or ornamental shelter. **3** a large ornamental building for public pleasure and entertainment.

paving N **1** stones or slabs used to pave a surface. **2** a paved surface.

paw N **1** the foot of a four-legged mammal. **2** COLLOQ a hand, esp when used clumsily.
➣ VB **1** to finger or handle something clumsily; to touch or caress someone with unwelcome familiarity. **2** (also **paw at sth**) of an animal: to scrape or strike it with a paw.

pawn¹ VB **1** to deposit (an article of value) with a pawnbroker as a pledge for money borrowed. **2** to pledge or stake something.
➣ N **1** the condition of being deposited as a pledge: **in pawn**. **2** an article so pledged.

pawn² N **1** CHESS a chess piece of lowest value. **2** a person manipulated by others.

pawnbroker N someone who lends money in exchange for pawned articles.

pawnshop N a pawnbroker's place of business.

pawpaw see under **papaw**

pay VB (**paid**) **1** TR & INTR to give (money) to someone in exchange for goods, services, etc. **2** TR & INTR to settle (a bill, debt, etc). **3** TR & INTR to give (wages or salary) to an employee. **4** TR & INTR to make a profit, or make something as profit: **businesses that don't pay**. **5** TR & INTR to benefit; to be worthwhile: **It pays one to be**

polite. **6** TR & INTR (also **pay for sth**) to suffer a penalty on account of it; to be punished for it. **7 a** to do someone the honour of (a visit or call): **paid her a visit**; **b** to offer someone (a compliment, one's respects, etc).
➤ N money given or received for work, etc.
◆ **pay sb back** to revenge oneself on them.
◆ **pay sth back** to return (money owed).
◆ **pay its way** to compensate adequately for initial outlay.
◆ **pay off** to have profitable results.
◆ **pay one's way** to pay all of one's own debts and living expenses.
◆ **pay sth off** to finish paying (a debt, etc).
◆ **pay through the nose** to pay a very high price.
◆ **pay up** COLLOQ to pay the full amount that is due, esp reluctantly.
◆ **put paid to sth** or **sb** COLLOQ to put an end to it or them.

payable ADJ that can or must be paid: **Make cheques payable to me** • **payable by 31st July.**

payee N someone to whom money is paid or a cheque is made out.

payload N **1** the part of a vehicle's load which earns revenue. **2** the operating equipment carried by a spaceship or satellite. **3** the quantity and strength of the explosive carried by a missile. **4** the quantity of goods, passengers, etc carried by an aircraft.

payment N **1** a sum of money paid. **2** the act of paying or process of being paid.

pay-off N, COLLOQ **1** a fruitful result; a good return. **2** a bribe. **3** a final settling of accounts.

payola N a bribe for promoting a product.

payphone N a telephone that is operated by coins, a phonecard or credit card.

payroll N a register of employees that lists the wage or salary due to each.

pay slip N a note of an employee's pay, showing deductions for tax, etc.

pazzazz or **pazazz** see **pizzazz**

PC ABBREV **1** personal computer. **2** Police Constable. **3** politically correct.

pc ABBREV per cent.

PE ABBREV physical education.

pea N **1** a climbing plant of the pulse family, cultivated for its edible seeds, which are produced in long pods. **2** the round protein-rich seed of this plant, eaten as a vegetable.

peace N **1** freedom from or absence of war. **2** a treaty ending a war. **3** freedom from or absence of noise, disturbance or disorder; quietness or calm. **4** freedom from mental agitation; serenity: **peace of mind.**
◆ **keep the peace 1** LAW to preserve law and order. **2** to prevent, or refrain from, fighting.
◆ **make peace** to end a war or quarrel, etc.

peaceable ADJ peace-loving; mild; placid.

peaceful ADJ **1** calm and quiet. **2** unworried; serene. **3** free from war, violence, disturbance, disorder, etc.

peacemaker N someone who makes or brings about peace between enemies.
■ **peacemaking** N, ADJ.

peach[1] N **1** a small deciduous tree, widely cultivated for its edible fruit or for ornament. **2** the large round fruit of this tree, consisting of a hard stone surrounded by sweet juicy yellow flesh and a yellowish-pink velvety skin. **3** the yellowish-pink colour of this fruit. **4** COLLOQ something delightful: **a peach of a day.**

peach[2] VB (always **peach on sb**) COLLOQ to betray or inform on them.

peacock N (*peacock* or *peacocks*) **1** a large bird, the male of which has a train of green and gold eyespot feathers which it fans showily during courtship. Also called **peafowl**. **2** the male peafowl (the female being the **peahen**). **3** DEROG a vain person.

peak[1] N **1 a** a sharp pointed summit; **b** a pointed mountain or hill. **2 a** a maximum, eg in consumer use: **Consumption reaches its peak at around 7pm**; **b** AS ADJ referring or relating to the period of highest use or demand: **peak viewing time. 3** a time of maximum achievement, etc: **His peak was in his early twenties. 4** the front projecting part of a cap.
➤ VB, INTR **1** to reach a maximum. **2** to reach the

heightof one's powers or popularity.

peak² VB, INTR to droop; to look thin or sickly.

peaky ADJ (*-ier, -iest*) ill-looking; pallid.

peal N **1** the ringing of a bell or set of bells. **2** NON-TECHNICAL a set of bells. **3** a burst of noise: **a peal of thunder**.
➤ VB **1** INTR to ring or resound. **2** to sound or signal (eg a welcome) by ringing.

pean see **paean**

peanut N **1** a low-growing plant of the pulse family, widely cultivated for its edible seeds which are produced under the ground in pods. **2** the protein-rich seed of this plant. **3** (**peanuts**) COLLOQ **a** something small or unimportant; **b** a paltry amount of money.

pear N **1** a deciduous tree, widely cultivated for its edible fruit and ornamental flowers. **2** the edible cone-shaped fruit of this tree.

pearl N **1** a bead of smooth hard lustrous material found inside the shell of certain molluscs, eg oysters, and used as a gem. **2** an artificial imitation of this. **3** mother-of-pearl. **4** something resembling a pearl. **5** something valued or precious: **pearls of wisdom**.
➤ ADJ **1** like a pearl in colour or shape. **2** made of or set with pearls or mother-of-pearl.

pearly ADJ (*-ier, -iest*) **1** like a pearl or pearl. **2** covered in pearl.

pearly gates PL N, COLLOQ the gates of Heaven.

peasant N **1** in poor agricultural societies: a farm worker or small farmer. **2** DEROG a rough unmannerly or culturally ignorant person. ■ **peasantry** N.

pea-souper N, COLLOQ a thick yellowish fog.

peat N **1** a mass of dark-brown or black fibrous plant material, produced by the compression of partially decomposed vegetation, used in compost and in dried form as a fuel. **2** a cut block of this material. ■ **peaty** ADJ (*-ier, -iest*).

pebble N a small fragment of rock, esp one worn round and smooth by the action of water.

➤ VB to cover with pebbles. ■ **pebbly** ADJ (*-ier, -iest*).

pebbledash N, BRIT a coating for exterior walls of cement or plaster with small stones embedded in it.

pec N (usu **pecs**) COLLOQ a pectoral muscle.

pecan N an oblong reddish-brown edible nut with a sweet oily kernel.

peccadillo N (*-os* or *-oes*) a minor misdeed.

peck¹ VB **1** (also **peck at sth**) of a bird: to strike, nip or pick at it with the beak: **pecked at the bark of the tree**. **2** to poke (a hole) with the beak. **3** to kiss someone or something in a quick or perfunctory way: **pecked her on the cheek**.
➤ N **1** a tap or nip with the beak. **2** a perfunctory kiss.
◆ **peck at sth** to eat (food) in a cursory or dainty way, without enjoyment or application.

peck² N **1** in the imperial system: a measure of capacity of dry goods, esp grain, equal to two gallons (9.1 litres) or a quarter of a bushel. **2** a measuring container holding this quantity.

pecker N, COLLOQ spirits; resolve: **keep one's pecker up**.

pecking order N any social hierarchy.

peckish ADJ, COLLOQ quite hungry.

pectin N, BIOCHEM a complex carbohydrate that functions as a cement-like material within and between plant cell-walls.

pectoral ADJ **1** referring or relating to the breast or chest. **2** worn on the breast.
➤ N **1** a pectoral muscle. **2** a pectoral fin. **3** a neck ornament worn covering the chest. **4** armour for the breast of a person or a horse.

peculate VB, TR & INTR, FORMAL to embezzle. ■ **peculation** N.

peculiar ADJ **1** strange; odd. **2** (**peculiar to sb** or **sth**) exclusively or typically belonging to or associated with them: **habits peculiar to cats**. **3** special; individual: **their own peculiar methods**. **4** especial; particular: **of peculiar interest**. ■ **peculiarly** ADV.

peculiarity N (*-ies*) **1** the quality of being

strange or odd. **2** an idiosyncrasy.

pecuniary ADJ relating to, concerning or consisting of money.

pedagogue N, OLD DEROG USE a teacher, esp a strict or pedantic one. ■ **pedagogic** ADJ.

pedagogy N the science or work of teaching.

pedal N a lever operated by the foot, eg on a machine, vehicle or musical instrument. ➤ VB (-*ll*-; or (esp N AMER) -*l*-) TR & INTR to move or operate by means of a pedal or pedals.

pedant N, DEROG someone who is over-concerned with correctness of detail, esp in academic matters. ■ **pedantic** ADJ.

pedantry N **1** excessive concern with correctness. **2** a pedantic expression.

peddle VB **1** TR & INTR to go from place to place selling (a selection of small goods). **2** COLLOQ to deal illegally in (narcotic drugs).

peddler N **1** the usual N AMER spelling of **pedlar**. **2** someone who deals illegally in narcotics.

pederasty or **paederasty** N sexual relations between adults and children. ■ **pederast** or **paederast** N.

pedestal N the base on which a vase, statue, column, etc is placed or mounted. ◆ **put** or **place sb on a pedestal** to admire or revere them extremely; to idolize them.

pedestrian N someone travelling on foot, esp in a street; someone who is walking. ➤ ADJ **1** referring to, or for, pedestrians. **2** dull; unimaginative; uninspired.

pedestrianize or **-ise** VB to convert (a shopping street, etc) into an area for pedestrians only by excluding through-traffic. ■ **pedestrianization** N.

pedicure N a medical or cosmetic treatment of the feet and toenails.

pedigree N **1** a person's or animal's line of descent, esp if long and distinguished, or proof of pure breeding. **2** a genealogical table showing this; a family tree.

pediment N, ARCHIT a wide triangular gable set over a portico or the face of a building.

pedlar or (chiefly N AMER) **peddler** N someone who peddles.

pedometer N a device that measures distance walked.

peduncle N **1** BOT a short stalk, eg one carrying an inflorescence or a single flower-head. **2** ANAT, PATHOL any stalk-like structure.

pee COLLOQ, VB (*peed, peeing*) INTR to urinate. ➤ N **1** an act of urinating. **2** urine.

peek VB, INTR (also **peek at sth**) to glance briefly and surreptitiously at it; to peep. ➤ N a brief furtive glance.

peel VB **1** to strip the skin or rind off (a fruit or vegetable). **2** INTR to be able to be peeled: *Grapes don't peel easily.* **3** (also **peel sth away** or **off**) to strip off (an outer layer). **4** INTR of a wall or other surface: to shed its outer coating in flaky strips. **5** INTR of skin, paint or other coverings: to flake off in patches. ➤ N the skin or rind of vegetables or fruit, esp citrus fruit: *candied peel.* ■ **peeler** N.

peep[1] VB, INTR **1** (often **peep at sth** or **sb** or **peep out**) to look quickly or covertly, eg through a narrow opening or from a place of concealment; to peek. **2** (also **peep out**) to emerge briefly or partially. ➤ N a quick covert look.

peep[2] N **1** the faint high-pitched cry of a baby bird, etc; a cheep. **2** the smallest utterance: *not another peep out of you!* ➤ VB, INTR of a young bird, etc: to cheep.

peephole N a hole, crack, aperture, etc through which to peep.

peepshow N a box with a peephole through which a series of moving pictures, esp erotic or pornographic ones, can be watched.

peer[1] N **1** a member of the nobility, such as, in Britain, a duke, marquess, earl, viscount or baron. **2 a** someone who is one's equal in age, rank, etc; a contemporary, companion or fellow; **b** AS ADJ: *peer group.*

peer[2] VB, INTR (also **peer at sth** or **sb**) to look hard at it or them, esp through narrowed eyes, as if having difficulty in seeing.

peerage N **1** the title or rank of a peer. **2** SING OR PL the members of the nobility as a group.

peerless ADJ without equal; excelling all.

peer pressure N compulsion to do or obtain the same things as others in one's peer group.

peeve VB, COLLOQ to irritate, annoy or offend. ■ **peeved** ADJ.

peevish ADJ irritable; cantankerous; inclined to whine or complain. ■ **peevishly** ADV.

peg N **1** a little shaft of wood, metal or plastic shaped for fixing, fastening or marking uses. **2** a coat hook fixed to a wall, etc. **3** a wooden or plastic clip for fastening washing to a line to dry; a clothes peg. **4** a small stake for securing tent ropes, marking a position, etc. **5** any of several wooden pins on a stringed instrument, which are turned to tune it. **6** COLLOQ a leg. ➤ VB (**-gg-**) **1** to insert a peg into something. **2** to fasten something with a peg or pegs. **3** to set or freeze (prices, incomes, etc) at a certain level. ◆ **off the peg** of clothes: ready to wear. ◆ **peg away** COLLOQ to work steadily. ◆ **peg out 1** COLLOQ to die. **2** to become exhausted. ◆ **peg sth out** to mark out (ground) with pegs. ◆ **take sb down a peg or two** COLLOQ to humiliate them; to humble them.

pejorative ADJ disapproving, derogatory, disparaging or uncomplimentary. ➤ N a word or affix with derogatory force.

pelican N (**pelican** or **pelicans**) a large aquatic bird that has an enormous beak with a pouch below it, and mainly white plumage.

pelican crossing N a pedestrian crossing with pedestrian-controlled traffic lights.

pelisse N, HIST **1** a long mantle of silk, velvet, etc, worn esp by women. **2** a fur or fur-lined garment, esp a military cloak.

pellagra N, MED a disease characterized by scaly discoloration of the skin, diarrhoea, and psychological disturbances.

pellet N **1** a small rounded mass of compressed material, eg paper. **2** a piece of small shot for an airgun, etc. **3** a ball of undigested material regurgitated by an owl or hawk.

pell-mell ADV headlong; in confused haste.

pellucid ADJ **1** transparent. **2** absolutely clear in expression and meaning.

pelmet N a strip of fabric or a narrow board fitted along the top of a window to conceal the curtain rail.

pelt[1] VB **1** to bombard with missiles. **2** INTR to rush along at top speed. ➤ N an act or spell of pelting. ◆ **at full pelt** as fast as possible. ◆ **pelt down** INTR of rain, hail, etc: to fall fast and heavily.

pelt[2] N **1** the skin of a dead animal, esp with the fur still on it. **2** the coat of a living animal. **3** a hide stripped of hair for tanning.

pelvic ADJ of or in the region of the pelvis.

pelvis N (**pelvises** or **pelves**) ANAT the basin-shaped cavity in the bones of the hips.

pen[1] N **1** a writing instrument that uses ink. **2** this instrument as a symbol of the writing profession. ➤ VB (**-nn-**) FORMAL to compose and write (a letter, poem, etc) with a pen.

pen[2] N **1** a small enclosure, esp for animals. **2** often IN COMPOUNDS any small enclosure or area of confinement: **a playpen**. ➤ VB (**penned** or **pent, penning**) (often **pen sb** or **sth in** or **up**) to enclose or confine them.

pen[3] N, N AMER COLLOQ a penitentiary.

pen[4] N a female swan.

penal ADJ relating to punishment, esp by law. ■ **penally** ADV.

penalize or **-ise** VB **1** to impose a penalty on someone, for wrongdoing, cheating, breaking a rule, committing a foul in sport, etc. **2** to disadvantage someone.

penalty N (**-ies**) **1** a punishment, such as imprisonment, a fine, etc, imposed for wrongdoing, breaking a contract or rule, etc. **2** a punishment that one brings on oneself through ill-advised action. **3** SPORT a handicap imposed on a competitor or team for an infringement of the rules, taking the form of an advantage awarded to the opposing side.

penance N repentance or atonement.

pence a plural of **penny**

penchant N a taste, liking, inclination or tendency: *a penchant for childish pranks.*

pencil N **1 a** a writing and drawing instrument consisting of a wooden shaft containing a stick of graphite or other material; **b** AS ADJ: **pencil drawing. 2** something with a similar function or shape, eg for medical or cosmetic purposes: **an eyebrow pencil.**
➤ VB (**-ll-**; N AMER **-l-**) to write, draw or mark something with a pencil.
◆ **pencil sth** or **sb in** to note down a provisional commitment in one's diary.

pendant or (sometimes) **pendent** N **1 a** an ornament suspended from a neck chain, necklace, bracelet, etc; **b** a necklace with such an ornament hanging from it. **2** any of several hanging articles, eg a ceiling light, etc.

pendent or (sometimes) **pendant** ADJ **1** hanging; suspended; dangling. **2** projecting; jutting; overhanging.

pending ADJ **1** waiting to be decided or dealt with. **2** of a patent: about to come into effect.
➤ PREP until; awaiting; during: **held in prison pending trial.**

pendulous ADJ hanging down loosely.

pendulum N **1** PHYS a weight, suspended from a fixed point, that swings freely back and forth. **2** a swinging lever used to regulate the movement of a clock. **3** anything that undergoes obvious and regular shifts or reversals in direction, attitude, opinion, etc.

penetrate VB **1** (also **penetrate into sth**) to find a way into it; to enter it, esp with difficulty. **2** to gain access into and influence within (a country, organization, market, etc) for political, financial, etc purposes. **3** to find a way through something; to pierce or permeate: **penetrate enemy lines. 4** to fathom, solve, or understand (a mystery). **5** of a man: to insert his penis into

the vagina of (a woman) or anus of (a man or a woman). ■ **penetrative** ADJ.

penetrating ADJ **1** of a voice, etc: all too loud and clear; strident; carrying. **2** of a person's mind: acute; discerning. **3** of the eyes or of a look: piercing; probing.

penetration N **1** the process of penetrating or being penetrated. **2** insight.

penguin N a flightless sea bird with a stout body, small almost featherless wings, short legs, black plumage, and a white belly.

penicillin N any of various antibiotics that are widely used to treat bacterial infections.

peninsula N a piece of land projecting into water from a larger landmass and almost completely surrounded by water.
■ **peninsular** ADJ.

penis N in higher vertebrates: the male organ of copulation used to transfer sperm to the female reproductive tract and also containing the urethra. ■ **penile** ADJ.

penitent ADJ regretful for wrong one has done, and feeling a desire to reform; repentant.
➤ N a repentant person. ■ **penitence** N.

penitential ADJ referring to, showing or constituting penance: **penitential psalms.**

penitentiary N (**-ies**) N AMER a federal or state prison.
➤ ADJ **1** of punishment or penance. **2** penal or reformatory.

penknife N a pocket knife with blades that fold into the handle.

pen name N a pseudonym used by a writer.

pennant N **1** NAUT a dangling line from the masthead, etc, with a block for tackle, etc. **2** NAUT a small narrow triangular flag, used on vessels for signalling. Also called **pennon.**

pennate ADJ, BIOL **1** winged; feathered; shaped like a wing. **2** pinnate.

penniless ADJ without money; very poor.

pennon N **1** HIST a long narrow flag with a tapering divided tip, eg borne on his lance by a knight. **2** same as **pennant** (N sense 2).

penny N (*pence* in senses 1 and 2, or *pennies*) **1** (SING and PL abbrev **p**) in the UK: a hundredth part of £1, or a bronze coin having this value. **2** (SING and PL symbol **d**) in the UK before decimalization in 1971: one twelfth of a shilling, or a bronze coin having this value. **3** N AMER one cent, or a coin having this value.
◆ **a pretty penny** IRONIC a huge sum.
◆ **the penny dropped** COLLOQ understanding about something finally came.
◆ **two a penny** or **ten a penny** very common; in abundant supply and of little value.

penny-pinching ADJ, DEROG too careful with one's money; miserly; stingy.

pen pusher N a clerk or minor official whose job includes much tedious paperwork.

pension N **1** a government allowance to a retired, disabled or widowed person. **2** a regular payment by an employer to a retired employee. **3** a regular payment from a private pension company to a person who contributed to a pension fund for much of their working life. **4** a boarding-house in continental Europe.
➤ VB to grant a pension to (a person).
■ **pensionable** ADJ. ■ **pensioner** N.
◆ **pension sb off** to put them into retirement, or make them redundant, on a pension.

pensive ADJ preoccupied with one's thoughts; thoughtful. ■ **pensively** ADV.

pentacle N a pentangle.

pentad N **1** a set of five things. **2** a period of five years or five days.

pentagon N, GEOM a plane figure with five sides and five angles. ■ **pentagonal** ADJ.

pentagram N **1** a figure in the shape of a star with five points and consisting of five lines. **2** such a figure used as a magic symbol.

pentahedron N (*-rons* or *-ra*) GEOM a five-faced solid figure. ■ **pentahedral** ADJ.

pentameter N, POETRY a line of verse with five metrical feet.

pentangle N a pentagram or similar figure or amulet used as a defence against demons.

pentathlon N an athletic competition comprising five events all of which the contestants must compete in.

penthouse N an apartment, esp a luxuriously appointed one, built on to the roof of a tall building. **Also** AS ADJ: **penthouse suite**.

pent-up (also **pent up**) ADJ of feelings, energy, etc: stifled; bursting to be released.

penultimate ADJ last but one.

penumbra N (*-ae* or *-as*) **1** the lighter outer shadow that surrounds the dark central shadow produced by a large unfocused light-source shining on an opaque object. **2** ASTRON the lighter area around the edge of a sunspot.
■ **penumbral** or **penumbrous** ADJ.

penury N extreme poverty. ■ **penurious** ADJ.

peon N **1** in India and Ceylon: an office messenger; an attendant. **2** in Latin America: a farm labourer.

people N, USU PL **1** a set or group of persons. **2** men and women in general. **3** a body of persons held together by belief in common origin, speech, culture, political union, or by common leadership, etc. **4** (**the people**) ordinary citizens without special rank; the general populace. **5** (**the people**) voters as a body. **6** subjects or supporters of a monarch, etc. **7** SING a nation or race: **a warlike people**. **8** COLLOQ one's parents or relations.
➤ VB **1** to fill or supply (a region, etc) with people; to populate. **2** to inhabit.

pep N, COLLOQ energy; vitality; go.
➤ VB (*-pp-*) (always **pep sb** or **sth up**) to enliven or invigorate them or it.

peplum N (*-lums* or *-la*) a short skirt-like section attached to the waistline of a garment.

pepper N **1 a** a climbing shrub, widely cultivated for its small red berries which are dried to form peppercorns; **b** a pungent seasoning prepared by grinding the dried berries of this plant. **2 a** a tropical shrub cultivated for its large red, green or yellow edible fruits; **b** the fruit of this plant, eaten raw in salads or cooked as a vegetable. Also called **capsicum, sweet pepper**.

➤ VB **1** to bombard something or someone (with missiles). **2** to sprinkle liberally. **3** to season (a dish, etc) with pepper.

peppercorn N **1** the dried berry of the pepper plant. **2** something of little value.

peppermint N **1** a species of mint with dark-green leaves, widely cultivated for its aromatic oil. **2** a food flavouring prepared from the aromatic oil produced by this plant. **3** a sweet flavoured with peppermint.

pepperoni or **peperoni** N (*pepperonies* or *peperonis*) a hard, spicy sausage.

peppery ADJ **1** well seasoned with pepper; tasting of pepper; hot-tasting or pungent. **2** short-tempered. ■ **pepperiness** N.

pepsin N, BIOCHEM a digestive enzyme.

pep talk N a brief talk to raise morale.

peptic ADJ **1** referring or relating to digestion. **2** referring or relating to the stomach. **3** referring or relating to pepsin.

peptide N, BIOCHEM a molecule that consists of a relatively short chain of amino acids.

per PREP **1** out of every: **two per thousand**. **2** for every: **£5 per head**. **3** in every: **60 miles per hour**. **4** through; by means of: **per post**.
◆ **as per ...** according to ...: **proceed as per instructions**.
◆ **as per usual** COLLOQ as always.

perambulate VB, FORMAL to stroll around. ■ **perambulation** N.

perambulator N, FORMAL a pram.

per annum ADV for each year; yearly.

per capita ADV, ADJ for each person.

perceive VB **1** to observe, notice, or discern. **2** to understand, interpret or view: **how one perceives one's role**. ■ **perceivable** ADJ.

per cent ADV, ADJ (symbol **%**) **1** in or for every 100: **Sales are 20 per cent down**. **2** on a scale of 1 to 100: **90 per cent certain**.
➤ N (usu **percent**) **1** a percentage or proportion. **2** one part in or on every 100.

percentage N **1** an amount, number or rate stated as a proportion of one hundred. **2** profit; advantage.

percentile N, STATISTICS one of the points or values that divide a collection of statistical data, arranged in order, into 100 equal parts.

perceptible ADJ able to be perceived; noticeable; detectable. ■ **perceptibly** ADV.

perception N **1** PSYCHOL the process whereby information about one's environment, received by the senses, is organized and interpreted so that it becomes meaningful. **2** one's powers of observation; discernment; insight. **3** one's view or interpretation of something.

perceptive ADJ quick to notice or discern.

perch[1] N **1** a branch or other narrow support above ground for a bird to rest or roost on. **2** a high position or vantage point.
➤ VB **1** INTR of a bird: to alight and rest on a perch. **2** INTR to sit, esp insecurely or temporarily. **3** TR & INTR to sit or place high up.

perch[2] N a freshwater fish which has a streamlined body and a silvery-white belly.

percipient ADJ perceptive; acutely observant; discerning. ■ **percipience** N.

percolate VB **1** TR & INTR to undergo or subject (a liquid) to the process of filtering, oozing or trickling. **2** INTR (also **percolate through**) COLLOQ of news or information: to trickle or spread slowly. **3** TR & INTR of coffee: to make or be made in a percolator.

percolator N a pot for making coffee, in which boiling water circulates up through a tube and down through ground coffee beans.

percussion N **1** the striking of one hard object against another. **2 a** musical instruments played by striking, eg drums, cymbals, xylophone, etc; **b** these instruments collectively as a section of an orchestra. ■ **percussionist** N. ■ **percussive** ADJ.

perdition N everlasting punishment after death; damnation; hell.

peregrinate VB, INTR, LITERARY to travel, voyage or roam; to wander abroad. ■ **peregrination** N.

peregrine N a large falcon with greyish-blue plumage on its back and wings and paler underparts. Also called **peregrine falcon**.

peremptory ADJ 1 of an order: made in expectation of immediate compliance. 2 of a tone or manner: arrogantly impatient. 3 of a statement, etc: allowing no denial or discussion.

perennial ADJ 1 BOT referring or relating to a plant that lives for several to many years. 2 lasting throughout the year.
➤ N a perennial plant.

perfect ADJ 1 complete in all essential elements. 2 faultless; flawless. 3 excellent; absolutely satisfactory. 4 exact: **a perfect circle**. 5 COLLOQ absolute; utter: **perfect nonsense**. 6 GRAM of the tense or aspect of a verb: denoting an action completed at some time in the past or prior to the time spoken of.
➤ VB 1 to improve something to one's satisfaction. 2 to finalize or complete. 3 to develop to a reliable standard. ■ **perfectible** ADJ. ■ **perfectly** ADV.

perfection N 1 the state of being perfect. 2 the process of making or being made perfect, complete, etc. 3 flawlessness. 4 COLLOQ an instance of absolute excellence.
◆ **to perfection** perfectly.

perfectionism N 1 the doctrine that perfection is attainable. 2 an expectation of the highest standard. ■ **perfectionist** ADJ, N.

perfidious ADJ treacherous, double-dealing or disloyal. ■ **perfidiously** ADV. ■ **perfidy** N.

perforate VB 1 to make holes in something. 2 to make a row of holes in something, for ease of tearing. ■ **perforation** N.

perforce ADV, chiefly OLD USE necessarily; inevitably or unavoidably.

perform VB 1 to carry out (a task, job, action, etc); to do or accomplish. 2 to fulfil (a function) or provide (a service, etc). 3 TR & INTR to act, sing, play, dance, etc (a play, song, dance, etc) to entertain an audience. 4 INTR eg of an engine: to function. 5 INTR to conduct oneself, esp when presenting oneself for assessment.
■ **performer** N. ■ **performing** ADJ.

performance N 1 a the performing of a play, part, dance, piece of music, etc before an audience; b a dramatic or artistic presentation or entertainment. 2 the act or process of performing a task, etc. 3 a level of achievement, success or, in commerce, profitability. 4 manner or efficiency of functioning.

perfume N 1 a sweet smell; a scent or fragrance. 2 a fragrant liquid prepared from the extracts of flowers, etc, for applying to the skin or clothes; scent.
➤ VB to give a sweet smell to something; to apply perfume to something. ■ **perfumed** ADJ. ■ **perfumery** N. ■ **perfumy** ADJ.

perfunctory ADJ done merely as a duty or routine, without genuine care or feeling.
■ **perfunctorily** ADV. ■ **perfunctoriness** N.

pergola N a framework constructed from slender branches, for plants to climb up; a trellis.

perhaps ADV possibly; maybe.

perianth N, BOT the outer part of a flower.

pericardium N (-ia) ANAT the sac that surrounds the heart. ■ **pericardiac** or **pericardial** ADJ.

perigee N the point in the orbit of the Moon or a satellite when it is closest to the Earth.

perihelion N (-ia) the point in the orbit of a planet when it is closest to the Sun.

peril N 1 grave danger. 2 a hazard.
■ **perilous** ADJ. ■ **perilously** ADV.
◆ **at one's peril** at the risk of one's safety.

perimeter N 1 a the boundary of an enclosed area; b AS ADJ: **perimeter fence**. 2 GEOM a the boundary or circumference of any plane figure; b the length of this boundary.

perinatal ADJ, MED denoting or relating to the period extending from the 28th week of pregnancy to about one month after childbirth.

perineum N (-nea) ANAT the region of the body between the genital organs and the anus. ■ **perineal** ADJ.

period N 1 a portion of time. 2 a phase or stage, eg in history, or in a person's life and

development, etc. **3** an interval of time at the end of which events recur in the same order. **4** GEOL a unit of geological time that is a subdivision of an era. **5** any of the sessions of equal length into which the school day is divided, and to which particular subjects or activities are assigned. **6** esp N AMER a full stop. **7** the periodic discharge of blood during a woman's menstrual cycle.
➤ ADJ dating from, or in the style of, the historical period in question: **period furniture**.

periodic ADJ happening at intervals, esp regular intervals. ■ **periodicity** N.

periodical N a magazine published weekly, monthly, quarterly, etc.
➤ ADJ referring or relating to such publications. ■ **periodically** ADV.

periodic table N, CHEM a table of all the chemical elements in order of increasing atomic number.

peripatetic ADJ **1** travelling about from place to place. **2** of a teacher: employed by several schools and so obliged to travel between them.

peripheral ADJ **1** relating or belonging to the outer edge or outer surface: **peripheral nerves**. **2** (**peripheral to sth**) not central to the issue in hand. **3** COMP supplementary.

periphery N (**-ies**) **1** the edge or boundary of something. **2** the external surface of something. **3** a surrounding region.

periscope N, OPTICS a system of prisms or mirrors that enables the user to view objects that are above eye-level, used in submarines, military tanks, etc.

perish VB **1** INTR to die; to be destroyed or ruined. **2 a** INTR of materials: to decay; **b** TR to cause (materials) to decay or rot.

perishable ADJ of commodities, esp food: liable to rot or go bad quickly.

perishing ADJ **1** COLLOQ of weather, etc: very cold. **2** OLD USE, COLLOQ damned.

peristalsis N (**-ses**) PHYSIOL in eg the intestines: the waves of involuntary muscle contractions that force the contents of the tube, eg food,

further forward. ■ **peristaltic** ADJ.

peritoneum N (**-nea** or **-neums**) ANAT a serous membrane that lines the abdominal cavity. ■ **peritoneal** ADJ.

peritonitis N, PATHOL inflammation of the peritoneum.

periwig N a man's wig of the 17c and 18c.

periwinkle N **1** a climbing plant with single bluish-purple flowers. **2** a small marine mollusc with a spirally coiled shell.

perjure VB (now always **perjure oneself**) to lie while under oath; to commit perjury.

perjury N (**-ies**) the crime of lying while under oath in a court of law. ■ **perjurer** N.

perk¹ VB, TR & INTR (always **perk up**) to become or make (someone) more lively and cheerful. ■ **perky** ADJ (**-ier, -iest**).

perk² N, COLLOQ a benefit, additional to income, derived from employment, such as membership of a health club, the use of a company car, etc.

perk³ VB, TR & INTR, COLLOQ to percolate (coffee).

perm N a hair treatment using chemicals that give a long-lasting wave or curl.
➤ VB to curl or wave (hair) with a perm.

permafrost N, GEOL an area of subsoil or rock that has remained frozen for at least a year.

permanent ADJ **1** lasting, or intended to last, indefinitely; not temporary. **2** of a condition, etc: unlikely to alter. ■ **permanence** N.

permanganate N, CHEM any of the salts of **permanganic acid** used as an oxidizing and bleaching agent and disinfectant.

permeable ADJ of a porous material or membrane: allowing certain liquids or gases to pass through it. ■ **permeability** N.

permeate VB (also **permeate through sth**) **1** of a liquid or gas: to pass, penetrate or diffuse through (a fine or porous material or a membrane). **2** TR & INTR of a smell, gas, etc: to spread through a room or other space; to fill or impregnate. ■ **permeation** N.

permissible ADJ allowable; permitted.

permission N consent or authorization.

permissive ADJ **1** tolerant; liberal. **2** allowing usu excessive freedom, esp in sexual matters: the permissive society. ■ **permissiveness** N.

permit VB (-*tt*-) **1** to consent to or give permission for something. **2** to give (someone) leave or authorization. **3** to allow someone something: permitted him access to his children. **4** (also **permit of sth**) FORMAL to enable it to happen or take effect.
➤ N a document that authorizes something: a fishing permit.

permutation N, MATH any of several different ways in which a set of objects or numbers can be arranged.

permute or **permutate** VB to rearrange (a set of things) in different orders, esp in every possible order in succession.

pernicious ADJ harmful; destructive; deadly.

pernickety ADJ **1** over-particular about small details; fussy. **2** tricky; intricate.

peroration N the concluding part of a speech, summing up the points.

peroxide N **1** CHEM a strong oxidizing agent that releases hydrogen peroxide when treated with acid, used in rocket fuels, antiseptics, disinfectants and bleaches. **2 a** a solution of hydrogen peroxide used as a bleach for hair and textiles; **b** AS ADJ: a peroxide blonde.
➤ VB to bleach (hair) with hydrogen peroxide.

perpendicular ADJ **1** vertical; upright; in the direction of gravity. **2** (also **perpendicular to sth**) at right angles; forming a right angle with (a particular line or surface). **3** of a cliff, etc: steep.
➤ N a perpendicular line, position or direction.
■ **perpendicularity** N.

perpetrate VB to commit, or be guilty of (a crime, misdeed, error, etc). ■ **perpetration** N.
■ **perpetrator** N.

perpetual ADJ **1** everlasting; eternal; continuous; permanent. **2** continual; continually recurring. ■ **perpetually** ADV.

perpetuate VB **1** to make something last or continue: perpetuate a species. **2** to preserve

the memory of (a name, etc). **3** to repeat and pass on (an error, etc). ■ **perpetuation** N.

perpetuity N (*-ies*) **1** the state of being perpetual. **2** eternity. **3** duration for an indefinite period.

perplex VB **1** to puzzle, confuse or baffle someone with intricacies or difficulties. **2** to complicate. ■ **perplexed** ADJ. ■ **perplexing** ADJ. ■ **perplexity** N.

perquisite N **1** same as **perk**². **2** a customary tip expected on some occasions.

perry N (*-ies*) an alcoholic drink made from fermented pear juice.

per se ADV in itself: not valuable per se.

persecute VB **1** to ill-treat, oppress, torment or put to death (a person or people), esp for their religious or political beliefs. **2** to harass, pester or bother someone continually.
■ **persecution** N. ■ **persecutor** N.

perseverance N the act or state of persevering; continued effort to achieve something one has begun, despite setbacks.

persevere VB, INTR (also **persevere in** or **with sth**) to keep on striving for it; to persist steadily with (an endeavour).

persiflage N banter; teasing; frivolous talk.

persimmon N **1** a tall tree, widely cultivated for its hard wood and edible fruits. **2** the plum-like fruit of this tree.

persist VB, INTR **1** (also **persist in** or **with sth**) to continue with it in spite of resistance, difficulty, etc. **2** of rain, etc: to continue steadily. **3** to continue to exist. ■ **persistence** N.

persistent ADJ **1** continuing with determination in spite of discouragement; tenacious. **2** constant; unrelenting: persistent questions.

person N (*persons* or in sense 1 also *people*) **1** an individual human being. **2** the body, often including clothes: A knife was found hidden on his person. **3** GRAM each of the three classes into which pronouns and verb forms fall, **first person** denoting the speaker, **second person** denoting the person(s) addressed,

and **third person** denoting the person(s) or thing(s) spoken about.
◆ **in person 1** actually present oneself. **2** doing something oneself.

persona N (*-ae* or *-as*) PSYCHOANAL one's character as one presents it to the world, masking one's inner thoughts, feelings, etc.

personable ADJ good-looking or likeable.

personage N a well-known, important or distinguished person.

personal ADJ **1** of a comment, opinion, etc: coming from someone as an individual, not from a group or organization: **my personal opinion**. **2** done, attended to, etc by the individual person in question, not by a substitute: **give it my personal attention**. **3** relating to oneself in particular: **a personal triumph**. **4** relating to one's private concerns: **details of her personal life**. **5** of remarks: referring, often disparagingly, to an individual's characteristics. **6** relating to the body: **personal hygiene**.

personal assistant N a secretary.

personal column N a newspaper column or section in which members of the public may place advertisements, enquiries, etc.

personal computer N (abbrev **PC** or **pc**) a small computer designed for use by one person and containing an entire **CPU** on a single microchip.

personality N (*-ies*) **1** a person's nature or disposition; the qualities that give one's character individuality. **2** strength or distinctiveness of character: **lots of personality**. **3** a well-known person; a celebrity.

personalize or **-ise** VB **1** to mark something distinctively, eg with name, initials, etc, as the property of a particular person. **2** to focus (a discussion, etc) on personalities instead of the matter in hand. **3** to personify.

personally ADV **1** as far as one is concerned: **Personally, I disapprove**. **2** in person. **3** as a person. **4** as directed against one: **take a remark personally**.

personal stereo N a small audio-cassette player with earphones, that can be worn attached to a belt or carried in a pocket.

personify VB (*-ies, -ied*) **1** in literature, etc: to represent (an abstract quality, etc) as a human being or as having human qualities. **2** of a figure in art, etc: to symbolize (a quality, etc). **3** to be the perfect example of something: **She's patience personified**. ■ **personification** N.

personnel PL N the people employed in a business company or other organization.

perspective N **1** the observer's view of objects in relation to one another, esp with regard to the way they seem smaller the more distant they are. **2** the representation of this phenomenon in drawing and painting. **3** the balanced or objective view of a situation, in which all its elements assume their due importance.

perspicacious ADJ shrewd; astute; perceptive or discerning. ■ **perspicacity** N.

perspicuous ADJ of speech or writing: clearly expressed and easily understood. ■ **perspicuity** N.

perspiration N the secretion of fluid by the sweat glands of the skin, usu in response to heat or physical exertion.

perspire VB, INTR to secrete fluid from the sweat glands of the skin; to sweat.

persuade VB **1** (also **persuade sb to do sth**) to urge successfully; to prevail on or induce someone. **2** (often **persuade sb of sth**) to convince them that it is true, advisable, etc.

persuasion N **1** the act of urging, coaxing or persuading. **2** a creed or set of beliefs, esp that of a political group or religious sect.

persuasive ADJ having the power to persuade; convincing or plausible.

pert ADJ **1** impudent; cheeky. **2** of clothing or style: jaunty; saucy. ■ **pertness** N.

pertain VB, INTR (often **pertain to sb** or **sth**) **1** to concern or relate to them or it; to have to do with them or it. **2** to belong to them or it: **skills pertaining to the job**.

pertinacious ADJ determined in one's purpose; dogged; tenacious.

pertinent ADJ (also **pertinent to sb** or **sth**) relating to or concerned with them or it; relevant. ■ **pertinence** N.

perturb VB to make someone anxious, agitated, worried, etc. ■ **perturbation** N.

peruse VB 1 to read through (a book, magazine, etc) carefully. 2 to browse through something casually. 3 to examine or study (eg someone's face) attentively. ■ **perusal** N.

pervade VB to spread or extend throughout something; to affect throughout something; to permeate. ■ **pervasion** N. ■ **pervasive** ADJ.

perverse ADJ 1 deliberately departing from what is normal and reasonable. 2 unreasonable; awkward. ■ **perversity** N.

perversion N 1 the process of perverting or condition of being perverted. 2 a distortion. 3 an abnormal sexual activity.

pervert VB 1 to divert something or someone illicitly from what is normal or right: **pervert the course of justice**. 2 to lead someone into evil or unnatural behaviour; to corrupt them. ➤ N someone who is morally or sexually perverted.

pesky ADJ (**-ier, -iest**) N AMER COLLOQ troublesome or infuriating. ■ **peskily** ADV.

peso N the standard unit of currency of many Central and S American countries.

pessary N (**-ies**) a vaginal suppository.

pessimism N the tendency to emphasize the gloomiest aspects of anything, and to expect the worst to happen. ■ **pessimist** N. ■ **pessimistic** ADJ.

pest N 1 a living organism, such as an insect, fungus or weed, that has a damaging effect on animal livestock, crop plants or stored produce. 2 COLLOQ a constant nuisance.

pester VB 1 to annoy constantly. 2 to harass or hound someone with requests.

pesticide N any of various chemical compounds, including insecticides, herbicides and fungicides, that are used to kill pests.

pestilence N a virulent epidemic or contagious disease. ■ **pestilential** ADJ.

pestilent ADJ 1 deadly, harmful or destructive. 2 COLLOQ, often FACETIOUS troublesome.

pestle N a club-shaped utensil for pounding, crushing and mixing substances in a mortar.

pet^1 N 1 a tame animal or bird kept as a companion. 2 someone's favourite: **the teacher's pet**. 3 a term of endearment. ➤ ADJ 1 kept as a pet: **a pet lamb**. 2 relating to pets or for pets: **pet food**. 3 favourite; own special: **her pet subject**. ➤ VB (**-tt-**) 1 to pat or stroke (an animal, etc). 2 to treat someone indulgently; to make a fuss of them. 3 INTR of two people: to fondle and caress for erotic pleasure. ■ **petting** N.

pet^2 N a fit of bad temper or sulks.

petal N, BOT in a flower: one of the modified leaves, often scented and brightly coloured, which in insect-pollinated plants attract passing insects.

petard N, HIST a small bomb for blasting a hole in a wall, door, etc.
◆ **hoist with one's own petard** be the victim of one's own trick or cunning.

peter VB, INTR (always **peter out**) to dwindle away to nothing.

petiole N 1 BOT the stalk that attaches a leaf to the stem of a plant. 2 ZOOL a stalk-like structure, esp that of the abdomen in wasps, etc.

petite ADJ of a woman or girl: small and dainty.

petition N 1 a formal written request to an authority to take some action, signed by a large number of people. 2 any appeal to a higher authority. 3 LAW an application to a court for some procedure to be set in motion. ➤ VB, TR & INTR (also **petition sb for** or **against sth**) to address a petition to; to make an appeal. ■ **petitionary** ADJ. ■ **petitioner** N.

petrel N a small seabird with a hooked bill and external tube-shaped nostrils.

petrifaction or **petrification** N, GEOL

1 a form of fossilization by which organic remains are turned into stone as tissue is replaced by minerals. **2** the state of being petrified.

petrify VB (*-ies, -ied*) **1** to terrify; to paralyse someone with fright. **2** TR & INTR to turn into stone by the process of petrifaction.

petrochemical N any organic chemical derived from petroleum or natural gas.

petrol N a volatile flammable liquid mixture of hydrocarbons, used as a fuel.

petroleum N a naturally occurring oil consisting of a thick dark liquid mixture of hydrocarbons, which yields liquid and gas fuels, asphalt, and raw materials for the manufacture of plastics, solvents, drugs, etc.

petrology N, GEOL the scientific study of the structure, origin, distribution and history of rocks.

petrol station N a filling station.

petticoat N a woman's underskirt.

pettifogger N, DEROG someone who argues over trivial details. ■ **pettifogging** N, ADJ.

pettish ADJ peevish; sulky.

petty ADJ (*-ier, -iest*) **1** being of minor importance; trivial. **2** small-minded or childishly spiteful. **3** of a low or subordinate rank. ■ **pettily** ADV. ■ **pettiness** N.

petty cash N money kept for small everyday expenses in an office, etc.

petulant ADJ ill-tempered; peevish. ■ **petulance** N. ■ **petulantly** ADV.

petunia N a plant with large funnel-shaped flowers in a range of bright colours.

pew N **1** one of the long benches with backs used as seating in a church. **2** COLLOQ a seat.

pewter N **1** a silvery alloy with a bluish tinge, composed of tin and lead, used to make tableware (eg tankards), jewellery and other decorative objects. **2** articles made of pewter. **3** AS ADJ made of pewter. ■ **pewterer** N.

PG ABBREV as a film classification: parental guidance (needed).

pH and **pH value** N, CHEM a measure of the relative acidity or alkalinity of a solution.

phagocyte N, BIOL a cell, esp a white blood cell, that engulfs and destroys micro-organisms and other foreign particles. ■ **phagocytic** ADJ.

phalanger N a nocturnal tree-dwelling marsupial. Also called **possum**.

phalanx N (*phalanxes* or *phalanges*) a solid body of people, esp one representing united support or opposition.

phallic ADJ relating to or resembling a phallus.

phallus N (*-luses* or *-li*) **1** a penis. **2** a representation or image of an erect penis, esp as a symbol of male reproductive power.

phantasm N **1** an illusion or fantasy. **2** a ghost or phantom. ■ **phantasmal** ADJ.

phantasmagoria N a fantastic succession of real or illusory images seen as if in a dream. ■ **phantasmagoric** or **phantasmagorical** ADJ.

phantom N **1** a ghost or spectre. **2** an illusory image or vision. ➤ ADJ **1** referring to the nature of a phantom; spectral. **2** imaginary; not real.

Pharaoh N the title of the kings of ancient Egypt.

pharmaceutical and **pharmaceutic** ADJ referring or relating to the preparation of drugs and medicines.

pharmaceutics SING N the preparation and dispensing of drugs and medicine.

pharmacist N someone who prepares and dispenses drugs and medicines.

pharmacology N the scientific study of medicines and drugs and their effects and uses. ■ **pharmacological** ADJ. ■ **pharmacologist** N.

pharmacopoeia N, MED a book that contains a list of drugs, with details of their properties, uses, side-effects, methods of preparation and recommended dosages.

pharmacy N (*-ies*) **1** the mixing and

dispensing of drugs and medicines.
2 a dispensary in a hospital, etc.

pharynx N (*pharynxes* or *pharynges*)
1 ANAT in mammals: the part of the alimentary
canal that links the mouth and nasal passages
with the oesophagus and trachea. **2** the throat.
■ **pharyngeal** ADJ.

phase N **1** a stage or period in growth or
development. **2** the appearance or aspect of
anything at any stage. **3** ASTRON any of the
different shapes assumed by the illuminated
surface of a celestial body, eg the Moon.
➤ VB to organize or carry out in stages.

PhD ABBREV: philosophiae doctor (Latin), Doctor
of Philosophy.

pheasant N (*pheasant* or *pheasants*) a
ground-dwelling bird, the male being brightly
coloured and having a long pointed tail.

phenobarbitone N a hypnotic and
sedative drug.

phenol N, CHEM **1** a colourless crystalline toxic
solid used in the manufacture of resins, nylon,
solvents, explosives, drugs, dyes and perfumes.
Also called **carbolic acid**. **2** any of a group of
weakly acidic organic chemical compounds,
many of which are used as antiseptics.

phenomenal ADJ **1** remarkable;
extraordinary; abnormal. **2** referring to the
nature of a phenomenon. **3** relating to
phenomena. ■ **phenomenally** ADV.

phenomenon N (-*mena*) **1** a happening
perceived through the senses, esp something
unusual. **2** an extraordinary or abnormal
person or thing; a prodigy. **3** a feature of life,
etc: **a work-related phenomenon**.

phenotype N, GENETICS the observable
characteristics of an organism.

phenyl N, CHEM an organic radical found in
benzene, phenol, etc.

pheromone N, ZOOL any chemical substance
secreted by an animal which has a specific
effect on the behaviour of other members of
the same species.

phew EXCLAM used to express relief,

astonishment or exhaustion.

phial or **vial** N a little medicine bottle.

philander VB, INTR of men: to flirt or have
casual love affairs with women; to womanize.
■ **philanderer** N.

philanthropy N a charitable regard for one's
fellow human beings, esp in the form of
benevolence to those in need.
■ **philanthropic** ADJ. ■ **philanthropist** N.

philately N the collecting of postage stamps.
■ **philatelic** ADJ. ■ **philatelist** N.

philharmonic ADJ dedicated to music.

philippic N a speech making a bitter attack.

philistine ADJ having no interest in or
appreciation of art, literature, music, etc, and
tending rather towards materialism.
➤ N a philistine person. ■ **philistinism** N.

philology N **1** the study of language, its history
and development. **2** the study of literary and
non-literary texts, esp older ones.
■ **philological** ADJ. ■ **philologist** N.

philosopher N someone who studies
philosophy.

philosophical or **philosophic** ADJ
1 referring or relating to philosophy or
philosophers. **2** calm and dispassionate.

philosophize or **-ise** VB, INTR **1** to form
philosophical theories. **2** to reason or
speculate in the manner of a philosopher.

philosophy N (-*ies*) **1** the search for truth and
knowledge concerning the universe, human
existence, perception and behaviour, pursued
by means of reflection, reasoning and
argument. **2** any particular system or set of
beliefs established as a result of this. **3** a set of
principles that serves as a basis for making
judgements and decisions.

philtre N a magic potion for arousing sexual
desire.

phlebitis N, PATHOL inflammation of the wall of
a vein.

phlegm N **1** a thick yellowish substance

produced by the mucous membrane that lines the air passages, brought up by coughing. **2** calmness or impassiveness; stolidity.

phlegmatic or **phlegmatical** ADJ **1** of a person: calm; not easily excited. **2** producing or having phlegm. ■ **phlegmatically** ADV.

phloem N, BOT the plant tissue that carries sugars and other nutrients from the leaves to all other parts of the plant.

phobia N an obsessive and persistent fear of a specific object or situation, representing a form of neurosis. ■ **phobic** ADJ.

phoenix N in Arabian legend: a bird which every 500 years sets itself on fire and is reborn from its ashes to live a further 500 years.

phone or **'phone** N a telephone.
➤ VB (also **phone sb up**) TR & INTR to telephone someone.

phoneme N, LING the smallest unit of sound in a language that has significance in distinguishing one word from another. ■ **phonemic** ADJ.

phonetic ADJ **1** referring or relating to the sounds of a spoken language. **2** eg of a spelling: intended to represent the pronunciation. ■ **phonetically** ADV.

phonetics SING N the branch of linguistics that deals with speech sounds, esp how they are produced and perceived. ■ **phonetician** N.

phoney or (US) **phony** ADJ (**-ier, -iest**) not genuine; fake, sham, bogus or insincere.
➤ N (**phoneys** or **phonies**) someone or something bogus; a fake or humbug.

phonograph N, N AMER, OLD USE a record-player.

phonology N (**-ies**) the study of speech sounds in general, or of those in any particular language. ■ **phonological** ADJ.

phooey EXCLAM, COLLOQ an exclamation of scorn, contempt, disbelief, etc.

phosgene N, CHEM a poisonous gas, carbonyl chloride, used in pesticides and dyes.

phosphate N, CHEM any salt or ester of phosphoric acid, found in living organisms and in many minerals, and used in fertilizers, detergents, etc.

phosphor N, CHEM any substance capable of phosphorescence. ■ **phosphoric** ADJ.

phosphorescence N the emission of light from a substance after it has absorbed energy from a source such as ultraviolet radiation, and which continues for some time after the energy source has been removed. ■ **phosphoresce** VB. ■ **phosphorescent** ADJ.

phosphorous ADJ, CHEM referring to or containing phosphorus in lower valency.

phosphorus N, CHEM a non-metallic element that exists as several different allotropes.

photo N, COLLOQ a photograph.

photocopier N a machine that makes copies of printed documents by any of various photographic techniques, esp xerography.

photocopy N (**-ies**) a photographic copy of a document, drawing, etc.
➤ VB (**-ies, -ied**) to make a photographic copy of (a document, etc).

photoelectric ADJ referring or relating to the electrical effects of light, eg the emission of electrons or a change in resistance. ■ **photoelectricity** N.

photoelectric cell N a light-sensitive device that converts light energy into electrical energy.

photogenic ADJ characterized by the quality of looking attractive in photographs.

photograph N a permanent record of an image that has been produced on photosensitive film or paper by the process of photography.
➤ VB, TR & INTR to take a photograph (of).

photographic ADJ **1** relating to or similar to photographs or photography. **2** of memory: retaining images in exact detail.

photography N the process of creating an image on light-sensitive film or some other sensitized material using visible light, X-rays, or some other form of radiant energy.

■ **photographer** N.

photojournalism N journalism consisting mainly of photographs to convey the meaning of the article. ■ **photojournalist** N.

photolithography N a process of lithographic printing from a photographically produced plate.

photometry N, PHYS the measurement of visible light and its flow. ■ **photometric** ADJ.

photon N, PHYS a particle of electromagnetic radiation that travels at the speed of light, used to explain phenomena that require light to behave as particles rather than as waves.

photophobia N, MED aversion to light.

photosensitive ADJ readily stimulated by light or some other form of radiant energy.

photosphere N, ASTRON the outermost visible layer of the Sun.

photosynthesis N, BOT the process whereby green plants manufacture carbohydrates from carbon dioxide and water, using the light energy from sunlight trapped by the pigment chlorophyll. ■ **photosynthesize** or **-ise** VB.

phototropism N, BOT the growth of the roots or shoots of plants in response to light.

phrasal verb N, GRAM a phrase consisting of a verb plus an adverb or preposition, or both, frequently with a meaning or meanings that cannot be determined from the meanings of the individual words, eg **let on**.

phrase N **1** a set of words expressing a single idea, forming part of a sentence though not constituting a clause. **2** an idiomatic expression: **What is the phrase she used? 3** manner or style of speech or expression: **ease of phrase. 4** MUS a run of notes making up an individually distinct part of a melody. ➤ VB **1** to express; to word something. **2** MUS to bring out the phrases in (music) as one plays. ■ **phrasal** ADJ.

phraseology N (**-ies**) **1** one's choice of words and way of combining them, in expressing oneself. **2** the language belonging to a particular subject, etc: **legal phraseology.**

phrenetic ADJ a variant of **frenetic**

phrenology N the practice of assessing someone's character and aptitudes by examining the shape of their skull. ■ **phrenological** ADJ. ■ **phrenologist** N.

phut N, COLLOQ the noise of a small explosion. ◆ **go phut 1** to break down or cease to function. **2** to go wrong.

phylum N (**phyla**) BIOL, ZOOL in taxonomy: any of the major groups into which the animal kingdom is divided and which in turn is subdivided into one or more classes.

physical ADJ **1** relating to the body rather than the mind; bodily: **physical strength. 2** relating to objects that can be seen or felt; material: **the physical world. 3** relating to nature or to the laws of nature: **physical features. 4** involving bodily contact. **5** relating to physics. ■ **physically** ADV.

physical education N instruction in sport and gymnastics.

physical training N instruction in sport and gymnastics, esp in the army.

physician N a registered medical practitioner who specializes in medical as opposed to surgical treatment of diseases and disorders.

physics SING N the scientific study of the properties and inter-relationships of matter, energy, force and motion. ■ **physicist** N.

physio N, COLLOQ **1** physiotherapy. **2** a physiotherapist.

physiognomy N (**-ies**) the face or features, esp seen as a key to someone's personality.

physiology N, BIOL the branch of biology that is concerned with the internal processes and functions of living organisms, as opposed to their structure. ■ **physiologic** or **physiological** ADJ. ■ **physiologist** N.

physiotherapy N, MED the treatment of injury and disease by external physical methods, such as remedial exercises, manipulation or massage, rather than by drugs or surgery. ■ **physiotherapist** N.

physique N the structure of the body with regard to size, shape and muscular development.

pi[1] N **1** the sixteenth letter of the Greek alphabet (Π, π). **2** MATH this symbol (π), representing the ratio of the circumference of a circle to its diameter, in numerical terms 3.14159.

pi[2] see **pie**[2]

pianissimo ADV, MUS performed very softly.

pianist N someone who plays the piano.

piano[1] N a large musical instrument with a keyboard, the keys being pressed down to operate a set of hammers that strike tautened wires to produce the sound.

piano[2] ADV, MUS softly.

piano accordion N an accordion whose melody is produced by means of a keyboard.

pianoforte N the full term for a **piano**[1].

Pianola N, TRADEMARK a mechanical, playerless piano.

piazza N **1** a public square in an Italian town. **2** mainly BRIT a covered walkway.

pibroch N a series of variations on a martial theme or lament, played on the bagpipes.

pic N (*pics* or *pix*) COLLOQ a photograph or picture.

picador N, BULLFIGHTING a toreador who weakens the bull by wounding it with a lance.

picaresque ADJ of a novel, etc: telling of the adventures of a usu likeable rogue in separate, only loosely connected, episodes.

piccalilli N a pickle consisting of mixed vegetables in a mustard sauce.

piccolo N a small flute pitched one octave higher than the standard flute.

pick[1] VB **1** TR & INTR to choose or select. **2** to detach and gather (flowers from a plant, fruit from a tree, etc). **3** to open (a lock) with a device other than a key, often to gain unauthorized entry. **4** to get, take or extract whatever is of use or value from something: **pick a bone clean. 5** to steal money or valuables from (someone's pocket). **6** to undo; to unpick: **pick a dress to pieces. 7** to make (a hole) by unpicking. **8** to provoke (a fight, quarrel, etc) with someone.
➤ N **1** the best of a group: **the pick of the bunch. 2** one's own preferred selection. ■ **picker** N.
◆ **pick at sth 1** to eat only small quantities of (one's food). **2** to keep pulling at (a scab, etc) with one's fingernails.
◆ **pick sb's brains** to ask someone for ideas, etc, and then use it as your own.
◆ **pick holes in sth** to find fault with it.
◆ **pick on sb 1** to blame them unfairly. **2** to bully them.
◆ **pick sb** or **sth to pieces** to criticize them or it severely.
◆ **pick up** to recover or improve.
◆ **pick up** or **pick sth up** to resume: **pick up where one left off.**
◆ **pick sb up 1** to arrest or seize them. **2** to go and fetch them from where they are waiting. **3** to stop one's vehicle for them and give them a lift. **4** COLLOQ to approach them and successfully invite them, eg to go home with one, esp with a view to sexual relations.
◆ **pick sb up on sth** to point out their error.
◆ **pick sth up 1** to lift or raise it. **2** to learn or acquire (a skill, language, etc) over a time. **3** to become aware of it: **picked up a faint odour. 4** to obtain or acquire it casually, by chance, etc: **pick up a bargain. 5** to go and fetch (something waiting to be collected). **6** COLLOQ to agree to pay (a bill, etc): **pick up the tab.**
◆ **pick up the pieces** to have to restore things to normality after some trouble.

pick[2] N **1** a tool with a long metal head pointed at one or both ends, for breaking ground, rock, ice, etc. **2** a poking or cleaning tool: **a toothpick. 3** a plectrum.

pickaxe N a large pick.

picket N **1** a person or group of people stationed outside a place of work to persuade other employees not to go in during a strike. **2** a body of soldiers on patrol or sentry duty. **3** a stake fixed in the ground, eg as part of a fence.
➤ VB **1** to station pickets or act as a picket at (a factory, etc). **2** to guard or patrol with, or as, a military picket. **3** to fence with pickets.

pickings PL N, COLLOQ profits made easily or casually from something: **rich pickings**.

pickle N 1 (also **pickles**) a preserve of vegetables, eg onions, in vinegar, salt water or a tart sauce. 2 a vegetable preserved in this way. 3 the liquid used for this preserve. 4 COLLOQ a mess; a predicament. ➤ VB to preserve something in vinegar, salt water, etc.

pick-me-up N 1 a stimulating drink, such as tea, a whisky, etc. 2 anything that revives.

pickpocket N a thief who steals from people's pockets, usu in crowded areas.

picky ADJ (*-ier, -iest*) COLLOQ choosy or fussy, esp excessively so; difficult to please.

picnic N 1 an outing on which one takes food for eating outside. 2 food eaten in this way. ➤ VB (*-icked, -icking*) INTR to have a picnic.

picot N 1 a loop in an ornamental edging. 2 EMBROIDERY a raised knot.

pictograph and **pictogram** N 1 a picture or symbol that represents a word, as in Chinese writing. 2 a pictorial or diagrammatic representation of values, statistics, etc. ■ **pictographic** ADJ. ■ **pictography** N.

pictorial ADJ relating to, or consisting of, pictures. ➤ N a periodical with a high proportion of pictures as opposed to text.

picture N 1 a representation of someone or something on a flat surface; a drawing, painting or photograph. 2 someone's portrait. 3 a view; a mental image: **a clear picture of the battle**. 4 a situation or outlook: **a gloomy financial picture**. 5 a person or thing strikingly like another: **She is the picture of her mother**. 6 a visible embodiment: **was the picture of happiness**. 7 an image of beauty: **looks a picture**. 8 the image received on a television screen: **We get a good picture**. 9 a film; a motion picture. 10 (**the pictures**) COLLOQ the cinema: **went to the pictures last night**. ➤ VB 1 to imagine or visualize. 2 to describe something or someone vividly. 3 to represent or show someone or something in a picture.

◆ **get the picture** COLLOQ to understand.
◆ **in the picture** informed of all the facts, etc.

picturesque ADJ 1 of places or buildings: charming to look at, esp if rather quaint. 2 of language: colourful, expressive or graphic.

piddle VB, INTR, COLLOQ to urinate. ➤ N 1 urine. 2 the act of urinating.

piddling ADJ trivial; trifling: **piddling excuses**.

pidgin N 1 a type of simplified language used esp for trading purposes between speakers of different languages, commonly used in the East and West Indies, Africa and the Americas. 2 (also **pigeon**) COLLOQ one's own affair, business or concern.

pie¹ N a savoury or sweet dish, usu cooked in a container, consisting of a quantity of food with a covering of pastry, a base of pastry, or both.
◆ **pie in the sky** some hoped-for but unguaranteed future prospect.

pie² or **pi** N 1 PRINTING confusedly mixed type. 2 a mixed state; confusion.

piebald ADJ having contrasting patches of colour, esp black and white. ➤ N a horse with black and white markings.

piece N 1 a portion of some material; a bit. 2 any of the sections into which something is divided; a portion taken from a whole. 3 a component part: **a jigsaw piece**. 4 an item in a set. 5 an individual member of a class of things represented by a collective noun: **a piece of clothing**. 6 a specimen or example of something: **a fine piece of Chippendale**. 7 an instance: **a piece of nonsense**. 8 a musical, artistic, literary or dramatic work. 9 an article in a newspaper, etc. 10 a coin: **a 50 pence piece**. 11 one of the tokens or men used in a board game. 12 a cannon or firearm.
◆ **all in one piece** undamaged, unhurt, intact.
◆ **go to pieces** COLLOQ to lose emotional control; to panic.
◆ **of a piece with sth** consistent with it.
◆ **a piece of one's mind** a frank and outspoken reprimand.
◆ **piece sth** or **things together** to join it or them together to form a whole.

◆ **say one's piece** to make one's contribution to a discussion.

piecemeal ADV a bit at a time.

piece of cake N something that is easy.

piecework N work paid for according to the amount done, not the time taken to do it.

pied ADJ of a bird: having variegated plumage, esp of black and white.

pier N **1 a** a structure built of stone, wood or iron, projecting into water for use as a landing-stage or breakwater; **b** such a structure used as a promenade with funfair-like sideshows, amusement arcades, etc. **2** a pillar supporting a bridge or arch. **3** the masonry between two openings in the wall of a building.

pierce VB (also **pierce through sth**) **1** of a sharp object or a person using one: to make a hole in or through; to puncture; to make (a hole) with something sharp. **2** to penetrate or force a way through or into something. **3** of light or sound: to burst through (darkness or silence). **4** to affect or touch (someone's heart, soul, etc) keenly or painfully.

pietism N pious feeling or an exaggerated show of piety. ■ **pietist** N.

piety N **1** dutifulness; devoutness. **2** the quality of being pious, dutiful or religiously devout.

piezoelectricity N electricity produced by stretching or compressing quartz crystals and other non-conducting crystals.
■ **piezoelectric** ADJ.

piffle N, COLLOQ nonsense; rubbish.

piffling ADJ, COLLOQ trivial, trifling or petty.

pig N **1** a hoofed omnivorous mammal with a stout heavy bristle-covered body and a protruding flattened snout, kept worldwide for its meat. **2** an abusive term for a person, esp someone greedy, dirty, selfish or brutal. **3** SLANG an unpleasant job or situation. **4** OFFENSIVE SLANG a policeman. **5 a** a quantity of metal cast into an oblong mass; **b** the mould into which it is run.
➤ VB (**-gg-**) **1** of a pig: to produce young. **2** TR & INTR of a person: to eat greedily.

◆ **make a pig of oneself** COLLOQ to eat greedily.
◆ **make a pig's ear of sth** COLLOQ to make a mess of it; to botch it.
◆ **a pig in a poke** COLLOQ a purchase made without first checking whether it is suitable.
◆ **pig out** to eat a large amount with relish and overindulgence; to overeat.

pigeon¹ N **1** a medium-sized bird with a plump body, a rounded tail and dense soft grey, brown or pink plumage. **2** SLANG a dupe or simpleton.

pigeon² see **pidgin** (sense 2)

pigeonhole N **1** any of a set of compartments, eg in a desk or on a wall, for filing letters or papers in. **2** a compartment of the mind.
➤ VB **1** to put something into a pigeonhole. **2** to put someone or something mentally into a category, esp too readily or rigidly.

pigeon-toed ADJ of a person: standing and walking with their toes turned in.

piggery N (**-ies**) **1** a place where pigs are bred. **2** COLLOQ greediness or otherwise disgusting behaviour.

piggish ADJ, DEROG greedy, dirty, selfish, mean or ill-mannered. ■ **piggishness** N.

piggyback N a ride on someone's back, with the legs supported by the bearer's arms.

piggy bank N a child's pig-shaped china container for saving money in.

pigheaded ADJ stupidly obstinate.

pig iron N, METALLURGY an impure form of iron produced by smelting iron in a blast furnace.

piglet N a young pig.

pigment N **1** any insoluble colouring matter that is used in suspension in water, oil or other liquids to give colour to paint, paper, etc. **2** a coloured substance that occurs naturally in living tissues.
➤ VB to colour something with pigment; to dye or stain. ■ **pigmentation** N.

pigmy see **pygmy**

pigskin N leather made from the skin of a pig.

pigsty N (*-ies*) **1** a pen where pigs are kept. **2** COLLOQ a filthy and disordered place.

pigtail N a plaited length of hair worn hanging at the sides or back of the head.

pike[1] N (*pike* or *pikes*) a large predatory freshwater fish with a narrow pointed head and a small number of large teeth in the lower jaw.

pike[2] N **1** HIST a weapon like a spear, consisting of a metal point mounted on a long shaft. **2** a point or spike. **3** N ENGLISH DIALECT a pointed hill or summit.

pike[3] N **1** a turnpike. **2** US a main road.

pikestaff N the shaft of a **pike**[2].
◆ **plain as a pikestaff** all too obvious.

pilau, **pilaf** or **pilaff** N an oriental dish of spiced rice with, or to accompany, chicken, fish, etc. Also AS ADJ: pilau rice.

pilchard N a small edible marine fish.

pile[1] N **1** a number of things lying on top of each other. **2** (**a pile** or **piles**) COLLOQ a large quantity. **3** COLLOQ a fortune: **made a pile on the horses**. **4** a massive or imposing building. **5** a pyre. **6** a nuclear reactor. Also called **atomic pile**.
➤ VB, TR & INTR (usu **pile up** or **pile sth up**) to accumulate into a pile.
◆ **pile in** or **into sth** or **pile off**, **out**, etc to move in a crowd or confused bunch into or off, etc.

pile[2] N a heavy wooden shaft, stone or concrete pillar, etc driven into the ground as a support for a building, bridge, etc.

pile[3] N **1** the raised cropped threads that give a soft thick surface to carpeting, velvet, etc. **2** soft fine hair, fur, wool, etc.

pile-driver N a machine for driving piles (see **pile**[2]) into the ground.

piles PL N haemorrhoids.

pile-up N a vehicle collision in which following vehicles also crash.

pilfer VB, TR & INTR to steal in small quantities.

pilgrim N **1** someone who makes a journey to a holy place as an act of reverence. **2** a traveller. ■ **pilgrimage** N.

pill N **1** a small ball or tablet of medicine, for swallowing. **2** something unpleasant that one must accept. **3** (**the pill**) an oral contraceptive for women.

pillage VB, TR & INTR to plunder or loot.
➤ N **1** the act of pillaging. **2** loot, plunder or booty. ■ **pillager** N.

pillar N **1** a vertical post of wood, stone, metal or concrete serving as a support to a main structure. **2** any slender vertical mass of something, eg of smoke, rock, etc. **3** a strong and reliable supporter of a cause, etc.
◆ **from pillar to post** from one place to another, esp moving between these in desperation, frustration, etc.

pillar box see **letter box**

pillbox N **1** a small round container for pills. **2** MIL a small, usu circular, concrete shelter for use as a lookout post and gun emplacement.

pillion N a seat for a passenger on a motorcycle or horse, behind the driver or rider.
➤ ADV on a pillion: **to ride pillion**.

pillock N, BRIT SLANG a stupid or foolish person.

pillory N (*-ies*) HIST a wooden frame with holes for the hands and head, into which wrongdoers were locked as a punishment and ridiculed.
➤ VB (*-ies*, *-ied*) **1** to hold someone up to public ridicule. **2** to put someone in a pillory.

pillow N **1** a cushion for the head, esp a large rectangular one on a bed. **2** anything that resembles a pillow in shape, feel or function.

pilot N **1** someone who flies an aircraft, hovercraft, spacecraft, etc. **2** someone employed to conduct or steer ships into and out of harbour. **3** someone who is qualified to act as pilot. **4** a guide. **5** AS ADJ of a scheme, programme, test, etc: serving as a preliminary test which may be modified before the final version is put into effect: **a pilot project**.
➤ VB **1** to act as pilot to someone. **2** to direct, guide or steer (a project, etc).

pilot light N 1 a small permanent gas flame, eg on a gas cooker, that ignites the main burners when they are turned on. 2 an indicator light on an electrical apparatus showing when it is on.

pimento N 1 a small tropical evergreen tree, cultivated mainly in Jamaica. 2 any of the dried unripe berries of this tree which are a source of allspice. Also called **allspice**. 3 the pimiento.

pimiento N 1 a variety of sweet pepper, widely cultivated for its mild-flavoured red fruit. 2 the fruit of this plant, eaten raw or cooked.

pimp N a man who finds customers for a prostitute or a brothel and lives off the earnings. ➤ VB, INTR to act as a pimp.

pimpernel N a small sprawling plant.

pimple N a small raised often pus-containing swelling on the skin. ■ **pimply** ADJ (*-ier, -iest*).

PIN ABBREV personal identification number, a multi-digit number used to authorize electronic transactions, such as cash withdrawal from a dispenser at a bank, access to an account via a telephone line, etc.

pin N 1 a short slender implement with a sharp point and small round head, usu made of stainless steel, for fastening, attaching, etc, and used esp in dressmaking. 2 IN COMPOUNDS a fastening device consisting of or incorporating a slender metal or wire shaft: **hatpin**. 3 a narrow brooch. 4 IN COMPOUNDS any of several cylindrical wooden or metal objects with various functions: **a rolling-pin**. 5 a peg. 6 any or either of the cylindrical or square-sectioned legs on an electric plug. 7 a club-shaped object set upright for toppling with a ball: **ten-pin bowling**. 8 the clip on a grenade, that is removed before it is thrown. 9 (**pins**) COLLOQ one's legs: **shaky on my pins**.
➤ VB (*-nn-*) to secure it with a pin.
◆ **pin sb down** to force a commitment or definite expression of opinion from them.
◆ **pin sth down** to identify it precisely.
◆ **pin sth** or **sb down** to hold them fast.
◆ **pin sth on sb** COLLOQ to put the blame for (a crime or offence) on them.

pinafore N 1 an apron, esp one with a bib.

2 (also **pinafore dress**) a sleeveless dress for wearing over a blouse, sweater, etc.

pinball N a game played on a slot machine, in which a small metal ball is propelled by flippers round a course, the score depending on what hazards it avoids and targets it hits.

pince-nez PL N spectacles that are held in position by a clip gripping the nose.

pincers PL N 1 a hinged tool with two claw-like jaws joined by a pivot, used for gripping objects, pulling nails, etc. 2 the modified claw-like appendage of a decapod crustacean, eg a crab or lobster, adapted for grasping.

pinch VB 1 to squeeze or nip the flesh of someone or something, between thumb and finger. 2 to compress or squeeze something painfully. 3 eg of cold or hunger: to affect someone or something painfully or injuriously. 4 TR & INTR of tight shoes: to hurt or chafe. 5 TR & INTR, COLLOQ to steal. 6 INTR to cause hardship. 7 INTR to economize: **had to pinch and scrape to get by**. 8 COLLOQ to arrest someone.
➤ N 1 an act of pinching; a nip or squeeze. 2 the quantity of something (eg salt) held between thumb and finger. 3 a very small amount. 4 a critical time of difficulty or hardship.
◆ **at a pinch** COLLOQ if absolutely necessary.
◆ **feel the pinch** COLLOQ to find life, work, etc difficult because of lack of money.

pinchbeck N a copper-zinc alloy with the appearance of gold, used in cheap jewellery.

pinched ADJ of a person's appearance: pale and haggard from tiredness, cold, etc.

pincushion N a pad into which to stick dressmaking pins for convenient storage.

pine[1] N 1 (also **pine tree**) an evergreen coniferous tree with narrow needle-like leaves. 2 (also **pinewood**) the pale durable wood of this tree, used to make furniture, and widely used in construction work.

pine[2] VB, INTR 1 (also **pine for sb** or **sth**) to long or yearn for them or it. 2 (also **pine away**) to waste away from grief or longing.

pineal gland and **pineal body** N, ANAT a small outgrowth from the roof of the forebrain, which produces hormones.

pineapple N **1** a tropical S American plant widely cultivated for its large edible fruit. **2** the fruit of this plant with sweet juicy yellow flesh covered by a yellowish-brown spiny skin.

ping N a sharp ringing sound like that made by plucking a taut wire, lightly striking glass, etc.

ping-pong N table tennis.

pinhead N **1** the little rounded or flattened head of a pin. **2** something that is very small. **3** SLANG a stupid person. ■ **pinheaded** ADJ.

pinhole N a tiny hole made by, or as if by, a pin.

pinion¹ VB **1** to immobilize someone by holding or binding their arms; to hold or bind (someone's arms). **2** to hold fast or bind.
➤ N **1** the extreme tip of a bird's wing. **2** a bird's flight feather.

pinion² N a small cogwheel that engages with a larger wheel or rack.

pink¹ N **1** a light or pale-red colour, between red and white. **2** a plant, eg a carnation, which has grass-like bluish-green leaves and flowers with five spreading toothed or slightly frilled petals. **3** a scarlet hunting-coat or its colour. **4** the highest point: **in the pink of condition**.
➤ ADJ **1** having, being or referring to the colour pink. **2** slightly left-wing. ■ **pinkness** N.
◆ **in the pink** COLLOQ in the best of health.

pink² VB to cut (cloth) with a serrated edge that frays less readily than a straight edge.

pinkie or **pinky** N (-ies) SCOT & N AMER the little finger.

pinking shears PL N scissors with a serrated blade for cutting a zig-zag edge in cloth.

pinnace N a small boat carried on a larger ship; a ship's boat.

pinnacle N **1** a slender spire crowning a buttress, gable, roof or tower. **2** a rocky peak. **3** a high point of achievement.

pinnate ADJ, BOT denoting a compound leaf that consists of pairs of leaflets arranged in two rows on either side of a central axis or midrib. ■ **pinnately** ADV.

pinny short for **pinafore** (sense 1).

pinpoint VB to place, define or identify something precisely.

pinprick N **1** a tiny hole made by, or as if by, a pin. **2** a slight irritation or annoyance.

pinstripe N **1** a very narrow stripe in cloth. **2** cloth with such stripes. ■ **pinstriped** ADJ.

pint N **1** in the UK, in the imperial system: a unit of liquid measure equivalent to on eighth of a gallon, equivalent to 0.568 litre (liquid or dry). **2** in the US: a unit of liquid measure equivalent to one eighth of a gallon, equivalent to 0.473 litre (liquid) and 0.551 litre (dry).

pint-size or **pint-sized** ADJ, HUMOROUS of a person: very small.

pin-up N a picture of a famous or glamorous person that one pins on one's wall.

pioneer N **1** an explorer of, or settler in, hitherto unknown or wild country. **2** someone who breaks new ground in anything; an innovator.
➤ VB **1** INTR to be a pioneer; to be innovative. **2** to explore and open up (a route, etc). **3** to try out, originate or develop (a technique, etc).

pious ADJ **1** religiously devout. **2** dutiful. **3** DEROG sanctimonious.

pip¹ N the small seed of a fruit such as an apple, pear, orange or grape. ■ **pipless** ADJ.

pip² N one of a series of short high-pitched signals on the radio, telephone, etc.

pip³ VB (-pp-) to defeat someone narrowly.
◆ **pipped at the post** COLLOQ overtaken narrowly in the closing stages of a contest, etc.

pip⁴ N **1** one of the emblems or spots on playing-cards, dice or dominoes. **2** MIL in the British army: a star on a uniform indicating rank.

pip⁵ N.
◆ **give sb the pip** COLLOQ to irritate them.

pipe¹ N **1** a tubular conveyance for water, gas, oil, etc. **2 a** a little bowl with a hollow stem for smoking tobacco, etc; **b** a quantity of tobacco smoked in one of these. **3** a wind instrument consisting of a simple tube. **4** (**the pipes**) the bagpipes. **5** any of the vertical metal tubes

through which sound is produced on an organ. **6** a boatswain's whistle. **7** a pipe-like vent forming part of a volcano.
➤ VB **1** to convey (gas, water, oil, etc) through pipes. **2** TR & INTR to play on a pipe or the pipes. **3** TR & INTR of a child: to speak or say in a small shrill voice. **4** INTR to sing shrilly as a bird does. **5 a** to use a bag with a nozzle in order to force (icing etc from the bag) into long strings for decorating a cake, etc; **b** to make (designs, etc) on a cake, etc this way.
◆ **pipe down** COLLOQ to stop talking; to be quiet: Will you please pipe down!

pipe² N **1** a cask or butt of varying capacity, but usu about 105 gallons in Britain (equal to 126 US gallons), used for wine or oil. **2** a measure of this amount.

pipe dream N a delightful fantasy of the kind indulged in while smoking a pipe, orig one filled with opium.

pipeline N a series of connected pipes laid underground to carry oil, natural gas, water, etc, across large distances.
◆ **in the pipeline** COLLOQ under consideration; forthcoming or in preparation.

piper N a player of a pipe or the bagpipes.

pipette N a small laboratory device usu consisting of a narrow tube into which liquid can be sucked.

piping N **1** a length of pipe, or a system or series of pipes conveying water, oil, etc. **2** covered cord forming a decorative edging on upholstery or clothing. **3** strings and knots of icing or cream decorating a cake or dessert. **4** the art of playing a pipe or the bagpipes.

pipistrelle N the smallest European bat.

pipit N a small ground-dwelling songbird with streaked brown plumage and a long tail.

pippin N any of several varieties of eating apple with a green or rosy skin.

pipsqueak N, DEROG COLLOQ someone or something insignificant or contemptible.

piquant ADJ **1** having a pleasantly spicy taste or tang. **2** amusing, intriguing, provocative or

stimulating. ■ **piquancy** N.

pique N resentment; hurt pride.
➤ VB **1** to hurt someone's pride; to offend or nettle them. **2** to arouse (curiosity or interest). **3** to pride (oneself) on something.

piracy N (**-ies**) **1** the activity of pirates, such as robbery on the high seas. **2** unauthorized reproduction of copyright material.

piranha or **piraña** N an extremely aggressive S American freshwater fish, with sharp saw-edged teeth.

pirate N **1** someone who attacks and robs ships at sea. **2** the ship used by pirates. **3** someone who publishes material without permission from the copyright-holder. **4** someone who runs a radio station without a licence.
➤ VB to publish, reproduce or use (someone else's literary or artistic work, or ideas) without legal permission. ■ **piratic** or **piratical** ADJ.

pirouette N a spin on tiptoe in dancing.
➤ VB, INTR to execute a pirouette.

piscatorial and **piscatory** ADJ, FORMAL relating to fish or fishing.

Pisces N, ASTROL the twelfth sign of the zodiac (the Fishes).

pisciculture N the rearing of fish by artificial methods or under controlled conditions. ■ **pisciculturist** N.

piscina N (**-ae** or **-as**) a stone basin with a drain, found in older churches, in which to empty water used for rinsing the sacred vessels.

piscine ADJ referring or relating to, or resembling, a fish or fishes.

piss VB **1** INTR, COARSE SLANG, SOMETIMES CONSIDERED TABOO to urinate. **2** to discharge something (eg blood) in the urine.
➤ N **1** urine. **2** an act of urinating.

pistachio N **1** a small deciduous tree with greenish flowers and reddish-brown nut-like fruits containing edible seeds. **2** the edible greenish seed of this tree.

piste N a ski slope of compacted snow.

pistil N, BOT in a flowering plant: the female reproductive structure.

pistol N a small gun held in one hand.

piston N, ENG a cylindrical device that moves up and down in the cylinder of an engine.

pit[1] N 1 a big deep hole in the ground. 2 a mine, esp a coalmine. 3 a cavity sunk into the ground from which to inspect vehicle engines, etc. 4 (**the pits**) MOTOR SPORT any of a set of areas beside a racetrack where vehicles can refuel, have wheel changes, etc. 5 an enclosure in which fighting animals or birds are put. 6 a the floor of the auditorium in a theatre; b the people sitting there. 7 ANAT a hollow, indentation or depression. 8 a scar left by a smallpox or acne pustule. 9 (**the pits**) SLANG an awful or intolerable situation, person, etc.
➤ VB (**-tt-**) to mark with scars and holes.
◆ **pit oneself against sb** to set or match oneself against them in competition.

pit[2] N, N AMER the stone in a peach, apricot, etc.
➤ VB (**-tt-**) to remove the stone from (fruit).

pit-a-pat N 1 a noise of pattering. 2 a succession of light taps.

pitch[1] VB 1 to set up (a tent or camp). 2 to throw or fling. 3 TR & INTR to fall or make someone or something fall heavily forward. 4 INTR of a ship: to plunge and lift alternately at bow and stern. 5 TR & INTR of a roof: to slope: **is pitched at a steep angle**. 6 to give a particular musical pitch to (one's voice or a note) in singing or playing, or to set (a song, etc) at a higher or lower level within a possible range: **The tune is pitched too high for me**. 7 to choose a level, eg of difficulty, etc at which to present (a talk, etc).
➤ N 1 the field or area of play in any of several sports. 2 an act or style of pitching or throwing. 3 a degree of intensity; a level: **reached such a pitch of excitement**. 4 a the angle of steepness of a slope; b such a slope. 5 MUS the degree of highness or lowness of a note that results from the frequency of the vibrations producing it. 6 a line in sales talk, esp one often made use of.
◆ **pitch in** COLLOQ 1 to begin enthusiastically. 2 to join in; to make a contribution.
◆ **pitch into sb** COLLOQ to rebuke or blame them angrily.

pitch[2] N a thick black sticky substance obtained from coal tar.

pitch-black or **pitch-dark** ADJ utterly, intensely or unrelievedly black or dark.

pitchblende N, GEOL a radioactive glossy brown or black form of uraninite, the main ore of uranium and radium.

pitcher[1] N a large earthenware jug with either one or two handles. ■ **pitcherful** N.

pitcher[2] N, BASEBALL the player who throws the ball to the person batting to hit.

pitchfork N a long-handled fork with two or three sharp prongs, for tossing hay.

piteous ADJ arousing one's pity; moving, poignant, heartrending or pathetic.

pitfall N a hidden danger, unsuspected hazard or unforeseen difficulty.

pith N 1 the soft white tissue that lies beneath the rind of many citrus fruits, eg orange. 2 BOT in the stem of many plants: a central cylinder of generally soft tissue. 3 the most important part of an argument, etc. 4 substance, forcefulness or vigour as a quality in writing, etc.

pithy ADJ (**-ier, -iest**) 1 of a saying, comment, etc: brief, forceful and to the point. 2 referring to, resembling or full of pith. ■ **pithily** ADV. ■ **pithiness** N.

pitiable ADJ 1 arousing pity. 2 miserably inadequate; contemptible.

pitiful ADJ arousing pity; wretched or pathetic. ■ **pitifully** ADV.

pitiless ADJ showing no pity; merciless, cruel or relentless. ■ **pitilessly** ADV.

piton N, MOUNTAINEERING a metal peg or spike with an eye for passing a rope through, hammered into a rockface.

pitstop N, MOTOR SPORT a pause made at a refuelling pit by a racing driver.

pitta N a Middle-Eastern slightly leavened bread, usu in a hollow oval shape.

pittance N a meagre allowance or wage.

pitter-patter N the sound of pattering.
➤ ADV with this sound.
➤ VB, INTR to make such a sound.

pituitary N (*-ies*) short form of **pituitary gland**.
➤ ADJ relating to this gland.

pituitary gland or **pituitary body** N, PHYSIOL an endocrine gland at the base of the brain producing important hormones.

pity N (*-ies*) **1** a feeling of sorrow for the troubles and sufferings of others; compassion. **2** a cause of sorrow or regret.
➤ VB (*-ies, -ied*) to feel or show pity for someone or something.

pivot N **1** a central pin, spindle or pointed shaft round which something revolves, balances or oscillates. **2** someone or something crucial, on which everything else depends.
➤ VB **1** INTR (often **pivot on sth**) **a** to turn, swivel or revolve; **b** to depend. **2** to mount something on a pivot.

pivotal ADJ **1** constructed as or acting like a pivot. **2** crucially important; critical.

pixel N, ELECTRONICS the smallest element of the image displayed on a computer or TV screen.

pixie or **pixy** N (*-ies*) MYTHOL a kind of fairy, traditionally with mischievous tendencies.

pizza N a circle of dough spread with cheese, tomatoes, etc and baked, made orig in Italy.

pizzazz, **pazzazz**, **pizazz** or **pazazz** N, COLLOQ a quality that is a combination of boldness, vigour, dash and flamboyance.

pizzeria N a restaurant specializing in pizzas.

pizzicato MUS, ADJ, ADV of stringed instruments: played using the fingers to pluck the strings.

placable ADJ easily appeased.

placard N a board or stiff card bearing a notice, advertisement, slogan, message of protest, etc, carried or displayed in public.
➤ VB **1** to put placards on (a wall, etc). **2** to announce (an event, etc) by placard.

placate VB to pacify or appease (someone who is angry, etc). ■ **placatory** ADJ.

place N **1** a portion of the Earth's surface, particularly one considered as a unit, such as an area, region, district, locality, etc. **2** a geographic area or position, such as a country, city, town, village, etc. **3** a building, room, piece of ground, etc, particularly one assigned to some purpose: **place of business**. **4** COLLOQ one's home or lodging: **Let's go to my place**. **5** IN COMPOUNDS somewhere with a specified association or function: **one's birthplace**. **6** a seat or space, eg at table: **lay three places**. **7** a seat in a theatre, on a train, bus, etc. **8** an area on the surface of something, eg on the body: **point to the sore place**. **9** the customary position of something or someone: **put it back in its place**. **10** a point reached, eg in a conversation, narrative, series of developments, etc: **a good place to stop**. **11** a point in a book, etc, esp where one stopped reading: **made me lose my place**. **12** a position within an order eg of competitors in a contest, a set of priorities, etc: **finished in third place**. **13** social or political rank: **know one's place**. **14** a vacancy at an institution, on a committee, in a firm, etc: **a university place**. **15** one's role, function, duty, etc. **16** an open square or a row of houses: **the market place**.
➤ VB **1** to put, position, etc in a particular place. **2** to submit: **place an order**. **3** to find a place, home, job, publisher, etc for someone. **4** to assign final positions to (contestants, etc): **was placed fourth**. **5** to identify or categorize: **a familiar voice that I couldn't quite place**. **6** COMMERCE to find a buyer for (stocks or shares). **7** to arrange (a bet, loan, etc). **8** INTR, esp N AMER to finish a race or competition (in a specified position or, if unspecified, in second position).
◆ **go places** COLLOQ **1** to travel. **2** to be successful.
◆ **in place of sth** or **sb** instead of it or them.
◆ **know one's place** to show proper subservience (to someone, etc).
◆ **lose one's place** to falter in following a text, etc; not to know what point has been reached.
◆ **out of place 1** not in the correct position. **2** inappropriate.
◆ **put** or **keep sb in their place** to humble

them as they deserve because of their arrogance, conceit, etc.
◆ **take one's place** to assume one's usual or rightful position.
◆ **take place** to happen, occur, be held, etc.

placebo N, MED a substance that is administered as a drug but has no medicinal content.

placement N **1** the act or process of placing or positioning. **2** the finding of a job or home for someone.

placename N the name of a town, hill, etc.

placenta N (*-tas* or *-tae*) in mammals: a disc-shaped organ attached to the lining of the uterus during pregnancy and through which the embryo obtains nutrients and oxygen.
■ **placental** ADJ.

placid ADJ calm; tranquil. ■ **placidity** or **placidness** N. ■ **placidly** ADV.

placket N, DRESSMAKING **1** an opening in a skirt for a pocket or at the fastening. **2** a piece of material sewn behind this.

plagiarize or **-ise** VB, TR & INTR to copy (ideas, passages of text, etc) from someone else's work and use them as if they were one's own.
■ **plagiarism** N. ■ **plagiarist** N.

plague N **1** MED **a** any of several epidemic diseases with a high mortality rate; **b** specifically, an infectious bacterial epidemic disease of rats and other rodents, transmitted to humans by flea bites. **2** an overwhelming intrusion by something unwelcome: **a plague of tourists**. **3** COLLOQ a nuisance. **4** an affliction regarded as a sign of divine displeasure.
➢ VB **1** to afflict someone: **plagued by headaches**. **2** to pester someone.

plaice N (PL *plaice*) a flatfish that has a brown upper surface covered with bright orange spots, and is an important food fish.

plaid N **1** tartan cloth. **2** a long piece of woollen cloth worn over the shoulder, usu as part of Scottish Highland dress.

plain ADJ **1** all of one colour; unpatterned; undecorated. **2** simple; unsophisticated;

without improvement, embellishment or pretensions: **plain food**. **3** obvious; clear. **4** straightforward; direct: **plain language**. **5** frank; open. **6** of a person: lacking beauty. **7** sheer; downright: **plain selfishness**.
➢ N **1** a large area of relatively smooth flat land without significant hills or valleys. **2** KNITTING the simpler of two basic stitches, with the wool passed round the front of the needle.
➢ ADV utterly; quite: **just plain stupid**.
■ **plainly** ADV. ■ **plainness** N.

plain clothes PL N ordinary clothes worn by police officers on duty, as distinct from uniform.
➢ ADJ (**plain-clothes** or **plain-clothed**) wearing ordinary clothes, not uniformed.

plain sailing N easy unimpeded progress.

plainsong N music for unaccompanied voices, sung in unison.

plaint N **1** POETIC an expression of woe; a lamentation. **2** LAW a written statement of grievance submitted to a court of law.

plaintiff N, LAW someone who brings a case against another person in a court of law.

plaintive ADJ mournful-sounding; sad; wistful.

plait VB to arrange something (esp hair) by interweaving three or more lengths of it.
➢ N a length of hair or other material interwoven in this way. ■ **plaited** ADJ.

plan N **1** a thought-out arrangement or method for doing something. **2** (usu **plans**) intentions: **What are your plans for today?** **3** a sketch, outline, scheme or set of guidelines. **4** a large-scale detailed drawing or diagram of a floor of a house, the streets of a town, etc done as though viewed from above.
➢ VB (*-nn-*) **1** (also **plan for sth**) to devise a scheme for it. **2** (also **plan for sth**) to make preparations or arrangements for it. **3** INTR to prepare; to make plans: **plan ahead**. **4** (also **plan on sth**) to intend or expect it. **5** to draw up plans for (eg a building); to design.

plane[1] N an aeroplane.

plane[2] N **1** MATH a flat surface, either real or imaginary, such that a straight line joining any two points lies entirely on it. **2** a level surface.

3 a level or standard: **on a higher plane**.
➤ ADJ **1** flat; level. **2** having the character of a plane. **3** MATH lying in one plane: **a plane figure** • **plane geometry**.
➤ VB, INTR **1** of a boat: to skim over the surface of the water. **2** of a bird: to wheel or soar with the wings motionless.

plane³ N a carpenter's tool for smoothing wood by shaving away unevennesses.
➤ VB (also **plane sth down**) to smooth (a surface, esp wood) with a plane.

plane⁴ N a large deciduous tree with thin bark which is shed in large flakes.

planet N, ASTRON a celestial body, in orbit around the Sun or another star.

planetarium N (**-ia** or **-iums**) **1** a special projector by means of which the positions and movements of stars and planets can be projected on to a hemispherical domed ceiling. **2** the building that houses such a projector.

planetary ADJ **1** ASTRON **a** relating to or resembling a planet; **b** consisting of or produced by planets; **c** revolving in an orbit. **2** ASTROL under the influence of a planet.

plangent ADJ of a sound: deep, ringing and mournful. ■ **plangency** N.

plank N **1** a long flat piece of timber thicker than a board. **2** any of the policies forming the platform or programme of a political party.
➤ VB to fit or cover something with planks.

plankton N, BIOL microscopic animals and plants that passively float or drift with the current in the surface waters of seas and lakes.

planner N **1** someone who draws up plans or designs. **2** a wall calendar showing the whole year, on which holidays, etc can be marked.

plant N **1** any living organism that is capable of manufacturing carbohydrates by the process of photosynthesis and that typically possesses cell walls containing cellulose. **2** a relatively small organism of this type, eg a herb or shrub as opposed to a tree. **3** the buildings, equipment and machinery used in the manufacturing or production industries, eg a factory, a power station, etc. **4** COLLOQ

something deliberately placed for others to find and be misled by. **5** COLLOQ a spy placed in an organization in order to gain information, etc.
➤ VB **1** to put (seeds or plants) into the ground to grow. **2** (often **plant sth out**) to put plants or seeds into (ground, a garden, bed, etc). **3** to introduce (an idea, doubt, etc) into someone's mind. **4** to place something firmly. **5** to post someone as a spy in an office, factory, etc. **6** COLLOQ to place something deliberately so as to mislead the finder, esp as a means of incriminating an innocent person.

plantain N a plant belonging to the banana family, widely cultivated for its edible fruit.

plantation N **1** an estate, esp in the tropics, that specializes in the large-scale production of a single cash crop, eg tea, coffee, cotton or rubber. **2** an area of land planted with a certain kind of tree for commercial purposes: **a conifer plantation**. **3** HIST a colony.

plaque N **1** a commemorative inscribed tablet fixed to or set into a wall. **2** a thin layer of food debris, bacteria and calcium salts that forms on teeth and may cause tooth decay.

plasma N, PHYSIOL the colourless liquid component of blood or lymph.

plaster N **1** a material consisting of lime, sand and water applied to walls when soft and drying to form a hard smooth surface. **Also AS ADJ**. **2** a strip of material with an adhesive backing used for covering and protecting small wounds. Also called **sticking-plaster**.
➤ VB **1** to apply plaster to (walls, etc). **2** (usu **plaster sth with** or **on sth**) COLLOQ to coat or spread thickly. **3** to fix something with some wet or sticky substance: **hair plastered to his skull**.
■ **plasterer** N. ■ **plastering** N.

plasterboard N hardened plaster faced on both sides with paper or thin board, used to form or line interior walls.

plastic N **1** any of a large number of synthetic materials that can be moulded by heat and/or pressure into a rigid or semi-rigid shape. **2** a credit card, or credit cards collectively.
➤ ADJ **1** made of plastic. **2** easily moulded or shaped; pliant. **3** easily influenced. **4** DEROG

artificial; lacking genuine substance. **5** of money: in the form of, or funded by, a credit card. **6** relating to sculpture and modelling. ■ **plasticity** N.

plasticizer or **-iser** N, CHEM an organic compound added to a rigid polymer to make it flexible and easily workable. ■ **plasticize** VB.

plastic surgery N, MED the branch of surgery concerned with the repair or reconstruction of deformed or damaged tissue or body parts, and cosmetic surgery. ■ **plastic surgeon** N.

plate N **1** a shallow dish, esp one made of earthenware or porcelain, for serving food on. Also IN COMPOUNDS: side plate • dinner plate. **2 a** the amount held by this; a plateful; **b** a portion served on a plate. **3** (also **collection plate**) a shallow vessel in which to take the collection in church. **4** a sheet of metal, glass or other rigid material. **5** a flat piece of metal, plastic, etc inscribed with a name, etc. Often IN COMPOUNDS: nameplate • bookplate. **6** gold and silver vessels or cutlery. **7 a** a gold or silver cup as the prize in a horse race, etc; **b** a race or contest for such a prize. **8** a thin coating of gold, silver or tin applied to a base metal. Also called **plating**. **9** an illustration on glossy paper in a book. **10** PHOTOG a sheet of glass prepared with a light-sensitive coating for receiving an image. **11 a** a sheet of metal with an image engraved on it; **b** a print taken from one of these. **12** a surface set up with type ready for printing. **13 a** a rigid plastic fitting to which false teeth are attached; **b** a denture. **14** GEOL any of the rigid sections that make up the Earth's crust. **15** ANAT a thin flat piece of bone or horn. **16** BASEBALL a white slab at the home base. ➤ VB **1** to coat (a base metal) with a thin layer of a precious one. **2** to cover something with metal plates. ■ **plateful** N.
◆ **have a lot on one's plate** COLLOQ to have a great deal of work, commitments, etc.
◆ **hand** or **give sb sth on a plate** COLLOQ to present them with it without their having to make the least effort.

plateau N (-teaux or -teaus) an extensive area of relatively flat high land.
➤ VB, INTR (sometimes **plateau out**) to reach a level; to even out.

plated ADJ **1** covered with plates of metal. **2** USU IN COMPOUNDS covered with a coating of another metal, esp gold or silver.

plate glass N a high-quality form of glass that has been ground and polished to remove defects, used in shop windows, mirrors, etc.

platelet N, PHYSIOL any of the small disc-shaped cell fragments responsible for starting the formation of a blood clot.

platen N **1** in some printing-presses: a plate that pushes the paper against the type. **2** the roller of a typewriter.

plate tectonics SING N a geological theory concerning the movements of the large plates of solid rock of which the Earth's crust is composed.

platform N **1** a raised floor for speakers, performers, etc. **2** the raised walkway alongside the track at a railway station. **3** a floating installation moored to the sea bed, for oil-drilling, etc. Often IN COMPOUNDS: oil platform • production platform. **4** an open step at the back of some buses, for passengers getting on or off. **5** a very thick rigid sole for a shoe. **6** the publicly declared principles of a political party, forming the basis of its policies.

plating N same as **plate** (noun sense 8).

platinum N, CHEM a silvery-white metallic element used to make jewellery, coins, etc.

platitude N an empty, unoriginal or redundant comment, esp one made as though it were important. ■ **platitudinous** ADJ.

platonic ADJ of human love: not involving sexual relations. ■ **platonically** ADV.

platoon N **1** MIL a subdivision of a company. **2** a squad of people acting in co-operation.

platter N a large flat dish.

platypus N an Australian egg-laying amphibious mammal with dense brown fur, a long flattened toothless snout and webbed feet. Also called **duck-billed platypus**.

plaudit N (usu **plaudits**) a commendation; an expression of praise.

plausible ADJ **1** credible, reasonable or likely. **2** of a person: characterized by having a pleasant and persuasive manner; smooth-tongued or glib. ■ **plausibility** N.

play VB **1** INTR to spend time in recreation, eg dancing about, kicking a ball around, doing things in make-believe, generally having fun, etc. **2** INTR to pretend for fun; to behave without seriousness. **3** (also **play at sth**) to take part in (a recreative pursuit, game, sport, match, round, etc): We played rounders. **4** to compete against in a game or sport: St Johnstone played Aberdeen. **5** INTR, COLLOQ to co-operate: He refuses to play. **6** SPORT to include someone as a team member: playing McGuire in goal. **7** SPORT to hit or kick (the ball), deliver (a shot), etc in a sport. **8** CARDS to use (a card) in the course of a game: played the three of clubs. **9** to speculate or gamble on (the stock exchange, etc): playing the market. **10** TR & INTR **a** to act or behave in a certain way: play it cool; **b** to pretend to be someone or something: play the dumb blonde. **11** to act (a particular role): play host to the delegates. **12** (usu **play in sth**) TR & INTR to perform a role in (a play): played Oliver in the school play. **13** TR & INTR to perform in (a particular place or venue): played Cardiff and Swansea. **14** INTR of a film, play, etc: to be shown or performed publicly: playing all next week. **15** MUS **a** to perform (a specified type of music) on an instrument: plays jazz on the saxophone; **b** to perform on (an instrument) **16** to turn on (a radio, a tape-recording, etc). **17** INTR **a** of recorded music, etc: to be heard from a radio, etc; **b** of a radio, etc: to produce sound. **18** ANGLING to allow (a fish) to tire itself by its struggles to get away. ➤ N **1** recreation; playing games for fun and amusement: children at play. **2** the playing of a game, performance in a sport, etc: rain stopped play. **3** COLLOQ behaviour; conduct: fair play. **4** a dramatic piece for the stage or a performance of it. **5** fun; jest: said in play. **6** range; scope: give full play to the imagination. **7** freedom of movement; looseness: too much play in the steering.

8 action or interaction: play of sunlight on water. **9** use: bring all one's cunning into play.
◆ **make a play for sth** to try to get (eg someone's attention).
◆ **play about** or **around with sth** to fiddle or meddle with it.
◆ **play sb along** to manipulate them.
◆ **play along with sb** to co-operate with them for the time being.
◆ **play ball** COLLOQ to co-operate.
◆ **play sth down** to represent it as unimportant.
◆ **play for time** to delay action or decision in the hope of more favourable conditions later.
◆ **play hard to get** to make a show of unwillingness to co-operate or lack of interest.
◆ **play into the hands of sb** to act so as to give, usu unintentionally, an advantage to them.
◆ **play it by ear** to improvise a plan of action to meet the situation as it develops.
◆ **play off 1** to replay a match, etc after a draw. **2** GOLF to play from the tee.
◆ **play one person off against another** to set them in rivalry.
◆ **play on sth 1** to exploit (someone's fears, feelings, sympathies, etc) for one's own benefit. **2** to make a pun on it: played on the two meanings of 'batter'.
◆ **play safe** to take no risks.
◆ **play up 1** COLLOQ to behave unco-operatively. **2** COLLOQ to cause one pain or discomfort. **3** COLLOQ of a machine, etc: to function faultily. **4** to try one's hardest.
◆ **play sth up** to give prominence to it.
◆ **play up to sb** to flatter them; to ingratiate oneself with them.
◆ **play with fire** to take foolish risks.
◆ **play with sth** to contemplate (an idea, plan, etc).

playboy N a man of wealth, leisure and frivolous lifestyle.

player N **1** someone who plays. **2** someone who participates in a game or sport, particularly as their profession. **3** COLLOQ a participant in a particular activity, esp a powerful one: a major player in the mafia scene. **4** OLD USE an actor.

playful ADJ **1** full of fun. **2** of a remark, etc:

humorous. ■ **playfully** ADV. ■ **playfulness** N.

playhouse N, OLD USE a theatre.

playing-card N a rectangular card belonging to a pack used in card games.

playmate N a companion to play with.

play-off N a match or game played to resolve a draw or other undecided contest.

playschool N a playgroup, or a school for children between the ages of two and five.

plaything N a toy, or a person or thing treated as if they were a toy.

playwright N an author of plays.

plaza N a large public square or market place.

PLC or **plc** ABBREV public limited company.

plea N 1 an earnest appeal. 2 LAW a statement made in a court of law by or on behalf of the defendant.

plead VB (*pleaded* or esp N AMER & SCOT *pled*) 1 (usu **plead with sb for sth**) to appeal earnestly to them for it: **pleading for mercy**. 2 INTR of an accused person: to state in a court of law that one is guilty or not guilty. 3 (also **plead for sth**) to argue in defence of it: **plead someone's case**. 4 to give something as an excuse: **plead ignorance**.

pleadings PL N, LAW the statements submitted by defendant and plaintiff in a lawsuit.

pleasant ADJ 1 giving pleasure; enjoyable; agreeable. 2 of a person: friendly; affable. ■ **pleasantly** ADV.

pleasantry N (*-ies*) 1 a remark made for the sake of politeness. 2 humour; teasing.

please VB 1 TR & INTR to give satisfaction, pleasure or enjoyment; to be agreeable to someone. 2 (WITH it as subject) FORMAL to be the inclination of someone or something: **if it should please you to join us**. 3 TR & INTR to choose; to like: **Do as you please**.
➤ ADV, EXCLAM used politely to accompany a request, acceptance of an offer, a call for attention, etc. ■ **pleased** ADJ. ■ **pleasing** ADJ.

pleasurable ADJ enjoyable; pleasant.

pleasure N 1 a feeling of enjoyment or satisfaction. 2 a source of such a feeling: **have the pleasure of your company**. 3 one's will, desire, wish or inclination. 4 recreation; enjoyment. Also AS ADJ: **a pleasure trip**. 5 gratification of a sensual kind.
◆ **with pleasure** gladly; willingly; of course.

pleat N a fold sewn or pressed into cloth, etc.
➤ VB to make pleats in (cloth, etc).

pleb N, DEROG someone who has coarse or vulgar tastes, manners or habits. ■ **plebby** ADJ.

plebeian N 1 a member of the common people, esp of ancient Rome. 2 DEROG someone who lacks refinement or culture.
➤ ADJ 1 referring or belonging to the common people. 2 DEROG coarse; vulgar; unrefined.

plebiscite N a vote of all the electors, taken to decide a matter of public importance.

plectrum N (*-rums* or *-ra*) a small flat implement of metal, plastic, horn, etc used for plucking the strings of a guitar.

pledge N 1 a solemn promise. 2 something left as security with someone to whom one owes money, etc. 3 something put into pawn. 4 a token or symbol.
➤ VB 1 to promise (money, loyalty, etc) to someone. 2 to bind or commit (oneself, etc). 3 to offer or give something as a pledge or guarantee.

plenary ADJ 1 full; complete: **plenary powers**. 2 of a meeting, assembly, council, etc: to be attended by all members, delegates, etc.

plenipotentiary ADJ entrusted with, or conveying, full authority to act on behalf of one's government or other organization.
➤ N (*-ies*) someone, eg an ambassador, invested with such authority.

plenitude N 1 abundance; profusion. 2 completeness; fullness.

plenteous ADJ, LITERARY plentiful; abundant.

plentiful ADJ in good supply; copious; abundant. ■ **plentifully** ADV.

plenty N 1 (often **plenty of sth**) a lot: **plenty of folk would agree**. 2 wealth or sufficiency; a

sufficient amount: **in times of plenty**.
➤ PRONOUN enough, or more than enough.

plenum N (*-nums* or *-na*) a meeting attended by all members.

plethora N a large or excessive amount.

pleura N (*-ae*) ANAT in mammals: the double membrane that covers the lungs and lines the chest cavity. ■ **pleural** ADJ.

pleurisy N, PATHOL, MED inflammation of the pleura. ■ **pleuritic** ADJ.

plexus N (*plexus* or *plexuses*) ANAT a network of nerves or blood vessels.

pliable ADJ 1 easily bent; flexible. 2 adaptable or alterable. 3 easily persuaded or influenced. ■ **pliability** N.

pliant ADJ 1 bending easily; pliable, flexible or supple. 2 easily influenced. ■ **pliancy** N.

pliers PL N a hinged tool with jaws for gripping small objects, bending or cutting wire, etc.

plight[1] N a danger, difficulty or situation of hardship that one finds oneself in.

plight[2] VB, OLD USE to promise solemnly.
◆ **plight one's troth** to pledge oneself in marriage.

plimsoll or **plimsole** N, OLD USE a light rubber-soled canvas shoe worn for gymnastics, etc. Also called **gym shoe**.

plinth N 1 ARCHIT a square block serving as the base of a column, pillar, etc. 2 a base or pedestal for a statue or other sculpture.

plod VB (*-dd-*) INTR 1 to walk slowly with a heavy tread. 2 to work slowly, methodically and thoroughly, if without inspiration. ■ **plodder** N.

plonk[1] COLLOQ, N the resounding thud made by a heavy object falling.
➤ VB 1 to put or place something with a thud. 2 INTR to place oneself or to fall with a plonk.
➤ ADV with a thud: **landed plonk beside her**.

plonk[2] N, COLLOQ cheap, undistinguished wine.

plop N the sound of a small object dropping into water without a splash.

➤ VB (*-pp-*) TR & INTR to drop with this sound.

plot[1] N 1 a secret plan, esp one laid jointly with others, for contriving something illegal or evil; a conspiracy. 2 the story of a play, novel, etc.
➤ VB (*-tt-*) 1 TR & INTR to plan something (esp something illegal or evil), usu with others. 2 to make a plan of something; to mark the course or progress of something. 3 MATH to mark (a series of individual points) on a graph, or to draw a curve through them.

plot[2] N, often IN COMPOUNDS a piece of ground for any of various uses: **vegetable plot**.

plough or (N AMER) **plow** N 1 a bladed farm implement used to turn over the surface of the soil and bury stubble, weeds, etc, in preparation for the cultivation of a crop. 2 any similar implement, esp a snowplough.
➤ VB 1 (also **plough sth up**) to till or turn over (soil, land, etc) with a plough. 2 INTR to make a furrow or to turn over the surface of the soil with a plough.
◆ **plough sth back** to re-invest (the profits of a business) in that business.
◆ **plough into sth** COLLOQ of a vehicle or its driver: to crash into it at speed.
◆ **plough on** COLLOQ to continue with something although progress is laborious.
◆ **plough through sth** 1 to move through it with a ploughing action. 2 COLLOQ to make steady but laborious progress with it.

ploughman or (N AMER) **plowman** N someone who steers a plough.

ploughshare or (N AMER) **plowshare** N a blade of a plough. Also called **share**.

plover N a wading bird with boldly patterned plumage and a short straight bill.

plow the N AMER spelling of **plough**

ploy N a stratagem, dodge or manoeuvre.

pluck VB 1 to pull the feathers off (a bird) before cooking it. 2 to pick (flowers or fruit) from a plant. 3 (often **pluck sth out**) to remove it by pulling. 4 to shape (the eyebrows) by removing hairs from them. 5 (also **pluck at sth**) to pull or tug it. 6 to sound (the strings of a violin, etc) using the fingers or a plectrum.

➤ N **1** courage; guts. **2** a little tug. **3** the heart, liver and lungs of an animal.

◆ **pluck up courage** to strengthen one's resolve for a difficult undertaking, etc.

plucky ADJ (*-ier, -iest*) COLLOQ courageous; spirited. ■ **pluckily** ADV. ■ **pluckiness** N.

plug N **1** a piece of rubber, plastic, etc shaped to fit a hole as a stopper, eg in a bath or sink. **2** often IN COMPOUNDS any device or piece of material for a similar purpose: **earplugs**. **3 a** the plastic or rubber device with metal pins, fitted to the end of the flex of an electrical apparatus, that is pushed into a socket to connect with the power supply; **b** LOOSELY the socket or power point. **4** COLLOQ a piece of favourable publicity given to a product, programme, etc, eg on television. **5** a spark plug. **6** an accumulation of solidified magma in the vent of a volcano.
➤ VB (*-gg-*) **1** (often **plug sth up**) to stop or block up (a hole, etc) with something. **2** COLLOQ to give favourable publicity to (a product, programme, etc), esp repeatedly: **plugged her new book**.

◆ **plug away** COLLOQ to work steadily.

plughole N the hole in a bath or sink through which water flows into the wastepipe.

plum N **1** a shrub or small tree, cultivated in temperate regions for its edible fruit, or for its ornamental flowers or foliage. **2** the smooth-skinned red, purple, green or yellow fruit of this tree, which has a hard central stone surrounded by sweet juicy flesh, eg damson, greengage. **3** IN COMPOUNDS a raisin used in cakes, etc: **plum pudding**. **4 a** COLLOQ something esp valued or sought; **b** AS ADJ: **a plum job**. **5** a deep dark-red colour.

plumage N a bird's feathers.

plumb N a lead weight, usu suspended from a line, used for measuring water depth or for testing a wall, etc for perpendicularity.
➤ ADJ straight, vertical or perpendicular.
➤ ADV **1** in a straight, vertical or perpendicular way. **2** COLLOQ exactly: **plumb in the middle**.
➤ VB **1** to measure the depth of (water), test (a structure) for verticality, or adjust something to the vertical, using a plumb. **2** to penetrate,

probe or understand (a mystery, etc). **3** (usu **plumb sth in**) to connect (a water-using appliance) to the water supply or waste pipe.

◆ **plumb the depths of sth** to experience the worst extreme of (a bad feeling, etc).

plumbago N, CHEM another name for **graphite**.

plumber N someone who fits and repairs water pipes, and water-using appliances.

plumbing N **1** the system of water and gas pipes in a building, etc. **2** the work of a plumber.

plumbline N a line with a plumb attached, used for testing for verticality.

plume N **1** a conspicuous feather of a bird. **2** a feather, or bunch of feathers, worn as an ornament or crest, represented in a coat of arms, etc. **3** a curling column (of smoke etc).
➤ VB **1** of a bird: to clean or preen (itself or its feathers). **2** to decorate with plumes. **3** (usu **plume oneself on sth**) to pride or congratulate oneself on it.

plummet VB, INTR to fall or drop rapidly; to plunge or hurtle downwards.
➤ N the weight on a plumbline or fishing-line.

plummy ADJ (*-ier, -iest*) DEROG of a voice: affectedly or excessively rich and deep.

plump¹ ADJ full, rounded or chubby; not unattractively fat.
➤ VB (often **plump sth up**) to shake (cushions or pillows) to give them their full soft bulk.

plump² COLLOQ, VB, TR & INTR (sometimes **plump down** or **plump sth down**) to put down, drop, fall or sit heavily.
➤ ADV **1** suddenly; with a plump. **2** in a blunt or direct way. **Also** AS ADJ.

◆ **plump for sb** or **sth** to choose them.

plunder VB, TR & INTR to steal (valuable goods) or loot (a place), esp with open force during a war; to rob or ransack.
➤ N the goods plundered; loot; booty.

plunge VB **1** INTR (usu **plunge in** or **into sth**) to dive, throw oneself, fall or rush headlong in or into it. **2** INTR (usu **plunge in** or **into sth**) to involve oneself rapidly and enthusiastically. **3** to

thrust or push something. **4** TR & INTR to put something or someone into a particular state or condition: **plunged into darkness. 5** to dip something briefly into water or other liquid. **6** INTR to dip steeply: **The ship plunged.**
➤ N **1** an act of plunging; a dive. **2** COLLOQ a dip or swim.
◆ **take the plunge** COLLOQ to take an irreversible decision.

plunger N a rubber suction cup at the end of a long handle, used to clear blocked drains, etc.

plunk VB **1** to pluck (the strings of a banjo, etc); to twang. **2** (often **plunk sth down**) to drop it.
➤ N the act of plunking or the sound this makes.

plural ADJ **1** GRAM denoting or referring to two or more people, things, etc as opposed to only one. **2** consisting of more than one, or of different kinds.
➤ N, GRAM a word or form of a word expressing the idea or involvement of two or more people, things, etc. ■ **pluralize** or **-ise** VB.

pluralism N the existence within a society of a variety of ethnic, cultural and religious groups. ■ **pluralist** N, ADJ. ■ **pluralistic** ADJ.

plurality N (-*ies*) **1** the state or condition of being plural. **2** a large number or variety.

plus PREP **1** MATH with the addition of (a specified number): **2 plus 5 equals 7. 2** in combination with something; with the added factor of (a specified thing).
➤ ADV after a specified amount: with something more besides: **Helen earns £20,000 plus.**
➤ ADJ **1** denoting the symbol '+': **the plus sign. 2** mathematically positive; above zero: **plus 3. 3** advantageous: **a plus factor. 4** in grades: denoting a slightly higher mark than the letter alone: **B plus. 5** PHYS, ELEC electrically positive.
➤ N **1** (also **plus sign**) the symbol '+', denoting addition or positive value. **2** COLLOQ something positive or good; a bonus, surplus, or extra.

plus fours PL N loose breeches gathered below the knee.

plush N a fabric with a long velvety pile.
➤ ADJ **1** made of plush. **2** COLLOQ plushy.

plushy ADJ (-*ier, -iest*) COLLOQ luxurious,

opulent, stylish or costly.

plutocracy N (-*ies*) **1** government or domination by the wealthy. **2** a state governed by the wealthy. **3** an influential group whose power is backed by their wealth.

plutocrat N **1** a member of a plutocracy. **2** COLLOQ a wealthy person. ■ **plutocratic** ADJ.

plutonium N, CHEM a dense highly poisonous silvery-grey radioactive metallic element, whose isotope plutonium-239 is used as an energy source for nuclear weapons.

pluvial ADJ of or characterized by rain; rainy.
➤ N, GEOL a period of prolonged rainfall.

ply[1] N (*plies*) **1 a** thickness of yarn, rope or wood, measured by the number of strands or layers that compose it; **b** IN COMPOUNDS, often AS ADJ specifying the number of strands or layers involved: **four-ply wool. 2** a strand or layer.

ply[2] VB (*plies, plied*) **1** (usu **ply sb with sth**) to keep supplying them with something or making a repeated, often annoying, onslaught on them: **plied them with drinks • plying me with questions. 2** TR & INTR to travel a route regularly; to go regularly to and fro between destinations. **3** DATED OR LITERARY to work at (a trade). **4** DATED OR LITERARY to use (a tool, etc): **ply one's needle.** ■ **plier** N.

plywood N wood which consists of thin layers glued together, widely used in building.

PM ABBREV Prime Minister.

p.m. or **pm** ABBREV **1** post meridiem.

PMT ABBREV premenstrual tension.

pneumatic ADJ **1** relating to air or gases. **2** containing or operated by compressed air.

pneumonia N, PATHOL inflammation of one or more lobes of the lungs.

PO ABBREV Post Office.

poach[1] VB, COOKERY **1** to cook (an egg without its shell) in or over boiling water. **2** to simmer (fish) in milk or other liquid.

poach[2] VB **1** TR & INTR to catch (game or fish)

illegally on someone else's property. **2** to steal (ideas, etc). **3** to lure away (personnel at a rival business, etc) to work for one. ■ **poacher** N.

pock N **1** a small inflamed area on the skin, containing pus, esp one caused by smallpox. **2** a pockmark.

pocket N **1** an extra piece sewn into or on to a garment to form a pouch for carrying things in. **2** any container similarly fitted or attached. **3** one's financial resources: **well beyond my pocket**. **4** in conditions of air turbulence: a place in the atmosphere where the air pressure drops or rises abruptly. **5** an isolated patch or area of something: **pockets of unemployment**. **6** BILLIARDS, ETC any of the holes, with pouches beneath them, situated around the edges of the table and into which balls are potted.
➤ VB **1** to put in one's pocket. **2** COLLOQ to take something dishonestly; to steal it. **3** BILLIARDS, ETC to drive (a ball) into a pocket. ■ **pocketful** N.
◆ **in** or **out of pocket** having gained, or lost, money on a transaction.
◆ **in sb's pocket** controlled by them.

pockmark N a small pit or hollow in the skin left by a pock, esp one caused by chickenpox or smallpox. ■ **pockmarked** ADJ.

pod N, BOT **a** the long dry fruit produced by leguminous plants, eg peas and beans, consisting of a seedcase which splits to release its seeds; **b** the seedcase itself.

podgy or **pudgy** ADJ (**-ier, -iest**) DEROG plump or chubby; short and squat.

podium N (**-iums** or **-ia**) a small platform for a public speaker, orchestra conductor, etc.

poem N **1** a literary composition, typically, but not necessarily, in verse, often with elevated and/or imaginatively expressed content. **2** an object, scene or creation of inspiring beauty.

poesy N (**-ies**) OLD USE poetry.

poet and **poetess** N a writer of poems.

poetic or **poetical** ADJ **1** relating or suitable to poets or poetry. **2** possessing grace, beauty or inspiration suggestive of poetry. **3** written in verse. ■ **poetically** ADV.

poet laureate N (**poets laureate** or **poet laureates**) in the UK: an officially appointed court poet, commissioned to produce poems for state occasions.

poetry N (**-ies**) **1** the art of composing poems. **2** poems collectively. **3** poetic quality, feeling, beauty or grace.

po-faced ADJ, DEROG COLLOQ wearing a disapproving or solemn expression.

pogo stick N a spring-mounted pole with a handlebar and foot rests, on which to bounce.

pogrom N an organized persecution or massacre of a particular group of people.

poignant ADJ **1** painful to the feelings: **a poignant reminder**. **2** deeply moving; full of pathos. **3** of words or expressions: sharp; penetrating. ■ **poignancy** N.

point N **1** a sharp or tapering end or tip. **2** a dot, eg inserted (either on the line or above it) before a decimal fraction. **3** a punctuation mark, esp a full stop. **4** GEOM a position found by means of coordinates. **5** a position, place or location. **6** a moment: **Sandy lost his temper at that point**. **7** a stage in a process, etc. **8** IN COMPOUNDS a stage, temperature, etc: **boiling-point**. **9** the right moment for doing something: **She lost courage when it came to the point**. **10** a feature or characteristic. **11** a detail, fact or particular used or mentioned. **12** aim or intention: **What is the point of this? 13** use or value: **no point in trying**. **14** the significance (of a remark, story, joke, etc). **15** a unit or mark in scoring. **16** any of the 32 directions marked on, or indicated by, a compass. **17** (often **points**) an adjustable tapering rail by means of which a train changes lines. **18** ELEC a socket or power point. **19** (usu **points**) BALLET **a** the tip of the toe; **b** a block inserted into the toe of a ballet shoe. **20** a headland or promontory.
➤ VB **1** to aim something. **2** TR & INTR **a** to extend (one's finger or a pointed object) towards someone or something, so as to direct attention there; **b** to indicate (a certain direction): **a weather vane pointing south**. **3** INTR to extend or face in a certain direction: **toes pointing upward**. **4** INTR of a gun dog: to stand

with the nose turned to where the dead game lies. **5** often FACETIOUS to direct someone: **point me to the grub. 6** (usu **point to sth** or **sb**) to indicate or suggest it or them: **It points to one solution. 7** in dancing, etc: to extend (the toes) to form a point. **8** to fill gaps or cracks in (stonework) with cement or mortar.

beside the point irrelevant.

in point of fact actually; in truth.

make a point of doing sth to be sure of doing it or take care to do it.

make one's point to state one's opinion forcefully.

on the point of doing sth about to do it.

point sth out to indicate it.

score points off sb to argue cleverly and successfully against them.

◆ **to the point** relevant.

up to a point to a limited degree.

point-blank ADJ **1** fired at very close range. **2** of a question, refusal, etc: blunt and direct. ➤ ADV **1** at close range. **2** in a blunt, direct manner: **refused point-blank.**

point duty N the task or station of a police officer or traffic warden who is directing traffic.

pointed ADJ **1** having or ending in a point. **2** of a remark, etc: intended for, though not directly addressed to, a particular person. **3** keen or incisive. ■ **pointedly** ADV.

pointer N **1** a rod used by a speaker for indicating positions on a wall map, chart, etc. **2** the indicating finger on a measuring instrument. **3** COLLOQ a suggestion or hint. **4** a gun dog trained to point its muzzle in the direction where the dead game lies.

pointing N the cement or mortar filling the gaps between the bricks or stones of a wall.

pointless ADJ **1** without a point. **2** lacking purpose or meaning. ■ **pointlessly** ADV.

point of view N (*points of view*) one's own particular way of looking at or attitude towards something.

point-to-point N a horse race across open country, from landmark to landmark.

poise N **1** self-confidence, calm or composure.

2 grace of posture or carriage. **3** a state of equilibrium, balance or stability. ➤ VB **1** TR & INTR, often IN PASSIVE to balance or suspend. **2** IN PASSIVE to be in a state of readiness: **poised to take over as leader.**

poison N **1** any substance that damages tissues or causes death when injected, absorbed or swallowed by living organisms. **2** any destructive or corrupting influence: **a poison spreading through society.** ➤ VB **1** to harm or kill with poison. **2** to put poison into (food, etc). **3** to contaminate or pollute: **rivers poisoned by effluents. 4** to corrupt or pervert (someone's mind). **5** to harm or spoil in an unpleasant or malicious way: **Jealousy poisoned their relationship.** ■ **poisoner** N.

poisonous ADJ **1** liable to cause injury or death if swallowed, inhaled or absorbed by the skin. **2** containing or capable of injecting a poison: **poisonous snakes. 3** COLLOQ of a person, remark, etc: malicious.

poke VB **1** (often **poke at sth**) to thrust: **Kevin poked at the hole with a stick. 2** to prod or jab. **3** to make (a hole) by prodding. **4** TR & INTR to project or make something project: **Her big toe poked through a hole in her sock. 5** to make (a fire) burn more brightly by stirring it with a poker. **6** INTR (esp **poke about** or **around**) to search; to pry or snoop. ➤ N a jab or prod.

◆ **poke fun at sb** to tease or laugh at them.

◆ **poke one's nose into sth** COLLOQ to pry into or interfere in it.

poker[1] N a metal rod for stirring a fire to make it burn better.

poker[2] N a card game in which players bet on the hands they hold, relying on bluff to outwit their opponents.

poker face N a blank expressionless face that shows no emotion. ■ **poker-faced** ADJ.

poky ADJ (*-ier, -iest*) **1** COLLOQ of a room, house, etc: small and confined or cramped. **2** US slow; dull. ■ **pokiness** N.

polar ADJ **1** of or relating to the North or South Pole, or the regions round them. **2** relating to or having electric or magnetic poles. **3** having polarity. **4** as different as possible: **polar opposites**.

polarity N (*-ies*) **1** the state of having two opposite poles: **magnetic polarity**. **2** the condition of having two properties that are opposite. **3** the tendency to develop differently in different directions along an axis. **4** PHYS the status, whether positive or negative, of the poles of a magnet, the terminals of an electrode, etc: **negative polarity**. **5** the tendency to develop, or be drawn, in opposite directions; oppositeness or an opposite.

polarize or **-ise** VB **1** to give magnetic or electrical polarity to something. **2** PHYS to restrict the vibrations of (electromagnetic waves, eg light) to one direction only by the process of polarization. **3** TR & INTR of people or opinions: to split according to opposing views. ■ **polarization** or **-isation** N.

polder N an area of low-lying land which has been reclaimed from the sea, a river or lake.

pole[1] N **1** either of two points representing the north and south ends of the axis about which the Earth rotates, known as the North Pole and South Pole respectively. **2** a magnetic pole. **3** either of the two terminals of a battery.
◆ **poles apart** COLLOQ widely different; as far apart as it is possible to be.

pole[2] N a rod, esp one that is cylindrical in section and fixed in the ground as a support.

poleaxe N a short-handled axe with a spike or hammer opposite the blade.
➤ VB to strike, fell or floor (an animal or person) with, or as if with, a poleaxe.

polecat N **1** a mammal resembling a large weasel that produces a foul-smelling discharge when alarmed or when marking territory. **2** N AMER, ESP US a skunk.

polemic N **1** a controversial speech or piece of writing that fiercely attacks or defends an idea, opinion, etc. **2** writing or oratory of this sort. **3** someone who argues in this way.
➤ ADJ (also **polemical**) relating to or involving polemics or controversy. ■ **polemicist** N.

polemics SING N the art of verbal debate.

pole vault N, ATHLETICS a field event in which athletes attempt to jump over a high horizontal bar with the help of a long flexible pole to haul themselves into the air. ■ **pole vaulter** N.

police PL N **1** the body of men and women employed by the government of a country to keep order, enforce the law, prevent crime, etc. **2** members of this body.
➤ VB **1** to keep law and order in (an area) using the police, army, etc. **2** to supervise (an operation, etc) to ensure that it is fairly or properly run.

policeman and **policewoman** N a male or female member of a police force.

police officer N a member of a police force.

policy[1] N (*-ies*) a plan of action, usu based on certain principles.

policy[2] N (*-ies*) **1** an insurance agreement. **2** a document confirming such an agreement.

polio N short form of **poliomyelitis**.

poliomyelitis N, PATHOL a viral disease of the brain and spinal cord, which can result in permanent paralysis.

polish VB **1** TR & INTR to make or become smooth and glossy by rubbing: **polishing my shoes**. **2** to improve or perfect.
➤ N **1** a substance used for polishing surfaces. **2** a smooth shiny finish; a gloss. **3** an act of polishing. **4** refinement or elegance.
◆ **polish off sth** or **polish sth off** to finish it quickly and completely, esp speedily.

polite ADJ **1** of a person or their actions, etc: well-mannered; considerate towards others; courteous. **2** well-bred, cultivated or refined. ■ **politely** ADV. ■ **politeness** N.

politic ADJ **1** prudent; wise; shrewd. **2** of a person: cunning; crafty.
➤ VB (also **politick**) (*-icked, -icking*) INTR, DEROG to indulge in politics, esp to strike political bargains or to gain votes for oneself.

political ADJ **1** relating or belonging to government or public affairs. **2** relating to politics. **3** interested or involved in politics. **4** of a course of action: made in the interests of gaining or keeping power. **5** of a map: showing political and social structure rather than physical features. ■ **politically** ADV.

political correctness N the avoidance of expressions or actions that may be understood to exclude or denigrate certain people or groups of people on the grounds of race, gender, disability, sexual orientation, etc.

political science N the study of politics and government.

politician N someone engaged in politics.

politicize or **-ise** VB **1** INTR to take part in political activities or discussion. **2** to give a political nature to something. **3** to make someone aware of or informed about politics. ■ **politicization** N.

politico N (**-os** or **-oes**) COLLOQ, USU DEROG a politician or someone who is keen on politics.

politics SING N **1** the science or business of government. **2** political science. **3** a political life as a career: **entered politics in 1961.**
➤ SING OR PL N political activities, wrangling, etc.
➤ PL N **1** moves and manoeuvres concerned with the acquisition of power or getting one's way, eg in business. **2** one's political sympathies: **What are your politics?**

polity N (**-ies**) **1** a politically organized body such as a state, church or association. **2** any form of political institution or government.

polka N a lively Bohemian dance usu performed with a partner, which has a pattern of three steps followed by a hop.
➤ VB (**-kaed, -kaing**) INTR to dance a polka.

polka dot N any one of numerous regularly-spaced dots forming a pattern on fabric, etc.

poll N **1** (**polls**) a political election: **another Tory disaster at the polls. 2** the voting or votes cast at an election: **a heavy poll. 3** (also **opinion poll**) a survey of public opinion carried out by directly questioning a representative sample of the populace. **4** OLD USE the head.
➤ VB **1** to win (a number of votes) in an election. **2** to register the votes of (a population). **3** TR &

INTR to cast (one's vote). **4** to conduct an opinion poll among (people, a specified group, etc).

pollard N a tree whose branches have been cut back, in order to produce a crown of shoots at the top of the trunk.
➤ VB to make a pollard of (a tree).

pollen N the fine, usu yellow, dust-like powder produced by the anthers of flowering plants, and by the male cones of cone-bearing plants.

pollinate VB, BOT in flowering and cone-bearing plants: to transfer pollen from anther to stigma, or from the male to the female cone in order to achieve fertilization and subsequent development of seed. ■ **pollination** N.

polling-station N the building where voters go to cast their votes during an election.

pollster N someone who organizes and carries out opinion polls.

poll tax N, FORMERLY in Britain: a tax levied on individuals to pay for local services. Also called **community charge**.

pollutant N any substance that pollutes.
➤ ADJ polluting: **pollutant emissions**.

pollute VB **1** to contaminate something with harmful substances or impurities; to cause pollution in something. **2** to corrupt (someone's mind, etc). **3** to defile. ■ **pollution** N.

polo N a game, similar to hockey, played on horseback by players using long-handled mallets to propel the ball along the ground.

polonaise N **1** a stately Polish marching dance. **2** a piece of music for this dance.

polo neck N **1** a high close-fitting neckband on a sweater or shirt, which is doubled over. **2** a sweater or shirt with such a neck. **3** Also AS ADJ: **polo-neck jumper**.

polo shirt N a short-sleeved open-necked casual shirt with a collar.

poltergeist N a type of ghost supposedly responsible for otherwise unaccountable noises and the movement of objects.

poltroon N, LITERARY OR OLD USE a coward.

polyandrous ADJ 1 having more than one husband at the same time. 2 BOT of a flower: having many stamens.

polyandry N the practice of having more than one husband at the same time.

polychromatic ADJ 1 polychrome. 2 of electromagnetic radiation: composed of a number of different wavelengths.

polychrome ADJ (also **polychromatic**) multicoloured.

polyester N a synthetic resin used to form strong durable crease-resistant artificial fibres, such as Terylene.

polygamy N the custom or practice of having more than one husband or wife at the same time. ■ **polygamist** N. ■ **polygamous** ADJ.

polyglot ADJ speaking, using or written in many languages.
➤ N someone who speaks many languages.

polygon N, GEOM a plane figure with a number of straight sides, usu more than three, eg a pentagon or a hexagon. ■ **polygonal** ADJ.

polygraph N, MED a device, sometimes used as a lie-detector, that monitors several body functions simultaneously, eg pulse, blood pressure and conductivity of the skin.

polygyny N the condition or custom of having more than one wife at the same time.

polyhedron N (-rons or -ra) GEOM a solid figure with four or more faces, all of which are polygons. ■ **polyhedral** ADJ.

polymath N someone who is well educated in a wide variety of subjects.

polymer N, CHEM a very large molecule consisting of a long chain of monomers linked end to end to form a series of repeating units. ■ **polymerization** or **-isation** N.

polyp N 1 ZOOL a sessile coelenterate with a more or less cylindrical body and a mouth surrounded by tentacles. 2 PATHOL a small abnormal but usu benign growth projecting from a mucous membrane.

polyphonic ADJ 1 having many voices.

2 relating to polyphony.

polyphony N (-ies) a style of musical composition in which each part or voice has an independent melodic value.

polysaccharide N, BIOCHEM a large carbohydrate molecule consisting of many monosaccharides linked together to form long chains, eg starch and cellulose.

polysemy N, LING the existence of more than one meaning for a single word, such as **table**. ■ **polysemous** ADJ.

polystyrene N, CHEM a tough transparent thermoplastic that is used in packaging, insulation, ceiling tiles, etc.

polysyllable N a word of three or more syllables. ■ **polysyllabic** ADJ.

polytechnic N, BRIT EDUCATION, FORMERLY a college of higher education providing courses in a large range of subjects.

polytheism N belief in more than one god. ■ **polytheist** N. ■ **polytheistic** ADJ.

polythene N a waxy translucent easily-moulded thermoplastic, used in the form of film or sheeting to package food products, clothing, etc, and to make pipes, moulded articles and electrical insulators.

polyunsaturated ADJ, CHEM of a compound, esp a fat or oil: containing two or more double bonds per molecule.

polyurethane N, CHEM a polymer that contains the urethane group, and is used in protective coatings, adhesives, paints, etc.

pomade N, HIST a perfumed ointment for the hair and scalp.

pomander N a perfumed ball composed of various aromatic substances, orig carried as scent or to ward off infection.

pomegranate N a round fruit with tough red or brown skin surrounding a mass of seeds, each enclosed by red juicy edible flesh.

pomelo N a round yellow citrus fruit.

pommel N 1 the raised forepart of a saddle.

2 a rounded knob at the end of a sword hilt.

pommy N (*-ies*) AUSTRAL & NZ DEROG COLLOQ a British person. Often shortened to **pom**.

pomp N **1** ceremonial grandeur. **2** ostentation.

pompom or **pompon** N a ball made of cut wool or other yarn, used as a trimming on clothes, etc.

pompous ADJ **1** solemnly self-important. **2** said of language: inappropriately grand and flowery; pretentious. ■ **pomposity** N.

ponce OFFENSIVE SLANG, N **1** a pimp. **2** an effeminate man.
➢ VB, INTR (USU **ponce about** or **around**) **1** to mince about in an effeminate manner. **2** to mess around.

poncho N an outer garment, orig S American, made of a large piece of cloth with a hole in the middle for the head to go through.

pond N a small area of still fresh water surrounded by land.

ponder VB, TR & INTR (often **ponder on** or **over sth**) to consider or contemplate it deeply.

ponderous ADJ **1** heavy-handed, laborious, over-solemn or pompous. **2** heavy or cumbersome; lumbering. **3** weighty; important. ■ **ponderously** ADV.

pong COLLOQ, N a stink; a bad smell.
➢ VB, INTR to smell badly.

pontiff N a title for the Pope.

pontifical ADJ **1** of or relating to a pontiff. **2** DEROG pompously opinionated; dogmatic.

pontificate VB, INTR **1** to pronounce one's opinion pompously and arrogantly. **2** to perform the duties of a pontiff.
➢ N the office of a pope.

pontoon N **1** any of a number of flat-bottomed craft, punts, barges, etc, anchored side by side across a river, to support a temporary bridge or platform. **2** CARDS a game in which the object is to collect sets of cards that add up to or close to 21.

pony N (*-ies*) **1** any of several small hardy

breeds of horse. **2** BRIT SLANG a sum of £25.

ponytail N a hairstyle in which a person's hair is drawn back and gathered at the back of the head, so that it hangs like a pony's tail.

poo see **poop**[2]

pooch N, COLLOQ a dog.

poodle N **1** a breed of lively pet dog of various sizes which has a narrow head with pendulous ears and a long curly coat, often clipped into an elaborate style. **2** DEROG a lackey.

poof and **poofter** N, OFFENSIVE SLANG a male homosexual. ■ **poofy** ADJ (*-ier, -iest*).

pooh EXCLAM, COLLOQ indicating scorn or disgust, esp at an offensive smell.

pool[1] N **1** a small area of still water. **2** a puddle; a patch of spilt liquid. **3** a swimming pool. **4** a deep part of a stream or river.

pool[2] N **1** a reserve of money, personnel, vehicles, etc used as a communal resource. **2** the combined stakes of those betting on something; a jackpot. **3** COMMERCE a group of businesses with a common arrangement to maintain high prices, so eliminating competition and preserving profits. **4** a game like billiards played with a white cue ball and usu 15 numbered coloured balls, the aim being to shoot specified balls into specified pockets using the cue ball.
➢ VB to put (money or other resources) into a common supply for general use.

poop[1] N, NAUT **1** the raised enclosed part at the stern of old sailing ships. **2** the high deck at the stern of a ship. Also called **poop deck**.

poop[2] and **poo** SLANG, N faeces.
➢ VB, INTR to defecate.

poor ADJ **1** not having sufficient money or means to live comfortably. **2** (**the poor**) poor people in general. **3** (**poor in sth**) not well supplied with it. **4** not good; weak; unsatisfactory: **poor eyesight**. **5** unsatisfactorily small or sparse: **a poor attendance**. **6** used in expressing pity or sympathy: **poor fellow!** ■ **poorness** N.

poorly ADV not well; badly.

➤ ADJ, COLLOQ OR DIALECT unwell.

pop¹ N **1** a sharp explosive noise, like that of a cork coming out of a bottle. **2** any sweet non-alcoholic fizzy drink such as ginger beer.
➤ VB (-*pp*-) **1** TR & INTR to make or cause something to make a pop. **2** TR & INTR to burst with a pop: **The balloon popped. 3** (esp **pop out** or **up**) to spring out or up; to protrude. **4** INTR, COLLOQ to go quickly in a direction specified: **I'll just pop next door for a second. 5** COLLOQ to put something somewhere quickly or briefly: **just pop it in the oven.**
➤ ADV with a pop.
◆ **pop the question** HUMOROUS, COLLOQ to propose marriage.
◆ **pop up** to appear or occur unexpectedly.

pop² N (in full **pop music**) a type of music, primarily commercial, usu with a strong beat and characterized by its use of electronic equipment such as guitars and keyboards.
➤ ADJ popular: **pop culture.**

pop³ N, INFORMAL, esp N AMER **1** father; dad. **2** often as a form of address: an elderly man.

popcorn N **1** (also **popping corn**) maize grains that puff up and burst open when heated. **2** these edible puffed-up kernels.

pope N **1** (often **Pope**) the Bishop of Rome, the head of the Roman Catholic Church. **2** a priest in the Eastern Orthodox Church.

popgun N a toy gun that fires a cork or pellet with a pop.

popinjay N, OLD USE, DEROG a vain or conceited person; a dandy or fop.

popish ADJ, OFFENSIVE of or relating to Roman Catholicism.

poplar N **1** a tall slender deciduous tree found in northern temperate regions, with broad simple leaves which tremble in a slight breeze. **2** the soft fine-grained wood of this tree.

poplin N a strong cotton cloth with a finely ribbed finish.

pop music see **pop²**

poppadum, poppadom or **pappadom** N a paper-thin pancake, grilled or fried till crisp, served with Indian dishes.

popper N **1** someone or something that pops. **2** INFORMAL a press stud.

poppet N **1** a term of endearment for someone lovable. **2** in vehicle engines: an unhinged valve that rises and falls in its housing.

poppy N (-*ies*) a plant with large brightly-coloured bowl-shaped flowers and a fruit in the form of a capsule.

poppycock N, COLLOQ nonsense.

populace N the body of ordinary citizens.

popular ADJ **1** liked or enjoyed by most people. **2** of beliefs, etc: accepted by many people: **a popular misconception. 3** catering for the tastes and abilities of ordinary people as distinct from specialists, etc: **a popular history of science. 4** of a person: generally liked and admired. **5** involving the will or preferences of the public in general: **by popular demand.**
■ **popularity** N. ■ **popularly** ADV.

popularize or **-ise** VB **1** to make something popular. **2** to present something in a simple easily-understood way, so as to have general appeal. ■ **popularization** N.

populate VB **1** of people, animals or plants: to inhabit or live in (a certain area). **2** to supply (uninhabited places) with inhabitants.

population N **1** all the people living in a particular country, etc. **2** the number of people or animals living in a particular area, etc.

populist N a person who believes in the right and ability of the common people to play a major part in government. ■ **populism** N.

populous ADJ densely inhabited.

pop-up ADJ **1** of a picture book, greetings card, etc: having cut-out parts designed to stand upright as the page is opened. **2** of appliances, etc: having a mechanism which causes a component to pop up.

porcelain N **1 a** a fine white translucent earthenware, orig made in China; **b** AS ADJ: **a porcelain dish. 2** objects made of this.

porch N **1** a structure that forms a covered

entrance to the doorway of a building. **2** N AMER a verandah.

porcine ADJ of or resembling a pig.

porcupine N a large nocturnal rodent with long black–and–white spikes or quills on the back and sides of its body.

pore[1] N a small, usu round opening in the surface of a living organism, through which fluids, gases and other substances can pass.

pore[2] VB, INTR (always **pore over sth**) to study (books, etc) with intense concentration.

pork N the flesh of a pig used as food.

porker N a pig reared for fresh meat.

porky ADJ (**-ier, -iest**) COLLOQ plump.

porn and **porno** COLLOQ, N pornography.
➤ ADJ pornographic.

pornography N books, pictures, films, etc designed to be sexually arousing.
■ **pornographer** N. ■ **pornographic** ADJ.

porous ADJ **1** of or relating to a material that contains pores or cavities. **2** capable of being permeated by liquids or gases. ■ **porosity** N.

porphyry N, GEOL **1** LOOSELY any igneous rock that contains large crystals surrounded by much smaller ones. **2** a very hard purple and white rock used in sculpture. ■ **porphyritic** ADJ.

porpoise N **1** a small whale with a blunt snout. **2** LOOSELY a dolphin.

porridge N **1** a dish of oatmeal or some other cereal which is boiled in water or milk until it thickens. **2** BRIT SLANG a jail sentence.

porringer N a bowl, with a handle, for soup or porridge.

port[1] N **1** a harbour. **2** a town with a harbour.

port[2] N the left side of a ship or aircraft.

port[3] N **1** an opening in a ship's side for loading, etc. **2** a porthole. **3** COMP a socket that connects the **CPU** of a computer to a peripheral device.

port[4] N a sweet fortified wine.

portable ADJ **1** easily carried or moved, and

usu designed to be so. **2** COMP of a program: adaptable for use in a variety of systems.
➤ N a portable radio, television, typewriter, etc.

portal N, FORMAL an entrance, gateway or doorway, esp an imposing or awesome one.

portcullis N, HIST a vertical iron or wooden grating fitted into a town gateway or castle entrance, lowered to keep intruders out.

portend VB to warn of (usu something bad).

portent N **1** a prophetic sign; an omen. **2** fateful significance. **3** a marvel or prodigy.

portentous ADJ **1** ominous or fateful; relating to portents. **2** weighty, solemn or pompous.

porter[1] N a doorman, caretaker or janitor at a college, office or factory.

porter[2] N **1** someone employed to carry luggage or parcels, eg at a railway station. **2** in a hospital: someone employed to move patients when required and to carry out other general duties. **3** a heavy dark–brown beer.

portfolio N **1** a flat case for carrying papers, drawings, etc. **2** POL the post of a government minister with responsibility for a specific department. **3** a list of the investments or securities held by an individual, company, etc.

porthole N an opening, usu a round one, in a ship's side to admit light and air.

portico N (**-os** or **-oes**) ARCHIT a colonnade forming a porch or covered way.

portion N **1** a piece or part of a whole: divided the cake into 12 equal portions. **2** a share; a part allotted. **3** an individual helping of food. **4** LITERARY one's destiny or fate.
➤ VB (now usu **portion sth out**) to divide it up.

portly ADJ (**-ier, -iest**) esp of a man: stout.

portmanteau N (**-teaus** or **-teaux**) a large travelling–bag that opens flat in two halves.

portmanteau word N a word formed by combining two separate words, eg brunch (for breakfast and lunch). Also called **blend**.

portrait N **1** a drawing, painting or photograph of a person, esp of the face only.

2 a written description, film depiction, etc of something: **a portrait of country life.**
➤ ADJ, PRINTING of a page, illustration, etc: taller than it is wide.

portraiture N **1** the art or act of making portraits. **2** a portrait, or portraits collectively.

portray VB **1** to make a portrait of someone or something. **2** to describe or depict something. **3** to act the part of (a character) in a play, film, etc. ■ **portrayal** N.

pose N **1** a position or attitude of the body: **a relaxed pose. 2** an artificial way of behaving, adopted for effect.
➤ VB **1** TR & INTR to take up a position oneself, or position (someone else), for a photograph, portrait, etc. **2** INTR, DEROG to behave in an exaggerated or artificial way so as to draw attention to oneself. **3** INTR (usu **pose as sb** or **sth**) to pretend to be someone or something that one is not. **4** to ask or put forward (a question). **5** to cause (a problem, etc) or present (a threat, etc).

poser[1] N, DEROG a poseur.

poser[2] N a puzzling or perplexing question.

poseur N, DEROG someone who behaves in an affected way, esp to impress others.

posh ADJ, COLLOQ **1** high-quality, expensive, smart or stylish. **2** upper-class.

posit VB to lay down or assume something as a basis for discussion; to postulate.

position N **1** a place where someone or something is. **2** the right or proper place: **out of position. 3** the relationship of things to one another in space; arrangement. **4** a way of sitting, standing, lying, facing, being held or placed, etc: **an upright position. 5** MIL a place occupied for strategic purposes. **6** one's opinion or viewpoint. **7** a job or post. **8** rank; status; importance in society: **wealth and position. 9** the place of a competitor in the finishing order, or at an earlier stage in a contest: **lying in fourth position. 10** SPORT an allotted place in a team, esp on the pitch or playing-area. **11** the set of circumstances in which one is placed: **not in a position to help.**

➤ VB to place; to put something or someone in position. ■ **positional** ADJ.

positive ADJ **1** sure; certain; convinced. **2** allowing no doubt: **positive proof of her guilt. 3** expressing agreement or approval. **4** optimistic: **feeling more positive. 5** forceful or determined; not tentative. **6** constructive; contributing to progress or improvement; helpful. **7** clear and explicit: **positive directions. 8** COLLOQ downright: **a positive scandal. 9** of the result of a chemical test: confirming the existence of the suspected condition. **10** MATH of a number or quantity: greater than zero. **11** PHYS, ELEC having a deficiency of electrons, and so being able to attract them, ie attracted by a negative charge. **12** PHOTOG of a photographic image: in which light and dark tones and colours correspond to those in the original subject.

positivism N a school of philosophy maintaining that knowledge can come only from observable phenomena and positive facts. ■ **positivist** N, ADJ.

positron N, PHYS a particle that has the same mass as an electron, and an equal but opposite charge.

posse N **1** N AMER, HIST a mounted troop of men at the service of a local sheriff. **2** COLLOQ any group or band of people, esp friends.

possess VB **1** to own. **2** to have something as a feature: **Frances possesses a quick mind. 3** to dominate the mind of someone: **What possessed you to do that?** ■ **possessor** N.

possessed ADJ **1** (**possessed of sth**) FORMAL owning it; having it: **possessed of great wealth. 2** FOLLOWING ITS NOUN controlled or driven by demons, etc: **screaming like a man possessed.**

possession N **1** the condition of possessing something; ownership: **It came into my possession. 2** the crime of possessing something illegally. **3** occupancy of property: **take possession of the house. 4** something owned. **5** (**possessions**) one's belongings.
◆ **be in possession of sth** to have it.

possessive ADJ **1** relating to possession. **2** of a

person or of character: unwilling to share, or allow others to use, things they own: **I'm very possessive about my car. 3** of a person or of character: inclined to dominate, monopolize and allow no independence to one's wife, husband, child, etc: **a possessive husband.**
■ **possessiveness** N.

possibility N (*-ies*) **1** something that is possible. **2** the state of being possible. **3** a candidate for selection, etc. **4** (**possibilities**) promise or potential.

possible ADJ **1** achievable; able to be done: **a possible target of 50%. 2** capable of happening: **the possible outcome. 3** imaginable; conceivable.
➤ N someone or something potentially selectable or attainable; a possibility.

possibly ADV **1** perhaps. **2** within the limits of possibility: **We'll do all we possibly can.**

possum N, COLLOQ **1** an opossum. **2** a phalanger.
◆ **play possum** to pretend to be unconscious, asleep or unaware of what is happening.

post[1] N **1** a shaft or rod fixed upright in the ground, as a support, etc. **2** a vertical timber supporting a horizontal one. **3** an upright pole marking the beginning or end of a race track.
➤ VB to put up (a notice, etc) on a post or board, etc for public viewing.

post[2] N **1** a job: **a teaching post. 2** a position to which one is assigned for military duty: **never left his post. 3** a settlement or establishment, esp one in a remote area. **4** MIL a bugle call summoning soldiers to their quarters at night.
➤ VB (usu **post sb to, at** or **in somewhere**) to station them there on duty; to transfer (personnel) to a new location.

post[3] N (esp **the post**) **1** the official system for the delivery of mail. **2** letters and parcels delivered by this system; mail. **3** a collection of mail, eg from a postbox: **catch the next post. 4** a delivery of mail: **came by the second post. 5** a place for mail collection; a postbox or post office: **took it to the post.**
➤ VB **1** to put (mail) into a postbox; to send

something by post. **2** to supply someone with the latest news: **keep us posted.**

postage N the charge for sending a letter, etc through the post.

postal ADJ **1** of or relating to the post office or to delivery of mail. **2** sent by post: **a postal vote.**

postal order N a money order available from, and payable by, a post office.

postbag N **1** a mailbag. **2** the letters received by eg a radio or TV programme, magazine, etc.

post box see **letter box**

postcard N a card for writing messages on, often with a picture on one side, designed for sending through the post without an envelope.

postcode N a code used to identify a postal address, made up of a combination of letters and numerals.

postdate VB **1** to put a future date on (a cheque, etc). **2** to assign a later date than that previously accepted to (an event, etc). **3** to occur at a later date than (a specified date).

poster N **1** a large notice or advertisement for public display. **2** a large printed picture.

posterior ADJ **1** placed behind, after or at the back of something. **2** FORMAL OR OLD USE coming after in time.
➤ N, FACETIOUS the buttocks.

posterity N **1** future generations. **2** one's descendants.

postern N, HIST a back door, back gate or private entrance.

postgraduate N **1** a person studying for an advanced degree or qualification after obtaining a first degree. **2** AS ADJ relating to such a person or degree: **postgraduate diploma.**

posthaste ADV with the utmost speed.

posthumous ADJ **1** of a work: published after the death of the author, composer, etc. **2** of a child: born after its father's death. **3** coming or occurring after death: **posthumous fame.**

postilion or **postillion** N, HIST a rider on the nearside horse of one of the pairs of horses drawing a carriage, who, in the absence of a coachman, guides the team.

postman and **postwoman** N a man or woman whose job is to deliver mail.

postmark N a mark stamped on mail by the post office, cancelling the stamp and showing the date and place of posting.

postmaster and **postmistress** N the man or woman in charge of a local post office.

post meridiem N after midday.

postmortem N 1 (in full **postmortem examination**) the examination of the internal organs of the body after death, to determine the cause of death. Also called **autopsy**. 2 COLLOQ an after-the-event discussion. ➤ ADJ coming or happening after death.

postnatal ADJ relating to or occurring during the period immediately after childbirth: postnatal depression. ■ **postnatally** ADV.

post office N a local office that handles postal business, the issuing of licences, etc.

postpone VB to delay or put off something till later. ■ **postponement** N.

postprandial ADJ, FACETIOUS following a meal.

postscript N a message added to a letter as an afterthought, after one's signature.

postulant N someone who asks or petitions for something, esp a candidate for holy orders or for admission to a religious community.

postulate VB 1 to assume or suggest something as the basis for discussion; to take it for granted. 2 to demand; to claim. ➤ N 1 a stipulation or prerequisite. 2 a position assumed as self-evident. ■ **postulation** N.

posture N 1 the way one holds one's body while standing, sitting or walking. 2 a particular position or attitude of the body. 3 an attitude adopted towards a particular issue, etc. 4 a pose adopted for effect. ➤ VB 1 to take up a particular bodily attitude. 2 INTR, DEROG to pose, strike attitudes, etc to draw attention to oneself. ■ **postural** ADJ.

postwar ADJ relating or belonging to the period following a war.

posy N (-ies) a small bunch of flowers.

pot[1] N 1 a domestic container, usu a deep round one, used as a cooking or serving utensil, or for storage. 2 (also **potful**) the amount a pot can hold: a pot of tea. 3 POTTERY any handmade container. 4 the pool of accumulated bets in any gambling game. 5 in snooker, billiards, pool, etc: a shot that pockets a ball. 6 a casual shot: take a pot at something. 7 a chamberpot. 8 a flowerpot. 9 (**pots**) COLLOQ a great deal, esp of money. 10 COLLOQ a trophy, esp a cup. 11 a potbelly. ➤ VB (-tt-) 1 to plant something in a plant pot. 2 to preserve (a type of food) in a pot. 3 in snooker, billiards, pool, etc: to shoot (a ball) into a pocket: couldn't pot the black. ◆ **go to pot** COLLOQ to degenerate badly.

pot[2] N, COLLOQ cannabis.

potable ADJ fit or suitable for drinking.

potash N a compound of potassium.

potassium N, CHEM a soft silvery-white metallic element.

potation N, FORMAL OR HUMOROUS 1 the act or an instance of drinking. 2 a drink, esp an alcoholic one. 3 a drinking binge.

potato N (-oes) 1 a plant that produces edible tubers and is a staple crop of temperate regions worldwide. 2 the starch-rich round or oval tuber of this plant, which is cooked for food. Also AS ADJ: potato salad.

potbelly N (-ies) COLLOQ a large overhanging belly. ■ **pot-bellied** ADJ.

potboiler N, DEROG an inferior work of literature or art produced by a writer or artist capable of better work, simply to make money and stay in the public view.

poteen N, IRISH illicitly distilled Irish whiskey.

potent ADJ 1 strong; effective; powerful. 2 of an argument, etc: persuasive; convincing. 3 of a drug or poison: powerful and swift in effect. 4 of a male: capable of sexual intercourse. ■ **potency** N (-ies).

potentate N, esp HIST OR LITERARY a powerful ruler; a monarch.

potential ADJ possible or likely, though as yet not tested or actual: **a potential customer**. ➤ N the range of capabilities that someone or something has; powers or resources not yet made use of: **fulfil your potential**. ■ **potentiality** N. ■ **potentially** ADV.

pother N a fuss or commotion.

pot-hole N 1 a roughly circular hole worn in the bedrock of a river as pebbles are swirled around by water eddies. 2 a vertical cave system or deep hole eroded in limestone. 3 a hole worn in a road surface.

potion N a draught of medicine, poison or some magic elixir.

pot luck N whatever happens to be available.

potpourri N 1 a fragrant mixture of dried flowers, leaves, etc used to scent rooms. 2 a medley or mixture.

potsherd N, ARCHAEOL a fragment of pottery.

pot shot N 1 an easy shot at close range. 2 a shot made without taking careful aim.

pottage N a thick soup.

potted ADJ 1 abridged: **a potted history**. 2 of food: preserved in a pot or jar: **potted meat**. 3 growing in a pot: **a potted begonia**.

potter[1] N someone who makes pottery.

potter[2] VB, INTR 1 (usu **potter about**) to busy oneself in a mild way with trifling tasks. 2 (usu **potter about** or **along**) to progress in an unhurried manner; to dawdle. ■ **potterer** N.

pottery N (*-ies*) 1 containers, pots or other objects of baked clay. 2 the art or craft of making such objects. 3 a factory where such objects are produced commercially.

potty[1] ADJ (*-ier, -iest*) COLLOQ 1 mad; crazy. 2 (usu **potty about sb** or **sth**) intensely interested in or keen on them or it.

potty[2] N (*-ies*) COLLOQ a child's chamberpot.

potty-train VB to teach (usu a toddler) to use a potty or the toilet. ■ **potty-trained** ADJ.

pouch N 1 a purse or small bag, or anything resembling a small bag: **a tobacco pouch**. 2 in marsupials such as the kangaroo: a pocket of skin on the belly, in which the young are carried until they are weaned.

pouffe or **pouf** N a firmly stuffed drum- or cube-shaped cushion for use as a low seat.

poulterer N a dealer in poultry and game.

poultice N, MED a hot, semi-liquid mixture spread on a bandage and applied to the skin to reduce inflammation.

poultry N 1 COLLECTIVE domesticated birds kept for their eggs or meat, or both, eg chickens, ducks, etc. 2 the meat of such birds.

pounce VB, INTR (often **pounce on sth** or **sb**) 1 to leap or swoop on (a victim or prey), esp when trying to capture them or it. 2 to seize on it or them; to grab eagerly. ➤ N an act of pouncing.

pound[1] N 1 the standard unit of currency of the UK. Also called **pound sterling**. 2 the principal currency unit in several other countries. 3 a measure of weight equal to 16 ounces (0.45 kilograms).

pound[2] N 1 an enclosure where stray animals or illegally parked cars that have been taken into police charge are kept for collection. 2 a place where people are confined.

pound[3] VB 1 TR & INTR (often **pound on** or **at sth**) to beat or bang it vigorously. 2 INTR to walk or run with heavy thudding steps. 3 to crush or grind something to a powder. 4 to thump.

pour VB 1 TR & INTR to flow or cause something to flow in a downward stream. 2 TR & INTR of a jug, teapot, etc: to discharge (liquid) in a certain way: **doesn't pour very well**. 3 (also **pour sth out**) to serve (a drink, etc) by pouring. 4 INTR to rain heavily. 5 INTR (usu **pour in** or **out**) to come or go in large numbers. 6 INTR (also **pour in** or **out, etc**) to flow or issue plentifully. ■ **pourer** N. ◆ **pour sth out** to reveal without inhibition: **poured out her feelings**.

poussin N a young chicken killed and eaten at the age of four to six weeks.

pout VB, TR & INTR to push the lower lip or both lips forward in sulkiness or seductiveness.
➤ N 1 an act of pouting. 2 a pouting expression.

poverty N 1 the condition of being poor; want. 2 poor quality. 3 inadequacy; deficiency: **poverty of imagination**.

POW ABBREV prisoner of war.

powder N 1 any substance in the form of fine dust–like particles: **talcum powder**. 2 (also **face powder**) a cosmetic that is patted on to the skin to give it a soft smooth appearance. 3 gunpowder.
➤ VB 1 to apply powder to (eg one's face); to sprinkle or cover something with powder. 2 to reduce something to a powder by crushing; to pulverize. ■ **powdery** ADJ.

powder keg N 1 a barrel of gunpowder. 2 a potentially dangerous or explosive situation.

powder room N a women's cloakroom or toilet in a restaurant, hotel, etc.

power N 1 control and influence exercised over others. 2 strength, vigour, force or effectiveness. 3 usu IN COMPOUNDS military strength: **sea power • air power**. 4 the physical ability, skill, opportunity or authority to do something. 5 an individual faculty or skill: **the power of speech**. 6 a right, privilege or responsibility: **the power of arrest**. 7 political control. 8 a state that has an influential role in international affairs. 9 a person or group exercising control or influence. 10 COLLOQ a great deal: **The rest did her a power of good**. 11 any form of energy, esp when used as the driving force for a machine. 12 MATH a number that indicates how many times a given quantity is to be multiplied by itself. 13 PHYS the rate of doing work or converting energy from one form into another. 14 **a** mechanical or electrical energy, as distinct from manual effort; **b** AS ADJ: **power tools**.
➤ VB 1 to supply something with power. 2 TR & INTR, COLLOQ to move or cause something to move with great force, energy or speed.
◆ **the powers that be** the people who are in control or in authority.

power cut N a temporary break or reduction

in an electricity supply.

powerful ADJ 1 having great power, strength or vigour. 2 very effective or efficient.
➤ ADV, DIALECT extremely: **powerful hot**.

power of attorney N the right to act for another person in legal and business matters.

power station N a building where electricity is generated on a large scale from coal, nuclear fuel, moving water, etc.

powwow N 1 COLLOQ a meeting for discussion. 2 a meeting of Native Americans.

pox N 1 MED, often IN COMPOUNDS an infectious viral disease that causes a skin rash consisting of pimples containing pus: **chickenpox**. 2 (often **the pox**) a former name for syphilis.

poxy ADJ (*-ier, -iest*) BRIT COLLOQ trashy.

pp ABBREV 1 pages: pp9–12. 2 usu written when signing a letter in the absence of the sender: **per procurationem** (Latin), for and on behalf of (the specified person). Also called **per pro**.

PR ABBREV 1 proportional representation. 2 public relations.

practicable ADJ capable of being done, used or successfully carried out; feasible.
■ **practicability** N. ■ **practicably** ADV.

practical ADJ 1 concerned with or involving action rather than theory: **put her knowledge to practical use**. 2 effective, or capable of being effective, in actual use. 3 eg of clothes: designed for tough or everyday use; sensibly plain. 4 of a person: **a** sensible and efficient in deciding and acting; **b** good at doing manual jobs. 5 in effect; virtual: **a practical walkover**.
➤ N a practical lesson or examination, eg in a scientific subject. ■ **practicality** N (*-ies*).

practical joke N a trick or prank which is played on someone, usu making them look silly.

practically ADV 1 almost; very nearly. 2 in a practical manner.

practice N 1 the process of carrying something out: **put ideas into practice**. 2 a habit, activity, procedure or custom: **Don't make a practice of it!** 3 repeated exercise to improve technique in an art or sport, etc. **4** the business or clientele of a doctor, dentist, lawyer, etc.

practise or (US) **practice** VB **1** TR & INTR to do exercises repeatedly in (an art or sport, etc) so as to improve one's performance. **2** to make a habit of something: practise self-control. **3** to go in for something as a custom: tribes that practise bigamy. **4** to work at or follow (an art or profession, esp medicine or law).

practised or (US) **practiced** ADJ (often **practised at sth**) skilled; experienced.

practitioner N someone who practises an art or profession, esp medicine.

pragmatism N **1** a practical approach to dealing with problems, etc. **2** PHILOS a school of thought that assesses concepts in terms of their practical implications. ■ **pragmatic** ADJ. ■ **pragmatist** N.

prairie N in N America: a large expanse of flat or rolling natural grassland, usu without trees.

praise VB **1** to express admiration or approval of someone or something. **2** to worship or glorify (God) with hymns or thanksgiving, etc. ➤ N **1** the expression of admiration or approval; commendation. **2** worship of God. ◆ **sing sb's praises** to commend them.

praiseworthy ADJ deserving praise; commendable.

praline N a sweet consisting of nuts in caramelized sugar.

pram N a wheeled baby carriage pushed by someone on foot.

prance VB **1** INTR esp of a horse: to walk with springing steps. **2** INTR to skip about. **3** INTR to parade about in a swaggering manner.

prandial ADJ, often FACETIOUS of or relating to dinner.

prang COLLOQ, VB **1** to crash (a vehicle). **2** to bomb something from the air. ➤ N **1** a vehicle crash. **2** a bombing raid.

prank N a playful trick. ■ **prankster** N.

prat N, SLANG **1** OFFENSIVE a fool. **2** the buttocks.

prate VB, TR & INTR to talk or utter foolishly.

prattle VB, TR & INTR to chatter or utter childishly or foolishly. ➤ N childish or foolish chatter. ■ **prattler** N.

prawn N a small edible shrimp-like marine crustacean.

pray VB (often **pray for sth** or **sb**) **1** now usu INTR to address one's god, making earnest requests or giving thanks. **2** OLD USE, TR & INTR to entreat or implore: Stop, I pray you! **3** TR & INTR to hope desperately. ➤ EXCLAM, OLD USE (now often uttered with quaint politeness or cold irony) please, or may I ask: Pray come in • Who asked you, pray?

prayer[1] N **1** an address to one's god, making a request or giving thanks. **2** the activity of praying. **3** an earnest hope, desire or entreaty.

prayer[2] N someone who prays.

prayerful ADJ **1** of someone: devout; tending to pray a lot or often. **2** said of a speech, etc: imploring.

praying mantis see under **mantis**

preach VB **1** TR & INTR to deliver (a sermon) as part of a religious service. **2** (often **preach at sb**) to give them advice in a tedious or obtrusive manner. **3** to advise or advocate something. ■ **preacher** N.

preamble N an introduction or preface, eg to a speech or document; an opening statement.

prearrange VB to arrange something in advance. ■ **prearrangement** N.

prebend N **1** an allowance paid out of the revenues of a cathedral or collegiate church to its canons or chapter members. **2** the piece of land, etc which is the source of such revenue. **3** a prebendary. ■ **prebendal** ADJ.

prebendary N (*-ies*) **1** a clergyman of a cathedral or collegiate church who is in receipt of a prebend. **2** C OF E the honorary holder of a prebend.

precancerous ADJ esp of cells: showing early indications of possible malignancy.

precarious ADJ **1** unsafe; insecure;

dangerous. **2** uncertain; chancy.

precaution N **1** a measure taken to ensure a satisfactory outcome, or to avoid a risk or danger. **2** caution exercised beforehand. ■ **precautionary** ADJ.

precede VB, TR & INTR to go or be before someone or something, in time, order, position, rank or importance.

precedence N **1** priority. **2** the right to precede others.

precedent N a previous incident or legal case, etc that has something in common with one under consideration, serving as a basis for a decision in the present one.

precentor N, RELIG someone who leads the singing of a church congregation, or the prayers in a synagogue.

precept N a rule or principle that is seen or used as a guide to behaviour.

preceptor and **preceptress** N a teacher or instructor. ■ **preceptorial** ADJ.

precession N **1** PHYS the gradual change in direction of the axis of rotation of a spinning body. **2** the act of preceding.

precinct N **1** (also **precincts**) the enclosed grounds of a large building, etc: the cathedral precinct. **2** (also **precincts**) the environs or neighbourhood of a place. **3** a pedestrian precinct.

precious ADJ **1** valuable. **2** dear; beloved. **3** DEROG of speech or manner: affected. ◆ **precious few** or **little** COLLOQ almost none.

precious metal N gold, silver or platinum.

precious stone N a gemstone, such as a diamond, valued for its beauty and rarity.

precipice N a steep, vertical or overhanging cliff or rock face.

precipitate VB **1** to cause something or hasten its advent: precipitated a war. **2** to throw or plunge. **3** CHEM, TR & INTR to form or cause something to form a suspension of small solid particles in a solution, as a result of certain chemical reactions. **4** METEOROL of moisture, etc:

to condense and fall as rain, snow, etc. ➤ ADJ of actions or decisions: recklessly hasty. ➤ N **1** CHEM a suspension of small solid particles formed in a solution as a result of certain chemical reactions. **2** METEOROL moisture deposited as rain or snow, etc.

precipitation N **1** rash haste. **2** METEOROL water that falls from clouds in the atmosphere to the Earth's surface in the form of rain, snow, etc. **3** the act of precipitating or process of being precipitated. **4** CHEM the formation of a precipitate.

precipitous ADJ **1** dangerously steep. **2** of actions or decisions: rash; precipitate.

précis N (PL **précis**) a summary of a piece of writing. ➤ VB to make a précis of something.

precise ADJ **1** exact; very: at this precise moment. **2** clear; detailed: precise instructions. **3** accurate: precise timing. **4** careful over details. ■ **precisely** ADV.

precision N **1** accuracy. **2** AS ADJ of tools, etc: designed to operate with minute accuracy.

preclude VB **1** to rule out or eliminate something or make it impossible. **2** (often **preclude sb from sth**) to prevent their involvement in it. ■ **preclusion** N. ■ **preclusive** ADJ.

precocious ADJ eg of a child: unusually advanced in mental development, speech, etc. ■ **precociousness** or **precocity** N.

precognition N the supposed ability to foresee events. ■ **precognitive** ADJ.

preconceive VB to form (an idea, etc) of something before having direct experience of it. ■ **preconceived** ADJ.

preconception N an assumption about something not yet experienced.

precondition N a condition to be satisfied in advance.

precursor N something that precedes, and is a sign of, an approaching event. ■ **precursive** or **precursory** ADJ.

predate VB **1** to write an earlier date on (a

document, cheque, etc). **2** to occur at an earlier date than (a specified date or event).

predation N the killing and eating of other animals for survival; the activity of preying.

predator N any animal that obtains food by catching, usu killing, and eating other animals.

predatory ADJ **1** of an animal: obtaining food by catching and eating other animals. **2** cruelly exploiting the weakness or goodwill of others.

predecessor N **1** the person who formerly held a job or position now held by someone else. **2** the previous version, model, etc of a particular thing or product. **3** an ancestor.

predestination N **1** the act of predestining or fact of being predestined. **2** RELIG the doctrine that whatever is to happen has been unalterably fixed by God.

predestine VB to ordain or decree by fate.

predetermine VB **1** to decide, settle or fix in advance. **2** to influence, shape or bias something in a certain way.
■ **predetermined** ADJ.

predicable ADJ able to be predicated.

predicament N **1** a difficulty, plight or dilemma. **2** LOGIC a category.

predicate VB **1** to assert. **2** to imply; to entail the existence of something. **3** LOGIC to state something as a property of the subject of a proposition. **4** (usu **predicate on** or **upon sth**) to make the viability of (an idea, etc) depend on something else being true: **Their success was predicated on the number of supporters they had.** ■ **predication** N.

predict VB to prophesy, foretell or forecast.

predictable ADJ **1** able to be predicted; easily foreseen. **2** DEROG boringly consistent in behaviour or reactions, etc; unoriginal.
■ **predictability** N. ■ **predictably** ADV.

prediction N **1** the act or art of predicting. **2** something foretold.

predilection N a special liking or preference for something.

predispose VB **1** to incline someone to react in a particular way. **2** to make someone susceptible to something (esp illness).
■ **predisposition** N.

predominant ADJ more numerous, prominent or powerful. ■ **predominance** N.

predominate VB, INTR **1** to be more numerous. **2** to be more noticeable or prominent. **3** to have more influence.

pre-eminent ADJ better than all others.
■ **pre-eminence** N. ■ **pre-eminently** ADV.

pre-empt VB **1** to do something ahead of someone else and so make pointless (an action they had planned). **2** to obtain something in advance. ■ **pre-emption** N.

pre-emptive ADJ **1** having the effect of pre-empting. **2** MIL of an attack: effectively destroying the enemy's weapons before they can be used: **a pre-emptive strike**.

preen VB **1** TR & INTR of a bird: to clean and smooth (feathers, etc) with its beak. **2** of a person: to groom (oneself, hair, clothes, etc).

prefab N a prefabricated building.

prefabricate VB to manufacture standard sections of (a building) for later quick assembly.

preface N **1** an explanatory statement at the beginning of a book. **2** anything of an introductory or preliminary character.
➤ VB to introduce or precede something with some preliminary matter.

prefatory ADJ introductory.

prefect N **1** in a school: a senior pupil with minor disciplinary powers. **2** in some countries: the senior official of an administrative district.

prefecture N **1** the office or term of office of a prefect. **2** the district presided over by a prefect. **3** the official residence of a prefect.

prefer VB (**-rr-**) **1** to like someone or something better than another: **I prefer tea to coffee.** **2** LAW to submit (a charge, accusation, etc) to a court of law for consideration. **3** FORMAL to promote someone, esp over their colleagues.

preferable ADJ more desirable, suitable or

advisable; better. ■ **preferably** ADV.

preference N 1 the preferring of one person, thing, etc to another. 2 one's choice of, or liking for, someone or something particular. 3 favourable consideration.
◆ **in preference to** rather than.

preferential ADJ bestowing special favours or advantages: **preferential treatment**.

preferment N promotion to a more responsible position.

prefix N 1 GRAM an element such as **un-, pre-, non-, de-**, etc which is added to the beginning of a word to create a new word. 2 a title such as **Mr, Dr, Ms**, etc.
➣ VB 1 to add something as an introduction. 2 to add (a prefix) to something.

pregnable ADJ capable of being taken by force; vulnerable.

pregnancy N (-ies) BIOL in female mammals: the period between conception and birth, during which an embryo is in the womb.

pregnant ADJ 1 of a female mammal: carrying a child or young in the womb. 2 of a remark or pause, etc: loaded with significance.

preheat VB to heat (an oven, etc) before use.

prehensile ADJ, DENOTING a part of an animal adapted for grasping.

prehistoric or **prehistorical** ADJ 1 of or relating to the period before written records. 2 COLLOQ completely outdated or very old-fashioned. ■ **prehistory** N.

prejudge VB 1 to form an opinion on (an issue, etc) without having all the relevant facts. 2 to condemn someone unheard.

prejudice N 1 a biased opinion, based on insufficient knowledge. 2 hostility, eg towards a particular racial or religious group. 3 LAW harm; detriment; disadvantage.
➣ VB 1 to make someone feel prejudice; to bias. 2 to harm or endanger.

prejudicial ADJ 1 causing prejudice. 2 harmful.

prelate N, CHRISTIANITY a bishop, abbot or other high-ranking ecclesiastic. ■ **prelacy** N (-ies).

preliminary ADJ occurring at the beginning; introductory or preparatory.
➣ N (-ies) 1 (usu **preliminaries**) something done or said by way of introduction. 2 a preliminary round in a competition.

prelude N 1 MUS an introductory passage or first movement, eg of a fugue or suite. 2 a name sometimes given to a short musical piece or a poetical composition, etc. 3 (esp **a prelude to sth**) some event that precedes, and prepares for, one of greater significance.

premarital ADJ belonging to or occurring in the period before marriage.

premature ADJ 1 MED of human birth: occurring less than 37 weeks after conception. 2 occurring before the usual or expected time. 3 over-hasty; impulsive.

premeditate VB to plan; to think something out beforehand. ■ **premeditated** ADJ. ■ **premeditation** N.

premenstrual ADJ 1 relating to or occurring during the days immediately before a menstrual period. 2 of a woman: in the days immediately before a menstrual period.

premier ADJ first in rank; leading.
➣ N a prime minister.

première or **premiere** N the first public performance of a play or showing of a film.
➣ VB 1 to present a première of (a film, etc). 2 INTR of a play, film, etc: to open.

premise N 1 (also **premiss**) something assumed to be true as a basis for stating something further. 2 LOGIC either of the propositions introducing a syllogism.

premises PL N a building and its grounds, esp as a place of business.

premium N 1 an amount paid, usu annually, on an insurance agreement. 2 an extra sum added to wages or to interest. 3 a prize. 4 AS ADJ finest; exceptional: **premium quality**.
◆ **be at a premium** to be scarce and greatly in demand.

premolar N any of the teeth between the canine teeth and the molars.

premonition N a feeling that something is about to happen, before it actually does; an intuition or presentiment.

prenatal ADJ relating to or occurring during the period before childbirth. ■ **prenatally** ADV.

preoccupation N 1 the state or condition of being preoccupied. 2 something that preoccupies.

preoccupied ADJ 1 lost in thought. 2 (often **preoccupied by** or **with sth**) having one's attention completely taken up; engrossed.

preoccupy VB to occupy the attention of someone wholly; to engross or obsess.

preordain VB to decide or determine beforehand.

prep N, COLLOQ 1 short for **preparation** (sense 3). 2 short for **preparatory**: prep school.

prepack VB to pack (food, etc) before offering it for sale.

preparation N 1 the process of preparing or being prepared. 2 (usu **preparations**) something done by way of preparing or getting ready. 3 BRIT, chiefly in public schools: school work done out of school hours, done either in school or as homework.

preparatory ADJ 1 serving to prepare for something. 2 introductory; preliminary.

prepare VB 1 TR & INTR to make or get ready. 2 to make (a meal). 3 to clean or chop (vegetables or fruit). 4 to get someone or oneself into a fit state to receive a shock, etc.

prepared ADJ 1 (usu **be prepared to do sth**) of a person: to be willing and able: I'm not prepared to lend any more. 2 (usu **prepared for sth**) expecting it or ready for it.

prepay VB to pay for something, esp postage, in advance. ■ **prepaid** ADJ.

preponderance N 1 the circumstance of predominating. 2 a superior number; a majority.

preponderate VB, INTR (often **preponderate over sth**) to be more numerous than it; to predominate.

preposition N, GRAM a word, or words, such as **to, from, into, out of**, etc, typically preceding nouns and pronouns, and describing their position, movement, etc in relation to other words in the sentence. ■ **prepositional** ADJ.

prepossess VB, RATHER FORMAL 1 to charm. 2 to win over; to incline or bias. 3 to preoccupy someone in a specified way.

prepossessing ADJ attractive; winning.

preposterous ADJ ridiculous, absurd or outrageous. ■ **preposterously** ADV.

preppy INFORMAL, esp N AMER, ADJ (**-ier, -iest**) of dress sense, etc: neat and conservative. ➤ N (**-ies**) someone who dresses in such a way.

preprandial ADJ, FACETIOUS preceding a meal.

prep school N (in full **preparatory school**) in the UK: a private school that prepares children for public school.

prepuce N, ANAT the fold of skin that covers the top of the penis. Also called **foreskin**.

prequel N a book or film produced after one that has been a popular success, but with the story beginning prior to the start of the original.

prerecord VB to record (a programme for radio or TV) in advance of its scheduled broadcasting time.

prerequisite N a preliminary requirement that must be satisfied. ➤ ADJ of a condition, etc: required to be satisfied beforehand.

prerogative N 1 an exclusive right or privilege arising from one's rank or position. 2 any right or privilege.

presage VB 1 to warn of or be a warning sign of something; to forebode or portend. 2 to have a premonition about something. ➤ N, FORMAL OR LITERARY 1 a portent, warning or omen. 2 a premonition.

presbyterian ADJ of or relating to church administration by presbyters or elders.

presbytery N (**-ies**) 1 in a presbyterian church: an area of local administration. 2 a body of ministers and elders. 3 the residence of a Roman Catholic priest.

preschool ADJ denoting or relating to children before they are old enough to attend school.

prescience N foreknowledge; foresight. ■ **prescient** ADJ.

prescribe VB 1 esp of a doctor: to advise (a medicine) as a remedy, esp by completing a prescription. 2 to recommend officially (eg a text for academic study). 3 to lay down or establish (a duty, penalty, etc) officially.

prescript N, FORMAL a law, rule, principle, etc.

prescription N 1 a a set of written instructions from a doctor to a pharmacist regarding the preparation and dispensing of a drug, etc for a particular patient; b the drug, etc prescribed in this way by a doctor. 2 a set of written instructions for an optician stating the type of lenses required to correct a patient's vision.

prescriptive ADJ 1 authoritative; laying down rules. 2 of a right, etc: established by custom.

presence N 1 the state or circumstance of being present. 2 someone's company or nearness. 3 physical bearing, esp if it is commanding or authoritative. 4 a being felt to be close by, esp in a supernatural way. 5 a situation or activity demonstrating influence or power in a place.

presence of mind N the ability to act calmly and sensibly, esp in an emergency.

present[1] ADJ 1 being at the place or occasion in question. 2 existing, detectable or able to be found. 3 existing now: **the present situation**. 4 now being considered: **the present subject**. 5 GRAM of the tense of a verb: indicating action that is taking place now, or action that is continuing or habitual, as in **I walk the dog every morning** and **He's going to school**. ➤ N the present time. ◆ **for the present** for the time being.

present[2] VB 1 to give or award something, esp formally or ceremonially: **presented them with gold medals**. 2 to introduce (a person), esp formally. 3 to introduce or compère (a TV or radio show). 4 to stage (a play), show (a film), etc. 5 to offer something for consideration; to

submit. 6 to pose; to set: **shouldn't present any problem**. 7 of an idea: to suggest (itself). 8 to hand over (a cheque) for acceptance or (a bill) for payment. 9 to set out something: **presents her work neatly**. 10 to depict or represent something or someone. ◆ **present arms** to hold a rifle or other weapon vertically in front of one as a salute.

present[3] N something given; a gift.

presentable ADJ 1 fit to be seen or to appear in company, etc. 2 passable; satisfactory.

presentation N 1 the act of presenting. 2 the manner in which something is presented, laid out, explained or advertised. 3 something performed for an audience, eg a play, show or other entertainment. 4 a formal report, usu delivered verbally.

present-day ADJ modern; contemporary.

presenter N, BROADCASTING someone who introduces a programme and provides a linking commentary between items.

presentiment N a feeling that something is about to happen, just before it does.

presently ADV 1 soon; shortly. 2 N AMER, ESP US at the present time; now.

preservative N a chemical substance that, when added to food or other perishable material, slows down or prevents its decay.

preserve VB 1 to save something from loss, damage, decay or deterioration. 2 to treat (food), eg by freezing, smoking, drying, etc, so that it will last. 3 to maintain (eg peace, the status quo, standards, etc). 4 to keep safe from danger or death. ➤ N 1 an area of work or activity that is restricted to certain people. 2 an area of land or water where creatures are protected for private hunting, shooting or fishing: **game preserve**. 3 a jam, pickle or other form in which fruit or vegetables are preserved by cooking in sugar, salt, vinegar, etc. ■ **preservation** N.

preset VB to adjust (a piece of equipment, etc) so that it will operate at the required time.

preside VB, INTR (often **preside at** or **over**

sth) **1** to take the lead at (an event), the chair at (a meeting, etc); to be in charge. **2** to dominate.

president N **1** (often **President**) the elected head of state in a republic. **2** the chief office-bearer in a society or club. **3** esp US the head of a business organization, eg the chairman of a company, governor of a bank, etc.
■ **presidency** N. ■ **presidential** ADJ.

press¹ VB **1 a** TR & INTR to push steadily, esp with the finger: press the bell; **b** (often **press against** or **on** or **down on sth**) to push it; to apply pressure to it. **2** to hold something firmly against something; to flatten. **3** to compress or squash. **4** to squeeze (eg someone's hand) affectionately. **5** to preserve (plants) by flattening and drying, eg between the pages of a book. **6 a** to squeeze (fruit) to extract juice; **b** to extract (juice) from fruit by squeezing. **7** to iron (clothes, etc). **8** to urge or compel someone; to ask them insistently. **9** to insist on something: press the point. **10** LAW to bring (charges) officially against someone.
➤ N **1** an act of pressing. **2** any apparatus for pressing, flattening, squeezing, etc. **3** a printing press. **4** the process or art of printing. **5** (**the press**) newspapers or journalists in general. **6** newspaper publicity or reviews received by a show, book, etc: got a poor press. **7** SCOT a cupboard.
◆ **go to press** to be sent for printing.
◆ **press on, ahead** or **forward** to hurry on; to continue, esp in spite of difficulties.
◆ **press sth on sb** to insist on giving it to them.

press² VB **1** to force (men) into the army or navy. **2** (esp **press sth** or **sb into service**) to put it or them to use.

press agent N someone who arranges newspaper advertising or publicity.

press conference and **news conference** N an interview granted to reporters by a politician, etc.

press cutting N a paragraph or article cut from a newspaper, etc.

pressed ADJ of a person: under pressure; in a hurry.
◆ **be hard pressed** to be in difficulties.

◆ **be pressed for sth** COLLOQ to be short of it.

pressgang N, HIST a gang employed to seize men and force them into the army or navy.
➤ VB **1** to force (men) into the army or navy. **2** FACETIOUS to coerce someone into something.

pressie or **prezzie** N, COLLOQ a gift.

pressing ADJ urgent: pressing engagements.

press stud N a type of button-like fastener, one part of which is pressed into the other.

press-up N an exercise performed face down, raising and lowering the body on the arms while keeping the trunk and legs rigid.

pressure N **1** PHYS the force exerted on a surface divided by the area of the surface to which it is applied. **2** the act of pressing or process of being pressed. **3** forceful persuasion. **4** urgency; strong demand: work under pressure. **5** tension or stress.
➤ VB to try to persuade; to coerce or force.

pressure cooker N a thick-walled pan with an airtight lid, in which food is cooked at speed by steam under high pressure.

pressure group N a number of people who join together to influence public opinion and government policy on some issue.

pressurize or **-ise** VB **1** to adjust the pressure within (an enclosed compartment such as an aircraft cabin) so that nearly normal atmospheric pressure is constantly maintained. **2** to put pressure on someone or something; to force or coerce.

prestidigitation N sleight of hand.

prestige N **1** fame, distinction or reputation due to rank or success. **2 a** influence; glamour: a job with prestige; **b** AS ADJ: prestige cars.
■ **prestigious** ADJ.

presto ADV, MUS in a very fast manner.

presumably ADV I suppose; probably.

presume VB **1** to suppose (something to be the case) without proof; to take something for granted: presumed he was dead. **2** to be bold enough; to venture: wouldn't presume to advise the experts. ■ **presumption** N.

◆ **presume on** or **upon sb** or **sth 1** to rely or count on them or it, esp unduly. **2** to take unfair advantage of (someone's good nature, etc).

presumptive ADJ **1** presumed rather than certain. **2** giving grounds for presuming.

presumptuous ADJ over-bold in behaviour, esp towards others; insolent or arrogant.

presuppose VB **1** to take for granted; to assume as true. **2** to imply the existence of something. ■ **presupposition** N.

pretence or (US) **pretense** N **1** the act of pretending. **2** make-believe. **3** an act someone puts on deliberately to mislead. **4** a claim, esp an unjustified one: **make no pretence to expert knowledge**. **5** show, affectation or ostentation. **6** (usu **pretences**) a misleading declaration of intention. **7** show or semblance.

pretend VB **1** TR & INTR to make believe; to act as if, or give the impression that, something is the case when it is not. **2** TR & INTR to imply or claim falsely: **pretended not to know**. **3** to claim to feel something; to profess something falsely: **pretend friendship towards someone**.
◆ **pretend to sth 1** to claim to have (a skill, etc), esp falsely. **2** HIST to lay claim, esp doubtful claim, to (eg the throne).

pretender N someone who pretends or pretended to something, esp the throne.

pretension N **1** foolish vanity, self-importance or affectation. **2** a claim or aspiration: **had no pretensions to elegance**.

pretentious ADJ **1** pompous, self-important or foolishly grandiose. **2** phoney or affected. **3** showy; ostentatious. ■ **pretentiousness** N.

preternatural ADJ **1** exceeding the normal; uncanny; extraordinary. **2** supernatural.

pretext N a false reason given for doing something in order to disguise the real one.

prettify VB (**-ies, -ied**) to attempt to make something or someone prettier by superficial ornamentation. ■ **prettification** N.

pretty ADJ (**-ier, -iest**) **1** usu of a woman or girl: facially attractive, esp in a feminine way. **2** charming to look at; decorative. **3** of music, sound, etc: delicately melodious. **4** neat, elegant or skilful: **a pretty solution**.
➤ ADV fairly; satisfactorily; rather; decidedly. ■ **prettily** ADV. ■ **prettiness** N.
◆ **pretty much** COLLOQ more or less.
◆ **pretty nearly** almost.

pretzel N a crisp salted biscuit in a knot shape.

prevail VB, INTR **1** (often **prevail over** or **against sb** or **sth**) to be victorious; to win through: **Common sense prevailed**. **2** to be the common, usual or generally accepted thing.
◆ **prevail on** or **upon sb** or **sth** to persuade them or appeal to it.

prevailing ADJ most common or frequent.

prevalent ADJ common; widespread. ■ **prevalence** N.

prevaricate VB, INTR to avoid stating the truth or coming directly to the point; to behave or speak evasively. ■ **prevarication** N.

prevent VB **1** to stop someone from doing something, or something from happening; to hinder. **2** to stop the occurrence of something beforehand or to make it impossible; to avert. ■ **preventable** or **preventible** ADJ. ■ **prevention** N. ■ **preventive** or **preventative** ADJ, N.

preview N **1** an advance view. **2** an advance showing of a film, play, exhibition, etc before it is presented to the general public.
➤ VB to show or view (a film, etc) in advance to a select audience.

previous ADJ **1** earlier: **a previous occasion**. **2** former: **the previous chairman**. **3** prior: **a previous engagement**. **4** FACETIOUS premature; over-hasty. **5** (usu **previous to sth**) before (an event, etc). ■ **previously** ADV.

prey SING OR PL N **1** an animal or animals hunted as food by another animal. **2** a victim or victims: **easy prey for muggers**. **3** (usu **a prey to sth**) someone liable to suffer from (an illness, etc).
➤ VB, INTR (now esp **prey on** or **upon sth** or **sb**) **1** of an animal: to hunt or catch (another animal) as food. **2 a** to bully, exploit or terrorize as victims; **b** to afflict them in an obsessive way.

price N 1 the amount, usu in money, for which a thing is sold or offered. 2 what must be given up or suffered in gaining something. 3 the sum by which someone may be bribed.
➤ VB 1 to fix a price for or mark a price on something. 2 to find out the price of something.
◆ **at a price** at great expense.
◆ **at any price** no matter what it costs, eg in terms of money, sacrifice, etc.
◆ **beyond** or **without price** invaluable.

priceless ADJ 1 too valuable to have a price; inestimably precious. 2 COLLOQ hilarious.

pricey or **pricy** ADJ (*-ier, -iest*) COLLOQ expensive.

prick VB 1 to pierce slightly with a fine point. 2 to make (a hole) by this means. 3 TR & INTR to hurt something or someone by this means. 4 TR & INTR to smart or make something smart: **feel one's eyes pricking**. 5 TR & INTR (also **prick up**) a of a dog, horse, etc: to stick (its ears) upright in response to sound; b of a dog's, etc ears: to stand erect in this way. 6 to trouble: **His conscience must be pricking him**. 7 to plant (seedlings, etc) in an area of soil that has had small holes marked out on it.
➤ N 1 an act of pricking or feeling of being pricked. 2 the pain of this. 3 a puncture made by pricking. 4 SLANG the penis. 5 DEROG SLANG an abusive term for a man.
◆ **prick up one's ears** COLLOQ to start listening attentively.

prickle N 1 a hard pointed structure growing from the surface of a plant or animal. 2 a pricking sensation.
➤ VB, TR & INTR to cause, affect something with or be affected with, a prickling sensation.

prickly ADJ (*-ier, -iest*) 1 covered with or full of prickles. 2 causing prickling. 3 COLLOQ over-sensitive. ■ **prickliness** N.

prickly heat N an itchy skin rash.

pride N 1 a feeling of pleasure and satisfaction at one's own or another's accomplishments, possessions, etc. 2 the source of this feeling: **That car is my pride and joy**. 3 self-respect; personal dignity. 4 an unjustified assumption of superiority; arrogance. 5 POETIC the finest state;

the prime. 6 the finest item: **the pride of the collection**. 7 a group of lions.
➤ VB (always **pride oneself on sth**) to congratulate oneself on account of it.
◆ **take pride** or **take a pride in sth** to be conscientious about maintaining high standards in (one's work, etc).

priest N 1 a in the Roman Catholic and Orthodox churches: an ordained minister authorized to administer the sacraments; b in the Anglican church: a minister ranking between deacon and bishop. 2 in non-Christian religions: an official who performs religious rites. ■ **priestly** ADJ.

priestess N in non-Christian religions: a female priest.

priesthood N 1 the office of a priest. 2 the character of a priest. 3 priests collectively.

prig N someone who is self-righteously moralistic. ■ **priggery** N. ■ **priggish** ADJ.

prim ADJ (*primmer, primmest*) 1 stiffly formal, over-modest or over-proper. 2 prudishly disapproving. ■ **primly** ADV. ■ **primness** N.

prima ballerina N the leading female dancer in a ballet company.

primacy N (*-ies*) 1 the condition of being first in rank, importance or order. 2 the rank, office or area of jurisdiction of a primate of the church.

prima donna N (*prima donnas*) 1 a leading female opera singer. 2 someone given to melodramatic tantrums when displeased.

primaeval see **primeval**

primal ADJ 1 relating to the beginnings of life; original. 2 basic; fundamental.

primarily ADV 1 mainly. 2 initially.

primary ADJ 1 first or most important; principal. 2 earliest in order or development. 3 basic; fundamental. 4 at the elementary stage or level. 5 of education, schools, classes etc: for children aged between 5 and 11. 6 of a bird's wing feather: outermost and longest. 7 firsthand; direct: **primary sources of information**. 8 of a product or industry: being or concerned with produce in its raw natural state.

➤ N (*-ies*) **1** something that is first or most important. **2** US a preliminary election, esp to select delegates for a presidential election. **3** BRIT COLLOQ a primary school.

primary colour N of pigments: the colours red, yellow and blue, which can be combined in various proportions to give all other colours.

primary school N a school, esp a state one, for pupils aged between 5 and 11.

primate N **1** ZOOL any member of an order of mammalian vertebrates which have a large brain, forward-facing eyes, nails instead of claws, and hands with grasping thumbs facing the other digits, eg a human, ape, etc. **2** CHRISTIANITY an archbishop.

prime ADJ **1** chief; fundamental. **2** the best quality. **3** excellent: **in prime condition**. **4** supremely typical: **a prime example**. **5** having the greatest potential for attracting interest or custom.
➤ N the best, most productive or active stage in the life of a person or thing: **cut down in her prime**.
➤ VB **1** to prepare (something, eg wood for painting by applying a sealing coat of size, a gun for firing by inserting the igniting material, etc). **2** to brief.

prime minister N the chief minister of a government.

prime number N, MATH a whole number that can only be divided by itself and 1.

primer N **1** a first or introductory book of instruction. **2** any material that is used to provide an initial coating for a surface before it is painted. **3** any device that ignites or detonates an explosive charge.

primeval or **primaeval** ADJ **1** relating or belonging to the Earth's beginnings. **2** primitive. **3** instinctive.

primitive ADJ **1** relating or belonging to earliest times or the earliest stages of development. **2** simple, rough, crude or rudimentary. **3** ART simple, naïve or unsophisticated in style. **4** BIOL original; belonging to an early stage of development.

➤ N **1** an unsophisticated person or thing. **2 a** a work by an artist in naïve style; **b** an artist who produces such a work. ■ **primitively** ADV. ■ **primitiveness** N.

primitivism N, ART the pursuit of strong effects found, for example, in African tribal or Oceanic art.

primogeniture N **1** the fact of being the firstborn child. **2** the right or principle of succession or inheritance of an eldest son.

primordial ADJ **1** existing from the beginning; formed earliest: **primordial matter**. **2** BIOL relating to an early stage in growth.

primp VB, TR & INTR to groom, preen or titivate.

primrose N **1** a small plant with a rosette of oval leaves, and long-stalked pale-yellow flowers. **2** (in full **primrose yellow**) **a** the pale-yellow colour of these flowers; **b** AS ADJ: **a primrose dress**.

primula N (*-ae* or *-as*) a plant with white, pink, purple or yellow flowers with five spreading petals, eg the primrose, cowslip and oxslip.

prince N **1** in the UK: the son of a sovereign. **2** a non-reigning male member of a royal or imperial family. **3** a sovereign of a small territory. **4** a nobleman in certain countries. **5** someone or something celebrated or outstanding within a type or class: **the prince of highwaymen**.

princedom N a principality; the estate, jurisdiction, sovereignty or rank of a prince.

princely ADJ **1** characteristic of or suitable for a prince. **2** lavish; generous.

princess N **1** the wife or daughter of a prince. **2** the daughter of a sovereign. **3** a female member of a royal family.

principal ADJ first in rank or importance; chief.
➤ N **1** the head of an educational institution. **2** a leading actor, dancer, etc in a theatrical production. **3** LAW the person on behalf of whom an agent is acting. **4** someone who commits or participates in a crime. **5** COMMERCE the original sum of money on which interest is paid. **6** MUS the leading player of each section of an orchestra. ■ **principally** ADV.

principality N (-*ies*) **1** a territory ruled by a prince, or one that he derives his title from. **2** (**the Principality**) in the UK: Wales.

principle N **1** a general truth or assumption from which to argue. **2** a scientific law, esp one that explains a natural phenomenon or the way a machine works. **3** a general rule of morality that guides conduct; the having of or holding to such rules: **a woman of principle**. **4** (**principles**) a set of such rules. **5** a fundamental element or source: **the vital principle**.
◆ **in principle** esp of agreement to a plan or decision: in theory; in general, although not necessarily in a particular case.
◆ **on principle** on the grounds of a particular principle of morality or wisdom.

principled ADJ holding, or proceeding from principles, esp high moral principles.

print VB **1** to reproduce (text or pictures) on paper with ink, using a printing–press or other mechanical means. **2** to publish (a book, article, etc). **3** TR & INTR to write in separate, as opposed to joined–up, letters. **4** to make (a positive photograph) from a negative. **5** to mark (a shape, pattern, etc) in or on a surface by pressure. **6** to mark designs on (fabric). **7** to fix (a scene) indelibly (on the memory, etc).
➢ N **1** often IN COMPOUNDS a mark made on a surface by the pressure of something in contact with it: **pawprint**. **2** a fingerprint. **3** hand–done lettering with each letter written separately. **4** mechanically printed text: **small print**. **5** a printed publication. **6** a design or picture printed from an engraved wood block or metal plate. **7** a positive photograph made from a negative. **8** a fabric with a printed design.
◆ **print sth out** to produce a printed version, eg of computer data.

printer N **1** a person or business engaged in printing books, newspapers, etc. **2** a machine that prints, eg photographs. **3** COMP a type of output device that produces printed copies of text or graphics on to paper.

printing N **1** the art or business of producing books, etc in print. **2** the run of books, etc printed all at one time. **3** the form of handwriting in which the letters are separately written.

printout N, COMP output from a computer system in the form of a printed paper copy.

prior[1] ADJ **1** of an engagement: already arranged for the time in question; previous. **2** more urgent or pressing: **a prior claim**.
◆ **prior to sth** before an event.

prior[2] N, CHRISTIANITY **1** the head of some communities of monks and friars. **2** in an abbey: the deputy of the abbot. ■ **prioress** N.

priority N (-*ies*) **1** the right to be or go first; precedence or preference. **2** something that must be attended to before anything else. ■ **prioritize** or **-ise** VB.

priory N (-*ies*) CHRISTIANITY a religious house under the supervision of a prior or prioress.

prise or (US) **prize** VB **1** to lever something open, off, out, etc, usu with some difficulty: **prised open the lid**. **2** to get with difficulty: **prised the truth out of her**.

prism N **1** GEOM a solid figure in which the two ends are matching parallel polygons (eg triangles or squares) and all other surfaces are parallelograms. **2** OPTICS a transparent block, usu of glass and with triangular ends and rectangular sides, that separates a beam of white light into the colours of the visible spectrum. ■ **prismatic** ADJ.

prison N **1** a building for the confinement of convicted criminals and certain accused persons awaiting trial. **2** any place of confinement or situation of intolerable restriction. **3** custody; imprisonment.

prisoner N **1** someone who is under arrest or confined in prison. **2** a captive, esp in war.

prisoner of war N someone taken prisoner during a war, esp from the armed forces.

prissy ADJ (-*ier*, -*iest*) insipidly prim and prudish.

pristine ADJ **1** fresh, clean, unused or untouched. **2** original; unchanged or unspoilt: **still in its pristine state**. **3** former.

privacy N **1 a** freedom from intrusion by the public; **b** someone's right to this: **should respect**

her privacy. **2** seclusion; secrecy.

private ADJ **1** not open to, or available for the use of, the general public. **2** of a person: not holding public office. **3** kept secret from others; confidential. **4** relating to someone's personal, as distinct from their professional, life: **a private engagement**. **5** of thoughts or opinions: personal and usu kept to oneself. **6** quiet and reserved by nature. **7** of a place: secluded. **8 a** not coming under the state system of education, healthcare, etc; **b** paid for or paying individually by fee, etc.
➤ N **1** a private soldier. **2** (**privates**) COLLOQ the private parts. ■ **privately** ADV.
◆ **in private** not in public; confidentially.

private detective and **private investigator** N someone who is not a member of the police force, engaged to do detective work. Also called **private eye**.

privateer N, HIST a privately owned ship engaged by a government to seize and plunder an enemy's ships in wartime.

private parts PL N, EUPHEMISTIC the external genitals and excretory organs.

private school N a school run independently by an individual or group, esp for profit.

privation N the condition of not having, or being deprived of, life's comforts or necessities; a lack of something particular.

privative ADJ lacking some quality that is usu, or expected to be, present.

privatize or **-ise** VB to transfer (a state-owned business) to private ownership. ■ **privatization** N.

privet N a shrub with glossy dark-green leaves, used esp in garden hedges.

privilege N **1** a right granted to an individual or a select few, bestowing an advantage not enjoyed by others. **2** advantages and power enjoyed by people of wealth and high social class. **3** an opportunity to do something that brings one delight; a pleasure or honour.
➤ VB, TR & INTR to grant a right, privilege or special favour to someone or something.

privy ADJ **1** (usu **privy to sth**) allowed to share in (secret discussions, etc) or know about secret plans, etc. **2** OLD USE secret; hidden.
➤ N (**-ies**) OLD USE a lavatory.

prize[1] N **1** something won in a competition, lottery, etc. **2** a reward given in recognition of excellence. **3** something striven for, or worth striving for. **4** something captured or taken by force, esp a ship in war; a trophy. **5** AS ADJ **a** deserving, or having won, a prize: **a prize bull**; **b** highly valued: **her prize possession**; **c** IRONIC perfect; great: **a prize fool**; **d** belonging or relating to, or given as, a prize: **prize money**.
➤ VB to value or regard highly.

prize[2] see **prise**

prizefight N a boxing-match fought for a money prize. ■ **prizefighter** N.

pro[1] PREP in favour of something.
➤ N a reason or choice in favour of something.

pro[2] N, COLLOQ **1** a professional. **2** a prostitute.

proactive ADJ actively initiating change in anticipation of future developments, rather than merely reacting to events as they occur.

probability N (**-ies**) **1** the state of being probable; likelihood. **2** something that is probable. **3** STATISTICS a mathematical expression of the likelihood or chance of a particular event occurring.
◆ **in all probability** most probably.

probable ADJ **1** likely to happen: **a probable outcome**. **2** likely to be the case; likely to have happened. **3** likely to be correct; feasible. ■ **probably** ADV.

probate N **1** LAW the process of establishing that a will is valid. **2** an official copy of a will, with the document certifying its validity.

probation N **1** the system whereby offenders, esp young or first offenders, are allowed their freedom under supervision, on condition of good behaviour. **2** a trial period during which a new employee is observed on the job, to confirm whether or not they can do it satisfactorily. ■ **probationary** ADJ.

probationer N someone on probation.

probe N 1 a long, slender instrument used by doctors to examine a wound, locate a bullet, etc. 2 a comprehensive investigation. 3 an act of probing; a poke or prod.
➤ VB (often **probe into sth**) 1 to investigate it closely. 2 TR & INTR to examine it with a probe. 3 TR & INTR to poke or prod it.

probity N integrity; honesty.

problem N 1 a situation or matter that is difficult to understand or deal with: **a problem with the software**. 2 someone or something that is difficult to deal with. 3 a puzzle or mathematical question set for solving. 4 AS ADJ of a child, etc: difficult to deal with, esp in being disruptive or anti-social.
◆ **no problem** COLLOQ 1 it's a pleasure, no trouble, etc. 2 easily: **found it, no problem**.

problematic and **problematical** ADJ 1 causing problems. 2 uncertain.

proboscis N (*proboscises* or *proboscides*) 1 ZOOL the flexible elongated snout of the elephant or tapir. 2 ENTOMOL the elongated tubular mouthparts of certain insects.

procedure N 1 the method and order followed in doing something. 2 an established routine for conducting business at a meeting or in a law case. 3 a course of action; a step or measure taken. ■ **procedural** ADJ.

proceed VB, INTR 1 FORMAL to make one's way: **I proceeded along the road**. 2 (often **proceed with sth**) to go on with it; to continue after stopping. 3 to set about a task, etc.

proceeding N 1 an action; a piece of behaviour. 2 (**proceedings**) a published record of the business done or papers read at a meeting of a society, etc. 3 (**proceedings**) legal action: **begin divorce proceedings**.

proceeds PL N money made by an event, sale, transaction, etc.

process N 1 a series of operations performed during manufacture, etc. 2 a series of stages which something passes through, resulting in the development or transformation of it. 3 an operation or procedure: **a slow process**.

4 ANAT a projection or outgrowth, esp one on a bone. 5 LAW a writ by which a person or matter is brought into court.
➤ VB 1 to put something through the required process; to deal with (eg an application) appropriately. 2 to prepare (agricultural produce) for marketing, eg by canning, bottling or treating it chemically. 3 COMP to perform operations on (data, etc).
◆ **in the process of sth** in the course of it.

procession N 1 a file of people or vehicles proceeding ceremonially. 2 this kind of succession or sequence. ■ **processional** ADJ.

processor N 1 a machine or person that processes something. 2 COMP a central processing unit.

pro-choice ADJ supporting the right of a woman to have an abortion.

proclaim VB 1 to announce something publicly. 2 to declare someone to be something: **was proclaimed a traitor**. 3 to attest or prove something all too clearly. ■ **proclaimer** N. ■ **proclamation** N. ■ **proclamatory** ADJ.

proclivity N (*-ies*) rather FORMAL a tendency, liking or preference.

procrastinate VB, INTR to put off doing something that should be done straight away. ■ **procrastination** N. ■ **procrastinator** N.

procreate VB, TR & INTR to produce (offspring); to reproduce. N. ■ **procreation** N.

proctor N in some English universities: an official whose functions include enforcement of discipline. ■ **proctorial** ADJ.

procurator N an agent with power of attorney in a law court.

procurator fiscal N, SCOT an official combining the roles of coroner and public prosecutor.

procure VB 1 to manage to obtain something or bring it about. 2 TR & INTR to get (women or girls) to act as prostitutes. ■ **procurement** N.

prod VB (*-dd-*) 1 (often **prod at sth**) to poke or jab it. 2 to nudge, prompt or spur (a person or animal) into action.

➤ N **1** a poke, jab or nudge. **2** a reminder. **3** a goad or similar pointed instrument.

prodigal ADJ **1** heedlessly extravagant or wasteful. **2** (often **prodigal of sth**) FORMAL OR OLD USE lavish in bestowing it; generous.
➤ N **1** a squanderer, wastrel or spendthrift. **2** (also **prodigal son**) a repentant ne'er-do-well or a returned wanderer. ■ **prodigality** N.

prodigious ADJ **1** extraordinary or marvellous. **2** enormous; vast. ■ **prodigiously** ADV.

prodigy N (**-ies**) a wonder; an extraordinary phenomenon.

produce VB **1** to bring out or present something to view. **2** to bear (children, young, leaves, etc). **3** TR & INTR to yield (crops, fruit, etc). **4** to secrete (a substance), give off (a smell), etc. **5** TR & INTR to make or manufacture something. **6** to give rise to or prompt (a reaction) from people. **7** to direct (a play), arrange (a radio or television programme) for presentation, or finance and schedule the making of (a film).
➤ N foodstuffs derived from crops or animal livestock, eg fruit, vegetables, eggs and dairy products. ■ **producer** N. ■ **producible** ADJ.

product N **1** something produced, eg through manufacture. **2** a result. **3** MATH the value obtained by multiplying two or more numbers.

production N **1 a** the act of producing; **b** the process of producing or being produced: **The new model goes into production next year.** **2** the quantity produced or rate of producing it. **3** something created; a literary or artistic work. **4** a particular presentation of a play, opera, ballet, etc.

productive ADJ **1** yielding a lot; fertile; fruitful. **2** useful; profitable: **a productive meeting.** **3** (usu **productive of sth**) giving rise to it; resulting in it: **productive of ideas.**

productivity N the rate and efficiency of work, esp in industrial production, etc.

prof N, COLLOQ a professor.

Prof. ABBREV Professor.

profane ADJ **1** showing disrespect for sacred things. **2** not sacred or spiritual; worldly. **3** esp of language: vulgar; blasphemous.
➤ VB **1** to treat (something sacred) irreverently. **2** to violate (what should be respected). ■ **profanation** N. ■ **profanity** N (**-ies**).

profess VB **1** to make an open declaration of (beliefs, etc). **2** to declare adherence to something. **3** to claim or pretend.

professed ADJ **1** self-acknowledged; self-confessed. **2** claimed by oneself; pretended. **3** having taken the vows of a religious order.

profession N **1** an occupation, esp one that requires specialist academic and practical training, eg medicine, teaching, etc. **2** the body of people engaged in a particular one of these. **3** an act of professing; a declaration: **a profession of loyalty.**

professional ADJ **1** earning a living in the performance, practice or teaching of something that is usu a pastime: **a professional golfer.** **2** belonging to a trained profession. **3** like, appropriate to or having the competence, expertise or conscientiousness of someone with professional training.
➤ N **1** someone who belongs to one of the skilled professions. **2** someone who makes their living in an activity, etc that is also carried on at an amateur level. ■ **professionalism** N.

professor N **1** a teacher of the highest rank in a university; the head of a university department. **2** N AMER, ESP US a university teacher. ■ **professorial** ADJ.

proffer VB to offer something for someone to accept; to tender.

proficient ADJ fully trained and competent.
➤ N an expert. ■ **proficiency** N.

profile N **1 a** a side view of something, esp of a face or head; **b** a representation of this. **2** a brief outline, sketch or assessment.
➤ VB **1** to represent in profile. **2** to give a brief outline (of a person, a company, etc).
◆ **keep a low profile** to maintain a unobtrusive presence.

profit N **1** the money gained from selling something for more than it originally cost. **2** an excess of income over expenses. **3** benefit.

➢ VB, INTR (often **profit from** or **by sth**) to benefit from it.

profitable ADJ 1 of a business, etc: making a profit. 2 useful; fruitful. ■ **profitability** N.

profiteer N someone who takes advantage of a shortage or other emergency to make exorbitant profits.

profligate ADJ 1 immoral and irresponsible; dissolute. 2 scandalously extravagant. ➢ N a profligate person. ■ **profligacy** N.

profound ADJ 1 radical, extensive, far–reaching: profound changes. 2 deep; far below the surface. 3 of a feeling: deeply felt or rooted. 4 of comments, etc: showing understanding or penetration. 5 penetrating deeply into knowledge. 6 intense: profound deafness. 7 of sleep: deep; sound. ■ **profoundly** ADV. ■ **profundity** N.

profuse ADJ 1 overflowing; excessive: profuse apologies. 2 copious: profuse bleeding. ■ **profusely** ADV. ■ **profusion** N.

progenitor N an ancestor or forefather.

progeny N (-ies) 1 children; offspring; descendants. 2 a result or conclusion.

progesterone N, BIOCHEM a steroid sex hormone that prepares the lining of the uterus for implantation of a fertilized egg.

prognosis N (-ses) 1 an informed forecast of developments in any situation. 2 a doctor's prediction regarding the probable course of a disease, disorder or injury.

prognostic ADJ serving as an informed forecast; foretelling.

prognosticate VB to foretell. ■ **prognostication** N. ■ **prognosticator** N.

programmable ADJ capable of being programmed to perform a task automatically.

programme or (N AMER) **program** N 1 **a** the schedule of proceedings for, and list of participants in, a theatre performance, entertainment, ceremony, etc; **b** a leaflet or booklet describing these. 2 an agenda, plan or schedule. 3 a series of planned projects to be undertaken. 4 a scheduled radio or TV presentation. 5 (usu **program**) COMP a set of coded instructions to a computer for the performance of a task or a series of operations, written in a programming language. ➢ VB 1 to include something in a programme; to schedule. 2 to draw up a programme for something. 3 to set (a computer) by program to perform a set of operations. 4 to prepare a program for a computer. 5 to set (a machine) so as to operate at the required time.

programmer N someone who writes computer programs.

progress N 1 movement while travelling in any direction. 2 course: followed the progress of the trial. 3 movement towards a destination, goal or state of completion: make slow progress. 4 advances or development. ➢ VB 1 INTR to move forwards or onwards; to proceed towards a goal. 2 INTR to advance or develop. 3 INTR to improve. 4 to put (something planned) into operation; to expedite. ◆ **in progress** in the course of being done.

progression N 1 an act or the process of moving forwards or advancing in stages. 2 improvement.

progressive ADJ 1 advanced in outlook; using or favouring new methods. 2 moving forward or advancing continuously or by stages. 3 of a disease: continuously increasing in severity or complication. 4 of taxation: increasing as the sum taxed increases. ➢ N someone with progressive ideas. ■ **progressively** ADV. ■ **progressivism** N.

prohibit VB 1 to forbid something, esp by law; to ban. 2 to prevent or hinder.

prohibition N 1 the act of prohibiting or state of being prohibited. 2 a law or decree that prohibits something. ■ **prohibitionist** N.

prohibitive or **prohibitory** ADJ 1 banning; prohibiting. 2 tending to prevent or discourage. 3 of prices, etc: unaffordably high.

project N 1 a plan, scheme or proposal. 2 a research or study assignment. ➢ VB 1 INTR to jut out; to protrude. 2 to throw something forwards; to propel. **3** to throw (a shadow, image, etc) on to a surface, screen, etc. **4** to propose or plan. **5** to forecast something from present trends and other known data. **6** to imagine (oneself) in another situation, esp a future one. **7** to cause (a sound, esp the voice) to be heard clearly at some distance.

projectile N an object designed to be projected by an external force, eg a guided missile, bullet, etc.

projection N **1** the act of projecting or process of being projected. **2** something that protrudes from a surface. **3** the process of showing of a film or transparencies on a screen. **4** a forecast based on present trends and other known data. ■ **projectionist** N.

projector N an instrument containing a system of lenses that projects an enlarged version of an illuminated image on to a screen.

prolapse N, PATHOL the slipping out of place or falling down of an organ, esp the slipping of the uterus into the vagina.
➤ VB of an organ: to slip out of place.

prolate ADJ, GEOM of something approximately spherical: more pointed at the poles.

proletarian ADJ of the proletariat.
➤ N a member of the proletariat.

proletariat N **1** the working class, esp unskilled labourers and industrial workers. **2** HIST in ancient Rome: the lowest class.

pro-life ADJ of a person or an organization: opposing abortion, euthanasia and experimentation on human embryos.

proliferate VB **1** INTR of a plant or animal species: to reproduce rapidly. **2** INTR to increase in numbers; to multiply. **3** to reproduce (cells, etc) rapidly. ■ **proliferation** N.

prolific ADJ **1** abundant in growth; producing plentiful fruit or offspring. **2** of a writer, artist, etc: constantly producing new work. **3** (often **prolific of** or **in sth**) productive of it; abounding in it. ■ **prolificacy** N.

prolix ADJ of speech or writing: tediously long-winded; wordy; verbose. ■ **prolixity** N.

prologue N **1** THEAT **a** a speech addressed to the audience at the beginning of a play; **b** the actor delivering it. **2** a preface to a literary work. **3** an event serving as an introduction.

prolong VB to make something longer; to extend or protract. ■ **prolongation** N.

prom N, COLLOQ **1** a walkway or promenade. **2** a promenade concert, at which the audience stands and are able to move about. **3** N AMER a formal school or college dance at the end of the academic year.

promenade N **1** a broad paved walk, esp along a seafront. **2** FACETIOUS a stately stroll.
➤ VB **1** INTR to stroll in a stately fashion. **2** to walk (the streets, etc). **3** to take someone out for some fresh air; to parade. ■ **promenader** N.

prominence N **1** the state or quality of being prominent. **2** a prominent point. **3** a protrusion.

prominent ADJ **1** jutting out; projecting; protruding; bulging. **2** noticeable; conspicuous. **3** leading; notable.

promiscuous ADJ **1** indulging in casual or indiscriminate sexual relations. **2** haphazardly mixed. ■ **promiscuity** N.

promise VB **1** TR & INTR to give an undertaking (to do or not do something). **2** to undertake to give something to someone. **3** to show signs of bringing something. **4** to look likely (to do something). **5** to assure or warn.
➤ N **1** an assurance to give, do or not do something. **2** a sign: **promise of spring in the air**. **3** signs of future excellence.

promising ADJ **1** showing promise; talented; apt. **2** seeming to bode well for the future: **a promising start**.

promissory ADJ containing, relating to or expressing a promise.

promontory N (**-ies**) a usu hilly part of a coastline that projects into the sea.

promote VB **1 a** to raise someone to a more senior position; **b** SPORT, esp FOOTBALL to transfer (a team) to a higher division or league. **2** to contribute to something: **Exercise promotes health**. **3** to work for the cause of something:

promote peace. **4** to publicize; to try to boost the sales of (a product) by advertising. ■ **promotion** N. ■ **promotional** ADJ.

promoter N the organizer or financer of a sporting event or other undertaking.

prompt ADJ **1** immediate; quick; punctual. **2** instantly willing; ready; unhesitating. ➤ ADV punctually. ➤ N **1** something serving as a reminder. **2** THEAT words supplied by a prompter to an actor. **3** THEAT a prompter. **4** COMP a sign on screen indicating that the computer is ready for input. ➤ VB **1** to cause, lead or remind someone to do something. **2** to produce or elicit (a reaction or response). **3** TR & INTR to help (an actor) to remember their next words by supplying the first few. ■ **prompter** N. ■ **promptitude** N. ■ **promptness** N.

promulgate VB **1** to make (a decree, etc) effective by means of an official public announcement. **2** to publicize or promote (an idea, theory, etc) widely. ■ **promulgation** N.

prone ADJ **1** lying flat, esp face downwards. **2** (often **prone to sth**) predisposed to it, or liable to suffer from it. **3** liable to do something.

prong N **1** a point or spike, esp one of those on a fork. **2** any pointed projection.

pronoun N, GRAM a word such as **she, him, they, it**, etc used in place of, and to refer to, a noun, phrase, clause, etc.

pronounce VB **1** to say or utter (words, sounds, letters, etc); to articulate or enunciate. **2** to declare something officially, formally or authoritatively: **pronounced her innocent**. **3** to pass or deliver (judgement). **4** INTR (usu **pronounce on sth**) to give an opinion or verdict on it. ■ **pronounceable** ADJ.

pronounced ADJ **1** noticeable; distinct: a **pronounced limp**. **2** spoken; articulated.

pronouncement N **1** an announcement. **2** a declaration of opinion; a verdict.

pronto ADV, COLLOQ immediately.

pronunciation N **1** the act or a manner of pronouncing words, sounds, letters, etc. **2** the

correct way of pronouncing a word, sound, etc in a given language.

proof N **1** evidence, esp conclusive evidence, that something is true or a fact. **2** LAW the accumulated evidence on which a verdict is based. **3** the activity or process of testing or proving. **4** a test, trial or demonstration. **5** MATH a step-by-step verification of a proposed mathematical statement. **6** PRINTING a trial copy of printed text used for examination. **7** a trial print from a photographic negative. **8** a trial impression from an engraved plate. **9** a measure of the alcohol content of a distilled liquid. ➤ ADJ, esp IN COMPOUNDS able or designed to withstand, deter or be free from or secure against a specified thing: **leakproof**. ➤ VB **1** to make something resistant to or proof against a specified thing. **2** to take a proof of (printed material). **3** to proof-read.

proof-read VB, TR & INTR to read and mark for correction the proofs of (a text, etc). ■ **proof-reader** N. ■ **proof-reading** N.

prop[1] N **1** a rigid support, esp a vertical one: a **clothes prop**. **2** a person or thing that one depends on for help or emotional support. **3** (also **prop forward**) RUGBY **a** the position at either end of the front row of the scrum; **b** a player in this position. ➤ VB (-*pp*-) **1** (often **prop sth up**) to support or hold it upright with, or as if with, a prop. **2** (usu **prop against sth**) to lean against it; to put something against something else. **3** to serve as a prop to something.

prop[2] N, COLLOQ (in full **property**) THEAT an object or piece of furniture used on stage.

propaganda N **1** the circulation by a political group, etc of information, misinformation, rumour or opinion, intended to influence public feeling. **2** the material circulated in this way. ■ **propagandist** N.

propagate VB **1** TR & INTR, BOT of a plant: to multiply. **2** BOT to grow (new plants), either by natural means or artificially. **3** to spread or popularize (ideas, etc). ■ **propagation** N. ■ **propagator** N.

propane N, CHEM a colourless odourless flammable gas, obtained from petroleum.

propel VB (*-ll-*) 1 to drive or push something forward. 2 to steer or send someone or something in a certain direction.

propellant N 1 CHEM a compressed inert gas in an aerosol that is used to release the liquid contents as a fine spray when the pressure is released. 2 ENG the fuel and oxidizer that are burned in a rocket in order to provide thrust.

propeller N a device consisting of a revolving hub with radiating blades that produce thrust or power, used to propel aircraft, ships, etc.

propensity N (*-ies*) a tendency or inclination.

proper ADJ 1 real; genuine; able to be correctly described as (a specified thing). 2 right; correct. 3 appropriate: **at the proper time**. 4 own; particular; correct: **in its proper place**. 5 socially accepted; respectable. 6 DEROG morally strict; prim. 7 (usu **proper to sth**) belonging or appropriate to it; suitable. 8 used immediately after a noun: strictly so called; itself, excluding others not immediately connected with it: **entering the city proper**. 9 COLLOQ utter; complete; out-and-out: **a proper idiot**.

properly ADV 1 suitably; appropriately; correctly. 2 with strict accuracy. 3 fully; thoroughly; completely.

proper noun and **proper name** N, GRAM the name of a particular person, place or thing.

property N (*-ies*) 1 something someone owns. 2 possessions collectively. 3 the concept of ownership. 4 a land or real estate; b an item of this. 5 a quality or attribute. 6 a theatrical prop.

prophecy N (*-ies*) 1 a the interpretation of divine will; b the act of revealing such interpretations. 2 a the foretelling of the future; b something foretold; a prediction.

prophesy VB (*-ies, -ied*) 1 TR & INTR to foretell (future happenings); to predict. 2 INTR to utter prophecies; to interpret divine will.

prophet N 1 someone who is able to express the will of God or a god. 2 someone who claims to be able to tell what will happen in the future. ■ **prophetess** N.

prophetic ADJ 1 foretelling the future. 2 relating or belonging to prophets or prophecy.

prophylactic ADJ guarding against or tending to prevent disease or other mishap.

propinquity N 1 nearness in place or time; proximity. 2 closeness of kinship.

propitiate VB to appease or placate (an angry or insulted person or god). ■ **propitiable** ADJ. ■ **propitiation** N. ■ **propitiator** N. ■ **propitiatory** ADJ.

propitious ADJ 1 favourable; auspicious; advantageous. 2 (often **propitious for** or **to sth**) likely to favour or encourage it.

proponent N an advocate of something; someone who argues in favour of their cause.

proportion N 1 a comparative part of a total: **a large proportion of the population**. 2 the size of one element or group in relation to the whole or total. 3 the size of one group or component in relation to another: **in a proportion of two parts to one**. 4 the correct balance between parts or elements: **out of proportion**. 5 (**proportions**) size; dimensions: **a garden of large proportions**. 6 MATH correspondence between the ratios of two pairs of quantities, as expressed in **2 is to 8 as 3 is to 12**.
◆ **in proportion to sth** 1 in relation to it. 2 in parallel with it; at the same rate.

proportional ADJ 1 corresponding or matching in size, rate, etc. 2 in correct proportion; proportionate.

proportionate ADJ due or in correct proportion. ■ **proportionately** ADV.

proposal N 1 the act of proposing something. 2 something proposed. 3 an offer of marriage.

propose VB 1 to offer (a plan, etc) for consideration; to suggest. 2 to suggest or nominate someone for a position, task, etc. 3 to be the proposer of (the motion in a debate). 4 to intend (to do something): **don't propose to**

sell. **5** to suggest (a specified person, topic, etc) as the subject of a toast. **6** INTR (often **propose to sb**) to make them an offer of marriage.

proposition N **1** a proposal or suggestion. **2** something to be dealt with or undertaken: **an awkward proposition**. **3** EUPHEMISTIC, COLLOQ an invitation to have sexual intercourse. **4** LOGIC a form of statement affirming or denying something, that can be true or false; a premise.

propound VB to put forward (an idea or theory, etc) for consideration or discussion.

proprietary ADJ **1** eg of rights: belonging to an owner or proprietor. **2** suggestive or indicative of ownership. **3** of medicines, etc: marketed under a tradename. **4** of a company etc: privately owned and managed.
➤ N (**-ies**) **1** a body of proprietors. **2** proprietorship.

proprietor and **proprietress** N an owner, esp of a business, etc. ■ **proprietorial** ADJ.

propriety N (**-ies**) **1** conformity to socially acceptable behaviour, esp between the sexes. **2** moral acceptability. **3** (**proprieties**) accepted standards of conduct.

propulsion N **1** the act of causing something to move forward. **2** a force exerted against a body which makes it move forward. ■ **propulsive** ADJ.

pro rata ADV in proportion; in accordance with a certain rate.

prorogue VB, FORMAL to discontinue the meetings of (a legislative assembly) for a time, without dissolving it. ■ **prorogation** N.

prosaic ADJ **1** unpoetic; unimaginative. **2** dull, ordinary and uninteresting. ■ **prosaically** ADV.

pros and cons PL N the advantages and disadvantages of a course of action, idea, etc.

proscenium N (**-iums** or **-ia**) THEAT **1** the part of a stage in front of the curtain. **2** (also **proscenium arch**) the arch framing the stage and separating it from the auditorium.

proscribe VB **1** to prohibit or condemn something. **2** HIST to outlaw or exile someone. ■ **proscription** N. ■ **proscriptive** ADJ.

prose N the form of written or spoken language as distinct from verse or poetry.

prosecute VB **1** TR & INTR to bring a criminal action against someone. **2** FORMAL to carry on or carry out something (eg enquiries). ■ **prosecutable** ADJ. ■ **prosecutor** N.

prosecution N **1** the act of prosecuting or process of being prosecuted. **2** the bringing of a criminal action against someone. **3 a** the prosecuting party in a criminal case; **b** the lawyers involved in this.

proselyte N a convert, esp a Gentile turning to Judaism. ■ **proselytism** N.

proselytize or **-ise** VB, TR & INTR to try to convert someone from one faith to another; to make converts. ■ **proselytizer** N.

prosody N the study of verse composition, esp poetic metre.

prospect N **1** an expectation of something due or likely to happen. **2** an outlook for the future. **3** (**prospects**) chances of success, recovery, etc. **4** (**prospects**) opportunities for advancement, promotion, etc. **5** a potential client or customer. **6** a broad view.
➤ VB, TR & INTR to search or explore (an area, region, etc) for gold or other minerals.
◆ **in prospect** expected soon.

prospective ADJ likely or expected; future.

prospector N someone prospecting for oil, gold, etc.

prospectus N **1** a brochure giving information about a school or other institution, esp the courses on offer. **2** a document outlining a proposal for something, eg an issue of shares.

prosper VB **1** of someone: INTR to do well, esp financially. **2** of a business, etc: to thrive or flourish. ■ **prosperity** N.

prosperous ADJ wealthy and successful.

prostate N (in full **prostate gland**) ANAT in male mammals: a muscular gland around the base of the bladder which produces an alkaline fluid that activates sperm.

prosthesis N (**-ses**) MED an artificial substitute

for a part of the body that is missing or non-functional. ■ **prosthetic** ADJ.

prosthetics SING N the branch of surgery concerned with fitting prostheses.

prostitute N 1 someone who performs sexual acts or intercourse in return for money. 2 someone who offers their skills or talents, etc for unworthy ends.
➤ VB 1 to offer (oneself or someone else) as a prostitute. 2 to put (eg one's talents) to an unworthy use. ■ **prostitution** N.

prostrate ADJ 1 lying face downwards in an attitude of abject submission, humility or adoration. 2 distraught with illness, grief, etc.
➤ VB 1 to throw (oneself) face down in submission or adoration. 2 of exhaustion, illness, grief, etc: to overwhelm someone physically or emotionally. ■ **prostration** N.

prosy ADJ (*-ier, -iest*) of speech or writing: 1 prose-like. 2 dull and tedious.

protagonist N 1 the main character in a play, story, film, etc. 2 any person at the centre of a story or event. 3 NON-STANDARD a leader or champion of a movement or cause, etc.

protean ADJ readily able to change shape or appearance; variable; changeable.

protect VB to shield someone or something from danger; to guard them or it against injury, destruction, etc; to keep safe.

protection N 1 the action of protecting or condition of being protected; shelter, refuge, cover, safety or care. 2 something that protects. 3 (also **protectionism**) the system of protecting home industries against foreign competition by taxing imports. 4 COLLOQ the criminal practice of extorting money from shop-owners, etc in return for leaving their premises unharmed. ■ **protectionist** N.

protective ADJ 1 giving or designed to give protection: **protective clothing**. 2 inclined or tending to protect. ■ **protectiveness** N.

protector and **protectress** N 1 someone or something that protects. 2 a patron or benefactor. 3 someone who rules a country during the absence of a sovereign.

protectorate N 1 the office or period of rule of a protector. 2 protectorship of a weak or backward country assumed by a more powerful one without actual annexation.

protégé and **protégée** N a person (male and female respectively) under the guidance of someone wiser or more important.

protein N, BIOCHEM any of thousands of different organic compounds, characteristic of all living organisms, that have large molecules consisting of long chains of amino acids.

protest VB 1 INTR to express an objection, disapproval, opposition or disagreement. 2 N AMER, ESP US to challenge or object to (eg a decision or measure). 3 to declare something solemnly, eg in response to an accusation.
➤ N 1 a declaration of disapproval or dissent; an objection. 2 a an organized public demonstration of disapproval; b AS ADJ: a **protest march**. 3 the act of protesting. ■ **protestation** N. ■ **protester** or **protestor** N.
◆ **under protest** reluctantly; unwillingly.

Protestant or **protestant** N 1 a member of any of the Christian churches which embraced the Reformation and separated from the Roman Catholic Church. 2 a member of any body descended from these.
➤ ADJ relating or belonging to Protestants. ■ **Protestantism** N.

protocol N 1 correct formal or diplomatic etiquette or procedure. 2 a first draft of a diplomatic document, eg one setting out the terms of a treaty.

proton N, PHYS any of the positively charged subatomic particles that are found inside the nucleus at the centre of an atom.

protoplasm N, BIOL the mass of protein material of which cells are composed, consisting of the cytoplasm and usu a nucleus. ■ **protoplasmic** ADJ.

prototype N 1 an original model from which later forms are copied, developed or derived. 2 a first working version, eg of a vehicle or aircraft. ■ **prototypical** ADJ.

protozoan N (-**zoa**) a single-celled organism, eg an amoeba.

protract VB **1** to prolong; to cause something to last a long time. **2** to lengthen something out.

protractor N, GEOM an instrument, usu a transparent plastic semicircle marked in degrees, used to draw and measure angles.

protrude VB **1** INTR to project; to stick out. **2** to push something out or forward. ■ **protrusion** N. ■ **protrusive** ADJ.

protuberant ADJ projecting; bulging; swelling out. ■ **protuberance** N.

proud ADJ **1** (often **proud of sb** or **sth**) feeling satisfaction, delight, etc with one's own or another's accomplishments, possessions, etc. **2** arrogant; conceited. **3** concerned for one's dignity and self-respect. **4** honoured; gratified; delighted. **5** splendid; imposing; distinguished: a proud sight. **6** TECHNICAL projecting slightly from the surrounding surface. ■ **proudly** ADV.
◆ **do sb proud** to entertain them grandly.

prove VB (PA P **proved** or **proven**) **1** to show something to be true, correct or a fact. **2** to show something to be (a specified thing): was proved innocent. **3** INTR to be found to be (a specified thing) when tried; to turn out to be the case. **4** to show (oneself) to be (of a specified type or quality, etc). **5** to show (oneself) capable or daring. **6** LAW to establish the validity of (a will). **7** of dough: to rise when baked. ■ **provable** or **proveable** ADJ.

proven ADJ shown to be true, worthy, etc: of proven ability.

provenance N the place of origin (of a work of art, archaeological find, etc).

provender N **1** dry food for livestock. **2** now usu FACETIOUS food.

proverb N a well-known neatly-expressed saying that gives advice or expresses a supposed truth.

proverbial ADJ **1** of or relating to a proverb. **2** referred to in a proverb; traditionally quoted: turned up like the proverbial bad penny.

provide VB **1** to supply. **2** of a circumstance or situation, etc: to offer (a specified thing): provide an opportunity. ■ **provider** N.
◆ **provide for sb** or **sth** to support or keep (a dependant, etc), or arrange the means to do so.

provided and **providing** CONJ **1** on the condition or understanding (that a specified thing happens, etc). **2** if and only if: Providing Joe gives me the money, I'll go.

providence N **1** (**Providence**) God or Nature regarded as an all-seeing protector of the world. **2** the quality of being provident.

provident ADJ **1** having foresight and making provisions for the future. **2** careful and thrifty.

providential ADJ due to providence; lucky.

province N **1** an administrative division of a country. **2** someone's allotted range of duties or field of knowledge, etc. **3** (**the provinces**) the parts of a country away from the capital.

provincial ADJ **1** belonging or relating to a province. **2** relating to the parts of a country away from the capital: a provincial accent. **3** DEROG supposedly typical of provinces in being culturally backward, unsophisticated or narrow in outlook: provincial attitudes. ■ **provincialism** N. ■ **provincially** ADV.

provision N **1** the act or process of providing. **2** something provided or made available; facilities. **3** preparations; measures taken in advance: make provision for the future. **4** (**provisions**) food and other necessities. **5** LAW a condition or requirement.

provisional ADJ temporary; for the time being or immediate purposes only; liable to be altered. ■ **provisionally** ADV.

proviso N **1** a condition or stipulation. **2** LAW a clause stating a condition. ■ **provisory** ADJ.

provocation N **1** the act of provoking or state of being provoked; incitement. **2** a cause of anger, irritation or indignation.

provocative ADJ **1** tending or intended to cause anger; deliberately infuriating. **2** sexually arousing or stimulating.

provoke VB **1** to annoy or infuriate someone. **2** to incite or goad. **3** to rouse (someone's anger, etc). **4** to cause, stir up or bring about something. ■ **provoking** ADJ.

provost N **1** the head of some university colleges. **2** in Scotland: **a** the chief councillor of a district council; **b** FORMERLY the chief magistrate of a burgh.

prow N the projecting front part of a ship.

prowess N skill; ability; expertise.

prowl VB, INTR **1** to go about stealthily, eg in search of prey. **2** to pace restlessly. ➤ N an act of prowling. ■ **prowler** N.

proximate ADJ **1** nearest. **2** immediately before or after in time, place or chronology.

proximity N (-ies) nearness in space or time.

proxy N (-ies) **1a** a person authorized to act or vote on another's behalf; **b** the agency of such a person; **c** AS ADJ: **a proxy vote**. **2 a** the authority to act or vote for someone else; **b** a document granting this.

prude N someone who is, or affects to be, shocked by improper behaviour, sexual matters, etc; a prim person. ■ **prudery** N. ■ **prudish** ADJ. ■ **prudishness** N.

prudent ADJ **1** wise or careful in conduct. **2** shrewd or thrifty in planning ahead. **3** wary; discreet. ■ **prudence** N.

prudential ADJ, OLD USE characterized by or exercising careful forethought.

prune[1] VB **1** to cut off (branches, etc) from (a tree or shrub) in order to stimulate its growth, etc. **2** to cut back on (expenses, etc). ➤ N an act of pruning. ■ **pruner** N.

prune[2] N **1** a plum that has been preserved by drying, which gives it a black wrinkled appearance. **2** COLLOQ a silly foolish person.

prurient ADJ **1** unhealthily or excessively interested in sexual matters. **2** tending to arouse such unhealthy interest. ■ **prurience** N.

pry[1] VB (*pries, pried*) INTR **1** (also **pry into sth**) to investigate, esp the personal affairs of others. **2** to peer or peep inquisitively.

pry[2] VB (*pries, pried*) N AMER, ESP US to prise.

PS ABBREV postscript.

psalm N a sacred song, esp one from the Book of Psalms in the Old Testament.

psalmody N (-ies) **1** the art of singing psalms. **2** a collected body of psalms.

psalter N a book containing psalms.

psaltery N (-ies) HIST, MUS a stringed instrument similar to a zither.

psephology N the statistical study of elections and voting patterns. ■ **psephological** ADJ. ■ **psephologist** N.

pseud N, BRIT COLLOQ a pretentious person.

pseudo- or (BEFORE A VOWEL) **pseud-** COMB FORM, FORMING NOUNS AND ADJS, DENOTING **1** false; pretending to be something: *pseudo-intellectuals*. **2** deceptively resembling: *pseudo-scientific jargon*.

pseudonym N a false or assumed name, esp one used by an author; a pen name or nom de plume. ■ **pseudonymous** ADJ.

psittacosis N, PATHOL a contagious disease of birds, esp parrots, that can be transmitted to human beings.

psoriasis N, PATHOL a skin disease characterized by red scaly patches.

psych or **psyche** VB, COLLOQ.
◆ **psych sb out** to undermine the confidence of (an opponent, etc).
◆ **psych oneself** or **sb up** to prepare or steel oneself, or them, for a challenge, etc.

psyche N the mind or spirit.

psychedelic ADJ **1** of a drug, esp LSD: inducing a state of altered consciousness characterized by an increase in perception, eg of colour, sound, etc, and hallucinations. **2** of perceived phenomena, eg colour, music, etc: startlingly clear and vivid, often with a complex dazzling pattern. ■ **psychedelically** ADV.

psychiatry N the branch of medicine concerned with the diagnosis, treatment and prevention of mental and emotional disorders. ■ **psychiatric** ADJ. ■ **psychiatrist** N.

psychic ADJ 1 (also **psychical**) relating to mental processes or experiences that are not scientifically explainable, eg telepathy. 2 of a person: sensitive to such experiences.
➤ N someone who possesses such powers.

psycho COLLOQ, N a psychopath.
➤ ADJ psychopathic.

psychoanalyse or (US) **psychoanalyze** VB to examine or treat someone by psychoanalysis.

psychoanalysis N, PSYCHOL a theory and method of treatment for mental and emotional disorders, which explores the effects of unconscious motivation and conflict on a person's behaviour. ■ **psychoanalyst** N. ■ **psychoanalytic** ADJ.

psychological ADJ 1 relating or referring to psychology. 2 relating or referring to the mind or mental processes. ■ **psychologically** ADV.

psychology N 1 the scientific study of the mind and behaviour of humans and animals. 2 the mental attitudes and behaviour characteristics of a certain individual or group. ■ **psychologist** N.

psychopath N someone with a personality disorder characterized by extreme callousness, who is liable to behave antisocially or violently in getting their own way, without any feelings of remorse. ■ **psychopathic** ADJ. ■ **psychopathically** ADV.

psychosis N (-ses) PSYCHOL one of the two divisions of psychiatric disorders, characterized by a loss of contact with reality, in the form of delusions or hallucinations and belief that only one's own actions are rational.

psychosomatic ADJ, MED of physical symptoms or disorders: strongly associated with psychological factors, esp mental stress.

psychotherapy N the treatment of mental disorders and emotional and behavioural problems by psychological means, rather than by drugs or surgery. ■ **psychotherapist** N.

psychotic ADJ relating to a psychosis.
➤ N someone suffering from a psychosis.

ptarmigan N a mountain-dwelling game-bird with white winter plumage.

pterodactyl N a former name for pterosaur.

pterosaur N an extinct flying reptile with narrow leathery wings.

PTO or **pto** ABBREV please turn over.

ptomaine N, BIOCHEM any of a group of nitrogenous organic compounds produced during the bacterial decomposition of dead animal and plant matter.

pub N, COLLOQ a public house.

puberty N, BIOL in humans and other primates: the onset of sexual maturity.

pubes N (PL *pubes*) 1 ANAT the pubic region of the lower abdomen; the groin. 2 (also COLLOQ treated as PL N) the hair that grows on this part from puberty onward.

pubescence N 1 the onset of puberty. 2 BIOL a soft downy covering. ■ **pubescent** ADJ.

pubic ADJ relating to the pubis or pubes.

pubis N (PL *pubes*) ANAT in most vertebrates: one of the two bones forming the lower front part of each side of the pelvis.

public ADJ 1 relating to or concerning all the people of a country or community: **public opinion**. 2 relating to the organization and administration of a community. 3 provided for the use of the community: **public library**. 4 well known through exposure in the media: **public figure**. 5 made, done or held, etc openly, for all to see, hear or participate in: **a public inquiry**. 6 known to all: **make one's views public**. 7 open to view; not private or secluded: **It's too public here**. 8 provided by or run by central or local government: **under public ownership**.
➤ SING OR PL N 1 the people or community. 2 a particular class of people: **the concert-going public**. 3 an author's or performer's, etc audience or group of devotees: **mustn't disappoint my public**.
◆ **go public** 1 BUSINESS to become a public company. 2 to make something previously private known to everyone.
◆ **in public** in the presence of other people.

◆ **in the public eye** of a person, etc: well known through media exposure.

publican N, BRIT the keeper of a public house.

publication N **1** the act of publishing a printed work; the process of publishing or of being published. **2** a book, magazine, newspaper or other printed and published work. **3** the act of making something known to the public.

public bar N in a public house: a bar which is less well furnished and serves drinks more cheaply than a lounge bar.

public convenience N a public toilet.

public house N, BRIT an establishment licensed to sell alcoholic drinks.

publicity N advertising or other activity designed to rouse public interest in something.

publicize or **-ise** VB **1** to make something generally or widely known. **2** to advertise.

public relations SING OR PL N the process of creating a good relationship between an organization, etc and the public.
➤ SING N the department within an organization that is responsible for this.

public school N **1** in the UK: a secondary school, run independently of the state, financed by endowments and by pupils' fees. **2** in the US: a school run by a public authority.

public-spirited ADJ acting from or showing concern for the good of the whole community.

public works N buildings, roads, etc built by the state for public use.

publish VB, TR & INTR **1** to prepare, produce and distribute (printed material, software, etc) for sale to the public. **2** TR & INTR of an author: to have (their work) published. **3** to publish the work of (an author). ■ **publishing** N.

publisher N **1** a person or company which publishes books, newspapers, music, etc. **2** N AMER a newspaper proprietor.

puce N a colour anywhere between deep purplish–pink and purplish–brown.

puck[1] N a goblin or mischievous sprite.
■ **puckish** ADJ.

puck[2] N, SPORT a thick disc of hard rubber used in ice hockey instead of a ball.

pucker VB, TR & INTR to gather into creases, folds or wrinkles; to wrinkle.
➤ N a wrinkle, fold or crease.

pud N, BRIT COLLOQ pudding.

pudding N **1** any of several sweet or savoury foods usu made with flour and eggs and cooked by steaming, boiling or baking. **2 a** any sweet food served as dessert; **b** the dessert course. **3** IN COMPOUNDS a type of sausage made with minced meat, spices, blood, etc.

puddle N a small pool, esp one of rainwater.

pudenda PL N (rarely SING *-dum*) the external sexual organs, esp those of a woman.

pudgy see **podgy**

puerile ADJ childish; silly. ■ **puerility** N.

puerperal ADJ referring to childbirth.

puff N **1 a** a small rush, gust or blast of air or wind, etc; **b** the sound made by it. **2** a small cloud of smoke, dust or steam emitted from something. **3** COLLOQ breath: **quite out of puff**. **4** an act of inhaling and exhaling smoke from a pipe or cigarette; a drag or draw. **5** IN COMPOUNDS a light pastry, often containing a sweet or savoury filling: **jam puffs**. **6** a powder puff.
➤ VB **1** TR & INTR to blow or breathe in small blasts. **2** INTR of smoke or steam, etc: to emerge in small gusts or blasts. **3** TR & INTR to inhale and exhale smoke from, or draw at (a cigarette, etc). **4** INTR of a train or boat, etc: to go along emitting puffs of steam. **5** INTR to pant, or go along panting: **puffing up the hill**. **6** (often **puff sb out**) COLLOQ to leave them breathless after exertion. **7** TR & INTR (also **puff out** or **up**) to swell or cause to swell. ■ **puffy** ADJ (**-ier, -iest**).

puff pastry N, COOKERY light flaky pastry made with a high proportion of fat.

pug N a small breed of dog with a flattened face with a wrinkled snout and a short curled tail.

pugilism N, OLD USE the art or practice of boxing or prizefighting. ■ **pugilist** N.

pugnacious ADJ quarrelsome, belligerent or combative. ■ **pugnacity** N.

pug nose N a short upturned nose. ■ **pug-nosed** ADJ.

puke COLLOQ, VB, TR & INTR to vomit. ➤ N **1** vomit. **2** an act of vomiting.

pukka ADJ, COLLOQ **1** superior; high-quality. **2** upper-class; well-bred. **3** genuine.

pulchritude N, LITERARY OR FORMAL beauty.

pull VB **1** TR & INTR to grip something or someone strongly and draw or force it or them towards oneself; to tug or drag. **2** (also **pull sth out** or **up**) to remove or extract (a cork, tooth, weeds, etc) with this action. **3** to operate (a trigger, lever or switch) with this action. **4** to draw (a trailer, etc). **5** to open or close (curtains or a blind). **6** (often **pull sth on sb**) to produce (a weapon) as a threat to them. **7 a** TR & INTR to row; **b** INTR (often **pull away, off,** etc) of a boat: to be rowed or made to move in a particular direction. **8** to draw (beer, etc) from a cask by operating a lever. **9** INTR **a** of a driver or vehicle: to steer or move (in a specified direction): **pulled right**; **b** of a vehicle or its steering: (towards a specified direction), usu because of some defect. **10** (usu **pull at** or **on sth**) to inhale and exhale smoke from (a cigarette, etc). **11** to attract (a crowd, votes, etc). **12** to strain (a muscle or tendon).
➤ N **1** an act of pulling. **2** attraction; attracting force. **3** useful influence: **has some pull with the education department**. **4** a drag at a pipe; a swallow of liquor, etc. **5** a tab, etc for pulling. **6** a stroke made with an oar.
◆ **pull a fast one** to trick or cheat someone.
◆ **pull sth down** to demolish (a building, etc).
◆ **pull in 1** of a train: to arrive and halt at a station. **2** of a driver or vehicle: to move to the side of the road.
◆ **pull sth off** COLLOQ to arrange or accomplish it successfully: **pull off a deal**.
◆ **pull over** of a driver or vehicle: to move to the side of or off the road and stop.
◆ **pull one's punches** to be deliberately less

hard-hitting than one might be.
◆ **pull round** or **through** to recover.
◆ **pull together** to work together towards a common aim; to co-operate.
◆ **pull up** of a driver, vehicle or horse: to stop.

pullet N a young hen in its first laying year.

pulley N a simple mechanism for lifting and lowering weights, consisting of a wheel with a grooved rim over which a rope or belt runs.

pullover N a knitted garment pulled on over the head.

pulmonary ADJ **1** of or relating to, or affecting, the lungs. **2** having the function of a lung.

pulp N **1** the flesh of a fruit or vegetable. **2** a soft wet mass. **3** DEROG **a** worthless literature printed on poor paper; **b** AS ADJ: **pulp fiction**. **4** ANAT the tissue in the cavity of a tooth, containing nerves.
➤ VB **1** TR & INTR to reduce or be reduced to a pulp. **2** to remove the pulp from (fruit, etc).
■ **pulpy** ADJ (**-ier, -iest**).

pulpit N a small enclosed platform in a church, from which the preacher delivers the sermon.

pulsar N, ASTRON in space: a source of electromagnetic radiation emitted in brief regular pulses, mainly at radio frequency, believed to be a rapidly revolving neutron star.

pulsate VB, INTR **1** to beat or throb. **2** to contract and expand rhythmically. **3** to vibrate.

pulse[1] N **1** PHYSIOL the rhythmic beat that can be detected in an artery, as the heart pumps blood around the body. **2** MED, etc **a** the rate of this beat, often measured as an indicator of a person's state of health; **b** AS ADJ: **pulse rate**. **3** a regular throbbing beat in music. **4** PHYS a signal, eg one of light or electric current, of very short duration. **5** the hum or bustle of a busy place. **6** a thrill of excitement, etc.
➤ VB **1** INTR to throb or pulsate. **2** to drive something by pulses.

pulse[2] N **1** the edible dried seed of a plant belonging to the pea family, eg pea, bean, lentil, etc. **2** any plant that bears this seed.

pulverize or **-ise** VB **1** TR & INTR to crumble or

crush to dust or powder. **2** COLLOQ to defeat utterly; to annihilate. ■ **pulverization** N.

puma N one of the large cats of America, with short yellowish-brown or reddish fur, found in mountain regions, forests, plains and deserts. Also called **cougar, mountain lion** or **panther**.

pumice N (also **pumice stone**) GEOL a very light porous form of solidified lava, used as an abrasive and polishing agent.

pummel VB (-*ll*-) to beat something repeatedly with the fists.

pump[1] N a piston-operated or other device for forcing or driving liquids or gases into or out of something, etc.
➤ VB **1** TR & INTR to raise, force or drive (a liquid or gas) out of or into something with a pump. **2** (USU **pump sth up**) to inflate (a tyre, etc) with a pump. **3** to force something in large gushes or flowing amounts. **4** to pour (money or other resources) into a project, etc. **5** to force out the contents of (someone's stomach) to rid it of a poison, etc. **6** to try to extract information from someone by persistent questioning. **7** to work something vigorously up and down, as though operating a pump handle. **8** to fire (bullets, etc), often into someone or something.

pump[2] N **1** a light dancing shoe. **2** a plain, low-cut flat shoe for women. **3** a gymshoe.

pumpernickel N a dark heavy coarse ryebread, eaten esp in Germany.

pumpkin N **1** a trailing or climbing plant which produces large round fruits at ground level. **2** the fruit of this plant, which contains pulpy flesh enclosed by a leathery orange rind.

pun N a form of joke consisting of the use of a word or phrase that can be understood in two different ways, esp one where an association is created between words of similar sound but different meaning.
➤ VB (-*nn*-) INTR to make a pun.

punch[1] VB **1** TR & INTR to hit someone or something with the fist. **2** esp US & AUSTRAL to poke or prod with a stick; to drive (cattle, etc). **3** to prod, poke or strike smartly, esp with a blunt object, the foot, etc.
➤ N **1** a blow with the fist. **2** vigour and effectiveness in speech or writing.

punch[2] N **1** a tool for cutting or piercing holes or notches, or stamping designs, in leather, paper, metal, etc. **2** a tool for driving nail-heads well down into a surface.
➤ VB to pierce, notch or stamp something with a punch.

punch[3] N a drink, usu an alcoholic one, made up of a mixture of other drinks.

punchline N the words that conclude a joke or funny story and contain its point.

punch-up N, COLLOQ a fight.

punchy ADJ (-*ier, -iest*) of speech or writing: vigorous and effective; forcefully expressed. ■ **punchily** ADV. ■ **punchiness** N.

punctilious ADJ carefully attentive to details of correct, polite or considerate behaviour; making a point of observing a rule or custom.

punctual ADJ **1** arriving or happening at the arranged time; not late. **2** of a person: making a habit of arriving on time. ■ **punctuality** N.

punctuate VB **1** TR & INTR to put punctuation marks into (a piece of writing). **2** to interrupt something repeatedly.

punctuation N **1** a system of conventional marks used in a text to clarify its meaning for the reader, indicating pauses, intonation, missing letters, etc. **2 a** the use of such marks; **b** the process of inserting them.

punctuation mark N any of the set of marks such as the full stop, comma, question mark, colon, etc that in written text conventionally indicate the pauses and intonations that would be used in speech.

puncture N **1** a small hole pierced in something with a sharp point. **2 a** a perforation in an inflated object, esp one in a pneumatic tyre; **b** the resulting lat tyre.
➤ VB **1** TR & INTR to make a puncture in something, or to be punctured. **2** to deflate (pride, etc).

pundit N an authority or supposed authority

on a particular subject, esp one who is regularly consulted.

pungent ADJ 1 of a taste or smell: sharp and strong. 2 of remarks or wit, etc: cleverly caustic or biting. 3 of grief or pain: keen or sharp. ■ **pungency** N. ■ **pungently** ADV.

punish VB 1 to cause (an offender) to suffer for an offence. 2 to impose a penalty for (an offence). 3 COLLOQ to treat something or someone roughly. 4 to beat or defeat (an opponent, etc) soundly. ■ **punishable** ADJ.

punishment N 1 the act of punishing or process of being punished. 2 a method of punishing; a type of penalty.

punitive ADJ 1 relating to, inflicting or intended to inflict punishment. 2 severe; inflicting hardship. ■ **punitively** ADV.

punk N 1 an anti-establishment youth movement, at its height in the mid- to late-70s, which was characterized by aggressive music and dress style, vividly coloured hair and the wearing of cheap utility articles (eg safety pins) as ornament on or through various parts of the body. 2 a follower of punk styles or punk rock. 3 (in full **punk rock**) a type of loud aggressive rock music, popular in the mid- to late-1970s. 4 N AMER a worthless or stupid person. ➤ ADJ 1 relating to or characteristic of punk as a movement. 2 N AMER worthless; inferior.

punnet N a small container for soft fruit.

punt[1] N a long, flat-bottomed open boat with square ends, propelled by a pole pushed against the bed of the river, etc. ➤ VB 1 INTR to travel by or operate a punt. 2 to propel (a punt, etc) with a pole.

punt[2] VB, INTR, COLLOQ to bet on horses.

punter N, COLLOQ 1 someone who bets; a gambler. 2 a the average consumer, customer or member of the public; b a prostitute's client.

puny ADJ (-ier, -iest) 1 small, weak or undersized. 2 feeble or ineffective.

pup N 1 a young dog. 2 the young of other animals, eg the seal, wolf and rat. ➤ VB (-pp-) INTR to give birth to pups.

pupa N (-ae or -as) ZOOL in the life cycle of certain insects, eg butterflies and moths: the inactive stage during which a larva is transformed into a sexually mature adult while enclosed in a protective case. ■ **pupal** ADJ.

pupil[1] N 1 someone who is being taught; a schoolchild or student. 2 someone studying under a particular expert, etc.

pupil[2] N, ANAT in the eye of vertebrates: the dark circular opening in the centre of the iris.

puppet N 1 a type of doll that can be moved in a number of ways, eg one operated by strings or sticks attached to its limbs, or one designed to fit over the hand and operated by the fingers and thumb. 2 a person, company, country, etc, who is being controlled or manipulated by someone or something else. ■ **puppeteer** N.

puppy N (-ies) a young dog.

purblind ADJ 1 nearly blind; dim-sighted. 2 dull-witted; obtuse.

purchase VB 1 to obtain something in return for payment; to buy. 2 to get or achieve something through labour, effort, sacrifice or risk. ➤ N 1 something that has been bought. 2 the act of buying. 3 firmness in holding or gripping; a sure grasp or foothold. ■ **purchaser** N.

purdah N in some Muslim and Hindu societies: the seclusion or veiling of women.

pure ADJ 1 consisting of itself only; unmixed with anything else. 2 unpolluted; uncontaminated; wholesome. 3 virtuous; chaste; free from sin or guilt. 4 utter; sheer: **pure lunacy**. 5 of mathematics or science: dealing with theory and abstractions rather than practical applications. 6 of unmixed blood or descent. 7 of sound, eg a sung note: clear, unwavering and exactly in tune. 8 absolutely true to type or style. ■ **purely** ADV. ■ **pureness** N. ◆ **pure and simple** nothing but; without anything else: **jealousy pure and simple**.

pure-bred ADJ of an animal or plant: having parents of the same breed or variety.

purée COOKERY, N a quantity of vegetables, fruit, meat, fish, etc reduced to a smooth pulp by liquidizing or rubbing through a sieve.

➤ VB (*purées, puréed, puréeing*) to reduce something to a purée.

purgative N 1 a medicine that causes the bowels to empty. 2 something that purifies.

purgatory N (*-ies*) 1 chiefly RC CHURCH a place or state into which the soul passes after death, where it is cleansed of pardonable sins before going to heaven. ■ **purgatorial** ADJ.

purge VB 1 a to rid (eg the soul or body) of unwholesome thoughts or substances; b to rid (anything) of impurities. 2 to rid (a political party, community, etc) of (undesirable members). 3 OLD USE a to empty (the bowels), esp by taking a laxative; b to make someone empty their bowels, esp by giving them a laxative. 4 LAW, RELIG, etc to rid (oneself) of guilt by atoning for an offence.
➤ N 1 an act of purging. 2 the process of purging a party or community of undesirable members.

purify VB (*-ies, -ied*) 1 TR & INTR to make or become pure. 2 to cleanse something of contaminating or harmful substances. ■ **purification** N. ■ **purifier** N.

purism N insistence on the traditional elements of the content and style of a particular subject, esp of language. ■ **purist** N.

puritan N someone of strict, esp over-strict, moral principles. ■ **puritanical** ADJ.

purity N 1 the state of being pure or unmixed. 2 freedom from contamination, pollution or unwholesome or intrusive elements. 3 chasteness or innocence.

purl[1] KNITTING, N a reverse plain stitch.
➤ VB to knit in purl.

purl[2] VB, INTR 1 to flow with a murmuring sound. 2 to eddy or swirl.

purlieu N 1 (usu **purlieus**) the surroundings or immediate neighbourhood of a place. 2 (usu **purlieus**) someone's usual haunts.

purlin or **purline** N, BUILDING a roof timber stretching across the principal rafters or between the tops of walls.

purloin VB to steal, filch or pilfer.

purple N 1 a colour that is a mixture of blue and red. 2 crimson cloth, or a robe made from it, worn eg by emperors and cardinals, symbolic of their authority. 3 (**the purple**) high rank.
➤ ADJ 1 purple-coloured. 2 of writing: especially fine in style; over-elaborate.

purple patch N 1 a passage in a piece of writing which is over-elaborate and ornate. 2 any period of time characterized by good luck.

purport VB 1 to profess by its appearance, etc (to be something). 2 to convey; to imply (that).
➤ N meaning, significance, point or gist.

purpose N 1 the object or aim in doing something. 2 the function for which something is intended. 3 the intentions, aspirations, aim or goal: **no purpose in life**. 4 determination; resolve: **a woman of purpose**.
➤ VB to intend (to do something).
■ **purposeless** ADJ. ■ **purposely** ADJ.
◆ **on purpose** intentionally; deliberately.

purpose-built ADJ designed or made to meet specific requirements.

purposeful ADJ determined; showing a sense of purpose. ■ **purposefully** ADV.

purr VB 1 INTR of a cat: to make a soft low vibrating sound associated with contentment. 2 INTR of a vehicle or machine: to make a sound similar to this, suggestive of good running order. 3 TR & INTR to say something in a tone vibrating with satisfaction.
➤ N a purring sound.

purse N 1 a small container carried in the pocket or handbag, for keeping cash, etc in. 2 N AMER a woman's handbag. 3 funds available for spending. 4 a sum of money offered as a present or prize.
➤ VB to draw (the lips) together in disapproval or deep thought.

purser N the ship's officer responsible for keeping the accounts and, on a passenger ship, seeing to the welfare of passengers.

purse strings PL N.
◆ **hold the purse strings** to be in charge of the financial side of things, eg in a family.

pursuance N the process of pursuing:

in pursuance of his duties.

pursue VB **1** TR & INTR to follow someone or something in order to overtake, capture or attack them or it, etc; to chase. **2** to proceed along (a course or route). **3** to put effort into achieving (a goal, aim, etc). **4** to occupy oneself with (one's career, etc). **5** to continue with or follow up (enquiries, etc). ■ **pursuer** N.

pursuit N **1** the act of pursuing or chasing. **2** an occupation or hobby.

purulent ADJ, MED etc belonging or relating to, or full of, pus. ■ **purulence** N.

purvey VB, TR & INTR to supply (food or provisions, etc) as a business. ■ **purveyor** N.

purview N, FORMAL OR TECHNICAL scope of responsibility or concern, eg of a court of law.

pus N the thick, usu yellowish liquid that forms in abscesses or infected wounds.

push VB **1** (often **push against, at** or **on sth**) to exert pressure to force it away from one; to press, thrust or shove it. **2** to hold (eg a wheelchair, trolley, pram, etc) and move it forward in front of one. **3** TR & INTR (often **push through, in** or **past, etc**) to force one's way, thrusting aside people or obstacles. **4** INTR to progress esp laboriously. **5** to force in a specified direction: **push up prices**. **6** (often **push sb into sth**) to coax, urge, persuade or goad them to do it: **pushed me into agreeing**. **7** to pressurize someone (or oneself) into working harder, achieving more, etc. **8** (usu **push for sth**) to recommend it strongly; to campaign or press for it. **9** to promote (products or ideas). **10** to sell (drugs) illegally.
➢ N **1** an act of pushing; a thrust or shove. **2** a burst of effort towards achieving something. **3** determination, aggression or drive.
◆ **at a push** COLLOQ if forced.
◆ **push sb around** or **about** COLLOQ **1** to bully them. **2** to order them about.
◆ **be pushed for sth** COLLOQ to be short of (eg time or money).
◆ **push off** or **along** COLLOQ to go away.
◆ **push on** to continue on one's way.
◆ **push sth through** to force acceptance

of (a proposal or bill, etc).

pushbike N, COLLOQ a bicycle propelled by pedals alone.

pushchair N a small folding wheeled chair for a toddler.

pusher N, COLLOQ someone who sells illegal drugs.

pushover N, COLLOQ someone who is easily defeated or outwitted.

pushy ADJ (**-ier, -iest**) COLLOQ aggressively self-assertive or ambitious.

pusillanimous ADJ timid, cowardly, weak-spirited or faint-hearted.

puss N, COLLOQ a cat.

pussy N (**-ies**) (also **pussycat**) COLLOQ a cat.

pussyfoot VB, INTR to behave indecisively.

pustule N a small inflammation on the skin, containing pus; a pimple. ■ **pustular** ADJ.

put VB (PA T & PA P **put,** PR P **putting**) **1** to place something or someone in or convey them or it to a specified position or situation. **2** to fit: **Put a new lock on the door**. **3** to cause someone or something to be in a specified state: **put him at ease**. **4** to apply. **5** to set or impose: **put an end to free lunches**. **6** to lay (blame, reliance, emphasis, etc) on something. **7** to set someone to work, etc or apply something to a good purpose, etc. **8** to translate: **Put this into French**. **9** to invest or pour (energy, money or other resources) into something. **10** to classify or categorize something or put it in order: **I put accuracy before speed**. **11** to submit (questions for answering or ideas for considering) to someone; to suggest: **I put it to her that she was lying**. **12** to express something. **13** COLLOQ to write or say: **don't know what to put**. **14** INTR, NAUT to sail in a certain direction: **put to sea**. **15** ATHLETICS to throw (the shot).
◆ **put about** NAUT to turn round.
◆ **put sth about** to spread (a rumour, etc).
◆ **put sth across** to communicate (ideas, etc).
◆ **put sth aside** to save (eg money) for future use.

◆ **put sb away** COLLOQ **1** to imprison them. **2** to confine them in a mental institution.

◆ **put sth away 1** to replace it tidily where it belongs. **2** to save it for future use. **3** COLLOQ to consume (food or drink), esp in large amounts. **4** OLD USE to reject, discard or renounce it.

◆ **put sth back 1** to replace it. **2** to postpone (a match or meeting, etc). **3** to adjust (a clock, etc) to an earlier time.

◆ **put sb down** to humiliate or snub them.

◆ **put sth down 1** to lay it on a surface after holding it, etc. **2** to crush (a revolt, etc). **3** to kill (an animal) painlessly, esp when it is suffering.

◆ **put sth in 1** to fit or install it. **2** to spend (time) working at something: **puts in four hours' violin practice daily**. **3** to submit (a claim, etc).

◆ **put it on** to feign or exaggerate.

◆ **put sb off 1** to cancel or postpone an engagement with them. **2** to make them lose concentration. **3** to cause them to lose enthusiasm or to feel disgust for something.

◆ **put sth off** to postpone (an event or arrangement).

◆ **put sth on 1** to switch on (an electrical device, etc). **2** to dress in it. **3** to gain (weight or speed). **4** to present (a play or show, etc). **5** to assume (an accent or manner, etc) for effect or to deceive. **6** to bet (money) on a horse, etc.

◆ **put one over on sb** COLLOQ to trick them.

◆ **put sb out** to inconvenience them. **2** to offend or annoy them.

◆ **put sth out 1** to extinguish (a light or fire). **2** to publish (a leaflet, etc). **3** to strain or dislocate (a part of the body).

◆ **put sth over** to communicate (an idea, etc) to someone else.

◆ **put up** to stay for the night.

◆ **put sb up** to give them a bed for the night.

◆ **put sth up 1** to build it; to erect it. **2** to raise (prices). **3** to present (a plan, etc). **4** to offer (a house, etc) for sale.

◆ **put sb** or **oneself up for sth** to offer or nominate them, or oneself, as a candidate.

◆ **put upon sb** to presume on their good will.

◆ **put sb up to sth** to urge them to do something they ought not to do.

◆ **put up with sb** or **sth** to tolerate them or it.

putative ADJ supposed; assumed.

put-down N, COLLOQ a snub or humiliation.

put-on ADJ of an accent or manner, etc: assumed; pretended.

putrefy VB (*-ies, -ied*) INTR of flesh or other organic matter: to go bad, rot or decay, esp with a foul smell. ■ **putrefaction** N.

putrescent ADJ decaying; rotting; putrefying.

putrid ADJ **1** of organic matter: decayed; rotten. **2** stinking; foul; disgusting. **3** COLLOQ repellent; worthless.

putsch N a secretly-planned sudden attempt to remove a government from power.

putt VB, TR & INTR, GOLF, PUTTING to send (the ball) gently forward on the green and into or nearer the hole.
➤ N a putting stroke.

puttee N a long strip of cloth worn by wrapping it around the leg from the ankle to the knee and used as protection or support.

putter N, GOLF **1** a club used for putting. **2** someone who putts.

putty N (*-ies*) a paste of ground chalk and linseed oil, used for fixing glass in window frames, filling holes in wood, etc.
➤ VB (*-ied*) to fix or fill something with putty.

puzzle VB **1** to perplex, mystify or baffle.
➤ N **1** a baffling problem. **2** a game or toy that takes the form of something for solving, designed to test knowledge, memory, powers of reasoning, manipulative skill, etc.
■ **puzzlement** N. ■ **puzzling** ADJ.

PVC ABBREV polyvinyl chloride.

pygmy or **pigmy** N (*-ies*) **1** an undersized person; a dwarf. **2** DEROG someone insignificant, esp in a specified field: **an intellectual pygmy**.
➤ ADJ belonging or relating to a small-sized breed: **pygmy hippopotamus**.

pyjamas or (N AMER) **pajamas** PL N **1** a sleeping-suit consisting of a loose jacket or top, and trousers. **2** loose-fitting trousers worn by either sex in the East.

pylon N a tall steel structure for supporting

electric power cables.

pyramid N **1** any of the huge ancient Egyptian royal tombs built on a square base, with four sloping triangular sides meeting in a common apex. **2** GEOM a solid of this shape, with a square or triangular base. **3** any structure or pile, etc of similar shape. ■ **pyramidal** ADJ.

pyre N a pile of wood on which a dead body is ceremonially cremated.

pyretic ADJ, MED relating to or producing fever.

Pyrex N, TRADEMARK a heat-resistant glass.

pyrite N, GEOL the commonest sulphide mineral, used in the production of sulphuric acid. Also

called **iron pyrites** or **fool's gold**.

pyrites N **1** GEOL pyrite. **2** CHEM any of a large class of mineral sulphides: **copper pyrites**.

pyromania N, PSYCHOL an obsessive urge to set fire to things. ■ **pyromaniac** N.

pyrotechnics SING OR PL N **1** a fireworks display. **2** a display of brilliance in speech or music, etc.

Pyrrhic victory N a victory won at so great a cost in lives, etc that it can hardly be regarded as a triumph at all.

python N a non-venomous egg-laying snake that coils around and suffocates its prey.

Qq

Q or **q** N (**Qs, Q's** or **q's**) the seventeenth letter of the English alphabet.

QC ABBREV, LAW Queen's Counsel.

QED ABBREV: **quod erat demonstrandum** (Latin), which was the thing that had to be proved.

quack[1] N the noise that a duck makes.
➣ VB, INTR of a duck: to make this noise.

quack[2] N **1** someone who claims to have medical knowledge, but who has no formal training. **2** COLLOQ, often DEROG a term for any doctor. ■ **quackery** N.

quad[1] N, COLLOQ **1** a quadruplet.
2 a quadrangle.

quad[2] COLLOQ, ADJ quadraphonic.
➣ N **1** quadraphonics. **2** quadraphony.

quadrangle N **1** GEOM a square, rectangle or other four-sided two-dimensional figure.
2 a rectangular courtyard, esp one in the grounds of a college, school, etc.
■ **quadrangular** ADJ.

quadrant N **1** GEOM **a** a quarter of the circumference of a circle; **b** a plane figure that is a quarter of a circle, ie an area bounded by two perpendicular radii and the arc between them; **c** a quarter of a sphere, ie a section cut by two planes that intersect at right angles at the centre. **2** any device or mechanical part in the shape of a 90° arc. ■ **quadrantal** ADJ.

quadraphonic or **quadrophonic** ADJ of a stereophonic recording or reproduction: using four loudspeakers that are fed by four separate channels. ■ **quadraphonics** N.

quadrate ADJ square or almost square in cross-section or face view.

quadratic N, MATH (in full **quadratic equation**) an algebraic equation that involves the square, but no higher power, of an unknown quantity or variable.

quadrennial ADJ **1** lasting four years.
2 occurring every four years.

quadriceps N (**-cepses** or **-ceps**) ANAT a large

four-part muscle at the front of the thigh.

quadrilateral GEOM, N a two-dimensional figure that has four sides.
➤ ADJ four-sided.

quadrille N 1 a square dance for four couples, in five or six movements. **2** music for this.

quadriplegia N, PATHOL paralysis that affects all four limbs. ■ **quadriplegic** ADJ, N.

quadruped N an animal, esp a mammal, that has its four limbs specially adapted for walking.

quadruple ADJ 1 four times as great, much or many. **2** made up of four parts or things. **3** MUS of time: having four beats to the bar.
➤ VB, TR & INTR to make or become four times as great, much or many.

quadruplet N one of four children or animals born to the same mother at the same time.

quaff VB, TR & INTR, LITERARY to drink eagerly or deeply. ■ **quaffer** N.

quagmire N 1 an area of soft marshy ground; a bog. **2** a dangerous or difficult situation.

quail¹ N (*quail* or *quails*) a small migratory game bird of the partridge family.

quail² VB, INTR to lose courage; to be apprehensive with fear; to flinch.

quaint ADJ old-fashioned, strange or unusual, esp in a charming, pretty or dainty, etc way. ■ **quaintness** N.

quake VB, INTR 1 of people: to tremble with fear, etc. **2** of a building, etc: to shudder.
➤ N, COLLOQ an earthquake.

qualification N 1 a an official record that one has completed a training or performed satisfactorily in an examination, etc; **b** a document or certificate, etc that confirms this. **2** a skill or ability that fits one for some job, etc. **3** the act, process or fact of qualifying. **4** an addition to a statement, etc that modifies, narrows or restricts its implications; a condition.

qualify VB (-ies, -ied) 1 INTR to complete a training or pass an examination, etc, esp in order to practise a specified profession, occupation, etc. **2 a** (often **qualify sb for sth**) to give or provide them with the necessary competency, ability or attributes, etc to do it; **b** to entitle. **3** INTR **a** to meet or fulfil the required conditions or guidelines, etc (in order to receive an award or privilege); **b** (usu **qualify as sth**) to have the right characteristics to be a specified thing. **4 a** to modify (a statement, etc) in such a way as to restrict, limit or moderate, etc it; **b** to add reservations to something; to tone down or restrict it. **5** TR & INTR, SPORT to proceed or allow someone to proceed to the later stages or rounds, etc (of a competition, etc), usu by doing well in a preliminary round.

qualitative ADJ relating to, affecting or concerned with distinctions of the quality or standard of something.

quality N (-ies) 1 the degree or extent of excellence of something: **inferior quality**. **2 a** general excellence; high standard: **articles of quality**; **b** AS ADJ of or exhibiting a high quality or standard: **the quality newspapers**. **3 a** a distinctive or distinguishing talent or attribute, etc; **b** the basic nature of something.

qualm N 1 a a sudden feeling of nervousness or apprehension; **b** a misgiving or pang of conscience. **2** a feeling of faintness or nausea.

quandary N (-ies) 1 a state of indecision, doubt or perplexity. **2** a situation that involves some kind of dilemma or predicament.

quango N a semi-public administrative body that functions outwith the civil service but which is government-funded.

quantify VB (-ies, -ied) to determine the quantity of something or to measure or express it as a quantity. ■ **quantifiable** ADJ. ■ **quantification** N.

quantitative ADJ 1 relating to quantity. **2** estimated, or measurable, in terms of quantity.

quantity N (-ies) 1 the property that things have that allows them to be measured or counted; size or amount. **2** a specified amount or number, etc: **a tiny quantity**. **3** largeness of amount; bulk: **buy in quantity**. **4** (**quantities**) a large amount: **quantities of food**. **5** MATH a value that may be expressed as a number, or the symbol or figure representing it.

quantum N (*quanta*) **1 a** an amount or quantity, esp a specified one; **b** a portion, part or share. **2** PHYS **a** the minimal indivisible amount of a specified physical property (eg momentum or electromagnetic radiation energy, etc) that can exist; **b** a unit of this, eg the photon. Often AS ADJ: quantum effect.

quarantine N **1** the isolation of people or animals to prevent the spread of any infectious disease that they could be developing. **2** the duration or place of such isolation.
➤ VB to put (a person or animal) into quarantine.

quark N, PHYS the smallest known bit of matter, being any of a group of subatomic particles thought to make up all protons and neutrons.

quarrel N **1** an angry disagreement or argument. **2** a cause of such disagreement; a complaint. **3** a break in a friendship; a breach.
➤ VB (*-ll-*; US *-l-*) INTR **1** to argue or dispute angrily. **2** to fall out; to disagree and remain on bad terms. **3** (usu **quarrel with sb** or **sth**) to find fault with them or it. ■ **quarrelsome** ADJ.

quarry¹ N (*-ies*) **1** an open excavation for extracting stone or slate. **2** a place from which stone, etc can be excavated.
➤ VB (*-ies, -ied*) **1** to extract (stone, etc) from a quarry. **2** to excavate a quarry in (land).

quarry² N (*-ies*) **1** an animal or bird that is hunted. **2** any object of pursuit.

quart N **1** in the UK: **a** in the imperial system: a liquid measure equivalent to one quarter of a gallon, two pints (1.136 litres); **b** a container that holds this amount. **2** in the US: **a** a unit of liquid measure that is equivalent to one quarter of a gallon, two pints (0.946 litres); **b** a unit of dry measure that is equivalent to two pints (1.101 litres).

quarter N **1 a** one of four equal parts that an object or quantity is or can be divided into; **b** the number one when it is divided by four. **2** any of the three-month divisions of the year, esp one that begins or ends on a quarter day. **3** N AMER **a** 25 cents; **b** a coin of this value. **4 a** a period of 15 minutes; **b** a point of time 15

minutes after or before any hour. **5** ASTRON **a** a fourth part of the Moon's cycle; **b** either of the two phases of the Moon when half its surface is lit and visible. **6** any of the four main compass directions; any direction. **7** a district of a city, etc: the Spanish quarter. **8** (also **quarters**) a section of the public or society, etc; certain people or a certain person: no sympathy from that quarter. **9** (**quarters**) lodgings or accommodation, eg for soldiers and their families: married quarters. **10** in the imperial system: **a** a unit of weight equal to a quarter of a hundredweight; **b** BRIT COLLOQ 4 ounces or a quarter of a pound; **c** BRIT a unit of measure for grain equal to eight bushels. **11** any of the four sections that an animal's or bird's carcass is divided into, each section having a leg or a wing. **12** mercy that is shown or offered, eg to a defeated enemy, etc: give no quarter. **13** SPORT any of the four equal periods that a game is divided into.
➤ VB **1** to divide something into quarters. **2 a** to accommodate or billet (troops, etc) in lodgings; **b** to be accommodated or billeted in lodgings. **3** HIST to divide (the body of a hanged traitor, etc) into four parts, each with a limb.

quarterback N, AMER FOOTBALL a player who directs the attacking play.

quarterdeck N, NAUT the stern part of a ship's upper deck which is usu reserved for officers.

quarter final N a match or the round that precedes the semi-final match or round in a competition.

quarterly ADJ produced, occurring, published, paid or due, etc once every quarter of a year.
➤ N (*-ies*) a quarterly publication.

quartermaster N **1** an army officer who is responsible for soldiers' accommodation, food and clothing. **2** NAUT a petty officer who is responsible for navigation and signals.

quarter note N, N AMER, MUS a crotchet.

quartet or **quartette** N **1** MUS **a** an ensemble of four singers or instrumentalists; **b** a piece of music for four performers. **2** any group or set of four.

quarto N, PRINTING a size of paper produced by folding a sheet in half twice to give four leaves or eight pages.

quartz N, GEOL a common colourless mineral that is often tinged with impurities that give a wide variety of shades.

quartzite N, GEOL **1** a highly durable rock that is composed largely or entirely of quartz. **2** a sandstone consisting of grains of quartz cemented together by silica.

quasar N, ASTRON a highly intense luminous star-like source of light and radio waves.

quash VB **1** to subdue, crush or suppress, etc (eg a rebellion or protest). **2** to reject (a verdict, etc) as invalid. **3** to annul (a law, etc).

quaternary ADJ **1** having or consisting of four parts. **2** fourth in a series.

quatrain N, POETRY a verse or poem of four lines which usu rhyme alternately.

quatrefoil N **1** BOT a flower or leaf composed of four petals or leaflets. **2** ARCHIT a four-lobed design, esp one that is used in open stonework.

quattrocento N the 15c, esp with reference to Italian Renaissance art.

quaver VB **1** INTR of a voice or a musical sound, etc: to be unsteady; to shake or tremble. **2** to say or sing something in a trembling voice. ➤ N **1** MUS a note that lasts half as long as a crotchet and usu represented in notation by ♪. **2** a tremble in the voice. ■ **quavering** ADJ.

quay N an artificial structure for the loading and unloading of ships.

quayside N the area around a quay, esp the edge along the water.

queasy ADJ (-ier, -iest) **1** of a person: feeling slightly sick. **2** of the stomach or digestion: easily upset. **3** of the conscience: readily made uneasy. ■ **queasily** ADV. ■ **queasiness** N.

queen N **1 a** a woman who rules a country, having inherited her position by birth; **b** (in full **queen consort**) the wife of a king; **c** (usu **Queen**) the title applied to someone who holds either of these positions. **2** a woman, place or thing considered supreme in some way: **queen of European cities**. **3** a large fertile female ant, bee or wasp that lays eggs. **4** CHESS a piece that is able to move in any direction, making it the most powerful piece on the board. **5** CARDS any of the four high-ranking face cards that have a picture of a queen on them. **6** DEROG an effeminate male homosexual. ■ **queenly** ADJ (-ier, -iest).

queen post N, ARCHIT in a trussed roof: one of two upright posts that connect the tie-beam to the principal rafters.

queer ADJ **1** SLANG of a man: homosexual. **2** odd, strange or unusual. **3** faint or ill. ➤ N, SLANG a homosexual. ■ **queerness** N. ◆ **in queer street** BRIT COLLOQ **1** in debt or financial difficulties. **2** in trouble. ◆ **queer sb's pitch** COLLOQ to spoil their plans.

quell VB **1 a** to crush or subdue (disturbances or opposition, etc); **b** to force (rebels or rioters, etc) to give in. **2** to suppress, overcome or alleviate (unwanted feelings, etc).

quench VB **1 a** to satisfy (thirst) by drinking; **b** to satisfy (a desire, etc). **2** to extinguish (a fire or light, etc). **3** to damp or crush (an emotion).

quenelle N, COOKERY an oval or sausage-shaped dumpling made from meat-paste.

quern N **1** a mill, usu consisting of two circular stones (**quernstones**) one on top of the other, used for grinding grain by hand. **2** a small hand mill for grinding pepper or mustard, etc.

querulous ADJ **1** inclined or ready to complain. **2** complaining, grumbling or whining.

query N (-ies) **1** a question, esp one that raises a doubt or objection, etc. **2** a request for information; an inquiry. **3** a less common name for a **question mark**. ➤ VB (-ies, -ied) **1** to raise a doubt about something. **2** to ask. **3** chiefly US to interrogate or question someone.

quest N **1** a search or hunt. **2** a journey that involves searching for something or achieving some goal. **3** the object of a search; an aim. ➤ VB, INTR **1** (usu **quest after** or **for sth**) to

search about; to roam around in search of it.
2 of a dog: to search for game.

question N **1 a** a written or spoken sentence that is worded in such a way as to request information or an answer; **b** the interrogative sentence or other form of words in which this is expressed. **2** a doubt or query. **3** a problem or difficulty: **the Northern Ireland question. 4** a problem set for discussion or solution in an examination paper, etc. **5** an investigation or search for information. **6** a matter, concern or issue: **a question of safety.**
➤ VB **1** to ask someone questions; to interrogate them. **2** to raise doubts about something; to query it. ■ **questioner** N.
◆ **in question 1** presently under discussion or being referred to: **was away at the time in question. 2** in doubt: **Her ability is in question.**
◆ **out of the question** impossible.

questionable ADJ **1** doubtful; debatable; ambiguous. **2** suspect; disreputable; obscure; shady. ■ **questionably** ADV.

questioning N an act or the process of asking a question or questions.
➤ ADJ **1** characterized by doubt or uncertainty; mildly confused: **exchanged questioning looks. 2** inquisitive; keen to learn.

question mark N **1** the punctuation mark (?) used to indicate that the sentence that comes before it is a question. **2** a doubt.

questionnaire N a set of questions specially formulated as a means of collecting information and surveying opinions, etc.

queue N **1** BRIT a line of people or vehicles, etc, esp ones that are waiting for something. **2** a list of items held in a computer system in the order in which they are to be processed.
➤ VB, INTR **a** to form a queue; **b** to line up or wait in a queue.

quibble VB, INTR to argue over trifles; to make petty objections.
➤ N a trifling objection.

quiche N a type of open tart made with a filling of eggs and various savoury flavourings.

quick ADJ **1** taking little time. **2** brief. **3** fast;

rapid; speedy. **4** not delayed; immediate. **5** intelligent; alert; sharp. **6** of the temper: easily roused to anger. **7** nimble, deft or brisk. **8** not reluctant or slow (to do something); apt, eager or ready: **quick to take offence.**
➤ ADV, INFORMAL rapidly.
➤ N **1** an area of sensitive flesh at the base of the fingernail or toenail. **2** the site where someone's feelings, etc are supposed to be located: **Her words wounded him to the quick. 3** OLD USE those who are alive: **the quick and the dead.** ■ **quickly** ADV. ■ **quickness** N.

quicken VB **1** TR & INTR to make or become quicker; to accelerate. **2** to stimulate, rouse or stir (interest or imagination, etc). **3** INTR of a baby in the womb: to begin to move perceptibly.

quick-fire ADJ **1** very rapid. **2** able to fire shots in rapid succession.

quicksand N (an area of) loose, wet sand that can suck down anything that lands on it.

quicksilver N mercury.
➤ ADJ of someone's mind or temper, etc: fast, esp unpredictably so; volatile.

quickstep N a fast modern ballroom dance in quadruple time.

quick-tempered ADJ easily angered.

quick-witted ADJ **1** having fast reactions. **2** able to grasp or understand situations, etc quickly; clever. ■ **quick-wittedness** N.

quid N (PL *quid*) COLLOQ a pound sterling.

quiddity N (*-ies*) **1** the essence of something; the distinctive qualities, etc that make a thing what it is. **2** a quibble; a trifling detail or point.

quid pro quo N something that is given or taken in exchange for something else of comparable value or status, etc.

quiescent ADJ quiet, silent, at rest or in an inactive state. ■ **quiescence** N.

quiet ADJ **1 a** making little or no noise; **b** of a sound or voice, etc: soft; not loud. **2** of a place, etc: peaceful; tranquil; without noise or bustle. **3** of someone or their nature or disposition: reserved; unassertive; shy. **4** of the weather or sea, etc: calm. **5** not disturbed by trouble or

excitement. **6** without fuss or publicity; informal. **7** of business or trade, etc: not flourishing or busy. **8** secret; private. **9** undisclosed or hidden: **took a quiet satisfaction in his luck**. **10** enjoyed in peace: **a quiet read**. **11** not showy or gaudy, etc: **quiet tones of beige**.
➤ N **1** absence of, or freedom from, noise or commotion, etc. **2** calm, tranquillity or repose.
■ **quietly** ADV. ■ **quietness** N.
◆ **keep quiet about sth** or **keep sth quiet** to remain silent or say nothing about it.
◆ **on the quiet** (also **on the q.t.**) discreetly.

quieten VB **1** (often **quieten down**) TR & INTR to make or become quiet. **2** to calm (doubts or fears, etc).

quietism N a state of calmness and passivity.

quietude N quietness; tranquillity.

quiff N a tuft of hair at the front of the head that is brushed up into a crest.

quill N **1 a** a large stiff feather from a bird's wing or tail; **b** the hollow base part of this. **2** a pen that is made by sharpening and splitting the end of a feather, esp a goose feather. **3** a porcupine's long spine.

quilt N **1** a type of bedcover that is made by sewing together two layers of fabric, usu with some kind of soft padding material etc in between them. **2** a bedspread that is made in this way but which tends to be thinner. **3** LOOSELY a duvet; a continental quilt.
➤ VB, TR & INTR **1** to sew (two layers of material, etc) together with a filling in between. **2** to cover or line something with padding.
■ **quilter** N. ■ **quilted** ADJ.

quin N, COLLOQ a shortened form of **quintuplet**.

quince N **1** a small Asian tree of the rose family. **2** the acidic hard yellow fruit of this tree, used in making jams and jellies, etc.

quincentenary N a 500th anniversary.
■ **quincentennial** ADJ.

quinine or (esp US) N **1** an alkaloid that is found in the bark of the cinchona. **2** MED a bitter-tasting toxic drug obtained from this alkaloid, widely used in treating malaria.

quinquennial ADJ **1** lasting for five years. **2** recurring once every five years.

quinquereme N, HIST a type of ancient Roman or Greek galley ship with five banks of oars.

quinsy N, PATHOL inflammation of, and formation of abscesses on, the tonsils and the area of the throat round about them.

quintessence N **1** a perfect example or embodiment of it. **2** the fundamental essential nature of something. **3** OLD USE the purest, most concentrated extract of a substance.
■ **quintessential** ADJ.

quintet or **quintette** N **1** a group of five singers or musicians. **2** a piece of music for five such performers. **3** any group or set of five.

quintuple ADJ **1** five times as great, much or many. **2** made up of five parts or things. **3** MUS having five beats to the bar.
➤ VB, TR & INTR to make or become five times as great, much or many.

quintuplet N one of five children or animals born to the same mother at the same time.

quip N **1** a witty saying. **2** a sarcastic remark.
➤ VB (-*pp*-) **1** INTR to make a quip or quips. **2** to answer someone with a quip.

quire N **1** a measure for paper that is equivalent to 25 (formerly 24) sheets and one-twentieth of a ream. **2 a** a set of four sheets of parchment or paper folded in half together to form eight leaves; **b** LOOSELY any set of folded sheets that is grouped together with other similar ones and bound into book form.

quirk N **1** an odd habit, mannerism or aspect of personality, etc. **2** an odd twist in affairs or turn of events; a strange coincidence.
■ **quirkiness** N. ■ **quirky** ADJ (-*ier*, -*iest*).

quisling N **1** a traitor. **2** someone who collaborates with an enemy.

quit VB (*quitted* or *quit, quitting*) **1** to leave or depart from (a place, etc). **2** TR & INTR to leave, give up or resign (a job). **3** to exit (a computer program, application, etc). **4** N AMER, COLLOQ to cease something. **5** TR & INTR of a tenant: to move out of rented premises.

➤ ADJ (usu **quit of sth**) free or rid of it.
■ **quitter** N.

quitch N (in full **quitch grass**; PL *quitches*) another name for **couch**[2].

quite ADV 1 completely; entirely: *It's not quite clear.* 2 to a high degree: **quite exceptional**. 3 rather; fairly; to some or a limited degree: *quite a nice day.* 4 (also **quite so**) used in a reply: I agree, see your point, etc.
◆ **quite a** or **an** a striking, impressive, challenging, etc: **That was quite a night.**
◆ **quite a few** COLLOQ a reasonably large number of (people or things, etc).
◆ **quite some** a considerably large amount of: *quite some time.*
◆ **quite something** very impressive.

quits ADJ, COLLOQ 1 on an equal footing. 2 even.

quittance N release from debt or obligation.

quiver[1] VB 1 (often **quiver with sth**) INTR to shake or tremble slightly because of it: **quivered with fear**. 2 INTR to shake or flutter.
➤ N a tremble or shiver.

quiver[2] N a long narrow case used for carrying arrows.

quixotic ADJ 1 absurdly generous or chivalrous. 2 naïvely romantic, idealistic or impractical, etc.

quiz N (*quizzes*) 1 (also **quiz show**) an entertainment in which the knowledge of a panel of contestants is tested through a series of questions. 2 any series of questions as a test of knowledge. 3 an interrogation.
➤ VB (**-zz-**) to question or interrogate someone.

quizzical ADJ of an expression, etc: mildly amused or perplexed; mocking; questioning.
■ **quizzically** ADV.

quoin N 1 the external angle of a wall or building. 2 a cornerstone. 3 a wedge.

quoit N 1 a ring made of metal, rubber or rope used in the game of quoits. 2 (**quoits**) a game that involves throwing these rings at pegs with the aim of encircling them.

quorate ADJ, BRIT of a meeting, etc: attended by

enough people to form a quorum.

quorum N the fixed minimum number of members of an organization or society, etc who must be present at a meeting for its business to be valid.

quota N 1 the proportional or allocated share or part that is, or that should be, done, paid or contributed, etc out of a total amount, sum, etc. 2 the maximum or prescribed number or quantity that is permitted or required, eg of imported goods, etc.

quotation N 1 a remark or a piece of writing, etc that is quoted. 2 the act or an instance of quoting. 3 BUSINESS an estimated price for a job submitted by a contractor to a client.

quotation marks PL N a pair of punctuation marks, which can be either single (' ') or double (" "), used to mark the beginning and end of a quoted passage or to indicate the title of an essay, article or song, etc. Also called **inverted commas**.

quote VB, TR & INTR 1 to cite or offer (someone else or the words or ideas, etc of someone else) to substantiate an argument. 2 to repeat in writing or speech (the exact words, etc of someone else). 3 to cite or repeat (figures or data, etc). 4 TR & INTR of a contractor: to submit or suggest (a price) for doing a specified job or for buying something: **quoted her £600 as a trade-in**. 5 to give (a racehorse) betting odds as specified. 6 **a** to put quotation marks around (a written passage, word, etc); **b** (also **quote ... unquote**) to indicate (in speech) a part that has been said by someone else.
➤ N 1 a quotation. 2 a price quoted. 3 (**quotes**) quotation marks. ■ **quotable** ADJ.

quotidian ADJ 1 everyday; commonplace. 2 daily. 3 recurring daily.

quotient N, MATH the result of a division sum, eg when 72 (the dividend) is divided by 12 (the divisor), the quotient is 6.

qv or **q.v.** ABBREV: quod vide (Latin), which see.

Rr

R or **r** N (*Rs, R's* or *r's*) the eighteenth letter of the English alphabet.

rabbi N 1 a Jewish religious leader. 2 a Jewish scholar or teacher of the law. ■ **rabbinical** ADJ.

rabbit N 1 a small burrowing herbivorous mammal with long ears and a small stubby tail. 2 its flesh as food. 3 its fur.
➢ VB, INTR 1 to hunt rabbits. 2 (usu **rabbit on** or **away**) COLLOQ to talk at great length.

rabble N 1 a noisy disorderly crowd or mob. 2 (**the rabble**) the lowest class of people.

rabble-rouser N someone who agitates for social change. ■ **rabble-rousing** ADJ, N.

rabid ADJ 1 suffering from rabies. 2 fanatical; unreasoning. ■ **rabidity** or **rabidness** N.

rabies N a potentially fatal viral disease, causing convulsions and paralysis.

raccoon or **racoon** N (*raccoons* or *raccoon*) 1 a nocturnal American mammal with black eye patches. 2 its dense fur.

race¹ N 1 a contest of speed between runners, cars, etc. 2 (usu **the races**) a series of such contests over a fixed course, esp for horses or dogs. 3 any contest, esp to be the first to do or get something: the space race. 4 a strong or rapid current of water. 5 a channel conveying water to and from a mill wheel.
➢ VB 1 INTR to take part in a race. 2 to have a race with. 3 to cause (a horse, car, etc) to race. 4 INTR (usu **race about** or **along** or **around**) to run or move quickly and energetically. 5 INTR of an engine, etc: to run too fast. ■ **racer** N.

race² N 1 any of the major divisions of

humankind distinguished by a particular set of physical characteristics. 2 a nation or similar group of people thought of as distinct from others. 3 (**the human race**) human beings as a group. 4 a distinctive group of animals or plants within a species.

raceme N, BOT a flower-head consisting of individual flowers attached to a main unbranched stem.

racial ADJ 1 relating to a particular race. 2 based on race. ■ **racialism** N. ■ **racialist** N.

racism N 1 hatred, rivalry or bad feeling between races. 2 belief in the inherent superiority of a particular race or races over others. 3 discriminatory treatment based on such a belief. ■ **racist** N, ADJ.

rack¹ N 1 a framework with rails, shelves, hooks, etc for holding or storing things. 2 a framework for holding hay, etc from which livestock can feed. 3 a cogged or toothed bar connecting with a cogwheel or pinion for changing the position of something, or converting linear motion into rotary motion, or vice versa. 4 (**the rack**) HIST a device for torturing people by stretching their bodies.
➢ VB 1 to put in a rack. 2 to move or adjust by rack and pinion. 3 HIST to torture on a rack. 4 to stretch or move forcibly or excessively. 5 to cause pain or suffering to.
◆ **rack one's brains** to think very hard.

rack² N.
◆ **go to rack and ruin** to get into a state of neglect and decay.

racket¹ or **racquet** N a bat with a handle ending in a rounded head with a network of strings used in tennis, badminton, squash, etc.

racket² N **1** COLLOQ a loud confused noise or disturbance; a din. **2** a fraudulent or illegal means of making money.

racketeer N someone who makes money in an illegal way. ■ **racketeering** N.

racoon see **raccoon**

racquet see **racket¹**

racy ADJ (*-ier, -iest*) **1** lively or spirited. **2** slightly indecent; risqué. ■ **racily** ADV. ■ **raciness** N.

radar N **1** a system for detecting the presence of ships, aircraft, etc by transmitting short pulses of high-frequency radio waves. **2** the equipment for this.

radial ADJ **1** spreading out like rays. **2** relating to rays, a radius or radii. **3** along or in the direction of a radius or radii. **4** ANAT relating to the radius.
➤ N **1** a radiating part. **2** (in full **radial-ply tyre**) a tyre with fabric cords laid at right angle to the tread, giving the walls flexibility.
■ **radially** ADV.

radian N, GEOM the SI unit of plane angular measurement.

radiant ADJ **1** emitting electromagnetic radiation, eg, rays of light or heat. **2** glowing or shining. **3** of a person: beaming with joy, love, hope or health. **4** transmitted by or as radiation.
➤ N a point or object which emits electromagnetic radiation, eg, light or heat.
■ **radiance** N. ■ **radiantly** ADV.

radiate VB **1** to send out rays of light, heat, electromagnetic radiation, etc. **2** INTR of light, heat, radiation, etc: to be emitted in rays. **3** of a person: to manifestly exhibit (happiness, good health, etc). **4** TR & INTR to spread or cause (something) to spread out from a central point.

radiation N **1** energy that is emitted from a source and travels in the form of waves or particles. **2** a stream of particles emitted by a radioactive substance.

radiator N **1** an apparatus for heating, consisting of a series of pipes through which hot water is circulated. **2** an apparatus for cooling an engine, eg, in a car, consisting of a series of water-filled tubes and a fan.

radical ADJ **1** concerning or relating to the basic nature or root of something. **2** far-reaching; thoroughgoing: **radical changes**. **3** in favour of or tending to produce reforms. **4** relating to a political, etc group or party in favour of extreme reforms. **5** MATH relating to the root of a number.
➤ N **1** a root or basis in any sense. **2** someone who is a member of a radical political, etc group, or who holds political views. **3** CHEM within a molecule: a group of atoms which remains unchanged during a series of chemical reactions, but is normally incapable of independent existence: **free radical**. **4** MATH the root of a number. ■ **radicalism** N.
■ **radicalize** or **-ise** VB. ■ **radically** ADV.

radicchio N a variety of chicory with reddish or purplish leaves used in salads.

radicle N, BOT the part of a plant embryo which develops into the main root.

radii plural of **radius**

radio N **1** the use of radio waves to transmit and receive information such as television or radio programmes, telecommunications, and computer data, without connecting wires. **2** a wireless device that receives, and may also transmit, information in this manner. **3** a message or broadcast that is transmitted in this manner. **4** the business or profession of sound broadcasting: **to work in radio**.
➤ ADJ **1** relating to radio. **2** for transmitting by, or transmitted by radio. **3** controlled by radio.
➤ VB **1** to send (a message) to someone by radio. **2** INTR to communicate by radio.

radioactive ADJ relating to radioactivity.

radioactivity N the spontaneous disintegration of the nuclei of certain atoms, accompanied by the emission of alpha particles, beta particles or gamma rays.

radiogram N, OLD USE an apparatus consisting of a radio and record-player.

radiography N, MED the examination of the interior of the body by means of recorded images, known as **radiographs**, which are produced by X-rays on photographic film. ■ **radiographer** N.

radiology N the branch of medicine concerned with the use of radiation (eg, X-rays) and radioactive isotopes to diagnose and treat diseases. ■ **radiologist** N.

radiophonic ADJ 1 of sound, esp of music: produced electronically. 2 producing electronic music. ■ **radiophonics** PL N.

radioscopy N the examination of the inside of the body, or of opaque objects, using X-rays.

radiotherapy N the treatment of disease, esp cancer, by radiation.

radio wave N, PHYS an electromagnetic wave that has a low frequency and a long wavelength, widely used for communication.

radish N a plant with pungent red-skinned white roots, which are eaten raw in salads.

radium N a silvery-white highly toxic radioactive metallic element.

radius N (-*dii* or -*diuses*) 1 GEOM **a** a straight line running from the centre of a circle or sphere to any point on its circumference; **b** the length of such a line. 2 a radiating line. 3 anything placed like a radius, such as the spoke of a wheel. 4 a distance from a central point, thought of as defining, limiting, etc an area. 5 ANAT **a** the shorter of the two bones in the human forearm, on the thumb side; **b** the equivalent bone in other animals.

radon N, CHEM a highly toxic, colourless, radioactive gas.

raffia N fibre obtained from the leaves of a palm, used for weaving mats, baskets, etc.

raffish ADJ 1 slightly shady or disreputable; rakish. 2 flashy; vulgar.

raffle N a lottery, often to raise money for charity, with prizes.
➢ VB (also **raffle off**) to offer in a raffle.

raft N a flat structure of logs, timber, etc, fastened together so as to float on water.

rafter N a sloping beam supporting a roof.

rag[1] N 1 a worn, torn or waste scrap of cloth. 2 a shred, scrap or tiny portion of something. 3 (usu **rags**) an old or tattered garment. ■ **ragged** ADJ.

rag[2] VB (-**gg**-) 1 to tease. 2 to scold.
➢ N, BRIT a series of events put on by university or college students to raise money for charity.

ragamuffin N a person, usu a child, dressed in rags.

rag-bag N 1 a bag for storing scraps of material. 2 COLLOQ a random collection.

rage N 1 anger. 2 a passionate outburst, esp of anger. 3 a violent, stormy action, esp of weather, the sea, etc. 4 an intense desire or passion for something. 5 COLLOQ a widespread, usu temporary, fashion or craze.
➢ VB, INTR 1 to be violently angry. 2 to speak wildly with anger or passion. 3 of the wind, the sea, a battle, etc: to be stormy. ■ **raging** ADJ, N.

raglan ADJ 1 of a sleeve: attached to a garment by two seams running diagonally from the neck to the armpit. 2 of a garment: having such sleeves.

ragout N a highly seasoned stew of meat and vegetables.

ragtime N a type of jazz piano music with a highly syncopated rhythm.

raid N 1 a sudden unexpected attack. 2 an incursion by police, etc for the purpose of making arrests, or searching for suspected criminals or illicit goods.
➢ VB 1 to make a raid on (a person, place, etc). 2 INTR to go on a raid. ■ **raider** N.

rail[1] N 1 a bar, usu horizontal and supported by vertical posts. 2 a horizontal bar used to hang things on: *a picture rail*. 3 either of a pair of lengths of metal forming a track for the wheels of a train, tramcar or other vehicle. 4 the railway as a means of travel or transport: *go by rail*.
➢ VB 1 to provide with rails. 2 (usu **rail in** or **off**) to enclose or separate (eg, a space) within a rail or rails.
◆ **off the rails** 1 mad; eccentric. 2 not functioning or behaving normally or properly.

rail[2] VB, INTR (usu **rail at** or **against**) to

complain or criticize abusively or bitterly.

rail³ N a bird with a short neck and wings and long legs, usu found near water.

railing N a fence or barrier made of upright rails secured by horizontal connections.

raillery N (*-ies*) good-humoured teasing.

railroad N, N AMER, ESP US a railway.
➤ VB to rush or force (someone or something) unfairly (into doing something).

railway N 1 a track or set of tracks for trains to run on. 2 a similar set of tracks for a different type of vehicle: **funicular railway**.

raiment N, ARCHAIC, POETIC clothing.

rain N 1 a condensed moisture falling as separate water droplets from the atmosphere; **b** a shower of this. 2 (**rains**) the season of heavy rainfall in tropical countries.
➤ VB 1 INTR of rain: to fall. 2 TR & INTR to fall or cause (something) to fall like rain.
◆ **right as rain** COLLOQ in perfect order.

rainbow N an arch of red, orange, yellow, green, blue, indigo and violet seen in the sky when falling raindrops reflect and refract sunlight.

rain check N.
◆ **take a rain check (on sth)** COLLOQ, ORIG N AMER to promise to accept (an invitation) at a later date.

raincoat N a water-resistant coat.

rainfall N 1 the amount of rain that falls in a certain place over a certain period, measured by depth of water. 2 a shower of rain.

rainforest N forest in tropical regions, which has heavy rainfall.

rainy ADJ (*-ier, -iest*) characterized by periods of rain or by the presence of much rain.
◆ **save** or **keep sth for a rainy day** to keep it for a future time of potential need.

raise VB 1 to move or lift to a higher position or level. 2 to put in an upright or standing position. 3 to build or erect. 4 to increase the value, amount or strength of something: **raise one's voice**. 5 to put forward for consideration or

discussion: **raise an objection**. 6 to gather together or assemble: **raise an army**. 7 to collect together or obtain (funds, money, etc). 8 to stir up or incite: **raise a protest**. 9 to bring into being; to provoke: **raise the alarm**. 10 to promote to a higher rank. 11 to awaken or arouse from sleep or death. 12 to grow (vegetables, a crop, etc). 13 to bring up or rear (a child, children, etc): **raise a family**. 14 to bring to an end or remove: **raise the siege**. 15 to cause (bread or dough) to rise with yeast. 16 to establish radio contact with. 17 MATH to increase (a quantity to a given power): **3 raised to the power of 4 is 81**. 18 CARDS to increase a bet.
➤ N 1 an act of raising a bet, etc. 2 COLLOQ, esp N AMER an increase in salary.
◆ **raise an eyebrow** or **one's eyebrows** to look surprised or shocked.
◆ **raise Cain** or **the roof** COLLOQ 1 to make a lot of noise. 2 to be extremely angry.

raisin N a dried grape.

raison d'être N (*raisons d'être*) a purpose or reason that justifies someone's or something's existence.

raja or **rajah** N, HIST an Indian king or prince.

rake¹ N 1 a long-handled garden tool with a comb-like part at one end, used for smoothing or breaking up earth, gathering leaves together, etc. 2 any tool with a similar shape or use, eg, by a croupier.
➤ VB 1 (usu **rake up** or **together**) to collect, gather or remove with, or as if with, a rake. 2 (usu **rake over**) to make smooth with a rake. 3 INTR to work with, or as if with a rake. 4 TR & INTR (often **rake through**) to search carefully. 5 to sweep gradually along (the length of something), esp with gunfire or one's eyes. 6 to scratch or scrape.
◆ **rake sth in** COLLOQ to earn or acquire it in large amounts: **must be raking it in**.
◆ **rake up** COLLOQ to revive or uncover (something forgotten or lost).

rake² N, OLD USE a fashionable man who lives a dissolute and immoral life. ■ **rakish** ADJ.

rake³ N 1 a sloping position, esp of a ship's

funnel or mast backwards towards the stern, or of a ship's bow or stern in relation to the keel. **2** THEAT the slope of a stage. **3** the amount by which something slopes.
➢ VB to set or construct at a sloping angle.

rake-off N, COLLOQ a share of the profits, esp when dishonest or illegal.

rallentando MUS, ADJ, ADV as a musical direction: becoming gradually slower.

rally VB (*-ies, -ied*) **1** to come or bring together again after being dispersed. **2** to come or bring together for some common cause or action. **3** INTR to revive (spirits, strength, abilities, etc) by making an effort. **4** INTR to recover lost health, fitness, strength, etc, esp after an illness. **5** INTR of share prices: to increase again after a fall.
➢ N (*-ies*) **1** a reassembling of forces to make a new effort. **2** a mass meeting of people with a common cause or interest. **3** a recovering of lost health, fitness, strength, etc, esp after an illness. **4** TENNIS a series of strokes between players. **5** a competition to test skill in driving.
◆ **rally round** (**sb**) to come together to offer support (to someone) at a time of crisis, etc.

RAM ABBREV, COMP random access memory, a temporary memory which allows programs to be loaded and run, and data to be changed.

ram N **1** an uncastrated male sheep; a tup. **2** a battering-ram. **3** the falling weight of a pile-driver. **4** the striking head of a steam hammer. **5 a** a piston or plunger operated by hydraulic or other power; **b** a machine with such a piston.
➢ VB (*-mm-*) **1** to force (something) down or into position by pushing hard. **2** to strike or crash (something) violently (against, into, etc something or someone).

Ramadan or **Ramadhan** N **1** the ninth month of the Muslim year, during which Muslims fast between sunrise and sunset. **2** the fast itself.

ramble VB, INTR **1** to go for a long walk or walks, esp in the countryside, for pleasure. **2** (often **ramble on**) to speak or write, often at length, in an aimless or confused way.
➢ N a walk, usu in the countryside, for pleasure.

rambler N **1** someone who rambles. **2** a climbing plant, esp a rose.

rambling N walking for pleasure.
➢ ADJ **1** wandering; nomadic. **2** of a building, etc: extending without any obvious plan or organization: **a large rambling castle**. **3** of speech, etc: confused, disorganized and often lengthy. **4** of a plant: climbing, trailing or spreading freely: **a rambling rose**.

ramekin N **1** a small round straight-sided baking dish. **2** food served in such a dish.

ramification N **1** a single part or section of a complex subject, plot, situation, etc. **2** (usu **ramifications**) a consequence, esp a serious, complicated and unwelcome one.

ramp N **1** a sloping surface between two different levels. **2** a set of movable stairs for entering and leaving an aircraft. **3** a low hump across a road, designed to slow traffic down.
➢ VB **1** to provide with a ramp. **2** INTR to slope from one level to another.

rampage VB INTR to rush about wildly.
➢ N (chiefly **on the rampage**) storming about or behaving wildly and violently in anger, excitement, exuberance, etc.

rampant ADJ **1** uncontrolled; unrestrained. **2** HERALDRY, FOLLOWING ITS NOUN of an animal: in profile and standing erect on the left hind leg with the other legs raised: **lion rampant**.

rampart N **1** a broad mound or wall for defence, usu with a wall or parapet on top. **2** anything which performs such a role.

ramrod N a rod for ramming charge down into, or for cleaning, the barrel of a gun.

ramshackle ADJ of a building, car, etc: badly made or poorly maintained.

ranch N **1** esp N AMER & AUSTRAL an extensive grassland stock-farm where sheep, cattle or horses are raised. **2** any large farm that specializes in the production of a particular crop or animal: **a mink ranch**.
➢ VB to farm on a ranch. ■ **rancher** N.

rancid ADJ of stale butter, oil, etc: tasting or smelling rank or sour. ■ **rancidity** N.

rancour or (N AMER) **rancor** N a long–lasting feeling of hatred. ■ **rancorous** ADJ.

rand N (*rand* or *rands*) the standard monetary unit in South Africa.

R & B ABBREV rhythm and blues.

random ADJ lacking a definite plan or order.

random access N, COMP a method of accessing data stored on a disk or in the memory of a computer without having to read any other data stored on the same device, ie, the data can be read out of sequence.

randy ADJ (*-ier, -iest*) COLLOQ sexually excited; lustful. ■ **randily** ADV. ■ **randiness** N.

range N 1 a an area between limits within which things may move, function, etc; b the limits forming this area. 2 a number of items, products, etc forming a distinct series. 3 MUS the distance between the lowest and highest notes which may be produced by a musical instrument or a singing voice. 4 the distance to which a gun may be fired or an object thrown. 5 an area where shooting may be practised and rockets tested: **firing range**. 6 a group of mountains forming a distinct series or row. 7 N AMER a large area of open land for grazing livestock. 8 the region over which a plant or animal is distributed. 9 MATH the set of values that a function or dependent variable may take. 10 an enclosed kitchen fireplace fitted with a large cooking stove with one or more ovens and a flat top for pans.
➤ VB 1 to put in a row or rows. 2 to put (someone, oneself, etc) into a specified category or group. 3 INTR to vary or change between specified limits. 4 (usu **range over** or **through**) to roam freely.

ranger N 1 someone who looks after a royal or national forest or park. 2 N AMER a member of a group of armed patrol or police force.

rangy ADJ (*-ier, -iest*) of a person: with long thin limbs and a slender body.

rank¹ N 1 a line or row of people or things. 2 a line of soldiers standing side by side. 3 a position of seniority within an organization, society, the armed forces, etc. See table on next page. 4 a distinct class or group, eg, according to ability. 5 high social position or status. 6 (**the ranks**) ordinary soldiers, eg, privates and corporals, as opposed to officers. 7 BRIT a place where taxis wait for passengers.
➤ VB 1 to arrange (people or things) in a row or line. 2 TR & INTR to give or have a particular grade, position or status in relation to others.
◆ **close ranks** of a group of people: to keep their solidarity.
◆ **pull rank** to use rank or status to achieve something.
◆ **the rank and file** the ordinary members of an organization or group.

rank² ADJ 1 of, eg, plants: coarsely overgrown and untidy. 2 offensively strong in smell or taste. 3 bold, open and shocking: **rank disobedience**. 4 complete: **a rank beginner**.

rankle VB, INTR to continue to cause feelings of annoyance or bitterness.

ransack VB 1 to search (a house, etc) thoroughly. 2 to plunder.

ransom N money demanded in return for the release of a kidnapped person, or for the return of property, etc.
➤ VB to pay, demand or accept a ransom.

rant VB, INTR to talk in a loud, angry way.
➤ N 1 loud, pompous, empty speech. 2 an angry tirade. ■ **ranting** N, ADJ.

rap¹ N 1 a a quick short tap or blow; b the sound made by this. 2 SLANG blame or punishment: **take the rap**. 3 a fast rhythmic monologue recited over a musical backing with a pronounced beat. 4 rap music.
➤ VB (*-pp-*) 1 to strike sharply. 2 INTR to make a sharp tapping sound. 3 to criticize sharply. ■ **rapper** N.

rap² N the least bit: **not care a rap**.

rapacious ADJ 1 greedy and grasping, esp for money. 2 of an animal or bird: living by catching prey. ■ **rapaciously** ADV. ■ **rapacity** N.

rape¹ N 1 the crime of forcing a person, esp a woman, to have sexual intercourse against their will. 2 violation, despoiling or abuse.
➤ VB to commit rape on. ■ **rapist** N.

rape² N oilseed rape.

rapid ADJ moving, acting or happening quickly. ➤ N (usu **rapids**) a part of a river where the water flows quickly, usu over rocks.

rapid-fire ADJ fired, asked, etc in quick succession.

rapier N a long thin sword for thrusting. ➤ ADJ sharp: **rapier wit**.

rap music N a style of music that has a strong background beat and rhythmic monologues.

rapport N a feeling of sympathy and understanding; a close emotional bond.

rapprochement N the establishment or renewal of a close, friendly relationship.

rapscallion N, OLD USE a rascal or scamp.

rapt ADJ 1 enraptured; entranced. 2 completely absorbed. ■ **raptly** ADV.

raptor N a bird of prey. ■ **raptorial** ADJ.

rapture N 1 great delight; ecstasy. 2 (**raptures**) great enthusiasm or pleasure. ■ **rapturous** ADJ.

rare¹ ADJ 1 not done, found or occurring very often; unusual. 2 excellent; unusually good: **a rare old treat**. 3 of a gas, etc: lacking the usual density. ■ **rarely** ADV. ■ **rareness** N.

rare² ADJ of meat, esp a steak: lightly cooked, and often still bloody.

rarebit see **Welsh rabbit**

rarefied ADJ 1 of the air: thin; with a very low oxygen content. 2 refined; select; exclusive.

raring ADJ, COLLOQ (**raring to go**) keen and enthusiastic; very willing and ready.

rarity N (-**ies**) 1 uncommonness. 2 something valued because it is rare.

rascal N 1 a rogue. 2 a cheeky or mischievous child. ■ **rascally** ADJ.

rase VB see **raze**

rash¹ ADJ 1 of an action, etc: **a** over-hasty; reckless; **b** done without considering the consequences. 2 of a person: lacking in caution; impetuous. ■ **rashness** N.

rash² N 1 an outbreak of red spots or patches on the skin. 2 a large number of instances (of something happening) at the same time or in the same place: **a rash of burglaries**.

rasher N a thin slice of bacon or ham.

rasp N 1 **a** a coarse, rough file; **b** any tool with a similar surface. 2 a harsh, rough, grating sound or feeling. ➤ VB 1 to scrape roughly, esp with a rasp. 2 to grate upon or irritate (eg, someone's nerves). 3 to speak or utter in a harsh, grating voice. ■ **rasping** ADJ.

raspberry N (-**ies**) 1 a cone-shaped berry, usu reddish in colour. 2 a deciduous shrub with thorny canes that is cultivated for these berries. 3 a sound expressing disapproval or contempt, made by blowing through the lips.

rat N 1 a rodent, similar to a mouse but larger. 2 any of various unrelated but similar rodents, eg, the kangaroo rat. 3 COLLOQ a despicable person. ➤ VB (-**tt**-) INTR 1 to hunt or chase rats. 2 (usu **rat on**) COLLOQ to betray or inform on (someone).

ratafia N 1 a liqueur flavoured with fruit kernels and almonds. 2 an almond-flavoured biscuit or small cake.

ratan see **rattan**

rat-a-tat-tat N a sound of knocking.

ratatouille N a vegetable dish made with tomatoes, peppers, courgettes, aubergines, onions and garlic simmered in olive oil.

ratchet N 1 a bar which fits into the notches of a toothed wheel causing the wheel to turn in one direction only. 2 (also **ratchet-wheel**) a wheel with a toothed rim. 3 the mechanism of such a bar and toothed wheel together.

rate¹ N 1 the number of times something happens, etc within a given period of time; the amount of something considered in relation to, or measured according to, another amount: **a high suicide rate**. 2 a price or charge, often measured per unit: **the rate of pay for the job**. 3 a price or charge fixed according to a standard scale: **rate of exchange**. 4 class or rank: **second-rate**. 5 the

speed of movement or change.
➤ VB **1** to give a value to. **2** to be worthy of: **an answer that doesn't rate full marks. 3** INTR (usu **rate as**) to be placed in a certain class or rank.
◆ **at any rate** in any case; anyway.

rate² VB to scold or rebuke severely.

rateable or **ratable** ADJ **1** HIST of property: liable to payment of rates. **2** able to be rated.

rates PL N in the UK: a tax paid by businesses, based on the value of property and land.

rather ADV **1 a** more readily; more willingly; **b** in preference: **I'd rather go to the cinema than watch TV. 2** more truly or correctly: **my parents, or rather my mother and stepfather. 3** to a limited degree; slightly: **It's rather good. 4** on the contrary: **She said she'd help me; rather, she just sat around watching TV.**

ratify VB (**-ies, -ied**) to give formal consent to (eg, a treaty, agreement, etc), esp by signature. ■ **ratification** N.

rating N **1** a classification according to order, rank or value. **2** BRIT an ordinary seaman. **3** an estimated value of a person's position, esp as regards credit. **4** a measure of a TV or radio programme's popularity based on its estimated audience.

ratio N the number or degree of one class of things in relation to another, or between one thing and another, expressed as a proportion.

ration N **1** a fixed allowance of food, clothing, petrol, etc, during a time of war or shortage.
2 (**rations**) a daily allowance of food.
➤ VB **1** (often **ration out**) to distribute or share out (esp something that is in short supply). **2** to restrict (the supply of provisions, etc).

rational ADJ **1** related to or based on reason or logic. **2** able to think, form opinions, make judgements, etc. **3** sensible; reasonable.
4 sane. **5** MATH of a quantity, ratio, root: able to be expressed as a ratio of whole numbers.
■ **rationality** N. ■ **rationally** ADV.

rationale N the underlying principle or reason on which something is based.

rationalism N the theory that an individual's

actions and beliefs should be based on reason rather than on intuition or the teachings of others. ■ **rationalist** N. ■ **rationalistic** ADJ.

rationalize or **-ise** VB **1** to attribute (something) to sensible, well-thought-out reasons or motives, esp after the event. **2** to make (an industry or organization) more efficient and profitable by reorganization to lower costs, etc. ■ **rationalization** N.

rat race N, COLLOQ the fierce, unending competition for success in business, society, etc.

rattan or **ratan** N **1** a climbing palm with very long thin tough stems. **2** a cane made from the stem of this palm.

rattle VB **1** INTR to make a series of short sharp hard sounds in quick succession. **2** to cause (eg, crockery) to make such a noise. **3** INTR (usu **rattle on**) to chatter thoughtlessly or idly.
4 COLLOQ to make anxious, nervous or upset.
➤ N **1** a series of short sharp sounds. **2** a baby's toy made of a container filled with small pellets which rattle when it is shaken.
◆ **rattle sth off** or **rattle through sth** to say, recite or write it rapidly.

rattlesnake N a poisonous American snake.

rattling ADJ, ADV, COLLOQ, OLD USE **1** brisk or briskly. **2** as a general intensifying word: good or well; very: **told us a rattling good yarn.**

ratty ADJ (**-ier, -iest**) **1** like a rat. **2** COLLOQ irritable.

raucous ADJ of a sound: hoarse; harsh.

raunchy ADJ (**-ier, -iest**) COLLOQ coarsely or openly sexual; lewd. ■ **raunchiness** N.

ravage VB, TR & INTR to destroy or damage.
➤ N (usu **ravages**) damage or destruction.

rave VB **1** INTR to talk wildly as if mad or delirious.
2 INTR (usu **rave about** or **over**) to talk enthusiastically about something.
➤ N, COLLOQ **1** extravagant praise.
2 a gathering in a large warehouse or open-air venue for dancing to dance, etc music.
➤ ADJ, COLLOQ extremely enthusiastic.

ravel VB (**-ll-**; US **-l-**) **1** TR & INTR to tangle or become tangled up. **2** INTR to fray.

raven N a large bird of the crow family.

ravenous ADJ 1 extremely hungry or greedy. 2 of hunger, a desire, etc: intensely strong. 3 of an animal, etc: living on prey; predatory.

raver N, COLLOQ 1 someone who leads a wild social life. 2 someone who attends a rave.

ravine N a deep narrow steep-sided gorge.

raving ADJ, ADV 1 frenzied; delirious. 2 COLLOQ great; extreme: a raving beauty.
➤ N (usu **ravings**) frenzied or delirious talk.

ravioli SING OR PL N small square pasta cases with a savoury filling of meat, cheese, etc.

ravish VB 1 to overwhelm with joy, delight, etc. 2 to rape.

ravishing ADJ delightful; lovely.

raw ADJ 1 of meat, vegetables, etc: not cooked. 2 not processed, purified or refined: raw silk. 3 of alcoholic spirit: undiluted. 4 of statistics, data, etc: not analysed. 5 of a person: not trained or experienced. 6 of a wound, etc: with a sore, inflamed surface. 7 of the weather: cold and damp. 8 sensitive: touched a raw nerve.
◆ **get a raw deal** get unfair treatment.
◆ **in the raw** in a natural or crude state.

rawhide N untanned leather.

ray[1] N 1 a narrow beam of light or radioactive particles. 2 a set of lines fanning out from a central point. 3 a small amount (of hope, understanding, etc).

ray[2] N a fish with a flattened body and extended pectoral fins.

ray[3] or **re** N, MUS in sol-fa notation: the second note of the major scale.

rayon N an artificial fibre or fabrics used to make clothing, conveyer belts, hoses, etc.

raze or **rase** VB to destroy (buildings, a town, etc) completely.

razor N a sharp-edged shaving instrument.
➤ VB 1 to use a razor on. 2 to shave or cut.

razorbill N a seabird with a sharp-edged bill.

razor edge N a very fine sharp edge.

RC ABBREV 1 Red Cross. 2 Roman Catholic.

RE ABBREV religious education.

re[1] PREP with regard to; concerning: re your letter of 18th.

re[2] see **ray**[3]

're VB contraction of **are**[1]: We're going to Paris.

reach VB 1 to arrive at or get as far as (a place, position, etc). 2 TR & INTR to be able to touch or get hold of. 3 TR & INTR to project or extend to a point. 4 INTR (usu **reach across**, **out**, **up**, etc) to stretch out one's arm to try to touch or get hold of (something). 5 to make contact with, esp by telephone: I couldn't reach her.
➤ N 1 the distance one can stretch one's arm, hand, etc: out of reach. 2 a distance that can be travelled easily: within reach of London. 3 an act of reaching out. 4 range of influence, power, understanding or abilities. 5 (usu **reaches**) a section with clear limits.

react VB 1 INTR (chiefly **react to**) to act in response to. 2 INTR (usu **react against**) a to respond to adversely; b to act in a contrary or opposing way. 3 INTR, PHYS to exert an equal force in the opposite direction. 4 TR & INTR, CHEM to undergo or cause to undergo chemical change produced by a reagent.

reaction N 1 a response to stimulus. 2 an action or change in the opposite direction. 3 a change of opinions, feelings, etc. 4 a response showing how someone feels or thinks. 5 opposition to change, esp political reform, etc. 6 a physical or psychological effect caused by a drug, allergy, etc. 7 CHEM a a chemical process in which the electrons surrounding the nuclei in the atoms of one or more elements or compounds react to form one or more new compounds; b chemical change. 8 PHYS the force offered by a body that is equal in magnitude but opposite in direction to the force applied to it.

reactionary ADJ of a person or policies: characterized by opposition to change.
➤ N (**-ies**) a reactionary person.

reactive ADJ showing a reaction; liable to react; sensitive to stimuli. ■ **reactivity** N.

read VB (*read*) **1** to look at and understand (printed or written words). **2** to speak (words which are printed or written). **3** to learn or gain knowledge of by reading. **4** INTR to pass one's leisure time reading, esp for pleasure. **5** to look at or be able to see (something) and get information. **6** to interpret or understand the meaning of: **read a map**. **7** to interpret or understand (signs, marks, etc) without using one's eyes: **read Braille**. **8** INTR to have a certain wording: **The letter reads as follows**. **9** TR & INTR to think that (a statement, etc) has a particular meaning: **read it as criticism**. **10** INTR of writing: to convey meaning in a specified way: **an essay that reads well**. **11** of a dial, instrument, etc: to show a particular measurement: **The barometer reads 'fair'**. **12** to replace (a word, phrase, etc) by another: **for 'three' read 'four'**. **13** to study (a subject) at university. ➤ N **1** a period or act of reading. **2** a book, magazine, etc considered in terms of how readable it is: **a good read**. ■ **reader** N. ◆ **read between the lines** to perceive a meaning that is not stated. ◆ **read up on sth** to learn a subject by reading books about it. ◆ **take sth as read** to accept or assume it.

readership N the total number of people who read a newspaper, etc.

reading N **1** the action of someone who reads. **2** the ability to read: **his reading is poor**. **3** any book, printed material, etc that can be read. **4** an event at which a play, poetry, etc is read to an audience, often by the author. **5** BRIT POL any one of the three stages in the passage of a bill through Parliament. **6** an understanding or interpretation of something written or said, etc.

readjust VB to alter; to return to a previous condition. ■ **readjustment** N.

read-out N, COMP a record or display of data from the main memory of a computer into an external storage device, eg, a disk or tape.

ready ADJ (*-ier, -iest*) **1** prepared and available for use or action. **2** willing; eager: **always ready to help**. **3** prompt; quick, usu too quick: **He's always ready to find fault**. **4** likely or about to: **a plant just ready to flower**.

➤ N (*readies*) COLLOQ short form of **ready money**.
➤ ADV prepared beforehand: **ready cooked**.
➤ VB (*-ies, -ied*) to make ready; to prepare.
■ **readily** ADJ. ■ **readiness** N.
◆ **at the ready 1** of a gun: aimed and ready to be fired. **2** ready for immediate action.

ready-made ADJ **1** (also **ready-to-wear**) of clothes: made to a standard size, not made-to-measure. **2** convenient: **a ready-made excuse**.

ready money N cash for immediate use.

reafforest VB to replant trees in a cleared area of land that was formerly forested.
■ **reafforestation** N.

reagent N, CHEM a chemical compound that participates in a chemical reaction.

real ADJ **1** actually or physically existing; not imaginary. **2** actual; true: **the real reason**. **3** not imitation; genuine; authentic: **real leather**. **4 a** great, important or serious; **b** deserving to be so called: **a real problem**. **5** LAW consisting of or relating to immoveable property, such as land and houses. **6** of income, etc: measured in terms of its buying power rather than its nominal value: **in real terms**.
◆ **for real** SLANG in reality; seriously.

realign VB **1** to put back into alignment. **2** to regroup politically. ■ **realignment** N.

realism N **1** the tendency to consider, accept or deal with things as they really are. **2** a style in art, literature, etc that represents things in a lifelike way. ■ **realist** N.

realistic ADJ **1** showing awareness or acceptance of things as they really are. **2** representing things as they are; lifelike.

reality N (*-ies*) **1** the state or fact of being real. **2** the real nature of something; the truth. **3** something that is not imaginary.
◆ **in reality** as a fact; actually.

realize or **-ise** VB **1** to become aware of; to know or understand. **2** to accomplish or bring into being. **3** to make real or appear real. **4** to cause to seem real. **5** to convert (property or goods) into money. **6** to make (a sum of money).

■ **realizable** ADJ. ■ **realization** N.

really ADV **1** actually; in fact. **2** very: a really lovely day.

realm N **1** a kingdom. **2** a domain, province or region. **3** a field of interest, study or activity.

real number N, MATH any rational or irrational number.

realtor N, N AMER an estate agent.

ream N **1** twenty quires of paper. **2** (**reams**) COLLOQ a large quantity: wrote reams.

reap VB **1** to cut or gather (grain, etc); to harvest. **2** to clear (a field) by cutting a crop. **3** to receive (esp an advantage or benefit) as a consequence of one's actions. ■ **reaper** N.

rear[1] N **1** the back part; the area at the back. **2** a position behind or to the back. **3** COLLOQ the buttocks.
➤ ADJ situated or positioned at the back.
◆ **bring up the rear** to come last.

rear[2] VB **1** to bring up (offspring). **2 a** to breed (animals); **b** to grow (crops). **3** to build or erect something. **4** INTR (also **rear up**) of an animal, esp a horse: to rise up on the hind legs. **5** INTR to reach a great height, esp in relation to surroundings. **6** to move or hold upwards.

rear admiral N a naval officer.

rearguard N a group of soldiers who protect the rear of an army.

rearm VB to arm again, esp with new or improved weapons. ■ **rearmament** N.

rearmost ADJ last of all; nearest the back.

rearward ADJ positioned in or at the rear.
➤ ADV (also **rearwards**) towards the back.

reason N **1** a justification or motive for an action, belief, etc. **2** an underlying explanation or cause. **3** the power to think, form opinions and judgements, reach logical conclusions, etc. **4** sanity; sound mind: lose your reason.
➤ VB, INTR to form opinions and judgements, reach logical conclusions, deduce, etc.
◆ **by reason of sth** because of it.
◆ **it stands to reason** it is obvious or logical.
◆ **reason with sb** to try to persuade them by means of reasonable argument.
◆ **within reason** in moderation.

reasonable ADJ **1** sensible; rational; showing reason or good judgement. **2** willing to listen to reason or argument. **3** in accordance with reason. **4** fair or just; moderate; not extreme or excessive: a reasonable price. **5** satisfactory or equal to what one might expect.

reasoned ADJ well thought out or argued.

reasoning N **1** the forming of judgements or opinions using reason or careful argument. **2** the act or process of deducing logically from evidence. **3** the opinions or judgements formed, or deductions made, in this way.

reassure VB **1** to dispel or alleviate the anxiety or worry of. **2** to confirm (someone) in opinion, etc: reassured him he was correct.
■ **reassurance** N. ■ **reassuring** ADJ.

rebate N **1** a refund of part of a sum of money paid. **2** a discount.
➤ VB to pay as a rebate.

rebel VB INTR (-**ll**-) (often **rebel against**) **1** to resist or fight against authority or oppressive conditions. **2** to refuse to conform to conventional rules of behaviour, dress, etc.
➤ N someone who rebels. ■ **rebellion** N.

rebellious ADJ **1** rebelling or having a tendency to rebel. **2** characteristic of a rebel.

reboot VB, COMP to restart (a computer) esp when the computer has crashed or hung.

rebound VB, INTR **1** to bounce or spring back after an impact. **2** to recover after a setback. **3** (also **rebound on** or **upon**) of an action: to have a bad effect (on the person performing the action).
➤ N an instance of rebounding; a recoil.

rebuff N **1** a slight or snub. **2** a refusal.
➤ VB to give a rebuff to.

rebuke VB to reprimand.
➤ N a stern reprimand or reproach.

rebus N a puzzle where pictures, etc represent words or syllables in order to form a phrase.

rebut VB (-**tt**-) **1** to disprove or refute (a charge or claim), esp by offering opposing evidence. **2** to drive back. ■ **rebuttal** N.

recalcitrant ADJ not willing to accept authority or discipline. ■ **recalcitrance** N.

recall VB **1** to call back. **2** to order to return. **3** to remember. **4** to cancel or revoke.
➤ N **1** an act of recalling. **2** the ability to remember accurately.

recant VB **1** INTR to revoke a former declaration, belief, etc. **2** TR & INTR to withdraw or retract (a statement, belief, etc). ■ **recantation** N.

recap VB, COLLOQ (-*pp*-) to recapitulate.

recapitulate VB **1** to go over the chief points of (an argument, statement, etc) again. **2** to summarize. ■ **recapitulation** N.

recapture VB **1** to capture again. **2** to convey, recreate or re-experience (an image, sensation, etc from the past).

recce COLLOQ, N reconnaissance.
➤ VB (**recced** or **recceed, recceing**) to reconnoitre.

recede VB, INTR **1** to go or move back or backwards. **2** to become more distant. **3** to bend or slope backwards. **4** of hair: to stop growing above the forehead and at the temples. ■ **receding** ADJ.

receipt N **1** a printed or written note acknowledging that money, goods, etc have been received. **2** the act of receiving or being received. **3** (usu **receipts**) money received during a given period of time.

receive VB **1** to get, be given or accept (something offered, sent, etc). **2** to experience, undergo or suffer: **receive injuries**. **3** to give attention to or consider: **receive a petition**. **4** to learn of or be informed of: **receive word of their arrival**. **5** to react to in a specified way: **The film was badly received**. **6** to admit or accept (an idea, principle, etc) as true. **7** to be awarded (an honour, etc). **8** to support or bear the weight of something. **9** TR & INTR to be at home to (guests or visitors). **10** to welcome or greet (guests), esp formally. **11** TR & INTR, chiefly BRIT to buy or deal in (goods one knows are stolen). **12** to change (radio or television

signals) into sounds or pictures.

received ADJ generally accepted: **received wisdom**.

receiver N **1** someone or something that receives. **2** (in full **official receiver**) a person appointed by a court to manage property under litigation, or take control of the business of someone who has gone bankrupt or who is certified insane. **3** the part of a telephone held to the ear. **4** the equipment in a telephone, radio or television that changes signals into sounds and pictures, or both. **5** chiefly BRIT a person who receives stolen goods.

receivership N (usu **in receivership**) the status of a business that is under the control of an official receiver.

recent ADJ **1** happening, done, having appeared, etc not long ago. **2** new. **3** modern.

receptacle N anything that receives or holds.

reception N **1** the act of receiving or fact of being received. **2** a response, reaction or welcome; the manner in which a person, information, an idea, etc is received: **a hostile reception**. **3** a formal party or social function to welcome guests, esp after a wedding. **4** the quality of radio or television signals received. **5** an area where visitors are welcomed.

receptionist N someone employed in a hotel, office, surgery, etc to deal with clients, visitors and guests, arrange appointments, etc.

receptive ADJ willing to accept new ideas, suggestions, etc. ■ **receptively** ADV. ■ **receptiveness** or **receptivity** N.

receptor N, BIOL a cell or body part adapted to respond to external stimuli.

recess N **1** a space, such as a niche or alcove, set in a wall. **2** (often **recesses**) a hidden, inner or secret place: **the dark recesses of her mind**. **3** a temporary break from work, esp of a law-court, Parliament, etc: **summer recess**.

recession N **1** the act of receding or state of being set back. **2** a temporary decline in economic activity, trade and prosperity.

recessive ADJ **1** tending to recede. **2** BIOL

denoting a characteristic that is only present when it comes from a gene that is paired with a gene that gives the same characteristic.

recherché ADJ **1** rare, exotic or particularly exquisite. **2** obscure and affected.

recidivism N the habit of relapsing into crime. ■ **recidivist** N, ADJ.

recipe N directions for making something, esp for preparing and cooking food, usu consisting of a list of ingredients and instructions.

recipient N a person or thing that receives. ➤ ADJ receiving; receptive.

reciprocal ADJ **a** giving and receiving, or given and received; mutual; **b** complementary. ➤ N **1** something that is reciprocal. **2** MATH the value obtained when 1 is divided by the number concerned, eg, the reciprocal of 5 is one fifth.

reciprocate VB **1 a** to give and receive mutually; to interchange; **b** to return (affection, love, etc). **2** INTR of part of a machine: to move backwards and forwards. ■ **reciprocation** N. ■ **reciprocity** N.

recital N **1** a public performance of music, usu by a soloist or a small group. **2** a detailed statement or list of something. **3** an act of reciting or repeating something learned or prepared. ■ **recitalist** N.

recitation N **1** an act or instance of reciting something. **2** something recited.

recitative N, MUS a style of singing resembling speech.

recite VB **1** to repeat aloud (a poem, etc) from memory. **2** to make a detailed statement; to list.

reckless ADJ without consideration of the consequences, danger, etc; rash.

reckon VB **1** (also **reckon up**) to calculate, compute or estimate. **2** to regard, consider or class as: **reckon him among my friends**. **3** (usu **reckon that**) COLLOQ to think or suppose: I reckon it's going to rain. ◆ **to be reckoned with** of considerable importance or power that is not to be ignored.

reckoning N **1** calculation; counting. **2** an account or bill.

reclaim VB **1** to seek to regain possession of. **2** to make (land) available for agricultural or commercial use. **3** to recover useful materials from industrial or domestic waste. ■ **reclamation** N.

recline VB, INTR to lean or lie back.

recluse N someone who lives alone and has little contact with society. ■ **reclusive** ADJ.

recognition N the act or state of recognizing or being recognized.

recognizance or **recognisance** N a legally binding promise made to a magistrate or court to do or not do something specified.

recognize or **-ise** VB **1** to identify (a person or thing known or experienced before). **2** to admit or be aware of. **3** to show approval of and gratitude for. **4** to acknowledge the status or legality of (esp a government or state). ■ **recognizable** ADJ.

recoil VB, INTR **1** to spring back or rebound. **2** of a gun: to spring powerfully backwards under the force of being fired. ➤ N an act of recoiling.

recollect VB to recall to memory; to remember, esp with an effort. ■ **recollection** N.

recommend VB **1** to suggest as being suitable, acceptable, etc. **2** to make acceptable, desirable or pleasing. **3** TR & INTR to advise as a particular course of action. ■ **recommendation** N.

recompense VB **1** to repay or reward for service, work done, etc. **2** to compensate for loss, injury or hardship suffered. ➤ N **1** repayment or reward. **2** compensation.

reconcile VB **1** to put on friendly terms again, esp after a quarrel. **2** to bring (two or more different aims, points of view, etc) into agreement. **3** to agree to accept (an unwelcome fact or situation). ■ **reconciliation** N.

recondite ADJ **1** of a subject or knowledge: difficult to understand; little known. **2** dealing with profound or abstruse knowledge.

recondition VB to repair or restore (an engine, etc) to original or good working condition.

reconnaissance N, MIL a survey, eg, of land or the position of troops, to obtain information about the enemy before advancing.

reconnoitre or (US) **reconnoiter** VB to examine or survey (land, enemy troops, etc).

reconsider VB to consider (a decision, opinion, etc) again, esp for a possible change or reversal. ■ **reconsideration** N.

reconstitute VB 1 to restore to the original form or constitution. 2 to form or make up again. ■ **reconstitution** N.

reconstruct VB 1 to construct or form again; to rebuild. 2 to create a description or idea of (a crime, past event, etc) from the evidence available. 3 to re-enact (an incident, esp a crime). ■ **reconstruction** N. ■ **reconstructive** ADJ.

record N 1 a formal written report or statement of facts, events or information. 2 (often **records**) information, facts, etc, collected usu over a fairly long period of time: **dental records**. 3 the state or fact of being recorded: **for the record**. 4 a thin plastic disc used as a recording medium for reproducing music or other sound. 5 esp in sports: a performance which is officially recognized as the best of a particular kind or in a particular class. 6 a description of the history and achievements of a person, institution, etc.
➤ VB 1 to set down in writing or some other permanent form, esp for use in the future. 2 TR & INTR to register (sound, music, speech, etc) so that it can be listened to in the future.
◆ **off the record** of information, statements, etc: not intended to be made public.
◆ **on record** officially recorded.

recorder N 1 a wooden or plastic wind instrument with a tapering mouthpiece and holes which are covered by the player's fingers. 2 someone who records. 3 a device for recording, eg, a video recorder.

recording N 1 the process of registering

sounds or images on a record, tape, video, etc. 2 sound or images which have been recorded.

recount VB to tell (a story, etc) in detail.

recoup VB 1 to recover or get back (something lost, eg, money). 2 to compensate or reimburse someone (eg, for something lost).

recourse N a an act of turning to someone, or resorting to a particular course of action, for help; b a source of help.

recover VB 1 to get or find again. 2 INTR to regain one's good health, spirits or composure. 3 INTR to regain a former condition. 4 to regain control of: **recover his senses**.

recovery N (-ies) an act, instance or process of recovering, or state of having recovered.

recreate or **re-create** VB to create something again; to reproduce. ■ **re-creation** N.

recreation N 1 a pleasant activity. 2 the process of having an enjoyable and often refreshing time. ■ **recreational** ADJ.

recrimination N the act of returning an accusation; a countercharge. ■ **recriminate** VB. ■ **recriminatory** ADJ.

recruit N a newly enlisted member of the armed forces, a society, company, etc.
➤ VB, TR & INTR 1 MIL a to enlist (people) as recruits; b to raise or reinforce (eg, an army) by enlisting recruits. 2 to enrol or obtain new members, employees, etc. ■ **recruitment** N.

rectangle N a four-sided plane figure with opposite sides of equal length and all its angles right angles. ■ **rectangular** ADJ.

rectify VB (-ies, -ied) a to put (a mistake, etc) right or correct; b to adjust.

rectilineal or **rectilinear** ADJ 1 in or forming a straight line or straight lines. 2 bounded by straight lines.

rectitude N 1 correctness of behaviour or judgement. 2 moral integrity.

recto N 1 the right-hand page of an open book. 2 the front of a sheet of printed paper.

rector N **1** in the Church of England: a clergyman in charge of a parish. **2** in the Roman Catholic Church: a priest in charge of a congregation or a religious house, esp a Jesuit seminary. **3** the headmaster of some schools and colleges, esp in Scotland.

rectory N (-**ies**) the house of a rector.

rectum N (-**ta** or -**tums**) the lower part of the alimentary canal, ending at the anus.

recumbent ADJ lying down; reclining.

recuperate VB **1** INTR to recover, esp from illness. **2** to recover (health, something lost, etc). ■ **recuperation** N. ■ **recuperative** ADJ.

recur VB (-**rr**-) INTR to happen again.

recurrent ADJ happening often or regularly. ■ **recurrence** N. ■ **recurrently** ADV.

recycle VB to process or treat (waste material, etc) for re-use. ■ **recyclable** ADJ. ■ **recycling** N.

red ADJ (*redder, reddest*) **1** having the colour of blood, or a colour similar to it. **2** of hair, fur, etc: between a golden brown and a deep reddish-brown colour. **3** of the eyes: bloodshot or with red rims. **4** having a red or flushed face, esp from shame or anger. **5** of wine: made with black grapes whose skins colour the wine red. **6** COLLOQ communist. ➤ N **1** the colour of blood, or a similar shade. **2** red dye or paint. **3** red material or clothes. **4** the red traffic light, a sign that cars should stop. **5** (usu **the red**) the debit side of an account; the state of being in debt, eg, to a bank. **6** COLLOQ (often **Red**) a communist or socialist. ■ **reddish** and (COLLOQ) **reddy** ADJ. ■ **redness** N.
◆ **see red** COLLOQ to become angry.

red alert N a state of readiness to deal with imminent crisis or emergency, eg, war.

red-blooded ADJ, COLLOQ full of vitality; virile.

red card N, FOOTBALL a piece of red card or plastic shown by the referee to a player to indicate that they are being sent off.

red carpet N special treatment given to an important person.

redcurrant N a widely cultivated European shrub, or its small edible red berry.

redden VB **1** to make red or redder. **2** INTR to become red; to blush.

redeem VB **1** to buy back. **2** to recover (eg, something that has been pawned or mortgaged) by payment or service. **3** to fulfil (a promise). **4** to set free or save (someone) by paying a ransom. **5** to free (someone or oneself) from blame or debt. **6** to free from sin. **7** to make up or compensate for (something bad or wrong). **8** to exchange for goods or cash. ■ **redeemable** ADJ. ■ **redeemer** N.

redemption N **1** the act of redeeming or state of being redeemed. **2** anything which redeems. ■ **redemptive** ADJ.

redeploy VB to transfer (soldiers, supplies, etc) to another place or job. ■ **redeployment** N.

red-handed ADJ in the very act of committing a crime or doing something wrong.

redhead N a person, esp a woman, with red hair. ■ **redheaded** ADJ.

red herring N a misleading or diverting subject, idea, clue, etc.

red-hot ADJ **1** of metal, etc: heated until it glows red. **2** feeling or showing passionate or intense emotion or excitement. **3** COLLOQ feeling or showing great enthusiasm. **4** strongly tipped to win: a red-hot favourite. **5** of news, etc: completely up to date.

red-letter day N a memorable day.

red light N a red warning light, esp the red traffic light at which vehicles have to stop.

red meat N dark-coloured meat, eg, beef.

redolent ADJ **1** fragrant. **2** (usu **redolent of** or **with**) **a** smelling strongly; **b** strongly suggestive or reminiscent. ■ **redolence** N.

redouble VB to make or become greater or more intense.

redoubt N a fortification, esp a temporary one defending a pass or hilltop.

redoubtable ADJ inspiring fear or respect;

formidable. ■ **redoubtably** ADV.

red pepper N 1 cayenne pepper. 2 a red capsicum or sweet pepper.

red rag N (usu **red rag to a bull**) something which is likely to provoke someone.

redress VB 1 to set right or compensate for (something wrong). 2 to make even or equal again: **redress the balance**.
➤ N the act of redressing or being redressed.

red tape N, COLLOQ unnecessary rules and regulations which result in delay; bureaucracy.

reduce VB 1 TR & INTR to make or become less, smaller, etc. 2 to change into a worse or less desirable state or form: **reduced her to tears**. 3 MIL to lower the rank, status or grade of: **reduced him to the ranks**. 4 to bring into a state of obedience; to subdue. 5 to make weaker or poorer. 6 to lower (the price of something). 7 INTR to lose weight by dieting. 8 to convert (a substance) into a simpler form. 9 to simplify. 10 TR & INTR, COOKERY to thicken (a sauce) by boiling off the excess liquid. ■ **reducible** ADJ.

reduction N 1 an act, instance or process of reducing; the state of being reduced. 2 the amount by which something is reduced.
■ **reductive** ADJ.

redundant ADJ 1 not needed; superfluous. 2 of an employee: no longer needed and therefore dismissed. ■ **redundancy** N.

redwood N an extremely tall and long-lived sequoia, native to California.

reed N 1 a a grass that grows in the margins of streams, lakes and ponds; b a stalk of one of these plants. 2 a thin piece of cane or metal in certain musical instruments which vibrates and makes a sound when air passes over it.

reedy ADJ (-ier, -iest) 1 full of reeds. 2 having a tone like a reed instrument, esp in being thin and piping. 3 thin and weak. ■ **reediness** N.

reef[1] N a mass of rock, coral, sand, etc that either projects above the surface at low tide, or is permanently covered by shallow water.

reef[2] N, NAUT a part of a sail which may be folded in or let out so as to alter the area of sail exposed to the wind.

reefer N 1 (in full **reefer jacket**) a thick woollen double-breasted jacket. 2 COLLOQ a cigarette containing marijuana.

reef knot N a knot consisting of two loops passing symmetrically through each other.

reek N 1 a strong, unpleasant smell. 2 SCOT & N ENGLISH DIALECT smoke.
➤ VB, INTR 1 to give off a strong, usu unpleasant smell. 2 SCOT & N ENGLISH DIALECT to give off smoke. 3 (often **reek of**) to suggest (something unpleasant).

reel N 1 a round wheel-shaped or cylindrical object on which thread, film, fishing-lines, etc can be wound. 2 the quantity of film, thread, etc wound on one of these. 3 a device for winding and unwinding a fishing-line. 4 a lively Scottish or Irish dance, or the music for it.
➤ VB 1 to wind something on a reel. 2 (usu **reel in** or **up**) to pull in or up using a reel. 3 INTR to stagger or sway; to move unsteadily. 4 INTR to whirl or appear to move. 5 INTR to be shaken physically or mentally. 6 INTR to dance a reel.
◆ **reel sth off** to say, repeat or write it rapidly and often with little effort or unthinkingly.

reeve N, HIST an official on a feudal manor.

ref N, COLLOQ a sports referee.

refectory N (-ies) a dining-hall, esp one in a monastery or university.

refer VB (-rr-) to fail (an examination candidate).
◆ **refer to sth** 1 INTR to mention or make allusion to it. 2 INTR to look to it for information, facts, etc: **referred to his notes**. ■ **referral** N.
◆ **refer sb to sb** or **sth** to direct them to them or it.
◆ **refer sth to sb** 1 to hand it over to them for consideration: **referred the query to the manager**. 2 to hand it back to the person from whom it came because it is unacceptable.

referee N 1 a person to whom reference is made to settle a question, dispute, etc. 2 an umpire or judge, eg, of a game or in a dispute. 3 someone who is willing to testify to a person's character, talents and abilities.

➤ VB (*-reed, -reeing*) TR & INTR to act as a referee in (a game, dispute, etc).

reference N 1 a mention of or an allusion to something. 2 a direction in a book to another passage or another book where information can be found. 3 a book or passage referred to. 4 the act of referring to a book or passage for information. 5 a written report on a person's character, talents, abilities, etc. 6 a the providing of facts and information; b a source of facts or information. 7 relation, correspondence or connection: with reference to your last letter. 8 a standard for measuring or judging: a point of reference.
➤ VB 1 to make a reference to something. 2 to provide (a book, etc) with references to other sources. ■ **referential** ADJ.

referendum N (*-dums* or *-da*) a chance for people to state their opinions on a particular matter by voting for or against it.

refill N a new filling for something which has become empty through use.
➤ VB to fill again. ■ **refillable** ADJ.

refine VB 1 to make pure by removing dirt, waste substances, etc. 2 TR & INTR to become or make more elegant, polished or subtle.

refined ADJ 1 very polite; well-mannered; elegant. 2 with all the dirt, waste substances, etc removed. 3 improved; polished.

refinement N 1 an act or the process of refining. 2 good manners or good taste; polite speech; elegance. 3 an improvement or perfection. 4 a subtle distinction.

refinery N (*-ies*) a plant where raw materials, esp sugar and oil, are purified.

refit VB (*-tt-*) 1 to repair or fit new parts to (esp a ship). 2 INTR of a ship: to undergo repair or the fitting of new parts.
➤ N the process of refitting or being refitted.

reflate VB to bring about reflation of (an economy).

reflation N an increase in economic activity and in the amount of money and credit available after a period of deflation.
■ **reflationary** ADJ.

reflect VB 1 TR & INTR of a surface: to send back (light, heat, sound, etc). 2 TR & INTR of a mirror, etc: to give an image of (someone or something). 3 INTR of a sound, image, etc: to be sent back. 4 to have as a cause or be a consequence of. 5 to show or give an idea of. 6 (also **reflect on** or **upon**) to consider carefully. ■ **reflection** N.
◆ **reflect on** or **upon sb** of an action, etc: to bring about a specified result, attitude, etc: His behaviour reflects well on him.

reflective ADJ 1 of a person: thoughtful; meditative. 2 of a surface: able to reflect images, light, sound, etc.

reflector N 1 a polished surface that reflects light, heat, etc. 2 a telescope that uses a mirror to produce images, or the mirror itself.

reflex N 1 (also **reflex action**) PHYSIOL a response to a sensory, physical or chemical stimulus. 2 the ability to respond rapidly to a stimulus.
➤ ADJ 1 occurring as an automatic response without being thought about. 2 bent or turned backwards. 3 directed back on the source; reflected. 4 MATH denoting an angle that is greater than 180° but less than 360°.

reflexive ADJ, PHYSIOL relating to a reflex.
■ **reflexivity** N.

reflexology N the massaging of points on the soles of the feet, the hands and the head as a form of therapy. ■ **reflexologist** N.

reform VB 1 to improve or remove faults from (a person, behaviour, etc). 2 to improve (a law, institution, etc) by making changes or corrections to it. 3 INTR to give up bad habits; to improve one's behaviour, etc.
➤ N 1 a correction or improvement, esp in some social or political system. 2 improvement in behaviour, morals, etc. ■ **reformative** ADJ.
■ **reformer** N.

re-form VB, TR & INTR to form again or in a different way. ■ **re-formation** N.

reformation N the act or process of reforming or being reformed.

reformatory N (*-ies*) OLD USE a school where young offenders were sent to be reformed.

refract VB of a medium, eg, water, glass: to deflect (a wave of light, sound, etc) when it crosses the boundary between this medium and another at a different angle. ■ **refraction** N. ■ **refractive** ADJ. ■ **refractor** N.

refractory ADJ difficult to control; stubborn.

refrain[1] N 1 a phrase or group of lines repeated at the end of each stanza or verse in a poem or song. 2 the music for this.

refrain[2] VB, INTR (usu **refrain from**) to desist, stop or avoid doing (something).

refrangible ADJ able to be refracted.

refresh VB 1 to make fresh again. 2 to make brighter or livelier again. 3 of drink, food, rest, etc: to give renewed strength, energy, enthusiasm, etc to. 4 to revive (someone, oneself, etc) with drink, food, rest, etc. 5 to make (one's memory) clearer and stronger by reading or listening to the source of information again. 6 COMP to update (esp a screen display) with data. ■ **refresher** N.

refreshing ADJ 1 giving new strength, energy and enthusiasm. 2 cooling. 3 particularly pleasing because of being different, unexpected, new, etc: His attitude was refreshing. ■ **refreshingly** ADV.

refreshment N 1 the act of refreshing or state of being refreshed. 2 anything that refreshes. 3 (**refreshments**) food and drink.

refrigerant N a fluid that vaporizes at low temperatures and is used in the cooling mechanism of refrigerators.

refrigerate VB a to freeze or make cold; b INTR to become cold. ■ **refrigeration** N.

refrigerator N an insulated cabinet or room for keeping food and drink cold and fresh.

refuel VB to supply (an aircraft, car, etc) with more fuel.

refuge N 1 shelter or protection from danger or trouble. 2 any place, person or thing offering help or shelter.

refugee N someone who seeks refuge, esp from religious or political persecution.

refund VB to pay (money, etc) back, esp because something bought or a service delivered, etc was not up to standard, etc. ➤ N 1 the paying back of money, etc. 2 money, etc that is paid back. ■ **refundable** ADJ.

refurbish VB 1 to renovate. 2 to redecorate or brighten something up. ■ **refurbishment** N.

refusal N 1 an act or instance of refusing. 2 (usu **first refusal**) the opportunity to buy, accept or refuse something before it is offered, given, sold, etc to anyone else.

refuse[1] VB 1 TR & INTR to indicate unwillingness. 2 to decline to accept: refuse the offer of help. 3 not to allow (someone or something) (access, permission, etc).

refuse[2] N 1 rubbish; waste. 2 anything that is thrown away.

refute VB 1 to prove that (a person, statement, theory, etc) is wrong. 2 COLLOQ to deny. ■ **refutable** ADJ. ■ **refutation** N.

regain VB 1 to get back again or recover: regained consciousness. 2 to get back to (a place, position, etc).

regal ADJ 1 of or suitable for a king or queen. 2 royal. ■ **regality** N. ■ **regally** ADV.

regale VB 1 (usu **regale with**) to amuse (eg, with stories, etc). 2 to entertain lavishly.

regalia PL N 1 the insignia of royalty, eg, the crown, sceptre and orb. 2 ceremonial clothes, etc, worn as a sign of authority.

regard VB 1 to consider in a specified way: regarded him as a friend. 2 to esteem or respect: regarded him highly. 3 a to pay attention to or take notice of; b to heed. 4 to look attentively or steadily at. 5 to have a connection with or to relate to. ➤ N 1 a esteem; b respect and affection. 2 thought or attention. 3 care or consideration. 4 a gaze or look. 5 connection or relation. 6 (**regards**) a greetings; b good wishes. ◆ **as regards** concerning. ◆ **with regard to 1** about or concerning. 2 as concerns.

regarding PREP about; concerning.

regardless ADV **1** not thinking or caring about (problems, dangers, etc). **2** nevertheless; in spite of everything.
➤ ADJ (usu **regardless of**) taking no notice of.

regatta N a yacht or boat race-meeting.

regency N (*-ies*) **1** government by a regent; any period when a regent rules or ruled. **2** the office of a regent.

regenerate VB **1** to produce again or anew. **2** TR & INTR to develop or give new life or energy to. **3** TR & INTR, PHYSIOL to regrow or cause (new tissue) to regrow.
➤ ADJ regenerated, esp morally, spiritually or physically. ■ **regeneration** N.
■ **regenerative** ADJ.

regent N someone who governs a country during a monarch's childhood, illness, etc.

reggae N popular music of W Indian origin with a strongly-accented upbeat.

regicide N **1** the killing of a king. **2** someone who kills a king. ■ **regicidal** ADJ.

regime or **régime** N **1** a particular administration. **2** a regimen, esp in medicine.

regimen N, MED a course of treatment, esp of diet and exercise.

regiment N, MIL a body of soldiers consisting of several companies, etc and commanded by a colonel.
➤ VB **1** to organize, group or control (people, etc) strictly. **2** MIL to form or group (soldiers, an army, etc) into a regiment or regiments.
■ **regimental** ADJ. ■ **regimentation** N.

region N an area of the world or of a country.
■ **regional** ADJ. ■ **regionalization** or **-isation** N. ■ **regionally** ADV.
◆ **in the region of** approximately; nearly.

register N **1 a** a written list or record of names, events, etc; **b** a book containing such a list. **2** a machine or device which records and lists information, eg a cash register. **3** MUS the range of tones produced by the human voice or a musical instrument. **4** MUS **a** an organ stop or stop-knob; **b** the set of pipes controlled by an organ stop. **5** a style of speech or language.

6 COMP a device storing small amounts of data.
➤ VB **1** to enter (an event, name, etc) in an official register. **2** INTR to enter one's name and address in a hotel register on arrival. **3** TR & INTR to enrol formally: **Please register for the conference by Friday. 4** to send (a letter, parcel, etc) by registered post. **5** of a device: to record and usu show (speed, information, etc) automatically. **6** of a person's face, expression, etc: to show (a particular feeling). **7** INTR, COLLOQ to make an impression on someone, eg, by being remembered: **The name didn't register. ■ registration** N.

registrar N **1** someone who keeps an official register, esp of births, deaths and marriages. **2** a senior administrator in a university, responsible for student records, enrolment, etc. **3** BRIT a middle-ranking hospital doctor who is training to become a specialist.
■ **registrarship** N.

registry N (*-ies*) **1** an office or place where registers are kept. **2** registration.

regress VB **1** INTR **a** to go back; **b** to return. **2** INTR to revert to a former less desirable state.
■ **regression** N. ■ **regressive** ADJ.

regret VB (*-tt-*) **1 a** to feel sorry, repentant, distressed, disappointed, etc about (something one has done or that has happened); **b** to wish that things had been otherwise. **2** to remember (someone or something) with a sense of loss.
➤ N **1 a** a feeling of sorrow, repentance, distress, disappointment, etc; **b** a wish that things had been otherwise. **2** a sense of loss.

regretful ADJ feeling or displaying regret.
■ **regretfully** ADV.

regrettable ADJ unwelcome; unfortunate.

regular ADJ **1** usual; normal; customary. **2** arranged, occurring, acting, etc in a fixed pattern of predictable or equal intervals of space or time: **at regular intervals. 3** agreeing with some rule, custom, established practice, etc, and commonly accepted as correct. **4** symmetrical or even. **5** of a geometric figure: having all the faces, sides, angles, etc the same. **6** of bowel movements or menstrual periods: occurring with normal frequency. **7** orig US

medium-sized: a regular portion of fries. **8** COLLOQ complete; absolute: a regular little monster. **9** MIL of troops, the army, etc: belonging to or forming a permanent professional body. **10 a** officially qualified or recognized; **b** professional.
➤ N **1** MIL a soldier in a professional permanent army. **2** COLLOQ a frequent customer, esp of a pub, bar, shop, etc. ■ **regularity** N.
■ **regularize** or **-ise** VB. ■ **regularly** ADV.

regulate VB **1** to control, direct or adjust. **2** INTR to make or lay down a rule. ■ **regulation** N.
■ **regulatory** ADJ. ■ **regulator** N.

regurgitate VB **1** to bring back (food) into the mouth after it has been swallowed. **2** to repeat exactly (something already said).
■ **regurgitation** N.

rehabilitate VB **1** to help (someone who has been ill, etc or a former prisoner) adapt to normal life again. **2** to lift (the reputation of someone or something) to a better status or rank. ■ **rehabilitation** N.

rehash VB, COLLOQ to rework or reuse (material which has been used before).

rehearse VB **1** TR & INTR to practise (a play, piece of music, etc) before performing it in front of an audience. **2** to train (a person) for performing in front of an audience. **3** to give a list of: rehearsed his grievances. **4** to repeat or say over again. ■ **rehearsal** N.

reign N **1** the period of time when a king or queen rules. **2** the period during which someone or something rules, is in control or dominates: reign of terror.
➤ VB, INTR **1** to be a ruling king or queen. **2** to prevail, exist or dominate: silence reigns.

reimburse VB **1** to repay (money spent). **2** to pay (a person) money to compensate for or cover (expenses, losses, etc).
■ **reimbursement** N.

rein N **1** (often **reins**) the strap, or either of the two halves of the strap, attached to a bridle and used to guide and control a horse. **2** (usu **reins**) a device with straps for guiding a small child. **3** any means of controlling or restraining.
➤ VB **1** to provide with reins. **2** to guide or control (esp a horse) with reins. **3** (usu **rein in**) to stop or restrain with, or as if with, reins. **4** (usu **rein in**) INTR to stop or slow up.

reincarnation N in some beliefs: the transference of someone's soul after death to another body. ■ **reincarnate** VB, ADJ.

reindeer N (*reindeer* or *reindeers*) a large deer, antlered in both sexes, found in arctic and subarctic regions of Europe and Asia.

reinforce VB **1** to strengthen or give additional support to something. **2** to stress or emphasize: reinforced his argument. **3** to make (an army, work force, etc) stronger by providing additional soldiers, weapons, workers, etc.
■ **reinforcement** N.

reinstate VB **1** to place in a previous position. **2** to restore (someone) to a position, status or rank formerly held. ■ **reinstatement** N.

reiterate VB to do or say again or repeatedly.

reject VB **1** to refuse to accept, agree to, admit, believe, etc. **2** to throw away or discard. **3** MED of the body: to fail to accept (new tissue or an organ from another body).
➤ N **1** someone or something that is rejected. **2** an imperfect article offered for sale at a discount. ■ **rejection** N.

rejig VB (*-gg-*) **1** to re-equip or refit (a factory, etc). **2** to rearrange or reorganize (something).

rejoice VB **1** INTR to feel, show or express great happiness or joy. **2** (usu **rejoice that**) to be glad. ■ **rejoicing** N.

rejoin VB **1 a** to say in reply, esp abruptly or wittily; **b** to retort. **2** INTR, LAW to reply to a charge or pleading. ■ **rejoinder** N.

rejuvenate VB to make young again.
■ **rejuvenation** N.

relapse VB, INTR **1** to sink or fall back into a former state or condition. **2** to become ill again after apparent or partial recovery.
➤ N an act or instance of relapsing.

relate VB **1** to tell or narrate (a story, anecdote, etc). **2** to show or form a connection between facts, events, etc.

◆ **relate to sb** COLLOQ **1** to get on well with them. **2** to react sympathetically to them.
◆ **relate to sth 1** to be about it or concerned with it. **2** to be show empathy towards it.

related ADJ **1** belonging to the same family, by birth or marriage. **2** connected.

relation N **1** a connection or relationship between one person or thing and another. **2** someone who belongs to the same family through birth or marriage. **3** kinship. **4** (**relations**) social, political or personal contact between people, countries, etc. **5** (**relations**) EUPHEMISTIC sexual intercourse.
◆ **in** or **with relation to sth** with respect to it.

relationship N **1** the state of being related. **2** the state of being related by birth or marriage. **3** the friendship, communications, etc which exist between people, countries, etc. **4** an emotional or sexual affair.

relative N a person who is related to someone else by birth or marriage.
➤ ADJ **1** compared with something else; comparative: **the relative speeds of a car and train**. **2** existing only in relation to something else: **'hot' and 'cold ' are relative terms**. **3** (chiefly **relative to**) in proportion to: **salary relative to experience**. **4** relevant: **information relative to the problem**. ■ **relatively** ADV.

relativity N **1** the condition of being relative to and therefore affected by something else. **2** two theories of motion, **special theory of relativity** and **general theory of relativity**, which recognize the dependence of space, time and other physical measurements on the position and motion of the observer who is making the measurements.

relax VB **1 a** to make (part of the body, muscles, one's grip, etc) less tense, stiff or rigid; **b** INTR of muscles, a grip, etc: to become less tense; to become looser or slacker. **2** TR & INTR to make or become less tense, nervous or worried. **3** INTR of a person: to become less stiff or formal. **4** TR & INTR of discipline, rules, etc: to make or become less strict or severe. **5** to lessen the strength or intensity of (something). ■ **relaxation** N.

■ **relaxed** ADJ. ■ **relaxing** ADJ.

relay N **1** a relay race. **2** ELECTRONICS an electrical switching device that, in response to a change in an electric circuit, opens or closes one or more contacts in the same or another circuit. **3** TELECOMM a device fitted at regular intervals along TV broadcasting networks, underwater telecommunications cables, etc to amplify weak signals and pass them on from one communication link to the next. **4 a** something which is relayed, esp a signal or broadcast; **b** the act of relaying it.
➤ VB to receive and pass on (news, a message, a TV programme, etc).

relay race N a race between teams of runners, swimmers, etc in which each member of the team covers part of the total distance.

release VB **1** to free (a prisoner, etc) from captivity. **2** to relieve (someone) of a duty, burden, etc. **3** to loosen one's grip and stop holding something. **4** to make (news, information, etc) known publicly. **5** to offer (a film, record, book, etc) for sale, performance, etc. **6** to move (a catch, brake, etc) so that it no longer prevents something from operating. **7** to give off or emit (heat, gas, etc).
➤ N **1** an act or the process of releasing or state of being released. **2** an item of news made public: **press release**.

relegate VB **1** to move down to a lower grade, position, status, etc. **2** SPORT, esp FOOTBALL to move (a team) down to a lower league or division. ■ **relegation** N.

relent VB, INTR **1** to become less severe or unkind; to soften. **2** to give way and agree to something one initially would not accept.

relentless ADJ **1 a** without pity; **b** harsh. **2** never stopping. ■ **relentlessly** ADV.

relevant ADJ directly connected with or related to the matter in hand. ■ **relevance** N.

reliable ADJ dependable; trustworthy. ■ **reliability** N. ■ **reliably** ADV.

reliance N the state of relying on someone or something: **overcame her reliance on drugs**.

relic N **1** a fragment or part of an object left after the rest has decayed. **2** an object valued as a memorial or souvenir of the past. **3** part of the body of a saint or martyr, preserved as an object of veneration.

relief N **1** the lessening or removal of pain, worry, oppression, distress, etc or the feeling that comes from this. **2** anything lessening pain, worry, boredom, etc. **3** help, often in the form of money, food, clothing and medicine, given to people in need. **4** someone who takes over a job or task from another person. **5** the freeing of a besieged or endangered town, fortress, etc.

relief map N a map which shows the variations in the height of the land by shading.

relieve VB **1** to lessen or stop (pain, worry, boredom, etc). **2** to remove (a physical or mental burden) (from someone). **3** to give help or assistance. **4** to make less monotonous or tedious, esp by providing a contrast. **5** to free or dismiss from a duty or restriction. **6** to take over a job or task from. **7** to come to the help of (a besieged town, fortress, military post, etc).
◆ **relieve oneself** to urinate or defecate.

religion N **1** a belief in, or the worship of, a god or gods. **2** a particular system of belief or worship, such as Christianity or Judaism.

religious ADJ **1** relating to religion.
2 a following the rules or forms of worship of a particular religion very closely; **b** pious; devout. **3** conscientious.
➤ N (PL *religious*) a person bound by monastic vows, eg, a monk or nun. ■ **religiously** ADV.

relinquish VB **1** to give up or abandon (a belief, task, etc). **2** to release one's hold of (something). **3** to renounce possession or control of (a claim, right, etc).

reliquary N (*-ies*) a container for holy relics.

relish VB to enjoy greatly or with discrimination.
➤ N **1** pleasure; enjoyment. **2 a** a spicy appetizing flavour; **b** a sauce or pickle which adds such a flavour to food.

relive VB **1** INTR to live again. **2** to experience again, esp in the imagination.

relocate VB **1** to locate again. **2** TR & INTR to move (oneself, a business, home, etc) from one place, town, etc to another. ■ **relocation** N.

reluctant ADJ unwilling or disinclined.
■ **reluctance** N. ■ **reluctantly** ADV.

rely VB (*-ied, -ies*) (always **rely on** or **upon**) **1** to depend on or need. **2** to trust.

remain VB, INTR **1** to be left after others, or other parts of the whole, have been used up, taken away, lost, etc. **2 a** to stay behind; **b** to stay in the same place. **3** to stay the same or unchanged. **4** to continue to need to be done.

remainder N **1** what is left after others, or other parts, have gone, been used up, taken away, etc; the rest. **2** MATH the amount left over when one number cannot be divided exactly by another number. **3** MATH the amount left when one number is subtracted from another.
➤ VB to sell (copies of a book) at a reduced price because sales have fallen off.

remains PL N **1** a dead body. **2** relics.

remake VB to make again or in a new way.
➤ N something that is made again, eg, a new version of an existing film.

remand VB to send (an accused person) back into custody to await trial.
◆ **on remand** awaiting trial.

remark VB **1** TR & INTR to notice and comment on. **2** to make a casual comment.
➤ N **1** a comment. **2** an observation.
3 noteworthiness.

remarkable ADJ **1** worth mentioning or commenting on. **2** very unusual or extraordinary. ■ **remarkably** ADV.

remedy N (*-ies*) **1** a drug or treatment which cures or controls a disease. **2** something which solves a problem. **3** legal redress.
➤ VB (*-ies, -ied*) **1** to cure or control (a disease, etc). **2** to put right or correct (a problem, error, etc). ■ **remediable** ADJ. ■ **remedial** ADJ.

remember VB **1** to bring from the past to mind. **2** to keep (a fact, idea, etc) in one's mind: remember to phone. **3** to commemorate.

remembrance N **1** the act of remembering or being remembered. **2 a** something which reminds a person of something or someone;

b a souvenir. **3** a memory or recollection.

remind VB **1** to cause (someone) to remember (something or to do something): **remind me to speak to him**. **2** to make (someone) think about.

reminder N **1** something that reminds or is meant to remind. **2** a memento.

reminisce VB, INTR to think, talk or write about things remembered from the past.

reminiscence N **1** the act of thinking, talking or writing about the past. **2** something from the past that is remembered. **3** (often **reminiscences**) a written account of things remembered from the past.

reminiscent ADJ (usu **reminiscent of**) similar: **a painting reminiscent of Turner**.

remiss ADJ careless; negligent.

remission N **1** a lessening in force or effect, esp in the symptoms of a disease such as cancer. **2** a reduction of a prison sentence. **3 a** pardon; **b** forgiveness from sin.

remit VB (-*tt*-) **1** to cancel or refrain from demanding (a debt, punishment, etc). **2** TR & INTR to make or become loose, slack or relaxed. **3** to send (money) in payment. **4** to refer (a matter for decision, etc) to some other authority. **5** LAW to refer (a case) to a lower court. **6** INTR to become less severe for a period of time.
➤ N the authority or terms of reference given to a committee, etc in dealing with a matter.

remittance N **1** the sending of money in payment. **2** the money sent.

remnant N (often **remnants**) **1** a remaining small piece or amount of something larger, or a small amount left from a larger quantity. **2** a remaining piece of fabric from the end of a roll. **3** a surviving trace or vestige.

remonstrate VB to protest forcefully.
■ **remonstrance** N. ■ **remonstration** N.
◆ **remonstrate with sb** to protest to them.

remorse N **1** a deep feeling of guilt, regret and bitterness for something wrong or bad. **2** compassion or pity. ■ **remorseful** ADJ.

remorseless ADJ **1** without remorse. **2** cruel.

3 relentless. ■ **remorselessness** N.

remote ADJ **1** far away; distant in time or place. **2** out of the way; far from civilization. **3** operated or controlled from a distance; remote-controlled. **4** COMP of a computer terminal: located separately from the main processor but having a communication link with it. **5** distantly related or connected. **6** very small, slight or faint: **a remote chance**. **7** aloof or distant. ■ **remotely** ADV. ■ **remoteness** N.

remote control N **1** the control of machinery or electrical devices from a distance, by electrical signals or radio waves. **2** a battery-operated device for transmitting such waves.
■ **remote-controlled** ADJ.

remould N a tyre that has had new tread bonded onto it. Also called **retread**.

removal N **1** the act or process of removing or state of being removed. **2** the moving of possessions, furniture, etc to a new house.

remove VB **1** to move to a different place. **2** to take off (a piece of clothing). **3** to get rid of. **4** to dismiss from a job, position, etc.
➤ N **1** a removal. **2** the degree, usu specified, of difference separating two things: **government only one remove from tyranny**. ■ **removable** ADJ. ■ **remover** N.

remunerate VB **1** to recompense. **2** to pay (someone) for services rendered.
■ **remuneration** N. ■ **remunerative** ADJ.

renaissance N a rebirth or revival.

renal ADJ relating to the kidneys.

rend VB (*rent*) OLD USE, TR & INTR to tear.

render VB **1** to cause (something) to be or become: **render things more agreeable**. **2** to give or provide (a service, help, etc). **3** to show (obedience, honour, etc). **4** to pay (money) or perform (a duty), esp in return for something. **5** to give back or return (something). **6** to give in return or exchange. **7** (also **render up**) to give up, release or yield. **8** to translate. **9** to perform (the role of a character in a play, a piece of music, etc). **10** to portray or reproduce, esp in painting or music. **11** to present or submit for payment, approval, consideration, etc. **12** to cover (brick or stone) with a coat of plaster. **13** to melt (fat), esp to clarify it. ■ **rendering** N.

rendezvous N (PL *rendezvous*) **a** an appointment to meet at a specified time and place; **b** the meeting itself; **c** the place where such a meeting is to be.
➤ VB, INTR to meet at a fixed place or time.

rendition N a performance or interpretation of a piece of music, a dramatic role, etc.

renegade N someone who deserts the religious, political, etc group which they belong to, and joins an enemy or rival group.

renege VB, INTR (often **renege on**) to go back on (one's word, a promise, deal, etc).

renew VB **1 a** to make fresh or like new again; **b** to restore to the original condition. **2 a** to begin to do again; **b** to repeat. **3** TR & INTR to begin (some activity) again after a break. **4** TR & INTR to make (a licence, lease, loan, etc) valid for a further period of time. **5** to replenish or replace. ■ **renewable** ADJ. ■ **renewal** N.

rennet N a substance that curdles milk.

renounce VB **1** to give up (a claim, title, right, etc), esp formally and publicly. **2** to refuse to recognize or associate with (someone). **3** to give up (a bad habit).

renovate VB **1** to renew or make new again. **2** to restore (esp a building) to a former and better condition. ■ **renovation** N.

renown N fame. ■ **renowned** ADJ.

rent[1] N money paid periodically in return for the use or occupation of a property.
➤ VB **1** to pay rent for (a building, house, flat, etc). **2** (also **rent out**) to allow someone the use of (property) in return for payment of rent. **3** INTR to be hired out for rent.

rent[2] N, OLD USE **1** an opening or split made by tearing or rending. **2** a fissure.

rental N **1** the act of renting. **2** money paid as rent.

rent boy N a young male prostitute.

renunciation N **1** an act of renouncing. **2** a formal declaration renouncing something.

rep[1] N, COLLOQ a representative, esp a travelling salesperson.

rep[2] see under **repertory**

repair[1] VB **1** to restore (something damaged or broken) to good working condition. **2** to put right (some wrong that has been done).
➤ N **1** an act or the process of repairing. **2** a condition or state: **in good repair**. **3** a part or place that has been repaired.

repair[2] VB, INTR (usu **repair to**) OLD USE to go or take oneself.

reparation N an act or instance of making up for some wrong that has been done.

repartee N **1** the practice or skill of making spontaneous witty retorts. **2** a quick witty retort. **3** conversation with many such replies.

repast N, FORMAL OR OLD USE a meal.

repatriate VB to send (a refugee, prisoner of war, etc) back to their country of origin. ■ **repatriation** N.

repay VB **1** to pay back or refund (money). **2** to do or give something (to someone) in return for something they have done or given. ■ **repayable** ADJ. ■ **repayment** N.

repeal VB to make (a law, etc) no longer valid.
➤ N the act of repealing (a law, etc).

repeat VB **1** to say, do, etc, again or several times. **2** to echo or say again exactly (the words already said by someone else). **3** to tell (something, esp a secret) to someone else. **4 a** to quote from memory; **b** to recite (a poem, etc). **5** INTR of food: to be tasted again some time after being swallowed. **6** INTR to occur again or several times; to recur. **7** (usu **repeat itself**) of an event, occurrence, etc: to happen in exactly the same way more than once. **8** INTR of a gun: to fire several times without being reloaded. **9** INTR of a clock: to strike the hour or quarter hour.
➤ N **1 a** the act of repeating; **b** a repetition. **2** something that is repeated, esp a television or radio programme which has been broadcast before.
➤ ADJ second or subsequent: **repeat visits**.
■ **repeated** ADJ. ■ **repeatedly** ADV.

repeater N someone or something that repeats.

repel VB (*-ll-*) **1 a** to force or drive back or away; **b** to repulse. **2** TR & INTR to provoke a feeling of disgust. **3** to fail to mix with, absorb or be attracted by. **4** to reject or rebuff.

repellent N something that drives away or discourages the presence of insects, etc. ➤ ADJ **1** forcing or driving back or away. **2** provoking a feeling of disgust or loathing.

repent VB, TR & INTR **a** (usu **repent of**) to feel great sorrow or regret for something one has done; **b** to wish (an action, etc) undone. ■ **repentance** N. ■ **repentant** ADJ.

repercussion N **1** (usu **repercussions**) a bad, unforeseen, indirect, etc result or consequence of some action, event, etc. **2** an echo or reverberation. ■ **repercussive** ADJ.

repertoire N **1** the list of songs, operas, plays, etc that a singer, performer, group of actors, etc is able or ready to perform. **2** the range or stock of skills, techniques, talents, etc that someone or something has.

repertory N (*-ies*) **1** a repertoire, esp of a theatre company. **2** the performance of a repertoire of plays at regular, short intervals. **3** a storehouse or repository. **4** short form of **repertory company**. **5** repertory theatres collectively. Often shortened to **rep**.

repertory company N a group of actors who perform a series of plays from their repertoire in a season at one theatre.

repetition N **1** the act of repeating or being repeated. **2** something that is repeated. **3** a copy or replica.

repetitious ADJ inclined to repetition, esp when tedious, boring, etc.

repetitive ADJ happening, done, said, etc over and over again. ■ **repetitively** ADV.

rephrase VB to express in different words.

replace VB **1** to put back in a previous or proper position. **2** to take the place of or be a substitute for. **3** to supplant. **4** to substitute (a person or thing) in place of (an existing one).

■ **replaceable** ADJ. ■ **replacement** N.

replay N **1** an act or instance of playing of a game, football match, etc again, usu because there was no clear winner the first time. **2** an act or instance of playing a recording. ➤ VB to play (a tape, recording, etc) again.

replenish VB to fill up or make complete again, esp a supply of something which has been used up. ■ **replenishment** N.

replete ADJ **1** (often **replete with**) completely or well supplied. **2** FORMAL having eaten enough or more than enough. ■ **repletion** N.

replica N **1** an exact copy, esp of a work of art. **2** a copy or model, esp a scaled–down one.

replicate VB **1** to make a replica of. **2** to repeat (a scientific experiment). ■ **replication** N.

reply VB (*-ies, -ied*) **1** INTR to answer or respond to in words or action. **2** to say or do in response. ➤ N (*-ies*) **1** an answer or response. **2** an act or instance of replying.

report N **1** a detailed statement, description or account, esp one made after some form of investigation. **2** a detailed and usu formal account of the discussions and decisions of a committee, etc. **3** an account of news, etc: *a newspaper report.* **4** a statement of a pupil's work and behaviour at school. **5** rumour; general talk. **6** character or reputation. **7** a loud explosive noise, eg, of a gun firing. ➤ VB **1** to bring back (information, etc) as an answer, news or account: *reported that fighting had broken out.* **2** INTR to state. **3** (often **report on**) to give a formal or official account of (findings, information, etc), esp after an investigation. **4 a** to give an account of (some matter of news, etc), esp for a newspaper, or TV or radio broadcast; **b** INTR to act as a newspaper, TV or radio reporter. **5** to make a complaint about someone. **6** INTR to present oneself at an appointed place or time or to a specified person: *report to reception.* **7** INTR (usu **report to**) to be under (a specified superior). **8** INTR to account for oneself in a particular way: *report sick.*

reported speech N, GRAM same as **indirect speech**

reporter N someone who reports, esp for a newspaper, TV or radio.

repose[1] N 1 a state of rest, calm or peacefulness. 2 composure.
➤ VB 1 INTR to rest. 2 to lay (oneself, one's head, etc) down to rest.

repose[2] VB to place (confidence, trust, etc) in (someone or something).

repository N (-*ies*) 1 a storage place or container. 2 **a** a place where things are stored for exhibition; **b** a museum. 3 a warehouse. 4 someone or something thought of as a store of information, knowledge, etc.

repossess VB of a creditor: to regain possession of (property or goods), esp because the debtor has defaulted on payment.

reprehensible ADJ deserving blame or criticism. ■ **reprehensibly** ADV.

represent VB 1 **a** to serve as a symbol or sign for: *letters represent sounds*; **b** to stand for or correspond to: *A thesis represents years of hard work*. 2 to speak or act on behalf of (someone else). 3 **a** to be a good example of; **b** to typify. 4 to present an image of or portray, esp through painting or sculpture. 5 to bring clearly to mind. 6 to describe in a specified way; to attribute a specified character or quality to (someone, something, oneself, etc). 7 to show, state or explain. 8 to be an elected member of Parliament for (a constituency). 9 to act out or play the part of on stage.

re-present VB to present something again.

representation N 1 an act or process of representing, or the state or fact of being represented. 2 a person or thing that represents someone or something else. 3 **a** an image; **b** a picture or painting. 4 a dramatic performance. 5 (often **representations**) a strong statement made to present facts, opinions, complaints or demands. ■ **representational** ADJ.

representative ADJ 1 representing. 2 **a** standing as a good example of something; **b** typical. 3 of government: comprised of elected people.
➤ N **a** someone who represents someone or something else, esp someone who represents, or sells the goods of, a business or company; **b** someone who acts as a person's agent or who speaks on their behalf.

repress VB 1 **a** to keep (an impulse, a desire to do something, etc) under control; **b** to restrain (an impulse, desire, etc). 2 to put down, esp using force. 3 PSYCHOL to exclude (thoughts, feelings, etc) from the conscious mind.
■ **repression** N. ■ **repressive** ADJ.

reprieve VB 1 to delay or cancel (punishment, esp the execution of a prisoner condemned to death). 2 to give temporary relief or respite from (trouble, difficulty, pain, etc).
➤ N **a** an act or instance or the process of delaying or cancelling a criminal sentence, esp a death sentence; **b** a warrant granting this.

reprimand VB to criticize or rebuke angrily or severely, esp publicly or formally.
➤ N an angry or severe rebuke.

reprint VB 1 to print more copies of (a book, etc). 2 INTR to have more copies printed.
➤ N 1 the act of reprinting. 2 a copy of a book, etc made by reprinting.

reprisal N revenge or retaliation.

reprise N, MUS the repeating of a passage.

reproach VB **a** to express disapproval of, or disappointment with; **b** to blame.
➤ N 1 an act of reproaching. 2 (often **reproaches**) a rebuke or expression of disappointment. 3 a cause of disgrace or shame. ■ **reproachful** ADJ.

reprobate N an immoral unprincipled person.
➤ ADJ immoral and unprincipled.
■ **reprobation** N.

reproduce VB 1 to make or produce again. 2 **a** to make or produce a copy of; **b** to duplicate. 3 TR & INTR to produce (offspring).

reproduction N 1 an act or the process of reproducing. 2 a copy or imitation, esp of a work of art. 3 the quality of reproduced sound.
➤ ADJ of furniture, etc: made in imitation of an earlier style. ■ **reproductive** ADJ.

reproof N 1 blame or censure. 2 a rebuke.

reprove VB 1 to rebuke. 2 to blame or condemn for a fault, wrongdoing, etc.

reptile N, ZOOL a cold-blooded scaly vertebrate animal, eg, a lizard, snake, etc. ■ **reptilian** ADJ, N.

republic N a form of government without a monarch and in which supreme power is held by the people or their elected representatives.

republican ADJ 1 relating to or characteristic of a republic. 2 in favour of or supporting the republic as a form of government. ➤ N someone who favours the republic as a form of government. ■ **republicanism** N.

repudiate VB 1 to deny or reject as unfounded: repudiate the suggestion. 2 to refuse to recognize or have anything to do with (a person). 3 to refuse or cease to acknowledge (a debt, etc). ■ **repudiation** N.

repugnant ADJ distasteful; disgusting. ■ **repugnance** N. ■ **repugnantly** ADV.

repulse VB 1 to drive or force back (an enemy, attacking force, etc). 2 to reject (someone's offer of help, kindness, etc) with coldness and discourtesy. 3 to bring on a feeling of disgust, horror or loathing in someone. ➤ N 1 an act or instance of repulsing or state of being repulsed. 2 a cold discourteous rejection. ■ **repulsion** N. ■ **repulsive** ADJ.

reputable ADJ well thought of.

reputation N 1 a generally held opinion about someone's abilities, moral character, etc. 2 (often **reputation for** or **of**) fame or notoriety. 3 a high opinion generally held about someone or something.

repute VB to consider (as having some specified quality, etc): She is reputed to be a fine tennis player. ➤ N 1 general opinion or impression. 2 reputation.

request N 1 an act or an instance of asking for something. 2 something asked for. ➤ VB to ask for, esp politely or as a favour.

requiem N 1 RC CHURCH a mass for the souls of the dead. 2 a piece of music written for this.

require VB 1 to need or wish to have. 2 to demand, exact or command by authority. 3 to have as a necessary or essential condition for success, fulfilment, etc.

requirement N 1 a a need; b something that is needed. 2 something that is asked for, ordered, etc. 3 a necessary condition.

requisite ADJ required or necessary. ➤ N something that is required or necessary.

requisition N 1 a formal authoritative demand for supplies or the use of something. 2 an official form on which such a demand is made. ➤ VB to demand (the use of something, etc) by official requisition.

requite VB, FORMAL 1 to make a suitable return in response to (someone's kindness or injury). 2 to repay (someone) for (something). 3 to repay (eg, good with good, evil with evil, hate with love, etc). ■ **requital** N.

reredos N an ornamental screen behind an altar.

rerun VB 1 to cause (a race, etc) to be run again or to run (a race, etc) again, eg, because of an unclear result, etc. 2 to broadcast (a TV or radio programme) for a second or subsequent time.

rescind VB to cancel, annul or revoke (an order, law, custom, etc). ■ **rescission** N.

rescue VB to save or set free from danger, etc. ➤ N an act or an instance or the process of rescuing or being rescued. ■ **rescuer** N.

research N detailed and careful investigation into some subject or area of study with the aim of discovering new facts or information. ➤ VB, TR & INTR to do research (on a specified subject, etc). ■ **researcher** N.

resemblance N 1 likeness or similarity or the degree of likeness or similarity. 2 appearance.

resemble VB to be like or similar to (someone or something else), esp in appearance.

resent VB 1 to take or consider as an insult or an affront. 2 to feel anger, bitterness or ill-will towards or about (someone or something).

■ **resentful** ADJ. ■ **resentment** N.

reservation N 1 an act of reserving something for future use. 2 **a** an act of booking or ordering, eg, a hotel room, a table in a restaurant, a ticket, etc, in advance; **b** something reserved or booked in advance. 3 (often **reservations**) a doubt or objection. 4 a limiting condition, proviso or exception to an agreement, etc. 5 an area of land set aside for a particular purpose.

reserve VB 1 to keep back or set aside, eg, for a future, special or particular use, etc. 2 to book or order (eg, a hotel room, a table in a restaurant, a ticket, etc) in advance. 3 to delay or postpone (a legal judgement, taking a decision, etc). 4 to maintain or secure. ➢ N 1 something kept back or set aside, esp for future use or possible need. 2 the state or condition of being reserved or an act of reserving. 3 an area of land set aside for a particular purpose, esp for the protection of wildlife: **a nature reserve. 4** coolness, distance or restraint of manner; diffidence or reticence. 5 SPORT **a** an extra player or participant who can take another's place if needed; **b** (usu **the reserves**) the second or B team. 6 (also **reserves**) MIL **a** part of an army or force kept out of immediate action to provide reinforcements when needed; **b** forces not usu in service but that may be called upon if necessary; **c** a member of such a force. 7 (often **reserves**) FINANCE a company's assets, or a country's gold and foreign currency, held at a bank to meet future liabilities. 8 (usu **reserves**) an unexploited supply of oil, gas, coal, etc.

reserved ADJ 1 kept back, set aside or destined for a particular use or for a particular person. 2 of a person or their manner: cool, distant or restrained; diffident or reticent.

reservist N, MIL a member of a reserve force.

reservoir N 1 a large natural or artificial lake, or a tank, in which water is collected and stored for public use, irrigation, etc. 2 a chamber in a machine, device, etc where liquid is stored.

reshuffle VB 1 to shuffle (cards) again or differently. 2 to reorganize or redistribute (esp government posts). ➢ N an act of reshuffling: **a cabinet reshuffle.**

reside VB, INTR 1 FORMAL to live or have one's home (in a place), esp permanently. 2 of power, authority, etc: to rest (with someone).

residence N 1 FORMAL a house or dwelling, esp a large, impressive and imposing one. 2 **a** an act or an instance of living in a particular place; **b** the period of time someone lives there.

resident N 1 someone who lives permanently in a particular place. 2 a registered guest in a hotel, esp one staying a relatively long time. ➢ ADJ 1 living or dwelling in a particular place. 2 living in the place where one works. 3 of birds and animals: not migrating.

residential ADJ 1 of a street, etc: containing private houses. 2 requiring residence in the same place as one works or studies: **a residential course. 3** used as a residence.

residual ADJ remaining; left over.

residue N 1 what is left over when a part has been taken away, used up, etc. 2 LAW what is left of a dead person's estate after debts and legacies have been paid. 3 CHEM a residuum.

resign VB 1 INTR to give up (a job, an official position, etc). 2 to give up or relinquish (a right, claim, etc). 3 (usu **resign oneself to**) to come to accept (a situation, etc) with patience, tolerance, etc. ■ **resigned** ADJ.

resignation N 1 an act of resigning from a job, official position, etc. 2 a signed notification of intention to resign from a job, post, etc. 3 uncomplaining acceptance of something unpleasant, inevitable, etc.

resilient ADJ 1 of a person: able to recover quickly from, or to deal readily with, illness, hardship, etc. 2 of an object, a material, etc: able to return quickly to its original shape, position, etc. ■ **resilience** N.

resin N a sticky aromatic substance secreted by various plants and trees. ■ **resinous** ADJ.

resist VB 1 TR & INTR to oppose or refuse to comply with. 2 to withstand (something damaging): **a metal which resists corrosion.**

3 to impede: **resisted arrest. 4** to refrain from or turn down: **can't resist chocolate.**

resistance N **1** an act or the process of resisting. **2** the ability or power to resist, esp the extent to which damage, etc can be withstood: **resistance is low during the winter months. 3** PHYS in damped harmonic motion: the ratio of the frictional forces to the speed. **4** ELEC a measure of the extent to which a material or an electrical device opposes the flow of an electric current through it. **5** a measure of the extent to which a material opposes the flow of heat through it. ■ **resistant** ADJ.

resistor N, ELEC a device which introduces a known value of resistance into a circuit.

resit VB, TR & INTR to take (an examination) again. ➤ N an act of taking an examination again.

resoluble ADJ able to be resolved.

resolute ADJ determined; with a fixed purpose or belief. ■ **resolutely** ADV.

resolution N **1** an act or instance or the process of making a firm decision. **2** a firm decision. **3** determination or resoluteness. **4** an act or instance or the process of solving a difficult question, etc. **5** an answer to a difficult question, etc. **6** the ability of a television screen, photographic film, etc to reproduce an image in very fine detail. **7** a formal decision, expression of opinion, etc by a group of people. **8** PHYS the ability of a microscope, telescope, etc to distinguish between objects which are very close together.

resolve VB **1** to decide firmly or make up one's mind. **2** to find an answer to (a problem, question, etc). **3** to take away or dispel (a doubt, difficulty, etc). **4** to bring (an argument, etc) to an end. **5** TR & INTR to decide, or pass (a resolution), esp formally. **6** of a television screen, photographic film, etc: to produce an image in fine detail. **7** of a microscope, telescope, etc: to distinguish clearly (eg, objects which are very close together). ➤ N **1** determination or firmness of purpose. **2** a firm decision. ■ **resolvable** ADJ.

resonant ADJ **1** of sounds: echoing; continuing to sound; resounding. **2** producing echoing sounds: **resonant walls. 3** full of or intensified by a ringing quality: **a resonant voice.** ■ **resonance** N. ■ **resonantly** ADV.

resonate VB, TR & INTR to resound or echo. ■ **resonator** N.

resort VB, INTR (usu **resort to**) to use (something) as a means of solving a problem. ➤ N **1** a place visited by many people. **2** someone or something looked to for help.

resound VB **1** INTR of sounds: to ring or echo. **2** INTR (**resound with** or **to**) to reverberate. **3** INTR to be widely known or celebrated. **4** of a place: to make (a sound) echo or ring.

resounding ADJ **1** echoing and ringing. **2** clear and decisive: **a resounding victory.**

resource N **1** someone or something that provides a source of help, support, etc when needed. **2** a means of solving difficulties, problems, etc. **3** skill at finding ways of solving difficulties, problems, etc. **4** something useful. **5** (usu **resources**) a means of support, esp money or property. **6** (usu **resources**) a country's, business's, etc source of wealth or income: **natural resources.** ➤ VB to provide with support, usu financial.

resourceful ADJ skilled in finding ways of overcoming difficulties, solving problems, etc.

respect N **1** admiration; good opinion: **held in great respect. 2** the state of being honoured, admired or well thought of. **3** (**respect for**) consideration, thoughtfulness or attention. **4** (often **respects**) FORMAL a polite expression of esteem. **5** a particular detail, feature or characteristic: **In what respect are they different? 6** reference, relation or connection. ➤ VB **1** to show or feel high regard for. **2** to show consideration for, or thoughtfulness or attention to: **respect her wishes. 3** to heed or pay proper attention to (a rule, law, etc). ■ **respecter** N. ◆ **in respect of** or **with respect to sth** with reference to, or in connection with (a particular matter, point, etc).

respectable ADJ **1** worthy of or deserving respect. **2** having a reasonably good social

standing or reputation. **3** fairly or relatively good or large: a respectable turnout.
■ **respectability** N.

respectful ADJ having or showing respect.
■ **respectfully** ADV. ■ **respectfulness** N.

respecting PREP about; with regard to.

respective ADJ belonging to or relating to each person or thing mentioned; particular; separate: our respective homes.

respiration N breathing.

respirator N **1** a mask worn over the mouth and nose, esp to prevent poisonous gas, dust, etc being breathed in. **2** MED an apparatus that does a sick person's breathing for them.

respire VB **1** TR & INTR to inhale and exhale (air, etc); to breathe. **2** INTR to undergo respiration.
■ **respiratory** ADJ.

respite N **1** a period of rest or relief from, or a temporary stopping of, something unpleasant, difficult, etc. **2** a temporary delay.

resplendent ADJ brilliant or splendid in appearance. ■ **resplendence** N.

respond VB **1** TR & INTR to answer or reply; to say or do in reply. **2** INTR (usu **respond to**) to react favourably or well: respond to treatment. **3** INTR, RELIG to utter liturgical responses.

respondent N, LAW a defendant, esp in a divorce suit.

response N **1** an act of responding, replying or reacting. **2** a reply or answer. **3** a reaction.

responsibility N (-*ies*) **1** the state of being responsible or of having important duties for which one is responsible. **2** something or someone for which one is responsible.

responsible ADJ **1** (usu **responsible for** or **to**) accountable: responsible to her immediate superior. **2** of a job, position, etc: with many important duties. **3** (often **responsible for**) being the main or identifiable cause. **4** of a person: **a** able to be trusted; **b** capable of rational and socially acceptable behaviour. ■ **responsibly** ADV.

responsive ADJ **1** reacting readily to stimulus.

2 reacting well or favourably: a disease responsive to drugs. **3** made as or constituting a response: a responsive smile.

rest[1] N **1** a period of relaxation or freedom from work, worry, etc. **2** sleep; repose. **3** calm; tranquillity. **4** a pause from some activity. **5** death, when seen as repose. **6** a prop or support, eg, for a snooker cue, etc. **7** a place or thing which holds or supports. **8** a pause in reading, speaking, etc. **9** MUS **a** an interval of silence in a piece of music: two bars' rest; **b** a mark indicating the duration of this.
➤ VB **1** TR & INTR to stop or cause to stop working or moving. **2** INTR to relax, esp by sleeping or stopping some activity. **3** TR & INTR to set, place or lie on or against, for support, etc: rested her arm on the chair. **4** INTR to be calm and free from worry. **5** TR & INTR to give or have as a basis or support. **6** INTR to depend or be based on. **7** INTR to be left without further attention, discussion or action. **8** INTR to lie dead or buried.
◆ **at rest 1** not moving or working; stationary. **2** free from trouble, etc. **3** asleep. **4** dead.
◆ **lay sb to rest** to bury or inter them.

rest[2] N (usu **the rest**) **1** what is left when part of something is taken away, used, finished, etc; the remainder. **2** the others.
➤ VB, INTR to remain: rest assured.

restaurant N an establishment where meals may be bought and eaten.

restaurateur N an owner or manager of a restaurant.

restful ADJ **1** bringing or giving rest, or producing a sensation of calm, peace and rest. **2** relaxed; at rest. ■ **restfulness** N.

restitution N **1** the act of giving something stolen, lost, etc back to its rightful owner. **2** compensation for loss or injury.

restive ADJ **1** restless; nervous; uneasy. **2** unwilling to accept control or authority.

restless ADJ **1** constantly moving about or fidgeting. **2** constantly active or in motion; unceasing. **3** giving no rest; disturbed: a restless night. **4** nervous and uneasy.

restoration N **1** an act or instance or the

process of restoring or being restored. **2** a model or reconstruction.

restorative ADJ tending or helping to restore or improve health, strength, spirits, etc. ➤ N a restorative food or medicine.

restore VB **1** to return (a building, painting, etc) to a former condition by repairing, cleaning, etc. **2** to bring (someone or something) back to a normal or proper state or condition. **3** to bring back (a normal, desirable, etc state): **restore discipline**. ■ **restorer** N.

restrain VB **1** to prevent (someone, oneself, etc) from doing something. **2** to keep (one's temper, ambition, etc) under control. **3** to confine.

restraint N **1** an act or instance of restraining or the state of being restrained. **2** a limit or restriction. **3** the avoidance of excess.

restrict VB **1** to keep within certain limits. **2** to limit or regulate; to withhold from general use. ■ **restricted** ADJ. ■ **restriction** N.

restrictive ADJ restricting or intended to restrict, esp excessively.

rest room N, N AMER a lavatory for public use.

restructuring N the reorganization of a business in order to improve efficiency, etc.

result N **1** an outcome or consequence of something. **2** COLLOQ (often **results**) a positive or favourable outcome or consequence: **His action got results**. **3** a number or quantity obtained by calculation, etc. **4** (**results**) a list of scores, examination outcomes, etc. ➤ VB, INTR **1** (usu **result from**) to be a consequence or outcome. **2** (usu **result in**) to lead (to a specified thing, condition, etc).

resultant ADJ resulting.

resume VB **1** TR & INTR to return to or begin again after an interruption. **2** to take back or return to (a former position, etc): **resume one's seat**. ■ **resumption** N.

résumé N **1** a summary. **2** N AMER a curriculum vitae.

resurgence N an act or instance of returning to a state of activity, importance, influence, etc

after a period of decline. ■ **resurgent** ADJ.

resurrect VB **1** to bring (someone) back to life from the dead. **2** to bring (a custom, memory, etc) back. ■ **resurrection** N.

resuscitate VB **1** to bring back to life or consciousness; to revive. **2** INTR to revive or regain consciousness. ■ **resuscitation** N.

retail N the sale of goods in small quantities to customers buying them for personal use. ➤ ADJ relating to, concerned with, or engaged in selling such goods. ➤ ADV **1** by retail. **2** at a retail price. ➤ VB **a** to sell (goods) in small quantities; **b** INTR to be sold in small quantities to customers. ■ **retailer** N.

retain VB **1** to keep or continue to have: **retain a sense of humour**. **2** to be able or continue to hold or contain: **retains moisture**. **3** to keep (facts, information, etc) in one's memory. **4** to hold back or keep in place. **5** to secure the services of (a person, esp a barrister) by paying a preliminary fee.

retainer N **1** a domestic servant who has been with a family for a long time. **2** a fee paid to secure professional services. **3** a reduced rent paid for property while it is not occupied in order to reserve it for future use.

retake VB **1 a** to take again; **b** to take back. **2** to capture (eg, a fortress) again. **3** to sit (an examination) again. **4** to film (eg, a scene) again.

retaliate VB, INTR to repay an injury, wrong, etc in kind; to take revenge. ■ **retaliation** N. ■ **retaliatory** ADJ.

retard VB to slow down or delay something.

retarded ADJ backward in physical or esp mental development. ■ **retardation** N.

retch VB, INTR to strain as if to vomit, but without actually doing so.

retention N **1** the act of retaining something or the state of being retained. **2** the power of retaining or capacity to retain something. **3** the ability to remember things learnt.

retentive ADJ **1** able to retain or keep, esp

memories or information. **2** tending to retain.

rethink VB to think about or consider (a plan, etc) again, usu with a view to changing one's mind about it or reaching a different conclusion.

reticent ADJ **1** not saying very much. **2** not willing to communicate; reserved. **3** not communicating everything that is known. ■ **reticence** N. ■ **reticently** ADV.

reticulate ADJ like a net or network, esp in having lines, veins, etc: **a reticulate leaf**.

retina N (*-nas* or *-nae*) the light-sensitive tissue that lines the back of the eyeball.

retinue N the servants, officials, aides, etc who travel with and attend an important person.

retire VB **1** TR & INTR to stop or make (someone) stop working permanently: **retired at 60**. **2** INTR, FORMAL to go to bed. **3** INTR, FORMAL to go away (from or to a place); to leave: **retire to the drawing room**. **4** TR & INTR to withdraw or make (someone) withdraw from a sporting contest.

retirement N **1** an act of retiring or the state of being retired from work. **2** seclusion.

retiring ADJ shy and reserved.

retort[1] VB **1** INTR to make a quick and clever or angry reply. **2** to turn (an argument, criticism, blame, etc) back on the originator.
➤ N **1** a quick and clever or angry reply. **2** an argument, criticism, blame, etc which is turned back on the originator.

retort[2] N a glass vessel with a long neck which curves downwards, used in distilling.

retouch VB to improve or repair (a photograph, negative, etc) by making small alterations.

retrace VB **1** to go back over (a route, path, etc). **2** to trace back to a source or origin. **3** to go over (events, etc) again in one's memory.

retract VB **1** to draw (something, esp an animal's body part) in or back. **2** TR & INTR to withdraw (a statement, claim, charge, etc). ■ **retractable** ADJ. ■ **retraction** N.

retractile ADJ of a cat's, etc claws: able to be drawn in, back or up.

retrain VB, INTR to learn new skills, esp with a view to finding alternative employment.

retread see **remould**

retreat VB **1** INTR of a military force, army, etc: to move back or away from the enemy or retire after defeat. **2** INTR to retire or withdraw to a place of safety or seclusion. **3** INTR to recede.
➤ N **1** MIL a signal to retreat, esp one given on a bugle. **2** a place of privacy, safety or seclusion. **3 a** a period of retirement or withdrawal from the world, esp for prayer; **b** a place for this.

retrench VB, TR & INTR to economize; to reduce (expenses). ■ **retrenchment** N.

retrial N a second trial for the same offence.

retribution N vengeance. ■ **retributive** ADJ.

retrieve VB **1** to get or bring back again. **2** to rescue or save: **retrieve the situation**. **3** COMP to recover (information) from storage in a computer memory. **4** to remember or recall to mind. **5** TR & INTR of a dog: to search for and bring back (shot game, or a thrown ball, stick, etc). ■ **retrievable** ADJ. ■ **retrieval** N.

retro ADJ imitating a style from the past.

retroactive ADJ applying to or affecting things from a date in the past: **retroactive legislation**. ■ **retroactively** ADV.

retrograde ADJ being, tending towards or causing a less desirable state.

retrogress VB, INTR **1** to go back to an earlier, worse or less advanced condition or state; to deteriorate. **2** to recede or move backwards. ■ **retrogression** N. ■ **retrogressive** ADJ.

retrospect N.
◆ **in retrospect** with the benefit of hindsight.

retrospective ADJ **1** of a law, etc: applying to the past as well as to the future. **2** of an art exhibition, etc: showing how the work of the artist, etc has developed over their career. **3** inclined to look back on past events.
➤ N a retrospective exhibition, etc.

retroussé ADJ of a nose: turned up at the end.

return VB **1** INTR to come or go back again to a former place, state or owner, etc. **2** to give,

send, put back, etc in a former position. **3** INTR to come back to in thought or speech. **4** to repay: **return the compliment**. **5** TR & INTR to answer or reply. **6** to report or state officially or formally. **7** to earn or produce (profit, interest, etc). **8** to elect as a Member of Parliament. **9** LAW of a jury: to deliver (a verdict).
➤ N **1** an act of coming back from a place, state, etc. **2** an act of returning something, esp to its former place, state, ownership, etc. **3** something returned. **4** profit from work, a business or investment. **5** a statement of income and allowances, used for calculating tax. **6** (usu **returns**) a statement of the votes polled in an election. **7** BRIT (in full **return ticket**) a ticket entitling a passenger to travel to a place and back to the starting point. ■ **returnable** ADJ.
◆ **in return** in exchange; in reply.

returning officer N an official in charge of running an election in a constituency, counting the votes and declaring the result.

reunion N **1** a meeting of people (eg, relatives, friends, former colleagues, etc) who have not met for some time. **2** an act of reuniting or state of being reunited.

reunite VB, TR & INTR to bring or come together again after being separated.

Rev or **Revd** ABBREV Reverend.

rev N, COLLOQ (often **revs**) the number of revolutions of an engine per minute.
➤ VB (-**vv**-) COLLOQ (also **rev up**) **1** to increase the speed of revolution of (a car engine, etc). **2** INTR of an engine or vehicle: to run faster.

revalue VB to adjust the exchange rate of (a currency). ■ **revaluation** N.

revamp VB to revise, renovate or improve.

reveal VB **1** to make (a secret, etc) known. **2** to show or allow to be seen. **3** of a deity: to make known through divine inspiration or by supernatural means. ■ **revealing** ADJ.

reveille N a military wake-up call, usu by a drum or bugle.

revel VB (-**ll**-) INTR to have fun in a lively way.
➤ N (usu **revels**) an occasion of revelling.
■ **reveller** N. ■ **revelry** N (-**ies**).

◆ **revel in sth** to take great delight in it.

revelation N **1** an act of revealing, showing or disclosing something previously unknown or unexpected. **2** something revealed or disclosed in this way.

revenge N **1** malicious injury, harm or wrong done in return for injury, harm or wrong received. **2** something that is done as a means of returning like injury, harm, etc. **3** the desire to do such injury, harm, etc.
➤ VB **1** to do similar injury, harm, etc in return for injury, harm, etc received. **2** to take revenge on behalf of oneself or someone else.

revengeful ADJ keen for or bent on revenge.

revenue N **1** money from a property, shares, etc. **2** money raised by the government of a country or state from taxes, etc.

reverberate VB **1** INTR of a sound, light, heat, etc: to be echoed, repeated or reflected repeatedly. **2** to echo, repeat or reflect (a sound, light, etc) repeatedly. **3** INTR of a story, scandal, etc: to circulate or be repeated many times. ■ **reverberation** N.

revere VB to feel or show great respect for.

reverence N **1** great respect or veneration. **2** a feeling of, such respect.

reverend ADJ deserving reverence.
➤ N, COLLOQ a member of the clergy.

reverent ADJ showing or feeling reverence.

reverential ADJ reverent or very respectful.

reverie N a state of dreamy and absented-minded thought.

revers N (PL **revers**) any part of a garment that is turned back, esp a lapel.

reverse VB **1** TR & INTR to move or make something move backwards or in an opposite direction: **He reversed the car**. **2** to run (a mechanism, piece of machinery, etc) backwards or in the opposite direction from normal. **3** to put or arrange in an opposite position, state, order, etc. **4** to turn (an item of clothing, etc) inside out. **5** to change (a policy, decision, etc) to the exact opposite.

➣ N **1** the opposite or contrary of something. **2** a change to an opposite or contrary position, direction, state, etc. **3** the back or rear side of something, eg, the back cover of a book. **4** the side of a coin, medal, note, etc that has a secondary design on it. **5** a mechanism, esp a car gear, which makes a vehicle, piece of machinery, etc move or operate in a backwards direction. ■ **reversal** N. ■ **reversible** ADJ.

reversion N **1** a return to an earlier state, belief, etc. **2** BIOL a return to an earlier ancestral type.

revert VB (usu **revert to**) **1** to return (to something in thought or conversation). **2** to return (to a former and usu worse state, etc).

review N **1** an act of examining, reviewing or revising, or the state of being examined, reviewed or revised. **2** a general survey of a particular subject, situation, etc. **3** a survey of the past and past events. **4** a critical report of a recent book, play, film, etc, in a newspaper, etc. **5** a magazine or newspaper, or a section of one, with reviews of books, etc and often feature articles on the arts. **6** a re-examination. **7** MIL a formal or official inspection of troops, ships, etc. **8** LAW a re-examination of a case. ➣ VB **1** to see or view again. **2** to examine or go over, esp critically or formally. **3** to look back on and examine (events in the past). **4** INTR to write reviews (of books, plays, films, etc), esp professionally. **5** MIL to inspect (troops, ships, etc), esp formally or officially. **6** LAW to re-examine (a case). ■ **reviewer** N.

revile VB **1** to abuse or criticize scornfully. **2** INTR to speak scornfully. ■ **reviler** N.

revise VB **1** to examine or re-examine (eg, a text, book, etc) in order to identify and correct faults, make improvements, etc. **2** TR & INTR to study or look at (a subject, notes, etc) again, esp in preparation for an examination. **3** to reconsider or amend (eg, an opinion, etc). ■ **revisory** ADJ.

revision N **1** an act or the result of revising, or the process of revising. **2** a revised book, edition, article, etc.

revitalize or **-ise** VB to give new life or energy to.

revival N **1** an act or the process of reviving or the state of being revived. **2** a renewed interest, esp in old customs, fashions, styles, etc. **3** a new production or performance, esp of an old play.

revivalism N the promotion of renewed religious faith. ■ **revivalist** N.

revive VB, TR & INTR **1** to come or bring back to consciousness, strength, health, vitality, etc. **2** to come or bring back into use or fashion, etc. **3** to perform (an old play) again.

revoke VB to cancel (a will, agreement, etc). ■ **revocation** N.

revolt VB **1** INTR to rebel or rise up (against a government, authority, etc). **2** TR & INTR to feel, or provoke a feeling of loathing or revulsion. ➣ N a rebellion or uprising.

revolting ADJ causing a feeling of disgust, loathing, etc; nauseating. ■ **revoltingly** ADV.

revolution N **1** the overthrow of a government or system. **2** any complete economic, social, etc change: the Industrial Revolution. **3 a** an act or the process of turning about an axis; **b** a single turn about an axis; **c** the time taken to make one such movement. **4** a cycle of events.

revolutionary ADJ **1** relating to or causing a revolution. **2** completely new or different. ➣ N (**-ies**) someone who takes part in or is in favour of a political, social, etc revolution.

revolutionize or **-ise** VB to bring about a great change: Computers have revolutionized many businesses.

revolve VB **1** TR & INTR to move or turn, or cause to move or turn, in a circle around a central point; to rotate. **2** INTR (usu **revolve around** or **about**) to have as a centre, focus or main point. **3** INTR to occur in cycles or at regular intervals. **4** to consider: revolve the ideas in her head. ■ **revolving** ADJ.

revolver N a pistol with a revolving cylinder holding several bullets.

revue N a humorous theatrical show, that includes songs, sketches, etc.

revulsion N **1** a feeling of complete disgust, distaste or repugnance. **2** a sudden and often violent change of feeling, esp from love to hate.

reward N **1** something given or received in return for a service rendered, good behaviour, etc. **2** a sum of money offered for finding or helping to find a criminal, stolen or lost property, etc. **3** something given or received in return for a good or evil deed, etc.
➤ VB to give as a show of gratitude or in recompense. ■ **rewarding** N.

rewind VB (*rewound*) to wind (thread, tape, film, etc) back.

rewire VB to fit (a house, etc) with new electrical wiring.

reword VB to express in different words.

rework VB **1** to alter or refashion something in order to use it again. **2** to revise or rewrite something. ■ **reworking** N.

rewrite VB to write something again or in different words.
➤ N **1** the action of rewriting. **2** something that is rewritten.

rhapsodize or **-ise** VB, TR & INTR to speak or write with great enthusiasm or emotion.

rhapsody N (*-ies*) **1** MUS a piece of music, emotional in character and usu written to suggest an improvisation. **2** an exaggeratedly enthusiastic and highly emotional speech, piece of writing, etc. ■ **rhapsodic** ADJ.

rhea N a S American flightless bird.

rhetoric N the art of using language elegantly, effectively or persuasively. ■ **rhetorician** N.

rhetorical ADJ **1** relating to or using rhetoric. **2** persuasive or insincere in style.

rhetorical question N a question that is asked for effect rather than to gain information.

rheum N a watery mucous discharge from the nose or eyes. ■ **rheumy** ADJ.

rheumatic ADJ **1** relating to, like or caused by rheumatism. **2** affected with rheumatism.
➤ N **1** someone who suffers from rheumatism. **2** (**rheumatics**) COLLOQ rheumatism or pain caused by it. ■ **rheumatically** ADV.

rheumatism N a disease causing painful swelling of the joints, muscles and fibrous tissues. ■ **rheumatoid** ADJ.

rhinestone N an imitation diamond.

rhino N (*rhinos* or *rhino*) short form of **rhinoceros**.

rhinoceros N (*rhinoceroses* or *rhinoceros*) a large herbivorous mammal with very thick skin and either one or two horns on its snout.

rhizome N, BOT a thick horizontal underground stem which produces both roots and shoots.

rhododendron N (*-drons* or *-dra*) a widely cultivated shrub with large colourful flowers.

rhomboid N a quadrilateral where only the opposite sides and angles are equal.

rhombus N (*-buses* or *-bi*) **1** GEOM a quadrilateral with four equal sides and two angles greater than and two angles smaller than a right angle. **2** a lozenge or diamond shape, or an object with this shape.

rhubarb N a plant with large poisonous leaves or its long fleshy edible leaf stalks.

rhumba see **rumba**

rhyme N **1** a pattern of words which have the same final sounds at the ends of lines in a poem. **2** the use of such patterns in poetry, etc. **3** a word which has the same final sound as another. **4** a short verse written in rhyme.
➤ VB **1** INTR of words: to have the same final sound. **2** to use (a word) as a rhyme for another. **3** INTR to write using rhymes. **4** to put (a story, etc) into rhyme.
◆ **without rhyme or reason** lacking sense, reason or logic.

rhythm N **1** a regularly repeated pattern, movement, beat, sequence of events, etc. **2 a** the regular arrangement of stress, notes of different lengths, and pauses in a piece of music; **b** a particular pattern of stress, notes, etc in music: **tango rhythm**. **3** a regular arrangement of sounds, and of stressed and unstressed syllables, giving a sense or feeling of movement. **4** ability to sing, speak, move, etc rhythmically. ■ **rhythmic** or **rhythmical** ADJ.

rhythm and blues SING N, MUS a style of popular music combining blues elements with more lively rhythms.

rib[1] N 1 in vertebrates: any of the curved paired bones that articulates with the spine, forming the chest wall and protecting the heart, lungs, etc. 2 a cut of meat containing one or more ribs. 3 a part or section of an object or structure that resembles a rib in form or function.
➤ VB (*-bb-*) 1 to provide, support or enclose (an object, structure, etc) with ribs. 2 KNITTING to knit ribs or in ribs. ■ **ribbed** ADJ. ■ **ribbing** N.

rib[2] VB (*-bb-*) COLLOQ to tease; to mock gently.

ribald ADJ of language, a speaker, humour, etc: humorous in an obscene, vulgar or indecently disrespectful way. ■ **ribaldry** N.

riband or **ribband** N a ribbon, esp as a prize in sport, etc.

ribbon N 1 a a fine, usu coloured, material such as silk, etc, formed into a long narrow strip or band; **b** a strip of such material used for decorating clothes, tying hair, parcels, etc. 2 a long narrow strip of anything: **a typewriter ribbon**.

ribcage N the chest wall, formed by the ribs.

ribonucleic acid N, BIOCHEM a nucleic acid, present in all living cells, that plays an important part in the synthesis of proteins.

rice N 1 an important cereal plant of the grassfamily, native to SE Asia. 2 its edible starchy seeds used as food.

rich ADJ 1 having a lot of money, property or possessions. 2 of decoration, furnishings, etc: luxurious, costly and elaborate: **rich clothes**. 3 high in value or quality: **a rich harvest**. 4 (**rich in** or **with**) abundant with (esp a natural resource): **rich in minerals**. 5 of soil, a region, etc: very productive. 6 of colour, sound, smell, etc: vivid and intense; deep: **rich red**. 7 **a** of food: heavily seasoned, strongly flavoured; **b** of food or a diet: containing a lot of fat, oil or dried fruit. 8 of a remark, suggestion, event, etc: ridiculous: **That's rich, coming from you!** 9 of the mixture in an internal combustion engine: with a high proportion of fuel to air.

■ **richly** ADV. ■ **richness** N.

riches PL N wealth in general, or a particular form of abundance or wealth: **family riches** • **architectural riches**.

rick[1] N a stack or heap, eg, of hay, corn, etc.

rick[2] VB to sprain or wrench (one's neck, back, etc).

rickets SING OR PL N a disease, esp of children, caused by vitamin D deficiency.

rickety ADJ unsteady and likely to collapse.

rickshaw or **ricksha** N a small two-wheeled hooded carriage, usu drawn by a person on foot.

ricochet VB, INTR (*-ted* or *-tt-*, *-ting* or *-tt-*) of an object, esp a bullet, projectile, etc: to hit or glance off a surface and rebound.

ricotta N a soft white Italian curd cheese.

rid VB (*rid* or (ARCHAIC) *-dd-*) (**rid of**) to free (someone, oneself, something or somewhere) from (something unwanted).

riddance N the act of getting rid of something. ◆ **good riddance** a welcome relief from someone or something undesirable or unwanted.

riddle[1] N 1 a short and usu humorous puzzle, often in the form of a question, which can only be solved or understood using ingenuity. 2 a person, thing or fact that is puzzling or difficult to understand.

riddle[2] N a large coarse sieve for sifting soil, grain, etc.
➤ VB 1 to pass through a riddle. 2 (usu **riddle with**) to pierce with many holes. 3 (usu **riddle with**) to spread through; to fill.

ride VB (*rode, ridden*) 1 to sit, usu astride, on and control the movements of (esp a horse, bicycle, motorbike, etc). 2 INTR to travel or be carried (on a horse, bicycle, etc or in a car, train or other vehicle). 3 chiefly N AMER to travel on (a vehicle). 4 INTR to go on horseback, esp regularly. 5 to ride (a horse) in a race. 6 to move across or be carried over (eg, the sea, sky, etc). 7 of a ship: **a** INTR to float at anchor; **b** to be

attached to (an anchor). **8** to travel by horse, car, etc: **rode across the desert on camels. 9** to bend before (a blow, punch, etc) to reduce its impact. **10** to infest or dominate: **ridden with remorse**.
➤ N **1 a** a journey or certain distance covered on horseback, on a bicycle or in a vehicle; **b** the duration of this: **a long ride home. 2** a horse, vehicle, etc as a means of transport. **3** an experience or series of events of a specified nature: **a rough ride. 4** esp N AMER a lift. **5** the type of movement a vehicle, etc gives: **a very smooth ride. 6** a path or track, esp one through a wood or across an area of countryside, reserved for horseback riding.
◆ **ride on sth** to depend completely upon it: It all rides on his answer.
◆ **ride out** to come through (a difficult period, situation, etc) successfully: **ride out the storm**.
◆ **take sb for a ride** COLLOQ to cheat them.

rider N **1** someone who rides. **2** an extra or subsequent clause, etc added to a document.

ridge N **1** a strip of ground raised either side of a ploughed furrow. **2** any long narrow raised area on an otherwise flat surface. **3** the top edge of something where two upward sloping surfaces meet, eg, on a roof. **4** a long narrow strip of relatively high ground with steep slopes on either side. **5** METEOROL a long narrow area of high atmospheric pressure. ■ **ridged** ADJ.

ridgepole N a horizontal pole at the top of a tent.

ridicule N contemptuous mockery or derision.
➤ VB to subject or expose (someone or something) to ridicule.

ridiculous ADJ **1** deserving or provoking ridicule. **2** absurd or unreasonable.
■ **ridiculously** ADV. ■ **ridiculousness** N.

rife ADJ **1** very common or numerous. **2** (**rife with**) teeming in (usu something bad or undesirable).

riff N, POP MUSIC a short passage of music played repeatedly.

riffle VB **1** TR & INTR (often **riffle through**) to turn (pages) rapidly. **2** to shuffle (playing-cards) by

dividing the pack into two equal piles and allowing them to fall together alternately.
➤ N an act or instance of riffling.

riff-raff N undesirable people.

rifle[1] N **1** a large gun with a long barrel with a spiral groove on the inside, usu fired from the shoulder. **2** (usu **rifles**) riflemen.
➤ VB to cut spiral grooves in (a gun or its barrel).

rifle[2] VB **1** TR & INTR (often **rifle through**) to search (through a house, safe, drawer, etc). **2** to steal and take away.

rift N **1** a split or crack, esp one in the earth or in rock. **2** a break in friendly relations.

rig VB (**-gg-**) **1** NAUT to fit (a ship, masts, etc) with ropes, sails and rigging. **2** AERONAUTICS to position correctly the various parts and components of (an aircraft, etc). **3** to control or manipulate for dishonest purposes, or for personal profit or advantage.
➤ N **1** NAUT the particular arrangement of sails, ropes and masts on a ship. **2** an oil rig. **3** gear or equipment, esp for a specific task. **4** N AMER a lorry or truck.
◆ **rig sth up** to build or prepare it, esp hastily and with whatever material is available.

rigging N the system of ropes, wires, etc which support and control a ship's masts and sails.

right ADJ **1** indicating, relating or referring to, or on, the side facing east from the point of view of someone or something facing north. **2** of a part of the body: on or towards the right side. **3** of an article of clothing, etc: worn on the right hand, foot, etc. **4 a** on, towards or close to an observer's right; **b** on a stage: on or towards the performers' right. **5** of a river bank: on the right side of a person facing downstream. **6** correct; true. **7** of a clock or watch: showing the correct time. **8** suitable; appropriate; proper. **9** most appropriate or favourable. **10** in a correct, proper or satisfactory state or condition. **11** sound or stable: **not in his right mind. 12** morally correct or good. **13** legally correct or good. **14** on the side of a fabric, garment, etc which is intended to be seen: **turn the dress right side out. 15** conservative; right-wing. **16** socially acceptable: **know all the**

right people. **17** BRIT COLLOQ complete; utter; real: **a right mess.**
➤ ADV **1** on or towards the right side.
2 correctly; properly; satisfactorily. **3** exactly or precisely: **It happened right there.**
4 immediately: **He'll be right over.**
5 completely; absolutely: **It went right out of my mind. 6** all the way: **went right through him.**
7 of movement, a direction, etc: straight; without deviating from a straight line: **right to the top.**
8 towards or on the right side: **He looked right before crossing the road. 9** favourably or satisfactorily: **It turned out right in the end.**
10 esp in religious titles: most; very: **right reverend.**
➤ N **1** (often **rights**) a power, privilege, title, etc. **2** (often **rights**) a just or legal claim.
3 fairness; truth; justice. **4** something that is correct, good or just: **the rights and wrongs of the case. 5** the political party, or a group of people within a party, etc which has the most conservative views. **6** the right side, part or direction of something. **7** BOXING **a** the right hand: **He was lethal with his right; b** a punch with the right hand. **8** a glove, shoe, etc worn on the right hand or foot: **Can I try on the right?**
9 (**rights**) the legal permission to print, publish, film, etc a book.
➤ VB **1** TR & INTR to put or come back to the correct or normal, esp upright, position: **They soon righted the boat. 2** to avenge or compensate for (some wrong done). **3** to correct. **4** to put in order or return to order.
➤ EXCLAM expressing agreement, assent or readiness. ■ **rightness** N.
◆ **by right** or **rights** rightfully; properly.
◆ **in the right** with justice, etc on one's side.
◆ **put** or **set right** or **to rights** to make correct or proper.
◆ **right away** immediately.

right angle N an angle of 90°, formed by two lines which are perpendicular to each other. ■ **right-angled** ADJ.

righteous ADJ **1** of a person: virtuous, free from sin or guilt. **2** of an action: morally good.
3 justifiable morally: **righteous indignation.**
■ **righteously** ADV. ■ **righteousness** N.

rightful ADJ **1** having a legally just claim. **2** held

legally. **3** fair; just; equitable.

rightism N **1** the political opinions of conservatives or the right. **2** support for and promotion of this. ■ **rightist** N, ADJ.

rightly ADV **1** correctly. **2** justly. **3** fairly; properly. **4** with good reason; justifiably.

right-on ADJ, SLANG **1** excellent. **2** up to date or politically correct.

right wing N **1** the more conservative members of a group or political party. **2** SPORT **a** the extreme right side of a pitch or team in a field game; **b** (also **right-winger**) the member of a team who plays in this position.
3 the right side of an army.

rigid ADJ **1** completely stiff and inflexible. **2** of a person: strictly and inflexibly adhering to ideas, opinions, rules, etc. ■ **rigidity** N. ■ **rigidly** ADV. ■ **rigidness** N.

rigmarole N **1** a long and complicated procedure. **2** a long rambling or confused statement or speech.

rigor mortis N a stiffening of the body soon after death.

rigorous ADJ **1** showing or having rigour; strict; harsh; severe. **2** strictly accurate.

rigour or (US) **rigor** N **1** stiffness; hardness.
2 strictness or severity of temper, behaviour or judgement. **3** strict enforcement of rules or the law. **4** (usu **rigours**) of a particular situation or circumstances, eg, of weather or climate: harshness or severity.

rig-out N a set of clothes.

rile VB to anger or annoy.

rill N a small stream or brook.

rim N **1** a raised edge or border, esp of something curved or circular. **2** the outer circular edge of a wheel to which the tyre is attached. ■ **rimless** ADJ. ■ **rimmed** ADJ.

rime[1] N thick white frost formed esp from fog.
➤ VB to cover with rime. ■ **rimy** ADJ (**-ier, -iest**).

rime[2] ARCHAIC variant of **rhyme**

rind N a thick hard outer layer or covering on

fruit, cheese or bacon. ■ **rindless** ADJ.

ring[1] N 1 a small circle of gold, silver, etc, worn on the finger. 2 a circle of metal, wood, plastic, etc, for holding, keeping in place, connecting, hanging, etc. 3 any object, mark or figure which is circular in shape. 4 a circular course or route. 5 a group of people or things arranged in a circle. 6 an enclosed and usu circular area in which circus acts are performed. 7 a square area on a platform, marked off by ropes, where boxers or wrestlers fight. 8 (**the ring**) boxing as a profession. 9 an enclosure for bookmakers at a race-course. 10 at agricultural shows, etc: an enclosure where cattle, horses, etc are paraded or exhibited for auction. 11 a group of people who act together: **a drugs ring**.
➤ VB 1 to make, form, draw, etc a ring round (something) or to form into a ring. 2 to cut into rings. 3 to put a ring on (a bird's leg) as a means of identifying it. ■ **ringed** ADJ.
◆ **make** or **run rings round sb** COLLOQ to beat them or be much better than them.

ring[2] VB (*rang, rung*) 1 a to sound (a bell, etc); b INTR of a bell: to sound. 2 a to make (a metal object, etc) give a resonant bell-like sound by striking it; b INTR of a metal object, etc: to sound in this way when struck. 3 INTR of a large building, etc: to resound; to be filled with a particular sound: **The theatre rang with laughter and applause.** 4 INTR of a sound or noise: to resound; to re-echo: **Applause rang round the theatre.** 5 INTR (usu **ring out**) to make a sudden clear loud sound: **Shots rang out.** 6 INTR to sound repeatedly; to resound: **Her criticisms rang in his ears.** 7 INTR of the ears: to be filled with a buzzing, humming or ringing sensation or sound. 8 (also **ring up**) chiefly BRIT to call by telephone.
➤ N 1 an act of ringing a bell. 2 an act or sound of ringing. 3 a clear resonant sound of a bell, etc. 4 BRIT a telephone call. 5 a suggestion or impression: **a ring of truth.** ■ **ringing** N, ADJ.
◆ **ring a bell** to stir a vague memory.
◆ **ring sb back** to telephone them again.
◆ **ring off** to end a telephone call.
◆ **ring the changes** to vary the way something is done, used, said, etc.
◆ **ring up** to record (the price of an item sold,

etc) on a cash register.

ringer N 1 someone or something that rings a bell, etc. 2 (also **dead ringer**) someone or something that is almost identical to another.

ringleader N a person who leads or incites a group, esp in wrongdoing.

ringlet N a long spiral curl of hair.

ringmaster N a person who presents and is in charge of performances in a circus ring.

ring pull N a metal ring on a can, etc, which, when pulled, breaks a seal.

ring road N, BRIT a road that bypasses a town centre and so keeps it relatively free of traffic.

ringside N the seating area immediately next to a boxing ring, circus ring, etc.

ringworm N a fungal infection that causes dry, red, itchy patches on the skin.

rink N 1 a an area of ice prepared for skating, curling or ice-hockey; b a building or enclosure containing this. 2 a an area of smooth floor for roller-skating; b a building or enclosure containing this. 3 BOWLS, CURLING a a strip of grass or ice allotted to a team or set of players in bowling and curling; b a team or set of players using such a strip of grass or ice.

rinse VB 1 to wash (soap, detergent, etc) out of (clothes, hair, dishes, etc) with clean water. 2 to remove (traces of dirt, etc) from by dipping in clean water, usu without soap. 3 (also **rinse out**) to clean or freshen (a cup, one's mouth, etc) with a swirl of water.
➤ N 1 an act or instance or the process of rinsing. 2 liquid used for rinsing. 3 a temporary tint for the hair.

riot N 1 a noisy public disturbance or disorder. 2 uncontrolled or wild revelry and feasting. 3 a striking display.
➤ VB, INTR 1 to take part in a riot. 2 to take part in boisterous revelry. ■ **rioter** N.
◆ **read the riot act** to give an angry warning.
◆ **run riot** 1 to act, speak, etc in a wild or unrestrained way. 2 of plants: to grow profusely or in an uncontrolled way.

riotous ADJ **1** participating in, likely to start, or like, a riot. **2** very active, noisy, cheerful and wild: *a riotous party*. **3** filled with wild revelry, parties, etc: *riotous living*. ■ **riotously** ADV.

RIP ABBREV: *requiescat* (or *requiescant*) *in pace* (Latin), may he, she (or they) rest in peace.

rip VB (*-pp-*) **1** TR & INTR to tear or come apart violently or roughly. **2** INTR, COLLOQ to rush along without restraint. **3 a** to make (a hole, etc) by tearing roughly; **b** to make a long tear.
➤ N **1** a violent or rough tear or split. **2** an unrestrained rush.
 ◆ **rip sb off** to steal from or exploit them.
 ◆ **rip sth up** to shred or tear it into pieces.

riparian ADJ relating to a riverbank.

ripcord N a cord which, when pulled, releases a parachute from its pack.

ripe ADJ **1** of fruit, grain, etc: fully matured and ready to be picked or harvested and eaten. **2** of cheese, wine, etc: having been allowed to age to develop a full flavour. **3** of a flavour or taste: rich or strong. **4** of a person's age: very advanced. ■ **ripeness** N.
 ◆ **ripe for sth** suitable or appropriate for a particular action or purpose: *ripe for reform*.

ripen VB, TR & INTR to make or become ripe.

rip-off N an act or instance of stealing, cheating or defrauding.

riposte N a quick sharp reply; a retort.
➤ VB, INTR to deliver a riposte.

ripple N **1** a slight wave or undulation, or a series of these, on the surface of water. **2** a similar wavy appearance or motion in material, hair, etc. **3** of laughter or applause: a sound that rises and falls quickly and gently.
➤ VB **1 a** to ruffle or agitate the surface of (water, etc); **b** to mark with ripples, or form ripples in (a surface, material, etc). **2** INTR to form ripples or move with an undulating motion. **3** INTR of a sound: to rise and fall quickly and gently. ■ **ripply** ADJ.

rip-roaring ADJ, COLLOQ wild, noisy and exciting. ■ **rip-roaringly** ADV.

rise VB (*rose, risen*) INTR **1** to get or stand up, from a sitting, etc position. **2** to get up from bed. **3** to move upwards. **4** to increase in size, amount, volume, strength, degree, intensity, etc. **5** of the Sun, Moon, planets, etc: to appear above the horizon. **6** to stretch or slope upwards. **7** to rebel. **8** to move from a lower position, rank, level, etc to a higher one. **9** to begin or originate: *a river that rises in the mountains*. **10** of a person's spirits: to become more cheerful. **11** of an animal's fur, a person's hair, etc: to become straight and stiff, esp from fear or anger. **12** of a committee, court, parliament, etc: to finish a session; to adjourn. **13** to come back to life. **14** of fish: to come to the surface of the water. **15** of birds: to fly up from the ground, etc. **16** of dough, a cake, etc: to swell up; to increase in volume. **17** to be built. **18** (usu **rise to**) to respond (to provocation, criticism, etc).
➤ N **1** an act of rising. **2** an increase in size, amount, volume, strength, status, rank, etc. **3** BRIT an increase in salary. **4** a piece of rising ground; a slope or hill. **5** a beginning or origin. **6** the vertical height of a step or flight of stairs.
 ◆ **give rise to sth** to cause it or bring it about.
 ◆ **rise above sth** to remain unaffected by teasing, provocation, criticism, etc.

riser N **1** someone who gets out of bed, usu at a specified time: *a late riser*. **2** a vertical part between the horizontal steps of a staircase.

risible ADJ laughable; ludicrous.

rising N a rebellion.
➤ ADJ **1** moving or sloping upwards; getting higher. **2** approaching greater status, reputation or importance.

rising damp N, BRIT wetness which rises up through the bricks or stones of a wall.

risk N **1** the chance or possibility of suffering loss, injury, damage, etc; danger. **2** someone or something likely to cause loss, injury, etc.
➤ VB **1** to expose (someone or something) to risk. **2** to act in spite of (something unfortunate): *risked being caught*. ■ **risky** ADJ.

risotto N an Italian dish of rice cooked in stock with meat or seafood, onions, tomatoes, etc.

risqué ADJ of a story, joke, etc: rather rude.

rissole N a small fried cake or ball of chopped meat coated in breadcrumbs.

rite N **1** a formal ceremony, esp a religious one. **2** the required words or actions for such a ceremony. **3** a body of such ceremonies which are characteristic of a particular church.

rite of passage N (*rites of passage*) a ritual event or ceremony marking an important transition in a person's life.

ritual N **1** a set order or words used in a religious ceremony. **2** a series of actions performed regularly, habitually, etc. ➤ ADJ relating to, like or used for religious, social or other rites or ritual. ■ **ritualize** or **-ise** VB.

ritualism N excessive belief in the importance of, or excessive practice of, ritual. ■ **ritualist** N. ■ **ritualistic** ADJ.

ritzy ADJ (*-ier, -iest*) COLLOQ **1** very smart and elegant. **2** ostentatiously rich; flashy.

rival N **1** a person or group of people competing with another. **2** someone or something that is comparable with or equals another in quality, ability, etc. ➤ VB (*-ll-*; US *-l-*) **1** to try to gain the same objective as; to be in competition with. **2** to try to equal or be better than. **3** to equal or be comparable with, in terms of quality, ability, etc. ■ **rivalry** N (*-ies*).

rive VB (PA P *rived* or *riven*) POETIC, ARCHAIC **1** to tear or tear apart: **a family riven by feuds**. **2** INTR to split.

river N **1** a large body of flowing water, emptying into a lake or the sea. **2** an abundant or plentiful stream or flow: **cried rivers**.

riverside N an area along a river.

rivet N a metal pin or bolt for joining pieces of metal, etc. ➤ VB **1** to fasten (pieces of metal, etc) with a rivet. **2** to fix securely. **3** to attract and hold (attention, etc). **4** to render motionless, esp with fascination, fear, etc: **I was riveted to the spot**.

riveting ADJ fascinating; enthralling.

riviera N a coastal area with a warm climate.

rivulet N a small river or stream.

RNA ABBREV, BIOCHEM ribonucleic acid.

roach¹ N (*roaches* or *roach*) a silvery freshwater fish of the carp family.

roach² N, N AMER COLLOQ a cockroach.

road N **1 a** an open way, usu specially surfaced or paved, for people, vehicles or animals to travel on; **b** the part of this designated for the use of vehicles. **2** a route or course: **the road to ruin**. **3** (usu **roads**) a relatively sheltered area of water near the shore where ships may be anchored.
◆ **one for the road** a final, usu alcoholic, drink before leaving.
◆ **on the road** travelling from place to place.

road-hog N, COLLOQ an aggressive, selfish or reckless driver.

roadhouse N a public house or inn at the side of a major road.

roadie N, COLLOQ a person who helps move and organize the instruments and equipment for a rock or pop group, esp on tour.

road rage N uncontrolled anger or aggression between road users.

roadside N the area beside or along a road.

roadster N, orig US, OLD USE an open sports car for two people.

road test N **1** a test of a vehicle's performance and roadworthiness. **2** a practical test of a product, etc. ➤ VB (**road-test**) **1** to test (a vehicle's roadworthiness). **2** to test out the practicalities, suitability, etc of (a new product, etc).

roadway N the part of a road used by traffic.

roadworks PL N the building or repairing of a road.

roadworthy ADJ of a vehicle: safe to be used on the road. ■ **roadworthiness** N.

roam VB **1** INTR to ramble or wander with no fixed purpose or direction. **2** to ramble or wander about, over, through, etc (a particular area) in no fixed direction: **roamed the streets**.

➢ N **1** the act of roaming. **2** a ramble.

roan ADJ of a horse, etc: having a coat that is flecked with many grey or white hairs.
➢ N a roan animal, esp a horse.

roar VB **1** INTR of a lion or other animal: to give a loud growling cry. **2** of a person: **a** INTR to give a deep loud cry, esp in anger, pain or exhilaration; **b** to say (something) with a deep loud cry, esp in anger. **3** INTR to laugh loudly and wildly. **4** INTR of cannons, busy traffic, wind or waves, a fiercely burning fire, etc: to make a deep loud reverberating sound. **5** to move or be moving very fast and noisily.
➢ N an act or the sound of roaring.

roast VB **1** to cook (meat, etc) by exposure to dry heat, esp in an oven. **2** to dry and brown by exposure to dry heat. **3** INTR to be cooked or dried and made brown by exposure to dry heat. **4** COLLOQ to criticize severely.
➢ N a piece of meat for roasting.

roasting ADJ extremely or uncomfortably hot.
➢ N a dose of severe criticism.

rob VB (-*bb*-) **1** to steal from (a person or place), esp by force or threats. **2** INTR to commit robbery. **3** to deprive of something expected as a right or due: **robbed her of her dignity.**
■ **robber** N.

robbery N (-*ies*) an act or instance or the process of robbing.

robe N **1** (often **robes**) a long loose flowing garment. **2** a dressing-gown or bathrobe.

robin N (also **robin redbreast**) a small brown European thrush with a red breast and white abdomen.

robot N **1** esp in science-fiction: a machine that vaguely resembles a human being and which can be programmed to carry out tasks. **2** an automatic machine that can be programmed to perform specific tasks. **3** COLLOQ someone who works efficiently but who lacks human warmth or sensitivity. ■ **robotic** ADJ.

robotics SING N the design, construction, operation and use of industrial robots.

robust ADJ **1** of a person: strong and healthy.

2 strongly constructed. **3** of exercise, etc: requiring strength and energy. **4** of language, humour, etc: rough, earthy, slightly risqué. **5** of wine, food, etc: with a full, rich quality.

roc N in Arabian legends: an enormous bird, strong enough to carry off an elephant.

rock¹ N **1** GEOL a loose or consolidated mass of one or more minerals that forms part of the Earth's crust, eg, granite, limestone, etc. **2** a large natural mass of this material. **3** a large stone or boulder. **4** someone or something that provides a firm foundation or support. **5** BRIT a hard sweet usu made in the form of long, cylindrical sticks.
◆ **on the rocks** COLLOQ **1** of a marriage: broken down; failed. **2** of an alcoholic drink: served with ice cubes.

rock² VB **1** TR & INTR to sway or make (something) sway gently backwards and forwards or from side to side: **rock the baby to sleep. 2** TR & INTR to move or make (something) shake violently. **3** COLLOQ to disturb, upset or shock. **4** INTR to dance to or play rock music.
➢ N **1** a rocking movement. **2** (also **rock music**) a form of popular music with a very strong beat, usu played on electronic instruments and derived from rock and roll. **3** rock and roll.
◆ **rock the boat** to destabilize or disturb something, esp unnecessarily or out of spite.

rock and roll or **rock 'n' roll** N a form of popular music deriving from jazz, country and western and blues music, with a lively jive beat and simple melodies.

rock bottom or **rock-bottom** N **1** bedrock. **2** COLLOQ the lowest possible level.
➢ ADJ, COLLOQ of prices: the lowest possible.

rocker N **1** a curved support on which a chair, cradle, etc rocks. **2** a rocking chair. **3** someone or something that rocks. **4** a device which is operated with a movement from side to side, backwards and forwards, or up and down. **5** a devotee of rock music or a rock musician.
◆ **off one's rocker** COLLOQ mad; crazy.

rockery N (-*ies*) a garden or an area in a garden with large stones placed in the earth, and rock plants growing between them.

rocket[1] N 1 a cylinder containing inflammable material, which, when ignited, is projected through the air, used for signalling, carrying a line to a ship in distress, in a firework display, etc. 2 a projectile or vehicle that obtains its thrust from a backward jet of hot gases. 3 a missile propelled by a rocket system.
➤ VB 1 to propel (a spacecraft, etc) by means of a rocket. 2 INTR to move, esp upwards, extremely quickly. 3 INTR of prices, etc: to rise very quickly. 4 to attack with rockets.

rocket[2] N a Mediterranean salad plant.

rocketry N the study and use of rockets.

rock plant N any plant, esp an alpine, which grows among rocks.

rock-solid ADJ very firmly fixed.

rocky[1] ADJ (-ier, -iest) 1 a full of rocks; b made of rock; c like rock. 2 COLLOQ full of problems and obstacles. ■ **rockiness** N.

rocky[2] ADJ (-ier, -iest) shaky; unstable; unsteady. ■ **rockily** ADV. ■ **rockiness** N.

rococo N (also **Rococo**) a style of architecture, decoration and furniture-making originating in France in the early 18c.
➤ ADJ relating to, or in, this style.

rod N 1 a long slender stick or bar of wood, metal, etc. 2 a stick used to beat people as a punishment. 3 a stick, wand or sceptre carried as a symbol of office or authority. 4 a fishing-rod. 5 in surveying: a unit of length equivalent to 5.5 yards (5.03 metres). ■ **rodlike** ADJ.

rodent N, ZOOL an animal, eg, a rat, mouse, squirrel, beaver, etc, with strong, continually growing incisors adapted for gnawing.

rodeo N 1 a round-up of cattle in order to count or brand them. 2 a place where cattle are assembled for this. 3 a show or contest of skills such as riding and lassoing.

roe[1] N 1 (also **hard roe**) the mass of mature eggs contained in the ovaries of a female fish. 2 (also **soft roe**) the testis of a male fish containing mature sperm.

roe[2] or **roe deer** N (roes or roe) a small European and Asian deer.

roentgen or **röntgen** N a former unit for measurement of X-rays or gamma rays.

rogation N, CHRISTIANITY (usu **rogations**) solemn supplication, esp in ceremonial form.

roger EXCLAM 1 in radio communications and signalling, etc: message received and understood. 2 COLLOQ I will; OK: Roger, will do.

rogue N 1 a dishonest or unscrupulous person. 2 someone, esp a child, who is playfully mischievous. 3 someone or something, esp a plant, which is not true to its type and is of inferior quality. 4 a vicious wild animal that lives apart from, or has been driven from, its herd. ■ **roguery** N (-ies).

roguish ADJ 1 characteristic of a rogue. 2 dishonest; unprincipled. 3 playfully mischievous: a roguish grin. ■ **roguishly** ADV.

roister VB, INTR to enjoy oneself noisily and boisterously. ■ **roisterer** N.

role or **rôle** N 1 an actor's part or character in a play, film, etc. 2 a function or task.

role model N someone whose life, behaviour, etc is taken as a good example to follow.

role-play or **role-playing** N assuming and performing of imaginary roles.

roll N 1 a cylinder or tube formed by rolling up anything flat. 2 a rolled document. 3 a small individually-baked portion of bread: a cheese roll. 4 a folded piece of pastry or cake with a filling: swiss roll • sausage roll. 5 a rolled mass of something: rolls of fat. 6 an undulation in a surface or of a landscape. 7 a an official list of names, eg, of school pupils, members of a club or people eligible to vote; b the total number registered on such a list. 8 an act of rolling. 9 a swaying or rolling movement, eg, in walking or dancing, or of a ship. 10 a long low prolonged sound: a roll of thunder. 11 (also **drum roll**) a series of quick beats on a drum. 12 a complete rotation around its longitudinal axis by an aircraft. 13 a roller or cylinder used to press, shape or apply something. 14 a an act or bout of rolling: Sparky had a roll in the sand;

b a gymnastic exercise similar to a somersault: *a backward roll*. **15** COLLOQ money, esp a wad of banknotes.

➤ VB **1** TR & INTR to move or make (something) move by turning over and over, as if on an axis, and often in a specified direction: *rolled the dice*. **2** TR & INTR to move or make (something) move on wheels, rollers, etc, or in a vehicle with wheels. **3** INTR (also **roll over**) of a person or animal, etc that is lying down: to turn with a rolling movement to face in another direction. **4** TR & INTR to move or make (something) move or flow steadily. **5** INTR to seem to move like or in waves: *a garden rolling down to the river*. **6** INTR of a ship: to sway or rock gently from side to side. **7** INTR to walk with a swaying movement. **8** TR & INTR to begin to operate or work: *the cameras rolled*. **9** TR & INTR to move or make (one's eyes) move in a circle. **10** TR & INTR to form, or form something, into a tube or cylinder by winding or being wound round and round. **11** (also **roll up**) **a** to wrap something by rolling: *rolled a cigarette*; **b** to curl around: *The hamster rolled up into a ball*. **12** (also **roll out**) to spread out or make flat or flatter: *rolled out the pastry*. **13** INTR to make a series of long low rumbling sounds. **14** to pronounce (esp an 'r' sound) with a trill.

◆ **roll by** of time: to pass steadily and often quickly: *The weeks rolled by*.
◆ **roll in** to come or arrive in large quantities.
◆ **roll on ...** may a specified event, time, etc come soon: *Roll on the weekend*.
◆ **roll up 1** COLLOQ to arrive. **2** to come in large numbers.

roll-call N an act or the process of calling out names from a list to check who is present.

roller N **1** a cylindrical object or machine used for flattening, spreading, printing, applying paint, etc. **2** a small cylinder on which hair is rolled to make it curl. **3** a long heavy sea wave.

rollercoaster N a raised railway with sharp curves and steep inclines and descents, ridden on for pleasure and excitement at funfairs, etc.

roller skate N a series of wheels attached to a framework which can be fitted onto a shoe, or a shoe with wheels attached to the sole.

➤ VB (**roller-skate**) INTR to move on roller skates.

rollicking ADJ boisterous; carefree.

rolling ADJ **1** of land, countryside, etc: with low, gentle hills and valleys. **2** COLLOQ extremely wealthy. **3** COLLOQ staggering with drunkenness. **4** of a contract: subject to review at regular intervals.

rolling-pin N a cylinder made of wood, marble, etc for flattening out pastry or dough.

rolling stock N the engines, wagons, coaches, etc used on a railway.

rolling stone N someone who leads a restless or unsettled life.

rollmop N a rolled fillet of raw pickled herring.

roll-on N a deodorant, etc contained in a bottle with a rotating ball at the top, by means of which the liquid is applied.

roll-on roll-off ADJ of a passenger ferry: with entrances at both the front and back of the ship, so that vehicles can be driven on through one entrance and off through the other.
➤ N a ship of this kind.

roll-top desk N a desk with a flexible cover of slats that may be rolled down when the desk is not in use.

roll-up N, BRIT COLLOQ a hand-rolled cigarette.

roly-poly ADJ round and podgy.
➤ N (*-ies*) suet pastry spread with jam and rolled up, then baked or steamed.

ROM ABBREV, COMP read-only memory, a permanent memory that does not allow data to be changed.

Roman ADJ **1** of Rome, or the Roman Empire. **2** (**roman**) ADJ, PRINTING of type: relating to or indicating the ordinary, upright kind most commonly used for printed material.
➤ N an inhabitant of Rome.

roman alphabet N the alphabet developed by the ancient Romans, now used for most European languages.

Roman candle N a firework that discharges

a succession of flaming sparks.

Roman Catholic ADJ of the Roman Catholic Church, the Christian church which recognizes the pope as its head.
➤ N a member of this church. ∎ **Roman Catholicism** N.

romance N 1 a love affair. 2 sentimentalized or idealized love. 3 the feelings or behaviour associated with romantic love. 4 a sentimental account, esp in writing or on film, of a love affair. 5 such writing, films, etc as a group or genre. 6 a fictitious story which deals with imaginary, adventurous and mysterious events, characters, places, etc. 7 a medieval verse narrative dealing with chivalry, highly idealized love and fantastic adventures.
➤ VB 1 to try to win someone's love. 2 INTR to talk or write extravagantly, romantically or fantastically. 3 INTR to lie. ∎ **romancing** N, ADJ.

Romanesque N a style of European architecture from the 9c to the 12c.
➤ ADJ in or relating to this style.

Roman nose N an aquiline nose.

Roman numeral N an upper case letter of the roman alphabet used to represent a cardinal number, eg, I = 1, V = 5, X = 10, etc.

romantic ADJ 1 characterized by or inclined towards sentimental and idealized love. 2 dealing with adventure, mystery and sentimentalized love: romantic fiction. 3 highly impractical or imaginative.
➤ N someone who has a romantic view of love, etc. ∎ **romantically** ADV.

romanticism or **Romanticism** N a late 18c and early 19c movement in the arts with an emphasis on feelings and emotions, often using imagery from nature. ∎ **romanticist** N.

romanticize or **-ise** VB 1 to make romantic. 2 TR & INTR to describe, think of or interpret an idealized and sometimes misleading way. 3 INTR to hold or indulge in romantic ideas or act in a romantic way. ∎ **romanticization** N.

Romany N (-ies) 1 a Gypsy. 2 the language spoken by Gypsies.
➤ ADJ of or relating to the Romanies.

Romeo N 1 an ardent young male lover. 2 a womanizer.

romp VB, INTR 1 to play or run about in a lively boisterous way. 2 (usu **romp through**) COLLOQ to complete (a task, etc) easily.
➤ N 1 boisterous playing or running about. 2 a light-hearted outing. 3 a swift pace.

rompers PL N (also **romper suit**) FORMERLY a baby's suit, with short-legged trousers.

rondeau N (-deaux) a poem of 13 or sometimes 10 lines with only two rhymes.

rondo N, MUS a piece of music with a recurring principal theme.

rood N 1 a cross or crucifix. 2 a former unit of area, equal to a quarter of an acre.

rood screen N in a church: an ornamental screen separating the choir from the nave.

roof N (roofs) 1 a the top outside covering of a building; b the structure at the top of a building that supports this. 2 a similar top or covering for a vehicle, etc. 3 the interior overhead surface of a room, vault, cave, etc. 4 a dwelling or home: two families under the same roof. 5 the top inner surface of something, eg, the mouth.
➤ VB 1 to cover or provide with a roof. 2 to serve as a roof or shelter for something.
∎ **roofed** ADJ. ∎ **roofless** ADJ.
◆ **go through the roof** COLLOQ of a price, etc: to become very expensive.
◆ **hit the roof** COLLOQ to become very angry.

roofing N materials for building a roof.

roof rack N a frame attached to the roof of a car or other vehicle for carrying luggage, etc.

roof tree N a beam along a roof's ridge.

rook¹ N a large, noisy crow-like bird.
➤ VB, COLLOQ 1 to cheat or defraud, esp at cards. 2 to charge (a customer) an excessive price.

rook² N, CHESS a castle.

rookery N (-ies) 1 a colony of rooks. 2 a colony of seals or sea birds, esp penguins.

rookie N, COLLOQ a new or raw recruit.

room N 1 an area within a building enclosed by

a ceiling, floor and walls. **2** sufficient or necessary space: **no room for all her books. 3** all the people present in a room: **The room suddenly became silent. 4** opportunity, scope or possibility: **room for improvement. 5** (**rooms**) rented lodgings, esp a set of rooms within a house, etc as an individual unit.

roommate N a person sharing a room or rooms with another or others.

room service N in a hotel: a facility for guests to be served food, drinks, etc in their rooms.

roomy ADJ (**-ier, -iest**) with plenty of room; spacious. ■ **roominess** N.

roost N a branch, etc on which a bird perches. ➢ VB, INTR of a bird: to settle on a roost.

rooster N, chiefly N AMER a farmyard cock.

root¹ N **1** a structure in a plant, usu beneath the soil surface, which anchors the plant in the soil and absorbs water and nutrients. **2** a part by which something, eg, a tooth, hair, nail, etc is attached to or embedded in something larger. **3** a basic cause, source or origin of something: **the root of the problem. 4** (**roots**) ancestry or family origins, etc: **go back to one's roots. 5** the basic element in a word to which affixes can be added, eg, **love** is the root of **lovable, lovely, lover** and **unloved. 6** MATH a factor of a quantity that, when multiplied by itself a specified number of times, produces that quantity, eg, 2 is the square root of 4 and the cube root of 8. ➢ VB **1** INTR to grow a root. **2** INTR to become firmly established. **3** (usu **root up** or **out**) to dig it up by the roots. **4** to fix with or as if with a root. **5** to provide with a root. ■ **rootless** ADJ.
◆ **root sth out** to remove it completely.
◆ **take** or **strike root 1** to grow roots. **2** to become firmly settled or established.

root² VB INTR **1** of pigs: to dig in the earth with the snout in search of food, truffles, etc. **2** INTR (usu **root around** or **about**) COLLOQ to look for by rummaging.

root³ VB, INTR (always **root for**) COLLOQ to cheer on or encourage (someone or something).

root canal N a passage through which the nerves and blood vessels of a tooth enter the pulp cavity.

rooted ADJ **1** fixed by or as if by roots. **2** firmly established.

rope N **1 a** strong thick cord made by twisting fibres of hemp, wire, etc together; **b** a length of this. **2** a number of objects, esp pearls or onions, strung together. **3** (**the rope**) **a** a hangman's noose; **b** execution by this means. **4** (**ropes**) the cords that mark off a boxing or wrestling ring, or the boundary of a cricket ground.
➢ VB **1** to tie, fasten or bind with rope or as if with rope. **2** (usu **rope in** or **off**) to enclose or divide with a rope. **3** MOUNTAINEERING to tie (climbers) together with a rope for safety. **4** chiefly N AMER to catch (an animal) with a rope.
◆ **know the ropes** to be thoroughly conversant with a particular thing.
◆ **rope in** or **into** to persuade to take part in some activity.

ropy or **ropey** ADJ (**-ier, -iest**) **1** rope–like. **2** COLLOQ poor in quality. **3** COLLOQ unwell.

rorqual N a baleen whale with a small dorsal fin near the tail.

rosaceous ADJ belonging to the rose family of plants or resembling a rose.

rosary N (**-ies**) **1** RC CHURCH a series of prayers with a set form and order. **2** RC CHURCH a string of beads used for counting such prayers.

rose N **1** a thorny shrub that produces large, often fragrant, flowers and berries known as hips. **2** a flower of this plant. **3** a flowering plant that superficially resembles a rose, eg, the Christmas rose. **4** a darkish pink colour. **5** a perforated nozzle, attached to the end of a hose, watering can, etc. **6** a circular fitting in a ceiling through which an electric light flex hangs.
➢ ADJ relating to or like a rose or roses.

rosé N a pale pink wine.

roseate ADJ **1** like a rose, esp in colour. **2** unrealistically hopeful or cheerful.

rosebud N the bud of a rose.

rose-coloured and **rose-tinted** ADJ 1 pink; rosy. 2 cheerful; overoptimistic.

rosehip N a red berry-like fruit of a rose.

rosemary N a fragrant evergreen shrub with stiff needle-like leaves.

rosette N 1 a badge or decoration made in coloured ribbon to resemble the form of a rose, awarded as a prize, worn to show membership of some group, etc. 2 ARCHIT a rose-shaped ornament on a wall or other surface. 3 a cluster of leaves radiating from a central point. 4 any rose-shaped structure, arrangement or figure.

rose-water N perfume distilled from roses.

rose window N a circular window with ornamental tracery radiating from the centre.

rosewood N 1 the valuable dark red or purplish wood of any of various tropical trees used in making high quality furniture. 2 a tree from which this wood is obtained.

rosin N a clear hard resin, produced by distilling turpentine.
➤ VB to rub rosin on (the bow of a violin, etc).

roster N a list of people's names showing when they are to do various duties, go on leave, etc.

rostrum N (*-rums* or *-ra*) a platform for a public speaker, orchestra conductor, etc.

rosy ADJ (*-ier, -iest*) 1 rose-coloured; pink. 2 a hopeful or optimistic, often overly so: **a rosy view of things**; b promising: **The situation looks quite rosy**. ■ **rosily** ADV. ■ **rosiness** N.

rot VB (*-tt-*) 1 TR & INTR to decay or cause to decay or become putrefied as a result of the activity of bacteria, fungi, etc. 2 INTR to become corrupt. 3 INTR to become physically weak, esp through being confined, etc: **left to rot in jail**.
➤ N 1 a decay; b something which has decayed or decomposed. 2 COLLOQ nonsense.

rota N, BRIT a list of duties to be done with the names and order of the people who are to take turns doing them; a roster.

rotary ADJ turning on an axis like a wheel.

rotate VB 1 TR & INTR to turn or cause (something) to turn about an axis like a wheel; to revolve.

2 to arrange in an ordered sequence. 3 INTR to change position, take turns in doing something, etc according to an ordered sequence. 4 to grow (different crops) in an ordered sequence on the same ground. ■ **rotatable** ADJ. ■ **rotation** N.

rote N habitual repetition: **learn by rote**.

rotisserie N a cooking apparatus with a spit on which meat, etc is cooked by direct heat.

rotor N 1 a rotating part of a machine, esp in an internal combustion engine. 2 a system of blades providing the force to lift and propel a helicopter.

rotten ADJ 1 gone bad, decayed, rotted. 2 falling or fallen to pieces from age, decay, etc. 3 morally corrupt. 4 COLLOQ miserably unwell. 5 COLLOQ unsatisfactory: **a rotten plan**.
➤ ADV, COLLOQ very much; extremely: **fancied him rotten**. ■ **rottenly** ADV. ■ **rottenness** N.

rotter N, DATED, BRIT SLANG a thoroughly depraved, worthless or despicable person.

rotund ADJ 1 plump and round. 2 of speech, language, etc: impressive or grandiloquent. ■ **rotundity** N. ■ **rotundly** ADV.

rotunda N a round, usu domed, building or hall.

rouble or **ruble** N the standard unit of currency in Russia.

roué N, OLD USE a debauched man; a rake.

rouge N, OLD USE a pink or red cosmetic for colouring the cheeks.
➤ VB to apply rouge to.

rough ADJ 1 of a surface or texture: not smooth, even or regular. 2 of ground: covered with stones, tall grass, bushes and/or scrub. 3 of an animal: with shaggy or coarse hair. 4 of a sound: harsh or grating. 5 of a person's character, behaviour, etc: noisy, coarse or violent. 6 of the sea, etc: stormy. 7 requiring hard work or considerable physical effort, or involving great difficulty, tension, etc: **a rough day at work**. 8 hard to bear: **a rough deal**. 9 of a guess, calculation, etc: approximate. 10 not polished or refined: **a rough draft**. 11 COLLOQ slightly unwell. 12 not well-kept: **a rough area**.

➤ N **1** (**the rough**) rough ground, esp the uncut grass at the side of a golf fairway. **2** the unpleasant or disagreeable side of something. **3** a rough or crude state. **4** a thug or hooligan.
➤ ADV roughly: **treated her rough**.
➤ VB to make rough; to roughen. ■ **roughly** ADV. ■ **roughness** N.
◆ **sleep rough** to sleep in the open without proper shelter.

roughage N dietary fibre.

rough-and-ready ADJ **1** quickly prepared and not polished or perfect, but usu good enough for the purpose. **2** of a person: friendly and pleasant but not polite or refined.

rough-and-tumble N disorderly but usu friendly fighting or scuffling.
➤ ADJ haphazard; disorderly.

roughcast N a mixture of plaster and small stones used on outside walls.
➤ VB (*roughcast*) to cover (a wall) with roughcast.

roughen VB, TR & INTR to make or become rough.

rough-hewn ADJ crude, unrefined.

roughhouse N, COLLOQ a brawl.

roughneck N, COLLOQ **1** a worker on an oil rig. **2** a rough and rowdy person.

roughshod ADJ.
◆ **ride roughshod over** to behave without regard to other people's feelings.

roulade N something, usu meat, cooked in the shape of a roll.

roulette N a gambling game in which a ball is dropped into a revolving wheel, the players betting on which of its small, numbered compartments the ball will come to rest in.

round ADJ **1** shaped like, or approximately like, a circle or a ball. **2** not angular; with a curved outline. **3** of a body or part of a body: curved and plump: **a round face**. **4** moving in or forming a circle. **5** of numbers: complete and exact: **a round dozen**. **6** of a number: without a fraction. **7** of a number: approximate.
➤ ADV **1** in a circular direction or with a circular or revolving movement. **2** in or to the opposite direction, position or opinion: **win someone round**. **3** in, by or along a circuitous or indirect route. **4** on all sides so as to surround: **gather round**. **5** from one person to another successively: **pass it round**. **6** in rotation, so as to return to the starting point: **wait until spring comes round**. **7** from place to place: **drive round**. **8** in circumference: **measures six feet round**. **9** to a particular place, esp someone's home: **come round for supper**.
➤ PREP **1** on all sides of so as to surround or enclose. **2** so as to move or revolve around a centre or axis and return to the starting point: **run round the field**. **3** COLLOQ having as a central point or basis: **a story built round her experiences**. **4** from place to place in: **We went round the town shopping**. **5** in all or various directions from somewhere; close to it. **6** so as to pass, or having passed, in a curved course: **drive round the corner**.
➤ N **1** something round, and often flat, in shape. **2 a** movement in a circle; **b** a complete revolution round a circuit or path. **3** a single slice of bread. **4** a sandwich made from two slices of bread. **5** GOLF the playing of all 18 holes on a course in a single session. **6** one of a recurring series of events, actions, etc; a session: **a round of talks**. **7** a series of regular activities; a daily routine: **the daily round**. **8** a regular route followed, esp for the sale or delivery of goods: **a milk round**. **9** (usu **rounds**) a sequence of visits, usu a regular one, made by a doctor to patients, either in a hospital or their homes. **10** a stage in a competition. **11** a single turn by every member of a group of people playing a game, eg, in a card game. **12** a single period of play, competition, etc in a group of such periods, eg, in boxing, wrestling, etc. **13** a burst of applause or cheering. **14** a single bullet or charge of ammunition. **15** a number of drinks bought at the same time for all the members of a group. **16** MUS an unaccompanied song in which different people all sing the same part continuously but start at different times.
➤ VB **1** TR & INTR to make or become round. **2** to go round something: **The car rounded the corner**. ■ **roundness** N.
◆ **go the rounds** of news, information, a cold,

etc: to be passed round from person to person.

◆ **in the round 1** with all details shown or considered. **2** THEAT with the audience seated on three, or often four, sides of the stage.

◆ **round about 1** on all sides; in a ring surrounding. **2** the other way about. **3** approximately: **round about four o'clock**.

◆ **round off 1** to make (corners, angles, etc) smooth. **2** to complete: **round off the meal with a brandy**.

◆ **round on** to turn on or attack.

◆ **round up 1** to raise (a number, etc) to the nearest convenient figure: **round 15.89 up to 16**. **2** to collect (animals, facts, etc) together.

roundabout N **1** BRIT a junction of several roads where traffic must travel in the same direction round a central traffic island. **2** BRIT a merry-go-round.
➢ ADJ not direct; circuitous.

roundel N **1** a small circular window or design. **2** a coloured, round identification disc on a military aircraft.

roundelay N a simple song with a refrain.

rounders N **1** a team game with a series of bases, similar to baseball, in which each team sends players in to bat in turn while the other team bowls and fields. **2** (**rounder**) a scoring run made by a batter running a complete circuit, touching all the bases.

roundly ADV **1** thoroughly: **was roundly defeated**. **2** bluntly: **told him roundly to go**.

round robin N **1** a petition or protest, esp one in which the names are written in a circle to conceal the ringleader. **2** SPORT a tournament in which every competitor plays each of the others in turn.

round-the-clock ADJ lasting through the day and night: **round-the-clock surveillance**.

round trip N a trip to a place and back again.

round-up N **1** a systematic gathering together of people or animals. **2** a summary or résumé of facts: **a round-up of the news**.

rouse VB **1** to arouse or awaken (oneself or someone else) from sleep, listlessness or lethargy. **2** INTR to awaken or become more

fully conscious or alert. **3** to excite or provoke: **The injustice of it roused her anger**. **4** INTR to become excited, provoked, etc.

rousing ADJ stirring; exciting.

roustabout N an unskilled labourer, eg, on an oil-rig or a farm.

rout¹ VB to defeat (an army, troops, a sporting team, etc) completely.
➢ N a complete and overwhelming defeat.

rout² VB **1** TR & INTR to dig up, esp with the snout. **2** (**rout out** or **up**) to find and drive out or fetch by searching.

route N **1** a way travelled on a regular journey. **2** a particular group of roads followed to get to a place.
➢ VB (-*teing* or -*ting*) **1** to arrange a route for (a journey, etc). **2** to send by a particular route.

routine N **1** a regular or unvarying series of actions or way of doing things: **a daily routine**. **2** regular or unvarying procedure. **3** a set series of movements or steps in a dance, a skating performance, etc. **4** a performer's act.
➢ ADJ **1** unvarying. **2** standard; ordinary: **a routine examination**. **3** done as part of a routine. ■ **routinely** ADV.

roux N (PL *roux*) COOKERY a cooked mixture of flour and fat used to thicken sauces.

rove VB **1** INTR to roam about aimlessly. **2** to wander over or through (a particular area, etc). **3** INTR of the eyes: to keep looking in different directions. ■ **rover** N.

row¹ N **1** a number of people or things arranged in a line. **2** in a cinema, theatre, etc: a line of seats. **3** a street with a continuous line of houses on one or both sides.

◆ **in a row 1** forming a row. **2** COLLOQ in succession: **three telephone calls in a row**.

row² VB **1** to move (a boat) through the water using oars. **2** to carry (people, goods, etc) in a rowing boat.
➢ N the action or an act of rowing a boat.
■ **rower** N. ■ **rowing** N.

row³ N **1** a noisy quarrel. **2** a loud unpleasant noise or disturbance. **3** a severe reprimand.

➤ VB, INTR to quarrel noisily.

rowan N 1 (also **rowan-tree**) a tree of the rose family, with small pinnate leaves. Also called **mountain ash**. 2 (also **rowan-berry**) the small red or pink fruit of this tree.

rowdy ADJ (-**ier**, -**iest**) loud and disorderly. ➤ N (-**ies**) COLLOQ a loud, disorderly person. ■ **rowdily** ADV. ■ **rowdiness** N.

rowel N a small spiked wheel attached to a spur.

rowing boat N, BRIT a boat moved by oars.

rowlock N a device that holds an oar in place and acts as a fulcrum for it.

royal ADJ 1 relating to or suitable for a king or queen. 2 (often **Royal**) under the patronage or in the service of a monarch: Royal Geographical Society. 3 regal; magnificent. ➤ N (often **Royal**) COLLOQ a member of a royal family. ■ **royally** ADV.

royal blue N a rich deep-coloured blue.

royalist or **Royalist** N 1 a supporter of monarchy or of a specified monarchy. 2 HIST during the English Civil War: a supporter of Charles I. ➤ ADJ relating to royalists. ■ **royalism** N.

royal jelly N a rich protein substance secreted by worker bees and fed to certain female larvae destined to become queen bees.

royalty N (-**ies**) 1 the character, state, office or power of a king or queen. 2 members of a royal family or families, either individually or collectively. 3 royal authority. 4 a percentage of the profits from each copy of a book, piece of music, invention, etc that is sold, publicly performed or used, which is paid to the author, composer, inventor, etc.

royal warrant N an official authorization to a tradesperson to supply goods to a royal household.

RSVP ABBREV often written on invitations: répondez s'il vous plaît (French), please reply.

rub VB (-**bb**-) 1 to apply pressure and friction to by moving one's hand or an object backwards and forwards. 2 INTR (usu **rub against**, **on** or **along**) to move backwards and forwards against, on or along with pressure and friction. 3 to apply (cream, ointment, polish, etc) to. 4 to clean, polish, dry, smooth, etc by applying pressure and friction. 5 TR & INTR to remove or be removed by pressure and friction. 6 TR & INTR to be sore or cause to be sore through pressure and friction. 7 TR & INTR to fray by pressure and friction. ➤ N 1 the process or an act of rubbing. 2 an obstacle or difficulty: It will cost a lot and there's the rub.

◆ **rub down** 1 to rub (one's body, a horse, etc) briskly from head to foot, eg, to dry it. 2 to prepare (a surface) to receive new paint or varnish by rubbing the old paint or varnish off.

◆ **rub in** COLLOQ to insist on talking about or emphasizing (an embarrassing fact).

◆ **rub off on sb** to have an effect on or be passed to someone by close association.

◆ **rub out** to remove by rubbing.

◆ **rub shoulders** to come into social contact.

◆ **rub sb up the wrong way** to annoy or irritate them.

rubber[1] N 1 a strong, elastic substance, obtained from the latex of certain plants, esp the rubber tree, or manufactured synthetically. 2 BRIT a small piece of rubber or plastic for rubbing out pencil marks. 3 SLANG a condom. 4 (**rubbers**) US galoshes. ■ **rubbery** ADJ.

rubber[2] N 1 BRIDGE, WHIST, ETC a match to play for the best of three or sometimes five games. 2 a series of games in any of various sports.

rubberneck VB 1 INTR to gape inquisitively. 2 to stare at (the aftermath of an accident, etc).

rubber stamp N 1 a device used to stamp a name, date, etc on books, papers, etc. 2 **a** an act or instance or the process of making an automatic, unthinking, etc agreement or authorization; **b** a person or group doing this. ➤ VB (**rubber-stamp**) COLLOQ to approve or authorize automatically.

rubbing N an impression or copy made by placing paper over a raised surface and rubbing the paper with crayon, wax, chalk, etc.

rubbish N **1** waste material; refuse; litter. **2** worthless or useless material or objects. **3** COLLOQ nonsense.
➤ VB, COLLOQ to criticize or dismiss as worthless.

rubble N pieces of broken stones, bricks, plaster, etc. ■ **rubbly** ADJ.

rub-down N an act of rubbing down.

rubella N, MED a viral disease characterized by a reddish-pink rash and swelling of the lymph glands. Also called **German measles**.

Rubicon N a boundary which, once crossed, signifies an irrevocable course of action.

rubicund ADJ of the complexion: red or rosy.

ruble see **rouble**

rubric N **1** a heading, esp one in a book or manuscript. **2** CHRISTIANITY a rule or direction for the conduct of divine service. **3** an authoritative rule or set of rules.

ruby N (-ies) **1** a valuable red gemstone. **2** a rich deep-red colour.

ruche N a pleated or gathered frill used as a trimming. ■ **ruched** ADJ.

ruck¹ N **1** a heap or mass of indistinguishable people or things. **2** RUGBY a loose scrum that forms around a ball on the ground.

ruck² N a wrinkle or crease.
➤ VB, TR & INTR to wrinkle or crease or become wrinkled or creased.

rucksack N a bag carried on the back with straps over the shoulders.

ruction N, COLLOQ **1** a noisy disturbance; uproar. **2** (**ructions**) a noisy and usu unpleasant or violent argument or reaction.

rudder N **1** a movable flat device fixed vertically to a ship's stern for steering. **2** a movable aerofoil attached to the fin of an aircraft for steering. ■ **rudderless** ADJ.

ruddy ADJ (-ier, -iest) **1** of the face, complexion, etc: glowing; with a healthy rosy or pink colour. **2** red; reddish. **3** chiefly BRIT, COLLOQ bloody: ruddy fool. ■ **ruddiness** N.

rude ADJ **1** impolite or discourteous. **2** roughly made: a rude shelter. **3** ignorant, uneducated or primitive. **4** sudden and unpleasant: a rude awakening. **5** vigorous; robust: rude health. **6** indecent. ■ **rudely** ADV. ■ **rudeness** N.

rudiment N **1** (usu **rudiments**) a fundamental fact, rule or skill of a subject: the rudiments of cooking. **2** (usu **rudiments**) the early and incomplete stage of something. **3** BIOL an organ or part which does not develop fully.
■ **rudimentary** ADJ.

rue¹ VB (*ruing* or *rueing*) to wish (something) had not been said, had not happened, etc: rued the day she ever met him.

rue² N an evergreen plant with bitter leaves.

rueful ADJ feeling or showing sorrow or regret.

ruff N **1** a circular pleated or frilled collar. **2 a** a fringe or frill of feathers growing on a bird's neck; **b** a similar fringe of hair on an animal's neck. **3** a type of ruffed domestic pigeon.

ruffian N a coarse, violent or lawless person.

ruffle VB **1** to wrinkle or make uneven. **2** TR & INTR to make or become irritated, annoyed or discomposed. **3** of a bird: to make (its feathers) erect, usu in anger or display. **4** to gather (lace, linen, etc) into a ruff or ruffle. **5** to flick or turn (pages of a book, etc) hastily.
➤ N a frill worn either round the neck or wrists.

rufous ADJ reddish in colour.

rug N **1** a thick heavy mat or small carpet. **2** a thick blanket or wrap.
◆ **pull the rug (out) from under sb** to leave them without defence, support, etc.

rugby or **rugby football** N a team game played with an oval ball which players may kick or carry.

rugged ADJ **1** of landscape, hills, ground, etc: rough, steep and rocky. **2** of facial features: irregular and furrowed. **3** of character: stern, austere and unbending. **4** of manners, etc: unsophisticated; unrefined. **5** sturdy; robust.

rugger N, COLLOQ rugby.

ruin N **1** a broken, destroyed, decayed or collapsed state. **2** (often **ruins**) the remains of

something which has been broken, destroyed or has decayed or collapsed, esp a building. **3 a** complete loss of wealth, position, power, etc; **b** a person that has suffered this; **c** something or someone that causes this.
➤ VB **1** to reduce or bring (someone or something) to ruin. **2** to spoil.
◆ **in ruins** completely wrecked or destroyed.

ruination N **1** an act or the process of ruining. **2** the state of having been ruined.

ruinous ADJ **1** likely to bring about ruin: **ruinous prices. 2** ruined; decayed; destroyed.

rule N **1** a governing or controlling principle, regulation, etc. **2 a** government or control; **b** the period during which government or control is exercised. **3** a general principle, standard, guideline or custom: **make it a rule always to be punctual. 4** CHRISTIANITY the laws and customs that are followed by all members of a religious order: **the Benedictine rule. 5** same as **ruler** (sense 2). **6** PRINTING a thin straight line or dash. **7** LAW an order made by a court and judge which applies to a particular case only.
➤ VB **1** TR & INTR to govern; to exercise authority over. **2** to keep control of or restrain. **3** to make an authoritative and usu official or judicial decision. **4** INTR to be common or prevalent: **chaos ruled. 5** to draw a straight line.
◆ **as a rule** usually.
◆ **rule sth out** to leave it out; to preclude it.

rule of thumb N a method of doing something, based on practical experience rather than theory or careful calculation.

ruler N **1** someone who rules or governs. **2** a strip of wood, metal or plastic with straight edges that is marked off in units and used for drawing straight lines and measuring.

ruling N an official or authoritative decision.
➤ ADJ **1** governing; controlling. **2** most important or strongest; predominant.

rum[1] N a spirit distilled from fermented sugar-cane juice or from molasses.

rum[2] ADJ (**rummer, rummest**) chiefly BRIT, COLLOQ strange; odd; bizarre.

rumba or **rhumba** N **1** a lively Afro-Cuban dance. **2** music for this dance.

rumble VB **1** INTR to make a deep low grumbling sound: **Her stomach rumbled. 2** INTR to move with a rumbling noise. **3** BRIT SLANG to detect the truth about (someone or something).
➤ N a deep low grumbling sound.

rumbustious ADJ, BRIT COLLOQ noisy and cheerful; boisterous.

ruminant N a mammal, eg, a cow, sheep, goat, etc that chews the cud.
➤ ADJ **1** of this group of mammals. **2** meditative or contemplative.

ruminate VB **1** INTR to chew the cud. **2** TR & INTR to think deeply about. ■ **rumination** N.
■ **ruminative** ADJ.

rummage VB **1** TR & INTR (usu **rummage through**) to search messily through (a collection of things, a cupboard, etc). **2** INTR (usu **rummage about** or **around**) to search: **rummage around for a pen.**
➤ N a search.

rummy N a card game in which each player tries to collect sets or sequences of cards.

rumour or (N AMER) **rumor** N **1** a piece of news or information passed from person to person and which may or may not be true. **2** general talk or gossip; hearsay.
➤ VB to report or spread (news, etc) by rumour.

rump N **1** the rear part of an animal's or bird's body. **2** a person's buttocks. **3** (also **rump steak**) a cut of beef from the rump.

rumple VB, TR & INTR to become or to make (hair, clothes, etc) untidy, creased or wrinkled.

rumpus N, COLLOQ a noisy disturbance.

run VB (**ran, run, running**) **1** INTR to move so quickly that both or all feet are off the ground together for an instant during part of each step. **2** to cover (a specified distance, etc) by running: **run the marathon. 3** to perform (an action) as if by running: **run an errand. 4** INTR of a vehicle: to move quickly and easily over a surface on, or as if on, wheels. **5** INTR to flee; to run away. **6** TR & INTR to move or make (something) move in a specified way or

direction or with a specified result: **run the car up the ramp. 7** INTR to race or finish a race in a specified position. **8** to enter (a contestant) in a race or as a candidate for office. **9** INTR, chiefly N AMER to stand as a candidate in an election. **10** INTR of water, etc: to flow. **11** to make or allow (liquid) to flow. **12** INTR of the nose or eyes: to discharge liquid or mucus. **13** of wax, etc: to melt and flow. **14** TR & INTR to give out or cause (a tap, container, etc) to give out liquid. **15** to fill with water: **run a hot bath. 16** TR & INTR to come to a specified state or condition by, or as if by, flowing or running: **run dry. 17** to be full of or flow with. **18** TR & INTR to operate or function. **19** COMP to execute (a program). **20** to organize, manage or be in control of: **runs her own business. 21** TR & INTR to travel or make (a vehicle) travel on a regular route: **a train running between Paris and Nice. 22** TR & INTR to continue or cause (something) to continue or extend in a specified direction, for a specified time or distance, or over a specified range: **a road running south. 23** INTR, LAW to continue to have legal force: **a lease with a year still to run. 24** COLLOQ to drive (someone or something) in a vehicle. **25** INTR to spread or diffuse: **The colour in his shirt ran. 26** INTR to have as wording: **The report runs as follows. 27** to be affected by or subjected to: **run a high temperature. 28** INTR to be inherent or recur frequently: **Blue eyes run in the family. 29** to own, drive and maintain (a vehicle). **30** to publish: **run the story in the magazine. 31** to show or broadcast (a programme, film, etc): **run a repeat of the series. 32** INTR **a** of stitches: to come undone; **b** of a garment, eg, tights: to have some of its stitches come undone and form a ladder. **33** to get past or through an obstacle, etc: **run a blockade. 34** to smuggle or deal illegally in something.
➢ N **1** an act or instance or the process of running. **2** the distance covered or time taken up by an act of running. **3** a rapid pace quicker than a walk: **break into a run. 4** a manner of running. **5** a mark, streak, etc made by the flowing of some liquid, eg, paint. **6** a trip in a vehicle, esp for pleasure: **a run to the seaside. 7** a continuous and unbroken period or series of something: **a run of bad luck. 8** freedom to

move about or come and go as one pleases: **have the run of the house. 9** a high or urgent demand for (a currency, money, a commodity, etc): **a run on the pound. 10** a route which is regularly travelled, eg, by public transport, or as a delivery round, etc. **11** same as **ladder** (N sense 2). **12** the average type or class of something: **the run of new students. 13** (**the runs**) COLLOQ diarrhoea. **14** the quantity produced in a single period of production: **a print run. 15** CRICKET a point scored, usu by a batsman running from one wicket to the other. **16** a unit of scoring in baseball made by the batter successfully completing a circuit of four bases. **17** an enclosure or pen for domestic fowls or animals: **a chicken-run. 18** COMP the complete execution of a program.
◆ **on the run** fleeing, esp from the police.
◆ **run across** or **into** to meet unexpectedly.
◆ **run along** COLLOQ to go away.
◆ **run down** of a clock, battery, etc: to cease to work because of a gradual loss of power.
◆ **run sb** or **sth down 1** of a vehicle or its driver: to knock them or it to the ground. **2** to speak badly of them or it. **3** to chase or search for them or it until they are found or captured.
◆ **run into 1** to collide with. **2** to suffer from or be beset by (a problem, difficulty, etc): **Our plans quickly ran into problems. 3** to reach as far as (an amount or quantity): **His debts run into hundreds.**
◆ **run off 1** to leave quickly; to run away. **2** to drain or cause (a liquid) to be drained. **3** to produce (printed material, etc) quickly.
◆ **run on sth** to use (a specified fuel).
◆ **run out** of a supply: to be used up.
◆ **run out of sth** to use up a supply of it.
◆ **run out on sb** COLLOQ to abandon them.
◆ **run over 1** to overflow. **2** to go beyond (a limit, etc).
◆ **run over** or **through sth** to read or perform a piece of music, a script, etc quickly, esp for practice or as a rehearsal.
◆ **run sb** or **sth over** of a vehicle or driver: to knock them or it down and injure or kill them.
◆ **run through sth** to use up (money, resources, etc) quickly and recklessly.
◆ **run to sth 1** to have enough money for it: **We can't run to a holiday this year. 2** of a text:

to extend to (a specified extent). **3** to tend towards it: **run to fat**.

◆ **run up 1** to make (clothing, etc) quickly or promptly. **2** to amass or accumulate (bills, debts, etc). **3** to hoist (a flag).

◆ **run up against** to be faced with (a challenging opponent or difficulty).

runabout N a small light car, boat or aircraft.

runaround N a runabout.
◆ **give sb the runaround** COLLOQ to behave in a deceptive or evasive way towards them.

runaway N a person or animal that has run away or fled.
➤ ADJ **1** out of control: **a runaway train. 2** of a race, victory, etc: easily won.

run down ADJ **1** of a person: in weakened health. **2** of a building: dilapidated.
➤ N (**rundown**) **1** a gradual reduction in numbers, size, etc. **2** a brief statement of the main points or items; a summary.

rune N **1** a letter of an early alphabet used by the Germanic peoples between about AD 200 and AD 600, found in inscriptions, etc. **2** a mystical symbol or inscription. ■ **runic** ADJ.

rung N **1** a step on a ladder. **2** a crosspiece on a chair.

run-in N **1** an approach. **2** COLLOQ a quarrel.

runnel N **1** a small stream. **2** a gutter.

runner N **1** someone or something that runs. **2** a messenger. **3** a groove or strip along which a drawer, sliding door, etc slides. **4** either of the strips of metal or wood running the length of a sledge, etc. **5** a blade on an ice skate. **6** a stem that grows horizontally along the surface of the ground, producing new plants. **7** a long narrow strip of cloth or carpet used to decorate or cover a table, dresser, floor, etc. **8** a smuggler: **a drugs runner**.

runner bean N **1** a climbing plant which produces bright red flowers and long green edible beans. **2** the bean this plant produces.

runner-up N (**runners-up**) a team or competitor that finishes in second place.

running ADJ **1** relating to or for running: **running shoes. 2** done or performed while running, working, etc: **running repairs. 3** continuous: **running battle. 4** consecutive: **two days running. 5** flowing: **running water. 6** of a wound or sore, etc: giving out pus.
◆ **in** or **out of the running** having, or not having, a chance of success.
◆ **make** or **take up the running** to take the lead or set the pace, eg, in a race.

runny ADJ (**-ier, -iest**) **1** tending to run or flow with liquid. **2** liquid; too watery. **3** of the nose: discharging mucus.

run-of-the-mill ADJ ordinary; not special.

runt N the smallest animal in a litter.

run-through N a practice or rehearsal.

run-up N an approach to something or period of preparation.

runway N a wide hard surface that aircraft take off from and land on.

rupee N the standard unit of currency in several countries including India and Pakistan.

rupture N **1 a** a breach; a breaking or bursting; **b** the state of being broken or burst. **2** a breach of harmony or friendly relations. **3** a hernia, esp in the abdominal region.
➤ VB **1** to break, tear or burst. **2** to breach or break off (friendly relations). **3** to cause a rupture in (an organ, tissue, etc).

rural ADJ relating to the countryside.

ruse N a clever stratagem or plan intended to deceive or trick.

rush¹ VB **1** INTR to hurry; to move forward or go quickly. **2** to hurry (someone or something) on. **3** to send, transport, etc (someone or something) quickly or urgently: **rushed her to hospital. 4** to perform or deal with (someone or something) too quickly or hurriedly. **5** INTR to come, flow, spread, etc quickly and suddenly: **Colour rushed to her cheeks. 6** to attack (someone or something) suddenly. **7** (usu **rush into**) to begin or enter into (a course of action, an agreement, etc) too hastily and often without due consideration. **8** to force (someone or something) to act or do something too quickly: **don't rush me.**

➤ N **1** a sudden quick movement, esp forwards. **2** a sudden general movement or migration of people: **a gold rush. 3** a sound or sensation of rushing. **4** haste; hurry. **5** a period of great activity. **6** a sudden demand for a commodity.

➤ ADJ done, or needing to be done, quickly: **a rush job.**

rush² N **1** a densely tufted plant, typically found in cold wet regions. **2** a stalk or stalklike leaf of this plant, often used as a material for making baskets, covering floors, etc. **3** rushes as a material. ■ **rushy** ADJ.

rushes PL N, CINEMATOG the first unedited prints of a scene or scenes.

rush hour N the period at the beginning or end of a working day when traffic is busiest.

rusk N a piece of bread which has been rebaked, or a hard dry biscuit resembling this, esp as a baby food.

russet N **1** a reddish-brown colour. **2** a variety of apple with a reddish-brown skin.

Russian roulette N an act of daring or bravado, esp that of spinning the cylinder of a revolver which is loaded with just one bullet, pointing the revolver at one's own head, and pulling the trigger.

rust N **1** a reddish-brown coating that forms on the surface of iron or steel that has been exposed to air and moisture. **2** a similar coating which forms on other metals. **3** the colour of rust, usu a reddish-brown. **4** a fungus disease of cereals, etc, characterized by the appearance of reddish-brown patches on the leaves, etc.

➤ VB **1** TR & INTR to become or cause (something) to become coated with rust. **2** INTR of a plant: to be affected by rust. **3** INTR to become weaker, inefficient etc, usu through lack of use.

rustic ADJ **1** relating to, characteristic of, or living in the country; rural. **2** simple and

unsophisticated. **3** awkward or uncouth. **4** made of rough untrimmed branches: **rustic furniture.**

➤ N a person from, or who lives in, the country. ■ **rusticity** N.

rusticate VB **1** BRIT to suspend (a student) temporarily from college or university. **2** INTR to live or go to live in the country. ■ **rustication** N.

rustle VB **1** INTR to make a soft whispering sound like that of dry leaves. **2** INTR to move with such a sound. **3** to make (something) move with, or make, such a sound: **rustled the newspaper. 4** TR & INTR, chiefly US to round up and steal (cattle or horses).

➤ N a rustling sound. ■ **rustler** N.

◆ **rustle up** to prepare, esp at short notice.

rustproof ADJ **1** tending not to rust. **2** preventing rusting.

➤ VB to make rustproof.

rusty ADJ (**-ier, -iest**) **1** covered with rust; rusted. **2** of a plant: affected by rust. **3** impaired by lack of use or practice: **His French was rusty. 4** rust-coloured. ■ **rustiness** N.

rut¹ N **1** a deep track or furrow in soft ground, esp one made by wheels. **2** an established and usu boring or dreary routine.

➤ VB (**-tt-**) to furrow (the ground) with ruts.

rut² N in male ruminants, eg, deer: a period of sexual excitement.

➤ VB (**-tt-**) INTR of male animals: to be in a period of sexual excitement.

ruthless ADJ without pity; merciless. ■ **ruthlessly** ADV. ■ **ruthlessness** N.

rye N **1 a** a cereal plant similar to barley but with longer, narrower ears; **b** its grain, used for making flour and in the distillation of whiskey, gin, vodka, etc. **2** esp US whiskey distilled from fermented rye. **3** US rye bread: **pastrami on rye.**

rye grass N a grass grown esp for fodder.

Ss

S¹ or **s** N (*Ss*, *S's* or *s's*) the nineteenth letter of the English alphabet.

S² ABBREV South.

's¹ SFX **1** a word-forming element used to form the possessive: **the children's**. **2** a word-forming element used to form the plural of numbers and symbols: **3's, X's**.

's² ABBREV **1** short form of **is**, as in **he's not here**. **2** short form of **has**, as in **she's taken it**. **3** short form of **us**, as in **let's go**.

Sabbath N a day of the week set aside for religious worship and rest from work.

sabbatical ADJ of or relating to a period of leave usu given to teachers in higher education. ➤ N a period of such leave.

sable N (*sables* or *sable*) **1** a small carnivorous European and Asian mammal. **2** the highly prized dark brown or black coat of this animal. ➤ ADJ **1** made of sable fur. **2** POETIC dark. **3** HERALDRY black.

sabotage N **1** deliberate or underhand damage or destruction, esp carried out for military or political reasons. **2** any action designed to disrupt a plan or scheme. ➤ VB to deliberately destroy, damage or disrupt something. ■ **saboteur** N.

sabre or (US) **saber** N **1** a curved single-edged cavalry sword. **2** a lightweight sword with a tapering blade used for fencing.

sac N, BIOL any bag-like part in a plant or animal.

saccharin N a white crystalline substance used as an artificial sweetener.

saccharine ADJ over-sentimental or sweet.

sacerdotal ADJ of or relating to priests.

sachet N a small sealed packet.

sack¹ N **1** a large bag used for storing or carrying. **2** a sackful. **3** (**the sack**) COLLOQ dismissal from employment. **4** (**the sack**) SLANG bed. ➤ VB **1** to put into a sack or sacks. **2** COLLOQ to dismiss from employment.

sack² VB to plunder and destroy a town. ➤ N the act of sacking a town.

sackcloth N **1** coarse cloth used to make sacks; sacking. **2** a garment made from this, formerly worn in mourning or as a penance. ◆ **sackcloth and ashes** a display of mourning, sorrow or remorse.

sacking N coarse cloth used to make sacks.

sacrament N, CHRISTIANITY **1** a religious rite or ceremony, eg marriage or baptism. **2** (**Sacrament**) the service of the Eucharist or Holy Communion. ■ **sacramental** ADJ.

sacred ADJ **1** devoted or dedicated to a deity, saint, etc. **2** connected with religion or worship: **sacred music**. **3** not to be challenged or breached in any circumstances.

sacrifice N **1 a** the offering of a slaughtered person or animal to a god; **b** such an offering. **2** any offering made to a god. **3** the destruction or giving up of something valued. ➤ VB **1** to offer someone or something as a sacrifice to a god. **2** to surrender or give up something for the sake of some other person or thing. ■ **sacrificial** ADJ.

sacrilege N a profanation or extreme disrespect for something holy or greatly respected. ■ **sacrilegious** ADJ.

sacristan N a person responsible for church contents.

sacristy N (-*ies*) a room in a church where sacred utensils and vestments are kept.

sacrosanct ADJ supremely holy or sacred.

sacrum N (*sacra*) ANAT a large triangular bone forming part of the pelvis.

SAD ABBREV seasonal affective disorder.

sad ADJ (*sadder, saddest*) 1 feeling unhappy or sorrowful. 2 causing unhappiness: sad news. 3 expressing or suggesting unhappiness: sad music. 4 very bad; deplorable: a sad state. 5 COLLOQ pathetic; inspiring ridicule. ■ **sadly** ADV. ■ **sadness** N.

sadden VB 1 to make someone sad. 2 INTR to become sad.

saddle N 1 a leather seat for horse-riding, which fits on the horse's back. 2 a fixed seat on a bicycle or motorcycle. 3 a cut of meat including part of the backbone with the ribs. ➤ VB 1 to put a saddle on (an animal). 2 INTR to climb into a saddle. 3 to burden someone with a problem, duty, etc.
◆ **in the saddle** in a position of control.

saddleback N 1 an animal or bird with a saddle-shaped marking on its back. 2 a hill with a dip in the middle. ■ **saddlebacked** ADJ.

saddler N a person who makes or sells saddles, harness, and related equipment.

saddlery N (-*ies*) 1 the occupation or profession of a saddler. 2 a saddler's shop.

sadhu N a nomadic Hindu holy man.

sadism N 1 the pleasure, esp sexual, gained by inflicting pain on others. 2 any infliction of suffering on others for one's own satisfaction. ■ **sadist** N. ■ **sadistic** ADJ.

sado-masochism N the practice of deriving sexual pleasure from inflicting pain and having pain inflicted on oneself. ■ **sado-masochist** N. ■ **sado-masochistic** ADJ.

sae ABBREV stamped addressed envelope.

safari N an expedition to hunt or observe wild animals, esp in Africa.

safari park N a large enclosed area in which wild animals, mostly non-native, roam freely.

safe ADJ 1 free from danger or harm. 2 unharmed. 3 involving no risk of loss; assured: a safe bet. ➤ N a sturdily constructed cabinet, usu made of metal, in which valuables can be locked away. ■ **safely** ADV. ■ **safeness** N. ■ **safety** N.

safe-deposit and **safety-deposit** N a place in which valuables can be locked away.

safeguard N a person, device or arrangement giving protection against danger. ➤ VB to protect from harm.

safekeeping N protection; safe custody.

safety catch N a catch protecting against the accidental firing of a gun.

safety glass N strengthened glass.

safety lamp N a miner's oil lamp designed to prevent ignition of any flammable gases.

safety match N a match that ignites only when struck on a specially prepared surface.

safety net N 1 a large net stretched beneath acrobats, tightrope walkers, etc in case they accidentally fall. 2 any precautionary measure or means of protecting against loss or failure.

safety pin N a U-shaped pin with an attached guard to cover the point.

safety razor N a shaving razor with the blade protected by a guard.

safety valve N a valve that opens when the pressure exceeds a certain level, and closes again when the pressure drops.

saffron N 1 a crocus which has lilac flowers with large orange stigmas. 2 the dried stigmas of this species, used to dye and flavour food. 3 a bright orange-yellow colour.

sag VB (-*gg*-) INTR to bend, sink, or hang down, esp in the middle, under or as if under weight. ➤ N a sagging state or condition. ■ **saggy** ADJ.

saga N 1 a medieval Scandinavian tale of the

deeds of legendary heroes. **2** COLLOQ any long detailed story or series of events.

sagacious ADJ, FORMAL wise or discerning. ■ **sagacity** N.

sage¹ N **1** a shrub with greyish-green aromatic leaves. **2** the leaves of this plant, used in cookery as a seasoning.

sage² N someone of great wisdom and knowledge, esp an ancient philosopher. ➤ ADJ very wise and prudent. ■ **sagely** ADJ.

Sagittarius N, ASTROL the ninth sign of the zodiac (the Archer).

sago N **1** a starchy grain or powder from the soft pith of the sago palm. **2** any of various species of palm that yield this.

sahib N in India: a term of respect formerly used to address or refer to a European man.

said ADJ, often FORMAL previously or already mentioned: **the said occasion.**

sail N **1** a sheet of canvas, or similar structure, spread to catch the wind as a means of propelling a ship. **2** a voyage or trip in a boat or ship with or without sails. ➤ VB **1** TR & INTR to travel by boat or ship. **2** to control (a boat or ship): **He sailed his ship around the world. 3** INTR to depart by boat or ship: **We sail at two-thirty.** ◆ **set sail** to begin a journey by boat or ship.

sailboard N a windsurfing board, like a surfboard with a sail attached.

sailcloth N **1** strong cloth used to make sails. **2** heavy cotton cloth used for garments.

sailor N **1** any member of a ship's crew. **2** someone regarded in terms of ability to tolerate travel on a ship: **a good sailor.**

sainfoin N a leguminous plant, widely cultivated as a fodder crop.

saint N **1** (often **Saint**) a person whose holiness is formally recognized after death by a Christian Church. **2** COLLOQ a very good and kind person. ■ **sainthood** N. ■ **saintlike** ADJ.

sainted ADJ **1** formally declared a saint. **2** greatly respected or revered; hallowed.

saintly ADJ (**-ier, -iest**) **1** similar to, characteristic of, or befitting a saint. **2** very good or holy. ■ **saintliness** N.

St Valentine's Day N 14 February, a day on which greetings cards are sent to sweethearts.

Saint Vitus's dance N, PATHOL chorea.

saithe N, BRIT the coley. Also called **coalfish**.

sake¹ N **1** benefit or advantage; behalf; account: **for my sake. 2** purpose; object or aim.

sake² or **saki** N a Japanese fermented alcoholic drink made from rice.

salaam N a greeting used in Eastern countries, esp by Muslims.

salacious ADJ **1** lecherous or lustful. **2** seeking to arouse sexual desire. ■ **salaciousness** N.

salad N a cold dish of vegetables or herbs, either raw or pre-cooked, eaten either on its own or as an accompaniment to a main meal.

salad days PL N, LITERARY years of youthful inexperience and carefree innocence.

salamander N a small amphibian resembling a lizard.

salami N a highly seasoned type of sausage.

salaried ADJ receiving or providing a salary.

salary N (**-ies**) a fixed regular payment, usu made monthly, for esp non-manual work. ➤ VB (**-ies, -ied**) to pay a salary to someone.

sale N **1** the exchange of anything for a specified amount of money. **2** an item sold. **3** a period during which goods in shops, etc are offered at reduced prices. **4** any event at which goods can be bought: **a book sale. 6** (**sales**) the operations associated with, or the staff responsible for, selling. ➤ ADJ intended for selling, esp at reduced prices or by auction: **sales items.** ◆ **for** or **on sale** available for buying.

saleable or (US) **salable** ADJ **1** suitable for selling. **2** in demand. ■ **saleability** N.

salesman, salesgirl, saleswoman and **salesperson** N **1** a person who sells goods to customers, esp in a shop. **2** a person representing a company, who often visits people's homes, offices, etc.

salesmanship N the techniques used by a salesman to persuade people to buy goods.

sales pitch N persuasive sales talk.

salient ADJ striking; outstanding or prominent. ➤ N a projecting angle or part, eg of a fortification or a defensive line of troops.

saline ADJ 1 of a substance: containing salt. 2 of medicines: containing or having the nature of the salts of alkali metals and magnesium. ➤ N (also **saline solution**) a solution of sodium chloride in water used in intravenous drips, etc. ■ **salinity** N.

saliva N a clear liquid produced by the salivary glands of the mouth, that softens the food and begins the process of digestion.

salivate VB, INTR 1 of the salivary glands: to produce a flow of saliva into the mouth. 2 to drool. ■ **salivation** N.

sallow ADJ of a person's complexion: being a pale yellowish colour. ■ **sallowness** N.

sally N (-**ies**) 1 a sudden forward rush of troops. 2 an outing. 3 a witty remark. ➤ VB (-**ies**, -**ied**) INTR 1 of troops: to carry out a sally. 2 HUMOROUS (also **sally forth**) to rush out or surge forward. 3 to set off on an excursion.

salmon N (**salmon** or **salmons**) 1 a large silvery fish that migrates to freshwater rivers and streams to spawn. 2 the reddish-orange flesh of this fish. 3 an orange-pink colour.

salmonella N 1 a form of bacteria that can cause food poisoning. 2 food poisoning caused by such bacteria.

salon N 1 a reception room. 2 a social gathering of distinguished people. 3 a shop where clients are beautified in some way.

saloon N 1 COLLOQ (in full **saloon car**) any motor car with two or four doors and an enclosed compartment. 2 a large public cabin or dining-room on a passenger ship. 3 (also **saloon bar**) a lounge bar.

salsa N 1 rhythmic dance music of Latin-

American origin, containing elements of jazz and rock. 2 COOKERY a spicy Mexican sauce.

salsify N (-**ies**) a plant with a long white cylindrical tap root eaten as a vegetable.

salt N 1 sodium chloride, esp as used to season and preserve food. 2 CHEM a chemical compound that is formed when an acid reacts with a base. 3 liveliness; interest, wit or good sense: **Her opinion added salt to the debate.** 4 (also **old salt**) an experienced sailor. ➤ ADJ containing, tasting of or preserved in salt. ➤ VB 1 to season or preserve (food) with salt. 2 to cover (an icy road) with salt to melt the ice. 3 to add piquancy, interest or wit to something. ◆ **rub salt in sb's wounds** to add to their discomfort, sorrow, shame, etc. ◆ **salt away** to store up for future use. ◆ **the salt of the earth** a consistently reliable or dependable person. ◆ **take sth with a pinch of salt** to treat a statement or proposition sceptically. ◆ **worth one's salt** competent or useful.

saltcellar N a container holding salt.

saltpetre or (US) **saltpeter** N potassium nitrate.

salty ADJ (-**ier**, -**iest**) 1 tasting strongly or of, or containing, salt. 2 of humour: sharp.

salubrious ADJ 1 FORMAL promoting health or well-being: **a salubrious climate**. 2 decent or respectable: **a salubrious neighbourhood**. ■ **salubriousness** or **salubrity** N.

salutary ADJ beneficial; timely.

salutation N a word, act, or gesture of greeting. ■ **salutatory** ADJ.

salute VB 1 to greet with friendly words or a gesture, esp a kiss. 2 to pay tribute to something or someone: **We salute your bravery**. 3 INTR, MIL to pay formal respect with a set gesture, esp with the right arm. ➤ N 1 a greeting. 2 a gesture of respect.

salvage N 1 the rescue of a ship or its cargo from the danger of loss. 2 the rescue of any property from fire or other danger. 3 the saving and utilization of waste material. ➤ VB to rescue (property or a ship) from potential loss. ■ **salvageable** ADJ.

salvation N 1 the act of saving someone or something from harm. 2 a person or thing that saves another from harm. 3 RELIG the liberation or saving of man from the influence of sin.

salve N 1 ointment or remedy to heal or soothe: lip salve. 2 anything that comforts or soothes. ➤ VB to ease: salve one's conscience.

salver N a small ornamented tray.

salvo N (-os or -oes) a burst of gunfire from several guns firing simultaneously.

sal volatile N a former name for ammonium carbonate, used as smelling salts.

Samaritan N (in full **Good Samaritan**) a kind, considerate or helpful person.

samarium N, CHEM a soft silvery metallic element, used to make magnets.

samba N a lively Brazilian dance in duple time.

same ADJ 1 identical or very similar: This is the same film we saw last week. 2 used as emphasis: He went home the very same day. 3 unchanged or unvaried: This town is still the same as ever. 4 previously mentioned; the actual one in question: this same man. ➤ PRONOUN the same person or thing, or the one previously referred to: She drank whisky, and I drank the same. ➤ ADV (**the same**) 1 similarly; likewise: I feel the same. 2 COLLOQ equally: We love each of you the same. ■ **sameness** N. ◆ **all** or **just the same** nevertheless; anyhow. ◆ **at the same time** still; however.

samey ADJ, COLLOQ boringly similar or unchanging; monotonous.

samosa N (-sas or -sa) a small deep-fried triangular pastry turnover, of Indian origin.

samovar N a decorated Russian water boiler, used for making tea, etc.

sampan N a small Oriental boat.

sample N a small portion or part used to represent the nature of others or of a whole. ➤ ADJ used as or serving as a sample. ➤ VB 1 to take or try as a sample. 2 to get

experience of something: sampled life abroad. 3 POP MUSIC to mix a short extract from one recording into a different backing track.

sampler N 1 a collection of samples. 2 a piece of embroidery produced as a show of skill.

samurai N (PL -rai) HIST (a member of) an aristocratic caste of Japanese warriors.

sanatorium N (-iums or -ia) 1 a hospital for the chronically ill or convalescents. 2 BRIT a sickroom in a boarding school, etc.

sanctify VB (-ies, -ied) to make or consider to be sacred or holy. ■ **sanctification** N.

sanctimonious ADJ affecting or simulating holiness or virtuousness, esp hypocritically. ■ **sanctimoniousness** or **sanctimony** N.

sanction N 1 official permission or authority. 2 the act of giving permission or authority. 3 aid; support. 4 (esp **sanctions**) POL an economic or military measure taken by one nation against another as a means of coercion. ➤ VB 1 to authorize or confirm. 2 to permit.

sanctity N (-ies) 1 the quality of being holy or sacred. 2 purity or godliness; inviolability.

sanctuary N (-ies) 1 a holy or sacred place. 2 a place providing protection from arrest, persecution, etc. 3 a nature reserve.

sanctum N (-tums or -ta) 1 a sacred place. 2 a private place.

sand N 1 GEOL tiny rounded particles or grains of rock, esp quartz. 2 (**sands**) an area of land covered with these particles or grains. ➤ ADJ 1 made of sand. 2 having the colour of sand, a light brownish-yellow colour. ➤ VB 1 to smooth or polish a surface with sandpaper or a sander. 2 to sprinkle, cover or mix with sand.

sandal N a type of lightweight shoe consisting of a sole attached to the foot by straps.

sandalwood N, BOT the hard pale fragrant timber obtained from an evergreen tree.

sandbag N a sack filled with sand or earth, used with others to form a protective barrier. ➤ VB to barricade with sandbags.

sandbank and **sandbar** N a bank of sand in a river, river mouth or sea, formed by currents and often above the water level at low tide.

sandblast VB to clean or engrave (glass, metal, stone surfaces, etc) with a jet of sand forced from a tube by air or steam pressure.

sander N a power-driven tool fitted with sandpaper or an abrasive disc.

S and M ABBREV sado-masochism.

sandpaper N abrasive paper with a coating orig of sand or crushed glass, glued to one side.
➤ VB to smooth or polish with sandpaper.

sandstone N, GEOL a sedimentary rock made of compacted sand.

sandwich N a snack consisting of two slices of bread or a roll filled with cheese, meat, etc.
➤ VB to place between two layers.

sandy ADJ (-ier, -iest) 1 covered with or containing sand. 2 having the light brownish-yellow colour of sand. ■ **sandiness** N.

sane ADJ 1 sound in mind; not mentally impaired. 2 sensible or rational; sound in judgement. ■ **sanely** ADV. ■ **saneness** N.

sangfroid N calmness or composure.

sanguinary ADJ 1 bloody. 2 bloodthirsty.

sanguine ADJ 1 cheerful, confident and full of hope. 2 of a complexion: ruddy.

sanitary ADJ concerned with and promoting hygiene, good health and the prevention of disease. ■ **sanitarily** ADV.

sanitary towel and (US) **sanitary napkin** N an absorbent pad worn during menstruation.

sanitation N 1 standards of public hygiene. 2 measures taken to promote public health.

sanitize or **-ise** VB 1 to make hygienic. 2 to make less controversial or more acceptable.

sanity N soundness of mind; rationality.

sanserif or **sans serif** N, PRINTING a type in which the letters have no serifs.

Sanskrit N the ancient Indo-European religious and literary language of India.

sap^1 N 1 BOT a vital liquid containing nutrients that circulates in plants. 2 energy or vitality. 3 SLANG a weak or easily fooled person.
➤ VB (-pp-) 1 to extract sap from something. 2 to drain energy from something.

sap^2 N a hidden trench by which an attack is made on an enemy position.

sapient ADJ, FORMAL, often IRONIC having or showing good judgement; wise. ■ **sapience** N. ■ **sapiently** ADV.

sapling N a young tree.

saponify VB (-ies, -ied) CHEM to use an alkali to convert fats into soap. ■ **saponification** N.

sapper N 1 BRIT a soldier in the Royal Engineers. 2 a soldier responsible for making saps.

sapphire N 1 a hard transparent blue gem, prized as a gemstone. 2 a deep blue colour.
➤ ADJ having the colour of sapphire.

sappy ADJ (-ier, -iest) 1 of plants: full of sap. 2 full of energy. 3 weak. ■ **sappiness** N.

saraband N a slow formal Spanish dance.

sarcasm N 1 an often ironical expression of scorn. 2 the use of such an expression.

sarcastic ADJ 1 containing sarcasm. 2 tending to use sarcasm. ■ **sarcastically** ADV.

sarcoma N (-mas or -mata) PATHOL a cancerous tumour arising in connective tissue.

sarcophagus N (-gi or -guses) a stone coffin or tomb.

sardine N (sardines or sardine) a young pilchard, an important food fish.

sardonic ADJ mocking or scornful; sneering. ■ **sardonically** ADV.

sargasso N (-os or -oes) a brown seaweed with branching ribbon-like fronds.

sari or **saree** N a traditional garment of Hindu women, consisting of a single long piece of fabric draped over one shoulder.

sarky ADJ (-ier, -iest) COLLOQ sarcastic.

sarnie N, COLLOQ a sandwich.

sarong N a Malay garment worn by both sexes, consisting of a long piece of fabric wrapped around the waist or chest.

sarsaparilla N 1 a climbing tropical American plant. 2 US a non-alcoholic drink flavoured with the aromatic root of this plant.

sartorial ADJ of or relating to a tailor, tailoring or clothes in general: *sartorial elegance*.

sash N a broad band of cloth, worn round the waist or over the shoulder.

sashay VB, INTR to move in a gliding way.

sashimi N a Japanese dish of sliced raw fish.

sash window N a window consisting of two glazed frames, one or either of which can slide vertically past the other.

sass N, US COLLOQ impertinent talk or behaviour. ■ **sassy** ADJ.

sassafras N the aromatic dried bark obtained from the roots of a deciduous N American tree, which yields a pungent oil.

Sat. ABBREV Saturday.

Satan N the Devil.

satanic and **satanical** ADJ 1 of or relating to Satan. 2 evil; abominable.

Satanism N (also **satanism**) the worship of Satan. ■ **Satanist** N, ADJ.

satchel N a small bag for schoolbooks.

sate VB to satisfy (a longing or appetite).

satellite N 1 a celestial body that orbits a much larger celestial body, eg the Moon is a satellite of the Earth. 2 a man-made device placed in orbit around a planet, esp the Earth, used for communication, photography, etc. 3 a nation or state dependent on a larger neighbour.

satellite dish N a saucer-shaped aerial for receiving TV signals broadcast by satellite.

satellite TV or **satellite television** N, TELECOMM the broadcasting of television by means of an artificial satellite.

satiate VB to gratify fully; to satisfy to excess. ■ **satiation** N. ■ **satiety** N.

satin N silk or rayon with a shiny finish. ➤ ADJ resembling satin. ■ **satiny** ADJ.

satinwood N 1 a light-coloured hardwood used for fine furniture. 2 the tree that yields it.

satire N 1 a literary composition which holds up follies and vices for criticism, ridicule and scorn. 2 the use of sarcasm, irony, wit, humour, etc in such compositions. 3 satirical writing as a genre. ■ **satirical** ADJ. ■ **satirist** N.

satirize or **-ise** VB 1 INTR to write satire. 2 to mock or criticize using satire. ■ **satirization** N.

satisfaction N 1 the act of satisfying, or the state of being satisfied. 2 something that satisfies. 3 compensation for mistreatment.

satisfactory ADJ 1 adequate or acceptable. 2 giving satisfaction. ■ **satisfactorily** ADV.

satisfy VB (*-ies, -ied*) 1 INTR to fulfil the needs, desires or expectations of someone. 2 to give enough to or be enough for someone or something. 3 to meet the requirements of someone or something. 4 to remove the doubts of someone. ■ **satisfying** ADJ.

satsuma N a type of mandarin orange.

saturate VB 1 to soak. 2 to fill or cover with a large amount of something. 3 to charge (air or vapour) with moisture to the fullest extent possible. 4 CHEM to add a solid, liquid or gas to (a solution) until no more can be dissolved at a given temperature. ■ **saturation** N.

Saturday N the seventh day of the week.

Saturn N, ASTRON the sixth planet from the Sun.

saturnalia N a rowdy celebration.

saturnine ADJ grave and gloomy.

satyr N 1 GR MYTHOL a lecherous woodland god, part man, part goat. 2 a lustful man.

sauce N 1 any liquid, often thickened, cooked or served with food. 2 anything that adds relish, interest or excitement. 3 COLLOQ impertinent language or behaviour; cheek.

saucepan N a deep cooking pot with a long handle and usu a lid.

saucer N 1 a shallow round dish. 2 anything of

a similar shape. ■ **saucerful** N.

saucy ADJ (*-ier, -iest*) COLLOQ **1** impertinent or cheeky; bold or forward. **2** referring to sex, esp in an amusing way: **saucy postcards**.
■ **saucily** ADV. ■ **sauciness** N.

sauerkraut N a dish consisting of shredded cabbage pickled in salt water.

sauna N a bath where the person is exposed to dry heat and short blasts of steam.

saunter VB, INTR to walk at a leisurely pace.
➤ N a leisurely walk or stroll.

sausage N **1** a mass of chopped or minced seasoned meat, esp pork or beef, stuffed into a tube of gut. **2** any object of a similar shape.

sauté VB (*-téed, -téing* or *-téeing*) to fry lightly for a short time.
➤ N a dish of sautéed food.
➤ ADJ fried in this way: **sauté potatoes**.

savage ADJ **1** of animals: untamed or undomesticated. **2** ferocious or furious: **He has a savage temper**. **3** of eg behaviour: uncivilized; coarse. **4** cruel; barbaric. **5** of land: uncultivated; wild and rugged.
➤ N **1** now OFFENSIVE a member of a primitive people. **2** an uncultured, fierce or cruel person.
➤ VB to attack ferociously. ■ **savagely** ADV.
■ **savageness** N.

savanna or **savannah** N an expanse of level grassland characteristic esp of Africa.

savant and **savante** N a wise and learned man or woman respectively.

save VB **1** to rescue, protect or preserve someone or something from danger, evil, loss or failure. **2** INTR to be economical, esp with money: **saving for the future**. **3** to reserve or store for later use. **4** to spare from potential unpleasantness or inconvenience: **That will save you having to make another trip**. **5** SPORT to prevent (a ball or shot) from reaching the goal. **6** TR & INTR, RELIG to deliver from the influence or consequences of sin. **7** COMP to transfer (data) onto a disk or tape for storage.
➤ N **1** an act of saving a ball or shot, or of preventing a goal. **2** COMP the saving of data onto a disk or tape.

➤ PREP (sometimes **save for**) except: **We found all the tickets save one**.
◆ **save up** to set money aside for future use.

saveloy N a spicy smoked pork sausage.

saving ADJ **1** protecting or preserving.
2 economical or frugal.
➤ N **1** something saved, esp an economy made. **2** (**savings**) money set aside.

saving grace N a desirable virtue or feature that compensates for undesirable ones.

saviour N **1** a person who saves someone or something else from danger or destruction.
2 (**the Saviour**) CHRISTIANITY Christ.

savoir-faire N instinctively knowing exactly what to do and how to do it; expertise.

savory N (*-ies*) BOT a plant whose leaves are used as a culinary herb.

savour or (US) **savor** N **1** the taste or smell of something. **2** an unmistakable quality.
➤ VB **1** to taste or smell with relish. **2** to take pleasure in something. **3** to flavour or season.
4 (chiefly **savour of sth**) to show signs of it.

savoury or (US) **savory** ADJ **1** having a salty, sharp or piquant taste or smell: **a savoury snack**. **2** having a good savour or relish.
3 pleasant or attractive, esp morally.
➤ N (*-ies*) a savoury course or snack.
■ **savouriness** N.

savoy N (in full **savoy cabbage**) a cabbage with a compact head and wrinkled leaves.

savvy SLANG, VB (*-ies, -ied*) TR & INTR to know or understand.
➤ N **1** general ability or common sense; shrewdness. **2** skill; know-how.

saw N any of various toothed cutting tools.
➤ VB (PA P **sawn** or **sawed**) **1** to cut with a saw.
2 to shape by sawing. **3** INTR to use a saw.

sawdust N small particles of wood, made by sawing.

sawmill N a factory in which timber is cut.

sawn-off and (esp US) **sawed off** ADJ shortened by cutting with a saw.

sax N, COLLOQ short for **saxophone**.

Saxon N a member of a Germanic people which invaded Britain in 5c and 6c.
➤ ADJ of or relating to the Saxons, the Anglo-Saxons, their language or culture.

saxophone N a single-reeded wind instrument with a long S-shaped metal body. ■ **saxophonist** N.

say VB (*said*) **1** to speak, utter or articulate: He said he would come. **2** to assert or declare; to state as an opinion: I say we should give it a try. **3** to suppose: Say he doesn't come, what do we do then? **4** to convey information: She talked for ages but didn't actually say much. **5** to indicate: The clock says 10 o'clock.
➤ N **1** a chance to express an opinion: You've had your say. **2** the right to an opinion; influence: to have no say in the matter.
➤ EXCLAM, N AMER, ESP US **1** an expression of surprise, protest or sudden joy. **2** a way of attracting attention.

saying N a proverb or maxim.

say-so N authorization.

scab N **1** a crust of dried blood formed over a healing wound. **2** DEROG, SLANG a worker who defies a union's instruction to strike.
➤ VB (*-bb-*) INTR (also **scab over**) to become covered by a scab.

scabbard N a sheath for a sword or dagger.

scabby ADJ (*-ier, -iest*) **1** covered with scabs. **2** COLLOQ contemptible. ■ **scabbiness** N.

scabies N, PATHOL a contagious skin disease caused by a secretion of a mite.

scabrous ADJ **1** of skin, etc: rough and flaky or scaly; scurfy. **2** bawdy; smutty or indecent.

scaffold N **1** a temporary framework of metal poles and planks used as a platform. **2** (**the scaffold**) a platform on which a person is executed. ■ **scaffolding** N.

scalar MATH, ADJ denoting a quantity that has magnitude but not direction, such as distance, speed and mass.
➤ N a scalar quantity.

scald VB **1** to injure with hot liquid or steam. **2** to treat with hot water so as to sterilize. **3** to cook or heat to just short of boiling point.
➤ N an injury caused by scalding.

scale[1] N **1** a series of markings or divisions at regular intervals, for use in measuring. **2** a system of such markings or divisions. **3** a measuring device with such markings. **4** the relationship between actual size and the size as represented on a model or drawing. **5** MUS **a** a sequence of definite notes; **b** (usu **scales**) a succession of these notes performed in ascending or descending order of pitch. **6** any graded system, eg of salaries. **7** MATH a numeral system: logarithmic scale. **8** extent or level relative to others: on a grand scale.
➤ VB **1** to climb. **2** (also **scale up** and **scale down**) to change something's size to scale, making it either bigger or smaller.
◆ **to scale** in proportion to the actual size.

scale[2] N **1** any of the small thin plates that provide a protective covering on the skin of fish and reptiles. **2** any readily or easily detached flake. **3** tartar on the teeth. **4** a crusty white deposit formed when hard water is heated.
➤ VB **1** to clear something of scales. **2** to remove in thin layers. **3** INTR to become encrusted with scale. ■ **scaly** ADJ.

scale[3] N **1** (**scales**) a device for weighing. **2** a pan of a balance.
➤ VB to weigh or weigh up.

scalene ADJ, GEOM of a triangle: having each side a different length.

scallion N a spring onion.

scallop, scollop and **escallop** N **1** a marine bivalve mollusc with a ribbed shell with wavy edges. **2** any of a series of curves forming a wavy edge. **3** COOKERY an escalope.
➤ VB to shape (an edge) into scallops or curves.

scallywag N, COLLOQ a rascal or scamp.

scalp N **1** the area of the head covered, or usu covered, by hair. **2** the skin itself on which the hair grows. **3** a piece of this skin with its hair.
➤ VB to remove the scalp of.

scalpel N a small surgical knife.

scam N, SLANG a trick or swindle.

scamp N a cheeky or mischievous child.

scamper VB, INTR to run or skip about briskly.
➤ N an act of scampering.

scampi PL N large prawns.
➤ SING N a dish of these prawns.

scan VB (*-nn-*) **1** to read through or examine something carefully or critically. **2** to look or glance over something quickly. **3** to analyse (verse) metrically. **4** INTR of verse: to conform to the rules of metre or rhythm. **5** MED to examine (parts, esp internal organs, of the body) using techniques such as ultrasound. **6** COMP to examine (data) eg on a magnetic disk.
➤ N **1** an act of scanning. **2** MED an image obtained by scanning.

scandal N **1** widespread public outrage and loss of reputation. **2** any event or fact causing this. **3** any extremely objectionable fact, situation, person or thing. **4** malicious gossip or slander; a false imputation. ■ **scandalous** ADJ.

scandalize or **-ise** VB **1** to give or cause scandal or offence. **2** to shock or outrage.

scandalmonger N someone who spreads or relishes malicious gossip.

scandium N, CHEM a soft silvery–white metallic element with a pinkish tinge.

scanner N **1** RADAR the rotating aerial by which the beam is made to scan an area. **2** COMP any device capable of recognizing characters, etc, in documents and generating signals corresponding to them, used esp to input text and graphics directly. **3** MED any device that produces an image of an internal organ.

scansion N **1** the act of scanning poetry. **2** the division of a verse into metrical feet.

scant ADJ in short supply; deficient.

scanty ADJ (*-ier, -iest*) small or lacking in size or amount; barely enough: *a scanty meal.*
■ **scantily** ADV. ■ **scantiness** N.

scapegoat N someone made to take the blame or punishment for the errors of others.

scapula N (*-lae* or *-las*) ANAT the broad flat triangular bone at the back of the shoulder. Also called **shoulder blade**.

scar[1] N **1** a mark left on the skin after a sore or wound has healed. **2** any permanent damaging emotional effect. **3** any blemish.
➤ VB (*-rr-*) TR & INTR to mark or become marked with a scar.

scar[2] N a steep rocky outcrop or crag on the side of a hill or mountain.

scarab N a dung beetle.

scarce ADJ **1** rare. **2** in short supply.
➤ ADV scarcely; hardly ever: **We could scarce see it through the mist.** ■ **scarcity** N.
◆ **make oneself scarce** COLLOQ to leave quickly or stay away.

scarcely ADV **1** only just. **2** hardly ever. **3** not really: **That's scarcely a reason to hit him.**

scare VB **1** TR & INTR to make or become afraid. **2** to startle.
➤ N **1** a fright or panic. **2** a sudden and often unwarranted public alarm: **a bomb scare.**

scarecrow N **1** a device, usu in the shape of a human figure, set up in fields to scare birds. **2** COLLOQ a shabbily dressed person.

scaremonger N someone who causes alarm by spreading rumours of disaster.
■ **scaremongering** N.

scarf[1] N (*scarves* or *scarfs*) a strip or square of fabric, worn around the neck or head.

scarf[2] N a joint made between two ends cut so as to look like a continuous surface.

scarify VB (*-ies, -ied*) **1** chiefly SURGERY to make a number of scratches or lacerations in (the skin, etc). **2** to break up the surface of soil with a wire rake, etc. **3** to hurt someone with criticism.
■ **scarification** N.

scarlatina N, PATHOL scarlet fever.

scarlet N a brilliant red colour.

scarlet fever N an acute infectious disease characterized by fever and a red rash.

scarp N **1** the steep side of a hill or rock. **2** the inner side of a defensive ditch.

scarper VB, INTR, COLLOQ to run away.

scary ADV (*-ier, -iest*) COLLOQ causing fear or anxiety. ■ **scarily** ADV. ■ **scariness** N.

scat[1] VB (*-tt-*) INTR, COLLOQ to go away; to run off.

scat[2] N a form of jazz singing consisting of improvised sounds rather than words.

scathing ADJ scornfully critical; detrimental.

scatology N preoccupation with excrement. ■ **scatological** ADJ.

scatter VB **1** to strew, sprinkle or throw around loosely. **2** TR & INTR to disperse.

scatterbrain N, COLLOQ a person incapable of organized thought. ■ **scatterbrained** ADJ.

scatty ADJ (*-ier, -iest*) BRIT COLLOQ mentally disorganized.

scavenge VB, TR & INTR to search among waste for (usable items).

scavenger N **1** a person who searches among waste for usable items. **2** an animal that feeds on refuse or decaying flesh.

scenario N **1** a rough outline of a dramatic work, film, etc. **2** any hypothetical situation.

scene N **1** the setting in which a real or imaginary event takes place. **2** the representation of action on the stage. **3** a division of a play. **4** a unit of action in a book or film. **5** a landscape, situation or picture: A **delightful scene met their eyes. 6** an unseemly display of emotion in public: **make a scene. 7** COLLOQ the publicity, action, etc surrounding a particular activity: **the current music scene. 8** COLLOQ a liked or preferred area of interest: **Rock concerts are just not my scene.**

scenery N (*-ies*) **1** a picturesque landscape. **2** the items making up a stage or film set.

scenic ADJ referring to, being or including attractive natural landscapes: **the scenic route.**

scent N **1** the distinctive smell of a person, animal or plant. **2** a trail of this left behind. **3** a series of clues leading to a discovery. **4** perfume.
➤ VB **1** to smell. **2** to sense. **3** INTR to give out a smell. **4** to perfume. ■ **scented** ADJ.
◆ **put** or **throw sb off the scent** to deliberately mislead them.

sceptic or (N AMER) **skeptic** N **1** someone with a tendency to disbelieve or doubt the veracity or validity of other people's motives, ideas, etc. **2** someone who questions widely accepted, esp religious, doctrines and beliefs. ■ **sceptical** ADJ. ■ **scepticism** N.

sceptre N a ceremonial staff or baton carried by a monarch as a symbol of sovereignty.

schedule N **1** a list of events or activities planned to take place at certain times. **2** the state of an event or activity occurring on time: **We are well behind schedule.**
➤ VB **1** to plan something to take place at a certain time. **2** to put something on a schedule.

schema N (*-mata*) **1** a scheme or plan. **2** a diagrammatic outline or synopsis.

schematic ADJ represented by a diagram or plan. ■ **schematically** ADV.

scheme N **1** a plan of action. **2** a system or programme: **a pension scheme. 3** a careful arrangement of different components: **a colour scheme. 4** a secret plan intended to cause harm or damage. **5** a diagram or table.
➤ VB, INTR to plan or act secretly and often maliciously. ■ **schemer** N. ■ **scheming** ADJ, N.

scherzo N (*-zos* or *-zi*) a lively piece of music, generally the second or third part of a symphony, sonata, etc, replacing the minuet.

schism N, RELIG a separation into groups, or from the main group. ■ **schismatic** ADJ.

schizo COLLOQ, N a schizophrenic person.
➤ ADJ schizophrenic.

schizoid ADJ displaying some symptoms of schizophrenia, such as tendency to fantasy.
➤ N a schizoid person.

schizophrenia N a severe mental disorder characterized by impairment of thought processes, a marked personality change and social withdrawal. ■ **schizophrenic** N, ADJ.

schmaltz N, COLLOQ extreme or excessive sentimentality. ■ **schmaltzy** ADJ.

schnapps N a strong dry alcoholic spirit.

schnitzel N a veal cutlet.

scholar N 1 a learned person, esp an academic. 2 a person who studies; a pupil or student. 3 a person receiving a scholarship. ■ **scholarliness** N. ■ **scholarly** ADJ.

scholarship N 1 the achievements or learning of a scholar. 2 a sum of money awarded for the purposes of further study.

scholastic ADJ referring or relating to learning institutions, such as schools or universities, and to their teaching and education methods.

school[1] N 1 a place or institution where education is received, esp primary or secondary education. 2 the work of such an institution. 3 the disciples or adherents of a particular teacher. 4 a group of painters, writers or other artists sharing the same style. ➤ VB 1 to educate in a school. 2 to give training or instruction to. ■ **schooling** N.

school[2] N a group of fish, whales or other marine animals swimming together.

schoolmaster or **schoolmistress** N respectively, a male or female schoolteacher.

schoolteacher N a person who teaches in a school.

schooner N 1 a fast sailing-ship with two or more masts. 2 BRIT a large sherry glass. 3 N AMER, ESP US a large beer glass.

schottische N (music for) a German folk dance, similar to a slow polka.

sciatic ADJ 1 referring or relating to the hip region. 2 affected by sciatica.

sciatica N, PATHOL pain in the lower back, buttocks and backs of the thighs caused by pressure on the sciatic nerve.

science N 1 the systematic observation and classification of natural phenomena in order to learn about them and bring them under general principles. 2 a department or branch of such knowledge developed in this way, eg astronomy, genetics. 3 any area of knowledge obtained using, or arranged by formal principles: political science. ■ **scientist** N.

science fiction N imaginative fiction presenting a view of life in the future.

scientific ADJ 1 referring or relating to, or used in, science. 2 displaying the kind of principled approach characteristic of science. ■ **scientifically** ADV.

sci-fi N, COLLOQ science fiction.

scimitar N a sword with a short curved single-edged blade, broadest at the point end.

scintilla N, LITERARY a hint or trace.

scintillate VB, INTR 1 to sparkle or emit sparks. 2 to impress with one's vitality or wit. ■ **scintillating** ADJ. ■ **scintillation** N.

scion N 1 BOT the detached shoot of a plant inserted into a cut in the outer stem of another plant. 2 a descendant or offspring.

scissors PL N a one-handed cutting device with two long blades pivoted in the middle so the cutting edges close and overlap.

sclera N the outer membrane of the eyeball.

sclerosis N, PATHOL abnormal hardening or thickening of an artery or other body part.

scoff[1] VB, INTR (often **scoff at sb** or **sth**) to express scorn or contempt for them; to jeer. ➤ N an expression of scorn. ■ **scoffing** N, ADJ.

scoff[2] VB, TR & INTR, COLLOQ to eat rapidly.

scold VB 1 to reprimand or rebuke. 2 INTR to use strong or offensive language. ➤ N, OLD USE a nagging or quarrelsome person, esp a woman. ■ **scolding** N.

scollop see **scallop**

scone N a small flattish plain cake.

scoop VB 1 to lift, dig or remove something with a sweeping circular movement. 2 to do better than (rival newspapers) in being the first to publish a story. ➤ N 1 a spoonlike implement for handling or serving food. 2 a hollow shovel or lipped container for lifting loose material. 3 a quantity scooped. 4 a news story printed by one newspaper in advance of all others.

scoot VB, INTR, COLLOQ to make off speedily.

scooter N 1 a child's toy vehicle consisting of a board on a two-wheeled frame, with tall handlebars connected to the front wheel, propelled by pushing against the ground with one foot. 2 (in full **motor-scooter**) a small-wheeled motorcycle.

scope N 1 the range of a subject covered. 2 the aim or purpose of something. 3 the limits within which there is the opportunity to act. 4 range of understanding: **beyond his scope**.

scorbutic ADJ, PATHOL relating to scurvy.

scorch VB 1 TR & INTR to burn or be burned slightly or superficially. 2 to dry up, parch or wither. ➢ N 1 an act of scorching. 2 a scorched area.

scorcher N, COLLOQ an extremely hot day.

scorching ADJ, COLLOQ 1 of the weather: very hot. 2 of a criticism, etc: harsh.

score N 1 a total number of points gained or achieved eg in a game. 2 an act of gaining or achieving a point, etc. 3 a scratch or shallow cut. 4 a set of twenty: **three score**. 5 (**scores**) very many; lots. 6 COLLOQ (**the score**) the current situation: **What's the score with your job?** 7 a written or printed copy of music for several parts. 8 the music from a film or play. 9 (**the score**) a reason; grounds: **rejected on the score of expense**. ➢ VB 1 TR & INTR to gain or achieve (a point) in a game. 2 INTR to keep a record of points gained during a game. 3 to make cuts or scratches in the surface of something. 4 to be equivalent to (a number of points): **black king scores three**. 5 MUS to adapt music for instruments or voices other than those orig intended. 6 to compose music for a film or play. 7 INTR to achieve a rating; to be judged or regarded: **This film scores high for excitement**. ■ **scorer** N.

scoreboard N a board on which the score in a game is displayed.

scorn N extreme or mocking contempt. ➢ VB 1 to treat someone or something with scorn; to express scorn for. 2 to refuse or reject with scorn. ■ **scornful** ADJ. ■ **scornfully** ADV.

Scorpio N, ASTROL the eighth sign of the zodiac (the Scorpion).

scorpion N an invertebrate animal, found in hot regions, with eight legs, pincers and a segmented abdomen or 'tail' bearing a poisonous sting.

Scot N a native or inhabitant of Scotland.

Scotch ADJ of things, esp products, but not usu of people: Scottish: **Scotch broth**. ➢ N Scotch whisky.

scotch VB 1 to ruin or hinder eg plans. 2 to reveal (something, esp rumours) to be untrue.

scot-free ADJ unpunished or unharmed.

Scots ADJ 1 Scottish by birth. 2 esp of law and language: Scottish. ■ **Scotsman** and **Scotswoman** N.

Scottish ADJ of Scotland.

scoundrel N a villainous rogue.

scour[1] VB 1 to clean or remove by hard rubbing. 2 to clean with a jet of water. ■ **scourer** N.

scour[2] VB 1 to make an exhaustive search of (an area). 2 to range over (an area).

scourge N 1 a cause of great suffering and affliction. 2 a whip used for punishing. ➢ VB 1 to cause suffering to; to afflict. 2 to whip.

Scouse N 1 the dialect of Liverpool. 2 an inhabitant of Liverpool. **Also** AS ADJ.

scout N 1 MIL a person or group sent out to observe the enemy and bring back information. 2 (often **Scout,** FORMERLY **Boy Scout**) a member of the Scout Association. 3 a talent scout. 4 COLLOQ a search. ➢ VB, INTR 1 to act as a scout. 2 (often **scout about** or **around**) COLLOQ to make a search.

scowl VB, INTR to look disapprovingly or angrily. ➢ N a scowling expression.

scrabble VB, INTR 1 to scratch, grope or struggle frantically. 2 to scrawl.

scrag N the thin part of a neck of mutton or veal, providing poor quality meat. **Also scrag-end**. ■ **scraggy** ADJ (**-ier, -iest**) scrawny.

scram VB (**-mm-**) INTR, COLLOQ to go away.

scramble VB 1 INTR to crawl or climb using hands and feet, esp hurriedly or frantically. 2 INTR to struggle violently against others: **starving people scrambling to find food.** 3 to cook (eggs) whisked up with milk, butter, etc. 4 to convert (a message) into distorted form. 5 INTR of military aircraft or air crew: to take off immediately in an emergency. ➤ N 1 an act of scrambling. 2 a dash or struggle to beat others. 3 a quick take-off in an emergency. 4 a cross-country motorcar or motorcycle race. ■ **scrambling** ADJ, N.

scrambler N, ELECTRONICS a device that modifies radio or telephone signals so that they can only be decoded by a special device.

scrap[1] N 1 a small piece; a fragment. 2 waste material, esp metal, for recycling or re-using. 3 (**scraps**) leftover pieces of food. ➤ VB (**-pp-**) to discard or cease to use.

scrap[2] COLLOQ, N a fight or quarrel, usu physical. ➤ VB (**-pp-**) INTR to fight or quarrel.

scrapbook N a book with blank pages for pasting in cuttings, pictures, etc.

scrape VB 1 (also **scrape sth along, over, etc sth**) to push or drag (esp a sharp object) along or over (a hard or rough surface). 2 INTR to move along a surface with a grazing action. 3 to graze (the skin) by a scraping action. 4 to move along (a surface) with a grating sound. 5 INTR to make a grating sound. 6 (also **scrape sth off**) to remove it with such an action. ➤ N 1 an instance, process or act of dragging or grazing. 2 a part damaged or cleaned by scraping. 3 a graze (of the skin). 4 COLLOQ a difficult or embarrassing situation. 5 COLLOQ a fight or quarrel. ■ **scraper** N.
◆ **scrape through** or **by** to manage or succeed in doing something narrowly.
◆ **scrape sth together** or **up** to collect it little by little, usu with difficulty.

scrappy ADJ (**-ier, -iest**) fragmentary or disjointed. ■ **scrappiness** N.

scratch VB 1 to draw a sharp or pointed object across (a surface), causing damage or making marks. 2 to make (a mark) by such action. 3 TR & INTR to rub the skin with the fingernails, esp to

relieve itching. 4 to dig or scrape with the claws. 5 (usu **scratch sth out** or **off**) to erase or cancel it. 6 INTR to make a grating noise. 7 INTR to withdraw from a contest. ➤ N 1 an act of scratching. 2 a mark made by scratching. 3 a scratching sound. 4 a superficial wound or minor injury. ➤ ADJ 1 casually or hastily got together; improvised: **a scratch meal.** 2 of a competitor: not given a handicap. ■ **scratchy** ADJ.
◆ **come up to scratch** COLLOQ to meet the required or expected standard.
◆ **from scratch** from the beginning.

scrawl VB, TR & INTR to write or draw illegibly. ➤ N untidy or illegible handwriting.

scrawny ADJ (**-ier, -iest**) unhealthily thin and bony. ■ **scrawniness** ADJ.

scream VB 1 TR & INTR to cry out in a loud high-pitched voice, as in fear, pain or anger. 2 INTR to laugh shrilly or uproariously. ➤ N 1 a sudden piercing cry. 2 COLLOQ an extremely amusing person or thing.

scree N, GEOL a sloping mass of rock debris.

screech N a harsh, shrill cry or noise. ➤ VB, TR & INTR to utter a screech or make a sound like a screech. ■ **screechy** ADJ.

screed N a long spoken or written passage.

screen N 1 a movable set of foldable hinged panels, used to partition off part of a room for privacy. 2 a single panel used for protection against strong heat or light. 3 a windscreen. 4 a wire netting placed over windows to keep out insects. 5 the wide end of a TV set on which the images are formed. 6 a white surface onto which films or slides are projected. 7 (**the screen**) the medium of cinema or television. ➤ VB 1 to shelter or conceal. 2 to subject someone to tests in order to discern their ability, reliability, worthiness, etc. 3 to test someone in order to check for the presence of disease. 4 to show or project (a film, programme, etc) at the cinema or on TV. ■ **screening** N.

screenplay N the script of a film.

screen printing and **screen process** N a stencil technique in which coloured ink is forced through a fine silk or nylon mesh.

screen-saver N, COMP a program which temporarily blanks out a screen display.

screen test N a filmed audition to test whether an actor or actress is suitable for cinema work.

screw N 1 a small fastening device consisting of a metal cylinder with a spiral ridge down the shaft and a slot in its head, driven into position in wood, etc by rotation using a screwdriver. 2 any object similar in shape or function. 3 the turn or twist of a screw. 4 SNOOKER, BILLIARDS a shot in which the cue ball is subjected to sidespin or backspin. 5 SLANG a prison officer. 6 COARSE SLANG an act of sexual intercourse. ➤ VB 1 to twist (a screw) into place. 2 to push or pull with a twisting action. 3 COLLOQ to swindle. 4 SNOOKER, BILLIARDS to put sidespin or backspin on (the cue ball). 5 TR & INTR, COARSE SLANG to have sexual intercourse with someone.
◆ **screw sth up** SLANG to bungle it.

screwdriver N a hand-held tool with a shaped end that fits into a screw's head.

screwed-up ADJ, SLANG extremely anxious, nervous or psychologically disturbed.

screwy ADJ (-ier, -iest) COLLOQ crazy.

scribble VB 1 TR & INTR to write quickly or untidily; to scrawl. 2 INTR to draw meaningless lines or shapes absent-mindedly. ➤ N 1 untidy handwriting. 2 meaningless written lines or shapes. ■ **scribbler** N.

scribe N 1 before printing was invented: a person employed to make handwritten copies of documents. 2 in biblical times: a Jewish lawyer or teacher of law.

scrimmage and **scrummage** N 1 a noisy struggle. 2 AMER FOOTBALL play between the teams beginning with the snap and ending when the ball is dead. 3 RUGBY a scrum.

scrimp VB, INTR to be frugal or sparing.

scrip N 1 COLLOQ a doctor's prescription. 2 COMMERCE a provisional certificate issued before a formal share certificate is drawn up.

script N 1 a piece of handwriting. 2 the printed text of a play, film or broadcast. 3 a set of

characters used for writing: Cyrillic script. ➤ VB to write the script of (a play, film, etc).

scripture or **Scripture** N the sacred writings of a religion. ■ **scriptural** ADJ.

scrofula N, PATHOL the former name for tuberculosis of the lymph nodes, esp of the neck. ■ **scrofulous** ADJ.

scroll N 1 a roll of paper or parchment usu containing an inscription. 2 a decorative spiral shape, eg carved in stonework. ➤ VB 1 to roll or cut into a scroll or scrolls. 2 TR & INTR, COMP (often **scroll up** or **down**) to move the text displayed on a VDU up or down.

Scrooge N a miserly person.

scrotum N (-ta or -tums) BIOL the sac of skin that encloses the testicles.

scrounge VB 1 TR & INTR, COLLOQ to get something by asking or begging; to cadge or sponge. 2 INTR (often **scrounge for sth**) to hunt or search around for it. ■ **scrounger** N.

scrub¹ VB (-bb-) 1 TR & INTR to rub (something) hard in order to remove dirt. 2 to clean by hard rubbing. 3 COLLOQ to cancel (plans, etc). ➤ N an act of scrubbing.
◆ **scrub up** of a surgeon, etc, before an operation: to wash the hands thoroughly.

scrub² N 1 vegetation consisting of stunted trees and evergreen shrubs collectively. 2 (also **scrubland**) an area with such vegetation.

scrubby ADJ (-ier, -iest) 1 covered with scrub. 2 of trees, shrubs, etc: stunted.

scruff N 1 the back or nape of the neck. 2 COLLOQ a dirty untidy person.

scruffy ADJ (-ier, -iest) shabby and untidy.

scrum N 1 RUGBY the restarting of play when the players from both teams hunch together and tightly interlock their arms and heads in readiness for the ball being thrown in by the player known as the scrum half. Also called **scrimmage**. 2 COLLOQ a riotous struggle.

scrummage see **scrimmage**

scrummy ADJ (-ier, -iest) chiefly BRIT COLLOQ delicious; scrumptious.

scrumptious ADJ, COLLOQ delicious.

scrumpy N (*-ies*) strong dry cider.

scrunch VB 1 TR & INTR to crunch or crush, esp with relation to the noise produced. 2 INTR to make a crunching sound.
➤ N an act or the sound of scrunching.

scruple N (usu **scruples**) a sense of moral responsibility.
➤ VB, INTR to be reluctant because of scruples: **I'd scruple to steal even if we were starving.**

scrupulous ADJ 1 having scruples; being careful to do nothing morally wrong. 2 extremely conscientious and meticulous.

scrutinize or **-ise** VB to subject to scrutiny.

scrutiny N (*-ies*) 1 a close, careful and thorough examination or inspection. 2 a penetrating or searching look.

scuba N a device used by skin-divers in **scuba diving**, consisting of one or two cylinders of air connected by a tube to a mouthpiece allowing underwater breathing.

scud VB (*-dd-*) INTR 1 esp of clouds: to sweep quickly across the sky. 2 of sailing vessels: to sail swiftly by the force of a wind.

scuff VB, TR & INTR 1 to drag (the feet) when walking. 2 to scrape (esp shoes or heels) while walking.
➤ N 1 the act of scuffing. 2 an area worn away by scuffing.

scuffle N a confused fight or struggle.
➤ VB, INTR to take part in a scuffle.

scull N 1 either of a pair of short light oars used by one rower. 2 a small light racing boat propelled by one rower using sculls. 3 a large single oar over the stern of a boat.
➤ VB to propel with a scull or sculls. ■ **sculler** N.

scullery N (*-ies*) a room attached to the kitchen where basic chores are carried out.

sculpt VB, TR & INTR to carve or model.

sculptor and **sculptress** N a person who practises the art of sculpture.

sculpture N 1 the art or act of carving or modelling with clay, wood, stone, plaster, etc. 2 a work, or works, of art produced in this way.
➤ VB 1 to carve, mould or sculpt. 2 to represent in sculpture. ■ **sculptural** ADJ.

scum N 1 dirt or waste matter floating on the surface of a liquid. 2 COLLOQ, DEROG a worthless or contemptible person or such people.
➤ VB (*-mm-*) 1 to remove the scum from. 2 INTR to form a scum. ■ **scummy** ADJ.

scupper VB 1 COLLOQ to ruin or put an end to (a plan, an idea, etc). 2 to deliberately sink (a ship).

scurf N 1 small flakes of dead skin, esp dandruff. 2 any flaking or peeling substance.

scurrilous ADJ indecently insulting or abusive, and unjustly damaging to the reputation.

scurry VB, INTR to move hurriedly or briskly.
➤ N (*-ies*) 1 an act of or the sound of scurrying. 2 a sudden brief gust or fall, eg of wind or snow.

scurvy N, PATHOL a disease caused by dietary deficiency of vitamin C.
➤ ADJ (*-ier, -iest*) vile; contemptible.

scut N a short tail, esp of a rabbit, hare or deer.

scuttle¹ N (in full **coal scuttle**) a container for holding coal, usu kept near a fire.

scuttle² VB, INTR to move quickly with haste.
➤ N a scuttling pace or movement.

scythe N a tool with a wooden handle and a long curved blade for cutting tall crops.
➤ VB to cut with a scythe.

sea N 1 (usu **the sea**) the large expanse of salt water covering the greater part of the Earth's surface. 2 any geographical division of this, eg the Mediterranean Sea. 3 an area of this with reference to its calmness or turbulence: **choppy seas.** 4 a large inland saltwater lake, eg the Dead Sea. 5 anything resembling the sea in its seemingly limitless mass: **a sea of paperwork.**

sea anemone N a marine invertebrate with a round brightly-coloured body.

seaboard N a coast.

sea dog N an old or experienced sailor.

seafaring ADJ travelling by or working at sea.

seafood N shellfish and other edible fish.

seafront N the side of the land, a town or a building facing the sea.

seagoing ADJ of a ship: suitable for sea travel.

seagull same as **gull**

sea horse N a small fish that swims in an upright position, with its elongated horse-like head bent at right angles to its body.

seal[1] N **1** a piece of wax, lead or other material, attached to a document and stamped with an official mark to show authenticity. **2** an engraved metal stamp for making such a mark eg on wax. **3** a similar piece of material for keeping something closed. **4** a piece of rubber or other material serving to keep a joint airtight or watertight.
➤ VB **1** to fix a seal to something. **2** to fasten or stamp something with a seal. **3** to decide or confirm: **seal someone's fate**. **4** to close.

seal[2] N **1** a marine mammal with a smooth-skinned or furry streamlined body and limbs modified to form webbed flippers. **2** sealskin.

sealant N any material used for sealing a gap to prevent the leaking of water, etc.

sea level N the mean level of the surface of the sea between high and low tides, therefore the point from which land height is measured.

sealskin N the prepared skin of a furry seal.

seam N **1** a join between edges, esp one that has been welded. **2** a similar join where pieces of fabric have been stitched together. **3** GEOL a layer of coal or ore in the earth.
➤ VB **1** to join edge to edge. **2** to scar or wrinkle. ■ **seamless** ADJ.

seaman N (*seamen*) a sailor below the rank of officer.

seamanship N sailing skills.

seamstress N a woman who sews.

seamy ADJ (*-ier, -iest*) sordid; disreputable.

séance or **seance** N a meeting at which a person, esp a spiritualist, attempts to contact the spirits of dead people.

seaplane N an aeroplane designed to take off from and land on water.

sear VB **1** to scorch. **2** to dry out or wither.
➤ N a mark made by scorching. ■ **searing** ADJ.

search VB **1** TR & INTR to explore something thoroughly in order to try to find someone or something. **2** to check the clothing or body of someone for concealed objects. **3** to examine closely or scrutinize: **search one's conscience**.
➤ N an act of searching.

searchlight N a powerful lamp for illuminating an area in darkness.

seashell N the empty shell of a marine invertebrate, esp a mollusc.

seashore N the land adjacent to the sea.

seasickness N nausea caused by the rolling or dipping motion of a ship. ■ **seasick** ADJ.

seaside N (usu **the seaside**) a coastal area.

season N **1** any of the four major periods into which the year is divided according to changes in weather patterns and other natural phenomena. **2** any period having particular characteristics: **our busy season**. **3** a period of the year during which a particular sport, activity, etc is carried out: **holiday season**.
➤ VB **1** to flavour (food) by adding salt, pepper and/or other herbs and spices. **2** to prepare something, esp timber, for use by drying it out. **3** to add interest or liveliness to something.
◆ **in season 1** of food, esp fruit and vegetables: readily available, as determined by its growing season. **2** of game animals: legally allowed to be hunted and killed, according to the time of year. **3** of a female animal: ready to mate; on heat.
◆ **out of season 1** of food, esp fruit and vegetables: not yet available. **2** of game animals: legally not yet to be hunted.

seasonal ADJ available, taking place or occurring only at certain times of the year.

seasoned ADJ **1** of food: flavoured. **2** matured or conditioned: **seasoned wood**. **3** experienced: **seasoned travellers**.

seasoning N any substance such as salt,

pepper, herbs, spices, etc used to season food.

season ticket N a ticket, usu bought at a reduced price, allowing a specified or unlimited number of visits or journeys in a fixed period.

seat N 1 anything designed or intended for sitting on, eg a chair, bench, saddle, etc. 2 the part of it on which a person sits. 3 a place for sitting, eg in a cinema or theatre. 4 the buttocks. 5 the part of a garment covering the buttocks. 6 the base of an object, or any part on which it rests or fits. 7 a government constituency. 8 a position on a committee or other administrative body. 9 a large country house. ➤ VB 1 to place on a seat. 2 to cause to sit down. 3 to assign a seat to someone, eg at a dinner table. 4 to provide seats for (a specified number of people): **My car seats five.**

seat belt N a safety belt for a passenger in a car, aeroplane, etc.

sea urchin N a small echinoderm with a spherical or heart-shaped shell covered by protective spines.

seaward ADJ facing the sea. ➤ ADV (also **seawards**) towards the sea.

seaweed N the common name for any of numerous species of marine algae.

seaworthy ADJ of a ship: fit for a voyage at sea. ■ **seaworthiness** N.

sebaceous ADJ secreting sebum.

sebum N, BIOL the oily substance that lubricates and waterproofs the hair and skin.

sec¹ N, COLLOQ short for **second²**: wait a sec.

sec² ABBREV secant.

secant N 1 GEOM a straight line that cuts a curve at one or more places. 2 MATH for a given angle in a right-angled triangle: the ratio of the length of the hypotenuse to the length of the side adjacent to the angle under consideration.

secateurs PL N small shears used for pruning.

secede VB, INTR to withdraw formally, eg from a political or religious body or alliance. ■ **secession** N.

seclude VB 1 to keep away from other contacts or influences. 2 to keep out of view.

secluded ADJ private and quiet; hidden.

seclusion N 1 the state of being secluded or the act of secluding. 2 a private place.

second¹ ADJ 1 in counting: next after or below the first, in order of sequence or importance. 2 alternate; other: **every second week.** 3 MUS singing or playing a part in harmony which is subordinate or slightly lower in pitch to another part: **second violin.** ➤ N 1 someone or something next in sequence after the first; someone or something of second class. 2 a place in the second class or rank. 3 a second-class honours degree. 4 a flawed or imperfect article sold at reduced price. ➤ VB 1 to declare formal support for (a proposal, or the person making it). 2 to give support to someone or something. ➤ ADV secondly.

second² N 1 a unit of time equal to one sixtieth of a minute. 2 GEOM a unit of angular measurement equal to of a degree or one sixtieth of a minute. 3 a moment.

second³ VB to transfer someone temporarily to a different post or duty. ■ **secondment** N.

secondary ADJ 1 being of lesser importance than the principal or primary concern; subordinate. 2 developed from something earlier or original: **a secondary infection.** 3 of education: between primary and higher or further, for pupils aged between 11 and 18. ➤ N (**-ies**) 1 a subordinate person or thing. 2 a delegate or deputy.

secondary colour N a colour obtained by mixing or superimposing two primary colours.

second best N the next after the best. ➤ ADJ (**second-best**): my second-best suit.

second class N the next class or category after the first in quality or worth. ➤ ADJ (**second-class**) 1 referring or relating to the class below the first. 2 being of a poor standard; inferior. 3 of mail: sent at a cheaper rate than first class, therefore taking longer. ➤ ADV by second-class mail or transport.

second cousin N a child of the first cousin of either parent.

second-degree ADJ 1 MED, DENOTING the second most serious of the three degrees of burning. 2 N AMER LAW, DENOTING unlawful killing with intent, but no premeditation.

seconder N a person who seconds a proposal or the person making it.

second hand N the pointer on a watch or clock indicates the time in seconds.

second-hand ADJ 1 previously owned or used by someone else. 2 not directly received or obtained, but known through an intermediary: **second-hand information**. ➤ ADV 1 in a second-hand state: **It's cheaper to buy second-hand**. 2 not directly, but from someone else: **They heard it second-hand**.

second lieutenant N an army or navy officer of the lowest commissioned rank.

secondly ADV in the second place; as a second consideration.

second nature N a habit or tendency so deeply ingrained as to seem innate.

second person see under **person**

second-rate ADJ inferior or mediocre.

second sight N the power believed to enable someone to see the future or events elsewhere.

second thoughts N doubts.

second wind N a burst of renewed energy.

secrecy N 1 the state or fact of being secret. 2 confidentiality: **I'm sworn to secrecy**. 3 the tendency to keep information secret.

secret ADJ 1 kept hidden or away from the knowledge of others. 2 unknown or unobserved by others: **a secret army**. 3 tending to conceal things from others; private or secretive. 4 guarded against discovery or observation: **a secret location**. ➤ N 1 something not disclosed to others. 2 an unrevealed method of achievement: **the secret of eternal youth**. 3 a central but elusive principle, etc: **the secret of a good**

marriage. ■ **secretly** ADV.
◆ **in secret** secretly; unknown to others.

secret agent N a spy.

secretariat N the administrative department of any council, organization or legislative body.

secretary N (-*ies*) 1 a person employed to perform administrative or clerical tasks for a company or individual. 2 the member of a club or society committee responsible for its correspondence and business records. 3 a senior civil servant assisting a government minister or ambassador. ■ **secretarial** ADJ.

secrete¹ VB, BIOL, ZOOL of a gland or similar organ: to form and release (a substance).

secrete² VB to hide away or conceal.

secretion N 1 the process whereby glands of the body discharge or release particular substances. 2 any of the substances produced by such glands, eg sweat, saliva, mucus, bile.

secretive ADJ inclined to or fond of secrecy. ■ **secretively** ADV. ■ **secretiveness** N.

secret police N a police force operating in secret against opposition to the government.

secret service N a government department responsible for espionage and national security matters.

sect N a religious or other group whose views differ from those of an established body.

sectarian ADJ 1 of or relating to a sect. 2 having or caused by hostility towards those outside one's group. ■ **sectarianism** N.

section N 1 the act or process of cutting. 2 any of the parts into which something is or can be divided or of which it may be composed. 3 GEOM the surface formed when a plane cuts through a solid figure. 4 the act of cutting through a solid figure. 5 a diagram showing an object as if it had been cut through. ➤ VB 1 to divide something into sections. 2 MED to issue an order for the admission of (a mentally ill person) to a psychiatric hospital.

sector N 1 GEOM a portion of a circle bounded by two radii and an arc. 2 a division or section of a nation's economic operations. **3** a part of an area divided up for military purposes.

secular ADJ **1** relating to the present world rather than to spiritual things. **2** not religious or ecclesiastical. ■ **secularize** or **-ise** VB.

secularism N the view or belief that society should not be influenced or controlled by religion or the Church. ■ **secularist** N.

secure ADJ **1** free from danger; providing safety. **2** free from trouble, worry or uncertainty. **3** firmly fixed or attached. **4** not likely to be lost or taken away; safe or assured: **a secure job.**
➤ VB **1** to fasten or attach firmly. **2** to get or assure possession of something. **3** to make free from danger or risk; to make safe. **4** to guarantee. ■ **securely** ADV.

security N (-ies) **1** the state of being secure. **2** protection from future financial difficulty, from physical harm or from theft. **3** the staff providing such protection against attack or theft. **4** something given as a guarantee, esp to a creditor giving them the right to recover a debt. **5** (usu **securities**) a certificate stating ownership of stocks or shares.
➤ ADJ providing security or comfort.

sedan N, N AMER a saloon car.

sedate ADJ **1** calm and dignified in manner. **2** slow and unexciting.
➤ VB to calm or quieten someone by means of a sedative. ■ **sedately** ADV. ■ **sedateness** N.

sedation N, MED the state of having been calmed, esp by means of sedatives.

sedative N, MED any agent, esp a drug, that has a calming effect.

sedentary ADJ involving or spending much time sitting.

sedge N a plant, resembling grass, which grows in bogs, fens, marshes, etc. ■ **sedgy** ADJ.

sediment N **1** insoluble solid particles that have settled at the bottom of a liquid. **2** GEOL solid material that has been deposited by the action of gravity, wind, water or ice.
■ **sedimentary** ADJ. ■ **sedimentation** N.

sedition N any action encouraging public disorder, esp rebellion. ■ **seditious** ADJ.

seduce VB **1** to lure or entice someone into having sexual intercourse. **2** to lead astray; to tempt, esp into wrongdoing. ■ **seducer** or **seductress** N. ■ **seduction** N.

seductive ADJ **1** sexually attractive and charming. **2** tempting; enticing.

sedulous ADJ, FORMAL steadily hardworking.

see[1] VB (PA T *saw*, PA P *seen*) **1** to perceive by the sense operated in the eyes. **2** INTR to have the power of vision. **3** TR & INTR to understand or realize: **Don't you see what she's trying to do? 4** to watch: **We're going to see a play. 5** to be aware of or know, esp by looking or reading: **I see from your letter that you're married. 6** to predict; to expect: **We could see what was going to happen. 7** to spend time with someone: **I haven't seen her for ages. 8** to speak to someone; to consult: **He's asking to see the manager. 9** to make sure of something: **See that you lock the door. 10** to consider: **I see her more as an acquaintance than a friend. 11** to encounter or experience: **She's seen too much pain in her life. 12** to be witness to something as a sight or event: **We're now seeing huge wage rises. 13** to escort: **I'll see you home. 14** to refer to (the specified page, etc) for information: **see page five.**
◆ **see sb off 1** to accompany them to their place of departure: **saw her off at the airport. 2** COLLOQ to get rid of them by force.
◆ **see sth out** to stay until the end of it.
◆ **see through sth 1** to discern what is implied by an idea or scheme, etc. **2** to detect or determine the truth underlying a lie.
◆ **see sth through** to do it to the end.

see[2] N the area under the religious authority of a bishop or archbishop.

seed N (*seeds* or *seed*) **1** BOT in flowering and cone-bearing plants: the structure that develops from the ovule after fertilization, and is capable of developing into a new plant. **2** a small hard fruit or part in a fruit; a pip. **3** a source or origin: **the seeds of the plan. 4** SPORT a seeded player: **He is number one seed.**

➤ VB **1** INTR of a plant: to produce seeds. **2** to sow or plant (seeds). **3** to remove seeds from (eg a fruit). **4** SPORT to arrange (a tournament) so that high-ranking players only meet each other in the later stages of the contest.
◆ **go** or **run to seed 1** BOT of a plant: to stop flowering prior to the development of a seed. **2** COLLOQ to allow oneself to become unkempt or unhealthy through lack of care.

seedling N a young plant grown from seed.

seedy ADJ, COLLOQ (*-ier, -iest*) **1** mildly ill or unwell. **2** shabby; dirty or disreputable: a seedy club. ■ **seediness** N.

seeing N the ability to see; the power of vision.
➤ CONJ (usu **seeing that**) given (that); since: Seeing you are opposed to the plan, I shall not pursue it.

seek VB (*sought*) **1** to look for. **2** to try to get or achieve. ■ **seeker** N.

seem VB, INTR **1** to be apparent: She seems happy today. **2** to think or believe oneself (to be, do, etc): I seem to know you.

seemly ADJ (*-ier, -iest*) fitting or suitable.

seep VB, INTR of a liquid: to escape slowly or ooze through, or as if through, a narrow opening. ■ **seepage** N.

seer N a person who predicts future events.

seersucker N lightweight Indian cotton or linen fabric with a crinkly appearance.

seesaw N a plaything consisting of a plank balanced in the middle allowing people on the ends to propel each other up and down.
➤ VB, INTR to move alternately up-and-down or back-and-forth.

seethe VB, INTR **1** to be extremely agitated or upset, esp with anger. **2** of a liquid: to churn and foam as if boiling. ■ **seething** ADJ.

segment N **1** a part, section or portion. **2** GEOM in a circle or ellipse: the region enclosed by an arc and its chord.
➤ VB to divide into segments. ■ **segmental** ADJ. ■ **segmentation** N.

segregate VB **1** to set apart or isolate. **2** INTR to separate out into a group or groups.
■ **segregation** N. ■ **segregationist** N.

seismic ADJ relating to earthquakes.

seismology N, GEOL the scientific study of earthquakes. ■ **seismological** or **seismologic** ADJ. ■ **seismologist** N.

seize VB **1** to take or grab suddenly, eagerly or forcibly. **2** to take by force; to capture. **3** to affect suddenly and deeply; to overcome: He was seized by panic. **4** to take legal possession of someone or something. **5** (often **seize on** or **upon sth**) to use it eagerly.
◆ **seize up** to become stiff.

seizure N **1** the act of seizing. **2** PATHOL a sudden attack of illness, esp producing spasms.

seldom ADV rarely.

select VB to choose from several.
➤ ADJ **1** picked out or chosen in preference to others. **2** restricted entrance or membership; exclusive. ■ **selector** N.

selection N **1** the act or process of selecting or being selected. **2** a thing or set of things selected. **3** a range from which to select.

selective ADJ **1** tending to select or choose; discriminating: a selective school. **2** involving only certain people or things; exclusive.
■ **selectively** ADJ. ■ **selectivity** N.

selenium N, CHEM a metalloid element that is a semiconductor.

self N (*selves*) **1** personality, or a particular aspect of it. **2** a person's awareness of their own identity; ego. **3** a person as a whole, comprising a combination of characteristics: He was his usual happy self.
➤ PRONOUN, COLLOQ myself, yourself, himself or herself.

self-appointed ADJ acting on one's own authority, without the approval of others.

self-assurance N self-confidence. ■ **self-assured** ADJ.

self-catering ADJ of accommodation, etc: providing facilities allowing guests and residents to prepare their own meals.

self-centred ADJ interested only in oneself.

self-coloured ADJ of the same colour all over.

self-confessed ADJ as openly acknowledged and admitted by oneself: a self-confessed cheat.

self-confidence N confidence in one's own abilities. ■ **self-confident** ADJ.

self-conscious ADJ believing oneself to be the subject of observation by others.

self-contained ADJ 1 of accommodation: having no part that is shared with others. 2 needing nothing added; complete in itself.

self-defence N the act or techniques of protecting or defending oneself from attack.

self-denial N the practice of denying one's own needs or desires. ■ **self-denying** ADJ.

self-determination N 1 the freedom to make one's own decisions without intervention from others. 2 a nation's freedom to decide its own government and political relations.

self-drive ADJ of a hired motor vehicle: to be driven by the hirer.

self-effacing ADJ tending to avoid making others aware of one's presence or achievements out of shyness or modesty.

self-employed ADJ working for oneself and under one's own control, rather than as an employee. ■ **self-employment** N.

self-esteem N one's good opinion of oneself.

self-evident ADJ clear or evident enough without need for proof or explanation.

self-explanatory ADJ easily understood or obvious; needing no further explanation.

self-government N a government run by the people of a nation without any outside control or interference. ■ **self-governing** ADJ.

self-image N one's perception of oneself.

self-important ADJ having an exaggerated sense of one's own importance or worth; arrogant or pompous. ■ **self-importance** N.

self-indulgent ADJ indulging in one's own whims or desires. ■ **self-indulgence** N.

self-interest N 1 regard for oneself and one's own interests. 2 one's own personal welfare or advantage. ■ **self-interested** ADJ.

selfish ADJ 1 concerned only with one's personal welfare, with total disregard to that of others. 2 of an act: revealing such a tendency. ■ **selfishly** ADV. ■ **selfishness** N.

selfless ADJ altruistic. ■ **selflessness** N.

self-made ADJ having achieved wealth or success by working one's way up.

self-possessed ADJ calm, controlled and collected. ■ **self-possession** N.

self-propelled ADJ of a vehicle or craft: having its own means of propulsion.

self-raising ADJ of flour: containing an ingredient to make dough or pastry rise.

self-reliant ADJ never needing or seeking help from others. ■ **self-reliance** N.

self-righteous ADJ having too high an opinion of one's own merits. ■ **self-righteousness** N.

self-sacrifice N the forgoing of one's own needs or happiness for the sake of others.

selfsame ADJ the very same; identical: He left that selfsame day.

self-satisfied ADJ feeling or showing complacent or arrogant satisfaction with oneself. ■ **self-satisfaction** N.

self-seeking ADJ preoccupied with one's own interests and opportunities for personal advantage. Also AS N. ■ **self-seeker** N.

self-service N a system in which customers serve themselves and pay at a checkout.

self-serving ADJ benefiting oneself.

self-starter N 1 in a vehicle's engine: an automatic electric starting device. 2 COLLOQ a person with initiative and motivation, therefore requiring little supervision in a job.

self-styled ADJ called or considered so only by oneself: a self-styled superstar.

self-sufficient ADJ able to provide for oneself. ■ **self-sufficiency** N.

self-willed ADJ stubbornly or obstinately determined to do or have what one wants.

sell VB (*sold*) **1** to give something to someone in exchange for money. **2** INTR to be in demand among customers; to be sold: **This style sells well. 3** to promote the sale of something: **The author's name sells the book. 5** to convince someone: **It was difficult to sell them the idea.** ➤ N **1** the act or process of selling. **2** the style of persuasion used in selling: **hard sell.** ■ **seller** N.
◆ **sell sth off** to dispose of remaining goods by selling them quickly and cheaply.
◆ **sell out** to betray one's principles.
◆ **sell out of sth** to sell one's entire stock of it.
◆ **sell up** to sell one's house or business.
◆ **sold on sth** COLLOQ convinced about it.

Sellotape or **sellotape** N, TRADEMARK a form of usu transparent adhesive tape.

selvage or **selvedge** N an edge of a length of fabric sewn so as to prevent fraying.

semantic ADJ **1** referring or relating to meaning, esp of words. **2** referring or relating to semantics. ■ **semantically** ADV.

semantics SING N the branch of linguistics that deals with the meaning of words.

semaphore N a system of signalling using flags or the arms to represent individual letters and numbers.
➤ VB, TR & INTR to signal using semaphore.

semblance N **1** outer appearance, esp when superficial or deceptive. **2** a hint or trace.

semen N a thick whitish liquid carrying spermatozoa, ejaculated from the penis.

semester N in certain universities: an academic term of half an academic year.

semi N **1** COLLOQ a semi-detached house. **2** a semifinal.

semi-automatic ADJ **1** partially automatic. **2** of a firearm: continuously reloading itself, but only firing one bullet at a time.

semibreve N, MUS the longest note in common use, equal to half a breve or two minims.

semicircle N **1** one half of a circle. **2** an arrangement of anything in this form. ■ **semicircular** ADJ.

semicolon N a punctuation mark (;) indicating a pause stronger than a comma.

semiconductor N, ELECTRONICS a crystalline material used as an electrical conductor or as an insulator, eg silicon.

semi-detached ADJ of a house: forming part of the same building, with another house on the other side of the shared wall.
➤ N a semi-detached house.

semifinal N either of two matches, the winners of which play each other in the final. ■ **semifinalist** N.

seminal ADJ **1** of or relating to seed, semen or reproduction in general. **2** of or relating to the beginnings or early developments of an idea, study, etc. **3** highly original and at the root of a trend or movement: **seminal writings.**

seminar N **1** a group of advanced students working under the supervision of a teacher. **2** any meeting set up to discuss a topic.

seminary N (*-ies*) a college for the training of priests, ministers and rabbis. ■ **seminarian** N.

semiotics and **semiology** SING N, LING the study of human communication, esp the relationship between words and the objects or concepts they represent. ■ **semiotic** ADJ.

semi-permeable ADJ, BIOL denoting a membrane through which only certain molecules can pass.

semiquaver N a musical note equal to half a quaver or one-sixteenth of a semibreve.

semitic ADJ Jewish.

semitone N, MUS **1** half a tone. **2** the interval between adjacent notes on a keyboard instrument, and the smallest interval in a normal musical scale.

semolina N the hard particles of wheat not ground into flour during milling.

Sen. ABBREV **1** senate. **2** senator. **3** senior.

senate N (often **Senate**) in the USA, Australia and other countries: a legislative body, esp the upper chamber of the national assembly.

senator N (often **Senator**) a member of a senate. ■ **senatorial** ADJ.

send VB (*sent*) **1** to cause, direct or order to go or be conveyed. **2** to dispatch: I sent the letter yesterday. **3** to force or propel: He sent me flying. **4** to cause to pass into a specified state: She sent him into fits of laughter. ■ **sender** N.
◆ **send sb** or **sth up** BRIT COLLOQ to make fun of or parody them.

send-off N a display of good wishes from a gathering of people to a departing person.

send-up N, BRIT COLLOQ a parody or satire.

senescent ADJ, FORMAL **1** growing old; ageing. **2** characteristic of old age. ■ **senescence** N.

senile ADJ displaying the feebleness of mind or body brought on by old age. ■ **senility** N.

senile dementia N a psychological disorder caused by irreversible degeneration of the brain, characterized by loss of memory and impaired intellectual ability.

senior ADJ **1** older than someone. **2** higher in rank or authority than someone. **3** for or pertaining to schoolchildren over the age of 11.
➣ N **1** a person who is older or of a higher rank. **2** a pupil in a senior school, or in the senior part of a school. **3** N AMER a final-year student.

senior citizen N an elderly person.

seniority N **1** the state or fact of being senior. **2** a privileged position earned through long service in a profession or with a company.

senior nursing officer N same as **matron** (sense 1).

senna N **1** a plant native to Africa and Arabia, with leaves divided into oval leaflets, and long clusters of yellow flowers. **2** the dried leaves or pods of these plants, used as a laxative.

sensation N **1** an awareness of an external or internal stimulus as a result of its perception by the senses. **2** a physical feeling: a burning

sensation. **3** an emotion or general feeling. **4** a widespread feeling of excitement.
■ **sensational** ADJ.

sensationalism N the practice of or methods used in deliberately setting out to cause widespread excitement, intense interest or shock. ■ **sensationalist** N, ADJ.
■ **sensationalize** or **-ise** VB.

sense N **1** any of the five main faculties used by an animal to obtain information about its external or internal environment, namely sight, hearing, smell, taste and touch. **2** an awareness or appreciation of some specified thing: a good sense of direction. **3** (**senses**) soundness of mind; one's wits or reason: lost his senses. **4** wisdom; practical worth: There's no sense in doing it now. **5** a general feeling or emotion: a sense of guilt. **6** meaning: They understood the sense of the poem.
➣ VB **1** to detect a stimulus by means of any of the five main senses. **2** to be aware of something: I sensed someone was behind me.
◆ **in a sense** in one respect; in a way.
◆ **make sense 1** to be understandable. **2** to be wise, rational or reasonable.

senseless ADJ **1** unconscious. **2** unwise; without good sense or foolish. Also AS ADV: He was beaten senseless.

sensibility N (**-ies**) **1** the ability or capacity to feel or have sensations or emotions. **2** a delicacy of emotional response; sensitivity: There was a general sensibility to his grief.

sensible ADJ **1** having or showing reasonableness or good judgement; wise. **2** perceptible by the senses. **3** having the power of sensation; sensitive: sensible to pain. ■ **sensibly** ADV.

sensitive ADJ **1** feeling or responding readily, strongly or painfully: sensitive to our feelings. **2** BIOL responding to a stimulus. **3** easily upset or offended. **4** stimulating much strong feeling or difference of opinion: sensitive issues. **5** of documents, etc: containing confidential information. **6** of scientific instruments: reacting to or recording extremely small changes.
■ **sensitivity** N.

sensor N, ELEC any of various devices that detect a change in a physical quantity.

sensory ADJ referring or relating to the senses.

sensual ADJ 1 relating to the senses and the body rather than the mind or the spirit. 2 of pleasures: gratifying the bodily senses. 3 pursuing physical pleasures.

sensuality N 1 the quality of being sensual. 2 indulgence in physical, esp sexual, pleasures.

sensuous ADJ 1 appealing to the senses aesthetically, with no suggestion of sexual pleasure. 2 affected by or pleasing to the senses. ■ **sensuously** ADV.

sentence N 1 a sequence of words forming a meaningful grammatical structure that can stand alone as a complete utterance, and which in written English usu begins with a capital letter and ends with a full stop, question mark or exclamation mark. 2 a punishment pronounced by a court or judge. ➤ VB 1 to announce the judgement or sentence to be given to someone. 2 to condemn someone to a punishment.

sententious ADJ 1 fond of using or full of sayings or proverbs; aphoristic. 2 tending to lecture others on morals.

sentient ADJ capable of sensation or feeling; conscious or aware: **sentient beings**.

sentiment N 1 a thought or emotion, esp when expressed. 2 emotion or emotional behaviour in general, esp when considered excessive. 3 (often **sentiments**) an opinion or view.

sentimental ADJ 1 readily feeling, indulging in or expressing tender emotions or sentiments, esp love, friendship and pity. 2 provoking or designed to provoke such emotions, esp in large measure and without subtlety. ■ **sentimentality** N. ■ **sentimentally** ADV.

sentimentalize or **-ise** VB 1 INTR to behave sentimentally. 2 to make sentimental.

sentinel N someone posted on guard.

sentry N (**-ies**) a person, usu a soldier, posted on guard to control entry or passage.

sepal N, BOT in a flower: one of the modified leaves that together form the calyx.

separable ADJ able to be separated.

separate VB 1 to take, force or keep apart (from others or each other): **A hedge separates the two fields.** 2 INTR of a couple: to cease to be together or live together. ➤ ADJ 1 divided. 2 distinctly different or individual: **That is a separate issue.** ■ **separately** ADV. ■ **separateness** N. ■ **separation** N.

separatist N a person who encourages, or takes action to achieve, independence from an established church, federation, organization, etc. ■ **separatism** N.

sepia N a rich reddish-brown pigment.

sepoy N, HIST an Indian soldier serving with a European (esp British) army.

sepsis N (**-ses**) MED the presence of disease-causing micro-organisms, esp viruses or bacteria, and their toxins in the body tissues.

sept N esp in Scotland or Ireland: a clan; a division of a tribe.

September N the ninth month of the year.

septennial ADJ 1 occurring once every seven years. 2 lasting seven years.

septet N 1 a group of seven musicians. 2 a piece of music for seven performers. 3 any group or set of seven.

septic ADJ 1 MED of a wound: contaminated with pathogenic bacteria. 2 putrefying.

septicaemia N, PATHOL blood-poisoning.

septuagenarian ADJ aged between 70 and 79 years old. ➤ N a septuagenarian person.

septum N (**septa**) BIOL, ANAT any partition between cavities, eg nostrils.

septuplet N any of seven children or animals born at one birth to the same mother.

sepulchral ADJ 1 of or relating to a tomb or burial. 2 gloomy or funereal.

sepulchre or (US) **sepulcher** N a tomb.

sequel N **1** a book, film or play that continues an earlier story. **2** anything that follows on from a previous event, etc.

sequence N **1** a series or succession of things in a specific order; the order they follow. **2** a succession of short pieces of action making up a scene in a film.

sequential ADJ in, having or following a particular order or sequence.

sequester VB **1** to set aside or isolate. **2** to set apart. **3** LAW to sequestrate.

sequestrate VB, LAW to remove (property) from someone's possession until a dispute has been settled. ■ **sequestration** N.

sequin N a small round shiny disc of foil or plastic, sewn on a garment for decoration.

sequoia N either of two species of massive evergreen trees, native to N America.

seraph N (*seraphs* or *seraphim*) an angel of the highest rank. ■ **seraphic** ADJ.

serenade N **1** a song or piece of music performed at night under a woman's window by her suitor. **2** any musical piece with a gentle tempo suggestive of romance.
➤ VB **1** to entertain (a person) with a serenade. **2** INTR to perform a serenade.

serendipity N the state of frequently making lucky or beneficial finds. ■ **serendipitous** ADJ.

serene ADJ calm and composed; at peace.
■ **serenely** ADV. ■ **serenity** N.

serf N in medieval Europe: a worker bought and sold with the land on which they worked.
■ **serfdom** N.

serge N a strong twilled fabric.

sergeant or **serjeant** N **1** a non-commissioned officer of the rank next above corporal. **2** in Britain: a police officer of the rank between constable and inspector.

sergeant-at-arms N an officer of a court or parliament responsible for keeping order.

sergeant-major N a non-commissioned officer of the highest rank in the armed forces.

serial N a story, television programme, etc published or broadcast in regular instalments.
➤ ADJ **1** appearing in instalments. **2** forming a series or part of a series. **3** in series; in a row.

serialize or **-ise** VB to publish or broadcast (a story, television programme, etc) in instalments.
■ **serialization** N.

serial killer N someone who commits a succession of similar murders.

serial number N the individual identification number on each of a series of products.

series N (PL *series*) **1** a number of similar, related or identical things arranged or produced in line or in succession. **2** a TV or radio programme in which the same characters appear, or a similar subject is addressed, in regular shows. **3** a set of things that differ progressively.

serif N, PRINTING a short decorative line or stroke on the end of a printed letter.

serious ADJ **1** grave or solemn; not inclined to flippancy or lightness of mood. **2** dealing with important issues: **a serious newspaper.** **3** severe: **a serious accident. 4** important; significant: **There were serious differences of opinion. 5** sincere or earnest: **I am serious about doing it.** ■ **seriously** ADV.
■ **seriousness** N.

serjeant see **sergeant**

sermon N **1** a public speech or discourse, esp one forming part of a church service.
2 a lengthy moral or advisory speech.

serotonin N, PHYSIOL a hormone that acts as a neurotransmitter in the central nervous system.

serous ADJ relating to or containing serum.

serpent N **1** a snake. **2** a sneaky, treacherous or malicious person.

serpentine ADJ **1** snake-like. **2** winding.

serrate ADJ notched like the blade of a saw.
➤ VB to notch. ■ **serration** N.

serried ADJ closely packed or grouped together: **soldiers in serried ranks.**

serum N (*serums* or *sera*) **1** ANAT the yellowish

fluid component of blood. **2** BOT the watery part of a plant fluid.

servant N **1** OLD USE a person employed by another to do household or menial work for them. **2** a person who acts for the good of others in any capacity. **3** a public servant.

serve VB **1** to work for someone as a domestic servant; to be in the service of someone. **2** INTR to be a servant. **3** to work for the benefit of someone or something; to aid: **He serves the community well. 4** TR & INTR to attend to customers in a shop, etc. **5** TR & INTR to attend to the needs or requirements of someone or something: **These shoes have served me well. 6** TR & INTR to bring, distribute or present (food or drink) to someone. **7** INTR to wait at table. **8** INTR to carry out duties as a member of some body or organization: **They serve on a committee • We served in the marines. 9** INTR to have a specific effect or result: **His speech just served to make matters worse. 10** to undergo as a requirement: **You have to serve an apprenticeship. 11** TR & INTR in racket sports: to put (the ball) into play. **12** LAW to deliver or present (a legal document): **serve with a writ.** ➤ N in racket sports: an act of serving.

server N **1** a person who serves. **2** in racket sports: the person who serves the ball. **3** in computer networks: a central computer that stores communal files, processes e-mail, etc.

service N **1** the condition or occupation of being a servant or someone who serves. **2** work carried out for or on behalf of others: **do someone a service. 3** the act or manner of serving. **4** an organization working to serve or benefit others in some way: **the civil service. 5** assistance given to customers in a shop, restaurant, etc. **6** a facility provided: **British Rail ran an excellent service. 7** an occasion of worship or other religious ceremony; the words, etc used on such an occasion: **the marriage service. 8** a complete set of cutlery and crockery: **a dinner service. 9** (usu **services**) the supply eg of water, public transport, etc. **10** a periodic check of the workings of a vehicle or other machine. **11** in racket sports: the act of putting the ball into play.

➤ VB **1** to subject (a vehicle, etc) to a check. **2** of a male animal: to mate with (a female).

serviceable ADJ capable of being used. ■ **serviceability** N.

service industry N an industry whose business is providing services rather than manufacturing products, eg transport, etc.

serviceman and **servicewoman** N a member of any of the armed forces.

service station N a petrol station providing facilities for motorists, eg car-wash, shop, etc.

serviette N a table napkin.

servile ADJ slavishly respectful or obedient; fawning or submissive. ■ **servility** N.

serving N a portion of food or drink.

servitude N slavery.

servo ADJ denoting a system in which the main mechanism is started by a subsidiary one.

sesame N **1** a plant with solitary white flowers, usu marked with purple or yellow. **2** the small edible seeds of this plant.

session N **1** a meeting of a court, council or parliament, or the period during which such meetings are regularly held. **2** COLLOQ a period of time spent engaged in any particular activity: **a drinking session. 3** an academic term or year. ■ **sessional** ADJ.

sestet N **1** the last six lines of a sonnet. **2** MUS a sextet.

set¹ VB (**set, setting**) **1** to put, place or fix into a specified position or condition: **set them straight. 2** to array or arrange: **Everything was set out beautifully. 3** TR & INTR to make or become solid, rigid, firm or motionless: **the jelly has set. 4** to fix, establish or settle: **Let's set a date. 5** to put into a state of readiness or preparation: **set the table. 6** to adjust (a measuring device, eg a clock) to the correct reading. **7** to put something upon a course or start it off: **set it going. 8** to fix (a broken bone) in its normal position for healing. **9** to impose or assign as an exercise or duty: **set a test. 10** to present or fix as a lead to be followed: **We must set an example. **11** INTR of the Sun or Moon: to disappear below the horizon. **12** to compose or fit music to (words). **13** to place (a novel, film, etc) in a specified period, location, etc: **The Great Gatsby is set in the 1920s.**

➣ N **1** the act or process of setting or the condition of being set. **2** a setting. **3** form; shape: **the set of his jaw. 4** habitual or temporary posture or bearing. **5** THEAT, CINEMATOG the scenery and props used to create a particular location. **6** a hairstyle.

➣ ADJ **1** fixed or rigid; allowing no alterations or variations: **a set menu • set in his ways. 2** predetermined or conventional: **set phrases. 3** ready or prepared: **We're all set to go. 4** due: **We're set for a pay rise. 5** assigned: These are the set texts for this year.

◆ **be set on sth** to be determined to do it.

◆ **set about sb** to attack them.

◆ **set about sth** to start or begin it.

◆ **set sth** or **sb apart** to separate or put them aside as different, esp superior.

◆ **set sth back 1** to delay or hinder its progress. **2** to cause it to return to a previous and less advanced stage. **3** SLANG to cost (in money): **How much did that set you back?**

◆ **set sth down** to record it in writing.

◆ **set in** to become firmly established: **We must leave before darkness sets in.**

◆ **set off** to start out on a journey.

◆ **set sb off** to provoke them into action of a specified kind: **He set us off laughing.**

◆ **set sth off 1** to detonate (an explosive). **2** to show it off to good advantage: **The colour of the dress sets off your eyes.**

◆ **set on sb** to attack them.

◆ **set sb** or **sth on sb** to order them to attack: I'll set the dogs on you!

◆ **set out 1** to begin a journey. **2** to intend (to do something): **set out to cause trouble.**

◆ **set sth out 1** to present or explain it: **She set out her ideas plainly. 2** to lay it out for display.

◆ **set to 1** to start working; to apply oneself to a task. **2** to start fighting or arguing.

◆ **set sb up 1** to put them into a position of guaranteed security: **The inheritance has set him up for life. 2** to enable them to begin a new career. **3** SLANG to trick them into becoming a target for blame, or into feeling foolish.

◆ **set sth up 1** to bring it into being or operation; to establish it: **He set the company up by himself. 2** to arrange it. **3** to put up or erect something: **Let's set the tents up here.**

set^2 N **1** a group of related people or things, esp of a kind that usu associate, occur or are used together: **a set of twins. 2** MATH a group of objects, or elements, that have at least one characteristic in common. **3** a complete collection of pieces needed for a particular activity: **a chess set. 4** the songs or tunes performed by a singer or a band at a concert. **5** TENNIS, DARTS, **etc** a group of games in which the winning player or players have to win a specified number, with a match lasting a certain number of sets. **6** a device for receiving or transmitting television or radio broadcasts.

set^3 or **sett** N a badger's burrow.

setback N a delay or reversal to progress.

set piece N **1** a carefully prepared musical or literary performance. **2** SPORT a sequence of movements, etc taken at a free-kick, etc.

set square N a right-angled triangular plate used as an aid for marking lines and angles.

settee N a long, soft indoor seat; a sofa.

setter N a large sporting dog with a long smooth coat.

setting N **1 a** a situation or background within or against which action takes place; **b** THEAT, CINEMATOG the scenery and props used in a single scene. **2** a set of cutlery, crockery and glassware laid out for use by one person. **3** the position of a machine's controls.

settle^1 VB **1** TR & INTR to make or become securely, comfortably or satisfactorily positioned or established. **2** TR & INTR (also **settle on sth**) to come to an agreement about it: **settle an argument • settle on a date. 3** INTR to come to rest. **4** to establish a practice or routine: **You'll soon settle into the job. 5** TR & INTR (also **settle down** or **settle sb down**) to make or become calm, quiet or disciplined after a period of noisy excitement or chaos. **6** to conclude or decide: **Let's settle this matter once and for all. 7** TR & INTR to establish or take

up a permanent home or residence. **8** TR & INTR (also **settle up**) to pay off or clear (a debt).
◆ **settle for sth** to accept it as a compromise or instead of something more suitable.
◆ **settle in** to adapt to a new environment.

settle² N a wooden bench with arms and a solid high back.

settlement N **1** the act of settling or the state of being settled. **2** a recently settled community or colony. **3** an agreement.

set-to N **1** COLLOQ a fight. **2** a fierce contest.

set-up N **1** COLLOQ an arrangement or set of arrangements. **2** SLANG a trick to make a person unjustly blamed, accused or embarrassed.

seven N **1 a** the cardinal number 7; **b** the quantity that this represents, being one more than six. **2** any symbol for this, eg 7 or VII. **3** something, eg a shoe, whose size is denoted by the number 7. **4** the seventh hour after midnight or midday: **Come at seven.**
➤ ADJ **1** totalling seven. **2** aged seven.

seventeen N **1 a** the cardinal number 17; **b** the quantity that this represents, being one more than sixteen, or the sum of ten and seven. **2** any symbol for this, eg 17 or XVII. **3** something whose size is denoted by the number 17.
➤ ADJ **1** totalling seventeen. **2** aged seventeen.
■ **seventeenth** ADJ, N.

seventh (often written **7ᵗʰ**) ADJ **1** in counting: **a** next after sixth; **b** last of seven. **2** in seventh position.
➤ N **1** one of seven equal parts. **2** a fraction equal to one divided by seven.

seventh heaven N a state of intense joy.

seventies (often written **70s** or **70's**) PL N **1** (**one's seventies**) the period of time between one's seventieth and eightieth birthdays. **2** (**the seventies**) the range of temperatures between seventy and eighty degrees. **3** (**the seventies**) the period of time between the seventieth and eightieth years of a century.

seventy N (-ies) **1 a** the cardinal number 70; **b** the quantity that this represents, being one more than sixty-nine, or the product of ten and

seven. **2** any symbol for this, eg 70 or LXX.
➤ ADJ **1** totalling seventy. **2** aged seventy.
■ **seventieth** ADJ, N.

sever VB **1** to cut off physically. **2** to separate or isolate. **3** to end (a relationship, etc).

several ADJ **1** more than a few, but not a great number: **I had several drinks. 2** various or assorted: **their several backgrounds.**
➤ PRONOUN quite a few people or things.

severe ADJ **1** extreme and difficult to endure. **2** very strict. **3** suggesting seriousness: **a severe appearance. 4** having serious consequences: **a severe injury.** ■ **severity** N.

sew VB (PA P **sewed** or **sewn**) **1** to stitch, attach or repair (esp fabric) with thread, either by hand with a needle or by machine. **2** to make (garments) by stitching pieces of fabric together. **3** INTR to work using a needle and thread, or sewing-machine. ■ **sewer** N.

sewage N any liquid-borne waste matter.

sewer N a large underground pipe that carries away sewage from drains and water from road surfaces.

sewerage N **1** a system or network of sewers. **2** drainage of sewage and surface water.

sex N **1** either of the two classes, male and female, into which animals and plants are divided according to their role in reproduction. **2** membership of one of these classes, or the characteristics that determine this. **3** sexual intercourse, or the activities, feelings, desires, etc associated with it.
➤ ADJ **1** referring or relating to sexual matters in general: **sex education. 2** due to the fact of being male or female: **sex discrimination.**

sexagenarian ADJ aged between 60 and 69.
➤ N a person of this age.

sex appeal N sexual attractiveness.

sexism N discrimination against a particular sex, usu women. ■ **sexist** N, ADJ.

sexology N the study of human sexual behaviour. ■ **sexologist** N.

sextant N a device used in navigation and surveying for measuring angular distances.

sextet N **1a** a group of six singers or musicians; **b** a piece of music for it. **2** any set of six.

sexton N someone responsible for a church's buildings and churchyard.

sextuplet N any of six children or animals born at the same time to the same mother.

sexual ADJ **1** concerned with or suggestive of sex. **2** referring or relating to sexual reproduction involving the fusion of two gametes. **3** relating to membership of the male or female sex. ■ **sexuality** N.

sexual intercourse N the insertion of a man's penis into a woman's vagina.

sexy ADJ (*-ier, -iest*) COLLOQ **1** of a person: sexually attractive; stimulating or arousing sexual desire. **2** of an object, idea, etc: currently popular or interesting; attractive or tempting: sexy products. ■ **sexily** ADV. ■ **sexiness** N.

shabby ADJ (*-ier, -iest*) **1** esp of clothes or furnishings: old and worn; threadbare or dingy. **2** of a person: wearing such clothes; scruffy. **3** of behaviour, etc: unworthy or contemptible. ■ **shabbily** ADV. ■ **shabbiness** N.

shack N a crudely built hut or shanty.

shackle N **1** (usu **shackles**) a metal ring locked round the ankle or wrist of a prisoner or slave to limit movement, usu one of a pair joined by a chain. **2** (usu **shackles**) anything that restricts freedom; a hindrance or constraint. ➤ VB **1** to restrain with or as if with shackles. **2** to connect or couple.

shad N (*shad* or *shads*) any of various marine fish resembling a large herring.

shade N **1** the blocking or partial blocking out of sunlight, or the relative darkness caused by this. **2** an area from which sunlight has been completely or partially blocked. **3** any device used to modify direct light, eg a lampshade. **4** a dark or shaded area in a drawing or painting. **5** the state of appearing less impressive than something or someone else: Her singing puts mine in the shade. **6** a colour,

esp one similar to but slightly different from a principal colour: a lighter shade of blue. **7** a small amount: It is a shade smaller than that. **8** (**shades**) COLLOQ sunglasses. **9** LITERARY a ghost. ➤ VB **1** to block or partially block out sunlight from someone or something. **2** to draw or paint so as to give the impression of shade.

shadow N **1** a dark shape cast on a surface when an object stands between the surface and the source of light. **2** an area darkened by the blocking out of light. **3** the darker areas of a picture. **4** a slight amount; a hint or trace: without a shadow of a doubt. **5** a sense of gloom, trouble or foreboding: The incident cast a shadow over the proceedings. ➤ VB **1** to put into darkness by blocking out light. **2** to cloud or darken. **3** to follow closely and secretively. ➤ ADJ, POL in the main opposition party: denoting a counterpart to a member or section of the government: shadow Chancellor.

shadow-boxing N boxing against an imaginary opponent. ■ **shadow-box** VB.

shadowy ADJ dark and shady.

shady ADJ (*-ier, -iest*) **1** sheltered or giving shelter from heat or sunlight. **2** COLLOQ underhand or disreputable, often dishonest or illegal: a shady character. **3** shadowy or mysterious; sinister. ■ **shadiness** N.

shaft N **1** the long straight handle of a weapon or tool. **2** the long straight part or handle of anything. **3** a ray or beam of light. **4** in vehicle engines: a rotating rod that transmits motion. **5** a vertical passageway in a building, esp one through which a lift moves. **6** a well-like excavation or passage, eg into a mine. ➤ VB, US SLANG to dupe, cheat or swindle.

shag[1] N **1** a ragged mass of hair. **2** a long coarse pile or nap on fabric. **3** a type of tobacco cut into coarse shreds.

shag[2] N a cormorant with glossy dark-green plumage and a long neck.

shag[3] COARSE SLANG, VB (*-gg-*) to have sexual intercourse with someone.

➤ N an act of sexual intercourse.

shaggy ADJ (*-ier, -iest*) **1** of hair, fur, etc: long and coarse; rough and untidy in appearance. **2** having shaggy hair or fur. ■ **shagginess** N.

shagreen N **1** a coarse granular leather. **2** the skin of a shark, ray, etc.

shah N, HIST a title of the former rulers of Iran and other Eastern countries.

shake VB (*shook, shaken*) **1** to move with quick, often forceful to-and-fro or up-and-down movements. **2** (also **shake sth up**) to mix it in this way. **3** TR & INTR to tremble or make something or someone tremble. **4** (also **shake sb** or **sth up**) to disturb or shock them greatly. **5** INTR to shake hands.
➤ N **1** an act or the action of shaking. **2** COLLOQ a very short while; a moment. **3** (**the shakes**) COLLOQ a fit of uncontrollable trembling. **4** a milk shake. ■ **shakeable** or **shakable** ADJ.
◆ **shake sth** or **sb off 1** to get rid of them; to free oneself from them. **2** to escape from them.
◆ **shake sb up** COLLOQ to stimulate them into action, esp from a state of lethargy or apathy.
◆ **shake sth up 1** to mix it. **2** COLLOQ to reorganize it thoroughly.

shakedown N, COLLOQ a makeshift bed.

shaker N **1** a container from which something, eg salt, is dispensed by shaking. **2** a container in which something is mixed by shaking.

Shakespearean or **Shakespearian** ADJ relating to or characteristic of the works of William Shakespeare.

shake-up N, COLLOQ a fundamental change, disturbance or reorganization.

shaky ADJ (*-ier, -iest*) **1** trembling or inclined to tremble with, or as if with, weakness, fear or illness. **2** COLLOQ wavering; not solid, sound or secure. ■ **shakily** ADV.

shale N, GEOL a fine-grained sedimentary rock.

shall AUXILIARY VERB expressing: **1** the future tense of other verbs, esp when the subject is I or we. **2** determination, intention, certainty, and obligation, esp when the subject is **you, he, she, it** or **they**: They shall succeed •You shall not kill. **3** a question implying future action, often with the sense of an offer or suggestion, esp when the subject is I or we: What shall we do? • Shall I give you a hand?

shallot N a small onion.

shallow ADJ **1** having no great depth. **2** not profound or sincere; superficial.
➤ N (often **shallows**) a shallow place or part, esp in water.

sham ADJ false, counterfeit or pretended.
➤ VB (*-mm-*) TR & INTR to pretend or feign.
➤ N **1** anything not genuine. **2** a person who shams, esp an impostor.

shaman N a doctor-priest or medicine man or woman using magic to cure illness, make contact with gods and spirits, etc.

shamble VB, INTR to walk with slow awkward tottering steps.
➤ N a shambling walk. ■ **shambling** N, ADJ.

shambles SING N, COLLOQ a confused mess or muddle; a state of total disorder.

shambolic ADJ, COLLOQ totally disorganized.

shame N **1** the humiliating feeling of having appeared unfavourably in one's own eyes, or those of others. **2** susceptibility to such a feeling or emotion. **3** disgrace or loss of reputation: He's brought shame on the whole family. **4** a regrettable or disappointing situation: It's such a shame that he failed his exam.
➤ VB **1** to make someone feel shame. **2** to bring disgrace on someone or something.
◆ **put sb to shame 1** to disgrace them. **2** to make them seem inadequate by comparison.

shamefaced ADJ showing embarrassment.

shameful ADJ bringing or deserving shame: shameful behaviour. ■ **shamefully** ADV.

shameless ADJ **1** incapable of feeling shame. **2** done without shame; brazen or immodest.

shammy N (*-ies*) COLLOQ a chamois leather.

shampoo N **1** a soapy liquid for washing the hair and scalp. **2** a similar liquid for cleaning carpets or upholstery. **3** the act or an instance of treating with either liquid.

➤ VB to wash or clean with shampoo.

shamrock N a plant with leaves divided into three rounded leaflets adopted as the national emblem of Ireland.

shandy N (*-ies*) a mixture of beer or lager with lemonade or ginger beer.

shanghai VB (*-hais, -haied, -haiing*) COLLOQ **1** to kidnap and send to sea as a sailor. **2** to trick into any unpleasant situation.

shank N **1** the lower leg between the knee and the foot. **2** the same part of the leg in an animal. **3** the main section of the handle of a tool.

shanks's pony and (US) **shank's mare** N, COLLOQ the use of one's own legs to travel.

shan't CONTRACTION, COLLOQ shall not.

shantung N a fabric of wild silk.

shanty[1] N (*-ies*) a roughly built hut or cabin.

shanty[2] N (*-ies*) a rhythmical song with chorus and solo verses, formerly sung by sailors.

shape N **1** the outline or form of anything. **2** a person's body or figure. **3** a form, person, etc: I had an assistant in the shape of my brother. **4** a desired form or condition: We like to keep in shape. **5** a general condition: in bad shape. **6** an unidentifiable figure: shapes lurking in the dark. **7** a geometric figure.
➤ VB **1** to fashion; to give a particular form to something. **2** to influence to an important extent: the event that shaped history.
◆ **shape up** COLLOQ **1** to appear to be developing in a particular way: This project is shaping up well. **2** to be promising; to progress or develop well. **3** to lose weight; to tone up.

shapely ADJ having a well-proportioned, attractive shape or figure. ■ **shapeliness** N.

shard N a fragment of something brittle.

share N **1** a part allotted, contributed, or owned by each of several people or groups. **2** a portion, section or division. **3** (usu **shares**) the fixed units into which the total wealth of a business company is divided.
➤ VB **1** to have in common. **2** to use something with someone else: We had to share a book in

class. **3** (also **share in sth**) to have possession of or responsibility for it, with others.
◆ **share sth out** to divide it into portions and distribute it among several people or groups.

shareholder N someone who owns shares in a company. ■ **shareholding** N.

shareware N, COMP software readily available for a nominal fee.

shark N **1** a large, usu fierce, fish with a long body and a prominent dorsal fin. **2** COLLOQ a ruthless or dishonest person, esp one who swindles, exploits or extorts.

sharp ADJ **1** having a thin edge or point that cuts or pierces. **2** having a bitter pungent taste. **3** severely felt: sharp pain. **4** sudden and acute: a sharp bend. **5** abrupt or harsh in speech; sarcastic. **6** easily perceived; clear-cut or well-defined: a sharp contrast. **7** keen or perceptive. **8** barely honest; cunning. **9** COLLOQ stylish: a sharp dresser. **10** MUS higher in pitch by a semitone: C sharp.
➤ N **1** MUS a note raised by a semitone, or the sign indicating this (♯). **2** MUS the key producing this note. **3** COLLOQ a practised cheat; a sharper: a card sharp.
➤ ADV **1** punctually; on the dot: at 9 o'clock sharp. **2** suddenly: pulled up sharp.
■ **sharply** ADV. ■ **sharpness** N.

sharpen VB, TR & INTR to make or become sharp. ■ **sharpener** N.

sharpish ADJ quite sharp.
➤ ADV quickly; promptly.

sharpshooter N an expert marksman.

shatter VB **1** TR & INTR to break into tiny fragments, usu suddenly or with force. **2** to destroy completely; to wreck. **3** to upset greatly. **4** COLLOQ to tire out or exhaust.
■ **shattering** ADJ.

shave VB **1** to cut off (hair) from (esp the face) with a razor or shaver. **2** INTR to remove one's facial hair in this way. **3** to graze the surface of something in passing.
➤ N an act or the process of shaving one's facial hair. ■ **shaving** N.

shaver N an electrical device with a moving

blade or set of blades for shaving hair.

shawl N a large single piece of fabric used to cover the head or shoulders or to wrap a baby.

she PRONOUN **1** a female person or animal already referred to. **2** a thing thought of as female (eg a ship).
➢ N a female person or animal.

sheaf N (*sheaves*) a bundle of things tied up.
➢ VB to tie up in a bundle.

shear VB (PA P *sheared* or *shorn*) **1** to clip or cut off something, esp with a large pair of clippers. **2** to cut the fleece off (a sheep). **3** (usu **shear sb of sth**) to strip or deprive them of it.
➢ N **1** the act of shearing. **2** (**shears**) a large pair of clippers, or a scissor-like cutting tool with a pivot or spring. ■ **shearer** N.

sheath N **1** a case or covering for the blade of a sword or knife. **2** a condom. **3** BIOL any protective or encasing structure.

sheathe VB to put into a sheath or case.

shebang N, orig US SLANG an affair or matter.

shebeen N **1** an illicit liquor-shop. **2** in Ireland: illicit and usu home-made alcohol.

shed[1] N a small outbuilding for working in, for storage or for shelter.

shed[2] VB (*shed, shedding*) **1** to release or make something flow: **shed tears**. **2** to get rid of or cast off something: **shed a skin**.
◆ **to shed light on sth** to cause (a problem, etc) to become easier to comprehend.

she'd CONTRACTION **1** she had. **2** she would.

sheen N shine, lustre or radiance; glossiness.

sheep N (PL *sheep*) **1** a herbivorous mammal with a stocky body covered with a thick woolly fleece, bred for its meat and wool. **2** a meek person, esp one who follows unquestioningly.

sheep-dip N a disinfectant insecticidal preparation used for washing sheep.

sheepdog N **1** a working dog that is used to guard sheep from wild animals or to assist in herding. **2** any of several breeds of dog orig developed to herd sheep.

sheepish ADJ embarrassed through having done something wrong or foolish.

sheer[1] ADJ **1** complete; absolute or downright: **sheer madness**. **2** of a cliff, etc: vertical or nearly vertical: **a sheer drop**. **3** eg of a fabric: so thin or fine as to be almost transparent.
➢ ADV **1** completely. **2** vertically.

sheer[2] VB to make something change course.
◆ **sheer off** or **away** to change course suddenly; to swerve or deviate.

sheet N **1** a large broad rectangular piece of fabric, esp for covering the mattress of a bed. **2** any large wide piece or expanse. **3** a piece of paper, esp if large and rectangular. **4** a pamphlet, broadsheet or newspaper.

sheeting N fabric used for making sheets.

sheikh or **sheik** N **1** the chief of an Arab tribe, village or family. **2** a Muslim leader.
■ **sheikhdom** N.

sheila N, AUSTRAL, NZ COLLOQ a woman or girl.

shelf N (*shelves*) **1** a usu narrow, flat board fixed to a wall or part of a cupboard, bookcase, etc, for storing or laying things on. **2** a ledge of land, rock, etc; a sandbank.
◆ **on the shelf 1** of a person or thing: too old or worn out to be of any use. **2** of a person, esp a woman: no longer likely to marry.

shell N **1** the hard protective structure covering an egg. **2** ZOOL the hard protective structure covering the body of certain animals, esp shellfish, snails and tortoises. **3** BOT the hard protective structure covering the seed or fruit of some plants. **4** the empty covering of eg a shellfish, found on the seashore. **5** any hard protective cover. **6** a round of ammunition for a large-bore gun, eg a mortar. **7** a shotgun cartridge. **8** COMP a program that acts as a user-friendly interface between an operating system and the user.
➢ VB **1** to remove the shell from something. **2** to bombard with (eg mortar) shells.
◆ **shell out** or **shell out for sth** COLLOQ to pay out (money) or spend (money) on it.

she'll CONTRACTION **1** she will. **2** she shall.

shellac N **1** a resin produced by the lac insect.

2 a solution of this used as a varnish.
➤ VB (*-lacked, -lacking*) to coat with shellac.

shellfish N (PL *shellfish*) a shelled edible aquatic invertebrate, eg prawn, crab, lobster.

shell-shock N a psychological disorder caused by prolonged exposure to military combat conditions.

shelter N **1** protection against weather or danger. **2** a place or structure providing this. **3** a place of refuge or temporary lodging. ➤ VB **1** to protect someone or something from the effects of weather or danger. **2** to give asylum or lodging. **3** INTR to take cover.

sheltered ADJ **1** protected from the weather. **2** away from the harsh realities of the world.

shelve VB **1** to place or store on a shelf. **2** to fit with shelves. **3** to postpone or put aside; to abandon. **4** to remove from active service.

shenanigans PL N, COLLOQ **1** foolish behaviour. **2** underhand dealings; trickery.

shepherd N **1** someone who looks after, or herds, sheep. **2** LITERARY a religious minister. ➤ VB **1** to watch over or herd sheep. **2** to guide or herd (a group or crowd).

shepherdess N, OLD USE a female shepherd.

shepherd's pie N a dish consisting of minced meat baked with mashed potatoes on the top.

sherbet N **1** a fruit-flavoured powder eaten as confectionery. **2** N AMER a kind of water-ice.

sheriff N **1** in a US county: the chief elected police officer mainly responsible for maintaining peace and order, attending courts, serving processes and executing judgements. **2** in England: the chief officer of the monarch in a shire or county, with ceremonial duties. **3** in Scotland: the chief judge of a sheriff court.

sheriff court N in a Scottish town or region: a court trying all but the most serious crimes.

sherry N (*-ies*) a fortified wine ranging in colour from pale gold to dark brown.

she's CONTRACTION **1** she is. **2** she has.

shiatsu or **shiatzu** N, MED a Japanese healing massage technique involving the application of pressure to parts of the body distant from the affected region.

shibboleth N **1** a common saying. **2** a slogan, catchphrase, custom or belief, esp if considered outdated. **3** a peculiarity of speech.

shield N **1** a piece of armour consisting of a broad plate, carried to deflect weapons. **2** a protective plate, screen, pad or other guard. **3** any shield-shaped design or object, esp one used as an emblem or coat of arms. ➤ VB **1** to protect from danger or harm. **2** to ward off something.

shift VB **1** TR & INTR to change the position or direction of something; to change position or direction. **2** to transfer, switch or redirect: **shift the blame**. **3** in a vehicle: to change (gear). **4** to remove or dislodge someone or something. **5** INTR, COLLOQ to move quickly. ➤ N **1** a change, or change of position. **2** one of a set of consecutive periods into which a 24-hour working day is divided. **3** the group of workers on duty during any one of these periods. **4** a loose, usu straight, dress.

shiftless ADJ **1** having no motivation. **2** inefficient.

shifty ADJ (*-ier, -iest*) **1** of a person or behaviour: sly, shady or dubious. **2** of a person or behaviour: evasive or tricky.

shilling N in the UK: a coin used before the introduction of decimal currency.

shilly-shally VB (*-ies, -ied*) INTR to be indecisive; to vacillate.

shim N a thin washer or slip of metal, wood, plastic, etc used to adjust or fill a gap between machine parts, esp gears.

shimmer VB, INTR to shine tremulously and quiveringly with reflected light; to glisten. ➤ N a tremulous or quivering gleam of reflected light. ■ **shimmery** ADJ.

shin N **1** the bony front part of the leg below the knee. **2** the lower part of a leg of beef. ➤ VB (*-nn-*) TR & INTR (usu **shin up**) to climb by gripping with the hands and legs.

shinbone N the tibia.

shindig N, COLLOQ **1** a lively party or celebration. **2** a noisy disturbance or row.

shine VB (*shone* or in sense 3 *shined*) **1** INTR to give out or reflect light; to beam with a steady radiance. **2** to direct the light from something: They shone the torch around the room. **3** to make bright and gleaming by polishing. **4** INTR to excel: She shines at maths.
➤ N **1** shining quality; brightness. **2** an act or process of polishing. ■ **shiny** ADJ (*-ier, -iest*).
◆ **take a shine to sb** COLLOQ to like or fancy them on first acquaintance.

shiner N, COLLOQ a black eye.

shingle[1] N **1** a thin rectangular tile, esp made of wood, laid with others in overlapping rows on a roof or wall. **2** these tiles collectively.

shingle[2] N, GEOL **1** small pebbles that have been worn smooth by water. **2** a beach, bank or bed covered in gravel or stones.

shingles SING N, MED a disease which produces a series of blisters along the path of the nerve, esp in the area of the waist and ribs.

shinty N (*-ies*) a game, orig Scottish, similar to hockey, played by two teams of 12.

ship N **1** a large engine-propelled vessel, intended for sea travel. **2** a large sailing vessel, esp a three-masted, square-rigged sailing vessel. **3** COLLOQ a spaceship or airship.
➤ VB (*-pp-*) **1** to send or transport by ship. **2** to send or transport by land or air.

shipbuilder N a person or company that constructs ships. ■ **shipbuilding** N.

shipmate N a fellow sailor.

shipment N **1** the act or practice of shipping cargo. **2** a cargo or consignment transported.

shipping N **1** the commercial transportation of freight, esp by ship. **2** ships as traffic.

shipshape ADJ in good order; neat and tidy.

shipwreck N **1** the accidental sinking or destruction of a ship. **2** the remains of a sunken or destroyed ship. **3** wreck or ruin; disaster.
➤ VB **1** TR & INTR to be or make someone the victim of a ship's accidental sinking or destruction. **2** to wreck or ruin (eg plans).

shipwright N a skilled wright or carpenter who builds or repairs (esp wooden) ships.

shipyard N a place where ships are built.

shire N a county.

shirk VB **1** to evade (work, a duty, etc). **2** INTR to avoid work, duty or responsibility. ■ **shirker** N.

shirt N a light garment for the upper body, typically with buttons down the front.

shirtwaister N a woman's tailored dress with a shirt-like bodice.

shirty ADJ (*-ier, -iest*) COLLOQ irritable.

shit and **shite** COARSE SLANG, N **1** excrement or faeces. **2** an act of defecating. **3** DEROG nonsense. **4** DEROG a despicable person.
➤ VB (*shit, shitted* or *shat, shitting*) INTR to defecate.

shiver[1] VB, INTR **1** to quiver or tremble, eg with fear. **2** to make an involuntary muscular movement in response to the cold.
➤ N **1** an act of shivering; a shivering movement or sensation. **2** (**the shivers**) COLLOQ a fit of shivering.

shiver[2] N a splinter or other small fragment.

shoal[1] N **1** a multitude of fish swimming together. **2** a huge crowd or swarm.
➤ VB, INTR to gather or move in a shoal; to swarm.

shoal[2] N **1** an area of shallow water in a river, lake or sea where sediment has accumulated. **2** such an accumulation of sediment.
➤ ADJ shallow.

shock[1] N **1** a strong emotional disturbance, esp a feeling of extreme surprise, outrage or disgust. **2** a cause of such a disturbance. **3** a heavy impact. **4** (in full **electric shock**) a convulsion caused by the passage of an electric current through the body. **5** MED a state of physical collapse, with lowered blood pressure and body temperature.
➤ VB **1** to give a shock to someone. **2** INTR to outrage feelings.

shock² N a bushy mass of hair.

shock absorber N in a vehicle: a device that damps vibrations caused by the wheels passing over bumps in the road.

shocking ADJ 1 giving a shock. 2 extremely surprising, outrageous or disgusting. 3 COLLOQ deplorably bad: *His handwriting is shocking*. ■ **shockingly** ADV.

shockproof ADJ protected against or resistant to the effects of shock or impact.

shock wave N 1 PHYS an exceptionally intense sound wave. 2 a feeling of shock which spreads through a community, etc.

shoddy ADJ (*-ier, -iest*) of poor quality; carelessly done or made. ■ **shoddiness** N.

shoe N 1 either of a pair of shaped outer coverings for the feet, esp ones made of leather or other stiff material, usu finishing below the ankle. 2 anything like this in shape or function. ➤ VB (*shod, shoeing*) 1 to provide with shoes. 2 to fit (a horse) with horseshoes. ◆ **in sb's shoes** in the same situation as them.

shoehorn N a curved piece of metal or plastic used to lever the heel into a shoe.

shoelace N a string or cord passed through eyelet holes to fasten a shoe.

shoestring N, N AMER a shoelace. ◆ **on a shoestring** COLLOQ with or using a very small or limited amount of money.

shoe tree N a support put inside a shoe to preserve its shape when it is not being worn.

shoo EXCLAM an expression used to scare or chase away a person or animal. ➤ VB (*shooed, shooing*) 1 INTR to cry 'Shoo!'. 2 (usu **shoo sb** or **sth away** or **off**) to chase them away by, or as if by, shouting 'Shoo!'.

shoot VB (*shot*) 1 TR & INTR to fire a gun or other weapon. 2 to fire bullets, arrows or other missiles. 3 to hit, wound or kill with a weapon or missile. 4 to let fly with force: *The geyser shot water high into the air*. 5 to launch or direct forcefully and rapidly: *He shot questions at them*. 6 TR & INTR, SPORT to strike (the ball, etc) at goal. 7 TR & INTR to film (motion pictures), or take photographs of someone or something. 8 INTR of pain: to dart with a stabbing sensation. 9 INTR to dart forth or forwards. 10 INTR to use a bow or gun in practice, competition, hunting, etc. ➤ N 1 an act of shooting. 2 a shooting match or party. 3 an outing or expedition to hunt animals with firearms. 4 the shooting of a film or a photographic modelling session. 5 a new or young plant growth. 6 the sprouting of a plant. ◆ **shoot through** SLANG to leave quickly. ◆ **shoot up** to grow or increase quickly.

shooter N 1 someone or something that shoots. 2 COLLOQ a gun.

shooting gallery N a long room fitted out with targets used for practice with firearms.

shooting star N a meteor.

shop N 1 a room or building where goods are sold or services are provided. 2 a place providing specific goods or services: *a barber's shop • a betting shop*. 3 a spell of shopping, esp for food or household items. ➤ VB (*-pp-*) 1 INTR to visit a shop or shops, esp in order to buy goods. 2 SLANG to betray or inform on someone to the police, etc. ◆ **all over the shop** COLLOQ scattered everywhere; in numerous places. ◆ **shop around** 1 to compare the price and quality of goods in various shops. 2 COLLOQ to explore the full range of options available. ◆ **talk shop** COLLOQ to talk about one's work or business, esp in a tedious way.

shop assistant N someone serving in a shop.

shop floor N 1 the part of a factory or workshop where the manual work is carried out. 2 the workers in a factory, as opposed to the management.

shopkeeper N someone who owns and manages a shop.

shoplift VB, TR & INTR to steal (goods) from shops. ■ **shoplifter** N. ■ **shoplifting** N.

shopper N 1 someone who shops. 2 a shopping bag or basket.

shopping N 1 the act of visiting shops to look at or buy goods. 2 goods bought in shops.

shop-soiled ADJ slightly dirty, faded or spoiled from being used as a display in a shop.

shop steward N a worker elected by others to be an official trade union representative.

shop window N 1 a window of a shop in which goods are arranged in a display. 2 any arrangement which displays something to advantage.

shore[1] N 1 a narrow strip of land bordering on the sea, a lake or any other large body of water. 2 land as opposed to the sea. 3 (**shores**) lands; countries: **foreign shores**.
➤ VB to set on shore: **shore a boat**.

shore[2] N a prop.
➤ VB (USU **shore sth up**) 1 to support it with props. 2 to sustain or strengthen it.

shoreline N the line where land meets water.

short ADJ 1 having little physical length; not long. 2 having little height. 3 having little extent or duration; brief; concise: **short day**. 4 indicating a seemingly short length of time: **For a few short weeks we could enjoy our time together**. 5 of a temper: quickly and easily lost. 6 rudely abrupt; curt: **She was very short with him**. 7 of the memory: tending not to retain things for long. 8 of pastry: crisp and crumbling easily. 9 fewer than needed: **We are two tickets short**. 10 lacking in money.
➤ ADV 1 abruptly; briefly: **stopped short**. 2 on the near side: **The dart fell short of the board**.
➤ N 1 something that is short. 2 shortness; abbreviation or summary. 3 COLLOQ a drink of an alcoholic spirit. 4 a short cinema film shown before the main film. 5 a short circuit.
➤ VB, TR & INTR to short-circuit. ■ **shortness** N.
♦ **in short supply** scarce.
♦ **short of** or **on sth** deficient; lacking in it.
♦ **short of sth** without going as far as it; except it: **tried everything short of threats**.

shortage N a lack or deficiency.

shortbread N a rich crumbly biscuit made with flour, butter and sugar.

shortcake N shortbread or other crumbly cake.

short-change VB 1 to give (a customer) less than the correct amount of change. 2 COLLOQ to treat dishonestly; to cheat.

short circuit N, ELECTRONICS a connection across an electric circuit with a very low resistance, which may damage electrical equipment or be a fire hazard.
➤ VB (**short-circuit**) 1 to cause a short circuit in something. 2 to provide with a bypass.

shortcoming N a fault or defect.

short cut N 1 a quicker route than normal between two places. 2 a method that saves time or effort.

shorten VB, TR & INTR to make or become shorter.

shortening N butter, lard or other fat used for making pastry more crumbly.

shortfall N 1 a failure to reach a desired or expected level or specification. 2 the amount or margin by which something is deficient: **There is a shortfall of £100**.

shorthand N any of various systems representing speech sounds and groups of sounds, used as a fast way of writing.

short-handed ADJ short of workers.

shortlist N (also **short leet**) a selection of the best candidates from the total number submitted or nominated, from which the successful candidate will be chosen.
➤ VB (**short-list**) to place on a shortlist.

short-lived ADJ lasting only for a short time.

shortly ADV 1 soon; within a short period of time: **He'll arrive shortly**. 2 in a curt manner.

short-range ADJ relating to a short distance or length of time: **short-range telescope**.

shorts PL N trousers extending from the waist to anywhere between the thigh and the knee.

short shrift N discourteously brief or disdainful consideration.

short-sighted ADJ 1 of a person: capable of seeing only near objects clearly. 2 of a person, plan, etc: lacking or showing a lack of foresight. ■ **short-sightedness** N.

short-staffed ADJ having insufficient staff.

short-term ADJ **1** concerned only with the near future. **2** lasting only a short time.

short wave N **1** a radio wave with a wavelength between 10 and 100 metres. **2** PHYS an electromagnetic wave with a wavelength no longer than that of visible light.

shot[1] N **1** an act of shooting or firing a gun. **2** the sound of a gun being fired. **3** small metal pellets collectively, fired in clusters from a shotgun. **4** a person considered in terms of their ability to fire a gun accurately: **a good shot**. **5** a photographic exposure. **6** a single piece of filmed action recorded without a break by one camera. **7** SPORT an act or instance of shooting or playing a stroke eg in tennis, snooker, etc. **8** ATHLETICS a heavy metal ball thrown in the shot put. **9** COLLOQ an attempt: **I'll have a shot at it**. **10** COLLOQ an injection. **11** N AMER, ESP US COLLOQ a small drink of alcoholic spirit; a dram.
◆ **a shot in the dark** a wild guess.
◆ **be** or **get shot of** COLLOQ be rid of.

shot[2] ADJ **1** of a fabric: woven with different-coloured threads in the warp and weft to give the effect of changing colours: **shot silk**. **2** streaked with a different colour.

shotgun N a gun with a long, wide, smooth barrel for firing small shot.

shot put N, ATHLETICS a field event in which a heavy metal ball is thrown from the shoulder as far as possible. ■ **shot-putter** N.

should AUXILIARY VERB expressing: **1** obligation, duty or recommendation; ought to: **You should brush your teeth regularly**. **2** likelihood or probability: **He should have left by now**. **3** a condition: **If she should die before you, what would happen? 4** WITH FIRST PERSON PRONOUNS a past tense of **shall** in reported speech: **I told them I should be back soon**. **5** statements in clauses with **that**, following expressions of feeling or mood: **It seems odd that we should both have had the same idea**.

shoulder N **1** in humans and animals: the part on either side of the body, just below the neck, where the arm or forelimb joins the trunk. **2** the part of a garment that covers this. **3** a cut of meat consisting of the animal's upper foreleg. **4** either edge of a road.
➤ VB **1** to bear (eg a responsibility). **2** to carry on one's shoulders. **3** to thrust with the shoulder.
◆ **rub shoulders with sb** COLLOQ to meet or associate with them.

shoulder blade N the scapula.

shouldn't CONTRACTION, COLLOQ should not.

shout N **1** a loud cry or call. **2** COLLOQ a turn to buy a round of drinks.
➤ VB **1** TR & INTR (also **shout out**) to utter a loud cry or call. **2** INTR to speak in raised tones.

shove VB **1** TR & INTR to push with force. **2** COLLOQ to put, esp roughly: **Shove it in the bag**.
➤ N a forceful push.
◆ **shove off** COLLOQ to go away.

shovel N **1** a tool with a deep-sided spade-like blade and a handle, for lifting and carrying loose material. **2** a machine, machine part or device with a scooping action.
➤ VB (-*ll*-) **1** to lift or carry with, or as if with, a shovel. **2** to move in large quantities: **shovelled food into her mouth**. ■ **shovelful** N.

show VB (PA P *shown* or *showed*) **1** TR & INTR to make or become visible, known or noticeable: **Does my embarrassment show? 2** to present to view. **3** to prove, indicate or reveal: **This shows us that man evolved from the ape. 4** to teach by demonstrating. **5** to lead, guide or escort: **I'll show you to the door. 6** to give: **Show him some respect. 7** INTR of a cinema film, theatre production, etc: to be part of a current programme: **films now showing at the local Odeon. 8** INTR, SLANG to appear or arrive: **What time did he show?**
➤ N **1** an act of showing. **2** any form of entertainment or spectacle. **3** an exhibition. **4** a pretence: **a show of friendship. 5** a sign or indication: **show of emotion**.
◆ **show off** to display oneself or one's talents, aimed at inviting attention or admiration.
◆ **show sth off 1** to display it proudly, inviting admiration. **2** to display it to good effect: **The cream rug shows off the red carpet nicely**.
◆ **show up 1** COLLOQ to arrive; to turn up. **2** to

be clearly visible.

◆ **show sb up** to embarrass them in public.

showbiz N, ADJ, COLLOQ show business.

show business N the entertainment industry.

showcase N **1** a glass case for displaying objects. **2** any setting in which someone or something is displayed to good advantage.

showdown N, COLLOQ a confrontation or fight by which a long-term dispute may be settled.

shower N **1** a device that produces a spray of water for bathing under, usu while standing. **2** a room or cubicle fitted with such a device or devices. **3** an act or an instance of bathing under such a device. **4** a sudden but short fall of rain, snow or hail. **5** a fall of drops of any liquid. **6** a sudden (esp heavy) burst or fall: **a shower of abuse**. **7** N AMER **a** an abundance of wedding gifts, gifts for a baby, etc; **b** N AMER a party at which such gifts are presented. **8** SLANG a worthless person or group.
➤ VB **1** TR & INTR to cover, bestow, fall or come abundantly. **2** INTR to bathe under a shower. **3** INTR to rain in showers. ■ **showery** ADJ.

showing N **1** an act of exhibiting or displaying. **2** a screening of a cinema film. **3** a display of behaviour as evidence of a fact: **On this showing, he certainly won't get the job.**

showjumping N a competitive sport in which riders on horseback take turns to jump a variety of obstacles. ■ **showjumper** N.

showman N **1** someone who owns or manages a circus, a fairground stall, or other entertainment. **2** someone skilled in displaying their personal abilities. ■ **showmanship** N.

show-off N, COLLOQ someone who shows off to attract attention; an exhibitionist.

showpiece N **1** an item on display; an exhibit. **2** an item presented as an excellent example of its type, to be copied or admired.

showroom N a room where examples of goods for sale are displayed.

show-stopper N an act or performance that is very well received by the audience.

showy ADJ (**-ier, -iest**) **1** making an impressive or exciting display. **2** impressively bright; flashy. ■ **showily** ADV. ■ **showiness** N.

shrapnel N fragments of an exploding shell.

shred N **1** a thin scrap or strip cut or ripped off. **2** a small piece or amount.
➤ VB (**-dd-**) to cut, tear or scrape into shreds. ■ **shredder** N.

shrew N **1** a small nocturnal mammal with velvety fur, small eyes and a pointed snout. **2** a quarrelsome or scolding woman.

shrewd ADJ possessing or showing keen judgement gained from practical experience; astute. ■ **shrewdly** ADV. ■ **shrewdness** N.

shriek VB, TR & INTR to emit a piercing scream.
➤ N such a piercing cry.

shrill ADJ of a voice, sound, etc: high-pitched. ■ **shrillness** N.

shrimp N a small edible crustacean.
➤ VB, INTR to fish for shrimps.

shrine N **1** a sacred place of worship. **2** the tomb or monument of a saint or other holy person. **3** any place or thing greatly respected because of its associations.

shrink VB (**shrank, shrunk**) **1** TR & INTR to make or become smaller in size or extent, esp through exposure to heat, cold or moisture. **2** TR & INTR to contract or make something contract. **3** INTR to shrivel or wither. **4** (often **shrink from sth**) to move away in horror or disgust. **5** (often **shrink from sth**) to be reluctant do it.
➤ N, COLLOQ a psychiatrist.

shrinkage N **1** the act of shrinking. **2** the amount by which something shrinks.

shrinking violet N, COLLOQ a shy person.

shrink-wrap VB to wrap (goods) in clear plastic film that is then shrunk to fit tightly.

shrivel VB (**-ll-**) TR & INTR to make or become shrunken and wrinkled, esp as a result of drying.

shroud N **1** a garment or cloth in which a corpse is wrapped. **2** anything that obscures, masks or hides: **shrouds of fog**.
➤ VB **1** to wrap in a shroud. **2** to obscure, mask

or hide: **proceedings shrouded in secrecy.**

Shrove Tuesday N in the Christian calendar: the day before Ash Wednesday.

shrub N, BOT a woody plant or bush, without any main trunk.

shrubbery N (*-ies*) **1** a place where shrubs are grown. **2** a collective name for shrubs.

shrug VB (*-gg-*) TR & INTR to raise up and drop the shoulders briefly as an indication of doubt, indifference, etc.
➤ N an act of shrugging.
◆ **shrug sth off 1** to get rid of it easily. **2** to dismiss (esp criticism) lightly.

shrunken ADJ having (been) shrunk.

shudder VB, INTR to shiver or tremble.
➤ N **1** such a trembling movement or feeling. **2** a heavy vibration. ■ **shuddering** ADJ.

shuffle VB **1** TR & INTR to move or drag (one's feet) with short quick sliding steps; to walk in this fashion. **2** INTR to walk awkwardly. **3** to rearrange roughly or carelessly: **shuffle papers. 4** TR & INTR to jumble up (playing cards).
➤ N **1** an act or sound of shuffling. **2** a short quick sliding of the feet in dancing.

shufti or **shufty** N, COLLOQ a look or glance.

shun VB (*-nn-*) to avoid someone or something.

shunt VB **1** to move (a train or carriage) from one track to another. **2** to bypass or sidetrack. **3** to get rid of (eg a task) on to someone else.
➤ N **1** an act of shunting or being shunted. **2** COLLOQ a minor collision between vehicles.

shush EXCLAM be quiet!

shut VB (*shut, shutting*) **1** TR & INTR to place or move so as to close an opening: **shut the door. 2** TR & INTR to close or make something close over, denying access to the contents or inside: **shut the book. 3** TR & INTR (often **shut up**) not to allow access to something; to forbid entrance into it: **shut up the building. 4** to fasten or bar; to lock. **5** to bring together the parts or outer parts of something: **I can't shut the clasp. 6** to confine: **He shuts himself in his room for hours. 7** to catch or pinch in a fastening: **I shut my finger in the window. 8** INTR of a business, etc:

to cease to operate at the end of the day.
➤ ADJ **1** not open; closed. **2** made fast; secure.
◆ **shut down** or **shut sth down** to stop or make it stop working or operating.
◆ **shut sth off** to stop the flow of it.
◆ **shut up** COLLOQ to stop speaking.
◆ **shut sb up 1** COLLOQ to make them stop speaking. **2** to confine them.

shuteye N, COLLOQ sleep.

shutter N **1** someone or something that shuts. **2** a movable internal or external cover for a window, esp one of a pair. **3** a device in a camera that regulates the opening and closing of the aperture, exposing the film to light.

shuttle N **1** WEAVING the device that carries the horizontal thread (the weft) backwards and forwards between the vertical threads (the warp). **2** an aircraft, train or bus that runs a frequent service between two places.
➤ VB, TR & INTR to convey or travel in a shuttle.

shuttlecock N a feathered cone hit backwards and forwards in badminton.

shy[1] ADJ **1** of a person: embarrassed or unnerved by the company or attention of others. **2** easily scared; timid. **3** (**shy of sth**) wary or distrustful of it. **4** warily reluctant.
➤ VB (*shies, shied*) INTR eg of a horse: to jump suddenly aside or back in fear; to be startled.
■ **shyly** ADV. ■ **shyness** N.
◆ **shy away** or **off** to shrink from something or recoil, showing reluctance.

shy[2] VB (*shies, shied*) to fling or throw.
➤ N (*shies*) a fling or throw.

shyster N, N AMER, ESP US, SLANG an unscrupulous person, esp a lawyer.

SI and **SI unit** ABBREV Système International d'Unités, the modern scientific system of units used in measurement.

Si SYMBOL, CHEM silicon.

Siamese twins N conjoined twins.

sibilant ADJ similar to, having or pronounced with a hissing sound.

sibling N a blood relation; a brother or sister.

sic ADV a term used in brackets after a word or phrase in a quotation to indicate that it is quoted accurately, even if it appears to be a mistake.

sick ADJ **1** vomiting; feeling the need to vomit. **2** ill; unwell. **3** referring or relating to ill health: sick pay. **4** (often **sick for sb** or **sth**) pining or longing for them or it. **5** (often **sick of sb** or **sth**) thoroughly weary or fed up with them or it. **6** of humour, etc: exploiting gruesome subjects in an unpleasant way.
➢ N, COLLOQ vomit.
➢ VB, TR & INTR (usu **sick up**) to vomit.

sicken VB **1** to make someone or something feel like vomiting. **2** to annoy greatly or disgust.
◆ **sicken for sth** to show symptoms of an illness: I'm sickening for the flu.

sickle N a tool with a short handle and a curved blade for cutting grain crops.

sickly ADJ (**-ier, -iest**) **1** susceptible or prone to illness; ailing or feeble. **2** unhealthy-looking; pallid. **3** weakly sentimental; mawkish.
➢ ADV to an extent that suggests illness: sickly pale. ■ **sickliness** N.

sickness N **1** the condition of being ill; an illness. **2** vomiting. **3** nausea.

side N **1** any of the usu flat or flattish surfaces that form the outer extent of something. **2** any of these surfaces other than the front, back, top or bottom. **3** an edge or border, or the area adjoining this: My car's at the side of the road. **4** either of the parts or areas produced when the whole is divided up the middle: I'll take the left side of the room. **5** the part of the body between the armpit and hip. **6** the area of space next to someone or something: He's round the side of the house. **7** any of the lines forming a geometric figure. **8** any of the groups or teams in a conflict or competition. **9** an aspect: We've seen a different side to him. **10** BRIT COLLOQ a television channel. **11** either of the playing surfaces of a record or cassette.
➢ ADJ **1** located at the side: side entrance. **2** subsidiary or subordinate: side road.
➢ VB (usu **side with sb**) to take on their position or point of view.
◆ **on** or **to one side** removed to a position away from the main concern; put aside.
◆ **on the side** in addition to or apart from ordinary occupation or income.
◆ **side by side** close together.

sideboard N **1** a large piece of furniture, often consisting of shelves or cabinets along with drawers or cupboards. **2** (**sideboards**) sideburns.

sideburn N (usu **sideburns**) the hair that grows on a man's face in front of the ears.

side effect N **1** an additional and usu undesirable effect, esp of a drug, eg nausea, drowsiness. **2** any undesired additional effect.

sidekick N, COLLOQ a close or special friend; a partner or deputy.

sideline N **1** a line marking either side boundary of a sports pitch. **2** a business, occupation or trade in addition to regular work.

sidelong ADJ, ADV from or to one side; not direct or directly: a sidelong glance.

sidereal ADJ of or relating to the stars.

side-saddle N a horse's saddle designed to enable a woman in a skirt to sit with both legs on the same side.

sideshow N **1** an exhibition or show subordinate to a larger one. **2** any subordinate or incidental activity or event.

side-splitting ADJ extremely funny; provoking uproarious and hysterical laughter.

sidestep VB **1** to avoid by, or as if by, stepping aside: You're sidestepping the issue. **2** INTR to step aside.
➢ N a step taken to one side.

sidetrack VB to divert the attention of away from the matter in hand.

sidewalk N, N AMER, ESP US a pavement.

sideways ADV, ADJ **1** from, to or towards one side. **2** with one side foremost.

siding N a short dead-end railway line onto which trains, wagons, etc can be shunted temporarily from the main line.

sidle VB, INTR to go or edge along sideways, esp

in a cautious, furtive and ingratiating manner.

siege N 1 the act or process of surrounding a fort or town with troops, cutting off its supplies and subjecting it to attack to force its surrender. 2 a similar police operation.

siemens N the SI unit of conductance.

sienna N a pigment obtained from a type of earth with a high clay and iron content.

siesta N in hot countries: a sleep or rest after the midday meal.

sieve N a utensil with a meshed or perforated bottom, used for straining solids from liquids or for sifting large particles from smaller ones. ➤ VB to strain or sift with a sieve.

sift VB 1 to pass through a sieve in order to separate out lumps or larger particles. 2 to examine closely and discriminatingly.

sigh VB 1 INTR to release a long deep audible breath, expressive of sadness, longing, or relief. 2 to express with such a sound. ➤ N an act or the sound of sighing.

sight N 1 the power or faculty of seeing; vision. 2 a thing or object seen; view or spectacle: It's a lovely sight. 3 someone's field of view or vision, or the opportunity to see things that this provides: out of sight. 4 (usu **sights**) places, buildings, etc that are particularly interesting or worth seeing: see the sights of the city. 5 a device on a firearm through or along which one looks to take aim. 6 a similar device used as a guide to the eye on an optical or other instrument. 7 COLLOQ a person or thing unpleasant to look at. ➤ VB 1 to get a look at or glimpse of someone or something. 2 to aim (a firearm) using the sight. ◆ **set one's sights on sth** to decide on it as an ambition or aim.

sighted ADJ not blind.

sightless ADJ blind.

sight-reading N playing or singing from printed music that one has not previously seen.

sightsee VB, INTR to visit places of interest, esp as a tourist. ■ **sightseer** N. ■ **sightseeing** N.

sign N 1 a printed mark with a meaning; a symbol: a multiplication sign. 2 MATH an indication of positive or negative value: the minus sign. 3 a gesture expressing a meaning; a signal. 4 an indication: signs of improvement. 5 a portent or omen; a miraculous token. 6 a board or panel displaying information for public view. 7 a board or panel displaying a shopkeeper's name, trade, etc. 8 MED any external evidence or indication of disease, perceptible to an examining doctor, etc. 9 ASTROL any of the twelve parts of the zodiac, bearing the name of a constellation. ➤ VB 1 TR & INTR to give a signal or indication. 2 to write a signature on something; to confirm one's assent to something with a signature. 3 to write (one's name) as a signature: sign a cheque. 4 TR & INTR to employ or become employed with the signing of a contract. 5 TR & INTR to communicate using sign language. 6 to cross or make the sign of the cross over (oneself or someone else). ◆ **sign off** 1 to bring a broadcast to an end. 2 to stop work, etc. ◆ **sign up** to enrol with an organization.

signal N 1 a message in the form of a gesture, light, sound, etc, conveying information or indicating the time for action, often over a distance. 2 (**signals**) the apparatus used to send such a message, eg coloured lights or movable arms or poles on a railway network. 3 an event marking the moment for action to be taken. 4 any set of transmitted electrical impulses received as a sound or image, eg in television; the message conveyed by them. ➤ VB (-ll-) 1 TR & INTR to transmit or convey (a message) using signals. 2 to indicate. ➤ ADJ notable: a signal triumph.

signatory N (-ies) a person, organization or state that is a party to a contract.

signature N 1 one's name written by oneself, or a representative symbol, as a formal mark of authorization, etc. 2 an indication of key or time at the beginning of a line of music. 3 a large sheet of paper with printed pages on it, each with a numeral or letter at the bottom, which when folded forms a section of a book.

signature tune N a tune used to identify or

introduce a specified radio or television programme or performer.

signet N a small seal used for stamping documents, etc.

significance N 1 meaning or importance. 2 the condition or quality of being significant.

significant ADJ 1 important; worth noting or considering. 2 having some meaning; indicating something. ■ **significantly** ADV.

signify VB (*-ies, -ied*) 1 to suggest or mean. 2 to denote. 3 INTR to be significant.

sign language N any form of communication using gestures to represent words and ideas.

signpost N 1 a post supporting a sign that gives information or directions to motorists or pedestrians. 2 an indication or clue.
➤ VB 1 to mark (a route) with signposts. 2 to give directions to someone.

Sikh N an adherent of the monotheistic religion established in the 16c by Guru Nanak.
➤ ADJ of or relating to the Sikhs, their beliefs or customs. ■ **Sikhism** N.

silage N animal fodder made from forage crops such as grass, maize, etc compressed and preserved by controlled fermentation.

sild N a young herring.

silence N 1 absence of sound or speech. 2 a time of such absence of sound or speech. 3 failure or abstention from communication.
➤ VB to make someone or something stop speaking, making a noise, or giving away information.

silencer N a device fitted to a gun barrel or engine exhaust to reduce the noise made.

silent ADJ 1 free from noise; unaccompanied by sound. 2 refraining from speech; not mentioning or divulging something. 3 unspoken but expressed: silent joy. 4 not pronounced: the silent p in pneumonia. 5 of a cinema film: having no soundtrack. ■ **silently** ADV.

silhouette N 1 a dark shape or shadow seen against a light background. 2 an outline drawing of a person, in profile.

➤ VB to make appear as a silhouette.

silica N, GEOL a hard white or colourless glassy solid that occurs naturally as quartz, sand and flint, and also as silicate compounds.

silicate N, CHEM a chemical compound containing silicon, oxygen and one or more metals.

silicon N a non-metallic element used as a semiconductor to make transistors and silicon chips, etc.

silicon chip N, ELECTRONICS, COMP a very thin piece of silicon or other semiconductor material on which all the components of an integrated circuit are arranged. Also called **chip, microchip**.

silicone N, CHEM a synthetic polymer, used in lubricants, electrical insulators, paints, adhesives and surgical breast implants.

silicosis N, PATHOL a lung disease caused by prolonged inhalation of dust containing silica.

silk N 1 a fine soft fibre produced by the larva of the silkworm. 2 an imitation made by forcing a viscous solution of modified cellulose through small holes. 3 thread or fabric made from such fibres. 4 a garment made from such fabric. 5 a the silk gown worn by a Queen's or King's Counsel; b the rank conferred by this.

silken ADJ, LITERARY 1 made of silk. 2 as soft or smooth as silk.

silkworm N the caterpillar of the silk moth, which spins a cocoon of unbroken silk thread.

silky ADJ (*-ier, -iest*) 1 soft and shiny like silk. 2 of a person's manner or voice: suave.

sill N 1 the bottom part of the framework around the inside of a window or door. 2 the ledge of wood, stone or metal forming this.

silly ADJ (*-ier, -iest*) not sensible; foolish; trivial or frivolous.
➤ N (*-ies*) COLLOQ a foolish person. ■ **silliness** N.

silo N 1 a tall round airtight tower for storing green crops and converting them into silage. 2 an underground chamber housing a missile ready for firing.

silt N fine sedimentary material consisting of very small rock fragments or mineral particles. ➤ VB, INTR (often **silt up**) to become blocked with silt.

silvan see **sylvan**

silver N 1 an element, a soft white lustrous precious metal that is an excellent conductor of heat and electricity, and is used in jewellery, ornaments, mirrors and coins. 2 coins made of this metal. 3 articles made of or coated with this metal, esp cutlery and other tableware. 4 a silver medal. ➤ ADJ 1 having a whitish-grey colour. 2 denoting a 25th anniversary. ➤ VB 1 to apply a thin coating of silver; to plate with silver. 2 to give a silvery sheen to something. 3 INTR to become silvery.

silverfish N a primitive wingless insect with a tapering body covered with silvery scales.

silver lining N a positive aspect of an otherwise unpleasant or unfortunate situation.

silver medal N esp in sporting competitions: a medal of silver awarded to the person or team in second place.

silverside N a fine cut of beef from the rump.

silversmith N someone who makes or repairs articles made of silver.

silverware N objects, esp cutlery or tableware, made from or coated with silver.

silvery ADJ 1 having the colour or shiny quality of silver. 2 having a light ringing sound.

silviculture N, BOT the cultivation of forest trees.

simian N a monkey or ape. ➤ ADJ belonging or relating to, or resembling, a monkey or ape.

similar ADJ 1 having a close resemblance to something; being of the same kind, but not identical. 2 GEOM exactly corresponding in shape, regardless of size. ■ **similarity** N. ■ **similarly** ADV.

simile N a figure of speech in which a thing is

described by being likened to something, usu using **as** or **like**, as in **eyes sparkling like diamonds**.

similitude N, FORMAL resemblance.

simmer VB 1 TR & INTR to cook gently at just below boiling point. 2 INTR to be close to an outburst of emotion, usu anger. ➤ N a simmering state.
◆ **simmer down** to calm down.

simnel N a sweet fruit cake covered with marzipan, traditionally made at Easter.

simony N the practice of buying or selling a religious post, benefice or privilege.

simper VB 1 INTR to smile in a weak affected manner. 2 to express while smiling in this way. ➤ N a simpering smile.

simple ADJ 1 easy; not difficult. 2 not complex or complicated; straightforward. 3 plain or basic: **a simple outfit**. 4 down-to-earth; unpretentious. 5 often IRONIC gullible; lacking intelligence. 6 consisting of one thing or element.

simple-minded ADJ 1 lacking intelligence. 2 guileless. ■ **simple-mindedness** N.

simpleton N a foolish or unintelligent person.

simplicity N a simple state or quality.

simplify VB (-ies, -ied) to make something less difficult or complicated; to make it easier to understand. ■ **simplification** N.

simplistic ADJ unrealistically straight-forward or uncomplicated. ■ **simplistically** ADV.

simply ADV 1 in an uncomplicated manner. 2 just: **It's simply not true**. 3 absolutely: **simply marvellous**.

simulate VB 1 to convincingly re-create (a set of conditions or a real-life event), esp for the purposes of training. 2 to assume a false appearance of someone or something. 3 to pretend to have, do or feel: **She simulated anger**. ■ **simulated** ADJ. ■ **simulation** N.

simulator N a device that simulates a system, process or set of conditions, esp in order to test it, or for training purposes: **flight simulator**.

simultaneous ADJ happening, or carried out, at exactly the same time.

sin[1] N 1 an act that breaches a moral and esp a religious law or teaching. 2 the condition of offending a deity by committing a moral offence. 3 an act that offends common standards of morality or decency; an outrage. ➤ VB (**-nn-**) INTR to commit a sin. ■ **sinner** N.

sin[2] ABBREV sine.

since CONJ 1 from the time that; seeing that. 2 as; because: **I'm not surprised you failed the exam since you did no work for it.** ➤ PREP during or throughout the period between now and some earlier stated time: **I've been there several times since it opened.** ➤ ADV 1 from that time onwards: **I haven't been back since.** 2 ago: **five years since.**

sincere ADJ genuine; not pretended or affected. ■ **sincerely** ADV. ■ **sincerity** N.

sine N, TRIG in a right-angled triangle: a function of an angle, defined as the length of the side opposite the angle divided by the length of the hypotenuse.

sinecure N a paid job involving little work.

sinew N 1 a strong piece of fibrous tissue joining a muscle to a bone; a tendon. 2 (**sinews**) physical strength. ■ **sinewy** ADJ.

sinful ADJ wicked; involving sin; morally wrong.

sing VB (PAT **sang,** PAP **sung**) 1 TR & INTR to utter (words, sounds, etc) in a melodic rhythmic fashion, esp to the accompaniment of music. 2 INTR to utter such sounds as a profession: **Her mother was a dancer, but she sings.** 3 to make someone or something pass into a state with such sound: **The mother sang her baby to sleep.** 4 INTR to make a sound like a musical voice; to hum, ring or whistle. 5 INTR to suffer a ringing sound: **a loud bang that made their ears sing.** 6 INTR of birds, specific insects, etc: to produce calls or sounds. ■ **singer** N.
◆ **sing out** to shout or call out.

singe VB (**singeing**) TR & INTR to burn lightly on the surface; to scorch or become scorched. ➤ N a light surface burn.

single ADJ 1 comprising only one part; solitary. 2 having no partner; unmarried, esp never having been married. 3 for use by one person only: **a single room.** 4 of a travel ticket: valid for an outward journey only. 5 unique. 6 even one: **Not a single person turned up.** ➤ N 1 (often **singles**) a person without a partner, either marital or otherwise. 2 a single room, eg in a guest house. 3 a ticket for an outward journey only. 4 a record or CD, usu with only one main track. 5 BRIT a pound coin or note. 6 US a one-dollar note. ➤ VB (always **single out**) to pick someone or something from among others.

single-breasted ADJ of a coat or jacket: having only one row of buttons at the front.

single-decker N a bus with only one deck.

single figures N the numbers from 1 to 9.

single file N a line of people, animals, etc standing or moving one behind the other.

single-handed ADJ, ADV done, carried out etc by oneself, without any help from others.

single-minded ADJ determinedly pursuing one specific aim or object.

singles N in tennis, etc: a match where one player competes against another.

singlet N a sleeveless vest or undershirt.

singleton N a solitary person or thing.

singly ADV 1 one at a time; individually. 2 alone.

singsong N an informal gathering at which friends, etc sing together for pleasure. ➤ ADJ of a speaking voice, etc: having a fluctuating intonation and rhythm.

singular ADJ 1 single; unique. 2 extraordinary; exceptional. 3 strange; odd. 4 GRAM denoting or referring to one person, thing, etc. ➤ N, GRAM a word or form of a word expressing the idea or involvement of one person, thing, etc. ■ **singularity** N. ■ **singularly** ADV.

sinister ADJ suggesting evil or danger.

sink VB (PAT **sank** or **sunk,** PAP **sunk**) 1 TR & INTR to fall or cause to fall and remain below the surface of water, either partially or completely.

2 INTR to collapse downwardly or inwardly; to subside. **3** INTR to be or become inwardly withdrawn or dejected. **4** to embed: **They sank the pole into the ground. 5** to pass steadily (and often dangerously) into a worse level or state: **He sank into depression. 6** to diminish or decline. **7** to invest (money) heavily: **We sank a lot of money into this project. 8** COLLOQ to ruin the plans of someone; to ruin (plans): **We are sunk. 9** COLLOQ to drink (esp alcohol) usu quickly: **We sank four beers within the hour. 10** COLLOQ to send (a ball) into a pocket in snooker, billiards, etc and into the hole in golf. **11** to excavate (a well, shaft, etc). **12** to abandon or abolish: **I'll sink the whole organization.**
> N a basin, wall-mounted or in a sink unit, with built-in water supply and drainage, for washing dishes, etc.
◆ **sink in 1** COLLOQ to be fully understood or realized: **The bad news took a few days to sink in. 2** to penetrate or be absorbed: **Wait for the ink to sink in first.**

sinuous ADJ wavy; winding. ■ **sinuosity** N.

sinus N, ANAT a cavity or depression filled with air, esp in the bones of mammals.

sinusitis N inflammation of the lining of the sinuses, esp the nasal ones.

sip VB (-*pp*-) TR & INTR to drink in small mouthfuls.
> N **1** an act of sipping. **2** an amount sipped at one time.

siphon or **syphon** N a tube held in an inverted U-shape that can be used to transfer liquid from one container at a higher level into another at a lower level, used to empty car petrol tanks, etc.
> VB (usu **siphon sth off**) **1** to transfer (liquid) from one container to another using such a device. **2** to take (money, funds, etc) slowly and continuously from a store or fund.

sir N **1** a polite and respectful address for a man. **2** (**Sir**) a title used before the Christian name of a knight or baronet.

sire N **1** the father of a horse or other animal. **2** HIST a term of respect used to a king.
> VB of an animal: to father (young).

siren N **1** a device that gives out a loud wailing noise, usu as a warning signal. **2** an irresistible woman thought capable of ruining men's lives.

sirloin N a fine cut of beef from the loin.

sirocco N in S Europe: a dry hot dusty wind blowing from N Africa.

sis N, COLLOQ short for **sister**.

sisal N a strong coarse durable yellowish fibre used to make ropes, twine, sacking, etc.

sissy or **cissy** N (-*ies*) DEROG a feeble, cowardly or effeminate male.
> ADJ having the characteristics of a sissy.

sister N **1** a female child of the same parents as another. **2** a nun. **3** a senior female nurse, esp one in charge of a ward. **4** a close female associate; a fellow female member of a profession, class or racial group.
> ADJ being of the same origin, model or design: **a sister ship.**

sister-in-law N (*sisters-in-law*) **1** the sister of one's husband or wife. **2** the wife of one's brother.

sisterly ADJ of a woman or her behaviour: like a sister, esp in being kind and affectionate.

sit VB (*sat, sitting*) **1** INTR to rest the body on the buttocks, with the upper body more or less vertical. **2** of an animal: to position itself on its hindquarters in a similar manner. **3** INTR of a bird: to perch or lie. **4** INTR of a bird: to brood. **5** INTR of an object: to lie, rest or hang. **5** INTR to lie unused. **6** INTR to hold a meeting or other session. **7** INTR to be a member, taking regular part in meetings: **sit on a committee. 8** to have a seat, as in parliament. **9** to have a specific position. **10** to take (an examination); to be a candidate for (a degree or other award). **11** to conduct to a seat; to assign a seat to someone. **12** INTR to be or exist in a specified comparison or relation: **His smoking sits awkwardly with his being a doctor. 13** INTR to pose as an artist's or photographer's model.
◆ **be sitting pretty** COLLOQ to be in a very advantageous position.
◆ **sit in for sb** to act as a substitute for them.
◆ **sit in on sth** to be present at it as a visitor or

observer, esp without participating.

◆ **sit on sth 1** to be a member of it: sit on a committee. **2** COLLOQ to delay taking action over it.

◆ **sit sth out** to take no part.

◆ **sit tight 1** to maintain one's position and opinion determinedly. **2** to wait patiently.

◆ **sit up 1** to move oneself from a slouching or lying position into an upright sitting position. **2** to take notice suddenly or show a sudden interest.

sitar N a guitar-like instrument of Indian origin, with a long neck, rounded body and two sets of strings.

sitcom N a situation comedy, a TV or radio comedy series in which the same characters appear in the same surroundings, but in different situations.

sit-down ADJ of a strike: in which the workers occupy the workplace until an agreement is reached.

site N **1** the place where something was, is, or is to be situated: the site of the museum. **2** an area set aside for a specific activity: a camping site.
➤ VB to position or situate.

sit-in N the occupation of a public building, factory, etc as a form of protest or as a means of applying pressure.

sitter N **1** a person who poses for an artist or photographer. **2** a babysitter.

sitting N **1** a period of continuous activity, usu while sitting or in a similar position: He wrote it at one sitting. **2** a turn to eat for any of two or more sections of a group too large to eat all at the same time in the same place, or the period set aside for each turn. **3** a period of posing for an artist or photographer. **4** a session or meeting of an official body.
➤ ADJ **1** currently holding office: the sitting MP. **2** seated: in a sitting position.

sitting duck N someone or something in a defenceless or exposed position.

sitting-room N a room, esp in a private house, for relaxing in, entertaining visitors, etc.

sitting tenant N, BRIT a tenant occupying a

property when it changes ownership.

situate VB to place in a certain position, context or set of circumstances.

situation N **1** a set of circumstances or state of affairs. **2** a place, position or location. **3** a job; employment: situations vacant.

sit-up N a physical exercise in which the body is raised up and over the thighs from a lying position, often with the hands behind the head.

six N **1 a** the cardinal number 6; **b** the quantity that this represents, being one more than five. **2** any symbol for this, eg 6 or VI. **3** something, esp a garment or a person, whose size is denoted by the number 6. **4** the sixth hour after midnight or midday: Come at six.
➤ ADJ **1** totalling six. **2** aged six.

◆ **at sixes and sevens** in a state of total disorder or confusion.

◆ **knock sb for six** COLLOQ **1** to defeat or ruin them completely. **2** to shock or surprise them completely.

◆ **six and half a dozen** equal; equally acceptable or unacceptable.

sixfold ADJ **1** equal to six times as much. **2** divided into or consisting of six parts.
➤ ADV by six times as much.

six-pack N a pack containing six items sold as one unit, esp a pack of six cans of beer.

sixpence N in Britain: a former small silver coin worth six old pennies.

sixteen N **1 a** the cardinal number 16; **b** the quantity that this represents, being one more than fifteen, or the sum of ten and six. **2** any symbol for this, eg 16 or XVI. **3** something, esp a garment or a person, whose size is denoted by the number 16.
➤ ADJ **1** totalling sixteen. **2** aged sixteen.
■ **sixteenth** ADJ, N.

sixth (often written **6**th) ADJ **1** in counting: **a** next after fifth; **b** last of six. **2** in sixth position.
➤ N **1** one of six equal parts. **2** a fraction equal to one divided by six.

sixth sense N an unexplained power of intuition by which one is aware of things that are not seen, heard, touched, smelled or tasted.

sixties (often written **60s** or **60's**) PL N
1 (**one's sixties**) the period of time between one's sixtieth and seventieth birthdays. **2** (**the sixties**) **a** the range of temperatures between sixty and seventy degrees. **3** (**the sixties**) the period of time between the sixtieth and seventieth years of a century.

sixty N **1 a** the cardinal number 60; **b** the quantity that this represents, being one more than fifty-nine, or the product of ten and six. **2** any symbol for this, eg **60** or **LX**. **3** something whose size is denoted by the number 60.
➤ ADJ **1** totalling sixty. **2** aged sixty. ■ **sixtieth** ADJ, N.

size¹ N **1** length, breadth, height or volume, or a combination of these; the dimensions of something. **2** largeness; magnitude: **We were amazed at its size. 3** any of a range of graded measurements.
➤ VB **1** to measure something in order to determine size. **2** to sort according to size.
◆ **size sb** or **sth up 1** to take a mental measurement of them or it. **2** COLLOQ to mentally judge their or its nature, quality or worth.

size² N a weak kind of glue used to stiffen paper and fabric, and to prepare walls for plastering and wallpapering.
➤ VB to cover or treat with size.

sizeable or **sizable** ADJ fairly large.

sized ADJ, USU IN COMPOUNDS having a particular size: **medium-sized.**

sizzle VB, INTR **1** to make a hissing sound when, or as if when, frying in hot fat. **2** to be extremely hot: **sizzling weather. 3** COLLOQ to be in a state of intense emotion, esp anger or excitement.
➤ N a sizzling sound.

skate¹ N one of a pair of boots with blades or wheels fixed to the soles for gliding over ice or rolling over ground.
➤ VB, INTR to move around on skates. ■ **skater** N. ■ **skating** N.
◆ **get one's skates on** COLLOQ to hurry up.
◆ **skate on thin ice** to risk danger, harm or embarrassment, esp through lack of care.
◆ **skate over** or **round sth** to avoid dealing with something or considering (a difficulty, etc).

skate² N (**skate** or **skates**) a large flatfish.

skateboard N a narrow shaped board mounted on sets of small wheels.

skating rink N **1** a large surface covered in ice for skating. **2** the building that houses this.

skedaddle VB, INTR, COLLOQ to leave quickly.
➤ N a hurried departure.

skein N **1** a loosely tied coil of wool or thread. **2** a flock of geese in flight.

skeletal ADJ **1** similar to or like a skeleton. **2** painfully or extremely thin.

skeleton N **1** the framework of bones that supports the body of an animal. **2** the supporting veins of a leaf. **3** an outline or framework: **the skeleton of the plot. 5** COLLOQ an unhealthily thin person or animal.

skeleton key N a key that can open many different locks.

skeptic an alternative N AMER spelling of **sceptic**.

skerry N (**-ies**) a reef of rock or a small rocky island.

sketch N **1** a rough drawing quickly done. **2** a rough plan. **3** a short account or outline. **4** a short piece of comedy.
➤ VB **1** TR & INTR to do a rough drawing or drawings of something. **2** to give a rough outline of something. ■ **sketcher** N.

sketchy ADJ (**-ier, -iest**) lacking detail; not complete or substantial. ■ **sketchily** ADV.

skew ADJ slanted; oblique; askew.
➤ VB, TR & INTR to slant or cause to slant.
➤ N a slanting position; obliquity: **on the skew.**

skewbald ADJ of an animal, esp a horse: marked with patches of white and another colour (other than black). **Also AS NOUN.**

skewer N a long wooden or metal pin pushed through chunks of meat or vegetables which are to be roasted.
➤ VB to pierce with, or as if with, a skewer.

ski N **1** one of a pair of long narrow runners of wood, metal or plastic, upturned at the front and

attached to each of a pair of boots or to a vehicle for gliding over snow. **2** a water-ski.
➤ VB (*skis, skied* or *ski'd, skiing*) INTR to move on skis. ■ **skier** N. ■ **skiing** N.

skid VB (*-dd-*) **1** INTR of a vehicle or person: to slip or slide at an angle, esp out of control. **2** to cause a vehicle to slide out of control.
➤ N an instance of skidding.

skidoo N a motorized sledge, fitted with tracks at the rear and steerable skis at the front.
➤ VB (*-dooed, -dooing*) to use a skidoo.

skiff N a small light boat.

skilful or (US) **skillful** ADJ having or showing skill. ■ **skilfully** ADV. ■ **skilfulness** N.

ski lift N a device for carrying skiers to the top of a slope so that they can ski down.

skill N **1** expertness; dexterity. **2** a talent, craft or accomplishment, naturally acquired or developed through training. **3** (**skills**) aptitudes and abilities appropriate for a specific job.

skilled ADJ **1** of people: possessing skills; trained or experienced. **2** of a job: requiring skill or showing the use of skill.

skillet N **1** a small long-handled saucepan. **2** esp N AMER a frying-pan.

skim VB (*-mm-*) **1** to remove floating matter from the surface of (a liquid). **2** (often **skim off**) to take something off by skimming. **3** TR & INTR to brush or cause something to brush against (a surface): **He skimmed the table as he went past. 4** to throw an object over a surface so as to make it bounce.
◆ **skim through sth 1** to glance through (eg a book). **2** to deal with or discuss it superficially.

skimp VB **1** INTR (often **skimp on sth**) to spend, use or give too little or only just enough of it. **2** INTR to stint or restrict. **3** to carry out hurriedly or recklessly.

skimpy ADJ (*-ier, -iest*) **1** inadequate; barely enough. **2** of clothes: leaving much of the body uncovered; scanty. ■ **skimpily** ADV.

skin N **1** the tough flexible waterproof covering of the human or animal body. **2** an animal hide, with or without the fur or hair attached. **3** the

outer covering of certain fruits and vegetables. **4** any outer covering. **5** complexion: **greasy skin. 6** a membrane, esp covering internal organs in animals. **7** a semi-solid coating or film on the surface of a liquid. **8** a container made from animal hide.
➤ VB (*-nn-*) **1** to remove or strip the skin from something. **2** to injure by scraping the skin: **He skinned his elbow when he fell. 3** SLANG to cheat or swindle.
◆ **by the skin of one's teeth** very narrowly.
◆ **get under sb's skin** COLLOQ **1** to greatly irritate them. **2** to become their obsession.

skin-deep ADJ superficial; shallow.
➤ ADV superficially.

skin-diving N underwater swimming with breathing equipment carried on the back, but with no wet suit and no connection to a boat. ■ **skin-diver** N.

skinflint N, COLLOQ a very ungenerous person.

skinhead N a person, esp a white youth and generally one of a gang, with closely cropped hair, and anti-establishment attitudes.

skinny ADJ (*-ier, -iest*) **1** of a person or animal: very thin; emaciated. **2** COLLOQ of a pullover, T-shirt, etc: tight-fitting.

skint ADJ, SLANG without money; hard up.

skin-tight ADJ of a piece of clothing: very tight-fitting.

skip[1] VB (*-pp-*) **1** INTR to move along with light springing or hopping steps on alternate feet. **2** INTR to make jumps over a skipping-rope. **3** to omit or pass over. **4** COLLOQ not to attend eg a class in school. **5** to make (a stone) skim a surface. **6** of a stone: to skim over a surface.
➤ N **1** a skipping movement. **2** the act of omitting or leaving something out.

skip[2] N **1** BRIT a large metal container for rubbish from eg building work. **2** a lift in a coal mine for raising minerals.

skipper N **1** a ship's captain. **2** the captain of an aeroplane. **3** the captain of a team.
➤ VB to act as skipper of something.

skipping-rope N a rope swung backwards

and forwards or twirled, for jumping over.

skirl SCOT, N the high-pitched sound of bagpipes.
➤ VB **1** INTR to make this sound. **2** TR & INTR to shriek or sing in a high-pitched manner.

skirmish N a minor fight or dispute.
➤ VB, INTR to engage in a skirmish.

skirt N **1** a woman's or girl's garment that hangs from the waist. **2** the part of a woman's dress, coat, etc from the waist down. **3** any part or attachment resembling a skirt. **4** the part of a hovercraft containing the air-cushion. **5** a cut of beef from the rear part of the belly.
➤ VB **1** to border something. **2** to pass along or around the edge of something. **3** to avoid confronting (eg a problem).

skit N a short satirical piece of writing or drama.

skittish ADJ **1** lively and playful; spirited. **2** frequently changing mood or opinion; fickle or capricious. **3** of a horse: easily frightened.

skittle N **1** each of the upright bottle-shaped targets used in a game of skittles. **2** (**skittles**) a game in which balls are rolled down an alley towards a set of these, the object being to knock over as many as possible.

skive VB, TR & INTR, BRIT COLLOQ (also **skive off**) to evade work or a duty, esp through laziness.
➤ N the act or an instance of skiving. ■ **skiver** N. ■ **skiving** N.

skivvy COLLOQ, N (-ies) derog a servant, esp a woman, who does unpleasant household jobs.
➤ VB (-ies, -ied) INTR to work as if a skivvy.

skua N a large predatory gull-like seabird.

skulduggery or (N AMER) **skullduggery** N (-ies) underhand or dishonest behaviour.

skulk VB, INTR **1** to sneak off out of the way. **2** to hide or lurk, planning mischief. ■ **skulking** N.

skull N **1** the hard cartilaginous or bony framework of the head. **2** COLLOQ, often DEROG the head or brain; intelligence.

skullcap N a small brimless cap fitting closely on the head.

skunk N (**skunk** or **skunks**) a small American mammal related to the weasel, best known for the foul-smelling liquid which it squirts from musk glands at the base of its tail.

sky N (**skies**) **1** the apparent dome of space in which the Sun, Moon and stars can be seen. **2** (**skies**) the heavens.

sky-diving N free-falling from an aircraft, with a long delay before the parachute is opened. ■ **sky-diver** N.

sky-high ADJ, ADV esp of prices: very high.

skylark N a small lark known for its loud clear warbling song performed in flight.

skylight N a window in a roof or ceiling.

skyline N the outline of buildings, hills and trees seen against the sky; the horizon.

skyrocket N a firework that explodes very high in the sky.

skyscraper N an extremely tall building.

skyward ADJ directed towards the sky.
➤ ADV (also **skywards**) towards the sky.

slab N **1** a thick flat rectangular piece of stone, etc. **2** a thick slice, esp of cake.
➤ VB (-bb-) to pave with concrete slabs.

slack¹ ADJ **1** limp or loose; not pulled or stretched tight. **2** not careful or diligent; remiss. **3** not busy. **4** of the tide, etc: still.
➤ ADV in a slack manner; partially.
➤ VB (also **slacken**) (often **slack off**) **1** INTR (also **slack off** or **up**) to become slower; to slow one's working pace through tiredness or laziness: Stop slacking! **2** TR & INTR to make or become looser. **3** INTR to become less busy: work is slackening off for the winter.

slack² N coal dust or tiny fragments of coal.

slacken see under **slack¹** (VB)

slacker N an idle person; a shirker.

slacks PL N, DATED a type of loose casual trousers, worn by both males and females.

slag¹ N waste material from coalmining or smelting metal ore.

slag² VB (-gg-) SLANG (usu **slag sb off**) to criticize or deride them harshly.

slag[3] N, DEROG SLANG a woman who has casual sex with many different people.

slake VB 1 LITERARY to satisfy or quench (thirst, desire or anger). 2 to cause (lime) to crumble by adding water.

slalom N a race, on skis or in canoes, in and out of obstacles on a winding course designed to test tactical skill.

slam[1] VB (-mm-) 1 TR & INTR to shut loudly and with violence. 2 TR & INTR (usu **slam against, down, into**, etc) COLLOQ to make or cause something to make loud heavy contact. ➤ N the act or sound of slamming.

slam[2] N short for **grand slam**.

slander N 1 LAW damaging defamation by spoken words, or by looks or gestures. 2 a false, malicious and damaging spoken statement about a person. 3 the making of such statements. ➤ VB to speak about someone in such a way. ■ **slanderer** N. ■ **slanderous** ADJ.

slang N very informal words and phrases used by any class, profession or set of people.

slant VB 1 INTR to be at an angle as opposed to horizontal or vertical; to slope. 2 to turn, strike or fall obliquely or at an angle. 3 to present (information, etc) in a biased way, or for a particular audience or readership. ➤ N 1 a sloping position, surface or line. 2 a point of view, opinion or way of looking at a particular thing. ➤ ADJ sloping; lying at an angle. ■ **slantwise** ADV, ADJ.

slap N 1 a blow with the palm of the hand or anything flat. 2 the sound made by such a blow, or by the impact of one flat surface with another. 3 a snub or rebuke. ➤ VB (-pp-) 1 to strike with the open hand or anything flat. 2 to bring or send with a slapping sound. 3 (often **slap sth on**) COLLOQ to apply carelessly: She slapped cream on her face. ➤ ADV, COLLOQ 1 exactly or precisely: slap in the middle. 2 heavily or suddenly; with a slap: He fell slap on his face.

slap and tickle N, HUMOROUS COLLOQ kissing and cuddling; sexual activity of any kind.

slap-bang ADV, COLLOQ 1 exactly or precisely: slap-bang in the middle. 2 directly and with force: He drove slap-bang into the wall.

slapdash ADV in a careless and hurried way. ➤ ADJ careless and hurried.

slap-happy ADJ, COLLOQ cheerfully carefree or careless; happy-go-lucky.

slapstick N comedy in which the humour is derived from boisterous antics of all kinds.

slap-up ADJ, COLLOQ of a meal: lavish.

slash VB 1 TR & INTR to make sweeping cuts or cutting strokes, esp repeatedly. 2 to cut by striking violently and often randomly. 3 to make long cuts or gashes in something. 4 COLLOQ to reduce (prices, etc) suddenly and drastically. ➤ N 1 a sweeping cutting stroke. 2 a long and sometimes deep cut. 3 a solidus.

slat N a thin strip, esp of wood or metal.

slate[1] N 1 GEOL a shiny dark grey metamorphic rock that is easily split into thin flat layers, formed by the compression of clays and shales, and used for roofing and flooring. 2 a roofing tile made of this. 3 FORMERLY a piece of this for writing on. 4 a record of credit given to a customer: put the cost on my slate. ➤ VB to cover (a roof) with slates. ➤ ADJ 1 made of slate. 2 slate-coloured. ■ **slaty** ADJ. ◆ **wipe the slate clean** to enable a person to make a fresh start.

slate[2] VB, COLLOQ to criticize extremely harshly; to abuse or reprimand. ■ **slating** N.

slattern N, OLD USE a woman of dirty or untidy appearance or habits; a slut. ■ **slatternly** ADJ.

slaughter N 1 the killing of animals, esp for food. 2 cruel and violent murder. 3 the large-scale indiscriminate killing of people or animals. ➤ VB 1 to subject to slaughter. 2 COLLOQ to defeat resoundingly; to trounce.

slaughterhouse N a place where animals are killed for food; an abattoir.

slave N 1 HIST someone owned by and acting

as servant to another, with no personal freedom. **2** a person who is submissive under domination. **3** a person who works extremely hard for another; a drudge. **4** (also **a slave to sth**) a person whose life is dominated by a specific activity or thing: **a slave to her work**. ➢ VB, INTR to work like or as a slave.

slaver N spittle running from the mouth. ➢ VB, INTR **1** to let spittle run from the mouth; to dribble. **2** (also **slaver over sb**) to fawn over them, esp lustfully. **3** COLLOQ to talk nonsense.

slavery N **1** the state of being a slave. **2** the practice of owning slaves. **3** toil or drudgery.

slavish ADJ **1** characteristic of, belonging to or befitting a slave. **2** very closely copied or imitated; unoriginal. ■ **slavishly** ADV.

slay VB (PA T *slew*, PA P *slain*) TR & INTR, ARCHAIC OR LITERARY to kill. ■ **slayer** N.

sleaze N, COLLOQ **1** sleaziness. **2** someone of low standards.

sleazy ADJ (*-ier, -iest*) COLLOQ **1** dirty and neglected-looking. **2** disreputable. ■ **sleaziness** N.

sledge and **sled** N **1** a vehicle with ski-like runners for travelling over snow, drawn by horses or dogs. **2** a smaller vehicle of a similar design for children, for sliding on the snow. ➢ VB, INTR **1** to travel by sledge. **2** to play on a sledge.

sledgehammer N a large heavy hammer swung with both arms.

sleek ADJ **1** of hair, fur, etc: smooth, soft and glossy. **2** having a prosperous appearance. ➢ VB to smooth (esp hair).

sleep N **1** a readily reversible state of natural unconsciousness during which the body's functional powers are restored, and physical movements are minimal. **2** a period of such rest. ➢ VB (*slept*) INTR **1** to rest in a state of sleep. **2** to be motionless, inactive or dormant. **3** to provide or contain sleeping accommodation for (the specified number). **4** COLLOQ to be in a dreamy state, not paying attention, etc.
◆ **put sb** or **sth to sleep 1** to anaesthetize them. **2** EUPHEMISTIC to kill (an animal) painlessly

with an injected drug.
◆ **sleep in** to sleep later than usual in the morning.
◆ **sleep sth off** to recover from it by sleeping.

sleeper N **1** someone who sleeps, esp in a specified way: **a heavy sleeper**. **2** any of the horizontal wooden or concrete beams supporting the rails on a railway track. **3 a** a railway carriage providing sleeping accommodation for passengers; **b** a train with such carriages.

sleeping-bag N a large quilted sack for sleeping in when camping, etc.

sleeping partner N a business partner who invests money in a business without taking part in its management.

sleeping policeman N, COLLOQ a low hump built into the surface of a road, intended to slow down traffic.

sleepless ADJ **1** characterized by an inability to sleep: **a sleepless night**. **2** unable to sleep. ■ **sleeplessly** ADV. ■ **sleeplessness** N.

sleepwalking N walking in one's sleep. ■ **sleepwalker** N. ■ **sleepwalking** N.

sleepy ADJ (*-ier, -iest*) **1** feeling the desire or need to sleep; drowsy. **2** suggesting sleep or drowsiness: **sleepy music**. **3** characterized by quietness and a lack of activity: **a sleepy village**. ■ **sleepily** ADV. ■ **sleepiness** N.

sleet N rain mixed with snow and/or hail. ➢ VB, INTR to rain and snow simultaneously.

sleeve N **1** the part of a garment that covers the arm. **2** ENG a tube, esp of a different metal, fitted inside a metal cylinder or tube, either as protection or to decrease the diameter. **3** the cardboard or paper envelope in which a record is stored. ■ **sleeveless** ADJ.
◆ **have sth up one's sleeve** have something in secret reserve, possibly for later use.

sleigh N, esp N AMER a large horse-drawn sledge.

sleight N dexterity; cunning or trickery.

sleight of hand N the quick movement of the

hands in the performing of magic tricks.

slender ADJ **1** attractively slim. **2** thin or narrow; slight. **3** meagre: **slender means**.

sleuth COLLOQ, N a detective.
➢ VB, INTR to work as a detective.

slew or **slue** VB, TR & INTR to twist or cause to twist or swing round, esp uncontrollably.
➢ N an instance of slewing.

slice N **1** a thin broad piece, wedge or segment that is cut off. **2** COLLOQ a share or portion: **a slice of the business**. **3** a kitchen utensil with a broad flat blade for sliding under and lifting solid food, esp fish. **4** a slash or swipe.
➢ VB **1** to cut up into slices. **2** (also **slice sth off**) to cut it off as or like a slice: **slice a piece off the end**. **3** INTR to cut deeply and easily; to move easily and forcefully: **a boat slicing through the water**. **4** INTR to slash.

slick ADJ **1** dishonestly or slyly clever. **2** glib; smooth-tongued or suave: **a slick operator**. **3** impressively and superficially smart or efficient: **a slick organization**. **4** esp of hair: smooth and glossy; sleek.
➢ VB (usu **slick sth back** or **down**) to smooth.
➢ N an oil slick.

slide VB (**slid**) **1** TR & INTR to move or cause to move or run smoothly along a surface. **2** INTR to lose one's footing, esp on a slippery surface; to slip. **3** TR & INTR to move or place softly and unobtrusively: **slid the letter into his pocket**. **4** INTR to pass gradually, esp through neglect or laziness; to lapse: **slid back into bad habits**.
➢ N **1** an act or instance of sliding. **2** a polished slippery track, eg on ice. **3** any part of something that glides smoothly, eg the moving part of a trombone. **4** a chute. **5** a small glass plate on which specimens are mounted to be viewed through a microscope. **6** a small transparent photograph viewed in magnified size by means of a projector. **7** a hair-clip.

slight ADJ **1** small in extent, significance or seriousness: **a slight problem**. **2** slim or slender. **3** lacking solidity, weight or significance; flimsy.
➢ VB to insult someone by ignoring or dismissing them abruptly; to snub them.
➢ N an insult by snubbing or showing

neglect. ■ **slightly** ADV.

slim ADJ (**slimmer, slimmest**) **1** of people: attractively thin; slender. **2** characterized by little thickness or width. **3** not great; slight or remote: **a slim chance**.
➢ VB (**-mm-**) INTR **1** (sometimes **slim down**) to make oneself slimmer. **2** to try to lose weight.
■ **slimmer** N. ■ **slimming** N.

slime N **1** any thin, unpleasantly slippery or gluey, mud-like substance. **2** any mucus-like substance secreted, eg by snails and slugs.

slimy ADJ (**-ier, -iest**) **1** similar to, covered with or consisting of slime. **2** COLLOQ exaggeratedly obedient or attentive; obsequious.

sling N **1** a cloth hoop that hangs from the neck to support an injured arm. **2 a** a weapon for hurling stones, consisting of a strap or pouch in which the stone is placed and swung round fast; **b** a catapult. **3** a strap or loop for hoisting, lowering or carrying a weight.
➢ VB (**slung**) **1** COLLOQ to throw, esp with force; to fling. **2** to hang something loosely: **a jacket slung over his shoulder**. **3** to hurl, fling or toss.

slink VB (**slunk**) INTR **1** to move sneakingly or ashamedly. **2** to move in a seductive manner.

slinky ADJ (**-ier, -iest**) COLLOQ of clothing: attractively close-fitting: **a slinky dress**.

slip[1] VB (**-pp-**) **1** INTR to lose one's footing and slide accidentally. **2** INTR to make a slight mistake inadvertently. **3** INTR to slide, move or drop accidentally. **4** to place smoothly, quietly or secretively. **5** TR & INTR to move or cause to move quietly, smoothly or unobtrusively with a sliding motion. **6** to pull free from someone or something smoothly and swiftly; to suddenly escape from them or it. **7** COLLOQ to give or pass secretly. **8** INTR, COLLOQ to lose one's former skill or expertise, or control of a situation.
➢ N **1** an instance of losing one's footing and sliding accidentally. **2** a minor and usu inadvertent mistake. **3** an escape. **4** a woman's undergarment, worn under a dress or skirt. **5** a loose covering for a pillow. **6** a slipway.
◆ **give sb the slip** COLLOQ to escape from them skilfully or adroitly.
◆ **let sth slip 1** to reveal it accidentally. **2** to

fail to take advantage of an opportunity.
◆ **slip up** to make a slight mistake.

slip² N **1** a small strip of paper. **2** a small pre-printed form. **3** a young or exceptionally slender person: **a slip of a girl**.

slip³ N a creamy mixture of clay and water used for decorating pottery.

slip-knot N a knot in a noose, which slips along the cord to adjust the tightness.

slip-on N a shoe or other item of clothing that has no laces, buttons or other fastenings.

slipped disc N a dislocation of one of the flat circular plates of cartilage situated between any of the vertebrae.

slipper N a soft loose laceless indoor shoe.

slippery ADJ **1** so smooth, wet, etc as to cause or allow slipping. **2** difficult to catch or keep hold of; elusive or evasive. **3** unpredictable or untrustworthy: **a slippery character**.

slippy ADJ (**-ier, -iest**) COLLOQ of a thing: liable to slip; slippery.

slipshod ADJ untidy and careless.

slipstream N a stream of air driven back by an aircraft propeller.

slipway N a ramp in a dock or shipyard that slopes into water, for launching boats.

slit N a long narrow cut or opening.
➤ VB (**slit, slitting**) to cut a slit in something, esp lengthwise.

slither VB, INTR **1** to slide or slip unsteadily while walking. **2** to move slidingly, like a snake.
➤ N a slithering movement. ■ **slithery** ADJ.

sliver N a long thin piece cut or broken off.
➤ VB, TR & INTR to break or cut into slivers.

slob N, COLLOQ a lazy, untidy person.

slobber VB, INTR to let saliva run from the mouth; to dribble.
➤ N dribbled saliva; slaver. ■ **slobbery** ADJ.

sloe N **1** the fruit of the blackthorn bush. **2** the bush itself.

slog COLLOQ, VB (**-gg-**) **1** to hit hard and wildly.

2 INTR to labour or toil.
➤ N **1** a hard wild blow or stroke. **2** extremely tiring work.

slogan N a phrase used to identify a group or organization, or to advertise a product.

sloop N a single-masted sailing boat.

slop VB (**-pp-**) (often **slop about** or **around**) TR & INTR to splash or cause to splash or spill.
➤ N **1** spilled liquid; a puddle. **2** (**slops**) waste food. **3** (**slops**) semi-liquid food fed to pigs.

slope N **1** a slanting surface; an incline. **2** a position or direction that is neither level nor upright.
➤ VB, INTR **1** to rise or fall at an angle. **2** to be slanted or inclined.

sloppy ADJ (**-ier, -iest**) **1** wet or muddy. **2** watery. **3** over-sentimental. **4** of language, work, etc: inaccurate or careless; shoddy.
■ **sloppily** ADV. ■ **sloppiness** N.

slosh VB, TR & INTR (often **slosh about** or **around**) to splash or cause to splash or spill.
➤ N the sound of splashing or spilling.

sloshed ADJ, COLLOQ drunk; intoxicated.

slot N **1** a long narrow rectangular opening into which something is fitted or inserted. **2** a slit. **3** a (usu regular) time, place or position within a schedule, eg of radio or TV broadcasts, or airport take-offs and landings.
➤ VB (**-tt-**) to make a slot in.
◆ **slot sth in** to fit or insert it, or place it in a slot.

sloth N **1** a tree-dwelling mammal with long slender limbs and hook-like claws, noted for its very slow movements. **2** the desire to avoid all activity or exertion; laziness; indolence.

slothful ADJ lazy; inactive.

slouch VB, INTR to sit, stand or walk with a tired, lazy or drooping posture.
➤ N such a posture.
◆ **no slouch at sth** COLLOQ able or competent in some respect: **He's no slouch at cooking.**

slough¹ N **1** a mud-filled hollow. **2** N AMER an area of boggy land; a marsh or mire. **3** LITERARY a state of deep and gloomy emotion.

slough² N any outer part of an animal cast off or moulted, esp a snake's dead skin.
➤ VB **1** to shed (eg a dead skin). **2** to cast off or dismiss (eg worries).

sloven N a person of shoddy appearance.

slovenly ADJ **1** careless, untidy or dirty in appearance. **2** careless or shoddy in habits or methods of working.
➤ ADV in a slovenly manner. ■ **slovenliness** N.

slow ADJ **1** having little speed or pace; not moving fast or swiftly. **2** taking a long time, or longer than usual or expected. **3** of a watch or clock: showing a time earlier than the correct time. **4** of a mind: unable to quickly and easily understand or appreciate. **5** of wit or intellect: dull; unexciting or uninteresting. **6** progressing at a tediously gentle pace: **a slow afternoon**. **7** boring or tedious: **a slow film**. **8** needing much provocation in order to do something: **He's slow to get angry**. **9** of business: slack.
➤ ADV in a slow manner.
➤ VB, TR & INTR (also **slow down** or **up**) to reduce or make something reduce speed, pace or rate of progress. ■ **slowly** ADV.
■ **slowness** N.

slowcoach N, COLLOQ someone who moves or works at a slow pace.

slow motion N in film or television: a speed of movement that is much slower than real-life movement, created by increasing the speed at which the camera records the action.

slowworm N a species of legless lizard.

sludge N **1** soft slimy mud or mire. **2** muddy sediment. **3** sewage. **4** slush. ■ **sludgy** ADJ.

slug¹ N a mollusc, similar to a snail, but which has a long fleshy body and little or no shell.

slug² N **1** COLLOQ a bullet. **2** PRINTING a solid line or section of metal type.

slug³ COLLOQ, N a heavy blow.
➤ VB (-**gg**-) to strike with a heavy blow.

sluggard N a habitually lazy person.

sluggish ADJ **1** unenergetic; habitually lazy or inactive. **2** less lively or responsive than usual.

sluice N **1** a channel or drain for water. **2** (in full **sluicegate**) a valve or sliding gate for regulating the flow of water in such a channel. **3** a trough for washing gold or other minerals out of sand, etc.
➤ VB **1** to let out or drain by means of a sluice. **2** to wash down or rinse by throwing water on.

slum N **1** a run-down, dirty and usu overcrowded house. **2** (often **slums**) an area or neighbourhood containing such housing.
➤ VB (-**mm**-) INTR to visit an area of slums, esp out of curiosity or for amusement. ■ **slummy** ADJ.

slumber chiefly POETIC, N sleep.
➤ VB, INTR to sleep.

slump VB, INTR **1** to drop or sink suddenly and heavily, eg with tiredness: **He slumped into an armchair**. **2** of prices, trade, etc: to decline suddenly and sharply.
➤ N **1** an act or instance of slumping. **2** a serious and usu long-term decline, esp in an economy.

slur VB (-**rr**-) **1** to pronounce (words) indistinctly. **2** to speak or write about something very disparagingly; to cast aspersions on it. **3** (often **slur over sth**) to mention it only briefly or deal with only superficially.
➤ N **1** a disparaging remark intended to damage a reputation. **2** a slurred word or slurring way of speaking.

slurp VB to eat or drink noisily with a sucking action.
➤ N a slurping sound.

slurry N (-**ies**) **1** a thin paste or semi-fluid mixture, esp watery concrete. **2** liquid manure treated so that it can be distributed on to fields.

slush N **1** half-melted snow. **2** any watery half-liquid substance, eg liquid mud. **3** sickly sentimentality. ■ **slushy** ADJ.

slut N, DEROG a woman who regularly engages in casual sex. ■ **sluttish** ADJ.

sly ADJ **1** of people: clever; cunning or wily. **2** surreptitious; secretively dishonest. **3** playfully mischievous: **a sly smile**. ■ **slyly** or **slily** ADV. ■ **slyness** N.

Sm SYMBOL, CHEM samarium.

smack¹ VB **1** to slap loudly and smartly, esp with the hand. **2** TR & INTR, COLLOQ to hit loudly and heavily. **3** to kiss loudly and noisily. **4** to part (the lips) loudly, with relish.
➤ N **1** an act, or the sound, of smacking. **2** a loud enthusiastic kiss.
➤ ADV, COLLOQ **1** directly and with force: **He drove smack into the tree. 2** precisely: **smack in the middle.**

smack² VB, INTR (always **smack of sth**) **1** to have the flavour of it. **2** to have a trace of it.
➤ N a hint or trace.

smack³ N a small single-masted fishing boat.

small ADJ **1** little in size or quantity. **2** little in extent, importance or worth; not great. **3** slender: **of small build. 4** humble: **small beginnings. 5** young: **a small child. 6** minor; insignificant: **a small problem. 7** of a printed or written letter: lower-case; not capital. **8** humiliated: **feel small.**
➤ N **1** the narrow part, esp of the back. **2** (**smalls**) COLLOQ underclothes.
➤ ADV into small pieces. ■ **smallness** N.

small fry SING OR PL N, COLLOQ a person or thing, or people or things, of little importance or influence.

smallholding N a small area of cultivated land. ■ **smallholder** N.

small-minded ADJ narrow-minded; petty.

smallpox N, PATHOL a highly contagious viral disease, characterized by fever, vomiting, backache and a rash that usu leaves pitted scars (pocks) on the skin.

small talk N polite conversation about trivial matters.

small-time ADJ operating on a small scale; unimportant or insignificant.

smarm VB **1** INTR, COLLOQ to be exaggeratedly and insincerely flattering; to fawn ingratiatingly. **2** (often **smarm sth down**) to smooth or flatten (the hair) with an oily substance.
➤ N, COLLOQ exaggerated or insincere flattery.

smarmy ADJ (**-ier, -iest**) COLLOQ nauseously suave. ■ **smarmily** ADV. ■ **smarminess** N.

smart ADJ **1** neat, trim and well-dressed. **2** clever; witty; astute or shrewd. **3** expensive, sophisticated and fashionable: **a smart hotel. 4** quick, adept and efficient in business. **5** of pain, etc: sharp and stinging. **6** brisk: **He walked at a smart pace. 7** COMP technologically advanced. **8** computer-guided or electronically controlled: **a smart bomb.**
➤ VB, INTR **1** to feel or be the cause of a sharp stinging pain. **2** to feel or be the cause of acute irritation or distress: **smarting from the insult.**
➤ N a sharp stinging pain.
➤ ADV in a smart manner. ■ **smartly** ADV. ■ **smartness** N.
◆ **look smart** to hurry up.

smarten VB, TR & INTR (usu **smarten up**) to make or become smarter.

smash VB **1** TR & INTR to break or shatter violently into pieces; to destroy or be destroyed in this way. **2** TR & INTR to strike with violence, often causing damage; to burst with great force: **They smashed through the door. 3** COLLOQ to break up or ruin completely: **Police have smashed an international drugs ring. 4** in racket sports: to hit (a ball) with a powerful overhead stroke. **5** to crash (a car).
➤ N **1** an act, or the sound, of smashing. **2** in racket sports: a powerful overhead stroke. **3** COLLOQ a road traffic accident.
➤ ADV with a smashing sound.

smasher N, COLLOQ someone or something very much liked or admired.

smashing ADJ, COLLOQ excellent; splendid.

smash-up N, COLLOQ a serious road accident.

smattering N **1** a few scraps of superficial knowledge. **2** a small scattered amount.

smear VB **1** to spread (something sticky or oily) thickly over (a surface). **2** TR & INTR to make or become blurred; to smudge. **3** to say or write abusive and damaging things about someone.
➤ N **1** a greasy mark or patch. **2** a damaging criticism or accusation; a slur. **3** an amount of a substance, esp of cervical tissue, placed on a slide for examination under a microscope.
■ **smeary** ADJ.

smell N **1** the sense that allows different odours to be recognized by specialized receptors in the mucous membranes of the nose. **2** the characteristic odour of a particular substance: **It has a strong smell. 3** an unpleasant odour: **What a smell! 4** an act of using this sense: **Have a smell of this. 5** a sense, savour or suggestion of something.
➤ VB (*smelled* or *smelt*) **1** to recognize (a substance) by its odour. **2** INTR to give off an unpleasant odour. **3** to give off a specified odour: **the perfume smells flowery. 4** to be aware of something by intuition: **I smell a government cover-up.**

smelly ADJ (*-ier, -iest*) COLLOQ having a strong or unpleasant smell. ■ **smelliness** N.

smelt¹ VB to process (an ore), esp by melting it, in order to separate out the crude metal.

smelt² N (*smelts* or *smelt*) a small fish of the salmon family, including several edible species.

smelter N an industrial plant where smelting is done.

smidgen, **smidgeon** or **smidgin**
N, COLLOQ a very small amount.

smile VB **1** INTR to turn up the corners of the mouth, often showing the teeth, usu as an expression of pleasure, favour or amusement. **2** to show or communicate with such an expression: **He smiled his agreement.**
➤ N an act or way of smiling. ■ **smiler** N.
■ **smiling** N, ADJ. ■ **smilingly** ADV.
◆ **smile on sb** or **sth** to show favour towards them.

smiley N, COMP SLANG a symbol created from a number of symbols on the keyboard, eg :-) intended to look like a smiling face (sideways on), used to indicate irony or pleasure.

smirch VB **1** to make dirty; to soil or stain. **2** to damage or sully (a reputation, etc).
➤ N **1** a stain. **2** a smear on a reputation.

smirk VB to smile in a self-satisfied manner.
➤ N such a smile. ■ **smirking** ADJ.

smite VB (PA T *smote*, PA P *smitten*) LITERARY **1** to strike or beat with a heavy blow or blows. **2** to afflict. **3** to cause someone to fall immediately and overpoweringly in love.

smith N **1** IN COMPOUNDS a person who makes articles in the specified metal: **silversmith**. **2** a blacksmith. **3** IN COMPOUNDS a person who makes skilful use of anything: **wordsmith**.

smithereens PL N, COLLOQ tiny fragments.

smithy N (*-ies*) a blacksmith's workshop.

smitten ADJ in love; obsessed.

smock N **1** any loose shirt-like garment worn over other clothes for protection esp by artists, etc. **2** a woman's long loose-fitting blouse. **3** HIST a loose-fitting overall of coarse linen worn by farm-workers.

smocking N honeycomb-patterned stitching used on gathered material for decoration.

smog N a mixture of smoke and fog, esp in urban or industrial areas, produced by motor vehicle exhaust fumes, the burning of coal or other fuels, etc. ■ **smoggy** ADJ.

smoke N **1** a visible cloud given off by a burning substance. **2** a cloud or column of fumes. **3** COLLOQ the act or process of smoking tobacco: **Got time for a smoke? 4** COLLOQ something that can be smoked, eg a cigar.
➤ VB **1** INTR to give off smoke, visible fumes or vapours. **2** TR & INTR to inhale and then exhale the smoke from burning tobacco or other substances in a cigarette, cigar, pipe, etc. **3** TR & INTR to do this frequently, esp as a habit that is hard to break. **4** to preserve or flavour food by exposing it to smoke. ■ **smoky** ADJ (*-ier, -iest*).

smokeless ADJ of a fuel: giving off little or no smoke when burned, eg coke.

smoker N someone who smokes tobacco products.

smokescreen N **1** a cloud of smoke used to conceal the movements of troops, etc. **2** anything said or done to hide or deceive.

smolt N a young salmon migrating from fresh water to the sea.

smooch VB, INTR, COLLOQ **1** to kiss and cuddle. **2** to dance slowly while in an embrace.

smoochy ADJ (*-ier, -iest*) of music:

sentimental and romantic.

smooth ADJ **1** having an even regular surface; not rough, coarse, bumpy or wavy. **2** having few or no lumps; having an even texture or consistency: **smooth sauce**. **3** free from problems or difficulties: **a smooth journey**. **4** characterized by steady movement and a lack of jolts and lurches: **a smooth ferry crossing**. **5** of skin: having no hair, spots, blemishes, etc. **6** extremely charming, esp excessively or insincerely so: **a smooth talker**. ➤ VB **1** to make smooth: **She smoothed the sheets on the bed**. **2** (often **smooth over sth**) to cause a difficulty, etc to seem less serious or important. **3** to free from lumps or roughness. **4** (often **smooth sth away**) to remove (esp problems) by smoothing; to calm or soothe. **5** to make easier. **6** INTR to become smooth. ➤ ADV smoothly. ➤ N **1** the act or process of smoothing. **2** the easy or pleasurable part or aspect (eg of a situation): **take the rough with the smooth**. ■ **smoothly** ADV. ■ **smoothness** N.

smorgasbord N a Swedish-style buffet of hot and cold savoury dishes.

smother VB **1** TR & INTR to kill with or die from lack of air, esp with an obstruction over the mouth and nose; to suffocate. **2** to extinguish (a fire) by cutting off the air supply, eg by throwing a blanket over it. **3** to cover or smear something with a thick layer. **4** to give an oppressive or stifling amount to someone; **smothered with love**. **5** to suppress or contain.

smoulder VB, INTR **1** to burn slowly or without flame. **2** of emotions: to linger on in a suppressed and often hidden state. **3** of a person: to harbour suppressed emotions.

smudge N **1** a mark or blot caused or spread by rubbing. **2** a faint or blurred shape, eg an object seen from afar. ➤ VB **1** to make a smudge on or of something. **2** INTR to become or cause a smudge: **These pens smudge easily**. ■ **smudgy** ADJ.

smug ADJ (*smugger, smuggest*) arrogantly self-complacent or self-satisfied. ■ **smugly** ADV. ■ **smugness** N.

smuggle VB **1** to take (goods) into or out of a country secretly and illegally, eg to avoid paying duty. **2** to bring, take or convey secretly, usu breaking a rule or restriction. ■ **smuggler** N. ■ **smuggling** N.

smut N **1** a speck of dirt, soot, etc. **2** mildly obscene language, jokes, pictures or images. **3 a** any of a group of parasitic fungi causing a serious disease of cereal crops, and characterized by the appearance of masses of black spores, resembling soot; **b** the disease caused by such a fungus.

smutty ADJ (*-ier, -iest*) **1** dirtied by smut. **2** mildly obscene: **a smutty sense of humour**. ■ **smuttiness** N.

snack N a light meal often taken quickly, or a bite to eat between meals. ➤ VB, INTR to eat a snack.

snack bar and **snack counter** N a café, kiosk or counter serving snacks.

snaffle N (in full **snaffle-bit**) a simple bridle-bit for a horse. ➤ VB **1** to fit (a horse) with a snaffle. **2** SLANG to take sneakily or without permission; to steal.

snag N **1** a problem or drawback. **2** a protruding sharp or jagged edge on which clothes, etc could get caught. **3** a hole or tear in clothes (esp tights, stockings, etc) caused by such catching. **4** a part of a tree submerged in water, hazardous to boats. ➤ VB (*-gg-*) to catch or tear on a snag.

snaggletooth N a broken, irregular or projecting tooth. ■ **snaggletoothed** ADJ.

snail N **1** a mollusc similar to a slug, but carrying a coiled or conical shell on its back, into which the whole body can be withdrawn. **2** a sluggish person or animal. ◆ **at a snail's pace** extremely slowly.

snake N **1** a limbless carnivorous reptile which has a long narrow body covered with scaly skin, and a forked tongue. **2** any long and flexible or winding thing or shape. **3** a snake in the grass. ➤ VB, INTR to follow a winding course.

snap VB (*-pp-*) **1** TR & INTR to break suddenly and

cleanly with a sharp cracking noise: **He snapped the stick over his knee. 2** TR & INTR to make or cause to make a sharp noise. **3** TR & INTR to move quickly and forcefully into place with a sharp sound: **The lid snapped shut. 4** INTR to speak sharply in sudden irritation. **5** COLLOQ to take a photograph of someone or something, esp spontaneously and with a hand-held camera. **6** INTR, COLLOQ to lose one's senses or self-control suddenly.
➤ N **1** the act or sound of snapping. **2** COLLOQ a photograph, esp taken spontaneously and with a hand-held camera. **3** a catch or other fastening that closes with a snapping sound. **4** a sudden bite. **5** a crisp biscuit or savoury. **6** a card game in which all the cards played are collected by the first player to shout 'snap' on spotting a pair of matching cards laid down by consecutive players.
➤ ADJ taken or made spontaneously, without long consideration: **a snap decision.**
➤ ADV with a snapping sound.
◆ **snap sb's head** or **nose off** to answer irritably and rudely.
◆ **snap out of it** COLLOQ to bring oneself out of a state or condition, eg of sulking or depression.
◆ **snap sth up** to acquire or seize it eagerly.

snappy ADJ (*-ier, -iest*) **1** irritable; inclined to snap. **2** smart and fashionable: **a snappy dresser. 3** lively: **a snappy tempo.** ■ **snappily** ADV. ■ **snappiness** N.

snapshot N, COLLOQ a photograph, esp one taken with a hand-held camera.

snare N **1** an animal trap, esp one with a string or wire noose to catch the animal's foot. **2** anything that traps or entangles. **3** anything that lures or tempts. **4** (in full **snare drum**) a medium-sized drum sitting horizontally, with a set of wires fitted to its underside that rattle sharply when the drum is struck.
➤ VB to trap or entangle in, or as if in, a snare.

snarl[1] VB **1** INTR of an animal: to growl angrily, showing the teeth. **2** TR & INTR to speak aggressively in anger or irritation.
➤ N **1** an act of snarling. **2** a snarling sound or facial expression.

snarl[2] N a knotted or tangled mass.
➤ VB, TR & INTR (also **snarl sb** or **sth up** or **snarl up**) to make or become knotted, tangled, confused or congested.

snarl-up N, COLLOQ any muddled or congested situation, esp a traffic jam.

snatch VB **1** to seize or grab suddenly. **2** INTR to make a sudden grabbing movement. **3** to pull suddenly and forcefully: **She snatched her hand away. 4** COLLOQ to take or have as soon as the opportunity arises: **snatch a bite to eat.**
➤ N **1** an act of snatching. **2** a fragment overheard or remembered: **snatches of conversation. 3** a brief period: **snatches of rest between long shifts. 4** COLLOQ a robbery.

snazzy ADJ (*-ier, -iest*) COLLOQ fashionably and often flashily smart or elegant. ■ **snazzily** ADV.

sneak VB (*sneaked* or (COLLOQ) *snuck*) **1** (often **sneak away, off, out,** etc) INTR to move, go or depart quietly, furtively and unnoticed. **2** to bring or take secretly: **He tried to sneak a look at the letter. 3** INTR, COLLOQ to inform about someone; to tell tales.
➤ N, COLLOQ a tell-tale.

sneakers PL N, esp US sports shoes; soft-soled, usu canvas, shoes.

sneaky ADJ (*-ier, -iest*) done or operating with secretive unfairness or dishonesty; underhand. ■ **sneakily** ADV. ■ **sneakiness** N

sneer VB **1** (often **sneer at sb** or **sth**) INTR to show scorn or contempt, esp by drawing the top lip up at one side. **2** INTR to express scorn or contempt. **3** to say contemptuously.
➤ N **1** an act of sneering. **2** an expression of scorn or contempt made with a raised lip.

sneeze VB, INTR to blow air out through the nose suddenly, violently and involuntarily, esp because of irritation in the nostrils.
➤ N an act or the sound of sneezing.
◆ **not to be sneezed at** COLLOQ not to be disregarded or overlooked lightly.

snib chiefly SCOT, N a small bolt or catch for a door or window-sash.
➤ VB (*-bb-*) to fasten with a snib.

snick N a small cut; a nick.

➤ VB to make a small cut in something.

snicker VB, INTR to snigger.
➤ N a giggle.

snide ADJ expressing criticism or disapproval in an offensive, sly or malicious manner.

sniff VB **1** to draw in air with the breath through the nose. **2** INTR to draw up mucus or tears escaping into the nose. **3** (often **sniff sth** or **sniff at sth**) TR & INTR to smell it in this way.
➤ N **1** an act or the sound of sniffing. **2** a smell. **3** a small quantity inhaled by the nose. **4** a slight intimation or suspicion.
◆ **not to be sniffed at** COLLOQ not to be disregarded or overlooked lightly.
◆ **sniff sb** or **sth out** to discover or detect them or it by, or as if by, the sense of smell.

sniffle VB, INTR to sniff repeatedly, eg because of having a cold.
➤ N **1** an act or the sound of sniffling. **2** (also **the sniffles**) a slight cold. ■ **sniffly** ADJ.

sniffy ADJ (**-ier, -iest**) COLLOQ contemptuous or disdainful, or inclined to be so. ■ **sniffiness** N.

snifter N **1** SLANG a drink of alcohol, esp alcoholic spirit. **2** US a brandy glass.

snigger VB, INTR to laugh in a stifled or suppressed way, often derisively or mockingly.
➤ N such a laugh. ■ **sniggering** N, ADJ.

snip VB (**-pp-**) to cut, esp with a single quick action or actions, with scissors.
➤ N **1** an act or the action of snipping. **2** the sound of a stroke of scissors while snipping. **3** a small shred or piece snipped off. **4** a small cut, slit or notch. **5** COLLOQ a bargain.

snipe N (**snipe** or **snipes**) **1** a wading bird with a long straight bill. **2** a sniping shot, ie a shot at someone from a hidden position. **3** a quick verbal attack or criticism.
➤ VB, INTR **1** to shoot snipe for sport. **2** (often **snipe at sb**) **a** to shoot at them from a hidden position; **b** to criticize them bad-temperedly.
■ **sniper** N. ■ **sniping** N.

snippet N a scrap, eg of information, news, etc.

snitch SLANG, N an informer.
➤ VB **1** INTR to inform on or betray others. **2** to

steal; to pilfer. ■ **snitcher** N.

snivel VB (**-ll-**) INTR **1** to whine or complain tearfully. **2** to have a runny nose. **3** to sniff.
➤ N an act of snivelling. ■ **sniveller** N.

snob N **1** someone who places too high a value on social status, treating those lower down the social ladder with condescension and contempt. **2** someone having similar pretensions as regards specific tastes: **an intellectual snob.** ■ **snobbery** N.
■ **snobbish** ADJ.

snog SLANG, VB (**-gg-**) INTR to embrace and kiss.
➤ N a kiss and cuddle.

snook N (USU **cock a snook**) the gesture of putting the thumb to the nose and waving the fingers as an expression of contempt.

snooker N **1** a game played with cues, 15 red balls, one white cue ball and six balls of other colours, on a large cloth-covered table, with pockets on its sides into which the coloured balls are struck. **2** in this game: a position in which the path between the white ball and the target ball is obstructed by another ball.
➤ VB **1** in snooker: to force (an opponent) to attempt to hit an obstructed target ball. **2** COLLOQ to thwart (a person or a plan).

snoop VB, INTR to go about sneakingly and inquisitively; to pry.
➤ N **1** an act of snooping. **2** someone who snoops. ■ **snooper** N.

snooty ADJ (**-ier, -iest**) COLLOQ haughty; snobbish. ■ **snootily** ADV. ■ **snootiness** N.

snooze VB, INTR to sleep lightly; to doze.
➤ N a brief period of light sleeping; a nap.

snore VB, INTR to breathe heavily and with a snorting sound while sleeping.
➤ N an act or the sound of snoring.

snorkel N a rigid tube through which air from above the surface of water can be drawn into the mouth while one is swimming just below the surface.
➤ VB (**-ll-**) INTR to swim with a snorkel.

snort VB **1** INTR to force air violently and noisily out or in through the nostrils. **2** TR & INTR to express contempt or anger in this way. **3** SLANG to inhale (a powdered drug) through the nose. ➤ N an act or the sound of snorting.

snot N mucus of the nose.

snotty ADJ (*-ier, -iest*) COLLOQ **1** covered or messy with nasal mucus. **2** haughty or stand-offish; having or showing contempt: **a snotty attitude**. ■ **snottily** ADV. ■ **snottiness** N.

snout N **1** the projecting nose and mouth parts of certain animals, eg the pig. **2** COLLOQ the human nose. **3** any projecting part.

snow N **1** precipitation in the form of ice crystals falling to the ground in soft white flakes, or lying on the ground as a soft white mass. **2** a fall of this: **There's been a lot of snow this year**. **3** COLLOQ a flickering speckled background on a TV or radar screen, caused by interference. ➤ VB, INTR of snow: to fall. ◆ **snowed under** overwhelmed with work.

snowball N a small mass of snow pressed hard together, often used for fun as a missile. ➤ VB, INTR to develop or increase rapidly and uncontrollably.

snowboard N a board used to travel downhill over snow and guided with movements of the feet and body. ➤ VB, INTR to ski on a snowboard.

snowbound ADJ shut in or prevented from travelling because of heavy falls of snow.

snowdrift N a bank of snow blown together by the wind.

snowdrop N a plant with small solitary drooping white bell-shaped flowers.

snowfall N **1** a fall of snow. **2** METEOROL an amount of fallen snow in a given time.

snowflake N any of the single small feathery clumps of crystals of snow.

snowman N a figure, resembling a person, made from packed snow.

snowmobile N a motorized vehicle, on skis or tracks, designed for travelling on snow.

snowplough N a vehicle or train fitted with a large shovel-like device for clearing snow

from roads or railway tracks.

snowshoe N either of a pair of racket-like frameworks strapped to the feet for walking over deep snow.

snowy ADJ (*-ier, -iest*) **1** abounding or covered with snow. **2** white like snow. **3** pure.

Snr or **snr** ABBREV senior.

snub VB (*-bb-*) to insult by openly ignoring, rejecting or otherwise showing contempt. ➤ N an act of snubbing. ➤ ADJ short and flat; blunt.

snub nose N a broad flat nose.

snuff[1] VB **1** INTR to draw in air violently through the nose. **2** to examine or detect by sniffing. ➤ N **1** a sniff. **2** powdered tobacco for inhaling through the nose.

snuff[2] VB to snip off the burnt part of a wick. ➤ N the burnt part of the wick of a lamp or candle. ◆ **snuff it** SLANG to die. ◆ **snuff sth out 1** to extinguish (a candle). **2** to put an end to it: **tried to snuff out all opposition**.

snuffle VB **1** INTR to breathe, esp breathe in, through a partially blocked nose. **2** TR & INTR to say or speak nasally. **3** INTR to snivel. ➤ N an act or the sound of snuffling.

snug ADJ (*snugger, snuggest*) **1** warm, cosy and comfortable. **2** well protected and sheltered; not exposed: **a snug boat**. **3** compact and comfortably organized: **a snug kitchen**. **4** comfortably off: **a snug income**. **5** close-fitting: **a snug dress**. ➤ N, BRIT a small room or compartment in a pub. ■ **snugly** ADV. ■ **snugness** N.

snuggle VB, INTR **1** (usu **snuggle down** or **in**) to settle oneself into a position of warmth and comfort. **2** (sometimes **snuggle up**) to hug close; to nestle.

so[1] ADV **1** to such an extent: **so expensive that nobody buys it**. **2** to this, that, or the same extent; as: **This one is lovely, but that one is not so nice**. **3** extremely: **She is so talented! 4** in that state or condition: **promised to be faithful, and has remained so**. **5** also; likewise: **She's**

my friend and so are you. **6** used to avoid repeating a previous statement: **You've to go upstairs because I said so.**

➢ CONJ **1** therefore; thereafter: **He insulted me, so I hit him. 2** (also **so that …**) in order that …: **Give me more time so I can finish it.**

➢ ADJ the case; true: **You think I'm mad, but it's not so.**

➢ EXCLAM used to express discovery: **So, that's what you've been doing!**

◆ **and so on** or **and so forth** or **and so on and so forth** and more of the same; continuing in the same way.

◆ **just so** neatly, precisely or perfectly: **with her hair arranged just so.**

◆ **or so** approximately: **five or so days ago.**

◆ **so as to …** in order to ….

◆ **so be it** used to express acceptance or defiant resignation.

◆ **so far so good** everything is fine up to this point.

◆ **so much** or **many 1** such a lot: **so much work to do! 2** just; mere: **politicians squabbling like so many children.**

◆ **so much for …** nothing has come of; that has been disposed of or ruined.

◆ **so to speak** or **to say** used as an apology for a slightly inappropriate expression.

◆ **so what?** COLLOQ that is of no importance.

so² see **soh**

soak VB **1** TR & INTR to stand or leave to stand in a liquid for some time. **2** to make someone or something thoroughly wet; to drench.

➢ N **1** an act of soaking. **2** a drenching. **3** COLLOQ a long period of lying in a bath.

■ **soaking** N, ADJ, ADV.

◆ **soak sth up** to absorb it.

so-and-so N (*so-and-sos*) COLLOQ

1 someone whose name one does not know or remember: **He's gone with so-and-so.**

2 a word in place of a vulgar word or oath: **You crafty little so-and-so!**

soap N **1** a cleaning agent consisting of a fatty acid that is soluble in water, in the form of a solid, liquid or powder. **2** COLLOQ a soap opera.

➢ VB to apply soap to something. ■ **soapy** ADJ.

soapbox N **1** a crate for packing soap. **2** an

improvised platform for public speech-making, orig an upturned crate for carrying soap.

soap opera N a radio or TV series concerning the domestic and emotional lives and troubles of a regular group of characters.

soapstone N a soft usu grey or brown variety of the mineral talc, widely used for ornamental carvings.

soar VB, INTR **1** to rise or fly high into the air. **2** to glide through the air at a high altitude. **3** to rise sharply to a great height or level: **soaring temperatures.** ■ **soaring** N, ADJ.

sob VB (*-bb-*) **1** INTR to cry uncontrollably with intermittent gulps for breath. **2** (often **sob out**) to say or tell something while crying in this way.

➢ N a gulp for breath between bouts of crying.

sober ADJ **1** not at all drunk. **2** serious, solemn or restrained; not frivolous or extravagant. **3** suggesting sedateness or seriousness rather than exuberance or frivolity: **sober colours. 4** plain; unembellished: **the sober truth.**

➢ VB, TR & INTR **1** (always **sober down** or **sober sb down**) to become, or make someone, quieter, less excited, etc. **2** (always **sober up** or **sober sb up**) to become, or make someone, free from the effects of alcohol.

sobriety N the state of being sober, esp not drunk.

sobriquet and **soubriquet** N, LITERARY a nickname.

sob-story N, COLLOQ a story of personal misfortune told in order to gain sympathy.

so-called ADJ known or presented as such with the implication that the term is wrongly or inappropriately used: **so-called experts.**

soccer see under **football**

sociable ADJ **1** fond of the company of others; friendly. **2** characterized by friendliness.

social ADJ **1** relating to or for people or society as a whole: **social policies. 2** relating to the organization and behaviour of people in societies or communities: **social studies. 3** tending or needing to live with others; not solitary: **social creatures. 4** intended for or promoting friendly gatherings of people: a social club. **5** convivial; jovial.

➤ N a social gathering, esp one organized by a club or other group. ■ **socially** ADV.

socialism N a political doctrine which aims to create a classless society by moving ownership of the nation's wealth out of private and into public hands. ■ **socialist** N, ADJ.

socialite N someone who mixes with people of high social status.

socialize or **-ise** VB **1** INTR to meet with people on an informal, friendly basis. **2** INTR to mingle or circulate among guests at a party; to behave sociably. **3** to organize into societies or communities. ■ **socialization** N.

social sciences PL N the subjects that deal with the organization and behaviour of people in societies and communities.

social security N a system by which payments are made to those who are unemployed, ill, disabled or elderly, from a common state fund.

society N (*-ies*) **1** humankind as a whole, or a part of it such as one nation, considered as a single community. **2** a division of humankind with common characteristics, eg of nationality, race or religion. **3** an organized group or association, meeting to share a common interest. **4 a** the rich and fashionable section of the upper class; **b** its social scene. **5** FORMAL company: **the society of women**.

socioeconomic ADJ of or relating to both social and economic aspects.

sociology N the scientific study of the nature, structure and workings of human society. ■ **sociological** ADJ. ■ **sociologist** N.

sock¹ N a fabric covering for the foot and ankle, sometimes reaching to or over the knee.
  ◆ **pull one's socks up** COLLOQ to make an effort to do better.
  ◆ **put a sock in it** SLANG to be quiet.

sock² SLANG, VB to hit with a powerful blow.
  ➤ N a powerful blow.

socket N **1** a specially shaped hole or set of

holes into which something is inserted or fitted: **an electrical socket**. **2** ANAT a hollow structure into which another part fits.

sod¹ N **1** a slab of earth with grass growing on it; a turf. **2** POETIC the ground.

sod² N, SLANG **1** a term of abuse for a person. **2** a person in general: **lucky sod**.
  ◆ **sod all** SLANG nothing at all.
  ◆ **sod off** SLANG go away.

soda N **1** a common name given to any of various compounds of sodium in everyday use. **2** COLLOQ soda water. **3** N AMER, ESP US a fizzy soft drink of any kind.

soda water N water made fizzy by the addition of carbon dioxide.

sodden ADJ **1** heavy with moisture; saturated; thoroughly soaked. **2** made lifeless or sluggish, esp through excessive consumption of alcohol: **a drink-sodden brain**.

sodium N, CHEM a soft silvery-white metallic element used in alloys.

sodomy N the sexual act of inserting the penis into the anus; buggery. ■ **sodomite** N. ■ **sodomize** or **-ise** VB.

sofa N an upholstered seat with a back and arms, for two or more people.

soft ADJ **1** easily yielding or changing shape when pressed. **2** easily yielding to pressure. **3** easily cut. **4** of fabric, etc: having a smooth surface or texture producing little or no friction. **5** soothing to the senses; quiet: **a soft voice**. **6** having little brightness; not glaring: **soft colours**. **7** kind or sympathetic, esp excessively so. **8** not able to endure rough treatment or hardship. **9** lacking strength of character; easily influenced. **10** COLLOQ weak in the mind; simple: **soft in the head**. **11** of a person: out of training; in an unfit condition. **12** weakly sentimental. **13** of water: low in or free from mineral salts and so lathering easily. **14** tender; loving or affectionate: **soft words**.
  ➤ ADV softly; gently: **speaks soft**. ■ **softly** ADV.
  ◆ **be soft on sb** COLLOQ **1** to be lenient towards them. **2** to be infatuated with them.

softball N a game similar to baseball, played

with a larger, softer ball which is pitched underarm, as opposed to overarm in baseball.

soft drink N a non-alcoholic drink.

soften VB, TR & INTR **1** to make or become soft or softer. **2** to make or become less severe.
◆ **soften sb up** COLLOQ to prepare them for an unwelcome or difficult request.

softener N a substance added to another to increase its softness, pliability, etc.

soft focus N, PHOTOG, CINEMATOG the deliberate slight blurring of a picture or scene.

soft fruit N, BRIT small stoneless edible fruit, such as berries, currants, etc.

soft furnishings PL N rugs, curtains, cushion covers and other articles made of fabric.

softly-softly ADJ cautious or careful; delicate: a softly-softly approach.

soft option N the easier or easiest of two or several alternative courses of action.

soft palate N, ANAT the fleshy muscular back part of the palate. Also called **velum**.

soft pedal N a pedal on a piano pressed to make the tone less lingering or ringing.
➤ VB (**soft-pedal**) **1** MUS to play (the piano) using the soft pedal. **2** COLLOQ to tone down, or avoid emphasizing or mentioning something.

soft sell N the use of gentle persuasion as a selling technique.
➤ ADJ of or relating to this kind of technique.

soft soap N **1** a semi-liquid soap containing potash. **2** COLLOQ flattery or blarney.
➤ VB (**soft-soap**) COLLOQ to flatter someone.

soft-spoken ADJ **1** having a soft voice, and usu a mild manner. **2** suave or smooth-tongued.

soft spot N, COLLOQ a special affection.

software N, COMP the programs that are used in a computer system, and the magnetic disks, tapes, etc, on which they are recorded.

softwood N, BOT the wood of a coniferous tree, eg pine, including some woods that are in fact very hard and durable.

softy or **softie** N (-**ies**) COLLOQ **1** someone who is easily upset. **2** a weakly sentimental, soft-hearted or silly person.

soggy ADJ (-**ier**, -**iest**) **1** thoroughly soaked or wet; saturated. **2** of ground: waterlogged; boggy. ■ **sogginess** N.

soh, **so** or **sol** N, MUS in sol-fa notation: the fifth note or **dominant** of a major or minor scale.

soil[1] N **1** the mixture of fragmented rock, plant and animal debris that lies on the surface of the Earth. **2** LITERARY country; land: on foreign soil.

soil[2] VB **1** to stain or make dirty. **2** to bring discredit on; to sully.
➤ N **1** a spot or stain. **2** dung; sewage.

soirée or **soiree** N a formal party held in the evening.

sojourn FORMAL, N a short stay.
➤ VB, INTR to stay for a short while.

sol[1] see **soh**

sol[2] N, CHEM a type of colloid that consists of small solid particles dispersed in a liquid.

solace N **1** comfort in time of disappointment or sorrow. **2** a source of comfort.
➤ VB to provide with such comfort.

solar ADJ **1** referring or relating to the Sun: **solar system**. **2** relating to, by or using energy from the Sun's rays: **solar powered**.

solarium N (-**iums** or -**ia**) a room or establishment equipped with sunbeds.

solar plexus N, ANAT an area in the abdomen in which there is a concentration of nerves radiating from a central point.

solar system N, ASTRON the Sun and the system of nine major planets, and the asteroids, comets and meteors that revolve around it.

solder N, ENG an alloy with a low melting point, applied when molten to the joint between two metals to form an airtight seal.
➤ VB to join (two pieces of metal) without melting them, by applying a layer of molten alloy to the joint between them and allowing it to cool and solidify.

soldier N **1** a member of a fighting force.
2 a member of an army below officer rank.
◆ **soldier on** to continue determinedly in spite of difficulty and discouragement.

sole[1] N **1** the underside of the foot. **2** the underside of a shoe or boot, esp the part not including the heel.
➤ VB to fit (a shoe or boot) with a sole.

sole[2] N (*sole* or *soles*) an edible flatfish with both eyes on the left side of the head.

sole[3] ADJ **1** alone; only. **2** exclusive: **has sole rights to the story**.

solecism N **1** a mistake in the use of language; a breach of syntax, grammar, etc. **2** an instance of bad or incorrect behaviour.

solely ADV **1** without others: **solely to blame**. **2** excluding all else: **done solely for profit**.

solemn ADJ **1** done, made or carried out in earnest and seriousness: **a solemn vow**. **2** being of a very serious and formal nature; suggesting seriousness: **a solemn occasion**. **3** accompanied or marked by special (esp religious) ceremonies, pomp or gravity.
■ **solemnly** ADV. ■ **solemnness** N.

solemnity N (*-ies*) **1** the state of being solemn. **2** a solemn ceremony.

solemnize or **-ise** VB **1** to perform (esp a marriage) with a formal or religious ceremony. **2** to make something solemn.

solenoid N, PHYS a cylindrical coil of wire that produces a magnetic field when an electric current is passed through it.

sol-fa N a system of musical notation, either written down or sung, in which the notes of a scale are represented by the syllables **doh, re, mi, fah, soh, la, ti**. Also called **tonic sol-fa**.

solicit VB **1** FORMAL to ask for something, or for something from someone: **solicited me for advice**. **2** INTR of a prostitute: to approach people with open offers of sex for money.
■ **solicitation** N. ■ **soliciting** N.

solicitor N **1** in Britain: a lawyer who prepares legal documents, gives legal advice and, in the lower courts only, speaks on behalf of

clients. **2** someone who solicits.

solicitous ADJ **1** (**solicitous about** or **for sb** or **sth**) anxious or concerned about them. **2** willing or eager to do something.
■ **solicitously** ADV.

solicitude N **1** anxiety or uneasiness of mind. **2** the state of being solicitous.

solid ADJ **1** in a form other than liquid or gas, and resisting changes in shape due to firmly cohering particles. **2** having the same nature or material throughout; uniform or pure: **solid oak**. **3** not hollow; full of material: **a solid chocolate egg**. **4** firmly constructed or attached; not easily breaking or loosening. **5** GEOM having or pertaining to three dimensions. **6** difficult to undermine or destroy; sound: **solid support**. **7** without breaks; continuous: **We waited for four solid hours**. **8** of a character: reliable; sensible. **9** of a character: weighty; worthy of credit. **10** financially secure.
➤ N **1** a solid substance or body. **2** GEOM a three-dimensional geometric figure. **4** (**solids**) non-liquid food. ■ **solidity** N.

solidarity N (*-ies*) mutual support and unity among members of a group.

solidify VB (*-ies, -ied*) TR & INTR to make or become solid. ■ **solidification** N.

solidus N (*-di*) a printed line sloping from right to left, eg separating alternatives, as in **and/or**.

soliloquy N (*-quies*) **1** an act of talking to oneself, esp a speech in a play, etc in which a character reveals thoughts or intentions to the audience by talking aloud. **2** the use of such speeches. ■ **soliloquize** or **-ise** VB.

solipsism N, PHILOS the theory that one's own existence is the only certainty. ■ **solipsist** N, ADJ. ■ **solipsistic** ADJ.

solitaire N **1** any of several games for one player only, esp one whose object is to eliminate pegs or marbles from a board and leave one. **2** a single gem in its own setting.

solitary ADJ **1** single; lone. **2** preferring to be alone. **3** without companions. **4** secluded.
➤ N, COLLOQ solitary confinement.
■ **solitariness** N.

solitude N the state of being alone or secluded, esp pleasantly.

solo N (-*los* or -*li*) **1** a piece of music, or a passage within it, for a single voice or instrument, with or without accompaniment. **2** any performance in which no other person or instrument participates.
➤ ADJ performed alone, without assistance or accompaniment.
➤ ADV alone: **fly solo**.
➤ VB, INTR **1** to fly solo. **2** to play a solo.
■ **soloist** N.

solstice N either of the times when the Sun is furthest from the equator: the longest day (**summer solstice**) and the shortest day (**winter solstice**). ■ **solstitial** ADJ.

soluble ADJ **1** denoting a substance that is capable of being dissolved in a liquid. **2** capable of being solved or resolved.

solute N, CHEM any substance that is dissolved in a solvent.

solution N **1** the process of finding an answer to a problem or puzzle. **2** the answer sought or found. **3** CHEM a homogeneous mixture consisting of a solid or gas (the solute) and the liquid (the solvent) in which it is completely dissolved. **4** MATH in an equation: the value that one or more of the variables must have for that equation to be valid.

solve VB **1** to discover the answer to (a puzzle) or a way out of (a problem). **2** to clear up or explain something. ■ **solvable** ADJ.

solvent ADJ able to pay all one's debts.
➤ N, CHEM **1** in a solution: the liquid in which a solid or gas is dissolved. **2** a substance which may act in this way, eg for dissolving and removing an unwanted substance such as glue. ■ **solvency** N.

somatic ADJ, MED, BIOL of or relating to the body rather than the mind.

sombre ADJ **1** sad and serious; grave. **2** dark and gloomy; melancholy. **3** eg of colours: dark; drab. ■ **sombrely** ADV. ■ **sombreness** N.

some ADJ **1** signifying an unknown or unspecified amount or number of something:
She owns some shares. **2** signifying a certain undetermined category: **Some films are better than others**. **3** having an unknown or unspecified nature or identity: **some problem with the engine**. **4** quite a lot of something: **We have been waiting for some time**. **5** at least a little: **try to feel some enthusiasm**.
➤ PRONOUN **1** certain unspecified things or people: **Some say he should resign**. **2** an unspecified amount or number: **Give me some**.
➤ ADV **1** to an unspecified extent: **play some more**. **2** approximately: **some six feet deep**.

somebody PRONOUN **1** an unknown or unspecified person; someone. **2** someone of importance: **He strove to be somebody**.

someday ADV at an unknown or unspecified time in the future.

somehow ADV **1** in some way not yet known. **2** for a reason not easy to explain. **3** (also **somehow or other**) in any way necessary or possible: **I'll get there somehow or other**.

someone PRONOUN somebody.

somersault N a leap or roll in which the whole body turns a complete circle forwards or backwards, leading with the head.
➤ VB, INTR to perform such a leap or roll.

something PRONOUN **1** a thing not known or not stated: **Take something to eat**. **2** an amount or number not known or not stated: **something short of 500 people**. **3** a person or thing of importance: **make something of oneself**. **4** a certain truth or value: **There is something in what you say**.
➤ ADV to some degree; rather: **The garden looks something like a scrapyard**.

sometime ADV at an unknown or unspecified time in the future or the past: **I'll finish sometime**.
➤ ADJ former; late: **the sometime king**.

sometimes ADV occasionally; now and then.

somewhat ADV rather; a little.

somewhere ADV in or to some place or degree not known or not specified.

somnambulism N sleepwalking.

somniferous and **somnific** ADJ causing sleep.

somnolent ADJ, FORMAL sleepy or drowsy; causing sleepiness or drowsiness. ■ **somnolence** N.

son N 1 a male child or offspring. 2 a male person closely associated with, or seen as developing from, a particular activity or set of circumstances: **a son of the Russian revolution.** 3 a familiar and sometimes patronizing term of address used to a boy or man.

sonar N a system that is used to locate underwater objects by transmitting ultrasound signals and measuring the time taken for their echoes to return from an obstacle.

sonata N a piece of classical music written in three or more movements for a solo instrument, esp the piano.

song N 1 a set of words, short poem, etc to be sung. 2 the music to which these words are set. 3 singing: **poetry and song.** 4 the musical call of certain birds.

songbird N a bird that has a musical call.

sonic ADJ relating to or using sound or sound waves.

son-in-law N (*sons-in-law*) the husband of one's daughter.

sonnet N a short poem with 14 lines of 10 or 11 syllables each and a regular rhyming pattern.

sonny N a familiar and often condescending term of address used to a boy or man.

sonorous ADJ 1 sounding impressively loud and deep. 2 giving out a deep clear ring or sound when struck. 3 of language: impressively eloquent. ■ **sonority** N.

soon ADV 1 in a short time from now or from a stated time. 2 quickly. 3 readily.
◆ **as soon as …** at or not before the moment when ….

sooner ADV 1 earlier than previously thought. 2 preferably: **I'd sooner die than go back.**

soot N a black powdery substance produced when coal or wood is imperfectly burned;

smut. ■ **sooty** (*-ier, -iest*) ADJ.

soothe VB 1 to bring relief from (a pain, etc); to allay. 2 to comfort, calm or compose someone. 3 INTR to have a calming, tranquillizing or relieving effect. ■ **soothing** N, ADJ. ■ **soothingly** ADV.

soothsayer N someone who predicts the future; a seer or diviner.

sop N 1 (often **sops**) a piece of food, esp bread, dipped or soaked in a liquid, eg soup. 2 something given or done as a bribe or in order to pacify someone. 3 a feeble or spineless person.
➤ VB (*-pp-*) TR & INTR to soak or become soaked.

sophism N a convincing but false argument or explanation, esp one intended to deceive. ■ **sophist** N. ■ **sophistic** ADJ.

sophisticate N a sophisticated person.

sophisticated ADJ 1 having or displaying a broad knowledge and experience of the world and its culture. 2 appealing to or frequented by people with such knowledge and experience. 3 of a person: accustomed to an elegant lifestyle. 4 esp of machines: with the most up-to-date devices: **sophisticated weaponry.** ■ **sophistication** N.

sophistry N (*-ies*) 1 plausibly deceptive or fallacious reasoning, or an instance of this. 2 the art of reasoning speciously.

sophomore N, N AMER, ESP US a second-year student at a school or university.

soporific ADJ 1 causing sleep or drowsiness. 2 slow and boring: **a soporific speech.**
➤ N a sleep-inducing drug.

sopping ADJ
➤ ADV (also **sopping wet**) thoroughly wet; soaking.

soppy ADJ (*-ier, -iest*) COLLOQ weakly sentimental. ■ **soppily** ADV. ■ **soppiness** N.

soprano N (*-nos* or *-ni*) 1 a singing voice of the highest pitch for a woman or a boy. 2 a person having this voice pitch. 3 a musical part for such a voice. 4 a musical instrument high in pitch in relation to others in its family.

➤ ADJ referring or relating to a soprano pitch.

sorbet N a water ice.

sorcery N **1** the art or use of magic, esp black magic that is associated with the power of evil spirits, supernatural forces, etc. **2** an instance of this kind of magic. ■ **sorcerer** or **sorceress** N.

sordid ADJ **1** repulsively filthy; squalid. **2** morally revolting or degraded: **a sordid affair**. ■ **sordidly** ADV. ■ **sordidness** N.

sore ADJ **1** of a wound, injury, part of the body, etc: painful or tender. **2** of a blow, bite, sting, etc: painful or causing physical pain. **3** causing mental anguish, grief or annoyance: **a sore point**. **4** N AMER, ESP US angry or resentful: **got sore at the kids**. **5** severe or urgent: **in sore need of attention**.
➤ N a diseased or injured spot or area, esp an ulcer or boil. ■ **soreness** N.

sorely ADV acutely; very much: **I'm sorely tempted to tell her**.

sorghum N a grass grown as a cereal crop and a source of syrup.

sorority N (**-ies**) a women's club or society, esp one affiliated to a US university or church.

sorrel N **1** a plant with spear-shaped leaves which give an acid taste. **2** the leaves of this plant, which are used in med and in cookery.

sorrow N **1** a feeling of grief or deep sadness, esp one that arises from loss or disappointment. **2** something that is the cause of this.
➤ VB, INTR to have or express such feeling. ■ **sorrowful** ADJ. ■ **sorrowfully** ADV.

sorry ADJ (**-ier, -iest**) **1** distressed or full of regret or shame, esp over something that one has done or said, something that has happened, etc: **I'm sorry if I hurt you**. **2** (usu **sorry for sb**) full of pity or sympathy. **3** pitifully bad: **in a sorry state**.
➤ EXCLAM **1** given as an apology. **2** used when asking for something that has just been said to be repeated.

sort N **1** a kind, type or class. **2** COLLOQ a person: **not a bad sort**.
➤ VB **1** to arrange into different groups according to some specified criterion. **2** COLLOQ to fix something: **tried to sort the car himself**. **3** (also **sort out**) COLLOQ to resolve (a problem, etc): **You caused the problem, so you better sort it**.
◆ **a sort of …** a thing like a …: **a cafetière is a sort of pot for making coffee**.
◆ **sort of** COLLOQ rather; in a way; to a certain extent: **feeling sort of embarrassed**.
◆ **sort sb out 1** COLLOQ to deal with them firmly and decisively and sometimes violently. **2** to put them right.
◆ **sort sth out 1** to separate things out from a mixed collection into a group or groups according to their kind. **2** to put things into order; to arrange them systematically or methodically: **sort out your priorities**.

sortie N **1** a sudden attack by besieged troops. **2** COLLOQ a short return trip.
➤ VB (**sortied, sortieing**) INTR to make a sortie.

SOS N **1** an internationally recognized distress call consisting of these three letters transmitted in Morse code. **2** COLLOQ any call for help.

so-so ADJ, COLLOQ neither very good nor very bad. Also AS ADV.

sot N, OLD USE someone who is drunk or who habitually drinks a lot of alcohol. ■ **sottish** ADJ.

soubriquet see **sobriquet**

soufflé N a light fluffy sweet or savoury dish that is made with stiffly beaten egg-whites.

sough[1] N a sighing, rustling or murmuring sound that is made by the wind blowing through trees, etc.
➤ VB, INTR usu of the wind: to make this sound.

sough[2] N a small gutter or drain that allows water, sewage, etc to run off.

sought-after ADJ desired; in demand.

souk N an open-air market or market-place in Muslim countries.

soul N **1 a** the spiritual, non-physical part of someone or something which is often regarded as the source of individuality, personality, morality, will, emotions and intellect, and which is widely believed to survive in some form after the death of the body; **b** this entity when thought of as having separated from the body after death, but which still retains its essence of individuality, etc. **2** emotional sensitivity; morality: **a singer with no soul**. **3** the essential nature or an energizing or motivating force (of or behind something): **Brevity is the soul of wit**. **4** COLLOQ a person or individual: **a kind soul**. **5** a type of music that has its roots in African American urban rhythm and blues.

soulful ADJ having, expressing, etc deep feelings, esp of sadness. ■ **soulfully** ADV.

soulless ADJ **1** having, showing, etc no emotional sensitivity, morality, etc. **2** of a place: bleak; lifeless. ■ **soullessly** ADV. ■ **soullessness** N.

sound¹ N **1** PHYS periodic vibrations that are propagated through a medium, eg air, as pressure waves, so that the medium is displaced from its equilibrium state. **2** the noise that is heard as a result of such periodic vibrations. **3** audible quality: **The guitar has a nice sound**. **4** the mental impression created by something heard: **don't like the sound of that**. **5** (also **sounds**) COLLOQ music, esp pop music: **the sounds of the 60s**.
➤ VB **1** TR & INTR to produce or cause to produce a sound: **The bugle sounded**. **2** INTR to create an impression in the mind: **sounds like fun**. **3** to pronounce: **doesn't sound his h's**. **4** to signal with a sound: **sound the alarm**.
◆ **sound off** COLLOQ to state one's opinions, complaints, etc forcefully or angrily.

sound² ADJ **1** not damaged or injured; in good condition; healthy: **The kitten was found safe and sound**. **2 a** sensible; well-founded; reliable: **a sound investment**; **b** of an argument, opinion, etc: well researched or thought through; convincing. **3** acceptable. **4** severe or thorough: **a sound beating**. **5** of sleep: deep and undisturbed.
➤ ADV deeply: **sound asleep**. ■ **soundly** ADV. ■ **soundness** N.

sound³ VB, TR & INTR **1** to measure the depth of (esp the sea). **2** MED to examine (a hollow organ, etc) with a probe.
➤ N a probe for examining hollow organs.

◆ **sound sb** or **sth out** to try to discover or to make an assessment of (opinions, etc).

sound⁴ N a narrow passage of water that connects two large bodies of water.

soundbite N a short and succinct statement quoted on TV or radio or in the press.

soundcard N, COMP a printed circuit added to a computer to provide sound effects.

sound effects PL N artificially produced sounds used in film, broadcasting, theatre, etc, eg for authenticating the action, intensifying the suspense, etc.

sounding N **1 a** the process of measuring depth, esp of the sea, eg by using echo; **b** an instance of doing this; **c** (**soundings**) measurements that are taken or recorded when doing this. **2** (usu **soundings**) a sampling of opinions or (eg voting) intentions.

sounding-board N a means of testing the acceptability or popularity of ideas or opinions.

soundtrack N the recorded sound that accompanies a motion picture.

soup N a liquid food that is made by boiling meat, vegetables, grains, etc together in a stock or in water.
➤ VB (usu **soup up**) COLLOQ to make changes to a vehicle in order to increase its power.
◆ **in the soup** SLANG in trouble or difficulty.

soupçon N, often HUMOROUS the slightest amount; a dash.

sour ADJ **1** having an acid taste or smell, similar to that of lemon juice or vinegar. **2** rancid or stale because of fermentation: **sour milk**. **3** sullen; miserable; embittered: **a sour expression**. **4** unpleasant, unsuccessful or inharmonious: **The marriage turned sour**.
➤ VB, TR & INTR to make or become sour.
■ **soured** ADJ: **soured cream**. ■ **sourly** ADV. ■ **sourness** N.

source N **1** the place, thing, person, circumstance, etc that something begins or develops from; the origin. **2** a spring or place where a river or stream begins. **3** a person, a book or other document that can be used to

provide information, evidence, etc.
➤ VB to originate in someone or something.

sour grapes N a hostile or indifferent attitude towards something or someone, esp when motivated by envy, bitterness, resentment, etc.

souse VB **1** to steep or cook something in vinegar or white wine. **2** to pickle. **3** to make thoroughly wet; to drench.
➤ N **1** an act of sousing. **2** the liquid in which food is soused.

soutane N, RC CHURCH a long plain robe or cassock that a priest wears.

south N (also **South** or **the South**) **1** the direction to one's right when one faces the rising sun in the N hemisphere. **2** the direction that is directly opposite north, ie 180° from the north and 90° from both east and west. **3** any part of the Earth, a town, etc that lies in this direction.
➤ ADV towards the south.
➤ ADJ **1** on the side that is on or nearest the south. **2** of a wind: blowing from the south.

southbound ADJ going towards the south.

south-east N **1** the direction that is midway between south and east. **2** an area lying in this direction.
➤ ADV in this direction.
➤ ADJ belonging to, facing, coming from, lying in, etc the south-east. ■ **south-easterly** ADJ, ADV, N. ■ **south-eastern** ADJ.

southeaster N a wind, usu a fairly strong one, that blows from the direction of the south-east.

southerly ADJ **1** of a wind, etc: coming from the south. **2** looking, being, etc towards the south.
➤ ADV **1** to the south. **2** from the south.
➤ N (**-ies**) a southerly wind.

southern ADJ **1** belonging, relating or referring to, or in, the south. **2** of winds etc: coming from the south. **3** being or facing in or directed towards the south. ■ **southernmost** ADJ.

southerner N someone who lives in or comes from the south.

southpaw N, COLLOQ someone whose left hand is more dominant than their right.

southward and **southwards** ADV, ADJ towards the south.

south-west N **1** the direction midway between south and west. **2** an area lying in this direction.
➤ ADV in this direction.
➤ ADJ belonging to, facing, coming from, lying in, etc the south-west. ■ **south-westerly** ADJ, ADV, N. ■ **south-western** ADJ.

south-wester N **1** a wind that blows from the south-west. **2** same as **sou'wester** (sense 1).

souvenir N something that is bought, kept or given as a reminder of a place, person, occasion, etc; a memento.

sou'wester N **1** a type of oilskin or waterproof hat that has a large flap at the back and which is usu worn by seamen. **2** same as **southwester** (sense 1).

sovereign N **1** a supreme ruler or head, esp a monarch. **2** a former British gold coin worth £1.
➤ ADJ **1** having supreme power or authority: a sovereign ruler. **2** politically independent: a sovereign state. **3** outstanding; unrivalled; utmost: sovereign intelligence. **4** effective: a sovereign remedy. ■ **sovereignly** ADV.

sovereignty N (**-ies**) **1** supreme political power or authority. **2** a politically independent state. **3** self-government.

soviet N **1** any of the councils that made up the local and national governments of the former Soviet Union. **2** (**Soviet**) a citizen or inhabitant of the former Soviet Union.
➤ ADJ (**Soviet**) of the former Soviet Union.

sow[1] VB (**sown** or **sowed**) TR & INTR **1** to scatter or place (plant seeds, a crop, etc) on or in the earth, in a plant pot, etc. **2** to plant (a piece of land) with seeds, a crop, etc: **sowed the upper field with barley**. **3** to introduce or arouse: **sowed the seeds of doubt**. ■ **sower** N.

sow[2] N an adult female pig.

soy N **1** (also **soy sauce**) a salty dark brown sauce that is made from soya beans which ferment for around six months and which is used esp in oriental fish dishes. **2** soya.

soya and **soy** N 1 a plant of the pulse family, widely cultivated for their edible seeds. 2 (also called **soya bean**) the edible protein-rich seed of this plant, which is used in making soya flour, soya milk, etc, and which yields an oil that is used as a cooking oil and in the manufacture of margarine, soap, paints, etc.

sozzled ADJ, COLLOQ drunk.

spa N 1 a mineral water spring. 2 a town where such a spring is or was once located.

space N 1 the limitless three-dimensional expanse where all matter exists. 2 a restricted portion of this; room: **no space in the garden for a pool**. 3 an interval of distance; a gap: **sign in the space below**. 4 any of a restricted number of seats, places, etc. 5 a period of time: **within the space of ten minutes**. 6 (also **outer space**) all the regions of the Universe that lie beyond the Earth's atmosphere.
➤ VB 1 to set or place at intervals: **spaced the interviews over three days**. 2 to separate or divide with a space or spaces, eg in printing, etc. ■ **spacing** N.

space age N (usu **the space age**) the present era, when space travel became possible.
➤ ADJ (**space-age**) 1 technologically very advanced. 2 having a futuristic appearance.

spacecraft N a manned or unmanned vehicle designed to travel in space.

spaced ADJ 1 (also **spaced out**) COLLOQ being, acting, appearing to be, etc in a dazed, euphoric, stupefied or dreamlike state, esp one that is or seems to be induced by drugs. 2 set, placed, arranged, occurring, etc at intervals.

spacial see **spatial**

spacious ADJ having ample room or space; extending over a large area. ■ **spaciously** ADV. ■ **spaciousness** N.

spade[1] N a long-handled digging tool with a broad metal blade which is designed to be pushed into the ground with the foot.
➤ VB to dig or turn over (ground) with a spade. ■ **spadeful** N.
◆ **call a spade a spade** to speak frankly.

spade[2] N, CARDS **a** (**spades**) one of the four suits of playing-card with a black spade-shaped symbol (♠); **b** a playing-card of this suit.

spadework N hard or boring preparatory work.

spadix N (**spadices**) BOT a spike-shaped structure that consists of numerous tiny flowers and which is usu enclosed by a spathe.

spaghetti N 1 a type of pasta in the form of long thin solid strands. 2 a dish made from this.

span N 1 the distance, interval, length, etc between two points in space or time. 2 the length between the supports of a bridge, arch, pier, ceiling, etc. 3 the extent to which, or the duration of time for which, someone can concentrate, process information, listen attentively, etc. 4 the maximum distance between the tip of one wing and the tip of the other, eg in birds and planes. 5 a measure of length equal to the distance between the tips of thumb and little finger on an extended hand, which is conventionally taken as 9in (23cm).
➤ VB (**-nn-**) 1 **a** of a bridge, pier, ceiling, rainbow, etc: to extend across or over, esp in an arched shape: **A rainbow spanned the sky**; **b** to bridge (a river, etc): **spanned the river using logs**. 2 to last: **The feud spanned more than 30 years**. 3 to measure or cover, eg by using an extended hand.

spangle N a small piece of glittering material. ■ **spangled** ADJ. ■ **spangly** ADJ.

spaniel N a dog with a wavy coat and long silky ears.

spank VB to smack, usu on the buttocks with the flat of the hand, a slipper, belt, etc.
➤ N such a smack.

spanking N an act of delivering a series of smacks, eg as a punishment.
➤ ADV, COLLOQ absolutely; strikingly: **a spanking new watch**.
➤ ADJ, COLLOQ 1 brisk: **a spanking pace**. 2 impressively fine: **a spanking new car**.

spanner N a metal hand tool that has an opening (sometimes an adjustable one) or various sizes of openings at one or both ends and which is used for gripping, tightening or loosening nuts, bolts, etc.

◆ **throw, put**, etc **a spanner in the works** to frustrate, annoy, irritate, etc, esp by disrupting a plan, system, etc.

spar[1] N a strong thick pole of wood or metal, esp one used as a mast or beam on a ship.

spar[2] VB (-rr-) INTR (often **spar with sb** or **sth**) **1 a** to box, esp in a way that deliberately avoids the exchange of heavy blows, eg for practice; **b** to box against an imaginary opponent, for practice. **2** to engage in lively and light-hearted argument, banter, etc. ➢ N **1** an act or instance of sparring. **2** a light-hearted argument, banter, etc.

spar[3] N any of various translucent non-metallic minerals that split easily into layers.

spare ADJ **1** kept for occasional use: **the spare room. 2** kept for use as a replacement: **a spare wheel. 3** available for use; additional; extra: **a spare seat next to me. 4** lean; thin. **5** frugal; scanty. **6** furious or distraught to the point of distraction: **went spare when he found out.** ➢ VB **1** to afford to give, give away or do without: **I can't spare the time. 2 a** to refrain from harming, punishing, killing or destroying: **spare their feelings; b** to avoid causing or bringing on something: **will spare your embarrassment. 3** to avoid incurring something: **no expense spared.** ➢ N a duplicate kept as a replacement.

◆ **to spare** surplus to what is required.

sparing ADJ inclined to be economical or frugal: **be sparing with the chocolate sauce.** ■ **sparingly** ADV.

spark[1] N **1** a tiny red-hot glowing fiery particle that jumps out from some burning material. **2 a** a flash of light that is produced by a discontinuous electrical discharge flashing across a short gap between two conductors; **b** this kind of electrical discharge, eg in the engine of a motor vehicle, etc where its function is to ignite the explosive mixture. **3** a trace, hint or glimmer: **a spark of recognition.** ➢ VB, INTR to emit sparks of fire or electricity.

◆ **spark off** to stimulate, provoke or start: **The film sparked off great controversy.**

spark[2] N, often IRONIC (usu **bright spark**) someone who is lively, witty, intelligent, etc: **What bright spark left the oven on?**

sparkle VB, INTR **1** to give off sparks. **2** to shine with tiny points of bright light: **Her eyes sparkled. 3** of wine, mineral water, etc: to give off bubbles of carbon dioxide; to effervesce. **4** to be lively or witty. ➢ N **1** a point of bright shiny light; an act of sparkling; sparkling appearance. **2** liveliness; vivacity; wit. ■ **sparkling** ADJ. ■ **sparkly** ADJ.

sparkler N **1** a type of small handheld firework that produces gentle showers of silvery sparks. **2** COLLOQ a diamond or other impressive jewel.

spark plug N a device that discharges a spark between the two electrodes at its end, igniting the mixture of fuel and air in the cylinder.

sparrow N a small grey or brown perching bird with a short conical beak.

sparse ADJ thinly scattered or dotted about; scanty. ■ **sparsely** ADV. ■ **sparseness** N.

spartan ADJ **1** belonging to or characteristic of ancient Sparta, its inhabitants, customs, etc. **2** of living conditions, etc: austere; frugal; harsh. ➢ N **1** someone who shows these qualities. **2** a citizen or inhabitant of ancient Sparta.

spasm N **1** a sudden uncontrollable contraction of a muscle or muscles. **2** a short period of activity; a spell. **3** a sudden burst (of emotion, etc): **spasm of anger.** ➢ VB to twitch or go into a spasm.

spasmodic ADJ **1** being or occurring in, or consisting of, short periods; not constant or regular; intermittent: **spasmodic gunfire. 2** relating to or consisting of spasms. ■ **spasmodically** ADV.

spastic N, OLD USE someone who suffers from cerebral palsy.

spat COLLOQ, N a trivial or petty fight or quarrel. ➢ VB (-tt-) INTR to engage in a trivial or petty fight or quarrel.

spate N a sudden rush or increased quantity; a burst: a spate of complaints.
◆ **in spate** of a river: in a fast-flowing state brought about by flooding or melting snow.

spathe N, BOT a large bract that surrounds and protects the inflorescence or spadix.

spatial or **spacial** ADJ belonging, referring or relating to space. ■ **spatially** ADV.

spats PL N, HIST a cloth covering that goes around the ankle and over the top of a shoe, orig to protect against splashes of mud.

spatter VB, TR & INTR **1** of mud, etc: to spray, cover, shower or splash in scattered drops or patches: The muddy water spattered the car. **2** to cause (mud, etc) to fly in scattered drops or patches: the wheels of the bike spattered mud everywhere.
➢ N **1** a quantity spattered; a sprinkling. **2** the act or process of spattering.

spatula N **1** COOKERY an implement that has a broad blunt and often flexible blade and which can be used for a variety of purposes. **2** MED a flat, usu wooden, implement that is used for holding down the tongue during a throat examination, etc.

spawn N **1** the jelly-like mass or stream of eggs that amphibians, fish, molluscs, crustaceans, etc lay in water. **2** DERISIVE something that is the product of or that is derived from something else and which, because it is not original, is regarded with a degree of contempt.
➢ VB **1** INTR of amphibians, fish, etc: to lay eggs. **2** to give rise to something: The film's success spawned several sequels.

spay VB to remove the ovaries from (esp a domestic animal) in order to prevent it from breeding. ■ **spayed** ADJ.

speak VB (spoke, spoken) **1** TR & INTR **a** to utter words in an ordinary voice, as opposed to shouting, singing, screaming, etc; **b** to talk: speaks a load of rubbish. **2** INTR to have a conversation: We spoke on the phone. **3** INTR to deliver a speech: spoke about rising urban crime. **4** to communicate, or be able to communicate, in (a particular language): He speaks French.
◆ **speak for 1** to give an opinion on behalf of (another or others). **2** to articulate in either spoken or written words the commonly held feelings, beliefs, views, opinions, etc of (others).
◆ **speak out 1** to speak openly; to state one's views forcefully. **2** to speak more loudly.
◆ **speak up** INTR **1** to speak more loudly. **2** to make something known: If you've any objections, speak up now.
◆ **speak up for sb** or **sth 1** to vouch for or defend them or it. **2** to represent them or it.
◆ **speak volumes** to be significant: His aggressive response to the question spoke volumes.

speakeasy N (-ies) COLLOQ a bar or other place where alcohol was sold illicitly, esp one that operated during the period when the US prohibition laws were in force.

speaker N **1** someone who speaks, esp someone who gives a formal speech. **2** short form of **loudspeaker**. **3** (usu **the Speaker**) the person who presides over debate in a law-making assembly such as the House of Commons.

speaking N an act, instance or the process of saying something.
➢ ADJ **1** able to produce speech: speaking clock. **2** from or with regard to a specified point of view: Roughly speaking, the total cost will be about £100.
◆ **be on speaking terms** to be sufficiently friendly or familiar to hold a conversation.

spear N **1** a weapon that consists of a long pole with a hard sharp point, usu a metal one, and which is thrown from the shoulder (eg at prey, fish or an enemy). **2** a spiky plant shoot, such as a blade of grass or broccoli shoot.
➢ VB to pierce with a spear or something similar to a spear.

spearhead N **1** the leading part or member of an attacking force. **2** the tip of a spear.
➢ VB to lead (a movement, attack, etc).

spearmint N a plant of the mint family with lance-shaped aromatic leaves from which an oil is obtained that is used as a flavouring.

spec N.
◆ **on spec** as a speculation or gamble: **wrote on spec, asking for a job.**

special ADJ **1** distinct from, and usu better than, others of the same or a similar kind; exceptional: **a special occasion. 2** designed for a particular purpose: **You can get a special program to do that. 3** not ordinary or common: **special circumstances. 4** particular; great: **make a special effort.**
➤ N **1** something that is special, eg an extra edition of a newspaper, etc, an extra train that is put on over and above the timetabled ones, an item offered at a low price, a dish on a menu, etc. **2** a special person, such as a member of the special police constabulary. ■ **specially** ADV. ■ **specialness** N.

special effects PL N, CINEMATOG **1** the particular techniques, such as those that involve computer–generated graphics, elaborate make–up and costumes, skilled camera work, etc used in the making of films and TV programmes. **2** the impact or illusion that these techniques produce.

specialist N **1** someone whose work, interest or expertise is concentrated on a particular subject. **2** a doctor who is trained in specific diseases, diseases and conditions of particular parts of the body, etc: **a heart specialist.**

speciality or (chiefly US) **specialty** N (-ies) **1** something such as a particular area of interest, a distinctive quality, a specified product, etc that a company, individual, etc has special knowledge of or that they esp excel in studying, teaching, writing about, producing, etc: **The restaurant's speciality is seafood. 2** a special feature, skill, service, etc.

specialize or **-ise** VB **1** (also **specialize in sth**) to be or become an expert in a particular activity, field of study, etc. **2** of an organism, body part, etc: to adapt or become adapted for a specified purpose or to particular surroundings. ■ **specialization** N.

specie N money in the form of coins.
◆ **in specie 1** in kind. **2** in coin.

species N (PL **species**) **1 a** BIOL any of the groups into which a genus is divided, the main criterion for grouping being that all the members should be capable of interbreeding and producing fertile offspring; **b** BIOL the members of one of these units of classification. **2** (usu **species of**) a kind or type.

specific ADJ **1** particular; exact; precisely identified. **2** precise in meaning; not vague.
➤ N **1** (usu **specifics**) a specific detail, factor or feature, eg of a plan, scheme, etc. **2** a drug that is used to treat one particular disease, etc. ■ **specifically** ADV. ■ **specificity** N.

specification N **1 a** (often **specifications**) a detailed description of the methods, materials, dimensions, quantities, etc that are used in the construction, manufacture, building, planning, etc of something; **b** the standard, quality, etc of the construction, manufacture, etc of something. **2** an act or instance or the process of specifying.

specify VB (*-ies, -ied*) **1** to refer to, name or identify precisely: **The report does not specify who was to blame. 2** (usu **specify that**) to state as a condition or requirement.

specimen N **1** a sample or example of something, esp one that will be studied or put in a collection. **2** MED a sample of blood, urine, tissue, etc that is taken so that tests can be carried out on it. **3** COLLOQ a person of a specified kind: **an ugly specimen.**

specious ADJ apparently convincing, sound or just, but really false, flawed or lacking in sincerity: **specious arguments.**

speck N **1** a small spot, stain or mark. **2** a particle or tiny piece of something.
➤ VB to mark with specks: **specked with grey.**

speckle N a little spot, esp one of several on a different–coloured background.
➤ VB to mark with speckles. ■ **speckled** ADJ.

specs PL N, COLLOQ short form of **spectacles**.

spectacle N **1** a sight, esp one that is impressive, wonderful, ridiculous, etc: **The roses make a lovely spectacle. 2** a display or exhibition, esp one that is put on for entertaining the public. **3** someone or something that attracts attention.

◆ **make a spectacle of oneself** to behave in a way that attracts attention, esp scorn.

spectacles PL N a frame that holds two lenses designed to correct defective vision, and which has two legs that hook over the ears.

spectacular ADJ **1** impressively striking to see or watch. **2** remarkable; dramatic; huge. ➤ N a spectacular show or display, esp one with lavish costumes, sets, music, etc: **an old-fashioned musical spectacular**. ■ **spectacularly** ADV.

spectate VB, INTR to be a spectator.

spectator N someone who watches an event or incident.

spectre or (US) **specter** N **1** a ghost or an apparition. **2** a haunting fear; the threat of something unpleasant: **The spectre of famine was never far away. ■ spectral** ADJ.

spectrometer N a device that is designed to produce spectra, esp one that can measure wavelength, energy and intensity.

spectroscope N, CHEM an optical device that is used to produce a spectrum for a chemical compound, for the purposes of analysis.

spectrum N (*-ra* or *-rums*) **1** PHYS (in full **visible spectrum**) the band of colours (red, orange, yellow, green, blue, indigo and violet) that is produced when white light is split into its constituent wavelengths by passing it through a prism. **2** a continuous band or a series of lines representing the wavelengths or frequencies of electromagnetic radiation (eg visible light, X-rays, radio waves) emitted or absorbed by a particular substance. **3** any full range: **the spectrum of human emotions. ■ spectral** ADJ.

speculate VB, INTR **1** (often **speculate on** or **about sth**) to consider the circumstances or possibilities regarding it, usu without coming to a definite conclusion. **2** to engage in risky financial transactions, usu in the hope of making a quick profit. ■ **speculation** N. ■ **speculative** ADJ. ■ **speculator** N.

speculum N (*-la* or *-lums*) MED a device that is used to enlarge the opening of a body cavity so that the interior may be inspected.

speech N **1** the act or an instance of speaking; the ability to speak. **2** a way of speaking: **slurred speech**. **3** something that is spoken. **4** spoken language, esp that of a particular group, region, etc: **Doric speech**. **5** a talk that is addressed to an audience.

speechify VB (*-ies, -ied*) INTR, COLLOQ to make a speech or speeches, esp of a long and tedious nature.

speechless ADJ **1** often EUPHEMISTIC temporarily unable to speak, because of surprise, shock, emotion, etc. **2** not able to speak at all.

speech therapy N the treatment of people with speech and language disorders. ■ **speech therapist** N.

speed N **1** rate of movement or action, esp distance travelled per unit of time. **2** quickness; rapidity: **with speed**. **3** a gear setting on a vehicle: **five-speed gearbox**. **4** a photographic film's sensitivity to light. **5** DRUG-TAKING SLANG an amphetamine. ➤ VB, INTR **1** (*sped*) to move quickly. **2** (*speeded*) to drive at a speed higher than the legal limit.

◆ **at speed** quickly.

◆ **speed up** or **speed sth up** to increase in speed or make it increase in speed.

speedboat N a motor boat that is capable of high speeds.

speeding N an act, instance or the process of going fast, esp faster than the speed limit. ➤ ADJ moving, acting, etc fast: **a speeding car**.

speedometer N a device which indicates the speed that a motor vehicle is travelling at, and which often incorporates an odometer that displays the total mileage.

speedway N **1** the sport or pastime of racing round a cinder track on lightweight motorcycles. **2** the track that is used for this.

speedwell N a plant with small bluish (or occasionally white) four-petalled flowers.

speedy ADJ (*-ier, -iest*) fast; prompt; without

delay. ■ **speedily** ADV. ■ **speediness** N.

speleology N **1** the scientific study of caves. **2** the activity of exploring caves.

spell¹ VB (*spelt* or *spelled*) **1** to write or name (the constituent letters of a word or words) in their correct order. **2** of letters: to form (a word) when written in sequence: I T spells 'it'. **3** to indicate something clearly: His angry expression spelt trouble.
◆ **spell sth out 1** to read, write or speak (the constituent letters of a word) one by one. **2** to explain something clearly and in detail.

spell² N **1** a set of words which, esp when spoken, is believed to have magical power: a magic spell. **2** any strong attracting influence: the spell of her personality.
◆ **under sb's spell** captivated by them.

spell³ N **1** (often **for a spell** or **a spell of**) a period or bout of illness, work, weather, etc often of a specified kind: hope this spell of sunshine continues. **2** now chiefly AUSTRAL, NZ & N ENGLISH DIALECT an interval or short break from work.
➤ VB, now chiefly AUSTRAL, NZ & N ENGLISH DIALECT **1** to replace or relieve someone at work. **2** INTR to take an interval or short break from work.

spellbinding ADJ captivating, enchanting, entrancing or fascinating. ■ **spellbound** ADJ.

spelling N **1** the ability to spell: His spelling is awful. **2** a way a word is spelt: an American spelling.

spelunker N someone who takes part in the sport or activity of exploring caves; a potholer.

spend VB (*spent*) **1** TR & INTR (often **spend on**) to pay out (money, etc) eg on buying something new, for a service, repair, etc. **2** to use or devote (eg time, energy, effort, etc): spent hours trying to fix the car. **3** to use up completely; to exhaust: Her anger soon spends itself.
➤ N an act or the process of spending (esp money): went on a massive spend after winning the Lottery. ■ **spending** N.

spendthrift N someone who spends money freely, extravagantly and often wastefully.

spent ADJ used up; exhausted: a spent match.

sperm N **1** a spermatozoon. **2** semen.

spermaceti N a white waxy substance obtained from the snout of the sperm whale, formerly used for making candles, soap, etc.

spermatozoon N (*-zoa*) ZOOL in male animals: the small male gamete that locates, penetrates and fertilizes the female gamete. Often shortened to **sperm**.

spermicide N a substance that can kill sperm and which is used in conjunction with various methods of barrier contraception, eg the diaphragm. ■ **spermicidal** ADJ.

spew VB, TR & INTR **1** to vomit. **2** to pour or cause to pour or stream out.
➤ N vomit.

sphagnum N (*-na*) a moss that grows on temperate boggy or marshy ground, and which forms peat when it decays.

sphere N **1** MATH a round three-dimensional figure where all points on the surface are an equal distance from the centre. **2** a globe or ball. **3** a field of activity: Rugby's not really my sphere. **4** a class or circle within society: We don't move in the same sphere any more.

spherical ADJ having the shape of a sphere.

spheroid N, GEOM a figure having almost the shape of a sphere.

sphincter N, ANAT a ring of muscle that, when it contracts, closes the entrance to a cavity in the body. ■ **sphincteral** ADJ.

sphinx N **1** (also **Sphinx**) any stone carving or other representation in the form of a human head and lion's body, esp the statue near the Egyptian pyramids at Giza. **2** a mysterious or enigmatic person. ■ **sphinxlike** ADJ.

spice N **1** an aromatic or pungent substance, such as pepper, ginger, nutmeg, etc that is derived from plants and used for flavouring food, eg in sauces, curries, etc, and for drinks such as punch. **2** such substances collectively. **3** something that adds interest or enjoyment.
➤ VB **1** to flavour with spice. **2** (also **spice up**) to add interest or enjoyment to something.

spick and span ADJ neat, clean and tidy.

spicy or **spicey** ADJ (*-ier, -iest*) **1** flavoured with or tasting or smelling of spices; pungent; piquant. **2** COLLOQ characterized by, or suggestive of, scandal, sensation, impropriety, bad taste, etc: **Got any spicy gossip?**

spider N **1** any of numerous species of invertebrate animals that have eight legs and two main body parts, many of which produce silk and spin webs to trap their prey. **2** a snooker rest which has long legs so that it can be used to arch over a ball. ■ **spidery** ADJ.

spiel N, COLLOQ a long rambling, often implausible, story, esp one given as sales patter.

spigot N **1** a peg or plug, esp one that is used for stopping the vent hole in a cask or barrel. **2 a** US a tap; **b** a tap for controlling the flow of liquid, eg in a cask, pipe, etc.

spike¹ N **1 a** any thin sharp point; **b** a pointed piece of metal, eg one of several on railings. **2** (**spikes**) a pair of running–shoes with spiked soles. **3** a large metal nail.
➤ VB **1** to strike, pierce or impale with a pointed object. **2** COLLOQ **a** to make (a drink) stronger by adding alcohol or extra alcohol; **b** to lace (a drink) with a drug. ■ **spiky** ADJ.

spike² N, BOT a pointed flower–head which consists of a cluster of small individual flowers growing around, or along one side of, an axis.

spill¹ VB (PA T, PA P *spilt* or *spilled*) **1** TR & INTR to run or flow or cause (a liquid, etc) to run or flow out from a container, esp accidentally. **2** INTR to come or go in large crowds, esp quickly: **The spectators spilled onto the pitch. 3** to shed (blood).
➤ N **1** an act of spilling. **2** COLLOQ a fall.
◆ **spill the beans** COLLOQ to reveal confidential information.

spill² N a thin strip of wood or twisted paper for lighting a fire, candle, pipe, etc.

spillage N **1** the act or process of spilling. **2** something that is spilt or an amount spilt.

spin VB (PA T, PA P *spun*, PR P *spinning*) **1** TR & INTR to rotate or cause to rotate repeatedly, esp quickly: **We spun a coin to see who would go first. 2** to draw out and twist (fibres, etc) into

thread. **3** of spiders, silkworms, etc: to construct (a web, cocoon, etc) from the silky thread they produce. **4 a** to bowl, throw, kick, strike, etc (a ball) so that it rotates while moving forward, causing a change in the expected direction or speed; **b** of a ball, etc: to be delivered in this way. **5** INTR of someone's head, etc: to have a disorientated sensation, esp one that is brought on by excitement, amazement, drugs or alcohol, etc. **6** to dry (washing) in a spin–dryer.
➤ N **1** an act or process of spinning or a spinning motion. **2** rotation in a ball thrown, struck, etc. **3** a nose–first spiral descent in an aircraft, esp one that is out of control. Also called **tailspin**. **4** COLLOQ a short trip in a vehicle, for pleasure. **5** of information, a news report, etc, esp that is of a political nature: a favourable bias.
■ **spinning** N, ADJ.
◆ **spin round** to turn around, esp quickly.
◆ **spin a yarn** to tell a story, esp a long improbable one.

spina bifida N, PATHOL a condition existing from birth in which there is a protrusion of the spinal column through the backbone, often causing permanent paralysis.

spinach N the young dark green crinkly or flat leaves of the spinach plant which are cooked as a vegetable or used raw in salads.

spinal column N the spine.

spinal cord N a cord–like structure of nerve tissue enclosed by the spinal column.

spindle N **1** a rod with a notched or tapered end that is designed for twisting the fibres in hand–spinning and which is the place where the spun thread is wound. **2** a pin or axis which turns, or around which something else turns.

spindly ADJ (*-ier, -iest*) COLLOQ long, thin and, often, frail–looking.

spin doctor N, COLLOQ someone, esp in politics, who tries to put a favourable bias on information when it is presented to the public.

spindrift N spray that is blown from the crests of waves.

spine N **1** in vertebrates: the flexible bony structure that surrounds and protects the spinal cord. **2** the narrow middle section in the cover of a book that hides the part where the pages are glued or stitched. **3** in certain plants and animals, eg cacti, hedgehogs, etc: one of many sharply pointed structures that protect the plant or animal against predators. ■ **spinal** ADJ.

spine-chiller N something, such as a frightening story, that sends shivers down one's spine. ■ **spine-chilling** ADJ.

spineless ADJ **1** invertebrate. **2** COLLOQ lacking courage or strength of character.

spinet N a small harpsichord.

spinnaker N a large triangular sail set at the front of a yacht.

spinner N **1** someone or something that spins. **2** an angler's lure that has a projecting wing which makes it spin in the water when the line is pulled. **3** CRICKET a ball that is bowled with spin.

spinney N a small wood or thicket, esp one that has a prickly undergrowth.

spin-off N **1** a side-effect or by-product. **2** something that comes about because of the success of an earlier product or idea.

spinster N a woman, esp one who is middle-aged or older, who has never been married. ■ **spinsterish** ADJ.

spiny ADJ (*-ier, -iest*) **1** covered with spines; prickly. **2** troublesome: **a spiny problem**.

spiral N **1** the pattern that is made by a line winding outwards from a central point in circles or near-circles of regularly increasing size. **2** a curve or course that makes this kind of a pattern. **3** a gradual but continuous rise or fall, eg of prices, wages, etc.
➤ ADJ being in or having the shape or nature of a spiral: **a spiral staircase**.
➤ VB (*-ll-*; or (US) *-l-*) **1** INTR to follow a spiral course or pattern. **2** INTR esp of prices, wages, etc: to go up or down, usu quickly: **Prices spiralled out of control**. ■ **spirally** ADV.

spire N a tall thin structure tapering upwards to a point, esp the top of a tower on a church roof.

spirit N **1** the animating or vitalizing essence or force that motivates, invigorates or energizes

someone or something. **2** this force as an independent part of a person, widely believed to survive the body after death. **3** a supernatural being without a body: **Evil spirits haunted the house**. **4 a** temperament, frame of mind, etc, usu of a specified kind: **She always had a very independent spirit**; **b** the dominant or prevalent mood, attitude, etc: **public spirit**; **c** the characteristic essence, nature, etc of something: **the spirit of Christmas**. **5** a distilled alcoholic drink, eg whisky, brandy, gin, etc.
➤ VB (usu **spirit sth** or **sb away** or **off**) to carry or convey them mysteriously or magically.
◆ **in good** or **high**, etc **spirits** in a happy, contented, etc mood.
◆ **in spirit** as a presence that is perceived to be there: **I'll be with you in spirit**.

spirited ADJ **1** full of courage or liveliness. **2** IN COMPOUNDS having or showing a specified kind of spirit, mood, attitude, etc: **high-spirited**.

spirit level N a device used for testing that horizontal or vertical surfaces are level.

spiritual ADJ **1** belonging, referring or relating to the spirit or soul rather than to the body or to physical things. **2** sacred, holy or divine. **3 a** belonging, relating to, or arising from, the mind or intellect; **b** highly refined in thought, feelings, etc. **4** of or relating to spirits, ghosts, etc: **the spiritual world**.
➤ N a type of religious song which developed from the communal singing traditions of African American people in the southern states of the USA. ■ **spirituality** N. ■ **spiritually** ADV.

spiritualism N the belief that it is possible to have communication with the spirits of dead people. ■ **spiritualist** N.

spirograph N, MED a device for measuring and recording breathing movements.

spirogyra N a green alga with filaments containing spiralling chloroplasts.

spit[1] VB (PA T, PA P *spat* or (US) *spit,* PR P *spitting*) **1 a** TR & INTR to expel (saliva or phlegm) from the mouth; **b** INTR to do this as a gesture of contempt: **spat in his face**. **2** (also **spit out**) to eject (eg food) forcefully out of the mouth. **3** of a fire, fat or oil in a pan, etc: to throw off (a spark

of hot coal, oil, etc) in a spurt or spurts. **4** to speak or utter with contempt, hate, violence, etc. **5** INTR of rain or snow: to fall in light intermittent drops or flakes.
➤ N **1** spittle. **2** same as **spitting image**.
◆ **spit it out** COLLOQ to say what one has been hesitating to say.

spit² N **1** a long thin metal rod on which meat is skewered and held over a fire or in an oven for roasting. **2** a long narrow strip of land that juts out into the water.

spit and polish N, COLLOQ, often DEROG exceptional cleanliness, tidiness, smartness, etc.

spite N **1** the desire to intentionally hurt or offend. **2** an instance of this; a grudge.
➤ VB, chiefly used in the infinitive form: to annoy, offend, etc: **did it to spite him**.
◆ **in spite of** regardless; notwithstanding: **decided to go in spite of the rain**.

spiteful ADJ motivated by spite; vengeful; malicious. ■ **spitefully** ADV. ■ **spitefulness** N.

spitfire N someone who has a quick or fiery temper, esp a woman or girl.

spitting image N, COLLOQ an exact likeness.

spittle N saliva; spit.

spittoon N a container for spitting into.

spiv N, COLLOQ a man who sells, deals in, or is otherwise involved in the trading of, illicit, blackmarket or stolen goods.

splash VB **1 a** to make (a liquid or semi-liquid substance) to fly around or land in drops; **b** INTR of a liquid or semi-liquid substance: to fly around or land in drops. **2** to make something wet or dirty (with drops of liquid or semi-liquid): **The bus splashed them with mud. 3** to print or display something boldly: **The photograph was splashed across the front page.**
➤ N **1** a sound of splashing. **2** an amount splashed. **3** an irregular spot or patch: **splashes of colour. 4** COLLOQ a small amount of liquid; a dash: **tea with just a splash of milk.**
◆ **splash out** or **splash out on sth** COLLOQ to spend a lot of money, esp extravagantly.

splat N the sound made by a soft wet object

striking a surface.
➤ VB (**-tt-**) to hit, fall, land, etc with a splat.

splatter VB **1** TR & INTR to make something dirty with lots of small scattered drops. **2** of water, mud, etc: to wet or dirty: **The mud splattered him from head to toe.**
➤ N a splash, eg of colour, mud, etc.

splay VB to spread (eg the fingers).

splay foot N a foot that turns outwards.
■ **splay-footed** ADJ.

spleen N **1** a delicate organ located beneath the diaphragm on the left side, and which destroys red blood cells that are no longer functional. **2** bad temper; anger.

splendid ADJ **1** very good; excellent. **2** magnificent; impressively grand or sumptuous. ■ **splendidly** ADV.

splendiferous ADJ, now COLLOQ, HUMOROUS splendid.

splendour or (US) **splendor** N magnificence, opulence or grandeur.

splenetic ADJ bad-tempered; spiteful.

splice VB **1** to join (two pieces of rope) by weaving the strands of one into the other. **2** to join (two pieces of timber, etc) by overlapping and securing the ends. **3** to join the neatened ends of (two pieces of film, magnetic tape, wire, etc) using solder, adhesive, etc.
➤ N a join made in one of these ways.

splint N a piece of rigid material that is strapped to a broken limb, etc to hold it in position while the bone heals.
➤ VB to bind or hold (a broken limb, etc) in position using a splint.

splinter N **1** a small thin sharp piece that has broken off a hard substance, eg wood or glass. **2** a fragment of an exploded shell, etc.
➤ VB, TR & INTR to break into splinters.
■ **splintery** ADJ.

split VB (*split, splitting*) **1** TR & INTR to divide or break or cause to divide or break apart or into, usu two, pieces, esp lengthways. **2** to divide or share, money, etc. **3** (also **split up**) TR & INTR **a** to divide or separate into smaller amounts,

groups, parts, etc; **b** to divide or separate or cause to divide or separate, eg because of disagreement, disharmony, etc: **European policy split the party.**
➢ N **1 a** an act or the process of separating or dividing; **b** a division, esp of money, etc.
2 a lengthways break or crack. **3** a division through disagreement. **4** a dessert that consists of fruit, esp a banana, sliced open and topped with cream and/or ice-cream, sauce, nuts, etc.
5 (**the splits**) an acrobatic leap or drop to the floor so that the legs form a straight line and each leg is at right angles to the torso.
➢ ADJ divided, esp in two.
◆ **split away** or **split off** to separate from; to diverge: **The road splits off to the right.**
◆ **split hairs** to make or argue about fine and trivial distinctions.
◆ **split one's sides** COLLOQ to laugh uncontrollably.

split infinitive N, GRAM an infinitive that has an adverb or other word coming in between the particle **to** and the verb, as in **to really believe, to boldly go**, etc.

split-level ADJ of a house, room, etc: being on or having more than one level or floor.

split second N a fraction of a second.

splodge and **splotch** N a large splash, stain or patch.
➢ VB, TR & INTR to mark with splodges.

splurge N **1** an ostentatious display. **2** a bout of extravagance, eg a spending spree.
➢ VB, TR & INTR to spend extravagantly.

splutter VB **1** INTR to put or throw out drops of liquid, bits of food, sparks, etc with spitting sounds. **2** INTR to make intermittent noises or movements, esp as a sign of something being wrong: **The car spluttered to a halt. 3** TR & INTR to speak or say haltingly or incoherently, eg through embarrassment: **could only splutter that he didn't know the answer.**
➢ N the act or noise of spluttering.

spoil VB (PA T, PA P *spoilt* or *spoiled*) **1** to impair, ruin or make useless or valueless. **2** to mar or make less enjoyable: **The contrived ending spoiled the film. 3** to harm (eg, the character of

a child) by the kind of over-indulgence that will lead to selfish behaviour, unreasonable expectations of others, etc: **She is spoiling that boy — he never has to do anything for himself.**
4 INTR of food: to become unfit to eat.
➢ N (always **spoils**) **1** possessions taken by force; plunder: **the spoils of war. 2** any benefits or rewards: **a company car — just one of the spoils of the new job.**
◆ **be spoiling for sth** to seek out (a fight, argument, etc) eagerly.
◆ **be spoiled** or **spoilt for choice** to have so many options that it is hard to choose.

spoilage N **1** decay or deterioration of food. **2** waste, esp waste paper.

spoiler N **1** a flap on an aircraft wing that is used for increasing drag and so assists in its descent by reducing the air speed. **2** a fixed horizontal structure on a car that is designed to put pressure on the wheels and so increase its roadholding capacity, esp at high speeds.
3 someone or something that spoils.

spoilsport N, COLLOQ someone who mars or detracts from the fun or enjoyment of others.

spoke N **1** any of the radiating rods or bars that fan out from the hub of a wheel and attach it to the the rim. **2** a rung of a ladder.
◆ **put a spoke in sb's wheel** to upset their plans, esp intentionally or maliciously.

spoken ADJ **1** uttered or expressed in speech. **2** IN COMPOUNDS speaking in a specified way: **well-spoken.**
◆ **be spoken for** to be married, engaged or in a steady relationship.

spokesperson N someone, a **spokesman** or **spokeswoman**, appointed to speak on behalf of other people, a government, etc.

spoliation N **1** an act, instance or the process of robbing, plundering, etc.

spondee N, PROSODY a metrical foot of two long syllables or two stressed syllables.
■ **spondaic** ADJ.

spondulicks PL N, COLLOQ, chiefly US money.

sponge N **1** an aquatic, usu marine, invertebrate animal consisting of a large cluster

of cells supported by an often porous skeleton. **2 a** a piece of the soft porous skeleton of this animal used for washing, bathing, cleaning, etc; **b** a piece of similarly absorbent synthetic material that is used in the same way. **3** sponge cake or pudding. **4** a wipe with a cloth or sponge in order to clean something: **gave the baby's face a quick sponge.**
➤ VB **1** to wash or clean with a cloth or sponge and water. **2** to mop up. **3** (usu **sponge off** or **on sb**) COLLOQ to borrow money, etc from them. ■ **sponger** N. ■ **spongy** ADJ (**-ier, -iest**).

sponsor N **1** a person or organization that finances an event or broadcast in return for advertising. **2 a** someone who promises a sum of money to a participant in a forthcoming fund-raising event; **b** a company that provides backing for a sporting team or individual, in return for the team or individual displaying the company's name or logo on their shirts. **3** someone who offers to be responsible for another, esp in acting as a godparent.
➤ VB to act as a sponsor for someone or something. ■ **sponsored** ADJ: **a sponsored walk**. ■ **sponsorship** N.

spontaneity N natural or unrestrained reaction.

spontaneous ADJ **1** unplanned and voluntary or instinctive, not provoked or invited by others. **2** occurring naturally or by itself, not caused or influenced from outside.

spoof COLLOQ, N **1** a satirical imitation; a parody. **2** a light-hearted hoax or trick.
➤ VB to parody; to play a hoax.

spook COLLOQ, N **1** a ghost. **2** N AMER a spy.
➤ VB **1** to frighten or startle. **2** to haunt. **3** to make someone feel nervous or uneasy. ■ **spooky** ADJ (**-ier, -iest**).

spool N a small cylinder, usu with a hole down the centre on which thread, photographic film, tape, etc is wound; a reel.

spoon N **1** a metal, wooden or plastic utensil that has a handle with a round or oval shallow bowl-like part at one end and which is used for eating, serving or stirring food. **2** the amount a spoon will hold.

➤ VB **1** to lift (food) with a spoon. **2** INTR, OLD USE to kiss and cuddle. ■ **spoonful** N.

spoonerism N a slip of the tongue where the first sounds in a pair of words are reversed, such as **par cark** for **car park**.

spoon-feed VB **1** to feed (eg a baby) with a spoon. **2** to supply someone with everything they need or require.

spoor N the track or scent left by an animal.

sporadic ADJ occurring from time to time, at irregular intervals. ■ **sporadically** ADV.

spore N one of the tiny reproductive bodies produced in vast quantities by certain micro-organisms and non-flowering plants, and which can develop into new individuals.

sporran N a pouch traditionally worn hanging from a belt in front of a Scottish kilt.

sport N **1 a** an activity, pastime, competition, etc that usu involves a degree of physical exertion, and which people take part in for exercise and/or pleasure; **b** such activities collectively: **enjoys watching sport on TV. 2** good-humoured fun: **It was just meant to be a bit of sport. 3** COLLOQ **a** someone who is thought of as being fair-minded, generous, easy-going, etc: **Be a sport and lend me your car; b** someone who behaves in a specified way, esp with regard to winning or losing: **Even when he loses, he's a good sport; c** AUSTRAL, NZ a form of address that is esp used between men: **How's it going, sport?**
➤ VB **1** to wear or display, esp proudly: **She sported a small tattoo. 2** BIOL to vary from, or produce a variation from, the parent stock.

sporting ADJ **1** of sport: **sporting dogs. 2** of someone, their behaviour, etc: characterized by fairness, generosity, etc: **It was sporting of him to lend me the car. 3** keen or willing to gamble or take a risk.

sporting chance N (usu **a sporting chance**) a reasonable possibility of success.

sportive ADJ playful.

sports SING N **1** BRIT in schools and colleges: a day or afternoon that each year is dedicated to competitive sport, esp athletics: **Parents may attend the school sports. 2** AS ADJ belonging, referring or relating to sport: **sports pavilion. 3** AS ADJ used in or suitable for sport: **sports holdall. 4** AS ADJ casual: **sports jacket.**

sports car N a small fast car, usu a two-seater, often with a low-slung body.

sports jacket N a man's casual jacket, often one made from tweed.

sportsman N **1** a male sportsperson. **2** someone who plays fair, sticks to the rules and accepts defeat without any rancour. ■ **sportsmanlike** ADJ. ■ **sportsmanship** N.

sportswear N clothes that are designed for or suitable for sport or for wearing casually.

sportswoman N a female sportsperson.

sporty ADJ (**-ier, -iest**) **1** of someone: habitually taking part in sport, or being esp fond of, good at, etc sport. **2** of clothes: casual; suitable for wearing when playing a sport. **3** of a car: looking, performing or handling like a sports car. ■ **sportily** ADJ. ■ **sportiness** N.

spot N **1** a small mark or stain. **2** a drop of liquid. **3** a small amount, esp of liquid. **4** an eruption on the skin; a pimple. **5** a place: **found a secluded spot. 6** COLLOQ a small amount of work: **did a spot of ironing. 7** a place or period in a schedule or programme: **a five-minute comedy spot. 8** COLLOQ a spotlight.
➤ VB (**-tt-**) **1** to mark with spots. **2** to see; to catch sight of something. **3** USU IN COMPOUNDS to watch for and record the sighting of (eg trains, planes, etc). **4** to search for (new talent). **5** INTR of rain: to fall lightly.
◆ **in a spot** COLLOQ in trouble or difficulty.
◆ **knock spots off sb** or **sth** COLLOQ to be overwhelmingly better than them.
◆ **on the spot 1** immediately: **fined on the spot. 2** at the scene of some notable event. **3** in an awkward situation.

spot check N an inspection made at random and without warning.
➤ VB (**spot-check**) to carry out a random check.

spotless ADJ **1** absolutely clean.

2 unblemished: **a spotless working record.**
■ **spotlessly** ADV. ■ **spotlessness** N.

spotlight N **1** a concentrated circle of light that can be directed onto a small area, esp of a theatre stage. **2** a lamp that casts this kind of light.
➤ VB (**spotlit** or **spotlighted**) **1** to illuminate with a spotlight. **2** to direct attention to something; to highlight.
◆ **be in the spotlight** to have the attention of others, the media, etc.

spot-on ADJ, BRIT COLLOQ precisely what is required; excellent; very accurate.

spotted ADJ **1** patterned or covered with spots. **2** marked: **a tie spotted with tomato sauce.**

spotty ADJ (**-ier, -iest**) **1** marked with a pattern of spots. **2** of someone's skin, esp that of the face, back, etc: covered in blemishes, pimples, etc. ■ **spottiness** N.

spouse N a husband or wife.

spout N **1** a projecting tube or lip, eg on a kettle, teapot, fountain, etc, that allows liquid to pass through or through which it can be poured. **2** a jet or stream of liquid, eg from a fountain or a whale's blowhole.
➤ VB **1** TR & INTR to flow or make something flow out in a jet or stream. **2** TR & INTR to speak or say, esp at length and boringly. **3** INTR of a whale: to squirt air through a blowhole.
◆ **up the spout** SLANG **1** ruined or damaged beyond repair; no longer a possibility. **2** pregnant.

sprain VB to injure (a joint) by the sudden overstretching or tearing of ligaments.
➤ N such an injury, usu causing painful swelling.

sprat N a small edible fish of the herring family.

sprawl VB, INTR **1** to sit or lie lazily, esp with the arms and legs spread out wide. **2** to fall in an ungainly way. **3** to spread or extend in an irregular, straggling or untidy way.
➤ N **1** a sprawling position. **2** a straggling expansion, esp one that is unregulated, uncontrolled, etc: **urban sprawl.**

spray[1] N **1** a fine mist of small flying drops of liquid. **2** a liquid designed to be applied as a mist: **body spray**. **3** a device for dispensing a liquid as a mist; an atomizer or aerosol. **4** a shower of small objects: **a spray of pellets**. ➤ VB **1** to squirt (a liquid) in the form of a mist. **2** to apply a liquid in the form of a spray to something. **3** to subject someone or something to a heavy burst: **sprayed the car with bullets**.

spray² N **1 a** a small branch of a tree or plant which has delicate leaves and flowers growing on it; **b** any decoration that is an imitation of this. **2** a small bouquet of flowers.

spread VB **1** TR & INTR to apply, or be capable of being applied, in a smooth coating over a surface: **spread the butter on the toast**. **2** (also **spread out** or **spread sth out**) to extend or make it extend or scatter, often more widely or more thinly. **3** (also **spread sth out**) to open it out or unfold it, esp to its full extent: **spread the sheet on the bed**. **4** TR & INTR to transmit or be transmitted: **Rumours began to spread**. ➤ N **1** the act, process or extent of spreading. **2** a food in paste form, for spreading on bread, etc. **3** a pair of facing pages in a newspaper or magazine. **4** COLLOQ a lavish meal. **5 a** N AMER a farm and its lands, usu one given over to cattle-rearing; **b** a large house with extensive grounds. **6** COLLOQ increased fatness around the waist and hips: **middle-age spread**. **7** a cover, esp for a bed.

spread-eagle ADJ (also **spread-eagled**) in a position where the arms and legs are stretched out away from the body.

spreadsheet N, COMP a program that displays a grid containing data in the form of figures, text, formulae, etc and whose function is to enable various mathematical, statistical, etc calculations to be done.

spree N a period of fun, extravagance or excess, esp one that involves spending a lot of money or drinking a lot of alcohol.

sprig N a small shoot or twig.

sprightly ADJ (**-ier, -iest**) lively; vivacious; quick-moving. ■ **sprightliness** N.

spring VB (PAT *sprang* or (US) *sprung*, PAP *sprung*) **1** INTR to leap with a sudden quick launching action. **2** INTR to move suddenly and swiftly, esp from a stationary position: **sprang into action**. **3** to set off (a trap, etc) suddenly. **4** to fit (eg a mattress) with springs. **5** (also **spring sth on sb**) to present or reveal something suddenly and unexpectedly: **sprang the idea on me**. **6** SLANG to engineer the escape of (a prisoner) from jail. ➤ N **1** a metal coil that can be stretched or compressed, and which will return to its original shape when the pull or pressure is released. **2** any place where water emerges from underground and flows on to the Earth's surface or into a body of water. **3** (also **Spring**) the season between winter and summer, when most plants begin to grow. **4** a sudden vigorous leap. **5 a** the ability of a material to return rapidly to its original shape after a distorting force, such as stretching, bending or compression, has been removed: **The elastic has lost its spring**; **b** a lively bouncing or jaunty quality: **a spring in his step**.

springboard N **1 a** a long narrow pliable board that projects over a swimming pool and which is used in diving to give extra lift; **b** a similar but shorter board that is used in gymnastics and which is placed in front of a piece of apparatus to give extra height and impetus. **2** anything that serves to get things moving.

springbok N (*springbok* or *springboks*) a type of South African antelope that is renowned for its high springing leap.

spring-clean VB, TR & INTR to clean and tidy (a house) thoroughly, esp at the end of the winter. ➤ N an act of this. ■ **spring-cleaning** N.

spring tide N a tidal pattern that occurs twice a month when the Moon is full and again when it is new.

springtime and **springtide** N the season of spring.

springy ADJ (**-ier, -iest**) having the ability to readily spring back to the original shape when any pressure that has been exerted is released; bouncy; elastic; resilient. ■ **springiness** N.

sprinkle VB **1** to scatter in, or cover with a scattering of, tiny drops or particles. **2** to arrange or distribute in a thin scattering: The hillside was sprinkled with houses.
➤ N **1** an act of sprinkling. **2** a small amount.

sprinkler N a person or device that sprinkles, esp one that sprinkles water over plants, a lawn, etc or one for extinguishing fires.

sprinkling N a small amount of something, esp when it is thinly scattered.

sprint N **1** ATHLETICS a race at high speed over a short distance. **2** a burst of speed at a particular point, usu the end, of a long race, eg in athletics, cycling, horse-racing, etc. **3** a fast run.
➤ VB, TR & INTR to run at full speed.

sprinter N **1** an athlete, cyclist, etc who sprints. **2** a small bus or train that travels short distances.

sprit N a small diagonal spar used to spread a sail.

sprite N **1** FOLKLORE a playful fairy; an elf or imp. **2** a number of pixels that can be moved around a screen in a group, eg those representing a figure in a computer game.

spritzer N a mix of white wine and soda water.

sprocket N **1** any of a set of teeth on the rim of a driving wheel, eg fitting into the links of a chain or the holes on a strip of film. **2** (also **sprocket wheel**) a wheel with sprockets.

sprog N, SLANG a child.

sprout VB **1** TR & INTR to develop (a new growth, eg of leaves or hair). **2** (also **sprout up**) to grow or develop; to spring up: Cybercafés are sprouting up everywhere.
➤ N **1** a new growth; a shoot or bud. **2** short form of **Brussels sprout**.

spruce[1] N **1** an evergreen pyramid-shaped tree which has needle-like leaves. **2** the valuable white-grained timber of this tree.

spruce[2] ADJ neat and smart, esp in appearance and dress.
➤ VB (usu **spruce up**) to make oneself, someone or something neat and tidy.

sprung ADJ fitted with a spring or springs.

spry ADJ **1** lively; active. **2** light on one's feet; nimble. ■ **spryly** ADV. ■ **spryness** N.

spud N, COLLOQ a potato.

spume N foam or froth, esp on the sea.

spun ADJ **1** made by a spinning process: spun gold. **2** IN COMPOUNDS: home-spun.

spunk N, COLLOQ mettle. ■ **spunky** ADJ.

spur N **1** a device with a spiky metal wheel, fitted to the heel of a horse-rider's boot, which is used for pressing into the horse's side to make it go faster. **2** anything that urges or encourages greater effort or progress. **3** a spike or pointed part, eg on a cock's leg. **4** a ridge of high land that projects out into a valley.
➤ VB (-**rr**-) **1** to urge: The crowd spurred their team to victory. **2** to press with spurs. **3** to hurry up.
◆ **earn** or **win one's spurs** FORMERLY to prove oneself worthy of a knighthood.
◆ **on the spur of the moment** suddenly; on an impulse.
◆ **spur sb** or **sth on** to incite, encourage, provoke, etc them.

spurious ADJ false, counterfeit or untrue, esp when superficially seeming to be genuine.

spurn VB to reject scornfully.
➤ N an act or instance of spurning.

spurt VB, TR & INTR to flow out or make something flow out in a sudden sharp jet.
➤ N **1** a jet of liquid that suddenly gushes out. **2** a short spell of intensified activity or increased speed: Business tends to come in spurts.

sputter same as **splutter**

sputum N (-**ta**) a mixture of saliva and mucus. Also called **phlegm**.

spy N (**spies**) **1** someone who is employed by a government or organization to gather information about political enemies, etc. **2** someone who observes others in secret.
➤ VB (**spies, spied**) **1** INTR to act or be employed as a spy. **2** to catch sight of someone or something; to spot.
◆ **spy on sb** or **sth** to keep a secret watch on them or it.

spyglass N a small hand-held telescope.

spyhole N a peephole.

squab N 1 a young unfledged bird, esp a pigeon. 2 a short fat person.

squabble VB, INTR to quarrel noisily, esp about something trivial.
➤ N a noisy quarrel, esp a petty one.
■ **squabbler** N.

squad N 1 a small group of soldiers, often twelve, who work together. 2 any group of people who work together in some specified field: **drug squad**. 3 a set of players from which a sporting team is selected.

squaddy or **squaddie** N (-ies) SLANG an ordinary soldier; a private.

squadron N the principal unit of an air force.

squalid ADJ 1 esp of places to live: disgustingly filthy and neglected. 2 morally repulsive; sordid: **gossip about their squalid affair**.

squall[1] N, METEOROL a sudden or short-lived violent gust of wind, usu accompanied by rain or sleet. ■ **squally** ADJ.

squall[2] VB, TR & INTR to yell.

squalor N the condition or quality of being disgustingly filthy.

squander VB to use up (money, time, etc) wastefully. ■ **squanderer** N.

square N 1 a two-dimensional figure with four sides of equal length and four right angles. 2 anything shaped like this. 3 an open space in a town, usu roughly square in shape, and the buildings that surround it. 4 an L-shaped or T-shaped instrument which is used for measuring angles, drawing straight lines, etc. 5 the number that is formed when a number is multiplied by itself, eg the square of 2 (usu written 2^2) is 4. 6 COLLOQ someone who has traditional or old-fashioned values, tastes, ideas, etc.
➤ ADJ 1 shaped like a square or, sometimes, like a cube. 2 used with a defining measurement to denote the area of something: **The area of a rectangle whose sides are 2 feet by 3 feet would be 6 square feet**. 3 angular; less rounded than normal: **a square jaw**.

4 measuring almost the same in breadth as in length or height. 5 fair; honest: **a square deal**. 6 of debts: completely paid off: **now we're square**. 7 set at right angles. 8 COLLOQ, OLD USE having traditional or old-fashioned values, etc.
➤ VB 1 to make square in shape, esp to make right-angled. 2 to multiply (a number) by itself. 3 to pay off or settle (a debt). 4 to make the scores level in (a match). 5 to mark with a pattern of squares.
➤ ADV 1 solidly and directly: **hit me square on the jaw**. 2 fairly; honestly. ■ **squarely** ADV.
■ **squareness** N.
◆ **all square** COLLOQ 1 equal. 2 not in debt; with each side owing nothing.
◆ **a square peg in a round hole** something or someone that cannot or does not perform its or their function very well; a misfit.
◆ **square up** to settle a bill, etc.
◆ **square up to sb** to prepare to fight them.
◆ **square sth with sb** to get their approval or permission for it.
◆ **square with sth** to agree with it.

square bracket N either of a pair of characters ([ ]), chiefly used in mathematical notation or to contain special information.

square deal N, COLLOQ an arrangement or transaction that is considered to be fair and honest by all the parties involved.

square meal N a good nourishing meal.

square-rigged ADJ of a sailing ship: fitted with large square sails set at right angles to the length of the ship.

square root N, MATH (symbol $\sqrt{}$) a number or quantity that when multiplied by itself gives one particular number, eg 2 is the square root of 4, and 3 is the square root of 9.

squash[1] VB 1 to crush or flatten by pressing or squeezing. 2 TR & INTR to force someone or something into a confined space: **managed to squash everything into one bag**. 3 to suppress or put down (eg a rebellion). 4 to force someone into silence with a cutting reply.
➤ N 1 a concentrated fruit syrup, or a drink made by diluting this. 2 a crushed or crowded state. 3 squash rackets. 4 **a** an act or the

process of squashing something; **b** the sound of something being squashed.

squash² N, N AMER, ESP US **1** any of various trailing plants widely cultivated for their marrow–like gourds. **2** the fruit of any of these plants which can be used as a vegetable.

squashy ADJ (**-ier, -iest**) soft and easily squashed.

squat VB (**-tt-**) INTR **1** to take up, or be sitting in, a low position with the knees fully bent and the weight on the soles of the feet. **2** usu of homeless people: to occupy an empty building without legal right.
➤ N **1** a squatting position. **2 a** a building or part of a building that is unlawfully occupied; **b** the unlawful occupation of such a building.
➤ ADJ short and broad or fat.

squatter N someone who unlawfully occupies a building, usu an empty one.

squawk N **1** a loud harsh screeching noise, esp one made by a bird, eg a parrot. **2** a loud protest or complaint.
➤ VB, INTR **1** to make a loud harsh screeching noise. **2** to complain loudly.

squeak N **1** a short high–pitched cry or sound, like that made by a mouse or a rusty gate. **2** (also **narrow squeak**) a narrow escape; a victory or success by a slim margin.
➤ VB, TR & INTR to utter a squeak or with a squeak. ■ **squeaky** ADJ (**-ier, -iest**).
◆ **squeak through sth** to succeed in it by a very narrow margin.

squeal N **1** a long high–pitched noise, cry or yelp, like that of a pig, a child, etc. **2** a screeching sound: **The squeal of brakes**.
➤ VB **1** TR & INTR to utter a squeal or with a squeal. **2** INTR, COLLOQ to inform (on someone) or to report an incident (to the police or other authority). **3** INTR to complain or protest loudly.

squeamish ADJ **1** slightly nauseous; easily made nauseous. **2** easily offended.

squeegee N a device with a rubber blade for scraping water off a surface, eg a window, etc.

squeeze VB **1** to grasp or embrace tightly. **2** to press forcefully, esp from at least two sides. **3** to press or crush so as to extract (liquid, juice, toothpaste, etc). **4** to press gently, esp as an indication of affection, reassurance, etc. **5** TR & INTR to force or be forced into a confined space. **6** to put under financial pressure.
➤ N **1** an act of squeezing. **2** a crowded or crushed state. **3** an amount (of fruit juice, etc) that is obtained by squeezing. **4** a restriction, esp on spending or borrowing money.
◆ **put the squeeze on sb** COLLOQ to pressurize them into paying something.
◆ **squeeze sth out 1** to force it from its place, container, etc. **2** to extract it, esp by exerting some form of pressure.

squeezy ADJ of a container, etc: soft so that its contents can be squeezed out.

squelch N a loud gurgling or sucking sound made by contact with a thick sticky substance.
➤ VB, INTR **1** to walk through wet ground or with water in one's shoes and so make this sound. **2** to make this sound.

squib N **1** a small firework that jumps around on the ground before exploding. **2** a satirical criticism or attack; a lampoon.

squid N (**squid** or **squids**) a marine mollusc related to the octopus and cuttlefish, which has a torpedo–shaped body, eight sucker–bearing arms and two longer tentacles.

squidgy ADJ (**-ier, -iest**) soft, pliant and sometimes soggy.

squiffy ADJ (**-ier, -iest**) OLD USE slightly drunk.

squiggle N a wavy scribbled line.
■ **squiggly** ADJ.

squint N **1** the condition of having one or both eyes set slightly off–centre, preventing parallel vision. **2** COLLOQ a quick look; a peep.
➤ VB, INTR **1** to be affected by a squint. **2** to look with eyes half–closed; to peer.
➤ ADJ **1** having a squint. **2** COLLOQ not being properly straight or centred.

squire N **1** HIST in England and Ireland: an owner of a large area of rural land, esp the chief landowner in a district. **2** FEUDALISM a young man of good family who ranked next to a knight and who would attend upon him.

squirm VB, INTR **1** to wriggle along. **2** to feel or show embarrassment, shame, etc often with slight wriggling movements of the body.

squirrel N a rodent that has a bushy tail and tufty ears, and usu lives in trees.

squirt VB **1 a** to shoot (a liquid, etc) out in a narrow jet; **b** INTR of a liquid, etc: to shoot out in a narrow jet: *Paint squirted everywhere.* **2** INTR to press the nozzle, trigger, etc of a container, etc so that liquid comes shooting out of it.
➤ N **1 a** an act or instance of squirting; **b** an amount of liquid squirted. **2** COLLOQ a small, insignificant or despicable person, esp one who behaves arrogantly.

squish N a gentle splashing or squelching sound.
➤ VB **1** INTR to make this sound; to move with this sound. **2** to crush (eg an insect, etc).

stab VB (-*bb*-) **1 a** to wound or pierce with a sharp or pointed instrument or weapon; **b** of a sharp instrument, etc: to wound or pierce; **c** to push (a sharp implement) into (someone or something). **2** (often **stab at sth**) to make a quick thrusting movement with something sharp at something.
➤ N **1** an act of stabbing. **2** a stabbing sensation: *felt a sudden stab of pain.*
■ **stabbing** N.
◆ **have** or **make a stab at sth** to try to do it.

stability N the state or quality of being stable.

stabilize or **-ise** VB, TR & INTR to make or become stable or more stable.

stabilizer or **-iser** N a device for stabilizing an aircraft, a ship or a child's bicycle.

stab in the back N a devious betrayal.
◆ **stab sb in the back** to carry out this kind of betrayal.

stable¹ ADJ **1** firmly balanced or fixed; not likely to wobble or fall over. **2** firmly established; not likely to be abolished, overthrown or destroyed: *a stable government • a stable relationship.* **3 a** regular or constant; not erratic or changing; under control: *The patient's condition is stable;* **b** of someone or their judgement, etc: not moody, impulsive, etc.

stable² N **1** a building where horses are kept. **2** a place where horses are bred and trained. **3** COLLOQ a number of people or things trained, organized or directed in a particular sport or activity by an individual or company.

staccato ADV, MUS in a short, abrupt manner.

stack N **1** a large pile. **2** a large pile of hay or straw. **3** (sometimes **stacks**) COLLOQ a large amount: *stacks of money.* **4** a large industrial chimney.
➤ VB **1** to arrange in a stack or stacks. **2** to arrange (circumstances, etc) to favour or disadvantage a particular person: *The odds were stacked against us.* **3** to arrange (aircraft that are waiting to land) into a queue in which each circles the airport at a different altitude.
◆ **stack sth up** to pile (things) up on top of each other.

stadium N (-*iums* or -*ia*) a large sports arena.

staff N (PL in senses 1–3 *staffs,* in senses 4–5 *staffs* or *staves*) **1 a** the total number of employees working in an organization; **b** the employees working for or assisting a manager. **2** the teachers, lecturers, etc of a school, college, university, etc as distinct from the students. **3** MIL the officers assisting a senior commander, AS ADJ: *staff sergeant.* **4** any stick or rod, esp one that is carried in the hand as a sign of authority, dignity, etc. **5** MUS a set of lines and spaces on which music is written. Also called **stave**.
➤ VB to provide (an establishment) with staff.

staff nurse N a qualified nurse of the rank below sister.

staff sergeant N, MIL the senior sergeant in an army company.

stag N an adult male deer, esp a red deer.

stage N **1** a platform on which a performance takes place, esp one in a theatre. **2** any raised area or platform. **3** the scene of a specified event: *view the stage of battle.* **4** any of several distinct and successive periods: *the planning stage.* **5** (**the stage**) the theatre as a profession or art form. **6 a** a part of a journey or route: *The last stage of the trip entails a short*

bus ride; **b** BRIT a major stop on a bus route, esp one that involves a change in ticket prices.
➤ VB **1** to present a performance of (a play). **2** to organize and put on something or set it in motion: **stage the festival**.

stagecoach N, FORMERLY a large horse-drawn coach carrying passengers and mail on a regular fixed route.

stage door N the back or side entrance to a theatre.

stage fright N nervousness felt by an actor or other performer or speaker when about to appear in front of an audience.

stagehand N someone who is responsible for moving scenery and props in a theatre.

stage-manage VB to prearrange for something to happen in a certain way, in order to create a particular effect.

stage name N a name assumed by an actor, performer, etc.

stage-struck ADJ having an overwhelming desire to become an actor or performer.

stage whisper N an actor's loud whisper that is intended to be heard by the audience.

stagey see **stagy**

stagger VB **1** INTR to walk or move unsteadily. **2** INFORMAL to cause extreme shock or surprise to someone. **3** to arrange (a series of things) so that they begin at different times.
➤ N the action or an act of staggering.
■ **staggering** ADJ. ■ **staggeringly** ADV.

stagnant ADJ **1** of water: not flowing; dirty and foul because of a lack of movement. **2** not moving or developing: **a stagnant market**.

stagnate VB, INTR to be or become stagnant.
■ **stagnation** N.

stag night and **stag party** N a night out for men only, esp one held to celebrate the end of bachelorhood of a man about to get married.

stagy or **stagey** ADJ, N AMER, esp US (**-ier, -iest**) theatrical; artificial or affected.

staid ADJ serious or sober, esp to the point of being dull.

stain VB **1** to make or become marked or discoloured, often permanently. **2** to change the colour of (eg wood) by applying a liquid chemical. **3** to tarnish or become tarnished: **The affair stained his previously good name**.
➤ N **1** a mark or discoloration. **2** a liquid chemical applied (eg to wood) to bring about a change of colour. **3** a cause of shame or dishonour: **a stain on his reputation**.

stained glass N decorative coloured glass used esp in church windows.

stainless steel N a type of rust-resistant steel with a high percentage of chromium.

stair N **1** any of a set of indoor steps connecting the floors of a building. **2** (also **stairs**) a set of these.

staircase N a set of stairs.

stairway N a way into a building or part of a building that involves going up a staircase.

stairwell N the vertical shaft containing a staircase.

stake¹ N **1** a stick or post, usu with one pointed end, that is knocked into the ground as a support, eg for a young tree or a fence. **2** (**the stake**) FORMERLY a post at which a person is tied and burned alive as a punishment.
◆ **stake a claim** to assert or establish a right or ownership, esp to a piece of land.

stake² N **1** a sum of money risked in betting. **2** an interest, esp a financial one: **have a stake in the project's success**.
➤ VB to risk, esp as a bet.
◆ **at stake** at risk; in danger.

stakeout N, COLLOQ an act or period of surveillance of a person, building, etc, usu carried out by the police or a private detective.

stalactite N an icicle-like mass of calcium carbonate found in caves.

stalagmite N a spiky mass of calcium carbonate that sticks up from the floor of a cave.

stale ADJ **1** of food: past its best because it has been kept too long; not fresh. **2** of air: not fresh; musty. **3** of words, phrases, ideas, etc: overused and no longer interesting or original. **4** of someone: lacking in energy because of overfamiliarity, boredom, etc with the job in hand. **5** of news, gossip, etc: out-of-date.

stalemate N **1** CHESS a position where either player cannot make a move without putting their king in check and which results in a draw. **2** a deadlock: **The staff and management had reached a stalemate over pay.**

stalk[1] N **1** BOT **a** the main stem of a plant; **b** a stem that attaches a leaf, flower or fruit to the plant. **2** any slender connecting part.

stalk[2] VB **1 a** to hunt, follow, or approach stealthily; **b** to follow someone persistently, esp for a sinister purpose. **2** INTR to walk or stride stiffly, proudly, disdainfully, etc. ■ **stalker** N.

stall[1] N **1** a compartment in a cowshed, stable, etc for housing a single animal. **2** a stand, often with a canopy, set up temporarily in a market place, bazaar, fête, etc for the selling of goods. **3** (**stalls**) the seats on the ground floor of a theatre or cinema.
➤ VB, TR & INTR of a motor vehicle or its engine: to cut out or make it cut out unintentionally.

stall[2] VB **1** to delay. **2** INTR to do something in order to delay something else; to be evasive.

stallion N an uncastrated adult male horse.

stalwart ADJ **1** strong and sturdy. **2** unwavering in commitment and support.
➤ N a long-standing and committed supporter, esp a political one: **the stalwarts of the right.**

stamen N (-*mens* or -*mina*) BOT in flowering plants: the male reproductive structure producing pollen.

stamina N energy and staying power, esp that needed to withstand prolonged exertion.

stammer VB, TR & INTR to speak or say something in a faltering or hesitant way, often by repeating words or parts of words.
➤ N a speech disorder that is characterized by this kind of faltering or hesitancy.

stamp VB **1** TR & INTR to bring (the foot) down with force: **stamped her feet in rage. 2** INTR to walk with a heavy tread. **3** to imprint or impress (a mark or design). **4** to fix or mark deeply: **The event was stamped on his memory. 5** to fix a postage or other stamp on something.
➤ N **1 a** a small piece of gummed paper bearing an official mark and indicating that a tax or fee has been paid, esp a postage stamp; **b** a similar piece of gummed paper that is given away free, eg by petrol stations, and which can be collected until the requisite number of them is held, when they can be exchanged for a gift. **2** a device for stamping a mark or design. **3** a characteristic mark or sign: **The crime bears the stamp of a professional.**
◆ **stamp sth out 1** to put an end to (an activity or practice, esp an illicit one): **tried to stamp out the use of drugs. 2** to eradicate (a disease).

stampede N **1** a sudden dash made by a group of startled animals, esp when they all go charging off in the same direction. **2** an excited or hysterical rush by a crowd of people.
➤ VB, TR & INTR to rush or make (animals or people) rush in a herd or crowd.

stance N **1** point of view; a specified attitude towards something. **2 a** the position that the body of a person or an animal takes up: **She has a very upright stance; b** a position or manner of standing.

stanchion N an upright beam or pole that functions as a support.

stand VB (*stood*) **1** INTR to be in, remain in or move into an upright position supported by the legs or a base. **2** TR & INTR to place or situate, or be placed or situated in a specified position: **stood the vase on the table. 3** INTR to be a specified height: **The tower stands 300 feet tall. 4** to tolerate or put up with someone or something: **How can you stand that awful noise? 5** INTR to continue to apply or be valid: **The decision stands. 6** to withstand or survive something: **stood the test of time.**
➤ N **1** a base on which something sits or is supported. **2** a stall that goods or services for sale are displayed on. **3 a** a structure at a sports ground, etc which has sitting or standing

accommodation for spectators; **b (the stand)** a witness box. **4** an opinion, attitude or course of action that is adopted resolutely: **took a stand against animal testing.**

◆ **stand by 1** to be in a state of readiness to act. **2** to look on without taking the required or expected action: **just stood by and never offered to help.**

stand by sb to give them loyalty or support, esp when they are in difficulty.

stand down to resign.

stand for sth 1 to be in favour of promoting it. **2** of a symbol, letter, device, etc: to represent, mean or signify something: **The red ribbon stands for AIDS awareness. 3** to tolerate it.

◆ **stand in for** to act as a substitute for.

stand one's ground to maintain a position resolutely; to refuse to give in.

stand out to be noticeable or prominent.

◆ **stand to reason** to be the logical or obvious assumption to make.

stand trial to go through the usual legal processes to establish guilt or innocence.

◆ **stand up 1** to assume a standing position. **2** to prove to be valid on examination: **an argument that will stand up in court.**

stand up for sb to back them in a dispute.

stand up for sth to support it.

◆ **stand up to sb** to face or resist them.

stand up to sth to withstand it.

standard N **1** an established or accepted model: **Size 14 is the standard for British women. 2** something that functions as a model of excellence for other similar things to be compared to, measured or judged against: **the standard by which all other dictionaries will be measured. 3** (often **standards**) **a** a degree or level of excellence, value, quality, etc: **Standards of living have fallen; b** a principle, eg of morality, integrity, etc: **moral standards. 4** a flag or other emblem, esp one carried on a pole: **the royal standard. 5** an upright pole or support.

➢ ADJ **1** having features that are generally accepted as normal or expected; typical: **A month's notice is standard practice. 2** accepted as supremely authoritative: **the standard text of Shakespeare.**

standard-bearer N **1** someone who carries a flag. **2** the leader of a movement or cause.

standardize or **-ise** VB to make (all the examples of something) conform in size, shape, etc. ■ **standardization** N.

standard lamp N a lamp at the top of a pole which has a base that sits on the floor.

standard of living N a measurement of the comparative wealth of a class or community, usu taken from their ability to afford certain commodities.

stand-by N **1 a** a state of readiness to act, eg in an emergency; **b** a person or thing that takes on this kind of role. **2** of air travel: a system of allocating spare seats to passengers who do not have reservations, after all the booked seats have been taken.

stand-in N a deputy or substitute.

standing N **1** position, status, or reputation. **2** the length of time something has been in existence, someone has been doing something, etc: **a professor of long standing.** ➢ ADJ done, taken, etc in or from a standing position: **a standing ovation.**

standing joke N a subject that causes hilarity or jeering whenever it is mentioned.

standing order N, FINANCE an instruction from an account-holder to a bank to make fixed payments from the account to a third party at regular intervals.

stand-off N a stalemate or the condition of being in stalemate.

stand-offish ADJ unfriendly or aloof.

standpipe N a vertical pipe leading from a water supply, esp one that provides an emergency supply in the street.

standpoint N a point of view.

standstill N a complete stop, with no progress being made at all.

stand-up ADJ **1** in a standing position. **2** of a verbal fight as well as a physical one: earnest; passionate; fervent. **3** of a comedian:

performing solo in front of a live audience and so likely to have to improvise.

stanza N a verse in poetry.

staple[1] N a squared-off U-shaped wire fastener for holding sheets of paper together.

staple[2] ADJ principal; main: **staple foods**.
➢ N **1** an economically important food, product, industry, export, etc. **2** a major constituent of a particular community's diet.

stapler N a device for driving staples through paper.

star N **1** any celestial body that can be seen in a clear night sky as a twinkling white light, which consists of a sphere of gaseous material which generates heat and light energy by means of nuclear fusion reactions deep within its interior. **2** a representation of such a body in the form of a figure with five or more radiating points, often used as a symbol of rank or excellence, as an award, etc. **3 a** a celebrity, esp in the world of entertainment or sport: **movie star**; **b** someone or something that is distinguished or thought well of in a specified field: **Her brilliant paper made her the star of the conference. 4** (**the stars**) **a** the planets regarded as an influence on people's fortunes: **believed his fate was in the stars**; **b** a horoscope. **5** an asterisk.
➢ VB (**-rr-**) TR & INTR to feature someone as a principal performer or to appear in (a film, TV programme, etc) as a principal performer.
◆ **see stars** to see spots of light before one's eyes, esp as a result of a blow to the head.

starboard N the right side of a ship or aircraft as you look towards the front of it.
➢ ADJ, ADV relating to, on or towards the right side.

starch N **1 a** BIOCHEM a carbohydrate that occurs in all green plants, where it serves as an energy store; **b** the fine white powder form of this substance that is extracted from potatoes and cereals and which is widely used in the food industry; **c** a preparation of this substance used to stiffen fabrics and to make paper. **2** stiffness of manner; over-formality.
➢ VB to stiffen with starch.

starchy ADJ (**-ier, -iest**) **1** like or containing starch. **2** of someone's manner, demeanour, etc: over-formal; solemn and prudish.

stardom N the state of being a celebrity.

stare VB, INTR of someone or their eyes: to look with a fixed gaze.
➢ N **1** an act of staring. **2** a fixed gaze.

starfish N the popular name for a star-shaped marine invertebrate animal.

stargaze VB, INTR to study the stars.
■ **stargazer** N. ■ **stargazing** N, ADJ.

stark ADJ **1** barren or severely bare; harsh or simple: **a stark landscape. 2** plain; unembellished: **the stark truth. 3** utter; downright: **an act of stark stupidity**.
➢ ADV completely: **stark staring bonkers**.

starkers ADJ, COLLOQ stark naked.

starlet N a young film actress, esp one who is thought to have the potential to become a star.

starlight N the light from the stars.

starling N a small common gregarious songbird which has dark glossy speckled feathers and a short tail.

starry ADJ (**-ier, -iest**) relating to or like a star or the stars; filled or decorated with stars.

starry-eyed ADJ naively idealistic.

star-studded ADJ **1** COLLOQ of the cast of a film, theatre production, etc: featuring many well-known performers. **2** covered with stars.

start VB **1** TR & INTR to begin; to bring or come into being. **2** TR & INTR to set or be set in motion, or put or be put into a working state: **She started the car. 3** to establish or set up: **started his own business. 4** to initiate or get going; to cause or set off: **Harry started the quarrel. 5** INTR to flinch suddenly, eg in fear or surprise.
➢ N **1** the first or early part. **2** a beginning, origin or cause. **3** the time or place at which something starts: **made an early start. 4** an advantage given or held at the beginning of a race or other contest: **gave her a two metre start. 5** sudden flinching or shrinking back.
◆ **start up** or **start sth up 1** of a car, engine,

etc: to run or get it running. **2** to establish it: **The mums started up their own playgroup.**

starter N **1** an official who gives the signal for a race to begin. **2** any of the competitors, horses, greyhounds, etc that assemble for the start of a race. **3** (also **starter motor**) an electric motor that is used to start the engine of a motor vehicle. **4** the first course of a meal.

startle VB, TR & INTR to be or cause someone or something to be slightly shocked or surprised. ■ **startling** ADJ.

starve VB **1** TR & INTR **a** to die or cause someone or something to die because of a long-term lack of food; **b** to suffer or cause someone or something to suffer because of a long-term lack of food. **2** INTR, COLLOQ to be very hungry. **3** to deprive of something that is vital: **starved the project of funds.** ■ **starvation** N.

stash N, SLANG a hidden supply or store of something.

state N **1** the condition, eg of health, appearance, emotions, etc that someone or something is in at a particular time. **2** a territory governed by a single political body; a nation. **3** any of a number of locally governed areas making up a nation or federation under the ultimate control of a central government, as in the US. **4** (**the States**) the United States of America. **5** (also **State** or **the State**) the political entity of a nation, including the government and all its apparatus, eg the civil service and the armed forces. **5** COLLOQ **a** an emotionally agitated condition: **He was in a right state**; **b** a confused or untidy condition: **What a state your room's in!**
➢ VB **1** to express clearly, either in written or spoken form; to affirm or assert. **2** to specify.
◆ **lie in state** of a dead person: to be ceremonially displayed to the public.

stately ADJ (**-ier, -iest**) noble, dignified and impressive in appearance or manner.

stately home N a large grand old house.

statement N **1** a thing stated, esp a formal written or spoken declaration: **made a statement to the press. 2 a** a record of

finances, esp one sent by a bank to an account-holder detailing the transactions within a particular period; **b** an account that gives details of the costs of materials, services, etc and the amount that is due to be paid.

state of the art N **1** the current level of advancement achieved by the most modern, up-to-date technology or thinking in a particular field. **2** (**state-of-the-art**) AS ADJ: **state-of-the-art technology.**

stateroom N **1** a large room in a palace, etc that is used for ceremonial occasions. **2** a large private cabin on a ship.

state school N a school that is state-funded and where the education is free.

statesman N a distinguished male politician. ■ **statesmanship** N.

static ADJ **1** not moving; stationary. **2** fixed; not portable. **3** relating to statics. **4** characteristic of or relating to TV or radio interference.
➢ N **1** (in full **static electricity**) an accumulation of electric charges that remain at rest instead of moving to form a flow of current, eg electricity produced by friction. **2** a sharp crackling or hissing sound that interferes with radio and television signals, and which is caused by static electricity or atmospheric disturbance.

statics SING N the branch of mechanics that deals with the action of balanced forces on bodies such that they remain at rest or in unaccelerated motion.

station N **1** a place where trains or buses regularly stop so that people can get off and on, goods can be loaded and unloaded, etc. **2** a local headquarters, eg of a police force, etc. **3** a building equipped for some particular purpose: **power station. 4** a radio or TV channel. **5** a position in a specified structure, organization, etc: **ideas above his station. 6** AUSTRAL & NZ a large farm that specializes in rearing sheep or cattle.
➢ VB to appoint to a post or place of duty.

stationary ADJ not moving; still.

stationer N a person or shop that sells stationery.

stationery N paper, envelopes, pens and other writing materials.

stationmaster N the official who is in charge of a railway station.

statistic N a specified piece of information or data. ■ **statistical** ADJ. ■ **statistically** ADV. ■ **statistician** N.

statistics PL N items of related information that have been collected, interpreted, analysed and presented to show particular trends. ➢ SING N the branch of mathematics concerned with drawing inferences from numerical data, based on probability theory, esp on the basis of an appropriate sample from a population.

statue N a sculpted, moulded or cast figure, esp of a person or animal, usu life–size or larger.

statuesque ADJ of someone's appearance: tall and well–proportioned.

statuette N a small statue.

stature N 1 the height of a person, animal, tree, etc. 2 greatness; eminence; importance. 3 the level of achievement someone has attained.

status N 1 rank or position in relation to others, within society, an organization, etc: social status. 2 legal standing, eg with regard to adulthood, marriage, citizenship, etc. 3 a high degree or level of importance; prestige: Her huge salary reflects the status of the job.

status quo N (usu **the status quo**) the existing situation at a given moment.

status symbol N a possession that represents wealth, high social standing, etc.

statute N 1 a a law made by the legislative assembly of a country and recorded in a formal document; b the formal document where such a law is recorded. 2 a permanent rule drawn up by an organization, esp one that governs its internal workings or the conduct of its members.

statutory ADJ required by law or a rule.

staunch[1] ADJ loyal; trusty; steadfast. ■ **staunchly** ADV. ■ **staunchness** N.

staunch[2] VB to stop the flow of (something, such as blood from a wound).

stave N 1 any of the vertical wooden strips that are joined together to form a barrel, tub, boat hull, etc. 2 MUS a staff. ➢ VB (*staved* or *stove*) 1 (often **stave in**) to smash (a hole, etc in something): The door was staved in. 2 (in this sense PA T only *staved*) (often **stave off**) a to delay the onset of something: tried to stave off his downfall by calling an election; b to ward off something: staved her hunger with an apple.

stay[1] VB, INTR 1 to remain in the same place or condition, without moving or changing. 2 to reside temporarily, eg as a guest. ➢ N 1 a period of temporary residence; a visit. 2 a postponement of a legally enforceable punishment: grant a stay of execution.

stay[2] N 1 a prop or support. 2 (**stays**) a corset stiffened with strips of bone or metal.

staying power N stamina; endurance.

stead N (usu **in sb's stead**) in place of them. ◆ **stand sb in good stead** to prove useful to them.

steadfast ADJ resolute. ■ **steadfastly** ADV.

steady ADJ (**-ier, -iest**) 1 firmly fixed or balanced; not wobbling. 2 regular; constant; unvarying: a steady job. 3 stable; not easily disrupted or undermined. 4 having a serious or sober character. 5 continuous: a steady stream. ➢ VB (**-ies, -ied**) TR & INTR to make or become steady or steadier. ■ **steadily** ADV. ■ **steadiness** N. ◆ **go steady with sb** COLLOQ to have a steady romantic relationship with them.

steak N 1 a fine quality beef for frying or grilling; b a thick slice of this: fillet steak. 2 beef that is cut into chunks and used for stewing or braising. 3 a thick slice of any meat or fish.

steal VB (PA T *stole*, PA P *stolen*) 1 TR & INTR to take away (another person's property) without permission or legal right, esp secretly. 2 to obtain something by cleverness or trickery: steal a kiss. 3 fraudulently to present (another

person's work, ideas, etc) as one's own. **4** INTR to go stealthily: **stole down to the basement.**
◆ **steal the show** to attract the most applause, attention, publicity, admiration, etc.

stealth N **1** softness and quietness of movement in order to avoid being noticed. **2** secretive or deceitful behaviour. ■ **stealthy** ADJ (*-ier, -iest*). ■ **stealthily** ADV.

steam N **a** the colourless gas formed by vaporizing water at 100°C; **b** any similar vapour, esp one that is produced when an aqueous liquid is heated.
➤ VB **1** INTR to give off steam. **2** to cook, etc using steam. **3** INTR, COLLOQ to go at speed: **steamed up the road to catch the bus.**
◆ **full steam ahead** forward as fast as possible or with as much energy, enthusiasm, gusto, etc as possible.
◆ **let off steam** to release bottled-up energy or emotions, eg anger.
◆ **run out of steam** to become depleted of energy, power, enthusiasm, etc.
◆ **under one's own steam** unassisted.

steamboat N a vessel that is driven by steam.

steam engine N **1** an engine that is powered by steam from a boiler that is heated by a furnace. **2** a steam locomotive engine.

steamer N **1** a ship whose engines are powered by steam. **2** a two-tier pot in which food in the upper tier is cooked by the action of steam from water heated in the lower tier.

steamroller N a large vehicle, orig and still often steam-driven, that has huge heavy solid metal cylinders for wheels so that when it is driven over newly made roads it smooths, flattens and compacts the surface.
➤ VB, COLLOQ to use overpowering force or persuasion to secure the speedy movement or progress of something.

steamy ADJ (*-ier, -iest*) **1** full of, clouded by, emitting, etc steam. **2** COLLOQ sexy; erotic.

steed N a horse, esp one that is lively and bold.

steel N an iron alloy that contains small amounts of carbon and, in some cases, additional elements.

➤ VB (usu **steel oneself**) to harden oneself or prepare oneself emotionally, esp for something unpleasant or unwelcome. ■ **steely** ADJ.

steel band N a group, orig in the West Indies, who play music on oil or petrol drums which have had the tops specially beaten.

steel wool N thin strands of steel in a woolly mass, used for scrubbing and scouring.

steelworks SING OR PL N a factory where steel is manufactured. ■ **steelworker** N.

steep[1] ADJ **1** sloping sharply. **2** COLLOQ of a price, etc: unreasonably high. ■ **steeply** ADV.

steep[2] VB, TR & INTR to soak something thoroughly in liquid.
◆ **be steeped in sth** to be deeply involved in it: **a castle steeped in history.**

steeple N **1** a tower, esp one with a spire, of a church or temple. **2** the spire itself.

steeplechase N **1** a horse race round a course with hurdles, usu in the form of man-made hedges. **2** a track running race where athletes have to jump hurdles and, usu, a water jump. ■ **steeplechaser** N.

steeplejack N someone whose job is to construct and repair steeples and tall chimneys.

steer[1] VB **1** TR & INTR to guide or control the direction of (a vehicle or vessel) using a steering wheel, rudder, etc. **2** INTR to tend towards a specified direction: **This car steers to the right. 3** to guide or encourage (someone, a conversation, etc) to move in a specified direction: **steered the conversation round to the subject of money.**
◆ **steer clear of sb** or **sth** COLLOQ to avoid them or it.

steer[2] N a young castrated bull or male ox.

steering-wheel N a wheel that is turned by hand to direct the wheels of a vehicle or the rudder of a vessel.

stellar ADJ **1** of, relating to or resembling a star or stars. **2** of or relating to the famous.

stem[1] N **1 a** the central part of a plant that grows upward from its root; **b** the part that connects a leaf, flower or fruit to a branch. **2** any long slender part, eg of a wine glass. ➤ VB (-*mm*-) INTR (**stem from sth** or **sb**) to originate or derive from it or them.

stem² VB (-*mm*-) to stop (a flow).

stench N a strong unpleasant smell.

stencil N **1** a card or plate that has shapes cut out of it to form a pattern, letter, etc and which is put onto a surface and ink or paint applied so that the cut-out design is transferred to the surface. **2** the design produced by this technique. ➤ VB (-*ll*- or (US) -*l*-) to mark or decorate (a surface) using a stencil.

stentorian ADJ, LITERARY of a voice: strong.

step N **1** a single complete action of lifting then placing down the foot in walking or running. **2** the distance covered in the course of such an action. **3** a movement of the foot (usu one of a pattern of movements) in dancing. **4** a single action or measure that is taken in proceeding towards an end or goal: **a step in the right direction. 5** (often **steps**) **a** a single (often outdoor) stair, or any stair-like support used to climb up or down; **b** a stepladder. **6** the sound or mark of a foot being laid on the ground, etc in walking. **7** a degree or stage in a scale or series: **moved up a step on the payscale.** ➤ VB (-*pp*-) INTR **1** to move by lifting up each foot alternately and setting it down in a different place. **2** to go or come on foot: **Step right this way.**

◆ **in step 1** walking, marching, etc in time with others or with the music. **2** in harmony, unison, agreement, etc with another or others.

◆ **out of step 1** not walking, marching, etc in time with others or with the music. **2** not in harmony, unison, etc with another or others.

◆ **step down** to resign.

◆ **step in** to intervene in an argument.

◆ **step up** to increase the rate, intensity, etc of something.

◆ **take steps to** to take action in order to.

◆ **watch one's step 1** to walk with careful steps. **2** to proceed with caution.

stepbrother and **stepsister** N a son or

daughter of someone's step-parent.

stepchild, **stepdaughter** and **stepson** N a child of someone's spouse or partner who is the offspring of a previous relationship.

stepfather N a husband or partner of a person's mother who is not that person's biological father.

stepladder N a short ladder with flat steps and with a supporting frame.

stepmother N a wife or partner of a person's father who is not that person's biological mother.

step-parent N a stepfather or stepmother.

steppe N an extensive dry grassy treeless plain, esp one found in SE Europe and Asia.

stepping-stone N **1** a large stone that has a surface which is above the water level of a stream, etc and which can be used for crossing over to the other side. **2** something that functions as a means of progress.

stepson see under **stepchild**

steradian N, GEOM the SI unit that is used for measuring solid (three-dimensional) angles.

stereo N **1** stereophonic reproduction of sound. **2** a cassette player, record player, hi-fi system, etc that gives a stereophonic reproduction of sound. ➤ ADJ a shortened form of **stereophonic**.

stereophonic ADJ of a system for reproducing or broadcasting sound: using two or more independent sound channels leading to separate loudspeakers, in order to simulate the depth and physical separation of different sounds that would be experienced at a live performance.

stereotype N **a** an over-generalized and preconceived idea or impression of what characterizes someone or something, esp one that does not allow for any individuality or variation; **b** someone or something that conforms to such an idea, etc. ➤ VB to attribute over-generalized and preconceived characteristics to someone or something. ■ **stereotypical** ADJ.

sterile ADJ 1 biologically incapable of producing offspring, fruit or seeds. 2 free of germs. ■ **sterility** N.

sterilize or **-ise** VB 1 to make something germ-free. 2 to make someone or something infertile. ■ **sterilization** N.

sterling N 1 British money. 2 a the official level of purity that silver must conform to; b AS ADJ: sterling silver.
➤ ADJ 1 good quality; reliable: a sterling performance. 2 genuine.

stern[1] ADJ 1 extremely strict; authoritarian. 2 harsh, severe or rigorous. ■ **sternly** ADV. ■ **sternness** N.

stern[2] N the rear of a ship or boat.

sternum N (*-nums* or *-na*) ANAT in humans: the broad vertical bone in the chest that the ribs and collarbone are attached to. Also called **breastbone**.

steroid N 1 BIOCHEM any of a large group of fat-soluble organic compounds that have a complex molecular structure (17-carbon-atom, four-linked ring system), and which are important both physiologically and pharmacologically. 2 MED a class of drug containing such a compound.

stethoscope N, MED an instrument that consists of a small concave disc that has hollow tubes attached to it and which, when it is placed on the body, carries sounds.

stetson N a man's broad-brimmed felt hat with a high crown, worn esp by cowboys.

stevedore N someone whose job is to load and unload ships; a docker.

stew VB 1 TR & INTR to cook (esp meat) by long simmering. 2 a to cause (tea) to become bitter and over-strong by letting it brew for too long; b INTR of tea: to become bitter and over-strong because it has been left brewing for too long. 3 INTR, COLLOQ to be in a state of worry.
➤ N 1 a dish of food, esp a mixture of meat and vegetables, that has been cooked by stewing. 2 COLLOQ a state of worry.

steward N 1 someone whose job is to look after the needs of passengers on a ship. 2 someone whose duties include supervising crowd movements during sporting events, gigs, etc. 3 someone whose job is to oversee the catering arrangements, etc in a hotel or club.

stewardess N a female steward on a ship.

stewed ADJ 1 of meat, vegetables, fruit, etc: cooked by stewing: **stewed prunes**. 2 of tea: bitter and over-strong because it has been brewed for too long. 3 COLLOQ drunk.

stick[1] N 1 a twig or thin branch of a tree. 2 a any long thin piece of wood; b IN COMPOUNDS a shaped piece of wood or other material which has a designated purpose: **hockey stick**. 3 a long thin piece of anything: **a stick of rock**. 4 COLLOQ verbal abuse, criticism or mockery. 5 (**the sticks**) COLLOQ a rural area that is considered remote or unsophisticated.
◆ **get hold of the wrong end of the stick** to misunderstand a situation, a statement, etc.

stick[2] VB (*stuck*) 1 to push or thrust (esp something long and thin or pointed). 2 to fasten by piercing with a pin or other sharp object: **stick it up with drawing-pins**. 3 TR & INTR to fix, or be or stay fixed, with an adhesive. 4 INTR to remain persistently: **an episode that sticks in my mind**. 5 TR & INTR to make or be unable to move: **The car got stuck in the snow**. 6 to confine: **stuck in the house all day**. 7 COLLOQ to place or put: **just stick it on the table**. 8 COLLOQ to bear or tolerate: **could not stick it any longer**. 9 to cause to be at a loss; to baffle: **He's never stuck for something to say**.
◆ **stick by sb** or **sth** to remain loyal or supportive towards them or it: **She sticks by him no matter what he does**.
◆ **stick out** 1 to project or protrude. 2 to be obvious or noticeable. 3 to endure.
◆ **stick out for sth** to continue to insist on it.
◆ **stick to sth** 1 to remain faithful to it, eg a promise: **stuck to the same story throughout the questioning**. 2 to keep to it, eg a matter under discussion without digressing.
◆ **stick up for sb** or **oneself** to speak or act in their or one's own defence.

sticker N a small adhesive label.

stick insect N a tropical insect with a long slender body and legs that are camouflaged to look like twigs.

stick-in-the-mud N, COLLOQ someone who is opposed to anything new or adventurous and is therefore seen as boring and dull.

stickleback N a small spiny-backed fish found in many northern rivers.

stickler N (usu **a stickler for sth**) someone who fastidiously insists on something.

sticky ADJ (-*ier, -iest*) 1 covered with something that is tacky or gluey. 2 of the weather: warm and humid; muggy. ∎ **stickiness** N.

sticky wicket N, COLLOQ a difficult situation.

stiff ADJ 1 not easily bent or folded; rigid. 2 of limbs, joints, etc: lacking suppleness. 3 of a punishment, etc: harsh. 4 of a task, etc: difficult. 5 of someone or their manner: not natural and relaxed. 6 thick in consistency; viscous. 7 COLLOQ of an alcoholic drink: not diluted or only lightly diluted; strong.
➤ N, SLANG a corpse. ∎ **stiffly** ADV. ∎ **stiffness** N.

stiffen VB 1 TR & INTR to make or become stiff or stiffer. 2 INTR to become nervous or tense.

stifle VB 1 **a** to suppress (a feeling or action): stifled a laugh; **b** to conceal: stifled the truth. 2 TR & INTR to experience or cause to experience difficulty in breathing, esp because of heat and lack of air. 3 to kill or nearly kill by stopping the breathing; to smother.

stifling ADJ 1 unpleasantly hot or airless. 2 overly oppressive. ∎ **stiflingly** ADV.

stigma N 1 shame or social disgrace. 2 BOT in a flowering plant: the sticky surface that receives pollen.

stigmata PL N, CHRISTIANITY marks that are said to have appeared on the bodies of certain holy people and are thought to resemble Christ's crucifixion wounds.

stigmatize or **-ise** VB to describe, regard, single out, etc someone as bad, shameful, etc.

stile N a step, or set of steps, that is incorporated into a fence or wall so that people can cross but animals cannot.

stiletto N (in full **stiletto heel**) a high thin heel on a woman's shoe.

still[1] ADJ 1 motionless; inactive; silent. 2 quiet and calm; tranquil. 3 of a drink: not having escaping bubbles of carbon dioxide.
➤ ADV 1 continuing as before, now or at some future time: Do you still live in Edinburgh? 2 up to the present time, or the time in question; yet: I still don't understand. 3 even then; nevertheless: knows the dangers but still smokes. 4 quietly and without movement: sit still. 5 to a greater degree; even: older still.
➤ VB 1 TR & INTR to make or become still, silent, etc. 2 to calm, appease, or end something.
➤ N 1 stillness; tranquillity: the still of the countryside. 2 a photograph, esp of an actor in, or a scene from, a cinema film. ∎ **stillness** N.

still[2] N an apparatus for the distillation of alcoholic spirit.

stillbirth N the birth of a dead baby or fetus.

stillborn ADJ of a baby: dead when born.

still life N 1 a painting, drawing or photograph of an object or objects, eg a bowl of fruit, rather than of a living thing. 2 this kind of art or photography.

stilt N 1 either of a pair of long poles that have supports for the feet so that someone can walk around high above the ground. 2 any of a set of props on which a building, jetty, etc is supported above ground or water level.

stilted ADJ 1 of language: unnatural-sounding and over-formal. 2 laboured or jarring; not flowing: a stilted conversation.

stimulant N 1 any substance, such as a drug, that produces an increase in the activity of a particular body organ or function, eg caffeine, nicotine, amphetamines. 2 anything that causes an increase in excitement, activity, interest, etc.
➤ ADJ stimulating.

stimulate VB 1 to cause physical activity, or increased activity, in (eg an organ of the body). 2 to excite or arouse the senses of someone. 3 to create interest and enthusiasm in someone or something. ■ **stimulation** N.

stimulating ADJ exciting; invigorating.

stimulus N (-*li*) **1** something that acts as an incentive, provocation, etc. **2** something, such as a drug, heat, light, etc, that causes a specific response in a cell, tissue, organ, etc.

sting N **1** a defensive puncturing organ that is found in certain animals and plants, which can inject poison or venom. **2** the injection of poison from an animal or plant. **3** a painful wound resulting from the sting of an animal or plant. **4** any sharp tingling pain.
➤ VB (*stung*) **1** to pierce, poison or wound with a sting. **2** INTR to produce a sharp tingling pain.

stingray N a flatfish with a long whip–like tail tipped with spikes that are capable of inflicting severe wounds.

stingy ADJ (-*ier, -iest*) ungenerous; mean; miserly. ■ **stingily** ADV. ■ **stinginess** N.

stink N **1** a strong and very unpleasant smell. **2** COLLOQ an angry complaint; a fuss.
➤ VB (PAT *stank* or *stunk*, PAP *stunk*) **1** INTR to give off an offensive smell. **2** INTR, COLLOQ to be contemptibly bad or unpleasant: **The idea of going with Harry stinks**.

stinker N, COLLOQ **1** a very difficult task, question, etc. **2** someone who behaves in a dishonest or otherwise unpleasant way.

stinking ADJ **1** offensively smelly. **2** COLLOQ very unpleasant, disgusting, etc.
➤ ADV, COLLOQ extremely: **stinking rich**.

stint VB (**stint on**) to be mean or grudging in giving something: **Don't stint on the sauce**.
➤ N **1** an allotted amount of work or a fixed time for it: **a ten hour stint**. **2** a turn: **did his stint**.

stipend N a salary or allowance, now esp one that is paid to a member of the clergy.

stipple VB to paint, engrave or draw something in dots or dabs as distinct from using lines or masses of colour.

stipulate VB in a contract, etc: to specify as a necessary condition. ■ **stipulation** N.

stir VB (-*rr*-) **1** to mix or agitate (a liquid or semi-liquid substance) by repeated circular strokes with a spoon or other utensil. **2** to arouse the emotions of someone. **3** to make a slight or single movement: **she stirred in her sleep**. **4** INTR to get up after sleeping. **5** to rouse (oneself) to action. **6** to evoke something: **The photos stirred happy memories**. **7** INTR, COLLOQ to make trouble.
➤ N **1** an act of stirring (a liquid, etc). **2** an excited reaction; a commotion.
◆ **stir up sth** to cause or provoke (eg trouble).

stir-crazy ADJ, orig N AMER SLANG emotionally disturbed through long confinement.

stir-fry VB to cook (food) lightly by brisk frying in a wok or large frying pan on a high heat.
➤ N a dish of food cooked in this way.

stirrer N, COLLOQ someone who deliberately goes about making trouble.

stirring ADJ **1** arousing strong emotions. **2** lively.

stirrup N either of a pair of leather or metal loops attached to a horse's saddle, which are used as footrests for the rider.

stitch N **1** a single interlinking loop of thread or yarn in sewing or knitting. **2** a sharp ache in the side resulting from physical exertion. **3** NON-TECHNICAL a **suture**.
➤ VB **1** to join, close, decorate, etc with stitches. **2** to sew. **3** NON-TECHNICAL to close a cut, wound, etc with stitches.
◆ **in stitches** COLLOQ helpless with laughter.
◆ **without a stitch** or **not a stitch** COLLOQ without any clothing or no clothing at all.

stoat N a small flesh–eating mammal that has a long slender body and reddish–brown fur with white underparts.

stock N **1** (sometimes **stocks**) goods or raw material that a shop, factory, warehouse, etc has on the premises at a given time. **2** a supply kept in reserve: **an impressive stock of fine wine**. **3** equipment or raw material in use. **4** liquid in which meat or vegetables have been cooked and is then used as a base for soup, a sauce, etc. **5** the shaped wooden or plastic part of a rifle or similar gun that the user rests

against their shoulder. **6** farm animals; livestock. **7** the money raised by a company through the selling of shares. **8** the total shares issued by a particular company or held by an individual shareholder. **9** ancestry; descent: **of peasant stock**. **10** any of various plants of the wallflower family cultivated for their bright flowers. **11** (**the stocks**) FORMERLY a wooden device that was used for securing offenders who were held by the head and wrists or by the wrists and ankles, so that they could be displayed for public ridicule as a punishment.
➤ ADJ **1** being of a standard type, size, etc, constantly in demand and always kept in stock. **2** of a phrase, etc: much used, esp so over-used as to be meaningless.
➤ VB **1** to keep a supply for sale. **2** to provide with a supply: **stocked the drinks cabinet**.
◆ **in stock** currently held for sale on the premises.
◆ **out of stock** not currently held for sale on the premises.
◆ **stock up on sth** to acquire or accumulate a large supply of it.
◆ **take stock of sth** to make an overall assessment of one's circumstances, etc.

stockade N a defensive fence or enclosure that is built of upright tall heavy posts.

stockbroker N someone whose profession is to buy and sell stocks and shares on behalf of customers in return for a fee.

stock car N a car that has been specially strengthened and modified for competing in a kind of track racing where deliberate ramming and colliding are allowed.

stock exchange N **1 a** a market where the trading of stocks and shares by professional dealers on behalf of customers goes on; **b** a building where this type of trading is done. **2** (usu **the stock exchange**) the level of prices in this type of market or the amount of activity that this type of market generates.

stocking N either of a pair of close-fitting coverings for women's legs which are made of fine semi-transparent nylon or silk.

stocking stitch N, KNITTING a way of joining loops together that involves the alternation of plain and purl rows.

stock-in-trade N something that is seen as fundamental to a particular trade or activity.

stockist N a person or shop that stocks a particular item or brand.

stock market N the stock exchange.

stockpile N a large reserve supply.
➤ VB to accumulate a large reserve supply.

stockroom N a storeroom, esp in a shop.

stock-still ADJ, ADV completely motionless.

stocktaking N **1** the process of making a detailed inventory and valuation of all the goods, raw materials, etc that are held on the premises of a shop, factory, etc at a particular time. **2** the process of making an overall assessment eg of the present situation with regard to one's future prospects, etc.

stocky ADJ (**-ier, -iest**) of a person or animal: broad, strong-looking and usu not very tall. ■ **stockily** ADV. ■ **stockiness** N.

stockyard N a large yard where livestock are kept temporarily, eg before being auctioned.

stodge N food that is heavy, filling and, usually, fairly tasteless.

stodgy ADJ (**-ier, -iest**) of food: heavy and filling but usu fairly tasteless and unappetizing.

stoic N someone who can repress emotions and show patient resignation under difficult circumstances. ■ **stoical** ADJ. ■ **stoicism** N.

stoke VB **1** to put coal or other fuel on (eg a fire, the furnace of a boiler). **2** to arouse or intensify (eg passion or enthusiasm). ■ **stoker** N.

stole N a woman's scarf-like garment, often made of fur, that is worn around the shoulders.

stolid ADJ showing little or no interest or emotion. ■ **stolidity** N. ■ **stolidly** ADV.

stomach N **1** in the alimentary canal of vertebrates: a large sac-like organ where food is temporarily stored until it is partially digested. **2** LOOSELY the area around the abdomen.
➤ VB, COLLOQ to bear or put up with: **can't**

stomach his arrogance.

◆ **have the stomach for sth** COLLOQ to have the inclination, desire, courage, etc for it: has the stomach for dangerous sports.

stomach pump N an apparatus used medically for sucking out the contents of the stomach, eg in cases of drug overdosing.

stone N (*stones* or in sense 7 *stone*) **1** the hard solid material that rocks are made of. **2 a** a small fragment of rock, eg a pebble; **b** anything that resembles this: **hailstone**. **3** USU IN COMPOUNDS a shaped piece of stone that has a designated purpose, eg paving stone, tombstone, etc. **4** a gemstone. **5** the hard woody middle part of some fruits, eg peach, plum, etc, which contains the seed. **6** a hard mass that sometimes forms in the gall bladder, kidney, etc, which often causes pain and which often requires surgical removal. **7** a UK measure of weight equal to 14 pounds.
➢ VB **1** to pelt with stones as a punishment. **2** to remove the stone from (fruit).
◆ **leave no stone unturned** to make every possible effort.
◆ **a stone's throw** COLLOQ a short distance.

stone-cold ADV completely: stone-cold sober.

stoned ADJ, SLANG **1** in a state of drug-induced euphoria. **2** of a fruit: with the stone removed.

stonemason N someone who is skilled in shaping stone for building work.

stonewall VB, TR & INTR to hold up progress, esp in parliament, intentionally, eg by obstructing discussion, giving long irrelevant speeches, etc.

stoneware N a type of hard coarse pottery made from clay that has a high proportion of silica, sand or flint in it.

stonewashed ADJ of new clothes or a fabric, esp denim: having a faded and worn appearance because of being washed with small pieces of pumice stone.

stonework N a structure or building part that has been made out of stone.

stony or **stoney** ADJ (*-ier, -iest*) **1** covered with stones. **2** unfriendly; unfeeling; callous: a stony expression. **3 a** fixed: a stony stare; **b** unrelenting: a stony silence. ■ **stonily** ADV.

stony-broke ADJ, BRIT COLLOQ penniless.

stooge N **1** a performer whose function is to provide a comedian with opportunities for making jokes and who is often also the butt of the jokes. **2** an assistant, esp one who is exploited in some way.

stool N **1** a seat without a back. **2** faeces.

stoop VB, INTR **1** to bend the upper body forward and down. **2** to walk with head and shoulders bent forward.
➢ N a bent posture: **walks with a stoop**.
◆ **stoop to sth 1** to degrade oneself to do it: **How could you stoop to stealing?** **2** to deign or condescend to do it.

stop VB (*-pp-*) **1** TR & INTR to bring or come to rest, a standstill or an end; to cease or cause to cease moving, operating or progressing. **2** to prevent. **3** to withhold or keep something back. **4** to block, plug or close something. **5** to instruct a bank not to honour (a cheque). **6** INTR, COLLOQ to stay or reside temporarily: **stopped the night with friends**.
➢ N **1** an act of stopping. **2** a regular stopping place, eg on a bus route. **3** the state of being stopped; a standstill. **4** a device that prevents further movement: **a door stop**. **5** a temporary stay, esp when it is en route for somewhere else. **6** PHONETICS a consonant sound that is made by the sudden release of air that has built up behind the lips, teeth, etc eg **c** in **cat**.
◆ **put a stop to sth** to cause it to end.
◆ **stop at nothing** to be prepared to do anything, no matter how unscrupulous, in order to achieve an aim, outcome, etc.
◆ **stop off**, **in** or **by** to visit, esp on the way to somewhere else.
◆ **stop over** to make a break in a journey.

stopcock N a valve that controls the flow of liquid, gas, steam, etc in a pipe.

stopgap N a temporary substitute.

stop-off and **stop-over** N a brief or temporary stop during a longer journey.

stoppage N **1** an act of stopping. **2** an

organized withdrawal of labour.

stopper N a cork, plug or bung.

stop press N late news that can be placed in a specially reserved space of a newspaper even after printing has begun.

stopwatch N a watch that is used for recording the elapsed time in races, etc.

storage N 1 the act of storing. 2 space reserved for storing things. 3 COMP the act or process of storing information in a computer's memory.

storage device N, COMP any piece of equipment, such as a magnetic disk, that data can be stored on.

storage heater N a device that accumulates and stores heat (usu generated from overnight off-peak electricity) which is then slowly released during the daytime.

store N 1 a supply, usu one that is kept in reserve for use in the future. 2 BRIT a shop, esp a large one that is part of a chain: **department store**. 3 (also **stores**) a place where stocks or supplies are kept, eg a warehouse. 4 a computer's memory.
➤ VB 1 (also **store away** or **store up**) to put aside for future use. 2 to put something, eg furniture, into a warehouse for safekeeping. 3 to put something into a computer's memory.
◆ **in store** imminent: **a surprise in store**.

store card N a credit card that is issued by a department store for exclusive use in that store or any of its branches.

storehouse N a place where things are stored.

storeroom N 1 a room that is used for keeping things in. 2 space for storing things.

storey or (N AMER, ESP US) **story** N (*storeys* or *stories*) a level, floor or tier of a building.

stork N a large wading bird with long legs, and a long bill and neck.

storm N 1 an outbreak of violent weather, with severe winds and heavy falls of rain, hail or snow that is often accompanied by thunder and lightning. 2 a violent reaction, outburst or show of feeling: **a storm of protest**.
➤ VB 1 INTR to go or come loudly and angrily: **stormed out of the meeting**. 2 to say or shout something angrily: **stormed abuse at him**. 3 MIL to make a sudden violent attack on something.
◆ **take sb** or **sth by storm** 1 to enthral or captivate them or it totally and instantly. 2 MIL to capture them or it by storming.

stormtrooper N, HIST a member of a parliamentary wing of the Nazi party.

stormy ADJ (*-ier, -iest*) 1 affected by storms or high winds. 2 of a person or their temperament, etc or of circumstances, etc: characterized by violence, passion, emotion, tantrums, etc.

story[1] N (*-ies*) 1 a written or spoken description of an event or series of events which can be real or imaginary. 2 the plot of a novel, play, film, etc. 3 an incident, event, etc that has the potential to be interesting, amusing, etc. 4 a news article.

story[2] see **storey**

storybook N a book that contains a tale or a collection of tales, esp one for children.

storyline N the plot of a novel, play or film.

story-teller N 1 someone who tells stories, esp someone who does this in conversation habitually or exceptionally well. 2 COLLOQ a liar.

stout ADJ 1 of someone: well-built; fattish. 2 hard-wearing; robust. 3 courageous; steadfastly reliable.
➤ N dark beer that has a strong malt flavour.
■ **stoutly** ADV. ■ **stoutness** N.

stout-hearted ADJ courageous.

stove[1] N 1 a domestic cooker. 2 any cooking or heating apparatus, eg an industrial kiln.

stove[2] see **stave**

stow VB (often **stow sth away**) to pack or store it, esp out of sight.
◆ **stow away** to hide on a ship, aircraft or vehicle in the hope of travelling free.

stowaway N someone who hides on a ship, aeroplane, etc in the hope of being able to get to the destination undetected and so avoid paying the fare.

straddle VB 1 to have one leg or part on either side of something or someone: **straddled the horse. 2** COLLOQ **a** to adopt a neutral or non-committal attitude towards something; **b** to seem to be in favour of or see the advantage of both sides of something at once.

strafe VB to attack someone or something with heavy machine-gun fire from a low-flying aircraft.

straggle VB, INTR 1 to grow or spread untidily. **2** to lag behind or stray from the main group or path, etc. ■ **straggler** N. ■ **straggly** ADJ.

straight ADJ 1 not curved, bent, curly or wavy, etc: **straight hair. 2** without deviations or detours; direct: **a straight road. 3** level; horizontal; not sloping, leaning, or twisted: **Is the picture straight? 4** frank; open; direct: **a straight answer. 5** respectable; legitimate; not dishonest or criminal: **a straight deal. 6** neat; tidy; in good order. **7** successive; in a row: **won three straight sets. 8** of a drink, esp alcoholic: undiluted; neat. **9** having all debts and favours paid back. **10** not comic; serious. **11** COLLOQ heterosexual.
➤ ADV **1** in or into a level, upright, etc position or posture. **2** following an undeviating course; directly: **went straight home. 3** immediately: **I'll come round straight after work. 4** honestly; frankly: **told him straight that it was over.**
■ **straightness** N.
◆ **straight away** immediately.
◆ **straight out** bluntly: **asked her straight out if she was seeing someone else.**
◆ **the straight and narrow** the honest, respectable, sober, etc way of life or behaving.

straighten VB, TR & INTR 1 to make or become straight. **2** (sometimes **straighten out sth**) to make something less complicated or put it into order. **3** INTR (often **straighten up**) to stand upright, esp after bending down.

straight face N an unsmiling expression which is usu hiding the desire to laugh.

straightforward ADJ 1 without difficulties or complications; simple. **2** frank.

strain[1] VB 1 to injure or weaken (oneself or a part of one's body) through over-exertion. **2** INTR to make violent efforts. **3** to make extreme use of or demands on something. **4** to pass something through or pour something into a sieve or colander. **5** to stretch or draw it tight. **6** (usu **strain at sth**) to tug it forcefully.
➤ N **1** an injury caused by over-exertion, esp a wrenching of the muscles. **2** an act of forceful mental or physical perseverance or effort: **Talking to her is such a strain. 3** the fatigue resulting from such an effort. **4** mental tension; stress. **5** (also **strains**) a melody or tune, or a snatch of one: **the strains of distant pipes.**
■ **strained** ADJ.

strain[2] N a group of animals (esp farm livestock) or plants (esp crops) that is maintained by inbreeding, etc so that particular characteristics can be retained.

strainer N a small sieve or colander.

strait N 1 (often **straits**) a narrow strip of water that links two larger areas of ocean or sea. **2** (**straits**) difficulty; hardship: **dire straits.**

straiten VB 1 to distress, esp financially. **2** to restrict. ■ **straitened** ADJ: **found themselves in straitened circumstances.**

straitjacket N a jacket which has very long sleeves that can be crossed over the chest and tied behind the back and which is used for restraining someone who has violent tendencies.

strait-laced ADJ of someone, their moral attitudes, opinions, etc: strictly correct; prudish.

strand[1] VB 1 to run (a ship) aground. **2** to leave someone helpless, eg without transport.

strand[2] N a single thread, fibre, length of hair, etc, either alone or twisted or plaited with others to form a rope, cord or braid.

strange ADJ 1 not known or experienced before. **2** unfamiliar or alien. **3** not usual, ordinary or predictable. ■ **strangely** ADV. ■ **strangeness** N.

stranger N 1 someone that one does not know. **2** someone who comes from a different place, home town, family, etc.

◆ **a stranger to sth** someone who is unfamiliar with or inexperienced in something.

strangle VB **1** to kill or attempt to kill by squeezing the throat with the hands, a cord, etc. **2** to hold back or suppress (eg a scream or laughter). **3** to hinder or stop (the development or expression of something): **The job strangled her creativity.** ■ **strangler** N.

stranglehold N a choking hold in wrestling.

strangulate VB **1** MED to press or squeeze so as to stop the flow of blood or air. **2** to strangle. ■ **strangulation** N.

strap N **1** a narrow strip of leather or fabric which can be used for hanging something from, carrying or fastening something, etc. **2** (also **shoulder strap**) either of a pair of strips of fabric by which a garment hangs from the shoulders. **3** a loop that hangs down on a bus or train to provide a hand-hold for a standing passenger.
➢ VB (**-pp-**) to fasten or bind something with a strap or straps. ■ **strapless** ADJ.

strap-hanger N, COLLOQ a standing passenger on a bus, train, etc, esp one who holds onto a strap.

strapped ADJ.
◆ **strapped for sth** in dire need of it.

strapping ADJ tall and strong-looking.

stratagem N a trick or plan, esp one for deceiving an enemy or gaining an advantage.

strategic ADJ **1** characteristic of or relating to strategy or a strategy. **2** of weapons: designed for a direct long-range attack on an enemy's homeland, rather than for close-range battlefield use. ■ **strategically** ADV.

strategy N (**-ies**) **1** the process of, or skill in, planning and conducting a military campaign. **2** a long-term plan for future success or development. ■ **strategist** N.

stratify VB (**-ies, -ied**) **1** GEOL to deposit (rock) in layers or strata. **2** to classify or arrange things into different grades, levels or social classes. ■ **stratified** ADJ. ■ **stratification** N.

stratosphere N, METEOROL the layer of the Earth's atmosphere that extends from about 12 kilometres to about 50 kilometres above the Earth's surface.

stratum N (**strata**) **1** a layer of sedimentary rock. **2** a layer of cells in living tissue. **3** a layer of the atmosphere or the ocean. **4** a level, grade or social class.

straw N **1** the parts of cereal crops that remain after threshing, which may be ploughed back into the soil, burned as stubble or used as litter or feedstuff for animals, for thatching and weaving into hats, baskets, etc. **2** a single stalk of dried grass or cereal crop. **3** a thin hollow tube for sucking up a drink.
◆ **clutch at straws** to resort to an alternative option, remedy, etc in desperation, although it is unlikely to succeed.
◆ **draw the short straw** to be the person chosen from a group to carry out an unpleasant task, etc.

strawberry N a juicy red fruit which consists of tiny pips embedded in the surface.

strawberry blonde ADJ of hair: reddish-blonde.
➢ N a woman who has hair of this colour.

strawberry mark N a reddish birthmark.

straw poll and **straw vote** N an unofficial vote, esp taken on the spot among a small number of people, to get some idea of general opinion on a specified issue.

stray VB, INTR **1** to wander away from the right path or place, usu unintentionally. **2** to move away unintentionally from the main or current topic in thought, speech or writing: **He usually strays a bit from the main topic during a lecture. 3** to depart from the accepted or required pattern of behaviour, living, etc.
➢ N an ownerless or lost pet, farm animal, etc.
➢ ADJ of a pet, etc: homeless; ownerless; lost.

streak N **1** a long irregular stripe. **2** a flash of lightning. **3** an element or characteristic: **a cowardly streak. 4** a short period; a spell: **a streak of bad luck.**
➢ VB **1** to mark with a streak or streaks. **2** INTR to move at great speed; to dash.

streaky ADJ (*-ier, -iest*) **1** marked with streaks. **2** of bacon: with layers of fat and meat.

stream N **1** a very narrow river; a brook, burn or rivulet. **2** any constant flow of liquid: **streams of tears**. **3** anything that moves continuously in a line or mass: **a stream of traffic**. **4** an uninterrupted and unrelenting burst or succession, eg of insults: **a stream of questions**. ➤ VB **1** INTR to flow or move continuously and in large quantities or numbers. **2** INTR to float or trail in the wind.

streamer N **1** a long paper ribbon used to decorate a room. **2** a roll of coloured paper that uncoils when thrown. **3** a long thin flag.

streamlined ADJ **1** of a vehicle, aircraft, or vessel: shaped so as to move smoothly and efficiently with minimum resistance to air or water. **2** of an organization, process, etc: extremely efficient, with little or no waste of resources, excess staff, etc.

street N **1** (also in addresses **Street**) a public road with pavements and buildings at the side or sides, esp one in a town. **2** the area between the opposite pavements that is used by traffic. ◆ **be right up** or **up sb's street** COLLOQ to be ideally suited to them. ◆ **streets ahead of sb** or **sth** COLLOQ much more advanced than or superior to them.

streetwise ADJ, COLLOQ experienced in and well able to survive the ruthlessness of modern urban life, esp in areas such as drugs, crime, etc.

strength N **1** the quality or degree of being physically or mentally strong. **2** the ability to withstand pressure or force. **3** degree or intensity, eg of emotion or light. **4** potency, eg of a drug or alcoholic drink. **5** forcefulness of an argument. **6** a highly valued quality or asset. **7** the number of people, etc needed or expected in a group, esp in comparison to those actually present or available: **with the workforce only at half strength**. ◆ **on the strength of sth** on the basis of it.

strengthen VB, TR & INTR to make or become strong or stronger.

strenuous ADJ **1** characterized by the need for or the use of great effort or energy. **2** performed with great effort or energy and therefore very tiring. ■ **strenuously** ADV.

streptococcus N (*-cocci*) any of several species of bacterium that cause conditions such as scarlet fever and throat infections. ■ **streptococcal** ADJ.

stress N **1** physical or mental overexertion. **2** importance, emphasis or weight laid on or attached to something: **The stress was on speed not quality**. **3** the comparatively greater amount of force that is used in the pronunciation of a particular syllable. ➤ VB **1** to emphasize or attach importance to something. **2** to pronounce (a sound, word, etc) with emphasis. ■ **stressful** ADJ.

stressed-out ADJ debilitated or afflicted by emotional, nervous or mental tension.

stretch VB **1** TR & INTR to make or become temporarily or permanently longer or wider by pulling or drawing out. **2** INTR to extend in space or time. **3** TR & INTR to straighten and extend the body or part of the body, eg when waking or reaching out. **4** TR & INTR to make or become tight or taut. **5** INTR to lie at full length. **6** INTR to be extendable without breaking. **7** TR & INTR to last or make something last longer through economical use. **8** (also **stretch out**) to prolong or last. **9** to make extreme demands (eg resources or physical abilities): **The course stretched even the brightest students**. ➤ N **1** an act of stretching, esp (a part of) the body. **2** a period of time; a spell. **3** an expanse, eg of land or water. **4** capacity to extend or expand. **5** HORSE-RACING a straight part on a race-track or course, esp the part that leads up to the finishing line. ◆ **stretch one's legs** to take a short walk to invigorate oneself after inactivity.

stretcher N a device that is used for carrying a sick or wounded person in a lying position.

stretchy ADJ (*-ier, -iest*) of materials, clothes, etc: having the ability to stretch.

strew VB (PA P *strewed* or *strewn*) **1** to scatter untidily: **Papers were strewn across the floor**. **2** to cover with an untidy scattering: **The floor**

was strewn with papers.

stria N (PL **stria**) GEOL, BIOL any of a series of parallel grooves in rock, or furrows or streaks of colour in plants and animals. ■ **striated** ADJ.

stricken ADJ, often IN COMPOUNDS 1 deeply affected, esp by grief, sorrow, panic, etc: horror-stricken. 2 afflicted by disease, injury, etc: a typhoid-stricken community.

strict ADJ 1 demanding obedience or close observance of rules; severe. 2 observing rules or practices very closely: strict Catholics. 3 exact: in the strict sense of the word. 4 meant or designated to be closely obeyed: strict instructions. 5 complete: in the strictest confidence. ■ **strictly** ADV. ■ **strictness** N.

stricture N a severe criticism.

stride N 1 a single long step in walking. 2 the length of such a step. 3 a way of walking in long steps. 4 (usu **strides**) a measure of progress or development: make great strides. 5 a rhythm, eg in working, playing a game, etc that someone or something aims for or settles into: soon got into his stride.
➤ VB (PA T *strode*, PA P *stridden*) 1 INTR to walk with long steps. 2 INTR to take a long step.
◆ **take sth in one's stride** to cope with it effortlessly, as if part of a regular routine.

strident ADJ 1 of a sound, esp a voice: loud and harsh. 2 loudly assertive: a strident clamour for reforms. ■ **stridency** N.

strife N 1 bitter conflict or fighting. 2 COLLOQ trouble of any sort; hassle.

strike VB (*struck*) 1 to hit someone or something. 2 to come or bring into heavy contact with someone or something: The car struck the lamppost. 3 to make a particular impression on someone: They struck me as a strange couple. 4 to come into one's mind: It struck me as strange. 5 to cause (a match) to ignite through friction. 6 TR & INTR of a clock: to indicate the time, eg on the hour, half-hour, quarter-hour, with chimes, etc. 7 INTR to happen suddenly: Disaster struck. 8 to find a source of (eg oil, gold, etc). 9 INTR to stop working as part of a collective protest against an employer, working conditions, pay, etc. 10 to adopt (a posture or attitude). 11 TR & INTR to draw (a line) in order to cross something out.
➤ N 1 an act of hitting or dealing a blow. 2 a situation where a labour force refuses to work in order to protest against an employer, working conditions, pay, etc in the hope that, by doing this, their demands will be met. 3 a prolonged refusal to engage in a regular or expected activity, such as eating, in order to make some kind of a protest: hunger strike. 4 a military attack, esp one that is carried out by aircraft: a pre-emptive strike on the ground troops. 5 a discovery of a source, eg of oil, etc. 6 CRICKET the position of being the batsman bowled at: take strike. 7 BASEBALL a ball that the batter has taken a swing at but missed.
◆ **strike back** to retaliate.
◆ **strike it lucky** or **rich** to enjoy luck or become rich suddenly and unexpectedly.
◆ **strike sb off** to remove (the name of a member of a professional body from the register, esp because of misconduct.
◆ **strike sth out** to draw a line through (eg a name, etc) in order to to show a removal, etc.
◆ **strike up** 1 of a band, etc: to begin to play. 2 to start (eg a conversation, friendship, etc).

striker N 1 someone who takes part in a strike. 2 FOOTBALL a player who has an attacking role.

striking ADJ 1 impressive; arresting; attractive, esp in an unconventional way. 2 noticeable; marked: a striking omission. 3 on strike.
◆ **be** or **come within striking distance** to be close, possible, achievable, etc.

strimmer N, TRADEMARK an electrically operated garden tool that trims grass by means of a plastic or metal cord revolving at high speed, designed for long grass around garden beds, alongside fences, etc.

string N 1 thin cord, or a piece of this. 2 any of a set of pieces of stretched wire, catgut or other material that can vibrate to produce sound in various musical instruments such as the guitar, violin, piano, etc. 3 (**strings**) the orchestral instruments in which sound is produced in this way, usu the violins, violas, cellos and double basses collectively. 4 a series or succession:

a string of disasters. **5** COMP a group of characters that a computer can handle as a single unit. **6** one of several pieces of taut gut, etc that are used in sports rackets. **7** a set of things threaded together, eg beads, etc. ➤ VB (*strung*) **1** to fit or provide with a string or strings. **2** to tie with string. **3** to thread (eg beads) onto a string.

stringent ADJ **1** of rules, terms, etc: severe; rigorous; strictly enforced. **2** marked by a lack of money. ■ **stringency** N.

stringy ADJ (*-ier, -iest*) **1** like string, esp thin and thread-like. **2** of meat or other food: full of chewy fibres.

strip¹ VB (*-pp-*) **1** to remove (a covering, etc) by peeling or pulling it off: **strip the beds**. **2** to remove the surface or contents of something: **stripped the varnish**. **3 a** to remove (the clothing) from someone: **they stripped him, then flogged him**. **b** INTR to take one's clothes off. **4** to dismantle: **stripped the engine**. ➤ N **1** an act of undressing. **2** a striptease performance.
◆ **strip sth down** to take it apart.
◆ **strip sb of sth** to take it away from them: **stripped her of her dignity**.

strip² N **1** a long narrow, usu flat, piece of material, paper, land, etc. **2** SPORT lightweight distinctive clothing that is worn by a team: **Aberdeen's home strip is red**.

strip cartoon see **cartoon** (sense 3)

stripe N **1** a band of colour. **2** a chevron or coloured band on a uniform that indicates rank. ➤ VB to mark with stripes.

strip lighting N lighting that is given off by tube-shaped fluorescent lights.

stripper N **1** COLLOQ a striptease artiste. **2 a** a substance or appliance for removing paint, etc; **b** IN COMPOUNDS: **paint-stripper**.

striptease N a type of titillating show where a performer slowly and gradually takes their clothes off one by one while moving to music.

stripy ADJ (*-ier, -iest*) marked with stripes.

strive VB, INTR (PA T *strove*, PA P *striven*) to try extremely hard; to struggle: **strive to be the best**.

stroboscope N an instrument that uses a flashing light to measure or set the speed of rotating shafts, propellers, etc.

stroganoff N, COOKERY a dish of strips of sautéed meat, onions and mushrooms in a white wine sauce.

stroke N **1 a** any act or way of striking; **b** a blow. **2** SPORT **a** an act of striking a ball: **took six strokes at the par four** ; **b** the way a ball is struck: **a well-timed ground stroke**. **3** a single movement with a pen, paintbrush, etc, or the line or daub produced. **4 a** a single complete movement in a repeated series, as in swimming or rowing; **b** USU IN COMPOUNDS a particular named style of swimming: **backstroke**. **5** the total linear distance travelled by a piston in the cylinder of an engine. **6 a** the action of a clock, etc striking, or the sound of this; **b** the time indicated or which would be indicated by a clock striking: **out the door on the stroke of five**. **7** a gentle caress or other touching movement, eg when patting a dog, etc. **8** a sloping line used to separate alternatives in writing or print. Also called **solidus**. **9** PATHOL a sudden interruption to the supply of blood to the brain that results in loss of consciousness, often with accompanying paralysis and loss of speech, caused by bleeding from an artery, tissue blockage of an artery or a blood clot. ➤ VB to caress in kindness or affection.
◆ **at a stroke** with a single action.
◆ **a stroke of sth** a significant or impressive instance of it, esp of genius or luck.

stroll VB, INTR to walk in a slow leisurely way. ➤ N a leisurely walk.

strong ADJ **1** exerting or capable of great force or power. **2** able to withstand rough treatment; robust. **3** of views, etc: firmly held or boldly expressed. **4** of taste, light, etc: sharply felt or experienced; powerful. **5** of coffee; alcoholic drink, etc: relatively undiluted with water or other liquid; concentrated. **6** of an argument, etc: having much force; convincing. **7** of language: bold or straightforward; rude or offensive. **8** of a colour: deep and intense. **9** of a wind: blowing hard. **10** impressive: **a strong candidate for the job. 11** characterized by ability, stamina, good technique, etc: **a strong swimmer. 12** of an urge, desire, feeling, etc: intense; powerful; overwhelming: **a strong feeling of distrust.** ■ **strongly** ADV.

strongarm ADJ, COLLOQ **1** aggressively forceful. **2** making use of violence or threats.

strongbox N a safe, or other sturdy, usu lockable, box for storing money or valuables in.

stronghold N **1** a fortified place of defence, eg a castle. **2** a place where there is strong support (eg for a political party).

strong point N something that someone is especially good at: **Maths is my strong point.**

strongroom N a room that is designed to be difficult to get into or out of so that valuables, prisoners, etc can be held for safekeeping.

strontium N, CHEM a soft silvery-white highly reactive metallic element that is a good conductor of electricity.

stroppy ADJ (**-ier, -iest**) COLLOQ quarrelsome, bad-tempered and awkward to deal with.

structural ADJ belonging or relating to structure or a basic structure or framework. ■ **structurally** ADV.

structure N **1** the way in which the parts of a thing are arranged or organized. **2** a thing built from many smaller parts. **3** a building. ➤ VB to put into an organized arrangement.

strudel N a baked roll of thin pastry with a filling of fruit, esp apple.

struggle VB, INTR **1** to strive vigorously or make a strenuous effort under difficult conditions. **2** to make one's way with great difficulty. **3** to fight or contend. **4** to move the body around violently, eg in an attempt to get free. ➤ N **1** an act of struggling. **2** a task requiring strenuous effort. **3** a fight or contest.

strum VB (**-mm-**) TR & INTR to play (a stringed musical instrument, such as a guitar, or a tune on it) with sweeps of the fingers or thumb rather than with precise plucking.

strung ADJ **1** of a musical instrument: fitted with strings. **2** IN COMPOUNDS, of a person or animal: having a specified type of temperament: **highly-strung.**

strut VB (**-tt-**) INTR to walk in a proud or self-important way. ➤ N **1** a strutting way of walking. **2** a bar or rod whose function is to support weight or take pressure; a prop.

strychnine N a deadly poison that is obtained from the seeds of a tropical Indian tree and which can be used medicinally in small quantities as a nerve or appetite stimulant.

stub N **1** a short piece of something that remains when the rest of it has been used up, eg a cigarette, a pencil, etc. **2** the part of a cheque, ticket, receipt, etc that the holder retains as a record, proof of purchase, etc. ➤ VB (**-bb-**) **1** to accidentally bump the end of (one's toe) against a hard surface. **2** (usu **stub out**) to extinguish (eg a cigarette) by pressing the end against a surface.

stubble N **1** the mass of short stalks left in the ground after a crop has been harvested. **2** a short early growth of beard.

stubborn ADJ **1** resolutely or unreasonably unwilling to change one's opinions, ways, plans, etc; obstinate. **2** determined; unyielding. **3** difficult to treat, remove, deal with, etc: **stubborn stains.** ■ **stubbornly** ADV. ■ **stubbornness** N.

stubby ADJ (**-ier, -iest**) **1** short and broad. **2** small and worn down: **a stubby pencil.**

stucco N (**-os** or **-oes**) **1** a fine plaster that is used for coating indoor walls and ceilings and for forming decorative cornices, mouldings, etc. **2** a rougher kind of plaster or cement used for coating outside walls.

stuck ADJ **1** unable to give an answer, reason, etc. **2** unable to move. ◆ **be stuck for sth** COLLOQ to be in need of it or at a loss for it.

stuck-up ADJ, COLLOQ snobbish; conceited.

stud[1] N **1** a rivet-like metal peg that is fitted on to a surface, eg of a garment, for decoration.

2 any of several peg-like projections on the sole of a sports boot or shoe that give added grip. **3** a type of small round earring or nose-ring that has a post that goes through a hole and which is usu fastened at the back. **4** a fastener consisting of two small discs on either end of a short bar or shank, eg for fixing a collar to a shirt. **5** a short form of **press stud**.
➤ VB (*-dd-*) to fasten or decorate with a stud or studs.

stud² N **1** a male animal, esp a horse, kept for breeding. **2** (also **stud farm**) a place where animals, esp horses, are bred. **3** COLLOQ a man who has, or who sees himself as having, great sexual energy and prowess.

student N a someone who is following a formal course of study, esp in higher or further education; **b** AS ADJ: **student nurse**.

studied ADJ of an attitude, expression, etc: carefully practised or thought through and adopted or produced for effect.

studio N **1** the workroom of an artist or photographer. **2** a room in which music recordings, or TV or radio programmes, are made. **3 a** a company that produces films; **b** the premises where films are produced.

studio couch N a couch, often backless, that converts into a bed.

studio flat N a small flat with a single open-plan room.

studious ADJ **1** characterized by a serious hard-working approach, esp to study. **2** carefully attentive. ■ **studiously** ADV.

study VB (*-ies, -ied*) **1** TR & INTR to set one's mind to acquiring knowledge and understanding, esp by reading, research, etc. **2** to take an educational course in (a subject): **studied French to A-level. 3** to examine closely, or think about carefully: **studied her face.**
➤ N (*-ies*) **1** the act or process of studying. **2** (**studies**) work done in the process of acquiring knowledge: **having to work interfered with her studies. 3** a careful and detailed examination or consideration: **undertook a study of the problem. 4** a work of

art produced for the sake of practice, or in preparation for a more complex or detailed work. **5** a private room where quiet work or study is carried out.

stuff N **1 a** any material or substance: **the stuff that dreams are made of; b** something that is suitable for, relates to, or is characterized by whatever is specified: **kids' stuff. 2** moveable belongings: **I'll just get my stuff.**
➤ VB **1** to cram or thrust: **stuffed the clothes in the wardrobe. 2** to fill to capacity; to overfill. **3** to put something away: **stuffed the letter in the drawer. 4** to fill the hollow or hollowed-out part of something (eg a chicken, pepper, etc) with a mixture of other foods. **5** to fill out the disembodied skin of (an animal, bird, fish, etc) to recreate its living shape. **6** to feed (oneself) greedily: **stuffed himself until he felt sick. 7** (also **stuff up**) to block or clog something, eg a hole, the nose with mucus, etc.

stuffed ADJ **1** having a filling: **stuffed aubergines. 2** of a dead animal, etc: having had its internal body parts replaced by stuffing: **a stuffed tiger. 3** of a toy, cushion, etc: filled with soft stuffing. **4** (also **stuffed-up**) of the nose: blocked with mucus.

stuffed shirt N a conservative person.

stuffing N **1** any material that cushions, animal skins, etc are filled with. **2** COOKERY any mixture used as a filling for poultry, vegetables, etc.

stuffy ADJ (*-ier, -iest*) **1** lacking fresh, cool air; badly ventilated. **2** staid; boringly formal, conventional or unadventurous; pompous. ■ **stuffiness** N.

stultify VB (*-ies, -ied*) **1** to cause something to be useless, worthless, futile, etc. **2** to dull the mind of someone, eg with tedious tasks. ■ **stultification** N.

stumble VB, INTR **1** to lose one's balance and trip forwards after accidentally catching or misplacing one's foot. **2** to walk unsteadily. **3** to speak with frequent hesitations and mistakes.
➤ N an act of stumbling.
◆ **stumble across**, **into** or **upon sth** to find, come across, etc it by chance.

stumbling-block N 1 an obstacle or difficulty. 2 a cause of failure or faltering.

stump N 1 the part of a felled or fallen tree that is left in the ground. 2 the short part of anything, eg a limb, that is left after the larger part has been removed, used up, etc: **a little stump of a pencil**. 3 CRICKET **a** any of the three thin vertical wooden posts that form the wicket; **b** (**stumps**) the whole wicket, including the bails.
➢ VB to baffle or perplex.
◆ **stump up** COLLOQ to pay.

stumpy ADJ (*-ier, -iest*) short and thick.

stun VB (*-nn-*) 1 to make someone unconscious, eg by a blow to the head. 2 to make someone unable to speak or think clearly, eg through shock. 3 COLLOQ to impress someone greatly.

stunner N, COLLOQ someone or something that is extraordinarily beautiful, attractive, etc.

stunning ADJ, COLLOQ 1 extraordinarily beautiful, attractive, etc. 2 extremely impressive. ■ **stunningly** ADV.

stunt[1] VB to curtail the growth or development of (something) to its full potential: **Lack of water stunted the plants.** ■ **stunted** ADJ.

stunt[2] N 1 a daring act or spectacular event that is intended to show off talent or attract publicity. 2 a dangerous or acrobatic feat that is performed as part of the action of a film or television programme, usu by a **stuntman** or **stuntwoman** standing in for an actor.

stupefaction N stunned surprise.

stupefy VB (*-ies, -ied*) 1 to stun with amazement, fear or bewilderment. 2 to make someone senseless, eg with drugs or alcohol.

stupendous ADJ 1 astounding. 2 COLLOQ astoundingly huge or excellent.

stupid ADJ 1 lacking common sense, comprehension, perception, etc: **a stupid mistake**. 2 slow to understand; dull-witted. 3 COLLOQ silly; trivial; unimportant; ridiculous; boring: **a stupid quarrel**. ■ **stupidity** N.

stupor N 1 a state of unconsciousness or near-unconsciousness, esp one caused by drugs, alcohol, etc. 2 COLLOQ a daze, esp one brought on by shock, lack of sleep, sadness, etc.

sturdy ADJ (*-ier, -iest*) 1 of limbs, etc: thick and strong-looking. 2 strongly built; robust. 3 healthy; vigorous; hardy. ■ **sturdiness** N.

sturgeon N a large long-snouted fish, the source of true caviar.

stutter VB, TR & INTR to speak or say something in a faltering or hesitant way.
➢ N this kind of faltering or hesitant speech.

sty[1] N (*sties*) a pen where pigs are kept.

sty[2] or **stye** N (*sties* or *styes*) an inflamed swelling on the eyelid at the base of the lash.

Stygian ADJ, LITERARY dark and gloomy.

style N 1 a manner or way of doing something, eg writing, speaking, etc. 2 a distinctive manner that characterizes a particular author, painter, film-maker, etc. 3 kind; type; make. 4 a striking quality that is considered desirable or admirable: **She dresses with style.** 5 the state of being fashionable: **gone out of style.**
➢ VB to design, shape, groom, etc something in a particular way.

stylish ADJ elegant; fashionable.

stylist N a trained hairdresser.

stylistic ADJ relating to artistic or literary style.

stylized ADJ conventionalized and unnaturalistic: **a highly stylized art form**.

stylus N (*-luses* or *-li*) a pointed device which picks up the sound from a record's grooves.

stymie VB (*stymieing* or *stymying*) to prevent, thwart, hinder or frustrate.

styptic ADJ, MED of a substance: having the effect of stopping, slowing down or preventing bleeding.

suave ADJ of someone, esp a man: charming and sophisticated, esp in an insincere way.

sub COLLOQ, N 1 a submarine. 2 a substitute player. 3 an advance payment, eg from someone's wages. 4 (usu **subs**) a subscription fee. 5 a subeditor.
➢ VB (*-bb-*) 1 INTR to act as a substitute. 2 to lend

(esp a small amount of money): **Can you sub me a quid till tomorrow?**

subaltern N any army officer below the rank of captain.

subaqua ADJ of or relating to underwater activities: **subaqua diving**.

subatomic ADJ smaller than an atom: **subatomic particle**.

subconscious N the part of the mind where memories, associations, experiences, feelings, etc are stored and can be retrieved to the level of conscious awareness.
➤ ADJ denoting mental processes which a person is not fully aware of.

subcontinent N a large part of a continent that is distinctive in some way, eg by its shape, culture, etc: **the Indian subcontinent**.

subcontract N a contract where the person or company that is initially hired to do a job then hires another to carry out the work.
➤ VB (also **subcontract out**) to employ (a worker) or pass on (work) under the terms of a subcontract. ■ **subcontractor** N.

subculture N a group within a society, esp one seen as an underclass, whose members share the same, often unconventional, beliefs, lifestyle, tastes, activities, etc.

subcutaneous ADJ, MED situated, used, introduced, etc under the skin.

subdivide VB to divide (esp something that is already divided) into even smaller parts.
■ **subdivision** N.

subdue VB to overpower and bring under control; to suppress.

subdued ADJ 1 of lighting, etc: not intense, bright, harsh, loud, etc; toned down. 2 of a person: quiet, shy, restrained or in low spirits.

subedit VB, TR & INTR to prepare (copy) for the ultimate sanction of the editor–in–chief, esp on a newspaper. ■ **subeditor** N.

subheading and **subhead** N a subordinate title in a book, article, etc.

subhuman ADJ of a person: barbaric; lacking in intelligence.

subject N 1 a matter, topic, person, etc that is under discussion or consideration or that features as the major theme in a book, film, play, etc. 2 an area of learning that forms a course of study. 3 someone or something that an artist, sculptor, photographer, etc chooses to represent. 4 someone who undergoes an experiment, operation, form of treatment, hypnosis, psychoanalysis, etc. 5 someone who is ruled by a monarch, government, etc; a citizen: **became an American subject**. 6 GRAM a word, phrase or clause which indicates the person or thing that performs the action of an active verb or that receives the action of a passive verb, eg **The doctor** is the subject in **The doctor saw us**, and **We** is the subject in **We were seen by the doctor**.
➤ ADJ (often **subject to sth**) liable; showing a tendency; prone: **subject to mood swings**.
➤ ADV (always **subject to**) conditionally upon something: **You may go, subject to your parent's permission**.
➤ VB 1 (usu **subject sb** or **sth to sth**) to cause them or it to undergo or experience something unwelcome, unpleasant, etc: **subjected them to years of abuse**. 2 to make (a person, a people, nation, etc) subordinate to or under the control of another.

subjection N an act of domination; the state of being dominated: **the subjection of women**.

subjective ADJ 1 based on personal opinion, etc; not impartial. 2 GRAM indicating or referring to the subject of a verb; nominative.

sub judice ADJ of a court case: under judicial consideration and therefore not to be publicly discussed or remarked on.

subjugate VB 1 esp of one country, people, etc in regard to another: to bring them under control. 2 to make someone obedient or submissive. ■ **subjugation** N.

subjunctive ADJ, GRAM of the mood of a verb: used in English for denoting the conditional or hypothetical (eg 'If he **were** in hospital, I would certainly visit him' or 'If I **were** you') or the mandatory (eg 'I insist he **leave** now'), although in other languages it has a wider application.

sublet VB, TR & INTR to rent out (property one is renting from someone else) to another person.

sublieutenant N a naval officer who is immediately below lieutenant in rank.

sublimate VB, PSYCHOL to channel a morally or socially unacceptable impulse towards something else that is considered more appropriate. ■ **sublimation** N.

sublime ADJ 1 of someone: displaying the highest or noblest nature, esp in terms of their morality, intellectuality, etc. 2 of something in nature or art: overwhelmingly great; supreme; awe-inspiring. 3 LOOSELY unsurpassed. ➤ N (**the sublime**) the ultimate or ideal example or instance. ■ **sublimely** ADV.

subliminal ADJ existing in, resulting from, or targeting the area of the mind that is below the threshold of ordinary awareness: subliminal advertising. ■ **subliminally** ADV.

submachine-gun N a lightweight portable machine-gun fired from the shoulder or hip.

submarine N a vessel, esp a military one, that is designed for underwater travel. ■ **submariner** N.

submerge and **submerse** VB 1 TR & INTR to plunge or sink or cause to plunge or sink under the surface of water or other liquid. 2 to overwhelm or inundate someone, eg with too much work. ■ **submersion** N.

submersible ADJ of a vessel: designed to operate under water. ➤ N a submersible vessel; a submarine.

submission N 1 an act of submitting. 2 something, eg a plan, proposal, view, etc, put forward for consideration or approval.

submissive ADJ willing or tending to submit; meek; obedient. ■ **submissively** ADV.

submit VB (-tt-) 1 INTR (also **submit to sb**) to surrender; to give in, esp to the wishes or control of another person. 2 TR & INTR to offer (oneself) as a subject for an experiment, treatment, etc. 3 to offer, suggest or present (something) for formal consideration by others.

subnormal ADJ esp of someone's level of intelligence: lower than normal.

subordinate ADJ (often **subordinate to sb**) lower in rank, importance, etc; secondary. ➤ N someone or something that is characterized by being lower or secondary in rank, status, importance, etc. ➤ VB 1 to regard or treat someone as being lower or secondary in rank, status, importance, etc. 2 to cause or force someone or something to become dependent, subservient, etc. ■ **subordination** N.

subordinate clause N, GRAM a clause which cannot stand on its own as an independent sentence and which functions in a sentence in the same way as a noun, adjective or adverb, eg 'The book that you gave me for Christmas was fascinating'.

suborn VB to persuade someone to commit perjury, a crime or other wrongful act.

subplot N a minor storyline that runs parallel to the main plot in a novel, etc.

subpoena N a legal document that orders someone to appear in a court of law at a specified time; a summons. ➤ VB (*subpoenaed* or *subpoena'd*) to serve with a subpoena.

subroutine N, COMP a self-contained part of a computer program which performs a specific task.

subscribe VB 1 TR & INTR to contribute or undertake to contribute (a sum of money), esp on a regular basis. 2 (usu **subscribe to sth**) to undertake to receive (regular issues of a magazine, etc) in return for payment. 3 (usu **subscribe to sth**) to agree with or believe in (a theory, idea, etc). ■ **subscriber** N.

subscription N 1 a an act or instance of subscribing; b a payment made in subscribing. 2 BRIT a set fee for membership of a society, club, etc. 3 an agreement to take a magazine, etc, usu for a specified number of issues.

subsequent ADJ (also **subsequent to sth**) following. ■ **subsequently** ADV.

subservient ADJ 1 ready or eager to submit to

the wishes of others, often excessively so.
2 (usu **subservient to sth**) functioning as a means to an end.

subset N, MATH a set that forms one part of a larger set, eg **set X** is a subset of **set Y** if all the members of **set X** can be included in **set Y**.

subside VB, INTR **1** to sink to a lower level; to settle. **2** to become less loud or intense; to die down. ■ **subsidence** N.

subsidiary ADJ **1** of secondary importance; subordinate. **2** serving as an addition or supplement; auxiliary.
➤ N (*-ies*) **1** a subsidiary person or thing. **2** a company controlled by another, usu larger, company or organization.

subsidize or **-ise** VB **1** to provide or support with a subsidy. **2** to pay a proportion of the cost of (a thing supplied) in order to reduce the price paid by the customer.

subsidy N (*-ies*) **1** a sum of money given, eg by a government to an industry, to help with running costs or to keep product prices low. **2** financial aid of this kind.

subsist VB, INTR (usu **subsist on sth**) to live or manage to stay alive by means of it. ■ **subsistence** N.

subsoil N, GEOL the layer of soil that lies beneath the topsoil.

substance N **1** the matter or material that a thing is made of. **2** a particular kind of matter with a definable quality: **a sticky substance**. **3** the essence or basic meaning of something spoken or written. **4** touchable reality; tangibility: **Ghosts have no substance**. **5** solid quality or worth: **food with no substance**. **6** foundation: **no substance in the rumours**. **7** wealth and influence: **woman of substance**.

substantial ADJ **1** considerable in amount, extent, importance, etc. **2** of real value or worth. **3** of food: nourishing. **4** solidly built. **5** existing as a touchable thing; material; corporeal. **6** essential. ■ **substantially** ADV.

substantiate VB to prove or support something; to confirm the truth or validity of something. ■ **substantiation** N.

substantive ADJ **1** having or displaying significant importance, value, validity, etc. **2** belonging or relating to the essential nature of something.

substitute N someone or something that takes the place of, or is used instead of, another.
➤ VB (usu **substitute sth for sth else**) to use or bring something into use as a replacement, etc for something else. ■ **substitution** N.

substratum N (*-ta*) **1** an underlying layer. **2** a foundation or foundation material. **3** a layer of soil or rock that lies just below the surface.

substructure N the part of a building or other construction that supports the framework.

subsume VB to include (an example, instance, idea, etc) in or regard it as part of a larger, more general group, category, rule, principle, etc.

subterfuge N a trick or deception that evades, conceals or obscures.

subterranean ADJ situated, existing, operating, etc underground.

subtext N **1** the implied message that the author, director, etc of a play, film, book, etc creates at a level below that of plot, character, language, etc. **2** MORE LOOSELY anything implied but not explicitly stated.

subtitle N **1** (usu **subtitles**) a printed translation of the dialogue of a foreign film that appears bit by bit at the bottom of the frame. **2** a subordinate title that usu expands on or explains the main title.
➤ VB to give a subtitle to (a play, film, etc).

subtle ADJ **1** not straightforwardly or obviously stated or displayed. **2** difficult to appreciate or perceive. **3** delicate; understated. **4** capable of making fine distinctions: **a subtle mind**. ■ **subtlety** N (*-ies*). ■ **subtly** ADV.

subtotal N the amount that a column of figures adds up to and which forms part of a larger total.

subtract VB to take (one number, quantity, etc) away from another. ■ **subtraction** N.

subtropics PL N the areas of the world that lie between the tropics and the temperate zone.

■ **subtropical** or **subtropic** ADJ.

suburb N **1** a residential district that lies on the edge of a town or city. **2** (**the suburbs**) the outlying districts of a city thought of collectively.

suburbia N the suburbs and its inhabitants and way of life thought of collectively as typical of the suburbs. ■ **suburban** ADJ.

subversion N **1** an act or instance of overthrowing a law, government, etc. **2** the act or practice of subverting (usu a government).

subversive ADJ characterized by a likelihood or tendency to undermine authority.

subvert VB to undermine or overthrow (a government or other legally established body).

subway N **1** an underground passage or tunnel that pedestrians or vehicles can use for crossing under a road, railway, river, etc. **2** chiefly N AMER an underground railway.

subzero ADJ below zero.

succeed VB **1** INTR to achieve an aim or purpose. **2** INTR to develop or turn out as planned. **3** INTR (also **succeed in sth**) to do well in a particular area or field: *succeeded in getting four A's.* **4** to come next after (something); to follow. **5** TR & INTR (also **succeed to sb** or **sth**) to take up a position, etc, following on from someone else: *The Queen succeeded her father* • *She succeeded to the throne.*

success N **1** the quality of succeeding or the state of having succeeded. **2** any favourable development or outcome. **3** someone who attains fame, power, wealth, etc or is judged favourably by others. **4** something that turns out well or that is judged favourably by others.

successful ADJ **1** achieving or resulting in the required outcome. **2** prosperous, flourishing: *a successful business.* ■ **successfully** ADV.

succession N **1 a** a series of people or things that come, happen, etc one after the other; **b** the process or an instance of this. **2 a** the right or order by which one person or thing succeeds another; **b** the process or act of doing this.

successive ADJ immediately following another or each other. ■ **successively** ADV.

successor N someone who follows another, esp in taking over their job, title, etc.

succinct ADJ brief, precise and to the point; concise. ■ **succinctly** ADV.

succour FORMAL, N **1** help or relief in time of distress or need. **2** someone or something that gives this kind of help.
➤ VB to give help or relief to someone or something.

succulent ADJ **1** full of juice; juicy; tender and tasty. **2** BOT of a plant: characterized by having thick fleshy leaves or stems. ■ **succulence** N.

succumb VB, INTR (often **succumb to sth**) **1** to give in to (eg pressure, temptation, desire, etc): *succumbed to her charms.* **2** to fall victim to or to die of (something, esp a disease, etc).

such ADJ **1** of that kind, or of the same or a similar kind: *You cannot reason with such a person.* **2** so great; of a more extreme type, degree, extent, etc than is usual, normal, etc: *You're such a good friend.* **3** of a type, degree, extent, etc that has already been indicated, spoken about, etc: *I did no such thing.*
➤ PRONOUN a person or thing, or people or things, like that or those which have just been mentioned; suchlike: *chimps, gorillas and such.*
◆ **as such** as is usu thought of, described, etc: *There's no spare bed as such, but you can use the sofa.*
◆ **such as** for example.

such-and-such ADJ of a particular but unspecified kind.
➤ PRONOUN a person or thing of this kind.

suchlike PRONOUN things of the same kind: *soap, toothpaste and suchlike.*
➤ ADJ of the same kind: *soap, toothpaste and suchlike things.*

suck VB **1** TR & INTR to draw (liquid) into the mouth. **2** to draw liquid from (eg a juicy fruit) with the mouth. **3** (also **suck sth in** or **up**) to draw in by suction or an action similar to suction. **4** to rub (eg one's thumb, etc) with the tongue and inside of the mouth, using an action similar to sucking in liquids. **5** to draw the flavour from (eg a sweet) with squeezing and rolling

movements inside the mouth. **6** to take milk (from a breast or udder) with the mouth. **7** INTR, N AMER SLANG to be very bad: *That film sucks!*
◆ **suck sb into sth** to drag them into it: *sucked him into the world of politics.*
◆ **suck up to sb** COLLOQ to flatter or be obsequious to them in order to gain favour.

sucker N **1** someone who is gullible or who can be easily deceived or taken advantage of. **2** (usu **sucker for sth**) COLLOQ someone who finds a specified type of thing or person irresistible: *a sucker for ice cream.* **3** ZOOL a specially adapted organ that helps an insect, sea creature, etc adhere to surfaces by suction. **4** a rubber cup-shaped device that adheres to a surface by creating a vacuum.

suckle VB **1** to feed (a baby or young mammal) with milk from the nipple or udder. **2** TR & INTR to suck milk from (a nipple or udder).

suckling N a baby or young animal that is still being fed with its mother's milk.

sucrose N, BIOCHEM a white soluble crystalline sugar.

suction N **1** an act, an instance or the process of sucking. **2 a** the production of an adhering or sucking force that is created by a difference or reduction in air pressure; **b** the amount of force that this creates.

sudden ADJ happening or done quickly, without warning or unexpectedly.
■ **suddenly** ADV. ■ **suddenness** N.
◆ **all of a sudden** without any warning.

sudden infant death syndrome N the sudden unexpected death of an apparently healthy baby.

suds PL N (also **soap-suds**) a mass of bubbles produced on water when soap or other detergent is dissolved.

sue VB, TR & INTR to take legal proceedings against (a person or company).

suede N a soft leather rubbed or brushed so that it has a velvety finish.

suet N hard fat from around the kidneys of sheep or cattle, used for making pastry, etc.

suffer VB **1** TR & INTR to undergo or endure (pain or other unpleasantness). **2** INTR to deteriorate (as a result of something). ■ **sufferer** N.
■ **suffering** N.

sufferance N.
◆ **on sufferance** with reluctant toleration.

suffice VB **1** INTR to be adequate, sufficient, etc for a particular purpose. **2** to satisfy.

sufficient ADJ enough; adequate.
■ **sufficiency** N. ■ **sufficiently** ADV.

suffix N, GRAM a word-forming element that can be added to the end of a word or to the base form of a word, such as **-ed** in **walked** or **-s** in **monkeys**.

suffocate VB **1** TR & INTR to kill or be killed by a lack of air, eg because the air passages are blocked. **2** INTR to experience difficulty in breathing because of heat and lack of air. **3** to subject to an oppressive amount of something.
■ **suffocating** ADJ. ■ **suffocation** N.

suffrage N the right to vote in political elections. ■ **suffragist** N.

suffragette N a woman in favour of or who campaigns for women having the same voting rights as men, esp one who acted militantly for this in Britain in the early years of the 20c.

suffuse VB (often **be suffused with sth**) to be covered or spread over or throughout with (colour, light, liquid, etc): *The sky was suffused with red.* ■ **suffusion** N.

sugar N **1** a white crystalline carbohydrate that is soluble in water, typically having a sweet taste and widely used as a sweetener in confectionery, desserts, soft drinks, etc. **2** the common name for sucrose.
➤ VB **1** to sweeten something with sugar. **2** to sprinkle or coat something with sugar.

sugar beet N a variety of beet whose root is an important source of sugar.

sugar cane N a tall tropical grass which is a main source of sugar.

sugary ADJ **1** like sugar in taste or appearance. **2** containing much sugar. **3** COLLOQ cloying.

suggest VB 1 (often **suggest that sth**) to put forward as a possibility or recommendation. 2 to create an impression of something; to evoke it: **a painting that suggests the artist's anguish**. 3 to give a hint of something: **an expression that suggests guilt**.

suggestible ADJ easily influenced by others' suggestions. ■ **suggestibility** N.

suggestion N 1 a something that is suggested; a proposal, plan, recommendation, etc; b the act of suggesting. 2 a hint or trace: **just a suggestion of coriander**. 3 a the creation of a belief or impulse in the mind; b the process by which an idea, belief, etc can be instilled in the mind of a hypnotized person.

suggestive ADJ 1 (often **suggestive of sth**) causing one to think of it. 2 capable of a tacitly erotic or provocative interpretation. ■ **suggestively** ADV.

suicidal ADJ 1 characterized by behaviour that might result in suicide or ruin. 2 of a person: inclined or likely to commit suicide.

suicide N 1 the act or an instance of killing oneself deliberately. 2 someone who deliberately kills or tries to kill himself or herself. 3 ruin or downfall, esp when it is unintentional: **The minister's speech was political suicide.**

suit N 1 a set of clothes designed to be worn together, usu made from the same or contrasting material and which consists of a jacket and either trousers or a skirt and sometimes a waistcoat. 2 (often IN COMPOUNDS) an outfit worn on specified occasions or for a specified activity: **wet suit**. 3 any of the four groups (clubs, diamonds, hearts or spades) that a pack of playing-cards is divided into. 4 a legal action taken against someone. ➤ VB 1 TR & INTR to be acceptable to or what is required by someone. 2 to be appropriate to or in harmony with someone or something. ◆ **follow suit** to do the same as someone else has done. ◆ **suit oneself** to do what one wants to do, esp without considering others.

suitable ADJ appropriate, fitting, proper, etc. ■ **suitability** N. ■ **suitably** ADV.

suitcase N a stiffened portable travelling case that is used for carrying clothes.

suite N 1 a set of rooms forming a self-contained unit within a larger building, esp a hotel: **bridal suite**. 2 a set of matching furniture, etc: **three-piece suite**. 3 MUS a set of instrumental movements in related keys.

suitor N, OLD USE a man who woos a woman, esp with the intention of asking her to marry him.

Sukkoth N a Jewish harvest festival commemorating when the Israelites lived in the desert during the Exodus from Egypt.

sulk VB, INTR to be silent, grumpy, unsociable, etc, esp because of some petty resentment, etc.

sulky ADJ (**-ier, -iest**) inclined to moodiness, esp when taking the form of grumpy silence, resentful unsociability, etc. ■ **sulkiness** N.

sullen ADJ 1 silently and stubbornly angry, serious, morose, moody or unsociable. 2 of skies, etc: heavy and dismal. ■ **sullenly** ADV. ■ **sullenness** N.

sully VB (**-ies, -ied**) to tarnish or mar (a reputation, etc). ■ **sullied** ADJ.

sulphate or (US) **sulfate** N a salt or ester of sulphuric acid.

sulphide or (US) **sulfide** N a compound that contains sulphur with another element.

sulphite or (US) **sulfite** N a salt or ester of sulphurous acid.

sulphonamide or (US) **sulfonamide** N, CHEM 1 an amide of a sulphonic acid. 2 MED any of a group of drugs containing such a compound that prevent the growth of bacteria.

sulphur or (US) **sulfur** N a yellow solid non-metallic element that is used in the vulcanization of rubber and the manufacture of sulphuric acid, fungicides, insecticides, gunpowder, matches, fertilizers and sulphonamide drugs. ■ **sulphuric** ADJ.

sulphur dioxide N, CHEM a colourless, pungent-smelling, toxic gas, used in the manufacture of sulphuric acid.

sulphuric acid or (US) **sulfuric acid** N,

CHEM a colourless odourless oily liquid widely used in the manufacture of organic chemicals, fertilizers, explosives, detergents, and dyes.

sulphurize or **-ise** or (US) **sulfurize** VB to combine or treat with sulphur.

sulphurous or (US) **sulfurous** ADJ of, containing or resembling sulphur.

sultan N a ruler in some Muslim countries.

sultana N 1 a a pale seedless raisin used in making cakes, puddings, etc. 2 the wife, concubine, mother, sister or daughter of a sultan.

sultry ADJ (**-ier, -iest**) 1 hot and humid; close. 2 characterized by a sensual, passionate or sexually suggestive appearance, manner, etc.

sum N 1 the total that is arrived at when two or more numbers, quantities, ideas, feelings, etc are added together. 2 an amount of money, often a specified or particular one: **the grand sum of 50p. 3 a** an arithmetical calculation, esp of a basic kind; **b** (**sums**) COLLOQ arithmetic.
➤ VB (**-mm-**) to calculate the sum of something.
◆ **sum up 1** to summarize before finishing a speech, argument, etc. 2 of a judge: to review the main points of a case for the jury.
◆ **sum up sb** or **sth 1** to express or embody the complete nature of them or it. 2 to make a quick assessment of (a person, situation, etc).

summarize or **-ise** VB to make, present or be a summary of something; to state it concisely.

summary N (**-ies**) a short account that outlines or picks out the main points.
➤ ADJ done or performed quickly and without the usual attention to details or formalities.
■ **summarily** ADV.

summation N 1 the process of finding the sum; addition. 2 a summary or summing-up.

summer N (also **Summer**) the warmest season of the year, between spring and autumn. ■ **summertime** N. ■ **summery** ADJ.

summerhouse N any small building or shelter in a park or garden where people can sit during warm weather.

summer school N, BRIT a course of study held during the summer vacation.

summer solstice N the longest day of the year, 21 June for the N hemisphere, or 22 December for the S hemisphere.

summing-up N a review of the main points of a legal case by the judge before members of the jury retire to consider their verdict.

summit N 1 the highest point of a mountain or hill. 2 the highest possible level of achievement or development. 3 a meeting between heads of government or other senior officials.

summon VB 1 to order someone to come or appear, eg in a court of law as a witness, defendant, etc. 2 to order or request someone to do something: **had to summon help**.
◆ **summon up sth** to gather or muster (eg one's strength or energy).

summons N (**summonses**) 1 a written order that legally obliges someone to attend a court of law at a specified time. 2 any authoritative order that requests someone to attend a meeting, etc or to do something specified.
➤ VB, LAW to serve someone with a summons.

sumo N a style of traditional Japanese wrestling where contestants of great bulk try to force an opponent out of the unroped ring.

sump N a small depression inside a vehicle's engine that acts as a reservoir so that lubricating oil can drain into it.

sumptuous ADJ wildly expensive.

sum total N the complete or final total.

sun N 1 (**the Sun**) the star that the planets revolve around and which gives out the heat and light energy necessary to enable living organisms to survive on Earth. 2 the heat and light of this star.
➤ VB (**-nn-**) to expose (something or oneself) to the sun's rays.

sunbathe VB, INTR to expose one's body to the sun in order to get a suntan. ■ **sunbather** N.
■ **sunbathing** N.

sunbeam N a ray of sunlight.

sunbed N 1 a device with sun-lamps on which someone can lie in order to artificially tan the body. 2 a sun-lounger.

sunblock N a lotion, etc that protects the skin from the harmful effects of the sun's rays.

sunburn N soreness and reddening of the skin caused by over-exposure to the sun's rays. ■ **sunburnt** or **sunburned** ADJ.

sundae N a portion of ice-cream topped with fruit, nuts, syrup, etc.

Sunday N the first day of the week and for most Christians the day of worship and rest.

Sunday school N a class for the religious instruction of children that is held on Sundays.

sundial N an instrument that uses sunlight to tell the time, by the changing position of the shadow that a vertical arm casts on a horizontal plate with markings that indicate the hours.

sundry ADJ various; assorted; miscellaneous. ➤ N (**sundries**) various small unspecified items; oddments. ◆ **all and sundry** everybody.

sunflower N a tall plant which produces large flattened circular flowerheads with closely-packed seeds (which yield **sunflower oil**) and yellow petals radiating outwards.

sunglasses PL N spectacles that have tinted lenses, worn to protect the eyes from sunlight.

sun-god and **sun-goddess** N the Sun when it is thought of as a deity.

sunken ADJ **1** situated at a lower level than the surrounding area: **a sunken bath**. **2** submerged in water: **sunken treasure**. **3** of eyes, cheeks, etc: abnormally fallen in, gaunt or hollow.

sun-lamp N an electric lamp that emits rays, esp ultraviolet rays, used therapeutically and for artificially tanning the skin.

sunlight N light from the Sun. ■ **sunlit** ADJ.

sun-lounger N, BRIT a lightweight plastic sunbathing seat.

sunny ADJ (**-ier, -iest**) **1** of a day, the weather, etc: characterized by long spells of sunshine. **2** of a place, etc: exposed to, lit or warmed by plenty of sunshine: **a lovely sunny room**.

sunrise N the Sun's appearance above the horizon in the morning.

sunroof N a transparent panel in the roof of a car that can usu open for ventilation.

sunscreen N a preparation that protects the skin and minimizes the possibility of sunburn by blocking out most of the sun's harmful rays.

sunset N the sun's disappearance below the horizon in the evening.

sunshade N anything used as protection in strong sunshine, eg a parasol or an awning.

sunshine N the light or heat of the sun.

sunspot N, ASTRON a relatively dark cool patch on the sun's surface.

sunstroke N a condition of collapse brought on by over-exposure to the sun.

suntan N a browning of the skin through exposure to the sun or a sun-lamp.

suntrap N, BRIT a sheltered sunny place.

sup VB (**-pp-**) to drink in small mouthfuls. ➤ N a small quantity of something liquid; a sip.

super ADJ, COLLOQ extremely good; excellent.

superannuated ADJ **1** of a post, vacancy, job, etc: with a pension as an integral part of the employment package. **2** pensioned off.

superannuation N **1** an amount that is regularly deducted from someone's wages as a contribution to a company pension. **2** the pension someone receives when they retire.

superb ADJ **1** COLLOQ outstandingly excellent. **2** magnificent; majestic; highly impressive.

supercharge VB to increase the power and performance of (a vehicle engine).

supercharger N, ENG a device used to increase the amount of air taken into the cylinder of an internal combustion engine.

supercilious ADJ arrogantly disdainful or contemptuous. ■ **superciliousness** N.

superconductivity N, PHYS the property of having no electrical resistance, displayed by many metals and alloys at temperatures close to absolute zero, and by other substances at higher temperatures. ■ **superconductor** N.

superficial ADJ 1 belonging or relating to, or on or near, the surface: **a superficial wound**. 2 not thorough or in-depth; cursory: **a superficial understanding**. 3 only apparent; not real or genuine: **a superficial attempt to apologize**. 4 lacking the capacity for sincere emotion or serious thought; shallow. ■ **superficiality** N (**-ies**). ■ **superficially** ADV.

superfluous ADJ more than is needed or wanted. ■ **superfluity** N.

superglue N a type of quick-acting extra-strong adhesive.

supergrass N, SLANG someone who gives the police so much information that a large number of arrests follow.

superhero N a character in a film, novel, cartoon, comic, etc that has extraordinary powers, esp for saving the world from disaster.

superhuman ADJ beyond ordinary human power, ability, knowledge, etc.

superimpose VB to lay or set (one thing) on top of another.

superintend VB, TR & INTR to look after and manage someone or something; to supervise.

superintendent N 1 BRIT a police officer above the rank of chief inspector. 2 someone whose job is to look after and manage, eg a department, a group of workers, etc.

superior ADJ (often **superior to sb** or **sth**) 1 better. 2 higher in rank or position: **reported him to his superior officer**. 3 of high quality. 4 arrogant; self-important.
➤ N 1 someone who is of higher rank or position. 2 the head of a religious community. ■ **superiority** N.

superlative ADJ 1 GRAM of adjectives or adverbs: expressing the highest degree of a particular quality, eg **nicest, best, most beautiful**. 2 superior to all others; supreme.
➤ N, GRAM 1 a superlative adjective or adverb. 2 the superlative form of a word.

superman N 1 PHILOS an ideal man as he will have evolved in the future. 2 someone who has exceptional strength or powers.

supermarket N a large self-service store that sells food, household goods, etc.

supermodel N an extremely highly-paid, usu female, fashion model.

supernatural ADJ belonging or relating to or being phenomena that cannot be explained by the laws of nature or physics.
➤ N (**the supernatural**) the world of unexplained phenomena.

supernova N (**-vae** or **-vas**) ASTRON a vast stellar explosion which results in the star becoming temporarily millions of times brighter.

superpower N a nation or state that has outstanding political, economic or military influence, esp the USA or the former USSR.

superscript PRINTING, ADJ of a character: set above the level of the line that the other characters sit on, eg the number 2 in 10^2.
➤ N a superscript character.

supersede VB to take the place of (something, esp something outdated or no longer valid).

supersonic ADJ 1 faster than the speed of sound. 2 of aircraft: able to travel at supersonic speeds.

superstar N a very famous celebrity.

superstition N 1 belief in an influence that certain (esp commonplace) objects, actions or occurrences have on events, people's lives, etc. 2 a particular opinion or practice based on such belief. ■ **superstitious** ADJ.

superstore N 1 a very large supermarket that often sells clothes, etc as well as food and household goods. 2 a very large store that sells a specified type of goods such as DIY products, furniture, etc.

superstructure N anything that is based on or built above another, usu more important, part, eg those parts of a ship above the main deck.

supertanker N a large ship for transporting oil or other liquid.

supervene VB, INTR to occur as an interruption

to some process. ■ **supervention** N.

supervise VB 1 to be in overall charge of (employees, etc). 2 to oversee (a task, project, etc). ■ **supervision** N. ■ **supervisor** N. ■ **supervisory** ADJ.

supine ADJ 1 lying on one's back. 2 lazy.

supper N an evening meal, esp a light one.

supplant VB to take the place of someone, often by force or unfair means.

supple ADJ bending easily; flexible. ■ **supplely** ADV. ■ **suppleness** N.

supplement N 1 something that is added to make something else complete or that makes up a deficiency: **vitamin supplement**. 2 an extra section added to a book to give additional information or to correct previous errors. 3 a separate part that comes with a newspaper, esp a Sunday one.
➤ VB (often **supplement by** or **with sth**) to add to something. ■ **supplementary** ADJ.

supplicate VB, TR & INTR 1 (usu **supplicate for sth**) to humbly and earnestly request it. 2 (usu **supplicate sb for sth**) to humbly and earnestly request it of them. ■ **supplicant** N. ■ **supplication** N.

supply VB (-*ies*, -*ied*) a to provide or furnish (something believed to be necessary): **I'll supply the wine if you bring some beers**; b (also **supply sb with sth**) to provide or furnish them with it: **The garden supplied them with all their vegetables**.
➤ N (-*ies*) 1 an act or instance of providing. 2 an amount provided, esp regularly. 3 an amount that can be drawn from and used; a stock. 4 (**supplies**) necessary food, equipment, etc that is stored, gathered, taken on a journey, etc. 5 ECON the total amount of a commodity that is produced. ■ **supplier** N.

support VB 1 to keep something upright or in place. 2 to keep from falling. 3 to bear the weight of someone or something. 4 to give active approval, encouragement, money, etc to (an institution, belief, theory, etc). 5 to provide someone or something with the means necessary for living or existing: **She supports a**

large family. 6 to maintain a loyal and active interest in the fortunes of (a particular sport or team). 7 to speak in favour of (a proposal, etc). 8 to play a part subordinate to (a leading actor). 9 to perform before (the main item in a concert, show, etc). 10 to tolerate something.
➤ N 1 the act of supporting. 2 someone or something that supports. 3 someone or something that helps, comforts, etc. 4 (often **the support**) a group, singer, film, etc that accompanies or comes on before the main attraction. ■ **supportive** ADJ.

supporter N someone who gives a specified institution such as a sport, a team, a political party, etc their active backing, etc.

suppose VB 1 to consider something likely, even when there is a lack of tangible evidence for it to be so. 2 to think, believe, agree, etc reluctantly, unwillingly (that something could be true). 3 to assume, often wrongly: **He supposed she wouldn't find out.**

supposed ADJ generally believed to be so or true, but considered doubtful by the speaker: **couldn't find him at his supposed address.** ■ **supposedly** ADV.
◆ **be supposed to be** or **do sth** to be expected or allowed to be or do it.

supposition N 1 the act of supposing. 2 something that is supposed; a mere possibility or assumption. 3 conjecture.

suppository N (-*ies*) MED a soluble preparation of medicine which dissolves when it is inserted into the rectum or vagina.

suppress VB 1 to hold back or restrain (feelings, laughter, a yawn, etc). 2 to put a stop to something. 3 to prevent (information, news, etc) from being broadcast or otherwise being made known. ■ **suppression** N.

suppurate VB, INTR of a wound, boil, ulcer, etc: to gather and release pus; to fester.

supremacy N 1 supreme power or authority. 2 the state or quality of being supreme.

supreme ADJ 1 highest in rank, power, importance, etc: **the Supreme Court.** 2 most excellent: **supreme effort.** 3 greatest in degree:

supreme stupidity. ■ **supremely** ADV.

supremo N, COLLOQ **1** a supreme head or leader. **2** a boss.

surcharge N an extra charge, often as a penalty for late payment of a bill.
➤ VB to impose a surcharge on someone.

surd MATH, ADJ of a number: unable to be expressed in finite terms; irrational.
➤ N an irrational number.

sure ADJ **1** confident beyond doubt in one's belief or knowledge; convinced: **felt sure he'd picked up the keys. 2** undoubtedly true or accurate: **a sure sign. 3** reliably stable or secure: **on a sure footing.** ■ **sureness** N.

sure-fire ADJ, COLLOQ infallible.

sure-footed ADJ **1** not stumbling or likely to stumble. **2** not likely to make mistakes.

surely ADV **1** without doubt; certainly. **2** used in questions and exclamations: to express incredulity: **Surely you knew he was joking?**

surety N (**-ies**) **1** someone who agrees to become legally responsible for another person's behaviour, debts, etc. **2** security, usu in the form of a sum of money, as a guarantee.

surf N **1** the sea as it breaks against the shore, a reef, etc. **2** the foam produced by breaking waves. **3** an act or instance of surfing.
➤ VB **1** INTR to take part in a sport or recreation where the object is to stand or lie on a long narrow board, try to catch the crest of a wave and ride it to the shore. **2** to browse through (the Internet). ■ **surfer** N. ■ **surfing** N.

surface N **1 a** the upper or outer side of anything; **b** the size or area of such a side. **2** the upper level of a body or container of liquid or of the land. **3** the external appearance of something, as opposed to its underlying reality: **On the surface everything seems fine. 4** MATH a two-dimensional geometric figure, having length and breadth but no depth.
➤ VB **1** INTR to rise to the surface of a liquid. **2** INTR to become apparent; to come to light: **The scandal first surfaced in the press. 3** INTR, COLLOQ to get out of bed.
◆ **come to the surface** to become known.

surface mail N mail that is sent overland or by ship, as distinct from airmail.

surfboard N a long narrow shaped fibreglass board that a surfer stands or lies on.

surfeit N (usu **surfeit of sth**) an excess.

surge N **1** a sudden powerful mass movement of a crowd, esp forwards. **2** a sudden sharp increase. **3** a sudden rush of emotion: **felt a surge of indignation. 4** a rising and falling of a large area of sea.
➤ VB, INTR **1** of the sea, waves, etc: to move up and down or swell with force. **2** of a crowd, etc: to move forward in a mass. **3** (also **surge up**) of an emotion, etc: to rise up suddenly and often uncontrollably: **sorrow surged up inside him. 4** of prices, etc: to increase suddenly.

surgeon N a person who is professionally qualified to practise surgery.

surgery N (**-ies**) **1** the branch of medicine that is concerned with treating disease, disorder or injury by cutting into the patient's body to operate directly on or remove the affected part. **2** the performance or an instance of this type of treatment: **The surgery took 10 hours. 3** BRIT **a** the place where a doctor, dentist, etc sees their patients; **b** the time when they are available for consultation. **4** BRIT a time when eg an MP, lawyer, etc can be consulted.

surgical ADJ of, or by means of, surgery: **surgical instruments.** ■ **surgically** ADV.

surgical spirit N methylated spirit used for cleaning wounds and sterilizing equipment.

surly ADJ (**-ier, -iest**) abrupt and impolite in manner or speech. ■ **surliness** N.

surmise VB to conclude something from the information available, esp when the information is incomplete or insubstantial.
➤ N a conclusion drawn from such information.

surmount VB to overcome (problems, obstacles, etc). ■ **surmountable** ADJ.

surname N a family name or last name.

surpass VB **1** to go or be beyond in degree or extent; to exceed. **2** to be better than: **a holiday that surpassed all expectations.**

surplice N a loose wide-sleeved white linen garment worn ceremonially by members of the clergy and choir singers over their robes.

surplus N an amount that exceeds the amount required or used.
➤ ADJ left over after needs have been met.

surprise N 1 a sudden, unexpected, astounding, amazing, etc event, factor, gift, etc. 2 a feeling of mental disorientation caused by something of this nature. 3 the act of catching someone unawares or off-guard.
➤ VB 1 to cause someone to experience surprise by presenting them with or subjecting them to something unexpected, amazing, etc: **surprised her with a kiss**. 2 to come upon something or someone unexpectedly or catch them or it unawares. ■ **surprised** ADJ.
■ **surprising** ADJ. ■ **surprisingly** ADV.

surreal ADJ 1 dreamlike; very odd or bizarre. 2 being in the style of Surrealism.

surrealism N (sometimes **Surrealism**) a movement in art and literature that sprang up between the first and second World Wars, and whose most prominent aim was to allow the artist's or writer's unconscious to be expressed with complete creative freedom. ■ **surrealist** ADJ, N. ■ **surrealistic** ADJ.

surrender VB 1 INTR to admit defeat by giving oneself up to an enemy. 2 to give or hand over someone or something, either voluntarily or under duress. 3 to give up something: **surrendered all hope of being rescued**.
➤ N an act or the process of surrendering.
◆ **surrender to sth** to give in to it.

surreptitious ADJ secret, sneaky, underhand.

surrogate N someone or something that takes the place of or is substituted for another: **surrogate mother**. ■ **surrogacy** N.

surround VB to extend all around; to encircle.
➤ N a border or edge, or an ornamental structure fitted round this. ■ **surrounding** ADJ.

surroundings PL N the places and/or things round about someone or something; environment: **rural surroundings**.

surtax N 1 an additional tax, esp one that is levied on incomes above a certain level. 2 an additional tax on something that already has a tax or duty levied on it.

surveillance N a close watch over something (eg for security purposes) or someone (eg a suspected criminal).

survey VB 1 to look at or examine at length or in detail, in order to get a general view. 2 to examine (a building) in order to assess its condition or value, esp on behalf of a prospective owner, mortgage lender, etc. 3 to measure land heights and distances in (an area) for the purposes of drawing a detailed map, plan, etc. 4 to canvass (public opinion) and make an assessment of the replies.
➤ N 1 a detailed examination or investigation, eg to find out public opinion or customer preference. 2 an inspection of a building to assess condition or value. 3 a the collecting of land measurements for map-making purposes, etc; b the map, plan, report, etc that is drawn up after this has been done. ■ **surveying** N.
■ **surveyor** N.

survival N the fact of continuing to live, esp after some risk that might have prevented this.

survive VB 1 TR & INTR a to remain alive, esp despite (some risk that might prevent this); b INFORMAL to come or get through (something arduous or unpleasant). 2 to live on after the death of someone: **survived her husband by 10 years**. 3 INTR to remain alive or in existence. ■ **survivor** N.

susceptible ADJ 1 (**susceptible to sth**) prone to being, or likely to be, affected by it: **always been susceptible to colds**. 2 capable of being affected by strong feelings, esp of love. 3 (**susceptible to sth**) capable of being influenced by something. ■ **susceptibility** N.

sushi N a Japanese dish of small rolls or balls of cold boiled rice topped with egg, raw fish or vegetables.

suspect VB 1 to consider or believe likely. 2 to think (a particular person) possibly guilty of a crime or other wrongdoing. 3 to doubt the truth or genuineness of someone or something.
➤ N someone who is suspected of

committing a crime, etc.
➤ ADJ dubious: **His excuse sounds pretty suspect to me.**

suspend VB 1 to hang or hang up something. 2 to bring a halt to something, esp temporarily. 3 to remove someone from a job, a team, etc temporarily, as punishment or during an investigation of a possible misdemeanour.

suspended sentence N a judicial sentence that is deferred for a set time during which the offender is required to be of good behaviour.

suspenders PL N elasticated straps that can be attached to the top of a stocking or sock to hold it in place.

suspense N 1 a state of nervous or excited tension or uncertainty. 2 tension or excitedness, esp as brought on by an eager desire to know the outcome of something.

suspension N 1 the act of suspending or the state of being suspended. 2 a temporary exclusion from an official position, work, school, college, etc, esp while allegations of misconduct are being investigated. 3 a temporary cessation. 4 in a vehicle: a system of springs and shock absorbers that absorbs some of the unwanted vibrations transmitted from the road surface. 5 a liquid or gas that contains small insoluble solid particles dispersed throughout it.

suspension bridge N a bridge that has a road or rail surface hanging from vertical cables attached to thicker cables stretched between towers.

suspicion N 1 an act, instance or feeling of suspecting. 2 a belief or opinion that is based on very little evidence. 3 a slight quantity.
◆ **above suspicion** too highly respected to be suspected of a crime or wrongdoing.
◆ **under suspicion** suspected of a crime or wrongdoing.

suspicious ADJ 1 inclined to suspect guilt, wrongdoing, etc: **a suspicious nature.** 2 inviting or arousing suspicion; dubious: **in suspicious circumstances.** ■ **suspiciously** ADV.

suss VB, SLANG (**-ss-**) to discover, assess or establish something, esp by investigation or intuition: **soon sussed how the video worked.**
◆ **suss sb** or **sth out** 1 to investigate, inspect or examine: **sussed out the nightlife.** 2 to work out or understand: **couldn't suss out his motives.**

sustain VB 1 to keep going. 2 to withstand or endure: **can sustain impacts even at high speed.** 3 to suffer or undergo (eg an injury, loss, etc). 4 to declare that an objection in court is valid. 5 to maintain or provide for something: **couldn't sustain her family on her salary.**

sustainable ADJ 1 capable of being sustained. 2 of economic development, renewable resources, etc: capable of being maintained at a set level.

sustenance N 1 **a** something that nourishes the body or that keeps up energy or spirits; **b** the action or an instance of nourishment. 2 something that maintains, supports or provides a livelihood.

suture N **a** a stitch that joins the edges of a wound, surgical incision, etc together; **b** the joining of such edges together.

svelte ADJ slim or slender.

swab N **a** a piece of cotton wool, gauze, etc that is used for cleaning wounds, applying antiseptics, taking a medical specimen, etc; **b** a medical specimen, eg of some bodily fluid, etc, that is taken for examination or testing.
➤ VB (**-bb-**) 1 to clean (a wound) with, or as if with, a swab. 2 to mop something (eg a wound, a ship's deck, etc).

swaddling-clothes PL N, HIST strips of cloth wrapped round a newborn baby.

swag N 1 SLANG stolen goods. 2 AUSTRAL a traveller's pack or rolled bundle of possessions.

swagger VB, INTR to walk with an air of self-importance.
➤ N 1 a swaggering way of walking or behaving. 2 COLLOQ the quality of being showily fashionable or smart.

swallow[1] VB 1 to perform a muscular movement to make (food or drink) go from the mouth, down the oesophagus and into the stomach. 2 INTR to move the muscles of the

throat involuntarily, esp as a sign of emotional distress. **3** (also **swallow sth up**) to engulf or absorb it. **4** to stifle or repress (eg pride, tears, etc). **5** COLLOQ to believe gullibly or unquestioningly.
➤ N **1** an act of swallowing. **2** an amount swallowed at one time.

swallow² N a small migratory insect–eating bird with long pointed wings and a forked tail.

swallowtail N a large colourful butterfly that has the back wings extended into slender tails.

swamp N an area of land that is permanently waterlogged.
➤ VB **1** to overwhelm or inundate. **2** to cause (a boat) to fill with water. **3** to flood.

swan N a large, generally white, aquatic bird with a long slender elegant neck, powerful wings and webbed feet.
➤ VB (-*nn*-) INTR, COLLOQ (usu **swan off, around,** etc) to spend time idly; to wander aimlessly or gracefully.

swank VB, INTR, COLLOQ to boast or show off. ■ **swanky** ADJ.

swan song N the last performance or piece of work that a musician, artist, etc gives before their death or retirement.

swap or **swop** VB (-*pp*-) TR & INTR to exchange or trade (something or someone) for another.
➤ N an exchange or trading.

swarm¹ N **1** a large group of bees, led by a queen, that have left their hive in order to set up a new home. **2** any large group, esp one that is on the move.
➤ VB, INTR to gather, move, go, etc in a swarm.
◆ **be swarming** or **be swarming with** of a place: to be crowded or overrun.

swarm² VB, TR & INTR (often **swarm up sth**) to climb (esp a rope or tree) by clasping with the hands and knees or feet.

swarthy ADJ (-*ier*, -*iest*) having a dark complexion. ■ **swarthiness** N.

swashbuckler N **1** a daring and flamboyant adventurer. **2** a type of highly stylized film,

novel, etc that portrays exciting scenes of adventure and which usu features scenes of swordsmanship. ■ **swashbuckling** ADJ.

swastika N a plain cross with arms of equal length bent at right angles, usu clockwise, at or close to their mid point, used as the adopted badge of the former German Nazi Party.

swat VB (-*tt*-) to hit (esp a fly) with a heavy slapping blow.

swatch N a small sample, esp of fabric but also of wallpaper, carpet, etc.

swathe VB to bind or wrap someone or something in strips of cloth, eg bandages.
➤ N a wrapping, esp a strip of cloth or fabric; a bandage.

sway VB **1** TR & INTR to swing, or make something swing, backwards and forwards or from side to side, esp slowly and smoothly. **2** TR & INTR to lean or bend, or make something lean or bend, to one side or in one direction. **3** to persuade someone to take a particular view or decision.
➤ N **1** a swaying motion. **2** control or influence.

swear VB (*swore, sworn*) **1** INTR to use indecent or blasphemous language. **2** to assert something solemnly or earnestly, sometimes with an oath. **3** to promise solemnly.
➤ N an act of swearing.
◆ **swear by sth** COLLOQ to have or put complete trust in it.
◆ **swear sb in** to introduce them formally into a post, or into the witness box, by requesting them to take an oath.
◆ **swear off sth** COLLOQ to promise to renounce it or give it up.

swear-word N a word regarded as obscene or blasphemous.

sweat N the salty liquid produced actively by the sweat glands and given out through the pores of the skin, esp in response to great heat, physical exertion, nervousness or fear.
➤ VB (*sweated* or *sweat*) INTR to give out sweat through the pores. ■ **sweaty** ADJ.
◆ **sweat sth off** to remove (weight, fat, etc) by exercise that makes one sweat.

sweatband N a strip of fabric worn around

the wrist or head to absorb sweat when playing sports.

sweater N a knitted jersey or pullover.

sweatshirt N a long-sleeved jersey of a thick soft cotton fabric, orig worn for sports.

sweatshop N a workshop where employees work long hours with poor pay and conditions.

swede N 1 a plant widely cultivated for its edible root. **2** the swollen edible root of this plant, which has orange-yellow or whitish flesh, and can be cooked and eaten as a vegetable.

sweep VB (*swept*) **1** to clean (a room, a floor, etc) with a brush or broom. **2** to remove (dirt, dust, etc) with a brush or broom. **3** (usu **sweep sth aside** or **away**) to dismiss (ideas, suggestions, etc) or remove (problems, errors, etc): **She swept aside their objections. 4** (often **sweep sb** or **sth away, off, past,** etc) to take, carry or push them suddenly and with irresistible force: **The current swept the boat through the narrows. 5** (often **sweep sb** or **sth off, up,** etc) to lift, gather or clear with a forceful scooping or brushing movement: **He swept the child into his arms. 6** INTR to walk, esp with garments flowing, impressively, arrogantly, angrily, etc: **She swept across the room in her robes. 7** TR & INTR to pass quickly over, making light contact: **Her dress swept the floor. 8** to cast or direct (eg one's gaze) with a scanning movement. **9** to make extensive searches over (an area, esp the sea).
➤ N **1** an act of sweeping. **2** a sweeping movement or action. **3** a sweeping line. **4** the range or area over which something moves, esp in a curving or circular path. **5** COLLOQ a sweepstake. **6** COLLOQ a chimney-sweep.
◆ **a clean sweep** the winning of all prizes, awards, political seats, etc.

sweeper N **1** a device or machine used for sweeping. **2** FOOTBALL a player covering the whole area behind a line of defenders.

sweeping ADJ **1** of a search, change, etc: wide-ranging and thorough. **2** of a statement: too generalized; indiscriminate. **3** of a victory, etc: impressive; decisive.

sweepstake N **1** a system of gambling in which the prize money is the sum of the stakes of all those betting. **2** a horse race in which the owner of the winning horse receives sums of money put up by the owners of all the other horses.

sweet ADJ **1** tasting like sugar; not sour, salty or bitter. **2** pleasing to any of the senses, esp smell and hearing. **3** likeable; charming. **4** of wine: having some taste of sugar or fruit. **5** COLLOQ (usu **sweet on sb**) fond of them.
➤ N **1** any small sugar-based confection that is sucked or chewed. **2** a pudding or dessert.
■ **sweetly** ADV. ■ **sweetness** N.

sweet-and-sour ADJ cooked in a sauce that includes both sugar and vinegar or lemon juice.
➤ N a sweet-and-sour dish.

sweetbread N the pancreas or thymus of a young animal, esp a calf, used as food.

sweetcorn N kernels of a variety of maize eaten young while still sweet.

sweeten VB **1** to make (food) sweet or sweeter. **2** (also **sweeten sb up**) COLLOQ to make them more agreeable or amenable, eg by flattery or bribery.

sweetener N **1** a substance used for sweetening food, esp one other than sugar. **2** COLLOQ an inducement, usu illicit, added to an offer to make it more attractive.

sweetheart N **a** a person one is in love with; **b** used as a term of endearment.

sweetie N, COLLOQ **1** a sweet for sucking or chewing. **2** (also **sweetie-pie**) a term of endearment. **3** a lovable person.

sweet nothings PL N the endearments that people in love say to each other.

sweet pea N a climbing plant with brightly coloured butterfly-shaped flowers.

sweet pepper N the hollow edible fruit of a tropical American plant, which can be eaten when red and ripe or when green and unripe.

sweet potato N the swollen edible root of a type of climbing plant, which has sweet-tasting flesh and can be eaten as a vegetable.

sweet talk COLLOQ, N words, often flattery, intended to coax or persuade.
➤ VB (**sweet-talk**) to coax or persuade, eg with flattering words.

sweet tooth N a fondness for sweet foods.

swell VB (PA P *swollen* or *swelled*) **1** TR & INTR to become, or make something, bigger or fatter through injury or infection, or by filling with liquid or air. **2** TR & INTR to increase or make something increase in number, size or intensity. **3** INTR to become visibly filled with emotion, esp pride. **4** INTR of the sea: to rise and fall in smooth masses without forming individual waves.
➤ N **1** a heaving of the sea without waves. **2** an increase in number, size or intensity.

swelling N an area of the body that is temporarily swollen.

swelter VB, INTR to sweat heavily or feel extremely hot. ■ **sweltering** ADJ.

swerve VB, INTR to turn or move aside suddenly and sharply, eg to avoid a collision.

swift ADJ **1** fast-moving; able to move fast. **2** done, given, etc quickly or promptly.
➤ N a small fast-flying bird that has long narrow pointed wings and a forked tail.
■ **swiftly** ADV. ■ **swiftness** N.

swig COLLOQ, VB (**-gg-**) TR & INTR to drink in gulps, esp from a bottle.
➤ N a large drink or gulp.

swill VB (also **swill sth out**) to rinse something by splashing water round or over it.
➤ N any mushy mixture of scraps fed to pigs.

swim VB (*swam, swum, swimming*) **1** INTR to propel oneself through water by moving the arms and legs or (in fish) the tail and fins. **2** INTR to be affected by dizziness: **His head was swimming**.
➤ N a spell of swimming. ■ **swimmer** N.
■ **swimming** N.

swimming-bath N or **swimming-baths** PL N a swimming-pool, usu indoors.

swimming-costume N a swimsuit.

swimmingly ADV, COLLOQ successfully.

swimming-pool N an artificial pool for swimming in.

swimsuit N a garment worn for swimming.

swindle VB to cheat or trick someone in order to obtain money from them.
➤ N an act of swindling. ■ **swindler** N.

swine N (*swine* in sense 1 or *swines* in sense 2) **1** a pig. **2** a despicable person.

swing VB (*swung*) **1** TR & INTR to move in a curving motion, pivoting from a fixed point: **The door swung shut**. **2** TR & INTR to move or turn with a sweeping or curving movement or movements: **swung himself into the saddle**. **3** TR & INTR to turn around a central axis: **She swung round, surprised**. **4** INTR to undergo, often suddenly or sharply, a change or changes of opinion, mood, fortune or direction. **5** to persuade somebody to have a certain opinion: **That should swing them round to our way of thinking**. **6** TR & INTR (often **swing at sb** or **sth**) **a** to attempt to hit or make a hit with a curving movement of a bat, etc: **swung wildly at the ball**; **b** COLLOQ to attempt to punch someone or make a punch with a curving arm movement.
➤ N **1** a seat suspended from a frame or branch for a child (or sometimes an adult) to swing on. **2** a change, usu a sudden and sharp change, eg in mood, support, success, etc. **3** a swinging stroke with a golf club, cricket bat, etc; the technique of a golfer. **4** a punch made with a curving movement. **5** MUS jazz or jazz-like dance music with a simple regular rhythm, popularized by bands in the 1930s. **6** CRICKET a curving movement of a bowled ball. **7** a change in the voting pattern of the electorate: **a swing of 40% to Labour**.
◆ **in full swing** at the height of liveliness.

swingeing ADJ hard to bear; severe.

swipe VB **1** to hit with a heavy sweeping blow. **2** (usu **swipe at sb** or **sth**) to try to hit them or it. **3** COLLOQ to steal. **4** to pass (a credit or debit card) through a device that electronically interprets the information encoded on the card.
➤ N a heavy sweeping blow.

swirl VB, TR & INTR to flow or cause to flow or move with a whirling or circling motion. ➤ N **1** a whirling or circling motion. **2** a curling shape. ■ **swirling** ADJ.

swish[1] VB, TR & INTR to move with a rustling, hissing or whooshing sound. ➤ N a rustling, hissing or whooshing sound.

swish[2] ADJ, COLLOQ smart and stylish.

switch N **1** a manually operated or automatic device that is used to open or close an electric circuit. **2** a change. **3** an exchange or change-over, esp as a deception. **4** a long flexible twig or cane, esp one for corporal punishment. ➤ VB, TR & INTR **1** to exchange (one thing or person for another), esp quickly and without notice in order to deceive. **2** to transfer or change over (eg to a different system). ◆ **switch sth off** or **on** to turn (an appliance) off or on by means of a switch.

switchback N a road with many twists and turns and upward and downward slopes.

switchboard N a board on which incoming telephone calls are connected.

swivel N a joint between two parts enabling one part to turn or pivot freely and independently of the other. ➤ VB (-*ll*-) TR & INTR to turn or pivot on a swivel or as if on a swivel.

swizz N, COLLOQ a thing that is disappointingly inferior to what was cheatingly promised.

swizzle-stick N a thin stick used to stir drinks.

swoon VB, INTR to faint, esp from over-excitement. ➤ N an act of swooning. ◆ **swoon over sb** or **sth** to go into raptures of adoration about them or it.

swoop VB, INTR **1** to fly down with a fast sweeping movement. **2** to make a sudden forceful attack; to pounce. **3** (usu **swoop at sb** or **sth**) to make a sudden and quick attempt to seize or get hold of them or it. ➤ N **1** an act of swooping. **2** a swooping movement or feeling. ◆ **in one fell swoop** in one decisive action.

swoosh N the noise of a rush of air or water, or any noise resembling this. ➤ VB, INTR to make or move with such a noise.

swop see **swap**

sword N a weapon like a large long knife, with a blade sharpened on one or both edges and usu ending in a point. ◆ **cross swords with sb** to encounter them as an opponent; to argue or fight with them.

swordfish N a large marine fish whose upper jaw is prolonged into a sword-shaped snout.

swordplay N the activity or art of fencing.

swordsman N a man skilled in fighting with a sword. ■ **swordsmanship** N.

sworn ADJ bound or confirmed by, or as if by, having taken an oath: **sworn enemies**.

swot COLLOQ, VB (-*tt*-) TR & INTR **1** to study hard and seriously. **2** (also **swot sth up**) to study it intensively, esp just before an exam. ➤ N someone who studies hard, esp single-mindedly or in order to impress a teacher.

sybarite N someone devoted to a life of luxury and pleasure. ■ **sybaritic** ADJ.

sycamore N a large tree with dark green leaves divided into five toothed lobes, and two-winged fruits.

sycophant N someone who flatters in a servile way; a crawler. ■ **sycophancy** N. ■ **sycophantic** ADJ.

syllable N a segment of a spoken word consisting of one sound or of two or more sounds said as a single unit of speech (**segment** has two syllables; **consisting** has three).

syllabub N a frothy dessert.

syllabus N (-*buses* or -*bi*) **1** a series of topics prescribed for a course of study. **2** a booklet or sheet listing these.

syllogism N an argument in which a conclusion, whether valid or invalid, is drawn from two independent statements using logic, as in **All dogs are animals, foxhounds are dogs, therefore foxhounds are animals.**

sylph N 1 in folklore: a spirit of the air. 2 a slender woman or girl. ■ **sylph-like** ADJ.

sylvan or **silvan** ADJ, LITERARY relating to woods or woodland.

symbiosis N (-*ses*) BIOL a close association between two organisms of different species, usu to the benefit of both partners, and often essential for mutual survival. ■ **symbiotic** ADJ.

symbol N 1 a thing that represents or stands for another, usu something concrete or material representing an idea or emotion, eg the colour red representing danger. 2 a letter or sign used to represent a quantity, idea, operation, etc, such as **£** for pound sterling.

symbolic ADJ 1 being a symbol of something; representing something. 2 relating to symbols or their use. ■ **symbolically** ADV.

symbolism N 1 the use of symbols, esp to express ideas or emotions in literature, cinema, etc. 2 a system of symbols. ■ **symbolist** N.

symbolize or **-ise** VB 1 to be a symbol of something; to stand for something. 2 to represent something by means of symbols.

symmetry N (-*ies*) 1 exact similarity between two parts or halves, as if one were a mirror image of the other. 2 the arrangement of parts in pleasing proportion to each other. ■ **symmetrical** ADJ.

sympathetic ADJ 1 (often **sympathetic to sb** or **sth**) feeling or expressing sympathy for them. 2 amiable, esp because of being kind-hearted. 3 acting or done out of sympathy; showing sympathy. 4 in keeping with one's mood or feelings; agreeable.

sympathize or **-ise** VB, INTR 1 (often **sympathize with sb**) to feel or express sympathy for them. 2 (often **sympathize with sb** or **sth**) to support or be in agreement with them. ■ **sympathizer** N.

sympathy N (-*ies*) 1 (often **sympathy for** or **with sb**) an understanding of and feeling for the sadness or suffering of others, often shown in expressions of sorrow or pity. 2 (often **sympathies**) loyal or approving support for, or agreement with, an organization or belief.

3 affection between people resulting from their understanding of each other.

symphony N (-*ies*) 1 a long musical work divided into several movements, played by a full orchestra. 2 an instrumental passage in a musical work which consists mostly of singing. ■ **symphonic** ADJ.

symphony orchestra N an orchestra that can play large-scale orchestral music.

symposium N (-*ia* or -*iums*) a conference held to discuss a particular subject.

symptom N 1 MED an indication of the presence of a disease or disorder, esp something perceived by the patient and not outwardly visible, eg pain, nausea, etc. 2 an indication of the existence of a, usu unwelcome, state or condition: **a symptom of moral decline**. ■ **symptomatic** ADJ.

synagogue N a Jewish place of worship and religious instruction.

synch or **sync** COLLOQ, N synchronization, esp of sound and picture in film and television. ➢ VB to synchronize.

synchromesh N a gear system which matches the speeds of the gear wheels before they are engaged, avoiding shock and noise in gear-changing.

synchronize or **-ise** VB 1 TR & INTR to happen or cause to happen, move or operate in exact time with (something else or each other). 2 to project (a film), or broadcast (a TV programme), so that the action, actors' lip movements, etc precisely match the sounds or words heard. 3 to set (clocks or watches) so that they all show the same time. ■ **synchronization** N.

synchronous ADJ occurring at the same time; recurring with the same frequency.

syncopate VB to alter (the rhythm of music) by putting the stress on beats not usu stressed.

syndicate N 1 any association of people or groups working together on a single project. 2 a group of business organizations jointly managing or financing a single venture. 3 an association of criminals organizing

widespread illegal activities. **4** an agency selling journalists' material to a number of newspapers for publication at the same time.
➤ VB **1** to form into a syndicate. **2 a** to sell (an article, photograph, etc) for publication by a number of newspapers; **b** in the US: to sell (a programme) for broadcasting by a number of TV stations. ■ **syndication** N.

syndrome N a group of signs or symptoms whose appearance together usu indicates the presence of a particular disease or disorder.

synergy N the combined action or effect of two or more compounds, factors, etc that is greater than the sum of the individual effects of each compound, factor, etc.

synod N a council of the clergy.

synonym N a word having the same, or very nearly the same, meaning as another.

synonymous ADJ (often **synonymous with sth**) **1** having the same meaning. **2** very closely associated in the mind.

synopsis N (-**ses**) a brief outline, eg of the plot of a book; a summary. ■ **synoptic** ADJ.

syntax N **a** the positioning of words in a sentence and their relationship to each other; **b** the grammatical rules governing this.
■ **syntactic** or **syntactical** ADJ.

synthesis N (-**ses**) **1** the process of putting together separate parts to form a complex whole. **2** the result of such a process. **3** CHEM any process whereby a complex chemical compound is formed from simpler compounds or elements.

synthesize or **-ise** VB **1** to combine (simple parts) to form (a complex whole). **2** CHEM to form (a compound, product, etc) by a process of chemical synthesis.

synthesizer or **-iser** N, MUS an instrument that produces sound electronically.

synthetic ADJ **1** referring or relating to, or

produced by, chemical synthesis; man-made. **2** not sincere; sham. ■ **synthetically** ADV.

syphilis N, MED a sexually transmitted disease caused by bacterial infection. ■ **syphilitic** ADJ.

syphon see **siphon**

syringe N a medical instrument for injecting or drawing off liquid, consisting of a hollow cylinder with a plunger inside and a thin hollow needle attached.
➤ VB to clean, spray or inject using a syringe.

syrup N **1** a sweet, sticky, almost saturated solution of sugar, eg golden syrup. **2** a solution of sugar in water. ■ **syrupy** ADJ.

system N **1** a set of interconnected or interrelated parts forming a complex whole: **the transport system**. **2** an arrangement of mechanical, electrical or electronic parts functioning as a unit: **a stereo system**.
3 a method or arrangement of organization or classification: **a more efficient filing system**.
4 efficiency of organization: **You need to get some system into your exam revision. 5** one's mind or body regarded as a set of interconnected parts: **get the anger out of your system. 6** (**the system**) society, or the network of institutions that control it, usu regarded as an oppressive force.

systematic ADJ **1** making use of, or carried out according to, a clearly worked-out plan or method. **2** methodical. ■ **systematically** ADV.

systematize or **-ise** VB to organize or arrange in a methodical way.

systems analysis N, COMP the detailed investigation and analysis of some human task in order to determine whether and how it can be computerized.

systole N, MED contraction of the heart muscle, during which blood is pumped from the ventricle into the arteries. ■ **systolic** ADJ.

Tt

T or **t** N (*Ts, T's* or *t's*) the twentieth letter of the English alphabet.
◆ **to a T** exactly; perfectly well.

ta EXCLAM, BRIT COLLOQ thank you.

tab¹ N **1** a small flap, tag, strip of material, etc attached to something, for hanging it up, opening, holding or identifying it, etc. **2** chiefly N AMER a bill, eg, in a bar, restaurant, etc.
➢ VB (*-bb-*) to fix a tab to.
◆ **keep tabs on** COLLOQ to keep a close watch or check on.

tab² N a key on a keyboard which sets and finds the position of margins and columns.

tabard N a short loose sleeveless jacket or tunic, worn esp by a medieval knight or by a herald.

tabbouleh N a Mediterranean salad made with cracked wheat and vegetables.

tabby N (*-ies*) (also **tabby cat**) a grey or brown cat with darker stripes.

tabernacle N **1** the tent carried by the Israelites across the desert during the Exodus. **2** RC CHURCH a receptacle where the consecrated bread and wine are kept.

table N **1** a piece of furniture consisting of a flat horizontal surface supported by one or more legs. **2** a group of words or figures, etc arranged in columns and rows.
3 a multiplication table.
➢ VB **1** BRIT to put forward for discussion.
2 N AMER to postpone discussion of (a bill, etc) indefinitely.
◆ **on the table** under discussion.
◆ **turn the tables on sb** to reverse a situation so that they are at a disadvantage where previously they had an advantage.

tablecloth N a cloth for covering a table.

tableland N a broad high plain or a plateau.

tablespoon N **1** a large spoon used for measuring and serving food. **2** the amount a tablespoon can hold. ■ **tablespoonful** N.

tablet N **1** a small solid measured amount of a medicine or drug. **2** a solid flat piece of something, eg, soap. **3** a slab of stone or wood on which an inscription may be carved.

table tennis N a game based on tennis played indoors on a table with small bats and a light hollow ball. Also called **ping-pong**.

tabloid N a newspaper with relatively small pages, usu having a sensationalist style.
➢ ADJ relating to this type of newspaper.

taboo or **tabu** N **1** something which is forbidden or disapproved of for religious reasons or by social custom. **2** a system in which certain actions, etc are forbidden.
➢ ADJ forbidden or prohibited as being a taboo.

tabular ADJ arranged in systematic columns.

tabulate VB to arrange (information) in tabular form. ■ **tabulation** N.

tabulator N a **tab²**.

tachograph N a device which keeps a record of a vehicle's speed, esp a lorry.

tachometer N a device which measures speed.

tacit ADJ **1** silent; unspoken. **2** understood but not actually stated.

taciturn ADJ saying little; quiet and

uncommunicative. ■ **taciturnity** N.

tack¹ N **1** a short nail with a sharp point and a broad flat head. **2** N AMER a drawing-pin. **3** a long loose temporary stitch. **4** a sailing ship's course, esp when taking advantage of winds from different directions. **5** a direction, course of action or policy.
➢ VB **1** to fasten with a tack or tacks. **2** to sew with long loose temporary stitches. **3** to add as a supplement. **4** INTR to use the wind direction to one's advantage when sailing.

tack² N a horse's riding harness, saddle, etc.

tackle N **1** SPORT an act of trying to get the ball away from an opposing player. **2** the equipment needed for a particular sport or occupation. **3** a system of ropes and pulleys for lifting heavy objects. **4** the ropes and rigging on a ship.
➢ VB **1** to grasp or seize and struggle with. **2** to question (someone) (about a disputed, etc issue). **3** to try to deal with or solve (a problem). **4** TR & INTR, SPORT to try to get the ball from (an opposing player).

tacky ADJ (*-ier, -iest*) **1** slightly sticky. **2** COLLOQ vulgar; in bad taste. ■ **tackiness** N.

taco N a rolled or folded tortilla with a filling.

tact N **1** an awareness of the best way to deal with others so as to avoid offence. **2** skill in handling difficult situations; diplomacy.
■ **tactful** ADJ. ■ **tactless** ADJ.

tactic N a tactical manoeuvre.

tactical ADJ **1** relating to or forming tactics. **2** skilful; well planned and well executed.

tactics SING OR PL N **1** the art of employing troops to gain an advantage over the enemy. **2** plans, procedures, etc used in achieving something.
■ **tactician** N.

tactile ADJ **1** relating to, or having, a sense of touch. **2** perceptible to the sense of touch.

tad N, COLLOQ a small amount.

tadpole N the larval stage of an amphibian.

tae kwon do N a Korean martial art.

taffeta N a stiff woven silk or silk-like material.

tag¹ N **1** a label attached to something and carrying information. **2** a device which transmits radio signals, used to monitor the movements of an offender outside prison.
➢ VB (*-gg-*) **1** to put a tag or tags on. **2** (usu **tag along** or **on**) INTR to follow, esp when uninvited.

tag² N a children's chasing game. Also called **tig**.
➢ VB (*-gg-*) to catch in the game of tag.

tagliatelle N pasta in the form of long ribbons.

t'ai chi N a Chinese system of exercise and self-defence involving extremely slow and controlled movements.

tail N **1** the part of an animal's body that projects from the lower or rear end. **2** the feathers that project from the rear of a bird's body. **3** anything which has a similar position as a creature's tail: **shirt tail**. **4** a lower, last or rear part. **5** the rear part of an aircraft. **6** ASTRON the trail of luminous particles following a comet. **7** (**tails**) the reverse side of a coin, which does not bear a portrait. **8** (**tails**) a tailcoat.
➢ VB **1** to remove the stalks (from fruit or vegetables). **2** to follow and watch very closely. ■ **tailless** ADJ.
◆ **tail off** to become gradually less or weaker.

tailback N a long queue of traffic stretching back from an accident or roadworks, etc.

tailboard N a hinged or removable flap at the rear of a lorry, etc.

tailcoat N a man's formal black jacket with a long divided tapering tail.

tailgate N a door which opens upwards at the back of an estate car or hatchback.

tailor N someone whose job is making suits, jackets, trousers, etc to measure, esp for men.
➢ VB **1** to make (garments) so that they fit well. **2** to make suitable for particular circumstances.

tailored ADJ of clothes: fitting exactly.

tailor-made ADJ **1** of clothes: made by a tailor to fit a particular person. **2** perfectly suited or adapted for a particular purpose.

tailplane N a small horizontal wing at the rear of an aircraft.

tailspin N a spinning movement made by an aircraft, either because it is out of the pilot's control or as part of an aeronautical display.

taint VB **1** to affect by pollution or contamination. **2** to affect or spoil slightly. ➢ N **1** a trace of decay, contamination or infection. **2** a corrupt or decayed condition. ■ **tainted** ADJ.

take VB (*took, taken*) **1** to reach out for and grasp, lift or pull, etc. **2** to carry, conduct or lead to another place. **3** to do or perform: **take a walk**. **4** to get, occupy, rent or buy. **5** to agree to have: **take advice**. **6** to accept as true or valid: **take her word for it**. **7** to commit oneself to: **take a decision**. **8** to put up with: **cannot take his arrogance**. **9** to require: **It will take all day**. **10** to use (eg a bus or train) as a means of transport. **11** to make a written note, etc of: **take the minutes**. **12** to photograph: **take a few slides**. **13** to study or teach (a subject, etc). **14** to remove, use or borrow without permission. **15** to proceed to occupy: **take a seat**. **16** to come or derive from: **a quotation taken from Shakespeare**. **17** to have room to hold or strength to support: **The shelf won't take any more books**. **18** to consider as an example. **19** to consider in a particular way: **Do you take me for a fool? 20** to capture or win. **21** to charm and delight: **was very taken with the little cottage**. **22** to eat or drink. **23** to lead: **This road will take you the station**. **24** to be in charge of: **take the meeting**. **25** to react to (news, etc) in a specified way. **26** to feel: **takes pride in her work**. **27** to derive (help or refuge, etc): **takes refuge in his religion**. **28** to subtract or remove. **29** to select (a route, etc): **took the first road on the left**. **30** to deal with: **take the first two questions together**. **31** INTR to have the expected or desired effect: **The vaccination didn't take**. **32** INTR of seeds, etc: to begin to send out roots and grow. **33** to measure: **take a temperature**. **34** INTR to become suddenly (ill, etc). **35** to understand: **I take him to mean he isn't coming**. ➢ N a scene filmed or a piece of music recorded, etc in a single, uninterrupted period.

◆ **take after** to resemble.
◆ **take against** to dislike immediately.
◆ **take sb apart** to criticize them severely.
◆ **take sth apart** to separate it into pieces.
◆ **take back 1** to make (someone) remember the past. **2** to resume relations with (esp a former partner, lover, etc) after an estrangement. **3** to withdraw or retract (a statement or promise). **4** to regain possession of (something). **5** to return (something bought from a shop) for an exchange or refund.
◆ **take sth down 1** to make a written note of it. **2** to demolish or dismantle it. **3** to lower it.
◆ **take sb in 1** to give them accommodation or shelter. **2** to deceive them.
◆ **take sth in 1** to include it. **2** to understand and remember it. **3** to make (a piece of clothing) smaller. **4** to include a visit to (a place).
◆ **take it out of sb** COLLOQ to exhaust them.
◆ **take it out on sb** COLLOQ to vent one's anger or frustration on them.
◆ **take it upon oneself** to assume responsibility.
◆ **take off 1** of an aircraft or its passengers: to leave the ground. **2** to depart or set out. **3** COLLOQ of a scheme or product, etc: to become successful and expand quickly.
◆ **take sb off** to imitate them for comic effect.
◆ **take off 1** to remove. **2** to deduct. **3** to spend a period of time away from work.
◆ **take sb on 1** to give them employment. **2** to challenge or compete with them.
◆ **take on 1** to agree to do or undertake (something). **2** to acquire (a new meaning, quality or appearance, etc).
◆ **take sb out** to escort them in public.
◆ **take sth out 1** to remove or extract it. **2** to obtain it on application: **take out a warrant**.
◆ **take over** to assume control, management or ownership of (a business, etc).
◆ **take to sb** to develop a liking for them.
◆ **take to sth 1** to develop a liking for it. **2** to begin to do it regularly.
◆ **take up 1** to lift or raise. **2** to use or occupy (space or time). **3** to become interested in (a sport, hobby, etc). **4** to shorten (a piece of clothing). **5** to resume (a story or account, etc) after a pause. **6** to assume or adopt: **take up residence**. **7** to accept (an offer).

◆ **take sb up on sth 1** to accept their offer, proposal or challenge, etc. **2** to discuss (a point or issue) first raised by them.
◆ **take up with sb** to become friendly with them; to begin to associate with them.
◆ **take sth up with sb** to discuss it with them.

takeaway N **1** a cooked meal prepared and bought in a restaurant but taken away and eaten somewhere else. **2** a restaurant which provides such meals. **Also** AS ADJ.

take-off N **1** an act or instance of an aircraft leaving the ground. **2** an act of mimicking.

takeover N an act of assuming control.

taker N someone who accepts an offer.

takings PL N the amount of money taken at a concert or in a shop, etc; receipts.

talc N **1** GEOL a mineral form of magnesium silicate. **2** talcum.

talcum N (in full **talcum powder**) a fine, often perfumed, powder made from purified talc.

tale N **1** a story or narrative. **2** a false or malicious story or piece of gossip; a lie.

talent N **1** a special or innate skill, aptitude or ability. **2** high general or mental ability. **3** a person or people with such skill or ability. ■ **talented** ADJ.

talent scout N someone whose job is to find and recruit talented people.

talisman N a small object, supposed to protect its owner from evil or bring good luck.

talk VB **1** INTR to express ideas, etc by spoken words, or by sign language, etc. **2** to discuss: **talk business**. **3** INTR to use or be able to use speech. **4** to utter: **Don't talk nonsense! 5** INTR to gossip. **6** INTR to give away secret information. **7** to use (a language): **talk Dutch**. **8** to get into a certain state by talking: **talked themselves hoarse**. **9** INTR to have influence: **Money talks**. **10** INTR to give a talk or lecture. ➢ N **1** a conversation or discussion. **2** (often **talks**) a formal discussion or series of negotiations. **3** an informal lecture. **4** gossip or rumour, or the subject of it: **the talk of the town**. **5** fruitless or impractical discussion or boasting:

His threats are just talk. ■ **talker** N.
◆ **talk back** to answer rudely or impudently.
◆ **talk sb down 1** to silence them by speaking more loudly. **2** to help (a pilot or aircraft) to land by sending instructions over the radio.
◆ **talk down to sb** to talk patronizingly or condescendingly to them.
◆ **talk sb into** or **out of sth** to persuade them to do or not to do it.
◆ **talk out** to resolve (a problem or difference of opinion) by discussion.
◆ **talk sth over** to discuss it thoroughly.
◆ **talk sb round** to bring them to another way of thinking by talking persuasively.

talkative ADJ fond of talking a lot; chatty.

talking-to N, COLLOQ a ticking-off or reproof.

talk show N, esp N AMER a chat show.

tall ADJ **1** above average height. **2** having a specified height: **six feet tall**. **3** difficult to believe: **a tall story**. **4** difficult or demanding: **a tall order**.

tallow N hard animal fat melted down and used to make candles, soap, etc.

tally N (**-ies**) a reckoning up (of work done, debts, or the score in a game). ➢ VB (**-ies, -ied**) **1** INTR to agree or match: **Our results don't tally**. **2** to count or mark (a number or score, etc) on, or as if on, a tally.

tally-ho EXCLAM a cry to the hounds at a hunt when a fox has been sighted.

Talmud N, JUDAISM the body of Jewish civil and canon law. ■ **Talmudist** N.

talon N a hooked claw, esp of a bird of prey.

tambour N a drum.

tambourine N a musical instrument consisting of a circular frame with a skin stretched over it and small jingling metal discs along the rim.

tame ADJ **1** of animals: living or working with people. **2** meek and submissive. **3** unexciting. ➢ VB **1** to make (an animal) used to living or working with people. **2** to make meek and humble. ■ **tamer** N.

tamper VB, INTR (usu **tamper with**) 1 to interfere or meddle, esp in a harmful way. 2 to attempt to corrupt or influence, esp by bribery.

tampon N a plug of absorbent material inserted into a cavity or wound to absorb blood and other secretions.

tan[1] N 1 a suntan. 2 a tawny-brown colour.
➤ ADJ tawny-brown in colour.
➤ VB (**-nn-**) 1 TR & INTR to make or become brown by exposure to ultraviolet light. 2 to convert (hide) into leather. 3 COLLOQ to beat or thrash.

tan[2] ABBREV, MATH tangent.

tandem N a bicycle for two people.
➤ ADV one behind the other, esp on a bicycle.

tandoori ADJ cooked over charcoal in a clay oven: **tandoori chicken**.

tang N 1 a strong or sharp taste, flavour or smell. 2 a trace or hint. ■ **tangy** ADJ (**-ier, -iest**).

tangent N 1 GEOM a straight or curved line or a curved surface that touches a curve, but does not pass through it. 2 TRIG a function of an angle in a right-angled triangle, defined as the length of the side opposite the angle divided by the length of the side adjacent to it.

tangerine N 1 a small edible citrus fruit, similar to an orange. 2 a reddish-orange colour.

tangible ADJ 1 able to be felt by touch. 2 able to be grasped by the mind. 3 real or definite; material. ■ **tangibility** N. ■ **tangibly** ADV.

tangle N 1 an untidy and confused or knotted state or mass, eg, of hair or fibres. 2 a confused or complicated state or situation.
➤ VB 1 to cause (hair, fibres, etc) to get into this state. 2 (usu **tangle with**) COLLOQ to become involved (esp in conflict, or an argument).
■ **tangled** ADJ.

tango N a Latin-American dance with stylized body positions and long pauses.
➤ VB (**-os** or **-oes**) INTR to perform this dance.

tank N 1 a large container for holding, storing or transporting liquids or gas. 2 a heavy steel-covered vehicle armed with guns and which moves on Caterpillar tracks.
◆ **tanked up** COLLOQ very drunk.

tankard N a large beer mug.

tanker N a ship or large lorry which transports liquid in bulk.

tannic ADJ relating to or containing tannin.

tannin N any of several substances used in tanning leather, and which occur in red wine and tea. Also called **tannic acid**.

tantalize or **-ise** VB to tease or torment, esp by offering but then withholding an object, etc that is much desired. ■ **tantalizing** ADJ.

tantamount ADJ (always **tantamount to**) producing the same effect or result as.

tantrum N an outburst of bad temper.

tap[1] N 1 a quick or light touch, knock or blow, or the sound made by this. 2 tap-dancing. 3 a piece of metal attached to the sole and heel of a tap-dancing shoe.
➤ VB (**-pp-**) 1 TR & INTR to strike or knock lightly, and often audibly. 2 (also **tap out**) to produce by tapping: **tap out a message**.

tap[2] N 1 a device attached to a pipe, barrel, etc for controlling the flow of liquid or gas. 2 a a concealed receiver for listening to and recording private telephone conversations; b an act of attaching such a receiver. 3 the withdrawal of fluid, eg, from a body cavity.
➤ VB (**-pp-**) 1 to get liquid from (a barrel or a cavity in the body, etc) using a tap or tap-like device. 2 to let out (liquid) by opening a tap or tap-like device. 3 to get sap from (a tree) by cutting into it. 4 to attach a concealed receiver to (a telephone, etc). 5 to start using (a source, supply, etc). 6 COLLOQ to obtain (money, etc) from: **tapped his mum for £10**.

tapas PL N savoury snacks of a Spanish style.

tap dance N a dance performed wearing shoes with metal attached to the soles and toes so that the steps can be heard clearly.
➤ VB (**tap-dance**) INTR to perform a tap dance. ■ **tap-dancer** N. ■ **tap-dancing** N.

tape N 1 a narrow strip of cloth used for tying, fastening, etc. 2 (also **magnetic tape**) a strip of thin plastic or metal used for recording sounds or images: **video tape**. 3 an audio or

video recording. **4** (also **adhesive tape**) a strip of thin paper or plastic with a sticky surface, used for fastening or sticking, etc. **5** a string, strip of paper or ribbon stretched above the finishing line on a race track.
➤ VB **1** to fasten, tie or seal with tape. **2** TR & INTR to record (sounds or images) on magnetic tape.
◆ **have sth** or **sb taped** COLLOQ to understand it or them.

tape measure N a strip of cloth or flexible metal used for measuring length.

taper N **1** a long thin candle. **2** a waxed wick for lighting candles, fires, etc. **3** a lessening of diameter or width towards one end.
➤ VB, TR & INTR (also **taper off**) **1** to make or become narrower towards one end. **2** to make or become gradually less.

tape recorder N a machine for recording and playing back sounds on magnetic tape.
■ **tape-recording** N.

tapestry N (**-ies**) **1** a thick woven textile with an ornamental design, often a picture, used for curtains, wall-hangings, chair coverings, etc. **2** embroidery, or an embroidery, imitating this.

tapeworm N a parasitic segmented flatworm living in the intestines of vertebrates.

tapioca N hard white grains of starch from the root of the cassava plant, used for puddings.

taproot N a long tapering main root.

tar[1] N **1** a dark sticky pungent distillation of coal, wood, etc, used in road construction, etc. **2** a similar substance, esp the residue formed from burning tobacco.
➤ VB (**-rr-**) to cover with tar. ■ **tarry** ADJ.
◆ **tar and feather** to cover with tar and then feathers as a punishment.
◆ **tarred with the same brush** possessing the same faults.

tar[2] N, OLD COLLOQ a sailor.

taramasalata N a creamy pink pâté made from smoked fish roe.

tarantula N **1** a large European spider. **2** a large tropical spider with long hairy legs.

tardy ADJ (**-ier, -iest**) slow to move, progress or

grow; sluggish. ■ **tardiness** N.

target N **1** an object aimed at in shooting practice, etc, esp a flat round board marked with concentric circles. **2** any object or area fired or aimed at. **3** someone or something that is the object of ridicule, criticism, abuse, etc. **4** something aimed for; a goal.
➤ VB **1** to direct or aim. **2** to make (a person, place or thing) a target.

tariff N a list of fixed prices.

tarmac N **1** TRADEMARK tarmacadam. **2** a surface covered with tarmac.

tarmacadam N, TRADEMARK a mixture of small stones bound together with tar, used to make road surfaces, etc.

tarnish VB **1 a** to make (metal) dull and discoloured; **b** INTR of metal: to become dull. **2** to spoil or damage (a reputation, etc).

tarot N a pack of 78 playing-cards, now used mainly in fortune-telling.

tarpaulin N **1** heavy canvas waterproofed with tar, etc. **2** a sheet of this material.

tarragon N a bushy plant whose leaves are used as a flavouring in salads, etc.

tarry VB (**-ies, -ied**) INTR **1** to linger or stay in a place. **2** to be slow or late in doing something.

tarsal ANAT, ADJ of the bones of the tarsus.
➤ N any of the bones of the tarsus.

tarsus N (**-si**) the bones forming the upper part of the human foot and ankle.

tart[1] ADJ **1** sharp or sour in taste. **2** of a remark, etc: brief and sarcastic; cutting.

tart[2] N a pastry case, esp one without a top, with a sweet or savoury filling.

tart[3] SLANG, N a prostitute.
➤ VB (always **tart up**) COLLOQ to decorate or embellish, esp in an ostentatious or tasteless way. ■ **tarty** ADJ (**-ier, -iest**).

tartan N a distinctive checked pattern, esp one peculiar to a specified Scottish clan.

tartar[1] N a hard deposit on the teeth.

tartar[2] N a fierce, ill-tempered, etc person.

tartar sauce or **tartare sauce** N mayonnaise with chopped pickles, capers, etc.

tartrazine N a yellow powder used as an artificial colouring in foods.

task N 1 a piece of work to be done. 2 an unpleasant or difficult job; a chore.
◆ **take sb to task** to scold or criticize them.

task force N, MIL a temporary grouping of different units that undertake a specific mission.

taskmaster or **taskmistress** N a man or woman who sets and supervises the work of others, esp strictly or severely.

tassel N a decorative bunch of dangling threads, etc attached to a curtain, cushion, etc.

taste VB 1 TR & INTR to perceive the flavour of (food, drink, etc) in the mouth. 2 to try or test (a food or drink) by having a small amount. 3 to be aware of or recognize the flavour of (something). 4 (**taste of sth**) to have a specified flavour: tastes of vanilla. 5 to experience: taste defeat.
➤ N 1 a the particular sensation produced when food, drink, etc is in the mouth; b the sense by which this is detected. 2 the quality or flavour of a food, drink, etc as perceived by this sense: the taste of onions. 3 an act of tasting or a small quantity of food or drink tasted. 5 a first, usu brief, experience of something: a taste of what was to come. 6 a liking: a taste for exotic holidays. 7 ability to judge and appreciate what is suitable, elegant or beautiful.

taste bud N a sensory organ on the surface of the tongue by which tastes are perceived.

tasteful ADJ showing, or done with, good judgement or taste. ■ **tastefully** ADV.

tasteless ADJ 1 lacking flavour. 2 showing, or done with, a lack of good judgement or taste. ■ **tastelessly** ADV.

taster N 1 someone whose job is to taste and judge the quality of food or drink. 2 a sample.

tasty ADJ (*-ier, -iest*) 1 having a good, esp savoury, flavour. 2 COLLOQ attractive.

tat N, BRIT COLLOQ rubbish or junk.

ta-ta EXCLAM, BRIT COLLOQ good-bye.

tatter N (usu **tatters**) a torn ragged shred of cloth, paper, etc.

tattered ADJ ragged or torn.

tattle N idle chatter or gossip.
➤ VB, INTR to chat or gossip idly.

tattoo[1] VB to mark (a coloured design, etc) on (a person or a part of the body) by pricking the skin and putting in indelible dyes.
➤ N a design tattooed on the skin. ■ **tattooer** or **tattooist** N.

tattoo[2] N 1 a signal by drum or bugle calling soldiers to quarters. 2 an outdoor military display. 3 a rhythmic beating or drumming.

tatty ADJ, COLLOQ (*-ier, -iest*) shabby and untidy.

taunt VB to tease, say unpleasant things to, or jeer at in a cruel and hurtful way.
➤ N a cruel, unpleasant and hurtful remark.

taupe N a brownish-grey colour.

Taurus N, ASTROL the second sign of the zodiac (the Bull).

taut ADJ 1 pulled or stretched tight. 2 showing nervous strain or anxiety.

tauten VB, TR & INTR to make or become taut.

tautology N (*-ies*) the use of words which repeat the meaning of words already used, as in I myself personally am a vegetarian.

tavern N an inn or public house.

tawdry ADJ (*-ier, -iest*) cheap, gaudy and of poor quality. ■ **tawdriness** N.

tawny N a yellowish-brown colour.
➤ ADJ (*-ier, -iest*) yellowish-brown.

tax N a compulsory contribution to state revenue levied on people's salaries, property, the sale of goods and services, etc.
➤ VB 1 to impose a tax on (a person, goods, etc) or take tax from (a salary, etc). 2 to put a strain on. ■ **taxable** N. ■ **taxing** ADJ.

taxation N the levying or payment of taxes.

taxi N (*taxis* or *taxies*) a car which may be hired along with its driver to carry passengers on usu short town journeys.

➤ VB (*taxis* or *taxies, taxiing* or *taxying*) INTR of an aircraft: to move slowly along the ground before take-off or after landing.

taxidermy N the art of preparing, stuffing and mounting the skins of dead animals, birds, etc. ■ **taxidermist** N.

taxonomy N (*-ies*) the science of classification, eg, of animals, plants, fossils, etc.

TB ABBREV tuberculosis.

T-bone steak N a large beef steak with a T-shaped bone.

te or **ti** N, MUS in sol-fa notation: the seventh note of the major scale.

tea N 1 a (in full **tea plant**) a small evergreen tree or shrub cultivated for its leaves; b its dried leaves; c a drink made by infusing these with boiling water. 2 a similar drink made from the leaves or flowers of other plants: **peppermint tea**. 3 (also **afternoon tea**) a light afternoon meal with tea, sandwiches, cakes, etc. 4 BRIT a a cooked meal served early in the evening; b a main evening meal.

tea bag N a small bag or sachet of tea, which is infused in boiling water.

teacake N, BRIT a currant bun, eaten toasted.

teach VB (*taught*) 1 to give knowledge to (an individual, class, etc). 2 TR & INTR to give lessons in (a subject), esp as a professional.
◆ **teach sb a lesson** to demonstrate and reinforce their mistake.

teacher N someone whose job is to teach.

teaching N 1 the work or profession of a teacher. 2 (often **teachings**) something that is taught, esp guidance or doctrine.

tea cosy N (*-ies*) a cover to keep a teapot warm.

teacup N 1 a medium-sized cup used for drinking tea. 2 the amount a teacup can hold.

teak N a heavy yellowish-brown durable wood, used in furniture-making, etc.

teal N (*teals* or *teal*) a small freshwater duck.

team N 1 a group of people who form one side in a game. 2 a group of people or animals working together.
➤ VB, TR & INTR (usu **team up with**) to form a team for some common action.

teamwork N co-operation between those who are working together on a task.

teapot N a pot with a spout and handle used for making and pouring tea.

tear[1] N 1 a drop of clear saline liquid, secreted by a gland, moistening and cleaning the eyeball, or flowing in response to irritation, emotion, etc. 2 any pear-shaped drop or blob.

tear[2] VB (*tore, torn*) 1 to pull or rip apart by force; to pull violently or with tearing movements. 2 to make (a hole, etc) by pulling or ripping. 3 INTR to come apart; to be pulled or ripped apart: **material that tears easily**. 4 INTR to rush; to move with speed or force.
➤ N 1 a hole or other damage caused by tearing. 2 damage: **wear and tear**.
◆ **tear sb away** to remove or take them by force; to force or persuade them to leave.
◆ **tear sth down** to demolish it using force.
◆ **tear into sb** to attack them.
◆ **tear sth up** to tear it into pieces.

tearaway N, BRIT COLLOQ an undisciplined and reckless young person.

teardrop N a single tear.

tearful ADJ inclined to cry or weep.

tear gas N a gas which causes stinging blinding tears used in the control of riots, etc.

tearing ADJ furious: **a tearing hurry**.

tear-jerker N, COLLOQ a sentimental play, film or book, etc intended to make people cry.

tearoom and **teashop** N a restaurant where tea, coffee and cakes, etc are served.

tease VB 1 to annoy or irritate deliberately or unkindly. 2 to laugh at or make fun of playfully. 3 to arouse sexually and fail to satisfy, usu deliberately. 4 to comb (wool, flax or hair, etc) to remove tangles and open out the fibres.
➤ N someone or something that teases.
◆ **tease out** 1 to separate. 2 to clarify (an

obscure point) by discussion, etc.

teaser N a puzzle or tricky problem.

teaspoon N 1 a small spoon for use with a teacup. 2 the amount a teaspoon can hold.

teat N 1 a nipple, esp of an animal. 2 a piece of rubber, etc shaped like a nipple, esp one attached to a baby's feeding bottle.

tea towel N a towel for drying dishes, etc.

tech N, COLLOQ 1 a technical college. 2 technology.

tech. ABBREV 1 technical. 2 technology.

technical ADJ 1 relating to a practical skill or applied science. 2 requiring knowledge of a particular subject to be understood. 3 according to a strict interpretation of the law or rules. 4 belonging or relating to, or showing a quality of, technique. ■ **technically** ADV.

technical college N a college of further education that teaches practical skills.

technical drawing N drawing of plans, etc done with compasses and rulers.

technicality N (-ies) a technical detail or term.

technician N 1 someone specialized or skilled in a practical art or science. 2 someone employed to do practical work in a laboratory.

technique N 1 proficiency or skill in the practical or formal aspects of something, eg painting, music, etc. 2 mechanical or practical skill or method: **the techniques of film-making**. 3 a way of achieving a purpose skilfully.

technology N (-ies) 1 the practical use of scientific knowledge in industry and everyday life. 2 practical sciences as a group. 3 the technical skills and achievements of a particular time in history, of a civilization or a group of people. ■ **technological** ADJ.

technophobe N someone who dislikes or fears, and usu tries to avoids using, technology. ■ **technophobia** N. ■ **technophobic** ADJ.

tectonics SING N, GEOL the study of the Earth's crust and the forces which change it.

teddy[1] N (-ies) (in full **teddy bear**) a stuffed toy bear.

teddy[2] N (-ies) a woman's one-piece undergarment.

tedious ADJ tiresomely long; monotonous.

tedium N tediousness; boredom.

tee N, GOLF 1 a small area of level ground at the start of each hole where the initial shot towards a green is taken. 2 a small peg, etc used to support a ball when this shot is taken. ➤ VB (*teed, teeing*) (often **tee up**) to place a golf ball on a tee ready to be played. ◆ **tee off** to play a first shot at the start of a golf hole.

tee-hee EXCLAM expressing amusement.

teem[1] VB, INTR 1 (usu **teem with**) to be full of or abound in: **teeming with tourists**. 2 to be plentiful: **Fish teem in this river**.

teem[2] VB, INTR (usu **teem down**) of water, esp rain: to pour in torrents.

teen N 1 (**teens**) the years of a person's life between the ages of 13 and 19. 2 (**teens**) the numbers from 13 to 19. 3 COLLOQ a teenager. ➤ ADJ for or relating to teenagers.

teenage ADJ 1 (also **teenaged**) between the ages of 13 and 19. 2 relating to or suitable for someone of this age. ■ **teenager** N.

teeny ADJ (-ier, -iest) COLLOQ tiny.

teenybopper N, COLLOQ a young teenage girl who follows the latest trends.

teeny-weeny ADJ, COLLOQ very tiny.

teepee see **tepee**

tee shirt see **T-shirt**

teeter VB, INTR 1 to stand or move unsteadily; to wobble. 2 to hesitate or waver.

teethe VB, INTR to develop or cut teeth, esp milk teeth. ■ **teething** N.

teething troubles PL N initial problems.

teetotal ADJ abstaining completely from alcoholic drink. ■ **teetotaller** N.

Teflon N, TRADEMARK a material used esp to coat

the surface of non-stick cooking utensils.

telecommunication N 1 communication over a distance using cable, telephone, broadcasting, telegraph, fax, e-mail, etc. 2 (**telecommunications**) the branch of technology dealing with these ways of communicating.

teleconference N a conference between people in two or more locations using video, audio and/or computer links.

telegram N, FORMERLY a message sent by telegraph and delivered in printed form.

telegraph N a system of, or instrument for, sending messages over a distance, esp by sending electrical impulses along a wire. ➢ VB TR & INTR to send (a message) (to someone) by telegraph. ■ **telegraphy** N.

telegraphy N the science or practice of sending messages by telegraph.

telekinesis N the moving of objects at a distance without using physical contact, eg, by willpower. ■ **telekinetic** ADJ.

telemarketing N the marketing of goods and services by telephone.

telepathy N the apparent communication of thoughts directly from one person's mind to another's without using any of the five known senses. ■ **telepathic** ADJ.

telephone N 1 an instrument for transmitting speech in the form of electrical signals or radio waves. 2 the system of communication that uses such instruments. ➢ VB to seek or establish contact and speak to (someone) by telephone.

telephonist N a telephone switchboard operator.

telephoto lens N a camera lens which produces magnified images of distant objects.

teleprinter N an apparatus which prints messages as they are received by telegraph and transmits them as they are typed.

telesales SING AND PL N the selling of goods or services by telephone.

telescope N an optical instrument that makes distant objects appear larger. ➢ VB, TR & INTR to collapse part within part. ■ **telescopic** ADJ.

teleshopping N the purchase of goods, using the telephone, Internet, etc.

teletext N a non-interactive news and information service able to be viewed on a TV set with a suitable receiver and decoder.

telethon N a TV programme, usu a day-long one, broadcast to raise money for charity.

televise VB to broadcast by television.

television N 1 an electronic system that converts moving images and sound into electrical signals, which are then transmitted to a distant receiver that converts these signals back to images and sound: **digital television**. 2 (also **television set**) a device with a picture tube and loudspeakers that is used to receive picture and sound signals transmitted in this way. 3 television broadcasting in general: **works in television**.

telex or **Telex** N 1 an international telecommunications network using teleprinters and radio and satellite links. 2 a teleprinter used in such a network. 3 a message received or sent by such a network. ➢ VB, TR & INTR to communicate by telex.

tell VB (**told**) 1 TR & INTR to relate (something) in speech or writing (to someone): **told him what happened**. 2 to command or instruct: **told her not to go**. 3 to express in words: **tell lies**. 4 TR & INTR to discover or distinguish: **You can tell it by its smell**. 5 (usu **tell on**) COLLOQ to inform against. 6 to make known or give away: **promised not to tell**. 7 (also **tell on**) INTR of an ordeal, etc: to have a noticeable effect. 8 TR & INTR to know or recognize definitely: **I can never tell when he's lying**. 9 to assure: **I'm telling you, that's exactly what he said**. 10 (usu **tell against**) INTR of evidence, circumstances, etc: to have an influence, effect, etc.
◆ **tell apart** to distinguish between.
◆ **tell off** to scold or reprimand.

teller N 1 someone who tells, esp stories.

2 a bank employee who receives money from and pays it out to members of the public.

telling ADJ producing a great or marked effect.

telling-off N a mild scolding.

tell-tale N someone who spreads gossip, esp about the private affairs or misdeeds of others. ➤ ADJ revealing or indicating: **tell-tale signs**.

telly N (*-ies*) COLLOQ television.

temerity N **1** rashness or impetuosity. **2** boldness or impudence.

temp N a temporary employee. ➤ VB, INTR to work as a temp.

temper N **1** a characteristic state of mind; mood or humour: **have an even temper**. **2** a state of calm; composure; self-control: **lose one's temper**. **3** a state of uncontrolled anger: **in a temper**. **4** a tendency to have fits of uncontrolled anger: **She has quite a temper**. ➤ VB **1** to soften or make less severe: **temper firmness with understanding**. **2** to bring (metal, clay, etc) to the desired consistency.

temperament N **1** someone's natural character or disposition. **2** a sensitive, creative or emotional personality.

temperamental ADJ **1** given to or showing extreme mood changes. **2** of a machine, etc: not working reliably or consistently.

temperance N moderation or self-restraint, esp in controlling one's appetite or desires.

temperate ADJ **1** moderate and self-restrained. **2** not excessive. **3** of a climate or region: characterized by mild temperatures.

temperature N **1** the degree of hotness or coldness of an object, body, medium, eg, air or water, etc as measured by a thermometer. **2** COLLOQ a body temperature above normal: **He was running a temperature**.

tempest N a violent storm with strong winds.

tempestuous ADJ **1** relating to or like a tempest; very stormy. **2** violently emotional; passionate: **a tempestuous love affair**.

template N a piece of metal, plastic or wood cut in a particular shape and used as a pattern when cutting out material, drawing, etc.

temple N **1** a building in which people, usu non-Christians, worship. **2** the flat part at either side of the head in front of the ears.

tempo N (*tempos* or *tempi*) **1** the speed at which a piece of music should be or is played. **2** rate or speed.

temporal ADJ **1** relating to time. **2** relating to worldly or secular life rather than spiritual life.

temporary ADJ lasting, acting or used etc for a limited period of time only. ■ **temporarily** ADV. ■ **temporariness** N.

tempt VB **1** to seek to persuade (someone) to do something wrong, foolish, etc. **2** to attract or allure. **3** to risk provoking, esp by doing something foolhardy: **tempt fate**.

temptation N **1** an act of tempting or the state of being tempted. **2** something that tempts.

tempting ADJ attractive; inviting; enticing.

ten N **1 a** the cardinal number 10; **b** the quantity that this represents, being one more than nine. **2** any symbol for this, eg, 10 or X. **3** something, esp a garment or a person, whose size is denoted by the number 10. **5** the tenth hour after midnight or midday: **Come at ten**. ➤ ADJ **1** totalling ten. **2** aged ten.

tenable ADJ able to be maintained.

tenacious ADJ **1** holding or sticking firmly. **2** determined. **3** of memory: retaining information extremely well. ■ **tenacity** N.

tenancy N (*-ies*) the status of being a tenant.

tenant N **1** someone who rents property or land. **2** an occupant.

tench N (*tench* or *tenches*) a European freshwater fish of the carp family.

tend VB **1** to take care of or look after. **2** to wait on, serve at, manage, etc: **tend bar**. **3** (**tend to**) to attend to. **4** INTR (usu **tend to**) to be inclined to: **He tends to be late**.

tendency N (*-ies*) **1** a likelihood of acting or thinking, or an inclination to act or think, in a particular way. **2** a general course, trend or drift. **3** a faction within a political party, etc.

tendentious ADJ characterized by a particular bias or underlying purpose.

tender[1] ADJ **1** soft and delicate; fragile. **2** of meat: easily chewed or cut. **3** easily damaged or grieved; sensitive: **a tender heart**. **4** easily hurt when touched, esp because of having been hurt before. **5** loving and gentle: **tender words**. **6** youthful and vulnerable: **of tender years**. ■ **tenderly** ADV.

tender[2] VB **1** to offer or present (an apology, resignation, etc). **2** (usu **tender for**) to make a formal offer (to do work or supply goods) at a stated amount of money, etc.
➤ N a formal offer, usu in writing, to do work or supply goods for a stated amount of money.

tender[3] N a person who looks after something or someone: **bartender**.

tenderize or **-ise** VB to make (meat) tender by pounding, marinading, etc.

tendon N a cord of strong fibrous tissue that joins a muscle to a bone or some other structure.

tendril N a long shoot-like extension that some climbing plants use for attaching themselves to objects for support. ■ **tendrilled** ADJ.

tenement N a large building divided into several self-contained flats or apartments.

tenet N a belief, opinion or doctrine.

tenfold ADJ **1** equal to ten times as much. **2** divided into or consisting of ten parts.
➤ ADV by ten times as much.

tenner N, COLLOQ **1** a £10 note. **2** US a $10 bill.

tennis N (also **lawn tennis**) a game in which two players or two pairs of players use rackets to hit a ball across a net.

tenon N a projection at the end of a piece of wood, etc, formed to fit into a socket in another piece of wood, etc.

tenor N **1 a** a singing voice of the highest normal range for an adult man; **b** a singer who has this voice. **2** an instrument, eg, a viola, recorder or saxophone, with a similar range.

tenpin bowling N a game in which ten skittles are set up at the end of an alley and a ball is rolled at them to knock them down.

tense[1] N, GRAM a form or set of forms of a verb showing the time of its action in relation to the time of speaking.

tense[2] ADJ **1** suffering emotional, nervous or mental strain. **2** tightly stretched; taut.
➤ VB, TR & INTR (also **tense up**) to make or become tense. ■ **tensely** ADV.

tensile ADJ **1** able to be stretched. **2** relating to or involving stretching or tension. ■ **tensility** N.

tension N **1** an act of stretching or the degree to which something is stretched. **2** mental or emotional strain. **3** strained relations between people, countries, etc.

tent N a movable shelter supported by poles or a frame and fastened with ropes and pegs.

tentacle N a long thin flexible appendage growing near the mouth of many invertebrates.

tentative ADJ uncertain; hesitant; cautious. ■ **tentatively** ADV. ■ **tentativeness** N.

tenterhooks PL N.
◆ **on tenterhooks** in a state of impatient suspense or anxiety.

tenth (OFTEN WRITTEN **10th**) ADJ **1** in counting: **a** next after ninth; **b** last of ten. **2** in tenth position.
➤ N **1** one of ten equal parts. **2** a fraction equal to one divided by ten.

tenuous ADJ slight; with little strength or substance.

tenure N **1** the holding of an office, position or property. **2** the length of time an office, position or property is held. **3** the holding of a position, esp a university teaching job, for a guaranteed length of time or permanently.

tepee or **teepee** N a conical tent formed by skins stretched over a frame of poles, used by some Native Americans.

tepid ADJ **1** slightly or only just warm. **2** unenthusiastic. ■ **tepidity** N.

tequila N a Mexican alcoholic spirit

obtained from the agave plant.

term N 1 a word or expression, esp one used with a precise meaning in a specialized field. 2 (**terms**) language used; a particular way of speaking: in no uncertain terms. 3 a clearly defined period of time: term of office. 4 the end of a particular time, esp of pregnancy. 5 (**terms**) a relationship between people or countries: on good terms. 6 (**terms**) the rules or conditions of an agreement. 7 (**terms**) fixed charges for work or a service. 8 one of the divisions into which an academic year is divided. 9 MATH a quantity which is joined to another by either addition or subtraction. 10 MATH one quantity in a series or sequence. ➢ VB to name or call.
◆ **come to terms with** 1 to come to an agreement or understanding with. 2 to find a way of living with or tolerating (some personal trouble or difficulty).
◆ **in terms of** in relation to.

termagant N a scolding woman.

terminable ADJ able to be brought to an end.

terminal ADJ of an illness: causing death; fatal. ➢ N 1 an arrival and departure building at an airport. 2 a large station at the end of a railway line or for long-distance buses and coaches. 3 a point in an electric circuit device at which the current leaves or enters it, or by which it may be connected to another device. 4 a device which connects with a remote computer. ■ **terminally** ADV.

terminate VB 1 TR & INTR to bring or come to an end. 2 to end (a pregnancy) artificially and before the fetus is viable. ■ **termination** N.

terminology N (-*ies*) the words and phrases used in a particular field.

terminus N (-*ni* or -*nuses*) **a** the end of a railway line or bus route, usu with a station; **b** the station at this point.

termite N an ant-like insect.

tern N a sea-bird with a long forked tail.

ternary ADJ 1 containing three parts. 2 MATH of a number system: using three as a base.

terrace N 1 each of a series of raised level earth banks on a hillside used for cultivation. 2 BRIT a row of usu identical and connected houses. 3 a raised level paved area by the side of a house. 4 (usu **terraces**) open tiered areas round a sports ground, where spectators stand.

terracotta N 1 an unglazed brownish-orange earthenware used for pottery, roof tiles, etc. 2 a brownish-orange colour.

terra firma N dry land.

terrain N a stretch of land, esp with regard to its physical features or as a battle area.

terrapin N a small freshwater turtle.

terrestrial ADJ 1 relating to dry land or to the Earth. 2 denoting animals or plants that live on dry land. 3 of broadcast signals: sent by a land transmitter as opposed to satellite.

terrible ADJ 1 COLLOQ very bad: a terrible singer. 2 COLLOQ very great; extreme: a terrible gossip. 3 causing great fear or terror. 4 causing suffering or hardship: a terrible struggle. 5 COLLOQ **a** ill: have flu and feel terrible; **b** regretful. ■ **terribly** ADV.

terrier N a breed of small dog.

terrific ADJ 1 COLLOQ marvellous; excellent. 2 COLLOQ very powerful: a terrific storm.

terrify VB (-*ies, -ied*) to make very frightened. ■ **terrified** ADJ. ■ **terrifying** ADJ.

territorial ADJ 1 relating to a territory. 2 of birds and animals: likely to establish and defend their own territory. ■ **territoriality** N.

territorial waters PL N the area of sea surrounding a state considered to belong to that state.

territory N (-*ies*) 1 a stretch of land; a region. 2 the land under the control of a ruler, government or state. 3 an area of knowledge, interest or activity. 4 an area or district in which a travelling salesman or distributor operates. 5 an area which a bird or animal treats as its own and defends against others.

terror N 1 very great fear or dread. 2 something which causes such fear. 3 COLLOQ a troublesome or mischievous person.

terrorism N the systematic use of violence and intimidation to force a government or community, etc to act in a certain way or accept certain demands. ■ **terrorist** N, ADJ.

terrorize or **-ise** VB 1 to frighten greatly. 2 to use terrorism against.

terry N (**-ies**) an absorbent fabric with uncut loops on one side, used esp for towels. Also AS ADJ: terry towelling.

terse ADJ 1 brief and concise. 2 abrupt.

tertiary ADJ third in order, importance, etc.

Terylene N, TRADEMARK a light tough synthetic fabric of polyester fibres.

test N 1 a a critical examination or trial of qualities, abilities, etc; b something used as the basis for this: a test of strength. 3 a short minor examination, esp in school. 4 SPORT a test match. 5 CHEM anything used to distinguish, detect or identify a substance; a reagent.
➣ VB 1 to examine, esp by trial. 2 TR & INTR to examine (a substance) to discover whether another substance is present or not. 3 INTR to achieve a stated result in a test: tested negative for the virus. ■ **testable** ADJ. ■ **tester** ADJ.

testament N 1 a a written statement of someone's wishes, esp of what they want to be done with their property after death; b a will. 2 proof, evidence or a tribute: a testament to her hard work. 3 (**Testament**) either of the two main divisions of the Bible, the Old Testament and the New Testament.

testate ADJ, LAW having made a valid will.

testator and **testatrix** N, LAW someone who leaves a will at death.

test case N, LAW a case whose outcome will serve as a precedent for future cases.

test drive N a trial drive of a car by a prospective owner to assess its performance.
➣ VB (**test-drive**) to take (a car) for a test drive.

testicle N a testis. ■ **testicular** ADJ.

testify VB (**-ies, -ied**) 1 INTR to give evidence in court. 2 (often **testify to**) to serve as evidence

or proof (of something). 3 INTR to make a solemn declaration (eg of one's faith).

testimonial N 1 a letter or certificate giving details of a person's character, conduct and qualifications. 2 SPORT a match held in honour of a player, who receives all the proceeds.

testimony N (**-ies**) 1 a statement made under oath, esp in a law court. 2 evidence: testimony to her love. 3 a declaration of truth or fact.

testing N the assessment of an individual level of knowledge or skill, etc.
➣ ADJ 1 troublesome; difficult: a testing time. 2 mentally taxing: a testing question.

testis N (**testes**) ANAT in male animals: either of the two glands that produce sperm.

test match N in various sports, esp cricket: a match between two international teams.

testosterone N, PHYSIOL the main male sex hormone, secreted primarily by the testes.

test pilot N a pilot who tests new aircraft.

test tube N a thin glass tube closed at one end, used in chemical tests or experiments.

testy ADJ (**-ier, -iest**) irritable; bad-tempered.

tetanus N an infectious and potentially fatal disease whose main symptoms are fever and painful muscle spasms. Also called **lockjaw**.

tetchy ADJ (**-ier, -iest**) irritable; peevish.

tête-à-tête N a private conversation between two people.

tether N a rope, etc for tying an animal to a post or confining it to a particular spot.
➣ VB to tie or restrain with a tether.
◆ **at the end of one's tether** having reached the limit of one's patience.

tetrahedron N (**-ra** or **-rons**) GEOM a solid figure with four triangular plane faces.

Teutonic ADJ 1 belonging or relating to the Germanic languages or peoples speaking these languages. 2 German.

Tex-Mex ADJ of food, music, etc: typically Mexican, but with Texan elements.

text N 1 the main body of printed words in a

book as opposed to the notes and illustrations, etc. **2** a short passage from the Bible taken as the starting-point for a sermon or quoted in authority. **3** a book, novel or play, etc that forms part of a course of study. **4** COMP the words written or displayed on a VDU. ■ **textual** ADJ.

textbook N a book that contains the standard principles and information of a subject.
➤ ADJ conforming or as if conforming to the guidance of a textbook: **a textbook case**.

textile N **1** a cloth or fabric made by weaving or knitting. **2** fibre or yarn, etc suitable for weaving into cloth.
➤ ADJ **1** relating to manufacturing cloth.
2 woven; suitable for being woven into cloth.

texture N **1** the way a surface feels. **2** the feel or appearance of cloth, etc, caused by the way it is woven, etc. **3** the structure of a substance as formed by the size and arrangement of the particles which form it.
➤ VB to give a particular texture to (food, fabric, etc). ■ **textural** ADJ.

thalamus N (*-mi*) ANAT in the forebrain of vertebrates: either of two masses of grey matter that relay sensory nerve impulses to the cerebral cortex.

thalidomide N a drug formerly used as a sedative but withdrawn in 1961 because it was found to cause malformation of the fetus if taken by the mother in early pregnancy.

than CONJ **1** used to introduce the second part of a comparison, or that part which is taken as the basis of a comparison: **He's better than me.**
2 used to introduce the second, usu less desirable, option in a statement of alternatives: **I'd rather walk than drive. 3** except; other than: **left with no alternative than to resign.**
➤ PREP in comparison with: **older than him.**

thank VB **1** to express gratitude to: **thanked him for his help. 2** to hold responsible for something: **has only himself to thank for it.**
➤ N (usu **thanks**) **1** gratitude or an expression of gratitude: **to express my thanks. 2** thank you.
◆ **thank God** or **goodness** or **heavens**, etc an expression of relief.
◆ **thanks to** as a result of; because of:

Thanks to Amy, we missed the train.
◆ **thank you** a polite expression acknowledging a gift, help or offer.

thankful ADJ grateful; relieved and happy.
■ **thankfully** ADV. ■ **thankfulness** N.

thankless ADJ bringing no thanks or pleasure.

thanksgiving N **1** a formal act of giving thanks, esp to God. **2** (**Thanksgiving** or **Thanksgiving Day**) N AMER a public holiday for giving thanks, occurring on the fourth Thursday in November in the USA and the second Monday in October in Canada.

that ADJ (PL *those*) **1** indicating the thing, person or idea already mentioned, specified or understood: **There's that girl I was telling you about. 2** indicating someone or something that is farther away or is in contrast: **not this book, but that one.**
➤ PRONOUN (PL *those*) **1** the person, thing or idea just mentioned, already spoken of or understood: **When did that happen?**
2 a relatively distant or more distant person, thing or idea: **I'll take this, you take that.**
➤ PRONOUN used instead of **which, who** or **whom**, to introduce a relative clause which defines, distinguishes or restricts the person or thing mentioned in the preceding clause: **All the children that were late received detention.**
➤ CONJ used to introduce a noun clause, or a clause showing reason, purpose, consequence or a result or expressing a wish or desire: **He spoke so quickly that I couldn't understand.**
➤ ADV **1** to the degree or extent shown or understood: **won't reach that far. 2** COLLOQ OR DIALECT to such a degree that; so: **He's that mean he never buys a round.**

thatch N a roof covering of straw or reeds, etc.
➤ VB, TR & INTR to cover (a roof or building) with thatch. ■ **thatcher** N.

thaw VB **1 a** INTR of snow, ice, frozen food, etc: to melt; **b** to make (snow, ice, frozen food, etc) melt. **2** TR & INTR, COLLOQ to make or become more friendly or relaxed.
➤ N an act or the process of thawing.

the DEFINITE ARTICLE **1** used to refer to a particular person or thing, or group of people or things,

already mentioned, implied or known: **Pass me the CD. 2** used to refer to a unique person or thing: **the Pope. 3** used before a singular noun to denote all the members of a group or class: **a history of the novel. 4 a** used before an adjective to denote a specified thing: **the paranormal; b** used before an adjective to denote collectively people or things who have the specified attribute, etc: **the poor. 5** used before certain titles and proper names. **6** used after a preposition to refer to a unit of quantity or time, etc: **paid by the hour.**
➤ ADV **1** used before comparative adjectives or adverbs to indicate (by) so much or (by) how much: **the sooner the better. 2** used before superlative adjectives and adverbs to indicate an amount beyond all others: **like this the best.**

theatre or (US) **theater** N **1** a building specially designed for the performance of plays, operas, etc. **2** a large room with seats rising in tiers, for lectures, etc. **3** (also **the theatre**) the writing and production of plays in general or the world and profession of actors and theatre companies. **5** BRIT a room in a hospital where surgery is performed.

theatrical ADJ **1** relating to theatres or acting. **2** of behaviour or a gesture, etc: done only for effect; artificial and exaggerated.

thee PRONOUN the objective form of **thou**[1].

theft N an act or instance of stealing.

their ADJ **1** belonging or relating to them: **their opinion. 2** his or her: **Has everyone got their books?**

theirs PRONOUN a person or thing that belongs to them: **That's theirs.**

them PRONOUN **1** the objective form of **they**: **met them. 2** COLLOQ him or her.

theme N **1** a subject of a discussion, speech or piece of writing, etc. **2** MUS a short melody in a piece of music which is developed and repeated with variations. **3** a repeated or recurring image or idea in literature or art. ■ **thematic** ADJ. ■ **thematically** ADV.

theme park N a large amusement park in which all of the rides and attractions are based

on a particular theme, eg, outer space.

theme song or **theme tune** N a song or melody that is played at the beginning and end of a film or a TV or radio programme, or which is associated with a particular person.

themselves PRONOUN **1** the reflexive form of **them:** helped themselves. **2** used for emphasis: **They, themselves, are to blame. 3** their normal selves: **not feeling themselves today. 4** COLLOQ himself or herself: **Nobody needs to blame themselves.**

then ADV **1** at that time. **2** soon or immediately after that: **I looked at him, then turned away. 3** in that case; that being so; as a necessary consequence: **If you're tired, then you should rest. 4** also; in addition: **Then there's the cost to take into account. 5** used to continue a narrative after a break. **6** used esp at the end of questions which ask for an explanation, opinion, etc, or which ask for or assume agreement: **Your mind is made up, then?**
➤ N that time: **Until then you should stay away.**
➤ ADJ being or acting at that time: **the then Prime Minister.**

thence ADV, OLD USE OR FORMAL **1** from that place or time. **2** from that cause; therefore.

thenceforth and **thenceforward** ADV, OLD USE OR FORMAL from that time forwards.

theocracy N government by a deity or by priests representing a deity.

theology N the study of God, religious belief and revelation. ■ **theologian** N. ■ **theological** ADJ.

theorem N a scientific or mathematical statement which makes certain assumptions in order to explain observed phenomena, and which has been proved to be correct.

theoretical or **theoretic** ADJ **1** concerned with or based on theory rather than practical knowledge or experience. **2** existing in theory only; hypothetical. ■ **theoretically** ADV.

theoretician N someone who specializes in or is concerned with the theoretical aspects of a subject rather than its practical use.

theorize or **-ise** VB, INTR to devise theories; to speculate. ■ **theorist** N.

theory N (*-ies*) **1** a series of ideas and general principles that seek to explain some aspect of the world: **theory of relativity. 2** an idea or explanation which has not yet been proved; a conjecture: **My theory is he's jealous! 3** the general and usu abstract principles or ideas of a subject: **theory of music. 4** abstract reasoning: **a good idea in theory.**

therapeutic ADJ **1** relating to, concerning or contributing to healing or curing disease, etc. **2** bringing a feeling of general well-being.

therapy N (*-ies*) the treatment of physical, social, psychiatric and psychological diseases and disorders by means other than surgery or drugs. ■ **therapist** N.

there ADV **1** at, in or to a place or position: **You can sit there. 2** at that point in speech, a piece of writing or a performance, etc: **Don't stop there. 3** in that respect: **I agree with him there. 4** used to begin a sentence when the subject of the verb follows the verb instead of coming before it: **There are no mistakes in this. 5** used at the beginning of a sentence to emphasize or call attention to that sentence: **There goes the last bus.**
➤ N that place or point.
➤ EXCLAM **1** used to express satisfaction, approval, triumph or encouragement, etc: **There! I knew he would come. 2** used to express sympathy or comfort, etc: **There, there! He's just not worth it.**

thereabouts or **thereabout** ADV near that place, number, amount, degree or time.

thereafter ADV, FORMAL from that time onwards.

thereby ADV, FORMAL by that means.

therefore ADV for that reason; as a consequence.

therein ADV, FORMAL in or into that place.

thereof ADV, FORMAL belonging or relating to, or from, that or it.

thereupon ADV, FORMAL **1** on that matter or point. **2** immediately after it or that.

therm N a unit of heat equal to 1.055×10^8 joules, used to measure gas.

thermal ADJ **1** relating to, caused by or producing heat. **2** of clothing: designed to prevent the loss of heat from the body.
➤ N **1** a rising current of warm air, used by birds, gliders, etc to move upwards. **2** (**thermals**) thermal clothing, esp underwear.

thermocouple N a device for measuring temperature, consisting of two different metallic conductors welded together to form a loop.

thermodynamics SING N the branch of physics concerned with the relationship between heat and other forms of energy, and the behaviour of physical systems in which temperature is an important factor. ■ **thermodynamic** ADJ.

thermoelectricity N an electric current generated by a difference in temperature in an electric circuit. ■ **thermoelectric** ADJ.

thermometer N an instrument for measuring temperature, usu a sealed glass tube filled with eg mercury or alcohol.

thermonuclear ADJ using or showing nuclear reactions occurring at extremely high temperatures: **thermonuclear weapons.**

thermoplastic N, CHEM a polymer that can be repeatedly softened by heat and hardened by cooling.

Thermos or **Thermos flask** N, TRADEMARK a kind of vacuum flask.

thermosphere N, METEOROL the layer of the Earth's atmosphere above the mesosphere, and including the ionosphere.

thermostat N a device used to maintain the temperature of a system at a constant level.

thesaurus N (*-ruses* or *-ri*) a book which lists words and their synonyms according to sense.

these plural of **this**

thesis N (*-ses*) a long written dissertation or report, esp one based on original research.

thespian N, FACETIOUS an actor or actress.

they PRONOUN **1** the people, animals or things already spoken about, being indicated, or known from the context. **2** people in general. **3** COLLOQ he or she: **Anyone can help if they want.**

they'd CONTRACTION **1** they had. **2** they would.

they'll CONTRACTION **1** they will. **2** they shall.

they're CONTRACTION they are.

they've CONTRACTION they have.

thick ADJ **1** having a relatively large distance between opposite sides. **2** having a specified distance between opposite sides: **one inch thick. 3** having a large diameter: **a thick rope. 4** of a liquid: containing a lot of solid matter. **5** having many single units placed very close together; dense: **thick hair. 6** difficult to see through: **thick fog. 7** of an accent: marked; pronounced. **8** COLLOQ of a person: stupid. **9** COLLOQ unfair: **That's a bit thick!**
➤ N the busiest, most active or most intense part: **in the thick of the fighting.**
◆ **as thick as thieves** very friendly.
◆ **thick and fast** frequently and in large numbers.
◆ **through thick and thin** whatever happens; in spite of any difficulties.

thicken VB **1** TR & INTR to make or become thick or thicker. **2** INTR to become more complicated.

thickening N **1** something used to thicken liquid. **2** the process of making or becoming thicker. **3** a thickened part.

thicket N a dense mass of bushes and trees.

thickness N **1** the state, quality or degree of being thick. **2** a layer.

thickset ADJ heavily built.

thick-skinned ADJ not easily hurt by criticism or insults; not sensitive.

thief N (*thieves*) a person who steals.

thieve VB, TR & INTR to steal or be a thief.
■ **thievery** N. ■ **thieving** ADJ.

thigh N the part of the leg between the knee and hip.

thimble N a cap worn on the finger to protect it and push the needle when sewing.

thin ADJ (*thinner, thinnest*) **1** having a relatively short distance between opposite sides. **2** having a relatively small diameter: **thin string. 3** of a person or animal: not fat; lean. **4** of a liquid: containing very little solid matter. **5** set far apart; sparse: **thin hair. 6** having a very low oxygen content: **thin air. 7** not convincing or believable: **a thin disguise.**
➤ VB (**-nn-**) TR & INTR (often **thin out**) to make or become thin, thinner, sparser or less dense.

thing N **1** an object, esp an inanimate one. **2** a object that cannot, need not or should not be named. **3** a fact, quality or idea, etc that can be thought about or referred to. **4** an event or circumstance: **Things are getting out of hand. 5** a quality: **Generosity is a great thing. 6** COLLOQ a person or animal, esp when thought of as an object of pity: **Poor thing! 7** a preoccupation or interest: **She's got a real thing about Brad Pitt! 8** what is needed or required: **It's just the thing. 9** an aim: **The thing is to do better next time. 10** (**things**) personal belongings: **I'll just get my things. 11** (**things**) affairs in general: **How are things?**

thingummy, **thingamy**, **thingummyjig** and **thingummybob** N (*thingummies,* etc) COLLOQ someone or something whose name is unknown, forgotten or deliberately not used.

think VB (*thought*) **1** TR & INTR **a** to have or form ideas in the mind; **b** to have as a thought in one's mind. **2** TR & INTR to consider, judge or believe: **They think of themselves as great singers. 3** TR & INTR to intend or plan; to form an idea of: **think about going to London. 4** TR & INTR to imagine, expect or suspect: **I didn't think there would be any trouble. 5** to keep in mind; to consider: **think of the children first. 6** TR & INTR to remember: **couldn't think of his name.**
■ **thinker** N.
◆ **think over** to consider all the advantages and disadvantages of (an action or decision).
◆ **think through** to think carefully about the possible consequences of (a plan or idea).

◆ **think twice** to hesitate before doing something; to decide in the end not to do it.

◆ **think sth up** to invent or devise it.

thinking N 1 the act of using one's mind to produce thoughts. 2 opinion or judgement: What is your thinking on this? ➤ ADJ of people: using or able to use the mind intelligently and constructively.

thinner N a liquid such as turpentine that is added to paint or varnish to dilute it.

thin-skinned ADJ sensitive; easily hurt.

third (OFTEN WRITTEN **3rd**) ADJ 1 in counting: **a** next after second; **b** last of three. 2 in third position. ➤ N 1 one of three equal parts. 2 a fraction equal to one divided by three. 3 a third-class university degree.

third class N 1 the class or rank next (esp in quality) after second. 2 (also **third**) a third-class honours degree from a university. ➤ ADJ (**third-class**) belonging or relating to the third class of anything.

third degree N (**the third degree**) prolonged and intensive interrogation, usu involving physical and mental intimidation. ➤ ADJ (**third-degree**) MED denoting the most serious of the three degrees of burning.

third party N, LAW someone who is indirectly involved, or involved by chance, in a legal action or contract, etc. ➤ ADJ (**third-party**) of insurance: covering damage done by or injury done to someone other than the insured.

third person see under **person**

third-rate ADJ inferior; sub-standard.

Third World N the developing countries in Africa, Asia and Latin America. Also called **Developing World**.

thirst N 1 a need to drink, or the feeling of dryness in the mouth that this causes. 2 a strong desire or longing: **a thirst for knowledge**. ➤ VB, INTR to have a great desire or long for.

thirsty ADJ (**-ier, -iest**) 1 needing or wanting to drink. 2 eager or longing. 3 causing thirst.

thirteen N 1 **a** the cardinal number 13; **b** the quantity that represents this, being one more than twelve, or the sum of ten and three. 2 any symbol for this, eg, 13 or XIII. 3 something, esp a garment or a person, whose size is denoted by the number 13. ➤ ADJ 1 totalling thirteen. 2 aged thirteen. ■ **thirteenth** ADJ, N.

thirties PL N (often written **30s** or **30's**) 1 (**one's thirties**) the period of time between one's thirtieth and fortieth birthdays. 2 (**the thirties**) the range of temperatures between thirty and forty degrees. 3 (**the thirties**) the period of time between the thirtieth and fortieth years of a century.

thirty N (**-ies**) 1 **a** the cardinal number 30; **b** the quantity that this represents, being one more than twenty-nine. 2 any symbol for this, eg, 30 or XXX. 3 something, esp a garment or person, whose size is denoted by the number 30. ➤ ADJ 1 totalling thirty. 2 aged thirty. ■ **thirtieth** ADJ, N.

this PRONOUN (**these**) 1 a person, animal, thing or idea already mentioned, about to be mentioned, indicated or otherwise understood from the context. 2 a person, animal, thing or idea which is nearby, esp which is closer to the speaker than someone or something else. 3 the present time or place. 4 an action, event or circumstance: What do you think of this? ➤ ADJ 1 being the person, animal, thing or idea which is nearby, esp closer than someone or something else: this book or that one. 2 being the person, animal, thing or idea just mentioned, about to be mentioned, indicated or otherwise understood. 3 relating to today, or time in the recent past ending today: this morning. ➤ ADV to this degree or extent: I didn't think it would be this easy.

thistle N a plant with prickly leaves and usu globular flowerheads.

thither ADV, OLD USE, LITERARY OR FORMAL to or towards that place.

thong N 1 a narrow strip of leather used for fastening, etc. 2 a type of skimpy undergarment similar to a G-string.

thorax N (*thoraxes* or *thoraces*) ANAT, ZOOL in humans and other vertebrates: the part of the body between the neck and abdomen; the chest. ■ **thoracal** or **thoracic** ADJ.

thorn N 1 a hard sharp point sticking out from the stem or branch of certain plants. 2 a constant irritation: a thorn in one's side.

thorny ADJ (*-ier, -iest*) 1 full of or covered with thorns. 2 difficult; causing trouble or problems.

thorough ADJ 1 of a person: extremely careful and attending to every detail. 2 complete; absolute: a thorough waste of time. ■ **thoroughly** ADV.

thoroughbred N an animal, esp a horse, bred from the best specimens carefully developed by selective breeding over many years. Also AS ADJ.

thoroughfare N 1 a public road or street. 2 a road or path that is open at both ends.

thoroughgoing ADJ 1 extremely thorough. 2 utter; out-and-out: a thoroughgoing villain.

those plural of **that**

thou[1] PRONOUN, OLD USE OR DIALECT, also RELIG you (singular).

thou[2] N (*thous* or *thou*) COLLOQ a thousand.

though CONJ 1 (often **even though**) despite the fact that: I ate it up though I didn't like it. 2 and yet; but: We like the new car, though not as much as the old one.
➤ ADV however; nevertheless.
◆ **as though** as if: It's as though I've known him all my life.

thought N 1 an idea, concept or opinion. 2 an act or the process of thinking. 3 serious and careful consideration.

thoughtful ADJ 1 thinking deeply; reflective. 2 showing careful thought: a thoughtful reply. ■ **thoughtfully** ADV. ■ **thoughtfulness** N.

thoughtless ADJ 1 inconsiderate. 2 showing a lack of careful thought; rash. ■ **thoughtlessly** ADV. ■ **thoughtlessness** N.

thousand N (*thousands* or *thousand*) 1a the number 1000; b the quantity that this represents, being the product of ten and one hundred. 2 any symbol for this, eg 1000 or M. 3 (usu **thousands**) COLLOQ a large unspecified number or amount.
➤ ADJ numbering 1000.

thousandth ADJ 1 the last of 1000 people or things. 2 in 1000th position.
➤ N one of 1000 equal parts.

thrash VB 1 to beat soundly, esp with blows or a whip. 2 to defeat thoroughly or decisively. 3 INTR to move around violently or wildly. ■ **thrashing** N.
◆ **thrash out** to discuss (a problem, etc) thoroughly to try to come to a solution.

thread N 1 a strand of silk, cotton, wool, etc for sewing. 2 a naturally formed strand of fibre, such as that spun by a spider. 3 the projecting spiral ridge round a screw or bolt, or in a nut. 4 a connecting element or theme in a story or argument, etc.
➤ VB 1 to pass a thread through the eye of (a needle). 2 (usu **thread through**) to pass (tape, film, etc) (into or through something). 3 to put (beads, etc) on a string, etc. 4 TR & INTR to make (one's way): threaded my way through the crowd.

threadbare ADJ 1 of material or clothes: worn thin; shabby. 2 of a word, excuse, etc: commonly used and meaningless; hackneyed.

threadworm N a parasitic worm living in the human large intestine.

threat N 1 a warning of impending hurt or punishment. 2 a sign that something dangerous or unpleasant is or may be about to happen. 3 a person or thing seen as dangerous.

threaten VB 1 to make or be a threat to. 2 to warn. 3 INTR of something unpleasant or dangerous: to seem likely to happen: The storm threatened all day. ■ **threatening** ADJ.

three N 1a the cardinal number 3; b the quantity that this represents, being one more than two. 2 any symbol for this, eg, 3 or III. 3 something, esp a garment or a person, whose size is denoted by the number 3. 4 the third hour after midnight or midday: Come at three.

➤ ADJ **1** totalling three. **2** aged three.

three-dimensional ADJ having or appearing to have three dimensions, ie, height, width and depth. Often shortened to **three-D** or **3-D**.

threefold ADJ **1** equal to three times as much. **2** divided into or consisting of three parts. ➤ ADV by three times as much.

three-legged race N a race run between pairs of runners who have their adjacent legs tied together.

three-ply N something with three layers or strands bound together, esp wood or wool. ➤ ADJ having three layers or strands.

three-point turn N a manoeuvre, usu done in three movements, in which a driver turns a motor vehicle using forward and reverse gears, to face in the opposite direction.

three-quarter ADJ consisting of three-quarters of the full amount, length, etc.

threesome N a group of three.

thresh VB **1** TR & INTR to separate grain or seeds from (corn, etc) by beating. **2** to beat or strike. ■ **thresher** N.

threshold N **1** a piece of wood or stone forming the bottom of a doorway. **2** a starting-point: **on the threshold of a new career**. **3** BIOL the point below which there is no response to a stimulus: **a low pain threshold**.

thrice ADV, OLD USE OR LITERARY three times.

thrift N careful spending, use or management of resources, esp money.

thrifty ADJ (**-ier, -iest**) showing thrift; economical; frugal. ■ **thriftily** ADV.

thrill VB, TR & INTR to feel or cause to feel exhilaration. ➤ N **1** a sudden tingling feeling of excitement, happiness or pleasure. **2** something causing this. ■ **thrilling** ADJ.

thriller N an exciting novel, play, film, etc, usu involving crime, espionage or adventure.

thrips N (PL **thrips**) a minute black insect, which feeds by sucking sap from plants.

thrive VB (**throve** or **thrived, thriven** or **thrived**) INTR **1** to grow strong and healthy. **2** to prosper or be successful, esp financially.

throat N **1** the top part of the windpipe or gullet. **2** the front part of the neck.

throaty ADJ (**-ier, -iest**) **1** of a voice: deep and hoarse; husky. **2** COLLOQ indicating a sore throat: **feeling a bit throaty**.

throb VB (**-bb-**) INTR **1** to beat or vibrate with a strong regular rhythm. ➤ N a regular beat; pulse.

throe N (usu **throes**) a violent pang or spasm, esp during childbirth or before death. ◆ **in the throes of** busy with, involved in or suffering under: **in the throes of the storm**.

thrombosis N (**-ses**) an abnormal congealing of the blood within a blood vessel.

throne N **1** a ceremonial chair of a monarch, bishop, etc. **2** the office or power of the sovereign: **come to the throne**.

throng N a crowd of people or things. ➤ VB **1** to crowd or fill: **people thronging the streets**. **2** INTR to move in a crowd: **The audience thronged into the theatre**.

throttle N a valve regulating the amount of fuel, steam, etc supplied to an engine. ➤ VB to injure or kill by choking or strangling.

through or (N AMER) **thru** PREP **1** going from one side or end of something to the other: **a road through the village**. **2** all over: **searched through the house**. **3** from the beginning to the end of: **read through the magazine**. **4** because of: **lost his job through his own stupidity**. **5** by way, means, or agency of: **related through marriage**. ➤ ADV **1** into and out of; from one side or end to the other: **go straight through**. **2** from the beginning to the end. **3** into a position of having completed: **sat the exam and got through**. **4** completely: **soaked through**. ➤ ADJ **1** of a journey, route, train or ticket, etc: going or allowing one to go all the way to one's destination without requiring a change. **2** of traffic: passing straight through an area or

town, etc without stopping. **3** going from one surface, side or end to another: **a through road**. **4** COLLOQ finished: **I'm through with the paper**.
◆ **through and through** completely.

throughout PREP **1** in all parts of: **decorated throughout the house**. **2** during the whole of: **chattered throughout the film**.
➤ ADV **1** in every part; everywhere: **a house with carpets throughout**. **2** during the whole time: **remain friends throughout**.

throw VB (*threw, thrown*) **1** TR & INTR to propel or hurl through the air with force. **2** to move or hurl into a specified position. **3** to direct, cast or emit: **throw a glance**. **4** COLLOQ to puzzle or confuse. **5** of a horse: to make (its rider) fall off. **6** WRESTLING, JUDO to bring (an opponent) to the ground. **7** to make (pottery) on a potter's wheel. **8** COLLOQ to lose (a contest) deliberately, esp in return for a bribe. **9 a** TR & INTR to roll (dice) on to a flat surface; **b** to obtain (a specified number) by throwing dice. **10** to have or suffer: **throw a tantrum**. **11** to give (a party). **12** to deliver (a punch). **13** to cause (one's voice) to appear to come from elsewhere.
➤ N **1** an act of throwing or instance of being thrown. **2** a decorative fabric covering a piece of furniture, etc.
◆ **throw sth away 1** to discard it or get rid of it. **2** to fail to take advantage of it.
  throw in 1 to include or add (something extra) as a gift or as part of a deal at no extra cost. **2** to contribute (a remark) to a discussion, esp casually.
  throw oneself into sth to begin doing it with great energy or enthusiasm.
  throw off to get rid of: **throw off a cold**.
  throw out 1 to expel: **threw the troublemakers out**. **2** to get rid of: **threw the old newspapers out**.
  throw over to abandon (esp a lover).
  throw people together of circumstances, etc: to bring them into contact by chance.
  throw sth together to construct it hurriedly or temporarily.
  throw up COLLOQ to vomit.

throwaway ADJ **1** meant to be thrown away

after use. **2** said or done casually or carelessly.

throwback N someone or something that shows or reverts to earlier characteristics.

throw-in N, SPORT in football, etc: an act of throwing the ball back into play from a sideline.

thru see **through**

thrum VB (*-mm-*) TR & INTR to strum idly on (a stringed instrument).

thrush[1] N a songbird, typically with brown feathers and a spotted chest.

thrush[2] N **1** a fungal infection causing white blisters in the mouth, throat and lips. **2** a similar infection in the vagina.

thrust VB (*thrust*) **1** to push suddenly and violently. **2** (usu **thrust on** or **upon**) to force (someone) to accept (something). **3** to make (one's way) forcibly.
➤ N **1** a sudden or violent movement forward; a push or lunge. **2** AERONAUTICS the force produced by a jet or rocket engine that propels an aircraft or rocket forward. **3** an attack or lunge with a pointed weapon; a stab. **4** the main message or gist, eg of an argument.

thud N a dull sound like something heavy falling to the ground.
➤ VB (*-dd-*) INTR to move or fall with a thud.

thug N a violent or brutal person. ■ **thuggery** N. ■ **thuggish** ADJ.

thumb N in humans: the opposable digit on the inner side of the hand.
➤ VB **1** (often **thumb through**) TR & INTR to turn the pages of (a book or magazine, etc) and glance at the contents. **2** (also **thumb a lift** or **ride**) TR & INTR to hitchhike.
◆ **thumbs down** a sign indicating failure, rejection or disapproval.
◆ **thumbs up** a sign indicating success, best wishes for success, satisfaction or approval.
◆ **under sb's thumb** completely controlled or dominated by them.

thumb nail N **1** the nail on the thumb. **2** COMP (also **thumbnail**) a small version of a picture.
➤ ADJ brief and concise: **a thumb-nail sketch**.

thumbscrew N, HIST an instrument of torture

which crushes the thumbs.

thump N a heavy blow, or the dull sound of a blow.
➤ VB **1** TR & INTR to beat or strike with heavy blows. **2** INTR to throb or beat violently.

thumping COLLOQ, ADJ very big: a thumping lie.
➤ ADV very: a pair of thumping great boots.

thunder N **1** a deep rumbling or loud cracking sound heard soon after a flash of lightning. **2** a loud deep rumbling noise.
➤ VB **1** INTR of thunder: to sound or rumble. **2** INTR to make a noise like thunder while moving: tanks thundering over a bridge. **3** to say or utter in a loud voice. ■ **thundery** ADJ.

thunderbolt N **1** a flash of lightning coming simultaneously with a crash of thunder. **2** a sudden and unexpected event.

thunderclap N a sudden crash of thunder.

thundering COLLOQ, ADJ very great: a thundering idiot.
➤ ADV very: a thundering great error.

thunderous ADJ like thunder, esp in being very loud: thunderous applause.

thunderstorm N a storm with thunder and lightning, usu accompanied by heavy rain.

thunderstruck ADJ overcome by surprise.

Thursday N the fifth day of the week.

thus ADV **1** in the way or manner shown or mentioned; in this manner. **2** to this degree, amount or distance: thus far. **3** therefore.

thwack N a blow with something flat, or the noise of this.
➤ VB to strike with such a noise.

thwart VB to prevent or hinder.

thy ADJ, OLD USE OR DIALECT, also RELIG belonging or relating to **thee**.

thyme N a herb or shrub with aromatic leaves used to season food.

thyroid N (in full **thyroid gland**) a gland in the neck that secretes hormones which control growth, development and metabolic rate.

ti see **te**

tiara N a woman's jewelled head-ornament.

tibia N (-*as* or -*ae*) **1** the inner and usu larger of the two human leg bones between the knee and ankle. **2** the corresponding bone in other vertebrates. ■ **tibial** ADJ.

tic N a habitual nervous involuntary movement or twitch of a muscle, esp of the face.

tick^1 N **1** a regular tapping or clicking sound, such as that made by a watch or clock. **2** BRIT COLLOQ a moment: Wait a tick. **3** a small mark, usu a downward-sloping line with the bottom part bent upwards, used to show that something is correct, to mark off items on a list once they are dealt with, etc.
➤ VB **1** INTR of a clock, etc: to make a tick or ticks. **2** to mark with a written tick. **3** (often **tick off**) to mark (an item on a list, etc) with a tick.
◆ **tick sb off** COLLOQ to scold them.
◆ **tick over 1** to function or work quietly and smoothly at a relatively gentle or moderate rate. **2** of an engine: to idle.

tick^2 N **1** a bloodsucking arachnid living on the skin of dogs, cattle, etc. **2** a bloodsucking fly living on the skin of sheep, birds, etc.

tick^3 N, BRIT COLLOQ credit: buy it on tick.

ticker N, COLLOQ the heart.

ticker tape N **1** continuous paper tape with messages, esp up-to-date share prices, printed by a telegraph instrument. **2** this type of paper thrown from windows into the streets to welcome a famous person.

ticket N **1** a card, etc entitling the holder to travel on a bus, train, etc, or to be admitted to a theatre, cinema, sports match, etc, or to use a library, etc. **2** an official notice stating that a traffic offence, eg, speeding or illegal parking, has been committed. **3** a tag or label showing the price, size, etc of the item to which it is attached. **4** COLLOQ exactly what is required, proper or best: just the ticket.

ticking N a strong coarse, usu striped, cotton fabric used to cover mattresses, bolsters, etc.

ticking-off N, BRIT COLLOQ a mild scolding.

tickle VB **1** to touch (a person or body part) lightly and provoke a tingling or light prickling sensation, laughter, jerky movements, etc. **2** COLLOQ to amuse or entertain.
➤ N **1** an act of tickling. **2** a tingling or light prickling sensation.
◆ **tickled pink** or **tickled to death** COLLOQ very pleased or amused.
◆ **tickle sb's fancy** to attract or amuse them.

ticklish ADJ **1** sensitive to tickling. **2** of a problem, etc: needing careful handling.

tidal ADJ relating to or affected by tides.

tidal wave N **1** an unusually large ocean wave. **2** a widespread show of feeling, etc: a tidal wave of protest.

tiddler N, BRIT COLLOQ **1** a small fish, eg a minnow. **2** a small person or thing.

tiddly ADJ (**-ier, -iest**) BRIT COLLOQ slightly drunk.

tiddlywinks SING N a game in which players try to flick small flat discs into a cup using larger discs.

tide N **1** the twice-daily rise and fall of the water level in the oceans and seas. **2** the level of water, esp the sea, as affected by this: **high tide**. **3** a sudden or marked trend: **tide of public opinion**. **4** IN COMPOUNDS a time or season, esp of some festival: **Whitsuntide**.
◆ **tide sb over** to help them to deal with a problem, a difficult situation, etc.

tidemark N **1** a mark showing the highest level that the tide has reached or usu reaches. **2** BRIT COLLOQ **a** a scummy ring round a bath indicating where the water had come up to; **b** a mark on the skin indicating the difference between a washed area and an unwashed one.

tidings PL N, OLD USE news.

tidy ADJ (**-ier, -iest**) **1** neat and in good order. **2** methodical. **3** COLLOQ large; considerable: **a tidy sum of money**.
➤ N (**-ies**) **1** often IN COMPOUNDS a receptacle for keeping odds and ends in: **a sink-tidy** • **a desk-tidy**. **2** an act or the process of tidying: **gave the room a quick tidy**.
➤ VB (**-ies, -ied**) to make neat. ■ **tidily** ADV. ■ **tidiness** N.

tie VB (**tying**) **1** to fasten with a string, ribbon, rope, etc. **2 a** to make (string, ribbon, etc) into a bow or knot; **b** to make (a bow or knot) in. **3** to be fastened in a specified way: **a dress that ties at the back**. **4** (usu **tie with**) INTR to have the same score or final position as (another competitor or entrant) in a game or contest, etc. **5** to limit or restrict.
➤ N **1** a narrow strip of material worn, esp by men, round the neck under a shirt collar and tied in a knot or bow at the front. **2** a strip of ribbon, rope, cord or chain, etc for binding and fastening. **3** something that limits or restricts. **4** a link or bond: **ties of friendship**. **5** a match or competition, etc in which the result is an equal score for both sides. **6** BRIT a game or match to be played, esp in a knockout competition: **The third round ties were all postponed**.
◆ **tie in** or **up with sth** to be in or be brought into connection with it; to correspond or be made to correspond with it.
◆ **tie sb up** to bind them securely.
◆ **tie sth up** to fasten (a parcel, etc) securely with string, etc.

tie-break or **tie-breaker** N an extra game, series of games, question, etc to decide a drawn match, etc.

tied cottage N, BRIT a cottage occupied by a tenant during the period that they are employed by its owner.

tie-dye N a technique of dyeing fabrics in which parts of the fabric are tied tightly to stop them absorbing the dye, so that a swirly pattern is produced.
➤ VB to dye like this.

tie-pin N an ornamental pin fixed to a tie to hold it in place.

tier N a level, rank, row, etc, esp one of several positioned one above another.

tiff N a slight petty quarrel.

tig see under **tag²**

tiger N **1** a large carnivorous Asian member of the cat family with a fawn or reddish coat, with black or brownish-black transverse stripes. **2** a fierce cruel person.

tight ADJ 1 fitting very or too closely. 2 stretched so as not to be loose; tense; taut. 3 fixed or held firmly in place: **a tight knot**. 4 USU IN COMPOUNDS preventing the passage of air, water, etc: **watertight**. 5 difficult or awkward: **in a tight spot**. 6 of a schedule or timetable, etc: not allowing much time. 7 COLLOQ mean; miserly. 8 COLLOQ drunk. 9 of money or some commodity: in short supply.
➢ ADV tightly; soundly; completely: **sleep tight**.
■ **tightly** ADV. ■ **tightness** N.

tighten VB, TR & INTR to make or become tight or tighter.

tight-fisted ADJ mean with money, etc.

tight-knit or **tightly-knit** ADJ closely organized or united: **a tight-knit family**.

tight-lipped ADJ saying or revealing nothing.

tightrope N a tightly stretched rope or wire on which acrobats perform.

tights PL N a close-fitting garment covering the feet, legs and body up to the waist, worn esp by women, dancers, acrobats, etc.

tigress N 1 a female tiger. 2 a fierce woman.

tikka ADJ of meat in Indian cookery: having been marinated in yoghurt and spices.

tilde N a mark (~) placed over **n** in Spanish to show that it is pronounced **ny** and over **a** and **o** in Portuguese to show they are nasalized.

tile N a flat thin slab of fired clay, or a similar one of cork or linoleum, used to cover roofs, floors and walls, etc.
➢ VB to cover with tiles. ■ **tiler** N. ■ **tiling** N.
◆ **on the tiles** having a wild social time.

till¹ PREP up to the time of: **wait till tomorrow**.
➢ CONJ up to the time when: **go on till you reach the station**.

till² N a container or drawer where money taken from customers is put.

till³ VB to prepare and cultivate (soil or land) for the growing of crops.

tiller N a lever used to turn the rudder of a boat.

tilt VB, TR & INTR to slope or cause to slope.

➢ N a sloping position or angle.
◆ **at full tilt** at full speed or with full force.

timber N 1 wood, esp when prepared for or used in building or carpentry. 2 trees suitable for this. 3 a wooden beam in the framework, esp of a ship or house. ■ **timbered** ADJ.

timbre N the distinctive quality of the tone produced by a musical instrument or voice.

time N 1 the continuous passing and succession of minutes, days and years, etc. 2 a particular point in time expressed in hours and minutes, or days, months and years, as shown on a clock, watch, calendar, etc. 3 (also **times**) a point or period of time: **at the time of her marriage**. 4 IN COMPOUNDS a period of time allocated to an activity, etc: **lunchtime**. 5 an unspecified interval or period: **stayed there for a time**. 6 one of a number or series of occasions or repeated actions: **been to Spain three times**. 7 a period or occasion of a specified kind: **a good time**. 8 COLLOQ a prison sentence: **do time**. 9 an apprenticeship: **served her time and became a motor mechanic**. 10 BRIT the time when a public house must close. 11 MUS a specified rhythm or speed: **waltz time**.
➢ VB 1 to measure the time taken by (an event or journey, etc). 2 to arrange, set or choose the time for (a journey, meeting, etc).
◆ **all in good time** in due course.
◆ **all the time** continually.
◆ **behind the times** old-fashioned.
◆ **for the time being** meanwhile.
◆ **from time to time** occasionally.
◆ **have no time for sb** or **sth** to have no interest in or patience with them or it.
◆ **have the time of one's life** to enjoy oneself very much.
◆ **in good time** early.
◆ **in no time** very quickly.
◆ **in one's own time** 1 in one's spare time when not at work. 2 at the speed one prefers.
◆ **in time** early enough.
◆ **keep time** 1 to correctly follow the required rhythm of a piece of music. 2 of a watch or clock: to function accurately.
◆ **kill time** to pass time aimlessly.
◆ **no time at all** COLLOQ a very short time.
◆ **on time** at the right time; not late.

◆ **take one's time** to work, etc as slowly as one wishes.

time bomb N a bomb that has been set to explode at a particular pre-set time.

time capsule N a container for objects typical of the current age, buried or preserved for discovery in the future.

time-consuming ADJ taking up a lot of time.

time-honoured ADJ respected and upheld because of custom or tradition.

timekeeper N 1 someone who records time, eg, as taken by a competitor in a game, etc. 2 a clock, watch, or person thought of in terms of accuracy or punctuality: **a good timekeeper**. ■ **timekeeping** N.

timeless ADJ 1 not belonging to or typical of any particular time or date. 2 unaffected by time; ageless; eternal. ■ **timelessness** N.

timely ADJ (*-ier, -iest*) coming at the right or a suitable moment; opportune. ■ **timeliness** N.

time out N, N AMER a brief pause or rest.

timepiece N an instrument for keeping time, such as a watch or clock.

timer N a device like a clock which switches an appliance on or off at pre-set times, or which makes a sound when a set amount of time has passed.

times PREP expressing multiplication: **three times two makes six**.

timescale N the time envisaged for the completion of a particular project.

time-served ADJ having completed an apprenticeship: **a time-served electrician**.

time-sharing N a scheme whereby someone buys the right to use a holiday home for the same specified period each year.

time signature N, MUS a sign, usu placed after a clef, indicating rhythm.

timetable N 1 a list of the departure and arrival times of trains, buses, etc. 2 a plan showing the order of events.

timeworn ADJ worn out through long use; old.

time zone N any one of the 24 more or less parallel sections into which the world is divided longitudinally, with all places within a given zone having the same standard time.

timid ADJ easily frightened or alarmed; nervous; shy. ■ **timidity** N.

timing N the regulating of actions, events, etc to achieve the best possible effect.

timorous ADJ very timid; frightened. ■ **timorousness** N.

timpani or **tympani** PL N a set of kettledrums. ■ **timpanist** or **tympanist** N.

tin N 1 CHEM a soft silvery-white metallic element used in alloys, eg, bronze, pewter and solder, and forming tin plate. 2 an airtight metal container for storing food: **a biscuit tin**. 3 a sealed container for preserving food: **a tin of baked beans**. ➤ VB (*-nn-*) to pack (food) in a tin. ■ **tinned** ADJ.

tincture N 1 a slight flavour, trace or addition. 2 a slight trace of colour; hue. 3 a solution of a drug in alcohol for medicinal use.

tinder N dry material, esp wood, which is easily set alight and can be used as kindling.

tine N a slender prong, eg of a fork.

tinfoil N aluminium or other metal in the form of thin, paper-like sheets.

tinge N a trace or hint. ➤ VB to give a trace or hint to.

tingle VB, TR & INTR to feel or cause to feel a prickling or slightly stinging sensation. ➤ N a prickling or slightly stinging sensation. ■ **tingling** ADJ.

tinker N 1 a travelling mender of pots, pans and other household utensils. 2 COLLOQ a mischievous or impish person, esp a child. ➤ VB, INTR to work in an unskilled way, esp in trying to make minor adjustments or improvements: **tinkering with that old car**.

tinkle VB, TR & INTR to make or cause to make a succession of jingling sounds. ➤ N 1 a jingling sound. 2 BRIT COLLOQ a telephone call. ■ **tinkly** ADJ.

tinnitus N, MED an abnormal ringing, buzzing or whistling, etc noise in the ears.

tinny ADJ (*-ier, -iest*) 1 relating to or resembling tin. 2 of sound: thin and high-pitched.

tin-opener N a device for opening food tins.

tin plate N sheet iron or steel coated with tin.
➤ VB (**tin-plate**) to cover with a layer of tin.

tinpot ADJ, BRIT COLLOQ cheap or poor quality; paltry or contemptible: **tinpot dictator**.

tinsel N a long decorative strip of glittering metal threads, used esp at Christmas.

tinsmith N a worker in tin and tin plate.

tint N 1 a variety or slightly different shade of a colour, esp one made lighter by adding white. 2 a pale or faint colour. 3 a hair dye.
➤ VB to give a tint to (hair, etc); to colour slightly.

tiny ADJ (*-ier, -iest*) very small.

tip[1] N 1 an end or furthermost point of something: **the tips of her fingers**. 2 a small piece forming an end or point.
➤ VB (*-pp-*) to put or form a tip on.
◆ **on the tip of one's tongue** about to be said, but not able to be because not quite remembered.

tip[2] VB (*-pp-*) 1 TR & INTR to lean or cause to lean. 2 (also **tip out**) to empty (from a container, etc): **tipped the dirty water out of the bucket**. 3 BRIT to dump (rubbish).
➤ N 1 a place for tipping rubbish, etc. 2 COLLOQ a very untidy place.

tip[3] N 1 money given to a servant or waiter, etc in return for service done well. 2 a piece of useful information.
➤ VB (*-pp-*) to give a tip to.
◆ **tip sb off** to give them a piece of useful or secret information.

tip-off N a piece of useful or secret information, or the disclosing of this.

tipple COLLOQ, VB, TR & INTR to drink (alcohol) regularly, esp in relatively small amounts.
➤ N alcoholic drink. ■ **tippler** N.

tipster N someone who gives tips, esp as to which horses to bet on.

tipsy ADJ, COLLOQ (*-ier, -iest*) slightly drunk.

tiptoe VB (*-toed, -toeing*) INTR to walk quietly or stealthily on the tips of the toes.
➤ N (often **tiptoes**) the tips of the toes.

tip-top ADJ, ADV, COLLOQ excellent; first-class.

tirade N a long angry speech.

tire[1] VB 1 TR & INTR to make or become physically or mentally weary. 2 (**tire of**) to lose patience with or become bored with.

tire[2] N the US spelling of **tyre**.

tired ADJ 1 wearied; exhausted. 2 lacking freshness or showing the effects of time and wear. ■ **tiredness** N.
◆ **be tired of** to have had enough of.

tireless ADJ never becoming weary or exhausted. ■ **tirelessly** ADV.

tiresome ADJ annoying; tedious.

'tis CONTRACTION, OLD USE OR POETIC it is.

tissue N 1 a group of plant or animal cells with a similar structure and particular function: **muscle tissue**. 2 thin soft disposable paper used as a handkerchief or as toilet paper or a piece of this. 3 (also **tissue paper**) fine thin soft paper, used for wrapping, etc. 4 an interwoven mass or collection: **a tissue of lies**.

tit[1] N a small songbird.

tit[2] N.
◆ **tit for tat** blow for blow; with repayment of an injury by an injury.

tit[3] N 1 SLANG a teat. 2 COARSE SLANG a woman's breast.

titan N someone or something of very great strength, size, intellect or importance.

titanic ADJ having great strength or size.

titanium N, CHEM a silvery-white metallic element used in making alloys for components of aircraft, missiles, etc.

titbit N a choice or small tasty morsel of something, eg, food or gossip.

tithe N 1 (often **tithes**) HIST a tenth part of someone's annual income or produce, paid as a tax to support the church. **2** a tenth part.

Titian ADJ of a bright reddish–gold colour.

titillate VB **1** to excite, esp in a mildly erotic way. **2** to tickle. ■ **titillating** ADJ. ■ **titillation** N.

titivate VB, TR & INTR, COLLOQ to smarten up or put the finishing touches to. ■ **titivation** N.

title N **1** the distinguishing name of a book, play, work of art, piece of music, etc. **2** an often descriptive heading, eg, of a chapter in a book or a legal document. **3** a word used before someone's name to show acquired or inherited rank, an honour, occupation, marital status, etc. **4** (**titles**) written material on film giving credits or dialogue, etc. **5** LAW a right to the possession of property. **6** SPORT a championship. ➤ VB to give a title to.

titled ADJ having a title of nobility or rank.

title deed N a document that proves legal ownership, esp of real property.

title role N the name of the character in a play, film, etc that gives it its title, eg, King Lear.

titter COLLOQ, VB, INTR to giggle or snigger in a stifled way. ➤ N an instance or noise of this.

tittle-tattle N idle or petty gossip or chatter. ➤ VB, INTR to gossip or chatter idly.

titular ADJ having the title of an office or position, but none of the authority or duties.

tizzy or **tizz** N (*tizzies* or *tizzes*) COLLOQ a nervous highly excited or confused state.

TLC ABBREV, COLLOQ tender loving care.

TNT ABBREV trinitrotoluene.

to PREP **1** towards; in the direction of, or with the destination of somewhere or something: **go to the shop. 2** used to express as a resulting condition, aim or purpose: **boil the fruit to a pulp • to my surprise. 3** as far as; until: **from beginning to end • bears the scars to this day. 4** used to introduce the indirect object of a verb: **He sent it to us. 5** used to express addition: **add one to ten. 6** used to express attachment, connection, contact or possession: **put his ear to the door. 7** before the hour of:

ten minutes to three. **8** used to express response or reaction to a situation or event, etc: **rise to the occasion • dance to the music. 9** used to express comparison or proportion: **won by two goals to one • second to none. 10** used before an infinitive: **asked her to stay.** ➤ ADV **1** in or into a nearly closed position: **pulled the window to. 2** back into consciousness: **He came to later.** ◆ **to and fro** backwards and forwards.

toad N a tailless amphibian, with a short squat head and body, and moist skin.

toad-in-the-hole N, BRIT a dish of sausages cooked in batter.

toadstool N a fungus with a stalk and a spore–bearing cap, most varieties of which are poisonous or inedible.

toady N (*-ies*) someone who flatters someone else, does everything they want and hangs on their every word; a sycophant. ➤ VB (*-ies, -ied*) TR & INTR (**toady to sb**) to behave obsequiously towards them. ■ **toadyism** N.

toast VB **1** to make (bread, cheese, etc) brown by exposing to direct heat. **2** TR & INTR to make or become warm by being exposed to heat. **3** to drink ceremonially in honour of or to the health or future success of. ➤ N **1** bread which has been browned by exposure to direct heat. **2** an act of toasting someone, etc. **3** a highly regarded person or thing: **the toast of the festival.**

toaster N a machine for toasting bread.

toastie N, COLLOQ a toasted sandwich.

toastmaster or **toastmistress** N a man or woman who proposes the toasts at a ceremonial dinner.

tobacco N (*-os* or *-oes*) **1** a plant with very large leaves. **2** the dried nicotine–containing leaves of this plant, used in making cigarettes, cigars, pipe tobacco and snuff.

tobacconist N a person or shop selling tobacco, cigarettes, cigars and pipes, etc.

-to-be ADJ, IN COMPOUNDS future; soon to

become: **a bride-to-be.**

toboggan N a long light sledge.
➤ VB, INTR to ride on a toboggan.

toby jug N a jug in the shape of a stout man wearing a three-cornered hat.

toccata N a piece of music for a keyboard instrument intended to show off the performer's skill.

tod N, BRIT COLLOQ.
◆ **on one's tod** alone.

today N 1 this day. 2 the present time.
➤ ADV 1 on or during this day. 2 nowadays; at the present time.

toddle VB, INTR to walk with unsteady steps, as or like a young child.
➤ N a toddling walk.

toddler N a child who is just beginning, or has just learned, to walk.

toddy N (-ies) an alcoholic drink with added sugar, hot water and lemon juice.

to-do N, COLLOQ a fuss, commotion or bustle.

toe N 1 a one of the five digits at the end of the human foot; b a corresponding digit in an animal. 2 a part of a shoe, sock, etc covering the toes.
➤ VB (**toed, toeing**) to kick, strike or touch with the toes.
◆ **on one's toes** alert and ready for action.
◆ **toe the line** COLLOQ to act by the rules.

toecap N a reinforced covering on the toe of a boot or shoe.

toehold N 1 a place where toes can grip, eg, when climbing. 2 a start or small beginning: **got a toehold in the web designing business.**

toenail N a nail covering the tip of a toe.

toerag N, BRIT COLLOQ 1 a rascal.
2 a despicable or contemptible person.

toff N, BRIT SLANG an upper-class person.

toffee N 1 a sticky sweet, made by boiling sugar and butter. 2 a piece of this.

toffee-nosed ADJ, BRIT COLLOQ stuck-up.

tofu N a curd made from soya beans.

tog[1] N (**togs**) clothes.

tog[2] N a unit for measuring the warmth of fabrics, clothes, duvets, etc.

toga N, HIST an ancient Roman's loose outer garment.

together ADV 1 with someone or something else; in company: **travel together.** 2 at the same time: **all arrived together.** 3 so as to be in contact, joined or united. 4 by action with one or more other people: **Together we managed to persuade him.** 5 in or into one place: **gather together.** 6 COLLOQ into a proper or suitable order: **get things together.**
➤ ADJ, COLLOQ well organized; competent.
◆ **together with sb** or **sth** as well or in addition to them or it.

togetherness N a feeling of closeness, mutual sympathy and understanding, and of belonging together.

toggle N 1 a fastening, eg, for garments, consisting of a small bar passed through a loop. 2 COMP a keyboard command which allows the user to switch between one mode and another.
➤ VB 1 to provide or fasten (something) with a toggle. 2 COMP to use a toggle to switch between one mode and another.

toil VB, INTR 1 to work long and hard. 2 to make progress or move forwards with great effort.

toilet N a lavatory.

toilet paper or **toilet tissue** N paper for cleaning oneself after urination and defecation.

toiletry N (-ies) an article or cosmetic used when washing, making up, etc.

toilet water N a light perfume.

token N 1 a mark, sign or distinctive feature. 2 something serving as a reminder, etc: **a token of my esteem.** 3 a voucher worth a specified amount that can be exchanged for goods to the same value: **book token.** 4 a small coin-like piece of metal or plastic, used instead of money, eg, in a gambling machine.
➤ ADJ 1 nominal; of no real value: **token gesture.** 2 present, included, etc only for the sake of

appearances: *a token woman*.
◆ **by the same token** also; in addition.

tokenism N the principle or practice of doing no more than the minimum in a particular area, in pretence that one is committed to it.

tolerable ADJ 1 able to be endured. 2 fairly good. ■ **tolerably** ADV.

tolerance N 1 the ability to be fair towards and accepting of other people's beliefs or opinions. 2 the ability to resist or endure pain or hardship. 3 MED someone's ability to adapt to the effects of a prescribed or illegal drug, so that increasingly larger doses are required to produce the same effect.

tolerant ADJ 1 tolerating the beliefs and opinions of others. 2 capable of enduring unfavourable conditions, etc. 3 indulgent; permissive. ■ **tolerantly** ADV.

tolerate VB 1 to endure. 2 to be able to resist the effects of (a drug). 3 to treat fairly and accept. ■ **toleration** N.

toll¹ VB, TR & INTR to ring (a bell) with slow measured strokes.

toll² N 1 a fee or tax paid for the use of something, eg a bridge. 2 a cost, eg in damage, injury, lives lost, esp in a war.

toluene N, CHEM a colourless flammable liquid used in the manufacture of explosives, etc.

tom N a male cat.

tomahawk N a small axe used as a weapon by some Native Americans.

tomato N (-oes) 1 a round fleshy red, orange or yellow fruit, eaten raw, in salads, etc, or cooked. 2 a plant of the nightshade family producing this fruit.

tomb N a chamber or vault for a dead body.

tombola N a lottery in which winning tickets are drawn from a revolving drum.

tomboy N a girl who dresses or behaves in a boyish way. ■ **tomboyish** ADJ.

tombstone N an ornamental stone placed over a grave.

tomcat N a male cat.

tome N a large, heavy and usu learned book.

tomfoolery N (-ies) 1 stupid or foolish behaviour; nonsense. 2 an instance of this.

tommygun N a type of submachine-gun.

tomorrow N 1 the day after today. 2 the future.
➤ ADV 1 on the day after today. 2 in the future.

tomtit N a tit, esp a bluetit.

tom-tom N a tall drum, usu with a small head, which is beaten with the hands.

ton N 1 (IN FULL **long ton**) BRIT a unit of weight equal to 2240 lb. 2 (in full **short ton**) N AMER a unit of weight equal to 2000 lb. 3 (in full **metric ton**) a unit of weight equal to 1000kg. Also called **tonne**. 4 (in full **displacement ton**) a unit used to measure the amount of water a ship displaces, equal to 2 240 lb or 35 cubic feet of seawater. 5 (in full **register ton**) a unit used to measure a ship's internal capacity, equal to 100 cubic feet. 6 (in full **freight ton**) a unit for measuring the space taken up by cargo, equal to 40 cubic feet. 7 (usu **tons**) COLLOQ a lot. 8 COLLOQ a speed, score or sum, etc of 100. See also **tonnage**.

tonal ADJ belonging or relating to tone.

tonality N (-ies) 1 MUS the organization of all of the notes and chords of a piece of music in relation to a single tonic. 2 the colour scheme and tones used in a painting, etc.

tone N 1 a musical or vocal sound with reference to its quality and pitch. 2 MUS a sound that has a definite pitch. 3 a quality or character of the voice expressing a particular feeling or mood, etc. 4 the general character or style of spoken or written expression. 5 MUS the interval between, or equivalent to that between, the first two notes of the major scale. 6 high quality, style or character: **His coarse jokes lowered the tone of the meeting**. 7 the quality, tint or shade of a colour. 8 firmness of the body.
➤ VB 1 (also **tone in**) INTR to fit in well; to harmonize. 2 to give tone or the correct tone to. ■ **toneless** ADJ.
◆ **tone down** to become or cause to

become softer or less harsh in tone, colour or force, etc.

tone-deaf ADJ unable to distinguish accurately between notes of different pitch.

tongs PL N 1 a tool, consisting of two joined arms, used for holding and lifting. 2 a similar tool used to curl the hair.

tongue N 1 a fleshy muscular organ in the mouth, used for tasting, licking and swallowing and, in humans, speech. 2 the tongue of some animals, eg, the ox and sheep, used as food. 3 a particular language. 4 a particular manner of speaking: **a sharp tongue**. 5 anything like a tongue in shape: **the tongue of a shoe**. 6 the clapper in a bell. 7 a projecting strip along the side of a board that fits into a groove in another.
◆ **hold one's tongue** to say nothing.
◆ **tongue in cheek** with ironic intention.

tongue-tied ADJ unable to speak, esp because of shyness or embarrassment.

tongue-twister N a phrase or sentence that is difficult to say quickly.

tonic N 1 a medicine that increases or revives strength, energy and general wellbeing. 2 anything that is refreshing or invigorating. 3 tonic water. 4 MUS the first note of a scale, the note on which a key is based.
➤ ADJ 1 increasing energy and wellbeing. 2 MUS belonging or relating to the tonic scale.

tonic sol-fa see **sol-fa**

tonic water N a carbonated soft drink flavoured with quinine.

tonight N the night of this present day.
➤ ADV on or during the night of the present day.

tonnage N the space available in a ship for carrying cargo, measured in tons.

tonne see **ton**

tonsil N either of two lumps of lymph tissue at the back of the mouth. ■ **tonsillar** ADJ.

tonsillitis N inflammation of the tonsils.

tonsorial ADJ, often FACETIOUS belonging or relating to barbers or hairdressing.

tonsure N 1 the shaving of the crown or the head, esp of a person entering a monastic order. 2 a patch or head so shaved.

too ADV 1 to a greater extent or more than is required or suitable: **too many things to do**. 2 in addition; also: **loves Keats and likes Shelley too**. 3 extremely: **You're too generous!**

tool N 1 an implement, esp one used by hand, for cutting or digging, etc, such as a spade or hammer, etc. 2 a thing used in or necessary to a particular trade or profession: **Words are the tools of a journalist's trade**. 3 someone who is used or manipulated by another.
➤ VB to work or engrave (stone, leather, etc) using tools.

toot N a quick sharp blast of a trumpet, whistle or horn, etc.
➤ VB, TR & INTR to sound or cause (a trumpet or horn, etc) to sound with a quick sharp blast.

tooth N (**teeth**) 1 in vertebrates: any of the hard structures, usu embedded in the upper and lower jaw bones, used for biting and chewing food. 2 anything like a tooth in shape, arrangement, function, etc: **the teeth of a comb**. 3 (**teeth**) enough power to be effective.
◆ **get one's teeth into sth** to tackle or deal with it vigorously or eagerly, etc.
◆ **in the teeth of sth** in opposition to it.
◆ **long in the tooth** COLLOQ old.
◆ **tooth and nail** fiercely.

toothache N pain in a tooth, usu as a result of decay.

toothbrush N a brush for cleaning the teeth.

toothpaste N a paste for cleaning the teeth.

toothpick N a small sharp piece of wood or plastic for removing food stuck between teeth.

toothsome ADJ appetizing; delicious.

toothy ADJ (**-ier, -iest**) showing or having a lot of teeth: **a toothy grin**.

tootle VB, INTR, COLLOQ to go about casually, esp by car.

top[1] N 1 the highest part, point or level of anything. 2 the highest or most important rank or position. 3 the upper edge or surface of something. **4** a lid or piece for covering the top of something. **5** a garment for covering the upper half of the body, esp a woman's body. **6** the highest or loudest degree or pitch: **the top of one's voice**. **7** (**the tops**) COLLOQ the very best person or thing.

➤ ADJ at or being the highest or most important.

➤ VB (*-pp-*) **1** to cover or form the top of, esp as a finishing touch. **2** to remove the top of (a plant, fruit, etc). **3** to rise above or be better than. **4** SLANG (**top oneself**) to commit suicide.

◆ **on top of sth 1** in control of it. **2** in addition to it. **3** very close to it.

◆ **top sth off** to put a finishing or decorative touch to it.

◆ **top the bill** to head the list of performers in a show, as the main attraction.

◆ **top up 1** to refill (someone's glass or a container, etc) that has been partly emptied. **2** to provide money to bring (a grant or money supply) to the required or desirable total.

top² N a wooden or metal toy which spins on a pointed base.

topaz N an aluminium silicate mineral, the pale yellow variety of which is used as a gemstone.

top brass N, COLLOQ the highest-ranking officers or personnel, esp in the military.

top dog N, COLLOQ the most important or powerful person in a group.

top drawer N, COLLOQ high social position.
➤ ADJ (**top-drawer**) of the highest quality.

top-dressing N manure or fertilizer spread on soil as opposed to being ploughed or dug in.

top-flight ADJ OF the best or highest quality.

top gear N, BRIT the highest gear in a motor car, bike, etc.

top hat N a tall cylindrical men's hat worn as part of formal dress.

top-heavy ADJ disproportionately heavy in the upper part in comparison with the lower.

topiary N the art of cutting trees, bushes and hedges into ornamental shapes. ■ **topiarist** N.

topic N a subject or theme for a book, film, discussion, etc.

topical ADJ relating to matters of current interest. ■ **topicality** N.

topknot N a tuft of hair on top of the head.

topless ADJ of a woman: with her breasts exposed.

topmost ADJ the very highest of all.

top-notch ADJ, COLLOQ the very best quality.

topography N (*-ies*) **1** a description or map or the features of a landscape. **2** these features collectively. ■ **topographic** or **topographical** ADJ.

topping N something that forms a covering or garnish for food: **cheese topping**.

topple VB, TR & INTR **1** (also **topple over**) to fall, or cause to fall. **2** to overthrow.

topsail N a square sail set across the topmast.

top-secret ADJ very secret.

topside N a lean cut of beef from the rump.

topsoil N the uppermost layer of soil, rich in organic matter.

topspin N a spin given to a ball to make it travel higher, further or faster.

topsy-turvy ADJ, ADV **1** upside down. **2** in confusion.

tor N a tower-like rocky peak.

torch N **1** BRIT a small portable battery-powered light. **2** a piece of wood or bundle of cloth, etc set alight and used as a source of light.
➤ VB, COLLOQ, esp N AMER to set fire to.
◆ **carry a torch for sb** to feel love, esp unrequited love, for them.

toreador N a bullfighter, esp one on horseback.

torment N great pain, suffering or anxiety.
➤ VB **1** to cause great pain, suffering or anxiety to. **2** to pester or harass. ■ **tormentor** N.

tornado N (*-oes*) a violently destructive storm characterized by a funnel-shaped rotating column of air. ■ **tornadic** ADJ.

torpedo N (*-oes* or *-os*) **1** a long self-propelling underwater missile which explodes

on impact with its target. **2** a similar device dropped from the air.
➤ VB (**-oes, -oed**) to attack with torpedoes.

torpid ADJ sluggish and dull; lacking energy.

torpor N the state of being torpid.

torque N **1** HIST a necklace made of metal twisted into a band. **2** PHYS force multiplied by the perpendicular distance from a point about which it causes rotation.

torrent N **1** a great rushing stream or downpour of water or lava, etc. **2** a strong flow (of abuse, etc). ■ **torrential** ADJ.

torrid ADJ **1** of the weather: so hot and dry as to scorch the land. **2** of a relationship, etc: passionate.

torsion N twisting by applying force to one end while the other is held firm or twisted in the opposite direction. ■ **torsional** ADJ.

torso N the main part of the human body, without the limbs and head; the trunk.

torte N (**torten** or **tortes**) a rich sweet cake, often garnished or filled with fruit, cream, etc.

tortilla N a thin Mexican maize cake.

tortoise N a slow-moving reptile with a high domed shell into which the head, short scaly legs and tail can be withdrawn for safety.

tortoiseshell N **1** the brown and yellow mottled shell of a sea turtle, used in making combs, jewellery, etc. **2** a domestic cat with a mottled orange and creamy-brown coat.
➤ ADJ made of or mottled like tortoiseshell.

tortuous ADJ **1** full of twists and turns. **2** devious or involved.

torture N **1** the infliction of severe pain or mental suffering, esp as a punishment or as a means of persuasion. **2 a** great physical or mental suffering; **b** a cause of this.
➤ VB **1** to subject to torture. **2** to cause to experience great physical or mental suffering.

Tory N (**-ies**) a member or supporter of the British Conservative Party.

toss VB **1** to throw up into the air. **2** to throw away casually or carelessly. **3** INTR to move restlessly or from side to side repeatedly. **4** TR & INTR to be thrown or cause to be thrown from side to side repeatedly and violently: **a ship tossed by the storm**. **5** to jerk (the head). **6** TR & INTR (also **toss up**) to throw (a spinning coin) into the air and guess which side will land facing up, as a way of making a decision. **7** to coat (food, esp salad) with oil or a dressing, etc by gently mixing or turning it.
➤ N **1** an act or an instance of tossing. **2** SLANG the slightest amount: **not give a toss**.
◆ **toss sth off 1** to drink it quickly, esp in a single swallow. **2** to produce it quickly and easily.

toss-up N **1** COLLOQ an even chance or risk; something doubtful. **2** an act of tossing a coin.

tot[1] N **1** a small child; a toddler. **2** a small amount of spirits: **a tot of whisky**.

tot[2] VB (**-tt-**) (esp **tot up**) to add together.

total ADJ whole; complete.
➤ N the whole or complete amount.
➤ VB (**-ll-**; US **-l-**) **1** TR & INTR to amount to (a specified sum): **The figures totalled 385**. **2** (also **total up**) to add (figures, etc) up to produce a total. ■ **totally** ADV.

totalitarian ADJ of a system of government by a single party which allows no opposition and which demands complete obedience. ■ **totalitarianism** N.

totality N (**-ies**) completeness.

tote VB, COLLOQ to carry, drag or wear (esp something heavy).

totem N **1** in Native American culture: a natural object, esp an animal, used as the badge of a tribe or an individual. **2** an image of this.

totem pole N in Native American culture: a large wooden pole that has totems on it.

totter VB, INTR to walk or move unsteadily, shakily or weakly.

touch VB **1** to bring (a hand, etc) into contact with something. **2 a** TR & INTR to be in physical contact or come into physical contact with, esp lightly; **b** to bring together in close physical contact: **They touched hands. 3** OFTEN WITH NEGATIVES **a** to injure, harm or hurt: **I never touched him! b** to have dealings with, be associated with or be a party to: **wouldn't touch that kind of job; c** to make use of: **He never touches alcohol; d** to use (eg money, etc): **I don't touch the money; e** to approach in excellence; to be as good as: **Nobody can touch her at chess. 4** to concern or affect; to make a difference to: **It's a matter that touches us all. 5** (usu **touch on** or **upon**) to deal with (a matter, subject, etc), esp not very thoroughly. **6** to affect with pity, sympathy, etc: **The story of his sad life touched her heart. 7** to reach or go as far as, esp temporarily: **The temperature touched 100. 8** (often **touch with**) to tinge, taint, mark, modify, etc slightly or delicately: **The sky was touched with pink.**

➤ N **1** an act of touching or the sensation of being touched. **2** the sense by which the existence, nature, texture and quality of objects can be perceived through physical contact with the hands, etc. **3** the particular texture and qualities of an object, etc: **the silky touch of the fabric. 4** a small amount, quantity, distance, etc: **move it left a touch. 5** a detail which adds to the general pleasing effect: **The flowers were an elegant touch. 6** a characteristic style or manner: **need the expert's touch. 7** SPORT in rugby, etc: the ground outside the touchlines. **8** SLANG someone who can be persuaded to give or lend money: **a soft touch.**

◆ **get in touch** (**with**) to make contact or communicate (with): **They got in touch by letter.**

◆ **in touch** (**with**) **1** in contact, communication, etc (with): **We still keep in touch with each other. 2** up to date: **keeps in touch with the news.**

◆ **lose touch** (**with**) **1** to be no longer in contact, communication, etc (with). **2** to be no longer familiar (with) or well-informed (about): **lost touch with what's happening.**

◆ **out of touch** (**with**) **1** not in contact, communication, etc (with). **2** not up to date (with): **out of touch with the new technology.**

◆ **touch down 1** of an aircraft, spacecraft, etc: to land. **2** RUGBY to carry the ball over the goal-line and touch the ground with it.

◆ **touch sth off** to cause it to begin; to trigger it: **Police brutality touched off the riots.**

◆ **touch on** to verge towards: **That touches on the surreal.**

◆ **touch up** (usu **touch up sth**) to improve it by adding small details, correcting or hiding minor faults, etc: **touched up the painting.**

touch and go ADJ very uncertain in outcome: **It was touch and go whether she'd survive.**

touchdown N an instance of an aircraft or spacecraft making contact with the ground when landing.

touché EXCLAM **1** FENCING acknowledgement of a hit. **2** a good-humoured acknowledgment of the validity of a point that is made in an argument.

touched ADJ having a feeling of pity, sympathy, quiet pleasure, etc.

touching ADJ causing feelings of sympathy.

touchline N, esp FOOTBALL & RUGBY either of two lines that mark the sides of the pitch.

touchpaper N paper steeped in saltpetre and used for lighting fireworks or gunpowder.

touch-type VB, INTR to type without looking at the keyboard.

touchy ADJ (*-ier, -iest*) COLLOQ **1** easily annoyed or offended. **2** needing to be handled or dealt with with care and tact: **a touchy subject.**

tough ADJ **1** strong and durable; not easily cut, broken, torn or worn out. **2** of food, esp meat: difficult to chew. **3** of a person, animal, etc: strong and fit and able to endure hardship. **4** difficult to deal with or overcome; testing: **a tough decision. 5** severe and determined; unyielding; resolute: **a tough customer. 6** rough and violent; criminal: **a tough area. 7** COLLOQ unlucky; unjust; unpleasant: **The divorce was tough on the kids.**

◆ **tough sth out** to withstand (a difficult, trying, etc situation).

toughen VB, TR & INTR (also **toughen up**) to become or cause to become tough or tougher.

tough luck EXCLAM expressing sympathy when something has gone wrong or not to plan.

toupee N a small wig or hair-piece, usu worn by men to cover a bald patch.

tour N 1 an extended journey with stops at various places of interest. 2 a visit round a particular place: **a tour of the cathedral**. 3 a journey with frequent stops for business or professional engagements, eg, by a theatre company, rock group, etc. 3 an official period of duty or military service, esp abroad: **did a tour of duty in Germany**.
➤ VB, TR & INTR 1 to travel round (a place). 2 of a theatre company, band, performer, etc: to travel from place to place giving performances. ■ **touring** ADJ, N.

tourism N the practice of travelling to and visiting places for pleasure and relaxation.

tourist N someone who travels for pleasure and relaxation; a holiday-maker.

tournament N 1 a competition, eg, in tennis or chess, that involves many players taking part in heats for a championship. 2 HIST (also **tourney**) in the Middle Ages: **a** a competition with jousting contests; **b** a meeting for this.

tourniquet N a compression device for stopping the flow of blood through an artery.

tousle VB 1 to make (esp hair) untidy. 2 to tangle or dishevel. ■ **tousled** ADJ.

tout VB 1 INTR (usu **tout for**) to solicit custom, support, etc persistently. 2 to solicit the custom of (someone) or for (something).
➤ N (in full **ticket tout**) someone who buys up large numbers of tickets for a popular sporting event, concert, etc and sells them on at inflated prices. ■ **touter** N.

tow VB to pull (a ship, car, caravan, etc) along by rope, chain, cable, etc.
◆ **in tow** following or accompanying: **arrived with several men in tow**.

towards or **toward** PREP 1 in the direction of: **turn towards him**. 2 in relation or regard to: **showed no respect toward her boss**. 3 as a contribution to: **donated £1000 towards the costs**. 4 near; just before: **towards midnight**.

towel N a piece of absorbent cloth, etc used for drying the body, dishes, etc.

➤ VB (-**ll**-; US -**l**-) to rub or dry with a towel.

towelling N a highly absorbent material formed from many uncut loops of cotton, etc.

tower N 1 a **a** tall narrow structure forming part of a larger, lower building, eg a church; **b** a similar free-standing structure. 2 a fortress, esp with one or more towers.
➤ VB, INTR (usu **tower above** or **over**) to reach a great height, or be vastly superior.

tower block N, BRIT a very tall building comprised of many residential flats or offices.

towering ADJ reaching a great height; very tall or elevated: **towering mountains**.

tower of strength N someone who is a great help or support.

town N 1 an urban area smaller than a city but larger than a village. 2 the central shopping or business area in a neighbourhood: **went into town to buy new shoes**.

town council N the elected governing body of a town. ■ **town councillor** N.

town crier N, HIST someone whose job was to make public announcements in the streets.

town hall N the building where the business of a town's administration is carried out.

town house N a terraced house.

township N 1 S AFR an urban area that was formerly set aside for non-white citizens. 2 a small town or settlement.

towpath N a path alongside a canal or river where a horse can walk while towing a barge.

toxaemia or (US) **toxemia** N, MED blood poisoning.

toxic ADJ poisonous. ■ **toxicity** N.

toxin N a poison produced by a micro-organism.

toy N 1 a an object for someone, esp a child, to play with; **b** AS ADJ imitation, esp of something that adults use: **a toy gun**. 2 something that is very small, esp a dwarf breed or variety of dog.
➤ VB, INTR (usu **toy with**) 1 to flirt or trifle: **toyed with the idea of getting a new car**. 2 to move

(something) in an idle, distracted, etc way: **toying with his food**.

toyboy N, COLLOQ a woman's much younger male lover.

trace N **1** a mark or sign that some person, animal or thing has been in a particular place. **2** a track or footprint. **3** a very small amount that can only just be detected.
➤ VB **1** to track and discover by, or as if by, following clues, a trail, etc. **2** to follow step by step: **trace the development of medicine**. **3** to make a copy of (a drawing, design, etc) by covering it with a sheet of semi-transparent paper and drawing over the visible lines. **4** to outline or sketch (an idea, plan, etc). **5** to investigate and discover the cause, origin, etc of: **traced her family back to Tudor times**.
■ **traceable** ADJ.

trace element N a chemical element only found or required in very small amounts.

tracery N (-*ies*) **1** ornamental open stonework, esp in the top part of a Gothic window. **2** a finely patterned decoration or design.

trachea N (-*eae*) an air tube extending from the larynx to the lungs.

tracheotomy N a surgical incision into the trachea to make an alternative airway.

tracing N **1** a copy of a drawing, etc that is made on semi-transparent paper. **2** an act, instance or the process of making such a copy.

tracing-paper N thin semi-transparent paper used for tracing drawings, etc.

track N **1 a** a mark or series of marks or footprints, etc left behind: **a tyre track**; **b** a course of action, thought, etc taken: **followed in her mother's tracks and studied medicine**. **2** a rough path. **3** a specially prepared course: **a race track**. **4** the branch of athletics that comprises all the running events. **5** a railway line. **6** a length of railing that a curtain, spotlight, etc moves along. **7** an individual song, etc on an album, CD, cassette, etc. **8** a line, path or course of travel, passage or movement: **followed the track of the storm**. **9** a line or course of thought, reasoning, etc: **couldn't follow the track of his**

argument. **10** a predetermined line of travel of an aircraft. **11** a continuous band that tanks, etc have instead of individual tyres.
➤ VB **1** to follow (marks, footprints, etc left behind). **2** to follow and usu plot the course of (a spacecraft, etc) by radar. **3** INTR (often **track in**, **out** or **back**) of a film camera or its operator: to move. ■ **tracker** N, ADJ.
◆ **keep** or **lose track of sth** or **sb** to keep, or fail to keep, oneself informed about the progress, whereabouts, etc of them or it: **lost all track of time**.
◆ **make tracks** COLLOQ to leave; to set out.
◆ **off the beaten track** away from busy roads and therefore difficult to access or find.
◆ **on the right** or **wrong track** pursuing the right or wrong line of inquiry.
◆ **track sb** or **sth down** to search for and find them or it after following clues, etc.

track and field N the branch of athletics that comprises all the running and jumping events plus the hammer, discus, javelin, shot put, etc.

track record N, COLLOQ someone's performance, achievements, etc in the past.

track shoe N a running shoe with a spiked sole.

tracksuit N a loose suit worn by athletes, footballers, etc when exercising.

tract[1] N **1** an area of land, usu of indefinite extent: **large tracts of wilderness**. **2** a system in the body with a specified function: **the digestive tract**.

tract[2] N a short essay or pamphlet, esp on religion, politics, etc.

tractable ADJ of a person, etc: easily managed, controlled, etc; docile.

traction N **1** the action or process of pulling. **2** the state of being pulled or the force used in pulling. **3** MED a treatment involving steady pulling on a muscle, limb, etc using a series of pulleys and weights: **had her leg in traction**.

traction engine N a heavy steam-powered vehicle formerly used for pulling heavy loads.

tractor N a motor vehicle for pulling farm machinery, heavy loads, etc.

trade N **1 a** an act or instance or the process of buying and selling; **b** buying and selling generally: **foreign trade**. **2 a** a job, etc that involves skilled work, esp as opposed to professional or unskilled work: **left school at 16 to learn a trade**; **b** the people and businesses that are involved in such work: **the building trade**. **3** customers: **the lunch-time trade**. **4** business at a specified time, for a specified market or of a specified nature: **the tourist trade**. **5** (**trades**) the trade winds.
➤ VB **1** INTR to buy and sell; to engage in trading: **trades in securities**. **2 a** to exchange (one commodity) for another; **b** to exchange (blows, insults, etc); **c** COLLOQ to swap. ■ **trader** N.
◆ **trade in** to give (a used car, domestic appliance, etc) in part payment.
◆ **trade off** to give in exchange, usu as a compromise.
◆ **trade on** to take unfair advantage of: **traded on his sister's popularity**.

trade-in N something, esp a used car, etc, given in part exchange for another.

trademark N **1** (in full **registered trademark**) a name, word or symbol, esp one that is officially registered and protected by law, with which a company or individual identifies goods made or sold by them. **2** a distinguishing characteristic or feature.

tradename N a name that is given to an article or product, or a group of these, by the trade which produces them.

trade-off N a balance or compromise that is struck, esp between two desirable but incompatible things, situations, etc.

trade price N a wholesale cost that a retailer pays for goods.

trade secret N an ingredient, technique, etc that a company or individual will not divulge.

tradesman or **tradeswoman** N someone who follows a skilled trade, eg a plumber, electrician, etc.

trade union or **trades union** N an organization for the employees of a specified profession, trade, etc that exists to protect members' interests.

trade wind N a wind that blows continually towards the equator.

tradition N **1 a** a doctrine, belief, custom, story, etc passed on from generation to generation, esp orally or by example; **b** the action or process of handing down something in this way. **2** a particular body of doctrines, beliefs, customs, etc.

traditional ADJ belonging, relating or referring to, based on or derived from tradition: **morris dancers in their traditional costumes**.

traditionalist N someone who subscribes to tradition, esp slavishly. ■ **traditionalism** N.

traduce VB to say or write unpleasant things about (someone or something).

traffic N **1** the vehicles that are moving along a route. **2** the movement of vehicles, passengers, etc along a route. **3** illegal or dishonest trade.
➤ VB (*trafficked*, *trafficking*) (usu **traffic in**) to deal or trade in, esp illegally or dishonestly. ■ **trafficker** N.

traffic calming N the intentional curbing of the speed of road vehicles by having humps, bends, narrowed passing places, etc on roads.

traffic cone N a large plastic cone used for guiding diverted traffic, etc.

traffic jam N a queue of vehicles that are at a standstill.

traffic lights PL N a system of red, amber and green lights controlling traffic at road junctions, pedestrian crossings, etc.

traffic warden N, BRIT someone whose job is controlling traffic flow and issuing parking tickets.

tragedian N **1** an actor specializing in tragic roles. **2** a writer of tragedies.

tragedienne N an actress specializing in tragic roles.

tragedy N (*-ies*) **1** a serious catastrophe, accident, etc. **2** COLLOQ a sad, disappointing, etc event: **an absolute tragedy when we lost that goal**. **3 a** a serious play, film, opera, etc portraying tragic events and with an unhappy ending; **b** such plays, etc as a genre. **4** LOOSELY any sad play, film, book, etc.

tragic ADJ **1** very sad; intensely distressing. **2** THEAT belonging or relating to tragedy. ■ **tragically** ADV.

tragicomedy N (*-ies*) **1** a play, film, event, etc that includes a mixture of both tragedy and comedy. **2** such plays, etc as a group or genre. ■ **tragicomic** or **tragicomical** ADJ.

trail VB **1** TR & INTR to drag or be dragged loosely along the ground or other surface. **2** TR & INTR to walk or move along slowly and wearily. **3** to drag (a limb, etc) esp slowly and wearily. **4** TR & INTR to fall or lag behind in a race, contest, etc: trailed their opponents by 20 points. **5** to follow the track of. **6** TR & INTR of a plant or plant part: to grow so long that it droops over or along a surface towards the ground. ➤ N **1** a track, series of marks, footprints, etc left by a passing person, animal or thing, esp one followed in hunting. **2** a rough path or track through a wild or mountainous area. ◆ **trail away** or **off** to become fainter.

trailblazer N **1** someone who makes inroads into new territory. **2** an innovator in a particular field or activity. ■ **trailblazing** N, ADJ.

trailer N **1** a cart that can be hooked up behind a car, etc and used for carrying small loads, transporting small boats, etc. **2** the rear section of an articulated lorry. **3** N AMER a mobile home or caravan. **4** CINEMA, TV, RADIO a promotional preview of a film, programmme, etc.

train N **1 a** a string of railway carriages or wagons with a locomotive; **b** LOOSELY a locomotive. **2** a back part of a long dress or robe that trails behind the wearer. **3** the attendants following or accompanying an important person. **4** a connected series of events, actions, thoughts, etc. ➤ VB **1** to teach or prepare (a person or animal) through instruction, practice, exercises, etc. **2** INTR to be taught through instruction, practice, exercises, etc: trained as a nurse. **3** (usu **train for**) to prepare (for a performance, eg, in a sport) through practice, exercise, diet, etc. **4** to point or aim (eg a gun) at or focus (eg a telescope) on (a particular object, etc).

trainee N someone who is being trained.

trainer N **1** someone who trains racehorses, athletes, etc. **2** (**trainers**) BRIT running shoes without spikes, often worn as casual shoes.

training N **1** an act or the process of preparing for something: go into training for the marathon. **2** the state of being physically fit: out of training.

train-spotter N someone whose hobby is noting the numbers of railway locomotives, etc. ■ **train-spotting** N.

traipse VB, INTR to walk or trudge along idly or wearily: traipsed round the shops.

trait N an identifying feature or quality.

traitor N **1** someone who betrays their country, sovereign, government, etc. **2** someone who betrays a trust. ■ **traitorous** ADJ.

trajectory N (*-ies*) PHYS the curved path that a moving object describes, eg when it is projected into the air.

tram N an electrically–powered passenger vehicle that runs on rails laid in the streets.

trammel N (usu **trammels**) something that hinders or prevents free action or movement: trapped by the trammels of convention. ➤ VB (*-ll-*; US *-l-*) to hinder or catch with or as if with trammels.

tramp VB **1** INTR to walk with firm heavy footsteps. **2** INTR to make a journey on foot, esp heavily or wearily: tramp over the hills. **3** to walk heavily and wearily on or through: tramp the streets. ➤ N **1** someone who has no fixed home or job. **2** a long, tiring walk.

trample VB, TR & INTR **1** to tread heavily. **2** (also **trample on** or **over**) to crush underfoot: trampled on the flowers. **3** (also **trample on** or **over**) to treat (someone or their feelings, etc) roughly, dismissively or with contempt.

trampoline N a piece of gymnastic equipment that consists of a sheet of tightly stretched canvas, etc attached to a framework

by strong springs and used for jumping on.
➤ VB, INTR to jump, turn somersaults, etc on a
trampoline. ■ **trampolinist** N.

trance N **1** a sleep-like or half-conscious state
in which the ability to react to stimuli is
temporarily lost. **2** a dazed or absorbed state.

tranquil ADJ serenely quiet or peaceful;
undisturbed. ■ **tranquillity** or (US)
tranquility N. ■ **tranquilly** ADV.

tranquillize, -ise or (US) **tranquilize** VB
(-*ll*-; -*l*-) to make or become calm, esp by
administering a drug.

tranquillizer, -iser or (US) **tranquilizer**
N a drug that has a tranquillizing effect.

transact VB to conduct or carry out (business).

transaction N a business deal, etc that is
settled or is in the process of being settled.

transatlantic ADJ **1** crossing, or designed for
or capable of crossing, the Atlantic. **2 a** N AMER
European; **b** BRIT American.

transceiver N a piece of radio equipment
designed to transmit and receive signals.

transcend VB **1** to be beyond the limits, scope,
range, etc of: transcends the bounds of human
decency. **2** to surpass or excel. **3** to overcome
or surmount: transcend all difficulties.

transcendent ADJ **1** excellent; surpassing
others of the same or similar kind. **2** beyond
ordinary human knowledge or experience.
■ **transcendence** N.

transcendental ADJ **1** going beyond usual
human knowledge or experience.
2 supernatural or mystical.

transcendental meditation N a method
of meditating that involves silent repetition of a
mantra to promote spiritual wellbeing.

transcribe VB **1** to write out (a text) in full, eg
from notes. **2** to copy (a text) from one place to
another: transcribed the poem into her album.
3 to write out (a spoken text). **4** to transliterate.

transcript N a written, typed or printed copy,
esp a legal record of court proceedings.

transcription N **1** an act or the process of
transcribing. **2** something transcribed.

transducer N any device that converts
energy from one form to another, eg, a
loudspeaker, where electrical energy is
converted into sound waves.

transept N in a church with a cross-shaped
floor plan: either of two arms at right angles to
the nave.

transfer VB (-*rr*-) **1** TR & INTR to move from one
place, person, group, etc to another. **2** INTR to
change from one vehicle, line, passenger
system, etc to another while travelling. **3** LAW to
hand over (a title, rights, property, etc) to
someone else by means of a legal document.
4 BRIT **a** INTR of a professional footballer, etc: to
change clubs; **b** of a football club, etc: to
arrange for (a player) to go to another club.
➤ N **1** an act, instance or the process of
transferring or the state of being transferred:
asked for a transfer to another department.
2 BRIT a design that can be transferred from one
surface to another. **3** someone or something
that is transferred. **4** LAW an act of handing over
(eg, the legal right to property, etc) from one
person to another. ■ **transferable** or
transferrable ADJ. ■ **transference** N.

transfiguration N a change in appearance,
esp when becoming more beautiful, glorious,
exalted, etc.

transfigure VB to change or cause to change
in appearance, esp in becoming more
beautiful, glorious, exalted, etc.

transfix VB **1** to immobilize through surprise,
fear, horror, etc. **2** to pierce with a pointed
weapon, etc.

transform VB **1 a** to change in appearance,
nature, function, etc, often completely and
dramatically; **b** INTR to undergo such a change.
2 ELECTRONICS to change the voltage or type of
(a current). ■ **transformation** N.

transformer N, ELEC an electromagnetic
device designed to transfer electrical energy
from one alternating current circuit to another,
with an increase or decrease in voltage.

transfuse VB, MED **a** to transfer (blood or plasma) from one person or animal to another; **b** to treat (a person or animal) with a transfusion of blood or other fluid.

transfusion N, MED the process of introducing blood, plasma, etc into the bloodstream of a person or animal.

transgress VB **1** to break, breach or violate (divine law, a rule, etc). **2** to go beyond or overstep (a limit or boundary). ■ **transgression** N. ■ **transgressor** N.

transient ADJ lasting, staying, visiting, etc for only a short time; passing quickly. ■ **transience** or **transiency** N.

transistor N **1** ELECTRONICS a semiconductor device that has three or more electrodes, acting as a switch, amplifier or detector of electric current. **2** a small portable radio that has transistors instead of valves and tubes.

transistorize or **-ise** VB to design or fit with a transistor or transistors rather than valves.

transit N **1 a** an act or the process of carrying or moving goods, passengers, etc from one place to another; **b** AS ADJ: transit lounge. **2** a route or passage. **3** ASTRON **a** the passage of a heavenly body across a meridian; **b** the passage of a smaller heavenly body across a larger one. ◆ **in transit** in the process of going or being taken from one place to another.

transition N a change or passage from one condition, state, subject, place, etc to another. ■ **transitional** or **transitionary** ADJ.

transitive ADJ, GRAM of a verb: taking a direct object, eg make in They make lots of money.

transitory ADJ lasting only for a short time.

translate VB **1** to express (a word, speech, written text, etc) in another language. **2** INTR of a written text, etc: to be able to be expressed in another language, format, etc: Poetry doesn't always translate well. **3** to put or express (an idea, etc) in other, usu simpler, terms. **4** to interpret: translated her expression as contempt. **5** TR & INTR to convert or be converted into: translate their ideas into reality.

■ **translatable** ADJ. ■ **translator** N.

translation N **1** a word, speech, written text, etc that has been put into one language from another. **2** an act or instance or the process of translating. ■ **translational** ADJ.

transliterate VB to replace (the characters of a word, etc) with the nearest equivalent characters of another alphabet. ■ **transliteration** N.

translucent ADJ **1** allowing light to pass diffusely. **2** clear. ■ **translucence** or **translucency** N.

transmigrate VB, INTR of a soul: to pass into another body at or just after death. ■ **transmigration** N.

transmission N **1** an act or the process of transmitting or the state of being transmitted. **2** something that is transmitted, esp a radio or TV broadcast. **3** the system of parts in a motor vehicle that transfers power from the engine to the wheels. ■ **transmissional** ADJ.

transmit VB (-*tt*-) **1** to pass or hand on (esp a message, or an infection or disease). **2** to convey (emotion, etc). **3** TR & INTR **a** to send out (signals) by radio waves; **b** to broadcast (a programme). ■ **transmissible** ADJ.

transmitter N **1** someone or something that transmits. **2** the equipment that transmits the signals in radio and TV broadcasting.

transmogrify VB (-*ies*, -*ied*) HUMOROUS to transform, esp in a surprising or bizarre way.

transmute VB **1** to change the form, substance or nature of. **2** ALCHEMY to change (base metal) into gold or silver. ■ **transmutation** N.

transom N **1** a horizontal bar of wood or stone across a window or the top of a door. **2** a lintel.

transparency N (-*ies*) **1** the quality or state of being transparent. **2** a small photograph on glass or rigid plastic mounted in a frame, to be viewed using a slide projector.

transparent ADJ **1** able to be seen through. **2** of a motive, etc: easily understood or recognized; obvious; evident. **3** of an excuse, etc: easily seen through. **4** frank and open;

candid. ■ **transparently** ADV.

transpire VB 1 INTR of a secret, etc: to become known; to come to light. 2 INTR, LOOSELY to happen. 3 TR & INTR, BOT of a plant: to release water vapour. ■ **transpiration** N.

transplant VB 1 to take (tissue, an organ, etc) from someone and use it as an implant, either at another site in the donor's own body or in the body of another person. 2 to move (a growing plant) from one place to another.
➤ N 1 SURGERY an operation which involves transplanting an organ, etc. 2 an organ, plant, etc which has been transplanted or which is ready to be transplanted.

transponder N a radio and radar device that receives a signal and then sends out its own signal in response.

transport VB 1 to carry (goods, passengers, etc) from one place to another. 2 to affect strongly or deeply: **was transported with grief.**
➤ N 1 a system or business for taking people, goods, etc from place to place: **public transport.** 2 a means of getting or being transported from place to place. 3 (often **transports**) strong emotion, esp of pleasure. ■ **transportable** ADJ.

transportation N 1 an act of transporting or the process of being transported. 2 a means of being transported; transport.

transport café N, BRIT an inexpensive roadside restaurant.

transporter N a vehicle that carries other vehicles, pieces of machinery, etc by road.

transpose VB 1 to cause (two or more things, letters, words, etc) to change places. 2 to change the position of (an item) in a sequence or series. ■ **transposition** N.

transputer N, COMP a chip capable of all the functions of a microprocessor.

transsexual N someone who is anatomically of one sex but who adopts the characteristics, behaviour, etc usu perceived as typical of the opposite sex. Also AS ADJ.

transubstantiation N, CHRISTIANITY esp in the Roman Catholic church: the conversion of consecrated Eucharistic bread and wine into the body and blood of Christ.

transverse ADJ placed, lying, built, etc in a crosswise direction. ■ **transversely** ADV.

transvestite N someone, esp a man, who dresses in clothes that are conventionally thought of as being exclusive to people of the opposite sex. ■ **transvestism** N.

trap N 1 a device or hole, usu baited, for catching animals, sometimes killing them in the process. 2 a plan or trick for surprising someone into speech or action, or catching them unawares: **a speed trap.** 3 a trapdoor. 4 one of the compartments that are set along the starting line of a greyhound race-track.
➤ VB (-**pp**-) 1 to catch (an animal) in a trap. 2 to catch (someone) out or unawares.

trapdoor N a small door or opening in a floor, ceiling, etc that is usu set flush with its surface.

trapeze N a swing-like apparatus consisting of a short horizontal bar hanging on two ropes, used by gymnasts and acrobats.

trapezium N (-**iums** or -**ia**) a four-sided geometric figure that has one pair of its opposite sides parallel.

trapezoid N a four-sided geometric figure that has no sides parallel.

trapper N someone who traps wild animals, usu with the intention of selling their fur.

trappings PL N ornamental accessories denoting office, status, etc.

trash N 1 **a** rubbish; waste material; **b** chiefly US domestic waste. 2 nonsense. 3 a worthless, contemptible, etc person or people: **white trash.** 4 **a** a worthless object or worthless objects; **b** art, literature, cinema, music, etc perceived as having no merit.
➤ VB 1 COLLOQ to wreck. 2 COLLOQ to give (a film, novel, play, performance, etc) a very adverse review. ■ **trashy** ADJ (-**ier**, -**iest**).

trattoria N (-**rias** or -**rie**) an informal Italian restaurant.

trauma N (-**mas** or -**mata**) 1 MED **a** a severe

physical injury or wound; **b** a state of shock brought on by this. **2 a** a severe emotional shock that may have long-term effects on behaviour or personality; **b** the condition that can result from this type of emotional shock. **3** LOOSELY any event, situation, etc that is stressful, upsetting, etc. ■ **traumatize** or **-ise** VB.

traumatic ADJ **1** relating to, resulting from or causing trauma. **2** COLLOQ distressing; emotionally upsetting. ■ **traumatically** ADV.

travail N painful or extremely hard labour.

travel VB (**-ll-**; **-l-**) **1** TR & INTR to go from place to place; to make a journey: **travelled through France. 2** to journey across (a stated distance). **3** INTR to be capable of withstanding a journey, esp a long one: **not a wine that travels well. 4** INTR to journey from place to place as a sales representative. **5** INTR to move: **Light travels in a straight line. 6** INTR to move or pass steadily, deliberately, etc: **Her eyes travelled over the horizon. 7** INTR, COLLOQ to move quickly. ➣ N **1** an act or the process of travelling. **2** (usu **travels**) a journey or tour, esp abroad.

travel agency N a business that makes arrangements for travellers, holidaymakers, etc. ■ **travel agent** N.

traveller N **1** someone who travels. **2** OLD USE a travelling salesman. **3** BRIT COLLOQ a Gypsy.

traveller's cheque N a cheque for a fixed sum that can be exchanged for currency, goods or services in another country.

travelogue N a film, talk, etc about travel.

traverse VB to go or lie across or through. ➣ N an act or the process of crossing.

travesty N (**-ies**) a ridiculous or crude distortion; a mockery or caricature: **a travesty of justice**.

trawl N **1** (in full **trawl-net**) a large bag-shaped net with a wide mouth, for catching fish at sea. **2** a wide-ranging or extensive search: **a trawl through the library**. ➣ VB, TR & INTR **1** to fish (the sea, an area of sea, etc) using a trawl-net. **2** to search through (a large number of things, people, etc) thoroughly: **trawl through hundreds of applications**.

trawler N **1** a fishing-boat used in trawling. **2** someone who trawls.

tray N a flat piece of wood, metal, plastic, etc, used for carrying dishes, etc.

treacherous ADJ **1** of someone, their conduct, etc: not to be trusted; ready or likely to betray. **2** hazardous or dangerous.

treachery N (**-ies**) **1** deceit, betrayal, cheating or treason. **2** an act or instance of this.

treacle N **1** the thick dark sticky liquid that remains after the crystallization and removal of sugar from extracts of sugar-cane or sugar-beet. **2** molasses. **3** cloying sentimentality.

tread VB (**trod, trodden** or **trod**) **1** INTR (usu **tread on**) to walk or step: **trod on the cat's tail. 2** to step or walk on, over or along: **trod the primrose path. 3** to crush or press (into the ground, etc) with a foot or feet: **treading ash into the carpet. 4** to wear or form (a path, hole, etc) by walking. **5** INTR to suppress or treat cruelly. ➣ N **1** a manner, style or sound of walking. **2** an act of treading. **3** the horizontal part of a stair. **4** a mark made by treading; a footprint or track. **5 a** the thick, grooved and patterned surface of a tyre that grips the road and disperses rain water; **b** the depth of this surface. ◆ **tread on sb's toes 1** to encroach on their sphere of influence, etc. **2** to offend them.

treadle N a foot pedal that can be pushed back and forward in a rhythmic motion and so produce the momentum to drive a machine, eg, a sewing-machine.

treadmill N **1** an apparatus for producing motion that consists of a large wheel turned by people or animals treading on steps inside or around it. **2** a similar piece of equipment used for exercising. **3** a monotonous routine.

treason N **1** (in full **high treason**) disloyalty to or betrayal of one's country, sovereign or government. **2** any betrayal of trust or act of disloyalty. ■ **treasonable** ADJ.

treasure N **1** wealth and riches, esp in the form of gold, silver, precious stones and jewels, etc which have been accumulated over a period of time and which can be hoarded. **2** anything of great value. **3** COLLOQ someone who is loved and valued, esp as a helper, friend, etc. ➤ VB to value greatly or think of as precious: **treasured him as a friend**. ■ **treasured** ADJ.

treasure hunt N **1** a game where the object is to find a prize by solving a series of clues about its hiding place. **2** a hunt for treasure.

treasurer N **1** a person in a club, society, etc who is in charge of the money and accounts. **2** an official who is responsible for public money, eg, in a local council.

treasure-trove N, LAW something valuable found hidden and of unknown ownership, and deemed to be the property of the Crown.

treasury N (-ies) **1** (**Treasury**) **a** the government department in charge of a country's finances, esp the planning and implementation of expenditure policies, the collection of taxes, etc; **b** the place where the money that this department collects is kept. **2** the income or funds of a state, government, organization, society, etc.

treat VB **1** to deal with or behave towards (someone or something) in a specified manner: **treat it as a joke**. **2** to care for or deal with (a person, illness, injury, etc) medically. **3** to put (something) through a process, etc: **treat the wood with creosote**. **4** to provide with (food, drink, a gift, etc) at one's own expense: **I'll treat you to lunch**. **5** TR & INTR (often **treat of**) to discuss. **6** INTR (usu **treat with**) to negotiate. ➤ N **1** an outing, meal, present, etc that one person treats another to. **2** a source of pleasure or enjoyment, esp when unexpected. ■ **treatable** ADJ.

treatise N a formal piece of writing that deals systematically and in depth with a subject.

treatment N **1** the medical or surgical care given to cure an illness or injury. **2** the manner of dealing with someone or something: **rough treatment**. **3** a way of presenting something, esp in literature, music, art, etc: **his sympathetic treatment of his women characters**.

treaty N (-ies) a formal agreement between states or governments.

treble N **1** something that is three times as much or as many. **2** MUS **a** a soprano; **b** someone, esp a boy, who has a soprano singing voice. **3** BETTING a bet on three horses from three different races where the original stake money plus any winnings from the first race goes on the horse from the second race, after which, if the second horse wins, the total is laid on the horse from the third race. **4** SPORT esp in football: the winning of three competitions in one season. ➤ ADJ **1** three times as much or as many. **2** relating to, being or having a treble voice. ➤ VB, TR & INTR to make or become three times as much or as many. ■ **trebly** ADV.

treble chance N, BRIT a type of football pool where draws, home wins and away wins are each accorded different values and winnings are paid out on the basis of how accurately punters can predict the number of matches falling into each of the three categories.

treble clef N, MUS in musical notation: a sign (𝄞) at the beginning of a piece of written music placing the note G (a fifth above middle C) on the second line of the staff.

tree N **1** BOT **a** a tall woody perennial plant that typically has one main stem or trunk and which, unlike a shrub, usu only begins to branch at some distance from the ground; **b** in extended use: any plant, eg the banana, palm, etc, that has a single non-woody stem which grows to a considerable height. **2** a frame or support: **shoe tree • a mug tree**. ■ **treeless** ADJ.

tree of knowledge N, BIBLE the tree in the garden of Eden that bore the forbidden fruit.

tree surgery N the treatment and preservation of diseased or damaged trees. ■ **tree surgeon** N.

trefoil N **1** a leaf which is divided into three sections. **2** a plant with such leaves, eg clover.

trek VB (-kk-) INTR to make a long hard journey. ➤ N a long hard journey: **a trek to the shops**.

trellis N (in full **trellis-work**) an open lattice framework, usu fixed to a wall, for supporting climbing plants, fruit trees, etc.

tremble VB, INTR **1** to shake or shudder

involuntarily, eg, with cold, fear, weakness, etc.
2 to quiver or vibrate. ■ **trembling** ADJ.

tremendous ADJ **1** COLLOQ extraordinary, very good, remarkable, enormous, etc: a tremendous relief. **2** awe-inspiring; terrible: a tremendous roar. ■ **tremendously** ADV.

tremolo N, MUS **1** a trembling effect achieved by rapidly repeating a note or notes, or by quickly alternating notes. **2** a similar effect in singing. **3** a device in an organ used for producing a tremolo.

tremor N **1** a shaking or quivering: **couldn't disguise the tremor in his voice**. **2** (in full **earth tremor**) a minor earthquake. **3** a thrill of fear or pleasure.

tremulous ADJ quivering, esp with fear, worry, excitement, etc. ■ **tremulously** ADV.

trench N **1** a long narrow ditch in the ground.
2 MIL **a** a large-scale version of this where the earth thrown up by the excavations is used to form a parapet to protect soldiers from enemy fire, shells, etc and which often incorporates rudimentary living quarters; **b** (**trenches**) a series of these that forms a defensive system.

trenchant ADJ **1** incisive; penetrating: a trenchant mind. **2** forthright; vigorous: a trenchant policy to improve efficiency.
3 POETIC cutting; keen. ■ **trenchancy** N.

trench coat N a military-style raincoat, usu double-breasted and with a belt.

trend N **1** a general direction or tendency. **2** the current general movement in fashion, style, taste, etc.
➤ VB, INTR to turn or have a tendency to turn in a specified direction.

trendsetter N someone who starts a fashion.

trendy ADJ (*-ier, -iest*) BRIT COLLOQ **1** of a person: following the latest fashions. **2** of clothes, music, clubs, bars, etc: fashionable at a particular time.
➤ N (*-ies*) someone who is trendy.

trepidation N nervousness or apprehension.

trespass VB, INTR **1** (usu **trespass on** or **upon**) to make an unlawful or unwarranted entry (on someone else's property). **2** (usu **trespass on**)

to intrude (on someone's time, privacy, rights, etc). **3** OLD USE to sin.
➤ N **1** an act or the process of entering someone else's property without the right or permission to do so. **2** OLD USE a sin.
■ **trespasser** N.

tress N **1** a long lock or plait of hair. **2** (**tresses**) a woman's or girl's long hair.

trestle N **1** a supporting framework with a horizontal beam the end of which rests on a pair of legs which slope outwards, used with a board on top to form a table. **2** (in full **trestle-table**) a table that consists of a board or boards supported by trestles.

trews PL N, BRIT trousers, esp tartan ones.

triad N **1** a group of three people or things.
2 (also **Triad**) **a** a Chinese secret society, often involved in organized crime, etc; **b** a member of such a society.

trial N **1** a legal process in which someone who stands accused of a crime is judged in a court of law. **2** an act or the process of trying or testing.
3 trouble, worry or vexation, or a cause of this: **Her son is a great trial to her**. **4** SPORT a preliminary test of the skill, fitness, etc of a player, athlete, etc, esp one to decide whether they should be offered a job, team place, etc.
5 a test of a vehicle's performance held esp over rough ground or a demanding course.
6 (usu **trials**) a competition in which the skills of animals are tested: **sheepdog trials**.
◆ **on trial 1** in the process of undergoing legal action in court: **on trial for murder**. **2** in the process of undergoing tests or examination before being permanently approved.
◆ **trial and error** the process of trying various methods, alternatives, etc until a correct or suitable one is found.

trial run N a test of a new product, etc prior to an official launch.

triangle N **1** GEOM a plane figure with three sides and three internal angles. **2** anything of a similar shape. **3** a simple musical percussion instrument made from a metal bar which has been bent into a triangular shape with one corner left open and which is played by striking it with a small metal hammer. **4** an emotional relationship or love affair that involves three people. ■ **triangular** ADJ.

triangulate VB to mark off (an area of land) into a network of triangular sections with a view to making a survey. ■ **triangulation** N.

triathlon N an athletic contest of three events, usu swimming, running and cycling.
■ **triathlete** N.

tribalism N **1** the system of tribes as a way of organizing society. **2** the feeling of belonging to a tribe.

tribe N **1** an organized, usu hierarchical, group of people, families, clans, etc who share ancestral, social, cultural, linguistic, religious, economic, etc ties. **2** a large group with a shared interest, profession, etc: **a tribe of protesters.** ■ **tribal** ADJ.

tribesman and **tribeswoman** N a man or woman who belongs to a tribe.

tribulation N **1** great sorrow, trouble, affliction, misery, etc. **2** a cause or source of this.

tribunal N **1** a court of justice. **2** BRIT a board of people appointed to look into a specified matter and to adjudicate on it.

tribune N a champion or defender of the rights of the common people.

tributary N (-**ies**) a stream or river that flows into a larger river or a lake.

tribute N **1** a speech, gift, etc given as an expression of praise, thanks, affection, etc. **2** a sign or evidence of something valuable, effective, etc; a testimony: **Her success was a tribute to all her hard work.**

trice N.
◆ **in a trice** in a very short time.

triceps N (*tricepses* or *triceps*) a muscle that is attached in three places, esp the large muscle at the back of the upper arm.

trick N **1** something done or said to cheat, deceive, fool or humiliate someone.
2 a deceptive appearance; an illusion.
3 a mischievous act or plan; a prank or joke.

4 a clever or skilful act which astonishes, puzzles or amuses. **5** a peculiar habit or mannerism: **He has a trick of always saying inappropriate things. 6** a special technique or knack: **a trick of the trade. 7** a feat of skill which can be learned. **8** the cards played in one round of a card game and which are won by one of the players.
➤ VB **1** to cheat, deceive or defraud. **2** (**trick into** or **out of**) to persuade or cheat by: **tricked her into believing him.** ■ **trickery** N.

trickle VB, TR & INTR **1** to flow or cause to flow in a thin slow stream or drops. **2** to move, come or go slowly and gradually.
➤ N a slow stream, flow or movement.

trick or treat N, chiefly N AMER the children's practice of dressing up on Hallowe'en to call at people's houses for small gifts, threatening to play a trick on them if they are not given one.

trickster N someone who deceives, cheats or plays tricks.

tricky ADJ (-**ier**, -**iest**) **1** difficult to handle or do; needing skill and care. **2** inclined to trickery; sly; deceitful. ■ **trickiness** N.

tricolour or (US) **tricolor** N a three-coloured flag, esp one with three bands of equal size in three different colours.

tricycle N a pedal-driven vehicle with two wheels at the back and one at the front.

trident N, HIST a spear with three prongs.

triennial ADJ **1** happening once every three years. **2** lasting for three years.

trier N **1** someone who perseveres at something, esp something they have little talent or aptitude for. **2** someone who tries out food.

trifle N **1** something of little or no value. **2** a very small amount. **3** BRIT a dessert of sponge-cake soaked in sherry, topped with jelly and fruit, and then custard and whipped cream.
➤ VB (usu **trifle with**) **a** to treat (someone, their feelings, etc) frivolously or insensitively; **b** to talk or think about (a proposition, idea, project, etc) idly or not very seriously.
◆ **a trifle** slightly, rather: **a trifle upset.**

trifling ADJ 1 unimportant; trivial. 2 frivolous.

trigger N 1 a small lever which, when squeezed and released, sets a mechanism going, esp one that fires a gun. 2 something that starts off a train of events, reactions, etc. ➤ VB 1 (also **trigger off**) to start (a train of events, reactions, etc) in motion. 2 to fire or set off (a gun, detonator, etc).

trigger-happy ADJ, COLLOQ liable to shoot a gun, etc, or to go into a rage, etc, with little provocation.

trigonometry N, MATH the branch of mathematics concerned with the relationships between the sides and angles of triangles.

trike N short form of **tricycle**.

trilateral ADJ three-sided.

trilby N (-*ies*) BRIT a soft felt hat with an indented crown and narrow brim.

trill N 1 MUS a sound produced by repeatedly playing or singing a note and a note above in rapid succession. 2 a warbling sound made by a songbird. ➤ VB, TR & INTR to play, sing, etc with a trill.

trillion N (PL *trillion*) 1 chiefly N AMER a million million (10). 2 chiefly BRIT a million million million (10). ■ **trillionth** ADJ, N.

trilogy N (-*ies*) a group of three related plays, novels, poems, operas, etc.

trim VB (-*mm*-) 1 to make (hair, etc) neat and tidy, esp by clipping. 2 (also **trim away**, **from** or **off**) to remove by, or as if by, cutting: **trim hundreds of pounds off the cost**. 3 to make less by, or as if by, cutting: **trim costs**. 4 to decorate with lace, ornaments, etc: **trimmed the dress with pink velvet**. 5 to arrange (a ship's sails) to suit the weather conditions. ➤ N 1 a a neatening haircut; b an act or the process of giving or having this type of haircut. 2 proper order or condition: **in good trim**. 3 material, ornaments, etc used as decoration. 4 the upholstery, colour schemes, and chrome and leather accessories, etc of a car. ➤ ADJ (*trimmer, trimmest*) 1 in good order; neat and tidy. 2 slim.

trimaran N a boat that has three hulls side by side.

trimester N a period of three months, esp one of the three such periods of human gestation or an academic term.

trimming N 1 decorative ribbon, lace, etc. 2 (**trimmings**) the traditional or usual accompaniments of a meal or specified dish: **turkey with all the trimmings**.

trinitrotoluene or **trinitrotoluol** N, CHEM a highly explosive yellow crystalline solid used as an explosive.

trinity N (-*ies*) 1 the state of being three. 2 a group of three. 3 (**Trinity**) CHRISTIANITY the unity of the Father, Son and Holy Spirit.

trinket N a small ornament of little value.

trio N 1 a group or set of three. 2 MUS a group of three instruments, players or singers.

trip VB (-*pp*-) 1 TR & INTR (also **trip over** or **up**) to stumble or cause to stumble. 2 TR & INTR (also **trip up**) to make or cause to make a mistake. 3 to catch (someone) out, eg, in a mistake. 4 INTR (often **trip along**) to walk, skip or dance with short light steps. 5 INTR to move or flow smoothly and easily: **words tripping off the tongue**. 6 INTR, COLLOQ to experience the hallucinatory effects of a drug, esp LSD. 8 TR & INTR to activate or cause (a device or mechanism) to be activated, esp suddenly. ➤ N 1 a a short journey or excursion, esp for pleasure; b a journey of any length. 2 a stumble; the process of accidentally catching the foot. 3 a short light step or skip. 4 a part or catch that can be struck in order to activate a mechanism. 5 an error or blunder. 6 COLLOQ a hallucinatory experience, esp one brought on by taking a drug, eg, LSD: **a bad trip**.

tripartite ADJ 1 divided into or composed of three parts. 2 of talks, an agreement, etc: involving three groups, people, etc.

tripe N 1 parts of the stomach of a cow or sheep, used as food. 2 COLLOQ nonsense.

triple ADJ 1 three times as great, as much or as many. 2 made up of three parts or things. 3 MUS having three beats to the bar.

➤ VB, TR & INTR to make or become three times as great, as much or as many.
➤ N **1 a** an amount that is three times greater than the original, usual, etc amount; **b** a measure (of spirits) that is three times greater than a single measure. **2** a group or series of three.
■ **triply** ADV.

triple jump N an athletic event that involves doing a hop, a skip and then a jump.

triplet N one of three children or animals born to the same mother at one birth.

triplicate ADJ **1** having three parts which are exactly alike. **2** being one of three identical copies. **3** tripled.
➤ VB **1** to make three copies of. **2** to multiply by three. ■ **triplication** N.

tripod N **1** a three-legged stand or support, eg. for a camera, etc. **2** a stool, table, etc with three legs or feet.

tripper N, BRIT someone who goes on a journey for pleasure; a tourist: **day trippers**.

triptych N a picture or carving that covers three joined panels to form a single work of art.

trip-wire N a hidden wire that sets off a mechanism, eg, of an alarm, bomb, etc, when someone trips over it.

trite ADJ of a remark, phrase, etc: having no meaning or effectiveness because of overuse.

tritium N, CHEM a radioactive isotope of hydrogen that has two neutrons as well as one proton in its nucleus, used in fusion reactors.

triumph N **1** a great or notable victory, success, achievement, etc. **2** the joy or elation that is felt after winning a great victory, etc.
➤ VB, INTR **1** (also **triumph over**) to win a victory or be successful; to prevail. **2** to rejoice in a feeling of triumph. ■ **triumphal** ADJ.

triumphant ADJ **1** having won a victory or achieved success. **2** feeling or showing great joy because of a success, etc.

triumvirate N a group of three people who share an official position, power, authority, etc equally. ■ **triumviral** ADJ.

trivalent ADJ, CHEM having a valency of three. ■ **trivalence** or **trivalency** N.

trivet N a three-legged stand or bracket for standing a hot dish, pot, teapot, etc on.

trivia PL N unimportant or petty details.

trivial ADJ **1** having or being of very little importance or value. **2** of a person: frivolous. ■ **triviality** N. ■ **trivially** ADV.

trivialize or **-ise** VB to make or treat as unimportant or worthless. ■ **trivialization** N.

trochee N, PROSODY a metrical foot of one long or stressed syllable followed by one short or unstressed one. ■ **trochaic** ADJ.

troglodyte N someone who lives in a cave.

troika N a Russian vehicle drawn by three horses abreast.

Trojan Horse N **1** HIST a hollow wooden horse that the Greeks used to infiltrate Troy. **2** someone or something that undermines an organization, etc, from within.

troll N, MYTHOL an ugly, evil-tempered, human-like creature that can take the form of either a dwarf or a giant.

trolley N **1** BRIT a small cart or basket on wheels for conveying luggage, shopping, etc. **2** BRIT a small wheeled table for conveying food, crockery, etc. **3** a wheeled stretcher for transporting patients in hospital. **4** BRIT a small wagon or truck running on rails.

trollop N **1 a** a promiscuous girl or woman; **b** a prostitute. **2** a slovenly girl or woman.

trombone N a large brass instrument with a sliding tube. ■ **trombonist** N.

trompe l'oeil N (*trompe l'oeils*) a painting or decoration which gives an illusion of reality.

troop N **1** (**troops**) armed forces; soldiers. **2** a group or collection, esp of people or animals. **3** a division of a cavalry or armoured squadron. **4** a large group of Scouts divided into patrols.
➤ VB, INTR to move as a group.
◆ **troop the colour** BRIT to parade a regiment's flag ceremonially.

trooper N a private soldier, esp one in a cavalry or armoured unit.

troop-ship N a ship designed for transporting military personnel.

trope N a word or expression used figuratively.

trophy N (-*ies*) **1** a cup, medal, plate, etc awarded as a prize for victory or success in a contest, esp in sport. **2** something which is kept in memory of a victory or success, eg, in hunting. ➤ ADJ of a person's partner, spouse, etc: elevating the person's status: **a trophy wife**.

tropic N **1** either of two lines of latitude that encircle the earth at 23° 27′ north (**tropic of Cancer**) and 23° 27′ south (**tropic of Capricorn**) of the equator. **2** (**the Tropics**) the parts of the Earth that lie between these two circles.

tropical ADJ **1** relating to, found in or originating from the tropics: **keeps tropical fish**. **2** very hot: **a tropical climate**. ■ **tropically** ADV.

troposphere N, METEOROL the lowest layer of the Earth's atmosphere, situated below the stratosphere. ■ **tropospheric** ADJ.

trot VB (-*tt*-) **1** INTR of a horse: to move at a steady, fairly fast pace, in a bouncy kind of walk. **2** to make (a horse) move in this way. **3** INTR to move at a steady, fairly brisk pace. ➤ N **1** an act or the process of trotting. **2** (**the trots**) COLLOQ a euphemistic name for an ongoing bout of diarrhoea.
◆ **on the trot** COLLOQ one after the other.
◆ **trot out** COLLOQ to produce (a story, article, etc): **trots out the same lectures every year**.

trotter N a pig's foot.

troubadour N, HIST one of a group of lyric poets in medieval France and Italy who wrote about a highly idealized form of love.

trouble N **1 a** distress, worry or concern; **b** a cause of this. **2** bother or effort, or a cause of this: **go to a lot of trouble** • **The dog was no trouble**. **3** a problem or difficulty: **Your trouble is that you're too generous**. **4** (usu **troubles**) public disturbances and unrest. **5 a** illness or weakness: **heart trouble**; **b** malfunction; failure: **engine trouble**. ➤ VB **1** to cause distress, worry, concern, anger, sadness, etc to: **What's troubling you?** **2** to cause physical distress or discomfort to: **The cough is troubling her**. **3** used esp in polite requests: to put to the inconvenience of (doing, saying, etc something): **Could I trouble you to hold this for me?** **4** INTR to make any effort or take pains: **He didn't even trouble to tell me**. ■ **troubled** ADJ.
◆ **in trouble** in difficulties, esp because of doing something wrong or illegal.

troublemaker N someone who continually, and usu deliberately, causes trouble.

troubleshoot VB **1 a** to trace and mend a fault (in machinery, etc); **b** to identify and solve problems. **2** to mediate (in disputes, etc). ■ **troubleshooter** N. ■ **troubleshooting** N.

troublesome ADJ slightly worrying.

trough N **1** a long narrow open container that animal feed or water is put into. **2** a channel, drain or gutter. **3** a long narrow hollow between the crests of two waves. **4** METEOROL a long narrow area of low atmospheric pressure.

trounce VB to beat or defeat completely; to thrash. ■ **trouncing** N.

troupe N a group or company of performers.

trouper N **1** a member of a troupe. **2** an experienced, hard-working and loyal colleague.

trousers PL N an outer garment for the lower part of the body, reaching from the waist and covering each leg separately.

trouser suit N a woman's suit, consisting of a jacket and trousers.

trousseau N (-*eaux* or -*eaus*) clothes, linen, etc that a woman collects and keeps for her wedding and married life.

trout N (**trout** or **trouts**) a freshwater fish of the salmon family, highly valued as food.

trowel N **1** a small hand-held tool with a flat blade for applying and spreading mortar, plaster, etc. **2** a similar tool for potting plants.

troy N (in full **troy weight**) a system of weights used for precious metals and gemstones in which a pound is made up of 12 ounces or 5760 grains.

truant N someone who stays away from school without permission.
➤ VB, INTR to be a truant. ■ **truancy** N.
◆ **play truant** to stay away from school without permission.

truce N an agreement to stop fighting.

truck[1] N 1 BRIT an open railway wagon for carrying goods. 2 chiefly N AMER a lorry.
■ **trucker** N, N AMER.

truck[2] N.
◆ **have no truck with sb** or **sth** to avoid or refuse to have anything to do with them or it.

truculent ADJ aggressively defiant, quarrelsome or discourteous. ■ **truculence** N.
■ **truculently** ADV.

trudge VB, INTR to walk with slow and weary steps: **trudged through the snow**.
➤ N a long and tiring walk.

true ADJ 1 agreeing with fact or reality; not false or wrong. 2 real; genuine; properly so called: **The spider is not a true insect**. 3 accurate or exact: **The photograph doesn't give a true idea of the size of the building**. 4 faithful; loyal: **a true friend • be true to one's word**. 5 conforming to a standard, pattern, type or expectation: **behaved true to type**. 6 in the correct position; well-fitting.
➤ ADV 1 certainly: **True, she isn't very happy here**. 2 truthfully. 3 faithfully. 4 honestly. 5 accurately or precisely.
◆ **come true** of a wish, etc: to be fulfilled.
◆ **out of true** not straight or properly balanced.

true-blue BRIT, ADJ extremely loyal; staunchly orthodox.
➤ N (**true blue**) someone of this type.

true north N the direction of the north pole, as opposed to magnetic north.

truffle N 1 a fungus that grows underground and is considered a delicacy. 2 a type of chocolate sweet with a soft centre of cream, butter, chocolate and often flavoured with rum.

truism N a statement that is so obviously true that it requires no discussion. ■ **truistic** ADJ.

truly ADV 1 really: **Truly, I have no idea ...** 2 genuinely; honestly: **truly sorry ... 3** faithfully. 4 accurately; exactly. 5 properly; rightly.

trump N 1 a (**trumps**) the suit of cards that is declared to be of a higher value than any other suit; b (also **trump card**) a card of this suit. 2 (usu **trump card**) a secret advantage.
➤ VB 1 to defeat by playing a trump. 2 to win a surprising victory or advantage over.
◆ **come up** or **turn up trumps** COLLOQ 1 to be unexpectedly useful or helpful. 2 to turn out to be better than expected.

trumped-up ADJ of evidence, etc: invented.

trumpery N (**-ies**) 1 flashy but worthless articles. 2 rubbish.

trumpet N 1 a a brass instrument with a narrow tube and flared bell and a set of valves; b a similar but simpler instrument used, esp by the military, for signalling, fanfares, etc. 2 any conical device designed to amplify sound, eg, an ear-trumpet. 3 the loud cry of an elephant.
➤ VB 1 INTR of an elephant: to make a loud cry. 2 INTR to blow a trumpet. 3 to proclaim loudly.
■ **trumpeter** N.

truncate VB to cut a part from (a tree, word, piece of writing, etc), esp in order to shorten.

truncheon N a short thick heavy stick that police officers carry, used in self-defence or for subduing the unruly, etc.

trundle VB, TR & INTR to move or roll, or cause to move or roll, heavily and clumsily.

trunk N 1 the main stem of a tree without the branches and roots. 2 the body of a person or animal, not including the head and limbs. 3 a large rigid chest for storing or transporting clothes, etc. 4 N AMER the boot of a car. 5 the long, prehensile nose of an elephant. 6 (**trunks**) men's close-fitting shorts or pants worn esp for swimming.

trunk road N a main road between towns.

truss N a belt, etc worn to support a hernia.
➤ VB (often **truss up**) to tie up or bind tightly.

trust N 1 belief or confidence in, or reliance on, the truth, goodness, character, power, ability, etc of someone or something. 2 charge or care: **The child was placed in my trust. 3** the state of being responsible for the conscientious performance of some task: **be in a position of trust. 4** an arrangement by which money or property is managed by one person for the benefit of someone else. **5** a group of business firms working together to control the market in a particular commodity, beat down competition, and maximize profits.
➤ VB **1** TR & INTR to have confidence or faith in; to depend or rely on: **We can trust her to do a good job. 2** (usu **trust with**) to allow (someone) to use or do (something) in the belief that they will behave responsibly, honestly, etc: **I wouldn't trust him with your new car. 3** to give (someone or something) into the care of (someone): **trusted the children to their grandfather. 4** TR & INTR to be confident; to hope or suppose: **I trust you had a good journey.**

trustee N **1** someone who manages money or property for someone else. **2** a member of a group of people managing the affairs and business of a company or institution.

trust fund N money or property held in trust.

trustworthy ADJ able to be trusted or depended on; reliable. ■ **trustworthiness** N.

trusty ADJ (**-ier, -iest**) OLD USE **1** able to be trusted or depended on: **my trusty sword. 2** loyal: **a trusty servant.**
➤ N (**-ies**) a trusted person, esp a convict who is granted special privileges for good behaviour.

truth N **1** the quality or state of being true, genuine or factual. **2** the state of being truthful; sincerity; honesty. **3** that which is true. **4** that which is established or generally accepted as true: **scientific truths.**

truthful ADJ **1** of a person: telling the truth. **2** true; realistic. ■ **truthfully** ADV. ■ **truthfulness** N.

try VB (**tries, tried**) **1** TR & INTR to attempt or make an effort; to seek to attain or achieve. **2** (also **try out**) to test or experiment with in order to make an assessment. **3** to conduct the legal trial of: **tried him for murder. 4** to exert strain or stress on: **try his patience.**
➤ N (**tries**) **1** an attempt or effort. **2** RUGBY an act of carrying the ball over the opponent's goal line and touching it down on the ground.
◆ **try it on** BRIT COLLOQ to attempt to deceive someone, or to test their patience or tolerance.
◆ **try on** to put on (clothes, shoes, etc) in order to check the fit, appearance, etc.
◆ **try out** to go, eg, to a football, rugby, hockey, etc team, and have trials in the hope of being asked to join the team.

trying ADJ causing strain or anxiety; stretching one's patience to the limit.

try-on N, BRIT COLLOQ an attempt to deceive or to test someone's patience.

try-out N, COLLOQ a test or trial.

tryst N, OLD USE OR LITERARY **1** an arrangement to meet someone, esp a lover. **2** the meeting itself. **3** (also **trysting-place**) a place where such a meeting takes place.

tsar, tzar or **czar** N, HIST the title of the former emperors of Russia.

tsarina, tzarina or **czarina** N, HIST the title of a former Russian empress.

tsetse N (in full **tsetse fly**) an African fly that feeds on human and animal blood and can transmit several dangerous diseases.

T-shirt or **tee shirt** N a short-sleeved collarless top, usu made from knitted cotton.

T-square N a T-shaped ruler for drawing and testing right angles.

tsunami N a fast-moving and often very destructive wave.

tub N **1** a large, low container for holding water, growing plants, etc. **2** a small container for cream, ice-cream, yoghurt, margarine, etc. **3** (also **bathtub**) a bath.

tuba N a bass brass instrument with valves and a wide bell that points upwards.

tubby ADJ (**-ier, -iest**) COLLOQ of a person: plump; podgy. ■ **tubbiness** N.

tube N **1** a long hollow flexible or rigid cylinder

for holding or conveying air, liquids, etc.
2 a similar structure in the body of an animal or plant. **3** a squeezable, approximately cylindrical container containing a paste, etc: **a tube of toothpaste. 4** BRIT an underground railway system, esp the London one. **5** a cathode ray tube.
➤ VB to enclose in a tube. ■ **tubeless** ADJ.

tuber N **1** a swollen underground stem or rhizome, such as that of the potato, with buds that are capable of developing into a new plant. **2** a similar structure formed from a root, eg, of a dahlia, but without buds.

tubercle N **1** a small round swelling or lump on a bone, etc. **2** a small round swelling in an organ, esp one in the lung which is characteristic of tuberculosis.

tubercular ADJ affected by tuberculosis.

tuberculin N a sterile liquid preparation used to test for tuberculosis.

tuberculosis N an infectious diseases of humans and animals caused by the tubercle bacillus and characterized by the formation of tubercles, esp on the lungs.

tubing N **1** a length of tube or a system of tubes. **2** material that tubes can be made from.

tub-thumper N, COLLOQ a passionate or ranting public speaker or preacher.

tubular ADJ **1** made or consisting of tubes or tube-shaped pieces. **2** shaped like a tube.

tubule N a small tube.

tuck VB **1** (usu **tuck in**, **into**, **under**, **up**, etc) to push or fold into a specified position: **tucked the note into the envelope. 2** to make a tuck or tucks in (a piece of material, clothing, etc).
➤ N **1** a flat pleat or fold sewn into a garment or piece of material. **2** BRIT COLLOQ food, esp sweets, cakes, etc, eaten as snacks.
3 a cosmetic operation to tighten a flabby part or remove fat: **a tummy tuck.**
◆ **tuck away** COLLOQ **1** to eat (large quantities of food), esp heartily and with enjoyment. **2** to store, esp in a place that is difficult to find.
◆ **tuck in** or **into** COLLOQ to eat heartily.
◆ **tuck in** COLLOQ to put (someone) to bed by pulling up the covers, duvet, etc snugly.

tucker[1] N, COLLOQ food.
◆ **best bib and tucker** COLLOQ best clothes.

tucker[2] VB (usu **tucker out**) to tire.

tuck shop N, BRIT a small shop that sells sweets, cakes, pastries, etc in or near a school.

Tuesday N the third day of the week.

tuft N a small bunch or clump of grass, hair, feathers, wool, etc attached at the base or growing together. ■ **tufted** ADJ.

tug VB (**-gg-**) TR & INTR **1** (also **tug at** or **on**) to pull sharply or strongly: **a dog tugging at the lead. 2** to tow (a ship, etc) with a tugboat.
➤ N **1 a** a strong sharp pull; **b** a sharp or sudden pang of emotion. **2** a hard struggle. **3** (in full **tugboat**) a small boat with a very powerful engine, for towing larger ships, oil platforms, etc.

tug-of-war N (**tugs-of-war**) a contest in which two people or teams pull at opposite ends of a rope and try to haul their opponents over a centre line.

tuition N teaching or instruction, esp when paid for: **driving tuition.**

tulip N **1** a spring-flowering bulbous plant that produces a single cup-shaped flower of various colours on a long stem. **2** a flower of this plant.

tulle N a delicate thin netted silk.

tum N, BRIT COLLOQ the stomach.

tumble VB **1** TR & INTR to fall or cause to fall headlong, esp suddenly or clumsily. **2** INTR to fall or collapse suddenly, esp in value or amount. **3** TR & INTR to roll helplessly or haphazardly: **The kids tumbled around in the garden. 4** INTR to perform as an acrobat, esp turning somersaults. **5** (also **tumble to**) COLLOQ to understand or realize, esp suddenly.
➤ N **1** a fall. **2** a somersault. **3** a confused or untidy state or heap.

tumbledown ADJ of a building, etc: falling to pieces; ramshackle.

tumble-dryer or **tumble-drier** N an electrically powered machine that dries wet laundry inside a heated rotating drum. ■ **tumble-dry** VB.

tumbler N **1** a flat-bottomed drinking cup without a stem or handle, usu of glass or plastic. **2** an acrobat, esp one who performs somersaults.

tumescent ADJ swollen or becoming swollen.

tumid ADJ of an organ or body part: swollen.

tummy N (-ies) COLLOQ the stomach.

tumour or (US) **tumor** N an abnormal growth of benign or malignant cells that develops in normal body tissue. ■ **tumorous** ADJ.

tumult N **1** a great or confused noise; an uproar. **2** a violent or angry commotion or disturbance. **3** a state of extreme confusion, agitation, etc: **a mind in tumult**.

tumultuous ADJ **1** noisy and enthusiastic: **a tumultuous welcome**. **2** disorderly; unruly.

tumulus N (-li) ARCHAEOL an ancient burial mound or barrow.

tuna N (**tuna** or **tunas**) **1** a large marine fish that lives in warm and tropical seas. **2** its flesh used as food.

tundra N a vast relatively flat treeless zone lying to the south of the polar ice cap in America and Eurasia with permanently frozen subsoil.

tune N **1** a pleasing succession of musical notes; a melody. **2** the correct, or a standard, musical pitch.
➤ VB **1** TR & INTR (also **tune up**) to adjust (a musical instrument or its keys or strings, etc) to the correct or a standard pitch. **2 a** to adjust (a radio, TV, video recorder, etc) so that it can pick up signals from a specified frequency or station; **b** INTR (usu **tune in to**) to have a radio adjusted to receive (a specified signal, station, DJ, etc) and listen to (it or them): **tune in to Radio 4**. **3** to adjust (an engine, machine, etc) so that it runs properly and efficiently. ■ **tuner** N.
◆ **change one's tune** to change one's attitude, opinions, approach or way of talking.
◆ **in tune 1** having or producing the correct or a required pitch: **sing and play in tune**.
2 having the same pitch as other instruments or voices: **The two guitars are not in tune**.

◆ **in tune with** aware of and able to relate to: **in tune with public opinion**.
◆ **out of tune 1** not having or producing the correct or a required pitch. **2** not having the same pitch as other instruments or voices.
◆ **out of tune with** not aware of and not able to relate to: **out of tune with the latest technology**.
◆ **to the tune of** COLLOQ to the (considerable) sum or total of.

tuneful ADJ **1** having a clear, pleasant, etc tune; melodious. **2** full of music.

tuneless ADJ lacking a good, pleasant, etc tune; not melodious.

tungsten N, CHEM a very hard silvery-white metallic element used in the manufacture of filaments of electric light bulbs, X-ray tubes and TV sets, etc and in alloying steel, etc.

tunic N **1** a close-fitting, usu belted jacket, often forming part of the uniform. **2** a loose garment, often sleeveless, worn in ancient Greece and Rome, or by men in the Middle Ages, etc.

tuning fork N a small two-pronged device used for tuning musical instruments.

tunnel N **1** a constructed passage through or under a hill, river, road, etc, allowing access for pedestrians, vehicles, trains, etc. **2** an underground passage that a mole, etc digs.
➤ VB (-ll-; (US) -l-) INTR (**tunnel through**, **under**, etc) to make a tunnel through, under, etc (a hill, river, road, etc).

tunnel vision N **1** a medical condition in which the field of vision is reduced. **2** the inability or unwillingness to consider other opinions, viewpoints, etc.

tunny N (-ies) esp BRIT tuna.

tup N, BRIT a ram.

tuppence see **twopence**

turban N a headdress worn esp by Muslim and Sikh men formed by wrapping a length of cloth around the head.

turbid ADJ of liquid, etc: cloudy; not clear.

turbine N a power-generating machine with a

rotating wheel driven by water, steam, gas, etc.

turbo N **1** a short form of **turbocharger**. **2** COLLOQ a car fitted with a turbocharger.

turbocharger N a supercharger driven by a turbine which is itself powered by the exhaust gases of the engine. ■ **turbocharged** ADJ.

turbofan N a jet engine driven by a gas turbine that increases thrust.

turbojet N a type of gas turbine that uses exhaust gases to provide the thrust, or an aircraft powered by this.

turboprop N a jet engine in which the turbine drives a propeller.

turbot N (*turbot* or *turbots*) a large scaleless flatfish with eyes on the left side of its head.

turbulence N **1** a disturbed, wild or unruly state. **2** stormy weather caused by disturbances in atmospheric pressure. **3** the jolting or bumpy effect caused by irregularity in the flow of air across an aircraft wing.

turbulent ADJ **1** violently disturbed; wild; unruly. **2** stormy.

tureen N a large deep dish with a cover for serving eg soup from at table.

turf N (*turfs* or *turves*) **1** the surface of an area of grassland that consists of a layer of grass, weeds, matted roots, etc plus the surrounding earth. **2** (**the turf**) horse-racing, a race-course or the racing world generally.
➢ VB to cover (an area of land) with turf.
◆ **turf out** BRIT COLLOQ to throw out.

turf accountant N, BRIT a bookmaker.

turgid ADJ **1** swollen; inflated or distended. **2** of language: pompous. ■ **turgidity** N.

turkey N **1** a large gamebird with dark plumage, a bald blue or red head with red wattles and, in the male, a fanlike tail. **2** its flesh used as food. **3** N AMER COLLOQ a stupid or inept person. **4** N AMER COLLOQ a play, film, etc that is a complete failure.

turmeric N the aromatic underground stem of a plant of the ginger family, powdered and used as a spice and as a yellow dye.

turmoil N wild confusion, agitation or disorder.

turn VB **1** TR & INTR to move or go round in a circle or with a circular movement: **turned the key and opened the door**. **2** TR & INTR to change or cause to change position so that a different side or part comes to the top, front, etc: **turn to face the sun**. **3** to put into a specified position by, or as if by, inverting; to tip out: **turned the dough on to the table**. **4** TR & INTR to change direction or take a new direction: **turn left at the corner** • **turned his thoughts to the problems at work**. **5** to go round: **turned the corner too fast**. **6** TR & INTR to become or cause to become: **Fame turned him into a real show-off** • **The shock turned his hair white**. **7** TR & INTR of milk, etc: to make or become sour. **8** to shape using a lathe or potter's wheel. **9** to perform with a rotating movement: **turn somersaults**. **10** INTR to move or swing around a point or pivot: **a gate turning on its hinge**. **11** to appeal to or have recourse to (someone or something) for help, support, relief, etc: **always turns to me for advice**. **12** TR & INTR **a** of the stomach: to feel nausea or queasiness; **b** to cause (the stomach) to become nauseous or queasy: **enough to turn your stomach**. **13** INTR of the tide: to begin to flow in the opposite direction.
➢ N **1** an act, instance or the process of turning; a complete or partial rotation: **a turn of the wheel**. **2** a change of direction, course or position: **a turn to the right** • **an unfortunate turn of events**. **3** a point or place where a change of direction occurs: **the turn in the road**. **4** an opportunity or duty that comes to each of several people in rotation or succession: **her turn to bat**. **5** inclination or tendency: **a pessimistic turn of mind**. **6** an act or service of a specified kind, usu good or malicious: **do good turns for others**. **7** COLLOQ a sudden feeling of illness, nervousness, faintness, etc: **gave her quite a turn**. **8 a** each of a series of short acts, eg, in a circus or variety theatre; **b** a performer who does one of these acts.
◆ **at every turn** everywhere, at every stage.
◆ **in turn** or **by turns** one after the other in an orderly or pre-arranged manner.
◆ **not know where** or **which way to turn** to be completely confused as to how to act.

on the turn 1 of the tide: starting to change direction. **2** of milk: on the point of going sour.

out of turn 1 out of the correct order or at the wrong time: **played his shot out of turn. 2** inappropriately: **speak out of turn.**

◆ **the turn of the century** the end of one century and the beginning of the next.

to a turn to exactly the right degree; to perfection: **The steak was done to a turn.**

turn (and turn) about one after the other.

turn against sb to become hostile or unfriendly towards them.

turn sb against sb else to make them become hostile or unfriendly towards them.

turn sb away to send them away.

turn back to begin to go in the opposite direction: **We turned back because of heavy snow.**

turn sb or **sth back** to make them or it begin to go in the opposite direction.

turn sth back to fold over or back.

turn down to refuse or reject (someone or something): **turned him down at the interview.**

turn in 1 to bend, fold, incline, etc inwards. **2** COLLOQ to go to bed. **3** to hand (someone or something) over, esp to someone in authority: **turned in the wallet he found to the police. 4** to give, achieve, etc (a specified kind of performance, score, etc).

turn in one's grave of a dead person: to be thought certain to have been distressed, had they been alive, by circumstances such as those now in question.

turn off 1 to leave a straight course or a main road: **The car turned off at the lights. 2** of a side road: to lead from (a main road). **3** COLLOQ to make (someone) feel dislike or disgust, or to lose interest: **The violent scenes really turned me off. 4** to stop (a flow of water, electricity, etc): **turned off the tap. 5** to make (a machine, appliance, etc) stop functioning, working, etc: **turned off the microwave.**

turn on sb or **sth 1** to attack them or it physically or verbally, usu suddenly: **The dogs turned on each other. 2** to depend on it: **The whole argument turns on a single point.**

turn sb on COLLOQ to make them feel excitement, pleasure, interest, etc.

turn sth on 1 to start (the flow of water, electricity, etc). **2** to make (a machine, appliance, etc) start functioning, working, etc.

◆ **turn one's back on sb** or **sth 1** to leave them or it for good. **2** to have no more to do with them or it: **he turned his back on drugs.**

◆ **turn the other cheek** to refuse to engage in any form of retaliation.

◆ **turn sb's head** to make them conceited.

◆ **turn out 1** to happen or prove: **She turned out to be right. 2** to finally be: **It turned out all right in the end. 3** to gather or assemble, for a public meeting, event, etc: **Hundreds of people turned out to vote. 4** to send away; to expel: **turned the troublemakers out of the club. 5** to dress, equip, groom, etc: **He always turns the kids out nicely. 6** to bend, fold, incline, etc outwards. **7** to switch off (a light, etc). **8** to make, manufacture, etc (usu specified quantities of goods or produce): **They turn out around 50 cars a week. 9** BRIT to empty, clear, etc: **The police made him turn out his pockets.**

◆ **turn over 1** of an engine: to start running at low speed. **2** COLLOQ to surrender or transfer: **turned the thief over to the police. 3** to start (an engine) running at low speed. **4** to turn so that a hidden or reverse side becomes visible or faces upwards: **turn over the page. 5** to consider, esp thoughtfully, carefully, etc: **turned over his proposal in her mind. 6** to handle or do business at (a specified amount): **The business turns over five million pounds per year.**

◆ **turn the tide** to cause a change or reversal, in events, thinking, etc.

◆ **turn to sb** or **sth** to use it or them, eg, as a form of comfort, etc: **turned to drugs.**

◆ **turn up 1** to appear or arrive: **Hardly anyone turned up for the match. 2 a** to be found, esp by accident or unexpectedly: **The kitten turned up safe and well; b** to discover or reveal. **3** to increase (the strength, volume, etc, eg, of sound, light, etc produced by a machine): **turned up the music.**

turnabout N a complete change or reversal of direction, opinion, policy, etc.

turnaround N **1** an act or the operation of processing something, eg through a manufacturing procedure. **2** an act or the operation of unloading and reloading a vehicle or ship. **3** same as **turnabout**.

turncoat N someone who turns against or leaves his or her political party, principles, etc and joins the opposing side.

turning N **1** a place where one road branches off from another. **2** a road which branches off from another.

turning-point N a time, place, event at which there is a significant change.

turnip N **1** a plant of the cabbage family. **2** its root used as a vegetable or for animal fodder.

turnkey N, HIST someone who keeps the keys in a prison; a gaoler.

turn-off N **1** a road that branches off from a main road. **2** COLLOQ someone or something that causes dislike, disgust or revulsion.

turn of phrase N (*turns of phrase*) a way of talking, esp when it is distinctive.

turn-on N, COLLOQ someone or something that causes excitement, esp of a sexual nature.

turn-out N the number of people who collectively attend a meeting, event, etc.

turnover N **1** the total value of sales in a business during a certain time. **2** the rate at which stock is sold and replenished. **3** the rate at which money, workers, etc pass through a business. **4** a small pastry with a fruit filling.

turnpike N **1** HIST **a** a toll gate or barrier; **b** a road that has a toll system. **2** N AMER a motorway where drivers must pay a toll.

turnstile N a gate that allows only one person to pass through at a time, used esp for controlling admissions, eg at a football ground.

turntable N a revolving platform, eg on a record-player.

turn-up N, BRIT the bottom of a trouser-leg folded back on itself.
♦ **a turn-up for the books** an unexpected and usu pleasant surprise.

turpentine N **1** a thick oily resin obtained from certain trees, eg, pines. **2** a clear oil distilled

from this resin and used in many commercial products, esp solvents, paint thinners and in medicine. Often shortened to **turps**.

turpitude N, FORMAL vileness; depravity.

turquoise N **1** an opaque semi-precious stone that comes in varying shades of light blue or greenish blue. **2** its greenish blue colour.

turret N **1** a small tower projecting from a wall of a castle, etc. **2** (in full **gun-turret**) a small revolving structure on a warship, tank, etc with a gun mounted on it.

turtle N a marine or freshwater reptile with a bony shell enclosing its body and which has flippers or webbed toes.

turtledove N a wild dove noted for its soft cooing and for the affection shown to its mate.

turtle-neck N a round close-fitting neckline coming about a third of the way up the neck.

tusk N one of a pair of long, curved, pointed teeth which project from the mouth area of certain animals, eg, the elephant, walrus, etc.

tussle N a verbal or physical struggle or fight.

tussock N a clump of grass or vegetation.

tut or **tut-tut** EXCLAM expressing mild disapproval, annoyance or rebuke.

tutelage N tuition or instruction.

tutelary ADJ **1** having the power or role of a guardian. **2** belonging or relating to a guardian.

tutor N **1** a university or college teacher who teaches undergraduate students individually or in small groups, or who is responsible for the general welfare and progress of a certain number of students. **2** a private teacher: *my piano tutor*. **3** BRIT an instruction book.
➤ VB, TR & INTR **1** to act or work as a tutor to. **2** to discipline. ■ **tutorship** N.

tutorial N **1** a period of instruction when a university or college tutor and an individual student or small group of students meet. **2** a printed or on-screen lesson that a learner works through at their own pace.

tutti-frutti N an ice cream or other sweet that

contains or is flavoured with mixed fruits.

tut-tut see **tut**

tutu N a very short protruding skirt consisting of layers of stiffened net frills and worn by female ballet dancers.

tuxedo N (**-os** or **-oes**) chiefly N AMER a **dinner-jacket**. Often shortened to **tux**.

TV ABBREV television.

twaddle N, COLLOQ nonsense.

twain N, ADJ, OLD USE two.

twang N **1** a sharp ringing sound like that produced by plucking a tightly-stretched string or wire. **2** a nasal quality or tone of voice.
➤ VB, TR & INTR **1** to make or cause to make a twang. **2** to play (a musical instrument or a tune) casually, informally, etc.

tweak VB **1** to get hold of and pull or twist with a sudden jerk. **2** to make fine adjustments.
➤ N an act or instance, or the process, of tweaking.

twee ADJ, BRIT COLLOQ, DISPARAGING affectedly or pretentiously pretty, sweet, cute, quaint, etc.

tweed N **1** a thick roughish woollen cloth, usu with coloured flecks: **Harris tweed**.
2 (**tweeds**) clothes made of this material.

tweedy ADJ (**-ier, -iest**) **1** relating to or like tweed. **2** relating to or typical of people who enjoy outdoor country activities and who are conventionally thought of as wearing tweed.

tweet N a melodious chirping sound made by a small bird.
➤ VB, INTR to chirp melodiously.

tweeter N, ELECTRONICS a loudspeaker that is designed to reproduce high-frequency sounds.

tweezers PL N a small pair of pincers for pulling out individual hairs, holding small objects, etc.

twelfth (OFTEN WRITTEN **12th**) ADJ **1** in counting: **a** next after eleventh; **b** last of twelve. **2** in twelfth position.
➤ N **1** one of twelve equal parts. **2** a fraction equal to one divided by twelve.

Twelfth Night N the evening before the twelfth day after Christmas (5 January) or the evening of the day itself (6 January).

twelve N **1 a** the cardinal number 12; **b** the quantity that this represents, being one more than eleven. **2** any symbol for this, eg, **12** or **XII**. **3** something, esp a garment or a person, whose size is denoted by the number 12. **4** midnight or midday: **stopped at twelve for lunch**. **5** BRIT a film that has been classified as being suitable only for people aged twelve or over.
➤ ADJ **1** totalling twelve. **2** aged twelve.

twenties PL N (often written **20s** or **20's**) **1** (**one's twenties**) the period of time between one's twentieth and thirtieth birthdays. **2** (**the twenties**) the range of temperatures between twenty and thirty degrees. **3** (**the twenties**) the period of time between the twentieth and thirtieth years of a century.

twenty N (**-ies**) **1 a** the cardinal number 20; **b** the quantity that this represents, being one more than 19. **2** any symbol for this, eg, **20** or **XX**. **3** something, esp a garment or a person, whose size is denoted by the number 20.
➤ ADJ **1** totalling twenty. **2** aged twenty.
■ **twentieth** ADJ, N.

twerp N, COLLOQ a contemptible person.

twice ADV two times: **Twice two is four**.

twiddle VB **1** to twist round and round: **twiddle the knob on the radio**. **2** to play with or twist round and round idly: **twiddling her hair**.
◆ **twiddle one's thumbs** to have nothing to do.

twig[1] N a small shoot or branch of a tree.

twig[2] VB (**-gg-**) TR & INTR, BRIT COLLOQ to understand (a joke, situation, etc), esp suddenly.

twilight N **1** a faint diffused light in the sky when the sun is just below the horizon, esp just after sunset. **2** the time of day when this occurs. **3** a period of decline: **the twilight of his life**.

twill N a strong fabric woven to give a surface pattern of parallel diagonal ridges.

twin N **1** either of two people or animals that are born at the same time to the same mother.

2 either of two people or things that are very like each other or closely associated.
➤ ADJ being twins or one of a pair or consisting of very similar or closely connected parts.
➤ VB (-*nn*-) to link (a town) with a counterpart in another country to encourage cultural, social, etc exchanges.

twin bed N one of a pair of single beds.

twine N strong string of twisted cotton, etc.
➤ VB **1** to twist together; to interweave. **2** to form by twisting or interweaving. **3** TR & INTR to twist or coil round.

twinge N **1** a sudden sharp stabbing or shooting pain. **2** a sudden sharp pang of emotional pain, bad conscience, etc.

twinkle VB **1** INTR of a star, etc: to shine with a bright, flickering light. **2** INTR of the eyes: to shine or sparkle with amusement, mischief, etc. **3** to give off (light) with a flicker.
➤ N **1** a gleam or sparkle in the eyes. **2** a flicker or glimmer of light. **3** an act of twinkling.
■ **twinkly** ADJ (-*ier*, -*iest*).
◆ **in the twinkling of an eye** in a moment.

twinset N, BRIT a woman's matching sweater and cardigan.

twirl VB, TR & INTR to turn, spin or twist round.
➤ N **1** an act of twirling. **2** a curly mark or ornament. ■ **twirly** ADJ (-*ier*, -*iest*).

twist VB **1** TR & INTR to wind or turn round, esp by moving only a single part or by moving different parts in opposite directions: **twist the knob**. **2** INTR to follow a winding course: **The road twists through the hills**. **3** TR & INTR to wind around or together: **twist the pieces of string together**. **4** to force or wrench out of the correct shape or position with a sharp turning movement: **twisted his ankle as he fell**. **5** to distort: **twisted her words**. **6** (often **twist off**) to remove or break off with a sharp turning movement. **7** to form by winding or weaving. **8** INTR to dance the twist.
➤ N **1** an act or the process of twisting. **2** something that is formed by twisting or being twisted. **3** a turn or coil; a bend. **4** a sharp turning movement which pulls something out of shape; a wrench. **5** an unexpected event,

development or change, eg, of direction: **a twist in the plot**. **6** a distortion of form, nature or meaning. **7** a curl of citrus peel used to flavour a drink: **a twist of lemon**. **8** (**the twist**) a 1960s dance which involves making twisting movements of the legs and hips.
◆ **twist sb's arm** COLLOQ to persuade them, usu by applying moral pressure.

twisted ADJ **1** coiled or distorted: **a tree with twisted branches**. **2** COLLOQ of someone or their mind: emotionally disturbed or perverted.

twister N **1** BRIT COLLOQ a dishonest or deceiving person. **2** N AMER COLLOQ a tornado.

twit N, COLLOQ a fool or idiot.

twitch VB to move or cause to move with a spasm or jerk.
➤ N a sudden spasm or jerk.

twitcher N, COLLOQ a bird–watcher whose aim is to spot as many rare birds as possible.

twitchy ADJ (-*ier*, -*iest*) **1** COLLOQ nervous, anxious or restless. **2** characterized by twitching: **a twitchy eye**. ■ **twitchily** ADV.

twitter N **1** a light repeated chirping sound made esp by small birds. **2** COLLOQ a nervous or excited state: **go all of a twitter**.
➤ VB **1** INTR to make a light repeated chirping sound. **2** to say or utter with such a chirping sound. **3** (also **twitter on** or **away**) to talk rapidly and often trivially. ■ **twitterer** N.

two N **1 a** the cardinal number 2; **b** the quantity that this represents, being one more than one. **2** any symbol for this, eg, 2 or II. **3** something, such as a shoe size, that is denoted by the number 2. **4** the second hour after midnight or midday: **The meeting is at two**.
➤ ADJ **1** totalling two. **2** aged two.
◆ **put two and two together** to come to a conclusion, usu an obvious one, from the available evidence.

two-dimensional ADJ **1** having, or appearing to have, breadth and length but no depth. **2** DISPARAGING having little depth.

two-faced ADJ hypocritical; insincere.

twofold ADJ **1** twice as much or as many.

2 divided into or consisting of two parts. ➤ ADV by twice as much.

twopence N, BRIT **1** (also **tuppence**) the sum of two pence, esp before the introduction of decimal coinage. **2** a decimal coin of the value of two pence. ◆ **not care** or **give tuppence** COLLOQ not to care at all.

two-piece ADJ of a suit, bathing costume, etc: consisting of two matching pieces or parts. ➤ N a two-piece suit, etc.

two-ply ADJ consisting of two strands or layers: two-ply wool • two-ply wood. ➤ N (*-ies*) knitting wool consisting of two strands twisted together.

twosome N **1** a game, dance, etc for two people. **2** a pair of people together.

two-step N a ballroom dance in duple time.

two-stroke ADJ of an internal-combustion engine: taking one upward movement and one downward movement of the piston to complete the power cycle.

two-time VB, TR & INTR, COLLOQ to deceive or be unfaithful to. ■ **two-timing** ADJ, N.

two-way ADJ **1** of a street, etc: having traffic moving in both directions. **2** of a radio, etc: able to send and receive messages. **3** of a mirror: designed so that one side is like a normal mirror but with the other side allowing someone to see through without being observed.

tycoon N a business magnate.

tyke N **1** a dog, esp a mongrel. **2** BRIT COLLOQ a small child, esp a naughty or cheeky one.

tympani see **timpani**

type N **1** a class or group of people, animals or things which share similar characteristics. **2** the general character, nature or form of a particular class or group; a kind or sort. **3** COLLOQ a person, esp of a specified kind: the silent type. **4** a person, animal or thing that is a characteristic example of its group or class. **5** PRINTING **a** a small metal block with a raised letter or character on one surface that is used for printing; **b** a set of such blocks; **c** a set of such blocks that give printing of a specified kind: italic type. **6** printed letters, words, etc. ➤ VB, TR & INTR to use a typewriter or word processor (to produce words, text, etc).

typecast VB to put (an actor or actress) regularly in the same kind of part.

typeface N, PRINTING **1** a set of letters, characters, etc of a specified design or style. **2** the part of the type that is inked or the impression this leaves.

typescript N a typewritten document.

typeset VB (*typeset, typesetting*) PRINTING to arrange (type) or set (a page, etc) in type ready for printing. ■ **typesetter** N.

typewriter N a machine with keys that the user strikes to produce characters on paper.

typhoid N (in full **typhoid fever**) MED a bacterial infection characterized by fever, a rash, abdominal pain and sometimes delirium.

typhoon N a cyclonic storm of the W Pacific.

typhus N, MED an infectious disease caused by parasitic micro-organisms and characterized by fever, severe headache, a reddish-purple rash and delirium.

typical ADJ **1** having or showing the usual features, traits, etc, or being a characteristic or representative example: not a typical day. **2 a** (often **typical of**) displaying the usual or expected behaviour, attitude, etc: It's typical of him to be late. ■ **typically** ADV.

typify VB (*-ies, -ied*) to be an excellent or characteristic example of.

typist N **1** someone whose job is to type. **2** someone who uses a typewriter or word processor: I'm not a very fast typist.

typo N, COLLOQ a typographical error.

typography N **1** the art or occupation of setting type and arranging texts for printing. **2** the style and appearance of printed matter. ■ **typographer** N. ■ **typographic** or **typographical** ADJ.

tyrannical ADJ **1** of or like a tyrant. **2** oppressive. ■ **tyrannically** ADV.

tyrannize or **-ise** VB, TR & INTR to rule or treat in a cruel, unjust and oppressive way.

tyrannosaurus or **tyrannosaur** N a huge flesh-eating dinosaur.

tyranny N (**-ies**) the use of cruelty, injustice, oppression, etc to enforce authority or power.

tyrant N **1** a cruel, unjust and oppressive ruler with absolute power. **2** someone who uses authority or power cruelly and unjustly.

tyre or (US) **tire** N **1** a rubber ring around the outside edge of a wheel, eg, on a bicycle, pram, etc. **2** (in full **pneumatic tyre**) a similar hollow structure with an inner tube filled with air on the wheel of a car, lorry, etc.

tyro N a novice or beginner.

tzar, tzarina see **tsar, tsarina**

Uu

U[1] or **u** N (*Us, U's* or *u's*) the twenty-first letter of the English alphabet.

U[2] ABBREV, BRIT universal, denoting a film designated as suitable for people of all ages.

ubiquitous ADJ existing, found or seeming to be found everywhere at the same time.

udder N in certain mammals, eg cows, goats, etc: the bag-like structure containing the mammary glands that secrete milk.

UFO or **ufo** N an unidentified flying object, an unrecognizable flying vehicle presumed to be from another planet.

ugli N, TRADEMARK (*uglis* or *uglies*) a large juicy citrus fruit that is a cross between a grapefruit, a Seville orange and a tangerine.

ugly ADJ (**-ier, -iest**) **1** unpleasant to look at; extremely unattractive. **2** morally repulsive or offensive. **3** threatening, or involving danger or violence: *an ugly situation*. **4** angry; bad-tempered: *an ugly mood*. ■ **ugliness** N.

ugly duckling N someone or something, initially thought ugly or worthless, that later turns out to be beautiful or highly valued.

UHT ABBREV ultra-heat-treated.

ukulele or **ukelele** N a small guitar.

ulcer N, PATHOL a persistent open sore on the surface of the skin or of the mucous membranes lining a body cavity.

ulterior ADJ of motives, etc: beyond or other than what is apparent or admitted.

ultimate ADJ **1** last or final in a series or process. **2** most important; greatest possible. **3** fundamental; basic. **4** COLLOQ best; most advanced.
➤ N **1** the final point; the end or conclusion. **2** (**the ultimate**) COLLOQ the best; the most advanced of its kind: *the ultimate in computer technology*. ■ **ultimately** ADV.

ultimatum N (**-tums** or **-ta**) in a dispute, negotiations, etc: a statement from one of the parties involved to another, declaring an intention to take hostile action unless specified conditions are fulfilled.

ultramarine N **1** a deep-blue pigment used in paints, orig made by grinding lapis lazuli. **2** the colour of this pigment. Also AS ADJ.

ultrasonic ADJ relating to or producing ultrasound. ■ **ultrasonically** ADV.

ultrasound N sound consisting of waves with frequencies higher than 20,000 hertz.

ultrasound scan N a medical examination

of an internal part, esp a fetus, by directing ultrasound waves through it to produce an image on a screen.

ultraviolet ADJ denoting electro-magnetic radiation with wavelengths in the range between violet light and X-rays.

ululate VB, INTR to howl, wail or screech. ■ **ululant** ADJ. ■ **ululation** N.

umber N 1 a dark yellowish-brown earthy mineral containing oxides of iron and manganese, used to make pigments. 2 any of these pigments or the brownish colours produced by them.

umbilical cord N a long flexible tube-like organ by which a fetus is attached to the placenta and through which it receives nourishment.

umbra N (-*brae* or -*bras*) ASTRON the shadow cast by the moon on the earth during an eclipse of the sun. ■ **umbral** ADJ.

umbrage N (esp **give** or **take umbrage**) annoyance; offence.

umbrella N a device carried to give shelter from rain, etc, consisting of a rounded fabric canopy supported on a lightweight, usu metal, collapsible framework of ribs fitted around a central stick or handle.
➤ ADJ referring to something that covers or protects a number of things: **an umbrella organization**.

umlaut N in Germanic languages: a mark consisting of two dots placed above a vowel (eg ö or ä) to indicate a change in pronunciation.

umpire N 1 an impartial person who supervises play in various sports, eg cricket and tennis, enforcing the rules and deciding disputes. 2 someone who judges or decides a dispute or deadlock; an arbitrator.
➤ VB, TR & INTR to act as umpire in a match, etc.

umpteen ADJ, COLLOQ very many; innumerable. ■ **umpteenth** N, ADJ.

UN ABBREV United Nations.

unaccompanied ADJ 1 not escorted or attended. 2 MUS without accompaniment.

unaccountable ADJ 1 impossible to explain. 2 not answerable or accountable. ■ **unaccountably** ADV.

unaccounted ADJ (usu **unaccounted for**) 1 unexplained. 2 not included in an account.

unaccustomed ADJ 1 not usual or customary; unfamiliar. 2 (usu **unaccustomed to sth**) not used or accustomed to it.

unaffected ADJ 1 sincere or genuine, not affected; free from pretentiousness. 2 not affected or influenced. ■ **unaffectedly** ADV.

unanimous ADJ 1 all in complete agreement; of one mind. 2 of a decision, etc: shared or arrived at by all, with none disagreeing.

unannounced ADJ without warning.

unapproachable ADJ 1 out of reach; inaccessible. 2 aloof; unfriendly.

unassuming ADJ modest or unpretentious.

unattached ADJ 1 not attached, associated or connected, esp to a particular group, organization, etc. 2 not in a steady romantic or sexual relationship.

unattended ADJ not accompanied or watched over.

unaware ADJ with no knowledge (of something); not aware or conscious (of it).

unawares ADV 1 unexpectedly; by surprise. 2 without knowing or realizing; inadvertently.

unbalanced ADJ 1 not in a state of physical balance. 2 lacking mental balance; deranged. 3 eg of a view or judgement: lacking impartiality; biased.

unbearable ADJ not bearable; unendurable.

unbecoming ADJ (also **unbecoming for** or **to sb**) 1 not suited to the wearer or showing them to advantage. 2 of behaviour, etc: not appropriate or fitting.

unbeknown or **unbeknownst** ADV (usu **unbeknown** or **unbeknownst to sb**) unknown to them; without their knowledge.

unbelievable ADJ 1 too unusual or

unexpected to be believed. **2** COLLOQ astonishing. ■ **unbelievably** ADV.

unbeliever N someone who does not believe, esp in a particular religion.

unbend VB, TR & INTR **1** to relax (one's mind, behaviour, etc) from stiffness or formality. **2** to straighten or release something from a bent or curved position.

unbending ADJ **1** unyielding or inflexible. **2** strict or severe.

unbiased or **unbiassed** ADJ unprejudiced or impartial.

unbidden ADJ **1** spontaneous or voluntary. **2** not invited or solicited.

unbind VB **1** to release or free someone from a bond or restraint. **2** to unfasten or undo.

unblinking ADJ without blinking; not showing emotion, esp fear.

unblushing ADJ unashamed; shameless.

unbound ADJ **1** not bound or restrained. **2** loose; not tied or fastened with a band, etc. **3** of a book: without binding.

unbounded ADJ **1** without bounds or limits. **2** unchecked; unrestrained.

unbowed ADJ **1** not bowed or bent. **2** not conquered or forced to yield.

unbridled ADJ said of speech, emotion, etc: fully and freely felt or expressed; unrestrained.

unbroken ADJ **1** intact. **2** uninterrupted; continuous or undisturbed. **3** undaunted; not subdued in spirit or health. **4** of a horse, etc: not broken in; untamed. **5** of a (sporting) record: not surpassed.

unburden VB (often **unburden oneself**) to relieve (oneself or one's mind) of worries, secrets, etc by confessing them.

uncalled-for ADJ of a remark, etc: not warranted or deserved.

uncanny ADJ **1** weird, strange or mysterious, esp in an unsettling or uneasy way. **2** eg of skill or ability: beyond what is considered normal. ■ **uncannily** ADV. ■ **uncanniness** N.

unceremonious ADJ **1** without ceremony; informal. **2** with no regard for politeness or dignity; direct and abrupt.

uncertain ADJ **1** not sure, certain or confident. **2** not definitely known or decided. **3** not to be depended upon. **4** likely to change. ■ **uncertainly** ADV. ■ **uncertainty** N (-*ies*).

uncharted ADJ **1** of territory, etc: **a** not fully explored or mapped in detail; **b** not shown on a map or chart. **2** of a subject area, etc: not yet examined or fully investigated.

unchecked ADJ **1** not restrained. **2** not checked or verified.

uncivil ADJ discourteous; rude or impolite.

uncivilized or **-ised** ADJ **1** of a people, tribe, etc: not civilized. **2** uncultured; rough.

unclassified ADJ **1** not classified. **2** of information: not classified as secret.

uncle N **1** the brother or brother-in-law of a father or mother. **2** the husband of an aunt.

unclean ADJ **1** morally or spiritually impure. **2** of an animal: regarded for religious reasons as impure and unfit to be eaten. **3** dirty or foul.

unclog VB to free something from an obstruction; to unblock it.

unclothe VB **1** to remove the clothes from someone. **2** to uncover or reveal something.

uncomfortable ADJ **1** not comfortable. **2** feeling or causing discomfort or unease.

uncommitted ADJ not bound or pledged to support any particular party, policy, action, etc.

uncommon ADJ rare or unusual. ■ **uncommonly** ADV.

uncommunicative ADJ not communicative; not inclined to talk, express opinions, etc.

uncompromising ADJ **1** unwilling to compromise or submit. **2** sheer; out-and-out.

unconcerned ADJ **1** lacking concern or interest; indifferent. **2** not anxious; untroubled.

unconditional ADJ **1** not conditional; with no conditions or limits imposed. **2** complete or absolute. ■ **unconditionally** ADV.

unconscious ADJ **1** in a state of insensibility, characterized by loss of awareness of the external environment, and inability to respond to sensory stimuli. **2** of an action, behaviour, etc: characterized by lack of awareness; unintentional; not deliberate. **3** PSYCHOL relating to or produced by the unconscious.
➤ N (**the unconscious**) PSYCHOL the part of the mind that contains memories, thoughts and feelings of which one is not consciously aware, but which may be manifested as dreams, psychosomatic symptoms or certain patterns of behaviour.

unconventional ADJ not conventional; not conforming to the normal or accepted standards, rules, etc; unusual.

uncountable ADJ **1** not able to be counted; innumerable. **2** LING of a noun: that cannot be used with the indefinite article or form a plural.

uncouple VB **1** to undo the coupling of, or between (two or more things); to disconnect. **2** INTR to become unfastened or disconnected.

uncouth ADJ coarse or awkward in behaviour, manners or language; uncultured or lacking refinement. ■ **uncouthness** N.

uncover VB **1** to remove the cover or top from something. **2** to reveal or expose something.

unctuous ADJ **1** insincerely and excessively charming. **2** oily; greasy. ■ **unctuously** ADV.

uncut ADJ **1** not cut. **2** of a book: **a** with the pages not (yet) cut open; **b** with the margins untrimmed. **3** of a book, film, etc: with no parts cut out; unabridged. **4** of a gemstone: not cut into a regular shape.

undaunted ADJ not daunted; not discouraged or put off. ■ **undauntedly** ADV.

undecided ADJ **1** of a problem, question, etc: not (yet) decided; not settled. **2** of a person: not (yet) having decided or not able to decide; hesitating or irresolute. ■ **undecidedly** ADV.

undeniable ADJ **1** not able to be denied; unquestionably or obviously true. **2** clearly and indisputably excellent. ■ **undeniably** ADV.

under PREP **1 a** below or beneath something but not in contact with it: **under the table**; **b** below or beneath something and in contact with it: **under the book**. **2** at the foot of: **under the column**. **3** less than; short of: **under 10 per cent**. **4** lower in rank than. **5** subjected to, receiving or sustaining: **under consideration** • **under pressure**. **6** in the category or classification of. **7** known by: **goes under the name of**. **8** according to: **under the terms of the agreement**. **9** in view of; because of: **under the circumstances**.
➤ ADV in or to a lower place, position or rank.
◆ **under way 1** of a process, activity, project, etc: in progress. **2** NAUT of a vessel: in motion.

underachieve VB, INTR to be less successful than expected, esp academically; to fail to fulfil one's potential. ■ **underachiever** N.

underactive ADJ denoting insufficient activity: **an underactive thyroid gland**.

under-age ADJ of a person: below an age required by law; too young.

underarm ADJ **1** of a style of bowling in cricket, etc, or of a service in tennis, etc: performed with the arm kept below the level of the shoulder. **2** relating to or for the armpit.

underbelly N **1** the part of an animal's belly that is nearest the ground. **2** (also **soft underbelly**) an unprotected, vulnerable part.

undercarriage N **1** the landing gear of an aircraft, including wheels, shock absorbers, etc. **2** the supporting framework or chassis of a carriage or vehicle.

underclass N a subordinate social class, esp a class of people disadvantaged in society through poverty, unemployment, etc.

undercoat N **1** paint applied as preparation for the top or finishing coat. **2** underfur.
➤ VB to apply an undercoat to (a surface).

undercover ADJ working, carried out, etc in secret: **an undercover agent**.
➤ ADV in secret: **working undercover**.

undercurrent N **1** an unseen current under the surface of a body of water. **2** an underlying trend or body of opinion.

undercut VB to offer goods or services at a lower price than (a competitor).

underdeveloped ADJ **1** insufficiently developed; immature or undersized. **2** of a country: with resources inadequately used and a low standard of living.

underdone ADJ of food: cooked insufficiently or (too) lightly.

underdog N the competitor in a contest, etc who is considered unlikely to win.

underestimate VB to make too low an estimate of (something's value, etc).
➤ N an estimate that is too low.

underexpose VB, PHOTOG to expose (a film, plate or paper) for too little time or to too little light, resulting in a darkened photograph.
■ **underexposure** N.

underfoot ADV **1** beneath the foot or feet; on the ground. **2** COLLOQ always present and causing inconvenience.

underfund VB to provide (an organization, public service, etc) with insufficient funding to carry out all the planned activities.
■ **underfunding** N.

undergo VB to endure, experience or be subjected to something.

undergraduate N someone studying for a first degree in a higher education establishment.

underground N **1** (often **the underground**) a system of electric trains running in tunnels below ground. **2** a secret paramilitary organization fighting a government or occupying force. **3** any artistic movement seeking to challenge or overturn established views and practices.
➤ ADJ **1** below the surface of the ground: **an underground station**. **2** of or relating to any political or artistic underground: **underground music**.
➤ ADV **1** below ground level. **2** into hiding.

undergrowth N a thick growth of shrubs and bushes among trees.

underhand ADJ **1** secretively deceitful or dishonest; sly. **2** SPORT underarm.

➤ ADV in an underhand way.

underhanded ADV underhand.
➤ ADJ **1** underhand. **2** short of workers.

underlay N a thing laid underneath another, esp felt or rubber matting laid under a carpet.

underline VB **1** to draw a line under (eg a word or piece of text). **2** to emphasize.

underling N, DEROG a subordinate.

underlying ADJ **1** lying under or beneath. **2** present though not immediately obvious. **3** fundamental: **the underlying causes**.

undermanned ADJ provided with too few workers; understaffed.

undermine VB to weaken or destroy something, esp gradually and imperceptibly.

underneath PREP, ADV beneath or below.
➤ N a lower or downward-facing part or surface.

undernourished ADJ living on less food than is necessary for normal health and growth.

underpants PL N a man's undergarment covering the body from the waist or hips to (esp the tops of) the thighs.

underpart N (usu **underparts**) the lower side of an animal, bird, etc.

underpass N, orig US **1** a tunnel for pedestrians under a road or railway; a subway. **2** a road or railway passing under another.

underpay VB to pay less than is required or deserved. ■ **underpayment** N.

underperform VB, INTR **1** to perform less well than expected. **2** of an investment: to be less profitable than expected.

underpin VB **1** to support (a structure) from beneath with brickwork or a prop. **2** to support or corroborate.

underplay VB **1** TR & INTR to underact; to perform (a role) in a deliberately restrained or understated way. **2** to understate or play down the importance of something.

underprivileged ADJ **1** deprived of the basic living standards and rights enjoyed by most people in society. **2 (the underprivileged)** underprivileged people in general.

underrate VB to rate or assess something at a lower worth or value than it deserves; to have too low an opinion of something.

underscore VB **1** to score or draw a line under something. **2** to stress or emphasize something. ➤ N a line drawn under a piece of text.

underseal N an anti-rusting substance painted on to the underside of a motor vehicle. ➤ VB to apply such a substance to (a vehicle) in order to seal the metal for protection.

under-secretary N a junior minister or senior civil servant in a government department.

undersell VB to sell goods or services at a lower price than (a competitor).

undershoot VB to land short of (a runway).

underside N the downward-facing side or surface.

undersigned ADJ whose names are signed below: we, the undersigned…

underskirt N a thin skirt-like undergarment worn under a dress or skirt; a petticoat.

understand VB **1** to grasp the meaning of (a subject, words, a person, a language, etc): I've never understood trigonometry. **2** to make out the significance, cause, etc of something: I don't understand what all the fuss is about. **3** to have sympathetic awareness of someone or something: I fully understand your point of view. **4** to infer from the available information: I understood that he'd resigned.
■ **understandable** ADJ.

understanding N **1** the act of understanding or the ability to understand. **2** someone's perception or interpretation of information received. **3** an informal agreement. **4** a condition agreed upon: You can continue on the understanding that you try harder. ➤ ADJ sympathetic to the feelings of others.

understate VB to describe something as being less or more moderate than is really the case. ■ **understatement** N.

understated ADJ of clothes, someone's appearance, etc: effective through simplicity.

understood ADJ **1** implied but not expressed or stated. **2** realized without being, or needing to be, openly stated.

understudy VB **1** to study or prepare (a role or part) so as to be able to replace the actor or actress who usu plays that part, in case of absence, etc. **2** TR & INTR to act as understudy to (an actor or actress). ➤ N (-ies) **1** an actor or actress who understudies a role. **2** any person who is trained to replace another in case of absence.

undertake VB **1** to accept (a duty, responsibility or task). **2** to promise or agree.

undertaker N a person whose job is to organize funerals and prepare the bodies of the dead for burial or cremation.

undertaking N **1** a duty, responsibility or task undertaken. **2** a promise or guarantee.

under-the-counter ADJ of goods: obtained or sold illicitly, surreptitiously, etc.

undertone N **1** a quiet tone of voice. **2** an underlying quality, emotion or atmosphere.

undertow N an undercurrent in the sea that flows in the opposite direction to the surface current.

undervalue VB **1** to place too low a value on something. **2** to appreciate something insufficiently.

underwater ADJ, ADV under the surface of the water.

underwear N clothes, eg bras, pants, etc, worn under shirts, trousers, and skirts, etc.

underweight ADJ **1** lacking in weight; not heavy enough. **2** of a person: weighing less than is normal for their height, build, etc.

underwired ADJ of a bra: with a thin band of wire under each cup.

underworld N **1** MYTHOL a world imagined to lie beneath the Earth's surface, the home of the souls of the dead. **2** a hidden sphere of life or stratum of society, etc, esp the world of criminals and organized crime.

underwrite VB **1** to write (words, figures, etc) beneath other written matter. **2** to agree to finance (a commercial venture) and accept the loss in the event of failure. **3** to issue (an insurance policy), accepting the risk involved. ■ **underwriter** N.

undesirable ADJ unpleasant or objectionable.

undies PL N, COLLOQ items of underwear, esp women's bras, pants, etc.

undo VB (*undoes, undid, undone*) **1** TR & INTR to open, unfasten or untie (something). **2** to cancel or reverse something, or its effect or result.

undoing N.
◆ **be the undoing of sb** to bring about their downfall.

undone ADJ **1** not done; not achieved; unfinished or incomplete. **2** unfastened, untied, etc. **3** reversed; annulled. **4** destroyed; ruined.

undoubted ADJ beyond doubt or question; clear; evident. ■ **undoubtedly** ADV.

undreamed or **undreamt** ADJ (usu **undreamed-of** or **undreamt-of**) thought never to be likely or possible.

undress VB **1** to take the clothes off oneself (or another person). **2** INTR to take one's clothes off. ➤ N nakedness, or near-nakedness.

undressed ADJ **1** of stone, animal hide, etc: not treated, prepared or processed for use. **2** not wearing clothes; partially or completely naked.

undue ADJ **1** unjustifiable; improper. **2** inappropriately or unjustifiably great; excessive: undue criticism. ■ **unduly** ADV.

undulate VB, TR & INTR to move or to make something move in or like waves.

undulation N **1** the action of undulating. **2** a wave-like motion or form. **3** a wave.

undying ADJ everlasting; eternal.

unearned ADJ not deserved or merited.

unearth VB **1** to dig something up out of the ground. **2** to discover something by investigation, or by searching or rummaging.

unearthly ADJ **1** not of this Earth; heavenly or sublime. **2** supernatural; weird; ghostly; mysterious. **3** COLLOQ ridiculous or outrageous, esp outrageously early: at an unearthly hour.

unease N discomfort or apprehension.

uneasy ADJ (*-ier, -iest*) **1** nervous, anxious or unsettled; ill at ease. **2** unlikely to prove lasting; unstable. **3** causing anxiety; unsettling. ■ **uneasily** ADV. ■ **uneasiness** N.

uneconomic ADJ not in accordance with sound economic principles, esp unprofitable.

uneconomical ADJ not economical; wasteful.

unemployed ADJ **1** without paid employment; jobless. **2** not in use or not made use of. **3** (**the unemployed**) unemployed people.

unemployment N **1** the state or condition of being unemployed. **2** the number or percentage of unemployed people in a particular region, country, etc.

unenviable ADJ not provoking envy, esp because unpleasant or disagreeable: an unenviable task.

unequal ADJ **1** not equal in quantity, value, rank, size, etc. **2** of a contest, etc: not evenly matched or balanced. **3** (usu **unequal to sth**) unable to carry it out, deal with it, etc; inadequate. ■ **unequally** ADV.

unequalled ADJ without equal; not matched by any other; supreme.

unequivocal ADJ clearly stated; unambiguous. ■ **unequivocally** ADV.

unerring ADJ **1** not missing the mark or target; sure or certain. **2** consistently true or accurate; never making an error. ■ **unerringly** ADV.

uneven ADJ **1** of a surface, etc: not smooth or flat; bumpy. **2** of a contest: with contestants or sides poorly matched; unequal. **3** not equal; not matched or corresponding. ■ **unevenly** ADV. ■ **unevenness** N.

uneventful ADJ during which nothing interesting or out of the ordinary happens; uninteresting or routine. ■ **uneventfully** ADV.

unexceptional ADJ **1** not admitting or forming an exception. **2** ordinary; run-of-the-mill.

unexpected ADJ surprising; unforeseen.

unfailing ADJ **1** remaining constant; never weakening or failing. **2** continuous. **3** certain; sure. ■ **unfailingly** ADV.

unfair ADJ **1** not fair or just. **2** involving dishonesty. ■ **unfairly** ADV. ■ **unfairness** N.

unfaithful ADJ **1** not faithful to a sexual partner, usu by having a sexual relationship with someone else. **2** not loyal. **3** not true to a promise. ■ **unfaithfully** ADV. ■ **unfaithfulness** N.

unfamiliar ADJ **1** not (already or previously) known, experienced, etc. **2** strange; unusual. **3** (usu **unfamiliar with sth**) of a person: not familiar or well acquainted with it. ■ **unfamiliarity** N.

unfasten VB **1** to undo or release something from a fastening. **2** INTR to open.

unfathomable ADJ unable to be understood or fathomed; incomprehensible.

unfavourable or (US) **unfavorable** ADJ not favourable; adverse or inauspicious. ■ **unfavourably** ADV.

unfazed ADJ, COLLOQ not disconcerted.

unfeeling ADJ **1** without physical feeling or sensation. **2** unsympathetic; hard-hearted.

unfettered ADJ not controlled or restrained.

unfit ADJ **1** (often **unfit for** or **to** or **to do sth**) of a person: not suitably qualified for it; not good enough; incompetent. **2** (often **unfit for sth**) of a thing: not suitable or appropriate for it. **3** not fit; not in good physical condition.

unflappable ADJ, COLLOQ never becoming agitated, flustered or alarmed.

unflinching ADJ not flinching; showing a fearless determination in the face of danger or difficulty. ■ **unflinchingly** ADV.

unfold VB **1** to open out the folds of something; to spread it out. **2** INTR to open out or be spread out. **3** to reveal (a mystery, idea, etc); to make something clear. **4** INTR to develop or be revealed gradually.

unforced ADJ **1** not compelled. **2** natural.

unfortunate ADJ **1** unlucky; suffering misfortune or ill-luck. **2** resulting from bad luck: *an unfortunate injury.* **3** regrettable.

unfortunately ADV **1** in an unfortunate way; unluckily. **2** it's unfortunate that . . .; I'm sorry to say . . .: *Unfortunately he can't come.*

unfounded ADJ of rumours, etc: not based on fact; without foundation; groundless.

unfriendly ADV **1** not friendly; somewhat hostile. **2** not favourable. ■ **unfriendliness** N.

unfrock VB to defrock; to deprive (someone in holy orders) of ecclesiastical office or function.

unfurl VB, TR & INTR to open, spread out or unroll something from a rolled-up or tied-up state.

ungainly ADJ (*-ier, -iest*) awkward and ungraceful in movement. ■ **ungainliness** N.

ungodly ADJ **1** wicked or sinful; irreligious. **2** COLLOQ outrageously early.

unguarded ADJ **1** without guard; unprotected. **2** showing a lack of caution or alertness.

unguent N ointment or salve.

unhallowed ADJ not formally hallowed or consecrated.

unhappy ADJ **1** sad; in low spirits. **2** bringing sadness: *an unhappy ending.* **3** inappropriate: *an unhappy choice of words.* ■ **unhappily** ADV. ■ **unhappiness** N.

unhealthy ADJ **1** not conducive to health; harmful. **2** suffering from, or showing evidence of, ill health. **3** corrupting moral standards. **4** causing or likely to cause anxiety or worry; psychologically damaging: *an unhealthy attitude.* **5** COLLOQ dangerous to life. ■ **unhealthily** ADV. ■ **unhealthiness** N.

unheard-of ADJ not known to have ever happened or been done before.

unhinge VB **1 a** to remove (a door, etc) from its hinges; **b** to remove the hinges from (a door, etc). **2** to unbalance or derange (a person or a person's mind). ■ **unhinged** ADJ.

unholy ADJ **1** not holy or sacred. **2** wicked; sinful; irreligious. **3** COLLOQ outrageous; dreadful. ■ **unholiness** N.

unhook VB **1** to remove or free something from a hook or hooks. **2** to unfasten the hook or hooks of (eg a dress or other garment). **3** INTR to unfasten or become unfastened.

uni N, COLLOQ short form of **university**.

Uniat or **Uniate** ADJ of any church in eastern Europe and the Near East that acknowledges papal supremacy but retains its own customs, practices, liturgy, etc. ■ **Uniatism** N.

unicameral ADJ of a parliamentary system: with only one law-making body or chamber.

unicellular ADJ, BIOL of organisms or structures: consisting of a single cell.

unicorn N a mythical animal in the form of a horse (usu a white one) with a long straight spiralled horn growing from its forehead.

unicycle N a cycle consisting of a single wheel with a seat and pedals attached.

unidentified ADJ **1** not identified. **2** too strange to identify. ■ **unidentifiable** ADJ.

unification N an act or the process of unifying or uniting.

uniform N **1** distinctive clothing, always of the same colour, cut, etc, worn by all members of a particular organization or profession. **2** a single set of such clothing. **3** the recognizable appearance, or a distinctive feature or way of dressing, that is typical of a particular group. ➤ ADJ **1** unchanging or unvarying in form, nature or appearance; always the same, regardless of changes in circumstances, etc. **2** alike all over or throughout. **3** with the same form, character, etc as another or others; alike or like. ■ **uniformly** ADV.

uniformity N the state or fact of being uniform; conformity or similarity between several things, constituent parts, etc; sameness.

unify VB (*-ies, -ied*) to bring (two or more

things) together to form a single unit or whole.

unilateral ADJ **1** occurring on, affecting or involving one side only. **2** affecting, involving or done by only one person or group among several: *unilateral disarmament*. ■ **unilateralism** N. ■ **unilaterally** ADV.

unimpeachable ADJ indisputably reliable or honest; impossible to find fault with, etc.

uninterested ADJ not interested; indifferent.

union N **1 a** the action or an act of uniting two or more things; **b** the state of being united. **2** a united whole. **3** FORMAL **a** marriage; the state of wedlock; **b** sexual intercourse. **4** an association, confederation, etc of people or groups for a common (esp political) purpose. **5** a league or association, esp a trade union. **6** (also **Union**) **a** an organization concerned with the interests and welfare of the students in a college, university, etc; **b** the building that houses such an organization.

unionism or **Unionism** N advocacy of combination into one body for the purposes of social or political organization. ■ **unionist** or **Unionist** N, ADJ.

unionize or **-ise** VB **1** to organize (a workforce) into a trade union or trade unions. **2** INTR to join or constitute a trade union. ■ **unionization** N.

Union Jack N (also **Union flag**) the national flag of the United Kingdom.

unique ADJ **1** of which there is only one. **2** referring to something that is the only one of its kind; without equal; unparalleled. **3** (usu **unique to sb** or **sth**) referring to something that belongs solely to, or is associated solely with, them or it. ■ **uniquely** ADV. ■ **uniqueness** N.

unisex ADJ suited to, for use by, or wearable by, both men and women: *a unisex sauna*.

unison N the state of acting all in the same way at the same time; agreement.

unit N **1** a single item or element regarded as the smallest subdivision of a whole; a single person or thing. **2** a set of mechanical or electrical parts, or a group of workers, performing a specific function within a larger construction or organization. **3** a standard measure of a physical quantity, such as time or distance, specified multiples of which are used to express its size. **4** any whole number less than 10. **5** any subdivision of a military force. **6 a** an item of furniture that combines with others to form a set; **b** a set of such items. **7** a standard measure used to calculate alcohol intake.

unit cost N the cost of producing one item.

unite VB **1** TR & INTR to make or become a single unit or whole. **2** TR & INTR to bring or come together in a common purpose or belief.

united ADJ **1** referring to something that has or has been united; joined together or combined. **2** relating to, or resulting from, two or more people or things in union or combination.

United Kingdom N (in full **United Kingdom of Great Britain and Northern Ireland**) the kingdom comprising England, Wales, Scotland and N Ireland.

United Nations SING OR PL N an association of independent states formed in 1945 to promote peace and co-operation.

United States SING OR PL N (in full **United States of America**) a federal republic mostly in N America, comprising 50 states and the District of Columbia.

unit price N the price per item of goods.

unit trust N an investment scheme in which clients' money is invested in various companies, with the combined shares purchased divided into units allocated in multiples to each client according to the individual amount invested.

unity N (-*ies*) **1** the state or quality of being one; oneness. **2** a single unified whole. **3** the act, state or quality of forming a single unified whole from two or more parts. **4** agreement; harmony; concord.

univalent ADJ, CHEM monovalent. ■ **univalence** or **univalency** N.

universal ADJ **1** relating to the universe. **2** relating to, typical of, affecting, etc the whole world or all people. **3** relating to, typical of, affecting, etc all the people or things in a particular group. **4** COLLOQ widespread; general: **won universal approval**. **5** (abbrev **U**) in film classification: suitable for everyone. ■ **universally** ADV.

universe N **1** ASTRON **a** (**the Universe**) all existing space, energy and matter; the cosmos; **b** a star system; a galaxy. **2** all people.

university N (-*ies*) **1** a higher education institution with the authority to award degrees and usu having research facilities. **2** the buildings, staff or students of such an institution.

unkempt ADJ of appearance: untidy.

unkind ADJ unsympathetic, cruel or harsh. ■ **unkindly** ADV. ■ **unkindness** N.

unknowing ADJ not knowing; ignorant. ■ **unknowingly** ADV.

unknown ADJ **1** not known; unfamiliar. **2** not at all famous.
➤ N **1** an unknown person or thing. **2** (usu **the unknown**) something that is unknown, undiscovered, unexplored, etc.

unknown quantity N a person or thing whose precise identity, nature or influence is not known or cannot be predicted.

unlace VB to undo or loosen the lace or laces of (shoes, a garment, etc).

unleaded ADJ (also **lead-free**) of petrol: free from lead additives.

unlearn VB **1** to try actively to forget something learned; to rid the memory of it. **2** to free oneself from (eg an acquired habit).

unlearned[1] ADJ uneducated.

unlearned[2] or **unlearnt** ADJ **1** of a lesson, etc: not learnt. **2** of a skill, etc: not acquired by learning; instinctive; innate.

unleash VB to release or give free expression to (eg anger).

unleavened ADJ of bread: not leavened; made without yeast.

unless CONJ if not; except if: Unless you come in now you won't get any tea.

unlettered ADJ 1 uneducated. 2 illiterate.

unlike PREP 1 different from: Unlike her, he's going shopping today. 2 not typical or characteristic of: It's unlike her to be late. ➤ ADJ not like or alike; different; dissimilar.

unlikely ADJ 1 not expected or likely to happen. 2 not obviously suitable; improbable. 3 probably untrue; implausible. ■ **unlikeliness** or **unlikelihood** N.

unlined ADJ 1 free from or not marked with lines. 2 of a garment, etc: without any lining.

unlisted ADJ 1 not entered on a list. 2 of a telephone number: ex-directory.

unload VB 1 TR & INTR to remove (a load or cargo) from (a vehicle, ship, etc). 2 to remove the ammunition from (a gun) without firing it. 3 to get rid of (something undesirable).

unlock VB 1 to undo the lock of (a door, etc). 2 to free someone from being locked up.

unlooked-for ADJ 1 unexpected. 2 not deliberately encouraged or invited.

unloose VB to set free; to release.

unlucky ADJ 1 bringing, resulting from or constituting bad luck. 2 having, or tending to have, bad luck. 3 regrettable.

unmade ADJ 1 not yet made. 2 of a bed: with bedclothes not arranged neatly.

unmanly ADJ 1 not manly; not virile or masculine. 2 weak or cowardly.

unmanned ADJ esp of a vehicle or spacecraft: without personnel or a crew.

unmapped ADJ 1 not appearing on a map. 2 unexplored; untried: unmapped territory.

unmask VB, TR & INTR to remove a mask or disguise from (oneself or someone else).

unmentionable ADJ not fit to be mentioned or talked about, esp because indecent. ➤ N (**unmentionables**) HUMOROUS underwear.

unmerciful ADJ 1 merciless; not merciful.

2 unpleasantly great or extreme. ■ **unmercifully** ADV.

unmissable ADJ of a TV programme, film, etc: too good to be missed.

unmistakable or **unmistakeable** ADJ too easily recognizable to be mistaken for anything or anyone else. ■ **unmistakably** or **unmistakeably** ADV.

unmitigated ADJ 1 not lessened or made less severe. 2 unqualified; absolute; out-and-out: an unmitigated disaster.

unmoved ADJ 1 still in the same place. 2 not persuaded. 3 not affected by emotion; calm.

unnatural ADJ 1 contrary to the way things usually happen in nature. 2 abnormal. 3 intensely cruel. 4 insincere; affected. ■ **unnaturally** ADV.

unnecessary ADJ 1 not necessary. 2 more than is expected or required: spoke with unnecessary caution. ■ **unnecessarily** ADV.

unnerve VB to deprive of strength or courage.

unoccupied ADJ 1 not doing any work or engaged in any activity; idle. 2 of a building, etc: without occupants or inhabitants; empty.

unofficial ADJ 1 not officially authorized or confirmed. 2 not official or formal in character. 3 of a strike: not called or sanctioned by the strikers' trade union. ■ **unofficially** ADV.

unorganized or **-ised** ADJ 1 not organized; not brought into an organized state. 2 of a workforce: not represented by a trade union.

unpack VB to empty (eg a suitcase, bag, etc) of packed contents.

unpalatable ADJ 1 of food, drink, etc: not having a pleasant taste. 2 of a suggestion, idea, film scene, etc: unacceptable; distasteful.

unparalleled ADJ having no equal or parallel.

unpick VB 1 to undo (stitches). 2 to take (a sewn or knitted article, seam, etc) to pieces by undoing the stitching.

unpleasant ADJ not pleasant; disagreeable. ■ **unpleasantly** ADV. ■ **unpleasantness** N.

unplug VB **1** to unblock or unstop (something that is plugged or blocked). **2** to disconnect (an electrical appliance) by removing its plug from a socket.

unplumbed ADJ **1** of a building, etc: without plumbing. **2** unfathomed; unsounded. **3** not fully understood.

unpolished ADJ **1** not polished. **2** unrefined; not cultured or sophisticated.

unpractised or (US) **unpracticed** ADJ **1** with little or no practice, experience or skill. **2** not, or not yet, put into practice.

unprecedented ADJ **1** without precedent. **2** unparalleled.

unprepossessing ADJ unappealing.

unprincipled ADJ without moral principles.

unprintable ADJ not fit to be printed, esp because of being obscene or libellous.

unprofessional ADJ not in accordance with the rules governing, or the standards of conduct expected of, members of a particular profession. ■ **unprofessionally** ADV.

unprotected ADJ **1** not protected. **2** of sexual intercourse: without the use of a condom.

unputdownable ADJ, COLLOQ of a book: so absorbing that it is difficult to stop reading it.

unqualified ADJ **1** not having any formal qualifications; lacking the formal qualifications required for a particular job, etc. **2** not limited or moderated in any way. **3** absolute; out-and-out: **an unqualified success**. **4** not competent.

unquestionable ADJ beyond doubt or question. ■ **unquestionably** ADV.

unquestioning ADJ not arguing or protesting; done, accepted, etc without argument, protest or thought. ■ **unquestioningly** ADV.

unquote VB to indicate (in speech) the end of something that was said by someone else.

unravel VB **1** to separate out the strands of (a fabric). **2** to take something out of a tangled state. **3** INTR to become unravelled.

unread ADJ **1** of a book, etc: not having been read. **2** of a person: not educated.

unreadable ADJ **1** too difficult or tedious to read. **2** illegible.

unready ADJ **1** not ready. **2** not acting quickly; hesitant. ■ **unreadily** ADV. ■ **unreadiness** N.

unreal ADJ **1** not real; illusory or imaginary. **2** COLLOQ **a** exceptionally strange; incredible; **b** amazing; excellent. ■ **unreality** N.

unreasonable ADJ **1** not based on, or in accordance with reason or good sense. **2** immoderate; beyond what is fair.

unreasoning ADJ not reasoning; showing lack of reasoning; irrational.

unrelenting ADJ **1** refusing to change viewpoint or a chosen course of action. **2** not softened by feelings of mercy or pity. **3** constant; relentless; never stopping.

unremitting ADJ **1** not easing off or abating. **2** constant; never stopping.

unrequited ADJ esp of love: not returned.

unreserved ADJ **1** not booked or reserved. **2** open and sociable in manner; showing no shyness or reserve. **3** not moderated or limited; unqualified. ■ **unreservedly** ADV.

unrest N **1** a state of (esp public) discontent bordering on riotousness. **2** anxiety; unease.

unripe ADJ **1** not (yet) fully developed; not matured. **2** of fruit, etc: not (yet) ready to be harvested or eaten; not ripe.

unrivalled or (US) **unrivaled** ADJ far better than any other; unequalled.

unruffled ADJ **1** of a surface: smooth or still. **2** of a person: not agitated or flustered.

unruly ADJ (*-ier, -iest*) disobedient or disorderly, esp habitually. ■ **unruliness** N.

unsaid ADJ not said, expressed, spoken, etc, esp when it should have been.

unsaturated ADJ, CHEM of an organic chemical compound: containing at least one double or triple bond between carbon atoms.

unsavoury or (US) **unsavory** ADJ unpleasant or distasteful; offensive.

unscathed ADJ not harmed or injured.

unschooled ADJ 1 not educated. 2 not skilled or trained in a specified field or area.

unscramble VB 1 to interpret (a coded or scrambled message). 2 to take something out of a jumbled state. ■ **unscrambler** N.

unscrew VB to remove or loosen something by taking out a screw, or with a twisting action.

unscrupulous ADJ without scruples or moral principles. ■ **unscrupulously** ADV.

unseasonable ADJ 1 (also **unseasonal**) esp of the weather: not appropriate to the time of year. 2 coming at a bad time; inopportune.

unseasoned ADJ 1 of food: without seasonings. 2 not matured: **unseasoned wood**.

unseat VB 1 of a horse: to throw or knock (its rider) off. 2 to remove someone from an official post or position.

unseeded ADJ, SPORT, esp TENNIS not placed among the top players in the preliminary rounds of a tournament.

unseemly ADJ (**-ier, -iest**) not becoming or fitting, esp because of being indecent.

unselfish ADJ 1 having or showing concern for others. 2 generous.

unsettle VB to make someone ill at ease.

unsettled ADJ 1 lacking stability. 2 frequently changing or moving from place to place. 3 unresolved. 4 of the weather: changeable; unpredictable.

unshackle VB to release someone from a shackle or shackles.

unsheathe VB to draw (esp a sword, knife, etc) from a sheath.

unsightly ADJ (**-ier, -iest**) not pleasant to look at; ugly. ■ **unsightliness** N.

unsociable ADJ 1 of a person: disliking or avoiding the company of other people. 2 not conducive to social intercourse.

unsocial ADJ 1 annoying, or likely to annoy, other people; antisocial. 2 of working hours: falling outside the normal working day.

unsophisticated ADJ 1 not experienced or worldly; naive. 2 free from insincerity or artificiality. 3 lacking refinement or complexity.

unsound ADJ 1 not reliable; not based on sound reasoning: **an unsound argument**. 2 not firm or solid. 3 not stable or healthy.

unsparing ADJ 1 giving generously or liberally. 2 showing no mercy; unrelenting.

unspeakable ADJ 1 not able to be expressed in words; indescribable. 2 too bad or obscene to be spoken about. ■ **unspeakably** ADV.

unsteady ADJ 1 not secure or firm. 2 of behaviour, character, etc: not steady or constant; erratic. 3 of movement, a manner of walking, etc: unsure or precarious.

unstructured ADJ without any formal structure or organization.

unstuck ADJ.
◆ **come unstuck** COLLOQ of a person, plan, etc: to suffer a setback; to go wrong.

unstudied ADJ not affected; natural and spontaneous.

unsubstantial ADJ 1 with no basis or foundation in fact. 2 without material substance. 3 lacking strength or firmness.

unsung ADJ of someone, an achievement, etc: not praised or recognized: **an unsung hero**.

unsuspected ADJ 1 not suspected; not under suspicion. 2 not known or supposed to exist.

unswerving ADJ not deviating from a belief or aim; steadfast. ■ **unswervingly** ADV.

untangle VB to disentangle something.

untenable ADJ of an opinion, theory, argument, etc: not able to be defended or justified.

unthinkable ADJ 1 too unusual to be likely; inconceivable. 2 too unpleasant to think about.

unthinking ADJ 1 inconsiderate; thoughtless. 2 careless. ■ **unthinkingly** ADV.

untidy ADJ not tidy; messy or disordered. ■ **untidily** ADV. ■ **untidiness** N.

untie VB **1** to undo (a knot, etc) from a tied state. **2** INTR of a knot, etc: to come unfastened.

until PREP **1** up to the time of: **worked until 8**. **2** up to the time of reaching (a place); as far as: **slept until Paris**. **3** WITH NEGATIVES before: **not until Wednesday**.
➤ CONJ **1** up to the time that: **He waited until she emerged with the money**. **2** WITH NEGATIVES before: **not until I say so**.

untimely ADJ **1** happening before the proper or expected time: **an untimely death**. **2** coming at an inappropriate or inconvenient time.

unto PREP, ARCHAIC OR LITERARY to.

untold ADJ **1** not told. **2** too severe to be described. **3** too many to be counted.

untouchable ADJ **1** not to be touched or handled. **2** discouraging physical contact. **3** above the law. **4** unrivalled.
➤ N an untouchable person or thing.

untoward ADJ **1** adverse; unfavourable. **2** unseemly; improper.

untrue ADJ **1** not true. **2** unfaithful.

untruth N **1** the fact or quality of being untrue. **2** something that is untrue; a lie.

untutored ADJ **1** uneducated; untaught. **2** unsophisticated.

unused ADJ **1** brand new; never used. **2** (always **unused to sth**) not used or accustomed to it.

unusual ADJ not usual; uncommon; rare.

unutterable ADJ so extreme or intense as to be impossible to express in words.

unvarnished ADJ **1** not exaggerated or embellished. **2** not covered with varnish.

unveil VB **1** to remove a veil from (one's own or someone else's face). **2** to remove a covering from (a plaque, monument, etc) as part of a formal opening ceremony. ■ **unveiling** N.

unversed ADJ (USU **unversed in sth**) not experienced in it.

unvoiced ADJ not spoken.

unwarranted ADJ not justified.

unwary ADJ not wary; careless or incautious.

unwell ADJ not well; ill.

unwholesome ADJ **1** not conducive to physical or moral health; harmful. **2** of a person: of dubious character or morals. **3** diseased; not healthy-looking. **4** of food: of poor quality.

unwieldy ADJ **1** of an object: large and awkward to carry or manage; cumbersome. **2** of a person: clumsy; not graceful.

unwilling ADJ **1** reluctant; loath. **2** done, said, etc reluctantly.

unwind VB **1** to undo, slacken, untwist, etc something that has been wound or coiled up. **2** INTR of something that has been wound or coiled up: to come undone, to slacken, untwist, etc. **3** COLLOQ to become relaxed.

unwise ADJ not prudent; ill-advised; foolish.

unwished ADJ (USU **unwished for**) **1** unwelcome; uninvited. **2** not wanted.

unwitting ADJ not realizing or being aware.

unwonted ADJ not usual or habitual.

unworldly ADJ **1** not relating or belonging to this world; otherwordly. **2** not concerned with material things. **3** unsophisticated; naive.

unworthy ADJ **1** (often **unworthy of sth**) not deserving or worthy of it. **2** (often **unworthy of sb** or **sth**) not worthy or befitting to (a person's character, etc). **3** of little or no merit or value. **4** of treatment, etc: not warranted; undeserved or worse than is deserved.

unwrap VB to remove the wrapping or covering from something.

unwritten ADJ **1** not recorded in writing. **2** of a rule or law: not formally enforceable, but traditionally accepted and followed.

unzip VB **1** to unfasten or open (a garment, etc) by undoing a zip. **2** INTR to open or come apart by means of a zip. **3** COMP to convert (data that has been compressed in order to save storage space) into a less compressed form.

up PREP at or to a higher position on, or a position further along: **walking up the road**.

➤ ADV **1** at or to a higher position or level: **lift it up** • **turn up** the volume. **2** at or to a place higher up, or a more northerly place. **3** in or to a more erect position: **stood up**. **4** fully or completely: **use up**. **5** into the state of being gathered together: **parcel up** the presents. **6** in or to a place of storage or lodging: **put them up** for the night. **7** out of bed: **got up**. **8** to or towards: **walked up** to him.

➤ ADJ (*upper*, *uppermost* or *upmost*) **1** placed in, or moving or directed to, a higher position. **2** out of bed: **He's not up yet**. **3** having an advantage; ahead: **two goals up**. **4** appearing in court: **up before the judge**. **5** of the sun: visible above the horizon.

➤ VB (*-pp-*) **1** to raise or increase something: **upped the price**. **2** INTR, COLLOQ to get up (and do something): **He upped and left her**.

➤ N **1** a success or advantage. **2** a spell of good luck or prosperity.

not up to much COLLOQ not good at all.
on the up-and-up COLLOQ steadily becoming more successful.
something's up something is wrong.
up against sb or **sth 1** pressed close against them. **2** facing the difficulties, etc associated with them.
up for sth 1 presented for (eg discussion or sale). **2** under consideration for (a job or post). **3** prepared and eager to do it.
◆ **up to sb** their responsibility; dependent on them: **It's up to you**.
up to sth 1 immersed or embedded as far as: **up to his eyes in work**. **2** capable of; equal to: **Are you up to meeting them?** **3** doing: **What are you up to?** **4** as good as: **not up to his usual standard**. **5** as many or as much as: **up to two weeks**.
◆ **up to the minute** completely up to date.
What's up? What's the matter?

up-and-coming ADJ beginning to become successful or well known.

up-and-down ADJ **1** undulating. **2** moving or working both, or alternately, up and down.

upbeat ADJ, COLLOQ cheerful; optimistic.
➤ N, MUS an unstressed beat, esp the last in a bar and so coming before the downbeat.

upbraid VB to scold or reproach someone.

upbringing N the all-round instruction and education of a child, which influences their character and values.

upcoming ADJ, COLLOQ, esp N AMER forthcoming; approaching.

update VB to make or bring something or someone up to date.
➤ N an act of updating.

up-end VB, TR & INTR to turn or place something, or become turned or placed, upside down.

upfront ADJ, COLLOQ (also **up-front**) **1** candid; open. **2** of money: paid in advance.
➤ ADV (also **up front**) **1** candidly; openly. **2** of money or a payment: in advance.

upgrade VB **1** to promote someone. **2** to improve the quality of (machinery, equipment, a computer or its memory, etc), esp by adding or replacing features, components, etc.
➤ N an act or the process of upgrading.

upheaval N a change or disturbance that brings about great disruption.

uphill ADJ **1** sloping upwards; ascending. **2** of a task, etc: requiring great and sustained effort.
➤ ADV **1** up a slope. **2** against difficulties.

uphold VB **1** to support (an action), defend (a right) or maintain (the law), esp against opposition. **2** to declare (eg a court judgement or verdict) to be correct or just; to confirm.

upholster VB to fit (chairs, sofas, etc) with upholstery. ■ **upholsterer** N.

upholstery N **1** the springs, stuffing and covers of a chair or sofa. **2** the work of an upholsterer.

upkeep N **1** the task or process of keeping something in good order or condition; maintenance. **2** the cost of doing this.

upland N (often **uplands**) a hilly region.
➤ ADJ relating to or situated in such a region.

uplift VB to fill (a person or people) with an invigorating happiness, optimism or awareness of the spiritual nature of things. ■ **uplifting** ADJ.

uplighter and **uplight** N a type of lamp or wall light placed or designed so as to throw light upwards.

upload VB, TR & INTR, COMP to send (data, files, etc) from one computer to another, eg by means of a telephone line and modem.

up-market ADJ relating to or suitable for the more expensive end of the market; high in price, quality or prestige.

upon PREP on or on to.

upper ADJ **1** higher; situated above. **2** high or higher in rank or status. **3** (WITH CAPITAL when part of a name) upstream, farther inland or situated to the north.
➤ N **1** the part of a shoe above the sole. **2** the higher of two people, objects, etc. **3** SLANG a drug that induces euphoria.
◆ **on one's uppers** COLLOQ destitute.

upper case ADJ, PRINTING referring or relating to capital letters, as opposed to small letters.

upper class N the highest social class; the aristocracy. Also AS ADJ: **upper-class etiquette.**

upper crust N, COLLOQ the upper class.

uppercut N an upward blow with the fist.

upper hand N (usu **the upper hand**) a position of advantage or dominance.

upper house and **upper chamber** N the higher but normally smaller part of a two-chamber (bicameral) parliament.

uppermost ADJ, ADV at, in or into the highest or most prominent position.

uppish ADJ **1** arrogant or snobbish. **2** pretentious. ■ **uppishness** N.

uppity ADJ, COLLOQ self-important; arrogant.

upright ADJ **1** standing straight up; erect or vertical. **2** possessing integrity or moral correctness.
➤ ADV into an upright position.
➤ N a vertical (usu supporting) post or pole.
■ **uprightness** N.

uprising N a rebellion or revolt.

uproar N an outbreak of noisy and boisterous behaviour, esp angry protest.

uproarious ADJ **1** making, or characterized by, an uproar. **2** of laughter: loud and unrestrained.

uproot VB **1** to displace (a person or people) from their usual surroundings or home. **2** to pull (a plant) out of the ground completely. **3** to move away from a usual location or home.

ups and downs PL N **1** rises and falls. **2** spells of alternating success and failure.

upset VB **1** to disturb or distress someone emotionally. **2** to ruin or spoil (eg plans, etc). **3** to disturb the proper balance or function of (a person's stomach or digestion). **4** to disturb something's normal balance or stability. **5** TR & INTR to knock something over or overturn.
➤ N **1** a disturbance or disorder, eg of plans, the digestion, etc. **2** an unexpected result or outcome, eg of a contest.
➤ ADJ **1** emotionally distressed, angry or offended, etc. **2** disturbed: **an upset stomach.**
■ **upsetting** ADJ.

upshot N (often **the upshot**) the final outcome or ultimate effect.

upside N **1** the upper part or side of anything. **2** COLLOQ a positive or favourable aspect.

upside down ADJ (also **upside-down**) **1** with the top part at the bottom; inverted. **2** COLLOQ in complete confusion or disorder.
➤ ADV **1** in an inverted way or manner. **2** in a completely confused or disordered way.

upsides ADV (usu **upsides with sb**), BRIT COLLOQ even with them, esp through revenge.

upstage ADV on, at or towards the back of a theatre stage.
➤ ADJ situated, occurring at or towards, or relating to, the back of a theatre stage.
➤ VB **1** of an actor: to move upstage and force (another actor) to turn their back to the audience. **2** COLLOQ to direct attention away from someone on to oneself; to outshine them.

upstairs ADV **1** up the stairs; to or on an upper floor or floors of a house, etc. **2** COLLOQ to or in a senior or more senior position.
➤ ADJ (also **upstair**) on or relating to an

upper floor or floors.

➤ N the upper floors of a building.

upstanding ADJ **1** standing up. **2** of a person: honest; respectable; trustworthy.

upstart N, DEROG someone who has suddenly acquired wealth or risen to a position of power, esp one who is considered arrogant.

upstream ADV towards the source of a river or stream and against the current.

➤ ADJ situated towards the source of a river or stream.

upsurge N a sudden sharp rise or increase.

upswing N, ECON a recovery in the trade cycle or a period during which this occurs.

uptake N the act of taking up or accepting something on offer, or the extent of this.

◆ **quick** or **slow on the uptake** COLLOQ quick or slow to understand something.

up-tempo ADJ, ADV, MUS with or at a fast tempo.

upthrust N an upward thrust or push.

uptight ADJ, COLLOQ **1** nervous; anxious; tense. **2** angry; irritated. **3** strait-laced; conventional.

up to date or **up-to-date** ADJ **1** containing all the latest facts or information. **2** knowing or reflecting the latest trends.

upturn N **1** an upheaval. **2** an increase in (esp economic) activity; an upward trend.

upward ADV (usu **upwards**) to or towards a higher place, a more important or senior position, or an earlier era.

➤ ADJ moving or directed upwards, to a higher position, etc. ■ **upwardly** ADV.

◆ **upwards of** more than.

upwardly mobile ADJ moving, or in a position to move, into a higher social class or income bracket. ■ **upward mobility** N.

upwind ADV **1** against the direction of the wind; into the wind. **2** in front in terms of wind direction; with the wind carrying one's scent towards eg an animal one is stalking.

uranium N, CHEM a dense silvery-white radioactive metallic element chiefly used to produce nuclear energy. ■ **uranic** ADJ.

Uranus N the seventh planet from the sun.

urban ADJ relating or belonging to, constituting, or characteristic of a city or town.

urbane ADJ **1** suave; courteous. **2** sophisticated; elegant. ■ **urbanity** N.

urbanize or **-ise** VB to make (an area) less rural and more town-like. ■ **urbanization** N.

urchin N **1** a mischievous child. **2** a dirty raggedly dressed child. **3** a sea urchin.

Urdu N the official language of Pakistan.

urea N, BIOCHEM a compound, white and crystalline when purified, formed during amino-acid breakdown in the liver of mammals, and excreted in the urine. ■ **ureal** or **ureic** ADJ.

ureter N, ANAT one of the two tubes through which urine is carried from the kidneys to the bladder.

urethra N, ANAT the tube through which urine passes from the bladder out of the body and which, in males, also conveys semen.

urge VB **1** (also **urge sb on**) to persuade someone forcefully or incite them (to do something). **2** to beg or entreat someone (to do something). **3 a** (usu **urge that**) to earnestly advise or recommend that; **b** (usu **urge sth**) to earnestly recommend it: urged prudence. **4** to drive or hurry (onwards, forwards, etc).

➤ N a strong impulse, desire or motivation (to do something).

urgent ADJ **1** requiring or demanding immediate attention, action, etc; pressing. **2** of a request, etc: forcefully and earnestly made. ■ **urgency** N. ■ **urgently** ADV.

uric acid N, BIOCHEM an organic acid present in urine and blood.

urinal N any receptacle, esp one attached to a wall, designed for men to urinate into.

urinary ADJ relating to urine or the passing of urine.

urinate VB, INTR to discharge urine. ■ **urination** N.

urine N the yellowish slightly acidic liquid consisting mainly of water and containing urea, uric acid, and other nitrogenous waste products filtered from the blood by the kidneys.

urn N **1** a vase or vessel with a rounded body, usu a small narrow neck and a base or foot. **2** such a vase used to contain the ashes of a dead person. **3** a large cylindrical metal container with a tap and an internal heating element, used for heating water.

ursine ADJ **1** belonging, relating or referring to a bear or bears. **2** bearlike.

urticaria N, MED an allergic skin reaction with raised red or white itchy patches. Also called **nettle rash** or **hives**. ■ **urticarial** ADJ.

us PRONOUN **1** the speaker or writer together with another person or other people; the object form of **we** : **asked us the way** • **give it to us**. **2** all or any people; one: **Computers can help us to work more efficiently**. **3** FORMAL used by monarchs, etc: me.

usage N **1** the act or way of using, or fact of being used; use; employment. **2** custom or practice. **3 a** the way that the vocabulary, constructions, etc of a language are actually used in practice; **b** an example of this.

use VB **1** to put to a particular purpose. **2** to consume; to take something as fuel. **3** to treat someone as a means to benefit oneself; to exploit them. **4** SLANG to take (eg drugs or alcohol) regularly.
➤ N **1** the act of using. **2** the state of being (able to be) used: **go out of use** • **not in use**. **3** a purpose a thing can be put to. **4** the quality of serving a practical purpose: **It's no use complaining** • **Is this spanner any use? 5** the ability or power to use something (eg a limb): **lost the use of her leg after the accident**. **6** the length of time a thing is, will be or has remained serviceable: **should give you plenty of use**. **7** the habit of using; custom.
◆ **used to sth** or **sb** accustomed to it or them: **The puppies haven't got used to us yet.**
◆ **use sth up 1** to exhaust supplies, etc. **2** to finish off an amount left over.

used ADJ not new; second-hand: **a used car**.

used to AUXILIARY VERB used with other verbs to express habitual actions or states that took place in the past: **They used to be friends.**

useful ADJ **1** able to be used advantageously; serving a helpful purpose; able to be put to various purposes. **2** COLLOQ proficient: **Beckham put in a useful performance.**

useless ADJ **1** serving no practical purpose. **2** (often **useless at sth**) COLLOQ not at all proficient. ■ **uselessly** ADV. ■ **uselessness** N.

user N **1** someone who uses a specified facility. **2** someone who regularly takes a specified drug: **a heroin user**.

user-friendly ADJ esp of a computer system: designed to be easy or pleasant to use, or easy to follow or understand.

usher N **1 a** someone whose job is to show people to their seats, eg in a theatre, cinema, etc; **b** someone whose function is to direct wedding guests to their seats in church, and to look after them. **2** an official in a court of law who guards the door and maintains order.
➤ VB **1** (usu **usher sb in** or **out**) to conduct or escort them, eg into or out of a building, room, etc. **2** (usu **usher sth in**) FORMAL OR LITERARY to be a portent of it; to herald it.

usherette N a woman who shows people to their seats in a theatre or cinema.

usual ADJ done, happening, etc most often; customary: **took the usual route to work**.
➤ N **1** something which is usual, customary, etc. **2** (usu **the** or **my usual**) COLLOQ the thing regularly requested, done, etc, esp the drink that someone regularly or most often orders. ■ **usually** ADV. ■ **usualness** N.
◆ **as usual** as regularly happens.

usurer N someone who lends money, esp at exorbitant rates of interest. ■ **usury** N.

usurp VB to take possession of (eg land) or assume (eg power, authority, a title, etc) by force, without right or unjustly. ■ **usurper** N.

utensil N an implement or tool, esp one for everyday or domestic use: **cooking utensils**.

uterus N (-**ri**) TECHNICAL the womb.

utilitarian ADJ **1** intended to be useful rather than beautiful. **2** strictly or severely functional.

utility N (*-ies*) **1** usefulness; practicality. **2** something that is useful. **3** a company which provides a supply eg of electricity, gas or water for a community. **4** COMP a program designed to carry out a routine function.

utility room N a room where things such as a washing machine, freezer, etc are kept.

utilize or **-ise** VB to make practical use of something; to use it. ■ **utilization** N.

utmost ADJ greatest possible in degree, number or amount: **of the utmost urgency**. ➢ N **1** (often **the utmost**) the greatest possible amount, degree or extent. **2** the best or greatest, eg in terms of power, ability, etc: **tried his utmost to win**.

Utopia or **utopia** N any imaginary place, state or society of idealized perfection.

Utopian or **utopian** ADJ relating to some unrealistically ideal place, society, etc.

utter[1] VB **1** to give audible vocal expression to (an emotion, etc); to emit (a sound) with the voice: **uttered a piercing cry**. **2** to speak or say; to express something in words.

utter[2] ADJ complete; total; absolute: **utter disbelief**. ■ **utterly** ADV. ■ **utterness** N.

utterance N **1** the act of uttering or expressing something with the voice. **2** something that is uttered or expressed.

uttermost ADJ, N utmost.

U-turn N **1** a manoeuvre in which a vehicle is turned to face the other way in a single continuous movement. **2** a complete reversal of direction, eg of government policy.

UV ABBREV ultraviolet.

uvula N (*-las* or *-lae*) ANAT the small fleshy part of the soft palate that hangs over the back of the tongue.

uxorial ADJ relating to a wife or wives.

uxorious ADJ excessively fond of one's wife.

Vv

V[1] or **v** N (*Vs, V's* or *v's*) the twenty-second letter of the English alphabet.

V[2] SYMBOL the Roman numeral for 5.

v or **v.** ABBREV versus.

vacancy N (*-ies*) **1** the state of being vacant; emptiness. **2** an unoccupied job or post. **3** an unoccupied room in a hotel or guesthouse.

vacant ADJ **1** empty or unoccupied. **2** having, showing or suggesting an absence of thought, concentration or intelligence.

vacate VB **1** to make something empty; to empty something out. **2** TR & INTR to leave or cease to occupy (a house or a position).

vacation N **1** N AMER, ESP US a holiday. **2** a holiday between terms at a university, college or court of law.

vaccinate VB to administer to a person or an animal a vaccine that gives immunity from a disease; to inoculate. ■ **vaccination** N.

vaccine N **1** MED a preparation containing killed or weakened bacteria or viruses, or serum containing specific antibodies, used in vaccination to confer temporary or permanent immunity to a bacterial or viral disease by stimulating the body to produce antibodies to a specific bacterium or virus. **2** COMP a piece of software designed to remove computer viruses from a floppy disk, program, etc.

vacillate VB, INTR to waver. ■ **vacillation** N.

vacuity N (*-ies*) the quality of being vacuous.

vacuous ADJ **1** unintelligent; stupid; inane. **2** of a look or expression: blank; conveying no feeling or meaning.

vacuum N (*vacuums* or TECHNICAL *vacua*) **1** a space from which all matter has been removed. **2** a space from which all air or other gas has been removed. **3** a feeling or state of emptiness. **4** a condition of isolation from outside influences. **5** COLLOQ a vacuum cleaner. ➤ VB, TR & INTR, COLLOQ to clean with a vacuum cleaner.

vacuum cleaner N an electrically powered cleaning device that lifts dirt by suction.

vacuum flask N a container for preserving the temperature of liquids, consisting of a double-skinned bottle with a vacuum sealed between the layers, fitted inside a protective metal or plastic container.

vacuum-packed ADJ of food: sealed in a container from which air has been removed.

vagabond N someone with no fixed home who lives an unsettled wandering life.

vagary N (*-ies*) an unpredictable and erratic act or turn of events.

vagina N (*-as* or *-ae*) in female mammals: the muscular canal that leads from the cervix to the exterior of the body. ■ **vaginal** ADJ.

vagrant N someone who has no permanent home or place of work. ■ **vagrancy** N.

vague ADJ **1** indistinct or imprecise. **2** thinking, expressing or remembering without clarity or precision. ■ **vaguely** ADV. ■ **vagueness** N.

vain ADJ **1** having too much pride in one's appearance, achievements, etc. **2** having no useful effect or result. ■ **vainly** ADV.
◆ **in vain** without success; fruitlessly.

vainglory N, LITERARY extreme boastfulness; excessive pride. ■ **vainglorious** ADJ.

valance N a decorative strip of fabric hung over a curtain rail, etc.

vale N, LITERARY a valley.

valediction N the act of saying farewell; a farewell. ■ **valedictory** ADJ.

valency or (esp N AMER) **valence** N CHEM a positive or negative whole number that denotes the combining power of an atom of a particular element, equal to the number of hydrogen atoms or their equivalent with which it could combine to form a compound.

valentine N **1** a card given, often anonymously, as a token of love or affection on St Valentine's Day. **2** the person it is given to.

valerian N **a** a small flowering plant with pink tubular flowers and rhizome roots; **b** a sedative drug derived from the root.

valet N **1** a man's personal servant, who attends to his clothes, dressing, etc. **2** a man who carries out similar duties in a hotel. ➤ VB **1** INTR to work as a valet. **2** to clean the body-work and interior of (a car) as a service.

valiant ADJ outstandingly brave and heroic. ■ **valiantly** ADV.

valid ADJ **1** of an argument, objection, etc: **a** based on truth or sound reasoning; **b** well-grounded; having some force. **2** of a ticket or official document: **a** legally acceptable for use; **b** not having reached its expiry date. **3** of a contract: drawn up according to proper legal procedure. ■ **validity** N.

validate VB **1** to make (a document, a ticket, etc) valid, eg by marking it with an official stamp. **2** to confirm the validity of something. ■ **validation** N.

valise N, now chiefly N AMER, ESP US a small overnight case or bag.

valley N a long flat area of land, usu containing a river or stream, flanked on both sides by higher land, eg hills or mountains.

valour or (N AMER) **valor** N courage or bravery, esp in battle. ■ **valorous** ADJ.

valuable ADJ having value or usefulness.

➤ N (usu **valuables**) personal possessions of high financial or other value.

valuation N 1 an assessment of the monetary value of something. 2 the value arrived at.

value N 1 worth in monetary terms. 2 the quality of being useful or desirable. 3 the quality of being a fair exchange: **value for money**. 4 (**values**) moral principles or standards. 5 MATH a quantity represented by a symbol or set of symbols.
➤ VB 1 to consider something to be of a certain value, esp a high value. 2 to assess the value of something. ■ **valued** ADJ. ■ **valuer** N.

value judgement N an assessment of worth based on personal opinion rather than fact.

valve N 1 a any device that regulates the flow of a liquid or gas through a pipe by opening or closing an aperture; b any such device that allows flow in one direction only. 2 ANAT a flap of membranous tissue that allows flow of a body fluid, such as blood, in one direction only. 3 any of a set of finger-operated devices that control the flow of air through some brass musical instruments.

vamp[1] COLLOQ, N a woman who flaunts her sexual charm, esp in order to exploit men.
➤ VB 1 to seduce (a man) with intent to exploit him. 2 INTR to behave like a vamp.

vamp[2] N.
◆ **vamp sth up** to refurbish it or do it up.

vampire N a dead person who supposedly rises at night to suck the blood of the living.

van N a commercial road vehicle with luggage space at the rear, lighter than a lorry.

vandal N someone who wantonly damages or destroys personal and public property. ■ **vandalism** N.

vandalize or **-ise** VB to inflict wilful and senseless damage on (property, etc).

vane N 1 a weathervane. 2 each of the blades of a windmill, propeller or revolving fan.

vanguard N 1 the part of a military force that advances first. 2 a person or group that leads the way, esp by setting standards.

vanilla N 1 a a Mexican climbing orchid having large fragrant white or yellow flowers followed by pod-like fruits; b (in full **vanilla pod**) its fruit. 2 a flavouring substance obtained from the pod, used in ice cream and other foods.
➤ ADJ flavoured with or like vanilla.

vanish VB, INTR 1 to disappear suddenly. 2 to cease to exist; to die out.

vanity N (**-ies**) 1 the quality of being vain or conceited. 2 a thing one is conceited about.

vanquish VB, LITERARY to defeat someone.

vantage point N a position affording a clear overall view or prospect.

vapid ADJ dull; uninteresting; insipid.

vapour or (N AMER) **vapor** N 1 a substance in the form of a mist, fume or smoke, esp one coming off from a solid or liquid. 2 CHEM a gas that can be condensed to a liquid by pressure alone: **water vapour**. ■ **vaporize** or **-ise** VB.

variable ADJ 1 referring to something that varies or tends to vary; not steady or regular; changeable. 2 referring to something that can be varied or altered.
➤ N 1 a thing that can vary unpredictably in nature or degree. 2 a factor which may change or be changed by another. 3 MATH a symbol, usu a letter, for which one or more quantities or values may be substituted. ■ **variably** ADV.

variance N (often **at variance**) the state of being different or inconsistent.

variant N 1 a form of a thing that varies from another form. 2 an example that differs from a standard.
➤ ADJ 1 different. 2 differing from a standard.

variation N 1 the act or process of varying or changing. 2 something that varies from a standard. 3 the extent to which something varies from a standard.

varicose ADJ, PATHOL of a superficial vein: abnormally swollen and twisted so that it produces a raised knot on the skin surface.

varied ADJ having variety; diverse.

variegated ADJ, BOT of leaves or flowers:

marked with patches of two or more colours.

variety N (-*ies*) **1** any of various types of the same thing; a kind or sort. **2** the quality of departing from a fixed pattern or routine; diversity. **3** a plant or animal differing from another in certain characteristics, but not enough to be classed as a separate species. **4** a form of theatrical entertainment consisting of a succession of acts of different kinds.

varifocals PL N a pair of glasses with **varifocal** lenses, whose variable focal lengths allow a wide range of focusing distances.

various ADJ **1** several different: **worked for various companies**. **2** different; disparate; diverse: **Their interests are many and various**. ■ **variously** ADV.

varnish N **1** a liquid containing resin, painted on a surface to give a hard transparent and often glossy finish. **2** any liquid providing a similar finish: **nail varnish**.
➤ VB to apply varnish to something.

varsity N (-*ies*) COLLOQ **1** BRIT a university, esp with reference to sport. **2** N AMER the principal team representing a college in a sport.

vary VB (-*ies, -ied*) **1** INTR to change, or be of different kinds, esp according to different circumstances. **2** TR & INTR to make or become more diverse. ■ **varying** N, ADJ.

vas N (*vasa*) ANAT, BIOL a vessel, tube or duct carrying liquid.

vascular ADJ, BIOL relating to the blood vessels of animals or the sap–conducting tissues (xylem and phloem) of plants.

vas deferens N (*vasa deferentia*) BIOL the duct from each testicle that carries spermatozoa to the penis.

vase N a glass or pottery container, esp one for holding cut flowers.

vasectomy N (-*ies*) MED a surgical operation involving the tying and cutting of the vas deferens as a means of sterilization.

Vaseline N, TRADEMARK an ointment consisting mainly of petroleum jelly.

vassal N, FEUDALISM someone acting as a servant to, and fighting on behalf of, a medieval lord in return for land or protection or both.

vast ADJ **1** extremely great in size, extent or amount. **2** COLLOQ considerable; appreciable: **a vast difference**. ■ **vastly** ADV. ■ **vastness** N.

vat N a large barrel or tank for holding liquids.

Vatican N (usu **the Vatican**) the palace and official residence of the pope in Rome.

vault[1] N **1** an arched roof or ceiling, esp in a church. **2** an underground chamber used for storage or as a burial tomb. **3** a fortified room for storing valuables, eg in a bank.

vault[2] VB, TR & INTR to spring or leap over something, esp assisted by the hands or a pole.
➤ N an act of vaulting.

vaulting ADJ esp referring to ambition or pride: excessive or immoderate.

vaunt VB, TR & INTR to boast about something.

VDU ABBREV visual display unit.

veal N the flesh of a calf, used as food.

vector N, MATH a quantity which has both magnitude and direction, eg force, velocity, or acceleration.

veer VB, INTR **1** to move abruptly in a different direction: **The car veered off the road into the ditch**. **2** of the wind: to change direction clockwise in the northern hemisphere and anticlockwise in the southern. **3** NAUT to change course, esp away from the wind.

veg N (PL **veg**) COLLOQ a vegetable.

vegan N someone who does not eat meat, fish, dairy products or any foods containing animal fats or extracts, often also avoiding using wool, leather and other animal–based substances.
➤ ADJ of or for vegans. ■ **veganism** N.

vegetable N **1 a** a plant or any of its parts, other than fruits and seeds, that is used for food, eg roots, tubers, stems or leaves; **b** the edible part of such a plant. **2** OFFENSIVE, COLLOQ a person almost totally incapable of any activity because of severe brain damage.

vegetable marrow see **marrow**

vegetable oil N an oil obtained from a plant, used esp in cooking and cosmetics.

vegetarian N someone who does not eat meat or fish.
➤ ADJ referring to or for vegetarians.
■ **vegetarianism** N.

vegetate VB, INTR of a person: to live a dull inactive life.

vegetation N, BOT 1 a collective term for plants. 2 the plants of a particular area.

vegetative ADJ 1 referring to plants or vegetation. 2 BIOL denoting asexual reproduction in plants or animals, as in bulbs, corms, yeasts, etc. 3 BIOL denoting unconscious or involuntary bodily functions as resembling the process of vegetable growth.

veggie or **vegie** N, COLLOQ 1 a vegetarian. 2 a vegetable. Also written **veggy**.

vehement ADJ expressed with strong feeling or firm conviction; forceful; emphatic.
■ **vehemence** N. ■ **vehemently** ADV.

vehicle N 1 a conveyance for transporting people or things, esp a self-powered one. 2 someone or something used as a means of communicating ideas or opinions. ■ **vehicular** ADJ.

veil N 1 a fabric covering for a woman's head or face, forming part of traditional dress in some societies or worn eg by a bride. 2 the hoodlike part of a nun's habit. 3 anything that covers or obscures something: **a veil of secrecy**.
➤ VB 1 to cover something, or cover the face of someone, with a veil. 2 to disguise or obscure something: **veiled his threats in pleasantries**.
■ **veiled** ADJ.
◆ **take the veil** to become a nun.

vein N 1 ANAT a blood vessel that carries deoxygenated blood back towards the heart. 2 a thin sheetlike deposit of one or more minerals, deposited in a fracture or joint in the surrounding rock. 3 a streak of different colour, eg in cheese. 4 in a leaf: any of a large number of thin tubes containing the vascular tissues. 5 a mood or tone: **written in a sarcastic vein**.

Velcro N, TRADEMARK a fastening material consisting of two nylon surfaces, one of tiny hooks, the other of thin fibres.

vellum N a fine kind of parchment.

velocity N (-ies) 1 TECHNICAL rate of motion, ie distance per unit of time, in a particular direction. 2 LOOSELY speed.

velour or **velours** N any fabric with a velvet-like pile, used esp for upholstery.

velvet N a fabric with a very short soft closely woven pile on one side.
➤ ADJ 1 made of velvet. 2 soft or smooth like velvet. ■ **velvety** ADJ.

velveteen N cotton fabric like velvet.

venal ADJ 1 of a person: willing to be persuaded by corrupt means, esp bribery. 2 of behaviour: dishonest; corrupt. ■ **venality** N.

vendetta N 1 a bitter feud in which the family of a murdered person takes revenge by killing the murderer or one of their relatives. 2 any long-standing bitter feud or quarrel.

vending machine N a coin-operated machine that dispenses small articles such as snacks, condoms, cigarettes.

vendor N, LAW a seller, esp of property.

veneer N 1 a thin layer of a fine material, esp wood, fixed to the surface of an inferior material to give an attractive finish. 2 a false or misleading external appearance.

venerable ADJ deserving respect, esp on account of age or religious association.

venerate VB to regard someone or something with deep respect or awe. ■ **veneration** N.

Venetian blind N a window blind consisting of horizontal slats strung together, one beneath the other, and tilted to let in or shut out light.

vengeance N punishment inflicted as a revenge; retribution.
◆ **with a vengeance** 1 forcefully or violently. 2 to a great degree.

vengeful ADJ 1 eager for revenge. 2 carried out in revenge.

venial sin N a sin that is excusable.

venison N the flesh of a deer, used as food.

venom N 1 a poisonous liquid that some creatures, including scorpions and certain snakes, inject in a bite or sting. 2 spitefulness. ■ **venomous** ADJ.

vent N 1 an opening that allows air, gas or liquid into or out of a confined space. 2 the passage inside a volcano through which lava and gases escape. 3 a chimney flue. 4 a slit in a garment, esp upwards from the hem at the back, for style or ease of movement.
➤ VB to release and express (esp emotion) freely: **vented his frustration shaking his fists.**

ventilate VB 1 to allow fresh air to circulate throughout (a room, building, etc). 2 to supply air to (the lungs). 3 to expose (an idea, etc) to public examination. ■ **ventilation** N.

ventilator N 1 a device that circulates or draws in fresh air. 2 a machine that ventilates the lungs of a person whose respiratory system is damaged.

ventricle N, ANAT in mammals: either of the two lower chambers of the heart which have thick muscular walls. ■ **ventricular** ADJ.

ventriloquism N the art of speaking in a way that makes the sound appear to come from elsewhere, esp a dummy's mouth. ■ **ventriloquist** N.

venture N 1 an exercise or operation involving danger or uncertainty. 2 a business project, esp one involving risk or speculation.
➤ VB 1 TR & INTR to be so bold as to; to dare: **ventured to criticize the chairman.** 2 to put forward or present (a suggestion, etc) in the face of possible opposition.

venturesome ADJ prepared to take risks.

venue N the chosen location for a sports event, a concert or other entertainment.

Venus N, ASTRON the second planet from the Sun.

veracious ADJ, FORMAL truthful.

veracity N, FORMAL truthfulness.

veranda or **verandah** N a sheltered terrace attached to a building.

verb N a word or group of words that belongs to a grammatical class denoting an action, experience, occurrence or state, eg **do, feel, happen, love.**

verbal ADJ 1 relating to or consisting of words: **verbal abuse.** 2 spoken, not written: **verbal communication.** ■ **verbally** ADV.

verbalize or **-ise** VB to express in words.

verbatim ADJ, ADV using exactly the same words; word-for-word.

verbiage N language that is needlessly wordy.

verbose ADJ using or containing too many words; boringly or irritatingly long-winded. ■ **verbosity** N.

verdant ADJ 1 covered with lush green grass or vegetation. 2 of a rich green colour.

verdict N 1 a decision arrived at in a court of law. 2 any decision, opinion or judgement.

verdigris N, CHEM a blueish-green coating of basic copper salts that forms as a result of corrosion when copper, brass or bronze surfaces are exposed to air.

verdure N, LITERARY lush green vegetation.

verge N 1 a limit, boundary or border. 2 a strip of grass bordering a road. 3 a point or stage immediately beyond or after which something exists or occurs: **on the verge of tears.**
◆ **verge on sth** to be close to being it.

verger N a church official who assists the minister and acts as caretaker.

verify VB (-**ies, -ied**) 1 to check or confirm the truth or accuracy of something. 2 to assert or prove the truth of something. ■ **verifiable** ADJ. ■ **verification** N.

verisimilitude N, FORMAL the appearance of being real or true.

veritable ADJ, FORMAL accurately described as such: **a veritable genius!** ■ **veritably** ADV.

vermicelli N 1 pasta in very thin strands, thinner

than spaghetti. **2** (also **chocolate vermicelli**) tiny splinters of chocolate used for decorating cakes, etc.

vermiform appendix N, ANAT a small blind tube leading off the caecum, part of the large intestine. Usually shortened to **appendix**.

vermilion N a bright scarlet colour.

vermin SING OR PL N **1** a collective name for wild animals that spread disease or generally cause a nuisance, esp rats and other rodents. **2** detestable people. ■ **verminous** ADJ.

vermouth N an alcoholic drink consisting of wine flavoured with aromatic herbs.

vernacular N (usu **the vernacular**) the form of a language as commonly spoken, as opposed to the formal or literary language.

vernal ADJ relating to or appropriate to spring; happening or appearing in spring.

verruca N (**-as** or **-ae**) **1** PATHOL a wart, esp one on the sole of the foot. **2** BOT a wartlike growth.

versatile ADJ **1** adapting easily to different tasks. **2** having numerous uses or abilities. ■ **versatility** N.

verse N **1** a division of a poem; a stanza. **2** poetry, as opposed to prose. **3** a poem. **4** a division of a song. **5** any of the numbered subdivisions of the chapters of the Bible.

versed ADJ (always **versed in sth**) familiar with it or skilled in it: **well versed in chemistry**.

version N any of several types or forms in which a thing exists or is available, eg one person's account of an incident.

versus PREP **1** in a contest or lawsuit: against. **2** (abbrev **v** or **vs**) COLLOQ in comparison to.

vertebra N (**vertebrae**) ANAT in vertebrates: any of the small bones or cartilaginous segments that form the backbone.

vertebrate N, ZOOL any animal, including fish, amphibians, reptiles, birds and mammals, that has a backbone.

vertex N (**-texes** or **-tices**) **1** the highest point; the peak. **2** GEOM **a** the point opposite the base of a geometric figure, eg the pointed tip of a cone; **b** the point where the two sides forming an angle meet in a polygon, or where three or more surfaces meet in a polyhedron; **c** the intersection of a curve with its axis.

vertical ADJ **1** perpendicular to the horizon; upright. **2** running from top to bottom. ➤ N a vertical line or direction. ■ **vertically** ADV.

vertigo N a whirling sensation felt when the sense of balance is disturbed.

verve N great liveliness or enthusiasm.

very ADV **1** to a high degree or extent: **very kind. 2** (used with own, same and with superlative adjectives) absolutely; truly: **my very own room • the very same day.** ➤ ADJ (USED FOR EMPHASIS) **1** absolute: **the very top. 2** precise; actual: **this very minute. 3** most suitable: **That's the very tool for the job. 4** mere: **shocked by the very thought.** ◆ **very good** or **very well** expressions of consent and approval.

vespers SING N an evening service in some Christian churches; evensong.

vessel N **1** a container, esp for liquid. **2** a ship or large boat. **3** a tube or duct carrying liquid, eg blood or sap, in animals and plants.

vest N **1** an undergarment for the top half of the body. **2** US, AUSTRAL a waistcoat. ◆ **vest sth in sb** or **sb with sth** to give or bestow legally or officially: **by the power vested in me.**

vested interest N an interest a person has in the fortunes of something because that person is directly affected, esp financially.

vestibule N an entrance hall.

vestige N **1** a slight amount; a hint or shred. **2** BIOL a small functionless part in an animal or plant, once a fully developed organ in ancestors. ■ **vestigial** ADJ.

vestment N a garment worn ceremonially by members of the clergy and church choir.

vestry N (**-ies**) a room in a church where the vestments are kept, often also used for meetings, Sunday school classes, etc.

vet[1] N short for **veterinary surgeon**.
➤ VB (*-tt-*) to check someone for suitability.

vet[2] N, COLLOQ N AMER, ESP US short for **veteran**: a war vet.

vetch N a climbing plant of the pea family. Also called **tare**.

veteran N 1 someone with many years of experience in a particular activity. 2 an old and experienced member of the armed forces. 3 N AMER, ESP US an ex–serviceman or –woman.

veteran car N a very old motor car, specifically one made before 1905.

veterinary ADJ concerned with diseases of animals.

veterinary surgeon or (N AMER) **veterinarian** N a person qualified to treat diseases of animals.

veto N (-oes) 1 a the right to formally reject a proposal or forbid an action; b the act of using such a right. 2 COLLOQ any prohibition or refusal of permission.
➤ VB (-oes, -oed) 1 to formally reject or forbid. 2 LOOSELY to forbid.

vex VB 1 to annoy or irritate someone. 2 to worry someone. ■ **vexation** N. ■ **vexing** ADJ.

vexatious ADJ vexing; annoying.

vexed ADJ 1 annoyed; angry; troubled. 2 of an issue, etc: much discussed or debated.

via PREP by way of or by means of; through.

viable ADJ 1 of a plan, etc: having a chance of success; feasible; practicable. 2 of a plant, etc: able to exist or grow in particular conditions. 3 of a fetus or baby: able to survive independently outside the womb.

viaduct N a bridge–like structure of stone arches supporting a road or railway across a valley, etc.

vial same as **phial**

viands PL N, FORMAL items of food; provisions.

vibes PL N (also **vibe** SING N) COLLOQ feelings, sensations or an atmosphere experienced or communicated: *bad vibes in the room*. Also (in full) **vibrations**.

vibrant ADJ 1 extremely lively or exciting; animated or energetic. 2 of a colour: strong and bright. 3 vibrating. ■ **vibrancy** N.

vibrate VB 1 TR & INTR to move a short distance back and forth very rapidly. 2 INTR to ring or resound when struck. 3 INTR to tremble.

vibration N 1 a vibrating motion. 2 a a single movement back and forth in vibrating; b either of the back or forward movements.

vibrato N, MUS a faint trembling effect in singing or the playing of string and wind instruments, achieved by vibrating the throat muscles or the fingers.

vibrator N any device that produces a vibrating motion.

vicar N 1 C OF E the minister of a parish. 2 RC CHURCH a bishop's deputy.

vicarage N a vicar's residence or benefice.

vicarious ADJ experienced not directly but through witnessing the experience of another person: *vicarious pleasure in seeing his children learn*.

vice[1] or (N AMER) **vise** N a tool with heavy movable metal jaws, usu fixed to a bench, for gripping an object being worked on.

vice[2] N 1 a habit or activity considered immoral, evil or depraved, esp involving prostitution or drugs. 2 such activities collectively. 3 a bad habit; a fault in one's character.

vice-admiral N an officer in the navy.

vice-chancellor N the deputy chancellor of a British university, responsible for most administrative duties.

vice-president N 1 a president's deputy or assistant. 2 an officer next below the president.

viceroy N a governor of a province or colony ruling in the name of, and with the authority of, a monarch or national government.

vice squad N a branch of the police force that investigates crimes relating to vice.

vice versa ADV the other way round: **from me to you and vice versa.**

vicinity N (*-ies*) **1** a neighbourhood. **2** the area immediately surrounding a place.

vicious ADJ **1** violent or ferocious. **2** spiteful or malicious. **3** extremely severe or harsh. ■ **viciously** ADV. ■ **viciousness** N.

vicious circle N a situation in which any attempt to resolve a problem creates others which in turn recreate the first one.

vicissitude N an unpredictable change of fortune or circumstance.

victim N a person or animal subjected to death, suffering, ill-treatment or trickery.

victimize or **-ise** VB to single someone or something out for hostile, unfair or vindictive treatment. ■ **victimization** N.

victor N the winner in a war or contest.

victoria N a large oval red and yellow variety of plum with a sweet flavour. Also called **victoria plum**.

Victorian ADJ **1** relating to or characteristic of Queen Victoria or her reign (1837–1901). **2 a** typical of the strictness, prudery or conventionality associated with this period; **b** typical of the hypocrisy and bigotry often thought to underlie these values.

Victoriana PL N objects, esp bric-à-brac from the Victorian period.

victorious ADJ **1** having won a war or contest: **the victorious army. 2** referring to, marking or representing a victory: **a victorious outcome.**

victory N (*-ies*) **1** success against an opponent in a war or contest. **2** an occurrence of this.

victuals PL N (occasionally **victual**) food.

videlicet see **viz**

video N **1** short for **video cassette**. **2** short for **video cassette recorder**. **3** a film or programme pre-recorded on video cassette: **now available as a video. 4** the process of recording, reproducing or broadcasting visual, esp televised, images on magnetic tape.

➢ ADJ relating to the process of or equipment for recording by video.
➢ VB to make a video cassette recording of (a TV programme, a film, etc).

video camera N, PHOTOG a portable camera that records moving visual images directly on to videotape.

video cassette N a cassette containing videotape, for use in a video cassette recorder.

video cassette recorder N a machine for recording and playing back TV broadcasts, and playing pre-recorded tapes of films.

video game N any electronically operated game involving the manipulation of images produced by a computer program.

videophone N a communication device like a telephone which transmits a visual image as well as sound.

video recorder N a video cassette recorder.

videotape N magnetic tape on which visual images and sound can be recorded.

vie VB (*vying*) INTR (often **vie with sb for sth**) to compete with them for some gain.

view N **1** an act or opportunity of seeing without obstruction: **a good view of the stage. 2** something, esp a landscape, seen from a particular point: **a magnificent view from the summit. 3** a range or field of vision: **out of view. 4** a scene recorded in photograph or picture form. **5** an opinion; a point of view.
➢ VB **1** to see or look at something. **2** to inspect or examine something: **viewed the house that was for sale. 3** to consider or regard something. **4** TR & INTR to watch (a programme) on TV; to watch TV. ■ **viewer** N.
◆ **take a dim view of sth** to regard it disapprovingly or unfavourably.
◆ **with a view to sth** with the intention of achieving it.

viewfinder N a device in a camera that shows the area covered by the lens.

viewing N an act or opportunity of seeing or inspecting something, eg a house for sale.

viewpoint N **1** an opinion or point of view; a standpoint. **2** a location which is particularly good for admiring scenery.

vigil N a period of staying awake, usu to guard or watch over a person or thing.

vigilance N the state of being watchful.

vigilant ADJ ready for possible trouble or danger; alert; watchful. ■ **vigilantly** ADV.

vigilante N a private citizen who assumes the task of keeping order in a community.

vignette N **1** a decorative design on a book's title page, traditionally of vine leaves. **2** a photographic portrait with the background deliberately faded. **3** a short literary essay, esp one describing a person's character.

vigorous ADJ **1** strong and active. **2** forceful; energetic. ■ **vigorously** ADV.

vigour or (N AMER) **vigor** N **1** great strength and energy of body or mind. **2** liveliness or forcefulness of action.

Viking N any of the Scandinavian seafaring peoples who raided and settled in much of NW Europe between the 8c and 11c.

vile ADJ **1** morally evil or wicked. **2** physically repulsive; disgusting. **3** COLLOQ extremely bad or unpleasant. ■ **vilely** ADV. ■ **vileness** N.

vilify VB (*-ies, -ied*) to say abusive things about someone or something. ■ **vilification** N.

villa N **1** a country residence. **2** a holiday home, esp one abroad.

village N a group of houses, shops and other buildings, smaller than a town and larger than a hamlet, esp in or near the countryside. ■ **villager** N.

villain N **1** the principal wicked character in a story. **2** any violent, wicked or unscrupulous person. **3** COLLOQ a criminal.

villainous ADJ like or worthy of a villain.

villainy N (*-ies*) wicked or vile behaviour.

vim N, COLLOQ energy; liveliness.

vinaigrette N a salad dressing made by mixing oil, vinegar and seasonings.

vindaloo N a hot Indian curry, usu made with meat, poultry or fish.

vindicate VB **1** to clear someone of blame or criticism. **2** to show something to have been worthwhile or justified. **3** to maintain or uphold (a point of view, cause, etc). ■ **vindication** N.

vindictive ADJ **1** feeling or showing spite or hatred. **2** seeking revenge.

vine N a climbing plant that produces grapes.

vinegar N a sour liquid produced by the fermentation of alcoholic beverages, used as a condiment and preservative.

vineyard N a plantation of grape-bearing vines, esp for wine-making.

vintage N **1** the grape-harvest of a particular year. **2** the wine produced from a year's harvest. **3** the time of year when grapes are harvested. **4** a particular period of origin: literature of a postwar vintage.
➤ ADJ **1** of wine: good quality and from a specified year. **2** typical of someone's best work or most characteristic behaviour: That remark was vintage Churchill.

vintage car N, BRIT an old motor car, specifically one built between 1919 and 1930.

vintner N, FORMAL a wine-merchant.

vinyl N **1** any of a group of tough plastics in various forms, eg paint additives and carpet fibres. **2 a** COLLOQ plastic records regarded collectively; **b** AS ADJ: vinyl record.

viol N a Renaissance stringed musical instrument played with a bow.

viola N a musical instrument of the violin family, larger than the violin and lower in pitch.

violate VB **1** to disregard or break (a law, agreement or oath). **2** to treat (something sacred or private) with disrespect. **3** to disturb or disrupt (eg a person's privacy). **4** to rape or sexually abuse someone. ■ **violation** N.

violence N **1** the state or quality of being violent. **2** violent behaviour.

violent ADJ **1** marked by or using extreme physical force. **2** using or involving the use of

such force to cause physical harm.
3 impulsively aggressive and unrestrained in nature or behaviour. **4** intense; extreme: *They took a violent dislike to me.* ■ **violently** ADV.

violet N **1** a plant with large purple, blue or white petals. **2** a bluish-purple colour.

violin N a four-stringed musical instrument with a shaped body, held with one end under the chin and played with a bow. ■ **violinist** N.

VIP ABBREV very important person.

viper N **1** a poisonous snake with long tubular fangs through which venom is injected into the prey. **2** an adder.

virago N (-**oes** or -**os**) LITERARY a loudly fierce or abusive woman.

viral ADJ belonging or relating to a virus.

virgin N a person, esp a woman, who has never had sexual intercourse.
➤ ADJ never having been used.

virginal ADJ **1** belonging or relating or appropriate to a virgin. **2** in a state of virginity.

Virgin Birth N, CHRISTIANITY the birth of Christ to the Virgin Mary, regarded as an act of God.

virginity N (-**ies**) the state of being a virgin.

Virgo N, ASTROL the sixth sign of the zodiac.

virile ADJ **1** of a man: having a high level of sexual desire. **2** displaying or requiring qualities regarded as typically masculine. **3** of a man: able to produce children. ■ **virility** N.

virtual ADJ **1** being so in effect or in practice, but not in name: *a virtual state of war.* **2** nearly so; almost but not quite: *the virtual collapse of the steel industry.* **3** COMP, SLANG referring or relating to interaction, use, etc via the Internet: *pay by virtual money.* ■ **virtually** ADJ.

virtual reality N a computer simulation of a real or artificial environment that gives the user the impression of actually being within the environment and interacting with it.

virtue N **1** a quality regarded as morally good. **2** moral goodness; righteousness. **3** an admirable quality or desirable feature: *The*

virtue of this one is its long life.
◆ **by virtue of sth** because of it.

virtuoso N **1 a** someone with remarkable artistic skill, esp a brilliant musical performer; **b** AS ADJ: *a virtuoso performance.* **2** someone with a great knowledge or collection of fine art. ■ **virtuosity** N.

virtuous ADJ **1** possessing or showing virtue; morally sound. **2** esp of a woman: chaste.

virulent ADJ **1** of a disease: having a rapidly harmful effect. **2** of a disease or the organism causing it: extremely infectious. **3** of a substance: highly poisonous. **4** bitterly hostile. ■ **virulence** N.

virus N **1** an infectious particle, only visible under an electron microscope, that invades the cells of animals, plants and bacteria, and can only survive and reproduce within such cells. **2** the organism that causes and transmits an infectious disease. **3** LOOSELY a disease caused by such an organism. **4** a self-replicating program that attaches to a computer system and when activated can corrupt or destroy data stored on the hard disk.

visa N a permit stamped into a passport, or a similar document, allowing the holder to enter or leave the country which issues it.

visage N, LITERARY **1** the face. **2** the usual expression of a face; a countenance.

vis-à-vis PREP in relation to.

viscera PL N, ANAT the internal organs of the body, esp those found in the abdominal cavity.

visceral ADJ **1** relating to the viscera. **2** relating to the feelings, esp the basic human instincts as distinct from the intellect.

viscid ADJ glutinous; sticky.

viscose N cellulose in a viscous state, able to be made into thread.

viscosity N (-**ies**) a measure of the resistance of a fluid to flow, caused by internal friction.

viscount N a member of the British nobility ranked below an earl and above a baron.

viscountess N **1** the wife or widow of a

viscount. **2** a woman of the rank of viscount in her own right.

viscous ADJ thick; semi-liquid.

vise see **vice**[1]

visibility N **1** the state or fact of being visible. **2** the range in which one can see clearly in given conditions of light and weather.

visible ADJ **1** able to be seen. **2** able to be realized or perceived; apparent: his visible discomfort. ■ **visibly** ADV.

vision N **1** the ability or faculty of perceiving with the eye; sight. **2** an image conjured up vividly in the imagination. **3** the ability to perceive what is likely, and plan wisely for it; foresight. **4** an image communicated supernaturally, esp by God; an apparition. **5 a** the picture on a TV screen; **b** the quality of such a picture. **6** someone or something of overwhelming beauty: a vision in pink taffeta.

visionary ADJ **1** showing great foresight or imagination. **2** possible only in the imagination; impracticable; fanciful.
➤ N (**-ies**) a visionary person.

visit VB **1** TR & INTR to go or come to see (a person or place) socially or professionally. **2** TR & INTR to go or come to stay with someone temporarily.
➤ N **1** an act of visiting. **2** a temporary stay. **3** a sightseeing excursion.

visitation N **1** an official visit or inspection. **2** an instance of seeing a supernatural vision.

visiting card N a card with one's name, address, etc printed on it, which is left instead of a visit. N Amer equivalent **calling card**.

visitor N someone who visits a person or place.

visor or **vizor** N **1** the movable part of a helmet, covering the face. **2** a flap at the top of a vehicle's windscreen that can be lowered to shield the driver's eyes from the Sun's rays. **3** a peaked shield that is worn on the head to protect the eyes from the Sun's rays.

vista N a view into the distance.

visual ADJ relating to or received through sight or vision: a visual image. ■ **visually** ADV.

visual aid N a picture, film or other visual material used as an aid to teaching or presenting information.

visual display unit N a screen on which information from a computer is displayed.

visualize or **-ise** VB to form a clear mental image of someone or something. ■ **visualization** N.

vital ADJ **1** relating to or essential for life: the vital organs. **2** determining life or death, or success or failure: a vital error. **3** essential; of the greatest importance. **4** full of life; energetic. ➤ N (**vitals**) the vital organs, including the brain, heart and lungs. ■ **vitally** ADV.

vitality N **1** liveliness and energy. **2** the state of being alive; the ability to stay alive.

vitalize or **-ise** VB to fill someone with life or energy. ■ **vitalization** N.

vital statistics PL N **1** statistics concerning births, marriages, deaths and other matters relating to population. **2** COLLOQ a woman's bust, waist and hip measurements.

vitamin N any of various organic compounds that occur in small amounts in many foods, are also manufactured synthetically and are essential in small amounts for the normal growth and functioning of the body.

vitiate VB **1** to impair the effectiveness or quality of (eg an argument). **2** to make (eg a legal contract) ineffectual or invalid.

vitriol N **1** concentrated sulphuric acid. **2** extremely bitter speech or criticism.

vitriolic ADJ extremely bitter or hateful.

vituperate VB **1** to attack someone with abusive criticism or disapproval. **2** INTR to use abusive language. ■ **vituperation** N. ■ **vituperative** ADJ.

viva EXCLAM long live (someone or something named): viva Rodriguez!

vivacious ADJ attractively lively and animated. ■ **vivacity** N.

vivid ADJ **1** of a colour: strong and bright. **2** creating or providing a clear and immediate mental picture: *gave a vivid account of the incident*. ■ **vividly** ADV. ■ **vividness** N.

vivify VB (*-ies, -ied*) **1** to endue something with life. **2** to make something more vivid or startling.

vivisection N the practice of dissecting living animals for experimental purposes.

vixen N **1** a female fox. **2** a fierce woman.

viz. ADV (in full **videlicet**) used esp in writing: namely; that is.

vizier N a high-ranking government official in certain Muslim countries.

vizor see **visor**

V-neck N **1** the open neck of a garment cut or formed to a point at the front. **2** a garment, esp a pullover, with such a neck.
➤ ADJ (also **V-necked**): *a V-neck jumper*.

vocabulary N (*-ies*) **1** the words used in speaking or writing a particular language. **2** the words known to or used by a particular person or group. **3** a list of words with translations in another language alongside.

vocal ADJ **1** relating to or produced by the voice. **2** expressing opinions or criticism freely and forcefully: *She was very vocal in her support for the homeless*.
➤ N (**vocals**) the parts of a musical composition that are sung, as distinct from the instrumental accompaniment. ■ **vocally** ADV.

vocal cords PL N, ANAT the two folds of tissue within the larynx that vibrate and produce sound when air is expelled from the lungs.

vocalist N a singer, esp in a pop or jazz band.

vocalize or **-ise** VB **1** to utter or produce something with the voice. **2** to express in words; to articulate. ■ **vocalization** N.

vocation N **1** a particular occupation or profession, esp one regarded as needing dedication and skill. **2** a feeling of being especially suited for a particular type of work. **3** RELIG a divine calling to adopt a religious life or perform good works. ■ **vocational** ADJ.

vociferous ADJ loud and forceful.

vodka N a clear alcoholic spirit of Russian origin, traditionally made from rye, but sometimes from potatoes.

vogue N (usu **the vogue**) the current fashion or trend in any sphere.

voice N **1** a sound produced by the vocal organs and uttered through the mouth, esp by humans in speech or song. **2** the ability to speak; the power of speech: *lost his voice*. **3** a way of speaking or singing peculiar to each individual: *couldn't recognize the voice*. **4** a tone of speech reflecting an emotion: *in a nervous voice*. **5** the sound of someone speaking: *heard a voice*. **6** the ability to sing, esp to sing well: *has a lovely voice*.
➤ VB to express something in speech: *He voiced his disapproval*.
◆ **with one voice** unanimously.

voice box N, COLLOQ the larynx.

voice-over N the voice of an unseen narrator in a film, TV advertisement or programme, etc.

void ADJ **1** not valid or legally binding: *declared the contract null and void*. **2** containing nothing; empty or unoccupied. **3** (usu **void of sth**) lacking in it: *void of humour*.
➤ N **1** an empty space. **2** a feeling of absence or emptiness strongly felt.
➤ VB to make empty or clear.

voile N any very thin semi-transparent fabric.

volatile ADJ **1** changing quickly from a solid or liquid into a vapour. **2** easily becoming angry or violent. **3** of a situation, etc: liable to change, esp verging on violence. ■ **volatility** N.

vol-au-vent N a small round puff-pastry case with a savoury filling.

volcanic ADJ relating to or produced by a volcano or volcanoes.

volcano N (*-oes*) a vent in the Earth's crust through which magma is forced out onto the surface, usu taking the form of a conical hill due to the build-up of solidified lava.

vole N a small rodent with a blunt snout.

volition N the act of willing or choosing; the exercising of one's will: She did it of her own volition. ■ **volitional** ADJ.

volley N 1 a a firing of several guns or other weapons simultaneously; b the bullets, missiles, etc discharged. 2 an aggressive outburst, esp of criticism or insults. 3 SPORT a striking of the ball before it bounces.
➤ VB 1 TR & INTR to fire (weapons) in a volley. 2 TR & INTR, SPORT to strike (a ball) before it bounces. 3 to utter (words) in an aggressive outburst.

volleyball N, SPORT a game for two teams of six players each, in which a ball is volleyed back and forth over a high net with the hands.

volt N in the SI system: a unit of electric potential, the difference in potential that will carry a current of one ampere across a resistance of one ohm.

voltage N, ELEC potential difference expressed as a number of volts.

volte-face N a sudden and complete reversal of opinion or policy.

voluble ADJ 1 speaking or spoken insistently, uninterruptedly or with ease. 2 tending to talk at great length. ■ **volubility** N. ■ **volubly** ADV.

volume N 1 the amount of three-dimensional space occupied by an object, gas or liquid. 2 a loudness of sound; b the control that adjusts it on a radio, etc. 3 a a book, whether complete in itself or one of several forming a larger work; b IN COMPOUNDS, AS ADJ: a six-volume encyclopedia. 4 an amount or quantity, esp when large: the volume of traffic.

voluminous ADJ of clothing: flowing or billowing out; ample.

voluntary ADJ 1 done or acting by free choice, not by compulsion. 2 working with no expectation of being paid or otherwise rewarded. 3 of work: unpaid. 4 of an organization: staffed by unpaid workers; supported by donations of money freely given. 5 of a movement, muscle or limb: produced or controlled by the will. ■ **voluntarily** ADV.

volunteer VB 1 TR & INTR (often **volunteer for sth**) to offer one's help or services freely, without being persuaded or forced. 2 INTR to go into military service by choice, without being conscripted. 3 to give (information, etc) unasked. 4 COLLOQ to assign someone to perform a task without first asking them: I'm volunteering you for playground duty.
➤ N 1 someone who volunteers. 2 someone carrying out voluntary work. 3 a member of a non-professional army of voluntary soldiers.

voluptuous ADJ 1 relating to or suggestive of sensual pleasure. 2 of a woman: full-figured and sexually attractive; curvaceous.

vomit VB 1 TR & INTR to eject the contents of the stomach forcefully through the mouth through a reflex action; to be sick. 2 to emit or throw something out with force or violence.

voodoo N witchcraft of a type orig practised by the Black peoples of the West Indies and southern US.

voracious ADJ 1 eating or craving food in large quantities. 2 extremely eager in some respect: a voracious reader. ■ **voracity** N.

vortex N (**vortexes** or **vortices**) 1 a whirlpool or whirlwind; any whirling mass or motion. 2 a situation into which all surrounding people or things are helplessly and dangerously drawn. ■ **vortical** ADJ.

vote N 1 a formal indication of choice or opinion, eg in an election or debate. 2 the right to express a choice or opinion, esp in a national election. 3 a choice or opinion expressed formally, eg by a show of hands, a mark on a ballot paper, etc.
➤ VB 1 INTR to cast a vote in an election: Have you voted yet? 2 to decide, state, grant or bring about something by a majority of votes: voted to accept the proposal. 3 COLLOQ to declare or pronounce by general consent: The show was voted a success. 4 COLLOQ to propose or suggest something: I vote that we go for a swim. ■ **voter** N.
◆ **vote for** or **against sth** or **sb** to cast a vote in favour of or in opposition to.

vouch VB 1 INTR (usu **vouch for sb** or **sth**) to give a firm assurance of their authenticity, trustworthiness, etc. 2 to give (evidence) in support of a statement, assertion, etc.

voucher N 1 a ticket or paper serving as proof, eg of the purchase or receipt of goods. 2 esp IN COMPOUNDS a ticket worth a specific amount of money, exchangeable for goods or services up to the same value: **gift voucher.**

vouchsafe VB, TR & INTR, LITERARY to agree or condescend to do, give, grant or allow.

vow N 1 a solemn and binding promise. 2 (often **vows**) a solemn or formal promise of fidelity or affection: **marriage vows.**
➤ VB, TR & INTR to promise or declare solemnly, or threaten emphatically; to swear.

vowel N 1 any speech-sound made with an open mouth and no contact between mouth, lips, teeth or tongue. 2 a letter of the alphabet, used alone or in combination, representing such a sound, in English, eg **a, e, i, o, u, ai, oa** and in some words **y.**

vox pop N, BROADCASTING 1 popular opinion derived from comments given informally by members of the public. 2 an interview in which such opinions are expressed.

voyage N 1 a long journey to a distant place, esp by air or sea. 2 a journey into space.
➤ VB, INTR to go on a voyage. ■ **voyager** N.

voyeur N someone who derives gratification from furtively watching the sexual attributes or activities of others. ■ **voyeurism** N.
■ **voyeuristic** ADJ.

vs or **vs**. ABBREV versus.

vulcanize or **-ise** VB to treat natural or artificial rubber with various concentrations of sulphur at high temperatures, so as to harden it and increase its elasticity.

vulgar ADJ marked by a lack of politeness or cultural refinement; coarse. ■ **vulgarly** ADV.

vulgar fraction N a fraction expressed in the form of a numerator above a denominator, rather than in decimal form.

vulgarity N (**-ies**) 1 coarseness in speech or behaviour. 2 an instance of it.

vulgarize or **-ise** VB 1 to make something vulgar. 2 to make something common or popular, or spoil it in this way.

vulnerable ADJ 1 easily hurt or harmed physically or emotionally. 2 easily tempted or persuaded. 3 (often **vulnerable to sth** or **sb**) unprotected against attack from them.
■ **vulnerability** N. ■ **vulnerably** ADV.

vulpine ADJ 1 belonging or relating to, or resembling, a fox. 2 FORMAL cunning.

vulture N 1 a large bird with a bare head and a strongly curved beak, which feeds on carrion. 2 someone who exploits the downfall or death of another.

vulva N, ANAT the two pairs of labia surrounding the opening to the vagina; the external female genitals.

W[1] or **w** N (**Ws, W's** or **w's**) the twenty-third letter of the English alphabet.

W[2] ABBREV West.

wacky or **whacky** ADJ (**-ier, -iest**) COLLOQ crazy; eccentric. ■ **wackiness** N.

wad N 1 a mass of soft material used for packing, etc. 2 a compact roll of banknotes.

wadding N material used as padding or stuffing.

waddle VB, INTR to sway from side to side in walking.
➢ N the act of waddling.

wade VB, TR & INTR to walk through (something, esp deep water, which does not allow easy movement of the feet).
◆ **wade in** to involve oneself unhesitatingly and enthusiastically in a task, etc.
◆ **wade through sth** to make one's way laboriously through it.

wader N 1 any long-legged bird that wades in marshes, or along the shore. 2 (**waders**) thigh-high waterproof boots used by anglers.

wafer N 1 a thin light finely layered biscuit. 2 CHRISTIANITY a thin disc of unleavened bread or rice paper served at Communion. 3 COMP a thin disc of silicon from which chips are cut.

waffle¹ N, COOKERY a light-textured cake made of batter, with a grid-like surface pattern.

waffle² COLLOQ, VB, INTR (also **waffle on**) to talk or write at length but to little purpose.
➢ N talk or writing of this kind.

waft VB, TR & INTR to float or make (something) float or drift gently, esp through the air.

wag VB (-gg-) TR & INTR to wave (something) to and fro vigorously.
➢ N 1 a wagging movement. 2 a habitual joker or a wit. ■ **waggish** ADJ.

wage VB to engage in or fight (a war or battle).
➢ N (often **wages**) a regular, esp weekly, payment from an employer to an employee.

wager N a bet on the result of something.
➢ VB, TR & INTR to bet; to stake in a bet.

waggle VB, TR & INTR to move or make (something) move to and fro.

wagon or **waggon** N 1 a four-wheeled vehicle, often horse-drawn, used esp for carrying loads; a cart. 2 an open truck or closed van for carrying railway freight.
◆ **on the wagon** COLLOQ abstaining from alcohol.

waif N 1 an orphaned, abandoned or homeless child. 2 any pathetically undernourished-looking person. ■ **waif-like** ADJ.

wail N a prolonged and high-pitched mournful or complaining cry.
➢ VB to make such a cry.

wainscot N wooden panelling or boarding covering the lower part of the walls of a room. ■ **wainscoting** or **wainscotting** N.

waist N 1 the narrow part of the human body between the ribs and hips. 2 the part of a garment that covers this.

waistband N the reinforced strip of cloth on a skirt, trousers, etc that fits round the waist.

waistcoat N a close-fitting sleeveless garment, worn esp by men under a jacket.

waistline N 1 the line marking the waist. 2 the measurement of a waist.

wait VB 1 to be or remain in a particular place in readiness. 2 INTR of a task, etc: to remain temporarily undealt with: **That can wait**. 3 INTR to serve as a waiter or waitress.
◆ **lie in wait** to be in hiding ready to surprise or ambush someone.

waiter and **waitress** N a man or woman who serves people with food at a restaurant.

waiting-list N a list of people waiting for something currently unavailable, eg surgery.

waiting-room N a room for people to wait in, eg at a doctor's surgery.

waive VB, LAW to voluntarily give up (a claim or right, etc).

waiver N 1 the act or an instance of waiving. 2 a written statement formally confirming this.

wake¹ VB (PA T *woke*, PA P *woken*) (also **wake (sb) up**) TR & INTR a to rouse (them) or be roused from sleep; b to stir or be stirred out of a state of inactivity or lethargy, etc.
➢ N a watch or vigil kept beside a corpse.
◆ **wake (sb) up to sth** to become or make (them) aware of a fact or situation, etc.

wake² N a trail of disturbed water left by a ship, or of disturbed air left by an aircraft.

◆ **in the wake of sb** or **sth** coming after them or it; resulting from them or it.

wakeful ADJ **1** not asleep or unable to sleep. **2** vigilant or alert. ■ **wakefulness** N.

waken VB, TR & INTR to wake.

walk VB **1** INTR to go on foot, moving one's feet alternately and always having one foot on the ground. **2** to go about on foot. **3** to lead, accompany or support (someone who is on foot). **4** to take (a dog) out for exercise. **5** INTR, COLLOQ to disappear: **my pen has walked.** ➤ N **1** the motion, or pace of walking. **2** an outing or journey on foot. **3** a distance walked or for walking. **4** a person's distinctive manner of walking. **5** a route for walking. **6** a path, esp a broad one; a promenade. ■ **walker** N.
◆ **walk on air** to feel light-hearted.
◆ **walk out 1** of factory workers, etc: to leave the workplace in a body. **2** to depart abruptly, esp in protest.
◆ **walk out on sb** to abandon them.

walkabout N a casual stroll through a crowd of ordinary people by a celebrity.

walkie-talkie N, COLLOQ a portable two-way radio carried by police, etc.

walking-stick N a stick or cane used for support or balance in walking.

walk-on ADJ of a part in a play or opera, etc: not involving any speaking or singing.

walkout N a sudden departure, esp of a workforce in declaration of a strike.

walkover N, COLLOQ an easy victory.

wall N **1** a solid vertical brick or stone construction serving as a barrier, division, protection, etc. **2** the vertical side of a building or room. **3** something similar to a wall: **a wall of fire. 4** BIOL **a** an outer covering, eg of a cell; **b** the side of a hollow organ or cavity. ➤ VB **1** to surround (something) with, or as if with, a wall. **2** (usu **wall sth off** or **in**) to separate or enclose it with a wall. ■ **walled** ADJ.
◆ **have one's back to the wall** to be in a desperate situation.

wallaby N (*wallabies* or *wallaby*) an

Australian marsupial of the kangaroo family.

wallet N **1** a flat folding case for holding banknotes, credit cards, etc. **2** any of various kinds of folders for holding papers, etc.

wallflower N **1** a sweet-smelling flowering plant. **2** COLLOQ someone who sits all evening at the edge of a dance floor, waiting in vain to be asked to dance.

wallop COLLOQ, VB to hit or strike vigorously. ➤ N a hit or whack.

walloping N a thrashing. ➤ ADJ great; whopping.

wallow VB, INTR (often **wallow in sth**) **1** to lie or roll about (in water or mud, etc). **2** to revel or luxuriate (in admiration, etc). **3** to indulge excessively (in self-pity, etc). ➤ N the act of wallowing.

wallpaper N paper, often coloured or patterned, used to decorate interior walls. ➤ VB to cover (walls) or the walls of (a room) with wallpaper.

wall-to-wall ADJ **1** covering the entire floor of a room. **2** continuous; uninterrupted.

wally N (*-ies*) BRIT, COLLOQ an ineffectual, stupid or foolish person.

walnut N **1** a deciduous tree, cultivated for its timber and edible nuts. **2** the round nut yielded by this tree. **3** the hard durable golden brown wood of this tree.

walrus N (*walruses* or *walrus*) a large carnivorous marine mammal related to the seal, with thick wrinkled skin and two long tusks.

waltz N **1** a ballroom dance in triple time, in which the dancers spin round the room. **2** a piece of music for this dance. ➤ VB, INTR **1** to dance a waltz. **2** (often **waltz in** or **off**) COLLOQ to go with easy confidence.

wan ADJ (*wanner, wannest*) pale and pinched-looking. ■ **wanly** ADV.

wand N **1** a slender rod used by magicians, conjurors and fairies, etc for performing magic. **2** a conductor's baton.

wander VB **1** to walk, move or travel about,

with no particular destination; to ramble. **2** to stray or deviate. **3** of thoughts, etc: to flit randomly.
➤ N a ramble or stroll. ■ **wanderer** N.
■ **wandering** N, ADJ.

wanderlust N an urge to rove or travel.

wane VB, INTR **1** of the Moon: to appear to grow narrower as the Sun illuminates less of its surface. **2** to decline in glory, power, etc.
➤ N the process of waning or declining.
■ **waning** ADJ.

wangle VB, COLLOQ to contrive or obtain something by persuasiveness.

wannabe or **wannabee** COLLOQ, N someone who aspires to be something.
➤ ADJ aspiring: **a wannabe rock star.**

want VB **1** to feel a need or desire for (something). **2** to need to be dealt with in a specified way: **The bin wants emptying.**
3 COLLOQ ought; need: **You want to take care.**
4 (often **want for sth**) to feel the lack of it: **That kid wants for nothing. 5** to require the presence of (someone or something): **You are wanted next door.**
➤ N **1** a need or requirement. **2** a lack: **a want of discretion. 3** a state of need; destitution.

wanted ADJ **1** needed or desired. **2** sought by the police.

wanting ADJ **1** missing; lacking. **2** not up to requirements: **has been found wanting.**

wanton ADJ **1** thoughtlessly and needlessly cruel. **2** motiveless: **wanton destruction.**
3 sexually immoral; lewd or licentious.

war N **1** an open state of armed conflict, esp between nations. **2** any long-continued struggle or campaign.
➤ VB (**-rr-**) INTR **1** to fight wars. **2** to be in conflict.
◆ **have been in the wars** COLLOQ to have, or show signs of having, sustained injuries.

warble VB, TR & INTR **1** of a bird: to sing melodiously. **2** of a person: to sing in a high tremulous voice.

warbler N a small songbird.

war crime N a crime committed during a war,

esp ill-treatment of prisoners or massacre of civilians, etc. ■ **war criminal** N.

war cry N a cry used to rally or encourage troops, or as a signal for charging.

ward N **1** a room in a hospital with beds for patients. **2** any of the areas into which a town, etc is divided for administration or elections.
3 LAW someone under the protection of a guardian or court.
➤ VB (usu **ward off**) to keep (trouble, hunger or disease, etc) away.

warden N **1** someone in charge of a hostel, student residence or old people's home, etc.
2 IN COMPOUNDS a public official responsible for maintaining order: **traffic warden. 3** N AMER the officer in charge of a prison.

warder and **wardress** N, BRIT a prison officer.

wardrobe N **1** a tall cupboard in which clothes are kept. **2** a stock of garments.

ware N **1** IN COMPOUNDS manufactured goods of a specified material or for a specified use: **kitchenware. 2** (**wares**) goods for sale.

warehouse N **1** a large building or room for storing goods. **2** a large, usu wholesale, shop.

warfare N **1** the activity or process of waging or engaging in war. **2** armed or violent conflict.

warhead N the front part of a missile or torpedo etc that contains the explosives.

warhorse N **1** HIST a horse on which a knight rode into battle. **2** an old soldier or politician.

warlike ADJ **1** fond of fighting; aggressive or belligerent. **2** relating to war; military.

warlock N a wizard or sorcerer.

warlord N a powerful military leader.

warm ADJ **1** moderately or pleasantly hot.
2 providing and preserving heat. **3** kind and affectionate. **4** welcoming and congenial.
5 enthusiastic. **6** of a colour: suggestive of heat, typically containing red or yellow.
➤ VB **1** TR & INTR to make or become warm or warmer. **2** (usu **warm to**) to gain in enthusiasm for (a task) as one performs it. ■ **warmly** ADV.

◆ **warm up 1** to become or make (something) warm or warmer. **2** to exercise the body gently in preparation for a strenuous workout or race. **3** to re-heat (food). **4** of a party, etc: to become livelier.

warm-blooded ADJ, ZOOL of an animal: capable of maintaining its internal body temperature, independent of fluctuations in the temperature of its environment.

war memorial N a monument erected to commemorate those who died in war.

warm front N, METEOROL the edge of a mass of warm air advancing against a mass of cold air.

warm-hearted ADJ kind, affectionate and generous; sympathetic.

warmonger N someone who tries to precipitate war.

warmth N **1** the condition of being warm. **2** affection or kind-heartedness.

warm-up N the act of gently exercising the body in preparation for a workout or race.

warn VB **1** (USU **warn sb of** or **about**) to make them aware of (possible or approaching danger or difficulty). **2** to advise (someone) strongly. **3** to rebuke or admonish (someone), with the threat of punishment for a repetition of the offence.
◆ **warn sb off** to order them to go or keep away, often with threats.

warning N **1** a caution against danger, etc. **2** something that happens, or is said or done, that serves to warn against this.
➤ ADJ intended to warn: **a warning shot**.

warp VB, TR & INTR **1** to become or cause (something) to become twisted out of shape through the shrinking and expanding effects of damp or heat, etc. **2** to become or make (something) distorted, corrupted or perverted.
➤ N **1** the state or fact of being warped. **2** an unevenness or twist in wood, etc. **3** a distorted or abnormal twist in personality, etc. **4** a shift or displacement in a continuous dimension, esp time. **5** WEAVING the set of threads stretched lengthways in a loom, under and over which the

weft or woof are passed.

warpaint N **1** paint put on the face and body by certain peoples when going to war. **2** COLLOQ make-up.

warpath N.
◆ **on the warpath** COLLOQ **a** in angry pursuit; **b** in an angry mood.

warrant N **1** a written legal authorization for doing something, eg for searching property. **2** a certificate that authorizes, guarantees or confirms something.
➤ VB **1** to justify (something). **2** to guarantee (goods, etc) as being of the specified quality or quantity. ■ **warrantor** or **warranter** N.

warrant officer N in the armed services: an officer ranked between a commissioned and non-commissioned officer.

warranty N (**-ies**) an assurance of the quality of goods being sold, usu with an acceptance of responsibility for repairs for an initial period.

warren N **1** an underground labyrinth of rabbit burrows. **2** any maze of passages.

warrior N **1** a skilled fighting man, esp one belonging to earlier times. **2** any distinguished soldier or veteran.

warship N a ship armed with guns, etc for use in naval battles.

wart N a small hard benign growth on the skin, transmitted by a virus. ■ **warty** ADJ.

warthog N a large wild pig with wart-like lumps on its face.

wartime N a period during which a war is going on.

wary ADJ (**-ier, -iest**) **1** alert, vigilant or cautious; on one's guard. **2** distrustful or apprehensive. **3** (often **wary of sth** or **sb**) suspicious of it or them. ■ **warily** ADV. ■ **wariness** N.

wash VB **1** to cleanse (someone or something) with water or other liquid. **2** INTR to cleanse (oneself, or one's hands and face) with water, etc. **3** (also **wash off** or **out**) **a** TR to remove (a stain, dirt, etc) esp by using soap and water; **b** INTR of a stain, dirt, etc: to be removed in this

way. **4** of a river, waves, etc: to flow against or over (a place or land feature, etc). **5** INTR, COLLOQ to bear investigation: *That excuse just won't wash.*
➤ N **1** the process of washing or being washed. **2** a quantity of clothes, etc for washing, or just washed. **4** the breaking of waves against something; the sound of this. **5** the rough water or disturbed air left by a ship or aircraft.
■ **washable** ADJ.
◆ **wash down 1** to wash (something) from top to bottom. **2** to ease (a pill) down one's throat, or accompany or follow (food), with a drink.
◆ **wash up** to wash (the dishes, etc).

washbasin and **washhand basin** N a shallow sink in which to wash oneself.

washed-out ADJ **1** COLLOQ worn out and pale. **2** faded by, or as if by, washing.

washed-up ADJ, SLANG done for; finished.

washer N **1** someone who washes. **2** a washing machine. **3** a flat ring of rubber or metal for keeping a joint or nut secure.

washing N **1** the act of cleansing, wetting or coating with liquid. **2** clothes to be, or which have just been, washed.

washing line N a clothesline.

washing machine N a machine for washing clothes and bed linen, etc.

washing powder and **washing liquid** N detergent for washing fabrics.

washing soda N sodium carbonate crystals used for washing and cleaning.

washing-up N **1** the washing of dishes and cutlery, etc after a meal. **2** dishes and cutlery, etc for washing.

washout N, COLLOQ a flop or failure.

washstand N, HIST a small table in a bedroom with a jug and basin for washing oneself.

wasp N a common stinging insect with a slender black-and-yellow striped body.

waspish ADJ sharp-tongued.

wastage N **1** the process of wasting. **2** the amount lost through wasting. **3** (esp **natural wastage**) reduction of staff through retirement or resignation.

waste VB **1** to use or spend (something) purposelessly or extravagantly. **2** INTR to be used to no, or little, purpose or effect. **3** to fail to use, make the best of or take advantage of (an opportunity, etc). **4** to throw away (something uneaten, etc). **5** (also **waste away**) TR & INTR to lose or cause to lose flesh or strength.
➤ ADJ **1** rejected as useless, unneeded or excess to requirements. **2** of ground: lying unused, uninhabited or uncultivated. **3** PHYSIOL denoting material excreted from the body.
➤ N **1** the act or an instance of wasting, or the condition of being wasted. **2** failure to take advantage of something. **3** material that is no longer needed in its present form, eg nuclear waste. **4** refuse; rubbish. **5** PHYSIOL matter excreted from the body.
◆ **go** or **run to waste** to be wasted.

wasted ADJ **1** not exploited; squandered. **2** shrunken or emaciated. **3** SLANG extremely drunk or high on drugs.

wasteful ADJ causing waste; extravagant.

wasteland N **1** a desolate and barren region. **2** a place or point in time that is culturally, intellectually and spiritually empty.

waste paper N discarded used paper.

waster N an idler or good-for-nothing.

wastrel N an idle spendthrift.

watch VB **1** TR & INTR to look at or focus one's attention on (someone or something) that is moving or doing something, etc. **2** TR & INTR to pass time looking at or observing (TV, a programme, etc). **3** to keep track of, follow or monitor (developments, progress, etc). **4** INTR to keep vigil; to remain awake or on the alert. **5** (also **watch for**) **a** to await one's chance; to be on the alert to take advantage of (an opportunity); **b** to look out for or guard against (something). **6** to pay proper attention to (something): *watch where you're going!*
➤ N **1** a small timepiece, nowadays usu worn

strapped to the wrist. **2** the activity or duty of watching or guarding. **3** a wake; a vigil kept beside a corpse. **4** NAUT any of the four–hour shifts during which particular crew members are on duty.
◆ **on the watch for sth** seeking or looking out for it.
◆ **watch out** to be careful.
◆ **watch out for sth** or **sb** to be on one's guard against them; to look out for them.
◆ **watch over sb** or **sth** to guard, look after or tend to them or it.

watchdog N **1** a dog kept to guard premises, etc. **2** a person or organization that guards against unacceptable standards, etc.

watchful ADJ alert, vigilant and wary. ■ **watchfully** ADV. ■ **watchfulness** N.

watchman N a man employed to guard premises at night.

watchtower N a tower from which a sentry keeps watch.

watchword N a catchphrase or slogan that encapsulates the principles of a party or profession, etc.

water N **1** a colourless odourless tasteless liquid that freezes to form ice at 0°C and boils to form steam at 100°C. **2** (also **waters**) an expanse of this; a sea, etc. **3** PHYSIOL any of several fluids secreted by the body, esp urine, sweat, etc. **4** (**waters**) the amniotic fluid that surrounds the fetus in the womb. **5** any liquid that resembles or contains water.
➤ VB **1** to wet, soak or sprinkle (something) with water. **2** to irrigate (land). **3** INTR of the mouth: to produce saliva in response to a stimulus activated by the expectation of food. **4** INTR of the eyes: to fill with tears in response to irritation. **5** TR to let (animals) drink: **fed and watered**. **6** to wet (plants) with water.
◆ **hold water** of an explanation, etc: to be valid.
◆ **in deep water** in trouble or difficulty.
◆ **water sth down 1** to dilute or thin it with water. **2** to reduce the impact of it.

waterbed N a waterproof mattress filled with water.

water biscuit N a thin plain biscuit made from water and flour, usu eaten with cheese, etc.

water cannon N a powerful water jet used for dispersing crowds.

water chestnut N the tuber of a Chinese sedge plant, eaten as a vegetable.

water closet N **1** a lavatory flushed mechanically with water. **2** a small room containing such a lavatory.

watercolour or (US) **watercolor** N **1** paint thinned with water rather than oil. **2** a painting done using such paint.

watercourse N **1** a stream, river or canal. **2** the bed or channel along which it flows.

watercress N **1** a plant with hollow creeping stems and dark–green leaves that grows in watery regions. **2** its sharp–tasting leaves used in salads and soups, etc.

water-diviner N someone who detects, or attempts to detect, underground sources of water, usu with a divining–rod.

watered-down ADJ **1** very diluted. **2** reduced in force or vigour.

waterfall N a sudden interruption in the course of a river or stream where water falls more or less vertically.

waterfowl SING N a bird that lives on or near water, esp a swimming bird.
➤ PL N swimming birds collectively.

waterfront N the buildings or part of a town lying along the edge of a river, lake or sea.

waterhole N (also **watering hole**) a pool or spring in a dried–up or desert area.

watering can N a container with a handle and spout used for watering plants.

watering hole N **1** a waterhole. **2** SLANG a public house.

water jump N in a steeplechase, etc: a jump over a water–filled ditch or pool, etc.

water lily N an aquatic plant with large flat circular leaves and white, pink, red or yellow flowers that float on the water's surface.

waterline N the level reached by the water on the hull of a floating vessel.

waterlogged ADJ saturated with water.

water main N a large underground pipe that carries a public water supply.

watermark N **1** the limit reached by the sea at high or low tide. **2** a manufacturer's distinctive mark in paper, visible only when the paper is held up to the light.

watermelon N a large round fruit with a hard leathery green skin and sweet juicy red flesh.

water polo N a ball game for swimmers, in which the object is to score goals by propelling the ball into the opposing team's goal.

water power N the power generated by moving water used to drive machinery.

waterproof ADJ impenetrable by water; treated or coated so as to resist water.
➤ VB to treat (fabric, etc) so as to make it waterproof.
➤ N a waterproof outer garment.

water rat N, BRIT any of various unrelated small rat-like rodents that live near water.

watershed N **1** the line that separates two river basins. **2** a crucial point after which events take a different turn.

water-ski N a ski on which to glide over water, towed by a powered boat.
➤ VB, INTR to travel on water skis. ■ **water-skier** N. ■ **water-skiing** N.

water softener N a substance or device used in water to remove minerals, esp calcium, that cause hardness and prevent lathering.

water sports PL N sports carried out in the water, eg swimming and water-skiing, etc.

watertight ADJ **1** so well sealed as to be impenetrable by water. **2** without any apparent flaw, ambiguity, etc.

water tower N a tower that supports an elevated water tank, from which water can be distributed at uniform pressure.

water vapour N water in the form of an air

dispersion, esp where evaporation has occurred at a temperature below boiling point.

water vole N a species of vole which burrows into the banks of streams and ponds.

waterway N a navigable channel used by ships or smaller boats for travel or transport.

waterwings PL N an inflatable device used by people learning to swim.

waterworks N **1** SING an installation where water is purified and stored for distribution to an area. **2** PL, EUPHEMISTIC one's bladder and urinary system. **3** PL, FACETIOUS tears; weeping.

watery ADJ (**-ier, -iest**) **1** of or containing water. **2** containing too much water; weak or thin. **3** of eyes: moist; inclined to water.

watt N, PHYS in the SI system: a unit of power, defined as the power that gives rise to the production of energy at the rate of one joule per second.

wattage N an amount of electrical power expressed in watts.

wattle N **1** woven rods or branches, etc forming eg a framework for a wall, fences or roofs. **2** a loose fold of skin hanging from the throat of certain birds and lizards. **3** an Australian acacia tree.

wattle and daub N wattle plastered with mud or clay, used as a building material.

wave VB **1** INTR to move (one's hand) to and fro in greeting, farewell or as a signal. **2** to hold up and move (some other object) in this way for this purpose. **3** TR & INTR to move or make (something) move or sway to and fro. **4** INTR of hair: to have a gentle curl or curls.
➤ N **1** any of a series of moving ridges on the surface of the sea or some other body of water. **2** an act of waving the hand, etc. **3** PHYS a regularly repeated disturbance or displacement in a medium, eg water or air. **4** any of the circles of disturbance moving outwards from the site of a shock, such as an earthquake. **5** a loose soft curl, or series of such curls, in the hair. **6** a surge or sudden feeling of an emotion or a physical symptom. **7** a sudden increase in something: **a heat wave**.

◆ **make waves** to cause trouble, etc.

waveband N, RADIO a range of frequencies occupied by radio or TV broadcasting transmission of a particular type.

wavelength N, PHYS 1 the distance between two successive peaks or two successive troughs of a wave. 2 the length of the radio wave used by a broadcasting station.
◆ **on the same wavelength** speaking or thinking in a way that is mutually compatible.

waver VB, INTR 1 to move to and fro. 2 to falter, lessen or weaken, etc. 3 to hesitate through indecision. 4 of the voice: to become unsteady through emotion, etc. ■ **wavering** ADJ.

wavy ADJ (-ier, -iest) 1 of hair: full of waves. 2 curving alternately upward and downward.

wax¹ N 1 CHEM any of various fatty substances of plant, animal or mineral origin that are typically shiny, have a low melting point, are easily moulded when warm, and are insoluble in water. 2 the sticky yellowish matter that forms in the ears.
➢ VB to use or apply a natural or mineral wax on (something), eg prior to polishing. ■ **waxy** ADJ.

wax² VB, INTR 1 of the Moon: to appear larger as more of its surface is illuminated by the Sun. 2 FACETIOUS to become (eloquent or lyrical) in one's description of something.
◆ **wax and wane** to increase and decrease in alternating sequence.

waxen ADJ made of, covered with, or like wax.

wax paper N paper covered with a thin layer of white wax to make it waterproof.

waxwork N 1 a lifelike wax model, esp of a famous person. 2 (**waxworks**) an exhibition of these.

way N 1 a a route, entrance or exit, etc that provides passage or access somewhere; b the passage or access provided. 2 the route, road or direction taken for a particular journey. 3 an established position: the wrong way up. 4 a distance: a little way ahead. 5 one's district: if you're round our way. 6 a means. 7 a distinctive manner or style. 8 a method. 9 (**ways**) customs or rituals. 10 a characteristic

piece of behaviour. 11 a respect: correct in some ways. 12 a state or condition. 13 progress; forward motion: made their way through the crowds.
➢ ADV, COLLOQ far; a long way: met way back in the 60s.
◆ **by the way** incidentally.
◆ **by way of** as a form or means of: grinned by way of apology.
◆ **get** or **have one's own way** to do, get or have what one wants.
◆ **give way** to collapse or subside.
◆ **go out of one's way** to make special efforts.
◆ **in a bad way** COLLOQ in a poor or serious condition.
◆ **in a way** from a certain viewpoint.
◆ **out of the way** 1 situated so as not to hinder or obstruct anyone. 2 remote.
◆ **under way** in motion; progressing.

waybill N a list that gives details of goods or passengers being carried by a public vehicle.

wayfarer N, OLD USE OR POETIC a traveller.

waylay VB to lie in wait for and ambush.

way-out ADJ, SLANG excitingly unusual or new.

ways and means PL N methods and resources for carrying out any purpose.

wayside N the edge or side of a road.
➢ ADJ situated near the edge of roads.
◆ **fall by the wayside** to fail or give up in one's attempt to do something.

wayward ADJ undisciplined or self-willed.

WC ABBREV (WCs or WC's) water closet.

we PRONOUN, used as the subject of a verb: 1 to refer to oneself in company with another or others: We went to a party last night. 2 to refer to people in general: the times we live in. 3 used by a royal person, and by writers and editors in formal use, to refer to themselves or the authority they represent.

weak ADJ 1 lacking physical strength. 2 lacking in moral or mental force. 3 not able to support or sustain a great weight. 4 not functioning effectively. 5 liable to give way. 6 lacking power. 7 too easily influenced or led by others.

8 yielding too easily to temptation. **9** lacking full flavour. **10** of an argument: unsound or unconvincing. ■ **weakly** ADV.

weaken VB, TR & INTR to make or become weaker.

weakling N a sickly or physically weak person or animal.

weak-minded ADJ **1** having feeble intelligence. **2** lacking will or determination.

weakness N **1** the condition of being weak. **2** a fault or failing; a shortcoming. **3** (often **a weakness for sth**) a liking for it.

weal N a long raised reddened mark on the skin caused eg by a slash with a whip or sword.

wealth N **1** riches, valuables and property, or the possession of them. **2** abundance of resources: **the country's mineral wealth**. **3** a large quantity: **a wealth of examples**.

wealthy ADJ (*-ier, -iest*) **1** possessing riches and property; rich or prosperous. **2** (**wealthy in sth**) well supplied with it; rich in it.

wean VB **1** to accustom (a baby) to taking food other than its mother's milk. **2** to gradually break someone of a bad habit, etc.

weapon N **1** a device used to kill or injure people. **2** something one can use to get the better of others: **Patience is our best weapon.**

weaponry N (*-ies*) weapons collectively.

wear VB (*wore, worn*) **1** to be dressed in (something), or have (it) on one's body. **2** to have (one's hair or beard, etc) cut a certain length or in a certain style. **3** to have (a certain expression). **4** INTR to become thin or threadbare through use. **5** to make (a hole or bare patch, etc) in something through heavy use. **6** COLLOQ to accept (an excuse or story, etc) or tolerate (a situation, etc). **7** to tire. ➢ N **1** the act of wearing or state of being worn. **2** clothes suitable for a specified purpose, person or occasion, etc: **evening wear**. **3** damage caused by use. ■ **wearer** N.
◆ **wear down** or **wear sth down** to become reduced or consumed, or to reduce or consume something, by constant use.

◆ **wear sb down** to tire or overcome them, esp with persistent objections or demands.
◆ **wearing thin 1** becoming thin or threadbare. **2** becoming unconvincing or ineffective through over-use.
◆ **wear off** of a feeling or pain, etc: to become less intense; to disappear gradually.
◆ **wear out** to become unusable or make it unusable through use.
◆ **wear sb out** to tire them completely.

wear and tear N damage sustained in the course of continual or normal use.

wearing ADJ exhausting or tiring.

weary ADJ (*-ier, -iest*) **1** tired out; exhausted. **2** (usu **weary of sth**) tired by it; fed up with it. ➢ VB (*-ies, -ied*) **1** TR & INTR to make or become weary. **2** (usu **weary of sth**) INTR to get tired of it. ■ **wearily** ADV. ■ **weariness** N.

weasel N a small carnivorous mammal with a slender body, short legs and reddish-brown fur with white underparts.

weather N the atmospheric conditions in any area at any time, with regard to sun, cloud, temperature, wind and rain, etc. ➢ VB **1** TR & INTR to expose or be exposed to the effects of wind, Sun and rain, etc; to alter or be altered in colour, texture and shape, etc through such exposure. **2** to come safely through (a storm or difficult situation).
◆ **under the weather** COLLOQ not in good health; slightly unwell.

weatherbeaten ADJ of the skin or face: tanned or lined by exposure to sun and wind.

weathercock N a weathervane in the form of a farmyard cock.

weather eye N.
◆ **keep a weather eye on** to be watchful for developments.

weatherproof ADJ designed or treated so as to keep out wind and rain.

weathervane N a revolving arrow that turns to point in the direction of the wind, mounted eg on a church spire.

weave[1] VB (*wove, woven*) **1** TR & INTR to make

(cloth or tapestry) in a loom, passing threads under and over the threads of a fixed warp. **2** to devise (a story or plot, etc).
➤ N the pattern, compactness or texture of the weaving in a fabric. ■ **weaver** N.

weave² VB, INTR to wind in and out.

web N **1** a network of slender threads constructed by a spider to trap insects. **2** a membrane that connects the toes of a swimming bird or animal. **3** any intricate network: a web of lies. **4 a** (**the Web**) short for **World Wide Web**; **b** AS ADJ: Web page. ■ **webbed** ADJ.

webbing N strong jute or nylon fabric woven into strips for use as belts, straps, etc.

weber N, PHYS in the SI system: a unit of magnetic flux (the size of a magnetic field).

web-footed and **web-toed** ADJ of swimming birds, etc: having webbed feet.

wed VB (*wedded* or *wed, wedding*) **1** TR & INTR, OLD USE to marry. **2** OLD USE to join (someone) in marriage. **3** (usu **wed one thing to** or **with another**) to unite or combine them.

we'd CONTRACTION OF we had, we would or we should.

wedded ADJ **1** married. **2** relating to marriage.
◆ **wedded to** devoted or committed to (a principle or activity, etc).

wedding N **1** a marriage ceremony, or the ceremony together with the associated celebrations. **2** IN COMPOUNDS any of the notable anniversaries of a marriage, eg **silver** wedding.

wedge N **1** a piece of solid wood, metal or other material, tapering to a thin edge, that is driven into eg wood to split it, pushed into a narrow gap between moving parts to immobilize them, or used to hold a door open, etc. **2** anything shaped like a wedge, usu cut from something circular. **3** GOLF a club with a wedge-shaped head for lofting the ball.
➤ VB **1** to fix or immobilize (something) in position with, or as if with, a wedge. **2** to thrust, insert or squeeze like a wedge: **wedged herself into the corner.**

◆ **the thin end of the wedge** the first sign of something bad which is to come in the future.

wedlock N marriage.

Wednesday N the fourth day of the week.

wee ADJ (*weer, weest*) esp SCOT small; tiny.

weed N **1** any plant growing where it is not wanted, esp one that is thought to hinder the growth of cultivated plants such as crops or garden plants. **2** DEROG a skinny, feeble or ineffectual man. **3** SLANG marijuana.
➤ VB **1** TR & INTR to uproot weeds from (a garden or flowerbed, etc). **2** (also **weed out**) to identify and eliminate (eg those who are unwanted or ineffective from an organization or other group). ■ **weeding** N.

weedkiller N a substance, usu a chemical preparation, used to kill weeds.

weedy ADJ (*-ier, -iest*) **1** overrun with weeds. **2** DEROG having a weak or lanky build.

week N **1** a sequence of seven consecutive days, usu beginning on Sunday. **2** any period of seven consecutive days. **3** (also **working week**) the working days of the week, as distinct from the weekend. **4** the period worked per week: **works a 45-hour week.**
➤ ADV by a period of seven days before or after a specified day: **Tuesday week.**

weekday N any day except Sunday, or except Saturday and Sunday.

weekend N the period from Friday evening to Sunday night.

weekly ADJ occurring, produced or issued every week, or once a week.
➤ ADV **1** every week. **2** once a week.
➤ N (*-ies*) a magazine or newspaper published once a week.

weep VB, INTR (*wept*) **1** to shed tears as an expression of grief or other emotion. **2** of a wound, etc: to exude matter.
➤ N a bout of weeping.

weeping willow N an ornamental Chinese willow with long drooping branches.

weepy or **weepie** ADJ (*-ier, -iest*) **1** tearful.

2 of a film, etc: poignant or sentimental.
➤ N (**-ies**) COLLOQ a film or novel, etc of this kind.

weevil N a beetle which can damage plants.

weft N, WEAVING the threads that are passed over and under the fixed threads of the warp in a loom (also called **woof**).

weigh VB **1** to measure the weight of (something). **2** TR & INTR to have (a certain weight). **3** (often **weigh sth out**) to measure out a specific weight of it. **4** (often **weigh up**) to consider or assess (facts or possibilities, etc).
◆ **weigh sb down** to burden, overload or oppress them.

weighbridge N an apparatus for weighing vehicles with their loads.

weigh-in N the official weighing of a wrestler, boxer or jockey.

weight N **1** the heaviness of something; the amount that it weighs. **2** PHYS the gravitational force, measured in newtons, acting on a body. **3** any system of units for measuring and expressing weight. **4** a piece of metal of a standard weight, against which to measure the weight of other objects. **5** a heavy load. **6** ATHLETICS a heavy object for lifting or tossing. **7** influence, authority or credibility.
➤ VB **1** to add weight to (something), eg to restrict movement. **2** (often **weight sth down**) to hold it down in this way. **3** to organize (something) so as to have an unevenness or bias: *a tax system weighted in favour of the wealthy.*
◆ **pull one's weight** to do one's full share of work, etc.

weighting N a supplement to a salary, usu to compensate for high living costs.

weightless ADJ **1** weighing nothing or almost nothing. **2** of an astronaut, etc in space: not subject to the Earth's gravity, so able to float freely. ■ **weightlessness** N.

weightlifting N a sport in which competitors lift, or attempt to lift, a barbell which is made increasingly heavier. ■ **weightlifter** N.

weight-training N muscle-strengthening exercises using weights and pulleys.

weighty ADJ (**-ier, -iest**) **1** heavy. **2** important or significant. **3** grave; worrying.

weir N a shallow dam constructed across a river to control its flow.

weird ADJ **1** eerie or supernatural; uncanny. **2** strange or bizarre. **3** COLLOQ odd or eccentric. ■ **weirdly** ADV. ■ **weirdness** N.

weirdo N (**-os** or **-oes**) DEROG, COLLOQ someone who behaves or dresses oddly.

welcome VB **1** to receive (a guest or visitor, etc) with a warm greeting or kind hospitality. **2** to invite (suggestions or contributions, etc).
➤ N a reception: *a cool welcome.*
➤ ADJ **1** warmly received. **2** gladly permitted or encouraged (to do or keep something). **3** much appreciated. ■ **welcoming** ADJ.
◆ **you're welcome!** used in response to thanks: not at all; it's a pleasure.

weld VB, ENG to join (two pieces of metal) by heating them to melting point and fusing them together, or by applying pressure alone, producing a stronger joint than soldering.
➤ N a joint between two metals formed by welding. ■ **welder** or **weldor** N.

welfare N **1** the health, comfort, and general wellbeing of a person or group, etc. **2** financial and other support given to those in need.

welfare state N a system in which the government uses tax revenue to look after citizens' welfare, with the provision of free healthcare, old-age pensions and financial support for the old, sick, unemployed, etc.

well[1] ADV (*better, best*) **1** competently; skilfully. **2** satisfactorily. **3** kindly or favourably. **4** thoroughly, properly or carefully. **5** fully or adequately. **6** intimately: *don't know her well.* **7** successfully; prosperously. **8** attractively. **9** by a long way: *well past midnight.* **10** understandably: *if she objects, as well she may.* **11** very much: *well worth doing.*
➤ ADJ (*better, best*) healthy.
➤ EXCLAM **1** used enquiringly in expectation of a response or explanation, etc. **2** used variously in conversation, eg to preface a reply, express surprise, indignation or doubt, etc.

◆ **all very well** COLLOQ acceptable but only up to a point: *It's all very well to criticize.*
◆ **as well 1** too; in addition. **2** for all the difference it makes: *I may as well tell you.* **3** (also **just as well**) a good thing: *just as well you came when you did.*
◆ **as well as ...** in addition to ...
◆ **well off 1** wealthy. **2** fortunate; successful.

well² N a lined shaft that is sunk from ground level to a considerable depth below ground in order to obtain a supply of water, oil or gas, etc. ➤ VB, INTR (often **well up**) of a liquid: to spring, flow or flood to the surface.

we'll CONTRACTION we will; we shall.

well-adjusted ADJ emotionally sound.

well-advised ADJ sensible; prudent.

well-appointed ADJ well furnished.

wellbeing N the state of being healthy and contented, etc; welfare.

well-bred ADJ showing good breeding.

well-built ADJ **1** strongly built. **2** with a muscular or well-proportioned body.

well-connected ADJ having influential or aristocratic friends and relations.

well-disposed ADJ inclined to be friendly.

well-earned ADJ thoroughly deserved.

well-founded ADJ of suspicions, etc: justified: *a well-founded belief.*

well-groomed ADJ of a person: with a smart and neat appearance.

well-grounded ADJ **1** of an argument, etc: soundly based. **2** (usu **well grounded in sth**) having had a good basic education in it.

wellhead N **1** the source of a stream; a spring. **2** an origin or source.

well-heeled ADJ, COLLOQ wealthy.

well-informed ADJ **1** having reliable information on something particular. **2** full of varied knowledge.

wellington and **wellington boot** N a waterproof rubber or plastic boot loosely covering the foot and calf.

well-known ADJ familiar or famous.

well-nigh ADV almost; nearly.

well-read ADJ having read and learnt much.

well-rounded ADJ **1** pleasantly plump. **2** having had a broad and balanced upbringing and education.

well-spoken ADJ having a courteous, fluent and usu refined way of speaking.

wellspring N **1** a spring or fountain. **2** any rich or bountiful source.

well-thumbed ADJ of a book: showing marks of repeated use and handling.

well-to-do ADJ wealthy.

well-trodden ADJ often followed or walked along; much used or frequented.

well-versed ADJ knowledgeable.

well-wisher N someone concerned for another's welfare.

well-worn ADJ **1** much worn or used; showing signs of wear. **2** of an expression, etc: over-familiar from frequent use.

welly or **wellie** N (*-ies*) COLLOQ a wellington.

Welsh N the official Celtic language of Wales. ➤ ADJ of Wales. ■ **Welshman** and **Welshwoman** N.

welsh or **welch** VB **1** INTR (usu **welsh on**) to fail to pay (one's debts) or fulfil (one's obligations). **2** INTR (usu **welsh on sb**) to fail to keep one's promise to them.

Welsh rabbit or **Welsh rarebit** N melted cheese, usu with butter, ale and seasoning mixed in, served on toast. Also called **rarebit**.

welt N **1** a reinforcing band or border fastened to an edge, eg the ribbing at the waist of a knitted garment. **2** a weal raised by a lash.

welter N a confused mass.

welterweight N **1** a class for boxers and wrestlers of not more than a specified weight (66.7 kilograms in professional boxing). **2** a boxer or wrestler of this weight class.

wen N, PATHOL a sebaceous cyst on the scalp.

wench N a girl; a woman.

wend VB
◆ **wend one's way** to go steadily and purposefully on a route or journey.

we're CONTRACTION we are.

weren't CONTRACTION were not.

werewolf N, FOLKLORE someone who changes into a wolf, usu at full moon.

the West N the countries of Europe and N America, in contrast to those of Asia.

west N 1 the direction in which the Sun sets. 2 the direction that is directly opposite east, ie 180° from the east and 90° from both north and south. 3 any part of the Earth, a country or town, etc lying in the direction of the west.
➢ ADJ 1 on the side that is on or nearer the west. 2 of a wind: blowing from the west.
➢ ADV toward the west.

westbound ADJ going towards the west.

westerly ADJ 1 of a wind: coming from the west. 2 being, lying, etc towards the west.
➢ ADV 1 to or towards the west. 2 from the west.
➢ N (-ies) a westerly wind.

western ADJ 1 situated in the west. 2 directed towards the west. 3 belonging to the west.
➢ N (**Western**) a film or novel featuring cowboys in the west of the USA, esp during the 19c. ■ **westernmost** ADJ.

westerner N someone who lives in or comes from the west.

westernize or **-ise** VB to make or become like the people of Europe and America in customs, or like their institutions, practices or ideas. ■ **westernization** N.

westward or **westwards** ADV, ADJ towards the west.

wet ADJ (**wetter, wettest**) 1 covered or soaked in water or other liquid. 2 of the weather: rainy. 3 of paint, cement or varnish, etc: not yet dried. 4 DEROG SLANG of a person: feeble; ineffectual.
➢ N moisture.
➢ VB (**wet** or **wetted, wetting**) 1 to make

(someone or something) wet. 2 to urinate involuntarily on (something). ■ **wetness** N.

wet blanket N a dreary person who dampens the enthusiasm of others.

wet nurse N a woman employed to breastfeed another's baby.

wet suit N a tight-fitting rubber suit that is permeable by water, worn by divers, etc.

we've CONTRACTION we have.

whack COLLOQ, VB to hit (something or someone) sharply and resoundingly.
➢ N 1 a sharp resounding blow. 2 one's share of the profits, etc: **haven't had their whack yet**.

whacking COLLOQ, N a beating.
➢ ADJ enormous.

whale N (*whale* or *whales*) a large marine mammal which has a torpedo-shaped body, and a blowhole on the head for breathing.
➢ VB, INTR to hunt whales. ■ **whaling** N.

whaler N a person or ship engaged in hunting and killing whales.

wham N a resounding noise made by a blow.

whammy N (-*ies*) orig US COLLOQ an unfortunate or malevolent influence.

wharf N (*wharfs* or *wharves*) a landing-stage built along a waterfront for loading and unloading vessels.

what ADJ, PRONOUN 1 used in questions, indirect questions and statements, identifying, or seeking to identify or classify, a thing or person: **What street are we in? 2** used in exclamations expressing surprise, sympathy or other emotions: **What! You didn't pass? 3** used as a relative pronoun or adjective: that or those which; whatever; anything that: **It is just what I thought. 4** used to introduce a suggestion or new information: **I know what — let's go to the zoo! 5** used to ask for a repetition or confirmation of something said: **What? I didn't catch what you said.**
➢ ADV used in questions, indirect questions and statements: to how great an extent or degree?: **What does that matter?**
◆ **what ... for?** for what reason ...? to what

purpose …?: **What did you do that for?**
◆ **what's up?** what's the matter?

whatever PRONOUN, ADJ **1** (also **what ever**) used as an emphatic form of **what**: **Whatever shall I do? 2** anything: **Take whatever you want. 3** no matter what: **I must finish, whatever happens. 4** WITH NEGATIVES at all: **has nothing whatever to do with you. 5** COLLOQ some or other: **has disappeared, for whatever reason. 6** used to express uncertainty: **a didgeridoo, whatever that is.**

whatnot N, COLLOQ and other similar things: **cakes, bread and whatnot.**

whatsoever ADJ, PRONOUN **1** OLD USE OR LITERARY whatever; what. **2** WITH NEGATIVES at all: **none whatsoever.**

wheat N **1** a cereal grass. **2** the grain of this plant, which provides flour, etc.

wheat germ N the vitamin-rich germ or embryo of wheat, present in the grain.

wheatmeal N wheat flour containing most of the powdered whole grain (bran and germ).

wheedle VB, TR & INTR to coax or cajole.

wheel N **1** a circular object or frame rotating on an axle, used eg for moving a vehicle along the ground. **2** such an object serving as part of a machine or mechanism. **3** an object similar to or functioning like a wheel, eg a spinning-wheel.
➤ VB **1** to fit (something) with a wheel or wheels. **2** to push (a wheeled vehicle or conveyance) or to push (someone or something) in or on it: **He wheeled the bike outside.**
◆ **wheel about** and **wheel round** to turn around suddenly.
◆ **wheel and deal** to engage in tough business dealing or bargaining.

wheelbarrow N a hand-pushed cart with a wheel in front and two handles at the rear.

wheelchair N a chair with wheels in which invalids or disabled people can be conveyed or convey themselves.

wheelhouse N the shelter on a ship's bridge in which the steering-gear is housed.

wheelie N, BRIT a trick performed on a

motorbike or bicycle in which the front wheel is lifted off the ground.

wheelie bin or **wheely bin** N, BRIT a large dustbin mounted on wheels.

wheelwright N a craftsman who makes and repairs wheels and wheeled carriages.

wheeze VB, INTR to breathe in a laboured way with a gasping or rasping noise.
➤ N **1** a wheezing breath or sound. **2** COLLOQ a bright idea; a clever scheme. ■ **wheezy** ADJ.

whelk N a large edible marine snail.

when ADV used in questions, indirect questions and statements: at what time?
➤ CONJ **1** at the time, or during the period, that. **2** as soon as. **3** at any time that; whenever. **4** at which time. **5** in spite of the fact that: **Why just watch when you could be dancing?**
➤ PRONOUN **1** what or which time: **They stayed talking, until when I can't say. 2** used as a relative pronoun: at, during, etc which time: **an era when life was harder.**

whence OLD USE, FORMAL OR LITERARY, ADV, CONJ **1** used in questions, indirect questions and statements: from what place?; from which place: **enquired whence they had come. 2** used esp in statements: from what cause or circumstance: **can't explain whence the mistake arose. 3** to the place from which: **returned whence they had come.**

whenever CONJ at any or every time that: **gets furious whenever he doesn't get his way** • **I'll be here whenever you need me.**
➤ ADV **1** an emphatic form of **when**: **Whenever could I have said that? 2** used to indicate that one does not know when: **at Pentecost, whenever that is.**

where ADV used in questions, indirect questions and statements: **1** in, at or to which place: **Where is she going? 2** in what respect: **showed me where I'd gone wrong. 3** from what source: **Where did you get that?**
➤ PRONOUN what place?: **Where are you?**
➤ CONJ **1** in, at or to the, or any, place that: **went where he pleased. 2** in any case in which: **keep families together where possible. 3** the

respect in which: **That's where you are wrong.**

whereabouts ADV (roughly) where?
➤ SING OR PL N the (rough) position of a person or thing.

whereas CONJ but, by contrast: **I'm a pessimist, whereas my husband is an optimist.**

whereby PRONOUN by means of which.

wherefore N a reason: **whys and wherefores.**

whereupon CONJ at which point.

wherever PRONOUN any or every place that: **I'll take it to wherever you like.**
➤ CONJ **1** in, at or to whatever place: **They were welcomed wherever they went. 2** no matter where: **I won't lose touch, wherever I go.**
➤ ADV **1** an emphatic form of **where**: **Wherever can they be? 2** used to indicate that one does not know where: **the Round House, wherever that is.**

wherewithal N (**the wherewithal**) the means or necessary resources, esp money.

whet VB (**-tt-**) **1** to sharpen (a bladed tool) by rubbing it against stone, etc. **2** to arouse or intensify (someone's appetite, interest or desire).

whether CONJ **1** used to introduce an indirect question: **asked whether it was raining. 2** used in constructions involving other possibilities: **was uncertain whether he liked her or not.**

whey N the watery content of milk, separated from the curd in making cheese, etc.

which ADJ, PRONOUN **1** used in questions, indirect questions and statements to identify or specify a thing or person, usu from a known group: **Which did you choose? 2** used to introduce a defining or identifying relative clause: **animals which hibernate. 3** used to introduce a commenting clause, used chiefly in reference to things or ideas rather than people: **The house, which lies back from the road, is painted red.**

whichever PRONOUN, ADJ **1** the one or ones that; any that: **Take whichever is suitable. 2** according to which: **at 10.00 or 10.30, whichever is more convenient. 3** no matter which: **I'll be satisfied, whichever you choose.**

whiff N **1** a puff or slight rush of air or smoke, etc. **2** a hint or trace: **at the first whiff of scandal.**

while CONJ **1** at the same time as: **She held the bowl while I stirred. 2** during the time that: **happened while we were abroad. 4** whereas: **He likes camping, while she prefers sailing.**
➤ ADV at or during which: **all the months while I was ill.**
➤ N a space or lapse of time: **after a while.**
➤ VB (often **while away**) to pass (time or hours, etc) in a leisurely or undemanding way.
◆ **worth** (**one's**) **while** worth one's time.

whilst CONJ while.

whim N a sudden fanciful idea; a caprice.

whimper VB **1** INTR to cry feebly or plaintively. **2** to say (something) in a whining manner.
➤ N a feebly plaintive cry.

whimsical ADJ **1** delicately fanciful or playful. **2** odd, weird or fantastic. ■ **whimsically** ADV.

whimsy or **whimsey** N (*whimsies* or *whimseys*) **1** quaint humour. **2** a whim.

whin N gorse.

whine VB, INTR **1** to whimper. **2** to complain peevishly or querulously.
➤ N **1** a whimper. **2** a continuous high-pitched noise. **3** a thin and ingratiating nasal tone of voice. ■ **whining** N, ADJ.

whinge VB (*whingeing*) INTR, COLLOQ to complain irritably; to whine.
➤ N a peevish complaint. ■ **whinger** N.

whinny VB (**-ies, -ied**) INTR to neigh softly.
➤ N (**-ies**) a gentle neigh.

whip N **1** a lash with a handle for driving animals or punishing people. **2** a stroke administered by, or as if by, such a lash. **3** POL a member of a parliamentary party responsible for members' discipline, and also for their attendance to vote on important issues. **4** POL a notice sent to members by a party whip requiring their attendance for a vote, urgency being indicated (IN COMPOUNDS) by the number of underlinings: **a three-line whip. 5** a dessert made with beaten egg-whites or cream.

➢ VB (-*pp*-) **1** to strike or thrash with a whip. **2** to punish (someone) with lashes or smacking. **3** (usu **whip sth off** or **out, etc**) to snatch it: whipped out a revolver. **4** to rouse or force into a certain state: whipped the crowd into a fury. **5** to beat (egg-whites or cream, etc) until stiff or frothy. ■ **whipping** N, ADJ.

◆ **whip up 1** to arouse (support, enthusiasm or other feelings) for something. **2** to prepare (a meal, etc) at short notice.

whip hand N (often **the whip hand**) the advantage in a situation.

whiplash N **1** the lash of a whip. **2** (also **whiplash injury**) a neck injury caused by the sudden jerking back of the head and neck.

whippersnapper N, COLLOQ an insignificant and cheeky young lad.

whippet N a small slender breed of dog.

whip-round N, COLLOQ a collection of money made, often hastily, among a group of people.

whirl VB **1** INTR to spin or revolve rapidly. **2** TR & INTR to move with a rapid circling or spiralling motion. **3** INTR of the head: to feel dizzy.
➢ N **1** a circling or spiralling movement or pattern. **2** a round of intense activity.
◆ **give sth a whirl** COLLOQ to try it out.

whirligig N a spinning toy, esp a top.

whirlpool N a violent circular eddy of water that occurs in a river or sea at a point where several strong opposing currents converge.

whirlwind N **1** a violently spiralling column of air over land or sea. **2** anything that moves in a similarly rapid and usu destructive way.
➢ ADJ referring or relating to anything that develops rapidly: a whirlwind courtship.

whirr N a rapid drawn-out whirling, humming or vibratory sound.
➢ VB **1** INTR to turn or spin with a whirring noise. **2** to make (something) move with this sound.

whisk VB **1** to transport (someone or something) rapidly: was whisked into hospital. **2** to beat (egg-whites or cream, etc).
➢ N **1** a whisking movement or action. **2** an implement for whisking egg-whites, etc.

whisker N **1** any of the long coarse hairs that grow round the mouth of a cat or mouse, etc. **2** (**whiskers**) a man's beard. **3** the tiniest possible margin: won by a whisker.

whisky or (IRISH & N AMER) **whiskey** N (*whiskies* or *whiskeys*) an alcoholic spirit distilled from a fermented mash of cereal grains, eg barley, wheat or rye.

whisper VB, TR & INTR to speak or say (something) quietly, breathing rather than voicing the words.
➢ N **1** a whispered level of speech. **2** (often **whispers**) a rumour or hint. ■ **whispering** N.

whist N a card game, usu for two pairs of players, the object being to take a majority of 13 tricks, each trick over six scoring one point.

whistle N **1 a** a shrill sound produced through pursed lips or through the teeth, used to signal, etc; **b** the act of making this sound. **2** a small hand-held device used for making a similar sound. **3** any of several devices which produce a similar sound by the use of steam, eg a kettle.
➢ VB **1** TR & INTR to produce (a tune, etc) by passing air through a narrow constriction in the mouth, esp through pursed lips. **2** TR & INTR to blow or play on a whistle. **3** INTR of a kettle or locomotive: to emit a whistling sound.

Whit N Whitsuntide.

white ADJ **1** having the colour of snow, the colour that reflects all light. **2** (often **White**) of people: belonging to one of the pale-skinned races. **3** abnormally pale, eg from shock or illness. **4** of hair: lacking pigment, as in old age. **5** of a variety of anything, eg grapes: pale-coloured, as distinct from darker types. **6** of wine: made from white grapes or from skinned black grapes. **7 a** of flour: having had the bran and wheat germ removed; **b** of bread: made with white flour. **8** of coffee or tea: with milk or cream added.
➢ N **1** the colour of snow. **2** (often **White**) a white person. **3** (in full **egg-white**) the clear fluid surrounding the yolk of an egg; albumen. **4** the white part of the eyeball, surrounding the iris. ■ **whiteness** N.

whitebait N (PL *whitebait*) the young of some

silvery fishes, eg herrings and sprats.

white-collar ADJ referring to or denoting a class of workers, eg clerks or other professions, who are not engaged in manual labour.

white dwarf N, ASTRON a small dense hot star that has reached the last stage of its life.

white elephant N a possession or piece of property that is useless or unwanted.

white fish N a general name for edible sea fish, including whiting, cod, sole and haddock.

white flag N the signal used for offering surrender or requesting a truce.

white gold N a pale lustrous alloy of gold containing platinum, palladium, nickel or silver.

white goods PL N large kitchen appliances such as washing machines, refrigerators, etc.

white horse N (often **white horses**) a wave with a white crest, seen esp on a choppy sea.

white-hot ADJ **1** of a metal, etc: so hot that white light is emitted. **2** intense; passionate.

white-knuckle ADJ, COLLOQ causing extreme fear: **a white-knuckle roller-coaster ride**.

white lie N a forgivable lie, esp one told to avoid hurting someone's feelings.

white light N light, such as that of the sun, that contains all the wavelengths in the visible range of the spectrum.

white meat N pale-coloured meat, eg veal.

whiten VB, TR & INTR to make or become white or whiter; to bleach. ■ **whitener** N.

white noise N sound waves that contain a large number of frequencies of roughly equal intensity.

white-out N a phenomenon in snowy weather when the overcast sky blends imperceptibly with the white landscape.

white paper N (also **White Paper**) in the UK: a government policy statement printed on white paper.

white pepper N pepper made from peppercorns with the dark outer husk removed.

white slave N a girl or woman forced into prostitution. ■ **white slavery** N.

white spirit N a colourless liquid distilled from petroleum, used as a solvent and thinner for paints and varnishes.

white tie N **1** a white bow tie worn as part of men's formal evening dress. **2** formal evening dress for men.

whitewash N **1** (also **limewash**) a mixture of lime and water, used to give a white coating to walls, esp outside walls. **2** measures taken to cover up a disreputable affair, etc.
➢ VB **1** to coat (something) with whitewash. **2** to clean up or conceal (eg a disreputable affair).

whiting N (PL *whiting*) a small edible fish native to the waters of northern Europe.

whitlow N an inflammation of the finger or toe, esp near the nail.

Whitsun and **Whitsuntide** N in the Christian church: the week beginning with Whit Sunday, particularly the first three days.

Whit Sunday or **Whitsunday** N Pentecost.

whittle VB **1** to cut, carve or pare (a stick or piece of wood, etc) with a knife. **2** to shape or fashion (something) by this means.
◆ **whittle sth away** to erode it.
◆ **whittle sth down** to reduce it gradually.

whizz or **whiz** VB, INTR **1** to fly through the air, esp with a whistling noise. **2** to move rapidly.
➢ N **1** a whistling sound. **2** COLLOQ someone with an exceptional and usu specific talent for something; an expert.

whizz kid N, COLLOQ someone who achieves success quickly and early.

who PRONOUN **1** used in questions, indirect questions and statements: which or what person; which or what people: **Who is at the door?** • **asked who he had seen**. **2** used as a relative pronoun to introduce a defining clause: **the boy who was on the train**. **3** used as a relative pronoun to add a commenting clause: **Julius Caesar, who was murdered in 44** BC.

whoa EXCLAM a command to stop.

who'd CONTRACTION **1** who would. **2** who had.

whodunit or **whodunnit** N, COLLOQ a detective novel or play, etc; a mystery.

whoever PRONOUN **1** used in questions, indirect questions and statements as an emphatic form of who or whom: **Whoever is that at the door?** • **ask whoever you like. 2** no matter who: **I don't want to see them, whoever they are. 3** used to indicate that one does not know who: **St Fiacre, whoever he was.**

whole N **1** all the constituents or components of something: **the whole of the time. 2** something complete in itself, esp something consisting of integrated parts.
➢ ADJ comprising all of something; no less than the whole; entire: **The whole street heard you.**
➢ ADV **1** COLLOQ completely; altogether; wholly: **found a whole new approach. 2** in one piece: **swallowed it whole. 3** unbroken: **only two cups left whole.** ■ **wholeness** N.
◆ **on the whole** considering everything.

wholefood N (sometimes **wholefoods**) food which is processed as little as possible.

wholehearted ADJ sincere and enthusiastic. ■ **wholeheartedly** ADV.

wholemeal and **wholewheat** ADJ **1** of flour: made from the entire wheat grain. **2** of bread: made from wholemeal flour.

whole number N, MATH an integral number, being one without fractions.

wholesale N the sale of goods in large quantities to a retailer.
➢ ADJ, ADV **1** buying and selling, or concerned with buying and selling in this way. **2** on a huge scale or indiscriminately: **wholesale destruction.** ■ **wholesaler** N.

wholesome ADJ **1** attractively healthy. **2** promoting health: **wholesome food.**

wholly ADV completely: **not wholly satisfied.**

whom PRONOUN used as the object of a verb or preposition (but often replaced by who, esp in less formal usage): **1** in seeking to identify a person: **To whom are you referring? 2** as a relative pronoun in a defining clause: **I am**
looking for the man whom I met earlier. **3** used as a relative pronoun to introduce a commenting clause: **The man, whom I met earlier, has left.**

whoop N a loud cry of delight, joy or triumph.
➢ VB, TR & INTR to say (something) with a whoop.

whoopee EXCLAM expressing delight.

whooping cough N, PATHOL a highly contagious disease that mainly affects children, characterized by bouts of violent coughing followed by a sharp drawing in of the breath which produces a 'whooping' sound.

whoops EXCLAM expressing surprise, concern or apology, eg when one has a slight accident.

whopper N, COLLOQ **1** anything very large of its kind. **2** a blatant lie.

whopping ADJ, COLLOQ huge; enormous.

whore N, OFFENSIVE **1** a prostitute. **2** a sexually immoral or promiscuous woman.

whorl N a twist or coil.

who's CONTRACTION **1** who is. **2** who has.

whose PRONOUN, ADJ **1** used in questions, indirect questions and statements: belonging to which person or people: **Whose is this jacket? 2** used as a relative adjective to introduce a defining clause: of whom or which: **buildings whose foundations are sinking. 3** used as a relative adjective to add a commenting clause: **my parents, whose help I appreciate.**

why ADV used in questions, indirect questions and statements: for what reason.
➢ CONJ for, or because of, which: **no reason why I should get involved.**
➢ EXCLAM expressing surprise, indignation, impatience, etc: **Why, you little monster!**
◆ **the whys and wherefores** the reasons.

wick N the twisted string through a candle or lamp which draws the fuel to the flame.
◆ **get on sb's wick** SLANG to be a source of irritation to them.

wicked ADJ **1** evil or sinful; immoral. **2** mischievous, playful or roguish. **3** SLANG excellent or cool; admirable. ■ **wickedly**

ADV. ■ **wickedness** N.

wicker ADJ of a fence or basket, etc: made of interwoven twigs, canes or rushes, etc.

wickerwork N articles made from wicker.

wicket N, CRICKET **a** a row of three small wooden posts stuck upright in the ground behind either crease; **b** the playing area between these; **c** a batsman's dismissal by the bowler: 45 runs for two wickets.

wicketkeeper N, CRICKET the fielder who stands immediately behind the wicket.

wide ADJ **1** large in extent from side to side. **2** measuring a specified amount from side to side: three feet wide. **3** of the eyes: open to the fullest extent. **4** of a range, etc: covering a great variety: a wide choice of films on. **5** extensive; widespread: wide support.
➢ ADV **1** to the fullest extent: with the door wide open. **2** off the mark: His aim went wide.
■ **widely** ADV.

wide-angle lens N, PHOTOG, CINEMATOG a camera lens which takes pictures that cover a wider area than a normal lens.

wide-eyed ADJ **1** showing surprise. **2** naive.

widen VB, TR & INTR to make, or become, wider.

wide-ranging ADJ of interests, discussions, etc: covering a large variety of subjects.

widespread ADJ **1** extending over a wide area. **2** involving large numbers of people.

widget N a gadget; any small manufactured item or component.

widow N a woman whose husband is dead and who has not remarried.
➢ VB to leave or make (someone) a widow or widower. ■ **widowhood** N.

widower N a man whose wife is dead and who has not remarried.

width N **1** extent from side to side; breadth. **2** the distance from side to side across a swimming-pool: swam ten widths.

wield VB **1** to brandish or use (a tool or weapon, etc). **2** to have or exert (power, influence, etc).

wife N (*wives*) the woman to whom a man is married; a married woman. ■ **wifely** ADJ.

wig N an artificial covering of natural or synthetic hair for the head.

wiggle VB, TR & INTR, COLLOQ to move or cause (something) to move, esp jerkily, from side to side or up and down.
➢ N a wiggling motion or line. ■ **wiggly** ADJ (*-ier*, *-iest*).

wigwam N a domed Native American dwelling made of a framework of arched poles covered with skins, bark or mats.

wild ADJ **1** of animals: untamed or undomesticated; not dependent on humans. **2** of plants: growing in a natural uncultivated state. **3** of country: desolate, rugged or uninhabitable. **4** of peoples: savage; uncivilized. **5** unrestrained; uncontrolled: wild fury. **6** frantically excited. **7** distraught: wild with grief. **8** of the eyes: staring; distracted or scared-looking. **9** of a guess: random.
➢ N **1** (**the wild**) a wild animal's or plant's natural environment or life in it: returned the cub to the wild. **2** (**wilds**) lonely, sparsely inhabited regions away from the city. ■ **wildly** ADV.
■ **wildness** N.
◆ **run wild 1** to revert to a wild, overgrown and uncultivated state. **2** to live a life of freedom, with little discipline or control.

wild card N **1** someone allowed to compete in a sports event, despite lacking the usual or stipulated qualifications. **2** COMP a symbol, eg an asterisk, that can be used to represent any character or set of characters in a certain position, in order to identify text strings with variable contents.

wildcat N (*wildcats* or *wildcat*) an undomesticated cat of Europe and Asia.
➢ ADJ of a business scheme: financially unsound or risky; speculative.

wildebeest N (*wildebeest* or *wildebeests*) the gnu.

wilderness N **1** an uncultivated or uninhabited region. **2** an overgrown tangle of weeds, etc.

wildfire N.
- ◆ **spread like wildfire** of disease or rumour, etc: to spread rapidly and extensively.

wildfowl SING OR PL N a game bird or game birds.

wild-goose chase N a search that is bound to be unsuccessful and fruitless.

wildlife N wild animals, birds and plants in general.

wild rice N a tall aquatic grass that yields rice-like seeds.

Wild West N, HIST the western US in the days of the first settlers, before the establishment of law and order.

wile N 1 (**wiles**) charming personal ways. 2 a cunning trick.

wilful or (US) **willful** ADJ 1 deliberate; intentional. 2 headstrong, obstinate or self-willed. ■ **wilfully** ADV. ■ **wilfulness** N.

will[1] AUXILIARY VERB expressing or indicating: 1 the future tense of other verbs, esp when the subject is **you, he, she, it** or **they**: They will no doubt succeed. 2 intention or determination, when the subject is **I** or **we**: We will not give in. 3 a request: Will you please shut the door?

will[2] N 1 the power of conscious decision and deliberate choice of action: **free will**. 2 one's own preferences, or one's determination in effecting them: **against my will**. 3 desire or determination: **the will to live**. 4 a wish or desire. 5 **a** instructions for the disposal of a person's property, etc after death; **b** the document containing these.
- ➢ VB to try to compel (someone) by, or as if by, exerting one's will: **willed herself to keep going**.

the willies PL N, COLLOQ the creeps; a feeling of anxiety or unease.

willing ADJ 1 ready, glad or not disinclined to do something. 2 eager and co-operative. ■ **will-ingly** ADV. ■ **willingness** N.

willow N 1 a deciduous tree or shrub that generally grows near water, and has slender flexible branches. 2 the wood of this tree, which is used to make cricket bats and furniture.

willowy ADJ slender and graceful.

willpower N the determination, persistence and self-discipline needed to do something.

willy-nilly ADV whether one wishes or not; regardless.

wilt VB, INTR 1 BOT of a plant organ or tissue: to droop or become limp because of lack of water. 2 to droop from fatigue or heat. 3 to lose courage or confidence.

wily ADJ (**-ier, -iest**) cunning; crafty or devious.

wimp COLLOQ, N a feeble person.
- ➢ VB, INTR (always **wimp out**) to back out (of doing something) through feebleness.
- ■ **wimpish** or **wimpy** ADJ.

wimple N a veil folded around the head, neck and cheeks, orig a women's fashion and still worn as part of a nun's dress.

win VB (**won, winning**) 1 TR & INTR to be victorious or come first in (a contest, race or bet, etc). 2 TR & INTR to beat an opponent or rivals in (a competition, conflict or election, etc). 3 to compete or fight for, and obtain (a victory or prize, etc). 4 to obtain by struggle or effort. 5 to earn and receive or obtain: **won plaudits**.
- ➢ N, COLLOQ a victory or success.
- ◆ **win sb over** or **round** to persuade them over to one's side or opinion.

wince VB, INTR to shrink back, start or grimace, eg in pain or anticipation of it; to flinch.
- ➢ N a start or grimace in reaction to pain, etc.

winch N 1 a reel or roller round which a rope or chain is wound for hoisting or hauling heavy loads. 2 a crank or handle for setting a wheel, axle or machinery in motion.
- ➢ VB to hoist or haul (something or someone) with a winch.

wind[1] N 1 the movement of air across the Earth's surface as a result of differences in atmospheric pressure between one location and another. 2 a current of air produced artificially, by a fan, etc. 3 one's breath or breath supply: **short of wind**. 4 gas built up in the intestines; flatulence.
- ➢ VB 1 to deprive (someone) of breath

temporarily, eg by a punch. **2** to burp (a baby).

◆ **break wind** to discharge intestinal gas through the anus.

◆ **get wind of sth** to have one's suspicions aroused or hear a rumour about it.

wind² VB (*wound*) **1** (often **wind round**) TR & INTR to wrap or coil, or be wrapped or coiled. **2** TR & INTR to move or cause to move with many twists and turns. **3** (also **wind sth up**) to tighten the spring of (a clock or watch) by turning a knob or key.

◆ **wind down 1** of a clock or clockwork device: to slow down and stop working. **2** of a person: to begin to relax.

◆ **wind sth down 1** to lower (it) by turning a handle. **2** to reduce the resources and activities of (a business or enterprise).

◆ **wind up** COLLOQ to end up: He wound up in jail.

◆ **wind sb up 1** to make them tense, nervous or excited. **2** to taunt or tease them.

◆ **wind sth up 1** to raise (it) by turning a handle. **2** to conclude or close down (a business or enterprise).

windbag N, COLLOQ an excessively talkative person who communicates little of any value.

windbreak N a barrier that provides protection from the wind.

windcheater N a windproof jacket with tightly fitting cuffs, neck and waistband.

windchill N, METEOROL the extra chill given to air temperature by the wind.

windfall N **1** a fruit, esp an apple, blown down from its tree. **2** an unexpected or sudden financial gain or other piece of good fortune.

wind farm N a concentration of wind-driven turbines generating electricity.

wind instrument N a musical instrument such as a clarinet, flute or trumpet, played by blowing air, esp the breath, through it.

windlass N a drum-shaped axle round which a rope or chain is wound for hauling or hoisting weights.

windmill N **1** a mechanical device operated by wind-driven sails that revolve about a fixed shaft, used for grinding grain, pumping water and generating electricity. **2** a toy with a set of plastic or paper sails, mounted on a stick, that revolve in the wind.

window N **1** an opening in a wall to look through, or let in light and air, consisting of a wooden or metal frame fitted with panes of glass; a pane. **2** the frame itself. **3** the area immediately behind a shop's window, in which goods on sale are displayed. **4** a gap in a schedule, etc available for some purpose. **5** an opening in the front of an envelope, allowing the address written on the letter inside to be visible. **6** COMP an enclosed rectangular area displayed on the VDU of a computer, which can be used as an independent screen.

window box N a box fitted along an exterior window ledge, for growing plants in.

window-dressing N **1** the art of arranging goods in a shop window. **2** the art or practice of giving something superficial appeal by skilful presentation. ■ **window-dresser** N.

windowpane N a sheet of glass set in a window.

window seat N **1** a seat placed in the recess of a window. **2** on a train or aeroplane, etc: a seat next to a window.

window-shopping N the activity of looking at goods in shop windows without buying them.

windowsill N the interior or exterior ledge that runs along the bottom of a window.

windpipe N the trachea.

windpower N a renewable energy source derived from winds in the Earth's atmosphere.

windscreen N the large sheet of curved glass at the front of the motor vehicle.

windscreen-wiper N a device fitted to the windscreen of a motor vehicle, consisting of a rubber blade on an arm which moves in an arc, to keep the windscreen clear of rain, snow, etc.

windsock N an open-ended cone of fabric flying from a mast, eg at an airport, which shows the direction and speed of the wind.

windsurfing N the sport of riding the waves on a sailboard; sailboarding. ■ **windsurfer** N.

windswept ADJ **1** exposed to strong winds. **2** dishevelled from exposure to the wind.

wind-up N taunting or teasing.

windy ADJ (*-ier, -iest*) **1** exposed to, or characterized by, strong wind. **2** COLLOQ of speech or writing: long-winded or pompous.

wine N **1** an alcoholic drink made from fermented grape juice. **2** the dark-red colour of red wine.

wine bar N a bar which specializes in the selling of wine and often food.

wine cellar N **1** a cellar in which to store wines. **2** the stock of wine stored there.

wing N **1** one of the two modified forelimbs of a bird or bat that are adapted for flight. **2** one of two or more membranous outgrowths that project from either side of the body of an insect enabling it to fly. **3** one of the flattened structures that project from either side of an aircraft body. **4** any of the corner sections of a vehicle body, covering the wheels. **5** a part of a building projecting from the central or main section: **the west wing. 6** SPORT in football and hockey, etc: **a** either edge of the pitch; **b** the player at either extreme of the forward line. **7** (**wings**) THEAT the area at each side of a stage, where performers wait to enter, out of sight of the audience. **8** a group with its own distinct views and character, within a political party or other body.
➤ VB **1** to make (one's way) by flying, or with speed. **2** to wound (a bird) in the wing or (a person) in the arm or shoulder.
◆ **under sb's wing** under their protection or guidance.

wing commander N an officer in the air force.

winger N, SPORT in football and hockey, etc: a player in wing position.

wing mirror N a rear-view mirror attached to the side of a motor vehicle.

wing nut N a metal nut turned on a bolt by the finger and thumb by means of its flattened projections. Also called **butterfly nut**.

wingspan N the distance from tip to tip of the wings of an aircraft, bird, insect, etc.

wink VB, TR & INTR to shut an eye briefly as an informal or cheeky gesture or greeting.
➤ N **1** an act of winking. **2** a short spell of something, esp sleep. See also **forty winks**.

winkle N a small edible snail-shaped shellfish.

winner N **1** a person, animal or vehicle, etc that wins a contest or race. **2** someone or something that is or is destined to be a success.

winning ADJ **1** attractive or charming; persuasive. **2** securing victory.
➤ N (**winnings**) money or prizes won.

winnow VB to separate (chaff) from (grain) by blowing a current of air through it.

winsome ADJ charming; captivating.

winter N (also **Winter**) the coldest season of the year, coming between autumn and spring.

wintergreen N an evergreen plant yielding an aromatic oil which can be used medicinally or as a flavouring.

winter solstice N the shortest day of the year, when the Sun reaches its lowest point in the N hemisphere (usu 21 December).

winter sports PL N open-air sports held on snow or ice, such as skiing and ice-skating.

wintry or **wintery** ADJ (*-ier, -iest*) of weather, etc: characteristic of winter.

wipe VB **1** to clean or dry (something) with a cloth, etc. **2** (**wipe sth away, off, out** or **up**) to remove it by wiping. **3** COMP, etc **a** to clear (magnetic tape or a disk) of its contents; **b** to erase (data) from a disk or magnetic tape. **4** to remove or get rid of (something): **wiped the incident from his memory.**
➤ N **1** the act of cleaning something by rubbing. **2** a piece of fabric or tissue, usu specially treated, for wiping and cleaning, eg wounds.

wiper N a windscreen-wiper.

wire N **1** metal drawn out into a narrow flexible

strand. **2** a length of this, usu wrapped in insulating material, used for carrying an electric current. **3** TELECOMM a cable that connects one point with another.
➤ VB (also **wire up**) to fit or connect up (an electrical apparatus or system, etc) with wires.
◆ **get one's wires crossed** to misunderstand or be confused about something.

wire-haired ADJ of a breed of dog: with a coarse, wiry coat.

wireless N, OLD USE a radio.

wiring N the arrangement of wires that connects the individual components of electric circuits into an operating system.

wiry ADJ (**-ier, -iest**) of a person: of slight build, but strong and agile.

wisdom N **1** the quality of being wise. **2** the ability to make sensible judgements and decisions, esp on the basis of one's knowledge and experience. **3** learning; knowledge.

wisdom tooth N in humans: any of the last four molar teeth to come through, at the back of each side of the upper and lower jaw.

wise¹ ADJ **1** having or showing wisdom; prudent; sensible. **2** learned. **3** astute, shrewd or sagacious. ■ **wisely** ADV.
◆ **wise up to sb** or **sth** COLLOQ to find out the facts about them or it.

wise² N, OLD USE way: **in no wise to blame**.

wisecrack N a clever or knowing remark.
➤ VB, INTR to make a wisecrack.

wise guy N, COLLOQ someone who is full of smart and cocky comments; a know-all.

wish VB **1** to want; to have a desire. **2** to desire, esp vainly or helplessly (that something were the case). **3** to express a desire for (luck, success, happiness, etc) to come to (someone). **4** to say (good afternoon, etc) to (someone).
➤ N **1** a desire. **2** (usu **wishes**) what one wants to be done, etc. **3** (**wishes**) a hope expressed for someone's welfare: **best wishes**.

wishbone N a V-shaped bone in the breast of poultry.

wishful thinking N an over-optimistic expectation that something will happen, arising from one's desire that it should.

wishy-washy ADJ pale and insipid; bland.

wisp N a strand; a thin fine tuft or shred.
■ **wispy** ADJ (**-ier, -iest**).

wisteria N a climbing shrub with long pendulous clusters of lilac or white flowers.

wistful ADJ sadly or vainly yearning.

wit¹ N **1** the ability to express oneself amusingly; humour. **2** someone who has this ability. **3** humorous speech or writing. **4** (also **wits**) common sense or intelligence or resourcefulness: **will he have the wit to phone?**
◆ **at one's wits' end** COLLOQ reduced to despair; completely at a loss.
◆ **have one's wits about one** to be alert.

wit² VB.
◆ **to wit** LAW that is to say; namely.

witch N **1** someone, esp a woman, supposed to have magical powers used usu, but not always, malevolently. **2** a frighteningly ugly or wicked old woman or hag. ■ **witchlike** ADJ.

witchcraft N **1** magic or sorcery of the kind practised by witches. **2** the use of this.

witch doctor N a member of a tribal society who is believed to have magical powers, and to be able to use them to cure or harm people.

witch hazel N an astringent lotion produced from the bark of a N American shrub.

witch-hunt N a concerted campaign against an individual or group believed to hold views or to be acting in ways harmful to society.

with PREP **1** in the company of (someone): **went with her**. **2** used after verbs of partnering, co-operating, associating, etc: **danced with him**. **3** used after verbs of mixing: **mingled with the crowd**. **4** by means of; using: **raised it with a crowbar**. **5** used after verbs of covering, filling, etc: **plastered with mud**. **6** used after verbs of providing: **equipped with firearms**. **7** as a result of (something): **shaking with fear**. **8** in the same direction as (something): **drift with the current**. **9** used after verbs of conflict:

quarrelled with her brother. **10** used after verbs of agreeing, disagreeing, and comparing: **compared with last year. 11** used in describing (someone or something): **a man with a limp. 12** in or under the specified circumstances: **I can't go abroad with my mother so ill. 13** regarding: **What shall we do with this? 14** loyal to or supporting (someone or something): **We're with you all the way.**

withdraw VB (*withdrew, withdrawn*) **1** INTR to move somewhere else, esp more private: **withdrew into her bedroom. 2** INTR to leave; to go away: **We tactfully withdrew. 3** INTR of troops: to move back or retreat. **4** to take (money) from a bank account for use. **5** TR & INTR to back out or pull (something) out of an activity or contest, etc. **6** to take back (a comment) that one regrets making. **7** INTR to become uncommunicative or unresponsive.

withdrawal N **1** the act or process of withdrawing. **2** a removal of funds from a bank account. **3** MED the breaking of an addiction to drugs, etc, with associated physical and psychological symptoms. **4** a retreat into silence and self-absorption.

withdrawn ADJ unresponsive or reserved.

wither VB **1** INTR of plants: to fade, dry up and die. **2** TR & INTR to shrivel or make (something) shrivel and decay. **3** to humble or disconcert (someone) with a glaring or scornful, etc expression. ■ **withered** ADJ.

withhold VB **1** to refuse to give or grant (something): **withheld evidence. 2** to hold back (something): **withholding payment.**

within PREP **1** inside; enclosed by something: **within these four walls. 2** not outside the limits of (something); not beyond: **within sight. 3** in less than (a certain time or distance): **finished within a week.**
➢ ADV inside: **apply within.**

without PREP **1** not having the company of (someone): **She went home without him. 2** deprived of: **He can't live without her. 3** not having (something): **a blue sky without a cloud. 4** not (behaving as expected or in a particular way): **answered without smiling. 5** not giving

or showing, etc (something): **complied without a murmur. 6** free from (something): **admitted it without shame. 7** not having (something required).

withstand VB **1** to maintain one's position against (someone or something). **2** to resist or brave (something): **withstood his insults.**

witless ADJ stupid or brainless; lacking wit.

witness N **1** someone who sees, and can therefore give a direct account of, an event or occurrence, etc. **2** someone who gives evidence in a court of law. **3** someone who adds their own signature to confirm the authenticity of a signature just put on a document, etc. **4** proof or evidence of anything.
➢ VB **1** to be present as an observer at (an event or occurrence, etc). **2** to add one's own signature to confirm the authenticity of (a signature on a document, etc).

witter VB, INTR (usu **witter on**) to talk or mutter ceaselessly and ineffectually.

witticism N a witty remark or comment.

wittingly ADV consciously; deliberately.

witty ADJ (*-ier, -iest*) able to express oneself cleverly and amusingly. ■ **wittily** ADV.

wizard N **1** someone, esp a man, supposed to have magic powers; a sorcerer. **2** DATED, COLLOQ someone extraordinarily skilled. ■ **wizardry** N.

wizened ADJ shrivelled or wrinkled.

woad N **1** a plant whose leaves yield a blue dye. **2** this dye.

wobble VB **1** TR & INTR to rock or make (something) rock, sway or shake unsteadily. **2** INTR of the voice: to be unsteady.

wobbly ADJ (*-ier, -iest*) unsteady; shaky.
➢ N (*-ies*) COLLOQ a fit of anger; a tantrum.

wodge N, COLLOQ a large lump, wad or chunk.

woe N **1** grief; misery. **2** (often **woes**) calamity.
◆ **woe betide ...** OLD USE, FACETIOUS may evil befall, or evil will befall (whoever offends or acts in some specified way): **Woe betide anyone who disturbs him.**

woebegone ADJ dismal, sad-looking.

woeful ADJ 1 mournful; sorrowful. 2 causing woe: a woeful story. 3 disgraceful; pitiful: a woeful lack of interest. ■ **woefully** ADV.

woggle N a ring through which Scouts, etc thread their neckerchiefs.

wok N a large metal bowl-shaped pan used in Chinese cookery.

wolf N (*wolves*) a carnivorous mammal of the dog family which hunts in packs.
➤ VB (usu **wolf sth down**) COLLOQ to gobble it quickly and greedily.
◆ **cry wolf** to give a false alarm.

wolfhound N a large domestic dog, such as the Irish wolfhound.

wolfram N, CHEM tungsten.

wolf whistle N a loud whistle used as an expression of admiration for a person's appearance.

wolverine or **wolverene** N a large carnivorous animal of the weasel family, which inhabits forests in N America and Eurasia.

woman N (*women*) an adult human female.
➤ ADJ female: a woman doctor.
■ **womanhood** N.

womanish ADJ of a man: effeminate.

womanize or **-ise** VB INTR of a man: to have casual affairs with women. ■ **womanizer** N.

womankind N (also **womanhood**) women generally; the female sex.

womanly ADJ (*-ier, -iest*) feminine.

womb N, ANAT the organ in female mammals in which the young develop after conception and remain till birth.

wombat N a nocturnal Australian marsupial.

womenfolk PL N 1 women generally. 2 the female members of a family or society.

women's liberation N (also with capitals) a movement aimed at freeing women from the disadvantages they suffer in a male-dominated society. Often shortened to **women's lib**.

wonder N 1 the state of mind produced by something extraordinary, new or unexpected; amazement or awe. 2 something that is a cause of awe, amazement or bafflement.
➤ VB 1 TR & INTR to be curious: wondering where you'd gone. 2 (**wonder at someone** or **sth**) to be amazed or surprised by them or it. 3 used politely to introduce requests: I wonder if you could help me? ■ **wonderment** N.

wonderful ADJ 1 extraordinary; arousing wonder. 2 excellent. ■ **wonderfully** ADV.

wonderland N 1 an imaginary place full of marvels. 2 a scene of unearthly beauty.

wondrous ADJ wonderful or awesome.

wonky ADJ (*-ier, -iest*) BRIT, COLLOQ 1 unsound, unsteady or wobbly. 2 crooked or awry.

wont chiefly FORMAL, LITERARY OR OLD USE, ADJ habitually inclined; accustomed: He is wont to retire to bed early.
➤ N a habit that one has: It was her wont to rise early.

won't CONTRACTION will not.

woo VB (*wooed*) 1 OLD USE of a man: to try to win the love and affection of (a woman) esp in the hope of marrying her. 2 to try to win the support of (someone): woo the voters.

wood N 1 BOT the hard tissue beneath the bark, that forms the bulk of woody trees and shrubs. 2 this material used for building timber, fencing and furniture- making, etc. 3 (also **woods**) an expanse of growing trees.

woodcut N 1 a design cut into a wooden block. 2 a print taken from this.

wooden ADJ 1 made of or resembling wood. 2 of an actor, performance, etc: stiff, unnatural and inhibited.

wooden spoon N a booby prize.

woodland N (also **woodlands**) an area of land with trees that are more widely spaced than those in a forest.

woodlouse N a crustacean with a grey oval plated body, found in damp places.

woodpecker N a bird which has a straight

pointed chisel-like bill that is used to bore into tree bark in search of insects.

woodpigeon N a common pigeon that lives in woods, with a white marking round its neck.

woodwind N the wind instruments in an orchestra, including the flute, oboe, etc.

woodwork N 1 the art of making things out of wood. 2 the wooden parts of any structure.

woodworm N (*woodworm* or *woodworms*) 1 the larva of any of several beetles, that bores into wood. 2 the condition of wood caused by this.

woody ADJ (*-ier, -iest*) similar to wood in texture, smell or taste, etc.

woof[1] N the sound of a dog's bark.

woof[2] N, WEAVING the weft.

woofer N, ELECTRONICS a large loudspeaker for reproducing low-frequency sounds.

wool N 1 the soft wavy hair of sheep and certain other animals. 2 this hair spun into yarn for knitting or weaving. 3 fabric or clothing woven or knitted from this yarn.

woollen or (US) **woolen** ADJ made of or relating to wool.
➢ N (often **woollens**) a woollen garment.

woolly or (US) **wooly** ADJ (*-ier, -iest*) 1 made of, similar to, or covered with wool or wool-like fibres, etc; fluffy and soft. 2 vague and muddled: **woolly-minded**.
➢ N (*-ies*) COLLOQ a woollen, usu knitted garment. ■ **woolliness** N.

woozy ADJ (*-ier, -iest*) COLLOQ 1 having blurred senses, due to drink or drugs, etc. 2 dizzy.

word N 1 the smallest unit of spoken or written language that can be used independently, usu separated off by spaces in writing and printing. 2 a brief conversation on a particular matter. 3 any brief statement or message: **a word of caution**. 4 news or notice: **any word of Jane?** 5 a rumour: **The word is he's bankrupt**. 6 one's solemn promise. 7 an order: **expects her word to be obeyed**. 8 (**words**) an argument or heated discussion: **We had words when he**

returned. 9 (**words**) **a** the lyrics of a song, etc; **b** the speeches an actor must learn for a particular part.
➢ VB to express in carefully chosen words.
◆ **in a word** briefly; in short.
◆ **in other words** saying the same thing in a different way.
◆ **take sb at their word** to take their offer or suggestion, etc literally.
◆ **take sb's word for it** to accept what they say as true, without verification.
◆ **the last word** 1 the final, esp conclusive, remark or comment in an argument. 2 the finest example of eg a particular quality, etc: **the last word in good taste**.
◆ **word for word** verbatim.

wording N the choice and arrangement of words used to express something.

word of honour N a promise or assurance which cannot be broken without disgrace.

word of mouth N.
◆ **by word of mouth** through spoken word or conversation.

word-perfect ADJ able to repeat something accurately from memory.

word processor N, COMP a computer application dedicated completely to the input, processing, storage and retrieval of text.

wordy ADJ (*-ier, -iest*) using or containing too many words; long-winded, esp pompously so.

work N 1 physical or mental effort made in order to achieve or make something, eg labour, study, research, etc. 2 employment: **out of work**. 3 one's place of employment: **He leaves work at 4.30**. 4 tasks to be done: **She often brings work home with her**. Also IN COMPOUNDS: **housework**. 5 the product of mental or physical labour: **His work has improved**. 6 **a** any literary, artistic, musical, or dramatic composition or creation; **b** (**works**) the entire collection of such material by an artist, composer or author, etc. 7 anything done, managed, made or achieved, etc: **works of charity**. 8 (**the works**) COLLOQ the whole lot: **She has a headache, fever, cold — the works!**
➢ VB 1 INTR to do work; to exert oneself mentally

or physically. **2** INTR to be employed or have a job. **3** to impose tasks on (someone): **She works her staff hard. 4** TR & INTR to operate, esp satisfactorily: **Does this radio work? 5** INTR of a plan or idea, etc: to be successful or effective. **6** INTR to function in a particular way: **That's not how life works. 7** COLLOQ to manipulate (a system or rules, etc) to one's advantage. **8** TR & INTR to make (one's way), or shift gradually: **worked the nail out of the wall.**
◆ **work out 1** to be successfully achieved or resolved: **It'll all work out in the end. 2** to perform a set of energetic physical exercises.
◆ **work sth out** to solve it.
◆ **work up** to summon up (an appetite, enthusiasm or energy, etc).
◆ **work up to sth** to approach (a difficult task or objective) by gradual stages.

workable ADJ of a scheme, etc: able to be carried out.

workaday ADJ ordinary or mundane.

workaholic N, COLLOQ someone addicted to work.

workbench N a table at which a mechanic, craftsman, etc works.

worker N **1** someone who works. **2** someone employed in manual work. **3** an employee as opposed to an employer.

workforce N **1** the number of workers engaged in a particular industry, factory, etc. **2** the number of workers potentially available.

working N (also **workings**) the operation or mode of operation of something.
➤ ADJ **1** of a period of time: devoted to work, or denoting that part that is devoted to work. **2** adequate for one's purposes: **a working knowledge of French.**

working class N the wage-earning section of the population, employed esp in manual labour. Also (**working-class**) AS ADJ.

working day N **1** a day on which people go to work as usual. **2** the part of the day during which work is done.

working party N a group appointed to investigate and report on something.

workload N the amount of work to be done by a person or machine, esp in a specified time.

workman N a man employed to do manual work.

workmanlike ADJ suitable to, or characteristic of, a good or skilful workman.

workmanship N the degree of expertise or skill shown in making something.

workmate N, COLLOQ someone who works with another or others in their place of work.

work of art N **1** a painting or sculpture of high quality. **2** anything constructed or composed with obvious skill and elegance.

workout N a session of physical exercise.

workshop N **1** a room or building where construction and repairs are carried out. **2** a course of study or work, esp of a creative kind, for a group of people on a particular project: **a theatre workshop.**

workshy ADJ lazy; inclined to avoid work.

workstation N an area in an office, etc where one person works, esp at a computer.

work surface and **worktop** N a flat surface along the top of kitchen installations for the preparation of food, etc.

work to rule VB, INTR of workers: to scrupulously observe all the regulations for the express purpose of slowing down work, as a form of industrial action. ■ **work-to-rule** N.

world N **1** the Earth. **2** the people inhabiting the Earth; humankind: **tell the world. 3** any other planet or potentially habitable heavenly body. **4** (also **World**) a group of countries characterized in a certain way: **the developing world. 5** someone's individual way of life or range of experience: **He's in a world of his own. 6** an atmosphere or environment: **enter a world of make-believe. 7** a particular area of activity: **the world of politics. 8** COLLOQ a great deal; a lot: **did her a world of good.**
◆ **in the world** used for emphasis: **without a care in the world.**
◆ **on top of the world** COLLOQ supremely happy.

◆ **out of this world** COLLOQ marvellous.

◆ **think the world of sb** to love or admire them immensely.

world-class ADJ being among those of the highest standard in the world.

worldly ADJ (*-ier, -iest*) **1** relating to this world; material, as opposed to spiritual or eternal: **worldly possessions**. **2** over–concerned with possessions, money, luxuries, etc; materialistic. **3** shrewd about the ways of the world.

worldly-wise ADJ knowledgeable about life.

worldweary ADJ bored with life.

worldwide ADJ, ADV extending or known throughout the world.

World Wide Web N a network of hypermedia files containing hyperlinks from one file to another over the Internet, which allows the user to browse files containing related information from all over the world.

worm N **1** ZOOL a small soft–bodied limbless invertebrates that is characteristically long and slender. **2** a mean, contemptible, weak or worthless person. **3** (**worms**) PATHOL any disease characterized by the presence of parasitic worms in the intestines.
➤ VB **1** (also **worm out**) to extract (information, etc) little by little: **wormed the secret out of them**. **2** to treat (an animal that has worms) esp to rid it of these.

◆ **worm one's way** to wriggle or manoeuvre oneself gradually: **wormed their way forward**.

◆ **worm one's way into sth** to insinuate oneself into someone's favour or affections, etc.

worn ADJ **1** haggard with weariness. **2** showing signs of deterioration through long use or wear. **3** exhausted.

worn out ADJ **1** damaged or rendered useless by wear. **2** extremely weary; exhausted.

worry VB (*-ies, -ied*) **1** INTR to be anxious; to fret. **2** to make (someone) anxious. **3** to bother, pester or harass (someone). **4** of a dog: to chase and bite (sheep, etc).
➤ N (*-ies*) **1** a state of anxiety. **2** a cause of

anxiety. ■ **worrier** N.

worry beads PL N a string of beads for fiddling with, as a means of relieving tension.

worse ADJ **1** more bad. **2** more ill. **3** more grave, serious or acute. **4** inferior in standard.
➤ N something worse: **Worse was to follow**.
➤ ADV less well; more badly.

◆ **worse off** in a worse situation, esp financially.

worsen VB, TR & INTR to make or become worse.

worship VB (*-pp-*) **1** TR & INTR to honour (God or a god) with praise, prayer, hymns, etc. **2** to love or admire (someone or something), esp blindly.
➤ N **1** the activity of worshipping. **2** a religious service in which God or a god is honoured: **morning worship**. ■ **worshipper** N.

worst ADJ **1** most bad, awful or unpleasant, etc. **2** most grave, severe, acute or dire. **3** most inferior; lowest in standard.
➤ N **1** the worst thing, part or possibility. **2** the most advanced degree of badness.
➤ ADV most severely; most badly.
➤ VB to defeat (someone).

worsted N **1** a fine strong yarn spun from combed wool. **2** fabric woven from this.

worth N **1** value, importance or usefulness. **2** financial value. **3** the quantity that can be bought for a certain sum, accomplished in a certain time, etc: **an hour's worth of work**.
➤ ADJ **1** having a value of a specified amount. **2** COLLOQ having money and property to a specified value. **3** justifying, deserving or warranting something: **worth consideration**.

worthless ADJ **1** having no value or significance. **2** having no merit or virtue; useless. ■ **worthlessness** N.

worthwhile ADJ **1** worth the time, money or energy expended. **2** useful or rewarding.

worthy ADJ (*-ier, -iest*) admirable, excellent or deserving.
➤ N (*-ies*) **1** often PATRONIZING an esteemed person; a dignitary. **2** someone of notable and eminent worth.

would AUXILIARY VERB, used: **1** in reported

speech, as the past tense of **will**[1]: said she would leave at 10. **2** to indicate willingness, readiness, or ability: **was asked to help, but wouldn't. 3** to indicate habitual action: **would always telephone at six. 4** to express frustration at some happening: **It would rain, just as we're setting out.**

would-be ADJ hoping, aspiring or professing to be a specified thing: **a would-be actor.**

wound N **1** any local injury to living tissue of a human, animal or plant, caused by an external physical means such as cutting, crushing or tearing. **2** an injury caused to pride, etc.
➤ VB, TR & INTR **1** to inflict a wound on (a person, creature or limb, etc). **2** to injure (feelings, etc). ■ **wounding** N, ADJ.

WPC ABBREV Woman Police Constable.

wrack N **1** a type of seaweed floating in the sea or cast up on the beach. **2** destruction.

wraith N a ghost; a spectre.

wrangle VB, INTR to quarrel, argue or debate noisily or bitterly.
➤ N a bitter dispute.

wrap VB (-*pp*-) **1** to fold or wind (something) round (someone or something). **2** (also **wrap up**) to cover or enfold (someone or something).
➤ N **1** a warm garment, esp a shawl or stole for the shoulders. **2** a protective covering. **3** a wrapper. **4** CINEMATOG, TV the completion of filming or recording.
◆ **keep sth under wraps** COLLOQ to keep it secret.
◆ **wrap round** COMP of text on a screen: to start a new line automatically as soon as the last character space on the previous line is filled.
◆ **wrap up 1** to dress warmly: **Wrap up warm before you leave! 2** SLANG to be quiet.
◆ **wrap sth up 1** COLLOQ to finish it off or settle it finally. **2** to put and secure wrapping paper around it, esp a gift.

wrapper N a paper or cellophane cover round a packet or sweet, etc.

wrapping N (usu **wrappings**) any of various types of cover or packing material.

wrath N violent anger; resentment or indignation. ■ **wrathful** ADJ.

wreak VB **1** (esp **wreak havoc**) to cause (damage, etc) on a disastrous scale. **2** to take (vengeance) ruthlessly (on someone).

wreath N **1** a ring-shaped garland of flowers and foliage placed on a grave or memorial. **2** a similar garland hung up as a decoration.

wreathe VB **1** to hang or encircle (something) with flowers, etc. **2** of smoke, mist, etc: to cover or surround (something).

wreck N **1** the destruction, esp accidental, of a ship at sea. **2** a hopelessly damaged sunken or grounded ship. **3** a crashed aircraft or a ruined vehicle. **4** COLLOQ someone in a pitiful state of fitness or mental health.
➤ VB **1** to break or destroy (something). **2** to spoil (plans, hopes, a holiday, relationship, etc). **3** to cause the wreck of (a ship, etc).

wreckage N the remains of things that have been wrecked.

wrecker N **1** someone or something that wrecks. **2** someone who ruins anything.

Wren N **1** a member of the Women's Royal Naval Service. **2** (**the Wrens**) the service itself.

wren N a very small songbird with short wings and a short erect tail.

wrench VB **1** (often **wrench off** or **out**) to pull or twist (something) violently. **2** to sprain (an ankle, etc). **3** to twist or distort (a meaning).
➤ N **1** an act or instance of wrenching. **2** a violent pull or twist. **3** an adjustable spanner-like tool for gripping and turning nuts and bolts, etc. **4** a painful parting or separation.

wrest VB **1** to turn or twist (something). **2** to pull or wrench (something) away, esp from someone else's grasp or possession.

wrestle VB **1** TR & INTR **a** to fight by trying to grip, throw and pinion one's opponent; **b** to force (someone) into some position in this way; **c** to do this as a sport. **2** (usu **wrestle with**) to apply oneself keenly to. ■ **wrestler** N.

wrestling N the sport or exercise in which two people wrestle.

wretch N **1** a miserable, unfortunate and pitiful person. **2** a worthless and despicable person.

wretched ADJ **1** pitiable. **2** miserable, unhappy, distressed or distraught.

wriggle VB, TR & INTR **1** to twist to and fro. **2** to make (one's way) by this means.
> **wriggle out of** to manage to evade or escape from (an obligation, etc).

wring VB (*wrung*) **1** (also **wring out**) to force liquid from (something) by twisting or squeezing. **2** to force (information or a consent, etc) from someone. **3** to break (the neck) of a bird, etc by twisting. **4** to keep clasping and twisting (one's hands) in distress or agitation.
> **wringing wet** soaking wet; saturated.

wrinkle N **1** a crease or line in the skin, esp of the face, appearing with advancing age. **2** a slight crease in any surface. **3** a minor problem or difficulty to be smoothed out.
> VB, TR & INTR to develop or make (something) develop wrinkles. ■ **wrinkly** ADJ.

wrist N, ANAT in terrestrial vertebrates: the joint between the forearm and the hand.

writ N a legal document by which someone is summoned, or required to do something.

write VB (PA T *wrote*, PA P *written*) **1** TR & INTR to mark or produce (letters, symbols, numbers, words, etc) on a surface, esp paper, usu using a pen or pencil. **2 a** to compose or create (a book, music, etc) in manuscript, typescript or on computer, etc; **b** to be the author or composer of (a book or music, etc). **3** TR & INTR to compose (a letter, etc): I must write to him. **4** COMP to transfer (data) to a memory or storage device.
> **write sth down** to record it in writing.
> **write off** to write and send a letter of request: I wrote off for a catalogue.
> **write sth off 1** to damage (a vehicle in a crash) beyond repair. **2** to cancel (a debt). **3** to discontinue (a project) because it is likely to fail.
> **write sth out 1** to write it in full. **2** to remove a character or scene from a film or serial, etc.
> **write up 1** to write or rewrite (something) in a final form. **2** to bring (a diary or accounts, etc) up to date. **3** to write about (something).

write-off N something that is written off, esp a motor vehicle involved in an accident.

writer N **1** someone who writes, esp as a living; an author. **2** someone who has written a particular thing.

write-up N an written or published account, esp a review in a newspaper or magazine, etc.

writhe VB, INTR **1** to twist violently, esp in pain or discomfort; to squirm. **2** COLLOQ to feel painfully embarrassed or humiliated.

writing N **1** written or printed words. **2** handwriting. **3** literary composition.
◆ **in writing** of a promise etc: in written form, esp as being firm proof of intention, etc.

written ADJ expressed in writing, and so undeniable: **written consent**.

wrong ADJ **1** not correct. **2** mistaken. **3** not appropriate or suitable. **4** not good or sensible; unjustifiable. **5** morally bad; wicked. **6** defective or faulty. **7** amiss; causing trouble, pain, etc. **8** of one side of a fabric or garment, etc: intended as the inner or unseen side.
> ADV **1** incorrectly. **2** improperly; badly.
> N **1** whatever is not right or just. **2** any injury done to someone else.
> VB **1** to treat (someone) unjustly; to do wrong to (someone). **2** to judge unfairly. ■ **wrongly** ADV.

wrongdoing N evil or wicked action or behaviour. ■ **wrongdoer** N.

wrongfoot VB **1** TENNIS, etc to catch (one's opponent) off balance by making an unpredictable shot, etc to a point away from the direction in which they are moving or preparing to move. **2** to contrive to place (an opponent in a dispute, etc) at a disadvantage.

wrongful ADJ unlawful. ■ **wrongfully** ADV.

wrong-headed ADJ stubborn.

wrought iron N a malleable form of iron with a very low carbon content.

wry ADJ **1** eg of a smile: slightly mocking or bitter; ironic. **2** of a facial expression: with the features distorted or twisted into a grimace, in reaction to a bitter taste, etc. **3** of humour: dry.
■ **wryly** ADV. ■ **wryness** N.

wuss N (*wusses*) SLANG a weakling; a feeble person.

WWW or (IN WEB ADDRESSES) **www** ABBREV World Wide Web.

WYSIWYG or **wysiwyg** ACRONYM, COMP what you see is what you get, indicating that the type and characters appearing on screen are as they will appear on the print-out.

Xx

X[1] or **x** N (*Xs*, *X's* or *x's*) **1** the twenty-fourth letter of the English alphabet. **2** an unknown or unnamed person.

X[2] SYMBOL **1** MATH (usu **x**) an unknown quantity; the first of a pair or group of unknown quantities. **2** the Roman numeral for 10. **3** a mark used: **a** to symbolize a kiss; **b** to indicate an error; **c** as the signature of an illiterate person, etc.

X-chromosome N, BIOL the sex chromosome that when present as one half of an identical pair determines the female sex in most animals.

xenon N, CHEM an element, a colourless odourless inert gas used in fluorescent lamps and lasers.

xenophobia N intense fear or dislike of foreigners or strangers. ■ **xenophobic** ADJ.

xerography N an electrostatic printing process used to make photocopies of printed documents or illustrations. ■ **xerographic** ADJ.

Xerox N, TRADEMARK **1** a type of xerographic process. **2** a copying-machine using this process. **3** a photocopy made by this. ➢ VB (usu **xerox**) to photocopy something using this process.

Xmas N, COLLOQ Christmas.

X-ray N **1** an electromagnetic ray which can pass through many substances that are opaque to light, producing on photographic film an image of the object passed through. **2** a photograph taken using X-rays. **3** a medical examination using X-rays. ➢ VB to take a photograph of something using X-rays.

xylophone N a musical instrument consisting of a series of wooden or sometimes metal bars of different lengths, played by being struck by wooden hammers. ■ **xylophonist** N.

Yy

Y[1] or **y** N (*Ys*, *Y's* or *y's*) the twenty-fifth letter of the English alphabet.

Y[2] SYMBOL, MATH (usu **y**) the second of two or three unknown quantities.

yacht N a boat or small ship, usu with sails and often with an engine, built for racing or cruising. ■ **yachting** N, ADJ.

yachtsman and **yachtswoman** N a person who sails a yacht.

yahoo EXCLAM expressing happiness, etc.

yak N (*yaks* or *yak*) a large ox-like Tibetan mammal with a thick shaggy black coat.

Yale lock N, TRADEMARK a lock operated by a flat key with a notched upper edge.

yam N **1** a climbing plant cultivated in tropical regions for its edible tubers. **2** the thick starchy tuber of this plant. **3** N AMER a sweet potato.

yammer VB **1** INTR to complain whiningly. **2** INTR to talk loudly and at length. ➤ N the act or sound of yammering.

yang see under **yin**

Yank N, COLLOQ a person from the USA.

yank COLLOQ, N a sudden sharp pull. ➤ VB, TR & INTR to pull suddenly and sharply.

Yankee N **1** BRIT COLLOQ a person from the US. **2** N AMER, ESP US a person from New England or from any of the northern states of America.

yap VB (*-pp-*) INTR **1** eg, of a small dog: to give a high-pitched bark. **2** DEROG, COLLOQ of a person: to talk continually in a shrill voice. ➤ N a short high-pitched bark.

yard[1] N **1** in the imperial system: a unit of length equal to 3 feet. **2** NAUT a long beam hung on a mast, from which to hang a sail.

yard[2] N **1** often IN COMPOUNDS an area of enclosed ground associated with a building. **2** an area of enclosed ground used for a special industrial purpose. **3** N AMER a garden.

yardstick N a standard for comparison.

yarmulka or **yarmulke** N a skullcap worn by Jewish men.

yarn N **1** thread spun from wool, cotton, etc. **2** a story, often a lengthy and incredible one.

yashmak N a veil worn by Muslim women that covers the face below the eyes.

yawn VB, INTR **1** to open one's mouth wide and take a deep involuntary breath when tired or bored. **2** of a hole, etc: to be wide open. ➤ N an act or an instance of yawning. ■ **yawning** ADJ.

Y-chromosome N, BIOL the smaller of the two sex chromosomes, whose presence determines the male sex in most animals.

ye PRONOUN, ARCHAIC OR DIALECT you (plural).

yea FORMAL OR OLD USE, EXCLAM yes. ➤ N **a** a yes; **b** a person who has voted yes.

yeah EXCLAM, COLLOQ yes.

year N **1 a** the period of time the Earth takes to go once round the Sun, about 365 days; **b** the equivalent time for any other planet. **2** (also **calendar year**) the period between 1 January and 31 December, 365 days in a normal year, 366 days in a leap year. **3** any period of twelve months. **4** a period of less than 12 months during which some activity is carried on: **an academic year**. **5** a period of study at school, college, etc over an academic year: **She's in third year now.**

yearbook N a book of information updated and published every year, esp one that records the events, etc of the previous year.

yearling N an animal which is a year old.

yearly ADJ **1** happening, etc every year. **2** valid for one year. ➤ ADV every year.

yearn VB, INTR **1** (**yearn for** or **after sth** or **to do sth**) to feel a great desire for it; to long for it. **2** to feel compassion. ■ **yearning** N, ADJ.

years PL N **1** age: **He is wise for his years.** **2** COLLOQ a very long time: **She's been coming for years.** **3** some period of time in the past or future: **in years gone by.**

yeast N any of various single-celled fungi that are capable of fermenting carbohydrates, widely used in brewing and baking.

yell N a loud shout or cry. ➤ VB, TR & INTR to shout or cry out.

yellow ADJ **1** of the colour of gold, butter, egg-

yolk, a lemon, etc. **2** DEROG, COLLOQ cowardly.
➤ N any shade of the colour of gold, etc.
➤ VB, TR & INTR to make or become yellow.
■ **yellowness** N. ■ **yellowy** ADJ.

yellow-belly N, SLANG a coward.
■ **yellow-bellied** ADJ.

yellow card N, FOOTBALL a yellow-coloured card shown by the referee to a player being cautioned for a violation of the rules.

yellow fever N, PATHOL a tropical viral disease transmitted by the bite of a mosquito and causing high fever and jaundice.

yellowhammer N a large brightly-coloured bunting with a yellow head.

Yellow Pages PL N, TRADEMARK a telephone directory printed on yellow paper, in which entries are classified according to the nature of the trade or profession of those listed.

yelp VB, INTR to give a sharp sudden cry.
➤ N such a cry.

yen[1] N (PL *yen*) the unit of currency of Japan.

yen[2] N, COLLOQ a desire.

yeoman N (*yeomen*) **1** HIST a farmer who owned and worked his own land. **2** MIL a member of the yeomanry.

yeoman of the guard N a member of the British sovereign's ceremonial bodyguard.

yeomanry N (*-ies*) **1** HIST the class of land-owning farmers. **2** MIL a former volunteer cavalry force formed in the 18c.

yes EXCLAM used to express agreement or consent.
➤ N (*yesses*) an expression of agreement or consent.

yes-man N, DEROG someone who always agrees with the opinions and follows the suggestions of a superior, employer, etc.

yesterday N **1** the day before today. **2** OFTEN IN PL the recent past.
➤ ADV **1** on the day before today. **2** in the recent past.

yet ADV **1** (also **as yet**) up till now or then: He had not yet arrived. **2** at this time; now: You can't leave yet. **3** at some time in the future: She may yet make a success of it. **4** (USED FOR EMPHASIS WITH **another, more,** or a comparative) even; still: **yet another mistake**.
➤ CONJ but; however; nevertheless.
◆ **yet again** once more.

yeti N an ape-like creature supposed to live in the Himalayas. Also called **abominable snowman**.

yew N **1** a cone-bearing evergreen tree with reddish-brown flaky bark and narrow leaves. **2** the hard reddish-brown wood of this tree.

Y-fronts PL N men's or boys' underpants with a Y-shaped front seam.

Yiddish N a language spoken by many Jews, based on medieval German, with elements from Hebrew and several other languages.

yield VB **1** to produce (an animal product such as meat or milk, or a crop). **2** FINANCE to give or produce (interest, etc): **Shares yield dividends**. **3** to produce (a specified quantity of a natural or financial product). **4** TR & INTR to give up or give in; to surrender. **5** INTR to break or give way under force or pressure.
➤ N the amount produced.

yielding ADJ **1** submissive. **2** flexible. **3** able or tending to give way.

yin N in traditional Chinese philosophy, religion, medicine, etc: one of the two opposing and complementary principles, being the negative, feminine, dark, cold and passive element or force (as opposed to the positive, masculine, light, warm and active **yang**).

yippee EXCLAM expressing delight, etc.

yob or **yobbo** N, SLANG a lout or hooligan.
■ **yobbish** ADJ.

yodel VB (*-ll-*) TR & INTR to sing (a melody, etc), changing frequently from a normal to a falsetto voice and back again.
➤ N an act of yodelling. ■ **yodeller** N.

yoga N **1** a system of Hindu philosophy showing how to free the soul from reincarnation and reunite it with God. **2** any of several systems of physical and mental discipline based on this, esp a particular system of physical exercises. ■ **yogic** ADJ.

yoghurt, **yogurt** or **yoghourt** N a type of semi-liquid food made from fermented milk.

yogi and **yogin** N a person who practises the yoga philosophy.

yoke N **1** a wooden frame placed over the necks of oxen to hold them together when they are pulling a plough, cart, etc. **2** a frame placed across a person's shoulders, for carrying buckets. **3** DRESSMAKING, ETC the part of a garment that fits over the shoulders and round the neck. **4** a pair of animals, esp oxen.

yolk N the yellow part of an egg.

Yom Kippur N an annual Jewish religious festival devoted to repentance for past sins.

yonder ADV in or at that place over there. ➤ ADJ situated over there.

yonks N, COLLOQ a long time.

yoo-hoo EXCLAM, COLLOQ used to attract someone's attention.

yore and **days of yore** N, LITERARY OR ARCHAIC times past or long ago.

yorker N, CRICKET a ball pitched to a point directly under the bat.

Yorkshire pudding N a baked pudding of unsweetened batter.

you PRONOUN **1** the person or people, etc spoken or written to, with or without others: When are you all coming to visit us? **2** any or every person: You don't often see that now.

you'd CONTRACTION **1** you would. **2** you had.

you'll CONTRACTION **1** you will. **2** you shall.

young ADJ in the first part of life, growth, development, etc; not old. ➤ N **1** (**the young**) young people in general. **2** usu of animals or birds: their, etc offspring: Some birds feed their young on insects. ◆ **with young** of animals: pregnant.

youngster N, COLLOQ a young person.

your ADJ **1** belonging to you. **2** COLLOQ, often DEROG usual; ordinary; typical: Your politicians nowadays have no principles.

you're CONTRACTION you are.

yours PRONOUN **1** something belonging to you. **2** (also **yours faithfully, sincerely** or **truly**) conventional expressions written before a signature at the end of a letter. ◆ **of yours** (a specified thing, relation, etc) belonging to you: that book of yours.

yourself PRONOUN (PL *yourselves*) **1** the reflexive form of **you**. **2** used for emphasis: you yourself • Are you coming yourself? **3** your normal self: don't seem yourself this morning. **4** (also **by yourself**) alone; without help.

yours truly PRONOUN, COLLOQ used to refer to oneself, esp with irony: Then yours truly had to go and fetch it.

youth SING N **1** the state, quality or fact of being young. **2** the early part of life, often that between childhood and adulthood. **3** (*youths*) a boy or young man. **4** (SING OR PL N) young people in general: The youth of today expect too much.

youth club N a place or organization providing leisure activities for young people.

youthful ADJ **1** young, esp in manner or appearance. **2** of someone who is not young: young-looking, or having the energy, etc of a young person. ■ **youthfulness** N.

youth hostel N a hostel providing simple overnight accommodation.

yowl VB, INTR to howl or cry sadly. ➤ N such a howl. ■ **yowling** N.

yo-yo N a toy consisting of a pair of discs joined at their centre, and with a piece of string attached, and the toy being repeatedly made to unwind from the string by the force of its weight and rewind by its momentum. ➤ VB (**yo-yoed**) INTR to fluctuate repeatedly.

yucca N a tropical plant with a short thick trunk, stiff narrow sword-shaped leaves and white flowers.

yuck or **yuk** COLLOQ, EXCLAM expressing

disgust. ■ **yucky** or **yukky** ADJ (*-ier, -iest*).

Yule N, OLD, LITERARY & DIALECT **1** Christmas. **2** (also **Yuletide**) the Christmas period.

yummy ADJ (*-ier, -iest*) COLLOQ delicious.

yum-yum EXCLAM expressing delight at or appreciative anticipation of delicious food.

yuppie or **yuppy** N (*-ies*) DEROG, COLLOQ an ambitious young professional person.

Zz

Z¹ or **z** N (**Zs, Z's** or **z's**) the twenty-sixth and last letter of the English alphabet.

Z² SYMBOL, MATH (usu **z**) the third of three unknown quantities.

zany ADJ (*-ier, -iest*) amusingly crazy.

zap VB (*-pp-*) COLLOQ **1** to hit, destroy or shoot something, esp suddenly. **2** COMP to delete all the data in (a file) or from (the main memory of a computer). **3** TR & INTR to move quickly or suddenly.

zeal N great, and sometimes excessive, enthusiasm or keenness.

zealot N a single-minded and determined supporter of a political cause, religion, etc. ■ **zealotry** N.

zealous ADJ enthusiastic. ■ **zealously** ADV.

zebra N (*zebras* or *zebra*) a stocky black-and-white striped African mammal with a stubby mane, related to the horse.

zebra crossing N, BRIT a pedestrian crossing marked by black and white stripes on the road.

Zeitgeist N (also **zeitgeist**) the spirit of the age; the attitudes of a specific period.

Zen and **Zen Buddhism** N a school of Buddhism which stresses the personal experience of enlightenment based on a simple way of life and simple methods of meditation.

zenith N **1** ASTRON the point on the celestial sphere diametrically opposite the nadir and directly above the observer. **2** the highest point.

zephyr N, LITERARY a light gentle breeze.

zeppelin or **Zeppelin** N a cigar-shaped airship.

zero N **1** the number, figure or symbol 0. **2** the point on a scale eg on a thermometer which is taken as the base from which measurements may be made: **5 degrees below zero.** ➢ ADJ **1** being of no measurable size. **2** COLLOQ not any; no: **She has zero confidence.** ➢ VB (*zeroes, zeroed*) to set or adjust something to zero. ◆ **zero in on sth 1** to aim for it; to move towards it. **2** to focus one's attention on it.

zero hour N **1** the exact time fixed for something to happen. **2** the time at which a military operation, etc is fixed to begin.

zero-rated ADJ of goods: on which the buyer pays no VAT, and on which the seller can claim back any VAT they have paid.

zest N **1** keen enjoyment; enthusiasm. **2** something that adds to one's enjoyment of something. **3** COOKERY the coloured outer layer of the peel of an orange or lemon used for flavouring. ■ **zestful** ADJ.

zigzag N (usu **zigzags**) two or more sharp bends to alternate sides in a path, etc. ➢ ADJ **1** having sharp bends to alternate sides. **2** bent from side to side alternately.

➤ VB (-*gg*-) INTR to move in a zigzag direction.
➤ ADV in a zigzag direction or manner.

zillion N, COLLOQ a very large number.

Zimmer, **zimmer** and **Zimmer frame** or **zimmer frame** N, TRADEMARK a tubular metal frame, used as a support for walking by the disabled or infirm.

zinc N, CHEM a brittle bluish-white metallic element used in dry batteries and various alloys, and to galvanize steel.

zing N 1 a short high-pitched humming sound, eg that made by a bullet or vibrating string. 2 COLLOQ zest or vitality.
➤ VB, INTR to move very quickly, esp while making a high-pitched hum.

Zionism N the movement which worked for the establishment of a national homeland in Palestine for Jews. ■ **Zionist** N, ADJ.

zip N 1 a zip fastener. 2 COLLOQ energy; vitality. 3 a whizzing sound.
➤ VB (-*pp*-) 1 TR & INTR (also **zip up**) to fasten, or be fastened, with a zip fastener. 2 INTR to make, or move with, a whizzing sound. 3 COMP to convert (a file, etc) into a compressed form in order to save storage space.

zip code N in the US: a postal code. Brit equivalent: **postcode**.

zip fastener N a device for fastening clothes, bags, etc, in which two rows of metal or nylon teeth are made to fit into each other when a sliding tab is pulled along them.

zippy ADJ (-*ier*, -*iest*) COLLOQ lively; quick.

zircon N, GEOL a hard mineral form of zirconium silicate, the colourless variety of which is used as a gemstone.

zirconium N, CHEM a silvery-grey metallic element that is resistant to corrosion.

zit N, SLANG a pimple.

zither N a musical instrument consisting of a flat wooden sound-box, one section of which has frets on it, over which strings are stretched.

zodiac N (**the zodiac**) the band of sky that extends 8° on either side of the Sun's ecliptic, divided into 12 equal parts called the **signs of the zodiac**, named from the constellations that they once contained, though some no longer do. 2 ASTROL a chart or diagram (usu a circular one), representing this band of sky.

zombie or **zombi** N (-*bies* or -*bis*) 1 DEROG, COLLOQ a slow-moving, stupid or apathetic person. 2 a corpse brought to life again by magic.

zone N an area or region of a country, town, etc, esp one marked out for a special purpose or by a particular feature.
➤ VB 1 (also **zone sth off**) to divide it into zones; to mark it as a zone. 2 to assign to a particular zone. ■ **zonal** ADJ.

zoo N a garden or park where wild animals are kept for the purpose of study, breeding of rare species for conservation, etc, and where they are usually on show to the public.

zoological garden N, FORMAL a zoo.

zoology N the scientific study of animals, including their structure, function, behaviour, ecology, evolution and classification. ■ **zoological** ADJ. ■ **zoologist** N.

zoom VB 1 TR & INTR (often **zoom over, past,** etc) to move or cause something to move very quickly, making a loud low-pitched buzzing noise. 2 INTR (usu **zoom off,** etc) to move very quickly.
◆ **zoom in** or **zoom in on sb** or **sth** of a camera or its operator: to close up on them using a zoom lens.

zoom lens N a camera lens which can be used to make a distant object appear gradually closer or further away without loss of focus.

Zulu N (*Zulu* or *Zulus*) 1 a Bantu people of S Africa. 2 an individual belonging to this people. 3 their language.

zygote N, BIOL the cell that is formed as a result of the fertilization of a female gamete by a male gamete. ■ **zygotic** ADJ.